Profiles
of
Florida

2005-2006

Profiles of Florida

A Universal Reference Book

Grey House Publishing

PUBLISHER: Leslie Mackenzie
EDITOR: David Garoogian
EDITORIAL DIRECTOR: Laura Mars-Proietti

MARKETING DIRECTOR: Jessica Moody

Grey House Publishing, Inc.
185 Millerton Road
Millerton, NY 12546
518.789.8700
FAX 518.789.0545
www.greyhouse.com
e-mail: books @greyhouse.com

First edition published 2005
Printed in the USA

10 9 8 7 6 5 4 3 2

ISBN 1-59237-110-8

Table of Contents

Introduction

This is the first edition of *Profiles of Florida – Facts, Figures & Statistics for all 941 Populated Places in Florida.* We built this work using content from Grey House Publishing's award-winning *Profiles of America* – a 4-volume compilation of data on more than 42,000 places in the United States. We have taken the Florida chapter from *Profiles of America,* and added entire chapters of demographic information and rankings, so that *Profiles of Florida* is the most comprehensive portrait of the state of Florida ever published.

Profiles of Florida provides data on all populated communities and counties in the state of Florida, from bustling urban centers to the hard-to-find hamlets. It includes six major chapters that cover everything from **Education** to **Ethnic Backgrounds** to **Weather**. All chapters include **Comparative Statistics** or **Rankings**, and 4-color **Maps** at the back of the book provide valuable information in a quickly processed, visual format. Here's an overview of each chapter:

1. Profiles
This chapter, organized by county, gives detailed profiles of 941 places plus 67 counties, and is based on the 2000 Census. However, this core Census data has been so extensively updated that nearly 80% of this chapter has 2004 statistics. These profiles pull together statistical and descriptive information on every Census-recognized place in the state. Major fields of information include:

Geography	*Housing*	*Education*	*Religion*
Ancestry	*Transportation*	*Population*	*Weather*
Economy	*Industry*	*Health*	*Safety*

In addition to place profiles, this chapter includes **Comparative Statistics** that compare Florida's 100 largest communities by dozens of data points, and an **Alphabetical Place Index.**

2. Education
This chapter begins with an *Educational State Profile*, summarizing number of schools, students, diplomas granted and educational dollars spent. Following this summary are detailed profiles of all *79 School Districts, NAEP Test Scores*, plus the all-important *FCAT Scores*.

Part Two provides **School District Rankings** on 16 topics ranging from *Teacher/Student Ratios* to *HS Drop-Out Rates*. Most data is from 2003, a number of data points from 2004, with some statistics as recent as June 2005.

3. Ancestry
This chapter offers valuable statistics regarding the ethnic make-up of Florida's population in several different ways. Part One lists places in alphabetical order, with the ethnic backgrounds that comprise its population, from *Acadian/Cajun* to *Yugoslavian.*

Part Two sorts more than 200 ethnic backgrounds in three ways:

Top 10 places by number of people
Top 10 places by percentage (regardless of population)
Top 10 places by percentage (10,000 or more population)

4. Hispanic Population

This chapter defines Florida's Hispanic population by 23 Hispanic backgrounds from *Argentinian* to *Venezuelan* and presents the information in several ways. Part One lists number of Hispanics by 15 categories from *Median Age* to *Median Home Value*.

Part Two ranks each category by Top 10 places. For example, you'll see that Hialeah Gardens has the highest number of *Cubans* who speak Spanish only at home . . . and Sunny Isles Beach has the most housing units rented by *Argentinians*.

5. Asian Population

Similar in format to the chapter on Hispanic Population, this chapter defines Florida's Asian population by 23 Asian backgrounds from *Bangladeshi* to *Vietnamese*. Part One lists number of Asians by 15 categories from *Median Age* to *Median Home Value*.

Part Two ranks categories by Top 10 places. As there are significantly less Asians than Hispanics in Florida, this section is smaller than the Rankings in Chapter 5, but you will learn that Jacksonville has the most of many *Asian* backgrounds (including *Cambodian, Chinese, Korean, Filipino*), and *Asians* in Pinecrest have the highest per capita income of all *Asians* in Florida.

6. Weather

This important topic in the Sunshine State is explored in detail in this chapter, which includes a *State Summary*, and profiles both *National and Cooperative Weather Stations*. In addition, you'll find *Weather Station Rankings*, where you'll see that the temperature has dipped into the single digits in 18 places over the last 30 years, and the most snowfall recorded was 0.2 inches in Santa Rosa County.

This chapter also includes current *Storm* data. You'll see, at a glance, the most destructive Florida *Storms* ranked by both the most fatalities and the most property damage, from 1995 to 2005.

Maps

For a more visual point of view, there are 16 maps of Florida, most in 4-color, at the back of the book. They provide information on topics such as Core-Based Statistical Areas and Counties, Congressional Districts, Population Demographics, Household Size, Age, Male/Female Ratio, Income, Educational Attainment, and another look at who voted for George Bush and John Kerry in 2004.

Note: The extensive **User's Guide** that follows this Introduction is segmented into six sections and examines, in some detail, each data field in the individual profiles and comparative sections for all six chapters. It provides sources for all data points and statistical definitions as necessary.

User's Guide: Profiles

PLACES COVERED

All 67 counties.

402 incorporated municipalities. Municipalities are incorporated as either cities, towns or villages.

484 census designated places (CDP). The U.S. Bureau of the Census defines a CDP as "a statistical entity, defined for each decennial census according to Census Bureau guidelines, comprising a densely settled concentration of population that is not within an incorporated place, but is locally identified by a name. CDPs are delineated cooperatively by state and local officials and the Census Bureau, following Census Bureau guidelines. Beginning with Census 2000 there are no size limits."

55 unincorporated communities. The communities included have both their own zip code and statistics for their ZIP Code Tabulation Area (ZCTA) available from the Census Bureau. They are referred to as "postal areas." A ZCTA is a statistical entity developed by the Census Bureau to approximate the delivery area for a US Postal Service 5-digit or 3-digit ZIP Code in the US and Puerto Rico. A ZCTA is an aggregation of census blocks that have the same predominant ZIP Code associated with the mailing addresses in the Census Bureau's Master Address File. Thus, the Postal Service's delivery areas have been adjusted to encompass whole census blocks so that the Census Bureau can tabulate census data for the ZCTAs. ZCTAs do not include all ZIP Codes used for mail delivery and therefore do not precisely depict the area within which mail deliveries associated with that ZIP Code occur. Additionally, some areas that are known by a unique name, although they are part of a larger incorporated place, are also included as "postal areas."

Important Notes

- *Profiles of Florida* uses the term "community" to refer to all places except counties. The term "county" is used to refer to counties and county-equivalents. All places are defined as of the 2000 Census.
- In Florida, most school districts serve an entire county. In each community profile, only school districts that have schools that are physically located within the community are shown. In addition, statistics for each school district cover the entire district, regardless of the physical location of the schools within the district.
- Special care should be taken when interpreting certain statistics for communities containing large colleges or universities. College students were counted as residents of the area in which they were living while attending college (as they have been since the 1950 census). One effect this may have is skewing the figures for population, income, housing, and educational attainment.
- Some information (e.g. unemployment rates) is available for both counties and individual communities. Other information is available for just counties (e.g. election results), or just individual communities (e.g. local newspapers).
- Some statistical information is available only for larger communities. In addition, the larger places are more apt to have services such as newspapers, airports, school districts, etc.
- For the most complete information on any community, you should also check the entry for the county in which the community is located. In addition, more information and services will be listed under the larger places in the county.
- For a more in-depth discussion of geographic areas, please refer to the Census Bureau's Geographic Areas Reference Manual at http://www.census.gov/geo/www/garm.html.

DATA SOURCES

CENSUS 2000

The parts of the data which are from the 2000 Decennial Census are from the following sources: *U.S. Bureau of the Census, Census of Population and Housing, 2000: Summary Files 1 and 3.* Summary File 3 (SF 3) consists of 813 detailed tables of Census 2000 social, economic and housing characteristics compiled from a sample of approximately 19 million housing units (about 1 in 6 households) that received the Census 2000 long-form questionnaire. Summary File 1 (SF 1) contains 286 tables focusing on age, sex, households, families, and housing units. This file presents 100-percent population and housing figures for the total population, for 63 race categories, and for many other race and Hispanic or Latino categories.

Comparing SF 3 Estimates with Corresponding Values in SF 1

As in earlier censuses, the responses from the sample of households reporting on long forms must be weighted to reflect the entire population. Specifically, each responding household represents, on average, six or seven other households who reported using short forms.

One consequence of the weighting procedures is that each estimate based on the long form responses has an associated confidence interval. These confidence intervals are wider (as a percentage of the estimate) for geographic areas with smaller populations and for characteristics that occur less frequently in the area being examined (such as the proportion of people in poverty in a middle-income neighborhood).

In order to release as much useful information as possible, statisticians must balance a number of factors. In particular, for Census 2000, the Bureau of the Census created weighting areas—geographic areas from which about two hundred or more long forms were completed—which are large enough to produce good quality estimates. If smaller weighting areas had been used, the confidence intervals around the estimates would have been significantly wider, rendering many estimates less useful due to their lower reliability.

The disadvantage of using weighting areas this large is that, for smaller geographic areas within them, the estimates of characteristics that are also reported on the short form will not match the counts reported in SF 1. Examples of these characteristics are the total number of people, the number of people reporting specific racial categories, and the number of housing units. The official values for items reported on the short form come from SF 1 and SF 2.

The differences between the long form estimates in SF 3 and values in SF 1 are particularly noticeable for the smallest places, tracts, and block groups. The long form estimates of total population and total housing units in SF 3 will, however, match the SF 1 counts for larger geographic areas such as counties and states, and will be essentially the same for medium and large cities.

SF 1 gives exact numbers even for very small groups and areas, whereas SF 3 gives estimates for small groups and areas such as tracts and small places that are less exact. The goal of SF 3 is to identify large differences among areas or large changes over time. Estimates for small areas and small population groups often do exhibit large changes from one census to the next, so having the capability to measure them is worthwhile.

2004 Estimates and 2009 Projections

Some 2000 Census data has been updated with data provided by Claritas. Founded in 1971, Claritas is the industry leader in applied demography and the preeminent provider of small-area demographic estimates.

INFORMATION FOR COMMUNITIES

PHYSICAL CHARACTERISTICS

Place Type: Lists the type of place (city, town, village, borough, special city, CDP, township, plantation, gore, district, grant, location, reservation, or postal area). *Source: U.S. Bureau of the Census, Census of Population and Housing, 2000: Summary File 1 and U.S. Postal Service, City State File.*

Land and Water Area: Land and water area in square miles. *Source: U.S. Bureau of the Census, Census of Population and Housing, 2000: Summary File 1.*

Latitude and Longitude: Latitude and longitude in degrees. *Source: U.S. Bureau of the Census, Census of Population and Housing, 2000: Summary File 1.*

Elevation: Elevation in feet. *Source: U.S. Geological Survey, Geographic Names Information System (GNIS).*

HISTORY

History: Historical information. *Source: Columbia University Press, The Columbia Gazetteer of North America; Original research.*

POPULATION

Population: 1990 and 2000 figures are a 100% count of population. 2004 estimates and 2009 projections were provided by Claritas. *Source: Claritas; U.S. Bureau of the Census, Census of Population and Housing, 2000: Summary File 1.*

Population by Race: 2004 estimates includes the U.S. Bureau of the Census categories of White alone; Black alone; Asian alone; and Hispanic of any race. Alone refers to the fact that these figures are not in combination with any other race.

The concept of race, as used by the Census Bureau, reflects self-identification by people according to the race or races with which they most closely identify. These categories are socio-political constructs and should not be interpreted as being scientific or anthropological in nature. Furthermore, the race categories include both racial and national-origin groups.

- **White.** A person having origins in any of the original peoples of Europe, the Middle East, or North Africa. It includes people who indicate their race as "White" or report entries such as Irish, German, Italian, Lebanese, Near Easterner, Arab, or Polish.
- **Black or African American.** A person having origins in any of the Black racial groups of Africa. It includes people who indicate their race as "Black, African American, or Negro," or provide written entries such as African American, Afro-American, Kenyan, Nigerian, or Haitian.
- **Asian.** A person having origins in any of the original peoples of the Far East, Southeast Asia, or the Indian subcontinent including, for example, Cambodia, China, India, Japan, Korea, Malaysia, Pakistan, the Philippine Islands, Thailand, and Vietnam. It includes "Asian Indian," "Chinese," "Filipino," "Korean," "Japanese," "Vietnamese," and "Other Asian."
- **Hispanic.** The data on the Hispanic or Latino population, which was asked of all people, were derived from answers to long-form questionnaire Item 5, and short-form questionnaire Item 7. The terms "Spanish," "Hispanic origin," and "Latino" are used interchangeably. Some respondents identify with all three terms, while others may identify with only one of these three specific terms. Hispanics or Latinos who identify with the terms "Spanish," "Hispanic," or "Latino" are those who classify themselves in one of the specific Hispanic or Latino categories listed on the questionnaire — "Mexican," "Puerto Rican," or "Cuban" — as well as those who indicate that they are "other Spanish, Hispanic, or Latino." People who do not identify with one of the specific origins listed on the questionnaire but indicate that they are "other Spanish, Hispanic, or Latino" are those whose origins are from Spain, the Spanish-speaking countries of Central or South America, the Dominican Republic, or people identifying themselves generally as Spanish, Spanish-American, Hispanic, Hispano, Latino, and so on. All write-in responses to the "other Spanish/Hispanic/Latino" category were coded. Origin can be viewed as the heritage, nationality group, lineage, or country of birth of the person or the person's parents or ancestors before their arrival in the United States. People who identify their origin as Spanish, Hispanic, or Latino may be of any race.

Population Density: 2004 population divided by the land area in square miles. *Source: Claritas; U.S. Bureau of the Census, Census of Population and Housing, 2000: Summary File 1.*

Average Household Size: Average household size was calculated by dividing the total population by the total number of households. Figures are 2004 estimates. *Source: Claritas.*

Median Age: Figures are 2004 estimates. *Source: Claritas.*

Male/Female Ratio: Number of males per 100 females. Figures are 2004 estimates. *Source: Claritas.*

Marital Status: Percentage of population never married, now married, widowed, or divorced. *Source: U.S. Bureau of the Census, Census of Population and Housing, 2000: Summary File 3.*

The marital status classification refers to the status at the time of enumeration. Data on marital status are tabulated only for the population 15 years old and over. Each person was asked whether they were "Now married," "Widowed," "Divorced," or "Never married." Couples who live together (for example, people in common-law marriages) were able to report the marital status they considered to be the most appropriate.

- **Never married**. Never married includes all people who have never been married, including people whose only marriage(s) was annulled.
- **Now married.** All people whose current marriage has not ended by widowhood or divorce. This category includes people defined as "separated."
- **Widowed**. This category includes widows and widowers who have not remarried.
- **Divorced.** This category includes people who are legally divorced and who have not remarried.

Foreign Born: Percentage of population who were not U.S. citizens at birth. Foreign-born people are those who indicated they were either a U.S. citizen by naturalization or they were not a citizen of the United States. *Source: U.S. Bureau of the Census, Census of Population and Housing, 2000: Summary File 3.*

Ancestry: Largest ancestry groups reported (up to five). Includes multiple ancestries. *Source: U.S. Bureau of the Census, Census of Population and Housing, 2000: Summary File 3.*

The data represent self-classification by people according to the ancestry group or groups with which they most closely identify. Ancestry refers to a person's ethnic origin or descent, "roots," heritage, or the place of birth of the person, the person's parents, or their ancestors before their arrival in the United States. Some ethnic identities, such as Egyptian or Polish, can be traced to geographic areas outside the United States, while other ethnicities such as Pennsylvania German or Cajun evolved in the United States.

The ancestry question was intended to provide data for groups that were not included in the Hispanic origin and race questions. Therefore, although data on all groups are collected, the ancestry data shown in these tabulations are for non-Hispanic and non-race groups. Hispanic and race groups are included in the "Other groups" category for the ancestry tables in these tabulations.

The ancestry question allowed respondents to report one or more ancestry groups, although only the first two were coded. If a response was in terms of a dual ancestry, for example, "Irish English," the person was assigned two codes, in this case one for Irish and another for English. However, in certain cases, multiple responses such as "French Canadian," "Greek Cypriote," and "Scotch Irish" were assigned a single code reflecting their status as unique groups. If a person reported one of these unique groups in addition to another group, for example, "Scotch Irish English," resulting in three terms, that person received one code for the unique group (Scotch-Irish) and another one for the remaining group (English). If a person reported "English Irish French," only English and Irish were coded. Certain combinations of ancestries where the ancestry group is a part of another, such as "German-Bavarian," were coded as a single ancestry using the more specific group (Bavarian). Also, responses such as "Polish-American" or "Italian-American" were coded and tabulated as a single entry (Polish or Italian).

The Census Bureau accepted "American" as a unique ethnicity if it was given alone, with an ambiguous response, or with state names. If the respondent listed any other ethnic identity such as "Italian-American," generally the "American" portion of the response was not coded. However, distinct groups such as "American Indian," "Mexican American," and "African American" were coded and identified separately because they represented groups who considered themselves different from those who reported as "Indian," "Mexican," or "African," respectively.

The data is based on the total number of ancestries reported and coded. Thus, the sum of the counts in this type of presentation is not the total population but the total of all responses.

ECONOMY

Unemployment Rate: 2004 annual average. Includes all civilians age 16 or over who were unemployed and looking for work. *Source: U.S. Department of Labor, Bureau of Labor Statistics, Local Area Unemployment Statistics (http://www.bls.gov/lau/home.htm).*

Total Civilian Labor Force: 2004 annual average. Includes all civilians age 16 or over who were either employed, or unemployed and looking for work. *Source: U.S. Department of Labor, Bureau of Labor Statistics, Local Area Unemployment Statistics (http://www.bls.gov/lau/home.htm).*

Single-Family Building Permits Issued: Building permits issued for new single-family housing units in 2004. *Source: U.S. Census Bureau, Manufacturing and Construction Division (http://www.census.gov/const/www/permitsindex.html).*

Multi-Family Building Permits Issued: Building permits issued for new multi-family housing units in 2004. *Source: U.S. Census Bureau, Manufacturing and Construction Division (http://www.census.gov/const/www/permitsindex.html).*

Statistics on housing units authorized by building permits include housing units issued in local permit-issuing jurisdictions by a building or zoning permit. Not all areas of the country require a building or zoning permit. The statistics only represent those areas that do require a permit. Current surveys indicate that construction is undertaken for all but a very small percentage of housing units authorized by building permits. A major portion typically get under way during the month of permit issuance and most of the remainder begin within the three following months. Because of this lag, the housing unit authorization statistics do not represent the number of units actually put into construction for the period shown, and should therefore not be directly interpreted as "housing starts."

Statistics are based upon reports submitted by local building permit officials in response to a mail survey. They are obtained using Form C-404 const/www/c404.pdf, "Report of New Privately-Owned Residential Building or Zoning Permits Issued." When a report is not received, missing data are either (1) obtained from the Survey of Use of Permits (SUP) which is used to collect information on housing starts, or (2) imputed based on the assumption that the ratio of current month authorizations to those of a year ago should be the same for reporting and non-reporting places.

Employment by Occupation: Percentage of the employed civilian population 16 years and over in management, professional, service, sales, farming, construction, and production occupations. *Source: U.S. Bureau of the Census, Census of Population and Housing, 2000: Summary File 3.*

- **Management** includes management, business, and financial operations occupations:
  - Management occupations, except farmers and farm managers
  - Farmers and farm managers
  - Business and financial operations occupations:
    - Business operations specialists
    - Financial specialists

- **Professional** includes professional and related occupations:
  - Computer and mathematical occupations
  - Architecture and engineering occupations:
    - Architects, surveyors, cartographers, and engineers
    - Drafters, engineering, and mapping technicians
  - Life, physical, and social science occupations
  - Community and social services occupations
  - Legal occupations
  - Education, training, and library occupations
  - Arts, design, entertainment, sports, and media occupations
  - Healthcare practitioners and technical occupations:
    - Health diagnosing and treating practitioners and technical occupations
    - Health technologists and technicians

- **Service** occupations include:
  - Healthcare support occupations
  - Protective service occupations:
    - Fire fighting, prevention, and law enforcement workers, including supervisors

Other protective service workers, including supervisors
Food preparation and serving related occupations
Building and grounds cleaning and maintenance occupations
Personal care and service occupations

- **Sales** and office occupations include:
  Sales and related occupations
  Office and administrative support occupations

- **Farming,** fishing, and forestry occupations

- **Construction,** extraction, and maintenance occupations include:
  Construction and extraction occupations:
  Supervisors, construction, and extraction workers
  Construction trades workers
  Extraction workers
  Installation, maintenance, and repair occupations

- **Production,** transportation, and material moving occupations include:
  Production occupations
  Transportation and material moving occupations:
  Supervisors, transportation, and material moving workers
  Aircraft and traffic control occupations
  Motor vehicle operators
  Rail, water, and other transportation occupations
  Material moving workers

INCOME

Per Capita Income: Per capita income is the mean income computed for every man, woman, and child in a particular group. It is derived by dividing the total income of a particular group by the total population in that group. Per capita income is rounded to the nearest whole dollar. Figures shown are 2004 estimates. *Source: Claritas.*

Median Household Income: Includes the income of the householder and all other individuals 15 years old and over in the household, whether they are related to the householder or not. The median divides the income distribution into two equal parts: one-half of the cases falling below the median income and one-half above the median. For households, the median income is based on the distribution of the total number of households including those with no income. Median income for households is computed on the basis of a standard distribution and is rounded to the nearest whole dollar. Figures shown are 2004 estimates. *Source: Claritas.*

Average Household Income: Average household income is obtained by dividing total household income by the total number of households. Figures shown are 2004 estimates. *Source: Claritas.*

Percent of Households with Income of $100,000 or more: Figures shown are 2004 estimates. *Source: Claritas.*

Poverty Rate: Percentage of population with income in 1999 below the poverty level. Based on individuals for whom poverty status is determined. Poverty status was determined for all people except institutionalized people, people in military group quarters, people in college dormitories, and unrelated individuals under 15 years old. *Source: U.S. Bureau of the Census, Census of Population and Housing, 2000: Summary File 3.*

The poverty status of families and unrelated individuals in 1999 was determined using 48 thresholds (income cutoffs) arranged in a two-dimensional matrix. The matrix consists of family size (from 1 person to 9 or more people) cross-classified by presence and number of family members under 18 years old (from no children present to 8 or more children present). Unrelated individuals and 2-person families were further differentiated by the age of the reference person (RP) (under 65 years old and 65 years old and over).

To determine a person's poverty status, one compares the person's total family income with the poverty threshold appropriate for that person's family size and composition. If the total income of that person's family is less than the threshold appropriate for that family, then the person is considered poor, together with every member of his or her family. If a person is not living with anyone related by birth, marriage, or adoption, then the person's own income is compared with his or her poverty threshold.

TAXES

Total City Taxes Per Capita: Total city taxes collected divided by the population of the city. *Source: U.S. Bureau of the Census, State and Local Government Finances, 2002 (http://www.census.gov/govs/www/estimate.html).*

Taxes include:

- Property Taxes
- Sales and Gross Receipts Taxes
- Federal Customs Duties
- General Sales and Gross Receipts Taxes
- Selective Sales Taxes (alcoholic beverages; amusements; insurance premiums; motor fuels; pari-mutuels; public utilities; tobacco products; other)
- License Taxes (alcoholic beverages; amusements; corporations in general; hunting and fishing; motor vehicles motor vehicle operators; public utilities; occupation and business, NEC; other)
- Income Taxes (individual income; corporation net income; other)
- Death and Gift
- Documentary & Stock Transfer
- Severance
- Taxes, NEC

Total City Property Taxes Per Capita: Total city property taxes collected divided by the population of the city. *Source: U.S. Bureau of the Census, State and Local Government Finances, 2002 (http://www.census.gov/govs/www/estimate.html).*

Property Taxes include general property taxes, relating to property as a whole, taxed at a single rate or at classified rates according to the class of property. Property refers to real property (e.g. land and structures) as well as personal property; personal property can be either tangible (e.g. automobiles and boats) or intangible (e.g. bank accounts and stocks and bonds). Special property taxes, levied on selected types of property (e.g. oil and gas properties, house trailers, motor vehicles, and intangibles) and subject to rates not directly related to general property tax rates. Taxes based on income produced by property as a measure of its value on the assessment date.

EDUCATION

Educational Attainment: Figures shown are 2004 estimates and show the percent of population age 25 and over with a:

- **High school diploma (including GED) or higher:** includes people whose highest degree was a high school diploma or its equivalent, people who attended college but did not receive a degree, and people who received a college, university, or professional degree. People who reported completing the 12th grade but not receiving a diploma are not high school graduates.
- **Bachelor's degree or higher**
- **Master's degree or higher:** Master's degrees include the traditional MA and MS degrees and field-specific degrees, such as MSW, MEd, MBA, MLS, and Meng. *Source: Claritas.*

School Districts: Lists the name of each school district, the grade range (PK=pre-kindergarten; KG=kindergarten), the student enrollment, and the district headquarters' phone number. In cases where a school district serve multiple communities, the entry is listed under the place where the school district headquarters is located. *Source: U.S. Department of Education, National Center for Educational Statistics, Directory of Public Elementary and Secondary Education Agencies, 2003-04.*

Four-year Colleges: Lists the name of each four-year college, the type of institution (private or public; for-profit or non-profit; religious affiliation; historically black college), the student enrollment, the phone number, and the annual tuition (including fees) for full-time, first-time undergraduate students (in-state and out-of-state). *Source: U.S. Department of Education, National Center for Educational Statistics, Directory of Postsecondary Institutions, 2003-04.*

Two-year Colleges: Lists the name of each two-year college, the type of institution (private or public; for-profit or non-profit; religious affiliation; historically black college), the student enrollment, the phone number, and the annual tuition (including fees) for full-time, first-time undergraduate students (in-state and out-of-state). *Source: U.S. Department of Education, National Center for Educational Statistics, Directory of Postsecondary Institutions, 2003-04.*

HOUSING

Homeownership Rate: Percentage of housing units that are owner-occupied. Figures shown are 2004 estimates. *Source: Claritas.*

Median Home Value: Median value of all owner-occupied housing units as reported by the owner. Figures shown are 2004 estimates. *Source: Claritas.*

Median Rent: Median monthly contract rent on specified renter-occupied and specified vacant-for-rent units. Specified renter-occupied and specified vacant-for-rent units exclude 1-family houses on 10 acres or more. Contract rent is the monthly rent agreed to or contracted for, regardless of any furnishings, utilities, fees, meals, or services that may be included. For vacant units, it is the monthly rent asked for the rental unit at the time of enumeration. *Source: U.S. Bureau of the Census, Census of Population and Housing, 2000: Summary File 3.*

Median Age of Housing: Median age of housing was calculated by subtracting median year structure built from 2000 (e.g. if the median year structure built is 1967, the median age of housing in that area is 33 years—2000 minus 1967). Year structure built refers to when the building was first constructed, not when it was remodeled, added to, or converted. For housing units under construction that met the housing unit definition—that is, all exterior windows, doors, and final usable floors were in place—the category "1999 or 2000" was used for tabulations. For mobile homes, houseboats, RVs, etc, the manufacturer's model year was assumed to be the year built. The data relate to the number of units built during the specified periods that were still in existence at the time of enumeration. *Source: U.S. Bureau of the Census, Census of Population and Housing, 2000: Summary File 3.*

HOSPITALS

Lists the hospital name and the number of licensed beds. *Source: Grey House Publishing, Directory of Hospital Personnel, 2005.*

SAFETY

Violent Crime Rate: Number of violent crimes reported per 10,000 population. Violent crimes include murder, forcible rape, robbery, and aggravated assault. *Source: Federal Bureau of Investigation, Uniform Crime Reports 2003 (http://www.fbi.gov/ucr/ucr.htm).*

Property Crime Rate: Number of property crimes reported per 10,000 population. Property crimes include burglary, larceny-theft, and motor vehicle theft. *Source: Federal Bureau of Investigation, Uniform Crime Reports 2003 (http://www.fbi.gov/ucr/ucr.htm).*

NEWSPAPERS

Lists the names of daily and weekly newspapers. Also includes the newspaper type and circulation, if available. *Source: BurrellesLuce MediaContacts 2005 (http://www.burrellesluce.com/MediaConnect).*

TRANSPORTATION

Commute to Work: Percentage of workers 16 years old and over that use the following means of transportation to commute to work: car; public transportation; walk; work from home. *Source: U.S. Bureau of the Census, Census of Population and Housing, 2000: Summary File 3.*

The means of transportation data for some areas may show workers using modes of public transportation that are not available in those areas (e.g. subway or elevated riders in a metropolitan area where there actually is no subway or elevated service). This result is largely due to people who worked during the reference week at a location that was different from their usual place of work (such as people away from home on business in an area where subway service was available) and people who used more than one means of transportation each day but whose principal means was unavailable where they lived (e.g. residents of non-metropolitan areas who drove to the fringe of a metropolitan area and took the commuter railroad most of the distance to work).

Travel Time to Work: Travel time to work for workers 16 years old and over. Reported for the following intervals: less than 15 minutes; 15 to 30 minutes; 30 to 45 minutes; 45 to 60 minutes; 60 minutes or more. *Source: U.S. Bureau of the Census, Census of Population and Housing, 2000: Summary File 3.*

Travel time to work refers to the total number of minutes that it usually took the person to get from home to work each day during the reference week. The elapsed time includes time spent waiting for public transportation, picking up passengers in carpools, and time spent in other activities related to getting to work.

Amtrak: Indicates if Amtrak service is available. Please note that the cities being served continually change. *Source: National Railroad Passenger Corporation, Amtrak National Timetable, 2005 (www.amtrak.com).*

AIRPORTS

Lists the local airport(s) along with type of service and hub size. *Source: U.S. Department of Transportation, Bureau of Transportation Statistics (http://www.bts.gov).*

ADDITIONAL INFORMATION CONTACTS

The following phone numbers are provided as sources of additional information: Chambers of Commerce; Economic Development Agencies; Boards of Realtors; Convention & Visitors Bureaus. Efforts have been made to provide the most recent area codes. However, area code changes may have occurred in listed numbers. *Source: Original research.*

INFORMATION FOR COUNTIES

PHYSICAL CHARACTERISTICS

Physical Location: Describes the physical location of the county. *Source: Columbia University Press, The Columbia Gazetteer of North America and original research.*

Land and Water Area: Land and water area in square miles. *Source: U.S. Bureau of the Census, Census of Population and Housing, 2000: Summary File 1.*

Time Zone: Lists the time zone. *Source: Original research.*

Year Organized: Year the county government was organized. *Source: National Association of Counties (www.naco.org).*

County Seat: Lists the county seat. If a county has more than one seat, then both are listed. *Source: National Association of Counties (www.naco.org).*

Metropolitan Area: Indicates the metropolitan area the county is located in. Also lists all the component counties of that metropolitan area. The Office of Management and Budget (OMB) defines metropolitan and micropolitan statistical areas. The current definitions are as of November 2004. *Source: U.S. Bureau of the Census (http://www.census.gov/population/www/estimates/metrodef.html).*

Climate: Includes all weather stations located within the county. Indicates the station name and elevation as well as the monthly average high and low temperatures, average precipitation, and average snowfall. The period of record is generally 1970-1999, however, certain weather stations contain averages going back as far as 1900. *Source: Grey House Publishing, Weather America: A Thirty-Year Summary of Statistical Weather Data and Rankings, 2001.*

POPULATION

Population: 1990 and 2000 figures are a 100% count of population. 2004 estimates and 2009 projections were provided by Claritas. *Source: Claritas; U.S. Bureau of the Census, Census of Population and Housing, 2000: Summary File 1.*

Population by Race: 2004 estimates includes the U.S. Bureau of the Census categories of White alone; Black alone; Asian alone; and Hispanic of any race. Alone refers to the fact that these figures are not in combination with any other race.

The concept of race, as used by the Census Bureau, reflects self-identification by people according to the race or races with which they most closely identify. These categories are socio-political constructs and should not be interpreted as being scientific or anthropological in nature. Furthermore, the race categories include both racial and national-origin groups.

- **White.** A person having origins in any of the original peoples of Europe, the Middle East, or North Africa. It includes people who indicate their race as "White" or report entries such as Irish, German, Italian, Lebanese, Near Easterner, Arab, or Polish.
- **Black or African American.** A person having origins in any of the Black racial groups of Africa. It includes people who indicate their race as "Black, African American, or Negro," or provide written entries such as African American, Afro-American, Kenyan, Nigerian, or Haitian.
- **Asian.** A person having origins in any of the original peoples of the Far East, Southeast Asia, or the Indian subcontinent including, for example, Cambodia, China, India, Japan, Korea, Malaysia, Pakistan, the Philippine Islands, Thailand, and Vietnam. It includes "Asian Indian," "Chinese," "Filipino," "Korean," "Japanese," "Vietnamese," and "Other Asian."
- **Hispanic.** The data on the Hispanic or Latino population, which was asked of all people, were derived from answers to long-form questionnaire Item 5, and short-form questionnaire Item 7. The terms "Spanish," "Hispanic origin," and "Latino" are used interchangeably. Some respondents identify with all three terms, while others may identify with only one of these three specific terms. Hispanics or Latinos who identify with the terms "Spanish," "Hispanic," or "Latino" are those who classify themselves in one of the specific Hispanic or Latino categories listed on the questionnaire — "Mexican," "Puerto Rican," or "Cuban" — as well as those who indicate that they are "other Spanish, Hispanic, or Latino." People who do not identify with one of the specific origins listed on the questionnaire but indicate that they are "other

Spanish, Hispanic, or Latino" are those whose origins are from Spain, the Spanish-speaking countries of Central or South America, the Dominican Republic, or people identifying themselves generally as Spanish, Spanish-American, Hispanic, Hispano, Latino, and so on. All write-in responses to the "other Spanish/Hispanic/Latino" category were coded. Origin can be viewed as the heritage, nationality group, lineage, or country of birth of the person or the person's parents or ancestors before their arrival in the United States. People who identify their origin as Spanish, Hispanic, or Latino may be of any race.

Population Density: 2004 population divided by the land area in square miles. *Source: Claritas; U.S. Bureau of the Census, Census of Population and Housing, 2000: Summary File 1.*

Average Household Size: Average household size was calculated by dividing the total population by the total number of households. Figures are 2004 estimates. *Source: Claritas.*

Median Age: Figures are 2004 estimates. *Source: Claritas.*

Male/Female Ratio: Number of males per 100 females. Figures are 2004 estimates. *Source: Claritas.*

RELIGION

Religion: Lists the largest religious groups (up to five) based on the number of adherents divided by the population of the county. Adherents are defined as "all members, including full members, their children and the estimated number of other regular participants who are not considered as communicant, confirmed or full members." The data is based on a study of 149 religious bodies sponsored by the Association of Statisticians of American Religious Bodies. The 149 bodies reported 268,254 congregations and 141,371,963 adherents. *Source: Glenmary Research Center, Religious Congregations & Membership in the United States 2000.*

ECONOMY

Unemployment Rate: 2004 annual average. Includes all civilians age 16 or over who were unemployed and looking for work. *Source: U.S. Department of Labor, Bureau of Labor Statistics, Local Area Unemployment Statistics (http://www.bls.gov/lau/home.htm).*

Total Civilian Labor Force: 2004 annual average. Includes all civilians age 16 or over who were either employed, or unemployed and looking for work. *Source: U.S. Department of Labor, Bureau of Labor Statistics, Local Area Unemployment Statistics (http://www.bls.gov/lau/home.htm).*

Leading Industries: Lists the three largest industries (excluding government) based on the number of employees. *Source: U.S. Bureau of the Census, County Business Patterns 2003 (http://www.census.gov/epcd/cbp/view/cbpview.html).*

Companies that Employ 500 or more persons: The numbers of companies that employ 500 or more persons. Includes private employers only. *Source: U.S. Bureau of the Census, County Business Patterns 2003 (http://www.census.gov/epcd/cbp/view/cbpview.html).*

Companies that Employ 100 - 499 persons: The numbers of companies that employ 100 - 499 persons. Includes private employers only. *Source: U.S. Bureau of the Census, County Business Patterns 2003 (http://www.census.gov/epcd/cbp/view/cbpview.html).*

Companies that Employ 1 - 99 persons: The numbers of companies that employ 1 - 99 persons. Includes private employers only. *Source: U.S. Bureau of the Census, County Business Patterns 2003 (http://www.census.gov/epcd/cbp/view/cbpview.html)*

Farms: The total number of farms and the total acreage they occupy. *Source: U.S. Department of Agriculture, National Agricultural Statistics Service, 2002 Census of Agriculture (http://www.nass.usda.gov/census).*

Minority Business Ownership Rate: Percentage of all businesses that are majority-owned by a member of a minority group. *Source: U.S. Bureau of the Census, 1997 Economic Census: Surveys of Minority- and Women-Owned Businesses (http://www.census.gov/csd/mwb/).* ***Note:*** Updated figures for Florida from the 2002 Economic Census were not available at time of publication. They are due to be released in early 2006.

Women Business Ownership Rate: Percentage of all businesses that are majority-owned by a woman. *Source: U.S. Bureau of the Census, 1997 Economic Census: Surveys of Minority- and Women-Owned Businesses* *(http://www.census.gov/csd/mwb/)*. ***Note:*** Updated figures for Florida from the 2002 Economic Census were not available at time of publication. They are due to be released in early 2006.

The Survey of Minority-Owned Business Enterprises (SMOBE) is conducted in conjunction with the Survey of Women-Owned Business Enterprises (SWOBE). The SMOBE and SWOBE provide basic economic data on businesses owned by Blacks, persons of Alaska Native, American Indian, Asian, or Pacific Islander descent, persons of Hispanic or Latin American ancestry, and women. These surveys are based on the entire firm rather than on individual locations of a firm. The published data cover number of firms, gross receipts, number of paid employees, and annual payroll. The data are presented by geographic area, industry, size of firm, and legal form of organization of firm.

The data in this report were compiled by combining data collected on business owners in the 1997 Economic Census Surveys of Minority- and Women-Owned Business Enterprises with data collected on the main economic census and administrative records. Included are all non-farm businesses filing 1997 tax forms as individual proprietorships, partnerships, and any type of corporation, and with receipts of $1,000 or more.

Minority/women ownership of a business was based on the race/ethnicity/gender of the person(s) owning majority interest in the business. Firms equally male-/female-owned were counted and tabulated as a separate category. The gender of sole proprietors and self-employed persons who were "single filers" was taken directly from administrative record data.

Businesses in which ownership was shared among minority and non-minority groups, with no single racial/ethnic group having majority interest, were tabulated as 50-percent minority-/50-percent non-minority-owned and were excluded from the minority business counts.

Businesses with publicly held stock whose ownership was indeterminate relative to gender, race, or ethnicity, and non-profit, foreign-owned, and mutual companies were tabulated separately and published in the "other" category.

Retail Sales per Capita: Total dollar amount of retail sales divided by the population of the county. Please note that a value of $0 indicates that data was suppressed to avoid disclosure of confidential information. *Source: U.S. Bureau of the Census, 1997 Economic Census (http://www.census.gov/epcd/www/econ97.html).* ***Note:*** Updated figures for Florida from the 2002 Economic Census were not available at time of publication.

Single-Family Building Permits Issued: Building permits issued for new, single-family housing units in 2004. *Source: U.S. Census Bureau, Manufacturing and Construction Division (http://www.census.gov/const/www/permitsindex.html).*

Multi-Family Building Permits Issued: Building permits issued for new, multi-family housing units in 2004. *Source: U.S. Census Bureau, Manufacturing and Construction Division (http://www.census.gov/const/www/permitsindex.html).*

Statistics on housing units authorized by building permits include housing units issued in local permit-issuing jurisdictions by a building or zoning permit. Not all areas of the country require a building or zoning permit. The statistics only represent those areas that do require a permit. Current surveys indicate that construction is undertaken for all but a very small percentage of housing units authorized by building permits. A major portion typically get under way during the month of permit issuance and most of the remainder begin within the three following months. Because of this lag, the housing unit authorization statistics do not represent the number of units actually put into construction for the period shown, and should therefore not be directly interpreted as "housing starts."

Statistics are based upon reports submitted by local building permit officials in response to a mail survey. They are obtained using Form C-404 const/www/c404.pdf, "Report of New Privately-Owned Residential Building or Zoning Permits Issued." When a report is not received, missing data are either (1) obtained from the Survey of Use of Permits (SUP) which is used to collect information on housing starts, or (2) imputed based on the assumption that the ratio of current month authorizations to those of a year ago should be the same for reporting and non-reporting places.

INCOME

Per Capita Income: Per capita income is the mean income computed for every man, woman, and child in a particular group. It is derived by dividing the total income of a particular group by the total population in that group. Per capita income is rounded to the nearest whole dollar. Figures shown are 2004 estimates. *Source: Claritas.*

Median Household Income: Includes the income of the householder and all other individuals 15 years old and over in the household, whether they are related to the householder or not. The median divides the income distribution into two equal parts: one-half of the cases falling below the median income and one-half above the median. For households, the median income is based on the distribution of the total number of households including those with no income. Median income for households is computed on the basis of a standard distribution and is rounded to the nearest whole dollar. Figures shown are 2004 estimates. *Source: Claritas.*

Average Household Income: Average household income is obtained by dividing total household income by the total number of households. Figures shown are 2004 estimates. *Source: Claritas.*

Percent of Households with Income of $100,000 or more: Figures shown are 2004 estimates. *Source: Claritas.*

Poverty Rate: Estimated percentage of population with income in 2002 below the poverty level. *Source: U.S. Bureau of the Census, Small Area Income & Poverty Estimates.*

Bankruptcy Rate: The personal bankruptcy filing rate is the number of bankruptcies per thousand residents in 2004. Personal bankruptcy filings include both Chapter 7 (liquidations) and Chapter 13 (reorganizations) based on the county of residence of the filer. *Source: Federal Deposit Insurance Corporation, Regional Economic Conditions (http://www2.fdic.gov/recon/index.html).*

TAXES

Total County Taxes Per Capita: Total county taxes collected divided by the population of the county. *Source: U.S. Bureau of the Census, State and Local Government Finances, 2002 (http://www.census.gov/govs/www/estimate.html).*

Taxes include:

- Property Taxes
- Sales and Gross Receipts Taxes
- Federal Customs Duties
- General Sales and Gross Receipts Taxes
- Selective Sales Taxes (alcoholic beverages; amusements; insurance premiums; motor fuels; pari-mutuels; public utilities; tobacco products; other)
- License Taxes (alcoholic beverages; amusements; corporations in general; hunting and fishing; motor vehicles motor vehicle operators; public utilities; occupation and business, NEC; other)
- Income Taxes (individual income; corporation net income; other)
- Death and Gift
- Documentary & Stock Transfer
- Severance
- Taxes, NEC

Total County Property Taxes Per Capita: Total county property taxes collected divided by the population of the county. *Source: U.S. Bureau of the Census, State and Local Government Finances, 2002 (http://www.census.gov/govs/www/estimate.html).*

Property Taxes include general property taxes, relating to property as a whole, taxed at a single rate or at classified rates according to the class of property. Property refers to real property (e.g. land and structures) as well as personal property; personal property can be either tangible (e.g. automobiles and boats) or intangible (e.g. bank accounts and stocks and bonds). Special property taxes, levied on selected types of property (e.g. oil and gas properties, house trailers, motor vehicles, and intangibles) and subject to rates not directly related to general property tax rates. Taxes based on income produced by property as a measure of its value on the assessment date.

EDUCATION

Educational Attainment: Figures shown are 2004 estimates and show the percent of population age 25 and over with a:

- **High school diploma (including GED) or higher:** includes people whose highest degree was a high school diploma or its equivalent, people who attended college but did not receive a degree, and people who received a college, university, or professional degree. People who reported completing the 12th grade but not receiving a diploma are not high school graduates.

- **Bachelor's degree or higher**
- **Master's degree or higher:** Master's degrees include the traditional MA and MS degrees and field-specific degrees, such as MSW, MEd, MBA, MLS, and Meng. *Source: Claritas.*

HOUSING

Homeownership Rate: Percentage of housing units that are owner-occupied. Figures shown are 2004 estimates. *Source: Claritas.*

Median Home Value: Median value of all owner-occupied housing units as reported by the owner. Figures shown are 2004 estimates. *Source: Claritas.*

Median Rent: Median monthly contract rent on specified renter-occupied and specified vacant-for-rent units. Specified renter-occupied and specified vacant-for-rent units exclude 1-family houses on 10 acres or more. Contract rent is the monthly rent agreed to or contracted for, regardless of any furnishings, utilities, fees, meals, or services that may be included. For vacant units, it is the monthly rent asked for the rental unit at the time of enumeration. *Source: U.S. Bureau of the Census, Census of Population and Housing, 2000: Summary File 3.*

Median Age of Housing: Median age of housing was calculated by subtracting median year structure built from 2000 (e.g. if the median year structure built is 1967, the median age of housing in that area is 33 years — 2000 minus 1967). Year structure built refers to when the building was first constructed, not when it was remodeled, added to, or converted. For housing units under construction that met the housing unit definition—that is, all exterior windows, doors, and final usable floors were in place—the category "1999 or 2000" was used for tabulations. For mobile homes, houseboats, RVs, etc, the manufacturer's model year was assumed to be the year built. The data relate to the number of units built during the specified periods that were still in existence at the time of enumeration. *Source: U.S. Bureau of the Census, Census of Population and Housing, 2000: Summary File 3.*

HEALTH AND VITAL STATISTICS

Birth Rate: Estimated number of births per 10,000 population in 2004. *Source: U.S. Census Bureau, Population Estimates, July 1, 2003 - July 1 , 2004 (http://www.census.gov/popest/births.html).*

Death Rate: Estimated number of deaths per 10,000 population in 2004. *Source: U.S. Census Bureau, Population Estimates, July 1, 2003 - July 1 , 2004 (http://www.census.gov/popest/births.html).*

Age-adjusted Cancer Mortality Rate: Number of age-adjusted deaths from cancer per 100,000 population in 2002. Cancer is defined as International Classification of Disease (ICD) codes C00 - D48.9 Neoplasms. *Source: Centers for Disease Control, CDC Wonder (http://wonder.cdc.gov).*

Age-adjusted death rates are weighted averages of the age-specific death rates, where the weights represent a fixed population by age. They are used because the rates of almost all causes of death vary by age. Age adjustment is a technique for "removing" the effects of age from crude rates, so as to allow meaningful comparisons across populations with different underlying age structures. For example, comparing the crude rate of heart disease in Florida to that of California is misleading, because the relatively older population in Florida will lead to a higher crude death rate, even if the age-specific rates of heart disease in Florida and California are the same. For such a comparison, age-adjusted rates would be preferable. Age-adjusted rates should be viewed as relative indexes rather than as direct or actual measures of mortality risk.

Death rates based on counts of twenty or less (<=20) are flagged as "Unreliable". Death rates based on fewer than three years of data for counties with populations of less than 100,000 in the 1990 Census counts, are also flagged as "Unreliable" if the number of deaths is five or less (<=5).

Air Quality Index: The percentage of days in 2004 the AQI fell into the Good (0-50), Moderate (51-100), Unhealthy for Sensitive Groups (101-150), and Unhealthy (151+) ranges. *Source: Air Quality Index Report, 2004, U.S. Environmental Protection Agency, Office of Air and Radiation (http://www.epa.gov/oar).*

The AQI is an index for reporting daily air quality. It tells you how clean or polluted your air is, and what associated health concerns you should be aware of. The AQI focuses on health effects that can happen within a few hours or days after breathing polluted air. EPA uses the AQI for five major air pollutants regulated by the Clean Air Act:

ground-level ozone, particulate matter, carbon monoxide, sulfur dioxide, and nitrogen dioxide. For each of these pollutants, EPA has established national air quality standards to protect against harmful health effects.

The AQI runs from 0 to 500. The higher the AQI value, the greater the level of air pollution and the greater the health danger. For example, an AQI value of 50 represents good air quality and little potential to affect public health, while an AQI value over 300 represents hazardous air quality. An AQI value of 100 generally corresponds to the national air quality standard for the pollutant, which is the level EPA has set to protect public health. So, AQI values below 100 are generally thought of as satisfactory. When AQI values are above 100, air quality is considered to be unhealthy—at first for certain sensitive groups of people, then for everyone as AQI values get higher. Each category corresponds to a different level of health concern. For example, when the AQI for a pollutant is between 51 and 100, the health concern is "Moderate." Here are the six levels of health concern and what they mean:

- "Good" The AQI value for your community is between 0 and 50. Air quality is considered satisfactory and air pollution poses little or no risk.
- "Moderate" The AQI for your community is between 51 and 100. Air quality is acceptable; however, for some pollutants there may be a moderate health concern for a very small number of individuals. For example, people who are unusually sensitive to ozone may experience respiratory symptoms.
- "Unhealthy for Sensitive Groups" Certain groups of people are particularly sensitive to the harmful effects of certain air pollutants. This means they are likely to be affected at lower levels than the general public. For example, children and adults who are active outdoors and people with respiratory disease are at greater risk from exposure to ozone, while people with heart disease are at greater risk from carbon monoxide. Some people may be sensitive to more than one pollutant. When AQI values are between 101 and 150, members of sensitive groups may experience health effects. The general public is not likely to be affected when the AQI is in this range.
- "Unhealthy" AQI values are between 151 and 200. Everyone may begin to experience health effects. Members of sensitive groups may experience more serious health effects.
- "Very Unhealthy" AQI values between 201 and 300 trigger a health alert, meaning everyone may experience more serious health effects.
- "Hazardous" AQI values over 300 trigger health warnings of emergency conditions. The entire population is more likely to be affected.

Number of Physicians: The number of active, non-federal physicians per 10,000 population in 2001. *Source: Area Resource File (ARF). February 2004. U.S. Department of Health and Human Services, Health Resources and Services Administration, Bureau of Health Professions, Rockville, MD.*

Number of Hospital Beds: The number of hospital beds per 10,000 population in 2002. *Source: Area Resource File (ARF). February 2004. U.S. Department of Health and Human Services, Health Resources and Services Administration, Bureau of Health Professions, Rockville, MD.*

Number of Hospital Admissions: The number of hospital admissions per 10,000 population in 2002. *Source: Area Resource File (ARF). February 2004. U.S. Department of Health and Human Services, Health Resources and Services Administration, Bureau of Health Professions, Rockville, MD.*

ELECTIONS

Elections: 2004 Presidential election results. *Source: Dave Leip's Atlas of U.S. Presidential Elections (http://www.uselectionatlas.org).*

NATIONAL AND STATE PARKS

Lists National and State parks located in the area. *Source: U.S. Geological Survey, Geographic Names Information System.*

ADDITIONAL INFORMATION CONTACTS

The following phone numbers are provided as sources of additional information: Chambers of Commerce; Economic Development Agencies; Boards of Realtors; Convention & Visitors Bureaus. Efforts have been made to provide the most recent area codes. However, area code changes may have occurred in listed numbers. *Source: Original research.*

User's Guide: Education

School District Profile

Shown below is a fictitious listing illustrating the kind of information that is or might be included in a School District Profile. Each numbered item of information is described in the paragraphs following the example. Data in the rankings section utilize the same criteria and follow the same guidelines.

❶ **Anniston City SD**
1425 Woodstock Ave • Anniston, AL 36207
Mailing Address: PO Box 432 • Anniston, AL 36207-5432
(256) 231-5000 • http://www.anniston.k12.fl.us
❷ **Grade Span:** KG-12; ❸ **Agency Type:** 4
❹ **Schools:** 10
6 Primary; 1 Middle; 2 High; 1 Other Level
8 Regular; 0 Special Education; 0 Vocational; 2 Alternative
1 Magnet; 0 Charter; 7 Title I Eligible; 6 School-wide Title I
❺ **Students:** 2,839 (52.1% male; 47.9% female)
Individual Education Program: 508 (17.9%)
English Language Learner: 17 (0.6%); Migrant: 0 (0.0%)
Eligible for Free Lunch Program: 2,063 (72.7%)
Eligible for Reduced-Price Lunch Program: 163 (5.7%)
❻ **Teachers:** 194.2 (15.1 to 1)
❼ **Librarians/Media Specialists:** 8.0 (354.9 to 1)
❽ **Guidance Counselors:** 8.1 (350.5 to 1)
❾ **Current Spending:** ($ per student per year)
Total: $6,136; Instruction: $3,625; Support Services: $2,037
❿ **Enrollment, Drop-out Rates, Diploma Recipients by Race/Eth.**

Category	Total	White	Black	Asian	AIAN	Hisp.
Enrollment (%)	100.0	8.3	90.3	0.1	0.0	1.1
Drop-out Rate (%)	7.4	5.8	8.6	1.3	n/a	2.0
H.S. Diplomas (#)	154	19	129	1	0	5

❶ **Name/Address/Phone/Web Site:** *Source: U.S. Department of Education, National Center for Education Statistics, Common Core of Data, Local Education Agency (School District) Universe Survey: School Year 2003-2003.* Web site addresses were researched by the editors. Abbreviations used: SD=School District; RD=Regional District; UD=Unified District; ED=Elementary District; ESD=Elementary School District; HSD=High School District; USD=Unified School District; ISD=Independent School District; CSD=Community School District; JSD=Joint School District; MSD=Municipal School District; PSD=Public School District; CCD=Community Consolidated District; CUD=Community Unit District; CISD=Consolidated Independent School District; UFSD=Unified School District; JUSD=Joint Unified School District; CUSD=Community Unit School District; CHSD=Community High School District; UHSD=Unified High School District; ICSD=Independent Community School District; JUHSD=Joint Union High School District; JUESD=Joint Union Elementary School District

❷ **Grade Span:** The span of grades intended to be served by this school or agency, whether or not there are students currently enrolled in all grades. If a high school also has a prekindergarten program, the grade span of the high school is reported as a high school, not as a PK-12 school. For example, if a school has PK, 9, 10, 11, and 12 grades, the grade span will be reported as Grades 9 through 12 (9-12). Also, the ungraded designation (UG) cannot be used in a grade span unless the whole school is ungraded students, and in this case the grade span is reported as UGUG. *Source: U.S. Department of Education, National Center for Education Statistics, Common Core of Data, Local Education Agency (School District) Universe Survey: School Year 2002-2003.*

❸ **Agency Type:**

1 = Local school district that is not a component of a supervisory union.
2 = Local school district component of a supervisory union sharing a superintendent and administrative services with other local school districts.
3 = Supervisory union administrative center, or a county superintendent serving the same purpose. Type 3 agencies generally do not report student membership, although Massachusetts and Vermont are exceptions.
4 = Regional education services agency, or a county superintendent serving the same purpose.
5 = State-operated institution charged, at least in part, with providing elementary and/or secondary instruction or services to a special need population.
6 = Federally-operated institution charged, at least in part, with providing elementary and/or secondary instruction or services to a special need population.
7 = Other education agencies that do not fit into the first six categories.
Source: U.S. Department of Education, National Center for Education Statistics, Common Core of Data, Local Education Agency (School District) Universe Survey: School Year 2002-2003.

❹ **Schools:** Total number of schools in the district. *Source: U.S. Department of Education, National Center for Education Statistics, Common Core of Data, Public Elementary/Secondary School Universe Survey: School Year 2002-2003.*

Grade Levels:

Primary: Low grade - prekindergarten through 3; high grade - prekindergarten through 8
Middle: Low grade - 4 through 7; high grade - 4 through 9
High: Low grade - 7 through 12; high grade - 12 only
Other Level: Any configuration not falling within the previous three, including ungraded schools

Curriculum:

Regular: A regular school is defined as a public elementary/secondary school that does not focus primarily on vocational, special, or alternative education.

Special Education: A special education school is defined as a public elementary/secondary school that focuses primarily on special education, including instruction for any of the following: autism, deaf-blindness, developmental delay, hearing impairment, mental retardation, multiple disabilities, orthopedic impairment, serious emotional disturbance, specific learning disability, speech or language impairment, traumatic brain injury, visually impaired, and other health impairments. These schools adapt curriculum, materials or instruction for students served.

Vocational: A vocational educational school is defined as a public elementary/secondary school that focuses primarily on providing formal preparation for semi-skilled, skilled, technical, or professional occupations for high school-aged students who have opted to develop or expand their employment opportunities, often in lieu of preparing for college entry.

Alternative: A public elementary/secondary school that addresses needs of students which typically cannot be met in a regular school; provides nontraditional education; serves as an adjunct to a regular school; and falls outside of the categories of regular, special education, or vocational education.

Type:

Magnet: A special school or program designed to attract students of different racial/ethnic backgrounds for the purpose of reducing, preventing or eliminating racial isolation (50 percent or more minority enrollment); and/or to provide an academic or social focus on a particular theme (e.g., science/math, performing arts, gifted/talented, or foreign language).

Charter: A school providing free public elementary and/or secondary education to eligible students under a specific charter granted by the state legislature or other appropriate authority, and designated by such authority to be a charter school.

Title I Eligible: A school designated under appropriate state and federal regulations as being eligible for participation in programs authorized by Title I of Public Law 103-382.

School-wide Title I: A school in which all the pupils in a school are designated under appropriate state and federal regulations as being eligible for participation in programs authorized by Title I of Public Law 103-382.

❺ **Students:** A student is an individual for whom instruction is provided in an elementary or secondary education program that is not an adult education program and is under the jurisdiction of a school, school system, or other education institution. The gender breakdown is shown in parentheses. *Sources: U.S. Department of Education, National Center for Education Statistics, Common Core of Data, Local Education Agency (School District) Universe Survey: School Year 2002-2003 and Public Elementary/Secondary School Universe Survey: School Year 2002-2003*

For the following five categories, the first value shown is the number of students, the second value (in parentheses) is the percent of the entire student population.

Individual Education Program (IEP): A written instructional plan for students with disabilities designated as special education students under IDEA-Part B. The written instructional plan includes a statement of present levels of educational performance of a child; statement of annual goals, including short-term instructional objectives; statement of specific educational services to be provided and the extent to which the child will be able to participate in regular educational programs; the projected date for initiation and anticipated duration of services; the appropriate objectives, criteria and evaluation procedures; and the schedules for determining, on at least an annual basis, whether instructional objectives are being achieved. *Source: U.S. Department of Education, National Center for Education Statistics, Common Core of Data, Local Education Agency (School District) Universe Survey: School Year 2002-2003*

English Language Learner (ELL): Formerly referred to as Limited English Proficient (LEP). Students being served in appropriate programs of language assistance (e.g., English as a Second Language, High Intensity Language Training, bilingual education). Does not include pupils enrolled in a class to learn a language other than English. Also Limited-English-Proficient students are individuals who were not born in the United States or whose native language is a language other than English; or individuals who come from environments where a language other than English is dominant; or individuals who are American Indians and Alaskan Natives and who come from environments where a language other than English has had a significant impact on their level of English language proficiency; and who, by reason thereof, have sufficient difficulty speaking, reading, writing, or understanding the English language, to deny such individuals the opportunity to learn successfully in classrooms where the language of instruction is English or to participate fully in our society. *Source: U.S. Department of Education, National Center for Education Statistics, Common Core of Data, Local Education Agency (School District) Universe Survey: School Year 2002-2003*

Migrant: A migrant student as defined under federal regulation 34 CFR 200.40: 1) (a) Is younger than 22 (and has not graduated from high school or does not hold a high school equivalency certificate), but (b), if the child is too young to attend school-sponsored educational programs, is old enough to benefit from an organized instructional program; and 2) A migrant agricultural worker or a migrant fisher or has a parent, spouse, or guardian who is a migrant agricultural worker or a migrant fisher; and 3) Performs, or has a parent, spouse, or guardian who performs qualifying agricultural or fishing employment as a principal means of livelihood; and 4) Has moved within the preceding 36 months to obtain or to accompany or join a parent, spouse, or guardian to obtain, temporary or seasonal employment in agricultural or fishing work; and 5) Has moved from one school district to another; or in a state that is comprised of a single school district, has moved from one administrative area to another within such district; or resides in a school district of more than 15,000 square miles, and migrates a distance of 20 miles or more to a temporary residence to engage in a fishing activity. Provision 5 currently applies only to Alaska. *Source: U.S. Department of Education, National Center for Education Statistics, Common Core of Data, Public Elementary/Secondary School Universe Survey: School Year 2002-2003*

Eligible for Free Lunch Program: The free lunch program is defined as a program under the National School Lunch Act that provides cash subsidies for free lunches to students based on family size and income criteria. *Source: U.S. Department of Education, National Center for Education Statistics, Common Core of Data, Public Elementary/Secondary School Universe Survey: School Year 2002-2003*

Eligible for Reduced-Price Lunch Program: A student who is eligible to participate in the Reduced-Price Lunch Program under the National School Lunch Act. *Source: U.S. Department of Education, National Center for Education Statistics, Common Core of Data, Public Elementary/Secondary School Universe Survey: School Year 2002-2003*

❻ **Teachers:** Teachers are defined as individuals who provide instruction to pre-kindergarten, kindergarten, grades 1 through 12, or ungraded classes, or individuals who teach in an environment other than a classroom setting, and who maintain daily student attendance records. Numbers reported are full-time equivalents. The students per teacher ratio is shown in parentheses. *Source: U.S. Department of Education, National Center for Education Statistics, Common Core of Data, Local Education Agency (School District) Universe Survey: School Year 2002-2003.*

❼ **Librarians/Media Specialists:** Library and media support staff are defined as staff members who render other professional library and media services; also includes library aides and those involved in library/media support. Their duties include selecting, preparing, caring for, and making available to instructional staff, equipment, films, filmstrips, transparencies, tapes, TV programs, and similar materials maintained separately or as part of an instructional materials center. Also included are activities in the audio-visual center, TV studio, related-work-study areas, and services provided by audio-visual personnel. Numbers reported are full-time equivalents. The students per librarian/media specialist ratio is shown in parentheses. *Source: U.S. Department of Education, National Center for Education Statistics, Common Core of Data, Local Education Agency (School District) Universe Survey: School Year 2002-2003.*

❽ **Guidance Counselors:** Professional staff assigned specific duties and school time for any of the following activities in an elementary or secondary setting: counseling with students and parents; consulting with other staff members on learning problems; evaluating student abilities; assisting students in making educational and career choices; assisting students in personal and social development; providing referral assistance; and/or working with other staff members in planning and conducting guidance programs for students. The state applies its own standards in apportioning the aggregate of guidance counselors/directors into the elementary and secondary level components. Numbers reported are full-time equivalents. The students per guidance counselor ratio is shown in parentheses. *Source: U.S. Department of Education, National Center for Education Statistics, Common Core of Data, Local Education Agency (School District) Universe Survey: School Year 2002-2003.*

➒ Current Spending

Total: Expenditure for Instruction, Support Services, and Other Elementary/Secondary Programs. Includes salaries, employee benefits, purchased services, and supplies, as well as payments made by states on behalf of school districts. Also includes transfers made by school districts into their own retirement system. Excludes expenditure for Non-Elementary/Secondary Programs, debt service, capital outlay, and transfers to other governments or school districts. This item is formally called "Current Expenditures for Public Elementary/Secondary Education."

Instruction: Includes payments from all funds for salaries, employee benefits, supplies, materials, and contractual services for elementary/secondary instruction. It excludes capital outlay, debt service, and interfund transfers for elementary/secondary instruction. Instruction covers regular, special, and vocational programs offered in both the regular school year and summer school. It excludes instructional support activities as well as adult education and community services. Instruction salaries includes salaries for teachers and teacher aides and assistants.

Support Services: Relates to support services functions (series 2000) defined in Financial Accounting for Local and State School Systems (National Center for Education Statistics 2000). Includes payments from all funds for salaries, employee benefits, supplies, materials, and contractual services. It excludes capital outlay, debt service, and interfund transfers. It includes expenditure for the following functions:

- Business/Central/Other Support Services
- General Administration
- Instructional Staff Support
- Operation and Maintenance
- Pupil Support Services
- Pupil Transportation Services
- School Administration
- Nonspecified Support Services

Values shown are dollars per pupil per year. They were calculated by dividing the total dollar amounts by the fall membership. Fall membership is comprised of the total student enrollment on October 1 (or the closest school day to October 1) for all grade levels (including prekindergarten and kindergarten) and ungraded pupils. Membership includes students both present and absent on the measurement day. *Source: U.S. Department of Education, National Center for Education Statistics, Common Core of Data, School District Finance Survey (F-33), Fiscal Year 2001.*

➓ Enrollment, Drop-out Rates, and Diploma Recipients by Race/Ethnicity:

Enrollment: Breakdown of student enrollment by race. *Source: U.S. Department of Education, National Center for Education Statistics, Common Core of Data, Public Elementary/Secondary School Universe Survey: School Year 2002-2003.*

Drop-out: A dropout is a student who was enrolled in school at some time during the previous school year; was not enrolled at the beginning of the current school year; has not graduated from high school or completed a state or district approved educational program; and does not meet any of the following exclusionary conditions: has transferred to another public school district, private school, or state- or district-approved educational program; is temporarily absent due to suspension or school-approved illness; or has died. The values shown are drop-out rates by race and cover grades 9 through 12. *Source: U.S. Department of Education, National Center for Education Statistics, Common Core of Data, Local Education Agency Universe Dropout File: School Year 2000-2001*

H.S. Diplomas: A student who has received a diploma during the previous school year or subsequent summer school. This category includes regular diploma recipients and other diploma recipients. A High School Diploma is a formal document certifying the successful completion of a secondary school program prescribed by the state education agency or other appropriate body. The values shown are the number of high school diploma recipients by race. *Source: U.S. Department of Education, National Center for Education Statistics, Common Core of Data, Local Education Agency (School District) Universe Survey: School Year 2002-2003.*

Race/Ethnicity:

White: A person having origins in any of the original peoples of Europe, North Africa, or the Middle East. Figures include non-Hispanic whites only.

Black: A person having origins in any of the black racial groups of Africa. Figures include non-Hispanic blacks only.

Asian (Asian/Pacific Islander): A person having origins in any of the original peoples of the Far east, Southeast Asia, the Indian subcontinent, or the Pacific Islands. This includes, for example, China, India, Japan, Korea, the Philippine Islands, and Samoa.

AIAN (American Indian/Alaskan Native): A person having origins in any of the original peoples of North America, and who maintains cultural identification through tribal affiliation or community recognition.

Hispanic: A person of Mexican, Puerto Rican, Cuban, Central or South American, or other Spanish culture or origin, regardless of race.

Figures exclude schools that did not report race/ethnicity data.

Note: n/a indicates data not available.

Florida Educational Profile

Please refer to the District Profile section in the front of this User's Guide for an explanation of data for all items except for the following:

Average Salary: The average teacher salary in 2002-2003. *Source: American Federation of Teachers, 2003 Survey & Analysis of Teacher Salary Trends*

College Entrance Exam Scores:

Scholastic Aptitude Test (SAT). *Source: The College Board, Mean SAT I Verbal and Math Scores by State (The College Board strongly discourages the comparison or ranking of states on the basis of SAT scores alone)*

American College Testing Program (ACT). *ACT, 2003 ACT National and State Scores*

Florida NAEP Test Scores

The National Assessment of Educational Progress (NAEP), also known as "the Nation's Report Card," is the only nationally representative and continuing assessment of what America's students know and can do in various subject areas.

The NAEP 2003 reading and mathematics assessments were administered to representative samples of fourth- and eighth-graders in participating states and other jurisdictions. In 2003, 50 states and 3 jurisdictions at grade 4 and grade 8 participated in both assessments and met student and school participation criteria for reporting results. Approximately 343,000 students from 13,000 schools were assessed. The national results reflect the performance of students attending both public and nonpublic schools, while the state and jurisdiction results reflect only the performance of students attending public schools.

The results of student performance are presented in two ways: as average scores on the NAEP mathematics/reading scale and as the percentages of students attaining NAEP mathematics/reading achievement levels. The average scale scores represent how students performed on the assessment. The achievement levels (basic, proficient, advanced) represent how that performance measured up against set expectations for achievement. Thus, the average scale scores represent what students know and can do, while the achievement-level results indicate the degree to which student performance meets expectations of what they should know and be able to do.

Mathematics

Average mathematics scale score results are based on the NAEP mathematics scale, which ranges from 0 to 500. The NAEP mathematics assessment is a composite combining separate scales for each of the mathematics content strands: (1) number sense, properties and operations; (2) measurement; (3) geometry and spatial sense; (4) data analysis, statistics and probability; and (5) algebra and functions. Average scale scores are computed for groups, not for individual students. The average scores are based on analyses of the percentages of students who answered each item successfully. While the score ranges at each grade in mathematics are identical, the scale was derived independently at each grade. Therefore, average scale scores across grades cannot be compared. For example, equal scale scores on the grade 4 and grade 8 scales do not imply equal levels of mathematics achievement.

Reading

Average reading scale score results are based on the NAEP reading scale, which ranges from 0 to 500. The NAEP reading assessment scale is a composite combining separate scales for each reading context specified by the reading framework (at grade 4, reading for literary experience and reading for information, and at grade 8, those contexts and reading to perform a task). Average scale scores are computed for groups, not for individual students. The average scores are based on analyses of the percentages of students who answered each item successfully. While the score ranges at each grade in reading are identical, the scale was derived independently at each grade. Therefore, average scale scores across grades cannot be compared. For example, equal scale scores on the grade 4 and grade 8 scales do not imply equal levels of reading achievement.

Standard Error

The average scores and percentages presented in this chapter are estimates because they are based on representative samples of students rather than on the entire population of students. Moreover, the collection of subject-area questions used at each grade level is but a sample of the many questions that could have been asked. As such, NAEP results are subject to a measure of uncertainty, reflected in the standard error of the estimates (appears in parentheses).

Rank

The state ranking appears in the column labeled Rank. In most cases, 50 states and the District of Columbia are ranked. However in cases where data was not available, fewer than 51 states may be ranked. For example, a ranking of 32/41 indicates that the state ranked number 32 out of the 41 states with available data. All rankings represent their corresponding values sorted in descending order.

Caution

Readers are cautioned against interpreting NAEP results as implying causal relations. Inferences related to subgroup performance or to the effectiveness of public and nonpublic schools, for example, should take into consideration the many socioeconomic and educational factors that may also impact performance. *Source: U.S. Department of Education, National Center for Education Statistics, The Nation's Report Card*

User's Guide: Ancestry

Places Covered

The first part of the Ancestry chapter covers 269 places in Florida with populations of 10,000 or more. The ranking tables are based on all 886 places in Florida (except were noted). Places covered fall into one of the following categories:

402 incorporated municipalities. Municipalities are incorporated as either cities, towns, or villages. A few municipalities have a form of government combined with another entity (e.g. county) and are listed as "special cities."

484 census designated places (CDP). The U.S. Bureau of the Census defines a CDP as "a statistical entity, defined for each decennial census according to Census Bureau guidelines, comprising a densely settled concentration of population that is not within an incorporated place, but is locally identified by a name. CDPs are delineated cooperatively by state and local officials and the Census Bureau, following Census Bureau guidelines. Beginning with Census 2000 there are no size limits."

Source of Data

The ancestries shown in this chapter were compiled from three different sections of the 2000 Census: Race; Hispanic Origin; and Ancestry. While the ancestries are sorted alphabetically for ease-of-use, it's important to note the origin of each piece of data. Data for Race and Hispanic Origin was taken from Summary File 1 (SF1) while Ancestry data was taken from Summary File 3 (SF3). The distinction is important because SF1 contains the 100-percent data, which is the information compiled from the questions asked of all people and about every housing unit. SF3 was compiled from a sample of approximately 19 million housing units (about 1 in 6 households) that received the Census 2000 long-form questionnaire.

Ancestries Based on Race

The data on race were derived from answers to the question on race that was asked of all people. The concept of race, as used by the Census Bureau, reflects self-identification by people according to the race or races with which they most closely identify. These categories are sociopolitical constructs and should not be interpreted as being scientific or anthropological in nature. Furthermore, the race categories include both racial and national-origin groups.

African-American/Black:
- Not Hispanic
- Hispanic

Alaska Native tribes, specified:
- Alaska Athabascan
- Aleut
- Eskimo
- Tlingit-Haida
- All other tribes

Alaska Native tribes, not specified

American Indian or Alaska Native tribes, not specified

American Indian tribes, specified:
- Apache
- Blackfeet
- Cherokee
- Cheyenne
- Chickasaw
- Chippewa
- Choctaw
- Colville
- Comanche
- Cree
- Creek
- Crow
- Delaware
- Houma
- Iroquois
- Kiowa
- Latin American Indians
- Lumbee
- Menominee
- Navajo
- Osage
- Ottawa
- Paiute
- Pima
- Potawatomi
- Pueblo
- Puget Sound Salish
- Seminole
- Shoshone
- Sioux
- Tohono O'Odham
- Ute
- Yakama
- Yaqui
- Yuman
- All other tribes

American Indian tribes, not specified

Asian:
- Bangladeshi
- Cambodian
- Chinese, except Taiwanese
- Filipino
- Hmong
- Indian
- Indonesian
- Japanese
- Korean
- Laotian
- Malaysian
- Pakistani
- Sri Lankan
- Taiwanese
- Thai
- Vietnamese
- Other Asian, specified
- Other Asian, not specified

Hawaii Native/Pacific Islander:
- Melanesian:
  - Fijian
  - Other Melanesian
- Micronesian:
  - Guamanian/Chamorro
  - Other Micronesian
- Polynesian:
  - Native Hawaiian
  - Samoan
  - Tongan
  - Other Polynesian
- Other Pacific Islander, specified
- Other Pacific Islander, not specified

White:
- Not Hispanic
- Hispanic

If an individual did not provide a race response, the race or races of the householder or other household members were assigned using specific rules of precedence of household relationship. For example, if race was missing for a natural-born child in the household, then either the race or races of the householder, another natural-born child, or the spouse of the householder were assigned. If race was not reported for anyone in the household, the race or races of a householder in a previously processed household were assigned.

African American or Black: A person having origins in any of the Black racial groups of Africa. It includes people who indicate their race as "Black, African Am., or Negro," or provide written entries such as African American, Afro American, Kenyan, Nigerian, or Haitian.

American Indian or Alaska Native: A person having origins in any of the original peoples of North and South America (including Central America) and who maintain tribal affiliation or community attachment. It includes people who classified themselves as described below.

American Indian - Includes people who indicated their race as "American Indian," entered the name of an Indian tribe, or reported such entries as Canadian Indian, French American Indian, or Spanish-American Indian.

Respondents who identified themselves as American Indian were asked to report their enrolled or principal tribe. Therefore, tribal data in tabulations reflect the written entries reported on the questionnaires. Some of the entries (for example, Iroquois, Sioux, Colorado River, and Flathead) represent nations or reservations. The information on tribe is based on self identification and therefore does not reflect any designation of federally or state-recognized tribe. Information on American Indian tribes is presented in summary files. The information for Census 2000 is derived from the American Indian Tribal Classification List for the 1990 census that was updated based on a December 1997 Federal Register Notice, entitled "Indian Entities Recognized and Eligible to Receive Service From the United States Bureau of Indian Affairs," Department of the Interior, Bureau of Indian Affairs, issued by the Office of Management and Budget.

Alaska Native - Includes written responses of Eskimos, Aleuts, and Alaska Indians, as well as entries such as Arctic Slope, Inupiat, Yupik, Alutiiq, Egegik, and Pribilovian. The Alaska tribes are the Alaskan Athabascan, Tlingit, and Haida. The information for Census 2000 is based on the American Indian Tribal Classification List for the 1990 census, which was expanded to list the individual Alaska Native Villages when provided as a written response for race.

Asian: A person having origins in any of the original peoples of the Far East, Southeast Asia, or the Indian subcontinent including, for example, Cambodia, China, India, Japan, Korea, Malaysia, Pakistan, the Philippine Islands, Thailand, and Vietnam. It includes "Asian Indian," "Chinese," "Filipino," "Korean," "Japanese," "Vietnamese," and "Other Asian."

Asian Indian - Includes people who indicated their race as "Asian Indian" or identified themselves as Bengalese, Bharat, Dravidian, East Indian, or Goanese.

Chinese - Includes people who indicate their race as "Chinese" or who identify themselves as Cantonese, or Chinese American.

Filipino - Includes people who indicate their race as "Filipino" or who report entries such as Philipino, Philipine, or Filipino American.

Japanese - Includes people who indicate their race as "Japanese" or who report entries such as Nipponese or Japanese American.

Korean - Includes people who indicate their race as "Korean" or who provide a response of Korean American.

Vietnamese - Includes people who indicate their race as "Vietnamese" or who provide a response of Vietnamese American.

Cambodian - Includes people who provide a response such as Cambodian or Cambodia.

Hmong - Includes people who provide a response such as Hmong, Laohmong, or Mong.

Laotian - Includes people who provide a response such as Laotian, Laos, or Lao.

Thai - Includes people who provide a response such as Thai, Thailand, or Siamese.

Other Asian - Includes people who provide a response of Bangladeshi; Bhutanese; Burmese; Indochinese; Indonesian; Iwo Jiman; Madagascar; Malaysian; Maldivian; Nepalese; Okinawan; Pakistani; Singaporean; Sri Lankan; or Other Asian, specified and Other Asian, not specified.

Native Hawaiian or Other Pacific Islander: A person having origins in any of the original peoples of Hawaii, Guam, Samoa, or other Pacific Islands. It includes people who indicate their race as "Native Hawaiian," "Guamanian or Chamorro," "Samoan," and "Other Pacific Islander."

Native Hawaiian - Includes people who indicate their race as "Native Hawaiian" or who identify themselves as "Part Hawaiian" or "Hawaiian."

Guamanian or Chamorro - Includes people who indicate their race as such, including written entries of Chamorro or Guam.

Samoan - Includes people who indicate their race as "Samoan" or who identify themselves as American Samoan or Western Samoan.

Other Pacific Islander - Includes people who provide a write-in response of a Pacific Islander group, such as Carolinian, Chuukese (Trukese), Fijian, Kosraean, Melanesian, Micronesian, Northern Mariana Islander, Palauan, Papua New Guinean, Pohnpeian, Polynesian, Solomon Islander, Tahitian, Tokelauan, Tongan, Yapese, or Pacific Islander, not specified.

White: A person having origins in any of the original peoples of Europe, the Middle East, or North Africa. It includes people who indicate their race as "White" or report entries such as Irish, German, Italian, Lebanese, Near Easterner, Arab, or Polish.

Ancestries Based on Hispanic Origin

- Hispanic or Latino:
  - Central American:
    - Costa Rican
    - Guatemalan
    - Honduran
    - Nicaraguan
    - Panamanian
    - Salvadoran
    - Other Central American
  - Cuban
  - Dominican Republic
  - Mexican
  - Puerto Rican
  - South American:
    - Argentinean
    - Bolivian
    - Chilean
    - Colombian
    - Ecuadorian
    - Paraguayan
    - Peruvian
    - Uruguayan
    - Venezuelan
    - Other South American
  - Other Hispanic/Latino

The data on the Hispanic or Latino population were derived from answers to a question that was asked of all people. The terms "Spanish," "Hispanic origin," and "Latino" are used interchangeably. Some respondents identify with all three terms while others may identify with only one of these three specific terms. Hispanics or Latinos who identify with the terms "Spanish," "Hispanic," or "Latino" are those who classify themselves in one of the specific Spanish, Hispanic, or Latino categories listed on the questionnaire ("Mexican," "Puerto Rican," or "Cuban") as well as those who indicate that they are "other Spanish/Hispanic/Latino." People who do not identify with one of the specific origins listed on the questionnaire but indicate that they are "other Spanish, Hispanic, or Latino" are those whose origins are from Spain, the Spanish-speaking countries of Central or South America, the Dominican Republic, or people identifying themselves generally as Spanish, Spanish-American, Hispanic, Hispano, Latino, and so on. All write-in responses to the "other Spanish/Hispanic/Latino" category were coded.

Origin can be viewed as the heritage, nationality group, lineage, or country of birth of the person or the person's parents or ancestors before their arrival in the United States. People who identify their origin as Spanish, Hispanic, or Latino may be of any race.

In all cases where the origin of households, families, or occupied housing units is classified as Spanish, Hispanic, or Latino, the origin of the householder is used. If an individual could not provide a Hispanic origin response, their origin was assigned using specific rules of precedence of household relationship. For example, if origin was missing for a natural-born daughter in the household, then either the origin of the householder, another natural-born child, or spouse of the householder was assigned. If Hispanic origin was not reported for anyone in the household, the Hispanic origin of a householder in a previously processed household with the same race was assigned.

Other Ancestries

Acadian/Cajun
Afghan
African, Subsaharan:
- African
- Cape Verdean
- Ethiopian
- Ghanian
- Kenyan
- Liberian
- Nigerian
- Senegalese
- Sierra Leonean
- Somalian
- South African
- Sudanese
- Ugandan
- Zairian
- Zimbabwean
- Other Subsaharan African

Albanian
Alsatian
Arab:
- Arab/Arabic
- Egyptian
- Iraqi
- Jordanian
- Lebanese
- Moroccan
- Palestinian
- Syrian
- Other Arab

Armenian
Assyrian/Chaldean/Syriac
Australian
Austrian
Basque
Belgian
Brazilian
British
Bulgarian
Canadian
Carpatho Rusyn
Celtic
Croatian
Cypriot
Czech
Czechoslovakian
Danish
Dutch
Eastern European
English
Estonian
European
Finnish
French, except Basque
French Canadian
German
German Russian
Greek
Guyanese
Hungarian
Icelander
Iranian
Irish
Israeli
Italian
Latvian
Lithuanian
Luxemburger
Macedonian
Maltese
New Zealander
Northern European
Norwegian
Pennsylvania German
Polish
Portuguese
Romanian
Russian
Scandinavian
Scotch-Irish
Scottish
Serbian
Slavic
Slovak
Slovene
Soviet Union
Swedish
Swiss
Turkish
Ukrainian
United States or American
Welsh
West Indian, excluding Hispanic:
- Bahamian
- Barbadian
- Belizean
- Bermudan
- British West Indian
- Dutch West Indian
- Haitian
- Jamaican
- Trinidadian and Tobagonian
- U.S. Virgin Islander
- West Indian
- Other West Indian

Yugoslavian

The data on ancestry were derived from answers to long-form questionnaire Item 10, which was asked of a sample of the population. The data represent self-classification by people according to the ancestry group or groups with which they most closely identify. Ancestry refers to a person's ethnic origin or descent, "roots," heritage, or the place of birth of the person, the person's parents, or their ancestors before their arrival in the United States. Some ethnic identities, such as Egyptian or Polish, can be traced to geographic areas outside the United States, while other ethnicities, such as Pennsylvania German or Cajun, evolved in the United States.

The intent of the ancestry question was not to measure the degree of attachment the respondent had to a particular ethnicity. For example, a response of "Irish" might reflect total involvement in an Irish community or only a memory of ancestors several generations removed from the individual. Also, the question was intended to provide data for groups that were not included in the Hispanic origin and race questions. Official Hispanic origin data come from long-form questionnaire Item 5, and official race data come from long-form questionnaire Item 6. Therefore, although data on all groups are collected, the ancestry data shown in these tabulations are for non-Hispanic and non-race groups.

The ancestry question allowed respondents to report one or more ancestry groups, although only the first two were coded. If a response was in terms of a dual ancestry, for example, "Irish English," the person was assigned two codes, in this case one for Irish and another for English. However, in certain cases, multiple responses such as "French Canadian," "Greek Cypriote," and "Scotch Irish" were assigned a single code reflecting their status as unique groups. If a person reported one of these unique groups in addition to another group, for example, "Scotch Irish English," resulting in three terms, that person received one code for the unique group (Scotch-Irish) and another one for the remaining group (English). If a person reported "English Irish French," only English and Irish were coded. Certain combinations of ancestries where the ancestry group is a part of another, such as "German-Bavarian," were coded as a single ancestry using the more specific group (Bavarian). Also, responses such as "Polish-American" or "Italian-American" were coded and tabulated as a single entry (Polish or Italian).

The Census Bureau accepted "American" as a unique ethnicity if it was given alone, with an ambiguous response, or with state names. If the respondent listed any other ethnic identity such as "Italian-American," generally the "American" portion of the response was not coded. However, distinct groups such as "American Indian," "Mexican American," and "African American" were coded and identified separately because they represented groups who considered themselves different from those who reported as "Indian," "Mexican," or "African," respectively.

Census 2000 tabulations on ancestry are presented using two types of data presentations — one using total people as the base, and the other using total responses as the base. This chapter uses total responses as the base and includes the total number of ancestries reported and coded. If a person reported a multiple ancestry such as "French Danish," that response was counted twice in the tabulations — once in the French category and again in the Danish category. Thus, the sum of the counts in this type of presentation is not the total population but the total of all responses.

An automated coding system was used for coding ancestry in Census 2000. This greatly reduced the potential for error associated with a clerical review. Specialists with knowledge of the subject matter reviewed, edited, coded, and resolved inconsistent or incomplete responses. The code list used in Census 2000, containing over 1,000 categories, reflects the results of the Census Bureau's experience with the 1990 ancestry question, research, and consultation with many ethnic experts. Many decisions were made to determine the classification of responses. These decisions affected the grouping of the tabulated data. For example, the Italian category includes the responses of Sicilian and Tuscan, as well as a number of other responses.

Although some people consider religious affiliation a component of ethnic identity, the ancestry question was not designed to collect any information concerning religion. Thus, if a religion was given as an answer to the ancestry question, it was listed in the "Other groups" category which is not shown in this chapter.

Ancestry should not be confused with a person's place of birth, although a person's place of birth and ancestry may be the same.

Profiles Section

In the profiles section of this chapter, each community profile shows the name of the place, the type of place, the county (if a place spans more than one county, the county that holds the majority of the population is shown), and the 2000 population (based on 100-percent data from Summary File 1). Column one displays the ancestry name, column two displays the number of people reporting each ancestry, and column three is the percent of the total population reporting each ancestry. The population figure shown is used to calculate the value in the "%" column for ancestries based on race and Hispanic origin. The sample population figure from Summary File 3 (not shown) is used to calculate the value in the "%" column for all other ancestries.

For ancestries based on race data (White and African American/Black), the value in the "Number" column represents the total number of people who reported each category alone or in combination with one or more other race categories. This number represents the maximum number of people reporting and therefore the individual race categories may add to more than the total population because people may be included in more than one category. Tables P8 and P10 from SF1 were used for these categories.

For ancestries based on race data (American Indian or Alaska Native), the value in the "Number" column represents the total number of people who reported American Indian or Alaska Native alone or in combination with one or more other races, and with one or more tribes reported. This number represents the maximum number of people reporting and therefore the individual ancestries may add to more than the total population because people may be included in more than one category. Tables PCT1 and PCT3 from SF1 were used for these ancestries.

For ancestries based on race data (Asian), the value in the "Number" column represents the total number of people who reported Asian alone or in combination with one or more other races, and with one or more Asian categories. This number represents the maximum number of people reporting and therefore the individual ancestries may add to more than the total population because people may be included in more than one category. Tables PCT5 and PCT7 from SF1 were used for these ancestries.

For ancestries based on race data (Native Hawaiian and Other Pacific Islander), the value in the "Number" column represents the total number of people who reported Native Hawaiian and Other Pacific Islander alone or in combination with one or more other races, and with one or more Native Hawaiian and Other Pacific Islander categories. This number represents the maximum number of people reporting and therefore the individual ancestries may add to more than the total population because people may be included in more than one category. Tables PCT8 and PCT10 from SF1 were used for these ancestries.

The figures in parentheses (only available for ancestries based on race data) show the number of people that reported that particular ancestry alone. For example, in Phoenix, the entry for Korean shows 1,877 in parentheses and 2,462 in the "Number" column. This means that 1,877 people reported being Korean alone and 2,462 people reported being Korean alone or in combination with one or more other races.

For ancestries based on Hispanic Origin, the value in the "Number" column represents the number of people who reported being Mexican, Puerto Rican, Cuban or other Spanish/Hispanic/Latino (all written-in responses were coded). Table PCT11 from SF1 was used for these categories.

For ancestries in the "other" ancestries group, the value in the "Number" column includes multiple ancestries reported. For example, if a person reported a multiple ancestry such as "French Danish," that response was counted twice in the tabulations, once in the French category and again in the Danish category. Thus, the sum of the counts is not the total population but the total of all responses. Table PCT18 from SF3 was used for these categories.

Ranking Section

In the ranking section of this chapter, each ancestry has three tables. The first table shows the top 10 places sorted by number (based on all places, regardless of population), the second table shows the top 10 places sorted by percent (based on all places, regardless of population), the third table shows the top 10 places sorted by percent (based on places with populations of 10,000 or more).

Within each table, column one displays the place name, the state, and the county (if a place spans more than one county, the county that holds the majority of the population is shown). Column two displays the number of people reporting each ancestry, and column three is the percent of the total population reporting each ancestry. For tables representing ancestries based on race or Hispanic origin, the 100-percent population figure from SF1 is used to calculate the value in the "%" column. For all other ancestries the sample population figure from SF3 is used to calculate the value in the "%" column.

Alphabetical Ancestry Cross-Reference Guide

Acadian/Cajun
Afghan
African *See African, sub-Saharan: African*
African American/Black
African American/Black: Hispanic
African American/Black: Not Hispanic
African, sub-Saharan
African, sub-Saharan: African
African, sub-Saharan: Cape Verdean
African, sub-Saharan: Ethiopian
African, sub-Saharan: Ghanian
African, sub-Saharan: Kenyan
African, sub-Saharan: Liberian
African, sub-Saharan: Nigerian
African, sub-Saharan: Other
African, sub-Saharan: Senegalese
African, sub-Saharan: Sierra Leonean
African, sub-Saharan: Somalian
African, sub-Saharan: South African
African, sub-Saharan: Sudanese
African, sub-Saharan: Ugandan
African, sub-Saharan: Zairian
African, sub-Saharan: Zimbabwean
Alaska Athabascan *See Alaska Native: Alaska Athabascan*
Alaska Native tribes, not specified
Alaska Native tribes, specified
Alaska Native: Alaska Athabascan
Alaska Native: Aleut
Alaska Native: All other tribes
Alaska Native: Eskimo
Alaska Native: Tlingit-Haida
Albanian
Aleut *See Alaska Native: Aleut*
Alsatian
American *See United States or American*
American Indian or Alaska Native tribes, not specified
American Indian tribes, not specified
American Indian tribes, specified
American Indian: All other tribes
American Indian: Apache
American Indian: Blackfeet
American Indian: Cherokee
American Indian: Cheyenne
American Indian: Chickasaw
American Indian: Chippewa
American Indian: Choctaw
American Indian: Colville
American Indian: Comanche
American Indian: Cree
American Indian: Creek
American Indian: Crow
American Indian: Delaware
American Indian: Houma
American Indian: Iroquois
American Indian: Kiowa
American Indian: Latin American Indians
American Indian: Lumbee
American Indian: Menominee
American Indian: Navajo
American Indian: Osage
American Indian: Ottawa
American Indian: Paiute
American Indian: Pima
American Indian: Potawatomi
American Indian: Pueblo
American Indian: Puget Sound Salish
American Indian: Seminole
American Indian: Shoshone
American Indian: Sioux
American Indian: Tohono O'Odham
American Indian: Ute
American Indian: Yakama
American Indian: Yaqui
American Indian: Yuman
Apache *See American Indian: Apache*
Arab
Arab/Arabic *See Arab: Arab/Arabic*
Arab: Arab/Arabic
Arab: Egyptian
Arab: Iraqi
Arab: Jordanian
Arab: Lebanese
Arab: Moroccan
Arab: Other
Arab: Palestinian
Arab: Syrian
Argentinean *See Hispanic: Argentinean*
Armenian
Asian
Asian: Bangladeshi
Asian: Cambodian
Asian: Chinese, except Taiwanese
Asian: Filipino
Asian: Hmong
Asian: Indian
Asian: Indonesian
Asian: Japanese
Asian: Korean
Asian: Laotian
Asian: Malaysian
Asian: Other Asian, not specified
Asian: Other Asian, specified
Asian: Pakistani
Asian: Sri Lankan
Asian: Taiwanese
Asian: Thai
Asian: Vietnamese
Assyrian/Chaldean/Syriac
Australian
Austrian
Bahamian *See West Indian: Bahamian, excluding Hispanic*
Bangladeshi *See Asian: Bangladeshi*
Barbadian *See West Indian: Barbadian, excluding Hispanic*
Basque
Belgian
Belizean *See West Indian: Belizean, excluding Hispanic*
Bermudan *See West Indian: Bermudan, excluding Hispanic*
Blackfeet *See American Indian: Blackfeet*
Bolivian *See Hispanic: Bolivian*
Brazilian
British
British West Indian *See West Indian: British West Indian, excluding Hispanic*
Bulgarian
Cambodian *See Asian: Cambodian*
Canadian
Cape Verdean *See African, sub-Saharan: Cape Verdean*
Carpatho Rusyn
Celtic
Central American: *See Hispanic: Central American*
Cherokee *See American Indian: Cherokee*
Cheyenne *See American Indian: Cheyenne*
Chickasaw *See American Indian: Chickasaw*
Chilean *See Hispanic: Chilean*
Chinese, except Taiwanese *See Asian: Chinese, except Taiwanese*
Chippewa *See American Indian: Chippewa*
Choctaw *See American Indian: Choctaw*
Colombian *See Hispanic: Colombian*
Colville *See American Indian: Colville*
Comanche *See American Indian: Comanche*
Costa Rican *See Hispanic: Costa Rican*
Cree *See American Indian: Cree*
Creek *See American Indian: Creek*
Croatian
Crow *See American Indian: Crow*
Cuban *See Hispanic: Cuban*
Cypriot
Czech
Czechoslovakian
Danish
Delaware *See American Indian: Delaware*
Dominican Republic *See Hispanic: Dominican Republic*
Dutch
Dutch West Indian *See West Indian: Dutch West Indian, excluding Hispanic*
Eastern European
Ecuadorian *See Hispanic: Ecuadorian*
Egyptian *See Arab: Egyptian*
English
Eskimo *See Alaska Native: Eskimo*
Estonian
Ethiopian *See African, sub-Saharan: Ethiopian*
European
Fijian *See Hawaii Native/Pacific Islander: Fijian*
Filipino *See Asian: Filipino*
Finnish
French Canadian
French, except Basque
German
German Russian
Ghanian *See African, sub-Saharan: Ghanian*
Greek
Guamanian or Chamorro *See Hawaii Native/Pacific Islander: Guamanian or Chamorro*
Guatemalan *See Hispanic: Guatemalan*
Guyanese
Haitian *See West Indian: Haitian, excluding Hispanic*
Hawaii Native/Pacific Islander
Hawaii Native/Pacific Islander: Fijian
Hawaii Native/Pacific Islander: Guamanian or Chamorro
Hawaii Native/Pacific Islander: Melanesian
Hawaii Native/Pacific Islander: Micronesian
Hawaii Native/Pacific Islander: Native Hawaiian
Hawaii Native/Pacific Islander: Other Melanesian
Hawaii Native/Pacific Islander: Other Micronesian

Hawaii Native/Pacific Islander: Other Pacific Islander, not specified
Hawaii Native/Pacific Islander: Other Pacific Islander, specified
Hawaii Native/Pacific Islander: Other Polynesian
Hawaii Native/Pacific Islander: Polynesian
Hawaii Native/Pacific Islander: Samoan
Hawaii Native/Pacific Islander: Tongan
Hispanic or Latino
Hispanic: Argentinean
Hispanic: Bolivian
Hispanic: Central American
Hispanic: Chilean
Hispanic: Colombian
Hispanic: Costa Rican
Hispanic: Cuban
Hispanic: Dominican Republic
Hispanic: Ecuadorian
Hispanic: Guatemalan
Hispanic: Honduran
Hispanic: Mexican
Hispanic: Nicaraguan
Hispanic: Other
Hispanic: Other Central American
Hispanic: Other South American
Hispanic: Panamanian
Hispanic: Paraguayan
Hispanic: Peruvian
Hispanic: Puerto Rican
Hispanic: Salvadoran
Hispanic: South American
Hispanic: Uruguayan
Hispanic: Venezuelan
Hmong *See Asian: Hmong*
Honduran *See Hispanic: Honduran*
Houma *See American Indian: Houma*
Hungarian
Icelander
Indian, American *See American Indian*
Indian, Asian *See Asian: Indian*
Indonesian *See Asian: Indonesian*
Iranian
Iraqi *See Arab: Iraqi*
Irish
Iroquois *See American Indian: Iroquois*
Israeli
Italian
Jamaican *See West Indian: Jamaican, excluding Hispanic*
Japanese *See Asian: Japanese*
Jordanian *See Arab: Jordanian*
Kenyan *See African, sub-Saharan: Kenyan*
Kiowa *See American Indian: Kiowa*
Korean *See Asian: Korean*
Laotian *See Asian: Laotian*
Latin American Indians *See American Indian: Latin American Indians*
Latino *See Hispanic or Latino*
Latvian
Lebanese *See Arab: Lebanese*
Liberian *See African, sub-Saharan: Liberian*
Lithuanian
Lumbee *See American Indian: Lumbee*
Luxemburger
Macedonian
Malaysian *See Asian: Malaysian*
Maltese
Melanesian: *See Hawaii Native/Pacific Islander: Melanesian*
Menominee *See American Indian: Menominee*
Mexican *See Hispanic: Mexican*
Micronesian: *See Hawaii Native/Pacific Islander: Micronesian*
Moroccan *See Arab: Moroccan*
Native Hawaiian *See Hawaii Native/Pacific Islander: Native Hawaiian*
Navajo *See American Indian: Navajo*
New Zealander
Nicaraguan *See Hispanic: Nicaraguan*
Nigerian *See African, sub-Saharan: Nigerian*
Northern European
Norwegian
Osage *See American Indian: Osage*
Ottawa *See American Indian: Ottawa*
Paiute *See American Indian: Paiute*
Pakistani *See Asian: Pakistani*
Palestinian *See Arab: Palestinian*
Panamanian *See Hispanic: Panamanian*
Paraguayan *See Hispanic: Paraguayan*
Pennsylvania German
Peruvian *See Hispanic: Peruvian*
Pima *See American Indian: Pima*
Polish
Polynesian: *See Hawaii Native/Pacific Islander: Polynesian*
Portuguese
Potawatomi *See American Indian: Potawatomi*
Pueblo *See American Indian: Pueblo*
Puerto Rican *See Hispanic: Puerto Rican*
Puget Sound Salish *See American Indian: Puget Sound Salish*
Romanian
Russian
Salvadoran *See Hispanic: Salvadoran*
Samoan *See Hawaii Native/Pacific Islander: Samoan*
Scandinavian
Scotch-Irish
Scottish
Seminole *See American Indian: Seminole*
Senegalese *See African, sub-Saharan: Senegalese*
Serbian
Shoshone *See American Indian: Shoshone*
Sierra Leonean *See African, sub-Saharan: Sierra Leonean*
Sioux *See American Indian: Sioux*
Slavic
Slovak
Slovene
Somalian *See African, sub-Saharan: Somalian*
South African *See African, sub-Saharan: South African*
South American: *See Hispanic: South American*
Soviet Union
Sri Lankan *See Asian: Sri Lankan*
sub-Saharan African *See African, sub-Saharan*
Sudanese *See African, sub-Saharan: Sudanese*
Swedish
Swiss
Syrian *See Arab: Syrian*
Taiwanese *See Asian: Taiwanese*
Thai *See Asian: Thai*
Tlingit-Haida *See Alaska Native: Tlingit-Haida*
Tohono O'Odham *See American Indian: Tohono O'Odham*
Tongan *See Hawaii Native/Pacific Islander: Tongan*
Trinidadian and Tobagonian *See West Indian: Trinidadian and Tobagonian, excluding Hispanic*
Turkish
U.S. Virgin Islander *See West Indian: U.S. Virgin Islander, excluding Hispanic*
Ugandan *See African, sub-Saharan: Ugandan*
Ukrainian
United States or American
Uruguayan *See Hispanic: Uruguayan*
Ute *See American Indian: Ute*
Venezuelan *See Hispanic: Venezuelan*
Vietnamese *See Asian: Vietnamese*
Welsh
West Indian, excluding Hispanic
West Indian: Bahamian, excluding Hispanic
West Indian: Barbadian, excluding Hispanic
West Indian: Belizean, excluding Hispanic
West Indian: Bermudan, excluding Hispanic
West Indian: British West Indian, excluding Hispanic
West Indian: Dutch West Indian, excluding Hispanic
West Indian: Haitian, excluding Hispanic
West Indian: Jamaican, excluding Hispanic
West Indian: Other, excluding Hispanic
West Indian: Trinidadian and Tobagonian, excluding Hispanic
West Indian: U.S. Virgin Islander, excluding Hispanic
West Indian: West Indian, excluding Hispanic
White
White: Hispanic
White: Not Hispanic
Yakama *See American Indian: Yakama*
Yaqui *See American Indian: Yaqui*
Yugoslavian
Yuman *See American Indian: Yuman*
Zairian *See African, sub-Saharan: Zairian*
Zimbabwean *See African, sub-Saharan: Zimbabwean*

User's Guide: Hispanic Population

Places Covered

United States and State of Florida

39 counties with populations over 99,999.

38 incorporated municipalities with populations over 49,999. Municipalities are incorporated as either cities, towns, or villages. A few municipalities have a form of government combined with another entity (e.g. county) and are listed as "special cities."

9 census designated places (CDP) with populations over 49,999. The U.S. Bureau of the Census defines a CDP as "a statistical entity, defined for each decennial census according to Census Bureau guidelines, comprising a densely settled concentration of population that is not within an incorporated place, but is locally identified by a name. CDPs are delineated cooperatively by state and local officials and the Census Bureau, following Census Bureau guidelines. Beginning with Census 2000 there are no size limits."

Note: *Ranking tables include all places in Florida with Hispanic residents. Places with no Hispanic residents have been excluded.*

For a more in-depth discussion of geographic areas, please refer to the Census Bureau's Geographic Areas Reference Manual at http://www.census.gov/geo/www/garm.html.

Source of Data

CENSUS 2000

Data for this section was derived from following source: *U.S. Bureau of the Census, Census of Population and Housing, 2000: Summary File 4.* Summary File 4 (SF 4) contains sample data, which is the information compiled from the questions asked of a sample (generally 1-in-6) of all people and housing units. Summary File 4 is repeated or iterated for the total population and 335 additional population groups. This chapter focuses on the following 24 population groups:

- Hispanic or Latino (of any race)
  - Central American
    - Costa Rican
    - Guatemalan
    - Honduran
    - Nicaraguan
    - Panamanian
    - Salvadoran
  - Cuban
  - Dominican (Dominican Republic)
  - Mexican
  - Puerto Rican
  - South American
    - Argentinian
    - Bolivian
    - Chilean
    - Colombian
    - Ecuadorian
    - Paraguayan
    - Peruvian
    - Uruguayan
    - Venezuelan
  - Spaniard
  - Other Hispanic or Latino

Please note that the above list only includes Spanish-speaking population groups. Groups such as Brazilian are not classified as Hispanic by the Bureau of the Census because they primarily speak Portugese.

In order for any of the tables for a specific group to be shown in Summary File 4, the data must meet a minimum population threshold. For Summary File 4, all tables are repeated for each race group, American Indian and Alaska Native tribe, and Hispanic or Latino group if the 100-percent count of people of that specific group in a particular geographic area is 100 or more. There also must be 50 or more unweighted people of that specific group in a particular geographic area. For example, if there are 100 or more 100-percent people tabulated as Chilean in County A, and there are 50 or more unweighted people, then all matrices for Chilean are shown in SF 4 for County A.

To maintain confidentiality, the Census Bureau applies statistical procedures that introduce some uncertainty into data for small geographic areas with small population groups. Therefore, tables may contain both sampling and nonsampling error.

In an iterated file such as SF 4, the universes *households, families,* and *occupied housing units* are classified by the race or ethnic group of the householder. In any population table where there is no note, the universe classification is always based on the race or ethnicity of the person. In all housing tables, the universe classification is based on the race or ethnicity of the householder.

Comparing SF 4 Estimates with Corresponding Values in SF 1 and SF 2

As in earlier censuses, the responses from the sample of households reporting on long forms must be weighted to reflect the entire population. Specifically, each responding household represents, on average, six or seven other households who reported using short forms. One consequence of the weighting procedures is that each estimate based on the long form responses has an associated confidence interval. These confidence intervals are wider (as a percentage of the estimate) for geographic areas with smaller populations and for characteristics that occur less frequently in the area being examined (such as the proportion of people in poverty in a middle-income neighborhood).

In order to release as much useful information as possible, statisticians must balance a number of factors. In particular, for Census 2000, the Bureau of the Census created weighting areas—geographic areas from which about two hundred or more long forms were completed—which are large enough to produce good quality estimates. If smaller weighting areas had been used, the confidence intervals around the estimates would have been significantly wider, rendering many estimates less useful due to their lower reliability. The disadvantage of using weighting areas this large is that, for smaller geographic areas within them, the estimates of characteristics that are also reported on the short form will not match the counts reported in SF 1 or SF 2. Examples of these characteristics are the total number of people, the number of people reporting specific racial categories, and the number of housing units. The official values for items reported on the short form come from SF 1 and SF 2. The differences between the long form estimates in SF 4 and values in SF 1 or SF 2 are particularly noticeable for the smallest places, tracts, and block groups. The long form estimates of total population and total housing units in SF 4 will, however, match the SF 1 and SF 2 counts for larger geographic areas such as counties and states, and will be essentially the same for medium and large cities. This phenomenon also occurred for the 1990 Census, although in that case, the weighting areas included relatively small places. As a result, the long form estimates matched the short form counts for those places, but the confidence intervals around the estimates of characteristics collected only on the long form were often significantly wider (as a percentage of the estimate). SF 1 gives exact numbers even for very small groups and areas; whereas, SF 4 gives estimates for small groups and areas such as tracts and small places that are less exact. The goal of SF 4 is to identify large differences among areas or large changes over time. Estimates for small areas and small population groups often do exhibit large changes from one census to the next, so having the capability to measure them is worthwhile.

Topics

POPULATION

Total Population: Sample count of total population.

Hispanic Population: The data on the Hispanic or Latino population, which was asked of all people, were derived from answers to long-form questionnaire Item 5, and short-form questionnaire Item 7. The terms "Spanish," "Hispanic origin," and "Latino" are used interchangeably. Some respondents identify with all three terms, while others may identify with only one of these three specific terms. Hispanics or Latinos who identify with the terms "Spanish," "Hispanic," or "Latino" are those who classify themselves in one of the specific Hispanic or Latino categories listed on the questionnaire — "Mexican," "Puerto Rican," or "Cuban" — as well as those who indicate that they are "other Spanish, Hispanic, or Latino." People who do not identify with one of the specific origins listed on the questionnaire but indicate that they are "other Spanish, Hispanic, or Latino" are those whose origins are from Spain, the Spanish-speaking countries of Central or South America, the Dominican Republic, or people identifying themselves generally as Spanish, Spanish-American, Hispanic, Hispano, Latino, and so on. All write-in responses to the "other Spanish/Hispanic/Latino" category were coded. Origin can be viewed as the heritage, nationality group, lineage, or country of birth of the person or the person's parents or ancestors before their arrival in the United States. People who identify their origin as Spanish, Hispanic, or Latino may be of any race.

Population groups whose primary language is not Spanish are not classified as Hispanic by the Bureau of the Census and are not included in this chapter (eg. Brazilian).

AGE

Median Age: Divides the age distribution into two equal parts: one-half of the cases falling below the median age and one-half above the median. Median age is computed on the basis of a single year of age standard distribution.

The data on age, which was asked of all people, were derived from answers to the long-form questionnaire Item 4 and short-form questionnaire Item 6. The age classification is based on the age of the person in complete years as of April 1, 2000. The age of the person usually was derived from their date of birth information. Their reported age was used only when date of birth information was unavailable.

HOUSEHOLD SIZE

Average Household Size: A measure obtained by dividing the number of people in households by the total number of households (or householders). In cases where household members are tabulated by race or Hispanic origin, household members are classified by the race or Hispanic origin of the householder rather than the race or Hispanic origin of each individual. Average household size is rounded to the nearest hundredth.

LANGUAGE SPOKEN AT HOME

English Only: Number and percentage of population 5 years and over who report speaking English-only at home.

Spanish: Number and percentage of population 5 years and over who report speaking Spanish at home.

Language spoken at home data were derived from answers to long-form questionnaire Items 11a and 11b, which were asked of a sample of the population. Data were edited to include in tabulations only the population 5 years old and over. Questions 11a and 11b referred to languages spoken at home in an effort to measure the current use of languages other than English. People who knew languages other than English but did not use them at home or who only used them elsewhere were excluded. Most people who reported speaking a language other than English at home also speak English. The questions did not permit determination of the primary or dominant language of people who spoke both English and another language.

FOREIGN-BORN

Foreign Born: Number and percentage of population who were not U.S. citizens at birth. Foreign-born people are those who indicated they were either a U.S. citizen by naturalization or they were not a citizen of the United States.

Foreign-Born Naturalized Citizens: Number and percentage of population who were not U.S. citizens at birth but became U.S. citizens by naturalization.

The data on place of birth were derived from answers to long-form questionnaire Item 12 which was asked of a sample of the population. Respondents were asked to report the U.S. state, Puerto Rico, U.S. Island Area, or foreign country where they were born. People not reporting a place of birth were assigned the state or country of birth of another family member or their residence 5 years earlier, or were imputed the response of another person with similar characteristics. People born outside the United States were asked to report their place of birth according to current international boundaries. Since numerous changes in boundaries of foreign countries have occurred in the last century, some people may have reported their place of birth in terms of boundaries that existed at the time of their birth or emigration, or in accordance with their own national preference.

EDUCATIONAL ATTAINMENT

High School Graduates: Number and percentage of the population age 25 and over who have a high school diploma or higher. This category includes people whose highest degree was a high school diploma or its equivalent, people who attended college but did not receive a degree, and people who received a college, university, or professional degree. People who reported completing the 12th grade but not receiving a diploma are not high school graduates.

4-Years College Graduates: Number and percentage of the population age 25 and over who have a 4-year college, university, or professional degree.

Data on educational attainment were derived from answers to long-form questionnaire Item 9, which was asked of a sample of the population. Data on attainment are tabulated for the population 25 years old and over.

The order in which degrees were listed on the questionnaire suggested that doctorate degrees were "higher" than professional school degrees, which were "higher" than master's degrees. The question included instructions for people currently enrolled in school to report the level of the previous grade attended or the highest degree received. Respondents who did not report educational attainment or enrollment level were assigned the attainment of a person of the same age, race, Hispanic or Latino origin, occupation and sex, where possible, who resided in the same or a nearby area. Respondents who filled more than one box were edited to the highest level or degree reported.

The question included a response category that allowed respondents to report completing the 12th grade without receiving a high school diploma. It allowed people who received either a high school diploma or the equivalent (Test of General Educational Development—G.E.D.) and did not attend college, to be reported as "high school graduate(s)." The category "Associate degree" included people whose highest degree is an associate degree, which generally requires 2 years of college level work and is either in an occupational program that prepares them for a specific occupation, or an academic program primarily in the arts and sciences. The course work may or may not be transferable to a bachelor's degree. Master's degrees include the traditional MA and MS degrees and field-specific degrees, such as MSW, MEd, MBA, MLS, and MEng. Some examples of professional degrees include medicine, dentistry, chiropractic, optometry, osteopathic medicine, pharmacy, podiatry, veterinary medicine, law, and theology. Vocational and technical training such as barber school training; business, trade, technical, and vocational schools; or other training for a specific trade, are specifically excluded.

INCOME AND POVERTY

Median Household Income (in dollars): Includes the income of the householder and all other individuals 15 years old and over in the household, whether they are related to the householder or not. The median divides the income distribution into two equal parts: one-half of the cases falling below the median income and one-half above the median. For households, the median income is based on the distribution of the total number of households including those with no income. Median income for households is computed on the basis of a standard distribution and is rounded to the nearest whole dollar.

Per Capita Income (in dollars): Per capita income is the mean income computed for every man, woman, and child in a particular group. It is derived by dividing the total income of a particular group by the total population in that group. Per capita income is rounded to the nearest whole dollar.

The data on income in 1999 were derived from answers to long-form questionnaire Items 31 and 32, which were asked of a sample of the population 15 years old and over. "Total income" is the sum of the amounts reported separately for wage or salary income; net self-employment income; interest, dividends, or net rental or royalty income or income from estates and trusts; social security or railroad retirement income; Supplemental Security Income (SSI); public assistance or welfare payments; retirement, survivor, or disability pensions; and all other income.

Receipts from the following sources are not included as income: capital gains, money received from the sale of property (unless the recipient was engaged in the business of selling such property); the value of income "in kind" from food stamps, public housing subsidies, medical care, employer contributions for individuals, etc.; withdrawal of bank deposits; money borrowed; tax refunds; exchange of money between relatives living in the same household; and gifts and lump-sum inheritances, insurance payments, and other types of lump-sum receipts.

The eight types of income reported in the census are defined as follows:

Wage or salary income. Wage or salary income includes total money earnings received for work performed as an employee during the calendar year 1999. It includes wages, salary, armed forces pay, commissions, tips, piece-rate payments, and cash bonuses earned before deductions were made for taxes, bonds, pensions, union dues, etc.

Self-employment income. Self-employment income includes both farm and nonfarm self-employment income. Nonfarm self-employment income includes net money income (gross receipts minus expenses) from one's own business, professional enterprise, or partnership. Gross receipts include the value of all goods sold and services rendered. Expenses include costs of goods purchased, rent, heat, light, power, depreciation charges, wages and salaries paid, business taxes (not personal income taxes), etc. Farm self-employment income includes net money income (gross receipts minus operating expenses) from the operation of a farm by a person on his or her own account, as an owner, renter, or sharecropper. Gross receipts include the value of all products sold, government farm programs, money received from the rental of farm equipment to others, and incidental receipts from the sale of wood, sand, gravel, etc. Operating expenses include cost of feed, fertilizer, seed, and other farming supplies, cash wages paid to farmhands, depreciation charges, cash rent, interest on farm mortgages, farm building repairs, farm taxes (not state and federal personal income taxes), etc. The value of fuel, food, or other farm products used for family living is not included as part of net income.

Interest, dividends, or net rental income. Interest, dividends, or net rental income includes interest on savings or bonds, dividends from stockholdings or membership in associations, net income from rental of property to others and receipts from boarders or lodgers, net royalties, and periodic payments from an estate or trust fund.

Social Security income. Social security income includes social security pensions and survivors benefits, permanent disability insurance payments made by the Social Security Administration prior to deductions for medical insurance, and railroad retirement insurance checks from the U.S. government. Medicare reimbursements are not included.

Supplemental Security Income (SSI). Supplemental Security Income (SSI) is a nationwide U.S. assistance program administered by the Social Security Administration that guarantees a minimum level of income for needy aged, blind, or disabled individuals. The census questionnaire for Puerto Rico asked about the receipt of SSI; however, SSI is not a federally administered program in Puerto Rico. Therefore, it is probably not being interpreted by most respondents as the same as SSI in the United States. The only way a resident of Puerto Rico could have appropriately reported SSI would have been if they lived in the United States at any time during calendar year 1999 and received SSI.

Public assistance income. Public assistance income includes general assistance and Temporary Assistance to Needy Families (TANF). Separate payments received for hospital or other medical care (vendor payments) are excluded. This does not include Supplemental Security Income (SSI).

Retirement income. Retirement income includes: (1) retirement pensions and survivor benefits from a former employer; labor union; or federal, state, or local government; and the U.S. military; (2) income from workers' compensation; disability income from companies or unions; federal, state, or local government; and the U.S. military; (3) periodic receipts from annuities and insurance; and (4) regular income from IRA and KEOGH plans. This does not include social security income.

All other income. All other income includes unemployment compensation, Veterans' Administration (VA) payments, alimony and child support, contributions received periodically from people not living in the household, military family allotments, and other kinds of periodic income other than earnings.

Poverty Status: Number and percentage of population with income in 1999 below the poverty level. Based on individuals for whom poverty status is determined. Poverty status was determined for all people except institutionalized people, people in military group quarters, people in college dormitories, and unrelated individuals under 15 years old.

The poverty status of families and unrelated individuals in 1999 was determined using 48 thresholds (income cutoffs) arranged in a two dimensional matrix. The matrix consists of family size (from 1 person to 9 or more people) cross-classified by presence and number of family members under 18 years old (from no children present to 8 or more children present). Unrelated individuals and 2-person families were further differentiated by the age of the reference person (RP) (under 65 years old and 65 years old and over).

To determine a person's poverty status, one compares the person's total family income with the poverty threshold appropriate for that person's family size and composition. If the total income of that person's family is less than the threshold appropriate for that family, then the person is considered poor, together with every member of his or her family. If a person is not living with anyone related by birth, marriage, or adoption, then the person's own income is compared with his or her poverty threshold.

HOUSING

Homeownership: Number and percentage of housing units that are owner-occupied.

The data on tenure, which was asked at all occupied housing units, were obtained from answers to long-form questionnaire Item 33, and short-form questionnaire Item 2. All occupied housing units are classified as either owner occupied or renter occupied.

A housing unit is owner occupied if the owner or co-owner lives in the unit even if it is mortgaged or not fully paid for. The owner or co-owner must live in the unit and usually is Person 1 on the questionnaire. The unit is "Owned by you or someone in this household with a mortgage or loan" if it is being purchased with a mortgage or some other debt arrangement, such as a deed of trust, trust deed, contract to purchase, land contract, or purchase agreement. The unit is also considered owned with a mortgage if it is built on leased land and there is a mortgage on the unit. Mobile homes occupied by owners with installment loans balances are also included in this category.

Median Gross Rent (in dollars): Median monthly gross rent on specified renter-occupied and specified vacant-for-rent units. Specified renter-occupied and specified vacant-for-rent units exclude 1-family houses on 10 acres or more.

The data on gross rent were obtained from answers to long-form questionnaire Items 45a-d, which were asked on a sample basis. Gross rent is the contract rent plus the estimated average monthly cost of utilities (electricity, gas, water and sewer) and fuels (oil, coal, kerosene, wood, etc.) if these are paid by the renter (or paid for the renter by someone else). Gross rent is intended to eliminate differentials that result from varying practices with respect to the inclusion of utilities and fuels as part of the rental payment. The estimated costs of utilities and fuels are reported on an annual basis but are converted to monthly figures for the tabulations. Renter units occupied without payment of cash rent are shown separately as "No cash rent" in the tabulations.

Housing units that are renter occupied without payment of cash rent are shown separately as "No cash rent" in census data products. The unit may be owned by friends or relatives who live elsewhere and who allow occupancy without charge. Rent-free houses or apartments may be provided to compensate caretakers, ministers, tenant farmers, sharecroppers, or others.

Contract rent is the monthly rent agreed to or contracted for, regardless of any furnishings, utilities, fees, meals, or services that may be included. For vacant units, it is the monthly rent asked for the rental unit at the time of enumeration.

If the contract rent includes rent for a business unit or for living quarters occupied by another household, only that part of the rent estimated to be for the respondent's unit was included. Excluded was any rent paid for additional units or for business premises.

If a renter pays rent to the owner of a condominium or cooperative, and the condominium fee or cooperative carrying charge also is paid by the renter to the owner, the condominium fee or carrying charge was included as rent.

If a renter receives payments from lodgers or roomers who are listed as members of the household, the rent without deduction for any payments received from the lodgers or roomers was to be reported. The respondent was to report the rent agreed to or contracted for even if paid by someone else such as friends or relatives living elsewhere, a church or welfare agency, or the government through subsidies or vouchers.

The median divides the rent distribution into two equal parts: one-half of the cases falling below the median contract rent and one-half above the median. Median contract rents are computed on the basis of a standard distribution and are rounded to the nearest whole dollar. Units reported as "No cash rent" are excluded.

Median Home Value (in dollars): Reported by the owner of specified owner-occupied or specified vacant-for-sale housing units. Specified owner-occupied and specified vacant-for-sale housing units include only 1-family houses on less than 10 acres without a business or medical office on the property. The data for "specified units" exclude mobile homes, houses with a business or medical office, houses on 10 or more acres, and housing units in multi-unit buildings.

The data on value (also referred to as "price asked" for vacant units) were obtained from answers to long-form questionnaire Item 51, which was asked on a sample basis at owner-occupied housing units and units that were being bought, or vacant for sale at the time of enumeration. Value is the respondent's estimate of how much the property (house and lot, mobile home and lot, or condominium unit) would sell for if it were for sale. If the house or mobile home was owned or being bought, but the land on which it sits was not, the respondent was asked to estimate the combined value of the house or mobile home and the land. For vacant units, value was the price asked for the property. Value was tabulated separately for all owner-occupied and vacant-for-sale housing units, owner-occupied and vacant-for-sale mobile homes, and specified owner-occupied and specified vacant-for-sale housing units.

The median divides the value distribution into two equal parts: one-half of the cases falling below the median value of the property (house and lot, mobile home and lot, or condominium unit) and one-half above the median. Median values are computed on the basis of a standard distribution and are rounded to the nearest hundred dollars.

How to Read the Tables

There are three types of tables located in Section I.

Type I (1 line per entry). Six tables fall into this category: Median Age; Average Household Size; Median Household Income; Per Capita Income; Median Gross Rent; Median Home Value.

Place	All households	Hispanic households	Argentinian	Bolivian
UNITED STATES	41,994	33,676	46,091	47,245
ALABAMA	34,135	30,366	-	-
Baldwin County	40,250	39,702	-	-
Calhoun County	31,768	30,442	-	-
Etowah County	31,170	27,560	-	-
Dothan (city)	35,000	28,333	-	-

← Each line represents a number (eg. median household income, median age, etc.)

For example:

The median household income of Bolivians in the U.S. is $47,245

Type II (3 lines per entry). One table falls into this category: Population.

Place	Total population	① Total Hispanic population	② Argentinian	Bolivian
UNITED STATES	281,421,906	35,238,481 12.52	107,275 0.30 0.04	45,188 0.13 0.02
ALABAMA	4,447,100	72,627 1.63	-	-
Baldwin County	140,415	2,341 1.67	-	-

← The first line shows the number of persons

← The second line shows the number as a percentage of the total Hispanic population (column 2)

← The third line shows the number as a percentage of the total population (column 1)

For example:

There are 45,188 Bolivians in the U.S.

Bolivians make up 0.13% of the total Hispanic population in the U.S.

Bolivians make up 0.02% of the total population of the U.S.

Type III (5 lines per entry). Eight tables fall into this category: Language Spoken at Home: English Only; Language Spoken at Home: Spanish; Foreign Born; Foreign-Born Naturalized Citizens; Educational Attainment: High School Graduates; Educational Attainment: Four-Year College Graduates; Poverty Status; Homeownership

Place	① Total population 25 years and over who are 4-year college grads.	② Hispanic population 25 years and over	③ Hispanics 25 years and over who are 4-year college graduates	Argentinian	Bolivian
UNITED STATES	44,462,605 24.40	18,270,377	1,908,039 10.44 10.44 4.29	27,118 35.26 1.42 0.15 0.06	8,127 28.81 0.43 0.04 0.02
ALABAMA	549,608 19.03	36,486	5,320 14.58 14.58 0.97	-	-

The first line shows the number of persons

The second line shows the number as a percentage rate

The third line shows the number as a percentage of column 3

The fourth line shows the number as a percentage of column 2

The fifth line shows the number as a percentage of column 1

EXAMPLE

There are 8,127 Bolivian 4-year college graduates in the U.S.

The Bolivian 4-year college graduation rate is 28.81% in the U.S.

0.43% of Hispanic 4-year college graduates in the U.S. are Bolivian

0.04% of Hispanics in the U.S. are Bolivian 4-year college graduates

0.02% of all 4-year college graduates in the U.S. are Bolivian

Note: all numbers are based on persons 25 years and over

General Note: A dash indicates that data for that specific population group within the associated geographic area is less than the threshold(s). The population threshold on Summary File 4 is 100. In addition, there must be at least 50 or more unweighted cases of the population group. However, numbers less than 100 may appear because the thresholds apply to the entire universe (e.g. Population 5 years and over), not the specific data element (e.g. Speak only English). In addition, numbers may not add up to totals and percentages may not add up to 100% within the same row.

User's Guide: Asian Population

Places Covered

United States and State of Florida

38 counties with populations over 49,999.

7 incorporated municipalities with populations over 9,999 whose Asian and/or Native Hawaiian and other Pacific Islander population rates are greater than the national average. Depending on the state, municipalities are incorporated as either cities, towns, villages, or boroughs. A few municipalities have a form of government combined with another entity (e.g. county) and are listed as "special cities."

8 census designated places (CDP) with populations over 9,999 whose Asian and/or Native Hawaiian and other Pacific Islander population rates are greater than the national average. The U.S. Bureau of the Census defines a CDP as "a statistical entity, defined for each decennial census according to Census Bureau guidelines, comprising a densely settled concentration of population that is not within an incorporated place, but is locally identified by a name. CDPs are delineated cooperatively by state and local officials and the Census Bureau, following Census Bureau guidelines. Beginning with Census 2000 there are no size limits."

Note: *Ranking tables include all places in Florida with Asian and/or Native Hawaiian and other Pacific Islander residents. Places with no Asian/Native Hawaiian and Other Pacific Islander residents have been excluded.*

Source of Data

CENSUS 2000

Data for this chapter was derived from following source: *U.S. Bureau of the Census, Census of Population and Housing, 2000: Summary File 4.* Summary File 4 (SF 4) contains sample data, which is the information compiled from the questions asked of a sample (generally 1-in-6) of all people and housing units. Summary File 4 is repeated or iterated for the total population and 335 additional population groups. This chapter focuses on the following 23 population groups:

Asian
- Asian Indian
- Bangladeshi
- Cambodian
- Chinese (except Taiwanese)
- Filipino
- Hmong
- Indonesian
- Japanese
- Korean
- Laotian
- Malaysian
- Pakistani
- Sri Lankan
- Taiwanese
- Thai
- Vietnamese

Native Hawaiian and Other Pacific Islander
- Fijian
- Guamanian or Chamorro
- Hawaiian, Native
- Samoan
- Tongan

Please note that this chapter only includes people who responded to the question on race by indicating only one race. These people are classified by the Census Bureau as the race *alone* population. For example, respondents reporting a single detailed Asian group, such as Korean or Filipino, would be included in the Asian *alone* population. Respondents reporting more than one detailed Asian group, such as Chinese and Japanese or Asian Indian and Chinese and Vietnamese would also be included in the Asian *alone* population. This is because all of the detailed groups in these example combinations are part of the larger Asian race category. The same criteria apply to the Native Hawaiian and Other Pacific Islander groups.

In order for any of the tables for a specific group to be shown in Summary File 4, the data must meet a minimum population threshold. For Summary File 4, all tables are repeated for each race group, American Indian and Alaska Native tribe, and Hispanic or Latino group if the 100-percent count of people of that specific group in a particular geographic area is 100 or more. There also must be 50 or more unweighted people of that specific group in a particular geographic area. For example, if there are 100 or more 100-percent people tabulated as Korean in County A, and there are 50 or more unweighted people, then all matrices for Korean are shown in SF 4 for County A.

To maintain confidentiality, the Census Bureau applies statistical procedures that introduce some uncertainty into data for small geographic areas with small population groups. Therefore, tables may contain both sampling and nonsampling error.

In an iterated file such as SF 4, the universes *households, families,* and *occupied housing units* are classified by the race or ethnic group of the householder. In any population table where there is no note, the universe classification is always based on the race or ethnicity of the person. In all housing tables, the universe classification is based on the race or ethnicity of the householder.

Comparing SF 4 Estimates with Corresponding Values in SF 1 and SF 2

As in earlier censuses, the responses from the sample of households reporting on long forms must be weighted to reflect the entire population. Specifically, each responding household represents, on average, six or seven other households who reported using short forms. One consequence of the weighting procedures is that each estimate based on the long form responses has an associated confidence interval. These confidence intervals are wider (as a percentage of the estimate) for geographic areas with smaller populations and for characteristics that occur less frequently in the area being examined (such as the proportion of people in poverty in a middle-income neighborhood). In order to release as much useful information as possible, statisticians must balance a number of factors. In particular, for Census 2000, the Bureau of the Census created weighting areas—geographic areas from which about two hundred or more long forms were completed—which are large enough to produce good quality estimates. If smaller weighting areas had been used, the confidence intervals around the estimates would have been significantly wider, rendering many estimates less useful due to their lower reliability. The disadvantage of using weighting areas this large is that, for smaller geographic areas within them, the estimates of characteristics that are also reported on the short form will not match the counts reported in SF 1 or SF 2. Examples of these characteristics are the total number of people, the number of people reporting specific racial categories, and the number of housing units. The official values for items reported on the short form come from SF 1 and SF 2. The differences between the long form estimates in SF 4 and values in SF 1 or SF 2 are particularly noticeable for the smallest places, tracts, and block groups. The long form estimates of total population and total housing units in SF 4 will, however, match the SF 1 and SF 2 counts for larger geographic areas such as counties and states, and will be essentially the same for medium and large cities. This phenomenon also occurred for the 1990 Census, although in that case, the weighting areas included relatively small places. As a result, the long form estimates matched the short form counts for those places, but the confidence intervals around the estimates of characteristics collected only on the long form were often significantly wider (as a percentage of the estimate). SF 1 gives exact numbers even for very small groups and areas; whereas, SF 4 gives estimates for small groups and areas such as tracts and small places that are less exact. The goal of SF 4 is to identify large differences among areas or large changes over time. Estimates for small areas and small population groups often do exhibit large changes from one census to the next, so having the capability to measure them is worthwhile.

Topics

POPULATION

Total Population: Sample count of total population of all races.

Asian Population: A person having origins in any of the original peoples of the Far East, Southeast Asia, or the Indian subcontinent including, for example, Cambodia, China, India, Japan, Korea, Malaysia, Pakistan, the Philippine Islands, Thailand, and Vietnam. It includes Asian Indian, Bangladeshi, Cambodian, Chinese (except Taiwanese), Filipino, Hmong, Indonesian, Japanese, Korean, Laotian, Malaysian, Pakistani, Sri Lankan, Taiwanese, Thai, and Vietnamese.

Native Hawaiian or Other Pacific Islander (NHPI) Population: A person having origins in any of the original peoples of Hawaii, Guam, Samoa, or other Pacific Islands. It includes people who indicate their race as Fijian, Guamanian or Chamorro, Native Hawaiian, Samoan, and Tongan.

The data on race, which was asked of all people, were derived from answers to long-form questionnaire Item 6 and short-form questionnaire Item 8. The concept of race, as used by the Census Bureau, reflects self-identification by people according to the race or races with which they most closely identify. These categories are socio-political constructs and should not be interpreted as being scientific or anthropological in nature. Furthermore, the race categories include both racial and national-origin groups.

If an individual did not provide a race response, the race or races of the householder or other household members were assigned using specific rules of precedence of household relationship. For example, if race was missing for a natural-born child in the household, then either the race or races of the householder, another natural-born child, or the spouse of the householder were assigned. If race was not reported for anyone in the household, the race or races of a householder in a previously processed household were assigned.

AGE

Median Age: Divides the age distribution into two equal parts: one-half of the cases falling below the median age and one-half above the median. Median age is computed on the basis of a single year of age standard distribution.

The data on age, which was asked of all people, were derived from answers to the long-form questionnaire Item 4 and short-form questionnaire Item 6. The age classification is based on the age of the person in complete years as of April 1, 2000. The age of the person usually was derived from their date of birth information. Their reported age was used only when date of birth information was unavailable.

HOUSEHOLD SIZE

Average Household Size: A measure obtained by dividing the number of people in households by the total number of households (or householders). In cases where household members are tabulated by race or Hispanic origin, household members are classified by the race or Hispanic origin of the householder rather than the race or Hispanic origin of each individual. Average household size is rounded to the nearest hundredth.

LANGUAGE SPOKEN AT HOME

English Only: Number and percentage of population 5 years and over who report speaking English-only at home.

Language spoken at home data were derived from answers to long-form questionnaire Items 11a and 11b, which were asked of a sample of the population. Data were edited to include in tabulations only the population 5 years old and over. Questions 11a and 11b referred to languages spoken at home in an effort to measure the current use of languages other than English. People who knew languages other than English but did not use them at home or who only used them elsewhere were excluded. Most people who reported speaking a language other than English at home also speak English. The questions did not permit determination of the primary or dominant language of people who spoke both English and another language.

FOREIGN-BORN

Foreign Born: Number and percentage of population who were not U.S. citizens at birth. Foreign-born people are those who indicated they were either a U.S. citizen by naturalization or they were not a citizen of the United States.

Foreign-Born Naturalized Citizens: Number and percentage of population who were not U.S. citizens at birth but became U.S. citizens by naturalization.

The data on place of birth were derived from answers to long-form questionnaire Item 12 which was asked of a sample of the population. Respondents were asked to report the U.S. state, Puerto Rico, U.S. Island Area, or foreign country where they were born. People not reporting a place of birth were assigned the state or country of birth of another family member or their residence 5 years earlier, or were imputed the response of another person with similar characteristics. People born outside the United States were asked to report their place of birth according to current international boundaries. Since numerous changes in boundaries of foreign countries have occurred in the last century, some people may have reported their place of birth in terms of boundaries that existed at the time of their birth or emigration, or in accordance with their own national preference.

EDUCATIONAL ATTAINMENT

High School Graduates: Number and percentage of the population age 25 and over who have a high school diploma or higher. This category includes people whose highest degree was a high school diploma or its equivalent, people who attended college but did not receive a degree, and people who received a college, university, or professional degree. People who reported completing the 12th grade but not receiving a diploma are not high school graduates.

Four-Year College Graduates: Number and percentage of the population age 25 and over who have a 4-year college, university, or professional degree.

Data on educational attainment were derived from answers to long-form questionnaire Item 9, which was asked of a sample of the population. Data on attainment are tabulated for the population 25 years old and over.

The order in which degrees were listed on the questionnaire suggested that doctorate degrees were "higher" than professional school degrees, which were "higher" than master's degrees. The question included instructions for people currently enrolled in school to report the level of the previous grade attended or the highest degree received. Respondents who did not report educational attainment or enrollment level were assigned the attainment of a person of the same age, race, Hispanic or Latino origin, occupation and sex, where possible, who resided in the same or a nearby area. Respondents who filled more than one box were edited to the highest level or degree reported.

The question included a response category that allowed respondents to report completing the 12th grade without receiving a high school diploma. It allowed people who received either a high school diploma or the equivalent (Test of General Educational Development—G.E.D.) and did not attend college, to be reported as "high school graduate(s)." The category "Associate degree" included people whose highest degree is an associate degree, which generally requires 2 years of college level work and is either in an occupational program that prepares them for a specific occupation, or an academic program primarily in the arts and sciences. The course work may or may not be transferable to a bachelor's degree. Master's degrees include the traditional MA and MS degrees and field-specific degrees, such as MSW, MEd, MBA, MLS, and MEng. Some examples of professional degrees include medicine, dentistry, chiropractic, optometry, osteopathic medicine, pharmacy, podiatry, veterinary medicine, law, and theology. Vocational and technical training such as barber school training; business, trade, technical, and vocational schools; or other training for a specific trade, are specifically excluded.

INCOME AND POVERTY

Median Household Income (in dollars): Includes the income of the householder and all other individuals 15 years old and over in the household, whether they are related to the householder or not. The median divides the income distribution into two equal parts: one-half of the cases falling below the median income and one-half above the median. For households, the median income is based on the distribution of the total number of households including those with no income. Median income for households is computed on the basis of a standard distribution and is rounded to the nearest whole dollar.

Per Capita Income (in dollars): Per capita income is the mean income computed for every man, woman, and child in a particular group. It is derived by dividing the total income of a particular group by the total population in that group. Per capita income is rounded to the nearest whole dollar.

The data on income in 1999 were derived from answers to long-form questionnaire Items 31 and 32, which were asked of a sample of the population 15 years old and over. "Total income" is the sum of the amounts reported separately for wage or salary income; net self-employment income; interest, dividends, or net rental or royalty income or income from estates and trusts; social security or railroad retirement income; Supplemental Security Income (SSI); public assistance or welfare payments; retirement, survivor, or disability pensions; and all other income.

Receipts from the following sources are not included as income: capital gains, money received from the sale of property (unless the recipient was engaged in the business of selling such property); the value of income "in kind" from food stamps, public housing subsidies, medical care, employer contributions for individuals, etc.; withdrawal of bank deposits; money borrowed; tax refunds; exchange of money between relatives living in the same household; and gifts and lump-sum inheritances, insurance payments, and other types of lump-sum receipts.

The eight types of income reported in the census are defined as follows:

Wage or salary income. Wage or salary income includes total money earnings received for work performed as an employee during the calendar year 1999. It includes wages, salary, armed forces pay, commissions, tips, piece-rate payments, and cash bonuses earned before deductions were made for taxes, bonds, pensions, union dues, etc.

Self-employment income. Self-employment income includes both farm and nonfarm self-employment income. Nonfarm self-employment income includes net money income (gross receipts minus expenses) from one's own business, professional enterprise, or partnership. Gross receipts include the value of all goods sold and services rendered. Expenses include costs of goods purchased, rent, heat, light, power, depreciation charges, wages and salaries paid, business taxes (not personal income taxes), etc. Farm self-employment income includes net money income (gross receipts minus operating expenses) from the operation of a farm by a person on his or her own account, as an owner, renter, or sharecropper. Gross receipts include the value of all products sold, government farm programs, money received from the rental of farm equipment to others, and incidental receipts from the sale of wood, sand, gravel, etc. Operating expenses include cost of feed, fertilizer, seed, and other farming supplies, cash wages paid to farmhands, depreciation charges, cash rent, interest on farm mortgages, farm building repairs, farm taxes (not state and federal personal income taxes), etc. The value of fuel, food, or other farm products used for family living is not included as part of net income.

Interest, dividends, or net rental income. Interest, dividends, or net rental income includes interest on savings or bonds, dividends from stockholdings or membership in associations, net income from rental of property to others and receipts from boarders or lodgers, net royalties, and periodic payments from an estate or trust fund.

Social Security income. Social security income includes social security pensions and survivors benefits, permanent disability insurance payments made by the Social Security Administration prior to deductions for medical insurance, and railroad retirement insurance checks from the U.S. government. Medicare reimbursements are not included.

Supplemental Security Income (SSI). Supplemental Security Income (SSI) is a nationwide U.S. assistance program administered by the Social Security Administration that guarantees a minimum level of income for needy aged, blind, or disabled individuals. The census questionnaire for Puerto Rico asked about the receipt of SSI; however, SSI is not a federally administered program in Puerto Rico. Therefore, it is probably not being interpreted by most respondents as the same as SSI in the United States. The only way a resident of Puerto Rico could have appropriately reported SSI would have been if they lived in the United States at any time during calendar year 1999 and received SSI.

Public assistance income. Public assistance income includes general assistance and Temporary Assistance to Needy Families (TANF). Separate payments received for hospital or other medical care (vendor payments) are excluded. This does not include Supplemental Security Income (SSI).

Retirement income. Retirement income includes: (1) retirement pensions and survivor benefits from a former employer; labor union; or federal, state, or local government; and the U.S. military; (2) income from workers' compensation; disability income from companies or unions; federal, state, or local government; and the U.S. military; (3) periodic receipts from annuities and insurance; and (4) regular income from IRA and KEOGH plans. This does not include social security income.

All other income. All other income includes unemployment compensation, Veterans' Administration (VA) payments, alimony and child support, contributions received periodically from people not living in the household, military family allotments, and other kinds of periodic income other than earnings.

Poverty Status: Number and percentage of population with income in 1999 below the poverty level. Based on individuals for whom poverty status is determined. Poverty status was determined for all people except institutionalized people, people in military group quarters, people in college dormitories, and unrelated individuals under 15 years old.

The poverty status of families and unrelated individuals in 1999 was determined using 48 thresholds (income cutoffs) arranged in a two dimensional matrix. The matrix consists of family size (from 1 person to 9 or more people) cross-classified by presence and number of family members under 18 years old (from no children present to 8 or more children present). Unrelated individuals and 2-person families were further differentiated by the age of the reference person (RP) (under 65 years old and 65 years old and over).

To determine a person's poverty status, one compares the person's total family income with the poverty threshold appropriate for that person's family size and composition. If the total income of that person's family is less than the threshold appropriate for that family, then the person is considered poor, together with every member of his or her family. If a person is not living with anyone related by birth, marriage, or adoption, then the person's own income is compared with his or her poverty threshold.

HOUSING

Homeownership: Number and percentage of housing units that are owner-occupied.

The data on tenure, which was asked at all occupied housing units, were obtained from answers to long-form questionnaire Item 33, and short-form questionnaire Item 2. All occupied housing units are classified as either owner occupied or renter occupied.

A housing unit is owner occupied if the owner or co-owner lives in the unit even if it is mortgaged or not fully paid for. The owner or co-owner must live in the unit and usually is Person 1 on the questionnaire. The unit is "Owned by you or someone in this household with a mortgage or loan" if it is being purchased with a mortgage or some other debt arrangement, such as a deed of trust, trust deed, contract to purchase, land contract, or purchase agreement. The unit is also considered owned with a mortgage if it is built on leased land and there is a mortgage on the unit. Mobile homes occupied by owners with installment loans balances are also included in this category.

Median Gross Rent (in dollars): Median monthly gross rent on specified renter-occupied and specified vacant-for-rent units. Specified renter-occupied and specified vacant-for-rent units exclude 1-family houses on 10 acres or more.

The data on gross rent were obtained from answers to long-form questionnaire Items 45a-d, which were asked on a sample basis. Gross rent is the contract rent plus the estimated average monthly cost of utilities (electricity, gas, water and sewer) and fuels (oil, coal, kerosene, wood, etc.) if these are paid by the renter (or paid for the renter by someone else). Gross rent is intended to eliminate differentials that result from varying practices with respect to the inclusion of utilities and fuels as part of the rental payment. The estimated costs of utilities and fuels are reported on an annual basis but are converted to monthly figures for the tabulations. Renter units occupied without payment of cash rent are shown separately as "No cash rent" in the tabulations.

Housing units that are renter occupied without payment of cash rent are shown separately as "No cash rent" in census data products. The unit may be owned by friends or relatives who live elsewhere and who allow occupancy without charge. Rent-free houses or apartments may be provided to compensate caretakers, ministers, tenant farmers, sharecroppers, or others.

Contract rent is the monthly rent agreed to or contracted for, regardless of any furnishings, utilities, fees, meals, or services that may be included. For vacant units, it is the monthly rent asked for the rental unit at the time of enumeration.

If the contract rent includes rent for a business unit or for living quarters occupied by another household, only that part of the rent estimated to be for the respondent's unit was included. Excluded was any rent paid for additional units or for business premises.

If a renter pays rent to the owner of a condominium or cooperative, and the condominium fee or cooperative carrying charge also is paid by the renter to the owner, the condominium fee or carrying charge was included as rent.

If a renter receives payments from lodgers or roomers who are listed as members of the household, the rent without deduction for any payments received from the lodgers or roomers was to be reported. The respondent was to report the rent agreed to or contracted for even if paid by someone else such as friends or relatives living elsewhere, a church or welfare agency, or the government through subsidies or vouchers.

The median divides the rent distribution into two equal parts: one-half of the cases falling below the median contract rent and one-half above the median. Median contract rents are computed on the basis of a standard distribution and are rounded to the nearest whole dollar. Units reported as "No cash rent" are excluded.

Median Home Value (in dollars): Reported by the owner of specified owner-occupied or specified vacant-for-sale housing units. Specified owner-occupied and specified vacant-for-sale housing units include only 1-family houses on less than 10 acres without a business or medical office on the property. The data for "specified units" exclude mobile homes, houses with a business or medical office, houses on 10 or more acres, and housing units in multi-unit buildings.

The data on value (also referred to as "price asked" for vacant units) were obtained from answers to long-form questionnaire Item 51, which was asked on a sample basis at owner-occupied housing units and units that were being bought, or vacant for sale at the time of enumeration. Value is the respondent's estimate of how much the property (house and lot, mobile home and lot, or condominium unit) would sell for if it were for sale. If the house or mobile home was owned or being bought, but the land on which it sits was not, the respondent was asked to estimate the combined value of the house or mobile home and the land. For vacant units, value was the price asked for the property. Value was tabulated separately for all owner-occupied and vacant-for-sale housing units, owner-occupied and vacant-for-sale mobile homes, and specified owner-occupied and specified vacant-for-sale housing units.

The median divides the value distribution into two equal parts: one-half of the cases falling below the median value of the property (house and lot, mobile home and lot, or condominium unit) and one-half above the median. Median values are computed on the basis of a standard distribution and are rounded to the nearest hundred dollars.

How to Read the Tables

There are three types of tables located in Section I.

Type I (1 line per entry). Six tables fall into this category: Median Age; Average Household Size; Median Household Income; Per Capita Income; Median Gross Rent; Median Home Value.

Place	All households	Asian households	NHPI¹ households	Asian Indian
UNITED STATES	41,994	51,908	42,717	63,669
ALABAMA	34,135	42,007	37,583	54,113
Baldwin County	40,250	53,864	-	-
Calhoun County	31,768	35,179	-	-
Etowah County	31,170	55,500	-	-
Houston County	34,431	32,083	-	-

Each line represents a number (eg. median household income, median age, etc.)

For example:
The median household income of Asian Indians in the U.S. is $63,669

Type II (3 lines per entry). One table falls into this category: Population.

Place	Total population	① Total Asian population	② Total NHPI¹ population	③ Asian Indian
UNITED STATES	281,421,906	10,171,820	378,782	1,645,510
				16.18
		3.61	0.13	0.58
ALABAMA	4,447,100	29,908	1,187	6,686
				22.36
		0.67	0.03	0.15
Baldwin County	140,415	535	-	-
		0.38		

The first line shows the number of persons.
The second line shows the number as a percentage of column 2 for Asian groups and as a percentage of column 3 for Native Hawaiian and Other Pacific Islander groups.
The third line shows the number as a percentage of the total population (column 1)

For example:
There are 1,645,510 Asian Indians in the U.S.
Asian Indians make up 16.18% of the total Asian population in the U.S.
Asian Indians make up 0.58% of the total population of the U.S.

Type III (5 lines per entry). Seven tables fall into this category: Language Spoken at Home: English Only; Foreign Born; Foreign-Born Naturalized Citizens; Educational Attainment: High School Graduates; Educational Attainment: Four-Year College Graduates; Poverty Status; Homeownership

Place	Total population 25 years and over who are 4-year college graduates	① Asian population 25 years and over	② Asians 25 years and over who are 4-year college graduates	③ NHPI¹ population 25 years and over	④ NHPIs¹ 25 years and over who are 4-year college graduates	⑤ Asian Indian
UNITED STATES	44,462,605	6,640,671	2,925,743	206,675	28,498	668,029
	24.40		44.06		13.79	63.89
						22.83
			44.06		13.79	10.06
			6.58		0.06	1.50
ALABAMA	549,608	18,999	9,173	639	101	2,961
	19.03		48.28		15.81	71.59
						32.28
			48.28		15.81	15.59
			1.67		0.02	0.54

The first line shows the number of persons
The second line shows the number as a percentage rate
The third line shows the number as a percentage of column 3 for Asian groups and as a percentage of column 5 for Native Hawaiian and Other Pacific Islander groups
The fourth line shows the number as a percentage of column 2 for Asian groups and as a percentage of column 4 for Native Hawaiian and Other Pacific Islander groups
The fifth line shows the number as a percentage of column 1

EXAMPLE
There are 668,029 Asian Indian 4-year college graduates in the U.S.
The Asian Indian 4-year college graduation rate is 63.89% in the U.S.
22.83% of Asian 4-year college graduates in the U.S. are Asian Indian
10.06% of Asians in the U.S. are Asian Indian 4-year college graduates
1.50% of all 4-year college graduates in the U.S. are Asian Indian

General Note: A dash indicates that data for that specific population group within the associated geographic area is less than the threshold(s). The population threshold on Summary File 4 is 100. In addition, there must be at least 50 or more unweighted cases of the population group. However, numbers less than 100 (including 0) may appear because the thresholds apply to the entire universe (e.g. Population 5 years and over), not the specific data element (e.g. Speak only English). In addition, numbers may not add up to totals and percentages may not add up to 100% within the same row.

User's Guide: Weather

Inclusion Criteria — How the Data and Stations Were Selected

There were two central goals in the preparation of the weather chapter. The first was to select those data elements which would have the broadest possible use by the greatest range of potential users. For most of the National Weather Service stations there is a substantial quantity and variety of climatological data that is collected, however for the majority of stations the data is more limited. After evaluating the available data set, the editors chose nine temperature measures, five precipitation measures, and heating and cooling degree days — sixteen key data elements that are widely requested and are believed to be of the greatest general interest.

The second goal was to provide data for as many weather stations as possible. Although there are over 10,000 stations in the United States, not every station collects data for both precipitation and temperature, and even among those that do, the data is not always complete for the last thirty years. As the editors used a different methodology than that of NCDC to compute data, a formal data sufficiency criteria was devised and applied to the source tapes in order to select stations for inclusion.

Sources of the Data

The data in the weather chapter is compiled from several sources. The majority comes from the original National Climactic Data Center computer tapes (TD-3220 Summary of Month Co-Operative). This data was used to create the entire table for each Cooperative station and part of each National Weather Service station. The remainder of the data for each NWS station comes from the International Station Meteorological Climate Summary, Version 4.0, September 1996, which is also available from the NCDC.

NCDC has two main classes or types of weather stations; first order stations which are staffed by professional meteorologists (13 stations in Florida) and cooperative stations which are staffed by volunteers. In the weather chapter all first order stations operated by the National Weather Service are included, as well as every cooperative station that met our selection criteria.

Potential cautions in using *Weather America*

First, as with any statistical reference work of this type, users need to be aware of the source of the data. The information here comes from NOAA, and it is the most comprehensive and reliable core data available. Although it is the best, it is not perfect. Most weather stations are staffed by volunteers, times of observation sometimes vary, stations occasionally are moved (especially over a thirty year period), equipment is changed or upgraded, and all of these factors affect the uniformity of the data. the weather chapter does not attempt to correct for these factors, and is not intended for either climatologists or atmospheric scientists. Users with concerns about data collection and reporting protocols are both referred to NCDC technical documentation, and also, they are perhaps better served by using the original computer tapes themselves as well.

Second, users need to be aware of the methodology used, which is described later in this User's Guide. Although this methodology has produced fully satisfactory results, it is not directly compatible with other methodologies, hence variances in the results published here and those which appear in other publications will doubtlessly arise.

Third, is the trap of that informal logical fallacy known as "hasty generalization," and its corollaries. This may involve presuming the future will be like the past (specifically, next year will be an average year), or it may involve misunderstanding the limitations of an arithmetic average, but more interestingly, it may involve those mistakes made most innocently by generalizing informally on too broad a basis. As weather is highly localized, the data should be taken in that context. A weather station collects data about climatic conditions at that spot, and that spot may or may not be an effective paradigm for an entire town or area. For example, the weather station in Burlington, Vermont is located at the airport about 3 miles east of the center of town. Most of Burlington is a lot closer to Lake Champlain, and that should mean to a careful user that there could be a significant difference between the temperature readings gathered at the weather station and readings that might be gathered at City Hall downtown. How much would this difference be? How could it be estimated? There are no answers here for these sorts of questions, but it is important for users of this book to raise them for themselves. (It is interesting to note that similar situations abound across the country. For example, compare different readings for the multiple stations in San Francisco, CA or for those around New York City.)

Our source of data has been consistent, so has our methodology. The data has been computed and reported consistently as well. As a result, the the weather chapter should prove valuable to the careful and informed reader.

Weather Station Tables

The weather station tables are grouped by type (National Weather Service and Cooperative) and then arranged alphabetically. The station name is almost always a place name, and is shown here just as it appears in NCDC data. The station name is followed by the county in which the station is located, the elevation of the station (at the time beginning of the thirty year period) and the latitude and longitude.

The National Weather Service Station tables contain 30 data elements which were compiled from two different sources, the International Station Meteorological Climate Summary (ISMCS) and NCDC TD-3220 data tapes. The following 14 elements are from the ISMCS: maximum precipitation, minimum precipitation, maximum 24-hour precipitation, maximum snowfall, maximum 24-hour snowfall, thunderstorm days, foggy days, predominant sky cover, relative humidity (morning and afternoon), dewpoint, wind speed and direction, and maximum wind gust. The remaining 16 elements come from the TD-3220 data tapes. The period of record (POR) for data from the TD-3220 data tapes is 1970-1999. The POR for ISMCS data varies from station to station.

NWS Station Name	POR
Apalachicola Municipal Airport	1948-1992
Daytona Beach Regional Airport	1948-1995
Fort Myers Page Field	1948-1995
Gainesville Regional Airport	1962-1995
Jacksonville Int'l Airport	1948-1995
Key West Int'l Airport	1948-1995
Miami Int'l Airport	1948-1995
Orlando Int'l Airport	1974-1995
Pensacola Regional Airport	1948-1995
Tallahassee Municipal Airport	1948-1995
Tampa Int'l Airport	1948-1995
Vero Beach	1949-1995
West Palm Beach Int'l Airport	1948-1995

The Cooperative Station tables contain 16 data elements which were all compiled from the TD-3220 data tapes with a POR of 1970-1999.

Weather Elements (National Weather Service and Cooperative Stations)

The following elements were compiled by the editor from the NCDC TD-3220 data tapes using a period of record of 1970-1999.

The average temperatures (maximum, minimum, and mean) are the average (see Methodology below) of those temperatures for all available values for a given month. For example, for a given station the average maximum temperature for July is the arithmetic average of all available maximum July temperatures for that station. (Maximum means the highest recorded temperature, minimum means the lowest recorded temperature, and mean means an arithmetic average temperature.)

The extreme maximum temperature is the highest temperature recorded in each month over the period 1970-1999. The extreme minimum temperature is the lowest temperature recorded in each month over the same time period.

The days for maximum temperature and minimum temperature are the average number of days those criteria were met for all available instances. The symbol >= means greater than or equal to, the symbol <= means less than or equal to. For example, for a given station, the number of days the maximum temperature was greater than or equal to 90°F in July, is just an arithmetic average of the number of days in all the available Julys for that station.

Heating and cooling degree days are based on the median temperature for a given day and its variance from 65°F. For example, for a given station if the day's high temperature was 50°F and the day's low temperature was 30°F, the median (midpoint) temperature was 40°F. 40°F is 25 degrees below 65°F, hence on this day there would be 25 heating degree days. The also applies for cooling degree days. For example, for a given station if the day's high temperature was 80°F and the day's low temperature was 70°F, the median (midpoint) temperature was 75°F. 75°F is 10 degrees above 65°F, hence on this day there would be 10 cooling degree days. All heating and/or cooling degree days in a month are summed for the month giving respective totals for each element for that month. These sums for a given month for a given station over the past thirty years are again summed and then arithmetically averaged. It should be noted that the heating and cooling degree days do not cancel each other out. It is possible to have both for a given station in the same month.

Precipitation data is computed the same as heating and cooling degree days. Mean precipitation and mean snowfall are arithmetic averages of cumulative totals for the month. All available values for the thirty year period for a given month for a given station are summed and then divided by the number of values. The same is true for days of greater than or equal to 0.1" and 1.0" of precipitation, and days of greater than or equal to 1.0" of snow depth on the ground. The word trace appears for precipitation and snowfall amounts that are too small to measure.

Finally, remember that all values presented in the tables and the rankings are averages of available data (see Methodology below) for that specific data element for the last thirty years (1970-1999).

Weather Elements (National Weather Service Stations Only)

The following elements were taken directly from the International Station Meteorological Climate Summary. The periods of records vary per station.

Maximum precipitation, minimum precipitation, maximum 24-hour precipitation, maximum snowfall, maximum 24-hour snowfall, thunderstorm days, foggy days, relative humidity (morning and afternoon), dewpoint, prevailing wind speed and direction, and maximum wind gust are all self-explanatory.

The word trace appears for precipitation and snowfall amounts that are too small to measure.

Predominant sky cover contains four possible entries: CLR (clear); SCT (scattered); BRK (broken); and OVR (overcast).

How Cooperative Stations Were Selected

The basic criteria is that a station must have data for temperature, precipitation, heating and cooling degree days of sufficient quantity in order to create a meaningful average. More specifically, the definition of sufficiency here has two parts. First, there must be 22 values for a given data element (with the exception of cooling degree days which required only 14 values in order to be considered sufficient- more about this later), and second, eight of the sixteen elements included in the table must pass this sufficiency test. For example, in regard to average maximum temperature (the first element on every data table), a given station needs to have a value for every month of at least 22 of the last thirty years in order to meet the criteria, and, in addition, every station included must have at least eight of the sixteen elements at least this minimal level of completeness in order to fulfill the criteria. By using this procedure, 3,933 stations met these requirements and are included here.

Methodology

The following discussion applies only to data compiled from the NCDC TD-3220 data tapes.

the weather chapter is based on an arithmetic average of all available data for a specific data element at a given station. For example, the average maximum daily high temperature during July for Bartow, Florida was abstracted from NCDC source tapes for the thirty Julys, starting in July, 1970 and ending in July, 1999. These thirty figures were then summed and divided by thirty to produce an arithmetic average. As might be expected, there were not thirty values for every data element on every table. For a variety of reasons, NCDC data is sometimes incomplete. Thus the following standards were established.

For those data elements where there were 26-30 values, the data was taken to be essentially complete and an average was computed. For data elements where there were 22-25 values, the data was taken as being partly complete but still valid enough to use to compute an average. Such averages are shown in ***bold italic*** type to indicate that there was less than 26 values. For the few data elements where there were not even 22 values, no average was computed and 'na' appears in the space. If any of the twelve months for a given data element reported a value of 'na', no annual average was computed and the annual average was reported as 'na' as well.

This procedure was followed for 15 of the 16 data elements. The one exception is cooling degree days. The collection of this data began in 1980 so the following standards were adopted: for those data elements where there were 17-20 values, the data was taken to be essentially complete and an average was computed. For data elements where there were 14-16 values, the data was taken as being partly complete but still valid enough to use to compute an average. Such averages are shown in ***bold italic*** type to indicate that there was 14-16 values. For the few data elements where there were not even 14 values, no average was computed and 'na' appears in the space. If any of the twelve months for a given data element reported a value of 'na', no annual average was computed and the annual average was reported as 'na' as well.

Thus the basic computational methodology of the weather chapter is to provide an arithmetic average. Because of this, such a pure arithmetic average is somewhat different from the special type of average (called a "normal") which NCDC procedures produces and appears in federal publications.

Perhaps the best outline of the contrasting normalization methodology is found in the following paragraph (which appears as part of an NCDC technical document titled, CLIM81 1961-1990 NORMALS TD-9641 prepared by Lewis France of NCDC in May, 1992):

Normals have been defined as the arithmetic mean of a climatological element computed over a long time period. International agreements eventually led to the decision that the appropriate time period would be three consecutive decades (Guttman, 1989). The data record should be consistent (have no changes in location, instruments, observation practices, etc.; these are identified here as "exposure changes") and have no missing values so a normal will reflect the actual average climatic conditions. If any significant exposure changes have occurred, the data record is said to be "inhomogeneous," and the normal may not reflect a true climatic average. Such data need to be adjusted to remove the nonclimatic inhomogeneities. The resulting (adjusted) record is then said to be "homogeneous." If no exposure changes have occurred at a station, the normal is calculated simply by averaging the appropriate 30 values from the 1961-1990 record.

In the main, there are two "inhomogeneities" that NCDC is correcting for with normalization: adjusting for variances in time of day of observation (at the so-called First Order stations data is based on midnight to midnight observation times and this practice is not necessarily followed at cooperative stations which are staffed by volunteers), and second, estimating data that is either missing or incongruent.

A long discussion of the normalization process is not required here but a short note concerning comparative results of the two methodologies is appropriate.

When the editors first started compiling the weather chapter a concern arose because the normalization process would not be replicated: would our methodology produce strikingly different results than NCDC's? To allay concerns, results of the two processes were compared for the time period normalized results are available (1961-1990). In short, what was found was that the answer to this question is no. Never-the-less, users should be aware that because of both the time period covered (1970-1999) and the methodology used, data in the weather chapter is not compatible with data from other sources.

Alachua County

Located in northern Florida; bounded on the north by the Santa Fe River; includes many lakes. Covers a land area of 874.20 square miles, a water area of 94.90 square miles, and is located in the Eastern Time Zone. The county government was organized in 1824. County seat is Gainesville.

Alachua County is part of the Gainesville, FL Metropolitan Statistical Area. The entire metro area includes: Alachua County, FL; Gilchrist County, FL

Weather Station: High Springs Elevation: 62 feet

	Jan	Feb	Mar	Apr	May	Jun	Jul	Aug	Sep	Oct	Nov	Dec
High	68	72	78	83	89	92	93	92	90	83	77	71
Low	40	43	49	53	62	69	71	71	68	58	49	43
Precip	4.4	3.8	4.5	3.4	3.8	6.8	7.3	8.2	4.4	3.1	2.2	2.7
Snow	tr	0.0	0.0	0.0	0.0	0.0	0.0	0.0	0.0	0.0	0.0	0.0

High and Low temperatures in degrees Fahrenheit; Precipitation and Snow in inches

Population: 181,596 (1990); 217,955 (2000); 231,663 (2004); 248,973 (2009 projected); Race: 71.5% White, 21.3% Black, 3.5% Asian, 5.6% Hispanic of any race (2004); Density: 265.0 persons per square mile (2004); Average household size: 2.50 (2004); Median age: 30.5 (2004); Male/female ratio: 95.5 (2004).
Religion: Five largest groups: 11.2% Southern Baptist Convention, 7.3% Catholic Church, 5.4% The United Methodist Church, 1.1% Episcopal Church, 1.1% Presbyterian Church (U.S.A.) (2000).
Economy: Unemployment rate: 2.5% (2004); Total civilian labor force: 118,613 (2004); Leading industries: 20.8% health care and social assistance; 16.6% retail trade; 11.9% accommodation & food services (2003); Companies that employ 500 or more persons: 8 (2003); Companies that employ 100 to 499 persons: 117 (2003); Companies that employ less than 100 persons: 5,242 (2003); Farms: 1,493 totaling 222,728 acres (2002); Minority business ownership rate: 11.4% (1997); Women business ownership rate: 36.2% (1997); Retail sales per capita: $9,791 (1997). Single-family building permits issued: 1,328 (2004); Multi-family building permits issued: 681 (2004).
Income: Per capita income: $20,878 (2004); Median household income: $33,852 (2004); Average household income: $50,640 (2004); Percent of households with income of $100,000 or more: 10.9% (2004); Poverty rate: 15.1% (2002); Bankruptcy rate: 2.98% (2004).
Taxes: Total county taxes per capita: $356 (2002); County property taxes per capita: $324 (2002).
Education: Percent of population age 25 and over with: High school diploma (including GED) or higher: 88.3% (2004); Bachelor's degree or higher: 39.4% (2004); Master's degree or higher: 19.2% (2004).
Housing: Homeownership rate: 54.9% (2004); Median home value: $117,597 (2004); Median rent: $465 per month (2000); Median age of housing: 20 years (2000).
Health: Birth rate: 114.5 per 10,000 population (2004); Death rate: 72.0 per 10,000 population (2004); Age adjusted cancer mortality rate: 207.5 deaths per 100,000 population (2002); Air Quality Index: 90.4% good, 9.6% moderate, 0.0% unhealthy for sensitive individuals, 0.0% unhealthy (percent of days in 2004); Number of physicians: 76.7 per 10,000 population (2001); Hospital beds: 74.9 per 10,000 population (2002); Hospital admissions: 2,916.6 per 10,000 population (2002).
Elections: 2004 Presidential election results: 42.9% Bush, 56.1% Kerry, 0.5% Nader, 0.3% Badnarik
National and State Parks: Devils Millhopper Geological State Park; Dudley Farm Historic State Park; Marjorie Kinnan Rawlings Historic State Park; Paynes Prairie Preserve State Park; San Felasco Hammock Preserve State Park; Sunland Center State Park
Additional Information Contacts
Alachua County Government Offices.................. (352) 374-5210
Alachua Chamber of Commerce .... (386) 462-3333
Fort White Chamber of Commerce .... (386) 462-8277
Gainesville Alachua County Association of Realtors ...... (352) 332-8850
Gainesville Chamber of Commerce................... (352) 334-7100
High Springs Chamber of Commerce .... (386) 454-3120
Newberry Chamber of Commerce.................... (352) 472-6611

Alachua County Communities

ALACHUA (city). Covers a land area of 28.897 square miles and a water area of 0.153 square miles. Located at 29.77° N. Lat.; 82.48° W. Long. Elevation is 85 feet.
History: Alachua was founded in 1884 when the Atlantic Coast Line Railroad was built through the area. The town became a shipping point for tobacco, cotton, and winter vegetables, and later for watermelons.
Population: 4,825 (1990); 6,098 (2000); 6,549 (2004); 7,083 (2009 projected); Race: 67.9% White, 28.5% Black, 1.2% Asian, 3.6% Hispanic of any race (2004); Density: 226.6 persons per square mile (2004); Average household size: 2.56 (2004); Median age: 37.5 (2004); Male/female ratio: 88.2 (2004); Marriage status: 25.8% never married, 53.4% now married, 9.8% widowed, 11.1% divorced (2000); Foreign born: 3.3% (2000); Ancestry (includes multiple ancestries): 35.0% Other groups, 12.6% Irish, 9.6% German, 8.3% English, 5.9% United States or American (2000).
Economy: Single-family building permits issued: 162 (2004); Multi-family building permits issued: 18 (2004); Employment by occupation: 10.7% management, 24.7% professional, 18.3% services, 28.0% sales, 1.2% farming, 6.0% construction, 11.1% production (2000).
Income: Per capita income: $21,055 (2004); Median household income: $43,165 (2004); Average household income: $53,691 (2004); Percent of households with income of $100,000 or more: 10.8% (2004); Poverty rate: 16.0% (2000).
Taxes: Total city taxes per capita: $319 (2002); City property taxes per capita: $180 (2002).
Education: Percent of population age 25 and over with: High school diploma (including GED) or higher: 83.0% (2004); Bachelor's degree or higher: 27.1% (2004); Master's degree or higher: 11.0% (2004).

School District(s)

Alachua County School District (PK-12)
2002-03 Enrollment: 29,345 .... (352) 955-7880
Housing: Homeownership rate: 77.0% (2004); Median home value: $113,922 (2004); Median rent: $299 per month (2000); Median age of housing: 17 years (2000).
Safety: Violent crime rate: 96.9 per 10,000 population; Property crime rate: 625.0 per 10,000 population (2003).
Transportation: Commute to work: 92.3% car, 0.0% public transportation, 1.7% walk, 3.9% work from home (2000); Travel time to work: 20.1% less than 15 minutes, 39.6% 15 to 30 minutes, 32.2% 30 to 45 minutes, 4.2% 45 to 60 minutes, 3.9% 60 minutes or more (2000)
Additional Information Contacts
Alachua Chamber of Commerce .... (386) 462-3333
Fort White Chamber of Commerce .... (386) 462-8277
Local Government Offices.......................... (386) 462-1231

ARCHER (city). Covers a land area of 2.375 square miles and a water area of 0 square miles. Located at 29.53° N. Lat.; 82.52° W. Long. Elevation is 88 feet.
History: First called Deer Hammock, Archer was founded in 1859 and named for Brigadier General James J. Archer, a Confederate leader. Among the early settlers was a group of Quakers from Ohio, attracted by the citrus groves.
Population: 1,456 (1990); 1,289 (2000); 1,211 (2004); 1,192 (2009 projected); Race: 54.2% White, 44.3% Black, 0.1% Asian, 2.2% Hispanic of any race (2004); Density: 509.8 persons per square mile (2004); Average household size: 2.64 (2004); Median age: 33.4 (2004); Male/female ratio: 83.2 (2004); Marriage status: 29.6% never married, 46.5% now married, 10.1% widowed, 13.8% divorced (2000); Foreign born: 2.3% (2000); Ancestry (includes multiple ancestries): 39.5% Other groups, 13.3% United States or American, 9.4% Irish, 7.6% English, 7.3% German (2000).
Economy: Employment by occupation: 7.6% management, 13.6% professional, 24.9% services, 29.0% sales, 0.8% farming, 12.6% construction, 11.5% production (2000).
Income: Per capita income: $14,193 (2004); Median household income: $30,368 (2004); Average household income: $37,446 (2004); Percent of households with income of $100,000 or more: 5.0% (2004); Poverty rate: 21.6% (2000).
Education: Percent of population age 25 and over with: High school diploma (including GED) or higher: 75.1% (2004); Bachelor's degree or higher: 12.1% (2004); Master's degree or higher: 4.4% (2004).

School District(s)

Alachua County School District (PK-12)
2002-03 Enrollment: 29,345 .... (352) 955-7880
Housing: Homeownership rate: 67.5% (2004); Median home value: $70,685 (2004); Median rent: $305 per month (2000); Median age of housing: 24 years (2000).
Transportation: Commute to work: 90.8% car, 0.0% public transportation, 2.7% walk, 2.3% work from home (2000); Travel time to work: 12.8% less

than 15 minutes, 32.9% 15 to 30 minutes, 41.0% 30 to 45 minutes, 9.8% 45 to 60 minutes, 3.4% 60 minutes or more (2000)

GAINESVILLE (city). Covers a land area of 48.182 square miles and a water area of 0.921 square miles. Located at 29.66° N. Lat.; 82.33° W. Long. Elevation is 183 feet.
History: A settlement called Hog Town grew up around a trading post established here in 1830. The town was named Gainesville in 1853 for General Edmund P. Gaines, a Seminole War leader, and was settled by cotton planters from Georgia, Alabama, and the Carolinas. The University of Florida opened in 1853 in Gainesville, and in 1905 several State-supported schools were consolidated with it.
Population: 90,519 (1990); 95,447 (2000); 96,546 (2004); 98,536 (2009 projected); Race: 65.9% White, 26.0% Black, 4.2% Asian, 6.2% Hispanic of any race (2004); Density: 2,003.8 persons per square mile (2004); Average household size: 2.56 (2004); Median age: 28.1 (2004); Male/female ratio: 96.1 (2004); Marriage status: 49.1% never married, 37.1% now married, 4.7% widowed, 9.1% divorced (2000); Foreign born: 8.7% (2000); Ancestry (includes multiple ancestries): 31.1% Other groups, 12.6% German, 10.7% Irish, 9.9% English, 5.6% United States or American (2000).
Economy: Unemployment rate: 3.0% (2004); Total civilian labor force: 53,814 (2004); Single-family building permits issued: 141 (2004); Multi-family building permits issued: 413 (2004); Employment by occupation: 10.7% management, 35.2% professional, 17.6% services, 26.3% sales, 0.3% farming, 4.4% construction, 5.5% production (2000).
Income: Per capita income: $18,469 (2004); Median household income: $30,227 (2004); Average household income: $45,621 (2004); Percent of households with income of $100,000 or more: 9.1% (2004); Poverty rate: 26.7% (2000).
Taxes: Total city taxes per capita: $292 (2002); City property taxes per capita: $131 (2002).
Education: Percent of population age 25 and over with: High school diploma (including GED) or higher: 87.8% (2004); Bachelor's degree or higher: 43.3% (2004); Master's degree or higher: 22.4% (2004).

School District(s)

Alachua County School District (PK-12)
2002-03 Enrollment: 29,345 . . . . (352) 955-7880

Four-year College(s)

City College Branch Campus
2003-04 Enrollment: 313 . . . . (352) 335-4000
2003-04 Tuition: In-state $7,440; Out-of-state $7,440
University of Florida (Public)
2003-04 Enrollment: 47,858 . . . . (352) 392-3261
2003-04 Tuition: In-state $2,780; Out-of-state $13,808

Two-year College(s)

Santa Fe Community College (Public)
2003-04 Enrollment: 13,865 . . . . (352) 395-5000
2003-04 Tuition: In-state $1,338; Out-of-state $4,986

Housing: Homeownership rate: 47.6% (2004); Median home value: $109,793 (2004); Median rent: $457 per month (2000); Median age of housing: 26 years (2000).
Hospitals: Malcom Randall VA Medical Center (323 beds); North Florida Regional Medical Center (278 beds); Shands at AGH (367 beds); Shands at Gainesville (40 beds); Shands at University of Florida (570 beds); Shands at Vista (81 beds)
Safety: Violent crime rate: 103.6 per 10,000 population; Property crime rate: 521.0 per 10,000 population (2003).
Newspapers: The Gainesville Sun (Circulation 48,467); The Record (General - Circulation 5,000)
Transportation: Commute to work: 82.0% car, 3.2% public transportation, 5.6% walk, 3.1% work from home (2000); Travel time to work: 43.2% less than 15 minutes, 43.2% 15 to 30 minutes, 7.7% 30 to 45 minutes, 2.6% 45 to 60 minutes, 3.3% 60 minutes or more (2000); Amtrak: Service available.
Airports: Gainesville Regional (primary service)
Additional Information Contacts
Gainesville Alachua County Association of Realtors . . . . . . (352) 332-8850
Gainesville Chamber of Commerce . . . . (352) 334-7100

HAWTHORNE (city). Aka Hawthorn. Covers a land area of 3.203 square miles and a water area of 0.150 square miles. Located at 29.59° N. Lat.; 82.08° W. Long. Elevation is 153 feet.
History: Hawthorne was incorporated in 1890 and named for James M. Hawthorn (no "e"), the owner of the site.
Population: 1,495 (1990); 1,415 (2000); 1,318 (2004); 1,270 (2009 projected); Race: 45.4% White, 53.0% Black, 0.1% Asian, 1.1% Hispanic of any race (2004); Density: 411.5 persons per square mile (2004); Average household size: 2.61 (2004); Median age: 38.1 (2004); Male/female ratio: 87.5 (2004); Marriage status: 25.6% never married, 47.9% now married, 13.5% widowed, 12.9% divorced (2000); Foreign born: 1.2% (2000); Ancestry (includes multiple ancestries): 30.5% Other groups, 14.1% United States or American, 8.7% English, 7.9% Irish, 6.4% German (2000).
Economy: Employment by occupation: 8.1% management, 17.7% professional, 24.4% services, 23.4% sales, 0.0% farming, 11.7% construction, 14.6% production (2000).
Income: Per capita income: $14,300 (2004); Median household income: $28,250 (2004); Average household income: $37,322 (2004); Percent of households with income of $100,000 or more: 4.8% (2004); Poverty rate: 23.8% (2000).
Education: Percent of population age 25 and over with: High school diploma (including GED) or higher: 71.8% (2004); Bachelor's degree or higher: 10.8% (2004); Master's degree or higher: 5.6% (2004).

School District(s)

Alachua County School District (PK-12)
2002-03 Enrollment: 29,345 . . . . (352) 955-7880

Housing: Homeownership rate: 72.1% (2004); Median home value: $69,885 (2004); Median rent: $269 per month (2000); Median age of housing: 31 years (2000).
Transportation: Commute to work: 91.3% car, 2.0% public transportation, 3.7% walk, 2.4% work from home (2000); Travel time to work: 21.8% less than 15 minutes, 19.8% 15 to 30 minutes, 34.0% 30 to 45 minutes, 17.3% 45 to 60 minutes, 7.1% 60 minutes or more (2000)

HIGH SPRINGS (city). Covers a land area of 18.454 square miles and a water area of 0.030 square miles. Located at 29.82° N. Lat.; 82.59° W. Long. Elevation is 69 feet.
History: High Springs began as a trading post in 1885, and was named for a hilltop spring. It grew as a center for an agricultural area where tobacco, corn, and peanuts were raised.
Population: 3,390 (1990); 3,863 (2000); 4,401 (2004); 5,069 (2009 projected); Race: 76.4% White, 21.2% Black, 0.3% Asian, 4.2% Hispanic of any race (2004); Density: 238.5 persons per square mile (2004); Average household size: 2.48 (2004); Median age: 39.9 (2004); Male/female ratio: 86.3 (2004); Marriage status: 20.1% never married, 55.2% now married, 10.6% widowed, 14.1% divorced (2000); Foreign born: 3.5% (2000); Ancestry (includes multiple ancestries): 24.5% Other groups, 12.2% German, 11.6% English, 10.4% United States or American, 9.3% Irish (2000).
Economy: Employment by occupation: 9.0% management, 22.4% professional, 16.8% services, 29.1% sales, 0.7% farming, 10.7% construction, 11.4% production (2000).
Income: Per capita income: $18,923 (2004); Median household income: $38,344 (2004); Average household income: $46,753 (2004); Percent of households with income of $100,000 or more: 6.7% (2004); Poverty rate: 12.0% (2000).
Education: Percent of population age 25 and over with: High school diploma (including GED) or higher: 82.8% (2004); Bachelor's degree or higher: 16.0% (2004); Master's degree or higher: 5.4% (2004).

School District(s)

Alachua County School District (PK-12)
2002-03 Enrollment: 29,345 . . . . (352) 955-7880

Housing: Homeownership rate: 80.2% (2004); Median home value: $87,206 (2004); Median rent: $370 per month (2000); Median age of housing: 21 years (2000).
Safety: Violent crime rate: 42.8 per 10,000 population; Property crime rate: 283.0 per 10,000 population (2003).
Newspapers: The High Springs Herald (General - Circulation 5,000)
Transportation: Commute to work: 94.8% car, 0.4% public transportation, 1.1% walk, 2.0% work from home (2000); Travel time to work: 19.7% less than 15 minutes, 32.1% 15 to 30 minutes, 34.1% 30 to 45 minutes, 11.1% 45 to 60 minutes, 3.0% 60 minutes or more (2000)
Additional Information Contacts
High Springs Chamber of Commerce . . . . (386) 454-3120

LA CROSSE (town). Covers a land area of 1.338 square miles and a water area of 0 square miles. Located at 29.84° N. Lat.; 82.40° W. Long. Elevation is 46 feet.
Population: 122 (1990); 143 (2000); 145 (2004); 148 (2009 projected); Race: 80.0% White, 17.9% Black, 0.0% Asian, 8.3% Hispanic of any race (2004); Density: 108.3 persons per square mile (2004); Average household size: 2.30 (2004); Median age: 44.7 (2004); Male/female ratio: 107.1

(2004); Marriage status: 35.1% never married, 49.5% now married, 2.7% widowed, 12.6% divorced (2000); Foreign born: 0.0% (2000); Ancestry (includes multiple ancestries): 32.3% Other groups, 16.2% United States or American, 10.8% German, 10.8% Irish, 4.6% French (except Basque) (2000).
Economy: Employment by occupation: 0.0% management, 26.4% professional, 15.1% services, 22.6% sales, 3.8% farming, 11.3% construction, 20.8% production (2000).
Income: Per capita income: $14,466 (2004); Median household income: $26,667 (2004); Average household income: $33,294 (2004); Percent of households with income of $100,000 or more: 1.6% (2004); Poverty rate: 28.5% (2000).
Education: Percent of population age 25 and over with: High school diploma (including GED) or higher: 67.0% (2004); Bachelor's degree or higher: 13.4% (2004); Master's degree or higher: 5.4% (2004).
Housing: Homeownership rate: 87.3% (2004); Median home value: $70,000 (2004); Median rent: $n/a per month (2000); Median age of housing: 19 years (2000).
Transportation: Commute to work: 88.7% car, 0.0% public transportation, 5.7% walk, 5.7% work from home (2000); Travel time to work: 26.0% less than 15 minutes, 28.0% 15 to 30 minutes, 16.0% 30 to 45 minutes, 24.0% 45 to 60 minutes, 6.0% 60 minutes or more (2000)

MICANOPY (town). Covers a land area of 1.034 square miles and a water area of 0.046 square miles. Located at 29.50° N. Lat.; 82.28° W. Long. Elevation is 125 feet.
History: Micanopy was named for the Seminole chief Micanope. Settlement began in 1817 when land was granted to Don Fernando de la Maza Arredondo of Cuba.
Population: 693 (1990); 653 (2000); 624 (2004); 587 (2009 projected); Race: 66.5% White, 30.8% Black, 0.3% Asian, 1.9% Hispanic of any race (2004); Density: 603.4 persons per square mile (2004); Average household size: 2.12 (2004); Median age: 43.8 (2004); Male/female ratio: 95.6 (2004); Marriage status: 24.0% never married, 48.6% now married, 12.6% widowed, 14.7% divorced (2000); Foreign born: 3.5% (2000); Ancestry (includes multiple ancestries): 25.8% Other groups, 15.1% United States or American, 10.4% English, 7.9% German, 6.6% Irish (2000).
Economy: Employment by occupation: 9.0% management, 26.5% professional, 18.7% services, 24.0% sales, 0.0% farming, 6.9% construction, 15.0% production (2000).
Income: Per capita income: $24,018 (2004); Median household income: $33,056 (2004); Average household income: $50,805 (2004); Percent of households with income of $100,000 or more: 11.2% (2004); Poverty rate: 15.7% (2000).
Education: Percent of population age 25 and over with: High school diploma (including GED) or higher: 75.9% (2004); Bachelor's degree or higher: 28.9% (2004); Master's degree or higher: 13.3% (2004).

School District(s)

Alachua County School District (PK-12)
2002-03 Enrollment: 29,345 . . . . (352) 955-7880
Housing: Homeownership rate: 68.5% (2004); Median home value: $84,615 (2004); Median rent: $359 per month (2000); Median age of housing: 34 years (2000).
Transportation: Commute to work: 90.4% car, 0.0% public transportation, 1.6% walk, 4.5% work from home (2000); Travel time to work: 13.4% less than 15 minutes, 54.4% 15 to 30 minutes, 26.2% 30 to 45 minutes, 2.3% 45 to 60 minutes, 3.7% 60 minutes or more (2000)

NEWBERRY (city). Covers a land area of 44.916 square miles and a water area of 1.055 square miles. Located at 29.64° N. Lat.; 82.60° W. Long. Elevation is 75 feet.
History: Newberry developed as a shipping center for the watermelons grown on nearby farms.
Population: 2,683 (1990); 3,316 (2000); 3,533 (2004); 3,809 (2009 projected); Race: 81.9% White, 16.1% Black, 0.3% Asian, 2.3% Hispanic of any race (2004); Density: 78.7 persons per square mile (2004); Average household size: 2.62 (2004); Median age: 35.6 (2004); Male/female ratio: 92.1 (2004); Marriage status: 22.3% never married, 56.9% now married, 7.9% widowed, 12.9% divorced (2000); Foreign born: 3.6% (2000); Ancestry (includes multiple ancestries): 22.2% Other groups, 13.0% United States or American, 12.7% Irish, 11.9% English, 8.0% German (2000).
Economy: Single-family building permits issued: 101 (2004); Multi-family building permits issued: 0 (2004); Employment by occupation: 9.1% management, 16.6% professional, 16.0% services, 30.6% sales, 0.6% farming, 15.2% construction, 11.9% production (2000).
Income: Per capita income: $17,068 (2004); Median household income: $35,504 (2004); Average household income: $44,634 (2004); Percent of households with income of $100,000 or more: 7.1% (2004); Poverty rate: 12.8% (2000).
Education: Percent of population age 25 and over with: High school diploma (including GED) or higher: 79.3% (2004); Bachelor's degree or higher: 13.6% (2004); Master's degree or higher: 4.5% (2004).

School District(s)

Alachua County School District (PK-12)
2002-03 Enrollment: 29,345 . . . . (352) 955-7880
Housing: Homeownership rate: 80.7% (2004); Median home value: $92,254 (2004); Median rent: $330 per month (2000); Median age of housing: 17 years (2000).
Transportation: Commute to work: 94.4% car, 0.8% public transportation, 1.1% walk, 2.1% work from home (2000); Travel time to work: 17.0% less than 15 minutes, 26.3% 15 to 30 minutes, 40.9% 30 to 45 minutes, 9.5% 45 to 60 minutes, 6.3% 60 minutes or more (2000)

Additional Information Contacts

Newberry Chamber of Commerce . . . . (352) 472-6611

WALDO (city). Covers a land area of 1.719 square miles and a water area of 0 square miles. Located at 29.79° N. Lat.; 82.17° W. Long. Elevation is 154 feet.
History: Waldo developed as a shipping center, with produce from around Lake Santa Fe brought by steamer on a canal constructed in 1870, and transferred to the Seaboard Air Line Railway at Waldo.
Population: 924 (1990); 821 (2000); 841 (2004); 866 (2009 projected); Race: 77.1% White, 13.9% Black, 0.5% Asian, 2.1% Hispanic of any race (2004); Density: 489.1 persons per square mile (2004); Average household size: 2.32 (2004); Median age: 37.1 (2004); Male/female ratio: 91.1 (2004); Marriage status: 25.9% never married, 49.5% now married, 9.5% widowed, 15.1% divorced (2000); Foreign born: 1.4% (2000); Ancestry (includes multiple ancestries): 27.9% United States or American, 26.7% Other groups, 9.1% English, 7.9% German, 5.3% Irish (2000).
Economy: Single-family building permits issued: 1 (2004); Multi-family building permits issued: 0 (2004); Employment by occupation: 5.8% management, 12.2% professional, 25.1% services, 31.5% sales, 0.6% farming, 16.5% construction, 8.3% production (2000).
Income: Per capita income: $16,424 (2004); Median household income: $28,605 (2004); Average household income: $38,051 (2004); Percent of households with income of $100,000 or more: 3.6% (2004); Poverty rate: 16.7% (2000).
Education: Percent of population age 25 and over with: High school diploma (including GED) or higher: 72.8% (2004); Bachelor's degree or higher: 9.0% (2004); Master's degree or higher: 3.8% (2004).

School District(s)

Alachua County School District (PK-12)
2002-03 Enrollment: 29,345 . . . . (352) 955-7880
Housing: Homeownership rate: 69.4% (2004); Median home value: $57,377 (2004); Median rent: $327 per month (2000); Median age of housing: 31 years (2000).
Safety: Violent crime rate: 48.9 per 10,000 population; Property crime rate: 195.6 per 10,000 population (2003).
Transportation: Commute to work: 92.9% car, 0.6% public transportation, 4.0% walk, 1.2% work from home (2000); Travel time to work: 11.2% less than 15 minutes, 35.4% 15 to 30 minutes, 34.2% 30 to 45 minutes, 12.7% 45 to 60 minutes, 6.5% 60 minutes or more (2000); Amtrak: Service available.

Baker County

Located in northern Florida; bounded on the north by Georgia; includes part of Okefenokee Swamp and Osceola National Forest. Covers a land area of 585.20 square miles, a water area of 3.70 square miles, and is located in the Eastern Time Zone. The county government was organized in 1861. County seat is Macclenny.

Baker County is part of the Jacksonville, FL Metropolitan Statistical Area. The entire metro area includes: Baker County, FL; Clay County, FL; Duval County, FL; Nassau County, FL; St. Johns County, FL

Population: 18,486 (1990); 22,259 (2000); 23,380 (2004); 24,799 (2009 projected); Race: 85.1% White, 12.9% Black, 0.5% Asian, 2.0% Hispanic of any race (2004); Density: 40.0 persons per square mile (2004); Average

household size: 3.13 (2004); Median age: 34.5 (2004); Male/female ratio: 108.0 (2004).
Religion: Five largest groups: 14.2% Southern Baptist Convention, 3.6% Assemblies of God, 2.3% The United Methodist Church, 2.3% The Church of Jesus Christ of Latter-day Saints, 2.2% Church of God (Cleveland, Tennessee) (2000).
Economy: Unemployment rate: 3.9% (2004); Total civilian labor force: 10,696 (2004); Leading industries: 32.9% health care and social assistance; 13.5% retail trade; 12.6% transportation & warehousing (2003); Companies that employ 500 or more persons: 2 (2003); Companies that employ 100 to 499 persons: 6 (2003); Companies that employ less than 100 persons: 323 (2003); Farms: 204 totaling 18,061 acres (2002); Minority business ownership rate: n/a (1997); Women business ownership rate: 14.7% (1997); Retail sales per capita: $4,597 (1997). Single-family building permits issued: 184 (2004); Multi-family building permits issued: 22 (2004).
Income: Per capita income: $16,823 (2004); Median household income: $42,571 (2004); Average household income: $50,550 (2004); Percent of households with income of $100,000 or more: 7.6% (2004); Poverty rate: 13.3% (2002); Bankruptcy rate: 4.48% (2004).
Education: Percent of population age 25 and over with: High school diploma (including GED) or higher: 72.1% (2004); Bachelor's degree or higher: 8.4% (2004); Master's degree or higher: 2.9% (2004).
Housing: Homeownership rate: 81.4% (2004); Median home value: $92,145 (2004); Median rent: $310 per month (2000); Median age of housing: 19 years (2000).
Health: Birth rate: 158.2 per 10,000 population (2004); Death rate: 71.2 per 10,000 population (2004); Age adjusted cancer mortality rate: 145.3 deaths per 100,000 population (2002); Air Quality Index: 96.8% good, 3.2% moderate, 0.0% unhealthy for sensitive individuals, 0.0% unhealthy (percent of days in 2004); Number of physicians: 7.0 per 10,000 population (2001); Hospital beds: 29.8 per 10,000 population (2002); Hospital admissions: 544.5 per 10,000 population (2002).
Elections: 2004 Presidential election results: 77.7% Bush, 21.9% Kerry, 0.2% Nader, 0.1% Badnarik
National and State Parks: Osceola National Forest
Additional Information Contacts
Baker County Government Offices . . . . (904) 259-3613
Baker County Chamber of Commerce. . . . . (904) 259-6433

Baker County Communities

GLEN SAINT MARY (town). Covers a land area of 0.420 square miles and a water area of 0 square miles. Located at 30.27° N. Lat.; 82.16° W. Long. Elevation is 134 feet.
Population: 504 (1990); 473 (2000); 490 (2004); 511 (2009 projected); Race: 97.8% White, 0.6% Black, 1.0% Asian, 2.2% Hispanic of any race (2004); Density: 1,167.6 persons per square mile (2004); Average household size: 2.57 (2004); Median age: 31.8 (2004); Male/female ratio: 86.3 (2004); Marriage status: 20.2% never married, 57.7% now married, 6.4% widowed, 15.7% divorced (2000); Foreign born: 1.3% (2000); Ancestry (includes multiple ancestries): 34.4% United States or American, 11.1% Other groups, 6.0% Irish, 4.2% English, 2.2% Scotch-Irish (2000).
Economy: Employment by occupation: 10.5% management, 11.4% professional, 27.6% services, 25.2% sales, 4.3% farming, 9.0% construction, 11.9% production (2000).
Income: Per capita income: $14,520 (2004); Median household income: $31,220 (2004); Average household income: $37,251 (2004); Percent of households with income of $100,000 or more: 4.2% (2004); Poverty rate: 18.2% (2000).
Education: Percent of population age 25 and over with: High school diploma (including GED) or higher: 68.6% (2004); Bachelor's degree or higher: 6.6% (2004); Master's degree or higher: 1.0% (2004).

School District(s)

Baker County School District (PK-12)
2002-03 Enrollment: 4,525 . . . . (904) 259-0401
Housing: Homeownership rate: 67.5% (2004); Median home value: $58,611 (2004); Median rent: $345 per month (2000); Median age of housing: 22 years (2000).
Transportation: Commute to work: 91.8% car, 0.0% public transportation, 2.9% walk, 0.5% work from home (2000); Travel time to work: 33.8% less than 15 minutes, 26.6% 15 to 30 minutes, 22.2% 30 to 45 minutes, 4.8% 45 to 60 minutes, 12.6% 60 minutes or more (2000)

MACCLENNY (city). Covers a land area of 3.291 square miles and a water area of 0 square miles. Located at 30.28° N. Lat.; 82.12° W. Long. Elevation is 131 feet.
History: MacClenny had an early reputation as Florida's "Gretna Green" for its many quick weddings. It was said that when the judge was absent, his wife would perform the ceremony.
Population: 4,070 (1990); 4,459 (2000); 4,575 (2004); 4,732 (2009 projected); Race: 75.5% White, 22.1% Black, 0.9% Asian, 2.8% Hispanic of any race (2004); Density: 1,390.1 persons per square mile (2004); Average household size: 2.85 (2004); Median age: 31.1 (2004); Male/female ratio: 89.8 (2004); Marriage status: 18.1% never married, 58.8% now married, 7.9% widowed, 15.2% divorced (2000); Foreign born: 1.3% (2000); Ancestry (includes multiple ancestries): 21.2% Other groups, 15.1% United States or American, 9.3% Irish, 7.1% English, 6.1% German (2000).
Economy: Single-family building permits issued: 46 (2004); Multi-family building permits issued: 18 (2004); Employment by occupation: 8.5% management, 17.6% professional, 22.8% services, 24.2% sales, 0.5% farming, 13.0% construction, 13.6% production (2000).
Income: Per capita income: $16,363 (2004); Median household income: $34,913 (2004); Average household income: $43,621 (2004); Percent of households with income of $100,000 or more: 5.3% (2004); Poverty rate: 20.9% (2000).
Taxes: Total city taxes per capita: $398 (2002); City property taxes per capita: $69 (2002).
Education: Percent of population age 25 and over with: High school diploma (including GED) or higher: 71.7% (2004); Bachelor's degree or higher: 13.9% (2004); Master's degree or higher: 5.2% (2004).

School District(s)

Baker County School District (PK-12)
2002-03 Enrollment: 4,525 . . . . (904) 259-0401
Housing: Homeownership rate: 67.2% (2004); Median home value: $91,280 (2004); Median rent: $348 per month (2000); Median age of housing: 26 years (2000).
Hospitals: Ed Fraser Memorial Hospital (25 beds); Northeast Florida State Hospital (1138 beds)
Newspapers: The Baker County Press (General - Circulation 5,400)
Transportation: Commute to work: 93.4% car, 0.0% public transportation, 0.9% walk, 3.3% work from home (2000); Travel time to work: 39.6% less than 15 minutes, 16.3% 15 to 30 minutes, 19.8% 30 to 45 minutes, 17.5% 45 to 60 minutes, 6.7% 60 minutes or more (2000)
Additional Information Contacts
Baker County Chamber of Commerce. . . . . (904) 259-6433

SANDERSON (unincorporated postal area, zip code 32087). Covers a land area of 110.442 square miles and a water area of 0.756 square miles. Located at 30.39° N. Lat.; 82.26° W. Long. Elevation is 156 feet.
History: Sanderson was named in 1859 for an early settler.
Population: 3,331 (2000); Race: 76.9% White, 21.3% Black, 0.0% Asian, 2.9% Hispanic of any race (2000); Density: 30.2 persons per square mile (2000); Age: 34.7% under 18, 8.6% over 64 (2000); Marriage status: 27.6% never married, 53.8% now married, 6.9% widowed, 11.7% divorced (2000); Foreign born: 0.0% (2000); Ancestry (includes multiple ancestries): 28.7% Other groups, 25.2% United States or American, 9.8% Irish, 3.7% German, 3.4% English (2000).
Economy: Employment by occupation: 5.5% management, 9.5% professional, 23.4% services, 22.9% sales, 2.4% farming, 17.4% construction, 19.0% production (2000).
Income: Per capita income: $13,887 (2000); Median household income: $34,432 (2000); Poverty rate: 16.1% (2000).
Education: Percent of population age 25 and over with: High school diploma (including GED) or higher: 69.7% (2000); Bachelor's degree or higher: 3.4% (2000).
Housing: Homeownership rate: 79.6% (2000); Median home value: $70,500 (2000); Median rent: $280 per month (2000); Median age of housing: 19 years (2000).
Transportation: Commute to work: 97.0% car, 0.7% public transportation, 0.0% walk, 1.8% work from home (2000); Travel time to work: 8.9% less than 15 minutes, 27.6% 15 to 30 minutes, 21.7% 30 to 45 minutes, 14.2% 45 to 60 minutes, 27.5% 60 minutes or more (2000)

Bay County

Located in northwestern Florida; bounded on the south by the Gulf of Mexico. Covers a land area of 763.70 square miles, a water area of

269.60 square miles, and is located in the Central Time Zone. The county government was organized in 1913. County seat is Panama City.

Bay County is part of the Panama City-Lynn Haven, FL Metropolitan Statistical Area. The entire metro area includes: Bay County, FL

Weather Station: Panama City 5 NE Elevation: 29 feet

	Jan	Feb	Mar	Apr	May	Jun	Jul	Aug	Sep	Oct	Nov	Dec
High	63	65	71	77	84	88	90	90	88	80	73	65
Low	40	42	48	54	62	69	72	71	68	56	48	41
Precip	6.0	4.9	6.2	3.9	4.0	6.1	8.9	7.5	6.2	3.7	4.6	4.1
Snow	tr	tr	0.0	0.0	0.0	0.0	0.0	0.0	0.0	0.0	0.0	0.0

High and Low temperatures in degrees Fahrenheit; Precipitation and Snow in inches

Population: 126,994 (1990); 148,217 (2000); 155,312 (2004); 164,296 (2009 projected); Race: 84.0% White, 10.9% Black, 1.8% Asian, 1.9% Hispanic of any race (2004); Density: 203.4 persons per square mile (2004); Average household size: 2.47 (2004); Median age: 38.1 (2004); Male/female ratio: 98.4 (2004).
Religion: Five largest groups: 18.8% Southern Baptist Convention, 6.5% The United Methodist Church, 4.7% Catholic Church, 2.6% Assemblies of God, 1.0% Lutheran Church—Missouri Synod (2000).
Economy: Unemployment rate: 4.8% (2004); Total civilian labor force: 73,525 (2004); Leading industries: 18.0% retail trade; 15.7% health care and social assistance; 15.4% accommodation & food services (2003); Companies that employ 500 or more persons: 7 (2003); Companies that employ 100 to 499 persons: 76 (2003); Companies that employ less than 100 persons: 4,269 (2003); Farms: 116 totaling 10,863 acres (2002); Minority business ownership rate: 7.8% (1997); Women business ownership rate: 27.5% (1997); Retail sales per capita: $10,228 (1997). Single-family building permits issued: 1,462 (2004); Multi-family building permits issued: 2,382 (2004).
Income: Per capita income: $20,890 (2004); Median household income: $39,591 (2004); Average household income: $51,025 (2004); Percent of households with income of $100,000 or more: 9.1% (2004); Poverty rate: 12.4% (2002); Bankruptcy rate: 4.21% (2004).
Taxes: Total county taxes per capita: $385 (2002); County property taxes per capita: $224 (2002).
Education: Percent of population age 25 and over with: High school diploma (including GED) or higher: 81.1% (2004); Bachelor's degree or higher: 17.8% (2004); Master's degree or higher: 6.7% (2004).
Housing: Homeownership rate: 69.0% (2004); Median home value: $115,680 (2004); Median rent: $442 per month (2000); Median age of housing: 19 years (2000).
Health: Birth rate: 135.9 per 10,000 population (2004); Death rate: 95.7 per 10,000 population (2004); Age adjusted cancer mortality rate: 212.4 deaths per 100,000 population (2002); Air Quality Index: 86.7% good, 12.5% moderate, 0.8% unhealthy for sensitive individuals, 0.0% unhealthy (percent of days in 2004); Number of physicians: 19.6 per 10,000 population (2001); Hospital beds: 36.0 per 10,000 population (2002); Hospital admissions: 1,631.3 per 10,000 population (2002).
Elections: 2004 Presidential election results: 71.2% Bush, 28.1% Kerry, 0.5% Nader, 0.1% Badnarik
National and State Parks: Camp Helen State Park; Pine Log State Forest; Saint Andrews State Park
Additional Information Contacts
Bay County Government Offices . . . . (850) 784-4015
Bay County Association of Realtors. . . . . (386) 763-8078
Panama City Chamber of Commerce . . . . (850) 785-5206

Bay County Communities

CALLAWAY (city). Aka Calloway. Covers a land area of 5.685 square miles and a water area of 0.412 square miles. Located at 30.14° N. Lat.; 85.57° W. Long. Elevation is 33 feet.
Population: 13,001 (1990); 14,233 (2000); 14,493 (2004); 14,863 (2009 projected); Race: 73.3% White, 18.4% Black, 3.3% Asian, 2.7% Hispanic of any race (2004); Density: 2,549.2 persons per square mile (2004); Average household size: 2.53 (2004); Median age: 34.5 (2004); Male/female ratio: 99.5 (2004); Marriage status: 23.0% never married, 58.7% now married, 5.1% widowed, 13.2% divorced (2000); Foreign born: 5.9% (2000); Ancestry (includes multiple ancestries): 30.2% Other groups, 13.9% United States or American, 10.4% Irish, 10.0% German, 8.4% English (2000).
Economy: Single-family building permits issued: 35 (2004); Multi-family building permits issued: 0 (2004); Employment by occupation: 7.4% management, 15.9% professional, 21.8% services, 31.9% sales, 0.6% farming, 10.0% construction, 12.4% production (2000).
Income: Per capita income: $18,302 (2004); Median household income: $38,804 (2004); Average household income: $46,372 (2004); Percent of households with income of $100,000 or more: 6.1% (2004); Poverty rate: 11.6% (2000).
Taxes: Total city taxes per capita: $145 (2002); City property taxes per capita: $0 (2002).
Education: Percent of population age 25 and over with: High school diploma (including GED) or higher: 83.3% (2004); Bachelor's degree or higher: 14.1% (2004); Master's degree or higher: 5.6% (2004).
Housing: Homeownership rate: 64.7% (2004); Median home value: $117,560 (2004); Median rent: $417 per month (2000); Median age of housing: 18 years (2000).
Transportation: Commute to work: 96.0% car, 0.4% public transportation, 0.9% walk, 1.6% work from home (2000); Travel time to work: 24.1% less than 15 minutes, 54.2% 15 to 30 minutes, 12.8% 30 to 45 minutes, 2.6% 45 to 60 minutes, 6.3% 60 minutes or more (2000)
Additional Information Contacts
Local Government Offices . . . . (850) 871-6000

CEDAR GROVE (town). Covers a land area of 9.375 square miles and a water area of 0 square miles. Located at 30.21° N. Lat.; 85.60° W. Long. Elevation is 30 feet.
Population: 4,329 (1990); 5,367 (2000); 5,674 (2004); 6,057 (2009 projected); Race: 83.9% White, 11.5% Black, 1.9% Asian, 1.7% Hispanic of any race (2004); Density: 605.2 persons per square mile (2004); Average household size: 2.55 (2004); Median age: 34.7 (2004); Male/female ratio: 92.2 (2004); Marriage status: 22.2% never married, 56.2% now married, 5.7% widowed, 15.9% divorced (2000); Foreign born: 3.0% (2000); Ancestry (includes multiple ancestries): 21.7% United States or American, 19.1% Other groups, 10.0% Irish, 8.8% German, 6.8% English (2000).
Economy: Employment by occupation: 4.4% management, 10.6% professional, 24.3% services, 29.4% sales, 0.4% farming, 17.9% construction, 13.0% production (2000).
Income: Per capita income: $15,296 (2004); Median household income: $30,894 (2004); Average household income: $38,740 (2004); Percent of households with income of $100,000 or more: 4.3% (2004); Poverty rate: 19.0% (2000).
Taxes: Total city taxes per capita: $93 (2002); City property taxes per capita: $0 (2002).
Education: Percent of population age 25 and over with: High school diploma (including GED) or higher: 72.3% (2004); Bachelor's degree or higher: 8.4% (2004); Master's degree or higher: 3.3% (2004).
Housing: Homeownership rate: 67.3% (2004); Median home value: $79,050 (2004); Median rent: $378 per month (2000); Median age of housing: 17 years (2000).
Safety: Violent crime rate: 39.7 per 10,000 population; Property crime rate: 326.8 per 10,000 population (2003).
Transportation: Commute to work: 93.0% car, 0.7% public transportation, 1.1% walk, 2.0% work from home (2000); Travel time to work: 37.0% less than 15 minutes, 41.7% 15 to 30 minutes, 14.6% 30 to 45 minutes, 4.3% 45 to 60 minutes, 2.5% 60 minutes or more (2000)

FOUNTAIN (unincorporated postal area, zip code 32438). Covers a land area of 72.899 square miles and a water area of 0.280 square miles. Located at 30.48° N. Lat.; 85.41° W. Long. Elevation is 184 feet.
Population: 3,365 (2000); Race: 94.6% White, 0.6% Black, 1.9% Asian, 4.1% Hispanic of any race (2000); Density: 46.2 persons per square mile (2000); Age: 27.2% under 18, 9.6% over 64 (2000); Marriage status: 15.8% never married, 65.5% now married, 5.7% widowed, 13.0% divorced (2000); Foreign born: 3.1% (2000); Ancestry (includes multiple ancestries): 25.3% United States or American, 15.2% Other groups, 14.2% German, 12.1% Irish, 6.1% English (2000).
Economy: Employment by occupation: 4.0% management, 5.3% professional, 21.9% services, 27.6% sales, 0.5% farming, 23.8% construction, 16.8% production (2000).
Income: Per capita income: $12,267 (2000); Median household income: $25,465 (2000); Poverty rate: 28.9% (2000).
Education: Percent of population age 25 and over with: High school diploma (including GED) or higher: 59.1% (2000); Bachelor's degree or higher: 4.6% (2000).
Housing: Homeownership rate: 90.3% (2000); Median home value: $42,500 (2000); Median rent: $278 per month (2000); Median age of housing: 18 years (2000).

Transportation: Commute to work: 93.8% car, 0.0% public transportation, 0.0% walk, 1.2% work from home (2000); Travel time to work: 9.1% less than 15 minutes, 11.2% 15 to 30 minutes, 48.5% 30 to 45 minutes, 19.7% 45 to 60 minutes, 11.5% 60 minutes or more (2000)

HILAND PARK (CDP). Covers a land area of 1.133 square miles and a water area of 0 square miles. Located at 30.20° N. Lat.; 85.62° W. Long. Elevation is 28 feet.
Population: 1,016 (1990); 999 (2000); 1,035 (2004); 1,074 (2009 projected); Race: 90.3% White, 6.6% Black, 2.0% Asian, 0.9% Hispanic of any race (2004); Density: 913.8 persons per square mile (2004); Average household size: 2.67 (2004); Median age: 38.5 (2004); Male/female ratio: 96.8 (2004); Marriage status: 18.1% never married, 49.7% now married, 8.5% widowed, 23.7% divorced (2000); Foreign born: 3.4% (2000); Ancestry (includes multiple ancestries): 20.4% United States or American, 15.9% Other groups, 6.9% Irish, 5.7% German, 4.4% English (2000).
Economy: Employment by occupation: 10.4% management, 18.3% professional, 20.3% services, 26.6% sales, 0.0% farming, 19.5% construction, 4.8% production (2000).
Income: Per capita income: $17,405 (2004); Median household income: $39,167 (2004); Average household income: $46,108 (2004); Percent of households with income of $100,000 or more: 7.0% (2004); Poverty rate: 19.3% (2000).
Education: Percent of population age 25 and over with: High school diploma (including GED) or higher: 81.8% (2004); Bachelor's degree or higher: 15.9% (2004); Master's degree or higher: 4.7% (2004).
Housing: Homeownership rate: 77.6% (2004); Median home value: $78,158 (2004); Median rent: $370 per month (2000); Median age of housing: 22 years (2000).
Transportation: Commute to work: 90.6% car, 0.0% public transportation, 6.1% walk, 1.3% work from home (2000); Travel time to work: 35.7% less than 15 minutes, 33.4% 15 to 30 minutes, 14.7% 30 to 45 minutes, 13.6% 45 to 60 minutes, 2.6% 60 minutes or more (2000)

LAGUNA BEACH (CDP). Covers a land area of 2.558 square miles and a water area of 0.141 square miles. Located at 30.25° N. Lat.; 85.94° W. Long. Elevation is 7 feet.
Population: 1,886 (1990); 2,909 (2000); 2,982 (2004); 3,109 (2009 projected); Race: 94.1% White, 1.1% Black, 1.7% Asian, 0.8% Hispanic of any race (2004); Density: 1,166.0 persons per square mile (2004); Average household size: 2.12 (2004); Median age: 45.2 (2004); Male/female ratio: 99.2 (2004); Marriage status: 21.1% never married, 56.2% now married, 6.4% widowed, 16.2% divorced (2000); Foreign born: 2.3% (2000); Ancestry (includes multiple ancestries): 17.8% English, 17.1% German, 17.0% United States or American, 16.0% Other groups, 11.8% Irish (2000).
Economy: Employment by occupation: 10.3% management, 12.1% professional, 22.5% services, 25.1% sales, 0.0% farming, 19.6% construction, 10.4% production (2000).
Income: Per capita income: $22,575 (2004); Median household income: $36,548 (2004); Average household income: $47,915 (2004); Percent of households with income of $100,000 or more: 7.3% (2004); Poverty rate: 14.8% (2000).
Education: Percent of population age 25 and over with: High school diploma (including GED) or higher: 84.6% (2004); Bachelor's degree or higher: 21.0% (2004); Master's degree or higher: 5.7% (2004).
Housing: Homeownership rate: 69.2% (2004); Median home value: $142,462 (2004); Median rent: $491 per month (2000); Median age of housing: 20 years (2000).
Transportation: Commute to work: 91.5% car, 0.8% public transportation, 1.5% walk, 1.1% work from home (2000); Travel time to work: 31.0% less than 15 minutes, 31.3% 15 to 30 minutes, 25.2% 30 to 45 minutes, 8.0% 45 to 60 minutes, 4.5% 60 minutes or more (2000)

LOWER GRAND LAGOON (CDP). Covers a land area of 2.174 square miles and a water area of 0.517 square miles. Located at 30.15° N. Lat.; 85.76° W. Long.
Population: 3,323 (1990); 4,082 (2000); 4,300 (2004); 4,565 (2009 projected); Race: 95.7% White, 1.4% Black, 0.7% Asian, 2.5% Hispanic of any race (2004); Density: 1,978.0 persons per square mile (2004); Average household size: 1.94 (2004); Median age: 42.5 (2004); Male/female ratio: 104.4 (2004); Marriage status: 27.4% never married, 47.6% now married, 9.2% widowed, 15.9% divorced (2000); Foreign born: 6.8% (2000); Ancestry (includes multiple ancestries): 15.2% German, 14.6% English, 14.6% Irish, 11.8% Other groups, 8.5% United States or American (2000).
Economy: Employment by occupation: 12.9% management, 14.3% professional, 23.1% services, 30.8% sales, 1.2% farming, 12.1% construction, 5.5% production (2000).
Income: Per capita income: $19,292 (2004); Median household income: $30,042 (2004); Average household income: $37,453 (2004); Percent of households with income of $100,000 or more: 4.2% (2004); Poverty rate: 16.3% (2000).
Education: Percent of population age 25 and over with: High school diploma (including GED) or higher: 89.7% (2004); Bachelor's degree or higher: 21.0% (2004); Master's degree or higher: 6.1% (2004).
Housing: Homeownership rate: 52.1% (2004); Median home value: $125,401 (2004); Median rent: $515 per month (2000); Median age of housing: 17 years (2000).
Transportation: Commute to work: 91.6% car, 0.0% public transportation, 2.4% walk, 2.3% work from home (2000); Travel time to work: 39.4% less than 15 minutes, 42.6% 15 to 30 minutes, 13.3% 30 to 45 minutes, 1.5% 45 to 60 minutes, 3.1% 60 minutes or more (2000)

LYNN HAVEN (city). Covers a land area of 8.150 square miles and a water area of 1.378 square miles. Located at 30.24° N. Lat.; 85.64° W. Long. Elevation is 10 feet.
Population: 10,502 (1990); 12,451 (2000); 13,689 (2004); 15,169 (2009 projected); Race: 86.3% White, 9.2% Black, 1.7% Asian, 1.4% Hispanic of any race (2004); Density: 1,679.6 persons per square mile (2004); Average household size: 2.50 (2004); Median age: 38.0 (2004); Male/female ratio: 93.6 (2004); Marriage status: 19.9% never married, 61.6% now married, 6.4% widowed, 12.2% divorced (2000); Foreign born: 2.8% (2000); Ancestry (includes multiple ancestries): 17.2% Other groups, 14.9% United States or American, 14.4% Irish, 12.9% German, 11.6% English (2000).
Economy: Manufacturing includes automotive disc brakes, feeders, table lamps, vinyl windows. Single-family building permits issued: 265 (2004); Multi-family building permits issued: 148 (2004); Employment by occupation: 12.7% management, 22.9% professional, 14.2% services, 29.6% sales, 0.6% farming, 9.7% construction, 10.3% production (2000).
Income: Per capita income: $23,555 (2004); Median household income: $47,552 (2004); Average household income: $58,917 (2004); Percent of households with income of $100,000 or more: 12.7% (2004); Poverty rate: 7.2% (2000).
Taxes: Total city taxes per capita: $250 (2002); City property taxes per capita: $114 (2002).
Education: Percent of population age 25 and over with: High school diploma (including GED) or higher: 86.0% (2004); Bachelor's degree or higher: 22.7% (2004); Master's degree or higher: 8.0% (2004).

School District(s)

Bay County School District (PK-12)
2002-03 Enrollment: 26,440 . . . . (850) 872-7700
Housing: Homeownership rate: 77.1% (2004); Median home value: $133,520 (2004); Median rent: $417 per month (2000); Median age of housing: 19 years (2000).
Safety: Violent crime rate: 33.3 per 10,000 population; Property crime rate: 353.1 per 10,000 population (2003).
Transportation: Commute to work: 95.1% car, 0.1% public transportation, 1.5% walk, 1.5% work from home (2000); Travel time to work: 35.6% less than 15 minutes, 48.0% 15 to 30 minutes, 12.1% 30 to 45 minutes, 1.4% 45 to 60 minutes, 2.9% 60 minutes or more (2000)
Additional Information Contacts
Local Government Offices . . . . (850) 265-2121

MEXICO BEACH (city). Covers a land area of 1.308 square miles and a water area of 0.015 square miles. Located at 29.94° N. Lat.; 85.40° W. Long. Elevation is 13 feet.
Population: 1,012 (1990); 1,017 (2000); 1,017 (2004); 1,022 (2009 projected); Race: 95.2% White, 1.5% Black, 0.9% Asian, 1.3% Hispanic of any race (2004); Density: 777.3 persons per square mile (2004); Average household size: 1.90 (2004); Median age: 55.0 (2004); Male/female ratio: 97.1 (2004); Marriage status: 11.0% never married, 64.7% now married, 10.3% widowed, 14.0% divorced (2000); Foreign born: 3.4% (2000); Ancestry (includes multiple ancestries): 22.8% United States or American, 19.0% German, 15.3% Irish, 14.2% English, 12.3% Other groups (2000).
Economy: Single-family building permits issued: 10 (2004); Multi-family building permits issued: 228 (2004); Employment by occupation: 18.4% management, 14.9% professional, 16.2% services, 27.4% sales, 0.5% farming, 12.0% construction, 10.6% production (2000).
Income: Per capita income: $24,880 (2004); Median household income: $34,824 (2004); Average household income: $47,294 (2004); Percent of

households with income of $100,000 or more: 10.8% (2004); Poverty rate: 11.5% (2000).
Education: Percent of population age 25 and over with: High school diploma (including GED) or higher: 83.9% (2004); Bachelor's degree or higher: 19.2% (2004); Master's degree or higher: 6.6% (2004).
Housing: Homeownership rate: 74.0% (2004); Median home value: $137,500 (2004); Median rent: $484 per month (2000); Median age of housing: 20 years (2000).
Safety: Violent crime rate: 19.4 per 10,000 population; Property crime rate: 425.9 per 10,000 population (2003).
Transportation: Commute to work: 86.8% car, 0.0% public transportation, 5.9% walk, 5.3% work from home (2000); Travel time to work: 46.2% less than 15 minutes, 28.5% 15 to 30 minutes, 13.4% 30 to 45 minutes, 7.0% 45 to 60 minutes, 4.8% 60 minutes or more (2000)

PANAMA CITY (city). Covers a land area of 20.519 square miles and a water area of 6.171 square miles. Located at 30.17° N. Lat.; 85.66° W. Long. Elevation is 33 feet.
History: In 1909 Panama City was united in incorporation with St. Andrews and Millville. St. Andrews had been a flourishing community in the early 1800's, when homesteaders who came during the Revolutionary War established indigo plantations and engaged in lumbering and fishing. Growth came to Panama City with the founding of paper mills in 1931.
Population: 36,193 (1990); 36,417 (2000); 37,037 (2004); 37,855 (2009 projected); Race: 73.4% White, 21.8% Black, 1.5% Asian, 2.5% Hispanic of any race (2004); Density: 1,805.0 persons per square mile (2004); Average household size: 2.45 (2004); Median age: 37.7 (2004); Male/female ratio: 95.5 (2004); Marriage status: 23.5% never married, 53.8% now married, 8.2% widowed, 14.5% divorced (2000); Foreign born: 3.2% (2000); Ancestry (includes multiple ancestries): 25.9% Other groups, 12.9% United States or American, 10.3% Irish, 9.8% German, 9.1% English (2000).
Economy: Unemployment rate: 5.8% (2004); Total civilian labor force: 19,709 (2004); Employment by occupation: 10.9% management, 21.2% professional, 20.8% services, 27.7% sales, 0.4% farming, 8.6% construction, 10.4% production (2000).
Income: Per capita income: $19,560 (2004); Median household income: $33,923 (2004); Average household income: $46,983 (2004); Percent of households with income of $100,000 or more: 8.0% (2004); Poverty rate: 17.2% (2000).
Taxes: Total city taxes per capita: $533 (2002); City property taxes per capita: $141 (2002).
Education: Percent of population age 25 and over with: High school diploma (including GED) or higher: 79.2% (2004); Bachelor's degree or higher: 19.0% (2004); Master's degree or higher: 7.5% (2004).

School District(s)

Bay County School District (PK-12)
2002-03 Enrollment: 26,440 . . . . (850) 872-7700

Four-year College(s)

Gooding Institute of Nurse Anesthesia (Public)
2003-04 Enrollment: 35 . . . . (850) 747-6918

Two-year College(s)

Gulf Coast Community College (Public)
2003-04 Enrollment: 6,058 . . . . (850) 769-1551
2003-04 Tuition: In-state $1,672; Out-of-state $6,234
Tom P Haney Technical Center (Public)
2003-04 Enrollment: 427 . . . . (850) 747-5500

Housing: Homeownership rate: 57.5% (2004); Median home value: $102,692 (2004); Median rent: $435 per month (2000); Median age of housing: 31 years (2000).
Hospitals: 325th Medical Group (AETC) (25 beds); Bay Medical Center (433 beds); Gulf Coast Medical Center (176 beds)
Safety: Violent crime rate: 101.1 per 10,000 population; Property crime rate: 753.6 per 10,000 population (2003).
Newspapers: The News Herald (Circulation 32,350)
Transportation: Commute to work: 93.9% car, 0.7% public transportation, 1.6% walk, 2.2% work from home (2000); Travel time to work: 44.1% less than 15 minutes, 40.2% 15 to 30 minutes, 10.3% 30 to 45 minutes, 2.6% 45 to 60 minutes, 2.8% 60 minutes or more (2000)
Airports: Panama City-Bay Co International (primary service); Tyndall AFB (primary service)

Additional Information Contacts

Bay County Association of Realtors. . . . . (386) 763-8078
Panama City Chamber of Commerce . . . . (850) 785-5206

PANAMA CITY BEACH (city). Covers a land area of 6.943 square miles and a water area of 0.100 square miles. Located at 30.20° N. Lat.; 85.85° W. Long. Elevation is 7 feet.
History: Panama City Beach developed as a resort and fishing center in an area where English soldiers were given land grants in the late 1700's.
Population: 4,306 (1990); 7,671 (2000); 8,403 (2004); 9,268 (2009 projected); Race: 96.0% White, 1.1% Black, 0.7% Asian, 1.8% Hispanic of any race (2004); Density: 1,210.4 persons per square mile (2004); Average household size: 2.16 (2004); Median age: 45.5 (2004); Male/female ratio: 100.8 (2004); Marriage status: 15.7% never married, 63.0% now married, 6.9% widowed, 14.5% divorced (2000); Foreign born: 4.1% (2000); Ancestry (includes multiple ancestries): 17.8% English, 17.4% German, 14.8% Irish, 11.1% United States or American, 8.1% Other groups (2000).
Economy: Single-family building permits issued: 230 (2004); Multi-family building permits issued: 1,464 (2004); Employment by occupation: 13.8% management, 18.8% professional, 20.4% services, 29.3% sales, 0.2% farming, 9.3% construction, 8.2% production (2000).
Income: Per capita income: $27,967 (2004); Median household income: $46,142 (2004); Average household income: $60,351 (2004); Percent of households with income of $100,000 or more: 13.0% (2004); Poverty rate: 5.0% (2000).
Taxes: Total city taxes per capita: $873 (2002); City property taxes per capita: $0 (2002).
Education: Percent of population age 25 and over with: High school diploma (including GED) or higher: 87.5% (2004); Bachelor's degree or higher: 24.4% (2004); Master's degree or higher: 9.0% (2004).

School District(s)

Bay County School District (PK-12)
2002-03 Enrollment: 26,440 . . . . (850) 872-7700

Housing: Homeownership rate: 73.3% (2004); Median home value: $144,261 (2004); Median rent: $589 per month (2000); Median age of housing: 14 years (2000).
Safety: Violent crime rate: 128.5 per 10,000 population; Property crime rate: 1,471.7 per 10,000 population (2003).
Transportation: Commute to work: 90.3% car, 0.0% public transportation, 5.0% walk, 3.0% work from home (2000); Travel time to work: 48.0% less than 15 minutes, 30.5% 15 to 30 minutes, 15.0% 30 to 45 minutes, 2.8% 45 to 60 minutes, 3.7% 60 minutes or more (2000)

Additional Information Contacts

Local Government Offices . . . . (850) 233-5100

PARKER (city). Covers a land area of 1.941 square miles and a water area of 0.488 square miles. Located at 30.13° N. Lat.; 85.60° W. Long. Elevation is 20 feet.
Population: 4,559 (1990); 4,623 (2000); 4,712 (2004); 4,847 (2009 projected); Race: 79.9% White, 13.3% Black, 2.8% Asian, 1.8% Hispanic of any race (2004); Density: 2,427.5 persons per square mile (2004); Average household size: 2.30 (2004); Median age: 38.3 (2004); Male/female ratio: 98.3 (2004); Marriage status: 20.3% never married, 55.9% now married, 6.9% widowed, 16.8% divorced (2000); Foreign born: 5.1% (2000); Ancestry (includes multiple ancestries): 21.4% United States or American, 21.0% Other groups, 12.3% Irish, 10.6% German, 10.0% English (2000).
Economy: Employment by occupation: 9.5% management, 17.8% professional, 21.8% services, 25.5% sales, 0.6% farming, 14.8% construction, 10.0% production (2000).
Income: Per capita income: $21,085 (2004); Median household income: $41,898 (2004); Average household income: $48,465 (2004); Percent of households with income of $100,000 or more: 7.9% (2004); Poverty rate: 12.2% (2000).
Education: Percent of population age 25 and over with: High school diploma (including GED) or higher: 82.3% (2004); Bachelor's degree or higher: 18.0% (2004); Master's degree or higher: 5.9% (2004).
Housing: Homeownership rate: 61.9% (2004); Median home value: $107,169 (2004); Median rent: $449 per month (2000); Median age of housing: 24 years (2000).
Safety: Violent crime rate: 48.4 per 10,000 population; Property crime rate: 174.8 per 10,000 population (2003).
Transportation: Commute to work: 93.1% car, 0.5% public transportation, 2.2% walk, 2.4% work from home (2000); Travel time to work: 30.4% less than 15 minutes, 47.2% 15 to 30 minutes, 11.8% 30 to 45 minutes, 4.3% 45 to 60 minutes, 6.4% 60 minutes or more (2000)

PRETTY BAYOU (CDP). Covers a land area of 1.974 square miles and a water area of 0.141 square miles. Located at 30.19° N. Lat.; 85.69° W. Long.
Population: 3,685 (1990); 3,519 (2000); 3,447 (2004); 3,367 (2009 projected); Race: 94.1% White, 2.8% Black, 1.3% Asian, 1.2% Hispanic of any race (2004); Density: 1,746.1 persons per square mile (2004); Average household size: 2.45 (2004); Median age: 47.4 (2004); Male/female ratio: 93.5 (2004); Marriage status: 16.7% never married, 62.0% now married, 9.9% widowed, 11.4% divorced (2000); Foreign born: 2.7% (2000); Ancestry (includes multiple ancestries): 17.1% German, 16.3% English, 14.2% United States or American, 10.1% Irish, 8.9% Other groups (2000).
Economy: Employment by occupation: 12.7% management, 23.9% professional, 15.5% services, 30.0% sales, 1.0% farming, 6.3% construction, 10.6% production (2000).
Income: Per capita income: $28,666 (2004); Median household income: $51,972 (2004); Average household income: $70,201 (2004); Percent of households with income of $100,000 or more: 17.7% (2004); Poverty rate: 6.0% (2000).
Education: Percent of population age 25 and over with: High school diploma (including GED) or higher: 84.9% (2004); Bachelor's degree or higher: 28.5% (2004); Master's degree or higher: 11.6% (2004).
Housing: Homeownership rate: 82.7% (2004); Median home value: $167,077 (2004); Median rent: $433 per month (2000); Median age of housing: 27 years (2000).
Transportation: Commute to work: 96.0% car, 0.0% public transportation, 0.4% walk, 3.2% work from home (2000); Travel time to work: 47.0% less than 15 minutes, 41.4% 15 to 30 minutes, 6.2% 30 to 45 minutes, 1.1% 45 to 60 minutes, 4.3% 60 minutes or more (2000)

SPRINGFIELD (city). Covers a land area of 3.962 square miles and a water area of 0.162 square miles. Located at 30.16° N. Lat.; 85.61° W. Long. Elevation is 32 feet.
Population: 9,120 (1990); 8,810 (2000); 8,883 (2004); 9,018 (2009 projected); Race: 65.9% White, 24.4% Black, 4.7% Asian, 2.2% Hispanic of any race (2004); Density: 2,242.0 persons per square mile (2004); Average household size: 2.55 (2004); Median age: 33.5 (2004); Male/female ratio: 91.8 (2004); Marriage status: 24.6% never married, 54.4% now married, 7.2% widowed, 13.8% divorced (2000); Foreign born: 5.0% (2000); Ancestry (includes multiple ancestries): 32.2% Other groups, 14.1% United States or American, 10.0% Irish, 7.4% English, 5.9% German (2000).
Economy: Employment by occupation: 6.4% management, 12.9% professional, 24.9% services, 26.5% sales, 0.3% farming, 15.2% construction, 13.8% production (2000).
Income: Per capita income: $14,249 (2004); Median household income: $30,778 (2004); Average household income: $36,103 (2004); Percent of households with income of $100,000 or more: 1.5% (2004); Poverty rate: 21.5% (2000).
Taxes: Total city taxes per capita: $4 (2002); City property taxes per capita: $0 (2002).
Education: Percent of population age 25 and over with: High school diploma (including GED) or higher: 68.8% (2004); Bachelor's degree or higher: 7.8% (2004); Master's degree or higher: 2.1% (2004).
Housing: Homeownership rate: 60.0% (2004); Median home value: $81,105 (2004); Median rent: $376 per month (2000); Median age of housing: 27 years (2000).
Safety: Violent crime rate: 144.0 per 10,000 population; Property crime rate: 406.6 per 10,000 population (2003).
Transportation: Commute to work: 97.7% car, 0.1% public transportation, 0.5% walk, 1.2% work from home (2000); Travel time to work: 31.6% less than 15 minutes, 48.0% 15 to 30 minutes, 15.4% 30 to 45 minutes, 2.5% 45 to 60 minutes, 2.5% 60 minutes or more (2000)
Additional Information Contacts
Local Government Offices . . . . (850) 872-7570

TYNDALL AFB (CDP). Covers a land area of 14.574 square miles and a water area of 0.064 square miles. Located at 30.07° N. Lat.; 85.57° W. Long.
Population: 4,321 (1990); 2,757 (2000); 2,334 (2004); 1,991 (2009 projected); Race: 75.7% White, 13.9% Black, 3.2% Asian, 6.6% Hispanic of any race (2004); Density: 160.1 persons per square mile (2004); Average household size: 4.18 (2004); Median age: 22.1 (2004); Male/female ratio: 120.2 (2004); Marriage status: 28.0% never married, 69.4% now married, 0.7% widowed, 1.9% divorced (2000); Foreign born: 4.6% (2000); Ancestry (includes multiple ancestries): 29.9% Other groups, 15.2% German, 10.4% Irish, 10.3% United States or American, 6.0% Italian (2000).
Economy: Employment by occupation: 6.3% management, 25.1% professional, 22.0% services, 39.5% sales, 0.0% farming, 4.4% construction, 2.7% production (2000).
Income: Per capita income: $13,494 (2004); Median household income: $39,461 (2004); Average household income: $48,296 (2004); Percent of households with income of $100,000 or more: 5.0% (2004); Poverty rate: 3.6% (2000).
Education: Percent of population age 25 and over with: High school diploma (including GED) or higher: 96.8% (2004); Bachelor's degree or higher: 22.5% (2004); Master's degree or higher: 7.9% (2004).

School District(s)

Bay County School District (PK-12)
2002-03 Enrollment: 26,440 . . . . (850) 872-7700
Housing: Homeownership rate: 1.4% (2004); Median home value: $233,333 (2004); Median rent: $694 per month (2000); Median age of housing: 33 years (2000).
Transportation: Commute to work: 91.3% car, 0.0% public transportation, 3.6% walk, 1.8% work from home (2000); Travel time to work: 66.3% less than 15 minutes, 26.7% 15 to 30 minutes, 6.1% 30 to 45 minutes, 0.5% 45 to 60 minutes, 0.5% 60 minutes or more (2000)

UPPER GRAND LAGOON (CDP). Covers a land area of 8.248 square miles and a water area of 7.674 square miles. Located at 30.17° N. Lat.; 85.75° W. Long.
Population: 7,855 (1990); 10,889 (2000); 11,931 (2004); 13,194 (2009 projected); Race: 93.7% White, 1.4% Black, 1.8% Asian, 1.9% Hispanic of any race (2004); Density: 1,446.5 persons per square mile (2004); Average household size: 2.35 (2004); Median age: 39.3 (2004); Male/female ratio: 104.8 (2004); Marriage status: 19.8% never married, 62.9% now married, 5.0% widowed, 12.3% divorced (2000); Foreign born: 3.8% (2000); Ancestry (includes multiple ancestries): 16.6% United States or American, 15.8% English, 15.0% Irish, 13.5% German, 10.7% Other groups (2000).
Economy: Employment by occupation: 15.4% management, 19.6% professional, 22.5% services, 26.1% sales, 1.0% farming, 8.2% construction, 7.2% production (2000).
Income: Per capita income: $26,479 (2004); Median household income: $44,331 (2004); Average household income: $61,173 (2004); Percent of households with income of $100,000 or more: 13.7% (2004); Poverty rate: 9.6% (2000).
Education: Percent of population age 25 and over with: High school diploma (including GED) or higher: 88.0% (2004); Bachelor's degree or higher: 23.1% (2004); Master's degree or higher: 9.2% (2004).
Housing: Homeownership rate: 69.5% (2004); Median home value: $158,679 (2004); Median rent: $525 per month (2000); Median age of housing: 14 years (2000).
Transportation: Commute to work: 92.3% car, 0.0% public transportation, 1.9% walk, 4.4% work from home (2000); Travel time to work: 49.6% less than 15 minutes, 33.6% 15 to 30 minutes, 11.9% 30 to 45 minutes, 1.7% 45 to 60 minutes, 3.2% 60 minutes or more (2000)

YOUNGSTOWN (unincorporated postal area, zip code 32466). Covers a land area of 123.232 square miles and a water area of 0.178 square miles. Located at 30.37° N. Lat.; 85.52° W. Long. Elevation is 88 feet.
Population: 5,546 (2000); Race: 93.5% White, 1.3% Black, 0.3% Asian, 1.5% Hispanic of any race (2000); Density: 45.0 persons per square mile (2000); Age: 28.5% under 18, 8.0% over 64 (2000); Marriage status: 17.1% never married, 65.4% now married, 5.6% widowed, 11.9% divorced (2000); Foreign born: 2.8% (2000); Ancestry (includes multiple ancestries): 27.3% United States or American, 17.3% Other groups, 11.8% Irish, 9.7% English, 8.0% German (2000).
Economy: Employment by occupation: 9.3% management, 12.4% professional, 14.9% services, 24.9% sales, 0.7% farming, 19.1% construction, 18.6% production (2000).
Income: Per capita income: $14,899 (2000); Median household income: $35,000 (2000); Poverty rate: 12.0% (2000).
Education: Percent of population age 25 and over with: High school diploma (including GED) or higher: 73.7% (2000); Bachelor's degree or higher: 5.7% (2000).

School District(s)

Bay County School District (PK-12)
2002-03 Enrollment: 26,440 . . . . (850) 872-7700

Housing: Homeownership rate: 91.3% (2000); Median home value: $84,000 (2000); Median rent: $433 per month (2000); Median age of housing: 14 years (2000).
Transportation: Commute to work: 93.0% car, 0.8% public transportation, 0.8% walk, 3.0% work from home (2000); Travel time to work: 11.1% less than 15 minutes, 35.0% 15 to 30 minutes, 31.7% 30 to 45 minutes, 12.4% 45 to 60 minutes, 9.8% 60 minutes or more (2000)

Bradford County

Located in northern Florida; bounded on the south by the Santa Fe River. Covers a land area of 293.10 square miles, a water area of 6.90 square miles, and is located in the Eastern Time Zone. The county government was organized in 1858. County seat is Starke.
Population: 22,515 (1990); 26,088 (2000); 26,760 (2004); 27,619 (2009 projected); Race: 76.1% White, 21.2% Black, 0.7% Asian, 2.5% Hispanic of any race (2004); Density: 91.3 persons per square mile (2004); Average household size: 3.08 (2004); Median age: 37.4 (2004); Male/female ratio: 128.3 (2004).
Religion: Five largest groups: 33.8% Southern Baptist Convention, 4.0% The United Methodist Church, 2.5% Church of God (Cleveland, Tennessee), 1.4% The Church of Jesus Christ of Latter-day Saints, 1.3% Presbyterian Church (U.S.A.) (2000).
Economy: Unemployment rate: 3.2% (2004); Total civilian labor force: 10,966 (2004); Leading industries: 21.1% health care and social assistance; 18.6% retail trade; 17.0% accommodation & food services (2003); Companies that employ 500 or more persons: 0 (2003); Companies that employ 100 to 499 persons: 10 (2003); Companies that employ less than 100 persons: 387 (2003); Farms: 378 totaling 44,819 acres (2002); Minority business ownership rate: n/a (1997); Women business ownership rate: 23.0% (1997); Retail sales per capita: $6,165 (1997). Single-family building permits issued: 84 (2004); Multi-family building permits issued: 0 (2004).
Income: Per capita income: $15,148 (2004); Median household income: $36,444 (2004); Average household income: $45,319 (2004); Percent of households with income of $100,000 or more: 5.9% (2004); Poverty rate: 17.8% (2002); Bankruptcy rate: 3.41% (2004).
Taxes: Total county taxes per capita: $296 (2002); County property taxes per capita: $177 (2002).
Education: Percent of population age 25 and over with: High school diploma (including GED) or higher: 74.2% (2004); Bachelor's degree or higher: 8.1% (2004); Master's degree or higher: 3.2% (2004).
Housing: Homeownership rate: 79.0% (2004); Median home value: $88,638 (2004); Median rent: $323 per month (2000); Median age of housing: 23 years (2000).
Health: Birth rate: 105.4 per 10,000 population (2004); Death rate: 107.2 per 10,000 population (2004); Age adjusted cancer mortality rate: 201.0 deaths per 100,000 population (2002); Number of physicians: 5.3 per 10,000 population (2001); Hospital beds: 11.4 per 10,000 population (2002); Hospital admissions: 422.5 per 10,000 population (2002).
Elections: 2004 Presidential election results: 69.6% Bush, 29.9% Kerry, 0.3% Nader, 0.1% Badnarik

Additional Information Contacts

Bradford County Government Offices . . . . (904) 964-6280
Starke Chamber of Commerce . . . . (904) 964-9675

Bradford County Communities

BROOKER (town). Covers a land area of 0.525 square miles and a water area of 0 square miles. Located at 29.88° N. Lat.; 82.33° W. Long. Elevation is 142 feet.
Population: 312 (1990); 352 (2000); 319 (2004); 292 (2009 projected); Race: 97.8% White, 0.6% Black, 0.0% Asian, 2.5% Hispanic of any race (2004); Density: 607.9 persons per square mile (2004); Average household size: 2.82 (2004); Median age: 40.9 (2004); Male/female ratio: 83.3 (2004); Marriage status: 27.1% never married, 59.7% now married, 7.5% widowed, 5.8% divorced (2000); Foreign born: 0.0% (2000); Ancestry (includes multiple ancestries): 12.0% United States or American, 10.8% Other groups, 9.4% German, 7.9% Irish, 5.6% English (2000).
Economy: Employment by occupation: 6.0% management, 9.9% professional, 13.9% services, 27.8% sales, 4.6% farming, 25.8% construction, 11.9% production (2000).
Income: Per capita income: $20,349 (2004); Median household income: $43,906 (2004); Average household income: $57,367 (2004); Percent of households with income of $100,000 or more: 8.0% (2004); Poverty rate: 14.0% (2000).
Education: Percent of population age 25 and over with: High school diploma (including GED) or higher: 64.0% (2004); Bachelor's degree or higher: 9.3% (2004); Master's degree or higher: 3.7% (2004).

School District(s)

Bradford County School District (PK-12)
2002-03 Enrollment: 4,034 . . . . (904) 966-6018
Housing: Homeownership rate: 83.2% (2004); Median home value: $57,143 (2004); Median rent: $275 per month (2000); Median age of housing: 27 years (2000).
Transportation: Commute to work: 93.4% car, 1.3% public transportation, 2.0% walk, 1.3% work from home (2000); Travel time to work: 6.7% less than 15 minutes, 36.9% 15 to 30 minutes, 32.9% 30 to 45 minutes, 3.4% 45 to 60 minutes, 20.1% 60 minutes or more (2000)

HAMPTON (city). Covers a land area of 1.033 square miles and a water area of 0 square miles. Located at 29.86° N. Lat.; 82.13° W. Long. Elevation is 146 feet.
Population: 317 (1990); 431 (2000); 417 (2004); 388 (2009 projected); Race: 85.6% White, 12.9% Black, 0.0% Asian, 1.4% Hispanic of any race (2004); Density: 403.5 persons per square mile (2004); Average household size: 2.66 (2004); Median age: 38.1 (2004); Male/female ratio: 94.0 (2004); Marriage status: 23.7% never married, 47.6% now married, 13.4% widowed, 15.4% divorced (2000); Foreign born: 1.6% (2000); Ancestry (includes multiple ancestries): 16.7% German, 12.8% Other groups, 11.6% French (except Basque), 10.4% English, 8.1% United States or American (2000).
Economy: Employment by occupation: 10.2% management, 9.6% professional, 24.0% services, 19.8% sales, 3.6% farming, 15.0% construction, 18.0% production (2000).
Income: Per capita income: $16,575 (2004); Median household income: $29,310 (2004); Average household income: $42,309 (2004); Percent of households with income of $100,000 or more: 8.3% (2004); Poverty rate: 26.6% (2000).
Education: Percent of population age 25 and over with: High school diploma (including GED) or higher: 64.6% (2004); Bachelor's degree or higher: 2.6% (2004); Master's degree or higher: 1.5% (2004).

School District(s)

Bradford County School District (PK-12)
2002-03 Enrollment: 4,034 . . . . (904) 966-6018
Housing: Homeownership rate: 78.3% (2004); Median home value: $54,000 (2004); Median rent: $228 per month (2000); Median age of housing: 26 years (2000).
Safety: Violent crime rate: 0.0 per 10,000 population; Property crime rate: 113.6 per 10,000 population (2003).
Transportation: Commute to work: 96.4% car, 0.0% public transportation, 3.6% walk, 0.0% work from home (2000); Travel time to work: 27.4% less than 15 minutes, 22.6% 15 to 30 minutes, 16.7% 30 to 45 minutes, 10.1% 45 to 60 minutes, 23.2% 60 minutes or more (2000)

LAWTEY (city). Covers a land area of 1.376 square miles and a water area of 0 square miles. Located at 30.04° N. Lat.; 82.07° W. Long. Elevation is 162 feet.
History: Lawtey grew as a shipping center for strawberries raised in Bradford County.
Population: 663 (1990); 656 (2000); 788 (2004); 950 (2009 projected); Race: 67.1% White, 29.9% Black, 0.0% Asian, 1.8% Hispanic of any race (2004); Density: 572.8 persons per square mile (2004); Average household size: 2.49 (2004); Median age: 33.3 (2004); Male/female ratio: 98.5 (2004); Marriage status: 23.8% never married, 57.1% now married, 9.2% widowed, 9.9% divorced (2000); Foreign born: 2.1% (2000); Ancestry (includes multiple ancestries): 24.9% United States or American, 23.1% Other groups, 8.0% German, 7.3% Irish, 6.6% English (2000).
Economy: Employment by occupation: 6.4% management, 14.5% professional, 23.6% services, 28.2% sales, 2.3% farming, 11.4% construction, 13.6% production (2000).
Income: Per capita income: $15,238 (2004); Median household income: $26,932 (2004); Average household income: $37,879 (2004); Percent of households with income of $100,000 or more: 4.7% (2004); Poverty rate: 22.8% (2000).
Taxes: Total city taxes per capita: $134 (2002); City property taxes per capita: $24 (2002).

Education: Percent of population age 25 and over with: High school diploma (including GED) or higher: 65.0% (2004); Bachelor's degree or higher: 8.1% (2004); Master's degree or higher: 2.2% (2004).

School District(s)

Bradford County School District (PK-12)
2002-03 Enrollment: 4,034 . . . . (904) 966-6018

Housing: Homeownership rate: 71.0% (2004); Median home value: $74,412 (2004); Median rent: $269 per month (2000); Median age of housing: 23 years (2000).
Transportation: Commute to work: 99.1% car, 0.0% public transportation, 0.0% walk, 0.9% work from home (2000); Travel time to work: 19.0% less than 15 minutes, 30.1% 15 to 30 minutes, 18.5% 30 to 45 minutes, 26.4% 45 to 60 minutes, 6.0% 60 minutes or more (2000)

STARKE (city). Covers a land area of 6.664 square miles and a water area of 0 square miles. Located at 29.94° N. Lat.; 82.10° W. Long. Elevation is 160 feet.
History: Starke was named for Starke Perry, governor of Florida from 1857-1861, and grew as the seat of Bradford County with strawberry growing and truck gardening as early industries.
Population: 5,226 (1990); 5,593 (2000); 5,623 (2004); 5,679 (2009 projected); Race: 68.5% White, 28.2% Black, 1.4% Asian, 2.3% Hispanic of any race (2004); Density: 843.8 persons per square mile (2004); Average household size: 2.77 (2004); Median age: 37.2 (2004); Male/female ratio: 85.7 (2004); Marriage status: 23.3% never married, 47.3% now married, 12.7% widowed, 16.6% divorced (2000); Foreign born: 3.5% (2000); Ancestry (includes multiple ancestries): 30.8% Other groups, 10.9% United States or American, 9.9% English, 7.8% German, 7.8% Irish (2000).
Economy: Employment by occupation: 8.4% management, 12.9% professional, 27.0% services, 25.0% sales, 1.6% farming, 12.4% construction, 12.7% production (2000).
Income: Per capita income: $14,222 (2004); Median household income: $28,930 (2004); Average household income: $37,705 (2004); Percent of households with income of $100,000 or more: 5.3% (2004); Poverty rate: 23.9% (2000).
Taxes: Total city taxes per capita: $422 (2002); City property taxes per capita: $304 (2002).
Education: Percent of population age 25 and over with: High school diploma (including GED) or higher: 77.8% (2004); Bachelor's degree or higher: 11.4% (2004); Master's degree or higher: 4.8% (2004).

School District(s)

Bradford County School District (PK-12)
2002-03 Enrollment: 4,034 . . . . (904) 966-6018

Two-year College(s)

Bradford Union Area Vocational Technical Center (Public)
2003-04 Enrollment: 117 . . . . (904) 966-6764
2003-04 Tuition: In-state $1,375; Out-of-state $4,975

Housing: Homeownership rate: 66.0% (2004); Median home value: $81,045 (2004); Median rent: $311 per month (2000); Median age of housing: 30 years (2000).
Hospitals: Shands at Starke (49 beds)
Safety: Violent crime rate: 64.5 per 10,000 population; Property crime rate: 350.5 per 10,000 population (2003).
Newspapers: Bradford County Telegraph (General - Circulation 9,500)
Transportation: Commute to work: 91.4% car, 0.5% public transportation, 2.6% walk, 0.7% work from home (2000); Travel time to work: 43.2% less than 15 minutes, 24.0% 15 to 30 minutes, 11.6% 30 to 45 minutes, 11.2% 45 to 60 minutes, 10.0% 60 minutes or more (2000)

Additional Information Contacts

Local Government Offices . . . . (904) 964-5027
Starke Chamber of Commerce . . . . (904) 964-9675

Brevard County

Located in central Florida, on the Atlantic coast; bounded on the east by barrier beaches; drained by the St. Johns River in the western marshy peat area. Covers a land area of 1,018.20 square miles, a water area of 538.80 square miles, and is located in the Eastern Time Zone. The county government was organized in 1844. County seat is Titusville.

Brevard County is part of the Palm Bay-Melbourne-Titusville, FL Metropolitan Statistical Area. The entire metro area includes: Brevard County, FL

Weather Station: Melbourne Regional Airport — Elevation: 32 feet

	Jan	Feb	Mar	Apr	May	Jun	Jul	Aug	Sep	Oct	Nov	Dec
High	72	73	77	81	85	89	90	90	88	83	78	73
Low	51	52	57	61	67	71	72	73	72	68	61	54
Precip	2.5	2.5	3.0	2.1	4.1	5.7	5.4	5.7	7.2	4.7	3.1	2.3
Snow	0.0	0.0	0.0	0.0	0.0	0.0	0.0	0.0	0.0	0.0	0.0	0.0

High and Low temperatures in degrees Fahrenheit; Precipitation and Snow in inches

Weather Station: Titusville — Elevation: 29 feet

	Jan	Feb	Mar	Apr	May	Jun	Jul	Aug	Sep	Oct	Nov	Dec
High	70	72	77	81	86	90	92	91	89	83	78	73
Low	48	50	55	59	65	70	72	72	71	65	58	51
Precip	2.5	2.8	3.8	2.8	3.7	6.2	7.3	7.5	6.8	4.4	3.5	2.5
Snow	tr	0.0	0.0	0.0	0.0	0.0	0.0	0.0	0.0	0.0	0.0	0.0

High and Low temperatures in degrees Fahrenheit; Precipitation and Snow in inches

Population: 398,978 (1990); 476,230 (2000); 509,694 (2004); 551,911 (2009 projected); Race: 85.9% White, 8.9% Black, 1.6% Asian, 5.2% Hispanic of any race (2004); Density: 500.6 persons per square mile (2004); Average household size: 2.39 (2004); Median age: 42.3 (2004); Male/female ratio: 96.5 (2004).
Religion: Five largest groups: 16.8% Catholic Church, 6.4% Southern Baptist Convention, 4.0% The United Methodist Church, 1.3% Independent, Charismatic Churches, 1.2% Presbyterian Church (U.S.A.) (2000).
Economy: Unemployment rate: 4.5% (2004); Total civilian labor force: 232,076 (2004); Leading industries: 15.5% retail trade; 14.9% health care and social assistance; 11.3% professional, scientific & technical services (2003); Companies that employ 500 or more persons: 28 (2003); Companies that employ 100 to 499 persons: 221 (2003); Companies that employ less than 100 persons: 11,928 (2003); Farms: 555 totaling 187,570 acres (2002); Minority business ownership rate: 6.8% (1997); Women business ownership rate: 28.3% (1997); Retail sales per capita: $8,495 (1997). Single-family building permits issued: 6,487 (2004); Multi-family building permits issued: 2,438 (2004).
Income: Per capita income: $24,033 (2004); Median household income: $43,979 (2004); Average household income: $56,811 (2004); Percent of households with income of $100,000 or more: 12.3% (2004); Poverty rate: 9.8% (2002); Bankruptcy rate: 4.34% (2004).
Taxes: Total county taxes per capita: $300 (2002); County property taxes per capita: $245 (2002).
Education: Percent of population age 25 and over with: High school diploma (including GED) or higher: 86.6% (2004); Bachelor's degree or higher: 24.0% (2004); Master's degree or higher: 8.5% (2004).
Housing: Homeownership rate: 74.9% (2004); Median home value: $119,350 (2004); Median rent: $516 per month (2000); Median age of housing: 19 years (2000).
Health: Birth rate: 95.7 per 10,000 population (2004); Death rate: 107.7 per 10,000 population (2004); Age adjusted cancer mortality rate: 206.6 deaths per 100,000 population (2002); Air Quality Index: 94.6% good, 5.4% moderate, 0.0% unhealthy for sensitive individuals, 0.0% unhealthy (percent of days in 2004); Number of physicians: 20.6 per 10,000 population (2001); Hospital beds: 28.8 per 10,000 population (2002); Hospital admissions: 1,431.1 per 10,000 population (2002).
Elections: 2004 Presidential election results: 57.7% Bush, 41.6% Kerry, 0.5% Nader, 0.2% Badnarik
National and State Parks: Canaveral National Seashore; Merritt Island National Wildlife Refuge; Saint Johns National Wildlife Refuge

Additional Information Contacts

Brevard County Government Offices . . . . (321) 264-6942
Cocoa Beach Chamber of Commerce . . . . (321) 459-2200
Melbourne Area Association of Realtors . . . . (321) 242-2211
Melbourne Chamber of Commerce . . . . (321) 724-5400
Palm Bay Area Chamber of Commerce. . . . . (321) 951-9998
Space Coast Association of Realtors. . . . . (321) 452-9490
Space Coast Economic Development Commerce . . . . (321) 269-3221
Titusville Chamber of Commerce. . . . . (321) 267-3036

Brevard County Communities

CAPE CANAVERAL (city). Aka Port Canaveral. Covers a land area of 2.331 square miles and a water area of 0.017 square miles. Located at 28.38° N. Lat.; 80.60° W. Long. Elevation is 9 feet.
Population: 8,007 (1990); 8,829 (2000); 9,435 (2004); 10,225 (2009 projected); Race: 94.7% White, 1.3% Black, 2.0% Asian, 3.6% Hispanic of any race (2004); Density: 4,048.0 persons per square mile (2004); Average

household size: 1.72 (2004); Median age: 47.3 (2004); Male/female ratio: 108.9 (2004); Marriage status: 25.2% never married, 44.3% now married, 8.5% widowed, 22.0% divorced (2000); Foreign born: 7.8% (2000); Ancestry (includes multiple ancestries): 22.0% German, 16.4% Irish, 15.4% English, 12.2% Other groups, 8.3% Italian (2000).
Economy: Manufacturing: metal products, fishing boats, machining, space shuttle components. Single-family building permits issued: 34 (2004); Multi-family building permits issued: 608 (2004); Employment by occupation: 13.2% management, 18.7% professional, 20.4% services, 24.7% sales, 0.4% farming, 12.8% construction, 9.8% production (2000).
Income: Per capita income: $26,089 (2004); Median household income: $33,498 (2004); Average household income: $44,884 (2004); Percent of households with income of $100,000 or more: 6.8% (2004); Poverty rate: 11.6% (2000).
Taxes: Total city taxes per capita: $314 (2002); City property taxes per capita: $89 (2002).
Education: Percent of population age 25 and over with: High school diploma (including GED) or higher: 87.2% (2004); Bachelor's degree or higher: 25.3% (2004); Master's degree or higher: 7.8% (2004).

School District(s)

Brevard County School District (PK-12)
2002-03 Enrollment: 72,601 . . . . (321) 631-1911
Housing: Homeownership rate: 50.2% (2004); Median home value: $110,590 (2004); Median rent: $497 per month (2000); Median age of housing: 24 years (2000).
Transportation: Commute to work: 88.5% car, 1.0% public transportation, 3.1% walk, 2.8% work from home (2000); Travel time to work: 36.2% less than 15 minutes, 32.4% 15 to 30 minutes, 17.6% 30 to 45 minutes, 4.9% 45 to 60 minutes, 8.9% 60 minutes or more (2000)
Additional Information Contacts
Local Government Offices . . . . (321) 868-1221

COCOA (city). Aka Cocoa-Rockledge. Covers a land area of 7.459 square miles and a water area of 2.065 square miles. Located at 28.36° N. Lat.; 80.74° W. Long. Elevation is 39 feet.
History: Cocoa was incorporated in 1895 and named for the coco plum growing in the area. It grew as a popular fishing spot, both from the Indian River bridge and in the ocean surf, and as a citrus shipping center.
Population: 17,762 (1990); 16,412 (2000); 16,417 (2004); 16,501 (2009 projected); Race: 59.4% White, 34.8% Black, 0.9% Asian, 6.0% Hispanic of any race (2004); Density: 2,201.0 persons per square mile (2004); Average household size: 2.35 (2004); Median age: 36.8 (2004); Male/female ratio: 91.1 (2004); Marriage status: 27.8% never married, 46.8% now married, 8.8% widowed, 16.5% divorced (2000); Foreign born: 5.8% (2000); Ancestry (includes multiple ancestries): 36.5% Other groups, 9.6% German, 9.1% United States or American, 9.0% Irish, 8.7% English (2000).
Economy: Single-family building permits issued: 84 (2004); Multi-family building permits issued: 0 (2004); Employment by occupation: 6.6% management, 15.7% professional, 21.7% services, 27.9% sales, 0.1% farming, 12.5% construction, 15.5% production (2000).
Income: Per capita income: $16,455 (2004); Median household income: $28,051 (2004); Average household income: $38,328 (2004); Percent of households with income of $100,000 or more: 5.6% (2004); Poverty rate: 24.1% (2000).
Education: Percent of population age 25 and over with: High school diploma (including GED) or higher: 75.6% (2004); Bachelor's degree or higher: 13.8% (2004); Master's degree or higher: 4.5% (2004).

School District(s)

Brevard County School District (PK-12)
2002-03 Enrollment: 72,601 . . . . (321) 631-1911

Two-year College(s)

Brevard Community College-Cocoa Campus (Public)
2003-04 Enrollment: 14,806 . . . . (321) 632-1111
2003-04 Tuition: In-state $1,356; Out-of-state $5,046
Housing: Homeownership rate: 58.0% (2004); Median home value: $83,810 (2004); Median rent: $403 per month (2000); Median age of housing: 32 years (2000).
Safety: Violent crime rate: 264.6 per 10,000 population; Property crime rate: 779.5 per 10,000 population (2003).
Transportation: Commute to work: 93.1% car, 0.6% public transportation, 2.5% walk, 0.8% work from home (2000); Travel time to work: 26.1% less than 15 minutes, 42.1% 15 to 30 minutes, 21.7% 30 to 45 minutes, 4.4% 45 to 60 minutes, 5.7% 60 minutes or more (2000)
Additional Information Contacts
Local Government Offices . . . . (321) 639-7556

COCOA BEACH (city). Covers a land area of 4.891 square miles and a water area of 10.149 square miles. Located at 28.33° N. Lat.; 80.61° W. Long. Elevation is 12 feet.
History: Cocoa Beach began as a small ocean resort built on a dune ridge along the shore.
Population: 12,083 (1990); 12,482 (2000); 12,518 (2004); 12,620 (2009 projected); Race: 96.5% White, 0.7% Black, 1.2% Asian, 2.5% Hispanic of any race (2004); Density: 2,559.4 persons per square mile (2004); Average household size: 1.89 (2004); Median age: 54.5 (2004); Male/female ratio: 100.2 (2004); Marriage status: 17.2% never married, 58.0% now married, 11.5% widowed, 13.3% divorced (2000); Foreign born: 8.6% (2000); Ancestry (includes multiple ancestries): 18.5% Irish, 18.4% German, 16.1% English, 9.3% Italian, 8.2% Other groups (2000).
Economy: Single-family building permits issued: 7 (2004); Multi-family building permits issued: 2 (2004); Employment by occupation: 18.1% management, 25.9% professional, 15.0% services, 26.5% sales, 0.5% farming, 5.7% construction, 8.3% production (2000).
Income: Per capita income: $32,431 (2004); Median household income: $46,632 (2004); Average household income: $61,354 (2004); Percent of households with income of $100,000 or more: 14.3% (2004); Poverty rate: 6.5% (2000).
Taxes: Total city taxes per capita: $635 (2002); City property taxes per capita: $370 (2002).
Education: Percent of population age 25 and over with: High school diploma (including GED) or higher: 93.5% (2004); Bachelor's degree or higher: 34.0% (2004); Master's degree or higher: 11.6% (2004).

School District(s)

Brevard County School District (PK-12)
2002-03 Enrollment: 72,601 . . . . (321) 631-1911
Housing: Homeownership rate: 73.0% (2004); Median home value: $157,834 (2004); Median rent: $555 per month (2000); Median age of housing: 27 years (2000).
Hospitals: Cape Canaveral Hospital (150 beds)
Safety: Violent crime rate: 95.8 per 10,000 population; Property crime rate: 713.6 per 10,000 population (2003).
Transportation: Commute to work: 91.2% car, 0.6% public transportation, 2.2% walk, 3.5% work from home (2000); Travel time to work: 34.8% less than 15 minutes, 31.0% 15 to 30 minutes, 19.1% 30 to 45 minutes, 7.1% 45 to 60 minutes, 8.1% 60 minutes or more (2000)
Airports: Patrick AFB
Additional Information Contacts
Local Government Offices . . . . (321) 868-3286

COCOA WEST (CDP). Covers a land area of 4.281 square miles and a water area of 0 square miles. Located at 28.36° N. Lat.; 80.76° W. Long.
Population: 6,048 (1990); 5,921 (2000); 5,643 (2004); 5,423 (2009 projected); Race: 53.7% White, 41.8% Black, 0.2% Asian, 4.2% Hispanic of any race (2004); Density: 1,318.1 persons per square mile (2004); Average household size: 2.62 (2004); Median age: 33.8 (2004); Male/female ratio: 98.4 (2004); Marriage status: 26.9% never married, 46.4% now married, 7.9% widowed, 18.8% divorced (2000); Foreign born: 2.9% (2000); Ancestry (includes multiple ancestries): 39.5% Other groups, 12.0% United States or American, 8.7% German, 8.2% English, 7.4% Irish (2000).
Economy: Employment by occupation: 8.6% management, 9.8% professional, 22.7% services, 25.4% sales, 1.2% farming, 19.2% construction, 13.2% production (2000).
Income: Per capita income: $13,128 (2004); Median household income: $28,406 (2004); Average household income: $34,424 (2004); Percent of households with income of $100,000 or more: 2.9% (2004); Poverty rate: 26.8% (2000).
Education: Percent of population age 25 and over with: High school diploma (including GED) or higher: 66.1% (2004); Bachelor's degree or higher: 6.8% (2004); Master's degree or higher: 1.5% (2004).
Housing: Homeownership rate: 59.8% (2004); Median home value: $69,725 (2004); Median rent: $422 per month (2000); Median age of housing: 31 years (2000).
Transportation: Commute to work: 93.5% car, 0.0% public transportation, 1.8% walk, 1.1% work from home (2000); Travel time to work: 25.4% less than 15 minutes, 39.8% 15 to 30 minutes, 20.7% 30 to 45 minutes, 5.1% 45 to 60 minutes, 8.9% 60 minutes or more (2000)

GRANT (unincorporated postal area, zip code 32949). Covers a land area of 2.077 square miles and a water area of 0 square miles. Located at 27.93° N. Lat.; 80.55° W. Long. Elevation is 8 feet.

Population: 735 (2000); Race: 93.3% White, 3.2% Black, 0.0% Asian, 1.8% Hispanic of any race (2000); Density: 353.9 persons per square mile (2000); Age: 18.3% under 18, 19.4% over 64 (2000); Marriage status: 12.7% never married, 78.3% now married, 4.7% widowed, 4.3% divorced (2000); Foreign born: 0.0% (2000); Ancestry (includes multiple ancestries): 20.7% German, 9.6% Scotch-Irish, 9.1% United States or American, 8.4% Other groups, 7.8% Italian (2000).
Economy: Employment by occupation: 10.3% management, 16.6% professional, 18.8% services, 31.0% sales, 4.1% farming, 10.7% construction, 8.5% production (2000).
Income: Per capita income: $24,906 (2000); Median household income: $36,875 (2000); Poverty rate: 16.8% (2000).
Education: Percent of population age 25 and over with: High school diploma (including GED) or higher: 73.5% (2000); Bachelor's degree or higher: 15.0% (2000).
Housing: Homeownership rate: 80.4% (2000); Median home value: $143,500 (2000); Median rent: $364 per month (2000); Median age of housing: 22 years (2000).
Transportation: Commute to work: 90.2% car, 0.0% public transportation, 0.0% walk, 9.8% work from home (2000); Travel time to work: 25.0% less than 15 minutes, 35.4% 15 to 30 minutes, 19.6% 30 to 45 minutes, 8.3% 45 to 60 minutes, 11.7% 60 minutes or more (2000)

INDIALANTIC (town). Covers a land area of 1.036 square miles and a water area of 0.201 square miles. Located at 28.08° N. Lat.; 80.56° W. Long. Elevation is 18 feet.
Population: 2,844 (1990); 2,944 (2000); 2,983 (2004); 3,058 (2009 projected); Race: 97.3% White, 0.3% Black, 0.7% Asian, 2.2% Hispanic of any race (2004); Density: 2,878.2 persons per square mile (2004); Average household size: 2.21 (2004); Median age: 46.5 (2004); Male/female ratio: 98.2 (2004); Marriage status: 23.1% never married, 58.3% now married, 7.3% widowed, 11.3% divorced (2000); Foreign born: 5.9% (2000); Ancestry (includes multiple ancestries): 18.9% German, 18.5% English, 16.4% Irish, 13.7% Italian, 5.5% Other groups (2000).
Economy: Manufacturing includes medical equipment, baked goods. Single-family building permits issued: 1 (2004); Multi-family building permits issued: 74 (2004); Employment by occupation: 14.1% management, 40.1% professional, 8.0% services, 22.2% sales, 0.5% farming, 10.5% construction, 4.5% production (2000).
Income: Per capita income: $46,935 (2004); Median household income: $73,841 (2004); Average household income: $103,940 (2004); Percent of households with income of $100,000 or more: 33.2% (2004); Poverty rate: 2.3% (2000).
Education: Percent of population age 25 and over with: High school diploma (including GED) or higher: 95.5% (2004); Bachelor's degree or higher: 51.7% (2004); Master's degree or higher: 24.6% (2004).

School District(s)

Brevard County School District (PK-12)
2002-03 Enrollment: 72,601 . . . . (321) 631-1911
Housing: Homeownership rate: 79.1% (2004); Median home value: $198,254 (2004); Median rent: $660 per month (2000); Median age of housing: 30 years (2000).
Safety: Violent crime rate: 69.6 per 10,000 population; Property crime rate: 464.0 per 10,000 population (2003).
Transportation: Commute to work: 90.5% car, 0.0% public transportation, 1.5% walk, 6.3% work from home (2000); Travel time to work: 45.6% less than 15 minutes, 38.8% 15 to 30 minutes, 9.4% 30 to 45 minutes, 1.4% 45 to 60 minutes, 4.8% 60 minutes or more (2000)

INDIAN HARBOUR BEACH (city). Covers a land area of 2.140 square miles and a water area of 0.491 square miles. Located at 28.15° N. Lat.; 80.59° W. Long. Elevation is 10 feet.
Population: 6,995 (1990); 8,152 (2000); 8,734 (2004); 9,477 (2009 projected); Race: 95.1% White, 1.0% Black, 1.7% Asian, 3.6% Hispanic of any race (2004); Density: 4,082.1 persons per square mile (2004); Average household size: 2.17 (2004); Median age: 47.3 (2004); Male/female ratio: 90.9 (2004); Marriage status: 17.7% never married, 60.3% now married, 10.3% widowed, 11.7% divorced (2000); Foreign born: 7.3% (2000); Ancestry (includes multiple ancestries): 20.5% German, 18.1% English, 16.1% Irish, 11.1% Other groups, 9.5% Italian (2000).
Economy: Manufacturing includes water and waste systems, communications equipment, and cosmetics. Single-family building permits issued: 3 (2004); Multi-family building permits issued: 24 (2004); Employment by occupation: 17.2% management, 29.8% professional, 10.8% services, 27.5% sales, 0.0% farming, 9.3% construction, 5.4% production (2000).
Income: Per capita income: $33,985 (2004); Median household income: $49,004 (2004); Average household income: $73,892 (2004); Percent of households with income of $100,000 or more: 19.6% (2004); Poverty rate: 5.5% (2000).
Taxes: Total city taxes per capita: $304 (2002); City property taxes per capita: $219 (2002).
Education: Percent of population age 25 and over with: High school diploma (including GED) or higher: 93.8% (2004); Bachelor's degree or higher: 39.7% (2004); Master's degree or higher: 17.8% (2004).

School District(s)

Brevard County School District (PK-12)
2002-03 Enrollment: 72,601 . . . . (321) 631-1911
Housing: Homeownership rate: 74.6% (2004); Median home value: $145,520 (2004); Median rent: $591 per month (2000); Median age of housing: 26 years (2000).
Safety: Violent crime rate: 11.6 per 10,000 population; Property crime rate: 138.4 per 10,000 population (2003).
Transportation: Commute to work: 91.4% car, 0.0% public transportation, 0.9% walk, 4.1% work from home (2000); Travel time to work: 26.5% less than 15 minutes, 49.7% 15 to 30 minutes, 14.0% 30 to 45 minutes, 4.5% 45 to 60 minutes, 5.3% 60 minutes or more (2000)
Additional Information Contacts
Local Government Offices . . . . (321) 773-7212

JUNE PARK (CDP). Covers a land area of 3.729 square miles and a water area of 0 square miles. Located at 28.07° N. Lat.; 80.68° W. Long. Elevation is 26 feet.
Population: 3,714 (1990); 4,367 (2000); 4,633 (2004); 4,980 (2009 projected); Race: 96.4% White, 0.9% Black, 1.4% Asian, 2.6% Hispanic of any race (2004); Density: 1,242.3 persons per square mile (2004); Average household size: 2.51 (2004); Median age: 43.6 (2004); Male/female ratio: 99.8 (2004); Marriage status: 17.4% never married, 66.1% now married, 7.0% widowed, 9.5% divorced (2000); Foreign born: 3.5% (2000); Ancestry (includes multiple ancestries): 22.4% German, 15.6% English, 15.0% Irish, 11.8% Other groups, 10.9% United States or American (2000).
Economy: Employment by occupation: 13.9% management, 17.8% professional, 14.5% services, 29.3% sales, 0.3% farming, 12.8% construction, 11.5% production (2000).
Income: Per capita income: $25,650 (2004); Median household income: $49,973 (2004); Average household income: $64,402 (2004); Percent of households with income of $100,000 or more: 16.0% (2004); Poverty rate: 4.9% (2000).
Education: Percent of population age 25 and over with: High school diploma (including GED) or higher: 81.7% (2004); Bachelor's degree or higher: 16.8% (2004); Master's degree or higher: 8.8% (2004).
Housing: Homeownership rate: 90.6% (2004); Median home value: $130,760 (2004); Median rent: $429 per month (2000); Median age of housing: 27 years (2000).
Transportation: Commute to work: 93.2% car, 0.0% public transportation, 0.5% walk, 2.5% work from home (2000); Travel time to work: 37.4% less than 15 minutes, 42.1% 15 to 30 minutes, 9.3% 30 to 45 minutes, 5.1% 45 to 60 minutes, 6.2% 60 minutes or more (2000)

MALABAR (town). Covers a land area of 10.631 square miles and a water area of 2.582 square miles. Located at 27.99° N. Lat.; 80.58° W. Long. Elevation is 27 feet.
History: Malabar developed around a sawmill, and was named for Cape Malabar on the African coast.
Population: 1,977 (1990); 2,622 (2000); 2,610 (2004); 2,612 (2009 projected); Race: 92.7% White, 3.7% Black, 1.1% Asian, 2.3% Hispanic of any race (2004); Density: 245.5 persons per square mile (2004); Average household size: 2.51 (2004); Median age: 43.7 (2004); Male/female ratio: 106.2 (2004); Marriage status: 18.2% never married, 63.6% now married, 8.2% widowed, 10.1% divorced (2000); Foreign born: 7.4% (2000); Ancestry (includes multiple ancestries): 19.3% English, 18.3% German, 15.1% Irish, 14.2% United States or American, 10.3% Other groups (2000).
Economy: Single-family building permits issued: 24 (2004); Multi-family building permits issued: 0 (2004); Employment by occupation: 11.8% management, 24.1% professional, 15.4% services, 23.5% sales, 0.7% farming, 17.9% construction, 6.6% production (2000).
Income: Per capita income: $27,393 (2004); Median household income: $53,264 (2004); Average household income: $68,653 (2004); Percent of

households with income of $100,000 or more: 18.8% (2004); Poverty rate: 10.7% (2000).
Taxes: Total city taxes per capita: $267 (2002); City property taxes per capita: $74 (2002).
Education: Percent of population age 25 and over with: High school diploma (including GED) or higher: 85.8% (2004); Bachelor's degree or higher: 21.2% (2004); Master's degree or higher: 7.5% (2004).
Housing: Homeownership rate: 92.0% (2004); Median home value: $160,374 (2004); Median rent: $450 per month (2000); Median age of housing: 17 years (2000).
Transportation: Commute to work: 94.2% car, 1.0% public transportation, 0.7% walk, 3.5% work from home (2000); Travel time to work: 32.3% less than 15 minutes, 43.2% 15 to 30 minutes, 18.4% 30 to 45 minutes, 0.8% 45 to 60 minutes, 5.3% 60 minutes or more (2000)

MELBOURNE (city). Covers a land area of 30.197 square miles and a water area of 5.292 square miles. Located at 28.11° N. Lat.; 80.63° W. Long. Elevation is 21 feet.
History: Melbourne was named for the Australian city by a resident who had immigrated from there. Melbourne attracted hunting parties going up the St. Johns River, as well as fresh and salt-water fishermen.
Population: 61,834 (1990); 71,382 (2000); 75,124 (2004); 80,059 (2009 projected); Race: 83.3% White, 10.0% Black, 2.5% Asian, 6.2% Hispanic of any race (2004); Density: 2,487.8 persons per square mile (2004); Average household size: 2.30 (2004); Median age: 40.4 (2004); Male/female ratio: 95.1 (2004); Marriage status: 24.3% never married, 53.3% now married, 9.0% widowed, 13.5% divorced (2000); Foreign born: 7.8% (2000); Ancestry (includes multiple ancestries): 20.2% Other groups, 16.7% German, 14.7% Irish, 12.8% English, 8.2% Italian (2000).
Economy: Unemployment rate: 5.1% (2004); Total civilian labor force: 35,213 (2004); Single-family building permits issued: 371 (2004); Multi-family building permits issued: 506 (2004); Employment by occupation: 10.9% management, 20.5% professional, 18.2% services, 28.9% sales, 0.3% farming, 10.2% construction, 11.0% production (2000).
Income: Per capita income: $21,184 (2004); Median household income: $36,947 (2004); Average household income: $47,883 (2004); Percent of households with income of $100,000 or more: 8.1% (2004); Poverty rate: 11.5% (2000).
Taxes: Total city taxes per capita: $395 (2002); City property taxes per capita: $149 (2002).
Education: Percent of population age 25 and over with: High school diploma (including GED) or higher: 85.5% (2004); Bachelor's degree or higher: 21.7% (2004); Master's degree or higher: 7.6% (2004).

School District(s)

Brevard County School District (PK-12)
2002-03 Enrollment: 72,601 . . . . (321) 631-1911

Four-year College(s)

Florida Institute of Technology-Melbourne
2003-04 Enrollment: 4,689 . . . . (321) 674-8000
2003-04 Tuition: In-state $22,600; Out-of-state $22,600
Florida Metropolitan University-Melbourne (Private, For-profit)
2003-04 Enrollment: 873 . . . . (321) 253-2929
2003-04 Tuition: In-state $8,820; Out-of-state $8,820

Two-year College(s)

Career Tech (Private, For-profit)
2003-04 Enrollment: n/a . . . . (321) 242-7555
Keiser College-Melbourne (Private, For-profit)
2003-04 Enrollment: n/a . . . . (321) 255-2255
2003-04 Tuition: In-state $10,920; Out-of-state $10,920
Melbourne Beauty School (Private, For-profit)
2003-04 Enrollment: 112 . . . . (321) 259-0001

Housing: Homeownership rate: 61.9% (2004); Median home value: $106,835 (2004); Median rent: $510 per month (2000); Median age of housing: 21 years (2000).
Hospitals: Circles of Care (52 beds); HealthSouth Sea Pines Rehabilitation Hospital (80 beds); Holmes Regional Medical Center (468 beds)
Safety: Violent crime rate: 78.9 per 10,000 population; Property crime rate: 482.7 per 10,000 population (2003).
Newspapers: Bay Bulletin (General - Circulation 30,524); Florida Today (Circulation 94,118); The Press Tribune (General - Circulation 38,022); The Times (General - Circulation 52,778)
Transportation: Commute to work: 94.3% car, 0.3% public transportation, 1.9% walk, 1.9% work from home (2000); Travel time to work: 36.2% less than 15 minutes, 43.3% 15 to 30 minutes, 11.5% 30 to 45 minutes, 4.0% 45 to 60 minutes, 5.0% 60 minutes or more (2000)
Airports: Melbourne International (primary service)

Additional Information Contacts

Melbourne Area Association of Realtors . . . . (321) 242-2211
Melbourne Chamber of Commerce . . . . (321) 724-5400

MELBOURNE BEACH (town). Covers a land area of 1.028 square miles and a water area of 0.255 square miles. Located at 28.06° N. Lat.; 80.56° W. Long. Elevation is 12 feet.
Population: 3,021 (1990); 3,335 (2000); 3,357 (2004); 3,425 (2009 projected); Race: 97.5% White, 0.1% Black, 1.0% Asian, 2.5% Hispanic of any race (2004); Density: 3,264.9 persons per square mile (2004); Average household size: 2.36 (2004); Median age: 46.4 (2004); Male/female ratio: 103.7 (2004); Marriage status: 15.6% never married, 64.6% now married, 7.9% widowed, 11.9% divorced (2000); Foreign born: 6.5% (2000); Ancestry (includes multiple ancestries): 16.9% German, 16.8% Irish, 16.5% English, 12.6% Italian, 7.3% Other groups (2000).
Economy: Light manufacturing. Single-family building permits issued: 2 (2004); Multi-family building permits issued: 0 (2004); Employment by occupation: 22.5% management, 29.8% professional, 10.8% services, 27.2% sales, 0.4% farming, 6.8% construction, 2.6% production (2000).
Income: Per capita income: $34,991 (2004); Median household income: $61,058 (2004); Average household income: $82,432 (2004); Percent of households with income of $100,000 or more: 19.7% (2004); Poverty rate: 3.8% (2000).
Education: Percent of population age 25 and over with: High school diploma (including GED) or higher: 93.8% (2004); Bachelor's degree or higher: 44.3% (2004); Master's degree or higher: 20.5% (2004).

School District(s)

Brevard County School District (PK-12)
2002-03 Enrollment: 72,601 . . . . (321) 631-1911

Housing: Homeownership rate: 84.1% (2004); Median home value: $212,281 (2004); Median rent: $622 per month (2000); Median age of housing: 30 years (2000).
Safety: Violent crime rate: 8.8 per 10,000 population; Property crime rate: 236.8 per 10,000 population (2003).
Transportation: Commute to work: 90.1% car, 0.0% public transportation, 1.9% walk, 5.8% work from home (2000); Travel time to work: 28.4% less than 15 minutes, 40.6% 15 to 30 minutes, 18.0% 30 to 45 minutes, 5.2% 45 to 60 minutes, 7.9% 60 minutes or more (2000)

MELBOURNE VILLAGE (town). Covers a land area of 0.570 square miles and a water area of 0 square miles. Located at 28.08° N. Lat.; 80.66° W. Long. Elevation is 25 feet.
Population: 591 (1990); 706 (2000); 700 (2004); 700 (2009 projected); Race: 99.4% White, 0.0% Black, 0.4% Asian, 1.3% Hispanic of any race (2004); Density: 1,228.9 persons per square mile (2004); Average household size: 2.29 (2004); Median age: 48.6 (2004); Male/female ratio: 93.4 (2004); Marriage status: 16.3% never married, 60.9% now married, 11.2% widowed, 11.6% divorced (2000); Foreign born: 5.6% (2000); Ancestry (includes multiple ancestries): 22.9% English, 20.1% German, 15.6% Irish, 12.0% United States or American, 7.9% Italian (2000).
Economy: Single-family building permits issued: 2 (2004); Multi-family building permits issued: 0 (2004); Employment by occupation: 20.7% management, 36.5% professional, 8.4% services, 22.4% sales, 0.0% farming, 5.4% construction, 6.7% production (2000).
Income: Per capita income: $30,964 (2004); Median household income: $50,446 (2004); Average household income: $70,833 (2004); Percent of households with income of $100,000 or more: 17.6% (2004); Poverty rate: 6.4% (2000).
Education: Percent of population age 25 and over with: High school diploma (including GED) or higher: 94.9% (2004); Bachelor's degree or higher: 41.7% (2004); Master's degree or higher: 18.4% (2004).
Housing: Homeownership rate: 90.2% (2004); Median home value: $159,783 (2004); Median rent: $584 per month (2000); Median age of housing: 37 years (2000).
Safety: Violent crime rate: 0.0 per 10,000 population; Property crime rate: 236.1 per 10,000 population (2003).
Transportation: Commute to work: 91.9% car, 0.0% public transportation, 0.7% walk, 6.8% work from home (2000); Travel time to work: 35.3% less than 15 minutes, 50.2% 15 to 30 minutes, 8.4% 30 to 45 minutes, 2.5% 45 to 60 minutes, 3.6% 60 minutes or more (2000)

MERRITT ISLAND (CDP). Covers a land area of 17.651 square miles and a water area of 29.400 square miles. Located at 28.35° N. Lat.; 80.68° W. Long. Elevation is 15 feet.
History: Merritt Island was named for an early settler who received the entire island as a land grant from Spain about 1800. The town of Merritt Island developed as the chief trading center on the island.
Population: 32,886 (1990); 36,090 (2000); 36,829 (2004); 37,941 (2009 projected); Race: 90.0% White, 5.2% Black, 1.8% Asian, 4.2% Hispanic of any race (2004); Density: 2,086.5 persons per square mile (2004); Average household size: 2.41 (2004); Median age: 43.4 (2004); Male/female ratio: 95.9 (2004); Marriage status: 19.6% never married, 58.3% now married, 9.0% widowed, 13.1% divorced (2000); Foreign born: 6.4% (2000); Ancestry (includes multiple ancestries): 19.6% German, 16.0% English, 15.5% Irish, 14.4% Other groups, 8.7% Italian (2000).
Economy: Employment by occupation: 13.9% management, 25.6% professional, 15.6% services, 25.9% sales, 0.5% farming, 9.1% construction, 9.5% production (2000).
Income: Per capita income: $26,803 (2004); Median household income: $47,354 (2004); Average household income: $63,672 (2004); Percent of households with income of $100,000 or more: 16.8% (2004); Poverty rate: 9.4% (2000).
Education: Percent of population age 25 and over with: High school diploma (including GED) or higher: 88.5% (2004); Bachelor's degree or higher: 28.5% (2004); Master's degree or higher: 10.2% (2004).

School District(s)

Brevard County School District (PK-12)
2002-03 Enrollment: 72,601 . . . . (321) 631-1911

Two-year College(s)

Advanced-Basic Hair Design Training Center (Private, For-profit)
2003-04 Enrollment: 46 . . . . (321) 452-8490

Housing: Homeownership rate: 75.3% (2004); Median home value: $145,745 (2004); Median rent: $503 per month (2000); Median age of housing: 30 years (2000).
Transportation: Commute to work: 94.2% car, 0.3% public transportation, 1.2% walk, 2.8% work from home (2000); Travel time to work: 33.0% less than 15 minutes, 38.4% 15 to 30 minutes, 16.7% 30 to 45 minutes, 5.8% 45 to 60 minutes, 6.2% 60 minutes or more (2000)

Additional Information Contacts

Cocoa Beach Chamber of Commerce . . . . (321) 459-2200
Space Coast Association of Realtors. . . . . (321) 452-9490

MICCO (CDP). Covers a land area of 9.405 square miles and a water area of 0.263 square miles. Located at 27.87° N. Lat.; 80.51° W. Long. Elevation is 23 feet.
History: Micco grew as a center for citrus growing and commercial fishing. The Sebastian River Bridge near Micco was the scene in 1924 of a confrontation between the Ashley gang, who had been robbing banks for 14 years, and the deputy sheriffs. This was the end of the Ashley gang.
Population: 8,757 (1990); 9,498 (2000); 9,419 (2004); 9,377 (2009 projected); Race: 98.8% White, 0.2% Black, 0.1% Asian, 1.6% Hispanic of any race (2004); Density: 1,001.5 persons per square mile (2004); Average household size: 1.80 (2004); Median age: 68.2 (2004); Male/female ratio: 88.9 (2004); Marriage status: 8.5% never married, 65.2% now married, 16.4% widowed, 10.0% divorced (2000); Foreign born: 5.0% (2000); Ancestry (includes multiple ancestries): 19.9% German, 18.9% Irish, 16.2% English, 10.4% Italian, 6.4% United States or American (2000).
Economy: Employment by occupation: 8.4% management, 11.3% professional, 19.0% services, 33.6% sales, 1.9% farming, 12.5% construction, 13.4% production (2000).
Income: Per capita income: $22,860 (2004); Median household income: $31,279 (2004); Average household income: $41,162 (2004); Percent of households with income of $100,000 or more: 4.6% (2004); Poverty rate: 10.1% (2000).
Education: Percent of population age 25 and over with: High school diploma (including GED) or higher: 77.5% (2004); Bachelor's degree or higher: 10.4% (2004); Master's degree or higher: 4.2% (2004).
Housing: Homeownership rate: 92.0% (2004); Median home value: $75,242 (2004); Median rent: $517 per month (2000); Median age of housing: 17 years (2000).
Transportation: Commute to work: 91.8% car, 0.4% public transportation, 2.2% walk, 2.7% work from home (2000); Travel time to work: 33.6% less than 15 minutes, 30.2% 15 to 30 minutes, 26.0% 30 to 45 minutes, 3.8% 45 to 60 minutes, 6.3% 60 minutes or more (2000)

MIMS (CDP). Covers a land area of 19.797 square miles and a water area of 5.913 square miles. Located at 28.66° N. Lat.; 80.84° W. Long. Elevation is 33 feet.
Population: 9,064 (1990); 9,147 (2000); 9,136 (2004); 9,237 (2009 projected); Race: 87.2% White, 10.4% Black, 0.2% Asian, 1.6% Hispanic of any race (2004); Density: 461.5 persons per square mile (2004); Average household size: 2.51 (2004); Median age: 41.8 (2004); Male/female ratio: 98.9 (2004); Marriage status: 20.7% never married, 58.4% now married, 8.6% widowed, 12.4% divorced (2000); Foreign born: 2.2% (2000); Ancestry (includes multiple ancestries): 19.0% Other groups, 16.4% United States or American, 11.8% German, 11.1% English, 10.5% Irish (2000).
Economy: Manufacturing includes liquified gases, heat-sealing products, fruit packing, structural steel fabrication, chemically treated fittings. Employment by occupation: 7.9% management, 17.9% professional, 18.2% services, 26.5% sales, 0.5% farming, 17.1% construction, 11.9% production (2000).
Income: Per capita income: $18,980 (2004); Median household income: $39,633 (2004); Average household income: $47,447 (2004); Percent of households with income of $100,000 or more: 7.1% (2004); Poverty rate: 15.6% (2000).
Education: Percent of population age 25 and over with: High school diploma (including GED) or higher: 77.2% (2004); Bachelor's degree or higher: 11.2% (2004); Master's degree or higher: 3.3% (2004).

School District(s)

Brevard County School District (PK-12)
2002-03 Enrollment: 72,601 . . . . (321) 631-1911

Housing: Homeownership rate: 85.8% (2004); Median home value: $82,673 (2004); Median rent: $412 per month (2000); Median age of housing: 25 years (2000).
Transportation: Commute to work: 97.4% car, 0.0% public transportation, 0.9% walk, 1.0% work from home (2000); Travel time to work: 27.4% less than 15 minutes, 32.5% 15 to 30 minutes, 23.5% 30 to 45 minutes, 9.4% 45 to 60 minutes, 7.2% 60 minutes or more (2000)

PALM BAY (city). Covers a land area of 63.645 square miles and a water area of 3.105 square miles. Located at 27.98° N. Lat.; 80.65° W. Long. Elevation is 19 feet.
Population: 62,587 (1990); 79,413 (2000); 86,027 (2004); 94,342 (2009 projected); Race: 79.0% White, 13.1% Black, 1.8% Asian, 9.9% Hispanic of any race (2004); Density: 1,351.7 persons per square mile (2004); Average household size: 2.59 (2004); Median age: 37.5 (2004); Male/female ratio: 95.5 (2004); Marriage status: 21.5% never married, 59.9% now married, 6.5% widowed, 12.0% divorced (2000); Foreign born: 9.5% (2000); Ancestry (includes multiple ancestries): 21.9% Other groups, 17.9% German, 14.6% Irish, 10.1% English, 9.2% Italian (2000).
Economy: Manufacturing includes aerospace and aircraft components, semiconductors and optical instruments. Unemployment rate: 4.7% (2004); Total civilian labor force: 37,830 (2004); Single-family building permits issued: 2,233 (2004); Multi-family building permits issued: 0 (2004); Employment by occupation: 9.6% management, 19.8% professional, 18.8% services, 27.5% sales, 0.2% farming, 12.1% construction, 12.1% production (2000).
Income: Per capita income: $18,315 (2004); Median household income: $39,350 (2004); Average household income: $47,171 (2004); Percent of households with income of $100,000 or more: 6.2% (2004); Poverty rate: 9.5% (2000).
Taxes: Total city taxes per capita: $357 (2002); City property taxes per capita: $178 (2002).
Education: Percent of population age 25 and over with: High school diploma (including GED) or higher: 83.7% (2004); Bachelor's degree or higher: 16.7% (2004); Master's degree or higher: 4.9% (2004).

School District(s)

Brevard County School District (PK-12)
2002-03 Enrollment: 72,601 . . . . (321) 631-1911

Two-year College(s)

Darlyne Mcgees Academy of Cosmetology (Private, For-profit)
2003-04 Enrollment: 58 . . . . (321) 951-0595

Housing: Homeownership rate: 74.9% (2004); Median home value: $98,965 (2004); Median rent: $536 per month (2000); Median age of housing: 15 years (2000).
Safety: Violent crime rate: 68.1 per 10,000 population; Property crime rate: 378.3 per 10,000 population (2003).
Transportation: Commute to work: 95.6% car, 0.4% public transportation, 0.4% walk, 2.1% work from home (2000); Travel time to work: 19.4% less

than 15 minutes, 47.1% 15 to 30 minutes, 21.0% 30 to 45 minutes, 6.7% 45 to 60 minutes, 5.8% 60 minutes or more (2000)
Additional Information Contacts
Palm Bay Area Chamber of Commerce. . . . . (321) 951-9998

PALM SHORES (town). Covers a land area of 0.494 square miles and a water area of 0 square miles. Located at 28.19° N. Lat.; 80.66° W. Long. Elevation is 18 feet.
Population: 310 (1990); 794 (2000); 911 (2004); 1,040 (2009 projected); Race: 84.7% White, 5.9% Black, 4.1% Asian, 5.2% Hispanic of any race (2004); Density: 1,845.4 persons per square mile (2004); Average household size: 2.46 (2004); Median age: 43.5 (2004); Male/female ratio: 99.8 (2004); Marriage status: 16.0% never married, 66.4% now married, 4.9% widowed, 12.8% divorced (2000); Foreign born: 14.6% (2000); Ancestry (includes multiple ancestries): 19.4% German, 17.5% Other groups, 16.7% English, 16.1% Irish, 7.0% French (except Basque) (2000).
Economy: Single-family building permits issued: 8 (2004); Multi-family building permits issued: 0 (2004); Employment by occupation: 21.2% management, 20.7% professional, 15.9% services, 28.7% sales, 0.0% farming, 4.8% construction, 8.8% production (2000).
Income: Per capita income: $26,265 (2004); Median household income: $50,455 (2004); Average household income: $64,669 (2004); Percent of households with income of $100,000 or more: 17.8% (2004); Poverty rate: 9.3% (2000).
Education: Percent of population age 25 and over with: High school diploma (including GED) or higher: 91.9% (2004); Bachelor's degree or higher: 23.0% (2004); Master's degree or higher: 7.7% (2004).
Housing: Homeownership rate: 82.4% (2004); Median home value: $120,050 (2004); Median rent: $475 per month (2000); Median age of housing: 8 years (2000).
Transportation: Commute to work: 93.2% car, 0.0% public transportation, 1.5% walk, 4.1% work from home (2000); Travel time to work: 21.8% less than 15 minutes, 56.5% 15 to 30 minutes, 13.2% 30 to 45 minutes, 3.5% 45 to 60 minutes, 5.1% 60 minutes or more (2000)

PATRICK AFB (unincorporated postal area, zip code 32925). Covers a land area of 3.134 square miles and a water area of 0 square miles. Located at 28.17° N. Lat.; 80.58° W. Long.
Population: 2,137 (2000); Race: 61.1% White, 21.8% Black, 3.3% Asian, 12.9% Hispanic of any race (2000); Density: 681.9 persons per square mile (2000); Age: 38.7% under 18, 0.1% over 64 (2000); Marriage status: 25.0% never married, 69.7% now married, 0.0% widowed, 5.3% divorced (2000); Foreign born: 4.0% (2000); Ancestry (includes multiple ancestries): 44.5% Other groups, 11.2% German, 9.8% United States or American, 9.4% Irish, 2.9% Italian (2000).
Economy: Employment by occupation: 12.2% management, 22.0% professional, 16.9% services, 42.2% sales, 0.0% farming, 4.1% construction, 2.6% production (2000).
Income: Per capita income: $12,547 (2000); Median household income: $40,282 (2000); Poverty rate: 4.2% (2000).
Education: Percent of population age 25 and over with: High school diploma (including GED) or higher: 97.2% (2000); Bachelor's degree or higher: 13.9% (2000).
Housing: Homeownership rate: 0.7% (2000); Median home value: $22,500 (2000); Median rent: $708 per month (2000); Median age of housing: 4 years (2000).
Transportation: Commute to work: 90.1% car, 0.0% public transportation, 4.2% walk, 4.2% work from home (2000); Travel time to work: 52.6% less than 15 minutes, 22.1% 15 to 30 minutes, 19.9% 30 to 45 minutes, 4.2% 45 to 60 minutes, 1.3% 60 minutes or more (2000)

PORT SAINT JOHN (CDP). Covers a land area of 3.818 square miles and a water area of 0 square miles. Located at 28.47° N. Lat.; 80.78° W. Long.
Population: 8,933 (1990); 12,112 (2000); 12,476 (2004); 13,009 (2009 projected); Race: 90.0% White, 5.5% Black, 0.8% Asian, 3.5% Hispanic of any race (2004); Density: 3,267.3 persons per square mile (2004); Average household size: 2.81 (2004); Median age: 37.5 (2004); Male/female ratio: 99.8 (2004); Marriage status: 17.8% never married, 63.5% now married, 4.9% widowed, 13.8% divorced (2000); Foreign born: 2.8% (2000); Ancestry (includes multiple ancestries): 17.6% German, 16.3% Irish, 14.6% Other groups, 13.6% English, 10.2% United States or American (2000).
Economy: Employment by occupation: 10.6% management, 22.9% professional, 15.3% services, 26.5% sales, 0.0% farming, 11.2% construction, 13.4% production (2000).
Income: Per capita income: $20,411 (2004); Median household income: $49,690 (2004); Average household income: $54,496 (2004); Percent of households with income of $100,000 or more: 8.8% (2004); Poverty rate: 6.6% (2000).
Education: Percent of population age 25 and over with: High school diploma (including GED) or higher: 88.6% (2004); Bachelor's degree or higher: 15.4% (2004); Master's degree or higher: 4.3% (2004).
Housing: Homeownership rate: 86.8% (2004); Median home value: $102,247 (2004); Median rent: $614 per month (2000); Median age of housing: 14 years (2000).
Transportation: Commute to work: 96.9% car, 0.1% public transportation, 0.8% walk, 1.4% work from home (2000); Travel time to work: 14.3% less than 15 minutes, 52.0% 15 to 30 minutes, 20.8% 30 to 45 minutes, 6.6% 45 to 60 minutes, 6.3% 60 minutes or more (2000)

ROCKLEDGE (city). Covers a land area of 10.703 square miles and a water area of 1.476 square miles. Located at 28.32° N. Lat.; 80.73° W. Long. Elevation is 43 feet.
Population: 16,297 (1990); 20,170 (2000); 22,748 (2004); 25,824 (2009 projected); Race: 80.3% White, 15.2% Black, 1.8% Asian, 3.6% Hispanic of any race (2004); Density: 2,125.3 persons per square mile (2004); Average household size: 2.55 (2004); Median age: 41.2 (2004); Male/female ratio: 91.3 (2004); Marriage status: 19.6% never married, 62.0% now married, 6.9% widowed, 11.5% divorced (2000); Foreign born: 4.6% (2000); Ancestry (includes multiple ancestries): 21.1% Other groups, 16.7% German, 14.4% English, 13.7% Irish, 7.9% United States or American (2000).
Economy: Single-family building permits issued: 404 (2004); Multi-family building permits issued: 144 (2004); Employment by occupation: 14.2% management, 23.6% professional, 15.1% services, 28.7% sales, 0.1% farming, 7.2% construction, 11.1% production (2000).
Income: Per capita income: $23,626 (2004); Median household income: $49,613 (2004); Average household income: $59,277 (2004); Percent of households with income of $100,000 or more: 12.7% (2004); Poverty rate: 6.5% (2000).
Taxes: Total city taxes per capita: $345 (2002); City property taxes per capita: $175 (2002).
Education: Percent of population age 25 and over with: High school diploma (including GED) or higher: 87.4% (2004); Bachelor's degree or higher: 24.4% (2004); Master's degree or higher: 8.4% (2004).

School District(s)

Brevard County School District (PK-12)
2002-03 Enrollment: 72,601 . . . . (321) 631-1911
Housing: Homeownership rate: 81.9% (2004); Median home value: $119,594 (2004); Median rent: $587 per month (2000); Median age of housing: 20 years (2000).
Hospitals: Wuesthoff Health Systems (295 beds)
Safety: Violent crime rate: 19.9 per 10,000 population; Property crime rate: 338.9 per 10,000 population (2003).
Transportation: Commute to work: 95.1% car, 0.3% public transportation, 0.8% walk, 2.7% work from home (2000); Travel time to work: 30.2% less than 15 minutes, 35.7% 15 to 30 minutes, 22.9% 30 to 45 minutes, 5.7% 45 to 60 minutes, 5.5% 60 minutes or more (2000)
Additional Information Contacts
Local Government Offices . . . . (321) 690-3978

SATELLITE BEACH (city). Covers a land area of 2.376 square miles and a water area of 0.989 square miles. Located at 28.17° N. Lat.; 80.59° W. Long. Elevation is 19 feet.
Population: 9,840 (1990); 9,577 (2000); 9,768 (2004); 10,084 (2009 projected); Race: 94.8% White, 1.1% Black, 1.5% Asian, 3.0% Hispanic of any race (2004); Density: 4,111.0 persons per square mile (2004); Average household size: 2.39 (2004); Median age: 45.9 (2004); Male/female ratio: 95.7 (2004); Marriage status: 19.0% never married, 62.6% now married, 8.0% widowed, 10.3% divorced (2000); Foreign born: 5.2% (2000); Ancestry (includes multiple ancestries): 20.4% German, 18.4% English, 17.9% Irish, 10.5% Italian, 8.2% Other groups (2000).
Economy: Single-family building permits issued: 44 (2004); Multi-family building permits issued: 2 (2004); Employment by occupation: 12.6% management, 30.3% professional, 15.4% services, 27.3% sales, 0.1% farming, 7.4% construction, 6.8% production (2000).
Income: Per capita income: $28,981 (2004); Median household income: $58,696 (2004); Average household income: $69,117 (2004); Percent of households with income of $100,000 or more: 17.9% (2004); Poverty rate: 4.5% (2000).

Taxes: Total city taxes per capita: $351 (2002); City property taxes per capita: $241 (2002).
Education: Percent of population age 25 and over with: High school diploma (including GED) or higher: 95.6% (2004); Bachelor's degree or higher: 37.6% (2004); Master's degree or higher: 14.5% (2004).

School District(s)

Brevard County School District (PK-12)
2002-03 Enrollment: 72,601 . . . . (321) 631-1911

Housing: Homeownership rate: 83.6% (2004); Median home value: $160,414 (2004); Median rent: $648 per month (2000); Median age of housing: 28 years (2000).
Safety: Violent crime rate: 28.8 per 10,000 population; Property crime rate: 253.2 per 10,000 population (2003).
Transportation: Commute to work: 92.0% car, 0.0% public transportation, 2.0% walk, 3.6% work from home (2000); Travel time to work: 29.2% less than 15 minutes, 45.1% 15 to 30 minutes, 14.0% 30 to 45 minutes, 4.2% 45 to 60 minutes, 7.5% 60 minutes or more (2000)

Additional Information Contacts

Local Government Offices . . . . (321) 773-4407

SHARPES (CDP). Covers a land area of 2.983 square miles and a water area of 3.303 square miles. Located at 28.44° N. Lat.; 80.76° W. Long. Elevation is 22 feet.
Population: 3,348 (1990); 3,415 (2000); 3,321 (2004); 3,287 (2009 projected); Race: 91.2% White, 3.8% Black, 0.7% Asian, 2.9% Hispanic of any race (2004); Density: 1,113.1 persons per square mile (2004); Average household size: 2.27 (2004); Median age: 42.5 (2004); Male/female ratio: 98.5 (2004); Marriage status: 18.7% never married, 55.6% now married, 7.8% widowed, 17.8% divorced (2000); Foreign born: 2.0% (2000); Ancestry (includes multiple ancestries): 18.4% United States or American, 17.2% Other groups, 17.0% Irish, 17.0% German, 9.7% English (2000).
Economy: Manufacturing includes rock and coquina mining and processing. Employment by occupation: 10.6% management, 12.7% professional, 17.9% services, 29.4% sales, 0.9% farming, 18.2% construction, 10.3% production (2000).
Income: Per capita income: $18,477 (2004); Median household income: $29,178 (2004); Average household income: $41,430 (2004); Percent of households with income of $100,000 or more: 8.1% (2004); Poverty rate: 18.7% (2000).
Education: Percent of population age 25 and over with: High school diploma (including GED) or higher: 77.9% (2004); Bachelor's degree or higher: 13.2% (2004); Master's degree or higher: 4.4% (2004).
Housing: Homeownership rate: 77.3% (2004); Median home value: $55,873 (2004); Median rent: $410 per month (2000); Median age of housing: 24 years (2000).
Transportation: Commute to work: 93.7% car, 0.0% public transportation, 2.1% walk, 3.0% work from home (2000); Travel time to work: 23.8% less than 15 minutes, 41.3% 15 to 30 minutes, 24.1% 30 to 45 minutes, 4.8% 45 to 60 minutes, 6.0% 60 minutes or more (2000)

SOUTH PATRICK SHORES (CDP). Aka Amherst. Covers a land area of 2.058 square miles and a water area of 1.669 square miles. Located at 28.20° N. Lat.; 80.60° W. Long.
Population: 10,298 (1990); 8,913 (2000); 8,496 (2004); 8,163 (2009 projected); Race: 91.1% White, 3.0% Black, 2.1% Asian, 5.1% Hispanic of any race (2004); Density: 4,128.7 persons per square mile (2004); Average household size: 2.45 (2004); Median age: 42.0 (2004); Male/female ratio: 98.2 (2004); Marriage status: 17.2% never married, 66.3% now married, 6.1% widowed, 10.4% divorced (2000); Foreign born: 6.0% (2000); Ancestry (includes multiple ancestries): 20.4% German, 17.6% Irish, 15.4% Other groups, 15.1% English, 9.2% Italian (2000).
Economy: Employment by occupation: 12.3% management, 26.4% professional, 18.7% services, 23.9% sales, 0.3% farming, 10.2% construction, 8.2% production (2000).
Income: Per capita income: $26,193 (2004); Median household income: $51,814 (2004); Average household income: $64,194 (2004); Percent of households with income of $100,000 or more: 13.5% (2004); Poverty rate: 4.6% (2000).
Education: Percent of population age 25 and over with: High school diploma (including GED) or higher: 91.9% (2004); Bachelor's degree or higher: 30.5% (2004); Master's degree or higher: 12.5% (2004).
Housing: Homeownership rate: 71.3% (2004); Median home value: $142,933 (2004); Median rent: $672 per month (2000); Median age of housing: 34 years (2000).
Transportation: Commute to work: 93.6% car, 0.5% public transportation, 1.0% walk, 2.5% work from home (2000); Travel time to work: 30.4% less than 15 minutes, 38.0% 15 to 30 minutes, 21.5% 30 to 45 minutes, 5.0% 45 to 60 minutes, 5.1% 60 minutes or more (2000)

TITUSVILLE (city). Covers a land area of 21.256 square miles and a water area of 4.651 square miles. Located at 28.59° N. Lat.; 80.82° W. Long. Elevation is 18 feet.
History: Titusville was named for Colonel H.T. Titus, an early resident. It was a flourishing port in the 1880's, situated at the head of navigation on the Indian River. A railroad with wooden tracks, powered by mules, carried goods inland.
Population: 39,970 (1990); 40,670 (2000); 41,313 (2004); 42,423 (2009 projected); Race: 82.4% White, 13.9% Black, 1.0% Asian, 3.8% Hispanic of any race (2004); Density: 1,943.6 persons per square mile (2004); Average household size: 2.34 (2004); Median age: 41.7 (2004); Male/female ratio: 91.5 (2004); Marriage status: 20.0% never married, 56.7% now married, 10.0% widowed, 13.3% divorced (2000); Foreign born: 4.8% (2000); Ancestry (includes multiple ancestries): 19.4% Other groups, 16.7% German, 13.4% Irish, 12.4% English, 8.9% United States or American (2000).
Economy: Unemployment rate: 4.4% (2004); Total civilian labor force: 23,055 (2004); Single-family building permits issued: 329 (2004); Multi-family building permits issued: 616 (2004); Employment by occupation: 10.1% management, 23.5% professional, 16.7% services, 25.9% sales, 0.1% farming, 10.8% construction, 13.0% production (2000).
Income: Per capita income: $21,010 (2004); Median household income: $38,175 (2004); Average household income: $48,597 (2004); Percent of households with income of $100,000 or more: 9.1% (2004); Poverty rate: 12.4% (2000).
Taxes: Total city taxes per capita: $379 (2002); City property taxes per capita: $180 (2002).
Education: Percent of population age 25 and over with: High school diploma (including GED) or higher: 84.4% (2004); Bachelor's degree or higher: 19.3% (2004); Master's degree or higher: 6.0% (2004).

School District(s)

Brevard County School District (PK-12)
2002-03 Enrollment: 72,601 . . . . (321) 631-1911

Housing: Homeownership rate: 68.0% (2004); Median home value: $93,737 (2004); Median rent: $445 per month (2000); Median age of housing: 27 years (2000).
Hospitals: Parrish Medical Center (210 beds)
Safety: Violent crime rate: 85.0 per 10,000 population; Property crime rate: 412.1 per 10,000 population (2003).
Transportation: Commute to work: 94.6% car, 0.3% public transportation, 1.8% walk, 2.0% work from home (2000); Travel time to work: 35.4% less than 15 minutes, 30.1% 15 to 30 minutes, 19.2% 30 to 45 minutes, 8.8% 45 to 60 minutes, 6.6% 60 minutes or more (2000)
Airports: Space Coast Regional

Additional Information Contacts

Space Coast Economic Development Commerce . . . . (321) 269-3221
Titusville Chamber of Commerce. . . . . (321) 267-3036

WEST MELBOURNE (city). Covers a land area of 7.823 square miles and a water area of 0.017 square miles. Located at 28.07° N. Lat.; 80.66° W. Long. Elevation is 32 feet.
Population: 8,881 (1990); 9,824 (2000); 12,197 (2004); 14,970 (2009 projected); Race: 92.5% White, 1.7% Black, 2.4% Asian, 4.5% Hispanic of any race (2004); Density: 1,559.1 persons per square mile (2004); Average household size: 2.15 (2004); Median age: 50.0 (2004); Male/female ratio: 86.4 (2004); Marriage status: 18.1% never married, 54.9% now married, 13.9% widowed, 13.1% divorced (2000); Foreign born: 8.3% (2000); Ancestry (includes multiple ancestries): 18.6% German, 17.9% English, 15.8% Irish, 13.3% Other groups, 10.0% United States or American (2000).
Economy: Manufacturing includes electrical and electronic products and equipment. Single-family building permits issued: 626 (2004); Multi-family building permits issued: 8 (2004); Employment by occupation: 12.8% management, 29.1% professional, 11.5% services, 27.0% sales, 0.0% farming, 7.6% construction, 12.0% production (2000).
Income: Per capita income: $26,036 (2004); Median household income: $42,412 (2004); Average household income: $54,888 (2004); Percent of households with income of $100,000 or more: 11.3% (2004); Poverty rate: 7.8% (2000).
Taxes: Total city taxes per capita: $365 (2002); City property taxes per capita: $0 (2002).

Education: Percent of population age 25 and over with: High school diploma (including GED) or higher: 87.3% (2004); Bachelor's degree or higher: 24.8% (2004); Master's degree or higher: 8.6% (2004).

School District(s)

Brevard County School District (PK-12)
2002-03 Enrollment: 72,601 . . . . (321) 631-1911

Four-year College(s)

Rollins College-Brevard Campus
2003-04 Enrollment: n/a . . . . (321) 726-0432
2003-04 Tuition: In-state $4,008; Out-of-state $4,008

Housing: Homeownership rate: 72.9% (2004); Median home value: $104,255 (2004); Median rent: $544 per month (2000); Median age of housing: 18 years (2000).

Safety: Violent crime rate: 86.2 per 10,000 population; Property crime rate: 499.5 per 10,000 population (2003).

Transportation: Commute to work: 93.6% car, 0.3% public transportation, 2.5% walk, 1.8% work from home (2000); Travel time to work: 43.7% less than 15 minutes, 38.9% 15 to 30 minutes, 11.2% 30 to 45 minutes, 2.3% 45 to 60 minutes, 3.9% 60 minutes or more (2000)

Additional Information Contacts

Local Government Offices . . . . (321) 727-7700

Broward County

Located in southern Florida, on the Atlantic coast. Covers a land area of 1,205.40 square miles, a water area of 114.20 square miles, and is located in the Eastern Time Zone. The county government was organized in 1915. County seat is Fort Lauderdale.

Broward County is part of the Miami-Fort Lauderdale-Miami Beach, FL Metropolitan Statistical Area. The entire metro area includes: Fort Lauderdale-Pompano Beach-Deerfield Beach, FL Metropolitan Division (Broward County, FL); Miami-Miami Beach-Kendall, FL Metropolitan Division (Miami-Dade County, FL); West Palm Beach-Boca Raton-Boynton Beach, FL Metropolitan Division (Palm Beach County, FL)

Weather Station: Fort Lauderdale — Elevation: 13 feet

	Jan	Feb	Mar	Apr	May	Jun	Jul	Aug	Sep	Oct	Nov	Dec
High	76	77	79	82	86	88	90	90	89	85	81	78
Low	59	59	63	66	71	74	75	76	75	72	66	61
Precip	3.0	2.8	3.0	3.8	6.4	9.9	6.6	7.0	8.3	6.2	4.6	2.5
Snow	0.0	0.0	0.0	0.0	0.0	0.0	0.0	0.0	0.0	0.0	0.0	0.0

High and Low temperatures in degrees Fahrenheit; Precipitation and Snow in inches

Population: 1,255,488 (1990); 1,623,018 (2000); 1,738,282 (2004); 1,883,683 (2009 projected); Race: 66.0% White, 23.1% Black, 2.8% Asian, 21.1% Hispanic of any race (2004); Density: 1,442.1 persons per square mile (2004); Average household size: 2.50 (2004); Median age: 38.3 (2004); Male/female ratio: 94.1 (2004).

Religion: Five largest groups: 21.1% Catholic Church, 13.1% Jewish Estimate, 3.6% Southern Baptist Convention, 1.1% The United Methodist Church, 0.8% Presbyterian Church in America (2000).

Economy: Unemployment rate: 5.0% (2004); Total civilian labor force: 903,676 (2004); Leading industries: 15.4% retail trade; 13.2% health care and social assistance; 10.8% administration, support, waste management, remediation services (2003); Companies that employ 500 or more persons: 78 (2003); Companies that employ 100 to 499 persons: 937 (2003); Companies that employ less than 100 persons: 52,855 (2003); Farms: 494 totaling 23,741 acres (2002); Minority business ownership rate: 25.0% (1997); Women business ownership rate: 24.6% (1997); Retail sales per capita: $12,174 (1997). Single-family building permits issued: 4,784 (2004); Multi-family building permits issued: 3,925 (2004).

Income: Per capita income: $25,750 (2004); Median household income: $46,022 (2004); Average household income: $63,879 (2004); Percent of households with income of $100,000 or more: 16.1% (2004); Poverty rate: 11.7% (2002); Bankruptcy rate: 4.49% (2004).

Taxes: Total county taxes per capita: $429 (2002); County property taxes per capita: $344 (2002).

Education: Percent of population age 25 and over with: High school diploma (including GED) or higher: 82.3% (2004); Bachelor's degree or higher: 25.1% (2004); Master's degree or higher: 8.9% (2004).

Housing: Homeownership rate: 69.8% (2004); Median home value: $147,662 (2004); Median rent: $676 per month (2000); Median age of housing: 23 years (2000).

Health: Birth rate: 135.6 per 10,000 population (2004); Death rate: 95.6 per 10,000 population (2004); Age adjusted cancer mortality rate: 183.4 deaths per 100,000 population (2002); Air Quality Index: 92.5% good, 7.5% moderate, 0.0% unhealthy for sensitive individuals, 0.0% unhealthy (percent of days in 2004); Number of physicians: 24.7 per 10,000 population (2001); Hospital beds: 33.5 per 10,000 population (2002); Hospital admissions: 1,332.3 per 10,000 population (2002).

Elections: 2004 Presidential election results: 34.6% Bush, 64.2% Kerry, 0.5% Nader, 0.2% Badnarik

National and State Parks: Hugh Taylor Birch State Park; John U Lloyd Beach State Park; Pan-American State Park

Additional Information Contacts

Broward County Government Offices . . . . (954) 357-7585
British American Chamber of Commerce . . . . (407) 428-6226
Christian Chamber of Commerce . . . . (954) 972-9256
Coconut Creek Chamber of Commerce. . . . . (954) 461-8792
Davie-Cooper City Chamber of Commerce . . . . (954) 581-0790
Deerfield Beach Chamber of Commerce. . . . . (954) 427-1050
Florida-Israel Chamber . . . . (561) 620-9288
Fort Lauderdale Chamber of Commerce . . . . (954) 462-6000
Greater Dania Chamber of Commerce . . . . (954) 926-2323
Greater Hollywood Chamber of Commerce. . . . . (954) 923-4000
Greater Pompano Beach Chamber . . . . (954) 941-2940
Lauderdale By-The-Sea Chamber. (954) 776-1000
North Broward Chamber of Commerce . . . . (954) 972-0818
Oakland Park-Wilton Chamber . . . . (954) 489-0370
Pembroke Pines Chamber of Commerce . . . . (954) 432-9808
Plantation Chamber of Commerce. (954) 587-1410
Realtor Association of Greater Fort Lauderdale . . . . (954) 563-7261
South Broward Association of Realtors . . . . (954) 431-5300
Sunrise Chamber of Commerce . . . . (954) 835-2428
Tamarac Chamber of Commerce . . . . (954) 722-1520

Broward County Communities

BONNIE LOCK-WOODSETTER NORTH (CDP). Covers a land area of 0.479 square miles and a water area of 0 square miles. Located at 26.28° N. Lat.; 80.13° W. Long.

Population: 3,398 (1990); 4,275 (2000); 4,494 (2004); 4,776 (2009 projected); Race: 37.6% White, 36.8% Black, 3.2% Asian, 20.5% Hispanic of any race (2004); Density: 9,385.8 persons per square mile (2004); Average household size: 3.41 (2004); Median age: 31.0 (2004); Male/female ratio: 102.3 (2004); Marriage status: 31.9% never married, 53.5% now married, 4.5% widowed, 10.1% divorced (2000); Foreign born: 42.9% (2000); Ancestry (includes multiple ancestries): 30.3% Other groups, 20.2% Haitian, 6.2% German, 6.1% United States or American, 5.5% Brazilian (2000).

Economy: Employment by occupation: 8.1% management, 8.2% professional, 25.0% services, 34.8% sales, 0.0% farming, 13.0% construction, 10.9% production (2000).

Income: Per capita income: $15,852 (2004); Median household income: $42,781 (2004); Average household income: $53,173 (2004); Percent of households with income of $100,000 or more: 11.2% (2004); Poverty rate: 10.7% (2000).

Education: Percent of population age 25 and over with: High school diploma (including GED) or higher: 68.5% (2004); Bachelor's degree or higher: 12.1% (2004); Master's degree or higher: 3.6% (2004).

Housing: Homeownership rate: 67.6% (2004); Median home value: $111,558 (2004); Median rent: $639 per month (2000); Median age of housing: 24 years (2000).

Transportation: Commute to work: 95.3% car, 2.0% public transportation, 0.5% walk, 0.4% work from home (2000); Travel time to work: 19.0% less than 15 minutes, 40.6% 15 to 30 minutes, 27.3% 30 to 45 minutes, 6.9% 45 to 60 minutes, 6.2% 60 minutes or more (2000)

BOULEVARD GARDENS (CDP). Covers a land area of 0.263 square miles and a water area of 0 square miles. Located at 26.12° N. Lat.; 80.18° W. Long.

Population: 1,515 (1990); 1,415 (2000); 1,228 (2004); 1,096 (2009 projected); Race: 1.9% White, 94.1% Black, 0.4% Asian, 3.0% Hispanic of any race (2004); Density: 4,666.0 persons per square mile (2004); Average household size: 3.06 (2004); Median age: 33.0 (2004); Male/female ratio: 95.9 (2004); Marriage status: 42.5% never married, 34.0% now married, 12.4% widowed, 11.1% divorced (2000); Foreign born: 10.1% (2000); Ancestry (includes multiple ancestries): 77.6% Other groups, 4.3% Jamaican, 2.8% United States or American, 1.9% Haitian, 0.9% Hungarian (2000).

Economy: Employment by occupation: 8.7% management, 7.5% professional, 29.3% services, 12.6% sales, 0.0% farming, 21.5% construction, 20.3% production (2000).
Income: Per capita income: $13,864 (2004); Median household income: $21,707 (2004); Average household income: $42,456 (2004); Percent of households with income of $100,000 or more: 8.0% (2004); Poverty rate: 37.4% (2000).
Education: Percent of population age 25 and over with: High school diploma (including GED) or higher: 51.8% (2004); Bachelor's degree or higher: 6.3% (2004); Master's degree or higher: 3.4% (2004).
Housing: Homeownership rate: 64.6% (2004); Median home value: $105,000 (2004); Median rent: $399 per month (2000); Median age of housing: 38 years (2000).
Transportation: Commute to work: 71.9% car, 17.9% public transportation, 10.1% walk, 0.0% work from home (2000); Travel time to work: 12.2% less than 15 minutes, 31.7% 15 to 30 minutes, 36.1% 30 to 45 minutes, 17.4% 45 to 60 minutes, 2.6% 60 minutes or more (2000)

BROADVIEW PARK (CDP). Covers a land area of 0.978 square miles and a water area of 0.044 square miles. Located at 26.09° N. Lat.; 80.20° W. Long. Elevation is 17 feet.
Population: 6,109 (1990); 6,798 (2000); 6,974 (2004); 7,260 (2009 projected); Race: 62.3% White, 19.4% Black, 2.4% Asian, 51.1% Hispanic of any race (2004); Density: 7,129.0 persons per square mile (2004); Average household size: 3.27 (2004); Median age: 31.6 (2004); Male/female ratio: 108.2 (2004); Marriage status: 31.5% never married, 52.1% now married, 5.3% widowed, 11.1% divorced (2000); Foreign born: 36.9% (2000); Ancestry (includes multiple ancestries): 49.3% Other groups, 10.5% United States or American, 6.5% German, 6.2% Irish, 5.1% English (2000).
Economy: Employment by occupation: 5.2% management, 11.0% professional, 17.9% services, 26.3% sales, 0.7% farming, 20.0% construction, 18.9% production (2000).
Income: Per capita income: $15,618 (2004); Median household income: $42,755 (2004); Average household income: $50,253 (2004); Percent of households with income of $100,000 or more: 8.3% (2004); Poverty rate: 14.8% (2000).
Education: Percent of population age 25 and over with: High school diploma (including GED) or higher: 62.4% (2004); Bachelor's degree or higher: 7.2% (2004); Master's degree or higher: 3.6% (2004).
Housing: Homeownership rate: 60.8% (2004); Median home value: $120,208 (2004); Median rent: $547 per month (2000); Median age of housing: 39 years (2000).
Transportation: Commute to work: 92.3% car, 4.0% public transportation, 0.8% walk, 1.2% work from home (2000); Travel time to work: 15.6% less than 15 minutes, 46.4% 15 to 30 minutes, 21.9% 30 to 45 minutes, 9.2% 45 to 60 minutes, 6.9% 60 minutes or more (2000)

BROADVIEW-POMPANO PARK (CDP). Covers a land area of 0.594 square miles and a water area of 0 square miles. Located at 26.20° N. Lat.; 80.21° W. Long.
Population: 4,156 (1990); 5,314 (2000); 5,219 (2004); 5,147 (2009 projected); Race: 54.0% White, 23.4% Black, 4.0% Asian, 44.1% Hispanic of any race (2004); Density: 8,787.9 persons per square mile (2004); Average household size: 3.49 (2004); Median age: 30.5 (2004); Male/female ratio: 104.3 (2004); Marriage status: 28.4% never married, 52.5% now married, 5.9% widowed, 13.2% divorced (2000); Foreign born: 40.7% (2000); Ancestry (includes multiple ancestries): 43.1% Other groups, 9.3% Irish, 7.6% Italian, 7.1% United States or American, 7.0% Haitian (2000).
Economy: Employment by occupation: 9.0% management, 9.2% professional, 17.6% services, 22.0% sales, 0.0% farming, 22.5% construction, 19.8% production (2000).
Income: Per capita income: $13,714 (2004); Median household income: $38,328 (2004); Average household income: $47,762 (2004); Percent of households with income of $100,000 or more: 7.0% (2004); Poverty rate: 15.5% (2000).
Education: Percent of population age 25 and over with: High school diploma (including GED) or higher: 62.6% (2004); Bachelor's degree or higher: 6.1% (2004); Master's degree or higher: 1.8% (2004).
Housing: Homeownership rate: 76.8% (2004); Median home value: $109,960 (2004); Median rent: $700 per month (2000); Median age of housing: 33 years (2000).
Transportation: Commute to work: 96.0% car, 0.0% public transportation, 0.4% walk, 2.0% work from home (2000); Travel time to work: 19.6% less than 15 minutes, 40.7% 15 to 30 minutes, 26.8% 30 to 45 minutes, 7.4% 45 to 60 minutes, 5.5% 60 minutes or more (2000)

BROWARD ESTATES (CDP). Covers a land area of 0.517 square miles and a water area of 0 square miles. Located at 26.12° N. Lat.; 80.19° W. Long.
Population: 3,631 (1990); 3,416 (2000); 3,243 (2004); 2,961 (2009 projected); Race: 0.7% White, 96.8% Black, 0.3% Asian, 1.5% Hispanic of any race (2004); Density: 6,276.6 persons per square mile (2004); Average household size: 3.38 (2004); Median age: 34.6 (2004); Male/female ratio: 88.7 (2004); Marriage status: 34.7% never married, 47.6% now married, 7.7% widowed, 10.0% divorced (2000); Foreign born: 5.5% (2000); Ancestry (includes multiple ancestries): 74.6% Other groups, 2.8% Jamaican, 2.6% Haitian, 1.6% United States or American, 1.2% African (2000).
Economy: Employment by occupation: 5.3% management, 11.8% professional, 21.5% services, 30.6% sales, 0.0% farming, 11.2% construction, 19.6% production (2000).
Income: Per capita income: $13,425 (2004); Median household income: $37,063 (2004); Average household income: $44,867 (2004); Percent of households with income of $100,000 or more: 7.9% (2004); Poverty rate: 23.2% (2000).
Education: Percent of population age 25 and over with: High school diploma (including GED) or higher: 61.5% (2004); Bachelor's degree or higher: 9.9% (2004); Master's degree or higher: 3.9% (2004).
Housing: Homeownership rate: 82.5% (2004); Median home value: $114,126 (2004); Median rent: $575 per month (2000); Median age of housing: 40 years (2000).
Transportation: Commute to work: 94.8% car, 4.2% public transportation, 0.5% walk, 0.6% work from home (2000); Travel time to work: 22.1% less than 15 minutes, 44.2% 15 to 30 minutes, 23.0% 30 to 45 minutes, 4.5% 45 to 60 minutes, 6.2% 60 minutes or more (2000)

CARVER RANCHES (CDP). Covers a land area of 0.674 square miles and a water area of 0 square miles. Located at 25.99° N. Lat.; 80.19° W. Long. Elevation is 12 feet.
Population: 3,882 (1990); 4,299 (2000); 4,839 (2004); 5,508 (2009 projected); Race: 1.8% White, 96.7% Black, 0.0% Asian, 1.9% Hispanic of any race (2004); Density: 7,177.4 persons per square mile (2004); Average household size: 3.21 (2004); Median age: 31.8 (2004); Male/female ratio: 86.5 (2004); Marriage status: 38.3% never married, 41.6% now married, 8.7% widowed, 11.4% divorced (2000); Foreign born: 5.8% (2000); Ancestry (includes multiple ancestries): 72.8% Other groups, 5.3% United States or American, 2.5% Bahamian, 2.4% African, 1.6% Haitian (2000).
Economy: Employment by occupation: 3.3% management, 14.4% professional, 24.8% services, 24.5% sales, 0.0% farming, 9.6% construction, 23.5% production (2000).
Income: Per capita income: $10,526 (2004); Median household income: $29,498 (2004); Average household income: $33,391 (2004); Percent of households with income of $100,000 or more: 1.2% (2004); Poverty rate: 25.3% (2000).
Education: Percent of population age 25 and over with: High school diploma (including GED) or higher: 65.5% (2004); Bachelor's degree or higher: 5.7% (2004); Master's degree or higher: 1.6% (2004).
Housing: Homeownership rate: 61.2% (2004); Median home value: $121,619 (2004); Median rent: $532 per month (2000); Median age of housing: 32 years (2000).
Transportation: Commute to work: 89.8% car, 4.9% public transportation, 2.6% walk, 0.7% work from home (2000); Travel time to work: 22.2% less than 15 minutes, 36.6% 15 to 30 minutes, 28.6% 30 to 45 minutes, 6.5% 45 to 60 minutes, 6.1% 60 minutes or more (2000)

CHAMBERS ESTATES (CDP). Covers a land area of 0.551 square miles and a water area of 0 square miles. Located at 26.05° N. Lat.; 80.20° W. Long.
Population: 3,073 (1990); 3,556 (2000); 3,731 (2004); 3,888 (2009 projected); Race: 72.2% White, 14.5% Black, 2.1% Asian, 33.0% Hispanic of any race (2004); Density: 6,773.6 persons per square mile (2004); Average household size: 2.66 (2004); Median age: 34.3 (2004); Male/female ratio: 96.3 (2004); Marriage status: 26.3% never married, 50.6% now married, 5.3% widowed, 17.8% divorced (2000); Foreign born: 24.9% (2000); Ancestry (includes multiple ancestries): 32.0% Other groups, 10.6% Italian, 10.3% United States or American, 8.9% Irish, 8.4% German (2000).

Economy: Employment by occupation: 6.6% management, 16.0% professional, 17.6% services, 30.8% sales, 2.3% farming, 10.2% construction, 16.5% production (2000).
Income: Per capita income: $20,855 (2004); Median household income: $42,770 (2004); Average household income: $55,337 (2004); Percent of households with income of $100,000 or more: 12.0% (2004); Poverty rate: 12.8% (2000).
Education: Percent of population age 25 and over with: High school diploma (including GED) or higher: 78.7% (2004); Bachelor's degree or higher: 15.3% (2004); Master's degree or higher: 5.4% (2004).
Housing: Homeownership rate: 56.6% (2004); Median home value: $115,432 (2004); Median rent: $680 per month (2000); Median age of housing: 27 years (2000).
Transportation: Commute to work: 86.0% car, 5.1% public transportation, 1.8% walk, 4.7% work from home (2000); Travel time to work: 23.7% less than 15 minutes, 32.5% 15 to 30 minutes, 30.5% 30 to 45 minutes, 5.8% 45 to 60 minutes, 7.6% 60 minutes or more (2000)

CHULA VISTA (CDP). Covers a land area of 0.088 square miles and a water area of 0 square miles. Located at 26.10° N. Lat.; 80.18° W. Long.
Population: 524 (1990); 573 (2000); 578 (2004); 584 (2009 projected); Race: 63.1% White, 17.6% Black, 2.8% Asian, 43.4% Hispanic of any race (2004); Density: 6,583.5 persons per square mile (2004); Average household size: 2.79 (2004); Median age: 35.0 (2004); Male/female ratio: 107.9 (2004); Marriage status: 25.9% never married, 50.7% now married, 8.3% widowed, 15.1% divorced (2000); Foreign born: 36.4% (2000); Ancestry (includes multiple ancestries): 31.5% Other groups, 12.6% German, 9.1% Irish, 4.3% French (except Basque), 3.4% West Indian (2000).
Economy: Employment by occupation: 2.6% management, 9.1% professional, 3.9% services, 28.0% sales, 0.0% farming, 25.0% construction, 31.5% production (2000).
Income: Per capita income: $15,048 (2004); Median household income: $34,674 (2004); Average household income: $42,017 (2004); Percent of households with income of $100,000 or more: 1.9% (2004); Poverty rate: 21.5% (2000).
Education: Percent of population age 25 and over with: High school diploma (including GED) or higher: 59.7% (2004); Bachelor's degree or higher: 1.6% (2004); Master's degree or higher: 1.6% (2004).
Housing: Homeownership rate: 59.9% (2004); Median home value: $134,524 (2004); Median rent: $519 per month (2000); Median age of housing: 28 years (2000).
Transportation: Commute to work: 96.9% car, 0.0% public transportation, 0.0% walk, 0.0% work from home (2000); Travel time to work: 29.3% less than 15 minutes, 41.8% 15 to 30 minutes, 28.9% 30 to 45 minutes, 0.0% 45 to 60 minutes, 0.0% 60 minutes or more (2000)

COCONUT CREEK (city). Covers a land area of 11.546 square miles and a water area of 0.238 square miles. Located at 26.27° N. Lat.; 80.18° W. Long. Elevation is 17 feet.
History: Named for its abundance of coconut palms and canals. Site of major suburban development since 1980.
Population: 27,509 (1990); 43,566 (2000); 49,172 (2004); 56,036 (2009 projected); Race: 80.9% White, 8.8% Black, 3.3% Asian, 15.9% Hispanic of any race (2004); Density: 4,258.8 persons per square mile (2004); Average household size: 2.22 (2004); Median age: 41.3 (2004); Male/female ratio: 88.6 (2004); Marriage status: 17.6% never married, 60.3% now married, 11.4% widowed, 10.7% divorced (2000); Foreign born: 18.3% (2000); Ancestry (includes multiple ancestries): 24.4% Other groups, 13.5% Italian, 10.7% German, 10.2% Irish, 6.8% Polish (2000).
Economy: Unemployment rate: 5.8% (2004); Total civilian labor force: 17,557 (2004); Single-family building permits issued: 3 (2004); Multi-family building permits issued: 0 (2004); Employment by occupation: 17.9% management, 19.7% professional, 12.9% services, 33.8% sales, 0.3% farming, 8.7% construction, 6.7% production (2000).
Income: Per capita income: $28,128 (2004); Median household income: $49,330 (2004); Average household income: $62,125 (2004); Percent of households with income of $100,000 or more: 14.9% (2004); Poverty rate: 7.1% (2000).
Taxes: Total city taxes per capita: $394 (2002); City property taxes per capita: $191 (2002).
Education: Percent of population age 25 and over with: High school diploma (including GED) or higher: 87.8% (2004); Bachelor's degree or higher: 27.9% (2004); Master's degree or higher: 9.2% (2004).

School District(s)
Broward County School District (PK-12)
2002-03 Enrollment: 267,925 . . . . (754) 321-2600
Two-year College(s)
Atlantic Technical Center (Public)
2003-04 Enrollment: 1,110 . . . . (754) 321-5100
2003-04 Tuition: In-state $1,530; Out-of-state $6,120
Housing: Homeownership rate: 74.7% (2004); Median home value: $137,131 (2004); Median rent: $824 per month (2000); Median age of housing: 13 years (2000).
Safety: Violent crime rate: 23.1 per 10,000 population; Property crime rate: 211.4 per 10,000 population (2003).
Transportation: Commute to work: 95.1% car, 0.7% public transportation, 0.5% walk, 2.8% work from home (2000); Travel time to work: 17.3% less than 15 minutes, 43.2% 15 to 30 minutes, 27.4% 30 to 45 minutes, 7.4% 45 to 60 minutes, 4.7% 60 minutes or more (2000)
Additional Information Contacts
Coconut Creek Chamber of Commerce. . . . . (954) 461-8792
Local Government Offices . . . . (954) 973-6770
North Broward Chamber of Commerce . . . . (954) 972-0818

COLLIER MANOR-CRESTHAVEN (CDP). Covers a land area of 1.158 square miles and a water area of 0 square miles. Located at 26.26° N. Lat.; 80.10° W. Long.
Population: 7,322 (1990); 7,741 (2000); 7,779 (2004); 7,913 (2009 projected); Race: 71.1% White, 15.9% Black, 1.3% Asian, 19.7% Hispanic of any race (2004); Density: 6,715.1 persons per square mile (2004); Average household size: 2.57 (2004); Median age: 36.4 (2004); Male/female ratio: 104.4 (2004); Marriage status: 27.4% never married, 53.3% now married, 6.0% widowed, 13.3% divorced (2000); Foreign born: 22.2% (2000); Ancestry (includes multiple ancestries): 23.3% Other groups, 15.0% Italian, 14.3% German, 14.2% Irish, 9.3% English (2000).
Economy: Employment by occupation: 5.3% management, 10.1% professional, 21.9% services, 25.5% sales, 0.0% farming, 21.9% construction, 15.3% production (2000).
Income: Per capita income: $16,868 (2004); Median household income: $38,536 (2004); Average household income: $43,359 (2004); Percent of households with income of $100,000 or more: 4.3% (2004); Poverty rate: 11.1% (2000).
Education: Percent of population age 25 and over with: High school diploma (including GED) or higher: 76.4% (2004); Bachelor's degree or higher: 10.6% (2004); Master's degree or higher: 3.1% (2004).
Housing: Homeownership rate: 71.6% (2004); Median home value: $119,898 (2004); Median rent: $586 per month (2000); Median age of housing: 37 years (2000).
Transportation: Commute to work: 94.3% car, 1.2% public transportation, 1.3% walk, 1.7% work from home (2000); Travel time to work: 27.9% less than 15 minutes, 40.9% 15 to 30 minutes, 23.5% 30 to 45 minutes, 4.4% 45 to 60 minutes, 3.4% 60 minutes or more (2000)

COOPER CITY (city). Covers a land area of 6.346 square miles and a water area of 0.350 square miles. Located at 26.04° N. Lat.; 80.29° W. Long. Elevation is 8 feet.
Population: 21,193 (1990); 27,939 (2000); 28,994 (2004); 30,544 (2009 projected); Race: 86.5% White, 3.9% Black, 5.1% Asian, 18.8% Hispanic of any race (2004); Density: 4,568.6 persons per square mile (2004); Average household size: 3.09 (2004); Median age: 36.8 (2004); Male/female ratio: 94.8 (2004); Marriage status: 22.0% never married, 66.7% now married, 3.5% widowed, 7.8% divorced (2000); Foreign born: 16.9% (2000); Ancestry (includes multiple ancestries): 26.8% Other groups, 14.7% German, 13.9% Irish, 12.5% Italian, 8.4% English (2000).
Economy: Site of major suburban development since 1990. Manufacturing. Unemployment rate: 2.7% (2004); Total civilian labor force: 16,637 (2004); Single-family building permits issued: 55 (2004); Multi-family building permits issued: 0 (2004); Employment by occupation: 18.1% management, 27.2% professional, 12.8% services, 29.3% sales, 0.1% farming, 6.8% construction, 5.7% production (2000).
Income: Per capita income: $31,759 (2004); Median household income: $84,362 (2004); Average household income: $98,244 (2004); Percent of households with income of $100,000 or more: 37.1% (2004); Poverty rate: 3.2% (2000).
Taxes: Total city taxes per capita: $393 (2002); City property taxes per capita: $220 (2002).

Education: Percent of population age 25 and over with: High school diploma (including GED) or higher: 92.1% (2004); Bachelor's degree or higher: 38.3% (2004); Master's degree or higher: 14.9% (2004).

School District(s)

Broward County School District (PK-12)
2002-03 Enrollment: 267,925 . . . . (754) 321-2600

Housing: Homeownership rate: 92.2% (2004); Median home value: $215,016 (2004); Median rent: $831 per month (2000); Median age of housing: 15 years (2000).
Safety: Violent crime rate: 21.4 per 10,000 population; Property crime rate: 243.5 per 10,000 population (2003).
Transportation: Commute to work: 95.5% car, 0.1% public transportation, 0.5% walk, 3.3% work from home (2000); Travel time to work: 17.1% less than 15 minutes, 34.8% 15 to 30 minutes, 27.8% 30 to 45 minutes, 12.2% 45 to 60 minutes, 8.1% 60 minutes or more (2000)
Additional Information Contacts
Local Government Offices . . . . (954) 434-4300

CORAL SPRINGS (city). Covers a land area of 23.909 square miles and a water area of 0.237 square miles. Located at 26.27° N. Lat.; 80.25° W. Long. Elevation is 13 feet.
History: Named for the local natural springs. Has grown rapidly along with the South Florida and Fort Lauderdale area. The population of Coral Springs nearly doubled between 1980 and 1990. Incorporated 1963.
Population: 78,602 (1990); 117,549 (2000); 129,110 (2004); 143,768 (2009 projected); Race: 76.4% White, 12.0% Black, 4.3% Asian, 19.8% Hispanic of any race (2004); Density: 5,400.1 persons per square mile (2004); Average household size: 2.96 (2004); Median age: 34.5 (2004); Male/female ratio: 95.6 (2004); Marriage status: 25.5% never married, 60.2% now married, 4.1% widowed, 10.3% divorced (2000); Foreign born: 21.3% (2000); Ancestry (includes multiple ancestries): 26.8% Other groups, 14.2% Italian, 11.9% German, 11.3% Irish, 6.5% United States or American (2000).
Economy: Largely residential. Unemployment rate: 3.6% (2004); Total civilian labor force: 61,863 (2004); Single-family building permits issued: 2 (2004); Multi-family building permits issued: 84 (2004); Employment by occupation: 18.7% management, 20.8% professional, 12.8% services, 32.9% sales, 0.1% farming, 7.6% construction, 7.0% production (2000).
Income: Per capita income: $28,163 (2004); Median household income: $63,882 (2004); Average household income: $82,868 (2004); Percent of households with income of $100,000 or more: 25.7% (2004); Poverty rate: 8.0% (2000).
Taxes: Total city taxes per capita: $403 (2002); City property taxes per capita: $189 (2002).
Education: Percent of population age 25 and over with: High school diploma (including GED) or higher: 89.8% (2004); Bachelor's degree or higher: 34.4% (2004); Master's degree or higher: 11.8% (2004).

School District(s)

Broward County School District (PK-12)
2002-03 Enrollment: 267,925 . . . . (754) 321-2600

Housing: Homeownership rate: 65.2% (2004); Median home value: $231,627 (2004); Median rent: $806 per month (2000); Median age of housing: 14 years (2000).
Hospitals: Coral Springs Medical Center (200 beds)
Safety: Violent crime rate: 22.7 per 10,000 population; Property crime rate: 276.7 per 10,000 population (2003).
Newspapers: Coral Springs-Parkland Forum (General - Circulation 30,000); Jewish Journal - Broward Central (General, Jewish - Circulation 25,000); Margate-Coconut Creek Forum (General - Circulation 22,000); Sunrise Forum (General - Circulation 19,000); Tamarac-North Lauderdale Forum (General - Circulation 25,000)
Transportation: Commute to work: 92.7% car, 1.0% public transportation, 1.2% walk, 3.9% work from home (2000); Travel time to work: 23.5% less than 15 minutes, 30.0% 15 to 30 minutes, 28.0% 30 to 45 minutes, 11.1% 45 to 60 minutes, 7.4% 60 minutes or more (2000)
Additional Information Contacts
Local Government Offices . . . . (954) 344-5906

COUNTRY ESTATES (CDP). Covers a land area of 3.999 square miles and a water area of 0 square miles. Located at 26.04° N. Lat.; 80.40° W. Long.
Population: 1,824 (1990); 1,910 (2000); 2,421 (2004); 3,028 (2009 projected); Race: 89.9% White, 3.6% Black, 1.7% Asian, 23.1% Hispanic of any race (2004); Density: 605.3 persons per square mile (2004); Average household size: 3.41 (2004); Median age: 38.3 (2004); Male/female ratio: 107.3 (2004); Marriage status: 20.2% never married, 68.2% now married, 0.9% widowed, 10.6% divorced (2000); Foreign born: 14.5% (2000); Ancestry (includes multiple ancestries): 35.5% Other groups, 20.2% Irish, 15.3% Italian, 14.8% German, 8.9% English (2000).
Economy: Employment by occupation: 23.0% management, 23.1% professional, 14.5% services, 24.1% sales, 0.7% farming, 10.6% construction, 4.0% production (2000).
Income: Per capita income: $38,816 (2004); Median household income: $105,450 (2004); Average household income: $128,574 (2004); Percent of households with income of $100,000 or more: 53.2% (2004); Poverty rate: 4.2% (2000).
Education: Percent of population age 25 and over with: High school diploma (including GED) or higher: 87.0% (2004); Bachelor's degree or higher: 29.8% (2004); Master's degree or higher: 10.5% (2004).
Housing: Homeownership rate: 98.6% (2004); Median home value: $346,245 (2004); Median rent: $n/a per month (2000); Median age of housing: 16 years (2000).
Transportation: Commute to work: 86.2% car, 0.0% public transportation, 0.7% walk, 12.4% work from home (2000); Travel time to work: 8.7% less than 15 minutes, 29.7% 15 to 30 minutes, 31.9% 30 to 45 minutes, 21.7% 45 to 60 minutes, 8.0% 60 minutes or more (2000)

DANIA BEACH (city). Aka Dania. Covers a land area of 6.090 square miles and a water area of 0.221 square miles. Located at 26.05° N. Lat.; 80.15° W. Long. Elevation is 5 feet.
Population: 18,021 (1990); 20,061 (2000); 21,004 (2004); 22,377 (2009 projected); Race: 67.3% White, 25.0% Black, 1.8% Asian, 15.3% Hispanic of any race (2004); Density: 3,449.0 persons per square mile (2004); Average household size: 2.21 (2004); Median age: 40.3 (2004); Male/female ratio: 100.5 (2004); Marriage status: 30.2% never married, 45.4% now married, 8.2% widowed, 16.2% divorced (2000); Foreign born: 18.1% (2000); Ancestry (includes multiple ancestries): 29.9% Other groups, 12.4% Italian, 10.2% Irish, 9.7% German, 7.1% United States or American (2000).
Economy: Single-family building permits issued: 22 (2004); Multi-family building permits issued: 109 (2004); Employment by occupation: 12.0% management, 15.1% professional, 19.4% services, 29.6% sales, 0.1% farming, 12.1% construction, 11.7% production (2000).
Income: Per capita income: $23,628 (2004); Median household income: $38,786 (2004); Average household income: $51,415 (2004); Percent of households with income of $100,000 or more: 11.2% (2004); Poverty rate: 18.3% (2000).
Education: Percent of population age 25 and over with: High school diploma (including GED) or higher: 77.8% (2004); Bachelor's degree or higher: 17.7% (2004); Master's degree or higher: 5.4% (2004).

School District(s)

Broward County School District (PK-12)
2002-03 Enrollment: 267,925 . . . . (754) 321-2600

Housing: Homeownership rate: 57.2% (2004); Median home value: $127,373 (2004); Median rent: $599 per month (2000); Median age of housing: 26 years (2000).
Safety: Violent crime rate: 71.4 per 10,000 population; Property crime rate: 326.8 per 10,000 population (2003).
Transportation: Commute to work: 88.8% car, 3.2% public transportation, 2.5% walk, 2.7% work from home (2000); Travel time to work: 30.1% less than 15 minutes, 38.9% 15 to 30 minutes, 19.1% 30 to 45 minutes, 6.4% 45 to 60 minutes, 5.5% 60 minutes or more (2000)
Additional Information Contacts
Greater Dania Chamber of Commerce . . . . (954) 926-2323
Local Government Offices . . . . (954) 924-3601

DAVIE (town). Covers a land area of 33.428 square miles and a water area of 0.741 square miles. Located at 26.08° N. Lat.; 80.28° W. Long. Elevation is 5 feet.
Population: 54,493 (1990); 75,720 (2000); 80,641 (2004); 87,179 (2009 projected); Race: 83.8% White, 5.7% Black, 3.5% Asian, 24.1% Hispanic of any race (2004); Density: 2,412.4 persons per square mile (2004); Average household size: 2.66 (2004); Median age: 35.9 (2004); Male/female ratio: 95.9 (2004); Marriage status: 25.5% never married, 55.1% now married, 5.7% widowed, 13.6% divorced (2000); Foreign born: 17.5% (2000); Ancestry (includes multiple ancestries): 28.2% Other groups, 14.0% Irish, 13.7% German, 12.5% Italian, 7.5% English (2000).
Economy: Suburb of Ft. Lauderdale. Unemployment rate: 4.3% (2004); Total civilian labor force: 38,814 (2004); Single-family building permits issued: 554 (2004); Multi-family building permits issued: 24 (2004);

Employment by occupation: 14.8% management, 19.3% professional, 15.3% services, 30.0% sales, 0.3% farming, 11.6% construction, 8.8% production (2000).
Income: Per capita income: $26,251 (2004); Median household income: $51,691 (2004); Average household income: $69,573 (2004); Percent of households with income of $100,000 or more: 19.9% (2004); Poverty rate: 9.8% (2000).
Taxes: Total city taxes per capita: $488 (2002); City property taxes per capita: $258 (2002).
Education: Percent of population age 25 and over with: High school diploma (including GED) or higher: 84.5% (2004); Bachelor's degree or higher: 26.1% (2004); Master's degree or higher: 9.8% (2004).

School District(s)

Broward County School District (PK-12)
2002-03 Enrollment: 267,925 . . . . (754) 321-2600

Two-year College(s)

Mcfatter Technical Center (Public)
2003-04 Enrollment: 1,065 . . . . (954) 370-8324
2003-04 Tuition: In-state $1,530; Out-of-state $6,120
Housing: Homeownership rate: 76.2% (2004); Median home value: $149,432 (2004); Median rent: $711 per month (2000); Median age of housing: 17 years (2000).
Safety: Violent crime rate: 43.7 per 10,000 population; Property crime rate: 401.3 per 10,000 population (2003).
Newspapers: Miramar Community News (General - Circulation 100,000); Plantation Community News (General - Circulation 23,000)
Transportation: Commute to work: 93.7% car, 0.9% public transportation, 1.2% walk, 2.6% work from home (2000); Travel time to work: 19.1% less than 15 minutes, 36.4% 15 to 30 minutes, 26.6% 30 to 45 minutes, 9.9% 45 to 60 minutes, 8.0% 60 minutes or more (2000)

Additional Information Contacts

Davie-Cooper City Chamber of Commerce . . . . (954) 581-0790
Local Government Offices . . . . (954) 797-1000

DEERFIELD BEACH (city). Covers a land area of 13.425 square miles and a water area of 1.502 square miles. Located at 26.30° N. Lat.; 80.12° W. Long. Elevation is 16 feet.
History: Named for the abundance of local deer. Incorporated 1925.
Population: 55,289 (1990); 64,583 (2000); 65,162 (2004); 66,513 (2009 projected); Race: 75.7% White, 16.0% Black, 1.7% Asian, 11.1% Hispanic of any race (2004); Density: 4,853.7 persons per square mile (2004); Average household size: 2.04 (2004); Median age: 45.5 (2004); Male/female ratio: 87.7 (2004); Marriage status: 23.5% never married, 50.8% now married, 13.5% widowed, 12.3% divorced (2000); Foreign born: 22.7% (2000); Ancestry (includes multiple ancestries): 23.2% Other groups, 10.8% Irish, 10.6% Italian, 9.6% German, 7.2% English (2000).
Economy: The development of high-technology industry and commerce has expanded the town and more than doubled its population from 1970 to 1990. Deerfield Beach has one of the largest retirement communities in the U.S. Unemployment rate: 4.4% (2004); Total civilian labor force: 29,469 (2004); Single-family building permits issued: 48 (2004); Multi-family building permits issued: 44 (2004); Employment by occupation: 15.3% management, 15.4% professional, 18.8% services, 30.3% sales, 0.5% farming, 10.3% construction, 9.4% production (2000).
Income: Per capita income: $25,507 (2004); Median household income: $36,770 (2004); Average household income: $51,368 (2004); Percent of households with income of $100,000 or more: 10.6% (2004); Poverty rate: 12.5% (2000).
Taxes: Total city taxes per capita: $406 (2002); City property taxes per capita: $296 (2002).
Education: Percent of population age 25 and over with: High school diploma (including GED) or higher: 79.5% (2004); Bachelor's degree or higher: 21.2% (2004); Master's degree or higher: 6.6% (2004).

School District(s)

Broward County School District (PK-12)
2002-03 Enrollment: 267,925 . . . . (754) 321-2600
Housing: Homeownership rate: 70.5% (2004); Median home value: $106,126 (2004); Median rent: $718 per month (2000); Median age of housing: 23 years (2000).
Safety: Violent crime rate: 53.7 per 10,000 population; Property crime rate: 253.6 per 10,000 population (2003).
Newspapers: Deerfield Beach/Lighthouse Point Observer (General - Circulation 27,500); Hi-Riser/Broward (General - Circulation 18,500); Jewish Journal - Broward South (Jewish - Circulation 26,000)
Transportation: Commute to work: 93.4% car, 1.2% public transportation, 1.4% walk, 2.4% work from home (2000); Travel time to work: 24.3% less than 15 minutes, 45.0% 15 to 30 minutes, 20.9% 30 to 45 minutes, 5.4% 45 to 60 minutes, 4.4% 60 minutes or more (2000); Amtrak: Service available.

Additional Information Contacts

Deerfield Beach Chamber of Commerce . . . . (954) 427-1050
Florida-Israel Chamber . . . . (561) 620-9288
Local Government Offices . . . . (954) 480-4213

EDGEWATER (CDP). Covers a land area of 0.230 square miles and a water area of 0 square miles. Located at 26.06° N. Lat.; 80.20° W. Long.
Population: 766 (1990); 803 (2000); 691 (2004); 650 (2009 projected); Race: 88.7% White, 1.9% Black, 0.6% Asian, 15.9% Hispanic of any race (2004); Density: 3,007.0 persons per square mile (2004); Average household size: 2.24 (2004); Median age: 43.4 (2004); Male/female ratio: 110.0 (2004); Marriage status: 24.6% never married, 48.4% now married, 11.4% widowed, 15.6% divorced (2000); Foreign born: 15.7% (2000); Ancestry (includes multiple ancestries): 27.6% Other groups, 20.3% Irish, 18.1% German, 11.4% United States or American, 11.0% European (2000).
Economy: Employment by occupation: 15.1% management, 0.0% professional, 24.5% services, 20.4% sales, 0.0% farming, 25.8% construction, 14.2% production (2000).
Income: Per capita income: $19,559 (2004); Median household income: $29,813 (2004); Average household income: $43,738 (2004); Percent of households with income of $100,000 or more: 10.7% (2004); Poverty rate: 23.3% (2000).
Education: Percent of population age 25 and over with: High school diploma (including GED) or higher: 75.4% (2004); Bachelor's degree or higher: 6.6% (2004); Master's degree or higher: 1.3% (2004).
Housing: Homeownership rate: 71.2% (2004); Median home value: $140,476 (2004); Median rent: $654 per month (2000); Median age of housing: 31 years (2000).
Transportation: Commute to work: 97.2% car, 0.0% public transportation, 0.0% walk, 2.8% work from home (2000); Travel time to work: 27.8% less than 15 minutes, 43.7% 15 to 30 minutes, 17.2% 30 to 45 minutes, 4.9% 45 to 60 minutes, 6.5% 60 minutes or more (2000)

ESTATES OF FORT LAUDERDALE (CDP). Covers a land area of 0.316 square miles and a water area of 0.088 square miles. Located at 26.05° N. Lat.; 80.18° W. Long.
Population: 1,666 (1990); 1,791 (2000); 1,831 (2004); 1,900 (2009 projected); Race: 86.4% White, 4.6% Black, 1.9% Asian, 15.7% Hispanic of any race (2004); Density: 5,793.8 persons per square mile (2004); Average household size: 2.06 (2004); Median age: 50.7 (2004); Male/female ratio: 82.2 (2004); Marriage status: 17.7% never married, 58.5% now married, 13.0% widowed, 10.8% divorced (2000); Foreign born: 22.4% (2000); Ancestry (includes multiple ancestries): 21.6% Italian, 14.0% Other groups, 10.9% Irish, 9.8% German, 7.3% English (2000).
Economy: Employment by occupation: 20.7% management, 10.7% professional, 19.7% services, 30.4% sales, 0.0% farming, 11.2% construction, 7.2% production (2000).
Income: Per capita income: $26,298 (2004); Median household income: $39,136 (2004); Average household income: $54,165 (2004); Percent of households with income of $100,000 or more: 9.7% (2004); Poverty rate: 7.5% (2000).
Education: Percent of population age 25 and over with: High school diploma (including GED) or higher: 73.7% (2004); Bachelor's degree or higher: 13.6% (2004); Master's degree or higher: 4.4% (2004).
Housing: Homeownership rate: 88.4% (2004); Median home value: $104,082 (2004); Median rent: $706 per month (2000); Median age of housing: 24 years (2000).
Transportation: Commute to work: 89.4% car, 1.4% public transportation, 1.5% walk, 6.3% work from home (2000); Travel time to work: 32.4% less than 15 minutes, 46.7% 15 to 30 minutes, 15.3% 30 to 45 minutes, 1.9% 45 to 60 minutes, 3.7% 60 minutes or more (2000)

FORT LAUDERDALE (city). Covers a land area of 31.729 square miles and a water area of 4.287 square miles. Located at 26.13° N. Lat.; 80.14° W. Long. Elevation is 8 feet.
History: The town of Fort Lauderdale was built on the site of a fort constructed in 1838 and named for its commander, Major William Lauderdale. It developed as a popular winter headquarters for yachtsmen and fishermen.

Population: 149,908 (1990); 152,397 (2000); 156,657 (2004); 163,036 (2009 projected); Race: 61.8% White, 30.1% Black, 1.2% Asian, 10.9% Hispanic of any race (2004); Density: 4,937.4 persons per square mile (2004); Average household size: 2.20 (2004); Median age: 40.2 (2004); Male/female ratio: 110.8 (2004); Marriage status: 35.3% never married, 43.3% now married, 7.3% widowed, 14.0% divorced (2000); Foreign born: 21.7% (2000); Ancestry (includes multiple ancestries): 27.5% Other groups, 10.4% German, 10.3% Irish, 8.2% English, 7.6% Italian (2000).
Economy: Unemployment rate: 6.2% (2004); Total civilian labor force: 111,021 (2004); Single-family building permits issued: 378 (2004); Multi-family building permits issued: 1,132 (2004); Employment by occupation: 15.5% management, 17.9% professional, 20.1% services, 27.4% sales, 0.3% farming, 9.1% construction, 9.8% production (2000).
Income: Per capita income: $30,446 (2004); Median household income: $41,638 (2004); Average household income: $65,820 (2004); Percent of households with income of $100,000 or more: 16.2% (2004); Poverty rate: 17.7% (2000).
Taxes: Total city taxes per capita: $791 (2002); City property taxes per capita: $460 (2002).
Education: Percent of population age 25 and over with: High school diploma (including GED) or higher: 78.9% (2004); Bachelor's degree or higher: 27.9% (2004); Master's degree or higher: 10.4% (2004).

School District(s)

Broward County School District (PK-12)
 2002-03 Enrollment: 267,925 . . . . (754) 321-2600

Four-year College(s)

Art Institute of Fort Lauderdale (Private, For-profit)
 2003-04 Enrollment: 3,641 . . . . (954) 463-3000
 2003-04 Tuition: In-state $15,665; Out-of-state $15,665
Atlantic Institute of Oriental Medicine
 2003-04 Enrollment: 92 . . . . (954) 763-9840
City College
 2003-04 Enrollment: 636 . . . . (954) 492-5353
 2003-04 Tuition: In-state $7,200; Out-of-state $7,200
Everglades College
 2003-04 Enrollment: 352 . . . . (954) 772-2655
 2003-04 Tuition: In-state $9,728; Out-of-state $9,728
ITT Technical Institute (Private, For-profit)
 2003-04 Enrollment: 624 . . . . (954) 476-9300
 2003-04 Tuition: In-state $12,492; Out-of-state $12,492
Keiser College (Private, For-profit)
 2003-04 Enrollment: 4,673 . . . . (954) 776-4456
 2003-04 Tuition: In-state $10,920; Out-of-state $10,920
Nova Southeastern University
 2003-04 Enrollment: 23,522 . . . . (954) 262-7300
 2003-04 Tuition: In-state $15,220; Out-of-state $15,220

Two-year College(s)

ATI Career Training Center (Private, For-profit)
 2003-04 Enrollment: 649 . . . . (954) 973-4760
Broward Community College (Public)
 2003-04 Enrollment: 32,030 . . . . (954) 761-7400
 2003-04 Tuition: In-state $1,536; Out-of-state $5,763
Coral Ridge Nurses Assistant Training School Inc (Private, For-profit)
 2003-04 Enrollment: 16 . . . . (954) 561-2022
Key College (Private, For-profit)
 2003-04 Enrollment: 104 . . . . (954) 581-2223
 2003-04 Tuition: In-state $6,885; Out-of-state $6,885

Housing: Homeownership rate: 55.3% (2004); Median home value: $179,383 (2004); Median rent: $577 per month (2000); Median age of housing: 35 years (2000).
Hospitals: Atlantic Shores Hospital (72 beds); Broward General Medical Center (744 beds); Florida Medical Center (459 beds); Fort Lauderdale Hospital (100 beds); HealthSouth Sunrise Rehabilitation Hospital (116 beds); Holy Cross Hospital (597 beds); Imperial Point Medical Center (204 beds); Kindred Hospital-Ft Lauderdale (70 beds); North Ridge Medical Center (332 beds)
Safety: Violent crime rate: 83.9 per 10,000 population; Property crime rate: 604.4 per 10,000 population (2003).
Newspapers: Broward Daily Business Review (Circulation 10,000); City Link (Alternative, General - Circulation 56,000); El Heraldo de Broward (Hispanic - Circulation 22,000); New Times - Broward/Palm Beach (Alternative, General - Circulation 70,000); South Florida Sun-Sentinel (Circulation 282,538); The Broward Times (Black, General - Circulation 25,000); Westside Gazette (General - Circulation 65,000)
Transportation: Commute to work: 86.5% car, 4.9% public transportation, 2.4% walk, 3.8% work from home (2000); Travel time to work: 29.7% less than 15 minutes, 38.5% 15 to 30 minutes, 19.7% 30 to 45 minutes, 5.8% 45 to 60 minutes, 6.4% 60 minutes or more (2000); Amtrak: Service available.
Airports: Fort Lauderdale Executive; Fort Lauderdale/Hollywood International (primary service/large hub)

Additional Information Contacts

British American Chamber of Commerce . . . . (407) 428-6226
Christian Chamber of Commerce . . . . (954) 972-9256
Fort Lauderdale Chamber of Commerce . . . . (954) 462-6000
Lauderdale By-The-Sea Chamber . . . . (954) 776-1000
Realtor Association of Greater Fort Lauderdale . . . . (954) 563-7261

FRANKLIN PARK (CDP). Covers a land area of 0.068 square miles and a water area of 0 square miles. Located at 26.13° N. Lat.; 80.17° W. Long.
Population: 1,099 (1990); 943 (2000); 938 (2004); 955 (2009 projected); Race: 0.4% White, 97.5% Black, 0.0% Asian, 1.8% Hispanic of any race (2004); Density: 13,744.2 persons per square mile (2004); Average household size: 3.04 (2004); Median age: 23.0 (2004); Male/female ratio: 84.6 (2004); Marriage status: 51.3% never married, 40.0% now married, 1.8% widowed, 6.9% divorced (2000); Foreign born: 2.7% (2000); Ancestry (includes multiple ancestries): 78.4% Other groups, 5.1% African, 3.4% German, 1.7% Jamaican, 1.6% United States or American (2000).
Economy: Employment by occupation: 1.9% management, 8.4% professional, 38.4% services, 21.9% sales, 0.0% farming, 7.7% construction, 21.6% production (2000).
Income: Per capita income: $8,326 (2004); Median household income: $23,455 (2004); Average household income: $25,275 (2004); Percent of households with income of $100,000 or more: 0.0% (2004); Poverty rate: 38.2% (2000).
Education: Percent of population age 25 and over with: High school diploma (including GED) or higher: 50.3% (2004); Bachelor's degree or higher: 0.0% (2004); Master's degree or higher: 0.0% (2004).
Housing: Homeownership rate: 8.7% (2004); Median home value: $74,444 (2004); Median rent: $394 per month (2000); Median age of housing: 42 years (2000).
Transportation: Commute to work: 83.5% car, 16.5% public transportation, 0.0% walk, 0.0% work from home (2000); Travel time to work: 19.5% less than 15 minutes, 36.7% 15 to 30 minutes, 17.2% 30 to 45 minutes, 6.4% 45 to 60 minutes, 20.2% 60 minutes or more (2000)

GODFREY ROAD (CDP). Covers a land area of 0.216 square miles and a water area of 0 square miles. Located at 26.29° N. Lat.; 80.22° W. Long.
Population: 69 (1990); 172 (2000); 193 (2004); 219 (2009 projected); Race: 81.3% White, 0.0% Black, 0.0% Asian, 9.8% Hispanic of any race (2004); Density: 892.8 persons per square mile (2004); Average household size: 3.11 (2004); Median age: 45.9 (2004); Male/female ratio: 91.1 (2004); Marriage status: 39.1% never married, 60.9% now married, 0.0% widowed, 0.0% divorced (2000); Foreign born: 22.1% (2000); Ancestry (includes multiple ancestries): 32.9% Irish, 26.3% Italian, 17.8% Hungarian, 15.5% Other groups, 8.5% French Canadian (2000).
Economy: Employment by occupation: 9.6% management, 25.4% professional, 21.9% services, 35.1% sales, 0.0% farming, 7.9% construction, 0.0% production (2000).
Income: Per capita income: $37,761 (2004); Median household income: $86,667 (2004); Average household income: $105,968 (2004); Percent of households with income of $100,000 or more: 37.1% (2004); Poverty rate: 0.0% (2000).
Education: Percent of population age 25 and over with: High school diploma (including GED) or higher: 70.8% (2004); Bachelor's degree or higher: 40.1% (2004); Master's degree or higher: 9.5% (2004).
Housing: Homeownership rate: 98.4% (2004); Median home value: $510,417 (2004); Median rent: $n/a per month (2000); Median age of housing: 22 years (2000).
Transportation: Commute to work: 71.1% car, 0.0% public transportation, 0.0% walk, 28.9% work from home (2000); Travel time to work: 9.9% less than 15 minutes, 50.6% 15 to 30 minutes, 13.6% 30 to 45 minutes, 0.0% 45 to 60 minutes, 25.9% 60 minutes or more (2000)

GOLDEN HEIGHTS (CDP). Covers a land area of 0.051 square miles and a water area of 0 square miles. Located at 26.14° N. Lat.; 80.17° W. Long.

Population: 533 (1990); 501 (2000); 485 (2004); 469 (2009 projected); Race: 1.2% White, 93.0% Black, 1.0% Asian, 0.6% Hispanic of any race (2004); Density: 9,518.4 persons per square mile (2004); Average household size: 2.80 (2004); Median age: 41.0 (2004); Male/female ratio: 90.9 (2004); Marriage status: 26.2% never married, 43.9% now married, 14.2% widowed, 15.8% divorced (2000); Foreign born: 2.6% (2000); Ancestry (includes multiple ancestries): 87.5% Other groups, 2.6% African, 1.5% United States or American, 1.3% Jamaican, 0.7% Egyptian (2000).
Economy: Employment by occupation: 8.3% management, 19.3% professional, 18.9% services, 28.9% sales, 3.0% farming, 11.3% construction, 10.3% production (2000).
Income: Per capita income: $19,732 (2004); Median household income: $50,798 (2004); Average household income: $55,318 (2004); Percent of households with income of $100,000 or more: 13.3% (2004); Poverty rate: 11.6% (2000).
Education: Percent of population age 25 and over with: High school diploma (including GED) or higher: 59.3% (2004); Bachelor's degree or higher: 25.0% (2004); Master's degree or higher: 10.5% (2004).
Housing: Homeownership rate: 85.0% (2004); Median home value: $118,382 (2004); Median rent: $525 per month (2000); Median age of housing: 36 years (2000).
Transportation: Commute to work: 91.7% car, 2.7% public transportation, 0.0% walk, 0.0% work from home (2000); Travel time to work: 14.3% less than 15 minutes, 49.2% 15 to 30 minutes, 31.9% 30 to 45 minutes, 0.0% 45 to 60 minutes, 4.7% 60 minutes or more (2000)

GREEN MEADOW (CDP). Covers a land area of 2.090 square miles and a water area of 0.006 square miles. Located at 26.05° N. Lat.; 80.36° W. Long.
Population: 1,592 (1990); 1,874 (2000); 1,984 (2004); 2,131 (2009 projected); Race: 88.9% White, 3.4% Black, 3.4% Asian, 24.0% Hispanic of any race (2004); Density: 949.3 persons per square mile (2004); Average household size: 3.33 (2004); Median age: 38.9 (2004); Male/female ratio: 102.7 (2004); Marriage status: 18.9% never married, 71.8% now married, 2.9% widowed, 6.4% divorced (2000); Foreign born: 11.7% (2000); Ancestry (includes multiple ancestries): 27.2% Other groups, 17.2% German, 16.8% Italian, 7.8% Irish, 6.7% English (2000).
Economy: Employment by occupation: 18.9% management, 24.3% professional, 6.6% services, 34.0% sales, 1.0% farming, 8.2% construction, 6.9% production (2000).
Income: Per capita income: $38,498 (2004); Median household income: $93,207 (2004); Average household income: $128,370 (2004); Percent of households with income of $100,000 or more: 43.7% (2004); Poverty rate: 0.6% (2000).
Education: Percent of population age 25 and over with: High school diploma (including GED) or higher: 93.3% (2004); Bachelor's degree or higher: 21.0% (2004); Master's degree or higher: 10.5% (2004).
Housing: Homeownership rate: 98.7% (2004); Median home value: $340,939 (2004); Median rent: $2,000+ per month (2000); Median age of housing: 21 years (2000).
Transportation: Commute to work: 99.3% car, 0.0% public transportation, 0.0% walk, 0.7% work from home (2000); Travel time to work: 15.9% less than 15 minutes, 24.9% 15 to 30 minutes, 32.6% 30 to 45 minutes, 16.9% 45 to 60 minutes, 9.7% 60 minutes or more (2000)

HALLANDALE (city). Aka Hallandale Beach. Covers a land area of 4.210 square miles and a water area of 0.345 square miles. Located at 25.98° N. Lat.; 80.14° W. Long. Elevation is 10 feet.
History: Named for the country of Holland by early Hollander settler. Settled 1897. Incorporated 1927.
Population: 30,997 (1990); 34,282 (2000); 34,425 (2004); 34,897 (2009 projected); Race: 73.9% White, 17.7% Black, 1.3% Asian, 23.8% Hispanic of any race (2004); Density: 8,177.0 persons per square mile (2004); Average household size: 1.92 (2004); Median age: 53.1 (2004); Male/female ratio: 86.5 (2004); Marriage status: 20.4% never married, 50.3% now married, 16.4% widowed, 12.9% divorced (2000); Foreign born: 36.1% (2000); Ancestry (includes multiple ancestries): 33.9% Other groups, 9.2% Italian, 5.9% German, 5.4% United States or American, 5.1% Russian (2000).
Economy: Retirement center, especially for French Canadians. Horse and greyhound racetracks are major sources of employment. A principal tourist attraction is Gulf Stream Park, site of the annual Florida Derby. Unemployment rate: 6.8% (2004); Total civilian labor force: 15,373 (2004); Single-family building permits issued: 15 (2004); Multi-family building permits issued: 496 (2004); Employment by occupation: 12.4% management, 15.3% professional, 20.5% services, 32.4% sales, 0.1% farming, 8.3% construction, 11.0% production (2000).
Income: Per capita income: $23,397 (2004); Median household income: $30,789 (2004); Average household income: $44,016 (2004); Percent of households with income of $100,000 or more: 7.6% (2004); Poverty rate: 16.8% (2000).
Education: Percent of population age 25 and over with: High school diploma (including GED) or higher: 73.1% (2004); Bachelor's degree or higher: 19.7% (2004); Master's degree or higher: 8.1% (2004).

School District(s)

Broward County School District (PK-12)
2002-03 Enrollment: 267,925 . . . . (754) 321-2600

Housing: Homeownership rate: 66.5% (2004); Median home value: $107,718 (2004); Median rent: $578 per month (2000); Median age of housing: 28 years (2000).
Safety: Violent crime rate: 126.3 per 10,000 population; Property crime rate: 495.0 per 10,000 population (2003).
Transportation: Commute to work: 88.2% car, 4.3% public transportation, 2.8% walk, 3.2% work from home (2000); Travel time to work: 24.2% less than 15 minutes, 34.7% 15 to 30 minutes, 23.7% 30 to 45 minutes, 8.8% 45 to 60 minutes, 8.7% 60 minutes or more (2000)

Additional Information Contacts

Local Government Offices . . . . (954) 457-1300

HILLSBORO BEACH (town). Covers a land area of 0.436 square miles and a water area of 1.199 square miles. Located at 26.29° N. Lat.; 80.07° W. Long. Elevation is 16 feet.
Population: 1,748 (1990); 2,163 (2000); 2,276 (2004); 2,433 (2009 projected); Race: 99.2% White, 0.2% Black, 0.2% Asian, 2.0% Hispanic of any race (2004); Density: 5,215.4 persons per square mile (2004); Average household size: 1.66 (2004); Median age: 64.8 (2004); Male/female ratio: 81.6 (2004); Marriage status: 9.4% never married, 63.4% now married, 14.6% widowed, 12.6% divorced (2000); Foreign born: 14.0% (2000); Ancestry (includes multiple ancestries): 17.4% German, 16.3% Italian, 14.3% English, 11.8% Irish, 7.0% Other groups (2000).
Economy: Single-family building permits issued: 4 (2004); Multi-family building permits issued: 10 (2004); Employment by occupation: 38.7% management, 13.0% professional, 6.6% services, 34.5% sales, 0.0% farming, 3.8% construction, 3.5% production (2000).
Income: Per capita income: $54,796 (2004); Median household income: $54,960 (2004); Average household income: $90,768 (2004); Percent of households with income of $100,000 or more: 23.1% (2004); Poverty rate: 8.0% (2000).
Education: Percent of population age 25 and over with: High school diploma (including GED) or higher: 94.8% (2004); Bachelor's degree or higher: 39.8% (2004); Master's degree or higher: 14.1% (2004).
Housing: Homeownership rate: 90.4% (2004); Median home value: $199,584 (2004); Median rent: $1,169 per month (2000); Median age of housing: 29 years (2000).
Safety: Violent crime rate: 4.3 per 10,000 population; Property crime rate: 82.1 per 10,000 population (2003).
Transportation: Commute to work: 83.4% car, 0.0% public transportation, 1.7% walk, 12.0% work from home (2000); Travel time to work: 29.5% less than 15 minutes, 39.9% 15 to 30 minutes, 21.7% 30 to 45 minutes, 5.1% 45 to 60 minutes, 3.8% 60 minutes or more (2000)

HILLSBORO PINES (CDP). Covers a land area of 0.224 square miles and a water area of 0 square miles. Located at 26.32° N. Lat.; 80.19° W. Long.
Population: 95 (1990); 406 (2000); 494 (2004); 600 (2009 projected); Race: 93.3% White, 2.8% Black, 0.6% Asian, 4.3% Hispanic of any race (2004); Density: 2,202.3 persons per square mile (2004); Average household size: 2.87 (2004); Median age: 37.8 (2004); Male/female ratio: 108.4 (2004); Marriage status: 22.7% never married, 57.1% now married, 6.4% widowed, 13.7% divorced (2000); Foreign born: 5.6% (2000); Ancestry (includes multiple ancestries): 30.7% Italian, 17.1% English, 15.1% Irish, 11.8% Polish, 11.8% German (2000).
Economy: Employment by occupation: 30.7% management, 12.2% professional, 5.0% services, 26.1% sales, 0.0% farming, 18.1% construction, 8.0% production (2000).
Income: Per capita income: $31,680 (2004); Median household income: $73,171 (2004); Average household income: $90,988 (2004); Percent of households with income of $100,000 or more: 29.1% (2004); Poverty rate: 1.6% (2000).

Education: Percent of population age 25 and over with: High school diploma (including GED) or higher: 91.8% (2004); Bachelor's degree or higher: 16.5% (2004); Master's degree or higher: 0.0% (2004).
Housing: Homeownership rate: 86.6% (2004); Median home value: $221,111 (2004); Median rent: $605 per month (2000); Median age of housing: 24 years (2000).
Transportation: Commute to work: 92.8% car, 0.0% public transportation, 3.6% walk, 3.6% work from home (2000); Travel time to work: 12.4% less than 15 minutes, 45.2% 15 to 30 minutes, 25.3% 30 to 45 minutes, 3.3% 45 to 60 minutes, 13.7% 60 minutes or more (2000)

HILLSBORO RANCHES (CDP). Covers a land area of 0.100 square miles and a water area of 0 square miles. Located at 26.32° N. Lat.; 80.18° W. Long.
Population: 13 (1990); 47 (2000); 57 (2004); 70 (2009 projected); Race: 98.2% White, 0.0% Black, 0.0% Asian, 0.0% Hispanic of any race (2004); Density: 572.0 persons per square mile (2004); Average household size: 3.00 (2004); Median age: 39.6 (2004); Male/female ratio: 103.6 (2004); Marriage status: 0.0% never married, 0.0% now married, 100.0% widowed, 0.0% divorced (2000); Foreign born: 0.0% (2000); **Income:** Per capita income: $10,395 (2004); Median household income: $30,000 (2004); Average household income: $31,184 (2004); Percent of households with income of $100,000 or more: 0.0% (2004); Poverty rate: 0.0% (2000).
Education: Percent of population age 25 and over with: High school diploma (including GED) or higher: 100.0% (2004); Bachelor's degree or higher: 0.0% (2004); Master's degree or higher: 0.0% (2004).
Housing: Homeownership rate: 78.9% (2004); Median home value: $562,500 (2004); Median rent: $n/a per month (2000); Median age of housing: 21 years (2000).

HOLLYWOOD (city). Covers a land area of 27.340 square miles and a water area of 3.456 square miles. Located at 26.02° N. Lat.; 80.17° W. Long. Elevation is 11 feet.
History: Named for Joseph W. Young, the city's founder, who had come with his associaes from California to establish a resort town. The town of Hollywood was founded in 1921 and planned as a winter resort town, founded during the real estate boom and promoted vigorously by its developers.
Population: 121,944 (1990); 139,357 (2000); 143,197 (2004); 149,134 (2009 projected); Race: 73.6% White, 14.5% Black, 2.4% Asian, 28.4% Hispanic of any race (2004); Density: 5,237.6 persons per square mile (2004); Average household size: 2.35 (2004); Median age: 39.7 (2004); Male/female ratio: 95.1 (2004); Marriage status: 25.5% never married, 50.7% now married, 9.5% widowed, 14.4% divorced (2000); Foreign born: 26.3% (2000); Ancestry (includes multiple ancestries): 33.5% Other groups, 9.5% Italian, 9.1% Irish, 8.6% German, 7.0% United States or American (2000).
Economy: Unemployment rate: 5.6% (2004); Total civilian labor force: 85,628 (2004); Single-family building permits issued: 58 (2004); Multi-family building permits issued: 430 (2004); Employment by occupation: 13.0% management, 18.4% professional, 16.9% services, 29.7% sales, 0.4% farming, 11.6% construction, 10.0% production (2000).
Income: Per capita income: $23,879 (2004); Median household income: $40,119 (2004); Average household income: $55,639 (2004); Percent of households with income of $100,000 or more: 11.8% (2004); Poverty rate: 13.2% (2000).
Taxes: Total city taxes per capita: $469 (2002); City property taxes per capita: $264 (2002).
Education: Percent of population age 25 and over with: High school diploma (including GED) or higher: 79.5% (2004); Bachelor's degree or higher: 21.7% (2004); Master's degree or higher: 8.3% (2004).

School District(s)

Broward County School District (PK-12)
2002-03 Enrollment: 267,925 . . . . (754) 321-2600

Two-year College(s)

Prospect Hall School of Business (Private, For-profit)
2003-04 Enrollment: n/a . . . . (954) 923-8100
Ross Medical Education Center
2003-04 Enrollment: 41 . . . . (954) 963-0043
Sheridan Technical Center (Public)
2003-04 Enrollment: 1,630 . . . . (954) 985-3220
2003-04 Tuition: In-state $1,530; Out-of-state $6,120

Housing: Homeownership rate: 61.9% (2004); Median home value: $141,876 (2004); Median rent: $619 per month (2000); Median age of housing: 32 years (2000).
Hospitals: Hollywood Medical Center (324 beds); Hollywood Pavilion (46 beds); Memorial Regional Hospital (684 beds)
Safety: Violent crime rate: 64.7 per 10,000 population; Property crime rate: 546.9 per 10,000 population (2003).
Transportation: Commute to work: 90.8% car, 3.1% public transportation, 1.8% walk, 2.8% work from home (2000); Travel time to work: 22.5% less than 15 minutes, 37.4% 15 to 30 minutes, 24.5% 30 to 45 minutes, 9.1% 45 to 60 minutes, 6.5% 60 minutes or more (2000); Amtrak: Service available.

Additional Information Contacts

Greater Hollywood Chamber of Commerce . . . . (954) 923-4000

IVANHOE ESTATES (CDP). Covers a land area of 0.210 square miles and a water area of 0.011 square miles. Located at 26.05° N. Lat.; 80.34° W. Long.
Population: 269 (1990); 279 (2000); 313 (2004); 355 (2009 projected); Race: 68.4% White, 10.9% Black, 12.5% Asian, 23.0% Hispanic of any race (2004); Density: 1,491.0 persons per square mile (2004); Average household size: 4.01 (2004); Median age: 30.2 (2004); Male/female ratio: 105.9 (2004); Marriage status: 24.2% never married, 59.5% now married, 4.6% widowed, 11.8% divorced (2000); Foreign born: 15.0% (2000); Ancestry (includes multiple ancestries): 36.8% Other groups, 18.2% Italian, 7.5% European, 7.1% United States or American, 2.4% French Canadian (2000).
Economy: Employment by occupation: 11.5% management, 12.5% professional, 9.4% services, 56.3% sales, 0.0% farming, 5.2% construction, 5.2% production (2000).
Income: Per capita income: $40,711 (2004); Median household income: $137,097 (2004); Average household income: $163,365 (2004); Percent of households with income of $100,000 or more: 79.5% (2004); Poverty rate: 2.0% (2000).
Education: Percent of population age 25 and over with: High school diploma (including GED) or higher: 95.9% (2004); Bachelor's degree or higher: 38.0% (2004); Master's degree or higher: 12.9% (2004).
Housing: Homeownership rate: 98.7% (2004); Median home value: $498,077 (2004); Median rent: $n/a per month (2000); Median age of housing: 14 years (2000).
Transportation: Commute to work: 92.7% car, 0.0% public transportation, 0.0% walk, 7.3% work from home (2000); Travel time to work: 42.7% less than 15 minutes, 32.6% 15 to 30 minutes, 21.3% 30 to 45 minutes, 3.4% 45 to 60 minutes, 0.0% 60 minutes or more (2000)

KENDALL GREEN (CDP). Covers a land area of 0.477 square miles and a water area of 0 square miles. Located at 26.26° N. Lat.; 80.12° W. Long. Elevation is 20 feet.
Population: 2,781 (1990); 3,084 (2000); 3,180 (2004); 3,319 (2009 projected); Race: 25.7% White, 51.1% Black, 1.1% Asian, 17.7% Hispanic of any race (2004); Density: 6,669.2 persons per square mile (2004); Average household size: 3.41 (2004); Median age: 32.0 (2004); Male/female ratio: 104.1 (2004); Marriage status: 36.8% never married, 44.7% now married, 5.7% widowed, 12.8% divorced (2000); Foreign born: 36.8% (2000); Ancestry (includes multiple ancestries): 26.6% Other groups, 23.0% Haitian, 7.8% German, 6.7% United States or American, 4.0% English (2000).
Economy: Employment by occupation: 7.0% management, 8.9% professional, 34.2% services, 21.8% sales, 0.0% farming, 15.4% construction, 12.8% production (2000).
Income: Per capita income: $12,547 (2004); Median household income: $36,957 (2004); Average household income: $42,811 (2004); Percent of households with income of $100,000 or more: 2.6% (2004); Poverty rate: 22.7% (2000).
Education: Percent of population age 25 and over with: High school diploma (including GED) or higher: 60.9% (2004); Bachelor's degree or higher: 7.3% (2004); Master's degree or higher: 2.1% (2004).
Housing: Homeownership rate: 64.5% (2004); Median home value: $112,789 (2004); Median rent: $566 per month (2000); Median age of housing: 32 years (2000).
Transportation: Commute to work: 92.1% car, 2.6% public transportation, 1.4% walk, 0.6% work from home (2000); Travel time to work: 23.5% less than 15 minutes, 42.9% 15 to 30 minutes, 25.1% 30 to 45 minutes, 5.4% 45 to 60 minutes, 3.1% 60 minutes or more (2000)

LAKE FOREST (CDP). Covers a land area of 0.654 square miles and a water area of 0.065 square miles. Located at 25.97° N. Lat.; 80.18° W. Long. Elevation is 7 feet.

Population: 4,812 (1990); 4,994 (2000); 4,885 (2004); 4,795 (2009 projected); Race: 51.9% White, 28.6% Black, 1.2% Asian, 39.1% Hispanic of any race (2004); Density: 7,473.7 persons per square mile (2004); Average household size: 3.31 (2004); Median age: 33.5 (2004); Male/female ratio: 95.3 (2004); Marriage status: 27.7% never married, 57.4% now married, 5.8% widowed, 9.2% divorced (2000); Foreign born: 31.4% (2000); Ancestry (includes multiple ancestries): 40.7% Other groups, 8.5% German, 8.2% United States or American, 6.6% Italian, 6.2% Irish (2000).
Economy: Employment by occupation: 8.4% management, 13.1% professional, 20.0% services, 29.7% sales, 0.4% farming, 12.5% construction, 16.0% production (2000).
Income: Per capita income: $14,378 (2004); Median household income: $37,843 (2004); Average household income: $46,733 (2004); Percent of households with income of $100,000 or more: 5.3% (2004); Poverty rate: 15.4% (2000).
Education: Percent of population age 25 and over with: High school diploma (including GED) or higher: 72.2% (2004); Bachelor's degree or higher: 10.4% (2004); Master's degree or higher: 3.4% (2004).
Housing: Homeownership rate: 85.5% (2004); Median home value: $121,477 (2004); Median rent: $626 per month (2000); Median age of housing: 41 years (2000).
Transportation: Commute to work: 94.2% car, 2.2% public transportation, 0.5% walk, 2.7% work from home (2000); Travel time to work: 19.1% less than 15 minutes, 43.9% 15 to 30 minutes, 24.7% 30 to 45 minutes, 6.5% 45 to 60 minutes, 5.8% 60 minutes or more (2000)

LAUDERDALE LAKES (city). Covers a land area of 3.590 square miles and a water area of 0.051 square miles. Located at 26.17° N. Lat.; 80.20° W. Long. Elevation is 7 feet.
Population: 27,341 (1990); 31,705 (2000); 32,030 (2004); 32,623 (2009 projected); Race: 17.0% White, 73.8% Black, 1.0% Asian, 5.7% Hispanic of any race (2004); Density: 8,922.7 persons per square mile (2004); Average household size: 2.66 (2004); Median age: 35.8 (2004); Male/female ratio: 82.3 (2004); Marriage status: 32.2% never married, 45.9% now married, 11.0% widowed, 10.9% divorced (2000); Foreign born: 40.5% (2000); Ancestry (includes multiple ancestries): 35.3% Other groups, 17.9% Jamaican, 15.0% Haitian, 5.7% United States or American, 2.5% Italian (2000).
Economy: Manufacturing includes furniture, commercial glass. Unemployment rate: 7.0% (2004); Total civilian labor force: 16,818 (2004); Single-family building permits issued: 0 (2004); Multi-family building permits issued: 0 (2004); Employment by occupation: 5.3% management, 14.8% professional, 26.8% services, 27.3% sales, 0.3% farming, 11.7% construction, 13.8% production (2000).
Income: Per capita income: $14,072 (2004); Median household income: $28,593 (2004); Average household income: $36,776 (2004); Percent of households with income of $100,000 or more: 3.7% (2004); Poverty rate: 22.5% (2000).
Taxes: Total city taxes per capita: $274 (2002); City property taxes per capita: $97 (2002).
Education: Percent of population age 25 and over with: High school diploma (including GED) or higher: 67.8% (2004); Bachelor's degree or higher: 12.6% (2004); Master's degree or higher: 4.4% (2004).

School District(s)

Broward County School District (PK-12)
2002-03 Enrollment: 267,925 .... (754) 321-2600

Two-year College(s)

Concorde Career Institute (Private, For-profit)
2003-04 Enrollment: 475 .... (954) 731-8880
Hope Career Institute
2003-04 Enrollment: 101 .... (954) 741-0088
School of Health Careers (Private, For-profit)
2003-04 Enrollment: 27 .... (954) 777-0083
Ultrasound Diagnostic School (Private, For-profit)
2003-04 Enrollment: 576 .... (954) 733-8900

Housing: Homeownership rate: 61.6% (2004); Median home value: $85,749 (2004); Median rent: $596 per month (2000); Median age of housing: 25 years (2000).
Safety: Violent crime rate: 74.7 per 10,000 population; Property crime rate: 248.7 per 10,000 population (2003).
Transportation: Commute to work: 90.2% car, 7.1% public transportation, 1.2% walk, 0.8% work from home (2000); Travel time to work: 11.5% less than 15 minutes, 42.5% 15 to 30 minutes, 29.5% 30 to 45 minutes, 8.3% 45 to 60 minutes, 8.2% 60 minutes or more (2000)

Additional Information Contacts
Local Government Offices .... (954) 535-2705

LAUDERDALE-BY-THE-SEA (town). Covers a land area of 0.505 square miles and a water area of 0.726 square miles. Located at 26.19° N. Lat.; 80.09° W. Long. Elevation is 2 feet.
Population: 2,990 (1990); 2,563 (2000); 2,476 (2004); 2,337 (2009 projected); Race: 95.5% White, 1.0% Black, 1.3% Asian, 6.6% Hispanic of any race (2004); Density: 4,900.1 persons per square mile (2004); Average household size: 1.67 (2004); Median age: 53.9 (2004); Male/female ratio: 99.2 (2004); Marriage status: 18.1% never married, 49.3% now married, 13.1% widowed, 19.5% divorced (2000); Foreign born: 16.2% (2000); Ancestry (includes multiple ancestries): 21.3% Irish, 17.3% Italian, 13.5% German, 13.2% English, 8.7% Other groups (2000).
Economy: Employment by occupation: 26.1% management, 22.3% professional, 10.4% services, 27.4% sales, 0.0% farming, 6.1% construction, 7.6% production (2000).
Income: Per capita income: $32,149 (2004); Median household income: $38,142 (2004); Average household income: $53,567 (2004); Percent of households with income of $100,000 or more: 13.7% (2004); Poverty rate: 8.4% (2000).
Taxes: Total city taxes per capita: $2,410 (2002); City property taxes per capita: $1,878 (2002).
Education: Percent of population age 25 and over with: High school diploma (including GED) or higher: 89.1% (2004); Bachelor's degree or higher: 29.8% (2004); Master's degree or higher: 11.1% (2004).
Housing: Homeownership rate: 59.8% (2004); Median home value: $239,952 (2004); Median rent: $675 per month (2000); Median age of housing: 36 years (2000).
Safety: Violent crime rate: 54.3 per 10,000 population; Property crime rate: 211.5 per 10,000 population (2003).
Transportation: Commute to work: 76.5% car, 3.1% public transportation, 8.1% walk, 9.5% work from home (2000); Travel time to work: 28.3% less than 15 minutes, 37.7% 15 to 30 minutes, 21.2% 30 to 45 minutes, 6.6% 45 to 60 minutes, 6.2% 60 minutes or more (2000)

LAUDERHILL (city). Covers a land area of 7.296 square miles and a water area of 0.037 square miles. Located at 26.16° N. Lat.; 80.23° W. Long. Elevation is 7 feet.
Population: 49,135 (1990); 57,585 (2000); 58,733 (2004); 60,654 (2009 projected); Race: 27.1% White, 64.6% Black, 1.7% Asian, 7.5% Hispanic of any race (2004); Density: 8,050.2 persons per square mile (2004); Average household size: 2.52 (2004); Median age: 35.5 (2004); Male/female ratio: 85.5 (2004); Marriage status: 30.3% never married, 48.5% now married, 9.7% widowed, 11.5% divorced (2000); Foreign born: 33.8% (2000); Ancestry (includes multiple ancestries): 33.8% Other groups, 17.0% Jamaican, 8.8% Haitian, 7.5% United States or American, 3.8% Italian (2000).
Economy: Manufacturing includes plastic products, furniture, commercial printing, shelving, motor vehicle parts. Unemployment rate: 5.2% (2004); Total civilian labor force: 34,829 (2004); Single-family building permits issued: 3 (2004); Multi-family building permits issued: 0 (2004); Employment by occupation: 10.1% management, 16.1% professional, 20.0% services, 32.3% sales, 0.3% farming, 10.4% construction, 10.8% production (2000).
Income: Per capita income: $17,467 (2004); Median household income: $32,987 (2004); Average household income: $43,411 (2004); Percent of households with income of $100,000 or more: 6.3% (2004); Poverty rate: 17.8% (2000).
Taxes: Total city taxes per capita: $217 (2002); City property taxes per capita: $125 (2002).
Education: Percent of population age 25 and over with: High school diploma (including GED) or higher: 75.7% (2004); Bachelor's degree or higher: 16.1% (2004); Master's degree or higher: 5.3% (2004).

School District(s)

Broward County School District (PK-12)
2002-03 Enrollment: 267,925 .... (754) 321-2600

Housing: Homeownership rate: 59.1% (2004); Median home value: $97,972 (2004); Median rent: $614 per month (2000); Median age of housing: 23 years (2000).
Safety: Violent crime rate: 82.3 per 10,000 population; Property crime rate: 353.9 per 10,000 population (2003).
Transportation: Commute to work: 90.9% car, 5.3% public transportation, 1.0% walk, 1.5% work from home (2000); Travel time to work: 14.2% less

than 15 minutes, 40.2% 15 to 30 minutes, 28.9% 30 to 45 minutes, 9.5% 45 to 60 minutes, 7.1% 60 minutes or more (2000)

Additional Information Contacts

Local Government Offices . . . . (954) 730-3000

LAZY LAKE (village). Covers a land area of 0.024 square miles and a water area of 0 square miles. Located at 26.15° N. Lat.; 80.14° W. Long. Elevation is 7 feet.

Population: 33 (1990); 38 (2000); 37 (2004); 37 (2009 projected); Race: 81.1% White, 16.2% Black, 0.0% Asian, 2.7% Hispanic of any race (2004); Density: 1,534.7 persons per square mile (2004); Average household size: 3.08 (2004); Median age: 39.2 (2004); Male/female ratio: 236.4 (2004); Marriage status: 69.4% never married, 11.1% now married, 0.0% widowed, 19.4% divorced (2000); Foreign born: 7.7% (2000); Ancestry (includes multiple ancestries): 28.2% German, 28.2% Irish, 15.4% Dutch, 12.8% Other groups, 10.3% Swiss (2000).

Economy: Employment by occupation: 16.7% management, 23.3% professional, 10.0% services, 6.7% sales, 0.0% farming, 23.3% construction, 20.0% production (2000).

Income: Per capita income: $43,108 (2004); Median household income: $150,000 (2004); Average household income: $132,917 (2004); Percent of households with income of $100,000 or more: 75.0% (2004); Poverty rate: 15.4% (2000).

Education: Percent of population age 25 and over with: High school diploma (including GED) or higher: 100.0% (2004); Bachelor's degree or higher: 46.2% (2004); Master's degree or higher: 19.2% (2004).

Housing: Homeownership rate: 66.7% (2004); Median home value: $221,875 (2004); Median rent: $950 per month (2000); Median age of housing: 40 years (2000).

Transportation: Commute to work: 70.0% car, 23.3% public transportation, 0.0% walk, 6.7% work from home (2000); Travel time to work: 10.7% less than 15 minutes, 64.3% 15 to 30 minutes, 25.0% 30 to 45 minutes, 0.0% 45 to 60 minutes, 0.0% 60 minutes or more (2000)

LEISUREVILLE (CDP). Covers a land area of 0.218 square miles and a water area of 0 square miles. Located at 26.26° N. Lat.; 80.12° W. Long.

Population: 1,034 (1990); 1,147 (2000); 1,197 (2004); 1,244 (2009 projected); Race: 77.4% White, 14.7% Black, 0.8% Asian, 5.4% Hispanic of any race (2004); Density: 5,484.4 persons per square mile (2004); Average household size: 1.60 (2004); Median age: 69.8 (2004); Male/female ratio: 74.2 (2004); Marriage status: 8.1% never married, 48.0% now married, 32.5% widowed, 11.3% divorced (2000); Foreign born: 25.4% (2000); Ancestry (includes multiple ancestries): 21.8% German, 17.0% English, 11.8% Italian, 9.9% Irish, 8.6% Haitian (2000).

Economy: Employment by occupation: 4.1% management, 13.8% professional, 41.8% services, 30.5% sales, 0.0% farming, 2.2% construction, 7.5% production (2000).

Income: Per capita income: $20,075 (2004); Median household income: $26,090 (2004); Average household income: $32,212 (2004); Percent of households with income of $100,000 or more: 2.7% (2004); Poverty rate: 6.1% (2000).

Education: Percent of population age 25 and over with: High school diploma (including GED) or higher: 66.0% (2004); Bachelor's degree or higher: 12.7% (2004); Master's degree or higher: 6.1% (2004).

Housing: Homeownership rate: 88.5% (2004); Median home value: $75,571 (2004); Median rent: $525 per month (2000); Median age of housing: 33 years (2000).

Transportation: Commute to work: 87.9% car, 2.2% public transportation, 2.9% walk, 7.0% work from home (2000); Travel time to work: 18.2% less than 15 minutes, 64.9% 15 to 30 minutes, 7.9% 30 to 45 minutes, 6.5% 45 to 60 minutes, 2.4% 60 minutes or more (2000)

LIGHTHOUSE POINT (city). Covers a land area of 2.293 square miles and a water area of 0.108 square miles. Located at 26.27° N. Lat.; 80.08° W. Long. Elevation is 6 feet.

Population: 10,378 (1990); 10,767 (2000); 11,046 (2004); 11,494 (2009 projected); Race: 96.4% White, 0.6% Black, 1.0% Asian, 5.3% Hispanic of any race (2004); Density: 4,816.6 persons per square mile (2004); Average household size: 2.08 (2004); Median age: 47.3 (2004); Male/female ratio: 93.1 (2004); Marriage status: 15.1% never married, 62.2% now married, 9.9% widowed, 12.8% divorced (2000); Foreign born: 13.6% (2000); Ancestry (includes multiple ancestries): 19.0% Irish, 17.7% Italian, 16.6% German, 15.0% English, 10.1% Other groups (2000).

Economy: Manufacturing includes flow pumps. Single-family building permits issued: 23 (2004); Multi-family building permits issued: 0 (2004); Employment by occupation: 20.9% management, 20.2% professional, 12.4% services, 32.3% sales, 0.4% farming, 8.7% construction, 5.0% production (2000).

Income: Per capita income: $43,957 (2004); Median household income: $60,925 (2004); Average household income: $91,509 (2004); Percent of households with income of $100,000 or more: 26.6% (2004); Poverty rate: 5.0% (2000).

Taxes: Total city taxes per capita: $624 (2002); City property taxes per capita: $340 (2002).

Education: Percent of population age 25 and over with: High school diploma (including GED) or higher: 90.4% (2004); Bachelor's degree or higher: 36.6% (2004); Master's degree or higher: 13.0% (2004).

Housing: Homeownership rate: 83.8% (2004); Median home value: $243,096 (2004); Median rent: $698 per month (2000); Median age of housing: 34 years (2000).

Safety: Violent crime rate: 14.2 per 10,000 population; Property crime rate: 210.0 per 10,000 population (2003).

Transportation: Commute to work: 89.5% car, 1.2% public transportation, 1.0% walk, 6.3% work from home (2000); Travel time to work: 28.7% less than 15 minutes, 40.4% 15 to 30 minutes, 20.6% 30 to 45 minutes, 4.8% 45 to 60 minutes, 5.4% 60 minutes or more (2000)

Additional Information Contacts

Local Government Offices . . . . (954) 943-6500

LOCH LOMOND (CDP). Covers a land area of 0.225 square miles and a water area of 0 square miles. Located at 26.27° N. Lat.; 80.13° W. Long.

Population: 2,848 (1990); 3,537 (2000); 3,599 (2004); 3,712 (2009 projected); Race: 36.6% White, 33.5% Black, 1.4% Asian, 27.7% Hispanic of any race (2004); Density: 15,986.6 persons per square mile (2004); Average household size: 2.57 (2004); Median age: 30.4 (2004); Male/female ratio: 119.3 (2004); Marriage status: 34.2% never married, 52.4% now married, 2.5% widowed, 10.9% divorced (2000); Foreign born: 58.5% (2000); Ancestry (includes multiple ancestries): 39.6% Other groups, 18.6% Haitian, 14.1% Brazilian, 4.4% German, 3.3% English (2000).

Economy: Employment by occupation: 3.1% management, 5.8% professional, 28.5% services, 19.5% sales, 0.0% farming, 27.5% construction, 15.6% production (2000).

Income: Per capita income: $11,229 (2004); Median household income: $23,408 (2004); Average household income: $28,195 (2004); Percent of households with income of $100,000 or more: 1.4% (2004); Poverty rate: 30.7% (2000).

Education: Percent of population age 25 and over with: High school diploma (including GED) or higher: 64.1% (2004); Bachelor's degree or higher: 11.3% (2004); Master's degree or higher: 5.5% (2004).

Housing: Homeownership rate: 15.7% (2004); Median home value: $48,772 (2004); Median rent: $577 per month (2000); Median age of housing: 27 years (2000).

Transportation: Commute to work: 81.4% car, 7.3% public transportation, 1.2% walk, 1.2% work from home (2000); Travel time to work: 20.1% less than 15 minutes, 44.7% 15 to 30 minutes, 24.0% 30 to 45 minutes, 1.4% 45 to 60 minutes, 9.9% 60 minutes or more (2000)

MARGATE (city). Covers a land area of 8.808 square miles and a water area of 0.173 square miles. Located at 26.24° N. Lat.; 80.21° W. Long. Elevation is 12 feet.

Population: 42,985 (1990); 53,909 (2000); 54,248 (2004); 55,152 (2009 projected); Race: 71.8% White, 16.0% Black, 3.5% Asian, 19.7% Hispanic of any race (2004); Density: 6,159.0 persons per square mile (2004); Average household size: 2.39 (2004); Median age: 41.1 (2004); Male/female ratio: 90.8 (2004); Marriage status: 21.7% never married, 56.4% now married, 11.3% widowed, 10.6% divorced (2000); Foreign born: 22.0% (2000); Ancestry (includes multiple ancestries): 27.6% Other groups, 12.8% Italian, 11.2% German, 11.2% Irish, 6.5% English (2000).

Economy: Manufacturing includes commercial printing and light manufacturing. Unemployment rate: 4.9% (2004); Total civilian labor force: 28,768 (2004); Single-family building permits issued: 339 (2004); Multi-family building permits issued: 11 (2004); Employment by occupation: 12.1% management, 15.4% professional, 15.4% services, 34.5% sales, 0.1% farming, 12.5% construction, 9.9% production (2000).

Income: Per capita income: $21,826 (2004); Median household income: $42,333 (2004); Average household income: $52,042 (2004); Percent of

households with income of $100,000 or more: 9.8% (2004); Poverty rate: 8.4% (2000).
Taxes: Total city taxes per capita: $409 (2002); City property taxes per capita: $207 (2002).
Education: Percent of population age 25 and over with: High school diploma (including GED) or higher: 80.2% (2004); Bachelor's degree or higher: 17.1% (2004); Master's degree or higher: 5.7% (2004).

School District(s)

Broward County School District (PK-12)
2002-03 Enrollment: 267,925 . . . . (754) 321-2600

Two-year College(s)

Margate School of Beauty Inc (Private, For-profit)
2003-04 Enrollment: 464 . . . . (954) 972-9630

Housing: Homeownership rate: 79.9% (2004); Median home value: $117,531 (2004); Median rent: $720 per month (2000); Median age of housing: 22 years (2000).
Hospitals: Northwest Medical Center (150 beds)
Safety: Violent crime rate: 33.3 per 10,000 population; Property crime rate: 199.1 per 10,000 population (2003).
Newspapers: Senior News (General, Senior Citizen - Circulation 20,000)
Transportation: Commute to work: 94.4% car, 1.3% public transportation, 0.9% walk, 1.8% work from home (2000); Travel time to work: 18.6% less than 15 minutes, 36.4% 15 to 30 minutes, 30.2% 30 to 45 minutes, 9.0% 45 to 60 minutes, 5.8% 60 minutes or more (2000)
Additional Information Contacts
Local Government Offices . . . . (954) 972-6454

MELROSE PARK (CDP). Covers a land area of 0.903 square miles and a water area of 0 square miles. Located at 26.11° N. Lat.; 80.19° W. Long. Elevation is 10 feet.
Population: 6,477 (1990); 7,114 (2000); 7,102 (2004); 7,173 (2009 projected); Race: 6.6% White, 85.5% Black, 0.8% Asian, 3.2% Hispanic of any race (2004); Density: 7,863.8 persons per square mile (2004); Average household size: 3.69 (2004); Median age: 31.7 (2004); Male/female ratio: 96.7 (2004); Marriage status: 38.8% never married, 48.7% now married, 4.0% widowed, 8.5% divorced (2000); Foreign born: 37.5% (2000); Ancestry (includes multiple ancestries): 35.1% Other groups, 22.5% Jamaican, 15.9% Haitian, 4.7% United States or American, 2.5% Irish (2000).
Economy: Employment by occupation: 5.7% management, 15.4% professional, 24.1% services, 27.1% sales, 0.0% farming, 10.5% construction, 17.1% production (2000).
Income: Per capita income: $14,864 (2004); Median household income: $50,296 (2004); Average household income: $54,362 (2004); Percent of households with income of $100,000 or more: 8.3% (2004); Poverty rate: 15.7% (2000).
Education: Percent of population age 25 and over with: High school diploma (including GED) or higher: 66.1% (2004); Bachelor's degree or higher: 8.3% (2004); Master's degree or higher: 1.6% (2004).
Housing: Homeownership rate: 82.7% (2004); Median home value: $131,454 (2004); Median rent: $504 per month (2000); Median age of housing: 41 years (2000).
Transportation: Commute to work: 90.5% car, 5.9% public transportation, 1.4% walk, 1.0% work from home (2000); Travel time to work: 12.9% less than 15 minutes, 43.1% 15 to 30 minutes, 28.0% 30 to 45 minutes, 6.4% 45 to 60 minutes, 9.5% 60 minutes or more (2000)

MIAMI GARDENS (CDP). Covers a land area of 0.405 square miles and a water area of 0 square miles. Located at 25.97° N. Lat.; 80.20° W. Long. Elevation is 10 feet.
Population: 2,506 (1990); 2,706 (2000); 2,837 (2004); 3,016 (2009 projected); Race: 44.9% White, 35.3% Black, 2.0% Asian, 45.5% Hispanic of any race (2004); Density: 6,996.4 persons per square mile (2004); Average household size: 3.26 (2004); Median age: 33.7 (2004); Male/female ratio: 100.9 (2004); Marriage status: 25.9% never married, 55.9% now married, 6.6% widowed, 11.7% divorced (2000); Foreign born: 44.1% (2000); Ancestry (includes multiple ancestries): 64.3% Other groups, 6.8% United States or American, 6.5% Jamaican, 4.9% Irish, 3.7% Haitian (2000).
Economy: Employment by occupation: 9.4% management, 11.0% professional, 18.9% services, 21.8% sales, 1.0% farming, 20.8% construction, 17.1% production (2000).
Income: Per capita income: $11,754 (2004); Median household income: $36,393 (2004); Average household income: $38,375 (2004); Percent of households with income of $100,000 or more: 3.1% (2004); Poverty rate: 14.0% (2000).
Education: Percent of population age 25 and over with: High school diploma (including GED) or higher: 62.9% (2004); Bachelor's degree or higher: 7.8% (2004); Master's degree or higher: 1.2% (2004).
Housing: Homeownership rate: 83.9% (2004); Median home value: $116,145 (2004); Median rent: $519 per month (2000); Median age of housing: 40 years (2000).
Transportation: Commute to work: 92.1% car, 1.1% public transportation, 2.1% walk, 1.5% work from home (2000); Travel time to work: 14.7% less than 15 minutes, 36.9% 15 to 30 minutes, 28.8% 30 to 45 minutes, 9.6% 45 to 60 minutes, 10.0% 60 minutes or more (2000)

MIRAMAR (city). Covers a land area of 29.499 square miles and a water area of 1.501 square miles. Located at 25.97° N. Lat.; 80.28° W. Long. Elevation is 6 feet.
History: Named for the Spanish translations of "look, behold!" and "sea". Incorporated 1955.
Population: 40,663 (1990); 72,739 (2000); 101,514 (2004); 134,731 (2009 projected); Race: 40.0% White, 45.5% Black, 3.5% Asian, 34.5% Hispanic of any race (2004); Density: 3,441.2 persons per square mile (2004); Average household size: 3.21 (2004); Median age: 31.8 (2004); Male/female ratio: 92.1 (2004); Marriage status: 27.6% never married, 58.1% now married, 4.2% widowed, 10.1% divorced (2000); Foreign born: 40.7% (2000); Ancestry (includes multiple ancestries): 47.8% Other groups, 15.5% Jamaican, 6.0% Haitian, 4.9% United States or American, 3.9% German (2000).
Economy: Residential community in the rapidly growing I-75 corridor. Unemployment rate: 4.5% (2004); Total civilian labor force: 32,014 (2004); Single-family building permits issued: 1,630 (2004); Multi-family building permits issued: 154 (2004); Employment by occupation: 12.9% management, 18.4% professional, 16.3% services, 33.1% sales, 0.4% farming, 9.2% construction, 9.9% production (2000).
Income: Per capita income: $21,454 (2004); Median household income: $57,171 (2004); Average household income: $68,639 (2004); Percent of households with income of $100,000 or more: 18.0% (2004); Poverty rate: 8.2% (2000).
Taxes: Total city taxes per capita: $507 (2002); City property taxes per capita: $243 (2002).
Education: Percent of population age 25 and over with: High school diploma (including GED) or higher: 82.9% (2004); Bachelor's degree or higher: 22.1% (2004); Master's degree or higher: 7.0% (2004).

School District(s)

Broward County School District (PK-12)
2002-03 Enrollment: 267,925 . . . . (754) 321-2600

Housing: Homeownership rate: 81.0% (2004); Median home value: $171,085 (2004); Median rent: $694 per month (2000); Median age of housing: 16 years (2000).
Safety: Violent crime rate: 40.5 per 10,000 population; Property crime rate: 328.4 per 10,000 population (2003).
Transportation: Commute to work: 94.7% car, 1.5% public transportation, 0.9% walk, 1.9% work from home (2000); Travel time to work: 12.1% less than 15 minutes, 32.0% 15 to 30 minutes, 31.9% 30 to 45 minutes, 14.3% 45 to 60 minutes, 9.6% 60 minutes or more (2000)
Additional Information Contacts
Local Government Offices . . . . (954) 602-3011

NORTH ANDREWS GARDENS (CDP). Aka North Andrews Terrace. Covers a land area of 1.087 square miles and a water area of 0 square miles. Located at 26.19° N. Lat.; 80.14° W. Long.
Population: 8,968 (1990); 9,656 (2000); 9,576 (2004); 9,605 (2009 projected); Race: 79.3% White, 6.8% Black, 1.4% Asian, 34.8% Hispanic of any race (2004); Density: 8,809.5 persons per square mile (2004); Average household size: 2.80 (2004); Median age: 36.3 (2004); Male/female ratio: 104.9 (2004); Marriage status: 27.2% never married, 53.6% now married, 6.0% widowed, 13.2% divorced (2000); Foreign born: 24.6% (2000); Ancestry (includes multiple ancestries): 30.2% Other groups, 16.5% Irish, 11.9% Italian, 11.1% German, 9.5% United States or American (2000).
Economy: Employment by occupation: 10.9% management, 8.7% professional, 19.6% services, 28.2% sales, 0.2% farming, 20.7% construction, 11.7% production (2000).
Income: Per capita income: $18,148 (2004); Median household income: $45,419 (2004); Average household income: $50,672 (2004); Percent of households with income of $100,000 or more: 6.5% (2004); Poverty rate: 8.6% (2000).

Education: Percent of population age 25 and over with: High school diploma (including GED) or higher: 74.4% (2004); Bachelor's degree or higher: 9.6% (2004); Master's degree or higher: 2.6% (2004).
Housing: Homeownership rate: 85.3% (2004); Median home value: $129,208 (2004); Median rent: $743 per month (2000); Median age of housing: 39 years (2000).
Transportation: Commute to work: 92.5% car, 2.1% public transportation, 1.3% walk, 1.3% work from home (2000); Travel time to work: 29.4% less than 15 minutes, 44.8% 15 to 30 minutes, 17.3% 30 to 45 minutes, 4.7% 45 to 60 minutes, 3.8% 60 minutes or more (2000)

NORTH LAUDERDALE (city). Covers a land area of 3.878 square miles and a water area of 0.033 square miles. Located at 26.21° N. Lat.; 80.22° W. Long. Elevation is 11 feet.
Population: 26,844 (1990); 32,264 (2000); 33,539 (2004); 35,323 (2009 projected); Race: 40.0% White, 43.0% Black, 3.2% Asian, 24.5% Hispanic of any race (2004); Density: 8,647.9 persons per square mile (2004); Average household size: 3.00 (2004); Median age: 30.7 (2004); Male/female ratio: 94.6 (2004); Marriage status: 32.9% never married, 51.6% now married, 4.7% widowed, 10.8% divorced (2000); Foreign born: 34.9% (2000); Ancestry (includes multiple ancestries): 36.9% Other groups, 11.4% Jamaican, 8.0% United States or American, 6.9% Italian, 6.9% Haitian (2000).
Economy: Manufacturing includes cabinets and commercial printing. Unemployment rate: 4.7% (2004); Total civilian labor force: 22,036 (2004); Single-family building permits issued: 227 (2004); Multi-family building permits issued: 292 (2004); Employment by occupation: 10.2% management, 13.4% professional, 19.1% services, 31.7% sales, 0.2% farming, 13.8% construction, 11.7% production (2000).
Income: Per capita income: $15,690 (2004); Median household income: $40,704 (2004); Average household income: $47,074 (2004); Percent of households with income of $100,000 or more: 5.4% (2004); Poverty rate: 13.7% (2000).
Taxes: Total city taxes per capita: $293 (2002); City property taxes per capita: $107 (2002).
Education: Percent of population age 25 and over with: High school diploma (including GED) or higher: 77.7% (2004); Bachelor's degree or higher: 13.6% (2004); Master's degree or higher: 3.1% (2004).

School District(s)

Broward County School District (PK-12)
2002-03 Enrollment: 267,925 . . . . (754) 321-2600

Housing: Homeownership rate: 62.7% (2004); Median home value: $123,572 (2004); Median rent: $696 per month (2000); Median age of housing: 21 years (2000).
Safety: Violent crime rate: 66.2 per 10,000 population; Property crime rate: 188.3 per 10,000 population (2003).
Transportation: Commute to work: 94.1% car, 2.6% public transportation, 0.6% walk, 1.9% work from home (2000); Travel time to work: 13.9% less than 15 minutes, 40.1% 15 to 30 minutes, 31.3% 30 to 45 minutes, 7.5% 45 to 60 minutes, 7.3% 60 minutes or more (2000)

Additional Information Contacts

Local Government Offices . . . . (954) 722-0900

OAK POINT (CDP). Covers a land area of 0.041 square miles and a water area of 0 square miles. Located at 26.04° N. Lat.; 80.18° W. Long.
Population: 172 (1990); 145 (2000); 148 (2004); 153 (2009 projected); Race: 93.9% White, 0.0% Black, 0.0% Asian, 0.7% Hispanic of any race (2004); Density: 3,646.8 persons per square mile (2004); Average household size: 3.02 (2004); Median age: 48.0 (2004); Male/female ratio: 89.7 (2004); Marriage status: 18.1% never married, 77.1% now married, 0.0% widowed, 4.9% divorced (2000); Foreign born: 4.4% (2000); Ancestry (includes multiple ancestries): 25.3% United States or American, 25.3% Ukrainian, 13.9% Russian, 10.1% Polish, 9.5% German (2000).
Economy: Employment by occupation: 0.0% management, 73.1% professional, 11.5% services, 15.4% sales, 0.0% farming, 0.0% construction, 0.0% production (2000).
Income: Per capita income: $76,723 (2004); Median household income: $191,667 (2004); Average household income: $231,735 (2004); Percent of households with income of $100,000 or more: 73.5% (2004); Poverty rate: 0.0% (2000).
Education: Percent of population age 25 and over with: High school diploma (including GED) or higher: 100.0% (2004); Bachelor's degree or higher: 84.2% (2004); Master's degree or higher: 70.3% (2004).
Housing: Homeownership rate: 100.0% (2004); Median home value: $475,000 (2004); Median rent: $n/a per month (2000); Median age of housing: 16 years (2000).
Transportation: Commute to work: 100.0% car, 0.0% public transportation, 0.0% walk, 0.0% work from home (2000); Travel time to work: 30.8% less than 15 minutes, 46.2% 15 to 30 minutes, 23.1% 30 to 45 minutes, 0.0% 45 to 60 minutes, 0.0% 60 minutes or more (2000)

OAKLAND PARK (city). Covers a land area of 6.301 square miles and a water area of 0.604 square miles. Located at 26.17° N. Lat.; 80.14° W. Long. Elevation is 8 feet.
Population: 26,326 (1990); 30,966 (2000); 31,533 (2004); 32,423 (2009 projected); Race: 58.3% White, 27.9% Black, 2.2% Asian, 21.1% Hispanic of any race (2004); Density: 5,004.6 persons per square mile (2004); Average household size: 2.30 (2004); Median age: 36.2 (2004); Male/female ratio: 109.4 (2004); Marriage status: 35.6% never married, 43.9% now married, 5.2% widowed, 15.2% divorced (2000); Foreign born: 29.6% (2000); Ancestry (includes multiple ancestries): 32.4% Other groups, 10.3% German, 9.6% Irish, 8.0% Italian, 7.4% Haitian (2000).
Economy: Unemployment rate: 4.3% (2004); Total civilian labor force: 22,870 (2004); Single-family building permits issued: 81 (2004); Multi-family building permits issued: 0 (2004); Employment by occupation: 10.3% management, 16.2% professional, 21.3% services, 27.0% sales, 0.2% farming, 11.8% construction, 13.2% production (2000).
Income: Per capita income: $20,828 (2004); Median household income: $38,107 (2004); Average household income: $47,150 (2004); Percent of households with income of $100,000 or more: 7.4% (2004); Poverty rate: 16.5% (2000).
Education: Percent of population age 25 and over with: High school diploma (including GED) or higher: 78.0% (2004); Bachelor's degree or higher: 21.3% (2004); Master's degree or higher: 6.5% (2004).

School District(s)

Broward County School District (PK-12)
2002-03 Enrollment: 267,925 . . . . (754) 321-2600

Two-year College(s)

ATI Career Training Center (Private, For-profit)
2003-04 Enrollment: 207 . . . . (954) 563-5899
2003-04 Tuition: In-state $10,180; Out-of-state $10,180

Housing: Homeownership rate: 50.9% (2004); Median home value: $132,387 (2004); Median rent: $606 per month (2000); Median age of housing: 29 years (2000).
Safety: Violent crime rate: 87.0 per 10,000 population; Property crime rate: 383.3 per 10,000 population (2003).
Transportation: Commute to work: 89.9% car, 4.4% public transportation, 2.3% walk, 2.0% work from home (2000); Travel time to work: 26.1% less than 15 minutes, 42.7% 15 to 30 minutes, 19.2% 30 to 45 minutes, 6.3% 45 to 60 minutes, 5.7% 60 minutes or more (2000)

Additional Information Contacts

Local Government Offices . . . . (954) 561-6250
Oakland Park-Wilton Chamber . . . . (954) 489-0370

PALM AIRE (CDP). Covers a land area of 0.223 square miles and a water area of 0 square miles. Located at 26.20° N. Lat.; 80.19° W. Long.
Population: 1,411 (1990); 1,539 (2000); 1,560 (2004); 1,602 (2009 projected); Race: 78.7% White, 13.5% Black, 1.6% Asian, 19.4% Hispanic of any race (2004); Density: 6,987.9 persons per square mile (2004); Average household size: 2.82 (2004); Median age: 36.8 (2004); Male/female ratio: 104.2 (2004); Marriage status: 20.6% never married, 63.9% now married, 6.0% widowed, 9.6% divorced (2000); Foreign born: 15.4% (2000); Ancestry (includes multiple ancestries): 30.7% Other groups, 15.6% Italian, 15.5% German, 12.1% Irish, 9.6% English (2000).
Economy: Employment by occupation: 16.7% management, 20.6% professional, 9.2% services, 24.3% sales, 0.0% farming, 18.1% construction, 11.1% production (2000).
Income: Per capita income: $22,218 (2004); Median household income: $59,395 (2004); Average household income: $62,563 (2004); Percent of households with income of $100,000 or more: 17.0% (2004); Poverty rate: 7.9% (2000).
Education: Percent of population age 25 and over with: High school diploma (including GED) or higher: 87.5% (2004); Bachelor's degree or higher: 20.4% (2004); Master's degree or higher: 9.6% (2004).
Housing: Homeownership rate: 94.2% (2004); Median home value: $161,787 (2004); Median rent: $1,125 per month (2000); Median age of housing: 26 years (2000).

Transportation: Commute to work: 97.9% car, 1.1% public transportation, 0.0% walk, 0.9% work from home (2000); Travel time to work: 25.2% less than 15 minutes, 42.4% 15 to 30 minutes, 19.1% 30 to 45 minutes, 4.1% 45 to 60 minutes, 9.1% 60 minutes or more (2000)

PARKLAND (city). Covers a land area of 10.198 square miles and a water area of 0.579 square miles. Located at 26.31° N. Lat.; 80.24° W. Long. Elevation is 15 feet.
Population: 4,201 (1990); 13,835 (2000); 19,916 (2004); 27,034 (2009 projected); Race: 88.5% White, 4.3% Black, 4.4% Asian, 10.7% Hispanic of any race (2004); Density: 1,953.0 persons per square mile (2004); Average household size: 3.18 (2004); Median age: 36.0 (2004); Male/female ratio: 99.2 (2004); Marriage status: 16.9% never married, 75.1% now married, 2.9% widowed, 5.0% divorced (2000); Foreign born: 16.7% (2000); Ancestry (includes multiple ancestries): 22.2% Other groups, 16.4% Italian, 12.9% German, 12.5% Irish, 9.3% United States or American (2000).
Economy: Single-family building permits issued: 347 (2004); Multi-family building permits issued: 160 (2004); Employment by occupation: 26.2% management, 25.1% professional, 7.4% services, 32.0% sales, 0.2% farming, 3.5% construction, 5.4% production (2000).
Income: Per capita income: $48,698 (2004); Median household income: $113,435 (2004); Average household income: $155,080 (2004); Percent of households with income of $100,000 or more: 56.6% (2004); Poverty rate: 2.4% (2000).
Taxes: Total city taxes per capita: $568 (2002); City property taxes per capita: $299 (2002).
Education: Percent of population age 25 and over with: High school diploma (including GED) or higher: 94.1% (2004); Bachelor's degree or higher: 53.0% (2004); Master's degree or higher: 19.4% (2004).

School District(s)

Broward County School District (PK-12)
2002-03 Enrollment: 267,925 .... (754) 321-2600
Housing: Homeownership rate: 88.5% (2004); Median home value: $384,539 (2004); Median rent: $958 per month (2000); Median age of housing: 6 years (2000).
Safety: Violent crime rate: 7.3 per 10,000 population; Property crime rate: 190.0 per 10,000 population (2003).
Transportation: Commute to work: 91.6% car, 0.4% public transportation, 0.1% walk, 7.1% work from home (2000); Travel time to work: 18.4% less than 15 minutes, 35.2% 15 to 30 minutes, 28.2% 30 to 45 minutes, 9.4% 45 to 60 minutes, 8.8% 60 minutes or more (2000)
Additional Information Contacts
Local Government Offices .... (954) 753-5040

PEMBROKE PARK (town). Aka Pembroke. Covers a land area of 1.411 square miles and a water area of 0.365 square miles. Located at 25.98° N. Lat.; 80.17° W. Long. Elevation is 10 feet.
Population: 5,240 (1990); 6,299 (2000); 6,548 (2004); 6,889 (2009 projected); Race: 33.7% White, 57.0% Black, 0.7% Asian, 15.9% Hispanic of any race (2004); Density: 4,642.1 persons per square mile (2004); Average household size: 2.33 (2004); Median age: 33.3 (2004); Male/female ratio: 86.4 (2004); Marriage status: 32.1% never married, 44.8% now married, 9.4% widowed, 13.7% divorced (2000); Foreign born: 28.6% (2000); Ancestry (includes multiple ancestries): 39.2% Other groups, 7.9% Jamaican, 7.0% United States or American, 6.5% Italian, 6.0% German (2000).
Economy: Single-family building permits issued: 0 (2004); Multi-family building permits issued: 34 (2004); Employment by occupation: 4.7% management, 16.1% professional, 21.9% services, 31.1% sales, 0.0% farming, 13.8% construction, 12.4% production (2000).
Income: Per capita income: $13,660 (2004); Median household income: $22,458 (2004); Average household income: $31,570 (2004); Percent of households with income of $100,000 or more: 3.8% (2004); Poverty rate: 24.0% (2000).
Taxes: Total city taxes per capita: $639 (2002); City property taxes per capita: $322 (2002).
Education: Percent of population age 25 and over with: High school diploma (including GED) or higher: 69.6% (2004); Bachelor's degree or higher: 6.9% (2004); Master's degree or higher: 2.4% (2004).

School District(s)

Broward County School District (PK-12)
2002-03 Enrollment: 267,925 .... (754) 321-2600
Housing: Homeownership rate: 45.0% (2004); Median home value: $57,815 (2004); Median rent: $625 per month (2000); Median age of housing: 24 years (2000).
Safety: Violent crime rate: 124.8 per 10,000 population; Property crime rate: 421.1 per 10,000 population (2003).
Transportation: Commute to work: 95.1% car, 1.9% public transportation, 0.6% walk, 0.3% work from home (2000); Travel time to work: 24.0% less than 15 minutes, 38.6% 15 to 30 minutes, 22.0% 30 to 45 minutes, 6.8% 45 to 60 minutes, 8.7% 60 minutes or more (2000)

PEMBROKE PINES (city). Covers a land area of 33.054 square miles and a water area of 1.382 square miles. Located at 26.01° N. Lat.; 80.31° W. Long. Elevation is 7 feet.
History: Named for the many pine trees in the area, and for Pembroke Road. Has grown and urbanized since 1970. Incorporated 1961.
Population: 66,095 (1990); 137,427 (2000); 151,196 (2004); 168,456 (2009 projected); Race: 69.6% White, 16.7% Black, 4.7% Asian, 35.8% Hispanic of any race (2004); Density: 4,574.2 persons per square mile (2004); Average household size: 2.65 (2004); Median age: 37.3 (2004); Male/female ratio: 87.8 (2004); Marriage status: 20.9% never married, 60.7% now married, 7.8% widowed, 10.6% divorced (2000); Foreign born: 29.0% (2000); Ancestry (includes multiple ancestries): 42.2% Other groups, 9.4% Italian, 8.2% Irish, 8.1% German, 6.1% United States or American (2000).
Economy: A major retirement community is here. Unemployment rate: 3.3% (2004); Total civilian labor force: 47,828 (2004); Single-family building permits issued: 11 (2004); Multi-family building permits issued: 0 (2004); Employment by occupation: 18.4% management, 22.3% professional, 12.5% services, 32.2% sales, 0.2% farming, 7.3% construction, 7.2% production (2000).
Income: Per capita income: $26,942 (2004); Median household income: $58,653 (2004); Average household income: $71,113 (2004); Percent of households with income of $100,000 or more: 21.5% (2004); Poverty rate: 5.4% (2000).
Taxes: Total city taxes per capita: $330 (2002); City property taxes per capita: $148 (2002).
Education: Percent of population age 25 and over with: High school diploma (including GED) or higher: 88.0% (2004); Bachelor's degree or higher: 28.9% (2004); Master's degree or higher: 10.1% (2004).

School District(s)

Broward County School District (PK-12)
2002-03 Enrollment: 267,925 .... (754) 321-2600

Two-year College(s)

Keiser Career College (Private, For-profit)
2003-04 Enrollment: n/a .... (954) 431-4300
2003-04 Tuition: In-state $10,920; Out-of-state $10,920
SER IBM Business Institute
2003-04 Enrollment: n/a .... (954) 983-5700
Housing: Homeownership rate: 80.4% (2004); Median home value: $171,085 (2004); Median rent: $856 per month (2000); Median age of housing: 10 years (2000).
Hospitals: Memorial Hospital Pembroke (301 beds); Memorial Hospital West (220 beds); South Florida State Hospital (350 beds)
Safety: Violent crime rate: 26.4 per 10,000 population; Property crime rate: 296.0 per 10,000 population (2003).
Newspapers: Observer (General - Circulation 10,000)
Transportation: Commute to work: 94.6% car, 0.9% public transportation, 0.6% walk, 3.0% work from home (2000); Travel time to work: 13.4% less than 15 minutes, 29.5% 15 to 30 minutes, 31.2% 30 to 45 minutes, 16.7% 45 to 60 minutes, 9.1% 60 minutes or more (2000)
Additional Information Contacts
Pembroke Pines Chamber of Commerce .... (954) 432-9808
South Broward Association of Realtors .... (954) 431-5300

PINE ISLAND RIDGE (CDP). Covers a land area of 0.782 square miles and a water area of 0.006 square miles. Located at 26.09° N. Lat.; 80.27° W. Long.
Population: 5,230 (1990); 5,199 (2000); 5,677 (2004); 6,292 (2009 projected); Race: 93.3% White, 1.5% Black, 1.9% Asian, 12.3% Hispanic of any race (2004); Density: 7,259.4 persons per square mile (2004); Average household size: 1.76 (2004); Median age: 57.8 (2004); Male/female ratio: 77.3 (2004); Marriage status: 16.4% never married, 52.6% now married, 17.3% widowed, 13.7% divorced (2000); Foreign born: 20.0% (2000); Ancestry (includes multiple ancestries): 20.6% Other groups, 14.0% Italian, 10.9% Irish, 10.4% German, 10.2% United States or American (2000).
Economy: Employment by occupation: 16.8% management, 23.1% professional, 11.3% services, 38.3% sales, 0.0% farming, 2.8% construction, 7.7% production (2000).

Income: Per capita income: $28,154 (2004); Median household income: $37,427 (2004); Average household income: $49,498 (2004); Percent of households with income of $100,000 or more: 8.4% (2004); Poverty rate: 3.5% (2000).
Education: Percent of population age 25 and over with: High school diploma (including GED) or higher: 87.9% (2004); Bachelor's degree or higher: 26.9% (2004); Master's degree or higher: 9.3% (2004).
Housing: Homeownership rate: 86.2% (2004); Median home value: $112,715 (2004); Median rent: $728 per month (2000); Median age of housing: 18 years (2000).
Transportation: Commute to work: 91.6% car, 0.0% public transportation, 1.2% walk, 3.2% work from home (2000); Travel time to work: 22.6% less than 15 minutes, 43.5% 15 to 30 minutes, 20.5% 30 to 45 minutes, 9.0% 45 to 60 minutes, 4.3% 60 minutes or more (2000)

PLANTATION (city). Covers a land area of 21.738 square miles and a water area of 0.193 square miles. Located at 26.12° N. Lat.; 80.24° W. Long. Elevation is 7 feet.
History: Named for its history as the plantation of Frederick C. Peters. Incorporated 1953.
Population: 66,997 (1990); 82,934 (2000); 84,421 (2004); 86,938 (2009 projected); Race: 73.0% White, 17.4% Black, 3.6% Asian, 15.9% Hispanic of any race (2004); Density: 3,883.6 persons per square mile (2004); Average household size: 2.48 (2004); Median age: 38.5 (2004); Male/female ratio: 91.1 (2004); Marriage status: 25.2% never married, 57.7% now married, 6.5% widowed, 10.7% divorced (2000); Foreign born: 22.4% (2000); Ancestry (includes multiple ancestries): 26.8% Other groups, 10.8% German, 10.2% Irish, 8.9% Italian, 8.0% United States or American (2000).
Economy: Major housing developments and the presence of banking companies mark Plantation's urban boom. Unemployment rate: 3.6% (2004); Total civilian labor force: 53,916 (2004); Single-family building permits issued: 157 (2004); Multi-family building permits issued: 0 (2004); Employment by occupation: 18.7% management, 24.2% professional, 12.0% services, 32.2% sales, 0.1% farming, 6.5% construction, 6.2% production (2000).
Income: Per capita income: $31,534 (2004); Median household income: $59,312 (2004); Average household income: $77,789 (2004); Percent of households with income of $100,000 or more: 23.9% (2004); Poverty rate: 6.4% (2000).
Taxes: Total city taxes per capita: $439 (2002); City property taxes per capita: $207 (2002).
Education: Percent of population age 25 and over with: High school diploma (including GED) or higher: 90.8% (2004); Bachelor's degree or higher: 36.2% (2004); Master's degree or higher: 13.3% (2004).

School District(s)

Broward County School District (PK-12)
2002-03 Enrollment: 267,925 .... (754) 321-2600

Four-year College(s)

American Intercontinental University (Private, For-profit)
2003-04 Enrollment: 1,273 .... (954) 446-6100
2003-04 Tuition: In-state $56,750; Out-of-state $56,750
University of Phoenix-Fort Lauderdale (Private, For-profit)
2003-04 Enrollment: 2,043 .... (954) 382-5303
2003-04 Tuition: In-state $8,850; Out-of-state $8,850

Two-year College(s)

Medvance Institute of Fort Lauderdale (Private, For-profit)
2003-04 Enrollment: 28 .... (954) 723-0266

Housing: Homeownership rate: 71.3% (2004); Median home value: $184,715 (2004); Median rent: $851 per month (2000); Median age of housing: 19 years (2000).
Hospitals: Columbia Westside Regional Medical Center (204 beds); Plantation General Hospital (264 beds)
Safety: Violent crime rate: 27.4 per 10,000 population; Property crime rate: 435.8 per 10,000 population (2003).
Transportation: Commute to work: 93.9% car, 1.2% public transportation, 0.6% walk, 3.4% work from home (2000); Travel time to work: 22.1% less than 15 minutes, 37.0% 15 to 30 minutes, 25.9% 30 to 45 minutes, 9.2% 45 to 60 minutes, 5.8% 60 minutes or more (2000)

Additional Information Contacts

Local Government Offices .... (954) 797-2237
Plantation Chamber of Commerce .... (954) 587-1410

POMPANO BEACH (city). Covers a land area of 20.553 square miles and a water area of 1.601 square miles. Located at 26.23° N. Lat.; 80.12° W. Long. Elevation is 13 feet.
History: Named for the abundance of fish found along its coast. Incorporated 1908.
Population: 72,400 (1990); 78,191 (2000); 79,006 (2004); 80,783 (2009 projected); Race: 65.6% White, 26.0% Black, 1.0% Asian, 12.6% Hispanic of any race (2004); Density: 3,844.1 persons per square mile (2004); Average household size: 2.21 (2004); Median age: 43.2 (2004); Male/female ratio: 98.3 (2004); Marriage status: 27.0% never married, 49.8% now married, 10.5% widowed, 12.7% divorced (2000); Foreign born: 20.3% (2000); Ancestry (includes multiple ancestries): 29.3% Other groups, 9.7% German, 9.7% Irish, 8.9% Italian, 6.5% English (2000).
Economy: Resort city with ocean beaches, excellent fishing, and a harness-racing track. Over 60% of the city's economy is based on tourism. Manufacturing includes precision and electronic equipment and various technological supplies. Unemployment rate: 5.9% (2004); Total civilian labor force: 48,520 (2004); Single-family building permits issued: 227 (2004); Multi-family building permits issued: 152 (2004); Employment by occupation: 13.5% management, 15.1% professional, 18.5% services, 30.0% sales, 0.5% farming, 11.4% construction, 11.0% production (2000).
Income: Per capita income: $26,189 (2004); Median household income: $39,419 (2004); Average household income: $56,120 (2004); Percent of households with income of $100,000 or more: 12.4% (2004); Poverty rate: 17.0% (2000).
Taxes: Total city taxes per capita: $697 (2002); City property taxes per capita: $334 (2002).
Education: Percent of population age 25 and over with: High school diploma (including GED) or higher: 77.2% (2004); Bachelor's degree or higher: 21.7% (2004); Master's degree or higher: 7.1% (2004).

School District(s)

Broward County School District (PK-12)
2002-03 Enrollment: 267,925 .... (754) 321-2600

Four-year College(s)

Florida Metropolitan University-Fort Lauderdale (Private, For-profit)
2003-04 Enrollment: 1,612 .... (954) 783-7339
2003-04 Tuition: In-state $8,640; Out-of-state $8,640

Two-year College(s)

Florida Barber Academy
2003-04 Enrollment: 36 .... (954) 781-6066
Florida College of Natural Health (Private, For-profit)
2003-04 Enrollment: 265 .... (954) 975-6400

Housing: Homeownership rate: 62.8% (2004); Median home value: $134,658 (2004); Median rent: $630 per month (2000); Median age of housing: 27 years (2000).
Hospitals: North Broward Medical Center (409 beds)
Safety: Violent crime rate: 79.7 per 10,000 population; Property crime rate: 344.9 per 10,000 population (2003).
Newspapers: Boca Thursday (General - Circulation 27,000); Boynton Beach Times (General - Circulation 27,000); Deerfield Beach/Lighthouse Point Thursday Times (General - Circulation 20,000); Delray Thursday Times (General - Circulation 19,000); Jewish Journal - Palm Beach South (General, Jewish - Circulation 22,000); Jewish Journal Broward North (General, Jewish - Circulation 21,000); Jewish Journal-Dade (General, Jewish - Circulation 20,000); The Jewish Journal-Palm Beach North (General, Jewish - Circulation 22,000); The Pompano Pelican (General - Circulation 10,000); West Boca Times (General - Circulation 24,000)
Transportation: Commute to work: 89.7% car, 2.7% public transportation, 2.2% walk, 2.6% work from home (2000); Travel time to work: 25.9% less than 15 minutes, 41.5% 15 to 30 minutes, 21.5% 30 to 45 minutes, 5.4% 45 to 60 minutes, 5.7% 60 minutes or more (2000)

Additional Information Contacts

Greater Pompano Beach Chamber .... (954) 941-2940
Local Government Offices .... (954) 786-4060

POMPANO BEACH HIGHLANDS (CDP). Covers a land area of 1.345 square miles and a water area of 0 square miles. Located at 26.28° N. Lat.; 80.10° W. Long. Elevation is 12 feet.
Population: 6,104 (1990); 6,505 (2000); 6,912 (2004); 7,456 (2009 projected); Race: 71.1% White, 11.7% Black, 3.0% Asian, 27.8% Hispanic of any race (2004); Density: 5,137.3 persons per square mile (2004); Average household size: 2.84 (2004); Median age: 34.7 (2004); Male/female ratio: 107.6 (2004); Marriage status: 27.1% never married, 53.7% now married, 5.1% widowed, 14.1% divorced (2000); Foreign born:

22.0% (2000); Ancestry (includes multiple ancestries): 32.5% Other groups, 14.3% Irish, 13.0% German, 10.5% Italian, 7.7% United States or American (2000).
Economy: Employment by occupation: 8.2% management, 13.5% professional, 18.3% services, 27.2% sales, 0.3% farming, 20.5% construction, 12.0% production (2000).
Income: Per capita income: $16,249 (2004); Median household income: $37,539 (2004); Average household income: $46,163 (2004); Percent of households with income of $100,000 or more: 6.1% (2004); Poverty rate: 12.9% (2000).
Education: Percent of population age 25 and over with: High school diploma (including GED) or higher: 73.8% (2004); Bachelor's degree or higher: 10.1% (2004); Master's degree or higher: 4.1% (2004).
Housing: Homeownership rate: 73.6% (2004); Median home value: $118,895 (2004); Median rent: $668 per month (2000); Median age of housing: 39 years (2000).
Transportation: Commute to work: 90.0% car, 3.0% public transportation, 0.0% walk, 3.7% work from home (2000); Travel time to work: 29.1% less than 15 minutes, 38.4% 15 to 30 minutes, 21.9% 30 to 45 minutes, 5.3% 45 to 60 minutes, 5.4% 60 minutes or more (2000)

POMPANO ESTATES (CDP). Covers a land area of 0.544 square miles and a water area of 0 square miles. Located at 26.28° N. Lat.; 80.11° W. Long.
Population: 3,286 (1990); 3,367 (2000); 3,154 (2004); 2,948 (2009 projected); Race: 26.8% White, 58.7% Black, 0.2% Asian, 11.5% Hispanic of any race (2004); Density: 5,801.2 persons per square mile (2004); Average household size: 3.56 (2004); Median age: 32.5 (2004); Male/female ratio: 94.1 (2004); Marriage status: 35.6% never married, 46.3% now married, 7.4% widowed, 10.7% divorced (2000); Foreign born: 36.4% (2000); Ancestry (includes multiple ancestries): 32.6% Other groups, 31.3% Haitian, 4.6% United States or American, 3.2% German, 2.5% Italian (2000).
Economy: Employment by occupation: 6.4% management, 12.0% professional, 22.9% services, 27.3% sales, 1.2% farming, 14.0% construction, 16.2% production (2000).
Income: Per capita income: $12,052 (2004); Median household income: $31,273 (2004); Average household income: $41,264 (2004); Percent of households with income of $100,000 or more: 5.4% (2004); Poverty rate: 32.5% (2000).
Education: Percent of population age 25 and over with: High school diploma (including GED) or higher: 58.3% (2004); Bachelor's degree or higher: 9.9% (2004); Master's degree or higher: 2.1% (2004).
Housing: Homeownership rate: 63.9% (2004); Median home value: $109,125 (2004); Median rent: $496 per month (2000); Median age of housing: 26 years (2000).
Transportation: Commute to work: 93.4% car, 1.1% public transportation, 0.3% walk, 2.3% work from home (2000); Travel time to work: 20.1% less than 15 minutes, 45.4% 15 to 30 minutes, 23.5% 30 to 45 minutes, 4.1% 45 to 60 minutes, 6.9% 60 minutes or more (2000)

RAMBLEWOOD EAST (CDP). Covers a land area of 0.093 square miles and a water area of 0 square miles. Located at 26.28° N. Lat.; 80.24° W. Long.
Population: 1,103 (1990); 1,395 (2000); 1,503 (2004); 1,643 (2009 projected); Race: 86.8% White, 3.9% Black, 2.1% Asian, 26.3% Hispanic of any race (2004); Density: 16,088.8 persons per square mile (2004); Average household size: 1.73 (2004); Median age: 47.7 (2004); Male/female ratio: 72.0 (2004); Marriage status: 21.1% never married, 42.8% now married, 25.1% widowed, 11.0% divorced (2000); Foreign born: 27.4% (2000); Ancestry (includes multiple ancestries): 33.4% Other groups, 13.0% Russian, 10.8% Italian, 7.9% Polish, 6.5% United States or American (2000).
Economy: Employment by occupation: 9.2% management, 15.3% professional, 14.1% services, 35.1% sales, 0.0% farming, 14.4% construction, 11.9% production (2000).
Income: Per capita income: $21,267 (2004); Median household income: $25,380 (2004); Average household income: $36,869 (2004); Percent of households with income of $100,000 or more: 3.9% (2004); Poverty rate: 14.4% (2000).
Education: Percent of population age 25 and over with: High school diploma (including GED) or higher: 75.9% (2004); Bachelor's degree or higher: 14.7% (2004); Master's degree or higher: 7.0% (2004).
Housing: Homeownership rate: 74.3% (2004); Median home value: $56,519 (2004); Median rent: $539 per month (2000); Median age of housing: 24 years (2000).
Transportation: Commute to work: 98.2% car, 1.8% public transportation, 0.0% walk, 0.0% work from home (2000); Travel time to work: 21.2% less than 15 minutes, 27.0% 15 to 30 minutes, 30.5% 30 to 45 minutes, 6.3% 45 to 60 minutes, 15.1% 60 minutes or more (2000)

RAVENSWOOD ESTATES (CDP). Covers a land area of 0.166 square miles and a water area of 0 square miles. Located at 26.05° N. Lat.; 80.17° W. Long.
Population: 929 (1990); 960 (2000); 1,018 (2004); 1,090 (2009 projected); Race: 90.9% White, 2.3% Black, 2.8% Asian, 9.5% Hispanic of any race (2004); Density: 6,122.4 persons per square mile (2004); Average household size: 2.20 (2004); Median age: 46.8 (2004); Male/female ratio: 94.6 (2004); Marriage status: 15.5% never married, 65.4% now married, 6.2% widowed, 12.9% divorced (2000); Foreign born: 18.5% (2000); Ancestry (includes multiple ancestries): 17.0% Italian, 15.1% German, 15.1% Irish, 12.3% Other groups, 10.7% Canadian (2000).
Economy: Employment by occupation: 11.1% management, 8.0% professional, 19.0% services, 35.2% sales, 0.0% farming, 22.2% construction, 4.6% production (2000).
Income: Per capita income: $22,738 (2004); Median household income: $45,538 (2004); Average household income: $49,995 (2004); Percent of households with income of $100,000 or more: 7.3% (2004); Poverty rate: 8.8% (2000).
Education: Percent of population age 25 and over with: High school diploma (including GED) or higher: 69.1% (2004); Bachelor's degree or higher: 8.1% (2004); Master's degree or higher: 2.6% (2004).
Housing: Homeownership rate: 89.2% (2004); Median home value: $91,311 (2004); Median rent: $589 per month (2000); Median age of housing: 17 years (2000).
Transportation: Commute to work: 91.5% car, 0.0% public transportation, 0.0% walk, 4.4% work from home (2000); Travel time to work: 16.8% less than 15 minutes, 47.3% 15 to 30 minutes, 29.0% 30 to 45 minutes, 5.1% 45 to 60 minutes, 1.8% 60 minutes or more (2000)

RIVERLAND VILLAGE (CDP). Covers a land area of 0.325 square miles and a water area of 0 square miles. Located at 26.09° N. Lat.; 80.19° W. Long.
Population: 2,077 (1990); 2,108 (2000); 2,140 (2004); 2,224 (2009 projected); Race: 80.7% White, 8.3% Black, 1.6% Asian, 33.0% Hispanic of any race (2004); Density: 6,575.4 persons per square mile (2004); Average household size: 2.83 (2004); Median age: 38.0 (2004); Male/female ratio: 105.4 (2004); Marriage status: 19.8% never married, 60.2% now married, 2.2% widowed, 17.8% divorced (2000); Foreign born: 27.7% (2000); Ancestry (includes multiple ancestries): 39.3% Other groups, 9.5% Irish, 8.3% English, 7.7% Italian, 6.7% German (2000).
Economy: Employment by occupation: 14.6% management, 11.3% professional, 20.9% services, 27.2% sales, 0.0% farming, 11.4% construction, 14.7% production (2000).
Income: Per capita income: $21,454 (2004); Median household income: $56,191 (2004); Average household income: $60,811 (2004); Percent of households with income of $100,000 or more: 10.9% (2004); Poverty rate: 5.5% (2000).
Education: Percent of population age 25 and over with: High school diploma (including GED) or higher: 81.2% (2004); Bachelor's degree or higher: 17.4% (2004); Master's degree or higher: 3.4% (2004).
Housing: Homeownership rate: 92.5% (2004); Median home value: $143,802 (2004); Median rent: $838 per month (2000); Median age of housing: 40 years (2000).
Transportation: Commute to work: 91.7% car, 3.4% public transportation, 0.8% walk, 3.2% work from home (2000); Travel time to work: 20.0% less than 15 minutes, 46.4% 15 to 30 minutes, 20.2% 30 to 45 minutes, 9.6% 45 to 60 minutes, 3.8% 60 minutes or more (2000)

ROCK ISLAND (CDP). Covers a land area of 0.614 square miles and a water area of 0 square miles. Located at 26.15° N. Lat.; 80.18° W. Long.
Population: 3,538 (1990); 3,076 (2000); 2,933 (2004); 2,766 (2009 projected); Race: 1.9% White, 96.0% Black, 0.3% Asian, 0.9% Hispanic of any race (2004); Density: 4,778.7 persons per square mile (2004); Average household size: 3.14 (2004); Median age: 34.2 (2004); Male/female ratio: 86.5 (2004); Marriage status: 32.6% never married, 47.9% now married, 8.4% widowed, 11.1% divorced (2000); Foreign born: 6.0% (2000); Ancestry (includes multiple ancestries): 69.5% Other groups, 8.7%

Jamaican, 3.7% United States or American, 2.5% African, 1.1% Bahamian (2000).
Economy: Employment by occupation: 5.2% management, 14.3% professional, 19.7% services, 31.7% sales, 0.0% farming, 9.0% construction, 20.2% production (2000).
Income: Per capita income: $13,017 (2004); Median household income: $31,523 (2004); Average household income: $39,647 (2004); Percent of households with income of $100,000 or more: 5.2% (2004); Poverty rate: 21.7% (2000).
Education: Percent of population age 25 and over with: High school diploma (including GED) or higher: 63.1% (2004); Bachelor's degree or higher: 9.2% (2004); Master's degree or higher: 2.0% (2004).
Housing: Homeownership rate: 73.5% (2004); Median home value: $109,960 (2004); Median rent: $461 per month (2000); Median age of housing: 31 years (2000).
Transportation: Commute to work: 93.3% car, 4.1% public transportation, 0.0% walk, 1.4% work from home (2000); Travel time to work: 11.7% less than 15 minutes, 63.7% 15 to 30 minutes, 13.6% 30 to 45 minutes, 4.4% 45 to 60 minutes, 6.5% 60 minutes or more (2000)

ROLLING OAKS (CDP). Covers a land area of 2.529 square miles and a water area of <.001 square miles. Located at 26.04° N. Lat.; 80.38° W. Long.
Population: 1,209 (1990); 1,291 (2000); 1,577 (2004); 1,919 (2009 projected); Race: 88.6% White, 4.4% Black, 0.9% Asian, 31.3% Hispanic of any race (2004); Density: 623.5 persons per square mile (2004); Average household size: 3.35 (2004); Median age: 39.2 (2004); Male/female ratio: 98.1 (2004); Marriage status: 24.9% never married, 66.1% now married, 3.6% widowed, 5.4% divorced (2000); Foreign born: 16.9% (2000); Ancestry (includes multiple ancestries): 39.4% Other groups, 16.7% English, 14.9% Italian, 11.8% United States or American, 10.0% Irish (2000).
Economy: Employment by occupation: 19.2% management, 19.4% professional, 24.7% services, 23.5% sales, 0.0% farming, 9.3% construction, 4.0% production (2000).
Income: Per capita income: $45,556 (2004); Median household income: $111,620 (2004); Average household income: $152,532 (2004); Percent of households with income of $100,000 or more: 53.5% (2004); Poverty rate: 7.3% (2000).
Education: Percent of population age 25 and over with: High school diploma (including GED) or higher: 86.2% (2004); Bachelor's degree or higher: 30.6% (2004); Master's degree or higher: 11.4% (2004).
Housing: Homeownership rate: 98.1% (2004); Median home value: $397,561 (2004); Median rent: $n/a per month (2000); Median age of housing: 21 years (2000).
Transportation: Commute to work: 91.0% car, 0.0% public transportation, 0.0% walk, 9.0% work from home (2000); Travel time to work: 6.2% less than 15 minutes, 36.5% 15 to 30 minutes, 22.6% 30 to 45 minutes, 21.6% 45 to 60 minutes, 13.1% 60 minutes or more (2000)

ROOSEVELT GARDENS (CDP). Covers a land area of 0.317 square miles and a water area of 0 square miles. Located at 26.14° N. Lat.; 80.18° W. Long.
Population: 2,231 (1990); 1,923 (2000); 1,970 (2004); 2,024 (2009 projected); Race: 0.6% White, 98.0% Black, 0.0% Asian, 0.1% Hispanic of any race (2004); Density: 6,216.5 persons per square mile (2004); Average household size: 2.84 (2004); Median age: 31.3 (2004); Male/female ratio: 90.3 (2004); Marriage status: 40.3% never married, 35.7% now married, 10.5% widowed, 13.5% divorced (2000); Foreign born: 3.5% (2000); Ancestry (includes multiple ancestries): 81.0% Other groups, 2.6% Jamaican, 1.4% West Indian, 1.2% United States or American, 0.9% Trinidadian and Tobagonian (2000).
Economy: Employment by occupation: 2.4% management, 7.0% professional, 32.8% services, 21.4% sales, 1.7% farming, 12.5% construction, 22.2% production (2000).
Income: Per capita income: $9,546 (2004); Median household income: $20,000 (2004); Average household income: $27,136 (2004); Percent of households with income of $100,000 or more: 1.3% (2004); Poverty rate: 33.2% (2000).
Education: Percent of population age 25 and over with: High school diploma (including GED) or higher: 55.4% (2004); Bachelor's degree or higher: 3.0% (2004); Master's degree or higher: 0.0% (2004).
Housing: Homeownership rate: 39.7% (2004); Median home value: $94,028 (2004); Median rent: $501 per month (2000); Median age of housing: 31 years (2000).
Transportation: Commute to work: 83.5% car, 8.9% public transportation, 1.5% walk, 0.0% work from home (2000); Travel time to work: 10.0% less than 15 minutes, 46.5% 15 to 30 minutes, 27.0% 30 to 45 minutes, 6.1% 45 to 60 minutes, 10.4% 60 minutes or more (2000)

ROYAL PALM RANCHES (CDP). Covers a land area of 0.292 square miles and a water area of 0 square miles. Located at 26.04° N. Lat.; 80.27° W. Long.
Population: 209 (1990); 294 (2000); 322 (2004); 358 (2009 projected); Race: 86.3% White, 0.6% Black, 5.3% Asian, 19.9% Hispanic of any race (2004); Density: 1,104.5 persons per square mile (2004); Average household size: 3.25 (2004); Median age: 39.6 (2004); Male/female ratio: 106.4 (2004); Marriage status: 16.8% never married, 70.5% now married, 1.8% widowed, 10.9% divorced (2000); Foreign born: 17.3% (2000); Ancestry (includes multiple ancestries): 32.2% German, 27.9% United States or American, 24.3% Other groups, 16.6% Italian, 10.6% Irish (2000).
Economy: Employment by occupation: 29.3% management, 20.4% professional, 5.4% services, 29.3% sales, 0.0% farming, 0.0% construction, 15.6% production (2000).
Income: Per capita income: $43,672 (2004); Median household income: $139,063 (2004); Average household income: $142,045 (2004); Percent of households with income of $100,000 or more: 62.6% (2004); Poverty rate: 0.0% (2000).
Education: Percent of population age 25 and over with: High school diploma (including GED) or higher: 93.4% (2004); Bachelor's degree or higher: 26.5% (2004); Master's degree or higher: 19.4% (2004).
Housing: Homeownership rate: 99.0% (2004); Median home value: $378,261 (2004); Median rent: $n/a per month (2000); Median age of housing: 17 years (2000).
Transportation: Commute to work: 78.2% car, 15.0% public transportation, 6.8% walk, 0.0% work from home (2000); Travel time to work: 12.2% less than 15 minutes, 8.8% 15 to 30 minutes, 40.8% 30 to 45 minutes, 38.1% 45 to 60 minutes, 0.0% 60 minutes or more (2000)

SAINT GEORGE (CDP). Covers a land area of 0.449 square miles and a water area of 0 square miles. Located at 26.13° N. Lat.; 80.19° W. Long.
Population: 2,626 (1990); 2,450 (2000); 2,239 (2004); 2,027 (2009 projected); Race: 1.3% White, 97.4% Black, 0.0% Asian, 1.3% Hispanic of any race (2004); Density: 4,990.0 persons per square mile (2004); Average household size: 3.22 (2004); Median age: 35.6 (2004); Male/female ratio: 90.2 (2004); Marriage status: 36.3% never married, 40.7% now married, 10.3% widowed, 12.7% divorced (2000); Foreign born: 12.1% (2000); Ancestry (includes multiple ancestries): 72.4% Other groups, 7.4% Jamaican, 1.3% Haitian, 1.0% Barbadian, 0.9% United States or American (2000).
Economy: Employment by occupation: 2.6% management, 12.6% professional, 23.4% services, 31.7% sales, 0.0% farming, 15.5% construction, 14.2% production (2000).
Income: Per capita income: $15,842 (2004); Median household income: $42,361 (2004); Average household income: $51,036 (2004); Percent of households with income of $100,000 or more: 10.5% (2004); Poverty rate: 10.9% (2000).
Education: Percent of population age 25 and over with: High school diploma (including GED) or higher: 67.8% (2004); Bachelor's degree or higher: 10.3% (2004); Master's degree or higher: 2.8% (2004).
Housing: Homeownership rate: 86.8% (2004); Median home value: $116,604 (2004); Median rent: $528 per month (2000); Median age of housing: 38 years (2000).
Transportation: Commute to work: 91.6% car, 6.6% public transportation, 0.0% walk, 0.9% work from home (2000); Travel time to work: 18.1% less than 15 minutes, 38.4% 15 to 30 minutes, 28.6% 30 to 45 minutes, 6.7% 45 to 60 minutes, 8.2% 60 minutes or more (2000)

SEA RANCH LAKES (village). Covers a land area of 0.181 square miles and a water area of 0.044 square miles. Located at 26.20° N. Lat.; 80.09° W. Long. Elevation is 5 feet.
Population: 619 (1990); 1,392 (2000); 1,276 (2004); 1,185 (2009 projected); Race: 97.4% White, 1.3% Black, 0.5% Asian, 9.5% Hispanic of any race (2004); Density: 7,048.7 persons per square mile (2004); Average household size: 1.99 (2004); Median age: 57.1 (2004); Male/female ratio: 83.9 (2004); Marriage status: 10.8% never married, 64.4% now married, 13.0% widowed, 11.9% divorced (2000); Foreign born: 15.1% (2000); Ancestry (includes multiple ancestries): 20.5% German, 16.9% Irish, 16.4% Italian, 12.6% English, 7.5% Russian (2000).

Economy: Single-family building permits issued: 0 (2004); Multi-family building permits issued: 0 (2004); Employment by occupation: 27.6% management, 30.9% professional, 0.8% services, 33.9% sales, 0.0% farming, 2.5% construction, 4.3% production (2000).
Income: Per capita income: $65,535 (2004); Median household income: $66,239 (2004); Average household income: $130,660 (2004); Percent of households with income of $100,000 or more: 30.6% (2004); Poverty rate: 7.0% (2000).
Education: Percent of population age 25 and over with: High school diploma (including GED) or higher: 93.3% (2004); Bachelor's degree or higher: 53.4% (2004); Master's degree or higher: 24.3% (2004).
Housing: Homeownership rate: 90.6% (2004); Median home value: $314,876 (2004); Median rent: $1,034 per month (2000); Median age of housing: 24 years (2000).
Safety: Violent crime rate: 0.0 per 10,000 population; Property crime rate: 41.8 per 10,000 population (2003).
Transportation: Commute to work: 92.1% car, 2.5% public transportation, 0.0% walk, 5.4% work from home (2000); Travel time to work: 24.2% less than 15 minutes, 40.8% 15 to 30 minutes, 18.3% 30 to 45 minutes, 9.6% 45 to 60 minutes, 7.0% 60 minutes or more (2000)

SUNRISE (city). Aka City of Sunrise. Covers a land area of 18.202 square miles and a water area of 0.229 square miles. Located at 26.15° N. Lat.; 80.28° W. Long. Elevation is 5 feet.
Population: 64,675 (1990); 85,779 (2000); 88,453 (2004); 92,416 (2009 projected); Race: 63.0% White, 24.7% Black, 3.7% Asian, 21.2% Hispanic of any race (2004); Density: 4,859.4 persons per square mile (2004); Average household size: 2.57 (2004); Median age: 37.2 (2004); Male/female ratio: 88.8 (2004); Marriage status: 24.1% never married, 55.2% now married, 10.0% widowed, 10.7% divorced (2000); Foreign born: 28.1% (2000); Ancestry (includes multiple ancestries): 33.8% Other groups, 10.3% Italian, 8.0% Jamaican, 7.4% Irish, 7.4% German (2000).
Economy: Major office and commercial center and site of Sawgrass Mills, one of the largest factory-outlet malls in US. Home of Florida Panthers National Hockey League team. Unemployment rate: 4.5% (2004); Total civilian labor force: 44,796 (2004); Single-family building permits issued: 46 (2004); Multi-family building permits issued: 52 (2004); Employment by occupation: 13.1% management, 18.6% professional, 15.7% services, 34.1% sales, 0.1% farming, 8.9% construction, 9.5% production (2000).
Income: Per capita income: $20,511 (2004); Median household income: $44,167 (2004); Average household income: $52,391 (2004); Percent of households with income of $100,000 or more: 9.8% (2004); Poverty rate: 9.7% (2000).
Taxes: Total city taxes per capita: $338 (2002); City property taxes per capita: $232 (2002).
Education: Percent of population age 25 and over with: High school diploma (including GED) or higher: 83.8% (2004); Bachelor's degree or higher: 20.2% (2004); Master's degree or higher: 6.5% (2004).

School District(s)

Broward County School District (PK-12)
2002-03 Enrollment: 267,925 . . . . (754) 321-2600
Housing: Homeownership rate: 73.1% (2004); Median home value: $133,436 (2004); Median rent: $759 per month (2000); Median age of housing: 19 years (2000).
Safety: Violent crime rate: 47.1 per 10,000 population; Property crime rate: 417.5 per 10,000 population (2003).
Transportation: Commute to work: 94.8% car, 1.7% public transportation, 1.1% walk, 1.8% work from home (2000); Travel time to work: 20.3% less than 15 minutes, 33.2% 15 to 30 minutes, 28.2% 30 to 45 minutes, 10.9% 45 to 60 minutes, 7.3% 60 minutes or more (2000)
Additional Information Contacts
Local Government Offices . . . . (954) 741-2580
Sunrise Chamber of Commerce . . . . (954) 835-2428

SUNSHINE ACRES (CDP). Covers a land area of 1.028 square miles and a water area of 0 square miles. Located at 26.05° N. Lat.; 80.29° W. Long.
Population: 894 (1990); 827 (2000); 860 (2004); 909 (2009 projected); Race: 86.3% White, 6.4% Black, 2.4% Asian, 10.7% Hispanic of any race (2004); Density: 836.7 persons per square mile (2004); Average household size: 3.48 (2004); Median age: 38.7 (2004); Male/female ratio: 109.2 (2004); Marriage status: 20.4% never married, 68.4% now married, 3.8% widowed, 7.3% divorced (2000); Foreign born: 16.7% (2000); Ancestry (includes multiple ancestries): 26.1% Other groups, 23.0% German, 20.3% English, 17.0% Irish, 15.3% Italian (2000).
Economy: Employment by occupation: 11.9% management, 16.1% professional, 23.2% services, 32.2% sales, 3.1% farming, 8.6% construction, 4.9% production (2000).
Income: Per capita income: $32,380 (2004); Median household income: $81,686 (2004); Average household income: $111,528 (2004); Percent of households with income of $100,000 or more: 37.2% (2004); Poverty rate: 4.3% (2000).
Education: Percent of population age 25 and over with: High school diploma (including GED) or higher: 82.0% (2004); Bachelor's degree or higher: 29.8% (2004); Master's degree or higher: 8.9% (2004).
Housing: Homeownership rate: 96.8% (2004); Median home value: $350,556 (2004); Median rent: $n/a per month (2000); Median age of housing: 19 years (2000).
Transportation: Commute to work: 87.9% car, 0.0% public transportation, 8.0% walk, 2.6% work from home (2000); Travel time to work: 27.6% less than 15 minutes, 35.8% 15 to 30 minutes, 12.9% 30 to 45 minutes, 0.0% 45 to 60 minutes, 23.6% 60 minutes or more (2000)

SUNSHINE RANCHES (CDP). Covers a land area of 4.171 square miles and a water area of 0 square miles. Located at 26.04° N. Lat.; 80.32° W. Long. Elevation is 4 feet.
Population: 1,405 (1990); 1,704 (2000); 2,163 (2004); 2,720 (2009 projected); Race: 90.9% White, 3.5% Black, 0.7% Asian, 21.7% Hispanic of any race (2004); Density: 518.5 persons per square mile (2004); Average household size: 3.12 (2004); Median age: 40.5 (2004); Male/female ratio: 95.7 (2004); Marriage status: 15.6% never married, 71.7% now married, 7.0% widowed, 5.7% divorced (2000); Foreign born: 19.4% (2000); Ancestry (includes multiple ancestries): 29.4% Other groups, 15.3% Italian, 13.0% Irish, 11.8% United States or American, 10.2% German (2000).
Economy: Employment by occupation: 28.9% management, 22.6% professional, 10.7% services, 26.4% sales, 2.5% farming, 3.0% construction, 5.9% production (2000).
Income: Per capita income: $41,592 (2004); Median household income: $98,258 (2004); Average household income: $128,755 (2004); Percent of households with income of $100,000 or more: 48.8% (2004); Poverty rate: 2.1% (2000).
Education: Percent of population age 25 and over with: High school diploma (including GED) or higher: 90.5% (2004); Bachelor's degree or higher: 42.1% (2004); Master's degree or higher: 19.5% (2004).
Housing: Homeownership rate: 94.4% (2004); Median home value: $477,143 (2004); Median rent: $1,875 per month (2000); Median age of housing: 18 years (2000).
Transportation: Commute to work: 90.0% car, 0.0% public transportation, 1.1% walk, 8.9% work from home (2000); Travel time to work: 8.9% less than 15 minutes, 34.4% 15 to 30 minutes, 29.0% 30 to 45 minutes, 12.8% 45 to 60 minutes, 14.9% 60 minutes or more (2000)

TAMARAC (city). Covers a land area of 11.391 square miles and a water area of 0.502 square miles. Located at 26.20° N. Lat.; 80.24° W. Long. Elevation is 11 feet.
Population: 45,366 (1990); 55,588 (2000); 57,385 (2004); 60,047 (2009 projected); Race: 76.2% White, 14.3% Black, 1.8% Asian, 19.2% Hispanic of any race (2004); Density: 5,037.6 persons per square mile (2004); Average household size: 2.03 (2004); Median age: 52.8 (2004); Male/female ratio: 82.0 (2004); Marriage status: 17.3% never married, 55.7% now married, 16.0% widowed, 11.0% divorced (2000); Foreign born: 21.3% (2000); Ancestry (includes multiple ancestries): 29.8% Other groups, 10.9% Italian, 9.1% United States or American, 7.9% Irish, 7.7% German (2000).
Economy: Manufacturing includes commercial printing, apparel, landscape equipment, trailers, optical glass. Unemployment rate: 5.4% (2004); Total civilian labor force: 24,718 (2004); Single-family building permits issued: 245 (2004); Multi-family building permits issued: 60 (2004); Employment by occupation: 13.2% management, 15.2% professional, 15.7% services, 36.0% sales, 0.1% farming, 10.6% construction, 9.0% production (2000).
Income: Per capita income: $23,445 (2004); Median household income: $36,640 (2004); Average household income: $47,104 (2004); Percent of households with income of $100,000 or more: 7.5% (2004); Poverty rate: 8.9% (2000).
Taxes: Total city taxes per capita: $325 (2002); City property taxes per capita: $213 (2002).
Education: Percent of population age 25 and over with: High school diploma (including GED) or higher: 83.7% (2004); Bachelor's degree or higher: 17.0% (2004); Master's degree or higher: 5.8% (2004).

School District(s)
Broward County School District (PK-12)
2002-03 Enrollment: 267,925 . . . . (754) 321-2600
Housing: Homeownership rate: 80.3% (2004); Median home value: $124,779 (2004); Median rent: $720 per month (2000); Median age of housing: 21 years (2000).
Hospitals: University Hospital & Medical Center (317 beds)
Safety: Violent crime rate: 31.3 per 10,000 population; Property crime rate: 150.9 per 10,000 population (2003).
Transportation: Commute to work: 94.2% car, 1.7% public transportation, 1.0% walk, 1.9% work from home (2000); Travel time to work: 19.9% less than 15 minutes, 36.2% 15 to 30 minutes, 29.2% 30 to 45 minutes, 8.3% 45 to 60 minutes, 6.4% 60 minutes or more (2000)
Additional Information Contacts
Local Government Offices . . . . (954) 724-1200
Tamarac Chamber of Commerce . . . . (954) 722-1520

TEDDER (CDP). Covers a land area of 0.278 square miles and a water area of 0 square miles. Located at 26.28° N. Lat.; 80.12° W. Long.
Population: 1,686 (1990); 2,079 (2000); 2,046 (2004); 1,935 (2009 projected); Race: 30.4% White, 47.2% Black, 1.4% Asian, 21.3% Hispanic of any race (2004); Density: 7,347.1 persons per square mile (2004); Average household size: 4.18 (2004); Median age: 35.3 (2004); Male/female ratio: 104.6 (2004); Marriage status: 40.7% never married, 45.1% now married, 6.2% widowed, 8.1% divorced (2000); Foreign born: 35.2% (2000); Ancestry (includes multiple ancestries): 34.5% Other groups, 25.1% Haitian, 7.2% German, 4.9% United States or American, 4.7% Irish (2000).
Economy: Employment by occupation: 8.7% management, 11.0% professional, 22.9% services, 27.9% sales, 0.8% farming, 10.9% construction, 17.8% production (2000).
Income: Per capita income: $10,483 (2004); Median household income: $39,527 (2004); Average household income: $41,431 (2004); Percent of households with income of $100,000 or more: 1.2% (2004); Poverty rate: 18.2% (2000).
Education: Percent of population age 25 and over with: High school diploma (including GED) or higher: 50.7% (2004); Bachelor's degree or higher: 8.6% (2004); Master's degree or higher: 2.8% (2004).
Housing: Homeownership rate: 82.0% (2004); Median home value: $120,427 (2004); Median rent: $586 per month (2000); Median age of housing: 35 years (2000).
Transportation: Commute to work: 97.0% car, 2.1% public transportation, 0.0% walk, 0.0% work from home (2000); Travel time to work: 25.5% less than 15 minutes, 49.9% 15 to 30 minutes, 18.5% 30 to 45 minutes, 5.5% 45 to 60 minutes, 0.6% 60 minutes or more (2000)

TERRA MAR (CDP). Covers a land area of 0.373 square miles and a water area of 0 square miles. Located at 26.21° N. Lat.; 80.09° W. Long. Elevation is 6 feet.
Population: 3,072 (1990); 2,631 (2000); 2,653 (2004); 2,712 (2009 projected); Race: 97.2% White, 0.7% Black, 0.3% Asian, 6.1% Hispanic of any race (2004); Density: 7,113.2 persons per square mile (2004); Average household size: 1.63 (2004); Median age: 60.9 (2004); Male/female ratio: 91.0 (2004); Marriage status: 15.4% never married, 55.1% now married, 14.3% widowed, 15.2% divorced (2000); Foreign born: 22.5% (2000); Ancestry (includes multiple ancestries): 16.4% German, 14.8% Italian, 12.1% Irish, 10.3% English, 8.7% Other groups (2000).
Economy: Employment by occupation: 14.3% management, 23.2% professional, 12.2% services, 37.0% sales, 0.0% farming, 7.9% construction, 5.4% production (2000).
Income: Per capita income: $51,054 (2004); Median household income: $54,140 (2004); Average household income: $83,351 (2004); Percent of households with income of $100,000 or more: 22.9% (2004); Poverty rate: 8.2% (2000).
Education: Percent of population age 25 and over with: High school diploma (including GED) or higher: 88.7% (2004); Bachelor's degree or higher: 37.9% (2004); Master's degree or higher: 17.2% (2004).
Housing: Homeownership rate: 76.7% (2004); Median home value: $214,658 (2004); Median rent: $1,074 per month (2000); Median age of housing: 30 years (2000).
Transportation: Commute to work: 88.2% car, 1.1% public transportation, 2.5% walk, 8.2% work from home (2000); Travel time to work: 19.6% less than 15 minutes, 37.6% 15 to 30 minutes, 28.2% 30 to 45 minutes, 10.4% 45 to 60 minutes, 4.2% 60 minutes or more (2000)

TWIN LAKES (CDP). Covers a land area of 0.260 square miles and a water area of 0.006 square miles. Located at 26.18° N. Lat.; 80.15° W. Long. Elevation is 10 feet.
Population: 1,786 (1990); 1,875 (2000); 1,871 (2004); 1,923 (2009 projected); Race: 71.1% White, 20.6% Black, 2.0% Asian, 19.2% Hispanic of any race (2004); Density: 7,195.5 persons per square mile (2004); Average household size: 2.88 (2004); Median age: 36.8 (2004); Male/female ratio: 113.1 (2004); Marriage status: 26.5% never married, 60.2% now married, 3.7% widowed, 9.6% divorced (2000); Foreign born: 21.9% (2000); Ancestry (includes multiple ancestries): 19.8% Other groups, 15.3% English, 14.6% German, 14.1% United States or American, 10.0% Irish (2000).
Economy: Employment by occupation: 15.6% management, 15.7% professional, 11.0% services, 30.1% sales, 0.0% farming, 17.6% construction, 10.0% production (2000).
Income: Per capita income: $19,365 (2004); Median household income: $45,605 (2004); Average household income: $55,828 (2004); Percent of households with income of $100,000 or more: 9.9% (2004); Poverty rate: 8.9% (2000).
Education: Percent of population age 25 and over with: High school diploma (including GED) or higher: 72.8% (2004); Bachelor's degree or higher: 13.0% (2004); Master's degree or higher: 3.5% (2004).
Housing: Homeownership rate: 78.6% (2004); Median home value: $138,182 (2004); Median rent: $597 per month (2000); Median age of housing: 34 years (2000).
Transportation: Commute to work: 92.8% car, 1.1% public transportation, 0.0% walk, 4.5% work from home (2000); Travel time to work: 33.5% less than 15 minutes, 34.6% 15 to 30 minutes, 23.0% 30 to 45 minutes, 3.1% 45 to 60 minutes, 5.7% 60 minutes or more (2000)

UTOPIA (CDP). Covers a land area of 0.307 square miles and a water area of 0 square miles. Located at 25.98° N. Lat.; 80.20° W. Long.
Population: 660 (1990); 714 (2000); 780 (2004); 866 (2009 projected); Race: 16.4% White, 68.1% Black, 0.5% Asian, 26.0% Hispanic of any race (2004); Density: 2,542.0 persons per square mile (2004); Average household size: 2.69 (2004); Median age: 30.5 (2004); Male/female ratio: 96.5 (2004); Marriage status: 39.9% never married, 42.4% now married, 5.0% widowed, 12.7% divorced (2000); Foreign born: 31.4% (2000); Ancestry (includes multiple ancestries): 65.9% Other groups, 12.6% Jamaican, 8.1% United States or American, 4.0% British West Indian, 2.1% U.S. Virgin Islander (2000).
Economy: Employment by occupation: 2.0% management, 14.0% professional, 16.4% services, 38.4% sales, 0.0% farming, 12.4% construction, 16.8% production (2000).
Income: Per capita income: $14,526 (2004); Median household income: $22,736 (2004); Average household income: $39,069 (2004); Percent of households with income of $100,000 or more: 6.2% (2004); Poverty rate: 28.4% (2000).
Education: Percent of population age 25 and over with: High school diploma (including GED) or higher: 59.0% (2004); Bachelor's degree or higher: 5.1% (2004); Master's degree or higher: 0.0% (2004).
Housing: Homeownership rate: 34.1% (2004); Median home value: $87,500 (2004); Median rent: $560 per month (2000); Median age of housing: 25 years (2000).
Transportation: Commute to work: 84.2% car, 13.3% public transportation, 2.5% walk, 0.0% work from home (2000); Travel time to work: 14.5% less than 15 minutes, 48.1% 15 to 30 minutes, 31.1% 30 to 45 minutes, 6.2% 45 to 60 minutes, 0.0% 60 minutes or more (2000)

VILLAGE PARK (CDP). Covers a land area of 0.178 square miles and a water area of 0 square miles. Located at 26.19° N. Lat.; 80.20° W. Long.
Population: 566 (1990); 895 (2000); 899 (2004); 917 (2009 projected); Race: 74.0% White, 7.1% Black, 5.3% Asian, 27.9% Hispanic of any race (2004); Density: 5,052.6 persons per square mile (2004); Average household size: 1.91 (2004); Median age: 50.2 (2004); Male/female ratio: 107.1 (2004); Marriage status: 18.0% never married, 44.2% now married, 14.8% widowed, 23.0% divorced (2000); Foreign born: 28.0% (2000); Ancestry (includes multiple ancestries): 27.2% Other groups, 15.8% Italian, 13.9% German, 11.9% Irish, 7.6% Canadian (2000).
Economy: Employment by occupation: 0.0% management, 6.5% professional, 18.4% services, 33.5% sales, 0.0% farming, 28.8% construction, 12.9% production (2000).

Income: Per capita income: $18,523 (2004); Median household income: $27,365 (2004); Average household income: $35,356 (2004); Percent of households with income of $100,000 or more: 2.3% (2004); Poverty rate: 16.4% (2000).
Education: Percent of population age 25 and over with: High school diploma (including GED) or higher: 64.0% (2004); Bachelor's degree or higher: 11.7% (2004); Master's degree or higher: 5.2% (2004).
Housing: Homeownership rate: 91.9% (2004); Median home value: $19,999 (2004); Median rent: $421 per month (2000); Median age of housing: 25 years (2000).
Transportation: Commute to work: 85.9% car, 9.1% public transportation, 2.6% walk, 0.0% work from home (2000); Travel time to work: 20.3% less than 15 minutes, 33.8% 15 to 30 minutes, 21.4% 30 to 45 minutes, 7.9% 45 to 60 minutes, 16.6% 60 minutes or more (2000)

WASHINGTON PARK (CDP). Covers a land area of 0.398 square miles and a water area of 0.017 square miles. Located at 26.13° N. Lat.; 80.17° W. Long.
Population: 1,524 (1990); 1,257 (2000); 1,247 (2004); 1,254 (2009 projected); Race: 0.0% White, 98.0% Black, 0.1% Asian, 0.7% Hispanic of any race (2004); Density: 3,136.9 persons per square mile (2004); Average household size: 3.01 (2004); Median age: 35.7 (2004); Male/female ratio: 90.7 (2004); Marriage status: 37.4% never married, 45.1% now married, 6.7% widowed, 10.7% divorced (2000); Foreign born: 9.1% (2000); Ancestry (includes multiple ancestries): 74.5% Other groups, 8.3% Jamaican, 6.9% United States or American, 1.0% Bahamian, 0.4% Belizean (2000).
Economy: Employment by occupation: 5.7% management, 12.7% professional, 32.8% services, 12.3% sales, 1.5% farming, 14.4% construction, 20.6% production (2000).
Income: Per capita income: $11,317 (2004); Median household income: $23,776 (2004); Average household income: $34,088 (2004); Percent of households with income of $100,000 or more: 4.3% (2004); Poverty rate: 28.5% (2000).
Education: Percent of population age 25 and over with: High school diploma (including GED) or higher: 50.9% (2004); Bachelor's degree or higher: 9.6% (2004); Master's degree or higher: 3.5% (2004).
Housing: Homeownership rate: 64.3% (2004); Median home value: $108,451 (2004); Median rent: $525 per month (2000); Median age of housing: 32 years (2000).
Transportation: Commute to work: 95.0% car, 5.0% public transportation, 0.0% walk, 0.0% work from home (2000); Travel time to work: 15.8% less than 15 minutes, 37.0% 15 to 30 minutes, 31.1% 30 to 45 minutes, 7.8% 45 to 60 minutes, 8.4% 60 minutes or more (2000)

WEST KEN-LARK (CDP). Covers a land area of 0.486 square miles and a water area of 0 square miles. Located at 26.14° N. Lat.; 80.19° W. Long.
Population: 3,413 (1990); 3,412 (2000); 3,493 (2004); 3,627 (2009 projected); Race: 1.2% White, 96.9% Black, 0.1% Asian, 1.9% Hispanic of any race (2004); Density: 7,192.2 persons per square mile (2004); Average household size: 3.44 (2004); Median age: 31.6 (2004); Male/female ratio: 86.5 (2004); Marriage status: 42.0% never married, 39.7% now married, 10.2% widowed, 8.2% divorced (2000); Foreign born: 3.9% (2000); Ancestry (includes multiple ancestries): 85.3% Other groups, 1.2% Jamaican, 0.8% Haitian, 0.5% West Indian, 0.4% African (2000).
Economy: Employment by occupation: 3.8% management, 11.0% professional, 29.1% services, 26.1% sales, 0.9% farming, 12.6% construction, 16.6% production (2000).
Income: Per capita income: $11,289 (2004); Median household income: $31,399 (2004); Average household income: $37,108 (2004); Percent of households with income of $100,000 or more: 1.4% (2004); Poverty rate: 33.3% (2000).
Education: Percent of population age 25 and over with: High school diploma (including GED) or higher: 51.8% (2004); Bachelor's degree or higher: 4.3% (2004); Master's degree or higher: 2.5% (2004).
Housing: Homeownership rate: 74.8% (2004); Median home value: $112,884 (2004); Median rent: $294 per month (2000); Median age of housing: 34 years (2000).
Transportation: Commute to work: 92.1% car, 5.6% public transportation, 1.6% walk, 0.0% work from home (2000); Travel time to work: 17.5% less than 15 minutes, 42.9% 15 to 30 minutes, 25.9% 30 to 45 minutes, 4.7% 45 to 60 minutes, 9.0% 60 minutes or more (2000)

WESTON (city). Covers a land area of 23.762 square miles and a water area of 2.516 square miles. Located at 26.10° N. Lat.; 80.38° W. Long.
Population: 10,099 (1990); 49,286 (2000); 68,571 (2004); 88,041 (2009 projected); Race: 85.1% White, 4.7% Black, 3.9% Asian, 35.6% Hispanic of any race (2004); Density: 2,885.8 persons per square mile (2004); Average household size: 3.04 (2004); Median age: 34.6 (2004); Male/female ratio: 94.7 (2004); Marriage status: 19.2% never married, 70.6% now married, 3.3% widowed, 6.9% divorced (2000); Foreign born: 28.0% (2000); Ancestry (includes multiple ancestries): 40.7% Other groups, 9.8% Italian, 9.2% German, 7.9% Irish, 6.8% United States or American (2000).
Economy: Single-family building permits issued: 183 (2004); Multi-family building permits issued: 597 (2004); Employment by occupation: 28.1% management, 23.6% professional, 10.1% services, 30.5% sales, 0.0% farming, 3.2% construction, 4.6% production (2000).
Income: Per capita income: $41,567 (2004); Median household income: $90,263 (2004); Average household income: $126,350 (2004); Percent of households with income of $100,000 or more: 44.5% (2004); Poverty rate: 5.0% (2000).
Taxes: Total city taxes per capita: $296 (2002); City property taxes per capita: $99 (2002).
Education: Percent of population age 25 and over with: High school diploma (including GED) or higher: 95.7% (2004), Bachelor's degree or higher: 52.5% (2004); Master's degree or higher: 21.8% (2004).

School District(s)

Broward County School District (PK-12)
2002-03 Enrollment: 267,925 . . . . (754) 321-2600
Housing: Homeownership rate: 83.4% (2004); Median home value: $269,626 (2004); Median rent: $969 per month (2000); Median age of housing: 5 years (2000).
Hospitals: Cleveland Clinic Hospital (150 beds)
Safety: Violent crime rate: 12.8 per 10,000 population; Property crime rate: 72.4 per 10,000 population (2003).
Newspapers: Pembroke Pines Community News (General - Circulation 27,000); Weston Community News (General - Circulation 18,000)
Transportation: Commute to work: 91.9% car, 0.6% public transportation, 0.8% walk, 5.7% work from home (2000); Travel time to work: 17.3% less than 15 minutes, 25.9% 15 to 30 minutes, 29.6% 30 to 45 minutes, 16.9% 45 to 60 minutes, 10.4% 60 minutes or more (2000)
Additional Information Contacts
Local Government Offices . . . . (954) 385-2000

WILTON MANORS (city). Aka Wilton Manor. Covers a land area of 1.943 square miles and a water area of 0 square miles. Located at 26.15° N. Lat.; 80.14° W. Long. Elevation is 8 feet.
Population: 11,804 (1990); 12,697 (2000); 12,840 (2004); 13,152 (2009 projected); Race: 74.6% White, 16.0% Black, 1.9% Asian, 11.8% Hispanic of any race (2004); Density: 6,608.9 persons per square mile (2004); Average household size: 2.13 (2004); Median age: 41.2 (2004); Male/female ratio: 123.5 (2004); Marriage status: 38.4% never married, 39.2% now married, 6.7% widowed, 15.7% divorced (2000); Foreign born: 20.5% (2000); Ancestry (includes multiple ancestries): 19.9% Other groups, 14.1% Irish, 13.3% German, 12.1% English, 9.1% Italian (2000).
Economy: Single-family building permits issued: 1 (2004); Multi-family building permits issued: 2 (2004); Employment by occupation: 12.5% management, 15.8% professional, 19.4% services, 30.8% sales, 0.1% farming, 10.5% construction, 10.8% production (2000).
Income: Per capita income: $25,728 (2004); Median household income: $43,024 (2004); Average household income: $53,043 (2004); Percent of households with income of $100,000 or more: 10.6% (2004); Poverty rate: 15.4% (2000).
Taxes: Total city taxes per capita: $466 (2002); City property taxes per capita: $231 (2002).
Education: Percent of population age 25 and over with: High school diploma (including GED) or higher: 83.7% (2004); Bachelor's degree or higher: 24.9% (2004); Master's degree or higher: 8.2% (2004).

School District(s)

Broward County School District (PK-12)
2002-03 Enrollment: 267,925 . . . . (754) 321-2600
Housing: Homeownership rate: 57.8% (2004); Median home value: $184,845 (2004); Median rent: $566 per month (2000); Median age of housing: 35 years (2000).
Safety: Violent crime rate: 48.8 per 10,000 population; Property crime rate: 511.6 per 10,000 population (2003).

Transportation: Commute to work: 88.2% car, 4.2% public transportation, 2.1% walk, 3.9% work from home (2000); Travel time to work: 33.1% less than 15 minutes, 39.7% 15 to 30 minutes, 16.4% 30 to 45 minutes, 5.5% 45 to 60 minutes, 5.3% 60 minutes or more (2000)

Additional Information Contacts

Local Government Offices . . . . (954) 390-2122

Calhoun County

Located in northwestern Florida; lowland area, drained by the Chipola River; bounded on the east by the Apalachicola River. Covers a land area of 567.30 square miles, a water area of 7.00 square miles, and is located in the Central Time Zone. The county government was organized in 1838. County seat is Blountstown.

Population: 11,011 (1990); 13,017 (2000); 12,847 (2004); 12,647 (2009 projected); Race: 81.7% White, 14.2% Black, 0.6% Asian, 3.7% Hispanic of any race (2004); Density: 22.6 persons per square mile (2004); Average household size: 2.97 (2004); Median age: 37.3 (2004); Male/female ratio: 116.0 (2004).

Religion: Five largest groups: 17.4% Southern Baptist Convention, 4.0% The United Methodist Church, 2.6% International Pentecostal Holiness Church, 2.5% Church of God (Cleveland, Tennessee), 1.6% Assemblies of God (2000).

Economy: Unemployment rate: 4.9% (2004); Total civilian labor force: 4,892 (2004); Leading industries: 28.5% retail trade; 19.6% health care and social assistance; 10.4% forestry, fishing, hunting, and agriculture support (2003); Companies that employ 500 or more persons: 0 (2003); Companies that employ 100 to 499 persons: 2 (2003); Companies that employ less than 100 persons: 207 (2003); Farms: 151 totaling 49,107 acres (2002); Minority business ownership rate: n/a (1997); Women business ownership rate: n/a (1997); Retail sales per capita: $6,545 (1997). Single-family building permits issued: 34 (2004); Multi-family building permits issued: 0 (2004).

Income: Per capita income: $12,639 (2004); Median household income: $28,391 (2004); Average household income: $36,774 (2004); Percent of households with income of $100,000 or more: 4.2% (2004); Poverty rate: 20.2% (2002); Bankruptcy rate: 3.30% (2004).

Taxes: Total county taxes per capita: $284 (2002); County property taxes per capita: $168 (2002).

Education: Percent of population age 25 and over with: High school diploma (including GED) or higher: 69.1% (2004); Bachelor's degree or higher: 7.5% (2004); Master's degree or higher: 3.0% (2004).

Housing: Homeownership rate: 80.4% (2004); Median home value: $74,200 (2004); Median rent: $248 per month (2000); Median age of housing: 21 years (2000).

Health: Birth rate: 138.0 per 10,000 population (2004); Death rate: 78.1 per 10,000 population (2004); Age adjusted cancer mortality rate: 150.2 deaths per 100,000 population (2002); Number of physicians: 6.9 per 10,000 population (2001); Hospital beds: 23.9 per 10,000 population (2002); Hospital admissions: 446.4 per 10,000 population (2002).

Elections: 2004 Presidential election results: 63.4% Bush, 35.5% Kerry, 0.6% Nader, 0.1% Badnarik

Additional Information Contacts

Calhoun County Government Offices . . . . (904) 674-4545
Calhoun Chamber of Commerce . . . . (850) 674-4519

Calhoun County Communities

ALTHA (town). Covers a land area of 1.426 square miles and a water area of 0.040 square miles. Located at 30.57° N. Lat.; 85.12° W. Long. Elevation is 209 feet.

History: Altha grew as a farming community with a cotton gin and gristmill. Corn, rice, pecans, and Satsuma oranges were grown in the area.

Population: 497 (1990); 506 (2000); 453 (2004); 421 (2009 projected); Race: 96.2% White, 0.2% Black, 0.2% Asian, 6.4% Hispanic of any race (2004); Density: 317.6 persons per square mile (2004); Average household size: 2.46 (2004); Median age: 38.3 (2004); Male/female ratio: 91.1 (2004); Marriage status: 26.5% never married, 48.6% now married, 10.6% widowed, 14.3% divorced (2000); Foreign born: 4.1% (2000); Ancestry (includes multiple ancestries): 39.7% United States or American, 12.9% Irish, 12.9% Other groups, 12.0% German, 4.5% English (2000).

Economy: Employment by occupation: 6.9% management, 12.2% professional, 21.6% services, 24.5% sales, 4.1% farming, 20.8% construction, 9.8% production (2000).

Income: Per capita income: $16,082 (2004); Median household income: $32,586 (2004); Average household income: $39,592 (2004); Percent of households with income of $100,000 or more: 5.4% (2004); Poverty rate: 17.3% (2000).

Education: Percent of population age 25 and over with: High school diploma (including GED) or higher: 70.7% (2004); Bachelor's degree or higher: 7.8% (2004); Master's degree or higher: 2.7% (2004).

School District(s)

Calhoun County School District (PK-12)
2002-03 Enrollment: 2,174 . . . . (850) 674-5927

Housing: Homeownership rate: 67.4% (2004); Median home value: $60,224 (2004); Median rent: $255 per month (2000); Median age of housing: 27 years (2000).

Safety: Violent crime rate: 39.2 per 10,000 population; Property crime rate: 19.6 per 10,000 population (2003).

Transportation: Commute to work: 89.2% car, 0.8% public transportation, 4.2% walk, 4.6% work from home (2000); Travel time to work: 25.8% less than 15 minutes, 39.3% 15 to 30 minutes, 13.5% 30 to 45 minutes, 10.9% 45 to 60 minutes, 10.5% 60 minutes or more (2000)

BLOUNTSTOWN (city). Covers a land area of 3.186 square miles and a water area of 0.009 square miles. Located at 30.44° N. Lat.; 85.04° W. Long. Elevation is 69 feet.

History: Blountstown was founded in 1823 and named for Seminole chief John Blount. Incorporated in 1925, the town developed as a lumber center along the Apalachicola River.

Population: 2,541 (1990); 2,444 (2000); 2,272 (2004); 2,146 (2009 projected); Race: 71.8% White, 25.3% Black, 0.3% Asian, 0.5% Hispanic of any race (2004); Density: 713.2 persons per square mile (2004); Average household size: 2.73 (2004); Median age: 46.1 (2004); Male/female ratio: 69.9 (2004); Marriage status: 25.1% never married, 50.4% now married, 14.0% widowed, 10.5% divorced (2000); Foreign born: 2.1% (2000); Ancestry (includes multiple ancestries): 33.0% Other groups, 18.2% United States or American, 6.3% English, 4.0% Irish, 3.6% German (2000).

Economy: Single-family building permits issued: 3 (2004); Multi-family building permits issued: 0 (2004); Employment by occupation: 10.3% management, 18.1% professional, 25.6% services, 25.3% sales, 2.7% farming, 8.4% construction, 9.7% production (2000).

Income: Per capita income: $12,221 (2004); Median household income: $23,017 (2004); Average household income: $31,645 (2004); Percent of households with income of $100,000 or more: 3.2% (2004); Poverty rate: 24.3% (2000).

Taxes: Total city taxes per capita: $228 (2002); City property taxes per capita: $26 (2002).

Education: Percent of population age 25 and over with: High school diploma (including GED) or higher: 70.1% (2004); Bachelor's degree or higher: 11.6% (2004); Master's degree or higher: 5.9% (2004).

School District(s)

Calhoun County School District (PK-12)
2002-03 Enrollment: 2,174 . . . . (850) 674-5927

Housing: Homeownership rate: 72.7% (2004); Median home value: $89,263 (2004); Median rent: $248 per month (2000); Median age of housing: 32 years (2000).

Hospitals: Calhoun-Liberty Hospital (36 beds)

Safety: Violent crime rate: 20.5 per 10,000 population; Property crime rate: 200.6 per 10,000 population (2003).

Newspapers: County Record (General - Circulation 3,000)

Transportation: Commute to work: 91.6% car, 1.7% public transportation, 5.6% walk, 0.0% work from home (2000); Travel time to work: 46.6% less than 15 minutes, 15.6% 15 to 30 minutes, 15.9% 30 to 45 minutes, 9.3% 45 to 60 minutes, 12.6% 60 minutes or more (2000)

Additional Information Contacts

Calhoun Chamber of Commerce . . . . (850) 674-4519

CLARKSVILLE (unincorporated postal area, zip code 32430). Covers a land area of 95.111 square miles and a water area of 0 square miles. Located at 30.43° N. Lat.; 85.24° W. Long. Elevation is 112 feet.

Population: 1,037 (2000); Race: 98.2% White, 0.0% Black, 0.0% Asian, 0.0% Hispanic of any race (2000); Density: 10.9 persons per square mile (2000); Age: 20.3% under 18, 18.6% over 64 (2000); Marriage status: 13.3% never married, 62.2% now married, 9.6% widowed, 15.0% divorced (2000); Foreign born: 0.9% (2000); Ancestry (includes multiple ancestries): 26.6% United States or American, 15.5% Other groups, 9.3% Irish, 6.5% German, 5.3% English (2000).

Economy: Employment by occupation: 8.6% management, 13.0% professional, 21.1% services, 20.4% sales, 2.5% farming, 27.1% construction, 7.4% production (2000).
Income: Per capita income: $17,622 (2000); Median household income: $32,670 (2000); Poverty rate: 5.3% (2000).
Education: Percent of population age 25 and over with: High school diploma (including GED) or higher: 83.4% (2000); Bachelor's degree or higher: 4.8% (2000).

School District(s)

Calhoun County School District (PK-12)
2002-03 Enrollment: 2,174 . . . . (850) 674-5927
Housing: Homeownership rate: 90.4% (2000); Median home value: $56,700 (2000); Median rent: $225 per month (2000); Median age of housing: 19 years (2000).
Transportation: Commute to work: 91.7% car, 0.0% public transportation, 0.0% walk, 6.8% work from home (2000); Travel time to work: 12.5% less than 15 minutes, 46.4% 15 to 30 minutes, 28.1% 30 to 45 minutes, 3.1% 45 to 60 minutes, 9.9% 60 minutes or more (2000)

KINARD (unincorporated postal area, zip code 32449). Covers a land area of 58.177 square miles and a water area of 1.345 square miles. Located at 30.28° N. Lat.; 85.21° W. Long. Elevation is 75 feet.
Population: 562 (2000); Race: 85.6% White, 0.0% Black, 0.0% Asian, 0.0% Hispanic of any race (2000); Density: 9.7 persons per square mile (2000); Age: 19.3% under 18, 19.7% over 64 (2000); Marriage status: 8.7% never married, 73.9% now married, 8.7% widowed, 8.7% divorced (2000); Foreign born: 0.0% (2000); Ancestry (includes multiple ancestries): 40.5% United States or American, 12.2% Other groups, 5.4% English, 4.2% German, 3.3% Irish (2000).
Economy: Employment by occupation: 10.4% management, 13.2% professional, 22.6% services, 23.1% sales, 9.0% farming, 14.2% construction, 7.5% production (2000).
Income: Per capita income: $10,731 (2000); Median household income: $20,787 (2000); Poverty rate: 24.0% (2000).
Education: Percent of population age 25 and over with: High school diploma (including GED) or higher: 57.7% (2000); Bachelor's degree or higher: 4.6% (2000).
Housing: Homeownership rate: 84.1% (2000); Median home value: $42,400 (2000); Median rent: $300 per month (2000); Median age of housing: 25 years (2000).
Transportation: Commute to work: 90.0% car, 0.0% public transportation, 3.0% walk, 7.0% work from home (2000); Travel time to work: 30.5% less than 15 minutes, 25.7% 15 to 30 minutes, 16.6% 30 to 45 minutes, 17.1% 45 to 60 minutes, 10.2% 60 minutes or more (2000)

Charlotte County

Located in southern Florida, on the Gulf of Mexico. Covers a land area of 693.60 square miles, a water area of 165.50 square miles, and is located in the Eastern Time Zone. The county government was organized in 1921. County seat is Punta Gorda.

Charlotte County is part of the Punta Gorda, FL Metropolitan Statistical Area. The entire metro area includes: Charlotte County, FL

Weather Station: Punta Gorda 4 ESE Elevation: 19 feet

	Jan	Feb	Mar	Apr	May	Jun	Jul	Aug	Sep	Oct	Nov	Dec
High	74	76	80	84	89	91	92	92	91	86	81	76
Low	52	53	57	60	66	71	73	73	72	66	60	54
Precip	2.3	2.4	3.0	1.7	3.4	8.5	7.7	7.8	6.6	3.1	1.9	1.8
Snow	0.0	0.0	0.0	0.0	0.0	0.0	0.0	0.0	0.0	0.0	0.0	0.0

High and Low temperatures in degrees Fahrenheit; Precipitation and Snow in inches

Population: 110,975 (1990); 141,627 (2000); 154,137 (2004); 169,894 (2009 projected); Race: 92.0% White, 4.9% Black, 1.1% Asian, 3.7% Hispanic of any race (2004); Density: 222.2 persons per square mile (2004); Average household size: 2.20 (2004); Median age: 53.9 (2004); Male/female ratio: 91.6 (2004).
Religion: Five largest groups: 18.4% Catholic Church, 3.0% The United Methodist Church, 2.4% Southern Baptist Convention, 1.8% Jewish Estimate, 1.4% Presbyterian Church (U.S.A.) (2000).
Economy: Unemployment rate: 5.1% (2004); Total civilian labor force: 54,830 (2004); Leading industries: 24.7% health care and social assistance; 23.9% retail trade; 11.2% accommodation & food services (2003); Companies that employ 500 or more persons: 4 (2003); Companies that employ 100 to 499 persons: 41 (2003); Companies that employ less than 100 persons: 3,387 (2003); Farms: 284 totaling 191,529 acres (2002); Minority business ownership rate: 9.5% (1997); Women business ownership rate: 27.9% (1997); Retail sales per capita: $8,035 (1997). Single-family building permits issued: 2,331 (2004); Multi-family building permits issued: 1,321 (2004).
Income: Per capita income: $24,332 (2004); Median household income: $40,395 (2004); Average household income: $53,105 (2004); Percent of households with income of $100,000 or more: 9.5% (2004); Poverty rate: 10.1% (2002); Bankruptcy rate: 3.82% (2004).
Taxes: Total county taxes per capita: $690 (2002); County property taxes per capita: $336 (2002).
Education: Percent of population age 25 and over with: High school diploma (including GED) or higher: 82.5% (2004); Bachelor's degree or higher: 18.0% (2004); Master's degree or higher: 6.8% (2004).
Housing: Homeownership rate: 84.1% (2004); Median home value: $127,237 (2004); Median rent: $520 per month (2000); Median age of housing: 17 years (2000).
Health: Birth rate: 68.2 per 10,000 population (2004); Death rate: 148.7 per 10,000 population (2004); Age adjusted cancer mortality rate: 172.6 deaths per 100,000 population (2002); Number of physicians: 23.3 per 10,000 population (2001); Hospital beds: 48.6 per 10,000 population (2002); Hospital admissions: 1,868.3 per 10,000 population (2002).
Elections: 2004 Presidential election results: 55.7% Bush, 42.9% Kerry, 0.7% Nader, 0.2% Badnarik
National and State Parks: Don Pedro Island State Park; Island Bay National Wildlife Refuge; Port Charlotte Beach State Park; Stump Pass Beach State Park

Additional Information Contacts

Charlotte County Government Offices . . . . (941) 743-1200
Economic Development Council . . . . (941) 627-3023
Port Charlotte Chamber of Commerce . . . . (941) 627-2222
Punta Gorda Chamber of Commerce . . . . (941) 639-2222
Punta Gorda-Port Charlotte-North Port Assn. of Realtors . . (941) 629-8261
Southwest Florida Tourist Info . . . . (941) 639-0007

Charlotte County Communities

CHARLOTTE HARBOR (CDP). Covers a land area of 2.181 square miles and a water area of 0.038 square miles. Located at 26.96° N. Lat.; 82.06° W. Long. Elevation is 4 feet.
History: Charlotte Harbor was established as a fishing village at the mouth of the Peace River. The name probably refers to the Calusa tribe which formerly inhabited this area.
Population: 3,061 (1990); 3,647 (2000); 3,756 (2004); 3,936 (2009 projected); Race: 92.3% White, 3.8% Black, 1.7% Asian, 3.8% Hispanic of any race (2004); Density: 1,721.8 persons per square mile (2004); Average household size: 2.02 (2004); Median age: 69.9 (2004); Male/female ratio: 74.7 (2004); Marriage status: 11.3% never married, 51.9% now married, 29.0% widowed, 7.7% divorced (2000); Foreign born: 4.9% (2000); Ancestry (includes multiple ancestries): 15.9% English, 14.3% German, 11.9% Irish, 10.9% United States or American, 8.9% Other groups (2000).
Economy: Employment by occupation: 1.3% management, 24.2% professional, 20.9% services, 32.8% sales, 1.3% farming, 11.9% construction, 7.6% production (2000).
Income: Per capita income: $25,573 (2004); Median household income: $31,131 (2004); Average household income: $45,848 (2004); Percent of households with income of $100,000 or more: 5.3% (2004); Poverty rate: 10.3% (2000).
Education: Percent of population age 25 and over with: High school diploma (including GED) or higher: 73.1% (2004); Bachelor's degree or higher: 15.5% (2004); Master's degree or higher: 6.2% (2004).

School District(s)

Charlotte County School District (PK-12)
2002-03 Enrollment: 17,714 . . . . (941) 255-0808
Housing: Homeownership rate: 63.8% (2004); Median home value: $82,980 (2004); Median rent: $626 per month (2000); Median age of housing: 20 years (2000).
Transportation: Commute to work: 95.2% car, 0.0% public transportation, 2.4% walk, 0.9% work from home (2000); Travel time to work: 42.6% less than 15 minutes, 31.9% 15 to 30 minutes, 14.2% 30 to 45 minutes, 6.5% 45 to 60 minutes, 4.7% 60 minutes or more (2000)

CHARLOTTE PARK (CDP). Covers a land area of 1.211 square miles and a water area of 0.155 square miles. Located at 26.90° N. Lat.; 82.04° W. Long. Elevation is 4 feet.

Population: 2,101 (1990); 2,182 (2000); 2,457 (2004); 2,799 (2009 projected); Race: 98.2% White, 0.2% Black, 0.2% Asian, 2.2% Hispanic of any race (2004); Density: 2,028.6 persons per square mile (2004); Average household size: 1.87 (2004); Median age: 64.4 (2004); Male/female ratio: 96.9 (2004); Marriage status: 10.2% never married, 64.9% now married, 12.0% widowed, 12.9% divorced (2000); Foreign born: 4.9% (2000); Ancestry (includes multiple ancestries): 26.3% German, 19.1% English, 18.9% Irish, 5.2% Other groups, 5.2% Italian (2000).
Economy: Employment by occupation: 5.7% management, 20.6% professional, 17.9% services, 29.0% sales, 1.2% farming, 13.5% construction, 12.0% production (2000).
Income: Per capita income: $23,533 (2004); Median household income: $32,106 (2004); Average household income: $43,970 (2004); Percent of households with income of $100,000 or more: 5.8% (2004); Poverty rate: 6.8% (2000).
Education: Percent of population age 25 and over with: High school diploma (including GED) or higher: 81.3% (2004); Bachelor's degree or higher: 16.1% (2004); Master's degree or higher: 3.6% (2004).
Housing: Homeownership rate: 90.7% (2004); Median home value: $107,151 (2004); Median rent: $533 per month (2000); Median age of housing: 23 years (2000).
Transportation: Commute to work: 88.7% car, 0.0% public transportation, 0.0% walk, 8.1% work from home (2000); Travel time to work: 53.5% less than 15 minutes, 22.7% 15 to 30 minutes, 4.4% 30 to 45 minutes, 6.9% 45 to 60 minutes, 12.6% 60 minutes or more (2000)

CLEVELAND (CDP). Covers a land area of 5.496 square miles and a water area of 0.050 square miles. Located at 26.95° N. Lat.; 81.99° W. Long. Elevation is 7 feet.
Population: 2,896 (1990); 3,268 (2000); 3,464 (2004); 3,721 (2009 projected); Race: 97.8% White, 0.5% Black, 0.2% Asian, 1.6% Hispanic of any race (2004); Density: 630.3 persons per square mile (2004); Average household size: 2.07 (2004); Median age: 53.1 (2004); Male/female ratio: 100.2 (2004); Marriage status: 15.3% never married, 60.0% now married, 13.2% widowed, 11.5% divorced (2000); Foreign born: 4.4% (2000); Ancestry (includes multiple ancestries): 22.4% German, 21.6% English, 11.1% Irish, 9.8% United States or American, 5.2% Italian (2000).
Economy: Employment by occupation: 9.2% management, 11.5% professional, 23.5% services, 29.7% sales, 0.5% farming, 11.8% construction, 13.9% production (2000).
Income: Per capita income: $24,664 (2004); Median household income: $35,237 (2004); Average household income: $51,130 (2004); Percent of households with income of $100,000 or more: 7.6% (2004); Poverty rate: 8.4% (2000).
Education: Percent of population age 25 and over with: High school diploma (including GED) or higher: 82.4% (2004); Bachelor's degree or higher: 15.7% (2004); Master's degree or higher: 5.9% (2004).
Housing: Homeownership rate: 83.1% (2004); Median home value: $77,361 (2004); Median rent: $439 per month (2000); Median age of housing: 23 years (2000).
Transportation: Commute to work: 95.3% car, 0.8% public transportation, 0.0% walk, 1.9% work from home (2000); Travel time to work: 31.3% less than 15 minutes, 35.0% 15 to 30 minutes, 17.0% 30 to 45 minutes, 9.6% 45 to 60 minutes, 7.2% 60 minutes or more (2000)

GROVE CITY (CDP). Covers a land area of 1.270 square miles and a water area of 0.057 square miles. Located at 26.91° N. Lat.; 82.32° W. Long. Elevation is 12 feet.
Population: 2,057 (1990); 2,092 (2000); 2,140 (2004); 2,217 (2009 projected); Race: 97.3% White, 0.6% Black, 1.1% Asian, 0.8% Hispanic of any race (2004); Density: 1,685.4 persons per square mile (2004); Average household size: 1.98 (2004); Median age: 56.8 (2004); Male/female ratio: 100.4 (2004); Marriage status: 9.6% never married, 63.0% now married, 11.0% widowed, 16.4% divorced (2000); Foreign born: 4.5% (2000); Ancestry (includes multiple ancestries): 19.1% German, 17.0% English, 14.0% United States or American, 12.9% Irish, 5.7% Polish (2000).
Economy: Manufacturing: commercial printing. Employment by occupation: 6.1% management, 15.1% professional, 28.1% services, 25.3% sales, 0.0% farming, 16.2% construction, 9.1% production (2000).
Income: Per capita income: $23,924 (2004); Median household income: $36,866 (2004); Average household income: $47,361 (2004); Percent of households with income of $100,000 or more: 8.9% (2004); Poverty rate: 9.6% (2000).
Education: Percent of population age 25 and over with: High school diploma (including GED) or higher: 79.4% (2004); Bachelor's degree or higher: 12.5% (2004); Master's degree or higher: 5.1% (2004).
Housing: Homeownership rate: 82.4% (2004); Median home value: $91,709 (2004); Median rent: $490 per month (2000); Median age of housing: 25 years (2000).
Transportation: Commute to work: 93.0% car, 1.2% public transportation, 0.8% walk, 4.6% work from home (2000); Travel time to work: 39.0% less than 15 minutes, 26.1% 15 to 30 minutes, 17.9% 30 to 45 minutes, 12.1% 45 to 60 minutes, 4.8% 60 minutes or more (2000)

HARBOUR HEIGHTS (CDP). Covers a land area of 2.196 square miles and a water area of 0.014 square miles. Located at 26.99° N. Lat.; 82.00° W. Long. Elevation is 10 feet.
Population: 2,498 (1990); 2,873 (2000); 2,995 (2004); 3,131 (2009 projected); Race: 93.0% White, 3.5% Black, 0.9% Asian, 4.6% Hispanic of any race (2004); Density: 1,363.8 persons per square mile (2004); Average household size: 2.29 (2004); Median age: 49.6 (2004); Male/female ratio: 87.8 (2004); Marriage status: 14.8% never married, 70.6% now married, 7.4% widowed, 7.2% divorced (2000); Foreign born: 7.9% (2000); Ancestry (includes multiple ancestries): 19.5% German, 13.4% Italian, 10.8% Irish, 10.0% United States or American, 9.8% English (2000).
Economy: Employment by occupation: 12.9% management, 19.2% professional, 12.8% services, 34.6% sales, 0.0% farming, 12.4% construction, 8.1% production (2000).
Income: Per capita income: $25,822 (2004); Median household income: $48,828 (2004); Average household income: $59,036 (2004); Percent of households with income of $100,000 or more: 13.2% (2004); Poverty rate: 2.7% (2000).
Education: Percent of population age 25 and over with: High school diploma (including GED) or higher: 85.3% (2004); Bachelor's degree or higher: 18.5% (2004); Master's degree or higher: 5.4% (2004).
Housing: Homeownership rate: 85.3% (2004); Median home value: $145,479 (2004); Median rent: $485 per month (2000); Median age of housing: 16 years (2000).
Transportation: Commute to work: 96.3% car, 0.6% public transportation, 0.0% walk, 2.4% work from home (2000); Travel time to work: 32.9% less than 15 minutes, 42.1% 15 to 30 minutes, 10.0% 30 to 45 minutes, 6.9% 45 to 60 minutes, 8.2% 60 minutes or more (2000)

MANASOTA KEY (CDP). Covers a land area of 1.065 square miles and a water area of 1.660 square miles. Located at 26.92° N. Lat.; 82.36° W. Long.
Population: 1,395 (1990); 1,345 (2000); 1,381 (2004); 1,438 (2009 projected); Race: 99.2% White, 0.1% Black, 0.3% Asian, 1.1% Hispanic of any race (2004); Density: 1,297.0 persons per square mile (2004); Average household size: 1.73 (2004); Median age: 66.4 (2004); Male/female ratio: 82.4 (2004); Marriage status: 4.0% never married, 75.0% now married, 13.7% widowed, 7.4% divorced (2000); Foreign born: 7.0% (2000); Ancestry (includes multiple ancestries): 23.5% German, 19.9% English, 13.4% Irish, 10.2% Scottish, 8.3% Polish (2000).
Economy: Employment by occupation: 15.6% management, 27.9% professional, 17.8% services, 19.0% sales, 3.1% farming, 5.5% construction, 11.0% production (2000).
Income: Per capita income: $40,306 (2004); Median household income: $46,729 (2004); Average household income: $69,753 (2004); Percent of households with income of $100,000 or more: 15.9% (2004); Poverty rate: 4.7% (2000).
Education: Percent of population age 25 and over with: High school diploma (including GED) or higher: 93.2% (2004); Bachelor's degree or higher: 35.5% (2004); Master's degree or higher: 16.2% (2004).
Housing: Homeownership rate: 80.6% (2004); Median home value: $229,783 (2004); Median rent: $657 per month (2000); Median age of housing: 18 years (2000).
Transportation: Commute to work: 75.2% car, 0.0% public transportation, 8.0% walk, 13.2% work from home (2000); Travel time to work: 47.3% less than 15 minutes, 29.0% 15 to 30 minutes, 1.8% 30 to 45 minutes, 12.7% 45 to 60 minutes, 9.2% 60 minutes or more (2000)

PLACIDA (unincorporated postal area, zip code 33946). Covers a land area of 3.446 square miles and a water area of 0.019 square miles. Located at 26.84° N. Lat.; 82.28° W. Long. Elevation is 3 feet.
History: Placida was built around an ancient Indian mound, with fishing as the primary occupation.

Population: 1,064 (2000); Race: 99.4% White, 0.0% Black, 0.0% Asian, 0.0% Hispanic of any race (2000); Density: 308.8 persons per square mile (2000); Age: 8.6% under 18, 47.5% over 64 (2000); Marriage status: 3.8% never married, 85.7% now married, 6.2% widowed, 4.3% divorced (2000); Foreign born: 3.8% (2000); Ancestry (includes multiple ancestries): 30.6% German, 24.3% English, 12.1% Irish, 7.2% Scottish, 6.5% Italian (2000).
Economy: Employment by occupation: 24.4% management, 26.3% professional, 3.8% services, 32.7% sales, 0.0% farming, 8.3% construction, 4.5% production (2000).
Income: Per capita income: $43,383 (2000); Median household income: $64,141 (2000); Poverty rate: 4.7% (2000).
Education: Percent of population age 25 and over with: High school diploma (including GED) or higher: 95.3% (2000); Bachelor's degree or higher: 40.6% (2000).
Housing: Homeownership rate: 97.8% (2000); Median home value: $264,300 (2000); Median rent: $225 per month (2000); Median age of housing: 14 years (2000).
Transportation: Commute to work: 66.7% car, 0.0% public transportation, 0.0% walk, 22.0% work from home (2000); Travel time to work: 7.7% less than 15 minutes, 62.4% 15 to 30 minutes, 16.2% 30 to 45 minutes, 13.7% 45 to 60 minutes, 0.0% 60 minutes or more (2000)

PORT CHARLOTTE (CDP). Covers a land area of 22.269 square miles and a water area of 1.590 square miles. Located at 26.99° N. Lat.; 82.10° W. Long. Elevation is 8 feet.
History: Planned residential community— one of several on a peninsula once owned by the Vanderbilt family. The town's population quadrupled between 1970 and 1990.
Population: 41,534 (1990); 46,451 (2000); 47,874 (2004); 50,019 (2009 projected); Race: 87.8% White, 7.8% Black, 1.4% Asian, 6.0% Hispanic of any race (2004); Density: 2,149.8 persons per square mile (2004); Average household size: 2.28 (2004); Median age: 48.1 (2004); Male/female ratio: 88.3 (2004); Marriage status: 15.8% never married, 61.8% now married, 11.8% widowed, 10.5% divorced (2000); Foreign born: 9.6% (2000); Ancestry (includes multiple ancestries): 19.3% German, 15.9% Irish, 12.6% English, 12.4% Other groups, 10.4% Italian (2000).
Economy: An important cultural center and large retired population are here. Employment by occupation: 8.0% management, 17.1% professional, 22.4% services, 29.5% sales, 0.2% farming, 13.1% construction, 9.8% production (2000).
Income: Per capita income: $20,282 (2004); Median household income: $35,979 (2004); Average household income: $45,888 (2004); Percent of households with income of $100,000 or more: 7.1% (2004); Poverty rate: 10.1% (2000).
Education: Percent of population age 25 and over with: High school diploma (including GED) or higher: 79.2% (2004); Bachelor's degree or higher: 14.9% (2004); Master's degree or higher: 6.0% (2004).

School District(s)

Charlotte County School District (PK-12)
2002-03 Enrollment: 17,714 . . . . (941) 255-0808

Two-year College(s)

Charlotte Technical Center (Public)
2003-04 Enrollment: 805 . . . . (941) 255-7500
2003-04 Tuition: In-state $2,040; Out-of-state $2,040

Housing: Homeownership rate: 80.4% (2004); Median home value: $113,480 (2004); Median rent: $535 per month (2000); Median age of housing: 21 years (2000).
Hospitals: Bon Secours St. Joseph Hospital (212 beds); Fawcett Memorial Hospital (238 beds)
Newspapers: Charlotte Sun Herald (Circulation 39,332)
Transportation: Commute to work: 95.0% car, 0.3% public transportation, 0.6% walk, 2.4% work from home (2000); Travel time to work: 42.6% less than 15 minutes, 35.0% 15 to 30 minutes, 10.1% 30 to 45 minutes, 6.7% 45 to 60 minutes, 5.6% 60 minutes or more (2000); Amtrak: Service available.

Additional Information Contacts

Economic Development Council . . . . (941) 627-3023
Port Charlotte Chamber of Commerce . . . . (941) 627-2222
Punta Gorda-Port Charlotte-North Port Assn. of Realtors . . (941) 629-8261

PUNTA GORDA (city). Covers a land area of 14.162 square miles and a water area of 4.314 square miles. Located at 26.91° N. Lat.; 82.04° W. Long. Elevation is 61 feet.
History: The name of Punta Gorda is Spanish for "flat point," referring to its location on the peninsula extending into Charlotte Harbor. The town was first named for Isaac Trabue of Kentucky, who purchased land here in 1880 and built a hotel and pier.
Population: 10,931 (1990); 14,344 (2000); 17,029 (2004); 20,236 (2009 projected); Race: 95.0% White, 2.6% Black, 1.1% Asian, 2.2% Hispanic of any race (2004); Density: 1,202.4 persons per square mile (2004); Average household size: 1.98 (2004); Median age: 63.6 (2004); Male/female ratio: 89.7 (2004); Marriage status: 6.6% never married, 74.8% now married, 10.6% widowed, 8.0% divorced (2000); Foreign born: 7.8% (2000); Ancestry (includes multiple ancestries): 23.7% German, 17.7% English, 16.8% Irish, 8.6% Italian, 6.7% Other groups (2000).
Economy: Single-family building permits issued: 124 (2004); Multi-family building permits issued: 231 (2004); Employment by occupation: 15.4% management, 18.7% professional, 18.3% services, 32.8% sales, 0.0% farming, 6.5% construction, 8.3% production (2000).
Income: Per capita income: $36,820 (2004); Median household income: $53,111 (2004); Average household income: $72,525 (2004); Percent of households with income of $100,000 or more: 17.3% (2004); Poverty rate: 6.5% (2000).
Taxes: Total city taxes per capita: $561 (2002); City property taxes per capita: $262 (2002).
Education: Percent of population age 25 and over with: High school diploma (including GED) or higher: 90.8% (2004); Bachelor's degree or higher: 32.8% (2004); Master's degree or higher: 12.8% (2004).

School District(s)

Charlotte County School District (PK-12)
2002-03 Enrollment: 17,714 . . . . (941) 255-0808

Housing: Homeownership rate: 87.6% (2004); Median home value: $244,613 (2004); Median rent: $481 per month (2000); Median age of housing: 16 years (2000).
Hospitals: Charlotte Regional Medical Center (208 beds)
Safety: Violent crime rate: 18.4 per 10,000 population; Property crime rate: 257.0 per 10,000 population (2003).
Transportation: Commute to work: 86.9% car, 0.0% public transportation, 1.0% walk, 9.2% work from home (2000); Travel time to work: 44.5% less than 15 minutes, 31.6% 15 to 30 minutes, 12.6% 30 to 45 minutes, 6.1% 45 to 60 minutes, 5.2% 60 minutes or more (2000)

Additional Information Contacts

Punta Gorda Chamber of Commerce . . . . (941) 639-2222
Southwest Florida Tourist Info . . . . (941) 639-0007

ROTONDA (CDP). Covers a land area of 11.005 square miles and a water area of 0.179 square miles. Located at 26.88° N. Lat.; 82.27° W. Long. Elevation is 5 feet.
Population: 3,576 (1990); 6,574 (2000); 7,718 (2004); 9,070 (2009 projected); Race: 98.1% White, 0.6% Black, 0.4% Asian, 1.5% Hispanic of any race (2004); Density: 701.3 persons per square mile (2004); Average household size: 2.05 (2004); Median age: 62.1 (2004); Male/female ratio: 89.4 (2004); Marriage status: 7.3% never married, 74.5% now married, 10.1% widowed, 8.1% divorced (2000); Foreign born: 9.2% (2000); Ancestry (includes multiple ancestries): 22.0% German, 17.0% Irish, 13.6% English, 11.9% Italian, 6.0% French (except Basque) (2000).
Economy: Employment by occupation: 10.2% management, 20.3% professional, 23.8% services, 31.8% sales, 0.8% farming, 6.6% construction, 6.4% production (2000).
Income: Per capita income: $23,715 (2004); Median household income: $40,095 (2004); Average household income: $48,447 (2004); Percent of households with income of $100,000 or more: 7.4% (2004); Poverty rate: 4.0% (2000).
Education: Percent of population age 25 and over with: High school diploma (including GED) or higher: 87.5% (2004); Bachelor's degree or higher: 22.3% (2004); Master's degree or higher: 7.3% (2004).
Housing: Homeownership rate: 82.9% (2004); Median home value: $151,473 (2004); Median rent: $495 per month (2000); Median age of housing: 12 years (2000).
Transportation: Commute to work: 93.2% car, 0.0% public transportation, 0.8% walk, 5.9% work from home (2000); Travel time to work: 22.5% less than 15 minutes, 41.2% 15 to 30 minutes, 20.0% 30 to 45 minutes, 10.3% 45 to 60 minutes, 6.0% 60 minutes or more (2000)

ROTONDA WEST (unincorporated postal area, zip code 33947). Covers a land area of 14.442 square miles and a water area of 0.015 square miles. Located at 26.88° N. Lat.; 82.26° W. Long.
Population: 5,238 (2000); Race: 96.6% White, 0.4% Black, 0.3% Asian, 2.1% Hispanic of any race (2000); Density: 362.7 persons per square mile (2000); Age: 13.9% under 18, 40.9% over 64 (2000); Marriage status: 9.0%

never married, 75.2% now married, 7.8% widowed, 8.0% divorced (2000); Foreign born: 8.5% (2000); Ancestry (includes multiple ancestries): 21.3% German, 18.0% Irish, 12.4% Italian, 12.2% English, 6.9% United States or American (2000).
Economy: Employment by occupation: 8.5% management, 20.7% professional, 27.0% services, 32.5% sales, 1.0% farming, 5.5% construction, 5.0% production (2000).
Income: Per capita income: $20,777 (2000); Median household income: $40,967 (2000); Poverty rate: 3.0% (2000).
Education: Percent of population age 25 and over with: High school diploma (including GED) or higher: 87.8% (2000); Bachelor's degree or higher: 21.7% (2000).

School District(s)

Charlotte County School District (PK-12)
2002-03 Enrollment: 17,714 . . . . (941) 255-0808
Housing: Homeownership rate: 88.9% (2000); Median home value: $112,600 (2000); Median rent: $568 per month (2000); Median age of housing: 12 years (2000).
Transportation: Commute to work: 95.4% car, 0.0% public transportation, 0.9% walk, 3.6% work from home (2000); Travel time to work: 22.5% less than 15 minutes, 41.0% 15 to 30 minutes, 21.3% 30 to 45 minutes, 9.6% 45 to 60 minutes, 5.6% 60 minutes or more (2000)

SOLANA (CDP). Covers a land area of 1.713 square miles and a water area of 0.058 square miles. Located at 26.94° N. Lat.; 82.02° W. Long. Elevation is 3 feet.
Population: 1,046 (1990); 1,011 (2000); 1,002 (2004); 1,004 (2009 projected); Race: 92.0% White, 5.3% Black, 1.4% Asian, 2.4% Hispanic of any race (2004); Density: 585.1 persons per square mile (2004); Average household size: 2.17 (2004); Median age: 42.9 (2004); Male/female ratio: 100.8 (2004); Marriage status: 25.0% never married, 43.5% now married, 12.2% widowed, 19.4% divorced (2000); Foreign born: 2.0% (2000); Ancestry (includes multiple ancestries): 22.8% German, 17.9% United States or American, 16.9% Irish, 10.3% Italian, 9.6% English (2000).
Economy: Employment by occupation: 5.2% management, 10.7% professional, 24.7% services, 24.9% sales, 0.0% farming, 22.5% construction, 12.0% production (2000).
Income: Per capita income: $16,370 (2004); Median household income: $24,434 (2004); Average household income: $35,503 (2004); Percent of households with income of $100,000 or more: 4.5% (2004); Poverty rate: 19.7% (2000).
Education: Percent of population age 25 and over with: High school diploma (including GED) or higher: 72.6% (2004); Bachelor's degree or higher: 12.0% (2004); Master's degree or higher: 2.2% (2004).
Housing: Homeownership rate: 63.0% (2004); Median home value: $71,519 (2004); Median rent: $418 per month (2000); Median age of housing: 29 years (2000).
Transportation: Commute to work: 83.6% car, 0.0% public transportation, 2.5% walk, 5.1% work from home (2000); Travel time to work: 35.9% less than 15 minutes, 38.3% 15 to 30 minutes, 14.8% 30 to 45 minutes, 5.6% 45 to 60 minutes, 5.3% 60 minutes or more (2000)

Citrus County

Located in central Florida; bounded on the west by the Gulf of Mexico, and on the north and east by the Withlacoochee River; includes a swampy coast and the Homosassa Islands. Covers a land area of 583.80 square miles, a water area of 189.30 square miles, and is located in the Eastern Time Zone. The county government was organized in 1887. County seat is Inverness.

Citrus County is part of the Homosassa Springs, FL Micropolitan Statistical Area. The entire metro area includes: Citrus County, FL

Weather Station: Inverness 3 SE — Elevation: 39 feet

	Jan	Feb	Mar	Apr	May	Jun	Jul	Aug	Sep	Oct	Nov	Dec
High	70	72	77	82	88	91	92	91	90	84	77	72
Low	44	46	51	56	63	70	71	72	70	62	53	47
Precip	3.6	3.1	4.3	2.4	3.5	7.3	6.9	7.8	5.9	2.7	2.3	2.6
Snow	0.0	0.0	0.0	0.0	0.0	0.0	0.0	0.0	0.0	0.0	0.0	0.0

High and Low temperatures in degrees Fahrenheit; Precipitation and Snow in inches

Population: 93,515 (1990); 118,085 (2000); 127,430 (2004); 139,209 (2009 projected); Race: 94.7% White, 2.6% Black, 1.0% Asian, 3.0% Hispanic of any race (2004); Density: 218.3 persons per square mile (2004); Average household size: 2.23 (2004); Median age: 52.1 (2004); Male/female ratio: 92.3 (2004).
Religion: Five largest groups: 14.5% Catholic Church, 5.6% Southern Baptist Convention, 3.5% The United Methodist Church, 1.6% Church of God (Cleveland, Tennessee), 1.3% Presbyterian Church in America (2000).
Economy: Unemployment rate: 5.1% (2004); Total civilian labor force: 42,428 (2004); Leading industries: 23.8% health care and social assistance; 21.4% retail trade; 9.3% accommodation & food services (2003); Companies that employ 500 or more persons: 4 (2003); Companies that employ 100 to 499 persons: 36 (2003); Companies that employ less than 100 persons: 2,476 (2003); Farms: 432 totaling 47,209 acres (2002); Minority business ownership rate: 4.1% (1997); Women business ownership rate: 24.8% (1997); Retail sales per capita: $7,191 (1997). Single-family building permits issued: 2,527 (2004); Multi-family building permits issued: 4 (2004).
Income: Per capita income: $20,619 (2004); Median household income: $33,977 (2004); Average household income: $45,439 (2004); Percent of households with income of $100,000 or more: 7.1% (2004); Poverty rate: 13.3% (2002); Bankruptcy rate: 4.94% (2004).
Taxes: Total county taxes per capita: $384 (2002); County property taxes per capita: $333 (2002).
Education: Percent of population age 25 and over with: High school diploma (including GED) or higher: 78.5% (2004); Bachelor's degree or higher: 13.3% (2004); Master's degree or higher: 5.0% (2004).
Housing: Homeownership rate: 85.9% (2004); Median home value: $95,270 (2004); Median rent: $388 per month (2000); Median age of housing: 16 years (2000).
Health: Birth rate: 68.7 per 10,000 population (2004); Death rate: 163.5 per 10,000 population (2004); Age adjusted cancer mortality rate: 205.9 deaths per 100,000 population (2002); Air Quality Index: 92.9% good, 6.3% moderate, 0.9% unhealthy for sensitive individuals, 0.0% unhealthy (percent of days in 2004); Number of physicians: 19.5 per 10,000 population (2001); Hospital beds: 24.2 per 10,000 population (2002); Hospital admissions: 1,335.9 per 10,000 population (2002).
Elections: 2004 Presidential election results: 56.9% Bush, 42.1% Kerry, 0.7% Nader, 0.2% Badnarik
National and State Parks: Crystal River State Archaeological Site; Fort Cooper State Park; Homosassa Springs Wildlife State Park; Withlacoochee Trail State Park; Yulee Sugar Mill Ruins Historic State Park
Additional Information Contacts
Citrus County Government Offices . . . . (352) 637-9400
Citrus County Chamber of Commerce . . . . (352) 726-2801
Crystal River Chamber of Commerce . . . . (352) 795-3149
Homosassa Chamber of Commerce . . . . (352) 628-2666
Nature Coast Visitors Guide . . . . (352) 344-1184
Realtors Association of Citrus County . . . . (352) 746-7550

Citrus County Communities

BEVERLY HILLS (CDP). Covers a land area of 2.846 square miles and a water area of 0 square miles. Located at 28.91° N. Lat.; 82.45° W. Long. Elevation is 100 feet.
Population: 7,015 (1990); 8,317 (2000); 8,543 (2004); 8,888 (2009 projected); Race: 95.3% White, 2.2% Black, 0.7% Asian, 4.8% Hispanic of any race (2004); Density: 3,001.4 persons per square mile (2004); Average household size: 1.91 (2004); Median age: 66.8 (2004); Male/female ratio: 81.3 (2004); Marriage status: 9.1% never married, 63.0% now married, 18.4% widowed, 9.5% divorced (2000); Foreign born: 9.2% (2000); Ancestry (includes multiple ancestries): 19.8% German, 16.5% Irish, 13.8% English, 12.5% Italian, 8.3% Other groups (2000).
Economy: Employment by occupation: 3.4% management, 11.3% professional, 33.9% services, 24.8% sales, 0.7% farming, 11.4% construction, 14.4% production (2000).
Income: Per capita income: $17,246 (2004); Median household income: $26,805 (2004); Average household income: $32,796 (2004); Percent of households with income of $100,000 or more: 2.1% (2004); Poverty rate: 12.4% (2000).
Education: Percent of population age 25 and over with: High school diploma (including GED) or higher: 77.2% (2004); Bachelor's degree or higher: 11.1% (2004); Master's degree or higher: 4.5% (2004).
Housing: Homeownership rate: 87.4% (2004); Median home value: $73,042 (2004); Median rent: $453 per month (2000); Median age of housing: 20 years (2000).
Newspapers: Beverly Hills Visitor (General - Circulation 10,600)

Transportation: Commute to work: 94.5% car, 0.3% public transportation, 2.3% walk, 1.8% work from home (2000); Travel time to work: 33.7% less than 15 minutes, 35.9% 15 to 30 minutes, 20.4% 30 to 45 minutes, 2.4% 45 to 60 minutes, 7.6% 60 minutes or more (2000)

BLACK DIAMOND (CDP). Covers a land area of 3.780 square miles and a water area of 0 square miles. Located at 28.91° N. Lat.; 82.49° W. Long.
Population: 309 (1990); 694 (2000); 811 (2004); 946 (2009 projected); Race: 92.5% White, 0.5% Black, 6.7% Asian, 0.7% Hispanic of any race (2004); Density: 214.6 persons per square mile (2004); Average household size: 2.81 (2004); Median age: 63.2 (2004); Male/female ratio: 78.2 (2004); Marriage status: 6.0% never married, 69.7% now married, 22.6% widowed, 1.8% divorced (2000); Foreign born: 16.0% (2000); Ancestry (includes multiple ancestries): 17.8% Other groups, 15.8% English, 9.4% Irish, 7.2% Italian, 6.9% German (2000).
Economy: Employment by occupation: 12.1% management, 57.8% professional, 6.0% services, 24.1% sales, 0.0% farming, 0.0% construction, 0.0% production (2000).
Income: Per capita income: $60,784 (2004); Median household income: $120,890 (2004); Average household income: $161,220 (2004); Percent of households with income of $100,000 or more: 60.6% (2004); Poverty rate: 3.7% (2000).
Education: Percent of population age 25 and over with: High school diploma (including GED) or higher: 83.6% (2004); Bachelor's degree or higher: 37.1% (2004); Master's degree or higher: 13.3% (2004).
Housing: Homeownership rate: 97.2% (2004); Median home value: $342,742 (2004); Median rent: $n/a per month (2000); Median age of housing: 4 years (2000).
Transportation: Commute to work: 87.1% car, 0.0% public transportation, 0.0% walk, 12.9% work from home (2000); Travel time to work: 26.7% less than 15 minutes, 73.3% 15 to 30 minutes, 0.0% 30 to 45 minutes, 0.0% 45 to 60 minutes, 0.0% 60 minutes or more (2000)

CITRUS HILLS (CDP). Covers a land area of 9.798 square miles and a water area of 0 square miles. Located at 28.88° N. Lat.; 82.42° W. Long.
Population: 2,291 (1990); 4,029 (2000); 4,634 (2004); 5,378 (2009 projected); Race: 91.3% White, 1.4% Black, 5.6% Asian, 3.6% Hispanic of any race (2004); Density: 473.0 persons per square mile (2004); Average household size: 2.24 (2004); Median age: 58.4 (2004); Male/female ratio: 94.6 (2004); Marriage status: 9.7% never married, 81.1% now married, 5.4% widowed, 3.8% divorced (2000); Foreign born: 11.0% (2000); Ancestry (includes multiple ancestries): 16.9% Irish, 16.8% English, 16.8% German, 12.5% Other groups, 11.6% Italian (2000).
Economy: Employment by occupation: 14.2% management, 30.6% professional, 12.7% services, 26.2% sales, 0.0% farming, 5.7% construction, 10.6% production (2000).
Income: Per capita income: $30,828 (2004); Median household income: $51,418 (2004); Average household income: $69,012 (2004); Percent of households with income of $100,000 or more: 15.7% (2004); Poverty rate: 6.5% (2000).
Education: Percent of population age 25 and over with: High school diploma (including GED) or higher: 89.7% (2004); Bachelor's degree or higher: 27.2% (2004); Master's degree or higher: 9.2% (2004).
Housing: Homeownership rate: 92.0% (2004); Median home value: $177,891 (2004); Median rent: $729 per month (2000); Median age of housing: 9 years (2000).
Transportation: Commute to work: 93.4% car, 0.0% public transportation, 0.0% walk, 5.2% work from home (2000); Travel time to work: 32.5% less than 15 minutes, 44.4% 15 to 30 minutes, 13.8% 30 to 45 minutes, 3.4% 45 to 60 minutes, 5.8% 60 minutes or more (2000)

CITRUS SPRINGS (CDP). Covers a land area of 21.274 square miles and a water area of 0 square miles. Located at 28.99° N. Lat.; 82.46° W. Long. Elevation is 43 feet.
Population: 3,058 (1990); 4,157 (2000); 4,729 (2004); 5,417 (2009 projected); Race: 93.6% White, 1.8% Black, 0.9% Asian, 6.0% Hispanic of any race (2004); Density: 222.3 persons per square mile (2004); Average household size: 2.31 (2004); Median age: 53.1 (2004); Male/female ratio: 88.6 (2004); Marriage status: 12.6% never married, 67.0% now married, 12.2% widowed, 8.2% divorced (2000); Foreign born: 4.9% (2000); Ancestry (includes multiple ancestries): 19.2% German, 14.3% Irish, 13.9% Italian, 11.2% Other groups, 11.1% English (2000).
Economy: Employment by occupation: 9.9% management, 24.4% professional, 16.3% services, 29.7% sales, 0.5% farming, 6.2% construction, 13.0% production (2000).
Income: Per capita income: $18,692 (2004); Median household income: $33,411 (2004); Average household income: $42,917 (2004); Percent of households with income of $100,000 or more: 5.2% (2004); Poverty rate: 7.8% (2000).
Education: Percent of population age 25 and over with: High school diploma (including GED) or higher: 76.7% (2004); Bachelor's degree or higher: 11.2% (2004); Master's degree or higher: 5.1% (2004).

School District(s)

Citrus County School District (PK-12)
2002-03 Enrollment: 15,355 . . . . (352) 726-1931
Housing: Homeownership rate: 90.6% (2004); Median home value: $99,568 (2004); Median rent: $437 per month (2000); Median age of housing: 16 years (2000).
Transportation: Commute to work: 93.9% car, 1.2% public transportation, 0.0% walk, 3.5% work from home (2000); Travel time to work: 20.6% less than 15 minutes, 43.4% 15 to 30 minutes, 20.9% 30 to 45 minutes, 6.7% 45 to 60 minutes, 8.4% 60 minutes or more (2000)

CRYSTAL RIVER (city). Covers a land area of 5.696 square miles and a water area of 0.574 square miles. Located at 28.90° N. Lat.; 82.59° W. Long. Elevation is 4 feet.
History: The town of Crystal River grew as a fish, oyster, and lumber center. It was established in an area of springs, some of them crystal clear.
Population: 4,069 (1990); 3,485 (2000); 3,605 (2004); 3,787 (2009 projected); Race: 84.0% White, 12.4% Black, 1.6% Asian, 3.6% Hispanic of any race (2004); Density: 632.8 persons per square mile (2004); Average household size: 2.31 (2004); Median age: 49.4 (2004); Male/female ratio: 92.0 (2004); Marriage status: 19.5% never married, 56.4% now married, 10.0% widowed, 14.2% divorced (2000); Foreign born: 3.1% (2000); Ancestry (includes multiple ancestries): 20.1% Other groups, 16.2% English, 15.2% Irish, 12.7% German, 6.4% Italian (2000).
Economy: Single-family building permits issued: 11 (2004); Multi-family building permits issued: 2 (2004); Employment by occupation: 8.4% management, 25.9% professional, 14.5% services, 27.1% sales, 1.2% farming, 9.9% construction, 12.9% production (2000).
Income: Per capita income: $28,404 (2004); Median household income: $40,271 (2004); Average household income: $62,800 (2004); Percent of households with income of $100,000 or more: 16.7% (2004); Poverty rate: 9.9% (2000).
Taxes: Total city taxes per capita: $878 (2002); City property taxes per capita: $507 (2002).
Education: Percent of population age 25 and over with: High school diploma (including GED) or higher: 80.6% (2004); Bachelor's degree or higher: 24.0% (2004); Master's degree or higher: 9.0% (2004).

School District(s)

Citrus County School District (PK-12)
2002-03 Enrollment: 15,355 . . . . (352) 726-1931
Housing: Homeownership rate: 70.5% (2004); Median home value: $103,534 (2004); Median rent: $345 per month (2000); Median age of housing: 22 years (2000).
Hospitals: Seven Rivers Community Hospital (128 beds)
Safety: Violent crime rate: 86.1 per 10,000 population; Property crime rate: 1,025.0 per 10,000 population (2003).
Newspapers: Citrus County Chronicle (Circulation 27,168)
Transportation: Commute to work: 96.3% car, 0.0% public transportation, 0.8% walk, 2.8% work from home (2000); Travel time to work: 50.5% less than 15 minutes, 31.2% 15 to 30 minutes, 10.9% 30 to 45 minutes, 3.2% 45 to 60 minutes, 4.2% 60 minutes or more (2000)
Additional Information Contacts
Crystal River Chamber of Commerce . . . . (352) 795-3149

FLORAL CITY (CDP). Covers a land area of 23.326 square miles and a water area of 1.593 square miles. Located at 28.74° N. Lat.; 82.29° W. Long. Elevation is 68 feet.
History: Floral City was established at the south end of Lake Tsala Apopka as a center for sportsmen who came to the nearby lakes and hunting grounds.
Population: 4,268 (1990); 4,989 (2000); 5,614 (2004); 6,372 (2009 projected); Race: 96.3% White, 1.8% Black, 0.1% Asian, 3.0% Hispanic of any race (2004); Density: 240.7 persons per square mile (2004); Average household size: 2.27 (2004); Median age: 48.7 (2004); Male/female ratio: 92.2 (2004); Marriage status: 14.4% never married, 64.9% now married,

9.6% widowed, 11.1% divorced (2000); Foreign born: 1.9% (2000); Ancestry (includes multiple ancestries): 24.7% German, 16.6% English, 13.1% Irish, 8.9% Other groups, 8.8% United States or American (2000).
Economy: Employment by occupation: 8.0% management, 17.1% professional, 20.3% services, 26.3% sales, 3.2% farming, 17.4% construction, 7.7% production (2000).
Income: Per capita income: $17,106 (2004); Median household income: $30,678 (2004); Average household income: $38,299 (2004); Percent of households with income of $100,000 or more: 4.0% (2004); Poverty rate: 15.1% (2000).
Education: Percent of population age 25 and over with: High school diploma (including GED) or higher: 74.2% (2004); Bachelor's degree or higher: 7.8% (2004); Master's degree or higher: 2.7% (2004).

School District(s)

Citrus County School District (PK-12)
2002-03 Enrollment: 15,355 . . . . (352) 726-1931
Housing: Homeownership rate: 89.3% (2004); Median home value: $83,223 (2004); Median rent: $358 per month (2000); Median age of housing: 19 years (2000).
Transportation: Commute to work: 89.8% car, 0.9% public transportation, 1.7% walk, 5.3% work from home (2000); Travel time to work: 16.0% less than 15 minutes, 38.2% 15 to 30 minutes, 17.1% 30 to 45 minutes, 15.3% 45 to 60 minutes, 13.5% 60 minutes or more (2000)

HERNANDO (CDP). Covers a land area of 31.478 square miles and a water area of 3.900 square miles. Located at 28.92° N. Lat.; 82.37° W. Long. Elevation is 50 feet.
History: Hernando was settled on the west shore of Lake Tsala Apopka in 1881, and named for Hernando de Soto, who had crossed through this area in the 1500's.
Population: 6,281 (1990); 8,253 (2000); 8,671 (2004); 9,231 (2009 projected); Race: 95.4% White, 2.4% Black, 0.6% Asian, 1.8% Hispanic of any race (2004); Density: 275.5 persons per square mile (2004); Average household size: 2.21 (2004); Median age: 49.9 (2004); Male/female ratio: 96.7 (2004); Marriage status: 14.1% never married, 62.7% now married, 9.0% widowed, 14.2% divorced (2000); Foreign born: 3.0% (2000); Ancestry (includes multiple ancestries): 21.0% German, 16.0% English, 15.5% Irish, 11.3% United States or American, 10.1% Other groups (2000).
Economy: Employment by occupation: 6.7% management, 14.1% professional, 19.7% services, 26.0% sales, 0.3% farming, 18.4% construction, 14.7% production (2000).
Income: Per capita income: $17,019 (2004); Median household income: $31,556 (2004); Average household income: $37,548 (2004); Percent of households with income of $100,000 or more: 3.3% (2004); Poverty rate: 15.4% (2000).
Education: Percent of population age 25 and over with: High school diploma (including GED) or higher: 73.1% (2004); Bachelor's degree or higher: 9.0% (2004); Master's degree or higher: 1.9% (2004).

School District(s)

Citrus County School District (PK-12)
2002-03 Enrollment: 15,355 . . . . (352) 726-1931
Housing: Homeownership rate: 83.6% (2004); Median home value: $72,218 (2004); Median rent: $346 per month (2000); Median age of housing: 19 years (2000).
Transportation: Commute to work: 92.1% car, 0.0% public transportation, 2.6% walk, 3.8% work from home (2000); Travel time to work: 20.8% less than 15 minutes, 42.7% 15 to 30 minutes, 18.7% 30 to 45 minutes, 5.5% 45 to 60 minutes, 12.2% 60 minutes or more (2000)

HOMOSASSA (CDP). Covers a land area of 7.946 square miles and a water area of 0.435 square miles. Located at 28.78° N. Lat.; 82.61° W. Long. Elevation is 4 feet.
Population: 2,576 (1990); 2,294 (2000); 2,446 (2004); 2,593 (2009 projected); Race: 98.7% White, 0.1% Black, 0.0% Asian, 0.8% Hispanic of any race (2004); Density: 307.8 persons per square mile (2004); Average household size: 2.00 (2004); Median age: 58.3 (2004); Male/female ratio: 98.9 (2004); Marriage status: 11.8% never married, 63.6% now married, 10.0% widowed, 14.6% divorced (2000); Foreign born: 1.5% (2000); Ancestry (includes multiple ancestries): 23.5% German, 18.4% English, 16.1% Irish, 6.5% Other groups, 6.0% Polish (2000).
Economy: Employment by occupation: 10.2% management, 19.0% professional, 17.1% services, 32.0% sales, 4.5% farming, 13.4% construction, 3.8% production (2000).
Income: Per capita income: $22,748 (2004); Median household income: $38,130 (2004); Average household income: $45,149 (2004); Percent of households with income of $100,000 or more: 8.1% (2004); Poverty rate: 10.8% (2000).
Education: Percent of population age 25 and over with: High school diploma (including GED) or higher: 83.6% (2004); Bachelor's degree or higher: 16.8% (2004); Master's degree or higher: 6.9% (2004).

School District(s)

Citrus County School District (PK-12)
2002-03 Enrollment: 15,355 . . . . (352) 726-1931
Housing: Homeownership rate: 88.3% (2004); Median home value: $146,277 (2004); Median rent: $448 per month (2000); Median age of housing: 18 years (2000).
Transportation: Commute to work: 92.9% car, 0.0% public transportation, 0.0% walk, 5.7% work from home (2000); Travel time to work: 21.2% less than 15 minutes, 39.6% 15 to 30 minutes, 24.1% 30 to 45 minutes, 6.1% 45 to 60 minutes, 8.9% 60 minutes or more (2000)
Additional Information Contacts
Homosassa Chamber of Commerce . . . . (352) 628-2666

HOMOSASSA SPRINGS (CDP). Covers a land area of 25.843 square miles and a water area of 0 square miles. Located at 28.80° N. Lat.; 82.55° W. Long. Elevation is 6 feet.
History: Homosassa Springs was established at the site of springs which were used to form a natural aquarium as part of a Federal fish preserve. This was the location of a hunting lodge operated by baseball pitcher Dazzy Vance.
Population: 10,235 (1990); 12,458 (2000); 13,135 (2004); 13,991 (2009 projected); Race: 96.4% White, 1.0% Black, 0.6% Asian, 2.4% Hispanic of any race (2004); Density: 508.3 persons per square mile (2004); Average household size: 2.36 (2004); Median age: 42.7 (2004); Male/female ratio: 97.8 (2004); Marriage status: 16.5% never married, 60.0% now married, 9.5% widowed, 14.0% divorced (2000); Foreign born: 2.7% (2000); Ancestry (includes multiple ancestries): 21.1% German, 17.4% Irish, 15.2% English, 11.4% United States or American, 10.4% Other groups (2000).
Economy: Employment by occupation: 5.9% management, 12.7% professional, 21.4% services, 25.9% sales, 1.4% farming, 16.5% construction, 16.3% production (2000).
Income: Per capita income: $15,959 (2004); Median household income: $30,878 (2004); Average household income: $37,597 (2004); Percent of households with income of $100,000 or more: 3.5% (2004); Poverty rate: 13.3% (2000).
Education: Percent of population age 25 and over with: High school diploma (including GED) or higher: 73.5% (2004); Bachelor's degree or higher: 6.8% (2004); Master's degree or higher: 2.7% (2004).
Housing: Homeownership rate: 83.6% (2004); Median home value: $68,932 (2004); Median rent: $369 per month (2000); Median age of housing: 15 years (2000).
Transportation: Commute to work: 96.7% car, 0.3% public transportation, 0.4% walk, 1.4% work from home (2000); Travel time to work: 30.3% less than 15 minutes, 41.9% 15 to 30 minutes, 14.1% 30 to 45 minutes, 4.1% 45 to 60 minutes, 9.7% 60 minutes or more (2000)

INVERNESS (city). Covers a land area of 7.286 square miles and a water area of 0.818 square miles. Located at 28.83° N. Lat.; 82.34° W. Long. Elevation is 50 feet.
History: Inverness, on Lake Tsala Apopka, was named by an early settler for his home town in Scotland. The town developed as the marketing center for a large rural area where citrus growing, truck farming, beekeeping, and dairying were early occupations.
Population: 5,913 (1990); 6,789 (2000); 7,034 (2004); 7,365 (2009 projected); Race: 91.8% White, 5.2% Black, 0.7% Asian, 4.9% Hispanic of any race (2004); Density: 965.3 persons per square mile (2004); Average household size: 2.12 (2004); Median age: 54.9 (2004); Male/female ratio: 77.2 (2004); Marriage status: 17.2% never married, 51.8% now married, 16.4% widowed, 14.6% divorced (2000); Foreign born: 3.7% (2000); Ancestry (includes multiple ancestries): 16.4% German, 13.8% Irish, 13.2% English, 12.7% Other groups, 8.7% United States or American (2000).
Economy: Single-family building permits issued: 31 (2004); Multi-family building permits issued: 2 (2004); Employment by occupation: 7.9% management, 19.2% professional, 23.8% services, 27.0% sales, 0.7% farming, 10.7% construction, 10.8% production (2000).
Income: Per capita income: $19,268 (2004); Median household income: $29,089 (2004); Average household income: $39,353 (2004); Percent of households with income of $100,000 or more: 5.1% (2004); Poverty rate: 14.8% (2000).

Taxes: Total city taxes per capita: $452 (2002); City property taxes per capita: $209 (2002).
Education: Percent of population age 25 and over with: High school diploma (including GED) or higher: 74.1% (2004); Bachelor's degree or higher: 12.0% (2004); Master's degree or higher: 4.2% (2004).

School District(s)

Citrus County School District (PK-12)
2002-03 Enrollment: 15,355 . . . . (352) 726-1931

Two-year College(s)

Withlacoochee Technical Institute (Public)
2003-04 Enrollment: 499 . . . . (352) 726-2430
2003-04 Tuition: In-state $1,639; Out-of-state $7,211

Housing: Homeownership rate: 67.6% (2004); Median home value: $86,674 (2004); Median rent: $371 per month (2000); Median age of housing: 17 years (2000).
Hospitals: Citrus Memorial Hospital (171 beds)
Safety: Violent crime rate: 30.4 per 10,000 population; Property crime rate: 251.7 per 10,000 population (2003).
Transportation: Commute to work: 87.4% car, 2.2% public transportation, 6.4% walk, 3.7% work from home (2000); Travel time to work: 50.2% less than 15 minutes, 21.4% 15 to 30 minutes, 9.0% 30 to 45 minutes, 7.8% 45 to 60 minutes, 11.6% 60 minutes or more (2000)

Additional Information Contacts

Citrus County Chamber of Commerce. . . . . (352) 726-2801
Local Government Offices . . . . (352) 726-2611
Nature Coast Visitors Guide . . . . (352) 344-1184

INVERNESS HIGHLANDS NORTH (CDP). Covers a land area of 1.917 square miles and a water area of 0.018 square miles. Located at 28.86° N. Lat.; 82.37° W. Long.
Population: 1,162 (1990); 1,470 (2000); 1,489 (2004); 1,512 (2009 projected); Race: 90.0% White, 7.9% Black, 0.3% Asian, 2.8% Hispanic of any race (2004); Density: 776.7 persons per square mile (2004); Average household size: 2.34 (2004); Median age: 41.7 (2004); Male/female ratio: 90.2 (2004); Marriage status: 16.6% never married, 62.4% now married, 8.7% widowed, 12.4% divorced (2000); Foreign born: 2.7% (2000); Ancestry (includes multiple ancestries): 19.6% Irish, 15.6% German, 12.6% Other groups, 11.3% English, 10.2% United States or American (2000).
Economy: Employment by occupation: 7.6% management, 6.2% professional, 30.3% services, 29.8% sales, 1.2% farming, 14.1% construction, 10.9% production (2000).
Income: Per capita income: $14,741 (2004); Median household income: $29,618 (2004); Average household income: $34,567 (2004); Percent of households with income of $100,000 or more: 2.2% (2004); Poverty rate: 14.0% (2000).
Education: Percent of population age 25 and over with: High school diploma (including GED) or higher: 69.7% (2004); Bachelor's degree or higher: 4.7% (2004); Master's degree or higher: 0.0% (2004).
Housing: Homeownership rate: 92.8% (2004); Median home value: $74,538 (2004); Median rent: $479 per month (2000); Median age of housing: 18 years (2000).
Transportation: Commute to work: 94.4% car, 0.0% public transportation, 1.1% walk, 3.2% work from home (2000); Travel time to work: 58.4% less than 15 minutes, 23.3% 15 to 30 minutes, 8.2% 30 to 45 minutes, 6.2% 45 to 60 minutes, 4.0% 60 minutes or more (2000)

INVERNESS HIGHLANDS SOUTH (CDP). Covers a land area of 5.642 square miles and a water area of 0.012 square miles. Located at 28.79° N. Lat.; 82.33° W. Long.
Population: 4,828 (1990); 5,781 (2000); 6,179 (2004); 6,681 (2009 projected); Race: 95.0% White, 2.1% Black, 1.0% Asian, 5.4% Hispanic of any race (2004); Density: 1,095.1 persons per square mile (2004); Average household size: 2.23 (2004); Median age: 49.1 (2004); Male/female ratio: 88.9 (2004); Marriage status: 12.5% never married, 66.0% now married, 12.4% widowed, 9.0% divorced (2000); Foreign born: 5.8% (2000); Ancestry (includes multiple ancestries): 22.3% German, 18.3% Italian, 17.3% Irish, 13.3% Other groups, 11.6% English (2000).
Economy: Employment by occupation: 4.6% management, 21.3% professional, 23.9% services, 25.5% sales, 0.0% farming, 13.3% construction, 11.5% production (2000).
Income: Per capita income: $20,332 (2004); Median household income: $32,759 (2004); Average household income: $45,292 (2004); Percent of households with income of $100,000 or more: 6.7% (2004); Poverty rate: 9.0% (2000).
Education: Percent of population age 25 and over with: High school diploma (including GED) or higher: 79.0% (2004); Bachelor's degree or higher: 11.3% (2004); Master's degree or higher: 5.2% (2004).
Housing: Homeownership rate: 90.0% (2004); Median home value: $93,837 (2004); Median rent: $425 per month (2000); Median age of housing: 16 years (2000).
Transportation: Commute to work: 95.3% car, 0.0% public transportation, 0.5% walk, 2.1% work from home (2000); Travel time to work: 41.2% less than 15 minutes, 28.4% 15 to 30 minutes, 17.0% 30 to 45 minutes, 6.5% 45 to 60 minutes, 7.0% 60 minutes or more (2000)

LECANTO (CDP). Covers a land area of 27.045 square miles and a water area of 0.009 square miles. Located at 28.84° N. Lat.; 82.48° W. Long. Elevation is 49 feet.
Population: 3,432 (1990); 5,161 (2000); 5,794 (2004); 6,583 (2009 projected); Race: 92.7% White, 4.1% Black, 0.8% Asian, 3.0% Hispanic of any race (2004); Density: 214.2 persons per square mile (2004); Average household size: 2.75 (2004); Median age: 45.5 (2004); Male/female ratio: 105.7 (2004); Marriage status: 17.4% never married, 61.0% now married, 11.1% widowed, 10.6% divorced (2000); Foreign born: 5.0% (2000); Ancestry (includes multiple ancestries): 17.2% Irish, 16.3% German, 14.6% English, 12.1% Other groups, 8.9% United States or American (2000).
Economy: Manufacturing includes building materials, furniture. Employment by occupation: 12.2% management, 13.7% professional, 18.5% services, 28.5% sales, 0.4% farming, 13.8% construction, 12.9% production (2000).
Income: Per capita income: $20,749 (2004); Median household income: $43,610 (2004); Average household income: $51,934 (2004); Percent of households with income of $100,000 or more: 8.6% (2004); Poverty rate: 9.1% (2000).
Education: Percent of population age 25 and over with: High school diploma (including GED) or higher: 75.3% (2004); Bachelor's degree or higher: 12.1% (2004); Master's degree or higher: 4.6% (2004).

School District(s)

Citrus County School District (PK-12)
2002-03 Enrollment: 15,355 . . . . (352) 726-1931

Housing: Homeownership rate: 86.0% (2004); Median home value: $105,713 (2004); Median rent: $405 per month (2000); Median age of housing: 14 years (2000).
Transportation: Commute to work: 89.9% car, 0.0% public transportation, 3.6% walk, 4.7% work from home (2000); Travel time to work: 29.0% less than 15 minutes, 45.0% 15 to 30 minutes, 9.2% 30 to 45 minutes, 6.5% 45 to 60 minutes, 10.4% 60 minutes or more (2000)

Additional Information Contacts

Realtors Association of Citrus County . . . . (352) 746-7550

PINE RIDGE (CDP). Covers a land area of 25.235 square miles and a water area of 0 square miles. Located at 28.94° N. Lat.; 82.47° W. Long.
Population: 3,374 (1990); 5,490 (2000); 6,198 (2004); 7,030 (2009 projected); Race: 94.0% White, 2.9% Black, 2.0% Asian, 3.2% Hispanic of any race (2004); Density: 245.6 persons per square mile (2004); Average household size: 2.34 (2004); Median age: 60.0 (2004); Male/female ratio: 87.0 (2004); Marriage status: 9.1% never married, 72.5% now married, 11.2% widowed, 7.3% divorced (2000); Foreign born: 11.8% (2000); Ancestry (includes multiple ancestries): 19.3% German, 15.9% Irish, 14.2% English, 9.6% Italian, 7.1% Other groups (2000).
Economy: Employment by occupation: 11.9% management, 27.0% professional, 21.0% services, 24.0% sales, 0.0% farming, 9.1% construction, 7.0% production (2000).
Income: Per capita income: $26,724 (2004); Median household income: $49,219 (2004); Average household income: $60,798 (2004); Percent of households with income of $100,000 or more: 12.9% (2004); Poverty rate: 5.9% (2000).
Education: Percent of population age 25 and over with: High school diploma (including GED) or higher: 82.8% (2004); Bachelor's degree or higher: 23.9% (2004); Master's degree or higher: 8.5% (2004).
Housing: Homeownership rate: 91.6% (2004); Median home value: $163,494 (2004); Median rent: $597 per month (2000); Median age of housing: 7 years (2000).
Transportation: Commute to work: 93.0% car, 0.0% public transportation, 0.0% walk, 5.1% work from home (2000); Travel time to work: 29.0% less than 15 minutes, 50.7% 15 to 30 minutes, 9.0% 30 to 45 minutes, 4.9% 45 to 60 minutes, 6.3% 60 minutes or more (2000)

SUGARMILL WOODS (CDP). Covers a land area of 26.369 square miles and a water area of 0.001 square miles. Located at 28.73° N. Lat.; 82.52° W. Long.
Population: 4,073 (1990); 6,409 (2000); 7,489 (2004); 8,780 (2009 projected); Race: 97.3% White, 1.2% Black, 1.0% Asian, 1.4% Hispanic of any race (2004); Density: 284.0 persons per square mile (2004); Average household size: 2.07 (2004); Median age: 64.7 (2004); Male/female ratio: 92.4 (2004); Marriage status: 7.9% never married, 76.2% now married, 9.8% widowed, 6.1% divorced (2000); Foreign born: 5.2% (2000); Ancestry (includes multiple ancestries): 25.6% German, 19.4% English, 17.0% Irish, 9.4% Italian, 5.6% Other groups (2000).
Economy: Employment by occupation: 18.6% management, 16.3% professional, 16.7% services, 30.1% sales, 0.0% farming, 10.2% construction, 8.2% production (2000).
Income: Per capita income: $27,011 (2004); Median household income: $46,648 (2004); Average household income: $55,768 (2004); Percent of households with income of $100,000 or more: 10.4% (2004); Poverty rate: 6.4% (2000).
Education: Percent of population age 25 and over with: High school diploma (including GED) or higher: 88.8% (2004); Bachelor's degree or higher: 21.1% (2004); Master's degree or higher: 8.3% (2004).
Housing: Homeownership rate: 92.9% (2004); Median home value: $144,063 (2004); Median rent: $586 per month (2000); Median age of housing: 13 years (2000).
Transportation: Commute to work: 94.8% car, 0.0% public transportation, 0.7% walk, 4.5% work from home (2000); Travel time to work: 14.0% less than 15 minutes, 46.5% 15 to 30 minutes, 23.4% 30 to 45 minutes, 5.1% 45 to 60 minutes, 11.0% 60 minutes or more (2000)

Clay County

Located in northeastern Florida; bounded on the east by the St. Johns River; includes many small lakes. Covers a land area of 601.10 square miles, a water area of 42.60 square miles, and is located in the Eastern Time Zone. The county government was organized in 1858. County seat is Green Cove Springs.

Clay County is part of the Jacksonville, FL Metropolitan Statistical Area. The entire metro area includes: Baker County, FL; Clay County, FL; Duval County, FL; Nassau County, FL; St. Johns County, FL

Population: 105,986 (1990); 140,814 (2000); 159,345 (2004); 182,637 (2009 projected); Race: 86.3% White, 7.2% Black, 2.3% Asian, 4.9% Hispanic of any race (2004); Density: 265.1 persons per square mile (2004); Average household size: 2.78 (2004); Median age: 36.3 (2004); Male/female ratio: 97.5 (2004).
Religion: Five largest groups: 18.0% Southern Baptist Convention, 9.7% Catholic Church, 4.5% The United Methodist Church, 1.6% Episcopal Church, 1.2% Presbyterian Church (U.S.A.) (2000).
Economy: Unemployment rate: 4.5% (2004); Total civilian labor force: 79,090 (2004); Leading industries: 24.2% retail trade; 16.3% health care and social assistance; 13.5% accommodation & food services (2003); Companies that employ 500 or more persons: 2 (2003); Companies that employ 100 to 499 persons: 50 (2003); Companies that employ less than 100 persons: 3,128 (2003); Farms: 340 totaling 78,542 acres (2002); Minority business ownership rate: 9.2% (1997); Women business ownership rate: 32.1% (1997); Retail sales per capita: $8,231 (1997). Single-family building permits issued: 2,935 (2004); Multi-family building permits issued: 213 (2004).
Income: Per capita income: $23,525 (2004); Median household income: $53,788 (2004); Average household income: $65,001 (2004); Percent of households with income of $100,000 or more: 15.4% (2004); Poverty rate: 6.7% (2002); Bankruptcy rate: 6.46% (2004).
Taxes: Total county taxes per capita: $489 (2002); County property taxes per capita: $267 (2002).
Education: Percent of population age 25 and over with: High school diploma (including GED) or higher: 86.7% (2004); Bachelor's degree or higher: 20.5% (2004); Master's degree or higher: 6.8% (2004).
Housing: Homeownership rate: 78.6% (2004); Median home value: $132,537 (2004); Median rent: $566 per month (2000); Median age of housing: 16 years (2000).
Health: Birth rate: 122.8 per 10,000 population (2004); Death rate: 70.9 per 10,000 population (2004); Age adjusted cancer mortality rate: 246.2 deaths per 100,000 population (2002); Number of physicians: 18.9 per 10,000 population (2001); Hospital beds: 17.4 per 10,000 population (2002); Hospital admissions: 1,277.8 per 10,000 population (2002).
Elections: 2004 Presidential election results: 76.2% Bush, 23.3% Kerry, 0.3% Nader, 0.1% Badnarik
National and State Parks: Camp Blanding State Wildlife Management Area; Mike Roess Gold Head Branch State Park
Additional Information Contacts
Clay County Government Offices . . . . (904) 284-6300
Clay County Development Authority . . . . (904) 264-7373
Orange Park Chamber of Commerce . . . . (904) 264-2651

Clay County Communities

ASBURY LAKE (CDP). Covers a land area of 3.361 square miles and a water area of 0.246 square miles. Located at 30.05° N. Lat.; 81.81° W. Long.
Population: 2,072 (1990); 2,228 (2000); 2,694 (2004); 3,270 (2009 projected); Race: 97.0% White, 0.3% Black, 0.8% Asian, 1.4% Hispanic of any race (2004); Density: 801.5 persons per square mile (2004); Average household size: 2.72 (2004); Median age: 45.0 (2004); Male/female ratio: 101.8 (2004); Marriage status: 15.8% never married, 72.4% now married, 3.7% widowed, 8.1% divorced (2000); Foreign born: 0.4% (2000); Ancestry (includes multiple ancestries): 19.2% German, 16.3% Irish, 16.2% United States or American, 13.8% English, 9.1% Other groups (2000).
Economy: Employment by occupation: 9.3% management, 19.3% professional, 5.7% services, 39.1% sales, 0.0% farming, 16.5% construction, 10.0% production (2000).
Income: Per capita income: $27,973 (2004); Median household income: $70,489 (2004); Average household income: $76,198 (2004); Percent of households with income of $100,000 or more: 23.6% (2004); Poverty rate: 3.8% (2000).
Education: Percent of population age 25 and over with: High school diploma (including GED) or higher: 92.5% (2004); Bachelor's degree or higher: 20.2% (2004); Master's degree or higher: 9.6% (2004).
Housing: Homeownership rate: 96.4% (2004); Median home value: $175,332 (2004); Median rent: $625 per month (2000); Median age of housing: 21 years (2000).
Transportation: Commute to work: 91.9% car, 1.6% public transportation, 0.0% walk, 5.9% work from home (2000); Travel time to work: 6.6% less than 15 minutes, 16.8% 15 to 30 minutes, 17.5% 30 to 45 minutes, 38.8% 45 to 60 minutes, 20.3% 60 minutes or more (2000)

BELLAIR-MEADOWBROOK TERRACE (CDP). Covers a land area of 5.603 square miles and a water area of 0 square miles. Located at 30.17° N. Lat.; 81.74° W. Long.
Population: 15,606 (1990); 16,539 (2000); 17,535 (2004); 18,919 (2009 projected); Race: 75.6% White, 13.0% Black, 4.0% Asian, 7.6% Hispanic of any race (2004); Density: 3,129.3 persons per square mile (2004); Average household size: 2.51 (2004); Median age: 34.0 (2004); Male/female ratio: 94.3 (2004); Marriage status: 24.1% never married, 58.9% now married, 4.7% widowed, 12.3% divorced (2000); Foreign born: 6.4% (2000); Ancestry (includes multiple ancestries): 26.7% Other groups, 12.1% German, 11.0% Irish, 10.8% United States or American, 10.3% English (2000).
Economy: Employment by occupation: 12.3% management, 16.2% professional, 17.6% services, 31.8% sales, 0.1% farming, 11.8% construction, 10.1% production (2000).
Income: Per capita income: $23,036 (2004); Median household income: $44,471 (2004); Average household income: $57,086 (2004); Percent of households with income of $100,000 or more: 11.0% (2004); Poverty rate: 7.5% (2000).
Education: Percent of population age 25 and over with: High school diploma (including GED) or higher: 87.1% (2004); Bachelor's degree or higher: 17.7% (2004); Master's degree or higher: 5.9% (2004).
Housing: Homeownership rate: 52.2% (2004); Median home value: $114,585 (2004); Median rent: $618 per month (2000); Median age of housing: 21 years (2000).
Transportation: Commute to work: 95.5% car, 0.1% public transportation, 1.5% walk, 1.6% work from home (2000); Travel time to work: 23.9% less than 15 minutes, 34.9% 15 to 30 minutes, 26.3% 30 to 45 minutes, 9.4% 45 to 60 minutes, 5.6% 60 minutes or more (2000)

GREEN COVE SPRINGS (city). Covers a land area of 6.816 square miles and a water area of 2.633 square miles. Located at 29.99° N. Lat.; 81.68° W. Long. Elevation is 17 feet.

History: Green Cove Springs was established around a spring and developed as a fashionable spa in the late 1870's and 1880's. Prominent property owners here were Gail Borden, condensed milk manufacturer, and J.C. Penney, department store owner. Nearby, Penney built the Penney Farms Memorial Home Community for retired religious leaders of all denominations.
Population: 4,646 (1990); 5,378 (2000); 5,608 (2004); 5,956 (2009 projected); Race: 71.7% White, 23.8% Black, 0.6% Asian, 6.1% Hispanic of any race (2004); Density: 822.7 persons per square mile (2004); Average household size: 2.67 (2004); Median age: 40.4 (2004); Male/female ratio: 99.9 (2004); Marriage status: 18.7% never married, 60.2% now married, 8.3% widowed, 12.8% divorced (2000); Foreign born: 5.4% (2000); Ancestry (includes multiple ancestries): 26.7% Other groups, 10.8% English, 9.5% United States or American, 9.3% Irish, 9.2% German (2000).
Economy: Single-family building permits issued: 67 (2004); Multi-family building permits issued: 0 (2004); Employment by occupation: 8.3% management, 13.4% professional, 19.1% services, 25.7% sales, 0.6% farming, 14.7% construction, 18.2% production (2000).
Income: Per capita income: $19,991 (2004); Median household income: $36,123 (2004); Average household income: $50,975 (2004); Percent of households with income of $100,000 or more: 11.7% (2004); Poverty rate: 19.1% (2000).
Taxes: Total city taxes per capita: $330 (2002); City property taxes per capita: $83 (2002).
Education: Percent of population age 25 and over with: High school diploma (including GED) or higher: 76.2% (2004); Bachelor's degree or higher: 16.0% (2004); Master's degree or higher: 6.2% (2004).

School District(s)

Clay County School District (PK-12)
2002-03 Enrollment: 29,861 . . . . (904) 284-6510

Housing: Homeownership rate: 70.8% (2004); Median home value: $103,145 (2004); Median rent: $322 per month (2000); Median age of housing: 26 years (2000).
Safety: Violent crime rate: 108.0 per 10,000 population; Property crime rate: 414.2 per 10,000 population (2003).
Transportation: Commute to work: 88.9% car, 0.6% public transportation, 2.4% walk, 2.2% work from home (2000); Travel time to work: 33.9% less than 15 minutes, 23.0% 15 to 30 minutes, 20.6% 30 to 45 minutes, 15.8% 45 to 60 minutes, 6.8% 60 minutes or more (2000)

Additional Information Contacts

Local Government Offices . . . . (904) 529-2200

KEYSTONE HEIGHTS (city). Covers a land area of 4.544 square miles and a water area of 0.085 square miles. Located at 29.78° N. Lat.; 82.03° W. Long. Elevation is 136 feet.
History: Keystone Heights developed as a resort town in the lake region. First known as Brookly, it was renamed in 1922 by J.J. Lawrence of Pennsylvania for his home Keystone State.
Population: 1,321 (1990); 1,349 (2000); 1,463 (2004); 1,604 (2009 projected); Race: 95.3% White, 0.5% Black, 0.7% Asian, 3.1% Hispanic of any race (2004); Density: 322.0 persons per square mile (2004); Average household size: 2.60 (2004); Median age: 37.9 (2004); Male/female ratio: 87.6 (2004); Marriage status: 22.9% never married, 57.6% now married, 8.7% widowed, 10.9% divorced (2000); Foreign born: 2.1% (2000); Ancestry (includes multiple ancestries): 18.3% English, 15.1% German, 12.7% Irish, 10.5% United States or American, 8.2% Other groups (2000).
Economy: Single-family building permits issued: 0 (2004); Multi-family building permits issued: 0 (2004); Employment by occupation: 10.4% management, 19.3% professional, 20.1% services, 30.4% sales, 0.3% farming, 10.7% construction, 8.9% production (2000).
Income: Per capita income: $21,728 (2004); Median household income: $44,175 (2004); Average household income: $56,170 (2004); Percent of households with income of $100,000 or more: 9.8% (2004); Poverty rate: 8.3% (2000).
Taxes: Total city taxes per capita: $121 (2002); City property taxes per capita: $50 (2002).
Education: Percent of population age 25 and over with: High school diploma (including GED) or higher: 90.3% (2004); Bachelor's degree or higher: 20.4% (2004); Master's degree or higher: 6.9% (2004).

School District(s)

Clay County School District (PK-12)
2002-03 Enrollment: 29,861 . . . . (904) 284-6510

Housing: Homeownership rate: 83.1% (2004); Median home value: $109,923 (2004); Median rent: $431 per month (2000); Median age of housing: 27 years (2000).
Newspapers: Lake Region Monitor (General - Circulation 2,175)
Transportation: Commute to work: 92.6% car, 0.0% public transportation, 3.2% walk, 3.5% work from home (2000); Travel time to work: 36.0% less than 15 minutes, 14.7% 15 to 30 minutes, 20.1% 30 to 45 minutes, 18.6% 45 to 60 minutes, 10.7% 60 minutes or more (2000)

LAKESIDE (CDP). Covers a land area of 15.155 square miles and a water area of 2.264 square miles. Located at 30.13° N. Lat.; 81.76° W. Long.
Population: 29,137 (1990); 30,927 (2000); 32,217 (2004); 34,142 (2009 projected); Race: 84.3% White, 7.9% Black, 2.9% Asian, 6.0% Hispanic of any race (2004); Density: 2,125.9 persons per square mile (2004); Average household size: 2.82 (2004); Median age: 35.8 (2004); Male/female ratio: 96.2 (2004); Marriage status: 20.7% never married, 64.4% now married, 4.4% widowed, 10.6% divorced (2000); Foreign born: 5.7% (2000); Ancestry (includes multiple ancestries): 20.8% Other groups, 14.7% German, 12.4% Irish, 11.9% United States or American, 10.9% English (2000).
Economy: Employment by occupation: 15.1% management, 19.3% professional, 12.2% services, 32.8% sales, 0.1% farming, 11.4% construction, 9.2% production (2000).
Income: Per capita income: $22,800 (2004); Median household income: $55,730 (2004); Average household income: $64,055 (2004); Percent of households with income of $100,000 or more: 15.2% (2004); Poverty rate: 4.5% (2000).
Education: Percent of population age 25 and over with: High school diploma (including GED) or higher: 90.1% (2004); Bachelor's degree or higher: 21.9% (2004); Master's degree or higher: 7.0% (2004).
Housing: Homeownership rate: 77.2% (2004); Median home value: $134,163 (2004); Median rent: $609 per month (2000); Median age of housing: 18 years (2000).
Transportation: Commute to work: 94.3% car, 0.2% public transportation, 0.8% walk, 2.9% work from home (2000); Travel time to work: 17.9% less than 15 minutes, 26.8% 15 to 30 minutes, 28.9% 30 to 45 minutes, 18.1% 45 to 60 minutes, 8.3% 60 minutes or more (2000)

MIDDLEBURG (CDP). Covers a land area of 18.284 square miles and a water area of 0 square miles. Located at 30.05° N. Lat.; 81.90° W. Long. Elevation is 29 feet.
History: Middleburg was a shipping port for cotton in the 1840's, where sea-going vessels could enter Black Creek.
Population: 6,223 (1990); 10,338 (2000); 11,881 (2004); 13,850 (2009 projected); Race: 93.0% White, 3.4% Black, 0.6% Asian, 2.8% Hispanic of any race (2004); Density: 649.8 persons per square mile (2004); Average household size: 2.93 (2004); Median age: 34.2 (2004); Male/female ratio: 100.0 (2004); Marriage status: 21.6% never married, 63.3% now married, 4.0% widowed, 11.1% divorced (2000); Foreign born: 2.2% (2000); Ancestry (includes multiple ancestries): 14.4% United States or American, 14.2% German, 13.4% English, 13.1% Irish, 12.7% Other groups (2000).
Economy: Employment by occupation: 10.2% management, 11.3% professional, 15.0% services, 32.0% sales, 0.8% farming, 16.5% construction, 14.2% production (2000).
Income: Per capita income: $19,584 (2004); Median household income: $49,165 (2004); Average household income: $57,452 (2004); Percent of households with income of $100,000 or more: 10.3% (2004); Poverty rate: 9.2% (2000).
Education: Percent of population age 25 and over with: High school diploma (including GED) or higher: 80.8% (2004); Bachelor's degree or higher: 8.8% (2004); Master's degree or higher: 2.3% (2004).

School District(s)

Clay County School District (PK-12)
2002-03 Enrollment: 29,861 . . . . (904) 284-6510

Housing: Homeownership rate: 88.4% (2004); Median home value: $106,385 (2004); Median rent: $453 per month (2000); Median age of housing: 11 years (2000).
Transportation: Commute to work: 97.0% car, 0.0% public transportation, 0.8% walk, 1.3% work from home (2000); Travel time to work: 10.5% less than 15 minutes, 20.0% 15 to 30 minutes, 26.7% 30 to 45 minutes, 20.0% 45 to 60 minutes, 22.8% 60 minutes or more (2000)

ORANGE PARK (town). Covers a land area of 3.896 square miles and a water area of 1.655 square miles. Located at 30.16° N. Lat.; 81.70° W. Long. Elevation is 24 feet.
History: Orange Park was established on land granted to Zephaniah Kingsley in 1790 by Spain. In the early 1800's Kingsley owned much land

on Fort George Island and engaged in an active slave trade, bringing slaves from Africa in his own ships. Orange Park was founded on part of the original Kingsley plantation.

Population: 9,491 (1990); 9,081 (2000); 9,139 (2004); 9,303 (2009 projected); Race: 82.2% White, 11.1% Black, 2.6% Asian, 5.3% Hispanic of any race (2004); Density: 2,346.0 persons per square mile (2004); Average household size: 2.61 (2004); Median age: 43.6 (2004); Male/female ratio: 91.1 (2004); Marriage status: 19.3% never married, 60.7% now married, 8.7% widowed, 11.3% divorced (2000); Foreign born: 5.8% (2000); Ancestry (includes multiple ancestries): 18.7% Other groups, 16.6% English, 14.6% German, 12.5% Irish, 11.1% United States or American (2000).

Economy: Single-family building permits issued: 10 (2004); Multi-family building permits issued: 8 (2004); Employment by occupation: 12.0% management, 21.3% professional, 15.4% services, 29.4% sales, 0.0% farming, 11.0% construction, 11.0% production (2000).

Income: Per capita income: $25,262 (2004); Median household income: $48,964 (2004); Average household income: $63,197 (2004); Percent of households with income of $100,000 or more: 14.3% (2004); Poverty rate: 7.5% (2000).

Education: Percent of population age 25 and over with: High school diploma (including GED) or higher: 87.4% (2004); Bachelor's degree or higher: 25.4% (2004); Master's degree or higher: 10.4% (2004).

School District(s)

Clay County School District (PK-12)
2002-03 Enrollment: 29,861 . . . . (904) 284-6510

Two-year College(s)

North Florida Institute
2003-04 Enrollment: 255 . . . . (904) 269-7086

Housing: Homeownership rate: 63.5% (2004); Median home value: $141,202 (2004); Median rent: $554 per month (2000); Median age of housing: 25 years (2000).

Hospitals: Orange Park Medical Center (224 beds)

Safety: Violent crime rate: 49.2 per 10,000 population; Property crime rate: 347.6 per 10,000 population (2003).

Newspapers: Clay Today (General - Circulation 10,000); The Jax Air News (General - Circulation 12,000)

Transportation: Commute to work: 91.6% car, 0.9% public transportation, 2.8% walk, 3.4% work from home (2000); Travel time to work: 27.9% less than 15 minutes, 29.8% 15 to 30 minutes, 27.6% 30 to 45 minutes, 10.8% 45 to 60 minutes, 3.9% 60 minutes or more (2000)

Additional Information Contacts

Clay County Development Authority . . . . (904) 264-7373
Local Government Offices . . . . (904) 278-3018
Orange Park Chamber of Commerce . . . . (904) 264-2651

PENNEY FARMS (town). Covers a land area of 1.399 square miles and a water area of 0 square miles. Located at 29.98° N. Lat.; 81.81° W. Long. Elevation is 92 feet.

Population: 660 (1990); 580 (2000); 624 (2004); 687 (2009 projected); Race: 93.4% White, 5.6% Black, 0.2% Asian, 0.3% Hispanic of any race (2004); Density: 446.2 persons per square mile (2004); Average household size: 2.17 (2004); Median age: 77.4 (2004); Male/female ratio: 64.2 (2004); Marriage status: 9.3% never married, 68.0% now married, 17.0% widowed, 5.8% divorced (2000); Foreign born: 5.2% (2000); Ancestry (includes multiple ancestries): 28.9% English, 14.3% German, 8.6% United States or American, 6.1% Scotch-Irish, 5.8% Other groups (2000).

Economy: Single-family building permits issued: 1 (2004); Multi-family building permits issued: 0 (2004); Employment by occupation: 6.6% management, 35.5% professional, 18.4% services, 25.0% sales, 3.9% farming, 6.6% construction, 3.9% production (2000).

Income: Per capita income: $24,836 (2004); Median household income: $39,227 (2004); Average household income: $48,876 (2004); Percent of households with income of $100,000 or more: 8.0% (2004); Poverty rate: 16.4% (2000).

Education: Percent of population age 25 and over with: High school diploma (including GED) or higher: 93.8% (2004); Bachelor's degree or higher: 57.0% (2004); Master's degree or higher: 34.2% (2004).

Housing: Homeownership rate: 32.4% (2004); Median home value: $105,625 (2004); Median rent: $392 per month (2000); Median age of housing: 37 years (2000).

Transportation: Commute to work: 88.2% car, 0.0% public transportation, 2.6% walk, 6.6% work from home (2000); Travel time to work: 35.2% less than 15 minutes, 36.6% 15 to 30 minutes, 15.5% 30 to 45 minutes, 12.7% 45 to 60 minutes, 0.0% 60 minutes or more (2000)

Collier County

Located in southern Florida, on the Gulf of Mexico; swampy area, including the Everglades and Ten Thousand Islands. Covers a land area of 2,025.30 square miles, a water area of 279.60 square miles, and is located in the Eastern Time Zone. The county government was organized in 1923. County seat is East Naples.

Collier County is part of the Naples-Marco Island, FL Metropolitan Statistical Area. The entire metro area includes: Collier County, FL

Weather Station: Immokalee 3 NNW — Elevation: 32 feet

	Jan	Feb	Mar	Apr	May	Jun	Jul	Aug	Sep	Oct	Nov	Dec
High	76	78	82	85	89	91	92	91	90	86	82	78
Low	52	53	56	59	65	70	72	72	72	66	60	54
Precip	2.3	2.3	3.0	2.4	4.2	7.9	7.0	7.5	6.4	2.8	2.3	1.8
Snow	0.0	0.0	0.0	0.0	0.0	0.0	0.0	0.0	0.0	0.0	0.0	0.0

High and Low temperatures in degrees Fahrenheit; Precipitation and Snow in inches

Weather Station: Naples — Elevation: 3 feet

	Jan	Feb	Mar	Apr	May	Jun	Jul	Aug	Sep	Oct	Nov	Dec
High	77	78	81	84	88	90	92	92	91	88	83	78
Low	54	55	58	62	67	72	73	73	73	68	62	56
Precip	2.1	2.2	2.5	2.0	4.3	8.2	8.0	7.7	8.2	3.7	2.0	1.5
Snow	0.0	0.0	0.0	0.0	0.0	0.0	0.0	0.0	0.0	0.0	0.0	0.0

High and Low temperatures in degrees Fahrenheit; Precipitation and Snow in inches

Population: 152,099 (1990); 251,377 (2000); 297,619 (2004); 355,671 (2009 projected); Race: 84.2% White, 5.0% Black, 0.7% Asian, 23.7% Hispanic of any race (2004); Density: 146.9 persons per square mile (2004); Average household size: 2.44 (2004); Median age: 44.1 (2004); Male/female ratio: 100.7 (2004).

Religion: Five largest groups: 19.3% Catholic Church, 3.8% Southern Baptist Convention, 2.1% The United Methodist Church, 1.7% Presbyterian Church (U.S.A.), 1.7% Jewish Estimate (2000).

Economy: Unemployment rate: 4.0% (2004); Total civilian labor force: 126,970 (2004); Leading industries: 18.7% retail trade; 14.8% accommodation & food services; 13.0% construction (2003); Companies that employ 500 or more persons: 5 (2003); Companies that employ 100 to 499 persons: 160 (2003); Companies that employ less than 100 persons: 9,327 (2003); Farms: 273 totaling 180,852 acres (2002); Minority business ownership rate: 10.0% (1997); Women business ownership rate: 23.4% (1997); Retail sales per capita: $13,624 (1997). Single-family building permits issued: 4,202 (2004); Multi-family building permits issued: 2,719 (2004).

Income: Per capita income: $33,437 (2004); Median household income: $53,126 (2004); Average household income: $80,522 (2004); Percent of households with income of $100,000 or more: 21.2% (2004); Poverty rate: 9.6% (2002); Bankruptcy rate: 2.82% (2004).

Taxes: Total county taxes per capita: $587 (2002); County property taxes per capita: $455 (2002).

Education: Percent of population age 25 and over with: High school diploma (including GED) or higher: 82.2% (2004); Bachelor's degree or higher: 28.3% (2004); Master's degree or higher: 9.9% (2004).

Housing: Homeownership rate: 76.0% (2004); Median home value: $199,506 (2004); Median rent: $669 per month (2000); Median age of housing: 13 years (2000).

Health: Birth rate: 126.6 per 10,000 population (2004); Death rate: 81.0 per 10,000 population (2004); Age adjusted cancer mortality rate: 141.6 deaths per 100,000 population (2002); Air Quality Index: 97.0% good, 3.0% moderate, 0.0% unhealthy for sensitive individuals, 0.0% unhealthy (percent of days in 2004); Number of physicians: 25.0 per 10,000 population (2001); Hospital beds: 20.3 per 10,000 population (2002); Hospital admissions: 1,200.1 per 10,000 population (2002).

Elections: 2004 Presidential election results: 65.0% Bush, 34.1% Kerry, 0.5% Nader, 0.1% Badnarik

National and State Parks: Barefoot Beach State Preserve; Big Cypress National Preserve; Collier-Seminole State Park; Delnor-Wiggins Pass State Park; Fakahatchee Strand Preserve State Park

Additional Information Contacts

Collier County Government Offices . . . . (941) 774-8097
Golden Gate Area Chamber of Commerce . . . . (941) 455-3100
Immokalee Chamber of Commerce . . . . (239) 657-3237
Marco Island Area Association of Realtors . . . . (239) 394-5616
Marco Island Chamber of Commerce . . . . (239) 394-7549
Naples Area Board of Realtors . . . . (239) 597-1666
Naples Area Chamber of Commerce . . . . (239) 262-6141

Collier County Communities

CHOKOLOSKEE (CDP). Covers a land area of 0.280 square miles and a water area of 0 square miles. Located at 25.81° N. Lat.; 81.36° W. Long. Elevation is 10 feet.
Population: 347 (1990); 404 (2000); 622 (2004); 869 (2009 projected); Race: 98.4% White, 0.0% Black, 0.0% Asian, 3.5% Hispanic of any race (2004); Density: 2,224.8 persons per square mile (2004); Average household size: 2.18 (2004); Median age: 52.0 (2004); Male/female ratio: 97.5 (2004); Marriage status: 5.2% never married, 75.0% now married, 5.5% widowed, 14.3% divorced (2000); Foreign born: 2.7% (2000); Ancestry (includes multiple ancestries): 50.3% United States or American, 10.9% English, 10.5% German, 8.9% Irish, 3.5% Hungarian (2000).
Economy: Employment by occupation: 11.1% management, 17.6% professional, 31.7% services, 23.6% sales, 4.5% farming, 4.0% construction, 7.5% production (2000).
Income: Per capita income: $22,677 (2004); Median household income: $36,447 (2004); Average household income: $49,491 (2004); Percent of households with income of $100,000 or more: 9.8% (2004); Poverty rate: 1.6% (2000).
Education: Percent of population age 25 and over with: High school diploma (including GED) or higher: 69.7% (2004); Bachelor's degree or higher: 13.9% (2004); Master's degree or higher: 3.7% (2004).
Housing: Homeownership rate: 84.2% (2004); Median home value: $108,621 (2004); Median rent: $333 per month (2000); Median age of housing: 27 years (2000).
Transportation: Commute to work: 81.4% car, 0.0% public transportation, 9.0% walk, 0.0% work from home (2000); Travel time to work: 72.4% less than 15 minutes, 12.1% 15 to 30 minutes, 8.0% 30 to 45 minutes, 4.0% 45 to 60 minutes, 3.5% 60 minutes or more (2000)

EVERGLADES (city). Aka Everglades City. Covers a land area of 0.933 square miles and a water area of 0.252 square miles. Located at 25.85° N. Lat.; 81.38° W. Long.
History: The city of Everglades developed on the Barron River, inland from the western boundary of the Everglades, as the seat of Collier County.
Population: 321 (1990); 479 (2000); 737 (2004); 1,030 (2009 projected); Race: 94.6% White, 1.5% Black, 0.5% Asian, 6.8% Hispanic of any race (2004); Density: 789.6 persons per square mile (2004); Average household size: 2.05 (2004); Median age: 57.2 (2004); Male/female ratio: 104.2 (2004); Marriage status: 11.4% never married, 71.7% now married, 5.8% widowed, 11.0% divorced (2000); Foreign born: 4.8% (2000); Ancestry (includes multiple ancestries): 17.2% German, 16.2% English, 14.9% Irish, 10.4% Other groups, 8.7% United States or American (2000).
Economy: Single-family building permits issued: 6 (2004); Multi-family building permits issued: 0 (2004); Employment by occupation: 7.1% management, 11.7% professional, 27.4% services, 26.9% sales, 13.7% farming, 4.6% construction, 8.6% production (2000).
Income: Per capita income: $24,647 (2004); Median household income: $38,229 (2004); Average household income: $50,599 (2004); Percent of households with income of $100,000 or more: 6.4% (2004); Poverty rate: 6.0% (2000).
Taxes: Total city taxes per capita: $712 (2002); City property taxes per capita: $349 (2002).
Education: Percent of population age 25 and over with: High school diploma (including GED) or higher: 83.1% (2004); Bachelor's degree or higher: 17.7% (2004); Master's degree or higher: 6.6% (2004).
Housing: Homeownership rate: 79.1% (2004); Median home value: $152,817 (2004); Median rent: $510 per month (2000); Median age of housing: 22 years (2000).
Transportation: Commute to work: 77.4% car, 0.0% public transportation, 13.8% walk, 5.6% work from home (2000); Travel time to work: 63.6% less than 15 minutes, 17.9% 15 to 30 minutes, 4.3% 30 to 45 minutes, 9.8% 45 to 60 minutes, 4.3% 60 minutes or more (2000)
Airports: Everglades Airpark

GOLDEN GATE (CDP). Aka Golden Gate Estates. Covers a land area of 4.036 square miles and a water area of 0.038 square miles. Located at 26.18° N. Lat.; 81.70° W. Long. Elevation is 11 feet.
Population: 14,116 (1990); 20,951 (2000); 23,071 (2004); 25,907 (2009 projected); Race: 71.3% White, 12.8% Black, 0.7% Asian, 50.3% Hispanic of any race (2004); Density: 5,716.0 persons per square mile (2004); Average household size: 3.29 (2004); Median age: 29.4 (2004); Male/female ratio: 112.8 (2004); Marriage status: 32.1% never married, 53.9% now married, 3.3% widowed, 10.7% divorced (2000); Foreign born: 33.5% (2000); Ancestry (includes multiple ancestries): 37.6% Other groups, 9.4% German, 7.8% Irish, 7.4% United States or American, 5.8% Haitian (2000).
Economy: Employment by occupation: 6.8% management, 9.4% professional, 25.0% services, 23.7% sales, 0.5% farming, 22.1% construction, 12.5% production (2000).
Income: Per capita income: $15,650 (2004); Median household income: $42,895 (2004); Average household income: $51,286 (2004); Percent of households with income of $100,000 or more: 7.5% (2004); Poverty rate: 14.1% (2000).
Education: Percent of population age 25 and over with: High school diploma (including GED) or higher: 67.9% (2004); Bachelor's degree or higher: 11.0% (2004); Master's degree or higher: 3.0% (2004).
Housing: Homeownership rate: 56.4% (2004); Median home value: $136,465 (2004); Median rent: $639 per month (2000); Median age of housing: 15 years (2000).
Transportation: Commute to work: 92.9% car, 0.3% public transportation, 1.6% walk, 1.6% work from home (2000); Travel time to work: 17.7% less than 15 minutes, 53.9% 15 to 30 minutes, 21.9% 30 to 45 minutes, 3.2% 45 to 60 minutes, 3.3% 60 minutes or more (2000)

GOODLAND (CDP). Aka Collier City. Covers a land area of 0.212 square miles and a water area of 0.190 square miles. Located at 25.92° N. Lat.; 81.64° W. Long. Elevation is 4 feet.
Population: 348 (1990); 320 (2000); 336 (2004); 360 (2009 projected); Race: 99.1% White, 0.3% Black, 0.3% Asian, 1.8% Hispanic of any race (2004); Density: 1,587.6 persons per square mile (2004); Average household size: 1.70 (2004); Median age: 53.5 (2004); Male/female ratio: 111.3 (2004); Marriage status: 13.8% never married, 49.2% now married, 14.8% widowed, 22.2% divorced (2000); Foreign born: 0.0% (2000); Ancestry (includes multiple ancestries): 18.6% Irish, 17.6% German, 11.8% English, 11.3% Czech, 7.2% Scottish (2000).
Economy: Employment by occupation: 23.8% management, 0.0% professional, 32.1% services, 15.5% sales, 0.0% farming, 19.0% construction, 9.5% production (2000).
Income: Per capita income: $26,161 (2004); Median household income: $31,304 (2004); Average household income: $44,394 (2004); Percent of households with income of $100,000 or more: 8.1% (2004); Poverty rate: 14.0% (2000).
Education: Percent of population age 25 and over with: High school diploma (including GED) or higher: 82.0% (2004); Bachelor's degree or higher: 22.9% (2004); Master's degree or higher: 4.9% (2004).
Housing: Homeownership rate: 76.8% (2004); Median home value: $229,730 (2004); Median rent: $604 per month (2000); Median age of housing: 29 years (2000).
Transportation: Commute to work: 89.2% car, 0.0% public transportation, 0.0% walk, 0.0% work from home (2000); Travel time to work: 91.9% less than 15 minutes, 0.0% 15 to 30 minutes, 0.0% 30 to 45 minutes, 8.1% 45 to 60 minutes, 0.0% 60 minutes or more (2000)

IMMOKALEE (CDP). Covers a land area of 8.070 square miles and a water area of 0.008 square miles. Located at 26.42° N. Lat.; 81.42° W. Long. Elevation is 35 feet.
History: A sawmill was built in Immokalee in 1884, at the location of an Episcopal Indian Mission School. The area was first known as Gopher Ridge. The name of Immokalee is of Indian origin meaning "tumbling water."
Population: 14,317 (1990); 19,763 (2000); 20,226 (2004); 21,266 (2009 projected); Race: 34.6% White, 17.5% Black, 0.2% Asian, 74.8% Hispanic of any race (2004); Density: 2,506.5 persons per square mile (2004); Average household size: 4.26 (2004); Median age: 24.8 (2004); Male/female ratio: 129.7 (2004); Marriage status: 43.8% never married, 47.9% now married, 3.3% widowed, 5.1% divorced (2000); Foreign born: 45.8% (2000); Ancestry (includes multiple ancestries): 60.8% Other groups, 10.8% Haitian, 3.3% United States or American, 0.9% Irish, 0.5% English (2000).
Economy: Employment by occupation: 6.9% management, 4.5% professional, 20.5% services, 12.7% sales, 27.0% farming, 14.8% construction, 13.5% production (2000).
Income: Per capita income: $9,035 (2004); Median household income: $25,896 (2004); Average household income: $34,191 (2004); Percent of households with income of $100,000 or more: 3.6% (2004); Poverty rate: 39.8% (2000).

Education: Percent of population age 25 and over with: High school diploma (including GED) or higher: 23.8% (2004); Bachelor's degree or higher: 2.2% (2004); Master's degree or higher: 0.4% (2004).

School District(s)

Collier County School District (PK-12)
2002-03 Enrollment: 38,110 . . . . (239) 254-4100

Housing: Homeownership rate: 38.0% (2004); Median home value: $77,772 (2004); Median rent: $327 per month (2000); Median age of housing: 20 years (2000).

Transportation: Commute to work: 73.6% car, 18.2% public transportation, 6.3% walk, 1.3% work from home (2000); Travel time to work: 23.7% less than 15 minutes, 17.5% 15 to 30 minutes, 22.2% 30 to 45 minutes, 16.1% 45 to 60 minutes, 20.5% 60 minutes or more (2000)

Airports: Immokalee

Additional Information Contacts

Immokalee Chamber of Commerce . . . . (239) 657-3237

LELY (CDP). Covers a land area of 1.462 square miles and a water area of 0.011 square miles. Located at 26.10° N. Lat.; 81.73° W. Long.

Population: 2,993 (1990); 3,857 (2000); 4,249 (2004); 4,787 (2009 projected); Race: 96.4% White, 0.9% Black, 0.6% Asian, 5.6% Hispanic of any race (2004); Density: 2,907.1 persons per square mile (2004); Average household size: 1.86 (2004); Median age: 65.1 (2004); Male/female ratio: 83.2 (2004); Marriage status: 7.4% never married, 65.0% now married, 18.0% widowed, 9.6% divorced (2000); Foreign born: 5.8% (2000); Ancestry (includes multiple ancestries): 21.2% German, 20.8% Irish, 17.3% English, 11.8% Italian, 5.8% Other groups (2000).

Economy: Employment by occupation: 20.3% management, 21.2% professional, 13.6% services, 30.6% sales, 0.0% farming, 7.1% construction, 7.3% production (2000).

Income: Per capita income: $34,409 (2004); Median household income: $48,199 (2004); Average household income: $60,533 (2004); Percent of households with income of $100,000 or more: 13.5% (2004); Poverty rate: 6.3% (2000).

Education: Percent of population age 25 and over with: High school diploma (including GED) or higher: 89.3% (2004); Bachelor's degree or higher: 28.0% (2004); Master's degree or higher: 11.0% (2004).

Housing: Homeownership rate: 76.8% (2004); Median home value: $150,494 (2004); Median rent: $1,397 per month (2000); Median age of housing: 16 years (2000).

Transportation: Commute to work: 95.1% car, 0.0% public transportation, 1.6% walk, 3.3% work from home (2000); Travel time to work: 30.9% less than 15 minutes, 42.3% 15 to 30 minutes, 22.8% 30 to 45 minutes, 3.0% 45 to 60 minutes, 1.0% 60 minutes or more (2000)

LELY RESORT (CDP). Covers a land area of 5.226 square miles and a water area of 0.004 square miles. Located at 26.08° N. Lat.; 81.70° W. Long.

Population: 56 (1990); 1,426 (2000); 2,114 (2004); 2,939 (2009 projected); Race: 81.0% White, 9.3% Black, 0.6% Asian, 32.8% Hispanic of any race (2004); Density: 404.5 persons per square mile (2004); Average household size: 2.30 (2004); Median age: 42.2 (2004); Male/female ratio: 105.6 (2004); Marriage status: 20.4% never married, 65.5% now married, 8.2% widowed, 5.9% divorced (2000); Foreign born: 19.0% (2000); Ancestry (includes multiple ancestries): 21.9% Other groups, 16.8% German, 14.6% Irish, 14.2% Italian, 7.6% Polish (2000).

Economy: Employment by occupation: 5.7% management, 13.6% professional, 15.8% services, 45.6% sales, 0.0% farming, 8.1% construction, 11.1% production (2000).

Income: Per capita income: $35,426 (2004); Median household income: $54,906 (2004); Average household income: $81,314 (2004); Percent of households with income of $100,000 or more: 18.3% (2004); Poverty rate: 6 9% (2000).

Education: Percent of population age 25 and over with: High school diploma (including GED) or higher: 88.2% (2004); Bachelor's degree or higher: 32.2% (2004); Master's degree or higher: 11.7% (2004).

Housing: Homeownership rate: 61.0% (2004); Median home value: $203,311 (2004); Median rent: $717 per month (2000); Median age of housing: 3 years (2000).

Transportation: Commute to work: 95.9% car, 0.0% public transportation, 0.0% walk, 4.1% work from home (2000); Travel time to work: 33.6% less than 15 minutes, 44.8% 15 to 30 minutes, 17.2% 30 to 45 minutes, 2.0% 45 to 60 minutes, 2.5% 60 minutes or more (2000)

MARCO ISLAND (city). Covers a land area of 10.574 square miles and a water area of 6.522 square miles. Located at 25.94° N. Lat.; 81.71° W. Long. Elevation is 5 feet.

Population: 9,772 (1990); 14,879 (2000); 15,454 (2004); 16,399 (2009 projected); Race: 97.9% White, 0.3% Black, 0.6% Asian, 5.6% Hispanic of any race (2004); Density: 1,461.5 persons per square mile (2004); Average household size: 2.07 (2004); Median age: 60.0 (2004); Male/female ratio: 96.7 (2004); Marriage status: 9.5% never married, 73.6% now married, 8.2% widowed, 8.7% divorced (2000); Foreign born: 12.3% (2000); Ancestry (includes multiple ancestries): 23.4% German, 19.3% Irish, 14.9% English, 13.4% Italian, 5.3% Other groups (2000).

Economy: Single-family building permits issued: 233 (2004); Multi-family building permits issued: 123 (2004); Employment by occupation: 18.8% management, 17.0% professional, 20.0% services, 32.8% sales, 0.4% farming, 6.2% construction, 4.8% production (2000).

Income: Per capita income: $45,216 (2004); Median household income: $60,986 (2004); Average household income: $93,093 (2004); Percent of households with income of $100,000 or more: 26.8% (2004); Poverty rate: 5.4% (2000).

Taxes: Total city taxes per capita: $518 (2002); City property taxes per capita: $380 (2002).

Education: Percent of population age 25 and over with: High school diploma (including GED) or higher: 92.6% (2004); Bachelor's degree or higher: 37.0% (2004); Master's degree or higher: 13.2% (2004).

School District(s)

Collier County School District (PK-12)
2002-03 Enrollment: 38,110 . . . . (239) 254-4100

Housing: Homeownership rate: 87.3% (2004); Median home value: $355,839 (2004); Median rent: $785 per month (2000); Median age of housing: 16 years (2000).

Safety: Violent crime rate: 7.1 per 10,000 population; Property crime rate: 170.0 per 10,000 population (2003).

Newspapers: Marco Island Eagle (General - Circulation 7,938)

Transportation: Commute to work: 86.3% car, 0.2% public transportation, 2.6% walk, 8.7% work from home (2000); Travel time to work: 62.9% less than 15 minutes, 16.2% 15 to 30 minutes, 10.4% 30 to 45 minutes, 4.6% 45 to 60 minutes, 5.9% 60 minutes or more (2000)

Airports: Marco Island

Additional Information Contacts

Marco Island Area Association of Realtors . . . . (239) 394-5616
Marco Island Chamber of Commerce . . . . (239) 394-7549

NAPLES (city). Covers a land area of 12.025 square miles and a water area of 2.379 square miles. Located at 26.15° N. Lat.; 81.79° W. Long. Elevation is 9 feet.

History: Naples was laid out as a winter resort in the 1880's, and named for the Italian city. The resort flourished after the railroad reached Naples.

Population: 19,903 (1990); 20,976 (2000); 21,374 (2004); 22,210 (2009 projected); Race: 91.7% White, 5.5% Black, 0.4% Asian, 2.9% Hispanic of any race (2004); Density: 1,777.4 persons per square mile (2004); Average household size: 1.93 (2004); Median age: 61.0 (2004); Male/female ratio: 86.3 (2004); Marriage status: 11.9% never married, 65.6% now married, 12.1% widowed, 10.4% divorced (2000); Foreign born: 8.9% (2000); Ancestry (includes multiple ancestries): 20.0% German, 18.7% English, 15.5% Irish, 7.3% Italian, 6.9% Other groups (2000).

Economy: Single-family building permits issued: 173 (2004); Multi-family building permits issued: 115 (2004); Employment by occupation: 26.5% management, 17.9% professional, 14.0% services, 30.4% sales, 0.2% farming, 6.4% construction, 4.6% production (2000).

Income: Per capita income: $62,030 (2004); Median household income: $71,505 (2004); Average household income: $119,469 (2004); Percent of households with income of $100,000 or more: 36.3% (2004); Poverty rate: 5.9% (2000).

Taxes: Total city taxes per capita: $1,007 (2002); City property taxes per capita: $416 (2002).

Education: Percent of population age 25 and over with: High school diploma (including GED) or higher: 92.8% (2004); Bachelor's degree or higher: 44.8% (2004); Master's degree or higher: 15.3% (2004).

School District(s)

Collier County School District (PK-12)
2002-03 Enrollment: 38,110 . . . . (239) 254-4100

Four-year College(s)

International College
2003-04 Enrollment: 1,500 . . . . (239) 513-1122
2003-04 Tuition: In-state $8,540; Out-of-state $8,540

Two-year College(s)

Lorenzo Walker Institute of Technology (Public)
2003-04 Enrollment: 819 . . . . (941) 430-6900

Housing: Homeownership rate: 79.3% (2004); Median home value: $475,735 (2004); Median rent: $621 per month (2000); Median age of housing: 24 years (2000).
Hospitals: NCH Healthcare System (446 beds); Willough at Naples (92 beds)
Safety: Violent crime rate: 25.1 per 10,000 population; Property crime rate: 503.0 per 10,000 population (2003).
Newspapers: Everglades Echo (General - Circulation 1,000); Golden Gate Gazette (General - Circulation 7,000); Naples Daily News (Circulation 66,976)
Transportation: Commute to work: 79.1% car, 0.5% public transportation, 4.3% walk, 12.6% work from home (2000); Travel time to work: 58.0% less than 15 minutes, 31.2% 15 to 30 minutes, 5.8% 30 to 45 minutes, 2.2% 45 to 60 minutes, 2.8% 60 minutes or more (2000)
Airports: Naples Municipal (primary service)

Additional Information Contacts

Golden Gate Area Chamber of Commerce . . . . (941) 455-3100
Naples Area Board of Realtors . . . . (239) 597-1666
Naples Area Chamber of Commerce. . . . . (239) 262-6141

NAPLES MANOR (CDP). Covers a land area of 0.693 square miles and a water area of 0.013 square miles. Located at 26.09° N. Lat.; 81.72° W. Long. Elevation is 6 feet.
Population: 3,022 (1990); 5,186 (2000); 6,093 (2004); 7,234 (2009 projected); Race: 40.6% White, 14.4% Black, 0.0% Asian, 80.7% Hispanic of any race (2004); Density: 8,791.7 persons per square mile (2004); Average household size: 4.82 (2004); Median age: 25.0 (2004); Male/female ratio: 127.8 (2004); Marriage status: 34.1% never married, 59.6% now married, 2.1% widowed, 4.3% divorced (2000); Foreign born: 52.9% (2000); Ancestry (includes multiple ancestries): 58.2% Other groups, 9.2% Haitian, 2.3% United States or American, 1.7% German, 1.1% English (2000).
Economy: Employment by occupation: 2.0% management, 3.2% professional, 37.8% services, 15.4% sales, 0.8% farming, 25.7% construction, 15.2% production (2000).
Income: Per capita income: $12,123 (2004); Median household income: $42,922 (2004); Average household income: $58,391 (2004); Percent of households with income of $100,000 or more: 11.5% (2004); Poverty rate: 26.5% (2000).
Education: Percent of population age 25 and over with: High school diploma (including GED) or higher: 32.1% (2004); Bachelor's degree or higher: 2.1% (2004); Master's degree or higher: 0.4% (2004).
Housing: Homeownership rate: 63.3% (2004); Median home value: $118,570 (2004); Median rent: $547 per month (2000); Median age of housing: 17 years (2000).
Transportation: Commute to work: 94.7% car, 0.5% public transportation, 1.4% walk, 0.0% work from home (2000); Travel time to work: 14.2% less than 15 minutes, 46.6% 15 to 30 minutes, 33.2% 30 to 45 minutes, 4.3% 45 to 60 minutes, 1.8% 60 minutes or more (2000)

NAPLES PARK (CDP). Covers a land area of 1.216 square miles and a water area of 0 square miles. Located at 26.26° N. Lat.; 81.80° W. Long. Elevation is 13 feet.
Population: 6,302 (1990); 6,741 (2000); 7,012 (2004); 7,451 (2009 projected); Race: 88.9% White, 1.9% Black, 1.1% Asian, 24.4% Hispanic of any race (2004); Density: 5,764.1 persons per square mile (2004); Average household size: 2.43 (2004); Median age: 37.1 (2004); Male/female ratio: 108.1 (2004); Marriage status: 26.0% never married, 53.2% now married, 6.4% widowed, 14.4% divorced (2000); Foreign born: 18.6% (2000); Ancestry (includes multiple ancestries): 21.5% Other groups, 16.1% Irish, 15.6% German, 13.6% Italian, 10.0% English (2000).
Economy: Employment by occupation: 10.0% management, 10.8% professional, 25.4% services, 26.3% sales, 0.0% farming, 19.2% construction, 8.3% production (2000).
Income: Per capita income: $23,257 (2004); Median household income: $44,957 (2004); Average household income: $56,502 (2004); Percent of households with income of $100,000 or more: 9.0% (2004); Poverty rate: 7.8% (2000).
Education: Percent of population age 25 and over with: High school diploma (including GED) or higher: 82.9% (2004); Bachelor's degree or higher: 18.2% (2004); Master's degree or higher: 4.4% (2004).
Housing: Homeownership rate: 63.2% (2004); Median home value: $185,622 (2004); Median rent: $691 per month (2000); Median age of housing: 22 years (2000).
Transportation: Commute to work: 89.6% car, 0.2% public transportation, 1.3% walk, 3.9% work from home (2000); Travel time to work: 30.4% less than 15 minutes, 48.5% 15 to 30 minutes, 16.3% 30 to 45 minutes, 2.8% 45 to 60 minutes, 2.0% 60 minutes or more (2000)

OCHOPEE (unincorporated postal area, zip code 34141). Covers a land area of 1,221.159 square miles and a water area of 156.272 square miles. Located at 25.87° N. Lat.; 81.16° W. Long. Elevation is 6 feet.
History: Ochopee developed as the center for tomato farms in a swampy region. Marsh buggies, with wheels 8-10 feet high, were developed here to operate within the swamps, on land or on water.
Population: 128 (2000); Race: 44.4% White, 37.0% Black, 0.0% Asian, 0.0% Hispanic of any race (2000); Density: 0.1 persons per square mile (2000); Age: 48.1% under 18, 14.8% over 64 (2000); Marriage status: 2.9% never married, 78.1% now married, 0.0% widowed, 19.0% divorced (2000); Foreign born: 1.9% (2000); Ancestry (includes multiple ancestries): 15.7% Other groups, 13.0% Italian, 9.3% United States or American, 6.5% German, 5.6% Scotch-Irish (2000).
Economy: Employment by occupation: 0.0% management, 0.0% professional, 61.5% services, 38.5% sales, 0.0% farming, 0.0% construction, 0.0% production (2000).
Income: Per capita income: $13,381 (2000); Median household income: $36,328 (2000); Poverty rate: 5.1% (2000).
Education: Percent of population age 25 and over with: High school diploma (including GED) or higher: 64.3% (2000); Bachelor's degree or higher: 16.1% (2000).
Housing: Homeownership rate: 83.3% (2000); Median home value: $75,000 (2000); Median rent: $475 per month (2000); Median age of housing: 26 years (2000).
Transportation: Commute to work: 76.9% car, 0.0% public transportation, 0.0% walk, 23.1% work from home (2000); Travel time to work: 70.0% less than 15 minutes, 0.0% 15 to 30 minutes, 30.0% 30 to 45 minutes, 0.0% 45 to 60 minutes, 0.0% 60 minutes or more (2000)

ORANGETREE (CDP). Covers a land area of 4.424 square miles and a water area of 0.007 square miles. Located at 26.28° N. Lat.; 81.58° W. Long.
Population: 221 (1990); 950 (2000); 1,313 (2004); 1,747 (2009 projected); Race: 95.2% White, 1.3% Black, 0.2% Asian, 12.9% Hispanic of any race (2004); Density: 296.8 persons per square mile (2004); Average household size: 3.00 (2004); Median age: 35.0 (2004); Male/female ratio: 101.7 (2004); Marriage status: 8.8% never married, 79.8% now married, 2.2% widowed, 9.2% divorced (2000); Foreign born: 5.0% (2000); Ancestry (includes multiple ancestries): 21.3% Other groups, 18.8% Irish, 17.2% English, 16.9% German, 10.2% Italian (2000).
Economy: Employment by occupation: 16.9% management, 24.5% professional, 24.3% services, 23.9% sales, 0.0% farming, 5.3% construction, 5.1% production (2000).
Income: Per capita income: $24,107 (2004); Median household income: $66,406 (2004); Average household income: $72,266 (2004); Percent of households with income of $100,000 or more: 21.0% (2004); Poverty rate: 1.7% (2000).
Education: Percent of population age 25 and over with: High school diploma (including GED) or higher: 92.0% (2004); Bachelor's degree or higher: 24.3% (2004); Master's degree or higher: 12.3% (2004).
Housing: Homeownership rate: 96.3% (2004); Median home value: $220,000 (2004); Median rent: $345 per month (2000); Median age of housing: 3 years (2000).
Transportation: Commute to work: 91.1% car, 0.0% public transportation, 2.6% walk, 5.0% work from home (2000); Travel time to work: 13.8% less than 15 minutes, 22.9% 15 to 30 minutes, 29.0% 30 to 45 minutes, 16.9% 45 to 60 minutes, 17.4% 60 minutes or more (2000)

PELICAN BAY (CDP). Covers a land area of 3.242 square miles and a water area of 0.175 square miles. Located at 26.23° N. Lat.; 81.80° W. Long.
Population: 2,035 (1990); 5,686 (2000); 7,423 (2004); 9,527 (2009 projected); Race: 99.2% White, 0.1% Black, 0.5% Asian, 1.2% Hispanic of any race (2004); Density: 2,289.8 persons per square mile (2004); Average

household size: 1.86 (2004); Median age: 67.5 (2004); Male/female ratio: 84.8 (2004); Marriage status: 6.2% never married, 79.0% now married, 9.4% widowed, 5.3% divorced (2000); Foreign born: 10.8% (2000); Ancestry (includes multiple ancestries): 21.9% German, 19.4% English, 17.1% Irish, 9.4% Italian, 4.3% Other groups (2000).
Economy: Employment by occupation: 30.8% management, 15.6% professional, 3.0% services, 47.3% sales, 0.0% farming, 3.2% construction, 0.0% production (2000).
Income: Per capita income: $88,347 (2004); Median household income: $108,736 (2004); Average household income: $163,791 (2004); Percent of households with income of $100,000 or more: 52.7% (2004); Poverty rate: 2.8% (2000).
Education: Percent of population age 25 and over with: High school diploma (including GED) or higher: 95.1% (2004); Bachelor's degree or higher: 59.9% (2004); Master's degree or higher: 22.3% (2004).
Housing: Homeownership rate: 94.5% (2004); Median home value: $517,732 (2004); Median rent: $1,082 per month (2000); Median age of housing: 8 years (2000).
Transportation: Commute to work: 74.2% car, 0.6% public transportation, 3.7% walk, 19.9% work from home (2000); Travel time to work: 53.8% less than 15 minutes, 32.4% 15 to 30 minutes, 9.2% 30 to 45 minutes, 0.9% 45 to 60 minutes, 3.8% 60 minutes or more (2000)

PINE RIDGE (CDP). Covers a land area of 1.767 square miles and a water area of 0.092 square miles. Located at 26.23° N. Lat.; 81.79° W. Long.
Population: 1,983 (1990); 1,965 (2000); 2,188 (2004); 2,484 (2009 projected); Race: 96.8% White, 1.5% Black, 0.5% Asian, 4.0% Hispanic of any race (2004); Density: 1,238.1 persons per square mile (2004); Average household size: 2.40 (2004); Median age: 44.1 (2004); Male/female ratio: 91.8 (2004); Marriage status: 11.9% never married, 65.2% now married, 8.1% widowed, 14.7% divorced (2000); Foreign born: 7.6% (2000); Ancestry (includes multiple ancestries): 19.8% English, 17.5% German, 8.7% Other groups, 8.6% Irish, 8.2% United States or American (2000).
Economy: Employment by occupation: 17.7% management, 16.4% professional, 4.1% services, 47.6% sales, 0.0% farming, 8.9% construction, 5.4% production (2000).
Income: Per capita income: $59,567 (2004); Median household income: $73,742 (2004); Average household income: $143,065 (2004); Percent of households with income of $100,000 or more: 40.1% (2004); Poverty rate: 1.9% (2000).
Education: Percent of population age 25 and over with: High school diploma (including GED) or higher: 93.0% (2004); Bachelor's degree or higher: 44.6% (2004); Master's degree or higher: 17.3% (2004).
Housing: Homeownership rate: 85.4% (2004); Median home value: $418,182 (2004); Median rent: $893 per month (2000); Median age of housing: 19 years (2000).
Transportation: Commute to work: 92.1% car, 0.0% public transportation, 2.4% walk, 3.3% work from home (2000); Travel time to work: 43.8% less than 15 minutes, 45.0% 15 to 30 minutes, 2.6% 30 to 45 minutes, 2.4% 45 to 60 minutes, 6.2% 60 minutes or more (2000)

PLANTATION ISLAND (CDP). Covers a land area of 0.587 square miles and a water area of 0 square miles. Located at 25.84° N. Lat.; 81.36° W. Long.
Population: 129 (1990); 202 (2000); 311 (2004); 433 (2009 projected); Race: 100.0% White, 0.0% Black, 0.0% Asian, 5.5% Hispanic of any race (2004); Density: 529.8 persons per square mile (2004); Average household size: 2.16 (2004); Median age: 49.7 (2004); Male/female ratio: 103.3 (2004); Marriage status: 26.5% never married, 54.7% now married, 6.6% widowed, 12.2% divorced (2000); Foreign born: 0.5% (2000); Ancestry (includes multiple ancestries): 28.6% United States or American, 19.7% Irish, 18.3% German, 12.7% English, 7.5% Other groups (2000).
Economy: Employment by occupation: 5.4% management, 17.4% professional, 31.5% services, 9.8% sales, 8.7% farming, 9.8% construction, 17.4% production (2000).
Income: Per capita income: $23,939 (2004); Median household income: $37,308 (2004); Average household income: $51,701 (2004); Percent of households with income of $100,000 or more: 9.7% (2004); Poverty rate: 14.6% (2000).
Education: Percent of population age 25 and over with: High school diploma (including GED) or higher: 83.6% (2004); Bachelor's degree or higher: 12.3% (2004); Master's degree or higher: 2.0% (2004).
Housing: Homeownership rate: 91.0% (2004); Median home value: $129,891 (2004); Median rent: $325 per month (2000); Median age of housing: 21 years (2000).
Transportation: Commute to work: 92.0% car, 0.0% public transportation, 2.3% walk, 5.7% work from home (2000); Travel time to work: 67.1% less than 15 minutes, 2.4% 15 to 30 minutes, 4.9% 30 to 45 minutes, 8.5% 45 to 60 minutes, 17.1% 60 minutes or more (2000)

VINEYARDS (CDP). Covers a land area of 2.261 square miles and a water area of 0 square miles. Located at 26.22° N. Lat.; 81.72° W. Long.
Population: 980 (1990); 2,232 (2000); 3,449 (2004); 4,887 (2009 projected); Race: 98.1% White, 0.7% Black, 0.3% Asian, 2.2% Hispanic of any race (2004); Density: 1,525.3 persons per square mile (2004); Average household size: 2.17 (2004); Median age: 59.5 (2004); Male/female ratio: 88.7 (2004); Marriage status: 7.1% never married, 79.6% now married, 5.5% widowed, 7.9% divorced (2000); Foreign born: 9.2% (2000); Ancestry (includes multiple ancestries): 20.2% German, 16.3% Irish, 14.6% Italian, 14.1% English, 5.2% Polish (2000).
Economy: Employment by occupation: 22.4% management, 13.3% professional, 13.0% services, 46.0% sales, 0.0% farming, 0.0% construction, 5.4% production (2000).
Income: Per capita income: $64,950 (2004); Median household income: $95,128 (2004); Average household income: $139,375 (2004); Percent of households with income of $100,000 or more: 46.9% (2004); Poverty rate: 6.9% (2000).
Education: Percent of population age 25 and over with: High school diploma (including GED) or higher: 96.0% (2004); Bachelor's degree or higher: 51.3% (2004); Master's degree or higher: 15.6% (2004).
Housing: Homeownership rate: 94.9% (2004); Median home value: $317,123 (2004); Median rent: $1,344 per month (2000); Median age of housing: 5 years (2000).
Transportation: Commute to work: 81.6% car, 0.0% public transportation, 1.7% walk, 13.8% work from home (2000); Travel time to work: 14.6% less than 15 minutes, 62.9% 15 to 30 minutes, 16.0% 30 to 45 minutes, 3.1% 45 to 60 minutes, 3.3% 60 minutes or more (2000)

Columbia County

Located in northern Florida; bounded on the north by Georgia, on the west by the Suwanee River; includes part of the Okefenokee Swamp and Osceola National Forest. Covers a land area of 797.00 square miles, a water area of 4.00 square miles, and is located in the Eastern Time Zone. The county government was organized in 1832. County seat is Lake City.

Columbia County is part of the Lake City, FL Micropolitan Statistical Area. The entire metro area includes: Columbia County, FL

Weather Station: Lake City 2 E — Elevation: 193 feet

	Jan	Feb	Mar	Apr	May	Jun	Jul	Aug	Sep	Oct	Nov	Dec
High	64	68	74	80	86	90	91	91	88	81	74	67
Low	42	44	50	55	62	68	71	71	68	59	51	44
Precip	4.5	3.8	5.1	3.3	3.8	6.8	6.7	7.4	4.6	2.9	2.4	3.0
Snow	tr	0.0	0.0	0.0	0.0	0.0	0.0	0.0	0.0	0.0	0.0	0.0

High and Low temperatures in degrees Fahrenheit; Precipitation and Snow in inches

Population: 42,613 (1990); 56,513 (2000); 59,502 (2004); 63,283 (2009 projected); Race: 79.3% White, 17.7% Black, 0.7% Asian, 2.9% Hispanic of any race (2004); Density: 74.7 persons per square mile (2004); Average household size: 2.71 (2004); Median age: 37.7 (2004); Male/female ratio: 103.7 (2004).
Religion: Five largest groups: 17.3% Southern Baptist Convention, 4.2% Catholic Church, 4.0% The United Methodist Church, 1.9% The Church of Jesus Christ of Latter-day Saints, 1.6% Church of God (Cleveland, Tennessee) (2000).
Economy: Unemployment rate: 4.3% (2004); Total civilian labor force: 26,201 (2004); Leading industries: 21.4% health care and social assistance; 17.4% retail trade; 11.8% accommodation & food services (2003); Companies that employ 500 or more persons: 3 (2003); Companies that employ 100 to 499 persons: 18 (2003); Companies that employ less than 100 persons: 1,159 (2003); Farms: 688 totaling 90,227 acres (2002); Minority business ownership rate: 6.3% (1997); Women business ownership rate: 17.3% (1997); Retail sales per capita: $10,764 (1997). Single-family building permits issued: 380 (2004); Multi-family building permits issued: 0 (2004).
Income: Per capita income: $15,727 (2004); Median household income: $32,485 (2004); Average household income: $41,784 (2004); Percent of

households with income of $100,000 or more: 5.6% (2004); Poverty rate: 17.2% (2002); Bankruptcy rate: 4.16% (2004).
Education: Percent of population age 25 and over with: High school diploma (including GED) or higher: 74.4% (2004); Bachelor's degree or higher: 10.8% (2004); Master's degree or higher: 4.0% (2004).
Housing: Homeownership rate: 77.6% (2004); Median home value: $89,783 (2004); Median rent: $344 per month (2000); Median age of housing: 18 years (2000).
Health: Birth rate: 144.8 per 10,000 population (2004); Death rate: 99.5 per 10,000 population (2004); Age adjusted cancer mortality rate: 206.0 deaths per 100,000 population (2002); Air Quality Index: 95.9% good, 4.1% moderate, 0.0% unhealthy for sensitive individuals, 0.0% unhealthy (percent of days in 2004); Number of physicians: 15.7 per 10,000 population (2001); Hospital beds: 87.9 per 10,000 population (2002); Hospital admissions: 2,482.8 per 10,000 population (2002).
Elections: 2004 Presidential election results: 67.1% Bush, 32.1% Kerry, 0.4% Nader, 0.2% Badnarik
National and State Parks: O'Leno State Park; River Rise Preserve State Park
Additional Information Contacts
Columbia County Government Offices . . . . (904) 755-4100
Lake City Board of Realtors . . . . (386) 755-3966
Lake City Chamber of Commerce . . . . (904) 752-3690

Columbia County Communities

FIVE POINTS (CDP). Covers a land area of 2.582 square miles and a water area of 0 square miles. Located at 30.21° N. Lat.; 82.64° W. Long. Elevation is 169 feet.
Population: 1,108 (1990); 1,362 (2000); 1,404 (2004); 1,486 (2009 projected); Race: 81.3% White, 17.4% Black, 0.2% Asian, 2.0% Hispanic of any race (2004); Density: 543.8 persons per square mile (2004); Average household size: 3.55 (2004); Median age: 32.8 (2004); Male/female ratio: 153.9 (2004); Marriage status: 12.8% never married, 46.1% now married, 13.3% widowed, 27.8% divorced (2000); Foreign born: 1.5% (2000); Ancestry (includes multiple ancestries): 19.0% United States or American, 10.5% Other groups, 3.5% English, 2.8% Irish, 1.7% French (except Basque) (2000).
Economy: Employment by occupation: 2.5% management, 6.0% professional, 26.8% services, 21.1% sales, 0.0% farming, 12.7% construction, 31.0% production (2000).
Income: Per capita income: $6,685 (2004); Median household income: $16,667 (2004); Average household income: $21,572 (2004); Percent of households with income of $100,000 or more: 2.0% (2004); Poverty rate: 43.8% (2000).
Education: Percent of population age 25 and over with: High school diploma (including GED) or higher: 50.4% (2004); Bachelor's degree or higher: 3.0% (2004); Master's degree or higher: 1.5% (2004).
Housing: Homeownership rate: 62.4% (2004); Median home value: $40,278 (2004); Median rent: $259 per month (2000); Median age of housing: 25 years (2000).
Transportation: Commute to work: 85.0% car, 0.0% public transportation, 1.8% walk, 0.0% work from home (2000); Travel time to work: 53.1% less than 15 minutes, 33.3% 15 to 30 minutes, 4.4% 30 to 45 minutes, 2.2% 45 to 60 minutes, 7.0% 60 minutes or more (2000)

FORT WHITE (town). Covers a land area of 2.313 square miles and a water area of 0 square miles. Located at 29.92° N. Lat.; 82.71° W. Long. Elevation is 72 feet.
History: The original Fort White, for which the town was named, was built during the Seminole Wars. The town of Fort White developed as a turkey-farming center.
Population: 381 (1990); 409 (2000); 442 (2004); 483 (2009 projected); Race: 47.1% White, 50.7% Black, 0.5% Asian, 3.6% Hispanic of any race (2004); Density: 191.1 persons per square mile (2004); Average household size: 2.66 (2004); Median age: 37.4 (2004); Male/female ratio: 78.9 (2004); Marriage status: 35.5% never married, 44.5% now married, 11.3% widowed, 8.7% divorced (2000); Foreign born: 0.0% (2000); Ancestry (includes multiple ancestries): 33.9% Other groups, 27.9% United States or American, 5.3% German, 4.8% English, 4.6% Irish (2000).
Economy: Employment by occupation: 8.9% management, 23.3% professional, 25.3% services, 26.7% sales, 0.0% farming, 6.8% construction, 8.9% production (2000).
Income: Per capita income: $12,698 (2004); Median household income: $25,882 (2004); Average household income: $33,810 (2004); Percent of households with income of $100,000 or more: 4.2% (2004); Poverty rate: 26.8% (2000).
Education: Percent of population age 25 and over with: High school diploma (including GED) or higher: 69.0% (2004); Bachelor's degree or higher: 11.2% (2004); Master's degree or higher: 3.6% (2004).

School District(s)
Columbia County School District (PK-12)
2002-03 Enrollment: 9,707 . . . . (386) 755-8000
Housing: Homeownership rate: 78.9% (2004); Median home value: $66,842 (2004); Median rent: $325 per month (2000); Median age of housing: 18 years (2000).
Transportation: Commute to work: 92.4% car, 0.0% public transportation, 4.1% walk, 1.4% work from home (2000); Travel time to work: 37.8% less than 15 minutes, 20.3% 15 to 30 minutes, 18.9% 30 to 45 minutes, 18.9% 45 to 60 minutes, 4.2% 60 minutes or more (2000)

LAKE CITY (city). Covers a land area of 10.563 square miles and a water area of 0.520 square miles. Located at 30.19° N. Lat.; 82.64° W. Long. Elevation is 188 feet.
History: Before 1859, Lake City was known as Alligator. From 1883 to 1905, this was the location of the State Agricultural College. Lumber, naval stores (rosin and turpentine used for calking ships), and tobacco were the basis of Lake City's early economy.
Population: 10,198 (1990); 9,980 (2000); 9,982 (2004); 10,186 (2009 projected); Race: 56.9% White, 40.2% Black, 1.1% Asian, 3.0% Hispanic of any race (2004); Density: 945.0 persons per square mile (2004); Average household size: 2.49 (2004); Median age: 38.3 (2004); Male/female ratio: 90.6 (2004); Marriage status: 27.4% never married, 45.9% now married, 12.8% widowed, 13.9% divorced (2000); Foreign born: 3.1% (2000); Ancestry (includes multiple ancestries): 37.8% Other groups, 11.9% United States or American, 7.3% German, 6.7% English, 5.8% Irish (2000).
Economy: Single-family building permits issued: 35 (2004); Multi-family building permits issued: 0 (2004); Employment by occupation: 8.0% management, 16.2% professional, 25.5% services, 26.4% sales, 0.8% farming, 11.1% construction, 12.0% production (2000).
Income: Per capita income: $15,400 (2004); Median household income: $27,217 (2004); Average household income: $37,543 (2004); Percent of households with income of $100,000 or more: 5.9% (2004); Poverty rate: 20.5% (2000).
Taxes: Total city taxes per capita: $604 (2002); City property taxes per capita: $133 (2002).
Education: Percent of population age 25 and over with: High school diploma (including GED) or higher: 75.3% (2004); Bachelor's degree or higher: 15.3% (2004); Master's degree or higher: 7.3% (2004).

School District(s)
Columbia County School District (PK-12)
2002-03 Enrollment: 9,707 . . . . (386) 755-8000

Two-year College(s)
Lake City Community College (Public)
2003-04 Enrollment: 2,695 . . . . (386) 754-1822
2003-04 Tuition: In-state $1,706; Out-of-state $6,306
Housing: Homeownership rate: 55.5% (2004); Median home value: $80,025 (2004); Median rent: $359 per month (2000); Median age of housing: 32 years (2000).
Hospitals: Lake City Medical Center (75 beds); Shands at Lake Shore (128 beds); Veterans Affairs Medical Center (319 beds)
Safety: Violent crime rate: 148.6 per 10,000 population; Property crime rate: 1,166.5 per 10,000 population (2003).
Newspapers: Lake City Reporter (Circulation 8,184)
Transportation: Commute to work: 93.5% car, 0.0% public transportation, 1.5% walk, 2.6% work from home (2000); Travel time to work: 60.8% less than 15 minutes, 19.7% 15 to 30 minutes, 9.3% 30 to 45 minutes, 4.6% 45 to 60 minutes, 5.7% 60 minutes or more (2000); Amtrak: Service available.
Additional Information Contacts
Lake City Board of Realtors . . . . (386) 755-3966
Lake City Chamber of Commerce . . . . (904) 752-3690
Local Government Offices . . . . (386) 758-5427

LULU (unincorporated postal area, zip code 32061). Covers a land area of 12.609 square miles and a water area of 0 square miles. Located at 30.10° N. Lat.; 82.50° W. Long. Elevation is 155 feet.
Population: 146 (2000); Race: 94.2% White, 0.0% Black, 0.0% Asian, 0.0% Hispanic of any race (2000); Density: 11.6 persons per square mile (2000); Age: 15.3% under 18, 16.8% over 64 (2000); Marriage status: 11.5% never married, 74.6% now married, 0.0% widowed, 13.9% divorced

(2000); Foreign born: 0.0% (2000); Ancestry (includes multiple ancestries): 33.6% United States or American, 17.5% Other groups, 7.3% German, 7.3% Irish, 5.8% English (2000).
Economy: Employment by occupation: 18.2% management, 0.0% professional, 22.7% services, 50.0% sales, 0.0% farming, 9.1% construction, 0.0% production (2000).
Income: Per capita income: $19,290 (2000); Median household income: $45,469 (2000); Poverty rate: 10.2% (2000).
Education: Percent of population age 25 and over with: High school diploma (including GED) or higher: 92.6% (2000); Bachelor's degree or higher: 7.4% (2000).
Housing: Homeownership rate: 100.0% (2000); Median home value: $55,000 (2000); Median rent: $n/a per month (2000); Median age of housing: 17 years (2000).
Transportation: Commute to work: 100.0% car, 0.0% public transportation, 0.0% walk, 0.0% work from home (2000); Travel time to work: 9.1% less than 15 minutes, 79.5% 15 to 30 minutes, 0.0% 30 to 45 minutes, 0.0% 45 to 60 minutes, 11.4% 60 minutes or more (2000)

WATERTOWN (CDP). Covers a land area of 2.391 square miles and a water area of 0.060 square miles. Located at 30.18° N. Lat.; 82.60° W. Long. Elevation is 191 feet.
History: Watertown developed as a center for lumbering, with railroad spur lines bringing logs to the sawmills.
Population: 3,069 (1990); 2,837 (2000); 2,877 (2004); 2,965 (2009 projected); Race: 67.2% White, 30.5% Black, 0.2% Asian, 1.4% Hispanic of any race (2004); Density: 1,203.0 persons per square mile (2004); Average household size: 2.42 (2004); Median age: 41.3 (2004); Male/female ratio: 92.3 (2004); Marriage status: 21.6% never married, 54.7% now married, 8.2% widowed, 15.4% divorced (2000); Foreign born: 1.2% (2000); Ancestry (includes multiple ancestries): 33.5% Other groups, 16.3% United States or American, 8.8% Irish, 8.2% English, 4.9% German (2000).
Economy: Employment by occupation: 4.7% management, 16.2% professional, 26.1% services, 19.8% sales, 1.1% farming, 14.0% construction, 18.1% production (2000).
Income: Per capita income: $15,483 (2004); Median household income: $31,806 (2004); Average household income: $37,399 (2004); Percent of households with income of $100,000 or more: 2.9% (2004); Poverty rate: 17.1% (2000).
Education: Percent of population age 25 and over with: High school diploma (including GED) or higher: 76.0% (2004); Bachelor's degree or higher: 7.5% (2004); Master's degree or higher: 3.0% (2004).
Housing: Homeownership rate: 72.5% (2004); Median home value: $73,682 (2004); Median rent: $296 per month (2000); Median age of housing: 31 years (2000).
Transportation: Commute to work: 89.9% car, 0.0% public transportation, 4.8% walk, 1.3% work from home (2000); Travel time to work: 51.7% less than 15 minutes, 24.3% 15 to 30 minutes, 13.1% 30 to 45 minutes, 4.4% 45 to 60 minutes, 6.5% 60 minutes or more (2000)

De Soto County

Located in south central Florida; partly swampy with many small lakes, drained by the Peace River. Covers a land area of 637.30 square miles, a water area of 2.20 square miles, and is located in the Eastern Time Zone. The county government was organized in 1887. County seat is Arcadia.

De Soto County is part of the Arcadia, FL Micropolitan Statistical Area. The entire metro area includes: DeSoto County, FL

Weather Station: Arcadia Elevation: 62 feet

	Jan	Feb	Mar	Apr	May	Jun	Jul	Aug	Sep	Oct	Nov	Dec
High	74	75	80	84	89	91	92	91	90	86	80	75
Low	49	50	54	57	63	69	71	71	70	64	57	52
Precip	2.2	2.6	3.3	1.7	4.2	8.0	7.4	7.0	6.8	2.9	2.1	1.8
Snow	0.0	0.0	0.0	0.0	0.0	0.0	0.0	0.0	0.0	0.0	0.0	0.0

High and Low temperatures in degrees Fahrenheit; Precipitation and Snow in inches

Population: 23,865 (1990); 32,209 (2000); 33,137 (2004); 34,321 (2009 projected); Race: 71.9% White, 11.9% Black, 0.4% Asian, 29.3% Hispanic of any race (2004); Density: 52.0 persons per square mile (2004); Average household size: 3.04 (2004); Median age: 36.1 (2004); Male/female ratio: 132.1 (2004).
Religion: Five largest groups: 15.0% Southern Baptist Convention, 5.2% The United Methodist Church, 2.6% Catholic Church, 1.5% Church of God (Cleveland, Tennessee), 1.4% Assemblies of God (2000).
Economy: Unemployment rate: 8.6% (2004); Total civilian labor force: 8,851 (2004); Leading industries: 28.7% retail trade; 21.5% health care and social assistance; 9.2% accommodation & food services (2003); Companies that employ 500 or more persons: 0 (2003); Companies that employ 100 to 499 persons: 6 (2003); Companies that employ less than 100 persons: 450 (2003); Farms: 1,153 totaling 388,177 acres (2002); Minority business ownership rate: n/a (1997); Women business ownership rate: 22.2% (1997); Retail sales per capita: $7,961 (1997). Single-family building permits issued: 149 (2004); Multi-family building permits issued: 0 (2004).
Income: Per capita income: $14,502 (2004); Median household income: $32,476 (2004); Average household income: $42,151 (2004); Percent of households with income of $100,000 or more: 5.2% (2004); Poverty rate: 21.3% (2002); Bankruptcy rate: 2.97% (2004).
Taxes: Total county taxes per capita: $352 (2002); County property taxes per capita: $210 (2002).
Education: Percent of population age 25 and over with: High school diploma (including GED) or higher: 64.0% (2004); Bachelor's degree or higher: 8.6% (2004); Master's degree or higher: 3.2% (2004).
Housing: Homeownership rate: 75.2% (2004); Median home value: $76,337 (2004); Median rent: $364 per month (2000); Median age of housing: 20 years (2000).
Health: Birth rate: 136.7 per 10,000 population (2004); Death rate: 90.3 per 10,000 population (2004); Age adjusted cancer mortality rate: 149.4 deaths per 100,000 population (2002); Number of physicians: 9.2 per 10,000 population (2001); Hospital beds: 14.9 per 10,000 population (2002); Hospital admissions: 839.5 per 10,000 population (2002).
Elections: 2004 Presidential election results: 58.1% Bush, 41.1% Kerry, 0.5% Nader, 0.1% Badnarik

Additional Information Contacts

De Soto County Government Offices. . . . . (863) 993-4800
Arcadia Chamber of Commerce . . . . (863) 494-4033
Desoto County Board of Realtors . . . . (863) 494-7700

De Soto County Communities

ARCADIA (city). Covers a land area of 4.038 square miles and a water area of 0.006 square miles. Located at 27.21° N. Lat.; 81.86° W. Long. Elevation is 57 feet.
History: Arcadia developed as the center of a cattle area, with numerous cow camps in the vicinity giving the town a frontier atmosphere in the early 1900's.
Population: 6,490 (1990); 6,604 (2000); 6,734 (2004); 6,837 (2009 projected); Race: 61.8% White, 26.3% Black, 1.1% Asian, 24.8% Hispanic of any race (2004); Density: 1,667.8 persons per square mile (2004); Average household size: 2.98 (2004); Median age: 32.2 (2004); Male/female ratio: 106.1 (2004); Marriage status: 31.5% never married, 50.6% now married, 6.1% widowed, 11.7% divorced (2000); Foreign born: 15.9% (2000); Ancestry (includes multiple ancestries): 50.5% Other groups, 11.6% United States or American, 8.4% English, 6.2% German, 5.9% Irish (2000).
Economy: Employment by occupation: 4.7% management, 16.2% professional, 22.5% services, 17.9% sales, 17.1% farming, 11.2% construction, 10.3% production (2000).
Income: Per capita income: $12,361 (2004); Median household income: $25,827 (2004); Average household income: $35,808 (2004); Percent of households with income of $100,000 or more: 3.8% (2004); Poverty rate: 25.9% (2000).
Taxes: Total city taxes per capita: $358 (2002); City property taxes per capita: $182 (2002).
Education: Percent of population age 25 and over with: High school diploma (including GED) or higher: 64.0% (2004); Bachelor's degree or higher: 10.0% (2004); Master's degree or higher: 3.5% (2004).

School District(s)

Desoto County School District (PK-12)
2002-03 Enrollment: 4,916 . . . . (863) 494-4222

Housing: Homeownership rate: 61.1% (2004); Median home value: $72,893 (2004); Median rent: $351 per month (2000); Median age of housing: 33 years (2000).
Hospitals: Desoto Memorial Hospital (82 beds)
Safety: Violent crime rate: 124.2 per 10,000 population; Property crime rate: 523.0 per 10,000 population (2003).
Newspapers: DeSoto Sun Herald (Circulation 3,900)
Transportation: Commute to work: 91.5% car, 1.5% public transportation, 2.3% walk, 1.7% work from home (2000); Travel time to work: 39.7% less

than 15 minutes, 25.0% 15 to 30 minutes, 22.3% 30 to 45 minutes, 6.7% 45 to 60 minutes, 6.3% 60 minutes or more (2000)

Additional Information Contacts

Arcadia Chamber of Commerce .... (863) 494-4033
Desoto County Board of Realtors .... (863) 494-7700
Local Government Offices .... (863) 494-4114

SOUTHEAST ARCADIA (CDP). Covers a land area of 7.305 square miles and a water area of 0 square miles. Located at 27.19° N. Lat.; 81.85° W. Long.

Population: 4,143 (1990); 6,064 (2000); 5,728 (2004); 5,426 (2009 projected); Race: 69.3% White, 3.5% Black, 0.4% Asian, 54.5% Hispanic of any race (2004); Density: 784.1 persons per square mile (2004); Average household size: 3.25 (2004); Median age: 30.3 (2004); Male/female ratio: 142.9 (2004); Marriage status: 22.1% never married, 64.1% now married, 6.0% widowed, 7.7% divorced (2000); Foreign born: 32.1% (2000); Ancestry (includes multiple ancestries): 39.6% Other groups, 15.4% United States or American, 6.0% German, 5.6% English, 4.2% Irish (2000).

Economy: Employment by occupation: 2.8% management, 5.3% professional, 16.9% services, 14.1% sales, 40.0% farming, 10.7% construction, 10.2% production (2000).

Income: Per capita income: $13,126 (2004); Median household income: $31,201 (2004); Average household income: $42,476 (2004); Percent of households with income of $100,000 or more: 5.7% (2004); Poverty rate: 33.8% (2000).

Education: Percent of population age 25 and over with: High school diploma (including GED) or higher: 54.7% (2004); Bachelor's degree or higher: 4.6% (2004); Master's degree or higher: 1.0% (2004).

Housing: Homeownership rate: 66.9% (2004); Median home value: $59,765 (2004); Median rent: $400 per month (2000); Median age of housing: 21 years (2000).

Transportation: Commute to work: 84.4% car, 12.7% public transportation, 0.8% walk, 0.9% work from home (2000); Travel time to work: 27.3% less than 15 minutes, 25.6% 15 to 30 minutes, 31.4% 30 to 45 minutes, 6.3% 45 to 60 minutes, 9.3% 60 minutes or more (2000)

Dixie County

Located in northern Florida; swampy area, bounded on the south and west by the Gulf of Mexico, and on the east by the Suwannee River. Covers a land area of 704.00 square miles, a water area of 159.60 square miles, and is located in the Eastern Time Zone. The county government was organized in 1921. County seat is Cross City.

Weather Station: Cross City 2 WNW — Elevation: 39 feet

	Jan	Feb	Mar	Apr	May	Jun	Jul	Aug	Sep	Oct	Nov	Dec
High	65	68	74	79	85	89	90	90	88	82	74	68
Low	40	43	49	53	60	67	70	70	68	57	49	42
Precip	4.5	3.6	4.7	3.5	3.2	6.3	8.9	9.8	5.8	3.0	2.4	3.4
Snow	0.0	0.0	0.0	0.0	0.0	0.0	0.0	0.0	0.0	0.0	0.0	0.0

High and Low temperatures in degrees Fahrenheit; Precipitation and Snow in inches

Population: 10,585 (1990); 13,827 (2000); 14,673 (2004); 15,742 (2009 projected); Race: 89.0% White, 8.7% Black, 0.3% Asian, 2.2% Hispanic of any race (2004); Density: 20.8 persons per square mile (2004); Average household size: 2.66 (2004); Median age: 40.8 (2004); Male/female ratio: 114.3 (2004).

Religion: Five largest groups: 30.8% Southern Baptist Convention, 3.7% The United Methodist Church, 2.2% International Pentecostal Holiness Church, 2.0% Church of God (Cleveland, Tennessee), 1.4% The Church of Jesus Christ of Latter-day Saints (200

Economy: Unemployment rate: 5.1% (2004); Total civilian labor force: 4,446 (2004); Leading industries: 25.7% manufacturing; 18.6% retail trade; 12.2% health care and social assistance (2003); Companies that employ 500 or more persons: 0 (2003); Companies that employ 100 to 499 persons: 2 (2003); Companies that employ less than 100 persons: 188 (2003); Farms: 215 totaling 31,249 acres (2002); Minority business ownership rate: n/a (1997); Women business ownership rate: 21.0% (1997); Retail sales per capita: $3,090 (1997). Single-family building permits issued: 48 (2004); Multi-family building permits issued: 16 (2004).

Income: Per capita income: $15,328 (2004); Median household income: $28,724 (2004); Average household income: $39,522 (2004); Percent of households with income of $100,000 or more: 5.4% (2004); Poverty rate: 20.8% (2002); Bankruptcy rate: 3.18% (2004).

Education: Percent of population age 25 and over with: High school diploma (including GED) or higher: 65.8% (2004); Bachelor's degree or higher: 6.7% (2004); Master's degree or higher: 3.1% (2004).

Housing: Homeownership rate: 86.9% (2004); Median home value: $65,355 (2004); Median rent: $231 per month (2000); Median age of housing: 19 years (2000).

Health: Birth rate: 121.7 per 10,000 population (2004); Death rate: 145.5 per 10,000 population (2004); Age adjusted cancer mortality rate: 247.9 deaths per 100,000 population (2002); Number of physicians: 2.1 per 10,000 population (2001); Hospital beds: 0.0 per 10,000 population (2002); Hospital admissions: 0.0 per 10,000 population (2002).

Elections: 2004 Presidential election results: 68.8% Bush, 30.4% Kerry, 0.5% Nader, 0.1% Badnarik

National and State Parks: Lower Suwannee National Wildlife Refuge

Additional Information Contacts

Dixie County Government Offices .... (352) 498-1206
Cross City Chamber of Commerce .... (352) 498-5454

Dixie County Communities

CROSS CITY (town). Covers a land area of 1.897 square miles and a water area of 0 square miles. Located at 29.63° N. Lat.; 83.12° W. Long. Elevation is 42 feet.

History: Cross City developed as a timber, turpentine, and fishing center, with cold-storage plants that prepared fish for shipment to northern markets.

Population: 2,041 (1990); 1,775 (2000); 1,579 (2004); 1,493 (2009 projected); Race: 70.7% White, 27.2% Black, 0.8% Asian, 0.7% Hispanic of any race (2004); Density: 832.2 persons per square mile (2004); Average household size: 2.58 (2004); Median age: 35.2 (2004); Male/female ratio: 84.0 (2004); Marriage status: 23.4% never married, 51.7% now married, 14.7% widowed, 10.3% divorced (2000); Foreign born: 1.1% (2000); Ancestry (includes multiple ancestries): 25.8% Other groups, 15.3% United States or American, 7.1% English, 5.6% German, 4.4% Irish (2000).

Economy: Employment by occupation: 8.6% management, 14.2% professional, 18.7% services, 21.1% sales, 6.3% farming, 9.8% construction, 21.4% production (2000).

Income: Per capita income: $12,938 (2004); Median household income: $21,143 (2004); Average household income: $32,786 (2004); Percent of households with income of $100,000 or more: 4.4% (2004); Poverty rate: 27.2% (2000).

Education: Percent of population age 25 and over with: High school diploma (including GED) or higher: 64.7% (2004); Bachelor's degree or higher: 7.7% (2004); Master's degree or higher: 2.4% (2004).

School District(s)

Dixie County School District (PK-12)
2002-03 Enrollment: 2,229 .... (352) 498-6131

Housing: Homeownership rate: 69.9% (2004); Median home value: $57,792 (2004); Median rent: $222 per month (2000); Median age of housing: 28 years (2000).

Safety: Violent crime rate: 67.4 per 10,000 population; Property crime rate: 618.0 per 10,000 population (2003).

Newspapers: Dixie County Advocate (General - Circulation 3,200)

Transportation: Commute to work: 91.9% car, 0.0% public transportation, 1.9% walk, 1.4% work from home (2000); Travel time to work: 55.5% less than 15 minutes, 15.8% 15 to 30 minutes, 7.2% 30 to 45 minutes, 4.0% 45 to 60 minutes, 17.4% 60 minutes or more (2000)

Additional Information Contacts

Cross City Chamber of Commerce .... (352) 498-5454

HORSESHOE BEACH (town). Covers a land area of 0.203 square miles and a water area of 0.041 square miles. Located at 29.44° N. Lat.; 83.28° W. Long. Elevation is 5 feet.

Population: 252 (1990); 206 (2000); 182 (2004); 174 (2009 projected); Race: 94.5% White, 5.5% Black, 0.0% Asian, 0.0% Hispanic of any race (2004); Density: 895.9 persons per square mile (2004); Average household size: 2.43 (2004); Median age: 49.1 (2004); Male/female ratio: 83.8 (2004); Marriage status: 20.6% never married, 66.1% now married, 7.3% widowed, 6.1% divorced (2000); Foreign born: 0.0% (2000); Ancestry (includes multiple ancestries): 24.8% United States or American, 16.3% Irish, 7.9% English, 5.9% German, 4.0% Other groups (2000).

Economy: Single-family building permits issued: 12 (2004); Multi-family building permits issued: 16 (2004); Employment by occupation: 24.7% management, 2.7% professional, 8.2% services, 23.3% sales, 21.9% farming, 11.0% construction, 8.2% production (2000).

Income: Per capita income: $21,937 (2004); Median household income: $42,500 (2004); Average household income: $53,233 (2004); Percent of households with income of $100,000 or more: 9.3% (2004); Poverty rate: 22.3% (2000).
Education: Percent of population age 25 and over with: High school diploma (including GED) or higher: 72.0% (2004); Bachelor's degree or higher: 6.4% (2004); Master's degree or higher: 2.4% (2004).
Housing: Homeownership rate: 90.7% (2004); Median home value: $97,500 (2004); Median rent: $375 per month (2000); Median age of housing: 17 years (2000).
Transportation: Commute to work: 80.8% car, 0.0% public transportation, 8.2% walk, 0.0% work from home (2000); Travel time to work: 69.9% less than 15 minutes, 9.6% 15 to 30 minutes, 6.8% 30 to 45 minutes, 4.1% 45 to 60 minutes, 9.6% 60 minutes or more (2000)

OLD TOWN (unincorporated postal area, zip code 32680). Covers a land area of 115.124 square miles and a water area of 2.006 square miles. Located at 29.64° N. Lat.; 82.99° W. Long. Elevation is 23 feet.
History: Old Town, once known as Suwannee Oldtown, was built on the site of a large Creek village. An early industry was a moss factory where Spanish moss was prepared for use in mattresses and upholstering.
Population: 7,748 (2000); Race: 97.3% White, 0.3% Black, 0.5% Asian, 1.8% Hispanic of any race (2000); Density: 67.3 persons per square mile (2000); Age: 22.0% under 18, 20.9% over 64 (2000); Marriage status: 16.7% never married, 61.9% now married, 9.1% widowed, 12.3% divorced (2000); Foreign born: 2.1% (2000); Ancestry (includes multiple ancestries): 21.7% United States or American, 11.0% Irish, 9.8% German, 9.4% English, 8.9% Other groups (2000).
Economy: Employment by occupation: 7.7% management, 11.0% professional, 20.1% services, 24.7% sales, 4.5% farming, 14.3% construction, 17.7% production (2000).
Income: Per capita income: $13,200 (2000); Median household income: $24,131 (2000); Poverty rate: 19.1% (2000).
Education: Percent of population age 25 and over with: High school diploma (including GED) or higher: 62.6% (2000); Bachelor's degree or higher: 6.7% (2000).

School District(s)

Dixie County School District (PK-12)
2002-03 Enrollment: 2,229 . . . . (352) 498-6131

Housing: Homeownership rate: 91.0% (2000); Median home value: $66,700 (2000); Median rent: $245 per month (2000); Median age of housing: 17 years (2000).
Transportation: Commute to work: 91.3% car, 0.5% public transportation, 0.0% walk, 6.4% work from home (2000); Travel time to work: 29.5% less than 15 minutes, 31.1% 15 to 30 minutes, 14.4% 30 to 45 minutes, 6.2% 45 to 60 minutes, 18.9% 60 minutes or more (2000)

Duval County

Located in northeastern Florida; partly swampy area, bounded on the east by the Atlantic Ocean; includes Little Talbot Island; drained by the St. Johns River. Covers a land area of 773.70 square miles, a water area of 144.60 square miles, and is located in the Eastern Time Zone. The county government was organized in 1822. County seat is Jacksonville.

Duval County is part of the Jacksonville, FL Metropolitan Statistical Area. The entire metro area includes: Baker County, FL; Clay County, FL; Duval County, FL; Nassau County, FL; St. Johns County, FL

Weather Station: Jacksonville Beach — Elevation: 9 feet

	Jan	Feb	Mar	Apr	May	Jun	Jul	Aug	Sep	Oct	Nov	Dec
High	64	66	71	77	83	87	90	88	86	80	72	67
Low	46	48	54	59	66	72	74	74	73	66	56	50
Precip	3.7	3.0	4.1	2.8	3.1	5.7	5.2	6.1	7.1	5.2	2.3	2.8
Snow	tr	tr	0.0	0.0	0.0	0.0	0.0	0.0	0.0	0.0	0.0	tr

High and Low temperatures in degrees Fahrenheit; Precipitation and Snow in inches

Weather Station: Jacksonville Int'l Airport — Elevation: 22 feet

	Jan	Feb	Mar	Apr	May	Jun	Jul	Aug	Sep	Oct	Nov	Dec
High	65	68	74	79	85	90	92	91	87	80	73	67
Low	42	44	50	55	63	69	72	72	69	60	51	44
Precip	3.7	3.4	4.2	3.1	3.5	5.4	6.0	7.0	7.6	4.0	2.3	2.6
Snow	tr	tr	tr	tr	0.0	tr	tr	0.0	0.0	0.0	0.0	tr

High and Low temperatures in degrees Fahrenheit; Precipitation and Snow in inches

Population: 672,971 (1990); 778,879 (2000); 831,263 (2004); 897,372 (2009 projected); Race: 62.6% White, 30.2% Black, 3.1% Asian, 4.5% Hispanic of any race (2004); Density: 1,074.4 persons per square mile (2004); Average household size: 2.55 (2004); Median age: 34.7 (2004); Male/female ratio: 94.4 (2004).
Religion: Five largest groups: 18.4% Southern Baptist Convention, 8.3% Catholic Church, 3.7% The United Methodist Church, 1.7% Presbyterian Church (U.S.A.), 1.7% Episcopal Church (2000).
Economy: Unemployment rate: 5.7% (2004); Total civilian labor force: 432,559 (2004); Leading industries: 13.0% finance & insurance; 12.2% health care and social assistance; 11.9% retail trade (2003); Companies that employ 500 or more persons: 78 (2003); Companies that employ 100 to 499 persons: 582 (2003); Companies that employ less than 100 persons: 21,397 (2003); Farms: 382 totaling 31,241 acres (2002); Minority business ownership rate: 11.8% (1997); Women business ownership rate: 27.0% (1997); Retail sales per capita: $11,003 (1997). Single-family building permits issued: 6,193 (2004); Multi-family building permits issued: 3,468 (2004).
Income: Per capita income: $22,973 (2004); Median household income: $44,272 (2004); Average household income: $57,961 (2004); Percent of households with income of $100,000 or more: 12.4% (2004); Poverty rate: 11.6% (2002); Bankruptcy rate: 6.88% (2004).
Education: Percent of population age 25 and over with: High school diploma (including GED) or higher: 83.0% (2004); Bachelor's degree or higher: 22.2% (2004); Master's degree or higher: 7.0% (2004).
Housing: Homeownership rate: 63.1% (2004); Median home value: $117,722 (2004); Median rent: $508 per month (2000); Median age of housing: 25 years (2000).
Health: Birth rate: 158.1 per 10,000 population (2004); Death rate: 83.0 per 10,000 population (2004); Age adjusted cancer mortality rate: 224.5 deaths per 100,000 population (2002); Air Quality Index: 68.7% good, 30.5% moderate, 0.8% unhealthy for sensitive individuals, 0.0% unhealthy (percent of days in 2004); Number of physicians: 29.6 per 10,000 population (2001); Hospital beds: 35.8 per 10,000 population (2002); Hospital admissions: 1,542.7 per 10,000 population (2002).
Elections: 2004 Presidential election results: 57.8% Bush, 41.6% Kerry, 0.3% Nader, 0.2% Badnarik
National and State Parks: Big Talbot Island State Park; Fort Caroline National Memorial; Fort George Island Cultural State Park; Kingsley Plantation State Historical Site; Little Talbot Island State Park; Yellow Bluff Fort Historic State Park
Additional Information Contacts
Duval County Government Offices . . . . (904) 630-2039
Jacksonville Beach Chamber of Commerce . . . . (904) 249-3868
Jacksonville Chamber of Commerce . . . . (904) 366-6600
Northeast Florida Association of Realtors . . . . (904) 394-9494

Duval County Communities

ATLANTIC BEACH (city). Covers a land area of 3.730 square miles and a water area of 9.252 square miles. Located at 30.33° N. Lat.; 81.40° W. Long. Elevation is 17 feet.
History: Named for the city's location on the Atlantic Ocean. Atlantic Beach developed as a summer resort, particularly for Jacksonville residents.
Population: 11,639 (1990); 13,368 (2000); 13,783 (2004); 14,381 (2009 projected); Race: 82.6% White, 12.5% Black, 1.8% Asian, 4.3% Hispanic of any race (2004); Density: 3,695.5 persons per square mile (2004); Average household size: 2.33 (2004); Median age: 39.9 (2004); Male/female ratio: 94.9 (2004); Marriage status: 24.5% never married, 55.2% now married, 7.0% widowed, 13.2% divorced (2000); Foreign born: 5.6% (2000); Ancestry (includes multiple ancestries): 19.7% Other groups, 15.7% German, 14.2% English, 13.3% Irish, 7.9% United States or American (2000).
Economy: Single-family building permits issued: 50 (2004); Multi-family building permits issued: 16 (2004); Employment by occupation: 15.9% management, 23.8% professional, 15.9% services, 24.2% sales, 0.5% farming, 9.8% construction, 9.9% production (2000).
Income: Per capita income: $33,188 (2004); Median household income: $52,354 (2004); Average household income: $76,585 (2004); Percent of households with income of $100,000 or more: 23.7% (2004); Poverty rate: 8.8% (2000).
Taxes: Total city taxes per capita: $268 (2002); City property taxes per capita: $116 (2002).

Education: Percent of population age 25 and over with: High school diploma (including GED) or higher: 89.2% (2004); Bachelor's degree or higher: 38.6% (2004); Master's degree or higher: 16.7% (2004).

School District(s)

Duval County School District (PK-12)
2002-03 Enrollment: 128,126 . . . . (904) 390-2115

Housing: Homeownership rate: 66.2% (2004); Median home value: $198,306 (2004); Median rent: $620 per month (2000); Median age of housing: 21 years (2000).
Safety: Violent crime rate: 47.1 per 10,000 population; Property crime rate: 355.8 per 10,000 population (2003).
Transportation: Commute to work: 89.4% car, 2.3% public transportation, 2.3% walk, 3.0% work from home (2000); Travel time to work: 25.9% less than 15 minutes, 27.2% 15 to 30 minutes, 28.7% 30 to 45 minutes, 12.2% 45 to 60 minutes, 6.0% 60 minutes or more (2000)

Additional Information Contacts

Local Government Offices . . . . (904) 247-5809

BALDWIN (town). Covers a land area of 2.130 square miles and a water area of 0.002 square miles. Located at 30.30° N. Lat.; 81.97° W. Long. Elevation is 86 feet.
History: Baldwin was once called Thigpen, but was renamed for Dr. A.S. Baldwin who arranged for the railroad to be built in the area in 1860. The Seaboard Air Line Railway established its freight yards in Baldwin.
Population: 1,456 (1990); 1,634 (2000); 1,704 (2004); 1,800 (2009 projected); Race: 68.9% White, 29.2% Black, 0.8% Asian, 0.8% Hispanic of any race (2004); Density: 800.1 persons per square mile (2004); Average household size: 2.57 (2004); Median age: 34.0 (2004); Male/female ratio: 88.1 (2004); Marriage status: 27.5% never married, 47.1% now married, 9.3% widowed, 16.1% divorced (2000); Foreign born: 1.3% (2000); Ancestry (includes multiple ancestries): 34.4% Other groups, 11.2% Irish, 10.8% United States or American, 7.9% English, 7.1% German (2000).
Economy: Single-family building permits issued: 5 (2004); Multi-family building permits issued: 0 (2004); Employment by occupation: 5.3% management, 8.9% professional, 21.2% services, 24.2% sales, 0.3% farming, 15.2% construction, 25.0% production (2000).
Income: Per capita income: $16,105 (2004); Median household income: $32,395 (2004); Average household income: $41,329 (2004); Percent of households with income of $100,000 or more: 6.6% (2004); Poverty rate: 17.7% (2000).
Education: Percent of population age 25 and over with: High school diploma (including GED) or higher: 66.9% (2004); Bachelor's degree or higher: 5.2% (2004); Master's degree or higher: 2.2% (2004).

School District(s)

Duval County School District (PK-12)
2002-03 Enrollment: 128,126 . . . . (904) 390-2115

Housing: Homeownership rate: 65.8% (2004); Median home value: $71,596 (2004); Median rent: $285 per month (2000); Median age of housing: 25 years (2000).
Safety: Violent crime rate: 120.4 per 10,000 population; Property crime rate: 590.0 per 10,000 population (2003).
Transportation: Commute to work: 92.8% car, 0.0% public transportation, 3.5% walk, 1.5% work from home (2000); Travel time to work: 21.9% less than 15 minutes, 28.3% 15 to 30 minutes, 33.7% 30 to 45 minutes, 6.7% 45 to 60 minutes, 9.3% 60 minutes or more (2000)

JACKSONVILLE (special city). Covers a land area of 757.678 square miles and a water area of 116.649 square miles. Located at 30.31° N. Lat.; 81.66° W. Long. Elevation is 12 feet.
History: Jacksonville was established in 1822 on the north bank of the St. Johns River, where a settlement named Cowford had grown up around a rowboat ferry maintained by John Brady. The new town was named Jacksonville in honor of Florida's governor, General Andrew Jackson. Growth was slow until 1842, when steamship service began and Jacksonville began to ship lumber and cotton from its harbor. Badly damaged by the Civil War, Jacksonville was rebuilt as a winter resort during the Reconstruction period.
Population: 635,221 (1990); 735,617 (2000); 787,027 (2004); 851,662 (2009 projected); Race: 61.1% White, 31.5% Black, 3.2% Asian, 4.5% Hispanic of any race (2004); Density: 1,038.7 persons per square mile (2004); Average household size: 2.57 (2004); Median age: 34.4 (2004); Male/female ratio: 94.2 (2004); Marriage status: 26.5% never married, 53.9% now married, 6.3% widowed, 13.3% divorced (2000); Foreign born: 5.9% (2000); Ancestry (includes multiple ancestries): 35.5% Other groups, 9.6% German, 9.3% United States or American, 9.0% Irish, 8.5% English (2000).
Economy: Unemployment rate: 5.8% (2004); Total civilian labor force: 405,805 (2004); Single-family building permits issued: 6,067 (2004); Multi-family building permits issued: 3,048 (2004); Employment by occupation: 13.6% management, 17.6% professional, 14.0% services, 32.6% sales, 0.2% farming, 9.5% construction, 12.4% production (2000).
Income: Per capita income: $22,467 (2004); Median household income: $43,762 (2004); Average household income: $57,167 (2004); Percent of households with income of $100,000 or more: 11.9% (2004); Poverty rate: 12.2% (2000).
Taxes: Total city taxes per capita: $802 (2002); City property taxes per capita: $485 (2002).
Education: Percent of population age 25 and over with: High school diploma (including GED) or higher: 82.6% (2004); Bachelor's degree or higher: 21.5% (2004); Master's degree or higher: 6.6% (2004).

School District(s)

Duval County School District (PK-12)
2002-03 Enrollment: 128,126 . . . . (904) 390-2115

Four-year College(s)

Edward Waters College
2003-04 Enrollment: 1,301 . . . . (904) 470-8000
2003-04 Tuition: In-state $8,344; Out-of-state $8,344
Florida Coastal School of Law (Private, For-profit)
2003-04 Enrollment: 685 . . . . (904) 680-7700
Florida Metropolitan University-Jacksonville (Private, For-profit)
2003-04 Enrollment: 955 . . . . (904) 731-4949
2003-04 Tuition: In-state $8,460; Out-of-state $8,460
ITT Technical Institute (Private, For-profit)
2003-04 Enrollment: 613 . . . . (904) 573-9100
2003-04 Tuition: In-state $12,492; Out-of-state $12,492
Jacksonville University
2003-04 Enrollment: 3,092 . . . . (904) 256-8000
2003-04 Tuition: In-state $17,700; Out-of-state $17,700
Jones College-Jacksonville
2003-04 Enrollment: 693 . . . . (904) 743-1122
2003-04 Tuition: In-state $5,490; Out-of-state $5,490
Remington College (Private, For-profit)
2003-04 Enrollment: 365 . . . . (904) 296-3435
2003-04 Tuition: In-state $29,280; Out-of-state $29,280
Trinity Baptist College
2003-04 Enrollment: 410 . . . . (904) 596-2400
2003-04 Tuition: In-state $4,900; Out-of-state $4,900
University of North Florida (Public)
2003-04 Enrollment: 13,966 . . . . (904) 620-1000
2003-04 Tuition: In-state $2,330; Out-of-state $10,614
University of Phoenix-Jacksonville (Private, For-profit)
2003-04 Enrollment: 1,662 . . . . (904) 636-6645
2003-04 Tuition: In-state $8,850; Out-of-state $8,850

Two-year College(s)

Advanced Career Training-Jacksonville Campus (Private, For-profit)
2003-04 Enrollment: n/a . . . . (904) 737-6911
Concorde Career Institute (Private, For-profit)
2003-04 Enrollment: 461 . . . . (904) 725-0525
Florida Community College At Jacksonville (Public)
2003-04 Enrollment: 25,692 . . . . (904) 632-3000
2003-04 Tuition: In-state $1,510; Out-of-state $5,304
Florida Technical College of Jacksonville Inc (Private, For-profit)
2003-04 Enrollment: 174 . . . . (904) 724-2229
Heritage Institute-Jacksonville (Private, For-profit)
2003-04 Enrollment: 359 . . . . (904) 332-0910
Jacksonville Beauty Institute
2003-04 Enrollment: 22 . . . . (904) 768-9001
Normandy Beauty School of Jacksonville (Private, For-profit)
2003-04 Enrollment: 55 . . . . (904) 786-6250
North Florida Institute-Jacksonville (Private, For-profit)
2003-04 Enrollment: 65 . . . . (904) 443-6300
Riverside Hairstyling Academy (Private, For-profit)
2003-04 Enrollment: 117 . . . . (904) 398-0502
Southeastern Sch of Neuromuscular & Massage Therapy-Jacksonvl (Private, For-profit)
2003-04 Enrollment: 57 . . . . (904) 448-9499
Stenotype Institute of Jacksonville Inc (Private, For-profit)
2003-04 Enrollment: 362 . . . . (904) 398-4141
2003-04 Tuition: In-state $8,400; Out-of-state $8,400

Tulsa Welding School-Jacksonville Campus (Private, For-profit)
2003-04 Enrollment: 96 .... (877) 935-3529
Ultrasound Diagnostic School (Private, For-profit)
2003-04 Enrollment: 570 .... (904) 363-6221
Housing: Homeownership rate: 63.1% (2004); Median home value: $114,607 (2004); Median rent: $501 per month (2000); Median age of housing: 25 years (2000).
Hospitals: Baptist Medical Center (601 beds); Baptist Medical Center-Beaches (120 beds); Brooks Health System (127 beds); Columbia Memorial Hospital of Jacksonville (353 beds); Mayo Clinic; Shands at Jacksonville (696 beds); Specialty Hospital Jacksonville (107 beds); St. Luke's Hospital (289 beds); St. Vincent's Medical Center (528 beds); Ten Broeck Hospital (99 beds); US Naval Hospital (176 beds)
Safety: Violent crime rate: 86.7 per 10,000 population; Property crime rate: 564.0 per 10,000 population (2003).
Newspapers: Financial News and Daily Record (Circulation 5,400); Florida Star (Black - Circulation 3,000); Jacksonville Advocate (Black, General - Circulation 36,000); Jacksonville Free Press (Black, General - Circulation 36,230); Mandarin News & St. Johns River Pilot (General - Circulation 5,000); The Florida Times-Union (Circulation 169,093); The Veteran Voice (General - Circulation 10,000)
Transportation: Commute to work: 92.6% car, 2.1% public transportation, 1.8% walk, 1.9% work from home (2000); Travel time to work: 21.2% less than 15 minutes, 43.7% 15 to 30 minutes, 24.1% 30 to 45 minutes, 6.4% 45 to 60 minutes, 4.6% 60 minutes or more (2000); Amtrak: Service available.
Airports: Craig Municipal; Herlong; Jacksonville International (primary service/medium hub); Jacksonville NAS/Towers Field (primary service/medium hub)
Additional Information Contacts
Jacksonville Chamber of Commerce .... (904) 366-6600
Northeast Florida Association of Realtors .... (904) 394-9494

JACKSONVILLE BEACH (city). Covers a land area of 7.682 square miles and a water area of 14.281 square miles. Located at 30.28° N. Lat.; 81.39° W. Long. Elevation is 12 feet.
History: Named for Andrew Jackson, seventh President of the United States. Jacksonville Beach developed as part of a large ocean front resort area, with a mile-long boardwalk and other amusements.
Population: 17,842 (1990); 20,990 (2000); 21,500 (2004); 22,246 (2009 projected); Race: 91.1% White, 4.3% Black, 1.7% Asian, 3.2% Hispanic of any race (2004); Density: 2,798.7 persons per square mile (2004); Average household size: 2.11 (2004); Median age: 39.3 (2004); Male/female ratio: 100.7 (2004); Marriage status: 27.3% never married, 50.9% now married, 7.0% widowed, 14.8% divorced (2000); Foreign born: 4.4% (2000); Ancestry (includes multiple ancestries): 15.9% Irish, 15.5% English, 13.0% German, 13.0% Other groups, 8.0% Italian (2000).
Economy: Single-family building permits issued: 55 (2004); Multi-family building permits issued: 402 (2004); Employment by occupation: 15.4% management, 23.0% professional, 16.0% services, 28.0% sales, 0.8% farming, 10.2% construction, 6.6% production (2000).
Income: Per capita income: $32,039 (2004); Median household income: $54,326 (2004); Average household income: $67,037 (2004); Percent of households with income of $100,000 or more: 18.2% (2004); Poverty rate: 7.2% (2000).
Taxes: Total city taxes per capita: $446 (2002); City property taxes per capita: $296 (2002).
Education: Percent of population age 25 and over with: High school diploma (including GED) or higher: 89.7% (2004); Bachelor's degree or higher: 29.9% (2004); Master's degree or higher: 9.3% (2004).

School District(s)

Duval County School District (PK-12)
2002-03 Enrollment: 128,126 .... (904) 390-2115
Housing: Homeownership rate: 59.5% (2004); Median home value: $179,960 (2004); Median rent: $636 per month (2000); Median age of housing: 25 years (2000).
Safety: Violent crime rate: 66.6 per 10,000 population; Property crime rate: 564.3 per 10,000 population (2003).
Newspapers: Sun Times Weekly (General - Circulation 11,000); The Beaches Leader (General - Circulation 22,500)
Transportation: Commute to work: 91.9% car, 1.0% public transportation, 1.7% walk, 3.9% work from home (2000); Travel time to work: 31.0% less than 15 minutes, 29.8% 15 to 30 minutes, 27.0% 30 to 45 minutes, 8.4% 45 to 60 minutes, 3.7% 60 minutes or more (2000)
Additional Information Contacts
Jacksonville Beach Chamber of Commerce .... (904) 249-3868
Local Government Offices .... (904) 247-6299

NEPTUNE BEACH (city). Covers a land area of 2.449 square miles and a water area of 4.386 square miles. Located at 30.31° N. Lat.; 81.40° W. Long. Elevation is 10 feet.
History: Neptune Beach was once a part of Jacksonville Beach, but later incorporated on its own.
Population: 6,813 (1990); 7,270 (2000); 7,249 (2004); 7,283 (2009 projected); Race: 95.8% White, 0.6% Black, 1.1% Asian, 2.1% Hispanic of any race (2004); Density: 2,960.3 persons per square mile (2004); Average household size: 2.22 (2004); Median age: 39.9 (2004); Male/female ratio: 103.7 (2004); Marriage status: 24.6% never married, 51.7% now married, 6.3% widowed, 17.4% divorced (2000); Foreign born: 3.9% (2000); Ancestry (includes multiple ancestries): 16.3% German, 13.7% Other groups, 13.7% English, 13.6% Irish, 9.9% United States or American (2000).
Economy: Single-family building permits issued: 16 (2004); Multi-family building permits issued: 2 (2004); Employment by occupation: 19.5% management, 28.3% professional, 12.7% services, 26.7% sales, 0.9% farming, 6.8% construction, 5.1% production (2000).
Income: Per capita income: $33,215 (2004); Median household income: $59,716 (2004); Average household income: $73,631 (2004); Percent of households with income of $100,000 or more: 21.3% (2004); Poverty rate: 2.5% (2000).
Taxes: Total city taxes per capita: $220 (2002); City property taxes per capita: $163 (2002).
Education: Percent of population age 25 and over with: High school diploma (including GED) or higher: 93.4% (2004); Bachelor's degree or higher: 40.2% (2004); Master's degree or higher: 13.3% (2004).

School District(s)

Duval County School District (PK-12)
2002-03 Enrollment: 128,126 .... (904) 390-2115
Housing: Homeownership rate: 63.4% (2004); Median home value: $199,953 (2004); Median rent: $660 per month (2000); Median age of housing: 29 years (2000).
Safety: Violent crime rate: 36.7 per 10,000 population; Property crime rate: 311.1 per 10,000 population (2003).
Transportation: Commute to work: 94.5% car, 1.1% public transportation, 0.2% walk, 1.8% work from home (2000); Travel time to work: 27.1% less than 15 minutes, 27.9% 15 to 30 minutes, 26.6% 30 to 45 minutes, 12.1% 45 to 60 minutes, 6.3% 60 minutes or more (2000)
Additional Information Contacts
Local Government Offices .... (904) 270-2400

Escambia County

Located in northwestern Florida; bounded on the north by Alabama, on the west by the Perdido River and the Alabama border, on the south by the Gulf of Mexico, and on the east by the Escambia River. Covers a land area of 662.40 square miles, a water area of 213.20 square miles, and is located in the Central Time Zone. The county government was organized in 1822. County seat is Pensacola.

Escambia County is part of the Pensacola-Ferry Pass-Brent, FL Metropolitan Statistical Area. The entire metro area includes: Escambia County, FL; Santa Rosa County, FL

Weather Station: Pensacola Regional Airport — Elevation: 111 feet

	Jan	Feb	Mar	Apr	May	Jun	Jul	Aug	Sep	Oct	Nov	Dec
High	61	64	70	76	83	89	90	90	87	79	70	64
Low	43	45	52	58	66	72	74	74	71	60	51	45
Precip	5.4	4.9	6.5	3.9	4.7	6.6	8.0	7.0	5.6	4.4	4.2	4.0
Snow	tr	tr	tr	0.0	0.0	0.0	tr	0.0	0.0	0.0	0.0	tr

High and Low temperatures in degrees Fahrenheit; Precipitation and Snow in inches

Population: 262,441 (1990); 294,410 (2000); 301,317 (2004); 310,168 (2009 projected); Race: 69.6% White, 23.7% Black, 2.5% Asian, 2.0% Hispanic of any race (2004); Density: 454.9 persons per square mile (2004); Average household size: 2.67 (2004); Median age: 35.7 (2004); Male/female ratio: 101.1 (2004).
Religion: Five largest groups: 20.3% Southern Baptist Convention, 8.5% Catholic Church, 5.0% The United Methodist Church, 3.2% Assemblies of God, 1.7% Episcopal Church (2000).
Economy: Unemployment rate: 4.6% (2004); Total civilian labor force: 130,401 (2004); Leading industries: 18.4% administration, support, waste

management, remediation services; 16.6% health care and social assistance; 14.0% retail trade (2003); Companies that employ 500 or more persons: 18 (2003); Companies that employ 100 to 499 persons: 118 (2003); Companies that employ less than 100 persons: 6,636 (2003); Farms: 674 totaling 64,581 acres (2002); Minority business ownership rate: 12.6% (1997); Women business ownership rate: 25.5% (1997); Retail sales per capita: $10,265 (1997). Single-family building permits issued: 1,766 (2004); Multi-family building permits issued: 847 (2004).
Income: Per capita income: $20,472 (2004); Median household income: $38,397 (2004); Average household income: $50,861 (2004); Percent of households with income of $100,000 or more: 9.3% (2004); Poverty rate: 15.4% (2002); Bankruptcy rate: 5.31% (2004).
Taxes: Total county taxes per capita: $421 (2002); County property taxes per capita: $243 (2002).
Education: Percent of population age 25 and over with: High school diploma (including GED) or higher: 82.4% (2004); Bachelor's degree or higher: 21.2% (2004); Master's degree or higher: 7.4% (2004).
Housing: Homeownership rate: 67.4% (2004); Median home value: $102,685 (2004); Median rent: $443 per month (2000); Median age of housing: 24 years (2000).
Health: Birth rate: 136.4 per 10,000 population (2004); Death rate: 99.2 per 10,000 population (2004); Age adjusted cancer mortality rate: 215.7 deaths per 100,000 population (2002); Air Quality Index: 69.2% good, 28.0% moderate, 2.7% unhealthy for sensitive individuals, 0.0% unhealthy (percent of days in 2004); Number of physicians: 24.6 per 10,000 population (2001); Hospital beds: 51.0 per 10,000 population (2002); Hospital admissions: 1,910.1 per 10,000 population (2002).
Elections: 2004 Presidential election results: 65.3% Bush, 33.7% Kerry, 0.4% Nader, 0.2% Badnarik
National and State Parks: Big Lagoon State Park; Fort Pickens State Park; Fort Pickens State Park Aquatic Preserve; Perdido Key State Park; Tarkiln Bayou Preserve State Park
Additional Information Contacts
Escambia County Government Offices . . . . (850) 595-4900
Pensacola Association of Realtors . . . . (850) 434-5507
Pensacola Chamber of Commerce . . . . (850) 438-4081
Pensacola Convention & Visitors Bureau . . . . (850) 434-1234

Escambia County Communities

BELLVIEW (CDP). Aka Belleview. Covers a land area of 11.822 square miles and a water area of 0.061 square miles. Located at 30.46° N. Lat.; 87.30° W. Long. Elevation is 73 feet.
Population: 19,386 (1990); 21,201 (2000); 21,297 (2004); 21,467 (2009 projected); Race: 77.0% White, 14.8% Black, 3.7% Asian, 1.7% Hispanic of any race (2004); Density: 1,801.4 persons per square mile (2004); Average household size: 2.57 (2004); Median age: 36.6 (2004); Male/female ratio: 92.6 (2004); Marriage status: 21.4% never married, 58.0% now married, 6.2% widowed, 14.4% divorced (2000); Foreign born: 4.1% (2000); Ancestry (includes multiple ancestries): 24.8% Other groups, 13.6% United States or American, 13.0% German, 11.0% Irish, 10.4% English (2000).
Economy: Employment by occupation: 9.8% management, 17.1% professional, 15.5% services, 31.4% sales, 0.5% farming, 11.7% construction, 13.9% production (2000).
Income: Per capita income: $19,800 (2004); Median household income: $41,932 (2004); Average household income: $50,843 (2004); Percent of households with income of $100,000 or more: 7.6% (2004); Poverty rate: 10.2% (2000).
Education: Percent of population age 25 and over with: High school diploma (including GED) or higher: 83.3% (2004); Bachelor's degree or higher: 13.6% (2004); Master's degree or higher: 5.5% (2004).
Housing: Homeownership rate: 76.0% (2004); Median home value: $94,680 (2004); Median rent: $489 per month (2000); Median age of housing: 20 years (2000).
Transportation: Commute to work: 95.7% car, 0.6% public transportation, 0.5% walk, 2.1% work from home (2000); Travel time to work: 21.0% less than 15 minutes, 53.6% 15 to 30 minutes, 16.7% 30 to 45 minutes, 3.5% 45 to 60 minutes, 5.1% 60 minutes or more (2000)

BRENT (CDP). Aka Brentwood. Covers a land area of 10.437 square miles and a water area of 0.087 square miles. Located at 30.47° N. Lat.; 87.24° W. Long. Elevation is 93 feet.
Population: 21,389 (1990); 22,257 (2000); 22,447 (2004); 22,850 (2009 projected); Race: 55.4% White, 38.3% Black, 2.7% Asian, 1.3% Hispanic of any race (2004); Density: 2,150.6 persons per square mile (2004); Average household size: 3.26 (2004); Median age: 25.2 (2004); Male/female ratio: 84.8 (2004); Marriage status: 38.9% never married, 43.8% now married, 6.0% widowed, 11.2% divorced (2000); Foreign born: 2.9% (2000); Ancestry (includes multiple ancestries): 35.0% Other groups, 8.7% United States or American, 5.3% German, 5.1% Irish, 4.2% English (2000).
Economy: Suburb. Employment by occupation: 6.0% management, 17.8% professional, 21.6% services, 30.5% sales, 0.5% farming, 11.2% construction, 12.4% production (2000).
Income: Per capita income: $11,935 (2004); Median household income: $29,454 (2004); Average household income: $35,881 (2004); Percent of households with income of $100,000 or more: 3.6% (2004); Poverty rate: 24.5% (2000).
Education: Percent of population age 25 and over with: High school diploma (including GED) or higher: 73.8% (2004); Bachelor's degree or higher: 11.9% (2004); Master's degree or higher: 4.2% (2004).
Housing: Homeownership rate: 63.1% (2004); Median home value: $73,062 (2004); Median rent: $389 per month (2000); Median age of housing: 31 years (2000).
Transportation: Commute to work: 77.7% car, 3.3% public transportation, 15.2% walk, 1.7% work from home (2000); Travel time to work: 46.1% less than 15 minutes, 35.2% 15 to 30 minutes, 11.8% 30 to 45 minutes, 2.4% 45 to 60 minutes, 4.4% 60 minutes or more (2000)

CANTONMENT (unincorporated postal area, zip code 32533). Covers a land area of 76.107 square miles and a water area of 0.126 square miles. Located at 30.60° N. Lat.; 87.32° W. Long. Elevation is 150 feet.
Population: 23,889 (2000); Race: 84.8% White, 11.3% Black, 0.7% Asian, 1.6% Hispanic of any race (2000); Density: 313.9 persons per square mile (2000); Age: 28.1% under 18, 10.3% over 64 (2000); Marriage status: 20.0% never married, 65.0% now married, 4.3% widowed, 10.7% divorced (2000); Foreign born: 2.0% (2000); Ancestry (includes multiple ancestries): 21.4% Other groups, 16.1% United States or American, 9.8% Irish, 9.5% English, 8.9% German (2000).
Economy: Employment by occupation: 12.1% management, 19.2% professional, 14.0% services, 29.3% sales, 0.2% farming, 12.7% construction, 12.4% production (2000).
Income: Per capita income: $19,852 (2000); Median household income: $44,191 (2000); Poverty rate: 11.1% (2000).
Education: Percent of population age 25 and over with: High school diploma (including GED) or higher: 83.5% (2000); Bachelor's degree or higher: 18.1% (2000).

School District(s)

Escambia County School District (PK-12)
2002-03 Enrollment: 44,019 . . . . (850) 469-6130
Housing: Homeownership rate: 86.6% (2000); Median home value: $107,200 (2000); Median rent: $374 per month (2000); Median age of housing: 16 years (2000).
Transportation: Commute to work: 94.5% car, 0.3% public transportation, 1.0% walk, 3.1% work from home (2000); Travel time to work: 21.2% less than 15 minutes, 43.2% 15 to 30 minutes, 23.2% 30 to 45 minutes, 6.1% 45 to 60 minutes, 6.3% 60 minutes or more (2000)

CENTURY (town). Aka South Flomaton. Covers a land area of 3.281 square miles and a water area of 0.061 square miles. Located at 30.97° N. Lat.; 87.26° W. Long. Elevation is 75 feet.
History: Century was named for the establishment in January 1900 of a large sawmill around which the settlement grew.
Population: 1,989 (1990); 1,714 (2000); 1,711 (2004); 1,715 (2009 projected); Race: 37.1% White, 58.9% Black, 0.8% Asian, 1.4% Hispanic of any race (2004); Density: 521.5 persons per square mile (2004); Average household size: 2.48 (2004); Median age: 35.3 (2004); Male/female ratio: 81.3 (2004); Marriage status: 27.7% never married, 49.9% now married, 11.3% widowed, 11.2% divorced (2000); Foreign born: 1.1% (2000); Ancestry (includes multiple ancestries): 45.4% Other groups, 11.9% United States or American, 9.4% African, 3.5% Irish, 2.3% English (2000).
Economy: Employment by occupation: 7.1% management, 10.1% professional, 21.5% services, 20.7% sales, 0.0% farming, 16.3% construction, 24.3% production (2000).
Income: Per capita income: $12,462 (2004); Median household income: $24,250 (2004); Average household income: $30,857 (2004); Percent of households with income of $100,000 or more: 2.7% (2004); Poverty rate: 30.1% (2000).
Taxes: Total city taxes per capita: $117 (2002); City property taxes per capita: $14 (2002).

Education: Percent of population age 25 and over with: High school diploma (including GED) or higher: 63.5% (2004); Bachelor's degree or higher: 5.2% (2004); Master's degree or higher: 1.8% (2004).

School District(s)

Escambia County School District (PK-12)
2002-03 Enrollment: 44,019 . . . . (850) 469-6130

Housing: Homeownership rate: 70.5% (2004); Median home value: $52,872 (2004); Median rent: $198 per month (2000); Median age of housing: 30 years (2000).

Transportation: Commute to work: 90.3% car, 2.8% public transportation, 2.5% walk, 2.7% work from home (2000); Travel time to work: 36.4% less than 15 minutes, 19.1% 15 to 30 minutes, 23.0% 30 to 45 minutes, 12.5% 45 to 60 minutes, 9.1% 60 minutes or more (2000)

ENSLEY (CDP). Covers a land area of 12.337 square miles and a water area of 0 square miles. Located at 30.52° N. Lat.; 87.27° W. Long. Elevation is 133 feet.

Population: 17,308 (1990); 18,752 (2000); 19,150 (2004); 19,688 (2009 projected); Race: 63.2% White, 31.8% Black, 1.3% Asian, 1.7% Hispanic of any race (2004); Density: 1,552.2 persons per square mile (2004); Average household size: 2.46 (2004); Median age: 35.9 (2004); Male/female ratio: 92.4 (2004); Marriage status: 23.3% never married, 54.7% now married, 7.2% widowed, 14.8% divorced (2000); Foreign born: 3.1% (2000); Ancestry (includes multiple ancestries): 36.3% Other groups, 11.4% United States or American, 9.6% Irish, 8.9% German, 8.0% English (2000).

Economy: Employment by occupation: 8.4% management, 15.3% professional, 17.4% services, 29.7% sales, 0.4% farming, 15.1% construction, 13.6% production (2000).

Income: Per capita income: $18,265 (2004); Median household income: $33,742 (2004); Average household income: $44,701 (2004); Percent of households with income of $100,000 or more: 6.4% (2004); Poverty rate: 15.7% (2000).

Education: Percent of population age 25 and over with: High school diploma (including GED) or higher: 78.8% (2004); Bachelor's degree or higher: 13.9% (2004); Master's degree or higher: 3.8% (2004).

Housing: Homeownership rate: 68.0% (2004); Median home value: $88,953 (2004); Median rent: $406 per month (2000); Median age of housing: 21 years (2000).

Transportation: Commute to work: 94.3% car, 0.7% public transportation, 1.5% walk, 2.0% work from home (2000); Travel time to work: 26.7% less than 15 minutes, 47.6% 15 to 30 minutes, 16.2% 30 to 45 minutes, 2.4% 45 to 60 minutes, 7.2% 60 minutes or more (2000)

FERRY PASS (CDP). Covers a land area of 14.084 square miles and a water area of 0.018 square miles. Located at 30.51° N. Lat.; 87.20° W. Long. Elevation is 37 feet.

Population: 24,919 (1990); 27,176 (2000); 28,417 (2004); 29,936 (2009 projected); Race: 80.7% White, 13.4% Black, 2.2% Asian, 2.0% Hispanic of any race (2004); Density: 2,017.8 persons per square mile (2004); Average household size: 2.36 (2004); Median age: 37.6 (2004); Male/female ratio: 87.4 (2004); Marriage status: 26.3% never married, 50.7% now married, 10.1% widowed, 13.0% divorced (2000); Foreign born: 4.3% (2000); Ancestry (includes multiple ancestries): 19.5% Other groups, 13.4% German, 12.1% United States or American, 11.0% Irish, 10.9% English (2000).

Economy: Employment by occupation: 11.6% management, 23.8% professional, 16.0% services, 30.8% sales, 0.2% farming, 9.3% construction, 8.3% production (2000).

Income: Per capita income: $24,229 (2004); Median household income: $41,600 (2004); Average household income: $54,015 (2004); Percent of households with income of $100,000 or more: 9.8% (2004); Poverty rate: 12.1% (2000).

Education: Percent of population age 25 and over with: High school diploma (including GED) or higher: 87.5% (2004); Bachelor's degree or higher: 29.7% (2004); Master's degree or higher: 11.9% (2004).

Housing: Homeownership rate: 55.4% (2004); Median home value: $116,085 (2004); Median rent: $523 per month (2000); Median age of housing: 17 years (2000).

Transportation: Commute to work: 94.4% car, 0.6% public transportation, 0.8% walk, 2.0% work from home (2000); Travel time to work: 28.7% less than 15 minutes, 49.0% 15 to 30 minutes, 15.5% 30 to 45 minutes, 2.4% 45 to 60 minutes, 4.4% 60 minutes or more (2000)

GONZALEZ (CDP). Aka Roberts. Covers a land area of 15.287 square miles and a water area of 0.054 square miles. Located at 30.57° N. Lat.; 87.29° W. Long. Elevation is 140 feet.

History: Gonzalez was first settled in the early 1800's and named for Don Manuel Gonzalez who had a land grant here. The town grew as a trading center for farmers.

Population: 7,949 (1990); 11,365 (2000); 11,754 (2004); 12,191 (2009 projected); Race: 85.3% White, 9.7% Black, 1.9% Asian, 1.3% Hispanic of any race (2004); Density: 768.9 persons per square mile (2004); Average household size: 2.76 (2004); Median age: 37.0 (2004); Male/female ratio: 96.6 (2004); Marriage status: 20.8% never married, 65.4% now married, 4.0% widowed, 9.8% divorced (2000); Foreign born: 2.9% (2000); Ancestry (includes multiple ancestries): 22.6% Other groups, 13.2% United States or American, 10.5% German, 10.1% Irish, 8.6% English (2000).

Economy: Employment by occupation: 11.7% management, 22.1% professional, 14.9% services, 30.6% sales, 0.0% farming, 10.7% construction, 10.0% production (2000).

Income: Per capita income: $24,025 (2004); Median household income: $54,725 (2004); Average household income: $66,218 (2004); Percent of households with income of $100,000 or more: 15.0% (2004); Poverty rate: 8.0% (2000).

Education: Percent of population age 25 and over with: High school diploma (including GED) or higher: 89.2% (2004); Bachelor's degree or higher: 20.9% (2004); Master's degree or higher: 6.2% (2004).

School District(s)

Escambia County School District (PK-12)
2002-03 Enrollment: 44,019 . . . . (850) 469-6130

Housing: Homeownership rate: 86.0% (2004); Median home value: $134,513 (2004); Median rent: $390 per month (2000); Median age of housing: 16 years (2000).

Transportation: Commute to work: 94.3% car, 0.5% public transportation, 0.9% walk, 3.2% work from home (2000); Travel time to work: 23.5% less than 15 minutes, 43.5% 15 to 30 minutes, 24.5% 30 to 45 minutes, 4.1% 45 to 60 minutes, 4.4% 60 minutes or more (2000)

GOULDING (CDP). Covers a land area of 1.231 square miles and a water area of 0 square miles. Located at 30.43° N. Lat.; 87.23° W. Long. Elevation is 75 feet.

History: Goulding developed as an industrial community with fertilizer factories and a chemical plant manufacturing rosin.

Population: 4,159 (1990); 4,484 (2000); 4,637 (2004); 4,873 (2009 projected); Race: 25.0% White, 72.5% Black, 0.7% Asian, 1.2% Hispanic of any race (2004); Density: 3,767.5 persons per square mile (2004); Average household size: 3.73 (2004); Median age: 39.1 (2004); Male/female ratio: 150.6 (2004); Marriage status: 41.3% never married, 33.5% now married, 15.2% widowed, 10.0% divorced (2000); Foreign born: 0.7% (2000); Ancestry (includes multiple ancestries): 40.7% Other groups, 3.9% African, 3.6% United States or American, 3.0% German, 2.5% Irish (2000).

Economy: Employment by occupation: 2.0% management, 7.8% professional, 30.1% services, 17.5% sales, 0.0% farming, 16.9% construction, 25.6% production (2000).

Income: Per capita income: $8,832 (2004); Median household income: $14,999 (2004); Average household income: $23,055 (2004); Percent of households with income of $100,000 or more: 2.3% (2004); Poverty rate: 30.4% (2000).

Education: Percent of population age 25 and over with: High school diploma (including GED) or higher: 57.8% (2004); Bachelor's degree or higher: 7.8% (2004); Master's degree or higher: 3.0% (2004).

Housing: Homeownership rate: 50.3% (2004); Median home value: $53,016 (2004); Median rent: $240 per month (2000); Median age of housing: 39 years (2000).

Transportation: Commute to work: 84.1% car, 7.7% public transportation, 6.0% walk, 0.8% work from home (2000); Travel time to work: 42.8% less than 15 minutes, 31.1% 15 to 30 minutes, 14.4% 30 to 45 minutes, 8.6% 45 to 60 minutes, 3.1% 60 minutes or more (2000)

MCDAVID (unincorporated postal area, zip code 32568). Covers a land area of 216.066 square miles and a water area of 0.157 square miles. Located at 30.87° N. Lat.; 87.47° W. Long. Elevation is 34 feet.

History: McDavid grew as a center for naval stores (rosen and turpentine used in calking boats).

Population: 3,225 (2000); Race: 84.8% White, 9.6% Black, 0.0% Asian, 0.8% Hispanic of any race (2000); Density: 14.9 persons per square mile (2000); Age: 26.3% under 18, 14.3% over 64 (2000); Marriage status:

19.6% never married, 64.8% now married, 5.6% widowed, 10.0% divorced (2000); Foreign born: 0.1% (2000); Ancestry (includes multiple ancestries): 23.1% United States or American, 18.3% Other groups, 6.4% German, 5.0% Irish, 4.7% English (2000).
Economy: Employment by occupation: 6.6% management, 16.1% professional, 16.7% services, 23.8% sales, 1.8% farming, 18.2% construction, 17.0% production (2000).
Income: Per capita income: $15,054 (2000); Median household income: $35,533 (2000); Poverty rate: 14.3% (2000).
Education: Percent of population age 25 and over with: High school diploma (including GED) or higher: 70.9% (2000); Bachelor's degree or higher: 7.1% (2000).
Housing: Homeownership rate: 88.1% (2000); Median home value: $70,700 (2000); Median rent: $260 per month (2000); Median age of housing: 23 years (2000).
Transportation: Commute to work: 93.1% car, 0.0% public transportation, 0.8% walk, 2.6% work from home (2000); Travel time to work: 15.4% less than 15 minutes, 28.5% 15 to 30 minutes, 21.7% 30 to 45 minutes, 18.0% 45 to 60 minutes, 16.5% 60 minutes or more (2000)

MOLINO (CDP). Covers a land area of 6.969 square miles and a water area of 0.029 square miles. Located at 30.72° N. Lat.; 87.32° W. Long. Elevation is 30 feet.
History: Molino was settled about 1820 and developed around the sawmills that had operated here as early as 1812.
Population: 1,192 (1990); 1,312 (2000); 1,340 (2004); 1,370 (2009 projected); Race: 67.8% White, 28.1% Black, 0.4% Asian, 0.6% Hispanic of any race (2004); Density: 192.3 persons per square mile (2004); Average household size: 2.77 (2004); Median age: 35.6 (2004); Male/female ratio: 105.8 (2004); Marriage status: 24.3% never married, 57.2% now married, 9.3% widowed, 9.3% divorced (2000); Foreign born: 0.4% (2000); Ancestry (includes multiple ancestries): 26.8% Other groups, 19.8% United States or American, 8.6% German, 7.2% Irish, 6.4% English (2000).
Economy: Employment by occupation: 4.4% management, 11.2% professional, 19.9% services, 17.0% sales, 2.0% farming, 18.5% construction, 27.1% production (2000).
Income: Per capita income: $16,194 (2004); Median household income: $39,167 (2004); Average household income: $44,835 (2004); Percent of households with income of $100,000 or more: 7.6% (2004); Poverty rate: 12.7% (2000).
Education: Percent of population age 25 and over with: High school diploma (including GED) or higher: 69.0% (2004); Bachelor's degree or higher: 4.8% (2004); Master's degree or higher: 0.4% (2004).

School District(s)

Escambia County School District (PK-12)
2002-03 Enrollment: 44,019 . . . . (850) 469-6130
Housing: Homeownership rate: 84.9% (2004); Median home value: $72,742 (2004); Median rent: $285 per month (2000); Median age of housing: 25 years (2000).
Transportation: Commute to work: 96.8% car, 0.0% public transportation, 1.8% walk, 0.0% work from home (2000); Travel time to work: 13.1% less than 15 minutes, 26.8% 15 to 30 minutes, 47.4% 30 to 45 minutes, 6.4% 45 to 60 minutes, 6.3% 60 minutes or more (2000)

MYRTLE GROVE (CDP). Covers a land area of 6.604 square miles and a water area of 0 square miles. Located at 30.42° N. Lat.; 87.30° W. Long. Elevation is 46 feet.
Population: 17,402 (1990); 17,211 (2000); 17,556 (2004); 17,998 (2009 projected); Race: 70.6% White, 17.5% Black, 5.6% Asian, 3.2% Hispanic of any race (2004); Density: 2,658.4 persons per square mile (2004); Average household size: 2.82 (2004); Median age: 32.3 (2004); Male/female ratio: 107.9 (2004); Marriage status: 28.6% never married, 53.3% now married, 6.0% widowed, 12.2% divorced (2000); Foreign born: 5.5% (2000); Ancestry (includes multiple ancestries): 33.1% Other groups, 12.4% Irish, 12.4% German, 9.5% United States or American, 9.2% English (2000).
Economy: Employment by occupation: 11.6% management, 17.7% professional, 18.3% services, 27.9% sales, 0.3% farming, 11.8% construction, 12.4% production (2000).
Income: Per capita income: $19,869 (2004); Median household income: $35,107 (2004); Average household income: $44,608 (2004); Percent of households with income of $100,000 or more: 5.7% (2004); Poverty rate: 14.2% (2000).
Education: Percent of population age 25 and over with: High school diploma (including GED) or higher: 84.1% (2004); Bachelor's degree or higher: 18.4% (2004); Master's degree or higher: 6.1% (2004).
Housing: Homeownership rate: 59.9% (2004); Median home value: $93,363 (2004); Median rent: $486 per month (2000); Median age of housing: 24 years (2000).
Transportation: Commute to work: 82.8% car, 0.8% public transportation, 13.4% walk, 1.4% work from home (2000); Travel time to work: 29.3% less than 15 minutes, 49.6% 15 to 30 minutes, 12.8% 30 to 45 minutes, 3.4% 45 to 60 minutes, 4.8% 60 minutes or more (2000)

PENSACOLA (city). Covers a land area of 22.696 square miles and a water area of 16.958 square miles. Located at 30.43° N. Lat.; 87.20° W. Long. Elevation is 32 feet.
History: Spanish and French forts and settlements were built around Pensacola Bay for several centuries. After Florida became a British colony in 1763, a town was laid out, which surrendered in 1781 to the Spanish. In 1814 both Spanish and British flags flew over Pensacola. When Florida was transfered to the United States in 1821, Andrew Jackson became provisional governor of the territory and took up residence in Pensacola, which was chartered as a city in 1822. Development began in earnest after the Civil War, when Pensacola's landlocked harbor was visited by ships from around the world.
Population: 58,906 (1990); 56,255 (2000); 54,392 (2004); 52,299 (2009 projected); Race: 63.3% White, 32.0% Black, 2.0% Asian, 1.5% Hispanic of any race (2004); Density: 2,396.6 persons per square mile (2004); Average household size: 2.27 (2004); Median age: 40.0 (2004); Male/female ratio: 89.6 (2004); Marriage status: 29.6% never married, 48.0% now married, 8.7% widowed, 13.6% divorced (2000); Foreign born: 3.6% (2000); Ancestry (includes multiple ancestries): 33.4% Other groups, 11.0% English, 10.5% German, 10.0% Irish, 7.7% United States or American (2000).
Economy: Unemployment rate: 5.1% (2004); Total civilian labor force: 29,106 (2004); Single-family building permits issued: 160 (2004); Multi-family building permits issued: 6 (2004); Employment by occupation: 13.3% management, 25.0% professional, 17.9% services, 26.8% sales, 0.6% farming, 7.7% construction, 8.7% production (2000).
Income: Per capita income: $23,286 (2004); Median household income: $36,983 (2004); Average household income: $52,616 (2004); Percent of households with income of $100,000 or more: 10.5% (2004); Poverty rate: 16.1% (2000).
Taxes: Total city taxes per capita: $611 (2002); City property taxes per capita: $199 (2002).
Education: Percent of population age 25 and over with: High school diploma (including GED) or higher: 84.8% (2004); Bachelor's degree or higher: 32.6% (2004); Master's degree or higher: 11.9% (2004).

School District(s)

Escambia County School District (PK-12)
2002-03 Enrollment: 44,019 . . . . (850) 469-6130

Four-year College(s)

The University of West Florida (Public)
2003-04 Enrollment: 9,452 . . . . (850) 474-2000
2003-04 Tuition: In-state $2,470; Out-of-state $10,660

Two-year College(s)

Florida Institute of Ultrasound Inc (Private, For-profit)
2003-04 Enrollment: 55 . . . . (850) 478-7611
George Stone Area Vocational Technical Center (Public)
2003-04 Enrollment: 716 . . . . (850) 941-6200
Medical Career Center (Private, For-profit)
2003-04 Enrollment: 383 . . . . (850) 436-8444
Pensacola Junior College (Public)
2003-04 Enrollment: 10,934 . . . . (850) 484-1000
2003-04 Tuition: In-state $1,337; Out-of-state $4,985
Housing: Homeownership rate: 63.3% (2004); Median home value: $118,348 (2004); Median rent: $455 per month (2000); Median age of housing: 33 years (2000).
Hospitals: Baptist Hospital (546 beds); Naval Hospital-Pensacola (65 beds); Sacred Heart Health System (431 beds); West Florida Regional Medical Center (531 beds)
Safety: Violent crime rate: 66.7 per 10,000 population; Property crime rate: 466.7 per 10,000 population (2003).
Newspapers: Escambia Sun Press (General - Circulation 4,800); Pensacola News Journal (Circulation 64,675); Pensacola Voice (Black - Circulation 36,584)
Transportation: Commute to work: 91.6% car, 2.1% public transportation, 1.7% walk, 3.0% work from home (2000); Travel time to work: 39.4% less than 15 minutes, 41.8% 15 to 30 minutes, 11.6% 30 to 45 minutes, 2.7%

45 to 60 minutes, 4.5% 60 minutes or more (2000); Amtrak: Service available.
Airports: Pensacola Regional (primary service/small hub)
Additional Information Contacts
Pensacola Association of Realtors . . . . (850) 434-5507
Pensacola Chamber of Commerce . . . . (850) 438-4081
Pensacola Convention & Visitors Bureau . . . . (850) 434-1234

WARRINGTON (CDP). Covers a land area of 6.572 square miles and a water area of 1.936 square miles. Located at 30.38° N. Lat.; 87.29° W. Long. Elevation is 20 feet.
Population: 15,984 (1990); 15,207 (2000); 14,644 (2004); 14,035 (2009 projected); Race: 68.0% White, 25.2% Black, 2.1% Asian, 2.0% Hispanic of any race (2004); Density: 2,228.4 persons per square mile (2004); Average household size: 2.30 (2004); Median age: 36.8 (2004); Male/female ratio: 93.2 (2004); Marriage status: 24.5% never married, 50.3% now married, 8.6% widowed, 16.6% divorced (2000); Foreign born: 3.4% (2000); Ancestry (includes multiple ancestries): 30.7% Other groups, 14.5% United States or American, 10.3% German, 9.6% Irish, 9.0% English (2000).
Economy: Although chiefly residential, it has shipyards and waterfront industries. Employment by occupation: 9.2% management, 13.8% professional, 22.1% services, 28.6% sales, 0.5% farming, 14.7% construction, 11.1% production (2000).
Income: Per capita income: $19,206 (2004); Median household income: $32,416 (2004); Average household income: $44,151 (2004); Percent of households with income of $100,000 or more: 6.1% (2004); Poverty rate: 20.6% (2000).
Education: Percent of population age 25 and over with: High school diploma (including GED) or higher: 79.2% (2004); Bachelor's degree or higher: 15.0% (2004); Master's degree or higher: 4.9% (2004).
Housing: Homeownership rate: 62.1% (2004); Median home value: $78,393 (2004); Median rent: $381 per month (2000); Median age of housing: 41 years (2000).
Transportation: Commute to work: 89.8% car, 3.4% public transportation, 1.2% walk, 2.7% work from home (2000); Travel time to work: 29.6% less than 15 minutes, 40.4% 15 to 30 minutes, 18.5% 30 to 45 minutes, 5.2% 45 to 60 minutes, 6.3% 60 minutes or more (2000)

WEST PENSACOLA (CDP). Covers a land area of 7.367 square miles and a water area of 0.076 square miles. Located at 30.42° N. Lat.; 87.26° W. Long. Elevation is 76 feet.
Population: 22,074 (1990); 21,939 (2000); 21,327 (2004); 20,607 (2009 projected); Race: 49.9% White, 41.6% Black, 3.7% Asian, 1.7% Hispanic of any race (2004); Density: 2,895.0 persons per square mile (2004); Average household size: 2.47 (2004); Median age: 34.9 (2004); Male/female ratio: 92.1 (2004); Marriage status: 29.1% never married, 44.5% now married, 9.6% widowed, 16.8% divorced (2000); Foreign born: 4.6% (2000); Ancestry (includes multiple ancestries): 37.6% Other groups, 10.2% United States or American, 7.1% Irish, 5.8% German, 5.5% English (2000).
Economy: Employment by occupation: 5.2% management, 12.3% professional, 26.0% services, 25.0% sales, 1.0% farming, 15.1% construction, 15.4% production (2000).
Income: Per capita income: $13,152 (2004); Median household income: $25,164 (2004); Average household income: $31,945 (2004); Percent of households with income of $100,000 or more: 2.4% (2004); Poverty rate: 25.3% (2000).
Education: Percent of population age 25 and over with: High school diploma (including GED) or higher: 69.3% (2004); Bachelor's degree or higher: 8.2% (2004); Master's degree or higher: 2.1% (2004).
Housing: Homeownership rate: 56.4% (2004); Median home value: $56,136 (2004); Median rent: $381 per month (2000); Median age of housing: 40 years (2000).
Transportation: Commute to work: 90.5% car, 3.3% public transportation, 1.8% walk, 1.9% work from home (2000); Travel time to work: 33.6% less than 15 minutes, 41.1% 15 to 30 minutes, 16.4% 30 to 45 minutes, 3.6% 45 to 60 minutes, 5.3% 60 minutes or more (2000)

Flagler County

Located in northeastern Florida; swampy area, bounded on the east by the Atlantic Ocean, and on the west by Crescent Lake. Covers a land area of 485.00 square miles, a water area of 85.80 square miles, and is located in the Eastern Time Zone. The county government was organized in 1917. County seat is Bunnell.

Flagler County is part of the Palm Coast, FL Micropolitan Statistical Area. The entire metro area includes: Flagler County, FL

Population: 28,701 (1990); 49,832 (2000); 62,950 (2004); 79,403 (2009 projected); Race: 87.3% White, 8.8% Black, 1.3% Asian, 5.8% Hispanic of any race (2004); Density: 129.8 persons per square mile (2004); Average household size: 2.32 (2004); Median age: 48.7 (2004); Male/female ratio: 93.0 (2004).
Religion: Five largest groups: 21.1% Catholic Church, 5.4% Southern Baptist Convention, 3.4% The United Methodist Church, 1.2% Episcopal Church, 1.2% Evangelical Lutheran Church in America (2000).
Economy: Unemployment rate: 5.5% (2004); Total civilian labor force: 22,714 (2004); Leading industries: 15.5% retail trade; 14.3% accommodation & food services; 13.6% manufacturing (2003); Companies that employ 500 or more persons: 2 (2003); Companies that employ 100 to 499 persons: 14 (2003); Companies that employ less than 100 persons: 1,342 (2003); Farms: 100 totaling 68,364 acres (2002); Minority business ownership rate: 17.6% (1997); Women business ownership rate: 23.3% (1997); Retail sales per capita: $5,435 (1997). Single-family building permits issued: 4,275 (2004); Multi-family building permits issued: 933 (2004).
Income: Per capita income: $24,618 (2004); Median household income: $44,299 (2004); Average household income: $56,900 (2004); Percent of households with income of $100,000 or more: 11.5% (2004); Poverty rate: 9.0% (2002); Bankruptcy rate: 5.50% (2004).
Taxes: Total county taxes per capita: $368 (2002); County property taxes per capita: $270 (2002).
Education: Percent of population age 25 and over with: High school diploma (including GED) or higher: 85.7% (2004); Bachelor's degree or higher: 20.9% (2004); Master's degree or higher: 7.7% (2004).
Housing: Homeownership rate: 84.1% (2004); Median home value: $142,885 (2004); Median rent: $592 per month (2000); Median age of housing: 11 years (2000).
Health: Birth rate: 79.8 per 10,000 population (2004); Death rate: 96.8 per 10,000 population (2004); Age adjusted cancer mortality rate: 186.5 deaths per 100,000 population (2002); Number of physicians: 11.5 per 10,000 population (2001); Hospital beds: 14.1 per 10,000 population (2002); Hospital admissions: 590.8 per 10,000 population (2002).
Elections: 2004 Presidential election results: 51.0% Bush, 48.3% Kerry, 0.5% Nader, 0.1% Badnarik
National and State Parks: Bulow Plantation Ruins Historic State Park; Gamble Rogers Memorial State Recreation Area; Relay State Wildlife Management Area; Washington Oaks Gardens State Park
Additional Information Contacts
Flagler County Government Offices. . . . . (386) 437-7414
Flagler Beach Chamber of Commerce . . . . (386) 439-0995
Flagler County Association of Realtors . . . . (386) 437-0095

Flagler County Communities

BEVERLY BEACH (town). Covers a land area of 0.358 square miles and a water area of 0.030 square miles. Located at 29.51° N. Lat.; 81.14° W. Long. Elevation is 6 feet.
Population: 312 (1990); 547 (2000); 688 (2004); 866 (2009 projected); Race: 97.2% White, 0.1% Black, 0.1% Asian, 0.0% Hispanic of any race (2004); Density: 1,921.1 persons per square mile (2004); Average household size: 1.72 (2004); Median age: 63.0 (2004); Male/female ratio: 90.6 (2004); Marriage status: 9.3% never married, 59.7% now married, 20.5% widowed, 10.5% divorced (2000); Foreign born: 4.3% (2000); Ancestry (includes multiple ancestries): 22.0% German, 17.5% English, 14.0% Irish, 9.6% Italian, 7.9% United States or American (2000).
Economy: Single-family building permits issued: 1 (2004); Multi-family building permits issued: 0 (2004); Employment by occupation: 8.6% management, 15.0% professional, 17.9% services, 30.0% sales, 0.0% farming, 20.7% construction, 7.9% production (2000).
Income: Per capita income: $23,714 (2004); Median household income: $32,164 (2004); Average household income: $40,788 (2004); Percent of households with income of $100,000 or more: 5.3% (2004); Poverty rate: 8.7% (2000).
Taxes: Total city taxes per capita: $194 (2002); City property taxes per capita: $95 (2002).
Education: Percent of population age 25 and over with: High school diploma (including GED) or higher: 79.4% (2004); Bachelor's degree or higher: 16.5% (2004); Master's degree or higher: 6.5% (2004).

Housing: Homeownership rate: 85.0% (2004); Median home value: $65,128 (2004); Median rent: $392 per month (2000); Median age of housing: 16 years (2000).
Transportation: Commute to work: 89.7% car, 0.0% public transportation, 7.4% walk, 2.9% work from home (2000); Travel time to work: 33.3% less than 15 minutes, 46.2% 15 to 30 minutes, 8.3% 30 to 45 minutes, 6.1% 45 to 60 minutes, 6.1% 60 minutes or more (2000)

BUNNELL (city). Covers a land area of 4.664 square miles and a water area of 0 square miles. Located at 29.46° N. Lat.; 81.25° W. Long. Elevation is 20 feet.
History: Bunnell developed as a lumber and turpentine town, situated in a potato-growing area. Another early industry was the cutting and shipping of palmetto leaves for use in Palm Sunday services.
Population: 1,911 (1990); 2,122 (2000); 2,885 (2004); 3,821 (2009 projected); Race: 67.6% White, 28.0% Black, 1.2% Asian, 5.3% Hispanic of any race (2004); Density: 618.6 persons per square mile (2004); Average household size: 2.50 (2004); Median age: 40.0 (2004); Male/female ratio: 90.1 (2004); Marriage status: 33.2% never married, 43.5% now married, 9.8% widowed, 13.5% divorced (2000); Foreign born: 2.2% (2000); Ancestry (includes multiple ancestries): 34.3% Other groups, 9.3% German, 8.5% English, 8.1% Irish, 6.0% Italian (2000).
Economy: Single-family building permits issued: 16 (2004); Multi-family building permits issued: 66 (2004); Employment by occupation: 6.4% management, 11.3% professional, 24.3% services, 24.9% sales, 1.6% farming, 15.0% construction, 16.5% production (2000).
Income: Per capita income: $14,909 (2004); Median household income: $24,125 (2004); Average household income: $35,214 (2004); Percent of households with income of $100,000 or more: 5.4% (2004); Poverty rate: 22.5% (2000).
Education: Percent of population age 25 and over with: High school diploma (including GED) or higher: 72.1% (2004); Bachelor's degree or higher: 10.4% (2004); Master's degree or higher: 2.2% (2004).

School District(s)

Flagler County School District (PK-12)
2002-03 Enrollment: 7,601 . . . . (386) 437-7526
Housing: Homeownership rate: 67.5% (2004); Median home value: $78,784 (2004); Median rent: $332 per month (2000); Median age of housing: 26 years (2000).
Safety: Violent crime rate: 153.4 per 10,000 population; Property crime rate: 285.0 per 10,000 population (2003).
Newspapers: The Flagler/Palm Coast News Tribune (General - Circulation 9,635)
Transportation: Commute to work: 90.0% car, 2.6% public transportation, 4.4% walk, 2.3% work from home (2000); Travel time to work: 38.8% less than 15 minutes, 37.9% 15 to 30 minutes, 13.1% 30 to 45 minutes, 5.0% 45 to 60 minutes, 5.2% 60 minutes or more (2000)
Airports: Flagler County
Additional Information Contacts
Flagler County Association of Realtors . . . . (386) 437-0095

FLAGLER BEACH (city). Covers a land area of 3.683 square miles and a water area of 0.402 square miles. Located at 29.47° N. Lat.; 81.12° W. Long. Elevation is 18 feet.
Population: 3,882 (1990); 4,954 (2000); 5,799 (2004); 6,869 (2009 projected); Race: 97.8% White, 0.6% Black, 0.7% Asian, 2.2% Hispanic of any race (2004); Density: 1,574.5 persons per square mile (2004); Average household size: 1.92 (2004); Median age: 52.8 (2004); Male/female ratio: 93.5 (2004); Marriage status: 15.3% never married, 60.4% now married, 12.0% widowed, 12.2% divorced (2000); Foreign born: 6.1% (2000); Ancestry (includes multiple ancestries): 19.7% Irish, 16.6% German, 16.5% English, 8.0% United States or American, 7.9% Italian (2000).
Economy: Resort town. Single-family building permits issued: 13 (2004); Multi-family building permits issued: 9 (2004); Employment by occupation: 13.3% management, 23.3% professional, 16.2% services, 24.1% sales, 0.0% farming, 11.8% construction, 11.4% production (2000).
Income: Per capita income: $28,931 (2004); Median household income: $41,863 (2004); Average household income: $55,407 (2004); Percent of households with income of $100,000 or more: 13.1% (2004); Poverty rate: 10.9% (2000).
Taxes: Total city taxes per capita: $557 (2002); City property taxes per capita: $142 (2002).
Education: Percent of population age 25 and over with: High school diploma (including GED) or higher: 89.9% (2004); Bachelor's degree or higher: 31.1% (2004); Master's degree or higher: 11.8% (2004).
Housing: Homeownership rate: 71.2% (2004); Median home value: $164,948 (2004); Median rent: $500 per month (2000); Median age of housing: 18 years (2000).
Safety: Violent crime rate: 20.5 per 10,000 population; Property crime rate: 285.8 per 10,000 population (2003).
Transportation: Commute to work: 89.5% car, 1.4% public transportation, 3.1% walk, 3.8% work from home (2000); Travel time to work: 29.4% less than 15 minutes, 39.4% 15 to 30 minutes, 17.9% 30 to 45 minutes, 8.8% 45 to 60 minutes, 4.5% 60 minutes or more (2000)
Additional Information Contacts
Flagler Beach Chamber of Commerce . . . . (386) 439-0995

MARINELAND (town). Covers a land area of 0.340 square miles and a water area of 0 square miles. Located at 29.66° N. Lat.; 81.21° W. Long. Elevation is 5 feet.
Population: 21 (1990); 6 (2000); 7 (2004); 8 (2009 projected); Race: 100.0% White, 0.0% Black, 0.0% Asian, 0.0% Hispanic of any race (2004); Density: 20.6 persons per square mile (2004); Average household size: 2.33 (2004); Median age: 30.0 (2004); Male/female ratio: 600.0 (2004); Marriage status: 66.7% never married, 33.3% now married, 0.0% widowed, 0.0% divorced (2000); Foreign born: 71.4% (2000); Ancestry (includes multiple ancestries): 71.4% Russian, 28.6% Welsh (2000).
Economy: Single-family building permits issued: 2 (2004); Multi-family building permits issued: 0 (2004); Employment by occupation: 0.0% management, 100.0% professional, 0.0% services, 0.0% sales, 0.0% farming, 0.0% construction, 0.0% production (2000).
Income: Per capita income: $13,929 (2004); Median household income: $32,500 (2004); Average household income: $32,500 (2004); Percent of households with income of $100,000 or more: 0.0% (2004); Poverty rate: 0.0% (2000).
Education: Percent of population age 25 and over with: High school diploma (including GED) or higher: 100.0% (2004); Bachelor's degree or higher: 100.0% (2004); Master's degree or higher: 40.0% (2004).
Housing: Homeownership rate: 0.0% (2004); Median home value: $n/a (2004); Median rent: $375 per month (2000); Median age of housing: 32 years (2000).
Transportation: Commute to work: 66.7% car, 0.0% public transportation, 33.3% walk, 0.0% work from home (2000); Travel time to work: 100.0% less than 15 minutes, 0.0% 15 to 30 minutes, 0.0% 30 to 45 minutes, 0.0% 45 to 60 minutes, 0.0% 60 minutes or more (2000)

PALM COAST (city). Covers a land area of 50.715 square miles and a water area of 0.981 square miles. Located at 29.53° N. Lat.; 81.22° W. Long. Elevation is 10 feet.
Population: 16,998 (1990); 32,732 (2000); 40,237 (2004); 49,763 (2009 projected); Race: 84.3% White, 10.9% Black, 1.7% Asian, 7.6% Hispanic of any race (2004); Density: 793.4 persons per square mile (2004); Average household size: 2.39 (2004); Median age: 49.1 (2004); Male/female ratio: 91.3 (2004); Marriage status: 12.9% never married, 70.8% now married, 9.2% widowed, 7.2% divorced (2000); Foreign born: 12.5% (2000); Ancestry (includes multiple ancestries): 17.5% Other groups, 16.9% Irish, 15.9% German, 15.3% Italian, 11.9% English (2000).
Economy: Manufacturing includes power-supply systems, electronic equipment, fiberglass boats and yachts. Unemployment rate: 5.5% (2004); Total civilian labor force: 10,157 (2004); Single-family building permits issued: 3,951 (2004); Multi-family building permits issued: 632 (2004); Employment by occupation: 12.5% management, 15.6% professional, 20.6% services, 29.9% sales, 0.1% farming, 10.6% construction, 10.8% production (2000).
Income: Per capita income: $24,270 (2004); Median household income: $46,050 (2004); Average household income: $57,569 (2004); Percent of households with income of $100,000 or more: 10.9% (2004); Poverty rate: 7.5% (2000).
Education: Percent of population age 25 and over with: High school diploma (including GED) or higher: 85.6% (2004); Bachelor's degree or higher: 19.5% (2004); Master's degree or higher: 7.2% (2004).

School District(s)

Flagler County School District (PK-12)
2002-03 Enrollment: 7,601 . . . . (386) 437-7526
Housing: Homeownership rate: 85.8% (2004); Median home value: $144,696 (2004); Median rent: $659 per month (2000); Median age of housing: 10 years (2000).
Hospitals: Memorial Hospital Flagler (81 beds)
Transportation: Commute to work: 94.2% car, 0.7% public transportation, 0.7% walk, 2.9% work from home (2000); Travel time to work: 36.6% less

than 15 minutes, 29.1% 15 to 30 minutes, 20.0% 30 to 45 minutes, 6.7% 45 to 60 minutes, 7.6% 60 minutes or more (2000)

Additional Information Contacts

Local Government Offices . . . . (386) 986-3700

Franklin County

Located in northwestern Florida; bounded on the south by the Gulf of Mexico, on the west by the Apalachicola River, and on the east by the Ochlockonee River; includes St. Vincent, St. George, and Dog Islands, enclosing St. Vincent Sound, Apalachicola Bay, and St. George Sound. Covers a land area of 544.30 square miles, a water area of 493.10 square miles, and is located in the Eastern Time Zone. The county government was organized in 1832. County seat is Apalachicola.

Weather Station: Apalachicola Municipal Airport Elevation: 19 feet

	Jan	Feb	Mar	Apr	May	Jun	Jul	Aug	Sep	Oct	Nov	Dec
High	62	65	70	76	83	88	90	89	87	80	72	65
Low	44	47	52	58	66	72	74	74	71	61	53	47
Precip	4.9	3.8	5.0	3.1	2.9	4.3	7.1	7.9	6.6	4.4	3.5	3.6
Snow	tr	tr	tr	0.0	0.0	0.0	0.0	0.0	0.0	0.0	0.0	tr

High and Low temperatures in degrees Fahrenheit; Precipitation and Snow in inches

Population: 8,967 (1990); 11,057 (2000); 10,368 (2004); 9,579 (2009 projected); Race: 85.8% White, 12.2% Black, 0.3% Asian, 1.8% Hispanic of any race (2004); Density: 19.0 persons per square mile (2004); Average household size: 2.90 (2004); Median age: 42.5 (2004); Male/female ratio: 129.1 (2004).

Religion: Five largest groups: 6.9% Southern Baptist Convention, 5.6% The United Methodist Church, 4.7% Assemblies of God, 4.0% Church of God (Cleveland, Tennessee), 2.1% International Pentecostal Holiness Church (2000).

Economy: Unemployment rate: 2.5% (2004); Total civilian labor force: 5,788 (2004); Leading industries: 21.9% accommodation & food services; 19.0% retail trade; 9.6% wholesale trade (2003); Companies that employ 500 or more persons: 0 (2003); Companies that employ 100 to 499 persons: 0 (2003); Companies that employ less than 100 persons: 362 (2003); Farms: 20 totaling n/a acres (2002); Minority business ownership rate: n/a (1997); Women business ownership rate: 14.9% (1997); Retail sales per capita: $5,643 (1997). Single-family building permits issued: 248 (2004); Multi-family building permits issued: 0 (2004).

Income: Per capita income: $18,679 (2004); Median household income: $31,551 (2004); Average household income: $43,555 (2004); Percent of households with income of $100,000 or more: 6.4% (2004); Poverty rate: 15.2% (2002); Bankruptcy rate: 3.75% (2004).

Taxes: Total county taxes per capita: $455 (2002); County property taxes per capita: $407 (2002).

Education: Percent of population age 25 and over with: High school diploma (including GED) or higher: 67.8% (2004); Bachelor's degree or higher: 12.3% (2004); Master's degree or higher: 6.2% (2004).

Housing: Homeownership rate: 79.1% (2004); Median home value: $107,645 (2004); Median rent: $300 per month (2000); Median age of housing: 21 years (2000).

Health: Birth rate: 90.9 per 10,000 population (2004); Death rate: 91.9 per 10,000 population (2004); Age adjusted cancer mortality rate: 161.8 deaths per 100,000 population (2002); Number of physicians: 9.8 per 10,000 population (2001); Hospital beds: 24.8 per 10,000 population (2002); Hospital admissions: 3,078.8 per 10,000 population (2002).

Elections: 2004 Presidential election results: 58.5% Bush, 40.5% Kerry, 0.6% Nader, 0.1% Badnarik

National and State Parks: Dr Julian G Bruce Saint George Island State Park; Fort Gadsden State Historic Site; Fort Gadsden State Park; John Gorrie Museum State Park; Saint Vincent National Wildlife Refuge

Additional Information Contacts

Franklin County Government Offices. . . . . (850) 653-8861
Apalachicola Bay Chamber of Commerce. . . . . (850) 653-9419
Carrabelle Chamber of Commerce . . . . (850) 697-2585
Realtor Association of Franklin & So. Gulf Counties . . . . . . (850) 653-3322

Franklin County Communities

APALACHICOLA (city). Covers a land area of 1.879 square miles and a water area of 0.780 square miles. Located at 29.72° N. Lat.; 84.99° W. Long. Elevation is 17 feet.

History: Apalachicola was founded in 1821 at the mouth of the Apalachicola (of Indian origin meaning "people on the other side") River. The town was incorporated as West Point in 1827, and renamed Apalachicola in 1831. This was a major cotton shipping port on the Gulf of Mexico until the Civil War, after which fishing became the dominant industry.

Population: 2,602 (1990); 2,334 (2000); 2,056 (2004); 1,783 (2009 projected); Race: 76.4% White, 22.2% Black, 0.5% Asian, 1.1% Hispanic of any race (2004); Density: 1,094.2 persons per square mile (2004); Average household size: 2.33 (2004); Median age: 45.9 (2004); Male/female ratio: 76.8 (2004); Marriage status: 26.8% never married, 47.9% now married, 12.3% widowed, 13.0% divorced (2000); Foreign born: 1.5% (2000); Ancestry (includes multiple ancestries): 41.2% Other groups, 7.8% Irish, 7.2% English, 6.1% United States or American, 6.0% German (2000).

Economy: Single-family building permits issued: 44 (2004); Multi-family building permits issued: 0 (2004); Employment by occupation: 9.8% management, 15.6% professional, 27.5% services, 21.2% sales, 5.9% farming, 5.6% construction, 14.4% production (2000).

Income: Per capita income: $16,451 (2004); Median household income: $28,254 (2004); Average household income: $38,135 (2004); Percent of households with income of $100,000 or more: 5.7% (2004); Poverty rate: 25.3% (2000).

Education: Percent of population age 25 and over with: High school diploma (including GED) or higher: 69.4% (2004); Bachelor's degree or higher: 15.4% (2004); Master's degree or higher: 4.1% (2004).

School District(s)

Franklin County School District (PK-12)
2002-03 Enrollment: 1,345 . . . . (850) 653-8831

Housing: Homeownership rate: 68.9% (2004); Median home value: $114,729 (2004); Median rent: $303 per month (2000); Median age of housing: 40 years (2000).

Hospitals: George E. Weems Memorial Hospital (25 beds)

Safety: Violent crime rate: 12.5 per 10,000 population; Property crime rate: 317.6 per 10,000 population (2003).

Newspapers: The Apalachicola Times (General - Circulation 4,500); The Carrabelle Times (General - Circulation 1,500)

Transportation: Commute to work: 87.5% car, 0.2% public transportation, 5.4% walk, 3.3% work from home (2000); Travel time to work: 72.0% less than 15 minutes, 13.7% 15 to 30 minutes, 6.1% 30 to 45 minutes, 1.7% 45 to 60 minutes, 6.5% 60 minutes or more (2000)

Additional Information Contacts

Apalachicola Bay Chamber of Commerce. . . . . (850) 653-9419
Realtor Association of Franklin & So. Gulf Counties . . . . . . (850) 653-3322

CARRABELLE (city). Covers a land area of 3.731 square miles and a water area of 1.078 square miles. Located at 29.85° N. Lat.; 84.66° W. Long. Elevation is 25 feet.

History: Carrabelle grew as a resort and fishing village, shipping shrimp, oysters, and fish to northern markets.

Population: 1,219 (1990); 1,303 (2000); 1,158 (2004); 970 (2009 projected); Race: 96.3% White, 1.8% Black, 0.0% Asian, 0.9% Hispanic of any race (2004); Density: 310.3 persons per square mile (2004); Average household size: 2.30 (2004); Median age: 46.4 (2004); Male/female ratio: 83.8 (2004); Marriage status: 16.9% never married, 55.5% now married, 9.4% widowed, 18.2% divorced (2000); Foreign born: 1.6% (2000); Ancestry (includes multiple ancestries): 22.1% United States or American, 15.1% Irish, 11.2% Other groups, 6.7% English, 6.0% German (2000).

Economy: Employment by occupation: 6.9% management, 10.5% professional, 28.1% services, 25.1% sales, 4.2% farming, 15.6% construction, 9.7% production (2000).

Income: Per capita income: $14,876 (2004); Median household income: $25,915 (2004); Average household income: $33,643 (2004); Percent of households with income of $100,000 or more: 3.0% (2004); Poverty rate: 19.4% (2000).

Taxes: Total city taxes per capita: $442 (2002); City property taxes per capita: $186 (2002).

Education: Percent of population age 25 and over with: High school diploma (including GED) or higher: 69.1% (2004); Bachelor's degree or higher: 7.5% (2004); Master's degree or higher: 2.7% (2004).

School District(s)

Franklin County School District (PK-12)
2002-03 Enrollment: 1,345 . . . . (850) 653-8831

Housing: Homeownership rate: 73.8% (2004); Median home value: $88,824 (2004); Median rent: $251 per month (2000); Median age of housing: 25 years (2000).

Safety: Violent crime rate: 14.9 per 10,000 population; Property crime rate: 515.3 per 10,000 population (2003).

Transportation: Commute to work: 91.2% car, 0.0% public transportation, 5.3% walk, 2.5% work from home (2000); Travel time to work: 43.5% less than 15 minutes, 19.3% 15 to 30 minutes, 26.5% 30 to 45 minutes, 5.0% 45 to 60 minutes, 5.7% 60 minutes or more (2000)
Additional Information Contacts
Carrabelle Chamber of Commerce . . . . (850) 697-2585

EASTPOINT (CDP). Covers a land area of 7.331 square miles and a water area of 0 square miles. Located at 29.74° N. Lat.; 84.87° W. Long. Elevation is 7 feet.
Population: 1,577 (1990); 2,158 (2000); 1,871 (2004); 1,557 (2009 projected); Race: 97.6% White, 0.5% Black, 0.2% Asian, 1.1% Hispanic of any race (2004); Density: 255.2 persons per square mile (2004); Average household size: 2.68 (2004); Median age: 38.5 (2004); Male/female ratio: 83.8 (2004); Marriage status: 15.9% never married, 58.1% now married, 7.9% widowed, 18.1% divorced (2000); Foreign born: 1.9% (2000); Ancestry (includes multiple ancestries): 21.5% Irish, 21.4% United States or American, 13.4% Other groups, 11.3% English, 8.0% German (2000).
Economy: Manufacturing includes seafood processing (especially oysters). Apalachicola National Forest to North, St. Vincent National Wildlife Refuge to West. Employment by occupation: 5.9% management, 6.8% professional, 22.4% services, 15.0% sales, 20.5% farming, 12.6% construction, 16.6% production (2000).
Income: Per capita income: $16,630 (2004); Median household income: $35,308 (2004); Average household income: $43,818 (2004); Percent of households with income of $100,000 or more: 3.6% (2004); Poverty rate: 12.1% (2000).
Education: Percent of population age 25 and over with: High school diploma (including GED) or higher: 63.9% (2004); Bachelor's degree or higher: 8.6% (2004); Master's degree or higher: 3.4% (2004).
School District(s)
Franklin County School District (PK-12)
2002-03 Enrollment: 1,345 . . . . (850) 653-8831
Housing: Homeownership rate: 83.7% (2004); Median home value: $79,506 (2004); Median rent: $196 per month (2000); Median age of housing: 17 years (2000).
Transportation: Commute to work: 93.8% car, 0.8% public transportation, 1.4% walk, 1.4% work from home (2000); Travel time to work: 41.2% less than 15 minutes, 39.2% 15 to 30 minutes, 11.7% 30 to 45 minutes, 0.0% 45 to 60 minutes, 7.9% 60 minutes or more (2000)

Gadsden County

Located in northwestern Florida; bounded on the north by Georgia, on the east and south by the Ochlockonee River and Lake Talquin, and on the west by the Apalachicola River. Covers a land area of 516.10 square miles, a water area of 12.40 square miles, and is located in the Eastern Time Zone. The county government was organized in 1823. County seat is Quincy.

Gadsden County is part of the Tallahassee, FL Metropolitan Statistical Area. The entire metro area includes: Gadsden County, FL; Jefferson County, FL; Leon County, FL; Wakulla County, FL

Weather Station: Quincy 3 SSW — Elevation: 242 feet

	Jan	Feb	Mar	Apr	May	Jun	Jul	Aug	Sep	Oct	Nov	Dec
High	62	66	72	78	85	89	91	90	87	80	72	65
Low	40	42	49	54	62	68	71	71	67	57	49	43
Precip	5.7	4.5	6.2	3.6	4.8	5.6	6.9	5.6	3.7	3.4	3.5	3.6
Snow	tr	tr	tr	0.0	0.0	0.0	0.0	0.0	0.0	0.0	0.0	0.0

High and Low temperatures in degrees Fahrenheit; Precipitation and Snow in inches

Population: 41,105 (1990); 45,087 (2000); 45,995 (2004); 47,163 (2009 projected); Race: 37.5% White, 58.4% Black, 0.3% Asian, 6.3% Hispanic of any race (2004); Density: 89.1 persons per square mile (2004); Average household size: 2.80 (2004); Median age: 36.2 (2004); Male/female ratio: 90.4 (2004).
Religion: Five largest groups: 15.0% Southern Baptist Convention, 4.1% The United Methodist Church, 3.9% National Primitive Baptist Convention, USA, 1.7% Presbyterian Church (U.S.A.), 0.9% Catholic Church (2000).
Economy: Unemployment rate: 4.8% (2004); Total civilian labor force: 19,707 (2004); Leading industries: 34.4% health care and social assistance; 15.0% manufacturing; 12.8% retail trade (2003); Companies that employ 500 or more persons: 1 (2003); Companies that employ 100 to 499 persons: 16 (2003); Companies that employ less than 100 persons: 568 (2003); Farms: 343 totaling 68,140 acres (2002); Minority business ownership rate: 27.8% (1997); Women business ownership rate: 33.4% (1997); Retail sales per capita: $4,076 (1997). Single-family building permits issued: 204 (2004); Multi-family building permits issued: 0 (2004).
Income: Per capita income: $16,030 (2004); Median household income: $33,967 (2004); Average household income: $43,274 (2004); Percent of households with income of $100,000 or more: 6.1% (2004); Poverty rate: 18.2% (2002); Bankruptcy rate: 5.97% (2004).
Taxes: Total county taxes per capita: $295 (2002); County property taxes per capita: $181 (2002).
Education: Percent of population age 25 and over with: High school diploma (including GED) or higher: 70.3% (2004); Bachelor's degree or higher: 12.8% (2004); Master's degree or higher: 4.9% (2004).
Housing: Homeownership rate: 78.3% (2004); Median home value: $80,448 (2004); Median rent: $271 per month (2000); Median age of housing: 22 years (2000).
Health: Birth rate: 166.4 per 10,000 population (2004); Death rate: 95.9 per 10,000 population (2004); Age adjusted cancer mortality rate: 247.2 deaths per 100,000 population (2002); Number of physicians: 8.4 per 10,000 population (2001); Hospital beds: 229.2 per 10,000 population (2002); Hospital admissions: 290.9 per 10,000 population (2002).
Elections: 2004 Presidential election results: 29.8% Bush, 69.7% Kerry, 0.3% Nader, 0.1% Badnarik
National and State Parks: Bear Creek State Park; Lake Talquin State Park
Additional Information Contacts
Gadsden County Government Offices . . . . (850) 875-8650
Gadsden County Board of Realtors . . . . (850) 875-8470
Quincy Chamber of Commerce . . . . (850) 627-9231

Gadsden County Communities

CHATTAHOOCHEE (city). Covers a land area of 5.454 square miles and a water area of 0.187 square miles. Located at 30.69° N. Lat.; 84.84° W. Long. Elevation is 151 feet.
History: The name of Chattahoochee is of Indian origin meaning "marked rock."
Population: 4,382 (1990); 3,287 (2000); 3,227 (2004); 3,182 (2009 projected); Race: 48.8% White, 48.5% Black, 1.2% Asian, 2.6% Hispanic of any race (2004); Density: 591.7 persons per square mile (2004); Average household size: 3.22 (2004); Median age: 41.7 (2004); Male/female ratio: 117.0 (2004); Marriage status: 27.9% never married, 52.8% now married, 8.8% widowed, 10.5% divorced (2000); Foreign born: 1.1% (2000); Ancestry (includes multiple ancestries): 29.4% Other groups, 12.8% United States or American, 5.0% English, 3.9% Irish, 2.8% German (2000).
Economy: Employment by occupation: 11.4% management, 21.4% professional, 30.4% services, 18.7% sales, 0.0% farming, 9.6% construction, 8.5% production (2000).
Income: Per capita income: $15,576 (2004); Median household income: $30,912 (2004); Average household income: $41,512 (2004); Percent of households with income of $100,000 or more: 6.3% (2004); Poverty rate: 26.1% (2000).
Education: Percent of population age 25 and over with: High school diploma (including GED) or higher: 68.9% (2004); Bachelor's degree or higher: 13.2% (2004); Master's degree or higher: 7.0% (2004).
School District(s)
Gadsden County School District (PK-12)
2002-03 Enrollment: 7,196 . . . . (850) 627-9651
Housing: Homeownership rate: 61.6% (2004); Median home value: $61,727 (2004); Median rent: $240 per month (2000); Median age of housing: 40 years (2000).
Hospitals: Florida State Hospital (2007 beds)
Safety: Violent crime rate: 35.5 per 10,000 population; Property crime rate: 266.2 per 10,000 population (2003).
Newspapers: Twin City News (General - Circulation 2,000)
Transportation: Commute to work: 91.7% car, 0.0% public transportation, 2.8% walk, 3.1% work from home (2000); Travel time to work: 54.4% less than 15 minutes, 7.9% 15 to 30 minutes, 14.0% 30 to 45 minutes, 12.5% 45 to 60 minutes, 11.2% 60 minutes or more (2000)

GREENSBORO (town). Covers a land area of 1.010 square miles and a water area of 0 square miles. Located at 30.56° N. Lat.; 84.74° W. Long. Elevation is 263 feet.
Population: 586 (1990); 619 (2000); 558 (2004); 508 (2009 projected); Race: 47.5% White, 38.0% Black, 2.0% Asian, 37.6% Hispanic of any race (2004); Density: 552.2 persons per square mile (2004); Average household

size: 2.95 (2004); Median age: 29.1 (2004); Male/female ratio: 96.5 (2004); Marriage status: 28.3% never married, 59.0% now married, 6.3% widowed, 6.3% divorced (2000); Foreign born: 23.7% (2000); Ancestry (includes multiple ancestries): 63.2% Other groups, 21.3% United States or American, 2.3% English, 1.0% Irish, 0.5% African (2000).
Economy: Employment by occupation: 3.3% management, 9.1% professional, 17.1% services, 21.8% sales, 15.3% farming, 15.6% construction, 17.8% production (2000).
Income: Per capita income: $13,123 (2004); Median household income: $33,676 (2004); Average household income: $38,743 (2004); Percent of households with income of $100,000 or more: 2.6% (2004); Poverty rate: 24.3% (2000).
Education: Percent of population age 25 and over with: High school diploma (including GED) or higher: 63.9% (2004); Bachelor's degree or higher: 9.9% (2004); Master's degree or higher: 3.8% (2004).

School District(s)

Gadsden County School District (PK-12)
2002-03 Enrollment: 7,196 . . . . (850) 627-9651
Housing: Homeownership rate: 69.8% (2004); Median home value: $62,222 (2004); Median rent: $358 per month (2000); Median age of housing: 42 years (2000).
Safety: Violent crime rate: 0.0 per 10,000 population; Property crime rate: 80.1 per 10,000 population (2003).
Transportation: Commute to work: 98.5% car, 0.0% public transportation, 0.4% walk, 0.0% work from home (2000); Travel time to work: 9.5% less than 15 minutes, 45.8% 15 to 30 minutes, 27.1% 30 to 45 minutes, 11.4% 45 to 60 minutes, 6.2% 60 minutes or more (2000)

GRETNA (city). Covers a land area of 1.885 square miles and a water area of 0 square miles. Located at 30.61° N. Lat.; 84.66° W. Long. Elevation is 301 feet.
Population: 2,058 (1990); 1,709 (2000); 2,078 (2004); 2,509 (2009 projected); Race: 6.1% White, 87.7% Black, 0.1% Asian, 10.9% Hispanic of any race (2004); Density: 1,102.5 persons per square mile (2004); Average household size: 3.33 (2004); Median age: 28.0 (2004); Male/female ratio: 91.7 (2004); Marriage status: 44.1% never married, 40.8% now married, 6.0% widowed, 9.1% divorced (2000); Foreign born: 6.8% (2000); Ancestry (includes multiple ancestries): 84.4% Other groups, 1.1% African, 0.8% United States or American, 0.4% English, 0.4% French (except Basque) (2000).
Economy: Single-family building permits issued: 1 (2004); Multi-family building permits issued: 0 (2004); Employment by occupation: 4.0% management, 10.3% professional, 33.7% services, 18.7% sales, 7.2% farming, 9.3% construction, 16.8% production (2000).
Income: Per capita income: $10,213 (2004); Median household income: $28,185 (2004); Average household income: $34,010 (2004); Percent of households with income of $100,000 or more: 2.7% (2004); Poverty rate: 30.6% (2000).
Education: Percent of population age 25 and over with: High school diploma (including GED) or higher: 59.1% (2004); Bachelor's degree or higher: 5.6% (2004); Master's degree or higher: 1.0% (2004).

School District(s)

Gadsden County School District (PK-12)
2002-03 Enrollment: 7,196 . . . . (850) 627-9651
Housing: Homeownership rate: 80.8% (2004); Median home value: $51,340 (2004); Median rent: $234 per month (2000); Median age of housing: 26 years (2000).
Transportation: Commute to work: 97.3% car, 0.4% public transportation, 1.2% walk, 0.0% work from home (2000); Travel time to work: 19.3% less than 15 minutes, 38.3% 15 to 30 minutes, 21.6% 30 to 45 minutes, 15.6% 45 to 60 minutes, 5.2% 60 minutes or more (2000)

HAVANA (town). Covers a land area of 1.857 square miles and a water area of 0 square miles. Located at 30.62° N. Lat.; 84.41° W. Long. Elevation is 245 feet.
History: Havana, named for the Cuban city, grew in an area of tobacco farms and cypress lumber and shingle mills.
Population: 1,654 (1990); 1,713 (2000); 1,676 (2004); 1,648 (2009 projected); Race: 42.4% White, 56.3% Black, 0.1% Asian, 1.0% Hispanic of any race (2004); Density: 902.6 persons per square mile (2004); Average household size: 2.38 (2004); Median age: 41.2 (2004); Male/female ratio: 83.4 (2004); Marriage status: 31.3% never married, 48.3% now married, 12.3% widowed, 8.1% divorced (2000); Foreign born: 0.2% (2000); Ancestry (includes multiple ancestries): 50.7% Other groups, 7.4% United States or American, 4.7% Irish, 4.3% English, 2.6% German (2000).
Economy: Employment by occupation: 8.4% management, 19.0% professional, 22.4% services, 33.8% sales, 0.6% farming, 8.1% construction, 7.7% production (2000).
Income: Per capita income: $20,917 (2004); Median household income: $30,611 (2004); Average household income: $47,663 (2004); Percent of households with income of $100,000 or more: 8.1% (2004); Poverty rate: 16.3% (2000).
Taxes: Total city taxes per capita: $92 (2002); City property taxes per capita: $23 (2002).
Education: Percent of population age 25 and over with: High school diploma (including GED) or higher: 70.9% (2004); Bachelor's degree or higher: 17.6% (2004); Master's degree or higher: 4.5% (2004).

School District(s)

Gadsden County School District (PK-12)
2002-03 Enrollment: 7,196 . . . . (850) 627-9651
Housing: Homeownership rate: 70.9% (2004); Median home value: $92,553 (2004); Median rent: $287 per month (2000); Median age of housing: 35 years (2000).
Safety: Violent crime rate: 190.6 per 10,000 population; Property crime rate: 485.3 per 10,000 population (2003).
Newspapers: Havana Herald (General - Circulation 3,100)
Transportation: Commute to work: 94.0% car, 0.0% public transportation, 4.0% walk, 1.4% work from home (2000); Travel time to work: 21.0% less than 15 minutes, 31.2% 15 to 30 minutes, 32.3% 30 to 45 minutes, 10.9% 45 to 60 minutes, 4.5% 60 minutes or more (2000)

MIDWAY (city). Covers a land area of 3.835 square miles and a water area of 0 square miles. Located at 30.49° N. Lat.; 84.46° W. Long. Elevation is 191 feet.
Population: 1,028 (1990); 1,446 (2000); 1,574 (2004); 1,733 (2009 projected); Race: 3.2% White, 96.0% Black, 0.3% Asian, 0.5% Hispanic of any race (2004); Density: 410.5 persons per square mile (2004); Average household size: 2.94 (2004); Median age: 30.2 (2004); Male/female ratio: 83.4 (2004); Marriage status: 37.0% never married, 43.4% now married, 7.8% widowed, 11.8% divorced (2000); Foreign born: 1.2% (2000); Ancestry (includes multiple ancestries): 80.8% Other groups, 1.1% United States or American, 1.1% African, 0.4% Irish, 0.1% Scotch-Irish (2000).
Economy: Single-family building permits issued: 49 (2004); Multi-family building permits issued: 0 (2004); Employment by occupation: 3.2% management, 9.7% professional, 30.7% services, 24.6% sales, 0.9% farming, 11.4% construction, 19.6% production (2000).
Income: Per capita income: $12,745 (2004); Median household income: $29,038 (2004); Average household income: $37,425 (2004); Percent of households with income of $100,000 or more: 3.0% (2004); Poverty rate: 31.3% (2000).
Taxes: Total city taxes per capita: $131 (2002); City property taxes per capita: $39 (2002).
Education: Percent of population age 25 and over with: High school diploma (including GED) or higher: 59.4% (2004); Bachelor's degree or higher: 5.6% (2004); Master's degree or higher: 1.1% (2004).
Housing: Homeownership rate: 80.8% (2004); Median home value: $84,286 (2004); Median rent: $218 per month (2000); Median age of housing: 16 years (2000).
Transportation: Commute to work: 98.4% car, 0.2% public transportation, 0.0% walk, 1.4% work from home (2000); Travel time to work: 7.7% less than 15 minutes, 48.1% 15 to 30 minutes, 30.6% 30 to 45 minutes, 8.8% 45 to 60 minutes, 4.7% 60 minutes or more (2000)

QUINCY (city). Covers a land area of 7.619 square miles and a water area of 0.012 square miles. Located at 30.58° N. Lat.; 84.58° W. Long. Elevation is 187 feet.
History: Quincy was settled about 1824 by tobacco planters. After the Civil War, many people of Swedish descent settled in Quincy.
Population: 7,468 (1990); 6,982 (2000); 6,544 (2004); 6,230 (2009 projected); Race: 28.9% White, 66.4% Black, 0.4% Asian, 7.8% Hispanic of any race (2004); Density: 859.0 persons per square mile (2004); Average household size: 2.58 (2004); Median age: 35.4 (2004); Male/female ratio: 80.4 (2004); Marriage status: 28.6% never married, 45.1% now married, 13.4% widowed, 12.9% divorced (2000); Foreign born: 4.8% (2000); Ancestry (includes multiple ancestries): 61.4% Other groups, 7.7% United States or American, 4.4% Irish, 4.1% English, 2.5% German (2000).
Economy: Single-family building permits issued: 9 (2004); Multi-family building permits issued: 0 (2004); Employment by occupation: 12.7% management, 15.4% professional, 21.6% services, 26.9% sales, 1.3% farming, 8.4% construction, 13.7% production (2000).

Income: Per capita income: $15,758 (2004); Median household income: $29,947 (2004); Average household income: $40,440 (2004); Percent of households with income of $100,000 or more: 5.4% (2004); Poverty rate: 19.1% (2000).
Taxes: Total city taxes per capita: $163 (2002); City property taxes per capita: $34 (2002).
Education: Percent of population age 25 and over with: High school diploma (including GED) or higher: 72.8% (2004); Bachelor's degree or higher: 14.7% (2004); Master's degree or higher: 5.8% (2004).

School District(s)

Gadsden County School District (PK-12)
2002-03 Enrollment: 7,196 . . . . (850) 627-9651
Housing: Homeownership rate: 72.0% (2004); Median home value: $78,578 (2004); Median rent: $299 per month (2000); Median age of housing: 35 years (2000).
Hospitals: Gadsden Community Hospital (51 beds)
Safety: Violent crime rate: 143.5 per 10,000 population; Property crime rate: 865.5 per 10,000 population (2003).
Newspapers: Gadsden County Times (General - Circulation 6,000)
Transportation: Commute to work: 94.5% car, 1.1% public transportation, 2.3% walk, 1.8% work from home (2000); Travel time to work: 39.6% less than 15 minutes, 18.7% 15 to 30 minutes, 23.4% 30 to 45 minutes, 12.6% 45 to 60 minutes, 5.7% 60 minutes or more (2000)
Additional Information Contacts
Gadsden County Board of Realtors . . . . (850) 875-8470
Local Government Offices . . . . (850) 875-7354
Quincy Chamber of Commerce . . . . (850) 627-9231

Gilchrist County

Located in northern Florida; bounded on the north by the Santa Fe River, and on the west by the Suwannee River; includes many small lakes. Covers a land area of 348.90 square miles, a water area of 6.60 square miles, and is located in the Eastern Time Zone. The county government was organized in 1925. County seat is Trenton.

Gilchrist County is part of the Gainesville, FL Metropolitan Statistical Area. The entire metro area includes: Alachua County, FL; Gilchrist County, FL

Population: 9,667 (1990); 14,437 (2000); 15,221 (2004); 16,212 (2009 projected); Race: 92.6% White, 5.2% Black, 0.2% Asian, 2.5% Hispanic of any race (2004); Density: 43.6 persons per square mile (2004); Average household size: 2.88 (2004); Median age: 36.4 (2004); Male/female ratio: 109.6 (2004).
Religion: Five largest groups: 32.0% Southern Baptist Convention, 2.7% Churches of Christ, 1.7% The United Methodist Church, 1.3% Church of God (Cleveland, Tennessee), 1.1% The American Baptist Association (2000).
Economy: Unemployment rate: 3.5% (2004); Total civilian labor force: 5,691 (2004); Leading industries: 25.6% health care and social assistance; 16.4% retail trade; 16.2% manufacturing (2003); Companies that employ 500 or more persons: 0 (2003); Companies that employ 100 to 499 persons: 1 (2003); Companies that employ less than 100 persons: 203 (2003); Farms: 408 totaling 81,489 acres (2002); Minority business ownership rate: n/a (1997); Women business ownership rate: 59.2% (1997); Retail sales per capita: $2,236 (1997). Single-family building permits issued: 214 (2004); Multi-family building permits issued: 0 (2004).
Income: Per capita income: $15,437 (2004); Median household income: $33,473 (2004); Average household income: $43,897 (2004); Percent of households with income of $100,000 or more: 5.6% (2004); Poverty rate: 16.6% (2002); Bankruptcy rate: 3.23% (2004).
Taxes: Total county taxes per capita: $309 (2002); County property taxes per capita: $241 (2002).
Education: Percent of population age 25 and over with: High school diploma (including GED) or higher: 72.2% (2004); Bachelor's degree or higher: 9.4% (2004); Master's degree or higher: 3.1% (2004).
Housing: Homeownership rate: 86.1% (2004); Median home value: $90,894 (2004); Median rent: $299 per month (2000); Median age of housing: 15 years (2000).
Health: Birth rate: 116.7 per 10,000 population (2004); Death rate: 83.0 per 10,000 population (2004); Age adjusted cancer mortality rate: 152.6 deaths per 100,000 population (2002); Number of physicians: 2.7 per 10,000 population (2001); Hospital beds: 0.0 per 10,000 population (2002); Hospital admissions: 0.0 per 10,000 population (2002).
Elections: 2004 Presidential election results: 70.4% Bush, 28.8% Kerry, 0.5% Nader, 0.2% Badnarik

Additional Information Contacts
Gilchrist County Government Offices. . . . . (352) 463-3170
Bell Chamber of Commerce. . . . . (352) 463-8923
Gilchrist County Chamber of Commerce . . . . (352) 463-3467

Gilchrist County Communities

BELL (town). Covers a land area of 1.634 square miles and a water area of 0 square miles. Located at 29.75° N. Lat.; 82.86° W. Long. Elevation is 70 feet.
Population: 280 (1990); 349 (2000); 342 (2004); 342 (2009 projected); Race: 96.5% White, 2.0% Black, 0.0% Asian, 0.9% Hispanic of any race (2004); Density: 209.2 persons per square mile (2004); Average household size: 2.74 (2004); Median age: 35.7 (2004); Male/female ratio: 89.0 (2004); Marriage status: 26.8% never married, 55.8% now married, 5.1% widowed, 12.3% divorced (2000); Foreign born: 2.0% (2000); Ancestry (includes multiple ancestries): 25.5% United States or American, 14.0% Irish, 11.5% Other groups, 7.4% German, 5.2% French (except Basque) (2000).
Economy: Employment by occupation: 5.8% management, 9.5% professional, 16.8% services, 30.7% sales, 6.6% farming, 10.2% construction, 20.4% production (2000).
Income: Per capita income: $13,596 (2004); Median household income: $32,045 (2004); Average household income: $37,200 (2004); Percent of households with income of $100,000 or more: 4.0% (2004); Poverty rate: 17.2% (2000).
Education: Percent of population age 25 and over with: High school diploma (including GED) or higher: 68.6% (2004); Bachelor's degree or higher: 12.9% (2004); Master's degree or higher: 3.3% (2004).

School District(s)

Gilchrist County School District (PK-12)
2002-03 Enrollment: 2,734 . . . . (352) 463-3200
Housing: Homeownership rate: 76.8% (2004); Median home value: $79,000 (2004); Median rent: $281 per month (2000); Median age of housing: 18 years (2000).
Transportation: Commute to work: 89.8% car, 1.5% public transportation, 0.7% walk, 1.5% work from home (2000); Travel time to work: 34.8% less than 15 minutes, 25.2% 15 to 30 minutes, 6.7% 30 to 45 minutes, 16.3% 45 to 60 minutes, 17.0% 60 minutes or more (2000)
Additional Information Contacts
Bell Chamber of Commerce. . . . . (352) 463-8923

TRENTON (city). Covers a land area of 2.594 square miles and a water area of 0 square miles. Located at 29.61° N. Lat.; 82.81° W. Long. Elevation is 56 feet.
Population: 1,363 (1990); 1,617 (2000); 1,810 (2004); 2,046 (2009 projected); Race: 86.2% White, 12.1% Black, 0.3% Asian, 1.3% Hispanic of any race (2004); Density: 697.8 persons per square mile (2004); Average household size: 2.68 (2004); Median age: 39.9 (2004); Male/female ratio: 81.5 (2004); Marriage status: 21.9% never married, 50.0% now married, 16.1% widowed, 12.0% divorced (2000); Foreign born: 1.7% (2000); Ancestry (includes multiple ancestries): 22.8% Other groups, 20.6% United States or American, 13.0% Irish, 8.4% English, 8.1% German (2000).
Economy: Lumbering, farming. Single-family building permits issued: 0 (2004); Multi-family building permits issued: 0 (2004); Employment by occupation: 4.6% management, 15.8% professional, 23.8% services, 30.8% sales, 3.8% farming, 9.1% construction, 12.1% production (2000).
Income: Per capita income: $14,165 (2004); Median household income: $28,036 (2004); Average household income: $37,012 (2004); Percent of households with income of $100,000 or more: 3.3% (2004); Poverty rate: 20.4% (2000).
Education: Percent of population age 25 and over with: High school diploma (including GED) or higher: 60.7% (2004); Bachelor's degree or higher: 8.1% (2004); Master's degree or higher: 3.1% (2004).

School District(s)

Gilchrist County School District (PK-12)
2002-03 Enrollment: 2,734 . . . . (352) 463-3200
Housing: Homeownership rate: 68.6% (2004); Median home value: $66,000 (2004); Median rent: $279 per month (2000); Median age of housing: 26 years (2000).
Safety: Violent crime rate: 82.4 per 10,000 population; Property crime rate: 664.7 per 10,000 population (2003).
Newspapers: Gilchrist County Journal (General - Circulation 4,000)
Transportation: Commute to work: 93.8% car, 0.0% public transportation, 4.1% walk, 1.5% work from home (2000); Travel time to work: 49.8% less

than 15 minutes, 16.0% 15 to 30 minutes, 12.2% 30 to 45 minutes, 13.9% 45 to 60 minutes, 8.1% 60 minutes or more (2000)
Additional Information Contacts
Gilchrist County Chamber of Commerce . . . . (352) 463-3467

Glades County

Located in southern Florida; bounded on the east by Lake Okeechobee; crossed by the Caloosahatchee River. Covers a land area of 773.60 square miles, a water area of 212.80 square miles, and is located in the Eastern Time Zone. The county government was organized in 1921. County seat is Moore Haven.

Weather Station: Moore Haven Lock 1 — Elevation: 32 feet

	Jan	Feb	Mar	Apr	May	Jun	Jul	Aug	Sep	Oct	Nov	Dec
High	74	76	80	83	88	90	92	91	90	85	80	75
Low	52	52	57	61	66	71	72	73	72	67	60	54
Precip	2.1	2.1	3.3	2.2	3.8	7.2	6.7	6.9	6.1	3.1	1.9	1.6
Snow	0.0	0.0	0.0	0.0	0.0	0.0	0.0	0.0	0.0	0.0	0.0	0.0

High and Low temperatures in degrees Fahrenheit; Precipitation and Snow in inches

Population: 7,617 (1990); 10,576 (2000); 10,822 (2004); 11,137 (2009 projected); Race: 75.7% White, 11.0% Black, 0.4% Asian, 17.0% Hispanic of any race (2004); Density: 14.0 persons per square mile (2004); Average household size: 2.81 (2004); Median age: 39.8 (2004); Male/female ratio: 126.9 (2004).
Religion: Five largest groups: 16.1% Catholic Church, 11.6% Southern Baptist Convention, 2.1% The United Methodist Church, 0.9% Church of God (Cleveland, Tennessee), 0.7% Christian Churches and Churches of Christ (2000).
Economy: Unemployment rate: 9.4% (2004); Total civilian labor force: 3,823 (2004); Leading industries: 11.1% accommodation & food services; 9.4% retail trade; 9.1% manufacturing (2003); Companies that employ 500 or more persons: 0 (2003); Companies that employ 100 to 499 persons: 1 (2003); Companies that employ less than 100 persons: 75 (2003); Farms: 231 totaling 407,950 acres (2002); Minority business ownership rate: 23.2% (1997); Women business ownership rate: n/a (1997); Retail sales per capita: $4,164 (1997). Single-family building permits issued: 48 (2004); Multi-family building permits issued: 0 (2004).
Income: Per capita income: $16,897 (2004); Median household income: $33,490 (2004); Average household income: $44,377 (2004); Percent of households with income of $100,000 or more: 7.7% (2004); Poverty rate: 15.5% (2002); Bankruptcy rate: 0.80% (2004).
Taxes: Total county taxes per capita: $673 (2002); County property taxes per capita: $378 (2002).
Education: Percent of population age 25 and over with: High school diploma (including GED) or higher: 69.8% (2004); Bachelor's degree or higher: 9.8% (2004); Master's degree or higher: 4.3% (2004).
Housing: Homeownership rate: 81.7% (2004); Median home value: $80,266 (2004); Median rent: $386 per month (2000); Median age of housing: 19 years (2000).
Health: Birth rate: 68.3 per 10,000 population (2004); Death rate: 88.9 per 10,000 population (2004); Age adjusted cancer mortality rate: 157.8 deaths per 100,000 population (2002); Number of physicians: 0.9 per 10,000 population (2001); Hospital beds: 0.0 per 10,000 population (2002); Hospital admissions: 0.0 per 10,000 population (2002).
Elections: 2004 Presidential election results: 58.3% Bush, 41.0% Kerry, 0.4% Nader, 0.1% Badnarik
Additional Information Contacts
Glades County Government Offices . . . . (863) 946-0949
Glades County Chamber of Commerce . . . . (863) 946-0440

Glades County Communities

BUCKHEAD RIDGE (CDP). Covers a land area of 1.304 square miles and a water area of 0.104 square miles. Located at 27.13° N. Lat.; 80.89° W. Long. Elevation is 16 feet.
Population: 1,279 (1990); 1,390 (2000); 1,402 (2004); 1,427 (2009 projected); Race: 98.4% White, 0.1% Black, 0.1% Asian, 0.9% Hispanic of any race (2004); Density: 1,075.5 persons per square mile (2004); Average household size: 2.00 (2004); Median age: 62.1 (2004); Male/female ratio: 101.4 (2004); Marriage status: 11.7% never married, 65.6% now married, 11.1% widowed, 11.6% divorced (2000); Foreign born: 0.0% (2000); Ancestry (includes multiple ancestries): 24.5% United States or American, 15.1% German, 14.9% English, 10.6% Irish, 5.0% French (except Basque) (2000).
Economy: Employment by occupation: 9.8% management, 16.3% professional, 18.1% services, 27.1% sales, 0.0% farming, 15.2% construction, 13.4% production (2000).
Income: Per capita income: $18,219 (2004); Median household income: $27,069 (2004); Average household income: $36,385 (2004); Percent of households with income of $100,000 or more: 6.3% (2004); Poverty rate: 19.4% (2000).
Education: Percent of population age 25 and over with: High school diploma (including GED) or higher: 72.5% (2004); Bachelor's degree or higher: 7.4% (2004); Master's degree or higher: 3.4% (2004).
Housing: Homeownership rate: 89.0% (2004); Median home value: $85,000 (2004); Median rent: $429 per month (2000); Median age of housing: 19 years (2000).
Transportation: Commute to work: 91.1% car, 0.0% public transportation, 0.0% walk, 3.1% work from home (2000); Travel time to work: 12.1% less than 15 minutes, 58.1% 15 to 30 minutes, 12.1% 30 to 45 minutes, 1.9% 45 to 60 minutes, 15.7% 60 minutes or more (2000)

MOORE HAVEN (city). Covers a land area of 1.084 square miles and a water area of 0.066 square miles. Located at 26.83° N. Lat.; 81.09° W. Long. Elevation is 18 feet.
History: Moore Haven grew on the southwestern shore of Lake Okeechobee as a trading and shipping center for produce and catfish.
Population: 1,432 (1990); 1,635 (2000); 1,537 (2004); 1,480 (2009 projected); Race: 59.3% White, 23.6% Black, 0.5% Asian, 29.8% Hispanic of any race (2004); Density: 1,418.3 persons per square mile (2004); Average household size: 2.86 (2004); Median age: 32.6 (2004); Male/female ratio: 110.0 (2004); Marriage status: 31.1% never married, 57.4% now married, 3.8% widowed, 7.7% divorced (2000); Foreign born: 13.4% (2000); Ancestry (includes multiple ancestries): 44.4% Other groups, 11.9% United States or American, 6.8% Irish, 6.0% English, 5.4% German (2000).
Economy: Single-family building permits issued: 9 (2004); Multi-family building permits issued: 0 (2004); Employment by occupation: 3.8% management, 8.2% professional, 18.5% services, 21.5% sales, 6.5% farming, 17.8% construction, 23.8% production (2000).
Income: Per capita income: $13,652 (2004); Median household income: $29,389 (2004); Average household income: $37,332 (2004); Percent of households with income of $100,000 or more: 4.5% (2004); Poverty rate: 23.8% (2000).
Taxes: Total city taxes per capita: $117 (2002); City property taxes per capita: $65 (2002).
Education: Percent of population age 25 and over with: High school diploma (including GED) or higher: 61.3% (2004); Bachelor's degree or higher: 6.6% (2004); Master's degree or higher: 2.8% (2004).

School District(s)

Glades County School District (PK-12)
2002-03 Enrollment: 998 . . . . (863) 946-2083
Housing: Homeownership rate: 76.0% (2004); Median home value: $56,238 (2004); Median rent: $347 per month (2000); Median age of housing: 19 years (2000).
Transportation: Commute to work: 91.3% car, 1.5% public transportation, 2.4% walk, 2.2% work from home (2000); Travel time to work: 43.7% less than 15 minutes, 26.4% 15 to 30 minutes, 12.8% 30 to 45 minutes, 5.9% 45 to 60 minutes, 11.2% 60 minutes or more (2000)
Additional Information Contacts
Glades County Chamber of Commerce . . . . (863) 946-0440

Gulf County

Located in northwestern Florida; swampy area, bounded on the south and west by the Gulf of Mexico, and on the east by the Apalachicola River. Covers a land area of 554.60 square miles, a water area of 190.00 square miles, and is located in the Central/Eastern Time Zone. The county government was organized in 1925. County seat is Port St. Joe.
Population: 11,504 (1990); 13,332 (2000); 15,373 (2004); 17,937 (2009 projected); Race: 74.5% White, 22.1% Black, 0.5% Asian, 3.4% Hispanic of any race (2004); Density: 27.7 persons per square mile (2004); Average household size: 2.71 (2004); Median age: 40.4 (2004); Male/female ratio: 133.4 (2004).
Religion: Five largest groups: 26.9% Southern Baptist Convention, 6.9% The United Methodist Church, 4.5% Assemblies of God, 2.4% International Pentecostal Holiness Church, 2.1% Catholic Church (2000).
Economy: Unemployment rate: 3.6% (2004); Total civilian labor force: 5,609 (2004); Leading industries: 18.7% health care and social assistance;

15.7% retail trade; 10.1% accommodation & food services (2003); Companies that employ 500 or more persons: 0 (2003); Companies that employ 100 to 499 persons: 2 (2003); Companies that employ less than 100 persons: 283 (2003); Farms: 30 totaling 4,521 acres (2002); Minority business ownership rate: n/a (1997); Women business ownership rate: n/a (1997); Retail sales per capita: $3,623 (1997). Single-family building permits issued: 183 (2004); Multi-family building permits issued: 0 (2004).
Income: Per capita income: $15,931 (2004); Median household income: $32,492 (2004); Average household income: $41,583 (2004); Percent of households with income of $100,000 or more: 5.1% (2004); Poverty rate: 18.9% (2002); Bankruptcy rate: 2.20% (2004).
Taxes: Total county taxes per capita: $476 (2002); County property taxes per capita: $429 (2002).
Education: Percent of population age 25 and over with: High school diploma (including GED) or higher: 72.7% (2004); Bachelor's degree or higher: 10.1% (2004); Master's degree or higher: 3.6% (2004).
Housing: Homeownership rate: 81.4% (2004); Median home value: $97,980 (2004); Median rent: $316 per month (2000); Median age of housing: 21 years (2000).
Health: Birth rate: 103.5 per 10,000 population (2004); Death rate: 99.2 per 10,000 population (2004); Age adjusted cancer mortality rate: 169.4 deaths per 100,000 population (2002); Number of physicians: 9.7 per 10,000 population (2001); Hospital beds: 20.3 per 10,000 population (2002); Hospital admissions: 633.6 per 10,000 population (2002).
Elections: 2004 Presidential election results: 66.0% Bush, 33.1% Kerry, 0.6% Nader, 0.1% Badnarik
National and State Parks: Constitution Convention Museum State Park; Dead Lakes State Park; Saint Joseph Peninsula State Park; T H Stone Memorial Saint Joseph Peninsula State Park
Additional Information Contacts
Gulf County Government Offices .... (850) 229-6106
Port St. Joe Chamber of Commerce .... (850) 227-1223
Wewahitchka Chamber of Commerce .... (850) 639-2130

Gulf County Communities

PORT SAINT JOE (city). Covers a land area of 3.321 square miles and a water area of 0 square miles. Located at 29.80° N. Lat.; 85.29° W. Long. Elevation is 5 feet.
History: Port St. Joe developed on the shore of St. Josephs Bay around a paper mill, opened in 1938, and plants manufacturing fish oil and fertilizers.
Population: 4,044 (1990); 3,644 (2000); 3,949 (2004); 4,332 (2009 projected); Race: 66.2% White, 32.9% Black, 0.2% Asian, 0.5% Hispanic of any race (2004); Density: 1,189.2 persons per square mile (2004); Average household size: 2.59 (2004); Median age: 42.3 (2004); Male/female ratio: 101.0 (2004); Marriage status: 19.8% never married, 57.4% now married, 12.4% widowed, 10.5% divorced (2000); Foreign born: 2.3% (2000); Ancestry (includes multiple ancestries): 34.5% Other groups, 13.6% United States or American, 10.6% Irish, 6.5% English, 5.0% German (2000).
Economy: Employment by occupation: 9.6% management, 20.5% professional, 23.0% services, 24.9% sales, 0.0% farming, 13.6% construction, 8.5% production (2000).
Income: Per capita income: $17,545 (2004); Median household income: $34,464 (2004); Average household income: $44,567 (2004); Percent of households with income of $100,000 or more: 4.8% (2004); Poverty rate: 13.0% (2000).
Taxes: Total city taxes per capita: $426 (2002); City property taxes per capita: $320 (2002).
Education: Percent of population age 25 and over with: High school diploma (including GED) or higher: 80.8% (2004); Bachelor's degree or higher: 14.7% (2004); Master's degree or higher: 4.5% (2004).

School District(s)

Gulf County School District (PK-12)
2002-03 Enrollment: 2,164 .... (850) 229-8256
Housing: Homeownership rate: 76.8% (2004); Median home value: $112,080 (2004); Median rent: $261 per month (2000); Median age of housing: 36 years (2000).
Hospitals: Gulf Pines Hospital (45 beds)
Safety: Violent crime rate: 54.0 per 10,000 population; Property crime rate: 178.3 per 10,000 population (2003).
Newspapers: Panhandle Beacon (General - Circulation 13,500); Panhandle Hook & Trigger (General - Circulation 13,500); The Star (General - Circulation 4,800)
Transportation: Commute to work: 95.1% car, 0.0% public transportation, 2.7% walk, 1.4% work from home (2000); Travel time to work: 59.8% less than 15 minutes, 11.9% 15 to 30 minutes, 9.6% 30 to 45 minutes, 7.8% 45 to 60 minutes, 10.9% 60 minutes or more (2000)
Additional Information Contacts
Port St. Joe Chamber of Commerce .... (850) 227-1223

WEWAHITCHKA (city). Covers a land area of 6.207 square miles and a water area of 1.221 square miles. Located at 30.11° N. Lat.; 85.19° W. Long. Elevation is 45 feet.
History: The name of Wewahitchka is of Indian origin meaning "water eyes," perhaps referring to two nearby small lakes of the same size. The town was known as a producer of tupelo honey made from the tupelo or cotton-gum trees that grow in the swamps.
Population: 1,779 (1990); 1,722 (2000); 1,785 (2004); 1,878 (2009 projected); Race: 85.9% White, 10.9% Black, 1.3% Asian, 1.5% Hispanic of any race (2004); Density: 287.6 persons per square mile (2004); Average household size: 2.45 (2004); Median age: 39.2 (2004); Male/female ratio: 100.3 (2004); Marriage status: 19.6% never married, 58.0% now married, 10.3% widowed, 12.1% divorced (2000); Foreign born: 1.5% (2000); Ancestry (includes multiple ancestries): 20.4% United States or American, 15.1% Other groups, 14.4% Irish, 8.3% English, 5.9% European (2000).
Economy: Employment by occupation: 7.2% management, 16.4% professional, 26.2% services, 21.3% sales, 0.3% farming, 16.1% construction, 12.4% production (2000).
Income: Per capita income: $15,238 (2004); Median household income: $27,815 (2004); Average household income: $37,236 (2004); Percent of households with income of $100,000 or more: 5.2% (2004); Poverty rate: 19.2% (2000).
Taxes: Total city taxes per capita: $127 (2002); City property taxes per capita: $37 (2002).
Education: Percent of population age 25 and over with: High school diploma (including GED) or higher: 68.5% (2004); Bachelor's degree or higher: 8.3% (2004); Master's degree or higher: 3.2% (2004).

School District(s)

Gulf County School District (PK-12)
2002-03 Enrollment: 2,164 .... (850) 229-8256
Housing: Homeownership rate: 75.5% (2004); Median home value: $72,857 (2004); Median rent: $222 per month (2000); Median age of housing: 25 years (2000).
Transportation: Commute to work: 90.6% car, 0.0% public transportation, 4.0% walk, 3.8% work from home (2000); Travel time to work: 41.3% less than 15 minutes, 11.5% 15 to 30 minutes, 21.5% 30 to 45 minutes, 15.7% 45 to 60 minutes, 10.0% 60 minutes or more (2000)
Additional Information Contacts
Wewahitchka Chamber of Commerce .... (850) 639-2130

Hamilton County

Located in northern Florida; bounded on the north by Georgia, on the south and east by the Suwannee River, and on the west by the Withlacoochee River; flatwoods area with swamps in the east; drained by the Alapaha River. Covers a land area of 514.90 square miles, a water area of 4.40 square miles, and is located in the Eastern Time Zone. The county government was organized in 1827. County seat is Jasper.

Weather Station: Jasper — Elevation: 144 feet

	Jan	Feb	Mar	Apr	May	Jun	Jul	Aug	Sep	Oct	Nov	Dec
High	64	67	74	79	86	90	92	91	89	81	74	66
Low	38	41	47	53	60	67	70	70	66	55	47	41
Precip	5.0	4.1	5.3	3.5	3.4	6.0	5.7	6.5	3.9	2.9	2.8	3.5
Snow	tr	tr	tr	0.0	0.0	0.0	0.0	0.0	0.0	0.0	0.0	tr

High and Low temperatures in degrees Fahrenheit; Precipitation and Snow in inches

Population: 10,930 (1990); 13,327 (2000); 14,132 (2004); 15,149 (2009 projected); Race: 58.6% White, 37.7% Black, 0.3% Asian, 6.7% Hispanic of any race (2004); Density: 27.4 persons per square mile (2004); Average household size: 3.26 (2004); Median age: 35.5 (2004); Male/female ratio: 148.9 (2004).
Religion: Five largest groups: 16.3% Southern Baptist Convention, 3.3% The United Methodist Church, 3.3% Church of God (Cleveland, Tennessee), 1.6% Christian Churches and Churches of Christ, 1.0% Presbyterian Church (U.S.A.) (2000).
Economy: Unemployment rate: 5.8% (2004); Total civilian labor force: 3,163 (2004); Leading industries: 19.5% retail trade; 19.2% health care and social assistance; 7.0% construction (2003); Companies that employ 500 or more persons: 0 (2003); Companies that employ 100 to 499 persons: 3 (2003); Companies that employ less than 100 persons: 178 (2003); Farms:

239 totaling 52,027 acres (2002); Minority business ownership rate: n/a (1997); Women business ownership rate: 19.9% (1997); Retail sales per capita: $4,293 (1997). Single-family building permits issued: 34 (2004); Multi-family building permits issued: 0 (2004).
Income: Per capita income: $10,503 (2004); Median household income: $25,726 (2004); Average household income: $33,366 (2004); Percent of households with income of $100,000 or more: 2.5% (2004); Poverty rate: 25.3% (2002); Bankruptcy rate: 4.06% (2004).
Taxes: Total county taxes per capita: $436 (2002); County property taxes per capita: $354 (2002).
Education: Percent of population age 25 and over with: High school diploma (including GED) or higher: 62.7% (2004); Bachelor's degree or higher: 7.1% (2004); Master's degree or higher: 2.0% (2004).
Housing: Homeownership rate: 77.9% (2004); Median home value: $64,218 (2004); Median rent: $209 per month (2000); Median age of housing: 20 years (2000).
Health: Birth rate: 138.2 per 10,000 population (2004); Death rate: 88.8 per 10,000 population (2004); Age adjusted cancer mortality rate: 205.2 deaths per 100,000 population (2002); Air Quality Index: 100.0% good, 0.0% moderate, 0.0% unhealthy for sensitive individuals, 0.0% unhealthy (percent of days in 2004); Number of physicians: 5.2 per 10,000 population (2001); Hospital beds: 30.6 per 10,000 population (2002); Hospital admissions: 587.9 per 10,000 population (2002).
Elections: 2004 Presidential election results: 55.0% Bush, 44.5% Kerry, 0.3% Nader, 0.0% Badnarik
National and State Parks: Big Shoals State Park; Stephen Foster Folk Culture Center State Park; Suwannee River State Park
Additional Information Contacts
Hamilton County Government Offices . . . . (386) 792-1288
Jasper Chamber of Commerce . . . . (386) 792-1300

Hamilton County Communities

JASPER (city). Covers a land area of 1.954 square miles and a water area of 0 square miles. Located at 30.51° N. Lat.; 82.95° W. Long. Elevation is 152 feet.
History: Jasper was established as a trading post in 1830 by families from South Carolina and Georgia, and was named for Sergeant William Jasper, a Revolutionary War soldier. Cotton was grown here, as well as tobacco.
Population: 2,105 (1990); 1,780 (2000); 1,684 (2004); 1,625 (2009 projected); Race: 53.0% White, 45.1% Black, 0.4% Asian, 2.9% Hispanic of any race (2004); Density: 862.0 persons per square mile (2004); Average household size: 2.35 (2004); Median age: 35.2 (2004); Male/female ratio: 79.0 (2004); Marriage status: 29.9% never married, 44.2% now married, 14.6% widowed, 11.4% divorced (2000); Foreign born: 0.8% (2000); Ancestry (includes multiple ancestries): 50.4% Other groups, 11.6% United States or American, 7.4% English, 4.9% Irish, 3.2% German (2000).
Economy: Employment by occupation: 9.1% management, 13.3% professional, 25.0% services, 24.4% sales, 2.0% farming, 5.5% construction, 20.8% production (2000).
Income: Per capita income: $12,867 (2004); Median household income: $18,525 (2004); Average household income: $30,262 (2004); Percent of households with income of $100,000 or more: 4.1% (2004); Poverty rate: 37.4% (2000).
Education: Percent of population age 25 and over with: High school diploma (including GED) or higher: 65.3% (2004); Bachelor's degree or higher: 12.2% (2004); Master's degree or higher: 3.2% (2004).

School District(s)

Hamilton County School District (PK-12)
2002-03 Enrollment: 2,065 . . . . (386) 792-6501
Housing: Homeownership rate: 59.6% (2004); Median home value: $63,788 (2004); Median rent: $185 per month (2000); Median age of housing: 32 years (2000).
Hospitals: Trinity Community Hospital (42 beds)
Safety: Violent crime rate: 113.9 per 10,000 population; Property crime rate: 461.0 per 10,000 population (2003).
Newspapers: The Jasper News (General - Circulation 2,300)
Transportation: Commute to work: 86.8% car, 0.0% public transportation, 6.2% walk, 1.4% work from home (2000); Travel time to work: 44.8% less than 15 minutes, 22.7% 15 to 30 minutes, 18.9% 30 to 45 minutes, 8.9% 45 to 60 minutes, 4.7% 60 minutes or more (2000)
Additional Information Contacts
Jasper Chamber of Commerce . . . . (386) 792-1300

JENNINGS (town). Covers a land area of 1.806 square miles and a water area of 0 square miles. Located at 30.60° N. Lat.; 83.10° W. Long. Elevation is 149 feet.
History: Jennings was named for George Jennings who settled here in the 1840's. For a time, Jennings was a cotton shipping center.
Population: 747 (1990); 833 (2000); 835 (2004); 838 (2009 projected); Race: 41.1% White, 44.2% Black, 1.2% Asian, 25.9% Hispanic of any race (2004); Density: 462.5 persons per square mile (2004); Average household size: 2.92 (2004); Median age: 32.8 (2004); Male/female ratio: 106.2 (2004); Marriage status: 26.8% never married, 54.1% now married, 7.2% widowed, 11.9% divorced (2000); Foreign born: 18.3% (2000); Ancestry (includes multiple ancestries): 56.9% Other groups, 6.6% United States or American, 4.2% German, 3.6% English, 2.8% Irish (2000).
Economy: Employment by occupation: 9.4% management, 10.6% professional, 22.1% services, 13.3% sales, 21.1% farming, 4.8% construction, 18.7% production (2000).
Income: Per capita income: $13,569 (2004); Median household income: $26,064 (2004); Average household income: $36,145 (2004); Percent of households with income of $100,000 or more: 4.9% (2004); Poverty rate: 30.8% (2000).
Education: Percent of population age 25 and over with: High school diploma (including GED) or higher: 53.2% (2004); Bachelor's degree or higher: 4.4% (2004); Master's degree or higher: 0.4% (2004).

School District(s)

Hamilton County School District (PK-12)
2002-03 Enrollment: 2,065 . . . . (386) 792-6501
Housing: Homeownership rate: 63.6% (2004); Median home value: $45,455 (2004); Median rent: $196 per month (2000); Median age of housing: 23 years (2000).
Safety: Violent crime rate: 23.8 per 10,000 population; Property crime rate: 178.1 per 10,000 population (2003).
Transportation: Commute to work: 72.2% car, 9.7% public transportation, 0.3% walk, 3.0% work from home (2000); Travel time to work: 34.6% less than 15 minutes, 31.8% 15 to 30 minutes, 26.5% 30 to 45 minutes, 2.2% 45 to 60 minutes, 5.0% 60 minutes or more (2000)

WHITE SPRINGS (town). Covers a land area of 1.836 square miles and a water area of 0.002 square miles. Located at 30.33° N. Lat.; 82.75° W. Long. Elevation is 133 feet.
History: White Springs was founded in 1826 on the Suwannee River, and grew as a health resort around medicinal springs. During the Civil War, the White Springs area was considered a place of refuge, where many plantation owners lived in safety from Union invasion.
Population: 823 (1990); 819 (2000); 841 (2004); 870 (2009 projected); Race: 32.3% White, 66.8% Black, 0.0% Asian, 0.4% Hispanic of any race (2004); Density: 458.0 persons per square mile (2004); Average household size: 2.37 (2004); Median age: 33.1 (2004); Male/female ratio: 89.8 (2004); Marriage status: 30.0% never married, 49.8% now married, 9.3% widowed, 10.8% divorced (2000); Foreign born: 1.4% (2000); Ancestry (includes multiple ancestries): 56.8% Other groups, 10.4% United States or American, 3.7% English, 2.8% German, 2.8% Irish (2000).
Economy: Employment by occupation: 3.3% management, 14.2% professional, 29.7% services, 15.3% sales, 6.7% farming, 14.7% construction, 16.1% production (2000).
Income: Per capita income: $14,985 (2004); Median household income: $26,705 (2004); Average household income: $35,500 (2004); Percent of households with income of $100,000 or more: 2.5% (2004); Poverty rate: 22.6% (2000).
Education: Percent of population age 25 and over with: High school diploma (including GED) or higher: 69.3% (2004); Bachelor's degree or higher: 8.9% (2004); Master's degree or higher: 2.6% (2004).

School District(s)

Hamilton County School District (PK-12)
2002-03 Enrollment: 2,065 . . . . (386) 792-6501
Housing: Homeownership rate: 73.5% (2004); Median home value: $59,859 (2004); Median rent: $163 per month (2000); Median age of housing: 28 years (2000).
Safety: Violent crime rate: 60.6 per 10,000 population; Property crime rate: 460.6 per 10,000 population (2003).
Transportation: Commute to work: 89.5% car, 0.0% public transportation, 5.9% walk, 1.7% work from home (2000); Travel time to work: 15.5% less than 15 minutes, 43.4% 15 to 30 minutes, 28.4% 30 to 45 minutes, 3.4% 45 to 60 minutes, 9.2% 60 minutes or more (2000)

Hardee County

Located in central Florida; rolling terrain, partly swampy, with many small lakes; drained by the Peace River. Covers a land area of 637.30 square miles, a water area of 1.00 square miles, and is located in the Eastern Time Zone. The county government was organized in 1921. County seat is Wauchula.

Hardee County is part of the Wauchula, FL Micropolitan Statistical Area. The entire metro area includes: Hardee County, FL

Weather Station: Wauchula Elevation: 59 feet

	Jan	Feb	Mar	Apr	May	Jun	Jul	Aug	Sep	Oct	Nov	Dec
High	74	76	80	84	89	91	92	92	91	86	80	75
Low	50	51	54	58	64	70	71	72	71	65	57	52
Precip	2.4	2.7	3.5	2.3	4.0	8.0	8.1	7.3	6.0	2.7	2.1	2.0
Snow	tr	0.0	0.0	0.0	0.0	0.0	0.0	0.0	0.0	0.0	0.0	0.0

High and Low temperatures in degrees Fahrenheit; Precipitation and Snow in inches

Population: 19,499 (1990); 26,938 (2000); 27,853 (2004); 29,017 (2009 projected); Race: 69.9% White, 8.2% Black, 0.4% Asian, 37.6% Hispanic of any race (2004); Density: 43.7 persons per square mile (2004); Average household size: 3.38 (2004); Median age: 33.0 (2004); Male/female ratio: 122.9 (2004).
Religion: Five largest groups: 34.2% Southern Baptist Convention, 18.4% Catholic Church, 3.6% The United Methodist Church, 3.1% Church of God (Cleveland, Tennessee), 2.6% Christian Churches and Churches of Christ (2000).
Economy: Unemployment rate: 8.5% (2004); Total civilian labor force: 9,433 (2004); Leading industries: 25.8% health care and social assistance; 21.6% retail trade; 8.7% accommodation & food services (2003); Companies that employ 500 or more persons: 0 (2003); Companies that employ 100 to 499 persons: 5 (2003); Companies that employ less than 100 persons: 400 (2003); Farms: 1,142 totaling 346,191 acres (2002); Minority business ownership rate: 27.9% (1997); Women business ownership rate: 21.0% (1997); Retail sales per capita: $5,544 (1997). Single-family building permits issued: 69 (2004); Multi-family building permits issued: 13 (2004).
Income: Per capita income: $13,275 (2004); Median household income: $31,963 (2004); Average household income: $43,701 (2004); Percent of households with income of $100,000 or more: 6.0% (2004); Poverty rate: 23.2% (2002); Bankruptcy rate: 2.53% (2004).
Taxes: Total county taxes per capita: $336 (2002); County property taxes per capita: $253 (2002).
Education: Percent of population age 25 and over with: High school diploma (including GED) or higher: 57.9% (2004); Bachelor's degree or higher: 8.3% (2004); Master's degree or higher: 2.8% (2004).
Housing: Homeownership rate: 73.3% (2004); Median home value: $74,672 (2004); Median rent: $334 per month (2000); Median age of housing: 24 years (2000).
Health: Birth rate: 167.6 per 10,000 population (2004); Death rate: 66.1 per 10,000 population (2004); Age adjusted cancer mortality rate: 152.4 deaths per 100,000 population (2002); Number of physicians: 4.1 per 10,000 population (2001); Hospital beds: 0.0 per 10,000 population (2002); Hospital admissions: 0.0 per 10,000 population (2002).
Elections: 2004 Presidential election results: 69.7% Bush, 29.6% Kerry, 0.5% Nader, 0.1% Badnarik
National and State Parks: Paynes Creek Historic State Park
Additional Information Contacts
Hardee County Government Offices .... (863) 773-6952
Hardee County Chamber of Commerce .... (863) 773-6967
Wauchula Board of Realtors .... (863) 773-0007

Hardee County Communities

BOWLING GREEN (city). Covers a land area of 1.416 square miles and a water area of 0.002 square miles. Located at 27.63° N. Lat.; 81.82° W. Long. Elevation is 117 feet.
History: The settlement here was first called Utica. It became Bowling Green in the late 1880's, when farmers from Bowling Green, Kentucky, purchased the land.
Population: 1,880 (1990); 2,892 (2000); 2,765 (2004); 2,686 (2009 projected); Race: 57.2% White, 11.1% Black, 0.6% Asian, 46.4% Hispanic of any race (2004); Density: 1,952.3 persons per square mile (2004); Average household size: 3.59 (2004); Median age: 29.0 (2004); Male/female ratio: 109.3 (2004); Marriage status: 31.3% never married, 55.1% now married, 5.3% widowed, 8.3% divorced (2000); Foreign born: 23.9% (2000); Ancestry (includes multiple ancestries): 46.4% Other groups, 10.3% United States or American, 3.6% German, 3.6% Irish, 2.4% English (2000).
Economy: Employment by occupation: 5.2% management, 8.3% professional, 16.3% services, 11.4% sales, 28.5% farming, 12.3% construction, 18.0% production (2000).
Income: Per capita income: $11,132 (2004); Median household income: $30,469 (2004); Average household income: $38,753 (2004); Percent of households with income of $100,000 or more: 3.9% (2004); Poverty rate: 30.5% (2000).
Education: Percent of population age 25 and over with: High school diploma (including GED) or higher: 47.6% (2004); Bachelor's degree or higher: 6.1% (2004); Master's degree or higher: 2.1% (2004).

School District(s)

Hardee County School District (PK-12)
2002-03 Enrollment: 5,175 .... (863) 773-9058
Housing: Homeownership rate: 73.2% (2004); Median home value: $64,930 (2004); Median rent: $316 per month (2000); Median age of housing: 26 years (2000).
Safety: Violent crime rate: 60.6 per 10,000 population; Property crime rate: 377.1 per 10,000 population (2003).
Transportation: Commute to work: 92.0% car, 2.6% public transportation, 2.3% walk, 0.5% work from home (2000); Travel time to work: 28.5% less than 15 minutes, 27.4% 15 to 30 minutes, 22.5% 30 to 45 minutes, 7.0% 45 to 60 minutes, 14.6% 60 minutes or more (2000)

ONA (unincorporated postal area, zip code 33865). Covers a land area of 140.742 square miles and a water area of 0.336 square miles. Located at 27.43° N. Lat.; 81.93° W. Long. Elevation is 90 feet.
Population: 681 (2000); Race: 86.8% White, 5.1% Black, 0.0% Asian, 12.5% Hispanic of any race (2000); Density: 4.8 persons per square mile (2000); Age: 17.1% under 18, 12.8% over 64 (2000); Marriage status: 19.0% never married, 65.9% now married, 6.8% widowed, 8.3% divorced (2000); Foreign born: 4.4% (2000); Ancestry (includes multiple ancestries): 27.2% Other groups, 21.9% Irish, 14.7% United States or American, 9.0% English, 7.2% German (2000).
Economy: Employment by occupation: 0.0% management, 20.5% professional, 22.8% services, 20.5% sales, 5.1% farming, 16.1% construction, 15.0% production (2000).
Income: Per capita income: $14,252 (2000); Median household income: $23,750 (2000); Poverty rate: 29.0% (2000).
Education: Percent of population age 25 and over with: High school diploma (including GED) or higher: 48.7% (2000); Bachelor's degree or higher: 10.8% (2000).
Housing: Homeownership rate: 65.1% (2000); Median home value: $62,900 (2000); Median rent: $275 per month (2000); Median age of housing: 24 years (2000).
Transportation: Commute to work: 79.9% car, 0.0% public transportation, 0.0% walk, 20.1% work from home (2000); Travel time to work: 26.1% less than 15 minutes, 20.7% 15 to 30 minutes, 35.5% 30 to 45 minutes, 7.9% 45 to 60 minutes, 9.9% 60 minutes or more (2000)

WAUCHULA (city). Covers a land area of 2.616 square miles and a water area of 0 square miles. Located at 27.54° N. Lat.; 81.81° W. Long. Elevation is 109 feet.
History: Wauchula began as Fort Hartsuff, built during the Seminole Wars. Wauchula was known as a supplier of frog's legs, gathered at night from the surrounding swamps and shipped to markets in the north.
Population: 3,400 (1990); 4,368 (2000); 4,474 (2004); 4,604 (2009 projected); Race: 71.0% White, 3.9% Black, 0.3% Asian, 44.6% Hispanic of any race (2004); Density: 1,710.1 persons per square mile (2004); Average household size: 3.09 (2004); Median age: 30.9 (2004); Male/female ratio: 99.5 (2004); Marriage status: 27.4% never married, 53.8% now married, 9.8% widowed, 9.0% divorced (2000); Foreign born: 19.6% (2000); Ancestry (includes multiple ancestries): 42.9% Other groups, 16.9% United States or American, 6.1% Irish, 5.8% English, 3.5% German (2000).
Economy: Employment by occupation: 5.4% management, 9.4% professional, 17.0% services, 22.1% sales, 22.2% farming, 10.8% construction, 13.1% production (2000).
Income: Per capita income: $11,004 (2004); Median household income: $27,112 (2004); Average household income: $32,949 (2004); Percent of households with income of $100,000 or more: 3.5% (2004); Poverty rate: 25.0% (2000).

Education: Percent of population age 25 and over with: High school diploma (including GED) or higher: 56.2% (2004); Bachelor's degree or higher: 7.6% (2004); Master's degree or higher: 3.8% (2004).

School District(s)

Hardee County School District (PK-12)
2002-03 Enrollment: 5,175 . . . . (863) 773-9058

Housing: Homeownership rate: 60.1% (2004); Median home value: $73,598 (2004); Median rent: $352 per month (2000); Median age of housing: 32 years (2000).

Hospitals: Florida Hospital Wauchula (25 beds)

Safety: Violent crime rate: 102.5 per 10,000 population; Property crime rate: 585.9 per 10,000 population (2003).

Newspapers: The Herald Advocate (General - Circulation 5,300)

Transportation: Commute to work: 90.9% car, 2.1% public transportation, 4.0% walk, 1.5% work from home (2000); Travel time to work: 44.7% less than 15 minutes, 12.0% 15 to 30 minutes, 22.3% 30 to 45 minutes, 6.0% 45 to 60 minutes, 15.0% 60 minutes or more (2000)

Additional Information Contacts

Hardee County Chamber of Commerce . . . . (863) 773-6967
Wauchula Board of Realtors . . . . (863) 773-0007

ZOLFO SPRINGS (town). Covers a land area of 1.510 square miles and a water area of 0 square miles. Located at 27.49° N. Lat.; 81.79° W. Long. Elevation is 64 feet.

History: Zolfo Springs was named for its large sulphur spring, by Italian laborers employed on the construction of the Atlantic Coast Line Railroad. Zolfo is Italian for sulphur.

Population: 1,219 (1990); 1,641 (2000); 1,663 (2004); 1,626 (2009 projected); Race: 67.0% White, 2.6% Black, 0.1% Asian, 55.0% Hispanic of any race (2004); Density: 1,101.1 persons per square mile (2004); Average household size: 3.31 (2004); Median age: 30.4 (2004); Male/female ratio: 103.5 (2004); Marriage status: 26.2% never married, 58.4% now married, 7.2% widowed, 8.1% divorced (2000); Foreign born: 27.2% (2000); Ancestry (includes multiple ancestries): 53.0% Other groups, 8.0% English, 7.9% United States or American, 4.3% German, 3.6% Irish (2000).

Economy: Employment by occupation: 4.6% management, 8.7% professional, 14.8% services, 18.5% sales, 24.2% farming, 17.3% construction, 11.9% production (2000).

Income: Per capita income: $12,150 (2004); Median household income: $28,313 (2004); Average household income: $39,950 (2004); Percent of households with income of $100,000 or more: 6.0% (2004); Poverty rate: 27.3% (2000).

Education: Percent of population age 25 and over with: High school diploma (including GED) or higher: 46.5% (2004); Bachelor's degree or higher: 3.2% (2004); Master's degree or higher: 1.1% (2004).

School District(s)

Hardee County School District (PK-12)
2002-03 Enrollment: 5,175 . . . . (863) 773-9058

Housing: Homeownership rate: 74.6% (2004); Median home value: $61,515 (2004); Median rent: $358 per month (2000); Median age of housing: 19 years (2000).

Safety: Violent crime rate: 17.8 per 10,000 population; Property crime rate: 41.5 per 10,000 population (2003).

Transportation: Commute to work: 91.1% car, 0.7% public transportation, 5.2% walk, 0.7% work from home (2000); Travel time to work: 36.7% less than 15 minutes, 21.2% 15 to 30 minutes, 23.0% 30 to 45 minutes, 9.3% 45 to 60 minutes, 9.8% 60 minutes or more (2000)

Hendry County

Located in southern Florida; Everglades area, crossed by the Caloosahatchee River. Covers a land area of 1,152.50 square miles, a water area of 37.30 square miles, and is located in the Eastern Time Zone. The county government was organized in 1923. County seat is La Belle.

Hendry County is part of the Clewiston, FL Micropolitan Statistical Area. The entire metro area includes: Hendry County, FL

Weather Station: Clewiston U.S. Engineers — Elevation: 19 feet

	Jan	Feb	Mar	Apr	May	Jun	Jul	Aug	Sep	Oct	Nov	Dec
High	73	75	80	84	88	90	92	91	90	85	80	75
Low	54	56	59	63	68	72	73	73	73	69	64	57
Precip	2.2	2.1	3.0	2.1	4.7	7.2	6.5	6.4	4.9	3.0	2.3	1.5
Snow	0.0	0.0	0.0	0.0	0.0	0.0	0.0	0.0	0.0	0.0	0.0	0.0

High and Low temperatures in degrees Fahrenheit; Precipitation and Snow in inches

Weather Station: La Belle — Elevation: 13 feet

	Jan	Feb	Mar	Apr	May	Jun	Jul	Aug	Sep	Oct	Nov	Dec
High	na	78	82	86	na	92	na	na	na	87	na	na
Low	na	52	55	59	64	69	na	na	na	65	na	na
Precip	2.4	2.2	3.3	2.3	4.1	8.9	7.7	7.8	6.3	3.4	2.3	1.7
Snow	tr	0.0	0.0	0.0	0.0	0.0	0.0	0.0	0.0	0.0	0.0	0.0

High and Low temperatures in degrees Fahrenheit; Precipitation and Snow in inches

Population: 25,773 (1990); 36,210 (2000); 36,679 (2004); 37,291 (2009 projected); Race: 65.4% White, 14.3% Black, 0.4% Asian, 43.0% Hispanic of any race (2004); Density: 31.8 persons per square mile (2004); Average household size: 3.44 (2004); Median age: 29.7 (2004); Male/female ratio: 127.1 (2004).

Religion: Five largest groups: 8.2% Southern Baptist Convention, 3.6% Catholic Church, 2.9% The United Methodist Church, 2.5% Assemblies of God, 2.3% Church of God (Cleveland, Tennessee) (2000).

Economy: Unemployment rate: 12.6% (2004); Total civilian labor force: 15,504 (2004); Leading industries: 25.5% retail trade; 14.3% health care and social assistance; 9.2% accommodation & food services (2003); Companies that employ 500 or more persons: 0 (2003); Companies that employ 100 to 499 persons: 9 (2003); Companies that employ less than 100 persons: 519 (2003); Farms: 456 totaling 552,352 acres (2002); Minority business ownership rate: 12.9% (1997); Women business ownership rate: 13.7% (1997); Retail sales per capita: $6,925 (1997). Single-family building permits issued: 133 (2004); Multi-family building permits issued: 0 (2004).

Income: Per capita income: $13,849 (2004); Median household income: $34,627 (2004); Average household income: $44,473 (2004); Percent of households with income of $100,000 or more: 6.1% (2004); Poverty rate: 18.7% (2002); Bankruptcy rate: 2.53% (2004).

Education: Percent of population age 25 and over with: High school diploma (including GED) or higher: 54.3% (2004); Bachelor's degree or higher: 8.6% (2004); Master's degree or higher: 2.3% (2004).

Housing: Homeownership rate: 72.8% (2004); Median home value: $73,398 (2004); Median rent: $380 per month (2000); Median age of housing: 18 years (2000).

Health: Birth rate: 173.5 per 10,000 population (2004); Death rate: 74.2 per 10,000 population (2004); Age adjusted cancer mortality rate: 220.0 deaths per 100,000 population (2002); Number of physicians: 6.3 per 10,000 population (2001); Hospital beds: 9.8 per 10,000 population (2002); Hospital admissions: 316.3 per 10,000 population (2002).

Elections: 2004 Presidential election results: 58.9% Bush, 40.5% Kerry, 0.2% Nader, 0.1% Badnarik

Additional Information Contacts

Hendry County Government Offices . . . . (863) 675-5220
Clewiston Chamber of Commerce . . . . (863) 983-7979
La Belle Chamber of Commerce . . . . (863) 675-0125

Hendry County Communities

CLEWISTON (city). Covers a land area of 4.678 square miles and a water area of 0.021 square miles. Located at 26.75° N. Lat.; 80.93° W. Long. Elevation is 18 feet.

History: Clewiston began in 1921 as a construction camp for the Moore Haven-Clewiston Railroad. The Clewiston Company Sugar Mill was built here to process sugar cane.

Population: 6,085 (1990); 6,460 (2000); 6,608 (2004); 6,789 (2009 projected); Race: 76.5% White, 12.0% Black, 1.1% Asian, 42.4% Hispanic of any race (2004); Density: 1,412.7 persons per square mile (2004); Average household size: 2.98 (2004); Median age: 32.4 (2004); Male/female ratio: 102.4 (2004); Marriage status: 26.3% never married, 57.4% now married, 7.4% widowed, 8.9% divorced (2000); Foreign born: 22.0% (2000); Ancestry (includes multiple ancestries): 50.1% Other groups, 12.2% United States or American, 7.0% German, 6.9% English, 6.7% Irish (2000).

Economy: Single-family building permits issued: 45 (2004); Multi-family building permits issued: 0 (2004); Employment by occupation: 11.7% management, 17.4% professional, 14.6% services, 20.5% sales, 9.1% farming, 13.3% construction, 13.4% production (2000).

Income: Per capita income: $15,610 (2004); Median household income: $36,618 (2004); Average household income: $45,950 (2004); Percent of households with income of $100,000 or more: 7.6% (2004); Poverty rate: 18.8% (2000).

Taxes: Total city taxes per capita: $273 (2002); City property taxes per capita: $110 (2002).

Education: Percent of population age 25 and over with: High school diploma (including GED) or higher: 65.4% (2004); Bachelor's degree or higher: 13.9% (2004); Master's degree or higher: 3.9% (2004).

School District(s)

Hendry County School District (PK-12)
2002-03 Enrollment: 7,673 . . . . (863) 674-4642

Housing: Homeownership rate: 66.5% (2004); Median home value: $93,113 (2004); Median rent: $382 per month (2000); Median age of housing: 26 years (2000).
Hospitals: Hendry Regional Medical Center (66 beds)
Safety: Violent crime rate: 151.4 per 10,000 population; Property crime rate: 793.9 per 10,000 population (2003).
Newspapers: The Clewiston News (General - Circulation 3,400)
Transportation: Commute to work: 86.9% car, 4.9% public transportation, 3.6% walk, 2.7% work from home (2000); Travel time to work: 56.4% less than 15 minutes, 16.4% 15 to 30 minutes, 19.5% 30 to 45 minutes, 2.2% 45 to 60 minutes, 5.5% 60 minutes or more (2000)

Additional Information Contacts

Clewiston Chamber of Commerce . . . . (863) 983-7979
Local Government Offices . . . . (863) 983-8399

HARLEM (CDP). Covers a land area of 0.968 square miles and a water area of 0 square miles. Located at 26.73° N. Lat.; 80.95° W. Long. Elevation is 19 feet.
Population: 3,053 (1990); 2,730 (2000); 2,090 (2004); 1,741 (2009 projected); Race: 1.9% White, 96.5% Black, 0.1% Asian, 2.1% Hispanic of any race (2004); Density: 2,159.6 persons per square mile (2004); Average household size: 3.06 (2004); Median age: 25.1 (2004); Male/female ratio: 87.9 (2004); Marriage status: 50.9% never married, 35.6% now married, 6.4% widowed, 7.0% divorced (2000); Foreign born: 10.7% (2000); Ancestry (includes multiple ancestries): 75.3% Other groups, 6.6% Jamaican, 1.5% German, 1.4% African, 1.3% United States or American (2000).
Economy: Employment by occupation: 0.8% management, 12.8% professional, 26.9% services, 16.0% sales, 4.7% farming, 15.5% construction, 23.2% production (2000).
Income: Per capita income: $9,123 (2004); Median household income: $21,040 (2004); Average household income: $27,958 (2004); Percent of households with income of $100,000 or more: 1.5% (2004); Poverty rate: 40.4% (2000).
Education: Percent of population age 25 and over with: High school diploma (including GED) or higher: 47.6% (2004); Bachelor's degree or higher: 2.5% (2004); Master's degree or higher: 0.0% (2004).
Housing: Homeownership rate: 63.5% (2004); Median home value: $65,804 (2004); Median rent: $257 per month (2000); Median age of housing: 22 years (2000).
Transportation: Commute to work: 95.2% car, 0.0% public transportation, 1.4% walk, 1.2% work from home (2000); Travel time to work: 64.3% less than 15 minutes, 23.6% 15 to 30 minutes, 5.7% 30 to 45 minutes, 3.7% 45 to 60 minutes, 2.8% 60 minutes or more (2000)

LABELLE (city). Covers a land area of 3.468 square miles and a water area of 0.086 square miles. Located at 26.76° N. Lat.; 81.43° W. Long. Elevation is 20 feet.
History: La Belle was named by Captain Francis Asbury Hendry (for whom the county was named) for his two daughters, Laura and Belle. The town developed around a sawmill and as a shipping point for cattle.
Population: 2,745 (1990); 4,210 (2000); 4,518 (2004); 4,769 (2009 projected); Race: 73.8% White, 9.8% Black, 0.4% Asian, 35.1% Hispanic of any race (2004); Density: 1,302.8 persons per square mile (2004); Average household size: 3.02 (2004); Median age: 37.0 (2004); Male/female ratio: 104.2 (2004); Marriage status: 20.7% never married, 59.2% now married, 10.2% widowed, 9.9% divorced (2000); Foreign born: 19.6% (2000); Ancestry (includes multiple ancestries): 42.5% Other groups, 10.4% United States or American, 8.6% English, 8.3% German, 6.9% Irish (2000).
Economy: Single-family building permits issued: 7 (2004); Multi-family building permits issued: n/a (2004); Employment by occupation: 9.6% management, 13.2% professional, 13.9% services, 26.1% sales, 12.2% farming, 14.2% construction, 10.8% production (2000).
Income: Per capita income: $15,485 (2004); Median household income: $33,793 (2004); Average household income: $44,746 (2004); Percent of households with income of $100,000 or more: 6.4% (2004); Poverty rate: 18.0% (2000).
Taxes: Total city taxes per capita: $281 (2002); City property taxes per capita: $74 (2002).
Education: Percent of population age 25 and over with: High school diploma (including GED) or higher: 61.3% (2004); Bachelor's degree or higher: 11.9% (2004); Master's degree or higher: 4.8% (2004).

School District(s)

Hendry County School District (PK-12)
2002-03 Enrollment: 7,673 . . . . (863) 674-4642

Housing: Homeownership rate: 75.5% (2004); Median home value: $64,934 (2004); Median rent: $422 per month (2000); Median age of housing: 19 years (2000).
Newspapers: Caloosa Belle (General - Circulation 6,500); Immokalee Bulletin (General - Circulation 3,500)
Transportation: Commute to work: 90.7% car, 5.1% public transportation, 1.9% walk, 0.9% work from home (2000); Travel time to work: 46.3% less than 15 minutes, 13.5% 15 to 30 minutes, 15.1% 30 to 45 minutes, 10.7% 45 to 60 minutes, 14.3% 60 minutes or more (2000)

Additional Information Contacts

La Belle Chamber of Commerce . . . . (863) 675-0125

PORT LA BELLE (CDP). Covers a land area of 8.615 square miles and a water area of 0.002 square miles. Located at 26.74° N. Lat.; 81.39° W. Long.
Population: 1,997 (1990); 3,050 (2000); 3,034 (2004); 3,124 (2009 projected); Race: 69.2% White, 9.5% Black, 0.6% Asian, 49.9% Hispanic of any race (2004); Density: 352.2 persons per square mile (2004); Average household size: 3.71 (2004); Median age: 27.1 (2004); Male/female ratio: 126.4 (2004); Marriage status: 31.2% never married, 58.1% now married, 4.5% widowed, 6.3% divorced (2000); Foreign born: 33.8% (2000); Ancestry (includes multiple ancestries): 48.2% Other groups, 8.3% Irish, 6.2% United States or American, 5.0% German, 4.1% English (2000).
Economy: Employment by occupation: 5.5% management, 7.1% professional, 13.9% services, 19.9% sales, 30.3% farming, 9.5% construction, 13.9% production (2000).
Income: Per capita income: $14,561 (2004); Median household income: $35,717 (2004); Average household income: $49,272 (2004); Percent of households with income of $100,000 or more: 7.7% (2004); Poverty rate: 22.5% (2000).
Education: Percent of population age 25 and over with: High school diploma (including GED) or higher: 54.3% (2004); Bachelor's degree or higher: 8.3% (2004); Master's degree or higher: 2.2% (2004).
Housing: Homeownership rate: 59.0% (2004); Median home value: $69,458 (2004); Median rent: $428 per month (2000); Median age of housing: 15 years (2000).
Transportation: Commute to work: 80.7% car, 12.7% public transportation, 0.6% walk, 2.0% work from home (2000); Travel time to work: 28.9% less than 15 minutes, 23.9% 15 to 30 minutes, 22.0% 30 to 45 minutes, 15.1% 45 to 60 minutes, 10.0% 60 minutes or more (2000)

Hernando County

Located in west central Florida; bounded on the east by the Withlacoochee River, and on the west by the Gulf of Mexico; lowland area with marshy coast and small lakes. Covers a land area of 478.30 square miles, a water area of 110.80 square miles, and is located in the Eastern Time Zone. The county government was organized in 1843. County seat is Brooksville.

Hernando County is part of the Tampa-St. Petersburg-Clearwater, FL Metropolitan Statistical Area. The entire metro area includes: Hernando County, FL; Hillsborough County, FL; Pasco County, FL; Pinellas County, FL

Weather Station: Brooksville Chin Hill — Elevation: 239 feet

	Jan	Feb	Mar	Apr	May	Jun	Jul	Aug	Sep	Oct	Nov	Dec
High	71	73	78	82	88	90	91	90	89	84	78	72
Low	49	50	55	59	65	70	72	72	70	64	56	51
Precip	3.4	3.4	4.4	2.7	3.4	7.0	6.9	8.5	6.1	2.4	2.4	2.5
Snow	0.0	0.0	0.0	0.0	0.0	0.0	0.0	0.0	0.0	0.0	0.0	0.0

High and Low temperatures in degrees Fahrenheit; Precipitation and Snow in inches

Weather Station: Weeki Wachee — Elevation: 19 feet

	Jan	Feb	Mar	Apr	May	Jun	Jul	Aug	Sep	Oct	Nov	Dec
High	70	72	77	82	87	90	92	91	90	85	79	73
Low	44	46	51	56	62	69	71	71	69	61	53	46
Precip	3.8	3.2	4.2	2.5	3.0	5.9	8.3	7.6	6.5	2.3	2.1	2.5
Snow	0.0	0.0	0.0	0.0	0.0	0.0	0.0	0.0	0.0	0.0	0.0	0.0

High and Low temperatures in degrees Fahrenheit; Precipitation and Snow in inches

Population: 101,115 (1990); 130,802 (2000); 142,865 (2004); 158,055 (2009 projected); Race: 92.4% White, 4.4% Black, 0.7% Asian, 6.1% Hispanic of any race (2004); Density: 298.7 persons per square mile (2004); Average household size: 2.36 (2004); Median age: 48.7 (2004); Male/female ratio: 91.0 (2004).
Religion: Five largest groups: 26.7% Catholic Church, 4.5% Southern Baptist Convention, 3.1% The United Methodist Church, 1.7% Assemblies of God, 1.2% Evangelical Lutheran Church in America (2000).
Economy: Unemployment rate: 5.2% (2004); Total civilian labor force: 53,826 (2004); Leading industries: 23.4% retail trade; 20.8% health care and social assistance; 12.0% accommodation & food services (2003); Companies that employ 500 or more persons: 4 (2003); Companies that employ 100 to 499 persons: 33 (2003); Companies that employ less than 100 persons: 2,646 (2003); Farms: 617 totaling 65,315 acres (2002); Minority business ownership rate: 6.9% (1997); Women business ownership rate: 19.8% (1997); Retail sales per capita: $6,626 (1997). Single-family building permits issued: 2,762 (2004); Multi-family building permits issued: 250 (2004).
Income: Per capita income: $20,488 (2004); Median household income: $36,579 (2004); Average household income: $47,723 (2004); Percent of households with income of $100,000 or more: 6.8% (2004); Poverty rate: 12.3% (2002); Bankruptcy rate: 5.30% (2004).
Taxes: Total county taxes per capita: $341 (2002); County property taxes per capita: $303 (2002).
Education: Percent of population age 25 and over with: High school diploma (including GED) or higher: 78.6% (2004); Bachelor's degree or higher: 12.8% (2004); Master's degree or higher: 4.6% (2004).
Housing: Homeownership rate: 86.7% (2004); Median home value: $117,316 (2004); Median rent: $453 per month (2000); Median age of housing: 15 years (2000).
Health: Birth rate: 87.9 per 10,000 population (2004); Death rate: 149.7 per 10,000 population (2004); Age adjusted cancer mortality rate: 212.6 deaths per 100,000 population (2002); Number of physicians: 15.1 per 10,000 population (2001); Hospital beds: 30.3 per 10,000 population (2002); Hospital admissions: 1,770.7 per 10,000 population (2002).
Elections: 2004 Presidential election results: 52.9% Bush, 46.2% Kerry, 0.6% Nader, 0.1% Badnarik
National and State Parks: Chassahowitzka National Wildlife Refuge
Additional Information Contacts
Hernando County Government Offices . . . . (352) 754-4000
Brooksville Chamber of Commerce . . . . (352) 796-0697
Hernando County Association of Realtors . . . . (352) 799-1971

Hernando County Communities

BAYPORT (CDP). Covers a land area of 0.663 square miles and a water area of 0 square miles. Located at 28.54° N. Lat.; 82.64° W. Long. Elevation is 10 feet.
Population: 30 (1990); 36 (2000); 36 (2004); 36 (2009 projected); Race: 97.2% White, 2.8% Black, 0.0% Asian, 0.0% Hispanic of any race (2004); Density: 54.3 persons per square mile (2004); Average household size: 2.25 (2004); Median age: 48.3 (2004); Male/female ratio: 89.5 (2004); Marriage status: 0.0% never married, 75.0% now married, 0.0% widowed, 25.0% divorced (2000); Foreign born: 0.0% (2000); Ancestry (includes multiple ancestries): 66.7% English, 41.7% German, 33.3% Other groups, 25.0% Scotch-Irish (2000).
Economy: Employment by occupation: 31.6% management, 36.8% professional, 0.0% services, 0.0% sales, 0.0% farming, 31.6% construction, 0.0% production (2000).
Income: Per capita income: $10,417 (2004); Median household income: $17,031 (2004); Average household income: $23,438 (2004); Percent of households with income of $100,000 or more: 0.0% (2004); Poverty rate: 25.0% (2000).
Education: Percent of population age 25 and over with: High school diploma (including GED) or higher: 100.0% (2004); Bachelor's degree or higher: 25.0% (2004); Master's degree or higher: 25.0% (2004).
Housing: Homeownership rate: 81.3% (2004); Median home value: $119,444 (2004); Median rent: $n/a per month (2000); Median age of housing: 19 years (2000).
Transportation: Commute to work: 68.4% car, 0.0% public transportation, 0.0% walk, 31.6% work from home (2000); Travel time to work: 61.5% less than 15 minutes, 38.5% 15 to 30 minutes, 0.0% 30 to 45 minutes, 0.0% 45 to 60 minutes, 0.0% 60 minutes or more (2000)

BROOKRIDGE (CDP). Covers a land area of 2.027 square miles and a water area of 0 square miles. Located at 28.54° N. Lat.; 82.49° W. Long.
Population: 2,805 (1990); 3,279 (2000); 3,519 (2004); 3,836 (2009 projected); Race: 98.7% White, 0.2% Black, 0.2% Asian, 1.1% Hispanic of any race (2004); Density: 1,736.1 persons per square mile (2004); Average household size: 1.79 (2004); Median age: 71.6 (2004); Male/female ratio: 82.1 (2004); Marriage status: 3.5% never married, 71.5% now married, 19.1% widowed, 5.9% divorced (2000); Foreign born: 4.6% (2000); Ancestry (includes multiple ancestries): 19.7% German, 17.2% English, 13.0% Irish, 6.9% Italian, 5.9% United States or American (2000).
Economy: Employment by occupation: 5.9% management, 6.6% professional, 15.3% services, 46.0% sales, 0.0% farming, 10.3% construction, 15.8% production (2000).
Income: Per capita income: $19,840 (2004); Median household income: $28,516 (2004); Average household income: $34,337 (2004); Percent of households with income of $100,000 or more: 2.1% (2004); Poverty rate: 5.7% (2000).
Education: Percent of population age 25 and over with: High school diploma (including GED) or higher: 73.9% (2004); Bachelor's degree or higher: 10.6% (2004); Master's degree or higher: 5.5% (2004).
Housing: Homeownership rate: 97.0% (2004); Median home value: $72,125 (2004); Median rent: $508 per month (2000); Median age of housing: 15 years (2000).
Transportation: Commute to work: 97.6% car, 0.0% public transportation, 0.0% walk, 2.4% work from home (2000); Travel time to work: 32.0% less than 15 minutes, 46.6% 15 to 30 minutes, 6.6% 30 to 45 minutes, 4.4% 45 to 60 minutes, 10.4% 60 minutes or more (2000)

BROOKSVILLE (city). Covers a land area of 4.943 square miles and a water area of 0.027 square miles. Located at 28.55° N. Lat.; 82.38° W. Long. Elevation is 209 feet.
History: Brooksville was named for Preston Brooks, a U.S. congressman from South Carolina. In the 1870's Brooksville was a stopover on the stage line from Gainesville to Tampa.
Population: 7,767 (1990); 7,264 (2000); 7,373 (2004); 7,579 (2009 projected); Race: 73.4% White, 22.7% Black, 1.5% Asian, 3.7% Hispanic of any race (2004); Density: 1,491.6 persons per square mile (2004); Average household size: 2.24 (2004); Median age: 43.9 (2004); Male/female ratio: 81.0 (2004); Marriage status: 19.3% never married, 50.9% now married, 16.6% widowed, 13.3% divorced (2000); Foreign born: 4.1% (2000); Ancestry (includes multiple ancestries): 28.0% Other groups, 13.8% Irish, 13.5% German, 11.1% English, 7.5% United States or American (2000).
Economy: Single-family building permits issued: 8 (2004); Multi-family building permits issued: 0 (2004); Employment by occupation: 10.7% management, 20.8% professional, 22.4% services, 21.3% sales, 0.3% farming, 11.1% construction, 13.3% production (2000).
Income: Per capita income: $17,398 (2004); Median household income: $28,010 (2004); Average household income: $37,510 (2004); Percent of households with income of $100,000 or more: 3.8% (2004); Poverty rate: 21.5% (2000).
Taxes: Total city taxes per capita: $424 (2002); City property taxes per capita: $239 (2002).
Education: Percent of population age 25 and over with: High school diploma (including GED) or higher: 76.1% (2004); Bachelor's degree or higher: 14.6% (2004); Master's degree or higher: 5.0% (2004).

School District(s)

Hernando County School District (PK-12)
2002-03 Enrollment: 18,605 . . . . (352) 797-7001
Housing: Homeownership rate: 64.5% (2004); Median home value: $57,429 (2004); Median rent: $345 per month (2000); Median age of housing: 22 years (2000).
Hospitals: Brooksville Regional Hospital (91 beds); Oak Hill Hospital (204 beds); Spring Brook Hospital (50 beds)
Safety: Violent crime rate: 179.0 per 10,000 population; Property crime rate: 853.4 per 10,000 population (2003).
Newspapers: Hernando Today (Circulation 16,395)
Transportation: Commute to work: 93.6% car, 0.4% public transportation, 3.1% walk, 2.0% work from home (2000); Travel time to work: 44.7% less than 15 minutes, 30.2% 15 to 30 minutes, 10.0% 30 to 45 minutes, 5.2% 45 to 60 minutes, 9.9% 60 minutes or more (2000)
Additional Information Contacts
Brooksville Chamber of Commerce . . . . (352) 796-0697
Hernando County Association of Realtors . . . . (352) 799-1971
Local Government Offices . . . . (352) 544-5435

HERNANDO BEACH (CDP). Covers a land area of 3.915 square miles and a water area of 0.057 square miles. Located at 28.48° N. Lat.; 82.65° W. Long.
Population: 1,788 (1990); 2,185 (2000); 2,303 (2004); 2,459 (2009 projected); Race: 97.8% White, 0.3% Black, 0.7% Asian, 2.6% Hispanic of any race (2004); Density: 588.3 persons per square mile (2004); Average household size: 2.20 (2004); Median age: 53.0 (2004); Male/female ratio: 98.4 (2004); Marriage status: 12.2% never married, 66.9% now married, 8.8% widowed, 12.1% divorced (2000); Foreign born: 5.7% (2000); Ancestry (includes multiple ancestries): 24.9% German, 15.0% English, 13.9% Other groups, 13.5% Irish, 12.5% Italian (2000).
Economy: Employment by occupation: 15.0% management, 23.6% professional, 13.2% services, 27.9% sales, 3.8% farming, 10.6% construction, 6.0% production (2000).
Income: Per capita income: $29,460 (2004); Median household income: $53,125 (2004); Average household income: $64,740 (2004); Percent of households with income of $100,000 or more: 17.8% (2004); Poverty rate: 6.6% (2000).
Education: Percent of population age 25 and over with: High school diploma (including GED) or higher: 86.7% (2004); Bachelor's degree or higher: 22.0% (2004); Master's degree or higher: 12.4% (2004).
Housing: Homeownership rate: 91.3% (2004); Median home value: $191,413 (2004); Median rent: $553 per month (2000); Median age of housing: 16 years (2000).
Transportation: Commute to work: 91.8% car, 0.0% public transportation, 0.0% walk, 5.5% work from home (2000); Travel time to work: 9.3% less than 15 minutes, 38.7% 15 to 30 minutes, 26.3% 30 to 45 minutes, 6.1% 45 to 60 minutes, 19.7% 60 minutes or more (2000)

HIGH POINT (CDP). Covers a land area of 2.940 square miles and a water area of 0.033 square miles. Located at 28.54° N. Lat.; 82.52° W. Long.
Population: 2,947 (1990); 2,973 (2000); 3,055 (2004); 3,176 (2009 projected); Race: 98.2% White, 0.2% Black, 0.4% Asian, 2.7% Hispanic of any race (2004); Density: 1,039.3 persons per square mile (2004); Average household size: 1.94 (2004); Median age: 65.8 (2004); Male/female ratio: 82.0 (2004); Marriage status: 8.7% never married, 64.4% now married, 19.1% widowed, 7.7% divorced (2000); Foreign born: 6.4% (2000); Ancestry (includes multiple ancestries): 20.6% German, 15.5% Irish, 9.2% United States or American, 9.0% English, 6.8% Italian (2000).
Economy: Employment by occupation: 6.7% management, 9.9% professional, 18.2% services, 36.5% sales, 0.0% farming, 10.8% construction, 18.0% production (2000).
Income: Per capita income: $19,344 (2004); Median household income: $28,629 (2004); Average household income: $37,616 (2004); Percent of households with income of $100,000 or more: 4.2% (2004); Poverty rate: 7.4% (2000).
Education: Percent of population age 25 and over with: High school diploma (including GED) or higher: 70.0% (2004); Bachelor's degree or higher: 5.7% (2004); Master's degree or higher: 2.8% (2004).
Housing: Homeownership rate: 93.8% (2004); Median home value: $65,825 (2004); Median rent: $441 per month (2000); Median age of housing: 18 years (2000).
Transportation: Commute to work: 94.9% car, 1.5% public transportation, 0.0% walk, 1.1% work from home (2000); Travel time to work: 29.9% less than 15 minutes, 45.2% 15 to 30 minutes, 11.1% 30 to 45 minutes, 4.4% 45 to 60 minutes, 9.3% 60 minutes or more (2000)

HILL 'N DALE (CDP). Covers a land area of 0.509 square miles and a water area of 0 square miles. Located at 28.52° N. Lat.; 82.29° W. Long. Elevation is 100 feet.
Population: 1,324 (1990); 1,436 (2000); 1,456 (2004); 1,488 (2009 projected); Race: 64.6% White, 30.1% Black, 0.5% Asian, 9.3% Hispanic of any race (2004); Density: 2,862.6 persons per square mile (2004); Average household size: 3.05 (2004); Median age: 28.3 (2004); Male/female ratio: 88.8 (2004); Marriage status: 28.2% never married, 53.2% now married, 4.9% widowed, 13.7% divorced (2000); Foreign born: 4.4% (2000); Ancestry (includes multiple ancestries): 28.2% Other groups, 18.0% United States or American, 15.3% German, 9.2% Irish, 8.2% English (2000).
Economy: Employment by occupation: 3.9% management, 13.7% professional, 22.4% services, 21.8% sales, 2.6% farming, 19.0% construction, 16.6% production (2000).
Income: Per capita income: $11,711 (2004); Median household income: $36,250 (2004); Average household income: $35,608 (2004); Percent of households with income of $100,000 or more: 0.4% (2004); Poverty rate: 18.5% (2000).
Education: Percent of population age 25 and over with: High school diploma (including GED) or higher: 70.4% (2004); Bachelor's degree or higher: 10.5% (2004); Master's degree or higher: 0.0% (2004).
Housing: Homeownership rate: 83.0% (2004); Median home value: $71,487 (2004); Median rent: $466 per month (2000); Median age of housing: 20 years (2000).
Transportation: Commute to work: 100.0% car, 0.0% public transportation, 0.0% walk, 0.0% work from home (2000); Travel time to work: 22.2% less than 15 minutes, 25.5% 15 to 30 minutes, 25.4% 30 to 45 minutes, 6.3% 45 to 60 minutes, 20.5% 60 minutes or more (2000)

ISTACHATTA (CDP). Covers a land area of 0.129 square miles and a water area of 0.020 square miles. Located at 28.66° N. Lat.; 82.27° W. Long. Elevation is 220 feet.
Population: 76 (1990); 65 (2000); 62 (2004); 61 (2009 projected); Race: 95.2% White, 3.2% Black, 0.0% Asian, 3.2% Hispanic of any race (2004); Density: 482.1 persons per square mile (2004); Average household size: 1.88 (2004); Median age: 59.0 (2004); Male/female ratio: 100.0 (2004); Marriage status: 18.9% never married, 81.1% now married, 0.0% widowed, 0.0% divorced (2000); Foreign born: 0.0% (2000); Ancestry (includes multiple ancestries): 49.2% Other groups, 36.1% German, 29.5% Irish (2000).
Economy: Employment by occupation: 0.0% management, 100.0% professional, 0.0% services, 0.0% sales, 0.0% farming, 0.0% construction, 0.0% production (2000).
Income: Per capita income: $13,427 (2004); Median household income: $24,167 (2004); Average household income: $25,227 (2004); Percent of households with income of $100,000 or more: 0.0% (2004); Poverty rate: 29.5% (2000).
Education: Percent of population age 25 and over with: High school diploma (including GED) or higher: 42.1% (2004); Bachelor's degree or higher: 0.0% (2004); Master's degree or higher: 0.0% (2004).
Housing: Homeownership rate: 87.9% (2004); Median home value: $51,000 (2004); Median rent: $n/a per month (2000); Median age of housing: 27 years (2000).
Transportation: Commute to work: 100.0% car, 0.0% public transportation, 0.0% walk, 0.0% work from home (2000); Travel time to work: 0.0% less than 15 minutes, 100.0% 15 to 30 minutes, 0.0% 30 to 45 minutes, 0.0% 45 to 60 minutes, 0.0% 60 minutes or more (2000)

LAKE LINDSEY (CDP). Covers a land area of 0.022 square miles and a water area of 0 square miles. Located at 28.63° N. Lat.; 82.36° W. Long.
Population: 59 (1990); 49 (2000); 53 (2004); 58 (2009 projected); Race: 100.0% White, 0.0% Black, 0.0% Asian, 0.0% Hispanic of any race (2004); Density: 2,387.0 persons per square mile (2004); Average household size: 2.12 (2004); Median age: 41.5 (2004); Male/female ratio: 89.3 (2004); Marriage status: 0.0% never married, 33.3% now married, 43.3% widowed, 23.3% divorced (2000); Foreign born: 0.0% (2000); Ancestry (includes multiple ancestries): 15.9% Norwegian, 15.9% German, 13.6% Irish (2000).
Economy: Employment by occupation: 0.0% management, 41.2% professional, 35.3% services, 0.0% sales, 0.0% farming, 23.5% construction, 0.0% production (2000).
Income: Per capita income: $10,896 (2004); Median household income: $26,154 (2004); Average household income: $23,100 (2004); Percent of households with income of $100,000 or more: 0.0% (2004); Poverty rate: 15.9% (2000).
Education: Percent of population age 25 and over with: High school diploma (including GED) or higher: 84.2% (2004); Bachelor's degree or higher: 0.0% (2004); Master's degree or higher: 0.0% (2004).
Housing: Homeownership rate: 80.0% (2004); Median home value: $31,111 (2004); Median rent: $375 per month (2000); Median age of housing: 20 years (2000).
Transportation: Commute to work: 100.0% car, 0.0% public transportation, 0.0% walk, 0.0% work from home (2000); Travel time to work: 0.0% less than 15 minutes, 58.8% 15 to 30 minutes, 41.2% 30 to 45 minutes, 0.0% 45 to 60 minutes, 0.0% 60 minutes or more (2000)

MASARYKTOWN (CDP). Covers a land area of 1.059 square miles and a water area of 0 square miles. Located at 28.44° N. Lat.; 82.46° W. Long. Elevation is 68 feet.
Population: 675 (1990); 920 (2000); 1,006 (2004); 1,111 (2009 projected); Race: 95.2% White, 0.3% Black, 0.4% Asian, 8.3% Hispanic of any race

(2004); Density: 949.9 persons per square mile (2004); Average household size: 2.41 (2004); Median age: 42.4 (2004); Male/female ratio: 92.0 (2004); Marriage status: 9.5% never married, 63.0% now married, 7.2% widowed, 20.3% divorced (2000); Foreign born: 6.7% (2000); Ancestry (includes multiple ancestries): 24.1% German, 10.6% Other groups, 10.0% Irish, 10.0% Italian, 9.1% English (2000).
Economy: Employment by occupation: 12.4% management, 8.5% professional, 18.9% services, 17.3% sales, 0.0% farming, 21.5% construction, 21.5% production (2000).
Income: Per capita income: $17,904 (2004); Median household income: $38,153 (2004); Average household income: $36,699 (2004); Percent of households with income of $100,000 or more: 0.0% (2004); Poverty rate: 13.8% (2000).
Education: Percent of population age 25 and over with: High school diploma (including GED) or higher: 76.1% (2004); Bachelor's degree or higher: 8.2% (2004); Master's degree or higher: 4.0% (2004).
Housing: Homeownership rate: 82.1% (2004); Median home value: $68,673 (2004); Median rent: $238 per month (2000); Median age of housing: 29 years (2000).
Transportation: Commute to work: 92.4% car, 0.0% public transportation, 0.0% walk, 5.0% work from home (2000); Travel time to work: 11.5% less than 15 minutes, 41.3% 15 to 30 minutes, 25.5% 30 to 45 minutes, 3.1% 45 to 60 minutes, 18.5% 60 minutes or more (2000)

NOBLETON (CDP). Covers a land area of 0.197 square miles and a water area of 0.012 square miles. Located at 28.64° N. Lat.; 82.26° W. Long. Elevation is 40 feet.
Population: 186 (1990); 160 (2000); 174 (2004); 191 (2009 projected); Race: 99.4% White, 0.0% Black, 0.0% Asian, 1.7% Hispanic of any race (2004); Density: 883.2 persons per square mile (2004); Average household size: 2.02 (2004); Median age: 45.5 (2004); Male/female ratio: 107.1 (2004); Marriage status: 0.0% never married, 69.0% now married, 9.5% widowed, 21.4% divorced (2000); Foreign born: 0.0% (2000); Ancestry (includes multiple ancestries): 23.5% United States or American, 7.6% French (except Basque), 6.8% German, 6.8% Irish, 6.8% Norwegian (2000).
Economy: Employment by occupation: 27.3% management, 0.0% professional, 0.0% services, 0.0% sales, 0.0% farming, 24.2% construction, 48.5% production (2000).
Income: Per capita income: $14,713 (2004); Median household income: $27,353 (2004); Average household income: $29,767 (2004); Percent of households with income of $100,000 or more: 0.0% (2004); Poverty rate: 50.8% (2000).
Education: Percent of population age 25 and over with: High school diploma (including GED) or higher: 66.4% (2004); Bachelor's degree or higher: 1.5% (2004); Master's degree or higher: 1.5% (2004).
Housing: Homeownership rate: 90.7% (2004); Median home value: $59,333 (2004); Median rent: $n/a per month (2000); Median age of housing: 25 years (2000).
Transportation: Commute to work: 72.7% car, 0.0% public transportation, 0.0% walk, 27.3% work from home (2000); Travel time to work: 33.3% less than 15 minutes, 37.5% 15 to 30 minutes, 29.2% 30 to 45 minutes, 0.0% 45 to 60 minutes, 0.0% 60 minutes or more (2000)

NORTH BROOKSVILLE (CDP). Covers a land area of 2.763 square miles and a water area of 0.002 square miles. Located at 28.56° N. Lat.; 82.40° W. Long.
Population: 1,438 (1990); 1,461 (2000); 1,416 (2004); 1,405 (2009 projected); Race: 89.5% White, 6.9% Black, 0.9% Asian, 3.3% Hispanic of any race (2004); Density: 512.4 persons per square mile (2004); Average household size: 2.65 (2004); Median age: 37.3 (2004); Male/female ratio: 85.8 (2004); Marriage status: 23.9% never married, 52.0% now married, 8.5% widowed, 15.6% divorced (2000); Foreign born: 2.7% (2000); Ancestry (includes multiple ancestries): 20.3% United States or American, 15.6% Other groups, 6.6% Italian, 6.5% English, 6.0% Irish (2000).
Economy: Employment by occupation: 4.4% management, 12.0% professional, 21.5% services, 24.8% sales, 1.4% farming, 20.0% construction, 15.9% production (2000).
Income: Per capita income: $15,098 (2004); Median household income: $30,242 (2004); Average household income: $37,607 (2004); Percent of households with income of $100,000 or more: 4.5% (2004); Poverty rate: 13.7% (2000).
Education: Percent of population age 25 and over with: High school diploma (including GED) or higher: 68.0% (2004); Bachelor's degree or higher: 8.8% (2004); Master's degree or higher: 3.8% (2004).
Housing: Homeownership rate: 70.5% (2004); Median home value: $79,138 (2004); Median rent: $387 per month (2000); Median age of housing: 25 years (2000).
Transportation: Commute to work: 95.3% car, 0.0% public transportation, 1.3% walk, 1.1% work from home (2000); Travel time to work: 53.6% less than 15 minutes, 23.6% 15 to 30 minutes, 11.3% 30 to 45 minutes, 1.0% 45 to 60 minutes, 10.5% 60 minutes or more (2000)

NORTH WEEKI WACHEE (CDP). Covers a land area of 7.357 square miles and a water area of 0.931 square miles. Located at 28.54° N. Lat.; 82.56° W. Long.
Population: 2,009 (1990); 4,253 (2000); 5,127 (2004); 6,197 (2009 projected); Race: 96.3% White, 1.4% Black, 0.5% Asian, 5.8% Hispanic of any race (2004); Density: 696.9 persons per square mile (2004); Average household size: 2.26 (2004); Median age: 54.5 (2004); Male/female ratio: 95.3 (2004); Marriage status: 10.3% never married, 72.8% now married, 8.5% widowed, 8.4% divorced (2000); Foreign born: 3.8% (2000); Ancestry (includes multiple ancestries): 18.9% German, 18.2% Irish, 13.3% English, 13.0% Italian, 11.7% United States or American (2000).
Economy: Employment by occupation: 16.4% management, 20.1% professional, 13.8% services, 27.2% sales, 0.7% farming, 13.1% construction, 8.7% production (2000).
Income: Per capita income: $26,050 (2004); Median household income: $37,775 (2004); Average household income: $58,833 (2004); Percent of households with income of $100,000 or more: 13.9% (2004); Poverty rate: 5.9% (2000).
Education: Percent of population age 25 and over with: High school diploma (including GED) or higher: 81.6% (2004); Bachelor's degree or higher: 17.1% (2004); Master's degree or higher: 4.4% (2004).
Housing: Homeownership rate: 90.1% (2004); Median home value: $131,472 (2004); Median rent: $487 per month (2000); Median age of housing: 10 years (2000).
Transportation: Commute to work: 92.8% car, 0.0% public transportation, 1.3% walk, 4.0% work from home (2000); Travel time to work: 30.3% less than 15 minutes, 35.9% 15 to 30 minutes, 15.7% 30 to 45 minutes, 5.9% 45 to 60 minutes, 12.2% 60 minutes or more (2000)

PINE ISLAND (CDP). Covers a land area of 0.068 square miles and a water area of 0 square miles. Located at 28.57° N. Lat.; 82.65° W. Long. Elevation is 1 feet.
Population: 53 (1990); 64 (2000); 65 (2004); 66 (2009 projected); Race: 84.6% White, 12.3% Black, 0.0% Asian, 0.0% Hispanic of any race (2004); Density: 960.4 persons per square mile (2004); Average household size: 2.24 (2004); Median age: 46.5 (2004); Male/female ratio: 91.2 (2004); Marriage status: 12.7% never married, 40.0% now married, 18.2% widowed, 29.1% divorced (2000); Foreign born: 0.0% (2000); Ancestry (includes multiple ancestries): 50.9% German, 21.8% Swedish, 21.8% Irish, 20.0% Dutch, 18.2% English (2000).
Economy: Employment by occupation: 0.0% management, 0.0% professional, 0.0% services, 100.0% sales, 0.0% farming, 0.0% construction, 0.0% production (2000).
Income: Per capita income: $16,346 (2004); Median household income: $39,688 (2004); Average household income: $36,638 (2004); Percent of households with income of $100,000 or more: 0.0% (2004); Poverty rate: 20.0% (2000).
Education: Percent of population age 25 and over with: High school diploma (including GED) or higher: 100.0% (2004); Bachelor's degree or higher: 24.5% (2004); Master's degree or higher: 0.0% (2004).
Housing: Homeownership rate: 72.4% (2004); Median home value: $182,143 (2004); Median rent: $625 per month (2000); Median age of housing: 17 years (2000).
Transportation: Commute to work: 100.0% car, 0.0% public transportation, 0.0% walk, 0.0% work from home (2000); Travel time to work: 0.0% less than 15 minutes, 0.0% 15 to 30 minutes, 0.0% 30 to 45 minutes, 0.0% 45 to 60 minutes, 100.0% 60 minutes or more (2000)

RIDGE MANOR (CDP). Covers a land area of 8.718 square miles and a water area of 0.309 square miles. Located at 28.49° N. Lat.; 82.18° W. Long. Elevation is 69 feet.
Population: 3,339 (1990); 4,108 (2000); 4,331 (2004); 4,635 (2009 projected); Race: 94.9% White, 2.4% Black, 0.3% Asian, 3.6% Hispanic of any race (2004); Density: 496.8 persons per square mile (2004); Average household size: 2.40 (2004); Median age: 44.1 (2004); Male/female ratio: 97.2 (2004); Marriage status: 17.3% never married, 61.4% now married, 9.7% widowed, 11.6% divorced (2000); Foreign born: 3.5% (2000);

Ancestry (includes multiple ancestries): 16.8% Irish, 14.7% German, 14.0% United States or American, 13.8% English, 13.5% Other groups (2000).
Economy: Employment by occupation: 8.6% management, 16.0% professional, 16.7% services, 27.7% sales, 0.0% farming, 11.2% construction, 19.8% production (2000).
Income: Per capita income: $18,821 (2004); Median household income: $33,678 (2004); Average household income: $45,260 (2004); Percent of households with income of $100,000 or more: 7.0% (2004); Poverty rate: 15.1% (2000).
Education: Percent of population age 25 and over with: High school diploma (including GED) or higher: 72.5% (2004); Bachelor's degree or higher: 9.3% (2004); Master's degree or higher: 2.6% (2004).
Housing: Homeownership rate: 87.1% (2004); Median home value: $92,931 (2004); Median rent: $410 per month (2000); Median age of housing: 19 years (2000).
Transportation: Commute to work: 93.7% car, 0.5% public transportation, 0.8% walk, 1.7% work from home (2000); Travel time to work: 14.0% less than 15 minutes, 42.3% 15 to 30 minutes, 14.3% 30 to 45 minutes, 9.2% 45 to 60 minutes, 20.1% 60 minutes or more (2000)

SOUTH BROOKSVILLE (CDP). Covers a land area of 3.506 square miles and a water area of 0.056 square miles. Located at 28.54° N. Lat.; 82.39° W. Long.
Population: 1,387 (1990); 1,376 (2000); 1,384 (2004); 1,402 (2009 projected); Race: 59.3% White, 37.1% Black, 0.5% Asian, 5.7% Hispanic of any race (2004); Density: 394.8 persons per square mile (2004); Average household size: 2.44 (2004); Median age: 35.9 (2004); Male/female ratio: 85.3 (2004); Marriage status: 17.5% never married, 51.3% now married, 12.8% widowed, 18.5% divorced (2000); Foreign born: 0.0% (2000); Ancestry (includes multiple ancestries): 40.9% Other groups, 14.9% United States or American, 9.9% German, 6.6% Irish, 5.8% Nigerian (2000).
Economy: Employment by occupation: 5.5% management, 11.2% professional, 29.1% services, 19.6% sales, 0.0% farming, 17.5% construction, 17.0% production (2000).
Income: Per capita income: $16,598 (2004); Median household income: $30,975 (2004); Average household income: $40,203 (2004); Percent of households with income of $100,000 or more: 4.9% (2004); Poverty rate: 16.1% (2000).
Education: Percent of population age 25 and over with: High school diploma (including GED) or higher: 62.0% (2004); Bachelor's degree or higher: 5.6% (2004); Master's degree or higher: 1.6% (2004).
Housing: Homeownership rate: 72.5% (2004); Median home value: $74,912 (2004); Median rent: $373 per month (2000); Median age of housing: 30 years (2000).
Transportation: Commute to work: 98.4% car, 0.0% public transportation, 0.0% walk, 1.6% work from home (2000); Travel time to work: 32.6% less than 15 minutes, 40.3% 15 to 30 minutes, 13.6% 30 to 45 minutes, 3.8% 45 to 60 minutes, 9.7% 60 minutes or more (2000)

SPRING HILL (CDP). Covers a land area of 53.134 square miles and a water area of 1.706 square miles. Located at 28.47° N. Lat.; 82.54° W. Long. Elevation is 209 feet.
Population: 50,663 (1990); 69,078 (2000); 77,042 (2004); 86,875 (2009 projected); Race: 92.7% White, 3.6% Black, 0.9% Asian, 8.2% Hispanic of any race (2004); Density: 1,450.0 persons per square mile (2004); Average household size: 2.44 (2004); Median age: 47.2 (2004); Male/female ratio: 90.0 (2004); Marriage status: 16.0% never married, 64.7% now married, 10.1% widowed, 9.2% divorced (2000); Foreign born: 6.7% (2000); Ancestry (includes multiple ancestries): 19.7% German, 18.0% Italian, 17.0% Irish, 12.8% Other groups, 11.0% English (2000).
Economy: Employment by occupation: 8.2% management, 17.5% professional, 19.3% services, 30.7% sales, 0.5% farming, 12.5% construction, 11.3% production (2000).
Income: Per capita income: $19,256 (2004); Median household income: $36,898 (2004); Average household income: $46,503 (2004); Percent of households with income of $100,000 or more: 6.0% (2004); Poverty rate: 9.5% (2000).
Education: Percent of population age 25 and over with: High school diploma (including GED) or higher: 78.9% (2004); Bachelor's degree or higher: 11.7% (2004); Master's degree or higher: 4.1% (2004).

School District(s)

Hernando County School District (PK-12)
2002-03 Enrollment: 18,605 . . . . (352) 797-7001

Housing: Homeownership rate: 86.5% (2004); Median home value: $122,837 (2004); Median rent: $510 per month (2000); Median age of housing: 14 years (2000).
Hospitals: Spring Hill Regional Hospital (75 beds)
Transportation: Commute to work: 96.3% car, 0.1% public transportation, 0.5% walk, 2.2% work from home (2000); Travel time to work: 27.6% less than 15 minutes, 36.6% 15 to 30 minutes, 16.0% 30 to 45 minutes, 7.1% 45 to 60 minutes, 12.8% 60 minutes or more (2000)

SPRING LAKE (CDP). Covers a land area of 3.375 square miles and a water area of 0.107 square miles. Located at 28.48° N. Lat.; 82.30° W. Long. Elevation is 122 feet.
Population: 304 (1990); 327 (2000); 354 (2004); 387 (2009 projected); Race: 98.3% White, 0.0% Black, 1.1% Asian, 7.3% Hispanic of any race (2004); Density: 104.9 persons per square mile (2004); Average household size: 2.62 (2004); Median age: 41.2 (2004); Male/female ratio: 86.3 (2004); Marriage status: 14.4% never married, 49.5% now married, 7.9% widowed, 28.2% divorced (2000); Foreign born: 4.1% (2000); Ancestry (includes multiple ancestries): 28.4% German, 23.5% United States or American, 16.0% English, 12.3% Irish, 10.8% Polish (2000).
Economy: Employment by occupation: 8.2% management, 4.1% professional, 10.2% services, 68.4% sales, 0.0% farming, 9.2% construction, 0.0% production (2000).
Income: Per capita income: $19,594 (2004); Median household income: $50,938 (2004); Average household income: $50,852 (2004); Percent of households with income of $100,000 or more: 4.4% (2004); Poverty rate: 3.4% (2000).
Education: Percent of population age 25 and over with: High school diploma (including GED) or higher: 84.3% (2004); Bachelor's degree or higher: 5.2% (2004); Master's degree or higher: 5.2% (2004).
Housing: Homeownership rate: 92.6% (2004); Median home value: $177,500 (2004); Median rent: $n/a per month (2000); Median age of housing: 15 years (2000).
Transportation: Commute to work: 100.0% car, 0.0% public transportation, 0.0% walk, 0.0% work from home (2000); Travel time to work: 0.0% less than 15 minutes, 66.3% 15 to 30 minutes, 7.1% 30 to 45 minutes, 18.4% 45 to 60 minutes, 8.2% 60 minutes or more (2000)

TIMBER PINES (CDP). Covers a land area of 2.378 square miles and a water area of 0 square miles. Located at 28.46° N. Lat.; 82.60° W. Long.
Population: 3,008 (1990); 5,840 (2000); 6,040 (2004); 6,336 (2009 projected); Race: 98.8% White, 0.5% Black, 0.3% Asian, 0.6% Hispanic of any race (2004); Density: 2,540.4 persons per square mile (2004); Average household size: 1.77 (2004); Median age: 72.0 (2004); Male/female ratio: 84.1 (2004); Marriage status: 2.0% never married, 82.0% now married, 13.0% widowed, 3.0% divorced (2000); Foreign born: 5.0% (2000); Ancestry (includes multiple ancestries): 26.0% German, 18.2% Irish, 17.9% English, 9.7% Italian, 6.9% Polish (2000).
Economy: Employment by occupation: 3.1% management, 31.5% professional, 6.8% services, 38.0% sales, 0.0% farming, 11.6% construction, 8.9% production (2000).
Income: Per capita income: $36,714 (2004); Median household income: $50,177 (2004); Average household income: $65,164 (2004); Percent of households with income of $100,000 or more: 11.8% (2004); Poverty rate: 2.6% (2000).
Education: Percent of population age 25 and over with: High school diploma (including GED) or higher: 89.9% (2004); Bachelor's degree or higher: 23.7% (2004); Master's degree or higher: 9.5% (2004).
Housing: Homeownership rate: 97.4% (2004); Median home value: $170,338 (2004); Median rent: $703 per month (2000); Median age of housing: 9 years (2000).
Transportation: Commute to work: 88.0% car, 0.0% public transportation, 0.0% walk, 12.0% work from home (2000); Travel time to work: 31.2% less than 15 minutes, 39.2% 15 to 30 minutes, 3.2% 30 to 45 minutes, 0.0% 45 to 60 minutes, 26.4% 60 minutes or more (2000)

WEEKI WACHEE (city). Aka Weekiwachee Springs. Covers a land area of 1.015 square miles and a water area of 0.024 square miles. Located at 28.51° N. Lat.; 82.57° W. Long. Elevation is 34 feet.
Population: 53 (1990); 12 (2000); 13 (2004); 14 (2009 projected); Race: 100.0% White, 0.0% Black, 0.0% Asian, 0.0% Hispanic of any race (2004); Density: 12.8 persons per square mile (2004); Average household size: 2.60 (2004); Median age: 30.0 (2004); Male/female ratio: 116.7 (2004); Marriage status: 0.0% never married, 100.0% now married, 0.0% widowed, 0.0% divorced (2000); Foreign born: 0.0% (2000); Ancestry (includes

multiple ancestries): 22.2% German, 22.2% Irish, 22.2% Other groups, 11.1% Italian, 11.1% French (except Basque) (2000).
Economy: Single-family building permits issued: 0 (2004); Multi-family building permits issued: 0 (2004); Employment by occupation: 0.0% management, 40.0% professional, 20.0% services, 0.0% sales, 0.0% farming, 0.0% construction, 40.0% production (2000).
Income: Per capita income: $16,346 (2004); Median household income: $54,167 (2004); Average household income: $42,500 (2004); Percent of households with income of $100,000 or more: 0.0% (2004); Poverty rate: 55.6% (2000).
Education: Percent of population age 25 and over with: High school diploma (including GED) or higher: 85.7% (2004); Bachelor's degree or higher: 42.9% (2004); Master's degree or higher: 0.0% (2004).
Housing: Homeownership rate: 80.0% (2004); Median home value: $60,000 (2004); Median rent: $475 per month (2000); Median age of housing: 17 years (2000).
Transportation: Commute to work: 80.0% car, 0.0% public transportation, 0.0% walk, 20.0% work from home (2000); Travel time to work: 0.0% less than 15 minutes, 0.0% 15 to 30 minutes, 0.0% 30 to 45 minutes, 50.0% 45 to 60 minutes, 50.0% 60 minutes or more (2000)

WEEKI WACHEE GARDENS (CDP). Covers a land area of 1.386 square miles and a water area of 0.011 square miles. Located at 28.53° N. Lat.; 82.62° W. Long.
Population: 1,170 (1990); 1,140 (2000); 1,155 (2004); 1,176 (2009 projected); Race: 98.1% White, 0.2% Black, 0.1% Asian, 1.2% Hispanic of any race (2004); Density: 833.4 persons per square mile (2004); Average household size: 2.02 (2004); Median age: 53.9 (2004); Male/female ratio: 108.1 (2004); Marriage status: 12.3% never married, 71.4% now married, 7.6% widowed, 8.7% divorced (2000); Foreign born: 3.4% (2000); Ancestry (includes multiple ancestries): 17.0% German, 16.6% English, 13.8% Other groups, 12.0% Irish, 8.3% United States or American (2000).
Economy: Employment by occupation: 17.1% management, 12.1% professional, 18.6% services, 25.6% sales, 1.5% farming, 12.9% construction, 12.3% production (2000).
Income: Per capita income: $23,963 (2004); Median household income: $33,737 (2004); Average household income: $48,472 (2004); Percent of households with income of $100,000 or more: 6.0% (2004); Poverty rate: 9.0% (2000).
Education: Percent of population age 25 and over with: High school diploma (including GED) or higher: 92.7% (2004); Bachelor's degree or higher: 17.4% (2004); Master's degree or higher: 6.0% (2004).
Housing: Homeownership rate: 87.7% (2004); Median home value: $129,237 (2004); Median rent: $420 per month (2000); Median age of housing: 24 years (2000).
Transportation: Commute to work: 94.8% car, 0.0% public transportation, 0.0% walk, 1.7% work from home (2000); Travel time to work: 21.6% less than 15 minutes, 34.9% 15 to 30 minutes, 22.5% 30 to 45 minutes, 7.3% 45 to 60 minutes, 13.7% 60 minutes or more (2000)

Highlands County

Located in south central Florida, partly in the Everglades; bounded on the east by the Kissimmee River; rolling terrain with many lakes, including Lake Istokpoga. Covers a land area of 1,028.30 square miles, a water area of 78.00 square miles, and is located in the Eastern Time Zone. The county government was organized in 1921. County seat is Sebring.

Highlands County is part of the Sebring, FL Micropolitan Statistical Area. The entire metro area includes: Highlands County, FL

Weather Station: Archbold Bio Station — Elevation: 137 feet

	Jan	Feb	Mar	Apr	May	Jun	Jul	Aug	Sep	Oct	Nov	Dec
High	74	76	81	85	90	92	93	93	91	87	81	76
Low	48	48	53	56	62	67	68	69	69	63	57	51
Precip	2.4	2.5	3.5	2.3	4.1	7.9	7.8	7.5	6.4	3.1	2.1	1.9
Snow	tr	0.0	0.0	0.0	0.0	0.0	0.0	0.0	0.0	0.0	0.0	0.0

High and Low temperatures in degrees Fahrenheit; Precipitation and Snow in inches

Weather Station: Avon Park 2 W — Elevation: 150 feet

	Jan	Feb	Mar	Apr	May	Jun	Jul	Aug	Sep	Oct	Nov	Dec
High	72	75	79	84	88	91	92	92	90	85	79	75
Low	48	50	55	59	65	70	71	72	71	64	57	51
Precip	2.6	2.5	3.2	2.2	3.8	8.2	7.1	7.2	6.0	3.1	2.3	1.8
Snow	tr	0.0	0.0	0.0	0.0	0.0	0.0	0.0	0.0	0.0	0.0	0.0

High and Low temperatures in degrees Fahrenheit; Precipitation and Snow in inches

Population: 68,432 (1990); 87,366 (2000); 91,200 (2004); 96,060 (2009 projected); Race: 82.2% White, 10.0% Black, 1.1% Asian, 13.9% Hispanic of any race (2004); Density: 88.7 persons per square mile (2004); Average household size: 2.34 (2004); Median age: 49.4 (2004); Male/female ratio: 95.4 (2004).
Religion: Five largest groups: 11.1% Southern Baptist Convention, 5.3% Catholic Church, 4.7% The United Methodist Church, 2.0% Seventh-day Adventist Church, 1.4% Associate Reformed Presbyterian Church (2000).
Economy: Unemployment rate: 5.6% (2004); Total civilian labor force: 31,495 (2004); Leading industries: 24.6% health care and social assistance; 22.0% retail trade; 11.2% accommodation & food services (2003); Companies that employ 500 or more persons: 4 (2003); Companies that employ 100 to 499 persons: 18 (2003); Companies that employ less than 100 persons: 1,812 (2003); Farms: 1,035 totaling 576,900 acres (2002); Minority business ownership rate: 13.7% (1997); Women business ownership rate: 23.9% (1997); Retail sales per capita: $8,239 (1997). Single-family building permits issued: 904 (2004); Multi-family building permits issued: 55 (2004).
Income: Per capita income: $18,624 (2004); Median household income: $32,500 (2004); Average household income: $43,160 (2004); Percent of households with income of $100,000 or more: 6.2% (2004); Poverty rate: 14.7% (2002); Bankruptcy rate: 2.98% (2004).
Taxes: Total county taxes per capita: $391 (2002); County property taxes per capita: $270 (2002).
Education: Percent of population age 25 and over with: High school diploma (including GED) or higher: 74.9% (2004); Bachelor's degree or higher: 13.7% (2004); Master's degree or higher: 5.3% (2004).
Housing: Homeownership rate: 80.1% (2004); Median home value: $82,338 (2004); Median rent: $372 per month (2000); Median age of housing: 18 years (2000).
Health: Birth rate: 100.5 per 10,000 population (2004); Death rate: 142.6 per 10,000 population (2004); Age adjusted cancer mortality rate: 173.7 deaths per 100,000 population (2002); Air Quality Index: 95.9% good, 4.1% moderate, 0.0% unhealthy for sensitive individuals, 0.0% unhealthy (percent of days in 2004); Number of physicians: 18.2 per 10,000 population (2001); Hospital beds: 34.7 per 10,000 population (2002); Hospital admissions: 1,775.9 per 10,000 population (2002).
Elections: 2004 Presidential election results: 62.4% Bush, 37.0% Kerry, 0.5% Nader, 0.1% Badnarik
National and State Parks: Highlands Hammock State Park; Lake June-in-Winter Scrub State Park
Additional Information Contacts
Highlands County Government Offices . . . . (863) 386-6517
Avon Park Area Board of Realtors. (863) 452-6777
Avon Park Chamber of Commerce . . . . (863) 453-3350
Highlands Association of Realtors . . . . (863) 385-6014
Lake Placid Board of Realtors . . . . (863) 465-3444
Lake Placid Chamber of Commerce . . . . (863) 465-4331
Sebring Chamber of Commerce . . . . (863) 385-8448

Highlands County Communities

AVON PARK (city). Covers a land area of 4.638 square miles and a water area of 1.017 square miles. Located at 27.59° N. Lat.; 81.50° W. Long. Elevation is 149 feet.
History: Avon Park was established in 1886 by the Florida Development Company. O.M. Crosby, president of the company, brought settlers from England who named the town for the Avon River in England. The town declined between 1885 and 1912, when construction of the Atlantic Coast Line Railroad brought new growth. Avon Park was incorporated in 1913.
Population: 8,134 (1990); 8,542 (2000); 8,436 (2004); 8,475 (2009 projected); Race: 55.5% White, 31.6% Black, 0.7% Asian, 22.2% Hispanic of any race (2004); Density: 1,819.0 persons per square mile (2004); Average household size: 2.69 (2004); Median age: 35.1 (2004); Male/female ratio: 98.0 (2004); Marriage status: 27.2% never married, 52.0% now married, 11.6% widowed, 9.2% divorced (2000); Foreign born: 14.3% (2000); Ancestry (includes multiple ancestries): 43.0% Other groups, 10.1% United States or American, 8.1% German, 7.3% Irish, 7.3% English (2000).
Economy: Single-family building permits issued: 12 (2004); Multi-family building permits issued: 0 (2004); Employment by occupation: 5.1% management, 9.5% professional, 26.7% services, 18.9% sales, 15.9% farming, 9.2% construction, 14.7% production (2000).
Income: Per capita income: $12,184 (2004); Median household income: $23,994 (2004); Average household income: $32,080 (2004); Percent of

households with income of $100,000 or more: 3.2% (2004); Poverty rate: 27.6% (2000).
Taxes: Total city taxes per capita: $377 (2002); City property taxes per capita: $143 (2002).
Education: Percent of population age 25 and over with: High school diploma (including GED) or higher: 62.1% (2004); Bachelor's degree or higher: 7.8% (2004); Master's degree or higher: 3.0% (2004).

School District(s)

Highlands County School District (PK-12)
2002-03 Enrollment: 11,428 . . . . (863) 471-5564

Two-year College(s)

South Florida Community College (Public)
2003-04 Enrollment: 2,634 . . . . (863) 453-6661
2003-04 Tuition: In-state $1,695; Out-of-state $6,395

Housing: Homeownership rate: 60.7% (2004); Median home value: $56,526 (2004); Median rent: $349 per month (2000); Median age of housing: 31 years (2000).
Safety: Violent crime rate: 88.7 per 10,000 population; Property crime rate: 367.5 per 10,000 population (2003).
Transportation: Commute to work: 93.1% car, 1.1% public transportation, 2.4% walk, 1.9% work from home (2000); Travel time to work: 37.8% less than 15 minutes, 33.6% 15 to 30 minutes, 15.8% 30 to 45 minutes, 3.9% 45 to 60 minutes, 8.9% 60 minutes or more (2000)
Airports: Avon Park Municipal

Additional Information Contacts

Avon Park Area Board of Realtors. (863) 452-6777
Avon Park Chamber of Commerce . . . . (863) 453-3350
Local Government Offices . . . . (863) 452-4400

LAKE PLACID (town). Covers a land area of 2.565 square miles and a water area of 0.270 square miles. Located at 27.29° N. Lat.; 81.36° W. Long. Elevation is 136 feet.
History: Lake Placid was called Lake Stearns when it was founded in 1924 as part of a land and citrus orchard development. It was later named for the Lake Placid Club of New York, which founded a branch here.
Population: 1,386 (1990); 1,668 (2000); 1,669 (2004); 1,680 (2009 projected); Race: 74.7% White, 10.3% Black, 0.8% Asian, 35.3% Hispanic of any race (2004); Density: 650.6 persons per square mile (2004); Average household size: 2.58 (2004); Median age: 33.8 (2004); Male/female ratio: 97.7 (2004); Marriage status: 22.8% never married, 56.6% now married, 7.0% widowed, 13.6% divorced (2000); Foreign born: 26.7% (2000); Ancestry (includes multiple ancestries): 47.2% Other groups, 9.7% German, 9.6% English, 8.1% United States or American, 6.2% Irish (2000).
Economy: Employment by occupation: 6.6% management, 9.5% professional, 20.5% services, 13.0% sales, 22.9% farming, 14.2% construction, 13.3% production (2000).
Income: Per capita income: $11,973 (2004); Median household income: $22,597 (2004); Average household income: $30,869 (2004); Percent of households with income of $100,000 or more: 4.3% (2004); Poverty rate: 34.7% (2000).
Taxes: Total city taxes per capita: $234 (2002); City property taxes per capita: $234 (2002).
Education: Percent of population age 25 and over with: High school diploma (including GED) or higher: 56.9% (2004); Bachelor's degree or higher: 7.1% (2004); Master's degree or higher: 2.2% (2004).

School District(s)

Highlands County School District (PK-12)
2002-03 Enrollment: 11,428 . . . . (863) 471-5564

Housing: Homeownership rate: 49.0% (2004); Median home value: $82,321 (2004); Median rent: $334 per month (2000); Median age of housing: 20 years (2000).
Hospitals: Florida Hospital Lake Placid
Safety: Violent crime rate: 138.6 per 10,000 population; Property crime rate: 871.8 per 10,000 population (2003).
Newspapers: Lake Placid Journal (General - Circulation 6,500)
Transportation: Commute to work: 90.6% car, 0.9% public transportation, 5.2% walk, 1.7% work from home (2000); Travel time to work: 34.6% less than 15 minutes, 42.9% 15 to 30 minutes, 17.1% 30 to 45 minutes, 1.8% 45 to 60 minutes, 3.7% 60 minutes or more (2000)

Additional Information Contacts

Lake Placid Board of Realtors . . . . (863) 465-3444
Lake Placid Chamber of Commerce . . . . (863) 465-4331

LORIDA (unincorporated postal area, zip code 33857). Covers a land area of 161.488 square miles and a water area of 0.785 square miles. Located at 27.39° N. Lat.; 81.14° W. Long. Elevation is 49 feet.
Population: 1,645 (2000); Race: 88.6% White, 8.0% Black, 0.0% Asian, 5.2% Hispanic of any race (2000); Density: 10.2 persons per square mile (2000); Age: 20.0% under 18, 28.2% over 64 (2000); Marriage status: 22.1% never married, 57.6% now married, 9.1% widowed, 11.1% divorced (2000); Foreign born: 2.2% (2000); Ancestry (includes multiple ancestries): 21.5% German, 21.3% Other groups, 16.2% Irish, 13.3% United States or American, 8.1% English (2000).
Economy: Employment by occupation: 0.0% management, 9.0% professional, 15.8% services, 27.6% sales, 14.8% farming, 8.1% construction, 24.6% production (2000).
Income: Per capita income: $12,998 (2000); Median household income: $23,500 (2000); Poverty rate: 16.8% (2000).
Education: Percent of population age 25 and over with: High school diploma (including GED) or higher: 62.9% (2000); Bachelor's degree or higher: 8.4% (2000).
Housing: Homeownership rate: 78.0% (2000); Median home value: $91,200 (2000); Median rent: $369 per month (2000); Median age of housing: 22 years (2000).
Transportation: Commute to work: 90.5% car, 0.0% public transportation, 5.3% walk, 4.1% work from home (2000); Travel time to work: 12.7% less than 15 minutes, 38.4% 15 to 30 minutes, 39.7% 30 to 45 minutes, 3.6% 45 to 60 minutes, 5.6% 60 minutes or more (2000)

PLACID LAKES (CDP). Covers a land area of 18.295 square miles and a water area of 0.024 square miles. Located at 27.25° N. Lat.; 81.40° W. Long.
Population: 2,045 (1990); 3,054 (2000); 3,071 (2004); 3,090 (2009 projected); Race: 87.1% White, 6.8% Black, 1.4% Asian, 12.7% Hispanic of any race (2004); Density: 167.9 persons per square mile (2004); Average household size: 2.27 (2004); Median age: 51.5 (2004); Male/female ratio: 92.4 (2004); Marriage status: 9.4% never married, 72.6% now married, 10.8% widowed, 7.3% divorced (2000); Foreign born: 7.5% (2000); Ancestry (includes multiple ancestries): 15.3% Other groups, 13.8% German, 11.8% United States or American, 10.9% Irish, 10.4% English (2000).
Economy: Employment by occupation: 11.9% management, 13.8% professional, 23.7% services, 29.4% sales, 1.7% farming, 6.6% construction, 13.0% production (2000).
Income: Per capita income: $19,071 (2004); Median household income: $34,230 (2004); Average household income: $43,223 (2004); Percent of households with income of $100,000 or more: 6.1% (2004); Poverty rate: 6.0% (2000).
Education: Percent of population age 25 and over with: High school diploma (including GED) or higher: 77.7% (2004); Bachelor's degree or higher: 12.8% (2004); Master's degree or higher: 3.6% (2004).
Housing: Homeownership rate: 84.7% (2004); Median home value: $108,313 (2004); Median rent: $451 per month (2000); Median age of housing: 15 years (2000).
Transportation: Commute to work: 98.5% car, 0.0% public transportation, 0.5% walk, 0.0% work from home (2000); Travel time to work: 32.0% less than 15 minutes, 38.9% 15 to 30 minutes, 12.6% 30 to 45 minutes, 7.0% 45 to 60 minutes, 9.5% 60 minutes or more (2000)

SEBRING (city). Covers a land area of 5.132 square miles and a water area of 5.875 square miles. Located at 27.49° N. Lat.; 81.44° W. Long. Elevation is 131 feet.
History: Sebring was founded in 1912 by George Eugene Sebring, a pottery manufacturer from Ohio who purchased the townsite and laid out the city with streets radiating from a central park.
Population: 9,238 (1990); 9,667 (2000); 9,638 (2004); 9,705 (2009 projected); Race: 72.9% White, 17.6% Black, 0.8% Asian, 12.7% Hispanic of any race (2004); Density: 1,878.0 persons per square mile (2004); Average household size: 2.46 (2004); Median age: 42.3 (2004); Male/female ratio: 92.4 (2004); Marriage status: 23.1% never married, 48.5% now married, 15.2% widowed, 13.2% divorced (2000); Foreign born: 7.5% (2000); Ancestry (includes multiple ancestries): 29.5% Other groups, 11.6% German, 10.7% Irish, 10.3% United States or American, 8.8% English (2000).
Economy: Single-family building permits issued: 48 (2004); Multi-family building permits issued: 12 (2004); Employment by occupation: 10.0%

management, 12.8% professional, 21.0% services, 29.4% sales, 5.3% farming, 9.4% construction, 12.2% production (2000).
Income: Per capita income: $16,112 (2004); Median household income: $25,583 (2004); Average household income: $38,127 (2004); Percent of households with income of $100,000 or more: 5.7% (2004); Poverty rate: 23.5% (2000).
Taxes: Total city taxes per capita: $453 (2002); City property taxes per capita: $203 (2002).
Education: Percent of population age 25 and over with: High school diploma (including GED) or higher: 67.9% (2004); Bachelor's degree or higher: 14.1% (2004); Master's degree or higher: 6.3% (2004).

School District(s)

Highlands County School District (PK-12)
2002-03 Enrollment: 11,428 . . . . (863) 471-5564
Housing: Homeownership rate: 59.1% (2004); Median home value: $71,093 (2004); Median rent: $359 per month (2000); Median age of housing: 31 years (2000).
Hospitals: Highlands Regional Medical Center (126 beds)
Safety: Violent crime rate: 147.4 per 10,000 population; Property crime rate: 747.2 per 10,000 population (2003).
Newspapers: Highlands Today (Circulation 41,200); The News-Sun (General - Circulation 18,100)
Transportation: Commute to work: 92.1% car, 0.6% public transportation, 3.6% walk, 1.3% work from home (2000); Travel time to work: 45.0% less than 15 minutes, 39.7% 15 to 30 minutes, 9.7% 30 to 45 minutes, 1.5% 45 to 60 minutes, 4.2% 60 minutes or more (2000); Amtrak: Service available.
Additional Information Contacts
Highlands Association of Realtors . . . . (863) 385-6014
Local Government Offices . . . . (863) 471-5100
Sebring Chamber of Commerce . . . . (863) 385-8448

SYLVAN SHORES (CDP). Covers a land area of 2.231 square miles and a water area of 0.584 square miles. Located at 27.31° N. Lat.; 81.35° W. Long.
Population: 2,067 (1990); 2,424 (2000); 2,416 (2004); 2,435 (2009 projected); Race: 95.2% White, 2.2% Black, 0.2% Asian, 6.5% Hispanic of any race (2004); Density: 1,082.8 persons per square mile (2004); Average household size: 2.09 (2004); Median age: 62.0 (2004); Male/female ratio: 88.2 (2004); Marriage status: 10.4% never married, 70.0% now married, 13.4% widowed, 6.2% divorced (2000); Foreign born: 5.7% (2000); Ancestry (includes multiple ancestries): 16.7% United States or American, 15.9% German, 15.2% Irish, 13.6% English, 13.0% Other groups (2000).
Economy: Employment by occupation: 7.9% management, 13.7% professional, 25.4% services, 31.4% sales, 8.0% farming, 8.7% construction, 4.9% production (2000).
Income: Per capita income: $18,931 (2004); Median household income: $32,215 (2004); Average household income: $39,634 (2004); Percent of households with income of $100,000 or more: 3.8% (2004); Poverty rate: 11.2% (2000).
Education: Percent of population age 25 and over with: High school diploma (including GED) or higher: 77.9% (2004); Bachelor's degree or higher: 9.5% (2004); Master's degree or higher: 2.7% (2004).
Housing: Homeownership rate: 94.1% (2004); Median home value: $73,132 (2004); Median rent: $468 per month (2000); Median age of housing: 19 years (2000).
Transportation: Commute to work: 88.0% car, 0.0% public transportation, 2.9% walk, 9.1% work from home (2000); Travel time to work: 51.1% less than 15 minutes, 28.6% 15 to 30 minutes, 11.0% 30 to 45 minutes, 0.6% 45 to 60 minutes, 8.6% 60 minutes or more (2000)

VENUS (unincorporated postal area, zip code 33960). Covers a land area of 176.301 square miles and a water area of 0.172 square miles. Located at 27.05° N. Lat.; 81.39° W. Long. Elevation is 105 feet.
History: The community of Venus was named for the Roman goddess of gardens and beauty.
Population: 701 (2000); Race: 90.5% White, 3.7% Black, 3.8% Asian, 7.5% Hispanic of any race (2000); Density: 4.0 persons per square mile (2000); Age: 22.0% under 18, 18.2% over 64 (2000); Marriage status: 15.1% never married, 70.2% now married, 5.2% widowed, 9.5% divorced (2000); Foreign born: 6.6% (2000); Ancestry (includes multiple ancestries): 21.0% United States or American, 13.8% Other groups, 10.7% Irish, 7.5% English, 6.6% Scotch-Irish (2000).
Economy: Employment by occupation: 12.8% management, 5.6% professional, 4.9% services, 23.4% sales, 14.8% farming, 14.8% construction, 23.7% production (2000).
Income: Per capita income: $16,981 (2000); Median household income: $27,875 (2000); Poverty rate: 22.5% (2000).
Education: Percent of population age 25 and over with: High school diploma (including GED) or higher: 62.4% (2000); Bachelor's degree or higher: 7.8% (2000).
Housing: Homeownership rate: 84.1% (2000); Median home value: $27,800 (2000); Median rent: $332 per month (2000); Median age of housing: 22 years (2000).
Transportation: Commute to work: 87.7% car, 0.0% public transportation, 7.6% walk, 4.7% work from home (2000); Travel time to work: 31.8% less than 15 minutes, 14.0% 15 to 30 minutes, 30.7% 30 to 45 minutes, 5.7% 45 to 60 minutes, 17.8% 60 minutes or more (2000)

Hillsborough County

Located in western Florida, on the Gulf Coast; bounded on the south and partly on the west by Tampa Bay; drained by the Hillsboro River; includes many small lakes. Covers a land area of 1,050.90 square miles, a water area of 215.30 square miles, and is located in the Eastern Time Zone. The county government was organized in 1834. County seat is Tampa.

Hillsborough County is part of the Tampa-St. Petersburg-Clearwater, FL Metropolitan Statistical Area. The entire metro area includes: Hernando County, FL; Hillsborough County, FL; Pasco County, FL; Pinellas County, FL

Weather Station: Plant City — Elevation: 118 feet

	Jan	Feb	Mar	Apr	May	Jun	Jul	Aug	Sep	Oct	Nov	Dec
High	73	75	79	84	89	91	92	91	90	85	80	75
Low	49	51	55	59	65	70	72	72	71	65	57	51
Precip	2.7	3.2	3.6	2.1	3.8	7.0	7.4	7.8	6.6	2.4	2.1	2.6
Snow	0.0	0.0	0.0	0.0	0.0	0.0	0.0	0.0	0.0	0.0	0.0	0.0

High and Low temperatures in degrees Fahrenheit; Precipitation and Snow in inches

Weather Station: Tampa Int'l Airport — Elevation: 16 feet

	Jan	Feb	Mar	Apr	May	Jun	Jul	Aug	Sep	Oct	Nov	Dec
High	71	72	77	82	87	90	91	91	89	84	78	73
Low	51	52	57	61	68	73	75	75	73	66	59	53
Precip	2.3	2.8	3.0	1.8	3.0	5.4	6.3	7.7	6.5	2.3	1.6	2.3
Snow	tr	0.0	tr	tr	0.0	0.0	tr	0.0	0.0	0.0	0.0	tr

High and Low temperatures in degrees Fahrenheit; Precipitation and Snow in inches

Population: 834,054 (1990); 998,948 (2000); 1,099,832 (2004); 1,226,798 (2009 projected); Race: 72.7% White, 16.2% Black, 2.5% Asian, 20.4% Hispanic of any race (2004); Density: 1,046.6 persons per square mile (2004); Average household size: 2.55 (2004); Median age: 35.7 (2004); Male/female ratio: 96.3 (2004).
Religion: Five largest groups: 16.6% Catholic Church, 10.3% Southern Baptist Convention, 3.3% The United Methodist Church, 2.0% Jewish Estimate, 1.0% Presbyterian Church (U.S.A.) (2000).
Economy: Unemployment rate: 3.8% (2004); Total civilian labor force: 639,337 (2004); Leading industries: 12.9% retail trade; 11.4% health care and social assistance; 10.8% administration, support, waste management, remediation services (2003); Companies that employ 500 or more persons: 96 (2003); Companies that employ 100 to 499 persons: 777 (2003); Companies that employ less than 100 persons: 28,169 (2003); Farms: 2,969 totaling 284,910 acres (2002); Minority business ownership rate: 21.9% (1997); Women business ownership rate: 25.4% (1997); Retail sales per capita: $12,018 (1997). Single-family building permits issued: 11,236 (2004); Multi-family building permits issued: 2,477 (2004).
Income: Per capita income: $24,307 (2004); Median household income: $45,001 (2004); Average household income: $61,288 (2004); Percent of households with income of $100,000 or more: 14.4% (2004); Poverty rate: 12.5% (2002); Bankruptcy rate: 6.00% (2004).
Taxes: Total county taxes per capita: $576 (2002); County property taxes per capita: $415 (2002).
Education: Percent of population age 25 and over with: High school diploma (including GED) or higher: 81.3% (2004); Bachelor's degree or higher: 25.9% (2004); Master's degree or higher: 8.7% (2004).
Housing: Homeownership rate: 64.0% (2004); Median home value: $133,340 (2004); Median rent: $532 per month (2000); Median age of housing: 20 years (2000).
Health: Birth rate: 144.2 per 10,000 population (2004); Death rate: 80.7 per 10,000 population (2004); Age adjusted cancer mortality rate: 205.7 deaths per 100,000 population (2002); Air Quality Index: 66.1% good, 33.1% moderate, 0.5% unhealthy for sensitive individuals, 0.3% unhealthy

(percent of days in 2004); Number of physicians: 30.2 per 10,000 population (2001); Hospital beds: 34.5 per 10,000 population (2002); Hospital admissions: 1,505.5 per 10,000 population (2002).
Elections: 2004 Presidential election results: 53.0% Bush, 46.2% Kerry, 0.4% Nader, 0.2% Badnarik
National and State Parks: Alafia River State Park; Egmont Key National Wildlife Refuge; Hillsborough River State Park; Little Manatee River State Park; Skyway Fishing Pier State Park; Ybor City Museum State Park
Additional Information Contacts
Hillsborough County Government Offices . . . . (813) 272-5750
Apollo Beach Chamber of Commerce . . . . (813) 645-1366
Brandon Chamber of Commerce . . . . (813) 689-1221
Florida Gulfcoast Commercial Association of Realtors . . . . (813) 969-4227
Greater Riverview Chamber . . . . (813) 643-8000
Greater Tampa Association of Realtors . . . . (813) 879-7010
Hispanic Chamber of Commerce . . . . (813) 414-9411
Land O' Lakes Board of Realtors . . . . (813) 962-1962
North Tampa Chamber of Commerce . . . . (813) 961-2420
Plant City Chamber of Commerce . . . . (813) 754-3707
Ruskin Chamber of Commerce . . . . (813) 645-3808
Seffner Chamber of Commerce . . . . (813)-627-8686
South Tampa Chamber of Commerce . . . . (813) 837-8972
Sun City Chamber of Commerce . . . . (813) 634-5111
Tampa Chamber of Commerce . . . . (813) 228-7777
Town 'n' Country Chamber of Commerce . . . . (813) 884-5344
West Tampa Chamber of Commerce . . . . (813) 253-2056
Ybor City Chamber of Commerce . . . . (813) 248-3712

Hillsborough County Communities

APOLLO BEACH (CDP). Covers a land area of 5.690 square miles and a water area of 0.215 square miles. Located at 27.77° N. Lat.; 82.41° W. Long.
Population: 6,025 (1990); 7,444 (2000); 7,787 (2004); 8,284 (2009 projected); Race: 92.7% White, 1.0% Black, 1.5% Asian, 9.0% Hispanic of any race (2004); Density: 1,368.6 persons per square mile (2004); Average household size: 2.35 (2004); Median age: 47.2 (2004); Male/female ratio: 100.1 (2004); Marriage status: 11.7% never married, 69.1% now married, 7.5% widowed, 11.8% divorced (2000); Foreign born: 7.8% (2000); Ancestry (includes multiple ancestries): 18.6% German, 16.5% Other groups, 16.1% Irish, 15.1% English, 7.6% Italian (2000).
Economy: Manufacturing includes marine rescue equipment. Employment by occupation: 19.9% management, 18.8% professional, 9.4% services, 33.4% sales, 0.2% farming, 7.7% construction, 10.6% production (2000).
Income: Per capita income: $32,076 (2004); Median household income: $57,824 (2004); Average household income: $75,460 (2004); Percent of households with income of $100,000 or more: 22.9% (2004); Poverty rate: 4.1% (2000).
Education: Percent of population age 25 and over with: High school diploma (including GED) or higher: 87.4% (2004); Bachelor's degree or higher: 21.0% (2004); Master's degree or higher: 7.5% (2004).
School District(s)
Hillsborough County School District (PK-12)
2002-03 Enrollment: 175,454 . . . . (813) 272-4050
Housing: Homeownership rate: 87.2% (2004); Median home value: $163,391 (2004); Median rent: $525 per month (2000); Median age of housing: 19 years (2000).
Transportation: Commute to work: 93.7% car, 0.2% public transportation, 0.4% walk, 4.3% work from home (2000); Travel time to work: 19.8% less than 15 minutes, 33.2% 15 to 30 minutes, 24.5% 30 to 45 minutes, 15.0% 45 to 60 minutes, 7.4% 60 minutes or more (2000)
Additional Information Contacts
Apollo Beach Chamber of Commerce . . . . (813) 645-1366

BLOOMINGDALE (CDP). Covers a land area of 7.829 square miles and a water area of 0.065 square miles. Located at 27.88° N. Lat.; 82.26° W. Long. Elevation is 54 feet.
Population: 14,129 (1990); 19,839 (2000); 20,890 (2004); 22,304 (2009 projected); Race: 86.3% White, 7.7% Black, 2.4% Asian, 7.9% Hispanic of any race (2004); Density: 2,668.2 persons per square mile (2004); Average household size: 2.99 (2004); Median age: 36.3 (2004); Male/female ratio: 98.2 (2004); Marriage status: 19.5% never married, 70.1% now married, 2.5% widowed, 7.9% divorced (2000); Foreign born: 6.5% (2000); Ancestry (includes multiple ancestries): 20.9% Other groups, 19.3% German, 16.2% Irish, 14.7% English, 8.7% Italian (2000).
Economy: Employment by occupation: 21.6% management, 24.5% professional, 10.1% services, 32.3% sales, 0.1% farming, 6.0% construction, 5.4% production (2000).
Income: Per capita income: $31,196 (2004); Median household income: $77,687 (2004); Average household income: $93,289 (2004); Percent of households with income of $100,000 or more: 33.4% (2004); Poverty rate: 3.3% (2000).
Education: Percent of population age 25 and over with: High school diploma (including GED) or higher: 94.9% (2004); Bachelor's degree or higher: 38.1% (2004); Master's degree or higher: 13.7% (2004).
Housing: Homeownership rate: 87.6% (2004); Median home value: $175,883 (2004); Median rent: $664 per month (2000); Median age of housing: 12 years (2000).
Transportation: Commute to work: 93.2% car, 1.0% public transportation, 0.5% walk, 4.3% work from home (2000); Travel time to work: 14.3% less than 15 minutes, 33.8% 15 to 30 minutes, 28.8% 30 to 45 minutes, 13.7% 45 to 60 minutes, 9.5% 60 minutes or more (2000)

BOYETTE (CDP). Covers a land area of 6.601 square miles and a water area of 0.288 square miles. Located at 27.84° N. Lat.; 82.28° W. Long. Elevation is 80 feet.
Population: 3,451 (1990); 5,895 (2000); 7,286 (2004); 8,963 (2009 projected); Race: 87.3% White, 6.6% Black, 1.4% Asian, 9.1% Hispanic of any race (2004); Density: 1,103.8 persons per square mile (2004); Average household size: 3.07 (2004); Median age: 36.0 (2004); Male/female ratio: 101.3 (2004); Marriage status: 19.0% never married, 63.9% now married, 5.8% widowed, 11.3% divorced (2000); Foreign born: 5.5% (2000); Ancestry (includes multiple ancestries): 19.9% Other groups, 16.8% German, 14.5% Irish, 13.4% English, 11.8% United States or American (2000).
Economy: Employment by occupation: 14.9% management, 18.1% professional, 8.3% services, 35.0% sales, 0.0% farming, 10.8% construction, 12.8% production (2000).
Income: Per capita income: $23,874 (2004); Median household income: $65,385 (2004); Average household income: $73,208 (2004); Percent of households with income of $100,000 or more: 22.0% (2004); Poverty rate: 5.9% (2000).
Education: Percent of population age 25 and over with: High school diploma (including GED) or higher: 83.3% (2004); Bachelor's degree or higher: 20.2% (2004); Master's degree or higher: 6.4% (2004).
Housing: Homeownership rate: 90.2% (2004); Median home value: $163,983 (2004); Median rent: $1,008 per month (2000); Median age of housing: 12 years (2000).
Transportation: Commute to work: 93.2% car, 0.9% public transportation, 0.9% walk, 4.6% work from home (2000); Travel time to work: 11.4% less than 15 minutes, 39.1% 15 to 30 minutes, 33.4% 30 to 45 minutes, 10.4% 45 to 60 minutes, 5.7% 60 minutes or more (2000)

BRANDON (CDP). Covers a land area of 28.719 square miles and a water area of 0.568 square miles. Located at 27.93° N. Lat.; 82.28° W. Long. Elevation is 48 feet.
History: Named for John Brandon, who moved to Florida in 1857 and homesteaded at this place in 1874. Experienced significant developmental and population growth, particularly due to the construction of new highways connecting it to other Florida urban centers.
Population: 57,304 (1990); 77,895 (2000); 89,337 (2004); 103,484 (2009 projected); Race: 77.4% White, 12.3% Black, 2.6% Asian, 15.7% Hispanic of any race (2004); Density: 3,110.8 persons per square mile (2004); Average household size: 2.67 (2004); Median age: 34.5 (2004); Male/female ratio: 94.5 (2004); Marriage status: 22.9% never married, 62.3% now married, 4.4% widowed, 10.4% divorced (2000); Foreign born: 7.6% (2000); Ancestry (includes multiple ancestries): 27.1% Other groups, 14.4% German, 12.5% Irish, 11.4% English, 8.5% United States or American (2000).
Economy: Chiefly a residential suburb, it is also a retail and service center. Citrus fruits and vegetables are grown in the area, which also has cattle and dairy farms. Employment by occupation: 15.3% management, 21.5% professional, 12.1% services, 34.9% sales, 0.3% farming, 7.2% construction, 8.7% production (2000).
Income: Per capita income: $24,619 (2004); Median household income: $56,614 (2004); Average household income: $65,182 (2004); Percent of households with income of $100,000 or more: 14.8% (2004); Poverty rate: 5.4% (2000).

Education: Percent of population age 25 and over with: High school diploma (including GED) or higher: 89.3% (2004); Bachelor's degree or higher: 25.9% (2004); Master's degree or higher: 7.4% (2004).

School District(s)

Hillsborough County School District (PK-12)
2002-03 Enrollment: 175,454 .... (813) 272-4050

Housing: Homeownership rate: 69.3% (2004); Median home value: $141,276 (2004); Median rent: $630 per month (2000); Median age of housing: 16 years (2000).

Hospitals: Brandon Regional Hospital (277 beds)

Newspapers: South Tampa News (General - Circulation 34,000)

Transportation: Commute to work: 94.8% car, 0.5% public transportation, 1.0% walk, 3.1% work from home (2000); Travel time to work: 22.9% less than 15 minutes, 34.5% 15 to 30 minutes, 25.8% 30 to 45 minutes, 10.8% 45 to 60 minutes, 6.0% 60 minutes or more (2000)

Additional Information Contacts

Brandon Chamber of Commerce .... (813) 689-1221

CHEVAL (CDP). Covers a land area of 6.683 square miles and a water area of 0.161 square miles. Located at 28.14° N. Lat.; 82.51° W. Long.

Population: 3,544 (1990); 7,602 (2000); 9,185 (2004); 11,103 (2009 projected); Race: 83.6% White, 5.6% Black, 6.1% Asian, 15.6% Hispanic of any race (2004); Density: 1,374.3 persons per square mile (2004); Average household size: 2.29 (2004); Median age: 36.2 (2004); Male/female ratio: 95.9 (2004); Marriage status: 22.5% never married, 58.6% now married, 5.7% widowed, 13.2% divorced (2000); Foreign born: 8.9% (2000); Ancestry (includes multiple ancestries): 25.9% Other groups, 17.5% German, 14.0% English, 13.2% Irish, 11.0% Italian (2000).

Economy: Employment by occupation: 23.1% management, 21.4% professional, 6.9% services, 36.7% sales, 0.7% farming, 4.6% construction, 6.8% production (2000).

Income: Per capita income: $40,480 (2004); Median household income: $63,694 (2004); Average household income: $92,559 (2004); Percent of households with income of $100,000 or more: 27.1% (2004); Poverty rate: 4.9% (2000).

Education: Percent of population age 25 and over with: High school diploma (including GED) or higher: 91.3% (2004); Bachelor's degree or higher: 41.3% (2004); Master's degree or higher: 12.6% (2004).

Housing: Homeownership rate: 41.7% (2004); Median home value: $259,468 (2004); Median rent: $631 per month (2000); Median age of housing: 10 years (2000).

Transportation: Commute to work: 96.5% car, 0.0% public transportation, 0.1% walk, 2.6% work from home (2000); Travel time to work: 11.1% less than 15 minutes, 34.2% 15 to 30 minutes, 31.6% 30 to 45 minutes, 16.2% 45 to 60 minutes, 7.0% 60 minutes or more (2000)

CITRUS PARK (CDP). Covers a land area of 10.572 square miles and a water area of 0.315 square miles. Located at 28.07° N. Lat.; 82.55° W. Long. Elevation is 45 feet.

Population: 15,020 (1990); 20,226 (2000); 21,637 (2004); 23,528 (2009 projected); Race: 79.4% White, 8.6% Black, 3.4% Asian, 23.6% Hispanic of any race (2004); Density: 2,046.5 persons per square mile (2004); Average household size: 2.84 (2004); Median age: 35.1 (2004); Male/female ratio: 97.0 (2004); Marriage status: 21.9% never married, 62.0% now married, 4.5% widowed, 11.5% divorced (2000); Foreign born: 11.8% (2000); Ancestry (includes multiple ancestries): 30.6% Other groups, 14.1% German, 11.0% Irish, 10.8% English, 10.4% United States or American (2000).

Economy: Employment by occupation: 17.2% management, 20.6% professional, 10.6% services, 35.8% sales, 0.3% farming, 7.2% construction, 8.4% production (2000).

Income: Per capita income: $25,288 (2004); Median household income: $61,710 (2004); Average household income: $71,524 (2004); Percent of households with income of $100,000 or more: 19.2% (2004); Poverty rate: 6.3% (2000).

Education: Percent of population age 25 and over with: High school diploma (including GED) or higher: 85.9% (2004); Bachelor's degree or higher: 29.2% (2004); Master's degree or higher: 7.9% (2004).

Housing: Homeownership rate: 83.6% (2004); Median home value: $145,794 (2004); Median rent: $636 per month (2000); Median age of housing: 14 years (2000).

Transportation: Commute to work: 94.2% car, 0.7% public transportation, 0.7% walk, 3.8% work from home (2000); Travel time to work: 14.6% less than 15 minutes, 40.8% 15 to 30 minutes, 28.4% 30 to 45 minutes, 10.9% 45 to 60 minutes, 5.3% 60 minutes or more (2000)

DOVER (CDP). Covers a land area of 2.613 square miles and a water area of 0.029 square miles. Located at 27.99° N. Lat.; 82.21° W. Long. Elevation is 102 feet.

Population: 2,606 (1990); 2,798 (2000); 2,857 (2004); 2,964 (2009 projected); Race: 75.5% White, 0.5% Black, 0.7% Asian, 58.4% Hispanic of any race (2004); Density: 1,093.3 persons per square mile (2004); Average household size: 3.82 (2004); Median age: 28.3 (2004); Male/female ratio: 114.7 (2004); Marriage status: 27.4% never married, 60.7% now married, 3.7% widowed, 8.3% divorced (2000); Foreign born: 29.5% (2000); Ancestry (includes multiple ancestries): 46.8% Other groups, 16.7% United States or American, 8.4% English, 4.4% German, 4.1% Irish (2000).

Economy: Employment by occupation: 4.9% management, 7.2% professional, 15.5% services, 15.5% sales, 11.9% farming, 28.8% construction, 16.2% production (2000).

Income: Per capita income: $10,153 (2004); Median household income: $32,937 (2004); Average household income: $37,543 (2004); Percent of households with income of $100,000 or more: 2.8% (2004); Poverty rate: 28.0% (2000).

Education: Percent of population age 25 and over with: High school diploma (including GED) or higher: 46.9% (2004); Bachelor's degree or higher: 4.1% (2004); Master's degree or higher: 1.8% (2004).

School District(s)

Hillsborough County School District (PK-12)
2002-03 Enrollment: 175,454 .... (813) 272-4050

Housing: Homeownership rate: 70.7% (2004); Median home value: $76,383 (2004); Median rent: $411 per month (2000); Median age of housing: 25 years (2000).

Transportation: Commute to work: 94.7% car, 0.0% public transportation, 0.0% walk, 1.6% work from home (2000); Travel time to work: 34.0% less than 15 minutes, 34.9% 15 to 30 minutes, 19.7% 30 to 45 minutes, 8.6% 45 to 60 minutes, 2.7% 60 minutes or more (2000)

EAST LAKE-ORIENT PARK (CDP). Covers a land area of 4.380 square miles and a water area of 0.276 square miles. Located at 27.97° N. Lat.; 82.37° W. Long.

Population: 6,171 (1990); 5,703 (2000); 5,445 (2004); 5,200 (2009 projected); Race: 58.7% White, 32.7% Black, 0.6% Asian, 14.0% Hispanic of any race (2004); Density: 1,243.1 persons per square mile (2004); Average household size: 2.84 (2004); Median age: 35.1 (2004); Male/female ratio: 97.4 (2004); Marriage status: 25.6% never married, 54.5% now married, 6.3% widowed, 13.6% divorced (2000); Foreign born: 6.5% (2000); Ancestry (includes multiple ancestries): 39.9% Other groups, 11.5% United States or American, 7.1% German, 6.9% Irish, 3.3% English (2000).

Economy: Employment by occupation: 4.1% management, 10.1% professional, 15.9% services, 30.9% sales, 0.6% farming, 13.8% construction, 24.7% production (2000).

Income: Per capita income: $15,849 (2004); Median household income: $36,508 (2004); Average household income: $44,931 (2004); Percent of households with income of $100,000 or more: 7.1% (2004); Poverty rate: 14.6% (2000).

Education: Percent of population age 25 and over with: High school diploma (including GED) or higher: 67.1% (2004); Bachelor's degree or higher: 7.6% (2004); Master's degree or higher: 1.8% (2004).

Housing: Homeownership rate: 76.7% (2004); Median home value: $85,780 (2004); Median rent: $434 per month (2000); Median age of housing: 33 years (2000).

Transportation: Commute to work: 91.3% car, 1.1% public transportation, 2.5% walk, 2.7% work from home (2000); Travel time to work: 25.7% less than 15 minutes, 42.6% 15 to 30 minutes, 19.0% 30 to 45 minutes, 6.4% 45 to 60 minutes, 6.4% 60 minutes or more (2000)

EGYPT LAKE-LETO (CDP). Covers a land area of 5.969 square miles and a water area of 0.217 square miles. Located at 28.01° N. Lat.; 82.50° W. Long.

Population: 28,830 (1990); 32,782 (2000); 35,932 (2004); 39,999 (2009 projected); Race: 72.6% White, 9.7% Black, 3.9% Asian, 51.5% Hispanic of any race (2004); Density: 6,019.4 persons per square mile (2004); Average household size: 2.42 (2004); Median age: 33.5 (2004); Male/female ratio: 95.6 (2004); Marriage status: 29.9% never married, 50.1% now married, 5.2% widowed, 14.8% divorced (2000); Foreign born: 27.3% (2000); Ancestry (includes multiple ancestries): 54.6% Other groups, 7.6% German, 6.8% Irish, 6.3% Italian, 5.5% United States or American (2000).

Economy: Employment by occupation: 11.2% management, 14.8% professional, 15.5% services, 35.4% sales, 0.1% farming, 9.1% construction, 13.7% production (2000).
Income: Per capita income: $18,963 (2004); Median household income: $36,875 (2004); Average household income: $45,901 (2004); Percent of households with income of $100,000 or more: 6.5% (2004); Poverty rate: 14.4% (2000).
Education: Percent of population age 25 and over with: High school diploma (including GED) or higher: 76.3% (2004); Bachelor's degree or higher: 18.9% (2004); Master's degree or higher: 6.7% (2004).
Housing: Homeownership rate: 44.1% (2004); Median home value: $117,382 (2004); Median rent: $559 per month (2000); Median age of housing: 22 years (2000).
Transportation: Commute to work: 94.6% car, 0.9% public transportation, 1.6% walk, 1.9% work from home (2000); Travel time to work: 27.5% less than 15 minutes, 42.0% 15 to 30 minutes, 21.5% 30 to 45 minutes, 5.3% 45 to 60 minutes, 3.7% 60 minutes or more (2000)

FISH HAWK (CDP). Covers a land area of 16.345 square miles and a water area of 0.060 square miles. Located at 27.85° N. Lat.; 82.20° W. Long.
Population: 1,232 (1990); 1,991 (2000); 4,052 (2004); 6,269 (2009 projected); Race: 89.6% White, 5.6% Black, 0.6% Asian, 7.0% Hispanic of any race (2004); Density: 247.9 persons per square mile (2004); Average household size: 2.94 (2004); Median age: 35.3 (2004); Male/female ratio: 98.4 (2004); Marriage status: 13.5% never married, 71.7% now married, 3.1% widowed, 11.6% divorced (2000); Foreign born: 4.4% (2000); Ancestry (includes multiple ancestries): 18.1% Other groups, 13.7% Irish, 11.7% German, 9.9% Italian, 9.7% English (2000).
Economy: Employment by occupation: 25.1% management, 22.3% professional, 9.8% services, 22.4% sales, 0.0% farming, 6.9% construction, 13.6% production (2000).
Income: Per capita income: $31,385 (2004); Median household income: $79,771 (2004); Average household income: $92,221 (2004); Percent of households with income of $100,000 or more: 31.4% (2004); Poverty rate: 3.3% (2000).
Education: Percent of population age 25 and over with: High school diploma (including GED) or higher: 87.6% (2004); Bachelor's degree or higher: 32.6% (2004); Master's degree or higher: 18.2% (2004).
Housing: Homeownership rate: 92.0% (2004); Median home value: $216,667 (2004); Median rent: $565 per month (2000); Median age of housing: 4 years (2000).
Transportation: Commute to work: 89.4% car, 1.1% public transportation, 1.3% walk, 7.0% work from home (2000); Travel time to work: 10.5% less than 15 minutes, 27.4% 15 to 30 minutes, 39.9% 30 to 45 minutes, 18.4% 45 to 60 minutes, 3.9% 60 minutes or more (2000)

GIBSONTON (CDP). Aka East Tampa. Covers a land area of 12.851 square miles and a water area of 0.836 square miles. Located at 27.83° N. Lat.; 82.37° W. Long. Elevation is 10 feet.
History: Gibsonton was settled along the southern bank of the Alafia River, and named for the pioneer Gibson family.
Population: 8,017 (1990); 8,752 (2000); 10,108 (2004); 11,780 (2009 projected); Race: 87.2% White, 1.8% Black, 0.7% Asian, 21.1% Hispanic of any race (2004); Density: 786.5 persons per square mile (2004); Average household size: 2.85 (2004); Median age: 32.3 (2004); Male/female ratio: 105.1 (2004); Marriage status: 25.4% never married, 54.1% now married, 6.3% widowed, 14.2% divorced (2000); Foreign born: 7.4% (2000); Ancestry (includes multiple ancestries): 23.4% Other groups, 11.9% German, 9.5% United States or American, 8.8% Irish, 5.5% English (2000).
Economy: Employment by occupation: 11.9% management, 7.8% professional, 11.9% services, 25.2% sales, 3.1% farming, 20.2% construction, 20.0% production (2000).
Income: Per capita income: $17,839 (2004); Median household income: $37,268 (2004); Average household income: $50,654 (2004); Percent of households with income of $100,000 or more: 8.7% (2004); Poverty rate: 18.3% (2000).
Education: Percent of population age 25 and over with: High school diploma (including GED) or higher: 64.3% (2004); Bachelor's degree or higher: 10.0% (2004); Master's degree or higher: 3.6% (2004).

School District(s)

Hillsborough County School District (PK-12)
2002-03 Enrollment: 175,454 . . . . (813) 272-4050

Housing: Homeownership rate: 62.4% (2004); Median home value: $81,488 (2004); Median rent: $444 per month (2000); Median age of housing: 20 years (2000).
Transportation: Commute to work: 92.4% car, 0.2% public transportation, 2.8% walk, 2.4% work from home (2000); Travel time to work: 21.6% less than 15 minutes, 41.1% 15 to 30 minutes, 21.0% 30 to 45 minutes, 10.9% 45 to 60 minutes, 5.4% 60 minutes or more (2000)

GREATER CARROLLWOOD (CDP). Covers a land area of 9.569 square miles and a water area of 0.715 square miles. Located at 28.05° N. Lat.; 82.51° W. Long.
Population: 29,062 (1990); 33,519 (2000); 35,291 (2004); 37,695 (2009 projected); Race: 82.5% White, 6.8% Black, 3.7% Asian, 21.8% Hispanic of any race (2004); Density: 3,687.9 persons per square mile (2004); Average household size: 2.38 (2004); Median age: 37.8 (2004); Male/female ratio: 92.1 (2004); Marriage status: 23.9% never married, 58.5% now married, 4.4% widowed, 13.2% divorced (2000); Foreign born: 13.5% (2000); Ancestry (includes multiple ancestries): 31.0% Other groups, 13.9% German, 12.7% Irish, 10.2% English, 8.9% Italian (2000).
Economy: Employment by occupation: 18.8% management, 25.4% professional, 10.5% services, 33.8% sales, 0.1% farming, 4.6% construction, 6.7% production (2000).
Income: Per capita income: $29,905 (2004); Median household income: $53,306 (2004); Average household income: $71,194 (2004); Percent of households with income of $100,000 or more: 18.8% (2004); Poverty rate: 5.0% (2000).
Education: Percent of population age 25 and over with: High school diploma (including GED) or higher: 91.8% (2004); Bachelor's degree or higher: 42.4% (2004); Master's degree or higher: 14.8% (2004).
Housing: Homeownership rate: 70.3% (2004); Median home value: $152,280 (2004); Median rent: $646 per month (2000); Median age of housing: 17 years (2000).
Transportation: Commute to work: 94.3% car, 0.6% public transportation, 1.0% walk, 3.0% work from home (2000); Travel time to work: 19.1% less than 15 minutes, 41.1% 15 to 30 minutes, 27.5% 30 to 45 minutes, 8.2% 45 to 60 minutes, 4.1% 60 minutes or more (2000)

GREATER NORTHDALE (CDP). Covers a land area of 7.897 square miles and a water area of 0.554 square miles. Located at 28.09° N. Lat.; 82.52° W. Long.
Population: 17,957 (1990); 20,461 (2000); 21,746 (2004); 23,419 (2009 projected); Race: 84.0% White, 6.4% Black, 3.9% Asian, 17.7% Hispanic of any race (2004); Density: 2,753.7 persons per square mile (2004); Average household size: 2.62 (2004); Median age: 36.5 (2004); Male/female ratio: 92.3 (2004); Marriage status: 25.7% never married, 58.9% now married, 4.3% widowed, 11.2% divorced (2000); Foreign born: 12.0% (2000); Ancestry (includes multiple ancestries): 27.0% Other groups, 16.7% German, 14.9% Irish, 11.5% English, 11.0% Italian (2000).
Economy: Employment by occupation: 19.3% management, 24.5% professional, 10.5% services, 35.3% sales, 0.1% farming, 4.5% construction, 5.8% production (2000).
Income: Per capita income: $28,599 (2004); Median household income: $62,673 (2004); Average household income: $74,410 (2004); Percent of households with income of $100,000 or more: 19.7% (2004); Poverty rate: 4.7% (2000).
Education: Percent of population age 25 and over with: High school diploma (including GED) or higher: 92.0% (2004); Bachelor's degree or higher: 33.9% (2004); Master's degree or higher: 9.2% (2004).
Housing: Homeownership rate: 71.7% (2004); Median home value: $164,658 (2004); Median rent: $711 per month (2000); Median age of housing: 15 years (2000).
Transportation: Commute to work: 94.1% car, 0.7% public transportation, 1.1% walk, 3.5% work from home (2000); Travel time to work: 16.0% less than 15 minutes, 33.5% 15 to 30 minutes, 31.9% 30 to 45 minutes, 12.3% 45 to 60 minutes, 6.3% 60 minutes or more (2000)

GREATER SUN CENTER (CDP). Covers a land area of 12.526 square miles and a water area of 0.284 square miles. Located at 27.71° N. Lat.; 82.36° W. Long.
Population: 10,697 (1990); 16,321 (2000); 17,435 (2004); 18,897 (2009 projected); Race: 98.8% White, 0.2% Black, 0.5% Asian, 1.5% Hispanic of any race (2004); Density: 1,392.0 persons per square mile (2004); Average household size: 1.74 (2004); Median age: 75.0 (2004); Male/female ratio: 75.5 (2004); Marriage status: 2.7% never married, 72.3% now married, 19.4% widowed, 5.6% divorced (2000); Foreign born: 6.5% (2000);

Ancestry (includes multiple ancestries): 22.9% German, 20.5% English, 14.7% Irish, 5.7% United States or American, 5.0% Italian (2000).
Economy: Employment by occupation: 14.4% management, 20.7% professional, 13.1% services, 37.8% sales, 1.0% farming, 1.0% construction, 12.1% production (2000).
Income: Per capita income: $29,260 (2004); Median household income: $38,974 (2004); Average household income: $46,983 (2004); Percent of households with income of $100,000 or more: 6.1% (2004); Poverty rate: 4.6% (2000).
Education: Percent of population age 25 and over with: High school diploma (including GED) or higher: 89.1% (2004); Bachelor's degree or higher: 28.9% (2004); Master's degree or higher: 11.3% (2004).
Housing: Homeownership rate: 89.9% (2004); Median home value: $124,334 (2004); Median rent: $1,357 per month (2000); Median age of housing: 15 years (2000).
Transportation: Commute to work: 86.8% car, 0.0% public transportation, 1.1% walk, 5.7% work from home (2000); Travel time to work: 52.3% less than 15 minutes, 21.2% 15 to 30 minutes, 14.6% 30 to 45 minutes, 8.6% 45 to 60 minutes, 3.4% 60 minutes or more (2000)

KEYSTONE (CDP). Covers a land area of 36.079 square miles and a water area of 3.164 square miles. Located at 28.12° N. Lat.; 82.58° W. Long. Elevation is 40 feet.
Population: 6,412 (1990); 14,627 (2000); 19,412 (2004); 25,102 (2009 projected); Race: 89.6% White, 4.5% Black, 2.8% Asian, 9.9% Hispanic of any race (2004); Density: 538.0 persons per square mile (2004); Average household size: 2.84 (2004); Median age: 38.2 (2004); Male/female ratio: 100.4 (2004); Marriage status: 17.2% never married, 73.8% now married, 3.1% widowed, 5.8% divorced (2000); Foreign born: 8.2% (2000); Ancestry (includes multiple ancestries): 20.4% German, 18.9% Other groups, 14.9% English, 13.9% Irish, 12.1% Italian (2000).
Economy: Employment by occupation: 25.4% management, 22.8% professional, 8.0% services, 31.8% sales, 0.5% farming, 5.3% construction, 6.2% production (2000).
Income: Per capita income: $41,245 (2004); Median household income: $92,916 (2004); Average household income: $116,952 (2004); Percent of households with income of $100,000 or more: 44.7% (2004); Poverty rate: 2.4% (2000).
Education: Percent of population age 25 and over with: High school diploma (including GED) or higher: 95.0% (2004); Bachelor's degree or higher: 43.1% (2004); Master's degree or higher: 13.1% (2004).
Housing: Homeownership rate: 94.7% (2004); Median home value: $263,394 (2004); Median rent: $800 per month (2000); Median age of housing: 6 years (2000).
Transportation: Commute to work: 90.4% car, 0.1% public transportation, 0.4% walk, 7.3% work from home (2000); Travel time to work: 8.5% less than 15 minutes, 32.9% 15 to 30 minutes, 37.6% 30 to 45 minutes, 13.6% 45 to 60 minutes, 7.4% 60 minutes or more (2000)

LAKE MAGDALENE (CDP). Covers a land area of 10.576 square miles and a water area of 1.109 square miles. Located at 28.08° N. Lat.; 82.47° W. Long.
Population: 28,791 (1990); 28,755 (2000); 28,750 (2004); 29,016 (2009 projected); Race: 84.7% White, 7.1% Black, 2.5% Asian, 16.0% Hispanic of any race (2004); Density: 2,718.4 persons per square mile (2004); Average household size: 2.36 (2004); Median age: 39.6 (2004); Male/female ratio: 92.2 (2004); Marriage status: 24.3% never married, 56.4% now married, 6.5% widowed, 12.8% divorced (2000); Foreign born: 9.7% (2000); Ancestry (includes multiple ancestries): 23.6% Other groups, 15.1% German, 13.5% Irish, 11.9% English, 8.3% Italian (2000).
Economy: Employment by occupation: 14.4% management, 23.9% professional, 11.7% services, 36.0% sales, 0.1% farming, 6.7% construction, 7.2% production (2000).
Income: Per capita income: $30,017 (2004); Median household income: $48,155 (2004); Average household income: $69,945 (2004); Percent of households with income of $100,000 or more: 16.7% (2004); Poverty rate: 7.2% (2000).
Education: Percent of population age 25 and over with: High school diploma (including GED) or higher: 89.2% (2004); Bachelor's degree or higher: 33.9% (2004); Master's degree or higher: 11.4% (2004).
Housing: Homeownership rate: 70.3% (2004); Median home value: $140,604 (2004); Median rent: $560 per month (2000); Median age of housing: 20 years (2000).
Transportation: Commute to work: 95.0% car, 0.6% public transportation, 0.7% walk, 2.8% work from home (2000); Travel time to work: 18.6% less than 15 minutes, 38.7% 15 to 30 minutes, 26.7% 30 to 45 minutes, 10.1% 45 to 60 minutes, 5.8% 60 minutes or more (2000)

LITHIA (unincorporated postal area, zip code 33547). Covers a land area of 190.922 square miles and a water area of 0.605 square miles. Located at 27.78° N. Lat.; 82.15° W. Long. Elevation is 105 feet.
Population: 8,527 (2000); Race: 94.6% White, 0.3% Black, 0.4% Asian, 6.5% Hispanic of any race (2000); Density: 44.7 persons per square mile (2000); Age: 27.2% under 18, 9.1% over 64 (2000); Marriage status: 19.0% never married, 65.2% now married, 6.6% widowed, 9.2% divorced (2000); Foreign born: 4.1% (2000); Ancestry (includes multiple ancestries): 19.9% Other groups, 12.4% German, 11.1% Irish, 10.4% English, 9.5% United States or American (2000).
Economy: Employment by occupation: 15.4% management, 14.2% professional, 11.3% services, 26.0% sales, 0.8% farming, 14.2% construction, 18.1% production (2000).
Income: Per capita income: $20,284 (2000); Median household income: $47,907 (2000); Poverty rate: 9.1% (2000).
Education: Percent of population age 25 and over with: High school diploma (including GED) or higher: 79.9% (2000); Bachelor's degree or higher: 14.5% (2000).

School District(s)

Hillsborough County School District (PK-12)
2002-03 Enrollment: 175,454 . . . . (813) 272-4050
Housing: Homeownership rate: 90.2% (2000); Median home value: $123,300 (2000); Median rent: $391 per month (2000); Median age of housing: 15 years (2000).
Transportation: Commute to work: 94.0% car, 1.3% public transportation, 0.7% walk, 3.4% work from home (2000); Travel time to work: 10.2% less than 15 minutes, 30.2% 15 to 30 minutes, 36.6% 30 to 45 minutes, 13.5% 45 to 60 minutes, 9.5% 60 minutes or more (2000)

LUTZ (CDP). Covers a land area of 21.470 square miles and a water area of 2.056 square miles. Located at 28.13° N. Lat.; 82.46° W. Long. Elevation is 71 feet.
Population: 13,403 (1990); 17,081 (2000); 19,411 (2004); 22,284 (2009 projected); Race: 91.3% White, 3.8% Black, 1.5% Asian, 9.1% Hispanic of any race (2004); Density: 904.1 persons per square mile (2004); Average household size: 2.70 (2004); Median age: 38.5 (2004); Male/female ratio: 99.6 (2004); Marriage status: 22.1% never married, 63.6% now married, 5.2% widowed, 9.2% divorced (2000); Foreign born: 5.5% (2000); Ancestry (includes multiple ancestries): 19.0% Other groups, 18.1% German, 16.4% Irish, 14.8% English, 10.1% United States or American (2000).
Economy: Manufacturing: neon signs, metal roofing; printing and publishing; hydraulic units. Employment by occupation: 20.5% management, 24.8% professional, 8.6% services, 31.3% sales, 0.1% farming, 9.1% construction, 5.6% production (2000).
Income: Per capita income: $33,608 (2004); Median household income: $68,661 (2004); Average household income: $90,404 (2004); Percent of households with income of $100,000 or more: 29.5% (2004); Poverty rate: 6.0% (2000).
Education: Percent of population age 25 and over with: High school diploma (including GED) or higher: 90.0% (2004); Bachelor's degree or higher: 34.6% (2004); Master's degree or higher: 13.6% (2004).

School District(s)

Hillsborough County School District (PK-12)
2002-03 Enrollment: 175,454 . . . . (813) 272-4050
Housing: Homeownership rate: 85.8% (2004); Median home value: $172,974 (2004); Median rent: $533 per month (2000); Median age of housing: 18 years (2000).
Newspapers: Brandon/Valrico Community News (General - Circulation 20,000); Carrollwood/Northdale/Cheval (General - Circulation 26,000); Riverview/Fishhawk/Apollo Beach Community News (General - Circulation 12,000); Temple Terrace Beacon (General - Circulation 22,000); The Laker (General - Circulation 15,000)
Transportation: Commute to work: 94.4% car, 0.0% public transportation, 0.4% walk, 4.0% work from home (2000); Travel time to work: 14.7% less than 15 minutes, 37.2% 15 to 30 minutes, 30.6% 30 to 45 minutes, 12.2% 45 to 60 minutes, 5.3% 60 minutes or more (2000)
Additional Information Contacts
Land O' Lakes Board of Realtors. . . . . (813) 962-1962

MANGO (CDP). Covers a land area of 4.588 square miles and a water area of 0.068 square miles. Located at 27.98° N. Lat.; 82.30° W. Long. Elevation is 56 feet.

Population: 8,700 (1990); 8,842 (2000); 9,114 (2004); 9,500 (2009 projected); Race: 85.6% White, 7.0% Black, 0.8% Asian, 11.3% Hispanic of any race (2004); Density: 1,986.4 persons per square mile (2004); Average household size: 2.67 (2004); Median age: 33.5 (2004); Male/female ratio: 100.9 (2004); Marriage status: 25.1% never married, 51.3% now married, 6.5% widowed, 17.1% divorced (2000); Foreign born: 3.5% (2000); Ancestry (includes multiple ancestries): 25.1% Other groups, 13.4% Irish, 13.0% United States or American, 12.0% German, 7.8% English (2000).
Economy: Employment by occupation: 6.5% management, 9.4% professional, 17.5% services, 32.0% sales, 0.4% farming, 17.6% construction, 16.6% production (2000).
Income: Per capita income: $16,898 (2004); Median household income: $37,054 (2004); Average household income: $45,117 (2004); Percent of households with income of $100,000 or more: 6.3% (2004); Poverty rate: 12.6% (2000).
Education: Percent of population age 25 and over with: High school diploma (including GED) or higher: 73.8% (2004); Bachelor's degree or higher: 8.2% (2004); Master's degree or higher: 1.8% (2004).
Housing: Homeownership rate: 66.7% (2004); Median home value: $92,778 (2004); Median rent: $466 per month (2000); Median age of housing: 21 years (2000).
Transportation: Commute to work: 93.4% car, 0.5% public transportation, 1.4% walk, 1.6% work from home (2000); Travel time to work: 24.5% less than 15 minutes, 41.1% 15 to 30 minutes, 19.3% 30 to 45 minutes, 7.3% 45 to 60 minutes, 7.8% 60 minutes or more (2000)

PALM RIVER-CLAIR MEL (CDP). Covers a land area of 11.705 square miles and a water area of 0.005 square miles. Located at 27.92° N. Lat.; 82.37° W. Long.
Population: 15,990 (1990); 17,589 (2000); 18,620 (2004); 19,956 (2009 projected); Race: 51.0% White, 37.0% Black, 1.4% Asian, 25.5% Hispanic of any race (2004); Density: 1,590.7 persons per square mile (2004); Average household size: 2.88 (2004); Median age: 32.1 (2004); Male/female ratio: 95.2 (2004); Marriage status: 27.6% never married, 51.5% now married, 6.3% widowed, 14.6% divorced (2000); Foreign born: 11.9% (2000); Ancestry (includes multiple ancestries): 53.1% Other groups, 9.6% United States or American, 6.0% German, 5.2% Irish, 5.0% English (2000).
Economy: Employment by occupation: 8.4% management, 11.9% professional, 16.1% services, 28.3% sales, 0.6% farming, 11.9% construction, 22.8% production (2000).
Income: Per capita income: $16,324 (2004); Median household income: $37,846 (2004); Average household income: $47,040 (2004); Percent of households with income of $100,000 or more: 7.2% (2004); Poverty rate: 17.4% (2000).
Education: Percent of population age 25 and over with: High school diploma (including GED) or higher: 69.2% (2004); Bachelor's degree or higher: 11.5% (2004); Master's degree or higher: 3.6% (2004).
Housing: Homeownership rate: 72.5% (2004); Median home value: $96,924 (2004); Median rent: $474 per month (2000); Median age of housing: 26 years (2000).
Transportation: Commute to work: 93.8% car, 1.9% public transportation, 0.9% walk, 1.2% work from home (2000); Travel time to work: 27.0% less than 15 minutes, 42.0% 15 to 30 minutes, 20.3% 30 to 45 minutes, 5.6% 45 to 60 minutes, 5.2% 60 minutes or more (2000)

PEBBLE CREEK (CDP). Covers a land area of 2.979 square miles and a water area of 0.005 square miles. Located at 28.15° N. Lat.; 82.34° W. Long.
Population: 1,665 (1990); 4,824 (2000); 5,707 (2004); 6,785 (2009 projected); Race: 80.4% White, 7.8% Black, 7.4% Asian, 11.1% Hispanic of any race (2004); Density: 1,916.0 persons per square mile (2004); Average household size: 2.79 (2004); Median age: 36.4 (2004); Male/female ratio: 94.8 (2004); Marriage status: 19.1% never married, 67.9% now married, 4.6% widowed, 8.3% divorced (2000); Foreign born: 10.4% (2000); Ancestry (includes multiple ancestries): 21.2% Other groups, 14.8% German, 11.6% English, 11.2% Irish, 10.1% Italian (2000).
Economy: Employment by occupation: 21.4% management, 32.6% professional, 10.9% services, 25.8% sales, 0.0% farming, 4.6% construction, 4.6% production (2000).
Income: Per capita income: $32,720 (2004); Median household income: $76,898 (2004); Average household income: $91,402 (2004); Percent of households with income of $100,000 or more: 31.2% (2004); Poverty rate: 1.7% (2000).
Education: Percent of population age 25 and over with: High school diploma (including GED) or higher: 92.6% (2004); Bachelor's degree or higher: 48.1% (2004); Master's degree or higher: 17.9% (2004).
Housing: Homeownership rate: 83.1% (2004); Median home value: $179,884 (2004); Median rent: $780 per month (2000); Median age of housing: 8 years (2000).
Transportation: Commute to work: 94.4% car, 0.0% public transportation, 0.6% walk, 4.0% work from home (2000); Travel time to work: 17.1% less than 15 minutes, 27.1% 15 to 30 minutes, 31.5% 30 to 45 minutes, 15.1% 45 to 60 minutes, 9.2% 60 minutes or more (2000)

PLANT CITY (city). Covers a land area of 22.630 square miles and a water area of 0.121 square miles. Located at 28.01° N. Lat.; 82.12° W. Long. Elevation is 130 feet.
History: Named for Henry B. Plant, owner of the South Florida Railroad. Plant City was called Ichepucksassa at first, and later changed to Cork by an Irish postmaster. When the town was incorporated in 1885 it was renamed for Plant, who had extended his South Florida Railroad to this area the year before. Strawberries were a leading product of Plant City.
Population: 23,296 (1990); 29,915 (2000); 31,872 (2004); 34,477 (2009 projected); Race: 69.5% White, 16.1% Black, 1.0% Asian, 20.4% Hispanic of any race (2004); Density: 1,408.4 persons per square mile (2004); Average household size: 2.76 (2004); Median age: 34.0 (2004); Male/female ratio: 93.7 (2004); Marriage status: 22.5% never married, 58.0% now married, 7.4% widowed, 12.1% divorced (2000); Foreign born: 9.8% (2000); Ancestry (includes multiple ancestries): 37.4% Other groups, 11.3% Irish, 11.0% German, 10.7% English, 9.2% United States or American (2000).
Economy: Unemployment rate: 3.8% (2004); Total civilian labor force: 15,711 (2004); Single-family building permits issued: 224 (2004); Multi-family building permits issued: 2 (2004); Employment by occupation: 10.9% management, 14.6% professional, 15.3% services, 28.1% sales, 2.5% farming, 10.1% construction, 18.5% production (2000).
Income: Per capita income: $20,523 (2004); Median household income: $43,141 (2004); Average household income: $56,363 (2004); Percent of households with income of $100,000 or more: 11.1% (2004); Poverty rate: 14.7% (2000).
Taxes: Total city taxes per capita: $478 (2002); City property taxes per capita: $431 (2002).
Education: Percent of population age 25 and over with: High school diploma (including GED) or higher: 72.2% (2004); Bachelor's degree or higher: 17.2% (2004); Master's degree or higher: 5.6% (2004).

School District(s)

Hillsborough County School District (PK-12)
2002-03 Enrollment: 175,454 . . . . (813) 272-4050

Housing: Homeownership rate: 66.1% (2004); Median home value: $122,889 (2004); Median rent: $445 per month (2000); Median age of housing: 20 years (2000).
Hospitals: South Florida Baptist Hospital (147 beds)
Safety: Violent crime rate: 85.3 per 10,000 population; Property crime rate: 617.3 per 10,000 population (2003).
Transportation: Commute to work: 94.7% car, 0.4% public transportation, 1.2% walk, 2.0% work from home (2000); Travel time to work: 34.6% less than 15 minutes, 30.6% 15 to 30 minutes, 21.8% 30 to 45 minutes, 7.5% 45 to 60 minutes, 5.5% 60 minutes or more (2000)

Additional Information Contacts

Local Government Offices . . . . (813) 659-4200
Plant City Chamber of Commerce . . . . (813) 754-3707

PROGRESS VILLAGE (CDP). Covers a land area of 3.366 square miles and a water area of 0 square miles. Located at 27.89° N. Lat.; 82.36° W. Long. Elevation is 18 feet.
Population: 2,495 (1990); 2,482 (2000); 2,786 (2004); 3,159 (2009 projected); Race: 8.0% White, 89.2% Black, 0.1% Asian, 3.1% Hispanic of any race (2004); Density: 827.7 persons per square mile (2004); Average household size: 2.85 (2004); Median age: 35.7 (2004); Male/female ratio: 84.9 (2004); Marriage status: 31.5% never married, 47.0% now married, 13.0% widowed, 8.5% divorced (2000); Foreign born: 2.2% (2000); Ancestry (includes multiple ancestries): 74.2% Other groups, 2.6% Italian, 2.5% African, 1.4% Jamaican, 1.0% Irish (2000).
Economy: Employment by occupation: 2.7% management, 11.3% professional, 21.6% services, 38.3% sales, 0.0% farming, 7.3% construction, 18.7% production (2000).
Income: Per capita income: $14,034 (2004); Median household income: $32,611 (2004); Average household income: $40,059 (2004); Percent of

households with income of $100,000 or more: 3.6% (2004); Poverty rate: 18.4% (2000).
Education: Percent of population age 25 and over with: High school diploma (including GED) or higher: 69.3% (2004); Bachelor's degree or higher: 6.5% (2004); Master's degree or higher: 0.9% (2004).
Housing: Homeownership rate: 83.0% (2004); Median home value: $80,818 (2004); Median rent: $459 per month (2000); Median age of housing: 35 years (2000).
Transportation: Commute to work: 95.7% car, 2.5% public transportation, 0.9% walk, 0.9% work from home (2000); Travel time to work: 19.6% less than 15 minutes, 28.1% 15 to 30 minutes, 31.6% 30 to 45 minutes, 10.1% 45 to 60 minutes, 10.6% 60 minutes or more (2000)

RIVERVIEW (CDP). Covers a land area of 9.144 square miles and a water area of 0.289 square miles. Located at 27.87° N. Lat.; 82.32° W. Long. Elevation is 3 feet.
History: Riverview was settled in 1856 on the Alafia River. First known as Peru, it developed as a center for truck gardening and citrus products.
Population: 6,843 (1990); 12,035 (2000); 15,360 (2004); 19,286 (2009 projected); Race: 81.9% White, 11.4% Black, 1.6% Asian, 10.7% Hispanic of any race (2004); Density: 1,679.7 persons per square mile (2004); Average household size: 2.74 (2004); Median age: 36.4 (2004); Male/female ratio: 98.4 (2004); Marriage status: 17.4% never married, 66.4% now married, 5.3% widowed, 11.0% divorced (2000); Foreign born: 4.5% (2000); Ancestry (includes multiple ancestries): 22.3% Other groups, 17.9% German, 11.1% English, 11.0% Irish, 10.3% United States or American (2000).
Economy: Employment by occupation: 17.9% management, 16.7% professional, 14.0% services, 32.0% sales, 0.4% farming, 8.6% construction, 10.5% production (2000).
Income: Per capita income: $27,677 (2004); Median household income: $60,965 (2004); Average household income: $75,543 (2004); Percent of households with income of $100,000 or more: 23.5% (2004); Poverty rate: 6.8% (2000).
Education: Percent of population age 25 and over with: High school diploma (including GED) or higher: 87.3% (2004); Bachelor's degree or higher: 26.5% (2004); Master's degree or higher: 8.3% (2004).

School District(s)

Hillsborough County School District (PK-12)
2002-03 Enrollment: 175,454 . . . . (813) 272-4050

Housing: Homeownership rate: 79.7% (2004); Median home value: $165,922 (2004); Median rent: $559 per month (2000); Median age of housing: 14 years (2000).
Transportation: Commute to work: 93.9% car, 0.2% public transportation, 1.0% walk, 3.4% work from home (2000); Travel time to work: 18.7% less than 15 minutes, 42.7% 15 to 30 minutes, 24.4% 30 to 45 minutes, 10.0% 45 to 60 minutes, 4.2% 60 minutes or more (2000)

Additional Information Contacts

Greater Riverview Chamber . . . . (813) 643-8000

RUSKIN (CDP). Covers a land area of 14.238 square miles and a water area of 1.184 square miles. Located at 27.71° N. Lat.; 82.43° W. Long. Elevation is 11 feet.
History: Ruskin was founded in 1910 as a socialist colony by George M. Miller, a Chicago lawyer and educator, and named for John Ruskin, English author and critic. Ruskin developed as a cooperative tomato-growing settlement at the mouth of the Little Manatee River.
Population: 7,762 (1990); 8,321 (2000); 9,611 (2004); 11,191 (2009 projected); Race: 77.6% White, 1.5% Black, 0.5% Asian, 41.2% Hispanic of any race (2004); Density: 675.0 persons per square mile (2004); Average household size: 2.85 (2004); Median age: 36.3 (2004); Male/female ratio: 104.4 (2004); Marriage status: 24.1% never married, 56.3% now married, 7.1% widowed, 12.4% divorced (2000); Foreign born: 13.3% (2000); Ancestry (includes multiple ancestries): 35.3% Other groups, 14.0% German, 9.6% English, 9.1% Irish, 7.6% United States or American (2000).
Economy: Employment by occupation: 7.7% management, 10.9% professional, 22.0% services, 20.2% sales, 8.4% farming, 15.0% construction, 15.8% production (2000).
Income: Per capita income: $13,405 (2004); Median household income: $30,739 (2004); Average household income: $37,985 (2004); Percent of households with income of $100,000 or more: 4.2% (2004); Poverty rate: 17.1% (2000).
Education: Percent of population age 25 and over with: High school diploma (including GED) or higher: 61.5% (2004); Bachelor's degree or higher: 7.1% (2004); Master's degree or higher: 2.9% (2004).

School District(s)

Hillsborough County School District (PK-12)
2002-03 Enrollment: 175,454 . . . . (813) 272-4050

Housing: Homeownership rate: 72.5% (2004); Median home value: $94,043 (2004); Median rent: $434 per month (2000); Median age of housing: 22 years (2000).
Hospitals: Columbia South Bay Hospital (112 beds)
Transportation: Commute to work: 93.5% car, 0.7% public transportation, 1.1% walk, 0.8% work from home (2000); Travel time to work: 36.8% less than 15 minutes, 28.3% 15 to 30 minutes, 13.5% 30 to 45 minutes, 10.9% 45 to 60 minutes, 10.5% 60 minutes or more (2000)

Additional Information Contacts

Ruskin Chamber of Commerce . . . . (813) 645-3808

SEFFNER (CDP). Covers a land area of 3.615 square miles and a water area of 0.111 square miles. Located at 27.99° N. Lat.; 82.27° W. Long. Elevation is 60 feet.
Population: 5,371 (1990); 5,467 (2000); 5,179 (2004); 4,897 (2009 projected); Race: 90.6% White, 3.3% Black, 1.2% Asian, 9.6% Hispanic of any race (2004); Density: 1,432.6 persons per square mile (2004); Average household size: 2.58 (2004); Median age: 37.8 (2004); Male/female ratio: 96.2 (2004); Marriage status: 21.8% never married, 58.6% now married, 6.8% widowed, 12.9% divorced (2000); Foreign born: 4.9% (2000); Ancestry (includes multiple ancestries): 22.3% Other groups, 15.0% German, 13.1% United States or American, 11.9% English, 11.2% Irish (2000).
Economy: Manufacturing includes fixtures, concrete products, printing and publishing. Employment by occupation: 10.8% management, 16.3% professional, 14.2% services, 34.9% sales, 0.0% farming, 12.5% construction, 11.3% production (2000).
Income: Per capita income: $22,675 (2004); Median household income: $46,469 (2004); Average household income: $57,955 (2004); Percent of households with income of $100,000 or more: 13.3% (2004); Poverty rate: 4.6% (2000).
Education: Percent of population age 25 and over with: High school diploma (including GED) or higher: 78.5% (2004); Bachelor's degree or higher: 13.8% (2004); Master's degree or higher: 3.1% (2004).

School District(s)

Hillsborough County School District (PK-12)
2002-03 Enrollment: 175,454 . . . . (813) 272-4050

Housing: Homeownership rate: 79.6% (2004); Median home value: $122,995 (2004); Median rent: $515 per month (2000); Median age of housing: 22 years (2000).
Transportation: Commute to work: 93.3% car, 0.6% public transportation, 2.3% walk, 2.4% work from home (2000); Travel time to work: 20.4% less than 15 minutes, 45.7% 15 to 30 minutes, 21.2% 30 to 45 minutes, 6.1% 45 to 60 minutes, 6.5% 60 minutes or more (2000)

Additional Information Contacts

Seffner Chamber of Commerce. . . . . (813)-627-8686

TAMPA (city). Covers a land area of 112.065 square miles and a water area of 58.534 square miles. Located at 27.97° N. Lat.; 82.46° W. Long. Elevation is 48 feet.
History: A post office called Tampa Bay was established in 1831 near the site of Fort Brooke, which had been built in 1823. Tampa became the center of a cattle industry, but activities of the Civil War caused severe damage. Rebuilding and expansion began about 1884 when Henry Plant's narrow-gauge South Florida Railroad reached Tampa, and when the Hillsborough River was bridged. Tampa was a deep-water port, shipping phosphate and cigars. Henry Plant, seeking to outdo Henry Flagler on the east coast, built the extravagant Tampa Bay Hotel in 1891 to establish Tampa as a winter resort.
Population: 279,960 (1990); 303,447 (2000); 325,584 (2004); 354,535 (2009 projected); Race: 61.9% White, 27.4% Black, 2.5% Asian, 21.2% Hispanic of any race (2004); Density: 2,905.3 persons per square mile (2004); Average household size: 2.43 (2004); Median age: 35.3 (2004); Male/female ratio: 95.9 (2004); Marriage status: 31.0% never married, 47.4% now married, 7.6% widowed, 14.0% divorced (2000); Foreign born: 12.2% (2000); Ancestry (includes multiple ancestries): 42.3% Other groups, 9.2% German, 8.4% Irish, 7.7% English, 6.2% United States or American (2000).
Economy: Unemployment rate: 4.8% (2004); Total civilian labor force: 203,355 (2004); Single-family building permits issued: 1,618 (2004); Multi-family building permits issued: 663 (2004); Employment by

occupation: 13.8% management, 20.2% professional, 16.3% services, 30.1% sales, 0.2% farming, 8.6% construction, 10.9% production (2000).
Income: Per capita income: $24,153 (2004); Median household income: $38,039 (2004); Average household income: $57,798 (2004); Percent of households with income of $100,000 or more: 12.7% (2004); Poverty rate: 18.1% (2000).
Taxes: Total city taxes per capita: $655 (2002); City property taxes per capita: $294 (2002).
Education: Percent of population age 25 and over with: High school diploma (including GED) or higher: 77.6% (2004); Bachelor's degree or higher: 26.4% (2004); Master's degree or higher: 9.5% (2004).

School District(s)

Hillsborough County School District (PK-12)
2002-03 Enrollment: 175,454 . . . . (813) 272-4050

Four-year College(s)

Argosy University-Tampa Campus (Private, For-profit)
2003-04 Enrollment: 390 . . . . (813) 246-4419
Faith Theological Seminary and Christian College
2003-04 Enrollment: 49 . . . . (813) 886-8492
2003-04 Tuition: In-state $1,050; Out-of-state $1,050
Florida Metropolitan University-Brandon (Private, For-profit)
2003-04 Enrollment: 1,384 . . . . (813) 621-0041
2003-04 Tuition: In-state $9,138; Out-of-state $9,138
Florida Metropolitan University-Tampa (Private, For-profit)
2003-04 Enrollment: 1,995 . . . . (813) 879-6000
2003-04 Tuition: In-state $8,460; Out-of-state $8,460
ITT Technical Institute (Private, For-profit)
2003-04 Enrollment: 595 . . . . (813) 885-2244
2003-04 Tuition: In-state $12,492; Out-of-state $12,492
International Academy of Design and Technology (Private, For-profit)
2003-04 Enrollment: 1,799 . . . . (813) 881-0007
2003-04 Tuition: In-state $15,120; Out-of-state $15,120
Remington College-Tampa Campus (Private, For-profit)
2003-04 Enrollment: 856 . . . . (813) 935-5700
2003-04 Tuition: In-state $13,071; Out-of-state $13,071
The University of Tampa
2003-04 Enrollment: 4,645 . . . . (813) 253-3333
2003-04 Tuition: In-state $17,572; Out-of-state $17,572
University of South Florida (Public)
2003-04 Enrollment: 40,945 . . . . (813) 974-2011
2003-04 Tuition: In-state $2,982; Out-of-state $14,011

Two-year College(s)

Brewster Technical Center (Public)
2003-04 Enrollment: 148 . . . . (813) 276-5448
Concorde Career Institute (Private, For-profit)
2003-04 Enrollment: 552 . . . . (813) 874-0094
D G Erwin Technical Center (Public)
2003-04 Enrollment: 911 . . . . (813) 231-1800
2003-04 Tuition: In-state $1,760; Out-of-state $6,875
Hillsborough Community College (Public)
2003-04 Enrollment: 22,006 . . . . (813) 253-7000
2003-04 Tuition: In-state $1,747; Out-of-state $6,513
Manhattan Beauty School (Private, For-profit)
2003-04 Enrollment: n/a . . . . (813) 264-3535
Manhattan Beauty School Inc Dba Manhattan Hair (Private, For-profit)
2003-04 Enrollment: 470 . . . . (813) 258-0505
Suncoast School (Private, For-profit)
2003-04 Enrollment: 72 . . . . (813) 287-1099
Ultrasound Diagnostic School (Private, For-profit)
2003-04 Enrollment: 408 . . . . (813) 621-0072
Webster Tech (Private, For-profit)
2003-04 Enrollment: 133 . . . . (813) 620-1446
2003-04 Tuition: In-state $9,605; Out-of-state $9,605

Housing: Homeownership rate: 54.6% (2004); Median home value: $123,118 (2004); Median rent: $486 per month (2000); Median age of housing: 34 years (2000).
Hospitals: 6th Medical Group (25 beds); H. Lee Moffitt Cancer Center & Research Institute (162 beds); James A. Haley Veterans' Hospital (581 beds); Kindred Hospital-Bay Area Tampa (73 beds); Kindred Hospital-Central Tampa (102 beds); Memorial Hospital of Tampa (172 beds); Northside Mental Health Center (16 beds); Shriners Hospitals for Children (60 beds); St. Joseph's Hospital (521 beds); Tampa General Healthcare (877 beds); Town and Country Hospital (201 beds); University Commmunity Hospital of Carrollwood (120 beds); University Community Hospital (551 beds)
Safety: Violent crime rate: 178.6 per 10,000 population; Property crime rate: 886.5 per 10,000 population (2003).
Newspapers: Florida Sentinel-Bulletin (Black, General - Circulation 23,000); La Gaceta (Hispanic - Circulation 18,000); Nuevo Siglo (Hispanic - Circulation 22,000); Tampa Tribune (Circulation 238,176); The Florida Dollar Stretcher (Black - Circulation 8,300); The Free Press (General - Circulation 1,500); Town 'n Country News (General - Circulation 23,700)
Transportation: Commute to work: 90.3% car, 2.7% public transportation, 2.3% walk, 2.6% work from home (2000); Travel time to work: 30.1% less than 15 minutes, 41.6% 15 to 30 minutes, 18.5% 30 to 45 minutes, 4.9% 45 to 60 minutes, 4.9% 60 minutes or more (2000); Amtrak: Service available.
Airports: Tampa International (primary service/large hub); Vandenberg (primary service/large hub)

Additional Information Contacts

Florida Gulfcoast Commercial Association of Realtors . . . . (813) 969-4227
Greater Tampa Association of Realtors . . . . (813) 879-7010
Hispanic Chamber of Commerce . . . . (813) 414-9411
North Tampa Chamber of Commerce . . . . (813) 961-2420
South Tampa Chamber of Commerce . . . . (813) 837-8972
Tampa Chamber of Commerce . . . . (813) 228-7777
West Tampa Chamber of Commerce . . . . (813) 253-2056
Ybor City Chamber of Commerce . . . . (813) 248-3712

TEMPLE TERRACE (city). Covers a land area of 6.856 square miles and a water area of 0.075 square miles. Located at 28.04° N. Lat.; 82.38° W. Long. Elevation is 56 feet.
Population: 18,960 (1990); 20,918 (2000); 22,420 (2004); 24,437 (2009 projected); Race: 76.9% White, 13.8% Black, 2.8% Asian, 12.9% Hispanic of any race (2004); Density: 3,270.3 persons per square mile (2004); Average household size: 2.36 (2004); Median age: 36.0 (2004); Male/female ratio: 92.2 (2004); Marriage status: 27.7% never married, 53.9% now married, 6.0% widowed, 12.4% divorced (2000); Foreign born: 11.6% (2000); Ancestry (includes multiple ancestries): 25.3% Other groups, 15.5% German, 12.3% English, 11.8% Irish, 8.3% Italian (2000).
Economy: Single-family building permits issued: 77 (2004); Multi-family building permits issued: 0 (2004); Employment by occupation: 17.0% management, 29.1% professional, 10.0% services, 32.4% sales, 0.1% farming, 5.1% construction, 6.3% production (2000).
Income: Per capita income: $27,170 (2004); Median household income: $46,733 (2004); Average household income: $63,812 (2004); Percent of households with income of $100,000 or more: 16.6% (2004); Poverty rate: 7.2% (2000).
Taxes: Total city taxes per capita: $488 (2002); City property taxes per capita: $222 (2002).
Education: Percent of population age 25 and over with: High school diploma (including GED) or higher: 90.4% (2004); Bachelor's degree or higher: 43.3% (2004); Master's degree or higher: 17.2% (2004).

School District(s)

Hillsborough County School District (PK-12)
2002-03 Enrollment: 175,454 . . . . (813) 272-4050

Four-year College(s)

Florida College
2003-04 Enrollment: 478 . . . . (813) 988-5131
2003-04 Tuition: In-state $9,400; Out-of-state $9,400
University of Phoenix-Tampa (Private, For-profit)
2003-04 Enrollment: 1,951 . . . . (813) 626-7911
2003-04 Tuition: In-state $8,850; Out-of-state $8,850

Housing: Homeownership rate: 59.4% (2004); Median home value: $143,342 (2004); Median rent: $631 per month (2000); Median age of housing: 19 years (2000).
Safety: Violent crime rate: 30.0 per 10,000 population; Property crime rate: 371.6 per 10,000 population (2003).
Transportation: Commute to work: 92.3% car, 0.8% public transportation, 1.4% walk, 4.1% work from home (2000); Travel time to work: 30.8% less than 15 minutes, 38.0% 15 to 30 minutes, 20.0% 30 to 45 minutes, 6.9% 45 to 60 minutes, 4.3% 60 minutes or more (2000)

Additional Information Contacts

Local Government Offices . . . . (813) 989-7100

THONOTOSASSA (CDP). Covers a land area of 16.665 square miles and a water area of 1.303 square miles. Located at 28.05° N. Lat.; 82.29° W. Long. Elevation is 48 feet.
History: In 1846 William Miley laid out a homestead at the site of Thonotosassa, on the lake named by the early inhabitants as the "place of

many flints." Orange groves here had been started by seeds dropped in 1835 by Major Dade and his troops.
Population: 5,960 (1990); 6,091 (2000); 6,358 (2004); 6,746 (2009 projected); Race: 90.5% White, 4.5% Black, 0.4% Asian, 7.4% Hispanic of any race (2004); Density: 381.5 persons per square mile (2004); Average household size: 2.79 (2004); Median age: 37.5 (2004); Male/female ratio: 100.1 (2004); Marriage status: 20.9% never married, 58.4% now married, 5.3% widowed, 15.4% divorced (2000); Foreign born: 4.3% (2000); Ancestry (includes multiple ancestries): 19.0% Other groups, 16.1% United States or American, 14.4% German, 11.0% English, 7.9% Irish (2000).
Economy: Employment by occupation: 10.9% management, 11.7% professional, 15.6% services, 31.1% sales, 0.0% farming, 14.8% construction, 15.9% production (2000).
Income: Per capita income: $20,139 (2004); Median household income: $47,599 (2004); Average household income: $55,253 (2004); Percent of households with income of $100,000 or more: 10.5% (2004); Poverty rate: 16.0% (2000).
Education: Percent of population age 25 and over with: High school diploma (including GED) or higher: 73.3% (2004); Bachelor's degree or higher: 11.1% (2004); Master's degree or higher: 3.6% (2004).

School District(s)

Hillsborough County School District (PK-12)
2002-03 Enrollment: 175,454 . . . . (813) 272-4050

Housing: Homeownership rate: 76.4% (2004); Median home value: $108,267 (2004); Median rent: $483 per month (2000); Median age of housing: 17 years (2000).
Transportation: Commute to work: 90.9% car, 0.3% public transportation, 1.8% walk, 4.9% work from home (2000); Travel time to work: 15.2% less than 15 minutes, 46.2% 15 to 30 minutes, 27.4% 30 to 45 minutes, 5.2% 45 to 60 minutes, 6.0% 60 minutes or more (2000)

TOWN 'N' COUNTRY (CDP). Covers a land area of 23.673 square miles and a water area of 0.744 square miles. Located at 28.01° N. Lat.; 82.57° W. Long.
Population: 60,978 (1990); 72,523 (2000); 76,301 (2004); 81,569 (2009 projected); Race: 75.0% White, 9.6% Black, 3.6% Asian, 34.0% Hispanic of any race (2004); Density: 3,223.1 persons per square mile (2004); Average household size: 2.50 (2004); Median age: 35.7 (2004); Male/female ratio: 95.6 (2004); Marriage status: 27.2% never married, 54.2% now married, 5.3% widowed, 13.3% divorced (2000); Foreign born: 17.6% (2000); Ancestry (includes multiple ancestries): 39.9% Other groups, 13.2% German, 10.3% Irish, 8.2% English, 7.3% Italian (2000).
Economy: Employment by occupation: 14.2% management, 17.1% professional, 14.4% services, 34.5% sales, 0.2% farming, 7.8% construction, 11.9% production (2000).
Income: Per capita income: $23,060 (2004); Median household income: $45,699 (2004); Average household income: $57,448 (2004); Percent of households with income of $100,000 or more: 11.3% (2004); Poverty rate: 8.6% (2000).
Education: Percent of population age 25 and over with: High school diploma (including GED) or higher: 83.0% (2004); Bachelor's degree or higher: 23.9% (2004); Master's degree or higher: 6.9% (2004).
Housing: Homeownership rate: 64.0% (2004); Median home value: $123,916 (2004); Median rent: $626 per month (2000); Median age of housing: 19 years (2000).
Transportation: Commute to work: 93.7% car, 1.3% public transportation, 1.1% walk, 2.3% work from home (2000); Travel time to work: 21.1% less than 15 minutes, 39.8% 15 to 30 minutes, 24.8% 30 to 45 minutes, 8.1% 45 to 60 minutes, 6.2% 60 minutes or more (2000)

Additional Information Contacts

Town 'n' Country Chamber of Commerce . . . . (813) 884-5344

UNIVERSITY (CDP). Covers a land area of 3.870 square miles and a water area of 0.012 square miles. Located at 28.07° N. Lat.; 82.43° W. Long.
Population: 23,760 (1990); 30,736 (2000); 32,634 (2004); 35,177 (2009 projected); Race: 45.5% White, 38.4% Black, 3.9% Asian, 22.0% Hispanic of any race (2004); Density: 8,431.7 persons per square mile (2004); Average household size: 2.24 (2004); Median age: 27.9 (2004); Male/female ratio: 97.7 (2004); Marriage status: 49.1% never married, 31.7% now married, 6.4% widowed, 12.8% divorced (2000); Foreign born: 15.0% (2000); Ancestry (includes multiple ancestries): 46.8% Other groups, 6.7% German, 6.1% Irish, 4.5% United States or American, 4.1% English (2000).
Economy: Employment by occupation: 7.5% management, 19.5% professional, 20.9% services, 32.5% sales, 0.4% farming, 9.7% construction, 9.5% production (2000).
Income: Per capita income: $13,763 (2004); Median household income: $23,142 (2004); Average household income: $28,823 (2004); Percent of households with income of $100,000 or more: 2.1% (2004); Poverty rate: 31.3% (2000).
Education: Percent of population age 25 and over with: High school diploma (including GED) or higher: 74.8% (2004); Bachelor's degree or higher: 21.8% (2004); Master's degree or higher: 7.2% (2004).
Housing: Homeownership rate: 11.5% (2004); Median home value: $76,948 (2004); Median rent: $481 per month (2000); Median age of housing: 20 years (2000).
Transportation: Commute to work: 87.0% car, 3.3% public transportation, 5.6% walk, 0.8% work from home (2000); Travel time to work: 26.4% less than 15 minutes, 33.7% 15 to 30 minutes, 23.8% 30 to 45 minutes, 9.2% 45 to 60 minutes, 6.9% 60 minutes or more (2000)

VALRICO (CDP). Part of the Census Designated Place of Brandon. Covers a land area of 5.592 square miles and a water area of 0.085 square miles. Located at 27.94° N. Lat.; 82.24° W. Long. Elevation is 55 feet.
Population: 5,174 (1990); 6,582 (2000); 8,002 (2004); 9,718 (2009 projected); Race: 87.1% White, 4.0% Black, 1.6% Asian, 15.9% Hispanic of any race (2004); Density: 1,430.9 persons per square mile (2004); Average household size: 2.50 (2004); Median age: 39.8 (2004); Male/female ratio: 95.6 (2004); Marriage status: 17.5% never married, 62.7% now married, 9.6% widowed, 10.2% divorced (2000); Foreign born: 6.9% (2000); Ancestry (includes multiple ancestries): 19.3% Other groups, 14.9% German, 13.8% United States or American, 11.4% Irish, 9.4% English (2000).
Economy: Employment by occupation: 14.1% management, 15.5% professional, 12.1% services, 31.1% sales, 1.9% farming, 9.8% construction, 15.5% production (2000).
Income: Per capita income: $23,155 (2004); Median household income: $43,997 (2004); Average household income: $57,456 (2004); Percent of households with income of $100,000 or more: 13.0% (2004); Poverty rate: 7.5% (2000).
Education: Percent of population age 25 and over with: High school diploma (including GED) or higher: 77.2% (2004); Bachelor's degree or higher: 18.4% (2004); Master's degree or higher: 4.7% (2004).

School District(s)

Hillsborough County School District (PK-12)
2002-03 Enrollment: 175,454 . . . . (813) 272-4050

Housing: Homeownership rate: 78.2% (2004); Median home value: $120,744 (2004); Median rent: $562 per month (2000); Median age of housing: 16 years (2000).
Transportation: Commute to work: 92.5% car, 0.9% public transportation, 0.7% walk, 4.2% work from home (2000); Travel time to work: 22.7% less than 15 minutes, 36.6% 15 to 30 minutes, 26.4% 30 to 45 minutes, 8.4% 45 to 60 minutes, 6.0% 60 minutes or more (2000)

WESTCHASE (CDP). Covers a land area of 10.748 square miles and a water area of 0.050 square miles. Located at 28.05° N. Lat.; 82.61° W. Long.
Population: 2,070 (1990); 11,116 (2000); 18,700 (2004); 27,555 (2009 projected); Race: 85.0% White, 6.0% Black, 4.8% Asian, 12.4% Hispanic of any race (2004); Density: 1,739.8 persons per square mile (2004); Average household size: 2.68 (2004); Median age: 34.1 (2004); Male/female ratio: 96.6 (2004); Marriage status: 16.6% never married, 73.2% now married, 3.7% widowed, 6.6% divorced (2000); Foreign born: 9.6% (2000); Ancestry (includes multiple ancestries): 25.1% Other groups, 18.2% German, 16.9% Irish, 12.7% English, 11.6% Italian (2000).
Economy: Employment by occupation: 27.8% management, 27.3% professional, 6.6% services, 30.5% sales, 0.0% farming, 4.3% construction, 3.5% production (2000).
Income: Per capita income: $42,704 (2004); Median household income: $92,151 (2004); Average household income: $114,653 (2004); Percent of households with income of $100,000 or more: 44.8% (2004); Poverty rate: 2.4% (2000).
Education: Percent of population age 25 and over with: High school diploma (including GED) or higher: 96.6% (2004); Bachelor's degree or higher: 49.3% (2004); Master's degree or higher: 14.8% (2004).
Housing: Homeownership rate: 87.7% (2004); Median home value: $244,385 (2004); Median rent: $832 per month (2000); Median age of housing: 4 years (2000).

Transportation: Commute to work: 93.3% car, 0.1% public transportation, 0.0% walk, 5.3% work from home (2000); Travel time to work: 13.0% less than 15 minutes, 32.3% 15 to 30 minutes, 34.6% 30 to 45 minutes, 14.1% 45 to 60 minutes, 6.0% 60 minutes or more (2000)

WIMAUMA (CDP). Covers a land area of 8.423 square miles and a water area of 0.389 square miles. Located at 27.71° N. Lat.; 82.31° W. Long. Elevation is 98 feet.
Population: 4,249 (1990); 4,246 (2000); 5,296 (2004); 6,534 (2009 projected); Race: 41.3% White, 6.4% Black, 0.2% Asian, 79.0% Hispanic of any race (2004); Density: 628.8 persons per square mile (2004); Average household size: 4.54 (2004); Median age: 23.6 (2004); Male/female ratio: 115.1 (2004); Marriage status: 30.6% never married, 56.0% now married, 4.5% widowed, 8.9% divorced (2000); Foreign born: 30.1% (2000); Ancestry (includes multiple ancestries): 58.2% Other groups, 3.7% United States or American, 3.7% German, 3.1% English, 2.5% African (2000).
Economy: Employment by occupation: 3.8% management, 6.1% professional, 19.8% services, 15.6% sales, 13.9% farming, 14.4% construction, 26.4% production (2000).
Income: Per capita income: $9,542 (2004); Median household income: $35,776 (2004); Average household income: $40,798 (2004); Percent of households with income of $100,000 or more: 4.5% (2004); Poverty rate: 31.7% (2000).
Education: Percent of population age 25 and over with: High school diploma (including GED) or higher: 37.8% (2004); Bachelor's degree or higher: 0.6% (2004); Master's degree or higher: 0.6% (2004).

School District(s)

Hillsborough County School District (PK-12)
2002-03 Enrollment: 175,454 . . . . (813) 272-4050

Housing: Homeownership rate: 60.1% (2004); Median home value: $95,729 (2004); Median rent: $251 per month (2000); Median age of housing: 17 years (2000).
Transportation: Commute to work: 93.9% car, 2.2% public transportation, 1.2% walk, 0.0% work from home (2000); Travel time to work: 22.0% less than 15 minutes, 40.5% 15 to 30 minutes, 21.0% 30 to 45 minutes, 12.3% 45 to 60 minutes, 4.3% 60 minutes or more (2000)

Holmes County

Located in northwestern Florida; bounded on the north by Alabama, and on the east by Holmes Creek; drained by the Choctawhatchee River. Covers a land area of 482.40 square miles, a water area of 6.30 square miles, and is located in the Central Time Zone. The county government was organized in 1848. County seat is Bonifay.
Population: 15,778 (1990); 18,564 (2000); 18,737 (2004); 18,967 (2009 projected); Race: 89.8% White, 6.1% Black, 0.5% Asian, 2.7% Hispanic of any race (2004); Density: 38.8 persons per square mile (2004); Average household size: 2.70 (2004); Median age: 38.1 (2004); Male/female ratio: 115.2 (2004).
Religion: Five largest groups: 35.4% Southern Baptist Convention, 9.9% Assemblies of God, 4.4% The United Methodist Church, 1.3% The Church of Jesus Christ of Latter-day Saints, 1.1% Catholic Church (2000).
Economy: Unemployment rate: 4.7% (2004); Total civilian labor force: 6,415 (2004); Leading industries: 24.7% health care and social assistance; 20.0% retail trade; 14.0% manufacturing (2003); Companies that employ 500 or more persons: 0 (2003); Companies that employ 100 to 499 persons: 1 (2003); Companies that employ less than 100 persons: 266 (2003); Farms: 672 totaling 90,875 acres (2002); Minority business ownership rate: n/a (1997); Women business ownership rate: 23.1% (1997); Retail sales per capita: $2,517 (1997). Single-family building permits issued: 49 (2004); Multi-family building permits issued: 0 (2004).
Income: Per capita income: $15,285 (2004); Median household income: $30,453 (2004); Average household income: $40,362 (2004); Percent of households with income of $100,000 or more: 5.2% (2004); Poverty rate: 20.5% (2002); Bankruptcy rate: 4.49% (2004).
Education: Percent of population age 25 and over with: High school diploma (including GED) or higher: 65.2% (2004); Bachelor's degree or higher: 8.7% (2004); Master's degree or higher: 3.0% (2004).
Housing: Homeownership rate: 81.9% (2004); Median home value: $73,881 (2004); Median rent: $273 per month (2000); Median age of housing: 22 years (2000).
Health: Birth rate: 122.0 per 10,000 population (2004); Death rate: 119.9 per 10,000 population (2004); Age adjusted cancer mortality rate: 181.4 deaths per 100,000 population (2002); Air Quality Index: 96.7% good, 3.3% moderate, 0.0% unhealthy for sensitive individuals, 0.0% unhealthy (percent of days in 2004); Number of physicians: 5.3 per 10,000 population (2001); Hospital beds: 13.4 per 10,000 population (2002); Hospital admissions: 416.6 per 10,000 population (2002).
Elections: 2004 Presidential election results: 77.3% Bush, 21.8% Kerry, 0.5% Nader, 0.2% Badnarik
National and State Parks: Ponce de Leon Springs State Park
Additional Information Contacts
Holmes County Government Offices . . . . (850) 547-1119
Holmes County Chamber of Commerce . . . . (850) 547-4682

Holmes County Communities

BONIFAY (city). Covers a land area of 3.619 square miles and a water area of 0 square miles. Located at 30.79° N. Lat.; 85.68° W. Long. Elevation is 160 feet.
History: Bonifay was established on Holmes Creek as a center for cattle, sheep, and hog farmers.
Population: 2,868 (1990); 4,078 (2000); 4,170 (2004); 4,286 (2009 projected); Race: 68.6% White, 24.4% Black, 1.5% Asian, 6.1% Hispanic of any race (2004); Density: 1,152.3 persons per square mile (2004); Average household size: 4.09 (2004); Median age: 35.4 (2004); Male/female ratio: 194.3 (2004); Marriage status: 32.7% never married, 39.9% now married, 11.4% widowed, 16.0% divorced (2000); Foreign born: 4.2% (2000); Ancestry (includes multiple ancestries): 29.0% Other groups, 23.9% United States or American, 7.5% Irish, 6.7% English, 5.0% German (2000).
Economy: Employment by occupation: 7.8% management, 16.6% professional, 23.4% services, 21.2% sales, 1.0% farming, 12.0% construction, 18.0% production (2000).
Income: Per capita income: $11,027 (2004); Median household income: $24,435 (2004); Average household income: $39,016 (2004); Percent of households with income of $100,000 or more: 8.7% (2004); Poverty rate: 21.7% (2000).
Taxes: Total city taxes per capita: $119 (2002); City property taxes per capita: $115 (2002).
Education: Percent of population age 25 and over with: High school diploma (including GED) or higher: 59.4% (2004); Bachelor's degree or higher: 10.2% (2004); Master's degree or higher: 4.2% (2004).

School District(s)

Holmes County School District (PK-12)
2002-03 Enrollment: 3,414 . . . . (850) 547-9341

Housing: Homeownership rate: 62.9% (2004); Median home value: $84,184 (2004); Median rent: $247 per month (2000); Median age of housing: 30 years (2000).
Hospitals: Doctors Memorial Hospital (34 beds)
Safety: Violent crime rate: 12.1 per 10,000 population; Property crime rate: 67.6 per 10,000 population (2003).
Transportation: Commute to work: 89.1% car, 0.0% public transportation, 6.1% walk, 4.0% work from home (2000); Travel time to work: 42.1% less than 15 minutes, 22.8% 15 to 30 minutes, 13.0% 30 to 45 minutes, 5.0% 45 to 60 minutes, 17.1% 60 minutes or more (2000)
Additional Information Contacts
Holmes County Chamber of Commerce . . . . (850) 547-4682

ESTO (town). Covers a land area of 2.202 square miles and a water area of 0.151 square miles. Located at 30.98° N. Lat.; 85.64° W. Long. Elevation is 241 feet.
Population: 253 (1990); 356 (2000); 341 (2004); 315 (2009 projected); Race: 91.5% White, 2.3% Black, 0.0% Asian, 3.2% Hispanic of any race (2004); Density: 154.8 persons per square mile (2004); Average household size: 2.45 (2004); Median age: 37.9 (2004); Male/female ratio: 110.5 (2004); Marriage status: 20.1% never married, 58.6% now married, 9.6% widowed, 11.6% divorced (2000); Foreign born: 0.0% (2000); Ancestry (includes multiple ancestries): 14.1% Irish, 14.1% United States or American, 13.2% English, 12.9% Other groups, 1.4% Dutch (2000).
Economy: Employment by occupation: 10.3% management, 5.6% professional, 15.0% services, 28.0% sales, 0.9% farming, 18.7% construction, 21.5% production (2000).
Income: Per capita income: $16,547 (2004); Median household income: $32,941 (2004); Average household income: $40,594 (2004); Percent of households with income of $100,000 or more: 2.9% (2004); Poverty rate: 12.5% (2000).
Taxes: Total city taxes per capita: $39 (2002); City property taxes per capita: $0 (2002).

Education: Percent of population age 25 and over with: High school diploma (including GED) or higher: 66.7% (2004); Bachelor's degree or higher: 5.9% (2004); Master's degree or higher: 2.3% (2004).
Housing: Homeownership rate: 84.2% (2004); Median home value: $59,444 (2004); Median rent: $275 per month (2000); Median age of housing: 25 years (2000).
Transportation: Commute to work: 96.9% car, 0.0% public transportation, 2.1% walk, 0.0% work from home (2000); Travel time to work: 9.3% less than 15 minutes, 27.8% 15 to 30 minutes, 23.7% 30 to 45 minutes, 25.8% 45 to 60 minutes, 13.4% 60 minutes or more (2000)

NOMA (town). Covers a land area of 1.094 square miles and a water area of 0 square miles. Located at 30.98° N. Lat.; 85.61° W. Long. Elevation is 207 feet.
Population: 222 (1990); 213 (2000); 204 (2004); 190 (2009 projected); Race: 79.9% White, 17.2% Black, 0.0% Asian, 2.0% Hispanic of any race (2004); Density: 186.5 persons per square mile (2004); Average household size: 2.32 (2004); Median age: 38.2 (2004); Male/female ratio: 94.3 (2004); Marriage status: 30.2% never married, 47.9% now married, 12.4% widowed, 9.5% divorced (2000); Foreign born: 0.9% (2000); Ancestry (includes multiple ancestries): 37.9% Other groups, 20.5% United States or American, 2.7% Irish, 2.3% English, 2.3% French (except Basque) (2000).
Economy: Employment by occupation: 2.5% management, 6.2% professional, 28.4% services, 18.5% sales, 0.0% farming, 11.1% construction, 33.3% production (2000).
Income: Per capita income: $13,064 (2004); Median household income: $28,846 (2004); Average household income: $30,284 (2004); Percent of households with income of $100,000 or more: 0.0% (2004); Poverty rate: 18.3% (2000).
Education: Percent of population age 25 and over with: High school diploma (including GED) or higher: 46.7% (2004); Bachelor's degree or higher: 2.9% (2004); Master's degree or higher: 0.0% (2004).
Housing: Homeownership rate: 78.4% (2004); Median home value: $40,588 (2004); Median rent: $172 per month (2000); Median age of housing: 23 years (2000).
Transportation: Commute to work: 93.4% car, 0.0% public transportation, 5.3% walk, 1.3% work from home (2000); Travel time to work: 12.0% less than 15 minutes, 36.0% 15 to 30 minutes, 28.0% 30 to 45 minutes, 12.0% 45 to 60 minutes, 12.0% 60 minutes or more (2000)

PONCE DE LEON (town). Covers a land area of 4.953 square miles and a water area of 0.011 square miles. Located at 30.72° N. Lat.; 85.93° W. Long. Elevation is 65 feet.
History: Ponce de Leon is on the site of Ponce de Leon Springs, one of many "fountains of youth" named for the Spanish explorer.
Population: 428 (1990); 457 (2000); 505 (2004); 555 (2009 projected); Race: 90.9% White, 2.8% Black, 0.0% Asian, 3.8% Hispanic of any race (2004); Density: 102.0 persons per square mile (2004); Average household size: 2.25 (2004); Median age: 41.6 (2004); Male/female ratio: 93.5 (2004); Marriage status: 14.0% never married, 64.0% now married, 9.3% widowed, 12.6% divorced (2000); Foreign born: 2.7% (2000); Ancestry (includes multiple ancestries): 24.7% United States or American, 17.3% Other groups, 12.8% Irish, 9.7% English, 7.6% German (2000).
Economy: Employment by occupation: 7.4% management, 5.3% professional, 24.7% services, 31.6% sales, 4.7% farming, 18.9% construction, 7.4% production (2000).
Income: Per capita income: $14,332 (2004); Median household income: $26,333 (2004); Average household income: $32,310 (2004); Percent of households with income of $100,000 or more: 1.3% (2004); Poverty rate: 19.3% (2000).
Taxes: Total city taxes per capita: $96 (2002); City property taxes per capita: $0 (2002).
Education: Percent of population age 25 and over with: High school diploma (including GED) or higher: 67.5% (2004); Bachelor's degree or higher: 2.9% (2004); Master's degree or higher: 0.6% (2004).

School District(s)

Holmes County School District (PK-12)
2002-03 Enrollment: 3,414 . . . . (850) 547-9341

Housing: Homeownership rate: 75.4% (2004); Median home value: $58,889 (2004); Median rent: $243 per month (2000); Median age of housing: 24 years (2000).
Transportation: Commute to work: 97.9% car, 0.0% public transportation, 1.1% walk, 1.1% work from home (2000); Travel time to work: 34.0% less than 15 minutes, 29.3% 15 to 30 minutes, 16.5% 30 to 45 minutes, 3.7% 45 to 60 minutes, 16.5% 60 minutes or more (2000)

WESTVILLE (town). Covers a land area of 7.274 square miles and a water area of 0.178 square miles. Located at 30.76° N. Lat.; 85.85° W. Long. Elevation is 66 feet.
Population: 257 (1990); 221 (2000); 236 (2004); 250 (2009 projected); Race: 98.7% White, 0.0% Black, 0.4% Asian, 1.7% Hispanic of any race (2004); Density: 32.4 persons per square mile (2004); Average household size: 2.34 (2004); Median age: 35.7 (2004); Male/female ratio: 81.5 (2004); Marriage status: 14.6% never married, 66.1% now married, 7.0% widowed, 12.3% divorced (2000); Foreign born: 0.0% (2000); Ancestry (includes multiple ancestries): 41.1% United States or American, 10.0% English, 9.5% Other groups, 5.6% Scottish, 3.5% Irish (2000).
Economy: Employment by occupation: 0.0% management, 14.1% professional, 16.5% services, 15.3% sales, 5.9% farming, 23.5% construction, 24.7% production (2000).
Income: Per capita income: $13,602 (2004); Median household income: $28,421 (2004); Average household income: $31,782 (2004); Percent of households with income of $100,000 or more: 2.0% (2004); Poverty rate: 13.9% (2000).
Education: Percent of population age 25 and over with: High school diploma (including GED) or higher: 68.8% (2004); Bachelor's degree or higher: 5.1% (2004); Master's degree or higher: 1.3% (2004).
Housing: Homeownership rate: 87.1% (2004); Median home value: $56,923 (2004); Median rent: $225 per month (2000); Median age of housing: 33 years (2000).
Transportation: Commute to work: 95.2% car, 0.0% public transportation, 0.0% walk, 0.0% work from home (2000); Travel time to work: 9.6% less than 15 minutes, 30.1% 15 to 30 minutes, 18.1% 30 to 45 minutes, 14.5% 45 to 60 minutes, 27.7% 60 minutes or more (2000)

Indian River County

Located in central Florida; bounded on the east by the Atlantic Ocean; coastal lowland area with a barrier beach enclosing Indian River Lagoon; includes Lake Wilmington. Covers a land area of 503.20 square miles, a water area of 113.70 square miles, and is located in the Eastern Time Zone. The county government was organized in 1925. County seat is Vero Beach.

Indian River County is part of the Vero Beach, FL Metropolitan Statistical Area. The entire metro area includes: Indian River County, FL

Population: 90,208 (1990); 112,947 (2000); 122,283 (2004); 134,047 (2009 projected); Race: 86.9% White, 8.4% Black, 0.9% Asian, 7.5% Hispanic of any race (2004); Density: 243.0 persons per square mile (2004); Average household size: 2.29 (2004); Median age: 47.2 (2004); Male/female ratio: 94.1 (2004).
Religion: Five largest groups: 26.7% Catholic Church, 6.0% Southern Baptist Convention, 3.7% The United Methodist Church, 2.4% United Church of Christ, 2.4% Episcopal Church (2000).
Economy: Unemployment rate: 8.0% (2004); Total civilian labor force: 55,712 (2004); Leading industries: 21.4% retail trade; 17.7% health care and social assistance; 10.4% accommodation & food services (2003); Companies that employ 500 or more persons: 5 (2003); Companies that employ 100 to 499 persons: 53 (2003); Companies that employ less than 100 persons: 3,626 (2003); Farms: 480 totaling 191,333 acres (2002); Minority business ownership rate: 4.6% (1997); Women business ownership rate: 28.9% (1997); Retail sales per capita: $11,683 (1997). Single-family building permits issued: 3,646 (2004); Multi-family building permits issued: 539 (2004).
Income: Per capita income: $29,520 (2004); Median household income: $43,418 (2004); Average household income: $66,887 (2004); Percent of households with income of $100,000 or more: 14.7% (2004); Poverty rate: 10.0% (2002); Bankruptcy rate: 2.63% (2004).
Taxes: Total county taxes per capita: $667 (2002); County property taxes per capita: $464 (2002).
Education: Percent of population age 25 and over with: High school diploma (including GED) or higher: 81.3% (2004); Bachelor's degree or higher: 22.9% (2004); Master's degree or higher: 7.9% (2004).
Housing: Homeownership rate: 78.0% (2004); Median home value: $125,110 (2004); Median rent: $521 per month (2000); Median age of housing: 17 years (2000).
Health: Birth rate: 91.1 per 10,000 population (2004); Death rate: 126.2 per 10,000 population (2004); Age adjusted cancer mortality rate: 195.3 deaths per 100,000 population (2002); Number of physicians: 27.3 per 10,000

population (2001); Hospital beds: 46.1 per 10,000 population (2002); Hospital admissions: 1,597.1 per 10,000 population (2002).
Elections: 2004 Presidential election results: 60.1% Bush, 39.0% Kerry, 0.5% Nader, 0.2% Badnarik
National and State Parks: Pelican Island National Wildlife Refuge; Sebastian Inlet State Park
Additional Information Contacts
Indian River County Government Offices .... (561) 567-8000
Indian River County Chamber .... (772) 567-3491
Realtors Association of Indian River County .... (772) 567-3510
Sebastian Chamber of Commerce..................... (772) 589-5969

Indian River County Communities

FELLSMERE (city). Covers a land area of 5.302 square miles and a water area of 0.103 square miles. Located at 27.76° N. Lat.; 80.59° W. Long. Elevation is 25 feet.
Population: 2,143 (1990); 3,813 (2000); 4,343 (2004); 4,930 (2009 projected); Race: 57.0% White, 6.1% Black, 0.1% Asian, 79.9% Hispanic of any race (2004); Density: 819.1 persons per square mile (2004); Average household size: 4.53 (2004); Median age: 26.2 (2004); Male/female ratio: 139.8 (2004); Marriage status: 24.2% never married, 67.5% now married, 4.3% widowed, 4.0% divorced (2000); Foreign born: 39.3% (2000); Ancestry (includes multiple ancestries): 59.2% Other groups, 3.5% United States or American, 2.5% English, 2.2% Irish, 2.0% German (2000).
Economy: Single-family building permits issued: 9 (2004); Multi-family building permits issued: 70 (2004); Employment by occupation: 4.2% management, 4.7% professional, 17.9% services, 12.6% sales, 28.7% farming, 14.7% construction, 17.1% production (2000).
Income: Per capita income: $10,838 (2004); Median household income: $34,519 (2004); Average household income: $42,239 (2004); Percent of households with income of $100,000 or more: 5.0% (2004); Poverty rate: 24.3% (2000).
Taxes: Total city taxes per capita: $212 (2002); City property taxes per capita: $50 (2002).
Education: Percent of population age 25 and over with: High school diploma (including GED) or higher: 28.9% (2004); Bachelor's degree or higher: 1.7% (2004); Master's degree or higher: 0.4% (2004).

School District(s)

Indian River County School District (PK-12)
2002-03 Enrollment: 15,986 .... (772) 564-3150

Four-year College(s)

Christ College of Florida
2003-04 Enrollment: 5 .... (772) 571-8833
2003-04 Tuition: In-state $1,350; Out-of-state $1,350
Reformation International College
2003-04 Enrollment: 5 .... (772) 571-8833
2003-04 Tuition: In-state $1,350; Out-of-state $1,350
Reformation International Theological Seminary
2003-04 Enrollment: 16 .... (772) 571-8833
2003-04 Tuition: In-state $1,760; Out-of-state $1,760

Housing: Homeownership rate: 69.8% (2004); Median home value: $76,259 (2004); Median rent: $396 per month (2000); Median age of housing: 16 years (2000).
Safety: Violent crime rate: 29.8 per 10,000 population; Property crime rate: 198.9 per 10,000 population (2003).
Transportation: Commute to work: 90.2% car, 4.7% public transportation, 1.8% walk, 0.1% work from home (2000); Travel time to work: 24.1% less than 15 minutes, 32.8% 15 to 30 minutes, 32.9% 30 to 45 minutes, 3.3% 45 to 60 minutes, 6.8% 60 minutes or more (2000)

FLORIDA RIDGE (CDP). Covers a land area of 10.798 square miles and a water area of 1.784 square miles. Located at 27.57° N. Lat.; 80.39° W. Long.
Population: 12,218 (1990); 15,217 (2000); 16,946 (2004); 19,080 (2009 projected); Race: 84.5% White, 12.2% Black, 0.9% Asian, 4.5% Hispanic of any race (2004); Density: 1,569.4 persons per square mile (2004); Average household size: 2.34 (2004); Median age: 42.7 (2004); Male/female ratio: 92.1 (2004); Marriage status: 17.1% never married, 61.1% now married, 9.8% widowed, 12.0% divorced (2000); Foreign born: 7.2% (2000); Ancestry (includes multiple ancestries): 19.1% Other groups, 16.0% Irish, 15.4% English, 14.4% German, 8.3% United States or American (2000).
Economy: Employment by occupation: 9.3% management, 12.9% professional, 23.0% services, 28.3% sales, 1.4% farming, 13.5% construction, 11.5% production (2000).
Income: Per capita income: $22,145 (2004); Median household income: $41,907 (2004); Average household income: $51,812 (2004); Percent of households with income of $100,000 or more: 7.8% (2004); Poverty rate: 9.5% (2000).
Education: Percent of population age 25 and over with: High school diploma (including GED) or higher: 80.6% (2004); Bachelor's degree or higher: 18.1% (2004); Master's degree or higher: 6.1% (2004).
Housing: Homeownership rate: 82.5% (2004); Median home value: $98,271 (2004); Median rent: $535 per month (2000); Median age of housing: 17 years (2000).
Transportation: Commute to work: 96.3% car, 0.3% public transportation, 0.6% walk, 1.5% work from home (2000); Travel time to work: 29.6% less than 15 minutes, 54.2% 15 to 30 minutes, 12.2% 30 to 45 minutes, 2.2% 45 to 60 minutes, 1.9% 60 minutes or more (2000)

GIFFORD (CDP). Covers a land area of 7.049 square miles and a water area of 0.455 square miles. Located at 27.67° N. Lat.; 80.41° W. Long. Elevation is 17 feet.
History: Gifford was named for F. Charles Gifford, who selected the site for Vero Beach, just south of Gifford.
Population: 6,278 (1990); 7,599 (2000); 8,211 (2004); 8,947 (2009 projected); Race: 41.4% White, 55.2% Black, 0.3% Asian, 7.8% Hispanic of any race (2004); Density: 1,164.9 persons per square mile (2004); Average household size: 2.46 (2004); Median age: 39.6 (2004); Male/female ratio: 84.1 (2004); Marriage status: 26.4% never married, 51.1% now married, 11.1% widowed, 11.4% divorced (2000); Foreign born: 8.4% (2000); Ancestry (includes multiple ancestries): 51.0% Other groups, 6.1% English, 5.2% German, 5.2% United States or American, 4.4% Irish (2000).
Economy: Employment by occupation: 7.5% management, 13.1% professional, 28.8% services, 21.9% sales, 5.7% farming, 7.1% construction, 16.0% production (2000).
Income: Per capita income: $22,771 (2004); Median household income: $31,267 (2004); Average household income: $54,796 (2004); Percent of households with income of $100,000 or more: 11.6% (2004); Poverty rate: 23.4% (2000).
Education: Percent of population age 25 and over with: High school diploma (including GED) or higher: 58.4% (2004); Bachelor's degree or higher: 16.3% (2004); Master's degree or higher: 5.6% (2004).
Housing: Homeownership rate: 51.7% (2004); Median home value: $135,861 (2004); Median rent: $323 per month (2000); Median age of housing: 14 years (2000).
Transportation: Commute to work: 90.6% car, 1.0% public transportation, 1.6% walk, 3.5% work from home (2000); Travel time to work: 45.4% less than 15 minutes, 35.6% 15 to 30 minutes, 14.3% 30 to 45 minutes, 2.1% 45 to 60 minutes, 2.6% 60 minutes or more (2000)

INDIAN RIVER SHORES (town). Covers a land area of 5.174 square miles and a water area of 1.985 square miles. Located at 27.70° N. Lat.; 80.38° W. Long. Elevation is 6 feet.
Population: 2,315 (1990); 3,448 (2000); 3,611 (2004); 3,768 (2009 projected); Race: 98.6% White, 0.1% Black, 0.9% Asian, 0.8% Hispanic of any race (2004); Density: 697.9 persons per square mile (2004); Average household size: 1.86 (2004); Median age: 68.6 (2004); Male/female ratio: 85.9 (2004); Marriage status: 3.4% never married, 78.4% now married, 12.5% widowed, 5.7% divorced (2000); Foreign born: 4.6% (2000); Ancestry (includes multiple ancestries): 27.9% English, 20.7% German, 16.7% Irish, 6.5% Scottish, 5.8% United States or American (2000).
Economy: Single-family building permits issued: 70 (2004); Multi-family building permits issued: 0 (2004); Employment by occupation: 34.8% management, 24.7% professional, 3.4% services, 31.2% sales, 1.6% farming, 3.4% construction, 0.9% production (2000).
Income: Per capita income: $98,722 (2004); Median household income: $118,429 (2004); Average household income: $183,377 (2004); Percent of households with income of $100,000 or more: 56.3% (2004); Poverty rate: 2.2% (2000).
Taxes: Total city taxes per capita: $629 (2002); City property taxes per capita: $477 (2002).
Education: Percent of population age 25 and over with: High school diploma (including GED) or higher: 98.9% (2004); Bachelor's degree or higher: 53.6% (2004); Master's degree or higher: 18.8% (2004).
Housing: Homeownership rate: 95.9% (2004); Median home value: $544,872 (2004); Median rent: $533 per month (2000); Median age of housing: 17 years (2000).
Safety: Violent crime rate: 0.0 per 10,000 population; Property crime rate: 56.4 per 10,000 population (2003).

Transportation: Commute to work: 82.0% car, 1.1% public transportation, 0.0% walk, 15.9% work from home (2000); Travel time to work: 38.5% less than 15 minutes, 46.9% 15 to 30 minutes, 7.5% 30 to 45 minutes, 5.8% 45 to 60 minutes, 1.3% 60 minutes or more (2000)

NORTH BEACH (CDP). Covers a land area of 3.088 square miles and a water area of 7.246 square miles. Located at 27.79° N. Lat.; 80.41° W. Long.

Population: 156 (1990); 243 (2000); 271 (2004); 305 (2009 projected); Race: 98.5% White, 0.7% Black, 0.0% Asian, 2.6% Hispanic of any race (2004); Density: 87.8 persons per square mile (2004); Average household size: 2.61 (2004); Median age: 51.3 (2004); Male/female ratio: 103.8 (2004); Marriage status: 8.1% never married, 91.9% now married, 0.0% widowed, 0.0% divorced (2000); Foreign born: 6.8% (2000); Ancestry (includes multiple ancestries): 24.4% English, 22.6% German, 18.6% Irish, 16.3% United States or American, 10.9% Norwegian (2000).

Economy: Employment by occupation: 26.6% management, 2.5% professional, 0.0% services, 58.2% sales, 0.0% farming, 6.3% construction, 6.3% production (2000).

Income: Per capita income: $60,987 (2004); Median household income: $66,176 (2004); Average household income: $158,918 (2004); Percent of households with income of $100,000 or more: 39.4% (2004); Poverty rate: 0.0% (2000).

Education: Percent of population age 25 and over with: High school diploma (including GED) or higher: 100.0% (2004); Bachelor's degree or higher: 45.5% (2004); Master's degree or higher: 14.1% (2004).

Housing: Homeownership rate: 89.4% (2004); Median home value: $601,563 (2004); Median rent: $n/a per month (2000); Median age of housing: 5 years (2000).

Transportation: Commute to work: 96.2% car, 0.0% public transportation, 0.0% walk, 3.8% work from home (2000); Travel time to work: 10.5% less than 15 minutes, 55.3% 15 to 30 minutes, 9.2% 30 to 45 minutes, 10.5% 45 to 60 minutes, 14.5% 60 minutes or more (2000)

ORCHID (town). Covers a land area of 1.230 square miles and a water area of 0.614 square miles. Located at 27.77° N. Lat.; 80.41° W. Long. Elevation is 3 feet.

Population: 10 (1990); 140 (2000); 156 (2004); 176 (2009 projected); Race: 100.0% White, 0.0% Black, 0.0% Asian, 0.6% Hispanic of any race (2004); Density: 126.8 persons per square mile (2004); Average household size: 2.03 (2004); Median age: 60.2 (2004); Male/female ratio: 95.0 (2004); Marriage status: 0.0% never married, 98.5% now married, 0.0% widowed, 1.5% divorced (2000); Foreign born: 2.9% (2000); Ancestry (includes multiple ancestries): 30.4% English, 29.0% German, 17.4% Irish, 6.5% Norwegian, 5.1% Scotch-Irish (2000).

Economy: Single-family building permits issued: 10 (2004); Multi-family building permits issued: 0 (2004); Employment by occupation: 52.9% management, 20.6% professional, 0.0% services, 17.6% sales, 8.8% farming, 0.0% construction, 0.0% production (2000).

Income: Per capita income: $156,266 (2004); Median household income: $325,000 (2004); Average household income: $316,591 (2004); Percent of households with income of $100,000 or more: 76.6% (2004); Poverty rate: 0.0% (2000).

Taxes: Total city taxes per capita: $2,764 (2002); City property taxes per capita: $1,929 (2002).

Education: Percent of population age 25 and over with: High school diploma (including GED) or higher: 98.6% (2004); Bachelor's degree or higher: 75.5% (2004); Master's degree or higher: 20.4% (2004).

Housing: Homeownership rate: 94.8% (2004); Median home value: $1 million+ (2004); Median rent: $625 per month (2000); Median age of housing: 2 years (2000).

Transportation: Commute to work: 64.7% car, 0.0% public transportation, 0.0% walk, 35.3% work from home (2000); Travel time to work: 31.8% less than 15 minutes, 40.9% 15 to 30 minutes, 27.3% 30 to 45 minutes, 0.0% 45 to 60 minutes, 0.0% 60 minutes or more (2000)

ROSELAND (CDP). Covers a land area of 1.987 square miles and a water area of 1.185 square miles. Located at 27.83° N. Lat.; 80.48° W. Long. Elevation is 21 feet.

Population: 1,651 (1990); 1,775 (2000); 1,879 (2004); 2,020 (2009 projected); Race: 96.6% White, 0.3% Black, 1.4% Asian, 1.2% Hispanic of any race (2004); Density: 945.6 persons per square mile (2004); Average household size: 2.08 (2004); Median age: 54.4 (2004); Male/female ratio: 93.5 (2004); Marriage status: 14.2% never married, 60.9% now married, 11.1% widowed, 13.8% divorced (2000); Foreign born: 3.9% (2000); Ancestry (includes multiple ancestries): 17.3% Irish, 13.4% German, 12.4% United States or American, 10.2% Other groups, 10.2% English (2000).

Economy: Manufacturing includes wire and cable, lead castings. Employment by occupation: 10.1% management, 15.1% professional, 21.5% services, 21.0% sales, 4.1% farming, 13.3% construction, 14.8% production (2000).

Income: Per capita income: $20,718 (2004); Median household income: $30,559 (2004); Average household income: $42,323 (2004); Percent of households with income of $100,000 or more: 7.5% (2004); Poverty rate: 18.7% (2000).

Education: Percent of population age 25 and over with: High school diploma (including GED) or higher: 72.3% (2004); Bachelor's degree or higher: 10.7% (2004); Master's degree or higher: 4.2% (2004).

Housing: Homeownership rate: 81.2% (2004); Median home value: $105,049 (2004); Median rent: $609 per month (2000); Median age of housing: 24 years (2000).

Transportation: Commute to work: 90.3% car, 0.0% public transportation, 2.6% walk, 4.9% work from home (2000); Travel time to work: 30.7% less than 15 minutes, 28.2% 15 to 30 minutes, 30.0% 30 to 45 minutes, 4.9% 45 to 60 minutes, 6.1% 60 minutes or more (2000)

SEBASTIAN (city). Covers a land area of 12.620 square miles and a water area of 0.927 square miles. Located at 27.78° N. Lat.; 80.48° W. Long. Elevation is 20 feet.

History: Sebastian began as a trading post on the Atlantic Coast, named for St. Sebastian. It developed as a tourist destination.

Population: 10,282 (1990); 16,181 (2000); 18,288 (2004); 20,865 (2009 projected); Race: 93.1% White, 3.8% Black, 0.8% Asian, 4.4% Hispanic of any race (2004); Density: 1,449.1 persons per square mile (2004); Average household size: 2.34 (2004); Median age: 46.7 (2004); Male/female ratio: 92.3 (2004); Marriage status: 15.5% never married, 64.6% now married, 9.5% widowed, 10.4% divorced (2000); Foreign born: 6.8% (2000); Ancestry (includes multiple ancestries): 19.8% German, 14.9% Irish, 13.7% English, 13.7% Italian, 10.1% Other groups (2000).

Economy: Single-family building permits issued: 565 (2004); Multi-family building permits issued: 186 (2004); Employment by occupation: 9.9% management, 14.0% professional, 26.0% services, 27.1% sales, 0.7% farming, 13.8% construction, 8.5% production (2000).

Income: Per capita income: $22,131 (2004); Median household income: $44,397 (2004); Average household income: $51,742 (2004); Percent of households with income of $100,000 or more: 7.5% (2004); Poverty rate: 6.3% (2000).

Taxes: Total city taxes per capita: $294 (2002); City property taxes per capita: $155 (2002).

Education: Percent of population age 25 and over with: High school diploma (including GED) or higher: 83.1% (2004); Bachelor's degree or higher: 14.2% (2004); Master's degree or higher: 4.2% (2004).

School District(s)

Indian River County School District (PK-12)
2002-03 Enrollment: 15,986 . . . . (772) 564-3150

Housing: Homeownership rate: 87.0% (2004); Median home value: $126,188 (2004); Median rent: $599 per month (2000); Median age of housing: 12 years (2000).

Hospitals: Sebastian River Medical Center (129 beds)

Safety: Violent crime rate: 30.9 per 10,000 population; Property crime rate: 263.9 per 10,000 population (2003).

Transportation: Commute to work: 93.4% car, 0.0% public transportation, 0.4% walk, 4.3% work from home (2000); Travel time to work: 24.5% less than 15 minutes, 50.8% 15 to 30 minutes, 16.3% 30 to 45 minutes, 3.7% 45 to 60 minutes, 4.6% 60 minutes or more (2000)

Additional Information Contacts

Sebastian Chamber of Commerce. (772) 589-5969

SOUTH BEACH (CDP). Covers a land area of 2.701 square miles and a water area of 4.188 square miles. Located at 27.59° N. Lat.; 80.33° W. Long.

Population: 2,754 (1990); 3,457 (2000); 3,735 (2004); 4,088 (2009 projected); Race: 97.9% White, 0.7% Black, 1.2% Asian, 1.5% Hispanic of any race (2004); Density: 1,382.7 persons per square mile (2004); Average household size: 2.12 (2004); Median age: 60.5 (2004); Male/female ratio: 93.2 (2004); Marriage status: 7.7% never married, 81.1% now married, 8.3% widowed, 3.0% divorced (2000); Foreign born: 4.3% (2000); Ancestry (includes multiple ancestries): 26.0% English, 19.2% Irish, 18.8% German, 7.6% Italian, 5.0% French (except Basque) (2000).

Economy: Employment by occupation: 26.5% management, 37.7% professional, 4.0% services, 23.9% sales, 0.0% farming, 2.6% construction, 5.2% production (2000).
Income: Per capita income: $88,238 (2004); Median household income: $127,615 (2004); Average household income: $184,267 (2004); Percent of households with income of $100,000 or more: 60.2% (2004); Poverty rate: 3.4% (2000).
Education: Percent of population age 25 and over with: High school diploma (including GED) or higher: 97.4% (2004); Bachelor's degree or higher: 58.4% (2004); Master's degree or higher: 26.4% (2004).
Housing: Homeownership rate: 95.8% (2004); Median home value: $392,289 (2004); Median rent: $625 per month (2000); Median age of housing: 16 years (2000).
Transportation: Commute to work: 79.6% car, 0.0% public transportation, 1.0% walk, 17.5% work from home (2000); Travel time to work: 47.8% less than 15 minutes, 35.7% 15 to 30 minutes, 6.7% 30 to 45 minutes, 3.4% 45 to 60 minutes, 6.4% 60 minutes or more (2000)

VERO BEACH (city). Covers a land area of 11.073 square miles and a water area of 1.853 square miles. Located at 27.64° N. Lat.; 80.39° W. Long. Elevation is 22 feet.
History: Vero Beach, extending across the Indian River to the ocean, developed as a citrus shipping point. In 1916 bones were found that were believed to be prehistoric, leading to the naming of the "Vero Beach Man." Though it was later thought that the bones were of more recent origin, other excavations revealed the remains of a mastodon.
Population: 17,403 (1990); 17,705 (2000); 17,400 (2004); 17,368 (2009 projected); Race: 92.1% White, 3.6% Black, 1.7% Asian, 6.9% Hispanic of any race (2004); Density: 1,571.3 persons per square mile (2004); Average household size: 2.06 (2004); Median age: 48.3 (2004); Male/female ratio: 92.9 (2004); Marriage status: 21.3% never married, 53.8% now married, 11.1% widowed, 13.8% divorced (2000); Foreign born: 8.8% (2000); Ancestry (includes multiple ancestries): 17.9% Irish, 16.4% German, 16.1% English, 11.4% Other groups, 8.7% Italian (2000).
Economy: Employment by occupation: 12.5% management, 20.9% professional, 19.8% services, 27.3% sales, 0.8% farming, 11.0% construction, 7.6% production (2000).
Income: Per capita income: $35,107 (2004); Median household income: $41,160 (2004); Average household income: $71,774 (2004); Percent of households with income of $100,000 or more: 17.1% (2004); Poverty rate: 9.1% (2000).
Education: Percent of population age 25 and over with: High school diploma (including GED) or higher: 84.2% (2004); Bachelor's degree or higher: 31.5% (2004); Master's degree or higher: 10.6% (2004).

School District(s)

Indian River County School District (PK-12)
2002-03 Enrollment: 15,986 . . . . (772) 564-3150

Two-year College(s)

Flight Safety International (Private, For-profit)
2003-04 Enrollment: 204 . . . . (772) 564-7600

Housing: Homeownership rate: 64.5% (2004); Median home value: $148,567 (2004); Median rent: $509 per month (2000); Median age of housing: 27 years (2000).
Hospitals: HealthSouth Treasure Coast Rehabilitation Hospital (90 beds); Indian River Hospital for Emotional & Behavioral Health (54 beds); Indian River Memorial Hospital (335 beds)
Safety: Violent crime rate: 52.7 per 10,000 population; Property crime rate: 415.6 per 10,000 population (2003).
Newspapers: Vero Beach Press-Journal (Circulation 32,712)
Transportation: Commute to work: 90.1% car, 0.5% public transportation, 3.0% walk, 4.4% work from home (2000); Travel time to work: 55.7% less than 15 minutes, 32.1% 15 to 30 minutes, 5.5% 30 to 45 minutes, 2.4% 45 to 60 minutes, 4.4% 60 minutes or more (2000)

Additional Information Contacts

Indian River County Chamber . . . . (772) 567-3491
Realtors Association of Indian River County . . . . (772) 567-3510

VERO BEACH SOUTH (CDP). Covers a land area of 10.337 square miles and a water area of 0.568 square miles. Located at 27.62° N. Lat.; 80.41° W. Long.
Population: 16,920 (1990); 20,362 (2000); 21,931 (2004); 23,833 (2009 projected); Race: 93.7% White, 2.8% Black, 1.2% Asian, 3.8% Hispanic of any race (2004); Density: 2,121.6 persons per square mile (2004); Average household size: 2.34 (2004); Median age: 42.9 (2004); Male/female ratio: 91.6 (2004); Marriage status: 17.2% never married, 62.3% now married, 8.7% widowed, 11.8% divorced (2000); Foreign born: 6.1% (2000); Ancestry (includes multiple ancestries): 19.4% Irish, 17.3% German, 15.8% English, 10.2% Other groups, 10.0% United States or American (2000).
Economy: Employment by occupation: 12.6% management, 17.6% professional, 19.8% services, 31.0% sales, 1.1% farming, 10.1% construction, 7.8% production (2000).
Income: Per capita income: $24,165 (2004); Median household income: $41,805 (2004); Average household income: $56,360 (2004); Percent of households with income of $100,000 or more: 11.7% (2004); Poverty rate: 7.6% (2000).
Education: Percent of population age 25 and over with: High school diploma (including GED) or higher: 86.2% (2004); Bachelor's degree or higher: 21.7% (2004); Master's degree or higher: 6.4% (2004).
Housing: Homeownership rate: 75.6% (2004); Median home value: $122,530 (2004); Median rent: $531 per month (2000); Median age of housing: 18 years (2000).
Transportation: Commute to work: 94.4% car, 0.0% public transportation, 1.1% walk, 2.8% work from home (2000); Travel time to work: 44.9% less than 15 minutes, 40.6% 15 to 30 minutes, 8.7% 30 to 45 minutes, 1.7% 45 to 60 minutes, 4.2% 60 minutes or more (2000)

WABASSO (CDP). Covers a land area of 2.423 square miles and a water area of 0 square miles. Located at 27.74° N. Lat.; 80.43° W. Long. Elevation is 14 feet.
History: Wabasso was named for Ossabaw Island, Georgia, but the name is spelled backwards. Wabasso developed as a citrus growing and packing area.
Population: 864 (1990); 918 (2000); 1,039 (2004); 1,190 (2009 projected); Race: 80.9% White, 6.0% Black, 1.6% Asian, 14.6% Hispanic of any race (2004); Density: 428.7 persons per square mile (2004); Average household size: 2.24 (2004); Median age: 42.8 (2004); Male/female ratio: 121.1 (2004); Marriage status: 14.9% never married, 47.7% now married, 19.6% widowed, 17.8% divorced (2000); Foreign born: 20.9% (2000); Ancestry (includes multiple ancestries): 17.8% Other groups, 15.5% United States or American, 14.5% Irish, 11.3% German, 7.4% English (2000).
Economy: Employment by occupation: 14.4% management, 6.6% professional, 19.5% services, 13.2% sales, 17.1% farming, 17.4% construction, 12.0% production (2000).
Income: Per capita income: $23,651 (2004); Median household income: $30,784 (2004); Average household income: $52,581 (2004); Percent of households with income of $100,000 or more: 8.6% (2004); Poverty rate: 25.9% (2000).
Education: Percent of population age 25 and over with: High school diploma (including GED) or higher: 62.6% (2004); Bachelor's degree or higher: 13.2% (2004); Master's degree or higher: 2.4% (2004).

School District(s)

Indian River County School District (PK-12)
2002-03 Enrollment: 15,986 . . . . (772) 564-3150

Housing: Homeownership rate: 63.5% (2004); Median home value: $108,511 (2004); Median rent: $507 per month (2000); Median age of housing: 28 years (2000).
Transportation: Commute to work: 91.9% car, 2.1% public transportation, 6.0% walk, 0.0% work from home (2000); Travel time to work: 21.9% less than 15 minutes, 45.2% 15 to 30 minutes, 19.8% 30 to 45 minutes, 3.0% 45 to 60 minutes, 10.2% 60 minutes or more (2000)

WABASSO BEACH (CDP). Covers a land area of 1.178 square miles and a water area of 0.016 square miles. Located at 27.76° N. Lat.; 80.40° W. Long. Elevation is 20 feet.
Population: 523 (1990); 1,075 (2000); 1,314 (2004); 1,609 (2009 projected); Race: 99.2% White, 0.0% Black, 0.1% Asian, 1.0% Hispanic of any race (2004); Density: 1,115.1 persons per square mile (2004); Average household size: 1.92 (2004); Median age: 64.0 (2004); Male/female ratio: 93.5 (2004); Marriage status: 9.7% never married, 72.4% now married, 9.1% widowed, 8.8% divorced (2000); Foreign born: 5.8% (2000); Ancestry (includes multiple ancestries): 22.4% German, 21.9% Irish, 20.2% English, 9.8% Italian, 7.1% Other groups (2000).
Economy: Employment by occupation: 23.9% management, 30.9% professional, 7.0% services, 32.9% sales, 0.0% farming, 0.0% construction, 5.3% production (2000).
Income: Per capita income: $51,197 (2004); Median household income: $67,647 (2004); Average household income: $98,065 (2004); Percent of households with income of $100,000 or more: 32.7% (2004); Poverty rate: 1.4% (2000).

Education: Percent of population age 25 and over with: High school diploma (including GED) or higher: 97.2% (2004); Bachelor's degree or higher: 60.6% (2004); Master's degree or higher: 22.4% (2004).
Housing: Homeownership rate: 92.0% (2004); Median home value: $274,632 (2004); Median rent: $847 per month (2000); Median age of housing: 13 years (2000).
Transportation: Commute to work: 91.7% car, 0.0% public transportation, 0.0% walk, 4.3% work from home (2000); Travel time to work: 14.6% less than 15 minutes, 65.6% 15 to 30 minutes, 14.2% 30 to 45 minutes, 0.0% 45 to 60 minutes, 5.6% 60 minutes or more (2000)

WEST VERO CORRIDOR (CDP). Covers a land area of 4.962 square miles and a water area of 0 square miles. Located at 27.64° N. Lat.; 80.49° W. Long.
Population: 6,605 (1990); 7,695 (2000); 8,277 (2004); 9,082 (2009 projected); Race: 98.0% White, 0.3% Black, 0.6% Asian, 2.5% Hispanic of any race (2004); Density: 1,668.1 persons per square mile (2004); Average household size: 1.78 (2004); Median age: 71.9 (2004); Male/female ratio: 78.4 (2004); Marriage status: 7.7% never married, 63.7% now married, 20.5% widowed, 8.1% divorced (2000); Foreign born: 6.0% (2000); Ancestry (includes multiple ancestries): 20.2% German, 18.8% English, 18.4% Irish, 8.6% United States or American, 8.4% Italian (2000).
Economy: Employment by occupation: 10.6% management, 14.4% professional, 25.6% services, 28.7% sales, 1.9% farming, 9.8% construction, 8.9% production (2000).
Income: Per capita income: $25,862 (2004); Median household income: $36,093 (2004); Average household income: $45,610 (2004); Percent of households with income of $100,000 or more: 5.4% (2004); Poverty rate: 7.3% (2000).
Education: Percent of population age 25 and over with: High school diploma (including GED) or higher: 83.3% (2004); Bachelor's degree or higher: 18.7% (2004); Master's degree or higher: 6.6% (2004).
Housing: Homeownership rate: 79.8% (2004); Median home value: $67,209 (2004); Median rent: $1,113 per month (2000); Median age of housing: 15 years (2000).
Transportation: Commute to work: 89.6% car, 0.0% public transportation, 1.2% walk, 5.7% work from home (2000); Travel time to work: 36.6% less than 15 minutes, 45.1% 15 to 30 minutes, 10.1% 30 to 45 minutes, 2.4% 45 to 60 minutes, 5.7% 60 minutes or more (2000)

WINTER BEACH (CDP). Covers a land area of 6.887 square miles and a water area of 0.013 square miles. Located at 27.71° N. Lat.; 80.42° W. Long. Elevation is 13 feet.
Population: 647 (1990); 965 (2000); 1,051 (2004); 1,160 (2009 projected); Race: 97.5% White, 0.9% Black, 1.0% Asian, 2.2% Hispanic of any race (2004); Density: 152.6 persons per square mile (2004); Average household size: 2.58 (2004); Median age: 47.8 (2004); Male/female ratio: 100.2 (2004); Marriage status: 14.6% never married, 68.5% now married, 5.6% widowed, 11.4% divorced (2000); Foreign born: 3.2% (2000); Ancestry (includes multiple ancestries): 19.6% German, 15.8% English, 15.7% Irish, 15.3% Italian, 9.9% Other groups (2000).
Economy: Employment by occupation: 21.1% management, 17.6% professional, 17.2% services, 26.0% sales, 1.5% farming, 5.7% construction, 10.8% production (2000).
Income: Per capita income: $42,955 (2004); Median household income: $88,924 (2004); Average household income: $110,411 (2004); Percent of households with income of $100,000 or more: 41.4% (2004); Poverty rate: 2.2% (2000).
Education: Percent of population age 25 and over with: High school diploma (including GED) or higher: 86.2% (2004); Bachelor's degree or higher: 29.5% (2004); Master's degree or higher: 9.2% (2004).
Housing: Homeownership rate: 86.8% (2004); Median home value: $230,769 (2004); Median rent: $363 per month (2000); Median age of housing: 15 years (2000).
Transportation: Commute to work: 97.8% car, 0.0% public transportation, 0.0% walk, 2.2% work from home (2000); Travel time to work: 47.8% less than 15 minutes, 36.3% 15 to 30 minutes, 10.4% 30 to 45 minutes, 2.3% 45 to 60 minutes, 3.2% 60 minutes or more (2000)

Jackson County

Located in northwestern Florida; bounded on the north by Alabama, and on the east by the Chattahoochee River and the Georgia border. Covers a land area of 915.60 square miles, a water area of 38.90 square miles, and is located in the Central Time Zone. The county government was organized in 1822. County seat is Marianna.
Population: 41,375 (1990); 46,755 (2000); 47,484 (2004); 48,429 (2009 projected); Race: 69.4% White, 27.4% Black, 0.5% Asian, 3.1% Hispanic of any race (2004); Density: 51.9 persons per square mile (2004); Average household size: 2.83 (2004); Median age: 38.1 (2004); Male/female ratio: 111.7 (2004).
Religion: Five largest groups: 22.9% Southern Baptist Convention, 5.8% The United Methodist Church, 5.0% Assemblies of God, 2.1% National Association of Free Will Baptists, 1.1% The Church of Jesus Christ of Latter-day Saints (2000).
Economy: Unemployment rate: 3.6% (2004); Total civilian labor force: 18,901 (2004); Leading industries: 21.5% retail trade; 18.1% health care and social assistance; 10.1% accommodation & food services (2003); Companies that employ 500 or more persons: 0 (2003); Companies that employ 100 to 499 persons: 10 (2003); Companies that employ less than 100 persons: 799 (2003); Farms: 920 totaling 226,890 acres (2002); Minority business ownership rate: 20.6% (1997); Women business ownership rate: 24.0% (1997); Retail sales per capita: $8,460 (1997). Single-family building permits issued: 152 (2004); Multi-family building permits issued: 6 (2004).
Income: Per capita income: $15,239 (2004); Median household income: $32,068 (2004); Average household income: $42,012 (2004); Percent of households with income of $100,000 or more: 6.2% (2004); Poverty rate: 17.0% (2002); Bankruptcy rate: 4.63% (2004).
Taxes: Total county taxes per capita: $299 (2002); County property taxes per capita: $148 (2002).
Education: Percent of population age 25 and over with: High school diploma (including GED) or higher: 69.1% (2004); Bachelor's degree or higher: 12.8% (2004); Master's degree or higher: 4.9% (2004).
Housing: Homeownership rate: 78.1% (2004); Median home value: $84,555 (2004); Median rent: $270 per month (2000); Median age of housing: 24 years (2000).
Health: Birth rate: 117.0 per 10,000 population (2004); Death rate: 102.3 per 10,000 population (2004); Age adjusted cancer mortality rate: 186.4 deaths per 100,000 population (2002); Number of physicians: 9.4 per 10,000 population (2001); Hospital beds: 23.9 per 10,000 population (2002); Hospital admissions: 807.2 per 10,000 population (2002).
Elections: 2004 Presidential election results: 61.2% Bush, 38.1% Kerry, 0.4% Nader, 0.1% Badnarik
National and State Parks: Florida Caverns State Park; Three Rivers State Park

Additional Information Contacts

Jackson County Government Offices	(850) 482-9633
Chipola Area Board of Realtors	(850) 526-4030
Graceville Chamber of Commerce	(850) 263-4289
Jackson County Chamber of Commerce	(850) 482-8061

Jackson County Communities

ALFORD (town). Covers a land area of 1.284 square miles and a water area of 0.023 square miles. Located at 30.69° N. Lat.; 85.39° W. Long. Elevation is 146 feet.
History: Alford was settled in an area of pecan groves.
Population: 472 (1990); 466 (2000); 500 (2004); 538 (2009 projected); Race: 95.8% White, 2.2% Black, 0.0% Asian, 2.6% Hispanic of any race (2004); Density: 389.4 persons per square mile (2004); Average household size: 2.34 (2004); Median age: 37.8 (2004); Male/female ratio: 81.2 (2004); Marriage status: 20.7% never married, 57.3% now married, 8.8% widowed, 13.2% divorced (2000); Foreign born: 2.0% (2000); Ancestry (includes multiple ancestries): 12.7% Irish, 12.4% Other groups, 10.0% United States or American, 8.0% English, 5.2% German (2000).
Economy: Employment by occupation: 7.2% management, 4.6% professional, 26.3% services, 26.8% sales, 0.0% farming, 21.6% construction, 13.4% production (2000).
Income: Per capita income: $13,230 (2004); Median household income: $21,364 (2004); Average household income: $30,911 (2004); Percent of households with income of $100,000 or more: 3.3% (2004); Poverty rate: 36.9% (2000).
Taxes: Total city taxes per capita: $47 (2002); City property taxes per capita: $0 (2002).
Education: Percent of population age 25 and over with: High school diploma (including GED) or higher: 53.1% (2004); Bachelor's degree or higher: 2.8% (2004); Master's degree or higher: 0.6% (2004).

Housing: Homeownership rate: 84.6% (2004); Median home value: $59,677 (2004); Median rent: $273 per month (2000); Median age of housing: 26 years (2000).
Transportation: Commute to work: 92.6% car, 0.0% public transportation, 2.1% walk, 4.2% work from home (2000); Travel time to work: 17.1% less than 15 minutes, 44.8% 15 to 30 minutes, 25.4% 30 to 45 minutes, 3.3% 45 to 60 minutes, 9.4% 60 minutes or more (2000)

BASCOM (town). Covers a land area of 0.236 square miles and a water area of 0 square miles. Located at 30.92° N. Lat.; 85.11° W. Long. Elevation is 144 feet.
Population: 90 (1990); 106 (2000); 86 (2004); 74 (2009 projected); Race: 100.0% White, 0.0% Black, 0.0% Asian, 0.0% Hispanic of any race (2004); Density: 363.7 persons per square mile (2004); Average household size: 2.53 (2004); Median age: 40.0 (2004); Male/female ratio: 115.0 (2004); Marriage status: 20.5% never married, 67.9% now married, 11.5% widowed, 0.0% divorced (2000); Foreign born: 0.0% (2000); Ancestry (includes multiple ancestries): 28.8% United States or American, 10.8% Other groups, 6.3% English, 4.5% Irish, 1.8% German (2000).
Economy: Employment by occupation: 2.1% management, 8.3% professional, 39.6% services, 14.6% sales, 0.0% farming, 22.9% construction, 12.5% production (2000).
Income: Per capita income: $14,913 (2004); Median household income: $31,000 (2004); Average household income: $37,721 (2004); Percent of households with income of $100,000 or more: 2.9% (2004); Poverty rate: 6.3% (2000).
Taxes: Total city taxes per capita: $47 (2002); City property taxes per capita: $0 (2002).
Education: Percent of population age 25 and over with: High school diploma (including GED) or higher: 63.0% (2004); Bachelor's degree or higher: 3.7% (2004); Master's degree or higher: 3.7% (2004).
Housing: Homeownership rate: 91.2% (2004); Median home value: $72,857 (2004); Median rent: $250 per month (2000); Median age of housing: 35 years (2000).
Transportation: Commute to work: 100.0% car, 0.0% public transportation, 0.0% walk, 0.0% work from home (2000); Travel time to work: 41.7% less than 15 minutes, 43.8% 15 to 30 minutes, 14.6% 30 to 45 minutes, 0.0% 45 to 60 minutes, 0.0% 60 minutes or more (2000)

CAMPBELLTON (town). Covers a land area of 0.889 square miles and a water area of 0.010 square miles. Located at 30.94° N. Lat.; 85.39° W. Long. Elevation is 152 feet.
History: Campbellton had its beginnings during the English occupation (1763-1783). Later, a grain elevator, lumber mill, and a grist mill processing corn and peanuts were established.
Population: 202 (1990); 212 (2000); 217 (2004); 222 (2009 projected); Race: 32.3% White, 67.3% Black, 0.0% Asian, 0.5% Hispanic of any race (2004); Density: 244.0 persons per square mile (2004); Average household size: 2.33 (2004); Median age: 42.9 (2004); Male/female ratio: 97.3 (2004); Marriage status: 28.8% never married, 51.7% now married, 15.1% widowed, 4.4% divorced (2000); Foreign born: 0.4% (2000); Ancestry (includes multiple ancestries): 29.5% Other groups, 7.0% United States or American, 4.1% German, 2.6% Irish, 1.5% British (2000).
Economy: Employment by occupation: 0.0% management, 10.5% professional, 26.3% services, 25.3% sales, 7.4% farming, 7.4% construction, 23.2% production (2000).
Income: Per capita income: $15,668 (2004); Median household income: $25,385 (2004); Average household income: $36,559 (2004); Percent of households with income of $100,000 or more: 4.3% (2004); Poverty rate: 16.6% (2000).
Taxes: Total city taxes per capita: $38 (2002); City property taxes per capita: $0 (2002).
Education: Percent of population age 25 and over with: High school diploma (including GED) or higher: 56.5% (2004); Bachelor's degree or higher: 3.2% (2004); Master's degree or higher: 1.9% (2004).
Housing: Homeownership rate: 79.6% (2004); Median home value: $58,750 (2004); Median rent: $213 per month (2000); Median age of housing: 24 years (2000).
Transportation: Commute to work: 95.6% car, 4.4% public transportation, 0.0% walk, 0.0% work from home (2000); Travel time to work: 16.5% less than 15 minutes, 31.9% 15 to 30 minutes, 28.6% 30 to 45 minutes, 18.7% 45 to 60 minutes, 4.4% 60 minutes or more (2000)

COTTONDALE (town). Covers a land area of 1.516 square miles and a water area of 0.178 square miles. Located at 30.79° N. Lat.; 85.37° W. Long. Elevation is 135 feet.
History: Cottondale developed as a farming, fishing, and hunting center. Early Cottondale residents claimed that the fish in their streams and lakes were so assertive, fishermen had to hide behind trees while baiting their hooks.
Population: 900 (1990); 869 (2000); 879 (2004); 894 (2009 projected); Race: 73.0% White, 22.4% Black, 0.6% Asian, 5.3% Hispanic of any race (2004); Density: 579.8 persons per square mile (2004); Average household size: 2.31 (2004); Median age: 35.3 (2004); Male/female ratio: 83.5 (2004); Marriage status: 27.8% never married, 49.1% now married, 12.8% widowed, 10.3% divorced (2000); Foreign born: 1.2% (2000); Ancestry (includes multiple ancestries): 22.0% Other groups, 15.8% United States or American, 8.6% Irish, 4.0% German, 3.3% English (2000).
Economy: Employment by occupation: 4.1% management, 26.2% professional, 24.3% services, 20.5% sales, 2.8% farming, 8.8% construction, 13.2% production (2000).
Income: Per capita income: $13,211 (2004); Median household income: $22,670 (2004); Average household income: $30,479 (2004); Percent of households with income of $100,000 or more: 2.6% (2004); Poverty rate: 27.4% (2000).
Taxes: Total city taxes per capita: $281 (2002); City property taxes per capita: $37 (2002).
Education: Percent of population age 25 and over with: High school diploma (including GED) or higher: 61.7% (2004); Bachelor's degree or higher: 12.4% (2004); Master's degree or higher: 5.0% (2004).

School District(s)

Jackson County School District (PK-12)
2002-03 Enrollment: 7,245 . . . . (850) 482-1200
Housing: Homeownership rate: 63.0% (2004); Median home value: $67,857 (2004); Median rent: $239 per month (2000); Median age of housing: 24 years (2000).
Transportation: Commute to work: 89.9% car, 0.0% public transportation, 5.5% walk, 4.5% work from home (2000); Travel time to work: 37.1% less than 15 minutes, 27.6% 15 to 30 minutes, 21.8% 30 to 45 minutes, 8.5% 45 to 60 minutes, 5.1% 60 minutes or more (2000)

GRACEVILLE (city). Covers a land area of 4.297 square miles and a water area of 0.100 square miles. Located at 30.95° N. Lat.; 85.51° W. Long. Elevation is 150 feet.
Population: 2,680 (1990); 2,402 (2000); 2,413 (2004); 2,393 (2009 projected); Race: 72.4% White, 25.0% Black, 0.2% Asian, 1.8% Hispanic of any race (2004); Density: 561.6 persons per square mile (2004); Average household size: 2.57 (2004); Median age: 36.7 (2004); Male/female ratio: 84.2 (2004); Marriage status: 24.3% never married, 54.1% now married, 12.3% widowed, 9.3% divorced (2000); Foreign born: 1.1% (2000); Ancestry (includes multiple ancestries): 20.5% Other groups, 15.0% United States or American, 7.4% Irish, 6.3% English, 4.2% African (2000).
Economy: Railroad terminus; peanut shelling, lumber milling. Employment by occupation: 8.6% management, 25.0% professional, 26.7% services, 20.3% sales, 0.4% farming, 7.6% construction, 11.4% production (2000).
Income: Per capita income: $16,031 (2004); Median household income: $25,923 (2004); Average household income: $40,549 (2004); Percent of households with income of $100,000 or more: 6.8% (2004); Poverty rate: 20.7% (2000).
Education: Percent of population age 25 and over with: High school diploma (including GED) or higher: 72.7% (2004); Bachelor's degree or higher: 21.1% (2004); Master's degree or higher: 8.0% (2004).

School District(s)

Jackson County School District (PK-12)
2002-03 Enrollment: 7,245 . . . . (850) 482-1200

Four-year College(s)

The Baptist College of Florida
2003-04 Enrollment: 624 . . . . (850) 263-3261
2003-04 Tuition: In-state $5,450; Out-of-state $5,450
Housing: Homeownership rate: 56.0% (2004); Median home value: $85,294 (2004); Median rent: $189 per month (2000); Median age of housing: 30 years (2000).
Safety: Violent crime rate: 12.4 per 10,000 population; Property crime rate: 288.8 per 10,000 population (2003).
Newspapers: The Graceville News (General - Circulation 1,700)
Transportation: Commute to work: 92.1% car, 0.0% public transportation, 5.8% walk, 1.7% work from home (2000); Travel time to work: 46.0% less

than 15 minutes, 17.5% 15 to 30 minutes, 23.7% 30 to 45 minutes, 7.0% 45 to 60 minutes, 5.8% 60 minutes or more (2000)

Additional Information Contacts

Graceville Chamber of Commerce. (850) 263-4289

GRAND RIDGE (town). Covers a land area of 2.171 square miles and a water area of 0.090 square miles. Located at 30.71° N. Lat.; 85.01° W. Long. Elevation is 32 feet.

Population: 741 (1990); 792 (2000); 803 (2004); 788 (2009 projected); Race: 93.0% White, 2.7% Black, 0.0% Asian, 1.5% Hispanic of any race (2004); Density: 369.9 persons per square mile (2004); Average household size: 2.53 (2004); Median age: 36.0 (2004); Male/female ratio: 90.3 (2004); Marriage status: 22.5% never married, 58.8% now married, 7.1% widowed, 11.6% divorced (2000); Foreign born: 0.8% (2000); Ancestry (includes multiple ancestries): 24.5% United States or American, 17.6% Other groups, 11.6% Irish, 8.0% German, 6.7% English (2000).

Economy: Manufacturing: animal feed. Employment by occupation: 9.7% management, 18.3% professional, 22.2% services, 22.2% sales, 0.6% farming, 11.4% construction, 15.8% production (2000).

Income: Per capita income: $15,489 (2004); Median household income: $32,188 (2004); Average household income: $39,235 (2004); Percent of households with income of $100,000 or more: 3.8% (2004); Poverty rate: 16.5% (2000).

Education: Percent of population age 25 and over with: High school diploma (including GED) or higher: 76.5% (2004); Bachelor's degree or higher: 8.8% (2004); Master's degree or higher: 4.2% (2004).

School District(s)

Jackson County School District (PK-12)
2002-03 Enrollment: 7,245 . . . . (850) 482-1200

Housing: Homeownership rate: 81.1% (2004); Median home value: $75,306 (2004); Median rent: $233 per month (2000); Median age of housing: 22 years (2000).

Transportation: Commute to work: 94.4% car, 0.0% public transportation, 1.4% walk, 2.2% work from home (2000); Travel time to work: 19.1% less than 15 minutes, 42.3% 15 to 30 minutes, 25.7% 30 to 45 minutes, 4.6% 45 to 60 minutes, 8.3% 60 minutes or more (2000)

GREENWOOD (town). Covers a land area of 4.795 square miles and a water area of 0 square miles. Located at 30.87° N. Lat.; 85.16° W. Long. Elevation is 115 feet.

Population: 612 (1990); 735 (2000); 711 (2004); 697 (2009 projected); Race: 64.7% White, 28.7% Black, 1.3% Asian, 2.5% Hispanic of any race (2004); Density: 148.3 persons per square mile (2004); Average household size: 2.49 (2004); Median age: 36.0 (2004); Male/female ratio: 89.1 (2004); Marriage status: 17.1% never married, 58.4% now married, 14.0% widowed, 10.5% divorced (2000); Foreign born: 2.2% (2000); Ancestry (includes multiple ancestries): 23.0% Other groups, 22.2% United States or American, 8.6% German, 8.4% English, 7.6% Irish (2000).

Economy: Employment by occupation: 8.2% management, 17.7% professional, 27.0% services, 26.3% sales, 0.0% farming, 5.1% construction, 15.7% production (2000).

Income: Per capita income: $16,599 (2004); Median household income: $31,311 (2004); Average household income: $39,930 (2004); Percent of households with income of $100,000 or more: 4.6% (2004); Poverty rate: 17.8% (2000).

Education: Percent of population age 25 and over with: High school diploma (including GED) or higher: 80.8% (2004); Bachelor's degree or higher: 14.1% (2004); Master's degree or higher: 7.4% (2004).

Housing: Homeownership rate: 79.3% (2004); Median home value: $73,585 (2004); Median rent: $310 per month (2000); Median age of housing: 25 years (2000).

Transportation: Commute to work: 97.5% car, 0.0% public transportation, 1.4% walk, 1.1% work from home (2000); Travel time to work: 29.1% less than 15 minutes, 47.8% 15 to 30 minutes, 14.0% 30 to 45 minutes, 1.8% 45 to 60 minutes, 7.2% 60 minutes or more (2000)

JACOB CITY (city). Aka Jacobs. Covers a land area of 3.099 square miles and a water area of 0.134 square miles. Located at 30.89° N. Lat.; 85.41° W. Long.

Population: 261 (1990); 281 (2000); 267 (2004); 262 (2009 projected); Race: 6.0% White, 94.0% Black, 0.0% Asian, 0.0% Hispanic of any race (2004); Density: 86.2 persons per square mile (2004); Average household size: 2.84 (2004); Median age: 34.1 (2004); Male/female ratio: 84.1 (2004); Marriage status: 28.0% never married, 57.5% now married, 9.3% widowed, 5.2% divorced (2000); Foreign born: 0.0% (2000); Ancestry (includes multiple ancestries): 76.9% Other groups, 3.3% United States or American, 1.5% African (2000).

Economy: Employment by occupation: 0.0% management, 0.0% professional, 39.7% services, 14.1% sales, 2.6% farming, 12.8% construction, 30.8% production (2000).

Income: Per capita income: $11,816 (2004); Median household income: $25,909 (2004); Average household income: $33,564 (2004); Percent of households with income of $100,000 or more: 2.1% (2004); Poverty rate: 26.0% (2000).

Taxes: Total city taxes per capita: $82 (2002); City property taxes per capita: $32 (2002).

Education: Percent of population age 25 and over with: High school diploma (including GED) or higher: 69.2% (2004); Bachelor's degree or higher: 5.0% (2004); Master's degree or higher: 1.9% (2004).

Housing: Homeownership rate: 89.4% (2004); Median home value: $52,800 (2004); Median rent: $171 per month (2000); Median age of housing: 13 years (2000).

Transportation: Commute to work: 100.0% car, 0.0% public transportation, 0.0% walk, 0.0% work from home (2000); Travel time to work: 7.1% less than 15 minutes, 18.6% 15 to 30 minutes, 51.4% 30 to 45 minutes, 20.0% 45 to 60 minutes, 2.9% 60 minutes or more (2000)

MALONE (town). Covers a land area of 3.129 square miles and a water area of 0 square miles. Located at 30.95° N. Lat.; 85.16° W. Long. Elevation is 138 feet.

Population: 988 (1990); 2,007 (2000); 1,902 (2004); 1,907 (2009 projected); Race: 42.8% White, 50.9% Black, 0.2% Asian, 9.2% Hispanic of any race (2004); Density: 607.8 persons per square mile (2004); Average household size: 6.82 (2004); Median age: 37.4 (2004); Male/female ratio: 441.9 (2004); Marriage status: 13.8% never married, 72.7% now married, 9.1% widowed, 4.4% divorced (2000); Foreign born: 0.6% (2000); Ancestry (includes multiple ancestries): 10.0% Other groups, 4.4% United States or American, 2.9% English, 2.4% Irish, 2.0% German (2000).

Economy: Employment by occupation: 12.1% management, 18.9% professional, 26.9% services, 21.5% sales, 2.7% farming, 8.4% construction, 9.4% production (2000).

Income: Per capita income: $6,403 (2004); Median household income: $31,290 (2004); Average household income: $41,676 (2004); Percent of households with income of $100,000 or more: 4.3% (2004); Poverty rate: 10.8% (2000).

Taxes: Total city taxes per capita: $65 (2002); City property taxes per capita: $0 (2002).

Education: Percent of population age 25 and over with: High school diploma (including GED) or higher: 44.4% (2004); Bachelor's degree or higher: 6.5% (2004); Master's degree or higher: 1.7% (2004).

School District(s)

Jackson County School District (PK-12)
2002-03 Enrollment: 7,245 . . . . (850) 482-1200

Housing: Homeownership rate: 79.6% (2004); Median home value: $80,833 (2004); Median rent: $204 per month (2000); Median age of housing: 35 years (2000).

Transportation: Commute to work: 92.4% car, 0.0% public transportation, 3.8% walk, 3.1% work from home (2000); Travel time to work: 31.6% less than 15 minutes, 30.5% 15 to 30 minutes, 24.5% 30 to 45 minutes, 6.4% 45 to 60 minutes, 7.1% 60 minutes or more (2000)

MARIANNA (city). Covers a land area of 8.028 square miles and a water area of 0.029 square miles. Located at 30.77° N. Lat.; 85.23° W. Long. Elevation is 117 feet.

History: Marianna was founded in 1829 on the Chipola River, and named for two daughters of a pioneer merchant. The town developed as the center of an agricultural area growing peanuts, corn, cotton, pecans, and fruit.

Population: 6,332 (1990); 6,230 (2000); 6,149 (2004); 6,097 (2009 projected); Race: 55.7% White, 41.2% Black, 1.0% Asian, 3.0% Hispanic of any race (2004); Density: 766.0 persons per square mile (2004); Average household size: 2.63 (2004); Median age: 36.1 (2004); Male/female ratio: 91.1 (2004); Marriage status: 31.2% never married, 44.7% now married, 14.3% widowed, 9.9% divorced (2000); Foreign born: 3.1% (2000); Ancestry (includes multiple ancestries): 34.2% Other groups, 13.2% United States or American, 4.9% English, 4.8% Irish, 3.6% German (2000).

Economy: Employment by occupation: 9.8% management, 24.6% professional, 25.0% services, 25.1% sales, 0.7% farming, 3.9% construction, 11.0% production (2000).

Income: Per capita income: $14,036 (2004); Median household income: $24,794 (2004); Average household income: $35,506 (2004); Percent of

households with income of $100,000 or more: 4.7% (2004); Poverty rate: 28.5% (2000).
Taxes: Total city taxes per capita: $385 (2002); City property taxes per capita: $46 (2002).
Education: Percent of population age 25 and over with: High school diploma (including GED) or higher: 74.7% (2004); Bachelor's degree or higher: 20.8% (2004); Master's degree or higher: 8.4% (2004).

School District(s)

Jackson County School District (PK-12)
2002-03 Enrollment: 7,245 . . . . (850) 482-1200

Four-year College(s)

Chipola College (Public)
2003-04 Enrollment: 2,274 . . . . (850) 526-2761
2003-04 Tuition: In-state $1,755; Out-of-state $5,325
Housing: Homeownership rate: 58.4% (2004); Median home value: $81,494 (2004); Median rent: $277 per month (2000); Median age of housing: 42 years (2000).
Hospitals: Jackson Hospital (100 beds)
Safety: Violent crime rate: 82.8 per 10,000 population; Property crime rate: 568.2 per 10,000 population (2003).
Newspapers: Jackson County Floridan (Circulation 6,413)
Transportation: Commute to work: 93.4% car, 0.3% public transportation, 2.6% walk, 2.1% work from home (2000); Travel time to work: 59.2% less than 15 minutes, 20.3% 15 to 30 minutes, 9.8% 30 to 45 minutes, 2.6% 45 to 60 minutes, 8.1% 60 minutes or more (2000)
Additional Information Contacts
Chipola Area Board of Realtors . . . . (850) 526-4030
Jackson County Chamber of Commerce . . . . (850) 482-8061
Local Government Offices . . . . (850) 482-4353

SNEADS (town). Covers a land area of 4.422 square miles and a water area of 0.211 square miles. Located at 30.71° N. Lat.; 84.92° W. Long. Elevation is 125 feet.
Population: 1,746 (1990); 1,919 (2000); 1,905 (2004); 1,893 (2009 projected); Race: 79.4% White, 16.5% Black, 0.1% Asian, 3.9% Hispanic of any race (2004); Density: 430.8 persons per square mile (2004); Average household size: 2.38 (2004); Median age: 37.7 (2004); Male/female ratio: 95.2 (2004); Marriage status: 23.6% never married, 57.2% now married, 8.0% widowed, 11.3% divorced (2000); Foreign born: 1.0% (2000); Ancestry (includes multiple ancestries): 31.6% United States or American, 20.6% Other groups, 7.3% English, 3.5% Irish, 3.3% German (2000).
Economy: Employment by occupation: 8.6% management, 21.9% professional, 27.8% services, 16.4% sales, 0.5% farming, 13.1% construction, 11.8% production (2000).
Income: Per capita income: $17,491 (2004); Median household income: $33,495 (2004); Average household income: $41,598 (2004); Percent of households with income of $100,000 or more: 5.0% (2004); Poverty rate: 17.2% (2000).
Education: Percent of population age 25 and over with: High school diploma (including GED) or higher: 74.8% (2004); Bachelor's degree or higher: 10.2% (2004); Master's degree or higher: 4.4% (2004).

School District(s)

Jackson County School District (PK-12)
2002-03 Enrollment: 7,245 . . . . (850) 482-1200
Housing: Homeownership rate: 75.3% (2004); Median home value: $71,010 (2004); Median rent: $234 per month (2000); Median age of housing: 26 years (2000).
Safety: Violent crime rate: 56.4 per 10,000 population; Property crime rate: 123.1 per 10,000 population (2003).
Transportation: Commute to work: 97.4% car, 0.0% public transportation, 1.8% walk, 0.8% work from home (2000); Travel time to work: 45.9% less than 15 minutes, 21.2% 15 to 30 minutes, 18.1% 30 to 45 minutes, 7.9% 45 to 60 minutes, 6.9% 60 minutes or more (2000)

Jefferson County

Located in northwestern Florida; bounded on the north by Georgia, on the south by the Gulf of Mexico, and on the east by the Aucilla River; lowland area, partly swampy, with Lake Miccosukee in the north. Covers a land area of 597.70 square miles, a water area of 38.90 square miles, and is located in the Eastern Time Zone. The county government was organized in 1827. County seat is Monticello.

Jefferson County is part of the Tallahassee, FL Metropolitan Statistical Area. The entire metro area includes: Gadsden County, FL; Jefferson County, FL; Leon County, FL; Wakulla County, FL

Weather Station: Monticello 3 W — Elevation: 144 feet

	Jan	Feb	Mar	Apr	May	Jun	Jul	Aug	Sep	Oct	Nov	Dec
High	62	66	72	78	85	89	91	90	87	80	72	65
Low	38	41	47	52	60	67	70	69	66	54	46	40
Precip	5.6	4.6	6.0	3.6	4.1	5.7	6.7	6.8	4.5	3.4	3.6	3.9
Snow	tr	tr	tr	0.0	0.0	0.0	0.0	0.0	0.0	0.0	0.0	tr

High and Low temperatures in degrees Fahrenheit; Precipitation and Snow in inches

Population: 11,296 (1990); 12,902 (2000); 13,885 (2004); 15,124 (2009 projected); Race: 59.2% White, 37.9% Black, 0.3% Asian, 4.1% Hispanic of any race (2004); Density: 23.2 persons per square mile (2004); Average household size: 2.75 (2004); Median age: 39.3 (2004); Male/female ratio: 114.4 (2004).
Religion: Five largest groups: 17.8% Southern Baptist Convention, 7.0% The United Methodist Church, 2.5% International Pentecostal Holiness Church, 2.1% Episcopal Church, 1.2% Catholic Church (2000).
Economy: Unemployment rate: 3.8% (2004); Total civilian labor force: 5,439 (2004); Leading industries: 21.3% retail trade; 20.2% health care and social assistance; 8.5% construction (2003); Companies that employ 500 or more persons: 0 (2003); Companies that employ 100 to 499 persons: 2 (2003); Companies that employ less than 100 persons: 252 (2003); Farms: 418 totaling 132,727 acres (2002); Minority business ownership rate: n/a (1997); Women business ownership rate: n/a (1997); Retail sales per capita: $3,942 (1997). Single-family building permits issued: 86 (2004); Multi-family building permits issued: 0 (2004).
Income: Per capita income: $18,835 (2004); Median household income: $35,869 (2004); Average household income: $50,135 (2004); Percent of households with income of $100,000 or more: 9.7% (2004); Poverty rate: 16.8% (2002); Bankruptcy rate: 4.23% (2004).
Education: Percent of population age 25 and over with: High school diploma (including GED) or higher: 73.1% (2004); Bachelor's degree or higher: 16.8% (2004); Master's degree or higher: 5.9% (2004).
Housing: Homeownership rate: 81.2% (2004); Median home value: $99,883 (2004); Median rent: $293 per month (2000); Median age of housing: 20 years (2000).
Health: Birth rate: 122.7 per 10,000 population (2004); Death rate: 89.6 per 10,000 population (2004); Age adjusted cancer mortality rate: 197.3 deaths per 100,000 population (2002); Number of physicians: 6.2 per 10,000 population (2001); Hospital beds: 0.0 per 10,000 population (2002); Hospital admissions: 0.0 per 10,000 population (2002).
Elections: 2004 Presidential election results: 44.1% Bush, 55.3% Kerry, 0.4% Nader, 0.1% Badnarik
Additional Information Contacts
Jefferson County Government Offices . . . . (850) 342-0218
Monticello Chamber of Commerce . . . . (850) 997-5552

Jefferson County Communities

LAMONT (unincorporated postal area, zip code 32336). Covers a land area of 80.203 square miles and a water area of 0.922 square miles. Located at 30.41° N. Lat.; 83.82° W. Long. Elevation is 63 feet.
History: Lamont was first called Lick Skillet, but was changed in 1890 by residents who desired a more dignified name and chose that of Vice-President Cornelius Lamont, who had been a recent visitor in the town.
Population: 1,130 (2000); Race: 49.2% White, 49.3% Black, 0.8% Asian, 0.0% Hispanic of any race (2000); Density: 14.1 persons per square mile (2000); Age: 20.0% under 18, 13.9% over 64 (2000); Marriage status: 33.3% never married, 49.6% now married, 8.0% widowed, 9.1% divorced (2000); Foreign born: 0.0% (2000); Ancestry (includes multiple ancestries): 53.2% Other groups, 9.0% English, 7.3% Irish, 7.2% United States or American, 5.3% German (2000).
Economy: Employment by occupation: 11.4% management, 5.4% professional, 27.0% services, 27.8% sales, 2.1% farming, 17.6% construction, 8.7% production (2000).
Income: Per capita income: $18,044 (2000); Median household income: $26,667 (2000); Poverty rate: 31.9% (2000).
Education: Percent of population age 25 and over with: High school diploma (including GED) or higher: 57.1% (2000); Bachelor's degree or higher: 8.6% (2000).

Housing: Homeownership rate: 85.3% (2000); Median home value: $79,600 (2000); Median rent: $158 per month (2000); Median age of housing: 17 years (2000).
Transportation: Commute to work: 95.0% car, 2.9% public transportation, 0.0% walk, 0.0% work from home (2000); Travel time to work: 18.0% less than 15 minutes, 24.3% 15 to 30 minutes, 34.8% 30 to 45 minutes, 16.8% 45 to 60 minutes, 6.1% 60 minutes or more (2000)

MONTICELLO (city). Covers a land area of 3.380 square miles and a water area of 0 square miles. Located at 30.54° N. Lat.; 83.86° W. Long. Elevation is 235 feet.
History: Monticello was founded in the early 1800's by planters from Georgia and the Carolinas, and named for Thomas Jefferson's home in Virginia. The courthouse built in the center of the town was modeled on Jefferson's house.
Population: 2,641 (1990); 2,533 (2000); 2,520 (2004); 2,583 (2009 projected); Race: 44.2% White, 53.4% Black, 0.7% Asian, 2.3% Hispanic of any race (2004); Density: 745.6 persons per square mile (2004); Average household size: 2.58 (2004); Median age: 39.0 (2004); Male/female ratio: 84.6 (2004); Marriage status: 30.0% never married, 45.4% now married, 11.7% widowed, 12.9% divorced (2000); Foreign born: 0.9% (2000); Ancestry (includes multiple ancestries): 49.5% Other groups, 9.7% United States or American, 7.4% English, 5.4% Irish, 3.4% German (2000).
Economy: Employment by occupation: 12.0% management, 15.5% professional, 21.2% services, 24.4% sales, 5.5% farming, 9.5% construction, 11.7% production (2000).
Income: Per capita income: $16,724 (2004); Median household income: $30,778 (2004); Average household income: $42,883 (2004); Percent of households with income of $100,000 or more: 7.6% (2004); Poverty rate: 22.2% (2000).
Education: Percent of population age 25 and over with: High school diploma (including GED) or higher: 74.4% (2004); Bachelor's degree or higher: 21.3% (2004); Master's degree or higher: 9.0% (2004).

School District(s)

Jefferson County School District (PK-12)
2002-03 Enrollment: 1,575 . . . . (850) 342-0100
Housing: Homeownership rate: 68.7% (2004); Median home value: $92,353 (2004); Median rent: $279 per month (2000); Median age of housing: 38 years (2000).
Safety: Violent crime rate: 88.8 per 10,000 population; Property crime rate: 204.6 per 10,000 population (2003).
Newspapers: Monticello News (General - Circulation 3,000)
Transportation: Commute to work: 95.7% car, 0.8% public transportation, 0.8% walk, 1.5% work from home (2000); Travel time to work: 42.9% less than 15 minutes, 9.1% 15 to 30 minutes, 22.2% 30 to 45 minutes, 20.9% 45 to 60 minutes, 4.9% 60 minutes or more (2000)
Additional Information Contacts
Monticello Chamber of Commerce . . . . (850) 997-5552

Lafayette County

Located in northern Florida; bounded on the east and northeast by the Suwanee River; swampy area, with many small lakes. Covers a land area of 542.80 square miles, a water area of 5.10 square miles, and is located in the Eastern Time Zone. The county government was organized in 1856. County seat is Mayo.

Weather Station: Mayo — Elevation: 62 feet

	Jan	Feb	Mar	Apr	May	Jun	Jul	Aug	Sep	Oct	Nov	Dec
High	65	69	75	81	87	91	92	92	89	82	75	67
Low	40	43	49	54	62	69	71	71	68	57	49	42
Precip	5.0	3.7	5.1	3.2	3.2	5.9	7.7	8.1	4.7	3.1	2.6	3.3
Snow	tr	0.0	0.0	0.0	0.0	0.0	0.0	0.0	0.0	0.0	0.0	0.0

High and Low temperatures in degrees Fahrenheit; Precipitation and Snow in inches

Population: 5,578 (1990); 7,022 (2000); 7,116 (2004); 7,239 (2009 projected); Race: 81.3% White, 11.3% Black, 0.2% Asian, 11.0% Hispanic of any race (2004); Density: 13.1 persons per square mile (2004); Average household size: 3.36 (2004); Median age: 35.2 (2004); Male/female ratio: 148.1 (2004).
Religion: Five largest groups: 41.2% Southern Baptist Convention, 4.0% The United Methodist Church, 2.6% Church of God (Cleveland, Tennessee), 1.7% Assemblies of God, 1.1% Churches of Christ (2000).
Economy: Unemployment rate: 1.8% (2004); Total civilian labor force: 2,897 (2004); Leading industries: 27.2% retail trade; 17.3% health care and social assistance; 14.1% manufacturing (2003); Companies that employ 500 or more persons: 0 (2003); Companies that employ 100 to 499 persons: 0 (2003); Companies that employ less than 100 persons: 82 (2003); Farms: 195 totaling 91,988 acres (2002); Minority business ownership rate: n/a (1997); Women business ownership rate: n/a (1997); Retail sales per capita: $1,604 (1997). Single-family building permits issued: 27 (2004); Multi-family building permits issued: 0 (2004).
Income: Per capita income: $13,553 (2004); Median household income: $31,744 (2004); Average household income: $42,122 (2004); Percent of households with income of $100,000 or more: 4.9% (2004); Poverty rate: 23.3% (2002); Bankruptcy rate: 1.63% (2004).
Taxes: Total county taxes per capita: $247 (2002); County property taxes per capita: $189 (2002).
Education: Percent of population age 25 and over with: High school diploma (including GED) or higher: 67.9% (2004); Bachelor's degree or higher: 7.0% (2004); Master's degree or higher: 2.7% (2004).
Housing: Homeownership rate: 80.7% (2004); Median home value: $84,821 (2004); Median rent: $296 per month (2000); Median age of housing: 23 years (2000).
Health: Birth rate: 93.6 per 10,000 population (2004); Death rate: 88.2 per 10,000 population (2004); Age adjusted cancer mortality rate: 234.4 (Unreliable rate as per CDC) deaths per 100,000 population (2002); Number of physicians: 2.8 per 10,000 population (2001); Hospital beds: 0.0 per 10,000 population (2002); Hospital admissions: 0.0 per 10,000 population (2002).
Elections: 2004 Presidential election results: 74.0% Bush, 25.4% Kerry, 0.3% Nader, 0.0% Badnarik
National and State Parks: Troy Spring State Park
Additional Information Contacts
Lafayette County Government Offices. . . . . (386) 294-1600
Lafayette County Chamber of Commerce . . . . (386) 294-2705

Lafayette County Communities

DAY (unincorporated postal area, zip code 32013). Covers a land area of 1.016 square miles and a water area of 0 square miles. Located at 30.19° N. Lat.; 83.29° W. Long. Elevation is 84 feet.
Population: 58 (2000); Race: 100.0% White, 0.0% Black, 0.0% Asian, 0.0% Hispanic of any race (2000); Density: 57.1 persons per square mile (2000); Age: 0.0% under 18, 0.0% over 64 (2000); Marriage status: 11.8% never married, 88.2% now married, 0.0% widowed, 0.0% divorced (2000); Foreign born: 0.0% (2000); Ancestry (includes multiple ancestries): 100.0% United States or American (2000).
Economy: Employment by occupation: 0.0% management, 0.0% professional, 23.5% services, 0.0% sales, 0.0% farming, 76.5% construction, 0.0% production (2000).
Income: Per capita income: $10,826 (2000); Median household income: $20,481 (2000); Poverty rate: 0.0% (2000).
Education: Percent of population age 25 and over with: High school diploma (including GED) or higher: 100.0% (2000); Bachelor's degree or higher: 0.0% (2000).
Housing: Homeownership rate: 100.0% (2000); Median home value: $n/a (2000); Median rent: $n/a per month (2000); Median age of housing: 17 years (2000).
Transportation: Commute to work: 100.0% car, 0.0% public transportation, 0.0% walk, 0.0% work from home (2000); Travel time to work: 0.0% less than 15 minutes, 100.0% 15 to 30 minutes, 0.0% 30 to 45 minutes, 0.0% 45 to 60 minutes, 0.0% 60 minutes or more (2000)

MAYO (town). Covers a land area of 0.817 square miles and a water area of 0 square miles. Located at 30.05° N. Lat.; 83.17° W. Long. Elevation is 79 feet.
Population: 917 (1990); 988 (2000); 971 (2004); 959 (2009 projected); Race: 67.9% White, 18.0% Black, 0.0% Asian, 22.6% Hispanic of any race (2004); Density: 1,188.3 persons per square mile (2004); Average household size: 2.94 (2004); Median age: 34.2 (2004); Male/female ratio: 93.0 (2004); Marriage status: 21.1% never married, 56.4% now married, 10.0% widowed, 12.5% divorced (2000); Foreign born: 16.4% (2000); Ancestry (includes multiple ancestries): 44.8% Other groups, 14.7% United States or American, 5.7% English, 3.6% Irish, 1.8% German (2000).
Economy: Lumbering; limestone quarrying. Employment by occupation: 5.9% management, 9.2% professional, 29.9% services, 9.5% sales, 19.9% farming, 5.9% construction, 19.7% production (2000).
Income: Per capita income: $13,488 (2004); Median household income: $27,679 (2004); Average household income: $38,447 (2004); Percent of

households with income of $100,000 or more: 5.2% (2004); Poverty rate: 34.6% (2000).
Education: Percent of population age 25 and over with: High school diploma (including GED) or higher: 52.3% (2004); Bachelor's degree or higher: 6.0% (2004); Master's degree or higher: 1.2% (2004).

School District(s)

Lafayette County School District (PK-12)
2002-03 Enrollment: 1,049 . . . . (386) 294-4107
Housing: Homeownership rate: 68.5% (2004); Median home value: $66,486 (2004); Median rent: $266 per month (2000); Median age of housing: 24 years (2000).
Newspapers: Mayo Free Press (General - Circulation 1,700)
Transportation: Commute to work: 89.4% car, 0.0% public transportation, 2.6% walk, 1.3% work from home (2000); Travel time to work: 47.1% less than 15 minutes, 28.3% 15 to 30 minutes, 13.9% 30 to 45 minutes, 2.1% 45 to 60 minutes, 8.6% 60 minutes or more (2000)
Additional Information Contacts
Lafayette County Chamber of Commerce . . . . (386) 294-2705

Lake County

Located in central Florida; bounded on the northeast by the St. Johns River; rolling terrain with many lakes; includes part of Apopka and Ocala National Forests. Covers a land area of 953.20 square miles, a water area of 203.20 square miles, and is located in the Eastern Time Zone. The county government was organized in 1887. County seat is Tavares.

Lake County is part of the Orlando-Kissimmee, FL Metropolitan Statistical Area. The entire metro area includes: Lake County, FL; Orange County, FL; Osceola County, FL; Seminole County, FL

Weather Station: Clermont 7 S — Elevation: 108 feet

	Jan	Feb	Mar	Apr	May	Jun	Jul	Aug	Sep	Oct	Nov	Dec
High	70	73	78	83	88	90	92	91	89	83	77	72
Low	49	51	55	59	65	70	72	72	71	65	58	52
Precip	3.2	2.7	4.0	2.2	3.8	7.9	6.8	6.9	5.8	2.5	2.4	2.4
Snow	tr	tr	0.0	0.0	0.0	0.0	0.0	0.0	0.0	0.0	0.0	0.0

High and Low temperatures in degrees Fahrenheit; Precipitation and Snow in inches

Weather Station: Lisbon — Elevation: 65 feet

	Jan	Feb	Mar	Apr	May	Jun	Jul	Aug	Sep	Oct	Nov	Dec
High	69	71	77	81	87	90	91	91	89	83	76	70
Low	47	49	53	58	65	71	72	72	71	63	55	49
Precip	3.4	3.0	4.2	2.8	4.2	6.1	5.5	6.3	5.6	2.6	2.5	2.6
Snow	tr	tr	0.0	0.0	0.0	0.0	0.0	0.0	0.0	0.0	0.0	0.0

High and Low temperatures in degrees Fahrenheit; Precipitation and Snow in inches

Population: 152,104 (1990); 210,528 (2000); 249,628 (2004); 298,713 (2009 projected); Race: 85.8% White, 8.8% Black, 1.1% Asian, 7.8% Hispanic of any race (2004); Density: 261.9 persons per square mile (2004); Average household size: 2.38 (2004); Median age: 44.7 (2004); Male/female ratio: 94.5 (2004).
Religion: Five largest groups: 12.2% Southern Baptist Convention, 9.1% Catholic Church, 4.7% The United Methodist Church, 2.5% Presbyterian Church (U.S.A.), 1.2% Church of God (Cleveland, Tennessee) (2000).
Economy: Unemployment rate: 4.3% (2004); Total civilian labor force: 102,324 (2004); Leading industries: 20.3% retail trade; 18.3% health care and social assistance; 10.6% construction (2003); Companies that employ 500 or more persons: 5 (2003); Companies that employ 100 to 499 persons: 91 (2003); Companies that employ less than 100 persons: 5,077 (2003); Farms: 1,798 totaling 180,245 acres (2002); Minority business ownership rate: 7.5% (1997); Women business ownership rate: 27.2% (1997); Retail sales per capita: $7,781 (1997). Single-family building permits issued: 5,642 (2004); Multi-family building permits issued: 571 (2004).
Income: Per capita income: $22,470 (2004); Median household income: $40,914 (2004); Average household income: $52,966 (2004); Percent of households with income of $100,000 or more: 9.9% (2004); Poverty rate: 10.8% (2002); Bankruptcy rate: 5.66% (2004).
Taxes: Total county taxes per capita: $396 (2002); County property taxes per capita: $203 (2002).
Education: Percent of population age 25 and over with: High school diploma (including GED) or higher: 80.2% (2004); Bachelor's degree or higher: 16.9% (2004); Master's degree or higher: 5.3% (2004).
Housing: Homeownership rate: 81.9% (2004); Median home value: $115,316 (2004); Median rent: $424 per month (2000); Median age of housing: 16 years (2000).
Health: Birth rate: 107.1 per 10,000 population (2004); Death rate: 117.3 per 10,000 population (2004); Age adjusted cancer mortality rate: 187.4 deaths per 100,000 population (2002); Air Quality Index: 88.7% good, 10.7% moderate, 0.6% unhealthy for sensitive individuals, 0.0% unhealthy (percent of days in 2004); Number of physicians: 17.9 per 10,000 population (2001); Hospital beds: 28.9 per 10,000 population (2002); Hospital admissions: 1,332.3 per 10,000 population (2002).
Elections: 2004 Presidential election results: 60.0% Bush, 38.9% Kerry, 0.5% Nader, 0.2% Badnarik
National and State Parks: General James A. Van Fleet Trail State Park; Hontoon Island State Park; Lake Griffin State Park; Lake Louisa State Park
Additional Information Contacts
Lake County Government Offices . . . . (352) 343-9850
Astor Chamber of Commerce . . . . (352) 759-2679
Clermont Chamber of Commerce . . . . (352) 394-4191
East Lake County Chamber of Commerce . . . . (352) 383-8801
Eustis Chamber of Commerce. . . . . (352) 357-3434
Greater Lake County Association of Realtors . . . . (352) 343-3003
Lady Lake Chamber of Commerce . . . . (352) 753-6029
Leesburg Area Chamber of Commerce. . . . . (352) 787-2131
Mount Dora Chamber of Commerce . . . . (352) 383-2165
Tavares Chamber of Commerce . . . . (352) 343-2531
Umatilla Chamber of Commerce . . . . (352) 669-3511

Lake County Communities

ALTOONA (CDP). Covers a land area of 0.448 square miles and a water area of 0.056 square miles. Located at 28.96° N. Lat.; 81.64° W. Long. Elevation is 103 feet.
Population: 52 (1990); 88 (2000); 98 (2004); 111 (2009 projected); Race: 99.0% White, 0.0% Black, 0.0% Asian, 1.0% Hispanic of any race (2004); Density: 218.8 persons per square mile (2004); Average household size: 2.28 (2004); Median age: 40.9 (2004); Male/female ratio: 88.5 (2004); Marriage status: 7.0% never married, 74.0% now married, 0.0% widowed, 19.0% divorced (2000); Foreign born: 0.0% (2000); Ancestry (includes multiple ancestries): 30.7% United States or American, 18.4% Other groups, 8.8% Irish (2000).
Economy: Employment by occupation: 0.0% management, 0.0% professional, 56.8% services, 0.0% sales, 22.7% farming, 0.0% construction, 20.5% production (2000).
Income: Per capita income: $18,776 (2004); Median household income: $33,500 (2004); Average household income: $42,791 (2004); Percent of households with income of $100,000 or more: 0.0% (2004); Poverty rate: 0.0% (2000).
Education: Percent of population age 25 and over with: High school diploma (including GED) or higher: 83.3% (2004); Bachelor's degree or higher: 1.4% (2004); Master's degree or higher: 1.4% (2004).

School District(s)

Lake County School District (PK-12)
2002-03 Enrollment: 31,782 . . . . (352) 253-6510
Housing: Homeownership rate: 67.4% (2004); Median home value: $95,000 (2004); Median rent: $296 per month (2000); Median age of housing: 26 years (2000).
Transportation: Commute to work: 77.3% car, 0.0% public transportation, 22.7% walk, 0.0% work from home (2000); Travel time to work: 22.7% less than 15 minutes, 0.0% 15 to 30 minutes, 77.3% 30 to 45 minutes, 0.0% 45 to 60 minutes, 0.0% 60 minutes or more (2000)

ASTATULA (town). Covers a land area of 2.186 square miles and a water area of 0.016 square miles. Located at 28.71° N. Lat.; 81.73° W. Long. Elevation is 92 feet.
Population: 1,064 (1990); 1,298 (2000); 1,479 (2004); 1,712 (2009 projected); Race: 85.0% White, 1.9% Black, 0.3% Asian, 21.4% Hispanic of any race (2004); Density: 676.5 persons per square mile (2004); Average household size: 2.64 (2004); Median age: 36.8 (2004); Male/female ratio: 93.3 (2004); Marriage status: 17.5% never married, 66.9% now married, 6.9% widowed, 8.6% divorced (2000); Foreign born: 11.5% (2000); Ancestry (includes multiple ancestries): 23.0% Other groups, 18.2% United States or American, 16.3% German, 12.8% English, 8.7% Irish (2000).
Economy: Employment by occupation: 8.3% management, 9.5% professional, 22.3% services, 20.1% sales, 9.5% farming, 12.7% construction, 17.6% production (2000).

Income: Per capita income: $17,813 (2004); Median household income: $35,060 (2004); Average household income: $46,961 (2004); Percent of households with income of $100,000 or more: 7.5% (2004); Poverty rate: 8.0% (2000).
Education: Percent of population age 25 and over with: High school diploma (including GED) or higher: 65.3% (2004); Bachelor's degree or higher: 4.0% (2004); Master's degree or higher: 1.9% (2004).

School District(s)

Lake County School District (PK-12)
2002-03 Enrollment: 31,782 . . . . (352) 253-6510
Housing: Homeownership rate: 85.0% (2004); Median home value: $85,429 (2004); Median rent: $400 per month (2000); Median age of housing: 16 years (2000).
Safety: Violent crime rate: 158.3 per 10,000 population; Property crime rate: 61.9 per 10,000 population (2003).
Transportation: Commute to work: 91.3% car, 0.6% public transportation, 0.4% walk, 5.2% work from home (2000); Travel time to work: 20.7% less than 15 minutes, 45.2% 15 to 30 minutes, 18.1% 30 to 45 minutes, 8.1% 45 to 60 minutes, 7.9% 60 minutes or more (2000)

ASTOR (CDP). Covers a land area of 2.465 square miles and a water area of 0.004 square miles. Located at 29.16° N. Lat.; 81.53° W. Long. Elevation is 6 feet.
Population: 1,283 (1990); 1,487 (2000); 1,685 (2004); 1,942 (2009 projected); Race: 96.3% White, 0.9% Black, 0.0% Asian, 13.6% Hispanic of any race (2004); Density: 683.6 persons per square mile (2004); Average household size: 2.35 (2004); Median age: 47.8 (2004); Male/female ratio: 97.3 (2004); Marriage status: 17.0% never married, 62.1% now married, 8.6% widowed, 12.2% divorced (2000); Foreign born: 8.0% (2000); Ancestry (includes multiple ancestries): 17.0% Other groups, 11.9% English, 9.6% German, 9.3% Irish, 8.6% United States or American (2000).
Economy: Employment by occupation: 6.4% management, 9.2% professional, 18.9% services, 29.4% sales, 9.5% farming, 14.1% construction, 12.4% production (2000).
Income: Per capita income: $15,620 (2004); Median household income: $31,609 (2004); Average household income: $36,657 (2004); Percent of households with income of $100,000 or more: 2.4% (2004); Poverty rate: 12.5% (2000).
Education: Percent of population age 25 and over with: High school diploma (including GED) or higher: 69.9% (2004); Bachelor's degree or higher: 11.7% (2004); Master's degree or higher: 2.4% (2004).
Housing: Homeownership rate: 84.4% (2004); Median home value: $82,642 (2004); Median rent: $335 per month (2000); Median age of housing: 19 years (2000).
Transportation: Commute to work: 90.1% car, 0.0% public transportation, 3.8% walk, 5.2% work from home (2000); Travel time to work: 47.1% less than 15 minutes, 10.1% 15 to 30 minutes, 10.1% 30 to 45 minutes, 10.0% 45 to 60 minutes, 22.7% 60 minutes or more (2000)
Additional Information Contacts
Astor Chamber of Commerce . . . . (352) 759-2679

CITRUS RIDGE (CDP). Covers a land area of 46.845 square miles and a water area of 3.741 square miles. Located at 28.33° N. Lat.; 81.64° W. Long.
Population: 4,090 (1990); 12,015 (2000); 18,380 (2004); 25,640 (2009 projected); Race: 83.6% White, 4.3% Black, 2.9% Asian, 21.1% Hispanic of any race (2004); Density: 392.4 persons per square mile (2004); Average household size: 2.41 (2004); Median age: 37.8 (2004); Male/female ratio: 97.8 (2004); Marriage status: 23.5% never married, 63.5% now married, 4.3% widowed, 8.7% divorced (2000); Foreign born: 12.2% (2000); Ancestry (includes multiple ancestries): 24.1% Other groups, 15.6% German, 13.1% Irish, 11.2% Italian, 9.7% English (2000).
Economy: Employment by occupation: 16.7% management, 15.3% professional, 24.3% services, 28.7% sales, 0.2% farming, 6.5% construction, 8.2% production (2000).
Income: Per capita income: $23,677 (2004); Median household income: $48,372 (2004); Average household income: $56,947 (2004); Percent of households with income of $100,000 or more: 9.2% (2004); Poverty rate: 5.2% (2000).
Education: Percent of population age 25 and over with: High school diploma (including GED) or higher: 89.0% (2004); Bachelor's degree or higher: 18.7% (2004); Master's degree or higher: 2.5% (2004).
Housing: Homeownership rate: 77.4% (2004); Median home value: $134,201 (2004); Median rent: $572 per month (2000); Median age of housing: 4 years (2000).
Transportation: Commute to work: 95.5% car, 0.1% public transportation, 1.6% walk, 2.2% work from home (2000); Travel time to work: 14.1% less than 15 minutes, 47.7% 15 to 30 minutes, 24.6% 30 to 45 minutes, 8.8% 45 to 60 minutes, 4.7% 60 minutes or more (2000)

CLERMONT (city). Covers a land area of 10.486 square miles and a water area of 0.979 square miles. Located at 28.54° N. Lat.; 81.75° W. Long. Elevation is 190 feet.
History: Clermont was named for Clermont, France, the birthplace of A.F. Wrotnoski, one of its founders. Diatomite was mined near Clermont and used in the manufacture of moisture-proof tops for salt shakers.
Population: 7,208 (1990); 9,333 (2000); 11,341 (2004); 13,853 (2009 projected); Race: 83.6% White, 11.2% Black, 1.2% Asian, 7.6% Hispanic of any race (2004); Density: 1,081.6 persons per square mile (2004); Average household size: 2.28 (2004); Median age: 48.4 (2004); Male/female ratio: 90.6 (2004); Marriage status: 18.2% never married, 62.0% now married, 11.4% widowed, 8.4% divorced (2000); Foreign born: 6.5% (2000); Ancestry (includes multiple ancestries): 19.9% Other groups, 19.8% German, 13.2% Irish, 12.9% English, 7.3% Italian (2000).
Economy: Employment by occupation: 14.0% management, 17.8% professional, 22.5% services, 25.6% sales, 0.5% farming, 9.3% construction, 10.4% production (2000).
Income: Per capita income: $24,359 (2004); Median household income: $43,488 (2004); Average household income: $54,398 (2004); Percent of households with income of $100,000 or more: 9.7% (2004); Poverty rate: 7.8% (2000).
Taxes: Total city taxes per capita: $471 (2002); City property taxes per capita: $177 (2002).
Education: Percent of population age 25 and over with: High school diploma (including GED) or higher: 87.0% (2004); Bachelor's degree or higher: 24.1% (2004); Master's degree or higher: 7.6% (2004).

School District(s)

Lake County School District (PK-12)
2002-03 Enrollment: 31,782 . . . . (352) 253-6510
Housing: Homeownership rate: 74.4% (2004); Median home value: $148,617 (2004); Median rent: $505 per month (2000); Median age of housing: 19 years (2000).
Newspapers: South Lake Press (General - Circulation 3,000)
Transportation: Commute to work: 90.1% car, 0.9% public transportation, 3.8% walk, 4.4% work from home (2000); Travel time to work: 28.8% less than 15 minutes, 19.1% 15 to 30 minutes, 30.5% 30 to 45 minutes, 15.0% 45 to 60 minutes, 6.7% 60 minutes or more (2000)
Additional Information Contacts
Clermont Chamber of Commerce . . . . (352) 394-4191
Local Government Offices . . . . (352) 241-9248

EUSTIS (city). Covers a land area of 8.354 square miles and a water area of 1.285 square miles. Located at 28.85° N. Lat.; 81.68° W. Long. Elevation is 67 feet.
History: Named for General Abram Eustis, a military leader in the Seminole Wars. Eustis was first known as Highlands and then as Pendryville. The town was settled in 1876 when A.S. Pendry planted a citrus grove and opened a hotel in which the post office was established.
Population: 13,440 (1990); 15,106 (2000); 16,401 (2004); 18,211 (2009 projected); Race: 75.0% White, 19.9% Black, 0.7% Asian, 9.0% Hispanic of any race (2004); Density: 1,963.3 persons per square mile (2004); Average household size: 2.36 (2004); Median age: 42.2 (2004); Male/female ratio: 85.2 (2004); Marriage status: 19.2% never married, 56.8% now married, 12.9% widowed, 11.2% divorced (2000); Foreign born: 4.3% (2000); Ancestry (includes multiple ancestries): 25.1% Other groups, 14.5% English, 13.5% German, 12.1% Irish, 9.7% United States or American (2000).
Economy: Single-family building permits issued: 110 (2004); Multi-family building permits issued: 8 (2004); Employment by occupation: 11.3% management, 20.7% professional, 19.3% services, 25.1% sales, 1.7% farming, 10.2% construction, 11.7% production (2000).
Income: Per capita income: $19,514 (2004); Median household income: $34,340 (2004); Average household income: $45,164 (2004); Percent of households with income of $100,000 or more: 8.2% (2004); Poverty rate: 15.3% (2000).
Taxes: Total city taxes per capita: $350 (2002); City property taxes per capita: $145 (2002).
Education: Percent of population age 25 and over with: High school diploma (including GED) or higher: 77.7% (2004); Bachelor's degree or higher: 18.0% (2004); Master's degree or higher: 5.7% (2004).

School District(s)

Lake County School District (PK-12)
2002-03 Enrollment: 31,782 . . . . (352) 253-6510

Two-year College(s)

Lake Technical Center (Public)
2003-04 Enrollment: 606 . . . . (352) 589-2250
2003-04 Tuition: In-state $1,700; Out-of-state $7,067

Housing: Homeownership rate: 68.7% (2004); Median home value: $101,796 (2004); Median rent: $401 per month (2000); Median age of housing: 22 years (2000).

Safety: Violent crime rate: 50.1 per 10,000 population; Property crime rate: 192.2 per 10,000 population (2003).

Transportation: Commute to work: 96.8% car, 0.0% public transportation, 0.4% walk, 2.5% work from home (2000); Travel time to work: 36.4% less than 15 minutes, 32.6% 15 to 30 minutes, 11.3% 30 to 45 minutes, 9.4% 45 to 60 minutes, 10.3% 60 minutes or more (2000)

Additional Information Contacts

Eustis Chamber of Commerce . . . . (352) 357-3434
Local Government Offices . . . . (352) 483-5430

FERNDALE (CDP). Covers a land area of 2.732 square miles and a water area of 0.107 square miles. Located at 28.61° N. Lat.; 81.70° W. Long. Elevation is 103 feet.

Population: 103 (1990); 233 (2000); 287 (2004); 355 (2009 projected); Race: 97.9% White, 0.3% Black, 0.0% Asian, 3.8% Hispanic of any race (2004); Density: 105.1 persons per square mile (2004); Average household size: 2.79 (2004); Median age: 36.6 (2004); Male/female ratio: 97.9 (2004); Marriage status: 11.6% never married, 69.7% now married, 3.0% widowed, 15.7% divorced (2000); Foreign born: 4.2% (2000); Ancestry (includes multiple ancestries): 20.1% German, 18.4% Italian, 17.7% United States or American, 14.6% Irish, 12.2% Other groups (2000).

Economy: Employment by occupation: 19.4% management, 9.7% professional, 10.3% services, 26.5% sales, 10.3% farming, 7.1% construction, 16.8% production (2000).

Income: Per capita income: $27,064 (2004); Median household income: $65,549 (2004); Average household income: $75,413 (2004); Percent of households with income of $100,000 or more: 17.5% (2004); Poverty rate: 0.0% (2000).

Education: Percent of population age 25 and over with: High school diploma (including GED) or higher: 64.9% (2004); Bachelor's degree or higher: 13.0% (2004); Master's degree or higher: 0.0% (2004).

Housing: Homeownership rate: 85.4% (2004); Median home value: $113,636 (2004); Median rent: $n/a per month (2000); Median age of housing: 18 years (2000).

Transportation: Commute to work: 82.6% car, 0.0% public transportation, 0.0% walk, 4.5% work from home (2000); Travel time to work: 10.8% less than 15 minutes, 37.8% 15 to 30 minutes, 18.9% 30 to 45 minutes, 16.9% 45 to 60 minutes, 15.5% 60 minutes or more (2000)

FRUITLAND PARK (city). Covers a land area of 2.917 square miles and a water area of 0.752 square miles. Located at 28.85° N. Lat.; 81.91° W. Long. Elevation is 113 feet.

History: Fruitland Park was founded in 1876 by Major O.P. Rooks, and named for the Fruitland Nurseries of Georgia, which specialized in rare fruits and flowers.

Population: 3,029 (1990); 3,186 (2000); 3,436 (2004); 3,782 (2009 projected); Race: 85.4% White, 10.0% Black, 1.7% Asian, 3.2% Hispanic of any race (2004); Density: 1,177.8 persons per square mile (2004); Average household size: 2.66 (2004); Median age: 35.3 (2004); Male/female ratio: 94.0 (2004); Marriage status: 21.0% never married, 57.9% now married, 7.9% widowed, 13.2% divorced (2000); Foreign born: 3.8% (2000); Ancestry (includes multiple ancestries): 18.0% Other groups, 14.5% Irish, 12.1% English, 11.8% German, 10.0% United States or American (2000).

Economy: Single-family building permits issued: 42 (2004); Multi-family building permits issued: 2 (2004); Employment by occupation: 9.8% management, 17.2% professional, 18.2% services, 28.5% sales, 1.2% farming, 11.9% construction, 13.3% production (2000).

Income: Per capita income: $19,195 (2004); Median household income: $43,355 (2004); Average household income: $50,970 (2004); Percent of households with income of $100,000 or more: 7.0% (2004); Poverty rate: 10.2% (2000).

Education: Percent of population age 25 and over with: High school diploma (including GED) or higher: 82.4% (2004); Bachelor's degree or higher: 9.5% (2004); Master's degree or higher: 2.9% (2004).

School District(s)

Lake County School District (PK-12)
2002-03 Enrollment: 31,782 . . . . (352) 253-6510

Housing: Homeownership rate: 73.3% (2004); Median home value: $94,576 (2004); Median rent: $398 per month (2000); Median age of housing: 26 years (2000).

Safety: Violent crime rate: 41.8 per 10,000 population; Property crime rate: 387.7 per 10,000 population (2003).

Newspapers: Lake News (General - Circulation 21,500)

Transportation: Commute to work: 96.2% car, 0.6% public transportation, 1.8% walk, 0.3% work from home (2000); Travel time to work: 38.2% less than 15 minutes, 38.1% 15 to 30 minutes, 12.0% 30 to 45 minutes, 5.3% 45 to 60 minutes, 6.5% 60 minutes or more (2000)

Additional Information Contacts

Leesburg Area Chamber of Commerce . . . . (352) 787-2131

GRAND ISLAND (unincorporated postal area, zip code 32735). Covers a land area of 5.092 square miles and a water area of 0.910 square miles. Located at 28.89° N. Lat.; 81.74° W. Long. Elevation is 106 feet.

History: Grand Island was settled in the late 1880's and named because the several lakes that surrounded it made it seem like an island.

Population: 2,532 (2000); Race: 96.0% White, 0.9% Black, 1.6% Asian, 3.2% Hispanic of any race (2000); Density: 497.3 persons per square mile (2000); Age: 19.0% under 18, 34.3% over 64 (2000); Marriage status: 5.9% never married, 77.7% now married, 9.1% widowed, 7.2% divorced (2000); Foreign born: 4.3% (2000); Ancestry (includes multiple ancestries): 17.3% German, 15.9% English, 15.7% United States or American, 14.5% Irish, 13.4% Other groups (2000).

Economy: Employment by occupation: 14.4% management, 23.9% professional, 15.5% services, 33.2% sales, 0.0% farming, 10.2% construction, 2.9% production (2000).

Income: Per capita income: $21,360 (2000); Median household income: $33,948 (2000); Poverty rate: 4.5% (2000).

Education: Percent of population age 25 and over with: High school diploma (including GED) or higher: 84.6% (2000); Bachelor's degree or higher: 15.4% (2000).

Housing: Homeownership rate: 94.7% (2000); Median home value: $90,300 (2000); Median rent: $367 per month (2000); Median age of housing: 12 years (2000).

Transportation: Commute to work: 93.9% car, 0.0% public transportation, 0.0% walk, 4.8% work from home (2000); Travel time to work: 25.7% less than 15 minutes, 47.2% 15 to 30 minutes, 8.6% 30 to 45 minutes, 7.2% 45 to 60 minutes, 11.4% 60 minutes or more (2000)

GROVELAND (city). Covers a land area of 2.631 square miles and a water area of 0.394 square miles. Located at 28.55° N. Lat.; 81.85° W. Long. Elevation is 107 feet.

History: Groveland was named for the large citrus groves that surrounded it when it was founded in the early 1900's. It was first called Taylorville, and was renamed Groveland in 1911. Many of Groveland's early residents were of Swedish descent.

Population: 2,405 (1990); 2,360 (2000); 3,192 (2004); 4,183 (2009 projected); Race: 67.3% White, 20.9% Black, 0.7% Asian, 19.5% Hispanic of any race (2004); Density: 1,213.4 persons per square mile (2004); Average household size: 2.75 (2004); Median age: 33.7 (2004); Male/female ratio: 98.9 (2004); Marriage status: 28.0% never married, 54.0% now married, 7.1% widowed, 10.8% divorced (2000); Foreign born: 5.9% (2000); Ancestry (includes multiple ancestries): 34.1% Other groups, 15.6% United States or American, 12.5% German, 9.7% Irish, 7.1% English (2000).

Economy: Single-family building permits issued: 210 (2004); Multi-family building permits issued: 6 (2004); Employment by occupation: 8.1% management, 8.3% professional, 22.7% services, 25.7% sales, 3.4% farming, 15.9% construction, 15.9% production (2000).

Income: Per capita income: $16,376 (2004); Median household income: $35,045 (2004); Average household income: $45,024 (2004); Percent of households with income of $100,000 or more: 7.0% (2004); Poverty rate: 18.8% (2000).

Taxes: Total city taxes per capita: $328 (2002); City property taxes per capita: $178 (2002).

Education: Percent of population age 25 and over with: High school diploma (including GED) or higher: 69.0% (2004); Bachelor's degree or higher: 8.9% (2004); Master's degree or higher: 3.4% (2004).

School District(s)

Lake County School District (PK-12)
2002-03 Enrollment: 31,782 . . . . (352) 253-6510

Housing: Homeownership rate: 68.4% (2004); Median home value: $107,857 (2004); Median rent: $351 per month (2000); Median age of housing: 30 years (2000).

Safety: Violent crime rate: 29.1 per 10,000 population; Property crime rate: 253.5 per 10,000 population (2003).

Transportation: Commute to work: 95.1% car, 0.2% public transportation, 0.8% walk, 2.2% work from home (2000); Travel time to work: 29.5% less than 15 minutes, 28.4% 15 to 30 minutes, 18.7% 30 to 45 minutes, 13.1% 45 to 60 minutes, 10.3% 60 minutes or more (2000)

HOWEY-IN-THE-HILLS (town). Aka Howey. Covers a land area of 1.768 square miles and a water area of 0.086 square miles. Located at 28.71° N. Lat.; 81.77° W. Long.

Population: 726 (1990); 956 (2000); 1,069 (2004); 1,212 (2009 projected); Race: 97.3% White, 0.6% Black, 0.7% Asian, 3.1% Hispanic of any race (2004); Density: 604.5 persons per square mile (2004); Average household size: 2.44 (2004); Median age: 45.6 (2004); Male/female ratio: 98.7 (2004); Marriage status: 16.2% never married, 68.3% now married, 5.9% widowed, 9.6% divorced (2000); Foreign born: 5.4% (2000); Ancestry (includes multiple ancestries): 21.1% German, 18.6% English, 14.8% United States or American, 13.0% Irish, 8.1% Other groups (2000).

Economy: Citrus-fruit packing and canning. Conference center. Single-family building permits issued: 15 (2004); Multi-family building permits issued: 0 (2004); Employment by occupation: 16.2% management, 21.2% professional, 11.9% services, 30.6% sales, 0.5% farming, 10.3% construction, 9.4% production (2000).

Income: Per capita income: $26,630 (2004); Median household income: $56,934 (2004); Average household income: $64,846 (2004); Percent of households with income of $100,000 or more: 15.9% (2004); Poverty rate: 5.7% (2000).

Education: Percent of population age 25 and over with: High school diploma (including GED) or higher: 87.5% (2004); Bachelor's degree or higher: 28.1% (2004); Master's degree or higher: 8.3% (2004).

Housing: Homeownership rate: 84.7% (2004); Median home value: $147,656 (2004); Median rent: $583 per month (2000); Median age of housing: 29 years (2000).

Safety: Violent crime rate: 46.9 per 10,000 population; Property crime rate: 93.9 per 10,000 population (2003).

Transportation: Commute to work: 88.0% car, 0.0% public transportation, 1.9% walk, 8.5% work from home (2000); Travel time to work: 24.0% less than 15 minutes, 37.6% 15 to 30 minutes, 16.2% 30 to 45 minutes, 12.1% 45 to 60 minutes, 10.1% 60 minutes or more (2000)

LADY LAKE (town). Covers a land area of 6.618 square miles and a water area of 0.135 square miles. Located at 28.92° N. Lat.; 81.93° W. Long. Elevation is 75 feet.

Population: 8,917 (1990); 11,828 (2000); 12,950 (2004); 14,468 (2009 projected); Race: 94.4% White, 3.9% Black, 0.4% Asian, 2.4% Hispanic of any race (2004); Density: 1,956.7 persons per square mile (2004); Average household size: 1.89 (2004); Median age: 68.3 (2004); Male/female ratio: 86.8 (2004); Marriage status: 6.8% never married, 73.7% now married, 13.4% widowed, 6.1% divorced (2000); Foreign born: 4.6% (2000); Ancestry (includes multiple ancestries): 19.1% German, 18.2% English, 15.2% Irish, 10.2% United States or American, 7.5% Italian (2000).

Economy: In citrus fruit and watermelon area. Fruit packing. Single-family building permits issued: 19 (2004); Multi-family building permits issued: 0 (2004); Employment by occupation: 7.1% management, 12.6% professional, 26.4% services, 29.8% sales, 0.3% farming, 11.4% construction, 12.4% production (2000).

Income: Per capita income: $24,509 (2004); Median household income: $36,557 (2004); Average household income: $45,878 (2004); Percent of households with income of $100,000 or more: 5.2% (2004); Poverty rate: 8.4% (2000).

Taxes: Total city taxes per capita: $325 (2002); City property taxes per capita: $98 (2002).

Education: Percent of population age 25 and over with: High school diploma (including GED) or higher: 82.6% (2004); Bachelor's degree or higher: 12.5% (2004); Master's degree or higher: 5.0% (2004).

School District(s)

Lake County School District (PK-12)
2002-03 Enrollment: 31,782 . . . . (352) 253-6510

Housing: Homeownership rate: 91.6% (2004); Median home value: $101,916 (2004); Median rent: $431 per month (2000); Median age of housing: 11 years (2000).

Safety: Violent crime rate: 21.9 per 10,000 population; Property crime rate: 181.7 per 10,000 population (2003).

Newspapers: The Daily Sun (Circulation 18,900)

Transportation: Commute to work: 91.4% car, 0.7% public transportation, 1.8% walk, 2.2% work from home (2000); Travel time to work: 39.9% less than 15 minutes, 36.6% 15 to 30 minutes, 12.3% 30 to 45 minutes, 5.3% 45 to 60 minutes, 5.9% 60 minutes or more (2000)

Additional Information Contacts

Lady Lake Chamber of Commerce . . . . (352) 753-6029
Local Government Offices . . . . (352) 751-1500

LAKE KATHRYN (CDP). Covers a land area of 2.800 square miles and a water area of 0.069 square miles. Located at 29.01° N. Lat.; 81.49° W. Long.

Population: 861 (1990); 845 (2000); 913 (2004); 1,005 (2009 projected); Race: 95.6% White, 1.0% Black, 0.2% Asian, 2.3% Hispanic of any race (2004); Density: 326.1 persons per square mile (2004); Average household size: 2.43 (2004); Median age: 39.3 (2004); Male/female ratio: 110.4 (2004); Marriage status: 28.5% never married, 41.9% now married, 10.1% widowed, 19.5% divorced (2000); Foreign born: 0.0% (2000); Ancestry (includes multiple ancestries): 30.6% Irish, 25.2% Other groups, 20.8% German, 12.7% Italian, 6.8% United States or American (2000).

Economy: Employment by occupation: 4.0% management, 9.3% professional, 30.8% services, 20.7% sales, 0.0% farming, 17.6% construction, 17.6% production (2000).

Income: Per capita income: $9,422 (2004); Median household income: $18,542 (2004); Average household income: $22,940 (2004); Percent of households with income of $100,000 or more: 0.0% (2004); Poverty rate: 36.9% (2000).

Education: Percent of population age 25 and over with: High school diploma (including GED) or higher: 46.1% (2004); Bachelor's degree or higher: 0.0% (2004); Master's degree or higher: 0.0% (2004).

Housing: Homeownership rate: 85.3% (2004); Median home value: $52,407 (2004); Median rent: $390 per month (2000); Median age of housing: 25 years (2000).

Transportation: Commute to work: 100.0% car, 0.0% public transportation, 0.0% walk, 0.0% work from home (2000); Travel time to work: 4.0% less than 15 minutes, 33.5% 15 to 30 minutes, 7.9% 30 to 45 minutes, 42.7% 45 to 60 minutes, 11.9% 60 minutes or more (2000)

LAKE MACK-FOREST HILLS (CDP). Covers a land area of 4.737 square miles and a water area of 0.302 square miles. Located at 28.99° N. Lat.; 81.42° W. Long.

Population: 923 (1990); 989 (2000); 1,040 (2004); 1,112 (2009 projected); Race: 94.2% White, 0.1% Black, 0.9% Asian, 5.6% Hispanic of any race (2004); Density: 219.6 persons per square mile (2004); Average household size: 2.47 (2004); Median age: 38.4 (2004); Male/female ratio: 101.6 (2004); Marriage status: 18.5% never married, 56.5% now married, 7.0% widowed, 18.0% divorced (2000); Foreign born: 2.1% (2000); Ancestry (includes multiple ancestries): 14.9% German, 11.9% Irish, 11.8% Other groups, 7.8% English, 6.4% United States or American (2000).

Economy: Employment by occupation: 6.1% management, 4.0% professional, 12.5% services, 10.6% sales, 7.7% farming, 39.1% construction, 19.9% production (2000).

Income: Per capita income: $14,957 (2004); Median household income: $29,524 (2004); Average household income: $36,948 (2004); Percent of households with income of $100,000 or more: 3.1% (2004); Poverty rate: 10.3% (2000).

Education: Percent of population age 25 and over with: High school diploma (including GED) or higher: 56.2% (2004); Bachelor's degree or higher: 0.8% (2004); Master's degree or higher: 0.8% (2004).

Housing: Homeownership rate: 81.5% (2004); Median home value: $52,237 (2004); Median rent: $288 per month (2000); Median age of housing: 23 years (2000).

Transportation: Commute to work: 100.0% car, 0.0% public transportation, 0.0% walk, 0.0% work from home (2000); Travel time to work: 6.6% less than 15 minutes, 33.8% 15 to 30 minutes, 21.8% 30 to 45 minutes, 19.7% 45 to 60 minutes, 18.1% 60 minutes or more (2000)

LEESBURG (city). Covers a land area of 18.666 square miles and a water area of 5.779 square miles. Located at 28.81° N. Lat.; 81.88° W. Long. Elevation is 79 feet.

History: Named for the Lee family of New York, the town's founders. Leesburg was founded in 1856 in an area that produced citrus fruit, berries, grapes, and watermelons.
Population: 15,039 (1990); 15,956 (2000); 16,838 (2004); 18,185 (2009 projected); Race: 62.0% White, 32.9% Black, 1.8% Asian, 5.4% Hispanic of any race (2004); Density: 902.1 persons per square mile (2004); Average household size: 2.33 (2004); Median age: 41.2 (2004); Male/female ratio: 84.4 (2004); Marriage status: 22.5% never married, 48.6% now married, 14.3% widowed, 14.5% divorced (2000); Foreign born: 5.6% (2000); Ancestry (includes multiple ancestries): 29.9% Other groups, 11.8% English, 11.8% German, 8.3% United States or American, 7.5% Irish (2000).
Economy: Single-family building permits issued: 229 (2004); Multi-family building permits issued: 176 (2004); Employment by occupation: 8.7% management, 16.2% professional, 24.1% services, 26.2% sales, 1.6% farming, 11.5% construction, 11.8% production (2000).
Income: Per capita income: $17,098 (2004); Median household income: $27,277 (2004); Average household income: $38,736 (2004); Percent of households with income of $100,000 or more: 4.8% (2004); Poverty rate: 19.8% (2000).
Taxes: Total city taxes per capita: $320 (2002); City property taxes per capita: $175 (2002).
Education: Percent of population age 25 and over with: High school diploma (including GED) or higher: 72.2% (2004); Bachelor's degree or higher: 13.8% (2004); Master's degree or higher: 5.2% (2004).

School District(s)

Lake County School District (PK-12)
2002-03 Enrollment: 31,782 . . . . (352) 253-6510

Four-year College(s)

Beacon College
2003-04 Enrollment: 82 . . . . (352) 787-7660
2003-04 Tuition: In-state $19,700; Out-of-state $19,700

Two-year College(s)

Lake-Sumter Community College (Public)
2003-04 Enrollment: 3,222 . . . . (352) 787-3747
2003-04 Tuition: In-state $1,731; Out-of-state $6,377

Housing: Homeownership rate: 58.4% (2004); Median home value: $81,138 (2004); Median rent: $380 per month (2000); Median age of housing: 26 years (2000).
Hospitals: Leesburg Regional Medical Center (294 beds)
Safety: Violent crime rate: 132.3 per 10,000 population; Property crime rate: 681.2 per 10,000 population (2003).
Newspapers: Daily Commercial (Circulation 29,718)
Transportation: Commute to work: 91.6% car, 0.7% public transportation, 3.5% walk, 1.7% work from home (2000); Travel time to work: 50.6% less than 15 minutes, 29.2% 15 to 30 minutes, 12.0% 30 to 45 minutes, 3.7% 45 to 60 minutes, 4.5% 60 minutes or more (2000)
Airports: Leesburg Regional
Additional Information Contacts
Local Government Offices . . . . (352) 728-9700

LISBON (CDP). Covers a land area of 1.883 square miles and a water area of 0.098 square miles. Located at 28.88° N. Lat.; 81.78° W. Long. Elevation is 82 feet.
Population: 179 (1990); 273 (2000); 320 (2004); 379 (2009 projected); Race: 88.8% White, 0.0% Black, 0.0% Asian, 13.8% Hispanic of any race (2004); Density: 169.9 persons per square mile (2004); Average household size: 2.58 (2004); Median age: 41.7 (2004); Male/female ratio: 110.5 (2004); Marriage status: 20.3% never married, 47.6% now married, 19.3% widowed, 12.8% divorced (2000); Foreign born: 6.7% (2000); Ancestry (includes multiple ancestries): 29.6% United States or American, 11.3% English, 11.3% German, 7.9% Other groups, 3.3% Italian (2000).
Economy: Employment by occupation: 8.4% management, 16.8% professional, 10.5% services, 28.4% sales, 2.1% farming, 15.8% construction, 17.9% production (2000).
Income: Per capita income: $13,672 (2004); Median household income: $25,909 (2004); Average household income: $35,282 (2004); Percent of households with income of $100,000 or more: 7.3% (2004); Poverty rate: 7.5% (2000).
Education: Percent of population age 25 and over with: High school diploma (including GED) or higher: 61.1% (2004); Bachelor's degree or higher: 4.8% (2004); Master's degree or higher: 0.0% (2004).
Housing: Homeownership rate: 77.4% (2004); Median home value: $78,571 (2004); Median rent: $340 per month (2000); Median age of housing: 10 years (2000).
Transportation: Commute to work: 100.0% car, 0.0% public transportation, 0.0% walk, 0.0% work from home (2000); Travel time to work: 16.8% less than 15 minutes, 48.4% 15 to 30 minutes, 34.7% 30 to 45 minutes, 0.0% 45 to 60 minutes, 0.0% 60 minutes or more (2000)

MASCOTTE (city). Covers a land area of 2.429 square miles and a water area of 0.389 square miles. Located at 28.57° N. Lat.; 81.88° W. Long. Elevation is 128 feet.
History: Mascotte developed around a railroad station as a trading center for citrus growers.
Population: 1,973 (1990); 2,687 (2000); 3,547 (2004); 4,535 (2009 projected); Race: 55.8% White, 4.8% Black, 0.7% Asian, 54.4% Hispanic of any race (2004); Density: 1,460.2 persons per square mile (2004); Average household size: 3.31 (2004); Median age: 26.4 (2004); Male/female ratio: 117.5 (2004); Marriage status: 28.6% never married, 56.0% now married, 4.2% widowed, 11.2% divorced (2000); Foreign born: 24.9% (2000); Ancestry (includes multiple ancestries): 48.7% Other groups, 13.9% United States or American, 5.8% German, 5.4% Irish, 5.1% English (2000).
Economy: Single-family building permits issued: 74 (2004); Multi-family building permits issued: 0 (2004); Employment by occupation: 5.3% management, 6.9% professional, 17.8% services, 17.1% sales, 11.7% farming, 25.9% construction, 15.2% production (2000).
Income: Per capita income: $14,608 (2004); Median household income: $42,535 (2004); Average household income: $47,929 (2004); Percent of households with income of $100,000 or more: 6.3% (2004); Poverty rate: 15.7% (2000).
Taxes: Total city taxes per capita: $117 (2002); City property taxes per capita: $82 (2002).
Education: Percent of population age 25 and over with: High school diploma (including GED) or higher: 51.9% (2004); Bachelor's degree or higher: 5.7% (2004); Master's degree or higher: 1.1% (2004).

School District(s)

Lake County School District (PK-12)
2002-03 Enrollment: 31,782 . . . . (352) 253-6510

Housing: Homeownership rate: 75.6% (2004); Median home value: $100,350 (2004); Median rent: $416 per month (2000); Median age of housing: 11 years (2000).
Safety: Violent crime rate: 23.5 per 10,000 population; Property crime rate: 264.4 per 10,000 population (2003).
Transportation: Commute to work: 91.3% car, 0.0% public transportation, 0.9% walk, 0.5% work from home (2000); Travel time to work: 10.3% less than 15 minutes, 29.0% 15 to 30 minutes, 21.7% 30 to 45 minutes, 20.0% 45 to 60 minutes, 19.1% 60 minutes or more (2000)

MINNEOLA (city). Covers a land area of 3.055 square miles and a water area of 0.173 square miles. Located at 28.57° N. Lat.; 81.74° W. Long. Elevation is 125 feet.
Population: 2,028 (1990); 5,435 (2000); 6,930 (2004); 8,742 (2009 projected); Race: 84.9% White, 7.2% Black, 1.8% Asian, 15.2% Hispanic of any race (2004); Density: 2,268.3 persons per square mile (2004); Average household size: 2.88 (2004); Median age: 32.6 (2004); Male/female ratio: 96.0 (2004); Marriage status: 17.5% never married, 71.0% now married, 3.9% widowed, 7.6% divorced (2000); Foreign born: 7.9% (2000); Ancestry (includes multiple ancestries): 19.4% Other groups, 16.0% German, 13.7% English, 12.4% Irish, 6.6% United States or American (2000).
Economy: Ships citrus fruit. Single-family building permits issued: 488 (2004); Multi-family building permits issued: 4 (2004); Employment by occupation: 13.8% management, 20.3% professional, 16.6% services, 28.5% sales, 0.3% farming, 11.7% construction, 8.7% production (2000).
Income: Per capita income: $21,853 (2004); Median household income: $51,511 (2004); Average household income: $62,611 (2004); Percent of households with income of $100,000 or more: 14.2% (2004); Poverty rate: 6.1% (2000).
Taxes: Total city taxes per capita: $201 (2002); City property taxes per capita: $81 (2002).
Education: Percent of population age 25 and over with: High school diploma (including GED) or higher: 84.3% (2004); Bachelor's degree or higher: 23.5% (2004); Master's degree or higher: 4.6% (2004).
Housing: Homeownership rate: 80.4% (2004); Median home value: $143,674 (2004); Median rent: $581 per month (2000); Median age of housing: 5 years (2000).
Transportation: Commute to work: 96.5% car, 0.0% public transportation, 0.9% walk, 1.2% work from home (2000); Travel time to work: 23.8% less than 15 minutes, 17.2% 15 to 30 minutes, 36.8% 30 to 45 minutes, 16.7% 45 to 60 minutes, 5.4% 60 minutes or more (2000)

Additional Information Contacts
Local Government Offices . . . . (352) 394-3598

MONTVERDE (town). Covers a land area of 1.571 square miles and a water area of 0.206 square miles. Located at 28.59° N. Lat.; 81.67° W. Long. Elevation is 110 feet.
History: Montverde developed as the center of a grape-growing area.
Population: 888 (1990); 882 (2000); 1,075 (2004); 1,313 (2009 projected); Race: 96.5% White, 2.0% Black, 0.3% Asian, 1.9% Hispanic of any race (2004); Density: 684.4 persons per square mile (2004); Average household size: 2.49 (2004); Median age: 40.7 (2004); Male/female ratio: 98.7 (2004); Marriage status: 9.6% never married, 71.5% now married, 7.2% widowed, 11.7% divorced (2000); Foreign born: 3.4% (2000); Ancestry (includes multiple ancestries): 25.6% German, 19.9% English, 15.7% Irish, 10.6% Italian, 8.2% United States or American (2000).
Economy: Employment by occupation: 14.2% management, 17.4% professional, 11.0% services, 31.2% sales, 1.1% farming, 13.3% construction, 11.7% production (2000).
Income: Per capita income: $22,830 (2004); Median household income: $51,786 (2004); Average household income: $56,811 (2004); Percent of households with income of $100,000 or more: 9.7% (2004); Poverty rate: 5.3% (2000).
Education: Percent of population age 25 and over with: High school diploma (including GED) or higher: 84.4% (2004); Bachelor's degree or higher: 14.5% (2004); Master's degree or higher: 4.9% (2004).
Housing: Homeownership rate: 86.1% (2004); Median home value: $136,644 (2004); Median rent: $504 per month (2000); Median age of housing: 18 years (2000).
Transportation: Commute to work: 88.8% car, 0.0% public transportation, 5.2% walk, 4.0% work from home (2000); Travel time to work: 19.8% less than 15 minutes, 16.6% 15 to 30 minutes, 36.1% 30 to 45 minutes, 17.1% 45 to 60 minutes, 10.4% 60 minutes or more (2000)

MOUNT DORA (city). Covers a land area of 4.917 square miles and a water area of 0.844 square miles. Located at 28.80° N. Lat.; 81.64° W. Long. Elevation is 175 feet.
History: Mount Dora was founded in 1882 on the shores of Lake Dora, named for Dora Ann Drawdy who lived in the area. The South Florida Chautauqua was established at Mount Dora in 1885.
Population: 7,670 (1990); 9,418 (2000); 10,449 (2004); 11,821 (2009 projected); Race: 75.3% White, 20.5% Black, 0.8% Asian, 9.0% Hispanic of any race (2004); Density: 2,125.0 persons per square mile (2004); Average household size: 2.25 (2004); Median age: 46.9 (2004); Male/female ratio: 86.7 (2004); Marriage status: 17.0% never married, 60.2% now married, 12.1% widowed, 10.7% divorced (2000); Foreign born: 5.4% (2000); Ancestry (includes multiple ancestries): 25.3% Other groups, 14.3% English, 14.2% German, 13.0% Irish, 8.6% United States or American (2000).
Economy: Single-family building permits issued: 116 (2004); Multi-family building permits issued: 220 (2004); Employment by occupation: 16.8% management, 21.5% professional, 14.4% services, 22.5% sales, 3.3% farming, 10.6% construction, 10.8% production (2000).
Income: Per capita income: $24,780 (2004); Median household income: $38,318 (2004); Average household income: $55,143 (2004); Percent of households with income of $100,000 or more: 11.8% (2004); Poverty rate: 15.6% (2000).
Education: Percent of population age 25 and over with: High school diploma (including GED) or higher: 81.6% (2004); Bachelor's degree or higher: 27.4% (2004); Master's degree or higher: 10.4% (2004).

School District(s)

Lake County School District (PK-12)
2002-03 Enrollment: 31,782 . . . . (352) 253-6510

Housing: Homeownership rate: 65.3% (2004); Median home value: $143,350 (2004); Median rent: $487 per month (2000); Median age of housing: 22 years (2000).
Newspapers: Eustis News (General - Circulation 1,500); Tavares Citizen (General - Circulation 1,000); The Mount Dora Topic (General - Circulation 1,500)
Transportation: Commute to work: 89.5% car, 1.1% public transportation, 2.4% walk, 5.5% work from home (2000); Travel time to work: 35.7% less than 15 minutes, 27.2% 15 to 30 minutes, 21.5% 30 to 45 minutes, 8.0% 45 to 60 minutes, 7.7% 60 minutes or more (2000)
Additional Information Contacts
Local Government Offices . . . . (352) 735-7100
Mount Dora Chamber of Commerce . . . . (352) 383-2165

MOUNT PLYMOUTH (CDP). Covers a land area of 2.784 square miles and a water area of 0.144 square miles. Located at 28.79° N. Lat.; 81.53° W. Long. Elevation is 83 feet.
Population: 2,221 (1990); 2,814 (2000); 3,232 (2004); 3,765 (2009 projected); Race: 90.0% White, 5.3% Black, 1.5% Asian, 5.1% Hispanic of any race (2004); Density: 1,161.0 persons per square mile (2004); Average household size: 2.57 (2004); Median age: 38.2 (2004); Male/female ratio: 95.8 (2004); Marriage status: 19.4% never married, 59.0% now married, 6.5% widowed, 15.1% divorced (2000); Foreign born: 4.1% (2000); Ancestry (includes multiple ancestries): 20.1% Other groups, 16.5% German, 13.1% English, 10.3% United States or American, 10.3% Irish (2000).
Economy: Employment by occupation: 12.9% management, 16.5% professional, 13.1% services, 34.0% sales, 2.7% farming, 12.6% construction, 8.2% production (2000).
Income: Per capita income: $19,878 (2004); Median household income: $45,714 (2004); Average household income: $51,150 (2004); Percent of households with income of $100,000 or more: 5.9% (2004); Poverty rate: 6.6% (2000).
Education: Percent of population age 25 and over with: High school diploma (including GED) or higher: 80.2% (2004); Bachelor's degree or higher: 13.8% (2004); Master's degree or higher: 5.4% (2004).
Housing: Homeownership rate: 90.2% (2004); Median home value: $117,651 (2004); Median rent: $627 per month (2000); Median age of housing: 14 years (2000).
Transportation: Commute to work: 93.5% car, 0.0% public transportation, 2.6% walk, 2.6% work from home (2000); Travel time to work: 11.8% less than 15 minutes, 38.5% 15 to 30 minutes, 23.1% 30 to 45 minutes, 14.7% 45 to 60 minutes, 11.9% 60 minutes or more (2000)

OKAHUMPKA (CDP). Covers a land area of 0.239 square miles and a water area of 0 square miles. Located at 28.74° N. Lat.; 81.90° W. Long. Elevation is 87 feet.
History: Okahumpka was founded in 1885 by Reverend Edmund Snyder of Pennsylvania. It grew as a lumber and turpentine community.
Population: 95 (1990); 251 (2000); 321 (2004); 410 (2009 projected); Race: 99.7% White, 0.3% Black, 0.0% Asian, 0.3% Hispanic of any race (2004); Density: 1,341.7 persons per square mile (2004); Average household size: 2.28 (2004); Median age: 40.5 (2004); Male/female ratio: 105.8 (2004); Marriage status: 16.9% never married, 48.3% now married, 9.3% widowed, 25.6% divorced (2000); Foreign born: 0.0% (2000); Ancestry (includes multiple ancestries): 36.3% Other groups, 22.1% United States or American, 17.2% English, 13.2% Irish, 6.9% German (2000).
Economy: Employment by occupation: 0.0% management, 0.0% professional, 29.3% services, 29.3% sales, 0.0% farming, 26.0% construction, 15.4% production (2000).
Income: Per capita income: $11,776 (2004); Median household income: $19,643 (2004); Average household income: $26,809 (2004); Percent of households with income of $100,000 or more: 0.0% (2004); Poverty rate: 31.4% (2000).
Education: Percent of population age 25 and over with: High school diploma (including GED) or higher: 67.8% (2004); Bachelor's degree or higher: 0.0% (2004); Master's degree or higher: 0.0% (2004).
Housing: Homeownership rate: 66.7% (2004); Median home value: $56,190 (2004); Median rent: $375 per month (2000); Median age of housing: 18 years (2000).
Transportation: Commute to work: 100.0% car, 0.0% public transportation, 0.0% walk, 0.0% work from home (2000); Travel time to work: 7.3% less than 15 minutes, 86.2% 15 to 30 minutes, 0.0% 30 to 45 minutes, 0.0% 45 to 60 minutes, 6.4% 60 minutes or more (2000)

PAISLEY (CDP). Covers a land area of 3.282 square miles and a water area of 0.148 square miles. Located at 28.98° N. Lat.; 81.53° W. Long. Elevation is 83 feet.
Population: 572 (1990); 734 (2000); 831 (2004); 958 (2009 projected); Race: 97.1% White, 0.0% Black, 0.7% Asian, 1.6% Hispanic of any race (2004); Density: 253.2 persons per square mile (2004); Average household size: 2.31 (2004); Median age: 43.0 (2004); Male/female ratio: 98.8 (2004); Marriage status: 10.8% never married, 54.1% now married, 14.4% widowed, 20.7% divorced (2000); Foreign born: 4.7% (2000); Ancestry (includes multiple ancestries): 29.4% Other groups, 22.1% United States or American, 16.6% Irish, 16.5% German, 5.6% English (2000).

Economy: Employment by occupation: 7.5% management, 10.4% professional, 25.4% services, 29.1% sales, 1.9% farming, 10.8% construction, 14.9% production (2000).
Income: Per capita income: $15,283 (2004); Median household income: $29,554 (2004); Average household income: $35,376 (2004); Percent of households with income of $100,000 or more: 5.6% (2004); Poverty rate: 17.4% (2000).
Education: Percent of population age 25 and over with: High school diploma (including GED) or higher: 83.5% (2004); Bachelor's degree or higher: 5.8% (2004); Master's degree or higher: 4.1% (2004).

School District(s)

Lake County School District (PK-12)
2002-03 Enrollment: 31,782 . . . . (352) 253-6510
Housing: Homeownership rate: 87.5% (2004); Median home value: $83,333 (2004); Median rent: $325 per month (2000); Median age of housing: 19 years (2000).
Transportation: Commute to work: 95.1% car, 4.9% public transportation, 0.0% walk, 0.0% work from home (2000); Travel time to work: 15.7% less than 15 minutes, 23.9% 15 to 30 minutes, 26.1% 30 to 45 minutes, 16.4% 45 to 60 minutes, 17.9% 60 minutes or more (2000)

PINE LAKES (CDP). Covers a land area of 1.551 square miles and a water area of 0.181 square miles. Located at 28.94° N. Lat.; 81.42° W. Long. Elevation is 52 feet.
Population: 533 (1990); 755 (2000); 864 (2004); 1,006 (2009 projected); Race: 95.8% White, 1.0% Black, 0.2% Asian, 3.2% Hispanic of any race (2004); Density: 557.1 persons per square mile (2004); Average household size: 2.64 (2004); Median age: 34.6 (2004); Male/female ratio: 105.7 (2004); Marriage status: 26.7% never married, 52.4% now married, 5.9% widowed, 15.0% divorced (2000); Foreign born: 3.2% (2000); Ancestry (includes multiple ancestries): 27.1% German, 14.5% English, 9.9% United States or American, 9.7% Irish, 7.4% Portuguese (2000).
Economy: Employment by occupation: 0.0% management, 9.8% professional, 13.7% services, 25.0% sales, 4.4% farming, 18.6% construction, 28.4% production (2000).
Income: Per capita income: $13,831 (2004); Median household income: $31,131 (2004); Average household income: $36,544 (2004); Percent of households with income of $100,000 or more: 2.8% (2004); Poverty rate: 32.4% (2000).
Education: Percent of population age 25 and over with: High school diploma (including GED) or higher: 60.1% (2004); Bachelor's degree or higher: 4.0% (2004); Master's degree or higher: 2.2% (2004).
Housing: Homeownership rate: 80.4% (2004); Median home value: $60,526 (2004); Median rent: $275 per month (2000); Median age of housing: 21 years (2000).
Transportation: Commute to work: 90.3% car, 5.1% public transportation, 4.6% walk, 0.0% work from home (2000); Travel time to work: 0.0% less than 15 minutes, 24.1% 15 to 30 minutes, 31.3% 30 to 45 minutes, 15.4% 45 to 60 minutes, 29.2% 60 minutes or more (2000)

PITTMAN (CDP). Covers a land area of 1.283 square miles and a water area of 0.017 square miles. Located at 28.99° N. Lat.; 81.64° W. Long. Elevation is 77 feet.
Population: 169 (1990); 192 (2000); 209 (2004); 231 (2009 projected); Race: 79.4% White, 15.3% Black, 0.0% Asian, 7.7% Hispanic of any race (2004); Density: 162.9 persons per square mile (2004); Average household size: 2.82 (2004); Median age: 37.4 (2004); Male/female ratio: 120.0 (2004); Marriage status: 41.0% never married, 28.2% now married, 0.0% widowed, 30.8% divorced (2000); Foreign born: 0.0% (2000); Ancestry (includes multiple ancestries): 43.6% Other groups, 16.7% English, 15.4% Irish, 14.1% Swiss, 12.8% German (2000).
Economy: Employment by occupation: 0.0% management, 0.0% professional, 32.4% services, 0.0% sales, 38.2% farming, 0.0% construction, 29.4% production (2000).
Income: Per capita income: $8,565 (2004); Median household income: $19,667 (2004); Average household income: $24,189 (2004); Percent of households with income of $100,000 or more: 0.0% (2004); Poverty rate: 28.2% (2000).
Education: Percent of population age 25 and over with: High school diploma (including GED) or higher: 35.6% (2004); Bachelor's degree or higher: 15.9% (2004); Master's degree or higher: 0.0% (2004).
Housing: Homeownership rate: 83.8% (2004); Median home value: $84,000 (2004); Median rent: $n/a per month (2000); Median age of housing: 23 years (2000).
Transportation: Commute to work: 100.0% car, 0.0% public transportation, 0.0% walk, 0.0% work from home (2000); Travel time to work: 0.0% less than 15 minutes, 70.6% 15 to 30 minutes, 0.0% 30 to 45 minutes, 0.0% 45 to 60 minutes, 29.4% 60 minutes or more (2000)

SILVER LAKE (CDP). Covers a land area of 2.449 square miles and a water area of 0.607 square miles. Located at 28.83° N. Lat.; 81.79° W. Long.
Population: 1,569 (1990); 1,882 (2000); 2,233 (2004); 2,683 (2009 projected); Race: 89.7% White, 3.9% Black, 4.5% Asian, 2.7% Hispanic of any race (2004); Density: 911.8 persons per square mile (2004); Average household size: 2.30 (2004); Median age: 46.5 (2004); Male/female ratio: 94.3 (2004); Marriage status: 20.8% never married, 59.9% now married, 8.8% widowed, 10.4% divorced (2000); Foreign born: 4.2% (2000); Ancestry (includes multiple ancestries): 19.7% English, 13.5% German, 11.6% United States or American, 10.6% Irish, 9.7% Other groups (2000).
Economy: Employment by occupation: 17.7% management, 23.3% professional, 3.7% services, 41.8% sales, 2.2% farming, 6.5% construction, 4.7% production (2000).
Income: Per capita income: $29,140 (2004); Median household income: $51,308 (2004); Average household income: $66,944 (2004); Percent of households with income of $100,000 or more: 18.6% (2004); Poverty rate: 8.8% (2000).
Education: Percent of population age 25 and over with: High school diploma (including GED) or higher: 91.0% (2004); Bachelor's degree or higher: 29.8% (2004); Master's degree or higher: 11.6% (2004).
Housing: Homeownership rate: 76.7% (2004); Median home value: $176,325 (2004); Median rent: $457 per month (2000); Median age of housing: 15 years (2000).
Transportation: Commute to work: 99.2% car, 0.0% public transportation, 0.0% walk, 0.8% work from home (2000); Travel time to work: 39.3% less than 15 minutes, 38.3% 15 to 30 minutes, 12.2% 30 to 45 minutes, 3.2% 45 to 60 minutes, 7.0% 60 minutes or more (2000)

SORRENTO (CDP). Covers a land area of 1.294 square miles and a water area of 0.016 square miles. Located at 28.80° N. Lat.; 81.56° W. Long. Elevation is 68 feet.
Population: 828 (1990); 765 (2000); 854 (2004); 967 (2009 projected); Race: 90.4% White, 0.5% Black, 0.0% Asian, 21.4% Hispanic of any race (2004); Density: 659.9 persons per square mile (2004); Average household size: 2.82 (2004); Median age: 34.8 (2004); Male/female ratio: 104.3 (2004); Marriage status: 20.9% never married, 59.2% now married, 9.5% widowed, 10.3% divorced (2000); Foreign born: 0.0% (2000); Ancestry (includes multiple ancestries): 21.0% United States or American, 15.2% English, 14.0% Irish, 12.1% Other groups, 11.7% German (2000).
Economy: Manufacturing includes egg processing, cedar chest manufacturing and printing and publishing. Employment by occupation: 3.0% management, 9.0% professional, 20.6% services, 24.4% sales, 12.1% farming, 16.2% construction, 14.6% production (2000).
Income: Per capita income: $17,954 (2004); Median household income: $42,845 (2004); Average household income: $50,602 (2004); Percent of households with income of $100,000 or more: 8.3% (2004); Poverty rate: 2.2% (2000).
Education: Percent of population age 25 and over with: High school diploma (including GED) or higher: 54.2% (2004); Bachelor's degree or higher: 7.3% (2004); Master's degree or higher: 3.6% (2004).

School District(s)

Lake County School District (PK-12)
2002-03 Enrollment: 31,782 . . . . (352) 253-6510
Housing: Homeownership rate: 72.6% (2004); Median home value: $86,102 (2004); Median rent: $388 per month (2000); Median age of housing: 28 years (2000).
Transportation: Commute to work: 100.0% car, 0.0% public transportation, 0.0% walk, 0.0% work from home (2000); Travel time to work: 23.4% less than 15 minutes, 46.2% 15 to 30 minutes, 14.8% 30 to 45 minutes, 8.1% 45 to 60 minutes, 7.4% 60 minutes or more (2000)
Additional Information Contacts
East Lake County Chamber of Commerce . . . . (352) 383-8801

TAVARES (city). Covers a land area of 7.089 square miles and a water area of 0.356 square miles. Located at 28.80° N. Lat.; 81.73° W. Long. Elevation is 76 feet.
History: Tavares was founded in 1875 by Alexander St.Clair Abrams and named for one of his Spanish ancestors. Abrahms planned the town as a resort community, but later built lumber mills and a cigar factory.

Population: 8,022 (1990); 9,700 (2000); 10,886 (2004); 12,475 (2009 projected); Race: 86.9% White, 9.1% Black, 1.1% Asian, 4.4% Hispanic of any race (2004); Density: 1,535.6 persons per square mile (2004); Average household size: 2.12 (2004); Median age: 55.9 (2004); Male/female ratio: 90.8 (2004); Marriage status: 15.0% never married, 59.9% now married, 12.8% widowed, 12.4% divorced (2000); Foreign born: 3.8% (2000); Ancestry (includes multiple ancestries): 18.2% German, 15.3% Other groups, 14.8% English, 10.3% United States or American, 9.8% Irish (2000).
Economy: Single-family building permits issued: 249 (2004); Multi-family building permits issued: 2 (2004); Employment by occupation: 10.8% management, 16.9% professional, 22.0% services, 28.1% sales, 0.6% farming, 10.7% construction, 10.9% production (2000).
Income: Per capita income: $22,537 (2004); Median household income: $33,099 (2004); Average household income: $45,582 (2004); Percent of households with income of $100,000 or more: 6.5% (2004); Poverty rate: 10.3% (2000).
Taxes: Total city taxes per capita: $484 (2002); City property taxes per capita: $133 (2002).
Education: Percent of population age 25 and over with: High school diploma (including GED) or higher: 77.8% (2004); Bachelor's degree or higher: 14.1% (2004); Master's degree or higher: 4.3% (2004).

School District(s)

Lake County School District (PK-12)
2002-03 Enrollment: 31,782 . . . . (352) 253-6510

Housing: Homeownership rate: 79.9% (2004); Median home value: $82,171 (2004); Median rent: $411 per month (2000); Median age of housing: 22 years (2000).
Hospitals: Florida Hospital Waterman (204 beds)
Safety: Violent crime rate: 26.5 per 10,000 population; Property crime rate: 224.0 per 10,000 population (2003).
Transportation: Commute to work: 95.5% car, 1.0% public transportation, 1.1% walk, 0.8% work from home (2000); Travel time to work: 39.6% less than 15 minutes, 33.9% 15 to 30 minutes, 11.6% 30 to 45 minutes, 7.9% 45 to 60 minutes, 7.1% 60 minutes or more (2000)

Additional Information Contacts

Greater Lake County Association of Realtors . . . . (352) 343-3003
Local Government Offices . . . . (352) 742-6209
Tavares Chamber of Commerce . . . . (352) 343-2531

UMATILLA (city). Covers a land area of 2.541 square miles and a water area of 0.516 square miles. Located at 28.93° N. Lat.; 81.66° W. Long. Elevation is 98 feet.
Population: 2,450 (1990); 2,214 (2000); 2,489 (2004); 2,850 (2009 projected); Race: 92.7% White, 3.9% Black, 0.3% Asian, 5.5% Hispanic of any race (2004); Density: 979.7 persons per square mile (2004); Average household size: 2.57 (2004); Median age: 39.2 (2004); Male/female ratio: 90.6 (2004); Marriage status: 18.3% never married, 57.7% now married, 14.2% widowed, 9.8% divorced (2000); Foreign born: 2.9% (2000); Ancestry (includes multiple ancestries): 22.5% United States or American, 12.7% Irish, 11.7% English, 11.2% German, 10.1% Other groups (2000).
Economy: Ships citrus fruit. Single-family building permits issued: 55 (2004); Multi-family building permits issued: 0 (2004); Employment by occupation: 8.6% management, 14.1% professional, 19.9% services, 24.2% sales, 2.6% farming, 13.0% construction, 17.4% production (2000).
Income: Per capita income: $18,107 (2004); Median household income: $32,083 (2004); Average household income: $45,201 (2004); Percent of households with income of $100,000 or more: 8.0% (2004); Poverty rate: 11.9% (2000).
Education: Percent of population age 25 and over with: High school diploma (including GED) or higher: 72.7% (2004); Bachelor's degree or higher: 10.9% (2004); Master's degree or higher: 5.1% (2004).

School District(s)

Lake County School District (PK-12)
2002-03 Enrollment: 31,782 . . . . (352) 253-6510

Housing: Homeownership rate: 69.3% (2004); Median home value: $89,764 (2004); Median rent: $323 per month (2000); Median age of housing: 26 years (2000).
Safety: Violent crime rate: 63.6 per 10,000 population; Property crime rate: 678.8 per 10,000 population (2003).
Newspapers: North Lake Outpost (General - Circulation 2,500)
Transportation: Commute to work: 95.7% car, 0.0% public transportation, 0.9% walk, 2.0% work from home (2000); Travel time to work: 33.2% less than 15 minutes, 35.9% 15 to 30 minutes, 15.0% 30 to 45 minutes, 7.3% 45 to 60 minutes, 8.6% 60 minutes or more (2000)

Additional Information Contacts

Umatilla Chamber of Commerce . . . . (352) 669-3511

YALAHA (CDP). Covers a land area of 6.250 square miles and a water area of 8.640 square miles. Located at 28.74° N. Lat.; 81.81° W. Long. Elevation is 80 feet.
Population: 1,168 (1990); 1,175 (2000); 1,414 (2004); 1,714 (2009 projected); Race: 85.7% White, 8.1% Black, 1.0% Asian, 6.9% Hispanic of any race (2004); Density: 226.3 persons per square mile (2004); Average household size: 2.21 (2004); Median age: 50.7 (2004); Male/female ratio: 94.8 (2004); Marriage status: 16.3% never married, 63.3% now married, 11.5% widowed, 8.9% divorced (2000); Foreign born: 1.5% (2000); Ancestry (includes multiple ancestries): 23.2% German, 18.4% English, 15.7% Other groups, 11.3% Irish, 9.5% United States or American (2000).
Economy: Employment by occupation: 14.5% management, 12.3% professional, 21.1% services, 32.1% sales, 4.7% farming, 6.2% construction, 9.1% production (2000).
Income: Per capita income: $19,466 (2004); Median household income: $32,897 (2004); Average household income: $42,680 (2004); Percent of households with income of $100,000 or more: 6.7% (2004); Poverty rate: 11.2% (2000).
Education: Percent of population age 25 and over with: High school diploma (including GED) or higher: 87.3% (2004); Bachelor's degree or higher: 23.3% (2004); Master's degree or higher: 2.7% (2004).
Housing: Homeownership rate: 89.0% (2004); Median home value: $141,008 (2004); Median rent: $450 per month (2000); Median age of housing: 26 years (2000).
Transportation: Commute to work: 88.8% car, 1.5% public transportation, 1.1% walk, 3.7% work from home (2000); Travel time to work: 16.6% less than 15 minutes, 24.2% 15 to 30 minutes, 32.9% 30 to 45 minutes, 11.4% 45 to 60 minutes, 15.0% 60 minutes or more (2000)

Lee County

Located in southwestern Florida, on the Gulf of Mexico; lowland area, drained by the Caloosahatchee River; bordered by a chain of barrier islands and lagoons. Covers a land area of 803.60 square miles, a water area of 408.30 square miles, and is located in the Eastern Time Zone. The county government was organized in 1887. County seat is Fort Myers.

Lee County is part of the Cape Coral-Fort Myers, FL Metropolitan Statistical Area. The entire metro area includes: Lee County, FL

Weather Station: Fort Myers Page Field — Elevation: 13 feet

	Jan	Feb	Mar	Apr	May	Jun	Jul	Aug	Sep	Oct	Nov	Dec
High	75	76	80	85	89	91	92	92	90	86	81	77
Low	54	55	59	63	68	73	74	75	74	69	62	56
Precip	2.4	2.1	3.3	1.6	3.6	9.7	9.0	9.6	7.8	2.5	1.8	1.6
Snow	0.0	0.0	0.0	0.0	0.0	0.0	0.0	0.0	0.0	0.0	0.0	0.0

High and Low temperatures in degrees Fahrenheit; Precipitation and Snow in inches

Population: 335,113 (1990); 440,888 (2000); 503,053 (2004); 581,167 (2009 projected); Race: 85.7% White, 7.3% Black, 0.9% Asian, 12.3% Hispanic of any race (2004); Density: 626.0 persons per square mile (2004); Average household size: 2.33 (2004); Median age: 44.8 (2004); Male/female ratio: 96.2 (2004).
Religion: Five largest groups: 17.1% Catholic Church, 4.1% Southern Baptist Convention, 3.1% Assemblies of God, 2.9% The United Methodist Church, 1.6% Presbyterian Church (U.S.A.) (2000).
Economy: Unemployment rate: 3.8% (2004); Total civilian labor force: 227,288 (2004); Leading industries: 18.0% retail trade; 14.0% health care and social assistance; 12.0% construction (2003); Companies that employ 500 or more persons: 15 (2003); Companies that employ 100 to 499 persons: 230 (2003); Companies that employ less than 100 persons: 13,964 (2003); Farms: 643 totaling 126,484 acres (2002); Minority business ownership rate: 8.2% (1997); Women business ownership rate: 27.4% (1997); Retail sales per capita: $11,320 (1997). Single-family building permits issued: 14,958 (2004); Multi-family building permits issued: 5,437 (2004).
Income: Per capita income: $27,826 (2004); Median household income: $46,069 (2004); Average household income: $64,142 (2004); Percent of households with income of $100,000 or more: 14.3% (2004); Poverty rate: 10.1% (2002); Bankruptcy rate: 4.41% (2004).
Taxes: Total county taxes per capita: $410 (2002); County property taxes per capita: $317 (2002).

Education: Percent of population age 25 and over with: High school diploma (including GED) or higher: 82.7% (2004); Bachelor's degree or higher: 21.4% (2004); Master's degree or higher: 7.7% (2004).
Housing: Homeownership rate: 76.7% (2004); Median home value: $138,841 (2004); Median rent: $554 per month (2000); Median age of housing: 17 years (2000).
Health: Birth rate: 109.9 per 10,000 population (2004); Death rate: 105.1 per 10,000 population (2004); Age adjusted cancer mortality rate: 181.3 deaths per 100,000 population (2002); Air Quality Index: 93.9% good, 6.1% moderate, 0.0% unhealthy for sensitive individuals, 0.0% unhealthy (percent of days in 2004); Number of physicians: 21.6 per 10,000 population (2001); Hospital beds: 37.6 per 10,000 population (2002); Hospital admissions: 1,563.9 per 10,000 population (2002).
Elections: 2004 Presidential election results: 59.9% Bush, 39.0% Kerry, 0.6% Nader, 0.2% Badnarik
National and State Parks: Caloosahatchee National Wildlife Refuge; Caloosahatchee River State Park; Cayo Costa State Park; Gasparilla Island State Park; J N Darling National Wildlife Refuge; Koreshan State Historic Site; Lovers Key State Park; Matlacha Pass National Wildlife Refuge; Mound Key Archaeological State Park; Pine Island National Wildlife Refuge

Additional Information Contacts

Lee County Government Offices . . . . (941) 335-2259
Bonita Springs Chamber of Commerce . . . . (239) 992-2943
Bonita Springs-Estero Association of Realtors . . . . (239) 992-6771
Cape Coral Association of Realtors . . . . (239) 542-6209
Cape Coral Chamber of Commerce . . . . (239) 549-6900
Christian Chamber of Commerce . . . . (239) 481-1411
Estero Chamber of Commerce . . . . (239) 948-7990
Fort Myers Beach Chamber of Commerce . . . . (239) 454-7500
Fort Myers Chamber of Commerce . . . . (239) 332-3624
Greater Pine Island Chamber . . . . (239) 283-0888
Hispanic Chamber of Commerce . . . . (239) 418-1441
Lehigh Acres Chamber of Commerce . . . . (239) 369-3322
Realtors Association of Greater Fort Myers & The Beach . . (239) 936-3537
SW Florida Chamber of Commerce . . . . (239) 418-1441
Sanibel and Captiva Islands Association of Realtors . . . . . . (239) 472-9353
Sanibel-Captiva Chamber of Commerce . . . . (239) 472-1080

Lee County Communities

ALVA (CDP). Covers a land area of 17.952 square miles and a water area of 0.843 square miles. Located at 26.71° N. Lat.; 81.62° W. Long. Elevation is 10 feet.
History: Alva developed along the Caloosahatchee River as a trading center for turkey farmers.
Population: 1,904 (1990); 2,182 (2000); 2,459 (2004); 2,813 (2009 projected); Race: 91.9% White, 2.0% Black, 0.2% Asian, 6.7% Hispanic of any race (2004); Density: 137.0 persons per square mile (2004); Average household size: 2.36 (2004); Median age: 47.4 (2004); Male/female ratio: 97.4 (2004); Marriage status: 13.0% never married, 65.6% now married, 9.0% widowed, 12.5% divorced (2000); Foreign born: 2.8% (2000); Ancestry (includes multiple ancestries): 19.5% English, 18.9% German, 15.2% United States or American, 15.1% Irish, 6.8% Other groups (2000).
Economy: Employment by occupation: 11.2% management, 16.2% professional, 14.4% services, 23.0% sales, 1.6% farming, 23.5% construction, 10.2% production (2000).
Income: Per capita income: $30,372 (2004); Median household income: $50,769 (2004); Average household income: $71,813 (2004); Percent of households with income of $100,000 or more: 17.6% (2004); Poverty rate: 7.8% (2000).
Education: Percent of population age 25 and over with: High school diploma (including GED) or higher: 81.6% (2004); Bachelor's degree or higher: 17.3% (2004); Master's degree or higher: 6.4% (2004).

School District(s)

Lee County School District (PK-12)
2002-03 Enrollment: 63,172 . . . . (239) 337-8301

Housing: Homeownership rate: 92.5% (2004); Median home value: $138,333 (2004); Median rent: $343 per month (2000); Median age of housing: 21 years (2000).
Transportation: Commute to work: 96.7% car, 0.6% public transportation, 0.9% walk, 1.1% work from home (2000); Travel time to work: 11.2% less than 15 minutes, 28.5% 15 to 30 minutes, 41.0% 30 to 45 minutes, 8.2% 45 to 60 minutes, 11.1% 60 minutes or more (2000)

BOKEELIA (CDP). Covers a land area of 8.846 square miles and a water area of 0.016 square miles. Located at 26.68° N. Lat.; 82.14° W. Long. Elevation is 3 feet.
Population: 1,491 (1990); 1,997 (2000); 2,357 (2004); 2,806 (2009 projected); Race: 97.8% White, 0.3% Black, 0.3% Asian, 19.2% Hispanic of any race (2004); Density: 266.4 persons per square mile (2004); Average household size: 2.19 (2004); Median age: 51.4 (2004); Male/female ratio: 111.0 (2004); Marriage status: 15.0% never married, 71.7% now married, 7.5% widowed, 5.8% divorced (2000); Foreign born: 13.0% (2000); Ancestry (includes multiple ancestries): 20.5% English, 20.5% Other groups, 16.5% German, 9.2% United States or American, 8.0% Irish (2000).
Economy: Employment by occupation: 10.8% management, 15.1% professional, 13.4% services, 27.9% sales, 12.7% farming, 9.4% construction, 10.8% production (2000).
Income: Per capita income: $28,691 (2004); Median household income: $40,704 (2004); Average household income: $62,966 (2004); Percent of households with income of $100,000 or more: 14.6% (2004); Poverty rate: 17.6% (2000).
Education: Percent of population age 25 and over with: High school diploma (including GED) or higher: 81.1% (2004); Bachelor's degree or higher: 17.7% (2004); Master's degree or higher: 6.6% (2004).
Housing: Homeownership rate: 81.8% (2004); Median home value: $131,633 (2004); Median rent: $339 per month (2000); Median age of housing: 19 years (2000).
Newspapers: Pine Island Eagle (General - Circulation 8,500)
Transportation: Commute to work: 80.2% car, 2.9% public transportation, 2.1% walk, 8.9% work from home (2000); Travel time to work: 30.8% less than 15 minutes, 23.6% 15 to 30 minutes, 25.5% 30 to 45 minutes, 7.2% 45 to 60 minutes, 13.0% 60 minutes or more (2000)

BONITA SPRINGS (city). Covers a land area of 35.289 square miles and a water area of 5.717 square miles. Located at 26.35° N. Lat.; 81.79° W. Long. Elevation is 12 feet.
Population: 17,511 (1990); 32,797 (2000); 33,119 (2004); 33,867 (2009 projected); Race: 86.3% White, 0.5% Black, 0.4% Asian, 22.9% Hispanic of any race (2004); Density: 938.5 persons per square mile (2004); Average household size: 2.20 (2004); Median age: 55.0 (2004); Male/female ratio: 104.0 (2004); Marriage status: 14.0% never married, 68.8% now married, 8.1% widowed, 9.1% divorced (2000); Foreign born: 16.0% (2000); Ancestry (includes multiple ancestries): 20.5% German, 19.4% Other groups, 14.8% English, 13.6% Irish, 6.2% United States or American (2000).
Economy: Manufacturing of shell novelties; fishing. Unemployment rate: 3.5% (2004); Total civilian labor force: 9,328 (2004); Single-family building permits issued: 855 (2004); Multi-family building permits issued: 689 (2004); Employment by occupation: 13.2% management, 11.4% professional, 21.7% services, 27.2% sales, 1.8% farming, 18.0% construction, 6.8% production (2000).
Income: Per capita income: $40,828 (2004); Median household income: $57,122 (2004); Average household income: $89,924 (2004); Percent of households with income of $100,000 or more: 23.4% (2004); Poverty rate: 6.7% (2000).
Education: Percent of population age 25 and over with: High school diploma (including GED) or higher: 84.2% (2004); Bachelor's degree or higher: 26.8% (2004); Master's degree or higher: 9.9% (2004).

School District(s)

Lee County School District (PK-12)
2002-03 Enrollment: 63,172 . . . . (239) 337-8301

Housing: Homeownership rate: 83.2% (2004); Median home value: $182,603 (2004); Median rent: $631 per month (2000); Median age of housing: 11 years (2000).
Transportation: Commute to work: 89.6% car, 0.5% public transportation, 1.6% walk, 5.8% work from home (2000); Travel time to work: 30.9% less than 15 minutes, 35.2% 15 to 30 minutes, 23.4% 30 to 45 minutes, 6.1% 45 to 60 minutes, 4.5% 60 minutes or more (2000)

Additional Information Contacts

Bonita Springs Chamber of Commerce . . . . (239) 992-2943
Bonita Springs-Estero Association of Realtors . . . . (239) 992-6771

BUCKINGHAM (CDP). Covers a land area of 18.964 square miles and a water area of <.001 square miles. Located at 26.65° N. Lat.; 81.73° W. Long. Elevation is 12 feet.

Population: 3,134 (1990); 3,742 (2000); 3,914 (2004); 4,154 (2009 projected); Race: 93.0% White, 2.7% Black, 0.6% Asian, 5.9% Hispanic of any race (2004); Density: 206.4 persons per square mile (2004); Average household size: 2.88 (2004); Median age: 41.1 (2004); Male/female ratio: 109.8 (2004); Marriage status: 27.8% never married, 56.9% now married, 4.7% widowed, 10.7% divorced (2000); Foreign born: 3.4% (2000); Ancestry (includes multiple ancestries): 18.8% German, 15.9% Irish, 15.2% English, 11.4% Other groups, 11.4% United States or American (2000).
Economy: Employment by occupation: 11.0% management, 19.7% professional, 10.7% services, 22.6% sales, 1.0% farming, 22.0% construction, 13.0% production (2000).
Income: Per capita income: $23,896 (2004); Median household income: $58,086 (2004); Average household income: $67,678 (2004); Percent of households with income of $100,000 or more: 19.2% (2004); Poverty rate: 16.8% (2000).
Education: Percent of population age 25 and over with: High school diploma (including GED) or higher: 75.0% (2004); Bachelor's degree or higher: 14.1% (2004); Master's degree or higher: 4.5% (2004).
Housing: Homeownership rate: 90.1% (2004); Median home value: $188,475 (2004); Median rent: $491 per month (2000); Median age of housing: 17 years (2000).
Transportation: Commute to work: 92.6% car, 0.2% public transportation, 2.9% walk, 4.2% work from home (2000); Travel time to work: 18.3% less than 15 minutes, 41.0% 15 to 30 minutes, 30.6% 30 to 45 minutes, 5.8% 45 to 60 minutes, 4.3% 60 minutes or more (2000)

BURNT STORE MARINA (CDP). Covers a land area of 1.221 square miles and a water area of 0.206 square miles. Located at 26.76° N. Lat.; 82.05° W. Long.
Population: 283 (1990); 1,271 (2000); 1,985 (2004); 2,828 (2009 projected); Race: 98.3% White, 1.3% Black, 0.1% Asian, 0.6% Hispanic of any race (2004); Density: 1,625.6 persons per square mile (2004); Average household size: 1.88 (2004); Median age: 63.2 (2004); Male/female ratio: 96.3 (2004); Marriage status: 4.1% never married, 81.9% now married, 6.1% widowed, 7.9% divorced (2000); Foreign born: 8.4% (2000); Ancestry (includes multiple ancestries): 27.0% German, 19.0% English, 16.9% Irish, 10.1% Italian, 7.7% United States or American (2000).
Economy: Employment by occupation: 17.8% management, 28.3% professional, 14.0% services, 29.7% sales, 0.0% farming, 6.6% construction, 3.5% production (2000).
Income: Per capita income: $55,640 (2004); Median household income: $71,630 (2004); Average household income: $104,588 (2004); Percent of households with income of $100,000 or more: 31.6% (2004); Poverty rate: 3.6% (2000).
Education: Percent of population age 25 and over with: High school diploma (including GED) or higher: 93.5% (2004); Bachelor's degree or higher: 40.0% (2004); Master's degree or higher: 16.4% (2004).
Housing: Homeownership rate: 94.5% (2004); Median home value: $247,774 (2004); Median rent: $894 per month (2000); Median age of housing: 8 years (2000).
Transportation: Commute to work: 71.2% car, 0.0% public transportation, 2.2% walk, 17.0% work from home (2000); Travel time to work: 26.2% less than 15 minutes, 29.8% 15 to 30 minutes, 15.1% 30 to 45 minutes, 20.0% 45 to 60 minutes, 8.9% 60 minutes or more (2000)

CAPE CORAL (city). Covers a land area of 105.188 square miles and a water area of 9.910 square miles. Located at 26.64° N. Lat.; 81.98° W. Long. Elevation is 5 feet.
History: Cape Coral has a cultural center and a historical Museum The city's population more than doubled between 1980 and 1990, and it was the fastest-growing city in the U.S. during that decade. Incorporated 1970.
Population: 75,507 (1990); 102,286 (2000); 121,513 (2004); 145,256 (2009 projected); Race: 90.7% White, 2.9% Black, 1.1% Asian, 11.6% Hispanic of any race (2004); Density: 1,155.2 persons per square mile (2004); Average household size: 2.51 (2004); Median age: 40.9 (2004); Male/female ratio: 95.0 (2004); Marriage status: 17.0% never married, 64.6% now married, 7.1% widowed, 11.3% divorced (2000); Foreign born: 8.7% (2000); Ancestry (includes multiple ancestries): 20.9% German, 15.9% Irish, 13.5% Other groups, 13.1% Italian, 11.9% English (2000).
Economy: There are 2 industrial parks in the vicinity, and boatbuilding is an industry. Unemployment rate: 3.7% (2004); Total civilian labor force: 51,861 (2004); Single-family building permits issued: 5,757 (2004); Multi-family building permits issued: 715 (2004); Employment by occupation: 12.2% management, 16.3% professional, 16.5% services, 32.3% sales, 0.3% farming, 12.8% construction, 9.5% production (2000).
Income: Per capita income: $24,888 (2004); Median household income: $50,446 (2004); Average household income: $62,114 (2004); Percent of households with income of $100,000 or more: 12.6% (2004); Poverty rate: 7.0% (2000).
Taxes: Total city taxes per capita: $401 (2002); City property taxes per capita: $278 (2002).
Education: Percent of population age 25 and over with: High school diploma (including GED) or higher: 85.5% (2004); Bachelor's degree or higher: 17.5% (2004); Master's degree or higher: 5.7% (2004).

School District(s)

Lee County School District (PK-12)
2002-03 Enrollment: 63,172 . . . . (239) 337-8301

Two-year College(s)

Cape Coral Beauty School (Private, For-profit)
2003-04 Enrollment: 27 . . . . (941) 549-1819
Lee County High Tech Center North (Public)
2003-04 Enrollment: 276 . . . . (239) 574-4440

Housing: Homeownership rate: 80.1% (2004); Median home value: $149,816 (2004); Median rent: $588 per month (2000); Median age of housing: 15 years (2000).
Safety: Violent crime rate: 27.1 per 10,000 population; Property crime rate: 327.3 per 10,000 population (2003).
Newspapers: Cape Coral Daily Breeze (Circulation 3,500)
Transportation: Commute to work: 94.7% car, 0.5% public transportation, 0.7% walk, 2.8% work from home (2000); Travel time to work: 25.5% less than 15 minutes, 41.4% 15 to 30 minutes, 21.1% 30 to 45 minutes, 5.8% 45 to 60 minutes, 6.2% 60 minutes or more (2000)

Additional Information Contacts

Cape Coral Association of Realtors . . . . (239) 542-6209
Cape Coral Chamber of Commerce . . . . (239) 549-6900
Greater Pine Island Chamber . . . . (239) 283-0888

CAPTIVA (CDP). Covers a land area of 1.242 square miles and a water area of 9.254 square miles. Located at 26.51° N. Lat.; 82.19° W. Long. Elevation is 3 feet.
Population: 469 (1990); 379 (2000); 374 (2004); 374 (2009 projected); Race: 98.1% White, 0.0% Black, 1.1% Asian, 0.5% Hispanic of any race (2004); Density: 301.2 persons per square mile (2004); Average household size: 1.97 (2004); Median age: 57.6 (2004); Male/female ratio: 95.8 (2004); Marriage status: 7.5% never married, 59.1% now married, 15.5% widowed, 17.9% divorced (2000); Foreign born: 10.2% (2000); Ancestry (includes multiple ancestries): 35.7% English, 30.1% German, 20.2% Irish, 13.0% Italian, 9.7% Scottish (2000).
Economy: Employment by occupation: 52.5% management, 11.5% professional, 11.5% services, 9.4% sales, 0.0% farming, 2.9% construction, 12.2% production (2000).
Income: Per capita income: $74,251 (2004); Median household income: $85,227 (2004); Average household income: $146,158 (2004); Percent of households with income of $100,000 or more: 43.2% (2004); Poverty rate: 0.0% (2000).
Education: Percent of population age 25 and over with: High school diploma (including GED) or higher: 93.1% (2004); Bachelor's degree or higher: 33.8% (2004); Master's degree or higher: 8.5% (2004).
Housing: Homeownership rate: 80.0% (2004); Median home value: $870,000 (2004); Median rent: $875 per month (2000); Median age of housing: 16 years (2000).
Transportation: Commute to work: 65.5% car, 0.0% public transportation, 0.0% walk, 30.2% work from home (2000); Travel time to work: 47.4% less than 15 minutes, 27.8% 15 to 30 minutes, 0.0% 30 to 45 minutes, 24.7% 45 to 60 minutes, 0.0% 60 minutes or more (2000)

CHARLESTON PARK (CDP). Covers a land area of 0.122 square miles and a water area of 0 square miles. Located at 26.70° N. Lat.; 81.58° W. Long.
Population: 251 (1990); 411 (2000); 454 (2004); 509 (2009 projected); Race: 0.9% White, 97.6% Black, 0.0% Asian, 2.4% Hispanic of any race (2004); Density: 3,733.0 persons per square mile (2004); Average household size: 3.63 (2004); Median age: 21.2 (2004); Male/female ratio: 86.1 (2004); Marriage status: 44.4% never married, 39.1% now married, 0.0% widowed, 16.5% divorced (2000); Foreign born: 5.4% (2000); Ancestry (includes multiple ancestries): 93.8% Other groups, 2.0% Haitian, 1.2% Jamaican (2000).
Economy: Employment by occupation: 3.1% management, 14.9% professional, 37.3% services, 14.3% sales, 0.0% farming, 15.5% construction, 14.9% production (2000).

Income: Per capita income: $9,730 (2004); Median household income: $30,735 (2004); Average household income: $35,340 (2004); Percent of households with income of $100,000 or more: 0.0% (2004); Poverty rate: 18.1% (2000).
Education: Percent of population age 25 and over with: High school diploma (including GED) or higher: 48.5% (2004); Bachelor's degree or higher: 4.5% (2004); Master's degree or higher: 0.0% (2004).
Housing: Homeownership rate: 53.6% (2004); Median home value: $71,600 (2004); Median rent: $192 per month (2000); Median age of housing: 25 years (2000).
Transportation: Commute to work: 100.0% car, 0.0% public transportation, 0.0% walk, 0.0% work from home (2000); Travel time to work: 3.7% less than 15 minutes, 42.9% 15 to 30 minutes, 26.1% 30 to 45 minutes, 24.2% 45 to 60 minutes, 3.1% 60 minutes or more (2000)

CYPRESS LAKE (CDP). Covers a land area of 3.977 square miles and a water area of 0.004 square miles. Located at 26.53° N. Lat.; 81.90° W. Long.
Population: 10,491 (1990); 12,072 (2000); 14,096 (2004); 16,621 (2009 projected); Race: 96.0% White, 1.3% Black, 0.7% Asian, 4.8% Hispanic of any race (2004); Density: 3,544.6 persons per square mile (2004); Average household size: 1.86 (2004); Median age: 56.6 (2004); Male/female ratio: 83.5 (2004); Marriage status: 15.8% never married, 58.6% now married, 13.4% widowed, 12.1% divorced (2000); Foreign born: 6.8% (2000); Ancestry (includes multiple ancestries): 23.1% German, 17.5% Irish, 17.5% English, 8.7% Italian, 7.4% United States or American (2000).
Economy: Employment by occupation: 15.5% management, 19.8% professional, 19.1% services, 32.3% sales, 0.4% farming, 7.5% construction, 5.5% production (2000).
Income: Per capita income: $26,459 (2004); Median household income: $38,485 (2004); Average household income: $48,861 (2004); Percent of households with income of $100,000 or more: 7.9% (2004); Poverty rate: 7.2% (2000).
Education: Percent of population age 25 and over with: High school diploma (including GED) or higher: 90.6% (2004); Bachelor's degree or higher: 27.3% (2004); Master's degree or higher: 9.6% (2004).
Housing: Homeownership rate: 78.6% (2004); Median home value: $127,748 (2004); Median rent: $662 per month (2000); Median age of housing: 17 years (2000).
Transportation: Commute to work: 93.3% car, 0.4% public transportation, 0.8% walk, 4.2% work from home (2000); Travel time to work: 30.8% less than 15 minutes, 44.7% 15 to 30 minutes, 16.2% 30 to 45 minutes, 4.7% 45 to 60 minutes, 3.7% 60 minutes or more (2000)

EAST DUNBAR (CDP). Covers a land area of 0.797 square miles and a water area of 0.010 square miles. Located at 26.63° N. Lat.; 81.84° W. Long.
Population: 2,485 (1990); 1,935 (2000); 1,842 (2004); 1,800 (2009 projected); Race: 3.7% White, 92.1% Black, 0.1% Asian, 3.5% Hispanic of any race (2004); Density: 2,310.7 persons per square mile (2004); Average household size: 3.01 (2004); Median age: 33.4 (2004); Male/female ratio: 93.7 (2004); Marriage status: 41.7% never married, 33.0% now married, 10.8% widowed, 14.6% divorced (2000); Foreign born: 1.1% (2000); Ancestry (includes multiple ancestries): 78.1% Other groups, 7.3% United States or American, 0.7% Haitian, 0.6% Irish, 0.6% African (2000).
Economy: Employment by occupation: 4.3% management, 11.6% professional, 32.5% services, 14.5% sales, 1.1% farming, 9.8% construction, 26.4% production (2000).
Income: Per capita income: $11,034 (2004); Median household income: $23,707 (2004); Average household income: $33,100 (2004); Percent of households with income of $100,000 or more: 4.2% (2004); Poverty rate: 37.3% (2000).
Education: Percent of population age 25 and over with: High school diploma (including GED) or higher: 52.5% (2004); Bachelor's degree or higher: 6.0% (2004); Master's degree or higher: 2.5% (2004).
Housing: Homeownership rate: 61.9% (2004); Median home value: $57,000 (2004); Median rent: $394 per month (2000); Median age of housing: 27 years (2000).
Transportation: Commute to work: 92.6% car, 2.2% public transportation, 1.0% walk, 0.0% work from home (2000); Travel time to work: 38.9% less than 15 minutes, 32.5% 15 to 30 minutes, 16.2% 30 to 45 minutes, 5.9% 45 to 60 minutes, 6.4% 60 minutes or more (2000)

ESTERO (CDP). Covers a land area of 21.085 square miles and a water area of 0.048 square miles. Located at 26.43° N. Lat.; 81.80° W. Long. Elevation is 11 feet.
History: In 1894 Estero was the site of the Koreshan Unity, a religious cooperative community established here by Cyrus R. Teed.
Population: 4,028 (1990); 9,503 (2000); 11,687 (2004); 14,290 (2009 projected); Race: 96.4% White, 0.9% Black, 0.5% Asian, 4.3% Hispanic of any race (2004); Density: 554.3 persons per square mile (2004); Average household size: 2.06 (2004); Median age: 60.2 (2004); Male/female ratio: 93.2 (2004); Marriage status: 9.6% never married, 75.1% now married, 7.6% widowed, 7.6% divorced (2000); Foreign born: 7.4% (2000); Ancestry (includes multiple ancestries): 22.7% German, 15.4% English, 13.1% Irish, 8.5% United States or American, 7.7% Italian (2000).
Economy: Employment by occupation: 18.1% management, 19.4% professional, 18.8% services, 31.2% sales, 0.3% farming, 8.2% construction, 4.0% production (2000).
Income: Per capita income: $37,572 (2004); Median household income: $51,928 (2004); Average household income: $76,805 (2004); Percent of households with income of $100,000 or more: 20.5% (2004); Poverty rate: 3.2% (2000).
Education: Percent of population age 25 and over with: High school diploma (including GED) or higher: 86.9% (2004); Bachelor's degree or higher: 29.4% (2004); Master's degree or higher: 10.3% (2004).

School District(s)

Lee County School District (PK-12)
2002-03 Enrollment: 63,172 . . . . (239) 337-8301

Housing: Homeownership rate: 86.7% (2004); Median home value: $171,774 (2004); Median rent: $683 per month (2000); Median age of housing: 6 years (2000).
Transportation: Commute to work: 90.8% car, 0.1% public transportation, 1.2% walk, 4.8% work from home (2000); Travel time to work: 24.1% less than 15 minutes, 35.5% 15 to 30 minutes, 26.5% 30 to 45 minutes, 8.3% 45 to 60 minutes, 5.6% 60 minutes or more (2000)

Additional Information Contacts

Estero Chamber of Commerce . . . . (239) 948-7990

FORT MYERS (city). Covers a land area of 31.829 square miles and a water area of 8.591 square miles. Located at 26.63° N. Lat.; 81.85° W. Long. Elevation is 10 feet.
History: Fort Myers began as a fort built by Federal troops in 1839 and named for Colonel Abraham C. Myers, then chief quartermaster in Florida. The community that grew up around the fort became an agricultural center and a headquarters for sportsmen fishing for tarpon. Thomas Edison came to Fort Myers in 1886 looking for a suitable fiber for the incandescent lamp he was developing. Edison continued to spend his winters here, along with his friend, Henry Ford, who bought an estate adjoining Edison's.
Population: 45,222 (1990); 48,208 (2000); 51,916 (2004); 56,810 (2009 projected); Race: 52.0% White, 36.1% Black, 1.2% Asian, 17.6% Hispanic of any race (2004); Density: 1,631.1 persons per square mile (2004); Average household size: 2.51 (2004); Median age: 32.0 (2004); Male/female ratio: 98.7 (2004); Marriage status: 33.6% never married, 43.2% now married, 8.8% widowed, 14.5% divorced (2000); Foreign born: 13.4% (2000); Ancestry (includes multiple ancestries): 38.5% Other groups, 10.7% German, 8.0% English, 7.7% Irish, 6.4% United States or American (2000).
Economy: Unemployment rate: 5.3% (2004); Total civilian labor force: 32,955 (2004); Single-family building permits issued: 483 (2004); Multi-family building permits issued: 567 (2004); Employment by occupation: 8.1% management, 17.5% professional, 23.4% services, 27.5% sales, 1.1% farming, 12.7% construction, 9.8% production (2000).
Income: Per capita income: $18,838 (2004); Median household income: $31,075 (2004); Average household income: $45,741 (2004); Percent of households with income of $100,000 or more: 8.1% (2004); Poverty rate: 21.8% (2000).
Taxes: Total city taxes per capita: $626 (2002); City property taxes per capita: $296 (2002).
Education: Percent of population age 25 and over with: High school diploma (including GED) or higher: 70.9% (2004); Bachelor's degree or higher: 18.1% (2004); Master's degree or higher: 6.4% (2004).

School District(s)

Lee County School District (PK-12)
2002-03 Enrollment: 63,172 . . . . (239) 337-8301

Four-year College(s)

Florida Gulf Coast University (Public)
2003-04 Enrollment: 5,972 .... (239) 590-1000
2003-04 Tuition: In-state $2,837; Out-of-state $13,192

Two-year College(s)

Edison Community College (Public)
2003-04 Enrollment: 10,341 .... (239) 489-9300
2003-04 Tuition: In-state $1,747; Out-of-state $6,513
Heritage Institute-Fort Myers (Private, For-profit)
2003-04 Enrollment: 182 .... (239) 936-5822
Lee County High Tech Center Central (Public)
2003-04 Enrollment: 653 .... (239) 334-4544
Southwest Florida College
2003-04 Enrollment: 1,809 .... (239) 939-4766
2003-04 Tuition: In-state $7,200; Out-of-state $7,200
Sunstate Academy of Hair Design (Private, For-profit)
2003-04 Enrollment: 101 .... (239) 278-1311

Housing: Homeownership rate: 37.6% (2004); Median home value: $103,629 (2004); Median rent: $508 per month (2000); Median age of housing: 26 years (2000).

Hospitals: Lee Memorial Health System (793 beds); Southwest Florida Regional Medical Center (400 beds)

Safety: Violent crime rate: 189.7 per 10,000 population; Property crime rate: 670.3 per 10,000 population (2003).

Newspapers: Community Voice (Black - Circulation 12,000); News-Press (Circulation 102,134)

Transportation: Commute to work: 90.0% car, 2.3% public transportation, 3.4% walk, 1.8% work from home (2000); Travel time to work: 33.5% less than 15 minutes, 38.9% 15 to 30 minutes, 15.6% 30 to 45 minutes, 5.8% 45 to 60 minutes, 6.1% 60 minutes or more (2000); Amtrak: Service available.

Airports: Page Field; Southwest Florida International (primary service/medium hub)

Additional Information Contacts

Christian Chamber of Commerce .... (239) 481-1411
Fort Myers Chamber of Commerce .... (239) 332-3624
Hispanic Chamber of Commerce .... (239) 418-1441
Realtors Association of Greater Fort Myers & The Beach . . (239) 936-3537
SW Florida Chamber of Commerce .... (239) 418-1441

FORT MYERS BEACH (town). Covers a land area of 2.864 square miles and a water area of 3.291 square miles. Located at 26.43° N. Lat.; 81.92° W. Long. Elevation is 8 feet.

Population: 5,836 (1990); 6,561 (2000); 6,970 (2004); 7,543 (2009 projected); Race: 96.4% White, 0.1% Black, 0.3% Asian, 4.8% Hispanic of any race (2004); Density: 2,433.7 persons per square mile (2004); Average household size: 1.88 (2004); Median age: 59.1 (2004); Male/female ratio: 98.4 (2004); Marriage status: 13.0% never married, 64.6% now married, 10.6% widowed, 11.8% divorced (2000); Foreign born: 8.8% (2000); Ancestry (includes multiple ancestries): 21.2% German, 18.1% English, 17.0% Irish, 7.0% Italian, 6.9% United States or American (2000).

Economy: Shrimp processing; light manufacturing. Resort on Gulf of Mexico. Single-family building permits issued: 19 (2004); Multi-family building permits issued: 163 (2004); Employment by occupation: 15.2% management, 14.8% professional, 23.4% services, 29.2% sales, 0.2% farming, 11.1% construction, 6.1% production (2000).

Income: Per capita income: $40,939 (2004); Median household income: $56,241 (2004); Average household income: $77,069 (2004); Percent of households with income of $100,000 or more: 22.1% (2004); Poverty rate: 7.2% (2000).

Education: Percent of population age 25 and over with: High school diploma (including GED) or higher: 90.4% (2004); Bachelor's degree or higher: 27.0% (2004); Master's degree or higher: 9.6% (2004).

School District(s)

Lee County School District (PK-12)
2002-03 Enrollment: 63,172 .... (239) 337-8301

Housing: Homeownership rate: 77.1% (2004); Median home value: $268,240 (2004); Median rent: $642 per month (2000); Median age of housing: 22 years (2000).

Newspapers: Fort Myers Beach Bulletin (General - Circulation 14,000)

Transportation: Commute to work: 78.7% car, 2.4% public transportation, 7.0% walk, 7.3% work from home (2000); Travel time to work: 38.7% less than 15 minutes, 25.3% 15 to 30 minutes, 20.6% 30 to 45 minutes, 11.0% 45 to 60 minutes, 4.4% 60 minutes or more (2000)

Additional Information Contacts

Fort Myers Beach Chamber of Commerce .... (239) 454-7500
Local Government Offices .... (239) 765-0202

FORT MYERS SHORES (CDP). Covers a land area of 2.146 square miles and a water area of 0.316 square miles. Located at 26.71° N. Lat.; 81.73° W. Long. Elevation is 10 feet.

Population: 5,460 (1990); 5,793 (2000); 6,029 (2004); 6,381 (2009 projected); Race: 80.9% White, 5.2% Black, 1.8% Asian, 24.5% Hispanic of any race (2004); Density: 2,809.2 persons per square mile (2004); Average household size: 2.65 (2004); Median age: 37.3 (2004); Male/female ratio: 95.0 (2004); Marriage status: 20.2% never married, 60.4% now married, 8.4% widowed, 11.0% divorced (2000); Foreign born: 6.5% (2000); Ancestry (includes multiple ancestries): 25.4% Other groups, 16.6% German, 13.0% United States or American, 11.1% Irish, 9.4% English (2000).

Economy: Employment by occupation: 7.9% management, 13.0% professional, 18.8% services, 30.5% sales, 0.2% farming, 20.0% construction, 9.6% production (2000).

Income: Per capita income: $21,765 (2004); Median household income: $43,546 (2004); Average household income: $57,655 (2004); Percent of households with income of $100,000 or more: 10.3% (2004); Poverty rate: 8.2% (2000).

Education: Percent of population age 25 and over with: High school diploma (including GED) or higher: 74.5% (2004); Bachelor's degree or higher: 12.9% (2004); Master's degree or higher: 5.3% (2004).

Housing: Homeownership rate: 79.4% (2004); Median home value: $119,410 (2004); Median rent: $452 per month (2000); Median age of housing: 23 years (2000).

Transportation: Commute to work: 97.4% car, 1.4% public transportation, 0.0% walk, 0.2% work from home (2000); Travel time to work: 18.9% less than 15 minutes, 39.4% 15 to 30 minutes, 30.3% 30 to 45 minutes, 5.2% 45 to 60 minutes, 6.3% 60 minutes or more (2000)

GATEWAY (CDP). Covers a land area of 8.551 square miles and a water area of 0.152 square miles. Located at 26.57° N. Lat.; 81.75° W. Long.

Population: 46 (1990); 2,943 (2000); 4,632 (2004); 6,611 (2009 projected); Race: 93.7% White, 2.0% Black, 2.2% Asian, 4.9% Hispanic of any race (2004); Density: 541.7 persons per square mile (2004); Average household size: 2.61 (2004); Median age: 40.1 (2004); Male/female ratio: 98.5 (2004); Marriage status: 10.1% never married, 77.8% now married, 4.0% widowed, 8.0% divorced (2000); Foreign born: 7.4% (2000); Ancestry (includes multiple ancestries): 19.5% German, 15.4% Irish, 11.1% Italian, 11.0% English, 10.2% Other groups (2000).

Economy: Employment by occupation: 25.3% management, 26.7% professional, 9.0% services, 33.3% sales, 0.4% farming, 2.7% construction, 2.7% production (2000).

Income: Per capita income: $47,211 (2004); Median household income: $98,825 (2004); Average household income: $123,340 (2004); Percent of households with income of $100,000 or more: 49.1% (2004); Poverty rate: 0.9% (2000).

Education: Percent of population age 25 and over with: High school diploma (including GED) or higher: 96.9% (2004); Bachelor's degree or higher: 48.1% (2004); Master's degree or higher: 17.0% (2004).

Housing: Homeownership rate: 92.1% (2004); Median home value: $253,303 (2004); Median rent: $1,121 per month (2000); Median age of housing: 4 years (2000).

Transportation: Commute to work: 92.7% car, 0.0% public transportation, 1.3% walk, 5.1% work from home (2000); Travel time to work: 16.3% less than 15 minutes, 51.8% 15 to 30 minutes, 20.5% 30 to 45 minutes, 2.3% 45 to 60 minutes, 9.1% 60 minutes or more (2000)

HARLEM HEIGHTS (CDP). Covers a land area of 0.794 square miles and a water area of 0 square miles. Located at 26.51° N. Lat.; 81.92° W. Long.

Population: 433 (1990); 1,065 (2000); 1,388 (2004); 1,790 (2009 projected); Race: 42.8% White, 34.3% Black, 0.2% Asian, 60.6% Hispanic of any race (2004); Density: 1,748.2 persons per square mile (2004); Average household size: 3.51 (2004); Median age: 29.1 (2004); Male/female ratio: 102.0 (2004); Marriage status: 43.2% never married, 34.3% now married, 6.9% widowed, 15.6% divorced (2000); Foreign born: 1.7% (2000); Ancestry (includes multiple ancestries): 92.7% Other groups, 1.8% United States or American, 1.0% Irish, 1.0% German (2000).

Economy: Employment by occupation: 0.0% management, 7.3% professional, 38.4% services, 31.3% sales, 0.0% farming, 12.3% construction, 10.6% production (2000).
Income: Per capita income: $9,890 (2004); Median household income: $31,948 (2004); Average household income: $34,753 (2004); Percent of households with income of $100,000 or more: 2.0% (2004); Poverty rate: 27.5% (2000).
Education: Percent of population age 25 and over with: High school diploma (including GED) or higher: 48.8% (2004); Bachelor's degree or higher: 3.6% (2004); Master's degree or higher: 0.0% (2004).
Housing: Homeownership rate: 82.8% (2004); Median home value: $77,156 (2004); Median rent: $341 per month (2000); Median age of housing: 21 years (2000).
Transportation: Commute to work: 97.6% car, 0.0% public transportation, 0.0% walk, 0.0% work from home (2000); Travel time to work: 38.0% less than 15 minutes, 23.5% 15 to 30 minutes, 27.6% 30 to 45 minutes, 8.2% 45 to 60 minutes, 2.6% 60 minutes or more (2000)

IONA (CDP). Covers a land area of 7.131 square miles and a water area of 3.077 square miles. Located at 26.51° N. Lat.; 81.95° W. Long. Elevation is 8 feet.
Population: 9,565 (1990); 11,756 (2000); 13,276 (2004); 15,218 (2009 projected); Race: 96.9% White, 0.4% Black, 0.6% Asian, 5.4% Hispanic of any race (2004); Density: 1,861.7 persons per square mile (2004); Average household size: 1.94 (2004); Median age: 58.0 (2004); Male/female ratio: 92.3 (2004); Marriage status: 11.9% never married, 65.9% now married, 11.3% widowed, 10.9% divorced (2000); Foreign born: 7.3% (2000); Ancestry (includes multiple ancestries): 25.1% German, 16.8% English, 15.8% Irish, 8.8% United States or American, 7.3% Other groups (2000).
Economy: Employment by occupation: 16.9% management, 20.0% professional, 19.3% services, 26.7% sales, 0.4% farming, 7.8% construction, 8.9% production (2000).
Income: Per capita income: $41,716 (2004); Median household income: $44,480 (2004); Average household income: $80,715 (2004); Percent of households with income of $100,000 or more: 19.3% (2004); Poverty rate: 10.0% (2000).
Education: Percent of population age 25 and over with: High school diploma (including GED) or higher: 86.4% (2004); Bachelor's degree or higher: 27.1% (2004); Master's degree or higher: 10.5% (2004).
Housing: Homeownership rate: 80.1% (2004); Median home value: $134,648 (2004); Median rent: $580 per month (2000); Median age of housing: 16 years (2000).
Transportation: Commute to work: 90.5% car, 0.2% public transportation, 2.0% walk, 4.8% work from home (2000); Travel time to work: 34.1% less than 15 minutes, 38.3% 15 to 30 minutes, 18.1% 30 to 45 minutes, 6.1% 45 to 60 minutes, 3.4% 60 minutes or more (2000)

LEHIGH ACRES (CDP). Covers a land area of 94.887 square miles and a water area of 1.094 square miles. Located at 26.60° N. Lat.; 81.63° W. Long. Elevation is 23 feet.
Population: 22,352 (1990); 33,430 (2000); 39,664 (2004); 47,354 (2009 projected); Race: 79.5% White, 11.7% Black, 0.9% Asian, 18.2% Hispanic of any race (2004); Density: 418.0 persons per square mile (2004); Average household size: 2.67 (2004); Median age: 37.3 (2004); Male/female ratio: 95.4 (2004); Marriage status: 17.3% never married, 63.2% now married, 9.2% widowed, 10.3% divorced (2000); Foreign born: 9.3% (2000); Ancestry (includes multiple ancestries): 22.4% Other groups, 15.1% German, 12.4% Irish, 11.9% United States or American, 10.6% English (2000).
Economy: Planned community surrounded by wilderness. Manufacturing includes building materials, printing and publishing. Employment by occupation: 9.0% management, 12.9% professional, 19.0% services, 30.5% sales, 0.2% farming, 16.3% construction, 12.1% production (2000).
Income: Per capita income: $19,536 (2004); Median household income: $44,145 (2004); Average household income: $51,776 (2004); Percent of households with income of $100,000 or more: 7.4% (2004); Poverty rate: 7.7% (2000).
Education: Percent of population age 25 and over with: High school diploma (including GED) or higher: 77.1% (2004); Bachelor's degree or higher: 11.1% (2004); Master's degree or higher: 4.2% (2004).

School District(s)

Lee County School District (PK-12)
2002-03 Enrollment: 63,172 . . . . (239) 337-8301

Housing: Homeownership rate: 84.0% (2004); Median home value: $113,964 (2004); Median rent: $513 per month (2000); Median age of housing: 17 years (2000).
Hospitals: East Pointe Hospital (88 beds)
Newspapers: Lehigh Acres News Star (General - Circulation 14,000)
Transportation: Commute to work: 95.2% car, 0.4% public transportation, 0.7% walk, 2.5% work from home (2000); Travel time to work: 18.9% less than 15 minutes, 30.7% 15 to 30 minutes, 32.3% 30 to 45 minutes, 11.1% 45 to 60 minutes, 7.0% 60 minutes or more (2000)

Additional Information Contacts

Lehigh Acres Chamber of Commerce . . . . (239) 369-3322

LOCHMOOR WATERWAY ESTATES (CDP). Covers a land area of 2.230 square miles and a water area of 0.528 square miles. Located at 26.64° N. Lat.; 81.91° W. Long.
Population: 3,671 (1990); 3,858 (2000); 4,128 (2004); 4,491 (2009 projected); Race: 94.8% White, 1.2% Black, 1.7% Asian, 4.9% Hispanic of any race (2004); Density: 1,850.9 persons per square mile (2004); Average household size: 2.33 (2004); Median age: 47.9 (2004); Male/female ratio: 93.1 (2004); Marriage status: 15.8% never married, 66.9% now married, 8.1% widowed, 9.1% divorced (2000); Foreign born: 5.4% (2000); Ancestry (includes multiple ancestries): 21.8% German, 16.8% Irish, 15.9% English, 7.9% Italian, 7.7% Other groups (2000).
Economy: Employment by occupation: 15.0% management, 21.5% professional, 13.2% services, 30.3% sales, 0.0% farming, 12.6% construction, 7.4% production (2000).
Income: Per capita income: $36,135 (2004); Median household income: $59,569 (2004); Average household income: $84,084 (2004); Percent of households with income of $100,000 or more: 23.3% (2004); Poverty rate: 3.2% (2000).
Education: Percent of population age 25 and over with: High school diploma (including GED) or higher: 89.2% (2004); Bachelor's degree or higher: 28.5% (2004); Master's degree or higher: 9.2% (2004).
Housing: Homeownership rate: 86.9% (2004); Median home value: $153,965 (2004); Median rent: $511 per month (2000); Median age of housing: 23 years (2000).
Transportation: Commute to work: 95.6% car, 0.8% public transportation, 0.4% walk, 3.1% work from home (2000); Travel time to work: 26.5% less than 15 minutes, 49.5% 15 to 30 minutes, 17.7% 30 to 45 minutes, 2.0% 45 to 60 minutes, 4.3% 60 minutes or more (2000)

MATLACHA (CDP). Covers a land area of 0.151 square miles and a water area of <.001 square miles. Located at 26.63° N. Lat.; 82.07° W. Long. Elevation is 3 feet.
Population: 742 (1990); 735 (2000); 774 (2004); 824 (2009 projected); Race: 97.9% White, 0.0% Black, 0.3% Asian, 1.8% Hispanic of any race (2004); Density: 5,137.6 persons per square mile (2004); Average household size: 1.79 (2004); Median age: 58.1 (2004); Male/female ratio: 106.4 (2004); Marriage status: 13.6% never married, 63.8% now married, 11.0% widowed, 11.6% divorced (2000); Foreign born: 2.7% (2000); Ancestry (includes multiple ancestries): 29.5% German, 17.8% Irish, 15.0% English, 11.4% Italian, 8.0% Other groups (2000).
Economy: Employment by occupation: 18.8% management, 17.1% professional, 19.9% services, 27.7% sales, 3.1% farming, 6.5% construction, 6.8% production (2000).
Income: Per capita income: $33,589 (2004); Median household income: $43,584 (2004); Average household income: $60,040 (2004); Percent of households with income of $100,000 or more: 9.2% (2004); Poverty rate: 9.2% (2000).
Education: Percent of population age 25 and over with: High school diploma (including GED) or higher: 90.1% (2004); Bachelor's degree or higher: 17.6% (2004); Master's degree or higher: 7.9% (2004).
Housing: Homeownership rate: 74.1% (2004); Median home value: $166,304 (2004); Median rent: $488 per month (2000); Median age of housing: 29 years (2000).
Transportation: Commute to work: 87.0% car, 0.0% public transportation, 3.8% walk, 7.5% work from home (2000); Travel time to work: 38.9% less than 15 minutes, 30.4% 15 to 30 minutes, 14.4% 30 to 45 minutes, 0.0% 45 to 60 minutes, 16.3% 60 minutes or more (2000)

MATLACHA ISLES-MATLACHA SHORES (CDP). Covers a land area of 0.218 square miles and a water area of 0.186 square miles. Located at 26.63° N. Lat.; 82.06° W. Long.
Population: 193 (1990); 304 (2000); 409 (2004); 532 (2009 projected); Race: 98.5% White, 0.0% Black, 0.2% Asian, 0.7% Hispanic of any race

(2004); Density: 1,872.2 persons per square mile (2004); Average household size: 1.89 (2004); Median age: 58.8 (2004); Male/female ratio: 109.7 (2004); Marriage status: 8.1% never married, 72.7% now married, 4.8% widowed, 14.4% divorced (2000); Foreign born: 7.4% (2000); Ancestry (includes multiple ancestries): 34.7% German, 18.5% United States or American, 12.2% English, 11.8% Irish, 10.7% French (except Basque) (2000).
Economy: Employment by occupation: 22.8% management, 20.5% professional, 13.4% services, 33.9% sales, 0.0% farming, 3.1% construction, 6.3% production (2000).
Income: Per capita income: $27,445 (2004); Median household income: $42,232 (2004); Average household income: $51,968 (2004); Percent of households with income of $100,000 or more: 7.4% (2004); Poverty rate: 4.8% (2000).
Education: Percent of population age 25 and over with: High school diploma (including GED) or higher: 95.1% (2004); Bachelor's degree or higher: 40.7% (2004); Master's degree or higher: 10.2% (2004).
Housing: Homeownership rate: 81.5% (2004); Median home value: $170,000 (2004); Median rent: $481 per month (2000); Median age of housing: 22 years (2000).
Transportation: Commute to work: 88.2% car, 0.0% public transportation, 0.0% walk, 11.8% work from home (2000); Travel time to work: 5.4% less than 15 minutes, 34.8% 15 to 30 minutes, 35.7% 30 to 45 minutes, 17.0% 45 to 60 minutes, 7.1% 60 minutes or more (2000)

MCGREGOR (CDP). Covers a land area of 2.563 square miles and a water area of 1.528 square miles. Located at 26.56° N. Lat.; 81.91° W. Long.
Population: 6,504 (1990); 7,136 (2000); 8,294 (2004); 9,732 (2009 projected); Race: 95.0% White, 1.3% Black, 1.9% Asian, 3.9% Hispanic of any race (2004); Density: 3,235.9 persons per square mile (2004); Average household size: 2.14 (2004); Median age: 52.4 (2004); Male/female ratio: 93.2 (2004); Marriage status: 11.7% never married, 67.2% now married, 10.8% widowed, 10.3% divorced (2000); Foreign born: 7.9% (2000); Ancestry (includes multiple ancestries): 21.6% German, 16.7% English, 14.8% Irish, 9.0% Italian, 8.2% Other groups (2000).
Economy: Employment by occupation: 18.4% management, 29.2% professional, 10.5% services, 32.1% sales, 0.0% farming, 4.7% construction, 5.0% production (2000).
Income: Per capita income: $47,872 (2004); Median household income: $67,731 (2004); Average household income: $102,305 (2004); Percent of households with income of $100,000 or more: 32.4% (2004); Poverty rate: 3.3% (2000).
Education: Percent of population age 25 and over with: High school diploma (including GED) or higher: 93.6% (2004); Bachelor's degree or higher: 49.6% (2004); Master's degree or higher: 19.5% (2004).
Housing: Homeownership rate: 89.6% (2004); Median home value: $195,592 (2004); Median rent: $624 per month (2000); Median age of housing: 22 years (2000).
Transportation: Commute to work: 93.8% car, 0.0% public transportation, 0.2% walk, 5.3% work from home (2000); Travel time to work: 32.8% less than 15 minutes, 47.3% 15 to 30 minutes, 14.8% 30 to 45 minutes, 3.0% 45 to 60 minutes, 2.1% 60 minutes or more (2000)

NORTH FORT MYERS (CDP). Covers a land area of 52.621 square miles and a water area of 1.967 square miles. Located at 26.70° N. Lat.; 81.88° W. Long. Elevation is 7 feet.
Population: 34,213 (1990); 40,214 (2000); 44,149 (2004); 49,310 (2009 projected); Race: 95.1% White, 1.5% Black, 0.6% Asian, 4.2% Hispanic of any race (2004); Density: 839.0 persons per square mile (2004); Average household size: 2.03 (2004); Median age: 59.1 (2004); Male/female ratio: 91.7 (2004); Marriage status: 11.6% never married, 64.4% now married, 13.2% widowed, 10.8% divorced (2000); Foreign born: 4.2% (2000); Ancestry (includes multiple ancestries): 20.0% German, 15.7% English, 14.0% Irish, 10.0% United States or American, 8.1% Other groups (2000).
Economy: Manufacturing includes signs, concrete products, shell products, coil winding. Employment by occupation: 9.4% management, 14.0% professional, 17.2% services, 30.6% sales, 0.4% farming, 16.7% construction, 11.7% production (2000).
Income: Per capita income: $23,253 (2004); Median household income: $36,807 (2004); Average household income: $46,944 (2004); Percent of households with income of $100,000 or more: 7.3% (2004); Poverty rate: 9.9% (2000).
Education: Percent of population age 25 and over with: High school diploma (including GED) or higher: 79.9% (2004); Bachelor's degree or higher: 14.1% (2004); Master's degree or higher: 5.8% (2004).

School District(s)

Lee County School District (PK-12)
2002-03 Enrollment: 63,172 . . . . (239) 337-8301
Housing: Homeownership rate: 86.7% (2004); Median home value: $79,349 (2004); Median rent: $480 per month (2000); Median age of housing: 18 years (2000).
Transportation: Commute to work: 92.2% car, 0.9% public transportation, 1.2% walk, 3.5% work from home (2000); Travel time to work: 23.0% less than 15 minutes, 43.4% 15 to 30 minutes, 19.7% 30 to 45 minutes, 7.2% 45 to 60 minutes, 6.7% 60 minutes or more (2000)

OLGA (CDP). Covers a land area of 4.249 square miles and a water area of 0.153 square miles. Located at 26.71° N. Lat.; 81.70° W. Long. Elevation is 7 feet.
Population: 1,163 (1990); 1,398 (2000); 1,568 (2004); 1,796 (2009 projected); Race: 86.5% White, 3.4% Black, 1.5% Asian, 12.7% Hispanic of any race (2004); Density: 369.0 persons per square mile (2004); Average household size: 2.70 (2004); Median age: 37.4 (2004); Male/female ratio: 96.7 (2004); Marriage status: 17.9% never married, 64.8% now married, 9.2% widowed, 8.1% divorced (2000); Foreign born: 6.2% (2000); Ancestry (includes multiple ancestries): 24.6% Other groups, 14.5% German, 14.1% English, 10.1% United States or American, 7.9% Irish (2000).
Economy: Employment by occupation: 14.8% management, 13.5% professional, 17.1% services, 27.6% sales, 0.8% farming, 19.0% construction, 7.2% production (2000).
Income: Per capita income: $30,182 (2004); Median household income: $64,562 (2004); Average household income: $81,595 (2004); Percent of households with income of $100,000 or more: 16.7% (2004); Poverty rate: 4.0% (2000).
Education: Percent of population age 25 and over with: High school diploma (including GED) or higher: 83.8% (2004); Bachelor's degree or higher: 15.7% (2004); Master's degree or higher: 5.7% (2004).
Housing: Homeownership rate: 83.6% (2004); Median home value: $120,080 (2004); Median rent: $471 per month (2000); Median age of housing: 17 years (2000).
Transportation: Commute to work: 94.4% car, 0.0% public transportation, 0.0% walk, 4.6% work from home (2000); Travel time to work: 13.9% less than 15 minutes, 31.8% 15 to 30 minutes, 27.7% 30 to 45 minutes, 7.2% 45 to 60 minutes, 19.3% 60 minutes or more (2000)

PAGE PARK (CDP). Covers a land area of 0.277 square miles and a water area of 0 square miles. Located at 26.57° N. Lat.; 81.86° W. Long. Elevation is 14 feet.
Population: 610 (1990); 524 (2000); 498 (2004); 492 (2009 projected); Race: 82.7% White, 4.2% Black, 0.2% Asian, 27.5% Hispanic of any race (2004); Density: 1,797.1 persons per square mile (2004); Average household size: 2.18 (2004); Median age: 32.2 (2004); Male/female ratio: 150.3 (2004); Marriage status: 28.5% never married, 42.1% now married, 2.6% widowed, 26.8% divorced (2000); Foreign born: 8.6% (2000); Ancestry (includes multiple ancestries): 21.7% German, 20.7% Other groups, 14.8% United States or American, 12.5% English, 10.7% French (except Basque) (2000).
Economy: Employment by occupation: 3.3% management, 9.5% professional, 22.5% services, 31.4% sales, 0.0% farming, 18.0% construction, 15.4% production (2000).
Income: Per capita income: $13,830 (2004); Median household income: $24,221 (2004); Average household income: $30,208 (2004); Percent of households with income of $100,000 or more: 0.9% (2004); Poverty rate: 13.2% (2000).
Education: Percent of population age 25 and over with: High school diploma (including GED) or higher: 76.9% (2004); Bachelor's degree or higher: 2.4% (2004); Master's degree or higher: 0.0% (2004).
Housing: Homeownership rate: 19.3% (2004); Median home value: $79,357 (2004); Median rent: $393 per month (2000); Median age of housing: 44 years (2000).
Transportation: Commute to work: 84.6% car, 2.1% public transportation, 6.6% walk, 0.0% work from home (2000); Travel time to work: 42.0% less than 15 minutes, 38.7% 15 to 30 minutes, 13.3% 30 to 45 minutes, 2.1% 45 to 60 minutes, 3.9% 60 minutes or more (2000)

PALMONA PARK (CDP). Covers a land area of 0.830 square miles and a water area of 0 square miles. Located at 26.68° N. Lat.; 81.89° W. Long.
Population: 1,392 (1990); 1,353 (2000); 1,324 (2004); 1,303 (2009 projected); Race: 93.6% White, 0.1% Black, 1.1% Asian, 17.2% Hispanic of any race (2004); Density: 1,596.0 persons per square mile (2004); Average household size: 2.43 (2004); Median age: 32.7 (2004); Male/female ratio: 112.2 (2004); Marriage status: 25.5% never married, 57.9% now married, 4.8% widowed, 11.8% divorced (2000); Foreign born: 4.0% (2000); Ancestry (includes multiple ancestries): 24.0% German, 23.0% Other groups, 16.9% Irish, 11.9% United States or American, 11.1% English (2000).
Economy: Employment by occupation: 4.7% management, 1.6% professional, 10.4% services, 34.7% sales, 2.7% farming, 29.8% construction, 16.2% production (2000).
Income: Per capita income: $16,520 (2004); Median household income: $23,963 (2004); Average household income: $40,207 (2004); Percent of households with income of $100,000 or more: 5.0% (2004); Poverty rate: 21.1% (2000).
Education: Percent of population age 25 and over with: High school diploma (including GED) or higher: 65.0% (2004); Bachelor's degree or higher: 3.6% (2004); Master's degree or higher: 1.5% (2004).
Housing: Homeownership rate: 56.1% (2004); Median home value: $63,723 (2004); Median rent: $424 per month (2000); Median age of housing: 27 years (2000).
Transportation: Commute to work: 85.3% car, 4.8% public transportation, 0.0% walk, 3.6% work from home (2000); Travel time to work: 33.9% less than 15 minutes, 48.7% 15 to 30 minutes, 10.6% 30 to 45 minutes, 6.8% 45 to 60 minutes, 0.0% 60 minutes or more (2000)

PINE ISLAND CENTER (CDP). Covers a land area of 4.298 square miles and a water area of 0.007 square miles. Located at 26.63° N. Lat.; 82.12° W. Long. Elevation is 9 feet.
Population: 1,395 (1990); 1,721 (2000); 1,967 (2004); 2,274 (2009 projected); Race: 96.1% White, 0.0% Black, 0.4% Asian, 2.6% Hispanic of any race (2004); Density: 457.6 persons per square mile (2004); Average household size: 2.29 (2004); Median age: 45.3 (2004); Male/female ratio: 103.2 (2004); Marriage status: 11.9% never married, 62.8% now married, 10.4% widowed, 14.9% divorced (2000); Foreign born: 0.9% (2000); Ancestry (includes multiple ancestries): 23.5% German, 17.1% Irish, 14.7% English, 10.4% United States or American, 7.3% French (except Basque) (2000).
Economy: Employment by occupation: 12.0% management, 16.5% professional, 12.5% services, 31.2% sales, 10.0% farming, 11.0% construction, 6.8% production (2000).
Income: Per capita income: $22,677 (2004); Median household income: $42,704 (2004); Average household income: $51,927 (2004); Percent of households with income of $100,000 or more: 11.4% (2004); Poverty rate: 9.6% (2000).
Education: Percent of population age 25 and over with: High school diploma (including GED) or higher: 88.1% (2004); Bachelor's degree or higher: 19.1% (2004); Master's degree or higher: 5.7% (2004).
Housing: Homeownership rate: 79.4% (2004); Median home value: $125,258 (2004); Median rent: $433 per month (2000); Median age of housing: 16 years (2000).
Transportation: Commute to work: 93.0% car, 0.0% public transportation, 0.0% walk, 4.7% work from home (2000); Travel time to work: 16.2% less than 15 minutes, 18.7% 15 to 30 minutes, 36.8% 30 to 45 minutes, 13.5% 45 to 60 minutes, 14.8% 60 minutes or more (2000)

PINE MANOR (CDP). Covers a land area of 0.425 square miles and a water area of 0 square miles. Located at 26.57° N. Lat.; 81.87° W. Long. Elevation is 10 feet.
Population: 3,166 (1990); 3,785 (2000); 4,184 (2004); 4,727 (2009 projected); Race: 56.9% White, 21.8% Black, 0.7% Asian, 55.7% Hispanic of any race (2004); Density: 9,840.0 persons per square mile (2004); Average household size: 3.15 (2004); Median age: 26.1 (2004); Male/female ratio: 121.5 (2004); Marriage status: 32.2% never married, 44.4% now married, 5.5% widowed, 17.8% divorced (2000); Foreign born: 27.9% (2000); Ancestry (includes multiple ancestries): 43.2% Other groups, 13.2% Irish, 8.1% United States or American, 8.0% German, 4.0% English (2000).
Economy: Employment by occupation: 3.9% management, 7.3% professional, 30.8% services, 18.5% sales, 1.2% farming, 25.9% construction, 12.4% production (2000).
Income: Per capita income: $9,952 (2004); Median household income: $26,375 (2004); Average household income: $29,561 (2004); Percent of households with income of $100,000 or more: 0.9% (2004); Poverty rate: 32.6% (2000).
Education: Percent of population age 25 and over with: High school diploma (including GED) or higher: 54.0% (2004); Bachelor's degree or higher: 6.9% (2004); Master's degree or higher: 4.0% (2004).
Housing: Homeownership rate: 16.2% (2004); Median home value: $59,684 (2004); Median rent: $423 per month (2000); Median age of housing: 29 years (2000).
Transportation: Commute to work: 84.2% car, 5.7% public transportation, 3.1% walk, 1.0% work from home (2000); Travel time to work: 23.4% less than 15 minutes, 34.6% 15 to 30 minutes, 25.6% 30 to 45 minutes, 8.9% 45 to 60 minutes, 7.5% 60 minutes or more (2000)

PINELAND (CDP). Covers a land area of 0.922 square miles and a water area of 0 square miles. Located at 26.66° N. Lat.; 82.14° W. Long. Elevation is 20 feet.
Population: 309 (1990); 444 (2000); 566 (2004); 719 (2009 projected); Race: 98.1% White, 0.0% Black, 0.0% Asian, 1.6% Hispanic of any race (2004); Density: 614.1 persons per square mile (2004); Average household size: 2.10 (2004); Median age: 56.5 (2004); Male/female ratio: 91.9 (2004); Marriage status: 10.0% never married, 72.0% now married, 5.3% widowed, 12.7% divorced (2000); Foreign born: 4.9% (2000); Ancestry (includes multiple ancestries): 23.6% English, 14.6% German, 13.9% Irish, 8.6% United States or American, 6.3% Scotch-Irish (2000).
Economy: Employment by occupation: 19.2% management, 52.6% professional, 8.3% services, 13.5% sales, 6.4% farming, 0.0% construction, 0.0% production (2000).
Income: Per capita income: $30,963 (2004); Median household income: $59,155 (2004); Average household income: $64,907 (2004); Percent of households with income of $100,000 or more: 15.6% (2004); Poverty rate: 3.0% (2000).
Education: Percent of population age 25 and over with: High school diploma (including GED) or higher: 95.3% (2004); Bachelor's degree or higher: 34.5% (2004); Master's degree or higher: 16.7% (2004).
Housing: Homeownership rate: 86.3% (2004); Median home value: $225,000 (2004); Median rent: $575 per month (2000); Median age of housing: 16 years (2000).
Transportation: Commute to work: 87.2% car, 0.0% public transportation, 8.3% walk, 4.5% work from home (2000); Travel time to work: 45.6% less than 15 minutes, 0.0% 15 to 30 minutes, 27.5% 30 to 45 minutes, 21.5% 45 to 60 minutes, 5.4% 60 minutes or more (2000)

PUNTA RASSA (CDP). Covers a land area of 2.356 square miles and a water area of 2.139 square miles. Located at 26.51° N. Lat.; 81.99° W. Long. Elevation is 4 feet.
History: Punta Rassa was established on the site of a military post built in 1837, and used again during the Civil War. The townsite of Punta Rassa was surveyed in 1866 by the International Ocean Telegraph Company, which established cable service between the U.S. and Cuba.
Population: 1,493 (1990); 1,731 (2000); 2,086 (2004); 2,528 (2009 projected); Race: 99.1% White, 0.5% Black, 0.2% Asian, 0.2% Hispanic of any race (2004); Density: 885.5 persons per square mile (2004); Average household size: 1.67 (2004); Median age: 79.4 (2004); Male/female ratio: 67.0 (2004); Marriage status: 6.9% never married, 58.0% now married, 31.3% widowed, 3.8% divorced (2000); Foreign born: 3.6% (2000); Ancestry (includes multiple ancestries): 30.0% English, 28.7% German, 8.9% Scottish, 8.5% Irish, 4.6% French (except Basque) (2000).
Economy: Employment by occupation: 12.1% management, 21.1% professional, 3.4% services, 63.4% sales, 0.0% farming, 0.0% construction, 0.0% production (2000).
Income: Per capita income: $48,205 (2004); Median household income: $51,872 (2004); Average household income: $77,210 (2004); Percent of households with income of $100,000 or more: 23.9% (2004); Poverty rate: 1.9% (2000).
Education: Percent of population age 25 and over with: High school diploma (including GED) or higher: 95.8% (2004); Bachelor's degree or higher: 52.1% (2004); Master's degree or higher: 18.8% (2004).
Housing: Homeownership rate: 43.0% (2004); Median home value: $247,260 (2004); Median rent: $1,074 per month (2000); Median age of housing: 21 years (2000).

Transportation: Commute to work: 86.0% car, 0.0% public transportation, 2.7% walk, 5.4% work from home (2000); Travel time to work: 23.9% less than 15 minutes, 42.4% 15 to 30 minutes, 28.4% 30 to 45 minutes, 2.9% 45 to 60 minutes, 2.5% 60 minutes or more (2000)

SAINT JAMES CITY (CDP). Covers a land area of 14.602 square miles and a water area of 0.168 square miles. Located at 26.53° N. Lat.; 82.09° W. Long. Elevation is 5 feet.
History: St. James City was settled in 1887 on Pine Island by a group of New Englanders, and developed as a resort. When the resort deteriorated, it was purchased by a sisal hemp company which began the manufacture of rope.
Population: 3,364 (1990); 4,105 (2000); 4,787 (2004); 5,637 (2009 projected); Race: 98.9% White, 0.1% Black, 0.3% Asian, 0.9% Hispanic of any race (2004); Density: 327.8 persons per square mile (2004); Average household size: 1.89 (2004); Median age: 62.8 (2004); Male/female ratio: 98.2 (2004); Marriage status: 6.3% never married, 72.1% now married, 13.1% widowed, 8.5% divorced (2000); Foreign born: 3.8% (2000); Ancestry (includes multiple ancestries): 23.6% German, 17.9% Irish, 17.4% English, 9.4% United States or American, 6.0% French (except Basque) (2000).
Economy: Employment by occupation: 11.7% management, 17.6% professional, 19.8% services, 30.6% sales, 3.3% farming, 8.7% construction, 8.3% production (2000).
Income: Per capita income: $31,175 (2004); Median household income: $43,564 (2004); Average household income: $58,963 (2004); Percent of households with income of $100,000 or more: 12.2% (2004); Poverty rate: 4.3% (2000).
Education: Percent of population age 25 and over with: High school diploma (including GED) or higher: 83.4% (2004); Bachelor's degree or higher: 17.7% (2004); Master's degree or higher: 7.0% (2004).
Housing: Homeownership rate: 91.9% (2004); Median home value: $133,714 (2004); Median rent: $629 per month (2000); Median age of housing: 19 years (2000).
Transportation: Commute to work: 86.1% car, 0.0% public transportation, 3.5% walk, 6.9% work from home (2000); Travel time to work: 36.4% less than 15 minutes, 15.8% 15 to 30 minutes, 23.2% 30 to 45 minutes, 20.2% 45 to 60 minutes, 4.4% 60 minutes or more (2000)

SAN CARLOS PARK (CDP). Covers a land area of 4.856 square miles and a water area of 0.209 square miles. Located at 26.47° N. Lat.; 81.81° W. Long. Elevation is 16 feet.
Population: 11,272 (1990); 16,317 (2000); 18,328 (2004); 20,869 (2009 projected); Race: 91.9% White, 1.8% Black, 0.8% Asian, 11.6% Hispanic of any race (2004); Density: 3,774.7 persons per square mile (2004); Average household size: 2.79 (2004); Median age: 33.0 (2004); Male/female ratio: 103.1 (2004); Marriage status: 21.5% never married, 60.8% now married, 4.3% widowed, 13.4% divorced (2000); Foreign born: 5.9% (2000); Ancestry (includes multiple ancestries): 25.5% German, 17.5% Irish, 14.2% Other groups, 11.1% Italian, 10.2% English (2000).
Economy: Employment by occupation: 10.3% management, 14.7% professional, 19.3% services, 29.9% sales, 0.2% farming, 15.5% construction, 10.1% production (2000).
Income: Per capita income: $21,631 (2004); Median household income: $53,292 (2004); Average household income: $60,278 (2004); Percent of households with income of $100,000 or more: 11.4% (2004); Poverty rate: 8.0% (2000).
Education: Percent of population age 25 and over with: High school diploma (including GED) or higher: 85.6% (2004); Bachelor's degree or higher: 13.7% (2004); Master's degree or higher: 4.6% (2004).
Housing: Homeownership rate: 79.3% (2004); Median home value: $136,177 (2004); Median rent: $612 per month (2000); Median age of housing: 13 years (2000).
Transportation: Commute to work: 96.8% car, 0.1% public transportation, 0.7% walk, 1.7% work from home (2000); Travel time to work: 16.1% less than 15 minutes, 44.6% 15 to 30 minutes, 26.6% 30 to 45 minutes, 7.8% 45 to 60 minutes, 4.9% 60 minutes or more (2000)

SANIBEL (city). Covers a land area of 17.207 square miles and a water area of 15.958 square miles. Located at 26.44° N. Lat.; 82.08° W. Long. Elevation is 6 feet.
Population: 5,468 (1990); 6,064 (2000); 6,192 (2004); 6,427 (2009 projected); Race: 97.9% White, 1.0% Black, 0.4% Asian, 1.6% Hispanic of any race (2004); Density: 359.9 persons per square mile (2004); Average household size: 1.96 (2004); Median age: 60.3 (2004); Male/female ratio: 90.5 (2004); Marriage status: 8.7% never married, 74.2% now married, 8.7% widowed, 8.5% divorced (2000); Foreign born: 7.4% (2000); Ancestry (includes multiple ancestries): 21.2% German, 21.2% English, 15.2% Irish, 7.9% Italian, 6.8% United States or American (2000).
Economy: Main settlement on Sanibel Island, a leading tourist area of Southwest Florida. Single-family building permits issued: 49 (2004); Multi-family building permits issued: 0 (2004); Employment by occupation: 28.5% management, 16.1% professional, 14.0% services, 29.6% sales, 0.2% farming, 5.2% construction, 6.6% production (2000).
Income: Per capita income: $68,054 (2004); Median household income: $91,608 (2004); Average household income: $133,690 (2004); Percent of households with income of $100,000 or more: 45.4% (2004); Poverty rate: 3.2% (2000).
Education: Percent of population age 25 and over with: High school diploma (including GED) or higher: 96.0% (2004); Bachelor's degree or higher: 54.9% (2004); Master's degree or higher: 22.3% (2004).

School District(s)

Lee County School District (PK-12)
2002-03 Enrollment: 63,172 . . . . (239) 337-8301

Housing: Homeownership rate: 86.6% (2004); Median home value: $496,292 (2004); Median rent: $929 per month (2000); Median age of housing: 21 years (2000).
Safety: Violent crime rate: 3.2 per 10,000 population; Property crime rate: 212.9 per 10,000 population (2003).
Newspapers: Captiva Current (General - Circulation 2,000); Island Reporter (General - Circulation 45,000); Island Sun (General - Circulation 12,000); Sanibel-Captiva Chronicle (General - Circulation 7,000)
Transportation: Commute to work: 78.0% car, 0.4% public transportation, 3.7% walk, 13.0% work from home (2000); Travel time to work: 54.4% less than 15 minutes, 26.2% 15 to 30 minutes, 10.3% 30 to 45 minutes, 5.9% 45 to 60 minutes, 3.3% 60 minutes or more (2000)

Additional Information Contacts

Local Government Offices . . . . (239) 395-2744
Sanibel and Captiva Islands Association of Realtors. . . . . . (239) 472-9353
Sanibel-Captiva Chamber of Commerce . . . . (239) 472-1080

SUNCOAST ESTATES (CDP). Covers a land area of 2.688 square miles and a water area of 0 square miles. Located at 26.71° N. Lat.; 81.86° W. Long.
Population: 4,469 (1990); 4,867 (2000); 5,212 (2004); 5,684 (2009 projected); Race: 94.0% White, 1.0% Black, 0.2% Asian, 7.3% Hispanic of any race (2004); Density: 1,939.3 persons per square mile (2004); Average household size: 2.64 (2004); Median age: 34.1 (2004); Male/female ratio: 109.6 (2004); Marriage status: 21.8% never married, 50.8% now married, 7.6% widowed, 19.8% divorced (2000); Foreign born: 2.7% (2000); Ancestry (includes multiple ancestries): 18.6% German, 17.3% Irish, 16.4% United States or American, 15.5% Other groups, 8.9% English (2000).
Economy: Employment by occupation: 3.3% management, 6.5% professional, 22.4% services, 26.2% sales, 1.0% farming, 27.9% construction, 12.6% production (2000).
Income: Per capita income: $12,258 (2004); Median household income: $28,804 (2004); Average household income: $32,332 (2004); Percent of households with income of $100,000 or more: 2.5% (2004); Poverty rate: 23.4% (2000).
Education: Percent of population age 25 and over with: High school diploma (including GED) or higher: 60.5% (2004); Bachelor's degree or higher: 4.0% (2004); Master's degree or higher: 1.8% (2004).
Housing: Homeownership rate: 62.0% (2004); Median home value: $54,851 (2004); Median rent: $426 per month (2000); Median age of housing: 22 years (2000).
Transportation: Commute to work: 95.1% car, 2.2% public transportation, 1.2% walk, 0.9% work from home (2000); Travel time to work: 19.8% less than 15 minutes, 42.0% 15 to 30 minutes, 19.8% 30 to 45 minutes, 8.4% 45 to 60 minutes, 10.0% 60 minutes or more (2000)

THREE OAKS (CDP). Covers a land area of 1.296 square miles and a water area of 0 square miles. Located at 26.46° N. Lat.; 81.79° W. Long.
Population: 665 (1990); 2,255 (2000); 2,765 (2004); 3,408 (2009 projected); Race: 95.1% White, 0.3% Black, 1.9% Asian, 5.8% Hispanic of any race (2004); Density: 2,132.9 persons per square mile (2004); Average household size: 3.04 (2004); Median age: 34.7 (2004); Male/female ratio: 97.1 (2004); Marriage status: 16.5% never married, 75.1% now married, 2.2% widowed, 6.3% divorced (2000); Foreign born: 3.9% (2000); Ancestry (includes multiple ancestries): 26.9% Irish, 21.8% English, 19.3% German, 14.7% Other groups, 11.1% Italian (2000).

Economy: Employment by occupation: 17.1% management, 22.3% professional, 11.1% services, 32.4% sales, 0.6% farming, 9.1% construction, 7.4% production (2000).
Income: Per capita income: $30,520 (2004); Median household income: $83,936 (2004); Average household income: $90,436 (2004); Percent of households with income of $100,000 or more: 31.9% (2004); Poverty rate: 1.6% (2000).
Education: Percent of population age 25 and over with: High school diploma (including GED) or higher: 95.3% (2004); Bachelor's degree or higher: 34.6% (2004); Master's degree or higher: 12.7% (2004).
Housing: Homeownership rate: 95.5% (2004); Median home value: $196,906 (2004); Median rent: $1,125 per month (2000); Median age of housing: 7 years (2000).
Transportation: Commute to work: 97.0% car, 0.5% public transportation, 0.0% walk, 2.4% work from home (2000); Travel time to work: 25.8% less than 15 minutes, 38.1% 15 to 30 minutes, 31.3% 30 to 45 minutes, 3.3% 45 to 60 minutes, 1.5% 60 minutes or more (2000)

TICE (CDP). Covers a land area of 1.140 square miles and a water area of 0.132 square miles. Located at 26.67° N. Lat.; 81.81° W. Long. Elevation is 15 feet.
Population: 3,971 (1990); 4,538 (2000); 4,640 (2004); 4,797 (2009 projected); Race: 58.3% White, 16.4% Black, 1.1% Asian, 52.4% Hispanic of any race (2004); Density: 4,068.7 persons per square mile (2004); Average household size: 2.98 (2004); Median age: 30.5 (2004); Male/female ratio: 111.6 (2004); Marriage status: 31.8% never married, 46.0% now married, 7.9% widowed, 14.3% divorced (2000); Foreign born: 17.7% (2000); Ancestry (includes multiple ancestries): 47.3% Other groups, 10.2% United States or American, 7.3% English, 5.6% German, 5.6% Irish (2000).
Economy: Employment by occupation: 5.3% management, 8.6% professional, 23.8% services, 18.7% sales, 2.1% farming, 23.9% construction, 17.7% production (2000).
Income: Per capita income: $12,723 (2004); Median household income: $27,364 (2004); Average household income: $37,939 (2004); Percent of households with income of $100,000 or more: 4.4% (2004); Poverty rate: 33.1% (2000).
Education: Percent of population age 25 and over with: High school diploma (including GED) or higher: 53.6% (2004); Bachelor's degree or higher: 5.5% (2004); Master's degree or higher: 1.6% (2004).
Housing: Homeownership rate: 60.0% (2004); Median home value: $83,271 (2004); Median rent: $441 per month (2000); Median age of housing: 34 years (2000).
Transportation: Commute to work: 91.0% car, 0.9% public transportation, 0.5% walk, 2.2% work from home (2000); Travel time to work: 22.6% less than 15 minutes, 39.2% 15 to 30 minutes, 19.1% 30 to 45 minutes, 10.6% 45 to 60 minutes, 8.4% 60 minutes or more (2000)

VILLAS (CDP). Covers a land area of 4.686 square miles and a water area of 0.119 square miles. Located at 26.55° N. Lat.; 81.86° W. Long.
Population: 9,898 (1990); 11,346 (2000); 12,952 (2004); 14,984 (2009 projected); Race: 92.2% White, 2.5% Black, 1.4% Asian, 8.3% Hispanic of any race (2004); Density: 2,763.7 persons per square mile (2004); Average household size: 1.97 (2004); Median age: 45.1 (2004); Male/female ratio: 89.1 (2004); Marriage status: 23.6% never married, 51.4% now married, 12.4% widowed, 12.6% divorced (2000); Foreign born: 9.0% (2000); Ancestry (includes multiple ancestries): 20.4% German, 17.3% English, 15.3% Irish, 11.6% Other groups, 10.1% Italian (2000).
Economy: Employment by occupation: 14.0% management, 18.3% professional, 18.8% services, 31.1% sales, 0.3% farming, 8.8% construction, 8.7% production (2000).
Income: Per capita income: $28,142 (2004); Median household income: $44,305 (2004); Average household income: $54,503 (2004); Percent of households with income of $100,000 or more: 9.0% (2004); Poverty rate: 6.5% (2000).
Education: Percent of population age 25 and over with: High school diploma (including GED) or higher: 87.4% (2004); Bachelor's degree or higher: 28.0% (2004); Master's degree or higher: 8.8% (2004).
Housing: Homeownership rate: 61.0% (2004); Median home value: $123,631 (2004); Median rent: $665 per month (2000); Median age of housing: 20 years (2000).
Transportation: Commute to work: 91.6% car, 0.5% public transportation, 2.4% walk, 3.9% work from home (2000); Travel time to work: 35.9% less than 15 minutes, 43.1% 15 to 30 minutes, 13.2% 30 to 45 minutes, 3.8% 45 to 60 minutes, 4.0% 60 minutes or more (2000)

WHISKEY CREEK (CDP). Covers a land area of 1.601 square miles and a water area of 0 square miles. Located at 26.57° N. Lat.; 81.89° W. Long.
Population: 5,063 (1990); 4,806 (2000); 5,179 (2004); 5,675 (2009 projected); Race: 95.6% White, 1.5% Black, 0.8% Asian, 3.1% Hispanic of any race (2004); Density: 3,235.1 persons per square mile (2004); Average household size: 2.18 (2004); Median age: 50.9 (2004); Male/female ratio: 88.2 (2004); Marriage status: 15.1% never married, 62.5% now married, 12.6% widowed, 9.7% divorced (2000); Foreign born: 5.3% (2000); Ancestry (includes multiple ancestries): 18.8% German, 16.2% Irish, 15.9% English, 10.8% United States or American, 9.9% Other groups (2000).
Economy: Employment by occupation: 16.5% management, 27.1% professional, 14.1% services, 26.0% sales, 0.9% farming, 9.3% construction, 6.1% production (2000).
Income: Per capita income: $32,463 (2004); Median household income: $55,240 (2004); Average household income: $70,850 (2004); Percent of households with income of $100,000 or more: 19.0% (2004); Poverty rate: 2.2% (2000).
Education: Percent of population age 25 and over with: High school diploma (including GED) or higher: 90.8% (2004); Bachelor's degree or higher: 34.1% (2004); Master's degree or higher: 12.2% (2004).
Housing: Homeownership rate: 93.7% (2004); Median home value: $153,333 (2004); Median rent: $542 per month (2000); Median age of housing: 23 years (2000).
Transportation: Commute to work: 94.9% car, 0.0% public transportation, 0.5% walk, 3.6% work from home (2000); Travel time to work: 32.7% less than 15 minutes, 44.4% 15 to 30 minutes, 12.1% 30 to 45 minutes, 3.1% 45 to 60 minutes, 7.6% 60 minutes or more (2000)

Leon County

Located in northwestern Florida; bounded on the north by Georgia, and on the west by the Ochlockonee River and Lake Talquin; includes many lakes and part of Apalachicola National Forest. Covers a land area of 666.70 square miles, a water area of 35.00 square miles, and is located in the Eastern Time Zone. The county government was organized in 1824. County seat is Tallahassee.

Leon County is part of the Tallahassee, FL Metropolitan Statistical Area. The entire metro area includes: Gadsden County, FL; Jefferson County, FL; Leon County, FL; Wakulla County, FL

Weather Station: Tallahassee Municipal Airport — Elevation: 52 feet

	Jan	Feb	Mar	Apr	May	Jun	Jul	Aug	Sep	Oct	Nov	Dec
High	64	67	74	80	86	91	92	91	89	81	73	66
Low	39	41	47	52	61	68	71	71	68	56	47	41
Precip	5.5	4.7	6.7	3.7	5.1	7.0	8.4	7.1	4.8	3.4	3.8	4.1
Snow	tr	tr	tr	0.0	0.0	tr	tr	0.0	tr	0.0	0.0	tr

High and Low temperatures in degrees Fahrenheit; Precipitation and Snow in inches

Population: 192,493 (1990); 239,452 (2000); 251,371 (2004); 266,457 (2009 projected); Race: 65.0% White, 30.6% Black, 1.9% Asian, 3.5% Hispanic of any race (2004); Density: 377.0 persons per square mile (2004); Average household size: 2.47 (2004); Median age: 30.8 (2004); Male/female ratio: 91.3 (2004).
Religion: Five largest groups: 12.5% Southern Baptist Convention, 5.7% Catholic Church, 4.7% The United Methodist Church, 2.2% National Primitive Baptist Convention, USA, 2.0% Episcopal Church (2000).
Economy: Unemployment rate: 3.1% (2004); Total civilian labor force: 141,562 (2004); Leading industries: 17.2% retail trade; 15.8% health care and social assistance; 12.4% accommodation & food services (2003); Companies that employ 500 or more persons: 7 (2003); Companies that employ 100 to 499 persons: 134 (2003); Companies that employ less than 100 persons: 6,706 (2003); Farms: 281 totaling 74,004 acres (2002); Minority business ownership rate: 12.3% (1997); Women business ownership rate: 25.5% (1997); Retail sales per capita: $10,476 (1997). Single-family building permits issued: 1,430 (2004); Multi-family building permits issued: 1,482 (2004).
Income: Per capita income: $23,057 (2004); Median household income: $40,096 (2004); Average household income: $55,766 (2004); Percent of households with income of $100,000 or more: 12.9% (2004); Poverty rate: 12.8% (2002); Bankruptcy rate: 3.71% (2004).
Taxes: Total county taxes per capita: $408 (2002); County property taxes per capita: $273 (2002).

Education: Percent of population age 25 and over with: High school diploma (including GED) or higher: 89.1% (2004); Bachelor's degree or higher: 41.9% (2004); Master's degree or higher: 17.8% (2004).
Housing: Homeownership rate: 57.1% (2004); Median home value: $131,768 (2004); Median rent: $489 per month (2000); Median age of housing: 18 years (2000).
Health: Birth rate: 131.2 per 10,000 population (2004); Death rate: 67.3 per 10,000 population (2004); Age adjusted cancer mortality rate: 209.5 deaths per 100,000 population (2002); Air Quality Index: 63.3% good, 35.1% moderate, 1.6% unhealthy for sensitive individuals, 0.0% unhealthy (percent of days in 2004); Number of physicians: 24.8 per 10,000 population (2001); Hospital beds: 33.4 per 10,000 population (2002); Hospital admissions: 1,450.9 per 10,000 population (2002).
Elections: 2004 Presidential election results: 37.8% Bush, 61.5% Kerry, 0.3% Nader, 0.2% Badnarik
National and State Parks: Alfred B Maclay Gardens State Park; Killearn Gardens State Park; Lake Jackson Mounds Archaeological State Park; Natural Bridge Battlefield Historic State Park
Additional Information Contacts
Leon County Government Offices . . . . (850) 488-4710
Tallahassee Board of Realtors. . . . . (850) 224-7713
Tallahassee Chamber of Commerce . . . . (850) 224-8116

Leon County Communities

TALLAHASSEE (city). Covers a land area of 95.708 square miles and a water area of 2.544 square miles. Located at 30.45° N. Lat.; 84.27° W. Long. Elevation is 188 feet.
History: Tallahassee was selected as the capital of Florida in 1824, before any town existed on the site. Settlers came in rapidly, however, and Tallahassee was incorporated as a city in 1825. The city became the center of an aristocratic society that made its money from cotton. Politics and education shaped the course of life for the residents, who set their calendars by the convening of the state legislature and by the opening of the school term.
Population: 128,014 (1990); 150,624 (2000); 158,930 (2004); 169,401 (2009 projected); Race: 58.7% White, 36.0% Black, 2.3% Asian, 4.2% Hispanic of any race (2004); Density: 1,660.6 persons per square mile (2004); Average household size: 2.37 (2004); Median age: 27.9 (2004); Male/female ratio: 89.8 (2004); Marriage status: 49.2% never married, 37.2% now married, 4.3% widowed, 9.3% divorced (2000); Foreign born: 5.5% (2000); Ancestry (includes multiple ancestries): 34.1% Other groups, 9.4% German, 9.2% English, 8.8% Irish, 5.3% United States or American (2000).
Economy: Unemployment rate: 3.8% (2004); Total civilian labor force: 90,459 (2004); Single-family building permits issued: 852 (2004); Multi-family building permits issued: 1,440 (2004); Employment by occupation: 15.3% management, 30.7% professional, 15.4% services, 28.7% sales, 0.1% farming, 4.6% construction, 5.2% production (2000).
Income: Per capita income: $20,699 (2004); Median household income: $31,998 (2004); Average household income: $47,577 (2004); Percent of households with income of $100,000 or more: 9.7% (2004); Poverty rate: 24.7% (2000).
Taxes: Total city taxes per capita: $390 (2002); City property taxes per capita: $115 (2002).
Education: Percent of population age 25 and over with: High school diploma (including GED) or higher: 89.7% (2004); Bachelor's degree or higher: 44.8% (2004); Master's degree or higher: 19.7% (2004).

School District(s)

Leon County School District (PK-12)
2002-03 Enrollment: 31,857 . . . . (850) 487-7147

Four-year College(s)

Florida Agricultural and Mechanical University (Public, Historically black)
2003-04 Enrollment: 13,013 . . . . (850) 599-3560
2003-04 Tuition: In-state $2,702; Out-of-state $13,058
Florida State University (Public)
2003-04 Enrollment: 36,884 . . . . (850) 644-2525
2003-04 Tuition: In-state $2,714; Out-of-state $13,742
Smith Chapel Bible College
2003-04 Enrollment: n/a . . . . (850) 656-5950

Two-year College(s)

Keiser College-Tallahassee (Private, For-profit)
2003-04 Enrollment: n/a . . . . (850) 906-9494
2003-04 Tuition: In-state $10,920; Out-of-state $10,920
Lively Technical Center (Public)
2003-04 Enrollment: 1,125 . . . . (850) 487-7555
2003-04 Tuition: In-state $2,300; Out-of-state $9,150
Tallahassee Community College (Public)
2003-04 Enrollment: 12,369 . . . . (850) 201-6200
2003-04 Tuition: In-state $1,320; Out-of-state $4,882
Housing: Homeownership rate: 44.0% (2004); Median home value: $129,663 (2004); Median rent: $490 per month (2000); Median age of housing: 21 years (2000).
Hospitals: Capital Regional Medical Center (198 beds); HealthSouth Rehabilitation Hospital of Tallahassee (70 beds); Tallahasse Memorial Health Care Foundation (770 beds)
Safety: Violent crime rate: 89.4 per 10,000 population; Property crime rate: 591.0 per 10,000 population (2003).
Newspapers: Capital Outlook (Black, General, Religious - Circulation 15,000); Tallahassee Democrat (Circulation 51,285)
Transportation: Commute to work: 91.3% car, 2.4% public transportation, 2.6% walk, 2.4% work from home (2000); Travel time to work: 37.6% less than 15 minutes, 45.4% 15 to 30 minutes, 12.3% 30 to 45 minutes, 2.0% 45 to 60 minutes, 2.7% 60 minutes or more (2000); Amtrak: Service available.
Airports: Tallahassee Regional (primary service/small hub)
Additional Information Contacts
Tallahassee Board of Realtors. . . . . (850) 224-7713
Tallahassee Chamber of Commerce . . . . (850) 224-8116

WOODVILLE (CDP). Covers a land area of 6.426 square miles and a water area of 0 square miles. Located at 30.30° N. Lat.; 84.25° W. Long. Elevation is 39 feet.
Population: 2,760 (1990); 3,006 (2000); 3,012 (2004); 3,095 (2009 projected); Race: 78.9% White, 18.8% Black, 0.1% Asian, 2.2% Hispanic of any race (2004); Density: 468.7 persons per square mile (2004); Average household size: 2.50 (2004); Median age: 37.6 (2004); Male/female ratio: 96.6 (2004); Marriage status: 20.8% never married, 62.8% now married, 4.1% widowed, 12.3% divorced (2000); Foreign born: 2.7% (2000); Ancestry (includes multiple ancestries): 31.8% Other groups, 16.5% United States or American, 8.3% Irish, 7.5% French (except Basque), 6.8% English (2000).
Economy: Employment by occupation: 10.0% management, 17.5% professional, 14.7% services, 31.4% sales, 0.0% farming, 12.9% construction, 13.4% production (2000).
Income: Per capita income: $22,429 (2004); Median household income: $42,465 (2004); Average household income: $55,969 (2004); Percent of households with income of $100,000 or more: 13.1% (2004); Poverty rate: 10.7% (2000).
Education: Percent of population age 25 and over with: High school diploma (including GED) or higher: 75.5% (2004); Bachelor's degree or higher: 18.1% (2004); Master's degree or higher: 7.9% (2004).

School District(s)

Leon County School District (PK-12)
2002-03 Enrollment: 31,857 . . . . (850) 487-7147
Housing: Homeownership rate: 83.4% (2004); Median home value: $82,308 (2004); Median rent: $373 per month (2000); Median age of housing: 17 years (2000).
Transportation: Commute to work: 96.2% car, 0.0% public transportation, 0.0% walk, 3.0% work from home (2000); Travel time to work: 13.6% less than 15 minutes, 43.9% 15 to 30 minutes, 28.1% 30 to 45 minutes, 11.3% 45 to 60 minutes, 3.2% 60 minutes or more (2000)

Levy County

Located in northern Florida; bounded partly on the south and west by the Gulf of Mexico, on the northwest by the Suwannee River, and on the south by the Withlacoochee River; flatwoods area, with many small lakes. Covers a land area of 1,118.40 square miles, a water area of 293.90 square miles, and is located in the Eastern Time Zone. The county government was organized in 1845. County seat is Bronson.

Weather Station: Usher Tower — Elevation: 32 feet

	Jan	Feb	Mar	Apr	May	Jun	Jul	Aug	Sep	Oct	Nov	Dec
High	68	71	77	82	88	91	92	91	90	84	76	70
Low	43	46	51	55	62	68	70	71	69	59	51	45
Precip	4.6	3.5	4.8	3.7	3.1	6.7	8.5	10.2	6.4	3.0	2.5	3.3
Snow	0.0	tr	0.0	0.0	0.0	0.0	0.0	0.0	0.0	0.0	0.0	0.0

High and Low temperatures in degrees Fahrenheit; Precipitation and Snow in inches

Population: 25,923 (1990); 34,450 (2000); 37,259 (2004); 40,799 (2009 projected); Race: 85.6% White, 11.2% Black, 0.4% Asian, 4.7% Hispanic of any race (2004); Density: 33.3 persons per square mile (2004); Average household size: 2.47 (2004); Median age: 41.5 (2004); Male/female ratio: 94.0 (2004).
Religion: Five largest groups: 21.0% Southern Baptist Convention, 3.8% The United Methodist Church, 2.0% Catholic Church, 1.9% Church of God (Cleveland, Tennessee), 1.8% Churches of Christ (2000).
Economy: Unemployment rate: 4.3% (2004); Total civilian labor force: 14,888 (2004); Leading industries: 25.1% retail trade; 15.5% accommodation & food services; 11.6% construction (2003); Companies that employ 500 or more persons: 0 (2003); Companies that employ 100 to 499 persons: 5 (2003); Companies that employ less than 100 persons: 663 (2003); Farms: 897 totaling 180,314 acres (2002); Minority business ownership rate: 10.2% (1997); Women business ownership rate: 26.1% (1997); Retail sales per capita: $7,541 (1997). Single-family building permits issued: 225 (2004); Multi-family building permits issued: 0 (2004).
Income: Per capita income: $16,079 (2004); Median household income: $29,772 (2004); Average household income: $39,352 (2004); Percent of households with income of $100,000 or more: 5.2% (2004); Poverty rate: 17.1% (2002); Bankruptcy rate: 3.73% (2004).
Taxes: Total county taxes per capita: $402 (2002); County property taxes per capita: $254 (2002).
Education: Percent of population age 25 and over with: High school diploma (including GED) or higher: 73.8% (2004); Bachelor's degree or higher: 10.5% (2004); Master's degree or higher: 3.7% (2004).
Housing: Homeownership rate: 83.7% (2004); Median home value: $77,504 (2004); Median rent: $307 per month (2000); Median age of housing: 17 years (2000).
Health: Birth rate: 128.0 per 10,000 population (2004); Death rate: 112.5 per 10,000 population (2004); Age adjusted cancer mortality rate: 229.6 deaths per 100,000 population (2002); Number of physicians: 6.5 per 10,000 population (2001); Hospital beds: 11.1 per 10,000 population (2002); Hospital admissions: 381.1 per 10,000 population (2002).
Elections: 2004 Presidential election results: 62.5% Bush, 36.5% Kerry, 0.6% Nader, 0.2% Badnarik
National and State Parks: Cedar Key Museum State Park; Cedar Key Scrub State Reserve; Cedar Key State Memorial; Cedar Keys National Wildlife Refuge; Fanning Springs State Park; Gulf Hammock State Wildlife Management Area; Manatee Springs State Park
Additional Information Contacts
Levy County Government Offices .... (352) 486-5100
Bronson Chamber of Commerce .... (352) 486-1003
Cedar Key Chamber of Commerce .... (352) 543-5600
Chiefland Chamber of Commerce .... (352) 493-1849
Dixie Gilchrist Levy Counties Board of Realtors .... (352) 493-9683
Inglis Chamber of Commerce .... (352) 447-3383
Williston Chamber of Commerce .... (352) 528-5552

Levy County Communities

ANDREWS (CDP). Covers a land area of 6.827 square miles and a water area of 0 square miles. Located at 29.53° N. Lat.; 82.88° W. Long.
Population: 462 (1990); 708 (2000); 807 (2004); 930 (2009 projected); Race: 96.9% White, 1.5% Black, 0.0% Asian, 2.6% Hispanic of any race (2004); Density: 118.2 persons per square mile (2004); Average household size: 2.39 (2004); Median age: 40.6 (2004); Male/female ratio: 98.8 (2004); Marriage status: 10.2% never married, 73.5% now married, 4.0% widowed, 12.4% divorced (2000); Foreign born: 2.1% (2000); Ancestry (includes multiple ancestries): 22.1% Irish, 13.2% English, 12.1% German, 11.3% Other groups, 8.6% United States or American (2000).
Economy: Employment by occupation: 2.1% management, 0.0% professional, 18.5% services, 44.4% sales, 0.0% farming, 15.4% construction, 19.6% production (2000).
Income: Per capita income: $12,748 (2004); Median household income: $28,261 (2004); Average household income: $30,436 (2004); Percent of households with income of $100,000 or more: 0.0% (2004); Poverty rate: 18.2% (2000).
Education: Percent of population age 25 and over with: High school diploma (including GED) or higher: 76.9% (2004); Bachelor's degree or higher: 3.7% (2004); Master's degree or higher: 0.0% (2004).
Housing: Homeownership rate: 83.1% (2004); Median home value: $74,478 (2004); Median rent: $366 per month (2000); Median age of housing: 13 years (2000).
Transportation: Commute to work: 96.3% car, 0.0% public transportation, 0.0% walk, 3.7% work from home (2000); Travel time to work: 31.7% less than 15 minutes, 34.0% 15 to 30 minutes, 15.1% 30 to 45 minutes, 3.9% 45 to 60 minutes, 15.4% 60 minutes or more (2000)

BRONSON (town). Covers a land area of 3.949 square miles and a water area of 0.089 square miles. Located at 29.44° N. Lat.; 82.63° W. Long. Elevation is 61 feet.
History: Bronson was originally called Chunky Pond, and adopted the name of Bronson from an early settler when it was incorporated in 1884.
Population: 875 (1990); 964 (2000); 1,049 (2004); 1,157 (2009 projected); Race: 70.0% White, 25.3% Black, 0.1% Asian, 9.6% Hispanic of any race (2004); Density: 265.7 persons per square mile (2004); Average household size: 2.60 (2004); Median age: 32.7 (2004); Male/female ratio: 82.8 (2004); Marriage status: 30.0% never married, 50.6% now married, 6.7% widowed, 12.7% divorced (2000); Foreign born: 0.0% (2000); Ancestry (includes multiple ancestries): 38.0% Other groups, 11.4% United States or American, 10.0% Irish, 8.3% English, 5.7% German (2000).
Economy: Employment by occupation: 6.4% management, 14.2% professional, 24.5% services, 25.5% sales, 1.0% farming, 10.1% construction, 18.3% production (2000).
Income: Per capita income: $14,495 (2004); Median household income: $29,730 (2004); Average household income: $37,636 (2004); Percent of households with income of $100,000 or more: 3.5% (2004); Poverty rate: 27.2% (2000).
Education: Percent of population age 25 and over with: High school diploma (including GED) or higher: 62.2% (2004); Bachelor's degree or higher: 6.7% (2004); Master's degree or higher: 2.4% (2004).
School District(s)
Levy County School District (PK-12)
2002-03 Enrollment: 6,113 .... (352) 486-5231
Housing: Homeownership rate: 73.8% (2004); Median home value: $62,727 (2004); Median rent: $321 per month (2000); Median age of housing: 19 years (2000).
Newspapers: Levy County Journal (General - Circulation 1,200)
Transportation: Commute to work: 89.6% car, 0.0% public transportation, 4.4% walk, 2.1% work from home (2000); Travel time to work: 31.7% less than 15 minutes, 22.0% 15 to 30 minutes, 32.3% 30 to 45 minutes, 11.4% 45 to 60 minutes, 2.6% 60 minutes or more (2000)
Additional Information Contacts
Bronson Chamber of Commerce .... (352) 486-1003

CEDAR KEY (city). Aka Cedar Keys. Covers a land area of 0.914 square miles and a water area of 1.129 square miles. Located at 29.14° N. Lat.; 83.04° W. Long. Elevation is 7 feet.
History: Cedar Key developed on an island three miles off the west coast of Florida in the Gulf of Mexico. First a fishing village, it later became a port and railroad transfer point to south Florida. The Atlantic, Gulf & West Indies Transit Company railroad was extended to Cedar Key in 1860.
Population: 707 (1990); 790 (2000); 926 (2004); 1,084 (2009 projected); Race: 97.4% White, 0.1% Black, 0.4% Asian, 1.8% Hispanic of any race (2004); Density: 1,013.6 persons per square mile (2004); Average household size: 1.91 (2004); Median age: 55.0 (2004); Male/female ratio: 92.1 (2004); Marriage status: 15.4% never married, 60.5% now married, 8.7% widowed, 15.5% divorced (2000); Foreign born: 4.5% (2000); Ancestry (includes multiple ancestries): 20.3% English, 18.2% German, 16.4% Irish, 12.1% United States or American, 6.2% Other groups (2000).
Economy: Single-family building permits issued: 13 (2004); Multi-family building permits issued: 0 (2004); Employment by occupation: 11.9% management, 20.6% professional, 17.7% services, 27.9% sales, 8.4% farming, 5.8% construction, 7.6% production (2000).
Income: Per capita income: $24,460 (2004); Median household income: $34,375 (2004); Average household income: $46,605 (2004); Percent of households with income of $100,000 or more: 8.6% (2004); Poverty rate: 11.1% (2000).
Taxes: Total city taxes per capita: $451 (2002); City property taxes per capita: $187 (2002).
Education: Percent of population age 25 and over with: High school diploma (including GED) or higher: 87.1% (2004); Bachelor's degree or higher: 34.5% (2004); Master's degree or higher: 15.7% (2004).
School District(s)
Levy County School District (PK-12)
2002-03 Enrollment: 6,113 .... (352) 486-5231

Housing: Homeownership rate: 77.2% (2004); Median home value: $168,581 (2004); Median rent: $394 per month (2000); Median age of housing: 20 years (2000).
Safety: Violent crime rate: 22.0 per 10,000 population; Property crime rate: 176.2 per 10,000 population (2003).
Newspapers: Cedar Key Beacon (General - Circulation 1,800)
Transportation: Commute to work: 70.3% car, 0.0% public transportation, 7.3% walk, 16.6% work from home (2000); Travel time to work: 70.0% less than 15 minutes, 5.9% 15 to 30 minutes, 3.5% 30 to 45 minutes, 7.3% 45 to 60 minutes, 13.2% 60 minutes or more (2000)
Additional Information Contacts
Cedar Key Chamber of Commerce . . . . (352) 543-5600

CHIEFLAND (city). Covers a land area of 3.911 square miles and a water area of 0 square miles. Located at 29.48° N. Lat.; 82.86° W. Long. Elevation is 38 feet.
History: The town of Chiefland began when Florida was a Territory, and became a shipping center for turpentine, rosin, livestock, and peanuts.
Population: 1,924 (1990); 1,993 (2000); 2,096 (2004); 2,232 (2009 projected); Race: 60.0% White, 34.3% Black, 2.5% Asian, 3.6% Hispanic of any race (2004); Density: 535.9 persons per square mile (2004); Average household size: 2.47 (2004); Median age: 34.1 (2004); Male/female ratio: 80.4 (2004); Marriage status: 26.7% never married, 43.7% now married, 15.8% widowed, 13.8% divorced (2000); Foreign born: 2.8% (2000); Ancestry (includes multiple ancestries): 33.2% Other groups, 10.6% United States or American, 6.3% English, 5.7% German, 4.1% Irish (2000).
Economy: Single-family building permits issued: 2 (2004); Multi-family building permits issued: 0 (2004); Employment by occupation: 6.6% management, 15.9% professional, 22.2% services, 30.0% sales, 3.8% farming, 9.1% construction, 12.3% production (2000).
Income: Per capita income: $10,760 (2004); Median household income: $17,421 (2004); Average household income: $25,555 (2004); Percent of households with income of $100,000 or more: 1.5% (2004); Poverty rate: 36.8% (2000).
Education: Percent of population age 25 and over with: High school diploma (including GED) or higher: 64.2% (2004); Bachelor's degree or higher: 9.2% (2004); Master's degree or higher: 1.7% (2004).
School District(s)
Levy County School District (PK-12)
2002-03 Enrollment: 6,113 . . . . (352) 486-5231
Housing: Homeownership rate: 53.8% (2004); Median home value: $71,193 (2004); Median rent: $240 per month (2000); Median age of housing: 23 years (2000).
Safety: Violent crime rate: 164.2 per 10,000 population; Property crime rate: 1,231.3 per 10,000 population (2003).
Newspapers: Chiefland Citizen (General - Circulation 3,650); Tri-County Bulletin (General - Circulation 22,000)
Transportation: Commute to work: 92.0% car, 0.0% public transportation, 4.3% walk, 1.3% work from home (2000); Travel time to work: 50.0% less than 15 minutes, 22.8% 15 to 30 minutes, 11.1% 30 to 45 minutes, 8.3% 45 to 60 minutes, 7.8% 60 minutes or more (2000)
Additional Information Contacts
Chiefland Chamber of Commerce . . . . (352) 493-1849
Dixie Gilchrist Levy Counties Board of Realtors . . . . (352) 493-9683

EAST BRONSON (CDP). Covers a land area of 11.462 square miles and a water area of 0 square miles. Located at 29.45° N. Lat.; 82.59° W. Long.
Population: 620 (1990); 1,075 (2000); 1,245 (2004); 1,451 (2009 projected); Race: 84.6% White, 6.7% Black, 0.3% Asian, 13.4% Hispanic of any race (2004); Density: 108.6 persons per square mile (2004); Average household size: 2.71 (2004); Median age: 35.6 (2004); Male/female ratio: 92.4 (2004); Marriage status: 17.9% never married, 67.7% now married, 5.8% widowed, 8.6% divorced (2000); Foreign born: 2.2% (2000); Ancestry (includes multiple ancestries): 18.5% Irish, 13.3% English, 13.2% Other groups, 11.0% German, 9.6% United States or American (2000).
Economy: Employment by occupation: 7.8% management, 17.4% professional, 22.3% services, 13.3% sales, 0.0% farming, 22.6% construction, 16.5% production (2000).
Income: Per capita income: $13,916 (2004); Median household income: $30,060 (2004); Average household income: $37,745 (2004); Percent of households with income of $100,000 or more: 4.8% (2004); Poverty rate: 15.2% (2000).
Education: Percent of population age 25 and over with: High school diploma (including GED) or higher: 60.2% (2004); Bachelor's degree or higher: 6.3% (2004); Master's degree or higher: 1.4% (2004).
Housing: Homeownership rate: 89.3% (2004); Median home value: $57,920 (2004); Median rent: $358 per month (2000); Median age of housing: 13 years (2000).
Transportation: Commute to work: 97.3% car, 0.0% public transportation, 0.0% walk, 2.7% work from home (2000); Travel time to work: 1.6% less than 15 minutes, 18.4% 15 to 30 minutes, 40.5% 30 to 45 minutes, 29.9% 45 to 60 minutes, 9.7% 60 minutes or more (2000)

EAST WILLISTON (CDP). Covers a land area of 3.110 square miles and a water area of 0 square miles. Located at 29.38° N. Lat.; 82.41° W. Long.
Population: 790 (1990); 966 (2000); 1,002 (2004); 1,056 (2009 projected); Race: 9.2% White, 87.9% Black, 0.0% Asian, 2.4% Hispanic of any race (2004); Density: 322.2 persons per square mile (2004); Average household size: 2.79 (2004); Median age: 30.6 (2004); Male/female ratio: 75.8 (2004); Marriage status: 41.7% never married, 35.2% now married, 9.3% widowed, 13.9% divorced (2000); Foreign born: 1.6% (2000); Ancestry (includes multiple ancestries): 68.8% Other groups, 5.4% Irish, 2.4% English, 1.7% German, 1.6% United States or American (2000).
Economy: Employment by occupation: 10.2% management, 13.8% professional, 36.2% services, 15.3% sales, 2.8% farming, 4.0% construction, 17.8% production (2000).
Income: Per capita income: $14,456 (2004); Median household income: $26,438 (2004); Average household income: $40,348 (2004); Percent of households with income of $100,000 or more: 10.3% (2004); Poverty rate: 28.7% (2000).
Education: Percent of population age 25 and over with: High school diploma (including GED) or higher: 72.7% (2004); Bachelor's degree or higher: 10.5% (2004); Master's degree or higher: 3.2% (2004).
Housing: Homeownership rate: 70.8% (2004); Median home value: $74,419 (2004); Median rent: $272 per month (2000); Median age of housing: 21 years (2000).
Transportation: Commute to work: 94.4% car, 0.0% public transportation, 1.4% walk, 2.5% work from home (2000); Travel time to work: 37.7% less than 15 minutes, 22.3% 15 to 30 minutes, 29.9% 30 to 45 minutes, 4.3% 45 to 60 minutes, 5.8% 60 minutes or more (2000)

FANNING SPRINGS (city). Aka Suwannee River. Covers a land area of 3.557 square miles and a water area of 0.138 square miles. Located at 29.58° N. Lat.; 82.92° W. Long. Elevation is 32 feet.
Population: 496 (1990); 737 (2000); 823 (2004); 929 (2009 projected); Race: 86.8% White, 6.6% Black, 0.5% Asian, 10.3% Hispanic of any race (2004); Density: 231.4 persons per square mile (2004); Average household size: 2.36 (2004); Median age: 37.4 (2004); Male/female ratio: 99.8 (2004); Marriage status: 16.8% never married, 56.6% now married, 9.4% widowed, 17.1% divorced (2000); Foreign born: 6.3% (2000); Ancestry (includes multiple ancestries): 14.4% Irish, 14.2% Other groups, 9.4% United States or American, 8.7% German, 8.2% English (2000).
Economy: Employment by occupation: 10.6% management, 10.6% professional, 24.5% services, 24.5% sales, 7.4% farming, 16.7% construction, 5.6% production (2000).
Income: Per capita income: $11,458 (2004); Median household income: $19,717 (2004); Average household income: $27,098 (2004); Percent of households with income of $100,000 or more: 0.9% (2004); Poverty rate: 30.5% (2000).
Education: Percent of population age 25 and over with: High school diploma (including GED) or higher: 66.0% (2004); Bachelor's degree or higher: 13.7% (2004); Master's degree or higher: 5.9% (2004).
Housing: Homeownership rate: 64.4% (2004); Median home value: $58,491 (2004); Median rent: $273 per month (2000); Median age of housing: 17 years (2000).
Transportation: Commute to work: 90.3% car, 0.0% public transportation, 3.2% walk, 2.8% work from home (2000); Travel time to work: 51.0% less than 15 minutes, 27.1% 15 to 30 minutes, 13.8% 30 to 45 minutes, 3.3% 45 to 60 minutes, 4.8% 60 minutes or more (2000)

INGLIS (town). Covers a land area of 3.653 square miles and a water area of 0.017 square miles. Located at 29.03° N. Lat.; 82.66° W. Long. Elevation is 15 feet.
Population: 1,241 (1990); 1,491 (2000); 1,478 (2004); 1,495 (2009 projected); Race: 99.0% White, 0.0% Black, 0.3% Asian, 2.4% Hispanic of any race (2004); Density: 404.6 persons per square mile (2004); Average

household size: 2.19 (2004); Median age: 47.1 (2004); Male/female ratio: 98.1 (2004); Marriage status: 16.1% never married, 57.5% now married, 8.8% widowed, 17.6% divorced (2000); Foreign born: 1.7% (2000); Ancestry (includes multiple ancestries): 17.2% German, 17.0% English, 14.4% United States or American, 13.3% Irish, 8.2% Other groups (2000).
Economy: Manufacturing: machine parts. Employment by occupation: 12.0% management, 13.8% professional, 13.4% services, 21.5% sales, 3.5% farming, 17.5% construction, 18.3% production (2000).
Income: Per capita income: $15,844 (2004); Median household income: $25,909 (2004); Average household income: $34,641 (2004); Percent of households with income of $100,000 or more: 4.1% (2004); Poverty rate: 22.3% (2000).
Taxes: Total city taxes per capita: $89 (2002); City property taxes per capita: $0 (2002).
Education: Percent of population age 25 and over with: High school diploma (including GED) or higher: 73.1% (2004); Bachelor's degree or higher: 9.8% (2004); Master's degree or higher: 2.3% (2004).

School District(s)

Levy County School District (PK-12)
2002-03 Enrollment: 6,113 . . . . (352) 486-5231

Housing: Homeownership rate: 78.4% (2004); Median home value: $69,667 (2004); Median rent: $232 per month (2000); Median age of housing: 18 years (2000).
Safety: Violent crime rate: 57.6 per 10,000 population; Property crime rate: 294.3 per 10,000 population (2003).
Transportation: Commute to work: 87.8% car, 0.4% public transportation, 4.2% walk, 5.4% work from home (2000); Travel time to work: 32.6% less than 15 minutes, 28.2% 15 to 30 minutes, 22.9% 30 to 45 minutes, 7.8% 45 to 60 minutes, 8.4% 60 minutes or more (2000)
Additional Information Contacts
Inglis Chamber of Commerce . . . . (352) 447-3383

MANATTEE ROAD (CDP). Covers a land area of 14.305 square miles and a water area of 0 square miles. Located at 29.50° N. Lat.; 82.92° W. Long.
Population: 1,618 (1990); 1,937 (2000); 1,908 (2004); 1,899 (2009 projected); Race: 96.2% White, 2.2% Black, 0.0% Asian, 1.8% Hispanic of any race (2004); Density: 133.4 persons per square mile (2004); Average household size: 2.26 (2004); Median age: 50.2 (2004); Male/female ratio: 94.1 (2004); Marriage status: 17.9% never married, 60.1% now married, 10.9% widowed, 11.1% divorced (2000); Foreign born: 0.5% (2000); Ancestry (includes multiple ancestries): 15.8% German, 14.7% Other groups, 12.4% English, 12.2% United States or American, 10.5% Irish (2000).
Economy: Employment by occupation: 1.2% management, 9.5% professional, 15.2% services, 32.8% sales, 1.6% farming, 23.9% construction, 15.8% production (2000).
Income: Per capita income: $16,226 (2004); Median household income: $24,543 (2004); Average household income: $36,639 (2004); Percent of households with income of $100,000 or more: 4.0% (2004); Poverty rate: 21.1% (2000).
Education: Percent of population age 25 and over with: High school diploma (including GED) or higher: 71.4% (2004); Bachelor's degree or higher: 8.6% (2004); Master's degree or higher: 2.0% (2004).
Housing: Homeownership rate: 91.2% (2004); Median home value: $67,500 (2004); Median rent: $263 per month (2000); Median age of housing: 16 years (2000).
Transportation: Commute to work: 88.9% car, 2.8% public transportation, 1.6% walk, 6.7% work from home (2000); Travel time to work: 30.7% less than 15 minutes, 27.1% 15 to 30 minutes, 15.2% 30 to 45 minutes, 8.6% 45 to 60 minutes, 18.5% 60 minutes or more (2000)

MORRISTON (unincorporated postal area, zip code 32668). Covers a land area of 151.141 square miles and a water area of 0.521 square miles. Located at 29.28° N. Lat.; 82.51° W. Long. Elevation is 63 feet.
Population: 3,881 (2000); Race: 93.7% White, 2.1% Black, 0.4% Asian, 2.9% Hispanic of any race (2000); Density: 25.7 persons per square mile (2000); Age: 21.3% under 18, 17.1% over 64 (2000); Marriage status: 18.6% never married, 61.8% now married, 10.1% widowed, 9.6% divorced (2000); Foreign born: 2.8% (2000); Ancestry (includes multiple ancestries): 17.6% German, 15.8% United States or American, 14.4% Irish, 13.2% Other groups, 12.0% English (2000).
Economy: Employment by occupation: 11.7% management, 7.3% professional, 19.1% services, 24.1% sales, 3.8% farming, 19.7% construction, 14.3% production (2000).
Income: Per capita income: $15,088 (2000); Median household income: $27,476 (2000); Poverty rate: 16.5% (2000).
Education: Percent of population age 25 and over with: High school diploma (including GED) or higher: 76.9% (2000); Bachelor's degree or higher: 7.9% (2000).
Housing: Homeownership rate: 91.8% (2000); Median home value: $107,500 (2000); Median rent: $313 per month (2000); Median age of housing: 13 years (2000).
Transportation: Commute to work: 92.3% car, 0.0% public transportation, 0.5% walk, 5.7% work from home (2000); Travel time to work: 6.7% less than 15 minutes, 32.4% 15 to 30 minutes, 27.5% 30 to 45 minutes, 17.1% 45 to 60 minutes, 16.2% 60 minutes or more (2000)

OTTER CREEK (town). Covers a land area of 1.428 square miles and a water area of 0.021 square miles. Located at 29.32° N. Lat.; 82.77° W. Long. Elevation is 29 feet.
History: Otter were hunted in the vicinity of Otter Creek through the 1800's, but the economy of the town developed around lumber. The manufacturing of hardwood slats for fruit crates was an early industry.
Population: 136 (1990); 121 (2000); 134 (2004); 148 (2009 projected); Race: 93.3% White, 2.2% Black, 0.0% Asian, 5.2% Hispanic of any race (2004); Density: 93.8 persons per square mile (2004); Average household size: 2.20 (2004); Median age: 48.8 (2004); Male/female ratio: 109.4 (2004); Marriage status: 16.7% never married, 59.8% now married, 7.8% widowed, 15.7% divorced (2000); Foreign born: 0.0% (2000); Ancestry (includes multiple ancestries): 22.0% English, 10.1% United States or American, 9.2% German, 8.3% Other groups, 7.3% Irish (2000).
Economy: Single-family building permits issued: 0 (2004); Multi-family building permits issued: 0 (2004); Employment by occupation: 0.0% management, 0.0% professional, 15.9% services, 31.8% sales, 11.4% farming, 13.6% construction, 27.3% production (2000).
Income: Per capita income: $10,784 (2004); Median household income: $18,421 (2004); Average household income: $23,689 (2004); Percent of households with income of $100,000 or more: 0.0% (2004); Poverty rate: 20.2% (2000).
Taxes: Total city taxes per capita: $91 (2002); City property taxes per capita: $58 (2002).
Education: Percent of population age 25 and over with: High school diploma (including GED) or higher: 56.3% (2004); Bachelor's degree or higher: 1.9% (2004); Master's degree or higher: 1.9% (2004).
Housing: Homeownership rate: 83.6% (2004); Median home value: $47,000 (2004); Median rent: $n/a per month (2000); Median age of housing: 30 years (2000).
Transportation: Commute to work: 97.7% car, 0.0% public transportation, 2.3% walk, 0.0% work from home (2000); Travel time to work: 11.4% less than 15 minutes, 29.5% 15 to 30 minutes, 18.2% 30 to 45 minutes, 18.2% 45 to 60 minutes, 22.7% 60 minutes or more (2000)

WILLISTON (city). Covers a land area of 6.061 square miles and a water area of 0.019 square miles. Located at 29.38° N. Lat.; 82.44° W. Long. Elevation is 76 feet.
History: Williston developed around limestone deposits from which rock is quarried.
Population: 2,279 (1990); 2,297 (2000); 2,315 (2004); 2,365 (2009 projected); Race: 70.2% White, 26.1% Black, 0.7% Asian, 4.1% Hispanic of any race (2004); Density: 382.0 persons per square mile (2004); Average household size: 2.73 (2004); Median age: 38.7 (2004); Male/female ratio: 86.8 (2004); Marriage status: 23.0% never married, 54.4% now married, 11.6% widowed, 11.0% divorced (2000); Foreign born: 3.2% (2000); Ancestry (includes multiple ancestries): 27.5% Other groups, 18.1% United States or American, 9.7% Irish, 7.9% German, 7.7% English (2000).
Economy: Single-family building permits issued: 15 (2004); Multi-family building permits issued: 0 (2004); Employment by occupation: 10.1% management, 12.7% professional, 21.6% services, 29.0% sales, 3.0% farming, 10.9% construction, 12.7% production (2000).
Income: Per capita income: $13,702 (2004); Median household income: $28,367 (2004); Average household income: $36,972 (2004); Percent of households with income of $100,000 or more: 4.3% (2004); Poverty rate: 22.6% (2000).
Taxes: Total city taxes per capita: $143 (2002); City property taxes per capita: $77 (2002).
Education: Percent of population age 25 and over with: High school diploma (including GED) or higher: 68.6% (2004); Bachelor's degree or higher: 10.2% (2004); Master's degree or higher: 3.5% (2004).

School District(s)
Levy County School District (PK-12)
2002-03 Enrollment: 6,113 . . . . (352) 486-5231
Housing: Homeownership rate: 68.5% (2004); Median home value: $75,957 (2004); Median rent: $318 per month (2000); Median age of housing: 28 years (2000).
Hospitals: Nature Coast Regional Hospital (40 beds)
Safety: Violent crime rate: 140.9 per 10,000 population; Property crime rate: 716.9 per 10,000 population (2003).
Transportation: Commute to work: 92.8% car, 0.0% public transportation, 5.7% walk, 0.7% work from home (2000); Travel time to work: 45.0% less than 15 minutes, 17.4% 15 to 30 minutes, 26.8% 30 to 45 minutes, 7.1% 45 to 60 minutes, 3.7% 60 minutes or more (2000)
Additional Information Contacts
Williston Chamber of Commerce . . . . (352) 528-5552

WILLISTON HIGHLANDS (CDP). Covers a land area of 11.241 square miles and a water area of 0 square miles. Located at 29.33° N. Lat.; 82.53° W. Long.
Population: 853 (1990); 1,386 (2000); 1,637 (2004); 1,946 (2009 projected); Race: 92.3% White, 5.1% Black, 0.2% Asian, 4.6% Hispanic of any race (2004); Density: 145.6 persons per square mile (2004); Average household size: 2.32 (2004); Median age: 46.2 (2004); Male/female ratio: 97.9 (2004); Marriage status: 17.4% never married, 64.9% now married, 5.4% widowed, 12.3% divorced (2000); Foreign born: 1.8% (2000); Ancestry (includes multiple ancestries): 19.4% United States or American, 15.7% German, 12.2% Other groups, 9.7% Irish, 5.9% English (2000).
Economy: Employment by occupation: 7.1% management, 12.1% professional, 21.5% services, 27.6% sales, 0.0% farming, 20.2% construction, 11.5% production (2000).
Income: Per capita income: $15,020 (2004); Median household income: $26,655 (2004); Average household income: $34,876 (2004); Percent of households with income of $100,000 or more: 4.5% (2004); Poverty rate: 21.1% (2000).
Education: Percent of population age 25 and over with: High school diploma (including GED) or higher: 77.4% (2004); Bachelor's degree or higher: 8.9% (2004); Master's degree or higher: 1.9% (2004).
Housing: Homeownership rate: 89.8% (2004); Median home value: $76,045 (2004); Median rent: $375 per month (2000); Median age of housing: 14 years (2000).
Transportation: Commute to work: 96.1% car, 0.0% public transportation, 0.0% walk, 2.1% work from home (2000); Travel time to work: 7.2% less than 15 minutes, 24.1% 15 to 30 minutes, 31.6% 30 to 45 minutes, 31.4% 45 to 60 minutes, 5.6% 60 minutes or more (2000)

YANKEETOWN (town). Covers a land area of 7.824 square miles and a water area of 12.481 square miles. Located at 29.03° N. Lat.; 82.72° W. Long. Elevation is 5 feet.
History: Yankeetown was founded by Judge A.F. Knotts as a sportsmen's resort.
Population: 635 (1990); 629 (2000); 673 (2004); 725 (2009 projected); Race: 96.3% White, 0.0% Black, 1.0% Asian, 0.4% Hispanic of any race (2004); Density: 86.0 persons per square mile (2004); Average household size: 2.01 (2004); Median age: 55.6 (2004); Male/female ratio: 104.6 (2004); Marriage status: 9.3% never married, 65.4% now married, 7.8% widowed, 17.5% divorced (2000); Foreign born: 4.5% (2000); Ancestry (includes multiple ancestries): 20.7% German, 19.9% English, 12.2% Other groups, 10.7% Irish, 6.0% Scotch-Irish (2000).
Economy: Employment by occupation: 13.1% management, 25.3% professional, 20.5% services, 11.8% sales, 5.2% farming, 12.7% construction, 11.4% production (2000).
Income: Per capita income: $26,248 (2004); Median household income: $39,180 (2004); Average household income: $52,889 (2004); Percent of households with income of $100,000 or more: 10.5% (2004); Poverty rate: 12.5% (2000).
Education: Percent of population age 25 and over with: High school diploma (including GED) or higher: 83.9% (2004); Bachelor's degree or higher: 26.2% (2004); Master's degree or higher: 14.4% (2004).
School District(s)
Levy County School District (PK-12)
2002-03 Enrollment: 6,113 . . . . (352) 486-5231
Housing: Homeownership rate: 82.9% (2004); Median home value: $134,322 (2004); Median rent: $365 per month (2000); Median age of housing: 29 years (2000).
Transportation: Commute to work: 86.0% car, 0.0% public transportation, 3.1% walk, 9.6% work from home (2000); Travel time to work: 24.2% less than 15 minutes, 37.2% 15 to 30 minutes, 22.2% 30 to 45 minutes, 4.8% 45 to 60 minutes, 11.6% 60 minutes or more (2000)

Liberty County

Located in northwestern Florida; bounded on the east by the Ochlockonee River, and on the west by the Apalachicola River; partly in Apalachicola National Forest. Covers a land area of 835.90 square miles, a water area of 7.30 square miles, and is located in the Eastern Time Zone. The county government was organized in 1855. County seat is Bristol.
Population: 5,569 (1990); 7,021 (2000); 7,013 (2004); 7,008 (2009 projected); Race: 79.4% White, 14.8% Black, 0.2% Asian, 5.9% Hispanic of any race (2004); Density: 8.4 persons per square mile (2004); Average household size: 3.22 (2004); Median age: 35.4 (2004); Male/female ratio: 148.0 (2004).
Religion: Five largest groups: 23.0% Southern Baptist Convention, 11.3% The Church of Jesus Christ of Latter-day Saints, 3.4% Assemblies of God, 3.3% Church of God (Cleveland, Tennessee), 2.2% The United Methodist Church (2000).
Economy: Unemployment rate: 2.5% (2004); Total civilian labor force: 3,332 (2004); Leading industries: 12.7% manufacturing; 9.8% forestry, fishing, hunting, and agriculture support; 9.3% health care and social assistance (2003); Companies that employ 500 or more persons: 0 (2003); Companies that employ 100 to 499 persons: 3 (2003); Companies that employ less than 100 persons: 77 (2003); Farms: 67 totaling 9,900 acres (2002); Minority business ownership rate: n/a (1997); Women business ownership rate: n/a (1997); Retail sales per capita: $1,766 (1997). Single-family building permits issued: 18 (2004); Multi-family building permits issued: 0 (2004).
Income: Per capita income: $18,469 (2004); Median household income: $31,948 (2004); Average household income: $45,911 (2004); Percent of households with income of $100,000 or more: 7.4% (2004); Poverty rate: 20.3% (2002); Bankruptcy rate: 4.47% (2004).
Taxes: Total county taxes per capita: $226 (2002); County property taxes per capita: $190 (2002).
Education: Percent of population age 25 and over with: High school diploma (including GED) or higher: 65.4% (2004); Bachelor's degree or higher: 7.1% (2004); Master's degree or higher: 3.2% (2004).
Housing: Homeownership rate: 81.9% (2004); Median home value: $73,177 (2004); Median rent: $265 per month (2000); Median age of housing: 22 years (2000).
Health: Birth rate: 108.0 per 10,000 population (2004); Death rate: 68.9 per 10,000 population (2004); Age adjusted cancer mortality rate: 259.3 (Unreliable rate as per CDC) deaths per 100,000 population (2002); Number of physicians: 1.4 per 10,000 population (2001); Hospital beds: 0.0 per 10,000 population (2002); Hospital admissions: 0.0 per 10,000 population (2002).
Elections: 2004 Presidential election results: 63.8% Bush, 35.4% Kerry, 0.5% Nader, 0.1% Badnarik
National and State Parks: Torreya State Park
Additional Information Contacts
Liberty County Government Offices . . . . (850) 643-5404
Bristol Chamber of Commerce . . . . (850) 643-2359

Liberty County Communities

BRISTOL (city). Covers a land area of 1.634 square miles and a water area of 0 square miles. Located at 30.42° N. Lat.; 84.97° W. Long. Elevation is 168 feet.
History: Bristol was founded about 1850, when it was called Riddeysville. The name was changed in 1858.
Population: 778 (1990); 845 (2000); 826 (2004); 799 (2009 projected); Race: 87.0% White, 2.5% Black, 0.0% Asian, 7.7% Hispanic of any race (2004); Density: 505.5 persons per square mile (2004); Average household size: 2.58 (2004); Median age: 39.3 (2004); Male/female ratio: 88.2 (2004); Marriage status: 18.8% never married, 54.4% now married, 14.4% widowed, 12.5% divorced (2000); Foreign born: 4.5% (2000); Ancestry (includes multiple ancestries): 39.7% United States or American, 15.2% Other groups, 8.8% Irish, 6.5% English, 5.0% German (2000).
Economy: Single-family building permits issued: 1 (2004); Multi-family building permits issued: 0 (2004); Employment by occupation: 7.9% management, 16.5% professional, 18.6% services, 19.2% sales, 7.9% farming, 14.8% construction, 15.1% production (2000).

Income: Per capita income: $18,325 (2004); Median household income: $33,293 (2004); Average household income: $46,039 (2004); Percent of households with income of $100,000 or more: 7.2% (2004); Poverty rate: 19.8% (2000).
Taxes: Total city taxes per capita: $71 (2002); City property taxes per capita: $38 (2002).
Education: Percent of population age 25 and over with: High school diploma (including GED) or higher: 74.6% (2004); Bachelor's degree or higher: 20.9% (2004); Master's degree or higher: 11.4% (2004).

School District(s)

Liberty County School District (PK-12)
2002-03 Enrollment: 1,383 . . . . (850) 643-2275
Housing: Homeownership rate: 72.8% (2004); Median home value: $76,786 (2004); Median rent: $233 per month (2000); Median age of housing: 29 years (2000).
Newspapers: The Calhoun-Liberty Journal (General - Circulation 5,000)
Transportation: Commute to work: 93.5% car, 0.0% public transportation, 2.7% walk, 3.1% work from home (2000); Travel time to work: 37.6% less than 15 minutes, 24.1% 15 to 30 minutes, 14.2% 30 to 45 minutes, 7.4% 45 to 60 minutes, 16.7% 60 minutes or more (2000)

Additional Information Contacts

Bristol Chamber of Commerce. . . . . (850) 643-2359

HOSFORD (unincorporated postal area, zip code 32334). Covers a land area of 147.569 square miles and a water area of 0.025 square miles. Located at 30.38° N. Lat.; 84.77° W. Long. Elevation is 95 feet.
Population: 1,548 (2000); Race: 98.3% White, 0.0% Black, 0.0% Asian, 0.0% Hispanic of any race (2000); Density: 10.5 persons per square mile (2000); Age: 25.8% under 18, 10.0% over 64 (2000); Marriage status: 20.8% never married, 52.6% now married, 9.6% widowed, 17.0% divorced (2000); Foreign born: 0.0% (2000); Ancestry (includes multiple ancestries): 29.6% United States or American, 22.7% Other groups, 9.3% Irish, 8.1% German, 6.2% English (2000).
Economy: Employment by occupation: 10.1% management, 7.2% professional, 17.1% services, 28.4% sales, 2.2% farming, 23.4% construction, 11.6% production (2000).
Income: Per capita income: $20,140 (2000); Median household income: $33,831 (2000); Poverty rate: 16.1% (2000).
Education: Percent of population age 25 and over with: High school diploma (including GED) or higher: 60.3% (2000); Bachelor's degree or higher: 4.8% (2000).

School District(s)

Liberty County School District (PK-12)
2002-03 Enrollment: 1,383 . . . . (850) 643-2275
Housing: Homeownership rate: 82.0% (2000); Median home value: $76,500 (2000); Median rent: $268 per month (2000); Median age of housing: 20 years (2000).
Transportation: Commute to work: 95.3% car, 0.0% public transportation, 0.6% walk, 3.3% work from home (2000); Travel time to work: 22.3% less than 15 minutes, 21.9% 15 to 30 minutes, 17.2% 30 to 45 minutes, 17.9% 45 to 60 minutes, 20.6% 60 minutes or more (2000)

Madison County

Located in northern Florida; bounded on the north by Georgia, on the west by the Aucilla River, on the northeast by the Withlacoochee River, and on the southeast by the Suwannee River; includes many lakes. Covers a land area of 691.80 square miles, a water area of 24.00 square miles, and is located in the Eastern Time Zone. The county government was organized in 1827. County seat is Madison.
Population: 16,563 (1990); 18,733 (2000); 18,470 (2004); 18,160 (2009 projected); Race: 57.2% White, 40.6% Black, 0.4% Asian, 3.7% Hispanic of any race (2004); Density: 26.7 persons per square mile (2004); Average household size: 2.81 (2004); Median age: 37.2 (2004); Male/female ratio: 106.2 (2004).
Religion: Five largest groups: 29.4% Southern Baptist Convention, 7.9% The United Methodist Church, 1.6% National Primitive Baptist Convention, USA, 1.0% Church of God (Cleveland, Tennessee), 0.8% Catholic Church (2000).
Economy: Unemployment rate: 5.6% (2004); Total civilian labor force: 6,701 (2004); Leading industries: 23.5% manufacturing; 22.6% health care and social assistance; 20.1% retail trade (2003); Companies that employ 500 or more persons: 1 (2003); Companies that employ 100 to 499 persons: 5 (2003); Companies that employ less than 100 persons: 312 (2003); Farms: 529 totaling 156,995 acres (2002); Minority business ownership rate: n/a (1997); Women business ownership rate: 12.2% (1997); Retail sales per capita: $3,653 (1997). Single-family building permits issued: 66 (2004); Multi-family building permits issued: 0 (2004).
Income: Per capita income: $13,664 (2004); Median household income: $28,047 (2004); Average household income: $37,800 (2004); Percent of households with income of $100,000 or more: 4.4% (2004); Poverty rate: 19.8% (2002); Bankruptcy rate: 4.72% (2004).
Taxes: Total county taxes per capita: $495 (2002); County property taxes per capita: $180 (2002).
Education: Percent of population age 25 and over with: High school diploma (including GED) or higher: 68.4% (2004); Bachelor's degree or higher: 9.9% (2004); Master's degree or higher: 3.5% (2004).
Housing: Homeownership rate: 78.7% (2004); Median home value: $71,064 (2004); Median rent: $237 per month (2000); Median age of housing: 23 years (2000).
Health: Birth rate: 137.7 per 10,000 population (2004); Death rate: 107.4 per 10,000 population (2004); Age adjusted cancer mortality rate: 247.7 deaths per 100,000 population (2002); Number of physicians: 6.9 per 10,000 population (2001); Hospital beds: 16.4 per 10,000 population (2002); Hospital admissions: 554.4 per 10,000 population (2002).
Elections: 2004 Presidential election results: 50.5% Bush, 48.8% Kerry, 0.5% Nader, 0.1% Badnarik

Additional Information Contacts

Madison County Government Offices . . . . (850) 973-3179
Madison Chamber of Commerce . . . . (850) 973-2788

Madison County Communities

GREENVILLE (town). Covers a land area of 1.314 square miles and a water area of 0 square miles. Located at 30.46° N. Lat.; 83.63° W. Long. Elevation is 98 feet.
History: Greenville was founded about 1850. It was first known as Sandy Ford, and later as Station Five for its location as the fifth railroad station east of Tallahassee. The town was later named for Greenville, South Carolina, the former home of many residents.
Population: 950 (1990); 837 (2000); 757 (2004); 709 (2009 projected); Race: 24.6% White, 75.0% Black, 0.1% Asian, 0.3% Hispanic of any race (2004); Density: 576.0 persons per square mile (2004); Average household size: 2.50 (2004); Median age: 36.5 (2004); Male/female ratio: 81.5 (2004); Marriage status: 35.1% never married, 43.1% now married, 12.6% widowed, 9.2% divorced (2000); Foreign born: 0.4% (2000); Ancestry (includes multiple ancestries): 60.6% Other groups, 8.1% United States or American, 7.4% Irish, 4.3% English, 2.8% German (2000).
Economy: Employment by occupation: 9.7% management, 10.8% professional, 22.6% services, 25.1% sales, 0.0% farming, 6.1% construction, 25.8% production (2000).
Income: Per capita income: $11,219 (2004); Median household income: $21,746 (2004); Average household income: $28,028 (2004); Percent of households with income of $100,000 or more: 1.7% (2004); Poverty rate: 32.9% (2000).
Education: Percent of population age 25 and over with: High school diploma (including GED) or higher: 53.0% (2004); Bachelor's degree or higher: 8.7% (2004); Master's degree or higher: 3.4% (2004).

School District(s)

Madison County School District (PK-12)
2002-03 Enrollment: 3,311 . . . . (850) 973-5022
Housing: Homeownership rate: 73.9% (2004); Median home value: $48,116 (2004); Median rent: $167 per month (2000); Median age of housing: 32 years (2000).
Transportation: Commute to work: 91.0% car, 0.0% public transportation, 6.5% walk, 0.7% work from home (2000); Travel time to work: 31.0% less than 15 minutes, 31.8% 15 to 30 minutes, 19.1% 30 to 45 minutes, 7.9% 45 to 60 minutes, 10.1% 60 minutes or more (2000)

LEE (town). Covers a land area of 1.223 square miles and a water area of 0.003 square miles. Located at 30.41° N. Lat.; 83.30° W. Long. Elevation is 94 feet.
Population: 330 (1990); 352 (2000); 339 (2004); 333 (2009 projected); Race: 95.9% White, 2.9% Black, 0.3% Asian, 2.9% Hispanic of any race (2004); Density: 277.1 persons per square mile (2004); Average household size: 2.67 (2004); Median age: 36.6 (2004); Male/female ratio: 92.6 (2004); Marriage status: 22.4% never married, 57.6% now married, 6.0% widowed, 14.0% divorced (2000); Foreign born: 0.0% (2000); Ancestry (includes multiple ancestries): 29.1% Other groups, 18.0% United States or American, 10.6% Irish, 9.7% German, 8.9% Scotch-Irish (2000).

Economy: Single-family building permits issued: 2 (2004); Multi-family building permits issued: 0 (2004); Employment by occupation: 5.9% management, 27.1% professional, 9.3% services, 22.0% sales, 7.6% farming, 1.7% construction, 26.3% production (2000).
Income: Per capita income: $16,268 (2004); Median household income: $29,722 (2004); Average household income: $43,425 (2004); Percent of households with income of $100,000 or more: 7.9% (2004); Poverty rate: 26.5% (2000).
Taxes: Total city taxes per capita: $153 (2002); City property taxes per capita: $68 (2002).
Education: Percent of population age 25 and over with: High school diploma (including GED) or higher: 72.9% (2004); Bachelor's degree or higher: 10.5% (2004); Master's degree or higher: 8.1% (2004).

School District(s)

Madison County School District (PK-12)
2002-03 Enrollment: 3,311 . . . . (850) 973-5022

Housing: Homeownership rate: 76.4% (2004); Median home value: $54,000 (2004); Median rent: $242 per month (2000); Median age of housing: 25 years (2000).
Transportation: Commute to work: 88.5% car, 0.0% public transportation, 3.5% walk, 4.4% work from home (2000); Travel time to work: 26.9% less than 15 minutes, 50.9% 15 to 30 minutes, 8.3% 30 to 45 minutes, 8.3% 45 to 60 minutes, 5.6% 60 minutes or more (2000)

MADISON (city). Covers a land area of 2.530 square miles and a water area of 0.047 square miles. Located at 30.46° N. Lat.; 83.41° W. Long. Elevation is 191 feet.
History: Madison was settled in 1838 by planters from South Carolina who grew sea-island cotton here.
Population: 3,428 (1990); 3,061 (2000); 2,908 (2004); 2,801 (2009 projected); Race: 35.2% White, 63.0% Black, 0.6% Asian, 2.5% Hispanic of any race (2004); Density: 1,149.2 persons per square mile (2004); Average household size: 2.47 (2004); Median age: 32.4 (2004); Male/female ratio: 82.0 (2004); Marriage status: 28.8% never married, 45.1% now married, 13.7% widowed, 12.4% divorced (2000); Foreign born: 1.0% (2000); Ancestry (includes multiple ancestries): 45.9% Other groups, 9.4% English, 6.0% United States or American, 4.0% Scotch-Irish, 1.6% German (2000).
Economy: Single-family building permits issued: 11 (2004); Multi-family building permits issued: 0 (2004); Employment by occupation: 7.7% management, 18.1% professional, 26.8% services, 21.6% sales, 0.8% farming, 5.4% construction, 19.6% production (2000).
Income: Per capita income: $10,750 (2004); Median household income: $16,090 (2004); Average household income: $24,792 (2004); Percent of households with income of $100,000 or more: 0.7% (2004); Poverty rate: 39.9% (2000).
Education: Percent of population age 25 and over with: High school diploma (including GED) or higher: 62.8% (2004); Bachelor's degree or higher: 17.9% (2004); Master's degree or higher: 7.3% (2004).

School District(s)

Madison County School District (PK-12)
2002-03 Enrollment: 3,311 . . . . (850) 973-5022

Two-year College(s)

North Florida Community College (Public)
2003-04 Enrollment: 1,120 . . . . (904) 973-2288
2003-04 Tuition: In-state $1,671; Out-of-state $6,141

Housing: Homeownership rate: 55.5% (2004); Median home value: $72,562 (2004); Median rent: $218 per month (2000); Median age of housing: 33 years (2000).
Hospitals: Madison County Memorial Hospital (42 beds)
Safety: Violent crime rate: 113.2 per 10,000 population; Property crime rate: 940.3 per 10,000 population (2003).
Newspapers: Enterprise-Recorder (General - Circulation 4,000)
Transportation: Commute to work: 91.0% car, 0.0% public transportation, 7.5% walk, 0.0% work from home (2000); Travel time to work: 59.0% less than 15 minutes, 24.0% 15 to 30 minutes, 6.4% 30 to 45 minutes, 6.3% 45 to 60 minutes, 4.3% 60 minutes or more (2000); Amtrak: Service available.
Additional Information Contacts
Madison Chamber of Commerce . . . . (850) 973-2788

PINETTA (unincorporated postal area, zip code 32350). Covers a land area of 36.601 square miles and a water area of 0.410 square miles. Located at 30.59° N. Lat.; 83.32° W. Long. Elevation is 148 feet.
Population: 1,173 (2000); Race: 82.8% White, 14.6% Black, 0.0% Asian, 0.0% Hispanic of any race (2000); Density: 32.0 persons per square mile (2000); Age: 29.1% under 18, 11.5% over 64 (2000); Marriage status: 24.9% never married, 51.2% now married, 8.1% widowed, 15.7% divorced (2000); Foreign born: 1.4% (2000); Ancestry (includes multiple ancestries): 17.0% English, 16.1% Other groups, 11.8% United States or American, 10.8% Irish, 5.5% German (2000).
Economy: Employment by occupation: 4.5% management, 10.8% professional, 27.0% services, 16.2% sales, 2.4% farming, 16.2% construction, 22.9% production (2000).
Income: Per capita income: $16,006 (2000); Median household income: $29,750 (2000); Poverty rate: 12.1% (2000).
Education: Percent of population age 25 and over with: High school diploma (including GED) or higher: 72.6% (2000); Bachelor's degree or higher: 6.0% (2000).

School District(s)

Madison County School District (PK-12)
2002-03 Enrollment: 3,311 . . . . (850) 973-5022

Housing: Homeownership rate: 83.0% (2000); Median home value: $35,000 (2000); Median rent: $199 per month (2000); Median age of housing: 17 years (2000).
Transportation: Commute to work: 96.0% car, 0.0% public transportation, 2.8% walk, 1.2% work from home (2000); Travel time to work: 6.7% less than 15 minutes, 43.2% 15 to 30 minutes, 31.2% 30 to 45 minutes, 4.5% 45 to 60 minutes, 14.5% 60 minutes or more (2000)

Manatee County

Located in western Florida, on the Gulf of Mexico; bounded on the west by Tampa Bay; drained by the Manatee and Myakka Rivers; includes several lakes, part of Sarasota Bay, Anna Maria Key, and other small islands. Covers a land area of 741.00 square miles, a water area of 151.70 square miles, and is located in the Eastern Time Zone. The county government was organized in 1855. County seat is Bradenton.

Manatee County is part of the Sarasota-Bradenton-Venice, FL Metropolitan Statistical Area. The entire metro area includes: Manatee County, FL; Sarasota County, FL

Weather Station: Bradenton 5 ESE — Elevation: 19 feet

	Jan	Feb	Mar	Apr	May	Jun	Jul	Aug	Sep	Oct	Nov	Dec
High	73	74	78	82	87	90	92	91	90	85	80	74
Low	50	51	56	59	65	71	72	73	72	65	58	52
Precip	3.0	2.7	3.5	1.8	3.0	7.4	8.5	9.4	7.2	3.0	2.3	2.4
Snow	0.0	0.0	0.0	0.0	0.0	0.0	0.0	0.0	0.0	0.0	0.0	0.0

High and Low temperatures in degrees Fahrenheit; Precipitation and Snow in inches

Weather Station: Parrish — Elevation: 59 feet

	Jan	Feb	Mar	Apr	May	Jun	Jul	Aug	Sep	Oct	Nov	Dec
High	73	74	78	83	88	90	91	91	90	85	80	75
Low	50	51	55	59	64	70	72	72	71	65	58	52
Precip	2.9	3.2	3.2	2.0	3.2	7.2	7.5	8.7	7.4	2.9	2.3	2.3
Snow	tr	0.0	0.0	0.0	0.0	0.0	0.0	0.0	0.0	0.0	0.0	0.0

High and Low temperatures in degrees Fahrenheit; Precipitation and Snow in inches

Population: 211,707 (1990); 264,002 (2000); 290,864 (2004); 324,669 (2009 projected); Race: 84.6% White, 9.0% Black, 1.2% Asian, 10.9% Hispanic of any race (2004); Density: 392.5 persons per square mile (2004); Average household size: 2.35 (2004); Median age: 43.4 (2004); Male/female ratio: 94.5 (2004).
Religion: Five largest groups: 13.3% Catholic Church, 8.0% Southern Baptist Convention, 3.1% The United Methodist Church, 1.5% Jewish Estimate, 1.2% Presbyterian Church (U.S.A.) (2000).
Economy: Unemployment rate: 3.6% (2004); Total civilian labor force: 144,348 (2004); Leading industries: 18.5% administration, support, waste management, remediation services; 16.2% retail trade; 12.7% health care and social assistance (2003); Companies that employ 500 or more persons: 10 (2003); Companies that employ 100 to 499 persons: 117 (2003); Companies that employ less than 100 persons: 6,268 (2003); Farms: 852 totaling 301,231 acres (2002); Minority business ownership rate: 9.3% (1997); Women business ownership rate: 24.0% (1997); Retail sales per capita: $9,110 (1997). Single-family building permits issued: 4,668 (2004); Multi-family building permits issued: 1,922 (2004).
Income: Per capita income: $25,356 (2004); Median household income: $43,414 (2004); Average household income: $58,591 (2004); Percent of households with income of $100,000 or more: 12.7% (2004); Poverty rate: 10.7% (2002); Bankruptcy rate: 4.39% (2004).
Taxes: Total county taxes per capita: $456 (2002); County property taxes per capita: $382 (2002).

Education: Percent of population age 25 and over with: High school diploma (including GED) or higher: 81.9% (2004); Bachelor's degree or higher: 21.3% (2004); Master's degree or higher: 7.4% (2004).
Housing: Homeownership rate: 74.3% (2004); Median home value: $137,207 (2004); Median rent: $539 per month (2000); Median age of housing: 21 years (2000).
Health: Birth rate: 121.6 per 10,000 population (2004); Death rate: 114.0 per 10,000 population (2004); Age adjusted cancer mortality rate: 174.8 deaths per 100,000 population (2002); Air Quality Index: 85.8% good, 13.4% moderate, 0.8% unhealthy for sensitive individuals, 0.0% unhealthy (percent of days in 2004); Number of physicians: 21.7 per 10,000 population (2001); Hospital beds: 28.1 per 10,000 population (2002); Hospital admissions: 1,184.4 per 10,000 population (2002).
Elections: 2004 Presidential election results: 56.6% Bush, 42.7% Kerry, 0.5% Nader, 0.1% Badnarik
National and State Parks: De Soto National Memorial; Lake Manatee State Park; Madira Bickel Mound State Archaeological Site; Passage Key National Wildlife Refuge
Additional Information Contacts
Manatee County Government Offices . . . . (941) 745-3700
Bradenton Beach Chamber of Commerce. . . . . (941) 778-1541
Bradenton Chamber of Commerce . . . . (941) 748-3411
Manatee Association of Realtors . . . . (941) 747-1818
Palmetto Convention & Visitors Bureau. . . . . (941) 729-9177

Manatee County Communities

ANNA MARIA (city). Covers a land area of 0.776 square miles and a water area of 0.210 square miles. Located at 27.53° N. Lat.; 82.73° W. Long. Elevation is 3 feet.
History: Anna Maria developed as a resort at the northern end of Anna Maria Key.
Population: 1,754 (1990); 1,814 (2000); 1,823 (2004); 1,852 (2009 projected); Race: 97.9% White, 0.4% Black, 0.3% Asian, 2.2% Hispanic of any race (2004); Density: 2,349.9 persons per square mile (2004); Average household size: 2.00 (2004); Median age: 55.4 (2004); Male/female ratio: 90.1 (2004); Marriage status: 15.3% never married, 63.2% now married, 12.1% widowed, 9.4% divorced (2000); Foreign born: 5.0% (2000); Ancestry (includes multiple ancestries): 22.0% German, 20.9% English, 17.2% Irish, 10.3% United States or American, 6.4% French (except Basque) (2000).
Economy: Single-family building permits issued: 12 (2004); Multi-family building permits issued: 0 (2004); Employment by occupation: 12.7% management, 23.1% professional, 20.3% services, 29.9% sales, 1.4% farming, 6.3% construction, 6.3% production (2000).
Income: Per capita income: $32,796 (2004); Median household income: $43,704 (2004); Average household income: $65,556 (2004); Percent of households with income of $100,000 or more: 15.5% (2004); Poverty rate: 10.5% (2000).
Education: Percent of population age 25 and over with: High school diploma (including GED) or higher: 93.4% (2004); Bachelor's degree or higher: 39.7% (2004); Master's degree or higher: 15.7% (2004).
Housing: Homeownership rate: 78.7% (2004); Median home value: $346,032 (2004); Median rent: $743 per month (2000); Median age of housing: 30 years (2000).
Transportation: Commute to work: 82.6% car, 0.0% public transportation, 2.7% walk, 9.1% work from home (2000); Travel time to work: 34.3% less than 15 minutes, 27.5% 15 to 30 minutes, 19.5% 30 to 45 minutes, 8.0% 45 to 60 minutes, 10.7% 60 minutes or more (2000)

BAYSHORE GARDENS (CDP). Covers a land area of 3.559 square miles and a water area of 0.024 square miles. Located at 27.43° N. Lat.; 82.57° W. Long. Elevation is 20 feet.
Population: 17,191 (1990); 17,350 (2000); 17,911 (2004); 18,738 (2009 projected); Race: 86.7% White, 5.7% Black, 1.5% Asian, 10.8% Hispanic of any race (2004); Density: 5,032.4 persons per square mile (2004); Average household size: 2.08 (2004); Median age: 44.0 (2004); Male/female ratio: 89.0 (2004); Marriage status: 19.7% never married, 52.3% now married, 14.1% widowed, 13.9% divorced (2000); Foreign born: 7.9% (2000); Ancestry (includes multiple ancestries): 18.6% German, 16.3% English, 14.8% Other groups, 12.8% Irish, 11.3% United States or American (2000).
Economy: Employment by occupation: 7.7% management, 13.6% professional, 16.9% services, 30.5% sales, 0.3% farming, 13.5% construction, 17.5% production (2000).
Income: Per capita income: $19,416 (2004); Median household income: $32,386 (2004); Average household income: $40,267 (2004); Percent of households with income of $100,000 or more: 4.5% (2004); Poverty rate: 10.1% (2000).
Education: Percent of population age 25 and over with: High school diploma (including GED) or higher: 78.9% (2004); Bachelor's degree or higher: 12.8% (2004); Master's degree or higher: 3.8% (2004).
Housing: Homeownership rate: 67.9% (2004); Median home value: $95,971 (2004); Median rent: $498 per month (2000); Median age of housing: 27 years (2000).
Transportation: Commute to work: 94.3% car, 0.7% public transportation, 3.0% walk, 0.9% work from home (2000); Travel time to work: 29.7% less than 15 minutes, 45.4% 15 to 30 minutes, 17.7% 30 to 45 minutes, 2.9% 45 to 60 minutes, 4.4% 60 minutes or more (2000)

BRADENTON (city). Covers a land area of 12.108 square miles and a water area of 2.335 square miles. Located at 27.48° N. Lat.; 82.57° W. Long. Elevation is 25 feet.
History: Dr. Joseph Braden built a house here in 1854, and when the post office was established in 1878, the town was named for him. At first the name was spelled Braidentown, later changed to Bradentown, and in 1924 to Bradenton.
Population: 43,699 (1990); 49,504 (2000); 52,762 (2004); 57,157 (2009 projected); Race: 75.7% White, 16.4% Black, 1.0% Asian, 13.3% Hispanic of any race (2004); Density: 4,357.6 persons per square mile (2004); Average household size: 2.32 (2004); Median age: 41.1 (2004); Male/female ratio: 91.7 (2004); Marriage status: 22.4% never married, 52.7% now married, 12.3% widowed, 12.6% divorced (2000); Foreign born: 8.5% (2000); Ancestry (includes multiple ancestries): 24.8% Other groups, 14.9% German, 12.0% English, 10.9% Irish, 6.7% United States or American (2000).
Economy: Unemployment rate: 4.2% (2004); Total civilian labor force: 29,940 (2004); Single-family building permits issued: 68 (2004); Multi-family building permits issued: 594 (2004); Employment by occupation: 10.0% management, 18.0% professional, 19.5% services, 26.3% sales, 1.8% farming, 10.6% construction, 13.7% production (2000).
Income: Per capita income: $22,321 (2004); Median household income: $38,684 (2004); Average household income: $49,605 (2004); Percent of households with income of $100,000 or more: 8.0% (2004); Poverty rate: 13.6% (2000).
Taxes: Total city taxes per capita: $417 (2002); City property taxes per capita: $157 (2002).
Education: Percent of population age 25 and over with: High school diploma (including GED) or higher: 80.3% (2004); Bachelor's degree or higher: 20.7% (2004); Master's degree or higher: 7.4% (2004).
School District(s)
Manatee County School District (PK-12)
2002-03 Enrollment: 39,132 . . . . (941) 708-8770
Two-year College(s)
Bradenton Beauty and Barber Academy (Private, For-profit)
2003-04 Enrollment: 90 . . . . (941) 761-4400
Manatee Community College (Public)
2003-04 Enrollment: 9,172 . . . . (941) 752-5000
2003-04 Tuition: In-state $1,741; Out-of-state $6,507
Manatee Technical Institute (Public)
2003-04 Enrollment: 2,224 . . . . (941) 751-7900
2003-04 Tuition: In-state $2,320; Out-of-state $9,000
Housing: Homeownership rate: 61.2% (2004); Median home value: $125,249 (2004); Median rent: $562 per month (2000); Median age of housing: 23 years (2000).
Hospitals: Blake Medical Center (383 beds); Manatee Glens Hospital (47 beds); Manatee Memorial Hospital (502 beds)
Safety: Violent crime rate: 87.0 per 10,000 population; Property crime rate: 634.8 per 10,000 population (2003).
Newspapers: Bradenton Herald (Circulation 51,113)
Transportation: Commute to work: 93.1% car, 1.0% public transportation, 1.4% walk, 2.3% work from home (2000); Travel time to work: 30.5% less than 15 minutes, 41.7% 15 to 30 minutes, 17.3% 30 to 45 minutes, 5.4% 45 to 60 minutes, 5.0% 60 minutes or more (2000); Amtrak: Service available.
Airports: Sarasota/Bradenton International (primary service/small hub)
Additional Information Contacts
Bradenton Chamber of Commerce . . . . (941) 748-3411
Manatee Association of Realtors . . . . (941) 747-1818

BRADENTON BEACH (city). Covers a land area of 0.548 square miles and a water area of 0.549 square miles. Located at 27.47° N. Lat.; 82.70° W. Long. Elevation is 5 feet.
Population: 1,657 (1990); 1,482 (2000); 1,458 (2004); 1,460 (2009 projected); Race: 98.5% White, 0.3% Black, 0.1% Asian, 1.8% Hispanic of any race (2004); Density: 2,661.1 persons per square mile (2004); Average household size: 1.80 (2004); Median age: 50.2 (2004); Male/female ratio: 103.1 (2004); Marriage status: 21.8% never married, 47.1% now married, 10.5% widowed, 20.7% divorced (2000); Foreign born: 3.4% (2000); Ancestry (includes multiple ancestries): 28.0% German, 17.5% English, 16.4% Irish, 7.5% Other groups, 6.4% United States or American (2000).
Economy: Manufacturing includes industrial prototypes. Single-family building permits issued: 2 (2004); Multi-family building permits issued: 42 (2004); Employment by occupation: 15.4% management, 18.0% professional, 25.4% services, 23.7% sales, 0.0% farming, 12.2% construction, 5.3% production (2000).
Income: Per capita income: $24,731 (2004); Median household income: $35,057 (2004); Average household income: $44,570 (2004); Percent of households with income of $100,000 or more: 6.7% (2004); Poverty rate: 7.3% (2000).
Taxes: Total city taxes per capita: $1,054 (2002); City property taxes per capita: $401 (2002).
Education: Percent of population age 25 and over with: High school diploma (including GED) or higher: 85.2% (2004); Bachelor's degree or higher: 24.5% (2004); Master's degree or higher: 11.3% (2004).
Housing: Homeownership rate: 57.1% (2004); Median home value: $158,197 (2004); Median rent: $618 per month (2000); Median age of housing: 34 years (2000).
Safety: Violent crime rate: 32.7 per 10,000 population; Property crime rate: 550.1 per 10,000 population (2003).
Transportation: Commute to work: 89.9% car, 0.0% public transportation, 2.4% walk, 3.3% work from home (2000); Travel time to work: 29.1% less than 15 minutes, 35.5% 15 to 30 minutes, 21.3% 30 to 45 minutes, 5.6% 45 to 60 minutes, 8.5% 60 minutes or more (2000)
Additional Information Contacts
Bradenton Beach Chamber of Commerce. . . . . (941) 778-1541

CORTEZ (CDP). Covers a land area of 2.193 square miles and a water area of 2.942 square miles. Located at 27.46° N. Lat.; 82.67° W. Long. Elevation is 4 feet.
History: Cortez developed as a fishing village.
Population: 4,509 (1990); 4,491 (2000); 4,781 (2004); 5,169 (2009 projected); Race: 98.0% White, 0.2% Black, 0.7% Asian, 1.5% Hispanic of any race (2004); Density: 2,179.9 persons per square mile (2004); Average household size: 1.87 (2004); Median age: 61.6 (2004); Male/female ratio: 91.6 (2004); Marriage status: 8.2% never married, 67.8% now married, 13.9% widowed, 10.1% divorced (2000); Foreign born: 6.5% (2000); Ancestry (includes multiple ancestries): 22.8% German, 16.8% English, 14.8% Irish, 9.4% United States or American, 7.1% Other groups (2000).
Economy: Employment by occupation: 9.8% management, 16.5% professional, 11.7% services, 38.5% sales, 1.9% farming, 11.8% construction, 9.9% production (2000).
Income: Per capita income: $28,842 (2004); Median household income: $39,880 (2004); Average household income: $53,912 (2004); Percent of households with income of $100,000 or more: 11.7% (2004); Poverty rate: 9.4% (2000).
Education: Percent of population age 25 and over with: High school diploma (including GED) or higher: 84.9% (2004); Bachelor's degree or higher: 22.1% (2004); Master's degree or higher: 8.3% (2004).
Housing: Homeownership rate: 85.1% (2004); Median home value: $143,887 (2004); Median rent: $529 per month (2000); Median age of housing: 25 years (2000).
Transportation: Commute to work: 90.6% car, 0.5% public transportation, 0.6% walk, 5.9% work from home (2000); Travel time to work: 26.1% less than 15 minutes, 46.1% 15 to 30 minutes, 17.5% 30 to 45 minutes, 2.8% 45 to 60 minutes, 7.5% 60 minutes or more (2000)

ELLENTON (CDP). Covers a land area of 3.668 square miles and a water area of 1.140 square miles. Located at 27.52° N. Lat.; 82.52° W. Long. Elevation is 9 feet.
History: It was in the Gamble plantation house in Ellenton that Judah Philip Benjamin, Secretary of State of the Confederacy, took refuge at the end of the Civil War. Federal gunboats came to Tampa Bay searching for Benjamin, but he disguised himself and sailed for England under the noses of the Federal officers.
Population: 2,597 (1990); 3,142 (2000); 3,680 (2004); 4,341 (2009 projected); Race: 88.5% White, 5.4% Black, 0.5% Asian, 11.0% Hispanic of any race (2004); Density: 1,003.4 persons per square mile (2004); Average household size: 2.26 (2004); Median age: 45.6 (2004); Male/female ratio: 90.1 (2004); Marriage status: 11.8% never married, 65.4% now married, 11.1% widowed, 11.7% divorced (2000); Foreign born: 6.2% (2000); Ancestry (includes multiple ancestries): 19.1% German, 14.3% Irish, 13.2% Other groups, 11.5% English, 11.0% United States or American (2000).
Economy: Employment by occupation: 7.3% management, 25.2% professional, 12.2% services, 25.3% sales, 2.1% farming, 15.0% construction, 12.9% production (2000).
Income: Per capita income: $19,587 (2004); Median household income: $33,774 (2004); Average household income: $43,552 (2004); Percent of households with income of $100,000 or more: 4.8% (2004); Poverty rate: 8.7% (2000).
Education: Percent of population age 25 and over with: High school diploma (including GED) or higher: 83.4% (2004); Bachelor's degree or higher: 11.7% (2004); Master's degree or higher: 2.6% (2004).
Housing: Homeownership rate: 75.2% (2004); Median home value: $114,459 (2004); Median rent: $508 per month (2000); Median age of housing: 21 years (2000).
Transportation: Commute to work: 89.3% car, 0.0% public transportation, 2.2% walk, 5.5% work from home (2000); Travel time to work: 37.6% less than 15 minutes, 32.8% 15 to 30 minutes, 16.8% 30 to 45 minutes, 7.5% 45 to 60 minutes, 5.3% 60 minutes or more (2000)

HOLMES BEACH (city). Covers a land area of 1.621 square miles and a water area of 0.110 square miles. Located at 27.51° N. Lat.; 82.71° W. Long. Elevation is 6 feet.
Population: 4,800 (1990); 4,966 (2000); 5,026 (2004); 5,148 (2009 projected); Race: 98.3% White, 0.2% Black, 0.4% Asian, 1.5% Hispanic of any race (2004); Density: 3,100.5 persons per square mile (2004); Average household size: 1.93 (2004); Median age: 53.7 (2004); Male/female ratio: 91.2 (2004); Marriage status: 12.3% never married, 58.5% now married, 13.3% widowed, 15.9% divorced (2000); Foreign born: 5.4% (2000); Ancestry (includes multiple ancestries): 20.7% German, 17.4% Irish, 15.0% English, 9.8% Italian, 7.1% Other groups (2000).
Economy: Single-family building permits issued: 22 (2004); Multi-family building permits issued: 14 (2004); Employment by occupation: 13.8% management, 16.1% professional, 23.9% services, 27.5% sales, 0.5% farming, 8.4% construction, 9.8% production (2000).
Income: Per capita income: $32,983 (2004); Median household income: $47,559 (2004); Average household income: $63,539 (2004); Percent of households with income of $100,000 or more: 14.6% (2004); Poverty rate: 3.6% (2000).
Taxes: Total city taxes per capita: $422 (2002); City property taxes per capita: $258 (2002).
Education: Percent of population age 25 and over with: High school diploma (including GED) or higher: 92.9% (2004); Bachelor's degree or higher: 29.4% (2004); Master's degree or higher: 11.2% (2004).
School District(s)
Manatee County School District (PK-12)
2002-03 Enrollment: 39,132 . . . . (941) 708-8770
Housing: Homeownership rate: 68.5% (2004); Median home value: $275,306 (2004); Median rent: $648 per month (2000); Median age of housing: 28 years (2000).
Safety: Violent crime rate: 5.9 per 10,000 population; Property crime rate: 515.7 per 10,000 population (2003).
Transportation: Commute to work: 84.9% car, 0.5% public transportation, 4.8% walk, 8.1% work from home (2000); Travel time to work: 38.6% less than 15 minutes, 25.3% 15 to 30 minutes, 16.8% 30 to 45 minutes, 7.0% 45 to 60 minutes, 12.3% 60 minutes or more (2000)

MEMPHIS (CDP). Covers a land area of 3.162 square miles and a water area of 0 square miles. Located at 27.54° N. Lat.; 82.56° W. Long. Elevation is 19 feet.
Population: 6,733 (1990); 7,264 (2000); 7,365 (2004); 7,613 (2009 projected); Race: 46.3% White, 42.1% Black, 0.3% Asian, 22.8% Hispanic of any race (2004); Density: 2,329.0 persons per square mile (2004); Average household size: 2.94 (2004); Median age: 33.0 (2004); Male/female ratio: 99.4 (2004); Marriage status: 30.1% never married, 51.2% now married, 8.0% widowed, 10.7% divorced (2000); Foreign born: 11.6% (2000); Ancestry (includes multiple ancestries): 48.0% Other

groups, 7.7% German, 5.5% English, 5.4% Irish, 4.2% United States or American (2000).
Economy: Employment by occupation: 5.9% management, 13.4% professional, 20.9% services, 26.3% sales, 2.7% farming, 12.6% construction, 18.1% production (2000).
Income: Per capita income: $16,494 (2004); Median household income: $36,453 (2004); Average household income: $45,404 (2004); Percent of households with income of $100,000 or more: 6.1% (2004); Poverty rate: 20.7% (2000).
Education: Percent of population age 25 and over with: High school diploma (including GED) or higher: 62.7% (2004); Bachelor's degree or higher: 13.7% (2004); Master's degree or higher: 5.6% (2004).
Housing: Homeownership rate: 74.8% (2004); Median home value: $104,914 (2004); Median rent: $416 per month (2000); Median age of housing: 22 years (2000).
Transportation: Commute to work: 93.0% car, 0.8% public transportation, 1.9% walk, 2.1% work from home (2000); Travel time to work: 23.9% less than 15 minutes, 47.3% 15 to 30 minutes, 20.6% 30 to 45 minutes, 4.8% 45 to 60 minutes, 3.4% 60 minutes or more (2000)

MYAKKA CITY (unincorporated postal area, zip code 34251). Covers a land area of 298.597 square miles and a water area of 0.282 square miles. Located at 27.39° N. Lat.; 82.23° W. Long. Elevation is 44 feet.
History: Myakka City grew as a trading center for truck farmers and citrus growers. The name Myakka is of Indian origin meaning "very large," referring to the river here.
Population: 4,239 (2000); Race: 97.4% White, 0.0% Black, 1.1% Asian, 13.7% Hispanic of any race (2000); Density: 14.2 persons per square mile (2000); Age: 30.2% under 18, 6.0% over 64 (2000); Marriage status: 15.2% never married, 73.8% now married, 2.3% widowed, 8.8% divorced (2000); Foreign born: 4.2% (2000); Ancestry (includes multiple ancestries): 13.4% English, 12.9% German, 11.3% United States or American, 10.9% Irish, 8.6% Other groups (2000).
Economy: Employment by occupation: 12.3% management, 14.4% professional, 19.2% services, 23.2% sales, 3.4% farming, 18.8% construction, 8.8% production (2000).
Income: Per capita income: $24,143 (2000); Median household income: $54,216 (2000); Poverty rate: 2.6% (2000).
Education: Percent of population age 25 and over with: High school diploma (including GED) or higher: 78.4% (2000); Bachelor's degree or higher: 11.9% (2000).

School District(s)

Manatee County School District (PK-12)
2002-03 Enrollment: 39,132 . . . . (941) 708-8770
Housing: Homeownership rate: 86.0% (2000); Median home value: $145,100 (2000); Median rent: $419 per month (2000); Median age of housing: 12 years (2000).
Transportation: Commute to work: 92.3% car, 0.0% public transportation, 0.5% walk, 7.3% work from home (2000); Travel time to work: 9.6% less than 15 minutes, 21.1% 15 to 30 minutes, 37.3% 30 to 45 minutes, 20.4% 45 to 60 minutes, 11.7% 60 minutes or more (2000)

PALMETTO (city). Covers a land area of 4.316 square miles and a water area of 0.134 square miles. Located at 27.52° N. Lat.; 82.57° W. Long. Elevation is 10 feet.
History: Palmetto developed on the north bank of the Manatee River as a packing and shipping center for fruits and vegetables. Palmetto's river-front harbor sheltered both fishing and pleasure boats.
Population: 9,534 (1990); 12,571 (2000); 13,310 (2004); 14,316 (2009 projected); Race: 74.2% White, 12.3% Black, 0.5% Asian, 30.5% Hispanic of any race (2004); Density: 3,084.2 persons per square mile (2004); Average household size: 2.86 (2004); Median age: 35.8 (2004); Male/female ratio: 101.3 (2004); Marriage status: 22.0% never married, 56.9% now married, 9.5% widowed, 11.6% divorced (2000); Foreign born: 13.3% (2000); Ancestry (includes multiple ancestries): 29.9% Other groups, 11.5% German, 11.3% English, 10.1% United States or American, 7.9% Irish (2000).
Economy: Single-family building permits issued: 144 (2004); Multi-family building permits issued: 0 (2004); Employment by occupation: 6.8% management, 14.3% professional, 20.2% services, 21.1% sales, 5.6% farming, 14.2% construction, 17.8% production (2000).
Income: Per capita income: $18,933 (2004); Median household income: $38,788 (2004); Average household income: $50,216 (2004); Percent of households with income of $100,000 or more: 7.8% (2004); Poverty rate: 13.9% (2000).
Taxes: Total city taxes per capita: $268 (2002); City property taxes per capita: $108 (2002).
Education: Percent of population age 25 and over with: High school diploma (including GED) or higher: 66.3% (2004); Bachelor's degree or higher: 11.5% (2004); Master's degree or higher: 4.5% (2004).

School District(s)

Manatee County School District (PK-12)
2002-03 Enrollment: 39,132 . . . . (941) 708-8770
Housing: Homeownership rate: 71.5% (2004); Median home value: $107,014 (2004); Median rent: $400 per month (2000); Median age of housing: 26 years (2000).
Safety: Violent crime rate: 141.0 per 10,000 population; Property crime rate: 530.3 per 10,000 population (2003).
Transportation: Commute to work: 90.5% car, 0.7% public transportation, 3.6% walk, 3.2% work from home (2000); Travel time to work: 30.1% less than 15 minutes, 37.5% 15 to 30 minutes, 23.6% 30 to 45 minutes, 5.1% 45 to 60 minutes, 3.6% 60 minutes or more (2000)
Additional Information Contacts
Palmetto Convention & Visitors Bureau. . . . . (941) 729-9177

PARRISH (unincorporated postal area, zip code 34219). Covers a land area of 80.450 square miles and a water area of 6.030 square miles. Located at 27.57° N. Lat.; 82.40° W. Long. Elevation is 44 feet.
History: Parrish developed as a citrus-fruit and vegetable shipping center.
Population: 5,812 (2000); Race: 93.4% White, 3.2% Black, 0.7% Asian, 5.6% Hispanic of any race (2000); Density: 72.2 persons per square mile (2000); Age: 18.3% under 18, 23.1% over 64 (2000); Marriage status: 13.1% never married, 74.0% now married, 6.4% widowed, 6.5% divorced (2000); Foreign born: 5.9% (2000); Ancestry (includes multiple ancestries): 18.9% German, 15.4% English, 13.5% Irish, 13.2% Other groups, 12.1% United States or American (2000).
Economy: Employment by occupation: 17.8% management, 18.7% professional, 13.9% services, 26.1% sales, 3.1% farming, 10.8% construction, 9.7% production (2000).
Income: Per capita income: $26,496 (2000); Median household income: $51,250 (2000); Poverty rate: 8.2% (2000).
Education: Percent of population age 25 and over with: High school diploma (including GED) or higher: 88.2% (2000); Bachelor's degree or higher: 23.0% (2000).
Housing: Homeownership rate: 92.2% (2000); Median home value: $178,400 (2000); Median rent: $439 per month (2000); Median age of housing: 7 years (2000).
Transportation: Commute to work: 89.0% car, 0.2% public transportation, 2.2% walk, 6.7% work from home (2000); Travel time to work: 19.9% less than 15 minutes, 37.6% 15 to 30 minutes, 28.1% 30 to 45 minutes, 10.0% 45 to 60 minutes, 4.4% 60 minutes or more (2000)

SAMOSET (CDP). Covers a land area of 1.927 square miles and a water area of 0 square miles. Located at 27.47° N. Lat.; 82.54° W. Long. Elevation is 28 feet.
Population: 3,135 (1990); 3,440 (2000); 3,556 (2004); 3,788 (2009 projected); Race: 53.5% White, 32.8% Black, 0.1% Asian, 23.3% Hispanic of any race (2004); Density: 1,845.2 persons per square mile (2004); Average household size: 3.12 (2004); Median age: 30.2 (2004); Male/female ratio: 98.7 (2004); Marriage status: 31.0% never married, 46.9% now married, 8.0% widowed, 14.1% divorced (2000); Foreign born: 6.0% (2000); Ancestry (includes multiple ancestries): 40.1% Other groups, 9.0% United States or American, 7.8% English, 5.2% Irish, 4.9% German (2000).
Economy: Quarrying: dolomite, limestone. Employment by occupation: 2.2% management, 6.9% professional, 16.5% services, 27.1% sales, 1.3% farming, 24.6% construction, 21.5% production (2000).
Income: Per capita income: $12,196 (2004); Median household income: $32,006 (2004); Average household income: $37,228 (2004); Percent of households with income of $100,000 or more: 1.8% (2004); Poverty rate: 22.5% (2000).
Education: Percent of population age 25 and over with: High school diploma (including GED) or higher: 58.4% (2004); Bachelor's degree or higher: 5.2% (2004); Master's degree or higher: 2.4% (2004).
Housing: Homeownership rate: 71.0% (2004); Median home value: $96,816 (2004); Median rent: $393 per month (2000); Median age of housing: 29 years (2000).
Transportation: Commute to work: 92.6% car, 1.1% public transportation, 2.6% walk, 0.0% work from home (2000); Travel time to work: 36.7% less

than 15 minutes, 39.5% 15 to 30 minutes, 15.0% 30 to 45 minutes, 6.3% 45 to 60 minutes, 2.5% 60 minutes or more (2000)

SOUTH BRADENTON (CDP). Covers a land area of 4.460 square miles and a water area of 0.078 square miles. Located at 27.45° N. Lat.; 82.57° W. Long.
Population: 20,264 (1990); 21,587 (2000); 22,747 (2004); 24,230 (2009 projected); Race: 86.8% White, 6.4% Black, 1.6% Asian, 11.3% Hispanic of any race (2004); Density: 5,100.5 persons per square mile (2004); Average household size: 2.02 (2004); Median age: 44.2 (2004); Male/female ratio: 88.7 (2004); Marriage status: 23.3% never married, 47.2% now married, 14.0% widowed, 15.5% divorced (2000); Foreign born: 9.0% (2000); Ancestry (includes multiple ancestries): 17.9% Other groups, 16.4% German, 14.0% English, 12.8% Irish, 8.0% United States or American (2000).
Economy: Employment by occupation: 6.5% management, 11.1% professional, 21.5% services, 30.4% sales, 1.4% farming, 10.6% construction, 18.4% production (2000).
Income: Per capita income: $18,268 (2004); Median household income: $29,546 (2004); Average household income: $36,514 (2004); Percent of households with income of $100,000 or more: 3.0% (2004); Poverty rate: 13.0% (2000).
Education: Percent of population age 25 and over with: High school diploma (including GED) or higher: 75.5% (2004); Bachelor's degree or higher: 13.1% (2004); Master's degree or higher: 3.8% (2004).
Housing: Homeownership rate: 59.0% (2004); Median home value: $79,698 (2004); Median rent: $488 per month (2000); Median age of housing: 26 years (2000).
Transportation: Commute to work: 93.8% car, 0.6% public transportation, 2.0% walk, 2.1% work from home (2000); Travel time to work: 36.2% less than 15 minutes, 43.3% 15 to 30 minutes, 13.7% 30 to 45 minutes, 2.5% 45 to 60 minutes, 4.4% 60 minutes or more (2000)

WEST BRADENTON (CDP). Aka Rosedale. Covers a land area of 1.365 square miles and a water area of 0.064 square miles. Located at 27.50° N. Lat.; 82.61° W. Long.
Population: 4,562 (1990); 4,444 (2000); 4,650 (2004); 4,943 (2009 projected); Race: 96.6% White, 0.8% Black, 1.0% Asian, 2.8% Hispanic of any race (2004); Density: 3,407.0 persons per square mile (2004); Average household size: 2.62 (2004); Median age: 40.6 (2004); Male/female ratio: 91.8 (2004); Marriage status: 17.0% never married, 65.7% now married, 5.9% widowed, 11.3% divorced (2000); Foreign born: 3.7% (2000); Ancestry (includes multiple ancestries): 23.4% German, 14.7% Irish, 13.9% English, 9.2% United States or American, 8.3% Other groups (2000).
Economy: Employment by occupation: 11.6% management, 26.2% professional, 17.0% services, 27.0% sales, 0.8% farming, 9.7% construction, 7.7% production (2000).
Income: Per capita income: $32,320 (2004); Median household income: $60,785 (2004); Average household income: $84,574 (2004); Percent of households with income of $100,000 or more: 21.7% (2004); Poverty rate: 5.2% (2000).
Education: Percent of population age 25 and over with: High school diploma (including GED) or higher: 89.3% (2004); Bachelor's degree or higher: 29.4% (2004); Master's degree or higher: 12.7% (2004).
Housing: Homeownership rate: 89.8% (2004); Median home value: $158,191 (2004); Median rent: $750 per month (2000); Median age of housing: 30 years (2000).
Transportation: Commute to work: 95.1% car, 0.0% public transportation, 1.0% walk, 2.9% work from home (2000); Travel time to work: 31.2% less than 15 minutes, 45.7% 15 to 30 minutes, 13.9% 30 to 45 minutes, 7.4% 45 to 60 minutes, 1.8% 60 minutes or more (2000)

WEST SAMOSET (CDP). Covers a land area of 1.372 square miles and a water area of 0 square miles. Located at 27.47° N. Lat.; 82.55° W. Long.
Population: 3,819 (1990); 5,507 (2000); 6,164 (2004); 6,987 (2009 projected); Race: 51.4% White, 34.0% Black, 0.8% Asian, 27.6% Hispanic of any race (2004); Density: 4,492.6 persons per square mile (2004); Average household size: 3.11 (2004); Median age: 28.5 (2004); Male/female ratio: 95.6 (2004); Marriage status: 32.1% never married, 46.3% now married, 11.9% widowed, 9.6% divorced (2000); Foreign born: 12.0% (2000); Ancestry (includes multiple ancestries): 47.5% Other groups, 9.2% United States or American, 7.6% German, 5.8% Irish, 3.9% English (2000).
Economy: Employment by occupation: 1.2% management, 5.7% professional, 18.3% services, 20.9% sales, 2.4% farming, 16.2% construction, 35.4% production (2000).
Income: Per capita income: $12,487 (2004); Median household income: $31,815 (2004); Average household income: $37,979 (2004); Percent of households with income of $100,000 or more: 3.3% (2004); Poverty rate: 18.8% (2000).
Education: Percent of population age 25 and over with: High school diploma (including GED) or higher: 56.6% (2004); Bachelor's degree or higher: 6.6% (2004); Master's degree or higher: 2.2% (2004).
Housing: Homeownership rate: 40.0% (2004); Median home value: $79,095 (2004); Median rent: $529 per month (2000); Median age of housing: 26 years (2000).
Transportation: Commute to work: 95.2% car, 1.8% public transportation, 1.6% walk, 0.0% work from home (2000); Travel time to work: 29.7% less than 15 minutes, 42.9% 15 to 30 minutes, 17.2% 30 to 45 minutes, 2.3% 45 to 60 minutes, 8.0% 60 minutes or more (2000)

WHITFIELD (CDP). Covers a land area of 1.404 square miles and a water area of 0.020 square miles. Located at 27.41° N. Lat.; 82.56° W. Long.
Population: 3,246 (1990); 2,984 (2000); 3,211 (2004); 3,474 (2009 projected); Race: 92.1% White, 4.7% Black, 0.9% Asian, 6.0% Hispanic of any race (2004); Density: 2,286.6 persons per square mile (2004); Average household size: 2.38 (2004); Median age: 44.3 (2004); Male/female ratio: 97.2 (2004); Marriage status: 20.9% never married, 63.0% now married, 5.4% widowed, 10.7% divorced (2000); Foreign born: 16.9% (2000); Ancestry (includes multiple ancestries): 23.5% German, 15.0% English, 13.0% Irish, 12.1% Other groups, 9.6% French (except Basque) (2000).
Economy: Employment by occupation: 11.5% management, 20.3% professional, 17.4% services, 23.2% sales, 0.0% farming, 13.8% construction, 13.8% production (2000).
Income: Per capita income: $28,550 (2004); Median household income: $55,679 (2004); Average household income: $67,906 (2004); Percent of households with income of $100,000 or more: 14.3% (2004); Poverty rate: 6.3% (2000).
Education: Percent of population age 25 and over with: High school diploma (including GED) or higher: 88.6% (2004); Bachelor's degree or higher: 26.2% (2004); Master's degree or higher: 11.7% (2004).
Housing: Homeownership rate: 87.3% (2004); Median home value: $182,964 (2004); Median rent: $599 per month (2000); Median age of housing: 27 years (2000).
Transportation: Commute to work: 94.2% car, 0.0% public transportation, 0.0% walk, 5.8% work from home (2000); Travel time to work: 37.2% less than 15 minutes, 43.8% 15 to 30 minutes, 12.5% 30 to 45 minutes, 2.8% 45 to 60 minutes, 3.8% 60 minutes or more (2000)

Marion County

Located in north central Florida; drained by the Oklawaha River; includes Lakes Weir and Kerr, and Ocala National Forest. Covers a land area of 1,578.90 square miles, a water area of 84.20 square miles, and is located in the Eastern Time Zone. The county government was organized in 1844. County seat is Ocala.

Marion County is part of the Ocala, FL Metropolitan Statistical Area. The entire metro area includes: Marion County, FL

Weather Station: Ocala — Elevation: 72 feet

	Jan	Feb	Mar	Apr	May	Jun	Jul	Aug	Sep	Oct	Nov	Dec
High	70	73	78	83	88	91	92	92	90	84	77	72
Low	46	47	52	56	63	69	71	71	69	61	54	47
Precip	3.6	3.3	4.2	2.9	3.8	7.1	6.4	6.1	5.5	2.8	2.4	2.7
Snow	tr	tr	0.0	0.0	0.0	0.0	0.0	0.0	0.0	0.0	0.0	0.0

High and Low temperatures in degrees Fahrenheit; Precipitation and Snow in inches

Population: 194,833 (1990); 258,916 (2000); 282,475 (2004); 312,143 (2009 projected); Race: 83.4% White, 11.9% Black, 0.8% Asian, 7.0% Hispanic of any race (2004); Density: 178.9 persons per square mile (2004); Average household size: 2.41 (2004); Median age: 44.2 (2004); Male/female ratio: 93.6 (2004).
Religion: Five largest groups: 11.5% Catholic Church, 9.3% Southern Baptist Convention, 4.0% The United Methodist Church, 1.4% Presbyterian Church (U.S.A.), 1.3% Church of God (Cleveland, Tennessee) (2000).
Economy: Unemployment rate: 4.2% (2004); Total civilian labor force: 108,829 (2004); Leading industries: 19.3% retail trade; 16.3% health care

and social assistance; 11.3% manufacturing (2003); Companies that employ 500 or more persons: 9 (2003); Companies that employ 100 to 499 persons: 103 (2003); Companies that employ less than 100 persons: 5,950 (2003); Farms: 2,930 totaling 270,562 acres (2002); Minority business ownership rate: 7.2% (1997); Women business ownership rate: 23.8% (1997); Retail sales per capita: $9,423 (1997). Single-family building permits issued: 5,268 (2004); Multi-family building permits issued: 158 (2004).
Income: Per capita income: $19,460 (2004); Median household income: $34,641 (2004); Average household income: $46,153 (2004); Percent of households with income of $100,000 or more: 7.1% (2004); Poverty rate: 14.8% (2002); Bankruptcy rate: 5.62% (2004).
Taxes: Total county taxes per capita: $291 (2002); County property taxes per capita: $242 (2002).
Education: Percent of population age 25 and over with: High school diploma (including GED) or higher: 78.4% (2004); Bachelor's degree or higher: 13.7% (2004); Master's degree or higher: 5.1% (2004).
Housing: Homeownership rate: 80.4% (2004); Median home value: $94,495 (2004); Median rent: $404 per month (2000); Median age of housing: 16 years (2000).
Health: Birth rate: 102.9 per 10,000 population (2004); Death rate: 132.7 per 10,000 population (2004); Age adjusted cancer mortality rate: 216.6 deaths per 100,000 population (2002); Air Quality Index: 91.5% good, 8.5% moderate, 0.0% unhealthy for sensitive individuals, 0.0% unhealthy (percent of days in 2004); Number of physicians: 17.0 per 10,000 population (2001); Hospital beds: 21.8 per 10,000 population (2002); Hospital admissions: 1,311.6 per 10,000 population (2002).
Elections: 2004 Presidential election results: 58.2% Bush, 41.0% Kerry, 0.5% Nader, 0.2% Badnarik
National and State Parks: Ocala National Forest; Rainbow Springs State Park; Silver River State Park
Additional Information Contacts
Marion County Government Offices . . . . (352) 620-3904
Belleview Chamber of Commerce . . . . (352) 245-2178
Dunnellon Chamber of Commerce . . . . (352) 489-2320
Lake Weir Chamber of Commerce . . . . (352) 288-3751
Ocala Chamber of Commerce . . . . (352) 629-8051
Ocala Marion County Association of Realtors . . . . (352) 629-2415

Marion County Communities

ANTHONY (unincorporated postal area, zip code 32617). Covers a land area of 20.077 square miles and a water area of 0.090 square miles. Located at 29.31° N. Lat.; 82.10° W. Long. Elevation is 85 feet.
Population: 3,546 (2000); Race: 83.2% White, 14.5% Black, 0.0% Asian, 4.8% Hispanic of any race (2000); Density: 176.6 persons per square mile (2000); Age: 25.6% under 18, 11.1% over 64 (2000); Marriage status: 24.6% never married, 59.2% now married, 5.3% widowed, 10.9% divorced (2000); Foreign born: 3.9% (2000); Ancestry (includes multiple ancestries): 28.3% Other groups, 13.2% United States or American, 11.5% Irish, 10.4% German, 9.5% English (2000).
Economy: Employment by occupation: 11.8% management, 13.6% professional, 17.0% services, 25.7% sales, 1.7% farming, 14.1% construction, 16.0% production (2000).
Income: Per capita income: $15,483 (2000); Median household income: $38,627 (2000); Poverty rate: 13.4% (2000).
Education: Percent of population age 25 and over with: High school diploma (including GED) or higher: 72.0% (2000); Bachelor's degree or higher: 10.6% (2000).

School District(s)

Marion County School District (PK-12)
2002-03 Enrollment: 39,710 . . . . (352) 671-7702
Housing: Homeownership rate: 83.1% (2000); Median home value: $93,100 (2000); Median rent: $398 per month (2000); Median age of housing: 17 years (2000).
Transportation: Commute to work: 91.2% car, 0.0% public transportation, 3.3% walk, 2.9% work from home (2000); Travel time to work: 14.7% less than 15 minutes, 48.4% 15 to 30 minutes, 26.6% 30 to 45 minutes, 6.2% 45 to 60 minutes, 4.1% 60 minutes or more (2000)

BELLEVIEW (city). Covers a land area of 1.825 square miles and a water area of 0.002 square miles. Located at 29.06° N. Lat.; 82.05° W. Long. Elevation is 82 feet.
History: Belleview developed around an area of citrus and pecan groves, with fruit packing plants and lumber mills.
Population: 3,310 (1990); 3,478 (2000); 3,505 (2004); 3,580 (2009 projected); Race: 90.8% White, 4.6% Black, 0.5% Asian, 8.8% Hispanic of any race (2004); Density: 1,920.3 persons per square mile (2004); Average household size: 2.16 (2004); Median age: 43.1 (2004); Male/female ratio: 89.4 (2004); Marriage status: 20.4% never married, 45.7% now married, 16.8% widowed, 17.2% divorced (2000); Foreign born: 3.5% (2000); Ancestry (includes multiple ancestries): 21.3% Other groups, 15.5% German, 14.2% Irish, 10.3% United States or American, 10.1% French (except Basque) (2000).
Economy: Single-family building permits issued: 71 (2004); Multi-family building permits issued: 0 (2004); Employment by occupation: 4.5% management, 16.6% professional, 15.1% services, 31.1% sales, 0.0% farming, 14.2% construction, 18.4% production (2000).
Income: Per capita income: $18,232 (2004); Median household income: $29,069 (2004); Average household income: $37,535 (2004); Percent of households with income of $100,000 or more: 2.8% (2004); Poverty rate: 12.3% (2000).
Taxes: Total city taxes per capita: $300 (2002); City property taxes per capita: $122 (2002).
Education: Percent of population age 25 and over with: High school diploma (including GED) or higher: 73.8% (2004); Bachelor's degree or higher: 8.4% (2004); Master's degree or higher: 3.4% (2004).

School District(s)

Marion County School District (PK-12)
2002-03 Enrollment: 39,710 . . . . (352) 671-7702
Housing: Homeownership rate: 68.5% (2004); Median home value: $73,346 (2004); Median rent: $361 per month (2000); Median age of housing: 20 years (2000).
Safety: Violent crime rate: 67.5 per 10,000 population; Property crime rate: 575.5 per 10,000 population (2003).
Newspapers: Voice of South Marion (General - Circulation 2,800)
Transportation: Commute to work: 89.6% car, 0.0% public transportation, 2.4% walk, 5.1% work from home (2000); Travel time to work: 26.1% less than 15 minutes, 37.9% 15 to 30 minutes, 24.5% 30 to 45 minutes, 4.2% 45 to 60 minutes, 7.3% 60 minutes or more (2000)
Additional Information Contacts
Belleview Chamber of Commerce . . . . (352) 245-2178

CITRA (unincorporated postal area, zip code 32113). Covers a land area of 88.893 square miles and a water area of 3.659 square miles. Located at 29.39° N. Lat.; 82.09° W. Long. Elevation is 75 feet.
History: Citra was founded in the early 1880's. The pineapple orange was developed near here.
Population: 6,891 (2000); Race: 81.4% White, 15.6% Black, 0.6% Asian, 2.8% Hispanic of any race (2000); Density: 77.5 persons per square mile (2000); Age: 22.8% under 18, 17.5% over 64 (2000); Marriage status: 19.0% never married, 57.1% now married, 6.5% widowed, 17.4% divorced (2000); Foreign born: 2.4% (2000); Ancestry (includes multiple ancestries): 21.5% Other groups, 19.0% United States or American, 9.9% Irish, 8.7% German, 6.8% English (2000).
Economy: Employment by occupation: 9.8% management, 10.4% professional, 20.8% services, 26.3% sales, 4.3% farming, 15.6% construction, 12.7% production (2000).
Income: Per capita income: $15,948 (2000); Median household income: $30,045 (2000); Poverty rate: 19.1% (2000).
Education: Percent of population age 25 and over with: High school diploma (including GED) or higher: 69.9% (2000); Bachelor's degree or higher: 7.2% (2000).

School District(s)

Marion County School District (PK-12)
2002-03 Enrollment: 39,710 . . . . (352) 671-7702
Housing: Homeownership rate: 83.6% (2000); Median home value: $66,400 (2000); Median rent: $358 per month (2000); Median age of housing: 19 years (2000).
Transportation: Commute to work: 91.7% car, 0.0% public transportation, 1.2% walk, 5.2% work from home (2000); Travel time to work: 11.4% less than 15 minutes, 37.7% 15 to 30 minutes, 37.1% 30 to 45 minutes, 8.6% 45 to 60 minutes, 5.3% 60 minutes or more (2000)

DUNNELLON (city). Covers a land area of 7.048 square miles and a water area of 0.381 square miles. Located at 29.05° N. Lat.; 82.45° W. Long. Elevation is 50 feet.
History: Dunnellon was established on the Withlacoochee River, and grew after 1889 as a center for the mining and shipping of phosphate and

limestone rock. Before that, Dunnellon was a trading center for planters and stockmen of the surrounding areas.
Population: 1,741 (1990); 1,898 (2000); 2,088 (2004); 2,328 (2009 projected); Race: 86.2% White, 11.6% Black, 0.5% Asian, 1.9% Hispanic of any race (2004); Density: 296.2 persons per square mile (2004); Average household size: 1.97 (2004); Median age: 52.6 (2004); Male/female ratio: 81.6 (2004); Marriage status: 15.1% never married, 52.7% now married, 17.6% widowed, 14.6% divorced (2000); Foreign born: 3.9% (2000); Ancestry (includes multiple ancestries): 17.9% Other groups, 17.6% German, 15.4% English, 11.5% Irish, 11.0% United States or American (2000).
Economy: Single-family building permits issued: 8 (2004); Multi-family building permits issued: 0 (2004); Employment by occupation: 8.3% management, 21.8% professional, 16.4% services, 21.7% sales, 1.9% farming, 10.5% construction, 19.5% production (2000).
Income: Per capita income: $20,084 (2004); Median household income: $28,797 (2004); Average household income: $39,487 (2004); Percent of households with income of $100,000 or more: 7.1% (2004); Poverty rate: 15.5% (2000).
Taxes: Total city taxes per capita: $516 (2002); City property taxes per capita: $253 (2002).
Education: Percent of population age 25 and over with: High school diploma (including GED) or higher: 84.0% (2004); Bachelor's degree or higher: 13.8% (2004); Master's degree or higher: 5.2% (2004).

School District(s)

Marion County School District (PK-12)
2002-03 Enrollment: 39,710 . . . . (352) 671-7702
Housing: Homeownership rate: 71.0% (2004); Median home value: $94,091 (2004); Median rent: $358 per month (2000); Median age of housing: 23 years (2000).
Safety: Violent crime rate: 59.5 per 10,000 population; Property crime rate: 346.9 per 10,000 population (2003).
Newspapers: Riverland News (General - Circulation 3,100)
Transportation: Commute to work: 91.9% car, 0.0% public transportation, 3.2% walk, 3.3% work from home (2000); Travel time to work: 38.0% less than 15 minutes, 19.3% 15 to 30 minutes, 23.4% 30 to 45 minutes, 13.8% 45 to 60 minutes, 5.4% 60 minutes or more (2000)
Additional Information Contacts
Dunnellon Chamber of Commerce . . . . (352) 489-2320

FORT MCCOY (unincorporated postal area, zip code 32134). Covers a land area of 225.356 square miles and a water area of 12.896 square miles. Located at 29.40° N. Lat.; 81.83° W. Long. Elevation is 75 feet.
Population: 7,950 (2000); Race: 95.9% White, 0.9% Black, 1.6% Asian, 2.1% Hispanic of any race (2000); Density: 35.3 persons per square mile (2000); Age: 20.2% under 18, 22.9% over 64 (2000); Marriage status: 12.2% never married, 62.5% now married, 12.2% widowed, 13.2% divorced (2000); Foreign born: 3.1% (2000); Ancestry (includes multiple ancestries): 15.3% United States or American, 14.1% German, 13.9% Other groups, 13.3% Irish, 11.5% English (2000).
Economy: Employment by occupation: 10.8% management, 7.3% professional, 16.1% services, 23.7% sales, 1.1% farming, 21.6% construction, 19.5% production (2000).
Income: Per capita income: $15,582 (2000); Median household income: $28,195 (2000); Poverty rate: 16.2% (2000).
Education: Percent of population age 25 and over with: High school diploma (including GED) or higher: 72.6% (2000); Bachelor's degree or higher: 8.1% (2000).

School District(s)

Marion County School District (PK-12)
2002-03 Enrollment: 39,710 . . . . (352) 671-7702
Housing: Homeownership rate: 88.5% (2000); Median home value: $62,500 (2000); Median rent: $334 per month (2000); Median age of housing: 21 years (2000).
Transportation: Commute to work: 95.6% car, 0.7% public transportation, 0.4% walk, 2.9% work from home (2000); Travel time to work: 13.5% less than 15 minutes, 12.4% 15 to 30 minutes, 34.0% 30 to 45 minutes, 21.9% 45 to 60 minutes, 18.2% 60 minutes or more (2000)

MCINTOSH (town). Covers a land area of 0.696 square miles and a water area of 0 square miles. Located at 29.44° N. Lat.; 82.22° W. Long. Elevation is 109 feet.
History: McIntosh developed in an area of citrus and pecan groves.
Population: 411 (1990); 453 (2000); 523 (2004); 610 (2009 projected); Race: 96.4% White, 3.3% Black, 0.0% Asian, 1.5% Hispanic of any race (2004); Density: 751.4 persons per square mile (2004); Average household size: 1.97 (2004); Median age: 52.5 (2004); Male/female ratio: 80.3 (2004); Marriage status: 14.8% never married, 62.7% now married, 7.5% widowed, 15.0% divorced (2000); Foreign born: 1.9% (2000); Ancestry (includes multiple ancestries): 15.8% Other groups, 13.7% English, 13.7% German, 11.6% Irish, 7.9% United States or American (2000).
Economy: Employment by occupation: 8.8% management, 29.3% professional, 6.3% services, 35.6% sales, 0.0% farming, 8.8% construction, 11.2% production (2000).
Income: Per capita income: $26,372 (2004); Median household income: $40,294 (2004); Average household income: $51,852 (2004); Percent of households with income of $100,000 or more: 11.7% (2004); Poverty rate: 6.3% (2000).
Taxes: Total city taxes per capita: $42 (2002); City property taxes per capita: $42 (2002).
Education: Percent of population age 25 and over with: High school diploma (including GED) or higher: 91.1% (2004); Bachelor's degree or higher: 26.3% (2004); Master's degree or higher: 13.8% (2004).

School District(s)

Marion County School District (PK-12)
2002-03 Enrollment: 39,710 . . . . (352) 671-7702
Housing: Homeownership rate: 80.1% (2004); Median home value: $106,250 (2004); Median rent: $395 per month (2000); Median age of housing: 25 years (2000).
Transportation: Commute to work: 99.0% car, 0.0% public transportation, 0.0% walk, 0.0% work from home (2000); Travel time to work: 11.2% less than 15 minutes, 41.0% 15 to 30 minutes, 40.5% 30 to 45 minutes, 2.4% 45 to 60 minutes, 4.9% 60 minutes or more (2000)

OCALA (city). Covers a land area of 38.633 square miles and a water area of 0 square miles. Located at 29.18° N. Lat.; 82.13° W. Long. Elevation is 73 feet.
History: Ocala began as a trading post established in 1825, and used during the Seminole Wars as a military post. The town became a trading and shipping center for truck gardeners and for phosphate and limestone mining companies.
Population: 42,851 (1990); 45,943 (2000); 47,466 (2004); 49,746 (2009 projected); Race: 71.7% White, 22.7% Black, 1.5% Asian, 6.9% Hispanic of any race (2004); Density: 1,228.6 persons per square mile (2004); Average household size: 2.48 (2004); Median age: 38.6 (2004); Male/female ratio: 91.1 (2004); Marriage status: 23.7% never married, 51.5% now married, 10.1% widowed, 14.6% divorced (2000); Foreign born: 4.6% (2000); Ancestry (includes multiple ancestries): 26.9% Other groups, 13.2% German, 11.8% Irish, 11.1% English, 6.8% United States or American (2000).
Economy: Unemployment rate: 4.5% (2004); Total civilian labor force: 25,132 (2004); Single-family building permits issued: 397 (2004); Multi-family building permits issued: 0 (2004); Employment by occupation: 11.7% management, 20.1% professional, 18.9% services, 27.1% sales, 0.8% farming, 9.4% construction, 12.0% production (2000).
Income: Per capita income: $18,918 (2004); Median household income: $32,139 (2004); Average household income: $45,227 (2004); Percent of households with income of $100,000 or more: 7.6% (2004); Poverty rate: 18.1% (2000).
Taxes: Total city taxes per capita: $535 (2002); City property taxes per capita: $251 (2002).
Education: Percent of population age 25 and over with: High school diploma (including GED) or higher: 79.4% (2004); Bachelor's degree or higher: 19.5% (2004); Master's degree or higher: 7.6% (2004).

School District(s)

Marion County School District (PK-12)
2002-03 Enrollment: 39,710 . . . . (352) 671-7702

Four-year College(s)

Webster College (Private, For-profit)
2003-04 Enrollment: 454 . . . . (352) 629-1941
2003-04 Tuition: In-state $9,605; Out-of-state $9,605

Two-year College(s)

Central Florida Community College (Public)
2003-04 Enrollment: 6,136 . . . . (352) 237-2111
2003-04 Tuition: In-state $1,381; Out-of-state $5,123
Marion County Comm Tech and Adult Edu Center (Public)
2003-04 Enrollment: 481 . . . . (352) 671-7200
2003-04 Tuition: In-state $1,800; Out-of-state $6,120

Housing: Homeownership rate: 56.9% (2004); Median home value: $95,722 (2004); Median rent: $430 per month (2000); Median age of housing: 24 years (2000).
Hospitals: Munroe Regional Medical Center (421 beds); Ocala Regional Medical Center (230 beds)
Safety: Violent crime rate: 135.0 per 10,000 population; Property crime rate: 768.8 per 10,000 population (2003).
Newspapers: Mahogany Revue (General, Hispanic - Circulation 30,000); Star-Banner (Circulation 49,660)
Transportation: Commute to work: 93.1% car, 0.4% public transportation, 2.1% walk, 2.6% work from home (2000); Travel time to work: 45.0% less than 15 minutes, 38.8% 15 to 30 minutes, 8.4% 30 to 45 minutes, 3.1% 45 to 60 minutes, 4.7% 60 minutes or more (2000); Amtrak: Service available.
Airports: Ocala Regional/Jim Taylor Field
Additional Information Contacts
Ocala Chamber of Commerce . . . . (352) 629-8051
Ocala Marion County Association of Realtors . . . . (352) 629-2415

REDDICK (town). Covers a land area of 1.245 square miles and a water area of 0 square miles. Located at 29.37° N. Lat.; 82.19° W. Long. Elevation is 75 feet.
Population: 554 (1990); 571 (2000); 591 (2004); 618 (2009 projected); Race: 50.8% White, 42.3% Black, 0.0% Asian, 8.1% Hispanic of any race (2004); Density: 474.7 persons per square mile (2004); Average household size: 2.77 (2004); Median age: 32.6 (2004); Male/female ratio: 96.3 (2004); Marriage status: 35.1% never married, 45.5% now married, 6.6% widowed, 12.8% divorced (2000); Foreign born: 6.7% (2000); Ancestry (includes multiple ancestries): 43.9% Other groups, 16.4% United States or American, 10.9% German, 6.3% Swedish, 5.1% English (2000).
Economy: Small-scale farming; limestone quarrying. Employment by occupation: 2.9% management, 10.0% professional, 22.9% services, 20.8% sales, 13.8% farming, 13.8% construction, 15.8% production (2000).
Income: Per capita income: $17,343 (2004); Median household income: $39,267 (2004); Average household income: $48,122 (2004); Percent of households with income of $100,000 or more: 8.5% (2004); Poverty rate: 18.3% (2000).
Taxes: Total city taxes per capita: $7 (2002); City property taxes per capita: $0 (2002).
Education: Percent of population age 25 and over with: High school diploma (including GED) or higher: 71.1% (2004); Bachelor's degree or higher: 8.0% (2004); Master's degree or higher: 3.8% (2004).
School District(s)
Marion County School District (PK-12)
2002-03 Enrollment: 39,710 . . . . (352) 671-7702
Housing: Homeownership rate: 77.0% (2004); Median home value: $77,500 (2004); Median rent: $350 per month (2000); Median age of housing: 29 years (2000).
Transportation: Commute to work: 91.2% car, 0.0% public transportation, 5.0% walk, 2.1% work from home (2000); Travel time to work: 32.1% less than 15 minutes, 20.9% 15 to 30 minutes, 38.0% 30 to 45 minutes, 5.6% 45 to 60 minutes, 3.4% 60 minutes or more (2000)

SILVER SPRINGS SHORES (CDP). Covers a land area of 4.774 square miles and a water area of 0.057 square miles. Located at 29.10° N. Lat.; 82.01° W. Long. Elevation is 80 feet.
Population: 6,421 (1990); 6,690 (2000); 7,025 (2004); 7,469 (2009 projected); Race: 58.6% White, 33.2% Black, 1.3% Asian, 12.8% Hispanic of any race (2004); Density: 1,471.4 persons per square mile (2004); Average household size: 2.33 (2004); Median age: 43.5 (2004); Male/female ratio: 81.1 (2004); Marriage status: 15.0% never married, 60.6% now married, 13.5% widowed, 10.9% divorced (2000); Foreign born: 18.1% (2000); Ancestry (includes multiple ancestries): 29.6% Other groups, 9.9% Jamaican, 9.5% Irish, 9.3% German, 8.5% Italian (2000).
Economy: Employment by occupation: 6.8% management, 18.5% professional, 17.8% services, 28.8% sales, 0.9% farming, 9.5% construction, 17.7% production (2000).
Income: Per capita income: $14,465 (2004); Median household income: $27,573 (2004); Average household income: $33,325 (2004); Percent of households with income of $100,000 or more: 3.5% (2004); Poverty rate: 12.0% (2000).
Education: Percent of population age 25 and over with: High school diploma (including GED) or higher: 74.6% (2004); Bachelor's degree or higher: 10.3% (2004); Master's degree or higher: 4.8% (2004).
Housing: Homeownership rate: 74.0% (2004); Median home value: $72,840 (2004); Median rent: $458 per month (2000); Median age of housing: 21 years (2000).
Transportation: Commute to work: 95.7% car, 1.3% public transportation, 0.4% walk, 0.4% work from home (2000); Travel time to work: 19.8% less than 15 minutes, 44.6% 15 to 30 minutes, 21.4% 30 to 45 minutes, 8.0% 45 to 60 minutes, 6.3% 60 minutes or more (2000)

WEIRSDALE (unincorporated postal area, zip code 32195). Covers a land area of 24.367 square miles and a water area of 2.343 square miles. Located at 29.00° N. Lat.; 81.89° W. Long. Elevation is 97 feet.
History: Weirsdale was established as a resort on the shores of Lake Weir, with citrus packing plants providing for the early economy of the town.
Population: 3,181 (2000); Race: 84.8% White, 11.7% Black, 2.4% Asian, 3.4% Hispanic of any race (2000); Density: 130.5 persons per square mile (2000); Age: 24.0% under 18, 16.4% over 64 (2000); Marriage status: 15.5% never married, 64.3% now married, 7.0% widowed, 13.2% divorced (2000); Foreign born: 5.9% (2000); Ancestry (includes multiple ancestries): 21.0% Other groups, 17.3% German, 11.9% Irish, 11.0% English, 9.6% United States or American (2000).
Economy: Employment by occupation: 8.3% management, 15.7% professional, 16.7% services, 27.6% sales, 2.4% farming, 16.8% construction, 12.4% production (2000).
Income: Per capita income: $21,543 (2000); Median household income: $40,410 (2000); Poverty rate: 13.7% (2000).
Education: Percent of population age 25 and over with: High school diploma (including GED) or higher: 70.9% (2000); Bachelor's degree or higher: 14.0% (2000).
School District(s)
Marion County School District (PK-12)
2002-03 Enrollment: 39,710 . . . . (352) 671-7702
Housing: Homeownership rate: 82.1% (2000); Median home value: $95,500 (2000); Median rent: $327 per month (2000); Median age of housing: 16 years (2000).
Transportation: Commute to work: 95.3% car, 0.0% public transportation, 2.4% walk, 1.6% work from home (2000); Travel time to work: 22.2% less than 15 minutes, 25.4% 15 to 30 minutes, 31.9% 30 to 45 minutes, 14.0% 45 to 60 minutes, 6.5% 60 minutes or more (2000)

Martin County

Located in southeastern Florida; bounded on the west by Lake Okeechobee, and on the east by the Atlantic Ocean and Jupiter Island. Covers a land area of 555.60 square miles, a water area of 197.20 square miles, and is located in the Eastern Time Zone. The county government was organized in 1925. County seat is Stuart.

Martin County is part of the Port St. Lucie-Fort Pierce, FL Metropolitan Statistical Area. The entire metro area includes: Martin County, FL; St. Lucie County, FL

Weather Station: Stuart 1 S — Elevation: 9 feet

	Jan	Feb	Mar	Apr	May	Jun	Jul	Aug	Sep	Oct	Nov	Dec
High	75	76	79	82	86	89	90	90	89	85	80	77
Low	55	55	60	64	69	73	74	74	74	70	64	58
Precip	3.1	3.4	4.6	2.8	5.4	6.9	6.3	6.4	8.2	6.4	4.2	2.7
Snow	0.0	0.0	0.0	0.0	0.0	0.0	0.0	0.0	0.0	0.0	0.0	0.0

High and Low temperatures in degrees Fahrenheit; Precipitation and Snow in inches

Population: 100,900 (1990); 126,731 (2000); 135,577 (2004); 146,737 (2009 projected); Race: 89.7% White, 5.0% Black, 0.6% Asian, 8.2% Hispanic of any race (2004); Density: 244.0 persons per square mile (2004); Average household size: 2.28 (2004); Median age: 47.9 (2004); Male/female ratio: 96.6 (2004).
Religion: Five largest groups: 28.0% Catholic Church, 3.8% The United Methodist Church, 3.2% Southern Baptist Convention, 2.9% Episcopal Church, 1.7% Jewish Estimate (2000).
Economy: Unemployment rate: 5.4% (2004); Total civilian labor force: 58,047 (2004); Leading industries: 20.2% retail trade; 14.9% health care and social assistance; 11.4% accommodation & food services (2003); Companies that employ 500 or more persons: 4 (2003); Companies that employ 100 to 499 persons: 71 (2003); Companies that employ less than 100 persons: 4,542 (2003); Farms: 418 totaling 206,198 acres (2002); Minority business ownership rate: 3.2% (1997); Women business ownership rate: 25.9% (1997); Retail sales per capita: $12,779 (1997).

Single-family building permits issued: 1,243 (2004); Multi-family building permits issued: 216 (2004).
Income: Per capita income: $31,749 (2004); Median household income: $47,285 (2004); Average household income: $71,374 (2004); Percent of households with income of $100,000 or more: 18.2% (2004); Poverty rate: 9.0% (2002); Bankruptcy rate: 2.47% (2004).
Taxes: Total county taxes per capita: $875 (2002); County property taxes per capita: $830 (2002).
Education: Percent of population age 25 and over with: High school diploma (including GED) or higher: 85.5% (2004); Bachelor's degree or higher: 26.6% (2004); Master's degree or higher: 9.0% (2004).
Housing: Homeownership rate: 80.2% (2004); Median home value: $156,590 (2004); Median rent: $557 per month (2000); Median age of housing: 18 years (2000).
Health: Birth rate: 89.7 per 10,000 population (2004); Death rate: 112.7 per 10,000 population (2004); Age adjusted cancer mortality rate: 184.6 deaths per 100,000 population (2002); Number of physicians: 29.1 per 10,000 population (2001); Hospital beds: 23.4 per 10,000 population (2002); Hospital admissions: 1,273.5 per 10,000 population (2002).
Elections: 2004 Presidential election results: 57.1% Bush, 41.7% Kerry, 0.6% Nader, 0.2% Badnarik
National and State Parks: Hobe Sound National Wildlife Refuge; Jonathan Dickinson State Park; Saint Lucie Inlet Preserve State Park; Seabranch Preserve State Park
Additional Information Contacts
Martin County Government Offices . . . . (561) 288-5420
Hobe Sound Chamber of Commerce. . . . . (561) 546-4724
Indiantown Chamber of Commerce . . . . (772) 597-3987
Jensen Beach Chamber of Commerce . . . . (772) 334-3444
Palm City Chamber of Commerce . . . . (561) 286-8121
Realtor Association of Martin County. . . . . (561) 627-4548
Stuart Chamber of Commerce . . . . (772) 287-1088

Martin County Communities

HOBE SOUND (CDP). Covers a land area of 5.462 square miles and a water area of 0.265 square miles. Located at 27.07° N. Lat.; 80.14° W. Long. Elevation is 24 feet.
Population: 11,507 (1990); 11,376 (2000); 11,480 (2004); 11,698 (2009 projected); Race: 92.5% White, 5.3% Black, 0.6% Asian, 2.3% Hispanic of any race (2004); Density: 2,101.8 persons per square mile (2004); Average household size: 2.18 (2004); Median age: 51.6 (2004); Male/female ratio: 93.6 (2004); Marriage status: 14.5% never married, 62.4% now married, 11.5% widowed, 11.6% divorced (2000); Foreign born: 4.8% (2000); Ancestry (includes multiple ancestries): 17.6% German, 15.1% Irish, 14.1% English, 11.1% Other groups, 8.6% United States or American (2000).
Economy: Resort town. Employment by occupation: 15.4% management, 15.2% professional, 21.9% services, 25.2% sales, 0.7% farming, 11.7% construction, 9.9% production (2000).
Income: Per capita income: $23,529 (2004); Median household income: $39,464 (2004); Average household income: $50,621 (2004); Percent of households with income of $100,000 or more: 10.8% (2004); Poverty rate: 5.5% (2000).
Education: Percent of population age 25 and over with: High school diploma (including GED) or higher: 82.8% (2004); Bachelor's degree or higher: 23.3% (2004); Master's degree or higher: 8.0% (2004).

School District(s)

Martin County School District (PK-12)
2002-03 Enrollment: 17,259 . . . . (772) 219-1200

Four-year College(s)

Hobe Sound Bible College
2003-04 Enrollment: 128 . . . . (772) 546-5534
2003-04 Tuition: In-state $4,240; Out-of-state $4,240
Housing: Homeownership rate: 80.9% (2004); Median home value: $127,676 (2004); Median rent: $529 per month (2000); Median age of housing: 18 years (2000).
Transportation: Commute to work: 89.0% car, 0.0% public transportation, 2.7% walk, 4.3% work from home (2000); Travel time to work: 36.2% less than 15 minutes, 29.9% 15 to 30 minutes, 19.8% 30 to 45 minutes, 7.3% 45 to 60 minutes, 6.7% 60 minutes or more (2000)
Additional Information Contacts
Hobe Sound Chamber of Commerce. . . . . (561) 546-4724

INDIANTOWN (CDP). Covers a land area of 5.969 square miles and a water area of 0 square miles. Located at 27.02° N. Lat.; 80.47° W. Long. Elevation is 30 feet.
Population: 4,794 (1990); 5,588 (2000); 5,699 (2004); 5,871 (2009 projected); Race: 45.7% White, 18.4% Black, 0.2% Asian, 50.8% Hispanic of any race (2004); Density: 954.8 persons per square mile (2004); Average household size: 3.44 (2004); Median age: 29.7 (2004); Male/female ratio: 121.9 (2004); Marriage status: 31.1% never married, 54.5% now married, 5.7% widowed, 8.6% divorced (2000); Foreign born: 32.1% (2000); Ancestry (includes multiple ancestries): 52.1% Other groups, 4.8% United States or American, 4.1% English, 4.0% Irish, 3.7% German (2000).
Economy: Manufacturing includes flour, concrete, beverages, and building equipment. Employment by occupation: 6.1% management, 9.8% professional, 31.3% services, 13.6% sales, 9.9% farming, 12.6% construction, 16.8% production (2000).
Income: Per capita income: $10,976 (2004); Median household income: $30,657 (2004); Average household income: $37,798 (2004); Percent of households with income of $100,000 or more: 2.4% (2004); Poverty rate: 23.8% (2000).
Education: Percent of population age 25 and over with: High school diploma (including GED) or higher: 52.1% (2004); Bachelor's degree or higher: 9.8% (2004); Master's degree or higher: 4.6% (2004).

School District(s)

Martin County School District (PK-12)
2002-03 Enrollment: 17,259 . . . . (772) 219-1200
Housing: Homeownership rate: 65.9% (2004); Median home value: $93,014 (2004); Median rent: $389 per month (2000); Median age of housing: 19 years (2000).
Transportation: Commute to work: 87.7% car, 2.9% public transportation, 0.0% walk, 1.8% work from home (2000); Travel time to work: 25.2% less than 15 minutes, 23.0% 15 to 30 minutes, 22.2% 30 to 45 minutes, 14.0% 45 to 60 minutes, 15.6% 60 minutes or more (2000)
Additional Information Contacts
Indiantown Chamber of Commerce . . . . (772) 597-3987

JENSEN BEACH (CDP). Covers a land area of 7.246 square miles and a water area of 0.880 square miles. Located at 27.23° N. Lat.; 80.23° W. Long. Elevation is 8 feet.
Population: 10,320 (1990); 11,100 (2000); 11,463 (2004); 11,962 (2009 projected); Race: 95.5% White, 2.3% Black, 0.4% Asian, 3.0% Hispanic of any race (2004); Density: 1,581.9 persons per square mile (2004); Average household size: 2.17 (2004); Median age: 44.9 (2004); Male/female ratio: 94.6 (2004); Marriage status: 18.1% never married, 57.5% now married, 10.5% widowed, 13.9% divorced (2000); Foreign born: 4.5% (2000); Ancestry (includes multiple ancestries): 20.9% German, 19.9% Irish, 17.2% English, 12.8% Italian, 9.5% Other groups (2000).
Economy: Employment by occupation: 14.4% management, 16.2% professional, 20.1% services, 26.9% sales, 0.5% farming, 13.2% construction, 8.7% production (2000).
Income: Per capita income: $24,949 (2004); Median household income: $40,953 (2004); Average household income: $53,693 (2004); Percent of households with income of $100,000 or more: 10.0% (2004); Poverty rate: 8.3% (2000).
Education: Percent of population age 25 and over with: High school diploma (including GED) or higher: 86.4% (2004); Bachelor's degree or higher: 19.8% (2004); Master's degree or higher: 5.7% (2004).

School District(s)

Martin County School District (PK-12)
2002-03 Enrollment: 17,259 . . . . (772) 219-1200
Housing: Homeownership rate: 76.2% (2004); Median home value: $122,248 (2004); Median rent: $518 per month (2000); Median age of housing: 22 years (2000).
Transportation: Commute to work: 94.1% car, 0.4% public transportation, 0.9% walk, 3.4% work from home (2000); Travel time to work: 29.6% less than 15 minutes, 43.3% 15 to 30 minutes, 15.1% 30 to 45 minutes, 5.4% 45 to 60 minutes, 6.6% 60 minutes or more (2000)
Additional Information Contacts
Jensen Beach Chamber of Commerce . . . . (772) 334-3444

JUPITER ISLAND (town). Covers a land area of 2.719 square miles and a water area of 0.900 square miles. Located at 27.05° N. Lat.; 80.11° W. Long. Elevation is 20 feet.

Population: 549 (1990); 620 (2000); 660 (2004); 711 (2009 projected); Race: 94.4% White, 1.1% Black, 0.0% Asian, 5.6% Hispanic of any race (2004); Density: 242.7 persons per square mile (2004); Average household size: 2.14 (2004); Median age: 60.8 (2004); Male/female ratio: 84.4 (2004); Marriage status: 15.2% never married, 59.5% now married, 15.8% widowed, 9.5% divorced (2000); Foreign born: 25.8% (2000); Ancestry (includes multiple ancestries): 28.5% English, 13.2% Irish, 11.1% Other groups, 6.3% German, 5.6% Portuguese (2000).
Economy: Single-family building permits issued: 12 (2004); Multi-family building permits issued: 0 (2004); Employment by occupation: 29.5% management, 13.8% professional, 40.7% services, 11.3% sales, 3.3% farming, 1.1% construction, 0.4% production (2000).
Income: Per capita income: $156,396 (2004); Median household income: $381,944 (2004); Average household income: $318,101 (2004); Percent of households with income of $100,000 or more: 75.0% (2004); Poverty rate: 8.1% (2000).
Taxes: Total city taxes per capita: $5,406 (2002); City property taxes per capita: $4,232 (2002).
Education: Percent of population age 25 and over with: High school diploma (including GED) or higher: 95.0% (2004); Bachelor's degree or higher: 48.2% (2004); Master's degree or higher: 15.5% (2004).
Housing: Homeownership rate: 91.9% (2004); Median home value: $1 million+ (2004); Median rent: $617 per month (2000); Median age of housing: 25 years (2000).
Safety: Violent crime rate: 15.6 per 10,000 population; Property crime rate: 545.2 per 10,000 population (2003).
Transportation: Commute to work: 23.6% car, 1.5% public transportation, 28.2% walk, 37.5% work from home (2000); Travel time to work: 50.6% less than 15 minutes, 30.2% 15 to 30 minutes, 6.2% 30 to 45 minutes, 4.3% 45 to 60 minutes, 8.6% 60 minutes or more (2000)

NORTH RIVER SHORES (CDP). Covers a land area of 1.300 square miles and a water area of 0.629 square miles. Located at 27.22° N. Lat.; 80.27° W. Long. Elevation is 12 feet.
Population: 3,238 (1990); 3,101 (2000); 3,039 (2004); 2,973 (2009 projected); Race: 97.7% White, 0.5% Black, 0.6% Asian, 2.0% Hispanic of any race (2004); Density: 2,338.1 persons per square mile (2004); Average household size: 2.17 (2004); Median age: 49.8 (2004); Male/female ratio: 90.3 (2004); Marriage status: 15.2% never married, 62.7% now married, 9.8% widowed, 12.3% divorced (2000); Foreign born: 2.8% (2000); Ancestry (includes multiple ancestries): 27.1% German, 20.3% Irish, 18.5% English, 14.9% Italian, 4.9% Other groups (2000).
Economy: Employment by occupation: 13.8% management, 26.6% professional, 16.5% services, 28.6% sales, 0.0% farming, 9.9% construction, 4.7% production (2000).
Income: Per capita income: $30,588 (2004); Median household income: $45,558 (2004); Average household income: $65,852 (2004); Percent of households with income of $100,000 or more: 17.7% (2004); Poverty rate: 5.3% (2000).
Education: Percent of population age 25 and over with: High school diploma (including GED) or higher: 89.3% (2004); Bachelor's degree or higher: 25.5% (2004); Master's degree or higher: 9.7% (2004).
Housing: Homeownership rate: 83.7% (2004); Median home value: $132,782 (2004); Median rent: $590 per month (2000); Median age of housing: 25 years (2000).
Transportation: Commute to work: 87.3% car, 0.5% public transportation, 1.7% walk, 8.2% work from home (2000); Travel time to work: 38.3% less than 15 minutes, 41.2% 15 to 30 minutes, 10.2% 30 to 45 minutes, 4.8% 45 to 60 minutes, 5.5% 60 minutes or more (2000)

OCEAN BREEZE PARK (town). Covers a land area of 0.171 square miles and a water area of 0.039 square miles. Located at 27.24° N. Lat.; 80.22° W. Long. Elevation is 25 feet.
Population: 519 (1990); 463 (2000); 482 (2004); 508 (2009 projected); Race: 98.5% White, 1.0% Black, 0.0% Asian, 0.8% Hispanic of any race (2004); Density: 2,817.6 persons per square mile (2004); Average household size: 1.38 (2004); Median age: 70.6 (2004); Male/female ratio: 83.3 (2004); Marriage status: 8.2% never married, 41.2% now married, 27.7% widowed, 22.8% divorced (2000); Foreign born: 4.4% (2000); Ancestry (includes multiple ancestries): 23.1% English, 20.4% German, 14.2% Irish, 8.9% United States or American, 4.9% Italian (2000).
Economy: Single-family building permits issued: 0 (2004); Multi-family building permits issued: 0 (2004); Employment by occupation: 8.2% management, 9.4% professional, 24.7% services, 29.4% sales, 0.0% farming, 8.2% construction, 20.0% production (2000).
Income: Per capita income: $18,257 (2004); Median household income: $17,340 (2004); Average household income: $25,143 (2004); Percent of households with income of $100,000 or more: 3.1% (2004); Poverty rate: 15.3% (2000).
Education: Percent of population age 25 and over with: High school diploma (including GED) or higher: 76.2% (2004); Bachelor's degree or higher: 15.9% (2004); Master's degree or higher: 4.4% (2004).
Housing: Homeownership rate: 90.6% (2004); Median home value: $19,999 (2004); Median rent: $241 per month (2000); Median age of housing: 34 years (2000).
Transportation: Commute to work: 84.3% car, 0.0% public transportation, 13.3% walk, 0.0% work from home (2000); Travel time to work: 33.7% less than 15 minutes, 48.2% 15 to 30 minutes, 13.3% 30 to 45 minutes, 0.0% 45 to 60 minutes, 4.8% 60 minutes or more (2000)

PALM CITY (CDP). Covers a land area of 14.634 square miles and a water area of 1.949 square miles. Located at 27.17° N. Lat.; 80.27° W. Long. Elevation is 5 feet.
Population: 11,139 (1990); 20,097 (2000); 23,343 (2004); 27,204 (2009 projected); Race: 96.1% White, 1.4% Black, 1.1% Asian, 3.0% Hispanic of any race (2004); Density: 1,595.2 persons per square mile (2004); Average household size: 2.36 (2004); Median age: 47.6 (2004); Male/female ratio: 92.2 (2004); Marriage status: 11.3% never married, 71.9% now married, 7.5% widowed, 9.4% divorced (2000); Foreign born: 5.6% (2000); Ancestry (includes multiple ancestries): 19.1% German, 17.3% Irish, 16.8% English, 14.9% Italian, 7.8% United States or American (2000).
Economy: Manufacturing includes medical laboratory instruments, water chlorination equipment, cable assemblies, resins. Employment by occupation: 17.9% management, 24.1% professional, 14.3% services, 32.4% sales, 0.2% farming, 6.1% construction, 5.0% production (2000).
Income: Per capita income: $39,207 (2004); Median household income: $68,291 (2004); Average household income: $91,927 (2004); Percent of households with income of $100,000 or more: 29.2% (2004); Poverty rate: 3.7% (2000).
Education: Percent of population age 25 and over with: High school diploma (including GED) or higher: 93.5% (2004); Bachelor's degree or higher: 35.8% (2004); Master's degree or higher: 11.6% (2004).

School District(s)

Martin County School District (PK-12)
2002-03 Enrollment: 17,259 . . . . (772) 219-1200
Housing: Homeownership rate: 86.2% (2004); Median home value: $240,557 (2004); Median rent: $817 per month (2000); Median age of housing: 11 years (2000).
Transportation: Commute to work: 92.4% car, 0.4% public transportation, 0.6% walk, 5.5% work from home (2000); Travel time to work: 27.5% less than 15 minutes, 43.2% 15 to 30 minutes, 16.4% 30 to 45 minutes, 5.8% 45 to 60 minutes, 7.2% 60 minutes or more (2000)

Additional Information Contacts

Palm City Chamber of Commerce . . . . (561) 286-8121

PORT SALERNO (CDP). Aka Salerno. Covers a land area of 3.618 square miles and a water area of 0.399 square miles. Located at 27.14° N. Lat.; 80.19° W. Long. Elevation is 14 feet.
Population: 7,786 (1990); 10,141 (2000); 10,801 (2004); 11,642 (2009 projected); Race: 88.6% White, 6.6% Black, 0.8% Asian, 9.2% Hispanic of any race (2004); Density: 2,985.6 persons per square mile (2004); Average household size: 2.24 (2004); Median age: 45.0 (2004); Male/female ratio: 92.9 (2004); Marriage status: 16.7% never married, 62.1% now married, 9.1% widowed, 12.1% divorced (2000); Foreign born: 6.5% (2000); Ancestry (includes multiple ancestries): 18.6% German, 17.5% Other groups, 17.1% Irish, 15.3% English, 9.5% Italian (2000).
Economy: Manufacturing includes marine hardware, tuna boat towers, machinery. Employment by occupation: 14.3% management, 14.2% professional, 19.3% services, 27.6% sales, 0.8% farming, 13.9% construction, 10.0% production (2000).
Income: Per capita income: $27,215 (2004); Median household income: $40,930 (2004); Average household income: $60,383 (2004); Percent of households with income of $100,000 or more: 13.7% (2004); Poverty rate: 9.6% (2000).
Education: Percent of population age 25 and over with: High school diploma (including GED) or higher: 85.3% (2004); Bachelor's degree or higher: 21.6% (2004); Master's degree or higher: 5.6% (2004).
Housing: Homeownership rate: 73.6% (2004); Median home value: $137,542 (2004); Median rent: $559 per month (2000); Median age of housing: 18 years (2000).

Transportation: Commute to work: 93.8% car, 0.6% public transportation, 1.0% walk, 2.9% work from home (2000); Travel time to work: 28.0% less than 15 minutes, 38.8% 15 to 30 minutes, 21.6% 30 to 45 minutes, 5.7% 45 to 60 minutes, 5.9% 60 minutes or more (2000)

RIO (CDP). Covers a land area of 0.400 square miles and a water area of 0.507 square miles. Located at 27.21° N. Lat.; 80.24° W. Long. Elevation is 9 feet.

Population: 1,054 (1990); 1,028 (2000); 966 (2004); 946 (2009 projected); Race: 98.2% White, 0.5% Black, 0.3% Asian, 1.8% Hispanic of any race (2004); Density: 2,413.6 persons per square mile (2004); Average household size: 2.07 (2004); Median age: 47.7 (2004); Male/female ratio: 100.4 (2004); Marriage status: 20.5% never married, 56.5% now married, 8.2% widowed, 14.7% divorced (2000); Foreign born: 1.0% (2000); Ancestry (includes multiple ancestries): 28.8% German, 16.4% Irish, 14.8% English, 13.3% Italian, 5.9% Dutch (2000).

Economy: Employment by occupation: 11.1% management, 30.2% professional, 19.1% services, 14.1% sales, 1.9% farming, 14.9% construction, 8.6% production (2000).

Income: Per capita income: $30,479 (2004); Median household income: $45,568 (2004); Average household income: $63,181 (2004); Percent of households with income of $100,000 or more: 13.3% (2004); Poverty rate: 11.9% (2000).

Education: Percent of population age 25 and over with: High school diploma (including GED) or higher: 85.3% (2004); Bachelor's degree or higher: 32.9% (2004); Master's degree or higher: 11.4% (2004).

Housing: Homeownership rate: 76.6% (2004); Median home value: $124,500 (2004); Median rent: $375 per month (2000); Median age of housing: 19 years (2000).

Transportation: Commute to work: 89.3% car, 0.0% public transportation, 0.0% walk, 5.8% work from home (2000); Travel time to work: 35.1% less than 15 minutes, 53.5% 15 to 30 minutes, 5.8% 30 to 45 minutes, 0.0% 45 to 60 minutes, 5.6% 60 minutes or more (2000)

SEWALL'S POINT (town). Covers a land area of 1.233 square miles and a water area of 2.903 square miles. Located at 27.19° N. Lat.; 80.19° W. Long.

Population: 1,588 (1990); 1,946 (2000); 2,166 (2004); 2,420 (2009 projected); Race: 98.7% White, 0.6% Black, 0.4% Asian, 1.7% Hispanic of any race (2004); Density: 1,756.6 persons per square mile (2004); Average household size: 2.59 (2004); Median age: 46.7 (2004); Male/female ratio: 98.4 (2004); Marriage status: 12.0% never married, 77.1% now married, 4.2% widowed, 6.7% divorced (2000); Foreign born: 6.5% (2000); Ancestry (includes multiple ancestries): 20.8% Irish, 20.1% German, 19.3% English, 13.8% Italian, 6.1% Other groups (2000).

Economy: Single-family building permits issued: 10 (2004); Multi-family building permits issued: 0 (2004); Employment by occupation: 25.3% management, 34.4% professional, 8.1% services, 25.1% sales, 0.0% farming, 2.4% construction, 4.7% production (2000).

Income: Per capita income: $54,897 (2004); Median household income: $98,136 (2004); Average household income: $142,064 (2004); Percent of households with income of $100,000 or more: 49.0% (2004); Poverty rate: 4.3% (2000).

Taxes: Total city taxes per capita: $661 (2002); City property taxes per capita: $316 (2002).

Education: Percent of population age 25 and over with: High school diploma (including GED) or higher: 96.6% (2004); Bachelor's degree or higher: 59.8% (2004); Master's degree or higher: 26.1% (2004).

Housing: Homeownership rate: 94.9% (2004); Median home value: $454,286 (2004); Median rent: $1,792 per month (2000); Median age of housing: 19 years (2000).

Safety: Violent crime rate: 0.0 per 10,000 population; Property crime rate: 57.7 per 10,000 population (2003).

Transportation: Commute to work: 88.2% car, 0.0% public transportation, 0.3% walk, 9.9% work from home (2000); Travel time to work: 37.3% less than 15 minutes, 34.9% 15 to 30 minutes, 9.4% 30 to 45 minutes, 8.6% 45 to 60 minutes, 9.8% 60 minutes or more (2000)

STUART (city). Covers a land area of 6.306 square miles and a water area of 2.220 square miles. Located at 27.19° N. Lat.; 80.24° W. Long. Elevation is 10 feet.

History: Stuart developed as a fishing center, with shark fishing predominating. All parts of the shark were valuable, the flesh, hides, teeth, bones, livers, fins, and eyes each having a market. Tiger, sand, nurse, hammerhead, and shovel-nose sharks were found in the waters here.

Population: 13,235 (1990); 14,633 (2000); 14,806 (2004); 15,107 (2009 projected); Race: 82.9% White, 12.0% Black, 0.6% Asian, 7.3% Hispanic of any race (2004); Density: 2,348.0 persons per square mile (2004); Average household size: 2.02 (2004); Median age: 49.0 (2004); Male/female ratio: 88.6 (2004); Marriage status: 21.6% never married, 46.6% now married, 16.5% widowed, 15.3% divorced (2000); Foreign born: 8.0% (2000); Ancestry (includes multiple ancestries): 19.5% Other groups, 15.7% Irish, 14.7% German, 14.2% English, 9.9% Italian (2000).

Economy: Single-family building permits issued: 71 (2004); Multi-family building permits issued: 38 (2004); Employment by occupation: 10.2% management, 19.4% professional, 19.8% services, 28.6% sales, 0.7% farming, 10.0% construction, 11.2% production (2000).

Income: Per capita income: $22,457 (2004); Median household income: $31,842 (2004); Average household income: $42,298 (2004); Percent of households with income of $100,000 or more: 6.4% (2004); Poverty rate: 11.2% (2000).

Education: Percent of population age 25 and over with: High school diploma (including GED) or higher: 81.0% (2004); Bachelor's degree or higher: 21.6% (2004); Master's degree or higher: 8.0% (2004).

School District(s)

Martin County School District (PK-12)
2002-03 Enrollment: 17,259 . . . . (772) 219-1200

Housing: Homeownership rate: 62.1% (2004); Median home value: $96,872 (2004); Median rent: $576 per month (2000); Median age of housing: 24 years (2000).

Hospitals: Martin Memorial Medical Center (336 beds)

Safety: Violent crime rate: 61.2 per 10,000 population; Property crime rate: 586.2 per 10,000 population (2003).

Newspapers: Flashes (General - Circulation 60,000); The Stuart News (Circulation 41,170)

Transportation: Commute to work: 91.5% car, 0.6% public transportation, 2.5% walk, 3.3% work from home (2000); Travel time to work: 43.5% less than 15 minutes, 28.9% 15 to 30 minutes, 16.8% 30 to 45 minutes, 5.0% 45 to 60 minutes, 5.9% 60 minutes or more (2000)

Airports: Witham Field

Additional Information Contacts

Realtor Association of Martin County. . . . . (561) 627-4548
Stuart Chamber of Commerce . . . . (772) 287-1088

Miami-Dade County

Covers a land area of 1,946.10 square miles, a water area of 485.20 square miles, and is located in the Eastern Time Zone. The county government was organized in 1836. County seat is Miami.

Miami-Dade County is part of the Miami-Fort Lauderdale-Miami Beach, FL Metropolitan Statistical Area. The entire metro area includes: Fort Lauderdale-Pompano Beach-Deerfield Beach, FL Metropolitan Division (Broward County, FL); Miami-Miami Beach-Kendall, FL Metropolitan Division (Miami-Dade County, FL); West Palm Beach-Boca Raton-Boynton Beach, FL Metropolitan Division (Palm Beach County, FL)

Weather Station: Hialeah — Elevation: 9 feet

	Jan	Feb	Mar	Apr	May	Jun	Jul	Aug	Sep	Oct	Nov	Dec
High	77	78	81	83	87	89	91	91	89	86	82	78
Low	58	59	64	67	71	75	76	76	75	71	67	61
Precip	2.5	2.3	3.2	3.8	6.3	10.4	7.0	9.0	8.9	6.4	3.8	2.4
Snow	0.0	0.0	0.0	0.0	0.0	0.0	0.0	0.0	0.0	0.0	0.0	0.0

High and Low temperatures in degrees Fahrenheit; Precipitation and Snow in inches

Weather Station: Miami Beach — Elevation: 3 feet

	Jan	Feb	Mar	Apr	May	Jun	Jul	Aug	Sep	Oct	Nov	Dec
High	74	75	77	79	83	86	87	88	86	83	79	76
Low	63	64	67	70	74	77	78	79	78	75	70	66
Precip	2.5	2.2	2.2	2.7	5.0	6.9	3.3	5.2	6.9	4.6	3.4	2.0
Snow	0.0	0.0	0.0	0.0	0.0	0.0	0.0	0.0	0.0	0.0	0.0	0.0

High and Low temperatures in degrees Fahrenheit; Precipitation and Snow in inches

Weather Station: Miami Int'l Airport — Elevation: 32 feet

	Jan	Feb	Mar	Apr	May	Jun	Jul	Aug	Sep	Oct	Nov	Dec
High	76	77	80	83	86	88	90	90	88	85	81	77
Low	60	61	65	68	72	76	77	77	76	73	68	63
Precip	2.0	2.1	2.6	3.3	5.8	8.6	5.8	8.5	8.3	5.7	3.4	2.0
Snow	0.0	0.0	0.0	0.0	tr	0.0	0.0	0.0	0.0	0.0	0.0	0.0

High and Low temperatures in degrees Fahrenheit; Precipitation and Snow in inches

Weather Station: Tamiami Trail 40 Mile Bend Elevation: 13 feet

	Jan	Feb	Mar	Apr	May	Jun	Jul	Aug	Sep	Oct	Nov	Dec
High	78	79	82	86	89	91	92	92	91	87	83	79
Low	57	57	60	63	67	72	74	75	75	71	65	59
Precip	1.9	2.0	2.3	2.4	5.0	8.5	7.6	6.9	6.6	4.5	2.3	1.6
Snow	0.0	0.0	0.0	0.0	0.0	0.0	0.0	0.0	0.0	0.0	0.0	0.0

High and Low temperatures in degrees Fahrenheit; Precipitation and Snow in inches

Population: 1,937,094 (1990); 2,253,362 (2000); 2,376,330 (2004); 2,531,816 (2009 projected); Race: 69.6% White, 20.0% Black, 1.3% Asian, 61.2% Hispanic of any race (2004); Density: 1,221.1 persons per square mile (2004); Average household size: 2.92 (2004); Median age: 37.0 (2004); Male/female ratio: 94.0 (2004).
Religion: Five largest groups: 24.1% Catholic Church, 5.5% Jewish Estimate, 3.6% Southern Baptist Convention, 0.8% Seventh-day Adventist Church, 0.8% The United Methodist Church (2000).
Economy: Unemployment rate: 5.6% (2004); Total civilian labor force: 1,107,950 (2004); Leading industries: 13.3% retail trade; 12.3% health care and social assistance; 10.3% accommodation & food services (2003); Companies that employ 500 or more persons: 113 (2003); Companies that employ 100 to 499 persons: 1,131 (2003); Companies that employ less than 100 persons: 69,443 (2003); Farms: 2,244 totaling 90,373 acres (2002); Minority business ownership rate: 58.2% (1997); Women business ownership rate: 23.6% (1997); Retail sales per capita: $9,718 (1997). Single-family building permits issued: 9,603 (2004); Multi-family building permits issued: 13,253 (2004).
Income: Per capita income: $19,859 (2004); Median household income: $38,537 (2004); Average household income: $57,143 (2004); Percent of households with income of $100,000 or more: 12.9% (2004); Poverty rate: 19.2% (2002); Bankruptcy rate: 5.54% (2004).
Taxes: Total county taxes per capita: $600 (2002); County property taxes per capita: $399 (2002).
Education: Percent of population age 25 and over with: High school diploma (including GED) or higher: 68.1% (2004); Bachelor's degree or higher: 21.8% (2004); Master's degree or higher: 9.4% (2004).
Housing: Homeownership rate: 58.0% (2004); Median home value: $159,022 (2004); Median rent: $572 per month (2000); Median age of housing: 27 years (2000).
Health: Birth rate: 146.1 per 10,000 population (2004); Death rate: 78.2 per 10,000 population (2004); Age adjusted cancer mortality rate: 162.3 deaths per 100,000 population (2002); Air Quality Index: 88.5% good, 10.7% moderate, 0.5% unhealthy for sensitive individuals, 0.3% unhealthy (percent of days in 2004); Number of physicians: 34.8 per 10,000 population (2001); Hospital beds: 38.3 per 10,000 population (2002); Hospital admissions: 1,493.3 per 10,000 population (2002).
Elections: 2004 Presidential election results: 46.6% Bush, 52.9% Kerry, 0.3% Nader, 0.1% Badnarik
National and State Parks: Bill Baggs Cape Florida State Park; Biscayne National Park; Grossman Hammock State Park; Oleta River State Park; The Barnacle Historic State Park
Additional Information Contacts
Miami-Dade County Government Offices . . . . (305) 375-5124
Allapattah Chamber of Commerce. . . . . (305) 638-0280
Argentine Florida Chamber . . . . (305) 858-1516
Aventura Chamber of Commerce . . . . (305) 935-2131
Brazilian-American Chamber. . . . . (305) 579-9030
British American Chamber of Commerce . . . . (305) 377-0992
Central America Us Chamber . . . . (305) 569-9113
Chile-US Chamber of Commerce . . . . (305) 447-0908
Coconut Grove Chamber of Commerce . . . . (305) 444-7270
Colombian American Chamber . . . . (305) 446-2542
Coral Gables Chamber of Commerce . . . . (305) 446-1657
Doral-Airport West Chamber . . . . (305) 592-5141
Ecuadorian-American Chamber. . . . . (305) 539-0010
Florida Gold Coast Chamber. . . . . (305) 866-6020
French-American Chamber of Commerce. . . . . (305) 442-2277
Greater Miami Chamber of Commerce . . . . (305) 350-7700
Greater Miami Convention & Visitors Bureau . . . . (305) 539-3000
Greater Miami Shores Chamber . . . . (305) 754-5466
Greater North Miami Chamber. . . . . (305) 891-7811
Homestead-Florida City Chamber . . . . (305) 247-2332
Italy America Chamber of Commerce . . . . (305) 577-9868
Key Biscayne Chamber of Commerce. . . . . (305) 361-5207
Korean American Chamber of Commerce. . . . . (305) 468-1718
Latin Chamber of Commerce. . . . . (305) 642-3870
Miami Beach Chamber of Commerce . . . . (305) 672-1270
Miami International Chamber. . . . . (305) 861-2000
Miami-Dade Chamber of Commerce . . . . (305) 751-8648
Nicaraguan-American Chamber of Commerce . . . . (305) 599-2737
North Dade Chamber of Commerce . . . . (305) 690-9123
North Miami Beach Chamber of Commerce . . . . (305) 944-8500
Northwestern Dade Association of Realtors . . . . (305) 557-1400
Peruvian U.S. Chamber of Commerce . . . . (305) 471-9434
Puerto Rico Convention Bureau . . . . (305) 471-0202
Realtor Association of Greater Miami & The Beaches. . . . . (305) 468-7000
Realtor Association of Miami-Dade County . . . . (305) 444-6528
South Beach Hispanic Chamber . . . . (305) 534-1903
South Miami Chamber of Commerce. . . . . (305) 661-1621
Swedish American Chamber of Commerce. . . . . (305) 443-3558
United States-Mexico Chamber of Commerce . . . . (305) 379-6090
Venezuelan American Chamber . . . . (305) 444-4336
Women's Chamber of Commerce . . . . (305) 446-6660

Miami-Dade County Communities

ANDOVER (CDP). Covers a land area of 1.676 square miles and a water area of 0.112 square miles. Located at 25.96° N. Lat.; 80.20° W. Long.
Population: 6,251 (1990); 8,489 (2000); 9,085 (2004); 9,835 (2009 projected); Race: 20.5% White, 72.2% Black, 0.9% Asian, 17.5% Hispanic of any race (2004); Density: 5,420.0 persons per square mile (2004); Average household size: 2.47 (2004); Median age: 35.0 (2004); Male/female ratio: 79.3 (2004); Marriage status: 32.7% never married, 42.9% now married, 7.6% widowed, 16.8% divorced (2000); Foreign born: 35.8% (2000); Ancestry (includes multiple ancestries): 45.7% Other groups, 16.6% Jamaican, 6.3% Haitian, 4.2% United States or American, 3.4% Bahamian (2000).
Economy: Employment by occupation: 11.2% management, 20.1% professional, 17.3% services, 32.6% sales, 0.1% farming, 8.4% construction, 10.3% production (2000).
Income: Per capita income: $17,001 (2004); Median household income: $31,275 (2004); Average household income: $41,753 (2004); Percent of households with income of $100,000 or more: 5.6% (2004); Poverty rate: 15.8% (2000).
Education: Percent of population age 25 and over with: High school diploma (including GED) or higher: 75.3% (2004); Bachelor's degree or higher: 15.9% (2004); Master's degree or higher: 4.9% (2004).
Housing: Homeownership rate: 48.5% (2004); Median home value: $104,337 (2004); Median rent: $541 per month (2000); Median age of housing: 25 years (2000).
Transportation: Commute to work: 91.1% car, 6.6% public transportation, 0.9% walk, 0.3% work from home (2000); Travel time to work: 9.7% less than 15 minutes, 40.4% 15 to 30 minutes, 30.2% 30 to 45 minutes, 10.1% 45 to 60 minutes, 9.7% 60 minutes or more (2000)

AVENTURA (city). Covers a land area of 2.704 square miles and a water area of 0.806 square miles. Located at 25.96° N. Lat.; 80.13° W. Long.
Population: 15,376 (1990); 25,267 (2000); 27,734 (2004); 30,768 (2009 projected); Race: 92.6% White, 2.1% Black, 1.3% Asian, 26.8% Hispanic of any race (2004); Density: 10,257.1 persons per square mile (2004); Average household size: 1.82 (2004); Median age: 54.1 (2004); Male/female ratio: 81.0 (2004); Marriage status: 19.3% never married, 53.6% now married, 15.8% widowed, 11.3% divorced (2000); Foreign born: 36.8% (2000); Ancestry (includes multiple ancestries): 30.8% Other groups, 11.9% Russian, 8.9% United States or American, 7.5% Polish, 4.7% German (2000).
Economy: Unemployment rate: 3.7% (2004); Total civilian labor force: 6,072 (2004); Single-family building permits issued: 2 (2004); Multi-family building permits issued: 2,236 (2004); Employment by occupation: 25.4% management, 23.1% professional, 9.5% services, 36.2% sales, 0.1% farming, 2.7% construction, 2.9% production (2000).
Income: Per capita income: $42,681 (2004); Median household income: $47,695 (2004); Average household income: $77,604 (2004); Percent of households with income of $100,000 or more: 21.5% (2004); Poverty rate: 9.1% (2000).
Education: Percent of population age 25 and over with: High school diploma (including GED) or higher: 89.5% (2004); Bachelor's degree or higher: 38.9% (2004); Master's degree or higher: 16.4% (2004).

School District(s)

Miami-Dade County School District (PK-12)

2002-03 Enrollment: 373,395 . . . . (305) 995-1428

Housing: Homeownership rate: 71.6% (2004); Median home value: $154,782 (2004); Median rent: $1,145 per month (2000); Median age of housing: 15 years (2000).

Hospitals: Aventura Hospital and Medical Center (407 beds)

Safety: Violent crime rate: 20.0 per 10,000 population; Property crime rate: 817.5 per 10,000 population (2003).

Transportation: Commute to work: 89.6% car, 2.0% public transportation, 1.8% walk, 5.7% work from home (2000); Travel time to work: 22.7% less than 15 minutes, 28.4% 15 to 30 minutes, 27.1% 30 to 45 minutes, 15.2% 45 to 60 minutes, 6.7% 60 minutes or more (2000)

Additional Information Contacts

Local Government Offices . . . . (305) 466-8900

BAL HARBOUR (village). Covers a land area of 0.338 square miles and a water area of 0.251 square miles. Located at 25.89° N. Lat.; 80.12° W. Long. Elevation is 5 feet.

Population: 3,045 (1990); 3,305 (2000); 3,268 (2004); 3,260 (2009 projected); Race: 93.5% White, 1.9% Black, 0.9% Asian, 29.6% Hispanic of any race (2004); Density: 9,681.8 persons per square mile (2004); Average household size: 1.75 (2004); Median age: 56.4 (2004); Male/female ratio: 76.5 (2004); Marriage status: 14.3% never married, 53.9% now married, 19.6% widowed, 12.2% divorced (2000); Foreign born: 40.0% (2000); Ancestry (includes multiple ancestries): 30.2% Other groups, 12.0% Russian, 8.9% Polish, 6.4% Irish, 6.2% French (except Basque) (2000).

Economy: Luxury resort community just North of Miami Beach. Upscale shopping and dining area, with many exclusive retailers. Single-family building permits issued: 2 (2004); Multi-family building permits issued: 0 (2004); Employment by occupation: 33.0% management, 29.6% professional, 8.2% services, 24.6% sales, 0.0% farming, 2.2% construction, 2.4% production (2000).

Income: Per capita income: $62,450 (2004); Median household income: $54,334 (2004); Average household income: $108,366 (2004); Percent of households with income of $100,000 or more: 29.1% (2004); Poverty rate: 9.2% (2000).

Taxes: Total city taxes per capita: $1,323 (2002); City property taxes per capita: $952 (2002).

Education: Percent of population age 25 and over with: High school diploma (including GED) or higher: 89.6% (2004); Bachelor's degree or higher: 46.3% (2004); Master's degree or higher: 21.3% (2004).

Housing: Homeownership rate: 49.5% (2004); Median home value: $359,596 (2004); Median rent: $1,068 per month (2000); Median age of housing: 29 years (2000).

Safety: Violent crime rate: 6.0 per 10,000 population; Property crime rate: 229.4 per 10,000 population (2003).

Transportation: Commute to work: 78.4% car, 2.2% public transportation, 6.4% walk, 12.5% work from home (2000); Travel time to work: 27.8% less than 15 minutes, 25.7% 15 to 30 minutes, 33.7% 30 to 45 minutes, 3.0% 45 to 60 minutes, 9.8% 60 minutes or more (2000)

BAY HARBOR ISLANDS (town). Covers a land area of 0.371 square miles and a water area of 0.241 square miles. Located at 25.88° N. Lat.; 80.13° W. Long. Elevation is 5 feet.

Population: 4,703 (1990); 5,146 (2000); 5,326 (2004); 5,571 (2009 projected); Race: 89.7% White, 2.0% Black, 1.4% Asian, 44.4% Hispanic of any race (2004); Density: 14,360.7 persons per square mile (2004); Average household size: 2.01 (2004); Median age: 43.2 (2004); Male/female ratio: 81.2 (2004); Marriage status: 23.3% never married, 48.7% now married, 11.0% widowed, 17.0% divorced (2000); Foreign born: 39.3% (2000); Ancestry (includes multiple ancestries): 44.1% Other groups, 9.5% Russian, 7.4% Italian, 6.9% Polish, 6.4% German (2000).

Economy: Residential area. Single-family building permits issued: 36 (2004); Multi-family building permits issued: 7 (2004); Employment by occupation: 18.9% management, 25.5% professional, 15.3% services, 31.4% sales, 0.0% farming, 4.9% construction, 4.0% production (2000).

Income: Per capita income: $30,557 (2004); Median household income: $41,177 (2004); Average household income: $61,345 (2004); Percent of households with income of $100,000 or more: 11.9% (2004); Poverty rate: 13.1% (2000).

Education: Percent of population age 25 and over with: High school diploma (including GED) or higher: 87.7% (2004); Bachelor's degree or higher: 35.5% (2004); Master's degree or higher: 14.5% (2004).

Housing: Homeownership rate: 52.9% (2004); Median home value: $145,551 (2004); Median rent: $743 per month (2000); Median age of housing: 37 years (2000).

Safety: Violent crime rate: 46.8 per 10,000 population; Property crime rate: 243.5 per 10,000 population (2003).

Transportation: Commute to work: 84.9% car, 3.5% public transportation, 6.1% walk, 5.2% work from home (2000); Travel time to work: 18.6% less than 15 minutes, 36.4% 15 to 30 minutes, 30.4% 30 to 45 minutes, 9.2% 45 to 60 minutes, 5.5% 60 minutes or more (2000)

Additional Information Contacts

Local Government Offices . . . . (305) 866-6241

BISCAYNE PARK (village). Covers a land area of 0.635 square miles and a water area of 0 square miles. Located at 25.88° N. Lat.; 80.18° W. Long. Elevation is 5 feet.

History: Incorporated 1932.

Population: 3,068 (1990); 3,269 (2000); 3,237 (2004); 3,228 (2009 projected); Race: 67.1% White, 22.7% Black, 2.4% Asian, 31.4% Hispanic of any race (2004); Density: 5,096.6 persons per square mile (2004); Average household size: 2.58 (2004); Median age: 37.9 (2004); Male/female ratio: 94.1 (2004); Marriage status: 25.5% never married, 56.6% now married, 8.0% widowed, 9.8% divorced (2000); Foreign born: 34.6% (2000); Ancestry (includes multiple ancestries): 34.5% Other groups, 12.7% English, 10.3% Haitian, 8.0% Italian, 8.0% Irish (2000).

Economy: Single-family building permits issued: 0 (2004); Multi-family building permits issued: 0 (2004); Employment by occupation: 13.1% management, 24.5% professional, 11.7% services, 36.6% sales, 0.0% farming, 6.4% construction, 7.7% production (2000).

Income: Per capita income: $26,434 (2004); Median household income: $54,774 (2004); Average household income: $68,290 (2004); Percent of households with income of $100,000 or more: 17.3% (2004); Poverty rate: 12.0% (2000).

Education: Percent of population age 25 and over with: High school diploma (including GED) or higher: 85.4% (2004); Bachelor's degree or higher: 34.2% (2004); Master's degree or higher: 12.9% (2004).

Housing: Homeownership rate: 70.2% (2004); Median home value: $185,070 (2004); Median rent: $609 per month (2000); Median age of housing: 47 years (2000).

Safety: Violent crime rate: 27.1 per 10,000 population; Property crime rate: 376.1 per 10,000 population (2003).

Transportation: Commute to work: 93.1% car, 0.0% public transportation, 0.5% walk, 5.7% work from home (2000); Travel time to work: 20.5% less than 15 minutes, 30.5% 15 to 30 minutes, 34.5% 30 to 45 minutes, 12.1% 45 to 60 minutes, 2.4% 60 minutes or more (2000)

BROWNSVILLE (CDP). Covers a land area of 2.294 square miles and a water area of 0.003 square miles. Located at 25.82° N. Lat.; 80.24° W. Long.

Population: 15,607 (1990); 14,393 (2000); 14,318 (2004); 14,329 (2009 projected); Race: 7.0% White, 89.3% Black, 0.0% Asian, 10.3% Hispanic of any race (2004); Density: 6,242.4 persons per square mile (2004); Average household size: 2.96 (2004); Median age: 30.6 (2004); Male/female ratio: 84.4 (2004); Marriage status: 48.4% never married, 27.3% now married, 10.7% widowed, 13.6% divorced (2000); Foreign born: 9.7% (2000); Ancestry (includes multiple ancestries): 74.6% Other groups, 3.8% United States or American, 2.1% African, 1.9% Bahamian, 0.8% Jamaican (2000).

Economy: Employment by occupation: 4.3% management, 9.7% professional, 31.9% services, 27.4% sales, 0.3% farming, 10.5% construction, 15.9% production (2000).

Income: Per capita income: $9,455 (2004); Median household income: $17,450 (2004); Average household income: $27,902 (2004); Percent of households with income of $100,000 or more: 2.3% (2004); Poverty rate: 42.7% (2000).

Education: Percent of population age 25 and over with: High school diploma (including GED) or higher: 53.6% (2004); Bachelor's degree or higher: 5.0% (2004); Master's degree or higher: 2.2% (2004).

Housing: Homeownership rate: 40.7% (2004); Median home value: $86,562 (2004); Median rent: $324 per month (2000); Median age of housing: 39 years (2000).

Transportation: Commute to work: 76.6% car, 17.7% public transportation, 2.6% walk, 0.8% work from home (2000); Travel time to work: 19.6% less than 15 minutes, 31.7% 15 to 30 minutes, 23.9% 30 to 45 minutes, 11.0% 45 to 60 minutes, 13.7% 60 minutes or more (2000)

BUNCHE PARK (CDP). Covers a land area of 0.758 square miles and a water area of 0 square miles. Located at 25.92° N. Lat.; 80.23° W. Long. Elevation is 5 feet.
Population: 4,388 (1990); 3,972 (2000); 4,023 (2004); 4,110 (2009 projected); Race: 1.9% White, 95.5% Black, 0.1% Asian, 4.2% Hispanic of any race (2004); Density: 5,307.3 persons per square mile (2004); Average household size: 2.91 (2004); Median age: 38.6 (2004); Male/female ratio: 84.5 (2004); Marriage status: 31.7% never married, 39.8% now married, 15.7% widowed, 12.9% divorced (2000); Foreign born: 7.5% (2000); Ancestry (includes multiple ancestries): 72.6% Other groups, 3.3% Bahamian, 2.5% United States or American, 2.4% Haitian, 2.1% African (2000).
Economy: Employment by occupation: 6.5% management, 15.5% professional, 27.7% services, 26.5% sales, 0.0% farming, 10.3% construction, 13.4% production (2000).
Income: Per capita income: $12,472 (2004); Median household income: $26,925 (2004); Average household income: $35,963 (2004); Percent of households with income of $100,000 or more: 5.9% (2004); Poverty rate: 27.0% (2000).
Education: Percent of population age 25 and over with: High school diploma (including GED) or higher: 60.8% (2004); Bachelor's degree or higher: 8.7% (2004); Master's degree or higher: 2.4% (2004).
Housing: Homeownership rate: 80.1% (2004); Median home value: $99,111 (2004); Median rent: $583 per month (2000); Median age of housing: 44 years (2000).
Transportation: Commute to work: 87.8% car, 8.6% public transportation, 1.0% walk, 2.0% work from home (2000); Travel time to work: 15.0% less than 15 minutes, 33.8% 15 to 30 minutes, 32.0% 30 to 45 minutes, 8.8% 45 to 60 minutes, 10.4% 60 minutes or more (2000)

CAROL CITY (CDP). Covers a land area of 7.625 square miles and a water area of 0.113 square miles. Located at 25.94° N. Lat.; 80.27° W. Long. Elevation is 8 feet.
Population: 53,331 (1990); 59,443 (2000); 63,841 (2004); 69,306 (2009 projected); Race: 38.9% White, 50.9% Black, 0.5% Asian, 45.0% Hispanic of any race (2004); Density: 8,372.8 persons per square mile (2004); Average household size: 3.62 (2004); Median age: 33.3 (2004); Male/female ratio: 92.7 (2004); Marriage status: 33.2% never married, 50.9% now married, 4.9% widowed, 10.9% divorced (2000); Foreign born: 37.2% (2000); Ancestry (includes multiple ancestries): 70.8% Other groups, 5.2% Jamaican, 4.8% United States or American, 2.3% Haitian, 0.8% African (2000).
Economy: The city has become a growing middle-class suburb. Pro Player Stadium, home of the Miami Dolphins football team and the Florida Marlins baseball team, and site of the New Year's Day Orange Bowl football game, is here. Employment by occupation: 6.6% management, 13.2% professional, 19.6% services, 29.9% sales, 0.3% farming, 11.6% construction, 18.9% production (2000).
Income: Per capita income: $13,489 (2004); Median household income: $40,366 (2004); Average household income: $47,960 (2004); Percent of households with income of $100,000 or more: 6.4% (2004); Poverty rate: 16.5% (2000).
Education: Percent of population age 25 and over with: High school diploma (including GED) or higher: 61.0% (2004); Bachelor's degree or higher: 9.7% (2004); Master's degree or higher: 3.7% (2004).

School District(s)

Miami-Dade County School District (PK-12)
2002-03 Enrollment: 373,395 . . . . (305) 995-1428

Housing: Homeownership rate: 82.6% (2004); Median home value: $123,313 (2004); Median rent: $620 per month (2000); Median age of housing: 27 years (2000).
Transportation: Commute to work: 94.1% car, 3.2% public transportation, 0.4% walk, 0.9% work from home (2000); Travel time to work: 11.7% less than 15 minutes, 33.5% 15 to 30 minutes, 33.8% 30 to 45 minutes, 11.5% 45 to 60 minutes, 9.4% 60 minutes or more (2000)

CORAL GABLES (city). Covers a land area of 13.133 square miles and a water area of 24.024 square miles. Located at 25.72° N. Lat.; 80.27° W. Long. Elevation is 10 feet.
History: Named for the town's first house, which had gables decorated with coral rock. Coral Gables developed quickly in the mid-1920s through the advertising of George Merrick, its founder. The University of Miami was established here in 1926.
Population: 41,660 (1990); 42,249 (2000); 42,765 (2004); 43,889 (2009 projected); Race: 91.6% White, 3.4% Black, 1.6% Asian, 49.5% Hispanic of any race (2004); Density: 3,256.2 persons per square mile (2004); Average household size: 2.51 (2004); Median age: 39.5 (2004); Male/female ratio: 88.4 (2004); Marriage status: 32.0% never married, 51.4% now married, 6.0% widowed, 10.6% divorced (2000); Foreign born: 37.9% (2000); Ancestry (includes multiple ancestries): 54.0% Other groups, 7.4% English, 7.0% German, 5.7% Irish, 5.3% Italian (2000).
Economy: Unemployment rate: 2.9% (2004); Total civilian labor force: 24,833 (2004); Single-family building permits issued: 50 (2004); Multi-family building permits issued: 244 (2004); Employment by occupation: 25.1% management, 34.8% professional, 9.4% services, 25.3% sales, 0.0% farming, 2.5% construction, 2.9% production (2000).
Income: Per capita income: $51,624 (2004); Median household income: $75,427 (2004); Average household income: $128,288 (2004); Percent of households with income of $100,000 or more: 39.0% (2004); Poverty rate: 6.9% (2000).
Taxes: Total city taxes per capita: $1,291 (2002); City property taxes per capita: $728 (2002).
Education: Percent of population age 25 and over with: High school diploma (including GED) or higher: 91.7% (2004); Bachelor's degree or higher: 58.4% (2004); Master's degree or higher: 31.1% (2004).

School District(s)

Miami-Dade County School District (PK-12)
2002-03 Enrollment: 373,395 . . . . (305) 995-1428

Four-year College(s)

University of Miami
2003-04 Enrollment: 15,235 . . . . (305) 284-2211
2003-04 Tuition: In-state $26,280; Out-of-state $26,280

Housing: Homeownership rate: 66.2% (2004); Median home value: $422,915 (2004); Median rent: $694 per month (2000); Median age of housing: 42 years (2000).
Safety: Violent crime rate: 36.4 per 10,000 population; Property crime rate: 609.1 per 10,000 population (2003).
Newspapers: Coral Gables Gazette (General - Circulation 8,600)
Transportation: Commute to work: 83.7% car, 2.9% public transportation, 6.7% walk, 5.5% work from home (2000); Travel time to work: 29.1% less than 15 minutes, 40.2% 15 to 30 minutes, 21.1% 30 to 45 minutes, 5.9% 45 to 60 minutes, 3.7% 60 minutes or more (2000)

Additional Information Contacts

Central America Us Chamber . . . . (305) 569-9113
Chile-US Chamber of Commerce . . . . (305) 447-0908
Colombian American Chamber . . . . (305) 446-2542
Coral Gables Chamber of Commerce . . . . (305) 446-1657
French-American Chamber of Commerce . . . . (305) 442-2277
Local Government Offices . . . . (305) 460-5209
Puerto Rico Convention Bureau . . . . (305) 471-0202
Realtor Association of Miami-Dade County . . . . (305) 444-6528
Swedish American Chamber of Commerce . . . . (305) 443-3558
Venezuelan American Chamber . . . . (305) 444-4336

CORAL TERRACE (CDP). Covers a land area of 3.429 square miles and a water area of 0.019 square miles. Located at 25.74° N. Lat.; 80.30° W. Long.
Population: 23,255 (1990); 24,380 (2000); 24,937 (2004); 25,765 (2009 projected); Race: 93.5% White, 1.3% Black, 0.5% Asian, 84.4% Hispanic of any race (2004); Density: 7,272.4 persons per square mile (2004); Average household size: 3.16 (2004); Median age: 43.2 (2004); Male/female ratio: 90.2 (2004); Marriage status: 21.8% never married, 57.5% now married, 8.7% widowed, 12.0% divorced (2000); Foreign born: 66.1% (2000); Ancestry (includes multiple ancestries): 79.5% Other groups, 2.4% United States or American, 1.7% Irish, 1.7% German, 1.7% English (2000).
Economy: Employment by occupation: 11.9% management, 14.7% professional, 15.0% services, 35.1% sales, 0.4% farming, 9.0% construction, 13.9% production (2000).
Income: Per capita income: $17,088 (2004); Median household income: $42,494 (2004); Average household income: $53,365 (2004); Percent of households with income of $100,000 or more: 11.1% (2004); Poverty rate: 11.2% (2000).
Education: Percent of population age 25 and over with: High school diploma (including GED) or higher: 62.1% (2004); Bachelor's degree or higher: 18.0% (2004); Master's degree or higher: 7.6% (2004).
Housing: Homeownership rate: 70.5% (2004); Median home value: $193,360 (2004); Median rent: $627 per month (2000); Median age of housing: 42 years (2000).

Transportation: Commute to work: 92.0% car, 2.7% public transportation, 1.2% walk, 3.1% work from home (2000); Travel time to work: 17.5% less than 15 minutes, 39.9% 15 to 30 minutes, 30.7% 30 to 45 minutes, 5.7% 45 to 60 minutes, 6.3% 60 minutes or more (2000)

COUNTRY CLUB (CDP). Covers a land area of 4.312 square miles and a water area of 0.196 square miles. Located at 25.93° N. Lat.; 80.31° W. Long.
Population: 23,164 (1990); 36,310 (2000); 41,543 (2004); 47,744 (2009 projected); Race: 62.0% White, 22.2% Black, 2.0% Asian, 65.2% Hispanic of any race (2004); Density: 9,634.1 persons per square mile (2004); Average household size: 2.84 (2004); Median age: 31.6 (2004); Male/female ratio: 90.7 (2004); Marriage status: 29.3% never married, 55.3% now married, 4.0% widowed, 11.5% divorced (2000); Foreign born: 47.0% (2000); Ancestry (includes multiple ancestries): 72.7% Other groups, 3.8% United States or American, 3.1% Haitian, 2.1% Irish, 2.1% Italian (2000).
Economy: Employment by occupation: 14.2% management, 17.3% professional, 13.9% services, 35.4% sales, 0.1% farming, 7.6% construction, 11.5% production (2000).
Income: Per capita income: $17,627 (2004); Median household income: $39,826 (2004); Average household income: $49,677 (2004); Percent of households with income of $100,000 or more: 7.3% (2004); Poverty rate: 13.1% (2000).
Education: Percent of population age 25 and over with: High school diploma (including GED) or higher: 80.2% (2004); Bachelor's degree or higher: 23.2% (2004); Master's degree or higher: 7.5% (2004).
Housing: Homeownership rate: 45.4% (2004); Median home value: $142,448 (2004); Median rent: $726 per month (2000); Median age of housing: 14 years (2000).
Transportation: Commute to work: 94.8% car, 1.7% public transportation, 0.7% walk, 1.9% work from home (2000); Travel time to work: 12.4% less than 15 minutes, 31.3% 15 to 30 minutes, 32.4% 30 to 45 minutes, 14.7% 45 to 60 minutes, 9.2% 60 minutes or more (2000)

COUNTRY WALK (CDP). Covers a land area of 2.746 square miles and a water area of 0.009 square miles. Located at 25.63° N. Lat.; 80.43° W. Long.
Population: 2,327 (1990); 10,653 (2000); 15,209 (2004); 20,466 (2009 projected); Race: 76.5% White, 10.9% Black, 2.2% Asian, 65.3% Hispanic of any race (2004); Density: 5,537.9 persons per square mile (2004); Average household size: 3.36 (2004); Median age: 32.1 (2004); Male/female ratio: 91.7 (2004); Marriage status: 21.0% never married, 67.7% now married, 2.6% widowed, 8.7% divorced (2000); Foreign born: 42.6% (2000); Ancestry (includes multiple ancestries): 65.4% Other groups, 6.4% German, 4.7% Jamaican, 4.5% Italian, 4.3% Irish (2000).
Economy: Employment by occupation: 20.9% management, 22.9% professional, 11.0% services, 32.4% sales, 0.2% farming, 5.3% construction, 7.2% production (2000).
Income: Per capita income: $23,282 (2004); Median household income: $70,021 (2004); Average household income: $77,365 (2004); Percent of households with income of $100,000 or more: 22.3% (2004); Poverty rate: 4.8% (2000).
Education: Percent of population age 25 and over with: High school diploma (including GED) or higher: 88.3% (2004); Bachelor's degree or higher: 31.4% (2004); Master's degree or higher: 11.8% (2004).
Housing: Homeownership rate: 92.2% (2004); Median home value: $191,563 (2004); Median rent: $917 per month (2000); Median age of housing: 6 years (2000).
Transportation: Commute to work: 92.8% car, 2.6% public transportation, 0.8% walk, 2.9% work from home (2000); Travel time to work: 8.7% less than 15 minutes, 26.3% 15 to 30 minutes, 26.6% 30 to 45 minutes, 16.9% 45 to 60 minutes, 21.5% 60 minutes or more (2000)

CUTLER (CDP). Covers a land area of 6.727 square miles and a water area of 0.024 square miles. Located at 25.62° N. Lat.; 80.32° W. Long.
Population: 15,548 (1990); 17,390 (2000); 18,099 (2004); 19,021 (2009 projected); Race: 88.6% White, 4.0% Black, 2.9% Asian, 31.8% Hispanic of any race (2004); Density: 2,690.4 persons per square mile (2004); Average household size: 3.06 (2004); Median age: 39.3 (2004); Male/female ratio: 95.5 (2004); Marriage status: 20.6% never married, 68.4% now married, 3.9% widowed, 7.1% divorced (2000); Foreign born: 23.7% (2000); Ancestry (includes multiple ancestries): 35.0% Other groups, 12.4% English, 12.2% German, 11.8% Irish, 7.9% Italian (2000).
Economy: Employment by occupation: 26.5% management, 30.2% professional, 8.7% services, 25.7% sales, 0.0% farming, 4.7% construction, 4.2% production (2000).
Income: Per capita income: $49,172 (2004); Median household income: $123,614 (2004); Average household income: $149,954 (2004); Percent of households with income of $100,000 or more: 61.1% (2004); Poverty rate: 5.2% (2000).
Education: Percent of population age 25 and over with: High school diploma (including GED) or higher: 92.9% (2004); Bachelor's degree or higher: 55.7% (2004); Master's degree or higher: 23.2% (2004).
Housing: Homeownership rate: 88.2% (2004); Median home value: $365,770 (2004); Median rent: $584 per month (2000); Median age of housing: 28 years (2000).
Transportation: Commute to work: 91.6% car, 2.7% public transportation, 0.3% walk, 4.4% work from home (2000); Travel time to work: 14.0% less than 15 minutes, 32.8% 15 to 30 minutes, 27.5% 30 to 45 minutes, 14.0% 45 to 60 minutes, 11.7% 60 minutes or more (2000)

CUTLER RIDGE (CDP). Covers a land area of 4.753 square miles and a water area of 0.111 square miles. Located at 25.58° N. Lat.; 80.34° W. Long. Elevation is 10 feet.
History: Named for Dr. C.F. Cutler of Massachusetts, who built a settlement and mill here in 1884. The town has grown and developed since the 1970s, and a large shopping center was constructed here. Sustained major devastation in 1992 when Hurricane Andrew struck; rebuilding effort completed by mid-1990s.
Population: 21,268 (1990); 24,781 (2000); 26,466 (2004); 28,586 (2009 projected); Race: 71.4% White, 17.0% Black, 1.5% Asian, 44.5% Hispanic of any race (2004); Density: 5,567.9 persons per square mile (2004); Average household size: 2.98 (2004); Median age: 35.8 (2004); Male/female ratio: 93.1 (2004); Marriage status: 24.6% never married, 57.4% now married, 6.5% widowed, 11.5% divorced (2000); Foreign born: 26.5% (2000); Ancestry (includes multiple ancestries): 49.4% Other groups, 8.6% Irish, 8.5% United States or American, 8.2% German, 5.7% English (2000).
Economy: Employment by occupation: 14.4% management, 18.1% professional, 13.0% services, 33.5% sales, 0.2% farming, 12.0% construction, 8.7% production (2000).
Income: Per capita income: $20,560 (2004); Median household income: $47,842 (2004); Average household income: $59,872 (2004); Percent of households with income of $100,000 or more: 14.1% (2004); Poverty rate: 11.5% (2000).
Education: Percent of population age 25 and over with: High school diploma (including GED) or higher: 82.3% (2004); Bachelor's degree or higher: 20.0% (2004); Master's degree or higher: 7.7% (2004).
Housing: Homeownership rate: 68.9% (2004); Median home value: $159,967 (2004); Median rent: $551 per month (2000); Median age of housing: 30 years (2000).
Transportation: Commute to work: 92.5% car, 3.0% public transportation, 0.7% walk, 2.3% work from home (2000); Travel time to work: 18.4% less than 15 minutes, 27.8% 15 to 30 minutes, 22.7% 30 to 45 minutes, 15.1% 45 to 60 minutes, 15.9% 60 minutes or more (2000)

DORAL (CDP). Covers a land area of 13.163 square miles and a water area of 0.478 square miles. Located at 25.80° N. Lat.; 80.35° W. Long.
Population: 6,267 (1990); 20,438 (2000); 28,117 (2004); 36,886 (2009 projected); Race: 85.1% White, 2.0% Black, 4.6% Asian, 75.2% Hispanic of any race (2004); Density: 2,136.0 persons per square mile (2004); Average household size: 2.73 (2004); Median age: 33.4 (2004); Male/female ratio: 97.3 (2004); Marriage status: 20.4% never married, 69.5% now married, 1.7% widowed, 8.5% divorced (2000); Foreign born: 62.6% (2000); Ancestry (includes multiple ancestries): 72.6% Other groups, 5.4% Italian, 3.3% United States or American, 2.6% Brazilian, 2.5% Irish (2000).
Economy: Single-family building permits issued: 0 (2004); Multi-family building permits issued: 0 (2004); Employment by occupation: 30.4% management, 19.4% professional, 7.1% services, 32.9% sales, 0.3% farming, 3.4% construction, 6.5% production (2000).
Income: Per capita income: $31,561 (2004); Median household income: $60,694 (2004); Average household income: $86,075 (2004); Percent of households with income of $100,000 or more: 25.0% (2004); Poverty rate: 11.7% (2000).
Education: Percent of population age 25 and over with: High school diploma (including GED) or higher: 91.9% (2004); Bachelor's degree or higher: 48.7% (2004); Master's degree or higher: 20.2% (2004).

Housing: Homeownership rate: 61.0% (2004); Median home value: $243,667 (2004); Median rent: $870 per month (2000); Median age of housing: 7 years (2000).
Transportation: Commute to work: 93.0% car, 0.8% public transportation, 1.9% walk, 4.1% work from home (2000); Travel time to work: 30.8% less than 15 minutes, 39.6% 15 to 30 minutes, 19.9% 30 to 45 minutes, 6.1% 45 to 60 minutes, 3.6% 60 minutes or more (2000)

EAST PERRINE (CDP). Covers a land area of 1.974 square miles and a water area of 0 square miles. Located at 25.60° N. Lat.; 80.34° W. Long.
Population: 6,526 (1990); 7,079 (2000); 7,296 (2004); 7,609 (2009 projected); Race: 70.4% White, 17.7% Black, 2.1% Asian, 35.7% Hispanic of any race (2004); Density: 3,696.1 persons per square mile (2004); Average household size: 3.11 (2004); Median age: 36.7 (2004); Male/female ratio: 91.5 (2004); Marriage status: 26.4% never married, 56.9% now married, 6.3% widowed, 10.4% divorced (2000); Foreign born: 30.2% (2000); Ancestry (includes multiple ancestries): 42.0% Other groups, 10.0% German, 9.8% United States or American, 8.2% Irish, 5.9% Jamaican (2000).
Economy: Employment by occupation: 17.3% management, 26.9% professional, 14.9% services, 24.4% sales, 0.0% farming, 10.5% construction, 6.0% production (2000).
Income: Per capita income: $27,124 (2004); Median household income: $69,379 (2004); Average household income: $83,841 (2004); Percent of households with income of $100,000 or more: 30.7% (2004); Poverty rate: 7.8% (2000).
Education: Percent of population age 25 and over with: High school diploma (including GED) or higher: 83.6% (2004); Bachelor's degree or higher: 31.0% (2004); Master's degree or higher: 12.6% (2004).
Housing: Homeownership rate: 74.6% (2004); Median home value: $206,879 (2004); Median rent: $627 per month (2000); Median age of housing: 27 years (2000).
Transportation: Commute to work: 89.6% car, 5.0% public transportation, 1.0% walk, 3.1% work from home (2000); Travel time to work: 21.5% less than 15 minutes, 24.1% 15 to 30 minutes, 22.1% 30 to 45 minutes, 15.2% 45 to 60 minutes, 17.1% 60 minutes or more (2000)

EL PORTAL (village). Covers a land area of 0.425 square miles and a water area of 0 square miles. Located at 25.85° N. Lat.; 80.19° W. Long. Elevation is 10 feet.
Population: 2,457 (1990); 2,505 (2000); 2,559 (2004); 2,594 (2009 projected); Race: 25.8% White, 62.5% Black, 0.7% Asian, 22.4% Hispanic of any race (2004); Density: 6,023.7 persons per square mile (2004); Average household size: 3.04 (2004); Median age: 38.2 (2004); Male/female ratio: 97.6 (2004); Marriage status: 38.9% never married, 39.9% now married, 7.7% widowed, 13.5% divorced (2000); Foreign born: 37.2% (2000); Ancestry (includes multiple ancestries): 42.3% Other groups, 22.1% Haitian, 8.1% Jamaican, 4.3% United States or American, 2.7% German (2000).
Economy: Single-family building permits issued: 3 (2004); Multi-family building permits issued: 0 (2004); Employment by occupation: 17.6% management, 17.6% professional, 23.3% services, 26.8% sales, 0.0% farming, 5.2% construction, 9.5% production (2000).
Income: Per capita income: $17,628 (2004); Median household income: $43,350 (2004); Average household income: $52,536 (2004); Percent of households with income of $100,000 or more: 11.9% (2004); Poverty rate: 22.2% (2000).
Education: Percent of population age 25 and over with: High school diploma (including GED) or higher: 75.6% (2004); Bachelor's degree or higher: 23.1% (2004); Master's degree or higher: 9.3% (2004).
Housing: Homeownership rate: 76.9% (2004); Median home value: $146,030 (2004); Median rent: $609 per month (2000); Median age of housing: 48 years (2000).
Safety: Violent crime rate: 55.0 per 10,000 population; Property crime rate: 428.0 per 10,000 population (2003).
Transportation: Commute to work: 86.5% car, 10.2% public transportation, 1.1% walk, 1.6% work from home (2000); Travel time to work: 14.7% less than 15 minutes, 41.2% 15 to 30 minutes, 28.3% 30 to 45 minutes, 8.4% 45 to 60 minutes, 7.3% 60 minutes or more (2000)

FISHER ISLAND (CDP). Covers a land area of 0.343 square miles and a water area of 0 square miles. Located at 25.76° N. Lat.; 80.14° W. Long.
Population: 204 (1990); 467 (2000); 476 (2004); 465 (2009 projected); Race: 92.2% White, 2.9% Black, 2.3% Asian, 12.6% Hispanic of any race (2004); Density: 1,388.9 persons per square mile (2004); Average household size: 2.13 (2004); Median age: 51.6 (2004); Male/female ratio: 99.2 (2004); Marriage status: 14.1% never married, 71.2% now married, 7.5% widowed, 7.2% divorced (2000); Foreign born: 27.7% (2000); Ancestry (includes multiple ancestries): 15.9% Russian, 13.3% English, 10.0% Other groups, 8.8% Iranian, 8.6% United States or American (2000).
Economy: Employment by occupation: 60.4% management, 26.6% professional, 7.9% services, 0.0% sales, 0.0% farming, 0.0% construction, 5.0% production (2000).
Income: Per capita income: $133,188 (2004); Median household income: $266,447 (2004); Average household income: $284,294 (2004); Percent of households with income of $100,000 or more: 69.5% (2004); Poverty rate: 0.0% (2000).
Education: Percent of population age 25 and over with: High school diploma (including GED) or higher: 97.3% (2004); Bachelor's degree or higher: 68.2% (2004); Master's degree or higher: 50.4% (2004).
Housing: Homeownership rate: 89.2% (2004); Median home value: $1 million+ (2004); Median rent: $1,698 per month (2000); Median age of housing: 11 years (2000).
Transportation: Commute to work: 56.8% car, 0.0% public transportation, 13.7% walk, 5.0% work from home (2000); Travel time to work: 52.3% less than 15 minutes, 31.1% 15 to 30 minutes, 16.7% 30 to 45 minutes, 0.0% 45 to 60 minutes, 0.0% 60 minutes or more (2000)

FLORIDA CITY (city). Covers a land area of 3.219 square miles and a water area of 0 square miles. Located at 25.45° N. Lat.; 80.48° W. Long. Elevation is 6 feet.
History: Florida City was incorporated in 1913. It was first called Detroit, but the postal authorities insisted on a different name.
Population: 5,896 (1990); 7,843 (2000); 8,714 (2004); 9,655 (2009 projected); Race: 28.4% White, 55.5% Black, 0.6% Asian, 35.9% Hispanic of any race (2004); Density: 2,706.7 persons per square mile (2004); Average household size: 3.59 (2004); Median age: 22.9 (2004); Male/female ratio: 94.9 (2004); Marriage status: 39.4% never married, 38.8% now married, 12.5% widowed, 9.4% divorced (2000); Foreign born: 20.9% (2000); Ancestry (includes multiple ancestries): 72.1% Other groups, 5.8% Haitian, 2.4% United States or American, 1.8% African, 1.0% Italian (2000).
Economy: Single-family building permits issued: 242 (2004); Multi-family building permits issued: 0 (2004); Employment by occupation: 6.0% management, 11.9% professional, 26.2% services, 24.8% sales, 4.9% farming, 9.3% construction, 16.9% production (2000).
Income: Per capita income: $8,000 (2004); Median household income: $17,242 (2004); Average household income: $27,635 (2004); Percent of households with income of $100,000 or more: 2.1% (2004); Poverty rate: 43.3% (2000).
Education: Percent of population age 25 and over with: High school diploma (including GED) or higher: 46.2% (2004); Bachelor's degree or higher: 6.9% (2004); Master's degree or higher: 2.1% (2004).

School District(s)

Miami-Dade County School District (PK-12)
2002-03 Enrollment: 373,395 . . . . (305) 995-1428
Housing: Homeownership rate: 40.6% (2004); Median home value: $95,141 (2004); Median rent: $431 per month (2000); Median age of housing: 18 years (2000).
Safety: Violent crime rate: 346.1 per 10,000 population; Property crime rate: 1,471.6 per 10,000 population (2003).
Transportation: Commute to work: 88.7% car, 4.6% public transportation, 1.6% walk, 3.9% work from home (2000); Travel time to work: 29.1% less than 15 minutes, 25.0% 15 to 30 minutes, 22.4% 30 to 45 minutes, 8.2% 45 to 60 minutes, 15.2% 60 minutes or more (2000)

Additional Information Contacts

Local Government Offices . . . . (305) 242-8132

FOUNTAINBLEAU (CDP). Covers a land area of 4.403 square miles and a water area of 0.114 square miles. Located at 25.77° N. Lat.; 80.34° W. Long.
Population: 46,661 (1990); 59,549 (2000); 63,895 (2004); 69,299 (2009 projected); Race: 86.9% White, 2.0% Black, 1.7% Asian, 88.3% Hispanic of any race (2004); Density: 14,511.8 persons per square mile (2004); Average household size: 2.85 (2004); Median age: 36.4 (2004); Male/female ratio: 87.4 (2004); Marriage status: 26.3% never married, 55.3% now married, 6.0% widowed, 12.3% divorced (2000); Foreign born:

73.1% (2000); Ancestry (includes multiple ancestries): 86.2% Other groups, 2.5% United States or American, 1.7% Italian, 0.8% German, 0.5% Irish (2000).
Economy: Employment by occupation: 13.0% management, 14.4% professional, 15.7% services, 37.6% sales, 0.2% farming, 6.7% construction, 12.4% production (2000).
Income: Per capita income: $15,980 (2004); Median household income: $37,709 (2004); Average household income: $45,501 (2004); Percent of households with income of $100,000 or more: 6.2% (2004); Poverty rate: 14.2% (2000).
Education: Percent of population age 25 and over with: High school diploma (including GED) or higher: 70.0% (2004); Bachelor's degree or higher: 22.2% (2004); Master's degree or higher: 10.3% (2004).
Housing: Homeownership rate: 52.0% (2004); Median home value: $124,345 (2004); Median rent: $705 per month (2000); Median age of housing: 18 years (2000).
Transportation: Commute to work: 92.0% car, 3.0% public transportation, 1.2% walk, 2.1% work from home (2000); Travel time to work: 15.9% less than 15 minutes, 41.5% 15 to 30 minutes, 27.0% 30 to 45 minutes, 9.6% 45 to 60 minutes, 6.0% 60 minutes or more (2000)

GLADEVIEW (CDP). Covers a land area of 2.541 square miles and a water area of 0 square miles. Located at 25.84° N. Lat.; 80.23° W. Long.
Population: 15,637 (1990); 14,468 (2000); 13,579 (2004); 12,563 (2009 projected); Race: 20.5% White, 72.8% Black, 0.2% Asian, 26.0% Hispanic of any race (2004); Density: 5,344.4 persons per square mile (2004); Average household size: 3.36 (2004); Median age: 27.6 (2004); Male/female ratio: 87.0 (2004); Marriage status: 47.8% never married, 32.2% now married, 9.5% widowed, 10.5% divorced (2000); Foreign born: 20.1% (2000); Ancestry (includes multiple ancestries): 74.4% Other groups, 2.2% United States or American, 1.5% Haitian, 1.0% African, 1.0% Bahamian (2000).
Economy: Employment by occupation: 4.2% management, 13.0% professional, 24.8% services, 24.7% sales, 0.5% farming, 9.0% construction, 23.8% production (2000).
Income: Per capita income: $7,984 (2004); Median household income: $16,214 (2004); Average household income: $25,851 (2004); Percent of households with income of $100,000 or more: 2.4% (2004); Poverty rate: 52.8% (2000).
Education: Percent of population age 25 and over with: High school diploma (including GED) or higher: 51.4% (2004); Bachelor's degree or higher: 4.0% (2004); Master's degree or higher: 1.0% (2004).
Housing: Homeownership rate: 42.6% (2004); Median home value: $72,402 (2004); Median rent: $278 per month (2000); Median age of housing: 38 years (2000).
Transportation: Commute to work: 80.9% car, 14.3% public transportation, 3.0% walk, 0.7% work from home (2000); Travel time to work: 16.0% less than 15 minutes, 34.5% 15 to 30 minutes, 31.4% 30 to 45 minutes, 7.5% 45 to 60 minutes, 10.6% 60 minutes or more (2000)

GLENVAR HEIGHTS (CDP). Covers a land area of 4.210 square miles and a water area of 0.175 square miles. Located at 25.70° N. Lat.; 80.31° W. Long.
Population: 14,823 (1990); 16,243 (2000); 16,842 (2004); 17,614 (2009 projected); Race: 86.8% White, 3.1% Black, 2.9% Asian, 63.1% Hispanic of any race (2004); Density: 4,000.7 persons per square mile (2004); Average household size: 2.27 (2004); Median age: 38.4 (2004); Male/female ratio: 88.1 (2004); Marriage status: 31.3% never married, 50.1% now married, 6.5% widowed, 12.1% divorced (2000); Foreign born: 45.4% (2000); Ancestry (includes multiple ancestries): 61.6% Other groups, 6.3% German, 5.5% English, 4.7% Irish, 4.2% Italian (2000).
Economy: Employment by occupation: 17.0% management, 25.8% professional, 13.1% services, 32.1% sales, 0.0% farming, 5.2% construction, 6.8% production (2000).
Income: Per capita income: $28,866 (2004); Median household income: $42,600 (2004); Average household income: $65,132 (2004); Percent of households with income of $100,000 or more: 16.2% (2004); Poverty rate: 12.7% (2000).
Education: Percent of population age 25 and over with: High school diploma (including GED) or higher: 87.5% (2004); Bachelor's degree or higher: 40.4% (2004); Master's degree or higher: 18.8% (2004).
Housing: Homeownership rate: 51.9% (2004); Median home value: $206,551 (2004); Median rent: $650 per month (2000); Median age of housing: 28 years (2000).
Transportation: Commute to work: 85.6% car, 6.5% public transportation, 1.5% walk, 4.8% work from home (2000); Travel time to work: 19.7% less than 15 minutes, 34.1% 15 to 30 minutes, 27.3% 30 to 45 minutes, 10.5% 45 to 60 minutes, 8.4% 60 minutes or more (2000)

GOLDEN BEACH (town). Covers a land area of 0.341 square miles and a water area of 0.059 square miles. Located at 25.96° N. Lat.; 80.12° W. Long. Elevation is 10 feet.
Population: 771 (1990); 919 (2000); 806 (2004); 738 (2009 projected); Race: 95.7% White, 0.1% Black, 1.1% Asian, 25.6% Hispanic of any race (2004); Density: 2,361.6 persons per square mile (2004); Average household size: 3.34 (2004); Median age: 38.2 (2004); Male/female ratio: 96.6 (2004); Marriage status: 20.4% never married, 66.8% now married, 4.8% widowed, 8.1% divorced (2000); Foreign born: 31.3% (2000); Ancestry (includes multiple ancestries): 31.2% Other groups, 11.9% United States or American, 11.0% Italian, 9.0% Russian, 7.4% Polish (2000).
Economy: Single-family building permits issued: 1 (2004); Multi-family building permits issued: 0 (2004); Employment by occupation: 35.6% management, 25.4% professional, 5.1% services, 29.8% sales, 0.0% farming, 1.5% construction, 2.5% production (2000).
Income: Per capita income: $65,071 (2004); Median household income: $157,778 (2004); Average household income: $217,624 (2004); Percent of households with income of $100,000 or more: 62.2% (2004); Poverty rate: 8.1% (2000).
Taxes: Total city taxes per capita: $2,992 (2002); City property taxes per capita: $2,499 (2002).
Education: Percent of population age 25 and over with: High school diploma (including GED) or higher: 96.5% (2004); Bachelor's degree or higher: 60.1% (2004); Master's degree or higher: 27.0% (2004).
Housing: Homeownership rate: 93.8% (2004); Median home value: $924,107 (2004); Median rent: $1,469 per month (2000); Median age of housing: 26 years (2000).
Safety: Violent crime rate: 0.0 per 10,000 population; Property crime rate: 116.2 per 10,000 population (2003).
Transportation: Commute to work: 83.9% car, 0.0% public transportation, 0.0% walk, 15.6% work from home (2000); Travel time to work: 25.0% less than 15 minutes, 30.0% 15 to 30 minutes, 31.9% 30 to 45 minutes, 10.3% 45 to 60 minutes, 2.8% 60 minutes or more (2000)

GOLDEN GLADES (CDP). Covers a land area of 4.917 square miles and a water area of 0.065 square miles. Located at 25.91° N. Lat.; 80.19° W. Long.
Population: 25,312 (1990); 32,623 (2000); 34,047 (2004); 35,967 (2009 projected); Race: 19.0% White, 69.6% Black, 1.3% Asian, 16.9% Hispanic of any race (2004); Density: 6,924.6 persons per square mile (2004); Average household size: 3.37 (2004); Median age: 32.7 (2004); Male/female ratio: 89.4 (2004); Marriage status: 35.6% never married, 46.7% now married, 6.9% widowed, 10.9% divorced (2000); Foreign born: 45.3% (2000); Ancestry (includes multiple ancestries): 36.4% Other groups, 32.0% Haitian, 5.4% Jamaican, 5.2% United States or American, 1.9% German (2000).
Economy: Site of freeway convergence (I-95, Florida's Turnpike, and Palmetto Expressway) considered to be one of the most complex in the U.S. Employment by occupation: 7.0% management, 14.9% professional, 25.7% services, 29.0% sales, 0.3% farming, 10.6% construction, 12.6% production (2000).
Income: Per capita income: $11,961 (2004); Median household income: $30,337 (2004); Average household income: $39,344 (2004); Percent of households with income of $100,000 or more: 4.9% (2004); Poverty rate: 20.9% (2000).
Education: Percent of population age 25 and over with: High school diploma (including GED) or higher: 63.4% (2004); Bachelor's degree or higher: 12.5% (2004); Master's degree or higher: 4.9% (2004).
Housing: Homeownership rate: 54.2% (2004); Median home value: $133,438 (2004); Median rent: $549 per month (2000); Median age of housing: 35 years (2000).
Transportation: Commute to work: 88.0% car, 8.7% public transportation, 0.7% walk, 1.4% work from home (2000); Travel time to work: 14.5% less than 15 minutes, 35.0% 15 to 30 minutes, 31.1% 30 to 45 minutes, 9.9% 45 to 60 minutes, 9.5% 60 minutes or more (2000)

GOULDS (CDP). Covers a land area of 2.964 square miles and a water area of 0.002 square miles. Located at 25.56° N. Lat.; 80.38° W. Long. Elevation is 10 feet.

History: Goulds grew around a packing plant that shipped citrus fruits, potatoes, and other truck garden produce.
Population: 7,284 (1990); 7,453 (2000); 7,951 (2004); 8,546 (2009 projected); Race: 17.1% White, 74.8% Black, 0.5% Asian, 20.3% Hispanic of any race (2004); Density: 2,682.6 persons per square mile (2004); Average household size: 3.35 (2004); Median age: 26.5 (2004); Male/female ratio: 87.1 (2004); Marriage status: 45.1% never married, 34.0% now married, 8.0% widowed, 12.9% divorced (2000); Foreign born: 15.2% (2000); Ancestry (includes multiple ancestries): 69.8% Other groups, 4.8% United States or American, 3.7% Jamaican, 2.5% Haitian, 1.8% Bahamian (2000).
Economy: Employment by occupation: 9.0% management, 15.9% professional, 26.5% services, 28.1% sales, 0.8% farming, 9.9% construction, 9.8% production (2000).
Income: Per capita income: $8,950 (2004); Median household income: $21,466 (2004); Average household income: $29,961 (2004); Percent of households with income of $100,000 or more: 3.0% (2004); Poverty rate: 43.6% (2000).
Education: Percent of population age 25 and over with: High school diploma (including GED) or higher: 50.4% (2004); Bachelor's degree or higher: 6.9% (2004); Master's degree or higher: 2.2% (2004).

School District(s)

Miami-Dade County School District (PK-12)
2002-03 Enrollment: 373,395 . . . . (305) 995-1428
Housing: Homeownership rate: 47.1% (2004); Median home value: $113,356 (2004); Median rent: $369 per month (2000); Median age of housing: 28 years (2000).
Transportation: Commute to work: 86.4% car, 9.5% public transportation, 0.6% walk, 1.4% work from home (2000); Travel time to work: 19.7% less than 15 minutes, 35.6% 15 to 30 minutes, 21.3% 30 to 45 minutes, 9.1% 45 to 60 minutes, 14.4% 60 minutes or more (2000)

HIALEAH (city). Covers a land area of 19.241 square miles and a water area of 0.501 square miles. Located at 25.86° N. Lat.; 80.29° W. Long. Elevation is 5 feet.
History: Named for the Seminole-Creek translations of "prairie" and "pretty". Hialeah was founded in the early 1920s by James Bright, a Missouri ranchman. In 1931 Joe Smoot built the Hialeah Park race track, attracting tourists in the Greater Miami area.
Population: 188,005 (1990); 226,419 (2000); 226,837 (2004); 228,483 (2009 projected); Race: 87.9% White, 2.6% Black, 0.4% Asian, 91.8% Hispanic of any race (2004); Density: 11,789.0 persons per square mile (2004); Average household size: 3.21 (2004); Median age: 39.4 (2004); Male/female ratio: 93.0 (2004); Marriage status: 22.3% never married, 58.5% now married, 7.3% widowed, 11.8% divorced (2000); Foreign born: 72.1% (2000); Ancestry (includes multiple ancestries): 85.0% Other groups, 2.6% United States or American, 0.7% Italian, 0.6% German, 0.5% Irish (2000).
Economy: Unemployment rate: 5.9% (2004); Total civilian labor force: 110,571 (2004); Single-family building permits issued: 14 (2004); Multi-family building permits issued: 31 (2004); Employment by occupation: 7.5% management, 9.0% professional, 14.2% services, 30.7% sales, 0.3% farming, 14.3% construction, 24.0% production (2000).
Income: Per capita income: $12,812 (2004); Median household income: $31,051 (2004); Average household income: $40,043 (2004); Percent of households with income of $100,000 or more: 5.1% (2004); Poverty rate: 18.6% (2000).
Taxes: Total city taxes per capita: $393 (2002); City property taxes per capita: $176 (2002).
Education: Percent of population age 25 and over with: High school diploma (including GED) or higher: 49.9% (2004); Bachelor's degree or higher: 10.4% (2004); Master's degree or higher: 4.4% (2004).

School District(s)

Miami-Dade County School District (PK-12)
2002-03 Enrollment: 373,395 . . . . (305) 995-1428

Two-year College(s)

Beauty Schools of America (Private, For-profit)
2003-04 Enrollment: 523 . . . . (305) 362-9003
Compu-Med Vocational Careers Corp (Private, For-profit)
2003-04 Enrollment: 492 . . . . (305) 888-9200
2003-04 Tuition: In-state $4,600; Out-of-state $4,600
Florida National College (Private, For-profit)
2003-04 Enrollment: 1,418 . . . . (305) 821-3333
2003-04 Tuition: In-state $8,185; Out-of-state $8,185
La Belle Beauty School (Private, For-profit)
2003-04 Enrollment: 431 . . . . (305) 558-0562
National School of Technology Inc (Private, For-profit)
2003-04 Enrollment: 1,548 . . . . (305) 558-9500
Housing: Homeownership rate: 50.6% (2004); Median home value: $146,179 (2004); Median rent: $537 per month (2000); Median age of housing: 27 years (2000).
Hospitals: Palmetto General Hospital (360 beds); Southern Winds Hospital (60 beds)
Safety: Violent crime rate: 61.5 per 10,000 population; Property crime rate: 465.1 per 10,000 population (2003).
Newspapers: El Sol de Hialeah (Hispanic - Circulation 24,000); La Voz Calle (Hispanic - Circulation 25,000)
Transportation: Commute to work: 93.1% car, 2.9% public transportation, 1.6% walk, 1.1% work from home (2000); Travel time to work: 18.4% less than 15 minutes, 38.4% 15 to 30 minutes, 27.8% 30 to 45 minutes, 8.4% 45 to 60 minutes, 6.9% 60 minutes or more (2000)

Additional Information Contacts

Northwestern Dade Association of Realtors . . . . (305) 557-1400

HIALEAH GARDENS (city). Covers a land area of 2.460 square miles and a water area of 0.065 square miles. Located at 25.87° N. Lat.; 80.34° W. Long. Elevation is 7 feet.
Population: 7,713 (1990); 19,297 (2000); 20,175 (2004); 21,288 (2009 projected); Race: 87.9% White, 2.1% Black, 0.6% Asian, 92.9% Hispanic of any race (2004); Density: 8,202.8 persons per square mile (2004); Average household size: 3.46 (2004); Median age: 35.4 (2004); Male/female ratio: 93.3 (2004); Marriage status: 21.4% never married, 63.1% now married, 4.6% widowed, 10.9% divorced (2000); Foreign born: 70.1% (2000); Ancestry (includes multiple ancestries): 88.9% Other groups, 1.9% United States or American, 1.1% Italian, 0.3% English, 0.3% German (2000).
Economy: Manufacturing includes figurines, wood products, building materials, apparel, marble products; textile printing. Single-family building permits issued: 94 (2004); Multi-family building permits issued: 0 (2004); Employment by occupation: 11.7% management, 8.7% professional, 11.8% services, 32.8% sales, 0.1% farming, 11.0% construction, 23.9% production (2000).
Income: Per capita income: $15,251 (2004); Median household income: $44,039 (2004); Average household income: $52,350 (2004); Percent of households with income of $100,000 or more: 9.1% (2004); Poverty rate: 13.3% (2000).
Education: Percent of population age 25 and over with: High school diploma (including GED) or higher: 60.3% (2004); Bachelor's degree or higher: 13.4% (2004); Master's degree or higher: 6.1% (2004).

School District(s)

Miami-Dade County School District (PK-12)
2002-03 Enrollment: 373,395 . . . . (305) 995-1428
Housing: Homeownership rate: 77.2% (2004); Median home value: $138,628 (2004); Median rent: $617 per month (2000); Median age of housing: 9 years (2000).
Safety: Violent crime rate: 22.7 per 10,000 population; Property crime rate: 495.5 per 10,000 population (2003).
Transportation: Commute to work: 92.9% car, 2.0% public transportation, 1.4% walk, 1.8% work from home (2000); Travel time to work: 13.9% less than 15 minutes, 39.3% 15 to 30 minutes, 28.8% 30 to 45 minutes, 10.7% 45 to 60 minutes, 7.2% 60 minutes or more (2000)

Additional Information Contacts

Local Government Offices . . . . (305) 558-4114

HOMESTEAD (city). Covers a land area of 14.284 square miles and a water area of 0.093 square miles. Located at 25.47° N. Lat.; 80.46° W. Long. Elevation is 9 feet.
History: Named for its history as an area open to homesteading by the U.S. government. Homestead developed as the trading center of the Redlands fruit and winter-vegetable area when the railroad arrived in 1904. In 1912 Colonel H.W. Johnston came to Homestead from Kentucky, and became interested in horticulture. On his estate he planted more than 8,000 varieties of tropical plants and trees, including more than 1,500 varieties of palms.
Population: 28,451 (1990); 31,909 (2000); 35,065 (2004); 38,903 (2009 projected); Race: 60.5% White, 22.1% Black, 0.7% Asian, 57.9% Hispanic of any race (2004); Density: 2,454.9 persons per square mile (2004); Average household size: 3.18 (2004); Median age: 28.6 (2004); Male/female ratio: 106.1 (2004); Marriage status: 36.7% never married, 48.5% now married, 4.8% widowed, 10.0% divorced (2000); Foreign born:

36.0% (2000); Ancestry (includes multiple ancestries): 62.2% Other groups, 5.2% United States or American, 4.8% Haitian, 4.2% Irish, 4.0% German (2000).
Economy: Unemployment rate: 5.3% (2004); Total civilian labor force: 13,786 (2004); Single-family building permits issued: 1,941 (2004); Multi-family building permits issued: 778 (2004); Employment by occupation: 7.0% management, 10.3% professional, 19.7% services, 21.4% sales, 14.3% farming, 17.5% construction, 9.8% production (2000).
Income: Per capita income: $11,800 (2004); Median household income: $27,315 (2004); Average household income: $36,492 (2004); Percent of households with income of $100,000 or more: 4.8% (2004); Poverty rate: 31.8% (2000).
Education: Percent of population age 25 and over with: High school diploma (including GED) or higher: 50.6% (2004); Bachelor's degree or higher: 10.0% (2004); Master's degree or higher: 3.1% (2004).

School District(s)

Miami-Dade County School District (PK-12)
2002-03 Enrollment: 373,395 . . . . (305) 995-1428
Housing: Homeownership rate: 36.8% (2004); Median home value: $117,637 (2004); Median rent: $444 per month (2000); Median age of housing: 19 years (2000).
Hospitals: Homestead Hospital (120 beds)
Safety: Violent crime rate: 180.5 per 10,000 population; Property crime rate: 909.6 per 10,000 population (2003).
Newspapers: South Dade News Leader (General - Circulation 15,000)
Transportation: Commute to work: 90.2% car, 2.9% public transportation, 1.6% walk, 1.0% work from home (2000); Travel time to work: 23.8% less than 15 minutes, 27.7% 15 to 30 minutes, 22.9% 30 to 45 minutes, 10.0% 45 to 60 minutes, 15.5% 60 minutes or more (2000)
Airports: Homestead AFB; Homestead General Aviation
Additional Information Contacts
Homestead-Florida City Chamber . . . . (305) 247-2332
Local Government Offices . . . . (305) 224-4400

HOMESTEAD BASE (CDP). Covers a land area of 4.353 square miles and a water area of 0 square miles. Located at 25.49° N. Lat.; 80.39° W. Long.
Population: 5,169 (1990); 446 (2000); 462 (2004); 514 (2009 projected); Race: 49.1% White, 39.6% Black, 0.6% Asian, 52.2% Hispanic of any race (2004); Density: 106.1 persons per square mile (2004); Average household size: 35.54 (2004); Median age: 30.0 (2004); Male/female ratio: 99.1 (2004); Marriage status: 40.0% never married, 41.6% now married, 7.9% widowed, 10.4% divorced (2000); Foreign born: 19.8% (2000); Ancestry (includes multiple ancestries): 44.0% Other groups, 10.6% United States or American, 3.0% Nigerian, 2.5% Italian, 1.7% German (2000).
Economy: Employment by occupation: 17.3% management, 0.0% professional, 26.7% services, 30.7% sales, 10.7% farming, 14.7% construction, 0.0% production (2000).
Income: Per capita income: $5,985 (2004); Median household income: $33,333 (2004); Average household income: $37,885 (2004); Percent of households with income of $100,000 or more: 0.0% (2004); Poverty rate: 65.5% (2000).
Education: Percent of population age 25 and over with: High school diploma (including GED) or higher: 29.4% (2004); Bachelor's degree or higher: 6.0% (2004); Master's degree or higher: 3.4% (2004).
Housing: Homeownership rate: 0.0% (2004); Median home value: $n/a (2004); Median rent: $175 per month (2000); Median age of housing: 35 years (2000).
Transportation: Commute to work: 37.3% car, 48.0% public transportation, 0.0% walk, 0.0% work from home (2000); Travel time to work: 0.0% less than 15 minutes, 21.3% 15 to 30 minutes, 0.0% 30 to 45 minutes, 14.7% 45 to 60 minutes, 64.0% 60 minutes or more (2000)

INDIAN CREEK (village). Covers a land area of 0.424 square miles and a water area of 0.029 square miles. Located at 25.87° N. Lat.; 80.13° W. Long.
Population: 44 (1990); 33 (2000); 28 (2004); 27 (2009 projected); Race: 100.0% White, 0.0% Black, 0.0% Asian, 10.7% Hispanic of any race (2004); Density: 66.1 persons per square mile (2004); Average household size: 2.33 (2004); Median age: 46.7 (2004); Male/female ratio: 100.0 (2004); Marriage status: 24.1% never married, 58.6% now married, 6.9% widowed, 10.3% divorced (2000); Foreign born: 55.9% (2000); Ancestry (includes multiple ancestries): 35.3% Other groups, 20.6% Dutch, 11.8% Brazilian, 11.8% Russian, 11.8% German (2000).
Economy: Single-family building permits issued: 0 (2004); Multi-family building permits issued: 0 (2004); Employment by occupation: 35.3% management, 29.4% professional, 23.5% services, 11.8% sales, 0.0% farming, 0.0% construction, 0.0% production (2000).
Income: Per capita income: $35,714 (2004); Median household income: $45,000 (2004); Average household income: $83,333 (2004); Percent of households with income of $100,000 or more: 16.7% (2004); Poverty rate: 29.4% (2000).
Taxes: Total city taxes per capita: $56,515 (2002); City property taxes per capita: $52,606 (2002).
Education: Percent of population age 25 and over with: High school diploma (including GED) or higher: 90.9% (2004); Bachelor's degree or higher: 31.8% (2004); Master's degree or higher: 13.6% (2004).
Housing: Homeownership rate: 75.0% (2004); Median home value: $1 million+ (2004); Median rent: $n/a per month (2000); Median age of housing: 37 years (2000).
Safety: Violent crime rate: 0.0 per 10,000 population; Property crime rate: 526.3 per 10,000 population (2003).
Transportation: Commute to work: 76.5% car, 0.0% public transportation, 11.8% walk, 11.8% work from home (2000); Travel time to work: 13.3% less than 15 minutes, 73.3% 15 to 30 minutes, 13.3% 30 to 45 minutes, 0.0% 45 to 60 minutes, 0.0% 60 minutes or more (2000)

ISLANDIA (city). Covers a land area of 6.452 square miles and a water area of 59.941 square miles. Located at 25.38° N. Lat.; 80.23° W. Long.
Population: 13 (1990); 6 (2000); 7 (2004); 8 (2009 projected); Race: 100.0% White, 0.0% Black, 0.0% Asian, 0.0% Hispanic of any race (2004); Density: 1.1 persons per square mile (2004); Average household size: 2.33 (2004); Median age: 27.5 (2004); Male/female ratio: 75.0 (2004); Marriage status: 50.0% never married, 50.0% now married, 0.0% widowed, 0.0% divorced (2000); Foreign born: 0.0% (2000); Ancestry (includes multiple ancestries): 50.0% Dutch, 50.0% German, 33.3% United States or American, 16.7% Norwegian, 16.7% Irish (2000).
Economy: Single-family building permits issued: 0 (2004); Multi-family building permits issued: 0 (2004); Employment by occupation: 0.0% management, 0.0% professional, 100.0% services, 0.0% sales, 0.0% farming, 0.0% construction, 0.0% production (2000).
Income: Per capita income: $20,000 (2004); Median household income: $42,500 (2004); Average household income: $46,667 (2004); Percent of households with income of $100,000 or more: 0.0% (2004); Poverty rate: 0.0% (2000).
Education: Percent of population age 25 and over with: High school diploma (including GED) or higher: 100.0% (2004); Bachelor's degree or higher: 100.0% (2004); Master's degree or higher: 0.0% (2004).
Housing: Homeownership rate: 0.0% (2004); Median home value: $n/a (2004); Median rent: $525 per month (2000); Median age of housing: 7 years (2000).
Transportation: Commute to work: 66.7% car, 0.0% public transportation, 0.0% walk, 0.0% work from home (2000); Travel time to work: 0.0% less than 15 minutes, 66.7% 15 to 30 minutes, 0.0% 30 to 45 minutes, 0.0% 45 to 60 minutes, 33.3% 60 minutes or more (2000)

IVES ESTATES (CDP). Covers a land area of 2.646 square miles and a water area of 0.153 square miles. Located at 25.96° N. Lat.; 80.18° W. Long.
Population: 13,531 (1990); 17,586 (2000); 18,568 (2004); 19,803 (2009 projected); Race: 43.6% White, 41.5% Black, 4.7% Asian, 27.3% Hispanic of any race (2004); Density: 7,017.0 persons per square mile (2004); Average household size: 2.57 (2004); Median age: 36.1 (2004); Male/female ratio: 84.4 (2004); Marriage status: 29.0% never married, 49.2% now married, 7.6% widowed, 14.2% divorced (2000); Foreign born: 40.7% (2000); Ancestry (includes multiple ancestries): 41.0% Other groups, 14.1% Haitian, 5.7% Jamaican, 5.3% United States or American, 4.1% Russian (2000).
Economy: Employment by occupation: 11.7% management, 21.7% professional, 16.7% services, 35.0% sales, 0.1% farming, 6.2% construction, 8.7% production (2000).
Income: Per capita income: $18,424 (2004); Median household income: $39,973 (2004); Average household income: $47,043 (2004); Percent of households with income of $100,000 or more: 6.0% (2004); Poverty rate: 8.6% (2000).
Education: Percent of population age 25 and over with: High school diploma (including GED) or higher: 85.0% (2004); Bachelor's degree or higher: 26.4% (2004); Master's degree or higher: 8.9% (2004).

Housing: Homeownership rate: 75.9% (2004); Median home value: $112,783 (2004); Median rent: $695 per month (2000); Median age of housing: 19 years (2000).
Transportation: Commute to work: 93.8% car, 1.4% public transportation, 1.1% walk, 2.5% work from home (2000); Travel time to work: 14.1% less than 15 minutes, 38.7% 15 to 30 minutes, 29.7% 30 to 45 minutes, 9.9% 45 to 60 minutes, 7.5% 60 minutes or more (2000)

KENDALE LAKES (CDP). Covers a land area of 8.173 square miles and a water area of 0.430 square miles. Located at 25.70° N. Lat.; 80.41° W. Long.
Population: 48,524 (1990); 56,901 (2000); 58,568 (2004); 60,849 (2009 projected); Race: 87.3% White, 2.0% Black, 1.6% Asian, 82.1% Hispanic of any race (2004); Density: 7,166.4 persons per square mile (2004); Average household size: 3.17 (2004); Median age: 36.9 (2004); Male/female ratio: 90.1 (2004); Marriage status: 23.9% never married, 58.4% now married, 6.4% widowed, 11.4% divorced (2000); Foreign born: 58.8% (2000); Ancestry (includes multiple ancestries): 79.4% Other groups, 2.8% United States or American, 2.3% Italian, 1.8% German, 1.7% English (2000).
Economy: Employment by occupation: 14.6% management, 16.8% professional, 13.1% services, 37.9% sales, 0.2% farming, 7.9% construction, 9.5% production (2000).
Income: Per capita income: $19,304 (2004); Median household income: $48,208 (2004); Average household income: $60,613 (2004); Percent of households with income of $100,000 or more: 13.5% (2004); Poverty rate: 10.3% (2000).
Education: Percent of population age 25 and over with: High school diploma (including GED) or higher: 78.6% (2004); Bachelor's degree or higher: 23.0% (2004); Master's degree or higher: 10.0% (2004).
Housing: Homeownership rate: 79.1% (2004); Median home value: $146,631 (2004); Median rent: $755 per month (2000); Median age of housing: 21 years (2000).
Transportation: Commute to work: 93.1% car, 2.1% public transportation, 1.1% walk, 3.3% work from home (2000); Travel time to work: 11.2% less than 15 minutes, 26.4% 15 to 30 minutes, 28.7% 30 to 45 minutes, 17.3% 45 to 60 minutes, 16.5% 60 minutes or more (2000)

KENDALL (CDP). Covers a land area of 16.126 square miles and a water area of 0.216 square miles. Located at 25.66° N. Lat.; 80.35° W. Long. Elevation is 10 feet.
Population: 69,644 (1990); 75,226 (2000); 78,094 (2004); 81,815 (2009 projected); Race: 86.5% White, 4.1% Black, 2.7% Asian, 57.3% Hispanic of any race (2004); Density: 4,842.7 persons per square mile (2004); Average household size: 2.66 (2004); Median age: 38.3 (2004); Male/female ratio: 88.9 (2004); Marriage status: 25.8% never married, 55.7% now married, 6.1% widowed, 12.4% divorced (2000); Foreign born: 42.6% (2000); Ancestry (includes multiple ancestries): 59.3% Other groups, 5.7% German, 5.4% United States or American, 5.1% Italian, 5.0% Irish (2000).
Economy: Major retail and business complexes abound, particularly around Dadeland where North Kendall Drive intersects the Palmetto Expressway and U.S. 1. Employment by occupation: 18.7% management, 26.2% professional, 11.8% services, 32.8% sales, 0.1% farming, 5.2% construction, 5.3% production (2000).
Income: Per capita income: $30,351 (2004); Median household income: $55,870 (2004); Average household income: $79,627 (2004); Percent of households with income of $100,000 or more: 23.2% (2004); Poverty rate: 8.6% (2000).
Education: Percent of population age 25 and over with: High school diploma (including GED) or higher: 88.3% (2004); Bachelor's degree or higher: 40.4% (2004); Master's degree or higher: 17.4% (2004).

School District(s)

Miami-Dade County School District (PK-12)
2002-03 Enrollment: 373,395 . . . . (305) 995-1428
Housing: Homeownership rate: 65.9% (2004); Median home value: $198,167 (2004); Median rent: $712 per month (2000); Median age of housing: 24 years (2000).
Transportation: Commute to work: 89.5% car, 4.5% public transportation, 1.0% walk, 4.2% work from home (2000); Travel time to work: 17.4% less than 15 minutes, 29.7% 15 to 30 minutes, 25.3% 30 to 45 minutes, 14.8% 45 to 60 minutes, 12.8% 60 minutes or more (2000)

KENDALL WEST (CDP). Covers a land area of 3.390 square miles and a water area of 0.259 square miles. Located at 25.70° N. Lat.; 80.44° W. Long.
Population: 16,857 (1990); 38,034 (2000); 44,317 (2004); 51,742 (2009 projected); Race: 83.7% White, 3.5% Black, 1.2% Asian, 84.4% Hispanic of any race (2004); Density: 13,071.9 persons per square mile (2004); Average household size: 3.31 (2004); Median age: 32.5 (2004); Male/female ratio: 90.1 (2004); Marriage status: 25.1% never married, 59.6% now married, 4.0% widowed, 11.4% divorced (2000); Foreign born: 59.4% (2000); Ancestry (includes multiple ancestries): 82.8% Other groups, 2.5% United States or American, 2.1% Italian, 1.6% German, 1.2% English (2000).
Economy: Employment by occupation: 12.5% management, 15.0% professional, 15.7% services, 37.6% sales, 0.2% farming, 9.7% construction, 9.4% production (2000).
Income: Per capita income: $15,769 (2004); Median household income: $40,722 (2004); Average household income: $51,837 (2004); Percent of households with income of $100,000 or more: 9.8% (2004); Poverty rate: 15.4% (2000).
Education: Percent of population age 25 and over with: High school diploma (including GED) or higher: 76.7% (2004); Bachelor's degree or higher: 21.3% (2004); Master's degree or higher: 8.5% (2004).
Housing: Homeownership rate: 63.2% (2004); Median home value: $149,270 (2004); Median rent: $691 per month (2000); Median age of housing: 13 years (2000).
Transportation: Commute to work: 92.3% car, 3.1% public transportation, 0.6% walk, 2.1% work from home (2000); Travel time to work: 8.5% less than 15 minutes, 20.8% 15 to 30 minutes, 30.4% 30 to 45 minutes, 19.5% 45 to 60 minutes, 20.7% 60 minutes or more (2000)

KEY BISCAYNE (village). Covers a land area of 1.277 square miles and a water area of 0.115 square miles. Located at 25.69° N. Lat.; 80.16° W. Long. Elevation is 4 feet.
Population: 8,854 (1990); 10,507 (2000); 10,352 (2004); 10,246 (2009 projected); Race: 95.0% White, 0.5% Black, 1.0% Asian, 54.0% Hispanic of any race (2004); Density: 8,103.6 persons per square mile (2004); Average household size: 2.48 (2004); Median age: 41.6 (2004); Male/female ratio: 89.1 (2004); Marriage status: 20.1% never married, 64.3% now married, 5.9% widowed, 9.7% divorced (2000); Foreign born: 50.4% (2000); Ancestry (includes multiple ancestries): 53.5% Other groups, 9.4% German, 6.9% English, 6.0% Italian, 4.8% Irish (2000).
Economy: Single-family building permits issued: 14 (2004); Multi-family building permits issued: 4 (2004); Employment by occupation: 37.9% management, 24.4% professional, 6.7% services, 27.8% sales, 0.2% farming, 0.9% construction, 2.0% production (2000).
Income: Per capita income: $57,933 (2004); Median household income: $94,323 (2004); Average household income: $143,956 (2004); Percent of households with income of $100,000 or more: 47.6% (2004); Poverty rate: 8.3% (2000).
Education: Percent of population age 25 and over with: High school diploma (including GED) or higher: 95.0% (2004); Bachelor's degree or higher: 65.2% (2004); Master's degree or higher: 31.5% (2004).

School District(s)

Miami-Dade County School District (PK-12)
2002-03 Enrollment: 373,395 . . . . (305) 995-1428
Housing: Homeownership rate: 70.5% (2004); Median home value: $517,857 (2004); Median rent: $1,609 per month (2000); Median age of housing: 25 years (2000).
Safety: Violent crime rate: 10.3 per 10,000 population; Property crime rate: 362.0 per 10,000 population (2003).
Newspapers: The Islander News (General - Circulation 3,800)
Transportation: Commute to work: 85.2% car, 1.7% public transportation, 2.0% walk, 9.4% work from home (2000); Travel time to work: 23.4% less than 15 minutes, 45.6% 15 to 30 minutes, 21.8% 30 to 45 minutes, 4.8% 45 to 60 minutes, 4.4% 60 minutes or more (2000)

Additional Information Contacts

Key Biscayne Chamber of Commerce. . . . . (305) 361-5207
Local Government Offices . . . . (305) 365-5511

LAKE LUCERNE (CDP). Covers a land area of 2.615 square miles and a water area of 0.014 square miles. Located at 25.96° N. Lat.; 80.25° W. Long.
Population: 9,478 (1990); 9,132 (2000); 9,756 (2004); 10,536 (2009 projected); Race: 10.5% White, 83.9% Black, 0.2% Asian, 15.0% Hispanic of any race (2004); Density: 3,730.9 persons per square mile (2004); Average household size: 3.44 (2004); Median age: 30.0 (2004); Male/female ratio: 88.4 (2004); Marriage status: 39.7% never married, 43.3% now married, 5.2% widowed, 11.9% divorced (2000); Foreign born:

20.0% (2000); Ancestry (includes multiple ancestries): 66.4% Other groups, 6.2% Jamaican, 5.3% United States or American, 3.1% Haitian, 2.6% Bahamian (2000).
Economy: Employment by occupation: 5.9% management, 13.6% professional, 19.7% services, 30.8% sales, 0.6% farming, 10.2% construction, 19.1% production (2000).
Income: Per capita income: $13,712 (2004); Median household income: $36,416 (2004); Average household income: $45,558 (2004); Percent of households with income of $100,000 or more: 7.3% (2004); Poverty rate: 16.5% (2000).
Education: Percent of population age 25 and over with: High school diploma (including GED) or higher: 63.0% (2004); Bachelor's degree or higher: 8.7% (2004); Master's degree or higher: 1.9% (2004).
Housing: Homeownership rate: 66.4% (2004); Median home value: $117,609 (2004); Median rent: $497 per month (2000); Median age of housing: 30 years (2000).
Transportation: Commute to work: 91.2% car, 6.9% public transportation, 0.4% walk, 0.4% work from home (2000); Travel time to work: 10.2% less than 15 minutes, 33.2% 15 to 30 minutes, 32.9% 30 to 45 minutes, 11.6% 45 to 60 minutes, 12.1% 60 minutes or more (2000)

LAKES BY THE BAY (CDP). Covers a land area of 4.852 square miles and a water area of 0.099 square miles. Located at 25.57° N. Lat.; 80.33° W. Long.
Population: 5,615 (1990); 9,055 (2000); 10,384 (2004); 11,958 (2009 projected); Race: 69.8% White, 17.2% Black, 2.7% Asian, 52.2% Hispanic of any race (2004); Density: 2,140.1 persons per square mile (2004); Average household size: 2.78 (2004); Median age: 33.9 (2004); Male/female ratio: 94.3 (2004); Marriage status: 21.6% never married, 62.5% now married, 4.4% widowed, 11.6% divorced (2000); Foreign born: 30.3% (2000); Ancestry (includes multiple ancestries): 54.5% Other groups, 8.0% Irish, 6.4% German, 5.4% United States or American, 4.2% Italian (2000).
Economy: Employment by occupation: 16.8% management, 20.0% professional, 13.2% services, 34.4% sales, 0.1% farming, 7.7% construction, 7.8% production (2000).
Income: Per capita income: $23,361 (2004); Median household income: $56,096 (2004); Average household income: $65,007 (2004); Percent of households with income of $100,000 or more: 17.3% (2004); Poverty rate: 10.1% (2000).
Education: Percent of population age 25 and over with: High school diploma (including GED) or higher: 83.7% (2004); Bachelor's degree or higher: 27.0% (2004); Master's degree or higher: 9.7% (2004).
Housing: Homeownership rate: 62.3% (2004); Median home value: $174,236 (2004); Median rent: $716 per month (2000); Median age of housing: 11 years (2000).
Transportation: Commute to work: 95.3% car, 1.7% public transportation, 0.9% walk, 1.2% work from home (2000); Travel time to work: 14.8% less than 15 minutes, 26.9% 15 to 30 minutes, 26.0% 30 to 45 minutes, 16.9% 45 to 60 minutes, 15.3% 60 minutes or more (2000)

LEISURE CITY (CDP). Covers a land area of 3.413 square miles and a water area of 0.019 square miles. Located at 25.49° N. Lat.; 80.43° W. Long.
Population: 19,378 (1990); 22,152 (2000); 23,546 (2004); 25,314 (2009 projected); Race: 64.7% White, 18.6% Black, 0.6% Asian, 69.2% Hispanic of any race (2004); Density: 6,898.4 persons per square mile (2004); Average household size: 3.73 (2004); Median age: 27.6 (2004); Male/female ratio: 101.2 (2004); Marriage status: 32.3% never married, 54.9% now married, 3.8% widowed, 9.0% divorced (2000); Foreign born: 39.4% (2000); Ancestry (includes multiple ancestries): 73.9% Other groups, 5.1% United States or American, 3.5% Haitian, 3.0% Irish, 2.9% German (2000).
Economy: Employment by occupation: 5.7% management, 10.0% professional, 21.4% services, 24.9% sales, 8.2% farming, 16.2% construction, 13.7% production (2000).
Income: Per capita income: $10,310 (2004); Median household income: $31,206 (2004); Average household income: $38,367 (2004); Percent of households with income of $100,000 or more: 3.7% (2004); Poverty rate: 25.0% (2000).
Education: Percent of population age 25 and over with: High school diploma (including GED) or higher: 48.6% (2004); Bachelor's degree or higher: 6.9% (2004); Master's degree or higher: 2.7% (2004).

School District(s)
Miami-Dade County School District (PK-12)
2002-03 Enrollment: 373,395 . . . . (305) 995-1428
Housing: Homeownership rate: 61.5% (2004); Median home value: $114,619 (2004); Median rent: $417 per month (2000); Median age of housing: 23 years (2000).
Transportation: Commute to work: 94.8% car, 2.0% public transportation, 1.2% walk, 0.8% work from home (2000); Travel time to work: 19.8% less than 15 minutes, 34.0% 15 to 30 minutes, 22.3% 30 to 45 minutes, 11.0% 45 to 60 minutes, 12.9% 60 minutes or more (2000)

MEDLEY (town). Covers a land area of 3.778 square miles and a water area of 0.520 square miles. Located at 25.85° N. Lat.; 80.33° W. Long. Elevation is 5 feet.
Population: 663 (1990); 1,098 (2000); 1,010 (2004); 983 (2009 projected); Race: 81.5% White, 7.2% Black, 2.8% Asian, 76.2% Hispanic of any race (2004); Density: 267.4 persons per square mile (2004); Average household size: 3.06 (2004); Median age: 40.8 (2004); Male/female ratio: 96.1 (2004); Marriage status: 20.4% never married, 56.1% now married, 5.4% widowed, 18.2% divorced (2000); Foreign born: 62.1% (2000); Ancestry (includes multiple ancestries): 72.4% Other groups, 4.4% United States or American, 2.4% Irish, 1.1% German, 0.7% Italian (2000).
Economy: Single-family building permits issued: 0 (2004); Multi-family building permits issued: 0 (2004); Employment by occupation: 4.5% management, 7.0% professional, 34.1% services, 14.2% sales, 0.6% farming, 21.8% construction, 17.9% production (2000).
Income: Per capita income: $13,058 (2004); Median household income: $24,872 (2004); Average household income: $35,174 (2004); Percent of households with income of $100,000 or more: 2.7% (2004); Poverty rate: 20.0% (2000).
Taxes: Total city taxes per capita: $7,063 (2002); City property taxes per capita: $4,756 (2002).
Education: Percent of population age 25 and over with: High school diploma (including GED) or higher: 48.1% (2004); Bachelor's degree or higher: 8.6% (2004); Master's degree or higher: 4.9% (2004).
Housing: Homeownership rate: 69.7% (2004); Median home value: $38,140 (2004); Median rent: $550 per month (2000); Median age of housing: 20 years (2000).
Safety: Violent crime rate: 151.2 per 10,000 population; Property crime rate: 2,348.8 per 10,000 population (2003).
Transportation: Commute to work: 89.0% car, 2.0% public transportation, 7.1% walk, 0.0% work from home (2000); Travel time to work: 24.6% less than 15 minutes, 48.4% 15 to 30 minutes, 14.7% 30 to 45 minutes, 7.9% 45 to 60 minutes, 4.2% 60 minutes or more (2000)

MIAMI (city). Covers a land area of 35.673 square miles and a water area of 19.593 square miles. Located at 25.78° N. Lat.; 80.22° W. Long. Elevation is 15 feet.
History: Miami owes its beginning to Julia S. Tuttle, who purchased property on both sides of the Miami River about 1870, and to Henry Flagler, who joined with her in 1896 to create a resort town and attact tourists and vacationers. Many people came for the game fishing. The first land boom occurred in the mid-1920's, when Florida real estate became prized across America, and skyrocketed in cost.
Population: 358,843 (1990); 362,470 (2000); 382,308 (2004); 407,786 (2009 projected); Race: 67.6% White, 20.9% Black, 0.6% Asian, 67.8% Hispanic of any race (2004); Density: 10,717.0 persons per square mile (2004); Average household size: 2.69 (2004); Median age: 39.4 (2004); Male/female ratio: 99.3 (2004); Marriage status: 32.2% never married, 46.7% now married, 8.3% widowed, 12.8% divorced (2000); Foreign born: 59.5% (2000); Ancestry (includes multiple ancestries): 71.3% Other groups, 5.0% Haitian, 3.1% United States or American, 1.4% Italian, 1.2% German (2000).
Economy: Unemployment rate: 8.2% (2004); Total civilian labor force: 191,207 (2004); Single-family building permits issued: 188 (2004); Multi-family building permits issued: 5,995 (2004); Employment by occupation: 10.4% management, 13.4% professional, 22.1% services, 26.2% sales, 0.5% farming, 13.6% construction, 13.8% production (2000).
Income: Per capita income: $16,381 (2004); Median household income: $24,978 (2004); Average household income: $42,532 (2004); Percent of households with income of $100,000 or more: 8.0% (2004); Poverty rate: 28.5% (2000).
Taxes: Total city taxes per capita: $639 (2002); City property taxes per capita: $389 (2002).

Education: Percent of population age 25 and over with: High school diploma (including GED) or higher: 52.8% (2004); Bachelor's degree or higher: 16.3% (2004); Master's degree or higher: 7.7% (2004).

School District(s)

Miami-Dade County School District (PK-12)
2002-03 Enrollment: 373,395 . . . . (305) 995-1428

Four-year College(s)

AI Miami International University of Art and Design (Private, For-profit)
2003-04 Enrollment: 1,277 . . . . (305) 428-5700
2003-04 Tuition: In-state $19,288; Out-of-state $19,288
Barry University
2003-04 Enrollment: 9,042 . . . . (800) 756-6000
2003-04 Tuition: In-state $20,320; Out-of-state $20,320
Carlos Albizu University-Miami Campus
2003-04 Enrollment: 850 . . . . (305) 593-1223
2003-04 Tuition: In-state $10,569; Out-of-state $10,569
City College
2003-04 Enrollment: 272 . . . . (305) 666-9242
2003-04 Tuition: In-state $8,160; Out-of-state $8,160
Florida International University (Public)
2003-04 Enrollment: 33,228 . . . . (305) 348-2000
2003-04 Tuition: In-state $2,668; Out-of-state $13,696
Florida Memorial College
2003-04 Enrollment: 2,176 . . . . (305) 626-3600
2003-04 Tuition: In-state $10,433; Out-of-state $10,433
ITT Technical Institute (Private, For-profit)
2003-04 Enrollment: 494 . . . . (305) 477-3080
2003-04 Tuition: In-state $12,492; Out-of-state $12,492
Jones College-Miami Campus
2003-04 Enrollment: 195 . . . . (305) 275-9996
2003-04 Tuition: In-state $5,490; Out-of-state $5,490
Miami Dade College (Public)
2003-04 Enrollment: 58,490 . . . . (305) 237-8888
2003-04 Tuition: In-state $1,583; Out-of-state $5,529
Saint John Vianney College Seminary
2003-04 Enrollment: 58 . . . . (305) 223-4561
2003-04 Tuition: In-state $11,000; Out-of-state $11,000
Saint Thomas University
2003-04 Enrollment: 2,520 . . . . (305) 625-6000
2003-04 Tuition: In-state $16,200; Out-of-state $16,200
Trinity International University
2003-04 Enrollment: 216 . . . . (305) 770-5100

Two-year College(s)

ATI Career Training Center (Private, For-profit)
2003-04 Enrollment: 662 . . . . (305) 573-1600
2003-04 Tuition: In-state $10,157; Out-of-state $10,157
ATI Health Education Center (Private, For-profit)
2003-04 Enrollment: 313 . . . . (305) 628-1000
2003-04 Tuition: In-state $27,000; Out-of-state $27,000
Acupuncture and Massage College
2003-04 Enrollment: 108 . . . . (305) 595-9500
Beauty Schools of America (Private, For-profit)
2003-04 Enrollment: 590 . . . . (305) 267-6604
College of Business and Technology (Private, For-profit)
2003-04 Enrollment: 141 . . . . (305) 273-4499
2003-04 Tuition: In-state $8,778; Out-of-state $8,778
Compu-Med Vocational Careers Corp (Private, For-profit)
2003-04 Enrollment: n/a . . . . (305) 888-9200
2003-04 Tuition: In-state $4,600; Out-of-state $4,600
Florida Career College (Private, For-profit)
2003-04 Enrollment: 2,131 . . . . (305) 553-6065
2003-04 Tuition: In-state $9,900; Out-of-state $9,900
Florida College of Natural Health (Private, For-profit)
2003-04 Enrollment: 168 . . . . (305) 597-9599
Florida Education Institute
2003-04 Enrollment: 157 . . . . (305) 444-1515
Florida National College-South Campus (Private, For-profit)
2003-04 Enrollment: n/a . . . . (305) 226-9999
2003-04 Tuition: In-state $8,185; Out-of-state $8,185
George T Baker Aviation School (Public)
2003-04 Enrollment: 386 . . . . (305) 871-3143
2003-04 Tuition: In-state $1,760; Out-of-state $1,760
Hi-Tech School of Miami (Private, For-profit)
2003-04 Enrollment: n/a . . . . (305) 221-3423
International Training Careers
2003-04 Enrollment: 238 . . . . (305) 263-9696
Keiser College- Kendall (Private, For-profit)
2003-04 Enrollment: n/a . . . . (305) 596-2226
2003-04 Tuition: In-state $10,920; Out-of-state $10,920
La Belle Beauty Academy (Private, For-profit)
2003-04 Enrollment: 338 . . . . (305) 649-2800
Lindsey Hopkins Technical Education Center (Public)
2003-04 Enrollment: 1,305 . . . . (305) 324-6070
2003-04 Tuition: In-state $2,215; Out-of-state $8,790
Mercy Hospital School of Practical Nursing
2003-04 Enrollment: 81 . . . . (305) 285-2777
Miami Lakes Educational Center (Public)
2003-04 Enrollment: 1,431 . . . . (305) 557-1100
2003-04 Tuition: In-state $1,741; Out-of-state $7,020
National School of Technology Inc (Private, For-profit)
2003-04 Enrollment: 1,754 . . . . (305) 893-0005
National School of Technology Inc (Private, For-profit)
2003-04 Enrollment: 1,563 . . . . (305) 949-9500
New Concept Massage and Beauty School
2003-04 Enrollment: 91 . . . . (305) 642-3020
New Professions Technical Institute (Private, For-profit)
2003-04 Enrollment: 190 . . . . (305) 461-2223
Nouvelle Institute (Private, For-profit)
2003-04 Enrollment: 390 . . . . (305) 643-3360
Praxis Institute (Private, For-profit)
2003-04 Enrollment: 288 . . . . (305) 642-4104
Professional Training Centers (Private, For-profit)
2003-04 Enrollment: 765 . . . . (305) 220-4120
Robert Morgan Educational Center (Public)
2003-04 Enrollment: 1,052 . . . . (305) 253-9920
2003-04 Tuition: In-state $1,950; Out-of-state $7,884
SER IBM Business Institute
2003-04 Enrollment: 119 . . . . (305) 871-2820
South Florida Institute of Technology (Private, For-profit)
2003-04 Enrollment: 16 . . . . (305) 649-2050
The English Center
2003-04 Enrollment: 661 . . . . (305) 445-7731
2003-04 Tuition: In-state $651; Out-of-state $2,550

Housing: Homeownership rate: 34.9% (2004); Median home value: $166,135 (2004); Median rent: $473 per month (2000); Median age of housing: 37 years (2000).

Hospitals: Baptist Hospital (577 beds); Cedars Medical Center (568 beds); Coral Gables Hospital (273 beds); HealthSouth Doctors' Hospital (285 beds); Hialeah Hospital (378 beds); Jackson Memorial Hospital (1567 beds); Jackson South Community Hospital (205 beds); Kendall Medical Center (412 beds); Mercy Health Systems (512 beds); Miami Childrens Hospital (268 beds); Miami Heart Institute and Medical Center (278 beds); Miami Jewish Home & Hospital for the Aged at Douglas Gardens (430 beds); Miami Veterans Affairs Medical Center (790 beds); Mount Sinai Medical Center (701 beds); North Shore Medical Center (357 beds); Palm Springs General Hospital (247 beds); Pan American Hospital (146 beds); South Miami Hospital (500 beds); South Shore Hospital & Medical Center (196 beds); University of Miami Hospital & Clinics (40 beds); University of Miami, Bascom Palmer Eye Institute (100 beds); Villa Maria Rehabilitation Hospital (272 beds); Westchester General Hospital (160 beds)

Safety: Violent crime rate: 187.5 per 10,000 population; Property crime rate: 690.9 per 10,000 population (2003).

Newspapers: Catalyst (General - Circulation 3,000); Diario las Americas (Circulation 69,100); El Especial (Hispanic, Senior Citizen - Circulation 35,000); El Nuevo Herald (Circulation 90,264); El Nuevo Patria (Hispanic - Circulation 28,000); Falcon Times (General - Circulation 2,000); Florida Newspaper (General - Circulation 20,000); Florida Review Newspaper (General - Circulation 32,000); Miami Daily Business Review (Circulation 10,000); Miami New Times (Alternative, General - Circulation 105,000); Prensa Grafica (Hispanic - Circulation 31,000); River Cities Gazette (General - Circulation 12,000); Sabor Magazine (Hispanic - Circulation 28,000); The Miami Herald (Circulation 306,943); The Miami Times (Black - Circulation 28,170); The Weekly News - TWN (Gay/Lesbian - Circulation 22,500)

Transportation: Commute to work: 80.8% car, 11.4% public transportation, 3.7% walk, 2.1% work from home (2000); Travel time to work: 20.0% less than 15 minutes, 38.9% 15 to 30 minutes, 24.8% 30 to 45 minutes, 6.6% 45 to 60 minutes, 9.6% 60 minutes or more (2000); Amtrak: Service available.

Airports: Dade-Collier Training and Transition; Kendall-Tamiami Executive; Miami (commercial service); Miami International (primary service/large hub); Opa Locka (primary service/large hub)

Additional Information Contacts

Allapattah Chamber of Commerce. . . . . (305) 638-0280
Argentine Florida Chamber . . . . . (305) 858-1516
Aventura Chamber of Commerce . . . . . (305) 935-2131
Brazilian-American Chamber. . . . . (305) 579-9030
British American Chamber of Commerce . . . . . (305) 377-0992
Coconut Grove Chamber of Commerce . . . . . (305) 444-7270
Doral-Airport West Chamber . . . . . (305) 592-5141
Ecuadorian-American Chamber. . . . . (305) 539-0010
Florida Gold Coast Chamber. . . . . (305) 866-6020
Greater Miami Chamber of Commerce . . . . . (305) 350-7700
Greater Miami Convention & Visitors Bureau . . . . . (305) 539-3000
Italy America Chamber of Commerce . . . . . (305) 577-9868
Korean American Chamber of Commerce. . . . . (305) 468-1718
Latin Chamber of Commerce. . . . . (305) 642-3870
Nicaraguan-American Chamber of Commerce . . . . . (305) 599-2737
North Dade Chamber of Commerce . . . . . (305) 690-9123
Peruvian U.S. Chamber of Commerce . . . . . (305) 471-9434
Realtor Association of Greater Miami & The Beaches. . . . . (305) 468-7000
United States-Mexico Chamber of Commerce . . . . . (305) 379-6090
Women's Chamber of Commerce . . . . . (305) 446-6660

MIAMI BEACH (city). Covers a land area of 7.033 square miles and a water area of 11.675 square miles. Located at 25.81° N. Lat.; 80.13° W. Long. Elevation is 5 feet.

History: Named for the Mayaimi Indian tribe. Miami Beach was made suitable for settlement by John S. Collins, a New Jersey horticulturist who first planted an avocado grove here. Collins dredged a canal, and organized the Miami Beach Improvement Company. A bridge across the bay to Miami was completed in 1913, and in 1915 Miami Beach was incorporated as a city.

Population: 92,639 (1990); 87,933 (2000); 89,972 (2004); 93,012 (2009 projected); Race: 87.0% White, 3.7% Black, 1.3% Asian, 57.8% Hispanic of any race (2004); Density: 12,792.0 persons per square mile (2004); Average household size: 1.91 (2004); Median age: 41.1 (2004); Male/female ratio: 105.0 (2004); Marriage status: 35.4% never married, 41.8% now married, 8.8% widowed, 14.0% divorced (2000); Foreign born: 55.5% (2000); Ancestry (includes multiple ancestries): 54.1% Other groups, 5.0% Italian, 5.0% United States or American, 4.3% German, 3.7% Russian (2000).

Economy: Unemployment rate: 6.6% (2004); Total civilian labor force: 46,992 (2004); Single-family building permits issued: 23 (2004); Multi-family building permits issued: 368 (2004); Employment by occupation: 17.7% management, 22.5% professional, 21.1% services, 26.9% sales, 0.2% farming, 4.8% construction, 6.8% production (2000).

Income: Per capita income: $30,514 (2004); Median household income: $31,643 (2004); Average household income: $57,824 (2004); Percent of households with income of $100,000 or more: 13.5% (2004); Poverty rate: 21.8% (2000).

Taxes: Total city taxes per capita: $1,470 (2002); City property taxes per capita: $780 (2002).

Education: Percent of population age 25 and over with: High school diploma (including GED) or higher: 78.8% (2004); Bachelor's degree or higher: 33.4% (2004); Master's degree or higher: 15.7% (2004).

School District(s)

Miami-Dade County School District (PK-12)
2002-03 Enrollment: 373,395 . . . . . (305) 995-1428

Four-year College(s)

Talmudic College of Florida
2003-04 Enrollment: 40 . . . . . (305) 534-7050
2003-04 Tuition: In-state $7,250; Out-of-state $7,250
Yeshivah Gedolah Rabbinical College
2003-04 Enrollment: 128 . . . . . (305) 673-5664
2003-04 Tuition: In-state $7,950; Out-of-state $7,950

Two-year College(s)

Miami Ad School (Private, For-profit)
2003-04 Enrollment: 185 . . . . . (305) 538-3193
2003-04 Tuition: In-state $10,500; Out-of-state $10,500

Housing: Homeownership rate: 36.5% (2004); Median home value: $183,235 (2004); Median rent: $581 per month (2000); Median age of housing: 37 years (2000).

Safety: Violent crime rate: 128.5 per 10,000 population; Property crime rate: 1,034.7 per 10,000 population (2003).

Transportation: Commute to work: 67.7% car, 11.4% public transportation, 10.3% walk, 5.4% work from home (2000); Travel time to work: 27.5% less than 15 minutes, 37.3% 15 to 30 minutes, 22.5% 30 to 45 minutes, 6.0% 45 to 60 minutes, 6.8% 60 minutes or more (2000)

Additional Information Contacts

Local Government Offices . . . . . (305) 673-7411
Miami Beach Chamber of Commerce . . . . . (305) 672-1270
Miami International Chamber. . . . . (305) 861-2000
South Beach Hispanic Chamber . . . . . (305) 534-1903

MIAMI LAKES (CDP). Covers a land area of 5.957 square miles and a water area of 0.431 square miles. Located at 25.91° N. Lat.; 80.32° W. Long.

Population: 14,033 (1990); 22,676 (2000); 24,075 (2004); 25,875 (2009 projected); Race: 89.1% White, 2.9% Black, 1.9% Asian, 75.4% Hispanic of any race (2004); Density: 4,041.2 persons per square mile (2004); Average household size: 2.87 (2004); Median age: 37.0 (2004); Male/female ratio: 93.2 (2004); Marriage status: 22.6% never married, 60.9% now married, 5.5% widowed, 10.9% divorced (2000); Foreign born: 47.6% (2000); Ancestry (includes multiple ancestries): 73.7% Other groups, 4.3% Irish, 3.8% United States or American, 3.8% German, 3.5% Italian (2000).

Economy: Manufacturing includes apparel, medical equipment, and plastic products. Employment by occupation: 21.2% management, 21.1% professional, 7.7% services, 37.4% sales, 0.2% farming, 3.8% construction, 8.4% production (2000).

Income: Per capita income: $29,736 (2004); Median household income: $65,298 (2004); Average household income: $84,793 (2004); Percent of households with income of $100,000 or more: 25.5% (2004); Poverty rate: 4.9% (2000).

Education: Percent of population age 25 and over with: High school diploma (including GED) or higher: 84.5% (2004); Bachelor's degree or higher: 34.7% (2004); Master's degree or higher: 14.4% (2004).

School District(s)

Miami-Dade County School District (PK-12)
2002-03 Enrollment: 373,395 . . . . . (305) 995-1428

Housing: Homeownership rate: 75.1% (2004); Median home value: $215,491 (2004); Median rent: $806 per month (2000); Median age of housing: 17 years (2000).

Safety: Violent crime rate: 39.1 per 10,000 population; Property crime rate: 439.3 per 10,000 population (2003).

Newspapers: Miami Laker (General - Circulation 27,000)

Transportation: Commute to work: 94.6% car, 1.1% public transportation, 0.2% walk, 3.7% work from home (2000); Travel time to work: 21.1% less than 15 minutes, 29.8% 15 to 30 minutes, 26.3% 30 to 45 minutes, 15.5% 45 to 60 minutes, 7.3% 60 minutes or more (2000)

MIAMI SHORES (village). Covers a land area of 2.455 square miles and a water area of 1.274 square miles. Located at 25.86° N. Lat.; 80.18° W. Long. Elevation is 8 feet.

History: Separated from Miami in 1932. Barry University is here.

Population: 9,891 (1990); 10,380 (2000); 10,382 (2004); 10,452 (2009 projected); Race: 62.0% White, 25.9% Black, 2.5% Asian, 26.4% Hispanic of any race (2004); Density: 4,228.4 persons per square mile (2004); Average household size: 2.92 (2004); Median age: 38.0 (2004); Male/female ratio: 95.4 (2004); Marriage status: 27.4% never married, 54.8% now married, 6.3% widowed, 11.5% divorced (2000); Foreign born: 27.7% (2000); Ancestry (includes multiple ancestries): 35.7% Other groups, 11.8% Irish, 9.3% Haitian, 9.2% German, 8.0% Italian (2000).

Economy: Single-family building permits issued: 1 (2004); Multi-family building permits issued: 14 (2004); Employment by occupation: 20.9% management, 28.8% professional, 15.3% services, 23.4% sales, 0.3% farming, 5.8% construction, 5.6% production (2000).

Income: Per capita income: $27,668 (2004); Median household income: $63,230 (2004); Average household income: $79,808 (2004); Percent of households with income of $100,000 or more: 25.8% (2004); Poverty rate: 8.8% (2000).

Taxes: Total city taxes per capita: $557 (2002); City property taxes per capita: $298 (2002).

Education: Percent of population age 25 and over with: High school diploma (including GED) or higher: 88.3% (2004); Bachelor's degree or higher: 42.3% (2004); Master's degree or higher: 17.8% (2004).

School District(s)
Miami-Dade County School District (PK-12)
2002-03 Enrollment: 373,395 . . . . (305) 995-1428
Housing: Homeownership rate: 89.5% (2004); Median home value: $222,830 (2004); Median rent: $679 per month (2000); Median age of housing: 47 years (2000).
Safety: Violent crime rate: 72.0 per 10,000 population; Property crime rate: 696.4 per 10,000 population (2003).
Transportation: Commute to work: 89.7% car, 2.9% public transportation, 1.9% walk, 4.8% work from home (2000); Travel time to work: 19.6% less than 15 minutes, 44.2% 15 to 30 minutes, 26.0% 30 to 45 minutes, 4.8% 45 to 60 minutes, 5.4% 60 minutes or more (2000)
Additional Information Contacts
Greater Miami Shores Chamber . . . . (305) 754-5466
Local Government Offices . . . . (305) 795-2207
Miami-Dade Chamber of Commerce . . . . (305) 751-8648

MIAMI SPRINGS (city). Covers a land area of 2.938 square miles and a water area of 0.041 square miles. Located at 25.82° N. Lat.; 80.29° W. Long. Elevation is 5 feet.
History: Named for the Mayaimi Indian tribe. Incorporated 1926.
Population: 13,268 (1990); 13,712 (2000); 13,582 (2004); 13,592 (2009 projected); Race: 90.7% White, 2.1% Black, 0.9% Asian, 67.7% Hispanic of any race (2004); Density: 4,622.5 persons per square mile (2004); Average household size: 2.74 (2004); Median age: 40.1 (2004); Male/female ratio: 93.0 (2004); Marriage status: 23.5% never married, 54.4% now married, 9.2% widowed, 12.9% divorced (2000); Foreign born: 43.6% (2000); Ancestry (includes multiple ancestries): 65.7% Other groups, 7.0% German, 6.3% Irish, 5.8% English, 4.3% United States or American (2000).
Economy: Miami International Airport is just South of the city. Single-family building permits issued: 4 (2004); Multi-family building permits issued: 0 (2004); Employment by occupation: 16.2% management, 18.5% professional, 11.1% services, 33.1% sales, 0.1% farming, 10.5% construction, 10.5% production (2000).
Income: Per capita income: $26,915 (2004); Median household income: $56,317 (2004); Average household income: $72,984 (2004); Percent of households with income of $100,000 or more: 19.9% (2004); Poverty rate: 9.7% (2000).
Education: Percent of population age 25 and over with: High school diploma (including GED) or higher: 82.4% (2004); Bachelor's degree or higher: 26.7% (2004); Master's degree or higher: 10.5% (2004).
School District(s)
Miami-Dade County School District (PK-12)
2002-03 Enrollment: 373,395 . . . . (305) 995-1428
Two-year College(s)
Technical Career Institute (Private, For-profit)
2003-04 Enrollment: 395 . . . . (305) 863-1818
2003-04 Tuition: In-state $7,900; Out-of-state $7,900
Housing: Homeownership rate: 64.5% (2004); Median home value: $220,821 (2004); Median rent: $547 per month (2000); Median age of housing: 44 years (2000).
Safety: Violent crime rate: 57.2 per 10,000 population; Property crime rate: 453.0 per 10,000 population (2003).
Transportation: Commute to work: 92.2% car, 1.9% public transportation, 1.2% walk, 3.8% work from home (2000); Travel time to work: 28.6% less than 15 minutes, 43.1% 15 to 30 minutes, 20.5% 30 to 45 minutes, 4.0% 45 to 60 minutes, 3.9% 60 minutes or more (2000)
Additional Information Contacts
Local Government Offices . . . . (305) 805-5000

NARANJA (CDP). Covers a land area of 1.520 square miles and a water area of 0.148 square miles. Located at 25.51° N. Lat.; 80.42° W. Long. Elevation is 10 feet.
History: Virtually destroyed by Hurricane Andrew in 1992.
Population: 5,790 (1990); 4,034 (2000); 4,328 (2004); 4,683 (2009 projected); Race: 33.5% White, 56.4% Black, 1.2% Asian, 32.6% Hispanic of any race (2004); Density: 2,848.1 persons per square mile (2004); Average household size: 3.45 (2004); Median age: 25.8 (2004); Male/female ratio: 91.2 (2004); Marriage status: 42.2% never married, 40.5% now married, 5.6% widowed, 11.7% divorced (2000); Foreign born: 23.3% (2000); Ancestry (includes multiple ancestries): 71.4% Other groups, 4.0% Haitian, 3.5% Jamaican, 2.5% United States or American, 2.5% Trinidadian and Tobagonian (2000).
Economy: Adjacent to Homestead Air Force Base. Employment by occupation: 8.6% management, 7.9% professional, 31.3% services, 33.1% sales, 0.8% farming, 11.4% construction, 7.0% production (2000).
Income: Per capita income: $7,393 (2004); Median household income: $19,147 (2004); Average household income: $23,101 (2004); Percent of households with income of $100,000 or more: 1.0% (2004); Poverty rate: 50.5% (2000).
Education: Percent of population age 25 and over with: High school diploma (including GED) or higher: 53.8% (2004); Bachelor's degree or higher: 5.1% (2004); Master's degree or higher: 1.4% (2004).
School District(s)
Miami-Dade County School District (PK-12)
2002-03 Enrollment: 373,395 . . . . (305) 995-1428
Housing: Homeownership rate: 35.5% (2004); Median home value: $85,258 (2004); Median rent: $430 per month (2000); Median age of housing: 21 years (2000).
Transportation: Commute to work: 79.5% car, 15.0% public transportation, 3.2% walk, 1.0% work from home (2000); Travel time to work: 17.7% less than 15 minutes, 29.7% 15 to 30 minutes, 25.4% 30 to 45 minutes, 13.1% 45 to 60 minutes, 14.0% 60 minutes or more (2000)

NORLAND (CDP). Covers a land area of 3.610 square miles and a water area of 0.040 square miles. Located at 25.94° N. Lat.; 80.21° W. Long. Elevation is 10 feet.
Population: 22,084 (1990); 22,995 (2000); 23,843 (2004); 25,018 (2009 projected); Race: 10.3% White, 82.1% Black, 0.9% Asian, 9.2% Hispanic of any race (2004); Density: 6,604.2 persons per square mile (2004); Average household size: 3.37 (2004); Median age: 32.0 (2004); Male/female ratio: 85.6 (2004); Marriage status: 36.3% never married, 46.3% now married, 5.9% widowed, 11.5% divorced (2000); Foreign born: 39.2% (2000); Ancestry (includes multiple ancestries): 42.2% Other groups, 21.1% Jamaican, 12.1% Haitian, 3.8% United States or American, 2.2% Bahamian (2000).
Economy: Employment by occupation: 7.9% management, 15.0% professional, 26.2% services, 28.5% sales, 0.3% farming, 10.3% construction, 11.9% production (2000).
Income: Per capita income: $13,803 (2004); Median household income: $37,290 (2004); Average household income: $45,564 (2004); Percent of households with income of $100,000 or more: 5.4% (2004); Poverty rate: 16.0% (2000).
Education: Percent of population age 25 and over with: High school diploma (including GED) or higher: 69.4% (2004); Bachelor's degree or higher: 12.4% (2004); Master's degree or higher: 4.2% (2004).
Housing: Homeownership rate: 65.3% (2004); Median home value: $123,677 (2004); Median rent: $546 per month (2000); Median age of housing: 36 years (2000).
Transportation: Commute to work: 88.1% car, 7.9% public transportation, 2.0% walk, 1.6% work from home (2000); Travel time to work: 14.4% less than 15 minutes, 32.8% 15 to 30 minutes, 31.9% 30 to 45 minutes, 11.0% 45 to 60 minutes, 9.9% 60 minutes or more (2000)

NORTH BAY VILLAGE (city). Covers a land area of 0.332 square miles and a water area of 0.505 square miles. Located at 25.84° N. Lat.; 80.15° W. Long. Elevation is 7 feet.
Population: 5,383 (1990); 6,733 (2000); 6,705 (2004); 6,731 (2009 projected); Race: 79.1% White, 5.4% Black, 3.4% Asian, 55.8% Hispanic of any race (2004); Density: 20,182.8 persons per square mile (2004); Average household size: 2.19 (2004); Median age: 36.6 (2004); Male/female ratio: 100.8 (2004); Marriage status: 31.9% never married, 48.6% now married, 5.1% widowed, 14.4% divorced (2000); Foreign born: 54.1% (2000); Ancestry (includes multiple ancestries): 52.5% Other groups, 6.7% Italian, 6.2% Brazilian, 5.0% United States or American, 4.7% German (2000).
Economy: Single-family building permits issued: 8 (2004); Multi-family building permits issued: 504 (2004); Employment by occupation: 13.5% management, 20.1% professional, 19.3% services, 31.6% sales, 0.0% farming, 5.7% construction, 9.7% production (2000).
Income: Per capita income: $21,880 (2004); Median household income: $35,712 (2004); Average household income: $47,513 (2004); Percent of households with income of $100,000 or more: 8.7% (2004); Poverty rate: 12.9% (2000).
Taxes: Total city taxes per capita: $378 (2002); City property taxes per capita: $205 (2002).

Education: Percent of population age 25 and over with: High school diploma (including GED) or higher: 86.5% (2004); Bachelor's degree or higher: 29.3% (2004); Master's degree or higher: 11.9% (2004).
Housing: Homeownership rate: 29.1% (2004); Median home value: $131,751 (2004); Median rent: $776 per month (2000); Median age of housing: 34 years (2000).
Safety: Violent crime rate: 33.5 per 10,000 population; Property crime rate: 375.9 per 10,000 population (2003).
Transportation: Commute to work: 88.6% car, 5.2% public transportation, 2.7% walk, 2.9% work from home (2000); Travel time to work: 12.9% less than 15 minutes, 40.9% 15 to 30 minutes, 35.3% 30 to 45 minutes, 5.5% 45 to 60 minutes, 5.3% 60 minutes or more (2000)
Additional Information Contacts
Local Government Offices . . . . (305) 756-7171

NORTH MIAMI (city). Covers a land area of 8.458 square miles and a water area of 1.531 square miles. Located at 25.89° N. Lat.; 80.18° W. Long. Elevation is 10 feet.
History: Named for its location north of Miami. Substantial retail development since the 1980s. Incorporated 1926.
Population: 50,721 (1990); 59,880 (2000); 60,049 (2004); 60,814 (2009 projected); Race: 30.2% White, 59.1% Black, 1.7% Asian, 23.6% Hispanic of any race (2004); Density: 7,099.9 persons per square mile (2004); Average household size: 2.97 (2004); Median age: 33.1 (2004); Male/female ratio: 93.0 (2004); Marriage status: 37.2% never married, 47.1% now married, 6.3% widowed, 9.4% divorced (2000); Foreign born: 48.5% (2000); Ancestry (includes multiple ancestries): 34.2% Other groups, 31.1% Haitian, 5.5% United States or American, 3.1% Jamaican, 2.4% German (2000).
Economy: Mainly residential. Manufacturing includes boats, wooden furniture, and aluminum products. Unemployment rate: 6.0% (2004); Total civilian labor force: 30,422 (2004); Single-family building permits issued: 8 (2004); Multi-family building permits issued: 0 (2004); Employment by occupation: 9.2% management, 15.0% professional, 25.0% services, 28.5% sales, 0.0% farming, 8.4% construction, 13.8% production (2000).
Income: Per capita income: $14,678 (2004); Median household income: $30,376 (2004); Average household income: $42,998 (2004); Percent of households with income of $100,000 or more: 6.7% (2004); Poverty rate: 23.9% (2000).
Taxes: Total city taxes per capita: $281 (2002); City property taxes per capita: $183 (2002).
Education: Percent of population age 25 and over with: High school diploma (including GED) or higher: 67.1% (2004); Bachelor's degree or higher: 15.9% (2004); Master's degree or higher: 6.9% (2004).

School District(s)

Miami-Dade County School District (PK-12)
2002-03 Enrollment: 373,395 . . . . (305) 995-1428

Four-year College(s)

Johnson & Wales University-Florida Campus
2003-04 Enrollment: 2,379 . . . . (305) 892-7000
2003-04 Tuition: In-state $19,194; Out-of-state $19,194
Housing: Homeownership rate: 50.5% (2004); Median home value: $120,893 (2004); Median rent: $547 per month (2000); Median age of housing: 35 years (2000).
Safety: Violent crime rate: 134.6 per 10,000 population; Property crime rate: 758.5 per 10,000 population (2003).
Transportation: Commute to work: 83.2% car, 10.6% public transportation, 2.7% walk, 2.0% work from home (2000); Travel time to work: 15.6% less than 15 minutes, 32.9% 15 to 30 minutes, 32.0% 30 to 45 minutes, 10.3% 45 to 60 minutes, 9.1% 60 minutes or more (2000)
Additional Information Contacts
Greater North Miami Chamber. . . . . (305) 891-7811
Local Government Offices . . . . (305) 893-6511

NORTH MIAMI BEACH (city). Covers a land area of 4.955 square miles and a water area of 0.335 square miles. Located at 25.93° N. Lat.; 80.17° W. Long. Elevation is 10 feet.
History: Named for its location north of Miami Beach. North Miami Beach was first known as Fulford, for an early settler. The town changed its name in the hope of becoming more closely associated with Miami Beach. The North Miami Zoo was established here.
Population: 34,812 (1990); 40,786 (2000); 41,085 (2004); 41,640 (2009 projected); Race: 43.1% White, 41.6% Black, 3.9% Asian, 33.5% Hispanic of any race (2004); Density: 8,291.0 persons per square mile (2004); Average household size: 2.97 (2004); Median age: 35.8 (2004); Male/female ratio: 92.1 (2004); Marriage status: 31.6% never married, 49.9% now married, 7.2% widowed, 11.3% divorced (2000); Foreign born: 49.7% (2000); Ancestry (includes multiple ancestries): 43.2% Other groups, 19.3% Haitian, 6.0% United States or American, 5.4% Jamaican, 3.0% Italian (2000).
Economy: Unemployment rate: 4.6% (2004); Total civilian labor force: 19,919 (2004); Single-family building permits issued: 109 (2004); Multi-family building permits issued: 4 (2004); Employment by occupation: 9.0% management, 13.0% professional, 22.6% services, 32.1% sales, 0.1% farming, 10.2% construction, 13.0% production (2000).
Income: Per capita income: $14,949 (2004); Median household income: $32,819 (2004); Average household income: $44,009 (2004); Percent of households with income of $100,000 or more: 6.1% (2004); Poverty rate: 20.5% (2000).
Taxes: Total city taxes per capita: $403 (2002); City property taxes per capita: $197 (2002).
Education: Percent of population age 25 and over with: High school diploma (including GED) or higher: 68.7% (2004); Bachelor's degree or higher: 14.4% (2004); Master's degree or higher: 6.0% (2004).

School District(s)

Miami-Dade County School District (PK-12)
2002-03 Enrollment: 373,395 . . . . (305) 995-1428

Four-year College(s)

Union Institute & University
2003-04 Enrollment: n/a . . . . (305) 653-7141
2003-04 Tuition: In-state $7,848; Out-of-state $7,848
Housing: Homeownership rate: 62.2% (2004); Median home value: $124,547 (2004); Median rent: $573 per month (2000); Median age of housing: 36 years (2000).
Hospitals: Parkway Regional Medical Center (382 beds)
Safety: Violent crime rate: 112.3 per 10,000 population; Property crime rate: 585.9 per 10,000 population (2003).
Transportation: Commute to work: 86.6% car, 9.5% public transportation, 1.3% walk, 1.6% work from home (2000); Travel time to work: 18.3% less than 15 minutes, 32.1% 15 to 30 minutes, 28.5% 30 to 45 minutes, 11.1% 45 to 60 minutes, 10.0% 60 minutes or more (2000)
Additional Information Contacts
Local Government Offices . . . . (305) 947-7581
North Miami Beach Chamber of Commerce . . . . (305) 944-8500

OJUS (CDP). Covers a land area of 2.786 square miles and a water area of 0.491 square miles. Located at 25.95° N. Lat.; 80.15° W. Long. Elevation is 5 feet.
History: Named for the Indian translation of "plentiful," referring to the vegetation in the area. Ojus began as a trading post.
Population: 15,141 (1990); 16,642 (2000); 16,741 (2004); 16,973 (2009 projected); Race: 81.6% White, 8.8% Black, 1.9% Asian, 39.7% Hispanic of any race (2004); Density: 6,008.7 persons per square mile (2004); Average household size: 2.33 (2004); Median age: 43.5 (2004); Male/female ratio: 87.4 (2004); Marriage status: 21.3% never married, 56.2% now married, 11.0% widowed, 11.6% divorced (2000); Foreign born: 41.6% (2000); Ancestry (includes multiple ancestries): 40.5% Other groups, 7.5% Russian, 7.0% United States or American, 5.0% Polish, 4.8% Italian (2000).
Economy: Employment by occupation: 18.1% management, 20.9% professional, 16.9% services, 32.4% sales, 0.0% farming, 5.4% construction, 6.3% production (2000).
Income: Per capita income: $26,042 (2004); Median household income: $36,206 (2004); Average household income: $59,887 (2004); Percent of households with income of $100,000 or more: 15.1% (2004); Poverty rate: 13.5% (2000).
Education: Percent of population age 25 and over with: High school diploma (including GED) or higher: 81.2% (2004); Bachelor's degree or higher: 30.6% (2004); Master's degree or higher: 15.5% (2004).
Housing: Homeownership rate: 84.8% (2004); Median home value: $87,492 (2004); Median rent: $569 per month (2000); Median age of housing: 32 years (2000).
Transportation: Commute to work: 90.4% car, 3.1% public transportation, 2.1% walk, 4.3% work from home (2000); Travel time to work: 22.0% less than 15 minutes, 32.2% 15 to 30 minutes, 26.9% 30 to 45 minutes, 11.9% 45 to 60 minutes, 7.1% 60 minutes or more (2000)

OLYMPIA HEIGHTS (CDP). Covers a land area of 2.722 square miles and a water area of 0.291 square miles. Located at 25.72° N. Lat.; 80.34° W. Long.

Population: 13,268 (1990); 13,452 (2000); 13,570 (2004); 13,852 (2009 projected); Race: 93.6% White, 0.9% Black, 0.7% Asian, 80.1% Hispanic of any race (2004); Density: 4,984.8 persons per square mile (2004); Average household size: 3.25 (2004); Median age: 43.4 (2004); Male/female ratio: 92.4 (2004); Marriage status: 21.4% never married, 59.4% now married, 7.8% widowed, 11.4% divorced (2000); Foreign born: 58.7% (2000); Ancestry (includes multiple ancestries): 75.9% Other groups, 3.6% Irish, 2.9% United States or American, 2.7% German, 2.6% English (2000).
Economy: Employment by occupation: 11.2% management, 16.1% professional, 14.9% services, 33.1% sales, 0.0% farming, 11.9% construction, 12.7% production (2000).
Income: Per capita income: $20,151 (2004); Median household income: $54,355 (2004); Average household income: $63,964 (2004); Percent of households with income of $100,000 or more: 16.9% (2004); Poverty rate: 6.9% (2000).
Education: Percent of population age 25 and over with: High school diploma (including GED) or higher: 69.0% (2004); Bachelor's degree or higher: 20.8% (2004); Master's degree or higher: 9.1% (2004).
Housing: Homeownership rate: 86.6% (2004); Median home value: $208,096 (2004); Median rent: $809 per month (2000); Median age of housing: 42 years (2000).
Transportation: Commute to work: 94.9% car, 1.7% public transportation, 0.7% walk, 1.9% work from home (2000); Travel time to work: 15.9% less than 15 minutes, 34.6% 15 to 30 minutes, 31.0% 30 to 45 minutes, 11.1% 45 to 60 minutes, 7.5% 60 minutes or more (2000)

OPA-LOCKA (city). Covers a land area of 4.331 square miles and a water area of 0.143 square miles. Located at 25.90° N. Lat.; 80.25° W. Long. Elevation is 7 feet.
Population: 15,283 (1990); 14,951 (2000); 14,708 (2004); 14,492 (2009 projected); Race: 24.3% White, 68.0% Black, 0.1% Asian, 30.8% Hispanic of any race (2004); Density: 3,395.8 persons per square mile (2004); Average household size: 3.04 (2004); Median age: 28.3 (2004); Male/female ratio: 85.9 (2004); Marriage status: 43.8% never married, 38.1% now married, 4.8% widowed, 13.2% divorced (2000); Foreign born: 23.6% (2000); Ancestry (includes multiple ancestries): 68.8% Other groups, 3.0% United States or American, 2.6% Jamaican, 2.4% Haitian, 1.3% African (2000).
Economy: Single-family building permits issued: 173 (2004); Multi-family building permits issued: 112 (2004); Employment by occupation: 6.4% management, 9.1% professional, 21.2% services, 30.0% sales, 2.6% farming, 11.8% construction, 18.9% production (2000).
Income: Per capita income: $9,737 (2004); Median household income: $19,049 (2004); Average household income: $28,456 (2004); Percent of households with income of $100,000 or more: 2.7% (2004); Poverty rate: 35.2% (2000).
Education: Percent of population age 25 and over with: High school diploma (including GED) or higher: 52.0% (2004); Bachelor's degree or higher: 5.4% (2004); Master's degree or higher: 2.4% (2004).

School District(s)

Miami-Dade County School District (PK-12)
2002-03 Enrollment: 373,395 . . . . (305) 995-1428

Housing: Homeownership rate: 35.3% (2004); Median home value: $98,876 (2004); Median rent: $395 per month (2000); Median age of housing: 35 years (2000).
Safety: Violent crime rate: 415.4 per 10,000 population; Property crime rate: 745.5 per 10,000 population (2003).
Transportation: Commute to work: 84.4% car, 10.2% public transportation, 3.3% walk, 0.5% work from home (2000); Travel time to work: 16.6% less than 15 minutes, 33.0% 15 to 30 minutes, 30.1% 30 to 45 minutes, 12.1% 45 to 60 minutes, 8.3% 60 minutes or more (2000)

Additional Information Contacts

Local Government Offices . . . . (305) 688-4611

OPA-LOCKA NORTH (CDP). Covers a land area of 2.174 square miles and a water area of 0.114 square miles. Located at 25.92° N. Lat.; 80.26° W. Long.
Population: 6,568 (1990); 6,224 (2000); 6,983 (2004); 7,855 (2009 projected); Race: 22.1% White, 72.5% Black, 0.5% Asian, 22.8% Hispanic of any race (2004); Density: 3,212.5 persons per square mile (2004); Average household size: 4.10 (2004); Median age: 26.0 (2004); Male/female ratio: 90.2 (2004); Marriage status: 38.5% never married, 44.7% now married, 4.7% widowed, 12.0% divorced (2000); Foreign born: 24.5% (2000); Ancestry (includes multiple ancestries): 65.6% Other groups, 6.4% Jamaican, 3.3% United States or American, 2.7% Haitian, 2.1% African (2000).
Economy: Employment by occupation: 4.3% management, 16.6% professional, 22.5% services, 31.2% sales, 0.0% farming, 9.1% construction, 16.3% production (2000).
Income: Per capita income: $11,496 (2004); Median household income: $37,911 (2004); Average household income: $44,509 (2004); Percent of households with income of $100,000 or more: 5.7% (2004); Poverty rate: 19.9% (2000).
Education: Percent of population age 25 and over with: High school diploma (including GED) or higher: 61.8% (2004); Bachelor's degree or higher: 7.2% (2004); Master's degree or higher: 2.9% (2004).
Housing: Homeownership rate: 68.7% (2004); Median home value: $115,391 (2004); Median rent: $588 per month (2000); Median age of housing: 38 years (2000).
Transportation: Commute to work: 82.3% car, 6.9% public transportation, 7.4% walk, 2.4% work from home (2000); Travel time to work: 17.8% less than 15 minutes, 29.4% 15 to 30 minutes, 29.5% 30 to 45 minutes, 8.9% 45 to 60 minutes, 14.4% 60 minutes or more (2000)

PALM SPRINGS NORTH (CDP). Covers a land area of 0.692 square miles and a water area of 0.098 square miles. Located at 25.93° N. Lat.; 80.33° W. Long.
Population: 5,300 (1990); 5,460 (2000); 5,276 (2004); 5,069 (2009 projected); Race: 92.4% White, 0.8% Black, 0.5% Asian, 72.2% Hispanic of any race (2004); Density: 7,619.5 persons per square mile (2004); Average household size: 3.35 (2004); Median age: 37.4 (2004); Male/female ratio: 96.1 (2004); Marriage status: 22.1% never married, 64.9% now married, 4.7% widowed, 8.3% divorced (2000); Foreign born: 36.6% (2000); Ancestry (includes multiple ancestries): 69.0% Other groups, 8.0% Irish, 6.0% United States or American, 4.8% English, 4.2% German (2000).
Economy: Employment by occupation: 10.9% management, 14.3% professional, 11.1% services, 38.8% sales, 0.0% farming, 14.0% construction, 10.9% production (2000).
Income: Per capita income: $24,241 (2004); Median household income: $71,940 (2004); Average household income: $80,380 (2004); Percent of households with income of $100,000 or more: 25.7% (2004); Poverty rate: 4.4% (2000).
Education: Percent of population age 25 and over with: High school diploma (including GED) or higher: 69.1% (2004); Bachelor's degree or higher: 15.7% (2004); Master's degree or higher: 5.4% (2004).
Housing: Homeownership rate: 93.3% (2004); Median home value: $196,564 (2004); Median rent: $951 per month (2000); Median age of housing: 34 years (2000).
Transportation: Commute to work: 95.1% car, 1.5% public transportation, 1.0% walk, 1.2% work from home (2000); Travel time to work: 13.8% less than 15 minutes, 30.0% 15 to 30 minutes, 33.0% 30 to 45 minutes, 13.8% 45 to 60 minutes, 9.5% 60 minutes or more (2000)

PALMETTO ESTATES (CDP). Covers a land area of 2.124 square miles and a water area of 0.024 square miles. Located at 25.62° N. Lat.; 80.36° W. Long.
Population: 12,293 (1990); 13,675 (2000); 14,314 (2004); 15,156 (2009 projected); Race: 36.4% White, 49.3% Black, 2.6% Asian, 33.5% Hispanic of any race (2004); Density: 6,738.1 persons per square mile (2004); Average household size: 3.43 (2004); Median age: 34.0 (2004); Male/female ratio: 92.5 (2004); Marriage status: 31.5% never married, 53.2% now married, 5.2% widowed, 10.2% divorced (2000); Foreign born: 41.2% (2000); Ancestry (includes multiple ancestries): 52.5% Other groups, 17.3% Jamaican, 4.1% United States or American, 3.4% Haitian, 3.2% German (2000).
Economy: Employment by occupation: 10.2% management, 19.7% professional, 18.9% services, 32.8% sales, 0.0% farming, 10.7% construction, 7.7% production (2000).
Income: Per capita income: $18,477 (2004); Median household income: $53,199 (2004); Average household income: $62,728 (2004); Percent of households with income of $100,000 or more: 13.6% (2004); Poverty rate: 10.9% (2000).
Education: Percent of population age 25 and over with: High school diploma (including GED) or higher: 81.5% (2004); Bachelor's degree or higher: 20.2% (2004); Master's degree or higher: 8.5% (2004).
Housing: Homeownership rate: 83.5% (2004); Median home value: $146,499 (2004); Median rent: $655 per month (2000); Median age of housing: 27 years (2000).

Transportation: Commute to work: 93.2% car, 4.1% public transportation, 0.7% walk, 1.2% work from home (2000); Travel time to work: 15.7% less than 15 minutes, 34.4% 15 to 30 minutes, 21.1% 30 to 45 minutes, 12.8% 45 to 60 minutes, 16.0% 60 minutes or more (2000)

PINECREST (village). Covers a land area of 7.538 square miles and a water area of 0.013 square miles. Located at 25.66° N. Lat.; 80.30° W. Long.
Population: 17,810 (1990); 19,055 (2000); 19,680 (2004); 20,557 (2009 projected); Race: 90.1% White, 1.7% Black, 4.6% Asian, 34.8% Hispanic of any race (2004); Density: 2,610.7 persons per square mile (2004); Average household size: 3.11 (2004); Median age: 38.5 (2004); Male/female ratio: 93.8 (2004); Marriage status: 21.5% never married, 67.3% now married, 4.7% widowed, 6.6% divorced (2000); Foreign born: 27.6% (2000); Ancestry (includes multiple ancestries): 41.7% Other groups, 9.9% English, 8.6% German, 6.9% Russian, 6.7% Irish (2000).
Economy: Single-family building permits issued: 52 (2004); Multi-family building permits issued: n/a (2004); Employment by occupation: 25.3% management, 34.7% professional, 7.5% services, 27.7% sales, 0.1% farming, 2.1% construction, 2.6% production (2000).
Income: Per capita income: $53,752 (2004); Median household income: $122,407 (2004); Average household income: $166,793 (2004); Percent of households with income of $100,000 or more: 56.8% (2004); Poverty rate: 4.1% (2000).
Education: Percent of population age 25 and over with: High school diploma (including GED) or higher: 94.2% (2004); Bachelor's degree or higher: 61.5% (2004); Master's degree or higher: 31.4% (2004).
Housing: Homeownership rate: 82.4% (2004); Median home value: $534,391 (2004); Median rent: $696 per month (2000); Median age of housing: 35 years (2000).
Safety: Violent crime rate: 25.8 per 10,000 population; Property crime rate: 353.3 per 10,000 population (2003).
Transportation: Commute to work: 86.7% car, 3.9% public transportation, 0.8% walk, 7.4% work from home (2000); Travel time to work: 20.6% less than 15 minutes, 27.3% 15 to 30 minutes, 32.2% 30 to 45 minutes, 12.6% 45 to 60 minutes, 7.3% 60 minutes or more (2000)
Additional Information Contacts
Local Government Offices . . . . (305) 234-2121

PINEWOOD (CDP). Covers a land area of 1.717 square miles and a water area of 0.177 square miles. Located at 25.87° N. Lat.; 80.21° W. Long.
Population: 15,518 (1990); 16,523 (2000); 16,738 (2004); 17,031 (2009 projected); Race: 19.7% White, 69.4% Black, 0.2% Asian, 24.6% Hispanic of any race (2004); Density: 9,746.6 persons per square mile (2004); Average household size: 3.30 (2004); Median age: 31.6 (2004); Male/female ratio: 92.6 (2004); Marriage status: 40.2% never married, 44.9% now married, 6.6% widowed, 8.4% divorced (2000); Foreign born: 38.1% (2000); Ancestry (includes multiple ancestries): 47.6% Other groups, 25.7% Haitian, 5.5% United States or American, 3.4% Jamaican, 1.8% Bahamian (2000).
Economy: Employment by occupation: 5.1% management, 10.2% professional, 30.2% services, 26.2% sales, 0.0% farming, 9.1% construction, 19.3% production (2000).
Income: Per capita income: $10,476 (2004); Median household income: $25,793 (2004); Average household income: $34,199 (2004); Percent of households with income of $100,000 or more: 3.0% (2004); Poverty rate: 33.5% (2000).
Education: Percent of population age 25 and over with: High school diploma (including GED) or higher: 50.4% (2004); Bachelor's degree or higher: 5.9% (2004); Master's degree or higher: 1.3% (2004).
Housing: Homeownership rate: 47.4% (2004); Median home value: $109,127 (2004); Median rent: $482 per month (2000); Median age of housing: 36 years (2000).
Transportation: Commute to work: 86.4% car, 11.8% public transportation, 0.5% walk, 0.5% work from home (2000); Travel time to work: 10.2% less than 15 minutes, 39.8% 15 to 30 minutes, 30.4% 30 to 45 minutes, 8.5% 45 to 60 minutes, 11.1% 60 minutes or more (2000)

PRINCETON (CDP). Covers a land area of 7.347 square miles and a water area of 0.004 square miles. Located at 25.53° N. Lat.; 80.39° W. Long.
History: Princeton was known as Modello until 1905, when a sawmill was established by several Princeton graduates who renamed the town for their university.
Population: 7,073 (1990); 10,090 (2000); 11,654 (2004); 13,548 (2009 projected); Race: 52.9% White, 32.5% Black, 1.0% Asian, 53.0% Hispanic of any race (2004); Density: 1,586.2 persons per square mile (2004); Average household size: 3.75 (2004); Median age: 29.0 (2004); Male/female ratio: 97.0 (2004); Marriage status: 33.3% never married, 55.2% now married, 5.4% widowed, 6.2% divorced (2000); Foreign born: 28.5% (2000); Ancestry (includes multiple ancestries): 73.9% Other groups, 3.7% German, 2.8% United States or American, 2.7% Irish, 2.7% Italian (2000).
Economy: Employment by occupation: 11.0% management, 14.4% professional, 18.8% services, 27.8% sales, 2.9% farming, 13.9% construction, 11.1% production (2000).
Income: Per capita income: $13,344 (2004); Median household income: $41,243 (2004); Average household income: $49,044 (2004); Percent of households with income of $100,000 or more: 7.5% (2004); Poverty rate: 23.8% (2000).
Education: Percent of population age 25 and over with: High school diploma (including GED) or higher: 67.7% (2004); Bachelor's degree or higher: 12.2% (2004); Master's degree or higher: 3.6% (2004).
Housing: Homeownership rate: 72.7% (2004); Median home value: $132,075 (2004); Median rent: $480 per month (2000); Median age of housing: 14 years (2000).
Transportation: Commute to work: 95.0% car, 1.8% public transportation, 0.5% walk, 1.8% work from home (2000); Travel time to work: 18.1% less than 15 minutes, 34.7% 15 to 30 minutes, 20.7% 30 to 45 minutes, 9.8% 45 to 60 minutes, 16.6% 60 minutes or more (2000)

RICHMOND HEIGHTS (CDP). Covers a land area of 1.655 square miles and a water area of 0 square miles. Located at 25.63° N. Lat.; 80.37° W. Long. Elevation is 10 feet.
Population: 8,583 (1990); 8,479 (2000); 8,347 (2004); 8,240 (2009 projected); Race: 13.3% White, 81.3% Black, 0.8% Asian, 14.8% Hispanic of any race (2004); Density: 5,044.5 persons per square mile (2004); Average household size: 3.14 (2004); Median age: 36.5 (2004); Male/female ratio: 84.5 (2004); Marriage status: 30.7% never married, 49.9% now married, 8.7% widowed, 10.7% divorced (2000); Foreign born: 12.8% (2000); Ancestry (includes multiple ancestries): 81.8% Other groups, 2.8% Jamaican, 2.7% United States or American, 1.5% African, 1.2% Bahamian (2000).
Economy: Richmond Heights Coast Guard facility located here. Employment by occupation: 7.5% management, 19.9% professional, 22.4% services, 30.6% sales, 0.2% farming, 7.2% construction, 12.3% production (2000).
Income: Per capita income: $17,558 (2004); Median household income: $43,340 (2004); Average household income: $54,163 (2004); Percent of households with income of $100,000 or more: 12.0% (2004); Poverty rate: 15.1% (2000).
Education: Percent of population age 25 and over with: High school diploma (including GED) or higher: 72.8% (2004); Bachelor's degree or higher: 15.4% (2004); Master's degree or higher: 5.4% (2004).

School District(s)

Miami-Dade County School District (PK-12)
2002-03 Enrollment: 373,395 . . . . (305) 995-1428
Housing: Homeownership rate: 83.5% (2004); Median home value: $120,921 (2004); Median rent: $537 per month (2000); Median age of housing: 33 years (2000).
Transportation: Commute to work: 89.3% car, 7.0% public transportation, 2.0% walk, 0.7% work from home (2000); Travel time to work: 17.2% less than 15 minutes, 31.9% 15 to 30 minutes, 24.3% 30 to 45 minutes, 12.7% 45 to 60 minutes, 13.9% 60 minutes or more (2000)

RICHMOND WEST (CDP). Covers a land area of 4.179 square miles and a water area of 0.088 square miles. Located at 25.61° N. Lat.; 80.42° W. Long.
Population: 6,224 (1990); 28,082 (2000); 35,211 (2004); 43,540 (2009 projected); Race: 77.7% White, 8.1% Black, 1.9% Asian, 77.5% Hispanic of any race (2004); Density: 8,426.6 persons per square mile (2004); Average household size: 3.67 (2004); Median age: 31.0 (2004); Male/female ratio: 95.7 (2004); Marriage status: 20.5% never married, 68.0% now married, 3.0% widowed, 8.4% divorced (2000); Foreign born: 45.6% (2000); Ancestry (includes multiple ancestries): 79.4% Other groups, 5.4% United States or American, 3.4% Jamaican, 2.7% Italian, 2.2% Irish (2000).
Economy: Employment by occupation: 15.1% management, 16.7% professional, 14.5% services, 36.7% sales, 0.4% farming, 8.7% construction, 7.9% production (2000).

Income: Per capita income: $20,157 (2004); Median household income: $64,448 (2004); Average household income: $73,963 (2004); Percent of households with income of $100,000 or more: 18.4% (2004); Poverty rate: 5.6% (2000).
Education: Percent of population age 25 and over with: High school diploma (including GED) or higher: 83.0% (2004); Bachelor's degree or higher: 22.6% (2004); Master's degree or higher: 7.7% (2004).
Housing: Homeownership rate: 93.8% (2004); Median home value: $178,200 (2004); Median rent: $929 per month (2000); Median age of housing: 4 years (2000).
Transportation: Commute to work: 95.8% car, 1.1% public transportation, 0.2% walk, 2.3% work from home (2000); Travel time to work: 8.5% less than 15 minutes, 22.8% 15 to 30 minutes, 27.6% 30 to 45 minutes, 17.4% 45 to 60 minutes, 23.7% 60 minutes or more (2000)

SCOTT LAKE (CDP). Covers a land area of 3.289 square miles and a water area of 0.059 square miles. Located at 25.93° N. Lat.; 80.23° W. Long.
Population: 14,588 (1990); 14,401 (2000); 14,487 (2004); 14,703 (2009 projected); Race: 4.3% White, 91.3% Black, 0.4% Asian, 5.7% Hispanic of any race (2004); Density: 4,404.5 persons per square mile (2004); Average household size: 3.53 (2004); Median age: 33.3 (2004); Male/female ratio: 87.1 (2004); Marriage status: 36.0% never married, 47.2% now married, 5.8% widowed, 11.0% divorced (2000); Foreign born: 24.1% (2000); Ancestry (includes multiple ancestries): 59.8% Other groups, 13.0% Jamaican, 5.5% Haitian, 2.2% United States or American, 1.5% Bahamian (2000).
Economy: Employment by occupation: 5.7% management, 16.7% professional, 22.5% services, 29.4% sales, 0.0% farming, 12.2% construction, 13.5% production (2000).
Income: Per capita income: $16,961 (2004); Median household income: $51,652 (2004); Average household income: $59,318 (2004); Percent of households with income of $100,000 or more: 13.3% (2004); Poverty rate: 16.4% (2000).
Education: Percent of population age 25 and over with: High school diploma (including GED) or higher: 75.6% (2004); Bachelor's degree or higher: 16.7% (2004); Master's degree or higher: 5.6% (2004).
Housing: Homeownership rate: 87.1% (2004); Median home value: $129,774 (2004); Median rent: $714 per month (2000); Median age of housing: 35 years (2000).
Transportation: Commute to work: 91.4% car, 6.0% public transportation, 0.5% walk, 1.2% work from home (2000); Travel time to work: 13.5% less than 15 minutes, 34.3% 15 to 30 minutes, 31.3% 30 to 45 minutes, 11.9% 45 to 60 minutes, 9.0% 60 minutes or more (2000)

SOUTH MIAMI (city). Covers a land area of 2.295 square miles and a water area of <.001 square miles. Located at 25.71° N. Lat.; 80.29° W. Long. Elevation is 9 feet.
History: Named for its location south of Miami. South Miami was first called Larkins for a man who operated a store here in the early days of the town. South Miami developed around a tomato packing plant and as a shipping center for citrus fruit and truck crops.
Population: 10,438 (1990); 10,741 (2000); 10,749 (2004); 10,860 (2009 projected); Race: 71.9% White, 22.5% Black, 1.2% Asian, 39.8% Hispanic of any race (2004); Density: 4,684.0 persons per square mile (2004); Average household size: 2.49 (2004); Median age: 38.8 (2004); Male/female ratio: 93.4 (2004); Marriage status: 31.5% never married, 46.8% now married, 6.1% widowed, 15.6% divorced (2000); Foreign born: 30.3% (2000); Ancestry (includes multiple ancestries): 54.9% Other groups, 6.5% Irish, 6.1% German, 5.9% English, 4.5% United States or American (2000).
Economy: Single-family building permits issued: 31 (2004); Multi-family building permits issued: 7 (2004); Employment by occupation: 15.0% management, 27.8% professional, 12.4% services, 34.5% sales, 0.0% farming, 4.3% construction, 5.9% production (2000).
Income: Per capita income: $28,297 (2004); Median household income: $47,223 (2004); Average household income: $70,155 (2004); Percent of households with income of $100,000 or more: 22.6% (2004); Poverty rate: 17.1% (2000).
Education: Percent of population age 25 and over with: High school diploma (including GED) or higher: 81.9% (2004); Bachelor's degree or higher: 38.4% (2004); Master's degree or higher: 18.4% (2004).

School District(s)

Miami-Dade County School District (PK-12)
2002-03 Enrollment: 373,395 .... (305) 995-1428

Housing: Homeownership rate: 62.1% (2004); Median home value: $236,143 (2004); Median rent: $609 per month (2000); Median age of housing: 40 years (2000).
Hospitals: Larkin Community Hospital (112 beds)
Safety: Violent crime rate: 104.7 per 10,000 population; Property crime rate: 789.3 per 10,000 population (2003).
Newspapers: Aventura News (General - Circulation 25,000); Coral Gables News (General - Circulation 15,000); Doral Tribune (General - Circulation 10,000); Kendall Gazette (General - Circulation 18,000); Pinecrest Tribune (General - Circulation 15,000); South Miami News (General - Circulation 7,500); Sunny Isles Beach Sun (General - Circulation 6,000)
Transportation: Commute to work: 84.6% car, 6.8% public transportation, 2.9% walk, 4.3% work from home (2000); Travel time to work: 23.0% less than 15 minutes, 33.1% 15 to 30 minutes, 27.5% 30 to 45 minutes, 7.8% 45 to 60 minutes, 8.7% 60 minutes or more (2000)

Additional Information Contacts

Local Government Offices .... (305) 663-6338
South Miami Chamber of Commerce .... (305) 661-1621

SOUTH MIAMI HEIGHTS (CDP). Covers a land area of 4.929 square miles and a water area of 0.004 square miles. Located at 25.58° N. Lat.; 80.38° W. Long.
Population: 30,030 (1990); 33,522 (2000); 35,549 (2004); 38,144 (2009 projected); Race: 55.7% White, 29.3% Black, 1.6% Asian, 60.7% Hispanic of any race (2004); Density: 7,211.6 persons per square mile (2004); Average household size: 3.41 (2004); Median age: 33.0 (2004); Male/female ratio: 93.5 (2004); Marriage status: 30.8% never married, 51.2% now married, 6.2% widowed, 11.8% divorced (2000); Foreign born: 44.1% (2000); Ancestry (includes multiple ancestries): 71.3% Other groups, 5.7% Jamaican, 4.4% United States or American, 1.7% English, 1.6% German (2000).
Economy: Employment by occupation: 8.5% management, 9.8% professional, 22.6% services, 30.8% sales, 0.6% farming, 14.2% construction, 13.5% production (2000).
Income: Per capita income: $13,268 (2004); Median household income: $36,775 (2004); Average household income: $44,949 (2004); Percent of households with income of $100,000 or more: 6.9% (2004); Poverty rate: 17.2% (2000).
Education: Percent of population age 25 and over with: High school diploma (including GED) or higher: 61.1% (2004); Bachelor's degree or higher: 9.0% (2004); Master's degree or higher: 3.4% (2004).
Housing: Homeownership rate: 62.4% (2004); Median home value: $128,167 (2004); Median rent: $518 per month (2000); Median age of housing: 25 years (2000).
Transportation: Commute to work: 91.0% car, 3.9% public transportation, 1.8% walk, 1.7% work from home (2000); Travel time to work: 17.3% less than 15 minutes, 31.4% 15 to 30 minutes, 23.5% 30 to 45 minutes, 12.8% 45 to 60 minutes, 14.9% 60 minutes or more (2000)

SUNNY ISLES BEACH (city). Covers a land area of 1.006 square miles and a water area of 0.401 square miles. Located at 25.94° N. Lat.; 80.12° W. Long. Elevation is 10 feet.
Population: 11,740 (1990); 15,315 (2000); 15,605 (2004); 15,922 (2009 projected); Race: 90.4% White, 2.4% Black, 1.5% Asian, 45.9% Hispanic of any race (2004); Density: 15,519.5 persons per square mile (2004); Average household size: 1.92 (2004); Median age: 51.4 (2004); Male/female ratio: 87.7 (2004); Marriage status: 19.7% never married, 51.3% now married, 15.7% widowed, 13.3% divorced (2000); Foreign born: 56.8% (2000); Ancestry (includes multiple ancestries): 41.7% Other groups, 9.5% Russian, 5.9% Italian, 5.0% Polish, 4.9% United States or American (2000).
Economy: Single-family building permits issued: 0 (2004); Multi-family building permits issued: 281 (2004); Employment by occupation: 20.8% management, 19.0% professional, 11.7% services, 37.5% sales, 0.5% farming, 5.0% construction, 5.5% production (2000).
Income: Per capita income: $29,854 (2004); Median household income: $34,249 (2004); Average household income: $57,151 (2004); Percent of households with income of $100,000 or more: 11.7% (2004); Poverty rate: 14.7% (2000).
Education: Percent of population age 25 and over with: High school diploma (including GED) or higher: 79.2% (2004); Bachelor's degree or higher: 28.7% (2004); Master's degree or higher: 12.6% (2004).
Housing: Homeownership rate: 58.6% (2004); Median home value: $143,561 (2004); Median rent: $833 per month (2000); Median age of housing: 25 years (2000).

Safety: Violent crime rate: 39.4 per 10,000 population; Property crime rate: 417.1 per 10,000 population (2003).
Transportation: Commute to work: 86.1% car, 3.8% public transportation, 3.5% walk, 4.5% work from home (2000); Travel time to work: 13.5% less than 15 minutes, 29.0% 15 to 30 minutes, 29.0% 30 to 45 minutes, 16.4% 45 to 60 minutes, 12.1% 60 minutes or more (2000)
Additional Information Contacts
Local Government Offices . . . . (305) 947-0606

SUNSET (CDP). Covers a land area of 3.558 square miles and a water area of 0.013 square miles. Located at 25.70° N. Lat.; 80.35° W. Long.
Population: 15,810 (1990); 17,150 (2000); 17,153 (2004); 17,185 (2009 projected); Race: 91.9% White, 1.3% Black, 2.1% Asian, 74.6% Hispanic of any race (2004); Density: 4,821.4 persons per square mile (2004); Average household size: 3.11 (2004); Median age: 39.2 (2004); Male/female ratio: 91.8 (2004); Marriage status: 25.0% never married, 57.4% now married, 6.8% widowed, 10.8% divorced (2000); Foreign born: 50.7% (2000); Ancestry (includes multiple ancestries): 74.4% Other groups, 4.6% German, 3.8% Italian, 3.5% Irish, 3.4% United States or American (2000).
Economy: Employment by occupation: 19.3% management, 21.9% professional, 13.0% services, 32.8% sales, 0.0% farming, 6.8% construction, 6.1% production (2000).
Income: Per capita income: $27,675 (2004); Median household income: $67,258 (2004); Average household income: $84,344 (2004); Percent of households with income of $100,000 or more: 27.0% (2004); Poverty rate: 7.1% (2000).
Education: Percent of population age 25 and over with: High school diploma (including GED) or higher: 81.6% (2004); Bachelor's degree or higher: 30.6% (2004); Master's degree or higher: 11.1% (2004).
Housing: Homeownership rate: 79.0% (2004); Median home value: $237,566 (2004); Median rent: $696 per month (2000); Median age of housing: 29 years (2000).
Transportation: Commute to work: 92.5% car, 2.0% public transportation, 0.6% walk, 4.2% work from home (2000); Travel time to work: 14.4% less than 15 minutes, 32.6% 15 to 30 minutes, 29.1% 30 to 45 minutes, 11.3% 45 to 60 minutes, 12.5% 60 minutes or more (2000)

SURFSIDE (town). Covers a land area of 0.505 square miles and a water area of 0.460 square miles. Located at 25.87° N. Lat.; 80.12° W. Long. Elevation is 10 feet.
Population: 4,108 (1990); 4,909 (2000); 4,857 (2004); 4,804 (2009 projected); Race: 93.6% White, 1.2% Black, 1.1% Asian, 50.4% Hispanic of any race (2004); Density: 9,618.8 persons per square mile (2004); Average household size: 2.24 (2004); Median age: 46.4 (2004); Male/female ratio: 88.3 (2004); Marriage status: 22.5% never married, 55.9% now married, 8.1% widowed, 13.5% divorced (2000); Foreign born: 50.7% (2000); Ancestry (includes multiple ancestries): 46.4% Other groups, 8.2% German, 6.8% Italian, 6.7% Polish, 6.7% Russian (2000).
Economy: Resort town. Single-family building permits issued: 1 (2004); Multi-family building permits issued: 0 (2004); Employment by occupation: 23.2% management, 29.1% professional, 9.9% services, 28.4% sales, 0.0% farming, 5.8% construction, 3.6% production (2000).
Income: Per capita income: $41,832 (2004); Median household income: $57,887 (2004); Average household income: $92,976 (2004); Percent of households with income of $100,000 or more: 28.2% (2004); Poverty rate: 11.5% (2000).
Education: Percent of population age 25 and over with: High school diploma (including GED) or higher: 87.0% (2004); Bachelor's degree or higher: 41.0% (2004); Master's degree or higher: 19.8% (2004).
Housing: Homeownership rate: 70.2% (2004); Median home value: $245,087 (2004); Median rent: $613 per month (2000); Median age of housing: 38 years (2000).
Safety: Violent crime rate: 72.1 per 10,000 population; Property crime rate: 446.9 per 10,000 population (2003).
Newspapers: The Tropical Tribune (General - Circulation 30,000)
Transportation: Commute to work: 88.7% car, 2.1% public transportation, 2.5% walk, 5.4% work from home (2000); Travel time to work: 16.3% less than 15 minutes, 32.4% 15 to 30 minutes, 30.1% 30 to 45 minutes, 12.7% 45 to 60 minutes, 8.4% 60 minutes or more (2000)

SWEETWATER (city). Covers a land area of 0.816 square miles and a water area of 0 square miles. Located at 25.76° N. Lat.; 80.37° W. Long. Elevation is 8 feet.
Population: 13,909 (1990); 14,226 (2000); 14,065 (2004); 13,982 (2009 projected); Race: 89.9% White, 0.9% Black, 0.1% Asian, 93.6% Hispanic of any race (2004); Density: 17,242.3 persons per square mile (2004); Average household size: 3.30 (2004); Median age: 38.0 (2004); Male/female ratio: 93.1 (2004); Marriage status: 24.2% never married, 59.6% now married, 6.5% widowed, 9.6% divorced (2000); Foreign born: 74.7% (2000); Ancestry (includes multiple ancestries): 85.0% Other groups, 2.3% United States or American, 0.5% Italian, 0.4% Irish, 0.4% Nigerian (2000).
Economy: Single-family building permits issued: 0 (2004); Multi-family building permits issued: 0 (2004); Employment by occupation: 6.5% management, 10.2% professional, 18.3% services, 36.9% sales, 0.1% farming, 12.5% construction, 15.4% production (2000).
Income: Per capita income: $11,863 (2004); Median household income: $30,227 (2004); Average household income: $39,140 (2004); Percent of households with income of $100,000 or more: 5.7% (2004); Poverty rate: 18.1% (2000).
Education: Percent of population age 25 and over with: High school diploma (including GED) or higher: 52.8% (2004); Bachelor's degree or higher: 12.8% (2004); Master's degree or higher: 6.0% (2004).
Housing: Homeownership rate: 50.6% (2004); Median home value: $133,596 (2004); Median rent: $581 per month (2000); Median age of housing: 24 years (2000).
Safety: Violent crime rate: 39.8 per 10,000 population; Property crime rate: 186.1 per 10,000 population (2003).
Transportation: Commute to work: 91.1% car, 5.2% public transportation, 3.0% walk, 0.5% work from home (2000); Travel time to work: 13.0% less than 15 minutes, 39.9% 15 to 30 minutes, 30.3% 30 to 45 minutes, 10.0% 45 to 60 minutes, 6.8% 60 minutes or more (2000)
Additional Information Contacts
Local Government Offices . . . . (305) 485-4528

TAMIAMI (CDP). Covers a land area of 7.343 square miles and a water area of 0.230 square miles. Located at 25.75° N. Lat.; 80.40° W. Long.
Population: 39,068 (1990); 54,788 (2000); 58,931 (2004); 64,038 (2009 projected); Race: 90.4% White, 0.9% Black, 0.5% Asian, 88.7% Hispanic of any race (2004); Density: 8,025.6 persons per square mile (2004); Average household size: 3.36 (2004); Median age: 38.4 (2004); Male/female ratio: 90.8 (2004); Marriage status: 23.3% never married, 60.2% now married, 6.2% widowed, 10.2% divorced (2000); Foreign born: 65.5% (2000); Ancestry (includes multiple ancestries): 88.0% Other groups, 1.9% United States or American, 1.3% Italian, 0.9% Irish, 0.9% German (2000).
Economy: Employment by occupation: 15.7% management, 16.0% professional, 13.2% services, 35.8% sales, 0.2% farming, 8.4% construction, 10.7% production (2000).
Income: Per capita income: $19,214 (2004); Median household income: $51,156 (2004); Average household income: $63,661 (2004); Percent of households with income of $100,000 or more: 15.2% (2004); Poverty rate: 9.4% (2000).
Education: Percent of population age 25 and over with: High school diploma (including GED) or higher: 70.9% (2004); Bachelor's degree or higher: 21.5% (2004); Master's degree or higher: 9.1% (2004).
Housing: Homeownership rate: 84.2% (2004); Median home value: $177,144 (2004); Median rent: $743 per month (2000); Median age of housing: 16 years (2000).
Transportation: Commute to work: 95.9% car, 0.7% public transportation, 0.6% walk, 2.2% work from home (2000); Travel time to work: 10.7% less than 15 minutes, 31.2% 15 to 30 minutes, 32.1% 30 to 45 minutes, 15.3% 45 to 60 minutes, 10.6% 60 minutes or more (2000)

THE CROSSINGS (CDP). Covers a land area of 3.736 square miles and a water area of 0.035 square miles. Located at 25.66° N. Lat.; 80.40° W. Long.
Population: 22,290 (1990); 23,557 (2000); 25,103 (2004); 27,045 (2009 projected); Race: 85.1% White, 4.6% Black, 3.1% Asian, 64.0% Hispanic of any race (2004); Density: 6,718.7 persons per square mile (2004); Average household size: 2.87 (2004); Median age: 36.8 (2004); Male/female ratio: 88.4 (2004); Marriage status: 25.7% never married, 56.2% now married, 4.5% widowed, 13.5% divorced (2000); Foreign born: 46.5% (2000); Ancestry (includes multiple ancestries): 67.1% Other groups, 4.8% German, 4.6% Irish, 4.6% Italian, 3.5% United States or American (2000).
Economy: Employment by occupation: 19.8% management, 23.0% professional, 11.4% services, 35.7% sales, 0.2% farming, 5.5% construction, 4.5% production (2000).
Income: Per capita income: $26,084 (2004); Median household income: $59,006 (2004); Average household income: $74,550 (2004); Percent of

households with income of $100,000 or more: 22.6% (2004); Poverty rate: 6.5% (2000).
Education: Percent of population age 25 and over with: High school diploma (including GED) or higher: 90.2% (2004); Bachelor's degree or higher: 36.4% (2004); Master's degree or higher: 13.7% (2004).
Housing: Homeownership rate: 80.8% (2004); Median home value: $161,447 (2004); Median rent: $869 per month (2000); Median age of housing: 19 years (2000).
Transportation: Commute to work: 92.8% car, 2.0% public transportation, 0.4% walk, 3.8% work from home (2000); Travel time to work: 14.6% less than 15 minutes, 27.9% 15 to 30 minutes, 24.2% 30 to 45 minutes, 17.5% 45 to 60 minutes, 15.8% 60 minutes or more (2000)

THE HAMMOCKS (CDP). Covers a land area of 7.861 square miles and a water area of 0.172 square miles. Located at 25.67° N. Lat.; 80.43° W. Long.
Population: 26,829 (1990); 47,379 (2000); 54,215 (2004); 62,366 (2009 projected); Race: 78.6% White, 6.3% Black, 2.9% Asian, 72.3% Hispanic of any race (2004); Density: 6,896.9 persons per square mile (2004); Average household size: 3.17 (2004); Median age: 32.6 (2004); Male/female ratio: 90.7 (2004); Marriage status: 26.6% never married, 58.4% now married, 4.4% widowed, 10.6% divorced (2000); Foreign born: 52.4% (2000); Ancestry (includes multiple ancestries): 75.5% Other groups, 4.0% Italian, 3.1% United States or American, 3.0% German, 3.0% Jamaican (2000).
Economy: Employment by occupation: 17.6% management, 19.6% professional, 12.4% services, 36.2% sales, 0.0% farming, 6.3% construction, 8.0% production (2000).
Income: Per capita income: $21,303 (2004); Median household income: $56,197 (2004); Average household income: $66,867 (2004); Percent of households with income of $100,000 or more: 16.4% (2004); Poverty rate: 8.6% (2000).
Education: Percent of population age 25 and over with: High school diploma (including GED) or higher: 87.1% (2004); Bachelor's degree or higher: 31.1% (2004); Master's degree or higher: 10.8% (2004).
Housing: Homeownership rate: 63.7% (2004); Median home value: $184,257 (2004); Median rent: $758 per month (2000); Median age of housing: 12 years (2000).
Transportation: Commute to work: 93.4% car, 2.2% public transportation, 0.6% walk, 2.9% work from home (2000); Travel time to work: 12.8% less than 15 minutes, 23.7% 15 to 30 minutes, 27.6% 30 to 45 minutes, 17.5% 45 to 60 minutes, 18.3% 60 minutes or more (2000)

THREE LAKES (CDP). Covers a land area of 3.263 square miles and a water area of 0.543 square miles. Located at 25.63° N. Lat.; 80.39° W. Long.
Population: 2,336 (1990); 6,955 (2000); 9,778 (2004); 13,055 (2009 projected); Race: 72.0% White, 15.5% Black, 3.5% Asian, 57.4% Hispanic of any race (2004); Density: 2,996.5 persons per square mile (2004); Average household size: 2.88 (2004); Median age: 31.8 (2004); Male/female ratio: 90.7 (2004); Marriage status: 26.2% never married, 61.1% now married, 3.0% widowed, 9.6% divorced (2000); Foreign born: 37.5% (2000); Ancestry (includes multiple ancestries): 60.0% Other groups, 7.6% German, 7.2% Jamaican, 6.7% Irish, 4.8% Italian (2000).
Economy: Employment by occupation: 17.6% management, 23.9% professional, 12.8% services, 33.6% sales, 0.4% farming, 4.9% construction, 6.7% production (2000).
Income: Per capita income: $25,966 (2004); Median household income: $62,994 (2004); Average household income: $74,676 (2004); Percent of households with income of $100,000 or more: 21.2% (2004); Poverty rate: 8.0% (2000).
Education: Percent of population age 25 and over with: High school diploma (including GED) or higher: 90.4% (2004); Bachelor's degree or higher: 32.0% (2004); Master's degree or higher: 13.7% (2004).
Housing: Homeownership rate: 69.3% (2004); Median home value: $170,924 (2004); Median rent: $863 per month (2000); Median age of housing: 7 years (2000).
Transportation: Commute to work: 92.6% car, 3.3% public transportation, 0.4% walk, 2.9% work from home (2000); Travel time to work: 15.1% less than 15 minutes, 25.2% 15 to 30 minutes, 23.5% 30 to 45 minutes, 19.2% 45 to 60 minutes, 16.9% 60 minutes or more (2000)

UNIVERSITY PARK (CDP). Covers a land area of 4.061 square miles and a water area of 0.039 square miles. Located at 25.74° N. Lat.; 80.36° W. Long.
Population: 24,524 (1990); 26,538 (2000); 26,930 (2004); 27,516 (2009 projected); Race: 88.3% White, 4.4% Black, 1.4% Asian, 83.3% Hispanic of any race (2004); Density: 6,631.6 persons per square mile (2004); Average household size: 3.03 (2004); Median age: 40.6 (2004); Male/female ratio: 84.5 (2004); Marriage status: 27.3% never married, 53.5% now married, 8.3% widowed, 10.9% divorced (2000); Foreign born: 66.6% (2000); Ancestry (includes multiple ancestries): 82.8% Other groups, 2.3% Italian, 1.4% United States or American, 1.0% German, 0.9% English (2000).
Economy: Employment by occupation: 14.0% management, 16.9% professional, 15.4% services, 33.7% sales, 0.1% farming, 10.2% construction, 9.6% production (2000).
Income: Per capita income: $19,103 (2004); Median household income: $43,391 (2004); Average household income: $57,109 (2004); Percent of households with income of $100,000 or more: 14.2% (2004); Poverty rate: 14.4% (2000).
Education: Percent of population age 25 and over with: High school diploma (including GED) or higher: 69.2% (2004); Bachelor's degree or higher: 22.7% (2004); Master's degree or higher: 8.7% (2004).
Housing: Homeownership rate: 62.6% (2004); Median home value: $200,097 (2004); Median rent: $600 per month (2000); Median age of housing: 23 years (2000).
Transportation: Commute to work: 91.8% car, 1.8% public transportation, 2.5% walk, 2.4% work from home (2000); Travel time to work: 13.5% less than 15 minutes, 32.1% 15 to 30 minutes, 32.8% 30 to 45 minutes, 14.2% 45 to 60 minutes, 7.4% 60 minutes or more (2000)

VIRGINIA GARDENS (village). Covers a land area of 0.300 square miles and a water area of 0 square miles. Located at 25.80° N. Lat.; 80.29° W. Long. Elevation is 5 feet.
Population: 2,212 (1990); 2,348 (2000); 2,427 (2004); 2,487 (2009 projected); Race: 83.8% White, 2.5% Black, 1.2% Asian, 74.9% Hispanic of any race (2004); Density: 8,083.7 persons per square mile (2004); Average household size: 2.67 (2004); Median age: 38.8 (2004); Male/female ratio: 97.6 (2004); Marriage status: 20.2% never married, 57.4% now married, 6.9% widowed, 15.5% divorced (2000); Foreign born: 50.3% (2000); Ancestry (includes multiple ancestries): 69.6% Other groups, 6.1% English, 5.9% Italian, 5.6% Irish, 5.6% United States or American (2000).
Economy: Single-family building permits issued: 0 (2004); Multi-family building permits issued: 0 (2004); Employment by occupation: 11.9% management, 14.3% professional, 14.1% services, 35.6% sales, 0.0% farming, 10.8% construction, 13.3% production (2000).
Income: Per capita income: $21,361 (2004); Median household income: $45,028 (2004); Average household income: $56,542 (2004); Percent of households with income of $100,000 or more: 11.2% (2004); Poverty rate: 11.3% (2000).
Taxes: Total city taxes per capita: $301 (2002); City property taxes per capita: $183 (2002).
Education: Percent of population age 25 and over with: High school diploma (including GED) or higher: 76.7% (2004); Bachelor's degree or higher: 22.3% (2004); Master's degree or higher: 7.7% (2004).
Housing: Homeownership rate: 50.7% (2004); Median home value: $180,571 (2004); Median rent: $579 per month (2000); Median age of housing: 41 years (2000).
Safety: Violent crime rate: 4.2 per 10,000 population; Property crime rate: 216.8 per 10,000 population (2003).
Transportation: Commute to work: 90.1% car, 4.9% public transportation, 1.9% walk, 2.3% work from home (2000); Travel time to work: 24.8% less than 15 minutes, 45.0% 15 to 30 minutes, 18.7% 30 to 45 minutes, 4.1% 45 to 60 minutes, 7.4% 60 minutes or more (2000)

WEST LITTLE RIVER (CDP). Covers a land area of 4.582 square miles and a water area of 0.047 square miles. Located at 25.85° N. Lat.; 80.23° W. Long.
Population: 33,575 (1990); 32,498 (2000); 32,397 (2004); 32,523 (2009 projected); Race: 35.7% White, 52.5% Black, 0.2% Asian, 45.2% Hispanic of any race (2004); Density: 7,071.2 persons per square mile (2004); Average household size: 3.40 (2004); Median age: 35.4 (2004); Male/female ratio: 95.9 (2004); Marriage status: 34.2% never married, 47.5% now married, 6.9% widowed, 11.4% divorced (2000); Foreign born: 35.0% (2000); Ancestry (includes multiple ancestries): 71.5% Other groups, 5.2% Haitian, 4.7% United States or American, 1.7% Jamaican, 1.7% African (2000).
Economy: Employment by occupation: 4.4% management, 9.0% professional, 23.7% services, 27.2% sales, 0.5% farming, 13.2% construction, 22.0% production (2000).

Income: Per capita income: $11,679 (2004); Median household income: $28,771 (2004); Average household income: $39,287 (2004); Percent of households with income of $100,000 or more: 5.4% (2004); Poverty rate: 29.0% (2000).
Education: Percent of population age 25 and over with: High school diploma (including GED) or higher: 50.9% (2004); Bachelor's degree or higher: 5.6% (2004); Master's degree or higher: 2.2% (2004).
Housing: Homeownership rate: 63.9% (2004); Median home value: $111,553 (2004); Median rent: $468 per month (2000); Median age of housing: 41 years (2000).
Transportation: Commute to work: 88.1% car, 8.0% public transportation, 1.3% walk, 0.4% work from home (2000); Travel time to work: 11.4% less than 15 minutes, 39.0% 15 to 30 minutes, 32.2% 30 to 45 minutes, 7.1% 45 to 60 minutes, 10.4% 60 minutes or more (2000)

WEST MIAMI (city). Covers a land area of 0.711 square miles and a water area of 0 square miles. Located at 25.75° N. Lat.; 80.29° W. Long. Elevation is 10 feet.
Population: 5,727 (1990); 5,863 (2000); 5,997 (2004); 6,230 (2009 projected); Race: 92.4% White, 0.8% Black, 0.4% Asian, 86.5% Hispanic of any race (2004); Density: 8,429.8 persons per square mile (2004); Average household size: 2.85 (2004); Median age: 45.2 (2004); Male/female ratio: 84.3 (2004); Marriage status: 20.4% never married, 56.7% now married, 10.1% widowed, 12.8% divorced (2000); Foreign born: 68.5% (2000); Ancestry (includes multiple ancestries): 83.6% Other groups, 2.7% United States or American, 2.4% Italian, 2.0% German, 1.5% English (2000).
Economy: Single-family building permits issued: 7 (2004); Multi-family building permits issued: 0 (2004); Employment by occupation: 11.7% management, 14.6% professional, 12.8% services, 37.0% sales, 0.4% farming, 11.5% construction, 12.0% production (2000).
Income: Per capita income: $19,620 (2004); Median household income: $41,178 (2004); Average household income: $54,987 (2004); Percent of households with income of $100,000 or more: 12.5% (2004); Poverty rate: 9.5% (2000).
Taxes: Total city taxes per capita: $401 (2002); City property taxes per capita: $303 (2002).
Education: Percent of population age 25 and over with: High school diploma (including GED) or higher: 63.3% (2004); Bachelor's degree or higher: 17.9% (2004); Master's degree or higher: 7.1% (2004).
Housing: Homeownership rate: 68.7% (2004); Median home value: $194,655 (2004); Median rent: $570 per month (2000); Median age of housing: 47 years (2000).
Safety: Violent crime rate: 35.9 per 10,000 population; Property crime rate: 305.2 per 10,000 population (2003).
Transportation: Commute to work: 94.1% car, 2.5% public transportation, 0.9% walk, 2.0% work from home (2000); Travel time to work: 13.1% less than 15 minutes, 44.9% 15 to 30 minutes, 30.8% 30 to 45 minutes, 6.8% 45 to 60 minutes, 4.3% 60 minutes or more (2000)
Additional Information Contacts
Local Government Offices . . . . (305) 266-1122

WEST PERRINE (CDP). Covers a land area of 1.731 square miles and a water area of 0 square miles. Located at 25.60° N. Lat.; 80.36° W. Long.
Population: 8,798 (1990); 8,600 (2000); 8,863 (2004); 9,233 (2009 projected); Race: 18.9% White, 72.1% Black, 1.0% Asian, 20.0% Hispanic of any race (2004); Density: 5,118.8 persons per square mile (2004); Average household size: 3.31 (2004); Median age: 31.9 (2004); Male/female ratio: 88.5 (2004); Marriage status: 41.4% never married, 39.5% now married, 8.1% widowed, 11.0% divorced (2000); Foreign born: 20.2% (2000); Ancestry (includes multiple ancestries): 68.1% Other groups, 4.8% Jamaican, 3.2% Haitian, 2.4% Trinidadian and Tobagonian, 2.4% English (2000).
Economy: Employment by occupation: 7.8% management, 16.4% professional, 26.0% services, 28.8% sales, 0.0% farming, 7.7% construction, 13.2% production (2000).
Income: Per capita income: $12,657 (2004); Median household income: $29,617 (2004); Average household income: $41,385 (2004); Percent of households with income of $100,000 or more: 8.9% (2004); Poverty rate: 34.4% (2000).
Education: Percent of population age 25 and over with: High school diploma (including GED) or higher: 67.7% (2004); Bachelor's degree or higher: 12.1% (2004); Master's degree or higher: 4.9% (2004).
Housing: Homeownership rate: 64.3% (2004); Median home value: $124,580 (2004); Median rent: $388 per month (2000); Median age of housing: 31 years (2000).
Transportation: Commute to work: 87.4% car, 6.1% public transportation, 2.0% walk, 1.4% work from home (2000); Travel time to work: 19.5% less than 15 minutes, 39.8% 15 to 30 minutes, 16.9% 30 to 45 minutes, 13.9% 45 to 60 minutes, 9.8% 60 minutes or more (2000)

WESTCHESTER (CDP). Covers a land area of 4.015 square miles and a water area of 0 square miles. Located at 25.74° N. Lat.; 80.33° W. Long.
Population: 29,883 (1990); 30,271 (2000); 30,493 (2004); 30,995 (2009 projected); Race: 94.3% White, 0.7% Black, 0.5% Asian, 87.2% Hispanic of any race (2004); Density: 7,595.2 persons per square mile (2004); Average household size: 3.07 (2004); Median age: 44.8 (2004); Male/female ratio: 87.7 (2004); Marriage status: 21.2% never married, 57.0% now married, 9.9% widowed, 11.9% divorced (2000); Foreign born: 69.0% (2000); Ancestry (includes multiple ancestries): 85.8% Other groups, 2.4% United States or American, 1.6% Italian, 1.1% English, 1.0% German (2000).
Economy: Employment by occupation: 13.5% management, 14.6% professional, 15.5% services, 34.7% sales, 0.6% farming, 10.1% construction, 10.9% production (2000).
Income: Per capita income: $19,478 (2004); Median household income: $44,473 (2004); Average household income: $58,825 (2004); Percent of households with income of $100,000 or more: 13.8% (2004); Poverty rate: 11.8% (2000).
Education: Percent of population age 25 and over with: High school diploma (including GED) or higher: 63.8% (2004); Bachelor's degree or higher: 21.5% (2004); Master's degree or higher: 9.3% (2004).
Housing: Homeownership rate: 69.0% (2004); Median home value: $205,267 (2004); Median rent: $629 per month (2000); Median age of housing: 37 years (2000).
Transportation: Commute to work: 93.7% car, 2.1% public transportation, 0.6% walk, 2.6% work from home (2000); Travel time to work: 13.7% less than 15 minutes, 40.0% 15 to 30 minutes, 28.1% 30 to 45 minutes, 10.8% 45 to 60 minutes, 7.4% 60 minutes or more (2000)

WESTVIEW (CDP). Covers a land area of 3.117 square miles and a water area of 0.110 square miles. Located at 25.88° N. Lat.; 80.23° W. Long.
Population: 9,668 (1990); 9,692 (2000); 9,996 (2004); 10,398 (2009 projected); Race: 17.2% White, 74.5% Black, 0.4% Asian, 21.5% Hispanic of any race (2004); Density: 3,206.8 persons per square mile (2004); Average household size: 3.33 (2004); Median age: 32.7 (2004); Male/female ratio: 88.7 (2004); Marriage status: 39.1% never married, 40.2% now married, 7.0% widowed, 13.7% divorced (2000); Foreign born: 30.3% (2000); Ancestry (includes multiple ancestries): 58.9% Other groups, 10.0% Haitian, 7.2% United States or American, 6.9% Jamaican, 1.7% African (2000).
Economy: Employment by occupation: 6.2% management, 13.8% professional, 26.7% services, 27.0% sales, 0.0% farming, 9.8% construction, 16.4% production (2000).
Income: Per capita income: $12,008 (2004); Median household income: $31,012 (2004); Average household income: $39,655 (2004); Percent of households with income of $100,000 or more: 4.5% (2004); Poverty rate: 26.0% (2000).
Education: Percent of population age 25 and over with: High school diploma (including GED) or higher: 61.0% (2004); Bachelor's degree or higher: 9.1% (2004); Master's degree or higher: 3.5% (2004).
Housing: Homeownership rate: 63.5% (2004); Median home value: $116,979 (2004); Median rent: $478 per month (2000); Median age of housing: 37 years (2000).
Transportation: Commute to work: 86.5% car, 11.2% public transportation, 1.0% walk, 0.8% work from home (2000); Travel time to work: 11.3% less than 15 minutes, 34.6% 15 to 30 minutes, 34.6% 30 to 45 minutes, 9.3% 45 to 60 minutes, 10.2% 60 minutes or more (2000)

WESTWOOD LAKES (CDP). Covers a land area of 1.723 square miles and a water area of 0.091 square miles. Located at 25.72° N. Lat.; 80.36° W. Long.
Population: 11,522 (1990); 12,005 (2000); 12,001 (2004); 12,103 (2009 projected); Race: 93.3% White, 0.8% Black, 0.9% Asian, 80.6% Hispanic of any race (2004); Density: 6,965.2 persons per square mile (2004); Average household size: 3.46 (2004); Median age: 41.4 (2004); Male/female ratio: 92.3 (2004); Marriage status: 20.8% never married, 60.6% now married,

7.5% widowed, 11.1% divorced (2000); Foreign born: 58.1% (2000); Ancestry (includes multiple ancestries): 74.3% Other groups, 4.3% United States or American, 3.7% Irish, 3.5% German, 2.6% English (2000).
Economy: Employment by occupation: 11.1% management, 12.2% professional, 17.6% services, 35.0% sales, 0.6% farming, 12.9% construction, 10.4% production (2000).
Income: Per capita income: $18,168 (2004); Median household income: $49,669 (2004); Average household income: $60,738 (2004); Percent of households with income of $100,000 or more: 14.3% (2004); Poverty rate: 9.6% (2000).
Education: Percent of population age 25 and over with: High school diploma (including GED) or higher: 66.1% (2004); Bachelor's degree or higher: 14.2% (2004); Master's degree or higher: 7.2% (2004).
Housing: Homeownership rate: 86.6% (2004); Median home value: $189,659 (2004); Median rent: $854 per month (2000); Median age of housing: 43 years (2000).
Transportation: Commute to work: 94.7% car, 1.6% public transportation, 0.8% walk, 2.6% work from home (2000); Travel time to work: 17.0% less than 15 minutes, 36.4% 15 to 30 minutes, 26.7% 30 to 45 minutes, 11.3% 45 to 60 minutes, 8.6% 60 minutes or more (2000)

Monroe County

Located in southern Florida, at the tip of a peninsula; Everglades area, with Cape Sable and Whitewater Bay; includes most of the Florida Keys, enclosing Florida Bay. Covers a land area of 996.90 square miles, a water area of 2,740.20 square miles, and is located in the Eastern Time Zone. The county government was organized in 1823. County seat is Key West.

Monroe County is part of the Key West-Marathon, FL Micropolitan Statistical Area. The entire metro area includes: Monroe County, FL

Weather Station: Flamingo Ranger Station — Elevation: 0 feet

	Jan	Feb	Mar	Apr	May	Jun	Jul	Aug	Sep	Oct	Nov	Dec
High	77	77	79	83	86	88	89	90	89	86	82	78
Low	56	57	60	64	69	73	74	74	73	69	64	59
Precip	2.0	1.6	1.9	2.1	5.0	7.3	4.9	7.5	7.3	4.3	2.5	1.5
Snow	0.0	0.0	0.0	0.0	0.0	0.0	0.0	0.0	0.0	0.0	0.0	0.0

High and Low temperatures in degrees Fahrenheit; Precipitation and Snow in inches

Weather Station: Key West Int'l Airport — Elevation: 3 feet

	Jan	Feb	Mar	Apr	May	Jun	Jul	Aug	Sep	Oct	Nov	Dec
High	75	76	79	82	85	88	89	89	88	85	80	77
Low	65	66	69	72	76	79	80	79	78	76	72	67
Precip	2.5	1.6	1.9	2.0	3.5	4.5	3.5	5.2	5.5	4.4	2.6	2.1
Snow	0.0	0.0	0.0	0.0	0.0	0.0	0.0	0.0	0.0	0.0	0.0	0.0

High and Low temperatures in degrees Fahrenheit; Precipitation and Snow in inches

Weather Station: Tavernier — Elevation: 6 feet

	Jan	Feb	Mar	Apr	May	Jun	Jul	Aug	Sep	Oct	Nov	Dec
High	77	78	80	84	87	89	91	90	89	86	82	78
Low	63	64	67	70	74	77	78	78	77	74	70	66
Precip	2.5	2.0	2.3	1.9	3.9	6.8	3.3	5.1	6.7	5.4	3.0	2.0
Snow	0.0	0.0	0.0	0.0	0.0	0.0	0.0	0.0	0.0	0.0	0.0	0.0

High and Low temperatures in degrees Fahrenheit; Precipitation and Snow in inches

Population: 78,024 (1990); 79,589 (2000); 80,915 (2004); 82,630 (2009 projected); Race: 90.4% White, 4.7% Black, 1.0% Asian, 18.7% Hispanic of any race (2004); Density: 81.2 persons per square mile (2004); Average household size: 2.25 (2004); Median age: 44.4 (2004); Male/female ratio: 114.4 (2004).
Religion: Five largest groups: 16.4% Catholic Church, 4.0% Southern Baptist Convention, 2.1% The United Methodist Church, 1.3% Episcopal Church, 1.2% Seventh-day Adventist Church (2000).
Economy: Unemployment rate: 2.2% (2004); Total civilian labor force: 49,465 (2004); Leading industries: 34.9% accommodation & food services; 20.9% retail trade; 8.3% health care and social assistance (2003); Companies that employ 500 or more persons: 1 (2003); Companies that employ 100 to 499 persons: 36 (2003); Companies that employ less than 100 persons: 3,727 (2003); Farms: 18 totaling 102 acres (2002); Minority business ownership rate: 17.0% (1997); Women business ownership rate: 22.0% (1997); Retail sales per capita: $11,300 (1997). Single-family building permits issued: 376 (2004); Multi-family building permits issued: 7 (2004).
Income: Per capita income: $29,058 (2004); Median household income: $46,741 (2004); Average household income: $65,010 (2004); Percent of households with income of $100,000 or more: 15.6% (2004); Poverty rate: 9.6% (2002); Bankruptcy rate: 2.57% (2004).
Taxes: Total county taxes per capita: $1,030 (2002); County property taxes per capita: $674 (2002).
Education: Percent of population age 25 and over with: High school diploma (including GED) or higher: 84.9% (2004); Bachelor's degree or higher: 25.5% (2004); Master's degree or higher: 8.8% (2004).
Housing: Homeownership rate: 62.6% (2004); Median home value: $261,212 (2004); Median rent: $735 per month (2000); Median age of housing: 23 years (2000).
Health: Birth rate: 96.3 per 10,000 population (2004); Death rate: 95.9 per 10,000 population (2004); Age adjusted cancer mortality rate: 206.1 deaths per 100,000 population (2002); Number of physicians: 25.5 per 10,000 population (2001); Hospital beds: 32.4 per 10,000 population (2002); Hospital admissions: 1,054.8 per 10,000 population (2002).
Elections: 2004 Presidential election results: 49.2% Bush, 49.7% Kerry, 0.7% Nader, 0.2% Badnarik
National and State Parks: Bahia Honda State Park; Crocodile Lake National Wildlife Refuge; Curry Hammock State Park; Dry Tortugas National Park; Everglades National Park; Fort Zachary Taylor Historic State Park; Great White Heron National Wildlife Refuge; Indian Key Historic State Park; John Pennekamp Coral Reef State Park; Key Largo Hammocks Botanical State Park; Key Largo National Marine Sanctuary; Key West National Wildlife Refuge; Lignumvitae Key Botanical State Park; Long Key State Park; Looe Key National Marine Sanctuary; National Key Deer Refuge; Windley Key Fossil Reef Geological State Park

Additional Information Contacts

Monroe County Government Offices . . . . (305) 294-4641
Big Pine Key Chamber of Commerce . . . . (305) 872-2411
Florida Keys Board of Realtors . . . . (305) 852-9294
Greater Marathon Chamber of Commerce . . . . (305) 743-5417
Islamorada Chamber of Commerce. . . . . (305) 664-4503
Key Largo Chamber of Commerce . . . . (305) 451-1414
Key West Association of Realtors . . . . (305) 296-8259
Key West Chamber of Commerce . . . . (305) 294-2587
Marathon And Lower Keys Association of Realtors. . . . . . . (305) 743-2485
Ocean Reef Business Council . . . . (305) 367-3646

Monroe County Communities

BIG COPPITT KEY (CDP). Covers a land area of 1.377 square miles and a water area of 0.096 square miles. Located at 24.59° N. Lat.; 81.65° W. Long.
Population: 2,388 (1990); 2,595 (2000); 2,638 (2004); 2,703 (2009 projected); Race: 93.0% White, 0.9% Black, 1.8% Asian, 19.8% Hispanic of any race (2004); Density: 1,916.4 persons per square mile (2004); Average household size: 2.37 (2004); Median age: 42.5 (2004); Male/female ratio: 119.7 (2004); Marriage status: 19.9% never married, 53.4% now married, 6.7% widowed, 20.0% divorced (2000); Foreign born: 13.5% (2000); Ancestry (includes multiple ancestries): 28.4% Other groups, 11.8% German, 11.0% English, 10.7% Irish, 8.1% United States or American (2000).
Economy: Employment by occupation: 10.6% management, 15.6% professional, 20.2% services, 25.1% sales, 5.1% farming, 13.4% construction, 9.8% production (2000).
Income: Per capita income: $27,091 (2004); Median household income: $51,974 (2004); Average household income: $64,094 (2004); Percent of households with income of $100,000 or more: 16.2% (2004); Poverty rate: 8.6% (2000).
Education: Percent of population age 25 and over with: High school diploma (including GED) or higher: 81.1% (2004); Bachelor's degree or higher: 18.8% (2004); Master's degree or higher: 7.9% (2004).
Housing: Homeownership rate: 66.2% (2004); Median home value: $244,633 (2004); Median rent: $746 per month (2000); Median age of housing: 18 years (2000).
Transportation: Commute to work: 93.1% car, 0.0% public transportation, 0.5% walk, 2.1% work from home (2000); Travel time to work: 33.3% less than 15 minutes, 49.7% 15 to 30 minutes, 13.5% 30 to 45 minutes, 1.0% 45 to 60 minutes, 2.5% 60 minutes or more (2000)

BIG PINE KEY (CDP). Covers a land area of 9.765 square miles and a water area of 0.183 square miles. Located at 24.68° N. Lat.; 81.36° W. Long. Elevation is 5 feet.
Population: 4,206 (1990); 5,032 (2000); 5,156 (2004); 5,306 (2009 projected); Race: 94.3% White, 1.3% Black, 0.7% Asian, 8.5% Hispanic of

any race (2004); Density: 528.0 persons per square mile (2004); Average household size: 2.21 (2004); Median age: 46.0 (2004); Male/female ratio: 110.6 (2004); Marriage status: 19.1% never married, 64.3% now married, 4.5% widowed, 12.1% divorced (2000); Foreign born: 9.5% (2000); Ancestry (includes multiple ancestries): 21.8% German, 17.0% English, 15.1% Other groups, 13.8% Irish, 8.8% Italian (2000).
Economy: Employment by occupation: 10.2% management, 13.1% professional, 22.0% services, 27.2% sales, 3.1% farming, 15.1% construction, 9.2% production (2000).
Income: Per capita income: $25,867 (2004); Median household income: $48,369 (2004); Average household income: $56,943 (2004); Percent of households with income of $100,000 or more: 10.8% (2004); Poverty rate: 9.5% (2000).
Education: Percent of population age 25 and over with: High school diploma (including GED) or higher: 86.6% (2004); Bachelor's degree or higher: 25.0% (2004); Master's degree or higher: 5.7% (2004).

School District(s)

Monroe County School District (PK-12)
2002-03 Enrollment: 9,218 . . . . (305) 293-1400
Housing: Homeownership rate: 76.7% (2004); Median home value: $225,461 (2004); Median rent: $836 per month (2000); Median age of housing: 19 years (2000).
Transportation: Commute to work: 85.9% car, 0.7% public transportation, 1.0% walk, 5.5% work from home (2000); Travel time to work: 30.7% less than 15 minutes, 14.1% 15 to 30 minutes, 27.9% 30 to 45 minutes, 20.9% 45 to 60 minutes, 6.4% 60 minutes or more (2000)
Additional Information Contacts
Big Pine Key Chamber of Commerce . . . . (305) 872-2411

CUDJOE KEY (CDP). Covers a land area of 5.238 square miles and a water area of 0.393 square miles. Located at 24.66° N. Lat.; 81.48° W. Long.
Population: 1,714 (1990); 1,695 (2000); 1,786 (2004); 1,885 (2009 projected); Race: 95.1% White, 1.2% Black, 1.5% Asian, 7.2% Hispanic of any race (2004); Density: 341.0 persons per square mile (2004); Average household size: 2.11 (2004); Median age: 49.5 (2004); Male/female ratio: 109.1 (2004); Marriage status: 20.2% never married, 62.5% now married, 3.3% widowed, 14.1% divorced (2000); Foreign born: 6.0% (2000); Ancestry (includes multiple ancestries): 23.9% Irish, 21.3% German, 16.0% English, 14.5% Other groups, 8.1% United States or American (2000).
Economy: Employment by occupation: 13.2% management, 13.6% professional, 13.9% services, 29.7% sales, 2.8% farming, 18.3% construction, 8.5% production (2000).
Income: Per capita income: $35,539 (2004); Median household income: $63,178 (2004); Average household income: $74,938 (2004); Percent of households with income of $100,000 or more: 22.4% (2004); Poverty rate: 5.8% (2000).
Education: Percent of population age 25 and over with: High school diploma (including GED) or higher: 92.6% (2004); Bachelor's degree or higher: 21.5% (2004); Master's degree or higher: 9.3% (2004).
Housing: Homeownership rate: 82.6% (2004); Median home value: $294,301 (2004); Median rent: $935 per month (2000); Median age of housing: 15 years (2000).
Transportation: Commute to work: 89.4% car, 0.0% public transportation, 0.0% walk, 5.0% work from home (2000); Travel time to work: 29.1% less than 15 minutes, 19.0% 15 to 30 minutes, 38.9% 30 to 45 minutes, 9.8% 45 to 60 minutes, 3.2% 60 minutes or more (2000)

DUCK KEY (CDP). Covers a land area of 0.862 square miles and a water area of 0.045 square miles. Located at 24.77° N. Lat.; 80.91° W. Long.
Population: 529 (1990); 443 (2000); 466 (2004); 494 (2009 projected); Race: 99.4% White, 0.2% Black, 0.0% Asian, 2.8% Hispanic of any race (2004); Density: 540.9 persons per square mile (2004); Average household size: 1.88 (2004); Median age: 54.6 (2004); Male/female ratio: 103.5 (2004); Marriage status: 10.4% never married, 79.3% now married, 7.5% widowed, 2.9% divorced (2000); Foreign born: 2.0% (2000); Ancestry (includes multiple ancestries): 26.4% Irish, 23.5% English, 17.7% German, 17.4% Russian, 9.2% Italian (2000).
Economy: Employment by occupation: 23.7% management, 22.5% professional, 11.9% services, 14.6% sales, 13.0% farming, 5.5% construction, 8.7% production (2000).
Income: Per capita income: $41,009 (2004); Median household income: $43,049 (2004); Average household income: $77,056 (2004); Percent of households with income of $100,000 or more: 20.6% (2004); Poverty rate: 16.6% (2000).
Education: Percent of population age 25 and over with: High school diploma (including GED) or higher: 98.5% (2004); Bachelor's degree or higher: 50.1% (2004); Master's degree or higher: 30.9% (2004).
Housing: Homeownership rate: 78.2% (2004); Median home value: $433,333 (2004); Median rent: $779 per month (2000); Median age of housing: 12 years (2000).
Transportation: Commute to work: 70.9% car, 0.0% public transportation, 3.3% walk, 15.2% work from home (2000); Travel time to work: 43.0% less than 15 minutes, 36.2% 15 to 30 minutes, 9.2% 30 to 45 minutes, 0.0% 45 to 60 minutes, 11.6% 60 minutes or more (2000)

ISLAMORADA (village). Covers a land area of 7.113 square miles and a water area of 0.141 square miles. Located at 24.93° N. Lat.; 80.61° W. Long. Elevation is 5 feet.
History: Islamorada, on the Upper Matecumbe Key, was the location of a camp of veterans working on the Overseas Highway when the devastating hurricane struck in 1935. The Hurricane Memorial was erected here in memory of the men who lost their lives in that storm.
Population: 6,720 (1990); 6,846 (2000); 6,920 (2004); 7,003 (2009 projected); Race: 96.7% White, 0.4% Black, 0.8% Asian, 7.8% Hispanic of any race (2004); Density: 972.9 persons per square mile (2004); Average household size: 2.13 (2004); Median age: 47.7 (2004); Male/female ratio: 113.1 (2004); Marriage status: 23.1% never married, 57.6% now married, 5.7% widowed, 13.6% divorced (2000); Foreign born: 6.7% (2000); Ancestry (includes multiple ancestries): 21.1% Irish, 19.3% German, 18.5% English, 9.8% Other groups, 8.0% United States or American (2000).
Economy: Employment by occupation: 11.6% management, 16.4% professional, 20.1% services, 30.0% sales, 3.9% farming, 7.0% construction, 10.9% production (2000).
Income: Per capita income: $31,791 (2004); Median household income: $44,191 (2004); Average household income: $67,405 (2004); Percent of households with income of $100,000 or more: 16.1% (2004); Poverty rate: 6.9% (2000).
Taxes: Total city taxes per capita: $641 (2002); City property taxes per capita: $525 (2002).
Education: Percent of population age 25 and over with: High school diploma (including GED) or higher: 92.0% (2004); Bachelor's degree or higher: 28.9% (2004); Master's degree or higher: 9.9% (2004).
Housing: Homeownership rate: 71.6% (2004); Median home value: $292,413 (2004); Median rent: $709 per month (2000); Median age of housing: 20 years (2000).
Transportation: Commute to work: 82.7% car, 0.1% public transportation, 7.8% walk, 7.3% work from home (2000); Travel time to work: 52.1% less than 15 minutes, 25.1% 15 to 30 minutes, 6.9% 30 to 45 minutes, 3.6% 45 to 60 minutes, 12.3% 60 minutes or more (2000)
Additional Information Contacts
Islamorada Chamber of Commerce. . . . . (305) 664-4503
Local Government Offices . . . . (305) 664-2345

KEY COLONY BEACH (city). Covers a land area of 0.508 square miles and a water area of 0.162 square miles. Located at 24.72° N. Lat.; 81.01° W. Long. Elevation is 4 feet.
Population: 993 (1990); 788 (2000); 831 (2004); 882 (2009 projected); Race: 99.0% White, 0.6% Black, 0.0% Asian, 6.3% Hispanic of any race (2004); Density: 1,634.3 persons per square mile (2004); Average household size: 1.86 (2004); Median age: 59.0 (2004); Male/female ratio: 102.2 (2004); Marriage status: 7.2% never married, 63.6% now married, 13.5% widowed, 15.8% divorced (2000); Foreign born: 11.8% (2000); Ancestry (includes multiple ancestries): 25.3% German, 22.0% English, 17.2% Irish, 14.2% Other groups, 7.3% French (except Basque) (2000).
Economy: Single-family building permits issued: 11 (2004); Multi-family building permits issued: 5 (2004); Employment by occupation: 14.4% management, 18.7% professional, 21.0% services, 32.7% sales, 2.3% farming, 6.2% construction, 4.7% production (2000).
Income: Per capita income: $39,434 (2004); Median household income: $46,111 (2004); Average household income: $73,475 (2004); Percent of households with income of $100,000 or more: 17.0% (2004); Poverty rate: 7.4% (2000).
Taxes: Total city taxes per capita: $1,246 (2002); City property taxes per capita: $1,041 (2002).
Education: Percent of population age 25 and over with: High school diploma (including GED) or higher: 92.6% (2004); Bachelor's degree or higher: 35.4% (2004); Master's degree or higher: 8.7% (2004).

Housing: Homeownership rate: 73.1% (2004); Median home value: $352,113 (2004); Median rent: $831 per month (2000); Median age of housing: 25 years (2000).
Transportation: Commute to work: 82.0% car, 0.0% public transportation, 4.7% walk, 6.7% work from home (2000); Travel time to work: 74.8% less than 15 minutes, 13.9% 15 to 30 minutes, 6.7% 30 to 45 minutes, 2.1% 45 to 60 minutes, 2.5% 60 minutes or more (2000)

KEY LARGO (CDP). Covers a land area of 12.152 square miles and a water area of 3.136 square miles. Located at 25.10° N. Lat.; 80.43° W. Long. Elevation is 6 feet.
Population: 11,302 (1990); 11,886 (2000); 11,943 (2004); 12,017 (2009 projected); Race: 94.0% White, 2.0% Black, 0.6% Asian, 21.0% Hispanic of any race (2004); Density: 982.8 persons per square mile (2004); Average household size: 2.28 (2004); Median age: 44.5 (2004); Male/female ratio: 108.8 (2004); Marriage status: 20.0% never married, 59.1% now married, 6.2% widowed, 14.7% divorced (2000); Foreign born: 15.9% (2000); Ancestry (includes multiple ancestries): 25.5% Other groups, 19.0% German, 14.4% English, 13.3% Irish, 8.5% Italian (2000).
Economy: Diversified light manufacturing, especially marine equipment. Employment by occupation: 12.7% management, 14.5% professional, 20.6% services, 25.3% sales, 2.1% farming, 15.0% construction, 9.7% production (2000).
Income: Per capita income: $28,356 (2004); Median household income: $46,831 (2004); Average household income: $64,621 (2004); Percent of households with income of $100,000 or more: 15.4% (2004); Poverty rate: 8.3% (2000).
Education: Percent of population age 25 and over with: High school diploma (including GED) or higher: 84.2% (2004); Bachelor's degree or higher: 24.1% (2004); Master's degree or higher: 8.2% (2004).

School District(s)

Monroe County School District (PK-12)
2002-03 Enrollment: 9,218 . . . . (305) 293-1400
Housing: Homeownership rate: 70.5% (2004); Median home value: $195,588 (2004); Median rent: $668 per month (2000); Median age of housing: 20 years (2000).
Transportation: Commute to work: 88.9% car, 1.1% public transportation, 2.3% walk, 3.9% work from home (2000); Travel time to work: 43.0% less than 15 minutes, 26.8% 15 to 30 minutes, 11.7% 30 to 45 minutes, 5.8% 45 to 60 minutes, 12.7% 60 minutes or more (2000)
Airports: Ocean Reef Club
Additional Information Contacts
Key Largo Chamber of Commerce . . . . (305) 451-1414
Ocean Reef Business Council . . . . (305) 367-3646

KEY WEST (city). Covers a land area of 5.946 square miles and a water area of 1.459 square miles. Located at 24.55° N. Lat.; 81.78° W. Long. Elevation is 8 feet.
History: Key West, at the tip of the string of coral islands off the southern coast of Florida, was visited by explorers and adventurers for several centuries before a permanent settlement was established after 1823. Families from New England, Virginia, and South Carolina came, and many turned to salvaging cargoes from vessels wrecked on the reefs. Fort Taylor was built here during the Mexican War of 1846-1848, and strengthened at the beginning of the Civil War. Though Key West citizens were Confederate sympathizers, the city was held by Federal forces throughout the war. For a time, Key West was the world's largest cigar manufacturer. The Overseas Extension of the Florida East Coast Railway was completed in 1912 to link Key West over the other keys with the mainland, but a 1935 hurricane destroyed it. In 1938 the Overseas Highway was built along the same route.
Population: 24,842 (1990); 25,478 (2000); 25,479 (2004); 25,534 (2009 projected); Race: 84.8% White, 9.2% Black, 1.5% Asian, 18.1% Hispanic of any race (2004); Density: 4,285.2 persons per square mile (2004); Average household size: 2.26 (2004); Median age: 40.9 (2004); Male/female ratio: 121.9 (2004); Marriage status: 33.8% never married, 45.5% now married, 5.4% widowed, 15.2% divorced (2000); Foreign born: 15.8% (2000); Ancestry (includes multiple ancestries): 27.4% Other groups, 12.4% English, 12.2% German, 11.3% Irish, 6.8% Italian (2000).
Economy: Unemployment rate: 2.2% (2004); Total civilian labor force: 15,925 (2004); Single-family building permits issued: 27 (2004); Multi-family building permits issued: 0 (2004); Employment by occupation: 14.7% management, 15.1% professional, 26.7% services, 26.2% sales, 2.2% farming, 9.1% construction, 6.0% production (2000).
Income: Per capita income: $30,617 (2004); Median household income: $49,287 (2004); Average household income: $68,512 (2004); Percent of households with income of $100,000 or more: 17.1% (2004); Poverty rate: 10.2% (2000).
Taxes: Total city taxes per capita: $524 (2002); City property taxes per capita: $409 (2002).
Education: Percent of population age 25 and over with: High school diploma (including GED) or higher: 84.8% (2004); Bachelor's degree or higher: 27.7% (2004); Master's degree or higher: 10.1% (2004).

School District(s)

Monroe County School District (PK-12)
2002-03 Enrollment: 9,218 . . . . (305) 293-1400

Two-year College(s)

Florida Keys Community College (Public)
2003-04 Enrollment: 1,283 . . . . (305) 296-9081
2003-04 Tuition: In-state $1,900; Out-of-state $6,390
Housing: Homeownership rate: 46.2% (2004); Median home value: $342,999 (2004); Median rent: $822 per month (2000); Median age of housing: 39 years (2000).
Hospitals: Lower Keys Medical Center (169 beds)
Safety: Violent crime rate: 59.1 per 10,000 population; Property crime rate: 730.1 per 10,000 population (2003).
Newspapers: Key West Citizen (Circulation 9,265)
Transportation: Commute to work: 66.7% car, 1.2% public transportation, 8.0% walk, 5.7% work from home (2000); Travel time to work: 64.7% less than 15 minutes, 29.3% 15 to 30 minutes, 3.8% 30 to 45 minutes, 0.8% 45 to 60 minutes, 1.4% 60 minutes or more (2000)
Airports: Key West International (primary service)
Additional Information Contacts
Key West Association of Realtors . . . . (305) 296-8259
Key West Chamber of Commerce . . . . (305) 294-2587

LAYTON (city). Aka Long Key. Covers a land area of 0.216 square miles and a water area of 0.028 square miles. Located at 24.82° N. Lat.; 80.81° W. Long. Elevation is 3 feet.
Population: 183 (1990); 186 (2000); 201 (2004); 220 (2009 projected); Race: 99.5% White, 0.0% Black, 0.5% Asian, 2.0% Hispanic of any race (2004); Density: 929.4 persons per square mile (2004); Average household size: 2.21 (2004); Median age: 52.1 (2004); Male/female ratio: 97.1 (2004); Marriage status: 28.9% never married, 55.0% now married, 7.3% widowed, 8.7% divorced (2000); Foreign born: 19.6% (2000); Ancestry (includes multiple ancestries): 34.6% English, 24.6% German, 17.1% French (except Basque), 17.1% Irish, 12.5% Other groups (2000).
Economy: Single-family building permits issued: 8 (2004); Multi-family building permits issued: 0 (2004); Employment by occupation: 23.1% management, 14.5% professional, 26.5% services, 26.5% sales, 0.0% farming, 7.7% construction, 1.7% production (2000).
Income: Per capita income: $30,970 (2004); Median household income: $53,125 (2004); Average household income: $68,407 (2004); Percent of households with income of $100,000 or more: 22.0% (2004); Poverty rate: 15.4% (2000).
Education: Percent of population age 25 and over with: High school diploma (including GED) or higher: 88.0% (2004); Bachelor's degree or higher: 21.0% (2004); Master's degree or higher: 4.8% (2004).
Housing: Homeownership rate: 67.0% (2004); Median home value: $342,593 (2004); Median rent: $600 per month (2000); Median age of housing: 25 years (2000).
Transportation: Commute to work: 76.9% car, 0.0% public transportation, 8.5% walk, 0.0% work from home (2000); Travel time to work: 45.3% less than 15 minutes, 28.2% 15 to 30 minutes, 8.5% 30 to 45 minutes, 8.5% 45 to 60 minutes, 9.4% 60 minutes or more (2000)

MARATHON (city). Covers a land area of 8.646 square miles and a water area of 0.997 square miles. Located at 24.72° N. Lat.; 81.04° W. Long. Elevation is 3 feet.
History: Marathon became the trading center of Key Vaca, chosen by settlers for its fertile land and fresh-water wells.
Population: 10,728 (1990); 10,255 (2000); 10,364 (2004); 10,527 (2009 projected); Race: 91.0% White, 4.5% Black, 0.6% Asian, 26.3% Hispanic of any race (2004); Density: 1,198.7 persons per square mile (2004); Average household size: 2.21 (2004); Median age: 45.6 (2004); Male/female ratio: 111.5 (2004); Marriage status: 20.7% never married, 57.6% now married, 6.1% widowed, 15.6% divorced (2000); Foreign born: 19.8% (2000); Ancestry (includes multiple ancestries): 28.8% Other groups, 17.2%

German, 15.7% Irish, 12.7% English, 5.8% United States or American (2000).
Economy: Single-family building permits issued: 84 (2004); Multi-family building permits issued: 0 (2004); Employment by occupation: 10.0% management, 12.5% professional, 25.3% services, 22.1% sales, 4.1% farming, 15.0% construction, 11.1% production (2000).
Income: Per capita income: $24,961 (2004); Median household income: $37,951 (2004); Average household income: $54,755 (2004); Percent of households with income of $100,000 or more: 11.0% (2004); Poverty rate: 14.2% (2000).
Education: Percent of population age 25 and over with: High school diploma (including GED) or higher: 80.5% (2004); Bachelor's degree or higher: 20.9% (2004); Master's degree or higher: 5.7% (2004).

School District(s)

Monroe County School District (PK-12)
2002-03 Enrollment: 9,218 .... (305) 293-1400
Housing: Homeownership rate: 63.3% (2004); Median home value: $192,692 (2004); Median rent: $628 per month (2000); Median age of housing: 24 years (2000).
Hospitals: Fishermen's Hospital (58 beds)
Newspapers: Florida Keys Keynoter (General - Circulation 11,000)
Transportation: Commute to work: 78.6% car, 2.2% public transportation, 8.0% walk, 3.6% work from home (2000); Travel time to work: 69.0% less than 15 minutes, 18.1% 15 to 30 minutes, 4.3% 30 to 45 minutes, 3.9% 45 to 60 minutes, 4.7% 60 minutes or more (2000)
Airports: The Florida Keys-Marathon
Additional Information Contacts
Greater Marathon Chamber of Commerce .... (305) 743-5417
Marathon And Lower Keys Association of Realtors....... (305) 743-2485

NORTH KEY LARGO (CDP). Covers a land area of 18.774 square miles and a water area of 0.889 square miles. Located at 25.29° N. Lat.; 80.30° W. Long.
Population: 1,490 (1990); 1,049 (2000); 907 (2004); 757 (2009 projected); Race: 98.8% White, 0.6% Black, 0.2% Asian, 2.6% Hispanic of any race (2004); Density: 48.3 persons per square mile (2004); Average household size: 1.82 (2004); Median age: 63.3 (2004); Male/female ratio: 95.1 (2004); Marriage status: 7.2% never married, 72.2% now married, 9.5% widowed, 11.2% divorced (2000); Foreign born: 4.3% (2000); Ancestry (includes multiple ancestries): 31.4% English, 20.9% German, 13.5% Irish, 7.1% Italian, 5.4% French (except Basque) (2000).
Economy: Employment by occupation: 40.2% management, 16.8% professional, 11.5% services, 17.1% sales, 2.4% farming, 11.9% construction, 0.0% production (2000).
Income: Per capita income: $72,274 (2004); Median household income: $90,761 (2004); Average household income: $131,368 (2004); Percent of households with income of $100,000 or more: 44.9% (2004); Poverty rate: 0.5% (2000).
Education: Percent of population age 25 and over with: High school diploma (including GED) or higher: 97.6% (2004); Bachelor's degree or higher: 58.1% (2004); Master's degree or higher: 20.7% (2004).
Housing: Homeownership rate: 85.8% (2004); Median home value: $1 million+ (2004); Median rent: $390 per month (2000); Median age of housing: 22 years (2000).
Transportation: Commute to work: 44.3% car, 0.0% public transportation, 13.3% walk, 32.2% work from home (2000); Travel time to work: 68.2% less than 15 minutes, 22.5% 15 to 30 minutes, 5.2% 30 to 45 minutes, 0.0% 45 to 60 minutes, 4.0% 60 minutes or more (2000)

STOCK ISLAND (CDP). Covers a land area of 0.896 square miles and a water area of 0.014 square miles. Located at 24.57° N. Lat.; 81.73° W. Long.
Population: 3,613 (1990); 4,410 (2000); 4,976 (2004); 5,645 (2009 projected); Race: 80.1% White, 10.5% Black, 1.3% Asian, 49.7% Hispanic of any race (2004); Density: 5,550.5 persons per square mile (2004); Average household size: 2.60 (2004); Median age: 38.2 (2004); Male/female ratio: 119.5 (2004); Marriage status: 30.5% never married, 47.0% now married, 4.6% widowed, 17.9% divorced (2000); Foreign born: 28.1% (2000); Ancestry (includes multiple ancestries): 52.2% Other groups, 8.7% United States or American, 7.5% English, 6.6% German, 5.8% Irish (2000).
Economy: Employment by occupation: 5.7% management, 9.7% professional, 29.1% services, 19.2% sales, 7.5% farming, 16.9% construction, 11.8% production (2000).
Income: Per capita income: $14,890 (2004); Median household income: $31,882 (2004); Average household income: $37,909 (2004); Percent of households with income of $100,000 or more: 3.1% (2004); Poverty rate: 20.5% (2000).
Education: Percent of population age 25 and over with: High school diploma (including GED) or higher: 66.6% (2004); Bachelor's degree or higher: 9.5% (2004); Master's degree or higher: 3.1% (2004).
Housing: Homeownership rate: 50.7% (2004); Median home value: $96,375 (2004); Median rent: $617 per month (2000); Median age of housing: 25 years (2000).
Transportation: Commute to work: 76.1% car, 2.3% public transportation, 4.7% walk, 1.2% work from home (2000); Travel time to work: 56.3% less than 15 minutes, 38.6% 15 to 30 minutes, 4.8% 30 to 45 minutes, 0.0% 45 to 60 minutes, 0.4% 60 minutes or more (2000)

SUMMERLAND KEY (unincorporated postal area, zip code 33042). Covers a land area of 27.945 square miles and a water area of 9.627 square miles. Located at 24.66° N. Lat.; 81.48° W. Long. Elevation is 10 feet.
Population: 6,097 (2000); Race: 97.0% White, 0.8% Black, 0.2% Asian, 6.3% Hispanic of any race (2000); Density: 218.2 persons per square mile (2000); Age: 15.7% under 18, 14.3% over 64 (2000); Marriage status: 17.0% never married, 65.4% now married, 2.6% widowed, 15.1% divorced (2000); Foreign born: 7.1% (2000); Ancestry (includes multiple ancestries): 20.9% Irish, 20.0% German, 17.4% English, 15.8% Other groups, 8.6% Italian (2000).
Economy: Employment by occupation: 12.2% management, 16.5% professional, 16.1% services, 29.2% sales, 3.0% farming, 14.9% construction, 8.0% production (2000).
Income: Per capita income: $28,353 (2000); Median household income: $53,409 (2000); Poverty rate: 6.6% (2000).
Education: Percent of population age 25 and over with: High school diploma (including GED) or higher: 89.6% (2000); Bachelor's degree or higher: 26.8% (2000).

School District(s)

Monroe County School District (PK-12)
2002-03 Enrollment: 9,218 .... (305) 293-1400
Housing: Homeownership rate: 80.1% (2000); Median home value: $270,600 (2000); Median rent: $834 per month (2000); Median age of housing: 16 years (2000).
Transportation: Commute to work: 90.5% car, 0.5% public transportation, 0.0% walk, 5.1% work from home (2000); Travel time to work: 26.7% less than 15 minutes, 23.5% 15 to 30 minutes, 36.2% 30 to 45 minutes, 9.8% 45 to 60 minutes, 3.9% 60 minutes or more (2000)

TAVERNIER (CDP). Covers a land area of 2.611 square miles and a water area of 0.094 square miles. Located at 25.01° N. Lat.; 80.51° W. Long. Elevation is 11 feet.
History: Tavernier, on the southern end of Key Largo, was named for a pirate friend of Jean La Fitte, who was said to have used this area as a hiding place. The land boom of the 1920's brought growth to Tavernier.
Population: 2,433 (1990); 2,173 (2000); 1,990 (2004); 1,780 (2009 projected); Race: 97.2% White, 0.9% Black, 0.5% Asian, 23.2% Hispanic of any race (2004); Density: 762.1 persons per square mile (2004); Average household size: 2.35 (2004); Median age: 44.5 (2004); Male/female ratio: 104.5 (2004); Marriage status: 16.4% never married, 62.4% now married, 5.4% widowed, 15.7% divorced (2000); Foreign born: 14.9% (2000); Ancestry (includes multiple ancestries): 29.2% Other groups, 20.5% Irish, 18.3% English, 17.3% German, 8.8% United States or American (2000).
Economy: Employment by occupation: 7.7% management, 12.5% professional, 21.1% services, 23.4% sales, 5.3% farming, 17.9% construction, 12.1% production (2000).
Income: Per capita income: $23,790 (2004); Median household income: $43,672 (2004); Average household income: $55,661 (2004); Percent of households with income of $100,000 or more: 11.3% (2004); Poverty rate: 9.9% (2000).
Education: Percent of population age 25 and over with: High school diploma (including GED) or higher: 87.9% (2004); Bachelor's degree or higher: 20.0% (2004); Master's degree or higher: 4.2% (2004).

School District(s)

Monroe County School District (PK-12)
2002-03 Enrollment: 9,218 .... (305) 293-1400
Housing: Homeownership rate: 65.3% (2004); Median home value: $217,308 (2004); Median rent: $638 per month (2000); Median age of housing: 19 years (2000).

Hospitals: Mariners Hospital (42 beds)
Newspapers: CBA: The Reporter (General - Circulation 8,000)
Transportation: Commute to work: 89.8% car, 0.0% public transportation, 1.8% walk, 4.4% work from home (2000); Travel time to work: 38.8% less than 15 minutes, 36.0% 15 to 30 minutes, 9.8% 30 to 45 minutes, 2.5% 45 to 60 minutes, 12.9% 60 minutes or more (2000)
Additional Information Contacts
Florida Keys Board of Realtors . . . . (305) 852-9294

Nassau County

Located in northeastern Florida; bounded on the east by the Atlantic Ocean, and on the north by the St. Marys River and the Georgia border; includes Amelia Barrier Island. Covers a land area of 651.60 square miles, a water area of 74.30 square miles, and is located in the Eastern Time Zone. The county government was organized in 1824. County seat is Fernandina Beach.

Nassau County is part of the Jacksonville, FL Metropolitan Statistical Area. The entire metro area includes: Baker County, FL; Clay County, FL; Duval County, FL; Nassau County, FL; St. Johns County, FL

Weather Station: Fernandina Beach — Elevation: 13 feet

	Jan	Feb	Mar	Apr	May	Jun	Jul	Aug	Sep	Oct	Nov	Dec
High	62	65	71	77	82	87	90	88	85	78	71	65
Low	43	46	51	58	65	71	74	74	72	64	54	47
Precip	3.9	3.3	4.2	2.8	3.0	5.3	5.9	5.5	7.4	4.5	2.5	2.7
Snow	tr	tr	tr	0.0	0.0	0.0	0.0	0.0	0.0	0.0	0.0	0.0

High and Low temperatures in degrees Fahrenheit; Precipitation and Snow in inches

Population: 43,941 (1990); 57,663 (2000); 63,454 (2004); 70,742 (2009 projected); Race: 90.4% White, 7.2% Black, 0.6% Asian, 1.7% Hispanic of any race (2004); Density: 97.4 persons per square mile (2004); Average household size: 2.61 (2004); Median age: 39.2 (2004); Male/female ratio: 98.0 (2004).
Religion: Five largest groups: 29.2% Southern Baptist Convention, 5.2% Catholic Church, 3.7% The United Methodist Church, 2.1% Church of God (Cleveland, Tennessee), 1.7% Presbyterian Church (U.S.A.) (2000).
Economy: Unemployment rate: 4.2% (2004); Total civilian labor force: 31,370 (2004); Leading industries: 21.6% accommodation & food services; 18.2% retail trade; 12.6% health care and social assistance (2003); Companies that employ 500 or more persons: 2 (2003); Companies that employ 100 to 499 persons: 20 (2003); Companies that employ less than 100 persons: 1,303 (2003); Farms: 315 totaling n/a acres (2002); Minority business ownership rate: n/a (1997); Women business ownership rate: 24.7% (1997); Retail sales per capita: $6,156 (1997). Single-family building permits issued: 1,252 (2004); Multi-family building permits issued: 35 (2004).
Income: Per capita income: $25,973 (2004); Median household income: $51,794 (2004); Average household income: $67,101 (2004); Percent of households with income of $100,000 or more: 15.9% (2004); Poverty rate: 8.3% (2002); Bankruptcy rate: 5.45% (2004).
Taxes: Total county taxes per capita: $506 (2002); County property taxes per capita: $342 (2002).
Education: Percent of population age 25 and over with: High school diploma (including GED) or higher: 81.1% (2004); Bachelor's degree or higher: 19.0% (2004); Master's degree or higher: 6.6% (2004).
Housing: Homeownership rate: 80.8% (2004); Median home value: $136,056 (2004); Median rent: $450 per month (2000); Median age of housing: 16 years (2000).
Health: Birth rate: 109.9 per 10,000 population (2004); Death rate: 88.7 per 10,000 population (2004); Age adjusted cancer mortality rate: 226.8 deaths per 100,000 population (2002); Air Quality Index: 89.9% good, 8.7% moderate, 1.1% unhealthy for sensitive individuals, 0.3% unhealthy (percent of days in 2004); Number of physicians: 11.7 per 10,000 population (2001); Hospital beds: 5.3 per 10,000 population (2002); Hospital admissions: 526.3 per 10,000 population (2002).
Elections: 2004 Presidential election results: 72.6% Bush, 26.2% Kerry, 0.6% Nader, 0.2% Badnarik
National and State Parks: Amelia Island State Park; Cary State Forest; Fernandina Plaza Historic State Park; Fort Clinch State Park; Nassau Sound Fishing Pier State Park
Additional Information Contacts
Nassau County Government Offices . . . . (904) 321-5700
Amelia Island-Greater Nassau County Association of Realtors. . . . . . (904) 261-8133
Fernandina Beach Chamber of Commerce . . . . (904) 261-3248

Nassau County Communities

BRYCEVILLE (unincorporated postal area, zip code 32009). Covers a land area of 91.626 square miles and a water area of 0.023 square miles. Located at 30.42° N. Lat.; 81.95° W. Long. Elevation is 70 feet.
History: Bryceville developed as a livestock and dairying center. Razorback hogs, allowed to roam the woods, were rounded up like cattle here.
Population: 2,730 (2000); Race: 97.8% White, 1.1% Black, 0.0% Asian, 0.5% Hispanic of any race (2000); Density: 29.8 persons per square mile (2000); Age: 30.1% under 18, 5.5% over 64 (2000); Marriage status: 18.2% never married, 69.6% now married, 3.1% widowed, 9.2% divorced (2000); Foreign born: 0.8% (2000); Ancestry (includes multiple ancestries): 25.4% United States or American, 7.3% English, 6.3% Irish, 6.0% Other groups, 5.4% German (2000).
Economy: Employment by occupation: 10.2% management, 13.6% professional, 11.9% services, 31.0% sales, 0.8% farming, 20.0% construction, 12.6% production (2000).
Income: Per capita income: $19,213 (2000); Median household income: $45,359 (2000); Poverty rate: 7.3% (2000).
Education: Percent of population age 25 and over with: High school diploma (including GED) or higher: 78.6% (2000); Bachelor's degree or higher: 8.7% (2000).

School District(s)

Nassau County School District (PK-12)
2002-03 Enrollment: 10,533 . . . . (904) 491-9901
Housing: Homeownership rate: 88.9% (2000); Median home value: $115,400 (2000); Median rent: $450 per month (2000); Median age of housing: 11 years (2000).
Transportation: Commute to work: 97.1% car, 0.0% public transportation, 0.0% walk, 2.1% work from home (2000); Travel time to work: 7.0% less than 15 minutes, 17.5% 15 to 30 minutes, 39.0% 30 to 45 minutes, 18.7% 45 to 60 minutes, 17.7% 60 minutes or more (2000)

CALLAHAN (town). Covers a land area of 1.327 square miles and a water area of 0 square miles. Located at 30.56° N. Lat.; 81.83° W. Long. Elevation is 21 feet.
History: Callahan was the site in 1778 of an attack by 300 American cavalry under Colonel Elijah Clarke on a larger group of British troops, in which the Americans lost 13 men and were forced to withdraw.
Population: 946 (1990); 962 (2000); 1,116 (2004); 1,300 (2009 projected); Race: 85.4% White, 11.3% Black, 0.4% Asian, 2.2% Hispanic of any race (2004); Density: 841.0 persons per square mile (2004); Average household size: 2.33 (2004); Median age: 32.8 (2004); Male/female ratio: 80.9 (2004); Marriage status: 25.6% never married, 47.4% now married, 14.6% widowed, 12.4% divorced (2000); Foreign born: 0.6% (2000); Ancestry (includes multiple ancestries): 24.8% United States or American, 15.9% Other groups, 12.1% Irish, 8.6% English, 6.2% German (2000).
Economy: Single-family building permits issued: 3 (2004); Multi-family building permits issued: 0 (2004); Employment by occupation: 8.0% management, 16.3% professional, 19.0% services, 28.1% sales, 0.0% farming, 10.7% construction, 17.9% production (2000).
Income: Per capita income: $16,257 (2004); Median household income: $26,859 (2004); Average household income: $37,448 (2004); Percent of households with income of $100,000 or more: 5.4% (2004); Poverty rate: 21.9% (2000).
Taxes: Total city taxes per capita: $134 (2002); City property taxes per capita: $115 (2002).
Education: Percent of population age 25 and over with: High school diploma (including GED) or higher: 69.6% (2004); Bachelor's degree or higher: 12.4% (2004); Master's degree or higher: 3.6% (2004).

School District(s)

Nassau County School District (PK-12)
2002-03 Enrollment: 10,533 . . . . (904) 491-9901
Housing: Homeownership rate: 48.0% (2004); Median home value: $102,703 (2004); Median rent: $327 per month (2000); Median age of housing: 19 years (2000).
Newspapers: Nassau County Record (General - Circulation 5,000)
Transportation: Commute to work: 88.2% car, 0.0% public transportation, 7.8% walk, 2.4% work from home (2000); Travel time to work: 23.7% less than 15 minutes, 33.6% 15 to 30 minutes, 26.7% 30 to 45 minutes, 12.9% 45 to 60 minutes, 3.0% 60 minutes or more (2000)

FERNANDINA BEACH (city). Covers a land area of 10.716 square miles and a water area of 0.003 square miles. Located at 30.66° N. Lat.; 81.45° W. Long. Elevation is 25 feet.

History: Named for Don Domingo Fernandez, who obtained a land grant in 1785. A Spanish post stood on the site of Fernandina Beach in the 1680s, when the island was called Santa Maria. It was renamed Amelia Island in 1735 by General James Oglethorpe of Georgia, when he established a fort here. When Florida was returned to Spain, a land grant given to Fernandez included the village of Fernandina. An important port in the 1800s, Fernandina Beach became an industrial city with shrimp and menhaden fisheries and pulp mills.

Population: 8,887 (1990); 10,549 (2000); 11,075 (2004); 11,809 (2009 projected); Race: 82.9% White, 14.6% Black, 0.7% Asian, 2.8% Hispanic of any race (2004); Density: 1,033.5 persons per square mile (2004); Average household size: 2.29 (2004); Median age: 44.5 (2004); Male/female ratio: 92.5 (2004); Marriage status: 22.1% never married, 58.0% now married, 9.0% widowed, 10.9% divorced (2000); Foreign born: 5.4% (2000); Ancestry (includes multiple ancestries): 19.1% Other groups, 16.4% English, 13.4% United States or American, 12.4% Irish, 11.4% German (2000).

Economy: Single-family building permits issued: 137 (2004); Multi-family building permits issued: 0 (2004); Employment by occupation: 15.3% management, 23.0% professional, 16.3% services, 23.6% sales, 0.3% farming, 10.5% construction, 11.2% production (2000).

Income: Per capita income: $28,512 (2004); Median household income: $46,942 (2004); Average household income: $63,952 (2004); Percent of households with income of $100,000 or more: 14.4% (2004); Poverty rate: 10.2% (2000).

Education: Percent of population age 25 and over with: High school diploma (including GED) or higher: 87.3% (2004); Bachelor's degree or higher: 32.9% (2004); Master's degree or higher: 12.3% (2004).

School District(s)

Nassau County School District (PK-12)
2002-03 Enrollment: 10,533 . . . . (904) 491-9901

Housing: Homeownership rate: 69.1% (2004); Median home value: $167,585 (2004); Median rent: $556 per month (2000); Median age of housing: 21 years (2000).

Hospitals: Baptist Medical Center Nassau (54 beds)

Safety: Violent crime rate: 18.7 per 10,000 population; Property crime rate: 331.5 per 10,000 population (2003).

Newspapers: News-Leader (General - Circulation 10,500)

Transportation: Commute to work: 91.0% car, 0.9% public transportation, 2.1% walk, 2.9% work from home (2000); Travel time to work: 50.3% less than 15 minutes, 20.3% 15 to 30 minutes, 12.3% 30 to 45 minutes, 10.6% 45 to 60 minutes, 6.5% 60 minutes or more (2000)

Airports: Fernandina Beach Municipal

Additional Information Contacts

Amelia Island-Greater Nassau County Association of Realtors . . . . . . (904) 261-8133
Fernandina Beach Chamber of Commerce . . . . (904) 261-3248
Local Government Offices . . . . (904) 277-7305

HILLIARD (town). Covers a land area of 5.495 square miles and a water area of 0 square miles. Located at 30.68° N. Lat.; 81.92° W. Long. Elevation is 69 feet.

History: Hilliard began as a trading post in the early 1800's, when cotton and tobacco were the leading crops.

Population: 2,486 (1990); 2,702 (2000); 3,063 (2004); 3,489 (2009 projected); Race: 84.4% White, 12.4% Black, 0.7% Asian, 1.0% Hispanic of any race (2004); Density: 557.4 persons per square mile (2004); Average household size: 2.80 (2004); Median age: 34.0 (2004); Male/female ratio: 87.9 (2004); Marriage status: 18.2% never married, 63.0% now married, 7.9% widowed, 10.9% divorced (2000); Foreign born: 1.0% (2000); Ancestry (includes multiple ancestries): 19.6% United States or American, 13.7% Irish, 12.7% Other groups, 11.0% English, 6.7% German (2000).

Economy: Single-family building permits issued: 45 (2004); Multi-family building permits issued: 8 (2004); Employment by occupation: 4.5% management, 8.0% professional, 17.4% services, 29.6% sales, 1.9% farming, 14.7% construction, 23.8% production (2000).

Income: Per capita income: $16,283 (2004); Median household income: $38,977 (2004); Average household income: $44,970 (2004); Percent of households with income of $100,000 or more: 7.3% (2004); Poverty rate: 11.7% (2000).

Education: Percent of population age 25 and over with: High school diploma (including GED) or higher: 67.8% (2004); Bachelor's degree or higher: 5.7% (2004); Master's degree or higher: 2.0% (2004).

School District(s)

Nassau County School District (PK-12)
2002-03 Enrollment: 10,533 . . . . (904) 491-9901

Housing: Homeownership rate: 59.2% (2004); Median home value: $85,517 (2004); Median rent: $396 per month (2000); Median age of housing: 23 years (2000).

Transportation: Commute to work: 92.3% car, 0.0% public transportation, 2.2% walk, 2.5% work from home (2000); Travel time to work: 25.7% less than 15 minutes, 8.2% 15 to 30 minutes, 26.6% 30 to 45 minutes, 19.3% 45 to 60 minutes, 20.2% 60 minutes or more (2000)

NASSAU VILLAGE-RATLIFF (CDP). Covers a land area of 14.812 square miles and a water area of 0 square miles. Located at 30.51° N. Lat.; 81.79° W. Long.

Population: 4,047 (1990); 4,667 (2000); 4,111 (2004); 3,600 (2009 projected); Race: 97.5% White, 0.3% Black, 0.4% Asian, 1.0% Hispanic of any race (2004); Density: 277.5 persons per square mile (2004); Average household size: 2.83 (2004); Median age: 37.2 (2004); Male/female ratio: 101.0 (2004); Marriage status: 18.5% never married, 66.8% now married, 5.8% widowed, 8.9% divorced (2000); Foreign born: 0.4% (2000); Ancestry (includes multiple ancestries): 35.7% United States or American, 8.8% English, 7.1% Other groups, 6.8% German, 6.5% Irish (2000).

Economy: Employment by occupation: 7.0% management, 9.5% professional, 14.1% services, 32.1% sales, 0.0% farming, 18.8% construction, 18.4% production (2000).

Income: Per capita income: $17,035 (2004); Median household income: $44,129 (2004); Average household income: $48,199 (2004); Percent of households with income of $100,000 or more: 3.6% (2004); Poverty rate: 6.8% (2000).

Education: Percent of population age 25 and over with: High school diploma (including GED) or higher: 72.8% (2004); Bachelor's degree or higher: 6.4% (2004); Master's degree or higher: 0.9% (2004).

Housing: Homeownership rate: 90.5% (2004); Median home value: $103,580 (2004); Median rent: $460 per month (2000); Median age of housing: 17 years (2000).

Transportation: Commute to work: 96.9% car, 0.0% public transportation, 1.5% walk, 1.6% work from home (2000); Travel time to work: 16.6% less than 15 minutes, 32.0% 15 to 30 minutes, 33.7% 30 to 45 minutes, 11.1% 45 to 60 minutes, 6.5% 60 minutes or more (2000)

YULEE (CDP). Covers a land area of 22.982 square miles and a water area of 0.020 square miles. Located at 30.63° N. Lat.; 81.57° W. Long. Elevation is 35 feet.

History: Yulee was named for David L. Yulee, U.S. Senator from Florida (1845-1851 and 1855-1861), whose name before his election was David Levy. After the Civil War, Yulee was arrested for aiding in the escape of Jefferson Davis, and was imprisoned briefly at Fort Pulaski, Georgia.

Population: 6,751 (1990); 8,392 (2000); 8,408 (2004); 8,472 (2009 projected); Race: 90.3% White, 6.7% Black, 0.6% Asian, 1.7% Hispanic of any race (2004); Density: 365.8 persons per square mile (2004); Average household size: 2.70 (2004); Median age: 36.1 (2004); Male/female ratio: 102.0 (2004); Marriage status: 18.5% never married, 63.9% now married, 5.2% widowed, 12.4% divorced (2000); Foreign born: 1.7% (2000); Ancestry (includes multiple ancestries): 18.5% Other groups, 17.8% United States or American, 10.1% Irish, 8.0% German, 6.8% English (2000).

Economy: Employment by occupation: 9.6% management, 11.8% professional, 15.5% services, 25.6% sales, 0.5% farming, 15.7% construction, 21.3% production (2000).

Income: Per capita income: $20,876 (2004); Median household income: $47,700 (2004); Average household income: $56,313 (2004); Percent of households with income of $100,000 or more: 9.8% (2004); Poverty rate: 10.6% (2000).

Education: Percent of population age 25 and over with: High school diploma (including GED) or higher: 78.6% (2004); Bachelor's degree or higher: 7.2% (2004); Master's degree or higher: 2.3% (2004).

School District(s)

Nassau County School District (PK-12)
2002-03 Enrollment: 10,533 . . . . (904) 491-9901

Housing: Homeownership rate: 82.3% (2004); Median home value: $111,419 (2004); Median rent: $398 per month (2000); Median age of housing: 15 years (2000).

Transportation: Commute to work: 94.3% car, 0.0% public transportation, 0.3% walk, 3.6% work from home (2000); Travel time to work: 14.1% less than 15 minutes, 45.7% 15 to 30 minutes, 23.2% 30 to 45 minutes, 12.9% 45 to 60 minutes, 4.2% 60 minutes or more (2000)

Okaloosa County

Located in northwestern Florida; bounded on the north by Alabama, and on the south by the Gulf of Mexico; drained by the Blackwater, Yellow, and Shoal Rivers; includes part of Choctawhatchee National Forest. Covers a land area of 935.60 square miles, a water area of 146.40 square miles, and is located in the Central Time Zone. The county government was organized in 1915. County seat is Crestview.

Okaloosa County is part of the Fort Walton Beach-Crestview-Destin, FL Metropolitan Statistical Area. The entire metro area includes: Okaloosa County, FL

Population: 143,776 (1990); 170,498 (2000); 181,471 (2004); 195,324 (2009 projected); Race: 82.2% White, 9.6% Black, 2.9% Asian, 4.2% Hispanic of any race (2004); Density: 194.0 persons per square mile (2004); Average household size: 2.55 (2004); Median age: 36.6 (2004); Male/female ratio: 102.5 (2004).
Religion: Five largest groups: 20.2% Southern Baptist Convention, 6.7% The United Methodist Church, 6.7% Catholic Church, 2.2% Assemblies of God, 1.3% Episcopal Church (2000).
Economy: Unemployment rate: 2.7% (2004); Total civilian labor force: 94,943 (2004); Leading industries: 20.7% retail trade; 17.2% accommodation & food services; 13.2% health care and social assistance (2003); Companies that employ 500 or more persons: 8 (2003); Companies that employ 100 to 499 persons: 81 (2003); Companies that employ less than 100 persons: 4,946 (2003); Farms: 465 totaling 55,119 acres (2002); Minority business ownership rate: 9.4% (1997); Women business ownership rate: 31.3% (1997); Retail sales per capita: $10,468 (1997). Single-family building permits issued: 1,737 (2004); Multi-family building permits issued: 974 (2004).
Income: Per capita income: $23,463 (2004); Median household income: $46,040 (2004); Average household income: $58,522 (2004); Percent of households with income of $100,000 or more: 12.3% (2004); Poverty rate: 9.4% (2002); Bankruptcy rate: 4.05% (2004).
Taxes: Total county taxes per capita: $259 (2002); County property taxes per capita: $193 (2002).
Education: Percent of population age 25 and over with: High school diploma (including GED) or higher: 88.0% (2004); Bachelor's degree or higher: 24.3% (2004); Master's degree or higher: 9.3% (2004).
Housing: Homeownership rate: 66.5% (2004); Median home value: $131,252 (2004); Median rent: $502 per month (2000); Median age of housing: 18 years (2000).
Health: Birth rate: 143.9 per 10,000 population (2004); Death rate: 72.1 per 10,000 population (2004); Age adjusted cancer mortality rate: 203.9 deaths per 100,000 population (2002); Number of physicians: 21.1 per 10,000 population (2001); Hospital beds: 27.5 per 10,000 population (2002); Hospital admissions: 1,301.2 per 10,000 population (2002).
Elections: 2004 Presidential election results: 77.6% Bush, 21.6% Kerry, 0.4% Nader, 0.2% Badnarik
National and State Parks: Fred Gannon Rocky Bayou State Park; Henderson Beach State Park; Rocky Bayou State Park Aquatic Preserve
Additional Information Contacts
Okaloosa County Government Offices . . . . (850) 689-5030
Crestview Area Association of Realtors . . . . (850) 682-7041
Crestview Chamber of Commerce . . . . (850) 682-3212
Destin Chamber of Commerce . . . . (850) 837-6241
Emerald Coast Association of Realtors . . . . (850) 243-6145
Greater Fort Walton Bch Chamber . . . . (850) 244-8191
Valparaiso Chamber of Commerce . . . . (850) 678-2323

Okaloosa County Communities

BAKER (unincorporated postal area, zip code 32531). Covers a land area of 229.191 square miles and a water area of 1.242 square miles. Located at 30.87° N. Lat.; 86.68° W. Long. Elevation is 249 feet.
Population: 4,278 (2000); Race: 95.4% White, 1.9% Black, 0.3% Asian, 0.4% Hispanic of any race (2000); Density: 18.7 persons per square mile (2000); Age: 26.7% under 18, 12.3% over 64 (2000); Marriage status: 16.1% never married, 73.1% now married, 3.9% widowed, 6.9% divorced (2000); Foreign born: 0.8% (2000); Ancestry (includes multiple ancestries): 17.0% United States or American, 14.4% Other groups, 13.0% Irish, 9.3% English, 7.6% German (2000).
Economy: Employment by occupation: 9.3% management, 17.9% professional, 14.0% services, 20.9% sales, 1.4% farming, 21.9% construction, 14.7% production (2000).
Income: Per capita income: $16,276 (2000); Median household income: $36,019 (2000); Poverty rate: 8.1% (2000).
Education: Percent of population age 25 and over with: High school diploma (including GED) or higher: 80.7% (2000); Bachelor's degree or higher: 12.4% (2000).

School District(s)

Okaloosa County School District (PK-12)
2002-03 Enrollment: 31,291 . . . . (850) 833-3109

Housing: Homeownership rate: 83.0% (2000); Median home value: $79,400 (2000); Median rent: $401 per month (2000); Median age of housing: 21 years (2000).
Transportation: Commute to work: 97.2% car, 0.0% public transportation, 1.3% walk, 1.5% work from home (2000); Travel time to work: 12.9% less than 15 minutes, 36.8% 15 to 30 minutes, 19.7% 30 to 45 minutes, 18.3% 45 to 60 minutes, 12.2% 60 minutes or more (2000)

CINCO BAYOU (town). Covers a land area of 0.178 square miles and a water area of 0 square miles. Located at 30.42° N. Lat.; 86.60° W. Long. Elevation is 10 feet.
Population: 322 (1990); 377 (2000); 404 (2004); 438 (2009 projected); Race: 77.2% White, 16.1% Black, 4.7% Asian, 3.2% Hispanic of any race (2004); Density: 2,267.5 persons per square mile (2004); Average household size: 1.76 (2004); Median age: 41.0 (2004); Male/female ratio: 99.0 (2004); Marriage status: 28.2% never married, 43.3% now married, 3.3% widowed, 25.2% divorced (2000); Foreign born: 7.2% (2000); Ancestry (includes multiple ancestries): 35.6% Other groups, 12.2% German, 11.9% United States or American, 10.2% English, 9.9% Irish (2000).
Economy: Employment by occupation: 11.7% management, 12.2% professional, 25.0% services, 31.7% sales, 0.0% farming, 16.7% construction, 2.8% production (2000).
Income: Per capita income: $27,739 (2004); Median household income: $31,983 (2004); Average household income: $48,308 (2004); Percent of households with income of $100,000 or more: 7.4% (2004); Poverty rate: 15.5% (2000).
Taxes: Total city taxes per capita: $562 (2002); City property taxes per capita: $361 (2002).
Education: Percent of population age 25 and over with: High school diploma (including GED) or higher: 91.3% (2004); Bachelor's degree or higher: 18.3% (2004); Master's degree or higher: 6.3% (2004).
Housing: Homeownership rate: 48.5% (2004); Median home value: $117,763 (2004); Median rent: $432 per month (2000); Median age of housing: 18 years (2000).
Transportation: Commute to work: 90.3% car, 1.0% public transportation, 1.0% walk, 6.6% work from home (2000); Travel time to work: 33.3% less than 15 minutes, 42.6% 15 to 30 minutes, 15.3% 30 to 45 minutes, 0.0% 45 to 60 minutes, 8.7% 60 minutes or more (2000)

CRESTVIEW (city). Covers a land area of 12.799 square miles and a water area of 0.029 square miles. Located at 30.75° N. Lat.; 86.57° W. Long. Elevation is 236 feet.
History: '
Population: 10,471 (1990); 14,766 (2000); 15,855 (2004); 17,271 (2009 projected); Race: 73.9% White, 17.9% Black, 3.1% Asian, 3.5% Hispanic of any race (2004); Density: 1,238.8 persons per square mile (2004); Average household size: 2.79 (2004); Median age: 33.4 (2004); Male/female ratio: 94.5 (2004); Marriage status: 23.7% never married, 58.3% now married, 6.9% widowed, 11.1% divorced (2000); Foreign born: 5.1% (2000); Ancestry (includes multiple ancestries): 25.7% Other groups, 14.3% United States or American, 11.1% German, 8.8% Irish, 8.6% English (2000).
Economy: Railroad junction; clothing factory, fruit cannery. Eglin Air Force Base is 20 miles South. Single-family building permits issued: 379 (2004); Multi-family building permits issued: 172 (2004); Employment by occupation: 8.5% management, 17.5% professional, 23.2% services, 27.7% sales, 0.1% farming, 13.2% construction, 9.8% production (2000).
Income: Per capita income: $17,499 (2004); Median household income: $39,369 (2004); Average household income: $47,713 (2004); Percent of households with income of $100,000 or more: 7.5% (2004); Poverty rate: 16.7% (2000).

Taxes: Total city taxes per capita: $330 (2002); City property taxes per capita: $178 (2002).
Education: Percent of population age 25 and over with: High school diploma (including GED) or higher: 79.2% (2004); Bachelor's degree or higher: 13.9% (2004); Master's degree or higher: 4.7% (2004).

School District(s)

Okaloosa County School District (PK-12)
2002-03 Enrollment: 31,291 . . . . (850) 833-3109
Housing: Homeownership rate: 66.6% (2004); Median home value: $108,536 (2004); Median rent: $367 per month (2000); Median age of housing: 15 years (2000).
Hospitals: North Okaloosa Medical Center (110 beds)
Safety: Violent crime rate: 38.4 per 10,000 population; Property crime rate: 371.6 per 10,000 population (2003).
Newspapers: Crestview News Bulletin (General - Circulation 2,500); News Extra (General - Circulation 12,361)
Transportation: Commute to work: 96.9% car, 0.2% public transportation, 0.7% walk, 1.0% work from home (2000); Travel time to work: 30.1% less than 15 minutes, 24.0% 15 to 30 minutes, 26.1% 30 to 45 minutes, 13.8% 45 to 60 minutes, 6.1% 60 minutes or more (2000); Amtrak: Service available.
Airports: Bob Sikes
Additional Information Contacts
Crestview Area Association of Realtors. . . . . (850) 682-7041
Crestview Chamber of Commerce. (850) 682-3212

DESTIN (city). Covers a land area of 7.528 square miles and a water area of 0.650 square miles. Located at 30.39° N. Lat.; 86.47° W. Long. Elevation is 25 feet.
Population: 7,689 (1990); 11,119 (2000); 12,083 (2004); 13,283 (2009 projected); Race: 95.8% White, 0.3% Black, 1.3% Asian, 2.8% Hispanic of any race (2004); Density: 1,605.2 persons per square mile (2004); Average household size: 2.25 (2004); Median age: 43.4 (2004); Male/female ratio: 102.6 (2004); Marriage status: 19.1% never married, 60.1% now married, 6.6% widowed, 14.2% divorced (2000); Foreign born: 5.1% (2000); Ancestry (includes multiple ancestries): 16.6% German, 14.8% English, 12.5% Irish, 11.1% United States or American, 10.9% Other groups (2000).
Economy: Manufacturing includes machinery, printing and publishing, transportation equipment, fabricated metal products. Apalachicola National Forest is nearby. Single-family building permits issued: 244 (2004); Multi-family building permits issued: 279 (2004); Employment by occupation: 19.2% management, 17.1% professional, 14.6% services, 28.4% sales, 2.0% farming, 10.7% construction, 8.1% production (2000).
Income: Per capita income: $35,506 (2004); Median household income: $58,138 (2004); Average household income: $79,335 (2004); Percent of households with income of $100,000 or more: 19.6% (2004); Poverty rate: 5.5% (2000).
Taxes: Total city taxes per capita: $500 (2002); City property taxes per capita: $339 (2002).
Education: Percent of population age 25 and over with: High school diploma (including GED) or higher: 91.9% (2004); Bachelor's degree or higher: 31.7% (2004); Master's degree or higher: 9.9% (2004).

School District(s)

Okaloosa County School District (PK-12)
2002-03 Enrollment: 31,291 . . . . (850) 833-3109
Housing: Homeownership rate: 75.3% (2004); Median home value: $192,428 (2004); Median rent: $678 per month (2000); Median age of housing: 14 years (2000).
Newspapers: Destin Log (General - Circulation 8,000)
Transportation: Commute to work: 92.9% car, 0.3% public transportation, 1.8% walk, 3.0% work from home (2000); Travel time to work: 41.5% less than 15 minutes, 33.3% 15 to 30 minutes, 17.1% 30 to 45 minutes, 3.5% 45 to 60 minutes, 4.5% 60 minutes or more (2000)
Airports: Destin-Fort Walton Beach
Additional Information Contacts
Destin Chamber of Commerce . . . . (850) 837-6241

EGLIN AFB (CDP). Covers a land area of 3.061 square miles and a water area of 0.138 square miles. Located at 30.45° N. Lat.; 86.55° W. Long.
Population: 8,347 (1990); 8,082 (2000); 8,602 (2004); 9,262 (2009 projected); Race: 72.3% White, 13.9% Black, 3.0% Asian, 11.5% Hispanic of any race (2004); Density: 2,810.0 persons per square mile (2004); Average household size: 3.48 (2004); Median age: 21.6 (2004); Male/female ratio: 101.2 (2004); Marriage status: 7.6% never married, 89.2% now married, 0.4% widowed, 2.7% divorced (2000); Foreign born: 4.7% (2000); Ancestry (includes multiple ancestries): 36.1% Other groups, 16.4% German, 11.5% United States or American, 9.2% Irish, 6.5% English (2000).
Economy: Employment by occupation: 8.4% management, 18.8% professional, 25.6% services, 30.8% sales, 0.0% farming, 9.1% construction, 7.3% production (2000).
Income: Per capita income: $11,395 (2004); Median household income: $33,353 (2004); Average household income: $38,972 (2004); Percent of households with income of $100,000 or more: 2.1% (2004); Poverty rate: 4.5% (2000).
Education: Percent of population age 25 and over with: High school diploma (including GED) or higher: 96.0% (2004); Bachelor's degree or higher: 19.4% (2004); Master's degree or higher: 6.0% (2004).

School District(s)

Okaloosa County School District (PK-12)
2002-03 Enrollment: 31,291 . . . . (850) 833-3109
Housing: Homeownership rate: 1.1% (2004); Median home value: $128,000 (2004); Median rent: $543 per month (2000); Median age of housing: 40 years (2000).
Transportation: Commute to work: 93.5% car, 0.5% public transportation, 0.9% walk, 2.6% work from home (2000); Travel time to work: 48.2% less than 15 minutes, 35.1% 15 to 30 minutes, 14.1% 30 to 45 minutes, 1.8% 45 to 60 minutes, 0.8% 60 minutes or more (2000)

FORT WALTON BEACH (city). Covers a land area of 7.444 square miles and a water area of 0.761 square miles. Located at 30.42° N. Lat.; 86.61° W. Long. Elevation is 18 feet.
History: The city grew around a fort constructed during the Seminole War (1835—1842). Its main growth came after 1941, when it developed as a resort center and the air force base was expanded. A national historic landmark here includes a Museum of Native American culture. Incorporated 1941.
Population: 21,548 (1990); 19,973 (2000); 20,306 (2004); 20,804 (2009 projected); Race: 77.8% White, 13.7% Black, 3.0% Asian, 3.8% Hispanic of any race (2004); Density: 2,727.8 persons per square mile (2004); Average household size: 2.33 (2004); Median age: 39.3 (2004); Male/female ratio: 96.8 (2004); Marriage status: 23.2% never married, 55.0% now married, 7.5% widowed, 14.3% divorced (2000); Foreign born: 5.7% (2000); Ancestry (includes multiple ancestries): 24.7% Other groups, 13.9% German, 12.3% English, 9.7% Irish, 9.3% United States or American (2000).
Economy: It is a year-round resort, with beaches and freshwater and deep-sea fishing. Manufacturing includes electronic equipment and small boats. Eglin Air Force Base, on the city's outskirts, contributes significantly to the economy. Single-family building permits issued: 27 (2004); Multi-family building permits issued: 93 (2004); Employment by occupation: 12.1% management, 18.2% professional, 21.6% services, 27.0% sales, 0.1% farming, 10.9% construction, 10.1% production (2000).
Income: Per capita income: $22,908 (2004); Median household income: $42,914 (2004); Average household income: $53,006 (2004); Percent of households with income of $100,000 or more: 9.8% (2004); Poverty rate: 9.9% (2000).
Taxes: Total city taxes per capita: $428 (2002); City property taxes per capita: $195 (2002).
Education: Percent of population age 25 and over with: High school diploma (including GED) or higher: 89.1% (2004); Bachelor's degree or higher: 21.3% (2004); Master's degree or higher: 7.3% (2004).

School District(s)

Okaloosa County School District (PK-12)
2002-03 Enrollment: 31,291 . . . . (850) 833-3109

Two-year College(s)

Okaloosa Applied Technology Center (Public)
2003-04 Enrollment: 470 . . . . (850) 833-3500
Housing: Homeownership rate: 63.6% (2004); Median home value: $120,377 (2004); Median rent: $482 per month (2000); Median age of housing: 31 years (2000).
Hospitals: Fort Walton Beach Medical Center (247 beds); Gulf Coast Treatment Center (24 beds)
Safety: Violent crime rate: 59.6 per 10,000 population; Property crime rate: 377.2 per 10,000 population (2003).
Newspapers: Northwest Florida Daily News (Circulation 40,562)
Transportation: Commute to work: 94.1% car, 0.2% public transportation, 2.3% walk, 1.8% work from home (2000); Travel time to work: 43.2% less

than 15 minutes, 36.9% 15 to 30 minutes, 12.3% 30 to 45 minutes, 3.1% 45 to 60 minutes, 4.5% 60 minutes or more (2000)

Additional Information Contacts

Emerald Coast Association of Realtors . . . . (850) 243-6145
Greater Fort Walton Bch Chamber . . . . (850) 244-8191

HOLT (unincorporated postal area, zip code 32564). Aka Holts. Covers a land area of 72.217 square miles and a water area of 0.083 square miles. Located at 30.71° N. Lat.; 86.77° W. Long. Elevation is 200 feet.

Population: 2,331 (2000); Race: 93.7% White, 0.3% Black, 1.0% Asian, 2.7% Hispanic of any race (2000); Density: 32.3 persons per square mile (2000); Age: 24.7% under 18, 12.7% over 64 (2000); Marriage status: 24.0% never married, 55.5% now married, 7.3% widowed, 13.3% divorced (2000); Foreign born: 1.7% (2000); Ancestry (includes multiple ancestries): 23.2% Other groups, 22.3% United States or American, 12.5% Irish, 10.0% English, 6.7% German (2000).

Economy: Employment by occupation: 7.2% management, 4.9% professional, 26.5% services, 23.3% sales, 0.7% farming, 23.1% construction, 14.2% production (2000).

Income: Per capita income: $13,694 (2000); Median household income: $35,385 (2000); Poverty rate: 16.2% (2000).

Education: Percent of population age 25 and over with: High school diploma (including GED) or higher: 68.6% (2000); Bachelor's degree or higher: 7.5% (2000).

Housing: Homeownership rate: 93.8% (2000); Median home value: $56,800 (2000); Median rent: $129 per month (2000); Median age of housing: 16 years (2000).

Transportation: Commute to work: 96.0% car, 1.1% public transportation, 0.0% walk, 0.0% work from home (2000); Travel time to work: 10.4% less than 15 minutes, 42.5% 15 to 30 minutes, 15.8% 30 to 45 minutes, 21.2% 45 to 60 minutes, 10.1% 60 minutes or more (2000)

HURLBURT FIELD (unincorporated postal area, zip code 32544). Aka Eglin Auxiliary Field No. 9. Covers a land area of 252.353 square miles and a water area of 0.154 square miles. Located at 30.42° N. Lat.; 86.69° W. Long.

Population: 3,093 (2000); Race: 66.8% White, 18.4% Black, 2.7% Asian, 8.8% Hispanic of any race (2000); Density: 12.3 persons per square mile (2000); Age: 31.3% under 18, 0.3% over 64 (2000); Marriage status: 33.6% never married, 62.4% now married, 0.0% widowed, 4.0% divorced (2000); Foreign born: 4.5% (2000); Ancestry (includes multiple ancestries): 38.4% Other groups, 12.8% Irish, 12.7% German, 8.8% English, 7.8% United States or American (2000).

Economy: Employment by occupation: 8.5% management, 9.6% professional, 28.2% services, 36.8% sales, 0.0% farming, 12.7% construction, 4.2% production (2000).

Income: Per capita income: $11,879 (2000); Median household income: $32,163 (2000); Poverty rate: 5.6% (2000).

Education: Percent of population age 25 and over with: High school diploma (including GED) or higher: 97.6% (2000); Bachelor's degree or higher: 14.4% (2000).

Housing: Homeownership rate: 2.0% (2000); Median home value: $n/a (2000); Median rent: $581 per month (2000); Median age of housing: 14 years (2000).

Transportation: Commute to work: 81.5% car, 0.5% public transportation, 11.9% walk, 2.1% work from home (2000); Travel time to work: 71.6% less than 15 minutes, 21.4% 15 to 30 minutes, 4.7% 30 to 45 minutes, 1.3% 45 to 60 minutes, 1.0% 60 minutes or more (2000)

LAKE LORRAINE (CDP). Covers a land area of 2.040 square miles and a water area of 0.317 square miles. Located at 30.44° N. Lat.; 86.57° W. Long.

Population: 6,779 (1990); 7,106 (2000); 7,245 (2004); 7,468 (2009 projected); Race: 81.8% White, 9.0% Black, 3.5% Asian, 5.5% Hispanic of any race (2004); Density: 3,551.3 persons per square mile (2004); Average household size: 2.38 (2004); Median age: 39.3 (2004); Male/female ratio: 97.5 (2004); Marriage status: 22.4% never married, 59.5% now married, 5.2% widowed, 12.8% divorced (2000); Foreign born: 6.1% (2000); Ancestry (includes multiple ancestries): 21.6% Other groups, 13.5% German, 13.3% United States or American, 10.9% English, 9.0% Irish (2000).

Economy: Employment by occupation: 10.6% management, 20.3% professional, 23.6% services, 30.1% sales, 0.5% farming, 8.8% construction, 6.1% production (2000).

Income: Per capita income: $25,884 (2004); Median household income: $51,310 (2004); Average household income: $61,688 (2004); Percent of households with income of $100,000 or more: 14.2% (2004); Poverty rate: 6.5% (2000).

Education: Percent of population age 25 and over with: High school diploma (including GED) or higher: 91.9% (2004); Bachelor's degree or higher: 30.3% (2004); Master's degree or higher: 14.3% (2004).

Housing: Homeownership rate: 65.2% (2004); Median home value: $152,025 (2004); Median rent: $575 per month (2000); Median age of housing: 21 years (2000).

Transportation: Commute to work: 94.5% car, 0.7% public transportation, 0.6% walk, 2.1% work from home (2000); Travel time to work: 30.2% less than 15 minutes, 53.3% 15 to 30 minutes, 9.7% 30 to 45 minutes, 3.7% 45 to 60 minutes, 3.1% 60 minutes or more (2000)

LAUREL HILL (city). Covers a land area of 3.139 square miles and a water area of 0 square miles. Located at 30.96° N. Lat.; 86.45° W. Long. Elevation is 289 feet.

Population: 556 (1990); 549 (2000); 614 (2004); 693 (2009 projected); Race: 79.8% White, 19.1% Black, 0.0% Asian, 1.1% Hispanic of any race (2004); Density: 195.6 persons per square mile (2004); Average household size: 2.45 (2004); Median age: 39.4 (2004); Male/female ratio: 92.5 (2004); Marriage status: 17.2% never married, 64.4% now married, 8.5% widowed, 9.8% divorced (2000); Foreign born: 2.0% (2000); Ancestry (includes multiple ancestries): 29.7% United States or American, 26.4% Other groups, 7.3% Irish, 6.0% German, 4.0% Scottish (2000).

Economy: Employment by occupation: 11.9% management, 9.1% professional, 14.2% services, 26.0% sales, 1.8% farming, 22.8% construction, 14.2% production (2000).

Income: Per capita income: $14,051 (2004); Median household income: $28,444 (2004); Average household income: $34,373 (2004); Percent of households with income of $100,000 or more: 3.2% (2004); Poverty rate: 21.6% (2000).

Education: Percent of population age 25 and over with: High school diploma (including GED) or higher: 62.7% (2004); Bachelor's degree or higher: 4.9% (2004); Master's degree or higher: 1.2% (2004).

School District(s)

Okaloosa County School District (PK-12)
2002-03 Enrollment: 31,291 . . . . (850) 833-3109

Housing: Homeownership rate: 80.9% (2004); Median home value: $55,714 (2004); Median rent: $263 per month (2000); Median age of housing: 24 years (2000).

Transportation: Commute to work: 85.1% car, 0.0% public transportation, 7.0% walk, 1.9% work from home (2000); Travel time to work: 13.7% less than 15 minutes, 18.0% 15 to 30 minutes, 24.6% 30 to 45 minutes, 11.4% 45 to 60 minutes, 32.2% 60 minutes or more (2000)

MARY ESTHER (city). Covers a land area of 1.539 square miles and a water area of 0 square miles. Located at 30.41° N. Lat.; 86.65° W. Long. Elevation is 22 feet.

Population: 4,139 (1990); 4,055 (2000); 4,165 (2004); 4,327 (2009 projected); Race: 82.6% White, 6.5% Black, 4.4% Asian, 3.9% Hispanic of any race (2004); Density: 2,706.4 persons per square mile (2004); Average household size: 2.46 (2004); Median age: 39.2 (2004); Male/female ratio: 102.2 (2004); Marriage status: 17.6% never married, 66.7% now married, 4.0% widowed, 11.8% divorced (2000); Foreign born: 6.7% (2000); Ancestry (includes multiple ancestries): 19.8% Other groups, 13.7% Irish, 13.3% German, 12.6% English, 11.8% United States or American (2000).

Economy: Employment by occupation: 11.4% management, 18.1% professional, 19.4% services, 32.7% sales, 0.0% farming, 9.4% construction, 9.0% production (2000).

Income: Per capita income: $24,164 (2004); Median household income: $46,241 (2004); Average household income: $59,483 (2004); Percent of households with income of $100,000 or more: 13.5% (2004); Poverty rate: 5.7% (2000).

Taxes: Total city taxes per capita: $307 (2002); City property taxes per capita: $144 (2002).

Education: Percent of population age 25 and over with: High school diploma (including GED) or higher: 92.0% (2004); Bachelor's degree or higher: 22.5% (2004); Master's degree or higher: 8.1% (2004).

School District(s)

Okaloosa County School District (PK-12)
2002-03 Enrollment: 31,291 . . . . (850) 833-3109

Housing: Homeownership rate: 74.6% (2004); Median home value: $126,371 (2004); Median rent: $521 per month (2000); Median age of housing: 27 years (2000).
Transportation: Commute to work: 94.8% car, 0.4% public transportation, 0.7% walk, 1.8% work from home (2000); Travel time to work: 48.4% less than 15 minutes, 30.4% 15 to 30 minutes, 15.0% 30 to 45 minutes, 2.1% 45 to 60 minutes, 4.1% 60 minutes or more (2000)

NICEVILLE (city). Covers a land area of 10.922 square miles and a water area of 0.407 square miles. Located at 30.51° N. Lat.; 86.47° W. Long. Elevation is 51 feet.
Population: 10,878 (1990); 11,684 (2000); 12,265 (2004); 13,041 (2009 projected); Race: 86.1% White, 4.7% Black, 3.8% Asian, 3.5% Hispanic of any race (2004); Density: 1,123.0 persons per square mile (2004); Average household size: 2.49 (2004); Median age: 40.0 (2004); Male/female ratio: 98.0 (2004); Marriage status: 21.4% never married, 63.4% now married, 5.2% widowed, 10.1% divorced (2000); Foreign born: 6.3% (2000); Ancestry (includes multiple ancestries): 21.6% Other groups, 14.4% German, 12.9% Irish, 12.9% United States or American, 11.4% English (2000).
Economy: Single-family building permits issued: 128 (2004); Multi-family building permits issued: 0 (2004); Employment by occupation: 12.6% management, 19.9% professional, 22.2% services, 27.0% sales, 0.1% farming, 10.4% construction, 7.8% production (2000).
Income: Per capita income: $23,409 (2004); Median household income: $50,133 (2004); Average household income: $58,090 (2004); Percent of households with income of $100,000 or more: 13.5% (2004); Poverty rate: 9.6% (2000).
Taxes: Total city taxes per capita: $149 (2002); City property taxes per capita: $0 (2002).
Education: Percent of population age 25 and over with: High school diploma (including GED) or higher: 88.6% (2004); Bachelor's degree or higher: 26.1% (2004); Master's degree or higher: 11.2% (2004).

School District(s)

Okaloosa County School District (PK-12)
2002-03 Enrollment: 31,291 . . . . (850) 833-3109

Two-year College(s)

Okaloosa-Walton Community College (Public)
2003-04 Enrollment: 7,272 . . . . (850) 678-5111
2003-04 Tuition: In-state $1,550; Out-of-state $5,980

Housing: Homeownership rate: 71.5% (2004); Median home value: $135,393 (2004); Median rent: $460 per month (2000); Median age of housing: 20 years (2000).
Hospitals: Twin Cities Hospital (65 beds)
Safety: Violent crime rate: 14.6 per 10,000 population; Property crime rate: 116.3 per 10,000 population (2003).
Newspapers: Bay Beacon (General - Circulation 2,000); Beacon Express (General - Circulation 13,250)
Transportation: Commute to work: 95.9% car, 0.3% public transportation, 0.7% walk, 1.3% work from home (2000); Travel time to work: 28.9% less than 15 minutes, 46.0% 15 to 30 minutes, 19.2% 30 to 45 minutes, 3.1% 45 to 60 minutes, 2.8% 60 minutes or more (2000)

Additional Information Contacts

Local Government Offices . . . . (850) 729-4008

OCEAN CITY (CDP). Covers a land area of 1.601 square miles and a water area of 0.308 square miles. Located at 30.44° N. Lat.; 86.60° W. Long. Elevation is 13 feet.
Population: 5,431 (1990); 5,594 (2000); 5,844 (2004); 6,162 (2009 projected); Race: 82.1% White, 7.7% Black, 3.9% Asian, 4.3% Hispanic of any race (2004); Density: 3,649.6 persons per square mile (2004); Average household size: 2.24 (2004); Median age: 38.9 (2004); Male/female ratio: 98.2 (2004); Marriage status: 23.5% never married, 54.6% now married, 7.2% widowed, 14.6% divorced (2000); Foreign born: 5.2% (2000); Ancestry (includes multiple ancestries): 18.5% Other groups, 13.8% United States or American, 11.7% German, 11.3% English, 10.3% Irish (2000).
Economy: Employment by occupation: 8.9% management, 20.3% professional, 19.4% services, 27.4% sales, 1.0% farming, 11.2% construction, 11.7% production (2000).
Income: Per capita income: $23,649 (2004); Median household income: $39,823 (2004); Average household income: $53,007 (2004); Percent of households with income of $100,000 or more: 8.4% (2004); Poverty rate: 8.6% (2000).
Education: Percent of population age 25 and over with: High school diploma (including GED) or higher: 90.3% (2004); Bachelor's degree or higher: 20.9% (2004); Master's degree or higher: 5.4% (2004).
Housing: Homeownership rate: 60.2% (2004); Median home value: $115,051 (2004); Median rent: $501 per month (2000); Median age of housing: 32 years (2000).
Transportation: Commute to work: 94.2% car, 0.0% public transportation, 1.5% walk, 3.5% work from home (2000); Travel time to work: 43.1% less than 15 minutes, 38.5% 15 to 30 minutes, 10.7% 30 to 45 minutes, 4.1% 45 to 60 minutes, 3.6% 60 minutes or more (2000)

SHALIMAR (town). Covers a land area of 0.294 square miles and a water area of 0 square miles. Located at 30.44° N. Lat.; 86.58° W. Long. Elevation is 16 feet.
Population: 345 (1990); 718 (2000); 716 (2004); 719 (2009 projected); Race: 87.4% White, 7.4% Black, 2.9% Asian, 1.5% Hispanic of any race (2004); Density: 2,434.8 persons per square mile (2004); Average household size: 2.46 (2004); Median age: 40.5 (2004); Male/female ratio: 93.0 (2004); Marriage status: 18.1% never married, 60.7% now married, 6.9% widowed, 14.3% divorced (2000); Foreign born: 4.8% (2000); Ancestry (includes multiple ancestries): 17.7% Other groups, 16.0% United States or American, 12.3% German, 10.9% Irish, 10.5% English (2000).
Economy: Employment by occupation: 27.6% management, 25.8% professional, 12.4% services, 24.2% sales, 0.0% farming, 3.9% construction, 6.1% production (2000).
Income: Per capita income: $34,983 (2004); Median household income: $67,572 (2004); Average household income: $86,074 (2004); Percent of households with income of $100,000 or more: 23.7% (2004); Poverty rate: 3.1% (2000).
Taxes: Total city taxes per capita: $469 (2002); City property taxes per capita: $249 (2002).
Education: Percent of population age 25 and over with: High school diploma (including GED) or higher: 95.5% (2004); Bachelor's degree or higher: 47.5% (2004); Master's degree or higher: 20.9% (2004).

School District(s)

Okaloosa County School District (PK-12)
2002-03 Enrollment: 31,291 . . . . (850) 833-3109

Housing: Homeownership rate: 81.4% (2004); Median home value: $211,667 (2004); Median rent: $769 per month (2000); Median age of housing: 10 years (2000).
Safety: Violent crime rate: 13.5 per 10,000 population; Property crime rate: 201.9 per 10,000 population (2003).
Transportation: Commute to work: 95.0% car, 0.3% public transportation, 2.5% walk, 2.2% work from home (2000); Travel time to work: 44.8% less than 15 minutes, 42.8% 15 to 30 minutes, 7.1% 30 to 45 minutes, 3.4% 45 to 60 minutes, 2.0% 60 minutes or more (2000)

VALPARAISO (city). Covers a land area of 11.937 square miles and a water area of 0.811 square miles. Located at 30.50° N. Lat.; 86.49° W. Long. Elevation is 55 feet.
Population: 4,654 (1990); 6,408 (2000); 6,506 (2004); 6,731 (2009 projected); Race: 77.6% White, 12.1% Black, 2.9% Asian, 10.1% Hispanic of any race (2004); Density: 545.0 persons per square mile (2004); Average household size: 3.23 (2004); Median age: 34.2 (2004); Male/female ratio: 161.4 (2004); Marriage status: 34.6% never married, 47.8% now married, 4.6% widowed, 13.0% divorced (2000); Foreign born: 6.7% (2000); Ancestry (includes multiple ancestries): 25.9% Other groups, 12.7% German, 12.5% Irish, 11.3% English, 8.6% United States or American (2000).
Economy: Eglin Air Force Base is just Southwest. Single-family building permits issued: 7 (2004); Multi-family building permits issued: 0 (2004); Employment by occupation: 11.4% management, 22.9% professional, 19.3% services, 26.0% sales, 0.3% farming, 11.8% construction, 8.4% production (2000).
Income: Per capita income: $19,680 (2004); Median household income: $40,236 (2004); Average household income: $49,245 (2004); Percent of households with income of $100,000 or more: 7.4% (2004); Poverty rate: 6.7% (2000).
Taxes: Total city taxes per capita: $230 (2002); City property taxes per capita: $59 (2002).
Education: Percent of population age 25 and over with: High school diploma (including GED) or higher: 90.6% (2004); Bachelor's degree or higher: 20.7% (2004); Master's degree or higher: 9.9% (2004).

School District(s)

Okaloosa County School District (PK-12)
2002-03 Enrollment: 31,291 . . . . (850) 833-3109

Housing: Homeownership rate: 69.5% (2004); Median home value: $106,791 (2004); Median rent: $379 per month (2000); Median age of housing: 28 years (2000).

Safety: Violent crime rate: 13.8 per 10,000 population; Property crime rate: 124.3 per 10,000 population (2003).

Transportation: Commute to work: 91.4% car, 0.8% public transportation, 4.3% walk, 1.4% work from home (2000); Travel time to work: 53.5% less than 15 minutes, 26.1% 15 to 30 minutes, 14.7% 30 to 45 minutes, 4.3% 45 to 60 minutes, 1.4% 60 minutes or more (2000)

Airports: Eglin AFB (primary service/small hub)

Additional Information Contacts

Local Government Offices . . . . (850) 729-5402
Valparaiso Chamber of Commerce . . . . (850) 678-2323

WRIGHT (CDP). Covers a land area of 5.469 square miles and a water area of 0.069 square miles. Located at 30.44° N. Lat.; 86.63° W. Long. Elevation is 46 feet.

Population: 18,927 (1990); 21,697 (2000); 23,685 (2004); 26,144 (2009 projected); Race: 73.5% White, 15.4% Black, 4.0% Asian, 5.2% Hispanic of any race (2004); Density: 4,330.5 persons per square mile (2004); Average household size: 2.34 (2004); Median age: 34.2 (2004); Male/female ratio: 101.1 (2004); Marriage status: 27.2% never married, 52.2% now married, 5.8% widowed, 14.8% divorced (2000); Foreign born: 7.2% (2000); Ancestry (includes multiple ancestries): 28.5% Other groups, 13.0% German, 12.3% Irish, 9.4% United States or American, 9.4% English (2000).

Economy: Employment by occupation: 10.8% management, 17.7% professional, 18.8% services, 26.9% sales, 0.4% farming, 14.2% construction, 11.2% production (2000).

Income: Per capita income: $21,131 (2004); Median household income: $41,315 (2004); Average household income: $48,625 (2004); Percent of households with income of $100,000 or more: 7.4% (2004); Poverty rate: 10.9% (2000).

Education: Percent of population age 25 and over with: High school diploma (including GED) or higher: 87.8% (2004); Bachelor's degree or higher: 21.1% (2004); Master's degree or higher: 7.2% (2004).

Housing: Homeownership rate: 54.9% (2004); Median home value: $115,156 (2004); Median rent: $496 per month (2000); Median age of housing: 16 years (2000).

Transportation: Commute to work: 95.1% car, 0.7% public transportation, 1.6% walk, 1.2% work from home (2000); Travel time to work: 44.4% less than 15 minutes, 39.3% 15 to 30 minutes, 9.5% 30 to 45 minutes, 3.1% 45 to 60 minutes, 3.7% 60 minutes or more (2000)

Okeechobee County

Located in central Florida; bounded on the west by the Kissimmee River, and on the south by Lake Okeechobee; contains many small lakes and swamps. Covers a land area of 773.90 square miles, a water area of 117.60 square miles, and is located in the Eastern Time Zone. The county government was organized in 1917. County seat is Okeechobee.

Okeechobee County is part of the Okeechobee, FL Micropolitan Statistical Area. The entire metro area includes: Okeechobee County, FL

Weather Station: Fort Drum 5 NW — Elevation: 68 feet

	Jan	Feb	Mar	Apr	May	Jun	Jul	Aug	Sep	Oct	Nov	Dec
High	75	76	80	84	88	90	91	91	90	86	80	76
Low	50	51	55	58	63	69	71	72	70	65	58	52
Precip	2.4	2.5	3.9	2.4	4.5	8.1	7.8	7.2	6.7	3.7	2.3	1.9
Snow	tr	0.0	0.0	0.0	0.0	0.0	0.0	0.0	0.0	0.0	0.0	0.0

High and Low temperatures in degrees Fahrenheit; Precipitation and Snow in inches

Population: 29,601 (1990); 35,910 (2000); 37,397 (2004); 39,283 (2009 projected); Race: 78.2% White, 7.8% Black, 0.6% Asian, 20.9% Hispanic of any race (2004); Density: 48.3 persons per square mile (2004); Average household size: 2.85 (2004); Median age: 36.8 (2004); Male/female ratio: 115.8 (2004).

Religion: Five largest groups: 15.9% Southern Baptist Convention, 7.7% Catholic Church, 1.9% The United Methodist Church, 1.7% Church of God (Cleveland, Tennessee), 1.3% Lutheran Church—Missouri Synod (2000).

Economy: Unemployment rate: 7.0% (2004); Total civilian labor force: 16,970 (2004); Leading industries: 22.3% retail trade; 20.7% health care and social assistance; 10.4% accommodation & food services (2003); Companies that employ 500 or more persons: 0 (2003); Companies that employ 100 to 499 persons: 8 (2003); Companies that employ less than 100 persons: 710 (2003); Farms: 638 totaling 392,495 acres (2002); Minority business ownership rate: 5.9% (1997); Women business ownership rate: 12.2% (1997); Retail sales per capita: $8,741 (1997). Single-family building permits issued: 182 (2004); Multi-family building permits issued: 3 (2004).

Income: Per capita income: $15,651 (2004); Median household income: $32,903 (2004); Average household income: $43,710 (2004); Percent of households with income of $100,000 or more: 6.5% (2004); Poverty rate: 16.7% (2002); Bankruptcy rate: 5.10% (2004).

Education: Percent of population age 25 and over with: High school diploma (including GED) or higher: 65.3% (2004); Bachelor's degree or higher: 8.9% (2004); Master's degree or higher: 2.8% (2004).

Housing: Homeownership rate: 75.2% (2004); Median home value: $88,102 (2004); Median rent: $418 per month (2000); Median age of housing: 19 years (2000).

Health: Birth rate: 146.5 per 10,000 population (2004); Death rate: 116.7 per 10,000 population (2004); Age adjusted cancer mortality rate: 242.0 deaths per 100,000 population (2002); Number of physicians: 12.1 per 10,000 population (2001); Hospital beds: 27.4 per 10,000 population (2002); Hospital admissions: 1,432.8 per 10,000 population (2002).

Elections: 2004 Presidential election results: 57.2% Bush, 42.3% Kerry, 0.3% Nader, 0.1% Badnarik

National and State Parks: Kissimmee Prairie Preserve State Park

Additional Information Contacts

Okeechobee County Government Offices . . . . (863) 763-6441
Okeechobee Chamber of Commerce . . . . (863) 763-6464
Okeechobee County Board of Realtors . . . . (863) 467-0004

Okeechobee County Communities

CYPRESS QUARTERS (CDP). Covers a land area of 2.706 square miles and a water area of 0 square miles. Located at 27.24° N. Lat.; 80.81° W. Long. Elevation is 25 feet.

Population: 1,343 (1990); 1,150 (2000); 1,122 (2004); 1,100 (2009 projected); Race: 36.2% White, 56.3% Black, 0.2% Asian, 8.9% Hispanic of any race (2004); Density: 414.7 persons per square mile (2004); Average household size: 2.71 (2004); Median age: 32.0 (2004); Male/female ratio: 95.8 (2004); Marriage status: 36.3% never married, 46.0% now married, 8.5% widowed, 9.2% divorced (2000); Foreign born: 2.3% (2000); Ancestry (includes multiple ancestries): 47.0% Other groups, 11.2% Irish, 6.5% English, 3.9% German, 3.0% United States or American (2000).

Economy: Employment by occupation: 7.1% management, 14.7% professional, 18.4% services, 25.3% sales, 7.1% farming, 12.4% construction, 14.9% production (2000).

Income: Per capita income: $16,355 (2004); Median household income: $32,679 (2004); Average household income: $44,124 (2004); Percent of households with income of $100,000 or more: 4.1% (2004); Poverty rate: 30.5% (2000).

Education: Percent of population age 25 and over with: High school diploma (including GED) or higher: 58.2% (2004); Bachelor's degree or higher: 7.7% (2004); Master's degree or higher: 2.8% (2004).

Housing: Homeownership rate: 69.8% (2004); Median home value: $75,915 (2004); Median rent: $242 per month (2000); Median age of housing: 29 years (2000).

Transportation: Commute to work: 92.0% car, 1.3% public transportation, 2.2% walk, 0.0% work from home (2000); Travel time to work: 47.1% less than 15 minutes, 24.2% 15 to 30 minutes, 4.9% 30 to 45 minutes, 6.0% 45 to 60 minutes, 17.8% 60 minutes or more (2000)

OKEECHOBEE (city). Covers a land area of 4.126 square miles and a water area of 0.037 square miles. Located at 27.24° N. Lat.; 80.83° W. Long. Elevation is 29 feet.

History: Okeechobee developed as a commercial center for the surrounding area of poultry and frog farms, and as the seat of Okeechobee County. The breeding of bullfrogs for the frog-leg market was a major early industry.

Population: 4,945 (1990); 5,376 (2000); 5,381 (2004); 5,431 (2009 projected); Race: 79.8% White, 8.8% Black, 0.8% Asian, 17.7% Hispanic of any race (2004); Density: 1,304.1 persons per square mile (2004); Average household size: 2.91 (2004); Median age: 36.9 (2004); Male/female ratio: 98.9 (2004); Marriage status: 21.4% never married, 53.8% now married, 10.2% widowed, 14.7% divorced (2000); Foreign born: 7.4% (2000);

Ancestry (includes multiple ancestries): 25.2% Other groups, 11.8% Irish, 11.2% United States or American, 10.7% German, 10.3% English (2000).
Economy: Single-family building permits issued: 24 (2004); Multi-family building permits issued: 3 (2004); Employment by occupation: 7.7% management, 14.6% professional, 23.9% services, 24.3% sales, 6.3% farming, 10.6% construction, 12.6% production (2000).
Income: Per capita income: $12,923 (2004); Median household income: $29,317 (2004); Average household income: $36,220 (2004); Percent of households with income of $100,000 or more: 4.0% (2004); Poverty rate: 19.0% (2000).
Taxes: Total city taxes per capita: $575 (2002); City property taxes per capita: $199 (2002).
Education: Percent of population age 25 and over with: High school diploma (including GED) or higher: 60.3% (2004); Bachelor's degree or higher: 10.1% (2004); Master's degree or higher: 4.7% (2004).

School District(s)

Okeechobee County School District (PK-12)
2002-03 Enrollment: 7,085 . . . . (863) 462-5000
Housing: Homeownership rate: 71.1% (2004); Median home value: $99,507 (2004); Median rent: $416 per month (2000); Median age of housing: 23 years (2000).
Safety: Violent crime rate: 84.0 per 10,000 population; Property crime rate: 819.9 per 10,000 population (2003).
Newspapers: Okeechobee News (Circulation 4,000)
Transportation: Commute to work: 92.3% car, 1.2% public transportation, 1.7% walk, 2.6% work from home (2000); Travel time to work: 55.6% less than 15 minutes, 20.4% 15 to 30 minutes, 11.9% 30 to 45 minutes, 3.5% 45 to 60 minutes, 8.5% 60 minutes or more (2000); Amtrak: Service available.
Additional Information Contacts
Local Government Offices . . . . (863) 763-3372
Okeechobee Chamber of Commerce . . . . (863) 763-6464
Okeechobee County Board of Realtors . . . . (863) 467-0004

TAYLOR CREEK (CDP). Covers a land area of 3.996 square miles and a water area of 0.150 square miles. Located at 27.21° N. Lat.; 80.79° W. Long.
Population: 4,081 (1990); 4,289 (2000); 4,401 (2004); 4,537 (2009 projected); Race: 93.9% White, 0.2% Black, 0.6% Asian, 6.0% Hispanic of any race (2004); Density: 1,101.3 persons per square mile (2004); Average household size: 2.13 (2004); Median age: 55.0 (2004); Male/female ratio: 103.5 (2004); Marriage status: 12.6% never married, 58.4% now married, 13.5% widowed, 15.4% divorced (2000); Foreign born: 6.6% (2000); Ancestry (includes multiple ancestries): 18.7% Other groups, 16.2% German, 13.7% English, 12.2% United States or American, 11.6% Irish (2000).
Economy: Employment by occupation: 7.6% management, 11.7% professional, 15.2% services, 28.9% sales, 4.6% farming, 21.0% construction, 11.1% production (2000).
Income: Per capita income: $17,506 (2004); Median household income: $26,276 (2004); Average household income: $36,818 (2004); Percent of households with income of $100,000 or more: 5.8% (2004); Poverty rate: 15.2% (2000).
Education: Percent of population age 25 and over with: High school diploma (including GED) or higher: 67.0% (2004); Bachelor's degree or higher: 6.1% (2004); Master's degree or higher: 1.3% (2004).
Housing: Homeownership rate: 80.9% (2004); Median home value: $78,601 (2004); Median rent: $445 per month (2000); Median age of housing: 20 years (2000).
Transportation: Commute to work: 95.2% car, 0.0% public transportation, 0.0% walk, 1.5% work from home (2000); Travel time to work: 42.9% less than 15 minutes, 24.4% 15 to 30 minutes, 12.9% 30 to 45 minutes, 4.7% 45 to 60 minutes, 15.1% 60 minutes or more (2000)

Orange County

Located in central Florida; bounded on the east by the St. Johns River; includes part of Lake Apopka. Covers a land area of 907.40 square miles, a water area of 96.70 square miles, and is located in the Eastern Time Zone. The county government was organized in 1824. County seat is Orlando.

Orange County is part of the Orlando-Kissimmee, FL Metropolitan Statistical Area. The entire metro area includes: Lake County, FL; Orange County, FL; Osceola County, FL; Seminole County, FL

Weather Station: Orlando Int'l Airport — Elevation: 95 feet

	Jan	Feb	Mar	Apr	May	Jun	Jul	Aug	Sep	Oct	Nov	Dec
High	71	74	78	83	88	91	92	92	90	84	79	73
Low	49	51	56	60	66	72	73	74	72	66	59	52
Precip	2.5	2.4	3.7	2.5	3.9	7.4	7.4	6.4	5.9	2.9	2.4	2.3
Snow	tr	0.0	tr	tr	tr	0.0	tr	tr	0.0	0.0	0.0	0.0

High and Low temperatures in degrees Fahrenheit; Precipitation and Snow in inches

Population: 677,491 (1990); 896,344 (2000); 993,758 (2004); 1,116,309 (2009 projected); Race: 64.6% White, 20.0% Black, 3.9% Asian, 21.9% Hispanic of any race (2004); Density: 1,095.1 persons per square mile (2004); Average household size: 2.66 (2004); Median age: 33.8 (2004); Male/female ratio: 98.3 (2004).
Religion: Five largest groups: 13.2% Catholic Church, 8.2% Southern Baptist Convention, 3.3% The United Methodist Church, 2.5% Assemblies of God, 1.6% Presbyterian Church (U.S.A.) (2000).
Economy: Unemployment rate: 4.7% (2004); Total civilian labor force: 565,056 (2004); Leading industries: 13.8% accommodation & food services; 11.1% retail trade; 11.0% administration, support, waste management, remediation services (2003); Companies that employ 500 or more persons: 120 (2003); Companies that employ 100 to 499 persons: 746 (2003); Companies that employ less than 100 persons: 27,336 (2003); Farms: 901 totaling 146,637 acres (2002); Minority business ownership rate: 19.7% (1997); Women business ownership rate: 26.9% (1997); Retail sales per capita: $13,312 (1997). Single-family building permits issued: 11,681 (2004); Multi-family building permits issued: 2,947 (2004).
Income: Per capita income: $22,889 (2004); Median household income: $44,929 (2004); Average household income: $60,432 (2004); Percent of households with income of $100,000 or more: 13.4% (2004); Poverty rate: 12.5% (2002); Bankruptcy rate: 5.33% (2004).
Taxes: Total county taxes per capita: $676 (2002); County property taxes per capita: $431 (2002).
Education: Percent of population age 25 and over with: High school diploma (including GED) or higher: 82.0% (2004); Bachelor's degree or higher: 26.3% (2004); Master's degree or higher: 7.9% (2004).
Housing: Homeownership rate: 60.4% (2004); Median home value: $137,668 (2004); Median rent: $605 per month (2000); Median age of housing: 18 years (2000).
Health: Birth rate: 148.8 per 10,000 population (2004); Death rate: 67.6 per 10,000 population (2004); Age adjusted cancer mortality rate: 203.6 deaths per 100,000 population (2002); Air Quality Index: 84.2% good, 15.8% moderate, 0.0% unhealthy for sensitive individuals, 0.0% unhealthy (percent of days in 2004); Number of physicians: 25.3 per 10,000 population (2001); Hospital beds: 43.2 per 10,000 population (2002); Hospital admissions: 2,206.6 per 10,000 population (2002).
Elections: 2004 Presidential election results: 49.6% Bush, 49.8% Kerry, 0.3% Nader, 0.2% Badnarik
National and State Parks: Rock Springs Run State Reserve; Wekiwa Springs State Park; William Beardall Tosohatchee State Preserve
Additional Information Contacts
Orange County Government Offices . . . . (407) 836-7350
African American Chamber of Commerce . . . . (407) 428-5850
Apopka Chamber of Commerce . . . . (407) 886-1441
Brazilian-American Chamber of Commerce . . . . (407) 425-0126
Downtown Orlando Partnership . . . . (407) 648-4010
East Orange Chamber of Commerce . . . . (407) 277-5951
Florida Association of Realtors . . . . (407) 438-1400
Maitland Chamber of Commerce . . . . (407) 644-0741
Orlando Chamber of Commerce . . . . (407) 275-3777
Orlando Regional Realtor Association . . . . (407) 691-7900
South Orange Chamber of Cmmrc . . . . (407) 854-4246
Winter Garden Chamber of Commerce . . . . (407) 656-1304
Winter Park Chamber of Commerce . . . . (407) 644-8281

Orange County Communities

APOPKA (city). Covers a land area of 24.042 square miles and a water area of 0.891 square miles. Located at 28.67° N. Lat.; 81.51° W. Long. Elevation is 145 feet.
History: Named for the Greek translations of "potato" and "eating place". Apopka was settled in 1856 when it was called The Lodge, for a Masonic lodge building erected here. Apopka became a trading and shipping center for fern growers.
Population: 17,031 (1990); 26,642 (2000); 31,482 (2004); 37,414 (2009 projected); Race: 69.2% White, 18.6% Black, 2.1% Asian, 21.5% Hispanic of any race (2004); Density: 1,309.4 persons per square mile (2004);

Average household size: 2.80 (2004); Median age: 33.8 (2004); Male/female ratio: 94.2 (2004); Marriage status: 22.1% never married, 59.6% now married, 5.1% widowed, 13.2% divorced (2000); Foreign born: 11.8% (2000); Ancestry (includes multiple ancestries): 30.1% Other groups, 12.6% German, 10.9% Irish, 8.9% United States or American, 7.9% English (2000).
Economy: Unemployment rate: 4.5% (2004); Total civilian labor force: 11,149 (2004); Single-family building permits issued: 917 (2004); Multi-family building permits issued: 6 (2004); Employment by occupation: 15.0% management, 18.8% professional, 12.8% services, 31.6% sales, 1.8% farming, 8.8% construction, 11.3% production (2000).
Income: Per capita income: $20,900 (2004); Median household income: $47,374 (2004); Average household income: $58,246 (2004); Percent of households with income of $100,000 or more: 12.2% (2004); Poverty rate: 9.5% (2000).
Taxes: Total city taxes per capita: $376 (2002); City property taxes per capita: $134 (2002).
Education: Percent of population age 25 and over with: High school diploma (including GED) or higher: 81.6% (2004); Bachelor's degree or higher: 22.2% (2004); Master's degree or higher: 7.3% (2004).

School District(s)

Orange County School District (PK-12)
2002-03 Enrollment: 158,718 . . . . (407) 317-3202

Two-year College(s)

Career Training Institute (Private, For-profit)
2003-04 Enrollment: 137 . . . . (407) 884-1816

Housing: Homeownership rate: 76.1% (2004); Median home value: $130,347 (2004); Median rent: $577 per month (2000); Median age of housing: 11 years (2000).
Hospitals: Florida Hospital Apopka (50 beds)
Safety: Violent crime rate: 105.6 per 10,000 population; Property crime rate: 550.9 per 10,000 population (2003).
Newspapers: Apopka Chief (General - Circulation 3,800); The Planter (General - Circulation 10,000)
Transportation: Commute to work: 94.6% car, 1.3% public transportation, 0.6% walk, 2.6% work from home (2000); Travel time to work: 18.6% less than 15 minutes, 30.4% 15 to 30 minutes, 30.5% 30 to 45 minutes, 12.4% 45 to 60 minutes, 8.2% 60 minutes or more (2000)

Additional Information Contacts

Apopka Chamber of Commerce . . . . (407) 886-1441
Local Government Offices . . . . (407) 703-1700

AZALEA PARK (CDP). Covers a land area of 3.210 square miles and a water area of 0.031 square miles. Located at 28.54° N. Lat.; 81.29° W. Long. Elevation is 97 feet.
Population: 8,924 (1990); 11,073 (2000); 11,483 (2004); 12,097 (2009 projected); Race: 63.9% White, 9.1% Black, 4.1% Asian, 46.5% Hispanic of any race (2004); Density: 3,577.8 persons per square mile (2004); Average household size: 2.81 (2004); Median age: 31.9 (2004); Male/female ratio: 97.5 (2004); Marriage status: 33.0% never married, 50.9% now married, 6.6% widowed, 9.4% divorced (2000); Foreign born: 15.2% (2000); Ancestry (includes multiple ancestries): 43.8% Other groups, 9.9% United States or American, 7.9% German, 7.2% English, 6.9% Irish (2000).
Economy: Employment by occupation: 6.2% management, 14.8% professional, 19.9% services, 32.9% sales, 0.1% farming, 13.6% construction, 12.5% production (2000).
Income: Per capita income: $13,799 (2004); Median household income: $32,409 (2004); Average household income: $38,176 (2004); Percent of households with income of $100,000 or more: 1.5% (2004); Poverty rate: 11.5% (2000).
Education: Percent of population age 25 and over with: High school diploma (including GED) or higher: 75.0% (2004); Bachelor's degree or higher: 13.1% (2004); Master's degree or higher: 3.3% (2004).
Housing: Homeownership rate: 56.2% (2004); Median home value: $110,241 (2004); Median rent: $611 per month (2000); Median age of housing: 26 years (2000).
Transportation: Commute to work: 92.9% car, 1.8% public transportation, 2.1% walk, 1.9% work from home (2000); Travel time to work: 16.2% less than 15 minutes, 41.8% 15 to 30 minutes, 26.7% 30 to 45 minutes, 9.9% 45 to 60 minutes, 5.3% 60 minutes or more (2000)

BAY HILL (CDP). Covers a land area of 2.540 square miles and a water area of 0.059 square miles. Located at 28.45° N. Lat.; 81.50° W. Long.
Population: 4,262 (1990); 5,177 (2000); 5,973 (2004); 6,951 (2009 projected); Race: 84.2% White, 2.6% Black, 9.7% Asian, 5.8% Hispanic of any race (2004); Density: 2,351.4 persons per square mile (2004); Average household size: 2.89 (2004); Median age: 41.9 (2004); Male/female ratio: 97.9 (2004); Marriage status: 21.0% never married, 71.0% now married, 2.4% widowed, 5.6% divorced (2000); Foreign born: 15.3% (2000); Ancestry (includes multiple ancestries): 21.2% Other groups, 13.4% German, 12.8% English, 11.8% Irish, 11.0% Italian (2000).
Economy: Employment by occupation: 34.5% management, 20.3% professional, 9.6% services, 30.4% sales, 0.3% farming, 1.3% construction, 3.6% production (2000).
Income: Per capita income: $52,148 (2004); Median household income: $107,841 (2004); Average household income: $150,766 (2004); Percent of households with income of $100,000 or more: 53.3% (2004); Poverty rate: 4.3% (2000).
Education: Percent of population age 25 and over with: High school diploma (including GED) or higher: 92.6% (2004); Bachelor's degree or higher: 50.9% (2004); Master's degree or higher: 15.0% (2004).
Housing: Homeownership rate: 92.8% (2004); Median home value: $319,500 (2004); Median rent: $1,500 per month (2000); Median age of housing: 15 years (2000).
Transportation: Commute to work: 92.4% car, 0.3% public transportation, 0.0% walk, 4.6% work from home (2000); Travel time to work: 23.8% less than 15 minutes, 45.6% 15 to 30 minutes, 18.4% 30 to 45 minutes, 5.5% 45 to 60 minutes, 6.7% 60 minutes or more (2000)

BAY LAKE (city). Covers a land area of 19.927 square miles and a water area of 1.193 square miles. Located at 28.39° N. Lat.; 81.56° W. Long. Elevation is 90 feet.
Population: 0 (1990); 23 (2000); 41 (2004); 63 (2009 projected); Race: 97.6% White, 2.4% Black, 0.0% Asian, 0.0% Hispanic of any race (2004); Density: 2.1 persons per square mile (2004); Average household size: 2.41 (2004); Median age: 40.5 (2004); Male/female ratio: 141.2 (2004); Marriage status: 33.3% never married, 59.3% now married, 0.0% widowed, 7.4% divorced (2000); Foreign born: 0.0% (2000); Ancestry (includes multiple ancestries): 59.0% Irish, 35.9% French (except Basque), 20.5% English, 20.5% German, 10.3% Other groups (2000).
Economy: Single-family building permits issued: 0 (2004); Multi-family building permits issued: 0 (2004); Employment by occupation: 0.0% management, 8.7% professional, 21.7% services, 43.5% sales, 0.0% farming, 13.0% construction, 13.0% production (2000).
Income: Per capita income: $41,890 (2004); Median household income: $85,417 (2004); Average household income: $101,029 (2004); Percent of households with income of $100,000 or more: 29.4% (2004); Poverty rate: 0.0% (2000).
Taxes: Total city taxes per capita: $52,348 (2002); City property taxes per capita: $52,348 (2002).
Education: Percent of population age 25 and over with: High school diploma (including GED) or higher: 92.9% (2004); Bachelor's degree or higher: 14.3% (2004); Master's degree or higher: 7.1% (2004).
Housing: Homeownership rate: 88.2% (2004); Median home value: $52,500 (2004); Median rent: $n/a per month (2000); Median age of housing: 16 years (2000).
Transportation: Commute to work: 100.0% car, 0.0% public transportation, 0.0% walk, 0.0% work from home (2000); Travel time to work: 77.8% less than 15 minutes, 0.0% 15 to 30 minutes, 22.2% 30 to 45 minutes, 0.0% 45 to 60 minutes, 0.0% 60 minutes or more (2000)

BELLE ISLE (city). Covers a land area of 1.925 square miles and a water area of 2.706 square miles. Located at 28.46° N. Lat.; 81.35° W. Long. Elevation is 97 feet.
Population: 5,243 (1990); 5,531 (2000); 5,799 (2004); 6,164 (2009 projected); Race: 93.8% White, 1.9% Black, 1.2% Asian, 7.1% Hispanic of any race (2004); Density: 3,012.4 persons per square mile (2004); Average household size: 2.48 (2004); Median age: 42.2 (2004); Male/female ratio: 100.7 (2004); Marriage status: 18.0% never married, 65.7% now married, 6.1% widowed, 10.2% divorced (2000); Foreign born: 6.3% (2000); Ancestry (includes multiple ancestries): 18.1% German, 15.6% English, 14.1% Irish, 12.2% Other groups, 8.5% United States or American (2000).
Economy: Seven miles South of Orlando, adjacent to Orlando International Airport. Employment by occupation: 18.4% management, 21.9% professional, 16.7% services, 26.0% sales, 0.0% farming, 7.4% construction, 9.6% production (2000).
Income: Per capita income: $31,224 (2004); Median household income: $65,549 (2004); Average household income: $77,380 (2004); Percent of

households with income of $100,000 or more: 23.2% (2004); Poverty rate: 2.9% (2000).
Taxes: Total city taxes per capita: $233 (2002); City property taxes per capita: $154 (2002).
Education: Percent of population age 25 and over with: High school diploma (including GED) or higher: 92.3% (2004); Bachelor's degree or higher: 36.7% (2004); Master's degree or higher: 15.1% (2004).
Housing: Homeownership rate: 88.6% (2004); Median home value: $185,181 (2004); Median rent: $475 per month (2000); Median age of housing: 29 years (2000).
Transportation: Commute to work: 91.7% car, 2.4% public transportation, 1.0% walk, 3.5% work from home (2000); Travel time to work: 16.8% less than 15 minutes, 53.6% 15 to 30 minutes, 18.3% 30 to 45 minutes, 8.0% 45 to 60 minutes, 3.3% 60 minutes or more (2000)
Additional Information Contacts
Local Government Offices . . . . (407) 851-7730

BITHLO (CDP). Covers a land area of 10.672 square miles and a water area of 0.203 square miles. Located at 28.55° N. Lat.; 81.10° W. Long. Elevation is 68 feet.
History: Derived from Native American word for "canoe."
Population: 4,834 (1990); 4,626 (2000); 5,553 (2004); 6,683 (2009 projected); Race: 92.4% White, 1.2% Black, 0.3% Asian, 10.3% Hispanic of any race (2004); Density: 520.3 persons per square mile (2004); Average household size: 2.80 (2004); Median age: 34.7 (2004); Male/female ratio: 107.0 (2004); Marriage status: 30.0% never married, 48.6% now married, 3.5% widowed, 17.9% divorced (2000); Foreign born: 1.5% (2000); Ancestry (includes multiple ancestries): 28.2% United States or American, 11.8% German, 11.8% Other groups, 8.5% Irish, 7.3% English (2000).
Economy: Employment by occupation: 6.6% management, 3.2% professional, 19.2% services, 27.3% sales, 0.4% farming, 27.1% construction, 16.0% production (2000).
Income: Per capita income: $17,168 (2004); Median household income: $40,096 (2004); Average household income: $48,075 (2004); Percent of households with income of $100,000 or more: 7.1% (2004); Poverty rate: 21.5% (2000).
Education: Percent of population age 25 and over with: High school diploma (including GED) or higher: 60.9% (2004); Bachelor's degree or higher: 2.2% (2004); Master's degree or higher: 0.0% (2004).
Housing: Homeownership rate: 72.6% (2004); Median home value: $74,691 (2004); Median rent: $427 per month (2000); Median age of housing: 20 years (2000).
Transportation: Commute to work: 95.3% car, 1.2% public transportation, 0.0% walk, 2.4% work from home (2000); Travel time to work: 15.0% less than 15 minutes, 22.3% 15 to 30 minutes, 26.4% 30 to 45 minutes, 20.4% 45 to 60 minutes, 15.8% 60 minutes or more (2000)

CHRISTMAS (CDP). Covers a land area of 3.572 square miles and a water area of 0 square miles. Located at 28.53° N. Lat.; 80.99° W. Long. Elevation is 44 feet.
Population: 1,121 (1990); 1,162 (2000); 1,336 (2004); 1,544 (2009 projected); Race: 94.9% White, 0.5% Black, 1.0% Asian, 2.1% Hispanic of any race (2004); Density: 374.0 persons per square mile (2004); Average household size: 2.74 (2004); Median age: 38.6 (2004); Male/female ratio: 107.5 (2004); Marriage status: 24.6% never married, 48.8% now married, 4.0% widowed, 22.6% divorced (2000); Foreign born: 1.3% (2000); Ancestry (includes multiple ancestries): 17.8% German, 15.6% United States or American, 13.6% Irish, 9.4% Other groups, 7.7% English (2000).
Economy: Light manufacturing. Employment by occupation: 8.5% management, 3.9% professional, 26.3% services, 25.7% sales, 0.0% farming, 25.3% construction, 10.4% production (2000).
Income: Per capita income: $15,303 (2004); Median household income: $33,885 (2004); Average household income: $41,982 (2004); Percent of households with income of $100,000 or more: 5.5% (2004); Poverty rate: 12.3% (2000).
Education: Percent of population age 25 and over with: High school diploma (including GED) or higher: 67.4% (2004); Bachelor's degree or higher: 4.7% (2004); Master's degree or higher: 1.6% (2004).
Housing: Homeownership rate: 80.7% (2004); Median home value: $69,733 (2004); Median rent: $460 per month (2000); Median age of housing: 16 years (2000).
Transportation: Commute to work: 90.1% car, 1.5% public transportation, 0.0% walk, 8.4% work from home (2000); Travel time to work: 4.3% less than 15 minutes, 33.6% 15 to 30 minutes, 30.0% 30 to 45 minutes, 18.7% 45 to 60 minutes, 13.4% 60 minutes or more (2000)

CONWAY (CDP). Covers a land area of 3.450 square miles and a water area of 0.172 square miles. Located at 28.49° N. Lat.; 81.33° W. Long. Elevation is 108 feet.
Population: 13,101 (1990); 14,394 (2000); 14,539 (2004); 14,845 (2009 projected); Race: 88.5% White, 3.2% Black, 2.1% Asian, 13.0% Hispanic of any race (2004); Density: 4,213.7 persons per square mile (2004); Average household size: 2.71 (2004); Median age: 38.5 (2004); Male/female ratio: 97.2 (2004); Marriage status: 22.7% never married, 62.9% now married, 5.1% widowed, 9.3% divorced (2000); Foreign born: 6.7% (2000); Ancestry (includes multiple ancestries): 23.3% Other groups, 16.6% English, 15.3% German, 12.8% Irish, 8.9% United States or American (2000).
Economy: Employment by occupation: 17.1% management, 23.3% professional, 11.3% services, 30.0% sales, 0.3% farming, 8.8% construction, 9.3% production (2000).
Income: Per capita income: $26,987 (2004); Median household income: $59,671 (2004); Average household income: $73,218 (2004); Percent of households with income of $100,000 or more: 19.9% (2004); Poverty rate: 5.0% (2000).
Education: Percent of population age 25 and over with: High school diploma (including GED) or higher: 89.0% (2004); Bachelor's degree or higher: 31.4% (2004); Master's degree or higher: 9.2% (2004).
Housing: Homeownership rate: 81.7% (2004); Median home value: $151,445 (2004); Median rent: $668 per month (2000); Median age of housing: 28 years (2000).
Transportation: Commute to work: 92.8% car, 1.3% public transportation, 2.0% walk, 3.2% work from home (2000); Travel time to work: 18.3% less than 15 minutes, 45.1% 15 to 30 minutes, 29.0% 30 to 45 minutes, 4.6% 45 to 60 minutes, 3.0% 60 minutes or more (2000)

DOCTOR PHILLIPS (CDP). Covers a land area of 3.400 square miles and a water area of 1.455 square miles. Located at 28.45° N. Lat.; 81.49° W. Long.
Population: 7,594 (1990); 9,548 (2000); 10,967 (2004); 12,717 (2009 projected); Race: 82.0% White, 3.4% Black, 9.7% Asian, 9.0% Hispanic of any race (2004); Density: 3,225.7 persons per square mile (2004); Average household size: 2.76 (2004); Median age: 39.5 (2004); Male/female ratio: 95.2 (2004); Marriage status: 23.9% never married, 64.9% now married, 3.0% widowed, 8.2% divorced (2000); Foreign born: 19.3% (2000); Ancestry (includes multiple ancestries): 20.8% Other groups, 15.6% German, 13.4% Irish, 12.1% English, 12.1% Italian (2000).
Economy: Suburb of Orlando, just East of Disney World. Employment by occupation: 23.7% management, 21.8% professional, 14.2% services, 33.5% sales, 0.0% farming, 1.8% construction, 5.0% production (2000).
Income: Per capita income: $36,055 (2004); Median household income: $77,675 (2004); Average household income: $99,652 (2004); Percent of households with income of $100,000 or more: 34.9% (2004); Poverty rate: 4.4% (2000).
Education: Percent of population age 25 and over with: High school diploma (including GED) or higher: 93.8% (2004); Bachelor's degree or higher: 50.2% (2004); Master's degree or higher: 17.2% (2004).
Housing: Homeownership rate: 80.9% (2004); Median home value: $201,933 (2004); Median rent: $1,000 per month (2000); Median age of housing: 14 years (2000).
Transportation: Commute to work: 92.2% car, 0.2% public transportation, 1.3% walk, 5.1% work from home (2000); Travel time to work: 24.3% less than 15 minutes, 49.3% 15 to 30 minutes, 16.8% 30 to 45 minutes, 5.5% 45 to 60 minutes, 4.0% 60 minutes or more (2000)

EATONVILLE (town). Covers a land area of 0.985 square miles and a water area of 0.101 square miles. Located at 28.61° N. Lat.; 81.38° W. Long. Elevation is 101 feet.
History: Eatonville was founded in 1886 and named for Captain Josiah Eaton of nearby Maitland. This was the home of novelist Zora Neale Hurston, author of "Their Eyes Were Watching God" (1937).
Population: 2,256 (1990); 2,432 (2000); 2,421 (2004); 2,433 (2009 projected); Race: 7.2% White, 89.5% Black, 0.4% Asian, 3.3% Hispanic of any race (2004); Density: 2,458.4 persons per square mile (2004); Average household size: 3.11 (2004); Median age: 32.3 (2004); Male/female ratio: 88.4 (2004); Marriage status: 43.0% never married, 39.7% now married, 5.9% widowed, 11.4% divorced (2000); Foreign born: 4.2% (2000); Ancestry (includes multiple ancestries): 78.6% Other groups, 3.9% United States or American, 2.6% African, 1.6% Dutch, 1.1% French (except Basque) (2000).

Economy: Single-family building permits issued: 2 (2004); Multi-family building permits issued: 0 (2004); Employment by occupation: 4.0% management, 14.9% professional, 24.4% services, 26.9% sales, 0.0% farming, 11.0% construction, 18.8% production (2000).
Income: Per capita income: $12,987 (2004); Median household income: $31,290 (2004); Average household income: $39,525 (2004); Percent of households with income of $100,000 or more: 5.8% (2004); Poverty rate: 25.0% (2000).
Education: Percent of population age 25 and over with: High school diploma (including GED) or higher: 66.2% (2004); Bachelor's degree or higher: 11.5% (2004); Master's degree or higher: 1.6% (2004).

School District(s)

Orange County School District (PK-12)
2002-03 Enrollment: 158,718 . . . . (407) 317-3202

Housing: Homeownership rate: 48.5% (2004); Median home value: $89,541 (2004); Median rent: $459 per month (2000); Median age of housing: 30 years (2000).
Safety: Violent crime rate: 133.2 per 10,000 population; Property crime rate: 347.2 per 10,000 population (2003).
Transportation: Commute to work: 86.7% car, 7.1% public transportation, 2.5% walk, 2.5% work from home (2000); Travel time to work: 36.3% less than 15 minutes, 35.6% 15 to 30 minutes, 17.3% 30 to 45 minutes, 1.2% 45 to 60 minutes, 9.6% 60 minutes or more (2000)

EDGEWOOD (city). Covers a land area of 1.214 square miles and a water area of 0.265 square miles. Located at 28.48° N. Lat.; 81.37° W. Long. Elevation is 90 feet.
Population: 1,738 (1990); 1,901 (2000); 1,976 (2004); 2,078 (2009 projected); Race: 86.7% White, 6.7% Black, 2.3% Asian, 8.8% Hispanic of any race (2004); Density: 1,627.9 persons per square mile (2004); Average household size: 2.38 (2004); Median age: 43.0 (2004); Male/female ratio: 97.2 (2004); Marriage status: 13.7% never married, 67.7% now married, 6.1% widowed, 12.5% divorced (2000); Foreign born: 7.3% (2000); Ancestry (includes multiple ancestries): 20.5% Other groups, 17.9% English, 12.9% Irish, 12.4% German, 5.8% United States or American (2000).
Economy: Single-family building permits issued: 2 (2004); Multi-family building permits issued: 0 (2004); Employment by occupation: 17.5% management, 28.1% professional, 9.6% services, 36.1% sales, 0.0% farming, 1.3% construction, 7.4% production (2000).
Income: Per capita income: $39,255 (2004); Median household income: $58,703 (2004); Average household income: $93,337 (2004); Percent of households with income of $100,000 or more: 26.0% (2004); Poverty rate: 6.2% (2000).
Taxes: Total city taxes per capita: $358 (2002); City property taxes per capita: $355 (2002).
Education: Percent of population age 25 and over with: High school diploma (including GED) or higher: 93.4% (2004); Bachelor's degree or higher: 40.1% (2004); Master's degree or higher: 14.4% (2004).
Housing: Homeownership rate: 80.2% (2004); Median home value: $180,597 (2004); Median rent: $559 per month (2000); Median age of housing: 26 years (2000).
Safety: Violent crime rate: 30.6 per 10,000 population; Property crime rate: 428.6 per 10,000 population (2003).
Transportation: Commute to work: 92.1% car, 0.3% public transportation, 1.6% walk, 3.8% work from home (2000); Travel time to work: 30.0% less than 15 minutes, 41.6% 15 to 30 minutes, 19.8% 30 to 45 minutes, 1.9% 45 to 60 minutes, 6.7% 60 minutes or more (2000)

FAIRVIEW SHORES (CDP). Covers a land area of 3.914 square miles and a water area of 0.548 square miles. Located at 28.59° N. Lat.; 81.39° W. Long. Elevation is 95 feet.
Population: 13,330 (1990); 13,898 (2000); 13,678 (2004); 13,572 (2009 projected); Race: 73.3% White, 16.6% Black, 3.1% Asian, 10.7% Hispanic of any race (2004); Density: 3,494.6 persons per square mile (2004); Average household size: 2.35 (2004); Median age: 37.0 (2004); Male/female ratio: 97.8 (2004); Marriage status: 29.4% never married, 44.8% now married, 8.5% widowed, 17.3% divorced (2000); Foreign born: 7.6% (2000); Ancestry (includes multiple ancestries): 27.0% Other groups, 15.0% German, 11.7% English, 11.3% Irish, 7.7% United States or American (2000).
Economy: Employment by occupation: 15.5% management, 15.9% professional, 15.4% services, 31.4% sales, 0.0% farming, 9.9% construction, 12.0% production (2000).
Income: Per capita income: $21,751 (2004); Median household income: $39,206 (2004); Average household income: $50,628 (2004); Percent of households with income of $100,000 or more: 9.4% (2004); Poverty rate: 13.6% (2000).
Education: Percent of population age 25 and over with: High school diploma (including GED) or higher: 82.6% (2004); Bachelor's degree or higher: 20.4% (2004); Master's degree or higher: 5.0% (2004).
Housing: Homeownership rate: 57.0% (2004); Median home value: $125,834 (2004); Median rent: $531 per month (2000); Median age of housing: 38 years (2000).
Transportation: Commute to work: 90.5% car, 3.1% public transportation, 1.3% walk, 3.1% work from home (2000); Travel time to work: 28.3% less than 15 minutes, 43.6% 15 to 30 minutes, 18.6% 30 to 45 minutes, 4.4% 45 to 60 minutes, 5.1% 60 minutes or more (2000)

GOLDENROD (CDP). Aka Golden Rod. Covers a land area of 2.593 square miles and a water area of 0.131 square miles. Located at 28.61° N. Lat.; 81.29° W. Long. Elevation is 80 feet.
Population: 12,380 (1990); 12,871 (2000); 13,294 (2004); 13,946 (2009 projected); Race: 78.1% White, 7.0% Black, 3.4% Asian, 22.0% Hispanic of any race (2004); Density: 5,126.3 persons per square mile (2004); Average household size: 2.34 (2004); Median age: 33.4 (2004); Male/female ratio: 103.3 (2004); Marriage status: 35.2% never married, 47.7% now married, 5.0% widowed, 12.1% divorced (2000); Foreign born: 9.8% (2000); Ancestry (includes multiple ancestries): 28.8% Other groups, 13.6% German, 13.3% Irish, 11.9% English, 6.8% Italian (2000).
Economy: Employment by occupation: 10.4% management, 20.8% professional, 15.4% services, 32.2% sales, 0.4% farming, 10.9% construction, 9.9% production (2000).
Income: Per capita income: $21,389 (2004); Median household income: $42,783 (2004); Average household income: $49,539 (2004); Percent of households with income of $100,000 or more: 7.8% (2004); Poverty rate: 10.9% (2000).
Education: Percent of population age 25 and over with: High school diploma (including GED) or higher: 89.5% (2004); Bachelor's degree or higher: 28.1% (2004); Master's degree or higher: 7.8% (2004).
Housing: Homeownership rate: 47.7% (2004); Median home value: $134,527 (2004); Median rent: $627 per month (2000); Median age of housing: 24 years (2000).
Transportation: Commute to work: 92.5% car, 1.8% public transportation, 1.4% walk, 3.1% work from home (2000); Travel time to work: 22.7% less than 15 minutes, 37.6% 15 to 30 minutes, 26.2% 30 to 45 minutes, 7.5% 45 to 60 minutes, 5.9% 60 minutes or more (2000)

Additional Information Contacts

Goldenrod Chamber of Commerce . . . . (407) 677-5980

GOTHA (CDP). Covers a land area of 1.760 square miles and a water area of 0.200 square miles. Located at 28.53° N. Lat.; 81.52° W. Long. Elevation is 121 feet.
Population: 265 (1990); 731 (2000); 988 (2004); 1,292 (2009 projected); Race: 86.8% White, 5.5% Black, 4.0% Asian, 8.7% Hispanic of any race (2004); Density: 561.5 persons per square mile (2004); Average household size: 2.92 (2004); Median age: 36.9 (2004); Male/female ratio: 98.0 (2004); Marriage status: 25.8% never married, 60.8% now married, 3.0% widowed, 10.4% divorced (2000); Foreign born: 7.3% (2000); Ancestry (includes multiple ancestries): 26.2% German, 19.1% English, 11.7% Italian, 9.5% Irish, 8.8% Other groups (2000).
Economy: Employment by occupation: 24.9% management, 16.1% professional, 16.6% services, 29.2% sales, 0.0% farming, 7.3% construction, 5.8% production (2000).
Income: Per capita income: $35,726 (2004); Median household income: $67,819 (2004); Average household income: $103,920 (2004); Percent of households with income of $100,000 or more: 31.4% (2004); Poverty rate: 20.0% (2000).
Education: Percent of population age 25 and over with: High school diploma (including GED) or higher: 100.0% (2004); Bachelor's degree or higher: 31.7% (2004); Master's degree or higher: 11.1% (2004).
Housing: Homeownership rate: 86.4% (2004); Median home value: $291,489 (2004); Median rent: $521 per month (2000); Median age of housing: 14 years (2000).
Transportation: Commute to work: 94.1% car, 0.0% public transportation, 0.0% walk, 5.9% work from home (2000); Travel time to work: 11.5% less than 15 minutes, 41.9% 15 to 30 minutes, 16.7% 30 to 45 minutes, 7.9% 45 to 60 minutes, 21.9% 60 minutes or more (2000)

HOLDEN HEIGHTS (CDP). Covers a land area of 1.273 square miles and a water area of 0.395 square miles. Located at 28.50° N. Lat.; 81.38° W. Long.
Population: 3,916 (1990); 3,856 (2000); 3,913 (2004); 4,054 (2009 projected); Race: 66.9% White, 21.4% Black, 3.1% Asian, 17.0% Hispanic of any race (2004); Density: 3,074.8 persons per square mile (2004); Average household size: 2.72 (2004); Median age: 40.7 (2004); Male/female ratio: 103.0 (2004); Marriage status: 23.1% never married, 58.4% now married, 5.9% widowed, 12.7% divorced (2000); Foreign born: 13.3% (2000); Ancestry (includes multiple ancestries): 26.1% Other groups, 11.6% German, 11.5% United States or American, 9.1% English, 8.3% Irish (2000).
Economy: Employment by occupation: 14.6% management, 19.8% professional, 14.6% services, 27.8% sales, 0.0% farming, 11.7% construction, 11.5% production (2000).
Income: Per capita income: $22,226 (2004); Median household income: $51,288 (2004); Average household income: $57,935 (2004); Percent of households with income of $100,000 or more: 9.9% (2004); Poverty rate: 16.6% (2000).
Education: Percent of population age 25 and over with: High school diploma (including GED) or higher: 81.1% (2004); Bachelor's degree or higher: 23.4% (2004); Master's degree or higher: 3.8% (2004).
Housing: Homeownership rate: 69.6% (2004); Median home value: $135,971 (2004); Median rent: $511 per month (2000); Median age of housing: 30 years (2000).
Transportation: Commute to work: 90.8% car, 3.8% public transportation, 0.9% walk, 2.8% work from home (2000); Travel time to work: 29.4% less than 15 minutes, 40.4% 15 to 30 minutes, 18.1% 30 to 45 minutes, 3.3% 45 to 60 minutes, 8.8% 60 minutes or more (2000)

HUNTERS CREEK (CDP). Covers a land area of 4.305 square miles and a water area of 0.003 square miles. Located at 28.35° N. Lat.; 81.42° W. Long.
Population: 1,241 (1990); 9,369 (2000); 12,603 (2004); 16,423 (2009 projected); Race: 80.0% White, 5.6% Black, 8.2% Asian, 13.5% Hispanic of any race (2004); Density: 2,927.8 persons per square mile (2004); Average household size: 2.75 (2004); Median age: 35.7 (2004); Male/female ratio: 98.0 (2004); Marriage status: 23.0% never married, 65.7% now married, 3.3% widowed, 8.0% divorced (2000); Foreign born: 19.9% (2000); Ancestry (includes multiple ancestries): 28.3% Other groups, 16.4% Irish, 15.6% German, 11.1% Italian, 10.8% English (2000).
Economy: Employment by occupation: 30.8% management, 21.0% professional, 13.9% services, 26.9% sales, 0.0% farming, 2.8% construction, 4.6% production (2000).
Income: Per capita income: $34,058 (2004); Median household income: $75,415 (2004); Average household income: $93,509 (2004); Percent of households with income of $100,000 or more: 32.5% (2004); Poverty rate: 4.2% (2000).
Education: Percent of population age 25 and over with: High school diploma (including GED) or higher: 93.3% (2004); Bachelor's degree or higher: 45.0% (2004); Master's degree or higher: 14.1% (2004).
Housing: Homeownership rate: 55.8% (2004); Median home value: $234,289 (2004); Median rent: $869 per month (2000); Median age of housing: 5 years (2000).
Transportation: Commute to work: 93.7% car, 0.6% public transportation, 1.3% walk, 3.1% work from home (2000); Travel time to work: 19.9% less than 15 minutes, 54.8% 15 to 30 minutes, 18.5% 30 to 45 minutes, 3.6% 45 to 60 minutes, 3.2% 60 minutes or more (2000)

LAKE BUENA VISTA (city). Covers a land area of 4.808 square miles and a water area of 0.088 square miles. Located at 28.37° N. Lat.; 81.52° W. Long. Elevation is 100 feet.
Population: 6 (1990); 16 (2000); 29 (2004); 45 (2009 projected); Race: 100.0% White, 0.0% Black, 0.0% Asian, 0.0% Hispanic of any race (2004); Density: 6.0 persons per square mile (2004); Average household size: 1.81 (2004); Median age: 53.2 (2004); Male/female ratio: 93.3 (2004); Marriage status: 0.0% never married, 68.8% now married, 18.8% widowed, 12.5% divorced (2000); Foreign born: 0.0% (2000); Ancestry (includes multiple ancestries): 37.5% German, 18.8% Irish, 18.8% United States or American, 12.5% French (except Basque) (2000).
Economy: Tourist center located adjacent to Walt Disney World. Single-family building permits issued: 0 (2004); Multi-family building permits issued: 0 (2004); Employment by occupation: 0.0% management, 40.0% professional, 40.0% services, 20.0% sales, 0.0% farming, 0.0% construction, 0.0% production (2000).
Income: Per capita income: $22,845 (2004); Median household income: $38,750 (2004); Average household income: $41,406 (2004); Percent of households with income of $100,000 or more: 0.0% (2004); Poverty rate: 0.0% (2000).
Taxes: Total city taxes per capita: $32,063 (2002); City property taxes per capita: $31,750 (2002).
Education: Percent of population age 25 and over with: High school diploma (including GED) or higher: 100.0% (2004); Bachelor's degree or higher: 24.0% (2004); Master's degree or higher: 12.0% (2004).
Housing: Homeownership rate: 87.5% (2004); Median home value: $95,000 (2004); Median rent: $475 per month (2000); Median age of housing: 14 years (2000).
Transportation: Commute to work: 100.0% car, 0.0% public transportation, 0.0% walk, 0.0% work from home (2000); Travel time to work: 40.0% less than 15 minutes, 0.0% 15 to 30 minutes, 60.0% 30 to 45 minutes, 0.0% 45 to 60 minutes, 0.0% 60 minutes or more (2000)

LAKE BUTTER (CDP). Covers a land area of 12.949 square miles and a water area of 7.545 square miles. Located at 28.49° N. Lat.; 81.53° W. Long.
Population: 4,050 (1990); 7,062 (2000); 8,833 (2004); 10,968 (2009 projected); Race: 88.6% White, 3.8% Black, 4.2% Asian, 5.2% Hispanic of any race (2004); Density: 682.1 persons per square mile (2004); Average household size: 3.14 (2004); Median age: 37.9 (2004); Male/female ratio: 99.0 (2004); Marriage status: 14.7% never married, 77.7% now married, 3.2% widowed, 4.5% divorced (2000); Foreign born: 8.1% (2000); Ancestry (includes multiple ancestries): 19.2% German, 16.9% English, 15.1% Irish, 11.7% Other groups, 7.6% United States or American (2000).
Economy: Employment by occupation: 34.8% management, 25.1% professional, 8.1% services, 27.8% sales, 0.0% farming, 1.4% construction, 2.8% production (2000).
Income: Per capita income: $55,491 (2004); Median household income: $129,990 (2004); Average household income: $174,370 (2004); Percent of households with income of $100,000 or more: 61.2% (2004); Poverty rate: 1.8% (2000).
Education: Percent of population age 25 and over with: High school diploma (including GED) or higher: 96.3% (2004); Bachelor's degree or higher: 55.9% (2004); Master's degree or higher: 20.5% (2004).
Housing: Homeownership rate: 95.9% (2004); Median home value: $380,087 (2004); Median rent: $629 per month (2000); Median age of housing: 10 years (2000).
Transportation: Commute to work: 91.2% car, 0.0% public transportation, 0.3% walk, 7.6% work from home (2000); Travel time to work: 17.7% less than 15 minutes, 42.6% 15 to 30 minutes, 30.1% 30 to 45 minutes, 4.9% 45 to 60 minutes, 4.8% 60 minutes or more (2000)

LAKE HART (CDP). Covers a land area of 1.368 square miles and a water area of 0.484 square miles. Located at 28.38° N. Lat.; 81.22° W. Long.
Population: 559 (1990); 557 (2000); 668 (2004); 804 (2009 projected); Race: 93.7% White, 0.4% Black, 1.9% Asian, 4.6% Hispanic of any race (2004); Density: 488.1 persons per square mile (2004); Average household size: 2.44 (2004); Median age: 43.1 (2004); Male/female ratio: 112.1 (2004); Marriage status: 28.9% never married, 58.0% now married, 0.0% widowed, 13.0% divorced (2000); Foreign born: 3.9% (2000); Ancestry (includes multiple ancestries): 17.1% English, 17.1% United States or American, 16.2% German, 15.6% Irish, 15.4% Other groups (2000).
Economy: Employment by occupation: 13.6% management, 15.3% professional, 14.9% services, 15.9% sales, 0.0% farming, 27.5% construction, 12.9% production (2000).
Income: Per capita income: $39,862 (2004); Median household income: $63,291 (2004); Average household income: $97,181 (2004); Percent of households with income of $100,000 or more: 24.1% (2004); Poverty rate: 6.9% (2000).
Education: Percent of population age 25 and over with: High school diploma (including GED) or higher: 87.7% (2004); Bachelor's degree or higher: 29.7% (2004); Master's degree or higher: 8.9% (2004).
Housing: Homeownership rate: 72.3% (2004); Median home value: $187,931 (2004); Median rent: $438 per month (2000); Median age of housing: 19 years (2000).
Transportation: Commute to work: 87.5% car, 0.0% public transportation, 3.4% walk, 9.2% work from home (2000); Travel time to work: 12.7% less

than 15 minutes, 35.4% 15 to 30 minutes, 34.7% 30 to 45 minutes, 7.1% 45 to 60 minutes, 10.1% 60 minutes or more (2000)

LOCKHART (CDP). Covers a land area of 4.368 square miles and a water area of 0.195 square miles. Located at 28.62° N. Lat.; 81.43° W. Long. Elevation is 97 feet.
Population: 11,636 (1990); 12,944 (2000); 14,103 (2004); 15,628 (2009 projected); Race: 68.3% White, 20.0% Black, 2.6% Asian, 18.7% Hispanic of any race (2004); Density: 3,229.0 persons per square mile (2004); Average household size: 2.78 (2004); Median age: 33.3 (2004); Male/female ratio: 98.7 (2004); Marriage status: 25.4% never married, 55.9% now married, 4.6% widowed, 14.1% divorced (2000); Foreign born: 9.7% (2000); Ancestry (includes multiple ancestries): 30.8% Other groups, 12.8% German, 10.5% Irish, 10.5% United States or American, 7.4% English (2000).
Economy: Light manufacturing. Employment by occupation: 11.2% management, 14.9% professional, 15.1% services, 29.7% sales, 0.1% farming, 14.6% construction, 14.4% production (2000).
Income: Per capita income: $17,877 (2004); Median household income: $41,895 (2004); Average household income: $49,608 (2004); Percent of households with income of $100,000 or more: 7.2% (2004); Poverty rate: 11.3% (2000).
Education: Percent of population age 25 and over with: High school diploma (including GED) or higher: 78.7% (2004); Bachelor's degree or higher: 15.4% (2004); Master's degree or higher: 4.1% (2004).
Housing: Homeownership rate: 69.2% (2004); Median home value: $111,759 (2004); Median rent: $557 per month (2000); Median age of housing: 21 years (2000).
Transportation: Commute to work: 95.9% car, 1.0% public transportation, 0.8% walk, 1.3% work from home (2000); Travel time to work: 20.5% less than 15 minutes, 37.7% 15 to 30 minutes, 25.8% 30 to 45 minutes, 10.4% 45 to 60 minutes, 5.6% 60 minutes or more (2000)

MAITLAND (city). Aka Lake Maitland. Covers a land area of 4.642 square miles and a water area of 1.033 square miles. Located at 28.62° N. Lat.; 81.36° W. Long. Elevation is 91 feet.
History: Maitland was established on the site of Fort Maitland, built in 1838 and named for Captain William S. Maitland of the U.S. Army. The town was incorporated in 1884.
Population: 10,220 (1990); 12,019 (2000); 12,253 (2004); 12,653 (2009 projected); Race: 82.9% White, 10.8% Black, 2.8% Asian, 7.4% Hispanic of any race (2004); Density: 2,639.5 persons per square mile (2004); Average household size: 2.48 (2004); Median age: 39.8 (2004); Male/female ratio: 90.7 (2004); Marriage status: 23.1% never married, 57.2% now married, 7.4% widowed, 12.3% divorced (2000); Foreign born: 7.4% (2000); Ancestry (includes multiple ancestries): 20.2% Other groups, 16.7% English, 14.2% German, 11.0% Irish, 7.5% United States or American (2000).
Economy: Single-family building permits issued: 14 (2004); Multi-family building permits issued: 0 (2004); Employment by occupation: 22.9% management, 28.1% professional, 10.0% services, 28.1% sales, 0.0% farming, 3.3% construction, 7.6% production (2000).
Income: Per capita income: $40,779 (2004); Median household income: $63,397 (2004); Average household income: $100,369 (2004); Percent of households with income of $100,000 or more: 29.6% (2004); Poverty rate: 6.4% (2000).
Taxes: Total city taxes per capita: $871 (2002); City property taxes per capita: $387 (2002).
Education: Percent of population age 25 and over with: High school diploma (including GED) or higher: 93.1% (2004); Bachelor's degree or higher: 50.9% (2004); Master's degree or higher: 19.3% (2004).

School District(s)

Orange County School District (PK-12)
2002-03 Enrollment: 158,718 . . . . (407) 317-3202

Four-year College(s)

ITT Technical Institute (Private, For-profit)
2003-04 Enrollment: 465 . . . . (407) 660-2900
2003-04 Tuition: In-state $12,492; Out-of-state $12,492
University of Phoenix-Orlando Campus (Private, For-profit)
2003-04 Enrollment: 1,604 . . . . (407) 667-0555
2003-04 Tuition: In-state $8,850; Out-of-state $8,850

Housing: Homeownership rate: 70.4% (2004); Median home value: $204,237 (2004); Median rent: $612 per month (2000); Median age of housing: 27 years (2000).
Safety: Violent crime rate: 31.1 per 10,000 population; Property crime rate: 387.0 per 10,000 population (2003).
Transportation: Commute to work: 89.9% car, 1.6% public transportation, 1.3% walk, 5.7% work from home (2000); Travel time to work: 23.9% less than 15 minutes, 47.7% 15 to 30 minutes, 17.3% 30 to 45 minutes, 4.9% 45 to 60 minutes, 6.1% 60 minutes or more (2000)

Additional Information Contacts

Local Government Offices . . . . (407) 539-6219
Maitland Chamber of Commerce . . . . (407) 644-0741

MEADOW WOODS (CDP). Covers a land area of 11.373 square miles and a water area of 0.036 square miles. Located at 28.37° N. Lat.; 81.36° W. Long.
Population: 5,514 (1990); 11,286 (2000); 15,274 (2004); 20,011 (2009 projected); Race: 64.9% White, 13.7% Black, 2.6% Asian, 59.0% Hispanic of any race (2004); Density: 1,343.0 persons per square mile (2004); Average household size: 3.30 (2004); Median age: 33.6 (2004); Male/female ratio: 94.4 (2004); Marriage status: 26.6% never married, 60.4% now married, 3.5% widowed, 9.5% divorced (2000); Foreign born: 20.5% (2000); Ancestry (includes multiple ancestries): 61.5% Other groups, 6.9% German, 6.5% Irish, 5.4% Italian, 4.3% English (2000).
Economy: Employment by occupation: 9.4% management, 13.7% professional, 21.9% services, 36.3% sales, 0.0% farming, 7.5% construction, 11.2% production (2000).
Income: Per capita income: $17,241 (2004); Median household income: $49,689 (2004); Average household income: $56,951 (2004); Percent of households with income of $100,000 or more: 9.0% (2004); Poverty rate: 7.5% (2000).
Education: Percent of population age 25 and over with: High school diploma (including GED) or higher: 81.1% (2004); Bachelor's degree or higher: 16.5% (2004); Master's degree or higher: 4.3% (2004).
Housing: Homeownership rate: 78.8% (2004); Median home value: $135,632 (2004); Median rent: $761 per month (2000); Median age of housing: 8 years (2000).
Transportation: Commute to work: 95.9% car, 1.2% public transportation, 0.2% walk, 2.2% work from home (2000); Travel time to work: 11.4% less than 15 minutes, 49.1% 15 to 30 minutes, 28.0% 30 to 45 minutes, 7.3% 45 to 60 minutes, 4.2% 60 minutes or more (2000)

OAK RIDGE (CDP). Covers a land area of 4.161 square miles and a water area of 0.153 square miles. Located at 28.47° N. Lat.; 81.42° W. Long.
Population: 15,388 (1990); 22,349 (2000); 24,764 (2004); 27,858 (2009 projected); Race: 37.5% White, 31.9% Black, 5.8% Asian, 43.9% Hispanic of any race (2004); Density: 5,951.3 persons per square mile (2004); Average household size: 3.08 (2004); Median age: 29.7 (2004); Male/female ratio: 101.3 (2004); Marriage status: 33.0% never married, 52.8% now married, 3.4% widowed, 10.8% divorced (2000); Foreign born: 35.5% (2000); Ancestry (includes multiple ancestries): 58.3% Other groups, 10.0% Haitian, 4.4% United States or American, 3.9% German, 3.5% Irish (2000).
Economy: Employment by occupation: 5.9% management, 8.9% professional, 30.8% services, 28.2% sales, 0.2% farming, 10.9% construction, 15.2% production (2000).
Income: Per capita income: $12,002 (2004); Median household income: $30,274 (2004); Average household income: $36,885 (2004); Percent of households with income of $100,000 or more: 3.1% (2004); Poverty rate: 19.6% (2000).
Education: Percent of population age 25 and over with: High school diploma (including GED) or higher: 67.2% (2004); Bachelor's degree or higher: 10.6% (2004); Master's degree or higher: 3.6% (2004).
Housing: Homeownership rate: 37.5% (2004); Median home value: $107,239 (2004); Median rent: $588 per month (2000); Median age of housing: 19 years (2000).
Transportation: Commute to work: 87.7% car, 7.4% public transportation, 1.6% walk, 1.4% work from home (2000); Travel time to work: 21.7% less than 15 minutes, 44.4% 15 to 30 minutes, 25.0% 30 to 45 minutes, 4.9% 45 to 60 minutes, 4.0% 60 minutes or more (2000)

OAKLAND (city). Covers a land area of 1.630 square miles and a water area of 0.002 square miles. Located at 28.55° N. Lat.; 81.63° W. Long. Elevation is 124 feet.
History: Oakland was founded in 1854 by settlers from South Carolina, and became an early industrial center with sawmills, sugar mills, and cotton gins. It was named for the large oak trees on the site.

Population: 783 (1990); 936 (2000); 1,051 (2004); 1,186 (2009 projected); Race: 69.7% White, 26.1% Black, 1.4% Asian, 3.4% Hispanic of any race (2004); Density: 644.7 persons per square mile (2004); Average household size: 2.74 (2004); Median age: 38.8 (2004); Male/female ratio: 94.3 (2004); Marriage status: 20.5% never married, 62.8% now married, 8.1% widowed, 8.5% divorced (2000); Foreign born: 1.6% (2000); Ancestry (includes multiple ancestries): 31.5% Other groups, 13.6% United States or American, 13.3% English, 9.8% German, 9.3% Irish (2000).
Economy: Employment by occupation: 17.2% management, 22.2% professional, 16.6% services, 26.3% sales, 1.6% farming, 8.6% construction, 7.5% production (2000).
Income: Per capita income: $26,974 (2004); Median household income: $62,216 (2004); Average household income: $73,828 (2004); Percent of households with income of $100,000 or more: 20.8% (2004); Poverty rate: 5.9% (2000).
Taxes: Total city taxes per capita: $799 (2002); City property taxes per capita: $163 (2002).
Education: Percent of population age 25 and over with: High school diploma (including GED) or higher: 80.9% (2004); Bachelor's degree or higher: 26.1% (2004); Master's degree or higher: 4.8% (2004).

School District(s)

Orange County School District (PK-12)
2002-03 Enrollment: 158,718 . . . . (407) 317-3202
Housing: Homeownership rate: 80.7% (2004); Median home value: $166,447 (2004); Median rent: $363 per month (2000); Median age of housing: 21 years (2000).
Safety: Violent crime rate: 29.5 per 10,000 population; Property crime rate: 697.4 per 10,000 population (2003).
Transportation: Commute to work: 94.6% car, 2.8% public transportation, 1.2% walk, 1.4% work from home (2000); Travel time to work: 20.8% less than 15 minutes, 28.1% 15 to 30 minutes, 37.6% 30 to 45 minutes, 8.3% 45 to 60 minutes, 5.2% 60 minutes or more (2000)

OCOEE (city). Covers a land area of 13.234 square miles and a water area of 0.819 square miles. Located at 28.57° N. Lat.; 81.53° W. Long. Elevation is 130 feet.
History: Named for the Cherokee translation of "apricot-vine place." Ocoee grew up around a camp established by Dr. J.S. Starke on the shore of Lake Starke. The settlement was called Starke until a town was platted in 1886.
Population: 14,479 (1990); 24,391 (2000); 28,144 (2004); 32,781 (2009 projected); Race: 76.5% White, 9.1% Black, 3.8% Asian, 17.4% Hispanic of any race (2004); Density: 2,126.7 persons per square mile (2004); Average household size: 3.00 (2004); Median age: 33.5 (2004); Male/female ratio: 97.6 (2004); Marriage status: 22.5% never married, 65.4% now married, 3.4% widowed, 8.8% divorced (2000); Foreign born: 12.4% (2000); Ancestry (includes multiple ancestries): 26.2% Other groups, 14.1% German, 11.3% Irish, 10.0% English, 9.9% United States or American (2000).
Economy: Unemployment rate: 5.0% (2004); Total civilian labor force: 10,317 (2004); Single-family building permits issued: 518 (2004); Multi-family building permits issued: 67 (2004); Employment by occupation: 15.5% management, 16.3% professional, 15.5% services, 29.7% sales, 0.7% farming, 12.0% construction, 10.1% production (2000).
Income: Per capita income: $24,032 (2004); Median household income: $62,254 (2004); Average household income: $71,931 (2004); Percent of households with income of $100,000 or more: 18.5% (2004); Poverty rate: 5.6% (2000).
Taxes: Total city taxes per capita: $372 (2002); City property taxes per capita: $179 (2002).
Education: Percent of population age 25 and over with: High school diploma (including GED) or higher: 81.6% (2004); Bachelor's degree or higher: 23.6% (2004); Master's degree or higher: 5.7% (2004).

School District(s)

Orange County School District (PK-12)
2002-03 Enrollment: 158,718 . . . . (407) 317-3202
Housing: Homeownership rate: 83.8% (2004); Median home value: $149,087 (2004); Median rent: $633 per month (2000); Median age of housing: 10 years (2000).
Hospitals: Health Central (141 beds)
Safety: Violent crime rate: 51.8 per 10,000 population; Property crime rate: 516.0 per 10,000 population (2003).
Transportation: Commute to work: 95.1% car, 0.6% public transportation, 0.6% walk, 3.0% work from home (2000); Travel time to work: 16.8% less than 15 minutes, 33.9% 15 to 30 minutes, 34.5% 30 to 45 minutes, 8.4% 45 to 60 minutes, 6.5% 60 minutes or more (2000)

Additional Information Contacts
Local Government Offices . . . . (407) 905-3100

ORLANDO (city). Covers a land area of 93.495 square miles and a water area of 7.459 square miles. Located at 28.53° N. Lat.; 81.37° W. Long. Elevation is 106 feet.
History: Orlando began in 1850 as Jernigan, an outgrowth of Fort Gatlin which had been abandoned by the army in 1848. The first residents were cattlemen who had been occupying the area for some years. Jernigan became the seat of Orange County in 1856, and was incorporated in 1875. The town's name was later changed to Orlando, perhaps for Shakespeare's hero in "As You Like It." The first commercial citrus grove near Orlando was planted by W.H. Holden in 1865, and citrus orchards soon replaced cattle lands.
Population: 161,172 (1990); 185,951 (2000); 195,770 (2004); 209,388 (2009 projected); Race: 57.0% White, 28.7% Black, 3.1% Asian, 20.5% Hispanic of any race (2004); Density: 2,093.9 persons per square mile (2004); Average household size: 2.27 (2004); Median age: 33.5 (2004); Male/female ratio: 94.5 (2004); Marriage status: 35.8% never married, 44.2% now married, 6.1% widowed, 13.8% divorced (2000); Foreign born: 14.4% (2000); Ancestry (includes multiple ancestries): 39.5% Other groups, 9.8% German, 8.7% Irish, 7.9% English, 6.7% United States or American (2000).
Economy: Unemployment rate: 5.0% (2004); Total civilian labor force: 132,763 (2004); Single-family building permits issued: 2,256 (2004); Multi-family building permits issued: 1,242 (2004); Employment by occupation: 14.4% management, 18.9% professional, 19.2% services, 30.0% sales, 0.2% farming, 7.5% construction, 9.8% production (2000).
Income: Per capita income: $22,951 (2004); Median household income: $38,304 (2004); Average household income: $51,622 (2004); Percent of households with income of $100,000 or more: 9.2% (2004); Poverty rate: 15.9% (2000).
Taxes: Total city taxes per capita: $766 (2002); City property taxes per capita: $371 (2002).
Education: Percent of population age 25 and over with: High school diploma (including GED) or higher: 82.3% (2004); Bachelor's degree or higher: 28.2% (2004); Master's degree or higher: 8.2% (2004).

Four-year College(s)

Devry University-Florida (Private, For-profit)
2003-04 Enrollment: 2,487 . . . . (407) 345-2800
2003-04 Tuition: In-state $10,590; Out-of-state $10,590
Florida College of Integrative Medicine (Private, For-profit)
2003-04 Enrollment: 103 . . . . (407) 888-8689
Florida Hospital College of Health Sciences
2003-04 Enrollment: 1,403 . . . . (407) 303-7742
2003-04 Tuition: In-state $5,050; Out-of-state $5,050
Florida Hospital School of Medical Technology
2003-04 Enrollment: n/a . . . . (407) 897-5600
Florida Metropolitan University-North Orlando (Private, For-profit)
2003-04 Enrollment: 1,667 . . . . (407) 628-5870
2003-04 Tuition: In-state $9,100; Out-of-state $9,100
Florida Metropolitan University-South Orlando (Private, For-profit)
2003-04 Enrollment: 2,217 . . . . (407) 851-2525
2003-04 Tuition: In-state $8,460; Out-of-state $8,460
International Academy of Design and Technology (Private, For-profit)
2003-04 Enrollment: 628 . . . . (407) 857-2300
2003-04 Tuition: In-state $31,500; Out-of-state $31,500
University of Central Florida (Public)
2003-04 Enrollment: 41,535 . . . . (407) 823-2000
2003-04 Tuition: In-state $3,013; Out-of-state $14,041

Two-year College(s)

Audio Recording Technology Institute (Private, For-profit)
2003-04 Enrollment: 131 . . . . (402) 423-2784
Clinton Technical Institute-Motorcycle/Marine Mech (Private, For-profit)
2003-04 Enrollment: 1,538 . . . . (407) 240-2422
Florida Technical College (Private, For-profit)
2003-04 Enrollment: 669 . . . . (407) 447-7300
High-Tech Institute-Orlando (Private, For-profit)
2003-04 Enrollment: 824 . . . . (407) 673-9900
Keiser College-Orlando (Private, For-profit)
2003-04 Enrollment: n/a . . . . (407) 273-5800
2003-04 Tuition: In-state $10,920; Out-of-state $10,920
Mid Florida Tech (Public)
2003-04 Enrollment: 1,743 . . . . (407) 855-5880

Orlando Culinary Academy (Private, For-profit)
2003-04 Enrollment: 993 . . . . (407) 888-4000
Orlando Tech (Public)
2003-04 Enrollment: 752 . . . . (407) 317-3431
Stenotype Institute of Jacksonville Inc (Private, For-profit)
2003-04 Enrollment: 228 . . . . (407) 816-5573
2003-04 Tuition: In-state $8,400; Out-of-state $8,400
Valencia Community College (Public)
2003-04 Enrollment: 29,269 . . . . (407) 299-2187
2003-04 Tuition: In-state $1,729; Out-of-state $6,494

Housing: Homeownership rate: 39.2% (2004); Median home value: $133,949 (2004); Median rent: $606 per month (2000); Median age of housing: 22 years (2000).
Hospitals: Arnold Palmer Hospital for Children & Women (281 beds); Florida Hospital E Orlando (123 beds); Florida Hospital Orlando (1783 beds); Orlando Regional Healthcare (1870 beds); Orlando Regional Medical Centre (267 beds); Sand Lake Hospital (153 beds)
Safety: Violent crime rate: 168.4 per 10,000 population; Property crime rate: 863.0 per 10,000 population (2003).
Newspapers: Central Florida Advocate (Black - Circulation 15,000); Latino International - Orlando Edition (Hispanic - Circulation 45,000); Orlando Times (Black - Circulation 10,000); Orlando Weekly (Alternative, General - Circulation 50,000); The Orlando Sentinel (Circulation 269,269)
Transportation: Commute to work: 90.1% car, 4.1% public transportation, 1.9% walk, 2.2% work from home (2000); Travel time to work: 21.7% less than 15 minutes, 43.7% 15 to 30 minutes, 23.6% 30 to 45 minutes, 5.9% 45 to 60 minutes, 5.1% 60 minutes or more (2000); Amtrak: Service available.
Airports: Executive; Kissimmee Municipal; Orlando International (primary service/large hub); Orlando Sanford (primary service/small hub)

Additional Information Contacts
African American Chamber of Commerce . . . . (407) 428-5850
Brazilian-American Chamber of Commerce . . . . . . (407) 425-0126
Downtown Orlando Partnership . . . . (407) 648-4010
East Orange Chamber of Commerce . . . . (407) 277-5951
Florida Association of Realtors . . . . (407) 438-1400
Orlando Chamber of Commerce . . . . (407) 275-3777
Orlando Regional Realtor Association . . . . (407) 691-7900
South Orange Chamber of Cmmrc . . . . (407) 854-4246

ORLOVISTA (CDP). Covers a land area of 1.930 square miles and a water area of 0.033 square miles. Located at 28.54° N. Lat.; 81.46° W. Long. Elevation is 109 feet.
History: Orlovista came into existence during the real estate boom of the 1920's. Near Orlovista was Deer Island Pit, constructed as a center for cock fighting.
Population: 5,438 (1990); 6,047 (2000); 6,237 (2004); 6,547 (2009 projected); Race: 50.7% White, 32.2% Black, 4.0% Asian, 16.9% Hispanic of any race (2004); Density: 3,231.5 persons per square mile (2004); Average household size: 2.88 (2004); Median age: 32.9 (2004); Male/female ratio: 100.3 (2004); Marriage status: 36.1% never married, 43.1% now married, 6.9% widowed, 13.8% divorced (2000); Foreign born: 14.3% (2000); Ancestry (includes multiple ancestries): 43.9% Other groups, 14.9% United States or American, 7.2% German, 6.3% Irish, 4.3% Italian (2000).
Economy: Employment by occupation: 9.2% management, 8.9% professional, 24.8% services, 23.8% sales, 0.4% farming, 16.0% construction, 16.9% production (2000).
Income: Per capita income: $15,000 (2004); Median household income: $36,265 (2004); Average household income: $40,281 (2004); Percent of households with income of $100,000 or more: 3.8% (2004); Poverty rate: 16.8% (2000).
Education: Percent of population age 25 and over with: High school diploma (including GED) or higher: 62.8% (2004); Bachelor's degree or higher: 5.9% (2004); Master's degree or higher: 1.9% (2004).
Housing: Homeownership rate: 60.8% (2004); Median home value: $89,385 (2004); Median rent: $553 per month (2000); Median age of housing: 28 years (2000).
Transportation: Commute to work: 93.2% car, 2.4% public transportation, 0.8% walk, 1.5% work from home (2000); Travel time to work: 21.9% less than 15 minutes, 34.3% 15 to 30 minutes, 27.3% 30 to 45 minutes, 9.5% 45 to 60 minutes, 7.0% 60 minutes or more (2000)

PARADISE HEIGHTS (CDP). Covers a land area of 0.472 square miles and a water area of 0 square miles. Located at 28.62° N. Lat.; 81.54° W. Long.
Population: 1,677 (1990); 1,310 (2000); 1,215 (2004); 1,167 (2009 projected); Race: 75.1% White, 3.7% Black, 0.6% Asian, 30.5% Hispanic of any race (2004); Density: 2,576.7 persons per square mile (2004); Average household size: 2.83 (2004); Median age: 32.8 (2004); Male/female ratio: 111.3 (2004); Marriage status: 29.3% never married, 52.7% now married, 9.2% widowed, 8.7% divorced (2000); Foreign born: 15.1% (2000); Ancestry (includes multiple ancestries): 31.1% Other groups, 30.6% United States or American, 11.6% Irish, 9.3% English, 8.6% German (2000).
Economy: Employment by occupation: 4.0% management, 5.3% professional, 18.8% services, 21.1% sales, 6.2% farming, 29.0% construction, 15.7% production (2000).
Income: Per capita income: $13,646 (2004); Median household income: $32,319 (2004); Average household income: $38,316 (2004); Percent of households with income of $100,000 or more: 4.4% (2004); Poverty rate: 14.9% (2000).
Education: Percent of population age 25 and over with: High school diploma (including GED) or higher: 61.9% (2004); Bachelor's degree or higher: 0.5% (2004); Master's degree or higher: 0.5% (2004).
Housing: Homeownership rate: 58.5% (2004); Median home value: $87,358 (2004); Median rent: $505 per month (2000); Median age of housing: 33 years (2000).
Transportation: Commute to work: 92.6% car, 0.0% public transportation, 1.9% walk, 1.0% work from home (2000); Travel time to work: 19.3% less than 15 minutes, 44.1% 15 to 30 minutes, 21.0% 30 to 45 minutes, 12.3% 45 to 60 minutes, 3.3% 60 minutes or more (2000)

PINE CASTLE (CDP). Covers a land area of 2.616 square miles and a water area of 0.213 square miles. Located at 28.46° N. Lat.; 81.37° W. Long. Elevation is 101 feet.
Population: 8,188 (1990); 8,803 (2000); 9,542 (2004); 10,510 (2009 projected); Race: 64.2% White, 15.2% Black, 2.7% Asian, 40.7% Hispanic of any race (2004); Density: 3,647.0 persons per square mile (2004); Average household size: 2.86 (2004); Median age: 33.5 (2004); Male/female ratio: 103.8 (2004); Marriage status: 27.2% never married, 56.6% now married, 4.2% widowed, 12.0% divorced (2000); Foreign born: 29.6% (2000); Ancestry (includes multiple ancestries): 38.7% Other groups, 8.1% German, 7.8% Irish, 7.2% English, 6.3% United States or American (2000).
Economy: Employment by occupation: 7.2% management, 9.9% professional, 21.9% services, 24.6% sales, 0.0% farming, 15.6% construction, 20.9% production (2000).
Income: Per capita income: $16,406 (2004); Median household income: $37,162 (2004); Average household income: $46,996 (2004); Percent of households with income of $100,000 or more: 5.6% (2004); Poverty rate: 15.0% (2000).
Education: Percent of population age 25 and over with: High school diploma (including GED) or higher: 72.1% (2004); Bachelor's degree or higher: 11.9% (2004); Master's degree or higher: 3.2% (2004).
Housing: Homeownership rate: 51.9% (2004); Median home value: $112,786 (2004); Median rent: $519 per month (2000); Median age of housing: 29 years (2000).
Transportation: Commute to work: 89.2% car, 4.5% public transportation, 2.0% walk, 2.4% work from home (2000); Travel time to work: 27.6% less than 15 minutes, 44.1% 15 to 30 minutes, 20.4% 30 to 45 minutes, 4.4% 45 to 60 minutes, 3.5% 60 minutes or more (2000)

PINE HILLS (CDP). Covers a land area of 7.682 square miles and a water area of 0.241 square miles. Located at 28.57° N. Lat.; 81.45° W. Long. Elevation is 115 feet.
Population: 34,712 (1990); 41,764 (2000); 42,618 (2004); 44,048 (2009 projected); Race: 24.5% White, 59.8% Black, 2.9% Asian, 14.4% Hispanic of any race (2004); Density: 5,547.9 persons per square mile (2004); Average household size: 3.18 (2004); Median age: 30.4 (2004); Male/female ratio: 93.3 (2004); Marriage status: 32.1% never married, 51.3% now married, 5.3% widowed, 11.2% divorced (2000); Foreign born: 22.4% (2000); Ancestry (includes multiple ancestries): 45.9% Other groups, 11.5% Haitian, 6.6% United States or American, 4.8% German, 4.2% Irish (2000).
Economy: Employment by occupation: 6.8% management, 11.4% professional, 23.7% services, 28.3% sales, 0.5% farming, 13.6% construction, 15.6% production (2000).

Income: Per capita income: $12,931 (2004); Median household income: $33,602 (2004); Average household income: $40,651 (2004); Percent of households with income of $100,000 or more: 3.8% (2004); Poverty rate: 18.5% (2000).
Education: Percent of population age 25 and over with: High school diploma (including GED) or higher: 71.3% (2004); Bachelor's degree or higher: 10.6% (2004); Master's degree or higher: 3.1% (2004).
Housing: Homeownership rate: 65.4% (2004); Median home value: $106,732 (2004); Median rent: $551 per month (2000); Median age of housing: 27 years (2000).
Transportation: Commute to work: 91.8% car, 4.6% public transportation, 0.8% walk, 1.2% work from home (2000); Travel time to work: 13.8% less than 15 minutes, 37.7% 15 to 30 minutes, 30.9% 30 to 45 minutes, 10.6% 45 to 60 minutes, 7.0% 60 minutes or more (2000)

SKY LAKE (CDP). Covers a land area of 1.260 square miles and a water area of 0.009 square miles. Located at 28.46° N. Lat.; 81.39° W. Long. Elevation is 100 feet.
Population: 6,202 (1990); 5,651 (2000); 6,751 (2004); 8,116 (2009 projected); Race: 65.2% White, 14.1% Black, 2.6% Asian, 40.2% Hispanic of any race (2004); Density: 5,356.6 persons per square mile (2004); Average household size: 2.94 (2004); Median age: 37.8 (2004); Male/female ratio: 95.3 (2004); Marriage status: 28.5% never married, 51.5% now married, 7.8% widowed, 12.2% divorced (2000); Foreign born: 21.3% (2000); Ancestry (includes multiple ancestries): 40.6% Other groups, 11.7% German, 11.4% Irish, 7.9% English, 4.4% United States or American (2000).
Economy: Employment by occupation: 5.6% management, 11.1% professional, 26.9% services, 34.6% sales, 0.4% farming, 8.8% construction, 12.7% production (2000).
Income: Per capita income: $17,490 (2004); Median household income: $40,487 (2004); Average household income: $50,387 (2004); Percent of households with income of $100,000 or more: 8.2% (2004); Poverty rate: 12.9% (2000).
Education: Percent of population age 25 and over with: High school diploma (including GED) or higher: 72.5% (2004); Bachelor's degree or higher: 12.1% (2004); Master's degree or higher: 3.6% (2004).
Housing: Homeownership rate: 72.0% (2004); Median home value: $114,061 (2004); Median rent: $549 per month (2000); Median age of housing: 33 years (2000).
Transportation: Commute to work: 90.9% car, 4.5% public transportation, 2.7% walk, 1.1% work from home (2000); Travel time to work: 25.8% less than 15 minutes, 40.9% 15 to 30 minutes, 22.0% 30 to 45 minutes, 4.5% 45 to 60 minutes, 6.8% 60 minutes or more (2000)

SOUTH APOPKA (CDP). Covers a land area of 2.747 square miles and a water area of 0.071 square miles. Located at 28.65° N. Lat.; 81.50° W. Long. Elevation is 115 feet.
Population: 5,584 (1990); 5,800 (2000); 5,902 (2004); 6,057 (2009 projected); Race: 26.8% White, 64.7% Black, 0.1% Asian, 13.9% Hispanic of any race (2004); Density: 2,148.3 persons per square mile (2004); Average household size: 3.26 (2004); Median age: 29.1 (2004); Male/female ratio: 93.4 (2004); Marriage status: 39.4% never married, 43.6% now married, 6.8% widowed, 10.2% divorced (2000); Foreign born: 6.8% (2000); Ancestry (includes multiple ancestries): 61.5% Other groups, 4.3% African, 4.2% United States or American, 3.5% English, 3.1% Irish (2000).
Economy: Employment by occupation: 4.1% management, 13.3% professional, 22.6% services, 18.8% sales, 6.6% farming, 16.7% construction, 18.0% production (2000).
Income: Per capita income: $11,173 (2004); Median household income: $27,889 (2004); Average household income: $36,161 (2004); Percent of households with income of $100,000 or more: 4.5% (2004); Poverty rate: 34.9% (2000).
Education: Percent of population age 25 and over with: High school diploma (including GED) or higher: 48.7% (2004); Bachelor's degree or higher: 5.8% (2004); Master's degree or higher: 1.2% (2004).
Housing: Homeownership rate: 64.8% (2004); Median home value: $86,342 (2004); Median rent: $343 per month (2000); Median age of housing: 29 years (2000).
Transportation: Commute to work: 88.7% car, 5.8% public transportation, 2.5% walk, 0.4% work from home (2000); Travel time to work: 21.0% less than 15 minutes, 31.8% 15 to 30 minutes, 27.2% 30 to 45 minutes, 7.0% 45 to 60 minutes, 13.0% 60 minutes or more (2000)

SOUTHCHASE (CDP). Covers a land area of 2.171 square miles and a water area of 0 square miles. Located at 28.39° N. Lat.; 81.38° W. Long.
Population: 441 (1990); 4,633 (2000); 5,490 (2004); 6,540 (2009 projected); Race: 52.0% White, 17.0% Black, 11.4% Asian, 40.1% Hispanic of any race (2004); Density: 2,528.6 persons per square mile (2004); Average household size: 3.45 (2004); Median age: 32.2 (2004); Male/female ratio: 95.0 (2004); Marriage status: 24.5% never married, 67.3% now married, 2.5% widowed, 5.7% divorced (2000); Foreign born: 14.6% (2000); Ancestry (includes multiple ancestries): 53.3% Other groups, 10.7% German, 8.5% Irish, 5.2% Italian, 5.0% English (2000).
Economy: Employment by occupation: 13.4% management, 18.3% professional, 12.4% services, 38.9% sales, 0.0% farming, 9.1% construction, 7.9% production (2000).
Income: Per capita income: $21,460 (2004); Median household income: $68,973 (2004); Average household income: $74,097 (2004); Percent of households with income of $100,000 or more: 17.9% (2004); Poverty rate: 3.0% (2000).
Education: Percent of population age 25 and over with: High school diploma (including GED) or higher: 90.3% (2004); Bachelor's degree or higher: 26.5% (2004); Master's degree or higher: 4.9% (2004).
Housing: Homeownership rate: 93.2% (2004); Median home value: $183,516 (2004); Median rent: $988 per month (2000); Median age of housing: 5 years (2000).
Transportation: Commute to work: 97.3% car, 0.0% public transportation, 1.2% walk, 1.5% work from home (2000); Travel time to work: 13.8% less than 15 minutes, 48.4% 15 to 30 minutes, 31.3% 30 to 45 minutes, 4.0% 45 to 60 minutes, 2.4% 60 minutes or more (2000)

TAFT (CDP). Covers a land area of 1.016 square miles and a water area of 0.027 square miles. Located at 28.42° N. Lat.; 81.36° W. Long. Elevation is 97 feet.
Population: 1,781 (1990); 1,938 (2000); 2,070 (2004); 2,249 (2009 projected); Race: 83.1% White, 4.9% Black, 2.4% Asian, 23.9% Hispanic of any race (2004); Density: 2,037.2 persons per square mile (2004); Average household size: 2.90 (2004); Median age: 35.4 (2004); Male/female ratio: 112.7 (2004); Marriage status: 25.4% never married, 51.8% now married, 7.3% widowed, 15.5% divorced (2000); Foreign born: 10.5% (2000); Ancestry (includes multiple ancestries): 23.8% Other groups, 18.7% United States or American, 10.2% German, 7.4% Irish, 5.3% Polish (2000).
Economy: Employment by occupation: 8.5% management, 8.1% professional, 14.1% services, 29.8% sales, 0.0% farming, 22.1% construction, 17.4% production (2000).
Income: Per capita income: $15,052 (2004); Median household income: $35,181 (2004); Average household income: $43,638 (2004); Percent of households with income of $100,000 or more: 6.2% (2004); Poverty rate: 14.3% (2000).
Education: Percent of population age 25 and over with: High school diploma (including GED) or higher: 59.5% (2004); Bachelor's degree or higher: 7.1% (2004); Master's degree or higher: 2.3% (2004).

School District(s)

Orange County School District (PK-12)
2002-03 Enrollment: 158,718 . . . . (407) 317-3202
Housing: Homeownership rate: 68.5% (2004); Median home value: $87,500 (2004); Median rent: $433 per month (2000); Median age of housing: 22 years (2000).
Transportation: Commute to work: 94.6% car, 3.5% public transportation, 0.0% walk, 1.9% work from home (2000); Travel time to work: 25.3% less than 15 minutes, 34.5% 15 to 30 minutes, 31.4% 30 to 45 minutes, 4.0% 45 to 60 minutes, 4.8% 60 minutes or more (2000)

TANGELO PARK (CDP). Covers a land area of 0.342 square miles and a water area of 0 square miles. Located at 28.45° N. Lat.; 81.44° W. Long. Elevation is 92 feet.
Population: 2,663 (1990); 2,430 (2000); 2,320 (2004); 2,204 (2009 projected); Race: 6.1% White, 90.1% Black, 0.2% Asian, 2.2% Hispanic of any race (2004); Density: 6,792.9 persons per square mile (2004); Average household size: 3.20 (2004); Median age: 31.2 (2004); Male/female ratio: 94.1 (2004); Marriage status: 39.4% never married, 42.0% now married, 7.0% widowed, 11.6% divorced (2000); Foreign born: 12.3% (2000); Ancestry (includes multiple ancestries): 73.3% Other groups, 6.2% Jamaican, 3.3% Haitian, 2.0% Ethiopian, 2.0% United States or American (2000).

Economy: Employment by occupation: 2.9% management, 4.9% professional, 25.5% services, 32.2% sales, 0.0% farming, 16.0% construction, 18.5% production (2000).
Income: Per capita income: $10,983 (2004); Median household income: $31,532 (2004); Average household income: $35,096 (2004); Percent of households with income of $100,000 or more: 1.0% (2004); Poverty rate: 13.9% (2000).
Education: Percent of population age 25 and over with: High school diploma (including GED) or higher: 70.8% (2004); Bachelor's degree or higher: 8.4% (2004); Master's degree or higher: 2.6% (2004).
Housing: Homeownership rate: 77.0% (2004); Median home value: $86,772 (2004); Median rent: $552 per month (2000); Median age of housing: 36 years (2000).
Transportation: Commute to work: 92.2% car, 4.5% public transportation, 0.8% walk, 1.6% work from home (2000); Travel time to work: 25.5% less than 15 minutes, 37.7% 15 to 30 minutes, 26.9% 30 to 45 minutes, 2.1% 45 to 60 minutes, 7.8% 60 minutes or more (2000)

TANGERINE (CDP). Covers a land area of 1.154 square miles and a water area of 0.649 square miles. Located at 28.75° N. Lat.; 81.63° W. Long. Elevation is 59 feet.
Population: 830 (1990); 826 (2000); 754 (2004); 697 (2009 projected); Race: 92.3% White, 2.3% Black, 2.1% Asian, 8.0% Hispanic of any race (2004); Density: 653.5 persons per square mile (2004); Average household size: 2.52 (2004); Median age: 42.7 (2004); Male/female ratio: 96.9 (2004); Marriage status: 8.9% never married, 80.2% now married, 2.6% widowed, 8.3% divorced (2000); Foreign born: 3.5% (2000); Ancestry (includes multiple ancestries): 20.7% English, 20.0% Other groups, 20.0% Irish, 8.7% German, 7.9% French (except Basque) (2000).
Economy: Employment by occupation: 18.4% management, 24.0% professional, 16.1% services, 22.9% sales, 2.1% farming, 14.1% construction, 2.4% production (2000).
Income: Per capita income: $25,106 (2004); Median household income: $50,647 (2004); Average household income: $63,311 (2004); Percent of households with income of $100,000 or more: 14.0% (2004); Poverty rate: 2.7% (2000).
Education: Percent of population age 25 and over with: High school diploma (including GED) or higher: 89.5% (2004); Bachelor's degree or higher: 30.9% (2004); Master's degree or higher: 7.7% (2004).
Housing: Homeownership rate: 91.3% (2004); Median home value: $154,412 (2004); Median rent: $n/a per month (2000); Median age of housing: 42 years (2000).
Transportation: Commute to work: 98.0% car, 0.0% public transportation, 0.0% walk, 2.0% work from home (2000); Travel time to work: 12.5% less than 15 minutes, 29.7% 15 to 30 minutes, 30.8% 30 to 45 minutes, 18.5% 45 to 60 minutes, 8.5% 60 minutes or more (2000)

TILDENVILLE (CDP). Covers a land area of 0.350 square miles and a water area of 0.058 square miles. Located at 28.53° N. Lat.; 81.60° W. Long. Elevation is 116 feet.
Population: 534 (1990); 513 (2000); 641 (2004); 789 (2009 projected); Race: 16.7% White, 75.8% Black, 0.0% Asian, 15.4% Hispanic of any race (2004); Density: 1,831.5 persons per square mile (2004); Average household size: 3.00 (2004); Median age: 32.6 (2004); Male/female ratio: 95.4 (2004); Marriage status: 34.3% never married, 52.8% now married, 0.0% widowed, 12.9% divorced (2000); Foreign born: 1.8% (2000); Ancestry (includes multiple ancestries): 86.1% Other groups, 6.9% African, 4.0% United States or American, 1.8% Jamaican (2000).
Economy: Employment by occupation: 12.0% management, 5.8% professional, 38.0% services, 23.9% sales, 1.4% farming, 14.5% construction, 4.3% production (2000).
Income: Per capita income: $14,770 (2004); Median household income: $38,871 (2004); Average household income: $44,241 (2004); Percent of households with income of $100,000 or more: 2.8% (2004); Poverty rate: 11.7% (2000).
Education: Percent of population age 25 and over with: High school diploma (including GED) or higher: 61.4% (2004); Bachelor's degree or higher: 7.7% (2004); Master's degree or higher: 0.0% (2004).
Housing: Homeownership rate: 79.9% (2004); Median home value: $81,042 (2004); Median rent: $382 per month (2000); Median age of housing: 12 years (2000).
Transportation: Commute to work: 85.9% car, 9.8% public transportation, 0.0% walk, 4.3% work from home (2000); Travel time to work: 20.8% less than 15 minutes, 21.2% 15 to 30 minutes, 46.9% 30 to 45 minutes, 11.0% 45 to 60 minutes, 0.0% 60 minutes or more (2000)

UNION PARK (CDP). Covers a land area of 2.987 square miles and a water area of 0.034 square miles. Located at 28.56° N. Lat.; 81.23° W. Long. Elevation is 82 feet.
Population: 6,861 (1990); 10,191 (2000); 11,907 (2004); 14,013 (2009 projected); Race: 72.3% White, 7.0% Black, 3.9% Asian, 32.1% Hispanic of any race (2004); Density: 3,986.0 persons per square mile (2004); Average household size: 2.75 (2004); Median age: 31.7 (2004); Male/female ratio: 100.3 (2004); Marriage status: 32.2% never married, 52.4% now married, 3.6% widowed, 11.8% divorced (2000); Foreign born: 10.2% (2000); Ancestry (includes multiple ancestries): 38.7% Other groups, 12.3% German, 10.5% Irish, 8.1% English, 6.8% United States or American (2000).
Economy: Employment by occupation: 10.2% management, 20.3% professional, 15.3% services, 30.7% sales, 0.3% farming, 11.8% construction, 11.4% production (2000).
Income: Per capita income: $20,299 (2004); Median household income: $48,329 (2004); Average household income: $55,681 (2004); Percent of households with income of $100,000 or more: 10.0% (2004); Poverty rate: 11.3% (2000).
Education: Percent of population age 25 and over with: High school diploma (including GED) or higher: 84.0% (2004); Bachelor's degree or higher: 21.0% (2004); Master's degree or higher: 4.8% (2004).
Housing: Homeownership rate: 65.8% (2004); Median home value: $123,081 (2004); Median rent: $675 per month (2000); Median age of housing: 17 years (2000).
Transportation: Commute to work: 96.8% car, 0.4% public transportation, 0.1% walk, 1.4% work from home (2000); Travel time to work: 16.2% less than 15 minutes, 34.7% 15 to 30 minutes, 32.9% 30 to 45 minutes, 11.3% 45 to 60 minutes, 4.9% 60 minutes or more (2000)

WEDGEFIELD (CDP). Covers a land area of 23.421 square miles and a water area of 0.079 square miles. Located at 28.48° N. Lat.; 81.08° W. Long.
Population: 1,091 (1990); 2,700 (2000); 3,339 (2004); 4,126 (2009 projected); Race: 76.3% White, 9.3% Black, 9.3% Asian, 10.8% Hispanic of any race (2004); Density: 142.6 persons per square mile (2004); Average household size: 2.85 (2004); Median age: 38.6 (2004); Male/female ratio: 104.8 (2004); Marriage status: 18.7% never married, 67.5% now married, 4.3% widowed, 9.6% divorced (2000); Foreign born: 15.2% (2000); Ancestry (includes multiple ancestries): 25.6% Other groups, 17.7% Irish, 13.9% German, 10.1% English, 10.1% United States or American (2000).
Economy: Employment by occupation: 21.2% management, 17.6% professional, 15.6% services, 30.6% sales, 0.0% farming, 7.7% construction, 7.2% production (2000).
Income: Per capita income: $27,903 (2004); Median household income: $70,870 (2004); Average household income: $79,562 (2004); Percent of households with income of $100,000 or more: 26.2% (2004); Poverty rate: 5.8% (2000).
Education: Percent of population age 25 and over with: High school diploma (including GED) or higher: 86.3% (2004); Bachelor's degree or higher: 24.4% (2004); Master's degree or higher: 9.3% (2004).
Housing: Homeownership rate: 83.2% (2004); Median home value: $174,205 (2004); Median rent: $888 per month (2000); Median age of housing: 10 years (2000).
Transportation: Commute to work: 94.8% car, 1.1% public transportation, 0.5% walk, 3.6% work from home (2000); Travel time to work: 3.0% less than 15 minutes, 32.1% 15 to 30 minutes, 26.4% 30 to 45 minutes, 27.0% 45 to 60 minutes, 11.5% 60 minutes or more (2000)

WILLIAMSBURG (CDP). Covers a land area of 3.680 square miles and a water area of 0.066 square miles. Located at 28.41° N. Lat.; 81.44° W. Long.
Population: 5,160 (1990); 6,736 (2000); 7,453 (2004); 8,386 (2009 projected); Race: 87.8% White, 2.2% Black, 4.9% Asian, 10.8% Hispanic of any race (2004); Density: 2,025.3 persons per square mile (2004); Average household size: 2.05 (2004); Median age: 52.1 (2004); Male/female ratio: 89.8 (2004); Marriage status: 21.0% never married, 57.2% now married, 10.4% widowed, 11.4% divorced (2000); Foreign born: 15.7% (2000); Ancestry (includes multiple ancestries): 21.6% Other groups, 14.8% German, 13.1% Italian, 12.5% Irish, 9.7% English (2000).
Economy: Employment by occupation: 16.6% management, 17.8% professional, 23.8% services, 32.4% sales, 0.6% farming, 3.7% construction, 5.1% production (2000).

Income: Per capita income: $28,920 (2004); Median household income: $50,602 (2004); Average household income: $59,215 (2004); Percent of households with income of $100,000 or more: 10.9% (2004); Poverty rate: 4.0% (2000).
Education: Percent of population age 25 and over with: High school diploma (including GED) or higher: 87.4% (2004); Bachelor's degree or higher: 29.5% (2004); Master's degree or higher: 8.9% (2004).
Housing: Homeownership rate: 86.3% (2004); Median home value: $150,345 (2004); Median rent: $797 per month (2000); Median age of housing: 14 years (2000).
Transportation: Commute to work: 97.0% car, 0.8% public transportation, 0.2% walk, 1.5% work from home (2000); Travel time to work: 24.6% less than 15 minutes, 56.4% 15 to 30 minutes, 13.4% 30 to 45 minutes, 3.7% 45 to 60 minutes, 2.0% 60 minutes or more (2000)

WINDERMERE (town). Covers a land area of 1.124 square miles and a water area of 0.002 square miles. Located at 28.49° N. Lat.; 81.53° W. Long. Elevation is 150 feet.
Population: 1,643 (1990); 1,897 (2000); 1,974 (2004); 2,099 (2009 projected); Race: 94.7% White, 1.8% Black, 2.3% Asian, 4.2% Hispanic of any race (2004); Density: 1,756.7 persons per square mile (2004); Average household size: 2.70 (2004); Median age: 40.9 (2004); Male/female ratio: 104.8 (2004); Marriage status: 18.9% never married, 67.9% now married, 5.5% widowed, 7.7% divorced (2000); Foreign born: 7.0% (2000); Ancestry (includes multiple ancestries): 21.8% German, 18.6% English, 14.4% Irish, 11.7% Other groups, 8.2% United States or American (2000).
Economy: Employment by occupation: 31.5% management, 26.2% professional, 8.9% services, 25.6% sales, 0.0% farming, 3.9% construction, 3.9% production (2000).
Income: Per capita income: $52,106 (2004); Median household income: $91,477 (2004); Average household income: $140,901 (2004); Percent of households with income of $100,000 or more: 45.9% (2004); Poverty rate: 3.1% (2000).
Taxes: Total city taxes per capita: $502 (2002); City property taxes per capita: $267 (2002).
Education: Percent of population age 25 and over with: High school diploma (including GED) or higher: 97.0% (2004); Bachelor's degree or higher: 54.6% (2004); Master's degree or higher: 17.4% (2004).

School District(s)

Orange County School District (PK-12)
2002-03 Enrollment: 158,718 . . . . (407) 317-3202

Housing: Homeownership rate: 88.6% (2004); Median home value: $418,125 (2004); Median rent: $817 per month (2000); Median age of housing: 27 years (2000).
Safety: Violent crime rate: 25.8 per 10,000 population; Property crime rate: 299.1 per 10,000 population (2003).
Transportation: Commute to work: 91.2% car, 0.6% public transportation, 1.2% walk, 6.2% work from home (2000); Travel time to work: 17.6% less than 15 minutes, 50.2% 15 to 30 minutes, 24.8% 30 to 45 minutes, 3.9% 45 to 60 minutes, 3.5% 60 minutes or more (2000)

WINTER GARDEN (city). Covers a land area of 12.057 square miles and a water area of 0.024 square miles. Located at 28.56° N. Lat.; 81.58° W. Long. Elevation is 126 feet.
History: Named for being a place to escape from cold winters. Winter Garden developed around citrus fruit packing plants.
Population: 11,437 (1990); 14,351 (2000); 19,978 (2004); 26,509 (2009 projected); Race: 73.9% White, 14.1% Black, 1.1% Asian, 20.8% Hispanic of any race (2004); Density: 1,656.9 persons per square mile (2004); Average household size: 2.66 (2004); Median age: 35.8 (2004); Male/female ratio: 92.8 (2004); Marriage status: 22.6% never married, 57.7% now married, 7.6% widowed, 12.1% divorced (2000); Foreign born: 9.7% (2000); Ancestry (includes multiple ancestries): 32.3% Other groups, 11.6% English, 11.4% German, 11.0% United States or American, 10.0% Irish (2000).
Economy: Single-family building permits issued: 1,219 (2004); Multi-family building permits issued: 282 (2004); Employment by occupation: 10.9% management, 16.4% professional, 19.5% services, 27.1% sales, 0.7% farming, 13.3% construction, 12.2% production (2000).
Income: Per capita income: $20,706 (2004); Median household income: $42,733 (2004); Average household income: $54,069 (2004); Percent of households with income of $100,000 or more: 11.6% (2004); Poverty rate: 12.0% (2000).
Taxes: Total city taxes per capita: $331 (2002); City property taxes per capita: $145 (2002).
Education: Percent of population age 25 and over with: High school diploma (including GED) or higher: 78.0% (2004); Bachelor's degree or higher: 18.5% (2004); Master's degree or higher: 4.9% (2004).

School District(s)

Orange County School District (PK-12)
2002-03 Enrollment: 158,718 . . . . (407) 317-3202

Two-year College(s)

Westside Tech (Public)
2003-04 Enrollment: 581 . . . . (407) 905-2018

Housing: Homeownership rate: 64.9% (2004); Median home value: $112,820 (2004); Median rent: $523 per month (2000); Median age of housing: 16 years (2000).
Safety: Violent crime rate: 59.2 per 10,000 population; Property crime rate: 366.3 per 10,000 population (2003).
Newspapers: The West Orange Times (General - Circulation 9,000)
Transportation: Commute to work: 94.9% car, 1.1% public transportation, 1.6% walk, 0.8% work from home (2000); Travel time to work: 22.5% less than 15 minutes, 37.8% 15 to 30 minutes, 29.3% 30 to 45 minutes, 6.1% 45 to 60 minutes, 4.3% 60 minutes or more (2000)

Additional Information Contacts

Local Government Offices . . . . (407) 656-4111
Winter Garden Chamber of Commerce . . . . (407) 656-1304

WINTER PARK (city). Covers a land area of 7.341 square miles and a water area of 1.313 square miles. Located at 28.59° N. Lat.; 81.34° W. Long. Elevation is 94 feet.
History: Named for being a place to escape from cold winters. Winter Park began as Lakeview, founded in 1858. The name was changed to Osceola in 1870, and to Winter Park in 1881 when a new townsite was laid out by a group of New Englanders. The town developed around Rollins College, founded in 1885 by the General Congregational Association.
Population: 24,339 (1990); 24,090 (2000); 24,931 (2004); 26,239 (2009 projected); Race: 84.2% White, 11.6% Black, 1.5% Asian, 5.0% Hispanic of any race (2004); Density: 3,396.1 persons per square mile (2004); Average household size: 2.20 (2004); Median age: 43.4 (2004); Male/female ratio: 84.9 (2004); Marriage status: 25.9% never married, 52.6% now married, 10.1% widowed, 11.4% divorced (2000); Foreign born: 6.6% (2000); Ancestry (includes multiple ancestries): 17.9% English, 17.3% Other groups, 15.3% German, 12.1% Irish, 6.1% United States or American (2000).
Economy: Unemployment rate: 3.3% (2004); Total civilian labor force: 15,785 (2004); Single-family building permits issued: 115 (2004); Multi-family building permits issued: 40 (2004); Employment by occupation: 22.0% management, 31.4% professional, 9.6% services, 27.3% sales, 0.0% farming, 4.2% construction, 5.5% production (2000).
Income: Per capita income: $42,583 (2004); Median household income: $52,953 (2004); Average household income: $93,071 (2004); Percent of households with income of $100,000 or more: 25.8% (2004); Poverty rate: 7.8% (2000).
Taxes: Total city taxes per capita: $705 (2002); City property taxes per capita: $339 (2002).
Education: Percent of population age 25 and over with: High school diploma (including GED) or higher: 92.1% (2004); Bachelor's degree or higher: 49.3% (2004); Master's degree or higher: 19.4% (2004).

School District(s)

Orange County School District (PK-12)
2002-03 Enrollment: 158,718 . . . . (407) 317-3202

Four-year College(s)

Herzing College (Private, For-profit)
2003-04 Enrollment: 110 . . . . (407) 478-0500
2003-04 Tuition: In-state $9,450; Out-of-state $9,450
Rollins College
2003-04 Enrollment: 3,829 . . . . (407) 646-2000
2003-04 Tuition: In-state $26,250; Out-of-state $26,250

Two-year College(s)

Central Florida College (Private, For-profit)
2003-04 Enrollment: 265 . . . . (407) 843-3984
Florida Institute of Animal Arts
2003-04 Enrollment: 61 . . . . (407) 657-5033
Full Sail Real World Education (Private, For-profit)
2003-04 Enrollment: 4,332 . . . . (407) 679-0100
Winter Park Tech (Public)
2003-04 Enrollment: 554 . . . . (407) 622-2900

Housing: Homeownership rate: 64.3% (2004); Median home value: $235,923 (2004); Median rent: $584 per month (2000); Median age of housing: 36 years (2000).
Hospitals: Winter Park Memorial Hospital (334 beds)
Safety: Violent crime rate: 27.2 per 10,000 population; Property crime rate: 392.7 per 10,000 population (2003).
Transportation: Commute to work: 87.6% car, 1.6% public transportation, 4.0% walk, 5.5% work from home (2000); Travel time to work: 30.7% less than 15 minutes, 42.3% 15 to 30 minutes, 19.7% 30 to 45 minutes, 4.1% 45 to 60 minutes, 3.1% 60 minutes or more (2000); Amtrak: Service available.

Additional Information Contacts
Local Government Offices .... (407) 599-3235
Winter Park Chamber of Commerce .... (407) 644-8281

ZELLWOOD (CDP). Covers a land area of 3.888 square miles and a water area of 0.184 square miles. Located at 28.72° N. Lat.; 81.59° W. Long. Elevation is 99 feet.
History: Zellwood was settled and named by Elwood Zell, a Philadelphia publisher, and became a winter destination for northern visitors.
Population: 2,813 (1990); 2,540 (2000); 2,529 (2004); 2,566 (2009 projected); Race: 94.3% White, 2.1% Black, 0.0% Asian, 10.2% Hispanic of any race (2004); Density: 650.4 persons per square mile (2004); Average household size: 1.97 (2004); Median age: 64.8 (2004); Male/female ratio: 86.8 (2004); Marriage status: 11.3% never married, 68.5% now married, 14.6% widowed, 5.6% divorced (2000); Foreign born: 9.1% (2000); Ancestry (includes multiple ancestries): 18.0% German, 15.4% Other groups, 14.6% English, 14.6% Irish, 8.8% United States or American (2000).
Economy: Employment by occupation: 12.8% management, 8.7% professional, 17.5% services, 33.7% sales, 1.2% farming, 11.6% construction, 14.4% production (2000).
Income: Per capita income: $22,798 (2004); Median household income: $31,667 (2004); Average household income: $43,694 (2004); Percent of households with income of $100,000 or more: 7.2% (2004); Poverty rate: 11.9% (2000).
Education: Percent of population age 25 and over with: High school diploma (including GED) or higher: 71.3% (2004); Bachelor's degree or higher: 12.0% (2004); Master's degree or higher: 1.3% (2004).

School District(s)
Orange County School District (PK-12)
2002-03 Enrollment: 158,718 .... (407) 317-3202
Housing: Homeownership rate: 90.0% (2004); Median home value: $87,566 (2004); Median rent: $443 per month (2000); Median age of housing: 17 years (2000).
Transportation: Commute to work: 87.3% car, 2.3% public transportation, 7.9% walk, 1.4% work from home (2000); Travel time to work: 20.7% less than 15 minutes, 20.3% 15 to 30 minutes, 41.9% 30 to 45 minutes, 3.0% 45 to 60 minutes, 14.1% 60 minutes or more (2000)

Osceola County

Located in central Florida; lowland area, includes Lakes Kissimmee, Tohopekaliga, East Tohopekaliga, and other lakes. Covers a land area of 1,321.90 square miles, a water area of 184.50 square miles, and is located in the Eastern Time Zone. The county government was organized in 1887. County seat is Kissimmee.

Osceola County is part of the Orlando-Kissimmee, FL Metropolitan Statistical Area. The entire metro area includes: Lake County, FL; Orange County, FL; Osceola County, FL; Seminole County, FL

Weather Station: Kissimmee 2 — Elevation: 59 feet

	Jan	Feb	Mar	Apr	May	Jun	Jul	Aug	Sep	Oct	Nov	Dec
High	73	75	79	83	88	91	92	92	90	85	80	75
Low	50	51	56	59	65	71	72	73	72	65	58	52
Precip	2.4	2.8	3.6	2.0	3.9	6.0	6.6	7.2	5.9	3.2	2.4	2.2
Snow	0.0	0.0	0.0	0.0	0.0	0.0	0.0	0.0	0.0	0.0	0.0	0.0

High and Low temperatures in degrees Fahrenheit; Precipitation and Snow in inches

Population: 107,728 (1990); 172,493 (2000); 207,559 (2004); 251,568 (2009 projected); Race: 73.8% White, 8.2% Black, 2.3% Asian, 35.3% Hispanic of any race (2004); Density: 157.0 persons per square mile (2004); Average household size: 2.84 (2004); Median age: 34.6 (2004); Male/female ratio: 98.1 (2004).
Religion: Five largest groups: 11.0% Catholic Church, 5.3% Southern Baptist Convention, 2.1% The United Methodist Church, 1.5% Christian Churches and Churches of Christ, 1.2% Assemblies of God (2000).
Economy: Unemployment rate: 5.1% (2004); Total civilian labor force: 107,184 (2004); Leading industries: 21.1% accommodation & food services; 18.2% retail trade; 12.8% health care and social assistance (2003); Companies that employ 500 or more persons: 7 (2003); Companies that employ 100 to 499 persons: 67 (2003); Companies that employ less than 100 persons: 3,909 (2003); Farms: 519 totaling 652,673 acres (2002); Minority business ownership rate: 15.5% (1997); Women business ownership rate: 25.5% (1997); Retail sales per capita: $9,579 (1997). Single-family building permits issued: 6,316 (2004); Multi-family building permits issued: 2,754 (2004).
Income: Per capita income: $18,093 (2004); Median household income: $41,008 (2004); Average household income: $50,970 (2004); Percent of households with income of $100,000 or more: 8.2% (2004); Poverty rate: 13.4% (2002); Bankruptcy rate: 6.59% (2004).
Taxes: Total county taxes per capita: $628 (2002); County property taxes per capita: $336 (2002).
Education: Percent of population age 25 and over with: High school diploma (including GED) or higher: 79.4% (2004); Bachelor's degree or higher: 15.9% (2004); Master's degree or higher: 4.9% (2004).
Housing: Homeownership rate: 68.4% (2004); Median home value: $127,092 (2004); Median rent: $610 per month (2000); Median age of housing: 13 years (2000).
Health: Birth rate: 135.4 per 10,000 population (2004); Death rate: 61.5 per 10,000 population (2004); Age adjusted cancer mortality rate: 172.1 deaths per 100,000 population (2002); Air Quality Index: 96.5% good, 3.5% moderate, 0.0% unhealthy for sensitive individuals, 0.0% unhealthy (percent of days in 2004); Number of physicians: 10.4 per 10,000 population (2001); Hospital beds: 11.8 per 10,000 population (2002); Hospital admissions: 775.0 per 10,000 population (2002).
Elections: 2004 Presidential election results: 52.5% Bush, 47.0% Kerry, 0.3% Nader, 0.1% Badnarik

Additional Information Contacts
Osceola County Government Offices .... (407) 847-1200
Kissimmee Osceola Chamber of Commerce .... (407) 847-3174
Osceola County Association of Realtors .... (407) 846-0117
St. Cloud/Greater Osceola Co. Chamber .... (407) 892-3671

Osceola County Communities

CAMPBELL (CDP). Covers a land area of 1.873 square miles and a water area of 0.027 square miles. Located at 28.26° N. Lat.; 81.45° W. Long. Elevation is 73 feet.
Population: 3,353 (1990); 2,677 (2000); 2,987 (2004); 3,397 (2009 projected); Race: 93.2% White, 1.1% Black, 1.0% Asian, 5.3% Hispanic of any race (2004); Density: 1,594.5 persons per square mile (2004); Average household size: 1.97 (2004); Median age: 66.1 (2004); Male/female ratio: 74.1 (2004); Marriage status: 16.1% never married, 49.4% now married, 24.7% widowed, 9.9% divorced (2000); Foreign born: 5.4% (2000); Ancestry (includes multiple ancestries): 20.0% English, 13.9% German, 10.4% United States or American, 10.1% Other groups, 7.4% Irish (2000).
Economy: Employment by occupation: 5.4% management, 6.7% professional, 25.9% services, 34.0% sales, 1.0% farming, 15.1% construction, 11.8% production (2000).
Income: Per capita income: $18,993 (2004); Median household income: $30,392 (2004); Average household income: $36,562 (2004); Percent of households with income of $100,000 or more: 4.0% (2004); Poverty rate: 13.5% (2000).
Education: Percent of population age 25 and over with: High school diploma (including GED) or higher: 76.8% (2004); Bachelor's degree or higher: 13.7% (2004); Master's degree or higher: 5.7% (2004).
Housing: Homeownership rate: 54.0% (2004); Median home value: $57,861 (2004); Median rent: $702 per month (2000); Median age of housing: 24 years (2000).
Transportation: Commute to work: 88.3% car, 0.0% public transportation, 0.0% walk, 4.4% work from home (2000); Travel time to work: 21.2% less than 15 minutes, 39.4% 15 to 30 minutes, 21.2% 30 to 45 minutes, 7.7% 45 to 60 minutes, 10.6% 60 minutes or more (2000)

CELEBRATION (CDP). Covers a land area of 10.669 square miles and a water area of 0.028 square miles. Located at 28.32° N. Lat.; 81.54° W. Long.

Population: 1,245 (1990); 2,736 (2000); 3,191 (2004); 3,758 (2009 projected); Race: 93.0% White, 2.0% Black, 2.6% Asian, 8.5% Hispanic of any race (2004); Density: 299.1 persons per square mile (2004); Average household size: 2.84 (2004); Median age: 36.6 (2004); Male/female ratio: 95.0 (2004); Marriage status: 22.2% never married, 67.6% now married, 5.8% widowed, 4.4% divorced (2000); Foreign born: 7.8% (2000); Ancestry (includes multiple ancestries): 16.9% Irish, 14.7% German, 14.5% Other groups, 11.6% Italian, 11.3% English (2000).
Economy: Employment by occupation: 33.5% management, 23.1% professional, 15.0% services, 18.2% sales, 0.0% farming, 4.7% construction, 5.5% production (2000).
Income: Per capita income: $47,315 (2004); Median household income: $84,916 (2004); Average household income: $133,458 (2004); Percent of households with income of $100,000 or more: 38.8% (2004); Poverty rate: 6.2% (2000).
Education: Percent of population age 25 and over with: High school diploma (including GED) or higher: 93.8% (2004); Bachelor's degree or higher: 57.4% (2004); Master's degree or higher: 21.7% (2004).

School District(s)

Osceola County School District (PK-12)
2002-03 Enrollment: 40,485 . . . . (407) 870-4008

Housing: Homeownership rate: 62.7% (2004); Median home value: $481,056 (2004); Median rent: $873 per month (2000); Median age of housing: 3 years (2000).
Transportation: Commute to work: 76.6% car, 0.0% public transportation, 5.6% walk, 15.9% work from home (2000); Travel time to work: 45.2% less than 15 minutes, 30.7% 15 to 30 minutes, 18.2% 30 to 45 minutes, 2.0% 45 to 60 minutes, 4.0% 60 minutes or more (2000)

KENANSVILLE

KENANSVILLE (unincorporated postal area, zip code 34739). Covers a land area of 353.332 square miles and a water area of 12.101 square miles. Located at 27.93° N. Lat.; 81.09° W. Long. Elevation is 74 feet.
Population: 828 (2000); Race: 97.5% White, 0.0% Black, 0.0% Asian, 9.4% Hispanic of any race (2000); Density: 2.3 persons per square mile (2000); Age: 20.5% under 18, 22.5% over 64 (2000); Marriage status: 17.7% never married, 64.8% now married, 8.4% widowed, 9.2% divorced (2000); Foreign born: 8.2% (2000); Ancestry (includes multiple ancestries): 19.2% Other groups, 15.3% Irish, 14.3% United States or American, 13.5% English, 10.5% German (2000).
Economy: Employment by occupation: 6.6% management, 4.3% professional, 16.9% services, 15.0% sales, 9.0% farming, 29.9% construction, 18.3% production (2000).
Income: Per capita income: $19,293 (2000); Median household income: $36,645 (2000); Poverty rate: 13.4% (2000).
Education: Percent of population age 25 and over with: High school diploma (including GED) or higher: 73.5% (2000); Bachelor's degree or higher: 9.2% (2000).
Housing: Homeownership rate: 75.2% (2000); Median home value: $133,300 (2000); Median rent: $310 per month (2000); Median age of housing: 17 years (2000).
Transportation: Commute to work: 82.3% car, 0.0% public transportation, 9.9% walk, 4.1% work from home (2000); Travel time to work: 29.5% less than 15 minutes, 23.8% 15 to 30 minutes, 15.7% 30 to 45 minutes, 10.7% 45 to 60 minutes, 20.3% 60 minutes or more (2000)

KISSIMMEE

KISSIMMEE (city). Covers a land area of 16.680 square miles and a water area of 0.636 square miles. Located at 28.30° N. Lat.; 81.41° W. Long. Elevation is 70 feet.
History: Named for the Seminole-Creek translation of "mulberry". The area around Kissimmee was settled by cattle ranchers who acquired Spanish land grants in the early 1800s. There was a trading post here in 1881, when the railroad was built from Orlando. Soon sugarcane plantations and sugar mills were established, and the settlement flourished.
Population: 32,042 (1990); 47,814 (2000); 52,198 (2004); 58,238 (2009 projected); Race: 62.4% White, 10.4% Black, 3.6% Asian, 50.9% Hispanic of any race (2004); Density: 3,129.5 persons per square mile (2004); Average household size: 2.80 (2004); Median age: 30.8 (2004); Male/female ratio: 99.3 (2004); Marriage status: 30.4% never married, 52.6% now married, 4.6% widowed, 12.4% divorced (2000); Foreign born: 19.5% (2000); Ancestry (includes multiple ancestries): 49.4% Other groups, 8.8% German, 7.1% Irish, 6.3% United States or American, 6.3% English (2000).
Economy: Unemployment rate: 5.9% (2004); Total civilian labor force: 34,119 (2004); Single-family building permits issued: 1,039 (2004); Multi-family building permits issued: 341 (2004); Employment by occupation: 8.9% management, 11.8% professional, 27.9% services, 29.7% sales, 0.2% farming, 11.2% construction, 10.3% production (2000).
Income: Per capita income: $15,270 (2004); Median household income: $34,304 (2004); Average household income: $42,485 (2004); Percent of households with income of $100,000 or more: 4.3% (2004); Poverty rate: 15.4% (2000).
Taxes: Total city taxes per capita: $283 (2002); City property taxes per capita: $127 (2002).
Education: Percent of population age 25 and over with: High school diploma (including GED) or higher: 78.5% (2004); Bachelor's degree or higher: 16.8% (2004); Master's degree or higher: 4.7% (2004).

School District(s)

Osceola County School District (PK-12)
2002-03 Enrollment: 40,485 . . . . (407) 870-4008

Four-year College(s)

Florida Christian College Inc
2003-04 Enrollment: 259 . . . . (407) 847-8966
2003-04 Tuition: In-state $8,390; Out-of-state $8,390

Two-year College(s)

Technical Education Center-Osceola (Public)
2003-04 Enrollment: 296 . . . . (407) 344-5080

Housing: Homeownership rate: 44.0% (2004); Median home value: $124,068 (2004); Median rent: $619 per month (2000); Median age of housing: 14 years (2000).
Hospitals: Florida Hospital Kissimmee (50 beds); Osceola Regional Medical Center (171 beds)
Safety: Violent crime rate: 106.6 per 10,000 population; Property crime rate: 607.7 per 10,000 population (2003).
Newspapers: Osceola News-Gazette (General - Circulation 29,000); South Orange News (General - Circulation 21,000)
Transportation: Commute to work: 93.3% car, 2.0% public transportation, 1.9% walk, 1.2% work from home (2000); Travel time to work: 21.8% less than 15 minutes, 41.2% 15 to 30 minutes, 25.2% 30 to 45 minutes, 6.6% 45 to 60 minutes, 5.2% 60 minutes or more (2000); Amtrak: Service available.

Additional Information Contacts

Kissimmee Osceola Chamber of Commerce. . . . . (407) 847-3174
Local Government Offices . . . . (407) 518-2308
Osceola County Association of Realtors . . . . (407) 846-0117

POINCIANA

POINCIANA (CDP). Covers a land area of 35.106 square miles and a water area of 0.238 square miles. Located at 28.15° N. Lat.; 81.47° W. Long.
Population: 4,687 (1990); 13,647 (2000); 21,246 (2004); 30,353 (2009 projected); Race: 60.7% White, 19.7% Black, 1.0% Asian, 46.4% Hispanic of any race (2004); Density: 605.2 persons per square mile (2004); Average household size: 3.32 (2004); Median age: 30.5 (2004); Male/female ratio: 96.1 (2004); Marriage status: 25.1% never married, 62.3% now married, 3.9% widowed, 8.7% divorced (2000); Foreign born: 15.2% (2000); Ancestry (includes multiple ancestries): 49.1% Other groups, 9.8% German, 8.6% Irish, 7.2% Italian, 4.4% English (2000).
Economy: Employment by occupation: 9.3% management, 10.3% professional, 28.2% services, 29.3% sales, 0.0% farming, 11.4% construction, 11.6% production (2000).
Income: Per capita income: $12,502 (2004); Median household income: $37,978 (2004); Average household income: $41,568 (2004); Percent of households with income of $100,000 or more: 2.3% (2004); Poverty rate: 12.8% (2000).
Education: Percent of population age 25 and over with: High school diploma (including GED) or higher: 77.7% (2004); Bachelor's degree or higher: 9.7% (2004); Master's degree or higher: 3.4% (2004).
Housing: Homeownership rate: 79.1% (2004); Median home value: $123,534 (2004); Median rent: $618 per month (2000); Median age of housing: 8 years (2000).
Transportation: Commute to work: 97.4% car, 0.7% public transportation, 0.4% walk, 0.3% work from home (2000); Travel time to work: 7.8% less than 15 minutes, 19.9% 15 to 30 minutes, 40.0% 30 to 45 minutes, 22.1% 45 to 60 minutes, 10.0% 60 minutes or more (2000)

SAINT CLOUD

SAINT CLOUD (city). Covers a land area of 9.163 square miles and a water area of 0.009 square miles. Located at 28.24° N. Lat.; 81.28° W. Long. Elevation is 75 feet.
History: Named for Saint Cloud, 524-560, grandson of King Clovis I of France. St. Cloud was founded in the early 1880s as a cattle shipping center. In 1909 many veterans of the Grand Army of the Republic settled

here, bringing the nickname of the G.A.R. Town to St. Cloud. The town was the center of a reclamation project that drained swamps to form pasture and crop lands.

Population: 13,703 (1990); 20,074 (2000); 22,616 (2004); 25,926 (2009 projected); Race: 88.0% White, 2.4% Black, 1.0% Asian, 17.8% Hispanic of any race (2004); Density: 2,468.2 persons per square mile (2004); Average household size: 2.62 (2004); Median age: 36.7 (2004); Male/female ratio: 92.3 (2004); Marriage status: 17.5% never married, 60.6% now married, 8.7% widowed, 13.2% divorced (2000); Foreign born: 6.2% (2000); Ancestry (includes multiple ancestries): 20.9% Other groups, 17.2% German, 16.4% Irish, 10.6% English, 8.8% United States or American (2000).

Economy: Single-family building permits issued: 524 (2004); Multi-family building permits issued: 9 (2004); Employment by occupation: 9.4% management, 13.9% professional, 21.2% services, 29.6% sales, 0.3% farming, 12.9% construction, 12.7% production (2000).

Income: Per capita income: $18,208 (2004); Median household income: $39,651 (2004); Average household income: $47,181 (2004); Percent of households with income of $100,000 or more: 6.2% (2004); Poverty rate: 8.1% (2000).

Taxes: Total city taxes per capita: $363 (2002); City property taxes per capita: $102 (2002).

Education: Percent of population age 25 and over with: High school diploma (including GED) or higher: 79.4% (2004); Bachelor's degree or higher: 14.0% (2004); Master's degree or higher: 3.7% (2004).

School District(s)

Osceola County School District (PK-12)
2002-03 Enrollment: 40,485 . . . . (407) 870-4008

Housing: Homeownership rate: 71.5% (2004); Median home value: $120,402 (2004); Median rent: $516 per month (2000); Median age of housing: 19 years (2000).

Hospitals: Orlando Regional St. Cloud Hospital (84 beds)

Safety: Violent crime rate: 51.0 per 10,000 population; Property crime rate: 481.9 per 10,000 population (2003).

Transportation: Commute to work: 94.3% car, 0.7% public transportation, 1.3% walk, 1.6% work from home (2000); Travel time to work: 24.1% less than 15 minutes, 26.1% 15 to 30 minutes, 31.5% 30 to 45 minutes, 11.0% 45 to 60 minutes, 7.3% 60 minutes or more (2000)

Additional Information Contacts

Local Government Offices . . . . (407) 957-7300
St. Cloud/Greater Osceola Co. Chamber . . . . (407) 892-3671

YEEHAW JUNCTION (CDP). Covers a land area of 5.596 square miles and a water area of 0.023 square miles. Located at 28.33° N. Lat.; 81.35° W. Long. Elevation is 67 feet.

Population: 14,383 (1990); 21,778 (2000); 25,805 (2004); 30,928 (2009 projected); Race: 57.9% White, 13.1% Black, 2.8% Asian, 61.6% Hispanic of any race (2004); Density: 4,611.7 persons per square mile (2004); Average household size: 3.18 (2004); Median age: 33.4 (2004); Male/female ratio: 94.4 (2004); Marriage status: 25.3% never married, 59.4% now married, 5.6% widowed, 9.7% divorced (2000); Foreign born: 19.8% (2000); Ancestry (includes multiple ancestries): 59.0% Other groups, 5.6% Irish, 5.1% German, 4.8% United States or American, 4.3% Italian (2000).

Economy: Employment by occupation: 8.9% management, 10.5% professional, 23.5% services, 31.7% sales, 0.2% farming, 11.5% construction, 13.8% production (2000).

Income: Per capita income: $15,839 (2004); Median household income: $41,589 (2004); Average household income: $49,848 (2004); Percent of households with income of $100,000 or more: 7.2% (2004); Poverty rate: 10.2% (2000).

Education: Percent of population age 25 and over with: High school diploma (including GED) or higher: 74.9% (2004); Bachelor's degree or higher: 13.3% (2004); Master's degree or higher: 3.5% (2004).

Housing: Homeownership rate: 73.7% (2004); Median home value: $122,472 (2004); Median rent: $653 per month (2000); Median age of housing: 13 years (2000).

Transportation: Commute to work: 96.2% car, 0.7% public transportation, 0.7% walk, 1.0% work from home (2000); Travel time to work: 12.4% less than 15 minutes, 45.7% 15 to 30 minutes, 30.6% 30 to 45 minutes, 5.1% 45 to 60 minutes, 6.2% 60 minutes or more (2000)

Palm Beach County

Located in southeastern Florida; bounded on the east by the Atlantic Ocean; includes Lake Okeechobee. Covers a land area of 1,974.10 square miles, a water area of 412.20 square miles, and is located in the Eastern Time Zone. The county government was organized in 1909. County seat is West Palm Beach.

Palm Beach County is part of the Miami-Fort Lauderdale-Miami Beach, FL Metropolitan Statistical Area. The entire metro area includes: Fort Lauderdale-Pompano Beach-Deerfield Beach, FL Metropolitan Division (Broward County, FL); Miami-Miami Beach-Kendall, FL Metropolitan Division (Miami-Dade County, FL); West Palm Beach-Boca Raton-Boynton Beach, FL Metropolitan Division (Palm Beach County, FL)

Weather Station: Belle Glade Exp. Station — Elevation: 13 feet

	Jan	Feb	Mar	Apr	May	Jun	Jul	Aug	Sep	Oct	Nov	Dec
High	75	76	80	84	87	90	91	91	90	86	81	76
Low	52	52	57	59	65	70	71	71	70	66	60	54
Precip	2.6	1.9	3.1	2.2	5.2	7.4	7.4	7.4	7.1	3.5	2.8	1.8
Snow	tr	0.0	0.0	0.0	0.0	0.0	0.0	0.0	0.0	0.0	0.0	0.0

High and Low temperatures in degrees Fahrenheit; Precipitation and Snow in inches

Weather Station: Canal Point USDA — Elevation: 29 feet

	Jan	Feb	Mar	Apr	May	Jun	Jul	Aug	Sep	Oct	Nov	Dec
High	74	76	80	84	88	90	92	92	90	86	81	76
Low	53	54	58	61	66	70	71	71	71	67	61	56
Precip	2.7	2.3	3.8	2.2	4.8	7.5	6.3	7.0	7.0	3.9	2.9	2.1
Snow	0.0	0.0	0.0	0.0	0.0	0.0	0.0	0.0	0.0	0.0	0.0	0.0

High and Low temperatures in degrees Fahrenheit; Precipitation and Snow in inches

Weather Station: West Palm Beach Int'l Airport — Elevation: 16 feet

	Jan	Feb	Mar	Apr	May	Jun	Jul	Aug	Sep	Oct	Nov	Dec
High	75	76	79	82	86	89	90	90	89	85	80	77
Low	57	58	62	65	70	74	75	75	75	71	66	60
Precip	3.9	2.6	4.0	3.5	5.6	7.8	5.9	6.7	8.1	5.4	5.4	3.1
Snow	tr	0.0	tr	0.0	0.0	0.0	0.0	tr	0.0	0.0	0.0	0.0

High and Low temperatures in degrees Fahrenheit; Precipitation and Snow in inches

Population: 863,518 (1990); 1,131,184 (2000); 1,231,398 (2004); 1,357,618 (2009 projected); Race: 76.5% White, 15.0% Black, 1.8% Asian, 15.4% Hispanic of any race (2004); Density: 623.8 persons per square mile (2004); Average household size: 2.39 (2004); Median age: 42.2 (2004); Male/female ratio: 94.0 (2004).

Religion: Five largest groups: 26.6% Catholic Church, 14.8% Jewish Estimate, 3.7% Southern Baptist Convention, 1.6% The United Methodist Church, 1.3% Independent, Non-Charismatic Churches (2000).

Economy: Unemployment rate: 5.5% (2004); Total civilian labor force: 601,066 (2004); Leading industries: 15.3% retail trade; 13.2% health care and social assistance; 10.7% accommodation & food services (2003); Companies that employ 500 or more persons: 67 (2003); Companies that employ 100 to 499 persons: 623 (2003); Companies that employ less than 100 persons: 38,895 (2003); Farms: 1,110 totaling 535,965 acres (2002); Minority business ownership rate: 12.7% (1997); Women business ownership rate: 26.4% (1997); Retail sales per capita: $11,561 (1997). Single-family building permits issued: 10,266 (2004); Multi-family building permits issued: 4,253 (2004).

Income: Per capita income: $31,340 (2004); Median household income: $49,358 (2004); Average household income: $74,309 (2004); Percent of households with income of $100,000 or more: 19.4% (2004); Poverty rate: 10.7% (2002); Bankruptcy rate: 3.19% (2004).

Taxes: Total county taxes per capita: $540 (2002); County property taxes per capita: $400 (2002).

Education: Percent of population age 25 and over with: High school diploma (including GED) or higher: 83.9% (2004); Bachelor's degree or higher: 28.0% (2004); Master's degree or higher: 10.2% (2004).

Housing: Homeownership rate: 75.1% (2004); Median home value: $152,861 (2004); Median rent: $648 per month (2000); Median age of housing: 19 years (2000).

Health: Birth rate: 119.9 per 10,000 population (2004); Death rate: 112.9 per 10,000 population (2004); Age adjusted cancer mortality rate: 175.7 deaths per 100,000 population (2002); Air Quality Index: 89.4% good, 10.6% moderate, 0.0% unhealthy for sensitive individuals, 0.0% unhealthy (percent of days in 2004); Number of physicians: 28.3 per 10,000 population (2001); Hospital beds: 33.7 per 10,000 population (2002); Hospital admissions: 1,460.0 per 10,000 population (2002).

Elections: 2004 Presidential election results: 39.1% Bush, 60.4% Kerry, 0.3% Nader, 0.1% Badnarik

National and State Parks: John D MacArthur Beach State Park; Loxahatchee National Wildlife Refuge; Mar-A-Lago National Historical Site; Pahokee State Park; Palm Beach Pines State Recreation Area

Additional Information Contacts

Palm Beach County Government Offices . . . . (561) 355-2001
Belle Glade Chamber of Commerce . . . . (561) 996-2745
Boca Raton Chamber of Commerce . . . . (561) 395-4433
Boynton Beach Chamber of Commerce . . . . (561) 732-9501
Delray Beach Chamber of Commerce . . . . (561) 278-0424
Hispanic Chamber of Commerce . . . . (561) 832-1986
Jupiter Chamber of Commerce . . . . (561) 746-7111
Jupiter Tequesta Hobe Sound Association of Realtors . . . . (561) 746-2707
Lake Worth Chamber of Commerce . . . . (561) 582-4401
Loxahatchee Chamber of Commerce . . . . (561) 790-6200
Pahokee Chamber of Commerce . . . . (561) 924-5579
Palm Beach Board of Realtors . . . . (561) 659-3810
Palm Beach Chamber of Commerce . . . . (561) 655-3282
Palm Beach Gardens Chamber of Commerce . . . . (561) 694-2300
Realtors Association of The Palm Beaches . . . . (561) 688-9294
West Palm Beach Chamber of Commerce . . . . (561) 833-3711

Palm Beach County Communities

ATLANTIS (city). Covers a land area of 1.371 square miles and a water area of 0.041 square miles. Located at 26.59° N. Lat.; 80.10° W. Long. Elevation is 15 feet.

Population: 1,658 (1990); 2,005 (2000); 2,154 (2004); 2,350 (2009 projected); Race: 96.6% White, 0.7% Black, 2.3% Asian, 2.9% Hispanic of any race (2004); Density: 1,571.7 persons per square mile (2004); Average household size: 1.92 (2004); Median age: 65.1 (2004); Male/female ratio: 87.0 (2004); Marriage status: 10.7% never married, 71.7% now married, 13.8% widowed, 3.8% divorced (2000); Foreign born: 12.6% (2000); Ancestry (includes multiple ancestries): 21.7% German, 18.1% English, 13.5% Irish, 10.0% Italian, 6.9% Other groups (2000).

Economy: Manufacturing of trophies and medical supplies. Heavily guarded community, fenced off from surrounding municipalities. Single-family building permits issued: 3 (2004); Multi-family building permits issued: 0 (2004); Employment by occupation: 21.6% management, 23.7% professional, 16.7% services, 29.9% sales, 0.8% farming, 4.3% construction, 2.9% production (2000).

Income: Per capita income: $53,883 (2004); Median household income: $73,005 (2004); Average household income: $103,261 (2004); Percent of households with income of $100,000 or more: 30.9% (2004); Poverty rate: 4.0% (2000).

Education: Percent of population age 25 and over with: High school diploma (including GED) or higher: 93.7% (2004); Bachelor's degree or higher: 40.4% (2004); Master's degree or higher: 18.6% (2004).

Two-year College(s)

Medvance Institute-Atlantis (Private, For-profit)
2003-04 Enrollment: 421 . . . . (561) 304-3466

Housing: Homeownership rate: 95.3% (2004); Median home value: $264,757 (2004); Median rent: $675 per month (2000); Median age of housing: 24 years (2000).

Hospitals: JFK Medical Center (387 beds)

Safety: Violent crime rate: 37.3 per 10,000 population; Property crime rate: 326.0 per 10,000 population (2003).

Transportation: Commute to work: 94.0% car, 0.0% public transportation, 0.0% walk, 6.0% work from home (2000); Travel time to work: 41.9% less than 15 minutes, 36.8% 15 to 30 minutes, 13.7% 30 to 45 minutes, 5.1% 45 to 60 minutes, 2.5% 60 minutes or more (2000)

BELLE GLADE (city). Covers a land area of 4.649 square miles and a water area of 0.009 square miles. Located at 26.68° N. Lat.; 80.67° W. Long. Elevation is 20 feet.

History: Named for a tourist's comment in 1921 — "belle of the Glades" referring to the Everglade section of the state. Belle Glade sprang into existence in 1925 and was destroyed just as quickly in 1928 by a hurricane. The town was rebuilt and grew as a trading center for a truck-farming area.

Population: 16,429 (1990); 14,906 (2000); 15,075 (2004); 15,409 (2009 projected); Race: 30.3% White, 50.4% Black, 0.2% Asian, 30.8% Hispanic of any race (2004); Density: 3,242.5 persons per square mile (2004); Average household size: 3.10 (2004); Median age: 30.0 (2004); Male/female ratio: 103.8 (2004); Marriage status: 38.1% never married, 48.6% now married, 6.4% widowed, 6.9% divorced (2000); Foreign born: 30.0% (2000); Ancestry (includes multiple ancestries): 53.7% Other groups, 9.8% Haitian, 8.5% United States or American, 3.0% English, 2.5% Jamaican (2000).

Economy: Single-family building permits issued: 9 (2004); Multi-family building permits issued: 2 (2004); Employment by occupation: 6.0% management, 16.1% professional, 15.3% services, 19.6% sales, 15.1% farming, 11.5% construction, 16.2% production (2000).

Income: Per capita income: $11,711 (2004); Median household income: $24,421 (2004); Average household income: $35,484 (2004); Percent of households with income of $100,000 or more: 4.7% (2004); Poverty rate: 32.9% (2000).

Taxes: Total city taxes per capita: $303 (2002); City property taxes per capita: $132 (2002).

Education: Percent of population age 25 and over with: High school diploma (including GED) or higher: 47.0% (2004); Bachelor's degree or higher: 10.0% (2004); Master's degree or higher: 3.8% (2004).

School District(s)

Palm Beach County School District (PK-12)
2002-03 Enrollment: 164,896 . . . . (561) 434-8200

Housing: Homeownership rate: 42.0% (2004); Median home value: $91,563 (2004); Median rent: $319 per month (2000); Median age of housing: 31 years (2000).

Hospitals: Glades General Hospital (73 beds)

Safety: Violent crime rate: 297.7 per 10,000 population; Property crime rate: 999.8 per 10,000 population (2003).

Transportation: Commute to work: 79.7% car, 14.3% public transportation, 3.0% walk, 0.9% work from home (2000); Travel time to work: 43.0% less than 15 minutes, 21.8% 15 to 30 minutes, 16.0% 30 to 45 minutes, 5.8% 45 to 60 minutes, 13.4% 60 minutes or more (2000)

Additional Information Contacts

Belle Glade Chamber of Commerce . . . . (561) 996-2745
Local Government Offices . . . . (561) 996-0100

BELLE GLADE CAMP (CDP). Covers a land area of 0.479 square miles and a water area of 0 square miles. Located at 26.66° N. Lat.; 80.68° W. Long.

Population: 1,616 (1990); 1,141 (2000); 996 (2004); 847 (2009 projected); Race: 19.7% White, 58.2% Black, 0.0% Asian, 34.0% Hispanic of any race (2004); Density: 2,077.8 persons per square mile (2004); Average household size: 3.98 (2004); Median age: 20.0 (2004); Male/female ratio: 90.1 (2004); Marriage status: 52.6% never married, 30.1% now married, 6.7% widowed, 10.6% divorced (2000); Foreign born: 21.9% (2000); Ancestry (includes multiple ancestries): 48.3% Other groups, 22.5% Haitian, 5.0% Jamaican, 2.1% United States or American, 1.6% African (2000).

Economy: Employment by occupation: 0.0% management, 9.3% professional, 17.6% services, 9.3% sales, 39.3% farming, 0.0% construction, 24.5% production (2000).

Income: Per capita income: $5,296 (2004); Median household income: $18,654 (2004); Average household income: $21,100 (2004); Percent of households with income of $100,000 or more: 0.0% (2004); Poverty rate: 62.1% (2000).

Education: Percent of population age 25 and over with: High school diploma (including GED) or higher: 24.9% (2004); Bachelor's degree or higher: 4.7% (2004); Master's degree or higher: 0.0% (2004).

Housing: Homeownership rate: 0.0% (2004); Median home value: $n/a (2004); Median rent: $308 per month (2000); Median age of housing: 28 years (2000).

Transportation: Commute to work: 75.5% car, 22.9% public transportation, 0.0% walk, 0.0% work from home (2000); Travel time to work: 21.7% less than 15 minutes, 18.0% 15 to 30 minutes, 22.3% 30 to 45 minutes, 12.7% 45 to 60 minutes, 25.4% 60 minutes or more (2000)

BOCA DEL MAR (CDP). Covers a land area of 4.021 square miles and a water area of 0 square miles. Located at 26.34° N. Lat.; 80.14° W. Long.

Population: 17,754 (1990); 21,832 (2000); 22,321 (2004); 23,111 (2009 projected); Race: 93.5% White, 1.5% Black, 2.1% Asian, 10.5% Hispanic of any race (2004); Density: 5,551.7 persons per square mile (2004); Average household size: 1.97 (2004); Median age: 47.3 (2004); Male/female ratio: 83.8 (2004); Marriage status: 20.6% never married, 53.4% now married, 12.7% widowed, 13.3% divorced (2000); Foreign born: 16.4% (2000);

Ancestry (includes multiple ancestries): 18.2% Other groups, 14.0% Italian, 12.7% German, 9.6% Irish, 9.5% Russian (2000).
Economy: Employment by occupation: 20.5% management, 24.0% professional, 13.0% services, 34.9% sales, 0.0% farming, 3.3% construction, 4.3% production (2000).
Income: Per capita income: $38,383 (2004); Median household income: $55,748 (2004); Average household income: $73,444 (2004); Percent of households with income of $100,000 or more: 21.3% (2004); Poverty rate: 4.3% (2000).
Education: Percent of population age 25 and over with: High school diploma (including GED) or higher: 94.9% (2004); Bachelor's degree or higher: 41.8% (2004); Master's degree or higher: 16.3% (2004).
Housing: Homeownership rate: 61.2% (2004); Median home value: $188,254 (2004); Median rent: $926 per month (2000); Median age of housing: 15 years (2000).
Transportation: Commute to work: 92.3% car, 0.3% public transportation, 0.3% walk, 5.9% work from home (2000); Travel time to work: 27.3% less than 15 minutes, 46.6% 15 to 30 minutes, 16.0% 30 to 45 minutes, 5.7% 45 to 60 minutes, 4.4% 60 minutes or more (2000)

BOCA POINTE (CDP). Covers a land area of 1.151 square miles and a water area of 0 square miles. Located at 26.33° N. Lat.; 80.16° W. Long.
Population: 2,147 (1990); 3,302 (2000); 3,595 (2004); 3,827 (2009 projected); Race: 98.3% White, 0.4% Black, 0.8% Asian, 4.5% Hispanic of any race (2004); Density: 3,122.2 persons per square mile (2004); Average household size: 1.81 (2004); Median age: 64.3 (2004); Male/female ratio: 79.8 (2004); Marriage status: 7.3% never married, 70.3% now married, 14.3% widowed, 8.1% divorced (2000); Foreign born: 11.5% (2000); Ancestry (includes multiple ancestries): 17.7% Russian, 16.6% Other groups, 12.1% United States or American, 10.9% Polish, 6.7% German (2000).
Economy: Employment by occupation: 25.4% management, 22.2% professional, 7.8% services, 44.0% sales, 0.0% farming, 0.6% construction, 0.0% production (2000).
Income: Per capita income: $71,849 (2004); Median household income: $92,389 (2004); Average household income: $130,387 (2004); Percent of households with income of $100,000 or more: 46.5% (2004); Poverty rate: 2.0% (2000).
Education: Percent of population age 25 and over with: High school diploma (including GED) or higher: 96.7% (2004); Bachelor's degree or higher: 39.6% (2004); Master's degree or higher: 15.2% (2004).
Housing: Homeownership rate: 94.4% (2004); Median home value: $274,359 (2004); Median rent: $1,511 per month (2000); Median age of housing: 14 years (2000).
Transportation: Commute to work: 83.7% car, 0.7% public transportation, 0.8% walk, 14.8% work from home (2000); Travel time to work: 38.1% less than 15 minutes, 34.5% 15 to 30 minutes, 14.9% 30 to 45 minutes, 5.5% 45 to 60 minutes, 7.1% 60 minutes or more (2000)

BOCA RATON (city). Covers a land area of 27.189 square miles and a water area of 1.931 square miles. Located at 26.36° N. Lat.; 80.10° W. Long. Elevation is 16 feet.
History: The Mediterranean architecture of Boca Raton was planned by architect Addison Mizner as his dream city during the 1920's land boom. The city's name comes from the Spanish for "mouth of rats," referring to the sharp rocks guarding the anchorage.
Population: 61,401 (1990); 74,764 (2000); 78,989 (2004); 84,703 (2009 projected); Race: 89.5% White, 4.3% Black, 2.2% Asian, 10.7% Hispanic of any race (2004); Density: 2,905.2 persons per square mile (2004); Average household size: 2.34 (2004); Median age: 43.6 (2004); Male/female ratio: 95.2 (2004); Marriage status: 22.1% never married, 60.6% now married, 7.4% widowed, 10.0% divorced (2000); Foreign born: 18.0% (2000); Ancestry (includes multiple ancestries): 15.5% Other groups, 14.4% German, 12.4% Italian, 12.0% Irish, 9.4% English (2000).
Economy: Unemployment rate: 3.5% (2004); Total civilian labor force: 46,175 (2004); Single-family building permits issued: 71 (2004); Multi-family building permits issued: 0 (2004); Employment by occupation: 23.3% management, 22.3% professional, 13.4% services, 30.9% sales, 0.1% farming, 5.2% construction, 4.8% production (2000).
Income: Per capita income: $50,779 (2004); Median household income: $67,772 (2004); Average household income: $117,187 (2004); Percent of households with income of $100,000 or more: 34.4% (2004); Poverty rate: 6.7% (2000).
Taxes: Total city taxes per capita: $918 (2002); City property taxes per capita: $488 (2002).
Education: Percent of population age 25 and over with: High school diploma (including GED) or higher: 92.0% (2004); Bachelor's degree or higher: 44.3% (2004); Master's degree or higher: 17.1% (2004).

School District(s)

Palm Beach County School District (PK-12)
2002-03 Enrollment: 164,896 . . . . (561) 434-8200

Four-year College(s)

Florida Atlantic University-Boca Raton (Public)
2003-04 Enrollment: 24,932 . . . . (561) 297-3000
2003-04 Tuition: In-state $2,354; Out-of-state $11,164
Lynn University
2003-04 Enrollment: 2,276 . . . . (561) 237-7000
2003-04 Tuition: In-state $22,600; Out-of-state $22,600

Housing: Homeownership rate: 75.5% (2004); Median home value: $261,337 (2004); Median rent: $770 per month (2000); Median age of housing: 23 years (2000).
Hospitals: Boca Raton Community Hospital (394 beds); West Boca Medical Center (185 beds)
Safety: Violent crime rate: 22.2 per 10,000 population; Property crime rate: 319.9 per 10,000 population (2003).
Newspapers: Boca Raton News (Circulation 23,105); Globe (General - Circulation 1,516,823); National Enquirer (General - Circulation 2,076,032); National Examiner (General - Circulation 600,000); Weekly World News (General - Circulation 380,000)
Transportation: Commute to work: 89.2% car, 0.9% public transportation, 2.0% walk, 6.1% work from home (2000); Travel time to work: 40.7% less than 15 minutes, 36.4% 15 to 30 minutes, 14.0% 30 to 45 minutes, 4.4% 45 to 60 minutes, 4.4% 60 minutes or more (2000)
Airports: Boca Raton

Additional Information Contacts

Boca Raton Chamber of Commerce . . . . (561) 395-4433
Local Government Offices . . . . (561) 393-7700

BOYNTON BEACH (city). Covers a land area of 15.877 square miles and a water area of 0.373 square miles. Located at 26.52° N. Lat.; 80.07° W. Long. Elevation is 30 feet.
History: Named for Major N.S. Boynton, who built a hotel on a local beach. Incorporated 1920 as Boynton.
Population: 48,285 (1990); 60,389 (2000); 66,755 (2004); 74,611 (2009 projected); Race: 67.1% White, 24.5% Black, 2.1% Asian, 11.8% Hispanic of any race (2004); Density: 4,204.4 persons per square mile (2004); Average household size: 2.31 (2004); Median age: 42.0 (2004); Male/female ratio: 88.6 (2004); Marriage status: 21.5% never married, 55.6% now married, 11.1% widowed, 11.8% divorced (2000); Foreign born: 17.4% (2000); Ancestry (includes multiple ancestries): 22.8% Other groups, 11.8% German, 11.6% Irish, 9.7% Italian, 9.0% English (2000).
Economy: Major suburban area, including manufacturing and retirement communities. Resort; vegetable-shipping point. Unemployment rate: 5.6% (2004); Total civilian labor force: 30,432 (2004); Single-family building permits issued: 379 (2004); Multi-family building permits issued: 838 (2004); Employment by occupation: 12.4% management, 17.2% professional, 21.1% services, 29.7% sales, 0.6% farming, 10.6% construction, 8.3% production (2000).
Income: Per capita income: $24,439 (2004); Median household income: $43,609 (2004); Average household income: $55,883 (2004); Percent of households with income of $100,000 or more: 10.8% (2004); Poverty rate: 10.2% (2000).
Taxes: Total city taxes per capita: $570 (2002); City property taxes per capita: $334 (2002).
Education: Percent of population age 25 and over with: High school diploma (including GED) or higher: 81.4% (2004); Bachelor's degree or higher: 21.7% (2004); Master's degree or higher: 6.7% (2004).

School District(s)

Palm Beach County School District (PK-12)
2002-03 Enrollment: 164,896 . . . . (561) 434-8200

Four-year College(s)

Saint Vincent De Paul Regional Seminary
2003-04 Enrollment: 85 . . . . (561) 732-4424

Housing: Homeownership rate: 73.1% (2004); Median home value: $122,710 (2004); Median rent: $707 per month (2000); Median age of housing: 21 years (2000).
Hospitals: Bethesda Memorial Hospital (362 beds)
Safety: Violent crime rate: 104.6 per 10,000 population; Property crime rate: 752.7 per 10,000 population (2003).

Transportation: Commute to work: 93.7% car, 1.5% public transportation, 1.1% walk, 2.6% work from home (2000); Travel time to work: 23.8% less than 15 minutes, 41.1% 15 to 30 minutes, 23.4% 30 to 45 minutes, 7.1% 45 to 60 minutes, 4.7% 60 minutes or more (2000)

Additional Information Contacts

Boynton Beach Chamber of Commerce . . . . (561) 732-9501
Local Government Offices . . . . (561) 369-3904

BRINY BREEZES (town). Covers a land area of 0.070 square miles and a water area of 0.024 square miles. Located at 26.50° N. Lat.; 80.05° W. Long. Elevation is 5 feet.
Population: 390 (1990); 411 (2000); 417 (2004); 429 (2009 projected); Race: 99.0% White, 0.0% Black, 0.7% Asian, 0.5% Hispanic of any race (2004); Density: 5,998.9 persons per square mile (2004); Average household size: 1.52 (2004); Median age: 70.8 (2004); Male/female ratio: 77.4 (2004); Marriage status: 8.3% never married, 57.3% now married, 23.2% widowed, 11.2% divorced (2000); Foreign born: 3.6% (2000); Ancestry (includes multiple ancestries): 22.3% English, 20.3% Irish, 18.2% German, 6.5% French (except Basque), 5.3% Other groups (2000).
Economy: Single-family building permits issued: 0 (2004); Multi-family building permits issued: 0 (2004); Employment by occupation: 11.2% management, 29.2% professional, 20.2% services, 25.8% sales, 0.0% farming, 4.5% construction, 9.0% production (2000).
Income: Per capita income: $38,076 (2004); Median household income: $41,000 (2004); Average household income: $57,947 (2004); Percent of households with income of $100,000 or more: 12.8% (2004); Poverty rate: 6.6% (2000).
Taxes: Total city taxes per capita: $88 (2002); City property taxes per capita: $51 (2002).
Education: Percent of population age 25 and over with: High school diploma (including GED) or higher: 87.4% (2004); Bachelor's degree or higher: 29.9% (2004); Master's degree or higher: 15.6% (2004).
Housing: Homeownership rate: 92.0% (2004); Median home value: $79,216 (2004); Median rent: $495 per month (2000); Median age of housing: 27 years (2000).
Transportation: Commute to work: 84.5% car, 0.0% public transportation, 2.4% walk, 0.0% work from home (2000); Travel time to work: 27.4% less than 15 minutes, 38.1% 15 to 30 minutes, 20.2% 30 to 45 minutes, 3.6% 45 to 60 minutes, 10.7% 60 minutes or more (2000)

CANAL POINT (CDP). Covers a land area of 1.547 square miles and a water area of 0 square miles. Located at 26.86° N. Lat.; 80.63° W. Long. Elevation is 26 feet.
History: Canal Point was built below the dike and along both banks of the West Palm Beach Canal. A sugar mill was the early industry here.
Population: 472 (1990); 525 (2000); 590 (2004); 667 (2009 projected); Race: 51.7% White, 12.9% Black, 0.5% Asian, 47.8% Hispanic of any race (2004); Density: 381.3 persons per square mile (2004); Average household size: 2.67 (2004); Median age: 34.8 (2004); Male/female ratio: 96.0 (2004); Marriage status: 19.9% never married, 57.0% now married, 11.9% widowed, 11.2% divorced (2000); Foreign born: 28.0% (2000); Ancestry (includes multiple ancestries): 58.7% Other groups, 15.6% United States or American, 7.3% English, 5.1% Jamaican, 4.2% Irish (2000).
Economy: Employment by occupation: 11.8% management, 16.3% professional, 11.8% services, 14.4% sales, 0.0% farming, 15.7% construction, 30.1% production (2000).
Income: Per capita income: $22,640 (2004); Median household income: $39,531 (2004); Average household income: $60,441 (2004); Percent of households with income of $100,000 or more: 11.8% (2004); Poverty rate: 14.4% (2000).
Education: Percent of population age 25 and over with: High school diploma (including GED) or higher: 55.0% (2004); Bachelor's degree or higher: 6.7% (2004); Master's degree or higher: 1.9% (2004).

School District(s)

Palm Beach County School District (PK-12)
2002-03 Enrollment: 164,896 . . . . (561) 434-8200

Housing: Homeownership rate: 47.5% (2004); Median home value: $89,444 (2004); Median rent: $349 per month (2000); Median age of housing: 41 years (2000).
Transportation: Commute to work: 100.0% car, 0.0% public transportation, 0.0% walk, 0.0% work from home (2000); Travel time to work: 40.5% less than 15 minutes, 39.9% 15 to 30 minutes, 3.9% 30 to 45 minutes, 15.7% 45 to 60 minutes, 0.0% 60 minutes or more (2000)

CENTURY VILLAGE (CDP). Covers a land area of 1.004 square miles and a water area of 0.073 square miles. Located at 26.71° N. Lat.; 80.12° W. Long.
Population: 8,528 (1990); 7,616 (2000); 6,952 (2004); 6,225 (2009 projected); Race: 97.9% White, 0.6% Black, 0.6% Asian, 4.4% Hispanic of any race (2004); Density: 6,926.5 persons per square mile (2004); Average household size: 1.35 (2004); Median age: 78.5 (2004); Male/female ratio: 60.7 (2004); Marriage status: 5.8% never married, 45.8% now married, 36.7% widowed, 11.7% divorced (2000); Foreign born: 16.3% (2000); Ancestry (includes multiple ancestries): 22.0% Other groups, 14.9% Russian, 9.3% Polish, 9.2% Italian, 5.7% United States or American (2000).
Economy: Employment by occupation: 5.2% management, 11.4% professional, 27.7% services, 42.1% sales, 0.0% farming, 5.6% construction, 8.0% production (2000).
Income: Per capita income: $19,389 (2004); Median household income: $19,720 (2004); Average household income: $26,173 (2004); Percent of households with income of $100,000 or more: 2.2% (2004); Poverty rate: 12.3% (2000).
Education: Percent of population age 25 and over with: High school diploma (including GED) or higher: 78.6% (2004); Bachelor's degree or higher: 13.8% (2004); Master's degree or higher: 5.0% (2004).
Housing: Homeownership rate: 91.5% (2004); Median home value: $31,052 (2004); Median rent: $420 per month (2000); Median age of housing: 26 years (2000).
Transportation: Commute to work: 87.0% car, 5.4% public transportation, 1.0% walk, 3.9% work from home (2000); Travel time to work: 27.3% less than 15 minutes, 43.9% 15 to 30 minutes, 14.4% 30 to 45 minutes, 9.8% 45 to 60 minutes, 4.5% 60 minutes or more (2000)

CLOUD LAKE (town). Covers a land area of 0.063 square miles and a water area of 0 square miles. Located at 26.67° N. Lat.; 80.07° W. Long. Elevation is 11 feet.
Population: 121 (1990); 167 (2000); 153 (2004); 146 (2009 projected); Race: 80.4% White, 4.6% Black, 13.1% Asian, 42.5% Hispanic of any race (2004); Density: 2,429.5 persons per square mile (2004); Average household size: 2.73 (2004); Median age: 38.8 (2004); Male/female ratio: 91.3 (2004); Marriage status: 18.0% never married, 63.1% now married, 6.3% widowed, 12.6% divorced (2000); Foreign born: 13.0% (2000); Ancestry (includes multiple ancestries): 24.4% Irish, 17.1% Other groups, 11.4% English, 10.6% United States or American, 10.6% German (2000).
Economy: Single-family building permits issued: 0 (2004); Multi-family building permits issued: 0 (2004); Employment by occupation: 2.2% management, 15.2% professional, 22.8% services, 28.3% sales, 0.0% farming, 28.3% construction, 3.3% production (2000).
Income: Per capita income: $25,605 (2004); Median household income: $56,250 (2004); Average household income: $69,955 (2004); Percent of households with income of $100,000 or more: 23.2% (2004); Poverty rate: 0.0% (2000).
Taxes: Total city taxes per capita: $36 (2002); City property taxes per capita: $0 (2002).
Education: Percent of population age 25 and over with: High school diploma (including GED) or higher: 87.6% (2004); Bachelor's degree or higher: 14.3% (2004); Master's degree or higher: 8.6% (2004).
Housing: Homeownership rate: 58.9% (2004); Median home value: $125,000 (2004); Median rent: $450 per month (2000); Median age of housing: 47 years (2000).
Transportation: Commute to work: 94.6% car, 5.4% public transportation, 0.0% walk, 0.0% work from home (2000); Travel time to work: 26.1% less than 15 minutes, 48.9% 15 to 30 minutes, 25.0% 30 to 45 minutes, 0.0% 45 to 60 minutes, 0.0% 60 minutes or more (2000)

CYPRESS LAKES (CDP). Covers a land area of 0.427 square miles and a water area of 0.026 square miles. Located at 26.72° N. Lat.; 80.12° W. Long.
Population: 1,177 (1990); 1,468 (2000); 1,667 (2004); 1,913 (2009 projected); Race: 97.1% White, 2.0% Black, 0.6% Asian, 2.8% Hispanic of any race (2004); Density: 3,905.1 persons per square mile (2004); Average household size: 1.69 (2004); Median age: 74.3 (2004); Male/female ratio: 78.5 (2004); Marriage status: 4.5% never married, 73.4% now married, 18.8% widowed, 3.3% divorced (2000); Foreign born: 5.4% (2000); Ancestry (includes multiple ancestries): 21.5% Italian, 17.2% Other groups, 11.3% United States or American, 9.3% Irish, 9.1% Russian (2000).

Economy: Employment by occupation: 34.5% management, 0.0% professional, 15.9% services, 33.6% sales, 0.0% farming, 0.0% construction, 15.9% production (2000).
Income: Per capita income: $29,858 (2004); Median household income: $32,033 (2004); Average household income: $50,582 (2004); Percent of households with income of $100,000 or more: 6.9% (2004); Poverty rate: 4.3% (2000).
Education: Percent of population age 25 and over with: High school diploma (including GED) or higher: 80.6% (2004); Bachelor's degree or higher: 11.5% (2004); Master's degree or higher: 3.0% (2004).
Housing: Homeownership rate: 97.3% (2004); Median home value: $122,667 (2004); Median rent: $n/a per month (2000); Median age of housing: 13 years (2000).
Transportation: Commute to work: 90.5% car, 0.0% public transportation, 0.0% walk, 9.5% work from home (2000); Travel time to work: 48.8% less than 15 minutes, 26.7% 15 to 30 minutes, 15.1% 30 to 45 minutes, 9.3% 45 to 60 minutes, 0.0% 60 minutes or more (2000)

DELRAY BEACH (city). Covers a land area of 15.368 square miles and a water area of 0.525 square miles. Located at 26.45° N. Lat.; 80.08° W. Long. Elevation is 20 feet.
History: Named, perhaps, for the Spanish translation of "of the king". Delray Beach was settled in 1895, and grew as a tourist resort area and the center of an agricultural area producing beans, peppers, tomatoes, sugar cane, and citrus fruit.
Population: 47,833 (1990); 60,020 (2000); 63,914 (2004); 69,065 (2009 projected); Race: 64.1% White, 27.9% Black, 1.3% Asian, 8.5% Hispanic of any race (2004); Density: 4,159.0 persons per square mile (2004); Average household size: 2.24 (2004); Median age: 44.8 (2004); Male/female ratio: 91.7 (2004); Marriage status: 24.6% never married, 51.6% now married, 11.5% widowed, 12.3% divorced (2000); Foreign born: 21.5% (2000); Ancestry (includes multiple ancestries): 21.5% Other groups, 10.6% Haitian, 10.5% German, 10.3% Irish, 8.1% English (2000).
Economy: Unemployment rate: 7.7% (2004); Total civilian labor force: 31,093 (2004); Single-family building permits issued: 301 (2004); Multi-family building permits issued: 163 (2004); Employment by occupation: 14.8% management, 18.8% professional, 22.1% services, 26.9% sales, 0.5% farming, 7.9% construction, 9.0% production (2000).
Income: Per capita income: $31,401 (2004); Median household income: $47,423 (2004); Average household income: $69,831 (2004); Percent of households with income of $100,000 or more: 18.1% (2004); Poverty rate: 11.8% (2000).
Taxes: Total city taxes per capita: $667 (2002); City property taxes per capita: $450 (2002).
Education: Percent of population age 25 and over with: High school diploma (including GED) or higher: 81.1% (2004); Bachelor's degree or higher: 29.6% (2004); Master's degree or higher: 10.2% (2004).

School District(s)

Palm Beach County School District (PK-12)
2002-03 Enrollment: 164,896 . . . . (561) 434-8200

Housing: Homeownership rate: 69.6% (2004); Median home value: $137,944 (2004); Median rent: $704 per month (2000); Median age of housing: 22 years (2000).
Hospitals: Delray Medical Center (343 beds); Pinecrest Rehabilitation Hospital (90 beds)
Safety: Violent crime rate: 82.2 per 10,000 population; Property crime rate: 636.5 per 10,000 population (2003).
Transportation: Commute to work: 90.5% car, 1.7% public transportation, 1.8% walk, 4.3% work from home (2000); Travel time to work: 32.9% less than 15 minutes, 41.5% 15 to 30 minutes, 15.4% 30 to 45 minutes, 5.2% 45 to 60 minutes, 5.0% 60 minutes or more (2000); Amtrak: Service available.

Additional Information Contacts

Delray Beach Chamber of Commerce . . . . (561) 278-0424
Local Government Offices . . . . (561) 243-7050

DUNES ROAD (CDP). Covers a land area of 0.517 square miles and a water area of 0 square miles. Located at 26.48° N. Lat.; 80.11° W. Long.
Population: 391 (1990); 391 (2000); 411 (2004); 440 (2009 projected); Race: 87.3% White, 10.2% Black, 0.7% Asian, 4.9% Hispanic of any race (2004); Density: 794.6 persons per square mile (2004); Average household size: 2.87 (2004); Median age: 40.2 (2004); Male/female ratio: 98.6 (2004); Marriage status: 10.1% never married, 55.9% now married, 11.4% widowed, 22.5% divorced (2000); Foreign born: 4.2% (2000); Ancestry (includes multiple ancestries): 48.2% German, 22.0% Palestinian, 19.7% Italian, 13.1% Czechoslovakian, 10.6% English (2000).
Economy: Employment by occupation: 44.9% management, 14.1% professional, 3.0% services, 27.8% sales, 0.0% farming, 5.1% construction, 5.1% production (2000).
Income: Per capita income: $38,400 (2004); Median household income: $94,022 (2004); Average household income: $110,367 (2004); Percent of households with income of $100,000 or more: 46.2% (2004); Poverty rate: 3.4% (2000).
Education: Percent of population age 25 and over with: High school diploma (including GED) or higher: 99.2% (2004); Bachelor's degree or higher: 26.7% (2004); Master's degree or higher: 6.0% (2004).
Housing: Homeownership rate: 97.2% (2004); Median home value: $336,765 (2004); Median rent: $n/a per month (2000); Median age of housing: 14 years (2000).
Transportation: Commute to work: 97.0% car, 0.0% public transportation, 0.0% walk, 3.0% work from home (2000); Travel time to work: 37.5% less than 15 minutes, 40.1% 15 to 30 minutes, 12.0% 30 to 45 minutes, 2.6% 45 to 60 minutes, 7.8% 60 minutes or more (2000)

FREMD VILLAGE-PADGETT ISLAND (CDP). Covers a land area of 1.182 square miles and a water area of 0 square miles. Located at 26.80° N. Lat.; 80.65° W. Long.
Population: 2,181 (1990); 2,264 (2000); 2,473 (2004); 2,731 (2009 projected); Race: 2.7% White, 92.7% Black, 0.1% Asian, 6.7% Hispanic of any race (2004); Density: 2,091.9 persons per square mile (2004); Average household size: 3.31 (2004); Median age: 19.9 (2004); Male/female ratio: 74.6 (2004); Marriage status: 57.5% never married, 30.3% now married, 5.9% widowed, 6.3% divorced (2000); Foreign born: 7.3% (2000); Ancestry (includes multiple ancestries): 75.2% Other groups, 1.8% United States or American, 1.6% Jamaican, 0.4% West Indian, 0.4% African (2000).
Economy: Employment by occupation: 2.9% management, 12.4% professional, 29.5% services, 24.1% sales, 7.2% farming, 3.1% construction, 20.8% production (2000).
Income: Per capita income: $7,683 (2004); Median household income: $16,361 (2004); Average household income: $25,435 (2004); Percent of households with income of $100,000 or more: 3.5% (2004); Poverty rate: 55.7% (2000).
Education: Percent of population age 25 and over with: High school diploma (including GED) or higher: 50.7% (2004); Bachelor's degree or higher: 6.1% (2004); Master's degree or higher: 0.0% (2004).
Housing: Homeownership rate: 9.0% (2004); Median home value: $86,111 (2004); Median rent: $269 per month (2000); Median age of housing: 27 years (2000).
Transportation: Commute to work: 81.0% car, 7.9% public transportation, 3.9% walk, 0.0% work from home (2000); Travel time to work: 39.0% less than 15 minutes, 27.5% 15 to 30 minutes, 9.2% 30 to 45 minutes, 14.9% 45 to 60 minutes, 9.5% 60 minutes or more (2000)

GLEN RIDGE (town). Covers a land area of 0.226 square miles and a water area of 0 square miles. Located at 26.67° N. Lat.; 80.07° W. Long. Elevation is 12 feet.
Population: 207 (1990); 276 (2000); 254 (2004); 241 (2009 projected); Race: 76.4% White, 12.2% Black, 0.0% Asian, 15.7% Hispanic of any race (2004); Density: 1,125.4 persons per square mile (2004); Average household size: 2.92 (2004); Median age: 35.8 (2004); Male/female ratio: 100.0 (2004); Marriage status: 21.3% never married, 42.6% now married, 11.1% widowed, 25.0% divorced (2000); Foreign born: 7.4% (2000); Ancestry (includes multiple ancestries): 19.9% Irish, 17.7% English, 17.3% French (except Basque), 13.3% German, 8.5% Other groups (2000).
Economy: Single-family building permits issued: 1 (2004); Multi-family building permits issued: 0 (2004); Employment by occupation: 14.0% management, 15.7% professional, 14.9% services, 32.2% sales, 0.0% farming, 11.6% construction, 11.6% production (2000).
Income: Per capita income: $20,906 (2004); Median household income: $46,719 (2004); Average household income: $61,034 (2004); Percent of households with income of $100,000 or more: 14.9% (2004); Poverty rate: 4.8% (2000).
Taxes: Total city taxes per capita: $18 (2002); City property taxes per capita: $0 (2002).
Education: Percent of population age 25 and over with: High school diploma (including GED) or higher: 83.5% (2004); Bachelor's degree or higher: 13.3% (2004); Master's degree or higher: 2.5% (2004).

Housing: Homeownership rate: 87.4% (2004); Median home value: $177,273 (2004); Median rent: $436 per month (2000); Median age of housing: 42 years (2000).
Transportation: Commute to work: 93.2% car, 0.0% public transportation, 0.0% walk, 4.2% work from home (2000); Travel time to work: 38.9% less than 15 minutes, 34.5% 15 to 30 minutes, 23.0% 30 to 45 minutes, 0.0% 45 to 60 minutes, 3.5% 60 minutes or more (2000)

GOLDEN LAKES (CDP). Covers a land area of 2.365 square miles and a water area of 0 square miles. Located at 26.70° N. Lat.; 80.16° W. Long.
Population: 3,867 (1990); 6,694 (2000); 9,050 (2004); 11,832 (2009 projected); Race: 58.7% White, 30.1% Black, 1.5% Asian, 23.3% Hispanic of any race (2004); Density: 3,827.4 persons per square mile (2004); Average household size: 2.18 (2004); Median age: 38.9 (2004); Male/female ratio: 85.3 (2004); Marriage status: 21.2% never married, 52.3% now married, 16.0% widowed, 10.5% divorced (2000); Foreign born: 21.0% (2000); Ancestry (includes multiple ancestries): 38.5% Other groups, 9.5% German, 6.2% Russian, 5.9% Irish, 5.5% Italian (2000).
Economy: Employment by occupation: 8.5% management, 17.9% professional, 26.2% services, 28.7% sales, 1.1% farming, 10.0% construction, 7.6% production (2000).
Income: Per capita income: $19,028 (2004); Median household income: $29,923 (2004); Average household income: $41,525 (2004); Percent of households with income of $100,000 or more: 6.1% (2004); Poverty rate: 13.0% (2000).
Education: Percent of population age 25 and over with: High school diploma (including GED) or higher: 75.2% (2004); Bachelor's degree or higher: 16.7% (2004); Master's degree or higher: 6.7% (2004).
Housing: Homeownership rate: 54.0% (2004); Median home value: $55,245 (2004); Median rent: $636 per month (2000); Median age of housing: 16 years (2000).
Transportation: Commute to work: 93.6% car, 2.9% public transportation, 0.0% walk, 2.1% work from home (2000); Travel time to work: 18.8% less than 15 minutes, 42.6% 15 to 30 minutes, 24.3% 30 to 45 minutes, 5.2% 45 to 60 minutes, 9.1% 60 minutes or more (2000)

GOLF (village). Covers a land area of 0.830 square miles and a water area of 0.014 square miles. Located at 26.50° N. Lat.; 80.10° W. Long.
Population: 234 (1990); 230 (2000); 251 (2004); 277 (2009 projected); Race: 96.0% White, 1.2% Black, 0.0% Asian, 2.8% Hispanic of any race (2004); Density: 302.5 persons per square mile (2004); Average household size: 1.89 (2004); Median age: 66.5 (2004); Male/female ratio: 93.1 (2004); Marriage status: 7.0% never married, 80.4% now married, 10.3% widowed, 2.3% divorced (2000); Foreign born: 5.0% (2000); Ancestry (includes multiple ancestries): 38.1% English, 23.8% Irish, 15.9% German, 10.5% Scottish, 6.7% Italian (2000).
Economy: Single-family building permits issued: 1 (2004); Multi-family building permits issued: 0 (2004); Employment by occupation: 28.6% management, 31.4% professional, 8.6% services, 31.4% sales, 0.0% farming, 0.0% construction, 0.0% production (2000).
Income: Per capita income: $153,745 (2004); Median household income: $238,636 (2004); Average household income: $290,150 (2004); Percent of households with income of $100,000 or more: 76.7% (2004); Poverty rate: 1.7% (2000).
Taxes: Total city taxes per capita: $2,413 (2002); City property taxes per capita: $1,939 (2002).
Education: Percent of population age 25 and over with: High school diploma (including GED) or higher: 99.1% (2004); Bachelor's degree or higher: 77.9% (2004); Master's degree or higher: 27.2% (2004).
Housing: Homeownership rate: 95.5% (2004); Median home value: $535,156 (2004); Median rent: $n/a per month (2000); Median age of housing: 25 years (2000).
Transportation: Commute to work: 84.3% car, 0.0% public transportation, 0.0% walk, 15.7% work from home (2000); Travel time to work: 30.5% less than 15 minutes, 50.8% 15 to 30 minutes, 11.9% 30 to 45 minutes, 0.0% 45 to 60 minutes, 6.8% 60 minutes or more (2000)

GREENACRES (city). Aka Greenacres City. Covers a land area of 4.659 square miles and a water area of 0.011 square miles. Located at 26.62° N. Lat.; 80.13° W. Long. Elevation is 23 feet.
Population: 20,225 (1990); 27,569 (2000); 31,142 (2004); 35,629 (2009 projected); Race: 78.2% White, 8.5% Black, 2.4% Asian, 28.3% Hispanic of any race (2004); Density: 6,684.5 persons per square mile (2004); Average household size: 2.28 (2004); Median age: 40.4 (2004); Male/female ratio: 88.5 (2004); Marriage status: 19.8% never married, 55.6% now married, 10.6% widowed, 14.1% divorced (2000); Foreign born: 19.3% (2000); Ancestry (includes multiple ancestries): 30.9% Other groups, 13.1% Italian, 12.0% German, 10.9% Irish, 7.4% English (2000).
Economy: Unemployment rate: 5.1% (2004); Total civilian labor force: 14,479 (2004); Single-family building permits issued: 277 (2004); Multi-family building permits issued: 32 (2004); Employment by occupation: 10.4% management, 14.4% professional, 21.4% services, 28.4% sales, 0.3% farming, 13.7% construction, 11.2% production (2000).
Income: Per capita income: $20,412 (2004); Median household income: $38,145 (2004); Average household income: $46,448 (2004); Percent of households with income of $100,000 or more: 6.1% (2004); Poverty rate: 7.2% (2000).
Taxes: Total city taxes per capita: $322 (2002); City property taxes per capita: $144 (2002).
Education: Percent of population age 25 and over with: High school diploma (including GED) or higher: 80.3% (2004); Bachelor's degree or higher: 18.1% (2004); Master's degree or higher: 7.5% (2004).

School District(s)

Palm Beach County School District (PK-12)
2002-03 Enrollment: 164,896 . . . . (561) 434-8200

Housing: Homeownership rate: 70.7% (2004); Median home value: $96,931 (2004); Median rent: $660 per month (2000); Median age of housing: 15 years (2000).
Safety: Violent crime rate: 75.2 per 10,000 population; Property crime rate: 493.3 per 10,000 population (2003).
Transportation: Commute to work: 95.0% car, 0.5% public transportation, 0.3% walk, 1.9% work from home (2000); Travel time to work: 17.3% less than 15 minutes, 40.4% 15 to 30 minutes, 28.5% 30 to 45 minutes, 7.9% 45 to 60 minutes, 5.9% 60 minutes or more (2000)

Additional Information Contacts

Local Government Offices . . . . (561) 642-2017

GULF STREAM (town). Covers a land area of 0.751 square miles and a water area of 0.080 square miles. Located at 26.49° N. Lat.; 80.06° W. Long. Elevation is 7 feet.
Population: 653 (1990); 716 (2000); 763 (2004); 819 (2009 projected); Race: 94.4% White, 1.3% Black, 1.8% Asian, 3.7% Hispanic of any race (2004); Density: 1,016.3 persons per square mile (2004); Average household size: 2.07 (2004); Median age: 55.8 (2004); Male/female ratio: 93.7 (2004); Marriage status: 14.6% never married, 64.8% now married, 10.1% widowed, 10.4% divorced (2000); Foreign born: 9.6% (2000); Ancestry (includes multiple ancestries): 22.6% English, 17.8% Irish, 16.8% German, 8.4% United States or American, 7.5% Italian (2000).
Economy: Employment by occupation: 34.4% management, 19.2% professional, 8.3% services, 27.5% sales, 1.4% farming, 7.6% construction, 1.4% production (2000).
Income: Per capita income: $107,133 (2004); Median household income: $152,679 (2004); Average household income: $221,524 (2004); Percent of households with income of $100,000 or more: 61.2% (2004); Poverty rate: 2.5% (2000).
Taxes: Total city taxes per capita: $2,116 (2002); City property taxes per capita: $1,897 (2002).
Education: Percent of population age 25 and over with: High school diploma (including GED) or higher: 95.6% (2004); Bachelor's degree or higher: 58.1% (2004); Master's degree or higher: 23.8% (2004).
Housing: Homeownership rate: 91.3% (2004); Median home value: $762,255 (2004); Median rent: $963 per month (2000); Median age of housing: 28 years (2000).
Safety: Violent crime rate: 0.0 per 10,000 population; Property crime rate: 214.2 per 10,000 population (2003).
Transportation: Commute to work: 69.3% car, 1.1% public transportation, 4.0% walk, 23.4% work from home (2000); Travel time to work: 36.2% less than 15 minutes, 33.8% 15 to 30 minutes, 18.1% 30 to 45 minutes, 5.7% 45 to 60 minutes, 6.2% 60 minutes or more (2000)

GUN CLUB ESTATES (CDP). Covers a land area of 0.118 square miles and a water area of 0 square miles. Located at 26.67° N. Lat.; 80.10° W. Long.
Population: 593 (1990); 711 (2000); 717 (2004); 705 (2009 projected); Race: 86.6% White, 1.3% Black, 0.0% Asian, 53.1% Hispanic of any race (2004); Density: 6,061.5 persons per square mile (2004); Average household size: 2.93 (2004); Median age: 33.8 (2004); Male/female ratio: 107.8 (2004); Marriage status: 38.1% never married, 37.9% now married, 1.6% widowed, 22.4% divorced (2000); Foreign born: 32.2% (2000);

Ancestry (includes multiple ancestries): 46.8% Other groups, 10.9% West Indian, 8.4% Italian, 7.6% German, 6.6% Irish (2000).
Economy: Employment by occupation: 9.1% management, 5.5% professional, 20.8% services, 35.2% sales, 0.0% farming, 20.3% construction, 9.1% production (2000).
Income: Per capita income: $14,923 (2004); Median household income: $34,423 (2004); Average household income: $43,673 (2004); Percent of households with income of $100,000 or more: 4.5% (2004); Poverty rate: 3.7% (2000).
Education: Percent of population age 25 and over with: High school diploma (including GED) or higher: 53.5% (2004); Bachelor's degree or higher: 0.0% (2004); Master's degree or higher: 0.0% (2004).
Housing: Homeownership rate: 87.3% (2004); Median home value: $99,322 (2004); Median rent: $570 per month (2000); Median age of housing: 45 years (2000).
Transportation: Commute to work: 97.4% car, 0.0% public transportation, 0.0% walk, 2.6% work from home (2000); Travel time to work: 14.6% less than 15 minutes, 69.4% 15 to 30 minutes, 7.7% 30 to 45 minutes, 8.2% 45 to 60 minutes, 0.0% 60 minutes or more (2000)

HAMPTONS AT BOCA RATON (CDP). Covers a land area of 2.486 square miles and a water area of 0.182 square miles. Located at 26.38° N. Lat.; 80.18° W. Long.
Population: 11,686 (1990); 11,306 (2000); 11,033 (2004); 10,775 (2009 projected); Race: 93.5% White, 2.2% Black, 1.5% Asian, 6.5% Hispanic of any race (2004); Density: 4,437.4 persons per square mile (2004); Average household size: 1.77 (2004); Median age: 71.6 (2004); Male/female ratio: 71.9 (2004); Marriage status: 9.4% never married, 56.6% now married, 27.9% widowed, 6.1% divorced (2000); Foreign born: 16.9% (2000); Ancestry (includes multiple ancestries): 24.2% Other groups, 10.0% Polish, 9.1% Russian, 8.3% United States or American, 7.6% Italian (2000).
Economy: Employment by occupation: 15.3% management, 19.1% professional, 15.5% services, 34.7% sales, 0.0% farming, 6.9% construction, 8.6% production (2000).
Income: Per capita income: $26,956 (2004); Median household income: $32,830 (2004); Average household income: $47,822 (2004); Percent of households with income of $100,000 or more: 10.0% (2004); Poverty rate: 7.3% (2000).
Education: Percent of population age 25 and over with: High school diploma (including GED) or higher: 82.3% (2004); Bachelor's degree or higher: 19.3% (2004); Master's degree or higher: 7.7% (2004).
Housing: Homeownership rate: 87.3% (2004); Median home value: $84,552 (2004); Median rent: $622 per month (2000); Median age of housing: 17 years (2000).
Transportation: Commute to work: 93.4% car, 1.4% public transportation, 0.0% walk, 3.7% work from home (2000); Travel time to work: 16.7% less than 15 minutes, 43.9% 15 to 30 minutes, 23.4% 30 to 45 minutes, 5.7% 45 to 60 minutes, 10.4% 60 minutes or more (2000)

HAVERHILL (town). Covers a land area of 0.574 square miles and a water area of 0 square miles. Located at 26.69° N. Lat.; 80.12° W. Long. Elevation is 19 feet.
Population: 1,127 (1990); 1,454 (2000); 1,375 (2004); 1,304 (2009 projected); Race: 70.8% White, 17.5% Black, 1.6% Asian, 28.9% Hispanic of any race (2004); Density: 2,397.0 persons per square mile (2004); Average household size: 2.76 (2004); Median age: 36.8 (2004); Male/female ratio: 101.6 (2004); Marriage status: 25.7% never married, 57.1% now married, 6.3% widowed, 10.9% divorced (2000); Foreign born: 19.3% (2000); Ancestry (includes multiple ancestries): 30.2% Other groups, 12.7% Irish, 12.3% German, 10.7% English, 7.6% United States or American (2000).
Economy: Single-family building permits issued: 3 (2004); Multi-family building permits issued: 0 (2004); Employment by occupation: 15.2% management, 17.6% professional, 18.0% services, 25.0% sales, 0.0% farming, 16.7% construction, 7.6% production (2000).
Income: Per capita income: $25,707 (2004); Median household income: $51,606 (2004); Average household income: $70,979 (2004); Percent of households with income of $100,000 or more: 15.7% (2004); Poverty rate: 8.3% (2000).
Taxes: Total city taxes per capita: $144 (2002); City property taxes per capita: $144 (2002).
Education: Percent of population age 25 and over with: High school diploma (including GED) or higher: 83.7% (2004); Bachelor's degree or higher: 23.2% (2004); Master's degree or higher: 7.9% (2004).
Housing: Homeownership rate: 80.7% (2004); Median home value: $158,553 (2004); Median rent: $588 per month (2000); Median age of housing: 27 years (2000).
Transportation: Commute to work: 93.0% car, 0.8% public transportation, 0.7% walk, 5.6% work from home (2000); Travel time to work: 24.1% less than 15 minutes, 41.7% 15 to 30 minutes, 21.9% 30 to 45 minutes, 7.2% 45 to 60 minutes, 5.1% 60 minutes or more (2000)

HIGH POINT (CDP). Covers a land area of 0.593 square miles and a water area of 0 square miles. Located at 26.46° N. Lat.; 80.12° W. Long.
Population: 2,003 (1990); 2,191 (2000); 2,167 (2004); 2,217 (2009 projected); Race: 88.2% White, 10.2% Black, 0.2% Asian, 2.8% Hispanic of any race (2004); Density: 3,653.5 persons per square mile (2004); Average household size: 1.67 (2004); Median age: 75.0 (2004); Male/female ratio: 78.2 (2004); Marriage status: 7.4% never married, 61.4% now married, 24.8% widowed, 6.4% divorced (2000); Foreign born: 9.6% (2000); Ancestry (includes multiple ancestries): 23.0% Other groups, 15.0% Russian, 9.5% Italian, 7.9% United States or American, 6.9% Polish (2000).
Economy: Employment by occupation: 11.6% management, 15.4% professional, 21.9% services, 49.2% sales, 0.0% farming, 0.0% construction, 1.9% production (2000).
Income: Per capita income: $22,945 (2004); Median household income: $33,067 (2004); Average household income: $38,307 (2004); Percent of households with income of $100,000 or more: 4.9% (2004); Poverty rate: 6.6% (2000).
Education: Percent of population age 25 and over with: High school diploma (including GED) or higher: 88.3% (2004); Bachelor's degree or higher: 17.9% (2004); Master's degree or higher: 6.3% (2004).
Housing: Homeownership rate: 89.4% (2004); Median home value: $71,538 (2004); Median rent: $707 per month (2000); Median age of housing: 16 years (2000).
Transportation: Commute to work: 96.1% car, 0.0% public transportation, 0.0% walk, 3.9% work from home (2000); Travel time to work: 19.1% less than 15 minutes, 58.9% 15 to 30 minutes, 16.1% 30 to 45 minutes, 2.7% 45 to 60 minutes, 3.3% 60 minutes or more (2000)

HIGHLAND BEACH (town). Covers a land area of 0.490 square miles and a water area of 0.641 square miles. Located at 26.40° N. Lat.; 80.06° W. Long. Elevation is 10 feet.
Population: 3,209 (1990); 3,775 (2000); 4,142 (2004); 4,610 (2009 projected); Race: 98.0% White, 0.5% Black, 0.4% Asian, 4.1% Hispanic of any race (2004); Density: 8,454.8 persons per square mile (2004); Average household size: 1.69 (2004); Median age: 66.1 (2004); Male/female ratio: 88.3 (2004); Marriage status: 8.7% never married, 68.0% now married, 15.8% widowed, 7.5% divorced (2000); Foreign born: 13.1% (2000); Ancestry (includes multiple ancestries): 12.0% German, 11.5% Russian, 11.0% Italian, 10.0% Other groups, 10.0% United States or American (2000).
Economy: Single-family building permits issued: 13 (2004); Multi-family building permits issued: 0 (2004); Employment by occupation: 33.7% management, 29.7% professional, 5.4% services, 24.4% sales, 0.0% farming, 3.0% construction, 3.8% production (2000).
Income: Per capita income: $65,934 (2004); Median household income: $75,648 (2004); Average household income: $110,413 (2004); Percent of households with income of $100,000 or more: 36.2% (2004); Poverty rate: 2.1% (2000).
Taxes: Total city taxes per capita: $1,113 (2002); City property taxes per capita: $878 (2002).
Education: Percent of population age 25 and over with: High school diploma (including GED) or higher: 94.6% (2004); Bachelor's degree or higher: 48.1% (2004); Master's degree or higher: 21.9% (2004).
Housing: Homeownership rate: 83.2% (2004); Median home value: $283,821 (2004); Median rent: $1,539 per month (2000); Median age of housing: 21 years (2000).
Safety: Violent crime rate: 10.0 per 10,000 population; Property crime rate: 116.9 per 10,000 population (2003).
Transportation: Commute to work: 84.4% car, 0.0% public transportation, 0.9% walk, 12.6% work from home (2000); Travel time to work: 34.8% less than 15 minutes, 45.7% 15 to 30 minutes, 13.2% 30 to 45 minutes, 1.1% 45 to 60 minutes, 5.3% 60 minutes or more (2000)

HYPOLUXO (town). Covers a land area of 0.595 square miles and a water area of 0.229 square miles. Located at 26.56° N. Lat.; 80.05° W. Long. Elevation is 9 feet.

History: Hypoluxo was settled in 1873 on Lake Worth. The name is of Indian origin meaning "round mound."
Population: 791 (1990); 2,015 (2000); 2,371 (2004); 2,805 (2009 projected); Race: 88.8% White, 4.6% Black, 2.4% Asian, 6.4% Hispanic of any race (2004); Density: 3,988.0 persons per square mile (2004); Average household size: 1.82 (2004); Median age: 49.7 (2004); Male/female ratio: 96.4 (2004); Marriage status: 19.8% never married, 54.9% now married, 9.6% widowed, 15.7% divorced (2000); Foreign born: 18.3% (2000); Ancestry (includes multiple ancestries): 19.8% German, 17.0% Irish, 13.8% English, 11.1% Italian, 10.9% Other groups (2000).
Economy: Single-family building permits issued: 18 (2004); Multi-family building permits issued: 0 (2004); Employment by occupation: 21.9% management, 24.3% professional, 12.7% services, 31.9% sales, 0.0% farming, 3.0% construction, 6.2% production (2000).
Income: Per capita income: $42,353 (2004); Median household income: $59,363 (2004); Average household income: $77,246 (2004); Percent of households with income of $100,000 or more: 23.0% (2004); Poverty rate: 7.1% (2000).
Taxes: Total city taxes per capita: $538 (2002); City property taxes per capita: $278 (2002).
Education: Percent of population age 25 and over with: High school diploma (including GED) or higher: 91.8% (2004); Bachelor's degree or higher: 37.9% (2004); Master's degree or higher: 13.4% (2004).

School District(s)

Palm Beach County School District (PK-12)
2002-03 Enrollment: 164,896 . . . . (561) 434-8200

Housing: Homeownership rate: 61.4% (2004); Median home value: $149,157 (2004); Median rent: $926 per month (2000); Median age of housing: 8 years (2000).
Safety: Violent crime rate: 15.5 per 10,000 population; Property crime rate: 473.4 per 10,000 population (2003).
Transportation: Commute to work: 94.0% car, 0.9% public transportation, 0.5% walk, 4.3% work from home (2000); Travel time to work: 18.1% less than 15 minutes, 43.8% 15 to 30 minutes, 23.4% 30 to 45 minutes, 6.7% 45 to 60 minutes, 8.0% 60 minutes or more (2000)

JUNO BEACH (town). Covers a land area of 1.395 square miles and a water area of 0.474 square miles. Located at 26.87° N. Lat.; 80.05° W. Long. Elevation is 5 feet.
Population: 2,340 (1990); 3,262 (2000); 3,426 (2004); 3,653 (2009 projected); Race: 97.5% White, 0.5% Black, 0.6% Asian, 4.6% Hispanic of any race (2004); Density: 2,456.8 persons per square mile (2004); Average household size: 1.81 (2004); Median age: 60.0 (2004); Male/female ratio: 85.0 (2004); Marriage status: 12.8% never married, 60.7% now married, 14.7% widowed, 11.8% divorced (2000); Foreign born: 7.3% (2000); Ancestry (includes multiple ancestries): 19.3% Irish, 18.2% German, 15.9% Italian, 13.4% English, 6.3% French (except Basque) (2000).
Economy: Single-family building permits issued: 0 (2004); Multi-family building permits issued: 0 (2004); Employment by occupation: 27.3% management, 19.0% professional, 13.5% services, 28.3% sales, 0.0% farming, 1.7% construction, 10.1% production (2000).
Income: Per capita income: $52,926 (2004); Median household income: $59,469 (2004); Average household income: $95,511 (2004); Percent of households with income of $100,000 or more: 25.7% (2004); Poverty rate: 4.5% (2000).
Taxes: Total city taxes per capita: $738 (2002); City property taxes per capita: $550 (2002).
Education: Percent of population age 25 and over with: High school diploma (including GED) or higher: 94.6% (2004); Bachelor's degree or higher: 40.8% (2004); Master's degree or higher: 14.4% (2004).

School District(s)

Palm Beach County School District (PK-12)
2002-03 Enrollment: 164,896 . . . . (561) 434-8200

Housing: Homeownership rate: 74.2% (2004); Median home value: $229,104 (2004); Median rent: $1,174 per month (2000); Median age of housing: 17 years (2000).
Safety: Violent crime rate: 8.8 per 10,000 population; Property crime rate: 377.2 per 10,000 population (2003).
Transportation: Commute to work: 84.5% car, 0.6% public transportation, 1.8% walk, 10.7% work from home (2000); Travel time to work: 31.4% less than 15 minutes, 44.2% 15 to 30 minutes, 10.4% 30 to 45 minutes, 11.1% 45 to 60 minutes, 2.9% 60 minutes or more (2000)

JUNO RIDGE (CDP). Covers a land area of 0.145 square miles and a water area of 0 square miles. Located at 26.84° N. Lat.; 80.06° W. Long.
Population: 802 (1990); 742 (2000); 679 (2004); 609 (2009 projected); Race: 91.9% White, 2.7% Black, 0.7% Asian, 7.2% Hispanic of any race (2004); Density: 4,667.7 persons per square mile (2004); Average household size: 1.83 (2004); Median age: 35.3 (2004); Male/female ratio: 116.2 (2004); Marriage status: 29.2% never married, 40.3% now married, 8.0% widowed, 22.6% divorced (2000); Foreign born: 10.8% (2000); Ancestry (includes multiple ancestries): 19.7% Irish, 18.7% Other groups, 13.7% English, 10.1% German, 7.2% Italian (2000).
Economy: Employment by occupation: 11.6% management, 14.0% professional, 20.9% services, 26.4% sales, 0.0% farming, 16.5% construction, 10.6% production (2000).
Income: Per capita income: $24,926 (2004); Median household income: $41,585 (2004); Average household income: $45,497 (2004); Percent of households with income of $100,000 or more: 3.8% (2004); Poverty rate: 9.4% (2000).
Education: Percent of population age 25 and over with: High school diploma (including GED) or higher: 92.0% (2004); Bachelor's degree or higher: 12.7% (2004); Master's degree or higher: 2.4% (2004).
Housing: Homeownership rate: 33.3% (2004); Median home value: $131,967 (2004); Median rent: $647 per month (2000); Median age of housing: 30 years (2000).
Transportation: Commute to work: 91.7% car, 0.0% public transportation, 5.8% walk, 1.6% work from home (2000); Travel time to work: 40.1% less than 15 minutes, 31.3% 15 to 30 minutes, 23.8% 30 to 45 minutes, 1.1% 45 to 60 minutes, 3.6% 60 minutes or more (2000)

JUPITER (town). Covers a land area of 19.999 square miles and a water area of 1.125 square miles. Located at 26.92° N. Lat.; 80.10° W. Long. Elevation is 8 feet.
Population: 30,117 (1990); 39,328 (2000); 45,619 (2004); 53,259 (2009 projected); Race: 93.5% White, 1.4% Black, 1.4% Asian, 10.2% Hispanic of any race (2004); Density: 2,281.1 persons per square mile (2004); Average household size: 2.34 (2004); Median age: 42.0 (2004); Male/female ratio: 97.7 (2004); Marriage status: 18.9% never married, 62.3% now married, 6.5% widowed, 12.3% divorced (2000); Foreign born: 10.5% (2000); Ancestry (includes multiple ancestries): 18.6% Irish, 17.9% German, 16.8% Italian, 13.6% English, 12.2% Other groups (2000).
Economy: Resort city experiencing much growth since 1970. Unemployment rate: 3.9% (2004); Total civilian labor force: 19,943 (2004); Single-family building permits issued: 591 (2004); Multi-family building permits issued: 87 (2004); Employment by occupation: 18.5% management, 21.9% professional, 16.0% services, 28.8% sales, 0.3% farming, 7.8% construction, 6.7% production (2000).
Income: Per capita income: $39,639 (2004); Median household income: $64,528 (2004); Average household income: $92,668 (2004); Percent of households with income of $100,000 or more: 27.7% (2004); Poverty rate: 4.8% (2000).
Taxes: Total city taxes per capita: $445 (2002); City property taxes per capita: $180 (2002).
Education: Percent of population age 25 and over with: High school diploma (including GED) or higher: 91.6% (2004); Bachelor's degree or higher: 34.9% (2004); Master's degree or higher: 12.3% (2004).

School District(s)

Palm Beach County School District (PK-12)
2002-03 Enrollment: 164,896 . . . . (561) 434-8200

Housing: Homeownership rate: 81.6% (2004); Median home value: $183,465 (2004); Median rent: $779 per month (2000); Median age of housing: 15 years (2000).
Hospitals: Jupiter Medical Center (156 beds)
Safety: Violent crime rate: 37.6 per 10,000 population; Property crime rate: 337.7 per 10,000 population (2003).
Newspapers: The Jupiter Courier (General - Circulation 8,000)
Transportation: Commute to work: 92.0% car, 0.4% public transportation, 0.8% walk, 4.9% work from home (2000); Travel time to work: 30.9% less than 15 minutes, 38.8% 15 to 30 minutes, 20.4% 30 to 45 minutes, 5.0% 45 to 60 minutes, 4.9% 60 minutes or more (2000)

Additional Information Contacts

Jupiter Chamber of Commerce . . . . (561) 746-7111
Jupiter Tequesta Hobe Sound Association of Realtors . . . . (561) 746-2707
Local Government Offices . . . . (561) 746-5134

JUPITER INLET COLONY (town). Covers a land area of 0.176 square miles and a water area of 0.052 square miles. Located at 26.94° N. Lat.; 80.07° W. Long.

Population: 434 (1990); 368 (2000); 390 (2004); 421 (2009 projected); Race: 99.7% White, 0.0% Black, 0.0% Asian, 0.0% Hispanic of any race (2004); Density: 2,215.1 persons per square mile (2004); Average household size: 2.03 (2004); Median age: 60.0 (2004); Male/female ratio: 100.0 (2004); Marriage status: 6.7% never married, 74.2% now married, 9.7% widowed, 9.4% divorced (2000); Foreign born: 6.2% (2000); Ancestry (includes multiple ancestries): 29.8% English, 20.2% Irish, 18.4% German, 12.2% Italian, 10.6% United States or American (2000).
Economy: Single-family building permits issued: 3 (2004); Multi-family building permits issued: 0 (2004); Employment by occupation: 29.1% management, 40.7% professional, 7.0% services, 17.4% sales, 0.0% farming, 0.0% construction, 5.8% production (2000).
Income: Per capita income: $59,538 (2004); Median household income: $61,842 (2004); Average household income: $120,938 (2004); Percent of households with income of $100,000 or more: 40.1% (2004); Poverty rate: 3.9% (2000).
Education: Percent of population age 25 and over with: High school diploma (including GED) or higher: 97.6% (2004); Bachelor's degree or higher: 56.1% (2004); Master's degree or higher: 21.5% (2004).
Housing: Homeownership rate: 94.3% (2004); Median home value: $630,556 (2004); Median rent: $2,000+ per month (2000); Median age of housing: 34 years (2000).
Safety: Violent crime rate: 0.0 per 10,000 population; Property crime rate: 51.3 per 10,000 population (2003).
Transportation: Commute to work: 91.4% car, 0.0% public transportation, 0.0% walk, 8.6% work from home (2000); Travel time to work: 23.0% less than 15 minutes, 44.6% 15 to 30 minutes, 21.6% 30 to 45 minutes, 5.4% 45 to 60 minutes, 5.4% 60 minutes or more (2000)

KINGS POINT (CDP). Covers a land area of 1.822 square miles and a water area of 0 square miles. Located at 26.44° N. Lat.; 80.14° W. Long.
Population: 12,428 (1990); 12,207 (2000); 12,374 (2004); 12,706 (2009 projected); Race: 98.9% White, 0.4% Black, 0.2% Asian, 1.5% Hispanic of any race (2004); Density: 6,790.2 persons per square mile (2004); Average household size: 1.50 (2004); Median age: 78.1 (2004); Male/female ratio: 67.1 (2004); Marriage status: 4.5% never married, 57.6% now married, 32.0% widowed, 5.9% divorced (2000); Foreign born: 10.8% (2000); Ancestry (includes multiple ancestries): 21.9% Other groups, 16.2% Russian, 10.9% Polish, 9.8% United States or American, 7.2% Italian (2000).
Economy: Employment by occupation: 9.5% management, 14.9% professional, 17.2% services, 43.6% sales, 0.6% farming, 2.0% construction, 12.2% production (2000).
Income: Per capita income: $24,029 (2004); Median household income: $28,034 (2004); Average household income: $35,822 (2004); Percent of households with income of $100,000 or more: 3.8% (2004); Poverty rate: 7.4% (2000).
Education: Percent of population age 25 and over with: High school diploma (including GED) or higher: 82.5% (2004); Bachelor's degree or higher: 13.0% (2004); Master's degree or higher: 5.1% (2004).
Housing: Homeownership rate: 91.2% (2004); Median home value: $56,993 (2004); Median rent: $523 per month (2000); Median age of housing: 22 years (2000).
Transportation: Commute to work: 94.2% car, 1.0% public transportation, 0.0% walk, 4.8% work from home (2000); Travel time to work: 37.0% less than 15 minutes, 41.5% 15 to 30 minutes, 16.4% 30 to 45 minutes, 2.3% 45 to 60 minutes, 2.7% 60 minutes or more (2000)

LAKE BELVEDERE ESTATES (CDP). Covers a land area of 0.579 square miles and a water area of 0.001 square miles. Located at 26.68° N. Lat.; 80.13° W. Long.
Population: 1,445 (1990); 1,525 (2000); 1,452 (2004); 1,351 (2009 projected); Race: 51.7% White, 38.6% Black, 1.6% Asian, 17.4% Hispanic of any race (2004); Density: 2,508.8 persons per square mile (2004); Average household size: 3.26 (2004); Median age: 34.2 (2004); Male/female ratio: 102.2 (2004); Marriage status: 31.9% never married, 49.3% now married, 4.5% widowed, 14.4% divorced (2000); Foreign born: 17.1% (2000); Ancestry (includes multiple ancestries): 32.4% Other groups, 11.7% German, 8.8% English, 8.2% Italian, 6.2% United States or American (2000).
Economy: Employment by occupation: 8.0% management, 13.0% professional, 17.4% services, 38.7% sales, 2.3% farming, 9.4% construction, 11.2% production (2000).
Income: Per capita income: $17,328 (2004); Median household income: $49,083 (2004); Average household income: $56,539 (2004); Percent of households with income of $100,000 or more: 7.6% (2004); Poverty rate: 17.9% (2000).
Education: Percent of population age 25 and over with: High school diploma (including GED) or higher: 76.9% (2004); Bachelor's degree or higher: 16.3% (2004); Master's degree or higher: 4.7% (2004).
Housing: Homeownership rate: 91.0% (2004); Median home value: $130,993 (2004); Median rent: $725 per month (2000); Median age of housing: 33 years (2000).
Transportation: Commute to work: 95.1% car, 1.1% public transportation, 0.7% walk, 3.1% work from home (2000); Travel time to work: 8.3% less than 15 minutes, 57.1% 15 to 30 minutes, 23.1% 30 to 45 minutes, 3.3% 45 to 60 minutes, 8.2% 60 minutes or more (2000)

LAKE CLARKE SHORES (town). Covers a land area of 0.975 square miles and a water area of 0.077 square miles. Located at 26.64° N. Lat.; 80.07° W. Long. Elevation is 10 feet.
Population: 3,364 (1990); 3,451 (2000); 3,402 (2004); 3,370 (2009 projected); Race: 91.1% White, 1.3% Black, 2.4% Asian, 23.8% Hispanic of any race (2004); Density: 3,488.7 persons per square mile (2004); Average household size: 2.43 (2004); Median age: 44.4 (2004); Male/female ratio: 99.9 (2004); Marriage status: 18.5% never married, 65.0% now married, 6.0% widowed, 10.5% divorced (2000); Foreign born: 19.5% (2000); Ancestry (includes multiple ancestries): 21.0% Other groups, 16.6% English, 15.1% German, 13.1% Irish, 8.8% Italian (2000).
Economy: Single-family building permits issued: 0 (2004); Multi-family building permits issued: 0 (2004); Employment by occupation: 21.5% management, 25.3% professional, 13.0% services, 25.1% sales, 0.0% farming, 7.7% construction, 7.4% production (2000).
Income: Per capita income: $33,732 (2004); Median household income: $66,933 (2004); Average household income: $82,087 (2004); Percent of households with income of $100,000 or more: 24.7% (2004); Poverty rate: 4.0% (2000).
Taxes: Total city taxes per capita: $362 (2002); City property taxes per capita: $223 (2002).
Education: Percent of population age 25 and over with: High school diploma (including GED) or higher: 89.7% (2004); Bachelor's degree or higher: 44.4% (2004); Master's degree or higher: 12.1% (2004).
Housing: Homeownership rate: 89.8% (2004); Median home value: $186,729 (2004); Median rent: $585 per month (2000); Median age of housing: 28 years (2000).
Safety: Violent crime rate: 5.6 per 10,000 population; Property crime rate: 230.1 per 10,000 population (2003).
Transportation: Commute to work: 91.8% car, 1.6% public transportation, 0.0% walk, 4.8% work from home (2000); Travel time to work: 28.3% less than 15 minutes, 48.6% 15 to 30 minutes, 17.3% 30 to 45 minutes, 4.5% 45 to 60 minutes, 1.3% 60 minutes or more (2000)

LAKE HARBOR (CDP). Covers a land area of 1.312 square miles and a water area of 0 square miles. Located at 26.68° N. Lat.; 80.80° W. Long. Elevation is 17 feet.
Population: 178 (1990); 195 (2000); 171 (2004); 146 (2009 projected); Race: 45.0% White, 38.6% Black, 4.1% Asian, 6.4% Hispanic of any race (2004); Density: 130.4 persons per square mile (2004); Average household size: 2.95 (2004); Median age: 36.9 (2004); Male/female ratio: 106.0 (2004); Marriage status: 24.7% never married, 59.7% now married, 0.0% widowed, 15.6% divorced (2000); Foreign born: 30.1% (2000); Ancestry (includes multiple ancestries): 33.3% Other groups, 31.2% African, 8.6% Scottish, 8.6% English, 3.2% Jamaican (2000).
Economy: Employment by occupation: 0.0% management, 0.0% professional, 16.7% services, 0.0% sales, 55.6% farming, 0.0% construction, 27.8% production (2000).
Income: Per capita income: $11,959 (2004); Median household income: $35,500 (2004); Average household income: $35,259 (2004); Percent of households with income of $100,000 or more: 0.0% (2004); Poverty rate: 9.7% (2000).
Education: Percent of population age 25 and over with: High school diploma (including GED) or higher: 50.5% (2004); Bachelor's degree or higher: 0.0% (2004); Master's degree or higher: 0.0% (2004).
Housing: Homeownership rate: 36.2% (2004); Median home value: $50,000 (2004); Median rent: $325 per month (2000); Median age of housing: 37 years (2000).
Transportation: Commute to work: 100.0% car, 0.0% public transportation, 0.0% walk, 0.0% work from home (2000); Travel time to work: 38.9% less than 15 minutes, 0.0% 15 to 30 minutes, 44.4% 30 to 45 minutes, 0.0% 45 to 60 minutes, 16.7% 60 minutes or more (2000)

LAKE PARK (town). Covers a land area of 2.170 square miles and a water area of 0.176 square miles. Located at 26.80° N. Lat.; 80.06° W. Long. Elevation is 5 feet.
Population: 7,362 (1990); 8,721 (2000); 8,907 (2004); 9,225 (2009 projected); Race: 34.6% White, 54.8% Black, 3.0% Asian, 6.8% Hispanic of any race (2004); Density: 4,104.5 persons per square mile (2004); Average household size: 2.60 (2004); Median age: 34.8 (2004); Male/female ratio: 96.8 (2004); Marriage status: 31.9% never married, 49.2% now married, 7.2% widowed, 11.6% divorced (2000); Foreign born: 24.8% (2000); Ancestry (includes multiple ancestries): 26.8% Other groups, 14.4% Haitian, 8.9% United States or American, 8.3% German, 7.4% Irish (2000).
Economy: Single-family building permits issued: 0 (2004); Multi-family building permits issued: 0 (2004); Employment by occupation: 10.8% management, 13.5% professional, 29.1% services, 24.5% sales, 0.6% farming, 10.5% construction, 11.0% production (2000).
Income: Per capita income: $17,778 (2004); Median household income: $33,542 (2004); Average household income: $45,300 (2004); Percent of households with income of $100,000 or more: 5.8% (2004); Poverty rate: 16.8% (2000).
Taxes: Total city taxes per capita: $655 (2002); City property taxes per capita: $439 (2002).
Education: Percent of population age 25 and over with: High school diploma (including GED) or higher: 74.3% (2004); Bachelor's degree or higher: 16.0% (2004); Master's degree or higher: 6.1% (2004).

School District(s)

Palm Beach County School District (PK-12)
2002-03 Enrollment: 164,896 .... (561) 434-8200

Housing: Homeownership rate: 46.3% (2004); Median home value: $123,337 (2004); Median rent: $596 per month (2000); Median age of housing: 31 years (2000).
Safety: Violent crime rate: 120.1 per 10,000 population; Property crime rate: 966.1 per 10,000 population (2003).
Newspapers: WeekDay (General - Circulation 11,500)
Transportation: Commute to work: 93.8% car, 1.9% public transportation, 1.1% walk, 1.4% work from home (2000); Travel time to work: 28.6% less than 15 minutes, 45.1% 15 to 30 minutes, 16.3% 30 to 45 minutes, 4.4% 45 to 60 minutes, 5.6% 60 minutes or more (2000)

Additional Information Contacts

Local Government Offices .... (561) 881-3300

LAKE WORTH (city). Covers a land area of 5.643 square miles and a water area of 0.820 square miles. Located at 26.62° N. Lat.; 80.05° W. Long. Elevation is 19 feet.
History: Named for General William Jenkins Worth, who saw service in the Seminole and Mexican Wars. The town of Lake Worth developed as a tourist town along both shores of the lake. The lake, too, was named for General Worth.
Population: 29,083 (1990); 35,133 (2000); 35,837 (2004); 37,032 (2009 projected); Race: 60.6% White, 20.0% Black, 0.8% Asian, 36.6% Hispanic of any race (2004); Density: 6,350.3 persons per square mile (2004); Average household size: 2.56 (2004); Median age: 35.6 (2004); Male/female ratio: 108.6 (2004); Marriage status: 31.9% never married, 47.4% now married, 7.3% widowed, 13.4% divorced (2000); Foreign born: 35.6% (2000); Ancestry (includes multiple ancestries): 34.6% Other groups, 8.7% German, 8.5% Irish, 7.8% Haitian, 6.1% English (2000).
Economy: Unemployment rate: 6.0% (2004); Total civilian labor force: 20,371 (2004); Single-family building permits issued: 44 (2004); Multi-family building permits issued: 213 (2004); Employment by occupation: 7.5% management, 14.4% professional, 25.3% services, 22.8% sales, 2.4% farming, 17.3% construction, 10.4% production (2000).
Income: Per capita income: $16,622 (2004); Median household income: $32,027 (2004); Average household income: $41,537 (2004); Percent of households with income of $100,000 or more: 5.5% (2004); Poverty rate: 20.0% (2000).
Taxes: Total city taxes per capita: $388 (2002); City property taxes per capita: $237 (2002).
Education: Percent of population age 25 and over with: High school diploma (including GED) or higher: 66.2% (2004); Bachelor's degree or higher: 16.3% (2004); Master's degree or higher: 5.4% (2004).

School District(s)

Palm Beach County School District (PK-12)
2002-03 Enrollment: 164,896 .... (561) 434-8200

Four-year College(s)

New Covenant International University
2003-04 Enrollment: n/a .... (561) 965-3132

Two-year College(s)

Academy of Healing Arts Massage & Facial Skin Care (Private, For-profit)
2003-04 Enrollment: 326 .... (561) 965-5550
Keiser Career College (Private, For-profit)
2003-04 Enrollment: 733 .... (561) 547-5472
2003-04 Tuition: In-state $10,920; Out-of-state $10,920
Palm Beach Community College (Public)
2003-04 Enrollment: 22,660 .... (561) 967-7222
2003-04 Tuition: In-state $1,950; Out-of-state $6,890

Housing: Homeownership rate: 52.7% (2004); Median home value: $104,568 (2004); Median rent: $484 per month (2000); Median age of housing: 38 years (2000).
Hospitals: Holley State Hospital, AG (100 beds)
Safety: Violent crime rate: 138.0 per 10,000 population; Property crime rate: 796.9 per 10,000 population (2003).
Newspapers: Beachcomber (General - Circulation 3,500); Coastal Observer (General - Circulation 38,000); Lake Worth Herald Press (General - Circulation 38,000)
Transportation: Commute to work: 90.7% car, 2.4% public transportation, 1.7% walk, 2.6% work from home (2000); Travel time to work: 19.4% less than 15 minutes, 43.9% 15 to 30 minutes, 23.4% 30 to 45 minutes, 6.5% 45 to 60 minutes, 6.8% 60 minutes or more (2000)

Additional Information Contacts

Lake Worth Chamber of Commerce .... (561) 582-4401
Local Government Offices .... (561) 586-1662

LAKE WORTH CORRIDOR (CDP). Covers a land area of 3.423 square miles and a water area of 0 square miles. Located at 26.62° N. Lat.; 80.10° W. Long.
Population: 14,533 (1990); 18,663 (2000); 18,651 (2004); 18,683 (2009 projected); Race: 54.2% White, 16.8% Black, 1.3% Asian, 51.3% Hispanic of any race (2004); Density: 5,449.2 persons per square mile (2004); Average household size: 3.22 (2004); Median age: 28.0 (2004); Male/female ratio: 115.3 (2004); Marriage status: 35.0% never married, 46.1% now married, 3.9% widowed, 15.0% divorced (2000); Foreign born: 29.9% (2000); Ancestry (includes multiple ancestries): 46.5% Other groups, 9.4% Irish, 8.1% German, 5.3% Italian, 5.0% United States or American (2000).
Economy: Employment by occupation: 5.6% management, 7.9% professional, 24.7% services, 23.2% sales, 2.7% farming, 23.2% construction, 12.6% production (2000).
Income: Per capita income: $12,762 (2004); Median household income: $33,505 (2004); Average household income: $40,146 (2004); Percent of households with income of $100,000 or more: 3.4% (2004); Poverty rate: 20.0% (2000).
Education: Percent of population age 25 and over with: High school diploma (including GED) or higher: 59.7% (2004); Bachelor's degree or higher: 6.2% (2004); Master's degree or higher: 2.2% (2004).
Housing: Homeownership rate: 39.9% (2004); Median home value: $106,135 (2004); Median rent: $564 per month (2000); Median age of housing: 27 years (2000).
Transportation: Commute to work: 92.3% car, 2.7% public transportation, 1.4% walk, 1.0% work from home (2000); Travel time to work: 17.1% less than 15 minutes, 39.5% 15 to 30 minutes, 30.9% 30 to 45 minutes, 6.2% 45 to 60 minutes, 6.3% 60 minutes or more (2000)

LAKESIDE GREEN (CDP). Covers a land area of 0.545 square miles and a water area of 0 square miles. Located at 26.73° N. Lat.; 80.11° W. Long.
Population: 2,994 (1990); 3,311 (2000); 3,139 (2004); 3,014 (2009 projected); Race: 68.6% White, 19.9% Black, 3.7% Asian, 12.5% Hispanic of any race (2004); Density: 5,761.9 persons per square mile (2004); Average household size: 2.39 (2004); Median age: 39.7 (2004); Male/female ratio: 84.3 (2004); Marriage status: 25.8% never married, 48.5% now married, 10.2% widowed, 15.5% divorced (2000); Foreign born: 12.5% (2000); Ancestry (includes multiple ancestries): 40.2% Other groups, 12.1% Irish, 11.4% Italian, 10.1% German, 6.3% English (2000).
Economy: Employment by occupation: 13.7% management, 30.9% professional, 18.2% services, 26.4% sales, 0.0% farming, 5.9% construction, 4.9% production (2000).
Income: Per capita income: $24,705 (2004); Median household income: $47,688 (2004); Average household income: $54,250 (2004); Percent of

households with income of $100,000 or more: 10.4% (2004); Poverty rate: 6.7% (2000).
Education: Percent of population age 25 and over with: High school diploma (including GED) or higher: 89.6% (2004); Bachelor's degree or higher: 31.5% (2004); Master's degree or higher: 10.0% (2004).
Housing: Homeownership rate: 69.3% (2004); Median home value: $128,914 (2004); Median rent: $791 per month (2000); Median age of housing: 15 years (2000).
Transportation: Commute to work: 94.4% car, 0.3% public transportation, 1.3% walk, 3.6% work from home (2000); Travel time to work: 23.3% less than 15 minutes, 48.2% 15 to 30 minutes, 19.0% 30 to 45 minutes, 4.3% 45 to 60 minutes, 5.2% 60 minutes or more (2000)

LANTANA (town). Covers a land area of 2.282 square miles and a water area of 0.624 square miles. Located at 26.58° N. Lat.; 80.05° W. Long. Elevation is 10 feet.
History: Lantana, a tourist community on Lake Worth, was named for a flowering shrub, common throughout Florida, called lantana.
Population: 8,392 (1990); 9,437 (2000); 9,740 (2004); 10,198 (2009 projected); Race: 74.7% White, 13.6% Black, 1.0% Asian, 22.0% Hispanic of any race (2004); Density: 4,267.6 persons per square mile (2004); Average household size: 2.49 (2004); Median age: 37.5 (2004); Male/female ratio: 104.9 (2004); Marriage status: 28.1% never married, 52.5% now married, 6.4% widowed, 13.1% divorced (2000); Foreign born: 21.5% (2000); Ancestry (includes multiple ancestries): 19.8% Other groups, 13.7% German, 13.7% Irish, 9.5% English, 6.5% Italian (2000).
Economy: Single-family building permits issued: 3 (2004); Multi-family building permits issued: 71 (2004); Employment by occupation: 7.9% management, 16.4% professional, 23.0% services, 26.8% sales, 1.2% farming, 15.2% construction, 9.5% production (2000).
Income: Per capita income: $22,762 (2004); Median household income: $38,707 (2004); Average household income: $56,173 (2004); Percent of households with income of $100,000 or more: 9.7% (2004); Poverty rate: 8.3% (2000).
Taxes: Total city taxes per capita: $487 (2002); City property taxes per capita: $271 (2002).
Education: Percent of population age 25 and over with: High school diploma (including GED) or higher: 75.9% (2004); Bachelor's degree or higher: 16.3% (2004); Master's degree or higher: 6.7% (2004).

School District(s)

Palm Beach County School District (PK-12)
2002-03 Enrollment: 164,896 .... (561) 434-8200

Housing: Homeownership rate: 67.8% (2004); Median home value: $120,460 (2004); Median rent: $530 per month (2000); Median age of housing: 31 years (2000).
Safety: Violent crime rate: 110.6 per 10,000 population; Property crime rate: 759.7 per 10,000 population (2003).
Transportation: Commute to work: 93.0% car, 2.4% public transportation, 0.6% walk, 2.1% work from home (2000); Travel time to work: 24.8% less than 15 minutes, 40.4% 15 to 30 minutes, 25.4% 30 to 45 minutes, 4.3% 45 to 60 minutes, 5.1% 60 minutes or more (2000)
Additional Information Contacts
Local Government Offices .... (561) 540-5000

LIMESTONE CREEK (CDP). Covers a land area of 0.453 square miles and a water area of 0 square miles. Located at 26.94° N. Lat.; 80.14° W. Long.
Population: 424 (1990); 569 (2000); 629 (2004); 703 (2009 projected); Race: 10.8% White, 84.6% Black, 0.8% Asian, 9.2% Hispanic of any race (2004); Density: 1,389.2 persons per square mile (2004); Average household size: 3.55 (2004); Median age: 27.1 (2004); Male/female ratio: 96.6 (2004); Marriage status: 27.7% never married, 49.0% now married, 13.7% widowed, 9.6% divorced (2000); Foreign born: 0.0% (2000); Ancestry (includes multiple ancestries): 72.4% Other groups, 14.5% Irish, 11.5% English, 6.0% United States or American (2000).
Economy: Employment by occupation: 22.8% management, 0.0% professional, 29.7% services, 19.0% sales, 0.0% farming, 16.5% construction, 12.0% production (2000).
Income: Per capita income: $11,626 (2004); Median household income: $32,845 (2004); Average household income: $41,314 (2004); Percent of households with income of $100,000 or more: 3.4% (2004); Poverty rate: 8.5% (2000).
Education: Percent of population age 25 and over with: High school diploma (including GED) or higher: 70.6% (2004); Bachelor's degree or higher: 0.0% (2004); Master's degree or higher: 0.0% (2004).
Housing: Homeownership rate: 84.7% (2004); Median home value: $118,116 (2004); Median rent: $n/a per month (2000); Median age of housing: 4 years (2000).
Transportation: Commute to work: 100.0% car, 0.0% public transportation, 0.0% walk, 0.0% work from home (2000); Travel time to work: 32.9% less than 15 minutes, 58.2% 15 to 30 minutes, 0.0% 30 to 45 minutes, 8.9% 45 to 60 minutes, 0.0% 60 minutes or more (2000)

LOXAHATCHEE (unincorporated postal area, zip code 33470). Covers a land area of 422.292 square miles and a water area of 0.300 square miles. Located at 26.75° N. Lat.; 80.30° W. Long. Elevation is 22 feet.
Population: 19,103 (2000); Race: 87.8% White, 5.6% Black, 1.2% Asian, 10.9% Hispanic of any race (2000); Density: 45.2 persons per square mile (2000); Age: 31.6% under 18, 4.6% over 64 (2000); Marriage status: 20.9% never married, 66.8% now married, 3.4% widowed, 8.8% divorced (2000); Foreign born: 10.0% (2000); Ancestry (includes multiple ancestries): 19.6% Other groups, 15.8% Irish, 15.4% German, 12.0% Italian, 8.2% English (2000).
Economy: Employment by occupation: 13.5% management, 16.0% professional, 14.9% services, 25.8% sales, 1.3% farming, 19.2% construction, 9.3% production (2000).
Income: Per capita income: $22,526 (2000); Median household income: $61,644 (2000); Poverty rate: 4.5% (2000).
Education: Percent of population age 25 and over with: High school diploma (including GED) or higher: 85.3% (2000); Bachelor's degree or higher: 15.7% (2000).

School District(s)

Palm Beach County School District (PK-12)
2002-03 Enrollment: 164,896 .... (561) 434-8200

Housing: Homeownership rate: 94.6% (2000); Median home value: $140,300 (2000); Median rent: $1,052 per month (2000); Median age of housing: 6 years (2000).
Hospitals: Palms West Hospital (117 beds)
Transportation: Commute to work: 94.3% car, 0.2% public transportation, 1.0% walk, 3.8% work from home (2000); Travel time to work: 9.4% less than 15 minutes, 20.2% 15 to 30 minutes, 29.4% 30 to 45 minutes, 18.0% 45 to 60 minutes, 23.0% 60 minutes or more (2000)
Additional Information Contacts
Loxahatchee Chamber of Commerce .... (561) 790-6200

MANALAPAN (town). Covers a land area of 0.450 square miles and a water area of 1.983 square miles. Located at 26.56° N. Lat.; 80.04° W. Long. Elevation is 4 feet.
Population: 312 (1990); 321 (2000); 322 (2004); 326 (2009 projected); Race: 97.5% White, 0.0% Black, 1.9% Asian, 3.7% Hispanic of any race (2004); Density: 714.9 persons per square mile (2004); Average household size: 1.92 (2004); Median age: 60.8 (2004); Male/female ratio: 94.0 (2004); Marriage status: 6.9% never married, 69.3% now married, 18.5% widowed, 5.3% divorced (2000); Foreign born: 15.5% (2000); Ancestry (includes multiple ancestries): 20.7% German, 18.0% Irish, 13.3% English, 7.1% Other groups, 5.3% Scottish (2000).
Economy: Single-family building permits issued: 2 (2004); Multi-family building permits issued: 0 (2004); Employment by occupation: 46.8% management, 24.7% professional, 7.8% services, 14.3% sales, 0.0% farming, 6.5% construction, 0.0% production (2000).
Income: Per capita income: $116,809 (2004); Median household income: $146,875 (2004); Average household income: $223,884 (2004); Percent of households with income of $100,000 or more: 58.9% (2004); Poverty rate: 5.9% (2000).
Taxes: Total city taxes per capita: $5,508 (2002); City property taxes per capita: $4,383 (2002).
Education: Percent of population age 25 and over with: High school diploma (including GED) or higher: 97.6% (2004); Bachelor's degree or higher: 43.4% (2004); Master's degree or higher: 17.0% (2004).
Housing: Homeownership rate: 95.8% (2004); Median home value: $1 million+ (2004); Median rent: $2,000+ per month (2000); Median age of housing: 26 years (2000).
Safety: Violent crime rate: 30.0 per 10,000 population; Property crime rate: 660.7 per 10,000 population (2003).
Transportation: Commute to work: 79.2% car, 0.0% public transportation, 3.9% walk, 16.9% work from home (2000); Travel time to work: 15.6% less than 15 minutes, 48.4% 15 to 30 minutes, 23.4% 30 to 45 minutes, 9.4% 45 to 60 minutes, 3.1% 60 minutes or more (2000)

MANGONIA PARK (town). Covers a land area of 0.709 square miles and a water area of 0 square miles. Located at 26.75° N. Lat.; 80.07° W. Long. Elevation is 14 feet.
Population: 1,453 (1990); 1,283 (2000); 1,320 (2004); 1,379 (2009 projected); Race: 8.0% White, 81.7% Black, 0.3% Asian, 10.7% Hispanic of any race (2004); Density: 1,861.9 persons per square mile (2004); Average household size: 2.95 (2004); Median age: 31.5 (2004); Male/female ratio: 88.6 (2004); Marriage status: 42.2% never married, 41.0% now married, 4.8% widowed, 12.0% divorced (2000); Foreign born: 24.7% (2000); Ancestry (includes multiple ancestries): 62.9% Other groups, 9.0% Haitian, 4.4% Irish, 3.9% Jamaican, 3.6% United States or American (2000).
Economy: Single-family building permits issued: 0 (2004); Multi-family building permits issued: 0 (2004); Employment by occupation: 4.2% management, 13.2% professional, 24.0% services, 29.3% sales, 1.7% farming, 12.5% construction, 15.1% production (2000).
Income: Per capita income: $17,741 (2004); Median household income: $40,463 (2004); Average household income: $52,388 (2004); Percent of households with income of $100,000 or more: 9.6% (2004); Poverty rate: 19.2% (2000).
Education: Percent of population age 25 and over with: High school diploma (including GED) or higher: 71.6% (2004); Bachelor's degree or higher: 8.6% (2004); Master's degree or higher: 0.9% (2004).
Housing: Homeownership rate: 50.8% (2004); Median home value: $96,053 (2004); Median rent: $554 per month (2000); Median age of housing: 28 years (2000).
Safety: Violent crime rate: 950.9 per 10,000 population; Property crime rate: 3,486.8 per 10,000 population (2003).
Transportation: Commute to work: 86.8% car, 8.6% public transportation, 3.5% walk, 0.5% work from home (2000); Travel time to work: 37.8% less than 15 minutes, 36.3% 15 to 30 minutes, 16.0% 30 to 45 minutes, 5.5% 45 to 60 minutes, 4.4% 60 minutes or more (2000)

MISSION BAY (CDP). Covers a land area of 0.773 square miles and a water area of 0 square miles. Located at 26.36° N. Lat.; 80.21° W. Long.
Population: 1,227 (1990); 2,926 (2000); 3,429 (2004); 4,035 (2009 projected); Race: 90.8% White, 1.7% Black, 3.4% Asian, 12.3% Hispanic of any race (2004); Density: 4,436.2 persons per square mile (2004); Average household size: 2.94 (2004); Median age: 38.3 (2004); Male/female ratio: 94.2 (2004); Marriage status: 16.8% never married, 73.3% now married, 3.6% widowed, 6.3% divorced (2000); Foreign born: 19.4% (2000); Ancestry (includes multiple ancestries): 26.7% Other groups, 15.7% Italian, 8.2% United States or American, 8.0% Irish, 7.5% Polish (2000).
Economy: Employment by occupation: 25.4% management, 31.8% professional, 8.2% services, 25.5% sales, 0.0% farming, 4.8% construction, 4.2% production (2000).
Income: Per capita income: $43,797 (2004); Median household income: $99,192 (2004); Average household income: $128,910 (2004); Percent of households with income of $100,000 or more: 49.4% (2004); Poverty rate: 2.3% (2000).
Education: Percent of population age 25 and over with: High school diploma (including GED) or higher: 97.6% (2004); Bachelor's degree or higher: 50.5% (2004); Master's degree or higher: 20.9% (2004).
Housing: Homeownership rate: 90.6% (2004); Median home value: $254,780 (2004); Median rent: $1,688 per month (2000); Median age of housing: 9 years (2000).
Transportation: Commute to work: 91.1% car, 1.7% public transportation, 0.0% walk, 5.1% work from home (2000); Travel time to work: 13.8% less than 15 minutes, 44.1% 15 to 30 minutes, 28.0% 30 to 45 minutes, 7.2% 45 to 60 minutes, 6.9% 60 minutes or more (2000)

NORTH PALM BEACH (village). Covers a land area of 3.561 square miles and a water area of 2.243 square miles. Located at 26.81° N. Lat.; 80.06° W. Long. Elevation is 25 feet.
Population: 12,009 (1990); 12,064 (2000); 12,677 (2004); 13,526 (2009 projected); Race: 95.2% White, 1.3% Black, 1.6% Asian, 4.6% Hispanic of any race (2004); Density: 3,560.1 persons per square mile (2004); Average household size: 1.91 (2004); Median age: 50.9 (2004); Male/female ratio: 94.6 (2004); Marriage status: 18.2% never married, 58.3% now married, 10.9% widowed, 12.6% divorced (2000); Foreign born: 8.7% (2000); Ancestry (includes multiple ancestries): 22.1% Irish, 20.4% German, 15.1% English, 11.5% Italian, 7.3% Other groups (2000).
Economy: Single-family building permits issued: 26 (2004); Multi-family building permits issued: 0 (2004); Employment by occupation: 18.2% management, 23.8% professional, 13.8% services, 30.1% sales, 0.2% farming, 8.6% construction, 5.4% production (2000).
Income: Per capita income: $43,220 (2004); Median household income: $58,764 (2004); Average household income: $82,658 (2004); Percent of households with income of $100,000 or more: 23.9% (2004); Poverty rate: 3.9% (2000).
Taxes: Total city taxes per capita: $713 (2002); City property taxes per capita: $416 (2002).
Education: Percent of population age 25 and over with: High school diploma (including GED) or higher: 92.6% (2004); Bachelor's degree or higher: 35.7% (2004); Master's degree or higher: 12.2% (2004).

School District(s)

Palm Beach County School District (PK-12)
2002-03 Enrollment: 164,896 . . . . (561) 434-8200
Housing: Homeownership rate: 77.1% (2004); Median home value: $164,555 (2004); Median rent: $723 per month (2000); Median age of housing: 28 years (2000).
Safety: Violent crime rate: 32.9 per 10,000 population; Property crime rate: 361.5 per 10,000 population (2003).
Transportation: Commute to work: 91.7% car, 0.4% public transportation, 1.3% walk, 5.4% work from home (2000); Travel time to work: 37.1% less than 15 minutes, 41.3% 15 to 30 minutes, 13.3% 30 to 45 minutes, 3.5% 45 to 60 minutes, 4.8% 60 minutes or more (2000)
Additional Information Contacts
Local Government Offices . . . . (561) 841-3355

OCEAN RIDGE (town). Covers a land area of 0.857 square miles and a water area of 1.141 square miles. Located at 26.52° N. Lat.; 80.05° W. Long. Elevation is 8 feet.
Population: 1,570 (1990); 1,636 (2000); 1,631 (2004); 1,652 (2009 projected); Race: 98.0% White, 0.1% Black, 0.6% Asian, 3.4% Hispanic of any race (2004); Density: 1,903.8 persons per square mile (2004); Average household size: 1.82 (2004); Median age: 56.4 (2004); Male/female ratio: 95.6 (2004); Marriage status: 11.9% never married, 63.3% now married, 13.1% widowed, 11.7% divorced (2000); Foreign born: 15.1% (2000); Ancestry (includes multiple ancestries): 19.7% Irish, 18.6% German, 14.2% English, 10.1% Italian, 8.5% Other groups (2000).
Economy: Single-family building permits issued: 4 (2004); Multi-family building permits issued: 0 (2004); Employment by occupation: 32.7% management, 18.6% professional, 10.2% services, 32.9% sales, 0.0% farming, 2.8% construction, 2.9% production (2000).
Income: Per capita income: $77,180 (2004); Median household income: $71,217 (2004); Average household income: $140,805 (2004); Percent of households with income of $100,000 or more: 40.4% (2004); Poverty rate: 4.7% (2000).
Education: Percent of population age 25 and over with: High school diploma (including GED) or higher: 94.3% (2004); Bachelor's degree or higher: 42.5% (2004); Master's degree or higher: 19.1% (2004).
Housing: Homeownership rate: 84.8% (2004); Median home value: $348,649 (2004); Median rent: $746 per month (2000); Median age of housing: 30 years (2000).
Safety: Violent crime rate: 11.7 per 10,000 population; Property crime rate: 410.3 per 10,000 population (2003).
Transportation: Commute to work: 78.8% car, 0.0% public transportation, 0.0% walk, 20.4% work from home (2000); Travel time to work: 26.9% less than 15 minutes, 39.9% 15 to 30 minutes, 21.6% 30 to 45 minutes, 4.6% 45 to 60 minutes, 7.0% 60 minutes or more (2000)

PAHOKEE (city). Covers a land area of 5.395 square miles and a water area of 0 square miles. Located at 26.82° N. Lat.; 80.66° W. Long. Elevation is 15 feet.
History: Pahokee developed on Lake Okeechobee as a shipping point for winter vegetables.
Population: 6,898 (1990); 5,985 (2000); 6,171 (2004); 6,453 (2009 projected); Race: 22.0% White, 55.5% Black, 0.5% Asian, 35.0% Hispanic of any race (2004); Density: 1,143.9 persons per square mile (2004); Average household size: 3.58 (2004); Median age: 25.4 (2004); Male/female ratio: 105.2 (2004); Marriage status: 33.1% never married, 49.3% now married, 9.5% widowed, 8.1% divorced (2000); Foreign born: 19.5% (2000); Ancestry (includes multiple ancestries): 67.8% Other groups, 5.6% United States or American, 2.4% Jamaican, 2.0% English, 1.5% Irish (2000).
Economy: Single-family building permits issued: 39 (2004); Multi-family building permits issued: 0 (2004); Employment by occupation: 7.1%

management, 10.2% professional, 21.8% services, 19.0% sales, 12.8% farming, 9.3% construction, 19.8% production (2000).
Income: Per capita income: $11,003 (2004); Median household income: $27,943 (2004); Average household income: $38,737 (2004); Percent of households with income of $100,000 or more: 5.6% (2004); Poverty rate: 32.0% (2000).
Education: Percent of population age 25 and over with: High school diploma (including GED) or higher: 46.3% (2004); Bachelor's degree or higher: 6.4% (2004); Master's degree or higher: 1.6% (2004).

School District(s)

Palm Beach County School District (PK-12)
2002-03 Enrollment: 164,896 . . . . (561) 434-8200
Housing: Homeownership rate: 57.9% (2004); Median home value: $70,791 (2004); Median rent: $249 per month (2000); Median age of housing: 30 years (2000).
Safety: Violent crime rate: 154.3 per 10,000 population; Property crime rate: 464.4 per 10,000 population (2003).
Transportation: Commute to work: 83.2% car, 8.6% public transportation, 4.4% walk, 0.6% work from home (2000); Travel time to work: 33.7% less than 15 minutes, 30.8% 15 to 30 minutes, 10.6% 30 to 45 minutes, 11.2% 45 to 60 minutes, 13.6% 60 minutes or more (2000)

Additional Information Contacts

Local Government Offices . . . . (561) 924-5534
Pahokee Chamber of Commerce . . . . (561) 924-5579

PALM BEACH (town). Covers a land area of 3.922 square miles and a water area of 6.518 square miles. Located at 26.71° N. Lat.; 80.03° W. Long. Elevation is 15 feet.
History: The first families to settle in what is now Palm Beach came in 1873 to the island formed by Lake Worth on the west and the Atlantic Ocean on the east. Captain Elisha Newton Dimick, who built a house on the island in 1876, is credited with being the founder of the town. In 1880 the Palm City post office was established, and soon the name was changed to Palm Beach. Luxurious hotels and lavish private residences made Palm Beach into an exclusive resort town.
Population: 9,814 (1990); 10,468 (2000); 10,579 (2004); 10,831 (2009 projected); Race: 94.8% White, 3.5% Black, 0.7% Asian, 2.9% Hispanic of any race (2004); Density: 2,697.5 persons per square mile (2004); Average household size: 1.79 (2004); Median age: 66.2 (2004); Male/female ratio: 79.8 (2004); Marriage status: 10.3% never married, 61.1% now married, 18.3% widowed, 10.4% divorced (2000); Foreign born: 15.4% (2000); Ancestry (includes multiple ancestries): 12.9% Other groups, 12.8% English, 11.5% German, 10.5% Russian, 8.7% Irish (2000).
Economy: Single-family building permits issued: 29 (2004); Multi-family building permits issued: 7 (2004); Employment by occupation: 32.0% management, 24.8% professional, 10.6% services, 30.7% sales, 0.0% farming, 1.2% construction, 0.7% production (2000).
Income: Per capita income: $99,112 (2004); Median household income: $101,006 (2004); Average household income: $177,818 (2004); Percent of households with income of $100,000 or more: 50.2% (2004); Poverty rate: 5.3% (2000).
Taxes: Total city taxes per capita: $3,735 (2002); City property taxes per capita: $2,511 (2002).
Education: Percent of population age 25 and over with: High school diploma (including GED) or higher: 95.7% (2004); Bachelor's degree or higher: 53.5% (2004); Master's degree or higher: 22.2% (2004).

School District(s)

Palm Beach County School District (PK-12)
2002-03 Enrollment: 164,896 . . . . (561) 434-8200
Housing: Homeownership rate: 83.7% (2004); Median home value: $488,142 (2004); Median rent: $844 per month (2000); Median age of housing: 29 years (2000).
Safety: Violent crime rate: 4.0 per 10,000 population; Property crime rate: 213.2 per 10,000 population (2003).
Newspapers: Palm Beach Daily News (Circulation 7,500)
Transportation: Commute to work: 67.4% car, 0.4% public transportation, 9.5% walk, 20.3% work from home (2000); Travel time to work: 51.4% less than 15 minutes, 30.2% 15 to 30 minutes, 10.3% 30 to 45 minutes, 4.8% 45 to 60 minutes, 3.3% 60 minutes or more (2000)

Additional Information Contacts

Local Government Offices . . . . (561) 838-5400
Palm Beach Board of Realtors. . . . . (561) 659-3810
Palm Beach Chamber of Commerce . . . . (561) 655-3282

PALM BEACH GARDENS (city). Covers a land area of 55.683 square miles and a water area of 0.251 square miles. Located at 26.82° N. Lat.; 80.11° W. Long. Elevation is 20 feet.
Population: 24,518 (1990); 35,058 (2000); 40,060 (2004); 46,190 (2009 projected); Race: 92.6% White, 3.0% Black, 2.5% Asian, 7.2% Hispanic of any race (2004); Density: 719.4 persons per square mile (2004); Average household size: 2.21 (2004); Median age: 45.8 (2004); Male/female ratio: 90.1 (2004); Marriage status: 18.4% never married, 60.2% now married, 8.1% widowed, 13.4% divorced (2000); Foreign born: 10.8% (2000); Ancestry (includes multiple ancestries): 17.2% German, 15.2% Irish, 13.7% Other groups, 13.3% English, 12.9% Italian (2000).
Economy: Industries include printing and publishing, diversified light manufacturing. Unemployment rate: 2.8% (2004); Total civilian labor force: 18,550 (2004); Single-family building permits issued: 1,426 (2004); Multi-family building permits issued: 1,157 (2004); Employment by occupation: 21.4% management, 25.5% professional, 12.3% services, 30.3% sales, 0.2% farming, 4.6% construction, 5.7% production (2000).
Income: Per capita income: $47,931 (2004); Median household income: $66,131 (2004); Average household income: $105,323 (2004); Percent of households with income of $100,000 or more: 29.9% (2004); Poverty rate: 5.6% (2000).
Education: Percent of population age 25 and over with: High school diploma (including GED) or higher: 94.0% (2004); Bachelor's degree or higher: 44.0% (2004); Master's degree or higher: 17.4% (2004).

School District(s)

Palm Beach County School District (PK-12)
2002-03 Enrollment: 164,896 . . . . (561) 434-8200
Housing: Homeownership rate: 80.1% (2004); Median home value: $181,207 (2004); Median rent: $846 per month (2000); Median age of housing: 14 years (2000).
Hospitals: Palm Beach Gardens Medical Center (204 beds)
Safety: Violent crime rate: 33.0 per 10,000 population; Property crime rate: 470.1 per 10,000 population (2003).
Transportation: Commute to work: 92.3% car, 0.3% public transportation, 1.1% walk, 5.4% work from home (2000); Travel time to work: 29.5% less than 15 minutes, 47.3% 15 to 30 minutes, 15.3% 30 to 45 minutes, 3.7% 45 to 60 minutes, 4.2% 60 minutes or more (2000)

Additional Information Contacts

Local Government Offices . . . . (561) 799-4100
Palm Beach Gardens Chamber of Commerce . . . . (561) 694-2300

PALM BEACH SHORES (town). Covers a land area of 0.253 square miles and a water area of 0.126 square miles. Located at 26.77° N. Lat.; 80.03° W. Long. Elevation is 10 feet.
Population: 1,040 (1990); 1,269 (2000); 1,345 (2004); 1,448 (2009 projected); Race: 84.4% White, 13.1% Black, 0.7% Asian, 3.2% Hispanic of any race (2004); Density: 5,310.6 persons per square mile (2004); Average household size: 1.80 (2004); Median age: 53.1 (2004); Male/female ratio: 100.1 (2004); Marriage status: 21.2% never married, 49.5% now married, 13.2% widowed, 16.1% divorced (2000); Foreign born: 12.8% (2000); Ancestry (includes multiple ancestries): 18.9% German, 16.5% Irish, 16.0% English, 7.3% Other groups, 7.2% Italian (2000).
Economy: Single-family building permits issued: 2 (2004); Multi-family building permits issued: 9 (2004); Employment by occupation: 18.5% management, 19.3% professional, 12.9% services, 32.6% sales, 0.0% farming, 10.6% construction, 6.2% production (2000).
Income: Per capita income: $36,699 (2004); Median household income: $43,321 (2004); Average household income: $66,166 (2004); Percent of households with income of $100,000 or more: 14.2% (2004); Poverty rate: 5.7% (2000).
Education: Percent of population age 25 and over with: High school diploma (including GED) or higher: 91.9% (2004); Bachelor's degree or higher: 34.7% (2004); Master's degree or higher: 14.3% (2004).
Housing: Homeownership rate: 69.2% (2004); Median home value: $219,760 (2004); Median rent: $608 per month (2000); Median age of housing: 38 years (2000).
Safety: Violent crime rate: 42.9 per 10,000 population; Property crime rate: 737.3 per 10,000 population (2003).
Transportation: Commute to work: 76.9% car, 1.7% public transportation, 7.4% walk, 11.0% work from home (2000); Travel time to work: 29.4% less than 15 minutes, 38.6% 15 to 30 minutes, 19.4% 30 to 45 minutes, 5.0% 45 to 60 minutes, 7.6% 60 minutes or more (2000)

PALM SPRINGS (village). Covers a land area of 1.611 square miles and a water area of 0.047 square miles. Located at 26.64° N. Lat.; 80.09° W. Long. Elevation is 15 feet.
Population: 10,799 (1990); 11,699 (2000); 11,536 (2004); 11,530 (2009 projected); Race: 80.2% White, 8.5% Black, 1.5% Asian, 33.0% Hispanic of any race (2004); Density: 7,159.9 persons per square mile (2004); Average household size: 2.30 (2004); Median age: 37.4 (2004); Male/female ratio: 90.3 (2004); Marriage status: 25.3% never married, 50.3% now married, 8.7% widowed, 15.7% divorced (2000); Foreign born: 26.2% (2000); Ancestry (includes multiple ancestries): 30.7% Other groups, 11.6% Irish, 11.2% German, 9.4% English, 8.6% Italian (2000).
Economy: Single-family building permits issued: 59 (2004); Multi-family building permits issued: 120 (2004); Employment by occupation: 10.6% management, 14.8% professional, 17.0% services, 30.7% sales, 0.0% farming, 12.8% construction, 14.1% production (2000).
Income: Per capita income: $19,833 (2004); Median household income: $37,480 (2004); Average household income: $45,523 (2004); Percent of households with income of $100,000 or more: 6.4% (2004); Poverty rate: 7.9% (2000).
Taxes: Total city taxes per capita: $256 (2002); City property taxes per capita: $103 (2002).
Education: Percent of population age 25 and over with: High school diploma (including GED) or higher: 82.2% (2004); Bachelor's degree or higher: 16.5% (2004); Master's degree or higher: 6.3% (2004).

School District(s)

Palm Beach County School District (PK-12)
2002-03 Enrollment: 164,896 . . . . (561) 434-8200
Housing: Homeownership rate: 64.3% (2004); Median home value: $88,916 (2004); Median rent: $610 per month (2000); Median age of housing: 24 years (2000).
Safety: Violent crime rate: 46.3 per 10,000 population; Property crime rate: 584.2 per 10,000 population (2003).
Transportation: Commute to work: 94.6% car, 0.6% public transportation, 1.3% walk, 1.9% work from home (2000); Travel time to work: 21.6% less than 15 minutes, 44.1% 15 to 30 minutes, 22.4% 30 to 45 minutes, 6.9% 45 to 60 minutes, 5.1% 60 minutes or more (2000)

PLANTATION MOBILE HOME PARK (CDP). Covers a land area of 0.257 square miles and a water area of 0.006 square miles. Located at 26.70° N. Lat.; 80.13° W. Long.
Population: 1,114 (1990); 1,218 (2000); 1,322 (2004); 1,460 (2009 projected); Race: 65.8% White, 17.1% Black, 0.4% Asian, 23.7% Hispanic of any race (2004); Density: 5,138.7 persons per square mile (2004); Average household size: 2.46 (2004); Median age: 33.9 (2004); Male/female ratio: 101.2 (2004); Marriage status: 34.0% never married, 47.9% now married, 7.4% widowed, 10.7% divorced (2000); Foreign born: 13.8% (2000); Ancestry (includes multiple ancestries): 21.7% Other groups, 15.5% German, 13.5% Irish, 12.4% United States or American, 9.2% English (2000).
Economy: Employment by occupation: 8.1% management, 9.1% professional, 27.5% services, 18.6% sales, 0.0% farming, 20.6% construction, 16.1% production (2000).
Income: Per capita income: $15,877 (2004); Median household income: $32,615 (2004); Average household income: $39,015 (2004); Percent of households with income of $100,000 or more: 3.2% (2004); Poverty rate: 20.8% (2000).
Education: Percent of population age 25 and over with: High school diploma (including GED) or higher: 68.4% (2004); Bachelor's degree or higher: 4.7% (2004); Master's degree or higher: 1.8% (2004).
Housing: Homeownership rate: 52.8% (2004); Median home value: $52,581 (2004); Median rent: $557 per month (2000); Median age of housing: 24 years (2000).
Transportation: Commute to work: 97.0% car, 0.8% public transportation, 2.2% walk, 0.0% work from home (2000); Travel time to work: 30.7% less than 15 minutes, 48.5% 15 to 30 minutes, 16.4% 30 to 45 minutes, 1.0% 45 to 60 minutes, 3.4% 60 minutes or more (2000)

RIVIERA BEACH (city). Covers a land area of 8.335 square miles and a water area of 1.515 square miles. Located at 26.78° N. Lat.; 80.06° W. Long. Elevation is 11 feet.
History: Named for the French coastal district. Incorporated 1922.
Population: 27,791 (1990); 29,884 (2000); 30,859 (2004); 32,234 (2009 projected); Race: 25.5% White, 69.4% Black, 1.2% Asian, 5.8% Hispanic of any race (2004); Density: 3,702.3 persons per square mile (2004); Average household size: 2.62 (2004); Median age: 35.9 (2004); Male/female ratio: 91.4 (2004); Marriage status: 32.3% never married, 46.4% now married, 8.5% widowed, 12.8% divorced (2000); Foreign born: 10.1% (2000); Ancestry (includes multiple ancestries): 57.1% Other groups, 4.4% German, 4.1% English, 3.8% Irish, 3.4% United States or American (2000).
Economy: Resort city. Research and development firms are located here. Unemployment rate: 9.7% (2004); Total civilian labor force: 19,170 (2004); Single-family building permits issued: 673 (2004); Multi-family building permits issued: 0 (2004); Employment by occupation: 8.8% management, 15.7% professional, 25.1% services, 26.1% sales, 0.2% farming, 9.3% construction, 14.7% production (2000).
Income: Per capita income: $19,819 (2004); Median household income: $33,846 (2004); Average household income: $51,371 (2004); Percent of households with income of $100,000 or more: 10.6% (2004); Poverty rate: 23.0% (2000).
Taxes: Total city taxes per capita: $750 (2002); City property taxes per capita: $479 (2002).
Education: Percent of population age 25 and over with: High school diploma (including GED) or higher: 72.9% (2004); Bachelor's degree or higher: 18.0% (2004); Master's degree or higher: 6.2% (2004).

School District(s)

Palm Beach County School District (PK-12)
2002-03 Enrollment: 164,896 . . . . (561) 434-8200
Housing: Homeownership rate: 59.1% (2004); Median home value: $122,986 (2004); Median rent: $503 per month (2000); Median age of housing: 27 years (2000).
Safety: Violent crime rate: 205.1 per 10,000 population; Property crime rate: 1,080.2 per 10,000 population (2003).
Transportation: Commute to work: 88.8% car, 4.3% public transportation, 2.2% walk, 2.3% work from home (2000); Travel time to work: 27.8% less than 15 minutes, 41.1% 15 to 30 minutes, 21.3% 30 to 45 minutes, 3.6% 45 to 60 minutes, 6.2% 60 minutes or more (2000)
Additional Information Contacts
Local Government Offices . . . . (561) 845-4000

ROYAL PALM BEACH (village). Covers a land area of 9.891 square miles and a water area of 0.179 square miles. Located at 26.70° N. Lat.; 80.22° W. Long. Elevation is 18 feet.
Population: 15,662 (1990); 21,523 (2000); 28,678 (2004); 37,141 (2009 projected); Race: 73.5% White, 17.4% Black, 3.2% Asian, 14.7% Hispanic of any race (2004); Density: 2,899.3 persons per square mile (2004); Average household size: 2.81 (2004); Median age: 37.2 (2004); Male/female ratio: 92.0 (2004); Marriage status: 19.4% never married, 65.3% now married, 7.6% widowed, 7.7% divorced (2000); Foreign born: 14.7% (2000); Ancestry (includes multiple ancestries): 24.4% Other groups, 14.0% German, 13.3% Italian, 11.8% Irish, 8.5% United States or American (2000).
Economy: Light manufacturing. Unemployment rate: 4.7% (2004); Total civilian labor force: 10,606 (2004); Single-family building permits issued: 239 (2004); Multi-family building permits issued: 0 (2004); Employment by occupation: 14.0% management, 20.4% professional, 13.5% services, 30.5% sales, 0.4% farming, 11.4% construction, 9.8% production (2000).
Income: Per capita income: $24,525 (2004); Median household income: $61,206 (2004); Average household income: $68,869 (2004); Percent of households with income of $100,000 or more: 18.2% (2004); Poverty rate: 4.3% (2000).
Taxes: Total city taxes per capita: $498 (2002); City property taxes per capita: $225 (2002).
Education: Percent of population age 25 and over with: High school diploma (including GED) or higher: 87.8% (2004); Bachelor's degree or higher: 24.8% (2004); Master's degree or higher: 8.0% (2004).

School District(s)

Palm Beach County School District (PK-12)
2002-03 Enrollment: 164,896 . . . . (561) 434-8200
Housing: Homeownership rate: 89.0% (2004); Median home value: $145,764 (2004); Median rent: $778 per month (2000); Median age of housing: 15 years (2000).
Safety: Violent crime rate: 50.9 per 10,000 population; Property crime rate: 658.4 per 10,000 population (2003).
Newspapers: The Observer (General - Circulation 21,000)
Transportation: Commute to work: 95.6% car, 0.1% public transportation, 0.8% walk, 2.4% work from home (2000); Travel time to work: 12.9% less than 15 minutes, 28.0% 15 to 30 minutes, 36.2% 30 to 45 minutes, 13.4% 45 to 60 minutes, 9.5% 60 minutes or more (2000)
Additional Information Contacts

Local Government Offices . . . . (561) 790-5100

ROYAL PALM ESTATES (CDP). Covers a land area of 0.805 square miles and a water area of 0 square miles. Located at 26.68° N. Lat.; 80.12° W. Long.
Population: 3,513 (1990); 3,583 (2000); 3,406 (2004); 3,170 (2009 projected); Race: 61.4% White, 19.5% Black, 1.5% Asian, 45.8% Hispanic of any race (2004); Density: 4,231.2 persons per square mile (2004); Average household size: 3.25 (2004); Median age: 30.8 (2004); Male/female ratio: 106.5 (2004); Marriage status: 40.5% never married, 40.7% now married, 2.6% widowed, 16.2% divorced (2000); Foreign born: 23.6% (2000); Ancestry (includes multiple ancestries): 45.2% Other groups, 8.1% United States or American, 7.6% Irish, 6.7% Italian, 4.6% German (2000).
Economy: Employment by occupation: 5.3% management, 12.9% professional, 21.1% services, 26.8% sales, 0.0% farming, 21.1% construction, 12.8% production (2000).
Income: Per capita income: $16,936 (2004); Median household income: $32,825 (2004); Average household income: $54,357 (2004); Percent of households with income of $100,000 or more: 7.6% (2004); Poverty rate: 22.2% (2000).
Education: Percent of population age 25 and over with: High school diploma (including GED) or higher: 66.6% (2004); Bachelor's degree or higher: 10.2% (2004); Master's degree or higher: 4.4% (2004).
Housing: Homeownership rate: 49.9% (2004); Median home value: $109,235 (2004); Median rent: $526 per month (2000); Median age of housing: 23 years (2000).
Transportation: Commute to work: 92.1% car, 1.7% public transportation, 0.8% walk, 1.5% work from home (2000); Travel time to work: 16.5% less than 15 minutes, 47.2% 15 to 30 minutes, 25.1% 30 to 45 minutes, 6.4% 45 to 60 minutes, 4.9% 60 minutes or more (2000)

SANDALFOOT COVE (CDP). Covers a land area of 2.968 square miles and a water area of 0 square miles. Located at 26.33° N. Lat.; 80.18° W. Long.
Population: 14,221 (1990); 16,582 (2000); 16,431 (2004); 16,329 (2009 projected); Race: 83.8% White, 5.1% Black, 3.6% Asian, 19.6% Hispanic of any race (2004); Density: 5,536.1 persons per square mile (2004); Average household size: 2.38 (2004); Median age: 39.9 (2004); Male/female ratio: 91.0 (2004); Marriage status: 20.7% never married, 58.7% now married, 7.0% widowed, 13.6% divorced (2000); Foreign born: 22.4% (2000); Ancestry (includes multiple ancestries): 22.7% Other groups, 15.0% Italian, 10.7% Irish, 10.7% German, 6.9% United States or American (2000).
Economy: Employment by occupation: 14.4% management, 19.4% professional, 15.1% services, 34.6% sales, 0.1% farming, 8.6% construction, 7.8% production (2000).
Income: Per capita income: $25,289 (2004); Median household income: $47,849 (2004); Average household income: $59,958 (2004); Percent of households with income of $100,000 or more: 12.5% (2004); Poverty rate: 5.0% (2000).
Education: Percent of population age 25 and over with: High school diploma (including GED) or higher: 84.3% (2004); Bachelor's degree or higher: 20.1% (2004); Master's degree or higher: 7.0% (2004).
Housing: Homeownership rate: 78.8% (2004); Median home value: $128,685 (2004); Median rent: $922 per month (2000); Median age of housing: 18 years (2000).
Transportation: Commute to work: 94.8% car, 0.6% public transportation, 0.3% walk, 3.3% work from home (2000); Travel time to work: 21.1% less than 15 minutes, 44.5% 15 to 30 minutes, 22.3% 30 to 45 minutes, 5.6% 45 to 60 minutes, 6.6% 60 minutes or more (2000)

SCHALL CIRCLE (CDP). Covers a land area of 0.318 square miles and a water area of 0 square miles. Located at 26.71° N. Lat.; 80.11° W. Long.
Population: 733 (1990); 965 (2000); 1,026 (2004); 1,106 (2009 projected); Race: 55.6% White, 34.8% Black, 0.9% Asian, 17.9% Hispanic of any race (2004); Density: 3,227.5 persons per square mile (2004); Average household size: 2.44 (2004); Median age: 31.1 (2004); Male/female ratio: 91.8 (2004); Marriage status: 44.1% never married, 41.2% now married, 3.5% widowed, 11.2% divorced (2000); Foreign born: 12.9% (2000); Ancestry (includes multiple ancestries): 47.6% Other groups, 10.4% Irish, 10.1% German, 9.0% United States or American, 4.1% English (2000).
Economy: Employment by occupation: 5.4% management, 8.6% professional, 51.7% services, 11.4% sales, 4.5% farming, 15.3% construction, 3.0% production (2000).
Income: Per capita income: $10,595 (2004); Median household income: $20,783 (2004); Average household income: $25,881 (2004); Percent of households with income of $100,000 or more: 0.0% (2004); Poverty rate: 33.0% (2000).
Education: Percent of population age 25 and over with: High school diploma (including GED) or higher: 55.4% (2004); Bachelor's degree or higher: 3.2% (2004); Master's degree or higher: 0.0% (2004).
Housing: Homeownership rate: 44.8% (2004); Median home value: $84,211 (2004); Median rent: $387 per month (2000); Median age of housing: 28 years (2000).
Transportation: Commute to work: 76.5% car, 13.6% public transportation, 4.5% walk, 5.4% work from home (2000); Travel time to work: 25.3% less than 15 minutes, 63.3% 15 to 30 minutes, 6.4% 30 to 45 minutes, 1.4% 45 to 60 minutes, 3.6% 60 minutes or more (2000)

SEMINOLE MANOR (CDP). Covers a land area of 0.407 square miles and a water area of 0 square miles. Located at 26.58° N. Lat.; 80.10° W. Long.
Population: 1,972 (1990); 2,546 (2000); 2,697 (2004); 2,883 (2009 projected); Race: 60.6% White, 21.9% Black, 1.1% Asian, 36.2% Hispanic of any race (2004); Density: 6,633.8 persons per square mile (2004); Average household size: 2.99 (2004); Median age: 33.6 (2004); Male/female ratio: 93.6 (2004); Marriage status: 27.2% never married, 53.3% now married, 3.7% widowed, 15.9% divorced (2000); Foreign born: 15.1% (2000); Ancestry (includes multiple ancestries): 29.0% Other groups, 10.5% Irish, 9.0% German, 8.9% Italian, 8.4% Haitian (2000).
Economy: Employment by occupation: 6.5% management, 10.5% professional, 22.2% services, 27.1% sales, 0.3% farming, 21.5% construction, 11.8% production (2000).
Income: Per capita income: $16,593 (2004); Median household income: $39,782 (2004); Average household income: $49,560 (2004); Percent of households with income of $100,000 or more: 6.2% (2004); Poverty rate: 12.3% (2000).
Education: Percent of population age 25 and over with: High school diploma (including GED) or higher: 70.3% (2004); Bachelor's degree or higher: 9.0% (2004); Master's degree or higher: 3.1% (2004).
Housing: Homeownership rate: 77.6% (2004); Median home value: $92,602 (2004); Median rent: $622 per month (2000); Median age of housing: 31 years (2000).
Transportation: Commute to work: 96.3% car, 2.3% public transportation, 0.7% walk, 0.6% work from home (2000); Travel time to work: 25.0% less than 15 minutes, 33.4% 15 to 30 minutes, 23.6% 30 to 45 minutes, 9.6% 45 to 60 minutes, 8.4% 60 minutes or more (2000)

SOUTH BAY (city). Covers a land area of 2.707 square miles and a water area of 1.004 square miles. Located at 26.66° N. Lat.; 80.71° W. Long. Elevation is 21 feet.
History: South Bay was established on the shores of Lake Okeechobee, and developed as the terminus of the Atlantic Coast Line and Florida East Coast Railway lines. Much of the town was destroyed in 1938 by a hurricane which blew waters inland from the lake.
Population: 3,614 (1990); 3,859 (2000); 3,948 (2004); 4,108 (2009 projected); Race: 25.1% White, 67.7% Black, 0.2% Asian, 18.0% Hispanic of any race (2004); Density: 1,458.3 persons per square mile (2004); Average household size: 4.84 (2004); Median age: 32.9 (2004); Male/female ratio: 176.7 (2004); Marriage status: 45.1% never married, 44.0% now married, 5.6% widowed, 5.4% divorced (2000); Foreign born: 11.5% (2000); Ancestry (includes multiple ancestries): 48.3% Other groups, 3.3% United States or American, 2.4% Jamaican, 0.5% African, 0.4% Bahamian (2000).
Economy: Single-family building permits issued: 10 (2004); Multi-family building permits issued: 0 (2004); Employment by occupation: 5.0% management, 16.2% professional, 18.2% services, 20.3% sales, 7.3% farming, 10.3% construction, 22.6% production (2000).
Income: Per capita income: $10,523 (2004); Median household income: $27,686 (2004); Average household income: $39,497 (2004); Percent of households with income of $100,000 or more: 6.6% (2004); Poverty rate: 36.7% (2000).
Taxes: Total city taxes per capita: $247 (2002); City property taxes per capita: $80 (2002).
Education: Percent of population age 25 and over with: High school diploma (including GED) or higher: 55.2% (2004); Bachelor's degree or higher: 7.2% (2004); Master's degree or higher: 1.9% (2004).

School District(s)

Palm Beach County School District (PK-12)
2002-03 Enrollment: 164,896 .... (561) 434-8200

Housing: Homeownership rate: 58.5% (2004); Median home value: $92,022 (2004); Median rent: $300 per month (2000); Median age of housing: 25 years (2000).

Safety: Violent crime rate: 235.4 per 10,000 population; Property crime rate: 563.3 per 10,000 population (2003).

Transportation: Commute to work: 87.2% car, 6.9% public transportation, 2.4% walk, 1.1% work from home (2000); Travel time to work: 36.5% less than 15 minutes, 29.1% 15 to 30 minutes, 18.3% 30 to 45 minutes, 6.0% 45 to 60 minutes, 10.0% 60 minutes or more (2000)

SOUTH PALM BEACH (town). Covers a land area of 0.134 square miles and a water area of 0.199 square miles. Located at 26.59° N. Lat.; 80.03° W. Long. Elevation is 20 feet.

Population: 1,480 (1990); 699 (2000); 703 (2004); 716 (2009 projected); Race: 99.1% White, 0.0% Black, 0.6% Asian, 3.4% Hispanic of any race (2004); Density: 5,234.1 persons per square mile (2004); Average household size: 1.51 (2004); Median age: 67.0 (2004); Male/female ratio: 76.2 (2004); Marriage status: 13.4% never married, 50.0% now married, 12.4% widowed, 24.2% divorced (2000); Foreign born: 20.9% (2000); Ancestry (includes multiple ancestries): 14.9% German, 14.6% Irish, 10.4% Other groups, 9.4% Russian, 8.0% Italian (2000).

Economy: Single-family building permits issued: 0 (2004); Multi-family building permits issued: 0 (2004); Employment by occupation: 19.8% management, 9.7% professional, 22.8% services, 40.9% sales, 0.0% farming, 4.2% construction, 2.5% production (2000).

Income: Per capita income: $39,065 (2004); Median household income: $40,671 (2004); Average household income: $58,932 (2004); Percent of households with income of $100,000 or more: 12.0% (2004); Poverty rate: 15.7% (2000).

Education: Percent of population age 25 and over with: High school diploma (including GED) or higher: 91.1% (2004); Bachelor's degree or higher: 40.1% (2004); Master's degree or higher: 18.0% (2004).

Housing: Homeownership rate: 85.2% (2004); Median home value: $128,597 (2004); Median rent: $760 per month (2000); Median age of housing: 25 years (2000).

Safety: Violent crime rate: 6.4 per 10,000 population; Property crime rate: 211.4 per 10,000 population (2003).

Transportation: Commute to work: 94.8% car, 0.0% public transportation, 5.2% walk, 0.0% work from home (2000); Travel time to work: 21.3% less than 15 minutes, 59.6% 15 to 30 minutes, 11.7% 30 to 45 minutes, 5.2% 45 to 60 minutes, 2.2% 60 minutes or more (2000)

STACEY STREET (CDP). Covers a land area of 0.115 square miles and a water area of 0 square miles. Located at 26.69° N. Lat.; 80.12° W. Long.

Population: 759 (1990); 958 (2000); 963 (2004); 954 (2009 projected); Race: 41.5% White, 53.2% Black, 0.3% Asian, 39.7% Hispanic of any race (2004); Density: 8,398.2 persons per square mile (2004); Average household size: 3.82 (2004); Median age: 24.9 (2004); Male/female ratio: 111.6 (2004); Marriage status: 49.3% never married, 37.0% now married, 2.1% widowed, 11.5% divorced (2000); Foreign born: 41.4% (2000); Ancestry (includes multiple ancestries): 58.6% Other groups, 13.4% Irish, 7.1% Jamaican, 6.0% Bahamian, 4.2% German (2000).

Economy: Employment by occupation: 3.1% management, 13.2% professional, 36.7% services, 21.0% sales, 0.0% farming, 17.6% construction, 8.4% production (2000).

Income: Per capita income: $9,377 (2004); Median household income: $28,333 (2004); Average household income: $34,921 (2004); Percent of households with income of $100,000 or more: 4.8% (2004); Poverty rate: 35.1% (2000).

Education: Percent of population age 25 and over with: High school diploma (including GED) or higher: 60.5% (2004); Bachelor's degree or higher: 6.7% (2004); Master's degree or higher: 4.4% (2004).

Housing: Homeownership rate: 8.3% (2004); Median home value: $78,750 (2004); Median rent: $603 per month (2000); Median age of housing: 21 years (2000).

Transportation: Commute to work: 81.1% car, 8.0% public transportation, 2.6% walk, 6.0% work from home (2000); Travel time to work: 17.0% less than 15 minutes, 46.8% 15 to 30 minutes, 18.2% 30 to 45 minutes, 4.9% 45 to 60 minutes, 13.1% 60 minutes or more (2000)

TEQUESTA (village). Covers a land area of 1.750 square miles and a water area of 0.458 square miles. Located at 26.96° N. Lat.; 80.09° W. Long. Elevation is 10 feet.

Population: 4,996 (1990); 5,273 (2000); 5,312 (2004); 5,430 (2009 projected); Race: 97.6% White, 0.5% Black, 0.9% Asian, 3.0% Hispanic of any race (2004); Density: 3,036.2 persons per square mile (2004); Average household size: 2.24 (2004); Median age: 48.3 (2004); Male/female ratio: 89.8 (2004); Marriage status: 15.6% never married, 63.5% now married, 11.4% widowed, 9.6% divorced (2000); Foreign born: 7.5% (2000); Ancestry (includes multiple ancestries): 20.1% German, 17.5% English, 16.5% Irish, 14.1% Italian, 7.9% United States or American (2000).

Economy: Light manufacturing. Single-family building permits issued: 14 (2004); Multi-family building permits issued: 5 (2004); Employment by occupation: 15.2% management, 25.3% professional, 14.0% services, 34.7% sales, 0.2% farming, 6.0% construction, 4.6% production (2000).

Income: Per capita income: $40,504 (2004); Median household income: $63,880 (2004); Average household income: $90,431 (2004); Percent of households with income of $100,000 or more: 26.9% (2004); Poverty rate: 3.2% (2000).

Education: Percent of population age 25 and over with: High school diploma (including GED) or higher: 95.5% (2004); Bachelor's degree or higher: 36.7% (2004); Master's degree or higher: 11.9% (2004).

Housing: Homeownership rate: 83.6% (2004); Median home value: $192,233 (2004); Median rent: $867 per month (2000); Median age of housing: 24 years (2000).

Safety: Violent crime rate: 3.6 per 10,000 population; Property crime rate: 268.9 per 10,000 population (2003).

Transportation: Commute to work: 91.2% car, 0.5% public transportation, 1.6% walk, 4.9% work from home (2000); Travel time to work: 36.9% less than 15 minutes, 28.7% 15 to 30 minutes, 20.2% 30 to 45 minutes, 7.3% 45 to 60 minutes, 6.9% 60 minutes or more (2000)

VILLAGES OF ORIOLE (CDP). Covers a land area of 1.026 square miles and a water area of 0 square miles. Located at 26.45° N. Lat.; 80.15° W. Long.

Population: 5,698 (1990); 4,758 (2000); 4,278 (2004); 3,861 (2009 projected); Race: 99.1% White, 0.4% Black, 0.0% Asian, 0.6% Hispanic of any race (2004); Density: 4,169.6 persons per square mile (2004); Average household size: 1.51 (2004); Median age: 78.3 (2004); Male/female ratio: 68.1 (2004); Marriage status: 2.8% never married, 63.2% now married, 29.4% widowed, 4.6% divorced (2000); Foreign born: 9.8% (2000); Ancestry (includes multiple ancestries): 25.0% Other groups, 17.5% Russian, 12.1% United States or American, 11.7% Polish, 4.3% Italian (2000).

Economy: Employment by occupation: 15.9% management, 3.5% professional, 21.5% services, 46.7% sales, 0.0% farming, 9.1% construction, 3.3% production (2000).

Income: Per capita income: $26,774 (2004); Median household income: $32,082 (2004); Average household income: $40,317 (2004); Percent of households with income of $100,000 or more: 4.0% (2004); Poverty rate: 7.0% (2000).

Education: Percent of population age 25 and over with: High school diploma (including GED) or higher: 87.8% (2004); Bachelor's degree or higher: 16.8% (2004); Master's degree or higher: 7.6% (2004).

Housing: Homeownership rate: 95.2% (2004); Median home value: $100,888 (2004); Median rent: $554 per month (2000); Median age of housing: 17 years (2000).

Transportation: Commute to work: 92.0% car, 0.0% public transportation, 2.2% walk, 5.8% work from home (2000); Travel time to work: 33.7% less than 15 minutes, 48.1% 15 to 30 minutes, 8.2% 30 to 45 minutes, 7.7% 45 to 60 minutes, 2.3% 60 minutes or more (2000)

WELLINGTON (village). Covers a land area of 31.053 square miles and a water area of 0.313 square miles. Located at 26.65° N. Lat.; 80.25° W. Long.

Population: 22,555 (1990); 38,216 (2000); 47,341 (2004); 58,224 (2009 projected); Race: 85.9% White, 6.9% Black, 2.3% Asian, 14.9% Hispanic of any race (2004); Density: 1,524.5 persons per square mile (2004); Average household size: 2.96 (2004); Median age: 36.7 (2004); Male/female ratio: 95.9 (2004); Marriage status: 20.3% never married, 67.6% now married, 3.8% widowed, 8.3% divorced (2000); Foreign born: 13.4% (2000); Ancestry (includes multiple ancestries): 19.0% Other groups, 15.1% Irish, 14.6% Italian, 13.6% German, 11.2% English (2000).

Economy: Unemployment rate: 3.0% (2004); Total civilian labor force: 15,803 (2004); Single-family building permits issued: 1,209 (2004); Multi-family building permits issued: 28 (2004); Employment by occupation: 19.4% management, 24.9% professional, 13.5% services, 30.7% sales, 0.6% farming, 5.0% construction, 5.8% production (2000).
Income: Per capita income: $34,018 (2004); Median household income: $77,170 (2004); Average household income: $100,566 (2004); Percent of households with income of $100,000 or more: 34.4% (2004); Poverty rate: 4.3% (2000).
Taxes: Total city taxes per capita: $362 (2002); City property taxes per capita: $139 (2002).
Education: Percent of population age 25 and over with: High school diploma (including GED) or higher: 92.2% (2004); Bachelor's degree or higher: 38.1% (2004); Master's degree or higher: 13.8% (2004).

School District(s)

Palm Beach County School District (PK-12)
2002-03 Enrollment: 164,896 . . . . (561) 434-8200
Housing: Homeownership rate: 82.1% (2004); Median home value: $212,052 (2004); Median rent: $867 per month (2000); Median age of housing: 11 years (2000).
Safety: Violent crime rate: 23.9 per 10,000 population; Property crime rate: 340.7 per 10,000 population (2003).
Newspapers: Greenacres/Lake Worth/Lantana Forum (General - Circulation 27,000); Town Crier (General - Circulation 20,500)
Transportation: Commute to work: 90.9% car, 0.6% public transportation, 0.6% walk, 6.6% work from home (2000); Travel time to work: 23.2% less than 15 minutes, 22.5% 15 to 30 minutes, 29.1% 30 to 45 minutes, 15.8% 45 to 60 minutes, 9.4% 60 minutes or more (2000)

Additional Information Contacts

Local Government Offices . . . . (561) 791-4000

WEST PALM BEACH (city). Covers a land area of 55.142 square miles and a water area of 3.059 square miles. Located at 26.71° N. Lat.; 80.06° W. Long. Elevation is 21 feet.
History: West Palm Beach was established on the western shore of Lake Worth, and grew as the business and railroad center for Palm Beach on the opposite shore. Later, West Palm Beach became a winter resort as well. West Palm Beach was developed by Henry Flagler, pioneer railroad builder, in the 1890's. When Palm Beach County was carved out of Dade County, West Palm Beach was chosen as the county seat.
Population: 68,172 (1990); 82,103 (2000); 88,904 (2004); 97,544 (2009 projected); Race: 54.4% White, 34.3% Black, 1.8% Asian, 20.7% Hispanic of any race (2004); Density: 1,612.3 persons per square mile (2004); Average household size: 2.35 (2004); Median age: 37.4 (2004); Male/female ratio: 97.1 (2004); Marriage status: 33.2% never married, 45.3% now married, 8.5% widowed, 13.0% divorced (2000); Foreign born: 24.7% (2000); Ancestry (includes multiple ancestries): 40.1% Other groups, 7.5% German, 7.0% Irish, 6.2% English, 5.2% United States or American (2000).
Economy: Unemployment rate: 6.9% (2004); Total civilian labor force: 52,756 (2004); Single-family building permits issued: 530 (2004); Multi-family building permits issued: 812 (2004); Employment by occupation: 12.4% management, 19.8% professional, 22.4% services, 25.7% sales, 0.8% farming, 9.0% construction, 10.0% production (2000).
Income: Per capita income: $26,113 (2004); Median household income: $40,341 (2004); Average household income: $59,844 (2004); Percent of households with income of $100,000 or more: 13.6% (2004); Poverty rate: 18.9% (2000).
Taxes: Total city taxes per capita: $835 (2002); City property taxes per capita: $499 (2002).
Education: Percent of population age 25 and over with: High school diploma (including GED) or higher: 75.9% (2004); Bachelor's degree or higher: 27.2% (2004); Master's degree or higher: 10.4% (2004).

School District(s)

Palm Beach County School District (PK-12)
2002-03 Enrollment: 164,896 . . . . (561) 434-8200

Four-year College(s)

Northwood University-Florida Education Center
2003-04 Enrollment: 959 . . . . (561) 478-5500
2003-04 Tuition: In-state $13,995; Out-of-state $13,995
Palm Beach Atlantic University-West Palm Beach
2003-04 Enrollment: 2,996 . . . . (561) 803-2000
2003-04 Tuition: In-state $14,890; Out-of-state $14,890
South University-West Palm Beach (Private, For-profit)
2003-04 Enrollment: 447 . . . . (561) 697-9200
2003-04 Tuition: In-state $10,185; Out-of-state $10,185

Two-year College(s)

Academy for Practical Nursing & Health Occupations
2003-04 Enrollment: 203 . . . . (561) 683-1400
Cooper Career Institute (Private, For-profit)
2003-04 Enrollment: 68 . . . . (561) 640-6999
New England Institute of Technology-Palm Beach (Private, For-profit)
2003-04 Enrollment: 1,238 . . . . (561) 842-8324
2003-04 Tuition: In-state $14,900; Out-of-state $14,900
Ross Medical Education Center (Private, For-profit)
2003-04 Enrollment: 70 . . . . (561) 433-1288
Summit Institute (Private, For-profit)
2003-04 Enrollment: 169 . . . . (561) 881-0220
2003-04 Tuition: In-state $12,930; Out-of-state $12,930
Housing: Homeownership rate: 52.1% (2004); Median home value: $132,311 (2004); Median rent: $582 per month (2000); Median age of housing: 26 years (2000).
Hospitals: Columbia Hospital (250 beds); Good Samaritan Medical Center (801 beds); St. Mary's Medical Center (460 beds); West Palm Beach Veterans Affairs Medical Center (270 beds)
Safety: Violent crime rate: 131.8 per 10,000 population; Property crime rate: 989.5 per 10,000 population (2003).
Newspapers: El Latino Semanal (Hispanic - Circulation 36,000); Palm Beach Daily Business Review (Circulation 9,072); Palm Beach Gazette (Black - Circulation 3,000); Palm Beach Jewish News (Jewish - Circulation 23,000); Semanario Accion (Hispanic - Circulation 25,000); The Palm Beach Post (Circulation 181,312)
Transportation: Commute to work: 89.8% car, 2.8% public transportation, 2.8% walk, 2.3% work from home (2000); Travel time to work: 29.6% less than 15 minutes, 44.1% 15 to 30 minutes, 17.3% 30 to 45 minutes, 4.1% 45 to 60 minutes, 4.9% 60 minutes or more (2000); Amtrak: Service available.
Airports: North Palm Beach County General Aviation; Palm Beach County Park; Palm Beach International (primary service/medium hub)

Additional Information Contacts

Hispanic Chamber of Commerce . . . . (561) 832-1986
Local Government Offices . . . . (561) 822-1210
Realtors Association of The Palm Beaches . . . . (561) 688-9294
West Palm Beach Chamber of Commerce . . . . (561) 833-3711

WESTGATE-BELVEDERE HOMES (CDP). Covers a land area of 2.062 square miles and a water area of 0 square miles. Located at 26.69° N. Lat.; 80.09° W. Long.
Population: 6,880 (1990); 8,134 (2000); 8,748 (2004); 9,508 (2009 projected); Race: 53.3% White, 30.2% Black, 0.9% Asian, 40.7% Hispanic of any race (2004); Density: 4,242.5 persons per square mile (2004); Average household size: 2.97 (2004); Median age: 30.1 (2004); Male/female ratio: 102.6 (2004); Marriage status: 31.6% never married, 49.6% now married, 4.4% widowed, 14.3% divorced (2000); Foreign born: 26.5% (2000); Ancestry (includes multiple ancestries): 45.4% Other groups, 9.5% United States or American, 7.1% Haitian, 7.0% Irish, 6.2% English (2000).
Economy: Employment by occupation: 5.7% management, 9.1% professional, 26.0% services, 23.8% sales, 3.1% farming, 18.9% construction, 13.3% production (2000).
Income: Per capita income: $12,575 (2004); Median household income: $30,165 (2004); Average household income: $37,258 (2004); Percent of households with income of $100,000 or more: 3.3% (2004); Poverty rate: 20.8% (2000).
Education: Percent of population age 25 and over with: High school diploma (including GED) or higher: 57.1% (2004); Bachelor's degree or higher: 6.9% (2004); Master's degree or higher: 2.3% (2004).
Housing: Homeownership rate: 55.6% (2004); Median home value: $83,518 (2004); Median rent: $534 per month (2000); Median age of housing: 31 years (2000).
Transportation: Commute to work: 93.0% car, 1.4% public transportation, 2.0% walk, 1.4% work from home (2000); Travel time to work: 22.7% less than 15 minutes, 43.8% 15 to 30 minutes, 20.0% 30 to 45 minutes, 5.6% 45 to 60 minutes, 8.0% 60 minutes or more (2000)

WHISPER WALK (CDP). Covers a land area of 1.002 square miles and a water area of 0 square miles. Located at 26.39° N. Lat.; 80.18° W. Long.

Population: 3,037 (1990); 5,135 (2000); 5,237 (2004); 5,417 (2009 projected); Race: 92.5% White, 2.6% Black, 3.2% Asian, 7.0% Hispanic of any race (2004); Density: 5,225.5 persons per square mile (2004); Average household size: 2.13 (2004); Median age: 64.1 (2004); Male/female ratio: 85.1 (2004); Marriage status: 8.1% never married, 74.8% now married, 11.8% widowed, 5.3% divorced (2000); Foreign born: 12.0% (2000); Ancestry (includes multiple ancestries): 21.3% Other groups, 12.6% Russian, 11.4% Italian, 11.2% Polish, 8.0% United States or American (2000).
Economy: Employment by occupation: 21.1% management, 19.9% professional, 13.0% services, 38.9% sales, 0.0% farming, 2.8% construction, 4.3% production (2000).
Income: Per capita income: $30,148 (2004); Median household income: $47,805 (2004); Average household income: $64,180 (2004); Percent of households with income of $100,000 or more: 17.3% (2004); Poverty rate: 4.7% (2000).
Education: Percent of population age 25 and over with: High school diploma (including GED) or higher: 87.0% (2004); Bachelor's degree or higher: 25.5% (2004); Master's degree or higher: 8.3% (2004).
Housing: Homeownership rate: 95.2% (2004); Median home value: $135,433 (2004); Median rent: $1,130 per month (2000); Median age of housing: 12 years (2000).
Transportation: Commute to work: 90.7% car, 0.0% public transportation, 0.0% walk, 9.3% work from home (2000); Travel time to work: 27.8% less than 15 minutes, 37.9% 15 to 30 minutes, 23.8% 30 to 45 minutes, 6.9% 45 to 60 minutes, 3.6% 60 minutes or more (2000)

Pasco County

Located in west central Florida; bounded on the west by the Gulf of Mexico; includes many small lakes. Covers a land area of 744.80 square miles, a water area of 123.10 square miles, and is located in the Eastern Time Zone. The county government was organized in 1887. County seat is Dade City.

Pasco County is part of the Tampa-St. Petersburg-Clearwater, FL Metropolitan Statistical Area. The entire metro area includes: Hernando County, FL; Hillsborough County, FL; Pasco County, FL; Pinellas County, FL

Weather Station: Saint Leo — Elevation: 187 feet

	Jan	Feb	Mar	Apr	May	Jun	Jul	Aug	Sep	Oct	Nov	Dec
High	72	74	79	84	89	91	92	92	91	85	79	74
Low	49	51	55	59	65	70	72	72	71	64	57	51
Precip	3.5	3.6	4.3	2.4	4.1	6.9	7.7	7.4	6.5	2.9	2.5	2.7
Snow	tr	0.0	0.0	0.0	0.0	0.0	0.0	0.0	0.0	0.0	0.0	0.0

High and Low temperatures in degrees Fahrenheit; Precipitation and Snow in inches

Population: 281,131 (1990); 344,765 (2000); 383,295 (2004); 431,760 (2009 projected); Race: 92.2% White, 2.8% Black, 1.2% Asian, 7.2% Hispanic of any race (2004); Density: 514.6 persons per square mile (2004); Average household size: 2.34 (2004); Median age: 44.0 (2004); Male/female ratio: 93.0 (2004).
Religion: Five largest groups: 16.1% Catholic Church, 4.4% Southern Baptist Convention, 2.2% The United Methodist Church, 1.3% Assemblies of God, 0.9% Church of God (Cleveland, Tennessee) (2000).
Economy: Unemployment rate: 5.1% (2004); Total civilian labor force: 160,412 (2004); Leading industries: 23.9% retail trade; 20.2% health care and social assistance; 11.2% accommodation & food services (2003); Companies that employ 500 or more persons: 7 (2003); Companies that employ 100 to 499 persons: 90 (2003); Companies that employ less than 100 persons: 6,836 (2003); Farms: 1,222 totaling 168,716 acres (2002); Minority business ownership rate: 8.0% (1997); Women business ownership rate: 29.2% (1997); Retail sales per capita: $7,057 (1997). Single-family building permits issued: 6,831 (2004); Multi-family building permits issued: 2,432 (2004).
Income: Per capita income: $21,239 (2004); Median household income: $38,057 (2004); Average household income: $49,299 (2004); Percent of households with income of $100,000 or more: 8.5% (2004); Poverty rate: 12.1% (2002); Bankruptcy rate: 5.88% (2004).
Taxes: Total county taxes per capita: $325 (2002); County property taxes per capita: $280 (2002).
Education: Percent of population age 25 and over with: High school diploma (including GED) or higher: 78.1% (2004); Bachelor's degree or higher: 13.8% (2004); Master's degree or higher: 4.5% (2004).
Housing: Homeownership rate: 82.9% (2004); Median home value: $98,323 (2004); Median rent: $432 per month (2000); Median age of housing: 19 years (2000).
Health: Birth rate: 99.8 per 10,000 population (2004); Death rate: 132.7 per 10,000 population (2004); Age adjusted cancer mortality rate: 205.6 deaths per 100,000 population (2002); Air Quality Index: 93.2% good, 6.8% moderate, 0.0% unhealthy for sensitive individuals, 0.0% unhealthy (percent of days in 2004); Number of physicians: 14.8 per 10,000 population (2001); Hospital beds: 29.3 per 10,000 population (2002); Hospital admissions: 1,461.3 per 10,000 population (2002).
Elections: 2004 Presidential election results: 54.1% Bush, 44.4% Kerry, 0.8% Nader, 0.3% Badnarik
National and State Parks: Anclote Key Preserve State Park; Anclote National Wildlife Refuge; Werner-Boyce Salt Springs State Park; Withlacoochee State Forest
Additional Information Contacts
Pasco County Government Offices .... (727) 847-8100
Dade City Chamber of Commerce.................... (352) 567-3769
East Pasco Association of Realtors.................. (813) 783-3794
Land O' Lakes Chamber of Commerce .... (813) 909-2722
New Port Richey Chamber of Commerce .... (727) 842-7651
West Pasco Board of Realtors...................... (727) 848-8507

Pasco County Communities

BAYONET POINT (CDP). Covers a land area of 5.604 square miles and a water area of 0.076 square miles. Located at 28.32° N. Lat.; 82.68° W. Long.
Population: 21,860 (1990); 23,577 (2000); 24,200 (2004); 25,010 (2009 projected); Race: 96.0% White, 1.1% Black, 0.7% Asian, 4.6% Hispanic of any race (2004); Density: 4,318.4 persons per square mile (2004); Average household size: 2.08 (2004); Median age: 57.3 (2004); Male/female ratio: 84.0 (2004); Marriage status: 12.9% never married, 59.6% now married, 18.9% widowed, 8.7% divorced (2000); Foreign born: 6.3% (2000); Ancestry (includes multiple ancestries): 21.5% German, 17.3% Irish, 16.2% Italian, 12.9% English, 7.6% Other groups (2000).
Economy: Manufacturing: printing. Employment by occupation: 8.9% management, 15.2% professional, 21.5% services, 30.8% sales, 0.2% farming, 13.1% construction, 10.4% production (2000).
Income: Per capita income: $18,773 (2004); Median household income: $31,652 (2004); Average household income: $38,534 (2004); Percent of households with income of $100,000 or more: 3.2% (2004); Poverty rate: 11.6% (2000).
Education: Percent of population age 25 and over with: High school diploma (including GED) or higher: 75.8% (2004); Bachelor's degree or higher: 10.3% (2004); Master's degree or higher: 3.8% (2004).
Housing: Homeownership rate: 84.7% (2004); Median home value: $86,635 (2004); Median rent: $468 per month (2000); Median age of housing: 22 years (2000).
Transportation: Commute to work: 95.7% car, 0.4% public transportation, 1.3% walk, 1.8% work from home (2000); Travel time to work: 36.6% less than 15 minutes, 32.5% 15 to 30 minutes, 13.2% 30 to 45 minutes, 6.2% 45 to 60 minutes, 11.5% 60 minutes or more (2000)

BEACON SQUARE (CDP). Aka Beacon Squier. Covers a land area of 1.999 square miles and a water area of 0.037 square miles. Located at 28.21° N. Lat.; 82.74° W. Long. Elevation is 9 feet.
Population: 6,265 (1990); 7,263 (2000); 7,746 (2004); 8,398 (2009 projected); Race: 93.8% White, 1.7% Black, 1.0% Asian, 5.2% Hispanic of any race (2004); Density: 3,875.0 persons per square mile (2004); Average household size: 2.09 (2004); Median age: 49.9 (2004); Male/female ratio: 84.6 (2004); Marriage status: 16.8% never married, 57.3% now married, 13.6% widowed, 12.2% divorced (2000); Foreign born: 8.1% (2000); Ancestry (includes multiple ancestries): 19.1% German, 16.6% Irish, 15.2% Italian, 10.6% English, 10.0% Other groups (2000).
Economy: Employment by occupation: 10.4% management, 16.1% professional, 18.4% services, 32.3% sales, 0.0% farming, 11.5% construction, 11.3% production (2000).
Income: Per capita income: $18,437 (2004); Median household income: $31,302 (2004); Average household income: $38,620 (2004); Percent of households with income of $100,000 or more: 3.8% (2004); Poverty rate: 9.5% (2000).
Education: Percent of population age 25 and over with: High school diploma (including GED) or higher: 77.3% (2004); Bachelor's degree or higher: 11.6% (2004); Master's degree or higher: 3.4% (2004).

Housing: Homeownership rate: 86.2% (2004); Median home value: $75,093 (2004); Median rent: $499 per month (2000); Median age of housing: 27 years (2000).
Transportation: Commute to work: 94.4% car, 0.3% public transportation, 0.5% walk, 2.9% work from home (2000); Travel time to work: 25.8% less than 15 minutes, 32.5% 15 to 30 minutes, 17.7% 30 to 45 minutes, 14.3% 45 to 60 minutes, 9.8% 60 minutes or more (2000)

CRYSTAL SPRINGS (CDP). Covers a land area of 5.553 square miles and a water area of 0 square miles. Located at 28.18° N. Lat.; 82.16° W. Long. Elevation is 73 feet.
Population: 1,028 (1990); 1,175 (2000); 1,233 (2004); 1,320 (2009 projected); Race: 91.1% White, 1.0% Black, 0.0% Asian, 7.1% Hispanic of any race (2004); Density: 222.0 persons per square mile (2004); Average household size: 2.73 (2004); Median age: 35.9 (2004); Male/female ratio: 103.1 (2004); Marriage status: 17.6% never married, 65.7% now married, 2.3% widowed, 14.4% divorced (2000); Foreign born: 0.5% (2000); Ancestry (includes multiple ancestries): 20.6% Irish, 18.3% United States or American, 15.9% Other groups, 15.8% English, 13.1% German (2000).
Economy: Employment by occupation: 3.0% management, 6.5% professional, 17.4% services, 33.2% sales, 1.8% farming, 16.5% construction, 21.6% production (2000).
Income: Per capita income: $19,236 (2004); Median household income: $44,578 (2004); Average household income: $52,472 (2004); Percent of households with income of $100,000 or more: 7.5% (2004); Poverty rate: 9.8% (2000).
Education: Percent of population age 25 and over with: High school diploma (including GED) or higher: 66.2% (2004); Bachelor's degree or higher: 3.8% (2004); Master's degree or higher: 1.2% (2004).
Housing: Homeownership rate: 82.5% (2004); Median home value: $84,659 (2004); Median rent: $439 per month (2000); Median age of housing: 16 years (2000).
Transportation: Commute to work: 86.1% car, 1.1% public transportation, 6.5% walk, 3.4% work from home (2000); Travel time to work: 20.8% less than 15 minutes, 35.4% 15 to 30 minutes, 19.9% 30 to 45 minutes, 7.3% 45 to 60 minutes, 16.7% 60 minutes or more (2000)

DADE CITY (city). Covers a land area of 3.282 square miles and a water area of 0.096 square miles. Located at 28.36° N. Lat.; 82.19° W. Long. Elevation is 104 feet.
History: Dade City began as a trading post and became the commercial center of a truck-farming and citrus-fruit district.
Population: 5,702 (1990); 6,188 (2000); 6,265 (2004); 6,462 (2009 projected); Race: 58.2% White, 27.5% Black, 0.7% Asian, 20.0% Hispanic of any race (2004); Density: 1,908.8 persons per square mile (2004); Average household size: 2.52 (2004); Median age: 35.6 (2004); Male/female ratio: 88.6 (2004); Marriage status: 25.6% never married, 48.9% now married, 12.3% widowed, 13.3% divorced (2000); Foreign born: 6.2% (2000); Ancestry (includes multiple ancestries): 45.4% Other groups, 11.0% German, 10.0% Irish, 9.2% English, 6.0% United States or American (2000).
Economy: Single-family building permits issued: 56 (2004); Multi-family building permits issued: 3 (2004); Employment by occupation: 7.9% management, 17.3% professional, 19.5% services, 22.6% sales, 5.0% farming, 12.2% construction, 15.5% production (2000).
Income: Per capita income: $17,145 (2004); Median household income: $31,343 (2004); Average household income: $41,843 (2004); Percent of households with income of $100,000 or more: 5.6% (2004); Poverty rate: 15.8% (2000).
Taxes: Total city taxes per capita: $425 (2002); City property taxes per capita: $184 (2002).
Education: Percent of population age 25 and over with: High school diploma (including GED) or higher: 72.8% (2004); Bachelor's degree or higher: 17.2% (2004); Master's degree or higher: 6.7% (2004).

School District(s)

Pasco County School District (PK-12)
2002-03 Enrollment: 54,957 .... (813) 794-2651

Housing: Homeownership rate: 57.4% (2004); Median home value: $85,020 (2004); Median rent: $416 per month (2000); Median age of housing: 26 years (2000).
Hospitals: Pasco Community Hospital (120 beds)
Safety: Violent crime rate: 77.2 per 10,000 population; Property crime rate: 703.8 per 10,000 population (2003).
Newspapers: Pasco News (General - Circulation 5,500); Wesley Chapel Connection (General - Circulation 36,000); Zephyr Hills Sun (General - Circulation 36,000)
Transportation: Commute to work: 91.7% car, 0.6% public transportation, 3.5% walk, 3.2% work from home (2000); Travel time to work: 43.3% less than 15 minutes, 24.6% 15 to 30 minutes, 14.0% 30 to 45 minutes, 8.4% 45 to 60 minutes, 9.8% 60 minutes or more (2000); Amtrak: Service available.

Additional Information Contacts

Dade City Chamber of Commerce.................... (352) 567-3769
Local Government Offices.......................... (352) 567-3721

DADE CITY NORTH (CDP). Covers a land area of 1.819 square miles and a water area of 0.018 square miles. Located at 28.37° N. Lat.; 82.19° W. Long.
Population: 3,052 (1990); 3,319 (2000); 3,296 (2004); 3,321 (2009 projected); Race: 48.2% White, 13.0% Black, 0.0% Asian, 66.0% Hispanic of any race (2004); Density: 1,811.6 persons per square mile (2004); Average household size: 3.64 (2004); Median age: 25.8 (2004); Male/female ratio: 121.8 (2004); Marriage status: 34.1% never married, 53.9% now married, 4.8% widowed, 7.2% divorced (2000); Foreign born: 33.5% (2000); Ancestry (includes multiple ancestries): 60.6% Other groups, 10.8% United States or American, 5.0% Irish, 3.0% English, 2.3% Dutch (2000).
Economy: Employment by occupation: 1.3% management, 3.4% professional, 14.3% services, 11.1% sales, 25.7% farming, 27.3% construction, 16.8% production (2000).
Income: Per capita income: $11,351 (2004); Median household income: $28,913 (2004); Average household income: $39,349 (2004); Percent of households with income of $100,000 or more: 4.4% (2004); Poverty rate: 29.1% (2000).
Education: Percent of population age 25 and over with: High school diploma (including GED) or higher: 30.6% (2004); Bachelor's degree or higher: 0.7% (2004); Master's degree or higher: 0.0% (2004).
Housing: Homeownership rate: 52.2% (2004); Median home value: $55,631 (2004); Median rent: $299 per month (2000); Median age of housing: 32 years (2000).
Transportation: Commute to work: 98.0% car, 0.0% public transportation, 1.5% walk, 0.0% work from home (2000); Travel time to work: 24.4% less than 15 minutes, 28.6% 15 to 30 minutes, 19.3% 30 to 45 minutes, 4.5% 45 to 60 minutes, 23.2% 60 minutes or more (2000)

ELFERS (CDP). Covers a land area of 3.510 square miles and a water area of 0.024 square miles. Located at 28.21° N. Lat.; 82.72° W. Long. Elevation is 41 feet.
Population: 12,153 (1990); 13,161 (2000); 13,783 (2004); 14,667 (2009 projected); Race: 93.8% White, 1.5% Black, 1.1% Asian, 6.0% Hispanic of any race (2004); Density: 3,926.4 persons per square mile (2004); Average household size: 2.33 (2004); Median age: 44.7 (2004); Male/female ratio: 83.7 (2004); Marriage status: 16.5% never married, 56.1% now married, 15.8% widowed, 11.6% divorced (2000); Foreign born: 6.0% (2000); Ancestry (includes multiple ancestries): 17.6% German, 16.4% Irish, 13.4% Italian, 13.1% English, 12.7% Other groups (2000).
Economy: Employment by occupation: 8.8% management, 11.1% professional, 20.3% services, 33.0% sales, 0.2% farming, 12.8% construction, 13.8% production (2000).
Income: Per capita income: $17,053 (2004); Median household income: $32,125 (2004); Average household income: $39,228 (2004); Percent of households with income of $100,000 or more: 3.2% (2004); Poverty rate: 12.9% (2000).
Education: Percent of population age 25 and over with: High school diploma (including GED) or higher: 72.8% (2004); Bachelor's degree or higher: 7.0% (2004); Master's degree or higher: 2.0% (2004).

School District(s)

Pasco County School District (PK-12)
2002-03 Enrollment: 54,957 .... (813) 794-2651

Housing: Homeownership rate: 85.6% (2004); Median home value: $74,280 (2004); Median rent: $460 per month (2000); Median age of housing: 26 years (2000).
Transportation: Commute to work: 93.1% car, 0.5% public transportation, 1.6% walk, 2.3% work from home (2000); Travel time to work: 29.2% less than 15 minutes, 29.2% 15 to 30 minutes, 18.5% 30 to 45 minutes, 12.1% 45 to 60 minutes, 11.0% 60 minutes or more (2000)

HOLIDAY (CDP). Covers a land area of 5.382 square miles and a water area of 0.345 square miles. Located at 28.18° N. Lat.; 82.74° W. Long. Elevation is 17 feet.
Population: 20,286 (1990); 21,904 (2000); 22,852 (2004); 24,212 (2009 projected); Race: 93.3% White, 2.3% Black, 1.1% Asian, 5.3% Hispanic of any race (2004); Density: 4,246.3 persons per square mile (2004); Average household size: 2.12 (2004); Median age: 47.5 (2004); Male/female ratio: 90.1 (2004); Marriage status: 16.9% never married, 57.9% now married, 13.5% widowed, 11.7% divorced (2000); Foreign born: 10.2% (2000); Ancestry (includes multiple ancestries): 18.6% German, 16.9% Irish, 11.5% Italian, 11.0% English, 9.2% Other groups (2000).
Economy: Manufacturing includes women's swimwear, kitchen cabinets, commercial printing, and industrial tools. Employment by occupation: 6.5% management, 14.3% professional, 19.3% services, 31.5% sales, 0.2% farming, 14.7% construction, 13.5% production (2000).
Income: Per capita income: $18,575 (2004); Median household income: $31,475 (2004); Average household income: $39,380 (2004); Percent of households with income of $100,000 or more: 3.2% (2004); Poverty rate: 11.4% (2000).
Education: Percent of population age 25 and over with: High school diploma (including GED) or higher: 74.3% (2004); Bachelor's degree or higher: 7.2% (2004); Master's degree or higher: 2.0% (2004).

School District(s)

Pasco County School District (PK-12)
2002-03 Enrollment: 54,957 . . . . (813) 794-2651

Four-year College(s)

Webster College Inc (Private, For-profit)
2003-04 Enrollment: 263 . . . . (727) 942-0069
2003-04 Tuition: In-state $9,605; Out-of-state $9,605

Housing: Homeownership rate: 82.6% (2004); Median home value: $74,108 (2004); Median rent: $464 per month (2000); Median age of housing: 27 years (2000).
Transportation: Commute to work: 94.5% car, 0.0% public transportation, 0.3% walk, 3.3% work from home (2000); Travel time to work: 24.7% less than 15 minutes, 31.3% 15 to 30 minutes, 21.0% 30 to 45 minutes, 13.4% 45 to 60 minutes, 9.5% 60 minutes or more (2000)

HUDSON (CDP). Covers a land area of 6.365 square miles and a water area of 0.018 square miles. Located at 28.36° N. Lat.; 82.68° W. Long. Elevation is 11 feet.
Population: 10,731 (1990); 12,765 (2000); 13,176 (2004); 13,811 (2009 projected); Race: 96.3% White, 0.6% Black, 1.1% Asian, 3.3% Hispanic of any race (2004); Density: 2,069.9 persons per square mile (2004); Average household size: 2.05 (2004); Median age: 56.5 (2004); Male/female ratio: 93.3 (2004); Marriage status: 13.4% never married, 62.0% now married, 13.8% widowed, 10.8% divorced (2000); Foreign born: 7.9% (2000); Ancestry (includes multiple ancestries): 19.9% German, 17.8% Irish, 13.3% English, 12.0% Italian, 7.8% Other groups (2000).
Economy: Manufacturing includes construction materials, furniture, lime rock processing. Employment by occupation: 10.5% management, 17.7% professional, 22.2% services, 25.4% sales, 0.5% farming, 14.6% construction, 9.1% production (2000).
Income: Per capita income: $22,980 (2004); Median household income: $37,319 (2004); Average household income: $46,691 (2004); Percent of households with income of $100,000 or more: 6.4% (2004); Poverty rate: 9.9% (2000).
Education: Percent of population age 25 and over with: High school diploma (including GED) or higher: 75.8% (2004); Bachelor's degree or higher: 12.9% (2004); Master's degree or higher: 4.2% (2004).

School District(s)

Pasco County School District (PK-12)
2002-03 Enrollment: 54,957 . . . . (813) 794-2651

Housing: Homeownership rate: 80.5% (2004); Median home value: $118,357 (2004); Median rent: $449 per month (2000); Median age of housing: 18 years (2000).
Hospitals: Regional Medical Center Bayonet Point (290 beds)
Transportation: Commute to work: 90.4% car, 0.8% public transportation, 1.4% walk, 3.9% work from home (2000); Travel time to work: 39.3% less than 15 minutes, 27.6% 15 to 30 minutes, 10.7% 30 to 45 minutes, 8.6% 45 to 60 minutes, 13.9% 60 minutes or more (2000)

JASMINE ESTATES (CDP). Covers a land area of 3.574 square miles and a water area of 0.064 square miles. Located at 28.29° N. Lat.; 82.69° W. Long.
Population: 17,133 (1990); 18,213 (2000); 17,944 (2004); 17,967 (2009 projected); Race: 92.7% White, 2.4% Black, 1.0% Asian, 7.8% Hispanic of any race (2004); Density: 5,021.2 persons per square mile (2004); Average household size: 2.18 (2004); Median age: 45.0 (2004); Male/female ratio: 87.0 (2004); Marriage status: 19.1% never married, 55.2% now married, 13.8% widowed, 11.9% divorced (2000); Foreign born: 8.5% (2000); Ancestry (includes multiple ancestries): 19.0% Italian, 16.4% German, 15.8% Irish, 11.3% Other groups, 8.2% United States or American (2000).
Economy: Employment by occupation: 8.2% management, 14.3% professional, 20.4% services, 35.6% sales, 0.0% farming, 10.0% construction, 11.5% production (2000).
Income: Per capita income: $15,908 (2004); Median household income: $29,482 (2004); Average household income: $34,689 (2004); Percent of households with income of $100,000 or more: 2.3% (2004); Poverty rate: 14.3% (2000).
Education: Percent of population age 25 and over with: High school diploma (including GED) or higher: 72.6% (2004); Bachelor's degree or higher: 8.3% (2004); Master's degree or higher: 2.7% (2004).
Housing: Homeownership rate: 76.9% (2004); Median home value: $85,313 (2004); Median rent: $473 per month (2000); Median age of housing: 22 years (2000).
Transportation: Commute to work: 96.0% car, 0.8% public transportation, 0.5% walk, 1.1% work from home (2000); Travel time to work: 35.1% less than 15 minutes, 31.4% 15 to 30 minutes, 12.7% 30 to 45 minutes, 8.8% 45 to 60 minutes, 12.1% 60 minutes or more (2000)

LACOOCHEE (CDP). Covers a land area of 2.852 square miles and a water area of 0 square miles. Located at 28.46° N. Lat.; 82.17° W. Long. Elevation is 74 feet.
Population: 2,072 (1990); 1,345 (2000); 1,181 (2004); 1,093 (2009 projected); Race: 62.0% White, 25.0% Black, 0.1% Asian, 43.4% Hispanic of any race (2004); Density: 414.1 persons per square mile (2004); Average household size: 3.17 (2004); Median age: 25.1 (2004); Male/female ratio: 103.3 (2004); Marriage status: 14.9% never married, 62.8% now married, 11.8% widowed, 10.5% divorced (2000); Foreign born: 16.5% (2000); Ancestry (includes multiple ancestries): 52.2% Other groups, 12.7% United States or American, 9.4% English, 7.4% Irish, 2.7% Scottish (2000).
Economy: Employment by occupation: 8.9% management, 10.5% professional, 22.0% services, 6.4% sales, 14.3% farming, 16.2% construction, 21.7% production (2000).
Income: Per capita income: $6,793 (2004); Median household income: $16,708 (2004); Average household income: $21,508 (2004); Percent of households with income of $100,000 or more: 1.1% (2004); Poverty rate: 51.2% (2000).
Education: Percent of population age 25 and over with: High school diploma (including GED) or higher: 40.9% (2004); Bachelor's degree or higher: 4.7% (2004); Master's degree or higher: 2.7% (2004).
Housing: Homeownership rate: 47.7% (2004); Median home value: $47,826 (2004); Median rent: $230 per month (2000); Median age of housing: 26 years (2000).
Transportation: Commute to work: 98.6% car, 0.0% public transportation, 1.4% walk, 0.0% work from home (2000); Travel time to work: 12.5% less than 15 minutes, 40.6% 15 to 30 minutes, 24.0% 30 to 45 minutes, 5.9% 45 to 60 minutes, 17.0% 60 minutes or more (2000)

LAND O' LAKES (CDP). Covers a land area of 18.616 square miles and a water area of 2.497 square miles. Located at 28.20° N. Lat.; 82.44° W. Long. Elevation is 81 feet.
Population: 13,062 (1990); 20,971 (2000); 26,561 (2004); 33,212 (2009 projected); Race: 92.2% White, 3.1% Black, 1.5% Asian, 10.3% Hispanic of any race (2004); Density: 1,426.8 persons per square mile (2004); Average household size: 2.73 (2004); Median age: 37.2 (2004); Male/female ratio: 98.5 (2004); Marriage status: 17.5% never married, 67.4% now married, 4.9% widowed, 10.2% divorced (2000); Foreign born: 4.2% (2000); Ancestry (includes multiple ancestries): 20.3% German, 18.9% Other groups, 14.7% Irish, 13.8% English, 8.7% United States or American (2000).
Economy: Employment by occupation: 14.7% management, 23.8% professional, 10.5% services, 31.7% sales, 0.1% farming, 11.0% construction, 8.2% production (2000).
Income: Per capita income: $27,716 (2004); Median household income: $67,317 (2004); Average household income: $75,310 (2004); Percent of households with income of $100,000 or more: 22.7% (2004); Poverty rate: 4.9% (2000).

Education: Percent of population age 25 and over with: High school diploma (including GED) or higher: 89.7% (2004); Bachelor's degree or higher: 28.0% (2004); Master's degree or higher: 9.1% (2004).

School District(s)

Pasco County School District (PK-12)
2002-03 Enrollment: 54,957 . . . . (813) 794-2651

Housing: Homeownership rate: 87.1% (2004); Median home value: $163,696 (2004); Median rent: $527 per month (2000); Median age of housing: 13 years (2000).

Transportation: Commute to work: 93.6% car, 0.4% public transportation, 0.8% walk, 4.1% work from home (2000); Travel time to work: 15.9% less than 15 minutes, 22.0% 15 to 30 minutes, 34.2% 30 to 45 minutes, 17.9% 45 to 60 minutes, 9.9% 60 minutes or more (2000)

Additional Information Contacts

Land O' Lakes Chamber of Commerce . . . . (813) 909-2722

NEW PORT RICHEY (city). Covers a land area of 4.510 square miles and a water area of 0.069 square miles. Located at 28.24° N. Lat.; 82.71° W. Long. Elevation is 14 feet.

History: Named for Old Port Richey, which was named for A.M. Richey, first settler and postmaster. New Port Richey developed as a resort town, about a mile from the Old Port Richey, which in the 1880s was a port of call for schooners between Cedar Keys and Key West.

Population: 14,615 (1990); 16,117 (2000); 16,492 (2004); 17,021 (2009 projected); Race: 92.5% White, 1.5% Black, 1.1% Asian, 7.0% Hispanic of any race (2004); Density: 3,656.5 persons per square mile (2004); Average household size: 2.21 (2004); Median age: 44.0 (2004); Male/female ratio: 89.1 (2004); Marriage status: 20.7% never married, 49.5% now married, 14.5% widowed, 15.3% divorced (2000); Foreign born: 9.3% (2000); Ancestry (includes multiple ancestries): 18.0% German, 16.8% Irish, 13.3% English, 11.8% Other groups, 11.2% Italian (2000).

Economy: Single-family building permits issued: 33 (2004); Multi-family building permits issued: 108 (2004); Employment by occupation: 7.0% management, 14.0% professional, 25.4% services, 26.1% sales, 0.3% farming, 13.6% construction, 13.6% production (2000).

Income: Per capita income: $18,075 (2004); Median household income: $28,766 (2004); Average household income: $38,550 (2004); Percent of households with income of $100,000 or more: 4.3% (2004); Poverty rate: 16.6% (2000).

Taxes: Total city taxes per capita: $407 (2002); City property taxes per capita: $171 (2002).

Education: Percent of population age 25 and over with: High school diploma (including GED) or higher: 73.7% (2004); Bachelor's degree or higher: 7.7% (2004); Master's degree or higher: 2.7% (2004).

School District(s)

Pasco County School District (PK-12)
2002-03 Enrollment: 54,957 . . . . (813) 794-2651

Two-year College(s)

Benes International School of Beauty (Private, For-profit)
2003-04 Enrollment: 148 . . . . (727) 848-8415
Pasco-Hernando Community College (Public)
2003-04 Enrollment: 6,909 . . . . (727) 847-2727
2003-04 Tuition: In-state $1,561; Out-of-state $5,780

Housing: Homeownership rate: 65.0% (2004); Median home value: $75,891 (2004); Median rent: $390 per month (2000); Median age of housing: 25 years (2000).

Hospitals: Community Hospital (414 beds); North Bay Medical Center (122 beds)

Safety: Violent crime rate: 91.9 per 10,000 population; Property crime rate: 580.9 per 10,000 population (2003).

Newspapers: The Suncoast News (General - Circulation 182,200); West Pasco Press (General - Circulation 1,500)

Transportation: Commute to work: 91.8% car, 0.2% public transportation, 4.7% walk, 1.0% work from home (2000); Travel time to work: 38.1% less than 15 minutes, 26.4% 15 to 30 minutes, 14.4% 30 to 45 minutes, 10.2% 45 to 60 minutes, 10.9% 60 minutes or more (2000)

Airports: Tampa Bay Executive

Additional Information Contacts

Local Government Offices . . . . (727) 841-4500
New Port Richey Chamber of Commerce . . . . (727) 842-7651
West Pasco Board of Realtors . . . . (727) 848-8507

NEW PORT RICHEY EAST (CDP). Covers a land area of 3.608 square miles and a water area of 0.056 square miles. Located at 28.26° N. Lat.; 82.69° W. Long.

Population: 9,300 (1990); 9,916 (2000); 9,861 (2004); 10,017 (2009 projected); Race: 94.2% White, 1.6% Black, 1.4% Asian, 6.1% Hispanic of any race (2004); Density: 2,732.8 persons per square mile (2004); Average household size: 2.20 (2004); Median age: 43.5 (2004); Male/female ratio: 90.6 (2004); Marriage status: 20.2% never married, 54.4% now married, 13.2% widowed, 12.2% divorced (2000); Foreign born: 6.2% (2000); Ancestry (includes multiple ancestries): 21.0% German, 16.8% Irish, 12.8% Italian, 10.9% Other groups, 10.1% English (2000).

Economy: Employment by occupation: 10.7% management, 15.6% professional, 16.1% services, 36.7% sales, 0.4% farming, 9.0% construction, 11.6% production (2000).

Income: Per capita income: $19,629 (2004); Median household income: $33,327 (2004); Average household income: $42,772 (2004); Percent of households with income of $100,000 or more: 5.2% (2004); Poverty rate: 10.8% (2000).

Education: Percent of population age 25 and over with: High school diploma (including GED) or higher: 81.9% (2004); Bachelor's degree or higher: 13.1% (2004); Master's degree or higher: 3.9% (2004).

Housing: Homeownership rate: 66.2% (2004); Median home value: $100,664 (2004); Median rent: $487 per month (2000); Median age of housing: 18 years (2000).

Transportation: Commute to work: 95.0% car, 0.0% public transportation, 1.0% walk, 2.5% work from home (2000); Travel time to work: 38.4% less than 15 minutes, 29.0% 15 to 30 minutes, 15.5% 30 to 45 minutes, 7.7% 45 to 60 minutes, 9.5% 60 minutes or more (2000)

ODESSA (CDP). Covers a land area of 5.298 square miles and a water area of 0.335 square miles. Located at 28.18° N. Lat.; 82.56° W. Long.

Population: 2,900 (1990); 3,173 (2000); 4,969 (2004); 7,082 (2009 projected); Race: 95.2% White, 1.0% Black, 0.9% Asian, 8.2% Hispanic of any race (2004); Density: 937.9 persons per square mile (2004); Average household size: 2.64 (2004); Median age: 38.5 (2004); Male/female ratio: 108.1 (2004); Marriage status: 19.1% never married, 63.9% now married, 6.8% widowed, 10.3% divorced (2000); Foreign born: 3.3% (2000); Ancestry (includes multiple ancestries): 16.0% Other groups, 11.3% United States or American, 10.5% German, 10.2% English, 9.7% Irish (2000).

Economy: Employment by occupation: 16.0% management, 13.8% professional, 13.6% services, 28.0% sales, 0.0% farming, 17.6% construction, 11.0% production (2000).

Income: Per capita income: $27,104 (2004); Median household income: $57,482 (2004); Average household income: $71,448 (2004); Percent of households with income of $100,000 or more: 21.1% (2004); Poverty rate: 6.7% (2000).

Education: Percent of population age 25 and over with: High school diploma (including GED) or higher: 81.3% (2004); Bachelor's degree or higher: 18.6% (2004); Master's degree or higher: 5.0% (2004).

Housing: Homeownership rate: 88.8% (2004); Median home value: $127,475 (2004); Median rent: $434 per month (2000); Median age of housing: 17 years (2000).

Transportation: Commute to work: 91.8% car, 1.9% public transportation, 0.0% walk, 5.5% work from home (2000); Travel time to work: 10.3% less than 15 minutes, 33.0% 15 to 30 minutes, 33.1% 30 to 45 minutes, 16.8% 45 to 60 minutes, 6.8% 60 minutes or more (2000)

PORT RICHEY (city). Covers a land area of 2.107 square miles and a water area of 0.630 square miles. Located at 28.27° N. Lat.; 82.72° W. Long. Elevation is 11 feet.

Population: 2,608 (1990); 3,021 (2000); 3,213 (2004); 3,441 (2009 projected); Race: 95.3% White, 0.9% Black, 1.4% Asian, 3.1% Hispanic of any race (2004); Density: 1,525.0 persons per square mile (2004); Average household size: 2.06 (2004); Median age: 48.2 (2004); Male/female ratio: 99.9 (2004); Marriage status: 17.1% never married, 52.2% now married, 14.8% widowed, 15.9% divorced (2000); Foreign born: 3.7% (2000); Ancestry (includes multiple ancestries): 26.8% German, 14.5% Irish, 12.7% Italian, 11.2% English, 7.8% Other groups (2000).

Economy: Single-family building permits issued: 13 (2004); Multi-family building permits issued: 0 (2004); Employment by occupation: 6.1% management, 19.9% professional, 20.1% services, 28.5% sales, 0.5% farming, 16.1% construction, 8.7% production (2000).

Income: Per capita income: $20,931 (2004); Median household income: $30,156 (2004); Average household income: $41,942 (2004); Percent of households with income of $100,000 or more: 6.9% (2004); Poverty rate: 16.1% (2000).

Education: Percent of population age 25 and over with: High school diploma (including GED) or higher: 78.1% (2004); Bachelor's degree or higher: 13.3% (2004); Master's degree or higher: 5.8% (2004).

School District(s)

Pasco County School District (PK-12)
2002-03 Enrollment: 54,957 . . . . (813) 794-2651

Housing: Homeownership rate: 68.1% (2004); Median home value: $113,546 (2004); Median rent: $395 per month (2000); Median age of housing: 23 years (2000).

Safety: Violent crime rate: 146.4 per 10,000 population; Property crime rate: 1,648.0 per 10,000 population (2003).

Transportation: Commute to work: 91.7% car, 0.0% public transportation, 1.7% walk, 4.6% work from home (2000); Travel time to work: 34.0% less than 15 minutes, 29.1% 15 to 30 minutes, 17.9% 30 to 45 minutes, 9.8% 45 to 60 minutes, 9.2% 60 minutes or more (2000)

SAINT LEO (town). Covers a land area of 1.609 square miles and a water area of 0.264 square miles. Located at 28.33° N. Lat.; 82.25° W. Long. Elevation is 178 feet.

History: St. Leo grew around an abbey established in 1889 by Benedictine monks and named for Pope Leo I.

Population: 1,241 (1990); 595 (2000); 604 (2004); 592 (2009 projected); Race: 82.8% White, 10.4% Black, 2.3% Asian, 11.4% Hispanic of any race (2004); Density: 375.4 persons per square mile (2004); Average household size: 12.85 (2004); Median age: 20.5 (2004); Male/female ratio: 93.6 (2004); Marriage status: 83.9% never married, 15.4% now married, 0.0% widowed, 0.7% divorced (2000); Foreign born: 6.4% (2000); Ancestry (includes multiple ancestries): 19.2% German, 17.6% United States or American, 15.3% Other groups, 14.3% Irish, 13.0% English (2000).

Economy: Single-family building permits issued: 6 (2004); Multi-family building permits issued: 0 (2004); Employment by occupation: 2.8% management, 27.1% professional, 19.4% services, 45.5% sales, 0.7% farming, 0.0% construction, 4.5% production (2000).

Income: Per capita income: $9,862 (2004); Median household income: $43,654 (2004); Average household income: $69,255 (2004); Percent of households with income of $100,000 or more: 23.4% (2004); Poverty rate: 19.9% (2000).

Education: Percent of population age 25 and over with: High school diploma (including GED) or higher: 85.1% (2004); Bachelor's degree or higher: 40.5% (2004); Master's degree or higher: 9.5% (2004).

Four-year College(s)

Saint Leo University
2003-04 Enrollment: 12,190 . . . . (352) 588-8200
2003-04 Tuition: In-state $13,150; Out-of-state $13,150

Housing: Homeownership rate: 72.3% (2004); Median home value: $307,143 (2004); Median rent: $267 per month (2000); Median age of housing: 17 years (2000).

Transportation: Commute to work: 35.3% car, 0.7% public transportation, 45.3% walk, 14.7% work from home (2000); Travel time to work: 74.7% less than 15 minutes, 13.9% 15 to 30 minutes, 7.6% 30 to 45 minutes, 1.3% 45 to 60 minutes, 2.5% 60 minutes or more (2000)

SAN ANTONIO (city). Covers a land area of 1.231 square miles and a water area of 0 square miles. Located at 28.33° N. Lat.; 82.27° W. Long. Elevation is 146 feet.

History: San Antonio was founded in the 1880's by Judge Edmund F. Dunne, former Chief Justice of Arizona, who named the town for the saint to whom he prayed when he was lost in the Arizona desert while prospecting for silver.

Population: 788 (1990); 655 (2000); 701 (2004); 757 (2009 projected); Race: 97.0% White, 0.0% Black, 1.4% Asian, 8.3% Hispanic of any race (2004); Density: 569.6 persons per square mile (2004); Average household size: 2.42 (2004); Median age: 36.9 (2004); Male/female ratio: 93.1 (2004); Marriage status: 21.2% never married, 65.4% now married, 3.9% widowed, 9.5% divorced (2000); Foreign born: 2.4% (2000); Ancestry (includes multiple ancestries): 19.0% Irish, 18.7% German, 16.3% English, 11.4% Other groups, 6.7% Italian (2000).

Economy: Single-family building permits issued: 24 (2004); Multi-family building permits issued: 0 (2004); Employment by occupation: 17.7% management, 28.6% professional, 13.5% services, 20.6% sales, 0.0% farming, 12.5% construction, 7.1% production (2000).

Income: Per capita income: $24,996 (2004); Median household income: $48,056 (2004); Average household income: $60,422 (2004); Percent of households with income of $100,000 or more: 16.9% (2004); Poverty rate: 10.1% (2000).

Taxes: Total city taxes per capita: $136 (2002); City property taxes per capita: $67 (2002).

Education: Percent of population age 25 and over with: High school diploma (including GED) or higher: 92.3% (2004); Bachelor's degree or higher: 28.0% (2004); Master's degree or higher: 8.1% (2004).

School District(s)

Pasco County School District (PK-12)
2002-03 Enrollment: 54,957 . . . . (813) 794-2651

Housing: Homeownership rate: 73.1% (2004); Median home value: $120,536 (2004); Median rent: $384 per month (2000); Median age of housing: 18 years (2000).

Transportation: Commute to work: 93.6% car, 0.0% public transportation, 3.5% walk, 2.9% work from home (2000); Travel time to work: 36.8% less than 15 minutes, 26.2% 15 to 30 minutes, 19.5% 30 to 45 minutes, 13.2% 45 to 60 minutes, 4.3% 60 minutes or more (2000)

SHADY HILLS (CDP). Covers a land area of 26.170 square miles and a water area of 1.225 square miles. Located at 28.40° N. Lat.; 82.54° W. Long.

Population: 7,197 (1990); 7,798 (2000); 8,402 (2004); 9,200 (2009 projected); Race: 96.2% White, 0.9% Black, 0.2% Asian, 4.7% Hispanic of any race (2004); Density: 321.1 persons per square mile (2004); Average household size: 2.74 (2004); Median age: 37.7 (2004); Male/female ratio: 98.0 (2004); Marriage status: 20.4% never married, 62.5% now married, 6.9% widowed, 10.1% divorced (2000); Foreign born: 4.6% (2000); Ancestry (includes multiple ancestries): 17.7% German, 16.2% Irish, 15.5% United States or American, 11.1% Other groups, 9.8% English (2000).

Economy: Employment by occupation: 9.8% management, 12.6% professional, 22.4% services, 24.2% sales, 0.2% farming, 16.9% construction, 13.9% production (2000).

Income: Per capita income: $17,710 (2004); Median household income: $41,526 (2004); Average household income: $48,611 (2004); Percent of households with income of $100,000 or more: 7.3% (2004); Poverty rate: 13.6% (2000).

Education: Percent of population age 25 and over with: High school diploma (including GED) or higher: 76.2% (2004); Bachelor's degree or higher: 7.7% (2004); Master's degree or higher: 2.4% (2004).

Housing: Homeownership rate: 87.0% (2004); Median home value: $107,112 (2004); Median rent: $404 per month (2000); Median age of housing: 16 years (2000).

Transportation: Commute to work: 93.1% car, 0.4% public transportation, 1.2% walk, 2.5% work from home (2000); Travel time to work: 10.5% less than 15 minutes, 28.5% 15 to 30 minutes, 28.5% 30 to 45 minutes, 12.2% 45 to 60 minutes, 20.3% 60 minutes or more (2000)

TRINITY (CDP). Covers a land area of 4.721 square miles and a water area of 0 square miles. Located at 28.17° N. Lat.; 82.67° W. Long.

Population: 1,141 (1990); 4,279 (2000); 5,284 (2004); 6,490 (2009 projected); Race: 95.1% White, 1.6% Black, 2.0% Asian, 3.2% Hispanic of any race (2004); Density: 1,119.2 persons per square mile (2004); Average household size: 2.52 (2004); Median age: 46.1 (2004); Male/female ratio: 93.1 (2004); Marriage status: 11.8% never married, 76.9% now married, 6.9% widowed, 4.3% divorced (2000); Foreign born: 9.4% (2000); Ancestry (includes multiple ancestries): 20.1% Italian, 17.6% Irish, 15.8% German, 14.7% English, 9.2% Other groups (2000).

Economy: Employment by occupation: 20.2% management, 25.4% professional, 8.9% services, 35.6% sales, 0.5% farming, 3.2% construction, 6.2% production (2000).

Income: Per capita income: $39,544 (2004); Median household income: $78,338 (2004); Average household income: $99,500 (2004); Percent of households with income of $100,000 or more: 34.9% (2004); Poverty rate: 2.1% (2000).

Education: Percent of population age 25 and over with: High school diploma (including GED) or higher: 92.7% (2004); Bachelor's degree or higher: 34.2% (2004); Master's degree or higher: 12.2% (2004).

Four-year College(s)

Trinity College of Florida
2003-04 Enrollment: 208 . . . . (727) 376-6911
2003-04 Tuition: In-state $7,256; Out-of-state $7,256

Housing: Homeownership rate: 98.0% (2004); Median home value: $259,519 (2004); Median rent: $1,110 per month (2000); Median age of housing: 3 years (2000).

Transportation: Commute to work: 93.8% car, 0.0% public transportation, 0.0% walk, 4.2% work from home (2000); Travel time to work: 11.5% less

than 15 minutes, 29.1% 15 to 30 minutes, 26.7% 30 to 45 minutes, 23.2% 45 to 60 minutes, 9.5% 60 minutes or more (2000)

WESLEY CHAPEL (CDP). Covers a land area of 6.057 square miles and a water area of 0.027 square miles. Located at 28.17° N. Lat.; 82.35° W. Long. Elevation is 100 feet.
Population: 1,928 (1990); 5,691 (2000); 8,365 (2004); 11,532 (2009 projected); Race: 74.3% White, 11.9% Black, 6.7% Asian, 15.7% Hispanic of any race (2004); Density: 1,381.0 persons per square mile (2004); Average household size: 2.86 (2004); Median age: 33.1 (2004); Male/female ratio: 95.9 (2004); Marriage status: 16.1% never married, 73.0% now married, 3.8% widowed, 7.0% divorced (2000); Foreign born: 11.5% (2000); Ancestry (includes multiple ancestries): 26.3% Other groups, 15.5% German, 14.4% Irish, 10.1% Italian, 9.1% English (2000).
Economy: Employment by occupation: 22.3% management, 30.2% professional, 8.5% services, 31.3% sales, 0.6% farming, 3.1% construction, 4.0% production (2000).
Income: Per capita income: $31,019 (2004); Median household income: $78,890 (2004); Average household income: $88,799 (2004); Percent of households with income of $100,000 or more: 29.9% (2004); Poverty rate: 1.9% (2000).
Education: Percent of population age 25 and over with: High school diploma (including GED) or higher: 95.4% (2004); Bachelor's degree or higher: 42.4% (2004); Master's degree or higher: 14.8% (2004).

School District(s)

Pasco County School District (PK-12)
2002-03 Enrollment: 54,957 . . . . (813) 794-2651

Housing: Homeownership rate: 97.4% (2004); Median home value: $184,671 (2004); Median rent: $1,069 per month (2000); Median age of housing: 4 years (2000).
Transportation: Commute to work: 96.8% car, 0.0% public transportation, 0.3% walk, 2.1% work from home (2000); Travel time to work: 10.6% less than 15 minutes, 31.2% 15 to 30 minutes, 31.4% 30 to 45 minutes, 13.2% 45 to 60 minutes, 13.6% 60 minutes or more (2000)

WESLEY CHAPEL SOUTH (CDP). Covers a land area of 11.131 square miles and a water area of 0.032 square miles. Located at 28.24° N. Lat.; 82.32° W. Long.
Population: 1,656 (1990); 3,245 (2000); 4,493 (2004); 5,977 (2009 projected); Race: 91.6% White, 2.1% Black, 2.2% Asian, 7.3% Hispanic of any race (2004); Density: 403.7 persons per square mile (2004); Average household size: 2.54 (2004); Median age: 39.8 (2004); Male/female ratio: 100.1 (2004); Marriage status: 18.5% never married, 66.0% now married, 4.1% widowed, 11.5% divorced (2000); Foreign born: 7.3% (2000); Ancestry (includes multiple ancestries): 20.4% Other groups, 19.0% German, 16.3% English, 14.5% United States or American, 13.4% Irish (2000).
Economy: Employment by occupation: 15.0% management, 21.9% professional, 15.3% services, 25.2% sales, 0.4% farming, 11.9% construction, 10.4% production (2000).
Income: Per capita income: $32,380 (2004); Median household income: $64,111 (2004); Average household income: $82,101 (2004); Percent of households with income of $100,000 or more: 22.0% (2004); Poverty rate: 6.6% (2000).
Education: Percent of population age 25 and over with: High school diploma (including GED) or higher: 86.9% (2004); Bachelor's degree or higher: 25.8% (2004); Master's degree or higher: 9.7% (2004).
Housing: Homeownership rate: 91.6% (2004); Median home value: $154,040 (2004); Median rent: $506 per month (2000); Median age of housing: 11 years (2000).
Transportation: Commute to work: 91.4% car, 0.0% public transportation, 0.0% walk, 4.9% work from home (2000); Travel time to work: 16.1% less than 15 minutes, 33.0% 15 to 30 minutes, 29.7% 30 to 45 minutes, 12.2% 45 to 60 minutes, 9.0% 60 minutes or more (2000)

ZEPHYRHILLS (city). Covers a land area of 6.268 square miles and a water area of 0.074 square miles. Located at 28.23° N. Lat.; 82.18° W. Long. Elevation is 97 feet.
History: The site of Zephyrhills was chosen by Captain H.B. Jefferies, a Union army officer, as a home for veterans. The town was known as Abbott's Station until 1915.
Population: 8,770 (1990); 10,833 (2000); 11,370 (2004); 12,088 (2009 projected); Race: 90.3% White, 4.0% Black, 1.4% Asian, 6.8% Hispanic of any race (2004); Density: 1,813.9 persons per square mile (2004); Average household size: 2.17 (2004); Median age: 48.2 (2004); Male/female ratio: 84.3 (2004); Marriage status: 12.6% never married, 59.2% now married, 14.7% widowed, 13.5% divorced (2000); Foreign born: 6.2% (2000); Ancestry (includes multiple ancestries): 19.2% German, 16.6% English, 13.0% United States or American, 12.6% Irish, 12.3% Other groups (2000).
Economy: Single-family building permits issued: 49 (2004); Multi-family building permits issued: 22 (2004); Employment by occupation: 9.8% management, 13.0% professional, 20.1% services, 34.0% sales, 0.9% farming, 10.6% construction, 11.6% production (2000).
Income: Per capita income: $18,952 (2004); Median household income: $30,600 (2004); Average household income: $40,080 (2004); Percent of households with income of $100,000 or more: 4.6% (2004); Poverty rate: 12.1% (2000).
Taxes: Total city taxes per capita: $423 (2002); City property taxes per capita: $203 (2002).
Education: Percent of population age 25 and over with: High school diploma (including GED) or higher: 74.6% (2004); Bachelor's degree or higher: 9.9% (2004); Master's degree or higher: 3.7% (2004).

School District(s)

Pasco County School District (PK-12)
2002-03 Enrollment: 54,957 . . . . (813) 794-2651

Housing: Homeownership rate: 69.7% (2004); Median home value: $88,267 (2004); Median rent: $376 per month (2000); Median age of housing: 21 years (2000).
Hospitals: East Pasco Medical Center (154 beds)
Safety: Violent crime rate: 41.8 per 10,000 population; Property crime rate: 624.2 per 10,000 population (2003).
Newspapers: Zephyrhills News (General - Circulation 5,000)
Transportation: Commute to work: 94.0% car, 0.1% public transportation, 2.7% walk, 2.5% work from home (2000); Travel time to work: 35.9% less than 15 minutes, 23.8% 15 to 30 minutes, 20.6% 30 to 45 minutes, 10.1% 45 to 60 minutes, 9.5% 60 minutes or more (2000)

Additional Information Contacts

East Pasco Association of Realtors . . . . (813) 783-3794
Local Government Offices . . . . (813) 780-0000

ZEPHYRHILLS NORTH (CDP). Covers a land area of 1.078 square miles and a water area of 0 square miles. Located at 28.25° N. Lat.; 82.16° W. Long.
Population: 2,272 (1990); 2,544 (2000); 2,628 (2004); 2,765 (2009 projected); Race: 92.8% White, 1.5% Black, 1.7% Asian, 4.5% Hispanic of any race (2004); Density: 2,437.9 persons per square mile (2004); Average household size: 1.95 (2004); Median age: 62.9 (2004); Male/female ratio: 81.6 (2004); Marriage status: 12.6% never married, 66.9% now married, 13.3% widowed, 7.2% divorced (2000); Foreign born: 5.1% (2000); Ancestry (includes multiple ancestries): 20.5% German, 15.9% English, 13.4% United States or American, 9.7% Irish, 8.4% French (except Basque) (2000).
Economy: Employment by occupation: 6.0% management, 13.9% professional, 17.2% services, 34.2% sales, 0.0% farming, 7.5% construction, 21.2% production (2000).
Income: Per capita income: $19,105 (2004); Median household income: $32,714 (2004); Average household income: $37,301 (2004); Percent of households with income of $100,000 or more: 3.2% (2004); Poverty rate: 10.7% (2000).
Education: Percent of population age 25 and over with: High school diploma (including GED) or higher: 75.1% (2004); Bachelor's degree or higher: 7.8% (2004); Master's degree or higher: 2.8% (2004).
Housing: Homeownership rate: 84.5% (2004); Median home value: $62,181 (2004); Median rent: $356 per month (2000); Median age of housing: 18 years (2000).
Transportation: Commute to work: 93.3% car, 0.0% public transportation, 3.5% walk, 0.0% work from home (2000); Travel time to work: 45.2% less than 15 minutes, 16.2% 15 to 30 minutes, 17.8% 30 to 45 minutes, 12.2% 45 to 60 minutes, 8.7% 60 minutes or more (2000)

ZEPHYRHILLS SOUTH (CDP). Covers a land area of 1.918 square miles and a water area of 0 square miles. Located at 28.21° N. Lat.; 82.18° W. Long.
Population: 3,461 (1990); 4,435 (2000); 4,916 (2004); 5,519 (2009 projected); Race: 95.1% White, 1.2% Black, 0.3% Asian, 3.5% Hispanic of any race (2004); Density: 2,562.6 persons per square mile (2004); Average household size: 2.00 (2004); Median age: 61.0 (2004); Male/female ratio: 93.2 (2004); Marriage status: 8.0% never married, 67.2% now married, 13.4% widowed, 11.4% divorced (2000); Foreign born: 6.9% (2000);

Ancestry (includes multiple ancestries): 15.7% German, 13.8% English, 12.5% Irish, 9.7% Other groups, 8.9% United States or American (2000).
Economy: Employment by occupation: 7.2% management, 10.7% professional, 19.7% services, 31.4% sales, 1.8% farming, 10.7% construction, 18.4% production (2000).
Income: Per capita income: $15,958 (2004); Median household income: $24,629 (2004); Average household income: $31,884 (2004); Percent of households with income of $100,000 or more: 1.8% (2004); Poverty rate: 12.5% (2000).
Education: Percent of population age 25 and over with: High school diploma (including GED) or higher: 70.1% (2004); Bachelor's degree or higher: 6.2% (2004); Master's degree or higher: 1.7% (2004).
Housing: Homeownership rate: 88.2% (2004); Median home value: $49,336 (2004); Median rent: $356 per month (2000); Median age of housing: 17 years (2000).
Transportation: Commute to work: 93.5% car, 0.5% public transportation, 2.9% walk, 1.8% work from home (2000); Travel time to work: 33.2% less than 15 minutes, 28.9% 15 to 30 minutes, 20.1% 30 to 45 minutes, 11.9% 45 to 60 minutes, 5.8% 60 minutes or more (2000)

ZEPHYRHILLS WEST (CDP). Covers a land area of 2.656 square miles and a water area of 0 square miles. Located at 28.23° N. Lat.; 82.20° W. Long.
Population: 4,746 (1990); 5,242 (2000); 5,496 (2004); 5,856 (2009 projected); Race: 97.2% White, 0.3% Black, 0.6% Asian, 2.8% Hispanic of any race (2004); Density: 2,069.0 persons per square mile (2004); Average household size: 1.87 (2004); Median age: 66.8 (2004); Male/female ratio: 86.4 (2004); Marriage status: 6.6% never married, 67.9% now married, 16.8% widowed, 8.7% divorced (2000); Foreign born: 6.8% (2000); Ancestry (includes multiple ancestries): 20.4% English, 18.0% German, 14.7% United States or American, 9.6% Irish, 5.7% French (except Basque) (2000).
Economy: Employment by occupation: 10.0% management, 10.3% professional, 20.8% services, 30.4% sales, 0.8% farming, 17.3% construction, 10.4% production (2000).
Income: Per capita income: $20,585 (2004); Median household income: $29,939 (2004); Average household income: $38,494 (2004); Percent of households with income of $100,000 or more: 3.5% (2004); Poverty rate: 10.7% (2000).
Education: Percent of population age 25 and over with: High school diploma (including GED) or higher: 74.6% (2004); Bachelor's degree or higher: 12.0% (2004); Master's degree or higher: 2.6% (2004).
Housing: Homeownership rate: 89.9% (2004); Median home value: $69,843 (2004); Median rent: $407 per month (2000); Median age of housing: 21 years (2000).
Transportation: Commute to work: 90.0% car, 0.0% public transportation, 2.1% walk, 4.9% work from home (2000); Travel time to work: 49.2% less than 15 minutes, 17.6% 15 to 30 minutes, 14.6% 30 to 45 minutes, 7.9% 45 to 60 minutes, 10.7% 60 minutes or more (2000)

Pinellas County

Located in western Florida; on the Pinellas Peninsula, bounded on the west by the Gulf of Mexico, and on the east by Tampa Bay; includes Long Key and a chain of barrier islands, and Butler Lake. Covers a land area of 279.90 square miles, a water area of 327.80 square miles, and is located in the Eastern Time Zone. The county government was organized in 1911. County seat is Clearwater.

Pinellas County is part of the Tampa-St. Petersburg-Clearwater, FL Metropolitan Statistical Area. The entire metro area includes: Hernando County, FL; Hillsborough County, FL; Pasco County, FL; Pinellas County, FL

Weather Station: Saint Petersburg — Elevation: 6 feet

	Jan	Feb	Mar	Apr	May	Jun	Jul	Aug	Sep	Oct	Nov	Dec
High	70	72	76	81	86	89	91	90	89	84	77	72
Low	54	56	60	65	71	75	77	77	76	70	63	57
Precip	2.8	3.0	3.5	1.9	2.9	6.0	6.3	8.1	7.5	2.7	2.0	2.6
Snow	tr	0.0	0.0	0.0	0.0	0.0	0.0	0.0	0.0	0.0	0.0	0.0

High and Low temperatures in degrees Fahrenheit; Precipitation and Snow in inches

Weather Station: Tarpon Springs Sewage Plant — Elevation: 6 feet

	Jan	Feb	Mar	Apr	May	Jun	Jul	Aug	Sep	Oct	Nov	Dec
High	71	73	77	82	87	90	91	91	90	85	79	74
Low	50	52	56	61	67	72	73	73	72	65	58	52
Precip	3.3	3.3	4.1	2.0	3.2	5.7	6.7	8.3	7.0	3.4	2.4	3.0
Snow	0.0	0.0	0.0	0.0	0.0	0.0	0.0	0.0	0.0	0.0	0.0	0.0

High and Low temperatures in degrees Fahrenheit; Precipitation and Snow in inches

Population: 851,659 (1990); 921,482 (2000); 937,398 (2004); 957,965 (2009 projected); Race: 83.7% White, 10.1% Black, 2.5% Asian, 5.7% Hispanic of any race (2004); Density: 3,348.8 persons per square mile (2004); Average household size: 2.22 (2004); Median age: 43.9 (2004); Male/female ratio: 91.4 (2004).
Religion: Five largest groups: 12.2% Catholic Church, 4.4% The United Methodist Church, 3.9% Southern Baptist Convention, 2.6% Jewish Estimate, 1.3% Presbyterian Church (U.S.A.) (2000).
Economy: Unemployment rate: 3.9% (2004); Total civilian labor force: 511,103 (2004); Leading industries: 16.7% administration, support, waste management, remediation services; 15.3% health care and social assistance; 12.9% retail trade (2003); Companies that employ 500 or more persons: 77 (2003); Companies that employ 100 to 499 persons: 523 (2003); Companies that employ less than 100 persons: 26,178 (2003); Farms: 111 totaling 1,589 acres (2002); Minority business ownership rate: 9.5% (1997); Women business ownership rate: 27.6% (1997); Retail sales per capita: $11,665 (1997). Single-family building permits issued: 2,252 (2004); Multi-family building permits issued: 1,317 (2004).
Income: Per capita income: $26,415 (2004); Median household income: $41,429 (2004); Average household income: $57,721 (2004); Percent of households with income of $100,000 or more: 12.5% (2004); Poverty rate: 11.4% (2002); Bankruptcy rate: 5.60% (2004).
Taxes: Total county taxes per capita: $442 (2002); County property taxes per capita: $319 (2002).
Education: Percent of population age 25 and over with: High school diploma (including GED) or higher: 84.1% (2004); Bachelor's degree or higher: 23.1% (2004); Master's degree or higher: 7.9% (2004).
Housing: Homeownership rate: 70.5% (2004); Median home value: $124,860 (2004); Median rent: $524 per month (2000); Median age of housing: 27 years (2000).
Health: Birth rate: 101.1 per 10,000 population (2004); Death rate: 133.7 per 10,000 population (2004); Age adjusted cancer mortality rate: 189.6 deaths per 100,000 population (2002); Air Quality Index: 80.9% good, 19.1% moderate, 0.0% unhealthy for sensitive individuals, 0.0% unhealthy (percent of days in 2004); Number of physicians: 28.2 per 10,000 population (2001); Hospital beds: 47.8 per 10,000 population (2002); Hospital admissions: 1,718.9 per 10,000 population (2002).
Elections: 2004 Presidential election results: 49.6% Bush, 49.5% Kerry, 0.5% Nader, 0.2% Badnarik
National and State Parks: Caladesi Island State Park; Honeymoon Island State Park; Pinellas County State Aquatic Preserve; Pinellas National Wildlife Refuge; Weedon Island State Preserve
Additional Information Contacts
Pinellas County Government Offices . . . . (727) 464-3377
Clearwater Beach Chamber. . . . . (727) 447-7600
Clearwater Chamber of Commerce . . . . (727) 461-0011
Dunedin Chamber of Commerce . . . . (727) 733-3197
Gulf Beaches Chamber of Commerce . . . . (727) 595-4575
Gulf Beaches-Tampa Bay Chamber . . . . (727) 391-7373
Largo Chamber of Commerce . . . . (727) 584-2321
Oldsmar Chamber of Commerce . . . . (813) 855-4233
Palm Harbor Area Chamber of Commerce . . . . (727) 784-4287
Pinellas Park Chamber of Commerce . . . . (727) 544-4777
Pinellas Suncoast Association of Realtors. . . . . (727) 347-7655
Safety Harbor Chamber of Commerce . . . . (727) 726-2890
Seminole Chamber of Commerce . . . . (727) 392-3245
St. Petersburg Chamber of Commerce . . . . (727) 821-4069
Suncoast Welcome Center . . . . (727) 573-1449
Tarpon Springs Chamber of Commerce . . . . (727) 937-6109

Pinellas County Communities

BAY PINES (CDP). Covers a land area of 1.394 square miles and a water area of 0.856 square miles. Located at 27.81° N. Lat.; 82.77° W. Long. Elevation is 13 feet.
Population: 3,698 (1990); 3,065 (2000); 3,073 (2004); 3,079 (2009 projected); Race: 97.5% White, 0.2% Black, 0.6% Asian, 2.8% Hispanic of any race (2004); Density: 2,204.7 persons per square mile (2004); Average

household size: 2.08 (2004); Median age: 50.8 (2004); Male/female ratio: 91.1 (2004); Marriage status: 15.9% never married, 59.0% now married, 10.8% widowed, 14.3% divorced (2000); Foreign born: 5.9% (2000); Ancestry (includes multiple ancestries): 19.7% German, 16.0% Irish, 13.0% English, 11.6% Italian, 8.3% Other groups (2000).
Economy: Employment by occupation: 14.1% management, 20.3% professional, 14.7% services, 29.1% sales, 0.0% farming, 11.7% construction, 10.2% production (2000).
Income: Per capita income: $23,934 (2004); Median household income: $37,530 (2004); Average household income: $49,797 (2004); Percent of households with income of $100,000 or more: 8.3% (2004); Poverty rate: 3.5% (2000).
Education: Percent of population age 25 and over with: High school diploma (including GED) or higher: 86.8% (2004); Bachelor's degree or higher: 21.3% (2004); Master's degree or higher: 6.1% (2004).
Housing: Homeownership rate: 91.8% (2004); Median home value: $123,256 (2004); Median rent: $479 per month (2000); Median age of housing: 32 years (2000).
Hospitals: Bay Pines Veterans Affairs Medical Center (563 beds)
Transportation: Commute to work: 93.8% car, 1.1% public transportation, 0.9% walk, 1.2% work from home (2000); Travel time to work: 30.6% less than 15 minutes, 45.4% 15 to 30 minutes, 18.4% 30 to 45 minutes, 3.8% 45 to 60 minutes, 1.8% 60 minutes or more (2000)

BELLEAIR (town). Covers a land area of 1.795 square miles and a water area of 1.019 square miles. Located at 27.93° N. Lat.; 82.81° W. Long. Elevation is 49 feet.
History: Belleair was incorporated in 1925, but the Belleview Hotel was built here in 1896 by Henry Plant with a spur of the Atlantic Coast Line Railroad running to the hotel entrance.
Population: 3,951 (1990); 4,067 (2000); 4,131 (2004); 4,227 (2009 projected); Race: 98.0% White, 0.2% Black, 0.5% Asian, 3.0% Hispanic of any race (2004); Density: 2,301.5 persons per square mile (2004); Average household size: 2.07 (2004); Median age: 52.8 (2004); Male/female ratio: 85.6 (2004); Marriage status: 13.2% never married, 65.4% now married, 13.7% widowed, 7.6% divorced (2000); Foreign born: 8.6% (2000); Ancestry (includes multiple ancestries): 21.9% English, 20.0% German, 15.9% Irish, 9.4% Other groups, 7.8% United States or American (2000).
Economy: Single-family building permits issued: 75 (2004); Multi-family building permits issued: 0 (2004); Employment by occupation: 24.4% management, 27.5% professional, 7.5% services, 32.4% sales, 0.0% farming, 3.4% construction, 4.8% production (2000).
Income: Per capita income: $57,620 (2004); Median household income: $73,731 (2004); Average household income: $116,724 (2004); Percent of households with income of $100,000 or more: 37.5% (2004); Poverty rate: 4.0% (2000).
Taxes: Total city taxes per capita: $754 (2002); City property taxes per capita: $533 (2002).
Education: Percent of population age 25 and over with: High school diploma (including GED) or higher: 95.7% (2004); Bachelor's degree or higher: 48.5% (2004); Master's degree or higher: 18.9% (2004).
Housing: Homeownership rate: 88.5% (2004); Median home value: $245,095 (2004); Median rent: $723 per month (2000); Median age of housing: 32 years (2000).
Safety: Violent crime rate: 4.8 per 10,000 population; Property crime rate: 88.8 per 10,000 population (2003).
Transportation: Commute to work: 87.7% car, 1.0% public transportation, 0.0% walk, 10.7% work from home (2000); Travel time to work: 41.7% less than 15 minutes, 31.4% 15 to 30 minutes, 11.9% 30 to 45 minutes, 8.2% 45 to 60 minutes, 6.8% 60 minutes or more (2000)

BELLEAIR BEACH (city). Covers a land area of 0.577 square miles and a water area of 1.152 square miles. Located at 27.92° N. Lat.; 82.83° W. Long. Elevation is 4 feet.
Population: 2,070 (1990); 1,751 (2000); 1,867 (2004); 2,009 (2009 projected); Race: 96.0% White, 0.3% Black, 1.9% Asian, 3.2% Hispanic of any race (2004); Density: 3,238.4 persons per square mile (2004); Average household size: 2.09 (2004); Median age: 52.6 (2004); Male/female ratio: 101.0 (2004); Marriage status: 12.6% never married, 68.7% now married, 6.6% widowed, 12.2% divorced (2000); Foreign born: 16.5% (2000); Ancestry (includes multiple ancestries): 23.8% German, 18.3% Irish, 15.2% English, 10.6% United States or American, 7.9% Other groups (2000).
Economy: Employment by occupation: 31.3% management, 20.6% professional, 13.1% services, 29.7% sales, 0.0% farming, 1.0% construction, 4.3% production (2000).
Income: Per capita income: $56,860 (2004); Median household income: $74,769 (2004); Average household income: $118,877 (2004); Percent of households with income of $100,000 or more: 36.3% (2004); Poverty rate: 7.8% (2000).
Education: Percent of population age 25 and over with: High school diploma (including GED) or higher: 95.4% (2004); Bachelor's degree or higher: 52.5% (2004); Master's degree or higher: 17.6% (2004).
Housing: Homeownership rate: 87.7% (2004); Median home value: $292,463 (2004); Median rent: $981 per month (2000); Median age of housing: 27 years (2000).
Safety: Violent crime rate: 0.0 per 10,000 population; Property crime rate: 174.3 per 10,000 population (2003).
Transportation: Commute to work: 96.0% car, 0.0% public transportation, 0.0% walk, 1.4% work from home (2000); Travel time to work: 24.8% less than 15 minutes, 44.8% 15 to 30 minutes, 17.4% 30 to 45 minutes, 10.3% 45 to 60 minutes, 2.8% 60 minutes or more (2000)

BELLEAIR BLUFFS (city). Covers a land area of 0.462 square miles and a water area of 0.164 square miles. Located at 27.92° N. Lat.; 82.81° W. Long. Elevation is 46 feet.
Population: 2,128 (1990); 2,243 (2000); 2,208 (2004); 2,148 (2009 projected); Race: 97.7% White, 0.2% Black, 1.3% Asian, 1.3% Hispanic of any race (2004); Density: 4,781.9 persons per square mile (2004); Average household size: 1.69 (2004); Median age: 59.1 (2004); Male/female ratio: 77.3 (2004); Marriage status: 15.5% never married, 50.9% now married, 17.3% widowed, 16.3% divorced (2000); Foreign born: 6.7% (2000); Ancestry (includes multiple ancestries): 18.9% English, 16.9% Irish, 16.9% German, 5.8% Italian, 5.5% United States or American (2000).
Economy: Employment by occupation: 19.2% management, 21.9% professional, 17.3% services, 26.8% sales, 0.0% farming, 6.8% construction, 8.1% production (2000).
Income: Per capita income: $33,621 (2004); Median household income: $35,463 (2004); Average household income: $56,472 (2004); Percent of households with income of $100,000 or more: 10.6% (2004); Poverty rate: 6.1% (2000).
Taxes: Total city taxes per capita: $320 (2002); City property taxes per capita: $221 (2002).
Education: Percent of population age 25 and over with: High school diploma (including GED) or higher: 90.1% (2004); Bachelor's degree or higher: 27.9% (2004); Master's degree or higher: 9.1% (2004).
Housing: Homeownership rate: 68.6% (2004); Median home value: $143,509 (2004); Median rent: $475 per month (2000); Median age of housing: 30 years (2000).
Safety: Violent crime rate: 17.5 per 10,000 population; Property crime rate: 253.5 per 10,000 population (2003).
Transportation: Commute to work: 89.0% car, 0.5% public transportation, 3.3% walk, 5.6% work from home (2000); Travel time to work: 35.2% less than 15 minutes, 38.9% 15 to 30 minutes, 12.4% 30 to 45 minutes, 9.1% 45 to 60 minutes, 4.4% 60 minutes or more (2000)

CLEARWATER (city). Covers a land area of 25.287 square miles and a water area of 12.437 square miles. Located at 27.97° N. Lat.; 82.76° W. Long. Elevation is 50 feet.
History: Named for the local waters of the Gulf of Mexico. Clearwater had its beginning in Fort Harrison, established here in 1841. The town was incorporated as Clearwater in 1891, and grew as a center for fruit and fruit juice canning. When Pinellas County was separated out from Hillsborough County in 1912, Clearwater acted faster than St. Petersburg in providing a courthouse, and became the county seat.
Population: 100,872 (1990); 108,787 (2000); 109,052 (2004); 109,396 (2009 projected); Race: 81.4% White, 11.0% Black, 1.9% Asian, 11.6% Hispanic of any race (2004); Density: 4,312.5 persons per square mile (2004); Average household size: 2.25 (2004); Median age: 42.8 (2004); Male/female ratio: 92.0 (2004); Marriage status: 24.4% never married, 50.9% now married, 9.9% widowed, 14.8% divorced (2000); Foreign born: 13.2% (2000); Ancestry (includes multiple ancestries): 21.5% Other groups, 16.9% German, 13.8% Irish, 11.9% English, 8.0% Italian (2000).
Economy: Unemployment rate: 4.2% (2004); Total civilian labor force: 60,557 (2004); Single-family building permits issued: 156 (2004); Multi-family building permits issued: 24 (2004); Employment by occupation: 14.5% management, 19.6% professional, 16.3% services, 31.0% sales, 0.3% farming, 7.8% construction, 10.5% production (2000).
Income: Per capita income: $25,039 (2004); Median household income: $40,422 (2004); Average household income: $54,855 (2004); Percent of

households with income of $100,000 or more: 11.5% (2004); Poverty rate: 12.3% (2000).
Taxes: Total city taxes per capita: $595 (2002); City property taxes per capita: $255 (2002).
Education: Percent of population age 25 and over with: High school diploma (including GED) or higher: 84.4% (2004); Bachelor's degree or higher: 23.9% (2004); Master's degree or higher: 8.4% (2004).

School District(s)

Pinellas County School District (PK-12)
2002-03 Enrollment: 114,772 . . . . (727) 588-6011

Four-year College(s)

Clearwater Christian College
2003-04 Enrollment: 623 . . . . (727) 726-1153
2003-04 Tuition: In-state $10,390; Out-of-state $10,390
Florida Metropolitan University-Pinellas (Private, For-profit)
2003-04 Enrollment: 1,147 . . . . (727) 725-2688
2003-04 Tuition: In-state $8,460; Out-of-state $8,460

Two-year College(s)

Edutech Centers (Private, For-profit)
2003-04 Enrollment: 278 . . . . (727) 535-0608
National Aviation Academy A & P School (Private, For-profit)
2003-04 Enrollment: 225 . . . . (727) 531-2080
Pinellas Technical Education Center-Clearwater (Public)
2003-04 Enrollment: 1,613 . . . . (727) 538-7167
2003-04 Tuition: In-state $2,295; Out-of-state $9,180
Sunstate Academy of Hair Design (Private, For-profit)
2003-04 Enrollment: 80 . . . . (727) 538-3827
Ultimate Medical Academy
2003-04 Enrollment: 30 . . . . (727) 298-8685

Housing: Homeownership rate: 61.5% (2004); Median home value: $132,064 (2004); Median rent: $538 per month (2000); Median age of housing: 27 years (2000).
Hospitals: Morton Plant Health System Rehabilitation Center (126 beds); Morton Plant Hospital (750 beds); Windmoor Healthcare of Clearwater (163 beds)
Safety: Violent crime rate: 105.4 per 10,000 population; Property crime rate: 505.2 per 10,000 population (2003).
Newspapers: Clearwater Gazette and Beach Views (General - Circulation 17,000)
Transportation: Commute to work: 86.7% car, 3.9% public transportation, 3.0% walk, 4.1% work from home (2000); Travel time to work: 31.1% less than 15 minutes, 39.6% 15 to 30 minutes, 18.8% 30 to 45 minutes, 6.0% 45 to 60 minutes, 4.5% 60 minutes or more (2000); Amtrak: Service available.

Additional Information Contacts

Clearwater Beach Chamber. . . . . (727) 447-7600
Clearwater Chamber of Commerce . . . . (727) 461-0011
Suncoast Welcome Center . . . . (727) 573-1449

CLEARWATER BEACH (unincorporated postal area, zip code 33767).

Covers a land area of 3.084 square miles and a water area of 0 square miles. Located at 27.96° N. Lat.; 82.82° W. Long. Elevation is 5 feet.
Population: 9,765 (2000); Race: 98.7% White, 0.0% Black, 0.3% Asian, 2.1% Hispanic of any race (2000); Density: 3,166.3 persons per square mile (2000); Age: 6.6% under 18, 36.9% over 64 (2000); Marriage status: 12.5% never married, 62.5% now married, 9.4% widowed, 15.6% divorced (2000); Foreign born: 14.2% (2000); Ancestry (includes multiple ancestries): 19.8% German, 16.6% Irish, 15.1% English, 8.8% Italian, 5.4% Other groups (2000).
Economy: Employment by occupation: 30.0% management, 20.5% professional, 9.6% services, 31.7% sales, 0.0% farming, 3.4% construction, 4.8% production (2000).
Income: Per capita income: $45,617 (2000); Median household income: $51,069 (2000); Poverty rate: 6.6% (2000).
Education: Percent of population age 25 and over with: High school diploma (including GED) or higher: 90.8% (2000); Bachelor's degree or higher: 37.6% (2000).
Housing: Homeownership rate: 72.1% (2000); Median home value: $331,200 (2000); Median rent: $765 per month (2000); Median age of housing: 24 years (2000).
Transportation: Commute to work: 75.8% car, 0.9% public transportation, 4.7% walk, 13.7% work from home (2000); Travel time to work: 25.2% less than 15 minutes, 33.4% 15 to 30 minutes, 20.6% 30 to 45 minutes, 13.0% 45 to 60 minutes, 7.8% 60 minutes or more (2000)

DUNEDIN (city).

Covers a land area of 10.381 square miles and a water area of 17.825 square miles. Located at 28.02° N. Lat.; 82.77° W. Long. Elevation is 39 feet.
History: Dunedin was settled in the late 1850s and was called Jonesboro until the post office was established in 1878. The name of Dunedin was chosen by J.L. Douglas and James Somerville who had come from Dunedin, Scotland. Dunedin was an early Gulf port where fruits and vegetables were shipped by schooner.
Population: 34,496 (1990); 35,691 (2000); 37,014 (2004); 38,583 (2009 projected); Race: 93.5% White, 2.6% Black, 1.5% Asian, 4.1% Hispanic of any race (2004); Density: 3,565.5 persons per square mile (2004); Average household size: 2.05 (2004); Median age: 49.1 (2004); Male/female ratio: 84.8 (2004); Marriage status: 18.6% never married, 53.6% now married, 12.8% widowed, 15.0% divorced (2000); Foreign born: 9.7% (2000); Ancestry (includes multiple ancestries): 21.3% German, 17.2% Irish, 14.6% English, 10.9% Other groups, 10.2% Italian (2000).
Economy: Unemployment rate: 3.4% (2004); Total civilian labor force: 19,378 (2004); Single-family building permits issued: 105 (2004); Multi-family building permits issued: 0 (2004); Employment by occupation: 15.1% management, 20.1% professional, 16.5% services, 33.0% sales, 0.3% farming, 7.8% construction, 7.3% production (2000).
Income: Per capita income: $26,687 (2004); Median household income: $38,356 (2004); Average household income: $53,293 (2004); Percent of households with income of $100,000 or more: 10.9% (2004); Poverty rate: 8.2% (2000).
Taxes: Total city taxes per capita: $310 (2002); City property taxes per capita: $137 (2002).
Education: Percent of population age 25 and over with: High school diploma (including GED) or higher: 86.5% (2004); Bachelor's degree or higher: 22.2% (2004); Master's degree or higher: 7.0% (2004).

School District(s)

Pinellas County School District (PK-12)
2002-03 Enrollment: 114,772 . . . . (727) 588-6011

Four-year College(s)

Schiller International University (Private, For-profit)
2003-04 Enrollment: 177 . . . . (727) 736-5082
2003-04 Tuition: In-state $14,400; Out-of-state $14,400

Housing: Homeownership rate: 71.4% (2004); Median home value: $122,682 (2004); Median rent: $501 per month (2000); Median age of housing: 26 years (2000).
Hospitals: Mease Dunedin Hospital (189 beds)
Safety: Violent crime rate: 21.7 per 10,000 population; Property crime rate: 266.2 per 10,000 population (2003).
Transportation: Commute to work: 91.3% car, 1.1% public transportation, 2.1% walk, 3.8% work from home (2000); Travel time to work: 31.4% less than 15 minutes, 35.9% 15 to 30 minutes, 20.3% 30 to 45 minutes, 6.8% 45 to 60 minutes, 5.5% 60 minutes or more (2000)

Additional Information Contacts

Dunedin Chamber of Commerce . . . . (727) 733-3197
Local Government Offices . . . . (727) 298-3000

EAST LAKE (CDP).

Covers a land area of 29.782 square miles and a water area of 1.983 square miles. Located at 28.10° N. Lat.; 82.69° W. Long.
Population: 12,669 (1990); 29,394 (2000); 33,276 (2004); 37,850 (2009 projected); Race: 93.5% White, 1.5% Black, 3.0% Asian, 4.7% Hispanic of any race (2004); Density: 1,117.3 persons per square mile (2004); Average household size: 2.51 (2004); Median age: 43.0 (2004); Male/female ratio: 94.9 (2004); Marriage status: 16.6% never married, 69.4% now married, 6.2% widowed, 7.8% divorced (2000); Foreign born: 9.6% (2000); Ancestry (includes multiple ancestries): 21.2% German, 16.7% Irish, 14.1% English, 13.9% Italian, 10.9% Other groups (2000).
Economy: Employment by occupation: 24.9% management, 24.2% professional, 11.5% services, 32.7% sales, 0.0% farming, 2.0% construction, 4.7% production (2000).
Income: Per capita income: $41,796 (2004); Median household income: $77,707 (2004); Average household income: $104,807 (2004); Percent of households with income of $100,000 or more: 36.5% (2004); Poverty rate: 3.9% (2000).
Education: Percent of population age 25 and over with: High school diploma (including GED) or higher: 94.0% (2004); Bachelor's degree or higher: 42.2% (2004); Master's degree or higher: 14.4% (2004).

Housing: Homeownership rate: 84.2% (2004); Median home value: $243,462 (2004); Median rent: $703 per month (2000); Median age of housing: 10 years (2000).
Transportation: Commute to work: 91.6% car, 0.4% public transportation, 0.6% walk, 5.8% work from home (2000); Travel time to work: 16.1% less than 15 minutes, 38.8% 15 to 30 minutes, 25.9% 30 to 45 minutes, 13.6% 45 to 60 minutes, 5.6% 60 minutes or more (2000)

FEATHER SOUND (CDP). Covers a land area of 4.211 square miles and a water area of 9.877 square miles. Located at 27.90° N. Lat.; 82.67° W. Long.
Population: 2,690 (1990); 3,597 (2000); 4,315 (2004); 5,151 (2009 projected); Race: 92.4% White, 2.9% Black, 3.0% Asian, 4.4% Hispanic of any race (2004); Density: 1,024.6 persons per square mile (2004); Average household size: 1.85 (2004); Median age: 39.8 (2004); Male/female ratio: 99.0 (2004); Marriage status: 28.9% never married, 52.5% now married, 3.1% widowed, 15.5% divorced (2000); Foreign born: 10.6% (2000); Ancestry (includes multiple ancestries): 17.7% German, 17.0% Irish, 14.9% Other groups, 12.2% Italian, 11.3% English (2000).
Economy: Employment by occupation: 28.3% management, 27.7% professional, 6.2% services, 32.9% sales, 0.0% farming, 1.9% construction, 3.2% production (2000).
Income: Per capita income: $64,513 (2004); Median household income: $81,283 (2004); Average household income: $119,422 (2004); Percent of households with income of $100,000 or more: 37.8% (2004); Poverty rate: 2.2% (2000).
Education: Percent of population age 25 and over with: High school diploma (including GED) or higher: 96.8% (2004); Bachelor's degree or higher: 58.1% (2004); Master's degree or higher: 19.6% (2004).
Housing: Homeownership rate: 49.7% (2004); Median home value: $228,897 (2004); Median rent: $788 per month (2000); Median age of housing: 14 years (2000).
Transportation: Commute to work: 92.7% car, 0.5% public transportation, 1.6% walk, 3.8% work from home (2000); Travel time to work: 27.8% less than 15 minutes, 44.7% 15 to 30 minutes, 16.0% 30 to 45 minutes, 6.1% 45 to 60 minutes, 5.2% 60 minutes or more (2000)

GANDY (CDP). Covers a land area of 2.548 square miles and a water area of 14.006 square miles. Located at 27.86° N. Lat.; 82.62° W. Long.
Population: 3,016 (1990); 2,031 (2000); 2,261 (2004); 2,553 (2009 projected); Race: 89.2% White, 4.0% Black, 2.9% Asian, 4.8% Hispanic of any race (2004); Density: 887.3 persons per square mile (2004); Average household size: 1.60 (2004); Median age: 49.8 (2004); Male/female ratio: 114.5 (2004); Marriage status: 19.1% never married, 41.4% now married, 13.6% widowed, 25.9% divorced (2000); Foreign born: 7.4% (2000); Ancestry (includes multiple ancestries): 16.9% German, 14.9% Irish, 12.7% United States or American, 11.8% Other groups, 10.6% English (2000).
Economy: Employment by occupation: 12.9% management, 24.0% professional, 15.5% services, 25.7% sales, 0.0% farming, 10.4% construction, 11.5% production (2000).
Income: Per capita income: $28,065 (2004); Median household income: $34,158 (2004); Average household income: $44,813 (2004); Percent of households with income of $100,000 or more: 6.6% (2004); Poverty rate: 5.2% (2000).
Education: Percent of population age 25 and over with: High school diploma (including GED) or higher: 79.1% (2004); Bachelor's degree or higher: 20.9% (2004); Master's degree or higher: 5.4% (2004).
Housing: Homeownership rate: 58.8% (2004); Median home value: $19,999 (2004); Median rent: $675 per month (2000); Median age of housing: 24 years (2000).
Transportation: Commute to work: 95.0% car, 3.0% public transportation, 0.0% walk, 2.0% work from home (2000); Travel time to work: 21.4% less than 15 minutes, 51.9% 15 to 30 minutes, 22.3% 30 to 45 minutes, 3.8% 45 to 60 minutes, 0.6% 60 minutes or more (2000)

GULFPORT (city). Aka Gulf Port. Covers a land area of 2.833 square miles and a water area of 1.009 square miles. Located at 27.75° N. Lat.; 82.70° W. Long. Elevation is 17 feet.
History: Named for its location on the Gulf of Mexico. Settled 1843. Incorporated 1913.
Population: 11,857 (1990); 12,527 (2000); 12,656 (2004); 12,829 (2009 projected); Race: 86.8% White, 9.3% Black, 0.6% Asian, 4.0% Hispanic of any race (2004); Density: 4,467.8 persons per square mile (2004); Average household size: 2.01 (2004); Median age: 47.9 (2004); Male/female ratio: 89.4 (2004); Marriage status: 23.0% never married, 50.5% now married, 11.8% widowed, 14.8% divorced (2000); Foreign born: 9.2% (2000); Ancestry (includes multiple ancestries): 17.3% German, 14.0% Other groups, 13.3% Irish, 12.8% English, 8.3% Italian (2000).
Economy: Single-family building permits issued: 15 (2004); Multi-family building permits issued: 0 (2004); Employment by occupation: 12.4% management, 16.6% professional, 17.8% services, 31.5% sales, 0.3% farming, 9.8% construction, 11.6% production (2000).
Income: Per capita income: $25,583 (2004); Median household income: $32,635 (2004); Average household income: $51,170 (2004); Percent of households with income of $100,000 or more: 9.8% (2004); Poverty rate: 13.3% (2000).
Education: Percent of population age 25 and over with: High school diploma (including GED) or higher: 81.7% (2004); Bachelor's degree or higher: 19.9% (2004); Master's degree or higher: 8.4% (2004).

School District(s)

Pinellas County School District (PK-12)
2002-03 Enrollment: 114,772 . . . . (727) 588-6011
Housing: Homeownership rate: 70.4% (2004); Median home value: $99,265 (2004); Median rent: $456 per month (2000); Median age of housing: 38 years (2000).
Safety: Violent crime rate: 60.2 per 10,000 population; Property crime rate: 493.0 per 10,000 population (2003).
Transportation: Commute to work: 89.9% car, 2.3% public transportation, 2.3% walk, 2.4% work from home (2000); Travel time to work: 32.2% less than 15 minutes, 37.8% 15 to 30 minutes, 17.6% 30 to 45 minutes, 5.5% 45 to 60 minutes, 6.8% 60 minutes or more (2000)
Additional Information Contacts
Local Government Offices . . . . (727) 893-1000

HARBOR BLUFFS (CDP). Covers a land area of 0.696 square miles and a water area of 0.258 square miles. Located at 27.90° N. Lat.; 82.82° W. Long.
Population: 2,614 (1990); 2,807 (2000); 2,716 (2004); 2,648 (2009 projected); Race: 96.2% White, 0.1% Black, 2.2% Asian, 2.1% Hispanic of any race (2004); Density: 3,899.7 persons per square mile (2004); Average household size: 2.41 (2004); Median age: 47.6 (2004); Male/female ratio: 93.4 (2004); Marriage status: 17.6% never married, 68.2% now married, 8.9% widowed, 5.3% divorced (2000); Foreign born: 7.0% (2000); Ancestry (includes multiple ancestries): 21.3% English, 20.9% Irish, 19.6% German, 9.7% United States or American, 6.5% Italian (2000).
Economy: Employment by occupation: 18.7% management, 27.2% professional, 10.2% services, 35.1% sales, 0.0% farming, 3.6% construction, 5.2% production (2000).
Income: Per capita income: $46,677 (2004); Median household income: $69,838 (2004); Average household income: $112,473 (2004); Percent of households with income of $100,000 or more: 30.6% (2004); Poverty rate: 5.7% (2000).
Education: Percent of population age 25 and over with: High school diploma (including GED) or higher: 93.2% (2004); Bachelor's degree or higher: 44.5% (2004); Master's degree or higher: 18.2% (2004).
Housing: Homeownership rate: 94.3% (2004); Median home value: $214,865 (2004); Median rent: $858 per month (2000); Median age of housing: 35 years (2000).
Transportation: Commute to work: 90.7% car, 0.0% public transportation, 0.9% walk, 7.0% work from home (2000); Travel time to work: 35.3% less than 15 minutes, 35.0% 15 to 30 minutes, 18.9% 30 to 45 minutes, 8.7% 45 to 60 minutes, 2.0% 60 minutes or more (2000)

INDIAN ROCKS BEACH (city). Covers a land area of 0.930 square miles and a water area of 0.465 square miles. Located at 27.89° N. Lat.; 82.84° W. Long. Elevation is 10 feet.
Population: 3,963 (1990); 5,072 (2000); 5,143 (2004); 5,258 (2009 projected); Race: 96.7% White, 0.4% Black, 0.8% Asian, 3.6% Hispanic of any race (2004); Density: 5,530.9 persons per square mile (2004); Average household size: 1.85 (2004); Median age: 48.9 (2004); Male/female ratio: 102.6 (2004); Marriage status: 16.9% never married, 56.3% now married, 6.9% widowed, 19.9% divorced (2000); Foreign born: 10.8% (2000); Ancestry (includes multiple ancestries): 26.3% German, 18.5% Irish, 17.5% English, 10.4% Italian, 9.2% Other groups (2000).
Economy: Single-family building permits issued: 12 (2004); Multi-family building permits issued: 30 (2004); Employment by occupation: 20.8% management, 22.5% professional, 13.8% services, 33.3% sales, 0.0% farming, 4.6% construction, 5.0% production (2000).
Income: Per capita income: $46,296 (2004); Median household income: $62,477 (2004); Average household income: $85,865 (2004); Percent of

households with income of $100,000 or more: 25.0% (2004); Poverty rate: 4.7% (2000).
Taxes: Total city taxes per capita: $224 (2002); City property taxes per capita: $197 (2002).
Education: Percent of population age 25 and over with: High school diploma (including GED) or higher: 94.4% (2004); Bachelor's degree or higher: 39.0% (2004); Master's degree or higher: 13.1% (2004).
Housing: Homeownership rate: 67.0% (2004); Median home value: $258,178 (2004); Median rent: $713 per month (2000); Median age of housing: 19 years (2000).
Safety: Violent crime rate: 22.8 per 10,000 population; Property crime rate: 341.9 per 10,000 population (2003).
Transportation: Commute to work: 87.4% car, 0.6% public transportation, 0.6% walk, 10.8% work from home (2000); Travel time to work: 25.0% less than 15 minutes, 37.4% 15 to 30 minutes, 19.4% 30 to 45 minutes, 7.8% 45 to 60 minutes, 10.3% 60 minutes or more (2000)
Additional Information Contacts
Gulf Beaches Chamber of Commerce . . . . (727) 595-4575
Local Government Offices . . . . (727) 595-2517

INDIAN SHORES (town). Aka Indian Rocks Beach South Shore. Covers a land area of 0.334 square miles and a water area of 0.611 square miles. Located at 27.85° N. Lat.; 82.84° W. Long. Elevation is 5 feet.
Population: 1,405 (1990); 1,705 (2000); 1,838 (2004); 1,984 (2009 projected); Race: 98.2% White, 0.3% Black, 0.4% Asian, 3.3% Hispanic of any race (2004); Density: 5,495.4 persons per square mile (2004); Average household size: 1.72 (2004); Median age: 56.6 (2004); Male/female ratio: 96.4 (2004); Marriage status: 13.0% never married, 52.2% now married, 15.0% widowed, 19.7% divorced (2000); Foreign born: 13.8% (2000); Ancestry (includes multiple ancestries): 22.6% German, 19.1% English, 17.9% Irish, 8.4% United States or American, 8.2% Italian (2000).
Economy: Single-family building permits issued: 6 (2004); Multi-family building permits issued: 8 (2004); Employment by occupation: 23.7% management, 23.5% professional, 13.8% services, 26.8% sales, 0.0% farming, 6.2% construction, 6.1% production (2000).
Income: Per capita income: $42,858 (2004); Median household income: $49,778 (2004); Average household income: $73,550 (2004); Percent of households with income of $100,000 or more: 21.2% (2004); Poverty rate: 6.9% (2000).
Taxes: Total city taxes per capita: $595 (2002); City property taxes per capita: $297 (2002).
Education: Percent of population age 25 and over with: High school diploma (including GED) or higher: 89.4% (2004); Bachelor's degree or higher: 33.6% (2004); Master's degree or higher: 14.0% (2004).
Housing: Homeownership rate: 60.8% (2004); Median home value: $222,973 (2004); Median rent: $648 per month (2000); Median age of housing: 22 years (2000).
Safety: Violent crime rate: 14.5 per 10,000 population; Property crime rate: 275.4 per 10,000 population (2003).
Transportation: Commute to work: 87.6% car, 1.2% public transportation, 1.4% walk, 6.8% work from home (2000); Travel time to work: 23.8% less than 15 minutes, 29.9% 15 to 30 minutes, 28.7% 30 to 45 minutes, 10.5% 45 to 60 minutes, 7.1% 60 minutes or more (2000)

KENNETH CITY (town). Covers a land area of 0.715 square miles and a water area of 0.004 square miles. Located at 27.81° N. Lat.; 82.71° W. Long. Elevation is 23 feet.
Population: 4,549 (1990); 4,400 (2000); 4,374 (2004); 4,291 (2009 projected); Race: 84.0% White, 4.9% Black, 6.4% Asian, 7.1% Hispanic of any race (2004); Density: 6,118.8 persons per square mile (2004); Average household size: 2.29 (2004); Median age: 46.3 (2004); Male/female ratio: 79.9 (2004); Marriage status: 19.0% never married, 53.5% now married, 15.8% widowed, 11.7% divorced (2000); Foreign born: 9.2% (2000); Ancestry (includes multiple ancestries): 17.5% Other groups, 17.2% Irish, 17.0% German, 12.1% English, 9.7% Italian (2000).
Economy: Single-family building permits issued: 0 (2004); Multi-family building permits issued: 0 (2004); Employment by occupation: 8.7% management, 15.0% professional, 11.8% services, 31.1% sales, 1.6% farming, 14.8% construction, 17.0% production (2000).
Income: Per capita income: $21,211 (2004); Median household income: $37,727 (2004); Average household income: $46,665 (2004); Percent of households with income of $100,000 or more: 7.3% (2004); Poverty rate: 9.4% (2000).
Education: Percent of population age 25 and over with: High school diploma (including GED) or higher: 81.3% (2004); Bachelor's degree or higher: 13.2% (2004); Master's degree or higher: 4.2% (2004).
Housing: Homeownership rate: 78.0% (2004); Median home value: $98,298 (2004); Median rent: $477 per month (2000); Median age of housing: 37 years (2000).
Safety: Violent crime rate: 51.2 per 10,000 population; Property crime rate: 487.6 per 10,000 population (2003).
Transportation: Commute to work: 95.6% car, 0.4% public transportation, 1.3% walk, 2.1% work from home (2000); Travel time to work: 29.8% less than 15 minutes, 49.1% 15 to 30 minutes, 13.6% 30 to 45 minutes, 4.6% 45 to 60 minutes, 2.9% 60 minutes or more (2000)

LARGO (city). Covers a land area of 15.663 square miles and a water area of 0.463 square miles. Located at 27.90° N. Lat.; 82.77° W. Long. Elevation is 40 feet.
History: Named for the Spanish translation of "long." Largo developed as a shipping center for citrus and truck gardeners, with citrus packing plants and fruit juice canneries.
Population: 70,008 (1990); 69,371 (2000); 70,311 (2004); 71,543 (2009 projected); Race: 90.7% White, 3.7% Black, 2.1% Asian, 5.2% Hispanic of any race (2004); Density: 4,489.1 persons per square mile (2004); Average household size: 2.03 (2004); Median age: 48.5 (2004); Male/female ratio: 87.3 (2004); Marriage status: 19.5% never married, 52.3% now married, 13.6% widowed, 14.7% divorced (2000); Foreign born: 9.4% (2000); Ancestry (includes multiple ancestries): 18.3% German, 15.4% Irish, 13.9% English, 11.2% Other groups, 9.6% Italian (2000).
Economy: Unemployment rate: 3.4% (2004); Total civilian labor force: 38,336 (2004); Single-family building permits issued: 327 (2004); Multi-family building permits issued: 527 (2004); Employment by occupation: 10.7% management, 18.5% professional, 16.6% services, 32.7% sales, 0.1% farming, 9.0% construction, 12.4% production (2000).
Income: Per capita income: $23,035 (2004); Median household income: $34,943 (2004); Average household income: $45,758 (2004); Percent of households with income of $100,000 or more: 6.4% (2004); Poverty rate: 9.1% (2000).
Taxes: Total city taxes per capita: $389 (2002); City property taxes per capita: $107 (2002).
Education: Percent of population age 25 and over with: High school diploma (including GED) or higher: 83.4% (2004); Bachelor's degree or higher: 16.3% (2004); Master's degree or higher: 5.7% (2004).

School District(s)

Pinellas County School District (PK-12)
2002-03 Enrollment: 114,772 . . . . (727) 588-6011

Four-year College(s)

Remington College-Largo Campus (Private, For-profit)
2003-04 Enrollment: 717 . . . . (727) 532-1999
2003-04 Tuition: In-state $29,280; Out-of-state $29,280
Housing: Homeownership rate: 67.7% (2004); Median home value: $89,637 (2004); Median rent: $539 per month (2000); Median age of housing: 25 years (2000).
Hospitals: Florida Youth Academy (132 beds); Largo Medical Center (256 beds); Sun Coast Hospital (300 beds)
Safety: Violent crime rate: 47.5 per 10,000 population; Property crime rate: 382.8 per 10,000 population (2003).
Newspapers: Bellair Bee (General - Circulation 8,300); Clearwater Leader (General - Circulation 12,988); Largo Leader (General - Circulation 20,500); Seminole Beacon (General - Circulation 35,000)
Transportation: Commute to work: 92.7% car, 1.3% public transportation, 2.0% walk, 2.2% work from home (2000); Travel time to work: 30.1% less than 15 minutes, 40.7% 15 to 30 minutes, 18.6% 30 to 45 minutes, 5.0% 45 to 60 minutes, 5.6% 60 minutes or more (2000)
Additional Information Contacts
Largo Chamber of Commerce . . . . (727) 584-2321
Local Government Offices . . . . (727) 587-6700

MADEIRA BEACH (city). Covers a land area of 1.027 square miles and a water area of 2.244 square miles. Located at 27.79° N. Lat.; 82.79° W. Long. Elevation is 6 feet.
Population: 4,229 (1990); 4,511 (2000); 4,493 (2004); 4,496 (2009 projected); Race: 96.8% White, 0.3% Black, 0.6% Asian, 2.4% Hispanic of any race (2004); Density: 4,374.5 persons per square mile (2004); Average household size: 1.76 (2004); Median age: 49.3 (2004); Male/female ratio: 111.0 (2004); Marriage status: 23.7% never married, 47.9% now married, 7.5% widowed, 20.9% divorced (2000); Foreign born: 6.4% (2000);

Ancestry (includes multiple ancestries): 19.7% German, 16.2% Irish, 13.5% English, 10.2% Italian, 7.4% Other groups (2000).
Economy: Employment by occupation: 18.2% management, 12.2% professional, 22.1% services, 28.9% sales, 0.7% farming, 10.6% construction, 7.2% production (2000).
Income: Per capita income: $37,114 (2004); Median household income: $42,919 (2004); Average household income: $65,189 (2004); Percent of households with income of $100,000 or more: 16.3% (2004); Poverty rate: 9.8% (2000).
Taxes: Total city taxes per capita: $503 (2002); City property taxes per capita: $214 (2002).
Education: Percent of population age 25 and over with: High school diploma (including GED) or higher: 87.4% (2004); Bachelor's degree or higher: 22.2% (2004); Master's degree or higher: 6.1% (2004).

School District(s)

Pinellas County School District (PK-12)
2002-03 Enrollment: 114,772 . . . . (727) 588-6011
Housing: Homeownership rate: 57.2% (2004); Median home value: $225,534 (2004); Median rent: $486 per month (2000); Median age of housing: 35 years (2000).
Safety: Violent crime rate: 96.4 per 10,000 population; Property crime rate: 762.2 per 10,000 population (2003).
Transportation: Commute to work: 84.2% car, 1.6% public transportation, 3.8% walk, 7.4% work from home (2000); Travel time to work: 29.6% less than 15 minutes, 34.1% 15 to 30 minutes, 26.6% 30 to 45 minutes, 6.2% 45 to 60 minutes, 3.5% 60 minutes or more (2000)

NORTH REDINGTON BEACH (town). Covers a land area of 0.303 square miles and a water area of 0.717 square miles. Located at 27.82° N. Lat.; 82.82° W. Long. Elevation is 3 feet.
Population: 1,135 (1990); 1,474 (2000); 1,481 (2004); 1,494 (2009 projected); Race: 95.9% White, 0.3% Black, 1.3% Asian, 3.8% Hispanic of any race (2004); Density: 4,889.7 persons per square mile (2004); Average household size: 1.84 (2004); Median age: 58.0 (2004); Male/female ratio: 85.8 (2004); Marriage status: 10.7% never married, 63.1% now married, 12.4% widowed, 13.8% divorced (2000); Foreign born: 8.9% (2000); Ancestry (includes multiple ancestries): 23.4% German, 16.1% English, 15.1% Italian, 13.5% Irish, 12.0% Other groups (2000).
Economy: Employment by occupation: 20.1% management, 23.5% professional, 14.7% services, 28.5% sales, 0.0% farming, 5.7% construction, 7.4% production (2000).
Income: Per capita income: $42,075 (2004); Median household income: $53,621 (2004); Average household income: $77,311 (2004); Percent of households with income of $100,000 or more: 23.7% (2004); Poverty rate: 4.2% (2000).
Taxes: Total city taxes per capita: $239 (2002); City property taxes per capita: $223 (2002).
Education: Percent of population age 25 and over with: High school diploma (including GED) or higher: 92.3% (2004); Bachelor's degree or higher: 33.7% (2004); Master's degree or higher: 14.2% (2004).
Housing: Homeownership rate: 55.6% (2004); Median home value: $288,182 (2004); Median rent: $732 per month (2000); Median age of housing: 26 years (2000).
Safety: Violent crime rate: 0.0 per 10,000 population; Property crime rate: 212.4 per 10,000 population (2003).
Transportation: Commute to work: 77.8% car, 1.2% public transportation, 6.4% walk, 8.3% work from home (2000); Travel time to work: 19.8% less than 15 minutes, 33.1% 15 to 30 minutes, 28.5% 30 to 45 minutes, 14.1% 45 to 60 minutes, 4.5% 60 minutes or more (2000)

OLDSMAR (city). Covers a land area of 8.916 square miles and a water area of 0.751 square miles. Located at 28.04° N. Lat.; 82.67° W. Long. Elevation is 8 feet.
Population: 8,104 (1990); 11,910 (2000); 13,195 (2004); 14,721 (2009 projected); Race: 88.1% White, 3.8% Black, 3.6% Asian, 8.0% Hispanic of any race (2004); Density: 1,480.0 persons per square mile (2004); Average household size: 2.61 (2004); Median age: 35.9 (2004); Male/female ratio: 93.4 (2004); Marriage status: 21.0% never married, 60.1% now married, 6.3% widowed, 12.6% divorced (2000); Foreign born: 11.6% (2000); Ancestry (includes multiple ancestries): 22.5% German, 18.9% Irish, 14.4% Other groups, 13.2% Italian, 12.1% English (2000).
Economy: Single-family building permits issued: 11 (2004); Multi-family building permits issued: 0 (2004); Employment by occupation: 19.1% management, 17.3% professional, 10.8% services, 33.9% sales, 0.0% farming, 7.0% construction, 11.9% production (2000).
Income: Per capita income: $24,376 (2004); Median household income: $55,757 (2004); Average household income: $63,319 (2004); Percent of households with income of $100,000 or more: 13.5% (2004); Poverty rate: 4.8% (2000).
Taxes: Total city taxes per capita: $550 (2002); City property taxes per capita: $208 (2002).
Education: Percent of population age 25 and over with: High school diploma (including GED) or higher: 86.5% (2004); Bachelor's degree or higher: 23.4% (2004); Master's degree or higher: 5.3% (2004).

School District(s)

Pinellas County School District (PK-12)
2002-03 Enrollment: 114,772 . . . . (727) 588-6011
Housing: Homeownership rate: 77.3% (2004); Median home value: $134,432 (2004); Median rent: $652 per month (2000); Median age of housing: 13 years (2000).
Safety: Violent crime rate: 27.0 per 10,000 population; Property crime rate: 462.3 per 10,000 population (2003).
Transportation: Commute to work: 93.3% car, 0.3% public transportation, 2.2% walk, 3.0% work from home (2000); Travel time to work: 26.2% less than 15 minutes, 34.4% 15 to 30 minutes, 25.9% 30 to 45 minutes, 9.0% 45 to 60 minutes, 4.5% 60 minutes or more (2000)

Additional Information Contacts

Local Government Offices . . . . (813) 855-4693
Oldsmar Chamber of Commerce . . . . (813) 855-4233

PALM HARBOR (CDP). Covers a land area of 17.917 square miles and a water area of 8.669 square miles. Located at 28.08° N. Lat.; 82.75° W. Long. Elevation is 50 feet.
History: Named for its abundance of palm trees. Palm Harbor was founded by real estate promoters in the 1880s, and was first called Sutherland, in the unfulfilled hope that the Duke of Sutherland, who lived in nearby Tarpon Springs, would lend financial support.
Population: 50,255 (1990); 59,248 (2000); 60,321 (2004); 61,688 (2009 projected); Race: 94.9% White, 1.3% Black, 1.6% Asian, 4.1% Hispanic of any race (2004); Density: 3,366.7 persons per square mile (2004); Average household size: 2.31 (2004); Median age: 43.8 (2004); Male/female ratio: 89.1 (2004); Marriage status: 18.2% never married, 61.6% now married, 10.3% widowed, 9.8% divorced (2000); Foreign born: 8.4% (2000); Ancestry (includes multiple ancestries): 19.5% German, 16.5% Irish, 13.9% English, 12.8% Italian, 8.9% Other groups (2000).
Economy: Employment by occupation: 17.7% management, 22.7% professional, 12.8% services, 32.7% sales, 0.1% farming, 7.0% construction, 7.0% production (2000).
Income: Per capita income: $30,391 (2004); Median household income: $50,145 (2004); Average household income: $68,762 (2004); Percent of households with income of $100,000 or more: 17.3% (2004); Poverty rate: 5.5% (2000).
Education: Percent of population age 25 and over with: High school diploma (including GED) or higher: 90.3% (2004); Bachelor's degree or higher: 28.3% (2004); Master's degree or higher: 9.5% (2004).

School District(s)

Pinellas County School District (PK-12)
2002-03 Enrollment: 114,772 . . . . (727) 588-6011

Two-year College(s)

Central Florida Institute
2003-04 Enrollment: 346 . . . . (727) 786-4707
Housing: Homeownership rate: 78.0% (2004); Median home value: $155,749 (2004); Median rent: $697 per month (2000); Median age of housing: 16 years (2000).
Transportation: Commute to work: 92.3% car, 0.8% public transportation, 0.9% walk, 4.9% work from home (2000); Travel time to work: 24.5% less than 15 minutes, 32.7% 15 to 30 minutes, 26.5% 30 to 45 minutes, 10.3% 45 to 60 minutes, 6.0% 60 minutes or more (2000)

Additional Information Contacts

Palm Harbor Area Chamber of Commerce . . . . (727) 784-4287

PINELLAS PARK (city). Covers a land area of 14.748 square miles and a water area of 0.190 square miles. Located at 27.85° N. Lat.; 82.70° W. Long. Elevation is 18 feet.
History: Named for the Spanish translation of "point of pines". Incorporated 1915.
Population: 45,348 (1990); 45,658 (2000); 45,714 (2004); 45,834 (2009 projected); Race: 86.3% White, 2.8% Black, 5.4% Asian, 7.6% Hispanic of any race (2004); Density: 3,099.6 persons per square mile (2004); Average household size: 2.35 (2004); Median age: 41.0 (2004); Male/female ratio:

91.4 (2004); Marriage status: 20.6% never married, 54.5% now married, 10.8% widowed, 14.1% divorced (2000); Foreign born: 9.5% (2000); Ancestry (includes multiple ancestries): 18.5% German, 17.8% Other groups, 15.8% Irish, 11.6% English, 8.4% Italian (2000).
Economy: Mainly residential. Some manufacturing: electronic equipment, plastics. Unemployment rate: 3.6% (2004); Total civilian labor force: 26,800 (2004); Single-family building permits issued: 114 (2004); Multi-family building permits issued: 0 (2004); Employment by occupation: 9.9% management, 13.3% professional, 15.1% services, 32.5% sales, 0.3% farming, 10.8% construction, 18.1% production (2000).
Income: Per capita income: $20,135 (2004); Median household income: $38,229 (2004); Average household income: $46,334 (2004); Percent of households with income of $100,000 or more: 5.7% (2004); Poverty rate: 9.3% (2000).
Taxes: Total city taxes per capita: $518 (2002); City property taxes per capita: $203 (2002).
Education: Percent of population age 25 and over with: High school diploma (including GED) or higher: 80.1% (2004); Bachelor's degree or higher: 11.9% (2004); Master's degree or higher: 3.5% (2004).

School District(s)

Pinellas County School District (PK-12)
2002-03 Enrollment: 114,772 . . . . (727) 588-6011

Four-year College(s)

Saint Petersburg College (Public)
2003-04 Enrollment: 23,859 . . . . (727) 341-4772
2003-04 Tuition: In-state $1,747; Out-of-state $6,513

Two-year College(s)

Humanities Ctr Inst of Allied Hlth Sch of Massage (Private, For-profit)
2003-04 Enrollment: 320 . . . . (727) 541-5200

Housing: Homeownership rate: 74.8% (2004); Median home value: $98,261 (2004); Median rent: $508 per month (2000); Median age of housing: 25 years (2000).
Safety: Violent crime rate: 59.5 per 10,000 population; Property crime rate: 602.6 per 10,000 population (2003).
Transportation: Commute to work: 92.7% car, 1.1% public transportation, 1.7% walk, 2.2% work from home (2000); Travel time to work: 31.5% less than 15 minutes, 47.3% 15 to 30 minutes, 13.5% 30 to 45 minutes, 3.9% 45 to 60 minutes, 3.7% 60 minutes or more (2000)

Additional Information Contacts

Local Government Offices . . . . (727) 541-0700
Pinellas Park Chamber of Commerce . . . . (727) 544-4777

REDINGTON BEACH (town).

Covers a land area of 0.364 square miles and a water area of 0.934 square miles. Located at 27.81° N. Lat.; 82.81° W. Long. Elevation is 4 feet.
Population: 1,626 (1990); 1,539 (2000); 1,591 (2004); 1,662 (2009 projected); Race: 96.6% White, 0.6% Black, 1.8% Asian, 3.6% Hispanic of any race (2004); Density: 4,371.4 persons per square mile (2004); Average household size: 2.13 (2004); Median age: 50.4 (2004); Male/female ratio: 86.5 (2004); Marriage status: 21.1% never married, 56.3% now married, 8.6% widowed, 14.0% divorced (2000); Foreign born: 12.5% (2000); Ancestry (includes multiple ancestries): 18.4% English, 18.3% German, 13.3% Irish, 8.0% Italian, 7.4% French (except Basque) (2000).
Economy: Employment by occupation: 23.1% management, 23.7% professional, 12.7% services, 25.1% sales, 0.0% farming, 6.4% construction, 8.9% production (2000).
Income: Per capita income: $44,153 (2004); Median household income: $64,848 (2004); Average household income: $94,166 (2004); Percent of households with income of $100,000 or more: 29.8% (2004); Poverty rate: 5.7% (2000).
Taxes: Total city taxes per capita: $207 (2002); City property taxes per capita: $201 (2002).
Education: Percent of population age 25 and over with: High school diploma (including GED) or higher: 88.3% (2004); Bachelor's degree or higher: 40.4% (2004); Master's degree or higher: 18.3% (2004).
Housing: Homeownership rate: 88.9% (2004); Median home value: $232,595 (2004); Median rent: $832 per month (2000); Median age of housing: 41 years (2000).
Safety: Violent crime rate: 6.4 per 10,000 population; Property crime rate: 338.7 per 10,000 population (2003).
Transportation: Commute to work: 91.0% car, 0.6% public transportation, 0.9% walk, 3.1% work from home (2000); Travel time to work: 20.2% less than 15 minutes, 35.7% 15 to 30 minutes, 25.1% 30 to 45 minutes, 12.5% 45 to 60 minutes, 6.5% 60 minutes or more (2000)

REDINGTON SHORES (town).

Covers a land area of 0.393 square miles and a water area of 0.807 square miles. Located at 27.82° N. Lat.; 82.83° W. Long. Elevation is 4 feet.
Population: 2,366 (1990); 2,338 (2000); 2,298 (2004); 2,287 (2009 projected); Race: 97.0% White, 0.3% Black, 0.6% Asian, 3.5% Hispanic of any race (2004); Density: 5,853.5 persons per square mile (2004); Average household size: 1.80 (2004); Median age: 55.6 (2004); Male/female ratio: 95.7 (2004); Marriage status: 18.1% never married, 54.0% now married, 11.9% widowed, 16.0% divorced (2000); Foreign born: 6.8% (2000); Ancestry (includes multiple ancestries): 20.9% German, 18.6% English, 16.1% Irish, 8.2% Italian, 6.0% Polish (2000).
Economy: Single-family building permits issued: 3 (2004); Multi-family building permits issued: 42 (2004); Employment by occupation: 15.7% management, 20.5% professional, 16.7% services, 32.0% sales, 0.3% farming, 8.3% construction, 6.6% production (2000).
Income: Per capita income: $36,089 (2004); Median household income: $44,800 (2004); Average household income: $64,943 (2004); Percent of households with income of $100,000 or more: 15.0% (2004); Poverty rate: 8.2% (2000).
Education: Percent of population age 25 and over with: High school diploma (including GED) or higher: 93.0% (2004); Bachelor's degree or higher: 27.0% (2004); Master's degree or higher: 6.3% (2004).
Housing: Homeownership rate: 75.3% (2004); Median home value: $204,310 (2004); Median rent: $704 per month (2000); Median age of housing: 26 years (2000).
Transportation: Commute to work: 89.7% car, 0.5% public transportation, 4.3% walk, 4.3% work from home (2000); Travel time to work: 23.8% less than 15 minutes, 31.6% 15 to 30 minutes, 28.8% 30 to 45 minutes, 8.5% 45 to 60 minutes, 7.3% 60 minutes or more (2000)

RIDGECREST (CDP).

Covers a land area of 0.563 square miles and a water area of 0.007 square miles. Located at 27.89° N. Lat.; 82.80° W. Long.
Population: 2,932 (1990); 2,453 (2000); 2,284 (2004); 2,164 (2009 projected); Race: 11.9% White, 85.3% Black, 0.1% Asian, 3.3% Hispanic of any race (2004); Density: 4,054.6 persons per square mile (2004); Average household size: 3.09 (2004); Median age: 28.1 (2004); Male/female ratio: 82.4 (2004); Marriage status: 39.4% never married, 46.1% now married, 9.6% widowed, 5.0% divorced (2000); Foreign born: 1.1% (2000); Ancestry (includes multiple ancestries): 71.9% Other groups, 3.2% German, 2.0% Irish, 1.3% English, 0.8% African (2000).
Economy: Employment by occupation: 2.3% management, 14.2% professional, 27.5% services, 33.9% sales, 0.0% farming, 10.9% construction, 11.2% production (2000).
Income: Per capita income: $15,372 (2004); Median household income: $35,227 (2004); Average household income: $42,142 (2004); Percent of households with income of $100,000 or more: 6.1% (2004); Poverty rate: 22.7% (2000).
Education: Percent of population age 25 and over with: High school diploma (including GED) or higher: 68.1% (2004); Bachelor's degree or higher: 11.5% (2004); Master's degree or higher: 8.5% (2004).
Housing: Homeownership rate: 61.9% (2004); Median home value: $90,940 (2004); Median rent: $427 per month (2000); Median age of housing: 27 years (2000).
Transportation: Commute to work: 91.6% car, 3.6% public transportation, 1.1% walk, 0.7% work from home (2000); Travel time to work: 29.5% less than 15 minutes, 33.9% 15 to 30 minutes, 31.2% 30 to 45 minutes, 2.1% 45 to 60 minutes, 3.4% 60 minutes or more (2000)

SAFETY HARBOR (city).

Covers a land area of 4.917 square miles and a water area of 0.132 square miles. Located at 28.00° N. Lat.; 82.69° W. Long. Elevation is 14 feet.
History: Named for its location as a sheltered harbor for seamen and ships. Safety Harbor, at the head of Old Tampa Bay, grew up around the mineral springs. Odet Philippe, a surgeon in Napoleon's navy, settled here in 1823. He planted citrus groves, grew tobacco, and made cigars.
Population: 16,155 (1990); 17,203 (2000); 17,412 (2004); 17,752 (2009 projected); Race: 91.3% White, 4.4% Black, 2.1% Asian, 4.1% Hispanic of any race (2004); Density: 3,540.8 persons per square mile (2004); Average household size: 2.40 (2004); Median age: 42.7 (2004); Male/female ratio: 91.5 (2004); Marriage status: 18.8% never married, 61.4% now married, 8.2% widowed, 11.6% divorced (2000); Foreign born: 7.3% (2000); Ancestry (includes multiple ancestries): 19.3% German, 16.2% Irish, 12.8% Other groups, 12.4% English, 9.7% Italian (2000).

Economy: Single-family building permits issued: 27 (2004); Multi-family building permits issued: 4 (2004); Employment by occupation: 16.8% management, 27.7% professional, 11.2% services, 31.9% sales, 0.1% farming, 5.3% construction, 7.1% production (2000).
Income: Per capita income: $32,475 (2004); Median household income: $58,490 (2004); Average household income: $76,334 (2004); Percent of households with income of $100,000 or more: 23.0% (2004); Poverty rate: 5.6% (2000).
Taxes: Total city taxes per capita: $361 (2002); City property taxes per capita: $132 (2002).
Education: Percent of population age 25 and over with: High school diploma (including GED) or higher: 89.5% (2004); Bachelor's degree or higher: 34.3% (2004); Master's degree or higher: 11.8% (2004).

School District(s)

Pinellas County School District (PK-12)
2002-03 Enrollment: 114,772 .... (727) 588-6011

Housing: Homeownership rate: 84.5% (2004); Median home value: $160,129 (2004); Median rent: $613 per month (2000); Median age of housing: 18 years (2000).
Hospitals: Mease Countryside Hospital (189 beds)
Safety: Violent crime rate: 15.3 per 10,000 population; Property crime rate: 218.2 per 10,000 population (2003).
Transportation: Commute to work: 92.5% car, 0.5% public transportation, 1.7% walk, 3.4% work from home (2000); Travel time to work: 23.5% less than 15 minutes, 37.8% 15 to 30 minutes, 28.0% 30 to 45 minutes, 7.3% 45 to 60 minutes, 3.4% 60 minutes or more (2000)

Additional Information Contacts

Local Government Offices .... (727) 724-1555
Safety Harbor Chamber of Commerce .... (727) 726-2890

SAINT PETE BEACH (city). Aka Saint Petersburg Beach. Covers a land area of 2.247 square miles and a water area of 17.632 square miles. Located at 27.72° N. Lat.; 82.74° W. Long. Elevation is 5 feet.
Population: 9,200 (1990); 9,929 (2000); 10,087 (2004); 10,281 (2009 projected); Race: 97.0% White, 1.0% Black, 0.7% Asian, 2.9% Hispanic of any race (2004); Density: 4,488.1 persons per square mile (2004); Average household size: 1.88 (2004); Median age: 54.1 (2004); Male/female ratio: 100.0 (2004); Marriage status: 16.3% never married, 56.5% now married, 12.8% widowed, 14.4% divorced (2000); Foreign born: 13.0% (2000); Ancestry (includes multiple ancestries): 18.5% German, 18.0% English, 17.9% Irish, 9.7% Italian, 7.0% Other groups (2000).
Economy: Single-family building permits issued: 12 (2004); Multi-family building permits issued: 179 (2004); Employment by occupation: 20.4% management, 22.8% professional, 15.2% services, 28.3% sales, 0.5% farming, 5.8% construction, 7.0% production (2000).
Income: Per capita income: $41,397 (2004); Median household income: $52,987 (2004); Average household income: $76,891 (2004); Percent of households with income of $100,000 or more: 19.7% (2004); Poverty rate: 7.4% (2000).
Taxes: Total city taxes per capita: $635 (2002); City property taxes per capita: $334 (2002).
Education: Percent of population age 25 and over with: High school diploma (including GED) or higher: 87.5% (2004); Bachelor's degree or higher: 34.5% (2004); Master's degree or higher: 11.6% (2004).
Housing: Homeownership rate: 69.8% (2004); Median home value: $242,595 (2004); Median rent: $566 per month (2000); Median age of housing: 32 years (2000).
Safety: Violent crime rate: 47.2 per 10,000 population; Property crime rate: 523.1 per 10,000 population (2003).
Transportation: Commute to work: 84.4% car, 1.7% public transportation, 5.5% walk, 5.6% work from home (2000); Travel time to work: 34.3% less than 15 minutes, 32.9% 15 to 30 minutes, 16.7% 30 to 45 minutes, 9.1% 45 to 60 minutes, 6.9% 60 minutes or more (2000)

Additional Information Contacts

Local Government Offices .... (727) 367-2735

SAINT PETERSBURG (city). Covers a land area of 59.627 square miles and a water area of 73.451 square miles. Located at 27.78° N. Lat.; 82.66° W. Long. Elevation is 44 feet.
History: St. Petersburg was founded by John C. Williams of Detroit, who bought land here in 1876. In 1888 he convinced Peter Demens to build a railroad, called the Orange Belt Line, to the community, which was named by Demens for the city in his native Russia. St. Petersburg, incorporated in 1892, was designed and promoted as a winter resort, capitalizing on its many days of sunshine each year.
Population: 238,846 (1990); 248,232 (2000); 251,151 (2004); 255,155 (2009 projected); Race: 68.0% White, 24.7% Black, 3.2% Asian, 4.9% Hispanic of any race (2004); Density: 4,212.0 persons per square mile (2004); Average household size: 2.27 (2004); Median age: 39.9 (2004); Male/female ratio: 91.8 (2004); Marriage status: 27.8% never married, 48.3% now married, 9.0% widowed, 14.9% divorced (2000); Foreign born: 9.1% (2000); Ancestry (includes multiple ancestries): 27.8% Other groups, 14.7% German, 12.4% Irish, 11.1% English, 6.8% Italian (2000).
Economy: Unemployment rate: 4.5% (2004); Total civilian labor force: 147,468 (2004); Single-family building permits issued: 781 (2004); Multi-family building permits issued: 256 (2004); Employment by occupation: 13.2% management, 20.8% professional, 16.7% services, 28.3% sales, 0.1% farming, 8.2% construction, 12.7% production (2000).
Income: Per capita income: $23,490 (2004); Median household income: $38,199 (2004); Average household income: $52,373 (2004); Percent of households with income of $100,000 or more: 10.2% (2004); Poverty rate: 13.3% (2000).
Taxes: Total city taxes per capita: $452 (2002); City property taxes per capita: $241 (2002).
Education: Percent of population age 25 and over with: High school diploma (including GED) or higher: 82.1% (2004); Bachelor's degree or higher: 23.1% (2004); Master's degree or higher: 8.1% (2004).

School District(s)

Pinellas County School District (PK-12)
2002-03 Enrollment: 114,772 .... (727) 588-6011

Four-year College(s)

Eckerd College
2003-04 Enrollment: 1,631 .... (727) 867-1166
2003-04 Tuition: In-state $22,538; Out-of-state $22,538
Florida Institute of Traditional Chinese Medicine (Private, For-profit)
2003-04 Enrollment: n/a .... (727) 546-6565
Saint Petersburg Theological Seminary
2003-04 Enrollment: 92 .... (727) 399-0276

Two-year College(s)

Loraines Academy Inc (Private, For-profit)
2003-04 Enrollment: 219 .... (727) 347-4247
Pinellas Technical Education Center (Public)
2003-04 Enrollment: 2,399 .... (727) 893-2500
2003-04 Tuition: In-state $1,836; Out-of-state $7,344
The Health Institute-Tampa Bay (Private, For-profit)
2003-04 Enrollment: 42 .... (727) 577-1497
2003-04 Tuition: In-state $11,900; Out-of-state $11,900

Housing: Homeownership rate: 62.6% (2004); Median home value: $115,740 (2004); Median rent: $478 per month (2000); Median age of housing: 37 years (2000).
Hospitals: All Children's Hospital (216 beds); Edward White Hospital (167 beds); Kindred Hospital-St. Petersburg (60 beds); Palms of Pasadena Hospital (307 beds); Saint Petersburg General Hospital (219 beds); St. Anthony's Hospital (405 beds)
Safety: Violent crime rate: 160.2 per 10,000 population; Property crime rate: 649.2 per 10,000 population (2003).
Newspapers: Pinellas News (General - Circulation 2,800); St. Petersburg Times (Circulation 311,680); Weekly Challenger (Black - Circulation 35,500)
Transportation: Commute to work: 90.0% car, 2.9% public transportation, 2.2% walk, 3.1% work from home (2000); Travel time to work: 30.8% less than 15 minutes, 41.1% 15 to 30 minutes, 17.9% 30 to 45 minutes, 5.7% 45 to 60 minutes, 4.5% 60 minutes or more (2000)
Airports: Saint Petersburg-Clearwater Int'l (primary service)

Additional Information Contacts

Gulf Beaches-Tampa Bay Chamber .... (727) 391-7373
Pinellas Suncoast Association of Realtors............. (727) 347-7655
St. Petersburg Chamber of Commerce .... (727) 821-4069

SEMINOLE (city). Covers a land area of 2.474 square miles and a water area of 0.243 square miles. Located at 27.83° N. Lat.; 82.78° W. Long. Elevation is 26 feet.
Population: 10,345 (1990); 10,890 (2000); 10,949 (2004); 11,109 (2009 projected); Race: 95.9% White, 0.6% Black, 1.0% Asian, 2.7% Hispanic of any race (2004); Density: 4,425.9 persons per square mile (2004); Average household size: 1.81 (2004); Median age: 59.2 (2004); Male/female ratio: 76.9 (2004); Marriage status: 15.9% never married, 48.7% now married, 22.1% widowed, 13.3% divorced (2000); Foreign born: 7.3% (2000); Ancestry (includes multiple ancestries): 22.2% German, 15.9% Irish, 14.6% English, 9.6% Italian, 7.4% United States or American (2000).

Economy: Single-family building permits issued: 63 (2004); Multi-family building permits issued: 120 (2004); Employment by occupation: 12.6% management, 14.4% professional, 17.6% services, 33.2% sales, 0.4% farming, 10.5% construction, 11.3% production (2000).
Income: Per capita income: $23,426 (2004); Median household income: $32,617 (2004); Average household income: $42,005 (2004); Percent of households with income of $100,000 or more: 5.8% (2004); Poverty rate: 9.0% (2000).
Taxes: Total city taxes per capita: $492 (2002); City property taxes per capita: $179 (2002).
Education: Percent of population age 25 and over with: High school diploma (including GED) or higher: 80.9% (2004); Bachelor's degree or higher: 16.0% (2004); Master's degree or higher: 5.7% (2004).

School District(s)

Pinellas County School District (PK-12)
2002-03 Enrollment: 114,772 .... (727) 588-6011

Housing: Homeownership rate: 77.4% (2004); Median home value: $95,430 (2004); Median rent: $577 per month (2000); Median age of housing: 28 years (2000).
Safety: Violent crime rate: 34.2 per 10,000 population; Property crime rate: 353.6 per 10,000 population (2003).
Transportation: Commute to work: 90.4% car, 1.3% public transportation, 2.8% walk, 4.2% work from home (2000); Travel time to work: 35.8% less than 15 minutes, 36.7% 15 to 30 minutes, 22.1% 30 to 45 minutes, 3.0% 45 to 60 minutes, 2.4% 60 minutes or more (2000)

Additional Information Contacts

Local Government Offices .... (727) 391-0204
Seminole Chamber of Commerce .... (727) 392-3245

SOUTH HIGHPOINT (CDP). Covers a land area of 2.176 square miles and a water area of 0 square miles. Located at 27.90° N. Lat.; 82.71° W. Long.
Population: 7,103 (1990); 8,839 (2000); 8,875 (2004); 9,004 (2009 projected); Race: 61.5% White, 28.5% Black, 4.2% Asian, 11.7% Hispanic of any race (2004); Density: 4,079.5 persons per square mile (2004); Average household size: 4.16 (2004); Median age: 32.5 (2004); Male/female ratio: 165.3 (2004); Marriage status: 31.1% never married, 47.3% now married, 4.3% widowed, 17.3% divorced (2000); Foreign born: 9.6% (2000); Ancestry (includes multiple ancestries): 24.6% Other groups, 8.6% German, 8.0% English, 6.6% Irish, 5.6% United States or American (2000).
Economy: Employment by occupation: 6.5% management, 12.6% professional, 19.6% services, 34.1% sales, 0.9% farming, 8.7% construction, 17.6% production (2000).
Income: Per capita income: $10,242 (2004); Median household income: $30,858 (2004); Average household income: $40,043 (2004); Percent of households with income of $100,000 or more: 5.3% (2004); Poverty rate: 22.2% (2000).
Education: Percent of population age 25 and over with: High school diploma (including GED) or higher: 70.3% (2004); Bachelor's degree or higher: 4.9% (2004); Master's degree or higher: 1.7% (2004).
Housing: Homeownership rate: 47.7% (2004); Median home value: $84,358 (2004); Median rent: $465 per month (2000); Median age of housing: 23 years (2000).
Transportation: Commute to work: 88.2% car, 3.2% public transportation, 2.0% walk, 2.7% work from home (2000); Travel time to work: 29.4% less than 15 minutes, 41.5% 15 to 30 minutes, 19.1% 30 to 45 minutes, 3.9% 45 to 60 minutes, 6.1% 60 minutes or more (2000)

SOUTH PASADENA (city). Aka Coreytown. Covers a land area of 0.677 square miles and a water area of 0.470 square miles. Located at 27.75° N. Lat.; 82.74° W. Long. Elevation is 8 feet.
Population: 5,644 (1990); 5,778 (2000); 5,795 (2004); 5,853 (2009 projected); Race: 98.1% White, 0.2% Black, 1.0% Asian, 1.9% Hispanic of any race (2004); Density: 8,555.7 persons per square mile (2004); Average household size: 1.58 (2004); Median age: 70.1 (2004); Male/female ratio: 64.4 (2004); Marriage status: 9.7% never married, 52.0% now married, 24.2% widowed, 14.1% divorced (2000); Foreign born: 13.0% (2000); Ancestry (includes multiple ancestries): 19.2% German, 16.8% Irish, 14.7% English, 8.2% Italian, 4.9% Other groups (2000).
Economy: Single-family building permits issued: 0 (2004); Multi-family building permits issued: 0 (2004); Employment by occupation: 16.4% management, 17.8% professional, 15.2% services, 39.8% sales, 0.0% farming, 4.5% construction, 6.3% production (2000).
Income: Per capita income: $30,090 (2004); Median household income: $30,962 (2004); Average household income: $46,382 (2004); Percent of households with income of $100,000 or more: 7.1% (2004); Poverty rate: 8.6% (2000).
Taxes: Total city taxes per capita: $299 (2002); City property taxes per capita: $83 (2002).
Education: Percent of population age 25 and over with: High school diploma (including GED) or higher: 85.8% (2004); Bachelor's degree or higher: 21.3% (2004); Master's degree or higher: 6.1% (2004).
Housing: Homeownership rate: 62.2% (2004); Median home value: $125,662 (2004); Median rent: $545 per month (2000); Median age of housing: 25 years (2000).
Safety: Violent crime rate: 22.1 per 10,000 population; Property crime rate: 330.0 per 10,000 population (2003).
Transportation: Commute to work: 86.5% car, 0.0% public transportation, 9.0% walk, 3.2% work from home (2000); Travel time to work: 29.6% less than 15 minutes, 40.4% 15 to 30 minutes, 16.9% 30 to 45 minutes, 8.4% 45 to 60 minutes, 4.6% 60 minutes or more (2000)

Additional Information Contacts

Local Government Offices .... (727) 343-4192

TARPON SPRINGS (city). Covers a land area of 9.143 square miles and a water area of 7.743 square miles. Located at 28.14° N. Lat.; 82.75° W. Long. Elevation is 17 feet.
History: Tarpon Springs was founded in 1876 and named for the mistaken belief that the fish that spawned in Spring Bayou were tarpon. A resort hotel was built here in the 1880s by Hamilton Disston, a manufacturer from Philadelphia. For several years, the Duke of Sutherland, cousin to Queen Victoria, was a neighbor.
Population: 18,361 (1990); 21,003 (2000); 22,703 (2004); 24,711 (2009 projected); Race: 89.1% White, 6.5% Black, 1.3% Asian, 5.5% Hispanic of any race (2004); Density: 2,483.0 persons per square mile (2004); Average household size: 2.29 (2004); Median age: 46.1 (2004); Male/female ratio: 92.3 (2004); Marriage status: 17.6% never married, 60.7% now married, 10.6% widowed, 11.0% divorced (2000); Foreign born: 10.1% (2000); Ancestry (includes multiple ancestries): 17.7% German, 14.9% Irish, 12.6% Other groups, 12.3% English, 11.8% Greek (2000).
Economy: Single-family building permits issued: 126 (2004); Multi-family building permits issued: 10 (2004); Employment by occupation: 14.2% management, 17.5% professional, 17.2% services, 30.8% sales, 0.2% farming, 10.1% construction, 9.9% production (2000).
Income: Per capita income: $26,223 (2004); Median household income: $43,451 (2004); Average household income: $59,584 (2004); Percent of households with income of $100,000 or more: 11.4% (2004); Poverty rate: 9.8% (2000).
Taxes: Total city taxes per capita: $521 (2002); City property taxes per capita: $201 (2002).
Education: Percent of population age 25 and over with: High school diploma (including GED) or higher: 81.5% (2004); Bachelor's degree or higher: 20.3% (2004); Master's degree or higher: 7.2% (2004).

School District(s)

Pinellas County School District (PK-12)
2002-03 Enrollment: 114,772 .... (727) 588-6011

Housing: Homeownership rate: 77.9% (2004); Median home value: $133,640 (2004); Median rent: $447 per month (2000); Median age of housing: 22 years (2000).
Hospitals: Helen Ellis Memorial Hospital (168 beds)
Safety: Violent crime rate: 60.9 per 10,000 population; Property crime rate: 315.6 per 10,000 population (2003).
Transportation: Commute to work: 91.2% car, 1.6% public transportation, 2.5% walk, 2.9% work from home (2000); Travel time to work: 27.0% less than 15 minutes, 29.2% 15 to 30 minutes, 22.0% 30 to 45 minutes, 12.4% 45 to 60 minutes, 9.3% 60 minutes or more (2000)

Additional Information Contacts

Local Government Offices .... (727) 938-3711
Tarpon Springs Chamber of Commerce .... (727) 937-6109

TIERRA VERDE (CDP). Covers a land area of 1.471 square miles and a water area of 3.076 square miles. Located at 27.68° N. Lat.; 82.72° W. Long. Elevation is 5 feet.
Population: 2,186 (1990); 3,574 (2000); 4,133 (2004); 4,773 (2009 projected); Race: 94.7% White, 2.5% Black, 1.2% Asian, 4.1% Hispanic of any race (2004); Density: 2,810.2 persons per square mile (2004); Average household size: 2.13 (2004); Median age: 48.5 (2004); Male/female ratio: 102.2 (2004); Marriage status: 15.7% never married, 67.5% now married,

3.1% widowed, 13.7% divorced (2000); Foreign born: 7.8% (2000); Ancestry (includes multiple ancestries): 23.2% German, 18.4% Irish, 13.1% English, 12.9% Italian, 10.7% Other groups (2000).
Economy: Employment by occupation: 30.0% management, 26.9% professional, 8.1% services, 30.5% sales, 0.0% farming, 2.1% construction, 2.5% production (2000).
Income: Per capita income: $58,617 (2004); Median household income: $91,522 (2004); Average household income: $124,942 (2004); Percent of households with income of $100,000 or more: 44.5% (2004); Poverty rate: 3.9% (2000).
Education: Percent of population age 25 and over with: High school diploma (including GED) or higher: 93.8% (2004); Bachelor's degree or higher: 47.9% (2004); Master's degree or higher: 14.4% (2004).
Housing: Homeownership rate: 86.8% (2004); Median home value: $296,957 (2004); Median rent: $996 per month (2000); Median age of housing: 13 years (2000).
Transportation: Commute to work: 90.9% car, 0.4% public transportation, 0.8% walk, 6.0% work from home (2000); Travel time to work: 14.1% less than 15 minutes, 46.4% 15 to 30 minutes, 25.2% 30 to 45 minutes, 7.1% 45 to 60 minutes, 7.2% 60 minutes or more (2000)

TREASURE ISLAND (city). Covers a land area of 1.592 square miles and a water area of 3.730 square miles. Located at 27.76° N. Lat.; 82.76° W. Long. Elevation is 5 feet.
Population: 7,266 (1990); 7,450 (2000); 7,547 (2004); 7,705 (2009 projected); Race: 97.3% White, 0.4% Black, 0.7% Asian, 2.6% Hispanic of any race (2004); Density: 4,740.0 persons per square mile (2004); Average household size: 1.79 (2004); Median age: 52.8 (2004); Male/female ratio: 96.0 (2004); Marriage status: 15.1% never married, 57.5% now married, 8.8% widowed, 18.6% divorced (2000); Foreign born: 7.8% (2000); Ancestry (includes multiple ancestries): 23.2% German, 19.5% Irish, 15.8% English, 9.6% Italian, 7.2% Other groups (2000).
Economy: Single-family building permits issued: 12 (2004); Multi-family building permits issued: 53 (2004); Employment by occupation: 19.5% management, 23.7% professional, 13.2% services, 32.0% sales, 0.5% farming, 6.4% construction, 4.8% production (2000).
Income: Per capita income: $39,339 (2004); Median household income: $46,390 (2004); Average household income: $70,320 (2004); Percent of households with income of $100,000 or more: 19.3% (2004); Poverty rate: 5.6% (2000).
Taxes: Total city taxes per capita: $395 (2002); City property taxes per capita: $213 (2002).
Education: Percent of population age 25 and over with: High school diploma (including GED) or higher: 89.6% (2004); Bachelor's degree or higher: 30.8% (2004); Master's degree or higher: 11.1% (2004).
Housing: Homeownership rate: 65.0% (2004); Median home value: $248,090 (2004); Median rent: $586 per month (2000); Median age of housing: 29 years (2000).
Safety: Violent crime rate: 31.5 per 10,000 population; Property crime rate: 454.8 per 10,000 population (2003).
Transportation: Commute to work: 87.5% car, 0.0% public transportation, 2.2% walk, 9.1% work from home (2000); Travel time to work: 26.7% less than 15 minutes, 42.1% 15 to 30 minutes, 15.4% 30 to 45 minutes, 7.8% 45 to 60 minutes, 8.0% 60 minutes or more (2000)
Additional Information Contacts
Local Government Offices . . . . (727) 547-4575

WEST AND EAST LEALMAN (CDP). Covers a land area of 4.729 square miles and a water area of 0.030 square miles. Located at 27.82° N. Lat.; 82.68° W. Long.
Population: 21,350 (1990); 21,753 (2000); 21,333 (2004); 20,968 (2009 projected); Race: 85.1% White, 4.5% Black, 5.3% Asian, 6.0% Hispanic of any race (2004); Density: 4,510.6 persons per square mile (2004); Average household size: 2.22 (2004); Median age: 41.5 (2004); Male/female ratio: 99.2 (2004); Marriage status: 21.0% never married, 48.6% now married, 11.7% widowed, 18.8% divorced (2000); Foreign born: 7.9% (2000); Ancestry (includes multiple ancestries): 17.8% Other groups, 17.0% German, 15.2% Irish, 12.5% English, 9.3% United States or American (2000).
Economy: Employment by occupation: 9.1% management, 10.1% professional, 17.4% services, 30.5% sales, 0.3% farming, 12.6% construction, 20.0% production (2000).
Income: Per capita income: $16,622 (2004); Median household income: $28,701 (2004); Average household income: $36,454 (2004); Percent of households with income of $100,000 or more: 3.6% (2004); Poverty rate: 17.4% (2000).
Education: Percent of population age 25 and over with: High school diploma (including GED) or higher: 67.6% (2004); Bachelor's degree or higher: 8.4% (2004); Master's degree or higher: 3.0% (2004).
Housing: Homeownership rate: 66.6% (2004); Median home value: $79,478 (2004); Median rent: $427 per month (2000); Median age of housing: 35 years (2000).
Transportation: Commute to work: 90.3% car, 2.4% public transportation, 2.3% walk, 2.3% work from home (2000); Travel time to work: 30.6% less than 15 minutes, 43.9% 15 to 30 minutes, 15.8% 30 to 45 minutes, 3.8% 45 to 60 minutes, 5.9% 60 minutes or more (2000)

Polk County

Located in central Florida; bounded on the east by the Kissimmee River, and on the north by the Withlacoochee River; drained by the Peace River. Covers a land area of 1,874.40 square miles, a water area of 135.60 square miles, and is located in the Eastern Time Zone. The county government was organized in 1861. County seat is Bartow.

Polk County is part of the Lakeland, FL Metropolitan Statistical Area. The entire metro area includes: Polk County, FL

Weather Station: Bartow — Elevation: 124 feet

	Jan	Feb	Mar	Apr	May	Jun	Jul	Aug	Sep	Oct	Nov	Dec
High	73	75	80	84	89	91	92	92	90	85	80	75
Low	50	52	56	60	66	71	72	73	72	65	59	52
Precip	2.6	2.9	3.3	2.5	4.0	6.8	8.4	6.6	6.6	2.7	2.2	2.4
Snow	0.0	0.0	0.0	0.0	0.0	0.0	0.0	0.0	0.0	0.0	0.0	0.0

High and Low temperatures in degrees Fahrenheit; Precipitation and Snow in inches

Weather Station: Lake Alfred Exp. Station — Elevation: 137 feet

	Jan	Feb	Mar	Apr	May	Jun	Jul	Aug	Sep	Oct	Nov	Dec
High	72	74	79	84	89	91	93	93	91	86	80	74
Low	47	49	54	58	64	70	72	72	70	63	56	50
Precip	2.6	2.8	3.7	2.0	4.2	6.9	7.2	7.3	6.5	3.0	2.3	2.2
Snow	tr	0.0	0.0	0.0	0.0	0.0	0.0	0.0	0.0	0.0	0.0	0.0

High and Low temperatures in degrees Fahrenheit; Precipitation and Snow in inches

Weather Station: Lakeland Linder Airport — Elevation: 209 feet

	Jan	Feb	Mar	Apr	May	Jun	Jul	Aug	Sep	Oct	Nov	Dec
High	72	74	80	84	89	92	93	92	91	85	79	74
Low	50	52	57	61	66	71	73	73	72	65	59	53
Precip	2.5	2.8	3.6	2.0	4.2	7.1	7.8	7.4	6.1	2.3	2.3	2.1
Snow	tr	0.0	0.0	0.0	0.0	0.0	0.0	0.0	0.0	0.0	0.0	0.0

High and Low temperatures in degrees Fahrenheit; Precipitation and Snow in inches

Weather Station: Mountain Lake — Elevation: 124 feet

	Jan	Feb	Mar	Apr	May	Jun	Jul	Aug	Sep	Oct	Nov	Dec
High	74	76	81	85	90	92	93	92	90	86	80	75
Low	49	50	55	59	64	70	71	71	70	64	57	51
Precip	2.4	2.5	3.3	2.0	4.0	7.5	7.5	6.6	5.8	2.5	2.2	2.1
Snow	tr	0.0	0.0	0.0	0.0	0.0	0.0	0.0	0.0	0.0	0.0	0.0

High and Low temperatures in degrees Fahrenheit; Precipitation and Snow in inches

Population: 405,382 (1990); 483,924 (2000); 513,989 (2004); 551,957 (2009 projected); Race: 77.6% White, 14.5% Black, 1.0% Asian, 11.3% Hispanic of any race (2004); Density: 274.2 persons per square mile (2004); Average household size: 2.58 (2004); Median age: 38.8 (2004); Male/female ratio: 96.3 (2004).
Religion: Five largest groups: 14.0% Southern Baptist Convention, 7.8% Catholic Church, 3.9% The United Methodist Church, 2.8% Assemblies of God, 1.6% Church of God (Cleveland, Tennessee) (2000).
Economy: Unemployment rate: 5.9% (2004); Total civilian labor force: 224,369 (2004); Leading industries: 13.8% retail trade; 12.7% health care and social assistance; 10.4% manufacturing (2003); Companies that employ 500 or more persons: 28 (2003); Companies that employ 100 to 499 persons: 237 (2003); Companies that employ less than 100 persons: 9,665 (2003); Farms: 3,114 totaling 626,634 acres (2002); Minority business ownership rate: 11.6% (1997); Women business ownership rate: 22.2% (1997); Retail sales per capita: $8,606 (1997). Single-family building permits issued: 8,715 (2004); Multi-family building permits issued: 1,527 (2004).
Income: Per capita income: $20,236 (2004); Median household income: $39,451 (2004); Average household income: $51,512 (2004); Percent of

households with income of $100,000 or more: 9.1% (2004); Poverty rate: 13.6% (2002); Bankruptcy rate: 6.39% (2004).
Taxes: Total county taxes per capita: $316 (2002); County property taxes per capita: $264 (2002).
Education: Percent of population age 25 and over with: High school diploma (including GED) or higher: 74.9% (2004); Bachelor's degree or higher: 15.0% (2004); Master's degree or higher: 4.9% (2004).
Housing: Homeownership rate: 74.0% (2004); Median home value: $93,427 (2004); Median rent: $400 per month (2000); Median age of housing: 20 years (2000).
Health: Birth rate: 137.4 per 10,000 population (2004); Death rate: 104.2 per 10,000 population (2004); Age adjusted cancer mortality rate: 193.2 deaths per 100,000 population (2002); Air Quality Index: 92.1% good, 7.9% moderate, 0.0% unhealthy for sensitive individuals, 0.0% unhealthy (percent of days in 2004); Number of physicians: 15.1 per 10,000 population (2001); Hospital beds: 27.4 per 10,000 population (2002); Hospital admissions: 1,269.1 per 10,000 population (2002).
Elections: 2004 Presidential election results: 58.6% Bush, 40.8% Kerry, 0.4% Nader, 0.1% Badnarik
National and State Parks: Lake Kissimmee State Park
Additional Information Contacts
Polk County Government Offices. . . . . (863) 534-6000
Auburndale Chamber of Commerce . . . . (863) 967-3400
Bartow Board of Realtors. . . . . (863) 534-1774
Bartow Chamber of Commerce . . . . (863) 533-7125
Davenport Chamber of Commerce . . . . (863) 422-3975
Dundee Area Chamber of Commerce . . . . (863) 439-3261
Eagle Lake Chamber of Commerce. . . . . (979) 234-2780
East Polk County Association of Realtors . . . . (863) 294-3163
Fort Meade Chamber of Commerce . . . . (863) 285-8253
Frostproof Chamber of Commerce . . . . (863) 635-9112
Greater Mulberry Chamber of Commerce . . . . (863) 425-4414
Haines City Chamber of Commerce . . . . (863) 422-3751
Lake Wales Association of Realtors . . . . (863) 676-1721
Lake Wales Chamber of Commerce . . . . (863) 676-3445
Lakeland Association of Realtors. . . . . (863) 687-6111
Lakeland Chamber of Commerce . . . . (863) 688-8551
Lakeland Economic Development Council . . . . (863) 687-3788
Winter Haven Chamber of Commerce. . . . . (863) 293-2138

Polk County Communities

AUBURNDALE (city). Covers a land area of 5.220 square miles and a water area of 4.078 square miles. Located at 28.06° N. Lat.; 81.79° W. Long. Elevation is 169 feet.
History: Auburndale was founded by a group seeking a healthful climate, who named the community Sanitaria. Later residents from Auburndale, Massachusetts, renamed the town.
Population: 9,597 (1990); 11,032 (2000); 11,484 (2004); 12,040 (2009 projected); Race: 77.2% White, 15.0% Black, 0.9% Asian, 9.9% Hispanic of any race (2004); Density: 2,200.1 persons per square mile (2004); Average household size: 2.69 (2004); Median age: 35.6 (2004); Male/female ratio: 92.1 (2004); Marriage status: 22.7% never married, 56.2% now married, 8.7% widowed, 12.4% divorced (2000); Foreign born: 5.8% (2000); Ancestry (includes multiple ancestries): 19.5% Other groups, 17.7% United States or American, 10.2% English, 9.6% German, 8.0% Irish (2000).
Economy: Single-family building permits issued: 128 (2004); Multi-family building permits issued: 2 (2004); Employment by occupation: 10.8% management, 13.4% professional, 18.3% services, 26.4% sales, 2.9% farming, 10.3% construction, 17.9% production (2000).
Income: Per capita income: $17,491 (2004); Median household income: $36,886 (2004); Average household income: $46,376 (2004); Percent of households with income of $100,000 or more: 7.6% (2004); Poverty rate: 17.3% (2000).
Taxes: Total city taxes per capita: $371 (2002); City property taxes per capita: $115 (2002).
Education: Percent of population age 25 and over with: High school diploma (including GED) or higher: 69.3% (2004); Bachelor's degree or higher: 11.2% (2004); Master's degree or higher: 3.4% (2004).
School District(s)
Polk County School District (PK-12)
2002-03 Enrollment: 82,179 . . . . (863) 534-0521
Housing: Homeownership rate: 67.2% (2004); Median home value: $91,738 (2004); Median rent: $372 per month (2000); Median age of housing: 25 years (2000).
Safety: Violent crime rate: 58.0 per 10,000 population; Property crime rate: 709.4 per 10,000 population (2003).
Transportation: Commute to work: 95.3% car, 1.3% public transportation, 0.7% walk, 1.0% work from home (2000); Travel time to work: 28.4% less than 15 minutes, 39.8% 15 to 30 minutes, 21.1% 30 to 45 minutes, 6.5% 45 to 60 minutes, 4.2% 60 minutes or more (2000)
Additional Information Contacts
Auburndale Chamber of Commerce . . . . (863) 967-3400

BABSON PARK (CDP). Covers a land area of 1.494 square miles and a water area of 0 square miles. Located at 27.83° N. Lat.; 81.52° W. Long. Elevation is 156 feet.
History: Babson Park was first called Crooked Lake for the nearby lake, but was renamed by Roger Babson who purchased the land in 1923.
Population: 1,125 (1990); 1,182 (2000); 1,366 (2004); 1,572 (2009 projected); Race: 78.3% White, 16.1% Black, 1.8% Asian, 7.9% Hispanic of any race (2004); Density: 914.6 persons per square mile (2004); Average household size: 3.22 (2004); Median age: 26.9 (2004); Male/female ratio: 102.4 (2004); Marriage status: 19.2% never married, 63.5% now married, 5.3% widowed, 12.0% divorced (2000); Foreign born: 1.3% (2000); Ancestry (includes multiple ancestries): 24.6% Other groups, 15.2% Irish, 13.9% English, 6.9% German, 5.2% Scottish (2000).
Economy: Employment by occupation: 5.9% management, 10.0% professional, 23.3% services, 27.9% sales, 10.2% farming, 13.6% construction, 9.2% production (2000).
Income: Per capita income: $12,732 (2004); Median household income: $32,170 (2004); Average household income: $38,709 (2004); Percent of households with income of $100,000 or more: 4.2% (2004); Poverty rate: 10.3% (2000).
Education: Percent of population age 25 and over with: High school diploma (including GED) or higher: 75.9% (2004); Bachelor's degree or higher: 15.8% (2004); Master's degree or higher: 8.6% (2004).
School District(s)
Polk County School District (PK-12)
2002-03 Enrollment: 82,179 . . . . (863) 534-0521
Four-year College(s)
Webber International University
2003-04 Enrollment: 656 . . . . (863) 638-1431
2003-04 Tuition: In-state $11,500; Out-of-state $11,500
Housing: Homeownership rate: 78.3% (2004); Median home value: $91,500 (2004); Median rent: $310 per month (2000); Median age of housing: 23 years (2000).
Transportation: Commute to work: 95.2% car, 0.0% public transportation, 0.0% walk, 4.8% work from home (2000); Travel time to work: 23.1% less than 15 minutes, 56.1% 15 to 30 minutes, 13.0% 30 to 45 minutes, 7.9% 45 to 60 minutes, 0.0% 60 minutes or more (2000)

BARTOW (city). Covers a land area of 11.226 square miles and a water area of 0.141 square miles. Located at 27.89° N. Lat.; 81.84° W. Long. Elevation is 116 feet.
History: The area around Bartow was settled in 1851 by planters on the site of Fort Blount, built during the Seminole Wars. The town was named in 1867 for Confederate General Francis Bartow.
Population: 14,829 (1990); 15,340 (2000); 15,330 (2004); 15,602 (2009 projected); Race: 64.9% White, 28.6% Black, 1.1% Asian, 9.7% Hispanic of any race (2004); Density: 1,365.6 persons per square mile (2004); Average household size: 2.74 (2004); Median age: 37.3 (2004); Male/female ratio: 96.5 (2004); Marriage status: 24.3% never married, 53.1% now married, 10.2% widowed, 12.4% divorced (2000); Foreign born: 5.4% (2000); Ancestry (includes multiple ancestries): 33.4% Other groups, 11.2% United States or American, 9.1% English, 7.7% Irish, 7.3% German (2000).
Economy: Single-family building permits issued: 96 (2004); Multi-family building permits issued: 164 (2004); Employment by occupation: 10.6% management, 19.1% professional, 15.1% services, 26.4% sales, 0.7% farming, 8.9% construction, 19.1% production (2000).
Income: Per capita income: $21,423 (2004); Median household income: $42,390 (2004); Average household income: $55,544 (2004); Percent of households with income of $100,000 or more: 10.4% (2004); Poverty rate: 13.1% (2000).
Education: Percent of population age 25 and over with: High school diploma (including GED) or higher: 78.2% (2004); Bachelor's degree or higher: 16.8% (2004); Master's degree or higher: 5.4% (2004).
School District(s)
Polk County School District (PK-12)
2002-03 Enrollment: 82,179 . . . . (863) 534-0521

Housing: Homeownership rate: 70.0% (2004); Median home value: $89,727 (2004); Median rent: $386 per month (2000); Median age of housing: 33 years (2000).
Hospitals: Bartow Memorial Hospital (56 beds)
Safety: Violent crime rate: 78.2 per 10,000 population; Property crime rate: 978.5 per 10,000 population (2003).
Newspapers: The Polk County Democrat (General - Circulation 4,405)
Transportation: Commute to work: 94.1% car, 0.3% public transportation, 3.3% walk, 1.0% work from home (2000); Travel time to work: 44.7% less than 15 minutes, 30.3% 15 to 30 minutes, 17.1% 30 to 45 minutes, 3.8% 45 to 60 minutes, 4.0% 60 minutes or more (2000)
Airports: Bartow Municipal
Additional Information Contacts
Bartow Board of Realtors. . . . . (863) 534-1774
Bartow Chamber of Commerce . . . . (863) 533-7125

COMBEE SETTLEMENT (CDP). Covers a land area of 2.121 square miles and a water area of 0 square miles. Located at 28.05° N. Lat.; 81.90° W. Long.
Population: 5,477 (1990); 5,436 (2000); 5,100 (2004); 4,766 (2009 projected); Race: 84.8% White, 7.6% Black, 0.6% Asian, 8.2% Hispanic of any race (2004); Density: 2,404.8 persons per square mile (2004); Average household size: 2.45 (2004); Median age: 36.3 (2004); Male/female ratio: 101.1 (2004); Marriage status: 22.1% never married, 52.8% now married, 9.2% widowed, 15.9% divorced (2000); Foreign born: 4.0% (2000); Ancestry (includes multiple ancestries): 20.2% United States or American, 18.7% Other groups, 12.0% Irish, 11.2% German, 10.8% English (2000).
Economy: Employment by occupation: 5.7% management, 13.3% professional, 17.0% services, 28.5% sales, 1.1% farming, 15.7% construction, 18.7% production (2000).
Income: Per capita income: $15,717 (2004); Median household income: $32,888 (2004); Average household income: $38,573 (2004); Percent of households with income of $100,000 or more: 4.0% (2004); Poverty rate: 19.5% (2000).
Education: Percent of population age 25 and over with: High school diploma (including GED) or higher: 75.5% (2004); Bachelor's degree or higher: 5.9% (2004); Master's degree or higher: 2.3% (2004).
Housing: Homeownership rate: 62.7% (2004); Median home value: $73,964 (2004); Median rent: $398 per month (2000); Median age of housing: 33 years (2000).
Transportation: Commute to work: 91.8% car, 0.9% public transportation, 3.0% walk, 0.8% work from home (2000); Travel time to work: 21.5% less than 15 minutes, 42.0% 15 to 30 minutes, 23.2% 30 to 45 minutes, 5.9% 45 to 60 minutes, 7.3% 60 minutes or more (2000)

CROOKED LAKE PARK (CDP). Covers a land area of 0.562 square miles and a water area of 0 square miles. Located at 27.83° N. Lat.; 81.59° W. Long. Elevation is 132 feet.
Population: 1,427 (1990); 1,682 (2000); 2,469 (2004); 3,348 (2009 projected); Race: 89.3% White, 5.4% Black, 0.3% Asian, 7.2% Hispanic of any race (2004); Density: 4,389.6 persons per square mile (2004); Average household size: 2.62 (2004); Median age: 39.1 (2004); Male/female ratio: 83.8 (2004); Marriage status: 21.3% never married, 59.3% now married, 11.1% widowed, 8.3% divorced (2000); Foreign born: 3.3% (2000); Ancestry (includes multiple ancestries): 24.8% United States or American, 12.3% English, 12.3% German, 11.7% Other groups, 10.4% Irish (2000).
Economy: Employment by occupation: 5.8% management, 21.5% professional, 12.3% services, 32.2% sales, 2.5% farming, 10.7% construction, 15.1% production (2000).
Income: Per capita income: $22,599 (2004); Median household income: $42,676 (2004); Average household income: $58,800 (2004); Percent of households with income of $100,000 or more: 10.0% (2004); Poverty rate: 5.3% (2000).
Education: Percent of population age 25 and over with: High school diploma (including GED) or higher: 79.4% (2004); Bachelor's degree or higher: 16.1% (2004); Master's degree or higher: 1.6% (2004).
Housing: Homeownership rate: 85.7% (2004); Median home value: $76,519 (2004); Median rent: $419 per month (2000); Median age of housing: 26 years (2000).
Transportation: Commute to work: 95.5% car, 0.0% public transportation, 4.0% walk, 0.5% work from home (2000); Travel time to work: 44.1% less than 15 minutes, 36.2% 15 to 30 minutes, 10.9% 30 to 45 minutes, 7.3% 45 to 60 minutes, 1.5% 60 minutes or more (2000)

CRYSTAL LAKE (CDP). Aka Lake Holloway. Covers a land area of 2.692 square miles and a water area of 0.118 square miles. Located at 28.03° N. Lat.; 81.91° W. Long.
Population: 5,270 (1990); 5,341 (2000); 5,432 (2004); 5,610 (2009 projected); Race: 76.7% White, 17.2% Black, 0.8% Asian, 8.5% Hispanic of any race (2004); Density: 2,017.7 persons per square mile (2004); Average household size: 2.49 (2004); Median age: 34.3 (2004); Male/female ratio: 97.0 (2004); Marriage status: 27.3% never married, 52.9% now married, 8.2% widowed, 11.6% divorced (2000); Foreign born: 6.9% (2000); Ancestry (includes multiple ancestries): 27.3% Other groups, 17.7% United States or American, 11.1% German, 9.8% English, 6.6% Irish (2000).
Economy: Employment by occupation: 5.3% management, 14.5% professional, 18.7% services, 30.0% sales, 0.0% farming, 14.0% construction, 17.5% production (2000).
Income: Per capita income: $16,196 (2004); Median household income: $32,538 (2004); Average household income: $40,338 (2004); Percent of households with income of $100,000 or more: 4.3% (2004); Poverty rate: 16.4% (2000).
Education: Percent of population age 25 and over with: High school diploma (including GED) or higher: 72.3% (2004); Bachelor's degree or higher: 9.5% (2004); Master's degree or higher: 2.7% (2004).
Housing: Homeownership rate: 56.7% (2004); Median home value: $72,091 (2004); Median rent: $418 per month (2000); Median age of housing: 28 years (2000).
Transportation: Commute to work: 94.3% car, 0.3% public transportation, 1.6% walk, 0.9% work from home (2000); Travel time to work: 29.9% less than 15 minutes, 42.7% 15 to 30 minutes, 17.9% 30 to 45 minutes, 2.3% 45 to 60 minutes, 7.2% 60 minutes or more (2000)

CYPRESS GARDENS (CDP). Covers a land area of 3.798 square miles and a water area of 0.491 square miles. Located at 28.00° N. Lat.; 81.69° W. Long. Elevation is 145 feet.
Population: 7,822 (1990); 8,844 (2000); 9,176 (2004); 9,658 (2009 projected); Race: 93.0% White, 2.7% Black, 1.7% Asian, 3.2% Hispanic of any race (2004); Density: 2,416.0 persons per square mile (2004); Average household size: 2.49 (2004); Median age: 45.2 (2004); Male/female ratio: 88.4 (2004); Marriage status: 14.3% never married, 65.2% now married, 9.9% widowed, 10.6% divorced (2000); Foreign born: 4.3% (2000); Ancestry (includes multiple ancestries): 19.5% German, 15.5% English, 13.7% Irish, 12.7% United States or American, 11.0% Other groups (2000).
Economy: Employment by occupation: 13.7% management, 27.2% professional, 12.7% services, 29.4% sales, 0.0% farming, 7.9% construction, 9.0% production (2000).
Income: Per capita income: $26,084 (2004); Median household income: $51,598 (2004); Average household income: $64,159 (2004); Percent of households with income of $100,000 or more: 13.9% (2004); Poverty rate: 3.2% (2000).
Education: Percent of population age 25 and over with: High school diploma (including GED) or higher: 87.2% (2004); Bachelor's degree or higher: 28.6% (2004); Master's degree or higher: 9.7% (2004).
Housing: Homeownership rate: 88.4% (2004); Median home value: $129,400 (2004); Median rent: $547 per month (2000); Median age of housing: 26 years (2000).
Transportation: Commute to work: 96.0% car, 0.0% public transportation, 1.0% walk, 2.3% work from home (2000); Travel time to work: 36.6% less than 15 minutes, 39.0% 15 to 30 minutes, 11.9% 30 to 45 minutes, 5.6% 45 to 60 minutes, 6.8% 60 minutes or more (2000)

DAVENPORT (city). Covers a land area of 1.564 square miles and a water area of 0.062 square miles. Located at 28.16° N. Lat.; 81.60° W. Long. Elevation is 136 feet.
History: Davenport developed as the center of a citrus region, with fruit-packing and canning plants. A citrus candy factory here made crystallized fruit peel.
Population: 1,625 (1990); 1,924 (2000); 2,091 (2004); 2,282 (2009 projected); Race: 87.9% White, 4.8% Black, 0.4% Asian, 13.2% Hispanic of any race (2004); Density: 1,337.4 persons per square mile (2004); Average household size: 2.68 (2004); Median age: 48.1 (2004); Male/female ratio: 89.6 (2004); Marriage status: 15.9% never married, 62.5% now married, 14.3% widowed, 7.3% divorced (2000); Foreign born: 5.9% (2000); Ancestry (includes multiple ancestries): 19.5% Other groups, 15.1% United States or American, 13.6% English, 12.8% German, 6.1% Irish (2000).
Economy: Single-family building permits issued: 13 (2004); Multi-family building permits issued: 2 (2004); Employment by occupation: 12.9%

management, 9.0% professional, 24.6% services, 27.9% sales, 0.0% farming, 20.0% construction, 5.6% production (2000).
Income: Per capita income: $16,004 (2004); Median household income: $33,864 (2004); Average household income: $40,749 (2004); Percent of households with income of $100,000 or more: 3.5% (2004); Poverty rate: 10.8% (2000).
Education: Percent of population age 25 and over with: High school diploma (including GED) or higher: 72.9% (2004); Bachelor's degree or higher: 10.9% (2004); Master's degree or higher: 1.7% (2004).

School District(s)

Osceola County School District (PK-12)
2002-03 Enrollment: 40,485 . . . . (407) 870-4008
Housing: Homeownership rate: 88.0% (2004); Median home value: $81,901 (2004); Median rent: $565 per month (2000); Median age of housing: 14 years (2000).
Hospitals: Heart of Florida Regional Medical Center (115 beds)
Safety: Violent crime rate: 10.1 per 10,000 population; Property crime rate: 311.9 per 10,000 population (2003).
Transportation: Commute to work: 96.3% car, 1.3% public transportation, 0.0% walk, 1.1% work from home (2000); Travel time to work: 16.7% less than 15 minutes, 36.5% 15 to 30 minutes, 27.6% 30 to 45 minutes, 10.9% 45 to 60 minutes, 8.2% 60 minutes or more (2000)

Additional Information Contacts

Davenport Chamber of Commerce . . . . (863) 422-3975

DUNDEE (town). Covers a land area of 3.931 square miles and a water area of 0.380 square miles. Located at 28.02° N. Lat.; 81.62° W. Long. Elevation is 175 feet.
History: Dundee grew as a community of citrus growers, whose groves are in the surrounding area.
Population: 2,342 (1990); 2,912 (2000); 3,037 (2004); 3,190 (2009 projected); Race: 65.4% White, 25.0% Black, 1.2% Asian, 13.5% Hispanic of any race (2004); Density: 772.5 persons per square mile (2004); Average household size: 2.59 (2004); Median age: 40.6 (2004); Male/female ratio: 92.7 (2004); Marriage status: 18.8% never married, 61.2% now married, 8.7% widowed, 11.3% divorced (2000); Foreign born: 7.2% (2000); Ancestry (includes multiple ancestries): 23.0% Other groups, 11.9% English, 11.4% United States or American, 10.3% Irish, 9.4% German (2000).
Economy: Single-family building permits issued: 35 (2004); Multi-family building permits issued: 0 (2004); Employment by occupation: 5.2% management, 10.1% professional, 20.0% services, 29.1% sales, 4.0% farming, 15.5% construction, 16.1% production (2000).
Income: Per capita income: $15,309 (2004); Median household income: $31,161 (2004); Average household income: $38,566 (2004); Percent of households with income of $100,000 or more: 2.9% (2004); Poverty rate: 12.8% (2000).
Taxes: Total city taxes per capita: $299 (2002); City property taxes per capita: $192 (2002).
Education: Percent of population age 25 and over with: High school diploma (including GED) or higher: 66.8% (2004); Bachelor's degree or higher: 5.3% (2004); Master's degree or higher: 1.1% (2004).

School District(s)

Polk County School District (PK-12)
2002-03 Enrollment: 82,179 . . . . (863) 534-0521
Housing: Homeownership rate: 79.8% (2004); Median home value: $83,771 (2004); Median rent: $343 per month (2000); Median age of housing: 21 years (2000).
Transportation: Commute to work: 96.2% car, 0.0% public transportation, 0.3% walk, 1.2% work from home (2000); Travel time to work: 27.2% less than 15 minutes, 48.8% 15 to 30 minutes, 10.6% 30 to 45 minutes, 6.6% 45 to 60 minutes, 6.8% 60 minutes or more (2000)

EAGLE LAKE (city). Covers a land area of 1.386 square miles and a water area of 0.046 square miles. Located at 27.98° N. Lat.; 81.75° W. Long. Elevation is 172 feet.
Population: 2,025 (1990); 2,496 (2000); 2,567 (2004); 2,609 (2009 projected); Race: 78.2% White, 6.3% Black, 0.3% Asian, 26.1% Hispanic of any race (2004); Density: 1,851.7 persons per square mile (2004); Average household size: 2.86 (2004); Median age: 33.3 (2004); Male/female ratio: 95.8 (2004); Marriage status: 23.0% never married, 58.1% now married, 8.1% widowed, 10.9% divorced (2000); Foreign born: 15.9% (2000); Ancestry (includes multiple ancestries): 35.8% Other groups, 16.4% United States or American, 8.7% German, 7.5% English, 6.9% Irish (2000).
Economy: Single-family building permits issued: 4 (2004); Multi-family building permits issued: 0 (2004); Employment by occupation: 6.4% management, 12.1% professional, 14.5% services, 20.2% sales, 8.2% farming, 17.1% construction, 21.5% production (2000).
Income: Per capita income: $14,430 (2004); Median household income: $32,405 (2004); Average household income: $41,044 (2004); Percent of households with income of $100,000 or more: 4.1% (2004); Poverty rate: 17.9% (2000).
Education: Percent of population age 25 and over with: High school diploma (including GED) or higher: 61.0% (2004); Bachelor's degree or higher: 8.9% (2004); Master's degree or higher: 3.2% (2004).

School District(s)

Polk County School District (PK-12)
2002-03 Enrollment: 82,179 . . . . (863) 534-0521
Housing: Homeownership rate: 67.6% (2004); Median home value: $75,429 (2004); Median rent: $353 per month (2000); Median age of housing: 28 years (2000).
Safety: Violent crime rate: 67.3 per 10,000 population; Property crime rate: 178.2 per 10,000 population (2003).
Transportation: Commute to work: 91.8% car, 0.7% public transportation, 5.1% walk, 1.5% work from home (2000); Travel time to work: 34.7% less than 15 minutes, 33.1% 15 to 30 minutes, 23.4% 30 to 45 minutes, 4.1% 45 to 60 minutes, 4.7% 60 minutes or more (2000)

Additional Information Contacts

Eagle Lake Chamber of Commerce. . . . . (979) 234-2780

FORT MEADE (city). Covers a land area of 4.975 square miles and a water area of 0.047 square miles. Located at 27.75° N. Lat.; 81.79° W. Long. Elevation is 129 feet.
History: The original Fort Meade was a military post built on the banks of the Peace River during the Seminole War, and named for Lieutenant George Gordon Meade, later acclaimed in the battle of Gettysburg. Stonewall Jackson was stationed at Fort Meade in 1851. The settlement here became a trading post with a traffic in alligator hides, with an order in 1881 for 5,000 hides from a Paris leather firm.
Population: 5,323 (1990); 5,691 (2000); 5,746 (2004); 5,866 (2009 projected); Race: 65.6% White, 23.2% Black, 0.1% Asian, 18.8% Hispanic of any race (2004); Density: 1,154.9 persons per square mile (2004); Average household size: 2.76 (2004); Median age: 35.4 (2004); Male/female ratio: 95.4 (2004); Marriage status: 23.6% never married, 54.7% now married, 10.4% widowed, 11.3% divorced (2000); Foreign born: 10.5% (2000); Ancestry (includes multiple ancestries): 35.0% Other groups, 15.6% United States or American, 6.6% Irish, 5.6% English, 4.9% German (2000).
Economy: Single-family building permits issued: 11 (2004); Multi-family building permits issued: 0 (2004); Employment by occupation: 9.0% management, 10.0% professional, 13.7% services, 25.0% sales, 3.4% farming, 16.5% construction, 22.4% production (2000).
Income: Per capita income: $16,469 (2004); Median household income: $34,985 (2004); Average household income: $45,134 (2004); Percent of households with income of $100,000 or more: 6.2% (2004); Poverty rate: 18.3% (2000).
Education: Percent of population age 25 and over with: High school diploma (including GED) or higher: 68.2% (2004); Bachelor's degree or higher: 6.0% (2004); Master's degree or higher: 2.2% (2004).

School District(s)

Polk County School District (PK-12)
2002-03 Enrollment: 82,179 . . . . (863) 534-0521
Housing: Homeownership rate: 74.0% (2004); Median home value: $71,234 (2004); Median rent: $303 per month (2000); Median age of housing: 31 years (2000).
Safety: Violent crime rate: 38.0 per 10,000 population; Property crime rate: 320.9 per 10,000 population (2003).
Newspapers: The Fort Meade Leader (General - Circulation 1,394)
Transportation: Commute to work: 95.3% car, 0.4% public transportation, 0.4% walk, 0.0% work from home (2000); Travel time to work: 29.8% less than 15 minutes, 28.4% 15 to 30 minutes, 21.1% 30 to 45 minutes, 10.8% 45 to 60 minutes, 9.9% 60 minutes or more (2000)

Additional Information Contacts

Fort Meade Chamber of Commerce . . . . (863) 285-8253
Local Government Offices . . . . (863) 285-1100

FROSTPROOF (city). Covers a land area of 2.486 square miles and a water area of 0.004 square miles. Located at 27.74° N. Lat.; 81.53° W. Long. Elevation is 102 feet.

History: Frostproof was named by early settlers who hoped that frost would never damage their citrus crops. Such was not the case, but the town grew around citrus packing and canning plants.
Population: 2,825 (1990); 2,975 (2000); 2,960 (2004); 3,031 (2009 projected); Race: 74.1% White, 4.7% Black, 0.0% Asian, 25.8% Hispanic of any race (2004); Density: 1,190.7 persons per square mile (2004); Average household size: 2.69 (2004); Median age: 34.9 (2004); Male/female ratio: 102.3 (2004); Marriage status: 22.8% never married, 60.0% now married, 7.4% widowed, 9.8% divorced (2000); Foreign born: 13.2% (2000); Ancestry (includes multiple ancestries): 30.6% Other groups, 17.6% United States or American, 8.0% English, 7.9% German, 6.7% Irish (2000).
Economy: Single-family building permits issued: 5 (2004); Multi-family building permits issued: 0 (2004); Employment by occupation: 7.9% management, 10.2% professional, 14.4% services, 30.1% sales, 7.1% farming, 11.1% construction, 19.2% production (2000).
Income: Per capita income: $16,932 (2004); Median household income: $33,497 (2004); Average household income: $45,481 (2004); Percent of households with income of $100,000 or more: 6.3% (2004); Poverty rate: 16.8% (2000).
Taxes: Total city taxes per capita: $215 (2002); City property taxes per capita: $215 (2002).
Education: Percent of population age 25 and over with: High school diploma (including GED) or higher: 62.7% (2004); Bachelor's degree or higher: 10.4% (2004); Master's degree or higher: 4.2% (2004).

School District(s)

Polk County School District (PK-12)
2002-03 Enrollment: 82,179 . . . . (863) 534-0521

Housing: Homeownership rate: 68.1% (2004); Median home value: $67,647 (2004); Median rent: $334 per month (2000); Median age of housing: 27 years (2000).
Safety: Violent crime rate: 30.1 per 10,000 population; Property crime rate: 454.7 per 10,000 population (2003).
Transportation: Commute to work: 92.1% car, 0.6% public transportation, 3.6% walk, 3.3% work from home (2000); Travel time to work: 45.0% less than 15 minutes, 15.1% 15 to 30 minutes, 23.0% 30 to 45 minutes, 7.7% 45 to 60 minutes, 9.2% 60 minutes or more (2000)

Additional Information Contacts

Frostproof Chamber of Commerce . . . . (863) 635-9112

FUSSELS CORNER (CDP). Covers a land area of 7.058 square miles and a water area of 0 square miles. Located at 28.06° N. Lat.; 81.85° W. Long.
Population: 4,329 (1990); 5,313 (2000); 5,805 (2004); 6,408 (2009 projected); Race: 88.2% White, 5.1% Black, 0.1% Asian, 6.7% Hispanic of any race (2004); Density: 822.4 persons per square mile (2004); Average household size: 2.33 (2004); Median age: 47.4 (2004); Male/female ratio: 99.6 (2004); Marriage status: 15.6% never married, 65.7% now married, 8.6% widowed, 10.0% divorced (2000); Foreign born: 6.5% (2000); Ancestry (includes multiple ancestries): 16.2% Other groups, 14.9% English, 13.4% German, 11.9% Irish, 9.6% United States or American (2000).
Economy: Employment by occupation: 5.6% management, 10.5% professional, 17.4% services, 30.9% sales, 0.8% farming, 12.0% construction, 22.8% production (2000).
Income: Per capita income: $21,006 (2004); Median household income: $38,883 (2004); Average household income: $49,011 (2004); Percent of households with income of $100,000 or more: 7.3% (2004); Poverty rate: 13.7% (2000).
Education: Percent of population age 25 and over with: High school diploma (including GED) or higher: 69.3% (2004); Bachelor's degree or higher: 11.3% (2004); Master's degree or higher: 3.9% (2004).
Housing: Homeownership rate: 82.9% (2004); Median home value: $70,021 (2004); Median rent: $325 per month (2000); Median age of housing: 10 years (2000).
Transportation: Commute to work: 95.5% car, 0.5% public transportation, 1.9% walk, 1.3% work from home (2000); Travel time to work: 26.0% less than 15 minutes, 45.5% 15 to 30 minutes, 17.5% 30 to 45 minutes, 5.1% 45 to 60 minutes, 5.8% 60 minutes or more (2000)

GIBSONIA (CDP). Covers a land area of 2.578 square miles and a water area of 0.648 square miles. Located at 28.11° N. Lat.; 81.97° W. Long. Elevation is 175 feet.
Population: 4,542 (1990); 4,507 (2000); 5,042 (2004); 5,686 (2009 projected); Race: 91.9% White, 3.5% Black, 0.8% Asian, 8.0% Hispanic of any race (2004); Density: 1,955.5 persons per square mile (2004); Average household size: 2.53 (2004); Median age: 39.3 (2004); Male/female ratio: 95.0 (2004); Marriage status: 18.8% never married, 63.0% now married, 6.6% widowed, 11.6% divorced (2000); Foreign born: 5.1% (2000); Ancestry (includes multiple ancestries): 21.0% Other groups, 14.8% German, 14.2% United States or American, 13.2% Irish, 8.2% English (2000).
Economy: Employment by occupation: 11.3% management, 13.2% professional, 17.3% services, 31.8% sales, 0.3% farming, 13.6% construction, 12.5% production (2000).
Income: Per capita income: $20,281 (2004); Median household income: $42,438 (2004); Average household income: $50,576 (2004); Percent of households with income of $100,000 or more: 7.7% (2004); Poverty rate: 10.6% (2000).
Education: Percent of population age 25 and over with: High school diploma (including GED) or higher: 83.9% (2004); Bachelor's degree or higher: 15.4% (2004); Master's degree or higher: 4.7% (2004).
Housing: Homeownership rate: 76.2% (2004); Median home value: $106,633 (2004); Median rent: $457 per month (2000); Median age of housing: 23 years (2000).
Transportation: Commute to work: 89.6% car, 0.5% public transportation, 2.1% walk, 5.3% work from home (2000); Travel time to work: 31.6% less than 15 minutes, 38.4% 15 to 30 minutes, 15.8% 30 to 45 minutes, 6.4% 45 to 60 minutes, 7.8% 60 minutes or more (2000)

HAINES CITY (city). Covers a land area of 8.292 square miles and a water area of 0.646 square miles. Located at 28.11° N. Lat.; 81.62° W. Long. Elevation is 200 feet.
History: First called Clay Cut, the community adopted the name of Haines City in 1887, in honor of Henry Haines. After this honor, Haines, a South Florida Railroad official, arranged for the railroad to erect a station here.
Population: 11,063 (1990); 13,174 (2000); 14,379 (2004); 15,808 (2009 projected); Race: 51.1% White, 33.8% Black, 0.4% Asian, 26.6% Hispanic of any race (2004); Density: 1,734.1 persons per square mile (2004); Average household size: 2.78 (2004); Median age: 35.8 (2004); Male/female ratio: 95.6 (2004); Marriage status: 22.8% never married, 57.3% now married, 9.1% widowed, 10.7% divorced (2000); Foreign born: 18.1% (2000); Ancestry (includes multiple ancestries): 47.6% Other groups, 8.8% German, 8.7% United States or American, 5.7% English, 4.9% Irish (2000).
Economy: Single-family building permits issued: 769 (2004); Multi-family building permits issued: 0 (2004); Employment by occupation: 5.4% management, 10.2% professional, 31.0% services, 21.9% sales, 5.1% farming, 12.2% construction, 14.1% production (2000).
Income: Per capita income: $14,617 (2004); Median household income: $29,807 (2004); Average household income: $40,355 (2004); Percent of households with income of $100,000 or more: 4.8% (2004); Poverty rate: 18.6% (2000).
Taxes: Total city taxes per capita: $389 (2002); City property taxes per capita: $176 (2002).
Education: Percent of population age 25 and over with: High school diploma (including GED) or higher: 59.4% (2004); Bachelor's degree or higher: 8.8% (2004); Master's degree or higher: 2.8% (2004).

School District(s)

Polk County School District (PK-12)
2002-03 Enrollment: 82,179 . . . . (863) 534-0521

Housing: Homeownership rate: 65.3% (2004); Median home value: $70,800 (2004); Median rent: $361 per month (2000); Median age of housing: 22 years (2000).
Safety: Violent crime rate: 65.9 per 10,000 population; Property crime rate: 871.8 per 10,000 population (2003).
Transportation: Commute to work: 91.6% car, 1.5% public transportation, 2.8% walk, 1.9% work from home (2000); Travel time to work: 28.3% less than 15 minutes, 26.1% 15 to 30 minutes, 32.1% 30 to 45 minutes, 6.8% 45 to 60 minutes, 6.6% 60 minutes or more (2000)

Additional Information Contacts

Dundee Area Chamber of Commerce . . . . (863) 439-3261
Haines City Chamber of Commerce . . . . (863) 422-3751

HIGHLAND CITY (CDP). Aka Highlands City. Covers a land area of 0.829 square miles and a water area of 0 square miles. Located at 27.96° N. Lat.; 81.87° W. Long. Elevation is 120 feet.
Population: 1,919 (1990); 2,051 (2000); 1,929 (2004); 1,787 (2009 projected); Race: 80.0% White, 13.4% Black, 0.9% Asian, 16.1% Hispanic of any race (2004); Density: 2,327.5 persons per square mile (2004); Average household size: 2.68 (2004); Median age: 30.7 (2004);

Male/female ratio: 92.3 (2004); Marriage status: 23.6% never married, 57.1% now married, 4.7% widowed, 14.6% divorced (2000); Foreign born: 1.8% (2000); Ancestry (includes multiple ancestries): 26.1% Other groups, 11.2% United States or American, 11.1% German, 10.6% Irish, 9.1% English (2000).
Economy: Manufacturing includes metal fabrication, fresh fruit processing; mailboxes, powder coatings. Employment by occupation: 5.3% management, 15.4% professional, 16.5% services, 39.6% sales, 0.0% farming, 9.3% construction, 14.0% production (2000).
Income: Per capita income: $14,557 (2004); Median household income: $34,664 (2004); Average household income: $39,000 (2004); Percent of households with income of $100,000 or more: 3.5% (2004); Poverty rate: 13.5% (2000).
Education: Percent of population age 25 and over with: High school diploma (including GED) or higher: 78.8% (2004); Bachelor's degree or higher: 5.1% (2004); Master's degree or higher: 2.2% (2004).

School District(s)

Polk County School District (PK-12)
2002-03 Enrollment: 82,179 . . . . (863) 534-0521
Housing: Homeownership rate: 64.2% (2004); Median home value: $77,372 (2004); Median rent: $358 per month (2000); Median age of housing: 19 years (2000).
Transportation: Commute to work: 93.8% car, 0.0% public transportation, 0.8% walk, 4.2% work from home (2000); Travel time to work: 33.0% less than 15 minutes, 41.5% 15 to 30 minutes, 18.6% 30 to 45 minutes, 0.9% 45 to 60 minutes, 6.0% 60 minutes or more (2000)

HIGHLAND PARK (village). Covers a land area of 0.448 square miles and a water area of 0.271 square miles. Located at 27.86° N. Lat.; 81.56° W. Long. Elevation is 115 feet.
Population: 155 (1990); 244 (2000); 246 (2004); 246 (2009 projected); Race: 92.7% White, 0.8% Black, 4.9% Asian, 0.8% Hispanic of any race (2004); Density: 548.6 persons per square mile (2004); Average household size: 2.14 (2004); Median age: 50.6 (2004); Male/female ratio: 90.7 (2004); Marriage status: 9.7% never married, 71.9% now married, 7.6% widowed, 10.8% divorced (2000); Foreign born: 3.8% (2000); Ancestry (includes multiple ancestries): 25.4% German, 19.9% English, 13.6% Scottish, 13.1% Irish, 9.3% Other groups (2000).
Economy: Employment by occupation: 17.3% management, 30.9% professional, 11.1% services, 23.5% sales, 0.0% farming, 3.7% construction, 13.6% production (2000).
Income: Per capita income: $33,252 (2004); Median household income: $44,886 (2004); Average household income: $71,130 (2004); Percent of households with income of $100,000 or more: 16.5% (2004); Poverty rate: 3.9% (2000).
Education: Percent of population age 25 and over with: High school diploma (including GED) or higher: 93.0% (2004); Bachelor's degree or higher: 42.2% (2004); Master's degree or higher: 18.9% (2004).
Housing: Homeownership rate: 86.1% (2004); Median home value: $108,333 (2004); Median rent: $567 per month (2000); Median age of housing: 29 years (2000).
Transportation: Commute to work: 87.7% car, 0.0% public transportation, 0.0% walk, 9.9% work from home (2000); Travel time to work: 45.2% less than 15 minutes, 32.9% 15 to 30 minutes, 6.8% 30 to 45 minutes, 2.7% 45 to 60 minutes, 12.3% 60 minutes or more (2000)

HILLCREST HEIGHTS (town). Covers a land area of 0.162 square miles and a water area of 0 square miles. Located at 27.82° N. Lat.; 81.53° W. Long. Elevation is 241 feet.
Population: 221 (1990); 266 (2000); 332 (2004); 408 (2009 projected); Race: 96.1% White, 2.1% Black, 0.9% Asian, 2.4% Hispanic of any race (2004); Density: 2,047.2 persons per square mile (2004); Average household size: 2.70 (2004); Median age: 40.1 (2004); Male/female ratio: 93.0 (2004); Marriage status: 15.1% never married, 70.7% now married, 5.9% widowed, 8.3% divorced (2000); Foreign born: 3.3% (2000); Ancestry (includes multiple ancestries): 26.2% English, 24.4% German, 10.7% Irish, 9.2% United States or American, 7.0% French (except Basque) (2000).
Economy: Employment by occupation: 23.0% management, 23.8% professional, 12.7% services, 24.6% sales, 0.8% farming, 10.3% construction, 4.8% production (2000).
Income: Per capita income: $27,538 (2004); Median household income: $65,878 (2004); Average household income: $74,329 (2004); Percent of households with income of $100,000 or more: 13.8% (2004); Poverty rate: 1.5% (2000).
Education: Percent of population age 25 and over with: High school diploma (including GED) or higher: 88.4% (2004); Bachelor's degree or higher: 25.9% (2004); Master's degree or higher: 10.7% (2004).
Housing: Homeownership rate: 88.6% (2004); Median home value: $132,692 (2004); Median rent: $420 per month (2000); Median age of housing: 40 years (2000).
Transportation: Commute to work: 99.2% car, 0.0% public transportation, 0.0% walk, 0.0% work from home (2000); Travel time to work: 30.6% less than 15 minutes, 52.4% 15 to 30 minutes, 7.3% 30 to 45 minutes, 6.5% 45 to 60 minutes, 3.2% 60 minutes or more (2000)

INWOOD (CDP). Aka West Winter Haven. Covers a land area of 1.917 square miles and a water area of 0.088 square miles. Located at 28.03° N. Lat.; 81.76° W. Long. Elevation is 150 feet.
Population: 6,764 (1990); 6,925 (2000); 6,566 (2004); 6,248 (2009 projected); Race: 61.7% White, 29.0% Black, 1.1% Asian, 9.2% Hispanic of any race (2004); Density: 3,424.8 persons per square mile (2004); Average household size: 2.45 (2004); Median age: 34.5 (2004); Male/female ratio: 97.1 (2004); Marriage status: 27.0% never married, 49.3% now married, 9.9% widowed, 13.8% divorced (2000); Foreign born: 9.9% (2000); Ancestry (includes multiple ancestries): 26.1% Other groups, 15.1% United States or American, 10.6% Irish, 7.7% German, 6.5% Haitian (2000).
Economy: Employment by occupation: 5.3% management, 12.0% professional, 24.0% services, 19.9% sales, 1.4% farming, 17.5% construction, 19.8% production (2000).
Income: Per capita income: $13,957 (2004); Median household income: $27,651 (2004); Average household income: $34,181 (2004); Percent of households with income of $100,000 or more: 2.6% (2004); Poverty rate: 19.1% (2000).
Education: Percent of population age 25 and over with: High school diploma (including GED) or higher: 65.2% (2004); Bachelor's degree or higher: 5.6% (2004); Master's degree or higher: 2.3% (2004).
Housing: Homeownership rate: 57.4% (2004); Median home value: $67,756 (2004); Median rent: $398 per month (2000); Median age of housing: 34 years (2000).
Transportation: Commute to work: 94.7% car, 0.3% public transportation, 1.0% walk, 1.6% work from home (2000); Travel time to work: 35.5% less than 15 minutes, 33.1% 15 to 30 minutes, 17.5% 30 to 45 minutes, 10.1% 45 to 60 minutes, 3.8% 60 minutes or more (2000)

JAN PHYL VILLAGE (CDP). Covers a land area of 4.716 square miles and a water area of 0.113 square miles. Located at 28.01° N. Lat.; 81.77° W. Long.
Population: 5,308 (1990); 5,633 (2000); 5,388 (2004); 5,157 (2009 projected); Race: 68.5% White, 23.4% Black, 1.9% Asian, 8.2% Hispanic of any race (2004); Density: 1,142.6 persons per square mile (2004); Average household size: 2.93 (2004); Median age: 33.0 (2004); Male/female ratio: 91.1 (2004); Marriage status: 22.9% never married, 61.5% now married, 6.6% widowed, 9.1% divorced (2000); Foreign born: 6.4% (2000); Ancestry (includes multiple ancestries): 29.4% Other groups, 21.6% United States or American, 10.6% English, 9.4% German, 8.5% Irish (2000).
Economy: Employment by occupation: 9.6% management, 14.4% professional, 13.3% services, 29.9% sales, 0.6% farming, 12.8% construction, 19.4% production (2000).
Income: Per capita income: $18,434 (2004); Median household income: $46,991 (2004); Average household income: $53,921 (2004); Percent of households with income of $100,000 or more: 8.8% (2004); Poverty rate: 8.5% (2000).
Education: Percent of population age 25 and over with: High school diploma (including GED) or higher: 77.2% (2004); Bachelor's degree or higher: 11.5% (2004); Master's degree or higher: 2.9% (2004).
Housing: Homeownership rate: 78.6% (2004); Median home value: $91,097 (2004); Median rent: $411 per month (2000); Median age of housing: 23 years (2000).
Transportation: Commute to work: 95.7% car, 0.0% public transportation, 0.0% walk, 3.5% work from home (2000); Travel time to work: 27.7% less than 15 minutes, 40.5% 15 to 30 minutes, 25.4% 30 to 45 minutes, 3.3% 45 to 60 minutes, 3.0% 60 minutes or more (2000)

KATHLEEN (CDP). Covers a land area of 3.325 square miles and a water area of 0 square miles. Located at 28.12° N. Lat.; 82.02° W. Long. Elevation is 142 feet.
Population: 2,743 (1990); 3,280 (2000); 3,786 (2004); 4,393 (2009 projected); Race: 91.8% White, 2.5% Black, 0.3% Asian, 9.7% Hispanic of any race (2004); Density: 1,138.6 persons per square mile (2004); Average

household size: 2.81 (2004); Median age: 35.7 (2004); Male/female ratio: 98.6 (2004); Marriage status: 20.7% never married, 58.9% now married, 7.2% widowed, 13.2% divorced (2000); Foreign born: 4.9% (2000); Ancestry (includes multiple ancestries): 31.4% United States or American, 14.4% Other groups, 12.2% Irish, 9.7% English, 8.5% German (2000).
Economy: Manufacturing includes cabinets. Employment by occupation: 12.9% management, 12.0% professional, 13.1% services, 26.1% sales, 0.5% farming, 16.2% construction, 19.3% production (2000).
Income: Per capita income: $18,466 (2004); Median household income: $44,756 (2004); Average household income: $51,941 (2004); Percent of households with income of $100,000 or more: 10.1% (2004); Poverty rate: 10.1% (2000).
Education: Percent of population age 25 and over with: High school diploma (including GED) or higher: 68.1% (2004); Bachelor's degree or higher: 7.7% (2004); Master's degree or higher: 3.8% (2004).
Housing: Homeownership rate: 83.3% (2004); Median home value: $88,359 (2004); Median rent: $376 per month (2000); Median age of housing: 18 years (2000).
Transportation: Commute to work: 95.7% car, 0.0% public transportation, 0.0% walk, 2.5% work from home (2000); Travel time to work: 14.3% less than 15 minutes, 52.4% 15 to 30 minutes, 15.4% 30 to 45 minutes, 8.0% 45 to 60 minutes, 9.9% 60 minutes or more (2000)

LAKE ALFRED (city). Covers a land area of 4.902 square miles and a water area of 3.684 square miles. Located at 28.09° N. Lat.; 81.72° W. Long. Elevation is 170 feet.
History: Lake Alfred was named for Alfred Parslow, an early landowner and franchiser for a local railroad. The town grew in an area of citrus groves, and was earlier known as Barton Junction, Chubb, and Fargo.
Population: 3,747 (1990); 3,890 (2000); 3,872 (2004); 3,886 (2009 projected); Race: 76.5% White, 18.7% Black, 0.8% Asian, 7.2% Hispanic of any race (2004); Density: 789.9 persons per square mile (2004); Average household size: 2.58 (2004); Median age: 37.8 (2004); Male/female ratio: 87.8 (2004); Marriage status: 19.2% never married, 62.4% now married, 7.2% widowed, 11.1% divorced (2000); Foreign born: 5.9% (2000); Ancestry (includes multiple ancestries): 25.7% Other groups, 13.7% German, 12.1% English, 12.0% United States or American, 11.7% Irish (2000).
Economy: Single-family building permits issued: 3 (2004); Multi-family building permits issued: 0 (2004); Employment by occupation: 13.6% management, 18.2% professional, 16.3% services, 24.7% sales, 1.7% farming, 11.8% construction, 13.8% production (2000).
Income: Per capita income: $18,960 (2004); Median household income: $38,958 (2004); Average household income: $48,098 (2004); Percent of households with income of $100,000 or more: 6.7% (2004); Poverty rate: 14.0% (2000).
Education: Percent of population age 25 and over with: High school diploma (including GED) or higher: 73.9% (2004); Bachelor's degree or higher: 15.6% (2004); Master's degree or higher: 5.5% (2004).

School District(s)

Polk County School District (PK-12)
2002-03 Enrollment: 82,179 . . . . (863) 534-0521
Housing: Homeownership rate: 72.4% (2004); Median home value: $100,518 (2004); Median rent: $397 per month (2000); Median age of housing: 28 years (2000).
Safety: Violent crime rate: 32.7 per 10,000 population; Property crime rate: 412.6 per 10,000 population (2003).
Transportation: Commute to work: 94.2% car, 0.3% public transportation, 2.3% walk, 1.4% work from home (2000); Travel time to work: 31.1% less than 15 minutes, 32.3% 15 to 30 minutes, 18.3% 30 to 45 minutes, 8.0% 45 to 60 minutes, 10.3% 60 minutes or more (2000)

LAKE HAMILTON (town). Covers a land area of 3.032 square miles and a water area of 0.881 square miles. Located at 28.04° N. Lat.; 81.62° W. Long. Elevation is 125 feet.
History: Lake Hamilton, on the shores of the lake for which it was named, grew around a citrus packing plant.
Population: 1,128 (1990); 1,304 (2000); 1,268 (2004); 1,254 (2009 projected); Race: 68.1% White, 27.1% Black, 0.4% Asian, 5.9% Hispanic of any race (2004); Density: 418.2 persons per square mile (2004); Average household size: 2.71 (2004); Median age: 38.9 (2004); Male/female ratio: 91.8 (2004); Marriage status: 23.9% never married, 63.2% now married, 6.5% widowed, 6.5% divorced (2000); Foreign born: 3.1% (2000); Ancestry (includes multiple ancestries): 36.1% Other groups, 10.2% English, 10.0% United States or American, 9.0% Irish, 8.4% German (2000).
Economy: Single-family building permits issued: 7 (2004); Multi-family building permits issued: 0 (2004); Employment by occupation: 9.9% management, 12.8% professional, 19.5% services, 18.3% sales, 4.1% farming, 16.6% construction, 18.9% production (2000).
Income: Per capita income: $17,701 (2004); Median household income: $34,398 (2004); Average household income: $44,685 (2004); Percent of households with income of $100,000 or more: 6.2% (2004); Poverty rate: 21.5% (2000).
Taxes: Total city taxes per capita: $339 (2002); City property taxes per capita: $181 (2002).
Education: Percent of population age 25 and over with: High school diploma (including GED) or higher: 66.0% (2004); Bachelor's degree or higher: 12.1% (2004); Master's degree or higher: 4.0% (2004).
Housing: Homeownership rate: 75.2% (2004); Median home value: $104,301 (2004); Median rent: $355 per month (2000); Median age of housing: 33 years (2000).
Safety: Violent crime rate: 80.1 per 10,000 population; Property crime rate: 982.5 per 10,000 population (2003).
Transportation: Commute to work: 96.5% car, 1.4% public transportation, 0.6% walk, 0.6% work from home (2000); Travel time to work: 22.9% less than 15 minutes, 38.0% 15 to 30 minutes, 25.8% 30 to 45 minutes, 7.1% 45 to 60 minutes, 6.2% 60 minutes or more (2000)

LAKE WALES (city). Covers a land area of 13.345 square miles and a water area of 0.665 square miles. Located at 27.90° N. Lat.; 81.58° W. Long. Elevation is 147 feet.
History: Lake Wales grew as a resort town on the lake of the same name. The name was originally Waels, for the Waels familly who settled here in the early 1900's. The spelling was changed when the town was platted in 1911.
Population: 10,130 (1990); 10,194 (2000); 10,560 (2004); 11,086 (2009 projected); Race: 56.6% White, 36.8% Black, 0.6% Asian, 11.8% Hispanic of any race (2004); Density: 791.3 persons per square mile (2004); Average household size: 2.53 (2004); Median age: 37.0 (2004); Male/female ratio: 88.9 (2004); Marriage status: 24.7% never married, 49.7% now married, 13.2% widowed, 12.4% divorced (2000); Foreign born: 7.9% (2000); Ancestry (includes multiple ancestries): 38.2% Other groups, 11.2% United States or American, 8.6% English, 7.8% German, 7.7% Irish (2000).
Economy: Single-family building permits issued: 290 (2004); Multi-family building permits issued: 284 (2004); Employment by occupation: 6.6% management, 18.3% professional, 17.8% services, 23.7% sales, 8.3% farming, 9.0% construction, 16.3% production (2000).
Income: Per capita income: $17,419 (2004); Median household income: $29,037 (2004); Average household income: $42,770 (2004); Percent of households with income of $100,000 or more: 7.1% (2004); Poverty rate: 21.4% (2000).
Taxes: Total city taxes per capita: $543 (2002); City property taxes per capita: $234 (2002).
Education: Percent of population age 25 and over with: High school diploma (including GED) or higher: 73.3% (2004); Bachelor's degree or higher: 18.2% (2004); Master's degree or higher: 6.3% (2004).

School District(s)

Polk County School District (PK-12)
2002-03 Enrollment: 82,179 . . . . (863) 534-0521

Four-year College(s)

Warner Southern College
2003-04 Enrollment: 989 . . . . (863) 638-1426
2003-04 Tuition: In-state $11,290; Out-of-state $11,290
Housing: Homeownership rate: 53.8% (2004); Median home value: $91,273 (2004); Median rent: $325 per month (2000); Median age of housing: 28 years (2000).
Hospitals: Lakes Wales Medical Center (154 beds)
Safety: Violent crime rate: 75.6 per 10,000 population; Property crime rate: 805.6 per 10,000 population (2003).
Newspapers: The Lake Wales News (General - Circulation 3,200)
Transportation: Commute to work: 90.7% car, 1.5% public transportation, 3.1% walk, 3.4% work from home (2000); Travel time to work: 44.8% less than 15 minutes, 23.6% 15 to 30 minutes, 15.5% 30 to 45 minutes, 8.0% 45 to 60 minutes, 7.9% 60 minutes or more (2000)

Additional Information Contacts

Lake Wales Association of Realtors . . . . (863) 676-1721
Lake Wales Chamber of Commerce . . . . (863) 676-3445

LAKELAND (city). Covers a land area of 45.842 square miles and a water area of 5.610 square miles. Located at 28.04° N. Lat.; 81.95° W. Long. Elevation is 190 feet.

History: Lakeland began when the South Florida Railroad was built here in 1884, and the town was incorporated in 1885. In 1894 Lakeland absorbed the town of Acton, established nearby by a group of Englishmen and named for British historian Lord Acton. Lakeland grew as the headquarters of the Florida Citrus Commission, and the location of many citrus producing and shipping companies.

Population: 73,375 (1990); 78,452 (2000); 82,714 (2004); 88,319 (2009 projected); Race: 71.7% White, 22.5% Black, 1.5% Asian, 7.4% Hispanic of any race (2004); Density: 1,804.3 persons per square mile (2004); Average household size: 2.33 (2004); Median age: 40.2 (2004); Male/female ratio: 86.6 (2004); Marriage status: 24.0% never married, 52.9% now married, 10.6% widowed, 12.5% divorced (2000); Foreign born: 5.7% (2000); Ancestry (includes multiple ancestries): 29.4% Other groups, 12.5% German, 11.1% English, 10.3% Irish, 9.9% United States or American (2000).

Economy: Unemployment rate: 5.4% (2004); Total civilian labor force: 39,164 (2004); Single-family building permits issued: 389 (2004); Multi-family building permits issued: 32 (2004); Employment by occupation: 11.3% management, 19.5% professional, 16.9% services, 28.6% sales, 0.4% farming, 7.6% construction, 15.7% production (2000).

Income: Per capita income: $21,257 (2004); Median household income: $35,696 (2004); Average household income: $48,538 (2004); Percent of households with income of $100,000 or more: 8.3% (2004); Poverty rate: 15.0% (2000).

Taxes: Total city taxes per capita: $364 (2002); City property taxes per capita: $135 (2002).

Education: Percent of population age 25 and over with: High school diploma (including GED) or higher: 79.5% (2004); Bachelor's degree or higher: 21.1% (2004); Master's degree or higher: 7.6% (2004).

School District(s)

Polk County School District (PK-12)
  2002-03 Enrollment: 82,179 . . . . (863) 534-0521

Four-year College(s)

Florida Metropolitan University-Lakeland (Private, For-profit)
  2003-04 Enrollment: 981 . . . . (863) 686-1444
  2003-04 Tuition: In-state $8,460; Out-of-state $8,460
Florida Southern College
  2003-04 Enrollment: 2,490 . . . . (863) 680-4111
  2003-04 Tuition: In-state $17,542; Out-of-state $17,542
Southeastern College Assemblies of God
  2003-04 Enrollment: 1,675 . . . . (863) 667-5000
  2003-04 Tuition: In-state $9,120; Out-of-state $9,120

Two-year College(s)

Florida Career Institute Inc (Private, For-profit)
  2003-04 Enrollment: 171 . . . . (863) 646-1400
  2003-04 Tuition: In-state $13,250; Out-of-state $13,250
Keiser College-Lakeland (Private, For-profit)
  2003-04 Enrollment: n/a . . . . (863) 701-7789
  2003-04 Tuition: In-state $10,920; Out-of-state $10,920
Travis Technical Center (Public)
  2003-04 Enrollment: 767 . . . . (863) 499-2700
  2003-04 Tuition: In-state $1,733; Out-of-state $7,200

Housing: Homeownership rate: 60.7% (2004); Median home value: $94,537 (2004); Median rent: $423 per month (2000); Median age of housing: 25 years (2000).

Hospitals: Lakeland Regional Medical Center (851 beds)

Safety: Violent crime rate: 58.8 per 10,000 population; Property crime rate: 588.6 per 10,000 population (2003).

Newspapers: The Ledger (Circulation 75,140)

Transportation: Commute to work: 91.9% car, 1.8% public transportation, 2.7% walk, 2.2% work from home (2000); Travel time to work: 37.1% less than 15 minutes, 39.4% 15 to 30 minutes, 13.0% 30 to 45 minutes, 5.3% 45 to 60 minutes, 5.2% 60 minutes or more (2000); Amtrak: Service available.

Airports: Lakeland Linder Regional

Additional Information Contacts

Lakeland Association of Realtors. (863) 687-6111
Lakeland Chamber of Commerce . . . . (863) 688-8551
Lakeland Economic Development Council . . . . (863) 687-3788

LAKELAND HIGHLANDS (CDP). Covers a land area of 5.584 square miles and a water area of 0.574 square miles. Located at 27.96° N. Lat.; 81.94° W. Long.

Population: 9,972 (1990); 12,557 (2000); 12,970 (2004); 13,559 (2009 projected); Race: 93.3% White, 3.2% Black, 1.7% Asian, 4.0% Hispanic of any race (2004); Density: 2,322.7 persons per square mile (2004); Average household size: 2.79 (2004); Median age: 40.6 (2004); Male/female ratio: 94.8 (2004); Marriage status: 17.3% never married, 70.9% now married, 5.8% widowed, 6.1% divorced (2000); Foreign born: 6.2% (2000); Ancestry (includes multiple ancestries): 17.3% German, 15.2% United States or American, 13.3% Irish, 13.3% English, 12.5% Other groups (2000).

Economy: Employment by occupation: 19.2% management, 30.4% professional, 10.1% services, 25.3% sales, 0.0% farming, 7.6% construction, 7.5% production (2000).

Income: Per capita income: $36,100 (2004); Median household income: $72,481 (2004); Average household income: $100,529 (2004); Percent of households with income of $100,000 or more: 30.4% (2004); Poverty rate: 3.3% (2000).

Education: Percent of population age 25 and over with: High school diploma (including GED) or higher: 93.0% (2004); Bachelor's degree or higher: 40.1% (2004); Master's degree or higher: 15.8% (2004).

Housing: Homeownership rate: 92.4% (2004); Median home value: $163,980 (2004); Median rent: $582 per month (2000); Median age of housing: 18 years (2000).

Transportation: Commute to work: 96.9% car, 0.0% public transportation, 0.1% walk, 2.3% work from home (2000); Travel time to work: 22.7% less than 15 minutes, 54.3% 15 to 30 minutes, 13.0% 30 to 45 minutes, 4.9% 45 to 60 minutes, 5.1% 60 minutes or more (2000)

LOUGHMAN (CDP). Covers a land area of 3.723 square miles and a water area of 0.046 square miles. Located at 28.24° N. Lat.; 81.56° W. Long. Elevation is 101 feet.

Population: 1,239 (1990); 1,385 (2000); 1,640 (2004); 1,954 (2009 projected); Race: 82.6% White, 10.5% Black, 0.6% Asian, 13.2% Hispanic of any race (2004); Density: 440.5 persons per square mile (2004); Average household size: 2.52 (2004); Median age: 37.6 (2004); Male/female ratio: 93.6 (2004); Marriage status: 26.4% never married, 56.8% now married, 7.3% widowed, 9.5% divorced (2000); Foreign born: 8.5% (2000); Ancestry (includes multiple ancestries): 28.3% Other groups, 17.3% German, 15.7% United States or American, 13.3% Irish, 8.4% English (2000).

Economy: Employment by occupation: 10.0% management, 12.1% professional, 25.4% services, 17.3% sales, 0.0% farming, 21.7% construction, 13.5% production (2000).

Income: Per capita income: $16,046 (2004); Median household income: $36,636 (2004); Average household income: $40,360 (2004); Percent of households with income of $100,000 or more: 6.1% (2004); Poverty rate: 18.0% (2000).

Education: Percent of population age 25 and over with: High school diploma (including GED) or higher: 66.0% (2004); Bachelor's degree or higher: 16.2% (2004); Master's degree or higher: 4.0% (2004).

Housing: Homeownership rate: 78.5% (2004); Median home value: $53,462 (2004); Median rent: $244 per month (2000); Median age of housing: 9 years (2000).

Transportation: Commute to work: 91.7% car, 0.0% public transportation, 1.6% walk, 4.0% work from home (2000); Travel time to work: 14.2% less than 15 minutes, 60.1% 15 to 30 minutes, 12.5% 30 to 45 minutes, 9.6% 45 to 60 minutes, 3.6% 60 minutes or more (2000)

MEDULLA (CDP). Covers a land area of 5.676 square miles and a water area of 0.018 square miles. Located at 27.96° N. Lat.; 81.98° W. Long. Elevation is 150 feet.

Population: 3,977 (1990); 6,637 (2000); 7,145 (2004); 7,789 (2009 projected); Race: 82.6% White, 12.9% Black, 0.7% Asian, 6.3% Hispanic of any race (2004); Density: 1,258.8 persons per square mile (2004); Average household size: 2.59 (2004); Median age: 33.9 (2004); Male/female ratio: 99.2 (2004); Marriage status: 25.1% never married, 61.6% now married, 4.0% widowed, 9.2% divorced (2000); Foreign born: 3.3% (2000); Ancestry (includes multiple ancestries): 17.8% United States or American, 17.2% Other groups, 12.7% German, 12.2% Irish, 8.7% English (2000).

Economy: Employment by occupation: 16.6% management, 20.7% professional, 14.6% services, 25.0% sales, 0.2% farming, 10.0% construction, 12.9% production (2000).

Income: Per capita income: $23,498 (2004); Median household income: $48,594 (2004); Average household income: $60,605 (2004); Percent of households with income of $100,000 or more: 13.8% (2004); Poverty rate: 6.0% (2000).
Education: Percent of population age 25 and over with: High school diploma (including GED) or higher: 87.5% (2004); Bachelor's degree or higher: 20.5% (2004); Master's degree or higher: 6.4% (2004).
Housing: Homeownership rate: 63.9% (2004); Median home value: $134,949 (2004); Median rent: $493 per month (2000); Median age of housing: 14 years (2000).
Transportation: Commute to work: 92.7% car, 0.7% public transportation, 0.8% walk, 4.1% work from home (2000); Travel time to work: 27.9% less than 15 minutes, 42.8% 15 to 30 minutes, 18.6% 30 to 45 minutes, 6.6% 45 to 60 minutes, 4.2% 60 minutes or more (2000)

MULBERRY (city). Covers a land area of 3.067 square miles and a water area of 0.141 square miles. Located at 27.89° N. Lat.; 81.97° W. Long. Elevation is 110 feet.
History: Mulberry grew up around a railroad loading station noted for a large mulberry tree growing beside the tracks where freight was unloaded. Pebble phosphate was mined here, and for several decades in the late 1800's and early 1900's Mulberry resembled a gold-mining town of the west.
Population: 3,084 (1990); 3,230 (2000); 3,547 (2004); 3,904 (2009 projected); Race: 77.2% White, 19.0% Black, 0.3% Asian, 5.2% Hispanic of any race (2004); Density: 1,156.7 persons per square mile (2004); Average household size: 2.40 (2004); Median age: 41.9 (2004); Male/female ratio: 92.8 (2004); Marriage status: 16.7% never married, 58.6% now married, 12.9% widowed, 11.8% divorced (2000); Foreign born: 3.6% (2000); Ancestry (includes multiple ancestries): 28.0% Other groups, 16.3% United States or American, 11.6% German, 10.2% English, 9.6% Irish (2000).
Economy: Single-family building permits issued: 8 (2004); Multi-family building permits issued: 0 (2004); Employment by occupation: 6.5% management, 14.4% professional, 15.7% services, 23.0% sales, 7.9% farming, 14.4% construction, 18.0% production (2000).
Income: Per capita income: $17,278 (2004); Median household income: $31,973 (2004); Average household income: $41,381 (2004); Percent of households with income of $100,000 or more: 4.7% (2004); Poverty rate: 16.6% (2000).
Taxes: Total city taxes per capita: $537 (2002); City property taxes per capita: $250 (2002).
Education: Percent of population age 25 and over with: High school diploma (including GED) or higher: 72.3% (2004); Bachelor's degree or higher: 7.2% (2004); Master's degree or higher: 2.0% (2004).

School District(s)

Polk County School District (PK-12)
2002-03 Enrollment: 82,179 . . . . (863) 534-0521

Four-year College(s)

Spurgeon Baptist Bible College
2003-04 Enrollment: 25 . . . . (863) 425-3429
2003-04 Tuition: In-state $7,200; Out-of-state $7,200

Housing: Homeownership rate: 75.5% (2004); Median home value: $61,306 (2004); Median rent: $340 per month (2000); Median age of housing: 20 years (2000).
Safety: Violent crime rate: 101.0 per 10,000 population; Property crime rate: 523.3 per 10,000 population (2003).
Newspapers: Polk County Press-Mulberry Edition (General - Circulation 3,000)
Transportation: Commute to work: 96.1% car, 0.0% public transportation, 0.6% walk, 1.8% work from home (2000); Travel time to work: 25.5% less than 15 minutes, 32.9% 15 to 30 minutes, 22.8% 30 to 45 minutes, 7.6% 45 to 60 minutes, 11.1% 60 minutes or more (2000)
Additional Information Contacts
Greater Mulberry Chamber of Commerce . . . . (863) 425-4414

POLK CITY (town). Covers a land area of 0.771 square miles and a water area of 0 square miles. Located at 28.18° N. Lat.; 81.82° W. Long. Elevation is 173 feet.
History: Polk City was founded in 1922 by Isasac Van Horn on the northern shore of Lake Agnes, one of many small lakes in the area.
Population: 1,493 (1990); 1,516 (2000); 1,608 (2004); 1,696 (2009 projected); Race: 93.3% White, 2.2% Black, 0.4% Asian, 10.3% Hispanic of any race (2004); Density: 2,085.5 persons per square mile (2004); Average household size: 2.77 (2004); Median age: 33.5 (2004); Male/female ratio: 97.3 (2004); Marriage status: 16.2% never married, 59.9% now married, 7.1% widowed, 16.8% divorced (2000); Foreign born: 2.1% (2000); Ancestry (includes multiple ancestries): 15.2% Other groups, 13.5% Irish, 12.6% English, 8.8% United States or American, 7.2% German (2000).
Economy: Single-family building permits issued: 5 (2004); Multi-family building permits issued: 0 (2004); Employment by occupation: 4.9% management, 8.9% professional, 17.4% services, 25.4% sales, 0.6% farming, 18.6% construction, 24.2% production (2000).
Income: Per capita income: $16,278 (2004); Median household income: $36,701 (2004); Average household income: $45,129 (2004); Percent of households with income of $100,000 or more: 4.1% (2004); Poverty rate: 13.4% (2000).
Taxes: Total city taxes per capita: $283 (2002); City property taxes per capita: $78 (2002).
Education: Percent of population age 25 and over with: High school diploma (including GED) or higher: 69.8% (2004); Bachelor's degree or higher: 6.2% (2004); Master's degree or higher: 1.1% (2004).

School District(s)

Polk County School District (PK-12)
2002-03 Enrollment: 82,179 . . . . (863) 534-0521

Housing: Homeownership rate: 76.7% (2004); Median home value: $75,426 (2004); Median rent: $325 per month (2000); Median age of housing: 16 years (2000).
Transportation: Commute to work: 94.9% car, 0.0% public transportation, 0.4% walk, 4.6% work from home (2000); Travel time to work: 14.4% less than 15 minutes, 32.6% 15 to 30 minutes, 37.3% 30 to 45 minutes, 8.3% 45 to 60 minutes, 7.4% 60 minutes or more (2000)

WAHNETA (CDP). Covers a land area of 2.421 square miles and a water area of 0 square miles. Located at 27.95° N. Lat.; 81.72° W. Long. Elevation is 133 feet.
Population: 4,050 (1990); 4,731 (2000); 4,990 (2004); 5,301 (2009 projected); Race: 63.4% White, 1.4% Black, 0.0% Asian, 56.5% Hispanic of any race (2004); Density: 2,061.3 persons per square mile (2004); Average household size: 3.61 (2004); Median age: 26.5 (2004); Male/female ratio: 119.8 (2004); Marriage status: 26.8% never married, 58.1% now married, 4.7% widowed, 10.3% divorced (2000); Foreign born: 24.0% (2000); Ancestry (includes multiple ancestries): 49.5% Other groups, 12.6% United States or American, 7.7% Irish, 4.7% English, 3.5% German (2000).
Economy: Manufacturing includes fiberglass boats and tanks. Employment by occupation: 7.9% management, 3.6% professional, 10.6% services, 13.3% sales, 14.9% farming, 24.1% construction, 25.7% production (2000).
Income: Per capita income: $8,432 (2004); Median household income: $23,423 (2004); Average household income: $30,445 (2004); Percent of households with income of $100,000 or more: 2.5% (2004); Poverty rate: 29.1% (2000).
Education: Percent of population age 25 and over with: High school diploma (including GED) or higher: 33.3% (2004); Bachelor's degree or higher: 0.9% (2004); Master's degree or higher: 0.6% (2004).
Housing: Homeownership rate: 62.2% (2004); Median home value: $51,396 (2004); Median rent: $376 per month (2000); Median age of housing: 27 years (2000).
Transportation: Commute to work: 93.0% car, 1.8% public transportation, 1.3% walk, 0.5% work from home (2000); Travel time to work: 30.4% less than 15 minutes, 31.0% 15 to 30 minutes, 16.6% 30 to 45 minutes, 3.7% 45 to 60 minutes, 18.3% 60 minutes or more (2000)

WAVERLY (CDP). Covers a land area of 3.544 square miles and a water area of 0.038 square miles. Located at 27.96° N. Lat.; 81.62° W. Long. Elevation is 129 feet.
Population: 1,994 (1990); 1,927 (2000); 1,935 (2004); 2,006 (2009 projected); Race: 64.5% White, 29.4% Black, 0.1% Asian, 5.8% Hispanic of any race (2004); Density: 546.1 persons per square mile (2004); Average household size: 2.27 (2004); Median age: 52.6 (2004); Male/female ratio: 91.2 (2004); Marriage status: 9.2% never married, 69.8% now married, 10.4% widowed, 10.7% divorced (2000); Foreign born: 2.3% (2000); Ancestry (includes multiple ancestries): 24.2% Other groups, 15.1% United States or American, 12.5% German, 10.0% Irish, 7.8% English (2000).
Economy: Manufacturing of fertilizer, insecticides; citrus-fruit packing. Employment by occupation: 1.5% management, 8.5% professional, 17.2% services, 38.6% sales, 1.4% farming, 11.9% construction, 20.8% production (2000).
Income: Per capita income: $16,447 (2004); Median household income: $24,026 (2004); Average household income: $37,397 (2004); Percent of

households with income of $100,000 or more: 7.1% (2004); Poverty rate: 15.2% (2000).
Education: Percent of population age 25 and over with: High school diploma (including GED) or higher: 62.6% (2004); Bachelor's degree or higher: 6.3% (2004); Master's degree or higher: 1.3% (2004).
Housing: Homeownership rate: 87.3% (2004); Median home value: $54,757 (2004); Median rent: $236 per month (2000); Median age of housing: 10 years (2000).
Transportation: Commute to work: 95.2% car, 0.0% public transportation, 1.6% walk, 1.6% work from home (2000); Travel time to work: 30.6% less than 15 minutes, 37.2% 15 to 30 minutes, 13.6% 30 to 45 minutes, 11.4% 45 to 60 minutes, 7.2% 60 minutes or more (2000)

WILLOW OAK (CDP). Covers a land area of 3.216 square miles and a water area of 0 square miles. Located at 27.92° N. Lat.; 82.02° W. Long. Elevation is 120 feet.
Population: 2,607 (1990); 4,917 (2000); 5,160 (2004); 5,464 (2009 projected); Race: 80.0% White, 8.4% Black, 0.6% Asian, 25.7% Hispanic of any race (2004); Density: 1,604.7 persons per square mile (2004); Average household size: 2.80 (2004); Median age: 30.4 (2004); Male/female ratio: 105.3 (2004); Marriage status: 22.9% never married, 61.5% now married, 3.9% widowed, 11.8% divorced (2000); Foreign born: 10.7% (2000); Ancestry (includes multiple ancestries): 32.4% Other groups, 20.7% United States or American, 11.4% German, 10.0% Irish, 5.5% English (2000).
Economy: Employment by occupation: 8.5% management, 11.9% professional, 15.0% services, 24.7% sales, 2.4% farming, 13.4% construction, 24.0% production (2000).
Income: Per capita income: $18,485 (2004); Median household income: $43,200 (2004); Average household income: $51,755 (2004); Percent of households with income of $100,000 or more: 7.4% (2004); Poverty rate: 13.4% (2000).
Education: Percent of population age 25 and over with: High school diploma (including GED) or higher: 72.9% (2004); Bachelor's degree or higher: 10.1% (2004); Master's degree or higher: 3.9% (2004).
Housing: Homeownership rate: 55.7% (2004); Median home value: $86,131 (2004); Median rent: $443 per month (2000); Median age of housing: 13 years (2000).
Transportation: Commute to work: 95.8% car, 0.0% public transportation, 0.0% walk, 3.2% work from home (2000); Travel time to work: 16.3% less than 15 minutes, 48.4% 15 to 30 minutes, 18.0% 30 to 45 minutes, 6.7% 45 to 60 minutes, 10.6% 60 minutes or more (2000)

WINSTON (CDP). Covers a land area of 5.449 square miles and a water area of 0.001 square miles. Located at 28.03° N. Lat.; 82.00° W. Long. Elevation is 138 feet.
Population: 9,033 (1990); 9,024 (2000); 9,299 (2004); 9,673 (2009 projected); Race: 57.3% White, 29.6% Black, 0.2% Asian, 18.7% Hispanic of any race (2004); Density: 1,706.7 persons per square mile (2004); Average household size: 2.77 (2004); Median age: 32.3 (2004); Male/female ratio: 98.2 (2004); Marriage status: 27.0% never married, 49.0% now married, 6.7% widowed, 17.3% divorced (2000); Foreign born: 9.0% (2000); Ancestry (includes multiple ancestries): 42.1% Other groups, 12.2% United States or American, 8.0% Irish, 6.8% German, 5.4% English (2000).
Economy: Employment by occupation: 5.1% management, 7.3% professional, 17.6% services, 24.6% sales, 0.9% farming, 16.4% construction, 28.1% production (2000).
Income: Per capita income: $12,755 (2004); Median household income: $28,207 (2004); Average household income: $34,952 (2004); Percent of households with income of $100,000 or more: 3.5% (2004); Poverty rate: 26.0% (2000).
Education: Percent of population age 25 and over with: High school diploma (including GED) or higher: 58.6% (2004); Bachelor's degree or higher: 4.8% (2004); Master's degree or higher: 2.0% (2004).
Housing: Homeownership rate: 60.7% (2004); Median home value: $54,583 (2004); Median rent: $370 per month (2000); Median age of housing: 27 years (2000).
Transportation: Commute to work: 92.7% car, 1.2% public transportation, 2.4% walk, 1.4% work from home (2000); Travel time to work: 31.0% less than 15 minutes, 42.1% 15 to 30 minutes, 15.0% 30 to 45 minutes, 6.9% 45 to 60 minutes, 5.0% 60 minutes or more (2000)

WINTER HAVEN (city). Covers a land area of 17.678 square miles and a water area of 7.738 square miles. Located at 28.03° N. Lat.; 81.72° W. Long. Elevation is 170 feet.
History: Winter Haven grew in the middle of citrus groves and a cluster of 97 lakes within a five-mile radius. The town developed around citrus packing houses and canneries.
Population: 26,334 (1990); 26,487 (2000); 26,547 (2004); 26,802 (2009 projected); Race: 68.9% White, 25.1% Black, 1.1% Asian, 5.7% Hispanic of any race (2004); Density: 1,501.7 persons per square mile (2004); Average household size: 2.24 (2004); Median age: 44.4 (2004); Male/female ratio: 85.7 (2004); Marriage status: 20.0% never married, 52.3% now married, 15.3% widowed, 12.5% divorced (2000); Foreign born: 5.9% (2000); Ancestry (includes multiple ancestries): 23.1% Other groups, 14.6% United States or American, 11.5% German, 10.6% English, 9.5% Irish (2000).
Economy: Unemployment rate: 5.4% (2004); Total civilian labor force: 13,041 (2004); Single-family building permits issued: 404 (2004); Multi-family building permits issued: 570 (2004); Employment by occupation: 10.9% management, 15.4% professional, 19.1% services, 29.2% sales, 1.2% farming, 10.2% construction, 14.1% production (2000).
Income: Per capita income: $20,703 (2004); Median household income: $33,912 (2004); Average household income: $45,438 (2004); Percent of households with income of $100,000 or more: 6.7% (2004); Poverty rate: 15.0% (2000).
Taxes: Total city taxes per capita: $562 (2002); City property taxes per capita: $211 (2002).
Education: Percent of population age 25 and over with: High school diploma (including GED) or higher: 75.7% (2004); Bachelor's degree or higher: 16.6% (2004); Master's degree or higher: 5.6% (2004).

School District(s)

Polk County School District (PK-12)
2002-03 Enrollment: 82,179 . . . . (863) 534-0521

Two-year College(s)

Polk Community College (Public)
2003-04 Enrollment: 7,080 . . . . (863) 297-1000
2003-04 Tuition: In-state $1,693; Out-of-state $6,254
Ridge Technical Center (Public)
2003-04 Enrollment: 1,049 . . . . (863) 419-3060
2003-04 Tuition: In-state $1,634; Out-of-state $6,930

Housing: Homeownership rate: 59.7% (2004); Median home value: $83,050 (2004); Median rent: $387 per month (2000); Median age of housing: 27 years (2000).
Hospitals: Winter Haven Hospital (579 beds)
Safety: Violent crime rate: 80.7 per 10,000 population; Property crime rate: 890.9 per 10,000 population (2003).
Newspapers: Homefinder (General - Circulation 14,500); Senior Lifestyles (General, Senior Citizen - Circulation 14,500); The News Chief (Circulation 11,226)
Transportation: Commute to work: 95.6% car, 0.8% public transportation, 1.0% walk, 1.1% work from home (2000); Travel time to work: 37.5% less than 15 minutes, 34.7% 15 to 30 minutes, 17.4% 30 to 45 minutes, 5.1% 45 to 60 minutes, 5.2% 60 minutes or more (2000); Amtrak: Service available.

Additional Information Contacts

East Polk County Association of Realtors . . . . (863) 294-3163
Winter Haven Chamber of Commerce. . . . . (863) 293-2138

Putnam County

Located in northern Florida; swampy area, drained by the St. Johns River; includes Lake George and Crescent Lake. Covers a land area of 721.90 square miles, a water area of 105.30 square miles, and is located in the Eastern Time Zone. The county government was organized in 1849. County seat is Palatka.

Putnam County is part of the Palatka, FL Micropolitan Statistical Area. The entire metro area includes: Putnam County, FL

Population: 65,070 (1990); 70,423 (2000); 71,876 (2004); 73,744 (2009 projected); Race: 77.2% White, 17.7% Black, 0.5% Asian, 6.3% Hispanic of any race (2004); Density: 99.6 persons per square mile (2004); Average household size: 2.52 (2004); Median age: 40.7 (2004); Male/female ratio: 98.2 (2004).
Religion: Five largest groups: 21.9% Southern Baptist Convention, 3.5% The United Methodist Church, 3.2% Catholic Church, 1.8% International Pentecostal Holiness Church, 1.5% The Church of Jesus Christ of Latter-day Saints (2000).
Economy: Unemployment rate: 5.6% (2004); Total civilian labor force: 30,686 (2004); Leading industries: 20.2% retail trade; 19.2% health care

and social assistance; 14.9% manufacturing (2003); Companies that employ 500 or more persons: 3 (2003); Companies that employ 100 to 499 persons: 13 (2003); Companies that employ less than 100 persons: 1,275 (2003); Farms: 466 totaling 92,619 acres (2002); Minority business ownership rate: n/a (1997); Women business ownership rate: 19.1% (1997); Retail sales per capita: $5,679 (1997). Single-family building permits issued: 222 (2004); Multi-family building permits issued: 10 (2004).
Income: Per capita income: $17,153 (2004); Median household income: $31,044 (2004); Average household income: $42,650 (2004); Percent of households with income of $100,000 or more: 6.5% (2004); Poverty rate: 19.3% (2002); Bankruptcy rate: 4.59% (2004).
Taxes: Total county taxes per capita: $326 (2002); County property taxes per capita: $290 (2002).
Education: Percent of population age 25 and over with: High school diploma (including GED) or higher: 70.2% (2004); Bachelor's degree or higher: 9.4% (2004); Master's degree or higher: 3.7% (2004).
Housing: Homeownership rate: 79.9% (2004); Median home value: $74,094 (2004); Median rent: $300 per month (2000); Median age of housing: 21 years (2000).
Health: Birth rate: 129.8 per 10,000 population (2004); Death rate: 131.6 per 10,000 population (2004); Age adjusted cancer mortality rate: 267.3 deaths per 100,000 population (2002); Air Quality Index: 98.4% good, 1.6% moderate, 0.0% unhealthy for sensitive individuals, 0.0% unhealthy (percent of days in 2004); Number of physicians: 10.4 per 10,000 population (2001); Hospital beds: 19.9 per 10,000 population (2002); Hospital admissions: 1,006.8 per 10,000 population (2002).
Elections: 2004 Presidential election results: 59.1% Bush, 40.1% Kerry, 0.4% Nader, 0.2% Badnarik
National and State Parks: Ocala National Recreation Trail; Ravine Gardens State Park
Additional Information Contacts
Putnam County Government Offices . . . . (386) 329-0200
Palatka Chamber of Commerce. . . . . (386) 328-1503
Putnam County Chamber of Commerce . . . . (386) 698-1657

Putnam County Communities

CRESCENT CITY (city). Covers a land area of 1.834 square miles and a water area of 0.303 square miles. Located at 29.43° N. Lat.; 81.51° W. Long. Elevation is 53 feet.
Population: 1,869 (1990); 1,776 (2000); 1,668 (2004); 1,594 (2009 projected); Race: 57.3% White, 35.1% Black, 0.8% Asian, 15.1% Hispanic of any race (2004); Density: 909.7 persons per square mile (2004); Average household size: 2.67 (2004); Median age: 40.5 (2004); Male/female ratio: 87.0 (2004); Marriage status: 27.4% never married, 47.5% now married, 13.6% widowed, 11.5% divorced (2000); Foreign born: 11.0% (2000); Ancestry (includes multiple ancestries): 46.9% Other groups, 12.7% English, 7.8% German, 5.9% United States or American, 5.5% Irish (2000).
Economy: Orange-growing center and resort. Employment by occupation: 6.4% management, 13.0% professional, 18.9% services, 30.0% sales, 10.3% farming, 6.2% construction, 15.2% production (2000).
Income: Per capita income: $14,957 (2004); Median household income: $25,842 (2004); Average household income: $38,782 (2004); Percent of households with income of $100,000 or more: 7.2% (2004); Poverty rate: 27.9% (2000).
Taxes: Total city taxes per capita: $378 (2002); City property taxes per capita: $216 (2002).
Education: Percent of population age 25 and over with: High school diploma (including GED) or higher: 62.5% (2004); Bachelor's degree or higher: 13.7% (2004); Master's degree or higher: 4.6% (2004).

School District(s)

Putnam County School District (PK-12)
2002-03 Enrollment: 12,483 . . . . (386) 329-0510
Housing: Homeownership rate: 60.6% (2004); Median home value: $94,231 (2004); Median rent: $220 per month (2000); Median age of housing: 34 years (2000).
Safety: Violent crime rate: 155.3 per 10,000 population; Property crime rate: 543.5 per 10,000 population (2003).
Newspapers: Courier-Journal (General - Circulation 3,000)
Transportation: Commute to work: 91.4% car, 0.5% public transportation, 2.9% walk, 3.1% work from home (2000); Travel time to work: 43.5% less than 15 minutes, 15.9% 15 to 30 minutes, 21.5% 30 to 45 minutes, 6.5% 45 to 60 minutes, 12.6% 60 minutes or more (2000)
Additional Information Contacts
Putnam County Chamber of Commerce . . . . (386) 698-1657

EAST PALATKA (CDP). Covers a land area of 3.207 square miles and a water area of 1.297 square miles. Located at 29.65° N. Lat.; 81.59° W. Long. Elevation is 16 feet.
History: East Palatka, established on the east bank of the St. Johns River, was the northern terminal of the St. Johns & Halifax Railway in 1886. When Henry Flagler purchased the railway in 1889, he extended the line to Ormond and Daytona, and began passenger service.
Population: 1,989 (1990); 1,707 (2000); 1,661 (2004); 1,667 (2009 projected); Race: 57.6% White, 39.4% Black, 1.3% Asian, 1.9% Hispanic of any race (2004); Density: 518.0 persons per square mile (2004); Average household size: 3.28 (2004); Median age: 37.3 (2004); Male/female ratio: 163.2 (2004); Marriage status: 37.8% never married, 46.4% now married, 5.1% widowed, 10.8% divorced (2000); Foreign born: 2.1% (2000); Ancestry (includes multiple ancestries): 24.6% Other groups, 12.4% United States or American, 8.2% English, 7.7% Irish, 5.9% German (2000).
Economy: Employment by occupation: 9.7% management, 14.9% professional, 16.5% services, 32.7% sales, 2.1% farming, 10.1% construction, 14.0% production (2000).
Income: Per capita income: $18,274 (2004); Median household income: $37,218 (2004); Average household income: $56,021 (2004); Percent of households with income of $100,000 or more: 13.4% (2004); Poverty rate: 17.4% (2000).
Education: Percent of population age 25 and over with: High school diploma (including GED) or higher: 62.8% (2004); Bachelor's degree or higher: 8.0% (2004); Master's degree or higher: 2.3% (2004).

School District(s)

Putnam County School District (PK-12)
2002-03 Enrollment: 12,483 . . . . (386) 329-0510
Housing: Homeownership rate: 78.1% (2004); Median home value: $76,986 (2004); Median rent: $349 per month (2000); Median age of housing: 32 years (2000).
Transportation: Commute to work: 96.1% car, 0.0% public transportation, 1.8% walk, 0.0% work from home (2000); Travel time to work: 57.5% less than 15 minutes, 22.9% 15 to 30 minutes, 9.9% 30 to 45 minutes, 3.6% 45 to 60 minutes, 6.1% 60 minutes or more (2000)

FLORAHOME (unincorporated postal area, zip code 32140). Covers a land area of 43.241 square miles and a water area of 1.336 square miles. Located at 29.76° N. Lat.; 81.85° W. Long. Elevation is 125 feet.
Population: 1,589 (2000); Race: 93.9% White, 1.6% Black, 0.0% Asian, 1.6% Hispanic of any race (2000); Density: 36.7 persons per square mile (2000); Age: 22.1% under 18, 10.1% over 64 (2000); Marriage status: 13.0% never married, 69.2% now married, 5.4% widowed, 12.4% divorced (2000); Foreign born: 0.7% (2000); Ancestry (includes multiple ancestries): 20.1% United States or American, 19.9% German, 12.9% Irish, 9.9% English, 8.0% Other groups (2000).
Economy: Employment by occupation: 16.7% management, 4.9% professional, 6.1% services, 24.3% sales, 2.8% farming, 25.6% construction, 19.6% production (2000).
Income: Per capita income: $16,733 (2000); Median household income: $32,955 (2000); Poverty rate: 9.7% (2000).
Education: Percent of population age 25 and over with: High school diploma (including GED) or higher: 64.2% (2000); Bachelor's degree or higher: 5.7% (2000).

School District(s)

Putnam County School District (PK-12)
2002-03 Enrollment: 12,483 . . . . (386) 329-0510
Housing: Homeownership rate: 93.6% (2000); Median home value: $59,900 (2000); Median rent: $467 per month (2000); Median age of housing: 17 years (2000).
Transportation: Commute to work: 97.8% car, 0.0% public transportation, 0.0% walk, 2.2% work from home (2000); Travel time to work: 8.8% less than 15 minutes, 30.8% 15 to 30 minutes, 29.2% 30 to 45 minutes, 11.4% 45 to 60 minutes, 19.8% 60 minutes or more (2000)

GEORGETOWN (unincorporated postal area, zip code 32139). Covers a land area of 7.787 square miles and a water area of 0.329 square miles. Located at 29.38° N. Lat.; 81.61° W. Long. Elevation is 24 feet.
Population: 607 (2000); Race: 77.8% White, 8.4% Black, 0.0% Asian, 13.8% Hispanic of any race (2000); Density: 78.0 persons per square mile (2000); Age: 11.9% under 18, 31.0% over 64 (2000); Marriage status: 10.3% never married, 72.0% now married, 10.0% widowed, 7.7% divorced (2000); Foreign born: 11.3% (2000); Ancestry (includes multiple

ancestries): 31.4% Other groups, 14.8% German, 12.9% Irish, 12.5% English, 2.7% Welsh (2000).
Economy: Employment by occupation: 0.0% management, 4.5% professional, 9.6% services, 24.9% sales, 22.0% farming, 18.1% construction, 20.9% production (2000).
Income: Per capita income: $39,665 (2000); Median household income: $25,508 (2000); Poverty rate: 15.2% (2000).
Education: Percent of population age 25 and over with: High school diploma (including GED) or higher: 61.9% (2000); Bachelor's degree or higher: 4.2% (2000).
Housing: Homeownership rate: 96.6% (2000); Median home value: $84,000 (2000); Median rent: $275 per month (2000); Median age of housing: 15 years (2000).
Transportation: Commute to work: 96.4% car, 0.0% public transportation, 0.0% walk, 3.6% work from home (2000); Travel time to work: 11.3% less than 15 minutes, 43.1% 15 to 30 minutes, 19.4% 30 to 45 minutes, 11.9% 45 to 60 minutes, 14.4% 60 minutes or more (2000)

INTERLACHEN (town). Covers a land area of 5.805 square miles and a water area of 0.646 square miles. Located at 29.62° N. Lat.; 81.89° W. Long. Elevation is 104 feet.
Population: 1,160 (1990); 1,475 (2000); 1,465 (2004); 1,449 (2009 projected); Race: 76.7% White, 5.8% Black, 0.3% Asian, 23.8% Hispanic of any race (2004); Density: 252.4 persons per square mile (2004); Average household size: 2.74 (2004); Median age: 35.8 (2004); Male/female ratio: 93.0 (2004); Marriage status: 24.3% never married, 57.4% now married, 7.8% widowed, 10.4% divorced (2000); Foreign born: 2.1% (2000); Ancestry (includes multiple ancestries): 35.5% Other groups, 12.6% United States or American, 7.1% English, 6.0% German, 5.4% Irish (2000).
Economy: Employment by occupation: 6.0% management, 16.1% professional, 14.6% services, 25.9% sales, 2.8% farming, 19.1% construction, 15.6% production (2000).
Income: Per capita income: $14,002 (2004); Median household income: $27,692 (2004); Average household income: $38,341 (2004); Percent of households with income of $100,000 or more: 5.2% (2004); Poverty rate: 27.5% (2000).
Taxes: Total city taxes per capita: $258 (2002); City property taxes per capita: $153 (2002).
Education: Percent of population age 25 and over with: High school diploma (including GED) or higher: 63.2% (2004); Bachelor's degree or higher: 7.4% (2004); Master's degree or higher: 2.7% (2004).

School District(s)

Putnam County School District (PK-12)
2002-03 Enrollment: 12,483 . . . . (386) 329-0510
Housing: Homeownership rate: 82.4% (2004); Median home value: $61,940 (2004); Median rent: $286 per month (2000); Median age of housing: 22 years (2000).
Safety: Violent crime rate: 86.6 per 10,000 population; Property crime rate: 1,099.3 per 10,000 population (2003).
Transportation: Commute to work: 92.0% car, 0.0% public transportation, 2.4% walk, 4.3% work from home (2000); Travel time to work: 20.4% less than 15 minutes, 22.2% 15 to 30 minutes, 24.0% 30 to 45 minutes, 9.7% 45 to 60 minutes, 23.8% 60 minutes or more (2000)

MELROSE (unincorporated postal area, zip code 32666). Covers a land area of 25.258 square miles and a water area of 3.534 square miles. Located at 29.73° N. Lat.; 82.01° W. Long. Elevation is 161 feet.
History: Melrose was settled in 1879 by Scottish pioneers who planted citrus groves on the shores of Santa Fe Lake. The town was named for Melrose, Scotland.
Population: 4,669 (2000); Race: 89.4% White, 6.5% Black, 1.2% Asian, 1.3% Hispanic of any race (2000); Density: 184.9 persons per square mile (2000); Age: 16.1% under 18, 22.9% over 64 (2000); Marriage status: 19.8% never married, 53.6% now married, 9.8% widowed, 16.8% divorced (2000); Foreign born: 2.7% (2000); Ancestry (includes multiple ancestries): 16.3% English, 16.0% United States or American, 12.4% Irish, 11.5% German, 10.3% Other groups (2000).
Economy: Employment by occupation: 13.9% management, 20.4% professional, 17.8% services, 22.2% sales, 0.7% farming, 12.8% construction, 12.1% production (2000).
Income: Per capita income: $22,637 (2000); Median household income: $36,903 (2000); Poverty rate: 8.0% (2000).
Education: Percent of population age 25 and over with: High school diploma (including GED) or higher: 85.6% (2000); Bachelor's degree or higher: 18.2% (2000).

School District(s)

Putnam County School District (PK-12)
2002-03 Enrollment: 12,483 . . . . (386) 329-0510
Housing: Homeownership rate: 87.7% (2000); Median home value: $98,200 (2000); Median rent: $426 per month (2000); Median age of housing: 22 years (2000).
Transportation: Commute to work: 92.7% car, 0.3% public transportation, 1.0% walk, 3.8% work from home (2000); Travel time to work: 13.7% less than 15 minutes, 19.0% 15 to 30 minutes, 32.9% 30 to 45 minutes, 17.4% 45 to 60 minutes, 17.0% 60 minutes or more (2000)

PALATKA (city). Covers a land area of 6.957 square miles and a water area of 0.577 square miles. Located at 29.64° N. Lat.; 81.65° W. Long. Elevation is 73 feet.
History: Palatka began as a trading post established in 1821 on the St. Johns River. The name is of Indian origin meaning "crossing over." Palatka became an important port in the 1870's, shipping citrus fruit and lumber from its cypress mill, as well as being a resort called on by passenger steamers from as far as the Mississippi River.
Population: 10,826 (1990); 10,033 (2000); 10,123 (2004); 10,307 (2009 projected); Race: 45.0% White, 52.4% Black, 0.5% Asian, 2.9% Hispanic of any race (2004); Density: 1,455.1 persons per square mile (2004); Average household size: 2.55 (2004); Median age: 34.7 (2004); Male/female ratio: 83.4 (2004); Marriage status: 31.1% never married, 44.5% now married, 11.9% widowed, 12.5% divorced (2000); Foreign born: 2.0% (2000); Ancestry (includes multiple ancestries): 40.2% Other groups, 10.2% United States or American, 5.5% English, 5.4% Irish, 4.4% German (2000).
Economy: Single-family building permits issued: 9 (2004); Multi-family building permits issued: 10 (2004); Employment by occupation: 6.6% management, 16.8% professional, 19.1% services, 26.1% sales, 2.4% farming, 10.5% construction, 18.4% production (2000).
Income: Per capita income: $12,149 (2004); Median household income: $19,413 (2004); Average household income: $29,261 (2004); Percent of households with income of $100,000 or more: 3.1% (2004); Poverty rate: 33.1% (2000).
Taxes: Total city taxes per capita: $401 (2002); City property taxes per capita: $169 (2002).
Education: Percent of population age 25 and over with: High school diploma (including GED) or higher: 66.2% (2004); Bachelor's degree or higher: 10.3% (2004); Master's degree or higher: 4.4% (2004).

School District(s)

Putnam County School District (PK-12)
2002-03 Enrollment: 12,483 . . . . (386) 329-0510

Two-year College(s)

Saint Johns River Community College (Public)
2003-04 Enrollment: 4,635 . . . . (386) 312-4200
2003-04 Tuition: In-state $1,585; Out-of-state $6,348
Housing: Homeownership rate: 51.6% (2004); Median home value: $71,311 (2004); Median rent: $273 per month (2000); Median age of housing: 30 years (2000).
Hospitals: Putnam Community Medical Center (141 beds)
Safety: Violent crime rate: 162.0 per 10,000 population; Property crime rate: 905.1 per 10,000 population (2003).
Newspapers: Daily News (Circulation 11,372)
Transportation: Commute to work: 90.9% car, 3.1% public transportation, 2.7% walk, 2.2% work from home (2000); Travel time to work: 51.6% less than 15 minutes, 28.3% 15 to 30 minutes, 9.6% 30 to 45 minutes, 4.4% 45 to 60 minutes, 6.2% 60 minutes or more (2000); Amtrak: Service available.

Additional Information Contacts

Palatka Chamber of Commerce. . . . . (386) 328-1503

POMONA PARK (town). Covers a land area of 2.930 square miles and a water area of 0.403 square miles. Located at 29.49° N. Lat.; 81.60° W. Long. Elevation is 67 feet.
Population: 663 (1990); 789 (2000); 792 (2004); 797 (2009 projected); Race: 86.0% White, 11.2% Black, 0.0% Asian, 4.4% Hispanic of any race (2004); Density: 270.3 persons per square mile (2004); Average household size: 2.28 (2004); Median age: 46.2 (2004); Male/female ratio: 99.5 (2004); Marriage status: 16.9% never married, 54.2% now married, 12.5% widowed, 16.3% divorced (2000); Foreign born: 5.8% (2000); Ancestry (includes multiple ancestries): 22.1% Other groups, 14.9% Irish, 13.9% German, 11.7% United States or American, 9.4% English (2000).
Economy: Employment by occupation: 9.6% management, 14.9% professional, 14.2% services, 31.0% sales, 4.6% farming, 7.7% construction, 18.0% production (2000).

Income: Per capita income: $17,507 (2004); Median household income: $27,500 (2004); Average household income: $37,220 (2004); Percent of households with income of $100,000 or more: 4.3% (2004); Poverty rate: 25.5% (2000).
Taxes: Total city taxes per capita: $186 (2002); City property taxes per capita: $108 (2002).
Education: Percent of population age 25 and over with: High school diploma (including GED) or higher: 68.5% (2004); Bachelor's degree or higher: 10.2% (2004); Master's degree or higher: 4.7% (2004).
Housing: Homeownership rate: 82.8% (2004); Median home value: $58,750 (2004); Median rent: $291 per month (2000); Median age of housing: 25 years (2000).
Transportation: Commute to work: 94.4% car, 0.0% public transportation, 2.4% walk, 0.8% work from home (2000); Travel time to work: 17.0% less than 15 minutes, 17.4% 15 to 30 minutes, 25.9% 30 to 45 minutes, 11.3% 45 to 60 minutes, 28.3% 60 minutes or more (2000)

SAN MATEO (unincorporated postal area, zip code 32187). Covers a land area of 24.116 square miles and a water area of 0.168 square miles. Located at 29.59° N. Lat.; 81.57° W. Long. Elevation is 85 feet.
History: San Mateo was established in a region of orange groves, where the land had been cultivated for more than a century. Between 1765 and 1783, a town called Rollestown, or Charlotia, existed near the site of San Mateo. Rolleston was founded by Denys Rolle, a member of the British parliament, who brought a group of people from the London slums, planning to rehabilitate them in the Utopia he created. In 1783 Rolles moved to the Bahamas.
Population: 2,037 (2000); Race: 77.9% White, 22.1% Black, 0.0% Asian, 1.2% Hispanic of any race (2000); Density: 84.5 persons per square mile (2000); Age: 26.4% under 18, 15.4% over 64 (2000); Marriage status: 19.9% never married, 62.3% now married, 7.1% widowed, 10.6% divorced (2000); Foreign born: 1.0% (2000); Ancestry (includes multiple ancestries): 27.0% Other groups, 15.6% United States or American, 13.8% English, 11.2% Irish, 7.3% German (2000).
Economy: Employment by occupation: 5.3% management, 19.8% professional, 18.5% services, 21.8% sales, 5.7% farming, 13.4% construction, 15.6% production (2000).
Income: Per capita income: $14,920 (2000); Median household income: $30,273 (2000); Poverty rate: 22.5% (2000).
Education: Percent of population age 25 and over with: High school diploma (including GED) or higher: 75.1% (2000); Bachelor's degree or higher: 10.6% (2000).

School District(s)

Putnam County School District (PK-12)
2002-03 Enrollment: 12,483 . . . . (386) 329-0510
Housing: Homeownership rate: 87.3% (2000); Median home value: $78,000 (2000); Median rent: $330 per month (2000); Median age of housing: 20 years (2000).
Transportation: Commute to work: 95.4% car, 2.2% public transportation, 1.0% walk, 1.4% work from home (2000); Travel time to work: 15.2% less than 15 minutes, 50.7% 15 to 30 minutes, 20.8% 30 to 45 minutes, 5.7% 45 to 60 minutes, 7.5% 60 minutes or more (2000)

SATSUMA (unincorporated postal area, zip code 32189). Covers a land area of 34.070 square miles and a water area of 0.267 square miles. Located at 29.55° N. Lat.; 81.64° W. Long. Elevation is 74 feet.
History: Satsuma developed as a trading center in a citrus and truck-farm area. The town was named for the Satsuma orange, a variety that withstands low temperatures.
Population: 5,866 (2000); Race: 92.7% White, 4.6% Black, 0.2% Asian, 2.2% Hispanic of any race (2000); Density: 172.2 persons per square mile (2000); Age: 17.8% under 18, 25.8% over 64 (2000); Marriage status: 11.3% never married, 63.7% now married, 9.5% widowed, 15.5% divorced (2000); Foreign born: 1.8% (2000); Ancestry (includes multiple ancestries): 17.0% United States or American, 13.4% Other groups, 12.1% Irish, 10.8% English, 9.6% German (2000).
Economy: Employment by occupation: 8.3% management, 10.9% professional, 17.8% services, 27.3% sales, 1.4% farming, 16.4% construction, 17.9% production (2000).
Income: Per capita income: $16,481 (2000); Median household income: $26,670 (2000); Poverty rate: 16.6% (2000).
Education: Percent of population age 25 and over with: High school diploma (including GED) or higher: 69.6% (2000); Bachelor's degree or higher: 7.1% (2000).
Housing: Homeownership rate: 88.5% (2000); Median home value: $74,600 (2000); Median rent: $355 per month (2000); Median age of housing: 17 years (2000).
Transportation: Commute to work: 96.5% car, 0.4% public transportation, 1.2% walk, 1.1% work from home (2000); Travel time to work: 12.6% less than 15 minutes, 34.8% 15 to 30 minutes, 23.4% 30 to 45 minutes, 11.4% 45 to 60 minutes, 17.9% 60 minutes or more (2000)

WELAKA (town). Covers a land area of 1.358 square miles and a water area of 0.043 square miles. Located at 29.48° N. Lat.; 81.67° W. Long. Elevation is 28 feet.
Population: 534 (1990); 586 (2000); 589 (2004); 595 (2009 projected); Race: 71.1% White, 25.1% Black, 0.0% Asian, 3.9% Hispanic of any race (2004); Density: 433.6 persons per square mile (2004); Average household size: 2.11 (2004); Median age: 52.2 (2004); Male/female ratio: 87.0 (2004); Marriage status: 15.2% never married, 58.8% now married, 12.1% widowed, 14.0% divorced (2000); Foreign born: 2.0% (2000); Ancestry (includes multiple ancestries): 22.3% Other groups, 14.2% United States or American, 7.7% English, 7.3% German, 7.0% Irish (2000).
Economy: Single-family building permits issued: 4 (2004); Multi-family building permits issued: 0 (2004); Employment by occupation: 8.7% management, 6.6% professional, 28.4% services, 29.0% sales, 3.8% farming, 12.0% construction, 11.5% production (2000).
Income: Per capita income: $16,824 (2004); Median household income: $28,587 (2004); Average household income: $34,946 (2004); Percent of households with income of $100,000 or more: 2.5% (2004); Poverty rate: 25.0% (2000).
Education: Percent of population age 25 and over with: High school diploma (including GED) or higher: 70.5% (2004); Bachelor's degree or higher: 10.4% (2004); Master's degree or higher: 1.3% (2004).
Housing: Homeownership rate: 73.5% (2004); Median home value: $63,714 (2004); Median rent: $250 per month (2000); Median age of housing: 19 years (2000).
Safety: Violent crime rate: 0.0 per 10,000 population; Property crime rate: 82.2 per 10,000 population (2003).
Transportation: Commute to work: 93.6% car, 0.0% public transportation, 3.5% walk, 1.7% work from home (2000); Travel time to work: 18.3% less than 15 minutes, 33.7% 15 to 30 minutes, 21.9% 30 to 45 minutes, 7.1% 45 to 60 minutes, 18.9% 60 minutes or more (2000)

Santa Rosa County

Located in northwestern Florida; bounded on the north by Georgia, on the south by the Gulf of Mexico, and on the west by the Escambia River; includes part of Pensacola Bay and Santa Rosa Sound; drained by the Blackwater and Yellow Rivers. Covers a land area of 1,016.90 square miles, a water area of 156.60 square miles, and is located in the Central Time Zone. The county government was organized in 1842. County seat is Milton.

Santa Rosa County is part of the Pensacola-Ferry Pass-Brent, FL Metropolitan Statistical Area. The entire metro area includes: Escambia County, FL; Santa Rosa County, FL

Weather Station: Milton Experiment Station Elevation: 216 feet

	Jan	Feb	Mar	Apr	May	Jun	Jul	Aug	Sep	Oct	Nov	Dec
High	61	65	72	78	85	90	92	91	88	80	71	64
Low	39	42	49	54	62	69	71	71	67	55	47	42
Precip	6.4	5.1	7.4	4.3	5.1	7.4	8.1	6.7	6.1	4.0	5.2	4.4
Snow	0.1	0.1	tr	0.0	0.0	0.0	0.0	0.0	0.0	0.0	0.0	0.0

High and Low temperatures in degrees Fahrenheit; Precipitation and Snow in inches

Population: 81,965 (1990); 117,743 (2000); 133,083 (2004); 152,365 (2009 projected); Race: 90.7% White, 4.2% Black, 1.5% Asian, 2.5% Hispanic of any race (2004); Density: 130.9 persons per square mile (2004); Average household size: 2.68 (2004); Median age: 37.3 (2004); Male/female ratio: 101.3 (2004).
Religion: Five largest groups: 16.7% Southern Baptist Convention, 7.9% The United Methodist Church, 5.7% Assemblies of God, 5.3% Catholic Church, 0.9% The Church of Jesus Christ of Latter-day Saints (2000).
Economy: Unemployment rate: 4.2% (2004); Total civilian labor force: 57,522 (2004); Leading industries: 19.2% retail trade; 15.3% health care and social assistance; 12.6% accommodation & food services (2003); Companies that employ 500 or more persons: 2 (2003); Companies that employ 100 to 499 persons: 25 (2003); Companies that employ less than 100 persons: 2,144 (2003); Farms: 505 totaling 83,790 acres (2002);

Minority business ownership rate: n/a (1997); Women business ownership rate: 23.9% (1997); Retail sales per capita: $4,932 (1997). Single-family building permits issued: 1,969 (2004); Multi-family building permits issued: 53 (2004).
Income: Per capita income: $23,158 (2004); Median household income: $47,322 (2004); Average household income: $61,499 (2004); Percent of households with income of $100,000 or more: 13.4% (2004); Poverty rate: 9.8% (2002); Bankruptcy rate: 4.63% (2004).
Taxes: Total county taxes per capita: $311 (2002); County property taxes per capita: $240 (2002).
Education: Percent of population age 25 and over with: High school diploma (including GED) or higher: 85.7% (2004); Bachelor's degree or higher: 23.2% (2004); Master's degree or higher: 8.0% (2004).
Housing: Homeownership rate: 80.6% (2004); Median home value: $122,676 (2004); Median rent: $441 per month (2000); Median age of housing: 15 years (2000).
Health: Birth rate: 119.4 per 10,000 population (2004); Death rate: 67.0 per 10,000 population (2004); Age adjusted cancer mortality rate: 194.9 deaths per 100,000 population (2002); Air Quality Index: 87.7% good, 12.3% moderate, 0.0% unhealthy for sensitive individuals, 0.0% unhealthy (percent of days in 2004); Number of physicians: 17.4 per 10,000 population (2001); Hospital beds: 16.5 per 10,000 population (2002); Hospital admissions: 727.5 per 10,000 population (2002).
Elections: 2004 Presidential election results: 77.3% Bush, 21.8% Kerry, 0.4% Nader, 0.1% Badnarik
National and State Parks: Blackwater Heritage Trail State Park; Blackwater River State Forest; Blackwater River State Park; Navarre Beach State Park
Additional Information Contacts
Santa Rosa County Government Offices . . . . (850) 623-0135
Gulf Breeze Area Chamber of Commerce . . . . (850) 932-7888
Gulf Breeze Chamber of Commerce . . . . (850) 932-1500
Milton Chamber of Commerce . . . . (850) 623-2339
Pace Area Chamber of Commerce . . . . (850) 994-9633
Santa Rosa County Board of Realtors . . . . (850) 623-5309

Santa Rosa County Communities

BAGDAD (CDP). Covers a land area of 3.520 square miles and a water area of 0.718 square miles. Located at 30.59° N. Lat.; 87.03° W. Long. Elevation is 17 feet.
History: Bagdad grew around the Bagdad Lumber Company, where pine and cypress were cut and shipped to New Orleans in the early 1850's.
Population: 1,457 (1990); 1,490 (2000); 1,650 (2004); 1,858 (2009 projected); Race: 83.3% White, 9.6% Black, 0.6% Asian, 1.6% Hispanic of any race (2004); Density: 468.8 persons per square mile (2004); Average household size: 2.51 (2004); Median age: 40.1 (2004); Male/female ratio: 96.4 (2004); Marriage status: 22.0% never married, 49.2% now married, 13.3% widowed, 15.5% divorced (2000); Foreign born: 1.0% (2000); Ancestry (includes multiple ancestries): 34.7% Other groups, 11.8% United States or American, 9.2% English, 7.6% Irish, 7.3% German (2000).
Economy: Employment by occupation: 5.4% management, 15.8% professional, 19.4% services, 24.3% sales, 0.0% farming, 18.9% construction, 16.2% production (2000).
Income: Per capita income: $18,196 (2004); Median household income: $36,676 (2004); Average household income: $43,988 (2004); Percent of households with income of $100,000 or more: 6.4% (2004); Poverty rate: 22.5% (2000).
Education: Percent of population age 25 and over with: High school diploma (including GED) or higher: 68.4% (2004); Bachelor's degree or higher: 13.0% (2004); Master's degree or higher: 2.6% (2004).
School District(s)
Santa Rosa County School District (PK-12)
2002-03 Enrollment: 23,645 . . . . (850) 983-5010
Housing: Homeownership rate: 78.8% (2004); Median home value: $83,077 (2004); Median rent: $408 per month (2000); Median age of housing: 31 years (2000).
Transportation: Commute to work: 96.9% car, 0.0% public transportation, 0.0% walk, 1.7% work from home (2000); Travel time to work: 31.7% less than 15 minutes, 48.6% 15 to 30 minutes, 12.8% 30 to 45 minutes, 3.8% 45 to 60 minutes, 3.2% 60 minutes or more (2000)

GULF BREEZE (city). Covers a land area of 4.752 square miles and a water area of 18.795 square miles. Located at 30.36° N. Lat.; 87.17° W. Long. Elevation is 14 feet.
Population: 5,530 (1990); 5,665 (2000); 6,116 (2004); 6,715 (2009 projected); Race: 97.4% White, 0.3% Black, 0.6% Asian, 1.2% Hispanic of any race (2004); Density: 1,286.9 persons per square mile (2004); Average household size: 2.34 (2004); Median age: 46.3 (2004); Male/female ratio: 90.4 (2004); Marriage status: 17.6% never married, 65.7% now married, 7.9% widowed, 8.8% divorced (2000); Foreign born: 3.0% (2000); Ancestry (includes multiple ancestries): 19.5% German, 16.7% English, 12.9% Irish, 10.6% Other groups, 9.7% United States or American (2000).
Economy: Major beach suburb of Pensacola, to which it is connected by bridge and causeway. Employment by occupation: 20.9% management, 32.4% professional, 9.5% services, 26.3% sales, 0.0% farming, 6.1% construction, 4.9% production (2000).
Income: Per capita income: $40,383 (2004); Median household income: $57,393 (2004); Average household income: $92,640 (2004); Percent of households with income of $100,000 or more: 23.5% (2004); Poverty rate: 4.2% (2000).
Education: Percent of population age 25 and over with: High school diploma (including GED) or higher: 95.7% (2004); Bachelor's degree or higher: 48.5% (2004); Master's degree or higher: 20.2% (2004).
School District(s)
Santa Rosa County School District (PK-12)
2002-03 Enrollment: 23,645 . . . . (850) 983-5010
Housing: Homeownership rate: 82.3% (2004); Median home value: $181,612 (2004); Median rent: $582 per month (2000); Median age of housing: 28 years (2000).
Hospitals: Friary (30 beds); Gulf Breeze Hospital (60 beds)
Safety: Violent crime rate: 18.1 per 10,000 population; Property crime rate: 232.1 per 10,000 population (2003).
Transportation: Commute to work: 91.7% car, 0.0% public transportation, 0.3% walk, 6.2% work from home (2000); Travel time to work: 23.4% less than 15 minutes, 52.3% 15 to 30 minutes, 16.7% 30 to 45 minutes, 2.1% 45 to 60 minutes, 5.5% 60 minutes or more (2000)
Additional Information Contacts
Gulf Breeze Area Chamber of Commerce . . . . (850) 932-7888
Gulf Breeze Chamber of Commerce . . . . (850) 932-1500
Local Government Offices . . . . (850) 934-5100

JAY (town). Covers a land area of 1.583 square miles and a water area of 0 square miles. Located at 30.95° N. Lat.; 87.15° W. Long. Elevation is 249 feet.
Population: 666 (1990); 579 (2000); 546 (2004); 527 (2009 projected); Race: 97.4% White, 0.4% Black, 0.2% Asian, 2.2% Hispanic of any race (2004); Density: 344.9 persons per square mile (2004); Average household size: 2.52 (2004); Median age: 42.3 (2004); Male/female ratio: 93.6 (2004); Marriage status: 18.4% never married, 54.0% now married, 12.5% widowed, 15.1% divorced (2000); Foreign born: 1.7% (2000); Ancestry (includes multiple ancestries): 40.1% United States or American, 10.5% Other groups, 8.8% English, 5.9% German, 4.4% Irish (2000).
Economy: Employment by occupation: 8.5% management, 21.8% professional, 19.7% services, 12.2% sales, 1.1% farming, 12.2% construction, 24.5% production (2000).
Income: Per capita income: $14,762 (2004); Median household income: $27,931 (2004); Average household income: $36,855 (2004); Percent of households with income of $100,000 or more: 5.5% (2004); Poverty rate: 16.5% (2000).
Education: Percent of population age 25 and over with: High school diploma (including GED) or higher: 64.5% (2004); Bachelor's degree or higher: 14.1% (2004); Master's degree or higher: 6.7% (2004).
School District(s)
Santa Rosa County School District (PK-12)
2002-03 Enrollment: 23,645 . . . . (850) 983-5010
Housing: Homeownership rate: 62.2% (2004); Median home value: $60,526 (2004); Median rent: $281 per month (2000); Median age of housing: 35 years (2000).
Hospitals: Jay Hospital (55 beds)
Transportation: Commute to work: 86.2% car, 0.0% public transportation, 4.3% walk, 5.9% work from home (2000); Travel time to work: 55.9% less than 15 minutes, 13.6% 15 to 30 minutes, 10.7% 30 to 45 minutes, 14.7% 45 to 60 minutes, 5.1% 60 minutes or more (2000)

MILTON (city). Covers a land area of 4.373 square miles and a water area of 0.210 square miles. Located at 30.63° N. Lat.; 87.04° W. Long. Elevation is 66 feet.

History: Milton began in 1825 as a trading post on the Blackwater River. A community grew up around several sawmills, and became a cotton shipping port during the Civil War.
Population: 7,537 (1990); 7,045 (2000); 7,114 (2004); 7,338 (2009 projected); Race: 78.3% White, 15.4% Black, 2.0% Asian, 3.6% Hispanic of any race (2004); Density: 1,626.9 persons per square mile (2004); Average household size: 2.62 (2004); Median age: 34.9 (2004); Male/female ratio: 87.1 (2004); Marriage status: 21.7% never married, 54.7% now married, 10.0% widowed, 13.5% divorced (2000); Foreign born: 3.1% (2000); Ancestry (includes multiple ancestries): 28.8% Other groups, 14.0% Irish, 12.4% German, 10.9% United States or American, 9.6% English (2000).
Economy: Employment by occupation: 7.1% management, 15.2% professional, 18.9% services, 28.0% sales, 0.0% farming, 13.4% construction, 17.4% production (2000).
Income: Per capita income: $16,591 (2004); Median household income: $32,100 (2004); Average household income: $41,341 (2004); Percent of households with income of $100,000 or more: 4.7% (2004); Poverty rate: 16.6% (2000).
Taxes: Total city taxes per capita: $239 (2002); City property taxes per capita: $76 (2002).
Education: Percent of population age 25 and over with: High school diploma (including GED) or higher: 79.4% (2004); Bachelor's degree or higher: 16.0% (2004); Master's degree or higher: 4.3% (2004).

School District(s)

Okaloosa County School District (PK-12)
2002-03 Enrollment: 31,291 . . . . (850) 833-3109

Two-year College(s)

Radford M Locklin Technical Center (Public)
2003-04 Enrollment: 310 . . . . (850) 983-5700
2003-04 Tuition: In-state $1,262; Out-of-state $4,970

Housing: Homeownership rate: 58.1% (2004); Median home value: $84,718 (2004); Median rent: $364 per month (2000); Median age of housing: 33 years (2000).
Hospitals: Santa Rosa Medical Center (129 beds); West Florida Community Care Center (100 beds)
Safety: Violent crime rate: 46.0 per 10,000 population; Property crime rate: 482.5 per 10,000 population (2003).
Newspapers: Press Gazette (General - Circulation 7,000); Santa Rosa Free Press (General - Circulation 7,000)
Transportation: Commute to work: 94.3% car, 0.3% public transportation, 1.9% walk, 1.3% work from home (2000); Travel time to work: 36.7% less than 15 minutes, 27.9% 15 to 30 minutes, 22.5% 30 to 45 minutes, 7.4% 45 to 60 minutes, 5.5% 60 minutes or more (2000)

Additional Information Contacts

Local Government Offices . . . . (850) 983-5401
Milton Chamber of Commerce . . . . (850) 623-2339
Santa Rosa County Board of Realtors . . . . (850) 623-5309

PACE (CDP). Covers a land area of 9.382 square miles and a water area of 0 square miles. Located at 30.59° N. Lat.; 87.15° W. Long. Elevation is 70 feet.
Population: 6,277 (1990); 7,393 (2000); 7,917 (2004); 8,616 (2009 projected); Race: 93.4% White, 1.5% Black, 1.3% Asian, 1.8% Hispanic of any race (2004); Density: 843.8 persons per square mile (2004); Average household size: 2.63 (2004); Median age: 35.7 (2004); Male/female ratio: 96.5 (2004); Marriage status: 19.7% never married, 62.9% now married, 4.7% widowed, 12.7% divorced (2000); Foreign born: 2.8% (2000); Ancestry (includes multiple ancestries): 19.6% United States or American, 17.5% Other groups, 14.2% Irish, 10.2% German, 8.2% English (2000).
Economy: Manufacturing includes fertilizers, boat interiors, industrial resins. Employment by occupation: 10.2% management, 18.0% professional, 15.6% services, 26.3% sales, 0.5% farming, 17.1% construction, 12.3% production (2000).
Income: Per capita income: $18,463 (2004); Median household income: $38,576 (2004); Average household income: $48,545 (2004); Percent of households with income of $100,000 or more: 8.3% (2004); Poverty rate: 12.3% (2000).
Education: Percent of population age 25 and over with: High school diploma (including GED) or higher: 85.6% (2004); Bachelor's degree or higher: 13.6% (2004); Master's degree or higher: 4.4% (2004).

School District(s)

Santa Rosa County School District (PK-12)
2002-03 Enrollment: 23,645 . . . . (850) 983-5010

Housing: Homeownership rate: 76.8% (2004); Median home value: $102,734 (2004); Median rent: $377 per month (2000); Median age of housing: 19 years (2000).
Transportation: Commute to work: 94.6% car, 0.2% public transportation, 0.5% walk, 2.8% work from home (2000); Travel time to work: 22.4% less than 15 minutes, 43.8% 15 to 30 minutes, 21.9% 30 to 45 minutes, 7.0% 45 to 60 minutes, 4.9% 60 minutes or more (2000)

Additional Information Contacts

Pace Area Chamber of Commerce . . . . (850) 994-9633

Sarasota County

Located in southwestern Florida; bounded on the west by the Gulf of Mexico, with barrier beaches and Sarasota Bay; lowland area, drained by the Myakka River. Covers a land area of 571.60 square miles, a water area of 153.60 square miles, and is located in the Eastern Time Zone. The county government was organized in 1921. County seat is Sarasota.

Sarasota County is part of the Sarasota-Bradenton-Venice, FL Metropolitan Statistical Area. The entire metro area includes: Manatee County, FL; Sarasota County, FL

Weather Station: Myakka River State Park — Elevation: 19 feet

	Jan	Feb	Mar	Apr	May	Jun	Jul	Aug	Sep	Oct	Nov	Dec
High	75	77	81	86	91	92	93	93	91	87	81	76
Low	49	51	55	58	63	69	71	72	71	65	58	52
Precip	3.2	2.9	3.6	2.1	3.4	8.9	9.6	9.6	8.1	3.2	2.2	2.3
Snow	0.0	0.0	0.0	0.0	0.0	0.0	0.0	0.0	0.0	0.0	0.0	tr

High and Low temperatures in degrees Fahrenheit; Precipitation and Snow in inches

Weather Station: Venice — Elevation: 6 feet

	Jan	Feb	Mar	Apr	May	Jun	Jul	Aug	Sep	Oct	Nov	Dec
High	72	74	77	82	86	90	91	91	90	86	80	74
Low	51	52	57	61	67	72	73	74	73	66	59	54
Precip	2.7	2.2	3.6	1.9	2.3	6.7	6.6	8.3	7.4	3.1	2.1	2.3
Snow	tr	0.0	0.0	0.0	0.0	0.0	0.0	0.0	0.0	0.0	0.0	0.0

High and Low temperatures in degrees Fahrenheit; Precipitation and Snow in inches

Population: 277,776 (1990); 325,957 (2000); 350,556 (2004); 381,572 (2009 projected); Race: 91.8% White, 4.5% Black, 1.0% Asian, 5.4% Hispanic of any race (2004); Density: 613.3 persons per square mile (2004); Average household size: 2.17 (2004); Median age: 50.4 (2004); Male/female ratio: 90.6 (2004).
Religion: Five largest groups: 19.9% Catholic Church, 4.9% Southern Baptist Convention, 4.1% Jewish Estimate, 3.4% The United Methodist Church, 3.0% Presbyterian Church (U.S.A.) (2000).
Economy: Unemployment rate: 3.2% (2004); Total civilian labor force: 173,002 (2004); Leading industries: 16.2% retail trade; 15.8% health care and social assistance; 11.2% administration, support, waste management, remediation services (2003); Companies that employ 500 or more persons: 11 (2003); Companies that employ 100 to 499 persons: 185 (2003); Companies that employ less than 100 persons: 11,918 (2003); Farms: 371 totaling 121,310 acres (2002); Minority business ownership rate: 6.4% (1997); Women business ownership rate: 24.3% (1997); Retail sales per capita: $12,011 (1997). Single-family building permits issued: 6,321 (2004); Multi-family building permits issued: 1,585 (2004).
Income: Per capita income: $31,531 (2004); Median household income: $46,707 (2004); Average household income: $67,460 (2004); Percent of households with income of $100,000 or more: 15.6% (2004); Poverty rate: 8.4% (2002); Bankruptcy rate: 4.47% (2004).
Taxes: Total county taxes per capita: $533 (2002); County property taxes per capita: $325 (2002).
Education: Percent of population age 25 and over with: High school diploma (including GED) or higher: 87.1% (2004); Bachelor's degree or higher: 27.4% (2004); Master's degree or higher: 10.3% (2004).
Housing: Homeownership rate: 79.4% (2004); Median home value: $152,282 (2004); Median rent: $626 per month (2000); Median age of housing: 21 years (2000).
Health: Birth rate: 85.7 per 10,000 population (2004); Death rate: 130.5 per 10,000 population (2004); Age adjusted cancer mortality rate: 171.1 deaths per 100,000 population (2002); Air Quality Index: 91.5% good, 7.4% moderate, 1.1% unhealthy for sensitive individuals, 0.0% unhealthy (percent of days in 2004); Number of physicians: 31.6 per 10,000 population (2001); Hospital beds: 39.1 per 10,000 population (2002); Hospital admissions: 1,597.1 per 10,000 population (2002).

Elections: 2004 Presidential election results: 53.5% Bush, 45.2% Kerry, 0.6% Nader, 0.3% Badnarik
National and State Parks: Myakka River State Park; Oscar Scherer State Park
Additional Information Contacts
Sarasota County Government Offices . . . . (941) 951-5344
Committee for Economic Development . . . . (941) 955-2508
Englewood Area Board of Realtors . . . . (941) 475-6656
Englewood Area Chamber of Commerce . . . . (941) 474-5511
Longboat Key Chamber of Commerce . . . . (941) 383-2466
North Port Chamber of Commerce . . . . (941) 423-5040
Sarasota Association of Realtors . . . . (941) 923-2315
Sarasota Chamber of Commerce . . . . (941) 955-8187
Siesta Key Chamber of Commerce . . . . (941) 349-3800
Venice Area Board of Realtors . . . . (941) 484-0614
Venice Chamber of Commerce . . . . (941) 488-2236

Sarasota County Communities

BEE RIDGE (CDP). Covers a land area of 3.907 square miles and a water area of 0 square miles. Located at 27.28° N. Lat.; 82.47° W. Long. Elevation is 35 feet.
Population: 6,406 (1990); 8,744 (2000); 9,630 (2004); 10,719 (2009 projected); Race: 96.8% White, 1.1% Black, 0.8% Asian, 3.7% Hispanic of any race (2004); Density: 2,464.8 persons per square mile (2004); Average household size: 2.24 (2004); Median age: 51.7 (2004); Male/female ratio: 80.9 (2004); Marriage status: 15.5% never married, 59.9% now married, 15.1% widowed, 9.5% divorced (2000); Foreign born: 8.0% (2000); Ancestry (includes multiple ancestries): 24.6% German, 14.4% English, 13.6% Irish, 9.4% Other groups, 8.6% Italian (2000).
Economy: Employment by occupation: 13.3% management, 23.0% professional, 19.3% services, 28.3% sales, 1.1% farming, 8.2% construction, 6.8% production (2000).
Income: Per capita income: $30,721 (2004); Median household income: $53,433 (2004); Average household income: $67,833 (2004); Percent of households with income of $100,000 or more: 18.5% (2004); Poverty rate: 5.5% (2000).
Education: Percent of population age 25 and over with: High school diploma (including GED) or higher: 89.0% (2004); Bachelor's degree or higher: 29.7% (2004); Master's degree or higher: 11.1% (2004).
Housing: Homeownership rate: 85.0% (2004); Median home value: $178,062 (2004); Median rent: $865 per month (2000); Median age of housing: 15 years (2000).
Transportation: Commute to work: 90.7% car, 1.2% public transportation, 2.0% walk, 4.9% work from home (2000); Travel time to work: 34.5% less than 15 minutes, 48.1% 15 to 30 minutes, 12.9% 30 to 45 minutes, 1.5% 45 to 60 minutes, 3.0% 60 minutes or more (2000)

DESOTO LAKES (CDP). Covers a land area of 1.261 square miles and a water area of 0 square miles. Located at 27.37° N. Lat.; 82.49° W. Long.
Population: 2,533 (1990); 3,198 (2000); 3,327 (2004); 3,479 (2009 projected); Race: 92.2% White, 4.1% Black, 1.2% Asian, 5.0% Hispanic of any race (2004); Density: 2,639.3 persons per square mile (2004); Average household size: 2.44 (2004); Median age: 42.4 (2004); Male/female ratio: 92.8 (2004); Marriage status: 17.8% never married, 63.4% now married, 5.2% widowed, 13.6% divorced (2000); Foreign born: 8.3% (2000); Ancestry (includes multiple ancestries): 18.3% German, 14.7% Other groups, 14.4% Irish, 12.8% English, 6.3% French (except Basque) (2000).
Economy: Employment by occupation: 15.3% management, 26.7% professional, 16.6% services, 25.8% sales, 0.0% farming, 7.6% construction, 8.0% production (2000).
Income: Per capita income: $31,136 (2004); Median household income: $62,684 (2004); Average household income: $76,113 (2004); Percent of households with income of $100,000 or more: 20.1% (2004); Poverty rate: 3.8% (2000).
Education: Percent of population age 25 and over with: High school diploma (including GED) or higher: 90.6% (2004); Bachelor's degree or higher: 29.1% (2004); Master's degree or higher: 9.5% (2004).
Housing: Homeownership rate: 89.1% (2004); Median home value: $154,952 (2004); Median rent: $751 per month (2000); Median age of housing: 19 years (2000).
Transportation: Commute to work: 95.3% car, 0.6% public transportation, 0.0% walk, 3.6% work from home (2000); Travel time to work: 31.8% less than 15 minutes, 48.3% 15 to 30 minutes, 14.6% 30 to 45 minutes, 1.8% 45 to 60 minutes, 3.6% 60 minutes or more (2000)

ENGLEWOOD (CDP). Covers a land area of 9.830 square miles and a water area of 3.001 square miles. Located at 26.96° N. Lat.; 82.35° W. Long. Elevation is 13 feet.
Population: 15,032 (1990); 16,196 (2000); 16,480 (2004); 16,971 (2009 projected); Race: 98.1% White, 0.2% Black, 0.4% Asian, 1.9% Hispanic of any race (2004); Density: 1,676.5 persons per square mile (2004); Average household size: 1.93 (2004); Median age: 62.4 (2004); Male/female ratio: 89.0 (2004); Marriage status: 9.5% never married, 65.8% now married, 14.8% widowed, 10.0% divorced (2000); Foreign born: 5.9% (2000); Ancestry (includes multiple ancestries): 24.3% German, 19.3% English, 14.5% Irish, 6.5% United States or American, 6.3% Italian (2000).
Economy: Employment by occupation: 11.1% management, 15.6% professional, 21.4% services, 27.6% sales, 0.6% farming, 13.9% construction, 9.8% production (2000).
Income: Per capita income: $25,065 (2004); Median household income: $34,613 (2004); Average household income: $48,186 (2004); Percent of households with income of $100,000 or more: 7.4% (2004); Poverty rate: 8.7% (2000).
Education: Percent of population age 25 and over with: High school diploma (including GED) or higher: 85.2% (2004); Bachelor's degree or higher: 16.0% (2004); Master's degree or higher: 6.2% (2004).

School District(s)

Sarasota County School District (PK-12)
2002-03 Enrollment: 38,057 . . . . (941) 927-9000
Housing: Homeownership rate: 85.5% (2004); Median home value: $113,904 (2004); Median rent: $488 per month (2000); Median age of housing: 21 years (2000).
Hospitals: Englewood Community Hospital (100 beds)
Newspapers: Englewood Review (General - Circulation 6,000); Englewood Sun (Circulation 31,000)
Transportation: Commute to work: 94.2% car, 0.7% public transportation, 1.3% walk, 0.8% work from home (2000); Travel time to work: 41.4% less than 15 minutes, 28.2% 15 to 30 minutes, 18.8% 30 to 45 minutes, 5.0% 45 to 60 minutes, 6.6% 60 minutes or more (2000)
Additional Information Contacts
Englewood Area Board of Realtors . . . . (941) 475-6656
Englewood Area Chamber of Commerce . . . . (941) 474-5511

FRUITVILLE (CDP). Covers a land area of 7.039 square miles and a water area of 0 square miles. Located at 27.33° N. Lat.; 82.46° W. Long. Elevation is 25 feet.
Population: 9,570 (1990); 12,741 (2000); 14,012 (2004); 15,577 (2009 projected); Race: 94.7% White, 1.6% Black, 1.6% Asian, 4.9% Hispanic of any race (2004); Density: 1,990.5 persons per square mile (2004); Average household size: 2.43 (2004); Median age: 38.6 (2004); Male/female ratio: 95.1 (2004); Marriage status: 21.2% never married, 61.6% now married, 7.6% widowed, 9.6% divorced (2000); Foreign born: 7.3% (2000); Ancestry (includes multiple ancestries): 23.3% German, 15.0% Irish, 13.3% English, 10.1% Other groups, 9.6% Italian (2000).
Economy: Employment by occupation: 14.0% management, 21.7% professional, 14.7% services, 29.5% sales, 0.3% farming, 11.4% construction, 8.5% production (2000).
Income: Per capita income: $28,304 (2004); Median household income: $55,390 (2004); Average household income: $67,995 (2004); Percent of households with income of $100,000 or more: 15.2% (2004); Poverty rate: 4.7% (2000).
Education: Percent of population age 25 and over with: High school diploma (including GED) or higher: 89.3% (2004); Bachelor's degree or higher: 29.4% (2004); Master's degree or higher: 8.9% (2004).
Housing: Homeownership rate: 73.6% (2004); Median home value: $169,749 (2004); Median rent: $715 per month (2000); Median age of housing: 13 years (2000).
Transportation: Commute to work: 95.0% car, 0.2% public transportation, 0.7% walk, 3.1% work from home (2000); Travel time to work: 32.1% less than 15 minutes, 48.4% 15 to 30 minutes, 12.4% 30 to 45 minutes, 2.2% 45 to 60 minutes, 4.8% 60 minutes or more (2000)

GULF GATE ESTATES (CDP). Covers a land area of 2.811 square miles and a water area of 0 square miles. Located at 27.25° N. Lat.; 82.50° W. Long.
Population: 11,622 (1990); 11,647 (2000); 11,717 (2004); 11,918 (2009 projected); Race: 95.8% White, 1.1% Black, 1.0% Asian, 4.1% Hispanic of

any race (2004); Density: 4,167.6 persons per square mile (2004); Average household size: 1.93 (2004); Median age: 50.9 (2004); Male/female ratio: 82.4 (2004); Marriage status: 18.9% never married, 52.2% now married, 14.4% widowed, 14.5% divorced (2000); Foreign born: 11.0% (2000); Ancestry (includes multiple ancestries): 19.4% German, 15.0% English, 13.9% Irish, 9.4% Italian, 8.4% Other groups (2000).
Economy: Employment by occupation: 11.5% management, 16.6% professional, 18.0% services, 34.9% sales, 0.0% farming, 9.7% construction, 9.2% production (2000).
Income: Per capita income: $27,072 (2004); Median household income: $38,639 (2004); Average household income: $51,873 (2004); Percent of households with income of $100,000 or more: 8.6% (2004); Poverty rate: 5.9% (2000).
Education: Percent of population age 25 and over with: High school diploma (including GED) or higher: 87.9% (2004); Bachelor's degree or higher: 25.1% (2004); Master's degree or higher: 10.3% (2004).
Housing: Homeownership rate: 65.1% (2004); Median home value: $142,703 (2004); Median rent: $672 per month (2000); Median age of housing: 25 years (2000).
Transportation: Commute to work: 92.4% car, 0.6% public transportation, 1.7% walk, 3.9% work from home (2000); Travel time to work: 39.1% less than 15 minutes, 41.9% 15 to 30 minutes, 14.6% 30 to 45 minutes, 1.2% 45 to 60 minutes, 3.2% 60 minutes or more (2000)

KENSINGTON PARK (CDP). Covers a land area of 1.345 square miles and a water area of 0 square miles. Located at 27.35° N. Lat.; 82.49° W. Long.
Population: 3,165 (1990); 3,720 (2000); 3,946 (2004); 4,240 (2009 projected); Race: 81.7% White, 9.4% Black, 1.8% Asian, 14.2% Hispanic of any race (2004); Density: 2,933.2 persons per square mile (2004); Average household size: 2.42 (2004); Median age: 41.6 (2004); Male/female ratio: 91.5 (2004); Marriage status: 19.9% never married, 55.2% now married, 9.5% widowed, 15.4% divorced (2000); Foreign born: 16.8% (2000); Ancestry (includes multiple ancestries): 24.1% Other groups, 17.0% German, 12.6% Irish, 10.9% English, 9.3% United States or American (2000).
Economy: Employment by occupation: 12.7% management, 13.3% professional, 19.8% services, 30.9% sales, 0.6% farming, 11.5% construction, 11.3% production (2000).
Income: Per capita income: $22,517 (2004); Median household income: $43,534 (2004); Average household income: $54,578 (2004); Percent of households with income of $100,000 or more: 10.4% (2004); Poverty rate: 10.0% (2000).
Education: Percent of population age 25 and over with: High school diploma (including GED) or higher: 84.4% (2004); Bachelor's degree or higher: 20.2% (2004); Master's degree or higher: 7.3% (2004).
Housing: Homeownership rate: 88.1% (2004); Median home value: $125,432 (2004); Median rent: $740 per month (2000); Median age of housing: 34 years (2000).
Transportation: Commute to work: 96.2% car, 0.7% public transportation, 0.0% walk, 1.3% work from home (2000); Travel time to work: 20.6% less than 15 minutes, 58.0% 15 to 30 minutes, 13.6% 30 to 45 minutes, 4.6% 45 to 60 minutes, 3.2% 60 minutes or more (2000)

LAKE SARASOTA (CDP). Covers a land area of 1.368 square miles and a water area of 0 square miles. Located at 27.29° N. Lat.; 82.43° W. Long.
Population: 3,898 (1990); 4,458 (2000); 4,646 (2004); 4,902 (2009 projected); Race: 95.5% White, 1.1% Black, 0.2% Asian, 5.0% Hispanic of any race (2004); Density: 3,395.6 persons per square mile (2004); Average household size: 2.88 (2004); Median age: 35.6 (2004); Male/female ratio: 99.6 (2004); Marriage status: 21.3% never married, 60.3% now married, 3.4% widowed, 15.0% divorced (2000); Foreign born: 5.2% (2000); Ancestry (includes multiple ancestries): 23.1% German, 16.2% Irish, 13.3% Other groups, 10.8% English, 7.6% Italian (2000).
Economy: Employment by occupation: 10.1% management, 19.2% professional, 23.2% services, 27.1% sales, 0.0% farming, 12.7% construction, 7.6% production (2000).
Income: Per capita income: $22,442 (2004); Median household income: $56,559 (2004); Average household income: $64,600 (2004); Percent of households with income of $100,000 or more: 13.4% (2004); Poverty rate: 3.0% (2000).
Education: Percent of population age 25 and over with: High school diploma (including GED) or higher: 90.6% (2004); Bachelor's degree or higher: 21.7% (2004); Master's degree or higher: 5.9% (2004).
Housing: Homeownership rate: 79.9% (2004); Median home value: $158,862 (2004); Median rent: $909 per month (2000); Median age of housing: 16 years (2000).
Transportation: Commute to work: 94.6% car, 0.8% public transportation, 0.4% walk, 2.9% work from home (2000); Travel time to work: 26.9% less than 15 minutes, 46.7% 15 to 30 minutes, 14.5% 30 to 45 minutes, 6.7% 45 to 60 minutes, 5.1% 60 minutes or more (2000)

LAUREL (CDP). Covers a land area of 5.215 square miles and a water area of 0.864 square miles. Located at 27.14° N. Lat.; 82.46° W. Long. Elevation is 8 feet.
Population: 8,245 (1990); 8,393 (2000); 8,446 (2004); 8,607 (2009 projected); Race: 95.6% White, 1.8% Black, 0.9% Asian, 1.6% Hispanic of any race (2004); Density: 1,619.7 persons per square mile (2004); Average household size: 1.98 (2004); Median age: 57.6 (2004); Male/female ratio: 91.5 (2004); Marriage status: 10.6% never married, 63.7% now married, 13.9% widowed, 11.8% divorced (2000); Foreign born: 6.2% (2000); Ancestry (includes multiple ancestries): 23.0% German, 18.5% English, 12.9% Irish, 8.5% Other groups, 8.4% United States or American (2000).
Economy: Employment by occupation: 11.9% management, 20.4% professional, 15.5% services, 32.4% sales, 0.9% farming, 9.3% construction, 9.6% production (2000).
Income: Per capita income: $36,523 (2004); Median household income: $48,761 (2004); Average household income: $72,411 (2004); Percent of households with income of $100,000 or more: 16.1% (2004); Poverty rate: 8.4% (2000).
Education: Percent of population age 25 and over with: High school diploma (including GED) or higher: 87.9% (2004); Bachelor's degree or higher: 25.6% (2004); Master's degree or higher: 9.6% (2004).
Housing: Homeownership rate: 85.7% (2004); Median home value: $165,707 (2004); Median rent: $556 per month (2000); Median age of housing: 24 years (2000).
Transportation: Commute to work: 91.5% car, 0.7% public transportation, 1.0% walk, 5.9% work from home (2000); Travel time to work: 41.4% less than 15 minutes, 35.1% 15 to 30 minutes, 16.6% 30 to 45 minutes, 2.9% 45 to 60 minutes, 3.9% 60 minutes or more (2000)

LONGBOAT KEY (town). Covers a land area of 4.916 square miles and a water area of 12.150 square miles. Located at 27.39° N. Lat.; 82.64° W. Long.
Population: 5,937 (1990); 7,603 (2000); 7,466 (2004); 7,357 (2009 projected); Race: 99.2% White, 0.1% Black, 0.5% Asian, 0.7% Hispanic of any race (2004); Density: 1,518.6 persons per square mile (2004); Average household size: 1.76 (2004); Median age: 67.8 (2004); Male/female ratio: 86.7 (2004); Marriage status: 4.4% never married, 77.7% now married, 13.1% widowed, 4.8% divorced (2000); Foreign born: 11.2% (2000); Ancestry (includes multiple ancestries): 17.1% German, 14.8% English, 13.0% Irish, 10.3% Russian, 6.5% Other groups (2000).
Economy: Single-family building permits issued: 30 (2004); Multi-family building permits issued: 10 (2004); Employment by occupation: 35.0% management, 20.6% professional, 8.2% services, 27.2% sales, 0.0% farming, 4.1% construction, 5.0% production (2000).
Income: Per capita income: $86,648 (2004); Median household income: $93,656 (2004); Average household income: $152,683 (2004); Percent of households with income of $100,000 or more: 47.2% (2004); Poverty rate: 2.9% (2000).
Education: Percent of population age 25 and over with: High school diploma (including GED) or higher: 94.4% (2004); Bachelor's degree or higher: 52.9% (2004); Master's degree or higher: 24.6% (2004).
Housing: Homeownership rate: 91.7% (2004); Median home value: $459,656 (2004); Median rent: $875 per month (2000); Median age of housing: 22 years (2000).
Safety: Violent crime rate: 1.3 per 10,000 population; Property crime rate: 120.9 per 10,000 population (2003).
Newspapers: The Longboat Observer (General - Circulation 20,000)
Transportation: Commute to work: 66.4% car, 1.5% public transportation, 4.6% walk, 20.1% work from home (2000); Travel time to work: 40.2% less than 15 minutes, 27.1% 15 to 30 minutes, 19.2% 30 to 45 minutes, 4.8% 45 to 60 minutes, 8.8% 60 minutes or more (2000)

Additional Information Contacts

Local Government Offices .... (941) 316-1999
Longboat Key Chamber of Commerce .... (941) 383-2466

NOKOMIS (CDP). Covers a land area of 1.668 square miles and a water area of 0.315 square miles. Located at 27.12° N. Lat.; 82.43° W. Long. Elevation is 10 feet.
History: The name of Nokomis is of Indian origin meaning "my grandmother."
Population: 3,301 (1990); 3,334 (2000); 3,387 (2004); 3,432 (2009 projected); Race: 97.3% White, 0.8% Black, 0.3% Asian, 2.5% Hispanic of any race (2004); Density: 2,030.3 persons per square mile (2004); Average household size: 2.12 (2004); Median age: 46.6 (2004); Male/female ratio: 100.8 (2004); Marriage status: 17.8% never married, 55.8% now married, 10.6% widowed, 15.7% divorced (2000); Foreign born: 2.7% (2000); Ancestry (includes multiple ancestries): 24.8% German, 15.0% English, 14.9% Irish, 9.2% United States or American, 8.5% Other groups (2000).
Economy: Employment by occupation: 8.4% management, 17.9% professional, 18.5% services, 30.3% sales, 1.2% farming, 16.3% construction, 7.3% production (2000).
Income: Per capita income: $25,903 (2004); Median household income: $38,146 (2004); Average household income: $54,704 (2004); Percent of households with income of $100,000 or more: 11.3% (2004); Poverty rate: 12.9% (2000).
Education: Percent of population age 25 and over with: High school diploma (including GED) or higher: 80.7% (2004); Bachelor's degree or higher: 13.0% (2004); Master's degree or higher: 6.1% (2004).

School District(s)

Sarasota County School District (PK-12)
2002-03 Enrollment: 38,057 . . . . (941) 927-9000
Housing: Homeownership rate: 79.1% (2004); Median home value: $91,603 (2004); Median rent: $452 per month (2000); Median age of housing: 26 years (2000).
Transportation: Commute to work: 93.6% car, 0.0% public transportation, 1.6% walk, 3.4% work from home (2000); Travel time to work: 37.8% less than 15 minutes, 35.8% 15 to 30 minutes, 16.0% 30 to 45 minutes, 4.1% 45 to 60 minutes, 6.2% 60 minutes or more (2000)

NORTH PORT (city). Aka North Port Charlotte. Covers a land area of 74.772 square miles and a water area of 0.766 square miles. Located at 27.06° N. Lat.; 82.17° W. Long. Elevation is 11 feet.
Population: 11,987 (1990); 22,797 (2000); 31,257 (2004); 41,057 (2009 projected); Race: 91.4% White, 5.1% Black, 0.6% Asian, 4.0% Hispanic of any race (2004); Density: 418.0 persons per square mile (2004); Average household size: 2.53 (2004); Median age: 40.5 (2004); Male/female ratio: 92.6 (2004); Marriage status: 15.6% never married, 63.8% now married, 9.5% widowed, 11.0% divorced (2000); Foreign born: 12.1% (2000); Ancestry (includes multiple ancestries): 21.8% German, 15.8% Irish, 11.9% English, 10.4% Other groups, 8.5% Italian (2000).
Economy: Contains Little Salt Springs archeological site. Unemployment rate: 3.6% (2004); Total civilian labor force: 6,451 (2004); Single-family building permits issued: 3,510 (2004); Multi-family building permits issued: 0 (2004); Employment by occupation: 8.4% management, 14.4% professional, 21.5% services, 29.8% sales, 0.1% farming, 14.8% construction, 11.0% production (2000).
Income: Per capita income: $19,124 (2004); Median household income: $41,137 (2004); Average household income: $48,004 (2004); Percent of households with income of $100,000 or more: 6.2% (2004); Poverty rate: 8.3% (2000).
Taxes: Total city taxes per capita: $434 (2002); City property taxes per capita: $157 (2002).
Education: Percent of population age 25 and over with: High school diploma (including GED) or higher: 80.7% (2004); Bachelor's degree or higher: 11.5% (2004); Master's degree or higher: 4.2% (2004).

School District(s)

Sarasota County School District (PK-12)
2002-03 Enrollment: 38,057 . . . . (941) 927-9000
Housing: Homeownership rate: 88.3% (2004); Median home value: $119,837 (2004); Median rent: $540 per month (2000); Median age of housing: 14 years (2000).
Safety: Violent crime rate: 38.1 per 10,000 population; Property crime rate: 304.9 per 10,000 population (2003).
Newspapers: North Port Sun (Circulation 5,500)
Transportation: Commute to work: 95.0% car, 0.4% public transportation, 0.4% walk, 2.5% work from home (2000); Travel time to work: 17.8% less than 15 minutes, 35.6% 15 to 30 minutes, 28.5% 30 to 45 minutes, 11.0% 45 to 60 minutes, 7.1% 60 minutes or more (2000)
Additional Information Contacts
North Port Chamber of Commerce . . . . (941) 423-5040

NORTH SARASOTA (CDP). Covers a land area of 3.783 square miles and a water area of 0 square miles. Located at 27.36° N. Lat.; 82.51° W. Long.
Population: 6,702 (1990); 6,738 (2000); 6,714 (2004); 6,795 (2009 projected); Race: 60.0% White, 33.9% Black, 0.5% Asian, 11.3% Hispanic of any race (2004); Density: 1,774.9 persons per square mile (2004); Average household size: 2.41 (2004); Median age: 42.2 (2004); Male/female ratio: 92.8 (2004); Marriage status: 22.2% never married, 54.5% now married, 8.1% widowed, 15.2% divorced (2000); Foreign born: 8.9% (2000); Ancestry (includes multiple ancestries): 33.0% Other groups, 14.1% German, 10.2% United States or American, 8.8% Irish, 8.3% English (2000).
Economy: Employment by occupation: 8.2% management, 13.1% professional, 23.2% services, 26.0% sales, 1.0% farming, 11.3% construction, 17.1% production (2000).
Income: Per capita income: $18,607 (2004); Median household income: $34,697 (2004); Average household income: $44,873 (2004); Percent of households with income of $100,000 or more: 7.7% (2004); Poverty rate: 17.2% (2000).
Education: Percent of population age 25 and over with: High school diploma (including GED) or higher: 74.0% (2004); Bachelor's degree or higher: 12.8% (2004); Master's degree or higher: 4.3% (2004).
Housing: Homeownership rate: 80.3% (2004); Median home value: $93,797 (2004); Median rent: $480 per month (2000); Median age of housing: 23 years (2000).
Transportation: Commute to work: 91.8% car, 0.9% public transportation, 0.4% walk, 2.6% work from home (2000); Travel time to work: 35.6% less than 15 minutes, 42.1% 15 to 30 minutes, 16.9% 30 to 45 minutes, 2.3% 45 to 60 minutes, 3.0% 60 minutes or more (2000)

OSPREY (CDP). Covers a land area of 5.455 square miles and a water area of 0.611 square miles. Located at 27.19° N. Lat.; 82.48° W. Long. Elevation is 14 feet.
History: Osprey developed as a fishing settlement. The town was named for the osprey, or fish hawk.
Population: 2,886 (1990); 4,143 (2000); 4,641 (2004); 5,252 (2009 projected); Race: 97.0% White, 0.2% Black, 1.2% Asian, 1.8% Hispanic of any race (2004); Density: 850.7 persons per square mile (2004); Average household size: 2.10 (2004); Median age: 53.9 (2004); Male/female ratio: 94.4 (2004); Marriage status: 11.1% never married, 71.5% now married, 7.3% widowed, 10.1% divorced (2000); Foreign born: 10.3% (2000); Ancestry (includes multiple ancestries): 24.2% German, 18.3% English, 14.5% Irish, 8.5% Italian, 7.2% United States or American (2000).
Economy: Employment by occupation: 14.8% management, 14.7% professional, 22.3% services, 33.6% sales, 0.0% farming, 9.6% construction, 5.1% production (2000).
Income: Per capita income: $54,927 (2004); Median household income: $70,339 (2004); Average household income: $115,556 (2004); Percent of households with income of $100,000 or more: 33.3% (2004); Poverty rate: 6.5% (2000).
Education: Percent of population age 25 and over with: High school diploma (including GED) or higher: 88.6% (2004); Bachelor's degree or higher: 35.6% (2004); Master's degree or higher: 13.0% (2004).

School District(s)

Sarasota County School District (PK-12)
2002-03 Enrollment: 38,057 . . . . (941) 927-9000
Housing: Homeownership rate: 88.8% (2004); Median home value: $254,965 (2004); Median rent: $525 per month (2000); Median age of housing: 15 years (2000).
Transportation: Commute to work: 83.8% car, 0.6% public transportation, 0.0% walk, 12.6% work from home (2000); Travel time to work: 24.7% less than 15 minutes, 50.0% 15 to 30 minutes, 18.4% 30 to 45 minutes, 2.2% 45 to 60 minutes, 4.7% 60 minutes or more (2000)

PLANTATION (CDP). Covers a land area of 2.448 square miles and a water area of 0.004 square miles. Located at 27.06° N. Lat.; 82.37° W. Long.
Population: 1,885 (1990); 4,168 (2000); 5,067 (2004); 6,135 (2009 projected); Race: 98.4% White, 0.2% Black, 0.4% Asian, 1.0% Hispanic of any race (2004); Density: 2,070.0 persons per square mile (2004); Average household size: 1.94 (2004); Median age: 67.2 (2004); Male/female ratio: 88.2 (2004); Marriage status: 5.7% never married, 82.3% now married, 7.8% widowed, 4.2% divorced (2000); Foreign born: 10.4% (2000);

Ancestry (includes multiple ancestries): 24.8% German, 19.8% English, 19.7% Irish, 8.4% Italian, 6.5% Polish (2000).
Economy: Employment by occupation: 19.7% management, 22.1% professional, 12.7% services, 30.6% sales, 0.0% farming, 3.7% construction, 11.2% production (2000).
Income: Per capita income: $36,656 (2004); Median household income: $58,289 (2004); Average household income: $71,218 (2004); Percent of households with income of $100,000 or more: 15.6% (2004); Poverty rate: 0.9% (2000).
Education: Percent of population age 25 and over with: High school diploma (including GED) or higher: 94.4% (2004); Bachelor's degree or higher: 30.9% (2004); Master's degree or higher: 11.8% (2004).
Housing: Homeownership rate: 96.5% (2004); Median home value: $227,793 (2004); Median rent: $744 per month (2000); Median age of housing: 10 years (2000).
Transportation: Commute to work: 94.6% car, 0.0% public transportation, 0.9% walk, 4.5% work from home (2000); Travel time to work: 33.3% less than 15 minutes, 42.0% 15 to 30 minutes, 16.8% 30 to 45 minutes, 5.2% 45 to 60 minutes, 2.7% 60 minutes or more (2000)

RIDGE WOOD HEIGHTS (CDP). Covers a land area of 1.429 square miles and a water area of 0.026 square miles. Located at 27.29° N. Lat.; 82.51° W. Long.
Population: 4,851 (1990); 5,028 (2000); 5,043 (2004); 5,115 (2009 projected); Race: 95.0% White, 1.1% Black, 1.1% Asian, 5.6% Hispanic of any race (2004); Density: 3,528.4 persons per square mile (2004); Average household size: 2.23 (2004); Median age: 39.2 (2004); Male/female ratio: 100.5 (2004); Marriage status: 23.0% never married, 54.8% now married, 4.8% widowed, 17.3% divorced (2000); Foreign born: 6.2% (2000); Ancestry (includes multiple ancestries): 27.7% German, 18.5% Irish, 15.2% English, 10.1% Other groups, 8.2% Italian (2000).
Economy: Employment by occupation: 12.6% management, 17.1% professional, 18.2% services, 28.8% sales, 0.0% farming, 14.0% construction, 9.4% production (2000).
Income: Per capita income: $24,594 (2004); Median household income: $47,220 (2004); Average household income: $54,758 (2004); Percent of households with income of $100,000 or more: 11.3% (2004); Poverty rate: 6.0% (2000).
Education: Percent of population age 25 and over with: High school diploma (including GED) or higher: 86.1% (2004); Bachelor's degree or higher: 21.1% (2004); Master's degree or higher: 5.7% (2004).
Housing: Homeownership rate: 71.5% (2004); Median home value: $136,816 (2004); Median rent: $621 per month (2000); Median age of housing: 25 years (2000).
Transportation: Commute to work: 94.4% car, 0.9% public transportation, 1.1% walk, 1.1% work from home (2000); Travel time to work: 38.3% less than 15 minutes, 46.1% 15 to 30 minutes, 8.6% 30 to 45 minutes, 3.1% 45 to 60 minutes, 3.9% 60 minutes or more (2000)

SARASOTA (city). Covers a land area of 14.892 square miles and a water area of 11.037 square miles. Located at 27.33° N. Lat.; 82.53° W. Long. Elevation is 27 feet.
History: Sarasota was settled in 1884 by sixty Scottish families, who kept the name of Sarasota by which the area had previously been known. A golf course was built in 1886, and with golf and fishing, Sarasota became popular as a winter resort. When Sarasota County was carved out of Manatee County by the legislature in 1921, Sarasota was named the county seat. John Ringling selected Sarasota as winter quarters for his circus in 1929 and made his home here.
Population: 51,400 (1990); 52,715 (2000); 54,031 (2004); 56,146 (2009 projected); Race: 74.6% White, 16.8% Black, 1.2% Asian, 15.4% Hispanic of any race (2004); Density: 3,628.2 persons per square mile (2004); Average household size: 2.24 (2004); Median age: 41.2 (2004); Male/female ratio: 95.4 (2004); Marriage status: 27.2% never married, 46.2% now married, 11.3% widowed, 15.4% divorced (2000); Foreign born: 13.9% (2000); Ancestry (includes multiple ancestries): 27.0% Other groups, 14.0% German, 10.5% English, 10.5% Irish, 6.2% United States or American (2000).
Economy: Unemployment rate: 4.0% (2004); Total civilian labor force: 35,961 (2004); Single-family building permits issued: 123 (2004); Multi-family building permits issued: 398 (2004); Employment by occupation: 11.2% management, 17.8% professional, 23.1% services, 26.6% sales, 0.4% farming, 11.1% construction, 9.8% production (2000).
Income: Per capita income: $25,148 (2004); Median household income: $37,015 (2004); Average household income: $54,516 (2004); Percent of households with income of $100,000 or more: 10.5% (2004); Poverty rate: 16.7% (2000).
Taxes: Total city taxes per capita: $800 (2002); City property taxes per capita: $225 (2002).
Education: Percent of population age 25 and over with: High school diploma (including GED) or higher: 80.2% (2004); Bachelor's degree or higher: 25.6% (2004); Master's degree or higher: 9.2% (2004).

School District(s)

Sarasota County School District (PK-12)
2002-03 Enrollment: 38,057 . . . . (941) 927-9000

Four-year College(s)

Argosy University- Sarasota Campus (Private, For-profit)
2003-04 Enrollment: 2,290 . . . . (941) 379-0404
East West College of Natural Medicine
2003-04 Enrollment: 151 . . . . (941) 955-4456
New College of Florida
2003-04 Enrollment: 671 . . . . (941) 359-4269
2003-04 Tuition: In-state $3,240; Out-of-state $16,473
Ringling School of Art and Design
2003-04 Enrollment: 989 . . . . (800) 255-7695
2003-04 Tuition: In-state $19,060; Out-of-state $19,060

Two-year College(s)

Fashion Focus Hair Academy (Private, For-profit)
2003-04 Enrollment: 71 . . . . (941) 921-4877
Florida College of Natural Health (Private, For-profit)
2003-04 Enrollment: 124 . . . . (941) 954-8999
Keiser College-Sarasota (Private, For-profit)
2003-04 Enrollment: n/a . . . . (941) 907-3900
2003-04 Tuition: In-state $10,920; Out-of-state $10,920
Sarasota County Technical Institute (Public)
2003-04 Enrollment: 80 . . . . (941) 924-1365
Sarasota School of Massage Therapy (Private, For-profit)
2003-04 Enrollment: 129 . . . . (941) 957-0577
Sunstate Academy of Hair Design (Private, For-profit)
2003-04 Enrollment: 49 . . . . (941) 377-4880

Housing: Homeownership rate: 58.3% (2004); Median home value: $138,797 (2004); Median rent: $566 per month (2000); Median age of housing: 30 years (2000).
Hospitals: Bayside Center for Behavorial Health at Sarasota Memorial (82 beds); Doctors Hospital of Sarasota (147 beds); HealthSouth Rehabilitation Hospital of Sarasota (70 beds); Sarasota Memorial Health Care Systems (845 beds)
Safety: Violent crime rate: 104.2 per 10,000 population; Property crime rate: 734.3 per 10,000 population (2003).
Newspapers: New York Staats Zeitung (Ethnic - Circulation 20,000); Pelican Press (General - Circulation 24,000); Sarasota Herald-Tribune (Circulation 116,044); Tempo News (General - Circulation 25,000); The Weekly (General - Circulation 50,000)
Transportation: Commute to work: 88.2% car, 2.5% public transportation, 2.7% walk, 3.5% work from home (2000); Travel time to work: 39.0% less than 15 minutes, 40.2% 15 to 30 minutes, 14.0% 30 to 45 minutes, 3.2% 45 to 60 minutes, 3.6% 60 minutes or more (2000); Amtrak: Service available.
Airports: Sarasota/Bradenton International (primary service/small hub)

Additional Information Contacts

Committee for Economic Development . . . . (941) 955-2508
Sarasota Association of Realtors . . . . (941) 923-2315
Sarasota Chamber of Commerce . . . . (941) 955-8187
Siesta Key Chamber of Commerce . . . . (941) 349-3800

SARASOTA SPRINGS (CDP). Covers a land area of 3.617 square miles and a water area of 0 square miles. Located at 27.31° N. Lat.; 82.47° W. Long.
Population: 16,088 (1990); 15,875 (2000); 15,809 (2004); 15,816 (2009 projected); Race: 94.8% White, 0.9% Black, 0.9% Asian, 6.1% Hispanic of any race (2004); Density: 4,371.3 persons per square mile (2004); Average household size: 2.37 (2004); Median age: 41.1 (2004); Male/female ratio: 92.9 (2004); Marriage status: 19.8% never married, 58.1% now married, 9.3% widowed, 12.8% divorced (2000); Foreign born: 5.9% (2000); Ancestry (includes multiple ancestries): 22.2% German, 14.1% Irish, 13.0% English, 11.0% Other groups, 9.3% United States or American (2000).
Economy: Employment by occupation: 10.8% management, 17.6% professional, 19.4% services, 30.6% sales, 0.3% farming, 12.7% construction, 8.7% production (2000).

Income: Per capita income: $24,273 (2004); Median household income: $46,219 (2004); Average household income: $57,432 (2004); Percent of households with income of $100,000 or more: 10.4% (2004); Poverty rate: 6.9% (2000).
Education: Percent of population age 25 and over with: High school diploma (including GED) or higher: 89.0% (2004); Bachelor's degree or higher: 20.2% (2004); Master's degree or higher: 6.5% (2004).
Housing: Homeownership rate: 82.9% (2004); Median home value: $132,762 (2004); Median rent: $675 per month (2000); Median age of housing: 25 years (2000).
Transportation: Commute to work: 95.5% car, 0.3% public transportation, 0.8% walk, 2.3% work from home (2000); Travel time to work: 30.2% less than 15 minutes, 50.7% 15 to 30 minutes, 12.5% 30 to 45 minutes, 2.1% 45 to 60 minutes, 4.4% 60 minutes or more (2000)

SIESTA KEY (CDP). Covers a land area of 2.292 square miles and a water area of 1.163 square miles. Located at 27.27° N. Lat.; 82.55° W. Long.
Population: 7,772 (1990); 7,150 (2000); 6,926 (2004); 6,658 (2009 projected); Race: 98.3% White, 0.1% Black, 0.6% Asian, 1.9% Hispanic of any race (2004); Density: 3,022.4 persons per square mile (2004); Average household size: 1.88 (2004); Median age: 59.5 (2004); Male/female ratio: 91.1 (2004); Marriage status: 11.1% never married, 66.4% now married, 11.7% widowed, 10.9% divorced (2000); Foreign born: 10.5% (2000); Ancestry (includes multiple ancestries): 21.4% German, 18.6% English, 15.1% Irish, 6.4% Other groups, 5.5% United States or American (2000).
Economy: Employment by occupation: 26.2% management, 28.7% professional, 10.7% services, 28.5% sales, 0.3% farming, 2.4% construction, 3.2% production (2000).
Income: Per capita income: $62,733 (2004); Median household income: $78,028 (2004); Average household income: $117,684 (2004); Percent of households with income of $100,000 or more: 36.2% (2004); Poverty rate: 4.4% (2000).
Education: Percent of population age 25 and over with: High school diploma (including GED) or higher: 95.7% (2004); Bachelor's degree or higher: 51.7% (2004); Master's degree or higher: 22.0% (2004).
Housing: Homeownership rate: 82.6% (2004); Median home value: $418,228 (2004); Median rent: $942 per month (2000); Median age of housing: 26 years (2000).
Transportation: Commute to work: 80.6% car, 0.3% public transportation, 3.6% walk, 12.2% work from home (2000); Travel time to work: 31.9% less than 15 minutes, 46.2% 15 to 30 minutes, 14.0% 30 to 45 minutes, 1.4% 45 to 60 minutes, 6.5% 60 minutes or more (2000)

SOUTH GATE RIDGE (CDP). Covers a land area of 1.811 square miles and a water area of 0 square miles. Located at 27.28° N. Lat.; 82.49° W. Long.
Population: 5,924 (1990); 5,655 (2000); 5,704 (2004); 5,817 (2009 projected); Race: 93.0% White, 0.8% Black, 2.4% Asian, 7.0% Hispanic of any race (2004); Density: 3,149.5 persons per square mile (2004); Average household size: 2.24 (2004); Median age: 42.3 (2004); Male/female ratio: 92.2 (2004); Marriage status: 19.4% never married, 56.7% now married, 9.3% widowed, 14.7% divorced (2000); Foreign born: 8.4% (2000); Ancestry (includes multiple ancestries): 17.9% German, 14.7% Irish, 14.3% English, 13.4% Italian, 11.2% Other groups (2000).
Economy: Employment by occupation: 14.6% management, 20.9% professional, 20.9% services, 22.9% sales, 0.0% farming, 12.9% construction, 7.9% production (2000).
Income: Per capita income: $29,010 (2004); Median household income: $51,310 (2004); Average household income: $64,810 (2004); Percent of households with income of $100,000 or more: 16.6% (2004); Poverty rate: 4.5% (2000).
Education: Percent of population age 25 and over with: High school diploma (including GED) or higher: 90.7% (2004); Bachelor's degree or higher: 28.6% (2004); Master's degree or higher: 10.1% (2004).
Housing: Homeownership rate: 75.1% (2004); Median home value: $141,806 (2004); Median rent: $670 per month (2000); Median age of housing: 24 years (2000).
Transportation: Commute to work: 93.8% car, 0.5% public transportation, 0.0% walk, 4.6% work from home (2000); Travel time to work: 36.3% less than 15 minutes, 44.3% 15 to 30 minutes, 11.8% 30 to 45 minutes, 2.3% 45 to 60 minutes, 5.3% 60 minutes or more (2000)

SOUTH SARASOTA (CDP). Covers a land area of 1.951 square miles and a water area of 0.372 square miles. Located at 27.28° N. Lat.; 82.53° W. Long.
Population: 5,174 (1990); 5,314 (2000); 5,261 (2004); 5,256 (2009 projected); Race: 95.1% White, 0.4% Black, 1.5% Asian, 5.0% Hispanic of any race (2004); Density: 2,697.1 persons per square mile (2004); Average household size: 2.08 (2004); Median age: 48.1 (2004); Male/female ratio: 95.6 (2004); Marriage status: 19.8% never married, 57.0% now married, 8.1% widowed, 15.1% divorced (2000); Foreign born: 8.5% (2000); Ancestry (includes multiple ancestries): 22.4% German, 18.2% English, 15.2% Irish, 9.5% Other groups, 8.1% Italian (2000).
Economy: Employment by occupation: 15.2% management, 24.2% professional, 14.6% services, 31.0% sales, 0.0% farming, 8.4% construction, 6.6% production (2000).
Income: Per capita income: $48,797 (2004); Median household income: $60,241 (2004); Average household income: $101,350 (2004); Percent of households with income of $100,000 or more: 29.7% (2004); Poverty rate: 6.6% (2000).
Education: Percent of population age 25 and over with: High school diploma (including GED) or higher: 90.4% (2004); Bachelor's degree or higher: 42.7% (2004); Master's degree or higher: 17.0% (2004).
Housing: Homeownership rate: 79.8% (2004); Median home value: $230,286 (2004); Median rent: $598 per month (2000); Median age of housing: 26 years (2000).
Transportation: Commute to work: 85.5% car, 0.9% public transportation, 5.2% walk, 6.3% work from home (2000); Travel time to work: 42.9% less than 15 minutes, 37.1% 15 to 30 minutes, 13.0% 30 to 45 minutes, 1.8% 45 to 60 minutes, 5.1% 60 minutes or more (2000)

SOUTH VENICE (CDP). Covers a land area of 6.213 square miles and a water area of 0.371 square miles. Located at 27.04° N. Lat.; 82.41° W. Long. Elevation is 17 feet.
Population: 11,999 (1990); 13,539 (2000); 14,076 (2004); 14,825 (2009 projected); Race: 97.3% White, 0.6% Black, 0.5% Asian, 2.2% Hispanic of any race (2004); Density: 2,265.6 persons per square mile (2004); Average household size: 2.31 (2004); Median age: 45.2 (2004); Male/female ratio: 94.3 (2004); Marriage status: 15.6% never married, 63.3% now married, 7.9% widowed, 13.2% divorced (2000); Foreign born: 5.2% (2000); Ancestry (includes multiple ancestries): 20.8% German, 17.6% Irish, 17.4% English, 9.6% Italian, 8.5% Other groups (2000).
Economy: Employment by occupation: 8.6% management, 15.2% professional, 22.1% services, 28.7% sales, 0.0% farming, 12.5% construction, 12.9% production (2000).
Income: Per capita income: $21,592 (2004); Median household income: $40,065 (2004); Average household income: $49,801 (2004); Percent of households with income of $100,000 or more: 5.7% (2004); Poverty rate: 5.7% (2000).
Education: Percent of population age 25 and over with: High school diploma (including GED) or higher: 82.8% (2004); Bachelor's degree or higher: 14.5% (2004); Master's degree or higher: 4.5% (2004).
Housing: Homeownership rate: 88.8% (2004); Median home value: $124,183 (2004); Median rent: $561 per month (2000); Median age of housing: 22 years (2000).
Transportation: Commute to work: 95.8% car, 0.3% public transportation, 0.8% walk, 2.2% work from home (2000); Travel time to work: 36.0% less than 15 minutes, 33.8% 15 to 30 minutes, 19.5% 30 to 45 minutes, 5.3% 45 to 60 minutes, 5.3% 60 minutes or more (2000)

SOUTHGATE (CDP). Aka Sarasota Southeast. Covers a land area of 2.044 square miles and a water area of 0.036 square miles. Located at 27.30° N. Lat.; 82.51° W. Long.
Population: 7,267 (1990); 7,455 (2000); 7,458 (2004); 7,580 (2009 projected); Race: 95.4% White, 1.1% Black, 1.2% Asian, 7.8% Hispanic of any race (2004); Density: 3,649.3 persons per square mile (2004); Average household size: 2.04 (2004); Median age: 47.8 (2004); Male/female ratio: 88.8 (2004); Marriage status: 15.0% never married, 59.6% now married, 9.0% widowed, 16.4% divorced (2000); Foreign born: 9.8% (2000); Ancestry (includes multiple ancestries): 24.0% German, 16.3% English, 13.3% Irish, 11.9% Other groups, 8.1% Italian (2000).
Economy: Employment by occupation: 12.4% management, 17.4% professional, 21.3% services, 31.3% sales, 0.5% farming, 9.6% construction, 7.5% production (2000).
Income: Per capita income: $27,265 (2004); Median household income: $44,967 (2004); Average household income: $55,422 (2004); Percent of

households with income of $100,000 or more: 11.7% (2004); Poverty rate: 6.8% (2000).
Education: Percent of population age 25 and over with: High school diploma (including GED) or higher: 87.5% (2004); Bachelor's degree or higher: 24.7% (2004); Master's degree or higher: 9.6% (2004).
Housing: Homeownership rate: 78.8% (2004); Median home value: $156,868 (2004); Median rent: $605 per month (2000); Median age of housing: 33 years (2000).
Transportation: Commute to work: 91.0% car, 0.7% public transportation, 2.0% walk, 4.3% work from home (2000); Travel time to work: 43.7% less than 15 minutes, 38.9% 15 to 30 minutes, 12.0% 30 to 45 minutes, 2.0% 45 to 60 minutes, 3.4% 60 minutes or more (2000)

THE MEADOWS (CDP). Covers a land area of 2.316 square miles and a water area of 0 square miles. Located at 27.36° N. Lat.; 82.47° W. Long.
Population: 3,665 (1990); 4,423 (2000); 4,724 (2004); 5,111 (2009 projected); Race: 95.7% White, 2.2% Black, 0.9% Asian, 1.6% Hispanic of any race (2004); Density: 2,039.7 persons per square mile (2004); Average household size: 1.81 (2004); Median age: 68.7 (2004); Male/female ratio: 80.2 (2004); Marriage status: 8.4% never married, 68.0% now married, 15.7% widowed, 7.9% divorced (2000); Foreign born: 12.8% (2000); Ancestry (includes multiple ancestries): 15.2% German, 15.0% English, 14.7% Irish, 8.5% Other groups, 8.5% Italian (2000).
Economy: Employment by occupation: 26.2% management, 21.0% professional, 14.8% services, 34.4% sales, 0.0% farming, 0.0% construction, 3.5% production (2000).
Income: Per capita income: $43,957 (2004); Median household income: $60,156 (2004); Average household income: $78,088 (2004); Percent of households with income of $100,000 or more: 22.0% (2004); Poverty rate: 3.4% (2000).
Education: Percent of population age 25 and over with: High school diploma (including GED) or higher: 96.5% (2004); Bachelor's degree or higher: 46.0% (2004); Master's degree or higher: 17.6% (2004).
Housing: Homeownership rate: 81.0% (2004); Median home value: $175,241 (2004); Median rent: $938 per month (2000); Median age of housing: 16 years (2000).
Transportation: Commute to work: 88.8% car, 0.0% public transportation, 0.7% walk, 9.9% work from home (2000); Travel time to work: 31.4% less than 15 minutes, 52.2% 15 to 30 minutes, 12.9% 30 to 45 minutes, 0.0% 45 to 60 minutes, 3.5% 60 minutes or more (2000)

VAMO (CDP). Covers a land area of 1.773 square miles and a water area of 0.316 square miles. Located at 27.22° N. Lat.; 82.49° W. Long. Elevation is 15 feet.
Population: 3,325 (1990); 5,285 (2000); 5,594 (2004); 5,958 (2009 projected); Race: 96.0% White, 1.0% Black, 1.4% Asian, 4.7% Hispanic of any race (2004); Density: 3,155.6 persons per square mile (2004); Average household size: 2.05 (2004); Median age: 50.8 (2004); Male/female ratio: 82.9 (2004); Marriage status: 19.9% never married, 50.4% now married, 15.3% widowed, 14.4% divorced (2000); Foreign born: 8.7% (2000); Ancestry (includes multiple ancestries): 17.0% German, 16.6% English, 13.9% Irish, 9.1% United States or American, 7.0% Other groups (2000).
Economy: Employment by occupation: 15.3% management, 17.8% professional, 23.4% services, 28.0% sales, 0.0% farming, 4.6% construction, 10.8% production (2000).
Income: Per capita income: $38,137 (2004); Median household income: $49,904 (2004); Average household income: $70,083 (2004); Percent of households with income of $100,000 or more: 17.4% (2004); Poverty rate: 5.6% (2000).
Education: Percent of population age 25 and over with: High school diploma (including GED) or higher: 92.5% (2004); Bachelor's degree or higher: 42.3% (2004); Master's degree or higher: 17.7% (2004).
Housing: Homeownership rate: 54.6% (2004); Median home value: $167,523 (2004); Median rent: $825 per month (2000); Median age of housing: 18 years (2000).
Transportation: Commute to work: 90.9% car, 0.3% public transportation, 2.8% walk, 2.5% work from home (2000); Travel time to work: 27.3% less than 15 minutes, 44.4% 15 to 30 minutes, 20.1% 30 to 45 minutes, 5.0% 45 to 60 minutes, 3.1% 60 minutes or more (2000)

VENICE (city). Covers a land area of 9.115 square miles and a water area of 0.548 square miles. Located at 27.09° N. Lat.; 82.43° W. Long. Elevation is 15 feet.
History: Venice came into existence during the Florida land boom of the 1920's. It was built by the Brotherhood of Locomotive Engineers, who laid out a city that had few residents until the mid-1930's.
Population: 18,380 (1990); 17,764 (2000); 18,946 (2004); 20,468 (2009 projected); Race: 97.9% White, 0.6% Black, 0.5% Asian, 1.3% Hispanic of any race (2004); Density: 2,078.5 persons per square mile (2004); Average household size: 1.81 (2004); Median age: 68.2 (2004); Male/female ratio: 77.3 (2004); Marriage status: 8.7% never married, 62.5% now married, 19.3% widowed, 9.5% divorced (2000); Foreign born: 6.8% (2000); Ancestry (includes multiple ancestries): 20.8% German, 19.1% English, 17.4% Irish, 7.9% Italian, 6.6% United States or American (2000).
Economy: Single-family building permits issued: 426 (2004); Multi-family building permits issued: 475 (2004); Employment by occupation: 14.0% management, 21.3% professional, 22.3% services, 29.1% sales, 0.1% farming, 6.5% construction, 6.6% production (2000).
Income: Per capita income: $31,268 (2004); Median household income: $40,366 (2004); Average household income: $54,857 (2004); Percent of households with income of $100,000 or more: 11.0% (2004); Poverty rate: 5.7% (2000).
Taxes: Total city taxes per capita: $568 (2002); City property taxes per capita: $260 (2002).
Education: Percent of population age 25 and over with: High school diploma (including GED) or higher: 89.9% (2004); Bachelor's degree or higher: 28.1% (2004); Master's degree or higher: 10.3% (2004).

School District(s)

Sarasota County School District (PK-12)
2002-03 Enrollment: 38,057 .... (941) 927-9000
Housing: Homeownership rate: 77.9% (2004); Median home value: $146,320 (2004); Median rent: $640 per month (2000); Median age of housing: 24 years (2000).
Hospitals: Bon Secours Venice Hospital (342 beds)
Safety: Violent crime rate: 19.5 per 10,000 population; Property crime rate: 278.8 per 10,000 population (2003).
Newspapers: The Venice Gondolier (General - Circulation 12,000)
Transportation: Commute to work: 87.6% car, 0.2% public transportation, 3.4% walk, 6.2% work from home (2000); Travel time to work: 46.2% less than 15 minutes, 27.1% 15 to 30 minutes, 17.3% 30 to 45 minutes, 4.6% 45 to 60 minutes, 4.7% 60 minutes or more (2000)
Additional Information Contacts
Venice Area Board of Realtors .... (941) 484-0614
Venice Chamber of Commerce .... (941) 488-2236

VENICE GARDENS (CDP). Covers a land area of 2.499 square miles and a water area of 0.188 square miles. Located at 27.07° N. Lat.; 82.40° W. Long. Elevation is 16 feet.
Population: 7,795 (1990); 7,466 (2000); 7,460 (2004); 7,509 (2009 projected); Race: 96.9% White, 0.5% Black, 1.6% Asian, 1.7% Hispanic of any race (2004); Density: 2,985.5 persons per square mile (2004); Average household size: 2.12 (2004); Median age: 55.0 (2004); Male/female ratio: 87.0 (2004); Marriage status: 12.1% never married, 64.0% now married, 12.6% widowed, 11.3% divorced (2000); Foreign born: 6.4% (2000); Ancestry (includes multiple ancestries): 21.0% German, 18.9% Irish, 17.9% English, 7.8% Other groups, 7.7% Italian (2000).
Economy: Employment by occupation: 8.7% management, 13.6% professional, 22.1% services, 33.2% sales, 0.0% farming, 13.6% construction, 8.7% production (2000).
Income: Per capita income: $23,983 (2004); Median household income: $43,128 (2004); Average household income: $50,958 (2004); Percent of households with income of $100,000 or more: 8.0% (2004); Poverty rate: 5.8% (2000).
Education: Percent of population age 25 and over with: High school diploma (including GED) or higher: 86.5% (2004); Bachelor's degree or higher: 18.7% (2004); Master's degree or higher: 6.8% (2004).
Housing: Homeownership rate: 87.0% (2004); Median home value: $136,398 (2004); Median rent: $577 per month (2000); Median age of housing: 26 years (2000).
Transportation: Commute to work: 92.9% car, 0.2% public transportation, 1.6% walk, 3.9% work from home (2000); Travel time to work: 38.6% less than 15 minutes, 36.3% 15 to 30 minutes, 14.7% 30 to 45 minutes, 7.3% 45 to 60 minutes, 3.0% 60 minutes or more (2000)

WARM MINERAL SPRINGS (CDP). Covers a land area of 2.623 square miles and a water area of 0.283 square miles. Located at 27.04° N. Lat.; 82.26° W. Long. Elevation is 9 feet.

Population: 4,027 (1990); 4,811 (2000); 5,400 (2004); 6,118 (2009 projected); Race: 98.5% White, 0.6% Black, 0.3% Asian, 1.0% Hispanic of any race (2004); Density: 2,058.7 persons per square mile (2004); Average household size: 1.77 (2004); Median age: 71.1 (2004); Male/female ratio: 83.5 (2004); Marriage status: 4.3% never married, 73.7% now married, 16.3% widowed, 5.7% divorced (2000); Foreign born: 13.6% (2000); Ancestry (includes multiple ancestries): 18.9% German, 15.7% English, 14.8% Irish, 7.3% Polish, 7.1% Italian (2000).
Economy: Employment by occupation: 6.4% management, 3.8% professional, 18.4% services, 46.4% sales, 0.0% farming, 11.4% construction, 13.6% production (2000).
Income: Per capita income: $25,627 (2004); Median household income: $34,014 (2004); Average household income: $45,299 (2004); Percent of households with income of $100,000 or more: 6.3% (2004); Poverty rate: 7.6% (2000).
Education: Percent of population age 25 and over with: High school diploma (including GED) or higher: 83.8% (2004); Bachelor's degree or higher: 19.2% (2004); Master's degree or higher: 6.9% (2004).
Housing: Homeownership rate: 93.2% (2004); Median home value: $97,843 (2004); Median rent: $477 per month (2000); Median age of housing: 17 years (2000).
Transportation: Commute to work: 92.3% car, 1.2% public transportation, 1.3% walk, 2.5% work from home (2000); Travel time to work: 22.6% less than 15 minutes, 45.0% 15 to 30 minutes, 22.7% 30 to 45 minutes, 3.0% 45 to 60 minutes, 6.7% 60 minutes or more (2000)

Seminole County

Located in east central Florida; bounded on the north and east by the St. Johns River; includes many lakes. Covers a land area of 308.20 square miles, a water area of 36.70 square miles, and is located in the Eastern Time Zone. The county government was organized in 1913. County seat is Sanford.

Seminole County is part of the Orlando-Kissimmee, FL Metropolitan Statistical Area. The entire metro area includes: Lake County, FL; Orange County, FL; Osceola County, FL; Seminole County, FL

Weather Station: Sanford Experiment Station   Elevation: 13 feet

	Jan	Feb	Mar	Apr	May	Jun	Jul	Aug	Sep	Oct	Nov	Dec
High	70	72	77	82	87	90	92	92	89	84	78	72
Low	48	49	54	58	64	70	72	72	71	64	57	51
Precip	3.0	3.1	3.9	2.6	3.6	6.5	6.8	7.4	5.7	3.7	3.0	2.6
Snow	0.0	0.0	0.0	0.0	0.0	0.0	0.0	0.0	0.0	0.0	0.0	0.0

High and Low temperatures in degrees Fahrenheit; Precipitation and Snow in inches

Population: 287,529 (1990); 365,196 (2000); 400,730 (2004); 445,460 (2009 projected); Race: 80.5% White, 10.3% Black, 2.9% Asian, 12.8% Hispanic of any race (2004); Density: 1,300.2 persons per square mile (2004); Average household size: 2.61 (2004); Median age: 37.0 (2004); Male/female ratio: 96.3 (2004).
Religion: Five largest groups: 16.5% Catholic Church, 5.3% Southern Baptist Convention, 2.6% The United Methodist Church, 2.6% Independent, Non-Charismatic Churches, 1.3% Lutheran Church—Missouri Synod (2000).
Economy: Unemployment rate: 4.4% (2004); Total civilian labor force: 230,889 (2004); Leading industries: 17.2% retail trade; 11.6% construction; 9.1% health care and social assistance (2003); Companies that employ 500 or more persons: 19 (2003); Companies that employ 100 to 499 persons: 196 (2003); Companies that employ less than 100 persons: 11,298 (2003); Farms: 376 totaling 27,987 acres (2002); Minority business ownership rate: 14.4% (1997); Women business ownership rate: 27.7% (1997); Retail sales per capita: $10,333 (1997). Single-family building permits issued: 3,854 (2004); Multi-family building permits issued: 227 (2004).
Income: Per capita income: $27,983 (2004); Median household income: $55,090 (2004); Average household income: $72,448 (2004); Percent of households with income of $100,000 or more: 19.8% (2004); Poverty rate: 8.2% (2002); Bankruptcy rate: 4.75% (2004).
Taxes: Total county taxes per capita: $423 (2002); County property taxes per capita: $262 (2002).
Education: Percent of population age 25 and over with: High school diploma (including GED) or higher: 88.7% (2004); Bachelor's degree or higher: 31.1% (2004); Master's degree or higher: 10.0% (2004).
Housing: Homeownership rate: 69.5% (2004); Median home value: $152,113 (2004); Median rent: $633 per month (2000); Median age of housing: 17 years (2000).
Health: Birth rate: 123.3 per 10,000 population (2004); Death rate: 69.6 per 10,000 population (2004); Age adjusted cancer mortality rate: 177.7 deaths per 100,000 population (2002); Air Quality Index: 90.6% good, 9.4% moderate, 0.0% unhealthy for sensitive individuals, 0.0% unhealthy (percent of days in 2004); Number of physicians: 17.7 per 10,000 population (2001); Hospital beds: 11.3 per 10,000 population (2002); Hospital admissions: 461.2 per 10,000 population (2002).
Elections: 2004 Presidential election results: 58.1% Bush, 41.3% Kerry, 0.3% Nader, 0.2% Badnarik
National and State Parks: Lower Wekiva River Preserve State Park
Additional Information Contacts
Seminole County Government Offices . . . . (407) 665-7219
Goldenrod Chamber of Commerce . . . . (407) 677-5980
Lake Mary-Heathrow Chamber of Commerce . . . . (407) 333-4748
Longwood Chamber of Commerce . . . . (407) 333-4748
Sanford Chamber of Commerce . . . . (407) 322-2212
Seminole County Regional Chamber of Commerce . . . . . . (407) 333-4748

Seminole County Communities

ALTAMONTE SPRINGS (city). Covers a land area of 8.896 square miles and a water area of 0.557 square miles. Located at 28.66° N. Lat.; 81.39° W. Long. Elevation is 87 feet.
Population: 36,355 (1990); 41,200 (2000); 42,292 (2004); 43,912 (2009 projected); Race: 76.2% White, 11.0% Black, 3.4% Asian, 18.7% Hispanic of any race (2004); Density: 4,753.8 persons per square mile (2004); Average household size: 2.18 (2004); Median age: 34.9 (2004); Male/female ratio: 93.0 (2004); Marriage status: 31.1% never married, 47.0% now married, 6.1% widowed, 15.8% divorced (2000); Foreign born: 12.7% (2000); Ancestry (includes multiple ancestries): 30.7% Other groups, 14.4% German, 12.5% Irish, 9.8% English, 8.3% Italian (2000).
Economy: Unemployment rate: 4.2% (2004); Total civilian labor force: 32,320 (2004); Single-family building permits issued: 35 (2004); Multi-family building permits issued: 89 (2004); Employment by occupation: 13.7% management, 25.3% professional, 13.4% services, 32.5% sales, 0.0% farming, 7.6% construction, 7.6% production (2000).
Income: Per capita income: $25,458 (2004); Median household income: $45,114 (2004); Average household income: $54,928 (2004); Percent of households with income of $100,000 or more: 10.6% (2004); Poverty rate: 7.4% (2000).
Taxes: Total city taxes per capita: $499 (2002); City property taxes per capita: $255 (2002).
Education: Percent of population age 25 and over with: High school diploma (including GED) or higher: 89.8% (2004); Bachelor's degree or higher: 31.4% (2004); Master's degree or higher: 9.1% (2004).

School District(s)

Seminole County School District (PK-12)
2002-03 Enrollment: 63,446 . . . . (407) 320-0006

Two-year College(s)

Florida College of Natural Health (Private, For-profit)
2003-04 Enrollment: 329 . . . . (407) 261-0319
Golf Academy of The South (Private, For-profit)
2003-04 Enrollment: 201 . . . . (800) 342-7342
2003-04 Tuition: In-state $8,863; Out-of-state $8,863
Housing: Homeownership rate: 41.2% (2004); Median home value: $135,218 (2004); Median rent: $646 per month (2000); Median age of housing: 18 years (2000).
Hospitals: Florida Hospital Altamonte
Safety: Violent crime rate: 35.7 per 10,000 population; Property crime rate: 424.9 per 10,000 population (2003).
Transportation: Commute to work: 93.5% car, 1.2% public transportation, 1.7% walk, 2.7% work from home (2000); Travel time to work: 25.5% less than 15 minutes, 39.6% 15 to 30 minutes, 22.5% 30 to 45 minutes, 7.8% 45 to 60 minutes, 4.6% 60 minutes or more (2000)
Additional Information Contacts
Local Government Offices . . . . (407) 571-8031
Seminole County Regional Chamber of Commerce . . . . . . (407) 333-4748

CASSELBERRY (city). Covers a land area of 6.662 square miles and a water area of 0.431 square miles. Located at 28.66° N. Lat.; 81.32° W. Long. Elevation is 64 feet.

Population: 21,488 (1990); 22,629 (2000); 23,527 (2004); 24,783 (2009 projected); Race: 83.7% White, 6.1% Black, 2.1% Asian, 17.6% Hispanic of any race (2004); Density: 3,531.3 persons per square mile (2004); Average household size: 2.29 (2004); Median age: 38.3 (2004); Male/female ratio: 93.9 (2004); Marriage status: 26.4% never married, 50.7% now married, 7.4% widowed, 15.5% divorced (2000); Foreign born: 10.0% (2000); Ancestry (includes multiple ancestries): 25.0% Other groups, 15.9% German, 14.4% Irish, 12.3% English, 8.5% Italian (2000).
Economy: Suburb of Orlando. Unemployment rate: 4.0% (2004); Total civilian labor force: 16,007 (2004); Single-family building permits issued: 72 (2004); Multi-family building permits issued: 0 (2004); Employment by occupation: 12.7% management, 15.6% professional, 15.9% services, 35.4% sales, 0.2% farming, 11.1% construction, 9.1% production (2000).
Income: Per capita income: $21,624 (2004); Median household income: $41,299 (2004); Average household income: $49,185 (2004); Percent of households with income of $100,000 or more: 8.1% (2004); Poverty rate: 8.8% (2000).
Education: Percent of population age 25 and over with: High school diploma (including GED) or higher: 84.7% (2004); Bachelor's degree or higher: 18.9% (2004); Master's degree or higher: 6.1% (2004).

School District(s)

Seminole County School District (PK-12)
2002-03 Enrollment: 63,446 . . . . (407) 320-0006

Two-year College(s)

City College
2003-04 Enrollment: 251 . . . . (407) 831-9816
2003-04 Tuition: In-state $8,160; Out-of-state $8,160
Housing: Homeownership rate: 61.2% (2004); Median home value: $113,162 (2004); Median rent: $625 per month (2000); Median age of housing: 22 years (2000).
Safety: Violent crime rate: 59.3 per 10,000 population; Property crime rate: 396.8 per 10,000 population (2003).
Transportation: Commute to work: 94.1% car, 1.1% public transportation, 1.9% walk, 1.9% work from home (2000); Travel time to work: 23.4% less than 15 minutes, 35.3% 15 to 30 minutes, 25.8% 30 to 45 minutes, 8.3% 45 to 60 minutes, 7.1% 60 minutes or more (2000)
Additional Information Contacts
Local Government Offices . . . . (407) 262-7700

CHULUOTA (CDP). Covers a land area of 1.804 square miles and a water area of 0.392 square miles. Located at 28.64° N. Lat.; 81.12° W. Long. Elevation is 58 feet.
Population: 1,398 (1990); 1,921 (2000); 2,356 (2004); 2,872 (2009 projected); Race: 94.4% White, 0.3% Black, 0.5% Asian, 5.5% Hispanic of any race (2004); Density: 1,305.7 persons per square mile (2004); Average household size: 2.77 (2004); Median age: 35.8 (2004); Male/female ratio: 93.9 (2004); Marriage status: 22.5% never married, 55.8% now married, 4.9% widowed, 16.8% divorced (2000); Foreign born: 2.8% (2000); Ancestry (includes multiple ancestries): 22.5% Other groups, 20.8% German, 14.7% Irish, 11.0% English, 9.9% United States or American (2000).
Economy: Employment by occupation: 10.1% management, 18.9% professional, 18.3% services, 21.8% sales, 0.0% farming, 20.3% construction, 10.6% production (2000).
Income: Per capita income: $18,140 (2004); Median household income: $47,665 (2004); Average household income: $50,279 (2004); Percent of households with income of $100,000 or more: 5.1% (2004); Poverty rate: 5.1% (2000).
Education: Percent of population age 25 and over with: High school diploma (including GED) or higher: 88.6% (2004); Bachelor's degree or higher: 12.9% (2004); Master's degree or higher: 1.6% (2004).
Housing: Homeownership rate: 85.2% (2004); Median home value: $123,955 (2004); Median rent: $511 per month (2000); Median age of housing: 20 years (2000).
Transportation: Commute to work: 96.9% car, 0.0% public transportation, 0.0% walk, 2.0% work from home (2000); Travel time to work: 4.4% less than 15 minutes, 33.5% 15 to 30 minutes, 22.0% 30 to 45 minutes, 24.9% 45 to 60 minutes, 15.2% 60 minutes or more (2000)

FERN PARK (CDP). Covers a land area of 2.051 square miles and a water area of 0.290 square miles. Located at 28.64° N. Lat.; 81.34° W. Long. Elevation is 99 feet.
Population: 8,080 (1990); 8,318 (2000); 8,254 (2004); 8,253 (2009 projected); Race: 83.0% White, 8.7% Black, 1.8% Asian, 14.4% Hispanic of any race (2004); Density: 4,024.1 persons per square mile (2004); Average household size: 2.29 (2004); Median age: 41.3 (2004); Male/female ratio: 91.9 (2004); Marriage status: 24.8% never married, 53.7% now married, 8.5% widowed, 13.0% divorced (2000); Foreign born: 10.1% (2000); Ancestry (includes multiple ancestries): 21.4% Other groups, 14.5% German, 14.1% Irish, 11.0% English, 8.6% United States or American (2000).
Economy: Manufacturing: printing and publishing. Employment by occupation: 11.2% management, 22.6% professional, 11.5% services, 39.0% sales, 0.1% farming, 8.1% construction, 7.5% production (2000).
Income: Per capita income: $26,585 (2004); Median household income: $47,405 (2004); Average household income: $60,772 (2004); Percent of households with income of $100,000 or more: 14.3% (2004); Poverty rate: 7.8% (2000).
Education: Percent of population age 25 and over with: High school diploma (including GED) or higher: 85.1% (2004); Bachelor's degree or higher: 30.1% (2004); Master's degree or higher: 9.1% (2004).

School District(s)

Seminole County School District (PK-12)
2002-03 Enrollment: 63,446 . . . . (407) 320-0006

Two-year College(s)

Americare School of Nursing
2003-04 Enrollment: 194 . . . . (407) 673-7406
Housing: Homeownership rate: 65.1% (2004); Median home value: $147,264 (2004); Median rent: $485 per month (2000); Median age of housing: 27 years (2000).
Transportation: Commute to work: 88.8% car, 3.3% public transportation, 1.2% walk, 3.7% work from home (2000); Travel time to work: 19.9% less than 15 minutes, 44.0% 15 to 30 minutes, 21.1% 30 to 45 minutes, 8.9% 45 to 60 minutes, 6.0% 60 minutes or more (2000)

FOREST CITY (CDP). Covers a land area of 4.271 square miles and a water area of 0.647 square miles. Located at 28.66° N. Lat.; 81.44° W. Long.
Population: 10,471 (1990); 12,612 (2000); 14,080 (2004); 15,932 (2009 projected); Race: 83.3% White, 5.5% Black, 4.0% Asian, 17.5% Hispanic of any race (2004); Density: 3,297.0 persons per square mile (2004); Average household size: 2.64 (2004); Median age: 36.7 (2004); Male/female ratio: 96.8 (2004); Marriage status: 23.1% never married, 61.0% now married, 5.4% widowed, 10.5% divorced (2000); Foreign born: 14.1% (2000); Ancestry (includes multiple ancestries): 23.2% Other groups, 15.2% German, 13.9% Irish, 11.5% English, 7.3% Italian (2000).
Economy: Employment by occupation: 16.9% management, 22.1% professional, 12.6% services, 30.9% sales, 0.6% farming, 9.1% construction, 7.6% production (2000).
Income: Per capita income: $28,673 (2004); Median household income: $57,257 (2004); Average household income: $74,786 (2004); Percent of households with income of $100,000 or more: 20.8% (2004); Poverty rate: 6.0% (2000).
Education: Percent of population age 25 and over with: High school diploma (including GED) or higher: 87.2% (2004); Bachelor's degree or higher: 26.3% (2004); Master's degree or higher: 8.8% (2004).
Housing: Homeownership rate: 68.7% (2004); Median home value: $142,954 (2004); Median rent: $662 per month (2000); Median age of housing: 18 years (2000).
Transportation: Commute to work: 92.7% car, 0.7% public transportation, 1.5% walk, 3.4% work from home (2000); Travel time to work: 20.1% less than 15 minutes, 37.4% 15 to 30 minutes, 26.7% 30 to 45 minutes, 8.5% 45 to 60 minutes, 7.3% 60 minutes or more (2000)

GENEVA (CDP). Covers a land area of 11.390 square miles and a water area of 1.036 square miles. Located at 28.73° N. Lat.; 81.11° W. Long. Elevation is 79 feet.
Population: 2,097 (1990); 2,601 (2000); 2,759 (2004); 2,971 (2009 projected); Race: 95.1% White, 2.0% Black, 1.2% Asian, 1.9% Hispanic of any race (2004); Density: 242.2 persons per square mile (2004); Average household size: 2.82 (2004); Median age: 39.7 (2004); Male/female ratio: 103.8 (2004); Marriage status: 21.0% never married, 66.2% now married, 4.2% widowed, 8.7% divorced (2000); Foreign born: 3.1% (2000); Ancestry (includes multiple ancestries): 22.0% German, 15.9% English, 13.4% Other groups, 12.5% Irish, 8.4% United States or American (2000).
Economy: Employment by occupation: 14.6% management, 20.0% professional, 13.1% services, 23.3% sales, 1.1% farming, 18.5% construction, 9.4% production (2000).
Income: Per capita income: $26,773 (2004); Median household income: $58,108 (2004); Average household income: $75,375 (2004); Percent of

households with income of $100,000 or more: 25.4% (2004); Poverty rate: 4.8% (2000).
Education: Percent of population age 25 and over with: High school diploma (including GED) or higher: 87.2% (2004); Bachelor's degree or higher: 20.9% (2004); Master's degree or higher: 8.6% (2004).

School District(s)

Seminole County School District (PK-12)
2002-03 Enrollment: 63,446 . . . . (407) 320-0006
Housing: Homeownership rate: 89.9% (2004); Median home value: $163,482 (2004); Median rent: $471 per month (2000); Median age of housing: 17 years (2000).
Transportation: Commute to work: 86.7% car, 1.6% public transportation, 2.2% walk, 6.4% work from home (2000); Travel time to work: 8.8% less than 15 minutes, 29.3% 15 to 30 minutes, 29.0% 30 to 45 minutes, 14.4% 45 to 60 minutes, 18.6% 60 minutes or more (2000)

HEATHROW (CDP). Covers a land area of 2.774 square miles and a water area of 0.531 square miles. Located at 28.77° N. Lat.; 81.37° W. Long. Elevation is 50 feet.
Population: 1,013 (1990); 4,068 (2000); 5,045 (2004); 6,216 (2009 projected); Race: 87.6% White, 4.1% Black, 5.6% Asian, 7.4% Hispanic of any race (2004); Density: 1,818.8 persons per square mile (2004); Average household size: 2.25 (2004); Median age: 42.9 (2004); Male/female ratio: 96.0 (2004); Marriage status: 17.4% never married, 68.6% now married, 4.7% widowed, 9.3% divorced (2000); Foreign born: 14.6% (2000); Ancestry (includes multiple ancestries): 19.2% Irish, 16.1% English, 14.0% German, 13.4% Other groups, 9.9% Italian (2000).
Economy: Employment by occupation: 37.2% management, 24.9% professional, 4.8% services, 29.3% sales, 0.0% farming, 1.4% construction, 2.4% production (2000).
Income: Per capita income: $62,761 (2004); Median household income: $96,358 (2004); Average household income: $141,478 (2004); Percent of households with income of $100,000 or more: 48.0% (2004); Poverty rate: 2.1% (2000).
Education: Percent of population age 25 and over with: High school diploma (including GED) or higher: 95.3% (2004); Bachelor's degree or higher: 52.5% (2004); Master's degree or higher: 20.1% (2004).
Housing: Homeownership rate: 73.3% (2004); Median home value: $284,323 (2004); Median rent: $966 per month (2000); Median age of housing: 5 years (2000).
Transportation: Commute to work: 94.2% car, 0.6% public transportation, 0.5% walk, 3.8% work from home (2000); Travel time to work: 28.1% less than 15 minutes, 39.5% 15 to 30 minutes, 21.1% 30 to 45 minutes, 4.4% 45 to 60 minutes, 6.9% 60 minutes or more (2000)

LAKE MARY (city). Covers a land area of 8.610 square miles and a water area of 1.063 square miles. Located at 28.75° N. Lat.; 81.32° W. Long. Elevation is 63 feet.
Population: 6,203 (1990); 11,458 (2000); 13,957 (2004); 16,946 (2009 projected); Race: 87.5% White, 4.2% Black, 4.6% Asian, 7.3% Hispanic of any race (2004); Density: 1,621.1 persons per square mile (2004); Average household size: 2.72 (2004); Median age: 39.1 (2004); Male/female ratio: 97.0 (2004); Marriage status: 17.8% never married, 68.6% now married, 5.3% widowed, 8.2% divorced (2000); Foreign born: 8.3% (2000); Ancestry (includes multiple ancestries): 22.4% German, 15.9% Other groups, 14.4% English, 14.0% Irish, 10.1% Italian (2000).
Economy: Manufacturing includes electrical equipment, computer peripherals, medical equipment, plastic molding, telephone switching equipment. Growth since 1990. Single-family building permits issued: 285 (2004); Multi-family building permits issued: 0 (2004); Employment by occupation: 21.0% management, 23.1% professional, 9.9% services, 33.0% sales, 0.1% farming, 7.5% construction, 5.3% production (2000).
Income: Per capita income: $35,461 (2004); Median household income: $79,331 (2004); Average household income: $95,733 (2004); Percent of households with income of $100,000 or more: 35.3% (2004); Poverty rate: 2.9% (2000).
Taxes: Total city taxes per capita: $778 (2002); City property taxes per capita: $352 (2002).
Education: Percent of population age 25 and over with: High school diploma (including GED) or higher: 92.2% (2004); Bachelor's degree or higher: 38.7% (2004); Master's degree or higher: 13.3% (2004).

School District(s)

Seminole County School District (PK-12)
2002-03 Enrollment: 63,446 . . . . (407) 320-0006
Housing: Homeownership rate: 83.6% (2004); Median home value: $223,587 (2004); Median rent: $683 per month (2000); Median age of housing: 10 years (2000).
Safety: Violent crime rate: 22.5 per 10,000 population; Property crime rate: 187.9 per 10,000 population (2003).
Transportation: Commute to work: 93.0% car, 0.1% public transportation, 1.2% walk, 3.8% work from home (2000); Travel time to work: 30.8% less than 15 minutes, 30.8% 15 to 30 minutes, 20.8% 30 to 45 minutes, 10.7% 45 to 60 minutes, 6.9% 60 minutes or more (2000)
Additional Information Contacts
Lake Mary-Heathrow Chamber of Commerce . . . . (407) 333-4748
Local Government Offices . . . . (407) 585-1400

LONGWOOD (city). Covers a land area of 5.320 square miles and a water area of 0.291 square miles. Located at 28.70° N. Lat.; 81.34° W. Long. Elevation is 75 feet.
History: Named for a district in Boston, home to E.W. Henck. Has experienced major growth since 1975.
Population: 13,724 (1990); 13,745 (2000); 13,850 (2004); 14,098 (2009 projected); Race: 85.3% White, 4.1% Black, 2.8% Asian, 12.8% Hispanic of any race (2004); Density: 2,603.4 persons per square mile (2004); Average household size: 2.71 (2004); Median age: 38.6 (2004); Male/female ratio: 94.0 (2004); Marriage status: 24.3% never married, 55.7% now married, 7.2% widowed, 12.7% divorced (2000); Foreign born: 10.5% (2000); Ancestry (includes multiple ancestries): 20.6% Other groups, 18.0% German, 16.0% Irish, 13.2% English, 9.2% Italian (2000).
Economy: Single-family building permits issued: 10 (2004); Multi-family building permits issued: 0 (2004); Employment by occupation: 14.7% management, 19.3% professional, 12.9% services, 30.4% sales, 0.0% farming, 11.4% construction, 11.3% production (2000).
Income: Per capita income: $24,255 (2004); Median household income: $57,208 (2004); Average household income: $64,868 (2004); Percent of households with income of $100,000 or more: 15.4% (2004); Poverty rate: 6.6% (2000).
Taxes: Total city taxes per capita: $509 (2002); City property taxes per capita: $227 (2002).
Education: Percent of population age 25 and over with: High school diploma (including GED) or higher: 86.2% (2004); Bachelor's degree or higher: 21.9% (2004); Master's degree or higher: 6.4% (2004).

School District(s)

Seminole County School District (PK-12)
2002-03 Enrollment: 63,446 . . . . (407) 320-0006
Housing: Homeownership rate: 75.3% (2004); Median home value: $137,143 (2004); Median rent: $629 per month (2000); Median age of housing: 22 years (2000).
Hospitals: Orlando Regional - South Seminole Hospital (206 beds)
Safety: Violent crime rate: 221.6 per 10,000 population; Property crime rate: 470.4 per 10,000 population (2003).
Newspapers: La Prensa (Hispanic - Circulation 30,000)
Transportation: Commute to work: 93.6% car, 0.2% public transportation, 0.3% walk, 3.6% work from home (2000); Travel time to work: 27.2% less than 15 minutes, 38.3% 15 to 30 minutes, 21.6% 30 to 45 minutes, 7.6% 45 to 60 minutes, 5.3% 60 minutes or more (2000)
Additional Information Contacts
Local Government Offices . . . . (407) 260-3440
Longwood Chamber of Commerce . . . . (407) 333-4748

MIDWAY (CDP). Covers a land area of 1.391 square miles and a water area of 0 square miles. Located at 28.79° N. Lat.; 81.22° W. Long. Elevation is 29 feet.
Population: 2,024 (1990); 1,714 (2000); 1,685 (2004); 1,668 (2009 projected); Race: 5.7% White, 91.2% Black, 0.8% Asian, 1.3% Hispanic of any race (2004); Density: 1,211.2 persons per square mile (2004); Average household size: 2.88 (2004); Median age: 34.6 (2004); Male/female ratio: 85.8 (2004); Marriage status: 37.8% never married, 32.6% now married, 12.9% widowed, 16.7% divorced (2000); Foreign born: 0.0% (2000); Ancestry (includes multiple ancestries): 75.3% Other groups, 2.5% African, 2.2% United States or American (2000).
Economy: Employment by occupation: 1.7% management, 4.8% professional, 25.3% services, 19.2% sales, 0.0% farming, 13.8% construction, 35.2% production (2000).
Income: Per capita income: $11,662 (2004); Median household income: $28,319 (2004); Average household income: $33,590 (2004); Percent of households with income of $100,000 or more: 1.7% (2004); Poverty rate: 26.0% (2000).

Education: Percent of population age 25 and over with: High school diploma (including GED) or higher: 51.7% (2004); Bachelor's degree or higher: 4.9% (2004); Master's degree or higher: 1.8% (2004).
Housing: Homeownership rate: 70.4% (2004); Median home value: $66,600 (2004); Median rent: $423 per month (2000); Median age of housing: 31 years (2000).
Transportation: Commute to work: 91.6% car, 6.8% public transportation, 0.0% walk, 0.3% work from home (2000); Travel time to work: 16.3% less than 15 minutes, 47.7% 15 to 30 minutes, 21.8% 30 to 45 minutes, 5.8% 45 to 60 minutes, 8.4% 60 minutes or more (2000)

OVIEDO (city). Covers a land area of 15.134 square miles and a water area of 0.320 square miles. Located at 28.66° N. Lat.; 81.19° W. Long. Elevation is 48 feet.
History: Named for the capital city of the Spanish province of Asturias. Incorporated 1925.
Population: 11,588 (1990); 26,316 (2000); 29,505 (2004); 33,490 (2009 projected); Race: 83.2% White, 8.1% Black, 2.8% Asian, 14.3% Hispanic of any race (2004); Density: 1,949.6 persons per square mile (2004); Average household size: 3.13 (2004); Median age: 33.0 (2004); Male/female ratio: 98.2 (2004); Marriage status: 22.9% never married, 67.1% now married, 3.1% widowed, 6.9% divorced (2000); Foreign born: 9.2% (2000); Ancestry (includes multiple ancestries): 24.0% Other groups, 18.1% German, 13.4% Irish, 11.7% English, 11.6% Italian (2000).
Economy: Unemployment rate: 3.4% (2004); Total civilian labor force: 8,724 (2004); Single-family building permits issued: 349 (2004); Multi-family building permits issued: 14 (2004); Employment by occupation: 17.9% management, 25.9% professional, 12.7% services, 30.1% sales, 0.1% farming, 6.7% construction, 6.5% production (2000).
Income: Per capita income: $27,790 (2004); Median household income: $73,100 (2004); Average household income: $86,738 (2004); Percent of households with income of $100,000 or more: 28.3% (2004); Poverty rate: 4.6% (2000).
Taxes: Total city taxes per capita: $391 (2002); City property taxes per capita: $199 (2002).
Education: Percent of population age 25 and over with: High school diploma (including GED) or higher: 93.3% (2004); Bachelor's degree or higher: 41.1% (2004); Master's degree or higher: 13.3% (2004).

School District(s)

Seminole County School District (PK-12)
2002-03 Enrollment: 63,446 .... (407) 320-0006
Housing: Homeownership rate: 86.0% (2004); Median home value: $175,505 (2004); Median rent: $776 per month (2000); Median age of housing: 8 years (2000).
Safety: Violent crime rate: 37.7 per 10,000 population; Property crime rate: 245.5 per 10,000 population (2003).
Newspapers: The Oviedo Voice (General - Circulation 4,500)
Transportation: Commute to work: 93.4% car, 0.1% public transportation, 0.4% walk, 4.1% work from home (2000); Travel time to work: 18.3% less than 15 minutes, 30.8% 15 to 30 minutes, 29.1% 30 to 45 minutes, 15.1% 45 to 60 minutes, 6.7% 60 minutes or more (2000)
Additional Information Contacts
Local Government Offices .... (407) 977-6001

SANFORD (city). Covers a land area of 19.107 square miles and a water area of 3.494 square miles. Located at 28.79° N. Lat.; 81.27° W. Long. Elevation is 35 feet.
History: Named for General Henry Shelton Sanford, President Lincoln's minister to Belgium. Sanford had its beginning as Mellonville, a trading post established in 1837 near Fort Mellon. The land on which the town was founded was purchased in 1871 by General Sanford, who planted citrus groves.
Population: 33,887 (1990); 38,291 (2000); 47,786 (2004); 59,036 (2009 projected); Race: 57.1% White, 33.2% Black, 1.2% Asian, 12.6% Hispanic of any race (2004); Density: 2,501.0 persons per square mile (2004); Average household size: 2.65 (2004); Median age: 33.2 (2004); Male/female ratio: 99.2 (2004); Marriage status: 30.6% never married, 47.6% now married, 6.5% widowed, 15.3% divorced (2000); Foreign born: 5.9% (2000); Ancestry (includes multiple ancestries): 38.8% Other groups, 10.7% German, 9.2% Irish, 9.1% English, 6.2% United States or American (2000).
Economy: Unemployment rate: 5.5% (2004); Total civilian labor force: 22,904 (2004); Single-family building permits issued: 686 (2004); Multi-family building permits issued: 42 (2004); Employment by occupation: 9.3% management, 15.8% professional, 18.3% services, 29.3% sales, 0.3% farming, 12.1% construction, 15.0% production (2000).
Income: Per capita income: $17,075 (2004); Median household income: $34,534 (2004); Average household income: $44,023 (2004); Percent of households with income of $100,000 or more: 6.5% (2004); Poverty rate: 17.8% (2000).
Education: Percent of population age 25 and over with: High school diploma (including GED) or higher: 77.0% (2004); Bachelor's degree or higher: 14.5% (2004); Master's degree or higher: 4.2% (2004).

School District(s)

Seminole County School District (PK-12)
2002-03 Enrollment: 63,446 .... (407) 320-0006

Two-year College(s)

Delta Connection Academy (Private, For-profit)
2003-04 Enrollment: 365 .... (407) 330-7020
Seminole Community College (Public)
2003-04 Enrollment: 12,108 .... (407) 328-4722
2003-04 Tuition: In-state $1,747; Out-of-state $6,513
Housing: Homeownership rate: 54.2% (2004); Median home value: $99,268 (2004); Median rent: $508 per month (2000); Median age of housing: 23 years (2000).
Hospitals: Central Florida Regional Hospital (226 beds)
Safety: Violent crime rate: 67.4 per 10,000 population; Property crime rate: 739.4 per 10,000 population (2003).
Newspapers: The Seminole Herald (General - Circulation 4,500)
Transportation: Commute to work: 93.2% car, 1.2% public transportation, 1.6% walk, 2.2% work from home (2000); Travel time to work: 28.7% less than 15 minutes, 35.1% 15 to 30 minutes, 19.8% 30 to 45 minutes, 8.4% 45 to 60 minutes, 8.0% 60 minutes or more (2000); Amtrak: Service available.
Additional Information Contacts
Local Government Offices .... (407) 330-5600
Sanford Chamber of Commerce .... (407) 322-2212

WEKIWA SPRINGS (CDP). Aka Wekiva Springs. Covers a land area of 8.641 square miles and a water area of 0.520 square miles. Located at 28.69° N. Lat.; 81.42° W. Long.
Population: 23,024 (1990); 23,169 (2000); 23,725 (2004); 24,608 (2009 projected); Race: 93.9% White, 1.6% Black, 2.5% Asian, 5.5% Hispanic of any race (2004); Density: 2,745.5 persons per square mile (2004); Average household size: 2.58 (2004); Median age: 42.4 (2004); Male/female ratio: 95.2 (2004); Marriage status: 20.6% never married, 66.8% now married, 4.7% widowed, 8.0% divorced (2000); Foreign born: 7.8% (2000); Ancestry (includes multiple ancestries): 19.4% German, 15.7% English, 14.9% Irish, 12.9% Other groups, 8.9% Italian (2000).
Economy: Employment by occupation: 24.3% management, 26.3% professional, 7.9% services, 33.1% sales, 0.0% farming, 4.3% construction, 4.1% production (2000).
Income: Per capita income: $41,097 (2004); Median household income: $76,726 (2004); Average household income: $105,893 (2004); Percent of households with income of $100,000 or more: 34.9% (2004); Poverty rate: 2.6% (2000).
Education: Percent of population age 25 and over with: High school diploma (including GED) or higher: 96.0% (2004); Bachelor's degree or higher: 49.6% (2004); Master's degree or higher: 17.4% (2004).
Housing: Homeownership rate: 79.1% (2004); Median home value: $202,529 (2004); Median rent: $908 per month (2000); Median age of housing: 18 years (2000).
Transportation: Commute to work: 91.2% car, 0.1% public transportation, 0.2% walk, 8.0% work from home (2000); Travel time to work: 18.3% less than 15 minutes, 37.5% 15 to 30 minutes, 28.4% 30 to 45 minutes, 10.1% 45 to 60 minutes, 5.6% 60 minutes or more (2000)

WINTER SPRINGS (city). Aka North Orlando. Covers a land area of 14.346 square miles and a water area of 0.138 square miles. Located at 28.69° N. Lat.; 81.27° W. Long. Elevation is 49 feet.
Population: 22,280 (1990); 31,666 (2000); 33,030 (2004); 34,946 (2009 projected); Race: 87.4% White, 5.1% Black, 2.1% Asian, 12.1% Hispanic of any race (2004); Density: 2,302.4 persons per square mile (2004); Average household size: 2.68 (2004); Median age: 38.2 (2004); Male/female ratio: 94.7 (2004); Marriage status: 20.9% never married, 64.1% now married, 5.2% widowed, 9.8% divorced (2000); Foreign born: 8.1% (2000); Ancestry (includes multiple ancestries): 19.0% Other groups, 18.2% German, 15.6% Irish, 12.8% English, 10.8% Italian (2000).

Economy: Manufacturing includes meat products. Unemployment rate: 3.7% (2004); Total civilian labor force: 17,691 (2004); Single-family building permits issued: 205 (2004); Multi-family building permits issued: 42 (2004); Employment by occupation: 18.8% management, 24.5% professional, 11.7% services, 30.4% sales, 0.1% farming, 7.6% construction, 6.9% production (2000).
Income: Per capita income: $30,169 (2004); Median household income: $61,507 (2004); Average household income: $80,716 (2004); Percent of households with income of $100,000 or more: 26.0% (2004); Poverty rate: 4.2% (2000).
Taxes: Total city taxes per capita: $276 (2002); City property taxes per capita: $115 (2002).
Education: Percent of population age 25 and over with: High school diploma (including GED) or higher: 92.3% (2004); Bachelor's degree or higher: 37.1% (2004); Master's degree or higher: 13.2% (2004).

School District(s)

Seminole County School District (PK-12)
2002-03 Enrollment: 63,446 . . . . (407) 320-0006

Housing: Homeownership rate: 80.5% (2004); Median home value: $164,484 (2004); Median rent: $631 per month (2000); Median age of housing: 15 years (2000).
Safety: Violent crime rate: 22.9 per 10,000 population; Property crime rate: 172.7 per 10,000 population (2003).
Transportation: Commute to work: 93.8% car, 0.3% public transportation, 0.3% walk, 4.5% work from home (2000); Travel time to work: 17.1% less than 15 minutes, 37.8% 15 to 30 minutes, 28.2% 30 to 45 minutes, 10.5% 45 to 60 minutes, 6.4% 60 minutes or more (2000)
Additional Information Contacts
Local Government Offices . . . . (407) 327-5957

Saint Johns County

Located in northeastern Florida; bounded on the west by the St. Johns River, and on the east by the Atlantic Ocean; lowland area, includes Anastasia Island and the Matanzas River. Covers a land area of 609.00 square miles, a water area of 212.40 square miles, and is located in the Eastern Time Zone. The county government was organized in 1822. County seat is St. Augustine.

Saint Johns County is part of the Jacksonville, FL Metropolitan Statistical Area. The entire metro area includes: Baker County, FL; Clay County, FL; Duval County, FL; Nassau County, FL; St. Johns County, FL

Weather Station: Saint Augustine — Elevation: 6 feet

	Jan	Feb	Mar	Apr	May	Jun	Jul	Aug	Sep	Oct	Nov	Dec
High	67	69	74	79	84	88	91	89	86	81	75	68
Low	46	48	53	58	65	71	72	72	71	64	56	49
Precip	3.2	3.0	3.7	2.7	3.2	5.2	4.6	5.9	6.6	4.6	2.3	2.9
Snow	tr	0.0	tr	0.0	0.0	0.0	0.0	0.0	0.0	0.0	0.0	0.0

High and Low temperatures in degrees Fahrenheit; Precipitation and Snow in inches

Population: 83,829 (1990); 123,135 (2000); 144,364 (2004); 171,020 (2009 projected); Race: 90.8% White, 6.3% Black, 1.1% Asian, 2.9% Hispanic of any race (2004); Density: 237.0 persons per square mile (2004); Average household size: 2.47 (2004); Median age: 40.8 (2004); Male/female ratio: 95.4 (2004).
Religion: Five largest groups: 16.3% Catholic Church, 8.7% Southern Baptist Convention, 4.5% Episcopal Church, 1.8% The United Methodist Church, 1.3% Presbyterian Church in America (2000).
Economy: Unemployment rate: 3.5% (2004); Total civilian labor force: 71,490 (2004); Leading industries: 18.6% retail trade; 16.1% accommodation & food services; 12.1% health care and social assistance (2003); Companies that employ 500 or more persons: 8 (2003); Companies that employ 100 to 499 persons: 44 (2003); Companies that employ less than 100 persons: 3,939 (2003); Farms: 204 totaling 37,653 acres (2002); Minority business ownership rate: 5.5% (1997); Women business ownership rate: 25.8% (1997); Retail sales per capita: $7,731 (1997). Single-family building permits issued: 4,119 (2004); Multi-family building permits issued: 905 (2004).
Income: Per capita income: $32,827 (2004); Median household income: $56,674 (2004); Average household income: $80,602 (2004); Percent of households with income of $100,000 or more: 23.1% (2004); Poverty rate: 7.5% (2002); Bankruptcy rate: 3.79% (2004).
Taxes: Total county taxes per capita: $508 (2002); County property taxes per capita: $403 (2002).
Education: Percent of population age 25 and over with: High school diploma (including GED) or higher: 87.3% (2004); Bachelor's degree or higher: 33.0% (2004); Master's degree or higher: 11.2% (2004).
Housing: Homeownership rate: 76.9% (2004); Median home value: $181,924 (2004); Median rent: $632 per month (2000); Median age of housing: 15 years (2000).
Health: Birth rate: 98.0 per 10,000 population (2004); Death rate: 81.2 per 10,000 population (2004); Age adjusted cancer mortality rate: 194.7 deaths per 100,000 population (2002); Number of physicians: 28.7 per 10,000 population (2001); Hospital beds: 19.9 per 10,000 population (2002); Hospital admissions: 976.9 per 10,000 population (2002).
Elections: 2004 Presidential election results: 68.6% Bush, 30.6% Kerry, 0.5% Nader, 0.3% Badnarik
National and State Parks: Anastasia State Park; Butler Beach State Park; Castillo de San Marcos National Monument; Faver-Dykes State Park; Fort Matanzas National Monument; Guana River State Park
Additional Information Contacts
St. Johns County Government Offices. . . . . (904) 823-2400
St. Augustine Chamber of Commerce . . . . (904) 829-5681
St. Augustine and St. Johns County Board of Realtors . . . . (904) 829-8738

Saint Johns County Communities

BUTLER BEACH (CDP). Covers a land area of 2.488 square miles and a water area of 0 square miles. Located at 29.80° N. Lat.; 81.26° W. Long.
Population: 3,349 (1990); 4,436 (2000); 5,140 (2004); 6,034 (2009 projected); Race: 97.8% White, 0.4% Black, 0.8% Asian, 1.3% Hispanic of any race (2004); Density: 2,066.0 persons per square mile (2004); Average household size: 2.01 (2004); Median age: 54.3 (2004); Male/female ratio: 95.2 (2004); Marriage status: 12.2% never married, 69.0% now married, 9.5% widowed, 9.3% divorced (2000); Foreign born: 6.6% (2000); Ancestry (includes multiple ancestries): 19.5% German, 17.9% Irish, 16.8% English, 10.4% Italian, 8.9% United States or American (2000).
Economy: Employment by occupation: 16.1% management, 26.2% professional, 14.7% services, 27.9% sales, 0.0% farming, 9.5% construction, 5.6% production (2000).
Income: Per capita income: $39,150 (2004); Median household income: $56,748 (2004); Average household income: $78,760 (2004); Percent of households with income of $100,000 or more: 18.4% (2004); Poverty rate: 6.3% (2000).
Education: Percent of population age 25 and over with: High school diploma (including GED) or higher: 95.0% (2004); Bachelor's degree or higher: 38.6% (2004); Master's degree or higher: 13.5% (2004).
Housing: Homeownership rate: 82.3% (2004); Median home value: $213,831 (2004); Median rent: $720 per month (2000); Median age of housing: 14 years (2000).
Transportation: Commute to work: 91.4% car, 0.5% public transportation, 2.3% walk, 5.4% work from home (2000); Travel time to work: 20.1% less than 15 minutes, 40.8% 15 to 30 minutes, 14.6% 30 to 45 minutes, 13.0% 45 to 60 minutes, 11.5% 60 minutes or more (2000)

CRESCENT BEACH (CDP). Covers a land area of 1.524 square miles and a water area of 0 square miles. Located at 29.76° N. Lat.; 81.25° W. Long. Elevation is 15 feet.
Population: 1,081 (1990); 985 (2000); 1,215 (2004); 1,505 (2009 projected); Race: 97.2% White, 0.1% Black, 0.4% Asian, 0.7% Hispanic of any race (2004); Density: 797.1 persons per square mile (2004); Average household size: 1.83 (2004); Median age: 57.0 (2004); Male/female ratio: 104.5 (2004); Marriage status: 20.2% never married, 47.9% now married, 6.8% widowed, 25.2% divorced (2000); Foreign born: 1.4% (2000); Ancestry (includes multiple ancestries): 19.4% German, 19.3% English, 17.0% Irish, 9.8% United States or American, 7.7% Scottish (2000).
Economy: Employment by occupation: 27.1% management, 15.1% professional, 5.5% services, 24.9% sales, 3.4% farming, 15.8% construction, 8.2% production (2000).
Income: Per capita income: $26,428 (2004); Median household income: $39,575 (2004); Average household income: $48,286 (2004); Percent of households with income of $100,000 or more: 7.1% (2004); Poverty rate: 8.9% (2000).
Education: Percent of population age 25 and over with: High school diploma (including GED) or higher: 83.1% (2004); Bachelor's degree or higher: 29.9% (2004); Master's degree or higher: 11.3% (2004).

Housing: Homeownership rate: 74.7% (2004); Median home value: $145,625 (2004); Median rent: $669 per month (2000); Median age of housing: 19 years (2000).
Transportation: Commute to work: 81.1% car, 0.0% public transportation, 7.9% walk, 7.7% work from home (2000); Travel time to work: 27.4% less than 15 minutes, 40.3% 15 to 30 minutes, 22.8% 30 to 45 minutes, 0.0% 45 to 60 minutes, 9.4% 60 minutes or more (2000)

ELKTON (unincorporated postal area, zip code 32033). Covers a land area of 78.595 square miles and a water area of 0.091 square miles. Located at 29.78° N. Lat.; 81.44° W. Long. Elevation is 36 feet.
Population: 2,171 (2000); Race: 87.0% White, 10.2% Black, 1.3% Asian, 3.6% Hispanic of any race (2000); Density: 27.6 persons per square mile (2000); Age: 20.7% under 18, 19.7% over 64 (2000); Marriage status: 15.0% never married, 67.1% now married, 10.7% widowed, 7.2% divorced (2000); Foreign born: 2.8% (2000); Ancestry (includes multiple ancestries): 21.3% Other groups, 18.0% Irish, 16.3% German, 11.6% English, 7.6% Italian (2000).
Economy: Employment by occupation: 13.2% management, 16.9% professional, 17.4% services, 31.3% sales, 0.6% farming, 13.3% construction, 7.4% production (2000).
Income: Per capita income: $20,047 (2000); Median household income: $40,156 (2000); Poverty rate: 12.2% (2000).
Education: Percent of population age 25 and over with: High school diploma (including GED) or higher: 80.4% (2000); Bachelor's degree or higher: 20.8% (2000).
Housing: Homeownership rate: 91.6% (2000); Median home value: $104,800 (2000); Median rent: $552 per month (2000); Median age of housing: 8 years (2000).
Transportation: Commute to work: 99.2% car, 0.0% public transportation, 0.8% walk, 0.0% work from home (2000); Travel time to work: 16.0% less than 15 minutes, 51.7% 15 to 30 minutes, 18.2% 30 to 45 minutes, 8.4% 45 to 60 minutes, 5.8% 60 minutes or more (2000)

FRUIT COVE (CDP). Covers a land area of 17.860 square miles and a water area of 0.005 square miles. Located at 30.10° N. Lat.; 81.61° W. Long. Elevation is 10 feet.
Population: 5,904 (1990); 16,077 (2000); 21,191 (2004); 27,358 (2009 projected); Race: 93.6% White, 2.9% Black, 1.8% Asian, 2.9% Hispanic of any race (2004); Density: 1,186.5 persons per square mile (2004); Average household size: 3.11 (2004); Median age: 36.9 (2004); Male/female ratio: 101.0 (2004); Marriage status: 16.7% never married, 73.3% now married, 3.9% widowed, 6.1% divorced (2000); Foreign born: 4.0% (2000); Ancestry (includes multiple ancestries): 18.9% German, 16.6% Irish, 14.7% English, 10.9% Other groups, 10.4% United States or American (2000).
Economy: Employment by occupation: 25.5% management, 23.8% professional, 9.6% services, 30.7% sales, 0.2% farming, 4.7% construction, 5.4% production (2000).
Income: Per capita income: $35,662 (2004); Median household income: $94,585 (2004); Average household income: $110,367 (2004); Percent of households with income of $100,000 or more: 45.9% (2004); Poverty rate: 1.9% (2000).
Education: Percent of population age 25 and over with: High school diploma (including GED) or higher: 95.8% (2004); Bachelor's degree or higher: 42.2% (2004); Master's degree or higher: 11.8% (2004).

School District(s)

St. Johns County School District (PK-12)
2002-03 Enrollment: 21,975 . . . . (904) 819-7502
Housing: Homeownership rate: 93.0% (2004); Median home value: $242,695 (2004); Median rent: $990 per month (2000); Median age of housing: 5 years (2000).
Transportation: Commute to work: 96.6% car, 0.3% public transportation, 0.0% walk, 2.5% work from home (2000); Travel time to work: 9.7% less than 15 minutes, 28.3% 15 to 30 minutes, 43.5% 30 to 45 minutes, 14.0% 45 to 60 minutes, 4.6% 60 minutes or more (2000)

HASTINGS (town). Covers a land area of 0.659 square miles and a water area of 0 square miles. Located at 29.71° N. Lat.; 81.50° W. Long. Elevation is 10 feet.
History: Hastings developed as a potato market town. In 1918 Hastings harvested a particularly large potato crop while the rest of the country had small crops, and the town was crowded with buyers paying cash for the potatoes. The town officials had to call out the Home Guards to protect the bank building because of the unusually large number of deposits.
Population: 595 (1990); 521 (2000); 517 (2004); 514 (2009 projected); Race: 48.4% White, 45.8% Black, 0.0% Asian, 6.8% Hispanic of any race (2004); Density: 784.4 persons per square mile (2004); Average household size: 2.42 (2004); Median age: 38.8 (2004); Male/female ratio: 84.6 (2004); Marriage status: 24.5% never married, 51.2% now married, 10.0% widowed, 14.3% divorced (2000); Foreign born: 4.7% (2000); Ancestry (includes multiple ancestries): 46.6% Other groups, 11.4% English, 7.5% United States or American, 7.5% German, 5.6% Irish (2000).
Economy: Employment by occupation: 7.3% management, 13.6% professional, 32.0% services, 22.3% sales, 5.3% farming, 12.1% construction, 7.3% production (2000).
Income: Per capita income: $14,739 (2004); Median household income: $28,261 (2004); Average household income: $35,502 (2004); Percent of households with income of $100,000 or more: 4.7% (2004); Poverty rate: 21.0% (2000).
Taxes: Total city taxes per capita: $518 (2002); City property taxes per capita: $184 (2002).
Education: Percent of population age 25 and over with: High school diploma (including GED) or higher: 75.8% (2004); Bachelor's degree or higher: 13.8% (2004); Master's degree or higher: 4.9% (2004).

School District(s)

St. Johns County School District (PK-12)
2002-03 Enrollment: 21,975 . . . . (904) 819-7502
Housing: Homeownership rate: 76.2% (2004); Median home value: $72,895 (2004); Median rent: $379 per month (2000); Median age of housing: 33 years (2000).
Transportation: Commute to work: 92.1% car, 0.0% public transportation, 5.0% walk, 3.0% work from home (2000); Travel time to work: 18.4% less than 15 minutes, 30.1% 15 to 30 minutes, 35.2% 30 to 45 minutes, 6.1% 45 to 60 minutes, 10.2% 60 minutes or more (2000)

PALM VALLEY (CDP). Covers a land area of 13.412 square miles and a water area of 0.586 square miles. Located at 30.20° N. Lat.; 81.38° W. Long. Elevation is 8 feet.
Population: 9,960 (1990); 19,860 (2000); 22,255 (2004); 25,370 (2009 projected); Race: 95.4% White, 1.5% Black, 1.4% Asian, 3.1% Hispanic of any race (2004); Density: 1,659.4 persons per square mile (2004); Average household size: 2.45 (2004); Median age: 39.5 (2004); Male/female ratio: 94.9 (2004); Marriage status: 19.5% never married, 64.7% now married, 4.2% widowed, 11.5% divorced (2000); Foreign born: 6.8% (2000); Ancestry (includes multiple ancestries): 18.1% English, 17.9% German, 17.0% Irish, 11.5% Other groups, 8.7% Italian (2000).
Economy: Employment by occupation: 26.7% management, 21.8% professional, 13.6% services, 28.8% sales, 0.0% farming, 4.8% construction, 4.3% production (2000).
Income: Per capita income: $48,998 (2004); Median household income: $79,049 (2004); Average household income: $119,120 (2004); Percent of households with income of $100,000 or more: 37.9% (2004); Poverty rate: 3.5% (2000).
Education: Percent of population age 25 and over with: High school diploma (including GED) or higher: 96.2% (2004); Bachelor's degree or higher: 53.6% (2004); Master's degree or higher: 17.7% (2004).
Housing: Homeownership rate: 68.5% (2004); Median home value: $318,394 (2004); Median rent: $784 per month (2000); Median age of housing: 10 years (2000).
Transportation: Commute to work: 92.1% car, 0.3% public transportation, 0.9% walk, 5.0% work from home (2000); Travel time to work: 30.5% less than 15 minutes, 27.8% 15 to 30 minutes, 28.8% 30 to 45 minutes, 8.7% 45 to 60 minutes, 4.2% 60 minutes or more (2000)

SAINT AUGUSTINE (city). Covers a land area of 8.372 square miles and a water area of 2.356 square miles. Located at 29.89° N. Lat.; 81.31° W. Long. Elevation is 5 feet.
History: Named for the saint's day, August 28, 1565, when land was first sighted by the Spaniards. St. Augustine is recognized as the oldest permanent European settlement in the United States. The site was chosen by the Spanish in 1565 because it could be easily defended, and the Spanish flavor has influenced successive groups of non-Spanish settlers. Don Pedro Menendez de Aviles, Spanish admiral, is credited with founding and naming St. Augustine. The town sustained a series of attacks by the British until 1763, when the Spanish fled and Florida came under British rule. During the Revolution, the city was a center of British operations against the southern colonies. After another period of Spanish rule, St. Augustine became an American town with the transfer of Florida to the United States.

Population: 11,874 (1990); 11,592 (2000); 11,807 (2004); 12,350 (2009 projected); Race: 81.5% White, 14.8% Black, 0.7% Asian, 3.2% Hispanic of any race (2004); Density: 1,410.3 persons per square mile (2004); Average household size: 2.25 (2004); Median age: 41.7 (2004); Male/female ratio: 84.2 (2004); Marriage status: 32.0% never married, 42.3% now married, 11.5% widowed, 14.2% divorced (2000); Foreign born: 5.8% (2000); Ancestry (includes multiple ancestries): 20.6% Other groups, 14.6% German, 13.8% Irish, 13.6% English, 6.6% United States or American (2000).
Economy: Single-family building permits issued: 60 (2004); Multi-family building permits issued: 22 (2004); Employment by occupation: 13.7% management, 18.3% professional, 21.0% services, 28.7% sales, 0.7% farming, 7.7% construction, 9.9% production (2000).
Income: Per capita income: $24,899 (2004); Median household income: $35,237 (2004); Average household income: $54,691 (2004); Percent of households with income of $100,000 or more: 12.5% (2004); Poverty rate: 15.8% (2000).
Taxes: Total city taxes per capita: $721 (2002); City property taxes per capita: $556 (2002).
Education: Percent of population age 25 and over with: High school diploma (including GED) or higher: 82.1% (2004); Bachelor's degree or higher: 29.0% (2004); Master's degree or higher: 11.2% (2004).

School District(s)

St. Johns County School District (PK-12)
2002-03 Enrollment: 21,975 . . . . (904) 819-7502

Four-year College(s)

Flagler College
2003-04 Enrollment: 2,034 . . . . (904) 829-6481
2003-04 Tuition: In-state $7,410; Out-of-state $7,410

Two-year College(s)

First Coast Technical Institute (Public)
2003-04 Enrollment: 777 . . . . (904) 824-4401

Housing: Homeownership rate: 60.5% (2004); Median home value: $145,680 (2004); Median rent: $545 per month (2000); Median age of housing: 48 years (2000).
Hospitals: Flagler Hospital (260 beds)
Safety: Violent crime rate: 94.1 per 10,000 population; Property crime rate: 696.9 per 10,000 population (2003).
Newspapers: St. Augustine Record (Circulation 15,804)
Transportation: Commute to work: 78.2% car, 1.3% public transportation, 12.0% walk, 4.0% work from home (2000); Travel time to work: 57.7% less than 15 minutes, 22.8% 15 to 30 minutes, 8.6% 30 to 45 minutes, 6.1% 45 to 60 minutes, 4.8% 60 minutes or more (2000)
Airports: Saint Augustine
Additional Information Contacts
St. Augustine Chamber of Commerce . . . . (904) 829-5681
St. Augustine and St. Johns County Board of Realtors . . . . (904) 829-8738

SAINT AUGUSTINE BEACH (city). Covers a land area of 1.941 square miles and a water area of 0 square miles. Located at 29.84° N. Lat.; 81.27° W. Long. Elevation is 10 feet.
History: There has been a lighthouse at St. Augustine Beach since the 1500's. In 1586 Sir Francis Drake sighted the Spanish signal-tower at this spot.
Population: 3,696 (1990); 4,683 (2000); 5,323 (2004); 6,129 (2009 projected); Race: 96.5% White, 0.4% Black, 1.3% Asian, 2.8% Hispanic of any race (2004); Density: 2,742.9 persons per square mile (2004); Average household size: 2.07 (2004); Median age: 44.1 (2004); Male/female ratio: 95.4 (2004); Marriage status: 25.9% never married, 53.1% now married, 5.1% widowed, 15.9% divorced (2000); Foreign born: 7.7% (2000); Ancestry (includes multiple ancestries): 19.7% German, 17.6% Irish, 17.1% English, 10.3% Other groups, 7.7% Italian (2000).
Economy: Single-family building permits issued: 86 (2004); Multi-family building permits issued: 24 (2004); Employment by occupation: 14.5% management, 21.5% professional, 18.4% services, 31.1% sales, 0.0% farming, 7.8% construction, 6.6% production (2000).
Income: Per capita income: $33,844 (2004); Median household income: $48,219 (2004); Average household income: $69,908 (2004); Percent of households with income of $100,000 or more: 15.5% (2004); Poverty rate: 8.7% (2000).
Taxes: Total city taxes per capita: $372 (2002); City property taxes per capita: $170 (2002).
Education: Percent of population age 25 and over with: High school diploma (including GED) or higher: 94.7% (2004); Bachelor's degree or higher: 43.1% (2004); Master's degree or higher: 18.5% (2004).
Housing: Homeownership rate: 61.2% (2004); Median home value: $195,691 (2004); Median rent: $647 per month (2000); Median age of housing: 16 years (2000).
Safety: Violent crime rate: 40.8 per 10,000 population; Property crime rate: 336.4 per 10,000 population (2003).
Transportation: Commute to work: 89.5% car, 0.2% public transportation, 2.1% walk, 4.4% work from home (2000); Travel time to work: 35.4% less than 15 minutes, 36.9% 15 to 30 minutes, 11.5% 30 to 45 minutes, 7.4% 45 to 60 minutes, 8.9% 60 minutes or more (2000)

SAINT AUGUSTINE SHORES (CDP). Covers a land area of 3.438 square miles and a water area of 0.030 square miles. Located at 29.81° N. Lat.; 81.31° W. Long.
Population: 4,411 (1990); 4,922 (2000); 5,516 (2004); 6,276 (2009 projected); Race: 94.9% White, 2.3% Black, 1.1% Asian, 3.5% Hispanic of any race (2004); Density: 1,604.4 persons per square mile (2004); Average household size: 2.13 (2004); Median age: 51.3 (2004); Male/female ratio: 84.2 (2004); Marriage status: 12.6% never married, 66.3% now married, 11.7% widowed, 9.4% divorced (2000); Foreign born: 7.6% (2000); Ancestry (includes multiple ancestries): 18.3% Irish, 16.1% German, 14.2% English, 9.9% United States or American, 9.1% Other groups (2000).
Economy: Employment by occupation: 13.1% management, 19.1% professional, 20.5% services, 32.7% sales, 0.0% farming, 7.5% construction, 7.0% production (2000).
Income: Per capita income: $22,868 (2004); Median household income: $43,041 (2004); Average household income: $48,629 (2004); Percent of households with income of $100,000 or more: 5.9% (2004); Poverty rate: 6.9% (2000).
Education: Percent of population age 25 and over with: High school diploma (including GED) or higher: 89.1% (2004); Bachelor's degree or higher: 23.2% (2004); Master's degree or higher: 10.1% (2004).
Housing: Homeownership rate: 82.8% (2004); Median home value: $134,449 (2004); Median rent: $712 per month (2000); Median age of housing: 19 years (2000).
Transportation: Commute to work: 93.6% car, 0.6% public transportation, 2.4% walk, 2.8% work from home (2000); Travel time to work: 33.0% less than 15 minutes, 47.5% 15 to 30 minutes, 9.6% 30 to 45 minutes, 7.8% 45 to 60 minutes, 2.1% 60 minutes or more (2000)

SAINT AUGUSTINE SOUTH (CDP). Covers a land area of 1.720 square miles and a water area of 0 square miles. Located at 29.84° N. Lat.; 81.31° W. Long.
Population: 4,218 (1990); 5,035 (2000); 5,486 (2004); 6,101 (2009 projected); Race: 96.6% White, 1.2% Black, 1.0% Asian, 3.2% Hispanic of any race (2004); Density: 3,189.5 persons per square mile (2004); Average household size: 2.58 (2004); Median age: 40.9 (2004); Male/female ratio: 92.4 (2004); Marriage status: 20.4% never married, 66.9% now married, 5.4% widowed, 7.2% divorced (2000); Foreign born: 6.0% (2000); Ancestry (includes multiple ancestries): 21.5% English, 16.1% Irish, 14.7% United States or American, 12.7% German, 11.4% Other groups (2000).
Economy: Employment by occupation: 12.6% management, 21.6% professional, 17.2% services, 29.1% sales, 0.5% farming, 8.4% construction, 10.6% production (2000).
Income: Per capita income: $25,851 (2004); Median household income: $56,852 (2004); Average household income: $65,902 (2004); Percent of households with income of $100,000 or more: 14.3% (2004); Poverty rate: 4.1% (2000).
Education: Percent of population age 25 and over with: High school diploma (including GED) or higher: 89.3% (2004); Bachelor's degree or higher: 21.8% (2004); Master's degree or higher: 6.2% (2004).
Housing: Homeownership rate: 89.7% (2004); Median home value: $153,775 (2004); Median rent: $832 per month (2000); Median age of housing: 17 years (2000).
Transportation: Commute to work: 96.9% car, 0.0% public transportation, 0.0% walk, 2.2% work from home (2000); Travel time to work: 35.6% less than 15 minutes, 33.8% 15 to 30 minutes, 7.6% 30 to 45 minutes, 9.8% 45 to 60 minutes, 13.2% 60 minutes or more (2000)

SAWGRASS (CDP). Covers a land area of 3.088 square miles and a water area of 0.143 square miles. Located at 30.19° N. Lat.; 81.37° W. Long.
Population: 2,999 (1990); 4,942 (2000); 5,324 (2004); 5,864 (2009 projected); Race: 97.1% White, 0.7% Black, 1.0% Asian, 2.0% Hispanic of any race (2004); Density: 1,724.1 persons per square mile (2004); Average household size: 2.01 (2004); Median age: 52.2 (2004); Male/female ratio:

86.7 (2004); Marriage status: 12.8% never married, 66.7% now married, 7.2% widowed, 13.4% divorced (2000); Foreign born: 5.2% (2000); Ancestry (includes multiple ancestries): 19.4% English, 16.4% German, 14.8% Irish, 7.8% Other groups, 7.0% United States or American (2000).
Economy: Employment by occupation: 35.9% management, 22.4% professional, 5.9% services, 30.3% sales, 0.0% farming, 1.9% construction, 3.7% production (2000).
Income: Per capita income: $64,775 (2004); Median household income: $89,500 (2004); Average household income: $130,185 (2004); Percent of households with income of $100,000 or more: 43.3% (2004); Poverty rate: 2.5% (2000).
Education: Percent of population age 25 and over with: High school diploma (including GED) or higher: 97.8% (2004); Bachelor's degree or higher: 61.2% (2004); Master's degree or higher: 19.6% (2004).
Housing: Homeownership rate: 80.3% (2004); Median home value: $345,052 (2004); Median rent: $965 per month (2000); Median age of housing: 13 years (2000).
Transportation: Commute to work: 93.8% car, 0.0% public transportation, 1.2% walk, 3.8% work from home (2000); Travel time to work: 25.8% less than 15 minutes, 23.8% 15 to 30 minutes, 39.2% 30 to 45 minutes, 9.4% 45 to 60 minutes, 1.8% 60 minutes or more (2000)

VILLANO BEACH (CDP). Covers a land area of 1.794 square miles and a water area of 0 square miles. Located at 29.93° N. Lat.; 81.30° W. Long.
Population: 1,867 (1990); 2,533 (2000); 2,945 (2004); 3,442 (2009 projected); Race: 97.1% White, 0.6% Black, 0.9% Asian, 1.0% Hispanic of any race (2004); Density: 1,641.4 persons per square mile (2004); Average household size: 2.11 (2004); Median age: 46.7 (2004); Male/female ratio: 93.5 (2004); Marriage status: 19.7% never married, 62.2% now married, 6.1% widowed, 11.9% divorced (2000); Foreign born: 4.4% (2000); Ancestry (includes multiple ancestries): 19.9% German, 15.7% English, 12.8% Irish, 11.7% Italian, 10.4% Other groups (2000).
Economy: Employment by occupation: 16.5% management, 24.3% professional, 18.5% services, 26.9% sales, 0.0% farming, 10.0% construction, 3.9% production (2000).
Income: Per capita income: $43,960 (2004); Median household income: $64,844 (2004); Average household income: $91,808 (2004); Percent of households with income of $100,000 or more: 31.8% (2004); Poverty rate: 4.9% (2000).
Education: Percent of population age 25 and over with: High school diploma (including GED) or higher: 92.2% (2004); Bachelor's degree or higher: 42.3% (2004); Master's degree or higher: 12.3% (2004).
Housing: Homeownership rate: 77.3% (2004); Median home value: $218,051 (2004); Median rent: $539 per month (2000); Median age of housing: 16 years (2000).
Transportation: Commute to work: 93.3% car, 0.0% public transportation, 1.1% walk, 2.8% work from home (2000); Travel time to work: 31.0% less than 15 minutes, 33.9% 15 to 30 minutes, 17.9% 30 to 45 minutes, 9.5% 45 to 60 minutes, 7.7% 60 minutes or more (2000)

Saint Lucie County

Located in southeastern Florida; swampy, lowland area bounded on the east by the Atlantic Ocean, with a barrier beach enclosing Indian River lagoon. Covers a land area of 572.40 square miles, a water area of 115.60 square miles, and is located in the Eastern Time Zone. The county government was organized in 1844. County seat is Fort Pierce.

Saint Lucie County is part of the Port St. Lucie-Fort Pierce, FL Metropolitan Statistical Area. The entire metro area includes: Martin County, FL; St. Lucie County, FL

Weather Station: Fort Pierce — Elevation: 22 feet

	Jan	Feb	Mar	Apr	May	Jun	Jul	Aug	Sep	Oct	Nov	Dec
High	74	75	79	82	86	89	91	91	89	85	80	76
Low	52	53	57	61	67	71	72	72	72	67	61	54
Precip	2.8	3.0	3.4	2.7	4.6	5.8	5.7	6.4	8.1	5.9	3.5	2.3
Snow	tr	0.0	0.0	0.0	0.0	0.0	0.0	0.0	0.0	0.0	0.0	0.0

High and Low temperatures in degrees Fahrenheit; Precipitation and Snow in inches

Population: 150,171 (1990); 192,695 (2000); 214,105 (2004); 241,037 (2009 projected); Race: 77.4% White, 16.4% Black, 1.1% Asian, 9.7% Hispanic of any race (2004); Density: 374.0 persons per square mile (2004); Average household size: 2.49 (2004); Median age: 42.1 (2004); Male/female ratio: 95.9 (2004).
Religion: Five largest groups: 23.4% Catholic Church, 4.3% Southern Baptist Convention, 2.0% The United Methodist Church, 1.6% Jewish Estimate, 0.7% Presbyterian Church (U.S.A.) (2000).
Economy: Unemployment rate: 8.2% (2004); Total civilian labor force: 92,886 (2004); Leading industries: 20.2% retail trade; 16.4% health care and social assistance; 10.0% accommodation & food services (2003); Companies that employ 500 or more persons: 8 (2003); Companies that employ 100 to 499 persons: 60 (2003); Companies that employ less than 100 persons: 4,247 (2003); Farms: 477 totaling 221,537 acres (2002); Minority business ownership rate: 13.6% (1997); Women business ownership rate: 20.7% (1997); Retail sales per capita: $7,818 (1997). Single-family building permits issued: 7,613 (2004); Multi-family building permits issued: 1,484 (2004).
Income: Per capita income: $20,970 (2004); Median household income: $39,984 (2004); Average household income: $51,756 (2004); Percent of households with income of $100,000 or more: 9.0% (2004); Poverty rate: 12.8% (2002); Bankruptcy rate: 3.90% (2004).
Taxes: Total county taxes per capita: $412 (2002); County property taxes per capita: $355 (2002).
Education: Percent of population age 25 and over with: High school diploma (including GED) or higher: 78.7% (2004); Bachelor's degree or higher: 15.5% (2004); Master's degree or higher: 5.4% (2004).
Housing: Homeownership rate: 79.1% (2004); Median home value: $120,668 (2004); Median rent: $518 per month (2000); Median age of housing: 16 years (2000).
Health: Birth rate: 108.2 per 10,000 population (2004); Death rate: 106.7 per 10,000 population (2004); Age adjusted cancer mortality rate: 186.9 deaths per 100,000 population (2002); Air Quality Index: 96.1% good, 3.9% moderate, 0.0% unhealthy for sensitive individuals, 0.0% unhealthy (percent of days in 2004); Number of physicians: 14.0 per 10,000 population (2001); Hospital beds: 36.2 per 10,000 population (2002); Hospital admissions: 1,517.8 per 10,000 population (2002).
Elections: 2004 Presidential election results: 47.6% Bush, 51.8% Kerry, 0.4% Nader, 0.1% Badnarik
National and State Parks: Avalon State Park; Fort Pierce Inlet State Park; Pepper Beach State Recreation Area; Savannas Preserve State Park
Additional Information Contacts
St. Lucie County Government Offices . . . . (561) 462-1400
St. Lucie Association of Realtors . . . . (772) 465-6080
St. Lucie County Chamber of Commerce . . . . (772) 398-1460

Saint Lucie County Communities

FORT PIERCE (city). Covers a land area of 14.742 square miles and a water area of 6.021 square miles. Located at 27.43° N. Lat.; 80.33° W. Long. Elevation is 5 feet.
History: The original Fort Pierce was built in 1838 as a link in a chain of east coast defenses. The town of Fort Pierce developed as a citrus and vegetable shipping center.
Population: 38,676 (1990); 37,516 (2000); 37,876 (2004); 38,748 (2009 projected); Race: 46.7% White, 42.5% Black, 1.0% Asian, 17.9% Hispanic of any race (2004); Density: 2,569.3 persons per square mile (2004); Average household size: 2.59 (2004); Median age: 35.4 (2004); Male/female ratio: 98.3 (2004); Marriage status: 29.7% never married, 48.0% now married, 10.0% widowed, 12.3% divorced (2000); Foreign born: 18.4% (2000); Ancestry (includes multiple ancestries): 42.8% Other groups, 8.2% Irish, 7.9% German, 6.9% English, 6.6% United States or American (2000).
Economy: Unemployment rate: 13.8% (2004); Total civilian labor force: 21,758 (2004); Single-family building permits issued: 41 (2004); Multi-family building permits issued: 635 (2004); Employment by occupation: 6.7% management, 13.2% professional, 19.3% services, 20.5% sales, 9.0% farming, 15.8% construction, 15.5% production (2000).
Income: Per capita income: $15,427 (2004); Median household income: $27,347 (2004); Average household income: $39,251 (2004); Percent of households with income of $100,000 or more: 5.7% (2004); Poverty rate: 30.9% (2000).
Education: Percent of population age 25 and over with: High school diploma (including GED) or higher: 62.0% (2004); Bachelor's degree or higher: 13.8% (2004); Master's degree or higher: 5.1% (2004).

School District(s)

St. Lucie County School District (PK-12)
2002-03 Enrollment: 31,554 . . . . (772) 429-3925

Two-year College(s)

Fort Pierce Beauty Academy (Private, For-profit)
2003-04 Enrollment: 26 .... (772) 464-4885
Indian River Community College (Public)
2003-04 Enrollment: 14,112 .... (772) 462-4700
2003-04 Tuition: In-state $1,650; Out-of-state $6,240

Housing: Homeownership rate: 54.5% (2004); Median home value: $82,404 (2004); Median rent: $413 per month (2000); Median age of housing: 27 years (2000).
Hospitals: Lawnwood Pavilion (36 beds); New Horizons of the Treasure Coast (30 beds)
Safety: Violent crime rate: 214.6 per 10,000 population; Property crime rate: 891.3 per 10,000 population (2003).
Newspapers: Tribune (Circulation 29,280)
Transportation: Commute to work: 89.9% car, 4.0% public transportation, 1.9% walk, 2.0% work from home (2000); Travel time to work: 30.9% less than 15 minutes, 31.9% 15 to 30 minutes, 25.2% 30 to 45 minutes, 4.1% 45 to 60 minutes, 7.8% 60 minutes or more (2000)
Airports: Saint Lucie County International

Additional Information Contacts

St. Lucie Association of Realtors .... (772) 465-6080
St. Lucie County Chamber of Commerce .... (772) 398-1460

FORT PIERCE NORTH (CDP).

Covers a land area of 4.470 square miles and a water area of 0.095 square miles. Located at 27.46° N. Lat.; 80.35° W. Long.
Population: 8,065 (1990); 7,386 (2000); 6,980 (2004); 6,566 (2009 projected); Race: 17.6% White, 77.7% Black, 0.0% Asian, 6.2% Hispanic of any race (2004); Density: 1,561.6 persons per square mile (2004); Average household size: 2.87 (2004); Median age: 34.5 (2004); Male/female ratio: 92.8 (2004); Marriage status: 32.7% never married, 47.8% now married, 7.9% widowed, 11.6% divorced (2000); Foreign born: 6.9% (2000); Ancestry (includes multiple ancestries): 52.3% Other groups, 9.2% African, 5.9% United States or American, 3.0% Irish, 2.8% German (2000).
Economy: Employment by occupation: 5.4% management, 15.2% professional, 25.8% services, 21.0% sales, 5.5% farming, 10.4% construction, 16.6% production (2000).
Income: Per capita income: $11,641 (2004); Median household income: $26,263 (2004); Average household income: $33,241 (2004); Percent of households with income of $100,000 or more: 2.8% (2004); Poverty rate: 22.1% (2000).
Education: Percent of population age 25 and over with: High school diploma (including GED) or higher: 59.5% (2004); Bachelor's degree or higher: 10.4% (2004); Master's degree or higher: 4.2% (2004).
Housing: Homeownership rate: 74.6% (2004); Median home value: $75,718 (2004); Median rent: $475 per month (2000); Median age of housing: 26 years (2000).
Transportation: Commute to work: 95.8% car, 2.3% public transportation, 1.2% walk, 0.0% work from home (2000); Travel time to work: 34.1% less than 15 minutes, 34.5% 15 to 30 minutes, 17.7% 30 to 45 minutes, 7.2% 45 to 60 minutes, 6.5% 60 minutes or more (2000)

FORT PIERCE SOUTH (CDP).

Covers a land area of 4.503 square miles and a water area of 0 square miles. Located at 27.41° N. Lat.; 80.35° W. Long.
Population: 4,899 (1990); 5,672 (2000); 5,656 (2004); 5,739 (2009 projected); Race: 70.3% White, 17.6% Black, 1.5% Asian, 23.0% Hispanic of any race (2004); Density: 1,256.0 persons per square mile (2004); Average household size: 2.84 (2004); Median age: 32.6 (2004); Male/female ratio: 96.9 (2004); Marriage status: 25.9% never married, 54.7% now married, 6.7% widowed, 12.8% divorced (2000); Foreign born: 14.1% (2000); Ancestry (includes multiple ancestries): 27.6% Other groups, 12.0% United States or American, 11.9% English, 10.3% Irish, 9.4% German (2000).
Economy: Employment by occupation: 8.3% management, 15.2% professional, 18.0% services, 22.8% sales, 3.3% farming, 17.4% construction, 15.0% production (2000).
Income: Per capita income: $17,502 (2004); Median household income: $33,127 (2004); Average household income: $49,515 (2004); Percent of households with income of $100,000 or more: 8.8% (2004); Poverty rate: 17.6% (2000).
Education: Percent of population age 25 and over with: High school diploma (including GED) or higher: 68.5% (2004); Bachelor's degree or higher: 12.4% (2004); Master's degree or higher: 4.9% (2004).
Housing: Homeownership rate: 64.3% (2004); Median home value: $93,257 (2004); Median rent: $470 per month (2000); Median age of housing: 27 years (2000).
Transportation: Commute to work: 94.5% car, 0.6% public transportation, 2.3% walk, 0.9% work from home (2000); Travel time to work: 42.8% less than 15 minutes, 33.3% 15 to 30 minutes, 13.4% 30 to 45 minutes, 4.0% 45 to 60 minutes, 6.6% 60 minutes or more (2000)

HUTCHINSON ISLAND SOUTH (CDP).

Covers a land area of 4.512 square miles and a water area of 43.560 square miles. Located at 27.28° N. Lat.; 80.22° W. Long.
Population: 3,893 (1990); 4,846 (2000); 6,166 (2004); 7,750 (2009 projected); Race: 98.9% White, 0.1% Black, 0.2% Asian, 0.8% Hispanic of any race (2004); Density: 1,366.7 persons per square mile (2004); Average household size: 1.69 (2004); Median age: 68.8 (2004); Male/female ratio: 87.7 (2004); Marriage status: 4.9% never married, 72.4% now married, 15.6% widowed, 7.0% divorced (2000); Foreign born: 9.0% (2000); Ancestry (includes multiple ancestries): 20.2% German, 19.8% English, 15.5% Irish, 11.4% Italian, 5.8% United States or American (2000).
Economy: Employment by occupation: 10.9% management, 23.9% professional, 15.7% services, 34.3% sales, 0.0% farming, 8.4% construction, 6.8% production (2000).
Income: Per capita income: $39,386 (2004); Median household income: $43,991 (2004); Average household income: $66,608 (2004); Percent of households with income of $100,000 or more: 14.3% (2004); Poverty rate: 4.5% (2000).
Education: Percent of population age 25 and over with: High school diploma (including GED) or higher: 86.7% (2004); Bachelor's degree or higher: 23.0% (2004); Master's degree or higher: 9.8% (2004).
Housing: Homeownership rate: 91.2% (2004); Median home value: $155,401 (2004); Median rent: $843 per month (2000); Median age of housing: 15 years (2000).
Transportation: Commute to work: 76.6% car, 0.0% public transportation, 9.3% walk, 11.0% work from home (2000); Travel time to work: 28.6% less than 15 minutes, 37.4% 15 to 30 minutes, 20.6% 30 to 45 minutes, 6.1% 45 to 60 minutes, 7.3% 60 minutes or more (2000)

INDIAN RIVER ESTATES (CDP).

Covers a land area of 5.537 square miles and a water area of 0.208 square miles. Located at 27.36° N. Lat.; 80.30° W. Long.
Population: 4,872 (1990); 5,793 (2000); 6,057 (2004); 6,438 (2009 projected); Race: 94.1% White, 3.2% Black, 0.5% Asian, 4.4% Hispanic of any race (2004); Density: 1,093.9 persons per square mile (2004); Average household size: 2.44 (2004); Median age: 44.1 (2004); Male/female ratio: 96.5 (2004); Marriage status: 13.8% never married, 66.8% now married, 8.5% widowed, 10.9% divorced (2000); Foreign born: 6.1% (2000); Ancestry (includes multiple ancestries): 17.7% German, 16.0% Irish, 11.6% English, 10.9% Italian, 10.9% United States or American (2000).
Economy: Employment by occupation: 13.1% management, 14.7% professional, 13.8% services, 33.2% sales, 0.6% farming, 15.9% construction, 8.7% production (2000).
Income: Per capita income: $17,997 (2004); Median household income: $38,607 (2004); Average household income: $43,619 (2004); Percent of households with income of $100,000 or more: 4.4% (2004); Poverty rate: 7.7% (2000).
Education: Percent of population age 25 and over with: High school diploma (including GED) or higher: 75.5% (2004); Bachelor's degree or higher: 8.7% (2004); Master's degree or higher: 2.8% (2004).
Housing: Homeownership rate: 91.9% (2004); Median home value: $115,996 (2004); Median rent: $558 per month (2000); Median age of housing: 15 years (2000).
Transportation: Commute to work: 93.8% car, 0.3% public transportation, 0.6% walk, 4.4% work from home (2000); Travel time to work: 21.3% less than 15 minutes, 50.1% 15 to 30 minutes, 18.5% 30 to 45 minutes, 4.6% 45 to 60 minutes, 5.5% 60 minutes or more (2000)

LAKEWOOD PARK (CDP).

Covers a land area of 6.697 square miles and a water area of 0.224 square miles. Located at 27.54° N. Lat.; 80.39° W. Long. Elevation is 22 feet.
Population: 9,240 (1990); 10,458 (2000); 10,548 (2004); 10,791 (2009 projected); Race: 90.1% White, 6.6% Black, 0.7% Asian, 3.1% Hispanic of any race (2004); Density: 1,575.0 persons per square mile (2004); Average household size: 2.27 (2004); Median age: 45.9 (2004); Male/female ratio: 95.2 (2004); Marriage status: 15.6% never married, 64.1% now married, 9.7% widowed, 10.5% divorced (2000); Foreign born: 5.2% (2000);

Ancestry (includes multiple ancestries): 16.9% Irish, 16.4% German, 13.2% English, 12.9% Other groups, 10.9% United States or American (2000).
Economy: Employment by occupation: 11.9% management, 12.4% professional, 16.1% services, 30.4% sales, 1.3% farming, 16.0% construction, 11.9% production (2000).
Income: Per capita income: $20,404 (2004); Median household income: $38,594 (2004); Average household income: $46,252 (2004); Percent of households with income of $100,000 or more: 6.3% (2004); Poverty rate: 9.5% (2000).
Education: Percent of population age 25 and over with: High school diploma (including GED) or higher: 81.1% (2004); Bachelor's degree or higher: 11.8% (2004); Master's degree or higher: 3.2% (2004).
Housing: Homeownership rate: 85.3% (2004); Median home value: $96,434 (2004); Median rent: $505 per month (2000); Median age of housing: 16 years (2000).
Transportation: Commute to work: 96.1% car, 0.0% public transportation, 0.7% walk, 1.5% work from home (2000); Travel time to work: 16.5% less than 15 minutes, 55.0% 15 to 30 minutes, 20.9% 30 to 45 minutes, 2.2% 45 to 60 minutes, 5.5% 60 minutes or more (2000)

PORT SAINT LUCIE (city). Covers a land area of 75.541 square miles and a water area of 1.149 square miles. Located at 27.27° N. Lat.; 80.35° W. Long. Elevation is 20 feet.
Population: 55,843 (1990); 88,769 (2000); 105,317 (2004); 125,342 (2009 projected); Race: 84.6% White, 9.5% Black, 1.5% Asian, 9.2% Hispanic of any race (2004); Density: 1,394.2 persons per square mile (2004); Average household size: 2.60 (2004); Median age: 39.6 (2004); Male/female ratio: 95.1 (2004); Marriage status: 18.4% never married, 64.3% now married, 6.9% widowed, 10.5% divorced (2000); Foreign born: 9.6% (2000); Ancestry (includes multiple ancestries): 17.4% Irish, 16.9% German, 15.7% Italian, 15.4% Other groups, 11.5% English (2000).
Economy: Unemployment rate: 6.4% (2004); Total civilian labor force: 37,075 (2004); Single-family building permits issued: 6,642 (2004); Multi-family building permits issued: 384 (2004); Employment by occupation: 10.6% management, 16.0% professional, 17.6% services, 32.0% sales, 0.5% farming, 12.5% construction, 10.7% production (2000).
Income: Per capita income: $20,134 (2004); Median household income: $44,402 (2004); Average household income: $52,150 (2004); Percent of households with income of $100,000 or more: 8.2% (2004); Poverty rate: 7.9% (2000).
Taxes: Total city taxes per capita: $233 (2002); City property taxes per capita: $106 (2002).
Education: Percent of population age 25 and over with: High school diploma (including GED) or higher: 83.8% (2004); Bachelor's degree or higher: 15.0% (2004); Master's degree or higher: 4.9% (2004).

School District(s)

St. Lucie County School District (PK-12)
2002-03 Enrollment: 31,554 . . . . (772) 429-3925

Two-year College(s)

Keiser Career College (Private, For-profit)
2003-04 Enrollment: n/a . . . . (772) 398-9990
2003-04 Tuition: In-state $10,920; Out-of-state $10,920
Housing: Homeownership rate: 83.5% (2004); Median home value: $129,797 (2004); Median rent: $627 per month (2000); Median age of housing: 12 years (2000).
Hospitals: Savannas Hospital (75 beds); St. Lucie Medical Center (194 beds)
Safety: Violent crime rate: 28.0 per 10,000 population; Property crime rate: 269.0 per 10,000 population (2003).
Transportation: Commute to work: 95.8% car, 0.3% public transportation, 0.5% walk, 2.2% work from home (2000); Travel time to work: 18.2% less than 15 minutes, 41.9% 15 to 30 minutes, 23.8% 30 to 45 minutes, 8.8% 45 to 60 minutes, 7.3% 60 minutes or more (2000)

PORT SAINT LUCIE-RIVER PARK (CDP). Covers a land area of 2.336 square miles and a water area of 0.176 square miles. Located at 27.32° N. Lat.; 80.33° W. Long.
Population: 4,954 (1990); 5,175 (2000); 5,401 (2004); 5,776 (2009 projected); Race: 88.7% White, 6.5% Black, 1.0% Asian, 8.5% Hispanic of any race (2004); Density: 2,312.2 persons per square mile (2004); Average household size: 2.17 (2004); Median age: 49.0 (2004); Male/female ratio: 93.7 (2004); Marriage status: 14.8% never married, 54.9% now married, 17.7% widowed, 12.5% divorced (2000); Foreign born: 7.2% (2000); Ancestry (includes multiple ancestries): 16.1% Italian, 15.6% German, 15.2% English, 14.2% Irish, 11.4% Other groups (2000).
Economy: Employment by occupation: 5.8% management, 13.3% professional, 19.5% services, 35.2% sales, 1.1% farming, 14.4% construction, 10.6% production (2000).
Income: Per capita income: $20,940 (2004); Median household income: $31,809 (2004); Average household income: $45,025 (2004); Percent of households with income of $100,000 or more: 7.4% (2004); Poverty rate: 9.2% (2000).
Education: Percent of population age 25 and over with: High school diploma (including GED) or higher: 78.5% (2004); Bachelor's degree or higher: 13.4% (2004); Master's degree or higher: 4.5% (2004).
Housing: Homeownership rate: 82.4% (2004); Median home value: $84,315 (2004); Median rent: $532 per month (2000); Median age of housing: 26 years (2000).
Transportation: Commute to work: 96.0% car, 0.0% public transportation, 0.1% walk, 3.2% work from home (2000); Travel time to work: 19.7% less than 15 minutes, 45.1% 15 to 30 minutes, 21.6% 30 to 45 minutes, 6.4% 45 to 60 minutes, 7.2% 60 minutes or more (2000)

SAINT LUCIE (village). Covers a land area of 0.810 square miles and a water area of 0 square miles. Located at 27.49° N. Lat.; 80.34° W. Long. Elevation is 24 feet.
Population: 634 (1990); 604 (2000); 685 (2004); 759 (2009 projected); Race: 96.8% White, 1.0% Black, 0.0% Asian, 3.1% Hispanic of any race (2004); Density: 846.2 persons per square mile (2004); Average household size: 2.16 (2004); Median age: 45.1 (2004); Male/female ratio: 105.7 (2004); Marriage status: 24.8% never married, 52.0% now married, 8.2% widowed, 15.1% divorced (2000); Foreign born: 1.9% (2000); Ancestry (includes multiple ancestries): 22.8% German, 17.7% Irish, 16.7% English, 9.1% Italian, 7.8% United States or American (2000).
Economy: Single-family building permits issued: 0 (2004); Multi-family building permits issued: 0 (2004); Employment by occupation: 15.9% management, 17.6% professional, 16.7% services, 25.6% sales, 0.6% farming, 17.0% construction, 6.6% production (2000).
Income: Per capita income: $31,394 (2004); Median household income: $43,973 (2004); Average household income: $67,839 (2004); Percent of households with income of $100,000 or more: 16.7% (2004); Poverty rate: 4.0% (2000).
Education: Percent of population age 25 and over with: High school diploma (including GED) or higher: 81.9% (2004); Bachelor's degree or higher: 24.3% (2004); Master's degree or higher: 7.8% (2004).
Housing: Homeownership rate: 75.4% (2004); Median home value: $152,778 (2004); Median rent: $504 per month (2000); Median age of housing: 33 years (2000).
Transportation: Commute to work: 93.8% car, 0.0% public transportation, 0.6% walk, 2.6% work from home (2000); Travel time to work: 33.8% less than 15 minutes, 40.2% 15 to 30 minutes, 15.7% 30 to 45 minutes, 3.0% 45 to 60 minutes, 7.3% 60 minutes or more (2000)

WHITE CITY (CDP). Covers a land area of 7.062 square miles and a water area of 0 square miles. Located at 27.38° N. Lat.; 80.33° W. Long. Elevation is 11 feet.
History: White City was settled in the 1890's by Danish immigrants from Chicago, interested in the citrus orchards.
Population: 3,792 (1990); 4,221 (2000); 4,724 (2004); 5,312 (2009 projected); Race: 92.1% White, 3.0% Black, 1.2% Asian, 5.8% Hispanic of any race (2004); Density: 668.9 persons per square mile (2004); Average household size: 2.72 (2004); Median age: 38.2 (2004); Male/female ratio: 98.7 (2004); Marriage status: 20.8% never married, 61.5% now married, 6.3% widowed, 11.4% divorced (2000); Foreign born: 4.4% (2000); Ancestry (includes multiple ancestries): 22.3% Irish, 17.5% English, 15.2% United States or American, 13.2% German, 11.6% Other groups (2000).
Economy: Employment by occupation: 10.1% management, 21.1% professional, 14.4% services, 23.9% sales, 1.4% farming, 17.1% construction, 11.9% production (2000).
Income: Per capita income: $24,417 (2004); Median household income: $47,459 (2004); Average household income: $65,806 (2004); Percent of households with income of $100,000 or more: 18.0% (2004); Poverty rate: 11.1% (2000).
Education: Percent of population age 25 and over with: High school diploma (including GED) or higher: 80.4% (2004); Bachelor's degree or higher: 17.5% (2004); Master's degree or higher: 6.4% (2004).
Housing: Homeownership rate: 83.8% (2004); Median home value: $133,125 (2004); Median rent: $514 per month (2000); Median age of housing: 25 years (2000).

Transportation: Commute to work: 95.9% car, 0.0% public transportation, 0.2% walk, 2.3% work from home (2000); Travel time to work: 35.8% less than 15 minutes, 34.6% 15 to 30 minutes, 18.9% 30 to 45 minutes, 5.3% 45 to 60 minutes, 5.3% 60 minutes or more (2000)

Sumter County

Located in central Florida; bounded partly on the west and south by the Withlacoochee River; includes Lake Panasoffkee and many other lakes. Covers a land area of 545.70 square miles, a water area of 34.60 square miles, and is located in the Eastern Time Zone. The county government was organized in 1853. County seat is Bushnell.

Sumter County is part of the The Villages, FL Micropolitan Statistical Area. The entire metro area includes: Sumter County, FL

Population: 31,577 (1990); 53,345 (2000); 64,844 (2004); 79,273 (2009 projected); Race: 82.0% White, 14.3% Black, 0.4% Asian, 7.3% Hispanic of any race (2004); Density: 118.8 persons per square mile (2004); Average household size: 2.54 (2004); Median age: 46.8 (2004); Male/female ratio: 116.2 (2004).
Religion: Five largest groups: 14.9% Southern Baptist Convention, 3.0% Church of God (Cleveland, Tennessee), 2.8% The United Methodist Church, 2.1% Assemblies of God, 2.1% Catholic Church (2000).
Economy: Unemployment rate: 3.6% (2004); Total civilian labor force: 19,845 (2004); Leading industries: 31.5% construction; 15.0% retail trade; 10.2% health care and social assistance (2003); Companies that employ 500 or more persons: 1 (2003); Companies that employ 100 to 499 persons: 16 (2003); Companies that employ less than 100 persons: 682 (2003); Farms: 902 totaling 187,373 acres (2002); Minority business ownership rate: n/a (1997); Women business ownership rate: 32.9% (1997); Retail sales per capita: $4,578 (1997). Single-family building permits issued: 4,153 (2004); Multi-family building permits issued: 0 (2004).
Income: Per capita income: $18,329 (2004); Median household income: $34,694 (2004); Average household income: $44,529 (2004); Percent of households with income of $100,000 or more: 6.4% (2004); Poverty rate: 15.0% (2002); Bankruptcy rate: 3.56% (2004).
Taxes: Total county taxes per capita: $363 (2002); County property taxes per capita: $218 (2002).
Education: Percent of population age 25 and over with: High school diploma (including GED) or higher: 78.6% (2004); Bachelor's degree or higher: 13.3% (2004); Master's degree or higher: 5.1% (2004).
Housing: Homeownership rate: 87.8% (2004); Median home value: $109,983 (2004); Median rent: $321 per month (2000); Median age of housing: 13 years (2000).
Health: Birth rate: 93.9 per 10,000 population (2004); Death rate: 128.2 per 10,000 population (2004); Age adjusted cancer mortality rate: 192.6 deaths per 100,000 population (2002); Number of physicians: 1.8 per 10,000 population (2001); Hospital beds: 0.0 per 10,000 population (2002); Hospital admissions: 0.0 per 10,000 population (2002).
Elections: 2004 Presidential election results: 62.2% Bush, 36.4% Kerry, 0.8% Nader, 0.1% Badnarik
National and State Parks: Dade Battlefield Historic State Park
Additional Information Contacts
Sumter County Government Offices .... (352) 793-0200
Sumter County Chamber of Commerce................ (352) 793-3099

Sumter County Communities

BUSHNELL (city). Covers a land area of 2.352 square miles and a water area of <.001 square miles. Located at 28.66° N. Lat.; 82.11° W. Long. Elevation is 79 feet.
History: Bushnell was named for the engineer who surveyed the railroad right-of-way through the area. The town developed as a shipping center for the surrounding citrus and agricultural area, and as the seat of Sumter County.
Population: 2,036 (1990); 2,050 (2000); 2,205 (2004); 2,403 (2009 projected); Race: 81.3% White, 14.8% Black, 0.8% Asian, 4.4% Hispanic of any race (2004); Density: 937.6 persons per square mile (2004); Average household size: 2.53 (2004); Median age: 37.2 (2004); Male/female ratio: 99.5 (2004); Marriage status: 13.2% never married, 64.1% now married, 12.4% widowed, 10.3% divorced (2000); Foreign born: 2.5% (2000); Ancestry (includes multiple ancestries): 18.1% Other groups, 13.4% United States or American, 11.2% German, 10.0% English, 8.8% Irish (2000).
Economy: Employment by occupation: 6.4% management, 19.3% professional, 14.6% services, 28.6% sales, 3.1% farming, 13.0% construction, 15.0% production (2000).
Income: Per capita income: $14,842 (2004); Median household income: $28,439 (2004); Average household income: $37,176 (2004); Percent of households with income of $100,000 or more: 2.5% (2004); Poverty rate: 14.7% (2000).
Taxes: Total city taxes per capita: $346 (2002); City property taxes per capita: $51 (2002).
Education: Percent of population age 25 and over with: High school diploma (including GED) or higher: 72.5% (2004); Bachelor's degree or higher: 10.0% (2004); Master's degree or higher: 2.5% (2004).

School District(s)

Sumter County School District (PK-12)
2002-03 Enrollment: 6,558 .... (352) 793-2315
Housing: Homeownership rate: 67.2% (2004); Median home value: $75,467 (2004); Median rent: $313 per month (2000); Median age of housing: 17 years (2000).
Safety: Violent crime rate: 14.3 per 10,000 population; Property crime rate: 181.5 per 10,000 population (2003).
Newspapers: Sumter County Times (General - Circulation 5,000)
Transportation: Commute to work: 92.5% car, 0.0% public transportation, 2.5% walk, 1.9% work from home (2000); Travel time to work: 40.1% less than 15 minutes, 21.4% 15 to 30 minutes, 13.9% 30 to 45 minutes, 8.0% 45 to 60 minutes, 16.6% 60 minutes or more (2000)
Additional Information Contacts
Sumter County Chamber of Commerce................ (352) 793-3099

CENTER HILL (city). Covers a land area of 1.711 square miles and a water area of 0.057 square miles. Located at 28.64° N. Lat.; 81.99° W. Long. Elevation is 102 feet.
History: Center Hill was settled in 1883 and became a shipping center for strawberries, watermelons, and green beans.
Population: 735 (1990); 910 (2000); 944 (2004); 995 (2009 projected); Race: 78.5% White, 5.3% Black, 0.7% Asian, 35.7% Hispanic of any race (2004); Density: 551.6 persons per square mile (2004); Average household size: 3.29 (2004); Median age: 26.8 (2004); Male/female ratio: 119.5 (2004); Marriage status: 24.2% never married, 59.4% now married, 7.0% widowed, 9.4% divorced (2000); Foreign born: 18.0% (2000); Ancestry (includes multiple ancestries): 40.0% Other groups, 9.5% Irish, 6.8% German, 6.0% English, 4.8% United States or American (2000).
Economy: Employment by occupation: 8.1% management, 11.8% professional, 18.0% services, 18.5% sales, 9.8% farming, 14.3% construction, 19.4% production (2000).
Income: Per capita income: $14,637 (2004); Median household income: $31,525 (2004); Average household income: $47,909 (2004); Percent of households with income of $100,000 or more: 7.3% (2004); Poverty rate: 26.2% (2000).
Taxes: Total city taxes per capita: $212 (2002); City property taxes per capita: $8 (2002).
Education: Percent of population age 25 and over with: High school diploma (including GED) or higher: 58.3% (2004); Bachelor's degree or higher: 5.4% (2004); Master's degree or higher: 1.4% (2004).
Housing: Homeownership rate: 75.6% (2004); Median home value: $58,475 (2004); Median rent: $303 per month (2000); Median age of housing: 28 years (2000).
Safety: Violent crime rate: 74.5 per 10,000 population; Property crime rate: 330.1 per 10,000 population (2003).
Transportation: Commute to work: 92.3% car, 0.0% public transportation, 4.5% walk, 2.6% work from home (2000); Travel time to work: 27.4% less than 15 minutes, 25.9% 15 to 30 minutes, 21.0% 30 to 45 minutes, 6.7% 45 to 60 minutes, 19.0% 60 minutes or more (2000)

COLEMAN (city). Covers a land area of 1.454 square miles and a water area of 0 square miles. Located at 28.80° N. Lat.; 82.06° W. Long. Elevation is 60 feet.
Population: 880 (1990); 647 (2000); 652 (2004); 656 (2009 projected); Race: 57.5% White, 38.8% Black, 0.0% Asian, 3.7% Hispanic of any race (2004); Density: 448.4 persons per square mile (2004); Average household size: 2.51 (2004); Median age: 31.0 (2004); Male/female ratio: 94.6 (2004); Marriage status: 23.3% never married, 44.9% now married, 13.0% widowed, 18.7% divorced (2000); Foreign born: 1.0% (2000); Ancestry (includes multiple ancestries): 40.6% Other groups, 15.5% United States or American, 9.5% English, 9.3% Irish, 5.0% German (2000).

Economy: Employment by occupation: 8.8% management, 10.3% professional, 28.6% services, 23.1% sales, 1.1% farming, 9.9% construction, 18.3% production (2000).
Income: Per capita income: $13,861 (2004); Median household income: $25,645 (2004); Average household income: $34,760 (2004); Percent of households with income of $100,000 or more: 5.0% (2004); Poverty rate: 22.7% (2000).
Taxes: Total city taxes per capita: $223 (2002); City property taxes per capita: $0 (2002).
Education: Percent of population age 25 and over with: High school diploma (including GED) or higher: 64.2% (2004); Bachelor's degree or higher: 7.4% (2004); Master's degree or higher: 2.6% (2004).
Housing: Homeownership rate: 76.9% (2004); Median home value: $65,625 (2004); Median rent: $297 per month (2000); Median age of housing: 29 years (2000).
Safety: Violent crime rate: 0.0 per 10,000 population; Property crime rate: 75.2 per 10,000 population (2003).
Transportation: Commute to work: 93.6% car, 0.7% public transportation, 1.5% walk, 4.1% work from home (2000); Travel time to work: 29.7% less than 15 minutes, 39.8% 15 to 30 minutes, 14.8% 30 to 45 minutes, 9.0% 45 to 60 minutes, 6.6% 60 minutes or more (2000)

LAKE PANASOFFKEE (CDP). Aka Panasoffkee. Covers a land area of 4.031 square miles and a water area of 0.014 square miles. Located at 28.79° N. Lat.; 82.13° W. Long. Elevation is 46 feet.
Population: 2,705 (1990); 3,413 (2000); 3,917 (2004); 4,570 (2009 projected); Race: 96.8% White, 0.9% Black, 0.5% Asian, 0.9% Hispanic of any race (2004); Density: 971.7 persons per square mile (2004); Average household size: 2.10 (2004); Median age: 46.0 (2004); Male/female ratio: 96.5 (2004); Marriage status: 11.3% never married, 63.0% now married, 10.6% widowed, 15.1% divorced (2000); Foreign born: 1.7% (2000); Ancestry (includes multiple ancestries): 21.5% United States or American, 17.1% Irish, 17.0% English, 16.1% German, 9.6% Other groups (2000).
Economy: Coleman Correctional Facility located here. Employment by occupation: 4.4% management, 9.6% professional, 26.0% services, 22.7% sales, 0.0% farming, 17.5% construction, 19.8% production (2000).
Income: Per capita income: $18,699 (2004); Median household income: $29,791 (2004); Average household income: $39,251 (2004); Percent of households with income of $100,000 or more: 5.1% (2004); Poverty rate: 12.0% (2000).
Education: Percent of population age 25 and over with: High school diploma (including GED) or higher: 69.0% (2004); Bachelor's degree or higher: 4.0% (2004); Master's degree or higher: 1.4% (2004).

School District(s)

Sumter County School District (PK-12)
2002-03 Enrollment: 6,558 . . . . (352) 793-2315

Housing: Homeownership rate: 84.5% (2004); Median home value: $61,901 (2004); Median rent: $302 per month (2000); Median age of housing: 22 years (2000).
Transportation: Commute to work: 93.6% car, 0.0% public transportation, 1.7% walk, 3.7% work from home (2000); Travel time to work: 20.8% less than 15 minutes, 31.3% 15 to 30 minutes, 20.1% 30 to 45 minutes, 9.1% 45 to 60 minutes, 18.8% 60 minutes or more (2000)

OXFORD (unincorporated postal area, zip code 34484). Covers a land area of 42.698 square miles and a water area of 0.237 square miles. Located at 28.90° N. Lat.; 82.06° W. Long. Elevation is 114 feet.
Population: 2,282 (2000); Race: 91.9% White, 6.3% Black, 0.0% Asian, 0.9% Hispanic of any race (2000); Density: 53.4 persons per square mile (2000); Age: 26.9% under 18, 13.2% over 64 (2000); Marriage status: 22.2% never married, 63.5% now married, 5.7% widowed, 8.7% divorced (2000); Foreign born: 0.3% (2000); Ancestry (includes multiple ancestries): 19.3% Other groups, 18.8% Irish, 15.4% United States or American, 11.1% English, 10.4% German (2000).
Economy: Employment by occupation: 10.8% management, 14.4% professional, 18.0% services, 24.7% sales, 1.6% farming, 17.3% construction, 13.2% production (2000).
Income: Per capita income: $18,201 (2000); Median household income: $37,741 (2000); Poverty rate: 11.5% (2000).
Education: Percent of population age 25 and over with: High school diploma (including GED) or higher: 82.6% (2000); Bachelor's degree or higher: 9.0% (2000).
Housing: Homeownership rate: 86.4% (2000); Median home value: $92,500 (2000); Median rent: $358 per month (2000); Median age of housing: 18 years (2000).
Transportation: Commute to work: 94.1% car, 0.0% public transportation, 0.8% walk, 4.0% work from home (2000); Travel time to work: 26.7% less than 15 minutes, 28.5% 15 to 30 minutes, 29.6% 30 to 45 minutes, 7.3% 45 to 60 minutes, 7.8% 60 minutes or more (2000)

SUMTERVILLE (unincorporated postal area, zip code 33585). Covers a land area of 17.122 square miles and a water area of 0.104 square miles. Located at 28.73° N. Lat.; 82.06° W. Long. Elevation is 75 feet.
Population: 777 (2000); Race: 83.5% White, 9.4% Black, 2.2% Asian, 6.8% Hispanic of any race (2000); Density: 45.4 persons per square mile (2000); Age: 22.2% under 18, 14.8% over 64 (2000); Marriage status: 16.7% never married, 62.7% now married, 9.9% widowed, 10.7% divorced (2000); Foreign born: 3.0% (2000); Ancestry (includes multiple ancestries): 25.5% United States or American, 24.1% Other groups, 11.6% Irish, 9.8% English, 9.5% German (2000).
Economy: Employment by occupation: 5.2% management, 9.6% professional, 13.0% services, 36.4% sales, 0.0% farming, 20.7% construction, 15.1% production (2000).
Income: Per capita income: $13,088 (2000); Median household income: $25,388 (2000); Poverty rate: 16.4% (2000).
Education: Percent of population age 25 and over with: High school diploma (including GED) or higher: 72.7% (2000); Bachelor's degree or higher: 10.2% (2000).
Housing: Homeownership rate: 78.9% (2000); Median home value: $51,400 (2000); Median rent: $302 per month (2000); Median age of housing: 20 years (2000).
Transportation: Commute to work: 93.8% car, 0.0% public transportation, 2.6% walk, 0.0% work from home (2000); Travel time to work: 33.2% less than 15 minutes, 33.6% 15 to 30 minutes, 13.7% 30 to 45 minutes, 6.2% 45 to 60 minutes, 13.4% 60 minutes or more (2000)

THE VILLAGES (CDP). Covers a land area of 5.190 square miles and a water area of 0.388 square miles. Located at 28.93° N. Lat.; 81.97° W. Long. Elevation is 75 feet.
Population: 627 (1990); 8,333 (2000); 13,703 (2004); 20,167 (2009 projected); Race: 98.2% White, 0.7% Black, 0.6% Asian, 1.5% Hispanic of any race (2004); Density: 2,640.1 persons per square mile (2004); Average household size: 1.90 (2004); Median age: 67.0 (2004); Male/female ratio: 89.5 (2004); Marriage status: 2.3% never married, 85.2% now married, 9.0% widowed, 3.6% divorced (2000); Foreign born: 5.8% (2000); Ancestry (includes multiple ancestries): 25.6% German, 20.0% English, 18.7% Irish, 10.6% Italian, 4.6% French (except Basque) (2000).
Economy: Employment by occupation: 9.8% management, 20.2% professional, 27.0% services, 34.1% sales, 0.0% farming, 4.7% construction, 4.3% production (2000).
Income: Per capita income: $30,110 (2004); Median household income: $45,277 (2004); Average household income: $56,989 (2004); Percent of households with income of $100,000 or more: 10.4% (2004); Poverty rate: 3.7% (2000).
Education: Percent of population age 25 and over with: High school diploma (including GED) or higher: 89.8% (2004); Bachelor's degree or higher: 23.6% (2004); Master's degree or higher: 10.0% (2004).

School District(s)

Sumter County School District (PK-12)
2002-03 Enrollment: 6,558 . . . . (352) 793-2315

Housing: Homeownership rate: 98.3% (2004); Median home value: $191,073 (2004); Median rent: $1,013 per month (2000); Median age of housing: 3 years (2000).
Transportation: Commute to work: 87.8% car, 0.0% public transportation, 0.0% walk, 5.6% work from home (2000); Travel time to work: 52.0% less than 15 minutes, 23.0% 15 to 30 minutes, 14.2% 30 to 45 minutes, 3.0% 45 to 60 minutes, 7.8% 60 minutes or more (2000)

WEBSTER (city). Covers a land area of 1.324 square miles and a water area of 0 square miles. Located at 28.61° N. Lat.; 82.05° W. Long. Elevation is 90 feet.
Population: 773 (1990); 805 (2000); 870 (2004); 958 (2009 projected); Race: 52.4% White, 37.4% Black, 0.3% Asian, 16.9% Hispanic of any race (2004); Density: 657.3 persons per square mile (2004); Average household size: 2.79 (2004); Median age: 30.8 (2004); Male/female ratio: 91.2 (2004); Marriage status: 28.0% never married, 45.6% now married, 11.7% widowed, 14.7% divorced (2000); Foreign born: 5.3% (2000); Ancestry (includes multiple ancestries): 46.9% Other groups, 12.9% United States or American, 7.8% German, 3.7% English, 3.1% Irish (2000).

Economy: Employment by occupation: 5.9% management, 8.9% professional, 27.4% services, 19.3% sales, 4.1% farming, 6.7% construction, 27.8% production (2000).
Income: Per capita income: $9,880 (2004); Median household income: $19,182 (2004); Average household income: $27,444 (2004); Percent of households with income of $100,000 or more: 1.9% (2004); Poverty rate: 30.6% (2000).
Education: Percent of population age 25 and over with: High school diploma (including GED) or higher: 52.5% (2004); Bachelor's degree or higher: 5.8% (2004); Master's degree or higher: 1.8% (2004).

School District(s)

Sumter County School District (PK-12)
2002-03 Enrollment: 6,558 . . . . (352) 793-2315
Housing: Homeownership rate: 67.3% (2004); Median home value: $57,692 (2004); Median rent: $246 per month (2000); Median age of housing: 20 years (2000).
Safety: Violent crime rate: 60.7 per 10,000 population; Property crime rate: 182.0 per 10,000 population (2003).
Transportation: Commute to work: 96.3% car, 0.0% public transportation, 0.0% walk, 2.6% work from home (2000); Travel time to work: 38.5% less than 15 minutes, 20.2% 15 to 30 minutes, 16.4% 30 to 45 minutes, 10.3% 45 to 60 minutes, 14.5% 60 minutes or more (2000)

WILDWOOD (city). Covers a land area of 5.165 square miles and a water area of 0.003 square miles. Located at 28.85° N. Lat.; 82.03° W. Long. Elevation is 64 feet.
History: Wildwood was named in 1878 by the telegraph operator at a station in the forest who headed his dispatches "Wildwood." The community developed around the Seaboard Air Line railroad yards.
Population: 3,622 (1990); 3,924 (2000); 3,770 (2004); 3,591 (2009 projected); Race: 62.1% White, 35.5% Black, 0.1% Asian, 2.9% Hispanic of any race (2004); Density: 729.9 persons per square mile (2004); Average household size: 2.40 (2004); Median age: 41.2 (2004); Male/female ratio: 84.3 (2004); Marriage status: 15.6% never married, 61.2% now married, 8.7% widowed, 14.6% divorced (2000); Foreign born: 1.9% (2000); Ancestry (includes multiple ancestries): 33.5% Other groups, 12.9% United States or American, 12.7% German, 11.1% English, 7.3% Irish (2000).
Economy: Single-family building permits issued: 16 (2004); Multi-family building permits issued: 0 (2004); Employment by occupation: 6.3% management, 11.3% professional, 20.6% services, 32.6% sales, 1.1% farming, 13.0% construction, 15.1% production (2000).
Income: Per capita income: $12,123 (2004); Median household income: $23,553 (2004); Average household income: $28,702 (2004); Percent of households with income of $100,000 or more: 0.8% (2004); Poverty rate: 21.7% (2000).
Taxes: Total city taxes per capita: $409 (2002); City property taxes per capita: $117 (2002).
Education: Percent of population age 25 and over with: High school diploma (including GED) or higher: 68.0% (2004); Bachelor's degree or higher: 9.0% (2004); Master's degree or higher: 2.7% (2004).

School District(s)

Sumter County School District (PK-12)
2002-03 Enrollment: 6,558 . . . . (352) 793-2315
Housing: Homeownership rate: 77.2% (2004); Median home value: $40,926 (2004); Median rent: $331 per month (2000); Median age of housing: 16 years (2000).
Safety: Violent crime rate: 105.0 per 10,000 population; Property crime rate: 530.4 per 10,000 population (2003).
Transportation: Commute to work: 95.3% car, 0.5% public transportation, 2.5% walk, 0.9% work from home (2000); Travel time to work: 31.9% less than 15 minutes, 37.5% 15 to 30 minutes, 14.1% 30 to 45 minutes, 11.3% 45 to 60 minutes, 5.2% 60 minutes or more (2000); Amtrak: Service available.

Suwannee County

Located in northern Florida; bounded on the west and south by the Suwannee River and on the south by the Santa Fe River; includes several lakes. Covers a land area of 687.60 square miles, a water area of 4.30 square miles, and is located in the Eastern Time Zone. The county government was organized in 1858. County seat is Live Oak.

Weather Station: Live Oak — Elevation: 118 feet

	Jan	Feb	Mar	Apr	May	Jun	Jul	Aug	Sep	Oct	Nov	Dec
High	67	71	77	82	88	92	93	92	90	83	76	69
Low	42	44	50	55	62	69	71	71	68	58	51	44
Precip	5.0	4.0	5.4	3.5	3.3	6.1	6.5	6.6	4.3	3.3	2.4	3.1
Snow	tr	tr	tr	0.0	0.0	0.0	0.0	0.0	0.0	0.0	0.0	0.1

High and Low temperatures in degrees Fahrenheit; Precipitation and Snow in inches

Population: 26,780 (1990); 34,844 (2000); 36,765 (2004); 39,194 (2009 projected); Race: 84.0% White, 12.6% Black, 0.6% Asian, 5.7% Hispanic of any race (2004); Density: 53.5 persons per square mile (2004); Average household size: 2.57 (2004); Median age: 40.2 (2004); Male/female ratio: 95.4 (2004).
Religion: Five largest groups: 34.3% Southern Baptist Convention, 3.1% Catholic Church, 3.0% The United Methodist Church, 2.6% Church of God (Cleveland, Tennessee), 1.5% The Church of Jesus Christ of Latter-day Saints (2000).
Economy: Unemployment rate: 3.9% (2004); Total civilian labor force: 13,927 (2004); Leading industries: 23.0% manufacturing; 19.4% retail trade; 14.5% health care and social assistance (2003); Companies that employ 500 or more persons: 1 (2003); Companies that employ 100 to 499 persons: 6 (2003); Companies that employ less than 100 persons: 623 (2003); Farms: 1,054 totaling 170,149 acres (2002); Minority business ownership rate: n/a (1997); Women business ownership rate: 15.0% (1997); Retail sales per capita: $6,438 (1997). Single-family building permits issued: 199 (2004); Multi-family building permits issued: 0 (2004).
Income: Per capita income: $15,942 (2004); Median household income: $31,708 (2004); Average household income: $40,614 (2004); Percent of households with income of $100,000 or more: 5.1% (2004); Poverty rate: 16.9% (2002); Bankruptcy rate: 3.88% (2004).
Taxes: Total county taxes per capita: $164 (2002); County property taxes per capita: $119 (2002).
Education: Percent of population age 25 and over with: High school diploma (including GED) or higher: 73.3% (2004); Bachelor's degree or higher: 10.5% (2004); Master's degree or higher: 3.3% (2004).
Housing: Homeownership rate: 81.1% (2004); Median home value: $80,844 (2004); Median rent: $280 per month (2000); Median age of housing: 17 years (2000).
Health: Birth rate: 120.8 per 10,000 population (2004); Death rate: 119.7 per 10,000 population (2004); Age adjusted cancer mortality rate: 243.9 deaths per 100,000 population (2002); Number of physicians: 3.4 per 10,000 population (2001); Hospital beds: 4.2 per 10,000 population (2002); Hospital admissions: 162.5 per 10,000 population (2002).
Elections: 2004 Presidential election results: 70.6% Bush, 28.6% Kerry, 0.5% Nader, 0.2% Badnarik
National and State Parks: Ichetucknee Springs State Park; Peacock Springs State Park
Additional Information Contacts
Suwannee County Government Offices. . . . . (386) 364-3450
Live Oak Chamber of Commerce . . . . (386) 935-3722

Suwannee County Communities

BRANFORD (town). Covers a land area of 0.829 square miles and a water area of 0 square miles. Located at 29.96° N. Lat.; 82.92° W. Long. Elevation is 40 feet.
Population: 670 (1990); 695 (2000); 679 (2004); 659 (2009 projected); Race: 87.9% White, 6.0% Black, 0.3% Asian, 12.5% Hispanic of any race (2004); Density: 819.2 persons per square mile (2004); Average household size: 2.56 (2004); Median age: 33.3 (2004); Male/female ratio: 91.3 (2004); Marriage status: 25.8% never married, 43.7% now married, 16.7% widowed, 13.8% divorced (2000); Foreign born: 7.5% (2000); Ancestry (includes multiple ancestries): 21.9% United States or American, 15.9% Other groups, 9.6% Irish, 8.0% German, 5.1% English (2000).
Economy: Manufacturing includes limestone, survey stakes. Some agriculture. Employment by occupation: 7.1% management, 13.4% professional, 21.2% services, 19.7% sales, 13.8% farming, 8.6% construction, 16.4% production (2000).
Income: Per capita income: $13,617 (2004); Median household income: $25,375 (2004); Average household income: $34,462 (2004); Percent of households with income of $100,000 or more: 3.4% (2004); Poverty rate: 21.0% (2000).
Education: Percent of population age 25 and over with: High school diploma (including GED) or higher: 64.1% (2004); Bachelor's degree or higher: 11.0% (2004); Master's degree or higher: 4.0% (2004).

School District(s)

Suwannee County School District (PK-12)
2002-03 Enrollment: 5,802 . . . . (386) 364-2604

Housing: Homeownership rate: 54.3% (2004); Median home value: $69,444 (2004); Median rent: $214 per month (2000); Median age of housing: 29 years (2000).

Newspapers: Branford News (General - Circulation 2,000)

Transportation: Commute to work: 87.9% car, 0.0% public transportation, 10.2% walk, 0.0% work from home (2000); Travel time to work: 40.9% less than 15 minutes, 7.6% 15 to 30 minutes, 31.8% 30 to 45 minutes, 11.4% 45 to 60 minutes, 8.3% 60 minutes or more (2000)

LIVE OAK (city). Covers a land area of 6.955 square miles and a water area of 0.002 square miles. Located at 30.29° N. Lat.; 82.98° W. Long. Elevation is 102 feet.

History: Live Oak was the location of a large bright-leaf tobacco market, with auction warehouses. The town's name referred to a large live oak tree near the place where the railroad station was later built. Live-oak timber was shipped from here in the 1830's.

Population: 6,346 (1990); 6,480 (2000); 6,809 (2004); 7,193 (2009 projected); Race: 56.5% White, 39.3% Black, 0.8% Asian, 10.4% Hispanic of any race (2004); Density: 979.0 persons per square mile (2004); Average household size: 2.72 (2004); Median age: 36.6 (2004); Male/female ratio: 94.0 (2004); Marriage status: 23.7% never married, 54.0% now married, 9.6% widowed, 12.7% divorced (2000); Foreign born: 6.9% (2000); Ancestry (includes multiple ancestries): 38.6% Other groups, 14.0% United States or American, 5.4% Irish, 5.1% English, 3.3% German (2000).

Economy: Single-family building permits issued: 10 (2004); Multi-family building permits issued: 0 (2004); Employment by occupation: 6.3% management, 15.1% professional, 20.8% services, 22.8% sales, 4.7% farming, 10.4% construction, 19.8% production (2000).

Income: Per capita income: $13,187 (2004); Median household income: $26,115 (2004); Average household income: $34,721 (2004); Percent of households with income of $100,000 or more: 3.4% (2004); Poverty rate: 23.9% (2000).

Taxes: Total city taxes per capita: $286 (2002); City property taxes per capita: $91 (2002).

Education: Percent of population age 25 and over with: High school diploma (including GED) or higher: 68.7% (2004); Bachelor's degree or higher: 11.9% (2004); Master's degree or higher: 3.3% (2004).

School District(s)

Suwannee County School District (PK-12)
2002-03 Enrollment: 5,802 . . . . (386) 364-2604

Two-year College(s)

Suwannee-Hamilton Technical Center (Public)
2003-04 Enrollment: 209 . . . . (386) 364-2750
2003-04 Tuition: In-state $2,327; Out-of-state $7,978

Housing: Homeownership rate: 65.9% (2004); Median home value: $72,270 (2004); Median rent: $250 per month (2000); Median age of housing: 31 years (2000).

Hospitals: Shands at Live Oak (30 beds)

Safety: Violent crime rate: 96.5 per 10,000 population; Property crime rate: 592.1 per 10,000 population (2003).

Newspapers: Suwannee Democrat (General - Circulation 5,400)

Transportation: Commute to work: 95.2% car, 0.0% public transportation, 2.6% walk, 1.5% work from home (2000); Travel time to work: 45.4% less than 15 minutes, 28.2% 15 to 30 minutes, 19.4% 30 to 45 minutes, 2.3% 45 to 60 minutes, 4.8% 60 minutes or more (2000)

Additional Information Contacts

Live Oak Chamber of Commerce . . . . (386) 935-3722
Local Government Offices . . . . (386) 362-2276

MCALPIN (unincorporated postal area, zip code 32062). Covers a land area of 60.398 square miles and a water area of 0.008 square miles. Located at 30.13° N. Lat.; 82.98° W. Long. Elevation is 101 feet.

Population: 1,994 (2000); Race: 92.1% White, 3.7% Black, 0.0% Asian, 5.4% Hispanic of any race (2000); Density: 33.0 persons per square mile (2000); Age: 29.8% under 18, 16.4% over 64 (2000); Marriage status: 21.0% never married, 64.6% now married, 6.8% widowed, 7.6% divorced (2000); Foreign born: 6.3% (2000); Ancestry (includes multiple ancestries): 22.3% United States or American, 13.8% Irish, 11.9% Other groups, 11.5% German, 11.3% English (2000).

Economy: Employment by occupation: 13.5% management, 25.6% professional, 12.9% services, 15.7% sales, 7.1% farming, 13.8% construction, 11.3% production (2000).

Income: Per capita income: $14,305 (2000); Median household income: $32,604 (2000); Poverty rate: 19.2% (2000).

Education: Percent of population age 25 and over with: High school diploma (including GED) or higher: 77.9% (2000); Bachelor's degree or higher: 11.0% (2000).

Housing: Homeownership rate: 89.5% (2000); Median home value: $70,900 (2000); Median rent: $303 per month (2000); Median age of housing: 16 years (2000).

Transportation: Commute to work: 87.2% car, 0.0% public transportation, 6.6% walk, 4.8% work from home (2000); Travel time to work: 18.6% less than 15 minutes, 29.5% 15 to 30 minutes, 28.9% 30 to 45 minutes, 10.2% 45 to 60 minutes, 12.8% 60 minutes or more (2000)

O'BRIEN (unincorporated postal area, zip code 32071). Covers a land area of 108.768 square miles and a water area of 0.007 square miles. Located at 30.03° N. Lat.; 82.94° W. Long. Elevation is 54 feet.

Population: 3,111 (2000); Race: 95.1% White, 3.5% Black, 0.5% Asian, 3.2% Hispanic of any race (2000); Density: 28.6 persons per square mile (2000); Age: 21.5% under 18, 14.0% over 64 (2000); Marriage status: 15.3% never married, 63.5% now married, 5.8% widowed, 15.4% divorced (2000); Foreign born: 3.1% (2000); Ancestry (includes multiple ancestries): 18.7% United States or American, 12.0% Irish, 11.7% Other groups, 11.6% German, 8.5% English (2000).

Economy: Employment by occupation: 9.2% management, 20.8% professional, 14.3% services, 21.2% sales, 4.3% farming, 16.6% construction, 13.6% production (2000).

Income: Per capita income: $16,202 (2000); Median household income: $32,237 (2000); Poverty rate: 11.4% (2000).

Education: Percent of population age 25 and over with: High school diploma (including GED) or higher: 75.2% (2000); Bachelor's degree or higher: 10.1% (2000).

Housing: Homeownership rate: 86.6% (2000); Median home value: $62,900 (2000); Median rent: $340 per month (2000); Median age of housing: 15 years (2000).

Transportation: Commute to work: 92.3% car, 0.0% public transportation, 0.0% walk, 6.4% work from home (2000); Travel time to work: 16.7% less than 15 minutes, 25.9% 15 to 30 minutes, 29.3% 30 to 45 minutes, 12.6% 45 to 60 minutes, 15.4% 60 minutes or more (2000)

WELLBORN (unincorporated postal area, zip code 32094). Covers a land area of 56.035 square miles and a water area of 0.469 square miles. Located at 30.20° N. Lat.; 82.81° W. Long. Elevation is 195 feet.

Population: 2,597 (2000); Race: 89.7% White, 5.1% Black, 0.0% Asian, 2.3% Hispanic of any race (2000); Density: 46.3 persons per square mile (2000); Age: 20.6% under 18, 16.1% over 64 (2000); Marriage status: 15.2% never married, 66.4% now married, 10.8% widowed, 7.6% divorced (2000); Foreign born: 1.8% (2000); Ancestry (includes multiple ancestries): 22.7% United States or American, 19.9% Other groups, 11.8% English, 9.3% German, 6.1% Irish (2000).

Economy: Employment by occupation: 7.2% management, 17.4% professional, 15.1% services, 22.3% sales, 4.0% farming, 20.9% construction, 13.1% production (2000).

Income: Per capita income: $16,257 (2000); Median household income: $31,745 (2000); Poverty rate: 16.7% (2000).

Education: Percent of population age 25 and over with: High school diploma (including GED) or higher: 75.2% (2000); Bachelor's degree or higher: 6.9% (2000).

Housing: Homeownership rate: 89.7% (2000); Median home value: $84,700 (2000); Median rent: $138 per month (2000); Median age of housing: 17 years (2000).

Transportation: Commute to work: 94.2% car, 0.0% public transportation, 1.1% walk, 3.1% work from home (2000); Travel time to work: 16.3% less than 15 minutes, 36.7% 15 to 30 minutes, 27.9% 30 to 45 minutes, 10.0% 45 to 60 minutes, 9.0% 60 minutes or more (2000)

Taylor County

Located in northern Florida; bounded on the south by the Gulf of Mexico, and on the west by the Aucilla River; includes many small lakes. Covers a land area of 1,041.90 square miles, a water area of 190.10 square miles, and is located in the Eastern Time Zone. The county government was organized in 1856. County seat is Perry.

Weather Station: Perry Elevation: 42 feet

	Jan	Feb	Mar	Apr	May	Jun	Jul	Aug	Sep	Oct	Nov	Dec
High	67	70	76	82	88	91	93	92	90	84	76	70
Low	41	43	49	54	62	68	71	70	67	57	49	43
Precip	4.9	4.0	5.6	3.4	3.5	6.0	8.5	8.9	5.0	3.2	2.7	3.4
Snow	tr	0.0	0.0	0.0	0.0	0.0	0.0	0.0	0.0	0.0	0.0	0.0

High and Low temperatures in degrees Fahrenheit; Precipitation and Snow in inches

Population: 17,117 (1990); 19,256 (2000); 19,822 (2004); 20,544 (2009 projected); Race: 77.8% White, 19.4% Black, 0.5% Asian, 1.6% Hispanic of any race (2004); Density: 19.0 persons per square mile (2004); Average household size: 2.71 (2004); Median age: 38.6 (2004); Male/female ratio: 110.0 (2004).

Religion: Five largest groups: 34.0% Southern Baptist Convention, 3.3% The United Methodist Church, 1.9% Catholic Church, 1.8% Churches of Christ, 1.6% Church of God (Cleveland, Tennessee) (2000).

Economy: Unemployment rate: 7.0% (2004); Total civilian labor force: 7,562 (2004); Leading industries: 33.1% manufacturing; 17.1% retail trade; 15.0% health care and social assistance (2003); Companies that employ 500 or more persons: 1 (2003); Companies that employ 100 to 499 persons: 7 (2003); Companies that employ less than 100 persons: 387 (2003); Farms: 101 totaling 53,720 acres (2002); Minority business ownership rate: 9.4% (1997); Women business ownership rate: 12.1% (1997); Retail sales per capita: $7,724 (1997). Single-family building permits issued: 71 (2004); Multi-family building permits issued: 14 (2004).

Income: Per capita income: $16,517 (2004); Median household income: $31,641 (2004); Average household income: $40,789 (2004); Percent of households with income of $100,000 or more: 6.2% (2004); Poverty rate: 17.3% (2002); Bankruptcy rate: 4.18% (2004).

Education: Percent of population age 25 and over with: High school diploma (including GED) or higher: 70.0% (2004); Bachelor's degree or higher: 8.8% (2004); Master's degree or higher: 3.6% (2004).

Housing: Homeownership rate: 80.0% (2004); Median home value: $76,090 (2004); Median rent: $263 per month (2000); Median age of housing: 21 years (2000).

Health: Birth rate: 127.5 per 10,000 population (2004); Death rate: 118.7 per 10,000 population (2004); Age adjusted cancer mortality rate: 239.0 deaths per 100,000 population (2002); Number of physicians: 9.4 per 10,000 population (2001); Hospital beds: 24.8 per 10,000 population (2002); Hospital admissions: 1,210.0 per 10,000 population (2002).

Elections: 2004 Presidential election results: 63.7% Bush, 35.5% Kerry, 0.5% Nader, 0.1% Badnarik

National and State Parks: Econfina River State Park; Forest Capital Museum State Park

Additional Information Contacts

Taylor County Government Offices . . . . (850) 838-3500
Perry Chamber of Commerce . . . . (850) 584-5366

Taylor County Communities

PERRY (city). Covers a land area of 9.287 square miles and a water area of 0 square miles. Located at 30.11° N. Lat.; 83.58° W. Long. Elevation is 42 feet.

History: Perry developed as a lumber town with sawmills along the railroad sidings. The post office was established in 1869. Prior to that the community was called Rosehead.

Population: 7,151 (1990); 6,847 (2000); 6,840 (2004); 6,812 (2009 projected); Race: 57.3% White, 40.0% Black, 0.5% Asian, 1.8% Hispanic of any race (2004); Density: 736.5 persons per square mile (2004); Average household size: 2.56 (2004); Median age: 36.2 (2004); Male/female ratio: 90.9 (2004); Marriage status: 28.1% never married, 49.1% now married, 9.2% widowed, 13.7% divorced (2000); Foreign born: 1.3% (2000); Ancestry (includes multiple ancestries): 40.2% Other groups, 10.3% United States or American, 7.3% Irish, 5.6% German, 5.4% English (2000).

Economy: Single-family building permits issued: 5 (2004); Multi-family building permits issued: 0 (2004); Employment by occupation: 9.1% management, 10.2% professional, 19.7% services, 22.1% sales, 4.0% farming, 10.1% construction, 24.8% production (2000).

Income: Per capita income: $13,885 (2004); Median household income: $26,563 (2004); Average household income: $35,208 (2004); Percent of households with income of $100,000 or more: 5.5% (2004); Poverty rate: 28.0% (2000).

Taxes: Total city taxes per capita: $335 (2002); City property taxes per capita: $110 (2002).

Education: Percent of population age 25 and over with: High school diploma (including GED) or higher: 67.5% (2004); Bachelor's degree or higher: 9.9% (2004); Master's degree or higher: 4.3% (2004).

School District(s)

Taylor County School District (PK-12)
2002-03 Enrollment: 3,593 . . . . (850) 838-2500

Two-year College(s)

Taylor Technical Institute (Public)
2003-04 Enrollment: 422 . . . . (850) 838-2545
2003-04 Tuition: In-state $1,443; Out-of-state $5,855

Housing: Homeownership rate: 67.7% (2004); Median home value: $78,599 (2004); Median rent: $233 per month (2000); Median age of housing: 32 years (2000).

Hospitals: Doctors Memorial Hospital (48 beds)

Safety: Violent crime rate: 120.9 per 10,000 population; Property crime rate: 568.1 per 10,000 population (2003).

Newspapers: Perry News-Herald (General - Circulation 5,200); Taco Times (General - Circulation 5,200)

Transportation: Commute to work: 92.1% car, 0.0% public transportation, 3.0% walk, 1.3% work from home (2000); Travel time to work: 63.8% less than 15 minutes, 22.2% 15 to 30 minutes, 6.8% 30 to 45 minutes, 1.3% 45 to 60 minutes, 5.8% 60 minutes or more (2000)

Airports: Perry-Foley

Additional Information Contacts

Local Government Offices . . . . (850) 584-7940
Perry Chamber of Commerce . . . . (850) 584-5366

SALEM (unincorporated postal area, zip code 32356). Covers a land area of 7.431 square miles and a water area of 0 square miles. Located at 29.90° N. Lat.; 83.42° W. Long. Elevation is 41 feet.

Population: 95 (2000); Race: 100.0% White, 0.0% Black, 0.0% Asian, 0.0% Hispanic of any race (2000); Density: 12.8 persons per square mile (2000); Age: 9.3% under 18, 14.7% over 64 (2000); Marriage status: 28.0% never married, 65.3% now married, 6.7% widowed, 0.0% divorced (2000); Foreign born: 0.0% (2000); Ancestry (includes multiple ancestries): 16.0% United States or American, 8.0% Scottish, 6.7% Other groups (2000).

Economy: Employment by occupation: 13.3% management, 0.0% professional, 31.1% services, 11.1% sales, 0.0% farming, 13.3% construction, 31.1% production (2000).

Income: Per capita income: $20,405 (2000); Median household income: $66,406 (2000); Poverty rate: 6.7% (2000).

Education: Percent of population age 25 and over with: High school diploma (including GED) or higher: 88.9% (2000); Bachelor's degree or higher: 11.1% (2000).

Housing: Homeownership rate: 100.0% (2000); Median home value: $n/a (2000); Median rent: $n/a per month (2000); Median age of housing: 29 years (2000).

Transportation: Commute to work: 86.7% car, 0.0% public transportation, 0.0% walk, 13.3% work from home (2000); Travel time to work: 0.0% less than 15 minutes, 35.9% 15 to 30 minutes, 48.7% 30 to 45 minutes, 0.0% 45 to 60 minutes, 15.4% 60 minutes or more (2000)

STEINHATCHEE (unincorporated postal area, zip code 32359). Aka Stephensville. Covers a land area of 88.776 square miles and a water area of 0.179 square miles. Located at 29.67° N. Lat.; 83.38° W. Long. Elevation is 15 feet.

Population: 1,453 (2000); Race: 98.7% White, 1.3% Black, 0.0% Asian, 0.4% Hispanic of any race (2000); Density: 16.4 persons per square mile (2000); Age: 15.3% under 18, 26.3% over 64 (2000); Marriage status: 11.5% never married, 63.4% now married, 12.1% widowed, 13.1% divorced (2000); Foreign born: 3.3% (2000); Ancestry (includes multiple ancestries): 19.9% United States or American, 13.5% Irish, 12.9% English, 10.4% German, 6.5% Other groups (2000).

Economy: Employment by occupation: 6.1% management, 15.9% professional, 28.3% services, 13.3% sales, 10.4% farming, 13.3% construction, 12.7% production (2000).

Income: Per capita income: $18,536 (2000); Median household income: $26,188 (2000); Poverty rate: 12.0% (2000).

Education: Percent of population age 25 and over with: High school diploma (including GED) or higher: 72.4% (2000); Bachelor's degree or higher: 12.1% (2000).

School District(s)

Taylor County School District (PK-12)
2002-03 Enrollment: 3,593 . . . . (850) 838-2500

Housing: Homeownership rate: 93.3% (2000); Median home value: $80,000 (2000); Median rent: $244 per month (2000); Median age of housing: 18 years (2000).
Transportation: Commute to work: 80.8% car, 2.7% public transportation, 7.2% walk, 4.4% work from home (2000); Travel time to work: 44.2% less than 15 minutes, 17.7% 15 to 30 minutes, 12.8% 30 to 45 minutes, 12.2% 45 to 60 minutes, 13.1% 60 minutes or more (2000)

Union County

Located in northern Florida; includes several lakes. Covers a land area of 240.30 square miles, a water area of 9.40 square miles, and is located in the Eastern Time Zone. The county government was organized in 1921. County seat is Lake Butler.
Population: 10,252 (1990); 13,442 (2000); 14,069 (2004); 14,863 (2009 projected); Race: 74.3% White, 22.0% Black, 0.5% Asian, 3.9% Hispanic of any race (2004); Density: 58.6 persons per square mile (2004); Average household size: 4.15 (2004); Median age: 36.3 (2004); Male/female ratio: 192.7 (2004).
Religion: Five largest groups: 19.5% Southern Baptist Convention, 2.8% The Church of Jesus Christ of Latter-day Saints, 2.2% Independent, Non-Charismatic Churches, 1.6% Christian Churches and Churches of Christ, 1.5% National Association of Free Wi
Economy: Unemployment rate: 3.3% (2004); Total civilian labor force: 4,111 (2004); Leading industries: 30.0% health care and social assistance; 14.2% transportation & warehousing; 12.1% manufacturing (2003); Companies that employ 500 or more persons: 0 (2003); Companies that employ 100 to 499 persons: 2 (2003); Companies that employ less than 100 persons: 117 (2003); Farms: 275 totaling 59,635 acres (2002); Minority business ownership rate: n/a (1997); Women business ownership rate: 50.7% (1997); Retail sales per capita: $2,185 (1997). Single-family building permits issued: 32 (2004); Multi-family building permits issued: 0 (2004).
Income: Per capita income: $13,261 (2004); Median household income: $36,960 (2004); Average household income: $45,463 (2004); Percent of households with income of $100,000 or more: 5.7% (2004); Poverty rate: 21.3% (2002); Bankruptcy rate: 2.40% (2004).
Taxes: Total county taxes per capita: $161 (2002); County property taxes per capita: $113 (2002).
Education: Percent of population age 25 and over with: High school diploma (including GED) or higher: 72.4% (2004); Bachelor's degree or higher: 7.5% (2004); Master's degree or higher: 2.7% (2004).
Housing: Homeownership rate: 74.8% (2004); Median home value: $79,900 (2004); Median rent: $278 per month (2000); Median age of housing: 18 years (2000).
Health: Birth rate: 103.6 per 10,000 population (2004); Death rate: 98.1 per 10,000 population (2004); Age adjusted cancer mortality rate: 402.8 deaths per 100,000 population (2002); Number of physicians: 10.2 per 10,000 population (2001); Hospital beds: 113.9 per 10,000 population (2002); Hospital admissions: 1,959.4 per 10,000 population (2002).
Elections: 2004 Presidential election results: 72.6% Bush, 26.8% Kerry, 0.3% Nader, 0.0% Badnarik
National and State Parks: Olustee Battlefield Historic State Park
Additional Information Contacts
Union County Government Offices . . . . (386) 496-4241

Union County Communities

LAKE BUTLER (city). Covers a land area of 1.719 square miles and a water area of 0.109 square miles. Located at 30.02° N. Lat.; 82.34° W. Long. Elevation is 136 feet.
History: The town of Lake Butler was named for Colonel Robert Butler who accepted East Florida from Spain in 1821. The principal early industry was the production of naval stores (rosin and turpentine originally used for calking ships).
Population: 2,116 (1990); 1,927 (2000); 1,897 (2004); 1,854 (2009 projected); Race: 64.6% White, 30.6% Black, 2.2% Asian, 3.8% Hispanic of any race (2004); Density: 1,103.7 persons per square mile (2004); Average household size: 2.64 (2004); Median age: 27.3 (2004); Male/female ratio: 83.3 (2004); Marriage status: 26.4% never married, 50.3% now married, 8.7% widowed, 14.6% divorced (2000); Foreign born: 3.1% (2000); Ancestry (includes multiple ancestries): 30.0% Other groups, 29.5% United States or American, 5.4% German, 5.0% Irish, 5.0% English (2000).
Economy: Employment by occupation: 9.5% management, 13.4% professional, 30.5% services, 23.1% sales, 2.8% farming, 6.1% construction, 14.5% production (2000).
Income: Per capita income: $16,132 (2004); Median household income: $27,611 (2004); Average household income: $42,076 (2004); Percent of households with income of $100,000 or more: 6.8% (2004); Poverty rate: 25.6% (2000).
Education: Percent of population age 25 and over with: High school diploma (including GED) or higher: 71.9% (2004); Bachelor's degree or higher: 9.4% (2004); Master's degree or higher: 4.9% (2004).

School District(s)

Union County School District (PK-12)
2002-03 Enrollment: 2,174 . . . . (386) 496-2045
Housing: Homeownership rate: 52.0% (2004); Median home value: $81,379 (2004); Median rent: $266 per month (2000); Median age of housing: 25 years (2000).
Hospitals: North Florida Reception Center Hospital (153 beds); Ramadan Hand Institute/Lake Butler Hospital (27 beds)
Newspapers: Union County Times (General - Circulation 2,500)
Transportation: Commute to work: 93.2% car, 0.0% public transportation, 2.5% walk, 3.2% work from home (2000); Travel time to work: 46.4% less than 15 minutes, 15.7% 15 to 30 minutes, 19.6% 30 to 45 minutes, 9.3% 45 to 60 minutes, 9.0% 60 minutes or more (2000)

RAIFORD (town). Covers a land area of 0.524 square miles and a water area of 0 square miles. Located at 30.06° N. Lat.; 82.23° W. Long. Elevation is 125 feet.
Population: 198 (1990); 187 (2000); 187 (2004); 182 (2009 projected); Race: 82.9% White, 15.0% Black, 0.0% Asian, 0.0% Hispanic of any race (2004); Density: 356.7 persons per square mile (2004); Average household size: 2.75 (2004); Median age: 30.2 (2004); Male/female ratio: 81.6 (2004); Marriage status: 23.1% never married, 62.7% now married, 6.7% widowed, 7.5% divorced (2000); Foreign born: 1.0% (2000); Ancestry (includes multiple ancestries): 31.3% United States or American, 16.2% Other groups, 12.1% German, 8.1% Irish, 6.6% English (2000).
Economy: Corn, vegetables. Florida State Prison nearby. Employment by occupation: 15.3% management, 18.6% professional, 30.5% services, 11.9% sales, 0.0% farming, 10.2% construction, 13.6% production (2000).
Income: Per capita income: $17,941 (2004); Median household income: $33,750 (2004); Average household income: $49,338 (2004); Percent of households with income of $100,000 or more: 7.4% (2004); Poverty rate: 36.4% (2000).
Education: Percent of population age 25 and over with: High school diploma (including GED) or higher: 60.0% (2004); Bachelor's degree or higher: 7.6% (2004); Master's degree or higher: 0.0% (2004).

School District(s)

Bradford County School District (PK-12)
2002-03 Enrollment: 4,034 . . . . (904) 966-6018
Housing: Homeownership rate: 77.9% (2004); Median home value: $67,222 (2004); Median rent: $240 per month (2000); Median age of housing: 34 years (2000).
Transportation: Commute to work: 93.4% car, 0.0% public transportation, 3.3% walk, 0.0% work from home (2000); Travel time to work: 29.5% less than 15 minutes, 42.6% 15 to 30 minutes, 14.8% 30 to 45 minutes, 6.6% 45 to 60 minutes, 6.6% 60 minutes or more (2000)

WORTHINGTON SPRINGS (town). Aka Worthington. Covers a land area of 0.360 square miles and a water area of 0 square miles. Located at 29.93° N. Lat.; 82.42° W. Long. Elevation is 84 feet.
Population: 178 (1990); 193 (2000); 207 (2004); 225 (2009 projected); Race: 88.4% White, 6.3% Black, 0.5% Asian, 2.4% Hispanic of any race (2004); Density: 575.6 persons per square mile (2004); Average household size: 2.72 (2004); Median age: 33.3 (2004); Male/female ratio: 91.7 (2004); Marriage status: 16.9% never married, 61.3% now married, 7.3% widowed, 14.5% divorced (2000); Foreign born: 0.0% (2000); Ancestry (includes multiple ancestries): 28.3% United States or American, 13.9% Other groups, 11.4% Irish, 11.4% English, 4.2% European (2000).
Economy: Employment by occupation: 9.4% management, 14.1% professional, 23.4% services, 23.4% sales, 0.0% farming, 20.3% construction, 9.4% production (2000).
Income: Per capita income: $13,792 (2004); Median household income: $26,667 (2004); Average household income: $37,566 (2004); Percent of households with income of $100,000 or more: 10.5% (2004); Poverty rate: 22.3% (2000).
Education: Percent of population age 25 and over with: High school diploma (including GED) or higher: 65.3% (2004); Bachelor's degree or higher: 16.5% (2004); Master's degree or higher: 8.3% (2004).

Housing: Homeownership rate: 68.4% (2004); Median home value: $64,286 (2004); Median rent: $317 per month (2000); Median age of housing: 23 years (2000).
Transportation: Commute to work: 85.9% car, 0.0% public transportation, 6.3% walk, 0.0% work from home (2000); Travel time to work: 39.1% less than 15 minutes, 39.1% 15 to 30 minutes, 15.6% 30 to 45 minutes, 0.0% 45 to 60 minutes, 6.3% 60 minutes or more (2000)

Volusia County

Located in northeastern Florida; bounded on the west by the St. Johns River, and on the east by the Atlantic Ocean; lowland area, with many lakes and lagoons, including Mosquito Lagoon. Covers a land area of 1,103.20 square miles, a water area of 329.20 square miles, and is located in the Eastern Time Zone. The county government was organized in 1854. County seat is De Land.

Volusia County is part of the Deltona-Daytona Beach-Ormond Beach, FL Metropolitan Statistical Area. The entire metro area includes: Volusia County, FL

Weather Station: Daytona Beach Regional Airport Elevation: 26 feet

	Jan	Feb	Mar	Apr	May	Jun	Jul	Aug	Sep	Oct	Nov	Dec
High	69	70	75	80	85	88	90	90	87	82	76	71
Low	48	49	54	59	65	71	73	73	72	66	57	51
Precip	3.2	2.8	3.7	2.6	3.2	5.7	5.1	6.1	6.3	4.6	3.0	2.7
Snow	tr	0.0	tr	0.0	0.0	tr	0.0	tr	0.0	0.0	0.0	tr

High and Low temperatures in degrees Fahrenheit; Precipitation and Snow in inches

Population: 370,712 (1990); 443,343 (2000); 472,690 (2004); 509,731 (2009 projected); Race: 84.9% White, 9.9% Black, 1.1% Asian, 8.0% Hispanic of any race (2004); Density: 428.5 persons per square mile (2004); Average household size: 2.40 (2004); Median age: 43.0 (2004); Male/female ratio: 94.9 (2004).
Religion: Five largest groups: 15.2% Catholic Church, 6.8% Southern Baptist Convention, 3.1% The United Methodist Church, 1.7% Jewish Estimate, 1.3% Presbyterian Church (U.S.A.) (2000).
Economy: Unemployment rate: 4.8% (2004); Total civilian labor force: 206,195 (2004); Leading industries: 18.7% retail trade; 15.3% health care and social assistance; 14.3% accommodation & food services (2003); Companies that employ 500 or more persons: 15 (2003); Companies that employ 100 to 499 persons: 188 (2003); Companies that employ less than 100 persons: 11,282 (2003); Farms: 1,114 totaling 93,842 acres (2002); Minority business ownership rate: 9.3% (1997); Women business ownership rate: 30.0% (1997); Retail sales per capita: $9,349 (1997). Single-family building permits issued: 4,820 (2004); Multi-family building permits issued: 1,616 (2004).
Income: Per capita income: $21,869 (2004); Median household income: $38,855 (2004); Average household income: $51,554 (2004); Percent of households with income of $100,000 or more: 9.5% (2004); Poverty rate: 12.2% (2002); Bankruptcy rate: 6.48% (2004).
Taxes: Total county taxes per capita: $373 (2002); County property taxes per capita: $315 (2002).
Education: Percent of population age 25 and over with: High school diploma (including GED) or higher: 82.3% (2004); Bachelor's degree or higher: 17.8% (2004); Master's degree or higher: 6.1% (2004).
Housing: Homeownership rate: 75.8% (2004); Median home value: $112,792 (2004); Median rent: $498 per month (2000); Median age of housing: 21 years (2000).
Health: Birth rate: 102.3 per 10,000 population (2004); Death rate: 130.9 per 10,000 population (2004); Age adjusted cancer mortality rate: 218.1 deaths per 100,000 population (2002); Air Quality Index: 95.2% good, 4.8% moderate, 0.0% unhealthy for sensitive individuals, 0.0% unhealthy (percent of days in 2004); Number of physicians: 19.1 per 10,000 population (2001); Hospital beds: 25.8 per 10,000 population (2002); Hospital admissions: 1,277.0 per 10,000 population (2002).
Elections: 2004 Presidential election results: 48.9% Bush, 50.5% Kerry, 0.4% Nader, 0.1% Badnarik
National and State Parks: Addison Blockhouse Historic State Park; Blue Spring State Park; Bulow Creek State Park; De Leon Springs State Park; Haw Creek Preserve State Park; Lake Woodruff National Wildlife Refuge; New Smyrna Sugar Mill Ruins State Historic Site; North Peninsula State Park; Ormond Tomb State Park; Tomoka State Park
Additional Information Contacts
Volusia County Government Offices . . . . (386) 736-5920
Daytona Beach Area Association of Realtors . . . . (386) 677-7131
Daytona Beach Chamber of Commerce . . . . (386) 255-0981
Daytona Beach Shores Chamber . . . . (386) 761-7163
De Land Chamber of Commerce . . . . (386) 734-4331
Deltona Chamber of Commerce . . . . (407) 574-5522
New Smyrna Beach Board of Realtors . . . . (386) 428-2104
New Smyrna Beach Chamber of Commerce . . . . (386) 428-2449
Orange City Chamber of Commerce . . . . (386) 775-2793
Ormond Beach Chamber of Commerce . . . . (386) 677-3454
West Volusia Association of Realtors . . . . (386) 774-6433

Volusia County Communities

DAYTONA BEACH (city). Covers a land area of 58.677 square miles and a water area of 6.254 square miles. Located at 29.20° N. Lat.; 81.03° W. Long. Elevation is 10 feet.
History: The town of Daytona Beach was laid out about 1870 in an area along the Halifax River (a tidewater lagoon on the Atlantic Ocean) where American colonists from Georgia had established plantations. The town was platted by Mathias Day, who named it Daytona. Transportation was a problem until 1887 when a bridge across the Halifax River made access to the ocean peninsula easier, and a bridge over the Tomoka River allowed the railroad to enter Daytona. Daytona developed as a resort, with some citrus industry. In 1926 the communities of Seabreeze and Daytona Beach, on the east shore of the peninsula, united with Daytona under the name of Daytona Beach. By this time, the Beach had become a motor speedway, with the cream of world racers breaking speed records here.
Population: 62,186 (1990); 64,112 (2000); 64,908 (2004); 66,482 (2009 projected); Race: 60.4% White, 34.2% Black, 2.0% Asian, 4.0% Hispanic of any race (2004); Density: 1,106.2 persons per square mile (2004); Average household size: 2.22 (2004); Median age: 37.7 (2004); Male/female ratio: 100.2 (2004); Marriage status: 34.7% never married, 41.9% now married, 9.6% widowed, 13.8% divorced (2000); Foreign born: 7.7% (2000); Ancestry (includes multiple ancestries): 33.1% Other groups, 11.0% German, 10.4% Irish, 8.3% English, 5.9% Italian (2000).
Economy: Unemployment rate: 6.4% (2004); Total civilian labor force: 36,027 (2004); Single-family building permits issued: 175 (2004); Multi-family building permits issued: 67 (2004); Employment by occupation: 8.9% management, 17.2% professional, 23.3% services, 29.4% sales, 0.2% farming, 8.4% construction, 12.6% production (2000).
Income: Per capita income: $18,693 (2004); Median household income: $27,657 (2004); Average household income: $40,097 (2004); Percent of households with income of $100,000 or more: 6.6% (2004); Poverty rate: 23.6% (2000).
Taxes: Total city taxes per capita: $499 (2002); City property taxes per capita: $229 (2002).
Education: Percent of population age 25 and over with: High school diploma (including GED) or higher: 80.4% (2004); Bachelor's degree or higher: 19.3% (2004); Master's degree or higher: 6.3% (2004).

School District(s)

Flagler County School District (PK-12)
2002-03 Enrollment: 7,601 . . . . (386) 437-7526

Four-year College(s)

Bethune Cookman College
2003-04 Enrollment: 2,794 . . . . (386) 481-2000
2003-04 Tuition: In-state $10,106; Out-of-state $10,106
Embry Riddle Aeronautical Univ-Extended Campus
2003-04 Enrollment: 9,568 . . . . (800) 522-6787
2003-04 Tuition: In-state $4,056; Out-of-state $4,056
Embry Riddle Aeronautical University-Daytona Beach
2003-04 Enrollment: 4,926 . . . . (800) 222-3728
2003-04 Tuition: In-state $21,360; Out-of-state $21,360

Two-year College(s)

American Motorcycle Institute (Private, For-profit)
2003-04 Enrollment: 485 . . . . (386) 255-0295
Daytona Beach Community College (Public)
2003-04 Enrollment: 12,262 . . . . (904) 255-8131
2003-04 Tuition: In-state $1,739; Out-of-state $6,530
Keiser College-Daytona (Private, For-profit)
2003-04 Enrollment: n/a . . . . (386) 274-5060
2003-04 Tuition: In-state $10,920; Out-of-state $10,920

Housing: Homeownership rate: 47.5% (2004); Median home value: $98,117 (2004); Median rent: $460 per month (2000); Median age of housing: 30 years (2000).
Hospitals: Halifax Medical Center (764 beds)

Safety: Violent crime rate: 184.5 per 10,000 population; Property crime rate: 933.5 per 10,000 population (2003).
Newspapers: Daytona Times (Black - Circulation 15,000); The Daytona Beach News-Journal (Circulation 107,251)
Transportation: Commute to work: 85.2% car, 3.8% public transportation, 5.7% walk, 2.1% work from home (2000); Travel time to work: 42.4% less than 15 minutes, 40.0% 15 to 30 minutes, 9.7% 30 to 45 minutes, 2.4% 45 to 60 minutes, 5.5% 60 minutes or more (2000); Amtrak: Service available.
Airports: Daytona Beach International (primary service)
Additional Information Contacts
Daytona Beach Chamber of Commerce . . . . (386) 255-0981
Daytona Beach Shores Chamber . . . . (386) 761-7163

DAYTONA BEACH SHORES (city). Aka Cottage Colony. Covers a land area of 0.910 square miles and a water area of 0.027 square miles. Located at 29.17° N. Lat.; 80.98° W. Long. Elevation is 23 feet.
Population: 2,813 (1990); 4,299 (2000); 4,867 (2004); 5,516 (2009 projected); Race: 96.2% White, 0.8% Black, 1.7% Asian, 1.1% Hispanic of any race (2004); Density: 5,346.1 persons per square mile (2004); Average household size: 1.76 (2004); Median age: 64.6 (2004); Male/female ratio: 89.7 (2004); Marriage status: 11.4% never married, 64.9% now married, 11.3% widowed, 12.5% divorced (2000); Foreign born: 13.6% (2000); Ancestry (includes multiple ancestries): 19.9% German, 17.8% English, 13.6% Irish, 8.9% Italian, 7.2% United States or American (2000).
Economy: Single-family building permits issued: 23 (2004); Multi-family building permits issued: 238 (2004); Employment by occupation: 20.8% management, 12.8% professional, 17.4% services, 35.9% sales, 0.8% farming, 6.2% construction, 6.1% production (2000).
Income: Per capita income: $38,717 (2004); Median household income: $46,115 (2004); Average household income: $67,953 (2004); Percent of households with income of $100,000 or more: 18.1% (2004); Poverty rate: 6.8% (2000).
Education: Percent of population age 25 and over with: High school diploma (including GED) or higher: 89.5% (2004); Bachelor's degree or higher: 25.0% (2004); Master's degree or higher: 9.0% (2004).
Housing: Homeownership rate: 80.3% (2004); Median home value: $174,130 (2004); Median rent: $731 per month (2000); Median age of housing: 15 years (2000).
Safety: Violent crime rate: 131.2 per 10,000 population; Property crime rate: 664.7 per 10,000 population (2003).
Transportation: Commute to work: 73.0% car, 0.7% public transportation, 10.9% walk, 13.9% work from home (2000); Travel time to work: 33.6% less than 15 minutes, 44.1% 15 to 30 minutes, 14.6% 30 to 45 minutes, 2.3% 45 to 60 minutes, 5.4% 60 minutes or more (2000)

DE BARY (city). Covers a land area of 18.223 square miles and a water area of 3.217 square miles. Located at 28.88° N. Lat.; 81.31° W. Long. Elevation is 76 feet.
Population: 9,671 (1990); 15,559 (2000); 16,195 (2004); 17,074 (2009 projected); Race: 94.0% White, 2.5% Black, 1.3% Asian, 4.9% Hispanic of any race (2004); Density: 888.7 persons per square mile (2004); Average household size: 2.42 (2004); Median age: 45.7 (2004); Male/female ratio: 92.4 (2004); Marriage status: 15.8% never married, 65.3% now married, 9.5% widowed, 9.5% divorced (2000); Foreign born: 5.0% (2000); Ancestry (includes multiple ancestries): 19.0% German, 15.3% English, 15.2% Irish, 10.5% Other groups, 10.4% United States or American (2000).
Economy: Employment by occupation: 15.6% management, 16.7% professional, 14.5% services, 29.8% sales, 0.0% farming, 13.1% construction, 10.4% production (2000).
Income: Per capita income: $26,684 (2004); Median household income: $50,339 (2004); Average household income: $64,333 (2004); Percent of households with income of $100,000 or more: 15.6% (2004); Poverty rate: 6.9% (2000).
Taxes: Total city taxes per capita: $244 (2002); City property taxes per capita: $108 (2002).
Education: Percent of population age 25 and over with: High school diploma (including GED) or higher: 82.6% (2004); Bachelor's degree or higher: 17.5% (2004); Master's degree or higher: 5.4% (2004).

School District(s)

Volusia County School District (PK-12)
2002-03 Enrollment: 63,000 . . . . (386) 734-7190
Housing: Homeownership rate: 88.2% (2004); Median home value: $120,785 (2004); Median rent: $524 per month (2000); Median age of housing: 16 years (2000).
Transportation: Commute to work: 94.1% car, 0.5% public transportation, 0.3% walk, 3.8% work from home (2000); Travel time to work: 17.7% less than 15 minutes, 31.5% 15 to 30 minutes, 27.0% 30 to 45 minutes, 12.1% 45 to 60 minutes, 11.7% 60 minutes or more (2000)
Additional Information Contacts
Local Government Offices . . . . (386) 668-2040

DE LAND (city). Covers a land area of 15.871 square miles and a water area of 0.186 square miles. Located at 29.02° N. Lat.; 81.30° W. Long. Elevation is 54 feet.
History: De Land was founded in 1876 by Henry A. DeLand, a baking powder manufacturer, who planted trees along all the proposed streets. DeLand also founded Stetson University (first called DeLand University) in 1886, with the financial backing of John B. Stetson, the hat manufacturer. Lue Gim Gong, known as the Luther Burbank of Florida, settled here in 1886 and gained recognition as a citrus culturist.
Population: 17,979 (1990); 20,904 (2000); 21,898 (2004); 23,317 (2009 projected); Race: 73.2% White, 20.0% Black, 0.9% Asian, 10.8% Hispanic of any race (2004); Density: 1,379.7 persons per square mile (2004); Average household size: 2.49 (2004); Median age: 37.7 (2004); Male/female ratio: 83.5 (2004); Marriage status: 23.2% never married, 51.7% now married, 13.0% widowed, 12.0% divorced (2000); Foreign born: 7.3% (2000); Ancestry (includes multiple ancestries): 27.7% Other groups, 12.1% German, 10.4% Irish, 10.2% English, 7.0% United States or American (2000).
Economy: Single-family building permits issued: 503 (2004); Multi-family building permits issued: 324 (2004); Employment by occupation: 10.5% management, 17.6% professional, 18.9% services, 24.6% sales, 2.0% farming, 10.8% construction, 15.6% production (2000).
Income: Per capita income: $17,583 (2004); Median household income: $31,463 (2004); Average household income: $41,013 (2004); Percent of households with income of $100,000 or more: 5.5% (2004); Poverty rate: 19.0% (2000).
Taxes: Total city taxes per capita: $485 (2002); City property taxes per capita: $208 (2002).
Education: Percent of population age 25 and over with: High school diploma (including GED) or higher: 78.0% (2004); Bachelor's degree or higher: 18.5% (2004); Master's degree or higher: 8.0% (2004).

School District(s)

Volusia County School District (PK-12)
2002-03 Enrollment: 63,000 . . . . (386) 734-7190

Four-year College(s)

Stetson University
2003-04 Enrollment: 3,439 . . . . (386) 822-7000
2003-04 Tuition: In-state $21,300; Out-of-state $21,300

Two-year College(s)

Angley College
2003-04 Enrollment: 78 . . . . (386) 740-1215
Housing: Homeownership rate: 54.0% (2004); Median home value: $90,684 (2004); Median rent: $458 per month (2000); Median age of housing: 27 years (2000).
Hospitals: Flordia Hospital DeLand (156 beds)
Safety: Violent crime rate: 67.3 per 10,000 population; Property crime rate: 623.5 per 10,000 population (2003).
Transportation: Commute to work: 90.1% car, 1.0% public transportation, 4.4% walk, 3.0% work from home (2000); Travel time to work: 43.1% less than 15 minutes, 26.4% 15 to 30 minutes, 16.1% 30 to 45 minutes, 7.1% 45 to 60 minutes, 7.3% 60 minutes or more (2000); Amtrak: Service available.
Additional Information Contacts
De Land Chamber of Commerce . . . . (386) 734-4331

DE LAND SOUTHWEST (CDP). Covers a land area of 0.628 square miles and a water area of 0 square miles. Located at 29.00° N. Lat.; 81.31° W. Long.
Population: 1,166 (1990); 1,169 (2000); 1,145 (2004); 1,135 (2009 projected); Race: 25.9% White, 69.0% Black, 0.4% Asian, 9.1% Hispanic of any race (2004); Density: 1,824.6 persons per square mile (2004); Average household size: 2.99 (2004); Median age: 39.9 (2004); Male/female ratio: 80.0 (2004); Marriage status: 32.5% never married, 33.6% now married, 19.8% widowed, 14.2% divorced (2000); Foreign born: 5.8% (2000); Ancestry (includes multiple ancestries): 47.3% Other groups, 3.9% African, 3.0% Jamaican, 0.9% West Indian, 0.6% Swedish (2000).

Economy: Employment by occupation: 2.3% management, 13.9% professional, 36.1% services, 20.0% sales, 1.9% farming, 12.9% construction, 12.9% production (2000).
Income: Per capita income: $9,023 (2004); Median household income: $14,999 (2004); Average household income: $22,095 (2004); Percent of households with income of $100,000 or more: 0.5% (2004); Poverty rate: 45.7% (2000).
Education: Percent of population age 25 and over with: High school diploma (including GED) or higher: 55.1% (2004); Bachelor's degree or higher: 8.0% (2004); Master's degree or higher: 4.5% (2004).
Housing: Homeownership rate: 61.9% (2004); Median home value: $68,113 (2004); Median rent: $340 per month (2000); Median age of housing: 33 years (2000).
Transportation: Commute to work: 89.0% car, 0.0% public transportation, 3.5% walk, 7.4% work from home (2000); Travel time to work: 31.0% less than 15 minutes, 48.8% 15 to 30 minutes, 17.8% 30 to 45 minutes, 0.0% 45 to 60 minutes, 2.4% 60 minutes or more (2000)

DE LEON SPRINGS (CDP). Covers a land area of 2.631 square miles and a water area of 0 square miles. Located at 29.12° N. Lat.; 81.35° W. Long. Elevation is 60 feet.
History: The village of De Leon Springs was established near the Ponce de Leon Springs, where the Spanish had erected a sugar mill previous to 1763. The site of the village was plantation land planted in corn, sugar cane, and indigo when Florida became a Territory in 1819.
Population: 1,467 (1990); 2,358 (2000); 2,438 (2004); 2,524 (2009 projected); Race: 56.5% White, 6.1% Black, 0.2% Asian, 53.0% Hispanic of any race (2004); Density: 926.6 persons per square mile (2004); Average household size: 3.24 (2004); Median age: 31.0 (2004); Male/female ratio: 101.3 (2004); Marriage status: 22.6% never married, 62.9% now married, 5.6% widowed, 8.8% divorced (2000); Foreign born: 24.0% (2000); Ancestry (includes multiple ancestries): 44.9% Other groups, 9.5% United States or American, 8.4% Irish, 5.5% English, 5.2% German (2000).
Economy: Employment by occupation: 6.4% management, 6.8% professional, 19.9% services, 18.4% sales, 13.5% farming, 15.5% construction, 19.5% production (2000).
Income: Per capita income: $13,328 (2004); Median household income: $32,536 (2004); Average household income: $43,208 (2004); Percent of households with income of $100,000 or more: 6.5% (2004); Poverty rate: 17.2% (2000).
Education: Percent of population age 25 and over with: High school diploma (including GED) or higher: 59.6% (2004); Bachelor's degree or higher: 7.2% (2004); Master's degree or higher: 2.5% (2004).

School District(s)

Volusia County School District (PK-12)
2002-03 Enrollment: 63,000 . . . . (386) 734-7190
Housing: Homeownership rate: 80.2% (2004); Median home value: $88,491 (2004); Median rent: $315 per month (2000); Median age of housing: 19 years (2000).
Transportation: Commute to work: 99.6% car, 0.0% public transportation, 0.0% walk, 0.0% work from home (2000); Travel time to work: 12.4% less than 15 minutes, 51.3% 15 to 30 minutes, 26.2% 30 to 45 minutes, 2.1% 45 to 60 minutes, 7.9% 60 minutes or more (2000)

DELTONA (city). Covers a land area of 35.778 square miles and a water area of 2.543 square miles. Located at 28.90° N. Lat.; 81.21° W. Long. Elevation is 50 feet.
Population: 49,242 (1990); 69,543 (2000); 77,005 (2004); 86,143 (2009 projected); Race: 80.6% White, 9.1% Black, 1.0% Asian, 22.2% Hispanic of any race (2004); Density: 2,152.3 persons per square mile (2004); Average household size: 2.84 (2004); Median age: 37.1 (2004); Male/female ratio: 94.6 (2004); Marriage status: 21.1% never married, 61.6% now married, 6.5% widowed, 10.8% divorced (2000); Foreign born: 7.1% (2000); Ancestry (includes multiple ancestries): 27.1% Other groups, 15.8% German, 14.5% Irish, 9.8% Italian, 9.7% English (2000).
Economy: Manufacturing includes transportation equipment, concrete. Unemployment rate: 5.4% (2004); Total civilian labor force: 27,848 (2004); Single-family building permits issued: 1,315 (2004); Multi-family building permits issued: 0 (2004); Employment by occupation: 10.6% management, 16.0% professional, 16.0% services, 31.1% sales, 0.1% farming, 13.8% construction, 12.4% production (2000).
Income: Per capita income: $18,369 (2004); Median household income: $44,091 (2004); Average household income: $51,730 (2004); Percent of households with income of $100,000 or more: 7.6% (2004); Poverty rate: 8.1% (2000).
Taxes: Total city taxes per capita: $166 (2002); City property taxes per capita: $86 (2002).
Education: Percent of population age 25 and over with: High school diploma (including GED) or higher: 82.5% (2004); Bachelor's degree or higher: 13.3% (2004); Master's degree or higher: 3.8% (2004).

School District(s)

Volusia County School District (PK-12)
2002-03 Enrollment: 63,000 . . . . (386) 734-7190
Housing: Homeownership rate: 87.2% (2004); Median home value: $111,552 (2004); Median rent: $580 per month (2000); Median age of housing: 15 years (2000).
Transportation: Commute to work: 95.6% car, 0.5% public transportation, 0.3% walk, 2.5% work from home (2000); Travel time to work: 14.8% less than 15 minutes, 28.5% 15 to 30 minutes, 27.6% 30 to 45 minutes, 14.7% 45 to 60 minutes, 14.5% 60 minutes or more (2000)
Additional Information Contacts
Deltona Chamber of Commerce . . . . (407) 574-5522

EDGEWATER (city). Covers a land area of 9.969 square miles and a water area of 0.374 square miles. Located at 28.96° N. Lat.; 80.90° W. Long. Elevation is 6 feet.
Population: 15,689 (1990); 18,668 (2000); 20,598 (2004); 22,971 (2009 projected); Race: 95.7% White, 1.9% Black, 0.6% Asian, 2.4% Hispanic of any race (2004); Density: 2,066.2 persons per square mile (2004); Average household size: 2.44 (2004); Median age: 42.5 (2004); Male/female ratio: 92.7 (2004); Marriage status: 17.2% never married, 61.9% now married, 8.8% widowed, 12.2% divorced (2000); Foreign born: 3.4% (2000); Ancestry (includes multiple ancestries): 16.9% German, 16.5% Irish, 14.1% English, 10.1% Other groups, 9.9% Italian (2000).
Economy: Resort city. Single-family building permits issued: 226 (2004); Multi-family building permits issued: 0 (2004); Employment by occupation: 9.5% management, 15.9% professional, 20.2% services, 27.9% sales, 0.3% farming, 13.9% construction, 12.2% production (2000).
Income: Per capita income: $19,553 (2004); Median household income: $39,462 (2004); Average household income: $47,547 (2004); Percent of households with income of $100,000 or more: 5.8% (2004); Poverty rate: 9.2% (2000).
Education: Percent of population age 25 and over with: High school diploma (including GED) or higher: 81.8% (2004); Bachelor's degree or higher: 10.5% (2004); Master's degree or higher: 3.8% (2004).

School District(s)

Volusia County School District (PK-12)
2002-03 Enrollment: 63,000 . . . . (386) 734-7190
Housing: Homeownership rate: 83.5% (2004); Median home value: $102,912 (2004); Median rent: $494 per month (2000); Median age of housing: 17 years (2000).
Safety: Violent crime rate: 30.8 per 10,000 population; Property crime rate: 350.3 per 10,000 population (2003).
Transportation: Commute to work: 94.8% car, 0.7% public transportation, 0.4% walk, 1.6% work from home (2000); Travel time to work: 31.8% less than 15 minutes, 31.1% 15 to 30 minutes, 22.6% 30 to 45 minutes, 7.5% 45 to 60 minutes, 6.9% 60 minutes or more (2000)
Additional Information Contacts
Local Government Offices . . . . (386) 424-2400

GLENCOE (CDP). Covers a land area of 7.646 square miles and a water area of 0.048 square miles. Located at 29.01° N. Lat.; 80.96° W. Long. Elevation is 20 feet.
Population: 1,908 (1990); 2,485 (2000); 2,715 (2004); 2,994 (2009 projected); Race: 97.7% White, 1.4% Black, 0.0% Asian, 1.0% Hispanic of any race (2004); Density: 355.1 persons per square mile (2004); Average household size: 2.51 (2004); Median age: 42.1 (2004); Male/female ratio: 99.9 (2004); Marriage status: 18.3% never married, 64.1% now married, 6.1% widowed, 11.5% divorced (2000); Foreign born: 2.5% (2000); Ancestry (includes multiple ancestries): 21.1% German, 18.8% English, 16.3% Irish, 11.7% United States or American, 7.5% Other groups (2000).
Economy: Employment by occupation: 12.4% management, 18.5% professional, 20.0% services, 24.0% sales, 0.5% farming, 14.8% construction, 9.9% production (2000).
Income: Per capita income: $24,132 (2004); Median household income: $42,699 (2004); Average household income: $60,546 (2004); Percent of households with income of $100,000 or more: 14.6% (2004); Poverty rate: 5.6% (2000).

Education: Percent of population age 25 and over with: High school diploma (including GED) or higher: 83.9% (2004); Bachelor's degree or higher: 19.2% (2004); Master's degree or higher: 6.8% (2004).
Housing: Homeownership rate: 92.9% (2004); Median home value: $128,516 (2004); Median rent: $585 per month (2000); Median age of housing: 18 years (2000).
Transportation: Commute to work: 91.4% car, 0.7% public transportation, 0.5% walk, 3.7% work from home (2000); Travel time to work: 39.1% less than 15 minutes, 30.8% 15 to 30 minutes, 21.6% 30 to 45 minutes, 2.1% 45 to 60 minutes, 6.3% 60 minutes or more (2000)

HOLLY HILL (city). Covers a land area of 3.892 square miles and a water area of 0.631 square miles. Located at 29.24° N. Lat.; 81.04° W. Long. Elevation is 15 feet.
History: Holly Hill was settled on the Turnbull land grant, and was named for the holly trees that once grew here. The town developed as a suburb of Daytona Beach.
Population: 11,401 (1990); 12,119 (2000); 13,012 (2004); 14,162 (2009 projected); Race: 84.5% White, 11.2% Black, 1.0% Asian, 4.6% Hispanic of any race (2004); Density: 3,342.9 persons per square mile (2004); Average household size: 2.15 (2004); Median age: 42.1 (2004); Male/female ratio: 92.2 (2004); Marriage status: 21.6% never married, 48.7% now married, 12.4% widowed, 17.2% divorced (2000); Foreign born: 4.9% (2000); Ancestry (includes multiple ancestries): 17.1% Other groups, 13.7% German, 12.1% Irish, 11.7% English, 11.3% United States or American (2000).
Economy: Single-family building permits issued: 23 (2004); Multi-family building permits issued: 16 (2004); Employment by occupation: 6.0% management, 13.7% professional, 23.6% services, 24.9% sales, 0.2% farming, 16.2% construction, 15.5% production (2000).
Income: Per capita income: $17,404 (2004); Median household income: $29,325 (2004); Average household income: $36,355 (2004); Percent of households with income of $100,000 or more: 3.2% (2004); Poverty rate: 16.5% (2000).
Taxes: Total city taxes per capita: $301 (2002); City property taxes per capita: $137 (2002).
Education: Percent of population age 25 and over with: High school diploma (including GED) or higher: 75.4% (2004); Bachelor's degree or higher: 9.6% (2004); Master's degree or higher: 3.0% (2004).

School District(s)

Volusia County School District (PK-12)
2002-03 Enrollment: 63,000 .... (386) 734-7190
Housing: Homeownership rate: 60.2% (2004); Median home value: $79,804 (2004); Median rent: $482 per month (2000); Median age of housing: 32 years (2000).
Safety: Violent crime rate: 99.3 per 10,000 population; Property crime rate: 838.8 per 10,000 population (2003).
Transportation: Commute to work: 90.6% car, 1.6% public transportation, 1.4% walk, 2.2% work from home (2000); Travel time to work: 41.1% less than 15 minutes, 36.0% 15 to 30 minutes, 14.6% 30 to 45 minutes, 3.0% 45 to 60 minutes, 5.4% 60 minutes or more (2000)
Additional Information Contacts
Daytona Beach Area Association of Realtors .... (386) 677-7131

LAKE HELEN (city). Covers a land area of 4.219 square miles and a water area of 0.103 square miles. Located at 28.98° N. Lat.; 81.23° W. Long. Elevation is 64 feet.
Population: 2,415 (1990); 2,743 (2000); 2,766 (2004); 2,821 (2009 projected); Race: 85.0% White, 12.3% Black, 0.3% Asian, 3.8% Hispanic of any race (2004); Density: 655.5 persons per square mile (2004); Average household size: 2.45 (2004); Median age: 43.1 (2004); Male/female ratio: 90.2 (2004); Marriage status: 18.9% never married, 59.9% now married, 8.4% widowed, 12.9% divorced (2000); Foreign born: 0.5% (2000); Ancestry (includes multiple ancestries): 19.9% English, 18.9% German, 14.4% Other groups, 13.0% Irish, 8.2% United States or American (2000).
Economy: In citrus-fruit-growing area. Single-family building permits issued: 8 (2004); Multi-family building permits issued: 0 (2004); Employment by occupation: 11.6% management, 20.9% professional, 14.9% services, 20.2% sales, 1.1% farming, 13.4% construction, 17.8% production (2000).
Income: Per capita income: $17,609 (2004); Median household income: $37,809 (2004); Average household income: $43,219 (2004); Percent of households with income of $100,000 or more: 4.1% (2004); Poverty rate: 9.7% (2000).
Education: Percent of population age 25 and over with: High school diploma (including GED) or higher: 79.3% (2004); Bachelor's degree or higher: 13.4% (2004); Master's degree or higher: 2.1% (2004).

School District(s)

Volusia County School District (PK-12)
2002-03 Enrollment: 63,000 .... (386) 734-7190
Housing: Homeownership rate: 86.1% (2004); Median home value: $88,144 (2004); Median rent: $471 per month (2000); Median age of housing: 24 years (2000).
Safety: Violent crime rate: 60.2 per 10,000 population; Property crime rate: 279.8 per 10,000 population (2003).
Transportation: Commute to work: 90.2% car, 1.7% public transportation, 2.5% walk, 4.1% work from home (2000); Travel time to work: 18.6% less than 15 minutes, 50.6% 15 to 30 minutes, 17.6% 30 to 45 minutes, 9.5% 45 to 60 minutes, 3.6% 60 minutes or more (2000)

NEW SMYRNA BEACH (city). Covers a land area of 27.686 square miles and a water area of 3.090 square miles. Located at 29.03° N. Lat.; 80.92° W. Long. Elevation is 8 feet.
History: Incorporated 1903.
Population: 18,261 (1990); 20,048 (2000); 20,732 (2004); 21,656 (2009 projected); Race: 91.5% White, 6.2% Black, 0.5% Asian, 1.7% Hispanic of any race (2004); Density: 748.8 persons per square mile (2004); Average household size: 2.02 (2004); Median age: 54.1 (2004); Male/female ratio: 89.8 (2004); Marriage status: 17.5% never married, 57.6% now married, 11.6% widowed, 13.3% divorced (2000); Foreign born: 5.5% (2000); Ancestry (includes multiple ancestries): 18.4% German, 16.9% English, 16.3% Irish, 11.5% Other groups, 8.8% Italian (2000).
Economy: Resort and tourist area. Citrus-fruit packing; commercial fishing; seafood processing. Light manufacturing. Single-family building permits issued: 146 (2004); Multi-family building permits issued: 331 (2004); Employment by occupation: 14.1% management, 17.1% professional, 20.2% services, 26.4% sales, 0.3% farming, 11.0% construction, 10.9% production (2000).
Income: Per capita income: $26,623 (2004); Median household income: $39,400 (2004); Average household income: $53,480 (2004); Percent of households with income of $100,000 or more: 10.6% (2004); Poverty rate: 10.8% (2000).
Education: Percent of population age 25 and over with: High school diploma (including GED) or higher: 85.1% (2004); Bachelor's degree or higher: 23.0% (2004); Master's degree or higher: 8.8% (2004).

School District(s)

Volusia County School District (PK-12)
2002-03 Enrollment: 63,000 .... (386) 734-7190
Housing: Homeownership rate: 74.8% (2004); Median home value: $136,163 (2004); Median rent: $497 per month (2000); Median age of housing: 24 years (2000).
Hospitals: Bert Fish Medical Center (116 beds)
Safety: Violent crime rate: 60.4 per 10,000 population; Property crime rate: 442.2 per 10,000 population (2003).
Newspapers: The Observer (Circulation 5,000)
Transportation: Commute to work: 89.6% car, 0.1% public transportation, 1.7% walk, 4.7% work from home (2000); Travel time to work: 40.1% less than 15 minutes, 26.8% 15 to 30 minutes, 18.8% 30 to 45 minutes, 5.6% 45 to 60 minutes, 8.6% 60 minutes or more (2000)
Airports: New Smyrna Beach Municipal
Additional Information Contacts
New Smyrna Beach Board of Realtors .... (386) 428-2104
New Smyrna Beach Chamber of Commerce .... (386) 428-2449

NORTH DE LAND (CDP). Covers a land area of 0.589 square miles and a water area of 0 square miles. Located at 29.04° N. Lat.; 81.29° W. Long.
Population: 1,379 (1990); 1,327 (2000); 1,388 (2004); 1,465 (2009 projected); Race: 89.8% White, 3.2% Black, 1.9% Asian, 9.3% Hispanic of any race (2004); Density: 2,357.3 persons per square mile (2004); Average household size: 2.51 (2004); Median age: 37.6 (2004); Male/female ratio: 96.3 (2004); Marriage status: 17.5% never married, 52.8% now married, 8.8% widowed, 20.9% divorced (2000); Foreign born: 9.0% (2000); Ancestry (includes multiple ancestries): 14.1% Other groups, 12.2% Irish, 11.0% German, 11.0% United States or American, 10.5% English (2000).
Economy: Employment by occupation: 12.6% management, 17.1% professional, 8.2% services, 28.1% sales, 2.1% farming, 11.2% construction, 20.7% production (2000).

Income: Per capita income: $19,200 (2004); Median household income: $34,000 (2004); Average household income: $48,192 (2004); Percent of households with income of $100,000 or more: 9.2% (2004); Poverty rate: 11.8% (2000).
Education: Percent of population age 25 and over with: High school diploma (including GED) or higher: 75.0% (2004); Bachelor's degree or higher: 15.7% (2004); Master's degree or higher: 6.0% (2004).
Housing: Homeownership rate: 77.9% (2004); Median home value: $87,756 (2004); Median rent: $483 per month (2000); Median age of housing: 39 years (2000).
Transportation: Commute to work: 92.9% car, 0.0% public transportation, 1.7% walk, 3.4% work from home (2000); Travel time to work: 51.5% less than 15 minutes, 20.0% 15 to 30 minutes, 10.5% 30 to 45 minutes, 3.9% 45 to 60 minutes, 14.2% 60 minutes or more (2000)

OAK HILL (city). Covers a land area of 6.377 square miles and a water area of 4.876 square miles. Located at 28.88° N. Lat.; 80.84° W. Long. Elevation is 10 feet.
History: Oak Hill developed as a shipping center for citrus fruit grown in the area, and for orange and palmetto honey from local apiaries.
Population: 1,164 (1990); 1,378 (2000); 1,394 (2004); 1,435 (2009 projected); Race: 84.1% White, 13.6% Black, 0.1% Asian, 0.9% Hispanic of any race (2004); Density: 218.6 persons per square mile (2004); Average household size: 2.47 (2004); Median age: 43.1 (2004); Male/female ratio: 106.5 (2004); Marriage status: 19.4% never married, 62.1% now married, 6.8% widowed, 11.7% divorced (2000); Foreign born: 5.0% (2000); Ancestry (includes multiple ancestries): 30.8% Other groups, 12.0% English, 9.7% German, 8.7% Irish, 8.3% United States or American (2000).
Economy: Single-family building permits issued: 18 (2004); Multi-family building permits issued: 0 (2004); Employment by occupation: 7.7% management, 12.5% professional, 21.5% services, 18.4% sales, 3.6% farming, 19.7% construction, 16.7% production (2000).
Income: Per capita income: $19,085 (2004); Median household income: $34,856 (2004); Average household income: $47,088 (2004); Percent of households with income of $100,000 or more: 5.3% (2004); Poverty rate: 14.4% (2000).
Education: Percent of population age 25 and over with: High school diploma (including GED) or higher: 71.5% (2004); Bachelor's degree or higher: 8.5% (2004); Master's degree or higher: 1.8% (2004).

School District(s)

Volusia County School District (PK-12)
2002-03 Enrollment: 63,000 . . . . (386) 734-7190
Housing: Homeownership rate: 80.2% (2004); Median home value: $94,304 (2004); Median rent: $369 per month (2000); Median age of housing: 23 years (2000).
Safety: Violent crime rate: 82.9 per 10,000 population; Property crime rate: 331.7 per 10,000 population (2003).
Transportation: Commute to work: 91.2% car, 0.0% public transportation, 3.7% walk, 3.5% work from home (2000); Travel time to work: 22.2% less than 15 minutes, 33.9% 15 to 30 minutes, 23.6% 30 to 45 minutes, 14.1% 45 to 60 minutes, 6.3% 60 minutes or more (2000)

ORANGE CITY (city). Covers a land area of 6.051 square miles and a water area of 0.065 square miles. Located at 28.94° N. Lat.; 81.29° W. Long. Elevation is 35 feet.
History: Orange City was founded in the 1870's by three families from Eau Claire, Wisconsin, who wanted to raise citrus crops. The settlement was first known as Wisconsin Settlement.
Population: 5,621 (1990); 6,604 (2000); 6,646 (2004); 6,764 (2009 projected); Race: 91.7% White, 4.3% Black, 0.6% Asian, 6.5% Hispanic of any race (2004); Density: 1,098.4 persons per square mile (2004); Average household size: 2.14 (2004); Median age: 50.3 (2004); Male/female ratio: 86.8 (2004); Marriage status: 13.7% never married, 61.1% now married, 12.1% widowed, 13.0% divorced (2000); Foreign born: 4.2% (2000); Ancestry (includes multiple ancestries): 17.8% German, 15.6% Irish, 15.1% English, 11.7% United States or American, 11.4% Other groups (2000).
Economy: Single-family building permits issued: 60 (2004); Multi-family building permits issued: 364 (2004); Employment by occupation: 10.5% management, 13.3% professional, 17.9% services, 31.9% sales, 0.0% farming, 11.2% construction, 15.2% production (2000).
Income: Per capita income: $17,235 (2004); Median household income: $29,431 (2004); Average household income: $36,174 (2004); Percent of households with income of $100,000 or more: 3.4% (2004); Poverty rate: 9.9% (2000).
Taxes: Total city taxes per capita: $469 (2002); City property taxes per capita: $235 (2002).
Education: Percent of population age 25 and over with: High school diploma (including GED) or higher: 80.3% (2004); Bachelor's degree or higher: 12.7% (2004); Master's degree or higher: 3.6% (2004).

School District(s)

Volusia County School District (PK-12)
2002-03 Enrollment: 63,000 . . . . (386) 734-7190
Housing: Homeownership rate: 75.5% (2004); Median home value: $74,715 (2004); Median rent: $417 per month (2000); Median age of housing: 20 years (2000).
Hospitals: Florida Hospital Fish Memorial (139 beds)
Safety: Violent crime rate: 91.3 per 10,000 population; Property crime rate: 911.8 per 10,000 population (2003).
Transportation: Commute to work: 92.8% car, 0.4% public transportation, 1.3% walk, 2.8% work from home (2000); Travel time to work: 28.9% less than 15 minutes, 32.3% 15 to 30 minutes, 19.9% 30 to 45 minutes, 12.3% 45 to 60 minutes, 6.6% 60 minutes or more (2000)
Additional Information Contacts
Local Government Offices . . . . (386) 775-5400
Orange City Chamber of Commerce . . . . (386) 775-2793
West Volusia Association of Realtors . . . . (386) 774-6433

ORMOND BEACH (city). Aka Ormond. Covers a land area of 25.750 square miles and a water area of 3.320 square miles. Located at 29.28° N. Lat.; 81.07° W. Long. Elevation is 6 feet.
History: Development began at Ormond Beach in 1875 when John Anderson built a home here which was later purchased by Henry M. Flagler, pioneer railroad and resort promoter. John D. Rockefeller (1839-1937) had a winter home in Ormond Beach, and spent much time here in his later years.
Population: 32,157 (1990); 36,301 (2000); 37,383 (2004); 38,861 (2009 projected); Race: 93.9% White, 2.9% Black, 1.6% Asian, 2.5% Hispanic of any race (2004); Density: 1,451.8 persons per square mile (2004); Average household size: 2.30 (2004); Median age: 48.1 (2004); Male/female ratio: 88.4 (2004); Marriage status: 17.4% never married, 61.0% now married, 10.1% widowed, 11.4% divorced (2000); Foreign born: 7.0% (2000); Ancestry (includes multiple ancestries): 17.6% German, 16.9% English, 14.8% Irish, 10.1% Other groups, 9.7% United States or American (2000).
Economy: Unemployment rate: 3.4% (2004); Total civilian labor force: 16,697 (2004); Single-family building permits issued: 340 (2004); Multi-family building permits issued: 58 (2004); Employment by occupation: 16.1% management, 24.3% professional, 14.9% services, 30.2% sales, 0.1% farming, 7.7% construction, 6.8% production (2000).
Income: Per capita income: $29,621 (2004); Median household income: $47,962 (2004); Average household income: $67,530 (2004); Percent of households with income of $100,000 or more: 16.6% (2004); Poverty rate: 6.1% (2000).
Education: Percent of population age 25 and over with: High school diploma (including GED) or higher: 88.0% (2004); Bachelor's degree or higher: 28.9% (2004); Master's degree or higher: 10.7% (2004).

School District(s)

Volusia County School District (PK-12)
2002-03 Enrollment: 63,000 . . . . (386) 734-7190
Housing: Homeownership rate: 81.7% (2004); Median home value: $135,207 (2004); Median rent: $621 per month (2000); Median age of housing: 21 years (2000).
Hospitals: Florida Hospital Ormond Memorial (205 beds); Memorial Hospital - Oceanside (119 beds)
Safety: Violent crime rate: 29.0 per 10,000 population; Property crime rate: 321.3 per 10,000 population (2003).
Transportation: Commute to work: 92.8% car, 0.9% public transportation, 1.1% walk, 3.4% work from home (2000); Travel time to work: 35.5% less than 15 minutes, 45.0% 15 to 30 minutes, 11.7% 30 to 45 minutes, 3.1% 45 to 60 minutes, 4.7% 60 minutes or more (2000)
Airports: Ormond Beach Municipal
Additional Information Contacts
Ormond Beach Chamber of Commerce . . . . (386) 677-3454

ORMOND-BY-THE-SEA (CDP). Covers a land area of 1.986 square miles and a water area of 0.005 square miles. Located at 29.33° N. Lat.; 81.06° W. Long. Elevation is 10 feet.
Population: 8,141 (1990); 8,430 (2000); 8,348 (2004); 8,340 (2009 projected); Race: 97.2% White, 0.4% Black, 0.6% Asian, 2.7% Hispanic of any race (2004); Density: 4,204.2 persons per square mile (2004); Average

household size: 1.94 (2004); Median age: 54.6 (2004); Male/female ratio: 87.7 (2004); Marriage status: 14.2% never married, 56.8% now married, 16.0% widowed, 13.0% divorced (2000); Foreign born: 7.1% (2000); Ancestry (includes multiple ancestries): 19.2% Irish, 19.0% German, 14.8% English, 12.6% Italian, 8.3% Other groups (2000).
Economy: Employment by occupation: 10.6% management, 21.8% professional, 18.1% services, 25.1% sales, 0.6% farming, 12.7% construction, 11.0% production (2000).
Income: Per capita income: $25,256 (2004); Median household income: $37,057 (2004); Average household income: $48,660 (2004); Percent of households with income of $100,000 or more: 7.3% (2004); Poverty rate: 9.8% (2000).
Education: Percent of population age 25 and over with: High school diploma (including GED) or higher: 85.7% (2004); Bachelor's degree or higher: 21.3% (2004); Master's degree or higher: 6.9% (2004).
Housing: Homeownership rate: 81.6% (2004); Median home value: $123,324 (2004); Median rent: $601 per month (2000); Median age of housing: 30 years (2000).
Transportation: Commute to work: 93.2% car, 0.4% public transportation, 1.3% walk, 2.7% work from home (2000); Travel time to work: 21.9% less than 15 minutes, 41.4% 15 to 30 minutes, 25.7% 30 to 45 minutes, 4.7% 45 to 60 minutes, 6.2% 60 minutes or more (2000)

OSTEEN (unincorporated postal area, zip code 32764). Covers a land area of 65.127 square miles and a water area of 0.929 square miles. Located at 28.83° N. Lat.; 81.09° W. Long. Elevation is 50 feet.
Population: 2,441 (2000); Race: 94.0% White, 4.4% Black, 0.0% Asian, 2.7% Hispanic of any race (2000); Density: 37.5 persons per square mile (2000); Age: 20.1% under 18, 26.2% over 64 (2000); Marriage status: 11.2% never married, 66.7% now married, 10.5% widowed, 11.6% divorced (2000); Foreign born: 3.7% (2000); Ancestry (includes multiple ancestries): 17.4% United States or American, 13.9% Irish, 13.5% English, 13.2% Other groups, 10.5% German (2000).
Economy: Employment by occupation: 14.9% management, 9.7% professional, 19.1% services, 23.9% sales, 0.8% farming, 17.4% construction, 14.2% production (2000).
Income: Per capita income: $23,566 (2000); Median household income: $36,830 (2000); Poverty rate: 10.4% (2000).
Education: Percent of population age 25 and over with: High school diploma (including GED) or higher: 82.8% (2000); Bachelor's degree or higher: 15.4% (2000).

School District(s)

Volusia County School District (PK-12)
2002-03 Enrollment: 63,000 . . . . (386) 734-7190
Housing: Homeownership rate: 92.5% (2000); Median home value: $102,700 (2000); Median rent: $347 per month (2000); Median age of housing: 18 years (2000).
Transportation: Commute to work: 94.9% car, 0.0% public transportation, 2.3% walk, 1.3% work from home (2000); Travel time to work: 4.2% less than 15 minutes, 29.5% 15 to 30 minutes, 37.9% 30 to 45 minutes, 12.6% 45 to 60 minutes, 15.8% 60 minutes or more (2000)

PIERSON (town). Covers a land area of 8.136 square miles and a water area of 0.604 square miles. Located at 29.24° N. Lat.; 81.45° W. Long. Elevation is 78 feet.
Population: 3,407 (1990); 2,596 (2000); 2,696 (2004); 2,839 (2009 projected); Race: 87.5% White, 3.8% Black, 0.0% Asian, 71.3% Hispanic of any race (2004); Density: 331.4 persons per square mile (2004); Average household size: 5.46 (2004); Median age: 29.2 (2004); Male/female ratio: 138.6 (2004); Marriage status: 15.6% never married, 73.8% now married, 5.6% widowed, 5.1% divorced (2000); Foreign born: 22.5% (2000); Ancestry (includes multiple ancestries): 33.0% Other groups, 4.5% English, 3.6% German, 3.6% United States or American, 2.7% Irish (2000).
Economy: Single-family building permits issued: 1 (2004); Multi-family building permits issued: 0 (2004); Employment by occupation: 6.2% management, 7.3% professional, 13.9% services, 14.1% sales, 36.9% farming, 10.6% construction, 11.0% production (2000).
Income: Per capita income: $13,576 (2004); Median household income: $29,653 (2004); Average household income: $38,745 (2004); Percent of households with income of $100,000 or more: 4.5% (2004); Poverty rate: 33.6% (2000).
Education: Percent of population age 25 and over with: High school diploma (including GED) or higher: 34.0% (2004); Bachelor's degree or higher: 4.4% (2004); Master's degree or higher: 1.4% (2004).

School District(s)

Volusia County School District (PK-12)
2002-03 Enrollment: 63,000 . . . . (386) 734-7190
Housing: Homeownership rate: 70.2% (2004); Median home value: $92,286 (2004); Median rent: $319 per month (2000); Median age of housing: 31 years (2000).
Transportation: Commute to work: 95.7% car, 0.0% public transportation, 0.9% walk, 2.7% work from home (2000); Travel time to work: 32.8% less than 15 minutes, 33.9% 15 to 30 minutes, 19.8% 30 to 45 minutes, 6.5% 45 to 60 minutes, 7.0% 60 minutes or more (2000)

PONCE INLET (town). Aka Ponce Park. Covers a land area of 4.332 square miles and a water area of 10.341 square miles. Located at 29.09° N. Lat.; 80.94° W. Long. Elevation is 10 feet.
Population: 1,704 (1990); 2,513 (2000); 2,896 (2004); 3,360 (2009 projected); Race: 97.6% White, 0.8% Black, 0.7% Asian, 1.7% Hispanic of any race (2004); Density: 668.6 persons per square mile (2004); Average household size: 2.06 (2004); Median age: 57.1 (2004); Male/female ratio: 94.9 (2004); Marriage status: 13.1% never married, 70.6% now married, 6.6% widowed, 9.7% divorced (2000); Foreign born: 7.0% (2000); Ancestry (includes multiple ancestries): 20.3% German, 15.1% Irish, 13.8% Italian, 13.4% English, 11.1% United States or American (2000).
Economy: Single-family building permits issued: 15 (2004); Multi-family building permits issued: 0 (2004); Employment by occupation: 24.6% management, 23.6% professional, 12.5% services, 28.5% sales, 0.2% farming, 4.9% construction, 5.8% production (2000).
Income: Per capita income: $40,024 (2004); Median household income: $59,644 (2004); Average household income: $82,616 (2004); Percent of households with income of $100,000 or more: 23.2% (2004); Poverty rate: 5.1% (2000).
Taxes: Total city taxes per capita: $641 (2002); City property taxes per capita: $573 (2002).
Education: Percent of population age 25 and over with: High school diploma (including GED) or higher: 92.2% (2004); Bachelor's degree or higher: 31.9% (2004); Master's degree or higher: 12.8% (2004).
Housing: Homeownership rate: 90.8% (2004); Median home value: $197,122 (2004); Median rent: $1,000 per month (2000); Median age of housing: 14 years (2000).
Safety: Violent crime rate: 22.0 per 10,000 population; Property crime rate: 205.0 per 10,000 population (2003).
Transportation: Commute to work: 86.3% car, 1.2% public transportation, 1.6% walk, 8.2% work from home (2000); Travel time to work: 14.9% less than 15 minutes, 48.6% 15 to 30 minutes, 18.9% 30 to 45 minutes, 9.4% 45 to 60 minutes, 8.3% 60 minutes or more (2000)

PORT ORANGE (city). Covers a land area of 24.706 square miles and a water area of 1.969 square miles. Located at 29.11° N. Lat.; 81.00° W. Long. Elevation is 20 feet.
History: Port Orange was established in 1861 and developed as a shrimp and oyster center on the west bank of the Halifax River. The Dunlawton Sugar Mill was built here in the 1700's and was still used as late as 1880.
Population: 37,779 (1990); 45,823 (2000); 51,528 (2004); 58,398 (2009 projected); Race: 94.9% White, 2.0% Black, 1.3% Asian, 2.9% Hispanic of any race (2004); Density: 2,085.6 persons per square mile (2004); Average household size: 2.31 (2004); Median age: 45.3 (2004); Male/female ratio: 91.5 (2004); Marriage status: 18.1% never married, 60.1% now married, 9.7% widowed, 12.1% divorced (2000); Foreign born: 5.7% (2000); Ancestry (includes multiple ancestries): 18.2% German, 15.7% Irish, 14.0% English, 11.1% Italian, 8.3% Other groups (2000).
Economy: Unemployment rate: 3.7% (2004); Total civilian labor force: 21,028 (2004); Single-family building permits issued: 504 (2004); Multi-family building permits issued: 40 (2004); Employment by occupation: 12.5% management, 17.6% professional, 17.6% services, 31.4% sales, 0.3% farming, 11.1% construction, 9.5% production (2000).
Income: Per capita income: $22,984 (2004); Median household income: $42,609 (2004); Average household income: $52,542 (2004); Percent of households with income of $100,000 or more: 8.8% (2004); Poverty rate: 7.6% (2000).
Taxes: Total city taxes per capita: $359 (2002); City property taxes per capita: $133 (2002).
Education: Percent of population age 25 and over with: High school diploma (including GED) or higher: 84.8% (2004); Bachelor's degree or higher: 17.3% (2004); Master's degree or higher: 5.7% (2004).

School District(s)

Volusia County School District (PK-12)
2002-03 Enrollment: 63,000 . . . . (386) 734-7190

Housing: Homeownership rate: 82.1% (2004); Median home value: $116,923 (2004); Median rent: $580 per month (2000); Median age of housing: 17 years (2000).
Safety: Violent crime rate: 8.8 per 10,000 population; Property crime rate: 202.9 per 10,000 population (2003).
Transportation: Commute to work: 95.0% car, 0.5% public transportation, 0.8% walk, 2.2% work from home (2000); Travel time to work: 28.0% less than 15 minutes, 48.4% 15 to 30 minutes, 13.8% 30 to 45 minutes, 3.0% 45 to 60 minutes, 6.7% 60 minutes or more (2000)

Additional Information Contacts

Local Government Offices . . . . (386) 756-5200

SAMSULA-SPRUCE CREEK (CDP).

Covers a land area of 19.918 square miles and a water area of 0.012 square miles. Located at 29.06° N. Lat.; 81.05° W. Long.
Population: 2,929 (1990); 4,877 (2000); 5,886 (2004); 7,003 (2009 projected); Race: 96.9% White, 0.4% Black, 0.8% Asian, 1.8% Hispanic of any race (2004); Density: 295.5 persons per square mile (2004); Average household size: 2.46 (2004); Median age: 47.8 (2004); Male/female ratio: 97.6 (2004); Marriage status: 15.8% never married, 68.2% now married, 5.8% widowed, 10.2% divorced (2000); Foreign born: 5.0% (2000); Ancestry (includes multiple ancestries): 24.4% German, 19.9% English, 13.0% Irish, 7.4% Other groups, 6.8% Italian (2000).
Economy: Employment by occupation: 16.3% management, 18.1% professional, 12.1% services, 26.1% sales, 2.2% farming, 14.2% construction, 11.0% production (2000).
Income: Per capita income: $38,833 (2004); Median household income: $70,167 (2004); Average household income: $95,557 (2004); Percent of households with income of $100,000 or more: 33.4% (2004); Poverty rate: 5.4% (2000).
Education: Percent of population age 25 and over with: High school diploma (including GED) or higher: 90.1% (2004); Bachelor's degree or higher: 30.7% (2004); Master's degree or higher: 10.5% (2004).
Housing: Homeownership rate: 91.4% (2004); Median home value: $230,725 (2004); Median rent: $535 per month (2000); Median age of housing: 13 years (2000).
Transportation: Commute to work: 89.0% car, 0.0% public transportation, 0.4% walk, 8.2% work from home (2000); Travel time to work: 16.9% less than 15 minutes, 53.1% 15 to 30 minutes, 20.7% 30 to 45 minutes, 2.1% 45 to 60 minutes, 7.2% 60 minutes or more (2000)

SEVILLE (unincorporated postal area, zip code 32190).

Covers a land area of 28.726 square miles and a water area of 3.739 square miles. Located at 29.33° N. Lat.; 81.50° W. Long. Elevation is 55 feet.
History: Seville was named for the small Seville orange which grew wild here. The trees, not native to the area, were reportedly planted by the Spaniards.
Population: 1,090 (2000); Race: 66.1% White, 19.5% Black, 0.0% Asian, 19.7% Hispanic of any race (2000); Density: 37.9 persons per square mile (2000); Age: 23.1% under 18, 19.6% over 64 (2000); Marriage status: 11.8% never married, 71.4% now married, 8.6% widowed, 8.2% divorced (2000); Foreign born: 8.1% (2000); Ancestry (includes multiple ancestries): 31.3% Other groups, 18.1% English, 13.6% Irish, 10.8% United States or American, 8.1% German (2000).
Economy: Employment by occupation: 9.8% management, 6.6% professional, 13.7% services, 24.9% sales, 15.1% farming, 5.9% construction, 23.8% production (2000).
Income: Per capita income: $14,029 (2000); Median household income: $29,821 (2000); Poverty rate: 10.1% (2000).
Education: Percent of population age 25 and over with: High school diploma (including GED) or higher: 75.1% (2000); Bachelor's degree or higher: 2.8% (2000).

School District(s)

Volusia County School District (PK-12)
2002-03 Enrollment: 63,000 . . . . (386) 734-7190

Housing: Homeownership rate: 84.3% (2000); Median home value: $70,600 (2000); Median rent: $200 per month (2000); Median age of housing: 28 years (2000).
Transportation: Commute to work: 92.6% car, 0.0% public transportation, 4.6% walk, 2.8% work from home (2000); Travel time to work: 41.1% less than 15 minutes, 36.1% 15 to 30 minutes, 10.7% 30 to 45 minutes, 5.5% 45 to 60 minutes, 6.7% 60 minutes or more (2000)

SOUTH DAYTONA (city).

Aka Blake. Covers a land area of 3.563 square miles and a water area of 1.277 square miles. Located at 29.16° N. Lat.; 81.00° W. Long. Elevation is 11 feet.
Population: 12,549 (1990); 13,177 (2000); 13,481 (2004); 13,886 (2009 projected); Race: 86.5% White, 9.9% Black, 1.3% Asian, 3.2% Hispanic of any race (2004); Density: 3,783.5 persons per square mile (2004); Average household size: 2.25 (2004); Median age: 40.4 (2004); Male/female ratio: 93.0 (2004); Marriage status: 24.4% never married, 51.2% now married, 8.6% widowed, 15.9% divorced (2000); Foreign born: 6.3% (2000); Ancestry (includes multiple ancestries): 16.5% Irish, 14.7% English, 14.5% German, 14.0% Other groups, 10.8% United States or American (2000).
Economy: Single-family building permits issued: 3 (2004); Multi-family building permits issued: 4 (2004); Employment by occupation: 11.4% management, 15.9% professional, 20.4% services, 31.2% sales, 0.4% farming, 9.9% construction, 10.8% production (2000).
Income: Per capita income: $19,055 (2004); Median household income: $33,280 (2004); Average household income: $42,728 (2004); Percent of households with income of $100,000 or more: 4.4% (2004); Poverty rate: 10.7% (2000).
Taxes: Total city taxes per capita: $308 (2002); City property taxes per capita: $128 (2002).
Education: Percent of population age 25 and over with: High school diploma (including GED) or higher: 83.5% (2004); Bachelor's degree or higher: 14.3% (2004); Master's degree or higher: 4.1% (2004).

School District(s)

Volusia County School District (PK-12)
2002-03 Enrollment: 63,000 . . . . (386) 734-7190

Two-year College(s)

International Academy (Private, For-profit)
2003-04 Enrollment: 150 . . . . (386) 767-4600

Housing: Homeownership rate: 67.7% (2004); Median home value: $102,340 (2004); Median rent: $498 per month (2000); Median age of housing: 26 years (2000).
Safety: Violent crime rate: 39.3 per 10,000 population; Property crime rate: 505.4 per 10,000 population (2003).
Transportation: Commute to work: 93.8% car, 0.8% public transportation, 1.7% walk, 2.2% work from home (2000); Travel time to work: 34.3% less than 15 minutes, 48.7% 15 to 30 minutes, 10.3% 30 to 45 minutes, 2.1% 45 to 60 minutes, 4.6% 60 minutes or more (2000)

Additional Information Contacts

Local Government Offices . . . . (386) 322-3000

WEST DE LAND (CDP).

Covers a land area of 2.337 square miles and a water area of 0 square miles. Located at 29.01° N. Lat.; 81.32° W. Long.
Population: 3,302 (1990); 3,424 (2000); 3,274 (2004); 3,127 (2009 projected); Race: 85.8% White, 8.8% Black, 0.4% Asian, 8.2% Hispanic of any race (2004); Density: 1,400.8 persons per square mile (2004); Average household size: 2.64 (2004); Median age: 38.2 (2004); Male/female ratio: 98.1 (2004); Marriage status: 23.1% never married, 57.0% now married, 9.6% widowed, 10.3% divorced (2000); Foreign born: 7.2% (2000); Ancestry (includes multiple ancestries): 19.5% German, 18.5% Irish, 15.3% Other groups, 14.0% English, 10.4% United States or American (2000).
Economy: Employment by occupation: 9.7% management, 15.1% professional, 13.6% services, 31.6% sales, 0.8% farming, 15.4% construction, 13.7% production (2000).
Income: Per capita income: $20,415 (2004); Median household income: $40,904 (2004); Average household income: $53,202 (2004); Percent of households with income of $100,000 or more: 10.2% (2004); Poverty rate: 9.4% (2000).
Education: Percent of population age 25 and over with: High school diploma (including GED) or higher: 81.8% (2004); Bachelor's degree or higher: 17.0% (2004); Master's degree or higher: 8.0% (2004).
Housing: Homeownership rate: 83.6% (2004); Median home value: $90,937 (2004); Median rent: $440 per month (2000); Median age of housing: 32 years (2000).
Transportation: Commute to work: 94.5% car, 0.7% public transportation, 0.9% walk, 3.4% work from home (2000); Travel time to work: 41.2% less than 15 minutes, 28.2% 15 to 30 minutes, 12.3% 30 to 45 minutes, 7.6% 45 to 60 minutes, 10.7% 60 minutes or more (2000)

Wakulla County

Located in northwestern Florida; bounded on the south by Apalachee Bay of the Gulf of Mexico; drained by the St. Marks and Wakulla Rivers; includes part of Apalachicola National Forest. Covers a land area of 606.70 square miles, a water area of 129.10 square miles, and is located in the Eastern Time Zone. The county government was organized in 1843. County seat is Crawfordville.

Wakulla County is part of the Tallahassee, FL Metropolitan Statistical Area. The entire metro area includes: Gadsden County, FL; Jefferson County, FL; Leon County, FL; Wakulla County, FL

Population: 14,202 (1990); 22,863 (2000); 25,810 (2004); 29,514 (2009 projected); Race: 84.1% White, 13.6% Black, 0.3% Asian, 2.2% Hispanic of any race (2004); Density: 42.5 persons per square mile (2004); Average household size: 2.71 (2004); Median age: 37.0 (2004); Male/female ratio: 111.9 (2004).
Religion: Five largest groups: 12.1% Southern Baptist Convention, 3.8% The United Methodist Church, 2.4% National Primitive Baptist Convention, USA, 1.5% The Church of Jesus Christ of Latter-day Saints, 1.2% Assemblies of God (2000).
Economy: Unemployment rate: 2.9% (2004); Total civilian labor force: 13,815 (2004); Leading industries: 20.3% retail trade; 11.9% accommodation & food services; 9.4% construction (2003); Companies that employ 500 or more persons: 0 (2003); Companies that employ 100 to 499 persons: 3 (2003); Companies that employ less than 100 persons: 368 (2003); Farms: 126 totaling 10,900 acres (2002); Minority business ownership rate: n/a (1997); Women business ownership rate: 20.1% (1997); Retail sales per capita: $3,127 (1997). Single-family building permits issued: 496 (2004); Multi-family building permits issued: 29 (2004).
Income: Per capita income: $20,287 (2004); Median household income: $42,331 (2004); Average household income: $52,414 (2004); Percent of households with income of $100,000 or more: 9.9% (2004); Poverty rate: 12.2% (2002); Bankruptcy rate: 4.54% (2004).
Taxes: Total county taxes per capita: $343 (2002); County property taxes per capita: $207 (2002).
Education: Percent of population age 25 and over with: High school diploma (including GED) or higher: 78.1% (2004); Bachelor's degree or higher: 15.6% (2004); Master's degree or higher: 5.6% (2004).
Housing: Homeownership rate: 84.1% (2004); Median home value: $115,763 (2004); Median rent: $383 per month (2000); Median age of housing: 15 years (2000).
Health: Birth rate: 109.6 per 10,000 population (2004); Death rate: 67.3 per 10,000 population (2004); Age adjusted cancer mortality rate: 178.4 deaths per 100,000 population (2002); Air Quality Index: 94.5% good, 5.5% moderate, 0.0% unhealthy for sensitive individuals, 0.0% unhealthy (percent of days in 2004); Number of physicians: 6.1 per 10,000 population (2001); Hospital beds: 0.0 per 10,000 population (2002); Hospital admissions: 0.0 per 10,000 population (2002).
Elections: 2004 Presidential election results: 57.6% Bush, 41.6% Kerry, 0.4% Nader, 0.2% Badnarik
National and State Parks: Apalachicola National Forest; Edward Ball Wakulla Springs State Park; Ochlockonee River State Park; Saint Marks National Wildlife Refuge; San Marcos De Apalache Historic State Park
Additional Information Contacts
Wakulla County Government Offices . . . . (850) 926-0919
Crawfordville Chamber of Commerce . . . . (850) 926-1848

Wakulla County Communities

PANACEA (unincorporated postal area, zip code 32346). Covers a land area of 39.879 square miles and a water area of 1.821 square miles. Located at 29.98° N. Lat.; 84.38° W. Long. Elevation is 5 feet.
History: Panacea was known as Smith Springs until 1893, when the land around the five springs was purchased by settlers from Boston and renamed for the curative properties of the spring waters. A salt plant was operated here during the Civil War.
Population: 2,165 (2000); Race: 92.5% White, 6.4% Black, 0.6% Asian, 0.3% Hispanic of any race (2000); Density: 54.3 persons per square mile (2000); Age: 20.5% under 18, 16.2% over 64 (2000); Marriage status: 16.9% never married, 53.4% now married, 9.3% widowed, 20.5% divorced (2000); Foreign born: 1.7% (2000); Ancestry (includes multiple ancestries): 19.9% United States or American, 19.6% Other groups, 12.5% English, 8.5% German, 6.2% Irish (2000).
Economy: Employment by occupation: 16.8% management, 10.2% professional, 16.2% services, 25.5% sales, 3.7% farming, 14.3% construction, 13.2% production (2000).
Income: Per capita income: $17,336 (2000); Median household income: $28,875 (2000); Poverty rate: 16.2% (2000).
Education: Percent of population age 25 and over with: High school diploma (including GED) or higher: 76.8% (2000); Bachelor's degree or higher: 20.0% (2000).
Housing: Homeownership rate: 79.6% (2000); Median home value: $119,900 (2000); Median rent: $354 per month (2000); Median age of housing: 22 years (2000).
Transportation: Commute to work: 89.6% car, 0.6% public transportation, 1.7% walk, 8.1% work from home (2000); Travel time to work: 34.3% less than 15 minutes, 21.2% 15 to 30 minutes, 7.7% 30 to 45 minutes, 11.3% 45 to 60 minutes, 25.5% 60 minutes or more (2000)

SAINT MARKS (city). Covers a land area of 1.929 square miles and a water area of 0.013 square miles. Located at 30.15° N. Lat.; 84.20° W. Long. Elevation is 7 feet.
History: St. Marks grew as a fishing village on an inlet of Apalachee Bay. Nearby was St. Marks Fort, built in 1739 by the Spanish and later used by the English.
Population: 307 (1990); 272 (2000); 314 (2004); 363 (2009 projected); Race: 94.3% White, 2.9% Black, 0.0% Asian, 0.3% Hispanic of any race (2004); Density: 162.8 persons per square mile (2004); Average household size: 1.97 (2004); Median age: 45.9 (2004); Male/female ratio: 107.9 (2004); Marriage status: 14.3% never married, 56.7% now married, 13.8% widowed, 15.2% divorced (2000); Foreign born: 2.5% (2000); Ancestry (includes multiple ancestries): 19.1% English, 13.0% German, 13.0% Irish, 10.5% Other groups, 7.9% United States or American (2000).
Economy: Employment by occupation: 17.9% management, 22.8% professional, 17.9% services, 10.6% sales, 1.6% farming, 17.9% construction, 11.4% production (2000).
Income: Per capita income: $16,298 (2004); Median household income: $25,882 (2004); Average household income: $32,186 (2004); Percent of households with income of $100,000 or more: 3.1% (2004); Poverty rate: 19.5% (2000).
Taxes: Total city taxes per capita: $379 (2002); City property taxes per capita: $151 (2002).
Education: Percent of population age 25 and over with: High school diploma (including GED) or higher: 75.1% (2004); Bachelor's degree or higher: 10.1% (2004); Master's degree or higher: 4.2% (2004).
School District(s)
Wakulla County School District (PK-12)
2002-03 Enrollment: 4,663 . . . . (850) 926-7131
Housing: Homeownership rate: 72.3% (2004); Median home value: $101,829 (2004); Median rent: $298 per month (2000); Median age of housing: 30 years (2000).
Transportation: Commute to work: 86.2% car, 0.0% public transportation, 8.1% walk, 4.1% work from home (2000); Travel time to work: 22.9% less than 15 minutes, 10.2% 15 to 30 minutes, 29.7% 30 to 45 minutes, 19.5% 45 to 60 minutes, 17.8% 60 minutes or more (2000)

SOPCHOPPY (city). Covers a land area of 1.519 square miles and a water area of 0 square miles. Located at 30.06° N. Lat.; 84.49° W. Long. Elevation is 28 feet.
History: Sopchoppy developed around a lumber mill on the Sopchoppy River.
Population: 427 (1990); 426 (2000); 494 (2004); 577 (2009 projected); Race: 75.9% White, 19.8% Black, 1.2% Asian, 4.7% Hispanic of any race (2004); Density: 325.2 persons per square mile (2004); Average household size: 2.35 (2004); Median age: 37.2 (2004); Male/female ratio: 89.3 (2004); Marriage status: 23.7% never married, 59.9% now married, 10.9% widowed, 5.4% divorced (2000); Foreign born: 0.0% (2000); Ancestry (includes multiple ancestries): 25.9% Other groups, 14.6% United States or American, 12.4% English, 6.1% German, 5.4% Irish (2000).
Economy: Employment by occupation: 6.8% management, 19.3% professional, 20.5% services, 24.2% sales, 1.9% farming, 15.5% construction, 11.8% production (2000).
Income: Per capita income: $20,369 (2004); Median household income: $34,259 (2004); Average household income: $47,917 (2004); Percent of households with income of $100,000 or more: 6.7% (2004); Poverty rate: 17.1% (2000).

Education: Percent of population age 25 and over with: High school diploma (including GED) or higher: 70.5% (2004); Bachelor's degree or higher: 10.0% (2004); Master's degree or higher: 4.1% (2004).

School District(s)

Wakulla County School District (PK-12)
2002-03 Enrollment: 4,663 . . . . (850) 926-7131

Housing: Homeownership rate: 74.8% (2004); Median home value: $80,476 (2004); Median rent: $373 per month (2000); Median age of housing: 30 years (2000).

Transportation: Commute to work: 94.3% car, 0.0% public transportation, 3.8% walk, 1.9% work from home (2000); Travel time to work: 23.7% less than 15 minutes, 37.2% 15 to 30 minutes, 14.1% 30 to 45 minutes, 13.5% 45 to 60 minutes, 11.5% 60 minutes or more (2000)

Walton County

Located in northwestern Florida; bounded on the east by the Choctawhatchee River, on the north by Alabama, and on the south by Choctawhatchee Bay on the Gulf of Mexico; includes the highest point in the state (345 ft), and part of Choctawhatchee Nati onal Forest. Covers a land area of 1,057.60 square miles, a water area of 180.50 square miles, and is located in the Central Time Zone. The county government was organized in 1824. County seat is De Funiak Springs.

Weather Station: De Funiak Springs — Elevation: 229 feet

	Jan	Feb	Mar	Apr	May	Jun	Jul	Aug	Sep	Oct	Nov	Dec
High	62	66	73	79	86	90	92	91	88	80	71	65
Low	38	41	47	52	60	67	70	70	65	54	45	41
Precip	5.4	5.8	6.4	4.0	5.0	6.9	8.0	7.0	5.9	3.6	4.7	4.4
Snow	tr	tr	tr	0.0	0.0	0.0	0.0	0.0	0.0	0.0	0.0	0.0

High and Low temperatures in degrees Fahrenheit; Precipitation and Snow in inches

Population: 27,760 (1990); 40,601 (2000); 47,866 (2004); 56,987 (2009 projected); Race: 89.6% White, 5.9% Black, 0.5% Asian, 2.3% Hispanic of any race (2004); Density: 45.3 persons per square mile (2004); Average household size: 2.45 (2004); Median age: 40.7 (2004); Male/female ratio: 104.3 (2004).

Religion: Five largest groups: 20.2% Southern Baptist Convention, 4.7% The United Methodist Church, 2.5% Catholic Church, 1.5% Assemblies of God, 1.2% Presbyterian Church (U.S.A.) (2000).

Economy: Unemployment rate: 2.9% (2004); Total civilian labor force: 22,309 (2004); Leading industries: 19.8% accommodation & food services; 19.7% retail trade; 12.8% construction (2003); Companies that employ 500 or more persons: 1 (2003); Companies that employ 100 to 499 persons: 12 (2003); Companies that employ less than 100 persons: 1,162 (2003); Farms: 540 totaling 79,910 acres (2002); Minority business ownership rate: n/a (1997); Women business ownership rate: 29.5% (1997); Retail sales per capita: $7,177 (1997). Single-family building permits issued: 1,682 (2004); Multi-family building permits issued: 910 (2004).

Income: Per capita income: $21,436 (2004); Median household income: $37,952 (2004); Average household income: $51,930 (2004); Percent of households with income of $100,000 or more: 9.4% (2004); Poverty rate: 15.0% (2002); Bankruptcy rate: 3.17% (2004).

Taxes: Total county taxes per capita: $954 (2002); County property taxes per capita: $594 (2002).

Education: Percent of population age 25 and over with: High school diploma (including GED) or higher: 77.0% (2004); Bachelor's degree or higher: 17.3% (2004); Master's degree or higher: 6.5% (2004).

Housing: Homeownership rate: 79.0% (2004); Median home value: $111,617 (2004); Median rent: $383 per month (2000); Median age of housing: 14 years (2000).

Health: Birth rate: 104.2 per 10,000 population (2004); Death rate: 98.4 per 10,000 population (2004); Age adjusted cancer mortality rate: 216.6 deaths per 100,000 population (2002); Number of physicians: 8.2 per 10,000 population (2001); Hospital beds: 7.8 per 10,000 population (2002); Hospital admissions: 385.9 per 10,000 population (2002).

Elections: 2004 Presidential election results: 73.2% Bush, 25.9% Kerry, 0.5% Nader, 0.1% Badnarik

National and State Parks: Basin Bayou State Recreation Area; Deer Lake State Park; Eden Gardens State Park; Grayton Beach State Park; Topsail Hill Preserve State Park

Additional Information Contacts

Walton County Government Offices . . . . (850) 892-8115
Walton County Chamber of Commerce. . . . . (850) 267-0683

Walton County Communities

DE FUNIAK SPRINGS (city). Covers a land area of 10.967 square miles and a water area of 0.276 square miles. Located at 30.72° N. Lat.; 86.11° W. Long. Elevation is 236 feet.

History: De Funiak Springs was named for Colonel Fred DeFuniak, an official of the Louisville & Nashville Railroad. A Confederate monument was erected in 1871 in De Funiak Springs.

Population: 5,173 (1990); 5,089 (2000); 5,534 (2004); 6,109 (2009 projected); Race: 75.9% White, 18.6% Black, 0.6% Asian, 3.8% Hispanic of any race (2004); Density: 504.6 persons per square mile (2004); Average household size: 2.45 (2004); Median age: 40.0 (2004); Male/female ratio: 86.7 (2004); Marriage status: 23.7% never married, 49.1% now married, 12.6% widowed, 14.6% divorced (2000); Foreign born: 4.0% (2000); Ancestry (includes multiple ancestries): 34.1% Other groups, 13.8% United States or American, 9.9% Irish, 7.6% German, 6.6% English (2000).

Economy: Single-family building permits issued: 19 (2004); Multi-family building permits issued: 0 (2004); Employment by occupation: 6.0% management, 14.7% professional, 22.0% services, 30.2% sales, 0.6% farming, 11.9% construction, 14.5% production (2000).

Income: Per capita income: $15,555 (2004); Median household income: $27,944 (2004); Average household income: $36,751 (2004); Percent of households with income of $100,000 or more: 4.9% (2004); Poverty rate: 18.4% (2000).

Taxes: Total city taxes per capita: $288 (2002); City property taxes per capita: $111 (2002).

Education: Percent of population age 25 and over with: High school diploma (including GED) or higher: 71.8% (2004); Bachelor's degree or higher: 13.0% (2004); Master's degree or higher: 4.6% (2004).

School District(s)

Walton County School District (PK-12)
2002-03 Enrollment: 6,303 . . . . (850) 892-8331

Housing: Homeownership rate: 64.1% (2004); Median home value: $89,568 (2004); Median rent: $277 per month (2000); Median age of housing: 36 years (2000).

Hospitals: Healthmark Regional Medical Center (50 beds)

Safety: Violent crime rate: 133.5 per 10,000 population; Property crime rate: 806.5 per 10,000 population (2003).

Transportation: Commute to work: 90.2% car, 1.0% public transportation, 5.3% walk, 1.6% work from home (2000); Travel time to work: 43.6% less than 15 minutes, 12.6% 15 to 30 minutes, 9.9% 30 to 45 minutes, 21.5% 45 to 60 minutes, 12.5% 60 minutes or more (2000)

Airports: Defuniak Springs

Additional Information Contacts

Local Government Offices . . . . (850) 892-8500
Walton County Chamber of Commerce. . . . . (850) 267-0683

FREEPORT (city). Covers a land area of 10.782 square miles and a water area of 0.027 square miles. Located at 30.50° N. Lat.; 86.13° W. Long. Elevation is 32 feet.

Population: 917 (1990); 1,190 (2000); 1,346 (2004); 1,544 (2009 projected); Race: 94.0% White, 1.9% Black, 0.1% Asian, 1.1% Hispanic of any race (2004); Density: 124.8 persons per square mile (2004); Average household size: 2.37 (2004); Median age: 37.1 (2004); Male/female ratio: 98.5 (2004); Marriage status: 18.5% never married, 59.6% now married, 11.1% widowed, 10.8% divorced (2000); Foreign born: 1.1% (2000); Ancestry (includes multiple ancestries): 22.2% United States or American, 18.0% Other groups, 13.4% Irish, 9.3% English, 5.8% German (2000).

Economy: Employment by occupation: 6.4% management, 10.0% professional, 22.3% services, 28.9% sales, 0.4% farming, 18.6% construction, 13.3% production (2000).

Income: Per capita income: $16,269 (2004); Median household income: $29,551 (2004); Average household income: $38,620 (2004); Percent of households with income of $100,000 or more: 5.8% (2004); Poverty rate: 21.4% (2000).

Taxes: Total city taxes per capita: $370 (2002); City property taxes per capita: $84 (2002).

Education: Percent of population age 25 and over with: High school diploma (including GED) or higher: 63.8% (2004); Bachelor's degree or higher: 8.4% (2004); Master's degree or higher: 3.1% (2004).

School District(s)

Walton County School District (PK-12)
2002-03 Enrollment: 6,303 . . . . (850) 892-8331

Housing: Homeownership rate: 67.5% (2004); Median home value: $79,038 (2004); Median rent: $282 per month (2000); Median age of housing: 18 years (2000).
Transportation: Commute to work: 91.9% car, 0.0% public transportation, 1.0% walk, 4.6% work from home (2000); Travel time to work: 28.3% less than 15 minutes, 18.7% 15 to 30 minutes, 35.0% 30 to 45 minutes, 10.4% 45 to 60 minutes, 7.6% 60 minutes or more (2000)

MIRAMAR BEACH (CDP). Covers a land area of 4.598 square miles and a water area of 0.120 square miles. Located at 30.38° N. Lat.; 86.35° W. Long. Elevation is 5 feet.
Population: 1,644 (1990); 2,435 (2000); 3,143 (2004); 3,981 (2009 projected); Race: 96.4% White, 0.6% Black, 1.1% Asian, 1.4% Hispanic of any race (2004); Density: 683.6 persons per square mile (2004); Average household size: 2.02 (2004); Median age: 53.0 (2004); Male/female ratio: 96.7 (2004); Marriage status: 11.6% never married, 72.0% now married, 5.9% widowed, 10.6% divorced (2000); Foreign born: 4.7% (2000); Ancestry (includes multiple ancestries): 21.0% German, 15.4% Irish, 14.5% English, 14.0% United States or American, 8.1% Other groups (2000).
Economy: Employment by occupation: 23.8% management, 16.9% professional, 17.9% services, 33.6% sales, 0.0% farming, 3.8% construction, 3.9% production (2000).
Income: Per capita income: $33,646 (2004); Median household income: $54,034 (2004); Average household income: $66,557 (2004); Percent of households with income of $100,000 or more: 17.1% (2004); Poverty rate: 6.9% (2000).
Education: Percent of population age 25 and over with: High school diploma (including GED) or higher: 92.3% (2004); Bachelor's degree or higher: 40.1% (2004); Master's degree or higher: 13.6% (2004).
Housing: Homeownership rate: 80.2% (2004); Median home value: $238,450 (2004); Median rent: $775 per month (2000); Median age of housing: 10 years (2000).
Transportation: Commute to work: 89.0% car, 0.0% public transportation, 1.9% walk, 6.3% work from home (2000); Travel time to work: 45.5% less than 15 minutes, 37.7% 15 to 30 minutes, 10.3% 30 to 45 minutes, 3.8% 45 to 60 minutes, 2.7% 60 minutes or more (2000)

PAXTON (town). Covers a land area of 3.907 square miles and a water area of 0.066 square miles. Located at 30.97° N. Lat.; 86.31° W. Long. Elevation is 314 feet.
Population: 600 (1990); 656 (2000); 702 (2004); 755 (2009 projected); Race: 93.9% White, 1.6% Black, 0.0% Asian, 1.9% Hispanic of any race (2004); Density: 179.7 persons per square mile (2004); Average household size: 2.48 (2004); Median age: 39.4 (2004); Male/female ratio: 87.7 (2004); Marriage status: 17.1% never married, 57.8% now married, 9.6% widowed, 15.6% divorced (2000); Foreign born: 0.9% (2000); Ancestry (includes multiple ancestries): 30.0% United States or American, 14.8% Other groups, 13.6% Irish, 10.0% English, 2.3% Scotch-Irish (2000).
Economy: Employment by occupation: 5.5% management, 18.8% professional, 20.7% services, 19.6% sales, 3.0% farming, 17.3% construction, 15.1% production (2000).
Income: Per capita income: $15,011 (2004); Median household income: $27,500 (2004); Average household income: $37,235 (2004); Percent of households with income of $100,000 or more: 3.5% (2004); Poverty rate: 12.3% (2000).
Taxes: Total city taxes per capita: $46 (2002); City property taxes per capita: $0 (2002).
Education: Percent of population age 25 and over with: High school diploma (including GED) or higher: 55.4% (2004); Bachelor's degree or higher: 6.1% (2004); Master's degree or higher: 0.9% (2004).

School District(s)

Walton County School District (PK-12)
2002-03 Enrollment: 6,303 . . . . (850) 892-8331
Housing: Homeownership rate: 86.9% (2004); Median home value: $58,154 (2004); Median rent: $314 per month (2000); Median age of housing: 29 years (2000).
Transportation: Commute to work: 94.3% car, 0.0% public transportation, 3.4% walk, 1.1% work from home (2000); Travel time to work: 37.6% less than 15 minutes, 10.5% 15 to 30 minutes, 24.0% 30 to 45 minutes, 15.9% 45 to 60 minutes, 12.0% 60 minutes or more (2000)

SANTA ROSA BEACH (unincorporated postal area, zip code 32459). Aka Santa Rosa. Covers a land area of 64.998 square miles and a water area of 0.823 square miles. Located at 30.36° N. Lat.; 86.18° W. Long. Elevation is 4 feet.
Population: 6,210 (2000); Race: 93.3% White, 0.0% Black, 0.8% Asian, 2.1% Hispanic of any race (2000); Density: 95.5 persons per square mile (2000); Age: 19.5% under 18, 14.4% over 64 (2000); Marriage status: 20.9% never married, 58.1% now married, 6.0% widowed, 15.0% divorced (2000); Foreign born: 4.3% (2000); Ancestry (includes multiple ancestries): 25.1% English, 18.0% German, 16.4% Irish, 13.3% Other groups, 10.9% United States or American (2000).
Economy: Employment by occupation: 16.2% management, 13.8% professional, 24.6% services, 25.6% sales, 2.0% farming, 12.2% construction, 5.6% production (2000).
Income: Per capita income: $28,132 (2000); Median household income: $42,359 (2000); Poverty rate: 6.8% (2000).
Education: Percent of population age 25 and over with: High school diploma (including GED) or higher: 90.0% (2000); Bachelor's degree or higher: 31.5% (2000).

School District(s)

Walton County School District (PK-12)
2002-03 Enrollment: 6,303 . . . . (850) 892-8331
Housing: Homeownership rate: 76.0% (2000); Median home value: $161,500 (2000); Median rent: $637 per month (2000); Median age of housing: 10 years (2000).
Newspapers: The Walton Sun (General - Circulation 14,000)
Transportation: Commute to work: 91.3% car, 0.4% public transportation, 1.5% walk, 4.4% work from home (2000); Travel time to work: 40.4% less than 15 minutes, 34.1% 15 to 30 minutes, 12.5% 30 to 45 minutes, 9.5% 45 to 60 minutes, 3.4% 60 minutes or more (2000)

Washington County

Located in northwestern Florida; bounded on the west by the Choctawhatchee River; includes many small lakes. Covers a land area of 579.90 square miles, a water area of 35.90 square miles, and is located in the Central Time Zone. The county government was organized in 1825. County seat is Chipley.

Weather Station: Chipley 3 E — Elevation: 127 feet

	Jan	Feb	Mar	Apr	May	Jun	Jul	Aug	Sep	Oct	Nov	Dec
High	60	65	72	78	85	90	91	91	88	80	71	63
Low	38	40	47	53	61	68	71	70	66	54	45	40
Precip	6.1	5.0	6.2	3.8	4.3	5.3	6.9	5.5	4.6	3.1	3.9	3.8
Snow	tr	0.0	0.0	0.0	0.0	0.0	0.0	0.0	0.0	0.0	0.0	0.0

High and Low temperatures in degrees Fahrenheit; Precipitation and Snow in inches

Population: 16,919 (1990); 20,973 (2000); 21,884 (2004); 23,039 (2009 projected); Race: 81.9% White, 14.1% Black, 0.4% Asian, 2.4% Hispanic of any race (2004); Density: 37.7 persons per square mile (2004); Average household size: 2.67 (2004); Median age: 39.3 (2004); Male/female ratio: 110.1 (2004).
Religion: Five largest groups: 24.8% Southern Baptist Convention, 4.2% Assemblies of God, 3.5% The United Methodist Church, 3.2% Catholic Church, 1.4% National Association of Free Will Baptists (2000).
Economy: Unemployment rate: 3.9% (2004); Total civilian labor force: 9,311 (2004); Leading industries: 20.2% health care and social assistance; 18.9% retail trade; 8.9% accommodation & food services (2003); Companies that employ 500 or more persons: 1 (2003); Companies that employ 100 to 499 persons: 5 (2003); Companies that employ less than 100 persons: 368 (2003); Farms: 391 totaling 53,251 acres (2002); Minority business ownership rate: n/a (1997); Women business ownership rate: 13.1% (1997); Retail sales per capita: $5,158 (1997). Single-family building permits issued: 126 (2004); Multi-family building permits issued: 0 (2004).
Income: Per capita income: $15,966 (2004); Median household income: $30,603 (2004); Average household income: $41,752 (2004); Percent of households with income of $100,000 or more: 6.3% (2004); Poverty rate: 18.0% (2002); Bankruptcy rate: 3.39% (2004).
Education: Percent of population age 25 and over with: High school diploma (including GED) or higher: 70.8% (2004); Bachelor's degree or higher: 9.0% (2004); Master's degree or higher: 3.5% (2004).
Housing: Homeownership rate: 82.2% (2004); Median home value: $92,267 (2004); Median rent: $278 per month (2000); Median age of housing: 20 years (2000).
Health: Birth rate: 90.7 per 10,000 population (2004); Death rate: 111.2 per 10,000 population (2004); Age adjusted cancer mortality rate: 200.4 deaths per 100,000 population (2002); Number of physicians: 7.1 per 10,000 population (2001); Hospital beds: 36.9 per 10,000 population (2002); Hospital admissions: 335.2 per 10,000 population (2002).

Elections: 2004 Presidential election results: 71.1% Bush, 28.1% Kerry, 0.5% Nader, 0.1% Badnarik
National and State Parks: Falling Waters State Park
Additional Information Contacts
Washington County Government Offices. . . . . (850) 638-6200
Chipley Chamber of Commerce. . . . . (850) 638-4157
Washington County Chamber of Commerce . . . . (724) 225-3010

Washington County Communities

CARYVILLE (town). Covers a land area of 3.023 square miles and a water area of 0.128 square miles. Located at 30.77° N. Lat.; 85.81° W. Long. Elevation is 53 feet.
Population: 660 (1990); 218 (2000); 198 (2004); 191 (2009 projected); Race: 73.2% White, 19.7% Black, 0.0% Asian, 7.6% Hispanic of any race (2004); Density: 65.5 persons per square mile (2004); Average household size: 2.51 (2004); Median age: 32.3 (2004); Male/female ratio: 117.6 (2004); Marriage status: 22.4% never married, 48.3% now married, 16.7% widowed, 12.6% divorced (2000); Foreign born: 1.9% (2000); Ancestry (includes multiple ancestries): 28.5% United States or American, 17.8% Other groups, 9.8% German, 9.3% Irish, 4.7% Dutch (2000).
Economy: Farming, lumbering. Employment by occupation: 0.0% management, 5.2% professional, 23.4% services, 23.4% sales, 0.0% farming, 28.6% construction, 19.5% production (2000).
Income: Per capita income: $11,591 (2004); Median household income: $22,500 (2004); Average household income: $29,051 (2004); Percent of households with income of $100,000 or more: 3.8% (2004); Poverty rate: 37.3% (2000).
Education: Percent of population age 25 and over with: High school diploma (including GED) or higher: 53.7% (2004); Bachelor's degree or higher: 3.3% (2004); Master's degree or higher: 0.0% (2004).
Housing: Homeownership rate: 78.5% (2004); Median home value: $58,000 (2004); Median rent: $275 per month (2000); Median age of housing: 18 years (2000).
Transportation: Commute to work: 93.5% car, 0.0% public transportation, 0.0% walk, 2.6% work from home (2000); Travel time to work: 26.7% less than 15 minutes, 25.3% 15 to 30 minutes, 26.7% 30 to 45 minutes, 2.7% 45 to 60 minutes, 18.7% 60 minutes or more (2000)

CHIPLEY (city). Covers a land area of 4.117 square miles and a water area of 0 square miles. Located at 30.77° N. Lat.; 85.53° W. Long. Elevation is 119 feet.
History: Chipley was founded in 1882 when the Pensacola & Atlantic Railroad arrived in the area. First called Orange, the town was later named for railroad official Colonel William D. Chipley.
Population: 3,894 (1990); 3,592 (2000); 3,564 (2004); 3,566 (2009 projected); Race: 66.7% White, 30.1% Black, 0.6% Asian, 1.4% Hispanic of any race (2004); Density: 865.7 persons per square mile (2004); Average household size: 2.51 (2004); Median age: 40.7 (2004); Male/female ratio: 84.8 (2004); Marriage status: 24.6% never married, 54.1% now married, 13.7% widowed, 7.6% divorced (2000); Foreign born: 1.0% (2000); Ancestry (includes multiple ancestries): 27.7% Other groups, 16.4% United States or American, 9.6% Irish, 7.7% English, 5.0% German (2000).
Economy: Employment by occupation: 6.9% management, 20.8% professional, 21.7% services, 19.6% sales, 2.9% farming, 14.9% construction, 13.1% production (2000).
Income: Per capita income: $14,155 (2004); Median household income: $23,924 (2004); Average household income: $35,376 (2004); Percent of households with income of $100,000 or more: 5.4% (2004); Poverty rate: 27.7% (2000).
Taxes: Total city taxes per capita: $295 (2002); City property taxes per capita: $100 (2002).
Education: Percent of population age 25 and over with: High school diploma (including GED) or higher: 66.2% (2004); Bachelor's degree or higher: 12.6% (2004); Master's degree or higher: 5.9% (2004).

School District(s)

Washington County School District (PK-12)
2002-03 Enrollment: 3,410 . . . . (850) 638-6222

Two-year College(s)

Washington-Holmes Technical Center (Public)
2003-04 Enrollment: 645 . . . . (850) 638-1180
Housing: Homeownership rate: 63.6% (2004); Median home value: $77,813 (2004); Median rent: $273 per month (2000); Median age of housing: 36 years (2000).
Hospitals: Northwest Florida Community Hospital (81 beds)
Safety: Violent crime rate: 30.1 per 10,000 population; Property crime rate: 469.9 per 10,000 population (2003).
Newspapers: Washington County News (General - Circulation 4,200)
Transportation: Commute to work: 93.7% car, 0.0% public transportation, 0.9% walk, 3.3% work from home (2000); Travel time to work: 54.2% less than 15 minutes, 17.7% 15 to 30 minutes, 7.5% 30 to 45 minutes, 9.7% 45 to 60 minutes, 10.9% 60 minutes or more (2000); Amtrak: Service available.
Additional Information Contacts
Chipley Chamber of Commerce. . . . . (850) 638-4157

EBRO (town). Covers a land area of 3.150 square miles and a water area of 0.050 square miles. Located at 30.44° N. Lat.; 85.88° W. Long. Elevation is 62 feet.
Population: 257 (1990); 250 (2000); 252 (2004); 253 (2009 projected); Race: 79.4% White, 2.8% Black, 0.0% Asian, 4.4% Hispanic of any race (2004); Density: 80.0 persons per square mile (2004); Average household size: 2.42 (2004); Median age: 37.3 (2004); Male/female ratio: 98.4 (2004); Marriage status: 26.2% never married, 48.9% now married, 6.2% widowed, 18.7% divorced (2000); Foreign born: 1.5% (2000); Ancestry (includes multiple ancestries): 26.2% United States or American, 18.1% English, 17.7% Other groups, 16.2% Irish, 2.6% French (except Basque) (2000).
Economy: Employment by occupation: 15.3% management, 6.6% professional, 16.1% services, 25.5% sales, 2.2% farming, 13.9% construction, 20.4% production (2000).
Income: Per capita income: $16,726 (2004); Median household income: $31,667 (2004); Average household income: $40,529 (2004); Percent of households with income of $100,000 or more: 5.8% (2004); Poverty rate: 21.0% (2000).
Taxes: Total city taxes per capita: $108 (2002); City property taxes per capita: $0 (2002).
Education: Percent of population age 25 and over with: High school diploma (including GED) or higher: 70.1% (2004); Bachelor's degree or higher: 2.4% (2004); Master's degree or higher: 2.4% (2004).
Housing: Homeownership rate: 72.1% (2004); Median home value: $70,625 (2004); Median rent: $266 per month (2000); Median age of housing: 17 years (2000).
Transportation: Commute to work: 88.9% car, 1.5% public transportation, 4.4% walk, 3.7% work from home (2000); Travel time to work: 40.0% less than 15 minutes, 8.5% 15 to 30 minutes, 21.5% 30 to 45 minutes, 17.7% 45 to 60 minutes, 12.3% 60 minutes or more (2000)

VERNON (city). Covers a land area of 4.723 square miles and a water area of 0.003 square miles. Located at 30.62° N. Lat.; 85.71° W. Long. Elevation is 47 feet.
Population: 778 (1990); 743 (2000); 811 (2004); 892 (2009 projected); Race: 78.7% White, 15.4% Black, 0.5% Asian, 1.4% Hispanic of any race (2004); Density: 171.7 persons per square mile (2004); Average household size: 2.53 (2004); Median age: 36.6 (2004); Male/female ratio: 82.7 (2004); Marriage status: 19.3% never married, 59.6% now married, 10.7% widowed, 10.4% divorced (2000); Foreign born: 0.7% (2000); Ancestry (includes multiple ancestries): 27.1% Other groups, 18.3% United States or American, 13.3% Irish, 10.3% German, 9.0% English (2000).
Economy: Employment by occupation: 8.3% management, 19.8% professional, 21.7% services, 18.2% sales, 3.6% farming, 13.8% construction, 14.6% production (2000).
Income: Per capita income: $13,725 (2004); Median household income: $22,652 (2004); Average household income: $33,201 (2004); Percent of households with income of $100,000 or more: 6.5% (2004); Poverty rate: 28.5% (2000).
Taxes: Total city taxes per capita: $168 (2002); City property taxes per capita: $31 (2002).
Education: Percent of population age 25 and over with: High school diploma (including GED) or higher: 60.0% (2004); Bachelor's degree or higher: 10.7% (2004); Master's degree or higher: 4.4% (2004).

School District(s)

Washington County School District (PK-12)
2002-03 Enrollment: 3,410 . . . . (850) 638-6222
Housing: Homeownership rate: 73.8% (2004); Median home value: $67,667 (2004); Median rent: $289 per month (2000); Median age of housing: 30 years (2000).
Transportation: Commute to work: 97.2% car, 0.0% public transportation, 0.8% walk, 0.8% work from home (2000); Travel time to work: 28.0% less than 15 minutes, 31.3% 15 to 30 minutes, 15.4% 30 to 45 minutes, 8.5% 45 to 60 minutes, 16.7% 60 minutes or more (2000)

Additional Information Contacts
Washington County Chamber of Commerce . . . . (724) 225-3010

WAUSAU (town). Covers a land area of 1.131 square miles and a water area of 0 square miles. Located at 30.63° N. Lat.; 85.58° W. Long. Elevation is 85 feet.
Population: 332 (1990); 398 (2000); 402 (2004); 404 (2009 projected); Race: 96.3% White, 0.0% Black, 0.0% Asian, 2.5% Hispanic of any race (2004); Density: 355.3 persons per square mile (2004); Average household size: 2.42 (2004); Median age: 37.3 (2004); Male/female ratio: 96.1 (2004); Marriage status: 17.1% never married, 57.3% now married, 9.2% widowed, 16.4% divorced (2000); Foreign born: 1.0% (2000); Ancestry (includes multiple ancestries): 24.9% United States or American, 11.6% Other groups, 11.1% Irish, 8.1% German, 7.1% French (except Basque) (2000).
Economy: Employment by occupation: 7.0% management, 17.5% professional, 17.5% services, 13.2% sales, 2.6% farming, 31.6% construction, 10.5% production (2000).
Income: Per capita income: $11,474 (2004); Median household income: $22,333 (2004); Average household income: $27,786 (2004); Percent of households with income of $100,000 or more: 2.4% (2004); Poverty rate: 29.2% (2000).
Education: Percent of population age 25 and over with: High school diploma (including GED) or higher: 59.8% (2004); Bachelor's degree or higher: 4.6% (2004); Master's degree or higher: 1.1% (2004).
Housing: Homeownership rate: 75.3% (2004); Median home value: $65,000 (2004); Median rent: $288 per month (2000); Median age of housing: 21 years (2000).
Transportation: Commute to work: 83.3% car, 0.0% public transportation, 11.1% walk, 0.0% work from home (2000); Travel time to work: 22.2% less than 15 minutes, 47.2% 15 to 30 minutes, 7.4% 30 to 45 minutes, 7.4% 45 to 60 minutes, 15.7% 60 minutes or more (2000)

COMPARATIVE STATISTICS

Population

Place	1990	2000	2004 Estimate	2009 Projection
Altamonte Springs (city)	36,355	41,200	42,292	43,912
Apopka (city)	17,031	26,642	31,482	37,414
Boca Raton (city)	61,401	74,764	78,989	84,703
Bonita Springs (city)	17,511	32,797	33,119	33,867
Boynton Beach (city)	48,285	60,389	66,755	74,611
Bradenton (city)	43,699	49,504	52,762	57,157
Brandon (CDP)	57,304	77,895	89,337	103,484
Cape Coral (city)	75,507	102,286	121,513	145,256
Carol City (CDP)	53,331	59,443	63,841	69,306
Clearwater (city)	100,872	108,787	109,052	109,396
Coconut Creek (city)	27,509	43,566	49,172	56,036
Coral Gables (city)	41,660	42,249	42,765	43,889
Coral Springs (city)	78,602	117,549	129,110	143,768
Country Club (CDP)	23,164	36,310	41,543	47,744
Davie (town)	54,493	75,720	80,641	87,179
Daytona Beach (city)	62,186	64,112	64,908	66,482
Deerfield Beach (city)	55,289	64,583	65,162	66,513
Delray Beach (city)	47,833	60,020	63,914	69,065
Deltona (city)	49,242	69,543	77,005	86,143
Dunedin (city)	34,496	35,691	37,014	38,583
East Lake (CDP)	12,669	29,394	33,276	37,850
Egypt Lake-Leto (CDP)	28,830	32,782	35,932	39,999
Fort Lauderdale (city)	149,908	152,397	156,657	163,036
Fort Myers (city)	45,222	48,208	51,916	56,810
Fort Pierce (city)	38,676	37,516	37,876	38,748
Fountainbleau (CDP)	46,661	59,549	63,895	69,299
Gainesville (city)	90,519	95,447	96,546	98,536
Golden Glades (CDP)	25,312	32,623	34,047	35,967
Grtr Carrollwood (CDP)	29,062	33,519	35,291	37,695
Greenacres (city)	20,225	27,569	31,142	35,629
Hallandale (city)	30,997	34,282	34,425	34,897
Hialeah (city)	188,005	226,419	226,837	228,483
Hollywood (city)	121,944	139,357	143,197	149,134
Homestead (city)	28,451	31,909	35,065	38,903
Jacksonville (special city)	635,221	735,617	787,027	851,662
Jupiter (town)	30,117	39,328	45,619	53,259
Kendale Lakes (CDP)	48,524	56,901	58,568	60,849
Kendall (CDP)	69,644	75,226	78,094	81,815
Kendall West (CDP)	16,857	38,034	44,317	51,742
Kissimmee (city)	32,042	47,814	52,198	58,238
Lake Worth (city)	29,083	35,133	35,837	37,032
Lakeland (city)	73,375	78,452	82,714	88,319
Lakeside (CDP)	29,137	30,927	32,217	34,142
Largo (city)	70,008	69,371	70,311	71,543
Lauderdale Lakes (city)	27,341	31,705	32,030	32,623
Lauderhill (city)	49,135	57,585	58,733	60,654
Lehigh Acres (CDP)	22,352	33,430	39,664	47,354
Margate (city)	42,985	53,909	54,248	55,152
Melbourne (city)	61,834	71,382	75,124	80,059

Place	1990	2000	2004 Estimate	2009 Projection
Merritt Island (CDP)	32,886	36,090	36,829	37,941
Miami (city)	358,843	362,470	382,308	407,786
Miami Beach (city)	92,639	87,933	89,972	93,012
Miramar (city)	40,663	72,739	101,514	134,731
North Fort Myers (CDP)	34,213	40,214	44,149	49,310
North Lauderdale (city)	26,844	32,264	33,539	35,323
North Miami (city)	50,721	59,880	60,049	60,814
North Miami Beach (city)	34,812	40,786	41,085	41,640
North Port (city)	11,987	22,797	31,257	41,057
Oakland Park (city)	26,326	30,966	31,533	32,423
Ocala (city)	42,851	45,943	47,466	49,746
Orlando (city)	161,172	185,951	195,770	209,388
Ormond Beach (city)	32,157	36,301	37,383	38,861
Oviedo (city)	11,588	26,316	29,505	33,490
Palm Bay (city)	62,587	79,413	86,027	94,342
Palm Bch Gardens (city)	24,518	35,058	40,060	46,190
Palm Coast (city)	16,998	32,732	40,237	49,763
Palm Harbor (CDP)	50,255	59,248	60,321	61,688
Panama City (city)	36,193	36,417	37,037	37,855
Pembroke Pines (city)	66,095	137,427	151,196	168,456
Pensacola (city)	58,906	56,255	54,392	52,299
Pine Hills (CDP)	34,712	41,764	42,618	44,048
Pinellas Park (city)	45,348	45,658	45,714	45,834
Plant City (city)	23,296	29,915	31,872	34,477
Plantation (city)	66,997	82,934	84,421	86,938
Pompano Beach (city)	72,400	78,191	79,006	80,783
Port Charlotte (CDP)	41,534	46,451	47,874	50,019
Port Orange (city)	37,779	45,823	51,528	58,398
Port Saint Lucie (city)	55,843	88,769	105,317	125,342
Richmond West (CDP)	6,224	28,082	35,211	43,540
Riviera Beach (city)	27,791	29,884	30,859	32,234
Saint Petersburg (city)	238,846	248,232	251,151	255,155
Sanford (city)	33,887	38,291	47,786	59,036
Sarasota (city)	51,400	52,715	54,031	56,146
South Miami Hgts (CDP)	30,030	33,522	35,549	38,144
Spring Hill (CDP)	50,663	69,078	77,042	86,875
Sunrise (city)	64,675	85,779	88,453	92,416
Tallahassee (city)	128,014	150,624	158,930	169,401
Tamarac (city)	45,366	55,588	57,385	60,047
Tamiami (CDP)	39,068	54,788	58,931	64,038
Tampa (city)	279,960	303,447	325,584	354,535
The Hammocks (CDP)	26,829	47,379	54,215	62,366
Titusville (city)	39,970	40,670	41,313	42,423
Town 'n' Country (CDP)	60,978	72,523	76,301	81,569
University (CDP)	23,760	30,736	32,634	35,177
Wellington (village)	22,555	38,216	47,341	58,224
West Little River (CDP)	33,575	32,498	32,397	32,523
West Palm Beach (city)	68,172	82,103	88,904	97,544
Westchester (CDP)	29,883	30,271	30,493	30,995
Weston (city)	10,099	49,286	68,571	88,041
Winter Springs (city)	22,280	31,666	33,030	34,946

Physical Characteristics

Place	Density (persons per square mile)	Land Area (square miles)	Water Area (square miles)	Elevation (feet)
Altamonte Springs (city)	4,753.8	8.90	0.56	87
Apopka (city)	1,309.4	24.04	0.89	145
Boca Raton (city)	2,905.2	27.19	1.93	16
Bonita Springs (city)	938.5	35.29	5.72	12
Boynton Beach (city)	4,204.4	15.88	0.37	30
Bradenton (city)	4,357.6	12.11	2.33	25
Brandon (CDP)	3,110.8	28.72	0.57	48
Cape Coral (city)	1,155.2	105.19	9.91	5
Carol City (CDP)	8,372.8	7.62	0.11	8
Clearwater (city)	4,312.5	25.29	12.44	50
Coconut Creek (city)	4,258.8	11.55	0.24	17
Coral Gables (city)	3,256.2	13.13	24.02	10
Coral Springs (city)	5,400.1	23.91	0.24	13
Country Club (CDP)	9,634.1	4.31	0.20	n/a
Davie (town)	2,412.4	33.43	0.74	5
Daytona Beach (city)	1,106.2	58.68	6.25	10
Deerfield Beach (city)	4,853.7	13.43	1.50	16
Delray Beach (city)	4,159.0	15.37	0.53	20
Deltona (city)	2,152.3	35.78	2.54	50
Dunedin (city)	3,565.5	10.38	17.83	39
East Lake (CDP)	1,117.3	29.78	1.98	n/a
Egypt Lake-Leto (CDP)	6,019.4	5.97	0.22	n/a
Fort Lauderdale (city)	4,937.4	31.73	4.29	8
Fort Myers (city)	1,631.1	31.83	8.59	10
Fort Pierce (city)	2,569.3	14.74	6.02	5
Fountainbleau (CDP)	14,511.8	4.40	0.11	n/a
Gainesville (city)	2,003.8	48.18	0.92	183
Golden Glades (CDP)	6,924.6	4.92	0.06	n/a
Grtr Carrollwood (CDP)	3,687.9	9.57	0.71	n/a
Greenacres (city)	6,684.5	4.66	0.01	23
Hallandale (city)	8,177.0	4.21	0.34	10
Hialeah (city)	11,789.0	19.24	0.50	5
Hollywood (city)	5,237.6	27.34	3.46	11
Homestead (city)	2,454.9	14.28	0.09	9
Jacksonville (special city)	1,038.7	757.68	116.65	12
Jupiter (town)	2,281.1	20.00	1.13	8
Kendale Lakes (CDP)	7,166.4	8.17	0.43	n/a
Kendall (CDP)	4,842.7	16.13	0.22	10
Kendall West (CDP)	13,071.9	3.39	0.26	n/a
Kissimmee (city)	3,129.5	16.68	0.64	70
Lake Worth (city)	6,350.3	5.64	0.82	19
Lakeland (city)	1,804.3	45.84	5.61	190
Lakeside (CDP)	2,125.9	15.15	2.26	n/a
Largo (city)	4,489.1	15.66	0.46	40
Lauderdale Lakes (city)	8,922.7	3.59	0.05	7
Lauderhill (city)	8,050.2	7.30	0.04	7
Lehigh Acres (CDP)	418.0	94.89	1.09	23
Margate (city)	6,159.0	8.81	0.17	12
Melbourne (city)	2,487.8	30.20	5.29	21

Place	Density (persons per square mile)	Land Area (square miles)	Water Area (square miles)	Elevation (feet)
Merritt Island (CDP)	2,086.5	17.65	29.40	15
Miami (city)	10,717.0	35.67	19.59	15
Miami Beach (city)	12,792.0	7.03	11.67	5
Miramar (city)	3,441.2	29.50	1.50	6
North Fort Myers (CDP)	839.0	52.62	1.97	7
North Lauderdale (city)	8,647.9	3.88	0.03	11
North Miami (city)	7,099.9	8.46	1.53	10
North Miami Beach (city)	8,291.0	4.96	0.34	10
North Port (city)	418.0	74.77	0.77	11
Oakland Park (city)	5,004.6	6.30	0.60	8
Ocala (city)	1,228.6	38.63	0.00	73
Orlando (city)	2,093.9	93.50	7.46	106
Ormond Beach (city)	1,451.8	25.75	3.32	6
Oviedo (city)	1,949.6	15.13	0.32	48
Palm Bay (city)	1,351.7	63.65	3.10	19
Palm Bch Gardens (city)	719.4	55.68	0.25	20
Palm Coast (city)	793.4	50.72	0.98	10
Palm Harbor (CDP)	3,366.7	17.92	8.67	50
Panama City (city)	1,805.0	20.52	6.17	33
Pembroke Pines (city)	4,574.2	33.05	1.38	7
Pensacola (city)	2,396.6	22.70	16.96	32
Pine Hills (CDP)	5,547.9	7.68	0.24	115
Pinellas Park (city)	3,099.6	14.75	0.19	18
Plant City (city)	1,408.4	22.63	0.12	130
Plantation (city)	3,883.6	21.74	0.19	7
Pompano Beach (city)	3,844.1	20.55	1.60	13
Port Charlotte (CDP)	2,149.8	22.27	1.59	8
Port Orange (city)	2,085.6	24.71	1.97	20
Port Saint Lucie (city)	1,394.2	75.54	1.15	20
Richmond West (CDP)	8,426.6	4.18	0.09	n/a
Riviera Beach (city)	3,702.3	8.34	1.51	11
Saint Petersburg (city)	4,212.0	59.63	73.45	44
Sanford (city)	2,501.0	19.11	3.49	35
Sarasota (city)	3,628.2	14.89	11.04	27
South Miami Hgts (CDP)	7,211.6	4.93	0.00	n/a
Spring Hill (CDP)	1,450.0	53.13	1.71	209
Sunrise (city)	4,859.4	18.20	0.23	5
Tallahassee (city)	1,660.6	95.71	2.54	188
Tamarac (city)	5,037.6	11.39	0.50	11
Tamiami (CDP)	8,025.6	7.34	0.23	n/a
Tampa (city)	2,905.3	112.07	58.53	48
The Hammocks (CDP)	6,896.9	7.86	0.17	n/a
Titusville (city)	1,943.6	21.26	4.65	18
Town 'n' Country (CDP)	3,223.1	23.67	0.74	n/a
University (CDP)	8,431.7	3.87	0.01	n/a
Wellington (village)	1,524.5	31.05	0.31	n/a
West Little River (CDP)	7,071.2	4.58	0.05	n/a
West Palm Beach (city)	1,612.3	55.14	3.06	21
Westchester (CDP)	7,595.2	4.01	0.00	n/a
Weston (city)	2,885.8	23.76	2.52	n/a
Winter Springs (city)	2,302.4	14.35	0.14	49

NOTE: Population and Population Density figures as of 2004. Land Area and Water Area figures as of 2000.

Population by Race/Hispanic Origin

Place	White Alone (%)	Black Alone (%)	Asian Alone (%)	Hispanic (%)
Altamonte Springs (city)	76.2	11.0	3.4	18.7
Apopka (city)	69.2	18.6	2.1	21.5
Boca Raton (city)	89.5	4.3	2.2	10.7
Bonita Springs (city)	86.3	0.5	0.4	22.9
Boynton Beach (city)	67.1	24.5	2.1	11.8
Bradenton (city)	75.7	16.4	1.0	13.3
Brandon (CDP)	77.4	12.3	2.6	15.7
Cape Coral (city)	90.7	2.9	1.1	11.6
Carol City (CDP)	38.9	50.9	0.5	45.0
Clearwater (city)	81.4	11.0	1.9	11.6
Coconut Creek (city)	80.9	8.8	3.3	15.9
Coral Gables (city)	91.6	3.4	1.6	49.5
Coral Springs (city)	76.4	12.0	4.3	19.8
Country Club (CDP)	62.0	22.2	2.0	65.2
Davie (town)	83.8	5.7	3.5	24.1
Daytona Beach (city)	60.4	34.2	2.0	4.0
Deerfield Beach (city)	75.7	16.0	1.7	11.1
Delray Beach (city)	64.1	27.9	1.3	8.5
Deltona (city)	80.6	9.1	1.0	22.2
Dunedin (city)	93.5	2.6	1.5	4.1
East Lake (CDP)	93.5	1.5	3.0	4.7
Egypt Lake-Leto (CDP)	72.6	9.7	3.9	51.5
Fort Lauderdale (city)	61.8	30.1	1.2	10.9
Fort Myers (city)	52.0	36.1	1.2	17.6
Fort Pierce (city)	46.7	42.5	1.0	17.9
Fountainbleau (CDP)	86.9	2.0	1.7	88.3
Gainesville (city)	65.9	26.0	4.2	6.2
Golden Glades (CDP)	19.0	69.6	1.3	16.9
Grtr Carrollwood (CDP)	82.5	6.8	3.7	21.8
Greenacres (city)	78.2	8.5	2.4	28.3
Hallandale (city)	73.9	17.7	1.3	23.8
Hialeah (city)	87.9	2.6	0.4	91.8
Hollywood (city)	73.6	14.5	2.4	28.4
Homestead (city)	60.5	22.1	0.7	57.9
Jacksonville (special city)	61.1	31.5	3.2	4.5
Jupiter (town)	93.5	1.4	1.4	10.2
Kendale Lakes (CDP)	87.3	2.0	1.6	82.1
Kendall (CDP)	86.5	4.1	2.7	57.3
Kendall West (CDP)	83.7	3.5	1.2	84.4
Kissimmee (city)	62.4	10.4	3.6	50.9
Lake Worth (city)	60.6	20.0	0.8	36.6
Lakeland (city)	71.7	22.5	1.5	7.4
Lakeside (CDP)	84.3	7.9	2.9	6.0
Largo (city)	90.7	3.7	2.1	5.2
Lauderdale Lakes (city)	17.0	73.8	1.0	5.7
Lauderhill (city)	27.1	64.6	1.7	7.5
Lehigh Acres (CDP)	79.5	11.7	0.9	18.2
Margate (city)	71.8	16.0	3.5	19.7
Melbourne (city)	83.3	10.0	2.5	6.2

Place	White Alone (%)	Black Alone (%)	Asian Alone (%)	Hispanic (%)
Merritt Island (CDP)	90.0	5.2	1.8	4.2
Miami (city)	67.6	20.9	0.6	67.8
Miami Beach (city)	87.0	3.7	1.3	57.8
Miramar (city)	40.0	45.5	3.5	34.5
North Fort Myers (CDP)	95.1	1.5	0.6	4.2
North Lauderdale (city)	40.0	43.0	3.2	24.5
North Miami (city)	30.2	59.1	1.7	23.6
North Miami Beach (city)	43.1	41.6	3.9	33.5
North Port (city)	91.4	5.1	0.6	4.0
Oakland Park (city)	58.3	27.9	2.2	21.1
Ocala (city)	71.7	22.7	1.5	6.9
Orlando (city)	57.0	28.7	3.1	20.5
Ormond Beach (city)	93.9	2.9	1.6	2.5
Oviedo (city)	83.2	8.1	2.8	14.3
Palm Bay (city)	79.0	13.1	1.8	9.9
Palm Bch Gardens (city)	92.6	3.0	2.5	7.2
Palm Coast (city)	84.3	10.9	1.7	7.6
Palm Harbor (CDP)	94.9	1.3	1.6	4.1
Panama City (city)	73.4	21.8	1.5	2.5
Pembroke Pines (city)	69.6	16.7	4.7	35.8
Pensacola (city)	63.3	32.0	2.0	1.5
Pine Hills (CDP)	24.5	59.8	2.9	14.4
Pinellas Park (city)	86.3	2.8	5.4	7.6
Plant City (city)	69.5	16.1	1.0	20.4
Plantation (city)	73.0	17.4	3.6	15.9
Pompano Beach (city)	65.6	26.0	1.0	12.6
Port Charlotte (CDP)	87.8	7.8	1.4	6.0
Port Orange (city)	94.9	2.0	1.3	2.9
Port Saint Lucie (city)	84.6	9.5	1.5	9.2
Richmond West (CDP)	77.7	8.1	1.9	77.5
Riviera Beach (city)	25.5	69.4	1.2	5.8
Saint Petersburg (city)	68.0	24.7	3.2	4.9
Sanford (city)	57.1	33.2	1.2	12.6
Sarasota (city)	74.6	16.8	1.2	15.4
South Miami Hgts (CDP)	55.7	29.3	1.6	60.7
Spring Hill (CDP)	92.7	3.6	0.9	8.2
Sunrise (city)	63.0	24.7	3.7	21.2
Tallahassee (city)	58.7	36.0	2.3	4.2
Tamarac (city)	76.2	14.3	1.8	19.2
Tamiami (CDP)	90.4	0.9	0.5	88.7
Tampa (city)	61.9	27.4	2.5	21.2
The Hammocks (CDP)	78.6	6.3	2.9	72.3
Titusville (city)	82.4	13.9	1.0	3.8
Town 'n' Country (CDP)	75.0	9.6	3.6	34.0
University (CDP)	45.5	38.4	3.9	22.0
Wellington (village)	85.9	6.9	2.3	14.9
West Little River (CDP)	35.7	52.5	0.2	45.2
West Palm Beach (city)	54.4	34.3	1.8	20.7
Westchester (CDP)	94.3	0.7	0.5	87.2
Weston (city)	85.1	4.7	3.9	35.6
Winter Springs (city)	87.4	5.1	2.1	12.1

NOTE: Data as of 2004; (1) Figures are not in combination with any other race; (2) Persons of Hispanic Origin may be of any race

Avg. Household Size, Median Age, Male/Female Ratio & Foreign Born

Place	Average Household Size (persons)	Median Age (years)	Male/Female Ratio (males per 100 females)	Foreign Born (%)
Altamonte Springs (city)	2.18	34.9	93.0	12.7
Apopka (city)	2.80	33.8	94.2	11.8
Boca Raton (city)	2.34	43.6	95.2	18.0
Bonita Springs (city)	2.20	55.0	104.0	16.0
Boynton Beach (city)	2.31	42.0	88.6	17.4
Bradenton (city)	2.32	41.1	91.7	8.5
Brandon (CDP)	2.67	34.5	94.5	7.6
Cape Coral (city)	2.51	40.9	95.0	8.7
Carol City (CDP)	3.62	33.3	92.7	37.2
Clearwater (city)	2.25	42.8	92.0	13.2
Coconut Creek (city)	2.22	41.3	88.6	18.3
Coral Gables (city)	2.51	39.5	88.4	37.9
Coral Springs (city)	2.96	34.5	95.6	21.3
Country Club (CDP)	2.84	31.6	90.7	47.0
Davie (town)	2.66	35.9	95.9	17.5
Daytona Beach (city)	2.22	37.7	100.2	7.7
Deerfield Beach (city)	2.04	45.5	87.7	22.7
Delray Beach (city)	2.24	44.8	91.7	21.5
Deltona (city)	2.84	37.1	94.6	7.1
Dunedin (city)	2.05	49.1	84.8	9.7
East Lake (CDP)	2.51	43.0	94.9	9.6
Egypt Lake-Leto (CDP)	2.42	33.5	95.6	27.3
Fort Lauderdale (city)	2.20	40.2	110.8	21.7
Fort Myers (city)	2.51	32.0	98.7	13.4
Fort Pierce (city)	2.59	35.4	98.3	18.4
Fountainbleau (CDP)	2.85	36.4	87.4	73.1
Gainesville (city)	2.56	28.1	96.1	8.7
Golden Glades (CDP)	3.37	32.7	89.4	45.3
Grtr Carrollwood (CDP)	2.38	37.8	92.1	13.5
Greenacres (city)	2.28	40.4	88.5	19.3
Hallandale (city)	1.92	53.1	86.5	36.1
Hialeah (city)	3.21	39.4	93.0	72.1
Hollywood (city)	2.35	39.7	95.1	26.3
Homestead (city)	3.18	28.6	106.1	36.0
Jacksonville (special city)	2.57	34.4	94.2	5.9
Jupiter (town)	2.34	42.0	97.7	10.5
Kendale Lakes (CDP)	3.17	36.9	90.1	58.8
Kendall (CDP)	2.66	38.3	88.9	42.6
Kendall West (CDP)	3.31	32.5	90.1	59.4
Kissimmee (city)	2.80	30.8	99.3	19.5
Lake Worth (city)	2.56	35.6	108.6	35.6
Lakeland (city)	2.33	40.2	86.6	5.7
Lakeside (CDP)	2.82	35.8	96.2	5.7
Largo (city)	2.03	48.5	87.3	9.4
Lauderdale Lakes (city)	2.66	35.8	82.3	40.5
Lauderhill (city)	2.52	35.5	85.5	33.8
Lehigh Acres (CDP)	2.67	37.3	95.4	9.3
Margate (city)	2.39	41.1	90.8	22.0
Melbourne (city)	2.30	40.4	95.1	7.8
Merritt Island (CDP)	2.41	43.4	95.9	6.4

Place	Average Household Size (persons)	Median Age (years)	Male/Female Ratio (males per 100 females)	Foreign Born (%)
Miami (city)	2.69	39.4	99.3	59.5
Miami Beach (city)	1.91	41.1	105.0	55.5
Miramar (city)	3.21	31.8	92.1	40.7
North Fort Myers (CDP)	2.03	59.1	91.7	4.2
North Lauderdale (city)	3.00	30.7	94.6	34.9
North Miami (city)	2.97	33.1	93.0	48.5
North Miami Beach (city)	2.97	35.8	92.1	49.7
North Port (city)	2.53	40.5	92.6	12.1
Oakland Park (city)	2.30	36.2	109.4	29.6
Ocala (city)	2.48	38.6	91.1	4.6
Orlando (city)	2.27	33.5	94.5	14.4
Ormond Beach (city)	2.30	48.1	88.4	7.0
Oviedo (city)	3.13	33.0	98.2	9.2
Palm Bay (city)	2.59	37.5	95.5	9.5
Palm Bch Gardens (city)	2.21	45.8	90.1	10.8
Palm Coast (city)	2.39	49.1	91.3	12.5
Palm Harbor (CDP)	2.31	43.8	89.1	8.4
Panama City (city)	2.45	37.7	95.5	3.2
Pembroke Pines (city)	2.65	37.3	87.8	29.0
Pensacola (city)	2.27	40.0	89.6	3.6
Pine Hills (CDP)	3.18	30.4	93.3	22.4
Pinellas Park (city)	2.35	41.0	91.4	9.5
Plant City (city)	2.76	34.0	93.7	9.8
Plantation (city)	2.48	38.5	91.1	22.4
Pompano Beach (city)	2.21	43.2	98.3	20.3
Port Charlotte (CDP)	2.28	48.1	88.3	9.6
Port Orange (city)	2.31	45.3	91.5	5.7
Port Saint Lucie (city)	2.60	39.6	95.1	9.6
Richmond West (CDP)	3.67	31.0	95.7	45.6
Riviera Beach (city)	2.62	35.9	91.4	10.1
Saint Petersburg (city)	2.27	39.9	91.8	9.1
Sanford (city)	2.65	33.2	99.2	5.9
Sarasota (city)	2.24	41.2	95.4	13.9
South Miami Hgts (CDP)	3.41	33.0	93.5	44.1
Spring Hill (CDP)	2.44	47.2	90.0	6.7
Sunrise (city)	2.57	37.2	88.8	28.1
Tallahassee (city)	2.37	27.9	89.8	5.5
Tamarac (city)	2.03	52.8	82.0	21.3
Tamiami (CDP)	3.36	38.4	90.8	65.5
Tampa (city)	2.43	35.3	95.9	12.2
The Hammocks (CDP)	3.17	32.6	90.7	52.4
Titusville (city)	2.34	41.7	91.5	4.8
Town 'n' Country (CDP)	2.50	35.7	95.6	17.6
University (CDP)	2.24	27.9	97.7	15.0
Wellington (village)	2.96	36.7	95.9	13.4
West Little River (CDP)	3.40	35.4	95.9	35.0
West Palm Beach (city)	2.35	37.4	97.1	24.7
Westchester (CDP)	3.07	44.8	87.7	69.0
Weston (city)	3.04	34.6	94.7	28.0
Winter Springs (city)	2.68	38.2	94.7	8.1

NOTE: Average Household Size, Median Age, and Male/Female Ratio figures as of 2004. Foreign Born figures as of 2000.

Five Largest Ancestry Groups

Place	Group 1	Group 2	Group 3	Group 4	Group 5
Altamonte Springs (city)	Other (30.7%)	German (14.4%)	Irish (12.5%)	English (9.8%)	Italian (8.3%)
Apopka (city)	Other (30.1%)	German (12.6%)	Irish (10.9%)	American (8.9%)	English (7.9%)
Boca Raton (city)	Other (15.5%)	German (14.4%)	Italian (12.4%)	Irish (12.0%)	English (9.4%)
Bonita Springs (city)	German (20.5%)	Other (19.4%)	English (14.8%)	Irish (13.6%)	American (6.2%)
Boynton Beach (city)	Other (22.8%)	German (11.8%)	Irish (11.6%)	Italian (9.7%)	English (9.0%)
Bradenton (city)	Other (24.8%)	German (14.9%)	English (12.0%)	Irish (10.9%)	American (6.7%)
Brandon (CDP)	Other (27.1%)	German (14.4%)	Irish (12.5%)	English (11.4%)	American (8.5%)
Cape Coral (city)	German (20.9%)	Irish (15.9%)	Other (13.5%)	Italian (13.1%)	English (11.9%)
Carol City (CDP)	Other (70.8%)	Jamaican (5.2%)	American (4.8%)	Haitian (2.3%)	African (0.8%)
Clearwater (city)	Other (21.5%)	German (16.9%)	Irish (13.8%)	English (11.9%)	Italian (8.0%)
Coconut Creek (city)	Other (24.4%)	Italian (13.5%)	German (10.7%)	Irish (10.2%)	Polish (6.8%)
Coral Gables (city)	Other (54.0%)	English (7.4%)	German (7.0%)	Irish (5.7%)	Italian (5.3%)
Coral Springs (city)	Other (26.8%)	Italian (14.2%)	German (11.9%)	Irish (11.3%)	American (6.5%)
Country Club (CDP)	Other (72.7%)	American (3.8%)	Haitian (3.1%)	Irish (2.1%)	Italian (2.1%)
Davie (town)	Other (28.2%)	Irish (14.0%)	German (13.7%)	Italian (12.5%)	English (7.5%)
Daytona Beach (city)	Other (33.1%)	German (11.0%)	Irish (10.4%)	English (8.3%)	Italian (5.9%)
Deerfield Beach (city)	Other (23.2%)	Irish (10.8%)	Italian (10.6%)	German (9.6%)	English (7.2%)
Delray Beach (city)	Other (21.5%)	Haitian (10.6%)	German (10.5%)	Irish (10.3%)	English (8.1%)
Deltona (city)	Other (27.1%)	German (15.8%)	Irish (14.5%)	Italian (9.8%)	English (9.7%)
Dunedin (city)	German (21.3%)	Irish (17.2%)	English (14.6%)	Other (10.9%)	Italian (10.2%)
East Lake (CDP)	German (21.2%)	Irish (16.7%)	English (14.1%)	Italian (13.9%)	Other (10.9%)
Egypt Lake-Leto (CDP)	Other (54.6%)	German (7.6%)	Irish (6.8%)	Italian (6.3%)	American (5.5%)
Fort Lauderdale (city)	Other (27.5%)	German (10.4%)	Irish (10.3%)	English (8.2%)	Italian (7.6%)
Fort Myers (city)	Other (38.5%)	German (10.7%)	English (8.0%)	Irish (7.7%)	American (6.4%)
Fort Pierce (city)	Other (42.8%)	Irish (8.2%)	German (7.9%)	English (6.9%)	American (6.6%)
Fountainbleau (CDP)	Other (86.2%)	American (2.5%)	Italian (1.7%)	German (0.8%)	Irish (0.5%)
Gainesville (city)	Other (31.1%)	German (12.6%)	Irish (10.7%)	English (9.9%)	American (5.6%)
Golden Glades (CDP)	Other (36.4%)	Haitian (32.0%)	Jamaican (5.4%)	American (5.2%)	German (1.9%)
Grtr Carrollwood (CDP)	Other (31.0%)	German (13.9%)	Irish (12.7%)	English (10.2%)	Italian (8.9%)
Greenacres (city)	Other (30.9%)	Italian (13.1%)	German (12.0%)	Irish (10.9%)	English (7.4%)
Hallandale (city)	Other (33.9%)	Italian (9.2%)	German (5.9%)	American (5.4%)	Russian (5.1%)
Hialeah (city)	Other (85.0%)	American (2.6%)	Italian (0.7%)	German (0.6%)	Irish (0.5%)
Hollywood (city)	Other (33.5%)	Italian (9.5%)	Irish (9.1%)	German (8.6%)	American (7.0%)
Homestead (city)	Other (62.2%)	American (5.2%)	Haitian (4.8%)	Irish (4.2%)	German (4.0%)
Jacksonville (special city)	Other (35.5%)	German (9.6%)	American (9.3%)	Irish (9.0%)	English (8.5%)
Jupiter (town)	Irish (18.6%)	German (17.9%)	Italian (16.8%)	English (13.6%)	Other (12.2%)
Kendale Lakes (CDP)	Other (79.4%)	American (2.8%)	Italian (2.3%)	German (1.8%)	English (1.7%)
Kendall (CDP)	Other (59.3%)	German (5.7%)	American (5.4%)	Italian (5.1%)	Irish (5.0%)
Kendall West (CDP)	Other (82.8%)	American (2.5%)	Italian (2.1%)	German (1.6%)	English (1.2%)
Kissimmee (city)	Other (49.4%)	German (8.8%)	Irish (7.1%)	American (6.3%)	English (6.3%)
Lake Worth (city)	Other (34.6%)	German (8.7%)	Irish (8.5%)	Haitian (7.8%)	English (6.1%)
Lakeland (city)	Other (29.4%)	German (12.5%)	English (11.1%)	Irish (10.3%)	American (9.9%)
Lakeside (CDP)	Other (20.8%)	German (14.7%)	Irish (12.4%)	American (11.9%)	English (10.9%)
Largo (city)	German (18.3%)	Irish (15.4%)	English (13.9%)	Other (11.2%)	Italian (9.6%)
Lauderdale Lakes (city)	Other (35.3%)	Jamaican (17.9%)	Haitian (15.0%)	American (5.7%)	Italian (2.5%)
Lauderhill (city)	Other (33.8%)	Jamaican (17.0%)	Haitian (8.8%)	American (7.5%)	Italian (3.8%)
Lehigh Acres (CDP)	Other (22.4%)	German (15.1%)	Irish (12.4%)	American (11.9%)	English (10.6%)
Margate (city)	Other (27.6%)	Italian (12.8%)	German (11.2%)	Irish (11.2%)	English (6.5%)
Melbourne (city)	Other (20.2%)	German (16.7%)	Irish (14.7%)	English (12.8%)	Italian (8.2%)

Place	Group 1	Group 2	Group 3	Group 4	Group 5
Merritt Island (CDP)	German (19.6%)	English (16.0%)	Irish (15.5%)	Other (14.4%)	Italian (8.7%)
Miami (city)	Other (71.3%)	Haitian (5.0%)	American (3.1%)	Italian (1.4%)	German (1.2%)
Miami Beach (city)	Other (54.1%)	Italian (5.0%)	American (5.0%)	German (4.3%)	Russian (3.7%)
Miramar (city)	Other (47.8%)	Jamaican (15.5%)	Haitian (6.0%)	American (4.9%)	German (3.9%)
North Fort Myers (CDP)	German (20.0%)	English (15.7%)	Irish (14.0%)	American (10.0%)	Other (8.1%)
North Lauderdale (city)	Other (36.9%)	Jamaican (11.4%)	American (8.0%)	Italian (6.9%)	Haitian (6.9%)
North Miami (city)	Other (34.2%)	Haitian (31.1%)	American (5.5%)	Jamaican (3.1%)	German (2.4%)
North Miami Beach (city)	Other (43.2%)	Haitian (19.3%)	American (6.0%)	Jamaican (5.4%)	Italian (3.0%)
North Port (city)	German (21.8%)	Irish (15.8%)	English (11.9%)	Other (10.4%)	Italian (8.5%)
Oakland Park (city)	Other (32.4%)	German (10.3%)	Irish (9.6%)	Italian (8.0%)	Haitian (7.4%)
Ocala (city)	Other (26.9%)	German (13.2%)	Irish (11.8%)	English (11.1%)	American (6.8%)
Orlando (city)	Other (39.5%)	German (9.8%)	Irish (8.7%)	English (7.9%)	American (6.7%)
Ormond Beach (city)	German (17.6%)	English (16.9%)	Irish (14.8%)	Other (10.1%)	American (9.7%)
Oviedo (city)	Other (24.0%)	German (18.1%)	Irish (13.4%)	English (11.7%)	Italian (11.6%)
Palm Bay (city)	Other (21.9%)	German (17.9%)	Irish (14.6%)	English (10.1%)	Italian (9.2%)
Palm Bch Gardens (city)	German (17.2%)	Irish (15.2%)	Other (13.7%)	English (13.3%)	Italian (12.9%)
Palm Coast (city)	Other (17.5%)	Irish (16.9%)	German (15.9%)	Italian (15.3%)	English (11.9%)
Palm Harbor (CDP)	German (19.5%)	Irish (16.5%)	English (13.9%)	Italian (12.8%)	Other (8.9%)
Panama City (city)	Other (25.9%)	American (12.9%)	Irish (10.3%)	German (9.8%)	English (9.1%)
Pembroke Pines (city)	Other (42.2%)	Italian (9.4%)	Irish (8.2%)	German (8.1%)	American (6.1%)
Pensacola (city)	Other (33.4%)	English (11.0%)	German (10.5%)	Irish (10.0%)	American (7.7%)
Pine Hills (CDP)	Other (45.9%)	Haitian (11.5%)	American (6.6%)	German (4.8%)	Irish (4.2%)
Pinellas Park (city)	German (18.5%)	Other (17.8%)	Irish (15.8%)	English (11.6%)	Italian (8.4%)
Plant City (city)	Other (37.4%)	Irish (11.3%)	German (11.0%)	English (10.7%)	American (9.2%)
Plantation (city)	Other (26.8%)	German (10.8%)	Irish (10.2%)	Italian (8.9%)	American (8.0%)
Pompano Beach (city)	Other (29.3%)	German (9.7%)	Irish (9.7%)	Italian (8.9%)	English (6.5%)
Port Charlotte (CDP)	German (19.3%)	Irish (15.9%)	English (12.6%)	Other (12.4%)	Italian (10.4%)
Port Orange (city)	German (18.2%)	Irish (15.7%)	English (14.0%)	Italian (11.1%)	Other (8.3%)
Port Saint Lucie (city)	Irish (17.4%)	German (16.9%)	Italian (15.7%)	Other (15.4%)	English (11.5%)
Richmond West (CDP)	Other (79.4%)	American (5.4%)	Jamaican (3.4%)	Italian (2.7%)	Irish (2.2%)
Riviera Beach (city)	Other (57.1%)	German (4.4%)	English (4.1%)	Irish (3.8%)	American (3.4%)
Saint Petersburg (city)	Other (27.8%)	German (14.7%)	Irish (12.4%)	English (11.1%)	Italian (6.8%)
Sanford (city)	Other (38.8%)	German (10.7%)	Irish (9.2%)	English (9.1%)	American (6.2%)
Sarasota (city)	Other (27.0%)	German (14.0%)	English (10.5%)	Irish (10.5%)	American (6.2%)
South Miami Hgts (CDP)	Other (71.3%)	Jamaican (5.7%)	American (4.4%)	English (1.7%)	German (1.6%)
Spring Hill (CDP)	German (19.7%)	Italian (18.0%)	Irish (17.0%)	Other (12.8%)	English (11.0%)
Sunrise (city)	Other (33.8%)	Italian (10.3%)	Jamaican (8.0%)	Irish (7.4%)	German (7.4%)
Tallahassee (city)	Other (34.1%)	German (9.4%)	English (9.2%)	Irish (8.8%)	American (5.3%)
Tamarac (city)	Other (29.8%)	Italian (10.9%)	American (9.1%)	Irish (7.9%)	German (7.7%)
Tamiami (CDP)	Other (88.0%)	American (1.9%)	Italian (1.3%)	Irish (0.9%)	German (0.9%)
Tampa (city)	Other (42.3%)	German (9.2%)	Irish (8.4%)	English (7.7%)	American (6.2%)
The Hammocks (CDP)	Other (75.5%)	Italian (4.0%)	American (3.1%)	German (3.0%)	Jamaican (3.0%)
Titusville (city)	Other (19.4%)	German (16.7%)	Irish (13.4%)	English (12.4%)	American (8.9%)
Town 'n' Country (CDP)	Other (39.9%)	German (13.2%)	Irish (10.3%)	English (8.2%)	Italian (7.3%)
University (CDP)	Other (46.8%)	German (6.7%)	Irish (6.1%)	American (4.5%)	English (4.1%)
Wellington (village)	Other (19.0%)	Irish (15.1%)	Italian (14.6%)	German (13.6%)	English (11.2%)
West Little River (CDP)	Other (71.5%)	Haitian (5.2%)	American (4.7%)	Jamaican (1.7%)	African (1.7%)
West Palm Beach (city)	Other (40.1%)	German (7.5%)	Irish (7.0%)	English (6.2%)	American (5.2%)
Westchester (CDP)	Other (85.8%)	American (2.4%)	Italian (1.6%)	English (1.1%)	German (1.0%)
Weston (city)	Other (40.7%)	Italian (9.8%)	German (9.2%)	Irish (7.9%)	American (6.8%)
Winter Springs (city)	Other (19.0%)	German (18.2%)	Irish (15.6%)	English (12.8%)	Italian (10.8%)

NOTE: Data as of 2000; "Other" includes Hispanic and race groups. Please refer to the User's Guide for more information.

Marriage Status

Place	Never Married (%)	Now Married (%)	Widowed (%)	Divorced (%)
Altamonte Springs (city)	31.1	47.0	6.1	15.8
Apopka (city)	22.1	59.6	5.1	13.2
Boca Raton (city)	22.1	60.6	7.4	10.0
Bonita Springs (city)	14.0	68.8	8.1	9.1
Boynton Beach (city)	21.5	55.6	11.1	11.8
Bradenton (city)	22.4	52.7	12.3	12.6
Brandon (CDP)	22.9	62.3	4.4	10.4
Cape Coral (city)	17.0	64.6	7.1	11.3
Carol City (CDP)	33.2	50.9	4.9	10.9
Clearwater (city)	24.4	50.9	9.9	14.8
Coconut Creek (city)	17.6	60.3	11.4	10.7
Coral Gables (city)	32.0	51.4	6.0	10.6
Coral Springs (city)	25.5	60.2	4.1	10.3
Country Club (CDP)	29.3	55.3	4.0	11.5
Davie (town)	25.5	55.1	5.7	13.6
Daytona Beach (city)	34.7	41.9	9.6	13.8
Deerfield Beach (city)	23.5	50.8	13.5	12.3
Delray Beach (city)	24.6	51.6	11.5	12.3
Deltona (city)	21.1	61.6	6.5	10.8
Dunedin (city)	18.6	53.6	12.8	15.0
East Lake (CDP)	16.6	69.4	6.2	7.8
Egypt Lake-Leto (CDP)	29.9	50.1	5.2	14.8
Fort Lauderdale (city)	35.3	43.3	7.3	14.0
Fort Myers (city)	33.6	43.2	8.8	14.5
Fort Pierce (city)	29.7	48.0	10.0	12.3
Fountainbleau (CDP)	26.3	55.3	6.0	12.3
Gainesville (city)	49.1	37.1	4.7	9.1
Golden Glades (CDP)	35.6	46.7	6.9	10.9
Grtr Carrollwood (CDP)	23.9	58.5	4.4	13.2
Greenacres (city)	19.8	55.6	10.6	14.1
Hallandale (city)	20.4	50.3	16.4	12.9
Hialeah (city)	22.3	58.5	7.3	11.8
Hollywood (city)	25.5	50.7	9.5	14.4
Homestead (city)	36.7	48.5	4.8	10.0
Jacksonville (special city)	26.5	53.9	6.3	13.3
Jupiter (town)	18.9	62.3	6.5	12.3
Kendale Lakes (CDP)	23.9	58.4	6.4	11.4
Kendall (CDP)	25.8	55.7	6.1	12.4
Kendall West (CDP)	25.1	59.6	4.0	11.4
Kissimmee (city)	30.4	52.6	4.6	12.4
Lake Worth (city)	31.9	47.4	7.3	13.4
Lakeland (city)	24.0	52.9	10.6	12.5
Lakeside (CDP)	20.7	64.4	4.4	10.6
Largo (city)	19.5	52.3	13.6	14.7
Lauderdale Lakes (city)	32.2	45.9	11.0	10.9
Lauderhill (city)	30.3	48.5	9.7	11.5
Lehigh Acres (CDP)	17.3	63.2	9.2	10.3
Margate (city)	21.7	56.4	11.3	10.6
Melbourne (city)	24.3	53.3	9.0	13.5
Merritt Island (CDP)	19.6	58.3	9.0	13.1

Place	Never Married (%)	Now Married (%)	Widowed (%)	Divorced (%)
Miami (city)	32.2	46.7	8.3	12.8
Miami Beach (city)	35.4	41.8	8.8	14.0
Miramar (city)	27.6	58.1	4.2	10.1
North Fort Myers (CDP)	11.6	64.4	13.2	10.8
North Lauderdale (city)	32.9	51.6	4.7	10.8
North Miami (city)	37.2	47.1	6.3	9.4
North Miami Beach (city)	31.6	49.9	7.2	11.3
North Port (city)	15.6	63.8	9.5	11.0
Oakland Park (city)	35.6	43.9	5.2	15.2
Ocala (city)	23.7	51.5	10.1	14.6
Orlando (city)	35.8	44.2	6.1	13.8
Ormond Beach (city)	17.4	61.0	10.1	11.4
Oviedo (city)	22.9	67.1	3.1	6.9
Palm Bay (city)	21.5	59.9	6.5	12.0
Palm Bch Gardens (city)	18.4	60.2	8.1	13.4
Palm Coast (city)	12.9	70.8	9.2	7.2
Palm Harbor (CDP)	18.2	61.6	10.3	9.8
Panama City (city)	23.5	53.8	8.2	14.5
Pembroke Pines (city)	20.9	60.7	7.8	10.6
Pensacola (city)	29.6	48.0	8.7	13.6
Pine Hills (CDP)	32.1	51.3	5.3	11.2
Pinellas Park (city)	20.6	54.5	10.8	14.1
Plant City (city)	22.5	58.0	7.4	12.1
Plantation (city)	25.2	57.7	6.5	10.7
Pompano Beach (city)	27.0	49.8	10.5	12.7
Port Charlotte (CDP)	15.8	61.8	11.8	10.5
Port Orange (city)	18.1	60.1	9.7	12.1
Port Saint Lucie (city)	18.4	64.3	6.9	10.5
Richmond West (CDP)	20.5	68.0	3.0	8.4
Riviera Beach (city)	32.3	46.4	8.5	12.8
Saint Petersburg (city)	27.8	48.3	9.0	14.9
Sanford (city)	30.6	47.6	6.5	15.3
Sarasota (city)	27.2	46.2	11.3	15.4
South Miami Hgts (CDP)	30.8	51.2	6.2	11.8
Spring Hill (CDP)	16.0	64.7	10.1	9.2
Sunrise (city)	24.1	55.2	10.0	10.7
Tallahassee (city)	49.2	37.2	4.3	9.3
Tamarac (city)	17.3	55.7	16.0	11.0
Tamiami (CDP)	23.3	60.2	6.2	10.2
Tampa (city)	31.0	47.4	7.6	14.0
The Hammocks (CDP)	26.6	58.4	4.4	10.6
Titusville (city)	20.0	56.7	10.0	13.3
Town 'n' Country (CDP)	27.2	54.2	5.3	13.3
University (CDP)	49.1	31.7	6.4	12.8
Wellington (village)	20.3	67.6	3.8	8.3
West Little River (CDP)	34.2	47.5	6.9	11.4
West Palm Beach (city)	33.2	45.3	8.5	13.0
Westchester (CDP)	21.2	57.0	9.9	11.9
Weston (city)	19.2	70.6	3.3	6.9
Winter Springs (city)	20.9	64.1	5.2	9.8

NOTE: Data as of 2000

Employment and Building Permits Issued

Place	Unemployment Rate (%)	Total Civilian Labor Force	Single-Family Building Permits	Multi-Family Building Permits
Altamonte Springs (city)	4.2	32,320	35	89
Apopka (city)	4.5	11,149	917	6
Boca Raton (city)	3.5	46,175	71	0
Bonita Springs (city)	3.5	9,328	855	689
Boynton Beach (city)	5.6	30,432	379	838
Bradenton (city)	4.2	29,940	68	594
Brandon (CDP)	n/a	n/a	n/a	n/a
Cape Coral (city)	3.7	51,861	5,757	715
Carol City (CDP)	n/a	n/a	n/a	n/a
Clearwater (city)	4.2	60,557	156	24
Coconut Creek (city)	5.8	17,557	3	0
Coral Gables (city)	2.9	24,833	50	244
Coral Springs (city)	3.6	61,863	2	84
Country Club (CDP)	n/a	n/a	n/a	n/a
Davie (town)	4.3	38,814	554	24
Daytona Beach (city)	6.4	36,027	175	67
Deerfield Beach (city)	4.4	29,469	48	44
Delray Beach (city)	7.7	31,093	301	163
Deltona (city)	5.4	27,848	1,315	0
Dunedin (city)	3.4	19,378	105	0
East Lake (CDP)	n/a	n/a	n/a	n/a
Egypt Lake-Leto (CDP)	n/a	n/a	n/a	n/a
Fort Lauderdale (city)	6.2	111,021	378	1,132
Fort Myers (city)	5.3	32,955	483	567
Fort Pierce (city)	13.8	21,758	41	635
Fountainbleau (CDP)	n/a	n/a	n/a	n/a
Gainesville (city)	3.0	53,814	141	413
Golden Glades (CDP)	n/a	n/a	n/a	n/a
Grtr Carrollwood (CDP)	n/a	n/a	n/a	n/a
Greenacres (city)	5.1	14,479	277	32
Hallandale (city)	6.8	15,373	15	496
Hialeah (city)	5.9	110,571	14	31
Hollywood (city)	5.6	85,628	58	430
Homestead (city)	5.3	13,786	1,941	778
Jacksonville (special city)	5.8	405,805	6,067	3,048
Jupiter (town)	3.9	19,943	591	87
Kendale Lakes (CDP)	n/a	n/a	n/a	n/a
Kendall (CDP)	n/a	n/a	n/a	n/a
Kendall West (CDP)	n/a	n/a	n/a	n/a
Kissimmee (city)	5.9	34,119	1,039	341
Lake Worth (city)	6.0	20,371	44	213
Lakeland (city)	5.4	39,164	389	32
Lakeside (CDP)	n/a	n/a	n/a	n/a
Largo (city)	3.4	38,336	327	527
Lauderdale Lakes (city)	7.0	16,818	0	0
Lauderhill (city)	5.2	34,829	3	0
Lehigh Acres (CDP)	n/a	n/a	n/a	n/a
Margate (city)	4.9	28,768	339	11
Melbourne (city)	5.1	35,213	371	506
Merritt Island (CDP)	n/a	n/a	n/a	n/a

Place	Unemployment Rate (%)	Total Civilian Labor Force	Single-Family Building Permits	Multi-Family Building Permits
Miami (city)	8.2	191,207	188	5,995
Miami Beach (city)	6.6	46,992	23	368
Miramar (city)	4.5	32,014	1,630	154
North Fort Myers (CDP)	n/a	n/a	n/a	n/a
North Lauderdale (city)	4.7	22,036	227	292
North Miami (city)	6.0	30,422	8	0
North Miami Beach (city)	4.6	19,919	109	4
North Port (city)	3.6	6,451	3,510	0
Oakland Park (city)	4.3	22,870	81	0
Ocala (city)	4.5	25,132	397	0
Orlando (city)	5.0	132,763	2,256	1,242
Ormond Beach (city)	3.4	16,697	340	58
Oviedo (city)	3.4	8,724	349	14
Palm Bay (city)	4.7	37,830	2,233	0
Palm Bch Gardens (city)	2.8	18,550	1,426	1,157
Palm Coast (city)	5.5	10,157	3,951	632
Palm Harbor (CDP)	n/a	n/a	n/a	n/a
Panama City (city)	5.8	19,709	n/a	n/a
Pembroke Pines (city)	3.3	47,828	11	0
Pensacola (city)	5.1	29,106	160	6
Pine Hills (CDP)	n/a	n/a	n/a	n/a
Pinellas Park (city)	3.6	26,800	114	0
Plant City (city)	3.8	15,711	224	2
Plantation (city)	3.6	53,916	157	0
Pompano Beach (city)	5.9	48,520	227	152
Port Charlotte (CDP)	n/a	n/a	n/a	n/a
Port Orange (city)	3.7	21,028	504	40
Port Saint Lucie (city)	6.4	37,075	6,642	384
Richmond West (CDP)	n/a	n/a	n/a	n/a
Riviera Beach (city)	9.7	19,170	673	0
Saint Petersburg (city)	4.5	147,468	781	256
Sanford (city)	5.5	22,904	686	42
Sarasota (city)	4.0	35,961	123	398
South Miami Hgts (CDP)	n/a	n/a	n/a	n/a
Spring Hill (CDP)	n/a	n/a	n/a	n/a
Sunrise (city)	4.5	44,796	46	52
Tallahassee (city)	3.8	90,459	852	1,440
Tamarac (city)	5.4	24,718	245	60
Tamiami (CDP)	n/a	n/a	n/a	n/a
Tampa (city)	4.8	203,355	1,618	663
The Hammocks (CDP)	n/a	n/a	n/a	n/a
Titusville (city)	4.4	23,055	329	616
Town 'n' Country (CDP)	n/a	n/a	n/a	n/a
University (CDP)	n/a	n/a	n/a	n/a
Wellington (village)	3.0	15,803	1,209	28
West Little River (CDP)	n/a	n/a	n/a	n/a
West Palm Beach (city)	6.9	52,756	530	812
Westchester (CDP)	n/a	n/a	n/a	n/a
Weston (city)	n/a	n/a	183	597
Winter Springs (city)	3.7	17,691	205	42

NOTE: Unemployment Rate and Total Civilian Labor Force are 2004 annual averages. Building permit data covers 2004.

Employment by Occupation

Place	Sales	Professional	Management	Services	Production	Construction
Altamonte Springs (city)	32.5	25.3	13.7	13.4	7.6	7.6
Apopka (city)	31.6	18.8	15.0	12.8	11.3	8.8
Boca Raton (city)	30.9	22.3	23.3	13.4	4.8	5.2
Bonita Springs (city)	27.2	11.4	13.2	21.7	6.8	18.0
Boynton Beach (city)	29.7	17.2	12.4	21.1	8.3	10.6
Bradenton (city)	26.3	18.0	10.0	19.5	13.7	10.6
Brandon (CDP)	34.9	21.5	15.3	12.1	8.7	7.2
Cape Coral (city)	32.3	16.3	12.2	16.5	9.5	12.8
Carol City (CDP)	29.9	13.2	6.6	19.6	18.9	11.6
Clearwater (city)	31.0	19.6	14.5	16.3	10.5	7.8
Coconut Creek (city)	33.8	19.7	17.9	12.9	6.7	8.7
Coral Gables (city)	25.3	34.8	25.1	9.4	2.9	2.5
Coral Springs (city)	32.9	20.8	18.7	12.8	7.0	7.6
Country Club (CDP)	35.4	17.3	14.2	13.9	11.5	7.6
Davie (town)	30.0	19.3	14.8	15.3	8.8	11.6
Daytona Beach (city)	29.4	17.2	8.9	23.3	12.6	8.4
Deerfield Beach (city)	30.3	15.4	15.3	18.8	9.4	10.3
Delray Beach (city)	26.9	18.8	14.8	22.1	9.0	7.9
Deltona (city)	31.1	16.0	10.6	16.0	12.4	13.8
Dunedin (city)	33.0	20.1	15.1	16.5	7.3	7.8
East Lake (CDP)	32.7	24.2	24.9	11.5	4.7	2.0
Egypt Lake-Leto (CDP)	35.4	14.8	11.2	15.5	13.7	9.1
Fort Lauderdale (city)	27.4	17.9	15.5	20.1	9.8	9.1
Fort Myers (city)	27.5	17.5	8.1	23.4	9.8	12.7
Fort Pierce (city)	20.5	13.2	6.7	19.3	15.5	15.8
Fountainbleau (CDP)	37.6	14.4	13.0	15.7	12.4	6.7
Gainesville (city)	26.3	35.2	10.7	17.6	5.5	4.4
Golden Glades (CDP)	29.0	14.9	7.0	25.7	12.6	10.6
Grtr Carrollwood (CDP)	33.8	25.4	18.8	10.5	6.7	4.6
Greenacres (city)	28.4	14.4	10.4	21.4	11.2	13.7
Hallandale (city)	32.4	15.3	12.4	20.5	11.0	8.3
Hialeah (city)	30.7	9.0	7.5	14.2	24.0	14.3
Hollywood (city)	29.7	18.4	13.0	16.9	10.0	11.6
Homestead (city)	21.4	10.3	7.0	19.7	9.8	17.5
Jacksonville (special city)	32.6	17.6	13.6	14.0	12.4	9.5
Jupiter (town)	28.8	21.9	18.5	16.0	6.7	7.8
Kendale Lakes (CDP)	37.9	16.8	14.6	13.1	9.5	7.9
Kendall (CDP)	32.8	26.2	18.7	11.8	5.3	5.2
Kendall West (CDP)	37.6	15.0	12.5	15.7	9.4	9.7
Kissimmee (city)	29.7	11.8	8.9	27.9	10.3	11.2
Lake Worth (city)	22.8	14.4	7.5	25.3	10.4	17.3
Lakeland (city)	28.6	19.5	11.3	16.9	15.7	7.6
Lakeside (CDP)	32.8	19.3	15.1	12.2	9.2	11.4
Largo (city)	32.7	18.5	10.7	16.6	12.4	9.0
Lauderdale Lakes (city)	27.3	14.8	5.3	26.8	13.8	11.7
Lauderhill (city)	32.3	16.1	10.1	20.0	10.8	10.4
Lehigh Acres (CDP)	30.5	12.9	9.0	19.0	12.1	16.3
Margate (city)	34.5	15.4	12.1	15.4	9.9	12.5
Melbourne (city)	28.9	20.5	10.9	18.2	11.0	10.2

Place	Sales	Professional	Management	Services	Production	Construction
Merritt Island (CDP)	25.9	25.6	13.9	15.6	9.5	9.1
Miami (city)	26.2	13.4	10.4	22.1	13.8	13.6
Miami Beach (city)	26.9	22.5	17.7	21.1	6.8	4.8
Miramar (city)	33.1	18.4	12.9	16.3	9.9	9.2
North Fort Myers (CDP)	30.6	14.0	9.4	17.2	11.7	16.7
North Lauderdale (city)	31.7	13.4	10.2	19.1	11.7	13.8
North Miami (city)	28.5	15.0	9.2	25.0	13.8	8.4
North Miami Beach (city)	32.1	13.0	9.0	22.6	13.0	10.2
North Port (city)	29.8	14.4	8.4	21.5	11.0	14.8
Oakland Park (city)	27.0	16.2	10.3	21.3	13.2	11.8
Ocala (city)	27.1	20.1	11.7	18.9	12.0	9.4
Orlando (city)	30.0	18.9	14.4	19.2	9.8	7.5
Ormond Beach (city)	30.2	24.3	16.1	14.9	6.8	7.7
Oviedo (city)	30.1	25.9	17.9	12.7	6.5	6.7
Palm Bay (city)	27.5	19.8	9.6	18.8	12.1	12.1
Palm Bch Gardens (city)	30.3	25.5	21.4	12.3	5.7	4.6
Palm Coast (city)	29.9	15.6	12.5	20.6	10.8	10.6
Palm Harbor (CDP)	32.7	22.7	17.7	12.8	7.0	7.0
Panama City (city)	27.7	21.2	10.9	20.8	10.4	8.6
Pembroke Pines (city)	32.2	22.3	18.4	12.5	7.2	7.3
Pensacola (city)	26.8	25.0	13.3	17.9	8.7	7.7
Pine Hills (CDP)	28.3	11.4	6.8	23.7	15.6	13.6
Pinellas Park (city)	32.5	13.3	9.9	15.1	18.1	10.8
Plant City (city)	28.1	14.6	10.9	15.3	18.5	10.1
Plantation (city)	32.2	24.2	18.7	12.0	6.2	6.5
Pompano Beach (city)	30.0	15.1	13.5	18.5	11.0	11.4
Port Charlotte (CDP)	29.5	17.1	8.0	22.4	9.8	13.1
Port Orange (city)	31.4	17.6	12.5	17.6	9.5	11.1
Port Saint Lucie (city)	32.0	16.0	10.6	17.6	10.7	12.5
Richmond West (CDP)	36.7	16.7	15.1	14.5	7.9	8.7
Riviera Beach (city)	26.1	15.7	8.8	25.1	14.7	9.3
Saint Petersburg (city)	28.3	20.8	13.2	16.7	12.7	8.2
Sanford (city)	29.3	15.8	9.3	18.3	15.0	12.1
Sarasota (city)	26.6	17.8	11.2	23.1	9.8	11.1
South Miami Hgts (CDP)	30.8	9.8	8.5	22.6	13.5	14.2
Spring Hill (CDP)	30.7	17.5	8.2	19.3	11.3	12.5
Sunrise (city)	34.1	18.6	13.1	15.7	9.5	8.9
Tallahassee (city)	28.7	30.7	15.3	15.4	5.2	4.6
Tamarac (city)	36.0	15.2	13.2	15.7	9.0	10.6
Tamiami (CDP)	35.8	16.0	15.7	13.2	10.7	8.4
Tampa (city)	30.1	20.2	13.8	16.3	10.9	8.6
The Hammocks (CDP)	36.2	19.6	17.6	12.4	8.0	6.3
Titusville (city)	25.9	23.5	10.1	16.7	13.0	10.8
Town 'n' Country (CDP)	34.5	17.1	14.2	14.4	11.9	7.8
University (CDP)	32.5	19.5	7.5	20.9	9.5	9.7
Wellington (village)	30.7	24.9	19.4	13.5	5.8	5.0
West Little River (CDP)	27.2	9.0	4.4	23.7	22.0	13.2
West Palm Beach (city)	25.7	19.8	12.4	22.4	10.0	9.0
Westchester (CDP)	34.7	14.6	13.5	15.5	10.9	10.1
Weston (city)	30.5	23.6	28.1	10.1	4.6	3.2
Winter Springs (city)	30.4	24.5	18.8	11.7	6.9	7.6

NOTE: Data as of 2000

Educational Attainment

Place	Percent of Population 25 Years and Over with:		
	High School Diploma including Equivalency	Bachelor's Degree or Higher	Masters's Degree or Higher
Altamonte Springs (city)	89.8	31.4	9.1
Apopka (city)	81.6	22.2	7.3
Boca Raton (city)	92.0	44.3	17.1
Bonita Springs (city)	84.2	26.8	9.9
Boynton Beach (city)	81.4	21.7	6.7
Bradenton (city)	80.3	20.7	7.4
Brandon (CDP)	89.3	25.9	7.4
Cape Coral (city)	85.5	17.5	5.7
Carol City (CDP)	61.0	9.7	3.7
Clearwater (city)	84.4	23.9	8.4
Coconut Creek (city)	87.8	27.9	9.2
Coral Gables (city)	91.7	58.4	31.1
Coral Springs (city)	89.8	34.4	11.8
Country Club (CDP)	80.2	23.2	7.5
Davie (town)	84.5	26.1	9.8
Daytona Beach (city)	80.4	19.3	6.3
Deerfield Beach (city)	79.5	21.2	6.6
Delray Beach (city)	81.1	29.6	10.2
Deltona (city)	82.5	13.3	3.8
Dunedin (city)	86.5	22.2	7.0
East Lake (CDP)	94.0	42.2	14.4
Egypt Lake-Leto (CDP)	76.3	18.9	6.7
Fort Lauderdale (city)	78.9	27.9	10.4
Fort Myers (city)	70.9	18.1	6.4
Fort Pierce (city)	62.0	13.8	5.1
Fountainbleau (CDP)	70.0	22.2	10.3
Gainesville (city)	87.8	43.3	22.4
Golden Glades (CDP)	63.4	12.5	4.9
Grtr Carrollwood (CDP)	91.8	42.4	14.8
Greenacres (city)	80.3	18.1	7.5
Hallandale (city)	73.1	19.7	8.1
Hialeah (city)	49.9	10.4	4.4
Hollywood (city)	79.5	21.7	8.3
Homestead (city)	50.6	10.0	3.1
Jacksonville (special city)	82.6	21.5	6.6
Jupiter (town)	91.6	34.9	12.3
Kendale Lakes (CDP)	78.6	23.0	10.0
Kendall (CDP)	88.3	40.4	17.4
Kendall West (CDP)	76.7	21.3	8.5
Kissimmee (city)	78.5	16.8	4.7
Lake Worth (city)	66.2	16.3	5.4
Lakeland (city)	79.5	21.1	7.6
Lakeside (CDP)	90.1	21.9	7.0
Largo (city)	83.4	16.3	5.7
Lauderdale Lakes (city)	67.8	12.6	4.4
Lauderhill (city)	75.7	16.1	5.3
Lehigh Acres (CDP)	77.1	11.1	4.2
Margate (city)	80.2	17.1	5.7
Melbourne (city)	85.5	21.7	7.6

Place	Percent of Population 25 Years and Over with: High School Diploma including Equivalency	Bachelor's Degree or Higher	Masters's Degree or Higher
Merritt Island (CDP)	88.5	28.5	10.2
Miami (city)	52.8	16.3	7.7
Miami Beach (city)	78.8	33.4	15.7
Miramar (city)	82.9	22.1	7.0
North Fort Myers (CDP)	79.9	14.1	5.8
North Lauderdale (city)	77.7	13.6	3.1
North Miami (city)	67.1	15.9	6.9
North Miami Beach (city)	68.7	14.4	6.0
North Port (city)	80.7	11.5	4.2
Oakland Park (city)	78.0	21.3	6.5
Ocala (city)	79.4	19.5	7.6
Orlando (city)	82.3	28.2	8.2
Ormond Beach (city)	88.0	28.9	10.7
Oviedo (city)	93.3	41.1	13.3
Palm Bay (city)	83.7	16.7	4.9
Palm Bch Gardens (city)	94.0	44.0	17.4
Palm Coast (city)	85.6	19.5	7.2
Palm Harbor (CDP)	90.3	28.3	9.5
Panama City (city)	79.2	19.0	7.5
Pembroke Pines (city)	88.0	28.9	10.1
Pensacola (city)	84.8	32.6	11.9
Pine Hills (CDP)	71.3	10.6	3.1
Pinellas Park (city)	80.1	11.9	3.5
Plant City (city)	72.2	17.2	5.6
Plantation (city)	90.8	36.2	13.3
Pompano Beach (city)	77.2	21.7	7.1
Port Charlotte (CDP)	79.2	14.9	6.0
Port Orange (city)	84.8	17.3	5.7
Port Saint Lucie (city)	83.8	15.0	4.9
Richmond West (CDP)	83.0	22.6	7.7
Riviera Beach (city)	72.9	18.0	6.2
Saint Petersburg (city)	82.1	23.1	8.1
Sanford (city)	77.0	14.5	4.2
Sarasota (city)	80.2	25.6	9.2
South Miami Heights (CDP)	61.1	9.0	3.4
Spring Hill (CDP)	78.9	11.7	4.1
Sunrise (city)	83.8	20.2	6.5
Tallahassee (city)	89.7	44.8	19.7
Tamarac (city)	83.7	17.0	5.8
Tamiami (CDP)	70.9	21.5	9.1
Tampa (city)	77.6	26.4	9.5
The Hammocks (CDP)	87.1	31.1	10.8
Titusville (city)	84.4	19.3	6.0
Town 'n' Country (CDP)	83.0	23.9	6.9
University (CDP)	74.8	21.8	7.2
Wellington (village)	92.2	38.1	13.8
West Little River (CDP)	50.9	5.6	2.2
West Palm Beach (city)	75.9	27.2	10.4
Westchester (CDP)	63.8	21.5	9.3
Weston (city)	95.7	52.5	21.8
Winter Springs (city)	92.3	37.1	13.2

NOTE: Data as of 2004

Income and Poverty

Place	Average Household Income ($)	Median Household Income ($)	Per Capita Income ($)	Households with income of $100,000+ (%)	Poverty Rate (%)
Altamonte Springs (city)	54,928	45,114	25,458	10.6	7.4
Apopka (city)	58,246	47,374	20,900	12.2	9.5
Boca Raton (city)	117,187	67,772	50,779	34.4	6.7
Bonita Springs (city)	89,924	57,122	40,828	23.4	6.7
Boynton Beach (city)	55,883	43,609	24,439	10.8	10.2
Bradenton (city)	49,605	38,684	22,321	8.0	13.6
Brandon (CDP)	65,182	56,614	24,619	14.8	5.4
Cape Coral (city)	62,114	50,446	24,888	12.6	7.0
Carol City (CDP)	47,960	40,366	13,489	6.4	16.5
Clearwater (city)	54,855	40,422	25,039	11.5	12.3
Coconut Creek (city)	62,125	49,330	28,128	14.9	7.1
Coral Gables (city)	128,288	75,427	51,624	39.0	6.9
Coral Springs (city)	82,868	63,882	28,163	25.7	8.0
Country Club (CDP)	49,677	39,826	17,627	7.3	13.1
Davie (town)	69,573	51,691	26,251	19.9	9.8
Daytona Beach (city)	40,097	27,657	18,693	6.6	23.6
Deerfield Beach (city)	51,368	36,770	25,507	10.6	12.5
Delray Beach (city)	69,831	47,423	31,401	18.1	11.8
Deltona (city)	51,730	44,091	18,369	7.6	8.1
Dunedin (city)	53,293	38,356	26,687	10.9	8.2
East Lake (CDP)	104,807	77,707	41,796	36.5	3.9
Egypt Lake-Leto (CDP)	45,901	36,875	18,963	6.5	14.4
Fort Lauderdale (city)	65,820	41,638	30,446	16.2	17.7
Fort Myers (city)	45,741	31,075	18,838	8.1	21.8
Fort Pierce (city)	39,251	27,347	15,427	5.7	30.9
Fountainbleau (CDP)	45,501	37,709	15,980	6.2	14.2
Gainesville (city)	45,621	30,227	18,469	9.1	26.7
Golden Glades (CDP)	39,344	30,337	11,961	4.9	20.9
Grtr Carrollwood (CDP)	71,194	53,306	29,905	18.8	5.0
Greenacres (city)	46,448	38,145	20,412	6.1	7.2
Hallandale (city)	44,016	30,789	23,397	7.6	16.8
Hialeah (city)	40,043	31,051	12,812	5.1	18.6
Hollywood (city)	55,639	40,119	23,879	11.8	13.2
Homestead (city)	36,492	27,315	11,800	4.8	31.8
Jacksonville (special city)	57,167	43,762	22,467	11.9	12.2
Jupiter (town)	92,668	64,528	39,639	27.7	4.8
Kendale Lakes (CDP)	60,613	48,208	19,304	13.5	10.3
Kendall (CDP)	79,627	55,870	30,351	23.2	8.6
Kendall West (CDP)	51,837	40,722	15,769	9.8	15.4
Kissimmee (city)	42,485	34,304	15,270	4.3	15.4
Lake Worth (city)	41,537	32,027	16,622	5.5	20.0
Lakeland (city)	48,538	35,696	21,257	8.3	15.0
Lakeside (CDP)	64,055	55,730	22,800	15.2	4.5
Largo (city)	45,758	34,943	23,035	6.4	9.1
Lauderdale Lakes (city)	36,776	28,593	14,072	3.7	22.5
Lauderhill (city)	43,411	32,987	17,467	6.3	17.8
Lehigh Acres (CDP)	51,776	44,145	19,536	7.4	7.7
Margate (city)	52,042	42,333	21,826	9.8	8.4
Melbourne (city)	47,883	36,947	21,184	8.1	11.5
Merritt Island (CDP)	63,672	47,354	26,803	16.8	9.4

Place	Average Household Income ($)	Median Household Income ($)	Per Capita Income ($)	Households with income of $100,000+ (%)	Poverty Rate (%)
Miami (city)	42,532	24,978	16,381	8.0	28.5
Miami Beach (city)	57,824	31,643	30,514	13.5	21.8
Miramar (city)	68,639	57,171	21,454	18.0	8.2
North Fort Myers (CDP)	46,944	36,807	23,253	7.3	9.9
North Lauderdale (city)	47,074	40,704	15,690	5.4	13.7
North Miami (city)	42,998	30,376	14,678	6.7	23.9
North Miami Beach (city)	44,009	32,819	14,949	6.1	20.5
North Port (city)	48,004	41,137	19,124	6.2	8.3
Oakland Park (city)	47,150	38,107	20,828	7.4	16.5
Ocala (city)	45,227	32,139	18,918	7.6	18.1
Orlando (city)	51,622	38,304	22,951	9.2	15.9
Ormond Beach (city)	67,530	47,962	29,621	16.6	6.1
Oviedo (city)	86,738	73,100	27,790	28.3	4.6
Palm Bay (city)	47,171	39,350	18,315	6.2	9.5
Palm Bch Gardens (city)	105,323	66,131	47,931	29.9	5.6
Palm Coast (city)	57,569	46,050	24,270	10.9	7.5
Palm Harbor (CDP)	68,762	50,145	30,391	17.3	5.5
Panama City (city)	46,983	33,923	19,560	8.0	17.2
Pembroke Pines (city)	71,113	58,653	26,942	21.5	5.4
Pensacola (city)	52,616	36,983	23,286	10.5	16.1
Pine Hills (CDP)	40,651	33,602	12,931	3.8	18.5
Pinellas Park (city)	46,334	38,229	20,135	5.7	9.3
Plant City (city)	56,363	43,141	20,523	11.1	14.7
Plantation (city)	77,789	59,312	31,534	23.9	6.4
Pompano Beach (city)	56,120	39,419	26,189	12.4	17.0
Port Charlotte (CDP)	45,888	35,979	20,282	7.1	10.1
Port Orange (city)	52,542	42,609	22,984	8.8	7.6
Port Saint Lucie (city)	52,150	44,402	20,134	8.2	7.9
Richmond West (CDP)	73,963	64,448	20,157	18.4	5.6
Riviera Beach (city)	51,371	33,846	19,819	10.6	23.0
Saint Petersburg (city)	52,373	38,199	23,490	10.2	13.3
Sanford (city)	44,023	34,534	17,075	6.5	17.8
Sarasota (city)	54,516	37,015	25,148	10.5	16.7
South Miami Hgts (CDP)	44,949	36,775	13,268	6.9	17.2
Spring Hill (CDP)	46,503	36,898	19,256	6.0	9.5
Sunrise (city)	52,391	44,167	20,511	9.8	9.7
Tallahassee (city)	47,577	31,998	20,699	9.7	24.7
Tamarac (city)	47,104	36,640	23,445	7.5	8.9
Tamiami (CDP)	63,661	51,156	19,214	15.2	9.4
Tampa (city)	57,798	38,039	24,153	12.7	18.1
The Hammocks (CDP)	66,867	56,197	21,303	16.4	8.6
Titusville (city)	48,597	38,175	21,010	9.1	12.4
Town 'n' Country (CDP)	57,448	45,699	23,060	11.3	8.6
University (CDP)	28,823	23,142	13,763	2.1	31.3
Wellington (village)	100,566	77,170	34,018	34.4	4.3
West Little River (CDP)	39,287	28,771	11,679	5.4	29.0
West Palm Beach (city)	59,844	40,341	26,113	13.6	18.9
Westchester (CDP)	58,825	44,473	19,478	13.8	11.8
Weston (city)	126,350	90,263	41,567	44.5	5.0
Winter Springs (city)	80,716	61,507	30,169	26.0	4.2

NOTE: Data as of 2004 except for Poverty Rate which is from 2000; (1) Percentage of population with income below the poverty level

Taxes

Place	Total City Taxes Per Capita ($)	City Property Taxes Per Capita ($)
Altamonte Springs (city)	499	255
Apopka (city)	376	134
Boca Raton (city)	918	488
Bonita Springs (city)	n/a	n/a
Boynton Beach (city)	570	334
Bradenton (city)	417	157
Brandon (CDP)	n/a	n/a
Cape Coral (city)	401	278
Carol City (CDP)	n/a	n/a
Clearwater (city)	595	255
Coconut Creek (city)	394	191
Coral Gables (city)	1,291	728
Coral Springs (city)	403	189
Country Club (CDP)	n/a	n/a
Davie (town)	488	258
Daytona Beach (city)	499	229
Deerfield Beach (city)	406	296
Delray Beach (city)	667	450
Deltona (city)	166	86
Dunedin (city)	310	137
East Lake (CDP)	n/a	n/a
Egypt Lake-Leto (CDP)	n/a	n/a
Fort Lauderdale (city)	791	460
Fort Myers (city)	626	296
Fort Pierce (city)	n/a	n/a
Fountainbleau (CDP)	n/a	n/a
Gainesville (city)	292	131
Golden Glades (CDP)	n/a	n/a
Grtr Carrollwood (CDP)	n/a	n/a
Greenacres (city)	322	144
Hallandale (city)	n/a	n/a
Hialeah (city)	393	176
Hollywood (city)	469	264
Homestead (city)	n/a	n/a
Jacksonville (special city)	802	485
Jupiter (town)	445	180
Kendale Lakes (CDP)	n/a	n/a
Kendall (CDP)	n/a	n/a
Kendall West (CDP)	n/a	n/a
Kissimmee (city)	283	127
Lake Worth (city)	388	237
Lakeland (city)	364	135
Lakeside (CDP)	n/a	n/a
Largo (city)	389	107
Lauderdale Lakes (city)	274	97
Lauderhill (city)	217	125
Lehigh Acres (CDP)	n/a	n/a
Margate (city)	409	207
Melbourne (city)	395	149

Place	Total City Taxes Per Capita ($)	City Property Taxes Per Capita ($)
Merritt Island (CDP)	n/a	n/a
Miami (city)	639	389
Miami Beach (city)	1,470	780
Miramar (city)	507	243
North Fort Myers (CDP)	n/a	n/a
North Lauderdale (city)	293	107
North Miami (city)	281	183
North Miami Beach (city)	403	197
North Port (city)	434	157
Oakland Park (city)	n/a	n/a
Ocala (city)	535	251
Orlando (city)	766	371
Ormond Beach (city)	n/a	n/a
Oviedo (city)	391	199
Palm Bay (city)	357	178
Palm Bch Gardens (city)	n/a	n/a
Palm Coast (city)	n/a	n/a
Palm Harbor (CDP)	n/a	n/a
Panama City (city)	533	141
Pembroke Pines (city)	330	148
Pensacola (city)	611	199
Pine Hills (CDP)	n/a	n/a
Pinellas Park (city)	518	203
Plant City (city)	478	431
Plantation (city)	439	207
Pompano Beach (city)	697	334
Port Charlotte (CDP)	n/a	n/a
Port Orange (city)	359	133
Port Saint Lucie (city)	233	106
Richmond West (CDP)	n/a	n/a
Riviera Beach (city)	750	479
Saint Petersburg (city)	452	241
Sanford (city)	n/a	n/a
Sarasota (city)	800	225
South Miami Hgts (CDP)	n/a	n/a
Spring Hill (CDP)	n/a	n/a
Sunrise (city)	338	232
Tallahassee (city)	390	115
Tamarac (city)	325	213
Tamiami (CDP)	n/a	n/a
Tampa (city)	655	294
The Hammocks (CDP)	n/a	n/a
Titusville (city)	379	180
Town 'n' Country (CDP)	n/a	n/a
University (CDP)	n/a	n/a
Wellington (village)	362	139
West Little River (CDP)	n/a	n/a
West Palm Beach (city)	835	499
Westchester (CDP)	n/a	n/a
Weston (city)	296	99
Winter Springs (city)	276	115

NOTE: Data as of 2002.

Housing

Place	Homeownership Rate (%)	Median Home Value ($)	Median Age of Housing (years)	Median Rent ($/month)
Altamonte Springs (city)	41.2	135,218	18	646
Apopka (city)	76.1	130,347	11	577
Boca Raton (city)	75.5	261,337	23	770
Bonita Springs (city)	83.2	182,603	11	631
Boynton Beach (city)	73.1	122,710	21	707
Bradenton (city)	61.2	125,249	23	562
Brandon (CDP)	69.3	141,276	16	630
Cape Coral (city)	80.1	149,816	15	588
Carol City (CDP)	82.6	123,313	27	620
Clearwater (city)	61.5	132,064	27	538
Coconut Creek (city)	74.7	137,131	13	824
Coral Gables (city)	66.2	422,915	42	694
Coral Springs (city)	65.2	231,627	14	806
Country Club (CDP)	45.4	142,448	14	726
Davie (town)	76.2	149,432	17	711
Daytona Beach (city)	47.5	98,117	30	460
Deerfield Beach (city)	70.5	106,126	23	718
Delray Beach (city)	69.6	137,944	22	704
Deltona (city)	87.2	111,552	15	580
Dunedin (city)	71.4	122,682	26	501
East Lake (CDP)	84.2	243,462	10	703
Egypt Lake-Leto (CDP)	44.1	117,382	22	559
Fort Lauderdale (city)	55.3	179,383	35	577
Fort Myers (city)	37.6	103,629	26	508
Fort Pierce (city)	54.5	82,404	27	413
Fountainbleau (CDP)	52.0	124,345	18	705
Gainesville (city)	47.6	109,793	26	457
Golden Glades (CDP)	54.2	133,438	35	549
Grtr Carrollwood (CDP)	70.3	152,280	17	646
Greenacres (city)	70.7	96,931	15	660
Hallandale (city)	66.5	107,718	28	578
Hialeah (city)	50.6	146,179	27	537
Hollywood (city)	61.9	141,876	32	619
Homestead (city)	36.8	117,637	19	444
Jacksonville (special city)	63.1	114,607	25	501
Jupiter (town)	81.6	183,465	15	779
Kendale Lakes (CDP)	79.1	146,631	21	755
Kendall (CDP)	65.9	198,167	24	712
Kendall West (CDP)	63.2	149,270	13	691
Kissimmee (city)	44.0	124,068	14	619
Lake Worth (city)	52.7	104,568	38	484
Lakeland (city)	60.7	94,537	25	423
Lakeside (CDP)	77.2	134,163	18	609
Largo (city)	67.7	89,637	25	539
Lauderdale Lakes (city)	61.6	85,749	25	596
Lauderhill (city)	59.1	97,972	23	614
Lehigh Acres (CDP)	84.0	113,964	17	513
Margate (city)	79.9	117,531	22	720
Melbourne (city)	61.9	106,835	21	510
Merritt Island (CDP)	75.3	145,745	30	503

Place	Homeownership Rate (%)	Median Home Value ($)	Median Age of Housing (years)	Median Rent ($/month)
Miami (city)	34.9	166,135	37	473
Miami Beach (city)	36.5	183,235	37	581
Miramar (city)	81.0	171,085	16	694
North Fort Myers (CDP)	86.7	79,349	18	480
North Lauderdale (city)	62.7	123,572	21	696
North Miami (city)	50.5	120,893	35	547
North Miami Beach (city)	62.2	124,547	36	573
North Port (city)	88.3	119,837	14	540
Oakland Park (city)	50.9	132,387	29	606
Ocala (city)	56.9	95,722	24	430
Orlando (city)	39.2	133,949	22	606
Ormond Beach (city)	81.7	135,207	21	621
Oviedo (city)	86.0	175,505	8	776
Palm Bay (city)	74.9	98,965	15	536
Palm Bch Gardens (city)	80.1	181,207	14	846
Palm Coast (city)	85.8	144,696	10	659
Palm Harbor (CDP)	78.0	155,749	16	697
Panama City (city)	57.5	102,692	31	435
Pembroke Pines (city)	80.4	171,085	10	856
Pensacola (city)	63.3	118,348	33	455
Pine Hills (CDP)	65.4	106,732	27	551
Pinellas Park (city)	74.8	98,261	25	508
Plant City (city)	66.1	122,889	20	445
Plantation (city)	71.3	184,715	19	851
Pompano Beach (city)	62.8	134,658	27	630
Port Charlotte (CDP)	80.4	113,480	21	535
Port Orange (city)	82.1	116,923	17	580
Port Saint Lucie (city)	83.5	129,797	12	627
Richmond West (CDP)	93.8	178,200	4	929
Riviera Beach (city)	59.1	122,986	27	503
Saint Petersburg (city)	62.6	115,740	37	478
Sanford (city)	54.2	99,268	23	508
Sarasota (city)	58.3	138,797	30	566
South Miami Hgts (CDP)	62.4	128,167	25	518
Spring Hill (CDP)	86.5	122,837	14	510
Sunrise (city)	73.1	133,436	19	759
Tallahassee (city)	44.0	129,663	21	490
Tamarac (city)	80.3	124,779	21	720
Tamiami (CDP)	84.2	177,144	16	743
Tampa (city)	54.6	123,118	34	486
The Hammocks (CDP)	63.7	184,257	12	758
Titusville (city)	68.0	93,737	27	445
Town 'n' Country (CDP)	64.0	123,916	19	626
University (CDP)	11.5	76,948	20	481
Wellington (village)	82.1	212,052	11	867
West Little River (CDP)	63.9	111,553	41	468
West Palm Beach (city)	52.1	132,311	26	582
Westchester (CDP)	69.0	205,267	37	629
Weston (city)	83.4	269,626	5	969
Winter Springs (city)	80.5	164,484	15	631

NOTE: Data as of 2004 except for Median Rent and Median Age of Housing which are from 2000.

Commute to Work

Place	Automobile (%)	Public Transportation (%)	Walk (%)	Work from Home (%)
Altamonte Springs (city)	93.5	1.2	1.7	2.7
Apopka (city)	94.6	1.3	0.6	2.6
Boca Raton (city)	89.2	0.9	2.0	6.1
Bonita Springs (city)	89.6	0.5	1.6	5.8
Boynton Beach (city)	93.7	1.5	1.1	2.6
Bradenton (city)	93.1	1.0	1.4	2.3
Brandon (CDP)	94.8	0.5	1.0	3.1
Cape Coral (city)	94.7	0.5	0.7	2.8
Carol City (CDP)	94.1	3.2	0.4	0.9
Clearwater (city)	86.7	3.9	3.0	4.1
Coconut Creek (city)	95.1	0.7	0.5	2.8
Coral Gables (city)	83.7	2.9	6.7	5.5
Coral Springs (city)	92.7	1.0	1.2	3.9
Country Club (CDP)	94.8	1.7	0.7	1.9
Davie (town)	93.7	0.9	1.2	2.6
Daytona Beach (city)	85.2	3.8	5.7	2.1
Deerfield Beach (city)	93.4	1.2	1.4	2.4
Delray Beach (city)	90.5	1.7	1.8	4.3
Deltona (city)	95.6	0.5	0.3	2.5
Dunedin (city)	91.3	1.1	2.1	3.8
East Lake (CDP)	91.6	0.4	0.6	5.8
Egypt Lake-Leto (CDP)	94.6	0.9	1.6	1.9
Fort Lauderdale (city)	86.5	4.9	2.4	3.8
Fort Myers (city)	90.0	2.3	3.4	1.8
Fort Pierce (city)	89.9	4.0	1.9	2.0
Fountainbleau (CDP)	92.0	3.0	1.2	2.1
Gainesville (city)	82.0	3.2	5.6	3.1
Golden Glades (CDP)	88.0	8.7	0.7	1.4
Grtr Carrollwood (CDP)	94.3	0.6	1.0	3.0
Greenacres (city)	95.0	0.5	0.3	1.9
Hallandale (city)	88.2	4.3	2.8	3.2
Hialeah (city)	93.1	2.9	1.6	1.1
Hollywood (city)	90.8	3.1	1.8	2.8
Homestead (city)	90.2	2.9	1.6	1.0
Jacksonville (special city)	92.6	2.1	1.8	1.9
Jupiter (town)	92.0	0.4	0.8	4.9
Kendale Lakes (CDP)	93.1	2.1	1.1	3.3
Kendall (CDP)	89.5	4.5	1.0	4.2
Kendall West (CDP)	92.3	3.1	0.6	2.1
Kissimmee (city)	93.3	2.0	1.9	1.2
Lake Worth (city)	90.7	2.4	1.7	2.6
Lakeland (city)	91.9	1.8	2.7	2.2
Lakeside (CDP)	94.3	0.2	0.8	2.9
Largo (city)	92.7	1.3	2.0	2.2
Lauderdale Lakes (city)	90.2	7.1	1.2	0.8
Lauderhill (city)	90.9	5.3	1.0	1.5
Lehigh Acres (CDP)	95.2	0.4	0.7	2.5
Margate (city)	94.4	1.3	0.9	1.8
Melbourne (city)	94.3	0.3	1.9	1.9

Place	Automobile (%)	Public Transportation (%)	Walk (%)	Work from Home (%)
Merritt Island (CDP)	94.2	0.3	1.2	2.8
Miami (city)	80.8	11.4	3.7	2.1
Miami Beach (city)	67.7	11.4	10.3	5.4
Miramar (city)	94.7	1.5	0.9	1.9
North Fort Myers (CDP)	92.2	0.9	1.2	3.5
North Lauderdale (city)	94.1	2.6	0.6	1.9
North Miami (city)	83.2	10.6	2.7	2.0
North Miami Beach (city)	86.6	9.5	1.3	1.6
North Port (city)	95.0	0.4	0.4	2.5
Oakland Park (city)	89.9	4.4	2.3	2.0
Ocala (city)	93.1	0.4	2.1	2.6
Orlando (city)	90.1	4.1	1.9	2.2
Ormond Beach (city)	92.8	0.9	1.1	3.4
Oviedo (city)	93.4	0.1	0.4	4.1
Palm Bay (city)	95.6	0.4	0.4	2.1
Palm Bch Gardens (city)	92.3	0.3	1.1	5.4
Palm Coast (city)	94.2	0.7	0.7	2.9
Palm Harbor (CDP)	92.3	0.8	0.9	4.9
Panama City (city)	93.9	0.7	1.6	2.2
Pembroke Pines (city)	94.6	0.9	0.6	3.0
Pensacola (city)	91.6	2.1	1.7	3.0
Pine Hills (CDP)	91.8	4.6	0.8	1.2
Pinellas Park (city)	92.7	1.1	1.7	2.2
Plant City (city)	94.7	0.4	1.2	2.0
Plantation (city)	93.9	1.2	0.6	3.4
Pompano Beach (city)	89.7	2.7	2.2	2.6
Port Charlotte (CDP)	95.0	0.3	0.6	2.4
Port Orange (city)	95.0	0.5	0.8	2.2
Port Saint Lucie (city)	95.8	0.3	0.5	2.2
Richmond West (CDP)	95.8	1.1	0.2	2.3
Riviera Beach (city)	88.8	4.3	2.2	2.3
Saint Petersburg (city)	90.0	2.9	2.2	3.1
Sanford (city)	93.2	1.2	1.6	2.2
Sarasota (city)	88.2	2.5	2.7	3.5
South Miami Hgts (CDP)	91.0	3.9	1.8	1.7
Spring Hill (CDP)	96.3	0.1	0.5	2.2
Sunrise (city)	94.8	1.7	1.1	1.8
Tallahassee (city)	91.3	2.4	2.6	2.4
Tamarac (city)	94.2	1.7	1.0	1.9
Tamiami (CDP)	95.9	0.7	0.6	2.2
Tampa (city)	90.3	2.7	2.3	2.6
The Hammocks (CDP)	93.4	2.2	0.6	2.9
Titusville (city)	94.6	0.3	1.8	2.0
Town 'n' Country (CDP)	93.7	1.3	1.1	2.3
University (CDP)	87.0	3.3	5.6	0.8
Wellington (village)	90.9	0.6	0.6	6.6
West Little River (CDP)	88.1	8.0	1.3	0.4
West Palm Beach (city)	89.8	2.8	2.8	2.3
Westchester (CDP)	93.7	2.1	0.6	2.6
Weston (city)	91.9	0.6	0.8	5.7
Winter Springs (city)	93.8	0.3	0.3	4.5

NOTE: Data as of 2000

Travel Time to Work

Place	Less than 15 Minutes (%)	15 to 30 Minutes (%)	30 to 45 Minutes (%)	45 to 60 Minutes (%)	60 Minutes or More (%)
Altamonte Springs (city)	25.5	39.6	22.5	7.8	4.6
Apopka (city)	18.6	30.4	30.5	12.4	8.2
Boca Raton (city)	40.7	36.4	14.0	4.4	4.4
Bonita Springs (city)	30.9	35.2	23.4	6.1	4.5
Boynton Beach (city)	23.8	41.1	23.4	7.1	4.7
Bradenton (city)	30.5	41.7	17.3	5.4	5.0
Brandon (CDP)	22.9	34.5	25.8	10.8	6.0
Cape Coral (city)	25.5	41.4	21.1	5.8	6.2
Carol City (CDP)	11.7	33.5	33.8	11.5	9.4
Clearwater (city)	31.1	39.6	18.8	6.0	4.5
Coconut Creek (city)	17.3	43.2	27.4	7.4	4.7
Coral Gables (city)	29.1	40.2	21.1	5.9	3.7
Coral Springs (city)	23.5	30.0	28.0	11.1	7.4
Country Club (CDP)	12.4	31.3	32.4	14.7	9.2
Davie (town)	19.1	36.4	26.6	9.9	8.0
Daytona Beach (city)	42.4	40.0	9.7	2.4	5.5
Deerfield Beach (city)	24.3	45.0	20.9	5.4	4.4
Delray Beach (city)	32.9	41.5	15.4	5.2	5.0
Deltona (city)	14.8	28.5	27.6	14.7	14.5
Dunedin (city)	31.4	35.9	20.3	6.8	5.5
East Lake (CDP)	16.1	38.8	25.9	13.6	5.6
Egypt Lake-Leto (CDP)	27.5	42.0	21.5	5.3	3.7
Fort Lauderdale (city)	29.7	38.5	19.7	5.8	6.4
Fort Myers (city)	33.5	38.9	15.6	5.8	6.1
Fort Pierce (city)	30.9	31.9	25.2	4.1	7.8
Fountainbleau (CDP)	15.9	41.5	27.0	9.6	6.0
Gainesville (city)	43.2	43.2	7.7	2.6	3.3
Golden Glades (CDP)	14.5	35.0	31.1	9.9	9.5
Grtr Carrollwood (CDP)	19.1	41.1	27.5	8.2	4.1
Greenacres (city)	17.3	40.4	28.5	7.9	5.9
Hallandale (city)	24.2	34.7	23.7	8.8	8.7
Hialeah (city)	18.4	38.4	27.8	8.4	6.9
Hollywood (city)	22.5	37.4	24.5	9.1	6.5
Homestead (city)	23.8	27.7	22.9	10.0	15.5
Jacksonville (special city)	21.2	43.7	24.1	6.4	4.6
Jupiter (town)	30.9	38.8	20.4	5.0	4.9
Kendale Lakes (CDP)	11.2	26.4	28.7	17.3	16.5
Kendall (CDP)	17.4	29.7	25.3	14.8	12.8
Kendall West (CDP)	8.5	20.8	30.4	19.5	20.7
Kissimmee (city)	21.8	41.2	25.2	6.6	5.2
Lake Worth (city)	19.4	43.9	23.4	6.5	6.8
Lakeland (city)	37.1	39.4	13.0	5.3	5.2
Lakeside (CDP)	17.9	26.8	28.9	18.1	8.3
Largo (city)	30.1	40.7	18.6	5.0	5.6
Lauderdale Lakes (city)	11.5	42.5	29.5	8.3	8.2
Lauderhill (city)	14.2	40.2	28.9	9.5	7.1
Lehigh Acres (CDP)	18.9	30.7	32.3	11.1	7.0
Margate (city)	18.6	36.4	30.2	9.0	5.8
Melbourne (city)	36.2	43.3	11.5	4.0	5.0

Place	Less than 15 Minutes (%)	15 to 30 Minutes (%)	30 to 45 Minutes (%)	45 to 60 Minutes (%)	60 Minutes or More (%)
Merritt Island (CDP)	33.0	38.4	16.7	5.8	6.2
Miami (city)	20.0	38.9	24.8	6.6	9.6
Miami Beach (city)	27.5	37.3	22.5	6.0	6.8
Miramar (city)	12.1	32.0	31.9	14.3	9.6
North Fort Myers (CDP)	23.0	43.4	19.7	7.2	6.7
North Lauderdale (city)	13.9	40.1	31.3	7.5	7.3
North Miami (city)	15.6	32.9	32.0	10.3	9.1
North Miami Beach (city)	18.3	32.1	28.5	11.1	10.0
North Port (city)	17.8	35.6	28.5	11.0	7.1
Oakland Park (city)	26.1	42.7	19.2	6.3	5.7
Ocala (city)	45.0	38.8	8.4	3.1	4.7
Orlando (city)	21.7	43.7	23.6	5.9	5.1
Ormond Beach (city)	35.5	45.0	11.7	3.1	4.7
Oviedo (city)	18.3	30.8	29.1	15.1	6.7
Palm Bay (city)	19.4	47.1	21.0	6.7	5.8
Palm Bch Gardens (city)	29.5	47.3	15.3	3.7	4.2
Palm Coast (city)	36.6	29.1	20.0	6.7	7.6
Palm Harbor (CDP)	24.5	32.7	26.5	10.3	6.0
Panama City (city)	44.1	40.2	10.3	2.6	2.8
Pembroke Pines (city)	13.4	29.5	31.2	16.7	9.1
Pensacola (city)	39.4	41.8	11.6	2.7	4.5
Pine Hills (CDP)	13.8	37.7	30.9	10.6	7.0
Pinellas Park (city)	31.5	47.3	13.5	3.9	3.7
Plant City (city)	34.6	30.6	21.8	7.5	5.5
Plantation (city)	22.1	37.0	25.9	9.2	5.8
Pompano Beach (city)	25.9	41.5	21.5	5.4	5.7
Port Charlotte (CDP)	42.6	35.0	10.1	6.7	5.6
Port Orange (city)	28.0	48.4	13.8	3.0	6.7
Port Saint Lucie (city)	18.2	41.9	23.8	8.8	7.3
Richmond West (CDP)	8.5	22.8	27.6	17.4	23.7
Riviera Beach (city)	27.8	41.1	21.3	3.6	6.2
Saint Petersburg (city)	30.8	41.1	17.9	5.7	4.5
Sanford (city)	28.7	35.1	19.8	8.4	8.0
Sarasota (city)	39.0	40.2	14.0	3.2	3.6
South Miami Hgts (CDP)	17.3	31.4	23.5	12.8	14.9
Spring Hill (CDP)	27.6	36.6	16.0	7.1	12.8
Sunrise (city)	20.3	33.2	28.2	10.9	7.3
Tallahassee (city)	37.6	45.4	12.3	2.0	2.7
Tamarac (city)	19.9	36.2	29.2	8.3	6.4
Tamiami (CDP)	10.7	31.2	32.1	15.3	10.6
Tampa (city)	30.1	41.6	18.5	4.9	4.9
The Hammocks (CDP)	12.8	23.7	27.6	17.5	18.3
Titusville (city)	35.4	30.1	19.2	8.8	6.6
Town 'n' Country (CDP)	21.1	39.8	24.8	8.1	6.2
University (CDP)	26.4	33.7	23.8	9.2	6.9
Wellington (village)	23.2	22.5	29.1	15.8	9.4
West Little River (CDP)	11.4	39.0	32.2	7.1	10.4
West Palm Beach (city)	29.6	44.1	17.3	4.1	4.9
Westchester (CDP)	13.7	40.0	28.1	10.8	7.4
Weston (city)	17.3	25.9	29.6	16.9	10.4
Winter Springs (city)	17.1	37.8	28.2	10.5	6.4

NOTE: Data as of 2000

Crime

Place	Violent Crime Rate (crimes per 10,000 population)	Property Crime Rate (crimes per 10,000 population)
Altamonte Springs (city)	35.7	424.9
Apopka (city)	105.6	550.9
Boca Raton (city)	22.2	319.9
Bonita Springs (city)	n/a	n/a
Boynton Beach (city)	104.6	752.7
Bradenton (city)	87.0	634.8
Brandon (CDP)	n/a	n/a
Cape Coral (city)	27.1	327.3
Carol City (CDP)	n/a	n/a
Clearwater (city)	105.4	505.2
Coconut Creek (city)	23.1	211.4
Coral Gables (city)	36.4	609.1
Coral Springs (city)	22.7	276.7
Country Club (CDP)	n/a	n/a
Davie (town)	43.7	401.3
Daytona Beach (city)	184.5	933.5
Deerfield Beach (city)	53.7	253.6
Delray Beach (city)	82.2	636.5
Deltona (city)	n/a	n/a
Dunedin (city)	21.7	266.2
East Lake (CDP)	n/a	n/a
Egypt Lake-Leto (CDP)	n/a	n/a
Fort Lauderdale (city)	83.9	604.4
Fort Myers (city)	189.7	670.3
Fort Pierce (city)	214.6	891.3
Fountainbleau (CDP)	n/a	n/a
Gainesville (city)	103.6	521.0
Golden Glades (CDP)	n/a	n/a
Grtr Carrollwood (CDP)	n/a	n/a
Greenacres (city)	75.2	493.3
Hallandale (city)	126.3	495.0
Hialeah (city)	61.5	465.1
Hollywood (city)	64.7	546.9
Homestead (city)	180.5	909.6
Jacksonville (special city)	86.7	564.0
Jupiter (town)	37.6	337.7
Kendale Lakes (CDP)	n/a	n/a
Kendall (CDP)	n/a	n/a
Kendall West (CDP)	n/a	n/a
Kissimmee (city)	106.6	607.7
Lake Worth (city)	138.0	796.9
Lakeland (city)	58.8	588.6
Lakeside (CDP)	n/a	n/a
Largo (city)	47.5	382.8
Lauderdale Lakes (city)	74.7	248.7
Lauderhill (city)	82.3	353.9
Lehigh Acres (CDP)	n/a	n/a
Margate (city)	33.3	199.1
Melbourne (city)	78.9	482.7

Place	Violent Crime Rate (crimes per 10,000 population)	Property Crime Rate (crimes per 10,000 population)
Merritt Island (CDP)	n/a	n/a
Miami (city)	187.5	690.9
Miami Beach (city)	128.5	1,034.7
Miramar (city)	40.5	328.4
North Fort Myers (CDP)	n/a	n/a
North Lauderdale (city)	66.2	188.3
North Miami (city)	134.6	758.5
North Miami Beach (city)	112.3	585.9
North Port (city)	38.1	304.9
Oakland Park (city)	87.0	383.3
Ocala (city)	135.0	768.8
Orlando (city)	168.4	863.0
Ormond Beach (city)	29.0	321.3
Oviedo (city)	37.7	245.5
Palm Bay (city)	68.1	378.3
Palm Bch Gardens (city)	33.0	470.1
Palm Coast (city)	n/a	n/a
Palm Harbor (CDP)	n/a	n/a
Panama City (city)	101.1	753.6
Pembroke Pines (city)	26.4	296.0
Pensacola (city)	66.7	466.7
Pine Hills (CDP)	n/a	n/a
Pinellas Park (city)	59.5	602.6
Plant City (city)	85.3	617.3
Plantation (city)	27.4	435.8
Pompano Beach (city)	79.7	344.9
Port Charlotte (CDP)	n/a	n/a
Port Orange (city)	8.8	202.9
Port Saint Lucie (city)	28.0	269.0
Richmond West (CDP)	n/a	n/a
Riviera Beach (city)	205.1	1,080.2
Saint Petersburg (city)	160.2	649.2
Sanford (city)	67.4	739.4
Sarasota (city)	104.2	734.3
South Miami Hgts (CDP)	n/a	n/a
Spring Hill (CDP)	n/a	n/a
Sunrise (city)	47.1	417.5
Tallahassee (city)	89.4	591.0
Tamarac (city)	31.3	150.9
Tamiami (CDP)	n/a	n/a
Tampa (city)	178.6	886.5
The Hammocks (CDP)	n/a	n/a
Titusville (city)	85.0	412.1
Town 'n' Country (CDP)	n/a	n/a
University (CDP)	n/a	n/a
Wellington (village)	23.9	340.7
West Little River (CDP)	n/a	n/a
West Palm Beach (city)	131.8	989.5
Westchester (CDP)	n/a	n/a
Weston (city)	12.8	72.4
Winter Springs (city)	22.9	172.7

NOTE: Data as of 2003.

A

B

C

D

E

EDUCATION

Florida Public School Educational Profile

Category	Value	Category	Value
Schools *(2002-2003)*	3,464	**Diploma Recipients** *(2002-2003)*	119,537
Instructional Level		White, Non-Hispanic	70,862
Primary	1,826	Black, Non-Hispanic	24,960
Middle	512	Asian/Pacific Islander	3,345
High	454	American Indian/Alaskan Native	303
Other Level	672	Hispanic	20,067
Curriculum		**High School Drop-out Rate** (%) *(2000-2001)*	4.4
Regular	3,114	White, Non-Hispanic	3.5
Special Education	127	Black, Non-Hispanic	5.9
Vocational	33	Asian/Pacific Islander	2.4
Alternative	190	American Indian/Alaskan Native	3.9
Type		Hispanic	5.6
Magnet	0	**Staff** *(2002-2003)*	287,091.0
Charter	226	Teachers	138,226.0
Title I Eligible	1,411	Average Salary ($)	40,281
School-wide Title I	1,335	Librarians/Media Specialists	2,666.0
Students *(2002-2003)*	2,541,478	Guidance Counselors	5,640.0
Gender (%)		**Ratios** *(2002-2003)*	
Male	51.5	Student/Teacher Ratio	18.4 to 1
Female	48.5	Student/Librarian Ratio	953.3 to 1
Race/Ethnicity (%)		Student/Counselor Ratio	450.6 to 1
White, Non-Hispanic	52.0	**Current Spending** *($ per student in FY 2001)*	6,213
Black, Non-Hispanic	24.5	Instruction	3,664
Asian/Pacific Islander	2.0	Support Services	2,240
American Indian/Alaskan Native	0.3	**College Entrance Exam Scores** *(2003)*	
Hispanic	21.2	Scholastic Aptitude Test (SAT)	
Classification (%)		Participation Rate (%)	61
Individual Education Program (IEP)	15.4	Mean SAT I Verbal Score	498
Migrant	1.9	Mean SAT I Math Score	498
English Language Learner (ELL)	8.0	American College Testing Program (ACT)	
Eligible for Free Lunch Program	36.6	Participation Rate (%)	41
Eligible for Reduced-Price Lunch Program	8.8	Average Composite Score	20.5

Note: *For an explanation of data, please refer to the User's Guide in the front of the book; n/a indicates data not available*

Florida NAEP 2003 Test Scores

Reading			Mathematics		
Grade/Category	**Value**	**Rank**	**Grade/Category**	**Value**	**Rank**
4th Grade			**4th Grade**		
Average Proficiency	218.0 (1.1)	32/51	Average Proficiency	233.7 (1.1)	32/51
Proficiency by Gender/Race/Ethnicity			Proficiency by Gender/Race/Ethnicity		
Male	213.8 (1.4)	32/51	Male	234.6 (1.2)	32/51
Female	222.3 (1.4)	29/51	Female	232.7 (1.1)	32/51
White, Non-Hispanic	229.1 (1.3)	11/51	White, Non-Hispanic	242.8 (1.2)	22/51
Black, Non-Hispanic	197.7 (1.9)	24/42	Black, Non-Hispanic	214.7 (1.5)	25/42
Asian, Non-Hispanic	210.8 (2.2)	6/41	Asian, Non-Hispanic	231.8 (1.3)	4/43
American Indian, Non-Hispanic	232.6 (6.2)	7/25	American Indian, Non-Hispanic	249.3 (3.9)	10/26
Hispanic	n/a	n/a	Hispanic	n/a	n/a
Proficiency by Class Size			Proficiency by Class Size		
Less than 16 Students	184.9 (7.3)	42/45	Less than 16 Students	212.2 (5.6)	42/47
16 to 18 Students	*193.1 (8.3)*	46/48	16 to 18 Students	*211.2 (4.0)*	47/48
19 to 20 Students	*210.7 (5.9)*	40/50	19 to 20 Students	*222.3 (3.1)*	47/50
21 to 25 Students	219.2 (2.2)	33/51	21 to 25 Students	234.0 (2.3)	34/51
Greater than 25 Students	221.9 (1.5)	17/49	Greater than 25 Students	237.7 (1.2)	16/49
Percent Attaining Achievement Levels			Percent Attaining Achievement Levels		
Below Basic	37.2 (1.4)	20/51	Below Basic	24.4 (1.4)	20/51
Basic or Above	62.8 (1.4)	32/51	Basic or Above	75.6 (1.4)	32/51
Proficient or Above	31.6 (1.4)	29/51	Proficient or Above	31.0 (1.3)	32/51
Advanced or Above	7.9 (0.8)	15/51	Advanced or Above	3.8 (0.5)	20/51
8th Grade			**8th Grade**		
Average Proficiency	257.3 (1.3)	41/51	Average Proficiency	271.4 (1.5)	38/51
Proficiency by Gender/Race/Ethnicity			Proficiency by Gender/Race/Ethnicity		
Male	251.0 (1.5)	41/51	Male	273.3 (1.9)	36/51
Female	263.4 (1.6)	38/51	Female	269.4 (1.5)	40/51
White, Non-Hispanic	268.4 (1.4)	31/50	White, Non-Hispanic	285.6 (1.5)	28/50
Black, Non-Hispanic	239.2 (2.1)	32/41	Black, Non-Hispanic	248.6 (1.9)	29/41
Asian, Non-Hispanic	251.1 (2.3)	7/37	Asian, Non-Hispanic	263.9 (2.6)	6/37
American Indian, Non-Hispanic	n/a	n/a	American Indian, Non-Hispanic	287.1 (4.4)	12/23
Hispanic	n/a	n/a	Hispanic	n/a	n/a
Proficiency by Parents Highest Level of Ed.			Proficiency by Parents Highest Level of Ed.		
Did Not Finish High School	250.5 (2.7)	9/50	Did Not Finish High School	255.0 (2.8)	31/50
Graduated High School	249.6 (2.1)	39/50	Graduated High School	264.2 (2.0)	37/50
Some Education After High School	265.6 (1.9)	31/50	Some Education After High School	280.4 (1.8)	28/50
Graduated College	265.3 (1.6)	40/50	Graduated College	279.8 (1.7)	39/50
Percent Attaining Achievement Levels			Percent Attaining Achievement Levels		
Below Basic	32.5 (1.5)	11/51	Below Basic	38.3 (1.8)	13/51
Basic or Above	67.5 (1.5)	41/51	Basic or Above	61.7 (1.8)	39/51
Proficient or Above	26.7 (1.3)	37/51	Proficient or Above	23.3 (1.5)	37/51
Advanced or Above	2.4 (0.6)	30/51	Advanced or Above	4.2 (0.6)	34/51

Note: *For an explanation of data, please refer to the User's Guide in the front of the book; values in italics indicate that the nature of the sample does not allow accurate determination of the variability of the statistic; n/a indicates data not available*

Alachua County

Alachua County SD
620 E University Ave • Gainesville, FL 32601-5498
(352) 955-7527 • http://www.sbac.edu/
Grade Span: PK-12; **Agency Type:** 1
Schools: 62
36 Primary; 10 Middle; 6 High; 10 Other Level
57 Regular; 3 Special Education; 0 Vocational; 2 Alternative
0 Magnet; 10 Charter; 31 Title I Eligible; 27 School-wide Title I
Students: 29,345 (50.5% male; 49.5% female)
Individual Education Program: 5,630 (19.2%);
English Language Learner: 439 (1.5%); Migrant: 54 (0.2%)
Eligible for Free Lunch Program: 12,195 (41.6%)
Eligible for Reduced-Price Lunch Program: 2,609 (8.9%)
Teachers: 1,657.0 (17.7 to 1)
Librarians/Media Specialists: 52.0 (564.3 to 1)
Guidance Counselors: 76.0 (386.1 to 1)
Current Spending: ($ per student per year):
Total: $6,038; Instruction: $3,230; Support Services: $2,487
Enrollment, Drop-out Rates and Diploma Recipients by Race/Ethnicity

Category	Total	White	Black	Asian	AIAN	Hisp.
Enrollment (%)	100.0	54.3	38.1	3.0	0.2	4.4
Drop-out Rate (%)	7.2	5.6	10.8	1.0	13.3	6.7
H.S. Diplomas (#)	1,651	1,126	404	49	4	68

Baker County

Baker County SD
392 S Blvd E • Macclenny, FL 32063-2799
(904) 259-0401 • http://prod.schoolcruiser.com/bcsd/
Grade Span: PK-12; **Agency Type:** 1
Schools: 8
4 Primary; 0 Middle; 0 High; 4 Other Level
6 Regular; 1 Special Education; 0 Vocational; 1 Alternative
0 Magnet; 0 Charter; 4 Title I Eligible; 4 School-wide Title I
Students: 4,525 (52.3% male; 47.7% female)
Individual Education Program: 580 (12.8%);
English Language Learner: 1 (<0.1%); Migrant: 13 (0.3%)
Eligible for Free Lunch Program: 1,446 (32.0%)
Eligible for Reduced-Price Lunch Program: 386 (8.5%)
Teachers: 240.0 (18.9 to 1)
Librarians/Media Specialists: 6.0 (754.2 to 1)
Guidance Counselors: 9.0 (502.8 to 1)
Current Spending: ($ per student per year):
Total: $5,543; Instruction: $2,855; Support Services: $2,367
Enrollment, Drop-out Rates and Diploma Recipients by Race/Ethnicity

Category	Total	White	Black	Asian	AIAN	Hisp.
Enrollment (%)	100.0	84.1	15.1	0.3	0.0	0.5
Drop-out Rate (%)	4.9	4.8	5.6	20.0	0.0	0.0
H.S. Diplomas (#)	223	194	26	2	1	0

Bay County

Bay County SD
1311 Balboa Ave • Panama City, FL 32401-2080
(850) 872-7700 • http://www.bay.k12.fl.us/district_schools.asp
Grade Span: PK-12; **Agency Type:** 1
Schools: 44
22 Primary; 6 Middle; 7 High; 9 Other Level
40 Regular; 3 Special Education; 1 Vocational; 0 Alternative
0 Magnet; 1 Charter; 21 Title I Eligible; 21 School-wide Title I
Students: 26,440 (51.5% male; 48.5% female)
Individual Education Program: 5,102 (19.3%);
English Language Learner: 218 (0.8%); Migrant: 122 (0.5%)
Eligible for Free Lunch Program: 9,384 (35.5%)
Eligible for Reduced-Price Lunch Program: 2,958 (11.2%)
Teachers: 1,526.0 (17.3 to 1)
Librarians/Media Specialists: 40.0 (661.0 to 1)
Guidance Counselors: 68.0 (388.8 to 1)
Current Spending: ($ per student per year):
Total: $5,992; Instruction: $3,472; Support Services: $2,164
Enrollment, Drop-out Rates and Diploma Recipients by Race/Ethnicity

Category	Total	White	Black	Asian	AIAN	Hisp.
Enrollment (%)	100.0	79.9	16.1	1.9	0.4	1.8
Drop-out Rate (%)	1.9	1.8	2.8	1.7	0.0	0.0
H.S. Diplomas (#)	1,230	1,043	141	29	4	13

Bradford County

Bradford County SD
501 W Washington St • Starke, FL 32091-2525
(904) 966-6018 • http://www.bradford.k12.fl.us/
Grade Span: PK-12; **Agency Type:** 1
Schools: 12
7 Primary; 1 Middle; 2 High; 2 Other Level
10 Regular; 1 Special Education; 1 Vocational; 0 Alternative
0 Magnet; 0 Charter; 5 Title I Eligible; 5 School-wide Title I
Students: 4,034 (52.0% male; 48.0% female)
Individual Education Program: 943 (23.4%);
English Language Learner: 23 (0.6%); Migrant: 9 (0.2%)
Eligible for Free Lunch Program: 1,806 (44.8%)
Eligible for Reduced-Price Lunch Program: 483 (12.0%)
Teachers: 241.0 (16.7 to 1)
Librarians/Media Specialists: 6.0 (672.3 to 1)
Guidance Counselors: 8.0 (504.3 to 1)
Current Spending: ($ per student per year):
Total: $6,078; Instruction: $3,356; Support Services: $2,408
Enrollment, Drop-out Rates and Diploma Recipients by Race/Ethnicity

Category	Total	White	Black	Asian	AIAN	Hisp.
Enrollment (%)	100.0	73.2	24.7	0.6	0.1	1.4
Drop-out Rate (%)	4.9	5.2	3.6	0.0	0.0	9.1
H.S. Diplomas (#)	214	167	45	1	0	1

Brevard County

Brevard County SD
2700 Judge Fran • Viera, FL 32940-6699
(321) 631-1911 • http://plx.brevard.k12.fl.us/bre/schools.pl
Grade Span: PK-12; **Agency Type:** 1
Schools: 110
64 Primary; 15 Middle; 12 High; 16 Other Level
96 Regular; 6 Special Education; 0 Vocational; 5 Alternative
0 Magnet; 10 Charter; 35 Title I Eligible; 34 School-wide Title I
Students: 72,601 (51.6% male; 48.4% female)
Individual Education Program: 12,196 (16.8%);
English Language Learner: 978 (1.3%); Migrant: 70 (0.1%)
Eligible for Free Lunch Program: 15,719 (21.7%)
Eligible for Reduced-Price Lunch Program: 4,471 (6.2%)
Teachers: 4,079.0 (17.8 to 1)
Librarians/Media Specialists: 115.0 (631.3 to 1)
Guidance Counselors: 145.0 (500.7 to 1)
Current Spending: ($ per student per year):
Total: $5,570; Instruction: $3,332; Support Services: $1,971
Enrollment, Drop-out Rates and Diploma Recipients by Race/Ethnicity

Category	Total	White	Black	Asian	AIAN	Hisp.
Enrollment (%)	100.0	78.9	13.9	1.6	0.3	5.3
Drop-out Rate (%)	2.6	2.2	5.9	0.5	3.7	3.0
H.S. Diplomas (#)	3,578	2,927	385	87	8	171

Broward County

Broward County SD
600 SE 3rd Ave • Fort Lauderdale, FL 33301-3125
(954) 765-6271 • http://www.browardschools.com/
Grade Span: PK-12; **Agency Type:** 1
Schools: 259
154 Primary; 43 Middle; 32 High; 27 Other Level
238 Regular; 9 Special Education; 2 Vocational; 7 Alternative
0 Magnet; 19 Charter; 100 Title I Eligible; 100 School-wide Title I
Students: 267,925 (51.7% male; 48.3% female)
Individual Education Program: 30,459 (11.4%);
English Language Learner: 30,139 (11.2%); Migrant: 1,026 (0.4%)
Eligible for Free Lunch Program: 83,267 (31.1%)
Eligible for Reduced-Price Lunch Program: 21,590 (8.1%)
Teachers: 13,264.0 (20.2 to 1)
Librarians/Media Specialists: 220.0 (1,217.8 to 1)
Guidance Counselors: 490.0 (546.8 to 1)
Current Spending: ($ per student per year):
Total: $5,853; Instruction: $3,262; Support Services: $2,358
Enrollment, Drop-out Rates and Diploma Recipients by Race/Ethnicity

Category	Total	White	Black	Asian	AIAN	Hisp.
Enrollment (%)	100.0	38.0	36.5	2.9	0.3	22.3
Drop-out Rate (%)	2.0	1.9	1.9	1.3	3.0	2.3
H.S. Diplomas (#)	11,654	5,119	3,864	464	38	2,169

Calhoun County

Calhoun County SD
20859 E Central Ave, G-20 • Blountstown, FL 32424-2264
(850) 674-5927 • http://www.paec.org/calhoun/district/
Grade Span: PK-12; **Agency Type:** 1
Schools: 7
2 Primary; 1 Middle; 1 High; 3 Other Level
7 Regular; 0 Special Education; 0 Vocational; 0 Alternative
0 Magnet; 0 Charter; 4 Title I Eligible; 4 School-wide Title I
Students: 2,174 (51.1% male; 48.9% female)
Individual Education Program: 451 (20.7%);
English Language Learner: 2 (0.1%); Migrant: 15 (0.7%)
Eligible for Free Lunch Program: 837 (38.5%)

Eligible for Reduced-Price Lunch Program: 245 (11.3%)
Teachers: 147.0 (14.8 to 1)
Librarians/Media Specialists: 6.0 (362.3 to 1)
Guidance Counselors: 8.0 (271.8 to 1)
Current Spending: ($ per student per year):
Total: $5,711; Instruction: $3,332; Support Services: $2,069
Enrollment, Drop-out Rates and Diploma Recipients by Race/Ethnicity

Category	Total	White	Black	Asian	AIAN	Hisp.
Enrollment (%)	100.0	83.5	14.1	0.7	0.2	1.4
Drop-out Rate (%)	3.3	3.1	4.1	0.0	33.3	0.0
H.S. Diplomas (#)	106	83	17	0	1	5

Charlotte County

Charlotte County SD
1445 Education Way • Port Charlotte, FL 33948-1053
(941) 255-0808 • http://www.ccps.k12.fl.us/
Grade Span: PK-12; **Agency Type:** 1
Schools: 24
11 Primary; 4 Middle; 5 High; 3 Other Level
21 Regular; 1 Special Education; 1 Vocational; 0 Alternative
0 Magnet; 0 Charter; 8 Title I Eligible; 8 School-wide Title I
Students: 17,714 (51.0% male; 49.0% female)
Individual Education Program: 3,443 (19.4%);
English Language Learner: 163 (0.9%); Migrant: 0 (0.0%)
Eligible for Free Lunch Program: 5,435 (30.7%)
Eligible for Reduced-Price Lunch Program: 2,434 (13.7%)
Teachers: 925.0 (19.2 to 1)
Librarians/Media Specialists: 21.0 (843.5 to 1)
Guidance Counselors: 38.0 (466.2 to 1)
Current Spending: ($ per student per year):
Total: $5,968; Instruction: $3,257; Support Services: $2,359
Enrollment, Drop-out Rates and Diploma Recipients by Race/Ethnicity

Category	Total	White	Black	Asian	AIAN	Hisp.
Enrollment (%)	100.0	84.9	8.6	1.5	0.3	4.8
Drop-out Rate (%)	4.0	4.1	3.2	1.1	0.0	4.0
H.S. Diplomas (#)	1,076	915	101	14	4	42

Citrus County

Citrus County SD
1007 W Main St • Inverness, FL 34450-4625
(352) 726-1931 • http://www.citrus.k12.fl.us/
Grade Span: PK-12; **Agency Type:** 1
Schools: 26
10 Primary; 4 Middle; 6 High; 6 Other Level
22 Regular; 1 Special Education; 2 Vocational; 1 Alternative
0 Magnet; 1 Charter; 8 Title I Eligible; 8 School-wide Title I
Students: 15,355 (51.9% male; 48.1% female)
Individual Education Program: 2,931 (19.1%);
English Language Learner: 85 (0.6%); Migrant: 65 (0.4%)
Eligible for Free Lunch Program: 4,992 (32.5%)
Eligible for Reduced-Price Lunch Program: 1,598 (10.4%)
Teachers: 926.0 (16.6 to 1)
Librarians/Media Specialists: 21.0 (731.2 to 1)
Guidance Counselors: 36.0 (426.5 to 1)
Current Spending: ($ per student per year):
Total: $5,791; Instruction: $3,230; Support Services: $2,323
Enrollment, Drop-out Rates and Diploma Recipients by Race/Ethnicity

Category	Total	White	Black	Asian	AIAN	Hisp.
Enrollment (%)	100.0	90.9	4.3	1.2	0.4	3.2
Drop-out Rate (%)	3.5	3.5	5.7	0.0	5.9	2.0
H.S. Diplomas (#)	830	750	41	15	1	23

Clay County

Clay County SD
900 Walnut St • Green Cove Springs, FL 32043-3129
(904) 284-6510 • http://www.clay.k12.fl.us/school_sites.htm
Grade Span: PK-12; **Agency Type:** 1
Schools: 32
20 Primary; 4 Middle; 6 High; 2 Other Level
31 Regular; 0 Special Education; 0 Vocational; 1 Alternative
0 Magnet; 0 Charter; 7 Title I Eligible; 5 School-wide Title I
Students: 29,861 (51.4% male; 48.6% female)
Individual Education Program: 5,829 (19.5%);
English Language Learner: 195 (0.7%); Migrant: 139 (0.5%)
Eligible for Free Lunch Program: 5,021 (16.8%)
Eligible for Reduced-Price Lunch Program: 2,198 (7.4%)
Teachers: 1,657.0 (18.0 to 1)
Librarians/Media Specialists: 36.0 (829.5 to 1)
Guidance Counselors: 74.0 (403.5 to 1)
Current Spending: ($ per student per year):
Total: $5,468; Instruction: $3,223; Support Services: $2,006
Enrollment, Drop-out Rates and Diploma Recipients by Race/Ethnicity

Category	Total	White	Black	Asian	AIAN	Hisp.
Enrollment (%)	100.0	83.3	10.1	2.1	0.2	4.3
Drop-out Rate (%)	3.0	2.8	6.1	2.7	0.0	0.7
H.S. Diplomas (#)	1,627	1,385	140	42	5	55

Collier County

Collier County SD
5775 Osceola Tr • Naples, FL 34109-0919
(239) 254-4100 • http://www.collier.k12.fl.us/
Grade Span: PK-12; **Agency Type:** 1
Schools: 53
26 Primary; 10 Middle; 6 High; 10 Other Level
46 Regular; 2 Special Education; 0 Vocational; 4 Alternative
0 Magnet; 2 Charter; 15 Title I Eligible; 12 School-wide Title I
Students: 38,110 (51.5% male; 48.5% female)
Individual Education Program: 5,922 (15.5%);
English Language Learner: 5,618 (14.7%); Migrant: 8,943 (23.5%)
Eligible for Free Lunch Program: 6,422 (16.9%)
Eligible for Reduced-Price Lunch Program: 2,210 (5.8%)
Teachers: 2,167.0 (17.6 to 1)
Librarians/Media Specialists: 42.0 (907.4 to 1)
Guidance Counselors: 119.0 (320.3 to 1)
Current Spending: ($ per student per year):
Total: $6,690; Instruction: $3,927; Support Services: $2,441
Enrollment, Drop-out Rates and Diploma Recipients by Race/Ethnicity

Category	Total	White	Black	Asian	AIAN	Hisp.
Enrollment (%)	100.0	52.3	11.5	0.9	0.4	34.9
Drop-out Rate (%)	4.9	3.3	4.7	6.7	12.1	8.8
H.S. Diplomas (#)	1,711	1,097	198	17	5	394

Columbia County

Columbia County SD
372 W Duval St • Lake City, FL 32055-3990
(386) 755-8000 • http://www.columbia.k12.fl.us/schools.html
Grade Span: PK-12; **Agency Type:** 1
Schools: 15
8 Primary; 1 Middle; 1 High; 5 Other Level
15 Regular; 0 Special Education; 0 Vocational; 0 Alternative
0 Magnet; 0 Charter; 8 Title I Eligible; 8 School-wide Title I
Students: 9,707 (51.2% male; 48.8% female)
Individual Education Program: 1,767 (18.2%);
English Language Learner: 32 (0.3%); Migrant: 29 (0.3%)
Eligible for Free Lunch Program: 4,271 (44.0%)
Eligible for Reduced-Price Lunch Program: 1,179 (12.1%)
Teachers: 569.0 (17.1 to 1)
Librarians/Media Specialists: 12.0 (808.9 to 1)
Guidance Counselors: 20.0 (485.4 to 1)
Current Spending: ($ per student per year):
Total: $5,869; Instruction: $3,395; Support Services: $2,153
Enrollment, Drop-out Rates and Diploma Recipients by Race/Ethnicity

Category	Total	White	Black	Asian	AIAN	Hisp.
Enrollment (%)	100.0	72.7	23.2	0.9	0.4	2.8
Drop-out Rate (%)	1.9	1.2	4.0	0.0	0.0	3.5
H.S. Diplomas (#)	441	327	97	6	1	10

De Soto County

Desoto County SD
PO Drawer 2000 • Arcadia, FL 34265-2000
(863) 494-4222 • http://www.desotoschools.com/web_site_links.htm
Grade Span: PK-12; **Agency Type:** 1
Schools: 13
4 Primary; 1 Middle; 1 High; 7 Other Level
11 Regular; 1 Special Education; 0 Vocational; 1 Alternative
0 Magnet; 0 Charter; 3 Title I Eligible; 3 School-wide Title I
Students: 4,916 (53.4% male; 46.6% female)
Individual Education Program: 1,024 (20.8%);
English Language Learner: 362 (7.4%); Migrant: 683 (13.9%)
Eligible for Free Lunch Program: 2,523 (51.3%)
Eligible for Reduced-Price Lunch Program: 471 (9.6%)
Teachers: 284.0 (17.3 to 1)
Librarians/Media Specialists: 6.0 (819.3 to 1)
Guidance Counselors: 9.0 (546.2 to 1)
Current Spending: ($ per student per year):
Total: $6,285; Instruction: $3,585; Support Services: $2,311
Enrollment, Drop-out Rates and Diploma Recipients by Race/Ethnicity

Category	Total	White	Black	Asian	AIAN	Hisp.
Enrollment (%)	100.0	54.3	19.7	0.4	0.1	25.5
Drop-out Rate (%)	4.3	4.2	4.2	0.0	0.0	4.9
H.S. Diplomas (#)	204	130	35	4	1	34

Dixie County

Dixie County SD

PO Box 890 • Cross City, FL 32628-0890
(352) 498-6131 • http://dixieschools.dixie.k12.fl.us/
Grade Span: PK-12; **Agency Type:** 1
Schools: 5
1 Primary; 0 Middle; 1 High; 3 Other Level
5 Regular; 0 Special Education; 0 Vocational; 0 Alternative
0 Magnet; 0 Charter; 3 Title I Eligible; 3 School-wide Title I
Students: 2,229 (51.7% male; 48.3% female)
Individual Education Program: 520 (23.3%);
English Language Learner: 0 (0.0%); Migrant: 85 (3.8%)
Eligible for Free Lunch Program: 1,231 (55.2%)
Eligible for Reduced-Price Lunch Program: 215 (9.6%)
Teachers: 128.0 (17.4 to 1)
Librarians/Media Specialists: 1.0 (2,229.0 to 1)
Guidance Counselors: 5.0 (445.8 to 1)
Current Spending: ($ per student per year):
Total: $6,216; Instruction: $3,319; Support Services: $2,512
Enrollment, Drop-out Rates and Diploma Recipients by Race/Ethnicity

Category	Total	White	Black	Asian	AIAN	Hisp.
Enrollment (%)	100.0	89.1	9.8	0.1	0.1	0.9
Drop-out Rate (%)	3.0	3.2	1.5	0.0	n/a	0.0
H.S. Diplomas (#)	150	138	11	0	0	1

Duval County

Duval County SD

1701 Prudential Dr • Jacksonville, FL 32207-8182
(904) 390-2115 • http://www.educationcentral.org/
Grade Span: PK-12; **Agency Type:** 1
Schools: 181
109 Primary; 28 Middle; 19 High; 23 Other Level
172 Regular; 3 Special Education; 0 Vocational; 4 Alternative
0 Magnet; 7 Charter; 73 Title I Eligible; 73 School-wide Title I
Students: 128,126 (50.8% male; 49.2% female)
Individual Education Program: 20,233 (15.8%);
English Language Learner: 2,557 (2.0%); Migrant: 194 (0.2%)
Eligible for Free Lunch Program: 41,797 (32.6%)
Eligible for Reduced-Price Lunch Program: 11,725 (9.2%)
Teachers: 6,620.0 (19.4 to 1)
Librarians/Media Specialists: 141.0 (908.7 to 1)
Guidance Counselors: 237.0 (540.6 to 1)
Current Spending: ($ per student per year):
Total: $5,665; Instruction: $3,227; Support Services: $2,159
Enrollment, Drop-out Rates and Diploma Recipients by Race/Ethnicity

Category	Total	White	Black	Asian	AIAN	Hisp.
Enrollment (%)	100.0	48.8	43.7	3.0	0.2	4.3
Drop-out Rate (%)	9.7	8.6	11.4	7.0	7.0	10.2
H.S. Diplomas (#)	5,260	2,922	1,871	237	10	220

Escambia County

Escambia County SD

215 W Garden St • Pensacola, FL 32501
(850) 469-6130 • http://www.escambia.k12.fl.us/schools.htm
Grade Span: PK-12; **Agency Type:** 1
Schools: 86
40 Primary; 13 Middle; 12 High; 16 Other Level
68 Regular; 6 Special Education; 1 Vocational; 6 Alternative
0 Magnet; 7 Charter; 51 Title I Eligible; 51 School-wide Title I
Students: 44,019 (51.2% male; 48.8% female)
Individual Education Program: 7,441 (16.9%);
English Language Learner: 314 (0.7%); Migrant: 392 (0.9%)
Eligible for Free Lunch Program: 20,272 (46.1%)
Eligible for Reduced-Price Lunch Program: 4,993 (11.3%)
Teachers: 2,393.0 (18.4 to 1)
Librarians/Media Specialists: 61.0 (721.6 to 1)
Guidance Counselors: 95.0 (463.4 to 1)
Current Spending: ($ per student per year):
Total: $5,757; Instruction: $3,139; Support Services: $2,247
Enrollment, Drop-out Rates and Diploma Recipients by Race/Ethnicity

Category	Total	White	Black	Asian	AIAN	Hisp.
Enrollment (%)	100.0	57.6	37.2	2.7	0.7	1.8
Drop-out Rate (%)	2.9	2.5	3.8	1.0	3.1	3.3
H.S. Diplomas (#)	2,320	1,473	699	101	15	32

Flagler County

Flagler County SD

PO Box 755 • Bunnell, FL 32110-0755
(386) 437-7526 • http://www.flagler.k12.fl.us/
Grade Span: PK-12; **Agency Type:** 1
Schools: 10
4 Primary; 1 Middle; 2 High; 3 Other Level
7 Regular; 0 Special Education; 0 Vocational; 3 Alternative
0 Magnet; 0 Charter; 3 Title I Eligible; 1 School-wide Title I
Students: 7,601 (51.4% male; 48.6% female)
Individual Education Program: 1,308 (17.2%);
English Language Learner: 201 (2.6%); Migrant: 21 (0.3%)
Eligible for Free Lunch Program: 2,102 (27.7%)
Eligible for Reduced-Price Lunch Program: 771 (10.1%)
Teachers: 453.0 (16.8 to 1)
Librarians/Media Specialists: 6.0 (1,266.8 to 1)
Guidance Counselors: 18.0 (422.3 to 1)
Current Spending: ($ per student per year):
Total: $6,073; Instruction: $3,215; Support Services: $2,591
Enrollment, Drop-out Rates and Diploma Recipients by Race/Ethnicity

Category	Total	White	Black	Asian	AIAN	Hisp.
Enrollment (%)	100.0	78.9	12.8	1.8	0.2	6.3
Drop-out Rate (%)	2.2	1.8	4.6	0.0	0.0	1.9
H.S. Diplomas (#)	385	301	59	2	0	23

Gadsden County

Gadsden County SD

35 Martin Luther King Blv • Quincy, FL 32351-4400
(850) 627-9651 • http://www.gcps.k12.fl.us/schs.html
Grade Span: PK-12; **Agency Type:** 1
Schools: 25
10 Primary; 2 Middle; 4 High; 7 Other Level
19 Regular; 2 Special Education; 1 Vocational; 1 Alternative
0 Magnet; 1 Charter; 15 Title I Eligible; 15 School-wide Title I
Students: 7,196 (50.8% male; 49.2% female)
Individual Education Program: 1,302 (18.1%);
English Language Learner: 386 (5.4%); Migrant: 530 (7.4%)
Eligible for Free Lunch Program: 4,739 (65.9%)
Eligible for Reduced-Price Lunch Program: 692 (9.6%)
Teachers: 421.0 (17.1 to 1)
Librarians/Media Specialists: 12.0 (599.7 to 1)
Guidance Counselors: 18.0 (399.8 to 1)
Current Spending: ($ per student per year):
Total: $6,689; Instruction: $3,637; Support Services: $2,615
Enrollment, Drop-out Rates and Diploma Recipients by Race/Ethnicity

Category	Total	White	Black	Asian	AIAN	Hisp.
Enrollment (%)	100.0	5.2	83.8	0.2	0.0	10.8
Drop-out Rate (%)	8.4	14.8	7.8	0.0	0.0	12.0
H.S. Diplomas (#)	346	21	312	0	0	13

Gilchrist County

Gilchrist County SD

310 NW 11th Ave • Trenton, FL 32693-3804
(352) 463-3200 • http://www.gilchristschools.org/
Grade Span: PK-12; **Agency Type:** 1
Schools: 4
1 Primary; 0 Middle; 0 High; 3 Other Level
4 Regular; 0 Special Education; 0 Vocational; 0 Alternative
0 Magnet; 0 Charter; 2 Title I Eligible; 2 School-wide Title I
Students: 2,734 (51.2% male; 48.8% female)
Individual Education Program: 647 (23.7%);
English Language Learner: 12 (0.4%); Migrant: 104 (3.8%)
Eligible for Free Lunch Program: 1,138 (41.6%)
Eligible for Reduced-Price Lunch Program: 356 (13.0%)
Teachers: 154.0 (17.8 to 1)
Librarians/Media Specialists: 4.0 (683.5 to 1)
Guidance Counselors: 7.0 (390.6 to 1)
Current Spending: ($ per student per year):
Total: $6,243; Instruction: $3,426; Support Services: $2,431
Enrollment, Drop-out Rates and Diploma Recipients by Race/Ethnicity

Category	Total	White	Black	Asian	AIAN	Hisp.
Enrollment (%)	100.0	93.0	4.8	0.1	0.3	1.9
Drop-out Rate (%)	3.9	3.7	5.7	n/a	n/a	10.0
H.S. Diplomas (#)	141	133	8	0	0	0

Gulf County

Gulf County SD

150 Middle School Rd • Port Saint Joe, FL 32456-2261
(850) 229-8256
Grade Span: PK-12; **Agency Type:** 1
Schools: 8
2 Primary; 2 Middle; 2 High; 2 Other Level
8 Regular; 0 Special Education; 0 Vocational; 0 Alternative
0 Magnet; 0 Charter; 2 Title I Eligible; 2 School-wide Title I
Students: 2,164 (51.9% male; 48.1% female)
Individual Education Program: 364 (16.8%);
English Language Learner: 3 (0.1%); Migrant: 0 (0.0%)
Eligible for Free Lunch Program: 761 (35.2%)

Eligible for Reduced-Price Lunch Program: 251 (11.6%)
Teachers: 130.0 (16.6 to 1)
Librarians/Media Specialists: 4.0 (541.0 to 1)
Guidance Counselors: 7.0 (309.1 to 1)
Current Spending: ($ per student per year):
Total: $6,645; Instruction: $3,665; Support Services: $2,670
Enrollment, Drop-out Rates and Diploma Recipients by Race/Ethnicity

Category	Total	White	Black	Asian	AIAN	Hisp.
Enrollment (%)	100.0	81.7	17.0	0.6	0.2	0.5
Drop-out Rate (%)	1.6	1.0	4.2	0.0	0.0	0.0
H.S. Diplomas (#)	117	91	23	1	0	2

Hamilton County

Hamilton County SD
4280 SW County Rd #152 • Jasper, FL 32052-3774
(386) 792-6501 •
http://www.firn.edu/schools/hamilton/hamilton/schools.htm
Grade Span: PK-12; **Agency Type:** 1
Schools: 7
3 Primary; 0 Middle; 1 High; 3 Other Level
6 Regular; 1 Special Education; 0 Vocational; 0 Alternative
0 Magnet; 0 Charter; 4 Title I Eligible; 4 School-wide Title I
Students: 2,065 (50.8% male; 49.2% female)
Individual Education Program: 369 (17.9%);
English Language Learner: 58 (2.8%); Migrant: 70 (3.4%)
Eligible for Free Lunch Program: 1,297 (62.8%)
Eligible for Reduced-Price Lunch Program: 200 (9.7%)
Teachers: 128.0 (16.1 to 1)
Librarians/Media Specialists: 4.0 (516.3 to 1)
Guidance Counselors: 6.0 (344.2 to 1)
Current Spending: ($ per student per year):
Total: $6,931; Instruction: $3,547; Support Services: $2,972
Enrollment, Drop-out Rates and Diploma Recipients by Race/Ethnicity

Category	Total	White	Black	Asian	AIAN	Hisp.
Enrollment (%)	100.0	43.3	48.0	0.4	0.1	8.2
Drop-out Rate (%)	2.5	2.4	2.8	0.0	0.0	0.0
H.S. Diplomas (#)	119	61	56	1	0	1

Hardee County

Hardee County SD
PO Drawer 1678 • Wauchula, FL 33873-1678
(863) 773-9058 • http://www.hardee.k12.fl.us/schools.htm
Grade Span: PK-12; **Agency Type:** 1
Schools: 9
4 Primary; 0 Middle; 1 High; 4 Other Level
8 Regular; 0 Special Education; 0 Vocational; 1 Alternative
0 Magnet; 0 Charter; 5 Title I Eligible; 5 School-wide Title I
Students: 5,175 (52.9% male; 47.1% female)
Individual Education Program: 1,088 (21.0%);
English Language Learner: 504 (9.7%); Migrant: 2,069 (40.0%)
Eligible for Free Lunch Program: 3,124 (60.4%)
Eligible for Reduced-Price Lunch Program: 379 (7.3%)
Teachers: 300.0 (17.3 to 1)
Librarians/Media Specialists: 7.0 (739.3 to 1)
Guidance Counselors: 9.0 (575.0 to 1)
Current Spending: ($ per student per year):
Total: $6,186; Instruction: $3,477; Support Services: $2,302
Enrollment, Drop-out Rates and Diploma Recipients by Race/Ethnicity

Category	Total	White	Black	Asian	AIAN	Hisp.
Enrollment (%)	100.0	41.4	8.3	0.9	0.0	49.4
Drop-out Rate (%)	7.9	4.5	4.6	0.0	0.0	14.1
H.S. Diplomas (#)	213	125	19	2	1	66

Hendry County

Hendry County SD
PO Box 1980 • La Belle, FL 33975-1980
(863) 674-4642 • http://www.hendry-schools.org/
Grade Span: PK-12; **Agency Type:** 1
Schools: 16
6 Primary; 0 Middle; 2 High; 8 Other Level
15 Regular; 1 Special Education; 0 Vocational; 0 Alternative
0 Magnet; 0 Charter; 8 Title I Eligible; 6 School-wide Title I
Students: 7,673 (52.0% male; 48.0% female)
Individual Education Program: 1,359 (17.7%);
English Language Learner: 597 (7.8%); Migrant: 2,746 (35.8%)
Eligible for Free Lunch Program: 4,706 (61.3%)
Eligible for Reduced-Price Lunch Program: 843 (11.0%)
Teachers: 373.0 (20.6 to 1)
Librarians/Media Specialists: 9.0 (852.6 to 1)
Guidance Counselors: 16.0 (479.6 to 1)
Current Spending: ($ per student per year):
Total: $6,135; Instruction: $3,269; Support Services: $2,464
Enrollment, Drop-out Rates and Diploma Recipients by Race/Ethnicity

Category	Total	White	Black	Asian	AIAN	Hisp.
Enrollment (%)	100.0	36.9	17.3	0.5	0.6	44.7
Drop-out Rate (%)	6.8	5.5	6.6	7.7	0.0	8.7
H.S. Diplomas (#)	290	155	39	5	0	91

Hernando County

Hernando County SD
919 N Broad St • Brooksville, FL 34601-2397
(352) 797-7001 • http://www.hcsb.k12.fl.us/
Grade Span: PK-12; **Agency Type:** 1
Schools: 23
11 Primary; 3 Middle; 3 High; 3 Other Level
19 Regular; 0 Special Education; 0 Vocational; 1 Alternative
0 Magnet; 0 Charter; 8 Title I Eligible; 8 School-wide Title I
Students: 18,605 (51.0% male; 49.0% female)
Individual Education Program: 3,204 (17.2%);
English Language Learner: 238 (1.3%); Migrant: 0 (0.0%)
Eligible for Free Lunch Program: 6,139 (33.0%)
Eligible for Reduced-Price Lunch Program: 2,046 (11.0%)
Teachers: 1,016.0 (18.3 to 1)
Librarians/Media Specialists: 20.0 (930.3 to 1)
Guidance Counselors: 54.0 (344.5 to 1)
Current Spending: ($ per student per year):
Total: $5,474; Instruction: $3,033; Support Services: $2,161
Enrollment, Drop-out Rates and Diploma Recipients by Race/Ethnicity

Category	Total	White	Black	Asian	AIAN	Hisp.
Enrollment (%)	100.0	84.1	7.4	0.9	0.3	7.5
Drop-out Rate (%)	2.2	2.2	2.8	0.0	20.0	0.7
H.S. Diplomas (#)	923	799	54	17	2	51

Highlands County

Highlands County SD
426 School St • Sebring, FL 33870-4048
(863) 471-5564 • http://www.highlands.k12.fl.us/
Grade Span: PK-12; **Agency Type:** 1
Schools: 18
7 Primary; 4 Middle; 3 High; 3 Other Level
16 Regular; 0 Special Education; 0 Vocational; 1 Alternative
0 Magnet; 0 Charter; 8 Title I Eligible; 8 School-wide Title I
Students: 11,428 (51.9% male; 48.1% female)
Individual Education Program: 2,077 (18.2%);
English Language Learner: 447 (3.9%); Migrant: 1,295 (11.3%)
Eligible for Free Lunch Program: 5,409 (47.3%)
Eligible for Reduced-Price Lunch Program: 1,216 (10.6%)
Teachers: 671.0 (17.0 to 1)
Librarians/Media Specialists: 14.0 (816.3 to 1)
Guidance Counselors: 26.0 (439.5 to 1)
Current Spending: ($ per student per year):
Total: $6,001; Instruction: $3,227; Support Services: $2,399
Enrollment, Drop-out Rates and Diploma Recipients by Race/Ethnicity

Category	Total	White	Black	Asian	AIAN	Hisp.
Enrollment (%)	100.0	59.2	20.0	1.0	0.6	19.3
Drop-out Rate (%)	6.3	5.5	8.5	7.7	10.0	7.1
H.S. Diplomas (#)	561	360	111	8	1	81

Hillsborough County

Hillsborough County SD
PO Box 3408 • Tampa, FL 33601-3408
(813) 272-4050 • http://apps.sdhc.k12.fl.us/sdhc2/schoolsite/
Grade Span: PK-12; **Agency Type:** 1
Schools: 229
129 Primary; 40 Middle; 26 High; 29 Other Level
209 Regular; 9 Special Education; 0 Vocational; 6 Alternative
0 Magnet; 16 Charter; 104 Title I Eligible; 104 School-wide Title I
Students: 175,454 (51.3% male; 48.7% female)
Individual Education Program: 27,127 (15.5%);
English Language Learner: 18,002 (10.3%); Migrant: 5,049 (2.9%)
Eligible for Free Lunch Program: 69,397 (39.6%)
Eligible for Reduced-Price Lunch Program: 16,394 (9.3%)
Teachers: 10,499.0 (16.7 to 1)
Librarians/Media Specialists: 214.0 (819.9 to 1)
Guidance Counselors: 435.0 (403.3 to 1)
Current Spending: ($ per student per year):
Total: $6,055; Instruction: $3,494; Support Services: $2,196
Enrollment, Drop-out Rates and Diploma Recipients by Race/Ethnicity

Category	Total	White	Black	Asian	AIAN	Hisp.
Enrollment (%)	100.0	49.6	23.8	2.3	0.3	23.9
Drop-out Rate (%)	3.1	2.5	4.9	1.5	6.1	3.3
H.S. Diplomas (#)	7,968	4,567	1,539	280	32	1,550

Holmes County

Holmes County SD

701 E Pennsylvania Ave • Bonifay, FL 32425-2349
(850) 547-9341 • http://www.firn.edu/schools/holmes/holmessb/
Grade Span: PK-12; **Agency Type:** 1
Schools: 9
2 Primary; 1 Middle; 2 High; 4 Other Level
9 Regular; 0 Special Education; 0 Vocational; 0 Alternative
0 Magnet; 0 Charter; 5 Title I Eligible; 5 School-wide Title I
Students: 3,414 (52.5% male; 47.5% female)
Individual Education Program: 546 (16.0%);
English Language Learner: 0 (0.0%); Migrant: 35 (1.0%)
Eligible for Free Lunch Program: 1,436 (42.1%)
Eligible for Reduced-Price Lunch Program: 466 (13.6%)
Teachers: 204.0 (16.7 to 1)
Librarians/Media Specialists: 7.0 (487.7 to 1)
Guidance Counselors: 9.0 (379.3 to 1)
Current Spending: ($ per student per year):
Total: $6,030; Instruction: $3,615; Support Services: $2,058
Enrollment, Drop-out Rates and Diploma Recipients by Race/Ethnicity

Category	Total	White	Black	Asian	AIAN	Hisp.
Enrollment (%)	100.0	95.0	2.8	1.0	0.1	1.2
Drop-out Rate (%)	3.0	3.0	0.0	0.0	0.0	10.0
H.S. Diplomas (#)	203	196	5	1	0	1

Indian River County

Indian River County SD

1990 25th St • Vero Beach, FL 32960-3395
(772) 564-3150 • http://www.indian-river.k12.fl.us/
Grade Span: PK-12; **Agency Type:** 1
Schools: 28
16 Primary; 4 Middle; 3 High; 5 Other Level
26 Regular; 2 Special Education; 0 Vocational; 0 Alternative
0 Magnet; 5 Charter; 12 Title I Eligible; 12 School-wide Title I
Students: 15,986 (51.2% male; 48.8% female)
Individual Education Program: 2,356 (14.7%);
English Language Learner: 662 (4.1%); Migrant: 904 (5.7%)
Eligible for Free Lunch Program: 4,815 (30.1%)
Eligible for Reduced-Price Lunch Program: 1,156 (7.2%)
Teachers: 393.0 (40.7 to 1)
Librarians/Media Specialists: 6.0 (2,664.3 to 1)
Guidance Counselors: 11.0 (1,453.3 to 1)
Current Spending: ($ per student per year):
Total: $6,161; Instruction: $3,430; Support Services: $2,379
Enrollment, Drop-out Rates and Diploma Recipients by Race/Ethnicity

Category	Total	White	Black	Asian	AIAN	Hisp.
Enrollment (%)	100.0	70.3	16.4	1.1	0.3	12.0
Drop-out Rate (%)	2.7	2.1	4.1	2.2	0.0	5.2
H.S. Diplomas (#)	821	620	129	8	2	62

Jackson County

Jackson County SD

PO Box 5958 • Marianna, FL 32447-5958
(850) 482-1200 • http://www.firn.edu/schools/jackson/jacksonsb/schools/
Grade Span: PK-12; **Agency Type:** 1
Schools: 21
5 Primary; 1 Middle; 3 High; 12 Other Level
17 Regular; 4 Special Education; 0 Vocational; 0 Alternative
0 Magnet; 1 Charter; 12 Title I Eligible; 12 School-wide Title I
Students: 7,245 (51.3% male; 48.7% female)
Individual Education Program: 1,468 (20.3%);
English Language Learner: 43 (0.6%); Migrant: 20 (0.3%)
Eligible for Free Lunch Program: 3,121 (43.1%)
Eligible for Reduced-Price Lunch Program: 878 (12.1%)
Teachers: 437.0 (16.6 to 1)
Librarians/Media Specialists: 12.0 (603.8 to 1)
Guidance Counselors: 24.0 (301.9 to 1)
Current Spending: ($ per student per year):
Total: $6,086; Instruction: $3,254; Support Services: $2,430
Enrollment, Drop-out Rates and Diploma Recipients by Race/Ethnicity

Category	Total	White	Black	Asian	AIAN	Hisp.
Enrollment (%)	100.0	65.2	31.9	0.4	0.5	1.9
Drop-out Rate (%)	1.8	1.9	1.6	0.0	0.0	3.4
H.S. Diplomas (#)	409	261	140	0	2	6

Jefferson County

Jefferson County SD

1490 W Washington St • Monticello, FL 32344-1100
(850) 342-0100 • http://www.paec.org/jefferson/Schools/schools.htm
Grade Span: PK-12; **Agency Type:** 1
Schools: 7
2 Primary; 1 Middle; 1 High; 2 Other Level
5 Regular; 1 Special Education; 0 Vocational; 0 Alternative
0 Magnet; 0 Charter; 1 Title I Eligible; 1 School-wide Title I
Students: 1,575 (51.2% male; 48.8% female)
Individual Education Program: 410 (26.0%);
English Language Learner: 2 (0.1%); Migrant: 4 (0.3%)
Eligible for Free Lunch Program: 989 (62.8%)
Eligible for Reduced-Price Lunch Program: 152 (9.7%)
Teachers: 103.0 (15.3 to 1)
Librarians/Media Specialists: 3.0 (525.0 to 1)
Guidance Counselors: 3.0 (525.0 to 1)
Current Spending: ($ per student per year):
Total: $7,130; Instruction: $3,755; Support Services: $2,977
Enrollment, Drop-out Rates and Diploma Recipients by Race/Ethnicity

Category	Total	White	Black	Asian	AIAN	Hisp.
Enrollment (%)	100.0	28.3	69.7	0.3	0.2	1.6
Drop-out Rate (%)	3.5	1.0	5.1	n/a	0.0	0.0
H.S. Diplomas (#)	65	27	38	0	0	0

Lake County

Lake County SD

201 W Burleigh Blvd • Tavares, FL 32778-2496
(352) 253-6510 • http://www.lake.k12.fl.us/
Grade Span: PK-12; **Agency Type:** 1
Schools: 53
23 Primary; 10 Middle; 8 High; 9 Other Level
45 Regular; 2 Special Education; 1 Vocational; 2 Alternative
0 Magnet; 7 Charter; 25 Title I Eligible; 14 School-wide Title I
Students: 31,782 (51.2% male; 48.8% female)
Individual Education Program: 5,402 (17.0%);
English Language Learner: 1,091 (3.4%); Migrant: 406 (1.3%)
Eligible for Free Lunch Program: 10,063 (31.7%)
Eligible for Reduced-Price Lunch Program: 2,704 (8.5%)
Teachers: 2,209.0 (14.4 to 1)
Librarians/Media Specialists: 42.0 (756.7 to 1)
Guidance Counselors: 76.0 (418.2 to 1)
Current Spending: ($ per student per year):
Total: $5,423; Instruction: $3,125; Support Services: $2,005
Enrollment, Drop-out Rates and Diploma Recipients by Race/Ethnicity

Category	Total	White	Black	Asian	AIAN	Hisp.
Enrollment (%)	100.0	72.4	16.2	1.1	0.3	10.0
Drop-out Rate (%)	5.2	5.1	5.2	3.5	14.3	7.0
H.S. Diplomas (#)	1,531	1,210	182	25	1	113

Lee County

Lee County SD

2055 Central Ave • Fort Myers, FL 33901-3916
(239) 337-8301 • http://www.lee.k12.fl.us/
Grade Span: PK-12; **Agency Type:** 1
Schools: 79
39 Primary; 12 Middle; 14 High; 14 Other Level
69 Regular; 4 Special Education; 3 Vocational; 3 Alternative
0 Magnet; 3 Charter; 25 Title I Eligible; 25 School-wide Title I
Students: 63,172 (51.4% male; 48.6% female)
Individual Education Program: 9,813 (15.5%);
English Language Learner: 6,707 (10.6%); Migrant: 1,443 (2.3%)
Eligible for Free Lunch Program: 23,006 (36.4%)
Eligible for Reduced-Price Lunch Program: 6,928 (11.0%)
Teachers: 3,200.0 (19.7 to 1)
Librarians/Media Specialists: 47.0 (1,344.1 to 1)
Guidance Counselors: 115.0 (549.3 to 1)
Current Spending: ($ per student per year):
Total: $6,070; Instruction: $3,289; Support Services: $2,501
Enrollment, Drop-out Rates and Diploma Recipients by Race/Ethnicity

Category	Total	White	Black	Asian	AIAN	Hisp.
Enrollment (%)	100.0	63.6	15.4	1.2	0.4	19.4
Drop-out Rate (%)	7.1	5.7	12.2	4.5	2.5	9.8
H.S. Diplomas (#)	2,846	2,105	352	56	10	323

Leon County

Leon County SD

2757 W Pensacola St • Tallahassee, FL 32304-2907
(850) 487-7147 •
http://www.leon.k12.fl.us/districtserver/Schools/Index.html
Grade Span: PK-12; **Agency Type:** 1
Schools: 58
27 Primary; 9 Middle; 6 High; 14 Other Level
49 Regular; 5 Special Education; 1 Vocational; 1 Alternative
0 Magnet; 2 Charter; 19 Title I Eligible; 19 School-wide Title I
Students: 31,857 (51.2% male; 48.8% female)
Individual Education Program: 6,455 (20.3%);
English Language Learner: 276 (0.9%); Migrant: 12 (<0.1%)

Eligible for Free Lunch Program: 8,735 (27.4%)
Eligible for Reduced-Price Lunch Program: 1,874 (5.9%)
Teachers: 1,711.0 (18.6 to 1)
Librarians/Media Specialists: 42.0 (758.5 to 1)
Guidance Counselors: 71.0 (448.7 to 1)
Current Spending: ($ per student per year):
Total: $6,326; Instruction: $3,485; Support Services: $2,572
Enrollment, Drop-out Rates and Diploma Recipients by Race/Ethnicity

Category	Total	White	Black	Asian	AIAN	Hisp.
Enrollment (%)	100.0	55.3	40.4	2.0	0.1	2.2
Drop-out Rate (%)	3.5	2.8	4.8	1.9	0.0	3.7
H.S. Diplomas (#)	1,788	1,173	543	32	3	37

Levy County

Levy County SD
PO Drawer 129 • Bronson, FL 32621-0129
(352) 486-5231 • http://www.levy.k12.fl.us/
Grade Span: PK-12; **Agency Type:** 1
Schools: 16
4 Primary; 2 Middle; 3 High; 7 Other Level
14 Regular; 0 Special Education; 0 Vocational; 2 Alternative
0 Magnet; 2 Charter; 11 Title I Eligible; 11 School-wide Title I
Students: 6,113 (51.9% male; 48.1% female)
Individual Education Program: 1,420 (23.2%);
English Language Learner: 140 (2.3%); Migrant: 252 (4.1%)
Eligible for Free Lunch Program: 2,836 (46.4%)
Eligible for Reduced-Price Lunch Program: 634 (10.4%)
Teachers: 366.0 (16.7 to 1)
Librarians/Media Specialists: 11.0 (555.7 to 1)
Guidance Counselors: 13.0 (470.2 to 1)
Current Spending: ($ per student per year):
Total: $6,103; Instruction: $3,447; Support Services: $2,308
Enrollment, Drop-out Rates and Diploma Recipients by Race/Ethnicity

Category	Total	White	Black	Asian	AIAN	Hisp.
Enrollment (%)	100.0	78.3	16.8	0.5	0.1	4.3
Drop-out Rate (%)	4.3	4.3	4.5	0.0	0.0	2.1
H.S. Diplomas (#)	301	237	53	3	0	8

Madison County

Madison County SD
312 NE Duval St • Madison, FL 32340-2552
(850) 973-5022 • http://janusgroup.com/madison/
Grade Span: PK-12; **Agency Type:** 1
Schools: 9
5 Primary; 0 Middle; 1 High; 3 Other Level
8 Regular; 0 Special Education; 0 Vocational; 1 Alternative
0 Magnet; 0 Charter; 4 Title I Eligible; 4 School-wide Title I
Students: 3,311 (54.8% male; 45.2% female)
Individual Education Program: 840 (25.4%);
English Language Learner: 8 (0.2%); Migrant: 19 (0.6%)
Eligible for Free Lunch Program: 1,819 (54.9%)
Eligible for Reduced-Price Lunch Program: 306 (9.2%)
Teachers: 173.0 (19.1 to 1)
Librarians/Media Specialists: 3.0 (1,103.7 to 1)
Guidance Counselors: 4.0 (827.8 to 1)
Current Spending: ($ per student per year):
Total: $6,147; Instruction: $3,444; Support Services: $2,307
Enrollment, Drop-out Rates and Diploma Recipients by Race/Ethnicity

Category	Total	White	Black	Asian	AIAN	Hisp.
Enrollment (%)	100.0	39.8	58.1	0.1	0.2	1.8
Drop-out Rate (%)	6.6	4.4	8.6	0.0	0.0	10.0
H.S. Diplomas (#)	180	100	75	3	0	2

Manatee County

Manatee County SD
PO Box 9069 • Bradenton, FL 34206-9069
(941) 741-7235 • http://www.manatee.k12.fl.us/school_sites.htm
Grade Span: PK-12; **Agency Type:** 1
Schools: 73
35 Primary; 9 Middle; 9 High; 19 Other Level
55 Regular; 8 Special Education; 1 Vocational; 8 Alternative
0 Magnet; 7 Charter; 15 Title I Eligible; 9 School-wide Title I
Students: 39,132 (51.7% male; 48.3% female)
Individual Education Program: 7,618 (19.5%);
English Language Learner: 2,552 (6.5%); Migrant: 1,607 (4.1%)
Eligible for Free Lunch Program: 13,024 (33.3%)
Eligible for Reduced-Price Lunch Program: 3,003 (7.7%)
Teachers: 2,159.0 (18.1 to 1)
Librarians/Media Specialists: 45.0 (869.6 to 1)
Guidance Counselors: 87.0 (449.8 to 1)
Current Spending: ($ per student per year):
Total: $6,193; Instruction: $3,629; Support Services: $2,265
Enrollment, Drop-out Rates and Diploma Recipients by Race/Ethnicity

Category	Total	White	Black	Asian	AIAN	Hisp.
Enrollment (%)	100.0	64.9	17.1	1.0	0.1	16.8
Drop-out Rate (%)	5.5	4.3	9.9	1.8	16.7	7.9
H.S. Diplomas (#)	1,709	1,309	258	23	2	117

Marion County

Marion County SD
PO Box 670 • Ocala, FL 34478-0670
(352) 671-7702 • http://www.marionschoolsk12.org/schooldir.htm
Grade Span: PK-12; **Agency Type:** 1
Schools: 65
32 Primary; 9 Middle; 8 High; 15 Other Level
53 Regular; 5 Special Education; 0 Vocational; 6 Alternative
0 Magnet; 2 Charter; 32 Title I Eligible; 32 School-wide Title I
Students: 39,710 (51.7% male; 48.3% female)
Individual Education Program: 6,957 (17.5%);
English Language Learner: 915 (2.3%); Migrant: 65 (0.2%)
Eligible for Free Lunch Program: 16,646 (41.9%)
Eligible for Reduced-Price Lunch Program: 4,528 (11.4%)
Teachers: 2,190.0 (18.1 to 1)
Librarians/Media Specialists: 46.0 (863.3 to 1)
Guidance Counselors: 78.0 (509.1 to 1)
Current Spending: ($ per student per year):
Total: $5,813; Instruction: $3,354; Support Services: $2,132
Enrollment, Drop-out Rates and Diploma Recipients by Race/Ethnicity

Category	Total	White	Black	Asian	AIAN	Hisp.
Enrollment (%)	100.0	68.1	21.2	0.9	0.3	9.4
Drop-out Rate (%)	4.4	3.9	5.7	1.7	3.4	5.8
H.S. Diplomas (#)	1,960	1,457	338	25	3	137

Martin County

Martin County SD
500 E Ocean Blvd • Stuart, FL 34994-2578
(772) 219-1200 • http://www.sbmc.org/
Grade Span: PK-12; **Agency Type:** 1
Schools: 29
14 Primary; 4 Middle; 2 High; 8 Other Level
21 Regular; 4 Special Education; 0 Vocational; 3 Alternative
0 Magnet; 0 Charter; 5 Title I Eligible; 4 School-wide Title I
Students: 17,259 (51.4% male; 48.6% female)
Individual Education Program: 2,942 (17.0%);
English Language Learner: 1,525 (8.8%); Migrant: 310 (1.8%)
Eligible for Free Lunch Program: 4,573 (26.5%)
Eligible for Reduced-Price Lunch Program: 1,034 (6.0%)
Teachers: 928.0 (18.6 to 1)
Librarians/Media Specialists: 18.0 (958.8 to 1)
Guidance Counselors: 40.0 (431.5 to 1)
Current Spending: ($ per student per year):
Total: $6,411; Instruction: $3,707; Support Services: $2,421
Enrollment, Drop-out Rates and Diploma Recipients by Race/Ethnicity

Category	Total	White	Black	Asian	AIAN	Hisp.
Enrollment (%)	100.0	73.5	10.5	1.1	0.2	14.7
Drop-out Rate (%)	0.6	0.4	1.2	0.0	0.0	2.4
H.S. Diplomas (#)	842	711	63	15	2	51

Miami-Dade County

Dade County SD
1450 NE 2nd Ave, #912 • Miami, FL 33132-1394
(305) 995-1428 • http://www.dade.k12.fl.us/schools/
Grade Span: PK-12; **Agency Type:** 1
Schools: 370
226 Primary; 54 Middle; 48 High; 38 Other Level
348 Regular; 5 Special Education; 2 Vocational; 11 Alternative
0 Magnet; 25 Charter; 174 Title I Eligible; 174 School-wide Title I
Students: 373,395 (51.3% male; 48.7% female)
Individual Education Program: 43,467 (11.6%);
English Language Learner: 66,084 (17.7%); Migrant: 2,612 (0.7%)
Eligible for Free Lunch Program: 200,001 (53.6%)
Eligible for Reduced-Price Lunch Program: 30,738 (8.2%)
Teachers: 18,656.0 (20.0 to 1)
Librarians/Media Specialists: 352.0 (1,060.8 to 1)
Guidance Counselors: 991.0 (376.8 to 1)
Current Spending: ($ per student per year):
Total: $6,552; Instruction: $3,872; Support Services: $2,372
Enrollment, Drop-out Rates and Diploma Recipients by Race/Ethnicity

Category	Total	White	Black	Asian	AIAN	Hisp.
Enrollment (%)	100.0	10.5	29.5	1.2	0.1	58.7
Drop-out Rate (%)	6.3	4.7	7.2	2.2	5.6	6.2
H.S. Diplomas (#)	16,638	2,424	4,864	321	13	9,016

Monroe County

Monroe County SD

PO Box 1788 • Key West, FL 33041-1788
(305) 293-1400 • http://www.monroe.k12.fl.us/district/schools.htm
Grade Span: PK-12; **Agency Type:** 1
Schools: 21
11 Primary; 1 Middle; 5 High; 2 Other Level
18 Regular; 0 Special Education; 0 Vocational; 1 Alternative
0 Magnet; 3 Charter; 7 Title I Eligible; 0 School-wide Title I
Students: 9,218 (52.8% male; 47.2% female)
Individual Education Program: 1,606 (17.4%);
English Language Learner: 581 (6.3%); Migrant: 26 (0.3%)
Eligible for Free Lunch Program: 2,622 (28.4%)
Eligible for Reduced-Price Lunch Program: 825 (8.9%)
Teachers: 688.0 (13.4 to 1)
Librarians/Media Specialists: 5.0 (1,843.6 to 1)
Guidance Counselors: 15.0 (614.5 to 1)
Current Spending: ($ per student per year):
Total: $7,151; Instruction: $3,890; Support Services: $2,931

Enrollment, Drop-out Rates and Diploma Recipients by Race/Ethnicity

Category	Total	White	Black	Asian	AIAN	Hisp.
Enrollment (%)	100.0	67.4	9.0	1.2	0.4	22.0
Drop-out Rate (%)	3.4	3.0	5.0	3.2	0.0	4.2
H.S. Diplomas (#)	486	346	46	6	0	88

Nassau County

Nassau County SD

1201 Atlantic Ave • Fernandina Beach, FL 32034-3499
(904) 321-5801 • http://www.nassau.k12.fl.us/
Grade Span: PK-12; **Agency Type:** 1
Schools: 19
7 Primary; 2 Middle; 2 High; 8 Other Level
18 Regular; 0 Special Education; 0 Vocational; 1 Alternative
0 Magnet; 0 Charter; 10 Title I Eligible; 0 School-wide Title I
Students: 10,533 (51.9% male; 48.1% female)
Individual Education Program: 1,680 (15.9%);
English Language Learner: 19 (0.2%); Migrant: 31 (0.3%)
Eligible for Free Lunch Program: 2,619 (24.9%)
Eligible for Reduced-Price Lunch Program: 957 (9.1%)
Teachers: 549.0 (19.2 to 1)
Librarians/Media Specialists: 16.0 (658.3 to 1)
Guidance Counselors: 22.0 (478.8 to 1)
Current Spending: ($ per student per year):
Total: $5,391; Instruction: $2,987; Support Services: $2,099

Enrollment, Drop-out Rates and Diploma Recipients by Race/Ethnicity

Category	Total	White	Black	Asian	AIAN	Hisp.
Enrollment (%)	100.0	88.8	9.3	0.5	0.3	1.2
Drop-out Rate (%)	5.5	5.0	7.4	33.3	0.0	20.0
H.S. Diplomas (#)	577	513	53	5	0	6

Okaloosa County

Okaloosa County SD

120 Lowery Place, SE • Fort Walton Beach, FL 32548-5595
(850) 833-3109 • http://www.okaloosa.k12.fl.us/schools/
Grade Span: PK-12; **Agency Type:** 1
Schools: 56
24 Primary; 8 Middle; 9 High; 14 Other Level
50 Regular; 1 Special Education; 2 Vocational; 2 Alternative
0 Magnet; 3 Charter; 15 Title I Eligible; 10 School-wide Title I
Students: 31,291 (52.1% male; 47.9% female)
Individual Education Program: 4,991 (16.0%);
English Language Learner: 169 (0.5%); Migrant: 13 (<0.1%)
Eligible for Free Lunch Program: 6,244 (20.0%)
Eligible for Reduced-Price Lunch Program: 2,580 (8.2%)
Teachers: 1,595.0 (19.6 to 1)
Librarians/Media Specialists: 36.0 (869.2 to 1)
Guidance Counselors: 56.0 (558.8 to 1)
Current Spending: ($ per student per year):
Total: $5,644; Instruction: $3,366; Support Services: $2,043

Enrollment, Drop-out Rates and Diploma Recipients by Race/Ethnicity

Category	Total	White	Black	Asian	AIAN	Hisp.
Enrollment (%)	100.0	80.3	12.8	2.7	0.5	3.6
Drop-out Rate (%)	4.3	3.8	8.1	3.8	0.0	2.5
H.S. Diplomas (#)	1,978	1,615	218	72	7	66

Okeechobee County

Okeechobee County SD

700 SW 2nd Ave • Okeechobee, FL 34974-5117
(863) 462-5000 • http://www.okee.k12.fl.us/web.nsf
Grade Span: PK-12; **Agency Type:** 1
Schools: 18
7 Primary; 1 Middle; 1 High; 9 Other Level
11 Regular; 2 Special Education; 0 Vocational; 5 Alternative
0 Magnet; 0 Charter; 5 Title I Eligible; 5 School-wide Title I
Students: 7,085 (52.0% male; 48.0% female)
Individual Education Program: 1,487 (21.0%);
English Language Learner: 429 (6.1%); Migrant: 1,230 (17.4%)
Eligible for Free Lunch Program: 3,186 (45.0%)
Eligible for Reduced-Price Lunch Program: 687 (9.7%)
Teachers: 415.0 (17.1 to 1)
Librarians/Media Specialists: 7.0 (1,012.1 to 1)
Guidance Counselors: 15.0 (472.3 to 1)
Current Spending: ($ per student per year):
Total: $5,801; Instruction: $3,219; Support Services: $2,232

Enrollment, Drop-out Rates and Diploma Recipients by Race/Ethnicity

Category	Total	White	Black	Asian	AIAN	Hisp.
Enrollment (%)	100.0	64.7	9.3	0.5	1.9	23.6
Drop-out Rate (%)	6.0	6.3	4.1	0.0	31.6	4.9
H.S. Diplomas (#)	339	248	28	2	3	58

Orange County

Orange County SD

PO Box 271 • Orlando, FL 32802-0271
(407) 317-3202 • http://www.ocps.k12.fl.us/schools/
Grade Span: PK-12; **Agency Type:** 1
Schools: 188
114 Primary; 27 Middle; 21 High; 24 Other Level
168 Regular; 5 Special Education; 4 Vocational; 9 Alternative
0 Magnet; 13 Charter; 79 Title I Eligible; 79 School-wide Title I
Students: 158,718 (51.6% male; 48.4% female)
Individual Education Program: 25,700 (16.2%);
English Language Learner: 19,613 (12.4%); Migrant: 1,510 (1.0%)
Eligible for Free Lunch Program: 53,942 (34.0%)
Eligible for Reduced-Price Lunch Program: 14,151 (8.9%)
Teachers: 9,128.0 (17.4 to 1)
Librarians/Media Specialists: 99.0 (1,603.2 to 1)
Guidance Counselors: 303.0 (523.8 to 1)
Current Spending: ($ per student per year):
Total: $5,721; Instruction: $3,143; Support Services: $2,271

Enrollment, Drop-out Rates and Diploma Recipients by Race/Ethnicity

Category	Total	White	Black	Asian	AIAN	Hisp.
Enrollment (%)	100.0	41.7	28.5	3.8	0.4	25.6
Drop-out Rate (%)	5.9	4.6	7.3	2.6	1.5	7.9
H.S. Diplomas (#)	7,361	3,737	1,713	401	34	1,476

Osceola County

Osceola County SD

817 Bill Beck Blvd • Kissimmee, FL 34744-4495
(407) 870-4008 • http://www.osceola.k12.fl.us/
Grade Span: PK-12; **Agency Type:** 1
Schools: 55
24 Primary; 8 Middle; 6 High; 17 Other Level
46 Regular; 1 Special Education; 0 Vocational; 8 Alternative
0 Magnet; 9 Charter; 21 Title I Eligible; 17 School-wide Title I
Students: 40,485 (51.5% male; 48.5% female)
Individual Education Program: 6,181 (15.3%);
English Language Learner: 6,527 (16.1%); Migrant: 127 (0.3%)
Eligible for Free Lunch Program: 15,941 (39.4%)
Eligible for Reduced-Price Lunch Program: 5,242 (12.9%)
Teachers: 1,853.0 (21.8 to 1)
Librarians/Media Specialists: 32.0 (1,265.2 to 1)
Guidance Counselors: 78.0 (519.0 to 1)
Current Spending: ($ per student per year):
Total: $5,543; Instruction: $2,993; Support Services: $2,280

Enrollment, Drop-out Rates and Diploma Recipients by Race/Ethnicity

Category	Total	White	Black	Asian	AIAN	Hisp.
Enrollment (%)	100.0	44.7	9.5	2.4	0.2	43.2
Drop-out Rate (%)	5.2	5.1	6.4	2.9	0.0	5.3
H.S. Diplomas (#)	1,853	979	172	71	1	630

Palm Beach County

Palm Beach County SD

3340 Forest Hill Blvd • West Palm Beach, FL 33406-5869
(561) 434-8200 • http://www.palmbeach.k12.fl.us/schools/
Grade Span: PK-12; **Agency Type:** 1
Schools: 208
114 Primary; 33 Middle; 27 High; 31 Other Level
186 Regular; 3 Special Education; 0 Vocational; 16 Alternative
0 Magnet; 23 Charter; 82 Title I Eligible; 82 School-wide Title I
Students: 164,896 (51.5% male; 48.5% female)
Individual Education Program: 23,875 (14.5%);
English Language Learner: 18,116 (11.0%); Migrant: 5,661 (3.4%)
Eligible for Free Lunch Program: 57,265 (34.7%)

Eligible for Reduced-Price Lunch Program: 10,851 (6.6%)
Teachers: 8,826.0 (18.7 to 1)
Librarians/Media Specialists: 153.0 (1,077.8 to 1)
Guidance Counselors: 382.0 (431.7 to 1)
Current Spending: ($ per student per year):
Total: $6,266; Instruction: $3,789; Support Services: $2,199
Enrollment, Drop-out Rates and Diploma Recipients by Race/Ethnicity

Category	Total	White	Black	Asian	AIAN	Hisp.
Enrollment (%)	100.0	47.5	29.7	2.2	0.5	20.0
Drop-out Rate (%)	3.0	2.1	4.2	1.2	0.7	4.2
H.S. Diplomas (#)	7,687	4,387	1,904	243	21	1,132

Pasco County

Pasco County SD

7227 Land O'lakes Blvd • Land O' Lakes, FL 34639-2899
(813) 794-2648 • http://www.pasco.k12.fl.us/schoollist.html
Grade Span: PK-12; **Agency Type:** 1
Schools: 72
35 Primary; 11 Middle; 8 High; 18 Other Level
70 Regular; 0 Special Education; 1 Vocational; 1 Alternative
0 Magnet; 6 Charter; 19 Title I Eligible; 19 School-wide Title I
Students: 54,957 (51.6% male; 48.4% female)
Individual Education Program: 10,639 (19.4%);
English Language Learner: 1,674 (3.0%); Migrant: 546 (1.0%)
Eligible for Free Lunch Program: 19,145 (34.8%)
Eligible for Reduced-Price Lunch Program: 6,240 (11.4%)
Teachers: 3,052.0 (18.0 to 1)
Librarians/Media Specialists: 73.0 (752.8 to 1)
Guidance Counselors: 133.0 (413.2 to 1)
Current Spending: ($ per student per year):
Total: $5,789; Instruction: $3,246; Support Services: $2,220
Enrollment, Drop-out Rates and Diploma Recipients by Race/Ethnicity

Category	Total	White	Black	Asian	AIAN	Hisp.
Enrollment (%)	100.0	85.8	4.0	1.2	0.3	8.7
Drop-out Rate (%)	5.4	5.1	8.7	1.7	0.0	8.7
H.S. Diplomas (#)	2,453	2,159	81	46	7	160

Pinellas County

Pinellas County SD

301 4th St SW • Largo, FL 33770-3536
(727) 588-6011 • http://www.pinellas.k12.fl.us/
Grade Span: PK-12; **Agency Type:** 1
Schools: 172
85 Primary; 25 Middle; 20 High; 39 Other Level
150 Regular; 8 Special Education; 2 Vocational; 9 Alternative
0 Magnet; 4 Charter; 52 Title I Eligible; 52 School-wide Title I
Students: 114,772 (51.5% male; 48.5% female)
Individual Education Program: 20,290 (17.7%);
English Language Learner: 2,871 (2.5%); Migrant: 0 (0.0%)
Eligible for Free Lunch Program: 33,946 (29.6%)
Eligible for Reduced-Price Lunch Program: 10,110 (8.8%)
Teachers: 6,516.0 (17.6 to 1)
Librarians/Media Specialists: 118.0 (972.6 to 1)
Guidance Counselors: 234.0 (490.5 to 1)
Current Spending: ($ per student per year):
Total: $6,150; Instruction: $3,591; Support Services: $2,279
Enrollment, Drop-out Rates and Diploma Recipients by Race/Ethnicity

Category	Total	White	Black	Asian	AIAN	Hisp.
Enrollment (%)	100.0	71.2	19.3	3.2	0.3	6.1
Drop-out Rate (%)	5.0	4.3	7.9	4.0	1.6	6.3
H.S. Diplomas (#)	5,413	4,332	672	207	12	190

Polk County

Polk County SD

PO Box 391 • Bartow, FL 33831-0391
(863) 534-0521 • http://www.pinellas.k12.fl.us/
Grade Span: PK-12; **Agency Type:** 1
Schools: 148
73 Primary; 21 Middle; 17 High; 33 Other Level
120 Regular; 3 Special Education; 2 Vocational; 19 Alternative
0 Magnet; 12 Charter; 61 Title I Eligible; 61 School-wide Title I
Students: 82,179 (52.1% male; 47.9% female)
Individual Education Program: 12,726 (15.5%);
English Language Learner: 3,756 (4.6%); Migrant: 1,989 (2.4%)
Eligible for Free Lunch Program: 36,545 (44.5%)
Eligible for Reduced-Price Lunch Program: 8,293 (10.1%)
Teachers: 4,801.0 (17.1 to 1)
Librarians/Media Specialists: 115.0 (714.6 to 1)
Guidance Counselors: 181.0 (454.0 to 1)
Current Spending: ($ per student per year):
Total: $5,882; Instruction: $3,418; Support Services: $2,090
Enrollment, Drop-out Rates and Diploma Recipients by Race/Ethnicity

Category	Total	White	Black	Asian	AIAN	Hisp.
Enrollment (%)	100.0	61.6	22.8	1.1	0.2	14.3
Drop-out Rate (%)	6.9	6.6	6.7	0.4	6.5	10.2
H.S. Diplomas (#)	3,815	2,594	832	67	5	317

Putnam County

Putnam County SD

200 S 7th St • Palatka, FL 32177-4615
(386) 329-0510 • http://www.putnamschools.org/
Grade Span: PK-12; **Agency Type:** 1
Schools: 21
10 Primary; 4 Middle; 3 High; 4 Other Level
18 Regular; 2 Special Education; 0 Vocational; 1 Alternative
0 Magnet; 0 Charter; 15 Title I Eligible; 15 School-wide Title I
Students: 12,483 (52.9% male; 47.1% female)
Individual Education Program: 2,266 (18.2%);
English Language Learner: 454 (3.6%); Migrant: 375 (3.0%)
Eligible for Free Lunch Program: 6,869 (55.0%)
Eligible for Reduced-Price Lunch Program: 1,210 (9.7%)
Teachers: 728.0 (17.1 to 1)
Librarians/Media Specialists: 17.0 (734.3 to 1)
Guidance Counselors: 35.0 (356.7 to 1)
Current Spending: ($ per student per year):
Total: $5,867; Instruction: $3,128; Support Services: $2,360
Enrollment, Drop-out Rates and Diploma Recipients by Race/Ethnicity

Category	Total	White	Black	Asian	AIAN	Hisp.
Enrollment (%)	100.0	63.3	26.8	0.5	0.1	9.3
Drop-out Rate (%)	2.8	2.4	2.9	0.0	0.0	6.7
H.S. Diplomas (#)	447	318	107	2	1	19

Santa Rosa County

Santa Rosa County SD

603 Canal St • Milton, FL 32570-6726
(850) 983-5010 • http://www.santarosa.k12.fl.us/
Grade Span: PK-12; **Agency Type:** 1
Schools: 37
15 Primary; 6 Middle; 9 High; 7 Other Level
35 Regular; 1 Special Education; 1 Vocational; 0 Alternative
0 Magnet; 1 Charter; 13 Title I Eligible; 10 School-wide Title I
Students: 23,645 (52.0% male; 48.0% female)
Individual Education Program: 3,863 (16.3%);
English Language Learner: 40 (0.2%); Migrant: 5 (<0.1%)
Eligible for Free Lunch Program: 5,395 (22.8%)
Eligible for Reduced-Price Lunch Program: 2,225 (9.4%)
Teachers: 1,230.0 (19.2 to 1)
Librarians/Media Specialists: 29.0 (815.3 to 1)
Guidance Counselors: 50.0 (472.9 to 1)
Current Spending: ($ per student per year):
Total: $5,771; Instruction: $3,257; Support Services: $2,215
Enrollment, Drop-out Rates and Diploma Recipients by Race/Ethnicity

Category	Total	White	Black	Asian	AIAN	Hisp.
Enrollment (%)	100.0	90.6	5.4	1.5	0.6	1.9
Drop-out Rate (%)	2.4	2.2	5.0	2.7	2.3	4.6
H.S. Diplomas (#)	1,333	1,221	45	22	12	33

Sarasota County

Sarasota County SD

1960 Landings Blvd • Sarasota, FL 34231-3331
(941) 927-9000 • http://www.sarasota.k12.fl.us/
Grade Span: PK-12; **Agency Type:** 1
Schools: 51
22 Primary; 7 Middle; 7 High; 12 Other Level
41 Regular; 3 Special Education; 1 Vocational; 3 Alternative
0 Magnet; 6 Charter; 11 Title I Eligible; 11 School-wide Title I
Students: 38,057 (51.2% male; 48.8% female)
Individual Education Program: 6,521 (17.1%);
English Language Learner: 1,545 (4.1%); Migrant: 115 (0.3%)
Eligible for Free Lunch Program: 9,362 (24.6%)
Eligible for Reduced-Price Lunch Program: 3,550 (9.3%)
Teachers: 2,139.0 (17.8 to 1)
Librarians/Media Specialists: 15.0 (2,537.1 to 1)
Guidance Counselors: 55.0 (691.9 to 1)
Current Spending: ($ per student per year):
Total: $6,606; Instruction: $3,831; Support Services: $2,467
Enrollment, Drop-out Rates and Diploma Recipients by Race/Ethnicity

Category	Total	White	Black	Asian	AIAN	Hisp.
Enrollment (%)	100.0	80.3	9.6	1.5	0.2	8.4
Drop-out Rate (%)	3.5	3.1	6.7	1.9	5.3	5.2
H.S. Diplomas (#)	1,895	1,634	118	47	1	95

Seminole County

Seminole County SD
400 E Lake Mary Blvd • Sanford, FL 32773-7127
(407) 320-0006 • http://www.scps.k12.fl.us/
Grade Span: PK-12; **Agency Type:** 1
Schools: 75
38 Primary; 12 Middle; 8 High; 14 Other Level
61 Regular; 3 Special Education; 0 Vocational; 8 Alternative
0 Magnet; 3 Charter; 20 Title I Eligible; 20 School-wide Title I
Students: 63,446 (51.3% male; 48.7% female)
Individual Education Program: 8,133 (12.8%);
English Language Learner: 1,953 (3.1%); Migrant: 0 (0.0%)
Eligible for Free Lunch Program: 13,512 (21.3%)
Eligible for Reduced-Price Lunch Program: 4,826 (7.6%)
Teachers: 3,411.0 (18.6 to 1)
Librarians/Media Specialists: 43.0 (1,475.5 to 1)
Guidance Counselors: 109.0 (582.1 to 1)
Current Spending: ($ per student per year):
Total: $5,511; Instruction: $3,340; Support Services: $1,914
Enrollment, Drop-out Rates and Diploma Recipients by Race/Ethnicity

Category	Total	White	Black	Asian	AIAN	Hisp.
Enrollment (%)	100.0	68.5	13.6	3.1	0.2	14.6
Drop-out Rate (%)	1.0	0.9	1.7	0.8	2.4	1.1
H.S. Diplomas (#)	3,420	2,516	355	138	9	402

St. Johns County

Saint Johns County SD
40 Orange St • Saint Augustine, FL 32084-3693
(904) 826-2101 • http://macserver.stjohns.k12.fl.us/
Grade Span: PK-12; **Agency Type:** 1
Schools: 36
15 Primary; 5 Middle; 7 High; 8 Other Level
34 Regular; 0 Special Education; 0 Vocational; 1 Alternative
0 Magnet; 5 Charter; 8 Title I Eligible; 5 School-wide Title I
Students: 21,975 (51.8% male; 48.2% female)
Individual Education Program: 3,490 (15.9%);
English Language Learner: 143 (0.7%); Migrant: 32 (0.1%)
Eligible for Free Lunch Program: 3,357 (15.3%)
Eligible for Reduced-Price Lunch Program: 1,081 (4.9%)
Teachers: 1,215.0 (18.1 to 1)
Librarians/Media Specialists: 27.0 (813.9 to 1)
Guidance Counselors: 51.0 (430.9 to 1)
Current Spending: ($ per student per year):
Total: $6,154; Instruction: $3,600; Support Services: $2,299
Enrollment, Drop-out Rates and Diploma Recipients by Race/Ethnicity

Category	Total	White	Black	Asian	AIAN	Hisp.
Enrollment (%)	100.0	86.8	9.5	1.2	0.1	2.3
Drop-out Rate (%)	2.8	2.6	5.4	0.0	0.0	0.7
H.S. Diplomas (#)	1,097	965	82	11	1	38

St. Lucie County

Saint Lucie County SD
2909 Delaware Ave • Fort Pierce, FL 34947-7299
(561) 468-5021 • http://plato.stlucie.k12.fl.us/
Grade Span: PK-12; **Agency Type:** 1
Schools: 43
22 Primary; 6 Middle; 5 High; 10 Other Level
35 Regular; 2 Special Education; 0 Vocational; 6 Alternative
0 Magnet; 0 Charter; 26 Title I Eligible; 26 School-wide Title I
Students: 31,554 (51.0% male; 49.0% female)
Individual Education Program: 4,528 (14.4%);
English Language Learner: 1,766 (5.6%); Migrant: 4,142 (13.1%)
Eligible for Free Lunch Program: 13,885 (44.0%)
Eligible for Reduced-Price Lunch Program: 3,190 (10.1%)
Teachers: 2,000.0 (15.8 to 1)
Librarians/Media Specialists: 37.0 (852.8 to 1)
Guidance Counselors: 81.0 (389.6 to 1)
Current Spending: ($ per student per year):
Total: $6,064; Instruction: $3,334; Support Services: $2,373
Enrollment, Drop-out Rates and Diploma Recipients by Race/Ethnicity

Category	Total	White	Black	Asian	AIAN	Hisp.
Enrollment (%)	100.0	56.5	29.1	1.3	0.3	12.7
Drop-out Rate (%)	2.1	1.7	3.2	0.9	0.0	1.2
H.S. Diplomas (#)	1,258	758	368	24	3	105

Sumter County

Sumter County SD
2680 Wc 476 • Bushnell, FL 33513-3574
(352) 793-2315 • http://www.sumter.k12.fl.us/
Grade Span: PK-12; **Agency Type:** 1
Schools: 13
6 Primary; 3 Middle; 2 High; 2 Other Level
11 Regular; 1 Special Education; 0 Vocational; 1 Alternative
0 Magnet; 2 Charter; 5 Title I Eligible; 5 School-wide Title I
Students: 6,558 (51.2% male; 48.8% female)
Individual Education Program: 1,197 (18.3%);
English Language Learner: 241 (3.7%); Migrant: 297 (4.5%)
Eligible for Free Lunch Program: 3,075 (46.9%)
Eligible for Reduced-Price Lunch Program: 676 (10.3%)
Teachers: 357.0 (18.4 to 1)
Librarians/Media Specialists: 12.0 (546.5 to 1)
Guidance Counselors: 13.0 (504.5 to 1)
Current Spending: ($ per student per year):
Total: $6,221; Instruction: $3,421; Support Services: $2,428
Enrollment, Drop-out Rates and Diploma Recipients by Race/Ethnicity

Category	Total	White	Black	Asian	AIAN	Hisp.
Enrollment (%)	100.0	70.2	21.8	0.6	0.2	7.2
Drop-out Rate (%)	3.3	2.7	4.9	0.0	0.0	5.7
H.S. Diplomas (#)	261	187	54	1	3	16

Suwannee County

Suwannee County SD
702 Second Street, NW • Live Oak, FL 32060-1608
(386) 364-2604 • http://www.suwannee.k12.fl.us/
Grade Span: PK-12; **Agency Type:** 1
Schools: 10
3 Primary; 1 Middle; 2 High; 4 Other Level
9 Regular; 0 Special Education; 1 Vocational; 0 Alternative
0 Magnet; 0 Charter; 3 Title I Eligible; 3 School-wide Title I
Students: 5,802 (53.0% male; 47.0% female)
Individual Education Program: 815 (14.0%);
English Language Learner: 101 (1.7%); Migrant: 142 (2.4%)
Eligible for Free Lunch Program: 2,382 (41.1%)
Eligible for Reduced-Price Lunch Program: 553 (9.5%)
Teachers: 309.0 (18.8 to 1)
Librarians/Media Specialists: 7.0 (828.9 to 1)
Guidance Counselors: 14.0 (414.4 to 1)
Current Spending: ($ per student per year):
Total: $5,865; Instruction: $3,418; Support Services: $2,125
Enrollment, Drop-out Rates and Diploma Recipients by Race/Ethnicity

Category	Total	White	Black	Asian	AIAN	Hisp.
Enrollment (%)	100.0	76.5	17.5	0.7	0.4	4.8
Drop-out Rate (%)	6.0	5.7	6.9	14.3	14.3	5.1
H.S. Diplomas (#)	284	228	46	2	1	7

Taylor County

Taylor County SD
318 N Clark St • Perry, FL 32347-2930
(850) 838-2500 • http://www.taylor.k12.fl.us/
Grade Span: PK-12; **Agency Type:** 1
Schools: 9
4 Primary; 1 Middle; 2 High; 2 Other Level
7 Regular; 0 Special Education; 1 Vocational; 1 Alternative
0 Magnet; 0 Charter; 4 Title I Eligible; 4 School-wide Title I
Students: 3,593 (51.3% male; 48.7% female)
Individual Education Program: 678 (18.9%);
English Language Learner: 2 (0.1%); Migrant: 1 (<0.1%)
Eligible for Free Lunch Program: 1,644 (45.8%)
Eligible for Reduced-Price Lunch Program: 286 (8.0%)
Teachers: 212.0 (16.9 to 1)
Librarians/Media Specialists: 4.0 (898.3 to 1)
Guidance Counselors: 5.0 (718.6 to 1)
Current Spending: ($ per student per year):
Total: $6,012; Instruction: $3,387; Support Services: $2,299
Enrollment, Drop-out Rates and Diploma Recipients by Race/Ethnicity

Category	Total	White	Black	Asian	AIAN	Hisp.
Enrollment (%)	100.0	74.8	23.0	0.5	0.6	1.1
Drop-out Rate (%)	2.1	1.8	3.3	0.0	0.0	0.0
H.S. Diplomas (#)	203	160	39	2	1	1

Union County

Union County SD
55 SW 6th St • Lake Butler, FL 32054-2599
(386) 496-2045 • http://www.union.k12.fl.us/
Grade Span: PK-12; **Agency Type:** 1
Schools: 6
1 Primary; 1 Middle; 1 High; 3 Other Level
5 Regular; 0 Special Education; 0 Vocational; 1 Alternative
0 Magnet; 0 Charter; 2 Title I Eligible; 2 School-wide Title I
Students: 2,174 (53.0% male; 47.0% female)
Individual Education Program: 374 (17.2%);
English Language Learner: 2 (0.1%); Migrant: 17 (0.8%)
Eligible for Free Lunch Program: 797 (36.7%)

Eligible for Reduced-Price Lunch Program: 167 (7.7%)
Teachers: 153.0 (14.2 to 1)
Librarians/Media Specialists: 2.0 (1,087.0 to 1)
Guidance Counselors: 3.0 (724.7 to 1)
Current Spending: ($ per student per year):
Total: $5,348; Instruction: $2,921; Support Services: $2,113

Enrollment, Drop-out Rates and Diploma Recipients by Race/Ethnicity

Category	Total	White	Black	Asian	AIAN	Hisp.
Enrollment (%)	100.0	79.9	17.8	0.3	0.0	1.9
Drop-out Rate (%)	4.0	4.0	4.5	0.0	n/a	0.0
H.S. Diplomas (#)	129	105	22	0	1	1

Volusia County

Volusia County SD

PO Box 2118 • Deland, FL 32721-2118
(386) 734-7190 • http://www.volusia.k12.fl.us/
Grade Span: PK-12; **Agency Type:** 1
Schools: 92
46 Primary; 11 Middle; 10 High; 24 Other Level
82 Regular; 2 Special Education; 0 Vocational; 7 Alternative
0 Magnet; 3 Charter; 47 Title I Eligible; 42 School-wide Title I
Students: 63,000 (51.6% male; 48.4% female)
Individual Education Program: 10,952 (17.4%);
English Language Learner: 1,907 (3.0%); Migrant: 1,109 (1.8%)
Eligible for Free Lunch Program: 19,089 (30.3%)
Eligible for Reduced-Price Lunch Program: 5,183 (8.2%)
Teachers: 3,824.0 (16.5 to 1)
Librarians/Media Specialists: 70.0 (900.0 to 1)
Guidance Counselors: 194.0 (324.7 to 1)
Current Spending: ($ per student per year):
Total: $5,810; Instruction: $3,426; Support Services: $2,112

Enrollment, Drop-out Rates and Diploma Recipients by Race/Ethnicity

Category	Total	White	Black	Asian	AIAN	Hisp.
Enrollment (%)	100.0	72.5	15.5	1.1	0.2	10.6
Drop-out Rate (%)	1.7	1.3	3.2	0.8	6.1	2.5
H.S. Diplomas (#)	3,386	2,675	396	59	3	253

Wakulla County

Wakulla County SD

PO Box 100 • Crawfordville, FL 32326-0100
(850) 926-7131 • http://www.firn.edu/schools/wakulla/wakulla/
Grade Span: PK-12; **Agency Type:** 1
Schools: 11
5 Primary; 2 Middle; 1 High; 3 Other Level
9 Regular; 0 Special Education; 0 Vocational; 2 Alternative
0 Magnet; 1 Charter; 5 Title I Eligible; 1 School-wide Title I
Students: 4,663 (52.1% male; 47.9% female)
Individual Education Program: 884 (19.0%);
English Language Learner: 9 (0.2%); Migrant: 0 (0.0%)
Eligible for Free Lunch Program: 1,202 (25.8%)
Eligible for Reduced-Price Lunch Program: 408 (8.7%)
Teachers: 251.0 (18.6 to 1)
Librarians/Media Specialists: 6.0 (777.2 to 1)
Guidance Counselors: 8.0 (582.9 to 1)
Current Spending: ($ per student per year):
Total: $5,777; Instruction: $3,169; Support Services: $2,322

Enrollment, Drop-out Rates and Diploma Recipients by Race/Ethnicity

Category	Total	White	Black	Asian	AIAN	Hisp.
Enrollment (%)	100.0	86.6	11.7	0.4	0.2	1.1
Drop-out Rate (%)	2.7	2.7	3.8	0.0	0.0	0.0
H.S. Diplomas (#)	233	198	30	1	2	2

Walton County

Walton County SD

145 Park Street, Ste #3 • Defuniak Springs, FL 32433-3344
(850) 892-8331 • http://www.walton.k12.fl.us/
Grade Span: PK-12; **Agency Type:** 1
Schools: 17
4 Primary; 2 Middle; 3 High; 7 Other Level
15 Regular; 0 Special Education; 1 Vocational; 0 Alternative
0 Magnet; 2 Charter; 7 Title I Eligible; 7 School-wide Title I
Students: 6,303 (52.3% male; 47.7% female)
Individual Education Program: 1,005 (15.9%);
English Language Learner: 74 (1.2%); Migrant: 23 (0.4%)
Eligible for Free Lunch Program: 2,425 (38.5%)
Eligible for Reduced-Price Lunch Program: 723 (11.5%)
Teachers: 354.0 (17.8 to 1)
Librarians/Media Specialists: 9.0 (700.3 to 1)
Guidance Counselors: 12.0 (525.3 to 1)
Current Spending: ($ per student per year):
Total: $6,108; Instruction: $3,511; Support Services: $2,263

Enrollment, Drop-out Rates and Diploma Recipients by Race/Ethnicity

Category	Total	White	Black	Asian	AIAN	Hisp.
Enrollment (%)	100.0	87.9	9.0	0.5	0.5	2.1
Drop-out Rate (%)	5.2	5.0	5.3	14.3	0.0	12.9
H.S. Diplomas (#)	246	221	20	0	1	4

Washington County

Washington County SD

652 Third St • Chipley, FL 32428-1442
(850) 638-6222 • http://www.firn.edu/schools/washington/wash/index.htm
Grade Span: PK-12; **Agency Type:** 1
Schools: 8
2 Primary; 2 Middle; 2 High; 2 Other Level
7 Regular; 0 Special Education; 0 Vocational; 1 Alternative
0 Magnet; 0 Charter; 6 Title I Eligible; 6 School-wide Title I
Students: 3,410 (51.7% male; 48.3% female)
Individual Education Program: 541 (15.9%);
English Language Learner: 0 (0.0%); Migrant: 1 (<0.1%)
Eligible for Free Lunch Program: 1,654 (48.5%)
Eligible for Reduced-Price Lunch Program: 359 (10.5%)
Teachers: 225.0 (15.2 to 1)
Librarians/Media Specialists: 5.0 (682.0 to 1)
Guidance Counselors: 10.0 (341.0 to 1)
Current Spending: ($ per student per year):
Total: $7,570; Instruction: $4,290; Support Services: $2,907

Enrollment, Drop-out Rates and Diploma Recipients by Race/Ethnicity

Category	Total	White	Black	Asian	AIAN	Hisp.
Enrollment (%)	100.0	79.1	19.0	0.4	0.7	0.8
Drop-out Rate (%)	2.9	3.4	0.6	0.0	16.7	0.0
H.S. Diplomas (#)	191	153	36	1	0	1

Number of Schools

Rank	Number	District Name	City
1	370	Dade County SD	Miami
2	259	Broward County SD	Fort Lauderdale
3	229	Hillsborough County SD	Tampa
4	208	Palm Beach County SD	West Palm Beach
5	188	Orange County SD	Orlando
6	181	Duval County SD	Jacksonville
7	172	Pinellas County SD	Largo
8	148	Polk County SD	Bartow
9	110	Brevard County SD	Viera
10	92	Volusia County SD	Deland
11	86	Escambia County SD	Pensacola
12	79	Lee County SD	Fort Myers
13	75	Seminole County SD	Sanford
14	73	Manatee County SD	Bradenton
15	72	Pasco County SD	Land O' Lakes
16	65	Marion County SD	Ocala
17	62	Alachua County SD	Gainesville
18	58	Leon County SD	Tallahassee
19	56	Okaloosa County SD	Ft Walton Beach
20	55	Osceola County SD	Kissimmee
21	53	Collier County SD	Naples
21	53	Lake County SD	Tavares
23	51	Sarasota County SD	Sarasota
24	44	Bay County SD	Panama City
25	43	Saint Lucie County SD	Fort Pierce
26	37	Santa Rosa County SD	Milton
27	36	Saint Johns County SD	Saint Augustine
28	32	Clay County SD	Green Cove Spgs
29	29	Martin County SD	Stuart
30	28	Indian River County SD	Vero Beach
31	26	Citrus County SD	Inverness
32	25	Gadsden County SD	Quincy
33	24	Charlotte County SD	Port Charlotte
34	23	Hernando County SD	Brooksville
35	21	Jackson County SD	Marianna
35	21	Monroe County SD	Key West
35	21	Putnam County SD	Palatka
38	19	Nassau County SD	Fernandina Bch
39	18	Highlands County SD	Sebring
39	18	Okeechobee County SD	Okeechobee
41	17	Walton County SD	Defuniak Spgs
42	16	Hendry County SD	La Belle
42	16	Levy County SD	Bronson
44	15	Columbia County SD	Lake City
45	13	Desoto County SD	Arcadia
45	13	Sumter County SD	Bushnell
47	12	Bradford County SD	Starke
48	11	Wakulla County SD	Crawfordville
49	10	Flagler County SD	Bunnell
49	10	Suwannee County SD	Live Oak
51	9	Hardee County SD	Wauchula
51	9	Holmes County SD	Bonifay
51	9	Madison County SD	Madison
51	9	Taylor County SD	Perry
55	8	Baker County SD	Macclenny
55	8	Gulf County SD	Port Saint Joe
55	8	Washington County SD	Chipley
58	7	Calhoun County SD	Blountstown
58	7	Hamilton County SD	Jasper
58	7	Jefferson County SD	Monticello
61	6	Union County SD	Lake Butler
62	5	Dixie County SD	Cross City
63	4	Gilchrist County SD	Trenton

Number of Teachers

Rank	Number	District Name	City
1	18,656	Dade County SD	Miami
2	13,264	Broward County SD	Fort Lauderdale
3	10,499	Hillsborough County SD	Tampa
4	9,128	Orange County SD	Orlando
5	8,826	Palm Beach County SD	West Palm Beach
6	6,620	Duval County SD	Jacksonville
7	6,516	Pinellas County SD	Largo
8	4,801	Polk County SD	Bartow
9	4,079	Brevard County SD	Viera
10	3,824	Volusia County SD	Deland
11	3,411	Seminole County SD	Sanford
12	3,200	Lee County SD	Fort Myers
13	3,052	Pasco County SD	Land O' Lakes
14	2,393	Escambia County SD	Pensacola
15	2,209	Lake County SD	Tavares
16	2,190	Marion County SD	Ocala
17	2,167	Collier County SD	Naples
18	2,159	Manatee County SD	Bradenton
19	2,139	Sarasota County SD	Sarasota
20	2,000	Saint Lucie County SD	Fort Pierce
21	1,853	Osceola County SD	Kissimmee
22	1,711	Leon County SD	Tallahassee
23	1,657	Alachua County SD	Gainesville
23	1,657	Clay County SD	Green Cove Spgs
25	1,595	Okaloosa County SD	Ft Walton Beach
26	1,526	Bay County SD	Panama City
27	1,230	Santa Rosa County SD	Milton
28	1,215	Saint Johns County SD	Saint Augustine
29	1,016	Hernando County SD	Brooksville
30	928	Martin County SD	Stuart
31	926	Citrus County SD	Inverness
32	925	Charlotte County SD	Port Charlotte
33	728	Putnam County SD	Palatka
34	688	Monroe County SD	Key West
35	671	Highlands County SD	Sebring
36	569	Columbia County SD	Lake City
37	549	Nassau County SD	Fernandina Bch
38	453	Flagler County SD	Bunnell
39	437	Jackson County SD	Marianna
40	421	Gadsden County SD	Quincy
41	415	Okeechobee County SD	Okeechobee
42	393	Indian River County SD	Vero Beach
43	373	Hendry County SD	La Belle
44	366	Levy County SD	Bronson
45	357	Sumter County SD	Bushnell
46	354	Walton County SD	Defuniak Spgs
47	309	Suwannee County SD	Live Oak
48	300	Hardee County SD	Wauchula
49	284	Desoto County SD	Arcadia
50	251	Wakulla County SD	Crawfordville
51	241	Bradford County SD	Starke
52	240	Baker County SD	Macclenny
53	225	Washington County SD	Chipley
54	212	Taylor County SD	Perry
55	204	Holmes County SD	Bonifay
56	173	Madison County SD	Madison
57	154	Gilchrist County SD	Trenton
58	153	Union County SD	Lake Butler
59	147	Calhoun County SD	Blountstown
60	130	Gulf County SD	Port Saint Joe
61	128	Dixie County SD	Cross City
61	128	Hamilton County SD	Jasper
63	103	Jefferson County SD	Monticello

Number of Students

Rank	Number	District Name	City
1	373,395	Dade County SD	Miami
2	267,925	Broward County SD	Fort Lauderdale
3	175,454	Hillsborough County SD	Tampa
4	164,896	Palm Beach County SD	West Palm Beach
5	158,718	Orange County SD	Orlando
6	128,126	Duval County SD	Jacksonville
7	114,772	Pinellas County SD	Largo
8	82,179	Polk County SD	Bartow
9	72,601	Brevard County SD	Viera
10	63,446	Seminole County SD	Sanford
11	63,172	Lee County SD	Fort Myers
12	63,000	Volusia County SD	Deland
13	54,957	Pasco County SD	Land O' Lakes
14	44,019	Escambia County SD	Pensacola
15	40,485	Osceola County SD	Kissimmee
16	39,710	Marion County SD	Ocala
17	39,132	Manatee County SD	Bradenton
18	38,110	Collier County SD	Naples
19	38,057	Sarasota County SD	Sarasota
20	31,857	Leon County SD	Tallahassee
21	31,782	Lake County SD	Tavares
22	31,554	Saint Lucie County SD	Fort Pierce
23	31,291	Okaloosa County SD	Ft Walton Beach
24	29,861	Clay County SD	Green Cove Spgs
25	29,345	Alachua County SD	Gainesville
26	26,440	Bay County SD	Panama City
27	23,645	Santa Rosa County SD	Milton
28	21,975	Saint Johns County SD	Saint Augustine
29	18,605	Hernando County SD	Brooksville
30	17,714	Charlotte County SD	Port Charlotte
31	17,259	Martin County SD	Stuart
32	15,986	Indian River County SD	Vero Beach
33	15,355	Citrus County SD	Inverness
34	12,483	Putnam County SD	Palatka
35	11,428	Highlands County SD	Sebring
36	10,533	Nassau County SD	Fernandina Bch
37	9,707	Columbia County SD	Lake City
38	9,218	Monroe County SD	Key West
39	7,673	Hendry County SD	La Belle
40	7,601	Flagler County SD	Bunnell
41	7,245	Jackson County SD	Marianna
42	7,196	Gadsden County SD	Quincy
43	7,085	Okeechobee County SD	Okeechobee
44	6,558	Sumter County SD	Bushnell
45	6,303	Walton County SD	Defuniak Spgs
46	6,113	Levy County SD	Bronson
47	5,802	Suwannee County SD	Live Oak
48	5,175	Hardee County SD	Wauchula
49	4,916	Desoto County SD	Arcadia
50	4,663	Wakulla County SD	Crawfordville
51	4,525	Baker County SD	Macclenny
52	4,034	Bradford County SD	Starke
53	3,593	Taylor County SD	Perry
54	3,414	Holmes County SD	Bonifay
55	3,410	Washington County SD	Chipley
56	3,311	Madison County SD	Madison
57	2,734	Gilchrist County SD	Trenton
58	2,229	Dixie County SD	Cross City
59	2,174	Calhoun County SD	Blountstown
59	2,174	Union County SD	Lake Butler
61	2,164	Gulf County SD	Port Saint Joe
62	2,065	Hamilton County SD	Jasper
63	1,575	Jefferson County SD	Monticello

Male Students

Rank	Percent	District Name	City
1	54.8	Madison County SD	Madison
2	53.4	Desoto County SD	Arcadia
3	53.0	Suwannee County SD	Live Oak
3	53.0	Union County SD	Lake Butler
5	52.9	Hardee County SD	Wauchula
5	52.9	Putnam County SD	Palatka
7	52.8	Monroe County SD	Key West
8	52.5	Holmes County SD	Bonifay
9	52.3	Baker County SD	Macclenny
9	52.3	Walton County SD	Defuniak Spgs
11	52.1	Okaloosa County SD	Ft Walton Beach
11	52.1	Polk County SD	Bartow
11	52.1	Wakulla County SD	Crawfordville
14	52.0	Bradford County SD	Starke
14	52.0	Hendry County SD	La Belle
14	52.0	Okeechobee County SD	Okeechobee
14	52.0	Santa Rosa County SD	Milton
18	51.9	Citrus County SD	Inverness
18	51.9	Gulf County SD	Port Saint Joe
18	51.9	Highlands County SD	Sebring
18	51.9	Levy County SD	Bronson
18	51.9	Nassau County SD	Fernandina Bch
23	51.8	Saint Johns County SD	Saint Augustine
24	51.7	Broward County SD	Fort Lauderdale
24	51.7	Dixie County SD	Cross City
24	51.7	Manatee County SD	Bradenton
24	51.7	Marion County SD	Ocala
24	51.7	Washington County SD	Chipley
29	51.6	Brevard County SD	Viera
29	51.6	Orange County SD	Orlando
29	51.6	Pasco County SD	Land O' Lakes
29	51.6	Volusia County SD	Deland
33	51.5	Bay County SD	Panama City
33	51.5	Collier County SD	Naples
33	51.5	Osceola County SD	Kissimmee
33	51.5	Palm Beach County SD	West Palm Beach
33	51.5	Pinellas County SD	Largo
38	51.4	Clay County SD	Green Cove Spgs
38	51.4	Flagler County SD	Bunnell
38	51.4	Lee County SD	Fort Myers
38	51.4	Martin County SD	Stuart
42	51.3	Dade County SD	Miami
42	51.3	Hillsborough County SD	Tampa
42	51.3	Jackson County SD	Marianna
42	51.3	Seminole County SD	Sanford
42	51.3	Taylor County SD	Perry
47	51.2	Columbia County SD	Lake City
47	51.2	Escambia County SD	Pensacola
47	51.2	Gilchrist County SD	Trenton
47	51.2	Indian River County SD	Vero Beach
47	51.2	Jefferson County SD	Monticello
47	51.2	Lake County SD	Tavares
47	51.2	Leon County SD	Tallahassee
47	51.2	Sarasota County SD	Sarasota
47	51.2	Sumter County SD	Bushnell
56	51.1	Calhoun County SD	Blountstown
57	51.0	Charlotte County SD	Port Charlotte
57	51.0	Hernando County SD	Brooksville
57	51.0	Saint Lucie County SD	Fort Pierce
60	50.8	Duval County SD	Jacksonville
60	50.8	Gadsden County SD	Quincy
60	50.8	Hamilton County SD	Jasper
63	50.5	Alachua County SD	Gainesville

Female Students

Rank	Percent	District Name	City
1	49.5	Alachua County SD	Gainesville
2	49.2	Duval County SD	Jacksonville
2	49.2	Gadsden County SD	Quincy
2	49.2	Hamilton County SD	Jasper
5	49.0	Charlotte County SD	Port Charlotte
5	49.0	Hernando County SD	Brooksville
5	49.0	Saint Lucie County SD	Fort Pierce
8	48.9	Calhoun County SD	Blountstown

9	48.8	Columbia County SD	Lake City
9	48.8	Escambia County SD	Pensacola
9	48.8	Gilchrist County SD	Trenton
9	48.8	Indian River County SD	Vero Beach
9	48.8	Jefferson County SD	Monticello
9	48.8	Lake County SD	Tavares
9	48.8	Leon County SD	Tallahassee
9	48.8	Sarasota County SD	Sarasota
9	48.8	Sumter County SD	Bushnell
18	48.7	Dade County SD	Miami
18	48.7	Hillsborough County SD	Tampa
18	48.7	Jackson County SD	Marianna
18	48.7	Seminole County SD	Sanford
18	48.7	Taylor County SD	Perry
23	48.6	Clay County SD	Green Cove Spgs
23	48.6	Flagler County SD	Bunnell
23	48.6	Lee County SD	Fort Myers
23	48.6	Martin County SD	Stuart
27	48.5	Bay County SD	Panama City
27	48.5	Collier County SD	Naples
27	48.5	Osceola County SD	Kissimmee
27	48.5	Palm Beach County SD	West Palm Beach
27	48.5	Pinellas County SD	Largo
32	48.4	Brevard County SD	Viera
32	48.4	Orange County SD	Orlando
32	48.4	Pasco County SD	Land O' Lakes
32	48.4	Volusia County SD	Deland
36	48.3	Broward County SD	Fort Lauderdale
36	48.3	Dixie County SD	Cross City
36	48.3	Manatee County SD	Bradenton
36	48.3	Marion County SD	Ocala
36	48.3	Washington County SD	Chipley
41	48.2	Saint Johns County SD	Saint Augustine
42	48.1	Citrus County SD	Inverness
42	48.1	Gulf County SD	Port Saint Joe
42	48.1	Highlands County SD	Sebring
42	48.1	Levy County SD	Bronson
42	48.1	Nassau County SD	Fernandina Bch
47	48.0	Bradford County SD	Starke
47	48.0	Hendry County SD	La Belle
47	48.0	Okeechobee County SD	Okeechobee
47	48.0	Santa Rosa County SD	Milton
51	47.9	Okaloosa County SD	Ft Walton Beach
51	47.9	Polk County SD	Bartow
51	47.9	Wakulla County SD	Crawfordville
54	47.7	Baker County SD	Macclenny
54	47.7	Walton County SD	Defuniak Spgs
56	47.5	Holmes County SD	Bonifay
57	47.2	Monroe County SD	Key West
58	47.1	Hardee County SD	Wauchula
58	47.1	Putnam County SD	Palatka
60	47.0	Suwannee County SD	Live Oak
60	47.0	Union County SD	Lake Butler
62	46.6	Desoto County SD	Arcadia
63	45.2	Madison County SD	Madison

Individual Education Program Students

Rank	Percent	District Name	City
1	26.0	Jefferson County SD	Monticello
2	25.4	Madison County SD	Madison
3	23.7	Gilchrist County SD	Trenton
4	23.4	Bradford County SD	Starke
5	23.3	Dixie County SD	Cross City
6	23.2	Levy County SD	Bronson
7	21.0	Hardee County SD	Wauchula
7	21.0	Okeechobee County SD	Okeechobee
9	20.8	Desoto County SD	Arcadia
10	20.7	Calhoun County SD	Blountstown
11	20.3	Jackson County SD	Marianna
11	20.3	Leon County SD	Tallahassee
13	19.5	Clay County SD	Green Cove Spgs
13	19.5	Manatee County SD	Bradenton
15	19.4	Charlotte County SD	Port Charlotte
15	19.4	Pasco County SD	Land O' Lakes
17	19.3	Bay County SD	Panama City
18	19.2	Alachua County SD	Gainesville
19	19.1	Citrus County SD	Inverness
20	19.0	Wakulla County SD	Crawfordville
21	18.9	Taylor County SD	Perry
22	18.3	Sumter County SD	Bushnell
23	18.2	Columbia County SD	Lake City
23	18.2	Highlands County SD	Sebring
23	18.2	Putnam County SD	Palatka
26	18.1	Gadsden County SD	Quincy
27	17.9	Hamilton County SD	Jasper
28	17.7	Hendry County SD	La Belle
28	17.7	Pinellas County SD	Largo
30	17.5	Marion County SD	Ocala
31	17.4	Monroe County SD	Key West
31	17.4	Volusia County SD	Deland
33	17.2	Flagler County SD	Bunnell
33	17.2	Hernando County SD	Brooksville
33	17.2	Union County SD	Lake Butler
36	17.1	Sarasota County SD	Sarasota
37	17.0	Lake County SD	Tavares
37	17.0	Martin County SD	Stuart
39	16.9	Escambia County SD	Pensacola
40	16.8	Brevard County SD	Viera
40	16.8	Gulf County SD	Port Saint Joe
42	16.3	Santa Rosa County SD	Milton
43	16.2	Orange County SD	Orlando
44	16.0	Holmes County SD	Bonifay
44	16.0	Okaloosa County SD	Ft Walton Beach
46	15.9	Nassau County SD	Fernandina Bch
46	15.9	Saint Johns County SD	Saint Augustine
46	15.9	Walton County SD	Defuniak Spgs
46	15.9	Washington County SD	Chipley
50	15.8	Duval County SD	Jacksonville
51	15.5	Collier County SD	Naples
51	15.5	Hillsborough County SD	Tampa
51	15.5	Lee County SD	Fort Myers
51	15.5	Polk County SD	Bartow
55	15.3	Osceola County SD	Kissimmee
56	14.7	Indian River County SD	Vero Beach
57	14.5	Palm Beach County SD	West Palm Beach
58	14.4	Saint Lucie County SD	Fort Pierce
59	14.0	Suwannee County SD	Live Oak
60	12.8	Baker County SD	Macclenny
60	12.8	Seminole County SD	Sanford
62	11.6	Dade County SD	Miami
63	11.4	Broward County SD	Fort Lauderdale

English Language Learner Students

Rank	Percent	District Name	City
1	17.7	Dade County SD	Miami
2	16.1	Osceola County SD	Kissimmee
3	14.7	Collier County SD	Naples
4	12.4	Orange County SD	Orlando
5	11.2	Broward County SD	Fort Lauderdale
6	11.0	Palm Beach County SD	West Palm Beach
7	10.6	Lee County SD	Fort Myers
8	10.3	Hillsborough County SD	Tampa
9	9.7	Hardee County SD	Wauchula
10	8.8	Martin County SD	Stuart
11	7.8	Hendry County SD	La Belle
12	7.4	Desoto County SD	Arcadia
13	6.5	Manatee County SD	Bradenton
14	6.3	Monroe County SD	Key West
15	6.1	Okeechobee County SD	Okeechobee
16	5.6	Saint Lucie County SD	Fort Pierce
17	5.4	Gadsden County SD	Quincy
18	4.6	Polk County SD	Bartow
19	4.1	Indian River County SD	Vero Beach
19	4.1	Sarasota County SD	Sarasota
21	3.9	Highlands County SD	Sebring
22	3.7	Sumter County SD	Bushnell
23	3.6	Putnam County SD	Palatka
24	3.4	Lake County SD	Tavares
25	3.1	Seminole County SD	Sanford
26	3.0	Pasco County SD	Land O' Lakes
26	3.0	Volusia County SD	Deland
28	2.8	Hamilton County SD	Jasper
29	2.6	Flagler County SD	Bunnell
30	2.5	Pinellas County SD	Largo
31	2.3	Levy County SD	Bronson
31	2.3	Marion County SD	Ocala
33	2.0	Duval County SD	Jacksonville
34	1.7	Suwannee County SD	Live Oak
35	1.5	Alachua County SD	Gainesville
36	1.3	Brevard County SD	Viera
36	1.3	Hernando County SD	Brooksville
38	1.2	Walton County SD	Defuniak Spgs
39	0.9	Charlotte County SD	Port Charlotte
39	0.9	Leon County SD	Tallahassee
41	0.8	Bay County SD	Panama City
42	0.7	Clay County SD	Green Cove Spgs
42	0.7	Escambia County SD	Pensacola
42	0.7	Saint Johns County SD	Saint Augustine
45	0.6	Bradford County SD	Starke
45	0.6	Citrus County SD	Inverness
45	0.6	Jackson County SD	Marianna
48	0.5	Okaloosa County SD	Ft Walton Beach
49	0.4	Gilchrist County SD	Trenton
50	0.3	Columbia County SD	Lake City
51	0.2	Madison County SD	Madison
51	0.2	Nassau County SD	Fernandina Bch
51	0.2	Santa Rosa County SD	Milton
51	0.2	Wakulla County SD	Crawfordville
55	0.1	Calhoun County SD	Blountstown
55	0.1	Gulf County SD	Port Saint Joe
55	0.1	Jefferson County SD	Monticello
55	0.1	Taylor County SD	Perry
55	0.1	Union County SD	Lake Butler
60	0.0	Baker County SD	Macclenny
61	0.0	Dixie County SD	Cross City
61	0.0	Holmes County SD	Bonifay
61	0.0	Washington County SD	Chipley

Migrant Students

Rank	Percent	District Name	City
1	40.0	Hardee County SD	Wauchula
2	35.8	Hendry County SD	La Belle
3	23.5	Collier County SD	Naples
4	17.4	Okeechobee County SD	Okeechobee
5	13.9	Desoto County SD	Arcadia
6	13.1	Saint Lucie County SD	Fort Pierce
7	11.3	Highlands County SD	Sebring
8	7.4	Gadsden County SD	Quincy
9	5.7	Indian River County SD	Vero Beach
10	4.5	Sumter County SD	Bushnell
11	4.1	Levy County SD	Bronson
11	4.1	Manatee County SD	Bradenton
13	3.8	Dixie County SD	Cross City
13	3.8	Gilchrist County SD	Trenton
15	3.4	Hamilton County SD	Jasper
15	3.4	Palm Beach County SD	West Palm Beach
17	3.0	Putnam County SD	Palatka
18	2.9	Hillsborough County SD	Tampa
19	2.4	Polk County SD	Bartow
19	2.4	Suwannee County SD	Live Oak
21	2.3	Lee County SD	Fort Myers
22	1.8	Martin County SD	Stuart
22	1.8	Volusia County SD	Deland
24	1.3	Lake County SD	Tavares
25	1.0	Holmes County SD	Bonifay
25	1.0	Orange County SD	Orlando
25	1.0	Pasco County SD	Land O' Lakes
28	0.9	Escambia County SD	Pensacola
29	0.8	Union County SD	Lake Butler
30	0.7	Calhoun County SD	Blountstown
30	0.7	Dade County SD	Miami
32	0.6	Madison County SD	Madison
33	0.5	Bay County SD	Panama City
33	0.5	Clay County SD	Green Cove Spgs
35	0.4	Broward County SD	Fort Lauderdale
35	0.4	Citrus County SD	Inverness
35	0.4	Walton County SD	Defuniak Spgs
38	0.3	Baker County SD	Macclenny
38	0.3	Columbia County SD	Lake City
38	0.3	Flagler County SD	Bunnell
38	0.3	Jackson County SD	Marianna
38	0.3	Jefferson County SD	Monticello
38	0.3	Monroe County SD	Key West
38	0.3	Nassau County SD	Fernandina Bch
38	0.3	Osceola County SD	Kissimmee
38	0.3	Sarasota County SD	Sarasota
47	0.2	Alachua County SD	Gainesville
47	0.2	Bradford County SD	Starke
47	0.2	Duval County SD	Jacksonville
47	0.2	Marion County SD	Ocala
51	0.1	Brevard County SD	Viera
51	0.1	Saint Johns County SD	Saint Augustine
53	0.0	Leon County SD	Tallahassee
53	0.0	Okaloosa County SD	Ft Walton Beach
53	0.0	Santa Rosa County SD	Milton
53	0.0	Taylor County SD	Perry
53	0.0	Washington County SD	Chipley
58	0.0	Charlotte County SD	Port Charlotte
58	0.0	Gulf County SD	Port Saint Joe
58	0.0	Hernando County SD	Brooksville
58	0.0	Pinellas County SD	Largo
58	0.0	Seminole County SD	Sanford
58	0.0	Wakulla County SD	Crawfordville

Students Eligible for Free Lunch

Rank	Percent	District Name	City
1	65.9	Gadsden County SD	Quincy
2	62.8	Hamilton County SD	Jasper
2	62.8	Jefferson County SD	Monticello
4	61.3	Hendry County SD	La Belle
5	60.4	Hardee County SD	Wauchula
6	55.2	Dixie County SD	Cross City
7	55.0	Putnam County SD	Palatka
8	54.9	Madison County SD	Madison
9	53.6	Dade County SD	Miami
10	51.3	Desoto County SD	Arcadia
11	48.5	Washington County SD	Chipley
12	47.3	Highlands County SD	Sebring
13	46.9	Sumter County SD	Bushnell
14	46.4	Levy County SD	Bronson
15	46.1	Escambia County SD	Pensacola
16	45.8	Taylor County SD	Perry
17	45.0	Okeechobee County SD	Okeechobee
18	44.8	Bradford County SD	Starke
19	44.5	Polk County SD	Bartow

20	44.0	Columbia County SD	Lake City
20	44.0	Saint Lucie County SD	Fort Pierce
22	43.1	Jackson County SD	Marianna
23	42.1	Holmes County SD	Bonifay
24	41.9	Marion County SD	Ocala
25	41.6	Alachua County SD	Gainesville
25	41.6	Gilchrist County SD	Trenton
27	41.1	Suwannee County SD	Live Oak
28	39.6	Hillsborough County SD	Tampa
29	39.4	Osceola County SD	Kissimmee
30	38.5	Calhoun County SD	Blountstown
30	38.5	Walton County SD	Defuniak Spgs
32	36.7	Union County SD	Lake Butler
33	36.4	Lee County SD	Fort Myers
34	35.5	Bay County SD	Panama City
35	35.2	Gulf County SD	Port Saint Joe
36	34.8	Pasco County SD	Land O' Lakes
37	34.7	Palm Beach County SD	West Palm Beach
38	34.0	Orange County SD	Orlando
39	33.3	Manatee County SD	Bradenton
40	33.0	Hernando County SD	Brooksville
41	32.6	Duval County SD	Jacksonville
42	32.5	Citrus County SD	Inverness
43	32.0	Baker County SD	Macclenny
44	31.7	Lake County SD	Tavares
45	31.1	Broward County SD	Fort Lauderdale
46	30.7	Charlotte County SD	Port Charlotte
47	30.3	Volusia County SD	Deland
48	30.1	Indian River County SD	Vero Beach
49	29.6	Pinellas County SD	Largo
50	28.4	Monroe County SD	Key West
51	27.7	Flagler County SD	Bunnell
52	27.4	Leon County SD	Tallahassee
53	26.5	Martin County SD	Stuart
54	25.8	Wakulla County SD	Crawfordville
55	24.9	Nassau County SD	Fernandina Bch
56	24.6	Sarasota County SD	Sarasota
57	22.8	Santa Rosa County SD	Milton
58	21.7	Brevard County SD	Viera
59	21.3	Seminole County SD	Sanford
60	20.0	Okaloosa County SD	Ft Walton Beach
61	16.9	Collier County SD	Naples
62	16.8	Clay County SD	Green Cove Spgs
63	15.3	Saint Johns County SD	Saint Augustine

Students Eligible for Reduced-Price Lunch

Rank	Percent	District Name	City
1	13.7	Charlotte County SD	Port Charlotte
2	13.6	Holmes County SD	Bonifay
3	13.0	Gilchrist County SD	Trenton
4	12.9	Osceola County SD	Kissimmee
5	12.1	Columbia County SD	Lake City
5	12.1	Jackson County SD	Marianna
7	12.0	Bradford County SD	Starke
8	11.6	Gulf County SD	Port Saint Joe
9	11.5	Walton County SD	Defuniak Spgs
10	11.4	Marion County SD	Ocala
10	11.4	Pasco County SD	Land O' Lakes
12	11.3	Calhoun County SD	Blountstown
12	11.3	Escambia County SD	Pensacola
14	11.2	Bay County SD	Panama City
15	11.0	Hendry County SD	La Belle
15	11.0	Hernando County SD	Brooksville
15	11.0	Lee County SD	Fort Myers
18	10.6	Highlands County SD	Sebring
19	10.5	Washington County SD	Chipley
20	10.4	Citrus County SD	Inverness
20	10.4	Levy County SD	Bronson
22	10.3	Sumter County SD	Bushnell
23	10.1	Flagler County SD	Bunnell
23	10.1	Polk County SD	Bartow
23	10.1	Saint Lucie County SD	Fort Pierce
26	9.7	Hamilton County SD	Jasper
26	9.7	Jefferson County SD	Monticello
26	9.7	Okeechobee County SD	Okeechobee
26	9.7	Putnam County SD	Palatka
30	9.6	Desoto County SD	Arcadia
30	9.6	Dixie County SD	Cross City
30	9.6	Gadsden County SD	Quincy
33	9.5	Suwannee County SD	Live Oak
34	9.4	Santa Rosa County SD	Milton
35	9.3	Hillsborough County SD	Tampa
35	9.3	Sarasota County SD	Sarasota
37	9.2	Duval County SD	Jacksonville
37	9.2	Madison County SD	Madison
39	9.1	Nassau County SD	Fernandina Bch
40	8.9	Alachua County SD	Gainesville
40	8.9	Monroe County SD	Key West
40	8.9	Orange County SD	Orlando
43	8.8	Pinellas County SD	Largo
44	8.7	Wakulla County SD	Crawfordville
45	8.5	Baker County SD	Macclenny
45	8.5	Lake County SD	Tavares
47	8.2	Dade County SD	Miami
47	8.2	Okaloosa County SD	Ft Walton Beach
47	8.2	Volusia County SD	Deland
50	8.1	Broward County SD	Fort Lauderdale
51	8.0	Taylor County SD	Perry
52	7.7	Manatee County SD	Bradenton
52	7.7	Union County SD	Lake Butler
54	7.6	Seminole County SD	Sanford
55	7.4	Clay County SD	Green Cove Spgs
56	7.3	Hardee County SD	Wauchula
57	7.2	Indian River County SD	Vero Beach
58	6.6	Palm Beach County SD	West Palm Beach
59	6.2	Brevard County SD	Viera
60	6.0	Martin County SD	Stuart
61	5.9	Leon County SD	Tallahassee
62	5.8	Collier County SD	Naples
63	4.9	Saint Johns County SD	Saint Augustine

Student/Teacher Ratio

Rank	Ratio	District Name	City
1	40.7	Indian River County SD	Vero Beach
2	21.8	Osceola County SD	Kissimmee
3	20.6	Hendry County SD	La Belle
4	20.2	Broward County SD	Fort Lauderdale
5	20.0	Dade County SD	Miami
6	19.7	Lee County SD	Fort Myers
7	19.6	Okaloosa County SD	Ft Walton Beach
8	19.4	Duval County SD	Jacksonville
9	19.2	Charlotte County SD	Port Charlotte
9	19.2	Nassau County SD	Fernandina Bch
9	19.2	Santa Rosa County SD	Milton
12	19.1	Madison County SD	Madison
13	18.9	Baker County SD	Macclenny
14	18.8	Suwannee County SD	Live Oak
15	18.7	Palm Beach County SD	West Palm Beach
16	18.6	Leon County SD	Tallahassee
16	18.6	Martin County SD	Stuart
16	18.6	Seminole County SD	Sanford
16	18.6	Wakulla County SD	Crawfordville
20	18.4	Escambia County SD	Pensacola
20	18.4	Sumter County SD	Bushnell
22	18.3	Hernando County SD	Brooksville
23	18.1	Manatee County SD	Bradenton
23	18.1	Marion County SD	Ocala
23	18.1	Saint Johns County SD	Saint Augustine
26	18.0	Clay County SD	Green Cove Spgs
26	18.0	Pasco County SD	Land O' Lakes
28	17.8	Brevard County SD	Viera
28	17.8	Gilchrist County SD	Trenton
28	17.8	Sarasota County SD	Sarasota
28	17.8	Walton County SD	Defuniak Spgs
32	17.7	Alachua County SD	Gainesville
33	17.6	Collier County SD	Naples
33	17.6	Pinellas County SD	Largo
35	17.4	Dixie County SD	Cross City
35	17.4	Orange County SD	Orlando
37	17.3	Bay County SD	Panama City
37	17.3	Desoto County SD	Arcadia
37	17.3	Hardee County SD	Wauchula
40	17.1	Columbia County SD	Lake City
40	17.1	Gadsden County SD	Quincy
40	17.1	Okeechobee County SD	Okeechobee
40	17.1	Polk County SD	Bartow
40	17.1	Putnam County SD	Palatka
45	17.0	Highlands County SD	Sebring
46	16.9	Taylor County SD	Perry
47	16.8	Flagler County SD	Bunnell
48	16.7	Bradford County SD	Starke
48	16.7	Hillsborough County SD	Tampa
48	16.7	Holmes County SD	Bonifay
48	16.7	Levy County SD	Bronson
52	16.6	Citrus County SD	Inverness
52	16.6	Gulf County SD	Port Saint Joe
52	16.6	Jackson County SD	Marianna
55	16.5	Volusia County SD	Deland
56	16.1	Hamilton County SD	Jasper
57	15.8	Saint Lucie County SD	Fort Pierce
58	15.3	Jefferson County SD	Monticello
59	15.2	Washington County SD	Chipley
60	14.8	Calhoun County SD	Blountstown
61	14.4	Lake County SD	Tavares
62	14.2	Union County SD	Lake Butler
63	13.4	Monroe County SD	Key West

Student/Librarian Ratio

Rank	Ratio	District Name	City
1	2,664.3	Indian River County SD	Vero Beach
2	2,537.1	Sarasota County SD	Sarasota
3	2,229.0	Dixie County SD	Cross City
4	1,843.6	Monroe County SD	Key West
5	1,603.2	Orange County SD	Orlando
6	1,475.5	Seminole County SD	Sanford
7	1,344.1	Lee County SD	Fort Myers
8	1,266.8	Flagler County SD	Bunnell
9	1,265.2	Osceola County SD	Kissimmee
10	1,217.8	Broward County SD	Fort Lauderdale
11	1,103.7	Madison County SD	Madison
12	1,087.0	Union County SD	Lake Butler
13	1,077.8	Palm Beach County SD	West Palm Beach
14	1,060.8	Dade County SD	Miami
15	1,012.1	Okeechobee County SD	Okeechobee
16	972.6	Pinellas County SD	Largo
17	958.8	Martin County SD	Stuart
18	930.3	Hernando County SD	Brooksville
19	908.7	Duval County SD	Jacksonville
20	907.4	Collier County SD	Naples
21	900.0	Volusia County SD	Deland
22	898.3	Taylor County SD	Perry
23	869.6	Manatee County SD	Bradenton
24	869.2	Okaloosa County SD	Ft Walton Beach
25	863.3	Marion County SD	Ocala
26	852.8	Saint Lucie County SD	Fort Pierce
27	852.6	Hendry County SD	La Belle
28	843.5	Charlotte County SD	Port Charlotte
29	829.5	Clay County SD	Green Cove Spgs
30	828.9	Suwannee County SD	Live Oak
31	819.9	Hillsborough County SD	Tampa
32	819.3	Desoto County SD	Arcadia
33	816.3	Highlands County SD	Sebring
34	815.3	Santa Rosa County SD	Milton
35	813.9	Saint Johns County SD	Saint Augustine
36	808.9	Columbia County SD	Lake City
37	777.2	Wakulla County SD	Crawfordville
38	758.5	Leon County SD	Tallahassee
39	756.7	Lake County SD	Tavares
40	754.2	Baker County SD	Macclenny
41	752.8	Pasco County SD	Land O' Lakes
42	739.3	Hardee County SD	Wauchula
43	734.3	Putnam County SD	Palatka
44	731.2	Citrus County SD	Inverness
45	721.6	Escambia County SD	Pensacola
46	714.6	Polk County SD	Bartow
47	700.3	Walton County SD	Defuniak Spgs
48	683.5	Gilchrist County SD	Trenton
49	682.0	Washington County SD	Chipley
50	672.3	Bradford County SD	Starke
51	661.0	Bay County SD	Panama City
52	658.3	Nassau County SD	Fernandina Bch
53	631.3	Brevard County SD	Viera
54	603.8	Jackson County SD	Marianna
55	599.7	Gadsden County SD	Quincy
56	564.3	Alachua County SD	Gainesville
57	555.7	Levy County SD	Bronson
58	546.5	Sumter County SD	Bushnell
59	541.0	Gulf County SD	Port Saint Joe
60	525.0	Jefferson County SD	Monticello
61	516.3	Hamilton County SD	Jasper
62	487.7	Holmes County SD	Bonifay
63	362.3	Calhoun County SD	Blountstown

Student/Counselor Ratio

Rank	Ratio	District Name	City
1	1,453.3	Indian River County SD	Vero Beach
2	827.8	Madison County SD	Madison
3	724.7	Union County SD	Lake Butler
4	718.6	Taylor County SD	Perry
5	691.9	Sarasota County SD	Sarasota
6	614.5	Monroe County SD	Key West
7	582.9	Wakulla County SD	Crawfordville
8	582.1	Seminole County SD	Sanford
9	575.0	Hardee County SD	Wauchula
10	558.8	Okaloosa County SD	Ft Walton Beach
11	549.3	Lee County SD	Fort Myers
12	546.8	Broward County SD	Fort Lauderdale
13	546.2	Desoto County SD	Arcadia
14	540.6	Duval County SD	Jacksonville
15	525.3	Walton County SD	Defuniak Spgs
16	525.0	Jefferson County SD	Monticello
17	523.8	Orange County SD	Orlando
18	519.0	Osceola County SD	Kissimmee
19	509.1	Marion County SD	Ocala
20	504.5	Sumter County SD	Bushnell
21	504.3	Bradford County SD	Starke
22	502.8	Baker County SD	Macclenny
23	500.7	Brevard County SD	Viera
24	490.5	Pinellas County SD	Largo
25	485.4	Columbia County SD	Lake City
26	479.6	Hendry County SD	La Belle
27	478.8	Nassau County SD	Fernandina Bch
28	472.9	Santa Rosa County SD	Milton

29	472.3	Okeechobee County SD	Okeechobee
30	470.2	Levy County SD	Bronson
31	466.2	Charlotte County SD	Port Charlotte
32	463.4	Escambia County SD	Pensacola
33	454.0	Polk County SD	Bartow
34	449.8	Manatee County SD	Bradenton
35	448.7	Leon County SD	Tallahassee
36	445.8	Dixie County SD	Cross City
37	439.5	Highlands County SD	Sebring
38	431.7	Palm Beach County SD	West Palm Beach
39	431.5	Martin County SD	Stuart
40	430.9	Saint Johns County SD	Saint Augustine
41	426.5	Citrus County SD	Inverness
42	422.3	Flagler County SD	Bunnell
43	418.2	Lake County SD	Tavares
44	414.4	Suwannee County SD	Live Oak
45	413.2	Pasco County SD	Land O' Lakes
46	403.5	Clay County SD	Green Cove Spgs
47	403.3	Hillsborough County SD	Tampa
48	399.8	Gadsden County SD	Quincy
49	390.6	Gilchrist County SD	Trenton
50	389.6	Saint Lucie County SD	Fort Pierce
51	388.8	Bay County SD	Panama City
52	386.1	Alachua County SD	Gainesville
53	379.3	Holmes County SD	Bonifay
54	376.8	Dade County SD	Miami
55	356.7	Putnam County SD	Palatka
56	344.5	Hernando County SD	Brooksville
57	344.2	Hamilton County SD	Jasper
58	341.0	Washington County SD	Chipley
59	324.7	Volusia County SD	Deland
60	320.3	Collier County SD	Naples
61	309.1	Gulf County SD	Port Saint Joe
62	301.9	Jackson County SD	Marianna
63	271.8	Calhoun County SD	Blountstown

Current Spending per Student in FY2001

Rank	Dollars	District Name	City
1	7,570	Washington County SD	Chipley
2	7,151	Monroe County SD	Key West
3	7,130	Jefferson County SD	Monticello
4	6,931	Hamilton County SD	Jasper
5	6,690	Collier County SD	Naples
6	6,689	Gadsden County SD	Quincy
7	6,645	Gulf County SD	Port Saint Joe
8	6,606	Sarasota County SD	Sarasota
9	6,552	Dade County SD	Miami
10	6,411	Martin County SD	Stuart
11	6,326	Leon County SD	Tallahassee
12	6,285	Desoto County SD	Arcadia
13	6,266	Palm Beach County SD	West Palm Beach
14	6,243	Gilchrist County SD	Trenton
15	6,221	Sumter County SD	Bushnell
16	6,216	Dixie County SD	Cross City
17	6,193	Manatee County SD	Bradenton
18	6,186	Hardee County SD	Wauchula
19	6,161	Indian River County SD	Vero Beach
20	6,154	Saint Johns County SD	Saint Augustine
21	6,150	Pinellas County SD	Largo
22	6,147	Madison County SD	Madison
23	6,135	Hendry County SD	La Belle
24	6,108	Walton County SD	Defuniak Spgs
25	6,103	Levy County SD	Bronson
26	6,086	Jackson County SD	Marianna
27	6,078	Bradford County SD	Starke
28	6,073	Flagler County SD	Bunnell
29	6,070	Lee County SD	Fort Myers
30	6,064	Saint Lucie County SD	Fort Pierce
31	6,055	Hillsborough County SD	Tampa
32	6,038	Alachua County SD	Gainesville
33	6,030	Holmes County SD	Bonifay
34	6,012	Taylor County SD	Perry
35	6,001	Highlands County SD	Sebring
36	5,992	Bay County SD	Panama City
37	5,968	Charlotte County SD	Port Charlotte
38	5,882	Polk County SD	Bartow
39	5,869	Columbia County SD	Lake City
40	5,867	Putnam County SD	Palatka
41	5,865	Suwannee County SD	Live Oak
42	5,853	Broward County SD	Fort Lauderdale
43	5,813	Marion County SD	Ocala
44	5,810	Volusia County SD	Deland
45	5,801	Okeechobee County SD	Okeechobee
46	5,791	Citrus County SD	Inverness
47	5,789	Pasco County SD	Land O' Lakes
48	5,777	Wakulla County SD	Crawfordville
49	5,771	Santa Rosa County SD	Milton
50	5,757	Escambia County SD	Pensacola
51	5,721	Orange County SD	Orlando
52	5,711	Calhoun County SD	Blountstown
53	5,665	Duval County SD	Jacksonville
54	5,644	Okaloosa County SD	Ft Walton Beach
55	5,570	Brevard County SD	Viera
56	5,543	Baker County SD	Macclenny
56	5,543	Osceola County SD	Kissimmee
58	5,511	Seminole County SD	Sanford
59	5,474	Hernando County SD	Brooksville
60	5,468	Clay County SD	Green Cove Spgs
61	5,423	Lake County SD	Tavares
62	5,391	Nassau County SD	Fernandina Bch
63	5,348	Union County SD	Lake Butler

Number of Diploma Recipients

Rank	Number	District Name	City
1	16,638	Dade County SD	Miami
2	11,654	Broward County SD	Fort Lauderdale
3	7,968	Hillsborough County SD	Tampa
4	7,687	Palm Beach County SD	West Palm Beach
5	7,361	Orange County SD	Orlando
6	5,413	Pinellas County SD	Largo
7	5,260	Duval County SD	Jacksonville
8	3,815	Polk County SD	Bartow
9	3,578	Brevard County SD	Viera
10	3,420	Seminole County SD	Sanford
11	3,386	Volusia County SD	Deland
12	2,846	Lee County SD	Fort Myers
13	2,453	Pasco County SD	Land O' Lakes
14	2,320	Escambia County SD	Pensacola
15	1,978	Okaloosa County SD	Ft Walton Beach
16	1,960	Marion County SD	Ocala
17	1,895	Sarasota County SD	Sarasota
18	1,853	Osceola County SD	Kissimmee
19	1,788	Leon County SD	Tallahassee
20	1,711	Collier County SD	Naples
21	1,709	Manatee County SD	Bradenton
22	1,651	Alachua County SD	Gainesville
23	1,627	Clay County SD	Green Cove Spgs
24	1,531	Lake County SD	Tavares
25	1,333	Santa Rosa County SD	Milton
26	1,258	Saint Lucie County SD	Fort Pierce
27	1,230	Bay County SD	Panama City
28	1,097	Saint Johns County SD	Saint Augustine
29	1,076	Charlotte County SD	Port Charlotte
30	923	Hernando County SD	Brooksville
31	842	Martin County SD	Stuart
32	830	Citrus County SD	Inverness
33	821	Indian River County SD	Vero Beach
34	577	Nassau County SD	Fernandina Bch
35	561	Highlands County SD	Sebring
36	486	Monroe County SD	Key West
37	447	Putnam County SD	Palatka
38	441	Columbia County SD	Lake City
39	409	Jackson County SD	Marianna
40	385	Flagler County SD	Bunnell
41	346	Gadsden County SD	Quincy
42	339	Okeechobee County SD	Okeechobee
43	301	Levy County SD	Bronson
44	290	Hendry County SD	La Belle
45	284	Suwannee County SD	Live Oak
46	261	Sumter County SD	Bushnell
47	246	Walton County SD	Defuniak Spgs
48	233	Wakulla County SD	Crawfordville
49	223	Baker County SD	Macclenny
50	214	Bradford County SD	Starke
51	213	Hardee County SD	Wauchula
52	204	Desoto County SD	Arcadia
53	203	Holmes County SD	Bonifay
53	203	Taylor County SD	Perry
55	191	Washington County SD	Chipley
56	180	Madison County SD	Madison
57	150	Dixie County SD	Cross City
58	141	Gilchrist County SD	Trenton
59	129	Union County SD	Lake Butler
60	119	Hamilton County SD	Jasper
61	117	Gulf County SD	Port Saint Joe
62	106	Calhoun County SD	Blountstown
63	65	Jefferson County SD	Monticello

High School Drop-out Rate

Rank	Percent	District Name	City
1	9.7	Duval County SD	Jacksonville
2	8.4	Gadsden County SD	Quincy
3	7.9	Hardee County SD	Wauchula
4	7.2	Alachua County SD	Gainesville
5	7.1	Lee County SD	Fort Myers
6	6.9	Polk County SD	Bartow
7	6.8	Hendry County SD	La Belle
8	6.6	Madison County SD	Madison
9	6.3	Dade County SD	Miami
9	6.3	Highlands County SD	Sebring
11	6.0	Okeechobee County SD	Okeechobee
11	6.0	Suwannee County SD	Live Oak
13	5.9	Orange County SD	Orlando
14	5.5	Manatee County SD	Bradenton
14	5.5	Nassau County SD	Fernandina Bch
16	5.4	Pasco County SD	Land O' Lakes
17	5.2	Lake County SD	Tavares
17	5.2	Osceola County SD	Kissimmee
17	5.2	Walton County SD	Defuniak Spgs
20	5.0	Pinellas County SD	Largo
21	4.9	Baker County SD	Macclenny
21	4.9	Bradford County SD	Starke
21	4.9	Collier County SD	Naples
24	4.4	Marion County SD	Ocala
25	4.3	Desoto County SD	Arcadia
25	4.3	Levy County SD	Bronson
25	4.3	Okaloosa County SD	Ft Walton Beach
28	4.0	Charlotte County SD	Port Charlotte
28	4.0	Union County SD	Lake Butler
30	3.9	Gilchrist County SD	Trenton
31	3.5	Citrus County SD	Inverness
31	3.5	Jefferson County SD	Monticello
31	3.5	Leon County SD	Tallahassee
31	3.5	Sarasota County SD	Sarasota
35	3.4	Monroe County SD	Key West
36	3.3	Calhoun County SD	Blountstown
36	3.3	Sumter County SD	Bushnell
38	3.1	Hillsborough County SD	Tampa
39	3.0	Clay County SD	Green Cove Spgs
39	3.0	Dixie County SD	Cross City
39	3.0	Holmes County SD	Bonifay
39	3.0	Palm Beach County SD	West Palm Beach
43	2.9	Escambia County SD	Pensacola
43	2.9	Washington County SD	Chipley
45	2.8	Putnam County SD	Palatka
45	2.8	Saint Johns County SD	Saint Augustine
47	2.7	Indian River County SD	Vero Beach
47	2.7	Wakulla County SD	Crawfordville
49	2.6	Brevard County SD	Viera
50	2.5	Hamilton County SD	Jasper
51	2.4	Santa Rosa County SD	Milton
52	2.2	Flagler County SD	Bunnell
52	2.2	Hernando County SD	Brooksville
54	2.1	Saint Lucie County SD	Fort Pierce
54	2.1	Taylor County SD	Perry
56	2.0	Broward County SD	Fort Lauderdale
57	1.9	Bay County SD	Panama City
57	1.9	Columbia County SD	Lake City
59	1.8	Jackson County SD	Marianna
60	1.7	Volusia County SD	Deland
61	1.6	Gulf County SD	Port Saint Joe
62	1.0	Seminole County SD	Sanford
63	0.6	Martin County SD	Stuart

FLORIDA COMPREHENSIVE ASSESSMENT TEST (FCAT) 2005

MATHEMATICS - Grade 3

			Total Test Scores								% AL3+	Mean Points Earned By Content				
						% in each Achievement Level										
Grade	District number	District Name	Number of Students	Mean Developmental Scale Score	Mean Scale Score (100-500)	1	2	3	4	5	Percent in Achievement Levels 3+	Number Sense	Measurement	Geometry	Algebraic Thinking	Data Analysis
Number of Points Possible												12	8	7	6	7
03	00	STATEWIDE AVERAGE	203,037	1380	317	15	17	34	25	9	68	7	5	4	4	5
03	01	ALACHUA	2,090	1398	321	15	16	32	25	12	69	7	5	4	4	5
03	02	BAKER	368	1405	323	10	17	36	28	9	73	7	6	5	3	5
03	03	BAY	1,996	1393	320	14	16	34	28	8	70	7	5	4	4	5
03	04	BRADFORD	292	1271	294	24	20	35	17	3	55	6	5	4	3	4
03	05	BREVARD	5,119	1452	333	9	13	35	31	12	78	8	6	4	4	5
03	06	BROWARD	21,050	1427	328	13	14	33	28	13	73	7	6	4	4	5
03	07	CALHOUN	144	1494	342	7	8	34	36	15	85	8	6	5	4	5
03	08	CHARLOTTE	1,209	1423	327	11	14	37	28	11	76	7	6	5	4	5
03	09	CITRUS	1,108	1427	328	8	15	40	28	9	77	7	6	4	4	5
03	10	CLAY	2,392	1446	332	7	15	36	30	11	77	7	6	4	4	5
03	11	COLLIER	3,346	1363	314	16	19	34	24	8	66	7	5	4	3	5
03	12	COLUMBIA	750	1347	310	15	20	37	24	5	65	7	5	4	3	4
03	13	MIAMI DADE	29,880	1345	310	18	18	33	22	8	63	6	5	4	3	5
03	14	DESOTO	389	1292	298	20	23	36	17	4	57	6	5	4	3	4
03	15	DIXIE	132	1348	310	20	19	25	30	7	61	7	5	4	3	4
03	16	DUVAL	10,185	1332	307	18	20	34	21	7	62	6	5	4	3	4
03	17	ESCAMBIA	3,208	1332	307	19	18	34	22	7	63	6	5	4	3	4
03	18	FLAGLER	733	1367	315	13	17	41	25	5	70	7	5	4	4	4
03	19	FRANKLIN	91	1241	287	25	18	37	15	4	57	6	5	3	3	4
03	20	GADSDEN	499	1264	292	22	25	37	14	2	53	5	5	4	3	4
03	21	GILCHRIST	227	1404	322	8	16	44	27	4	76	7	6	4	3	5
03	22	GLADES	104	1292	298	21	20	39	16	3	59	6	5	4	3	4
03	23	GULF	135	1385	318	16	13	37	24	9	70	7	6	4	3	4
03	24	HAMILTON	165	1223	283	28	24	32	15	2	48	5	4	3	3	4
03	25	HARDEE	441	1345	310	18	19	34	23	6	63	6	5	4	3	5
03	26	HENDRY	514	1278	295	22	21	35	18	3	57	6	5	4	3	4
03	27	HERNANDO	1,585	1411	324	10	15	39	28	8	75	7	6	4	4	5
03	28	HIGHLANDS	919	1360	313	17	17	34	25	8	66	7	5	4	3	5
03	29	HILLSBOROUGH	14,708	1362	313	17	18	33	23	9	64	7	5	4	3	4
03	30	HOLMES	263	1255	290	21	25	37	15	2	54	6	5	3	3	4
03	31	INDIAN RIVER	1,224	1442	331	10	15	32	30	12	75	7	6	5	4	5
03	32	JACKSON	536	1413	324	14	15	28	31	12	71	7	6	4	4	5
03	33	JEFFERSON	91	1171	272	36	24	31	5	3	40	5	4	3	3	4
03	34	LAFAYETTE	92	1372	316	16	16	30	27	10	67	7	6	5	3	5
03	35	LAKE	2,751	1365	314	17	16	33	26	8	67	7	5	4	4	4
03	36	LEE	5,598	1376	317	14	18	36	24	8	68	7	5	4	4	5
03	37	LEON	2,433	1467	336	10	13	32	29	16	77	8	6	4	4	5
03	38	LEVY	483	1303	301	16	28	37	17	2	56	6	5	4	3	4
03	39	LIBERTY	80	1409	323	6	18	49	21	6	76	7	5	4	3	5
03	40	MADISON	179	1291	298	21	21	36	17	4	58	6	5	4	3	4
03	41	MANATEE	3,146	1346	310	15	20	38	21	6	65	7	5	4	3	4
03	42	MARION	3,071	1340	309	17	18	38	21	5	65	6	5	4	3	4
03	43	MARTIN	1,237	1468	336	7	13	34	33	13	80	8	6	5	4	5
03	44	MONROE	621	1421	326	10	13	39	29	9	78	7	6	4	4	5
03	45	NASSAU	780	1452	333	8	12	38	33	10	81	7	6	5	4	5
03	46	OKALOOSA	2,167	1502	344	5	10	35	35	14	85	8	6	5	4	5
03	47	OKEECHOBEE	563	1363	314	14	17	38	24	7	68	7	6	4	3	4
03	48	ORANGE	13,713	1360	313	18	16	33	24	9	66	7	5	4	3	4
03	49	OSCEOLA	3,672	1276	295	24	20	34	19	4	56	6	5	4	3	4
03	50	PALM BEACH	13,393	1386	319	15	16	34	25	10	69	7	5	4	4	5
03	51	PASCO	4,924	1324	305	17	20	39	20	4	63	6	5	4	3	4
03	52	PINELLAS	8,312	1408	323	13	15	33	27	11	71	7	5	4	4	5
03	53	POLK	6,842	1342	309	16	21	35	22	6	63	6	5	4	3	4
03	54	PUTNAM	920	1344	310	17	18	38	23	5	65	6	5	4	3	4
03	55	ST. JOHNS	1,867	1474	338	9	12	32	33	14	79	8	6	4	4	5
03	56	ST. LUCIE	2,618	1338	308	18	18	35	22	6	64	7	5	4	3	4
03	57	SANTA ROSA	1,713	1496	342	5	11	35	36	13	84	8	6	5	4	5
03	58	SARASOTA	3,223	1437	330	11	14	34	28	13	75	7	6	4	4	5
03	59	SEMINOLE	5,006	1467	336	9	13	33	31	14	78	8	6	5	4	5
03	60	SUMTER	542	1379	317	13	18	36	26	6	68	7	5	4	4	5
03	61	SUWANNEE	375	1292	298	19	22	39	17	2	58	6	5	4	3	4
03	62	TAYLOR	252	1374	316	11	20	40	23	5	69	6	6	4	4	5
03	63	UNION	165	1480	339	9	6	36	35	14	85	8	6	5	4	5
03	64	VOLUSIA	4,882	1410	324	12	15	34	28	11	73	7	6	4	4	5
03	65	WAKULLA	354	1485	340	6	12	36	34	13	82	8	6	5	4	5
03	66	WALTON	494	1373	316	14	18	38	21	8	68	7	5	4	3	5
03	67	WASHINGTON	258	1406	323	12	12	39	28	8	75	7	5	4	4	5
03	68	FSDB	32	987	232	66	16	13	3	3	19	3	3	3	2	3
03	72	FAU HENDERSON	71	1582	361	3	3	25	51	18	94	9	6	5	4	5
03	73	FSU SCH	190	1501	343	6	11	28	41	13	83	8	6	5	4	5
03	74	FAMU SCH	34	1355	312	15	15	53	18	0	71	6	6	4	3	4
03	75	UF PK YONGE	58	1465	336	7	12	34	38	9	81	8	6	4	4	5
03	78	FL CONNECTIONS	14	1328	306	14	14	57	14	0	71	6	6	4	3	4
03	79	FL VIRTUAL SCHO	19	1473	337	11	5	32	37	16	84	8	7	4	4	5

Note: *Percentages in "Level 3 and Above" may differ from the sum of % in levels 3 - 5 due to rounding.*

Source: *Florida Department of Education, Office of Assessment and School Performance, May 2005*

FLORIDA COMPREHENSIVE ASSESSMENT TEST (FCAT) 2005
SUNSHINE STATE STANDARDS

MATHEMATICS - Grade 4

			Total Test Scores			% in each Achievement Level					% AL3+	Mean Points Earned By Content					Results for Students Matched to Previous Year			
Grade	District number	District Name	Number of Students	Mean Developmental Scale Score (0-3000)	Mean Scale Score (100-500)	1	2	3	4	5	Percent in Achievement Levels 3 and Above	Number Sense	Measurement	Geometry	Algebraic Thinking	Data Analysis	Percent Matched to 2004	Mean Developmental Scale Score (2005)	Mean Developmental Scale Score (2004)	Mean DSS Change for Matched Students Math (2005 - 2004)
Number of Points Possible												11	8	7	7	7				
04	00	STATEWIDE TOTAL	195,866	1509	312	15	21	38	21	6	64	7	5	4	4	4	87	1522	1391	132
04	01	ALACHUA	1,995	1502	311	19	21	30	21	8	59	7	5	4	4	4	90	1507	1374	133
04	02	BAKER	358	1452	299	25	24	31	16	5	52	6	5	4	4	4	90	1452	1435	17
04	03	BAY	1,828	1528	316	12	21	40	22	5	67	7	5	4	5	4	87	1535	1432	103
04	04	BRADFORD	250	1406	289	22	33	34	10	1	44	6	4	4	4	3	92	1419	1336	83
04	05	BREVARD	5,359	1563	325	10	17	39	26	8	72	7	5	4	5	4	85	1573	1454	118
04	06	BROWARD	21,331	1542	320	13	19	37	23	8	69	7	5	4	5	4	88	1555	1415	140
04	07	CALHOUN	161	1515	314	13	16	49	18	4	71	7	5	4	4	4	88	1526	1452	75
04	08	CHARLOTTE	1,151	1517	314	13	21	40	22	4	66	7	5	4	4	4	84	1527	1403	124
04	09	CITRUS	1,107	1513	313	11	24	41	21	3	65	7	5	4	4	4	88	1518	1396	122
04	10	CLAY	2,201	1557	323	9	19	42	24	7	72	7	5	4	5	4	85	1570	1462	108
04	11	COLLIER	3,217	1527	316	14	18	38	22	7	67	7	5	4	4	4	87	1543	1384	159
04	12	COLUMBIA	742	1422	292	20	30	38	11	1	50	6	4	3	4	3	90	1431	1339	93
04	13	MIAMI-DADE	26,770	1493	309	16	22	38	19	5	61	6	5	4	4	4	91	1508	1352	156
04	14	DESOTO	367	1490	308	16	21	40	18	4	62	6	5	4	4	4	93	1499	1364	135
04	15	DIXIE	159	1440	296	26	25	30	14	4	48	6	5	4	4	3	94	1442	1318	125
04	16	DUVAL	9,452	1479	305	18	22	38	18	4	60	7	5	4	4	4	85	1503	1362	141
04	17	ESCAMBIA	3,387	1460	301	20	23	37	16	4	57	6	5	4	4	4	88	1464	1343	121
04	18	FLAGLER	739	1492	308	14	23	41	18	3	62	6	5	4	5	4	80	1498	1388	110
04	19	FRANKLIN	88	1441	297	16	35	39	6	5	49	6	4	3	4	3	86	1449	1401	48
04	20	GADSDEN	434	1400	287	26	31	33	10	1	44	5	4	4	4	3	91	1409	1243	165
04	21	GILCHRIST	187	1528	317	10	19	44	24	3	71	7	5	4	4	4	91	1534	1415	119
04	22	GLADES	104	1388	285	24	34	29	10	4	42	6	4	4	4	3	87	1393	1255	138
04	23	GULF	146	1497	310	13	27	39	15	5	60	6	5	4	4	4	90	1509	1407	101
04	24	HAMILTON	136	1422	292	21	34	34	11	1	46	6	4	4	4	3	91	1427	1301	127
04	25	HARDEE	390	1451	299	17	25	42	15	2	58	6	5	4	4	4	89	1462	1327	135
04	26	HENDRY	578	1457	300	19	23	43	13	2	58	6	5	4	4	3	89	1471	1299	173
04	27	HERNANDO	1,502	1512	313	14	20	41	20	5	66	7	5	4	4	4	82	1531	1402	129
04	28	HIGHLANDS	882	1476	305	17	22	40	18	2	61	6	5	4	4	4	89	1491	1368	123
04	29	HILLSBOROUGH	14,205	1493	309	17	23	36	19	5	60	6	5	4	4	4	86	1506	1399	107
04	30	HOLMES	249	1456	300	16	29	39	16	0	56	6	5	4	4	4	89	1453	1331	123
04	31	INDIAN RIVER	1,265	1545	320	11	18	39	25	7	71	7	5	5	4	4	89	1553	1404	149
04	32	JACKSON	486	1523	315	13	22	38	20	7	65	7	5	4	4	4	92	1527	1397	130
04	33	JEFFERSON	90	1266	257	49	27	22	1	1	24	5	3	3	3	2	88	1268	1210	58
04	34	LAFAYETTE	76	1606	334	7	17	33	30	13	76	8	5	5	5	5	95	1622	1552	70
04	35	LAKE	2,775	1499	310	15	22	39	20	4	63	7	5	4	4	4	84	1509	1389	120
04	36	LEE	5,296	1506	312	14	22	40	19	5	64	7	5	4	4	4	84	1521	1398	123
04	37	LEON	2,240	1569	326	11	17	38	24	10	72	7	5	4	5	4	90	1579	1474	105
04	38	LEVY	284	1418	291	23	33	31	12	2	44	6	5	4	4	3	88	1420	1319	101
04	39	LIBERTY	83	1523	315	11	19	52	14	4	70	7	5	4	4	4	92	1529	1413	116
04	40	MADISON	212	1333	272	37	37	21	5	0	26	5	4	3	4	3	89	1330	1263	67
04	41	MANATEE	3,192	1477	305	17	24	38	18	4	59	6	5	4	4	4	83	1491	1367	124
04	42	MARION	3,093	1510	312	13	22	41	20	4	65	6	5	4	4	4	89	1519	1374	145
04	43	MARTIN	1,260	1592	331	8	14	41	28	10	78	7	6	5	5	5	89	1602	1473	129
04	44	MONROE	580	1552	322	10	18	40	25	7	72	7	5	4	5	4	87	1566	1426	141
04	45	NASSAU	772	1532	317	10	21	41	24	4	69	7	5	4	5	4	89	1535	1413	121
04	46	OKALOOSA	2,167	1611	335	6	14	38	33	10	80	8	6	5	5	5	86	1623	1497	125
04	47	OKEECHOBEE	492	1489	308	15	21	42	18	3	64	7	5	4	4	4	84	1501	1346	155
04	48	ORANGE	12,987	1479	305	19	22	35	19	5	59	7	5	4	4	4	82	1500	1364	136
04	49	OSCEOLA	3,565	1437	296	23	25	33	16	3	52	6	4	4	4	3	78	1463	1314	148
04	50	PALM BEACH	13,043	1521	315	15	19	38	22	7	66	7	5	4	4	4	87	1535	1386	149
04	51	PASCO	4,632	1469	303	18	26	37	16	3	56	6	5	4	4	4	87	1475	1374	101
04	52	PINELLAS	8,302	1525	316	14	20	37	23	7	66	7	5	4	5	4	89	1536	1384	152
04	53	POLK	6,448	1471	304	17	24	38	17	3	58	6	5	4	4	4	87	1488	1366	122
04	54	PUTNAM	918	1456	300	20	26	37	14	3	54	6	4	4	4	4	91	1465	1344	121
04	55	ST. JOHNS	1,839	1591	331	7	15	40	30	9	78	8	5	4	5	5	85	1596	1480	116
04	56	ST. LUCIE	2,696	1472	304	18	26	38	15	4	56	6	5	4	4	4	80	1484	1367	117
04	57	SANTA ROSA	1,719	1585	330	7	16	40	30	7	77	7	6	4	5	4	87	1593	1496	97
04	58	SARASOTA	3,142	1554	322	11	18	37	27	7	71	7	5	4	5	4	87	1563	1472	91
04	59	SEMINOLE	5,006	1573	327	10	15	39	28	8	75	7	5	5	5	4	87	1588	1494	94
04	60	SUMTER	568	1525	316	13	20	39	23	5	67	7	5	4	5	4	84	1524	1424	99
04	61	SUWANNEE	410	1454	300	20	27	36	16	1	54	6	5	4	4	3	89	1457	1336	122
04	62	TAYLOR	229	1443	297	19	28	40	10	3	53	6	5	4	4	3	93	1444	1357	87
04	63	UNION	155	1492	308	17	21	40	18	4	62	7	5	4	4	4	84	1504	1370	134
04	64	VOLUSIA	4,906	1518	314	14	19	39	23	5	67	7	5	4	5	4	88	1527	1399	129
04	65	WAKULLA	315	1565	325	8	13	47	27	5	79	7	5	4	5	4	92	1576	1500	76
04	66	WALTON	485	1521	315	13	21	40	20	6	66	7	5	4	4	4	86	1520	1396	123
04	67	WASHINGTON	243	1521	315	14	21	35	24	6	65	7	5	4	4	4	93	1523	1380	142
04	68	FSDB	22	1055	208	77	18	5	0	0	5	4	2	2	3	2	45	1068	929	139
04	72	FAU HENDERSON	70	1588	330	6	17	43	26	9	77	7	5	4	5	5	84	1603	1556	47
04	73	FSU SCH	186	1593	331	7	15	41	29	8	78	7	6	5	5	4	92	1597	1435	161
04	74	FAMU SCH	35	1415	291	20	29	43	9	0	51	6	4	3	4	3	83	1411	1347	64
04	75	UF PK YONGE	60	1469	303	20	25	38	10	7	55	7	5	4	4	3	93	1453	1373	80
04	78	FL CONNECTIONS	20	1442	297	30	15	40	15	0	55	6	5	3	4	3	10	1344	1397	-53
04	79	FL VIRTUAL SCHO	27	1529	317	22	19	19	30	11	59	7	5	4	5	4	4	1963	1739	224

Note: *Percentages in "Level 3 and Above" may differ from the sum of % in levels 3 - 5 due to rounding.*

Source: *Florida Department of Education, Office of Assessment and School Performance, May 2005*

FLORIDA COMPREHENSIVE ASSESSMENT TEST (FCAT) 2005
SUNSHINE STATE STANDARDS

MATHEMATICS - Grade 5

			Total Test Scores			% in each Achievement Level					% AL3+	Mean Points Earned By Content					Results for Students Matched to Previous Year			
Grade	District number	District Name	Number of Students	Mean Developmental Scale Score (0-3000)	Mean Scale Score (100-500)	1	2	3	4	5	Percent in Achievement Levels 3 and Above	Number Sense	Measurement	Geometry	Algebraic Thinking	Data Analysis	Percent Matched to 2004	Mean Developmental Scale Score (2005)	Mean Developmental Scale Score (2004)	Mean DSS Change for Matched Students Math (2005 - 2004)
Number of Points Possible												13	11	13	11	12				
05	00	STATEWIDE TOTAL	181,434	1648	329	16	27	27	24	6	57	6	6	7	6	6	87	1662	1518	144
05	01	ALACHUA	1,818	1659	331	18	25	23	24	10	57	6	6	7	6	6	90	1666	1527	140
05	02	BAKER	328	1593	317	23	30	24	19	4	47	6	6	6	6	5	91	1590	1512	79
05	03	BAY	1,971	1649	329	16	27	29	23	5	58	6	6	7	6	6	88	1656	1528	128
05	04	BRADFORD	236	1580	314	24	28	28	18	2	48	5	5	6	5	6	92	1579	1427	153
05	05	BREVARD	5,556	1686	337	12	22	29	29	8	65	7	7	7	6	7	85	1696	1563	133
05	06	BROWARD	19,378	1677	335	14	25	26	28	8	61	6	6	7	6	6	89	1689	1552	137
05	07	CALHOUN	155	1697	339	10	28	30	24	8	62	6	7	7	7	7	94	1695	1577	118
05	08	CHARLOTTE	1,112	1679	335	13	24	30	25	7	63	7	6	7	6	6	86	1687	1524	163
05	09	CITRUS	1,102	1651	329	13	30	31	22	3	57	6	6	7	6	6	88	1660	1509	151
05	10	CLAY	2,349	1660	331	13	28	29	24	6	59	6	6	7	6	6	87	1668	1543	125
05	11	COLLIER	2,646	1673	334	15	23	28	26	8	62	6	6	7	6	6	86	1692	1556	135
05	12	COLUMBIA	690	1563	311	27	31	24	15	3	42	5	5	6	5	5	90	1573	1427	146
05	13	MIAMI-DADE	22,606	1645	328	17	27	27	24	6	57	6	6	7	6	6	91	1664	1504	160
05	14	DESOTO	333	1593	317	21	32	29	16	2	47	5	5	7	5	6	90	1605	1449	155
05	15	DIXIE	114	1581	314	25	26	29	18	2	48	5	5	6	6	5	89	1582	1473	108
05	16	DUVAL	9,007	1608	320	20	29	27	20	4	51	6	6	7	6	6	87	1630	1469	162
05	17	ESCAMBIA	2,996	1600	318	22	30	24	19	4	48	5	6	6	6	6	88	1610	1486	123
05	18	FLAGLER	720	1604	319	19	30	28	20	3	50	5	6	6	6	6	80	1615	1505	111
05	19	FRANKLIN	83	1628	324	14	31	37	16	1	54	5	6	6	5	6	89	1628	1434	195
05	20	GADSDEN	463	1522	302	29	40	22	9	0	31	4	5	6	5	5	89	1524	1402	122
05	21	GILCHRIST	209	1656	330	15	24	31	24	6	61	6	6	7	6	6	86	1662	1556	107
05	22	GLADES	94	1531	304	36	26	23	13	2	38	4	5	6	5	5	77	1541	1453	88
05	23	GULF	153	1604	319	20	31	24	23	2	49	6	6	6	6	5	92	1602	1437	165
05	24	HAMILTON	115	1518	301	33	39	17	9	3	28	4	4	5	5	5	91	1528	1437	91
05	25	HARDEE	336	1600	318	19	34	26	17	5	47	5	5	7	5	6	90	1608	1455	153
05	26	HENDRY	513	1625	324	19	28	26	22	5	53	6	6	7	6	6	88	1638	1454	184
05	27	HERNANDO	1,422	1634	326	17	28	30	23	3	55	6	6	6	6	6	82	1648	1537	111
05	28	HIGHLANDS	843	1600	318	20	31	26	21	3	49	5	6	7	6	6	86	1610	1462	148
05	29	HILLSBOROUGH	13,752	1640	327	18	27	26	23	6	55	6	6	7	6	6	87	1656	1504	152
05	30	HOLMES	233	1564	311	28	28	26	15	2	43	5	5	5	6	5	88	1575	1474	100
05	31	INDIAN RIVER	1,124	1672	334	15	25	27	26	8	61	6	6	7	6	6	88	1684	1517	167
05	32	JACKSON	468	1650	329	18	23	29	25	5	59	6	6	7	6	6	91	1650	1533	117
05	33	JEFFERSON	79	1467	290	47	27	16	10	0	27	4	4	5	4	4	92	1463	1392	72
05	34	LAFAYETTE	75	1597	318	17	33	37	11	1	49	5	6	5	6	6	91	1607	1591	15
05	35	LAKE	2,605	1651	329	15	27	28	25	5	58	6	6	7	6	6	84	1660	1510	150
05	36	LEE	4,915	1665	332	14	25	27	27	6	60	6	6	7	6	6	84	1682	1516	166
05	37	LEON	2,349	1694	338	11	26	26	28	9	63	7	7	7	6	7	89	1703	1583	120
05	38	LEVY	261	1605	319	16	35	30	20	0	49	5	6	6	6	6	90	1609	1451	158
05	39	LIBERTY	89	1593	317	18	31	38	11	1	51	5	5	6	5	6	89	1612	1522	90
05	40	MADISON	170	1481	293	41	27	20	11	1	32	4	5	5	5	4	94	1485	1361	124
05	41	MANATEE	2,878	1623	323	18	29	28	21	4	53	6	6	7	6	6	85	1636	1481	155
05	42	MARION	2,882	1624	324	17	30	28	21	4	53	6	6	6	6	6	88	1636	1516	120
05	43	MARTIN	1,288	1701	340	11	21	30	30	8	68	7	7	8	7	7	90	1711	1582	130
05	44	MONROE	623	1660	331	14	26	27	28	4	60	6	6	7	6	6	91	1669	1521	148
05	45	NASSAU	732	1660	331	11	27	32	24	5	61	6	6	7	6	6	89	1667	1512	156
05	46	OKALOOSA	2,214	1708	341	9	23	31	29	8	68	7	7	7	7	7	87	1714	1580	134
05	47	OKEECHOBEE	545	1600	319	20	33	26	17	3	47	5	6	7	5	6	89	1610	1457	153
05	48	ORANGE	11,846	1622	323	20	27	25	22	6	53	6	6	7	6	6	82	1646	1504	142
05	49	OSCEOLA	3,318	1547	307	29	31	24	14	2	40	5	5	6	5	5	77	1574	1452	122
05	50	PALM BEACH	12,000	1658	331	16	25	27	25	7	59	6	6	7	6	6	89	1670	1538	132
05	51	PASCO	3,998	1628	324	17	30	29	20	3	53	6	6	6	6	6	86	1640	1497	143
05	52	PINELLAS	7,567	1673	334	14	25	27	26	8	61	6	6	7	6	7	90	1684	1509	175
05	53	POLK	6,065	1605	320	21	29	26	20	4	50	5	6	7	6	6	86	1620	1459	161
05	54	PUTNAM	846	1583	315	23	34	25	15	3	43	5	5	6	5	5	88	1589	1462	127
05	55	ST. JOHNS	1,796	1691	338	12	24	26	29	9	64	7	7	7	6	7	85	1697	1572	125
05	56	ST. LUCIE	2,401	1646	328	16	29	26	23	6	55	6	6	7	6	6	79	1657	1518	139
05	57	SANTA ROSA	1,791	1683	336	12	24	29	30	6	64	7	6	7	7	6	87	1693	1578	115
05	58	SARASOTA	2,952	1699	340	11	23	28	28	10	66	7	7	7	7	7	86	1711	1580	131
05	59	SEMINOLE	4,845	1695	339	11	22	28	30	8	66	7	7	7	6	7	87	1709	1580	128
05	60	SUMTER	518	1696	339	14	22	27	30	8	65	7	7	7	6	6	90	1705	1571	134
05	61	SUWANNEE	403	1578	314	26	29	28	15	1	45	5	5	6	6	5	85	1576	1454	122
05	62	TAYLOR	221	1535	305	29	41	19	9	2	30	4	5	5	5	5	93	1538	1440	99
05	63	UNION	155	1564	311	28	28	25	16	4	45	5	5	6	5	5	93	1560	1462	98
05	64	VOLUSIA	4,607	1667	333	14	26	29	26	6	61	6	6	7	6	7	89	1677	1528	148
05	65	WAKULLA	338	1682	336	13	20	36	23	8	67	6	6	7	7	7	91	1697	1538	158
05	66	WALTON	455	1635	326	16	31	29	21	4	53	6	6	6	6	6	88	1646	1507	138
05	67	WASHINGTON	250	1600	319	21	31	27	18	3	48	5	6	6	5	6	94	1602	1506	96
05	68	FSDB	23	1162	226	83	17	0	0	0	0	2	2	3	3	2	83	1176	1134	42
05	72	FAU HENDERSON	75	1714	343	5	21	40	25	8	73	7	7	7	6	7	81	1715	1548	167
05	73	FSU SCH	189	1722	344	6	23	31	33	7	71	7	7	8	7	7	95	1721	1599	122
05	74	FAMU SCH	38	1501	297	37	47	8	8	0	16	3	4	5	5	5	76	1512	1413	99
05	75	UF PK YONGE	59	1649	329	19	24	31	22	5	58	6	6	7	6	5	97	1644	1433	211
05	78	FL CONNECTIONS	18	1592	317	11	50	33	6	0	39	5	5	6	5	5	0			
05	79	FL VIRTUAL SCHO	30	1710	342	7	10	47	37	0	83	7	7	7	7	7	3	1829	1578	251

Note: *Percentages in "Level 3 and Above" may differ from the sum of % in levels 3 - 5 due to rounding.*
Source: *Florida Department of Education, Office of Assessment and School Performance, May 2005*

FLORIDA COMPREHENSIVE ASSESSMENT TEST (FCAT) 2005
SUNSHINE STATE STANDARDS

MATHEMATICS - Grade 6

			Total Test Scores			% in each Achievement Level					% AL3+	Mean Points Earned By Content					Results for Students Matched to Previous Year			
Grade	District number	District Name	Number of Students	Mean Developmental Scale Score (0-3000)	Mean Scale Score (100-500)	1	2	3	4	5	Percent in Achievement Levels 3 and Above	Number Sense	Measurement	Geometry	Algebraic Thinking	Data Analysis	Percent Matched to 2004	Mean Developmental Scale Score (2005)	Mean Developmental Scale Score (2004)	Mean DSS Change for Matched Students Math (2005 - 2004)
Number of Points Possible												9	9	9	8	9				
06	00	STATEWIDE TOTAL	201,550	1653	305	31	22	26	15	6	47	5	4	6	3	5	87	1666	1624	42
06	01	ALACHUA	2,131	1643	303	34	19	24	16	7	47	5	4	5	3	5	89	1649	1626	24
06	02	BAKER	361	1687	313	27	20	25	20	8	53	5	4	6	3	5	89	1689	1620	70
06	03	BAY	1,982	1667	308	27	25	30	14	4	48	5	4	6	3	5	89	1672	1633	39
06	04	BRADFORD	294	1607	294	34	28	26	10	3	38	4	3	5	3	5	90	1616	1536	79
06	05	BREVARD	5,525	1775	333	15	16	32	24	13	69	5	5	6	4	6	85	1792	1685	107
06	06	BROWARD	20,965	1698	316	26	20	27	18	9	54	5	4	6	4	5	89	1712	1663	49
06	07	CALHOUN	193	1674	310	24	24	31	18	4	52	5	4	6	3	5	96	1679	1643	36
06	08	CHARLOTTE	1,339	1695	315	24	21	29	19	6	55	5	4	6	3	5	85	1704	1651	53
06	09	CITRUS	1,172	1656	306	30	25	26	14	5	45	5	4	5	3	5	88	1667	1626	41
06	10	CLAY	2,622	1723	321	20	22	32	19	8	58	5	4	6	4	6	87	1734	1685	50
06	11	COLLIER	3,116	1652	305	32	21	25	16	6	47	5	4	5	3	5	86	1667	1625	42
06	12	COLUMBIA	807	1579	288	40	24	27	8	1	36	4	3	5	3	4	89	1589	1563	27
06	13	MIAMI-DADE	27,173	1600	293	39	21	24	12	4	40	4	4	5	3	5	91	1615	1579	35
06	14	DESOTO	354	1666	308	28	24	29	14	5	48	5	4	6	3	5	94	1676	1625	51
06	15	DIXIE	166	1524	275	46	26	21	5	2	28	3	3	5	3	4	92	1521	1492	29
06	16	DUVAL	10,201	1602	293	38	24	25	10	3	38	4	3	5	3	5	86	1621	1599	23
06	17	ESCAMBIA	3,385	1583	289	40	24	22	11	3	36	4	3	5	3	5	90	1589	1556	33
06	18	FLAGLER	778	1660	307	27	24	28	17	4	48	5	4	6	3	5	80	1667	1605	61
06	19	FRANKLIN	127	1669	309	29	24	28	14	5	47	5	4	6	3	5	88	1677	1523	154
06	20	GADSDEN	512	1556	283	45	26	22	7	0	29	4	3	5	2	4	89	1563	1496	66
06	21	GILCHRIST	195	1667	308	30	19	31	14	5	50	5	4	6	3	5	89	1683	1665	18
06	22	GLADES	110	1619	297	32	33	22	12	2	35	4	3	5	3	5	85	1633	1508	125
06	23	GULF	172	1709	318	20	23	34	19	4	57	5	4	6	3	6	85	1705	1634	71
06	24	HAMILTON	145	1630	300	34	17	29	18	3	50	4	4	6	3	5	91	1634	1508	126
06	25	HARDEE	385	1587	290	38	27	23	10	2	35	4	3	5	3	5	91	1607	1571	35
06	26	HENDRY	574	1598	292	36	25	25	11	3	39	4	3	5	3	5	91	1611	1572	39
06	27	HERNANDO	1,632	1639	302	31	25	26	15	3	44	4	4	5	3	5	86	1646	1633	13
06	28	HIGHLANDS	928	1611	295	33	25	28	11	4	43	4	3	6	3	5	89	1622	1548	74
06	29	HILLSBOROUGH	14,428	1661	307	31	22	26	15	6	47	5	4	6	3	5	87	1675	1636	38
06	30	HOLMES	263	1621	298	34	25	25	12	4	41	4	3	5	3	5	86	1633	1619	14
06	31	INDIAN RIVER	1,263	1666	308	30	21	26	16	7	49	5	4	6	3	5	90	1673	1653	20
06	32	JACKSON	587	1614	296	35	24	26	12	3	41	4	3	5	3	5	92	1617	1606	11
06	33	JEFFERSON	84	1482	265	57	26	13	4	0	17	3	3	4	2	3	95	1477	1433	45
06	34	LAFAYETTE	77	1594	291	38	23	31	8	0	39	4	3	5	3	5	90	1621	1536	85
06	35	LAKE	2,756	1660	307	28	23	30	14	4	49	5	4	6	3	5	84	1670	1633	37
06	36	LEE	5,446	1652	305	30	24	27	14	5	46	4	4	6	3	5	84	1670	1642	28
06	37	LEON	2,462	1706	318	23	21	29	18	8	55	5	4	6	4	5	87	1720	1684	37
06	38	LEVY	546	1579	288	38	24	27	9	2	38	4	3	5	3	4	89	1584	1579	5
06	39	LIBERTY	105	1599	293	34	26	30	10	1	40	4	3	5	3	5	93	1615	1557	58
06	40	MADISON	178	1507	271	54	21	17	7	1	25	4	3	5	2	4	87	1515	1467	48
06	41	MANATEE	3,061	1643	303	31	23	29	13	4	46	4	4	5	3	5	85	1656	1623	33
06	42	MARION	3,125	1633	301	32	24	27	13	3	44	4	4	6	3	5	88	1643	1610	33
06	43	MARTIN	1,335	1732	323	20	19	28	23	10	61	5	5	6	4	6	88	1748	1701	48
06	44	MONROE	679	1676	310	24	24	33	15	4	52	5	4	6	3	5	87	1691	1657	33
06	45	NASSAU	817	1685	312	23	26	34	14	2	50	5	4	6	3	5	88	1690	1643	47
06	46	OKALOOSA	2,341	1754	328	17	21	29	24	10	62	5	5	6	4	6	86	1766	1720	46
06	47	OKEECHOBEE	566	1621	298	32	27	28	9	3	40	4	4	5	3	5	86	1630	1573	57
06	48	ORANGE	13,466	1642	303	33	22	26	14	6	46	4	4	5	3	5	80	1664	1591	72
06	49	OSCEOLA	3,598	1580	288	41	23	24	10	2	36	4	3	5	3	5	77	1600	1533	67
06	50	PALM BEACH	13,269	1672	310	28	23	27	15	7	49	5	4	6	3	5	87	1685	1631	54
06	51	PASCO	4,660	1629	300	34	26	26	11	3	40	4	3	5	3	5	86	1634	1605	29
06	52	PINELLAS	8,315	1659	307	31	22	26	16	6	47	5	4	6	3	5	89	1669	1630	39
06	53	POLK	6,633	1587	290	41	24	23	10	3	36	4	3	5	3	4	87	1598	1588	10
06	54	PUTNAM	976	1608	295	35	25	28	9	3	40	4	3	5	3	5	89	1617	1573	44
06	55	ST. JOHNS	1,922	1722	321	24	18	27	22	10	58	5	4	6	4	6	86	1725	1695	30
06	56	ST. LUCIE	2,747	1625	299	36	23	25	13	4	41	4	4	5	3	5	80	1634	1599	35
06	57	SANTA ROSA	1,970	1729	323	20	20	32	20	8	60	5	4	6	4	6	86	1741	1673	68
06	58	SARASOTA	3,230	1676	311	29	22	26	16	8	49	5	4	5	3	5	86	1686	1680	6
06	59	SEMINOLE	5,170	1731	323	20	21	29	21	9	59	5	5	6	4	6	87	1745	1692	53
06	60	SUMTER	579	1684	312	26	19	30	15	9	55	5	4	6	3	5	87	1692	1636	56
06	61	SUWANNEE	442	1617	297	36	27	23	11	3	37	4	4	5	3	4	86	1619	1559	60
06	62	TAYLOR	266	1627	299	31	23	32	11	3	46	4	4	6	3	5	91	1642	1554	87
06	63	UNION	169	1649	304	28	23	33	12	3	49	5	4	6	3	5	92	1655	1561	94
06	64	VOLUSIA	4,904	1660	307	27	24	31	14	4	49	4	4	6	3	5	89	1669	1656	13
06	65	WAKULLA	388	1703	317	23	21	34	16	6	56	5	4	6	3	5	90	1714	1698	16
06	66	WALTON	548	1589	290	39	25	24	10	1	35	4	3	5	3	5	86	1607	1602	5
06	67	WASHINGTON	258	1674	310	24	26	32	15	4	51	5	4	6	3	5	92	1680	1619	61
06	68	FSDB	43	1279	218	86	9	5	0	0	5	2	2	3	2	2	65	1293	1104	189
06	72	FAU HENDERSON	75	1809	341	13	15	28	35	9	72	6	5	7	4	6	87	1816	1781	35
06	73	FSU SCH	256	1811	342	8	18	35	28	11	74	6	5	7	4	6	84	1832	1770	61
06	74	FAMU SCH	54	1614	296	31	30	33	6	0	39	4	3	5	3	5	85	1627	1565	62
06	75	UF PK YONGE	114	1733	324	14	23	39	19	4	63	5	4	6	3	6	86	1725	1707	18
06	78	FL CONNECTIONS	17	1674	310	41	24	0	24	12	35	5	4	5	4	5	6	1502	1598	-96
06	79	FL VIRTUAL SCHO	18	1782	335	22	6	44	17	11	72	5	6	6	5	6	11	1937	1877	60

Note: *Percentages in "Level 3 and Above" may differ from the sum of % in levels 3 - 5 due to rounding.*

Source: *Florida Department of Education, Office of Assessment and School Performance, May 2005*

FLORIDA COMPREHENSIVE ASSESSMENT TEST (FCAT) 2005
SUNSHINE STATE STANDARDS

MATHEMATICS - Grade 7

Grade	District number	District Name	Total Test Scores: Number of Students	Mean Developmental Scale Score (0-3000)	Mean Scale Score (100-500)	% in each Achievement Level: 1	2	3	4	5	% AL3+: Percent in Achievement Levels 3 and Above	Mean Points Earned By Content: Number Sense	Measurement	Geometry	Algebraic Thinking	Data Analysis	Results for Students Matched to Previous Year: Percent Matched to 2004	Mean Developmental Scale Score (2005)	Mean Developmental Scale Score (2004)	Mean DSS Change for Matched Students Math (2005 - 2004)
Number of Points Possible												9	9	8	9	9				
07	00	STATEWIDE TOTAL	202,361	1778	303	26	22	28	17	8	53	5	4	5	4	5	87	1791	1655	136
07	01	ALACHUA	2,089	1768	301	30	19	22	17	11	51	5	4	5	4	5	90	1772	1637	134
07	02	BAKER	375	1751	297	29	20	29	17	6	51	4	4	5	4	5	90	1751	1651	101
07	03	BAY	2,046	1794	307	23	22	31	17	7	55	5	4	5	4	5	88	1797	1675	122
07	04	BRADFORD	283	1698	284	36	24	26	11	3	40	4	3	4	4	4	91	1700	1608	92
07	05	BREVARD	5,879	1856	323	15	17	32	24	12	68	5	5	5	5	5	84	1870	1768	102
07	06	BROWARD	21,132	1817	313	21	21	28	19	11	58	5	4	5	5	5	89	1829	1700	128
07	07	CALHOUN	178	1817	313	17	22	36	19	7	61	5	4	5	4	5	94	1824	1678	147
07	08	CHARLOTTE	1,386	1833	317	20	16	30	22	12	64	5	4	5	5	6	88	1845	1702	144
07	09	CITRUS	1,297	1772	302	24	24	32	15	5	52	5	4	5	4	5	88	1780	1651	129
07	10	CLAY	2,624	1806	310	20	24	31	17	8	56	5	4	5	4	5	87	1815	1692	123
07	11	COLLIER	3,146	1779	304	25	21	28	18	8	54	5	4	5	4	5	87	1792	1655	137
07	12	COLUMBIA	836	1730	291	29	26	29	12	4	45	4	3	5	4	5	91	1738	1611	127
07	13	MIAMI-DADE	27,765	1726	290	34	22	26	13	5	44	4	3	5	4	5	90	1738	1580	158
07	14	DESOTO	319	1733	292	31	24	29	12	3	45	4	3	5	4	5	87	1732	1608	124
07	15	DIXIE	150	1748	296	26	30	29	10	5	44	4	3	4	4	5	91	1748	1611	137
07	16	DUVAL	9,739	1754	297	29	23	28	15	5	48	4	4	5	4	5	85	1770	1626	144
07	17	ESCAMBIA	3,569	1709	286	34	25	25	12	3	41	4	3	4	4	4	89	1715	1579	136
07	18	FLAGLER	794	1761	299	24	27	32	12	5	50	4	4	5	4	5	79	1768	1647	121
07	19	FRANKLIN	96	1700	284	32	22	36	7	2	46	4	3	4	4	4	85	1691	1638	53
07	20	GADSDEN	503	1662	275	42	28	24	5	1	30	4	2	4	3	4	92	1663	1515	148
07	21	GILCHRIST	222	1805	310	16	27	30	19	9	57	5	4	5	4	5	90	1813	1731	82
07	22	GLADES	104	1685	280	38	30	26	6	0	32	4	2	4	4	4	88	1685	1516	169
07	23	GULF	178	1799	309	17	29	34	16	3	53	5	4	5	4	5	93	1796	1663	132
07	24	HAMILTON	163	1632	267	52	17	20	10	1	31	4	3	4	3	4	93	1630	1494	136
07	25	HARDEE	426	1719	289	33	23	27	15	3	45	4	3	4	4	4	91	1730	1606	124
07	26	HENDRY	604	1705	285	35	25	27	10	3	40	4	3	4	4	4	92	1717	1610	108
07	27	HERNANDO	1,712	1751	297	27	25	30	13	4	48	4	4	5	4	4	81	1763	1608	154
07	28	HIGHLANDS	923	1760	299	25	20	35	14	5	54	5	4	5	4	5	88	1770	1631	138
07	29	HILLSBOROUGH	14,337	1790	306	25	22	28	17	9	53	5	4	5	4	5	86	1807	1679	128
07	30	HOLMES	265	1782	304	27	22	28	18	6	51	5	4	5	4	5	91	1786	1633	152
07	31	INDIAN RIVER	1,327	1807	310	22	20	28	19	11	58	5	4	5	4	5	90	1816	1635	180
07	32	JACKSON	595	1756	298	25	27	31	14	3	49	4	3	5	4	5	92	1758	1632	126
07	33	JEFFERSON	81	1701	284	32	33	25	10	0	35	4	3	4	4	5	91	1708	1462	245
07	34	LAFAYETTE	78	1738	293	28	18	33	15	5	54	4	4	5	4	5	87	1777	1614	163
07	35	LAKE	2,817	1779	304	23	22	32	17	6	55	5	4	5	4	5	84	1792	1656	135
07	36	LEE	5,489	1775	303	24	23	31	16	6	53	5	4	5	4	5	84	1792	1658	133
07	37	LEON	2,394	1830	316	18	22	28	21	11	60	5	4	5	5	5	90	1847	1727	120
07	38	LEVY	506	1756	298	25	25	34	13	3	50	4	3	5	4	5	87	1768	1613	155
07	39	LIBERTY	94	1787	306	15	34	35	12	4	51	4	4	5	4	5	89	1810	1679	131
07	40	MADISON	216	1676	278	41	26	25	6	1	32	4	3	4	3	4	88	1682	1512	170
07	41	MANATEE	3,015	1770	301	25	24	30	17	5	52	5	4	5	4	5	84	1782	1644	138
07	42	MARION	3,150	1765	300	24	24	30	16	6	52	5	4	5	4	5	86	1780	1659	121
07	43	MARTIN	1,428	1851	322	17	17	28	24	14	66	5	5	5	5	6	90	1865	1717	148
07	44	MONROE	654	1785	305	23	22	33	17	5	54	5	4	5	4	5	88	1788	1681	107
07	45	NASSAU	839	1813	312	19	21	33	20	7	60	5	4	5	5	5	87	1818	1692	126
07	46	OKALOOSA	2,315	1884	330	10	19	34	24	14	72	6	5	6	5	6	87	1897	1774	122
07	47	OKEECHOBEE	539	1734	292	30	24	30	11	5	46	4	3	5	4	4	88	1744	1683	62
07	48	ORANGE	12,628	1777	303	26	21	28	17	8	53	5	4	5	4	5	80	1799	1647	152
07	49	OSCEOLA	3,714	1713	287	34	25	26	12	3	41	4	3	4	4	4	80	1730	1585	145
07	50	PALM BEACH	13,206	1793	307	24	21	28	18	9	55	5	4	5	4	5	87	1808	1681	127
07	51	PASCO	4,625	1772	302	25	25	30	14	6	50	5	4	5	4	5	86	1780	1644	136
07	52	PINELLAS	8,524	1783	305	26	21	27	17	8	53	5	4	5	4	5	89	1796	1654	142
07	53	POLK	6,611	1711	287	35	24	26	12	3	42	4	3	4	4	4	84	1723	1599	124
07	54	PUTNAM	902	1738	293	29	22	30	14	5	49	4	4	5	4	5	88	1748	1625	122
07	55	ST. JOHNS	1,878	1845	320	17	18	30	23	12	65	5	5	5	5	5	87	1855	1713	142
07	56	ST. LUCIE	2,780	1749	296	29	23	30	13	5	48	4	3	5	4	5	81	1755	1625	130
07	57	SANTA ROSA	2,047	1851	321	15	18	33	23	11	66	5	4	5	5	6	86	1858	1725	133
07	58	SARASOTA	3,263	1811	312	22	21	27	18	11	57	5	4	5	5	5	87	1821	1687	134
07	59	SEMINOLE	5,223	1851	321	16	19	30	23	13	66	5	5	5	5	5	88	1868	1741	127
07	60	SUMTER	606	1798	308	21	22	29	21	8	57	5	4	5	4	5	89	1809	1665	144
07	61	SUWANNEE	449	1763	300	27	24	28	15	6	49	4	3	5	4	5	89	1772	1610	162
07	62	TAYLOR	246	1779	304	25	23	34	11	7	52	4	4	5	4	5	87	1797	1690	107
07	63	UNION	195	1758	298	29	19	29	17	6	52	4	4	5	4	5	90	1783	1579	204
07	64	VOLUSIA	5,092	1780	304	24	22	32	16	6	54	5	4	5	4	5	88	1787	1668	119
07	65	WAKULLA	392	1848	321	17	17	35	21	10	67	5	5	5	5	5	90	1859	1732	127
07	66	WALTON	525	1772	302	23	27	31	15	4	50	5	4	5	4	5	89	1781	1650	131
07	67	WASHINGTON	293	1755	298	26	22	31	16	5	53	5	3	5	4	5	93	1758	1613	145
07	68	FSDB	53	1429	217	87	13	0	0	0	0	2	1	3	2	2	83	1409	1166	243
07	72	FAU HENDERSON	65	1960	348	3	9	29	43	15	88	6	6	6	6	6	86	1984	1845	139
07	73	FSU SCH	167	1929	341	4	13	34	34	16	84	6	5	6	6	6	93	1933	1751	183
07	74	FAMU SCH	41	1702	285	34	39	20	5	2	27	4	3	4	4	4	88	1704	1587	117
07	75	UF PK YONGE	110	1894	332	5	19	39	24	14	76	6	5	6	5	6	98	1896	1714	183
07	78	FL CONNECTIONS	19	1856	323	11	11	58	11	11	79	5	4	5	5	5	0			
07	79	FL VIRTUAL SCHO	30	1804	310	20	23	23	27	7	57	5	4	5	5	5	3	2011	2160	-149

Note: *Percentages in "Level 3 and Above" may differ from the sum of % in levels 3 - 5 due to rounding.*

Source: *Florida Department of Education, Office of Assessment and School Performance, May 2005*

FLORIDA COMPREHENSIVE ASSESSMENT TEST (FCAT) 2005
SUNSHINE STATE STANDARDS

MATHEMATICS - Grade 8

Grade	District number	District Name	Total Test Scores: Number of Students	Mean Developmental Scale Score (0-3000)	Mean Scale Score (100-500)	% in each Achievement Level: 1	2	3	4	5	% AL3+: Percent in Achievement Levels 3 and Above	Mean Points Earned By Content: Number Sense	Measurement	Geometry	Algebraic Thinking	Data Analysis	Results for Students Matched to Previous Year: Percent Matched to 2004	Mean Developmental Scale Score (2005)	Mean Developmental Scale Score (2004)	Mean DSS Change for Matched Students Math (2005 - 2004)
Number of Points Possible												12	12	12	12	12				
08	00	STATEWIDE TOTAL	201,488	1866	313	21	20	32	15	11	59	7	5	4	6	6	87	1880	1778	101
08	01	ALACHUA	2,181	1860	311	27	17	25	14	17	56	7	5	5	6	6	90	1873	1773	100
08	02	BAKER	361	1853	310	22	19	37	16	7	59	7	5	4	6	6	85	1864	1787	77
08	03	BAY	2,050	1877	316	18	22	36	15	10	60	7	5	4	6	6	86	1886	1789	97
08	04	BRADFORD	302	1816	300	25	24	32	14	5	51	6	4	4	5	6	89	1825	1719	107
08	05	BREVARD	5,787	1930	329	12	16	35	21	16	73	7	6	5	7	7	85	1945	1864	81
08	06	BROWARD	21,003	1894	320	19	18	30	17	15	63	7	6	5	6	7	89	1907	1821	86
08	07	CALHOUN	166	1898	321	11	25	33	22	9	63	7	5	5	6	7	90	1912	1813	99
08	08	CHARLOTTE	1,448	1918	326	14	17	34	19	16	69	7	6	5	6	7	88	1926	1830	96
08	09	CITRUS	1,297	1870	314	17	23	35	18	7	60	7	5	5	6	6	87	1880	1766	114
08	10	CLAY	2,627	1899	321	16	20	34	18	13	64	7	6	5	6	7	88	1908	1809	99
08	11	COLLIER	3,216	1867	313	22	18	31	16	12	59	7	5	5	6	6	88	1880	1783	98
08	12	COLUMBIA	755	1832	304	23	23	36	12	6	54	6	5	4	5	6	90	1842	1750	91
08	13	MIAMI-DADE	28,393	1819	301	30	21	29	12	8	49	6	5	4	5	6	90	1831	1715	116
08	14	DESOTO	344	1798	296	30	20	32	13	5	50	6	4	3	5	6	90	1801	1748	53
08	15	DIXIE	154	1843	307	23	23	38	14	3	55	6	5	3	5	6	92	1840	1688	152
08	16	DUVAL	9,222	1845	308	24	22	31	14	9	54	6	5	4	5	6	85	1862	1743	119
08	17	ESCAMBIA	3,416	1813	299	27	24	31	12	5	48	6	4	4	5	6	89	1822	1727	95
08	18	FLAGLER	829	1874	315	17	21	36	17	8	62	7	5	4	6	6	80	1887	1796	91
08	19	FRANKLIN	98	1815	300	30	20	42	4	4	50	6	4	4	5	5	88	1832	1758	73
08	20	GADSDEN	468	1744	282	42	26	26	5	1	31	5	3	3	4	5	89	1755	1670	85
08	21	GILCHRIST	201	1910	324	13	21	29	19	17	65	7	6	5	6	7	92	1925	1808	116
08	22	GLADES	103	1798	296	27	28	36	5	4	45	6	4	4	5	5	83	1798	1697	101
08	23	GULF	203	1842	307	19	22	45	12	2	59	7	5	4	5	6	90	1845	1772	73
08	24	HAMILTON	147	1726	277	46	20	25	7	1	34	5	4	2	4	5	91	1727	1657	69
08	25	HARDEE	391	1808	298	28	23	31	11	7	49	6	4	4	5	6	90	1821	1728	93
08	26	HENDRY	589	1785	293	34	21	30	11	4	45	6	4	4	5	5	91	1791	1687	104
08	27	HERNANDO	1,676	1850	309	22	23	34	15	7	55	7	5	4	6	6	82	1863	1743	120
08	28	HIGHLANDS	923	1860	312	22	21	33	14	11	58	7	5	5	6	6	88	1878	1774	104
08	29	HILLSBOROUGH	14,029	1893	320	17	20	33	16	13	62	7	5	5	6	7	87	1910	1812	98
08	30	HOLMES	274	1891	319	19	12	31	24	14	69	7	6	6	6	6	93	1899	1799	100
08	31	INDIAN RIVER	1,262	1878	316	20	19	33	18	11	62	7	6	4	6	7	90	1887	1779	108
08	32	JACKSON	537	1850	309	19	24	36	14	7	57	7	5	4	5	6	92	1851	1769	83
08	33	JEFFERSON	81	1732	279	44	26	21	2	6	30	5	4	3	4	4	93	1739	1645	95
08	34	LAFAYETTE	83	1833	304	20	28	33	8	11	52	6	5	4	6	6	92	1841	1768	72
08	35	LAKE	2,665	1867	313	19	22	35	15	9	59	7	5	4	6	6	84	1879	1782	97
08	36	LEE	5,171	1863	312	21	20	34	15	10	59	7	5	4	6	6	83	1881	1775	106
08	37	LEON	2,163	1927	328	13	16	33	21	17	71	8	6	5	7	7	91	1938	1858	80
08	38	LEVY	512	1839	306	24	21	34	15	5	55	6	5	4	5	6	86	1850	1725	125
08	39	LIBERTY	78	1881	317	17	14	41	19	9	69	7	5	4	6	7	95	1897	1822	75
08	40	MADISON	217	1755	285	37	24	24	10	5	39	6	3	3	5	5	91	1754	1664	91
08	41	MANATEE	2,993	1859	311	20	22	35	15	8	58	7	5	4	6	6	85	1872	1779	93
08	42	MARION	3,270	1858	311	20	21	36	15	9	60	7	5	4	6	6	87	1872	1785	88
08	43	MARTIN	1,421	1918	326	15	15	33	21	16	70	8	6	5	7	7	90	1927	1844	83
08	44	MONROE	687	1883	317	17	20	35	18	10	63	7	5	4	6	7	87	1885	1785	100
08	45	NASSAU	899	1900	321	15	20	36	16	13	65	7	5	5	6	7	90	1913	1813	100
08	46	OKALOOSA	2,259	1981	342	6	12	36	24	23	82	8	7	6	7	8	86	1993	1907	86
08	47	OKEECHOBEE	529	1824	302	24	27	32	14	3	49	6	4	4	5	6	85	1830	1756	73
08	48	ORANGE	13,166	1855	310	24	19	30	16	11	57	7	5	4	6	6	80	1880	1758	122
08	49	OSCEOLA	3,676	1809	299	29	23	32	12	5	49	6	4	4	5	6	80	1823	1705	118
08	50	PALM BEACH	13,119	1884	317	19	19	32	16	14	62	7	5	5	6	6	87	1898	1802	96
08	51	PASCO	4,730	1851	309	22	23	34	13	8	55	6	5	4	6	6	87	1863	1763	101
08	52	PINELLAS	8,761	1873	315	21	20	32	16	11	60	7	5	4	6	7	88	1888	1783	105
08	53	POLK	6,337	1820	301	28	22	30	12	8	50	6	5	4	5	6	84	1830	1724	106
08	54	PUTNAM	979	1821	302	27	22	30	15	6	50	6	5	4	5	6	87	1828	1727	101
08	55	ST. JOHNS	1,901	1948	334	10	14	35	23	18	76	8	6	6	7	7	88	1959	1851	108
08	56	ST. LUCIE	2,740	1839	306	25	21	33	14	7	54	7	5	4	5	6	82	1851	1753	98
08	57	SANTA ROSA	2,008	1938	331	11	14	36	21	18	75	8	6	5	7	7	87	1942	1855	88
08	58	SARASOTA	3,152	1904	323	17	17	34	17	15	66	7	6	5	6	7	89	1911	1818	94
08	59	SEMINOLE	5,289	1921	327	13	16	35	19	16	70	7	6	5	7	7	89	1931	1840	91
08	60	SUMTER	581	1824	302	24	22	34	13	8	54	6	4	4	5	6	88	1830	1739	92
08	61	SUWANNEE	432	1841	307	27	17	34	16	6	56	7	5	4	5	6	87	1847	1760	87
08	62	TAYLOR	239	1881	317	16	21	41	16	6	63	7	5	4	5	6	89	1892	1775	117
08	63	UNION	157	1847	308	22	21	27	23	8	57	7	5	4	5	6	92	1847	1742	105
08	64	VOLUSIA	5,112	1852	309	20	23	35	15	7	57	7	5	4	6	6	89	1860	1771	89
08	65	WAKULLA	360	1904	323	16	15	36	19	14	69	7	6	5	6	7	91	1921	1823	98
08	66	WALTON	534	1871	314	16	21	38	18	6	63	7	5	4	6	6	88	1884	1793	91
08	67	WASHINGTON	269	1864	312	20	16	41	15	7	63	7	5	4	6	6	89	1875	1776	98
08	68	FSDB	62	1546	232	82	8	6	2	2	10	3	2	2	3	3	87	1561	1392	169
08	72	FAU HENDERSON	50	2025	353	4	4	38	32	22	92	9	7	6	8	8	94	2045	1975	70
08	73	FSU SCH	166	1938	331	4	17	48	21	9	78	8	6	5	7	7	96	1940	1856	84
08	74	FAMU SCH	41	1814	300	32	34	27	5	2	34	6	3	4	5	6	85	1804	1732	72
08	75	UF PK YONGE	114	1967	339	4	13	39	32	13	83	8	6	6	7	8	99	1967	1850	117
08	78	FL CONNECTIONS	4									.	.	.	.	.				
08	79	FL VIRTUAL SCHO	29	1936	331	3	28	34	21	14	69	7	6	5	7	7	3	1965	2051	-86

Note: *Percentages in "Level 3 and Above" may differ from the sum of % in levels 3 - 5 due to rounding.*
Source: *Florida Department of Education, Office of Assessment and School Performance, May 2005*

FLORIDA COMPREHENSIVE ASSESSMENT TEST (FCAT) 2005
SUNSHINE STATE STANDARDS

MATHEMATICS - Grade 9

			Total Test Scores			% in each Achievement Level					% AL3+	Mean Points Earned By Content					Results for Students Matched to Previous Year			
Grade	District number	District Name	Number of Students	Mean Developmental Scale Score (0-3000)	Mean Scale Score (100-500)	1	2	3	4	5	Percent in Achievement Levels 3 and Above	Number Sense	Measurement	Geometry	Algebraic Thinking	Data Analysis	Percent Matched to 2004	Mean Developmental Scale Score (2005)	Mean Developmental Scale Score (2004)	Mean DSS Change for Matched Students Math (2005 - 2004)
Number of Points Possible												8	7	11	10	8				
09	00	STATEWIDE TOTAL	214,360	1918	300	20	21	30	20	9	59	4	3	5	6	4	83	1929	1870	60
09	01	ALACHUA	2,394	1932	305	21	19	23	21	16	60	4	4	5	6	5	87	1942	1885	57
09	02	BAKER	403	1886	291	24	22	32	18	4	54	4	3	5	6	4	84	1892	1842	50
09	03	BAY	2,185	1937	306	15	21	34	21	9	64	4	3	5	6	5	83	1941	1874	67
09	04	BRADFORD	291	1866	285	27	23	30	15	4	49	4	3	4	5	4	87	1868	1804	64
09	05	BREVARD	6,169	1991	322	9	17	32	27	16	75	5	4	6	7	5	82	2000	1938	63
09	06	BROWARD	21,434	1935	305	18	21	30	21	11	62	4	3	5	6	5	85	1951	1894	58
09	07	CALHOUN	186	1956	312	14	20	35	20	11	66	5	4	5	6	5	91	1968	1923	44
09	08	CHARLOTTE	1,535	1962	313	13	18	34	25	11	70	4	4	6	7	5	84	1969	1928	41
09	09	CITRUS	1,320	1931	304	15	21	34	22	8	64	4	3	5	6	5	86	1944	1895	50
09	10	CLAY	2,666	1962	313	11	18	35	25	10	70	5	4	6	6	5	87	1967	1913	54
09	11	COLLIER	3,412	1918	300	21	20	30	19	10	59	4	3	5	6	5	82	1933	1883	50
09	12	COLUMBIA	837	1881	289	24	24	31	16	5	52	4	3	5	6	4	86	1889	1833	57
09	13	MIAMI-DADE	30,498	1870	286	28	24	27	15	6	48	4	3	5	5	4	85	1882	1812	70
09	14	DESOTO	343	1856	282	29	24	31	14	2	47	4	3	4	5	4	87	1862	1770	92
09	15	DIXIE	186	1877	288	23	26	34	14	3	52	4	3	5	5	4	88	1881	1807	74
09	16	DUVAL	10,405	1902	296	23	21	29	19	8	56	4	3	5	6	4	83	1915	1836	79
09	17	ESCAMBIA	3,448	1878	288	26	23	28	17	6	51	4	3	5	6	4	83	1886	1828	58
09	18	FLAGLER	874	1951	310	14	20	35	22	9	66	4	4	5	6	5	75	1968	1922	46
09	19	FRANKLIN	102	1810	269	38	21	28	11	2	41	3	2	4	5	3	88	1826	1772	53
09	20	GADSDEN	374	1839	277	29	33	27	9	2	38	3	2	4	5	4	87	1854	1772	83
09	21	GILCHRIST	220	1950	310	12	16	39	23	10	71	4	4	5	7	5	88	1968	1941	27
09	22	GLADES	76	1858	283	29	28	25	17	1	43	4	2	4	5	4	80	1898	1829	69
09	23	GULF	218	1935	305	17	21	32	22	9	62	4	3	5	6	5	91	1937	1875	62
09	24	HAMILTON	180	1809	268	41	23	29	5	3	37	3	2	3	5	3	93	1811	1725	87
09	25	HARDEE	351	1882	290	24	27	30	14	5	49	4	3	4	5	4	92	1883	1818	65
09	26	HENDRY	609	1871	286	27	23	31	15	4	50	4	3	4	5	4	84	1881	1810	71
09	27	HERNANDO	1,805	1892	293	20	26	33	16	4	53	4	3	4	6	4	81	1903	1844	59
09	28	HIGHLANDS	1,114	1893	293	22	23	33	16	6	55	4	3	5	6	4	86	1900	1848	52
09	29	HILLSBOROUGH	13,348	1953	311	13	21	31	23	11	66	4	4	6	6	5	84	1964	1920	44
09	30	HOLMES	267	1931	304	13	23	34	24	6	64	4	3	5	6	5	91	1932	1885	47
09	31	INDIAN RIVER	1,480	1937	306	17	22	31	20	10	62	4	3	5	6	5	85	1940	1865	75
09	32	JACKSON	570	1934	305	16	21	32	25	6	63	4	4	5	6	5	87	1943	1887	57
09	33	JEFFERSON	110	1814	270	32	37	25	6	0	31	3	2	3	5	4	84	1832	1752	81
09	34	LAFAYETTE	83	1926	303	19	19	31	28	2	61	4	3	5	6	4	94	1925	1877	49
09	35	LAKE	2,865	1908	297	20	23	30	20	7	57	4	3	5	6	4	83	1920	1864	57
09	36	LEE	5,656	1917	300	19	22	32	19	8	59	4	3	5	6	5	77	1933	1882	52
09	37	LEON	2,606	1965	314	12	20	31	25	12	68	5	4	6	7	5	84	1969	1925	45
09	38	LEVY	514	1885	290	25	22	31	18	5	54	4	3	4	6	4	85	1901	1847	53
09	39	LIBERTY	85	1922	302	15	22	36	24	2	62	4	3	5	6	5	92	1925	1870	55
09	40	MADISON	234	1831	275	35	29	22	9	5	36	3	2	4	5	4	88	1828	1749	79
09	41	MANATEE	3,108	1911	298	20	23	30	19	9	57	4	3	5	6	5	81	1926	1873	53
09	42	MARION	3,311	1917	300	19	21	31	21	7	60	4	3	5	6	5	83	1926	1870	56
09	43	MARTIN	1,639	1961	313	13	15	32	28	11	72	5	4	6	7	5	80	1970	1920	50
09	44	MONROE	715	1939	306	16	17	34	24	9	67	4	4	5	6	5	80	1952	1882	70
09	45	NASSAU	883	1952	310	12	19	36	22	10	68	4	4	5	6	5	88	1964	1915	49
09	46	OKALOOSA	2,533	1989	321	9	17	32	28	15	75	5	4	6	7	5	84	2003	1955	48
09	47	OKEECHOBEE	524	1886	291	26	19	30	20	5	56	4	3	5	5	4	86	1897	1830	66
09	48	ORANGE	13,778	1904	296	24	21	27	19	10	56	4	3	5	6	4	75	1925	1862	63
09	49	OSCEOLA	4,263	1874	287	26	25	29	15	5	49	4	3	5	5	4	75	1889	1811	78
09	50	PALM BEACH	15,210	1925	303	20	20	29	20	11	60	4	3	5	6	4	81	1938	1876	62
09	51	PASCO	5,173	1908	297	19	24	31	19	7	57	4	3	5	6	4	84	1917	1859	58
09	52	PINELLAS	9,939	1918	300	21	20	29	20	9	58	4	3	5	6	4	84	1924	1867	57
09	53	POLK	6,612	1875	288	27	24	27	16	6	49	4	3	5	5	4	83	1885	1823	62
09	54	PUTNAM	909	1896	294	23	23	31	17	7	54	4	3	5	6	4	86	1909	1845	64
09	55	ST. JOHNS	2,067	1990	322	10	15	32	28	16	75	5	4	6	7	5	82	2000	1939	62
09	56	ST. LUCIE	2,703	1907	297	20	25	30	18	7	55	4	3	5	6	4	81	1917	1855	62
09	57	SANTA ROSA	2,072	1982	319	9	15	34	28	14	75	5	4	6	7	5	85	1991	1950	41
09	58	SARASOTA	3,456	1958	312	15	19	30	24	13	67	5	4	6	6	5	82	1965	1916	50
09	59	SEMINOLE	5,738	1970	316	13	18	30	26	14	69	5	4	6	7	5	84	1979	1931	48
09	60	SUMTER	562	1923	302	19	19	28	24	10	62	4	3	5	6	5	77	1918	1834	84
09	61	SUWANNEE	493	1891	292	24	20	32	19	4	56	4	3	5	6	4	86	1904	1850	54
09	62	TAYLOR	228	1903	296	18	29	31	20	3	54	4	3	5	6	5	93	1911	1864	47
09	63	UNION	168	1881	289	23	30	27	14	6	48	4	3	4	6	4	90	1897	1835	62
09	64	VOLUSIA	5,171	1915	299	19	21	33	20	8	60	4	3	5	6	4	84	1922	1872	51
09	65	WAKULLA	429	1913	299	20	21	34	19	7	59	4	3	5	6	5	90	1919	1886	34
09	66	WALTON	532	1926	303	16	22	33	22	7	61	4	3	5	6	5	81	1925	1873	52
09	67	WASHINGTON	287	1949	309	13	20	33	26	8	68	5	4	5	6	5	90	1955	1893	61
09	68	FSDB	65	1676	229	74	11	8	8	0	15	2	1	3	3	2	78	1662	1573	89
09	72	FAU HENDERSON	14	2066	344	0	0	36	50	14	100	6	5	8	8	7	43	2093	2043	49
09	73	FSU SCH	153	2026	332	2	12	37	36	14	86	5	4	7	7	6	92	2035	2008	27
09	74	FAMU SCH	39	1824	273	33	36	28	3	0	31	3	2	3	5	4	85	1848	1827	21
09	75	UF PK YONGE	133	2033	334	2	13	37	32	17	86	5	4	7	7	6	90	2037	1964	73

Note: *Percentages in "Level 3 and Above" may differ from the sum of % in levels 3 - 5 due to rounding.*

Source: *Florida Department of Education, Office of Assessment and School Performance, May 2005*

FLORIDA COMPREHENSIVE ASSESSMENT TEST (FCAT) 2005

SUNSHINE STATE STANDARDS

MATHEMATICS - Grade 10

			Total Test Scores									% AL3+	Mean Points Earned By Content					Results for Students Matched to Previous Year			
							% in each Achievement Level														
Grade	District number	District Name	Number of Students	Mean Developmental Scale Score (0-3000)	Mean Scale Score (100-500)	Percent Passing	1	2	3	4	5	Percent in Achievement Levels 3 and Above	Number Sense	Measurement	Geometry	Algebraic Thinking	Data Analysis	Percent Matched to 2004	Mean Developmental Scale Score (2005)	Mean Developmental Scale Score (2004)	Mean DSS Change for Matched Students Math (2005 - 2004)
Number of Points Possible													11	10	14	14	11				
10		STATEWIDE TOTAL	178,530	1979	322	77	15	22	27	28	8	63	7	4	5	6	5	87	1994	1945	49
10	01	ALACHUA	2,225	1980	322	75	17	19	23	29	13	64	7	4	5	7	5	89	1999	1960	39
10	02	BAKER	275	1963	318	79	15	21	35	25	4	63	7	4	4	5	5	92	1972	1939	34
10	03	BAY	1,867	2003	328	82	11	21	28	32	8	68	7	4	5	7	5	89	2011	1966	45
10	04	BRADFORD	255	1917	307	69	22	27	31	19	2	51	6	3	3	5	4	92	1929	1885	44
10	05	BREVARD	5,520	2036	336	87	7	17	28	36	13	76	7	5	6	7	6	88	2044	2005	39
10	06	BROWARD	19,067	1977	321	76	15	22	28	27	8	63	7	4	5	6	5	88	1989	1950	40
10	07	CALHOUN	141	2031	335	85	11	15	26	38	11	74	7	5	6	7	6	96	2033	1988	45
10	08	CHARLOTTE	1,332	2003	328	82	11	19	29	34	7	70	7	4	5	6	5	89	2012	1966	46
10	09	CITRUS	1,085	1999	327	81	10	22	29	31	8	67	7	4	5	6	5	88	2008	1973	35
10	10	CLAY	2,429	2006	329	81	11	20	28	33	9	69	7	4	5	7	5	90	2014	1974	40
10	11	COLLIER	2,748	1979	322	78	14	23	29	27	8	63	6	4	5	6	5	84	2003	1954	49
10	12	COLUMBIA	571	1947	314	74	17	25	29	23	5	58	6	4	4	6	5	91	1952	1911	41
10	13	DADE	26,378	1935	311	68	22	24	27	22	5	54	6	4	4	5	4	87	1948	1884	65
10	14	DESOTO	303	1951	315	73	16	25	34	22	2	59	6	4	4	5	4	92	1960	1915	45
10	15	DIXIE	149	1916	307	66	21	31	27	18	3	48	6	3	4	5	4	91	1928	1879	49
10	16	DUVAL	7,105	1983	323	79	14	21	29	30	7	66	7	4	5	6	5	87	1999	1941	58
10	17	ESCAMBIA	2,862	1941	313	71	20	23	26	25	6	57	6	4	4	6	5	88	1961	1926	35
10	18	FLAGLER	682	2006	329	82	11	20	30	33	7	70	7	4	5	7	5	82	2020	1972	48
10	19	FRANKLIN	95	1891	301	57	26	37	21	15	1	37	5	3	3	4	4	91	1902	1872	30
10	20	GADSDEN	310	1896	302	66	22	35	31	12	0	43	6	3	3	4	4	85	1914	1875	39
10	21	GILCHRIST	193	2022	333	84	9	13	31	38	9	78	7	5	5	7	6	93	2027	1983	44
10	22	GLADES	67	1907	304	60	30	19	30	21	0	51	6	3	4	5	4	90	1927	1900	27
10	23	GULF	156	2002	328	83	9	18	37	29	8	73	7	4	5	6	5	94	2003	1948	55
10	24	HAMILTON	103	1870	295	61	28	25	24	19	3	47	6	3	3	4	4	86	1878	1836	42
10	25	HARDEE	325	1956	316	77	14	26	33	25	2	60	6	4	5	5	4	90	1972	1925	46
10	26	HENDRY	568	1897	302	59	26	34	23	16	2	40	5	3	3	4	4	88	1912	1872	40
10	27	HERNANDO	1,483	1968	319	78	14	24	31	27	4	62	6	4	4	6	5	83	1988	1930	58
10	28	HIGHLANDS	727	1985	324	82	13	20	33	29	6	68	7	4	5	6	5	89	2003	1963	40
10	29	HILLSBOROUGH	11,813	2001	327	81	12	21	27	31	9	68	7	4	5	7	5	87	2017	1977	41
10	30	HOLMES	250	1974	321	77	14	22	29	28	7	64	7	4	5	6	5	94	1980	1932	48
10	31	INDIAN RIVER	1,128	2003	328	81	11	21	26	34	8	67	7	4	5	6	5	89	2010	1962	47
10	32	JACKSON	477	1973	321	79	15	19	32	30	4	66	7	4	4	6	5	94	1981	1933	48
10	33	JEFFERSON	76	1903	303	63	28	34	29	8	1	38	5	3	3	4	4	92	1905	1849	57
10	34	LAFAYETTE	65	1985	323	85	11	14	38	34	3	75	7	4	4	7	5	92	2002	1982	20
10	35	LAKE	2,582	1954	316	74	18	23	28	26	4	59	6	4	4	6	5	84	1967	1919	47
10	36	LEE	4,510	1974	321	77	14	24	29	27	6	62	6	4	5	6	5	81	1992	1941	51
10	37	LEON	1,917	2041	337	89	6	16	30	34	14	78	8	5	6	7	6	92	2050	2013	37
10	38	LEVY	408	1962	318	74	15	26	30	23	6	58	6	4	5	5	5	85	1978	1920	58
10	39	LIBERTY	70	1983	323	84	13	23	41	20	3	64	6	4	4	5	5	94	1984	1955	29
10	40	MADISON	224	1822	284	50	37	25	25	13	0	38	5	3	3	4	4	91	1828	1783	45
10	41	MANATEE	2,756	1956	316	73	18	25	25	25	7	58	6	4	4	6	5	86	1969	1925	44
10	42	MARION	2,941	1974	321	78	14	22	29	29	6	64	7	4	5	6	5	86	1999	1959	40
10	43	MARTIN	1,266	2039	337	88	7	14	30	36	13	79	8	5	6	7	6	90	2052	2003	49
10	44	MONROE	598	2021	332	84	9	18	26	37	10	73	7	5	6	7	6	87	2033	1981	52
10	45	NASSAU	740	2019	332	88	6	19	35	33	7	74	7	4	5	6	5	93	2027	1973	54
10	46	OKALOOSA	2,198	2048	339	89	6	15	27	39	13	79	8	5	6	7	6	86	2058	2012	46
10	47	OKEECHOBEE	478	1944	314	76	17	24	29	27	3	59	6	4	4	5	5	87	1948	1914	34
10	48	ORANGE	12,270	1958	317	72	19	22	25	26	8	58	6	4	4	6	5	78	1988	1935	53
10	49	OSCEOLA	2,780	1941	313	73	19	24	27	26	4	57	6	4	4	5	5	76	1964	1919	45
10	50	PALM BEACH	10,897	2013	330	83	11	18	27	34	11	71	7	5	6	7	5	86	2033	1987	46
10	51	PASCO	3,725	1975	321	77	14	23	29	27	6	62	6	4	4	6	5	83	1996	1955	41
10	52	PINELLAS	8,118	2002	328	80	12	21	28	30	10	67	7	4	5	7	5	90	2012	1954	58
10	53	POLK	5,503	1941	313	70	20	25	28	23	5	55	6	4	4	5	5	88	1951	1903	48
10	54	PUTNAM	750	1943	313	70	20	27	24	26	3	54	6	4	4	5	4	92	1954	1901	53
10	55	ST. JOHNS	1,874	2030	334	87	8	17	28	34	13	75	7	5	6	7	6	88	2040	1987	53
10	56	ST. LUCIE	2,361	1944	314	70	20	25	27	23	4	54	6	4	4	5	4	79	1965	1923	42
10	57	SANTA ROSA	1,800	2030	334	88	7	16	29	38	10	77	8	5	5	7	6	89	2037	2003	34
10	58	SARASOTA	2,965	2012	330	82	11	19	27	32	11	70	7	5	5	7	5	87	2025	1981	44
10	59	SEMINOLE	4,756	2044	338	87	8	16	24	38	14	76	8	5	6	7	6	91	2049	1998	52
10	60	SUMTER	490	1968	319	75	13	26	29	27	6	61	6	4	5	6	5	80	1961	1916	45
10	61	SUWANNEE	337	1974	321	81	12	25	29	26	8	63	7	4	4	6	5	90	1983	1938	45
10	62	TAYLOR	208	1941	313	67	19	33	23	21	4	48	6	4	4	5	5	91	1948	1889	59
10	63	UNION	140	1976	321	79	16	21	32	26	4	63	6	4	4	6	5	94	1981	1912	69
10	64	VOLUSIA	4,658	1972	320	76	15	22	28	27	8	63	7	4	5	6	5	90	1981	1939	42
10	65	WAKULLA	319	1978	322	78	14	19	36	26	5	66	7	4	4	6	5	90	1993	1936	56
10	66	WALTON	465	1955	316	76	15	26	35	23	2	60	6	4	4	5	5	86	1965	1922	42
10	67	WASHINGTON	215	1955	316	74	14	26	28	30	2	60	6	4	4	6	5	90	1961	1916	46
10	68	FSDB	53	1710	257	23	66	21	11	2	0	13	3	2	2	2	3	75	1673	1653	20
10	72	FAU HENDERSON	4	.	.	.	.	.	.	.	.	.	.	.	.	.	.	.	.	.	.
10	73	FSU SCH	144	2064	343	95	0	15	30	44	10	85	8	5	6	8	6	98	2065	2029	36
10	74	FAMU SCH	38	1940	312	68	16	29	45	11	0	55	6	3	3	5	4	82	1929	1874	55
10	75	UF PK YONGE	123	2057	341	98	2	12	33	44	9	86	8	5	6	8	6	94	2052	1996	57
10	79	FL VIRTUAL SCHO	2	.	.	.	.	.	.	.	.	.	.	.	.	.	.	.	.	.	.
10	80	COMM. COLLEGES	17	2025	333	88	0	18	59	18	6	82	7	4	5	7	6	29	2051	2048	3

Note: *Percentages in "Level 3 and Above" may differ from the sum of % in levels 3 - 5 due to rounding.*

Source: *Florida Department of Education, Office of Assessment and School Performance, May 2005*

FLORIDA COMPREHENSIVE ASSESSMENT TEST (FCAT) 2005

READING - Grade 3

			Total Test Scores									Mean Points Earned by Content			
						% in each Achievement Level					% AL3+				
Grade	District number	District Name	Number of Students	Mean Developmental Scale Score	Mean Scale Score (100-500)	1	2	3	4	5	Percent in Achievement Levels 3+	Words / Phrases	Main Idea / Purpose	Comparisons	Reference / Research
Number of Points Possible												6	26	8	5
03	00	STATEWIDE TOTALS	202,975	1333	305	20	13	33	28	6	67	3	16	6	3
03	01	ALACHUA	2,101	1371	312	17	13	31	29	9	69	4	17	6	3
03	02	BAKER	369	1369	311	14	16	35	31	5	70	3	17	6	3
03	03	BAY	1,996	1411	318	13	11	36	32	9	77	4	17	6	3
03	04	BRADFORD	294	1329	305	19	13	33	29	6	67	4	16	6	3
03	05	BREVARD	5,113	1431	322	13	9	32	36	9	78	4	18	6	3
03	06	BROWARD	21,039	1334	306	20	13	32	28	7	67	3	17	6	3
03	07	CALHOUN	144	1446	324	10	8	33	38	10	81	4	18	6	4
03	08	CHARLOTTE	1,210	1411	318	15	9	32	35	8	76	4	18	6	3
03	09	CITRUS	1,108	1433	322	12	11	35	33	9	78	4	18	6	3
03	10	CLAY	2,389	1421	320	12	10	35	36	7	78	4	18	6	3
03	11	COLLIER	3,347	1307	301	21	15	33	26	5	64	3	16	6	3
03	12	COLUMBIA	749	1346	308	17	14	37	26	7	69	4	17	6	3
03	13	MIAMI DADE	29,885	1262	294	25	14	33	23	4	61	3	16	5	3
03	14	DESOTO	389	1196	283	30	17	33	17	2	52	3	14	5	3
03	15	DIXIE	132	1274	296	26	8	37	26	3	66	3	16	6	3
03	16	DUVAL	10,202	1334	306	20	13	34	27	6	67	3	17	6	3
03	17	ESCAMBIA	3,207	1298	300	23	12	32	27	6	64	3	16	6	3
03	18	FLAGLER	732	1394	315	14	11	37	32	6	76	4	17	6	3
03	19	FRANKLIN	90	1306	301	19	12	39	23	7	69	4	16	6	3
03	20	GADSDEN	499	1198	283	30	19	33	17	1	52	3	14	5	3
03	21	GILCHRIST	227	1336	306	16	12	35	34	3	72	4	17	6	3
03	22	GLADES	104	1296	299	19	17	42	17	4	63	3	15	6	3
03	23	GULF	135	1431	322	16	8	31	35	10	76	4	17	6	4
03	24	HAMILTON	165	1212	285	30	18	28	23	2	53	3	15	5	3
03	25	HARDEE	442	1250	292	25	14	36	22	3	61	3	15	6	3
03	26	HENDRY	514	1228	288	25	16	36	20	3	58	3	15	5	3
03	27	HERNANDO	1,588	1357	309	17	13	37	28	6	71	4	17	6	3
03	28	HIGHLANDS	917	1301	300	21	12	36	27	4	67	3	16	6	3
03	29	HILLSBOROUGH	14,703	1330	305	21	13	31	27	7	66	3	16	6	3
03	30	HOLMES	263	1278	296	20	18	37	22	3	62	3	16	6	3
03	31	INDIAN RIVER	1,224	1405	317	14	10	32	35	8	75	4	18	6	4
03	32	JACKSON	537	1376	312	17	12	30	34	7	71	4	17	6	3
03	33	JEFFERSON	89	1236	290	25	22	35	17	1	53	3	15	5	3
03	34	LAFAYETTE	93	1257	293	26	16	31	25	2	58	3	15	6	3
03	35	LAKE	2,760	1350	308	19	12	33	30	7	69	4	16	6	3
03	36	LEE	5,598	1355	309	17	13	35	28	7	70	3	17	6	3
03	37	LEON	2,433	1419	320	15	12	31	32	11	73	4	17	6	3
03	38	LEVY	483	1285	297	20	14	36	26	3	65	3	16	6	3
03	39	LIBERTY	81	1372	312	16	16	31	32	5	68	4	17	6	3
03	40	MADISON	179	1331	305	16	18	35	28	3	66	3	16	6	3
03	41	MANATEE	3,149	1308	301	21	15	35	24	6	65	3	16	6	3
03	42	MARION	3,073	1298	300	21	14	35	26	4	65	3	16	6	3
03	43	MARTIN	1,236	1434	322	11	10	36	35	9	80	4	18	6	3
03	44	MONROE	611	1416	319	14	10	32	36	9	76	4	18	6	3
03	45	NASSAU	780	1439	323	11	10	32	39	7	79	4	18	6	4
03	46	OKALOOSA	2,168	1465	327	10	10	33	38	10	81	4	18	6	4
03	47	OKEECHOBEE	563	1254	292	25	15	38	19	4	61	3	15	6	3
03	48	ORANGE	13,713	1304	301	22	13	34	25	6	65	3	16	6	3
03	49	OSCEOLA	3,672	1254	292	24	15	35	22	4	61	3	15	5	3
03	50	PALM BEACH	13,375	1325	304	20	13	33	27	6	67	3	16	6	3
03	51	PASCO	4,935	1305	301	21	14	35	26	5	66	3	16	6	3
03	52	PINELLAS	8,308	1346	308	19	13	32	29	7	68	4	17	6	3
03	53	POLK	6,771	1296	299	22	15	34	25	5	64	3	16	6	3
03	54	PUTNAM	919	1301	300	20	17	33	25	5	63	3	16	6	3
03	55	ST. JOHNS	1,867	1463	327	12	10	29	37	12	79	4	18	6	3
03	56	ST. LUCIE	2,621	1332	305	20	14	33	27	6	66	3	16	6	3
03	57	SANTA ROSA	1,713	1505	334	8	8	30	41	12	84	4	19	6	4
03	58	SARASOTA	3,227	1405	317	15	11	31	33	9	74	4	17	6	3
03	59	SEMINOLE	5,009	1452	325	12	9	32	36	11	79	4	18	6	4
03	60	SUMTER	543	1326	304	20	13	32	29	5	66	3	16	6	3
03	61	SUWANNEE	376	1303	300	20	12	37	26	5	68	3	16	6	3
03	62	TAYLOR	252	1325	304	22	9	35	29	5	69	3	16	6	3
03	63	UNION	166	1391	315	16	10	36	34	5	75	4	17	6	3
03	64	VOLUSIA	4,875	1368	311	16	12	36	30	7	72	4	17	6	3
03	65	WAKULLA	354	1443	324	13	8	34	36	10	79	4	18	6	4
03	66	WALTON	494	1402	317	13	12	36	30	9	75	4	17	6	3
03	67	WASHINGTON	258	1395	316	14	11	36	31	7	75	4	17	6	3
03	68	FDSB	32	765	212	81	3	9	6	0	16	2	9	3	2
03	72	FAU HENDERSON	71	1564	343	3	4	31	52	10	93	4	20	7	4
03	73	FSU SCH	189	1493	332	9	8	30	40	12	83	4	19	6	4
03	74	FAMU SCH	34	1310	302	9	26	35	26	3	65	3	17	6	3
03	75	UF PK YONGE	58	1536	339	7	2	34	48	9	91	5	20	6	4
03	78	FL CONNECTIONS	14	1517	336	0	14	43	21	21	86	4	18	7	4
03	79	FL VIRTUAL SCHO	19	1534	339	5	0	42	37	16	95	4	19	7	4

Note: *Percentages in "Level 3 and Above" may differ from the sum of % in levels 3 - 5 due to rounding.*

Source: *Florida Department of Education, Office of Assessment and School Performance, May 2005*

FLORIDA COMPREHENSIVE ASSESSMENT TEST (FCAT) 2005
SUNSHINE STATE STANDARDS

READING - Grade 4

Grade	District number	District Name	Total Test Scores: Number of Students	Mean Developmental Scale Score (0-3000)	Mean Scale Score (100-500)	% in each Achievement Level: 1	2	3	4	5	% AL3+: Percent in Achievement Levels 3+	Mean Points Earned By Content: Words / Phrases	Main Idea / Purpose	Comparisons	Reference / Research	Results for Students Matched to Previous Year: Percent Matched to 2004	Mean Developmental Scale Score (2005)	Mean Developmental Scale Score (2004)	Mean DSS Change for Matched Students Reading (2005 - 2004)
Number of Points Possible												7	23	19	2				
04	00	STATEWIDE TOTAL	195,678	1575	319	15	13	35	29	8	71	5	16	12	1	87	1593	1380	213
04	01	ALACHUA	1,996	1585	320	18	14	29	29	10	68	5	16	12	1	91	1590	1398	192
04	02	BAKER	358	1575	318	15	17	34	28	7	68	5	15	12	1	89	1580	1424	156
04	03	BAY	1,826	1622	327	12	11	35	33	9	77	5	16	13	1	87	1631	1453	178
04	04	BRADFORD	251	1522	309	20	14	40	22	4	66	4	15	12	1	92	1538	1361	178
04	05	BREVARD	5,345	1659	333	10	9	33	36	12	81	5	17	13	1	85	1671	1464	207
04	06	BROWARD	21,307	1561	316	17	14	35	27	7	69	5	16	12	1	89	1575	1364	211
04	07	CALHOUN	161	1610	325	14	6	39	31	10	80	5	16	13	1	88	1623	1430	193
04	08	CHARLOTTE	1,152	1600	323	13	13	35	33	6	74	5	16	13	1	84	1616	1416	200
04	09	CITRUS	1,106	1622	327	11	11	37	32	8	78	5	16	13	1	88	1621	1428	193
04	10	CLAY	2,204	1657	332	8	12	34	36	10	80	5	17	13	1	85	1671	1475	196
04	11	COLLIER	3,219	1566	317	17	14	33	29	8	69	5	16	12	1	87	1587	1362	224
04	12	COLUMBIA	737	1559	316	14	14	38	30	4	72	5	16	12	1	90	1573	1402	171
04	13	MIAMI-DADE	26,741	1547	314	17	14	35	27	6	69	4	16	12	1	92	1572	1328	244
04	14	DESOTO	367	1561	316	14	14	36	31	4	71	4	16	12	1	93	1565	1318	247
04	15	DIXIE	159	1542	313	19	12	42	19	8	69	4	15	11	1	94	1547	1309	238
04	16	DUVAL	9,461	1583	320	14	15	35	29	8	71	5	16	12	1	85	1616	1394	223
04	17	ESCAMBIA	3,382	1527	310	19	16	34	25	5	65	4	15	12	1	89	1532	1335	197
04	18	FLAGLER	735	1600	323	14	12	34	33	7	75	5	16	12	1	80	1610	1402	207
04	19	FRANKLIN	88	1542	313	16	13	49	18	5	72	5	15	12	1	85	1546	1309	237
04	20	GADSDEN	434	1447	297	27	18	38	15	2	55	4	14	11	1	91	1456	1186	270
04	21	GILCHRIST	186	1618	326	10	10	34	39	6	80	5	17	12	1	91	1624	1383	241
04	22	GLADES	104	1485	303	15	27	37	17	4	58	4	14	11	1	86	1471	1290	180
04	23	GULF	146	1536	312	18	10	42	24	6	72	5	15	12	1	90	1557	1382	175
04	24	HAMILTON	136	1457	298	26	15	35	18	4	58	4	14	11	1	90	1473	1310	163
04	25	HARDEE	391	1488	304	21	17	39	19	4	62	4	15	11	1	89	1504	1302	203
04	26	HENDRY	576	1509	307	20	16	36	23	5	64	4	15	11	1	90	1531	1311	219
04	27	HERNANDO	1,496	1576	319	13	13	39	28	6	73	5	16	12	1	82	1600	1404	196
04	28	HIGHLANDS	882	1548	314	16	13	39	26	5	71	5	15	12	1	90	1563	1361	202
04	29	HILLSBOROUGH	14,204	1559	316	17	15	34	27	8	68	5	15	12	1	87	1574	1382	192
04	30	HOLMES	250	1552	315	14	16	34	31	5	70	5	16	12	1	90	1549	1374	175
04	31	INDIAN RIVER	1,262	1629	328	11	11	34	34	10	78	5	17	13	1	89	1638	1396	242
04	32	JACKSON	486	1615	325	12	12	35	34	8	76	5	16	13	1	92	1619	1411	208
04	33	JEFFERSON	90	1372	284	38	18	30	13	1	44	4	13	10	1	89	1387	1231	155
04	34	LAFAYETTE	76	1623	327	8	12	41	28	12	80	5	17	13	1	95	1652	1467	185
04	35	LAKE	2,771	1570	318	15	13	37	31	5	73	5	16	12	1	85	1579	1379	200
04	36	LEE	5,296	1578	319	15	14	36	28	7	71	5	16	12	1	85	1599	1399	200
04	37	LEON	2,244	1646	331	11	11	34	32	12	78	5	17	13	1	90	1657	1465	193
04	38	LEVY	291	1529	311	16	14	40	26	3	70	5	15	12	1	89	1535	1335	200
04	39	LIBERTY	83	1582	320	10	10	47	27	7	81	5	16	12	1	93	1605	1414	191
04	40	MADISON	212	1432	294	28	17	38	14	2	54	4	14	11	1	91	1420	1260	160
04	41	MANATEE	3,189	1563	316	15	14	38	26	6	71	4	16	12	1	84	1583	1374	210
04	42	MARION	3,096	1563	316	15	14	38	27	6	71	5	16	12	1	89	1575	1364	212
04	43	MARTIN	1,258	1668	334	9	10	33	36	13	82	5	17	13	1	89	1687	1466	220
04	44	MONROE	580	1621	326	12	12	34	33	9	76	5	16	13	1	87	1640	1432	208
04	45	NASSAU	772	1628	328	11	9	38	34	9	80	5	17	13	1	89	1636	1448	187
04	46	OKALOOSA	2,168	1682	337	7	10	33	37	13	83	5	17	13	1	86	1697	1504	193
04	47	OKEECHOBEE	495	1527	310	19	15	35	27	5	66	4	15	12	1	85	1544	1324	220
04	48	ORANGE	12,902	1555	315	16	14	36	27	7	70	5	16	12	1	83	1582	1350	231
04	49	OSCEOLA	3,568	1513	308	19	15	36	25	5	65	4	15	11	1	78	1549	1333	216
04	50	PALM BEACH	13,013	1572	318	16	13	34	28	8	71	5	16	12	1	88	1591	1365	226
04	51	PASCO	4,634	1566	317	15	14	38	27	6	71	5	16	12	1	87	1577	1354	223
04	52	PINELLAS	8,303	1587	321	15	13	34	30	9	73	5	16	12	1	90	1600	1382	218
04	53	POLK	6,444	1525	310	19	15	36	25	5	66	4	15	12	1	87	1545	1356	189
04	54	PUTNAM	920	1540	313	16	17	39	25	4	67	4	15	12	1	91	1552	1334	218
04	55	ST. JOHNS	1,838	1687	338	9	8	30	39	14	83	5	17	13	1	85	1697	1486	211
04	56	ST. LUCIE	2,698	1560	316	16	15	36	27	6	69	5	16	12	1	80	1573	1357	216
04	57	SANTA ROSA	1,718	1705	341	6	6	33	41	14	88	5	18	14	1	86	1715	1516	199
04	58	SARASOTA	3,137	1641	330	11	10	33	34	11	78	5	17	13	1	87	1651	1473	177
04	59	SEMINOLE	5,004	1649	331	10	9	35	36	10	81	5	17	13	1	87	1667	1489	179
04	60	SUMTER	568	1586	320	15	11	36	29	8	74	5	16	12	1	83	1577	1390	187
04	61	SUWANNEE	411	1550	314	18	15	35	26	6	67	4	15	12	1	90	1555	1376	179
04	62	TAYLOR	229	1587	321	13	15	41	25	7	72	5	16	12	1	93	1588	1435	153
04	63	UNION	157	1570	318	15	14	32	36	3	71	4	16	12	1	85	1599	1414	185
04	64	VOLUSIA	4,902	1595	322	12	12	37	32	7	76	5	16	12	1	89	1607	1397	210
04	65	WAKULLA	315	1652	332	7	9	37	37	9	84	5	17	13	1	92	1670	1490	180
04	66	WALTON	484	1630	328	11	10	37	34	9	80	5	17	13	1	86	1644	1451	193
04	67	WASHINGTON	243	1557	315	15	16	30	33	6	69	5	16	12	1	93	1557	1363	193
04	68	FSDB	22	975	216	86	5	9	0	0	9	3	9	6	0	45	975	766	209
04	72	FAU HENDERSON	70	1605	324	16	17	27	27	13	67	5	16	12	1	83	1601	1465	136
04	73	FSU SCH	186	1666	334	6	10	41	32	12	84	5	17	13	1	87	1671	1491	180
04	74	FAMU SCH	35	1539	312	11	20	46	20	3	69	4	15	12	1	80	1549	1327	222
04	75	UF PK YONGE	60	1638	329	7	15	35	42	2	78	5	17	13	1	93	1630	1488	142
04	78	FL CONNECTIONS	21	1635	329	5	19	29	43	5	76	5	16	13	1	14	1424	1302	122
04	79	FL VIRTUAL SCHO	27	1688	338	7	19	22	37	15	74	5	17	13	1	7	1812	1771	42

Note: *Percentages in "Level 3 and Above" may differ from the sum of % in levels 3 - 5 due to rounding.*

Source: *Florida Department of Education, Office of Assessment and School Performance, May 2005*

FLORIDA COMPREHENSIVE ASSESSMENT TEST (FCAT) 2005
SUNSHINE STATE STANDARDS

READING - Grade 5

			Total Test Scores			% in each Achievement Level					% AL3+	Mean Points Earned By Content				Results for Students Matched to Previous Year			
Grade	District number	District Name	Number of Students	Mean Developmental Scale Score (0-3000)	Mean Scale Score (100-500)	1	2	3	4	5	Percent in Achievement Levels 3 and Above	Words / Phrases	Main Idea / Purpose	Comparisons	Reference / Research	Percent Matched to 2004	Mean Developmental Scale Score (2005)	Mean Developmental Scale Score (2004)	Mean DSS Change for Matched Students Reading (2005 - 2004)
Number of Points Possible												8	20	13	4				
05	00	STATEWIDE TOTAL	181,651	1611	303	18	16	34	25	7	66	6	14	10	3	87	1633	1579	53
05	01	ALACHUA	1,813	1651	310	19	14	29	27	11	67	6	15	10	3	90	1660	1620	39
05	02	BAKER	328	1568	295	22	17	31	23	6	61	6	14	9	3	91	1566	1610	-44
05	03	BAY	1,970	1660	312	13	14	35	30	8	72	6	15	10	3	88	1672	1608	63
05	04	BRADFORD	236	1546	292	24	20	30	20	6	56	5	13	9	3	92	1554	1509	45
05	05	BREVARD	5,571	1707	320	11	12	33	32	12	77	6	15	10	3	85	1722	1653	69
05	06	BROWARD	19,389	1604	302	19	17	34	24	7	65	6	14	10	3	89	1622	1575	48
05	07	CALHOUN	155	1689	317	11	13	37	28	11	76	6	15	10	3	94	1686	1630	55
05	08	CHARLOTTE	1,113	1657	311	15	13	33	30	8	72	6	15	10	3	85	1671	1614	58
05	09	CITRUS	1,098	1652	310	14	16	35	27	8	70	6	15	10	3	89	1666	1596	70
05	10	CLAY	2,351	1669	314	14	14	35	28	9	73	6	15	10	3	87	1684	1634	50
05	11	COLLIER	2,648	1623	305	18	15	33	25	9	67	6	14	10	3	86	1656	1597	60
05	12	COLUMBIA	690	1579	297	20	17	37	22	5	63	6	14	10	3	91	1588	1538	50
05	13	MIAMI-DADE	22,608	1578	297	20	16	35	23	6	64	5	14	10	3	91	1611	1553	57
05	14	DESOTO	333	1543	291	21	19	38	19	3	60	5	14	9	3	90	1556	1502	54
05	15	DIXIE	114	1584	298	15	24	38	19	4	61	6	14	10	3	88	1580	1561	19
05	16	DUVAL	9,018	1590	299	19	17	35	23	6	64	6	14	10	3	87	1621	1562	60
05	17	ESCAMBIA	3,001	1587	299	20	19	32	23	6	61	6	14	9	3	87	1600	1556	44
05	18	FLAGLER	719	1630	307	15	15	36	29	5	70	6	14	10	3	80	1645	1599	46
05	19	FRANKLIN	84	1560	294	21	20	35	20	4	58	6	14	9	3	89	1553	1493	60
05	20	GADSDEN	462	1404	266	33	32	27	7	1	35	5	12	8	2	89	1409	1395	13
05	21	GILCHRIST	209	1622	305	17	11	39	29	5	73	6	15	10	3	86	1643	1586	56
05	22	GLADES	94	1499	283	31	14	35	16	4	55	5	13	9	3	77	1525	1487	38
05	23	GULF	151	1590	299	21	15	35	24	5	64	6	14	9	3	91	1602	1502	100
05	24	HAMILTON	115	1497	283	32	19	24	23	2	49	5	13	9	3	91	1505	1522	-17
05	25	HARDEE	338	1501	283	29	19	32	15	5	52	5	13	9	3	91	1525	1494	32
05	26	HENDRY	512	1523	287	26	20	29	19	6	54	5	13	9	3	89	1545	1512	33
05	27	HERNANDO	1,428	1610	303	17	16	38	24	6	67	6	14	10	3	82	1627	1583	44
05	28	HIGHLANDS	844	1574	297	20	16	36	23	5	64	5	14	10	3	87	1585	1538	47
05	29	HILLSBOROUGH	13,741	1585	298	21	18	32	23	7	61	6	14	10	3	87	1605	1559	46
05	30	HOLMES	233	1598	301	21	16	30	27	6	63	6	14	10	3	88	1599	1567	32
05	31	INDIAN RIVER	1,125	1653	311	13	17	34	26	10	70	6	15	10	3	88	1678	1616	62
05	32	JACKSON	469	1633	307	15	16	35	28	6	69	6	14	10	3	91	1639	1591	48
05	33	JEFFERSON	78	1443	273	29	26	31	13	1	45	5	12	9	2	90	1446	1406	40
05	34	LAFAYETTE	75	1538	290	24	17	37	19	3	59	5	13	10	3	89	1536	1566	-29
05	35	LAKE	2,604	1615	304	17	17	35	24	8	66	6	14	10	3	85	1628	1574	55
05	36	LEE	4,914	1615	304	16	17	35	25	7	67	6	14	10	3	84	1638	1580	58
05	37	LEON	2,349	1689	317	13	15	32	27	12	71	6	15	10	3	90	1699	1648	51
05	38	LEVY	263	1571	296	22	14	40	20	4	64	6	14	9	3	89	1570	1535	36
05	39	LIBERTY	88	1605	302	18	13	35	27	7	69	6	14	10	3	92	1637	1590	48
05	40	MADISON	170	1480	280	29	23	29	16	3	48	5	13	9	3	94	1490	1459	31
05	41	MANATEE	2,902	1587	299	19	18	34	24	6	63	6	14	10	3	84	1607	1564	44
05	42	MARION	2,889	1600	301	18	17	34	25	6	65	6	14	10	3	88	1618	1556	61
05	43	MARTIN	1,288	1711	321	12	12	31	33	11	75	6	15	10	3	90	1727	1652	75
05	44	MONROE	624	1634	307	14	19	32	27	8	67	6	15	10	3	91	1645	1602	42
05	45	NASSAU	731	1668	313	11	16	37	27	9	73	6	15	10	3	89	1676	1621	55
05	46	OKALOOSA	2,215	1737	326	9	12	33	33	13	79	6	16	10	3	87	1746	1658	87
05	47	OKEECHOBEE	545	1532	289	23	21	34	17	5	56	5	13	9	3	88	1545	1481	64
05	48	ORANGE	11,947	1584	298	20	17	34	22	7	63	6	14	9	3	82	1618	1558	60
05	49	OSCEOLA	3,330	1524	288	25	19	32	19	5	56	5	13	9	3	77	1563	1514	49
05	50	PALM BEACH	12,001	1609	303	19	16	33	24	8	65	6	14	10	3	89	1629	1578	51
05	51	PASCO	3,997	1618	304	16	15	37	25	7	69	6	14	10	3	86	1634	1586	48
05	52	PINELLAS	7,569	1634	307	16	15	33	27	8	68	6	15	10	3	90	1650	1598	52
05	53	POLK	6,068	1544	291	24	17	33	20	6	59	5	13	9	3	85	1568	1525	42
05	54	PUTNAM	847	1565	295	20	18	35	22	5	62	6	14	9	3	89	1582	1526	56
05	55	ST. JOHNS	1,798	1695	318	13	13	33	30	12	75	6	15	10	3	86	1703	1666	37
05	56	ST. LUCIE	2,404	1600	301	19	17	34	25	6	65	6	14	10	3	80	1619	1578	41
05	57	SANTA ROSA	1,790	1743	327	9	11	32	34	13	79	6	16	10	3	87	1757	1677	80
05	58	SARASOTA	2,954	1692	318	13	12	33	31	10	75	6	15	10	3	87	1709	1670	39
05	59	SEMINOLE	4,844	1694	318	12	12	34	31	11	76	6	15	10	3	87	1714	1648	65
05	60	SUMTER	518	1678	315	14	13	33	31	9	73	6	15	10	3	90	1687	1599	89
05	61	SUWANNEE	401	1597	301	17	19	36	23	4	64	6	14	10	3	86	1607	1531	76
05	62	TAYLOR	221	1556	293	21	21	33	20	5	58	6	14	10	3	92	1570	1551	19
05	63	UNION	156	1573	296	24	14	29	23	9	62	6	14	9	3	92	1572	1539	34
05	64	VOLUSIA	4,633	1646	309	14	15	37	27	8	71	6	15	10	3	89	1661	1603	58
05	65	WAKULLA	338	1681	316	16	11	31	31	12	74	6	15	10	3	91	1696	1622	73
05	66	WALTON	456	1676	315	12	14	33	32	9	74	6	15	10	3	88	1692	1630	62
05	67	WASHINGTON	252	1563	295	22	17	34	22	5	61	6	14	10	3	93	1568	1541	27
05	68	FSDB	23	1044	202	74	22	4	0	0	4	4	8	6	1	83	1097	966	131
05	72	FAU HENDERSON	75	1683	316	9	17	36	24	13	73	6	15	10	3	81	1656	1631	25
05	73	FSU SCH	189	1738	326	5	16	35	33	11	79	6	16	10	3	95	1741	1684	57
05	74	FAMU SCH	38	1448	274	42	18	26	13	0	39	5	12	9	3	79	1475	1409	67
05	75	UF PK YONGE	59	1595	300	17	19	47	12	5	64	6	14	10	3	97	1596	1581	15
05	78	FL CONNECTIONS	18	1720	323	11	0	39	44	6	89	6	16	11	3	0			
05	79	FL VIRTUAL SCHO	30	1797	336	3	7	33	40	17	90	7	16	11	3	7	1473	1299	174

Note: Percentages in "Level 3 and Above" may differ from the sum of % in levels 3 - 5 due to rounding.

Source: *Florida Department of Education, Office of Assessment and School Performance, May 2005*

FLORIDA COMPREHENSIVE ASSESSMENT TEST (FCAT) 2005
SUNSHINE STATE STANDARDS

READING - Grade 6

Grade	District number	District Name	Total Test Scores: Number of Students	Total Test Scores: Mean Developmental Scale Score (0-3000)	Total Test Scores: Mean Scale Score (100-500)	% in each Achievement Level: 1	% in each Achievement Level: 2	% in each Achievement Level: 3	% in each Achievement Level: 4	% in each Achievement Level: 5	% AL3+: Percent in Achievement Levels 3 and Above	Mean Points Earned By Content: Words / Phrases	Mean Points Earned By Content: Main Idea / Purpose	Mean Points Earned By Content: Comparisons	Mean Points Earned By Content: Reference / Research	Results for Students Matched to Previous Year: Percent Matched to 2004	Results for Students Matched to Previous Year: Mean Developmental Scale Score (2005)	Results for Students Matched to Previous Year: Mean Developmental Scale Score (2004)	Results for Students Matched to Previous Year: Mean DSS Change for Matched Students Reading (2005 - 2004)
Number of Points Possible												7	20	11	7				
06	00	STATEWIDE TOTAL	201,609	1644	299	25	20	31	19	5	56	5	12	7	4	87	1656	1570	86
06	01	ALACHUA	2,132	1662	302	25	19	29	20	7	56	5	12	7	4	89	1664	1591	73
06	02	BAKER	361	1659	302	22	22	30	20	6	56	5	12	7	4	89	1657	1581	76
06	03	BAY	1,985	1708	311	18	18	36	22	6	64	5	13	7	5	89	1710	1634	76
06	04	BRADFORD	294	1586	289	29	24	28	17	2	47	5	11	6	4	90	1600	1543	58
06	05	BREVARD	5,508	1788	325	11	15	34	30	10	74	5	14	7	5	85	1805	1694	111
06	06	BROWARD	20,962	1659	302	23	20	32	19	6	57	5	12	7	4	89	1672	1579	93
06	07	CALHOUN	194	1666	303	21	19	34	20	6	60	5	12	7	4	97	1667	1579	88
06	08	CHARLOTTE	1,343	1688	307	19	18	35	22	6	63	5	13	7	5	85	1693	1605	88
06	09	CITRUS	1,174	1676	305	19	19	35	23	4	62	5	13	7	4	88	1685	1623	62
06	10	CLAY	2,626	1739	316	13	18	37	25	7	69	5	13	7	5	87	1746	1652	94
06	11	COLLIER	3,116	1628	296	26	20	29	19	5	53	5	12	6	4	86	1645	1553	92
06	12	COLUMBIA	808	1608	293	25	25	30	16	4	50	5	12	7	4	90	1618	1550	68
06	13	MIAMI-DADE	27,137	1548	282	35	21	27	14	3	44	4	11	6	4	91	1565	1472	93
06	14	DESOTO	352	1597	291	27	23	29	18	3	50	4	12	6	4	93	1614	1543	71
06	15	DIXIE	165	1546	282	38	21	25	15	2	41	4	11	6	4	92	1545	1450	95
06	16	DUVAL	10,239	1636	298	26	21	31	18	5	53	5	12	7	4	86	1655	1565	91
06	17	ESCAMBIA	3,388	1594	290	30	20	29	17	4	50	5	11	6	4	89	1599	1541	58
06	18	FLAGLER	779	1660	302	20	20	35	20	5	60	5	12	7	5	80	1669	1590	79
06	19	FRANKLIN	127	1678	305	21	22	31	20	6	57	5	12	7	4	88	1680	1528	152
06	20	GADSDEN	512	1496	272	39	26	28	7	0	35	4	10	6	3	89	1496	1404	92
06	21	GILCHRIST	195	1700	309	21	18	30	24	7	61	5	13	7	4	88	1713	1609	104
06	22	GLADES	110	1540	280	32	23	29	15	1	45	4	11	6	4	85	1532	1484	48
06	23	GULF	172	1707	311	19	18	31	27	6	63	5	13	7	5	85	1689	1582	107
06	24	HAMILTON	145	1565	285	32	23	30	12	4	46	4	11	6	4	91	1560	1451	108
06	25	HARDEE	385	1542	281	33	22	31	12	2	45	4	11	6	4	90	1565	1464	101
06	26	HENDRY	574	1535	280	36	22	27	12	3	42	4	11	6	4	91	1546	1490	56
06	27	HERNANDO	1,638	1641	299	25	20	31	19	5	55	5	12	7	4	85	1648	1591	56
06	28	HIGHLANDS	927	1614	294	27	21	31	18	4	52	5	12	7	4	89	1624	1544	80
06	29	HILLSBOROUGH	14,432	1639	298	26	20	29	19	6	54	5	12	7	4	87	1653	1578	74
06	30	HOLMES	264	1643	299	26	18	32	20	3	56	5	12	7	4	87	1647	1569	78
06	31	INDIAN RIVER	1,262	1678	305	22	18	33	21	7	60	5	13	7	4	90	1687	1596	91
06	32	JACKSON	586	1627	296	27	20	31	18	5	53	5	12	7	4	91	1628	1591	36
06	33	JEFFERSON	84	1473	268	43	27	23	7	0	30	4	10	6	3	95	1466	1363	103
06	34	LAFAYETTE	77	1632	297	25	17	38	18	3	58	5	12	6	4	90	1657	1562	96
06	35	LAKE	2,763	1671	304	21	19	35	20	5	60	5	13	7	4	84	1678	1593	85
06	36	LEE	5,466	1641	299	25	19	32	19	5	56	5	12	7	4	84	1657	1584	72
06	37	LEON	2,468	1732	315	16	19	34	23	9	66	5	13	7	5	87	1745	1674	71
06	38	LEVY	547	1581	288	32	20	29	17	3	49	5	11	6	4	88	1592	1547	45
06	39	LIBERTY	105	1679	306	22	19	23	30	7	59	5	13	7	4	93	1689	1573	116
06	40	MADISON	178	1537	280	35	22	26	13	3	43	4	11	6	4	85	1535	1508	27
06	41	MANATEE	3,061	1651	300	22	22	32	19	5	56	5	12	7	4	86	1664	1604	60
06	42	MARION	3,130	1625	296	25	22	31	18	4	53	5	12	7	4	88	1633	1571	62
06	43	MARTIN	1,333	1752	319	15	15	33	27	10	70	5	14	7	5	88	1770	1671	99
06	44	MONROE	679	1694	308	19	18	32	24	6	63	5	13	7	5	87	1705	1631	74
06	45	NASSAU	819	1713	312	15	18	38	25	4	68	5	13	7	5	88	1717	1641	76
06	46	OKALOOSA	2,343	1778	323	12	15	36	28	10	73	5	14	7	5	85	1793	1721	71
06	47	OKEECHOBEE	567	1607	293	27	22	32	16	3	51	5	12	6	4	86	1612	1522	90
06	48	ORANGE	13,473	1629	296	26	21	31	18	5	54	5	12	6	4	80	1651	1532	118
06	49	OSCEOLA	3,604	1580	288	31	22	29	15	3	47	4	11	6	4	78	1603	1502	101
06	50	PALM BEACH	13,263	1645	299	25	20	31	19	6	55	5	12	7	4	87	1657	1559	98
06	51	PASCO	4,659	1654	301	22	20	34	20	4	58	5	12	7	4	86	1660	1573	87
06	52	PINELLAS	8,312	1674	305	22	18	32	20	7	59	5	13	7	4	89	1684	1599	84
06	53	POLK	6,638	1591	290	30	21	29	15	4	48	5	11	6	4	87	1601	1534	67
06	54	PUTNAM	978	1588	289	30	25	28	13	4	45	4	11	6	4	89	1599	1534	66
06	55	ST. JOHNS	1,929	1767	321	14	14	33	28	10	72	5	14	7	5	86	1769	1673	95
06	56	ST. LUCIE	2,747	1631	297	26	20	32	18	4	54	5	12	7	4	80	1643	1544	99
06	57	SANTA ROSA	1,970	1773	323	13	14	35	28	10	74	5	14	7	5	87	1790	1709	80
06	58	SARASOTA	3,231	1687	307	22	17	31	22	8	61	5	13	7	4	86	1696	1631	65
06	59	SEMINOLE	5,173	1736	316	15	17	34	25	8	68	5	13	7	5	87	1748	1677	71
06	60	SUMTER	580	1669	304	22	20	31	21	7	58	5	12	7	4	87	1677	1609	68
06	61	SUWANNEE	441	1635	298	27	18	33	18	5	55	5	12	7	4	86	1629	1548	82
06	62	TAYLOR	266	1714	312	15	17	41	20	6	67	5	13	7	5	91	1726	1582	144
06	63	UNION	170	1624	296	26	21	28	20	5	52	5	12	7	4	91	1631	1563	68
06	64	VOLUSIA	4,891	1674	305	20	19	35	20	6	60	5	13	7	4	89	1682	1621	62
06	65	WAKULLA	388	1731	315	15	19	35	25	6	66	5	13	7	5	90	1738	1695	43
06	66	WALTON	549	1637	298	22	22	32	20	3	55	5	12	7	4	86	1654	1635	19
06	67	WASHINGTON	258	1665	303	22	17	33	25	2	61	5	12	7	4	92	1669	1578	91
06	68	FSDB	43	1247	228	72	9	14	5	0	19	3	7	4	3	65	1279	1031	249
06	72	FAU HENDERSON	75	1842	335	8	15	35	27	16	77	5	15	8	5	87	1838	1710	129
06	73	FSU SCH	256	1813	330	6	16	36	32	10	78	5	14	8	5	84	1837	1735	102
06	74	FAMU SCH	54	1583	288	33	13	43	9	2	54	5	11	6	4	85	1583	1544	39
06	75	UF PK YONGE	114	1756	319	11	17	35	33	4	72	5	14	7	5	87	1734	1699	35
06	78	FL CONNECTIONS	17	1872	340	12	29	12	24	24	59	6	14	8	4	6	1510	1627	-117
06	79	FL VIRTUAL SCHO	18	1938	352	11	0	22	44	22	89	6	15	9	6	11	2248	2081	167

Note: *Percentages in "Level 3 and Above" may differ from the sum of % in levels 3 - 5 due to rounding.*

Source: *Florida Department of Education, Office of Assessment and School Performance, May 2005*

FLORIDA COMPREHENSIVE ASSESSMENT TEST (FCAT) 2005
SUNSHINE STATE STANDARDS

READING - Grade 7

Grade	District number	District Name	Total Test Scores: Number of Students	Mean Developmental Scale Score (0-3000)	Mean Scale Score (100-500)	% in each Achievement Level: 1	2	3	4	5	% AL3+: Percent in Achievement Levels 3 and Above	Mean Points Earned By Content: Words / Phrases	Main Idea / Purpose	Comparisons	Reference / Research	Results for Students Matched to Previous Year: Percent Matched to 2004	Mean Developmental Scale Score (2005)	Mean Developmental Scale Score (2004)	Mean DSS Change for Matched Students Reading (2005 - 2004)
Number of Points Possible												6	21	10	8				
07	00	STATEWIDE TOTAL	202,520	1712	299	27	21	30	17	5	53	4	14	6	5	87	1728	1651	77
07	01	ALACHUA	2,105	1725	301	27	19	28	19	7	54	4	14	6	5	90	1735	1662	73
07	02	BAKER	379	1674	291	30	21	27	18	3	49	4	13	6	4	89	1670	1622	49
07	03	BAY	2,049	1769	310	20	20	35	20	6	60	4	14	6	5	88	1772	1727	46
07	04	BRADFORD	283	1637	284	37	24	22	14	3	39	4	12	5	4	91	1632	1591	40
07	05	BREVARD	5,885	1814	318	15	17	35	25	8	68	5	15	7	5	84	1831	1816	15
07	06	BROWARD	21,160	1742	304	24	21	31	19	6	56	4	14	6	5	89	1755	1661	94
07	07	CALHOUN	178	1721	300	23	25	31	15	6	52	4	14	6	5	94	1727	1682	46
07	08	CHARLOTTE	1,393	1758	308	22	20	31	20	7	59	4	14	6	5	88	1771	1692	78
07	09	CITRUS	1,299	1720	300	24	21	35	16	4	56	4	14	6	5	88	1729	1689	40
07	10	CLAY	2,630	1755	307	19	23	33	20	5	58	4	14	6	5	87	1763	1735	28
07	11	COLLIER	3,146	1704	297	28	20	30	17	5	53	4	14	6	5	87	1722	1635	87
07	12	COLUMBIA	837	1696	296	25	24	32	14	5	51	4	13	6	5	90	1702	1643	60
07	13	MIAMI-DADE	27,796	1629	283	37	21	26	13	4	43	4	13	5	4	90	1647	1531	116
07	14	DESOTO	311	1644	286	33	19	34	12	2	48	4	13	5	4	87	1644	1576	68
07	15	DIXIE	153	1645	286	35	22	25	15	4	44	4	13	5	4	92	1646	1625	21
07	16	DUVAL	9,766	1711	298	26	22	32	16	4	52	4	14	6	5	86	1730	1631	99
07	17	ESCAMBIA	3,563	1654	288	33	23	27	13	4	44	4	13	6	4	89	1660	1613	47
07	18	FLAGLER	793	1725	301	24	21	33	17	5	55	4	14	6	5	79	1740	1704	36
07	19	FRANKLIN	97	1628	283	36	20	32	7	5	44	4	12	6	4	84	1620	1657	-37
07	20	GADSDEN	503	1530	264	46	27	22	4	1	26	3	11	5	4	92	1536	1446	90
07	21	GILCHRIST	223	1729	302	20	24	34	18	4	57	4	14	6	5	90	1737	1729	8
07	22	GLADES	104	1593	276	44	16	27	8	5	39	4	11	5	4	88	1584	1531	53
07	23	GULF	178	1775	311	19	23	29	23	7	58	5	15	6	5	94	1762	1685	76
07	24	HAMILTON	163	1522	262	53	15	21	10	1	32	3	11	5	3	93	1534	1482	52
07	25	HARDEE	429	1581	274	42	23	24	10	2	35	3	12	5	4	91	1597	1542	55
07	26	HENDRY	604	1617	281	36	22	29	11	2	42	4	12	5	4	92	1632	1580	52
07	27	HERNANDO	1,714	1685	294	29	20	32	14	5	50	4	13	6	5	81	1690	1638	52
07	28	HIGHLANDS	923	1688	294	26	26	31	13	4	48	4	13	6	4	89	1704	1631	72
07	29	HILLSBOROUGH	14,355	1698	296	29	21	29	17	5	50	4	13	6	5	87	1716	1660	56
07	30	HOLMES	265	1692	295	30	19	30	15	5	51	4	13	6	4	91	1691	1649	42
07	31	INDIAN RIVER	1,330	1735	303	24	21	30	18	7	55	4	14	6	5	90	1746	1654	92
07	32	JACKSON	596	1710	298	26	20	32	17	4	54	4	14	6	5	92	1712	1661	51
07	33	JEFFERSON	81	1569	271	38	28	26	6	1	33	4	12	5	3	93	1590	1469	122
07	34	LAFAYETTE	78	1692	295	31	23	23	18	5	46	4	13	6	5	87	1727	1708	20
07	35	LAKE	2,825	1720	300	24	20	34	17	5	55	4	14	6	5	84	1738	1681	56
07	36	LEE	5,484	1727	301	25	20	32	18	6	55	4	14	6	5	84	1751	1669	82
07	37	LEON	2,400	1805	316	17	20	32	23	9	64	4	15	7	5	90	1824	1757	67
07	38	LEVY	506	1654	288	31	25	30	11	2	44	4	13	5	4	87	1659	1639	21
07	39	LIBERTY	94	1709	298	26	18	38	16	2	56	4	14	6	4	89	1736	1733	4
07	40	MADISON	215	1646	286	35	26	23	12	4	39	4	13	5	4	88	1645	1555	90
07	41	MANATEE	3,014	1708	298	26	22	31	17	4	52	4	14	6	5	85	1724	1675	48
07	42	MARION	3,149	1694	295	26	23	32	15	5	51	4	13	6	5	86	1710	1658	52
07	43	MARTIN	1,431	1820	319	18	15	31	24	11	67	4	15	7	5	90	1837	1746	91
07	44	MONROE	654	1749	306	22	20	31	20	6	58	4	14	6	5	88	1750	1692	58
07	45	NASSAU	836	1773	310	19	21	35	21	5	61	4	15	6	5	88	1778	1723	54
07	46	OKALOOSA	2,315	1850	325	11	18	35	26	10	71	5	15	7	5	87	1866	1812	54
07	47	OKEECHOBEE	539	1685	294	27	23	34	13	4	50	4	13	6	4	88	1695	1656	39
07	48	ORANGE	12,633	1727	301	25	20	31	18	6	55	4	14	6	5	80	1757	1639	117
07	49	OSCEOLA	3,692	1658	288	33	21	28	14	3	46	4	13	6	4	80	1681	1600	81
07	50	PALM BEACH	13,207	1714	299	27	20	30	17	6	53	4	14	6	5	87	1732	1642	90
07	51	PASCO	4,629	1720	300	24	22	31	17	5	54	4	14	6	5	86	1731	1685	46
07	52	PINELLAS	8,512	1734	303	25	20	30	18	7	55	4	14	6	5	89	1751	1680	71
07	53	POLK	6,619	1640	285	34	22	28	13	3	44	4	13	5	4	85	1651	1600	51
07	54	PUTNAM	899	1667	290	30	23	31	13	2	46	4	13	6	4	88	1671	1623	48
07	55	ST. JOHNS	1,879	1822	320	16	17	33	24	10	67	4	15	7	5	87	1831	1773	58
07	56	ST. LUCIE	2,778	1687	294	29	21	31	15	4	50	4	13	6	5	82	1695	1627	68
07	57	SANTA ROSA	2,049	1825	320	15	17	34	24	9	67	5	15	7	5	86	1836	1792	44
07	58	SARASOTA	3,267	1747	305	24	19	31	19	7	56	4	14	6	5	87	1756	1707	49
07	59	SEMINOLE	5,232	1796	315	18	19	34	22	8	64	4	15	6	5	88	1814	1746	67
07	60	SUMTER	607	1709	298	27	19	32	18	5	54	4	14	6	5	89	1714	1651	63
07	61	SUWANNEE	450	1691	295	27	25	29	13	6	48	4	13	6	5	89	1705	1666	40
07	62	TAYLOR	251	1765	309	21	21	35	15	8	58	4	14	6	5	88	1789	1730	59
07	63	UNION	195	1680	293	29	24	29	16	2	47	4	13	6	5	91	1699	1628	71
07	64	VOLUSIA	5,095	1743	305	22	20	35	18	5	58	4	14	6	5	88	1752	1698	54
07	65	WAKULLA	392	1814	318	15	18	36	25	7	67	5	15	7	5	90	1830	1774	55
07	66	WALTON	525	1710	298	23	22	36	14	4	54	4	13	6	5	89	1719	1715	5
07	67	WASHINGTON	293	1718	300	26	23	27	20	4	51	4	14	6	5	92	1718	1678	39
07	68	FSDB	53	1205	202	91	6	4	0	0	4	2	7	3	3	83	1201	1052	149
07	72	FAU HENDERSON	65	1920	338	3	11	49	26	11	86	5	17	7	6	86	1937	1833	104
07	73	FSU SCH	167	1874	330	5	19	43	26	7	76	5	16	7	5	93	1875	1786	90
07	74	FAMU SCH	41	1650	287	32	34	27	7	0	34	4	13	6	4	90	1653	1556	97
07	75	UF PK YONGE	110	1858	327	5	25	40	24	7	71	5	16	7	5	98	1857	1792	65
07	78	FL CONNECTIONS	19	1848	325	11	5	53	11	21	84	4	17	7	6	0			
07	79	FL VIRTUAL SCHO	30	1823	320	13	23	30	27	7	63	5	16	6	5	3	2049	2225	-176

Note: *Percentages in "Level 3 and Above" may differ from the sum of % in levels 3 - 5 due to rounding.*

Source: *Florida Department of Education, Office of Assessment and School Performance, May 2005*

FLORIDA COMPREHENSIVE ASSESSMENT TEST (FCAT) 2005
SUNSHINE STATE STANDARDS

READING - Grade 8			Total Test Scores									Mean Points Earned By Content				Results for Students Matched to Previous Year			
						% in each Achievement Level					% AL3+								
Grade	District number	District Name	Number of Students	Mean Developmental Scale Score (0-3000)	Mean Scale Score (100-500)	1	2	3	4	5	Percent in Achievement Levels 3 and Above	Words/ Phrases	Main Idea/ Purpose	Comparisons	Reference / Research	Percent Matched to 2004	Mean Developmental Scale Score (2005)	Mean Developmental Scale Score (2004)	Mean DSS Change for Matched Students Reading (2005 - 2004)
Number of Points Possible												7	24	13	7				
08	00	STATEWIDE TOTAL	201,758	1824	297	27	30	30	12	2	44	5	14	8	4	87	1838	1731	107
08	01	ALACHUA	2,177	1829	298	29	27	25	15	4	44	5	14	8	4	90	1840	1737	103
08	02	BAKER	364	1800	292	25	38	29	8	1	37	5	14	7	4	86	1807	1720	88
08	03	BAY	2,049	1867	306	18	32	35	13	2	50	5	15	8	4	86	1873	1805	68
08	04	BRADFORD	301	1814	295	27	35	26	9	3	38	5	14	8	4	90	1824	1725	99
08	05	BREVARD	5,780	1904	314	14	28	37	17	3	57	5	16	8	4	85	1920	1854	66
08	06	BROWARD	21,010	1845	301	24	29	31	13	3	47	5	15	8	4	89	1859	1754	105
08	07	CALHOUN	166	1882	309	17	30	36	16	1	54	5	15	8	4	90	1898	1777	121
08	08	CHARLOTTE	1,454	1877	308	18	32	33	15	3	50	5	15	8	4	88	1885	1791	94
08	09	CITRUS	1,299	1821	296	23	34	32	10	1	42	5	14	8	4	87	1830	1744	86
08	10	CLAY	2,629	1862	305	20	32	33	13	3	48	5	15	8	4	88	1870	1792	78
08	11	COLLIER	3,214	1816	295	28	28	30	12	2	44	5	14	8	4	88	1830	1720	111
08	12	COLUMBIA	754	1818	296	25	33	29	11	1	42	5	14	8	4	90	1824	1740	84
08	13	MIAMI-DADE	28,404	1753	282	37	29	24	8	1	34	4	13	7	4	90	1771	1631	140
08	14	DESOTO	347	1731	277	37	32	22	8	1	31	4	12	7	3	91	1734	1670	65
08	15	DIXIE	157	1808	294	27	37	25	8	2	36	5	13	8	4	92	1807	1713	94
08	16	DUVAL	9,260	1823	297	26	32	30	10	2	42	5	14	8	4	85	1841	1711	129
08	17	ESCAMBIA	3,426	1792	290	29	33	27	9	1	38	5	14	7	4	89	1799	1713	87
08	18	FLAGLER	825	1856	304	21	32	34	12	2	48	5	15	8	4	80	1872	1786	87
08	19	FRANKLIN	99	1774	286	27	36	26	8	2	36	5	13	7	4	88	1796	1746	50
08	20	GADSDEN	468	1677	266	48	38	13	2	0	15	4	12	6	3	88	1689	1581	109
08	21	GILCHRIST	201	1860	305	20	29	33	16	1	51	5	15	8	4	92	1873	1776	97
08	22	GLADES	102	1756	283	34	38	17	9	2	27	5	13	7	3	83	1759	1660	98
08	23	GULF	203	1816	295	27	28	36	8	1	46	5	14	8	4	90	1819	1779	40
08	24	HAMILTON	145	1686	268	46	32	15	8	0	23	4	12	7	3	90	1690	1556	133
08	25	HARDEE	389	1739	279	39	29	23	8	1	32	4	13	7	3	91	1752	1638	114
08	26	HENDRY	589	1723	276	40	30	24	5	1	30	4	12	7	3	91	1729	1628	101
08	27	HERNANDO	1,672	1822	297	25	32	31	11	1	43	5	14	8	4	82	1835	1713	122
08	28	HIGHLANDS	926	1816	295	27	32	30	10	2	41	5	14	8	4	88	1830	1740	90
08	29	HILLSBOROUGH	14,036	1835	299	25	30	29	12	2	44	5	14	8	4	87	1850	1735	115
08	30	HOLMES	274	1848	302	22	31	31	14	1	46	5	14	8	4	93	1854	1792	62
08	31	INDIAN RIVER	1,262	1854	303	22	29	34	13	2	49	5	15	8	4	90	1864	1771	94
08	32	JACKSON	538	1833	299	23	34	30	12	1	43	5	14	8	4	92	1832	1758	74
08	33	JEFFERSON	83	1713	274	42	31	20	5	1	27	4	12	7	3	92	1723	1586	137
08	34	LAFAYETTE	83	1783	288	27	35	33	4	2	39	5	13	8	3	90	1791	1723	67
08	35	LAKE	2,674	1823	297	25	32	31	10	2	43	5	14	8	4	84	1837	1753	84
08	36	LEE	5,317	1825	297	26	30	31	11	2	44	5	14	8	4	84	1845	1739	105
08	37	LEON	2,159	1911	315	16	26	35	19	4	58	5	16	9	4	91	1922	1859	63
08	38	LEVY	512	1779	288	29	35	27	8	1	36	5	13	7	4	86	1796	1677	119
08	39	LIBERTY	78	1887	310	26	13	31	27	4	62	5	16	8	4	95	1912	1863	49
08	40	MADISON	217	1724	276	36	35	22	6	0	29	4	13	7	3	91	1732	1613	119
08	41	MANATEE	2,992	1825	297	25	31	32	10	1	44	5	14	8	4	85	1841	1751	89
08	42	MARION	3,274	1812	294	25	32	31	11	1	43	5	14	8	4	87	1827	1738	88
08	43	MARTIN	1,429	1901	313	19	24	31	20	5	56	5	16	8	4	90	1913	1807	106
08	44	MONROE	686	1842	301	24	29	32	13	2	48	5	15	8	4	86	1846	1774	72
08	45	NASSAU	900	1868	306	19	33	35	11	3	49	5	15	8	4	91	1876	1789	87
08	46	OKALOOSA	2,258	1968	327	8	23	41	23	5	69	6	17	9	5	87	1978	1923	55
08	47	OKEECHOBEE	526	1760	284	35	33	24	6	1	31	4	13	7	3	85	1773	1681	93
08	48	ORANGE	13,174	1813	295	28	30	29	11	2	42	5	14	8	4	80	1839	1702	137
08	49	OSCEOLA	3,684	1769	286	34	30	27	8	1	36	5	13	7	4	80	1787	1666	121
08	50	PALM BEACH	13,138	1821	296	27	29	30	12	2	44	5	14	8	4	87	1836	1727	109
08	51	PASCO	4,739	1820	296	25	33	31	10	1	42	5	14	8	4	87	1831	1744	88
08	52	PINELLAS	8,754	1851	303	24	29	30	14	3	47	5	14	8	4	88	1868	1759	110
08	53	POLK	6,331	1778	287	33	30	26	9	1	36	5	13	7	4	84	1788	1671	117
08	54	PUTNAM	975	1772	286	34	33	25	7	1	33	5	13	7	3	88	1776	1664	111
08	55	ST. JOHNS	1,900	1933	320	13	25	37	21	5	62	5	16	9	4	88	1943	1855	88
08	56	ST. LUCIE	2,747	1809	294	28	32	28	11	1	41	5	14	8	4	82	1822	1725	96
08	57	SANTA ROSA	2,005	1927	319	13	24	39	20	4	63	5	16	9	4	87	1933	1881	52
08	58	SARASOTA	3,148	1862	305	23	27	32	16	3	51	5	15	8	4	88	1869	1786	83
08	59	SEMINOLE	5,292	1894	312	17	28	35	17	3	55	5	16	8	4	89	1904	1813	91
08	60	SUMTER	580	1808	294	26	33	29	10	2	41	5	14	8	4	88	1815	1675	141
08	61	SUWANNEE	433	1820	296	27	31	30	11	2	42	5	14	8	4	87	1823	1729	94
08	62	TAYLOR	239	1818	296	24	38	26	10	2	37	5	14	8	4	89	1826	1747	78
08	63	UNION	157	1838	300	20	31	38	8	3	48	5	14	8	4	92	1834	1740	95
08	64	VOLUSIA	5,125	1830	298	25	32	30	12	2	44	5	14	8	4	89	1838	1770	68
08	65	WAKULLA	360	1860	305	20	34	31	13	3	47	5	15	8	4	91	1882	1811	71
08	66	WALTON	536	1846	302	23	29	35	13	1	49	5	14	8	4	88	1859	1798	62
08	67	WASHINGTON	269	1832	299	25	32	29	12	2	43	5	14	8	4	90	1840	1757	83
08	68	FSDB	59	1396	207	80	10	7	3	0	10	3	8	4	2	88	1407	1233	174
08	72	FAU HENDERSON	50	2041	343	6	10	50	18	16	84	6	18	10	5	94	2065	1972	93
08	73	FSU SCH	166	1936	320	6	36	39	16	4	58	5	16	9	4	95	1941	1861	80
08	74	FAMU SCH	41	1790	290	29	37	27	7	0	34	5	13	7	4	85	1781	1727	54
08	75	UF PK YONGE	114	1973	328	5	25	42	27	1	70	6	17	9	5	98	1971	1867	104
08	78	FL CONNECTIONS	4																
08	79	FL VIRTUAL SCHO	30	1957	325	10	20	47	20	3	70	6	17	9	5	7	2117	2020	97

Note: *Percentages in "Level 3 and Above" may differ from the sum of % in levels 3 - 5 due to rounding.*

Source: *Florida Department of Education, Office of Assessment and School Performance, May 2005*

FLORIDA COMPREHENSIVE ASSESSMENT TEST (FCAT) 2005
SUNSHINE STATE STANDARDS

READING - Grade 9

Grade	District number	District Name	Total Test Scores: Number of Students	Mean Developmental Scale Score (0-3000)	Mean Scale Score (100-500)	% in each Achievement Level: 1	2	3	4	5	% AL3+: Percent in Achievement Levels 3 and Above	Mean Points Earned By Content: Words/ Phrases	Main Idea/ Purpose	Comparisons	Reference / Research	Results for Students Matched to Previous Year: Percent Matched to 2004	Mean Developmental Scale Score (2005)	Mean Developmental Scale Score (2004)	Mean DSS Change for Matched Students Reading (2005 - 2004)
Number of Points Possible												6	16	11	12				
09	00	STATEWIDE TOTAL	214,984	1860	301	35	28	21	10	6	36	4	10	8	7	83	1874	1824	50
09	01	ALACHUA	2,384	1894	307	35	24	19	11	11	41	4	10	8	7	88	1901	1846	55
09	02	BAKER	403	1814	292	43	30	16	8	3	27	3	10	7	6	85	1820	1745	75
09	03	BAY	2,193	1914	310	27	31	25	11	6	42	4	11	8	7	83	1918	1860	58
09	04	BRADFORD	290	1783	286	45	28	19	6	2	27	3	10	7	6	88	1789	1773	17
09	05	BREVARD	6,177	1975	322	20	29	27	14	10	51	4	12	8	7	82	1984	1915	70
09	06	BROWARD	21,525	1870	302	34	29	21	10	6	37	4	10	8	7	85	1891	1849	43
09	07	CALHOUN	186	1925	313	26	30	26	9	8	44	4	11	8	7	91	1938	1896	42
09	08	CHARLOTTE	1,535	1938	315	23	32	26	12	7	45	4	11	8	7	84	1945	1909	36
09	09	CITRUS	1,316	1889	306	31	30	24	9	6	39	4	11	8	7	86	1900	1853	47
09	10	CLAY	2,681	1925	313	25	32	25	11	7	43	4	11	8	7	87	1930	1872	58
09	11	COLLIER	3,400	1837	296	38	27	21	8	6	34	4	10	7	6	82	1857	1816	41
09	12	COLUMBIA	836	1837	296	38	28	21	9	5	34	4	10	7	6	87	1841	1801	39
09	13	MIAMI-DADE	30,615	1785	287	46	26	17	7	4	28	3	9	7	6	86	1806	1746	60
09	14	DESOTO	344	1751	280	49	27	16	7	2	24	3	9	7	6	87	1770	1701	70
09	15	DIXIE	186	1790	288	43	30	18	5	4	27	4	10	7	6	88	1791	1801	-10
09	16	DUVAL	10,455	1845	298	37	29	20	9	5	33	4	10	8	6	83	1860	1785	75
09	17	ESCAMBIA	3,448	1837	296	37	29	20	9	5	34	4	10	7	6	83	1843	1807	36
09	18	FLAGLER	874	1915	311	26	33	25	11	5	41	4	11	8	7	75	1937	1911	26
09	19	FRANKLIN	103	1705	272	55	27	15	3	0	17	3	9	7	5	87	1721	1689	31
09	20	GADSDEN	376	1705	272	59	27	12	2	1	15	3	8	7	5	87	1721	1713	8
09	21	GILCHRIST	222	1887	305	30	32	22	8	7	37	4	11	8	7	88	1916	1884	31
09	22	GLADES	78	1765	283	51	31	13	3	3	18	3	9	7	5	81	1807	1779	28
09	23	GULF	217	1891	306	35	26	20	13	6	39	4	10	8	6	91	1891	1859	31
09	24	HAMILTON	180	1725	276	57	27	11	2	3	16	3	9	7	5	93	1724	1672	53
09	25	HARDEE	350	1745	279	49	28	14	7	2	23	3	9	7	5	92	1740	1698	42
09	26	HENDRY	607	1761	282	48	28	15	6	3	24	3	9	7	6	84	1776	1749	27
09	27	HERNANDO	1,808	1858	300	34	31	22	9	4	36	4	10	8	6	81	1872	1807	64
09	28	HIGHLANDS	1,113	1827	294	40	29	20	8	4	31	4	10	7	6	86	1833	1810	23
09	29	HILLSBOROUGH	13,370	1893	307	31	30	22	11	6	39	4	11	8	7	84	1904	1868	36
09	30	HOLMES	267	1864	301	33	34	21	6	6	33	4	10	8	6	91	1859	1836	23
09	31	INDIAN RIVER	1,479	1918	311	28	30	24	11	7	42	4	11	8	7	85	1923	1846	76
09	32	JACKSON	568	1877	304	33	30	21	10	7	37	4	11	8	7	88	1885	1855	30
09	33	JEFFERSON	111	1722	275	60	26	11	2	1	14	3	8	7	5	84	1736	1676	60
09	34	LAFAYETTE	83	1859	300	35	29	29	5	2	36	4	10	8	6	95	1857	1788	69
09	35	LAKE	2,880	1844	297	36	30	20	9	5	34	4	10	7	6	83	1862	1826	37
09	36	LEE	5,650	1864	301	35	28	22	9	6	37	4	10	8	7	77	1883	1845	38
09	37	LEON	2,606	1947	317	27	27	22	14	11	47	4	11	8	7	84	1948	1904	44
09	38	LEVY	508	1789	287	44	28	18	7	2	27	4	10	7	6	84	1809	1778	31
09	39	LIBERTY	84	1909	309	26	29	33	10	2	45	4	11	8	7	92	1900	1884	17
09	40	MADISON	233	1755	281	50	27	12	7	3	22	3	9	7	6	89	1733	1671	62
09	41	MANATEE	3,128	1852	299	37	29	20	8	6	34	4	10	7	6	82	1867	1833	34
09	42	MARION	3,320	1847	298	38	29	21	8	5	34	4	10	7	6	83	1854	1832	22
09	43	MARTIN	1,627	1962	319	25	23	26	16	10	52	4	11	8	7	80	1971	1926	45
09	44	MONROE	717	1919	311	27	27	26	11	8	45	4	11	8	7	80	1938	1865	74
09	45	NASSAU	883	1906	309	25	35	24	10	5	40	4	11	8	7	87	1918	1879	38
09	46	OKALOOSA	2,534	1982	323	20	27	26	16	10	53	4	12	8	8	84	2000	1935	65
09	47	OKEECHOBEE	525	1815	292	42	26	20	8	5	32	4	10	7	6	86	1831	1754	77
09	48	ORANGE	13,850	1843	297	38	28	19	9	6	34	4	10	7	6	75	1869	1804	65
09	49	OSCEOLA	4,263	1815	292	41	29	19	7	4	29	4	10	7	6	75	1834	1758	75
09	50	PALM BEACH	15,273	1853	299	36	29	20	9	6	36	4	10	8	7	81	1866	1805	61
09	51	PASCO	5,195	1862	301	33	32	21	9	4	34	4	10	7	6	84	1872	1827	45
09	52	PINELLAS	9,987	1876	303	34	28	22	10	6	38	4	10	8	7	84	1878	1839	39
09	53	POLK	6,635	1795	288	45	28	17	6	4	27	4	10	7	6	82	1802	1770	32
09	54	PUTNAM	910	1821	293	41	30	17	8	4	28	4	10	7	6	87	1833	1797	35
09	55	ST. JOHNS	2,076	1992	325	20	26	26	16	11	54	4	12	8	8	82	1998	1936	62
09	56	ST. LUCIE	2,712	1847	298	36	31	21	8	4	33	4	10	7	6	81	1866	1828	37
09	57	SANTA ROSA	2,073	1986	324	19	29	27	15	10	52	4	12	8	8	86	1994	1951	43
09	58	SARASOTA	3,466	1916	311	29	27	23	13	8	44	4	11	8	7	82	1922	1867	55
09	59	SEMINOLE	5,754	1940	315	25	28	26	13	9	47	4	11	8	7	85	1948	1900	48
09	60	SUMTER	562	1836	296	36	31	18	10	5	33	4	10	8	6	77	1830	1793	37
09	61	SUWANNEE	498	1807	291	42	29	17	10	2	29	3	10	7	6	87	1821	1806	15
09	62	TAYLOR	229	1833	296	45	23	19	10	3	32	4	10	7	6	94	1837	1822	15
09	63	UNION	168	1824	294	38	33	18	8	3	29	4	10	7	6	90	1839	1809	30
09	64	VOLUSIA	5,203	1877	304	34	28	21	11	6	38	4	10	8	7	85	1883	1845	39
09	65	WAKULLA	430	1863	301	34	31	20	9	6	35	4	10	7	6	89	1869	1874	-5
09	66	WALTON	533	1892	306	30	33	20	11	6	37	4	11	8	7	81	1883	1846	37
09	67	WASHINGTON	289	1901	308	32	26	25	12	5	42	4	11	8	7	90	1907	1871	36
09	68	FSDB	64	1410	218	84	11	2	0	3	5	2	6	4	4	78	1367	1275	92
09	72	FAU HENDERSON	14	2152	354	0	0	50	43	7	100	5	14	10	10	43	2164	2016	148
09	73	FSU SCH	153	2034	333	8	35	31	18	8	57	5	12	9	8	92	2039	1969	70
09	74	FAMU SCH	39	1752	281	59	31	3	3	5	10	3	8	7	5	85	1771	1739	32
09	75	UF PK YONGE	133	1987	324	14	34	31	15	7	53	4	12	9	8	90	1987	1977	10

Note: *Percentages in "Level 3 and Above" may differ from the sum of % in levels 3 - 5 due to rounding.*

Source: *Florida Department of Education, Office of Assessment and School Performance, May 2005*

FLORIDA COMPREHENSIVE ASSESSMENT TEST (FCAT) 2005

SUNSHINE STATE STANDARDS

READING - Grade 10

Grade	District number	District Name	Total Test Scores: Number of Students	Mean Developmental Scale Score (0-3000)	Mean Scale Score (100-500)	Percent Passing	% in each Achievement Level: 1	2	3	4	5	% AL3+: Percent in Achievement Levels 3 and Above	Mean Points Earned By Content: Words / Phrases	Main Idea / Purpose	Comparisons	Reference / Research	Results for Students Matched to Previous Year: Percent Matched to 2004	Mean Developmental Scale Score (2005)	Mean Developmental Scale Score (2004)	Mean DSS Change for Matched Students Reading (2005 - 2004)
Number of Points Possible													7	19	10	15				
10	00	STATEWIDE TOTAL	179,354	1906	296	52	39	29	17	7	8	32	4	11	6	8	87	1930	1890	40
10	01	ALACHUA	2,233	1929	300	56	37	23	17	8	14	39	5	11	7	8	89	1958	1915	44
10	02	BAKER	273	1920	299	49	38	33	16	6	7	29	4	11	6	8	92	1932	1897	35
10	03	BAY	1,873	1956	306	58	33	31	20	9	8	37	5	11	7	9	89	1968	1934	34
10	04	BRADFORD	252	1837	283	40	48	30	13	5	4	22	4	10	6	8	92	1859	1838	22
10	05	BREVARD	5,512	2003	314	65	25	33	20	10	12	42	5	12	7	9	88	2015	1987	28
10	06	BROWARD	19,129	1894	294	49	41	30	16	6	7	29	4	11	6	8	88	1913	1884	30
10	07	CALHOUN	141	1986	311	62	29	33	19	7	11	38	5	12	7	9	96	1990	1952	37
10	08	CHARLOTTE	1,350	1963	307	61	30	33	20	9	8	37	5	12	7	9	89	1976	1918	58
10	09	CITRUS	1,084	1928	300	54	34	34	18	7	7	32	5	11	7	8	88	1939	1913	26
10	10	CLAY	2,425	1973	309	60	30	32	20	9	10	38	5	12	7	9	90	1984	1938	46
10	11	COLLIER	2,746	1887	293	49	42	29	16	6	7	29	4	11	6	8	84	1928	1879	49
10	12	COLUMBIA	571	1861	288	46	45	28	15	5	7	27	4	10	6	8	90	1869	1857	12
10	13	MIAMI-DADE	26,519	1829	282	41	50	27	14	5	5	23	4	10	6	8	87	1853	1802	51
10	14	DESOTO	309	1844	285	41	48	30	13	6	4	22	4	10	6	8	92	1856	1824	32
10	15	DIXIE	150	1791	275	37	53	24	9	8	6	23	4	10	6	7	91	1815	1784	30
10	16	DUVAL	7,164	1923	299	53	37	31	17	7	8	32	5	11	7	8	86	1948	1902	46
10	17	ESCAMBIA	2,863	1889	293	51	40	30	17	7	7	31	4	11	6	8	88	1918	1897	21
10	18	FLAGLER	688	1944	303	58	33	34	20	7	7	33	5	11	7	9	82	1966	1926	41
10	19	FRANKLIN	99	1795	276	34	56	28	7	5	4	16	4	9	6	7	91	1804	1769	35
10	20	GADSDEN	317	1731	264	27	63	30	7	0	1	8	4	8	6	7	88	1757	1784	-27
10	21	GILCHRIST	191	1979	310	64	29	28	26	12	6	43	5	12	7	9	93	1983	1902	80
10	22	GLADES	68	1741	266	40	51	32	10	0	6	16	4	9	6	7	88	1772	1787	-14
10	23	GULF	157	1960	306	55	34	33	18	5	10	33	5	11	7	9	93	1963	1905	58
10	24	HAMILTON	103	1798	276	34	59	18	14	8	1	22	4	9	6	7	87	1797	1753	44
10	25	HARDEE	327	1815	279	38	53	26	12	6	3	21	4	10	6	7	91	1831	1828	3
10	26	HENDRY	580	1723	262	30	61	24	10	3	2	15	4	9	6	7	89	1741	1745	-5
10	27	HERNANDO	1,491	1916	298	54	36	32	19	6	7	32	5	11	7	8	84	1948	1911	37
10	28	HIGHLANDS	730	1903	296	54	35	36	19	5	5	29	5	11	7	8	89	1931	1903	28
10	29	HILLSBOROUGH	11,857	1939	302	55	35	31	18	7	9	34	5	11	7	8	87	1963	1912	51
10	30	HOLMES	250	1899	295	47	42	33	13	5	7	25	4	11	7	8	94	1906	1843	62
10	31	INDIAN RIVER	1,128	1964	307	60	31	33	19	7	10	36	5	11	7	9	89	1975	1933	42
10	32	JACKSON	480	1889	293	50	41	33	15	5	7	27	4	11	7	8	94	1901	1874	26
10	33	JEFFERSON	76	1813	279	39	51	41	5	1	1	8	4	9	6	7	93	1816	1789	27
10	34	LAFAYETTE	65	1875	290	52	40	32	15	5	8	28	4	11	6	8	92	1917	1873	45
10	35	LAKE	2,597	1870	290	49	41	31	15	6	7	28	4	10	6	8	85	1893	1861	32
10	36	LEE	4,691	1905	296	51	40	30	16	6	8	30	5	11	6	8	82	1938	1899	39
10	37	LEON	1,912	2027	319	66	25	28	21	12	15	47	5	12	7	9	92	2039	2009	30
10	38	LEVY	412	1864	288	44	47	27	12	6	7	25	4	10	6	8	84	1884	1844	41
10	39	LIBERTY	72	1894	294	42	43	32	19	1	4	25	4	10	7	8	99	1897	1845	52
10	40	MADISON	223	1706	259	32	60	22	13	4	2	18	4	9	6	7	91	1709	1698	11
10	41	MANATEE	2,765	1872	290	48	43	28	16	6	7	30	4	11	6	8	87	1893	1873	19
10	42	MARION	2,941	1875	290	48	42	30	17	6	6	28	4	10	6	8	86	1910	1895	14
10	43	MARTIN	1,267	2016	317	67	24	30	23	10	13	46	5	12	7	9	90	2036	1965	71
10	44	MONROE	599	1969	308	62	30	27	21	10	12	43	5	12	7	9	88	1992	1938	53
10	45	NASSAU	742	1969	308	59	31	35	19	6	9	34	5	11	7	9	92	1986	1939	47
10	46	OKALOOSA	2,210	2026	318	69	22	32	22	10	13	46	5	12	7	9	86	2041	1995	45
10	47	OKEECHOBEE	480	1835	283	46	45	32	16	4	4	23	4	10	6	8	88	1839	1848	-10
10	48	ORANGE	12,356	1869	289	47	44	27	15	6	7	28	4	10	6	8	78	1912	1872	40
10	49	OSCEOLA	2,776	1848	286	46	44	30	16	5	5	26	4	10	6	8	76	1883	1853	30
10	50	PALM BEACH	10,927	1947	304	57	34	30	18	8	10	36	5	11	7	9	86	1979	1933	46
10	51	PASCO	3,756	1901	295	52	37	33	18	6	6	30	4	11	6	8	83	1937	1916	20
10	52	PINELLAS	8,165	1966	307	59	33	29	19	8	11	38	5	11	7	9	89	1985	1922	62
10	53	POLK	5,501	1843	285	45	46	27	15	5	6	26	4	10	6	8	88	1857	1818	40
10	54	PUTNAM	755	1833	283	41	49	29	13	5	4	22	4	10	6	7	90	1853	1826	27
10	55	ST. JOHNS	1,876	2012	316	67	24	30	23	10	13	46	5	12	7	9	88	2025	1992	34
10	56	ST. LUCIE	2,380	1856	287	45	46	29	15	5	5	25	4	10	6	8	78	1889	1853	36
10	57	SANTA ROSA	1,797	2018	317	69	23	32	23	11	11	45	5	12	7	9	89	2031	1998	33
10	58	SARASOTA	2,961	1958	306	59	32	29	19	10	10	39	5	11	7	9	87	1974	1948	26
10	59	SEMINOLE	4,762	2013	316	65	26	30	21	10	13	44	5	12	7	9	91	2023	1978	45
10	60	SUMTER	490	1879	291	47	42	31	16	4	7	26	4	10	6	8	80	1854	1791	64
10	61	SUWANNEE	339	1893	294	49	41	32	16	4	7	27	5	11	6	8	89	1908	1877	30
10	62	TAYLOR	208	1853	286	42	48	30	12	4	5	22	4	10	6	8	93	1856	1824	32
10	63	UNION	141	1907	296	51	38	29	20	9	4	33	4	11	7	8	94	1906	1863	43
10	64	VOLUSIA	4,672	1908	297	54	37	30	18	8	8	33	5	11	6	8	90	1924	1901	23
10	65	WAKULLA	318	1935	302	58	34	31	23	7	6	36	5	11	7	8	90	1971	1927	44
10	66	WALTON	466	1890	293	50	41	30	17	7	6	29	5	11	6	8	85	1911	1899	12
10	67	WASHINGTON	218	1887	293	51	38	33	20	3	7	29	4	11	6	8	87	1900	1825	75
10	68	FSDB	53	1439	210	9	85	9	4	2	0	6	3	6	4	5	79	1423	1460	-36
10	72	FAU HENDERSON	4	.	.	.	.	.	.	.	.	.	.	.	.	.	.	.	.	.
10	73	FSU SCH	143	2026	318	71	17	41	26	9	8	43	5	12	7	9	98	2027	1991	36
10	74	FAMU SCH	38	1830	282	32	53	32	13	3	0	16	4	10	6	8	82	1795	1784	11
10	75	UF PK YONGE	123	2037	320	73	20	35	28	11	7	46	5	12	7	10	94	2030	1935	95
10	79	FL VIRTUAL SCHO	2	.	.	.	.	.	.	.	.	.	.	.	.	.	.	.	.	.
10	80	COMM. COLLEGES	15	2068	326	93	7	40	40	7	7	53	6	13	8	9	27	2127	2077	49

Note: *Percentages in "Level 3 and Above" may differ from the sum of % in levels 3 - 5 due to rounding.*

Source: *Florida Department of Education, Office of Assessment and School Performance, May 2005*

FLORIDA COMPREHENSIVE ASSESSMENT TEST (FCAT) 2005
SUNSHINE STATE STANDARDS

SCIENCE - Grade 5					Mean Points Earned by Content			
Grade	District number	District Name	Number of Students	Mean Scale Score (100-500)	Physical and Chemical	Earth and Space	Life and Environmental	Scientific Thinking
Number of Points Possible					13	13	13	12
5	0	STATE TOTALS	180,453	296	8	7	8	7
5	1	ALACHUA	1,805	307	8	8	8	7
5	2	BAKER	326	286	8	7	7	6
5	3	BAY	1,960	300	8	7	8	7
5	4	BRADFORD	235	288	7	7	7	7
5	5	BREVARD	5,541	322	9	8	9	8
5	6	BROWARD	19,291	295	8	7	8	7
5	7	CALHOUN	154	310	8	7	8	7
5	8	CHARLOTTE	1,103	302	8	7	8	7
5	9	CITRUS	1,091	308	8	7	8	7
5	10	CLAY	2,335	314	9	8	8	7
5	11	COLLIER	2,634	302	8	7	8	7
5	12	COLUMBIA	687	293	8	7	7	7
5	13	DADE	22,569	286	8	6	7	7
5	14	DESOTO	332	280	7	6	7	6
5	15	DIXIE	114	289	8	6	7	7
5	16	DUVAL	8,899	288	8	7	7	7
5	17	ESCAMBIA	2,986	290	8	7	7	7
5	18	FLAGLER	705	303	8	7	8	7
5	19	FRANKLIN	84	296	8	7	8	7
5	20	GADSDEN	462	261	7	5	6	6
5	21	GILCHRIST	208	303	8	7	8	7
5	22	GLADES	94	282	8	6	8	6
5	23	GULF	154	299	8	7	8	7
5	24	HAMILTON	114	271	7	6	7	6
5	25	HARDEE	336	277	7	6	7	6
5	26	HENDRY	503	274	7	6	7	6
5	27	HERNANDO	1,409	297	8	7	8	7
5	28	HIGHLANDS	833	289	8	7	8	7
5	29	HILLSBOROUGH	13,662	290	8	7	7	7
5	30	HOLMES	232	289	8	7	7	7
5	31	INDIAN RIVER	1,123	301	8	7	8	7
5	32	JACKSON	466	294	8	7	8	7
5	33	JEFFERSON	76	249	6	5	6	6
5	34	LAFAYETTE	75	282	8	7	7	6
5	35	LAKE	2,564	302	8	7	8	7
5	36	LEE	4,870	298	8	7	8	7
5	37	LEON	2,335	308	8	8	8	7
5	38	LEVY	259	297	8	7	7	7
5	39	LIBERTY	91	277	7	6	7	6
5	40	MADISON	171	269	7	6	7	6
5	41	MANATEE	2,884	293	8	7	8	7
5	42	MARION	2,851	294	8	7	8	7
5	43	MARTIN	1,270	313	9	8	8	8
5	44	MONROE	618	306	8	8	8	7
5	45	NASSAU	724	299	8	7	8	7
5	46	OKALOOSA	2,205	319	9	8	9	8
5	47	OKEECHOBEE	540	287	8	7	7	7
5	48	ORANGE	11,874	290	8	7	7	7
5	49	OSCEOLA	3,314	283	7	7	7	7
5	50	PALM BEACH	11,976	303	8	7	8	7
5	51	PASCO	3,949	297	8	7	8	7
5	52	PINELLAS	7,531	294	8	7	7	7
5	53	POLK	6,005	284	7	7	7	7
5	54	PUTNAM	841	289	8	7	7	7
5	55	ST. JOHNS	1,784	315	8	8	8	8
5	56	ST. LUCIE	2,375	294	8	7	8	7
5	57	SANTA ROSA	1,777	317	9	8	9	7
5	58	SARASOTA	2,917	315	8	8	9	8
5	59	SEMINOLE	4,800	313	9	8	8	7
5	60	SUMTER	512	309	8	8	9	7
5	61	SUWANNEE	390	297	8	7	8	7
5	62	TAYLOR	217	293	8	7	8	7
5	63	UNION	156	288	8	7	7	6
5	64	VOLUSIA	4,588	304	8	7	8	7
5	65	WAKULLA	337	303	8	7	8	7
5	66	WALTON	454	309	9	8	8	7
5	67	WASHINGTON	251	288	8	7	7	7
5	68	FL SCH DEAF/BLI	22	204	5	4	4	4
5	72	FAU HENDERSON	74	312	8	8	9	7
5	73	FSU SCH	188	313	8	8	8	7
5	74	FAMU SCH	37	263	7	5	6	6
5	75	UF PK YONGE	58	312	9	8	8	7
5	78	FL CONNECTIONS	15	314	8	8	9	7
5	79	FL VIRTUAL SCHO	31	320	9	8	9	8

Source: *Florida DOE, Office of Assessment and School Performance, May 2005*

FLORIDA COMPREHENSIVE ASSESSMENT TEST (FCAT) 2005
SUNSHINE STATE STANDARDS

SCIENCE - Grade 8

Grade	District number	District Name	Number of Students	Mean Scale Score (100-500)	Mean Points Earned by Content: Physical and Chemical	Earth and Space	Life and Environmental	Scientific Thinking
Number of Points Possible					13	12	13	13
8	0	STATE TOTALS	198,670	291	7	6	7	6
8	1	ALACHUA	2,142	299	7	6	7	7
8	2	BAKER	355	279	7	5	7	6
8	3	BAY	2,024	300	7	6	8	7
8	4	BRADFORD	297	284	7	5	7	6
8	5	BREVARD	5,736	323	8	7	8	8
8	6	BROWARD	20,764	292	7	5	7	6
8	7	CALHOUN	166	299	7	6	8	6
8	8	CHARLOTTE	1,400	302	7	6	7	7
8	9	CITRUS	1,278	297	7	6	7	7
8	10	CLAY	2,596	306	7	6	8	7
8	11	COLLIER	3,166	291	7	6	7	6
8	12	COLUMBIA	730	289	6	6	7	6
8	13	DADE	28,128	272	6	5	6	6
8	14	DESOTO	341	267	6	5	6	5
8	15	DIXIE	144	283	6	5	7	6
8	16	DUVAL	8,968	285	7	5	7	6
8	17	ESCAMBIA	3,371	281	6	5	7	6
8	18	FLAGLER	812	301	7	6	8	7
8	19	FRANKLIN	97	286	6	5	7	6
8	20	GADSDEN	461	243	5	4	5	5
8	21	GILCHRIST	199	315	8	7	8	7
8	22	GLADES	102	263	6	5	6	5
8	23	GULF	201	279	6	5	7	6
8	24	HAMILTON	141	252	5	4	6	5
8	25	HARDEE	391	268	6	5	6	5
8	26	HENDRY	583	262	6	5	6	5
8	27	HERNANDO	1,645	290	7	5	7	6
8	28	HIGHLANDS	910	287	7	5	7	6
8	29	HILLSBOROUGH	13,781	294	7	6	7	6
8	30	HOLMES	272	295	7	6	7	7
8	31	INDIAN RIVER	1,244	292	7	6	7	7
8	32	JACKSON	532	289	7	6	7	6
8	33	JEFFERSON	78	269	6	5	7	5
8	34	LAFAYETTE	82	273	6	5	7	6
8	35	LAKE	2,650	298	7	6	7	7
8	36	LEE	5,160	290	7	5	7	6
8	37	LEON	2,150	312	8	6	8	7
8	38	LEVY	505	286	7	5	7	6
8	39	LIBERTY	79	313	7	6	8	7
8	40	MADISON	209	257	5	4	6	5
8	41	MANATEE	2,954	291	7	6	7	6
8	42	MARION	3,233	291	7	6	7	6
8	43	MARTIN	1,412	313	7	6	8	7
8	44	MONROE	668	303	7	6	8	7
8	45	NASSAU	881	294	7	6	7	6
8	46	OKALOOSA	2,242	332	8	7	9	8
8	47	OKEECHOBEE	520	276	6	5	7	6
8	48	ORANGE	12,942	286	7	5	7	6
8	49	OSCEOLA	3,631	278	6	5	7	6
8	50	PALM BEACH	13,057	294	7	6	7	6
8	51	PASCO	4,632	293	7	6	7	6
8	52	PINELLAS	8,551	292	7	6	7	6
8	53	POLK	6,211	276	6	5	7	6
8	54	PUTNAM	948	282	6	5	7	6
8	55	ST. JOHNS	1,886	322	8	7	8	7
8	56	ST. LUCIE	2,684	288	7	5	7	6
8	57	SANTA ROSA	1,983	320	8	7	8	7
8	58	SARASOTA	3,121	305	7	6	8	7
8	59	SEMINOLE	5,207	308	7	6	8	7
8	60	SUMTER	563	287	7	5	7	6
8	61	SUWANNEE	427	297	7	6	7	6
8	62	TAYLOR	238	293	7	6	7	6
8	63	UNION	157	302	8	6	8	7
8	64	VOLUSIA	5,018	293	7	6	7	6
8	65	WAKULLA	359	304	7	6	7	7
8	66	WALTON	533	306	7	6	8	7
8	67	WASHINGTON	268	290	7	6	7	6
8	68	FL SCH DEAF/BLI	58	211	4	3	5	4
8	72	FAU HENDERSON	51	343	9	7	9	9
8	73	FSU SCH	157	311	7	6	8	7
8	74	FAMU SCH	41	263	5	4	6	5
8	75	UF PK YONGE	113	328	8	7	9	8
8	78	FL CONNECTIONS	14	312	7	7	9	7
8	79	FL VIRTUAL SCHO	20	343	8	8	9	8

Source: *Florida DOE, Office of Assessment and School Performance, May 2005*

FLORIDA COMPREHENSIVE ASSESSMENT TEST (FCAT) 2005
SUNSHINE STATE STANDARDS

SCIENCE - Grade 11

Grade	District number	District Name	Number of Students	Mean Scale Score (100-500)	Mean Points Earned by Content: Physical and Chemical	Earth and Space	Life and Environmental	Scientific Thinking
Number of Points Possible					14	11	14	12
11	0	STATE TOTALS	142,353	293	6	6	6	7
11	1	ALACHUA	1,823	304	7	6	7	7
11	2	BAKER	183	300	6	6	6	7
11	3	BAY	1,533	303	6	6	6	8
11	4	BRADFORD	178	286	6	6	6	6
11	5	BREVARD	4,993	321	8	7	7	8
11	6	BROWARD	14,982	290	6	5	6	7
11	7	CALHOUN	134	312	7	6	7	8
11	8	CHARLOTTE	1,120	304	6	6	6	8
11	9	CITRUS	996	309	7	6	6	8
11	10	CLAY	2,103	293	6	6	6	7
11	11	COLLIER	2,088	291	6	5	6	7
11	12	COLUMBIA	421	289	6	5	6	7
11	13	DADE	19,540	275	5	5	5	6
11	14	DESOTO	274	265	5	4	4	6
11	15	DIXIE	112	299	6	6	6	7
11	16	DUVAL	5,495	297	6	6	6	7
11	17	ESCAMBIA	2,441	293	6	6	6	7
11	18	FLAGLER	499	303	6	6	6	7
11	19	FRANKLIN	70	279	5	5	6	6
11	20	GADSDEN	269	246	4	3	4	5
11	21	GILCHRIST	150	290	5	6	6	7
11	22	GLADES	43	277	5	5	5	6
11	23	GULF	127	299	6	6	6	7
11	24	HAMILTON	84	265	4	5	5	6
11	25	HARDEE	221	276	5	5	5	6
11	26	HENDRY	395	273	5	5	5	6
11	27	HERNANDO	1,051	292	6	6	6	7
11	28	HIGHLANDS	691	294	6	6	6	7
11	29	HILLSBOROUGH	10,420	298	6	6	6	7
11	30	HOLMES	200	281	5	5	6	6
11	31	INDIAN RIVER	896	300	6	6	6	7
11	32	JACKSON	388	292	6	5	6	7
11	33	JEFFERSON	61	277	5	5	5	6
11	34	LAFAYETTE	71	273	5	5	5	6
11	35	LAKE	1,843	296	6	6	6	7
11	36	LEE	3,375	290	6	6	6	7
11	37	LEON	1,763	314	7	6	7	8
11	38	LEVY	282	295	5	6	6	7
11	39	LIBERTY	59	275	5	5	5	6
11	40	MADISON	184	259	5	4	5	6
11	41	MANATEE	2,108	294	6	6	6	7
11	42	MARION	2,169	292	6	6	6	7
11	43	MARTIN	1,105	314	7	6	7	8
11	44	MONROE	494	311	7	6	7	8
11	45	NASSAU	576	293	6	6	6	7
11	46	OKALOOSA	2,015	315	7	6	7	8
11	47	OKEECHOBEE	366	282	5	5	6	6
11	48	ORANGE	9,341	291	6	5	6	7
11	49	OSCEOLA	2,867	280	5	5	5	6
11	50	PALM BEACH	10,789	287	6	5	6	7
11	51	PASCO	2,290	304	6	6	6	7
11	52	PINELLAS	5,813	298	6	6	6	7
11	53	POLK	4,300	285	5	5	6	7
11	54	PUTNAM	556	278	5	5	5	6
11	55	ST. JOHNS	1,557	317	7	6	7	8
11	56	ST. LUCIE	1,589	281	5	5	5	6
11	57	SANTA ROSA	1,533	313	7	6	7	8
11	58	SARASOTA	2,240	307	7	6	7	8
11	59	SEMINOLE	4,183	314	7	6	7	8
11	60	SUMTER	299	275	5	5	5	6
11	61	SUWANNEE	305	290	6	6	6	7
11	62	TAYLOR	153	287	6	5	6	7
11	63	UNION	128	287	5	5	5	7
11	64	VOLUSIA	2,881	297	6	6	6	7
11	65	WAKULLA	221	299	6	6	6	7
11	66	WALTON	375	298	6	6	6	7
11	67	WASHINGTON	211	288	6	5	5	7
11	68	FL SCH DEAF/BLI	41	224	3	3	4	4
11	72	FAU HENDERSON	6					
11	73	FSU SCH	136	315	7	6	7	8
11	74	FAMU SCH	35	266	5	4	5	5
11	75	UF PK YONGE	107	326	8	7	7	8
11	80	COMM. COLLEGES	6					

Source: *Florida DOE, Office of Assessment and School Performance, May 2005*

FLORIDA COMPREHENSIVE ASSESSMENT TEST (FCAT) 2005

WRITING - Grade 4

Grade	District Number	District Name	Type of Writing	Number of Students	Mean Score	Percent Earning Each Score Point: 1	1.5	2	2.5	3	3.5	4	4.5	5	5.5	6	Percent 3 or Above	Percent 3.5 or Above	Mean of Percent 3 and Above and Percent 3.5 and Above
04	00	STATEWIDE AVERAGE	Expository	97,245	3.7	1	1	3	4	18	20	32	13	6	2	1	91	73	82
04	00	STATEWIDE AVERAGE	Narrative	97,416	3.7	1	1	3	5	15	18	33	14	6	2	1	90	74	82
04	00	STATEWIDE AVERAGE	Combined	194,661	3.7	1	1	3	4	17	19	33	13	6	2	1	90	74	82
04	01	ALACHUA	Expository	992	3.9	0	1	2	5	15	15	29	17	10	4	2	91	76	84
04	01	ALACHUA	Narrative	996	3.8	1	1	3	5	15	20	29	13	8	3	2	90	75	82
04	01	ALACHUA	Combined	1,988	3.8	1	1	3	5	15	18	29	15	9	3	2	90	75	83
04	02	BAKER	Expository	178	3.5	1	1	3	6	25	27	21	8	4	2	1	88	63	76
04	02	BAKER	Narrative	175	3.4	1	1	6	13	26	21	21	7	2	0	2	79	53	66
04	02	BAKER	Combined	353	3.4	1	1	5	9	26	24	21	8	3	1	1	84	58	71
04	03	BAY	Expository	906	3.5	1	1	4	6	23	21	31	8	3	1	0	88	65	76
04	03	BAY	Narrative	903	3.5	2	1	5	6	18	21	32	11	4	1	0	86	68	77
04	03	BAY	Combined	1,809	3.5	2	1	4	6	20	21	32	10	4	1	0	87	67	77
04	04	BRADFORD	Expository	120	3.9	0	0	4	2	10	20	35	18	7	3	1	93	83	88
04	04	BRADFORD	Narrative	125	3.6	4	1	3	3	14	22	31	16	6	0	0	89	75	82
04	04	BRADFORD	Combined	245	3.8	2	0	4	2	12	21	33	17	6	1	0	91	79	85
04	05	BREVARD	Expository	2,652	3.8	1	1	2	3	15	17	35	16	7	3	1	93	78	86
04	05	BREVARD	Narrative	2,649	3.8	1	1	2	4	14	17	35	15	7	3	1	92	78	85
04	05	BREVARD	Combined	5,301	3.8	1	1	2	3	14	17	35	15	7	3	1	92	78	85
04	06	BROWARD	Expository	10,627	3.8	1	0	2	3	14	19	35	14	7	3	1	94	79	87
04	06	BROWARD	Narrative	10,607	3.9	1	1	2	3	11	16	38	16	8	2	1	93	82	87
04	06	BROWARD	Combined	21,234	3.9	1	0	2	3	13	17	37	15	8	3	1	93	80	87
04	07	CALHOUN	Expository	81	3.4	1	4	5	5	32	21	14	14	4	1	0	85	53	69
04	07	CALHOUN	Narrative	79	3.6	0	1	5	10	16	19	27	18	3	1	0	84	67	75
04	07	CALHOUN	Combined	160	3.5	1	3	5	8	24	20	20	16	3	1	0	84	60	72
04	08	CHARLOTTE	Expository	563	3.9	0	1	3	4	12	17	28	19	8	7	2	92	80	86
04	08	CHARLOTTE	Narrative	563	3.8	2	1	3	4	13	19	26	15	9	6	2	89	76	82
04	08	CHARLOTTE	Combined	1,126	3.9	1	1	3	4	12	18	27	17	8	6	2	90	78	84
04	09	CITRUS	Expository	554	3.7	0	1	3	7	20	22	24	12	6	3	1	88	68	78
04	09	CITRUS	Narrative	546	3.6	1	1	5	6	20	19	25	12	6	4	1	87	67	77
04	09	CITRUS	Combined	1,100	3.7	0	1	4	7	20	21	25	12	6	3	1	87	68	78
04	10	CLAY	Expository	1,099	3.8	1	1	3	5	17	19	28	14	7	3	2	91	74	82
04	10	CLAY	Narrative	1,095	3.9	0	1	2	4	14	19	32	15	7	4	1	93	79	86
04	10	CLAY	Combined	2,194	3.8	0	1	3	4	16	19	30	15	7	3	2	92	76	84
04	11	COLLIER	Expository	1,587	3.6	1	1	3	4	22	21	32	10	4	2	0	91	69	80
04	11	COLLIER	Narrative	1,603	3.7	1	1	4	5	16	17	36	12	6	2	0	89	72	80
04	11	COLLIER	Combined	3,190	3.6	1	1	3	5	19	19	34	11	5	2	0	90	71	80
04	12	COLUMBIA	Expository	368	3.6	1	1	4	6	21	23	21	13	7	1	1	87	66	76
04	12	COLUMBIA	Narrative	375	3.5	1	2	4	6	21	25	22	11	5	2	0	86	65	75
04	12	COLUMBIA	Combined	743	3.5	1	1	4	6	21	24	22	12	6	1	0	87	65	76
04	13	DADE	Expository	13,286	3.8	1	1	2	3	14	18	37	15	6	2	1	93	79	86
04	13	DADE	Narrative	13,308	3.8	1	1	2	3	11	16	39	16	7	2	1	92	81	87
04	13	DADE	Combined	26,594	3.8	1	1	2	3	13	17	38	15	7	2	1	92	80	86
04	14	DESOTO	Expository	181	3.6	3	1	2	3	16	24	24	18	7	1	0	90	73	81
04	14	DESOTO	Narrative	185	3.6	2	1	4	6	19	23	29	12	4	1	0	88	69	78
04	14	DESOTO	Combined	366	3.6	2	1	3	5	18	24	26	15	5	1	0	89	71	80
04	15	DIXIE	Expository	79	3.7	0	4	5	8	13	14	25	11	18	0	1	82	70	76
04	15	DIXIE	Narrative	77	3.3	6	4	6	3	23	17	25	12	3	0	0	79	56	68
04	15	DIXIE	Combined	156	3.5	3	4	6	5	18	15	25	12	10	0	1	81	63	72
04	16	DUVAL	Expository	4,681	3.6	1	1	2	5	20	23	35	10	3	1	0	91	72	81
04	16	DUVAL	Narrative	4,698	3.7	1	1	3	4	14	17	38	14	6	2	0	91	77	84
04	16	DUVAL	Combined	9,379	3.7	1	1	3	4	17	20	37	12	4	1	0	91	74	83
04	17	ESCAMBIA	Expository	1,690	3.6	1	1	3	5	22	20	32	11	3	1	0	89	67	78
04	17	ESCAMBIA	Narrative	1,681	3.6	2	2	4	6	19	18	34	10	4	1	0	87	68	77
04	17	ESCAMBIA	Combined	3,371	3.6	1	1	3	5	21	19	33	10	4	1	0	88	67	78
04	18	FLAGLER	Expository	366	3.5	1	1	4	6	27	23	25	7	2	2	0	87	60	74
04	18	FLAGLER	Narrative	366	3.6	2	1	3	6	21	21	25	13	5	2	0	87	66	77
04	18	FLAGLER	Combined	732	3.5	2	1	4	6	24	22	25	10	4	2	0	87	63	75
04	19	FRANKLIN	Expository	43	3.1	5	0	5	16	28	21	16	7	0	0	0	72	44	58
04	19	FRANKLIN	Narrative	46	3.1	7	2	9	20	13	20	15	7	2	4	0	61	48	54
04	19	FRANKLIN	Combined	89	3.1	6	1	7	18	20	20	16	7	1	2	0	66	46	56
04	20	GADSDEN	Expository	213	3.7	1	1	1	4	16	24	33	13	5	0	0	92	76	84
04	20	GADSDEN	Narrative	217	3.4	1	1	3	10	19	20	34	6	3	0	0	82	63	73

FLORIDA COMPREHENSIVE ASSESSMENT TEST (FCAT) 2005

WRITING - **Grade 4** - *continued*

Grade	District Number	District Name	Type of Writing	Number of Students	Mean Score	Percent Earning Each Score Point											Percent 3 or Above	Percent 3.5 or Above	Mean of Percent 3 and Above and Percent 3.5 and Above
						1	1.5	2	2.5	3	3.5	4	4.5	5	5.5	6			
04	00	STATEWIDE AVERAGE	Expository	97,245	3.7	1	1	3	4	18	20	32	13	6	2	1	91	73	82
04	00	STATEWIDE AVERAGE	Narrative	97,416	3.7	1	1	3	5	15	18	33	14	6	2	1	90	74	82
04	00	STATEWIDE AVERAGE	Combined	194,661	3.7	1	1	3	4	17	19	33	13	6	2	1	90	74	82
04	20	GADSDEN	Combined	430	3.5	1	1	2	7	18	22	33	9	4	0	0	87	70	78
04	21	GILCHRIST	Expository	92	3.6	1	1	8	8	20	15	23	13	8	3	1	83	63	73
04	21	GILCHRIST	Narrative	93	3.6	1	1	8	9	8	24	30	12	6	2	0	82	74	78
04	21	GILCHRIST	Combined	185	3.6	1	1	8	8	14	19	26	12	7	3	1	82	69	75
04	22	GLADES	Expository	52	3.2	4	0	6	2	31	25	29	2	0	0	0	87	56	71
04	22	GLADES	Narrative	53	3.3	6	0	8	2	25	23	28	8	2	0	0	85	60	73
04	22	GLADES	Combined	105	3.3	5	0	7	2	28	24	29	5	1	0	0	86	58	72
04	23	GULF	Expository	74	3.3	0	0	12	5	30	22	22	4	5	0	0	82	53	68
04	23	GULF	Narrative	71	3.4	7	0	3	6	27	20	24	10	4	0	0	85	58	71
04	23	GULF	Combined	145	3.4	3	0	8	6	28	21	23	7	5	0	0	83	55	69
04	24	HAMILTON	Expository	67	3.9	0	0	4	4	9	13	24	22	16	1	1	88	79	84
04	24	HAMILTON	Narrative	67	3.9	1	0	6	1	4	16	40	10	13	3	1	90	85	87
04	24	HAMILTON	Combined	134	3.9	1	0	5	3	7	15	32	16	15	2	1	89	82	85
04	25	HARDEE	Expository	191	3.6	2	1	3	5	20	20	30	12	5	2	1	89	69	79
04	25	HARDEE	Narrative	198	3.3	3	1	5	9	20	26	21	9	4	1	0	80	60	70
04	25	HARDEE	Combined	389	3.5	3	1	4	7	20	23	25	10	4	1	0	85	65	75
04	26	HENDRY	Expository	288	3.4	1	1	4	7	26	21	26	9	2	1	0	85	59	72
04	26	HENDRY	Narrative	288	3.3	0	2	4	8	27	21	21	10	3	0	0	83	56	69
04	26	HENDRY	Combined	576	3.4	1	2	4	8	26	21	24	10	3	1	0	84	58	71
04	27	HERNANDO	Expository	747	3.6	0	1	2	6	22	22	27	13	5	2	0	91	69	80
04	27	HERNANDO	Narrative	744	3.7	1	1	2	6	18	24	26	13	7	2	0	89	71	80
04	27	HERNANDO	Combined	1,491	3.6	1	1	2	6	20	23	26	13	6	2	0	90	70	80
04	28	HIGHLANDS	Expository	444	3.4	2	1	6	6	24	26	21	8	4	2	0	85	61	73
04	28	HIGHLANDS	Narrative	438	3.3	4	1	8	10	26	20	17	9	3	1	0	76	51	64
04	28	HIGHLANDS	Combined	882	3.4	3	1	7	8	25	23	19	8	4	1	0	81	56	68
04	29	HILLSBOROUGH	Expository	7,034	3.8	1	1	2	4	16	19	31	15	8	3	1	92	77	84
04	29	HILLSBOROUGH	Narrative	7,058	3.7	1	1	3	5	17	20	31	12	6	2	1	89	72	81
04	29	HILLSBOROUGH	Combined	14,092	3.7	1	1	3	4	16	20	31	14	7	2	1	91	75	83
04	30	HOLMES	Expository	123	3.3	2	3	4	7	33	23	18	7	2	0	0	84	50	67
04	30	HOLMES	Narrative	123	3.3	7	2	7	8	24	22	12	11	6	1	0	76	52	64
04	30	HOLMES	Combined	246	3.3	4	2	6	8	29	22	15	9	4	0	0	80	51	66
04	31	INDIAN RIVER	Expository	641	3.8	0	1	3	5	15	21	25	16	8	4	2	90	75	83
04	31	INDIAN RIVER	Narrative	627	3.8	1	1	2	5	17	21	25	16	6	4	2	91	74	83
04	31	INDIAN RIVER	Combined	1,268	3.8	1	1	3	5	16	21	25	16	7	4	2	91	75	83
04	32	JACKSON	Expository	246	3.4	1	2	4	4	30	21	27	7	3	0	0	89	59	74
04	32	JACKSON	Narrative	242	3.5	2	1	4	9	24	22	19	9	7	1	0	83	59	71
04	32	JACKSON	Combined	488	3.4	2	2	4	6	27	21	23	8	5	1	0	86	59	72
04	33	JEFFERSON	Expository	45	3.1	2	0	18	4	36	16	16	2	2	2	0	73	38	56
04	33	JEFFERSON	Narrative	45	2.7	18	2	9	18	18	16	18	0	2	0	0	53	36	44
04	33	JEFFERSON	Combined	90	2.9	10	1	13	11	27	16	17	1	2	1	0	63	37	50
04	34	LAFAYETTE	Expository	38	3.8	3	0	3	5	18	18	18	18	13	3	0	89	71	80
04	34	LAFAYETTE	Narrative	38	3.9	0	0	5	3	13	13	37	13	11	0	5	92	79	86
04	34	LAFAYETTE	Combined	76	3.9	1	0	4	4	16	16	28	16	12	1	3	91	75	83
04	35	LAKE	Expository	1,366	3.5	1	1	3	5	25	23	26	10	4	1	1	90	65	77
04	35	LAKE	Narrative	1,370	3.5	1	1	3	7	21	22	28	11	4	1	0	87	66	77
04	35	LAKE	Combined	2,736	3.5	1	1	3	6	23	23	27	10	4	1	0	88	66	77
04	36	LEE	Expository	2,623	3.6	1	1	3	4	21	19	33	11	4	2	1	91	70	81
04	36	LEE	Narrative	2,609	3.7	1	1	3	4	14	17	38	12	5	2	1	89	75	82
04	36	LEE	Combined	5,232	3.7	1	1	3	4	18	18	36	12	5	2	1	90	72	81
04	37	LEON	Expository	1,117	3.8	0	0	2	3	15	19	38	15	6	2	1	95	80	88
04	37	LEON	Narrative	1,104	3.8	1	1	2	3	15	18	38	13	6	1	0	92	77	85
04	37	LEON	Combined	2,221	3.8	1	1	2	3	15	18	38	14	6	2	1	94	79	86
04	38	LEVY	Expository	245	3.4	0	2	4	11	23	23	26	7	3	1	0	82	60	71
04	38	LEVY	Narrative	238	3.3	2	3	5	11	26	27	18	3	2	2	0	79	53	66
04	38	LEVY	Combined	483	3.3	1	2	5	11	24	25	22	5	3	1	0	81	56	68
04	39	LIBERTY	Expository	41	3.2	2	0	10	7	32	15	27	2	2	0	0	78	46	62
04	39	LIBERTY	Narrative	40	3.5	3	0	5	8	20	20	30	13	3	0	0	85	65	75
04	39	LIBERTY	Combined	81	3.3	2	0	7	7	26	17	28	7	2	0	0	81	56	69
04	40	MADISON	Expository	107	3	3	2	9	16	37	19	6	7	0	0	0	69	32	50

FLORIDA COMPREHENSIVE ASSESSMENT TEST (FCAT) 2005

WRITING - Grade 4 - *continued*

Grade	District Number	District Name	Type of Writing	Number of Students	Mean Score	Percent Earning Each Score Point											Percent 3 or Above	Percent 3.5 or Above	Mean of Percent 3 and Above and Percent 3.5 and Above
						1	1.5	2	2.5	3	3.5	4	4.5	5	5.5	6			
04	00	STATEWIDE AVERAGE	Expository	97,245	3.7	1	1	3	4	18	20	32	13	6	2	1	91	73	82
04	00	STATEWIDE AVERAGE	Narrative	97,416	3.7	1	1	3	5	15	18	33	14	6	2	1	90	74	82
04	00	STATEWIDE AVERAGE	Combined	194,661	3.7	1	1	3	4	17	19	33	13	6	2	1	90	74	82
04	40	MADISON	Narrative	104	3.1	4	0	9	20	26	16	14	6	1	3	0	66	40	53
04	40	MADISON	Combined	211	3	3	1	9	18	32	18	10	7	0	1	0	68	36	52
04	41	MANATEE	Expository	1,573	3.6	1	1	3	4	20	20	35	10	3	2	0	91	70	81
04	41	MANATEE	Narrative	1,592	3.7	2	1	4	4	14	17	34	14	6	2	1	89	74	82
04	41	MANATEE	Combined	3,165	3.7	1	1	3	4	17	19	35	12	4	2	1	90	72	81
04	42	MARION	Expository	1,521	3.5	1	1	4	7	25	20	27	10	3	1	0	87	62	74
04	42	MARION	Narrative	1,551	3.5	1	1	5	8	22	22	25	9	5	1	0	84	62	73
04	42	MARION	Combined	3,072	3.5	1	1	5	7	23	21	26	10	4	1	0	85	62	73
04	43	MARTIN	Expository	616	4	0	1	1	4	11	19	25	18	13	5	2	92	82	87
04	43	MARTIN	Narrative	631	4	0	0	2	3	15	19	22	17	13	5	3	94	79	87
04	43	MARTIN	Combined	1,247	4	0	1	2	3	13	19	23	17	13	5	2	93	81	87
04	44	MONROE	Expository	293	3.6	0	0	4	5	24	26	25	11	3	2	0	91	67	79
04	44	MONROE	Narrative	290	3.6	2	1	5	6	22	22	20	14	5	2	1	86	64	75
04	44	MONROE	Combined	583	3.6	1	1	4	5	23	24	22	13	4	2	1	89	66	77
04	45	NASSAU	Expository	378	3.7	1	0	4	5	21	23	24	13	6	3	1	91	70	80
04	45	NASSAU	Narrative	389	3.7	1	1	3	3	19	23	26	15	6	2	1	92	74	83
04	45	NASSAU	Combined	767	3.7	1	1	3	4	20	23	25	14	6	2	1	92	72	82
04	46	OKALOOSA	Expository	1,079	3.8	0	1	2	3	17	20	32	13	8	3	1	95	78	86
04	46	OKALOOSA	Narrative	1,083	3.7	1	1	2	5	18	20	27	15	8	2	1	90	72	81
04	46	OKALOOSA	Combined	2,162	3.8	1	1	2	4	18	20	30	14	8	3	1	92	75	84
04	47	OKEECHOBEE	Expository	245	3.5	2	2	5	4	22	23	28	9	4	2	0	87	65	76
04	47	OKEECHOBEE	Narrative	252	3.4	4	2	4	7	20	21	24	9	5	2	0	82	62	72
04	47	OKEECHOBEE	Combined	497	3.5	3	2	5	5	21	22	26	9	4	2	0	84	63	74
04	48	ORANGE	Expository	6,430	3.6	1	1	3	4	20	20	32	11	5	2	0	90	69	79
04	48	ORANGE	Narrative	6,442	3.6	2	1	4	6	17	18	31	13	5	2	1	87	70	78
04	48	ORANGE	Combined	12,872	3.6	2	1	3	5	19	19	31	12	5	2	0	88	70	79
04	49	OSCEOLA	Expository	1,767	3.4	2	2	4	6	28	23	23	8	3	1	0	85	57	71
04	49	OSCEOLA	Narrative	1,753	3.4	2	2	5	8	23	22	23	9	3	1	0	82	59	71
04	49	OSCEOLA	Combined	3,520	3.4	2	2	5	7	25	23	23	8	3	1	0	83	58	71
04	50	PALM BEACH	Expository	6,489	3.8	1	0	2	2	16	20	37	13	5	2	0	94	78	86
04	50	PALM BEACH	Narrative	6,479	3.8	1	1	2	3	12	17	38	15	7	2	1	93	81	87
04	50	PALM BEACH	Combined	12,968	3.8	1	1	2	3	14	18	37	14	6	2	0	93	79	86
04	51	PASCO	Expository	2,290	3.6	1	1	4	5	20	22	31	10	4	1	0	89	68	78
04	51	PASCO	Narrative	2,302	3.5	2	2	5	6	21	21	28	9	4	1	0	85	64	75
04	51	PASCO	Combined	4,592	3.5	2	1	4	6	21	22	30	9	4	1	0	87	66	77
04	52	PINELLAS	Expository	4,069	3.7	1	1	3	4	17	19	30	14	8	3	1	91	74	83
04	52	PINELLAS	Narrative	4,193	3.6	2	1	4	6	19	20	29	12	5	2	1	87	68	78
04	52	PINELLAS	Combined	8,262	3.7	1	1	3	5	18	19	30	13	6	2	1	89	71	80
04	53	POLK	Expository	3,194	3.7	1	1	3	3	18	20	35	12	5	2	1	92	74	83
04	53	POLK	Narrative	3,184	3.8	2	1	2	4	12	18	37	15	6	2	1	91	79	85
04	53	POLK	Combined	6,378	3.7	1	1	2	4	15	19	36	13	6	2	1	91	76	84
04	54	PUTNAM	Expository	459	3.7	1	1	4	7	16	19	29	13	6	4	0	88	72	80
04	54	PUTNAM	Narrative	454	3.6	2	1	2	6	20	20	29	10	4	4	1	89	69	79
04	54	PUTNAM	Combined	913	3.7	1	1	3	6	18	20	29	12	5	4	1	88	70	79
04	55	ST. JOHNS	Expository	920	3.7	0	1	3	5	18	20	25	13	7	4	2	90	71	80
04	55	ST. JOHNS	Narrative	906	3.9	1	1	2	5	13	21	24	19	10	4	2	92	79	86
04	55	ST. JOHNS	Combined	1,826	3.8	1	1	2	5	16	20	24	16	8	4	2	91	75	83
04	56	ST. LUCIE	Expository	1,337	3.6	1	1	3	6	23	23	25	12	5	2	1	90	66	78
04	56	ST. LUCIE	Narrative	1,335	3.6	1	1	3	6	20	20	29	12	6	1	1	89	69	79
04	56	ST. LUCIE	Combined	2,672	3.6	1	1	3	6	22	22	27	12	5	2	1	89	67	78
04	57	SANTA ROSA	Expository	847	3.9	1	1	2	3	11	16	39	15	9	3	1	94	83	88
04	57	SANTA ROSA	Narrative	867	3.8	1	0	2	2	14	19	38	16	6	2	1	94	81	88
04	57	SANTA ROSA	Combined	1,714	3.9	1	0	2	3	12	18	38	16	7	2	1	94	82	88
04	58	SARASOTA	Expository	1,563	4	1	0	2	2	12	16	32	17	9	4	2	94	82	88
04	58	SARASOTA	Narrative	1,570	4	1	1	3	4	10	14	31	18	10	5	2	92	81	86
04	58	SARASOTA	Combined	3,133	4	1	1	3	3	11	15	32	18	10	5	2	93	81	87
04	59	SEMINOLE	Expository	2,493	3.6	1	1	2	5	22	21	29	12	5	2	0	90	69	80
04	59	SEMINOLE	Narrative	2,489	3.7	2	1	3	5	19	19	28	14	7	2	1	89	70	80
04	59	SEMINOLE	Combined	4,982	3.7	1	1	3	5	20	20	28	13	6	2	1	90	70	80

FLORIDA COMPREHENSIVE ASSESSMENT TEST (FCAT) 2005

WRITING - **Grade 4** - *continued*

Grade	District Number	District Name	Type of Writing	Number of Students	Mean Score	Percent Earning Each Score Point											Percent 3 or Above	Percent 3.5 or Above	Mean of Percent 3 and Above and Percent 3.5 and Above
						1	1.5	2	2.5	3	3.5	4	4.5	5	5.5	6			
04	00	STATEWIDE AVERAGE	Expository	97,245	3.7	1	1	3	4	18	20	32	13	6	2	1	91	73	82
04	00	STATEWIDE AVERAGE	Narrative	97,416	3.7	1	1	3	5	15	18	33	14	6	2	1	90	74	82
04	00	STATEWIDE AVERAGE	Combined	194,661	3.7	1	1	3	4	17	19	33	13	6	2	1	90	74	82
04	60	SUMTER	Expository	283	3.5	2	2	3	7	26	23	19	10	5	2	0	86	60	73
04	60	SUMTER	Narrative	281	3.5	1	2	5	10	21	21	20	14	4	2	0	81	60	71
04	60	SUMTER	Combined	564	3.5	2	2	4	9	23	22	19	12	4	2	0	84	60	72
04	61	SUWANNEE	Expository	202	3.4	1	1	7	9	25	18	20	11	3	2	0	80	55	68
04	61	SUWANNEE	Narrative	202	3.7	1	1	6	6	21	16	21	13	8	4	1	85	64	74
04	61	SUWANNEE	Combined	404	3.5	1	1	7	8	23	17	21	12	6	3	1	82	59	71
04	62	TAYLOR	Expository	114	3.6	0	3	4	4	18	27	28	10	4	3	0	90	72	81
04	62	TAYLOR	Narrative	113	3.5	1	1	4	5	30	20	19	12	4	2	0	88	58	73
04	62	TAYLOR	Combined	227	3.6	0	2	4	4	24	24	24	11	4	2	0	89	65	77
04	63	UNION	Expository	76	4	0	5	1	3	13	9	30	18	9	9	1	91	78	84
04	63	UNION	Narrative	78	3.9	0	1	0	3	12	24	36	17	5	1	1	96	85	90
04	63	UNION	Combined	154	3.9	0	3	1	3	12	17	33	18	7	5	1	94	81	87
04	64	VOLUSIA	Expository	2,431	3.6	1	1	4	5	20	20	29	11	5	2	0	87	68	78
04	64	VOLUSIA	Narrative	2,419	3.5	2	2	4	6	18	21	28	11	5	2	0	85	67	76
04	64	VOLUSIA	Combined	4,850	3.6	2	2	4	6	19	20	29	11	5	2	0	86	67	77
04	65	WAKULLA	Expository	158	3.7	0	0	4	8	19	19	33	11	4	0	2	89	70	79
04	65	WAKULLA	Narrative	151	3.7	1	0	2	7	23	22	26	13	3	3	1	91	68	79
04	65	WAKULLA	Combined	309	3.7	0	0	3	7	21	20	30	12	4	2	1	90	69	79
04	66	WALTON	Expository	240	3.9	0	0	2	3	14	19	33	16	6	5	0	94	80	87
04	66	WALTON	Narrative	241	3.7	2	0	2	5	20	17	33	13	4	2	0	91	71	81
04	66	WALTON	Combined	481	3.8	1	0	2	4	17	18	33	15	5	4	0	92	75	84
04	67	WASHINGTON	Expository	120	3.3	3	3	3	8	30	20	23	6	1	2	1	82	52	67
04	67	WASHINGTON	Narrative	123	3.4	5	1	5	10	19	23	24	6	2	3	2	79	60	70
04	67	WASHINGTON	Combined	243	3.3	4	2	4	9	24	21	23	6	2	2	1	80	56	68
04	68	FL SCH DEAF/BLI	Expository	8															
04	68	FL SCH DEAF/BLI	Narrative	12	1.8	33	17	17	8	0	8	8	0	0	0	0	17	17	17
04	68	FL SCH DEAF/BLI	Combined	20	1.8	35	15	20	10	0	10	5	0	0	0	0	15	15	15
04	72	FAU HENDERSON	Expository	34	3.3	0	0	3	3	47	24	21	3	0	0	0	94	47	71
04	72	FAU HENDERSON	Narrative	36	3.7	0	3	6	8	14	22	31	3	6	3	6	83	69	76
04	72	FAU HENDERSON	Combined	70	3.5	0	1	4	6	30	23	26	3	3	1	3	89	59	74
04	73	FSU SCH	Expository	97	3.7	0	0	2	3	20	25	34	11	4	1	0	95	75	85
04	73	FSU SCH	Narrative	88	3.8	0	0	5	6	10	26	33	10	9	0	1	90	80	85
04	73	FSU SCH	Combined	185	3.7	0	0	3	4	15	25	34	11	6	1	1	92	77	85
04	74	FAMU SCH	Expository	17	3.7	0	0	0	0	35	12	35	18	0	0	0	100	65	82
04	74	FAMU SCH	Narrative	18	3.4	0	0	0	22	39	0	17	17	6	0	0	78	39	58
04	74	FAMU SCH	Combined	35	3.5	0	0	0	11	37	6	26	17	3	0	0	89	51	70
04	75	UF PK YONGE	Expository	30	3.9	0	0	3	3	7	20	43	20	3	0	0	93	87	90
04	75	UF PK YONGE	Narrative	30	3.6	0	0	3	3	20	27	40	7	0	0	0	93	73	83
04	75	UF PK YONGE	Combined	60	3.7	0	0	3	3	13	23	42	13	2	0	0	93	80	87
04	78	FLORIDA CONNECT	Expository	9															
04	78	FLORIDA CONNECT	Narrative	9															
04	78	FLORIDA CONNECT	Combined	18	3.2	0	0	11	11	33	22	22	0	0	0	0	78	44	61
04	79	FLORIDA VIRTUAL	Expository	16	3.3	0	0	13	0	44	13	31	0	0	0	0	88	44	66
04	79	FLORIDA VIRTUAL	Narrative	9															
04	79	FLORIDA VIRTUAL	Combined	25	3.1	0	0	8	4	44	8	32	0	0	0	0	84	40	62

Note: *No data were reported when fewer than 10 students were tested or all students received the same score.*

Source: *Florida Department of Education, Office of Assessment and School Performance, May 2005*

FLORIDA COMPREHENSIVE ASSESSMENT TEST (FCAT) 2005

WRITING - Grade 8

Grade	District Number	District Name	Type of Writing	Number of Students	Mean Score	Percent Earning Each Score Point											Percent 3 or Above	Percent 3.5 or Above	Mean of Percent 3 and Above and Percent 3.5 and Above
						1	1.5	2	2.5	3	3.5	4	4.5	5	5.5	6			
08	00	STATEWIDE AVERAGE	Expository	100,304	3.9	1	1	2	3	16	18	29	16	9	4	2	93	78	85
08	00	STATEWIDE AVERAGE	Persuasive	100,153	3.7	1	1	3	4	15	19	33	13	7	3	1	90	75	82
08	00	STATEWIDE AVERAGE	Combined	200,457	3.8	1	1	2	4	16	18	31	14	8	3	1	92	76	84
08	01	ALACHUA	Expository	1,075	3.9	1	1	3	3	15	16	24	16	11	5	3	92	76	84
08	01	ALACHUA	Persuasive	1,073	3.7	1	2	4	5	15	19	31	11	7	3	2	88	72	80
08	01	ALACHUA	Combined	2,148	3.8	1	2	3	4	15	18	28	14	9	4	3	90	74	82
08	02	BAKER	Expository	181	3.6	1	1	4	6	22	25	20	12	6	3	0	88	66	77
08	02	BAKER	Persuasive	178	3.6	1	1	3	5	21	26	31	8	4	1	0	90	70	80
08	02	BAKER	Combined	359	3.6	1	1	4	5	21	26	26	10	5	2	0	89	68	78
08	03	BAY	Expository	1,015	3.8	0	0	1	2	18	21	35	13	6	2	0	96	77	87
08	03	BAY	Persuasive	1,004	3.7	0	0	2	4	21	21	33	11	6	2	0	93	72	83
08	03	BAY	Combined	2,019	3.8	0	0	2	3	19	21	34	12	6	2	0	94	75	85
08	04	BRADFORD	Expository	154	3.5	1	3	2	3	28	19	33	6	4	1	0	91	63	77
08	04	BRADFORD	Persuasive	145	3.4	3	1	1	8	22	23	30	8	2	0	0	86	63	74
08	04	BRADFORD	Combined	299	3.5	2	2	2	5	25	21	32	7	3	0	0	88	63	76
08	05	BREVARD	Expository	2,859	3.9	1	1	2	2	15	17	29	17	9	5	2	95	80	87
08	05	BREVARD	Persuasive	2,884	3.8	1	1	2	3	15	18	36	13	6	3	2	93	78	85
08	05	BREVARD	Combined	5,743	3.9	1	1	2	3	15	17	33	15	8	4	2	94	79	86
08	06	BROWARD	Expository	10,453	4	1	1	1	3	13	16	30	17	11	5	2	95	82	88
08	06	BROWARD	Persuasive	10,415	3.9	1	1	2	3	13	17	33	15	9	4	2	93	80	86
08	06	BROWARD	Combined	20,868	3.9	1	1	1	3	13	17	32	16	10	4	2	94	81	87
08	07	CALHOUN	Expository	86	3.6	2	1	2	6	26	19	21	10	8	3	1	88	63	76
08	07	CALHOUN	Persuasive	83	3.9	0	0	1	6	11	17	43	13	6	1	1	93	82	87
08	07	CALHOUN	Combined	169	3.7	1	1	2	6	18	18	32	12	7	2	1	91	72	81
08	08	CHARLOTTE	Expository	719	4.3	1	1	1	2	9	13	22	19	19	9	5	95	87	91
08	08	CHARLOTTE	Persuasive	723	4	2	1	4	4	11	15	24	19	12	7	2	90	79	85
08	08	CHARLOTTE	Combined	1,442	4.1	1	1	2	3	10	14	23	19	15	8	4	93	83	88
08	09	CITRUS	Expository	642	3.7	2	1	3	5	19	21	23	15	7	3	1	89	70	80
08	09	CITRUS	Persuasive	646	3.5	1	2	4	9	20	19	29	11	4	1	1	84	65	75
08	09	CITRUS	Combined	1,288	3.6	1	1	4	7	19	20	26	13	6	2	1	87	67	77
08	10	CLAY	Expository	1,296	3.8	1	0	2	3	20	19	27	15	8	3	2	93	74	84
08	10	CLAY	Persuasive	1,309	3.8	1	1	3	4	17	21	30	12	7	3	1	92	74	83
08	10	CLAY	Combined	2,605	3.8	1	1	3	4	18	20	28	13	7	3	1	92	74	83
08	11	COLLIER	Expository	1,611	3.8	1	1	1	3	16	18	32	16	8	3	1	93	77	85
08	11	COLLIER	Persuasive	1,582	3.7	1	1	2	5	16	19	32	13	6	2	1	90	74	82
08	11	COLLIER	Combined	3,193	3.8	1	1	2	4	16	18	32	15	7	3	1	92	75	83
08	12	COLUMBIA	Expository	377	3.4	1	1	3	6	33	21	21	7	4	2	0	88	55	72
08	12	COLUMBIA	Persuasive	377	3.4	2	1	8	10	22	19	23	9	4	1	0	78	56	67
08	12	COLUMBIA	Combined	754	3.4	2	1	6	8	28	20	22	8	4	1	0	83	55	69
08	13	DADE	Expository	14,319	3.7	1	1	2	3	17	19	30	15	7	2	1	91	75	83
08	13	DADE	Persuasive	14,221	3.6	2	2	3	5	17	20	33	11	5	2	1	88	71	80
08	13	DADE	Combined	28,540	3.7	1	1	3	4	17	19	32	13	6	2	1	90	73	81
08	14	DESOTO	Expository	174	3.5	2	1	2	5	22	23	28	10	3	3	0	89	67	78
08	14	DESOTO	Persuasive	164	3.4	4	2	4	8	14	18	36	10	1	1	0	80	66	73
08	14	DESOTO	Combined	338	3.5	3	1	3	7	18	21	32	10	2	2	0	85	67	76
08	15	DIXIE	Expository	80	4	0	1	0	3	15	16	33	20	9	3	1	96	81	89
08	15	DIXIE	Persuasive	73	3.6	0	1	1	8	22	26	27	8	4	1	0	89	67	78
08	15	DIXIE	Combined	153	3.8	0	1	1	5	18	21	30	14	7	2	1	93	75	84
08	16	DUVAL	Expository	4,554	3.7	1	1	2	3	20	21	29	13	7	3	1	93	73	83
08	16	DUVAL	Persuasive	4,542	3.6	1	1	3	5	18	21	35	9	5	2	1	90	72	81
08	16	DUVAL	Combined	9,096	3.7	1	1	2	4	19	21	32	11	6	2	1	92	72	82
08	17	ESCAMBIA	Expository	1,689	3.7	1	1	2	2	18	21	33	13	6	2	0	94	76	85
08	17	ESCAMBIA	Persuasive	1,701	3.6	2	0	4	6	18	22	31	11	4	2	1	88	70	79
08	17	ESCAMBIA	Combined	3,390	3.7	1	1	3	4	18	22	32	12	5	2	0	91	73	82
08	18	FLAGLER	Expository	409	3.9	0	1	1	3	18	19	27	15	10	3	1	94	76	85
08	18	FLAGLER	Persuasive	408	3.7	0	1	3	5	15	20	34	10	7	3	0	90	75	82
08	18	FLAGLER	Combined	817	3.8	0	1	2	4	17	20	31	13	8	3	1	92	76	84
08	19	FRANKLIN	Expository	49	3.5	2	2	6	4	22	18	33	10	2	0	0	86	63	74
08	19	FRANKLIN	Persuasive	46	3.3	4	0	13	13	20	11	20	13	2	2	2	70	50	60
08	19	FRANKLIN	Combined	95	3.4	3	1	9	8	21	15	26	12	2	1	1	78	57	67
08	20	GADSDEN	Expository	233	3.4	1	3	3	3	24	25	30	8	1	0	0	89	64	77
08	20	GADSDEN	Persuasive	222	3.4	3	1	5	4	23	26	31	6	1	0	0	86	64	75
08	20	GADSDEN	Combined	455	3.4	2	2	4	4	24	25	30	7	1	0	0	87	64	76
08	21	GILCHRIST	Expository	97	3.5	1	1	1	7	33	20	20	9	6	2	0	90	57	73
08	21	GILCHRIST	Persuasive	103	3.4	2	1	4	7	25	27	23	4	6	1	0	86	61	74

FLORIDA COMPREHENSIVE ASSESSMENT TEST (FCAT) 2005

WRITING - Grade 8 - *continued*

Grade	District Number	District Name	Type of Writing	Number of Students	Mean Score	Percent Earning Each Score Point											Percent 3 or Above	Percent 3.5 or Above	Mean of Percent 3 and Above and Percent 3.5 and Above
						1	1.5	2	2.5	3	3.5	4	4.5	5	5.5	6			
08	00	STATEWIDE AVERAGE	Expository	100,304	3.9	1	1	2	3	16	18	29	16	9	4	2	93	78	85
08	00	STATEWIDE AVERAGE	Persuasive	100,153	3.7	1	1	3	4	15	19	33	13	7	3	1	90	75	82
08	00	STATEWIDE AVERAGE	Combined	200,457	3.8	1	1	2	4	16	18	31	14	8	3	1	92	76	84
08	21	GILCHRIST	Combined	200	3.5	2	1	3	7	29	24	22	7	6	2	0	88	59	74
08	22	GLADES	Expository	55	3.6	2	0	5	4	20	22	25	11	11	0	0	89	69	79
08	22	GLADES	Persuasive	47	3.4	0	0	11	11	26	13	28	9	2	2	0	79	53	66
08	22	GLADES	Combined	102	3.5	1	0	8	7	23	18	26	10	7	1	0	84	62	73
08	23	GULF	Expository	97	3.6	2	2	2	4	23	16	28	14	6	2	0	90	67	78
08	23	GULF	Persuasive	105	3.5	1	1	6	8	26	16	19	18	4	1	1	85	59	72
08	23	GULF	Combined	202	3.6	1	1	4	6	24	16	23	16	5	1	0	87	63	75
08	24	HAMILTON	Expository	68	3.4	4	3	3	6	18	24	31	10	1	0	0	84	66	75
08	24	HAMILTON	Persuasive	74	3.2	3	4	8	7	23	24	26	4	1	0	0	78	55	67
08	24	HAMILTON	Combined	142	3.3	4	4	6	6	20	24	28	7	1	0	0	81	61	71
08	25	HARDEE	Expository	190	3.8	2	2	6	2	15	18	21	14	12	6	2	88	73	80
08	25	HARDEE	Persuasive	197	3.6	3	4	3	6	13	20	38	7	5	1	2	85	72	78
08	25	HARDEE	Combined	387	3.7	2	3	4	4	14	19	29	10	8	3	2	86	72	79
08	26	HENDRY	Expository	301	3.5	2	2	5	7	23	19	21	12	5	2	2	83	61	72
08	26	HENDRY	Persuasive	290	3.2	5	4	3	11	26	20	22	5	3	0	0	76	50	63
08	26	HENDRY	Combined	591	3.4	4	3	4	9	24	19	21	9	4	1	1	80	56	68
08	27	HERNANDO	Expository	822	3.8	1	1	2	3	19	20	24	16	7	4	1	92	73	82
08	27	HERNANDO	Persuasive	824	3.6	1	2	4	4	18	23	31	11	5	2	0	89	71	80
08	27	HERNANDO	Combined	1,646	3.7	1	2	3	4	18	21	27	13	6	3	1	90	72	81
08	28	HIGHLANDS	Expository	458	3.7	1	1	2	4	20	22	24	15	7	4	1	92	72	82
08	28	HIGHLANDS	Persuasive	465	3.7	1	1	3	4	16	25	29	11	6	2	1	91	75	83
08	28	HIGHLANDS	Combined	923	3.7	1	1	2	4	18	23	27	13	7	3	1	91	73	82
08	29	HILLSBOROUGH	Expository	6,957	4.2	0	0	1	2	8	13	25	21	17	8	4	96	88	92
08	29	HILLSBOROUGH	Persuasive	6,938	4	1	1	2	4	10	15	32	18	10	5	3	93	83	88
08	29	HILLSBOROUGH	Combined	13,895	4.1	1	1	1	3	9	14	28	19	13	7	4	95	85	90
08	30	HOLMES	Expository	134	3.7	1	2	1	4	21	20	23	14	6	4	2	90	69	80
08	30	HOLMES	Persuasive	136	3.4	1	4	5	9	24	21	19	11	7	0	0	81	57	69
08	30	HOLMES	Combined	270	3.6	1	3	3	7	22	20	21	13	6	2	1	86	63	74
08	31	INDIAN RIVER	Expository	619	3.9	1	1	4	4	13	20	25	13	11	5	2	90	77	84
08	31	INDIAN RIVER	Persuasive	623	3.8	1	1	2	6	15	20	28	14	7	4	1	89	74	82
08	31	INDIAN RIVER	Combined	1,242	3.8	1	1	3	5	14	20	27	14	9	4	2	90	76	83
08	32	JACKSON	Expository	266	3.6	1	2	3	2	24	27	24	11	5	2	1	93	69	81
08	32	JACKSON	Persuasive	272	3.5	1	1	3	4	25	23	31	9	1	0	1	92	66	79
08	32	JACKSON	Combined	538	3.6	1	1	3	3	25	25	28	10	3	1	1	92	68	80
08	33	JEFFERSON	Expository	43	3.6	0	2	5	2	26	12	33	9	7	0	2	88	63	76
08	33	JEFFERSON	Persuasive	41	3.2	5	2	5	7	32	27	17	2	2	0	0	80	49	65
08	33	JEFFERSON	Combined	84	3.4	2	2	5	5	29	19	25	6	5	0	1	85	56	70
08	34	LAFAYETTE	Expository	42	3.2	0	0	7	7	38	19	19	5	2	0	0	83	45	64
08	34	LAFAYETTE	Persuasive	39	3	3	0	8	23	28	23	13	3	0	0	0	67	38	53
08	34	LAFAYETTE	Combined	81	3.1	1	0	7	15	33	21	16	4	1	0	0	75	42	59
08	35	LAKE	Expository	1,314	3.7	1	1	1	3	20	21	30	13	5	2	1	93	73	83
08	35	LAKE	Persuasive	1,319	3.6	2	1	3	4	20	20	35	10	4	1	0	90	70	80
08	35	LAKE	Combined	2,633	3.7	1	1	2	3	20	21	33	11	5	2	0	92	71	81
08	36	LEE	Expository	2,638	3.9	1	1	2	3	16	17	29	17	10	4	2	94	78	86
08	36	LEE	Persuasive	2,631	3.7	1	1	3	5	15	18	36	11	6	3	1	90	75	82
08	36	LEE	Combined	5,269	3.8	1	1	2	4	15	18	33	14	8	3	1	92	77	84
08	37	LEON	Expository	1,059	4.1	0	1	0	1	11	15	36	19	10	5	2	97	86	92
08	37	LEON	Persuasive	1,073	4	1	1	1	2	11	17	35	15	10	5	3	95	84	89
08	37	LEON	Combined	2,132	4	1	1	1	2	11	16	35	17	10	5	2	96	85	90
08	38	LEVY	Expository	250	3.9	1	0	2	3	17	22	24	17	8	4	2	94	77	85
08	38	LEVY	Persuasive	254	3.6	2	1	2	7	19	26	27	9	6	1	0	88	70	79
08	38	LEVY	Combined	504	3.7	1	1	2	5	18	24	26	13	7	2	1	91	73	82
08	39	LIBERTY	Expository	38	4.2	3	3	0	0	5	8	32	24	18	3	5	95	89	92
08	39	LIBERTY	Persuasive	39	4	0	3	0	3	5	23	33	23	5	3	3	95	90	92
08	39	LIBERTY	Combined	77	4.1	1	3	0	1	5	16	32	23	12	3	4	95	90	92
08	40	MADISON	Expository	108	3.4	1	4	5	6	27	27	18	6	1	6	1	85	58	72
08	40	MADISON	Persuasive	100	3.2	2	7	6	12	19	24	9	13	4	2	0	71	52	62
08	40	MADISON	Combined	208	3.3	1	5	5	9	23	25	13	10	2	4	0	78	55	67
08	41	MANATEE	Expository	1,483	3.8	1	1	2	3	17	18	32	15	7	2	1	92	75	84
08	41	MANATEE	Persuasive	1,492	3.6	2	1	2	5	17	21	34	11	5	1	1	90	72	81
08	41	MANATEE	Combined	2,975	3.7	1	1	2	4	17	19	33	13	6	2	1	91	74	82
08	42	MARION	Expository	1,626	3.8	2	1	2	4	19	19	26	15	7	4	1	92	72	82

FLORIDA COMPREHENSIVE ASSESSMENT TEST (FCAT) 2005

WRITING - Grade 8 - *continued*

Grade	District Number	District Name	Type of Writing	Number of Students	Mean Score	Percent Earning Each Score Point											Percent 3 or Above	Percent 3.5 or Above	Mean of Percent 3 and Above and Percent 3.5 and Above
						1	1.5	2	2.5	3	3.5	4	4.5	5	5.5	6			
08	00	STATEWIDE AVERAGE	Expository	100,304	3.9	1	1	2	3	16	18	29	16	9	4	2	93	78	85
08	00	STATEWIDE AVERAGE	Persuasive	100,153	3.7	1	1	3	4	15	19	33	13	7	3	1	90	75	82
08	00	STATEWIDE AVERAGE	Combined	200,457	3.8	1	1	2	4	16	18	31	14	8	3	1	92	76	84
08	42	MARION	Persuasive	1,610	3.6	2	1	2	5	19	20	32	10	4	2	1	88	69	79
08	42	MARION	Combined	3,236	3.7	2	1	2	4	19	19	29	13	6	3	1	90	71	80
08	43	MARTIN	Expository	708	3.9	0	0	2	2	18	18	25	16	12	5	1	95	77	86
08	43	MARTIN	Persuasive	710	3.9	1	1	3	6	13	17	26	15	10	5	3	90	77	83
08	43	MARTIN	Combined	1,418	3.9	1	1	2	4	15	18	25	15	11	5	2	92	77	85
08	44	MONROE	Expository	345	3.7	1	1	4	4	20	25	22	10	8	3	1	90	70	80
08	44	MONROE	Persuasive	337	3.7	1	1	3	5	16	21	34	10	4	2	1	90	73	81
08	44	MONROE	Combined	682	3.7	1	1	4	4	18	23	28	10	6	3	1	90	72	81
08	45	NASSAU	Expository	448	4.2	0	0	1	2	14	17	21	18	13	10	4	97	83	90
08	45	NASSAU	Persuasive	435	4.1	0	1	2	3	10	13	33	19	11	4	4	94	84	89
08	45	NASSAU	Combined	883	4.1	0	1	1	2	12	15	27	18	12	7	4	96	84	90
08	46	OKALOOSA	Expository	1,135	4.2	0	0	0	1	8	16	27	22	14	8	3	98	90	94
08	46	OKALOOSA	Persuasive	1,122	4	0	0	1	1	10	19	35	18	8	5	2	97	87	92
08	46	OKALOOSA	Combined	2,257	4.1	0	0	1	1	9	17	31	20	11	6	3	98	88	93
08	47	OKEECHOBEE	Expository	259	3.9	1	1	2	2	20	16	23	13	12	7	3	93	73	83
08	47	OKEECHOBEE	Persuasive	265	3.6	1	2	4	4	17	20	31	12	5	3	1	88	71	80
08	47	OKEECHOBEE	Combined	524	3.8	1	1	3	3	18	18	27	12	8	5	2	90	72	81
08	48	ORANGE	Expository	6,516	3.8	1	1	2	4	17	20	29	13	7	3	1	92	74	83
08	48	ORANGE	Persuasive	6,537	3.7	2	1	3	4	17	20	32	12	6	2	1	90	72	81
08	48	ORANGE	Combined	13,053	3.7	1	1	2	4	17	20	31	13	6	3	1	91	73	82
08	49	OSCEOLA	Expository	1,829	3.7	2	1	3	3	21	21	25	11	6	4	1	90	69	80
08	49	OSCEOLA	Persuasive	1,821	3.5	2	1	4	6	20	18	29	10	4	2	1	85	65	75
08	49	OSCEOLA	Combined	3,650	3.6	2	1	4	5	21	20	27	11	5	3	1	88	67	77
08	50	PALM BEACH	Expository	6,549	3.9	1	1	2	2	15	18	31	16	9	3	2	94	79	87
08	50	PALM BEACH	Persuasive	6,549	3.8	1	1	2	3	15	19	34	13	6	3	1	91	77	84
08	50	PALM BEACH	Combined	13,098	3.8	1	1	2	3	15	19	33	14	8	3	1	93	78	85
08	51	PASCO	Expository	2,333	3.9	1	1	2	3	17	19	27	15	9	4	1	93	76	85
08	51	PASCO	Persuasive	2,356	3.6	1	1	3	6	19	20	31	11	5	2	1	89	70	79
08	51	PASCO	Combined	4,689	3.7	1	1	2	4	18	20	29	13	7	3	1	91	73	82
08	52	PINELLAS	Expository	4,354	4.1	1	0	1	2	11	14	30	17	14	5	3	96	84	90
08	52	PINELLAS	Persuasive	4,336	3.9	1	1	2	4	13	18	33	15	8	4	2	92	79	86
08	52	PINELLAS	Combined	8,690	4	1	1	2	3	12	16	31	16	11	5	3	94	82	88
08	53	POLK	Expository	3,150	3.8	2	1	2	3	15	18	30	16	9	3	1	92	77	85
08	53	POLK	Persuasive	3,159	3.7	2	2	3	4	14	19	37	11	5	2	1	89	75	82
08	53	POLK	Combined	6,309	3.8	2	1	3	3	14	18	34	14	7	3	1	90	76	83
08	54	PUTNAM	Expository	476	3.7	1	1	3	4	21	23	23	14	7	3	1	91	70	80
08	54	PUTNAM	Persuasive	497	3.4	1	2	4	11	22	20	23	10	5	0	1	81	59	70
08	54	PUTNAM	Combined	973	3.6	1	2	3	7	22	22	23	12	6	2	1	86	64	75
08	55	ST. JOHNS	Expository	941	4	0	0	2	3	13	20	24	19	11	6	3	95	82	89
08	55	ST. JOHNS	Persuasive	950	3.9	1	1	2	5	12	17	29	16	10	3	4	91	79	85
08	55	ST. JOHNS	Combined	1,891	4	1	0	2	4	12	18	27	17	10	5	3	93	81	87
08	56	ST. LUCIE	Expository	1,362	3.8	1	1	3	3	18	20	28	15	8	2	1	92	74	83
08	56	ST. LUCIE	Persuasive	1,380	3.6	1	1	3	6	19	21	34	9	4	1	0	89	70	80
08	56	ST. LUCIE	Combined	2,742	3.7	1	1	3	4	19	21	31	12	6	1	1	91	72	81
08	57	SANTA ROSA	Expository	1,012	4.1	0	1	1	2	10	13	35	20	12	4	1	96	86	91
08	57	SANTA ROSA	Persuasive	990	3.9	1	1	1	3	12	17	35	17	9	4	1	95	82	88
08	57	SANTA ROSA	Combined	2,002	4	0	1	1	2	11	15	35	18	11	4	1	95	84	90
08	58	SARASOTA	Expository	1,549	3.9	1	0	2	3	16	17	32	15	9	4	1	94	78	86
08	58	SARASOTA	Persuasive	1,584	3.7	1	1	4	4	17	19	33	13	5	2	1	90	73	82
08	58	SARASOTA	Combined	3,133	3.8	1	1	3	4	17	18	32	14	7	3	1	92	76	84
08	59	SEMINOLE	Expository	2,617	4	1	0	1	3	16	17	26	17	10	5	3	95	78	86
08	59	SEMINOLE	Persuasive	2,621	3.8	1	1	2	4	15	18	31	14	9	3	2	91	77	84
08	59	SEMINOLE	Combined	5,238	3.9	1	1	2	4	15	17	29	15	9	4	2	93	78	85
08	60	SUMTER	Expository	286	3.6	1	0	5	6	20	20	22	14	8	2	0	87	66	77
08	60	SUMTER	Persuasive	285	3.5	4	2	4	7	15	21	29	10	5	1	1	82	67	75
08	60	SUMTER	Combined	571	3.6	2	1	5	7	18	21	25	12	6	2	1	84	67	76
08	61	SUWANNEE	Expository	217	3.5	1	0	3	8	27	23	15	12	6	2	1	86	59	73
08	61	SUWANNEE	Persuasive	217	3.4	1	3	6	9	22	24	17	7	10	1	0	81	59	70
08	61	SUWANNEE	Combined	434	3.5	1	2	4	9	24	23	16	10	8	2	1	83	59	71
08	62	TAYLOR	Expository	123	3.6	0	2	2	3	24	21	30	12	3	2	0	93	68	80
08	62	TAYLOR	Persuasive	111	3.5	1	1	5	7	18	25	33	5	2	1	0	85	67	76
08	62	TAYLOR	Combined	234	3.5	0	1	4	5	21	23	32	9	3	1	0	89	68	78

FLORIDA COMPREHENSIVE ASSESSMENT TEST (FCAT) 2005

WRITING - Grade 8 - *continued*

Grade	District Number	District Name	Type of Writing	Number of Students	Mean Score	Percent Earning Each Score Point											Percent 3 or Above	Percent 3.5 or Above	Mean of Percent 3 and Above and Percent 3.5 and Above
						1	1.5	2	2.5	3	3.5	4	4.5	5	5.5	6			
08	00	STATEWIDE AVERAGE	Expository	100,304	3.9	1	1	2	3	16	18	29	16	9	4	2	93	78	85
08	00	STATEWIDE AVERAGE	Persuasive	100,153	3.7	1	1	3	4	15	19	33	13	7	3	1	90	75	82
08	00	STATEWIDE AVERAGE	Combined	200,457	3.8	1	1	2	4	16	18	31	14	8	3	1	92	76	84
08	63	UNION	Expository	79	3.9	3	1	0	1	11	23	34	11	13	3	0	95	84	89
08	63	UNION	Persuasive	78	3.9	3	0	1	3	14	18	36	14	5	5	1	94	79	87
08	63	UNION	Combined	157	3.9	3	1	1	2	13	20	35	13	9	4	1	94	82	88
08	64	VOLUSIA	Expository	2,554	3.9	1	1	2	3	12	15	29	17	11	5	2	92	80	86
08	64	VOLUSIA	Persuasive	2,540	3.8	2	2	3	5	13	17	33	14	7	3	1	89	75	82
08	64	VOLUSIA	Combined	5,094	3.9	2	1	3	4	13	16	31	15	9	4	2	90	78	84
08	65	WAKULLA	Expository	181	3.9	0	1	3	3	14	16	33	13	9	6	2	93	78	86
08	65	WAKULLA	Persuasive	177	3.9	0	1	4	4	15	15	34	14	9	5	0	92	77	84
08	65	WAKULLA	Combined	358	3.9	0	1	4	4	15	15	34	13	9	6	1	92	78	85
08	66	WALTON	Expository	264	3.9	1	1	2	3	15	16	29	16	11	5	1	94	79	86
08	66	WALTON	Persuasive	270	3.9	1	0	2	4	10	23	34	14	8	2	3	93	84	89
08	66	WALTON	Combined	534	3.9	1	0	2	3	12	19	32	15	9	4	2	93	81	87
08	67	WASHINGTON	Expository	139	3.8	2	1	1	1	14	27	24	15	8	4	1	94	79	86
08	67	WASHINGTON	Persuasive	135	3.7	1	1	3	2	18	23	31	16	4	0	0	92	74	83
08	67	WASHINGTON	Combined	274	3.7	2	1	2	2	16	25	28	16	6	2	0	93	77	85
08	68	FL SCH DEAF/BLI	Expository	39	2.5	8	13	13	3	23	13	8	5	5	0	0	54	31	42
08	68	FL SCH DEAF/BLI	Persuasive	23	2	26	17	22	17	4	9	4	0	0	0	0	17	13	15
08	68	FL SCH DEAF/BLI	Combined	62	2.3	15	15	16	8	16	11	6	3	3	0	0	40	24	32
08	72	FAU HENDERSON	Expository	26	4.1	0	0	0	0	12	15	38	23	4	8	0	100	88	94
08	72	FAU HENDERSON	Persuasive	25	4.2	0	0	0	0	8	24	20	20	28	0	0	100	92	96
08	72	FAU HENDERSON	Combined	51	4.1	0	0	0	0	10	20	29	22	16	4	0	100	90	95
08	73	FSU SCH	Expository	81	4	0	0	0	0	16	23	21	26	7	4	2	100	84	92
08	73	FSU SCH	Persuasive	81	4	0	0	1	1	15	19	33	20	6	2	2	98	83	90
08	73	FSU SCH	Combined	162	4	0	0	1	1	15	21	27	23	7	3	2	99	83	91
08	74	FAMU SCH	Expository	20	3.6	0	0	0	0	30	30	35	5	0	0	0	100	70	85
08	74	FAMU SCH	Persuasive	20	3.7	5	0	0	0	20	5	60	5	5	0	0	95	75	85
08	74	FAMU SCH	Combined	40	3.6	3	0	0	0	25	18	48	5	3	0	0	98	73	85
08	75	UF PK YONGE	Expository	57	4.2	0	0	0	0	9	11	28	37	16	0	0	100	91	96
08	75	UF PK YONGE	Persuasive	57	4	0	0	0	0	9	16	47	19	9	0	0	100	91	96
08	75	UF PK YONGE	Combined	114	4.1	0	0	0	0	9	13	38	28	12	0	0	100	91	96
08	78	FLORIDA CONNECT	Expository	4															
08	78	FLORIDA CONNECT	Persuasive	7															
08	78	FLORIDA CONNECT	Combined	11	3.5	0	0	9	0	9	18	18	27	9	0	0	82	73	77
08	79	FLORIDA VIRTUAL	Expository	11	4	0	0	0	9	18	18	9	18	18	9	0	91	73	82
08	79	FLORIDA VIRTUAL	Persuasive	10	3.6	0	0	0	0	20	50	30	0	0	0	0	100	80	90
08	79	FLORIDA VIRTUAL	Combined	21	3.8	0	0	0	5	19	33	19	10	10	5	0	95	76	86

Note: *No data were reported when fewer than 10 students were tested or all students received the same score.*

Source: *Florida Department of Education, Office of Assessment and School Performance, May 2005*

FLORIDA COMPREHENSIVE ASSESSMENT TEST (FCAT) 2005

WRITING - Grade 10

Grade	District Number	District Name	Type of Writing	Number of Students	Mean Score	Percent Earning Each Score Point											Percent 3 or Above	Percent 3.5 or Above	Mean of Percent 3 and Above and Percent 3.5 and Above
						1	1.5	2	2.5	3	3.5	4	4.5	5	5.5	6			
10	00	STATEWIDE AVERAGE	Expository	91710	3.7	1	1	4	6	14	19	29	14	7	3	2	88	74	81
10	00	STATEWIDE AVERAGE	Persuasive	91753	4	1	1	2	3	7	13	39	18	11	3	1	91	85	88
10	00	STATEWIDE AVERAGE	Combined	183463	3.8	1	1	3	5	10	16	34	16	9	3	1	90	79	85
10	01	ALACHUA	Expository	1120	3.9	3	1	2	5	13	18	21	15	12	6	3	88	75	82
10	01	ALACHUA	Persuasive	1141	4	2	1	3	3	7	12	34	19	12	5	1	90	83	87
10	01	ALACHUA	Combined	2261	3.9	2	1	3	4	10	15	28	17	12	6	2	89	79	84
10	02	BAKER	Expository	132	3.7	2	2	3	3	22	23	22	14	4	4	2	91	69	80
10	02	BAKER	Persuasive	140	3.9	0	0	1	6	10	16	40	20	4	0	1	92	82	87
10	02	BAKER	Combined	272	3.8	1	1	2	5	16	19	31	17	4	2	2	92	76	84
10	03	BAY	Expository	955	3.8	1	0	3	4	14	20	33	15	5	3	2	92	78	85
10	03	BAY	Persuasive	945	3.9	1	0	3	3	7	13	46	17	8	1	0	93	86	90
10	03	BAY	Combined	1,900	3.9	1	0	3	4	11	17	40	16	7	2	1	93	82	87
10	04	BRADFORD	Expository	131	3.6	2	1	2	5	18	21	32	8	5	2	1	89	70	79
10	04	BRADFORD	Persuasive	126	3.7	1	3	9	4	9	18	33	13	8	2	0	83	75	79
10	04	BRADFORD	Combined	257	3.6	1	2	5	4	14	20	32	11	7	2	0	86	72	79
10	05	BREVARD	Expository	2,760	3.9	1	0	2	3	11	20	30	15	9	5	3	93	82	87
10	05	BREVARD	Persuasive	2,794	4.1	1	1	1	2	5	10	41	21	13	4	2	96	91	94
10	05	BREVARD	Combined	5,554	4	1	0	2	3	8	15	36	18	11	4	2	94	87	91
10	06	BROWARD	Expository	9,595	3.8	1	1	3	5	13	19	31	14	7	3	2	90	77	83
10	06	BROWARD	Persuasive	9,539	4	1	1	2	3	6	12	40	19	13	3	1	93	87	90
10	06	BROWARD	Combined	19,134	3.9	1	1	3	4	10	15	35	17	10	3	1	91	82	87
10	07	CALHOUN	Expository	72	3.8	0	0	6	8	19	14	21	17	4	8	3	86	67	76
10	07	CALHOUN	Persuasive	72	4	0	0	4	6	6	18	32	18	10	6	1	90	85	88
10	07	CALHOUN	Combined	144	3.9	0	0	5	7	13	16	26	17	7	7	2	88	76	82
10	08	CHARLOTTE	Expository	691	3.7	1	1	6	9	13	20	21	13	9	4	3	83	70	77
10	08	CHARLOTTE	Persuasive	648	4	1	1	2	5	10	13	29	19	14	4	3	91	81	86
10	08	CHARLOTTE	Combined	1,339	3.9	1	1	4	7	12	17	25	16	11	4	3	87	75	81
10	09	CITRUS	Expository	551	3.7	1	1	6	10	15	21	16	13	9	5	3	82	67	75
10	09	CITRUS	Persuasive	543	3.8	1	2	4	7	12	20	27	13	7	4	2	87	75	81
10	09	CITRUS	Combined	1,094	3.7	1	1	5	8	14	21	22	13	8	5	3	84	71	78
10	10	CLAY	Expository	1,211	3.8	1	0	3	6	15	19	28	14	7	4	1	88	74	81
10	10	CLAY	Persuasive	1,178	4	1	1	2	3	7	13	38	21	11	3	1	93	86	90
10	10	CLAY	Combined	2,389	3.9	1	1	3	5	11	16	33	17	9	4	1	91	80	85
10	11	COLLIER	Expository	1,393	3.8	2	2	3	6	14	17	29	14	7	4	2	87	74	80
10	11	COLLIER	Persuasive	1,417	3.9	2	1	4	3	6	12	40	17	10	2	1	90	83	86
10	11	COLLIER	Combined	2,810	3.8	2	1	3	4	10	14	35	16	9	3	1	89	78	83
10	12	COLUMBIA	Expository	280	3.4	1	1	5	13	19	26	19	8	4	1	2	78	59	69
10	12	COLUMBIA	Persuasive	289	3.7	3	3	2	7	9	17	31	18	8	1	0	85	76	80
10	12	COLUMBIA	Combined	569	3.6	2	2	4	10	14	22	25	13	6	1	1	82	68	75
10	13	DADE	Expository	14,088	3.7	2	1	4	6	13	19	32	13	6	3	1	87	74	80
10	13	DADE	Persuasive	14,106	3.9	2	1	3	3	6	12	42	17	10	2	1	91	84	88
10	13	DADE	Combined	28,194	3.8	2	1	3	4	10	15	37	15	8	3	1	89	79	84
10	14	DESOTO	Expository	160	3.3	1	4	7	9	24	25	18	7	2	3	1	78	54	66
10	14	DESOTO	Persuasive	159	3.5	1	1	8	8	10	27	33	9	3	0	0	82	72	77
10	14	DESOTO	Combined	319	3.4	1	2	7	8	17	26	25	8	2	1	0	80	63	71
10	15	DIXIE	Expository	73	3.6	3	3	5	8	10	16	22	19	11	1	0	79	70	75
10	15	DIXIE	Persuasive	76	3.7	1	0	8	8	13	11	29	18	9	1	0	82	68	75
10	15	DIXIE	Combined	149	3.6	2	1	7	8	11	13	26	19	10	1	0	81	69	75
10	16	DUVAL	Expository	3,792	3.8	1	1	3	5	14	18	33	15	7	2	1	90	76	83
10	16	DUVAL	Persuasive	3,739	4	1	2	2	3	5	12	44	18	10	3	1	92	86	89
10	16	DUVAL	Combined	7,531	3.9	1	1	3	4	10	15	38	16	8	3	1	91	81	86
10	17	ESCAMBIA	Expository	1,405	3.9	1	1	2	4	11	15	37	15	8	4	2	91	80	85
10	17	ESCAMBIA	Persuasive	1,413	4	2	1	2	2	4	9	42	21	13	3	1	92	89	90
10	17	ESCAMBIA	Combined	2,818	4	1	1	2	3	7	12	39	18	11	3	1	91	84	88
10	18	FLAGLER	Expository	347	3.7	0	0	3	10	18	22	23	11	7	3	1	87	68	78
10	18	FLAGLER	Persuasive	340	3.8	0	1	3	5	10	19	35	14	10	2	1	91	80	85
10	18	FLAGLER	Combined	687	3.8	0	0	3	7	14	21	29	12	8	3	1	89	74	81
10	19	FRANKLIN	Expository	50	3.4	0	0	8	16	18	28	14	10	2	4	0	76	58	67
10	19	FRANKLIN	Persuasive	50	3.4	2	6	12	10	20	10	16	6	10	4	4	70	50	60
10	19	FRANKLIN	Combined	100	3.4	1	3	10	13	19	19	15	8	6	4	2	73	54	64
10	20	GADSDEN	Expository	160	3.5	2	2	4	8	19	28	20	12	3	1	0	84	64	74
10	20	GADSDEN	Persuasive	158	3.9	3	1	3	3	7	18	32	18	14	2	0	91	84	87

FLORIDA COMPREHENSIVE ASSESSMENT TEST (FCAT) 2005

WRITING - Grade 10 - *continued*

Grade	District Number	District Name	Type of Writing	Number of Students	Mean Score	Percent Earning Each Score Point: 1	1.5	2	2.5	3	3.5	4	4.5	5	5.5	6	Percent 3 or Above	Percent 3.5 or Above	Mean of Percent 3 and Above and Percent 3.5 and Above
10	00	STATEWIDE AVERAGE	Expository	91710	3.7	1	1	4	6	14	19	29	14	7	3	2	88	74	81
10	00	STATEWIDE AVERAGE	Persuasive	91753	4	1	1	2	3	7	13	39	18	11	3	1	91	85	88
10	00	STATEWIDE AVERAGE	Combined	183463	3.8	1	1	3	5	10	16	34	16	9	3	1	90	79	85
10	20	GADSDEN	Combined	318	3.7	2	1	4	5	13	23	26	15	8	2	0	87	74	81
10	21	GILCHRIST	Expository	100	3.5	1	0	5	10	21	27	21	8	7	0	0	84	63	74
10	21	GILCHRIST	Persuasive	96	3.6	1	1	7	2	14	23	33	10	5	2	0	88	74	81
10	21	GILCHRIST	Combined	196	3.5	1	1	6	6	17	25	27	9	6	1	0	86	68	77
10	22	GLADES	Expository	32	2.9	9	6	6	3	28	19	22	3	0	0	0	72	44	58
10	22	GLADES	Persuasive	33	3.6	0	3	3	3	15	24	42	9	0	0	0	91	76	83
10	22	GLADES	Combined	65	3.3	5	5	5	3	22	22	32	6	0	0	0	82	60	71
10	23	GULF	Expository	76	3.7	0	0	8	5	18	28	17	9	8	3	4	87	68	78
10	23	GULF	Persuasive	78	3.9	0	0	1	4	10	22	36	13	9	4	1	95	85	90
10	23	GULF	Combined	154	3.8	0	0	5	5	14	25	27	11	8	3	3	91	77	84
10	24	HAMILTON	Expository	46	3.5	2	2	7	11	13	13	43	4	0	0	4	78	65	72
10	24	HAMILTON	Persuasive	57	3.6	4	5	0	7	5	26	35	5	12	0	0	84	79	82
10	24	HAMILTON	Combined	103	3.6	3	4	3	9	9	20	39	5	7	0	2	82	73	77
10	25	HARDEE	Expository	169	3.6	1	1	6	12	21	17	20	12	5	4	2	80	59	70
10	25	HARDEE	Persuasive	152	3.7	1	1	4	7	14	20	27	12	8	3	3	87	72	80
10	25	HARDEE	Combined	321	3.6	1	1	5	9	18	18	23	12	6	4	2	83	65	74
10	26	HENDRY	Expository	280	3	5	3	11	13	24	22	15	5	1	0	0	66	43	54
10	26	HENDRY	Persuasive	285	3.3	6	3	7	10	14	20	26	7	5	1	1	74	60	67
10	26	HENDRY	Combined	565	3.2	5	3	9	11	19	21	21	6	3	1	0	70	51	61
10	27	HERNANDO	Expository	778	3.6	2	1	4	7	18	20	22	14	6	3	2	85	66	76
10	27	HERNANDO	Persuasive	784	3.8	1	2	4	6	10	19	33	15	7	3	1	87	77	82
10	27	HERNANDO	Combined	1,562	3.7	1	1	4	7	14	20	27	14	6	3	1	86	72	79
10	28	HIGHLANDS	Expository	371	3.6	1	2	5	9	17	22	19	13	6	5	1	83	66	74
10	28	HIGHLANDS	Persuasive	375	3.9	2	2	2	5	11	18	27	17	11	3	2	90	79	84
10	28	HIGHLANDS	Combined	746	3.8	1	2	3	7	14	20	23	15	9	4	1	87	72	79
10	29	HILLSBOROUGH	Expository	5,997	3.9	1	1	2	4	11	19	31	17	8	4	3	92	81	87
10	29	HILLSBOROUGH	Persuasive	5,956	4.2	1	1	1	2	5	11	32	24	17	5	1	95	90	92
10	29	HILLSBOROUGH	Combined	11,953	4	1	1	2	3	8	15	31	20	13	4	2	93	86	89
10	30	HOLMES	Expository	124	3.8	2	2	5	9	16	15	17	13	11	6	4	82	66	74
10	30	HOLMES	Persuasive	127	3.7	2	5	7	7	12	20	14	14	8	7	4	79	67	73
10	30	HOLMES	Combined	251	3.7	2	3	6	8	14	18	16	14	10	6	4	80	67	74
10	31	INDIAN RIVER	Expository	567	3.7	0	1	4	8	15	22	23	12	7	4	2	86	71	78
10	31	INDIAN RIVER	Persuasive	581	3.9	1	1	2	6	9	17	35	14	9	4	2	90	81	86
10	31	INDIAN RIVER	Combined	1,148	3.8	0	1	3	7	12	19	29	13	8	4	2	88	76	82
10	32	JACKSON	Expository	241	3.7	1	2	6	10	16	22	16	12	6	7	2	81	66	73
10	32	JACKSON	Persuasive	242	4	1	0	3	6	10	17	24	16	11	7	4	89	79	84
10	32	JACKSON	Combined	483	3.8	1	1	4	8	13	20	20	14	8	7	3	85	72	79
10	33	JEFFERSON	Expository	38	3.4	3	0	5	11	18	24	29	5	5	0	0	82	63	72
10	33	JEFFERSON	Persuasive	43	3.5	5	5	2	7	9	28	23	14	7	0	0	81	72	77
10	33	JEFFERSON	Combined	81	3.5	4	2	4	9	14	26	26	10	6	0	0	81	68	75
10	34	LAFAYETTE	Expository	31	3.6	0	0	6	6	6	35	29	16	0	0	0	87	81	84
10	34	LAFAYETTE	Persuasive	31	3.6	0	0	3	3	26	10	23	26	6	0	0	90	65	77
10	34	LAFAYETTE	Combined	62	3.6	0	0	5	5	16	23	26	21	3	0	0	89	73	81
10	35	LAKE	Expository	1,269	3.5	3	1	4	6	20	25	24	10	4	1	1	85	65	75
10	35	LAKE	Persuasive	1,295	3.7	3	2	3	4	10	17	38	15	6	2	0	88	78	83
10	35	LAKE	Combined	2,564	3.6	3	1	4	5	15	21	31	12	5	1	0	87	71	79
10	36	LEE	Expository	2,312	3.8	1	1	3	5	14	18	31	14	7	4	2	89	76	82
10	36	LEE	Persuasive	2,305	4	1	1	3	4	6	11	39	17	12	3	1	90	84	87
10	36	LEE	Combined	4,617	3.9	1	1	3	5	10	15	35	15	10	4	1	90	80	85
10	37	LEON	Expository	991	4.1	0	1	1	2	8	15	36	19	9	5	4	96	88	92
10	37	LEON	Persuasive	972	4.2	0	0	1	1	4	10	42	22	14	4	1	97	93	95
10	37	LEON	Combined	1,963	4.1	0	0	1	1	6	12	39	21	11	4	3	97	91	94
10	38	LEVY	Expository	202	3.6	1	0	5	6	22	26	22	8	4	2	2	88	65	76
10	38	LEVY	Persuasive	214	3.7	2	2	2	8	9	20	35	16	4	1	1	86	77	82
10	38	LEVY	Combined	416	3.6	1	1	3	7	15	23	28	13	4	2	1	87	71	79
10	39	LIBERTY	Expository	35	3.4	0	3	3	14	20	34	11	6	3	6	0	80	60	70
10	39	LIBERTY	Persuasive	33	3.7	0	3	3	0	15	21	48	3	6	0	0	94	79	86
10	39	LIBERTY	Combined	68	3.6	0	3	3	7	18	28	29	4	4	3	0	87	69	78
10	40	MADISON	Expository	111	3.1	6	4	9	14	19	14	15	5	6	3	1	63	44	54

FLORIDA COMPREHENSIVE ASSESSMENT TEST (FCAT) 2005

WRITING - Grade 10 - *continued*

Grade	District Number	District Name	Type of Writing	Number of Students	Mean Score	Percent Earning Each Score Point: 1	1.5	2	2.5	3	3.5	4	4.5	5	5.5	6	Percent 3 or Above	Percent 3.5 or Above	Mean of Percent 3 and Above and Percent 3.5 and Above
10	00	STATEWIDE AVERAGE	Expository	91710	3.7	1	1	4	6	14	19	29	14	7	3	2	88	74	81
10	00	STATEWIDE AVERAGE	Persuasive	91753	4	1	1	2	3	7	13	39	18	11	3	1	91	85	88
10	00	STATEWIDE AVERAGE	Combined	183463	3.8	1	1	3	5	10	16	34	16	9	3	1	90	79	85
10	40	MADISON	Persuasive	117	3.3	6	3	9	8	15	16	21	14	5	2	1	74	58	66
10	40	MADISON	Combined	228	3.2	6	4	9	11	17	15	18	10	6	2	1	68	51	60
10	41	MANATEE	Expository	1,367	3.6	2	1	4	7	15	18	28	13	6	3	2	85	70	77
10	41	MANATEE	Persuasive	1,374	3.8	3	2	3	3	9	14	37	16	10	2	0	89	80	84
10	41	MANATEE	Combined	2,741	3.7	2	1	4	5	12	16	32	14	8	3	1	87	75	81
10	42	MARION	Expository	1,520	3.5	2	1	6	9	19	22	20	12	6	2	1	81	62	72
10	42	MARION	Persuasive	1,497	3.7	2	1	4	5	11	16	38	15	6	2	0	88	77	82
10	42	MARION	Combined	3,017	3.6	2	1	5	7	15	19	29	13	6	2	0	84	69	77
10	43	MARTIN	Expository	631	3.9	1	0	3	6	15	19	22	15	9	7	3	90	74	82
10	43	MARTIN	Persuasive	648	4.1	0	1	2	3	8	17	29	18	13	5	3	93	85	89
10	43	MARTIN	Combined	1,279	4	1	1	2	5	12	18	25	17	11	6	3	91	80	86
10	44	MONROE	Expository	311	3.7	1	1	4	6	18	20	25	13	7	4	2	88	70	79
10	44	MONROE	Persuasive	319	3.7	1	1	6	4	11	22	30	16	6	2	1	88	77	82
10	44	MONROE	Combined	630	3.7	1	1	5	5	14	21	27	14	7	3	1	88	74	81
10	45	NASSAU	Expository	368	3.8	1	0	4	6	16	23	24	14	6	5	2	89	74	82
10	45	NASSAU	Persuasive	366	4.1	1	1	1	2	6	14	34	22	16	3	1	95	89	92
10	45	NASSAU	Combined	734	3.9	1	0	2	4	11	18	29	18	11	4	1	92	81	87
10	46	OKALOOSA	Expository	1,093	4	0	1	2	4	13	16	28	16	11	7	3	93	80	87
10	46	OKALOOSA	Persuasive	1,110	4.2	0	0	2	2	5	10	34	23	16	6	2	96	91	93
10	46	OKALOOSA	Combined	2,203	4.1	0	0	2	3	9	13	31	20	13	6	2	94	86	90
10	47	OKEECHOBEE	Expository	248	3.5	4	2	6	6	15	19	25	11	7	2	1	81	67	74
10	47	OKEECHOBEE	Persuasive	248	3.7	4	2	4	6	8	13	31	19	8	4	1	83	75	79
10	47	OKEECHOBEE	Combined	496	3.6	4	2	5	6	11	16	28	15	8	3	1	82	71	77
10	48	ORANGE	Expository	6,145	3.6	1	2	5	7	16	20	28	11	5	3	1	84	68	76
10	48	ORANGE	Persuasive	6,183	3.9	2	1	3	4	7	13	41	16	9	2	1	90	83	86
10	48	ORANGE	Combined	12,328	3.7	1	1	4	5	12	17	35	14	7	2	1	87	75	81
10	49	OSCEOLA	Expository	1,751	3.5	2	1	5	7	19	24	23	11	5	2	1	84	65	75
10	49	OSCEOLA	Persuasive	1,763	3.7	2	2	4	5	9	16	39	15	6	1	0	86	77	82
10	49	OSCEOLA	Combined	3,514	3.6	2	2	4	6	14	20	31	13	5	2	1	85	71	78
10	50	PALM BEACH	Expository	5,555	3.8	1	1	3	4	12	19	34	15	7	4	1	91	79	85
10	50	PALM BEACH	Persuasive	5,549	4	1	1	1	2	4	10	46	20	10	3	1	94	90	92
10	50	PALM BEACH	Combined	11,104	3.9	1	1	2	3	8	14	40	17	9	3	1	93	84	89
10	51	PASCO	Expository	1,864	3.6	1	1	6	6	18	21	27	11	4	2	1	85	67	76
10	51	PASCO	Persuasive	1,870	3.8	1	1	3	5	7	14	39	16	10	2	1	89	82	85
10	51	PASCO	Combined	3,734	3.7	1	1	4	6	13	18	33	14	7	2	1	87	74	81
10	52	PINELLAS	Expository	4,230	3.8	1	1	3	6	14	19	27	15	8	4	2	89	75	82
10	52	PINELLAS	Persuasive	4,233	4.1	1	1	2	3	7	13	33	20	14	5	1	94	87	90
10	52	PINELLAS	Combined	8,463	4	1	1	3	5	10	16	30	17	11	5	2	91	81	86
10	53	POLK	Expository	2,764	3.7	2	1	4	6	14	19	31	12	5	3	1	86	72	79
10	53	POLK	Persuasive	2,819	3.9	2	2	3	3	8	13	41	16	9	2	1	90	83	86
10	53	POLK	Combined	5,583	3.8	2	2	3	4	11	16	36	14	7	2	1	88	77	83
10	54	PUTNAM	Expository	383	3.4	1	2	8	14	18	22	16	13	4	2	1	75	58	67
10	54	PUTNAM	Persuasive	383	3.6	2	3	5	9	16	20	26	12	5	2	1	82	66	74
10	54	PUTNAM	Combined	766	3.5	1	2	6	11	17	21	21	12	5	2	1	79	62	70
10	55	ST. JOHNS	Expository	943	3.8	0	0	3	7	14	21	21	16	8	5	2	88	74	81
10	55	ST. JOHNS	Persuasive	922	4	1	1	2	4	10	15	32	17	12	4	2	93	83	88
10	55	ST. JOHNS	Combined	1,865	3.9	0	1	3	6	12	18	27	16	10	5	2	90	78	84
10	56	ST. LUCIE	Expository	1,171	3.6	1	1	3	7	18	26	26	10	4	2	1	87	69	78
10	56	ST. LUCIE	Persuasive	1,178	3.8	1	1	3	5	8	15	40	16	7	1	1	90	82	86
10	56	ST. LUCIE	Combined	2,349	3.7	1	1	3	6	13	21	33	13	5	2	1	88	75	82
10	57	SANTA ROSA	Expository	898	4	0	1	2	3	11	16	32	18	9	5	3	95	84	89
10	57	SANTA ROSA	Persuasive	896	4.2	1	0	1	1	3	8	46	22	13	4	0	97	93	95
10	57	SANTA ROSA	Combined	1,794	4.1	0	0	1	2	7	12	39	20	11	5	2	96	88	92
10	58	SARASOTA	Expository	1,528	3.8	1	1	4	6	15	18	31	13	6	4	2	89	74	81
10	58	SARASOTA	Persuasive	1,527	4	1	1	3	4	7	12	40	18	10	3	1	92	84	88
10	58	SARASOTA	Combined	3,055	3.9	1	1	3	5	11	15	36	15	8	3	1	90	79	85
10	59	SEMINOLE	Expository	2,534	3.9	0	1	3	4	13	20	28	17	8	5	1	92	79	86
10	59	SEMINOLE	Persuasive	2,508	4	1	1	2	4	7	13	36	21	11	4	1	93	86	89
10	59	SEMINOLE	Combined	5,042	4	0	1	2	4	10	16	32	19	10	5	1	92	82	87

FLORIDA COMPREHENSIVE ASSESSMENT TEST (FCAT) 2005

WRITING - Grade 10 - *continued*

Grade	District Number	District Name	Type of Writing	Number of Students	Mean Score	Percent Earning Each Score Point: 1	1.5	2	2.5	3	3.5	4	4.5	5	5.5	6	Percent 3 or Above	Percent 3.5 or Above	Mean of Percent 3 and Above and Percent 3.5 and Above
10	00	STATEWIDE AVERAGE	Expository	91710	3.7	1	1	4	6	14	19	29	14	7	3	2	88	74	81
10	00	STATEWIDE AVERAGE	Persuasive	91753	4	1	1	2	3	7	13	39	18	11	3	1	91	85	88
10	00	STATEWIDE AVERAGE	Combined	183463	3.8	1	1	3	5	10	16	34	16	9	3	1	90	79	85
10	60	SUMTER	Expository	243	3.6	2	1	5	8	19	17	21	12	9	3	2	83	64	73
10	60	SUMTER	Persuasive	250	3.8	2	3	2	5	9	22	26	17	8	4	1	88	79	83
10	60	SUMTER	Combined	493	3.7	2	2	4	6	14	20	24	15	9	3	2	85	71	78
10	61	SUWANNEE	Expository	178	3.5	1	2	10	11	21	16	15	10	8	4	2	75	54	65
10	61	SUWANNEE	Persuasive	180	3.6	3	2	6	8	13	21	24	11	6	3	2	81	68	74
10	61	SUWANNEE	Combined	358	3.5	2	2	8	9	17	19	20	10	7	3	2	78	61	69
10	62	TAYLOR	Expository	101	3.4	1	3	4	7	23	28	24	7	4	0	0	85	62	74
10	62	TAYLOR	Persuasive	107	3.7	1	3	6	7	6	20	37	16	5	0	1	84	79	81
10	62	TAYLOR	Combined	208	3.6	1	3	5	7	14	24	31	12	4	0	0	85	71	78
10	63	UNION	Expository	74	4.4	1	0	1	1	8	12	19	19	22	9	7	96	88	92
10	63	UNION	Persuasive	72	4.3	0	0	1	6	8	15	11	17	31	7	4	93	85	89
10	63	UNION	Combined	146	4.3	1	0	1	3	8	14	15	18	26	8	5	95	86	90
10	64	VOLUSIA	Expository	2,395	3.7	2	1	5	6	15	20	28	13	6	3	2	85	71	78
10	64	VOLUSIA	Persuasive	2,428	3.9	1	1	3	4	7	11	36	19	12	3	1	90	82	86
10	64	VOLUSIA	Combined	4,823	3.8	2	1	4	5	11	16	32	16	9	3	1	88	77	82
10	65	WAKULLA	Expository	159	3.6	2	2	6	4	21	16	31	10	6	1	0	86	65	75
10	65	WAKULLA	Persuasive	162	4.1	1	1	1	2	6	7	40	27	13	2	1	96	90	93
10	65	WAKULLA	Combined	321	3.8	1	1	3	3	14	12	36	18	10	2	0	91	77	84
10	66	WALTON	Expository	224	3.6	1	1	6	6	16	24	24	13	5	2	1	85	69	77
10	66	WALTON	Persuasive	221	3.9	1	0	3	4	10	23	29	19	10	1	1	92	83	88
10	66	WALTON	Combined	445	3.7	1	1	4	5	13	23	26	16	7	2	1	89	76	82
10	67	WASHINGTON	Expository	105	3.7	1	2	4	5	13	31	20	14	4	1	5	89	75	82
10	67	WASHINGTON	Persuasive	114	3.8	2	1	3	5	11	15	46	11	5	2	1	89	79	84
10	67	WASHINGTON	Combined	219	3.7	1	1	3	5	12	23	33	12	5	1	3	89	77	83
10	68	FL SCH DEAF/BLI	Expository	33	2.5	6	24	21	12	15	3	9	6	3	0	0	36	21	29
10	68	FL SCH DEAF/BLI	Persuasive	21	2.5	14	14	14	10	24	14	10	0	0	0	0	48	24	36
10	68	FL SCH DEAF/BLI	Combined	54	2.5	9	20	19	11	19	7	9	4	2	0	0	41	22	31
10	72	FAU HENDERSON	Expository	2															
10	72	FAU HENDERSON	Persuasive	2															
10	72	FAU HENDERSON	Combined	4															
10	73	FSU SCH	Expository	74	3.9	0	0	0	1	14	31	31	9	8	4	1	99	85	92
10	73	FSU SCH	Persuasive	72	4	0	0	0	1	8	14	47	18	10	1	0	99	90	94
10	73	FSU SCH	Combined	146	4	0	0	0	1	11	23	39	14	9	3	1	99	88	93
10	74	FAMU SCH	Expository	19	3.7	0	0	0	0	32	21	32	5	11	0	0	100	68	84
10	74	FAMU SCH	Persuasive	19	4.1	0	0	0	5	5	5	53	16	11	5	0	95	89	92
10	74	FAMU SCH	Combined	38	3.9	0	0	0	3	18	13	42	11	11	3	0	97	79	88
10	75	UF PK YONGE	Expository	60	4.1	0	0	2	0	5	20	38	23	7	5	0	98	93	96
10	75	UF PK YONGE	Persuasive	62	4.4	0	0	0	2	2	6	32	29	23	3	3	98	97	98
10	75	UF PK YONGE	Combined	122	4.2	0	0	1	1	3	13	35	26	15	4	2	98	95	97
10	79	FLORIDA VIRTUAL	Expository	2															
10	79	FLORIDA VIRTUAL	Persuasive	1															
10	79	FLORIDA VIRTUAL	Combined	3															
10	80	COMM. COLLEGES	Expository	1															
10	80	COMM. COLLEGES	Combined	1															

Note: *No data were reported when fewer than 10 students were tested or all students received the same score.*

Source: *Florida Department of Education, Office of Assessment and School Performance, May 2005*

Altamonte Springs

Place Type: City
County: Seminole
Population: 41,200

Ancestry/Race	Number	%
African American/Black:	4,400	10.68
Not Hispanic (3,795)	4,081	9.91
Hispanic (209)	319	0.77
African, sub-Saharan:	132	0.32
African	107	0.26
Ghanian	10	0.02
Nigerian	8	0.02
Other sub-Saharan African	7	0.02
Am. Ind. or Alaska Nat., not spec.	115	0.28
Albanian	38	0.09
Alsatian	23	0.06
American Indian tribes, specified:	223	0.54
Apache (3)	5	0.01
Blackfeet (5)	15	0.04
Cherokee (39)	97	0.24
Chickasaw (2)	5	0.01
Chippewa (7)	7	0.02
Choctaw (1)	5	0.01
Comanche	2	0.00
Creek (2)	4	0.01
Crow	1	0.00
Delaware	1	0.00
Iroquois (4)	15	0.04
Latin American Indians (9)	27	0.07
Lumbee (3)	3	0.01
Menominee (1)	1	0.00
Navajo (1)	3	0.01
Potawatomi (2)	2	0.00
Pueblo (2)	2	0.00
Puget Sound Salish	2	0.00
Seminole (1)	5	0.01
Shoshone	1	0.00
Sioux (1)	7	0.02
All other tribes (8)	13	0.03
American Indian tribes, not spec.	16	0.04
Arab:	472	1.14
Arab/Arabic	55	0.13
Egyptian	204	0.49
Jordanian	7	0.02
Lebanese	121	0.29
Syrian	38	0.09
Other Arab	47	0.11
Armenian	33	0.08
Asian:	1,534	3.72
Bangladeshi (7)	14	0.03
Cambodian (5)	5	0.01
Chinese, ex. Taiwanese (150)	185	0.45
Filipino (149)	227	0.55
Indian (524)	577	1.40
Indonesian	3	0.01
Japanese (32)	65	0.16
Korean (193)	209	0.51
Laotian (9)	9	0.02
Malaysian (1)	2	0.00
Pakistani (24)	30	0.07
Sri Lankan	2	0.00
Taiwanese (7)	13	0.03
Thai (13)	15	0.04
Vietnamese (56)	77	0.19
Other Asian, specified (1)	2	0.00
Other Asian, not specified (21)	99	0.24
Australian	51	0.12
Austrian	187	0.45
Basque	22	0.05
Belgian	63	0.15
Brazilian	40	0.10
British	318	0.77
Bulgarian	22	0.05
Canadian	143	0.35
Croatian	76	0.18
Czech	63	0.15
Czechoslovakian	62	0.15
Danish	137	0.33
Dutch	576	1.39
Eastern European	71	0.17
English	4,071	9.83
European	255	0.62
Finnish	46	0.11
French, except Basque	1,269	3.07
French Canadian	454	1.10
German	5,951	14.37
Greek	212	0.51
Guyanese	33	0.08
Hawaii Native/Pacific Islander:	77	0.19
Micronesian: (6)	7	0.02
Guamanian/Chamorro (1)	2	0.00
Other Micronesian (5)	5	0.01
Polynesian: (7)	31	0.08
Native Hawaiian (7)	25	0.06
Tongan	3	0.01
Other Polynesian	3	0.01
Other Pac. Isl., not spec. (2)	39	0.09
Hispanic or Latino:	6,563	15.93
Central American:	262	0.64
Costa Rican	32	0.08
Guatemalan	23	0.06
Honduran	36	0.09
Nicaraguan	50	0.12
Panamanian	70	0.17
Salvadoran	36	0.09
Other Central American	15	0.04
Cuban	467	1.13
Dominican Republic	299	0.73
Mexican	485	1.18
Puerto Rican	3,007	7.30
South American:	958	2.33
Argentinean	65	0.16
Bolivian	17	0.04
Chilean	15	0.04
Colombian	459	1.11
Ecuadorian	84	0.20
Paraguayan	1	0.00
Peruvian	115	0.28
Uruguayan	7	0.02
Venezuelan	147	0.36
Other South American	48	0.12
Other Hispanic or Latino	1,085	2.63
Hungarian	300	0.72
Iranian	38	0.09
Irish	5,163	12.47
Israeli	15	0.04
Italian	3,422	8.27
Lithuanian	139	0.34
Luxemburger	8	0.02
Macedonian	8	0.02
Maltese	11	0.03
Norwegian	406	0.98
Pennsylvania German	14	0.03
Polish	1,218	2.94
Portuguese	134	0.32
Romanian	34	0.08
Russian	585	1.41
Scandinavian	66	0.16
Scotch-Irish	794	1.92
Scottish	1,075	2.60
Serbian	10	0.02
Slavic	10	0.02
Slovak	106	0.26
Slovene	43	0.10
Swedish	536	1.29
Swiss	152	0.37
Turkish	22	0.05
Ukrainian	112	0.27
United States or American	2,052	4.96
Welsh	343	0.83
West Indian, excl. Hispanic:	872	2.11
Bahamian	56	0.14
Barbadian	12	0.03
British West Indian	25	0.06
Haitian	80	0.19
Jamaican	437	1.06
Trinidadian and Tobagonian	107	0.26
U.S. Virgin Islander	34	0.08
West Indian	121	0.29
White:	33,601	81.56
Not Hispanic (28,623)	29,243	70.98
Hispanic (4,019)	4,358	10.58
Yugoslavian	11	0.03

Apopka

Place Type: City
County: Orange
Population: 26,642

Ancestry/Race	Number	%
African American/Black:	4,403	16.53
Not Hispanic (4,033)	4,243	15.93
Hispanic (112)	160	0.60
African, sub-Saharan:	116	0.44
African	83	0.32
Ethiopian	14	0.05
South African	19	0.07
Alaska Native tribes, specified:	3	0.01
Aleut (1)	1	0.00
Eskimo (1)	1	0.00
Tlingit-Haida	1	0.00
Am. Ind. or Alaska Nat., not spec.	64	0.24
American Indian tribes, specified:	127	0.48
Apache (1)	3	0.01
Blackfeet	3	0.01
Cherokee (20)	50	0.19
Chippewa (3)	4	0.02
Choctaw	4	0.02
Creek (2)	5	0.02
Iroquois	1	0.00
Kiowa (1)	1	0.00
Latin American Indians (22)	27	0.10
Ottawa (3)	3	0.01
Pueblo (1)	1	0.00
Seminole (3)	5	0.02
Sioux	2	0.01
Ute	1	0.00
All other tribes (11)	17	0.06
American Indian tribes, not spec.	4	0.02
Arab:	51	0.20
Egyptian	19	0.07
Lebanese	32	0.12
Armenian	34	0.13
Asian:	623	2.34
Bangladeshi (6)	6	0.02
Chinese, ex. Taiwanese (60)	76	0.29
Filipino (81)	105	0.39
Indian (94)	129	0.48
Indonesian (3)	3	0.01
Japanese (11)	22	0.08
Korean (71)	75	0.28
Laotian (23)	23	0.09
Pakistani (2)	2	0.01
Sri Lankan (8)	8	0.03
Thai (11)	11	0.04
Vietnamese (123)	137	0.51
Other Asian, not specified (9)	26	0.10
Austrian	95	0.36
Basque	18	0.07
Belgian	48	0.18
Brazilian	10	0.04
British	41	0.16
Bulgarian	55	0.21
Canadian	127	0.49
Czech	30	0.12
Czechoslovakian	21	0.08
Danish	69	0.26
Dutch	508	1.95
Eastern European	16	0.06
English	2,069	7.93
European	64	0.25
Finnish	18	0.07
French, except Basque	789	3.03
French Canadian	188	0.72
German	3,294	12.63
Greek	39	0.15
Guyanese	20	0.08
Hawaii Native/Pacific Islander:	38	0.14
Micronesian: (4)	6	0.02
Guamanian/Chamorro (4)	6	0.02
Polynesian: (4)	9	0.03

Notes: 1. Figures in the "Number" column do not add up to the total population due to: a) Ancestry/Race overlap — e.g. persons can report being both White and Irish, b) persons of Hispanic origin can report being any race, c) persons reporting two ancestries are counted in both categories. 2. Numbers in parentheses indicate the number of persons reporting this ancestry/race alone, not in combination with any other ancestry/race. 3. Refer to the User's Guide in the front of the book for more detailed information.

Native Hawaiian (3)	8	0.03
Samoan (1)	1	0.00
Other Pac. Isl., not spec. (16)	23	0.09
Hispanic or Latino:	4,817	18.08
Central American:	143	0.54
Costa Rican	17	0.06
Guatemalan	25	0.09
Honduran	36	0.14
Nicaraguan	11	0.04
Panamanian	23	0.09
Salvadoran	22	0.08
Other Central American	9	0.03
Cuban	161	0.60
Dominican Republic	114	0.43
Mexican	1,883	7.07
Puerto Rican	1,704	6.40
South American:	273	1.02
Argentinean	5	0.02
Bolivian	2	0.01
Chilean	8	0.03
Colombian	132	0.50
Ecuadorian	49	0.18
Peruvian	21	0.08
Uruguayan	3	0.01
Venezuelan	44	0.17
Other South American	9	0.03
Other Hispanic or Latino	539	2.02
Hungarian	129	0.49
Icelander	8	0.03
Iranian	46	0.18
Irish	2,844	10.90
Italian	1,451	5.56
Latvian	7	0.03
Lithuanian	55	0.21
Maltese	13	0.05
Northern European	11	0.04
Norwegian	179	0.69
Pennsylvania German	17	0.07
Polish	510	1.96
Portuguese	104	0.40
Romanian	41	0.16
Russian	81	0.31
Scotch-Irish	384	1.47
Scottish	660	2.53
Slovak	52	0.20
Swedish	220	0.84
Ukrainian	70	0.27
United States or American	2,328	8.93
Welsh	163	0.62
West Indian, excl. Hispanic:	974	3.73
Barbadian	6	0.02
British West Indian	54	0.21
Haitian	143	0.55
Jamaican	417	1.60
Trinidadian and Tobagonian	174	0.67
U.S. Virgin Islander	15	0.06
West Indian	165	0.63
White:	20,261	76.05
Not Hispanic (16,780)	17,066	64.06
Hispanic (2,895)	3,195	11.99
Yugoslavian	43	0.16

Atlantic Beach

Place Type: City
County: Duval
Population: 13,368

Ancestry/Race	Number	%
African American/Black:	1,757	13.14
Not Hispanic (1,669)	1,726	12.91
Hispanic (28)	31	0.23
African, sub-Saharan:	49	0.36
African	27	0.20
Cape Verdean	7	0.05
South African	7	0.05
Other sub-Saharan African	8	0.06
Am. Ind. or Alaska Nat., not spec.	19	0.14
Alsatian	9	0.07
American Indian tribes, specified:	63	0.47
Cherokee (6)	23	0.17
Chippewa (2)	3	0.02
Comanche (1)	4	0.03
Creek (2)	3	0.02
Houma (1)	1	0.01
Iroquois (1)	4	0.03
Latin American Indians (7)	7	0.05
Lumbee	1	0.01
Navajo	1	0.01
Pueblo (2)	2	0.01
Seminole (1)	5	0.04
Sioux (1)	3	0.02
All other tribes (4)	6	0.04
American Indian tribes, not spec.	5	0.04
Arab:	110	0.82
Arab/Arabic	32	0.24
Egyptian	44	0.33
Lebanese	12	0.09
Palestinian	18	0.13
Syrian	4	0.03
Asian:	349	2.61
Cambodian	1	0.01
Chinese, ex. Taiwanese (9)	13	0.10
Filipino (175)	221	1.65
Indian (6)	10	0.07
Indonesian (1)	1	0.01
Japanese (9)	17	0.13
Korean (8)	9	0.07
Laotian (2)	2	0.01
Malaysian	8	0.06
Sri Lankan (5)	5	0.04
Taiwanese (1)	1	0.01
Thai (3)	6	0.04
Vietnamese (21)	24	0.18
Other Asian, specified (3)	3	0.02
Other Asian, not specified (25)	28	0.21
Austrian	35	0.26
Belgian	77	0.57
Brazilian	22	0.16
British	102	0.76
Canadian	45	0.33
Croatian	14	0.10
Czech	21	0.16
Czechoslovakian	11	0.08
Danish	67	0.50
Dutch	224	1.66
Eastern European	16	0.12
English	1,910	14.18
Estonian	9	0.07
European	152	1.13
Finnish	25	0.19
French, except Basque	457	3.39
French Canadian	146	1.08
German	2,122	15.75
Greek	124	0.92
Hawaii Native/Pacific Islander:	24	0.18
Micronesian: (2)	3	0.02
Guamanian/Chamorro (2)	3	0.02
Polynesian: (2)	5	0.04
Native Hawaiian	3	0.02
Samoan (2)	2	0.01
Other Pac. Isl., not spec.	16	0.12
Hispanic or Latino:	559	4.18
Central American:	30	0.22
Costa Rican	1	0.01
Honduran	2	0.01
Nicaraguan	2	0.01
Panamanian	21	0.16
Salvadoran	4	0.03
Cuban	50	0.37
Dominican Republic	4	0.03
Mexican	132	0.99
Puerto Rican	208	1.56
South American:	37	0.28
Argentinean	4	0.03
Chilean	3	0.02
Colombian	18	0.13
Ecuadorian	1	0.01
Peruvian	4	0.03
Venezuelan	2	0.01
Other South American	5	0.04
Other Hispanic or Latino	98	0.73
Hungarian	103	0.76
Iranian	8	0.06
Irish	1,796	13.33
Italian	746	5.54
Lithuanian	34	0.25
Norwegian	181	1.34
Polish	317	2.35
Portuguese	60	0.45
Romanian	30	0.22
Russian	91	0.68
Scandinavian	14	0.10
Scotch-Irish	421	3.12
Scottish	613	4.55
Serbian	8	0.06
Slovak	24	0.18
Swedish	81	0.60
Swiss	46	0.34
Turkish	34	0.25
Ukrainian	104	0.77
United States or American	1,063	7.89
Welsh	135	1.00
West Indian, excl. Hispanic:	41	0.30
British West Indian	23	0.17
Trinidadian and Tobagonian	5	0.04
Other West Indian	13	0.10
White:	11,171	83.57
Not Hispanic (10,627)	10,778	80.63
Hispanic (365)	393	2.94
Yugoslavian	9	0.07

Auburndale

Place Type: City
County: Polk
Population: 11,032

Ancestry/Race	Number	%
African American/Black:	1,453	13.17
Not Hispanic (1,339)	1,430	12.96
Hispanic (14)	23	0.21
African, sub-Saharan:	88	0.78
African	88	0.78
Am. Ind. or Alaska Nat., not spec.	24	0.22
American Indian tribes, specified:	47	0.43
Apache	2	0.02
Blackfeet	2	0.02
Cherokee (4)	17	0.15
Chickasaw (1)	1	0.01
Chippewa	1	0.01
Choctaw (2)	2	0.02
Creek	1	0.01
Houma (4)	4	0.04
Iroquois (2)	2	0.02
Latin American Indians (1)	3	0.03
Lumbee (1)	1	0.01
Pima (3)	3	0.03
Seminole	2	0.02
Sioux (2)	2	0.02
All other tribes (1)	4	0.04
American Indian tribes, not spec.	3	0.03
Arab:	24	0.21
Lebanese	16	0.14
Moroccan	8	0.07
Asian:	120	1.09
Chinese, ex. Taiwanese (5)	6	0.05
Filipino (8)	12	0.11
Indian (30)	34	0.31
Japanese (3)	7	0.06
Korean (1)	3	0.03
Pakistani (1)	1	0.01
Taiwanese (1)	3	0.03
Vietnamese (41)	41	0.37
Other Asian, specified	1	0.01
Other Asian, not specified (6)	12	0.11
Austrian	11	0.10
Belgian	10	0.09
British	11	0.10
Canadian	23	0.21
Czech	9	0.08
Danish	20	0.18
Dutch	161	1.44
English	1,144	10.20

Notes: 1. Figures in the "Number" column do not add up to the total population due to: a) Ancestry/Race overlap — e.g. persons can report being both White and Irish, b) persons of Hispanic origin can report being any race, c) persons reporting two ancestries are counted in both categories. 2. Numbers in parentheses indicate the number of persons reporting this ancestry/race alone, not in combination with any other ancestry/race. 3. Refer to the User's Guide in the front of the book for more detailed information.

European	14	0.12
French, except Basque	246	2.19
French Canadian	64	0.57
German	1,082	9.65
Greek	15	0.13
Hawaii Native/Pacific Islander:	9	0.08
Micronesian: (5)	5	0.05
Guamanian/Chamorro (5)	5	0.05
Polynesian:	2	0.02
Native Hawaiian	2	0.02
Other Pac. Isl., not spec.	2	0.02
Hispanic or Latino:	894	8.10
Central American:	10	0.09
Guatemalan	4	0.04
Panamanian	1	0.01
Salvadoran	5	0.05
Cuban	35	0.32
Dominican Republic	2	0.02
Mexican	582	5.28
Puerto Rican	130	1.18
South American:	9	0.08
Chilean	1	0.01
Ecuadorian	2	0.02
Peruvian	1	0.01
Venezuelan	5	0.05
Other Hispanic or Latino	126	1.14
Hungarian	38	0.34
Icelander	7	0.06
Irish	902	8.04
Italian	252	2.25
Lithuanian	4	0.04
Norwegian	34	0.30
Pennsylvania German	13	0.12
Polish	163	1.45
Portuguese	11	0.10
Russian	33	0.29
Scotch-Irish	172	1.53
Scottish	181	1.61
Slovak	16	0.14
Swedish	48	0.43
Swiss	46	0.41
United States or American	1,984	17.69
Welsh	25	0.22
West Indian, excl. Hispanic:	163	1.45
Haitian	102	0.91
Jamaican	61	0.54
White:	9,101	82.50
Not Hispanic (8,508)	8,611	78.05
Hispanic (442)	490	4.44
Yugoslavian	7	0.06

Aventura

Place Type: City
County: Miami-Dade
Population: 25,267

Ancestry/Race	Number	%
African American/Black:	499	1.97
Not Hispanic (395)	454	1.80
Hispanic (35)	45	0.18
African, sub-Saharan:	132	0.52
African	35	0.14
South African	88	0.35
Other sub-Saharan African	9	0.04
Am. Ind. or Alaska Nat., not spec.	32	0.13
American Indian tribes, specified:	23	0.09
Cherokee (2)	7	0.03
Chickasaw	1	0.00
Choctaw (1)	1	0.00
Iroquois (1)	1	0.00
Latin American Indians (4)	6	0.02
Potawatomi	1	0.00
Pueblo	1	0.00
Seminole	1	0.00
All other tribes (2)	4	0.02
American Indian tribes, not spec.	4	0.02
Arab:	505	2.00
Arab/Arabic	80	0.32
Egyptian	6	0.02
Iraqi	27	0.11
Lebanese	81	0.32
Moroccan	76	0.30
Palestinian	38	0.15
Syrian	182	0.72
Other Arab	15	0.06
Armenian	8	0.03
Asian:	377	1.49
Bangladeshi (4)	4	0.02
Chinese, ex. Taiwanese (110)	128	0.51
Filipino (32)	39	0.15
Indian (69)	80	0.32
Indonesian (1)	2	0.01
Japanese (30)	31	0.12
Korean (31)	33	0.13
Laotian (2)	3	0.01
Pakistani (7)	11	0.04
Taiwanese (5)	5	0.02
Thai (4)	5	0.02
Vietnamese (7)	12	0.05
Other Asian, not specified (2)	24	0.09
Australian	17	0.07
Austrian	422	1.67
Belgian	52	0.21
Brazilian	463	1.83
British	115	0.46
Bulgarian	26	0.10
Canadian	192	0.76
Croatian	26	0.10
Czech	47	0.19
Czechoslovakian	59	0.23
Danish	20	0.08
Dutch	148	0.59
Eastern European	297	1.18
English	470	1.86
European	282	1.12
Finnish	23	0.09
French, except Basque	348	1.38
French Canadian	79	0.31
German	1,189	4.71
Greek	114	0.45
Hawaii Native/Pacific Islander:	11	0.04
Micronesian: (1)	2	0.01
Guamanian/Chamorro (1)	2	0.01
Polynesian: (3)	3	0.01
Native Hawaiian (2)	2	0.01
Samoan (1)	1	0.00
Other Pac. Isl., not spec. (1)	6	0.02
Hispanic or Latino:	5,218	20.65
Central American:	260	1.03
Costa Rican	47	0.19
Guatemalan	38	0.15
Honduran	56	0.22
Nicaraguan	30	0.12
Panamanian	66	0.26
Salvadoran	15	0.06
Other Central American	8	0.03
Cuban	731	2.89
Dominican Republic	102	0.40
Mexican	325	1.29
Puerto Rican	316	1.25
South American:	2,289	9.06
Argentinean	424	1.68
Bolivian	19	0.08
Chilean	50	0.20
Colombian	1,075	4.25
Ecuadorian	87	0.34
Paraguayan	2	0.01
Peruvian	236	0.93
Uruguayan	24	0.09
Venezuelan	331	1.31
Other South American	41	0.16
Other Hispanic or Latino	1,195	4.73
Hungarian	378	1.50
Iranian	69	0.27
Irish	559	2.21
Israeli	580	2.30
Italian	1,097	4.34
Latvian	26	0.10
Lithuanian	150	0.59
Norwegian	51	0.20
Polish	1,893	7.49
Portuguese	72	0.28
Romanian	446	1.77
Russian	2,998	11.87
Scotch-Irish	93	0.37
Scottish	122	0.48
Slovak	21	0.08
Soviet Union	7	0.03
Swedish	75	0.30
Swiss	7	0.03
Turkish	140	0.55
Ukrainian	136	0.54
United States or American	2,252	8.91
Welsh	17	0.07
West Indian, excl. Hispanic:	227	0.90
Bahamian	13	0.05
Barbadian	6	0.02
British West Indian	6	0.02
Haitian	98	0.39
Jamaican	65	0.26
Trinidadian and Tobagonian	16	0.06
West Indian	23	0.09
White:	24,092	95.35
Not Hispanic (18,954)	19,206	76.01
Hispanic (4,741)	4,886	19.34

Azalea Park

Place Type: Census Designated Place
County: Orange
Population: 11,073

Ancestry/Race	Number	%
African American/Black:	866	7.82
Not Hispanic (635)	699	6.31
Hispanic (112)	167	1.51
African, sub-Saharan:	24	0.22
African	24	0.22
Alaska Native tribes, specified:	2	0.02
All other tribes (2)	2	0.02
Am. Ind. or Alaska Nat., not spec.	31	0.28
American Indian tribes, specified:	67	0.61
Apache	1	0.01
Blackfeet (2)	6	0.05
Cherokee (14)	26	0.23
Chippewa (3)	3	0.03
Choctaw	3	0.03
Iroquois	1	0.01
Latin American Indians (4)	15	0.14
Menominee	1	0.01
Ottawa	1	0.01
Pueblo (2)	2	0.02
Yaqui (1)	1	0.01
All other tribes (6)	7	0.06
American Indian tribes, not spec.	5	0.05
Arab:	189	1.70
Arab/Arabic	44	0.40
Egyptian	20	0.18
Lebanese	79	0.71
Other Arab	46	0.41
Asian:	498	4.50
Bangladeshi (1)	1	0.01
Cambodian	1	0.01
Chinese, ex. Taiwanese (32)	49	0.44
Filipino (56)	75	0.68
Indian (71)	89	0.80
Japanese (18)	25	0.23
Korean (19)	28	0.25
Laotian	1	0.01
Pakistani (23)	23	0.21
Taiwanese (1)	1	0.01
Thai (5)	6	0.05
Vietnamese (159)	174	1.57
Other Asian, not specified (3)	25	0.23
Brazilian	7	0.06
British	29	0.26
Canadian	24	0.22
Danish	14	0.13
Dutch	93	0.84
English	801	7.19
European	40	0.36
Finnish	25	0.22
French, except Basque	140	1.26
French Canadian	120	1.08

Notes: 1. Figures in the "Number" column do not add up to the total population due to: a) Ancestry/Race overlap — e.g. persons can report being both White and Irish, b) persons of Hispanic origin can report being any race, c) persons reporting two ancestries are counted in both categories. 2. Numbers in parentheses indicate the number of persons reporting this ancestry/race alone, not in combination with any other ancestry/race. 3. Refer to the User's Guide in the front of the book for more detailed information.

German	879	7.89
Greek	45	0.40
Guyanese	31	0.28
Hawaii Native/Pacific Islander:	29	0.26
Micronesian: (2)	5	0.05
Guamanian/Chamorro (2)	5	0.05
Polynesian: (6)	11	0.10
Native Hawaiian (3)	5	0.05
Samoan (1)	3	0.03
Other Polynesian (2)	3	0.03
Other Pac. Isl., not spec.	13	0.12
Hispanic or Latino:	4,315	38.97
Central American:	145	1.31
Costa Rican	15	0.14
Guatemalan	28	0.25
Honduran	39	0.35
Nicaraguan	20	0.18
Panamanian	12	0.11
Salvadoran	26	0.23
Other Central American	5	0.05
Cuban	383	3.46
Dominican Republic	186	1.68
Mexican	138	1.25
Puerto Rican	2,745	24.79
South American:	261	2.36
Argentinean	10	0.09
Chilean	13	0.12
Colombian	136	1.23
Ecuadorian	48	0.43
Peruvian	18	0.16
Uruguayan	2	0.02
Venezuelan	24	0.22
Other South American	10	0.09
Other Hispanic or Latino	457	4.13
Hungarian	31	0.28
Iranian	13	0.12
Irish	772	6.93
Italian	334	3.00
Lithuanian	13	0.12
Norwegian	204	1.83
Polish	266	2.39
Portuguese	42	0.38
Romanian	4	0.04
Russian	36	0.32
Scotch-Irish	155	1.39
Scottish	159	1.43
Slavic	10	0.09
Slovak	68	0.61
Swedish	6	0.05
Swiss	6	0.05
United States or American	1,102	9.90
Welsh	61	0.55
West Indian, excl. Hispanic:	140	1.26
Barbadian	45	0.40
Haitian	79	0.71
Jamaican	16	0.14
White:	8,168	73.77
Not Hispanic (5,472)	5,637	50.91
Hispanic (2,305)	2,531	22.86
Yugoslavian	12	0.11

Bartow

Place Type: City
County: Polk
Population: 15,340

Ancestry/Race	Number	%
Acadian/Cajun	6	0.04
African American/Black:	4,400	28.68
Not Hispanic (4,321)	4,361	28.43
Hispanic (34)	39	0.25
African, sub-Saharan:	56	0.37
African	56	0.37
Alaska Native tribes, specified:	6	0.04
Aleut (1)	1	0.01
Eskimo (5)	5	0.03
Am. Ind. or Alaska Nat., not spec.	39	0.25
American Indian tribes, specified:	81	0.53
Apache	1	0.01
Blackfeet	1	0.01
Cherokee (17)	43	0.28
Chippewa (2)	2	0.01
Choctaw (1)	2	0.01
Creek (7)	9	0.06
Iroquois (2)	2	0.01
Latin American Indians (2)	8	0.05
Lumbee	1	0.01
Navajo	5	0.03
Potawatomi	2	0.01
Pueblo (1)	1	0.01
Seminole (1)	2	0.01
All other tribes	2	0.01
American Indian tribes, not spec.	9	0.06
Arab:	25	0.16
Other Arab	25	0.16
Armenian	9	0.06
Asian:	164	1.07
Chinese, ex. Taiwanese (3)	9	0.06
Filipino (18)	23	0.15
Indian (56)	59	0.38
Japanese (7)	7	0.05
Korean (5)	8	0.05
Laotian (39)	42	0.27
Taiwanese (3)	3	0.02
Thai (2)	4	0.03
Vietnamese (4)	4	0.03
Other Asian, not specified (3)	5	0.03
British	70	0.46
Bulgarian	12	0.08
Celtic	13	0.08
Czech	11	0.07
Czechoslovakian	7	0.05
Danish	9	0.06
Dutch	282	1.84
English	1,390	9.06
European	50	0.33
French, except Basque	257	1.68
French Canadian	123	0.80
German	1,126	7.34
Greek	19	0.12
Hawaii Native/Pacific Islander:	17	0.11
Micronesian: (1)	3	0.02
Guamanian/Chamorro (1)	3	0.02
Polynesian: (10)	13	0.08
Native Hawaiian (2)	4	0.03
Samoan (8)	9	0.06
Other Pac. Isl., not spec. (1)	1	0.01
Hispanic or Latino:	1,244	8.11
Central American:	13	0.08
Costa Rican	1	0.01
Guatemalan	1	0.01
Honduran	3	0.02
Nicaraguan	1	0.01
Panamanian	6	0.04
Other Central American	1	0.01
Cuban	72	0.47
Mexican	914	5.96
Puerto Rican	92	0.60
South American:	10	0.07
Chilean	3	0.02
Colombian	2	0.01
Ecuadorian	1	0.01
Peruvian	1	0.01
Venezuelan	3	0.02
Other Hispanic or Latino	143	0.93
Hungarian	56	0.37
Irish	1,186	7.73
Italian	286	1.86
Norwegian	46	0.30
Polish	90	0.59
Portuguese	15	0.10
Russian	30	0.20
Scandinavian	9	0.06
Scotch-Irish	255	1.66
Scottish	213	1.39
Slovak	29	0.19
Swedish	33	0.22
Swiss	27	0.18
Ukrainian	10	0.07
United States or American	1,719	11.21
Welsh	65	0.42
West Indian, excl. Hispanic:	128	0.83
British West Indian	18	0.12
Haitian	13	0.08
Jamaican	97	0.63
White:	10,393	67.75
Not Hispanic (9,445)	9,557	62.30
Hispanic (666)	836	5.45

Bayonet Point

Place Type: Census Designated Place
County: Pasco
Population: 23,577

Ancestry/Race	Number	%
Afghan	4	0.02
African American/Black:	207	0.88
Not Hispanic (142)	182	0.77
Hispanic (17)	25	0.11
Am. Ind. or Alaska Nat., not spec.	52	0.22
American Indian tribes, specified:	99	0.42
Apache (1)	11	0.05
Blackfeet (2)	4	0.02
Cherokee (15)	37	0.16
Chippewa (7)	8	0.03
Choctaw	3	0.01
Comanche	1	0.00
Cree	3	0.01
Creek (2)	3	0.01
Houma (2)	2	0.01
Iroquois (3)	4	0.02
Latin American Indians (1)	1	0.00
Lumbee	1	0.00
Osage	1	0.00
Seminole	2	0.01
Shoshone (1)	1	0.00
Sioux (1)	3	0.01
All other tribes (7)	14	0.06
American Indian tribes, not spec.	8	0.03
Arab:	62	0.26
Egyptian	24	0.10
Jordanian	8	0.03
Lebanese	8	0.03
Syrian	22	0.09
Asian:	192	0.81
Chinese, ex. Taiwanese (11)	17	0.07
Filipino (37)	47	0.20
Indian (38)	46	0.20
Japanese (5)	13	0.06
Korean (14)	19	0.08
Pakistani	1	0.00
Thai (4)	4	0.02
Vietnamese (28)	34	0.14
Other Asian, not specified (1)	11	0.05
Austrian	137	0.58
Belgian	42	0.18
Brazilian	10	0.04
British	47	0.20
Canadian	201	0.85
Croatian	31	0.13
Czech	73	0.31
Czechoslovakian	70	0.30
Danish	97	0.41
Dutch	480	2.03
English	3,046	12.87
European	72	0.30
Finnish	117	0.49
French, except Basque	970	4.10
French Canadian	329	1.39
German	5,079	21.46
Greek	246	1.04
Hawaii Native/Pacific Islander:	11	0.05
Micronesian:	1	0.00
Guamanian/Chamorro	1	0.00
Polynesian: (4)	6	0.03
Native Hawaiian (4)	6	0.03
Other Pac. Isl., not spec. (3)	4	0.02
Hispanic or Latino:	826	3.50
Central American:	39	0.17
Costa Rican	4	0.02
Guatemalan	9	0.04
Honduran	13	0.06
Nicaraguan	2	0.01

Notes: 1. Figures in the "Number" column do not add up to the total population due to: a) Ancestry/Race overlap — e.g. persons can report being both White and Irish, b) persons of Hispanic origin can report being any race, c) persons reporting two ancestries are counted in both categories. 2. Numbers in parentheses indicate the number of persons reporting this ancestry/race alone, not in combination with any other ancestry/race. 3. Refer to the User's Guide in the front of the book for more detailed information.

Panamanian	2	0.01
Salvadoran	8	0.03
Other Central American	1	0.00
Cuban	62	0.26
Dominican Republic	16	0.07
Mexican	88	0.37
Puerto Rican	344	1.46
South American:	54	0.23
Argentinean	1	0.00
Bolivian	4	0.02
Chilean	3	0.01
Colombian	22	0.09
Ecuadorian	11	0.05
Peruvian	5	0.02
Uruguayan	2	0.01
Venezuelan	5	0.02
Other South American	1	0.00
Other Hispanic or Latino	223	0.95
Hungarian	192	0.81
Irish	4,083	17.25
Italian	3,823	16.15
Lithuanian	122	0.52
Maltese	34	0.14
New Zealander	6	0.03
Norwegian	302	1.28
Pennsylvania German	36	0.15
Polish	1,492	6.30
Portuguese	84	0.35
Romanian	8	0.03
Russian	278	1.17
Scandinavian	32	0.14
Scotch-Irish	447	1.89
Scottish	603	2.55
Slavic	32	0.14
Slovak	77	0.33
Slovene	18	0.08
Swedish	330	1.39
Swiss	67	0.28
Ukrainian	88	0.37
United States or American	1,743	7.36
Welsh	236	1.00
West Indian, excl. Hispanic:	14	0.06
Jamaican	14	0.06
White:	23,054	97.78
Not Hispanic (22,203)	22,384	94.94
Hispanic (629)	670	2.84
Yugoslavian	21	0.09

Bayshore Gardens

Place Type: Census Designated Place
County: Manatee
Population: 17,350

Ancestry/Race	Number	%
African American/Black:	791	4.56
Not Hispanic (677)	761	4.39
Hispanic (13)	30	0.17
African, sub-Saharan:	61	0.35
African	48	0.28
Cape Verdean	13	0.07
Am. Ind. or Alaska Nat., not spec.	50	0.29
American Indian tribes, specified:	87	0.50
Apache	2	0.01
Blackfeet (4)	7	0.04
Cherokee (7)	33	0.19
Cheyenne (2)	2	0.01
Chippewa (3)	4	0.02
Choctaw (5)	9	0.05
Iroquois	2	0.01
Latin American Indians (7)	8	0.05
Lumbee (2)	2	0.01
Sioux (1)	5	0.03
All other tribes (8)	13	0.07
American Indian tribes, not spec.	8	0.05
Arab:	8	0.05
Lebanese	8	0.05
Armenian	12	0.07
Asian:	299	1.72
Bangladeshi	5	0.03
Cambodian (21)	21	0.12
Chinese, ex. Taiwanese (29)	33	0.19
Filipino (35)	56	0.32
Indian (29)	38	0.22
Indonesian (2)	2	0.01
Japanese (5)	13	0.07
Korean (6)	17	0.10
Laotian (7)	11	0.06
Malaysian	1	0.01
Pakistani (1)	1	0.01
Thai (11)	17	0.10
Vietnamese (65)	75	0.43
Other Asian, not specified	9	0.05
Austrian	47	0.27
Belgian	14	0.08
British	18	0.10
Canadian	76	0.44
Celtic	8	0.05
Croatian	36	0.21
Czech	76	0.44
Czechoslovakian	19	0.11
Danish	69	0.40
Dutch	435	2.50
English	2,826	16.26
European	64	0.37
Finnish	41	0.24
French, except Basque	727	4.18
French Canadian	175	1.01
German	3,225	18.55
German Russian	6	0.03
Greek	43	0.25
Hawaii Native/Pacific Islander:	28	0.16
Micronesian: (2)	2	0.01
Guamanian/Chamorro (2)	2	0.01
Polynesian: (10)	17	0.10
Native Hawaiian (6)	13	0.07
Other Polynesian (4)	4	0.02
Other Pac. Isl., not spec. (5)	9	0.05
Hispanic or Latino:	1,426	8.22
Central American:	85	0.49
Costa Rican	2	0.01
Guatemalan	37	0.21
Honduran	24	0.14
Nicaraguan	6	0.03
Panamanian	1	0.01
Salvadoran	10	0.06
Other Central American	5	0.03
Cuban	98	0.56
Dominican Republic	11	0.06
Mexican	537	3.10
Puerto Rican	354	2.04
South American:	119	0.69
Argentinean	4	0.02
Chilean	7	0.04
Colombian	60	0.35
Ecuadorian	20	0.12
Peruvian	17	0.10
Uruguayan	4	0.02
Venezuelan	3	0.02
Other South American	4	0.02
Other Hispanic or Latino	222	1.28
Hungarian	147	0.85
Irish	2,220	12.77
Italian	1,104	6.35
Latvian	10	0.06
Lithuanian	35	0.20
Northern European	20	0.12
Norwegian	189	1.09
Pennsylvania German	31	0.18
Polish	474	2.73
Portuguese	71	0.41
Romanian	47	0.27
Russian	139	0.80
Scandinavian	5	0.03
Scotch-Irish	299	1.72
Scottish	474	2.73
Serbian	26	0.15
Slavic	9	0.05
Slovak	52	0.30
Slovene	9	0.05
Swedish	259	1.49
Swiss	35	0.20
Ukrainian	47	0.27
United States or American	1,960	11.28
Welsh	77	0.44
West Indian, excl. Hispanic:	105	0.60
Haitian	31	0.18
Jamaican	74	0.43
White:	15,903	91.66
Not Hispanic (14,689)	14,913	85.95
Hispanic (903)	990	5.71
Yugoslavian	14	0.08

Bellair-Meadowbrook Terrace

Place Type: Census Designated Place
County: Clay
Population: 16,539

Ancestry/Race	Number	%
Afghan	14	0.08
African American/Black:	2,022	12.23
Not Hispanic (1,782)	1,925	11.64
Hispanic (67)	97	0.59
African, sub-Saharan:	46	0.28
African	46	0.28
Am. Ind. or Alaska Nat., not spec.	55	0.33
American Indian tribes, specified:	148	0.89
Apache (1)	1	0.01
Blackfeet	2	0.01
Cherokee (22)	80	0.48
Cheyenne	1	0.01
Chickasaw	5	0.03
Chippewa (3)	3	0.02
Creek (5)	11	0.07
Crow	2	0.01
Iroquois (5)	5	0.03
Latin American Indians (5)	6	0.04
Lumbee (3)	3	0.02
Navajo (6)	12	0.07
Osage	1	0.01
Potawatomi (4)	4	0.02
Seminole	3	0.02
Sioux	1	0.01
All other tribes (7)	8	0.05
American Indian tribes, not spec.	7	0.04
Arab:	85	0.51
Arab/Arabic	22	0.13
Lebanese	23	0.14
Syrian	27	0.16
Other Arab	13	0.08
Asian:	799	4.83
Cambodian (4)	5	0.03
Chinese, ex. Taiwanese (20)	37	0.22
Filipino (344)	436	2.64
Hmong (2)	2	0.01
Indian (57)	69	0.42
Japanese (36)	61	0.37
Korean (58)	68	0.41
Laotian (1)	1	0.01
Pakistani (4)	5	0.03
Sri Lankan (7)	7	0.04
Taiwanese (1)	2	0.01
Thai (8)	10	0.06
Vietnamese (42)	46	0.28
Other Asian, specified	1	0.01
Other Asian, not specified (15)	49	0.30
Australian	7	0.04
Austrian	55	0.33
Belgian	6	0.04
Brazilian	20	0.12
British	43	0.26
Canadian	72	0.43
Czech	72	0.43
Czechoslovakian	21	0.13
Danish	45	0.27
Dutch	182	1.10
English	1,698	10.25
European	142	0.86
Finnish	16	0.10
French, except Basque	655	3.95
French Canadian	125	0.75
German	1,998	12.06

Notes: 1. Figures in the "Number" column do not add up to the total population due to: a) Ancestry/Race overlap — e.g. persons can report being both White and Irish, b) persons of Hispanic origin can report being any race, c) persons reporting two ancestries are counted in both categories. 2. Numbers in parentheses indicate the number of persons reporting this ancestry/race alone, not in combination with any other ancestry/race. 3. Refer to the User's Guide in the front of the book for more detailed information.

Greek	26	0.16
Hawaii Native/Pacific Islander:	50	0.30
Micronesian: (10)	16	0.10
Guamanian/Chamorro (10)	16	0.10
Polynesian: (8)	23	0.14
Native Hawaiian (6)	21	0.13
Samoan (1)	1	0.01
Other Polynesian (1)	1	0.01
Other Pac. Isl., not spec.	11	0.07
Hispanic or Latino:	1,112	6.72
Central American:	48	0.29
Costa Rican	5	0.03
Guatemalan	2	0.01
Honduran	4	0.02
Nicaraguan	5	0.03
Panamanian	19	0.11
Salvadoran	10	0.06
Other Central American	3	0.02
Cuban	58	0.35
Dominican Republic	17	0.10
Mexican	256	1.55
Puerto Rican	410	2.48
South American:	90	0.54
Argentinean	8	0.05
Bolivian	4	0.02
Chilean	14	0.08
Colombian	35	0.21
Ecuadorian	6	0.04
Paraguayan	2	0.01
Peruvian	17	0.10
Uruguayan	1	0.01
Venezuelan	1	0.01
Other South American	2	0.01
Other Hispanic or Latino	233	1.41
Hungarian	77	0.46
Irish	1,823	11.01
Italian	797	4.81
Latvian	5	0.03
Lithuanian	17	0.10
Norwegian	182	1.10
Pennsylvania German	6	0.04
Polish	413	2.49
Portuguese	37	0.22
Romanian	10	0.06
Russian	29	0.18
Scotch-Irish	324	1.96
Scottish	442	2.67
Slavic	10	0.06
Slovak	9	0.05
Slovene	26	0.16
Swedish	106	0.64
Swiss	7	0.04
Ukrainian	20	0.12
United States or American	1,785	10.78
Welsh	241	1.45
West Indian, excl. Hispanic:	187	1.13
Bahamian	4	0.02
British West Indian	12	0.07
Haitian	109	0.66
Jamaican	12	0.07
U.S. Virgin Islander	12	0.07
West Indian	38	0.23
White:	13,448	81.31
Not Hispanic (12,502)	12,849	77.69
Hispanic (522)	599	3.62
Yugoslavian	8	0.05

Belle Glade

Place Type: City
County: Palm Beach
Population: 14,906

Ancestry/Race	Number	%
African American/Black:	8,653	58.05
Not Hispanic (7,471)	8,546	57.33
Hispanic (84)	107	0.72
African, sub-Saharan:	156	1.04
African	156	1.04
Alaska Native tribes, specified:	1	0.01
Aleut	1	0.01
Am. Ind. or Alaska Nat., not spec.	26	0.17
American Indian tribes, specified:	11	0.07
Cherokee	4	0.03
Latin American Indians	3	0.02
All other tribes (4)	4	0.03
American Indian tribes, not spec.	3	0.02
Arab:	141	0.94
Arab/Arabic	115	0.77
Other Arab	26	0.17
Asian:	54	0.36
Bangladeshi	3	0.02
Chinese, ex. Taiwanese	3	0.02
Filipino (1)	4	0.03
Indian (18)	19	0.13
Korean (7)	12	0.08
Thai	1	0.01
Other Asian, not specified (2)	12	0.08
British	39	0.26
Canadian	15	0.10
Danish	6	0.04
Dutch	42	0.28
English	451	3.01
French, except Basque	27	0.18
French Canadian	5	0.03
German	202	1.35
Hawaii Native/Pacific Islander:	145	0.97
Polynesian: (2)	7	0.05
Native Hawaiian (2)	6	0.04
Samoan	1	0.01
Other Pac. Isl., not spec. (4)	138	0.93
Hispanic or Latino:	4,110	27.57
Central American:	204	1.37
Costa Rican	8	0.05
Guatemalan	18	0.12
Honduran	55	0.37
Nicaraguan	76	0.51
Panamanian	1	0.01
Salvadoran	42	0.28
Other Central American	4	0.03
Cuban	891	5.98
Dominican Republic	73	0.49
Mexican	2,302	15.44
Puerto Rican	257	1.72
South American:	19	0.13
Chilean	3	0.02
Colombian	10	0.07
Ecuadorian	3	0.02
Peruvian	1	0.01
Venezuelan	2	0.01
Other Hispanic or Latino	364	2.44
Hungarian	7	0.05
Irish	254	1.69
Italian	64	0.43
Polish	13	0.09
Portuguese	15	0.10
Scotch-Irish	30	0.20
Scottish	40	0.27
Swedish	9	0.06
United States or American	1,271	8.47
Welsh	11	0.07
West Indian, excl. Hispanic:	1,988	13.25
Bahamian	110	0.73
Barbadian	21	0.14
Haitian	1,476	9.84
Jamaican	381	2.54
White:	4,744	31.83
Not Hispanic (2,058)	2,168	14.54
Hispanic (2,457)	2,576	17.28

Bellview

Place Type: Census Designated Place
County: Escambia
Population: 21,201

Ancestry/Race	Number	%
Acadian/Cajun	42	0.20
African American/Black:	2,581	12.17
Not Hispanic (2,474)	2,568	12.11
Hispanic (5)	13	0.06
African, sub-Saharan:	32	0.15
African	32	0.15
Alaska Native tribes, specified:	1	0.00
Aleut (1)	1	0.00
Am. Ind. or Alaska Nat., not spec.	109	0.51
American Indian tribes, specified:	327	1.54
Apache (1)	1	0.00
Blackfeet (1)	4	0.02
Cherokee (36)	90	0.42
Chickasaw	2	0.01
Chippewa (7)	7	0.03
Choctaw (9)	20	0.09
Colville	1	0.00
Creek (80)	135	0.64
Crow	1	0.00
Delaware (1)	2	0.01
Houma (11)	11	0.05
Latin American Indians (1)	2	0.01
Navajo (5)	8	0.04
Ottawa (1)	1	0.00
Paiute (4)	4	0.02
Potawatomi (2)	3	0.01
Pueblo (1)	2	0.01
Puget Sound Salish (6)	6	0.03
Seminole	2	0.01
Sioux (8)	10	0.05
All other tribes (2)	15	0.07
American Indian tribes, not spec.	8	0.04
Arab:	25	0.12
Arab/Arabic	7	0.03
Egyptian	13	0.06
Lebanese	5	0.02
Armenian	8	0.04
Asian:	917	4.33
Chinese, ex. Taiwanese (19)	36	0.17
Filipino (438)	585	2.76
Indian (13)	19	0.09
Indonesian	1	0.00
Japanese (46)	73	0.34
Korean (23)	31	0.15
Malaysian	9	0.04
Pakistani (1)	1	0.00
Sri Lankan	1	0.00
Taiwanese (3)	3	0.01
Thai (7)	11	0.05
Vietnamese (122)	134	0.63
Other Asian, specified (1)	1	0.00
Other Asian, not specified (7)	12	0.06
Austrian	29	0.14
Brazilian	8	0.04
British	98	0.47
Bulgarian	15	0.07
Canadian	61	0.29
Croatian	8	0.04
Czech	17	0.08
Czechoslovakian	7	0.03
Danish	76	0.36
Dutch	215	1.02
English	2,186	10.38
European	238	1.13
Finnish	5	0.02
French, except Basque	688	3.27
French Canadian	107	0.51
German	2,749	13.05
Greek	56	0.27
Hawaii Native/Pacific Islander:	58	0.27
Micronesian: (16)	24	0.11
Guamanian/Chamorro (16)	24	0.11
Polynesian: (10)	24	0.11
Native Hawaiian (9)	23	0.11
Samoan (1)	1	0.00
Other Pac. Isl., not spec. (6)	10	0.05
Hispanic or Latino:	509	2.40
Central American:	21	0.10
Guatemalan	1	0.00
Honduran	1	0.00
Nicaraguan	1	0.00
Panamanian	16	0.08
Salvadoran	2	0.01
Cuban	19	0.09
Mexican	169	0.80
Puerto Rican	134	0.63
South American:	25	0.12
Argentinean	5	0.02

Notes: 1. Figures in the "Number" column do not add up to the total population due to: a) Ancestry/Race overlap — e.g. persons can report being both White and Irish, b) persons of Hispanic origin can report being any race, c) persons reporting two ancestries are counted in both categories. 2. Numbers in parentheses indicate the number of persons reporting this ancestry/race alone, not in combination with any other ancestry/race. 3. Refer to the User's Guide in the front of the book for more detailed information.

Bolivian	1	0.00
Chilean	3	0.01
Colombian	10	0.05
Ecuadorian	4	0.02
Peruvian	1	0.00
Venezuelan	1	0.00
Other Hispanic or Latino	141	0.67
Hungarian	75	0.36
Irish	2,321	11.02
Italian	1,007	4.78
Norwegian	130	0.62
Polish	360	1.71
Portuguese	49	0.23
Romanian	15	0.07
Russian	63	0.30
Scandinavian	14	0.07
Scotch-Irish	547	2.60
Scottish	366	1.74
Slovak	39	0.19
Swedish	313	1.49
Swiss	21	0.10
Ukrainian	34	0.16
United States or American	2,863	13.59
Welsh	188	0.89
West Indian, excl. Hispanic:	21	0.10
Trinidadian and Tobagonian	10	0.05
West Indian	11	0.05
White:	17,575	82.90
Not Hispanic (16,771)	17,207	81.16
Hispanic (329)	368	1.74
Yugoslavian	22	0.10

Bloomingdale

Place Type: Census Designated Place
County: Hillsborough
Population: 19,839

Ancestry/Race	Number	%
African American/Black:	1,358	6.85
Not Hispanic (1,237)	1,322	6.66
Hispanic (29)	36	0.18
African, sub-Saharan:	158	0.79
African	54	0.27
Cape Verdean	53	0.27
South African	41	0.21
Zimbabwean	10	0.05
Am. Ind. or Alaska Nat., not spec.	35	0.18
Albanian	8	0.04
American Indian tribes, specified:	104	0.52
Apache	4	0.02
Blackfeet (3)	3	0.02
Cherokee (11)	39	0.20
Chippewa (1)	2	0.01
Choctaw (2)	3	0.02
Cree	1	0.01
Creek (3)	6	0.03
Iroquois (2)	3	0.02
Latin American Indians (1)	4	0.02
Lumbee (2)	2	0.01
Navajo	3	0.02
Pueblo (1)	1	0.01
Puget Sound Salish	6	0.03
Sioux	2	0.01
All other tribes (9)	25	0.13
American Indian tribes, not spec.	9	0.05
Arab:	136	0.68
Arab/Arabic	33	0.17
Egyptian	3	0.02
Lebanese	92	0.46
Syrian	8	0.04
Armenian	9	0.05
Asian:	602	3.03
Chinese, ex. Taiwanese (70)	96	0.48
Filipino (70)	111	0.56
Hmong (6)	6	0.03
Indian (144)	163	0.82
Japanese (17)	39	0.20
Korean (53)	80	0.40
Pakistani	4	0.02
Taiwanese (3)	3	0.02
Thai (15)	18	0.09
Vietnamese (38)	45	0.23
Other Asian, not specified (23)	37	0.19
Australian	9	0.05
Austrian	23	0.12
Brazilian	28	0.14
British	73	0.37
Canadian	135	0.68
Croatian	68	0.34
Czech	46	0.23
Czechoslovakian	41	0.21
Danish	89	0.45
Dutch	356	1.79
Eastern European	7	0.04
English	2,928	14.69
European	241	1.21
Finnish	63	0.32
French, except Basque	721	3.62
French Canadian	148	0.74
German	3,849	19.31
Greek	193	0.97
Guyanese	5	0.03
Hawaii Native/Pacific Islander:	33	0.17
Micronesian: (3)	7	0.04
Guamanian/Chamorro (3)	7	0.04
Polynesian: (2)	10	0.05
Native Hawaiian (1)	7	0.04
Samoan (1)	3	0.02
Other Pac. Isl., not spec. (9)	16	0.08
Hispanic or Latino:	1,375	6.93
Central American:	67	0.34
Costa Rican	8	0.04
Guatemalan	5	0.03
Honduran	14	0.07
Nicaraguan	5	0.03
Panamanian	23	0.12
Salvadoran	12	0.06
Cuban	215	1.08
Dominican Republic	19	0.10
Mexican	136	0.69
Puerto Rican	554	2.79
South American:	80	0.40
Argentinean	6	0.03
Bolivian	1	0.01
Chilean	2	0.01
Colombian	39	0.20
Ecuadorian	6	0.03
Peruvian	11	0.06
Venezuelan	8	0.04
Other South American	7	0.04
Other Hispanic or Latino	304	1.53
Hungarian	109	0.55
Irish	3,238	16.25
Israeli	9	0.05
Italian	1,735	8.71
Lithuanian	37	0.19
Norwegian	207	1.04
Pennsylvania German	10	0.05
Polish	935	4.69
Portuguese	133	0.67
Romanian	20	0.10
Russian	166	0.83
Scandinavian	9	0.05
Scotch-Irish	449	2.25
Scottish	616	3.09
Slavic	18	0.09
Slovak	18	0.09
Slovene	7	0.04
Swedish	362	1.82
Swiss	40	0.20
Turkish	18	0.09
Ukrainian	54	0.27
United States or American	1,387	6.96
Welsh	165	0.83
West Indian, excl. Hispanic:	136	0.68
Haitian	2	0.01
Jamaican	120	0.60
West Indian	14	0.07
White:	17,779	89.62
Not Hispanic (16,421)	16,651	83.93
Hispanic (1,062)	1,128	5.69
Yugoslavian	25	0.13

Boca Del Mar

Place Type: Census Designated Place
County: Palm Beach
Population: 21,832

Ancestry/Race	Number	%
African American/Black:	324	1.48
Not Hispanic (256)	305	1.40
Hispanic (13)	19	0.09
African, sub-Saharan:	98	0.46
Nigerian	9	0.04
South African	89	0.42
Am. Ind. or Alaska Nat., not spec.	22	0.10
American Indian tribes, specified:	18	0.08
Blackfeet	3	0.01
Cherokee	6	0.03
Iroquois	2	0.01
Latin American Indians (1)	3	0.01
All other tribes (3)	4	0.02
American Indian tribes, not spec.	6	0.03
Arab:	190	0.89
Arab/Arabic	18	0.08
Lebanese	43	0.20
Moroccan	41	0.19
Syrian	39	0.18
Other Arab	49	0.23
Armenian	43	0.20
Asian:	474	2.17
Bangladeshi (10)	11	0.05
Chinese, ex. Taiwanese (112)	122	0.56
Filipino (23)	33	0.15
Hmong (1)	1	0.00
Indian (167)	177	0.81
Indonesian (1)	2	0.01
Japanese (30)	34	0.16
Korean (31)	37	0.17
Pakistani	4	0.02
Sri Lankan (2)	2	0.01
Taiwanese (6)	6	0.03
Thai (9)	9	0.04
Vietnamese (13)	13	0.06
Other Asian, specified (1)	1	0.00
Other Asian, not specified (2)	22	0.10
Austrian	281	1.31
Belgian	18	0.08
Brazilian	171	0.80
British	87	0.41
Canadian	115	0.54
Cypriot	12	0.06
Czech	129	0.60
Czechoslovakian	112	0.52
Danish	64	0.30
Dutch	262	1.22
Eastern European	250	1.17
English	1,625	7.58
European	188	0.88
Finnish	18	0.08
French, except Basque	537	2.51
French Canadian	102	0.48
German	2,730	12.74
Greek	195	0.91
Guyanese	57	0.27
Hawaii Native/Pacific Islander:	12	0.05
Melanesian:	3	0.01
Fijian	3	0.01
Micronesian:	1	0.00
Guamanian/Chamorro	1	0.00
Polynesian: (3)	4	0.02
Native Hawaiian (3)	4	0.02
Other Pac. Isl., not spec. (3)	4	0.02
Hispanic or Latino:	1,782	8.16
Central American:	68	0.31
Costa Rican	9	0.04
Guatemalan	10	0.05
Honduran	17	0.08
Nicaraguan	13	0.06
Panamanian	13	0.06
Salvadoran	5	0.02
Other Central American	1	0.00
Cuban	213	0.98

Notes: 1. Figures in the "Number" column do not add up to the total population due to: a) Ancestry/Race overlap — e.g. persons can report being both White and Irish, b) persons of Hispanic origin can report being any race, c) persons reporting two ancestries are counted in both categories. 2. Numbers in parentheses indicate the number of persons reporting this ancestry/race alone, not in combination with any other ancestry/race. 3. Refer to the User's Guide in the front of the book for more detailed information.

Dominican Republic	38	0.17
Mexican	114	0.52
Puerto Rican	225	1.03
South American:	626	2.87
Argentinean	60	0.27
Bolivian	5	0.02
Chilean	29	0.13
Colombian	262	1.20
Ecuadorian	32	0.15
Paraguayan	2	0.01
Peruvian	116	0.53
Uruguayan	9	0.04
Venezuelan	85	0.39
Other South American	26	0.12
Other Hispanic or Latino	498	2.28
Hungarian	382	1.78
Iranian	53	0.25
Irish	2,063	9.63
Israeli	58	0.27
Italian	2,999	14.00
Latvian	19	0.09
Lithuanian	155	0.72
Macedonian	15	0.07
Northern European	17	0.08
Norwegian	157	0.73
Pennsylvania German	26	0.12
Polish	1,604	7.49
Portuguese	43	0.20
Romanian	208	0.97
Russian	2,027	9.46
Scandinavian	19	0.09
Scotch-Irish	224	1.05
Scottish	316	1.47
Slavic	40	0.19
Slovak	52	0.24
Slovene	16	0.07
Soviet Union	15	0.07
Swedish	117	0.55
Swiss	29	0.14
Turkish	54	0.25
Ukrainian	244	1.14
United States or American	1,306	6.09
Welsh	83	0.39
West Indian, excl. Hispanic:	184	0.86
Bahamian	9	0.04
Haitian	98	0.46
Jamaican	60	0.28
U.S. Virgin Islander	17	0.08
White:	20,849	95.50
Not Hispanic (19,136)	19,280	88.31
Hispanic (1,480)	1,569	7.19
Yugoslavian	49	0.23

Boca Raton

Place Type: City
County: Palm Beach
Population: 74,764

Ancestry/Race	Number	%
African American/Black:	3,251	4.35
Not Hispanic (2,725)	3,131	4.19
Hispanic (85)	120	0.16
African, sub-Saharan:	356	0.47
African	104	0.14
Cape Verdean	14	0.02
Ethiopian	55	0.07
Kenyan	5	0.01
Nigerian	6	0.01
South African	163	0.22
Other sub-Saharan African	9	0.01
Alaska Native tribes, specified:	3	0.00
Tlingit-Haida (1)	3	0.00
Am. Ind. or Alaska Nat., not spec.	106	0.14
Albanian	36	0.05
Alsatian	19	0.03
American Indian tribes, specified:	159	0.21
Blackfeet (2)	6	0.01
Cherokee (19)	62	0.08
Chickasaw	1	0.00
Chippewa (1)	3	0.00
Choctaw	2	0.00
Creek	3	0.00
Iroquois (8)	18	0.02
Latin American Indians (20)	32	0.04
Lumbee (2)	3	0.00
Potawatomi (2)	4	0.01
Pueblo (4)	4	0.01
Seminole (1)	1	0.00
Sioux	1	0.00
All other tribes (11)	19	0.03
American Indian tribes, not spec.	22	0.03
Arab:	704	0.93
Arab/Arabic	80	0.11
Egyptian	71	0.09
Iraqi	11	0.01
Jordanian	29	0.04
Lebanese	375	0.50
Moroccan	39	0.05
Palestinian	7	0.01
Syrian	48	0.06
Other Arab	44	0.06
Armenian	132	0.17
Asian:	1,879	2.51
Bangladeshi (18)	24	0.03
Cambodian (5)	10	0.01
Chinese, ex. Taiwanese (387)	450	0.60
Filipino (159)	215	0.29
Indian (537)	623	0.83
Indonesian (4)	10	0.01
Japanese (52)	97	0.13
Korean (84)	97	0.13
Malaysian (3)	6	0.01
Pakistani (33)	41	0.05
Sri Lankan (11)	17	0.02
Taiwanese (5)	6	0.01
Thai (32)	41	0.05
Vietnamese (102)	119	0.16
Other Asian, specified (7)	14	0.02
Other Asian, not specified (33)	109	0.15
Australian	26	0.03
Austrian	786	1.04
Basque	26	0.03
Belgian	70	0.09
Brazilian	788	1.04
British	558	0.74
Bulgarian	75	0.10
Canadian	582	0.77
Celtic	32	0.04
Croatian	80	0.11
Cypriot	52	0.07
Czech	396	0.52
Czechoslovakian	136	0.18
Danish	240	0.32
Dutch	1,241	1.64
Eastern European	518	0.69
English	7,127	9.43
Estonian	21	0.03
European	735	0.97
Finnish	210	0.28
French, except Basque	2,105	2.78
French Canadian	628	0.83
German	10,855	14.36
Greek	1,065	1.41
Guyanese	6	0.01
Hawaii Native/Pacific Islander:	89	0.12
Micronesian: (7)	18	0.02
Guamanian/Chamorro (7)	18	0.02
Polynesian: (13)	24	0.03
Native Hawaiian (9)	19	0.03
Samoan (4)	4	0.01
Other Polynesian	1	0.00
Other Pac. Isl., specified	4	0.01
Other Pac. Isl., not spec. (9)	43	0.06
Hispanic or Latino:	6,359	8.51
Central American:	397	0.53
Costa Rican	32	0.04
Guatemalan	98	0.13
Honduran	108	0.14
Nicaraguan	57	0.08
Panamanian	42	0.06
Salvadoran	44	0.06
Other Central American	16	0.02
Cuban	1,099	1.47
Dominican Republic	167	0.22
Mexican	778	1.04
Puerto Rican	762	1.02
South American:	1,662	2.22
Argentinean	159	0.21
Bolivian	27	0.04
Chilean	95	0.13
Colombian	685	0.92
Ecuadorian	139	0.19
Paraguayan	10	0.01
Peruvian	202	0.27
Uruguayan	15	0.02
Venezuelan	242	0.32
Other South American	88	0.12
Other Hispanic or Latino	1,494	2.00
Hungarian	1,054	1.39
Iranian	202	0.27
Irish	9,075	12.00
Israeli	237	0.31
Italian	9,386	12.42
Latvian	72	0.10
Lithuanian	343	0.45
Macedonian	70	0.09
Maltese	45	0.06
New Zealander	17	0.02
Northern European	69	0.09
Norwegian	796	1.05
Pennsylvania German	6	0.01
Polish	4,521	5.98
Portuguese	450	0.60
Romanian	365	0.48
Russian	4,066	5.38
Scandinavian	110	0.15
Scotch-Irish	915	1.21
Scottish	1,816	2.40
Serbian	39	0.05
Slavic	51	0.07
Slovak	186	0.25
Slovene	23	0.03
Swedish	1,045	1.38
Swiss	215	0.28
Turkish	147	0.19
Ukrainian	417	0.55
United States or American	4,229	5.59
Welsh	452	0.60
West Indian, excl. Hispanic:	1,352	1.79
Bahamian	34	0.04
Barbadian	23	0.03
British West Indian	7	0.01
Dutch West Indian	7	0.01
Haitian	928	1.23
Jamaican	201	0.27
Trinidadian and Tobagonian	119	0.16
West Indian	33	0.04
White:	68,870	92.12
Not Hispanic (62,925)	63,558	85.01
Hispanic (4,926)	5,312	7.11
Yugoslavian	111	0.15

Bonita Springs

Place Type: City
County: Lee
Population: 32,797

Ancestry/Race	Number	%
Afghan	10	0.03
African American/Black:	169	0.52
Not Hispanic (101)	135	0.41
Hispanic (17)	34	0.10
Alaska Native tribes, not specified	1	0.00
Am. Ind. or Alaska Nat., not spec.	63	0.19
American Indian tribes, specified:	114	0.35
Apache (3)	3	0.01
Blackfeet (1)	4	0.01
Cherokee (6)	30	0.09
Chippewa (2)	4	0.01
Creek (1)	2	0.01
Iroquois (1)	2	0.01

Notes: 1. Figures in the "Number" column do not add up to the total population due to: a) Ancestry/Race overlap — e.g. persons can report being both White and Irish, b) persons of Hispanic origin can report being any race, c) persons reporting two ancestries are counted in both categories. 2. Numbers in parentheses indicate the number of persons reporting this ancestry/race alone, not in combination with any other ancestry/race. 3. Refer to the User's Guide in the front of the book for more detailed information.

Kiowa (1)	1	0.00
Latin American Indians (22)	48	0.15
Lumbee (1)	1	0.00
Ottawa (1)	1	0.00
Seminole (2)	2	0.01
Sioux (5)	5	0.02
Tohono O'Odham	1	0.00
All other tribes (3)	10	0.03
American Indian tribes, not spec.	4	0.01
Arab:	84	0.26
Egyptian	19	0.06
Lebanese	34	0.10
Syrian	31	0.09
Armenian	13	0.04
Asian:	175	0.53
Chinese, ex. Taiwanese (47)	54	0.16
Filipino (22)	40	0.12
Indian (18)	23	0.07
Japanese (5)	12	0.04
Korean (12)	15	0.05
Laotian	1	0.00
Pakistani	1	0.00
Thai (1)	2	0.01
Vietnamese (8)	9	0.03
Other Asian, specified (1)	1	0.00
Other Asian, not specified (3)	17	0.05
Australian	6	0.02
Austrian	125	0.38
Belgian	42	0.13
British	117	0.36
Bulgarian	5	0.02
Canadian	299	0.91
Croatian	91	0.28
Cypriot	12	0.04
Czech	276	0.84
Czechoslovakian	103	0.31
Danish	211	0.64
Dutch	695	2.11
Eastern European	24	0.07
English	4,884	14.84
European	91	0.28
Finnish	50	0.15
French, except Basque	1,126	3.42
French Canadian	538	1.63
German	6,740	20.48
Greek	68	0.21
Hawaii Native/Pacific Islander:	59	0.18
Micronesian: (22)	31	0.09
Guamanian/Chamorro (22)	31	0.09
Polynesian: (6)	21	0.06
Native Hawaiian (3)	16	0.05
Samoan (3)	5	0.02
Other Pac. Isl., not spec.	7	0.02
Hispanic or Latino:	5,615	17.12
Central American:	663	2.02
Costa Rican	34	0.10
Guatemalan	393	1.20
Honduran	98	0.30
Nicaraguan	6	0.02
Panamanian	1	0.00
Salvadoran	128	0.39
Other Central American	3	0.01
Cuban	163	0.50
Dominican Republic	15	0.05
Mexican	3,955	12.06
Puerto Rican	135	0.41
South American:	143	0.44
Argentinean	30	0.09
Bolivian	1	0.00
Chilean	9	0.03
Colombian	76	0.23
Ecuadorian	5	0.02
Peruvian	12	0.04
Uruguayan	6	0.02
Venezuelan	2	0.01
Other South American	2	0.01
Other Hispanic or Latino	541	1.65
Hungarian	383	1.16
Iranian	16	0.05
Irish	4,475	13.60
Israeli	21	0.06
Italian	1,925	5.85
Latvian	7	0.02
Lithuanian	155	0.47
Luxemburger	9	0.03
Northern European	7	0.02
Norwegian	405	1.23
Pennsylvania German	49	0.15
Polish	1,294	3.93
Portuguese	82	0.25
Romanian	53	0.16
Russian	301	0.91
Scandinavian	76	0.23
Scotch-Irish	626	1.90
Scottish	888	2.70
Serbian	31	0.09
Slavic	12	0.04
Slovak	147	0.45
Slovene	35	0.11
Swedish	630	1.91
Swiss	196	0.60
Turkish	24	0.07
Ukrainian	101	0.31
United States or American	2,057	6.25
Welsh	250	0.76
West Indian, excl. Hispanic:	32	0.10
Jamaican	5	0.02
Trinidadian and Tobagonian	27	0.08
White:	29,787	90.82
Not Hispanic (26,669)	26,851	81.87
Hispanic (2,687)	2,936	8.95
Yugoslavian	8	0.02

Boynton Beach

Place Type: City
County: Palm Beach
Population: 60,389

Ancestry/Race	Number	%
Acadian/Cajun	22	0.04
African American/Black:	14,838	24.57
Not Hispanic (13,585)	14,528	24.06
Hispanic (237)	310	0.51
African, sub-Saharan:	339	0.57
African	221	0.37
Cape Verdean	4	0.01
Liberian	85	0.14
Nigerian	23	0.04
South African	6	0.01
Alaska Native tribes, specified:	2	0.00
Tlingit-Haida (1)	2	0.00
Am. Ind. or Alaska Nat., not spec.	107	0.18
Albanian	11	0.02
Alsatian	21	0.04
American Indian tribes, specified:	126	0.21
Apache (2)	3	0.00
Blackfeet (1)	4	0.01
Cherokee (19)	43	0.07
Chippewa (2)	6	0.01
Choctaw (1)	1	0.00
Comanche (1)	1	0.00
Creek (2)	3	0.00
Iroquois (5)	6	0.01
Latin American Indians (20)	30	0.05
Navajo (4)	6	0.01
Osage	1	0.00
Paiute	1	0.00
Potawatomi	1	0.00
Pueblo	1	0.00
Seminole (4)	7	0.01
Shoshone	1	0.00
Sioux (3)	4	0.01
All other tribes (2)	7	0.01
American Indian tribes, not spec.	20	0.03
Arab:	164	0.27
Egyptian	15	0.03
Iraqi	12	0.02
Lebanese	118	0.20
Syrian	19	0.03
Armenian	32	0.05
Asian:	1,156	1.91
Bangladeshi (33)	50	0.08
Chinese, ex. Taiwanese (207)	254	0.42
Filipino (132)	168	0.28
Indian (371)	415	0.69
Indonesian (4)	5	0.01
Japanese (15)	29	0.05
Korean (31)	47	0.08
Malaysian	1	0.00
Pakistani (7)	8	0.01
Sri Lankan (2)	2	0.00
Taiwanese (1)	3	0.00
Thai (27)	32	0.05
Vietnamese (41)	56	0.09
Other Asian, specified	3	0.00
Other Asian, not specified (30)	83	0.14
Australian	24	0.04
Austrian	322	0.54
Belgian	74	0.12
Brazilian	56	0.09
British	213	0.36
Canadian	201	0.34
Croatian	75	0.13
Czech	188	0.31
Czechoslovakian	92	0.15
Danish	131	0.22
Dutch	932	1.55
Eastern European	66	0.11
English	5,415	9.03
Estonian	11	0.02
European	198	0.33
Finnish	222	0.37
French, except Basque	1,598	2.67
French Canadian	449	0.75
German	7,057	11.77
Greek	304	0.51
Guyanese	25	0.04
Hawaii Native/Pacific Islander:	108	0.18
Micronesian: (15)	27	0.04
Guamanian/Chamorro (15)	27	0.04
Polynesian: (8)	12	0.02
Native Hawaiian (6)	10	0.02
Samoan (2)	2	0.00
Other Pac. Isl., not spec. (7)	69	0.11
Hispanic or Latino:	5,564	9.21
Central American:	525	0.87
Costa Rican	44	0.07
Guatemalan	164	0.27
Honduran	56	0.09
Nicaraguan	60	0.10
Panamanian	2	0.00
Salvadoran	182	0.30
Other Central American	17	0.03
Cuban	530	0.88
Dominican Republic	183	0.30
Mexican	1,199	1.99
Puerto Rican	1,652	2.74
South American:	592	0.98
Argentinean	64	0.11
Bolivian	10	0.02
Chilean	13	0.02
Colombian	271	0.45
Ecuadorian	60	0.10
Paraguayan	3	0.00
Peruvian	93	0.15
Uruguayan	14	0.02
Venezuelan	52	0.09
Other South American	12	0.02
Other Hispanic or Latino	883	1.46
Hungarian	627	1.05
Iranian	27	0.05
Irish	6,976	11.64
Israeli	22	0.04
Italian	5,829	9.72
Latvian	21	0.04
Lithuanian	215	0.36
Macedonian	34	0.06
Norwegian	379	0.63
Pennsylvania German	50	0.08
Polish	2,027	3.38
Portuguese	135	0.23
Romanian	208	0.35

Notes: 1. Figures in the "Number" column do not add up to the total population due to: a) Ancestry/Race overlap — e.g. persons can report being both White and Irish, b) persons of Hispanic origin can report being any race, c) persons reporting two ancestries are counted in both categories. 2. Numbers in parentheses indicate the number of persons reporting this ancestry/race alone, not in combination with any other ancestry/race. 3. Refer to the User's Guide in the front of the book for more detailed information.

Russian	1,420	2.37
Scandinavian	19	0.03
Scotch-Irish	774	1.29
Scottish	1,197	2.00
Serbian	44	0.07
Slavic	50	0.08
Slovak	196	0.33
Swedish	702	1.17
Swiss	84	0.14
Turkish	86	0.14
Ukrainian	226	0.38
United States or American	3,112	5.19
Welsh	309	0.52
West Indian, excl. Hispanic:	5,221	8.71
Bahamian	84	0.14
Barbadian	67	0.11
Bermudan	5	0.01
British West Indian	53	0.09
Haitian	4,040	6.74
Jamaican	856	1.43
Trinidadian and Tobagonian	62	0.10
U.S. Virgin Islander	6	0.01
West Indian	48	0.08
White:	43,133	71.43
Not Hispanic (38,897)	39,275	65.04
Hispanic (3,590)	3,858	6.39
Yugoslavian	39	0.07

Bradenton

Place Type: City
County: Manatee
Population: 49,504

Ancestry/Race	Number	%
Acadian/Cajun	21	0.04
African American/Black:	7,835	15.83
Not Hispanic (7,381)	7,665	15.48
Hispanic (100)	170	0.34
African, sub-Saharan:	330	0.66
African	302	0.61
Nigerian	2	0.00
South African	12	0.02
Zimbabwean	14	0.03
Alaska Native tribes, specified:	7	0.01
Eskimo (2)	3	0.01
Tlingit-Haida (3)	4	0.01
Alaska Native tribes, not specified	1	0.00
Am. Ind. or Alaska Nat., not spec.	101	0.20
American Indian tribes, specified:	178	0.36
Apache (3)	9	0.02
Blackfeet (5)	24	0.05
Cherokee (26)	67	0.14
Cheyenne (1)	1	0.00
Chippewa (4)	7	0.01
Choctaw	3	0.01
Comanche	1	0.00
Creek (1)	1	0.00
Delaware	1	0.00
Iroquois (2)	8	0.02
Latin American Indians (16)	18	0.04
Lumbee (4)	4	0.01
Navajo (7)	7	0.01
Seminole (1)	4	0.01
Shoshone (1)	1	0.00
Sioux (5)	7	0.01
All other tribes (11)	15	0.03
American Indian tribes, not spec.	16	0.03
Arab:	148	0.30
Arab/Arabic	9	0.02
Egyptian	37	0.07
Lebanese	55	0.11
Moroccan	25	0.05
Palestinian	8	0.02
Syrian	14	0.03
Armenian	32	0.06
Asian:	508	1.03
Bangladeshi (6)	6	0.01
Cambodian (24)	26	0.05
Chinese, ex. Taiwanese (116)	127	0.26
Filipino (51)	76	0.15
Indian (103)	129	0.26
Indonesian	2	0.00
Japanese (20)	30	0.06
Korean (24)	26	0.05
Laotian (3)	7	0.01
Taiwanese (1)	1	0.00
Thai (19)	20	0.04
Vietnamese (15)	18	0.04
Other Asian, specified (3)	5	0.01
Other Asian, not specified (4)	35	0.07
Australian	4	0.01
Austrian	181	0.36
Belgian	20	0.04
British	220	0.44
Canadian	138	0.28
Croatian	88	0.18
Czech	149	0.30
Czechoslovakian	76	0.15
Danish	85	0.17
Dutch	1,185	2.37
English	5,996	12.01
Estonian	10	0.02
European	150	0.30
Finnish	69	0.14
French, except Basque	1,868	3.74
French Canadian	394	0.79
German	7,444	14.92
Greek	190	0.38
Guyanese	25	0.05
Hawaii Native/Pacific Islander:	55	0.11
Micronesian: (2)	7	0.01
Guamanian/Chamorro (2)	7	0.01
Polynesian: (19)	28	0.06
Native Hawaiian (6)	13	0.03
Samoan (4)	6	0.01
Tongan (5)	5	0.01
Other Polynesian (4)	4	0.01
Other Pac. Isl., specified	2	0.00
Other Pac. Isl., not spec. (2)	18	0.04
Hispanic or Latino:	5,574	11.26
Central American:	326	0.66
Costa Rican	2	0.00
Guatemalan	78	0.16
Honduran	130	0.26
Nicaraguan	42	0.08
Panamanian	11	0.02
Salvadoran	40	0.08
Other Central American	23	0.05
Cuban	234	0.47
Dominican Republic	46	0.09
Mexican	3,507	7.08
Puerto Rican	663	1.34
South American:	159	0.32
Argentinean	16	0.03
Chilean	11	0.02
Colombian	55	0.11
Ecuadorian	13	0.03
Paraguayan	3	0.01
Peruvian	19	0.04
Uruguayan	3	0.01
Venezuelan	25	0.05
Other South American	14	0.03
Other Hispanic or Latino	639	1.29
Hungarian	375	0.75
Iranian	16	0.03
Irish	5,420	10.86
Israeli	33	0.07
Italian	2,705	5.42
Latvian	16	0.03
Lithuanian	126	0.25
Luxemburger	9	0.02
Macedonian	7	0.01
Norwegian	474	0.95
Pennsylvania German	109	0.22
Polish	1,299	2.60
Portuguese	60	0.12
Romanian	16	0.03
Russian	313	0.63
Scandinavian	39	0.08
Scotch-Irish	920	1.84
Scottish	1,220	2.44
Serbian	27	0.05
Slavic	12	0.02
Slovak	137	0.27
Slovene	15	0.03
Swedish	613	1.23
Swiss	192	0.38
Turkish	10	0.02
Ukrainian	158	0.32
United States or American	3,338	6.69
Welsh	501	1.00
West Indian, excl. Hispanic:	548	1.10
Bahamian	68	0.14
Barbadian	5	0.01
Haitian	325	0.65
Jamaican	117	0.23
Trinidadian and Tobagonian	28	0.06
West Indian	5	0.01
White:	39,326	79.44
Not Hispanic (35,450)	35,821	72.36
Hispanic (3,232)	3,505	7.08
Yugoslavian	31	0.06

Brandon

Place Type: Census Designated Place
County: Hillsborough
Population: 77,895

Ancestry/Race	Number	%
African American/Black:	7,766	9.97
Not Hispanic (6,924)	7,358	9.45
Hispanic (289)	408	0.52
African, sub-Saharan:	197	0.25
African	162	0.21
Cape Verdean	7	0.01
Ghanian	12	0.02
Other sub-Saharan African	16	0.02
Alaska Native tribes, specified:	4	0.01
Alaska Athabascan (1)	1	0.00
Eskimo (1)	1	0.00
Tlingit-Haida	2	0.00
Am. Ind. or Alaska Nat., not spec.	202	0.26
American Indian tribes, specified:	471	0.60
Apache (1)	6	0.01
Blackfeet (5)	26	0.03
Cherokee (72)	219	0.28
Cheyenne (1)	1	0.00
Chickasaw (1)	3	0.00
Chippewa (3)	9	0.01
Choctaw (11)	22	0.03
Comanche (3)	3	0.00
Cree	3	0.00
Creek (22)	24	0.03
Delaware	1	0.00
Iroquois (10)	14	0.02
Latin American Indians (11)	27	0.03
Lumbee (4)	5	0.01
Menominee (1)	1	0.00
Navajo (1)	1	0.00
Ottawa (2)	3	0.00
Potawatomi (2)	3	0.00
Pueblo (1)	2	0.00
Seminole (19)	26	0.03
Shoshone	1	0.00
Sioux (20)	28	0.04
Tohono O'Odham	1	0.00
All other tribes (13)	42	0.05
American Indian tribes, not spec.	52	0.07
Arab:	345	0.44
Arab/Arabic	7	0.01
Egyptian	42	0.05
Lebanese	84	0.11
Moroccan	9	0.01
Palestinian	149	0.19
Syrian	24	0.03
Other Arab	30	0.04
Armenian	57	0.07
Asian:	2,438	3.13
Cambodian (4)	4	0.01
Chinese, ex. Taiwanese (187)	256	0.33
Filipino (438)	602	0.77
Indian (566)	629	0.81
Indonesian (13)	19	0.02

Notes: 1. Figures in the "Number" column do not add up to the total population due to: a) Ancestry/Race overlap — e.g. persons can report being both White and Irish, b) persons of Hispanic origin can report being any race, c) persons reporting two ancestries are counted in both categories. 2. Numbers in parentheses indicate the number of persons reporting this ancestry/race alone, not in combination with any other ancestry/race. 3. Refer to the User's Guide in the front of the book for more detailed information.

Japanese (76)	130	0.17
Korean (235)	313	0.40
Laotian	4	0.01
Malaysian	2	0.00
Pakistani (10)	14	0.02
Taiwanese (1)	4	0.01
Thai (101)	140	0.18
Vietnamese (158)	184	0.24
Other Asian, specified	3	0.00
Other Asian, not specified (54)	134	0.17
Australian	8	0.01
Austrian	115	0.15
Belgian	132	0.17
Brazilian	107	0.14
British	556	0.72
Canadian	267	0.34
Croatian	93	0.12
Cypriot	17	0.02
Czech	272	0.35
Czechoslovakian	127	0.16
Danish	139	0.18
Dutch	1,352	1.74
Eastern European	44	0.06
English	8,848	11.38
European	856	1.10
Finnish	78	0.10
French, except Basque	2,988	3.84
French Canadian	688	0.89
German	11,195	14.40
Greek	352	0.45
Guyanese	8	0.01
Hawaii Native/Pacific Islander:	153	0.20
Melanesian: (1)	1	0.00
Fijian (1)	1	0.00
Micronesian: (20)	29	0.04
Guamanian/Chamorro (16)	25	0.03
Other Micronesian (4)	4	0.01
Polynesian: (34)	66	0.08
Native Hawaiian (14)	38	0.05
Samoan (11)	15	0.02
Tongan (3)	3	0.00
Other Polynesian (6)	10	0.01
Other Pac. Isl., specified	3	0.00
Other Pac. Isl., not spec. (16)	54	0.07
Hispanic or Latino:	9,882	12.69
Central American:	378	0.49
Costa Rican	23	0.03
Guatemalan	30	0.04
Honduran	76	0.10
Nicaraguan	55	0.07
Panamanian	122	0.16
Salvadoran	60	0.08
Other Central American	12	0.02
Cuban	1,078	1.38
Dominican Republic	232	0.30
Mexican	923	1.18
Puerto Rican	4,599	5.90
South American:	658	0.84
Argentinean	35	0.04
Bolivian	9	0.01
Chilean	25	0.03
Colombian	310	0.40
Ecuadorian	67	0.09
Paraguayan	1	0.00
Peruvian	85	0.11
Uruguayan	7	0.01
Venezuelan	89	0.11
Other South American	30	0.04
Other Hispanic or Latino	2,014	2.59
Hungarian	463	0.60
Icelander	9	0.01
Iranian	50	0.06
Irish	9,678	12.45
Italian	5,377	6.92
Lithuanian	260	0.33
Luxemburger	7	0.01
Northern European	14	0.02
Norwegian	699	0.90
Polish	2,333	3.00
Portuguese	424	0.55
Romanian	61	0.08
Russian	494	0.64
Scandinavian	128	0.16
Scotch-Irish	1,380	1.78
Scottish	1,884	2.42
Serbian	23	0.03
Slavic	47	0.06
Slovak	188	0.24
Slovene	17	0.02
Swedish	719	0.92
Swiss	131	0.17
Turkish	52	0.07
Ukrainian	191	0.25
United States or American	6,631	8.53
Welsh	458	0.59
West Indian, excl. Hispanic:	1,124	1.45
Bahamian	9	0.01
Barbadian	17	0.02
Belizean	48	0.06
British West Indian	52	0.07
Dutch West Indian	32	0.04
Haitian	76	0.10
Jamaican	630	0.81
Trinidadian and Tobagonian	165	0.21
U.S. Virgin Islander	26	0.03
West Indian	69	0.09
White:	65,406	83.97
Not Hispanic (57,398)	58,481	75.08
Hispanic (6,400)	6,925	8.89
Yugoslavian	130	0.17

Brent

Place Type: Census Designated Place
County: Escambia
Population: 22,257

Ancestry/Race	Number	%
Acadian/Cajun	5	0.02
African American/Black:	7,760	34.87
Not Hispanic (7,591)	7,715	34.66
Hispanic (31)	45	0.20
African, sub-Saharan:	240	1.08
African	240	1.08
Alaska Native tribes, specified:	1	0.00
All other tribes	1	0.00
Am. Ind. or Alaska Nat., not spec.	83	0.37
American Indian tribes, specified:	246	1.11
Apache (3)	4	0.02
Blackfeet (4)	12	0.05
Cherokee (20)	80	0.36
Cheyenne	1	0.00
Chippewa (3)	3	0.01
Choctaw (4)	16	0.07
Creek (71)	98	0.44
Houma (3)	4	0.02
Iroquois (2)	3	0.01
Latin American Indians (3)	6	0.03
Navajo (1)	6	0.03
Osage	1	0.00
Potawatomi	2	0.01
Pueblo	1	0.00
Puget Sound Salish (2)	2	0.01
Seminole	1	0.00
Sioux (1)	3	0.01
All other tribes	3	0.01
American Indian tribes, not spec.	43	0.19
Armenian	5	0.02
Asian:	652	2.93
Cambodian (39)	41	0.18
Chinese, ex. Taiwanese (45)	72	0.32
Filipino (141)	185	0.83
Indian (31)	49	0.22
Indonesian (12)	16	0.07
Japanese (14)	30	0.13
Korean (57)	68	0.31
Laotian (11)	11	0.05
Malaysian	2	0.01
Pakistani (1)	2	0.01
Taiwanese (2)	7	0.03
Thai (8)	14	0.06
Vietnamese (128)	131	0.59
Other Asian, specified (2)	4	0.02
Other Asian, not specified (2)	20	0.09
Austrian	7	0.03
Belgian	39	0.18
British	47	0.21
Canadian	27	0.12
Czech	14	0.06
Czechoslovakian	7	0.03
Danish	14	0.06
Dutch	238	1.07
English	941	4.25
European	104	0.47
Finnish	21	0.09
French, except Basque	268	1.21
French Canadian	39	0.18
German	1,169	5.28
Greek	37	0.17
Hawaii Native/Pacific Islander:	103	0.46
Melanesian:	3	0.01
Other Melanesian	3	0.01
Micronesian: (42)	64	0.29
Guamanian/Chamorro (29)	44	0.20
Other Micronesian (13)	20	0.09
Polynesian: (16)	26	0.12
Native Hawaiian (3)	10	0.04
Samoan (13)	16	0.07
Other Pac. Isl., specified	2	0.01
Other Pac. Isl., not spec. (2)	8	0.04
Hispanic or Latino:	433	1.95
Central American:	27	0.12
Costa Rican	3	0.01
Guatemalan	4	0.02
Honduran	8	0.04
Nicaraguan	1	0.00
Panamanian	10	0.04
Salvadoran	1	0.00
Cuban	32	0.14
Dominican Republic	3	0.01
Mexican	127	0.57
Puerto Rican	117	0.53
South American:	24	0.11
Argentinean	6	0.03
Bolivian	1	0.00
Chilean	1	0.00
Colombian	6	0.03
Ecuadorian	2	0.01
Peruvian	3	0.01
Venezuelan	2	0.01
Other South American	3	0.01
Other Hispanic or Latino	103	0.46
Hungarian	36	0.16
Irish	1,131	5.11
Italian	363	1.64
Norwegian	118	0.53
Pennsylvania German	5	0.02
Polish	141	0.64
Portuguese	36	0.16
Romanian	10	0.05
Russian	47	0.21
Scotch-Irish	338	1.53
Scottish	163	0.74
Slavic	8	0.04
Slovak	6	0.03
Swedish	111	0.50
Swiss	19	0.09
United States or American	1,926	8.69
Welsh	144	0.65
West Indian, excl. Hispanic:	27	0.12
Bahamian	7	0.03
Barbadian	4	0.02
Jamaican	6	0.03
Trinidadian and Tobagonian	10	0.05
White:	13,704	61.57
Not Hispanic (13,082)	13,405	60.23
Hispanic (244)	299	1.34

Brownsville

Place Type: Census Designated Place
County: Miami-Dade
Population: 14,393

Ancestry/Race	Number	%

Notes: 1. Figures in the "Number" column do not add up to the total population due to: a) Ancestry/Race overlap — e.g. persons can report being both White and Irish, b) persons of Hispanic origin can report being any race, c) persons reporting two ancestries are counted in both categories. 2. Numbers in parentheses indicate the number of persons reporting this ancestry/race alone, not in combination with any other ancestry/race. 3. Refer to the User's Guide in the front of the book for more detailed information.

African American/Black:	13,249	92.05
Not Hispanic (12,974)	13,069	90.80
Hispanic (157)	180	1.25
African, sub-Saharan:	307	2.12
African	307	2.12
Am. Ind. or Alaska Nat., not spec.	48	0.33
American Indian tribes, specified:	27	0.19
Blackfeet	1	0.01
Cherokee	17	0.12
Latin American Indians (2)	3	0.02
Pueblo	1	0.01
Seminole	5	0.03
American Indian tribes, not spec.	2	0.01
Asian:	18	0.13
Indian (3)	8	0.06
Other Asian, specified	2	0.01
Other Asian, not specified	8	0.06
British	13	0.09
Canadian	16	0.11
English	16	0.11
German	3	0.02
Hawaii Native/Pacific Islander:	29	0.20
Polynesian: (1)	4	0.03
Native Hawaiian	3	0.02
Samoan (1)	1	0.01
Other Pac. Isl., specified	2	0.01
Other Pac. Isl., not spec. (1)	23	0.16
Hispanic or Latino:	1,183	8.22
Central American:	261	1.81
Costa Rican	1	0.01
Guatemalan	6	0.04
Honduran	75	0.52
Nicaraguan	151	1.05
Panamanian	4	0.03
Salvadoran	8	0.06
Other Central American	16	0.11
Cuban	446	3.10
Dominican Republic	64	0.44
Mexican	16	0.11
Puerto Rican	81	0.56
South American:	27	0.19
Argentinean	5	0.03
Chilean	1	0.01
Colombian	15	0.10
Peruvian	2	0.01
Uruguayan	1	0.01
Venezuelan	3	0.02
Other Hispanic or Latino	288	2.00
Irish	5	0.03
Italian	21	0.15
Norwegian	3	0.02
Polish	8	0.06
Romanian	9	0.06
Russian	23	0.16
Scotch-Irish	6	0.04
United States or American	550	3.81
West Indian, excl. Hispanic:	544	3.76
Bahamian	279	1.93
Barbadian	8	0.06
Belizean	33	0.23
British West Indian	21	0.15
Haitian	52	0.36
Jamaican	114	0.79
Trinidadian and Tobagonian	17	0.12
West Indian	20	0.14
White:	921	6.40
Not Hispanic (102)	131	0.91
Hispanic (727)	790	5.49

Callaway

Place Type: City
County: Bay
Population: 14,233

Ancestry/Race	Number	%
Acadian/Cajun	21	0.15
African American/Black:	2,390	16.79
Not Hispanic (2,227)	2,357	16.56
Hispanic (24)	33	0.23
African, sub-Saharan:	154	1.08
African	154	1.08
Alaska Native tribes, specified:	2	0.01
Alaska Athabascan (1)	1	0.01
Eskimo	1	0.01
Am. Ind. or Alaska Nat., not spec.	48	0.34
American Indian tribes, specified:	147	1.03
Apache	3	0.02
Blackfeet	14	0.10
Cherokee (24)	54	0.38
Cheyenne (1)	2	0.01
Choctaw (2)	3	0.02
Comanche	1	0.01
Creek (21)	30	0.21
Delaware	2	0.01
Houma (2)	2	0.01
Latin American Indians (1)	5	0.04
Navajo (5)	5	0.04
Paiute (1)	1	0.01
Potawatomi (2)	2	0.01
Seminole (2)	3	0.02
Sioux (1)	4	0.03
Yaqui	1	0.01
All other tribes (12)	15	0.11
American Indian tribes, not spec.	18	0.13
Arab:	35	0.25
Egyptian	30	0.21
Lebanese	5	0.04
Asian:	701	4.93
Chinese, ex. Taiwanese (17)	37	0.26
Filipino (170)	257	1.81
Indian (8)	14	0.10
Indonesian	1	0.01
Japanese (30)	58	0.41
Korean (88)	125	0.88
Laotian (1)	1	0.01
Pakistani	4	0.03
Taiwanese (2)	5	0.04
Thai (52)	76	0.53
Vietnamese (84)	94	0.66
Other Asian, specified	1	0.01
Other Asian, not specified (15)	28	0.20
Australian	8	0.06
Austrian	8	0.06
Basque	9	0.06
British	97	0.68
Canadian	38	0.27
Celtic	64	0.45
Croatian	9	0.06
Czechoslovakian	22	0.15
Danish	22	0.15
Dutch	155	1.09
English	1,198	8.41
European	169	1.19
French, except Basque	315	2.21
French Canadian	190	1.33
German	1,420	9.96
Greek	16	0.11
Hawaii Native/Pacific Islander:	39	0.27
Micronesian: (5)	6	0.04
Guamanian/Chamorro (5)	6	0.04
Polynesian: (5)	23	0.16
Native Hawaiian (5)	21	0.15
Samoan	2	0.01
Other Pac. Isl., not spec. (2)	10	0.07
Hispanic or Latino:	509	3.58
Central American:	21	0.15
Honduran	2	0.01
Panamanian	18	0.13
Other Central American	1	0.01
Cuban	25	0.18
Dominican Republic	1	0.01
Mexican	189	1.33
Puerto Rican	163	1.15
South American:	12	0.08
Bolivian	3	0.02
Chilean	5	0.04
Colombian	1	0.01
Peruvian	1	0.01
Other South American	2	0.01
Other Hispanic or Latino	98	0.69
Hungarian	40	0.28
Icelander	12	0.08
Irish	1,485	10.42
Israeli	5	0.04
Italian	659	4.62
Norwegian	80	0.56
Pennsylvania German	31	0.22
Polish	230	1.61
Portuguese	21	0.15
Scandinavian	17	0.12
Scotch-Irish	298	2.09
Scottish	232	1.63
Serbian	18	0.13
Slovak	14	0.10
Swedish	112	0.79
Swiss	19	0.13
Turkish	12	0.08
United States or American	1,977	13.87
Welsh	22	0.15
West Indian, excl. Hispanic:	53	0.37
Dutch West Indian	9	0.06
Trinidadian and Tobagonian	44	0.31
White:	11,120	78.13
Not Hispanic (10,501)	10,802	75.89
Hispanic (268)	318	2.23

Cape Coral

Place Type: City
County: Lee
Population: 102,286

Ancestry/Race	Number	%
African American/Black:	2,424	2.37
Not Hispanic (1,831)	2,142	2.09
Hispanic (215)	282	0.28
African, sub-Saharan:	87	0.09
African	19	0.02
Cape Verdean	22	0.02
Liberian	22	0.02
South African	24	0.02
Am. Ind. or Alaska Nat., not spec.	191	0.19
Albanian	6	0.01
Alsatian	16	0.02
American Indian tribes, specified:	448	0.44
Apache (6)	12	0.01
Blackfeet (4)	25	0.02
Cherokee (56)	162	0.16
Cheyenne	1	0.00
Chickasaw (3)	5	0.00
Chippewa (10)	26	0.03
Choctaw (4)	22	0.02
Comanche	1	0.00
Cree	6	0.01
Creek (1)	7	0.01
Crow (1)	1	0.00
Delaware (2)	5	0.00
Houma (1)	1	0.00
Iroquois (24)	38	0.04
Latin American Indians (24)	31	0.03
Lumbee (1)	1	0.00
Navajo (2)	6	0.01
Osage	1	0.00
Potawatomi (7)	13	0.01
Pueblo	6	0.01
Puget Sound Salish (1)	2	0.00
Seminole (4)	13	0.01
Sioux (10)	32	0.03
Ute (1)	1	0.00
Yaqui	1	0.00
All other tribes (11)	29	0.03
American Indian tribes, not spec.	27	0.03
Arab:	245	0.24
Arab/Arabic	7	0.01
Egyptian	17	0.02
Lebanese	113	0.11
Moroccan	20	0.02
Syrian	80	0.08
Other Arab	8	0.01
Armenian	26	0.03
Asian:	1,288	1.26
Bangladeshi (11)	16	0.02
Cambodian (2)	2	0.00
Chinese, ex. Taiwanese (114)	157	0.15

Notes: 1. Figures in the "Number" column do not add up to the total population due to: a) Ancestry/Race overlap — e.g. persons can report being both White and Irish, b) persons of Hispanic origin can report being any race, c) persons reporting two ancestries are counted in both categories. 2. Numbers in parentheses indicate the number of persons reporting this ancestry/race alone, not in combination with any other ancestry/race. 3. Refer to the User's Guide in the front of the book for more detailed information.

Filipino (362)	461	0.45
Indian (112)	169	0.17
Indonesian (2)	14	0.01
Japanese (43)	98	0.10
Korean (103)	141	0.14
Laotian (23)	28	0.03
Malaysian (2)	6	0.01
Pakistani (4)	4	0.00
Taiwanese (1)	2	0.00
Thai (23)	40	0.04
Vietnamese (92)	106	0.10
Other Asian, specified (5)	14	0.01
Other Asian, not specified (10)	30	0.03
Australian	45	0.04
Austrian	370	0.36
Basque	4	0.00
Belgian	160	0.16
Brazilian	18	0.02
British	413	0.40
Bulgarian	24	0.02
Canadian	508	0.50
Croatian	298	0.29
Czech	509	0.50
Czechoslovakian	239	0.23
Danish	473	0.46
Dutch	1,991	1.95
Eastern European	25	0.02
English	12,127	11.87
Estonian	8	0.01
European	439	0.43
Finnish	315	0.31
French, except Basque	4,300	4.21
French Canadian	1,058	1.04
German	21,385	20.92
Greek	670	0.66
Guyanese	23	0.02
Hawaii Native/Pacific Islander:	128	0.13
Micronesian: (12)	13	0.01
Guamanian/Chamorro (8)	9	0.01
Other Micronesian (4)	4	0.00
Polynesian: (31)	69	0.07
Native Hawaiian (28)	62	0.06
Samoan (3)	7	0.01
Other Pac. Isl., specified	8	0.01
Other Pac. Isl., not spec. (12)	38	0.04
Hispanic or Latino:	8,521	8.33
Central American:	432	0.42
Costa Rican	54	0.05
Guatemalan	88	0.09
Honduran	78	0.08
Nicaraguan	49	0.05
Panamanian	41	0.04
Salvadoran	88	0.09
Other Central American	34	0.03
Cuban	1,408	1.38
Dominican Republic	380	0.37
Mexican	822	0.80
Puerto Rican	2,715	2.65
South American:	1,109	1.08
Argentinean	60	0.06
Bolivian	9	0.01
Chilean	31	0.03
Colombian	576	0.56
Ecuadorian	159	0.16
Paraguayan	4	0.00
Peruvian	149	0.15
Uruguayan	22	0.02
Venezuelan	54	0.05
Other South American	45	0.04
Other Hispanic or Latino	1,655	1.62
Hungarian	936	0.92
Icelander	6	0.01
Iranian	12	0.01
Irish	16,271	15.92
Israeli	7	0.01
Italian	13,437	13.15
Latvian	9	0.01
Lithuanian	398	0.39
Luxemburger	8	0.01
Macedonian	12	0.01
Maltese	141	0.14
New Zealander	23	0.02
Northern European	15	0.01
Norwegian	1,299	1.27
Pennsylvania German	110	0.11
Polish	5,055	4.95
Portuguese	536	0.52
Romanian	227	0.22
Russian	855	0.84
Scandinavian	144	0.14
Scotch-Irish	1,735	1.70
Scottish	2,012	1.97
Serbian	101	0.10
Slavic	45	0.04
Slovak	529	0.52
Slovene	138	0.14
Swedish	1,598	1.56
Swiss	336	0.33
Turkish	39	0.04
Ukrainian	370	0.36
United States or American	7,841	7.67
Welsh	773	0.76
West Indian, excl. Hispanic:	491	0.48
Bahamian	11	0.01
Bermudan	17	0.02
British West Indian	10	0.01
Haitian	180	0.18
Jamaican	191	0.19
Trinidadian and Tobagonian	29	0.03
West Indian	53	0.05
White:	96,532	94.37
Not Hispanic (89,535)	90,436	88.41
Hispanic (5,598)	6,096	5.96
Yugoslavian	104	0.10

Carol City

Place Type: Census Designated Place
County: Miami-Dade
Population: 59,443

Ancestry/Race	Number	%
African American/Black:	31,944	53.74
Not Hispanic (29,560)	30,062	50.57
Hispanic (1,410)	1,882	3.17
African, sub-Saharan:	622	1.05
African	505	0.85
Ethiopian	6	0.01
Ghanian	19	0.03
Nigerian	84	0.14
Other sub-Saharan African	8	0.01
Alaska Native tribes, specified:	1	0.00
Aleut	1	0.00
Am. Ind. or Alaska Nat., not spec.	132	0.22
American Indian tribes, specified:	82	0.14
Apache (4)	4	0.01
Blackfeet (2)	4	0.01
Cherokee (10)	26	0.04
Chippewa	1	0.00
Choctaw	3	0.01
Iroquois	1	0.00
Latin American Indians (12)	28	0.05
Paiute	1	0.00
Potawatomi (1)	3	0.01
Pueblo	2	0.00
Sioux (3)	4	0.01
All other tribes (1)	5	0.01
American Indian tribes, not spec.	19	0.03
Arab:	138	0.23
Arab/Arabic	48	0.08
Egyptian	21	0.04
Lebanese	40	0.07
Palestinian	20	0.03
Syrian	9	0.02
Armenian	4	0.01
Asian:	504	0.85
Bangladeshi (4)	4	0.01
Chinese, ex. Taiwanese (60)	111	0.19
Filipino (85)	99	0.17
Indian (132)	188	0.32
Japanese (6)	16	0.03
Korean (2)	5	0.01
Pakistani (20)	33	0.06
Thai	3	0.01
Vietnamese (5)	7	0.01
Other Asian, specified	3	0.01
Other Asian, not specified (7)	35	0.06
Austrian	6	0.01
Brazilian	43	0.07
British	78	0.13
Canadian	22	0.04
Celtic	5	0.01
Czech	6	0.01
Czechoslovakian	10	0.02
Danish	6	0.01
Dutch	20	0.03
English	255	0.43
European	14	0.02
Finnish	7	0.01
French, except Basque	168	0.28
French Canadian	27	0.05
German	353	0.59
German Russian	8	0.01
Greek	5	0.01
Guyanese	155	0.26
Hawaii Native/Pacific Islander:	75	0.13
Micronesian: (8)	10	0.02
Guamanian/Chamorro (8)	10	0.02
Polynesian: (6)	7	0.01
Native Hawaiian (2)	3	0.01
Samoan (1)	1	0.00
Tongan (2)	2	0.00
Other Polynesian (1)	1	0.00
Other Pac. Isl., specified	3	0.01
Other Pac. Isl., not spec. (10)	55	0.09
Hispanic or Latino:	24,965	42.00
Central American:	2,460	4.14
Costa Rican	128	0.22
Guatemalan	217	0.37
Honduran	428	0.72
Nicaraguan	1,305	2.20
Panamanian	206	0.35
Salvadoran	134	0.23
Other Central American	42	0.07
Cuban	11,146	18.75
Dominican Republic	1,785	3.00
Mexican	377	0.63
Puerto Rican	2,745	4.62
South American:	2,210	3.72
Argentinean	84	0.14
Bolivian	19	0.03
Chilean	92	0.15
Colombian	1,279	2.15
Ecuadorian	318	0.53
Paraguayan	1	0.00
Peruvian	253	0.43
Uruguayan	9	0.02
Venezuelan	131	0.22
Other South American	24	0.04
Other Hispanic or Latino	4,242	7.14
Hungarian	24	0.04
Irish	401	0.67
Israeli	2	0.00
Italian	405	0.68
Lithuanian	6	0.01
Norwegian	14	0.02
Polish	101	0.17
Portuguese	23	0.04
Romanian	36	0.06
Russian	38	0.06
Scotch-Irish	15	0.03
Scottish	38	0.06
Slovak	9	0.02
Swedish	35	0.06
Swiss	18	0.03
Turkish	5	0.01
Ukrainian	17	0.03
United States or American	2,830	4.76
West Indian, excl. Hispanic:	5,829	9.81
Bahamian	437	0.74
Barbadian	54	0.09
Belizean	85	0.14
British West Indian	327	0.55
Haitian	1,357	2.28

Notes: 1. Figures in the "Number" column do not add up to the total population due to: a) Ancestry/Race overlap — e.g. persons can report being both White and Irish, b) persons of Hispanic origin can report being any race, c) persons reporting two ancestries are counted in both categories. 2. Numbers in parentheses indicate the number of persons reporting this ancestry/race alone, not in combination with any other ancestry/race. 3. Refer to the User's Guide in the front of the book for more detailed information.

Jamaican	3,111	5.23
Trinidadian and Tobagonian	282	0.47
U.S. Virgin Islander	20	0.03
West Indian	122	0.21
Other West Indian	34	0.06
White:	23,995	40.37
Not Hispanic (3,798)	4,020	6.76
Hispanic (18,855)	19,975	33.60

Casselberry

Place Type: City
County: Seminole
Population: 22,629

Ancestry/Race	Number	%
Acadian/Cajun	27	0.12
African American/Black:	1,351	5.97
Not Hispanic (1,137)	1,241	5.48
Hispanic (81)	110	0.49
African, sub-Saharan:	12	0.05
African	12	0.05
Am. Ind. or Alaska Nat., not spec.	45	0.20
Albanian	27	0.12
American Indian tribes, specified:	149	0.66
Apache (1)	2	0.01
Blackfeet (2)	6	0.03
Cherokee (14)	64	0.28
Chippewa	4	0.02
Choctaw (2)	3	0.01
Creek (1)	12	0.05
Iroquois (4)	7	0.03
Latin American Indians (4)	18	0.08
Menominee	1	0.00
Seminole	1	0.00
Sioux (7)	8	0.04
Yaqui	11	0.05
All other tribes (5)	12	0.05
American Indian tribes, not spec.	12	0.05
Arab:	143	0.65
Arab/Arabic	17	0.08
Iraqi	7	0.03
Jordanian	13	0.06
Lebanese	60	0.27
Moroccan	6	0.03
Palestinian	26	0.12
Syrian	14	0.06
Armenian	48	0.22
Asian:	546	2.41
Bangladeshi (3)	3	0.01
Cambodian (1)	1	0.00
Chinese, ex. Taiwanese (95)	114	0.50
Filipino (72)	99	0.44
Indian (77)	94	0.42
Indonesian (1)	2	0.01
Japanese (13)	25	0.11
Korean (32)	39	0.17
Laotian (2)	5	0.02
Pakistani (4)	5	0.02
Taiwanese (4)	5	0.02
Thai (7)	9	0.04
Vietnamese (111)	122	0.54
Other Asian, specified	2	0.01
Other Asian, not specified (2)	21	0.09
Australian	6	0.03
Austrian	53	0.24
Basque	18	0.08
Brazilian	11	0.05
British	78	0.35
Canadian	83	0.37
Croatian	20	0.09
Czech	79	0.36
Czechoslovakian	41	0.19
Danish	141	0.64
Dutch	349	1.57
Eastern European	16	0.07
English	2,720	12.27
European	96	0.43
Finnish	18	0.08
French, except Basque	802	3.62
French Canadian	275	1.24
German	3,532	15.94
Greek	153	0.69
Guyanese	77	0.35
Hawaii Native/Pacific Islander:	37	0.16
Micronesian: (3)	4	0.02
Guamanian/Chamorro (3)	4	0.02
Polynesian: (4)	17	0.08
Native Hawaiian (2)	12	0.05
Samoan (2)	5	0.02
Other Pac. Isl., specified	2	0.01
Other Pac. Isl., not spec. (2)	14	0.06
Hispanic or Latino:	3,424	15.13
Central American:	110	0.49
Costa Rican	16	0.07
Guatemalan	23	0.10
Honduran	19	0.08
Nicaraguan	8	0.04
Panamanian	24	0.11
Salvadoran	16	0.07
Other Central American	4	0.02
Cuban	243	1.07
Dominican Republic	106	0.47
Mexican	278	1.23
Puerto Rican	1,869	8.26
South American:	350	1.55
Argentinean	47	0.21
Bolivian	9	0.04
Chilean	11	0.05
Colombian	157	0.69
Ecuadorian	47	0.21
Peruvian	26	0.11
Venezuelan	46	0.20
Other South American	7	0.03
Other Hispanic or Latino	468	2.07
Hungarian	143	0.65
Iranian	9	0.04
Irish	3,187	14.38
Italian	1,881	8.49
Latvian	23	0.10
Lithuanian	31	0.14
Macedonian	11	0.05
Norwegian	171	0.77
Pennsylvania German	14	0.06
Polish	815	3.68
Portuguese	152	0.69
Romanian	25	0.11
Russian	202	0.91
Scandinavian	32	0.14
Scotch-Irish	401	1.81
Scottish	550	2.48
Serbian	49	0.22
Slavic	18	0.08
Slovak	37	0.17
Swedish	234	1.06
Swiss	83	0.37
Turkish	25	0.11
Ukrainian	81	0.37
United States or American	1,664	7.51
Welsh	169	0.76
West Indian, excl. Hispanic:	255	1.15
Belizean	39	0.18
Bermudan	16	0.07
Jamaican	86	0.39
Trinidadian and Tobagonian	50	0.23
U.S. Virgin Islander	8	0.04
West Indian	49	0.22
Other West Indian	7	0.03
White:	19,867	87.79
Not Hispanic (17,145)	17,452	77.12
Hispanic (2,236)	2,415	10.67
Yugoslavian	110	0.50

Citrus Park

Place Type: Census Designated Place
County: Hillsborough
Population: 20,226

Ancestry/Race	Number	%
African American/Black:	1,680	8.31
Not Hispanic (1,478)	1,588	7.85
Hispanic (54)	92	0.45
African, sub-Saharan:	137	0.68
African	102	0.51
Cape Verdean	35	0.17
Am. Ind. or Alaska Nat., not spec.	40	0.20
American Indian tribes, specified:	92	0.45
Cherokee (18)	35	0.17
Chippewa (6)	6	0.03
Choctaw (2)	3	0.01
Creek (1)	4	0.02
Houma (2)	2	0.01
Iroquois (6)	7	0.03
Kiowa (1)	2	0.01
Latin American Indians (3)	6	0.03
Menominee	1	0.00
Navajo	1	0.00
Osage (2)	2	0.01
Puget Sound Salish (1)	1	0.00
Seminole (1)	3	0.01
Sioux (5)	8	0.04
All other tribes (4)	11	0.05
American Indian tribes, not spec.	13	0.06
Arab:	32	0.16
Lebanese	32	0.16
Armenian	31	0.15
Asian:	797	3.94
Bangladeshi (6)	6	0.03
Cambodian (1)	1	0.00
Chinese, ex. Taiwanese (68)	86	0.43
Filipino (86)	121	0.60
Indian (185)	216	1.07
Indonesian (2)	9	0.04
Japanese (11)	31	0.15
Korean (125)	142	0.70
Pakistani (4)	4	0.02
Taiwanese (8)	9	0.04
Thai (25)	32	0.16
Vietnamese (94)	103	0.51
Other Asian, specified (2)	2	0.01
Other Asian, not specified (21)	35	0.17
Austrian	50	0.25
Belgian	26	0.13
Brazilian	32	0.16
British	100	0.50
Canadian	62	0.31
Czech	22	0.11
Czechoslovakian	55	0.27
Danish	57	0.28
Dutch	327	1.63
English	2,176	10.82
European	95	0.47
Finnish	15	0.07
French, except Basque	515	2.56
French Canadian	231	1.15
German	2,842	14.14
Greek	160	0.80
Guyanese	105	0.52
Hawaii Native/Pacific Islander:	42	0.21
Micronesian: (1)	1	0.00
Guamanian/Chamorro (1)	1	0.00
Polynesian: (14)	23	0.11
Native Hawaiian (7)	13	0.06
Samoan (6)	9	0.04
Other Polynesian (1)	1	0.00
Other Pac. Isl., not spec.	18	0.09
Hispanic or Latino:	4,098	20.26
Central American:	109	0.54
Costa Rican	8	0.04
Guatemalan	15	0.07
Honduran	34	0.17
Nicaraguan	20	0.10
Panamanian	22	0.11
Salvadoran	9	0.04
Other Central American	1	0.00
Cuban	944	4.67
Dominican Republic	78	0.39
Mexican	165	0.82
Puerto Rican	1,442	7.13
South American:	453	2.24
Argentinean	11	0.05
Bolivian	5	0.02
Chilean	6	0.03
Colombian	228	1.13

Notes: 1. Figures in the "Number" column do not add up to the total population due to: a) Ancestry/Race overlap — e.g. persons can report being both White and Irish, b) persons of Hispanic origin can report being any race, c) persons reporting two ancestries are counted in both categories. 2. Numbers in parentheses indicate the number of persons reporting this ancestry/race alone, not in combination with any other ancestry/race. 3. Refer to the User's Guide in the front of the book for more detailed information.

Ecuadorian	23	0.11
Paraguayan	3	0.01
Peruvian	103	0.51
Venezuelan	49	0.24
Other South American	25	0.12
Other Hispanic or Latino	907	4.48
Hungarian	98	0.49
Iranian	25	0.12
Irish	2,202	10.95
Israeli	13	0.06
Italian	1,815	9.03
Latvian	11	0.05
Lithuanian	38	0.19
Norwegian	78	0.39
Pennsylvania German	20	0.10
Polish	665	3.31
Portuguese	56	0.28
Romanian	23	0.11
Russian	259	1.29
Scotch-Irish	235	1.17
Scottish	404	2.01
Serbian	28	0.14
Slovak	17	0.08
Slovene	10	0.05
Swedish	163	0.81
Swiss	32	0.16
Turkish	14	0.07
Ukrainian	19	0.09
United States or American	2,089	10.39
Welsh	121	0.60
West Indian, excl. Hispanic:	182	0.91
Belizean	7	0.03
British West Indian	10	0.05
Dutch West Indian	11	0.05
Haitian	24	0.12
Jamaican	87	0.43
Trinidadian and Tobagonian	19	0.09
U.S. Virgin Islander	9	0.04
Other West Indian	15	0.07
White:	16,924	83.67
Not Hispanic (13,566)	13,807	68.26
Hispanic (2,918)	3,117	15.41
Yugoslavian	24	0.12

Citrus Ridge

Place Type: Census Designated Place
County: Lake
Population: 12,015

Ancestry/Race	Number	%
Acadian/Cajun	2	0.02
African American/Black:	524	4.36
Not Hispanic (394)	464	3.86
Hispanic (35)	60	0.50
African, sub-Saharan:	25	0.22
African	18	0.16
Nigerian	7	0.06
Am. Ind. or Alaska Nat., not spec.	57	0.47
American Indian tribes, specified:	45	0.37
Apache	1	0.01
Blackfeet (1)	7	0.06
Cherokee (2)	16	0.13
Cheyenne (1)	1	0.01
Chippewa	1	0.01
Choctaw	3	0.02
Creek (1)	1	0.01
Iroquois (1)	1	0.01
Latin American Indians (4)	8	0.07
Navajo	1	0.01
Seminole	1	0.01
Shoshone (1)	1	0.01
All other tribes (1)	3	0.02
American Indian tribes, not spec.	2	0.02
Arab:	106	0.93
Arab/Arabic	27	0.24
Lebanese	22	0.19
Moroccan	27	0.24
Palestinian	21	0.18
Syrian	9	0.08
Asian:	358	2.98
Cambodian (1)	1	0.01
Chinese, ex. Taiwanese (88)	110	0.92
Filipino (44)	76	0.63
Indian (65)	70	0.58
Indonesian (2)	2	0.02
Japanese (12)	25	0.21
Korean (14)	19	0.16
Pakistani (7)	7	0.06
Taiwanese (10)	10	0.08
Thai (4)	4	0.03
Vietnamese (16)	21	0.17
Other Asian, not specified (5)	13	0.11
Austrian	64	0.56
Belgian	22	0.19
British	175	1.53
Canadian	96	0.84
Croatian	21	0.18
Czech	60	0.53
Czechoslovakian	8	0.07
Danish	29	0.25
Dutch	171	1.50
Eastern European	6	0.05
English	1,113	9.75
European	91	0.80
Finnish	37	0.32
French, except Basque	401	3.51
French Canadian	203	1.78
German	1,779	15.58
Greek	39	0.34
Hawaii Native/Pacific Islander:	27	0.22
Micronesian: (2)	2	0.02
Guamanian/Chamorro (2)	2	0.02
Polynesian: (4)	8	0.07
Native Hawaiian (4)	8	0.07
Other Pac. Isl., not spec. (4)	17	0.14
Hispanic or Latino:	1,874	15.60
Central American:	63	0.52
Costa Rican	4	0.03
Guatemalan	15	0.12
Honduran	10	0.08
Nicaraguan	11	0.09
Panamanian	17	0.14
Salvadoran	3	0.02
Other Central American	3	0.02
Cuban	99	0.82
Dominican Republic	53	0.44
Mexican	139	1.16
Puerto Rican	1,027	8.55
South American:	237	1.97
Argentinean	16	0.13
Bolivian	1	0.01
Chilean	1	0.01
Colombian	121	1.01
Ecuadorian	24	0.20
Paraguayan	1	0.01
Peruvian	39	0.32
Uruguayan	2	0.02
Venezuelan	28	0.23
Other South American	4	0.03
Other Hispanic or Latino	256	2.13
Hungarian	60	0.53
Icelander	2	0.02
Irish	1,495	13.09
Italian	1,283	11.23
Lithuanian	36	0.32
Maltese	10	0.09
Northern European	9	0.08
Norwegian	117	1.02
Pennsylvania German	29	0.25
Polish	390	3.42
Portuguese	102	0.89
Russian	127	1.11
Scandinavian	11	0.10
Scotch-Irish	105	0.92
Scottish	363	3.18
Slavic	2	0.02
Slovak	13	0.11
Slovene	12	0.11
Swedish	126	1.10
Turkish	7	0.06
Ukrainian	58	0.51
United States or American	1,033	9.05
Welsh	62	0.54
West Indian, excl. Hispanic:	122	1.07
Haitian	65	0.57
Jamaican	46	0.40
Trinidadian and Tobagonian	11	0.10
White:	10,706	89.11
Not Hispanic (9,213)	9,381	78.08
Hispanic (1,228)	1,325	11.03

Clearwater

Place Type: City
County: Pinellas
Population: 108,787

Ancestry/Race	Number	%
Acadian/Cajun	11	0.01
African American/Black:	11,315	10.40
Not Hispanic (10,361)	10,931	10.05
Hispanic (290)	384	0.35
African, sub-Saharan:	606	0.56
African	431	0.40
Ghanian	13	0.01
Kenyan	10	0.01
Nigerian	33	0.03
South African	66	0.06
Sudanese	19	0.02
Other sub-Saharan African	34	0.03
Alaska Native tribes, specified:	3	0.00
Eskimo (2)	2	0.00
Tlingit-Haida (1)	1	0.00
Am. Ind. or Alaska Nat., not spec.	260	0.24
Albanian	211	0.20
Alsatian	9	0.01
American Indian tribes, specified:	494	0.45
Apache (10)	20	0.02
Blackfeet (3)	28	0.03
Cherokee (50)	175	0.16
Cheyenne	1	0.00
Chickasaw (2)	6	0.01
Chippewa (12)	17	0.02
Choctaw (9)	23	0.02
Comanche (2)	3	0.00
Cree (1)	3	0.00
Creek (5)	20	0.02
Delaware	2	0.00
Iroquois (22)	36	0.03
Latin American Indians (43)	67	0.06
Lumbee (7)	8	0.01
Menominee (1)	1	0.00
Navajo (4)	7	0.01
Ottawa (5)	8	0.01
Potawatomi	3	0.00
Pueblo (5)	5	0.00
Puget Sound Salish (1)	1	0.00
Seminole (1)	10	0.01
Shoshone	1	0.00
Sioux (5)	12	0.01
Yuman	1	0.00
All other tribes (18)	36	0.03
American Indian tribes, not spec.	45	0.04
Arab:	809	0.75
Arab/Arabic	97	0.09
Egyptian	119	0.11
Iraqi	36	0.03
Jordanian	22	0.02
Lebanese	338	0.31
Moroccan	96	0.09
Palestinian	20	0.02
Syrian	73	0.07
Other Arab	8	0.01
Armenian	152	0.14
Asian:	2,152	1.98
Bangladeshi (4)	5	0.00
Cambodian (15)	19	0.02
Chinese, ex. Taiwanese (234)	309	0.28
Filipino (334)	427	0.39
Hmong (27)	27	0.02
Indian (468)	509	0.47
Indonesian (8)	15	0.01
Japanese (97)	131	0.12

Notes: 1. Figures in the "Number" column do not add up to the total population due to: a) Ancestry/Race overlap — e.g. persons can report being both White and Irish, b) persons of Hispanic origin can report being any race, c) persons reporting two ancestries are counted in both categories. 2. Numbers in parentheses indicate the number of persons reporting this ancestry/race alone, not in combination with any other ancestry/race. 3. Refer to the User's Guide in the front of the book for more detailed information.

Korean (127)	161	0.15
Laotian (46)	52	0.05
Malaysian (4)	4	0.00
Pakistani (10)	13	0.01
Sri Lankan (1)	1	0.00
Taiwanese (24)	27	0.02
Thai (57)	72	0.07
Vietnamese (254)	282	0.26
Other Asian, specified (3)	9	0.01
Other Asian, not specified (36)	89	0.08
Australian	70	0.06
Austrian	451	0.42
Belgian	118	0.11
Brazilian	71	0.07
British	877	0.81
Bulgarian	58	0.05
Canadian	570	0.53
Celtic	39	0.04
Croatian	120	0.11
Czech	489	0.45
Czechoslovakian	289	0.27
Danish	405	0.38
Dutch	1,684	1.56
Eastern European	25	0.02
English	12,820	11.88
Estonian	6	0.01
European	526	0.49
Finnish	317	0.29
French, except Basque	3,814	3.53
French Canadian	1,290	1.20
German	18,191	16.86
Greek	1,934	1.79
Hawaii Native/Pacific Islander:	160	0.15
Melanesian: (2)	2	0.00
Fijian (2)	2	0.00
Micronesian: (15)	24	0.02
Guamanian/Chamorro (13)	19	0.02
Other Micronesian (2)	5	0.00
Polynesian: (39)	65	0.06
Native Hawaiian (19)	41	0.04
Samoan (19)	23	0.02
Tongan (1)	1	0.00
Other Pac. Isl., specified	5	0.00
Other Pac. Isl., not spec. (19)	64	0.06
Hispanic or Latino:	9,754	8.97
Central American:	274	0.25
Costa Rican	43	0.04
Guatemalan	45	0.04
Honduran	58	0.05
Nicaraguan	18	0.02
Panamanian	42	0.04
Salvadoran	50	0.05
Other Central American	18	0.02
Cuban	469	0.43
Dominican Republic	108	0.10
Mexican	4,771	4.39
Puerto Rican	1,924	1.77
South American:	891	0.82
Argentinean	60	0.06
Bolivian	10	0.01
Chilean	20	0.02
Colombian	394	0.36
Ecuadorian	76	0.07
Paraguayan	8	0.01
Peruvian	131	0.12
Uruguayan	9	0.01
Venezuelan	140	0.13
Other South American	43	0.04
Other Hispanic or Latino	1,317	1.21
Hungarian	810	0.75
Iranian	56	0.05
Irish	14,935	13.84
Israeli	173	0.16
Italian	8,685	8.05
Latvian	52	0.05
Lithuanian	446	0.41
Luxemburger	122	0.11
Macedonian	37	0.03
Maltese	53	0.05
New Zealander	11	0.01
Northern European	61	0.06
Norwegian	1,234	1.14
Pennsylvania German	134	0.12
Polish	3,844	3.56
Portuguese	404	0.37
Romanian	174	0.16
Russian	1,353	1.25
Scandinavian	226	0.21
Scotch-Irish	2,091	1.94
Scottish	2,555	2.37
Serbian	72	0.07
Slavic	43	0.04
Slovak	280	0.26
Slovene	16	0.01
Swedish	1,863	1.73
Swiss	414	0.38
Turkish	66	0.06
Ukrainian	507	0.47
United States or American	5,737	5.32
Welsh	616	0.57
West Indian, excl. Hispanic:	612	0.57
British West Indian	8	0.01
Haitian	19	0.02
Jamaican	353	0.33
Trinidadian and Tobagonian	160	0.15
West Indian	72	0.07
White:	92,947	85.44
Not Hispanic (85,015)	86,260	79.29
Hispanic (6,208)	6,687	6.15
Yugoslavian	585	0.54

Cocoa Beach

Place Type: City
County: Brevard
Population: 12,482

Ancestry/Race	Number	%
African American/Black:	101	0.81
Not Hispanic (71)	89	0.71
Hispanic (7)	12	0.10
African, sub-Saharan:	15	0.12
South African	15	0.12
Am. Ind. or Alaska Nat., not spec.	20	0.16
Albanian	17	0.14
American Indian tribes, specified:	41	0.33
Blackfeet (1)	1	0.01
Cherokee (4)	21	0.17
Cheyenne (1)	1	0.01
Creek	1	0.01
Iroquois	1	0.01
Latin American Indians (2)	2	0.02
Osage (1)	2	0.02
Pueblo (3)	3	0.02
Seminole (6)	6	0.05
Sioux	1	0.01
All other tribes (2)	2	0.02
American Indian tribes, not spec.	5	0.04
Arab:	182	1.47
Egyptian	103	0.83
Iraqi	41	0.33
Lebanese	38	0.31
Armenian	6	0.05
Asian:	182	1.46
Cambodian (1)	1	0.01
Chinese, ex. Taiwanese (41)	46	0.37
Filipino (28)	46	0.37
Indian (24)	31	0.25
Japanese (11)	17	0.14
Korean (5)	7	0.06
Malaysian	2	0.02
Pakistani (1)	1	0.01
Taiwanese (1)	1	0.01
Thai (9)	14	0.11
Vietnamese (5)	7	0.06
Other Asian, specified	1	0.01
Other Asian, not specified (5)	8	0.06
Austrian	65	0.52
Belgian	12	0.10
Brazilian	7	0.06
British	64	0.52
Canadian	58	0.47
Croatian	19	0.15
Czech	27	0.22
Czechoslovakian	59	0.48
Danish	85	0.68
Dutch	214	1.72
English	2,002	16.13
Estonian	5	0.04
European	116	0.93
Finnish	17	0.14
French, except Basque	648	5.22
French Canadian	151	1.22
German	2,285	18.41
Greek	155	1.25
Hawaii Native/Pacific Islander:	19	0.15
Micronesian: (1)	1	0.01
Guamanian/Chamorro (1)	1	0.01
Polynesian: (6)	15	0.12
Native Hawaiian (6)	14	0.11
Samoan	1	0.01
Other Pac. Isl., not spec.	3	0.02
Hispanic or Latino:	314	2.52
Central American:	9	0.07
Costa Rican	1	0.01
Guatemalan	2	0.02
Honduran	2	0.02
Panamanian	2	0.02
Other Central American	2	0.02
Cuban	60	0.48
Mexican	68	0.54
Puerto Rican	44	0.35
South American:	49	0.39
Argentinean	9	0.07
Chilean	3	0.02
Colombian	14	0.11
Ecuadorian	10	0.08
Peruvian	2	0.02
Uruguayan	1	0.01
Venezuelan	7	0.06
Other South American	3	0.02
Other Hispanic or Latino	84	0.67
Hungarian	120	0.97
Irish	2,300	18.53
Italian	1,152	9.28
Lithuanian	56	0.45
Northern European	2	0.02
Norwegian	198	1.60
Pennsylvania German	12	0.10
Polish	441	3.55
Portuguese	52	0.42
Romanian	34	0.27
Russian	203	1.64
Scotch-Irish	471	3.79
Scottish	431	3.47
Slavic	7	0.06
Slovak	45	0.36
Soviet Union	10	0.08
Swedish	233	1.88
Swiss	24	0.19
Turkish	12	0.10
Ukrainian	44	0.35
United States or American	876	7.06
Welsh	153	1.23
West Indian, excl. Hispanic:	12	0.10
Jamaican	12	0.10
White:	12,187	97.64
Not Hispanic (11,805)	11,911	95.43
Hispanic (257)	276	2.21
Yugoslavian	9	0.07

Cocoa

Place Type: City
County: Brevard
Population: 16,412

Ancestry/Race	Number	%
African American/Black:	5,446	33.18
Not Hispanic (5,222)	5,357	32.64
Hispanic (76)	89	0.54
African, sub-Saharan:	87	0.53
African	87	0.53

Notes: 1. Figures in the "Number" column do not add up to the total population due to: a) Ancestry/Race overlap — e.g. persons can report being both White and Irish, b) persons of Hispanic origin can report being any race, c) persons reporting two ancestries are counted in both categories. 2. Numbers in parentheses indicate the number of persons reporting this ancestry/race alone, not in combination with any other ancestry/race. 3. Refer to the User's Guide in the front of the book for more detailed information.

Alaska Native tribes, specified:	1	0.01
Eskimo	1	0.01
Am. Ind. or Alaska Nat., not spec.	79	0.48
American Indian tribes, specified:	114	0.69
Apache	4	0.02
Blackfeet (1)	3	0.02
Cherokee (35)	64	0.39
Chippewa (1)	2	0.01
Choctaw (2)	4	0.02
Cree	1	0.01
Creek	1	0.01
Delaware	1	0.01
Iroquois (2)	2	0.01
Latin American Indians	4	0.02
Lumbee (8)	8	0.05
Navajo (1)	1	0.01
Potawatomi (1)	2	0.01
Seminole	5	0.03
Sioux	1	0.01
All other tribes (5)	11	0.07
American Indian tribes, not spec.	10	0.06
Arab:	92	0.56
Arab/Arabic	8	0.05
Iraqi	16	0.10
Lebanese	32	0.19
Syrian	19	0.12
Other Arab	17	0.10
Asian:	216	1.32
Bangladeshi (1)	1	0.01
Chinese, ex. Taiwanese (9)	15	0.09
Filipino (36)	49	0.30
Indian (29)	39	0.24
Indonesian (1)	1	0.01
Japanese (10)	21	0.13
Korean (13)	20	0.12
Pakistani (1)	1	0.01
Taiwanese (1)	1	0.01
Thai (4)	6	0.04
Vietnamese (41)	43	0.26
Other Asian, specified (2)	7	0.04
Other Asian, not specified (1)	12	0.07
Austrian	14	0.08
Belgian	9	0.05
Brazilian	22	0.13
British	130	0.79
Canadian	34	0.21
Croatian	6	0.04
Czech	46	0.28
Czechoslovakian	64	0.39
Danish	32	0.19
Dutch	160	0.97
English	1,428	8.65
European	73	0.44
Finnish	8	0.05
French, except Basque	547	3.32
French Canadian	138	0.84
German	1,579	9.57
Greek	4	0.02
Hawaii Native/Pacific Islander:	60	0.37
Micronesian: (35)	38	0.23
Guamanian/Chamorro (35)	38	0.23
Polynesian: (3)	14	0.09
Native Hawaiian (3)	12	0.07
Samoan	2	0.01
Other Pac. Isl., specified	4	0.02
Other Pac. Isl., not spec.	4	0.02
Hispanic or Latino:	809	4.93
Central American:	164	1.00
Costa Rican	1	0.01
Guatemalan	123	0.75
Honduran	12	0.07
Nicaraguan	6	0.04
Panamanian	8	0.05
Salvadoran	10	0.06
Other Central American	4	0.02
Cuban	52	0.32
Dominican Republic	14	0.09
Mexican	199	1.21
Puerto Rican	196	1.19
South American:	47	0.29
Argentinean	4	0.02
Chilean	1	0.01
Colombian	27	0.16
Ecuadorian	3	0.02
Peruvian	2	0.01
Venezuelan	8	0.05
Other South American	2	0.01
Other Hispanic or Latino	137	0.83
Hungarian	76	0.46
Icelander	6	0.04
Irish	1,480	8.97
Italian	927	5.62
Lithuanian	24	0.15
Northern European	14	0.08
Norwegian	32	0.19
Pennsylvania German	10	0.06
Polish	203	1.23
Portuguese	68	0.41
Romanian	5	0.03
Russian	32	0.19
Scotch-Irish	239	1.45
Scottish	199	1.21
Slovak	13	0.08
Swedish	96	0.58
Swiss	70	0.42
Turkish	19	0.12
Ukrainian	52	0.32
United States or American	1,499	9.08
Welsh	135	0.82
West Indian, excl. Hispanic:	94	0.57
Bahamian	31	0.19
British West Indian	7	0.04
Jamaican	37	0.22
Trinidadian and Tobagonian	11	0.07
West Indian	8	0.05
White:	10,501	63.98
Not Hispanic (9,839)	10,055	61.27
Hispanic (413)	446	2.72
Yugoslavian	15	0.09

Coconut Creek

Place Type: City
County: Broward
Population: 43,566

Ancestry/Race	Number	%
African American/Black:	2,963	6.80
Not Hispanic (2,584)	2,823	6.48
Hispanic (101)	140	0.32
African, sub-Saharan:	222	0.51
African	111	0.26
Cape Verdean	52	0.12
Ghanian	9	0.02
Nigerian	18	0.04
Senegalese	32	0.07
Alaska Native tribes, specified:	1	0.00
Tlingit-Haida (1)	1	0.00
Am. Ind. or Alaska Nat., not spec.	61	0.14
American Indian tribes, specified:	75	0.17
Apache (1)	3	0.01
Blackfeet (1)	1	0.00
Cherokee (5)	18	0.04
Chippewa (4)	10	0.02
Creek	2	0.00
Delaware	1	0.00
Iroquois (8)	11	0.03
Latin American Indians (12)	16	0.04
Lumbee	1	0.00
Navajo	1	0.00
Ottawa	1	0.00
Potawatomi (1)	1	0.00
Seminole (1)	1	0.00
Sioux (1)	2	0.00
Ute	1	0.00
Yuman (1)	1	0.00
All other tribes	4	0.01
American Indian tribes, not spec.	3	0.01
Arab:	459	1.06
Arab/Arabic	88	0.20
Egyptian	13	0.03
Iraqi	6	0.01
Lebanese	236	0.54
Moroccan	20	0.05
Palestinian	14	0.03
Syrian	64	0.15
Other Arab	18	0.04
Armenian	48	0.11
Asian:	1,323	3.04
Bangladeshi (5)	9	0.02
Chinese, ex. Taiwanese (296)	348	0.80
Filipino (96)	144	0.33
Indian (307)	378	0.87
Indonesian (3)	7	0.02
Japanese (29)	48	0.11
Korean (44)	60	0.14
Laotian (4)	4	0.01
Malaysian (3)	5	0.01
Pakistani (49)	72	0.17
Sri Lankan (2)	2	0.00
Taiwanese (4)	4	0.01
Thai (29)	37	0.08
Vietnamese (124)	136	0.31
Other Asian, specified	5	0.01
Other Asian, not specified (18)	64	0.15
Australian	8	0.02
Austrian	491	1.13
Belgian	16	0.04
Brazilian	589	1.36
British	264	0.61
Bulgarian	15	0.03
Canadian	338	0.78
Croatian	27	0.06
Czech	155	0.36
Czechoslovakian	33	0.08
Danish	86	0.20
Dutch	559	1.29
Eastern European	151	0.35
English	2,950	6.81
European	189	0.44
Finnish	48	0.11
French, except Basque	1,068	2.46
French Canadian	467	1.08
German	4,650	10.73
Greek	338	0.78
Guyanese	17	0.04
Hawaii Native/Pacific Islander:	60	0.14
Micronesian: (2)	2	0.00
Guamanian/Chamorro (2)	2	0.00
Polynesian: (16)	32	0.07
Native Hawaiian (9)	20	0.05
Samoan (4)	8	0.02
Tongan (3)	4	0.01
Other Pac. Isl., specified	4	0.01
Other Pac. Isl., not spec. (5)	22	0.05
Hispanic or Latino:	5,076	11.65
Central American:	264	0.61
Costa Rican	42	0.10
Guatemalan	46	0.11
Honduran	45	0.10
Nicaraguan	38	0.09
Panamanian	24	0.06
Salvadoran	57	0.13
Other Central American	12	0.03
Cuban	435	1.00
Dominican Republic	182	0.42
Mexican	688	1.58
Puerto Rican	1,120	2.57
South American:	1,402	3.22
Argentinean	95	0.22
Bolivian	22	0.05
Chilean	54	0.12
Colombian	557	1.28
Ecuadorian	106	0.24
Paraguayan	2	0.00
Peruvian	279	0.64
Uruguayan	26	0.06
Venezuelan	216	0.50
Other South American	45	0.10
Other Hispanic or Latino	985	2.26
Hungarian	566	1.31
Iranian	74	0.17
Irish	4,439	10.25
Israeli	130	0.30

Notes: 1. Figures in the "Number" column do not add up to the total population due to: a) Ancestry/Race overlap — e.g. persons can report being both White and Irish, b) persons of Hispanic origin can report being any race, c) persons reporting two ancestries are counted in both categories. 2. Numbers in parentheses indicate the number of persons reporting this ancestry/race alone, not in combination with any other ancestry/race. 3. Refer to the User's Guide in the front of the book for more detailed information.

Italian	5,841	13.48
Latvian	32	0.07
Lithuanian	162	0.37
Luxemburger	16	0.04
Macedonian	8	0.02
Maltese	49	0.11
Norwegian	259	0.60
Pennsylvania German	13	0.03
Polish	2,954	6.82
Portuguese	291	0.67
Romanian	257	0.59
Russian	2,804	6.47
Scandinavian	37	0.09
Scotch-Irish	379	0.87
Scottish	518	1.20
Serbian	8	0.02
Slavic	8	0.02
Slovak	97	0.22
Slovene	11	0.03
Swedish	358	0.83
Swiss	15	0.03
Turkish	186	0.43
Ukrainian	230	0.53
United States or American	2,390	5.52
Welsh	173	0.40
West Indian, excl. Hispanic:	1,402	3.24
Bahamian	33	0.08
British West Indian	33	0.08
Haitian	224	0.52
Jamaican	834	1.92
Trinidadian and Tobagonian	226	0.52
U.S. Virgin Islander	12	0.03
West Indian	32	0.07
Other West Indian	8	0.02
White:	38,303	87.92
Not Hispanic (33,909)	34,369	78.89
Hispanic (3,679)	3,934	9.03

Conway

Place Type: Census Designated Place
County: Orange
Population: 14,394

Ancestry/Race	Number	%
Acadian/Cajun	7	0.05
African American/Black:	450	3.13
Not Hispanic (340)	399	2.77
Hispanic (28)	51	0.35
African, sub-Saharan:	5	0.03
African	5	0.03
Alaska Native tribes, specified:	1	0.01
Aleut	1	0.01
Am. Ind. or Alaska Nat., not spec.	23	0.16
American Indian tribes, specified:	80	0.56
Apache (1)	1	0.01
Blackfeet	4	0.03
Cherokee (17)	31	0.22
Cheyenne (1)	1	0.01
Chippewa (3)	8	0.06
Choctaw (1)	3	0.02
Comanche (3)	3	0.02
Cree	1	0.01
Creek (1)	3	0.02
Crow	1	0.01
Iroquois	4	0.03
Latin American Indians (2)	11	0.08
Lumbee (1)	1	0.01
Shoshone	1	0.01
Sioux (1)	2	0.01
Yaqui (1)	1	0.01
All other tribes	4	0.03
American Indian tribes, not spec.	8	0.06
Arab:	170	1.19
Arab/Arabic	70	0.49
Iraqi	8	0.06
Lebanese	57	0.40
Moroccan	10	0.07
Palestinian	25	0.17
Armenian	13	0.09
Asian:	378	2.63
Cambodian (5)	5	0.03
Chinese, ex. Taiwanese (33)	54	0.38
Filipino (92)	100	0.69
Indian (53)	77	0.53
Indonesian (1)	3	0.02
Japanese (21)	36	0.25
Korean (23)	27	0.19
Pakistani (11)	15	0.10
Taiwanese (10)	19	0.13
Thai (7)	8	0.06
Vietnamese (18)	21	0.15
Other Asian, not specified (2)	13	0.09
Australian	12	0.08
Austrian	27	0.19
Basque	10	0.07
Belgian	35	0.24
Brazilian	20	0.14
British	43	0.30
Canadian	52	0.36
Croatian	9	0.06
Czech	75	0.52
Czechoslovakian	51	0.36
Danish	17	0.12
Dutch	285	1.99
English	2,370	16.59
European	89	0.62
Finnish	19	0.13
French, except Basque	541	3.79
French Canadian	139	0.97
German	2,185	15.29
Greek	69	0.48
Guyanese	37	0.26
Hawaii Native/Pacific Islander:	20	0.14
Micronesian: (4)	7	0.05
Guamanian/Chamorro (4)	7	0.05
Polynesian: (3)	6	0.04
Native Hawaiian (2)	5	0.03
Samoan (1)	1	0.01
Other Pac. Isl., not spec. (1)	7	0.05
Hispanic or Latino:	1,661	11.54
Central American:	43	0.30
Costa Rican	2	0.01
Guatemalan	3	0.02
Honduran	14	0.10
Nicaraguan	11	0.08
Panamanian	7	0.05
Salvadoran	6	0.04
Cuban	209	1.45
Dominican Republic	57	0.40
Mexican	92	0.64
Puerto Rican	819	5.69
South American:	178	1.24
Argentinean	18	0.13
Bolivian	2	0.01
Chilean	12	0.08
Colombian	102	0.71
Ecuadorian	26	0.18
Peruvian	4	0.03
Venezuelan	14	0.10
Other Hispanic or Latino	263	1.83
Hungarian	135	0.94
Irish	1,829	12.80
Italian	884	6.19
Lithuanian	46	0.32
Northern European	14	0.10
Norwegian	211	1.48
Pennsylvania German	8	0.06
Polish	412	2.88
Portuguese	5	0.03
Russian	69	0.48
Scandinavian	30	0.21
Scotch-Irish	400	2.80
Scottish	382	2.67
Serbian	5	0.03
Slovak	70	0.49
Slovene	7	0.05
Swedish	203	1.42
Swiss	65	0.45
Ukrainian	27	0.19
United States or American	1,268	8.87
Welsh	126	0.88
West Indian, excl. Hispanic:	96	0.67
Dutch West Indian	8	0.06
Haitian	46	0.32
Jamaican	20	0.14
Trinidadian and Tobagonian	6	0.04
West Indian	16	0.11
White:	13,235	91.95
Not Hispanic (11,862)	11,995	83.33
Hispanic (1,121)	1,240	8.61
Yugoslavian	26	0.18

Cooper City

Place Type: City
County: Broward
Population: 27,939

Ancestry/Race	Number	%
African American/Black:	994	3.56
Not Hispanic (846)	959	3.43
Hispanic (18)	35	0.13
African, sub-Saharan:	150	0.54
African	34	0.12
Nigerian	107	0.39
Other sub-Saharan African	9	0.03
Alaska Native tribes, specified:	4	0.01
Aleut	1	0.00
Eskimo	2	0.01
Tlingit-Haida	1	0.00
Am. Ind. or Alaska Nat., not spec.	35	0.13
Albanian	26	0.09
American Indian tribes, specified:	53	0.19
Apache (1)	1	0.00
Cherokee (7)	22	0.08
Chippewa (1)	3	0.01
Choctaw (4)	4	0.01
Cree (3)	3	0.01
Creek	2	0.01
Latin American Indians	6	0.02
Menominee (1)	1	0.00
Osage (2)	2	0.01
Pueblo (3)	3	0.01
Sioux	1	0.00
All other tribes (3)	5	0.02
American Indian tribes, not spec.	10	0.04
Arab:	395	1.43
Arab/Arabic	127	0.46
Iraqi	32	0.12
Lebanese	157	0.57
Palestinian	28	0.10
Syrian	34	0.12
Other Arab	17	0.06
Armenian	9	0.03
Asian:	1,359	4.86
Bangladeshi (13)	21	0.08
Chinese, ex. Taiwanese (240)	306	1.10
Filipino (94)	120	0.43
Indian (475)	545	1.95
Indonesian (7)	8	0.03
Japanese (17)	26	0.09
Korean (121)	128	0.46
Laotian (1)	1	0.00
Malaysian (1)	1	0.00
Pakistani (26)	37	0.13
Sri Lankan (5)	5	0.02
Taiwanese (12)	20	0.07
Thai (34)	37	0.13
Vietnamese (50)	57	0.20
Other Asian, specified (4)	4	0.01
Other Asian, not specified (15)	43	0.15
Australian	9	0.03
Austrian	184	0.66
Basque	10	0.04
Belgian	35	0.13
Brazilian	108	0.39
British	76	0.27
Canadian	209	0.75
Croatian	20	0.07
Czech	57	0.21
Czechoslovakian	83	0.30
Danish	43	0.16
Dutch	532	1.92

Notes: 1. Figures in the "Number" column do not add up to the total population due to: a) Ancestry/Race overlap — e.g. persons can report being both White and Irish, b) persons of Hispanic origin can report being any race, c) persons reporting two ancestries are counted in both categories. 2. Numbers in parentheses indicate the number of persons reporting this ancestry/race alone, not in combination with any other ancestry/race. 3. Refer to the User's Guide in the front of the book for more detailed information.

Eastern European	202	0.73
English	2,337	8.44
European	239	0.86
Finnish	71	0.26
French, except Basque	655	2.37
French Canadian	220	0.79
German	4,082	14.74
Greek	179	0.65
Guyanese	23	0.08
Hawaii Native/Pacific Islander:	31	0.11
Polynesian: (10)	17	0.06
Native Hawaiian (8)	13	0.05
Samoan (2)	4	0.01
Other Pac. Isl., not spec. (1)	14	0.05
Hispanic or Latino:	4,349	15.57
Central American:	169	0.60
Costa Rican	19	0.07
Guatemalan	32	0.11
Honduran	31	0.11
Nicaraguan	45	0.16
Panamanian	21	0.08
Salvadoran	12	0.04
Other Central American	9	0.03
Cuban	1,477	5.29
Dominican Republic	115	0.41
Mexican	139	0.50
Puerto Rican	714	2.56
South American:	922	3.30
Argentinean	67	0.24
Bolivian	5	0.02
Chilean	50	0.18
Colombian	496	1.78
Ecuadorian	65	0.23
Paraguayan	4	0.01
Peruvian	131	0.47
Uruguayan	11	0.04
Venezuelan	73	0.26
Other South American	20	0.07
Other Hispanic or Latino	813	2.91
Hungarian	411	1.48
Iranian	77	0.28
Irish	3,855	13.92
Israeli	233	0.84
Italian	3,460	12.50
Latvian	24	0.09
Lithuanian	110	0.40
Macedonian	30	0.11
Northern European	12	0.04
Norwegian	102	0.37
Pennsylvania German	17	0.06
Polish	1,510	5.45
Portuguese	65	0.23
Romanian	176	0.64
Russian	1,453	5.25
Scotch-Irish	332	1.20
Scottish	377	1.36
Slavic	7	0.03
Slovak	61	0.22
Slovene	34	0.12
Swedish	142	0.51
Swiss	100	0.36
Turkish	23	0.08
Ukrainian	83	0.30
United States or American	1,820	6.57
Welsh	198	0.72
West Indian, excl. Hispanic:	593	2.14
Bahamian	11	0.04
British West Indian	10	0.04
Haitian	165	0.60
Jamaican	280	1.01
Trinidadian and Tobagonian	64	0.23
U.S. Virgin Islander	21	0.08
West Indian	42	0.15
White:	25,300	90.55
Not Hispanic (21,147)	21,368	76.48
Hispanic (3,746)	3,932	14.07
Yugoslavian	80	0.29

Coral Gables

Place Type: City
County: Miami-Dade
Population: 42,249

Ancestry/Race	Number	%
African American/Black:	1,518	3.59
Not Hispanic (1,290)	1,367	3.24
Hispanic (104)	151	0.36
African, sub-Saharan:	160	0.38
African	128	0.30
Nigerian	32	0.08
Am. Ind. or Alaska Nat., not spec.	39	0.09
American Indian tribes, specified:	82	0.19
Blackfeet (1)	3	0.01
Cherokee (6)	26	0.06
Choctaw (1)	2	0.00
Creek (2)	3	0.01
Iroquois	1	0.00
Latin American Indians (17)	29	0.07
Navajo (1)	4	0.01
Potawatomi (1)	2	0.00
Seminole (1)	2	0.00
All other tribes (2)	10	0.02
American Indian tribes, not spec.	4	0.01
Arab:	571	1.35
Arab/Arabic	75	0.18
Iraqi	4	0.01
Lebanese	402	0.95
Moroccan	15	0.04
Syrian	46	0.11
Other Arab	29	0.07
Armenian	58	0.14
Asian:	878	2.08
Cambodian (1)	1	0.00
Chinese, ex. Taiwanese (179)	226	0.53
Filipino (63)	90	0.21
Indian (270)	294	0.70
Indonesian (3)	5	0.01
Japanese (61)	88	0.21
Korean (42)	51	0.12
Malaysian (2)	2	0.00
Pakistani (17)	20	0.05
Sri Lankan (3)	3	0.01
Taiwanese (15)	19	0.04
Thai (10)	11	0.03
Vietnamese (18)	23	0.05
Other Asian, specified (1)	1	0.00
Other Asian, not specified (14)	44	0.10
Australian	8	0.02
Austrian	134	0.32
Basque	82	0.19
Belgian	28	0.07
Brazilian	198	0.47
British	287	0.68
Bulgarian	36	0.09
Canadian	145	0.34
Celtic	6	0.01
Croatian	42	0.10
Cypriot	9	0.02
Czech	70	0.17
Czechoslovakian	37	0.09
Danish	61	0.14
Dutch	429	1.02
Eastern European	244	0.58
English	3,132	7.42
Estonian	14	0.03
European	406	0.96
Finnish	40	0.09
French, except Basque	943	2.23
French Canadian	124	0.29
German	2,963	7.02
Greek	234	0.55
Guyanese	22	0.05
Hawaii Native/Pacific Islander:	31	0.07
Micronesian: (1)	1	0.00
Guamanian/Chamorro (1)	1	0.00
Polynesian: (10)	14	0.03
Native Hawaiian (9)	13	0.03
Samoan (1)	1	0.00
Other Pac. Isl., not spec. (4)	16	0.04
Hispanic or Latino:	19,703	46.64
Central American:	936	2.22
Costa Rican	98	0.23
Guatemalan	64	0.15
Honduran	138	0.33
Nicaraguan	400	0.95
Panamanian	113	0.27
Salvadoran	99	0.23
Other Central American	24	0.06
Cuban	12,136	28.72
Dominican Republic	227	0.54
Mexican	482	1.14
Puerto Rican	887	2.10
South American:	2,586	6.12
Argentinean	297	0.70
Bolivian	40	0.09
Chilean	155	0.37
Colombian	961	2.27
Ecuadorian	206	0.49
Paraguayan	26	0.06
Peruvian	286	0.68
Uruguayan	44	0.10
Venezuelan	496	1.17
Other South American	75	0.18
Other Hispanic or Latino	2,449	5.80
Hungarian	226	0.54
Iranian	97	0.23
Irish	2,425	5.75
Israeli	66	0.16
Italian	2,225	5.27
Latvian	9	0.02
Lithuanian	116	0.27
Luxemburger	47	0.11
Northern European	19	0.05
Norwegian	289	0.68
Pennsylvania German	22	0.05
Polish	1,156	2.74
Portuguese	163	0.39
Romanian	132	0.31
Russian	1,050	2.49
Scandinavian	51	0.12
Scotch-Irish	337	0.80
Scottish	806	1.91
Serbian	16	0.04
Slavic	34	0.08
Slovak	39	0.09
Swedish	371	0.88
Swiss	114	0.27
Turkish	51	0.12
Ukrainian	85	0.20
United States or American	2,115	5.01
Welsh	138	0.33
West Indian, excl. Hispanic:	473	1.12
Bahamian	30	0.07
Belizean	7	0.02
British West Indian	31	0.07
Haitian	163	0.39
Jamaican	165	0.39
Trinidadian and Tobagonian	32	0.08
U.S. Virgin Islander	20	0.05
West Indian	25	0.06
White:	39,357	93.15
Not Hispanic (20,168)	20,397	48.28
Hispanic (18,630)	18,960	44.88

Coral Springs

Place Type: City
County: Broward
Population: 117,549

Ancestry/Race	Number	%
Acadian/Cajun	5	0.00
African American/Black:	11,955	10.17
Not Hispanic (10,412)	11,434	9.73
Hispanic (354)	521	0.44
African, sub-Saharan:	389	0.33
African	141	0.12
Cape Verdean	66	0.06
Nigerian	40	0.03
South African	114	0.10

Notes: 1. Figures in the "Number" column do not add up to the total population due to: a) Ancestry/Race overlap — e.g. persons can report being both White and Irish, b) persons of Hispanic origin can report being any race, c) persons reporting two ancestries are counted in both categories. 2. Numbers in parentheses indicate the number of persons reporting this ancestry/race alone, not in combination with any other ancestry/race. 3. Refer to the User's Guide in the front of the book for more detailed information.

Other sub-Saharan African	28	0.02
Alaska Native tribes, specified:	3	0.00
Tlingit-Haida (2)	3	0.00
Am. Ind. or Alaska Nat., not spec.	161	0.14
Albanian	9	0.01
Alsatian	17	0.01
American Indian tribes, specified:	270	0.23
Apache (1)	8	0.01
Blackfeet (1)	10	0.01
Cherokee (32)	98	0.08
Cheyenne	3	0.00
Chickasaw (2)	2	0.00
Chippewa (1)	2	0.00
Choctaw (7)	7	0.01
Comanche (4)	4	0.00
Creek (1)	1	0.00
Iroquois (6)	16	0.01
Latin American Indians (43)	72	0.06
Menominee (1)	2	0.00
Navajo	1	0.00
Ottawa	1	0.00
Potawatomi (1)	1	0.00
Pueblo (1)	2	0.00
Seminole (5)	5	0.00
Sioux (2)	10	0.01
All other tribes (9)	25	0.02
American Indian tribes, not spec.	32	0.03
Arab:	1,247	1.06
Arab/Arabic	194	0.17
Egyptian	189	0.16
Iraqi	26	0.02
Jordanian	53	0.05
Lebanese	511	0.43
Moroccan	35	0.03
Palestinian	51	0.04
Syrian	77	0.07
Other Arab	111	0.09
Armenian	191	0.16
Asian:	4,925	4.19
Bangladeshi (17)	28	0.02
Cambodian (4)	5	0.00
Chinese, ex. Taiwanese (922)	1,092	0.93
Filipino (303)	413	0.35
Indian (1,922)	2,149	1.83
Indonesian (10)	24	0.02
Japanese (68)	125	0.11
Korean (326)	357	0.30
Laotian (5)	5	0.00
Pakistani (176)	239	0.20
Sri Lankan (15)	18	0.02
Taiwanese (43)	47	0.04
Thai (30)	45	0.04
Vietnamese (170)	184	0.16
Other Asian, specified (16)	19	0.02
Other Asian, not specified (69)	175	0.15
Australian	50	0.04
Austrian	821	0.70
Basque	27	0.02
Belgian	99	0.08
Brazilian	901	0.77
British	653	0.56
Bulgarian	27	0.02
Canadian	599	0.51
Carpatho Rusyn	11	0.01
Croatian	111	0.09
Czech	441	0.38
Czechoslovakian	172	0.15
Danish	357	0.30
Dutch	992	0.84
Eastern European	508	0.43
English	7,115	6.06
Estonian	13	0.01
European	944	0.80
Finnish	210	0.18
French, except Basque	2,802	2.39
French Canadian	709	0.60
German	14,034	11.95
German Russian	7	0.01
Greek	976	0.83
Guyanese	147	0.13
Hawaii Native/Pacific Islander:	167	0.14
Micronesian: (16)	21	0.02
Guamanian/Chamorro (12)	17	0.01
Other Micronesian (4)	4	0.00
Polynesian: (33)	53	0.05
Native Hawaiian (19)	36	0.03
Samoan (7)	8	0.01
Other Polynesian (7)	9	0.01
Other Pac. Isl., not spec. (29)	93	0.08
Hispanic or Latino:	18,233	15.51
Central American:	804	0.68
Costa Rican	118	0.10
Guatemalan	121	0.10
Honduran	118	0.10
Nicaraguan	124	0.11
Panamanian	143	0.12
Salvadoran	157	0.13
Other Central American	23	0.02
Cuban	2,017	1.72
Dominican Republic	630	0.54
Mexican	1,603	1.36
Puerto Rican	4,163	3.54
South American:	5,261	4.48
Argentinean	498	0.42
Bolivian	54	0.05
Chilean	162	0.14
Colombian	2,408	2.05
Ecuadorian	441	0.38
Paraguayan	6	0.01
Peruvian	869	0.74
Uruguayan	99	0.08
Venezuelan	568	0.48
Other South American	156	0.13
Other Hispanic or Latino	3,755	3.19
Hungarian	1,134	0.97
Icelander	8	0.01
Iranian	247	0.21
Irish	13,257	11.28
Israeli	320	0.27
Italian	16,709	14.22
Latvian	99	0.08
Lithuanian	450	0.38
Luxemburger	8	0.01
Macedonian	5	0.00
Maltese	37	0.03
New Zealander	19	0.02
Northern European	19	0.02
Norwegian	894	0.76
Pennsylvania German	25	0.02
Polish	6,741	5.74
Portuguese	848	0.72
Romanian	611	0.52
Russian	5,710	4.86
Scandinavian	152	0.13
Scotch-Irish	1,013	0.86
Scottish	1,441	1.23
Serbian	78	0.07
Slavic	65	0.06
Slovak	172	0.15
Slovene	40	0.03
Swedish	1,324	1.13
Swiss	224	0.19
Turkish	192	0.16
Ukrainian	428	0.36
United States or American	7,594	6.46
Welsh	461	0.39
West Indian, excl. Hispanic:	7,065	6.01
Bahamian	237	0.20
Barbadian	49	0.04
Belizean	47	0.04
British West Indian	158	0.13
Haitian	2,856	2.43
Jamaican	3,019	2.57
Trinidadian and Tobagonian	433	0.37
West Indian	240	0.20
Other West Indian	26	0.02
White:	97,897	83.28
Not Hispanic (82,149)	83,258	70.83
Hispanic (13,711)	14,639	12.45
Yugoslavian	183	0.16

Coral Terrace

Place Type: Census Designated Place
County: Miami-Dade
Population: 24,380

Ancestry/Race	Number	%
Acadian/Cajun	5	0.02
African American/Black:	330	1.35
Not Hispanic (109)	118	0.48
Hispanic (172)	212	0.87
African, sub-Saharan:	55	0.23
African	45	0.18
South African	10	0.04
Am. Ind. or Alaska Nat., not spec.	21	0.09
Albanian	9	0.04
American Indian tribes, specified:	19	0.08
Apache	1	0.00
Cherokee (3)	6	0.02
Cheyenne (1)	1	0.00
Latin American Indians (7)	9	0.04
All other tribes (2)	2	0.01
American Indian tribes, not spec.	5	0.02
Arab:	181	0.74
Arab/Arabic	10	0.04
Lebanese	82	0.34
Moroccan	4	0.02
Palestinian	69	0.28
Syrian	9	0.04
Other Arab	7	0.03
Asian:	184	0.75
Chinese, ex. Taiwanese (45)	68	0.28
Filipino (22)	30	0.12
Indian (27)	35	0.14
Japanese (3)	5	0.02
Korean (8)	8	0.03
Pakistani (2)	5	0.02
Sri Lankan (5)	5	0.02
Taiwanese (3)	5	0.02
Thai (4)	8	0.03
Vietnamese (8)	9	0.04
Other Asian, not specified (1)	6	0.02
Assyrian/Chaldean/Syriac	6	0.02
Austrian	25	0.10
Basque	6	0.02
Brazilian	31	0.13
British	63	0.26
Canadian	31	0.13
Croatian	7	0.03
Czech	13	0.05
Danish	27	0.11
Dutch	59	0.24
English	413	1.70
European	8	0.03
French, except Basque	279	1.15
French Canadian	10	0.04
German	423	1.74
Greek	53	0.22
Hawaii Native/Pacific Islander:	10	0.04
Polynesian: (1)	7	0.03
Samoan (1)	7	0.03
Other Pac. Isl., not spec. (1)	3	0.01
Hispanic or Latino:	20,015	82.10
Central American:	1,057	4.34
Costa Rican	62	0.25
Guatemalan	87	0.36
Honduran	219	0.90
Nicaraguan	553	2.27
Panamanian	33	0.14
Salvadoran	82	0.34
Other Central American	21	0.09
Cuban	15,084	61.87
Dominican Republic	131	0.54
Mexican	111	0.46
Puerto Rican	453	1.86
South American:	1,043	4.28
Argentinean	64	0.26
Bolivian	31	0.13
Chilean	72	0.30
Colombian	414	1.70
Ecuadorian	63	0.26

Notes: 1. Figures in the "Number" column do not add up to the total population due to: a) Ancestry/Race overlap — e.g. persons can report being both White and Irish, b) persons of Hispanic origin can report being any race, c) persons reporting two ancestries are counted in both categories. 2. Numbers in parentheses indicate the number of persons reporting this ancestry/race alone, not in combination with any other ancestry/race. 3. Refer to the User's Guide in the front of the book for more detailed information.

Paraguayan	7	0.03
Peruvian	213	0.87
Uruguayan	30	0.12
Venezuelan	144	0.59
Other South American	5	0.02
Other Hispanic or Latino	2,136	8.76
Hungarian	30	0.12
Icelander	7	0.03
Irish	425	1.74
Italian	345	1.42
Latvian	5	0.02
Lithuanian	27	0.11
Norwegian	33	0.14
Polish	112	0.46
Portuguese	10	0.04
Russian	26	0.11
Scotch-Irish	93	0.38
Scottish	66	0.27
Swedish	65	0.27
Swiss	4	0.02
Turkish	13	0.05
Ukrainian	38	0.16
United States or American	589	2.42
Welsh	35	0.14
West Indian, excl. Hispanic:	107	0.44
Haitian	79	0.32
Jamaican	17	0.07
West Indian	11	0.05
White:	23,219	95.24
Not Hispanic (4,030)	4,098	16.81
Hispanic (18,657)	19,121	78.43

Country Club

Place Type: Census Designated Place
County: Miami-Dade
Population: 36,310

Ancestry/Race	Number	%
African American/Black:	8,534	23.50
Not Hispanic (7,337)	7,633	21.02
Hispanic (655)	901	2.48
African, sub-Saharan:	300	0.82
African	216	0.59
Cape Verdean	16	0.04
Nigerian	60	0.16
South African	8	0.02
Am. Ind. or Alaska Nat., not spec.	99	0.27
American Indian tribes, specified:	76	0.21
Blackfeet	5	0.01
Cherokee (3)	23	0.06
Chippewa (1)	1	0.00
Choctaw	2	0.01
Latin American Indians (13)	34	0.09
Navajo (2)	2	0.01
Pueblo	1	0.00
Sioux	2	0.01
All other tribes (1)	6	0.02
American Indian tribes, not spec.	13	0.04
Arab:	255	0.70
Arab/Arabic	51	0.14
Egyptian	11	0.03
Iraqi	8	0.02
Lebanese	119	0.33
Moroccan	8	0.02
Palestinian	28	0.08
Syrian	30	0.08
Armenian	29	0.08
Asian:	1,049	2.89
Chinese, ex. Taiwanese (153)	205	0.56
Filipino (170)	203	0.56
Indian (258)	303	0.83
Japanese (19)	36	0.10
Korean (73)	82	0.23
Laotian (9)	10	0.03
Pakistani (36)	89	0.25
Sri Lankan (1)	1	0.00
Taiwanese (4)	5	0.01
Thai (9)	16	0.04
Vietnamese (41)	44	0.12
Other Asian, specified	1	0.00
Other Asian, not specified (22)	54	0.15
Austrian	9	0.02
Belgian	7	0.02
Brazilian	91	0.25
British	45	0.12
Canadian	37	0.10
Carpatho Rusyn	9	0.02
Croatian	19	0.05
Czechoslovakian	5	0.01
Danish	86	0.24
Dutch	123	0.34
English	575	1.58
European	62	0.17
Finnish	9	0.02
French, except Basque	297	0.82
French Canadian	22	0.06
German	691	1.90
Greek	43	0.12
Guyanese	61	0.17
Hawaii Native/Pacific Islander:	71	0.20
Melanesian: (1)	1	0.00
Fijian (1)	1	0.00
Micronesian: (6)	10	0.03
Guamanian/Chamorro (6)	10	0.03
Polynesian: (6)	10	0.03
Native Hawaiian (1)	4	0.01
Samoan (4)	4	0.01
Other Polynesian (1)	2	0.01
Other Pac. Isl., specified	1	0.00
Other Pac. Isl., not spec. (8)	49	0.13
Hispanic or Latino:	21,903	60.32
Central American:	1,398	3.85
Costa Rican	99	0.27
Guatemalan	135	0.37
Honduran	219	0.60
Nicaraguan	585	1.61
Panamanian	240	0.66
Salvadoran	82	0.23
Other Central American	38	0.10
Cuban	7,251	19.97
Dominican Republic	1,309	3.61
Mexican	387	1.07
Puerto Rican	2,152	5.93
South American:	4,843	13.34
Argentinean	175	0.48
Bolivian	41	0.11
Chilean	138	0.38
Colombian	3,134	8.63
Ecuadorian	326	0.90
Paraguayan	2	0.01
Peruvian	454	1.25
Uruguayan	56	0.15
Venezuelan	456	1.26
Other South American	61	0.17
Other Hispanic or Latino	4,563	12.57
Hungarian	34	0.09
Iranian	22	0.06
Irish	769	2.11
Israeli	5	0.01
Italian	756	2.08
Lithuanian	8	0.02
Norwegian	94	0.26
Pennsylvania German	18	0.05
Polish	259	0.71
Portuguese	104	0.29
Romanian	18	0.05
Russian	148	0.41
Scandinavian	10	0.03
Scotch-Irish	98	0.27
Scottish	83	0.23
Slovak	8	0.02
Slovene	18	0.05
Swedish	51	0.14
Swiss	27	0.07
Turkish	37	0.10
Ukrainian	12	0.03
United States or American	1,401	3.85
Welsh	23	0.06
West Indian, excl. Hispanic:	2,555	7.02
Bahamian	313	0.86
Barbadian	21	0.06
British West Indian	88	0.24
Haitian	1,111	3.05
Jamaican	745	2.05
Trinidadian and Tobagonian	123	0.34
U.S. Virgin Islander	52	0.14
West Indian	92	0.25
Other West Indian	10	0.03
White:	24,358	67.08
Not Hispanic (5,643)	5,923	16.31
Hispanic (17,429)	18,435	50.77

Country Walk

Place Type: Census Designated Place
County: Miami-Dade
Population: 10,653

Ancestry/Race	Number	%
Acadian/Cajun	11	0.10
African American/Black:	1,314	12.33
Not Hispanic (1,065)	1,209	11.35
Hispanic (71)	105	0.99
African, sub-Saharan:	95	0.89
African	11	0.10
Nigerian	81	0.76
Sierra Leonean	3	0.03
Am. Ind. or Alaska Nat., not spec.	8	0.08
American Indian tribes, specified:	21	0.20
Cherokee (1)	7	0.07
Creek	4	0.04
Delaware	1	0.01
Latin American Indians (5)	5	0.05
Navajo	2	0.02
Pueblo (1)	1	0.01
All other tribes	1	0.01
American Indian tribes, not spec.	2	0.02
Arab:	86	0.81
Lebanese	45	0.42
Moroccan	41	0.38
Asian:	432	4.06
Bangladeshi	10	0.09
Chinese, ex. Taiwanese (122)	198	1.86
Filipino (31)	41	0.38
Indian (67)	114	1.07
Indonesian (2)	2	0.02
Japanese (9)	14	0.13
Korean (4)	4	0.04
Malaysian	1	0.01
Pakistani (5)	5	0.05
Thai (1)	2	0.02
Vietnamese (12)	21	0.20
Other Asian, not specified (4)	20	0.19
Austrian	13	0.12
Belgian	6	0.06
Brazilian	57	0.54
British	51	0.48
Canadian	29	0.27
Danish	24	0.23
Dutch	66	0.62
Eastern European	9	0.08
English	293	2.75
European	57	0.54
French, except Basque	201	1.89
French Canadian	12	0.11
German	681	6.39
Greek	10	0.09
Guyanese	21	0.20
Hawaii Native/Pacific Islander:	11	0.10
Polynesian: (4)	5	0.05
Native Hawaiian	1	0.01
Samoan (4)	4	0.04
Other Pac. Isl., not spec. (1)	6	0.06
Hispanic or Latino:	5,980	56.13
Central American:	364	3.42
Costa Rican	23	0.22
Guatemalan	27	0.25
Honduran	51	0.48
Nicaraguan	185	1.74
Panamanian	43	0.40
Salvadoran	30	0.28
Other Central American	5	0.05
Cuban	2,366	22.21
Dominican Republic	228	2.14

Notes: 1. Figures in the "Number" column do not add up to the total population due to: a) Ancestry/Race overlap — e.g. persons can report being both White and Irish, b) persons of Hispanic origin can report being any race, c) persons reporting two ancestries are counted in both categories. 2. Numbers in parentheses indicate the number of persons reporting this ancestry/race alone, not in combination with any other ancestry/race. 3. Refer to the User's Guide in the front of the book for more detailed information.

Mexican	78	0.73
Puerto Rican	589	5.53
South American:	1,243	11.67
Argentinean	66	0.62
Bolivian	18	0.17
Chilean	83	0.78
Colombian	594	5.58
Ecuadorian	93	0.87
Paraguayan	1	0.01
Peruvian	183	1.72
Uruguayan	8	0.08
Venezuelan	178	1.67
Other South American	19	0.18
Other Hispanic or Latino	1,112	10.44
Hungarian	22	0.21
Iranian	25	0.23
Irish	456	4.28
Italian	480	4.51
Norwegian	73	0.69
Polish	67	0.63
Romanian	11	0.10
Russian	126	1.18
Scotch-Irish	10	0.09
Scottish	74	0.69
Swedish	75	0.70
Swiss	34	0.32
Turkish	7	0.07
United States or American	436	4.09
Welsh	11	0.10
West Indian, excl. Hispanic:	980	9.20
Barbadian	18	0.17
British West Indian	27	0.25
Haitian	190	1.78
Jamaican	498	4.67
Trinidadian and Tobagonian	190	1.78
West Indian	57	0.54
White:	8,574	80.48
Not Hispanic (3,049)	3,163	29.69
Hispanic (5,218)	5,411	50.79

Crestview

Place Type: City
County: Okaloosa
Population: 14,766

Ancestry/Race	Number	%
African American/Black:	2,844	19.26
Not Hispanic (2,695)	2,801	18.97
Hispanic (24)	43	0.29
African, sub-Saharan:	247	1.67
African	247	1.67
Am. Ind. or Alaska Nat., not spec.	38	0.26
American Indian tribes, specified:	141	0.95
Apache (1)	5	0.03
Blackfeet	7	0.05
Cherokee (30)	57	0.39
Cheyenne (1)	2	0.01
Chickasaw	1	0.01
Chippewa (3)	5	0.03
Choctaw (1)	4	0.03
Comanche	1	0.01
Cree	1	0.01
Creek (12)	25	0.17
Iroquois (6)	7	0.05
Latin American Indians (2)	3	0.02
Navajo (1)	1	0.01
Ottawa (1)	1	0.01
Potawatomi	2	0.01
Pueblo	2	0.01
Seminole (1)	2	0.01
Shoshone	1	0.01
Sioux (1)	3	0.02
Ute	1	0.01
Yaqui (1)	1	0.01
All other tribes (4)	9	0.06
American Indian tribes, not spec.	9	0.06
Arab:	45	0.30
Lebanese	38	0.26
Moroccan	7	0.05
Asian:	508	3.44
Chinese, ex. Taiwanese (18)	27	0.18
Filipino (165)	249	1.69
Indian (17)	28	0.19
Indonesian (2)	3	0.02
Japanese (16)	37	0.25
Korean (58)	87	0.59
Taiwanese (1)	1	0.01
Thai (26)	36	0.24
Vietnamese (20)	26	0.18
Other Asian, specified	1	0.01
Other Asian, not specified (8)	13	0.09
Australian	11	0.07
British	93	0.63
Canadian	6	0.04
Danish	11	0.07
Dutch	153	1.03
English	1,277	8.62
European	114	0.77
French, except Basque	273	1.84
French Canadian	192	1.30
German	1,645	11.10
Greek	26	0.18
Hawaii Native/Pacific Islander:	42	0.28
Micronesian: (7)	12	0.08
Guamanian/Chamorro (7)	12	0.08
Polynesian: (15)	25	0.17
Native Hawaiian (15)	25	0.17
Other Pac. Isl., specified	1	0.01
Other Pac. Isl., not spec.	4	0.03
Hispanic or Latino:	481	3.26
Central American:	37	0.25
Costa Rican	1	0.01
Guatemalan	1	0.01
Honduran	5	0.03
Nicaraguan	2	0.01
Panamanian	22	0.15
Other Central American	6	0.04
Cuban	15	0.10
Dominican Republic	12	0.08
Mexican	156	1.06
Puerto Rican	127	0.86
South American:	15	0.10
Colombian	12	0.08
Peruvian	1	0.01
Other South American	2	0.01
Other Hispanic or Latino	119	0.81
Hungarian	8	0.05
Irish	1,310	8.84
Italian	648	4.37
Lithuanian	41	0.28
Luxemburger	7	0.05
Northern European	42	0.28
Norwegian	133	0.90
Pennsylvania German	8	0.05
Polish	279	1.88
Russian	9	0.06
Scandinavian	26	0.18
Scotch-Irish	193	1.30
Scottish	293	1.98
Swedish	96	0.65
Swiss	8	0.05
Turkish	24	0.16
United States or American	2,121	14.31
Welsh	38	0.26
West Indian, excl. Hispanic:	45	0.30
Bahamian	3	0.02
Barbadian	6	0.04
Haitian	36	0.24
White:	11,364	76.96
Not Hispanic (10,774)	11,073	74.99
Hispanic (258)	291	1.97

Cutler

Place Type: Census Designated Place
County: Miami-Dade
Population: 17,390

Ancestry/Race	Number	%
African American/Black:	777	4.47
Not Hispanic (645)	727	4.18
Hispanic (34)	50	0.29
African, sub-Saharan:	63	0.36
African	63	0.36
Am. Ind. or Alaska Nat., not spec.	8	0.05
American Indian tribes, specified:	40	0.23
Apache	1	0.01
Blackfeet	2	0.01
Cherokee (10)	23	0.13
Chippewa (3)	3	0.02
Creek	5	0.03
Latin American Indians (4)	5	0.03
Paiute	1	0.01
American Indian tribes, not spec.	1	0.01
Arab:	144	0.82
Egyptian	33	0.19
Lebanese	106	0.60
Syrian	5	0.03
Armenian	14	0.08
Asian:	627	3.61
Cambodian (5)	5	0.03
Chinese, ex. Taiwanese (220)	271	1.56
Filipino (41)	49	0.28
Indian (148)	170	0.98
Japanese (33)	39	0.22
Korean (30)	31	0.18
Laotian (1)	1	0.01
Malaysian	2	0.01
Pakistani (11)	16	0.09
Thai (13)	13	0.07
Vietnamese (10)	11	0.06
Other Asian, not specified (8)	19	0.11
Australian	8	0.05
Austrian	101	0.57
Basque	96	0.54
Belgian	7	0.04
Brazilian	110	0.62
British	159	0.90
Bulgarian	10	0.06
Canadian	63	0.36
Croatian	18	0.10
Czech	107	0.61
Czechoslovakian	41	0.23
Danish	60	0.34
Dutch	189	1.07
Eastern European	132	0.75
English	2,187	12.39
European	319	1.81
French, except Basque	360	2.04
French Canadian	87	0.49
German	2,152	12.19
Greek	204	1.16
Guyanese	14	0.08
Hawaii Native/Pacific Islander:	6	0.03
Micronesian: (2)	2	0.01
Guamanian/Chamorro (2)	2	0.01
Polynesian: (2)	2	0.01
Samoan (2)	2	0.01
Other Pac. Isl., not spec. (1)	2	0.01
Hispanic or Latino:	4,555	26.19
Central American:	354	2.04
Costa Rican	22	0.13
Guatemalan	38	0.22
Honduran	45	0.26
Nicaraguan	120	0.69
Panamanian	36	0.21
Salvadoran	68	0.39
Other Central American	25	0.14
Cuban	1,824	10.49
Dominican Republic	70	0.40
Mexican	144	0.83
Puerto Rican	309	1.78
South American:	978	5.62
Argentinean	107	0.62
Bolivian	33	0.19
Chilean	129	0.74
Colombian	343	1.97
Ecuadorian	78	0.45
Paraguayan	3	0.02
Peruvian	131	0.75
Uruguayan	14	0.08
Venezuelan	130	0.75
Other South American	10	0.06

Notes: 1. Figures in the "Number" column do not add up to the total population due to: a) Ancestry/Race overlap — e.g. persons can report being both White and Irish, b) persons of Hispanic origin can report being any race, c) persons reporting two ancestries are counted in both categories. 2. Numbers in parentheses indicate the number of persons reporting this ancestry/race alone, not in combination with any other ancestry/race. 3. Refer to the User's Guide in the front of the book for more detailed information.

Other Hispanic or Latino	876	5.04
Hungarian	217	1.23
Iranian	132	0.75
Irish	2,091	11.84
Israeli	18	0.10
Italian	1,390	7.87
Latvian	7	0.04
Lithuanian	36	0.20
Luxemburger	4	0.02
Maltese	31	0.18
Norwegian	100	0.57
Polish	524	2.97
Portuguese	119	0.67
Romanian	201	1.14
Russian	745	4.22
Scandinavian	39	0.22
Scotch-Irish	260	1.47
Scottish	472	2.67
Serbian	12	0.07
Slovak	6	0.03
Slovene	8	0.05
Swedish	212	1.20
Swiss	96	0.54
Turkish	65	0.37
Ukrainian	34	0.19
United States or American	978	5.54
Welsh	99	0.56
West Indian, excl. Hispanic:	211	1.20
Jamaican	165	0.93
Trinidadian and Tobagonian	28	0.16
West Indian	18	0.10
White:	15,782	90.75
Not Hispanic (11,405)	11,554	66.44
Hispanic (4,108)	4,228	24.31
Yugoslavian	15	0.08

Cutler Ridge

Place Type: Census Designated Place
County: Miami-Dade
Population: 24,781

Ancestry/Race	Number	%
African American/Black:	4,280	17.27
Not Hispanic (3,639)	3,936	15.88
Hispanic (246)	344	1.39
African, sub-Saharan:	71	0.29
African	62	0.25
Other sub-Saharan African	9	0.04
Am. Ind. or Alaska Nat., not spec.	69	0.28
American Indian tribes, specified:	85	0.34
Apache	1	0.00
Blackfeet	3	0.01
Cherokee (4)	16	0.06
Cheyenne (1)	1	0.00
Chippewa (1)	2	0.01
Choctaw (2)	4	0.02
Cree (1)	1	0.00
Creek	6	0.02
Crow	1	0.00
Latin American Indians (17)	26	0.10
Navajo (2)	4	0.02
Osage (1)	1	0.00
Seminole	1	0.00
Sioux (4)	9	0.04
Ute	2	0.01
All other tribes (5)	7	0.03
American Indian tribes, not spec.	5	0.02
Arab:	130	0.53
Arab/Arabic	28	0.11
Lebanese	55	0.22
Moroccan	24	0.10
Syrian	23	0.09
Armenian	10	0.04
Asian:	624	2.52
Bangladeshi (4)	4	0.02
Cambodian (1)	1	0.00
Chinese, ex. Taiwanese (74)	131	0.53
Filipino (33)	64	0.26
Indian (209)	297	1.20
Indonesian (3)	3	0.01
Japanese (10)	23	0.09
Korean (14)	14	0.06
Pakistani (6)	6	0.02
Taiwanese (1)	1	0.00
Thai (29)	30	0.12
Vietnamese (32)	32	0.13
Other Asian, specified (1)	1	0.00
Other Asian, not specified (6)	17	0.07
Australian	7	0.03
Austrian	94	0.38
Belgian	7	0.03
Brazilian	54	0.22
British	165	0.67
Canadian	131	0.53
Croatian	19	0.08
Czech	60	0.24
Czechoslovakian	8	0.03
Danish	63	0.26
Dutch	213	0.86
English	1,408	5.71
European	130	0.53
Finnish	43	0.17
French, except Basque	570	2.31
French Canadian	101	0.41
German	2,014	8.16
Greek	122	0.49
Guyanese	24	0.10
Hawaii Native/Pacific Islander:	58	0.23
Micronesian: (1)	1	0.00
Guamanian/Chamorro (1)	1	0.00
Polynesian: (8)	20	0.08
Native Hawaiian (1)	11	0.04
Samoan (4)	5	0.02
Other Polynesian (3)	4	0.02
Other Pac. Isl., not spec. (9)	37	0.15
Hispanic or Latino:	9,107	36.75
Central American:	701	2.83
Costa Rican	47	0.19
Guatemalan	31	0.13
Honduran	129	0.52
Nicaraguan	355	1.43
Panamanian	55	0.22
Salvadoran	64	0.26
Other Central American	20	0.08
Cuban	3,312	13.37
Dominican Republic	411	1.66
Mexican	332	1.34
Puerto Rican	1,625	6.56
South American:	1,051	4.24
Argentinean	80	0.32
Bolivian	15	0.06
Chilean	63	0.25
Colombian	472	1.90
Ecuadorian	94	0.38
Paraguayan	12	0.05
Peruvian	147	0.59
Uruguayan	22	0.09
Venezuelan	117	0.47
Other South American	29	0.12
Other Hispanic or Latino	1,675	6.76
Hungarian	196	0.79
Icelander	6	0.02
Iranian	17	0.07
Irish	2,133	8.65
Israeli	28	0.11
Italian	1,095	4.44
Latvian	6	0.02
Lithuanian	14	0.06
Maltese	6	0.02
Norwegian	206	0.83
Polish	361	1.46
Portuguese	49	0.20
Romanian	13	0.05
Russian	187	0.76
Scotch-Irish	342	1.39
Scottish	240	0.97
Slavic	13	0.05
Slovak	32	0.13
Swedish	138	0.56
Swiss	37	0.15
Turkish	12	0.05
Ukrainian	43	0.17
United States or American	2,104	8.53
Welsh	83	0.34
West Indian, excl. Hispanic:	1,374	5.57
Bahamian	21	0.09
Barbadian	5	0.02
Bermudan	5	0.02
British West Indian	93	0.38
Haitian	384	1.56
Jamaican	634	2.57
Trinidadian and Tobagonian	154	0.62
U.S. Virgin Islander	9	0.04
West Indian	69	0.28
White:	18,894	76.24
Not Hispanic (11,008)	11,234	45.33
Hispanic (7,260)	7,660	30.91
Yugoslavian	13	0.05

Cypress Lake

Place Type: Census Designated Place
County: Lee
Population: 12,072

Ancestry/Race	Number	%
Acadian/Cajun	7	0.06
African American/Black:	145	1.20
Not Hispanic (112)	123	1.02
Hispanic (14)	22	0.18
Alaska Native tribes, specified:	2	0.02
Tlingit-Haida	2	0.02
Am. Ind. or Alaska Nat., not spec.	13	0.11
American Indian tribes, specified:	25	0.21
Apache (1)	1	0.01
Cherokee (3)	10	0.08
Iroquois	1	0.01
Latin American Indians (4)	4	0.03
Lumbee (3)	3	0.02
Seminole (2)	2	0.02
Shoshone	2	0.02
All other tribes (1)	2	0.02
American Indian tribes, not spec.	3	0.02
Arab:	77	0.64
Egyptian	44	0.36
Lebanese	8	0.07
Palestinian	25	0.21
Asian:	95	0.79
Chinese, ex. Taiwanese (18)	21	0.17
Filipino (12)	17	0.14
Indian (12)	15	0.12
Indonesian (1)	1	0.01
Japanese (5)	6	0.05
Korean (6)	6	0.05
Thai (2)	3	0.02
Vietnamese (7)	10	0.08
Other Asian, not specified (10)	16	0.13
Austrian	71	0.59
Belgian	73	0.60
British	87	0.72
Canadian	61	0.50
Celtic	9	0.07
Croatian	44	0.36
Czech	55	0.45
Czechoslovakian	49	0.40
Danish	75	0.62
Dutch	164	1.36
English	2,121	17.53
Estonian	18	0.15
European	44	0.36
Finnish	41	0.34
French, except Basque	493	4.07
French Canadian	129	1.07
German	2,793	23.08
Greek	87	0.72
Guyanese	9	0.07
Hawaii Native/Pacific Islander:	7	0.06
Polynesian:	1	0.01
Other Polynesian	1	0.01
Other Pac. Isl., not spec. (4)	6	0.05
Hispanic or Latino:	437	3.62
Central American:	19	0.16

Notes: 1. Figures in the "Number" column do not add up to the total population due to: a) Ancestry/Race overlap — e.g. persons can report being both White and Irish, b) persons of Hispanic origin can report being any race, c) persons reporting two ancestries are counted in both categories. 2. Numbers in parentheses indicate the number of persons reporting this ancestry/race alone, not in combination with any other ancestry/race. 3. Refer to the User's Guide in the front of the book for more detailed information.

Costa Rican	9	0.07
Guatemalan	5	0.04
Honduran	1	0.01
Panamanian	3	0.02
Salvadoran	1	0.01
Cuban	43	0.36
Dominican Republic	13	0.11
Mexican	72	0.60
Puerto Rican	160	1.33
South American:	45	0.37
Argentinean	3	0.02
Chilean	2	0.02
Colombian	14	0.12
Ecuadorian	1	0.01
Peruvian	7	0.06
Uruguayan	1	0.01
Venezuelan	8	0.07
Other South American	9	0.07
Other Hispanic or Latino	85	0.70
Hungarian	66	0.55
Irish	2,122	17.54
Italian	1,052	8.69
Latvian	9	0.07
Lithuanian	14	0.12
Luxemburger	9	0.07
Maltese	10	0.08
Northern European	8	0.07
Norwegian	188	1.55
Pennsylvania German	15	0.12
Polish	650	5.37
Portuguese	81	0.67
Romanian	28	0.23
Russian	160	1.32
Scandinavian	29	0.24
Scotch-Irish	184	1.52
Scottish	340	2.81
Serbian	7	0.06
Slavic	11	0.09
Slovak	38	0.31
Slovene	8	0.07
Swedish	193	1.60
Swiss	122	1.01
Turkish	10	0.08
Ukrainian	51	0.42
United States or American	893	7.38
Welsh	95	0.79
West Indian, excl. Hispanic:	14	0.12
British West Indian	5	0.04
Jamaican	3	0.02
West Indian	6	0.05
White:	11,773	97.52
Not Hispanic (11,358)	11,421	94.61
Hispanic (311)	352	2.92
Yugoslavian	18	0.15

Dania Beach

Place Type: City
County: Broward
Population: 20,061

Ancestry/Race	Number	%
African American/Black:	4,927	24.56
Not Hispanic (4,623)	4,748	23.67
Hispanic (140)	179	0.89
African, sub-Saharan:	289	1.44
African	282	1.40
South African	7	0.03
Am. Ind. or Alaska Nat., not spec.	37	0.18
Albanian	9	0.04
American Indian tribes, specified:	97	0.48
Apache	1	0.00
Blackfeet (2)	4	0.02
Cherokee (14)	46	0.23
Choctaw	1	0.00
Comanche (4)	4	0.02
Creek	1	0.00
Delaware (1)	3	0.01
Iroquois (2)	2	0.01
Latin American Indians (8)	14	0.07
Potawatomi (3)	3	0.01
Seminole (3)	4	0.02
Shoshone (1)	1	0.00
Sioux (1)	4	0.02
All other tribes (4)	9	0.04
American Indian tribes, not spec.	5	0.02
Arab:	264	1.31
Arab/Arabic	47	0.23
Iraqi	22	0.11
Lebanese	120	0.60
Moroccan	7	0.03
Palestinian	43	0.21
Syrian	11	0.05
Other Arab	14	0.07
Armenian	17	0.08
Asian:	372	1.85
Chinese, ex. Taiwanese (38)	58	0.29
Filipino (60)	71	0.35
Indian (86)	99	0.49
Indonesian	4	0.02
Japanese (10)	19	0.09
Korean (57)	60	0.30
Laotian (1)	1	0.00
Pakistani (2)	5	0.02
Taiwanese (2)	2	0.01
Thai (3)	5	0.02
Vietnamese (7)	8	0.04
Other Asian, not specified (5)	40	0.20
Austrian	40	0.20
Basque	7	0.03
Belgian	46	0.23
Brazilian	102	0.51
British	128	0.64
Canadian	147	0.73
Celtic	14	0.07
Czech	57	0.28
Czechoslovakian	42	0.21
Danish	80	0.40
Dutch	171	0.85
Eastern European	7	0.03
English	1,055	5.24
Estonian	43	0.21
European	137	0.68
Finnish	33	0.16
French, except Basque	549	2.73
French Canadian	491	2.44
German	1,955	9.72
Greek	137	0.68
Guyanese	41	0.20
Hawaii Native/Pacific Islander:	24	0.12
Micronesian: (2)	5	0.02
Guamanian/Chamorro (1)	1	0.00
Other Micronesian (1)	4	0.02
Polynesian: (3)	10	0.05
Native Hawaiian (3)	8	0.04
Samoan	2	0.01
Other Pac. Isl., not spec. (1)	9	0.04
Hispanic or Latino:	2,410	12.01
Central American:	173	0.86
Costa Rican	33	0.16
Guatemalan	22	0.11
Honduran	27	0.13
Nicaraguan	34	0.17
Panamanian	21	0.10
Salvadoran	35	0.17
Other Central American	1	0.00
Cuban	340	1.69
Dominican Republic	45	0.22
Mexican	171	0.85
Puerto Rican	669	3.33
South American:	446	2.22
Argentinean	43	0.21
Bolivian	3	0.01
Chilean	11	0.05
Colombian	223	1.11
Ecuadorian	31	0.15
Paraguayan	1	0.00
Peruvian	71	0.35
Uruguayan	5	0.02
Venezuelan	49	0.24
Other South American	9	0.04
Other Hispanic or Latino	566	2.82
Hungarian	81	0.40
Irish	2,048	10.18
Israeli	49	0.24
Italian	2,490	12.38
Latvian	11	0.05
Lithuanian	24	0.12
Macedonian	18	0.09
Maltese	21	0.10
Norwegian	123	0.61
Polish	518	2.57
Portuguese	156	0.78
Romanian	46	0.23
Russian	151	0.75
Scandinavian	39	0.19
Scotch-Irish	168	0.84
Scottish	157	0.78
Serbian	11	0.05
Slovak	28	0.14
Swedish	150	0.75
Swiss	23	0.11
Turkish	11	0.05
Ukrainian	50	0.25
United States or American	1,428	7.10
Welsh	92	0.46
West Indian, excl. Hispanic:	839	4.17
Bahamian	122	0.61
Barbadian	34	0.17
British West Indian	11	0.05
Haitian	341	1.69
Jamaican	285	1.42
Trinidadian and Tobagonian	38	0.19
West Indian	8	0.04
White:	14,375	71.66
Not Hispanic (12,352)	12,540	62.51
Hispanic (1,718)	1,835	9.15
Yugoslavian	21	0.10

Davie

Place Type: Town
County: Broward
Population: 75,720

Ancestry/Race	Number	%
Acadian/Cajun	5	0.01
Afghan	13	0.02
African American/Black:	3,967	5.24
Not Hispanic (3,207)	3,613	4.77
Hispanic (247)	354	0.47
African, sub-Saharan:	216	0.29
African	117	0.15
Nigerian	44	0.06
South African	45	0.06
Other sub-Saharan African	10	0.01
Alaska Native tribes, specified:	6	0.01
Alaska Athabascan (1)	1	0.00
Eskimo (2)	5	0.01
Am. Ind. or Alaska Nat., not spec.	138	0.18
Albanian	36	0.05
Alsatian	8	0.01
American Indian tribes, specified:	287	0.38
Apache (2)	5	0.01
Blackfeet (8)	31	0.04
Cherokee (23)	92	0.12
Chickasaw (3)	4	0.01
Chippewa (4)	6	0.01
Choctaw (9)	10	0.01
Cree	1	0.00
Creek (2)	7	0.01
Delaware	1	0.00
Houma (2)	2	0.00
Iroquois (7)	13	0.02
Latin American Indians (10)	34	0.04
Lumbee (1)	1	0.00
Navajo (5)	7	0.01
Paiute (2)	2	0.00
Potawatomi	1	0.00
Pueblo	2	0.00
Seminole (23)	27	0.04
Sioux (4)	10	0.01
Yaqui (1)	3	0.00

Notes: 1. Figures in the "Number" column do not add up to the total population due to: a) Ancestry/Race overlap — e.g. persons can report being both White and Irish, b) persons of Hispanic origin can report being any race, c) persons reporting two ancestries are counted in both categories. 2. Numbers in parentheses indicate the number of persons reporting this ancestry/race alone, not in combination with any other ancestry/race. 3. Refer to the User's Guide in the front of the book for more detailed information.

All other tribes (8)	28	0.04
American Indian tribes, not spec.	13	0.02
Arab:	541	0.71
Arab/Arabic	54	0.07
Egyptian	85	0.11
Iraqi	6	0.01
Jordanian	11	0.01
Lebanese	350	0.46
Moroccan	10	0.01
Syrian	25	0.03
Armenian	19	0.03
Asian:	2,634	3.48
Bangladeshi (22)	26	0.03
Cambodian (8)	9	0.01
Chinese, ex. Taiwanese (493)	619	0.82
Filipino (225)	299	0.39
Indian (728)	880	1.16
Indonesian (5)	18	0.02
Japanese (65)	103	0.14
Korean (170)	188	0.25
Laotian (4)	6	0.01
Malaysian	5	0.01
Pakistani (122)	155	0.20
Taiwanese (44)	45	0.06
Thai (28)	39	0.05
Vietnamese (131)	149	0.20
Other Asian, specified (8)	10	0.01
Other Asian, not specified (30)	83	0.11
Australian	43	0.06
Austrian	273	0.36
Basque	9	0.01
Belgian	40	0.05
Brazilian	305	0.40
British	404	0.53
Bulgarian	40	0.05
Canadian	396	0.52
Celtic	6	0.01
Croatian	88	0.12
Cypriot	11	0.01
Czech	295	0.39
Czechoslovakian	121	0.16
Danish	218	0.29
Dutch	827	1.09
Eastern European	123	0.16
English	5,660	7.48
Estonian	12	0.02
European	326	0.43
Finnish	41	0.05
French, except Basque	2,368	3.13
French Canadian	833	1.10
German	10,389	13.73
Greek	544	0.72
Guyanese	136	0.18
Hawaii Native/Pacific Islander:	91	0.12
Micronesian: (5)	12	0.02
Guamanian/Chamorro (5)	12	0.02
Polynesian: (12)	21	0.03
Native Hawaiian (5)	13	0.02
Samoan (7)	8	0.01
Other Pac. Isl., specified	1	0.00
Other Pac. Isl., not spec. (13)	57	0.08
Hispanic or Latino:	14,270	18.85
Central American:	871	1.15
Costa Rican	74	0.10
Guatemalan	144	0.19
Honduran	151	0.20
Nicaraguan	190	0.25
Panamanian	94	0.12
Salvadoran	177	0.23
Other Central American	41	0.05
Cuban	3,275	4.33
Dominican Republic	441	0.58
Mexican	782	1.03
Puerto Rican	3,285	4.34
South American:	2,984	3.94
Argentinean	190	0.25
Bolivian	54	0.07
Chilean	117	0.15
Colombian	1,304	1.72
Ecuadorian	307	0.41
Paraguayan	12	0.02
Peruvian	482	0.64
Uruguayan	30	0.04
Venezuelan	389	0.51
Other South American	99	0.13
Other Hispanic or Latino	2,632	3.48
Hungarian	622	0.82
Iranian	80	0.11
Irish	10,617	14.03
Israeli	83	0.11
Italian	9,477	12.52
Latvian	79	0.10
Lithuanian	138	0.18
Luxemburger	11	0.01
Maltese	28	0.04
Norwegian	512	0.68
Pennsylvania German	59	0.08
Polish	3,184	4.21
Portuguese	434	0.57
Romanian	407	0.54
Russian	2,365	3.12
Scandinavian	91	0.12
Scotch-Irish	990	1.31
Scottish	1,252	1.65
Slavic	57	0.08
Slovak	97	0.13
Slovene	34	0.04
Swedish	730	0.96
Swiss	153	0.20
Turkish	81	0.11
Ukrainian	197	0.26
United States or American	5,248	6.93
Welsh	214	0.28
West Indian, excl. Hispanic:	1,553	2.05
Bahamian	97	0.13
Barbadian	83	0.11
Belizean	7	0.01
British West Indian	33	0.04
Haitian	355	0.47
Jamaican	696	0.92
Trinidadian and Tobagonian	114	0.15
U.S. Virgin Islander	7	0.01
West Indian	119	0.16
Other West Indian	42	0.06
White:	67,335	88.93
Not Hispanic (54,676)	55,419	73.19
Hispanic (11,240)	11,916	15.74
Yugoslavian	97	0.13

Daytona Beach

Place Type: City
County: Volusia
Population: 64,112

Ancestry/Race	Number	%
Acadian/Cajun	10	0.02
African American/Black:	21,462	33.48
Not Hispanic (20,813)	21,234	33.12
Hispanic (181)	228	0.36
African, sub-Saharan:	788	1.23
African	604	0.94
Ethiopian	9	0.01
Ghanian	6	0.01
Kenyan	10	0.02
Liberian	41	0.06
Nigerian	82	0.13
Other sub-Saharan African	36	0.06
Alaska Native tribes, specified:	4	0.01
Aleut (2)	2	0.00
Eskimo (1)	2	0.00
Alaska Native tribes, not specified	4	0.01
Am. Ind. or Alaska Nat., not spec.	158	0.25
American Indian tribes, specified:	331	0.52
Apache (3)	9	0.01
Blackfeet (4)	25	0.04
Cherokee (51)	149	0.23
Cheyenne (2)	4	0.01
Chickasaw	1	0.00
Chippewa (2)	4	0.01
Choctaw (4)	7	0.01
Comanche	2	0.00
Cree	4	0.01
Creek (1)	6	0.01
Crow	2	0.00
Delaware	1	0.00
Iroquois (13)	30	0.05
Kiowa (1)	1	0.00
Latin American Indians (4)	9	0.01
Lumbee (1)	1	0.00
Navajo (1)	6	0.01
Osage (1)	1	0.00
Potawatomi	1	0.00
Pueblo (1)	1	0.00
Puget Sound Salish (1)	2	0.00
Seminole (3)	17	0.03
Shoshone (1)	2	0.00
Sioux (3)	5	0.01
Ute (1)	2	0.00
Yakama	1	0.00
Yaqui (3)	4	0.01
All other tribes (15)	34	0.05
American Indian tribes, not spec.	32	0.05
Arab:	486	0.76
Arab/Arabic	93	0.15
Egyptian	41	0.06
Jordanian	15	0.02
Lebanese	84	0.13
Moroccan	65	0.10
Palestinian	59	0.09
Syrian	41	0.06
Other Arab	88	0.14
Armenian	60	0.09
Asian:	1,375	2.14
Cambodian (2)	6	0.01
Chinese, ex. Taiwanese (139)	163	0.25
Filipino (112)	138	0.22
Indian (436)	490	0.76
Indonesian (1)	4	0.01
Japanese (78)	98	0.15
Korean (181)	202	0.32
Laotian (3)	3	0.00
Malaysian (1)	3	0.00
Pakistani (20)	21	0.03
Sri Lankan (19)	19	0.03
Taiwanese (9)	13	0.02
Thai (14)	28	0.04
Vietnamese (61)	80	0.12
Other Asian, specified	10	0.02
Other Asian, not specified (19)	97	0.15
Australian	17	0.03
Austrian	127	0.20
Basque	38	0.06
Belgian	42	0.07
Brazilian	88	0.14
British	338	0.53
Bulgarian	12	0.02
Canadian	238	0.37
Croatian	33	0.05
Czech	393	0.61
Czechoslovakian	116	0.18
Danish	186	0.29
Dutch	746	1.16
Eastern European	28	0.04
English	5,345	8.34
Estonian	8	0.01
European	343	0.54
Finnish	78	0.12
French, except Basque	1,814	2.83
French Canadian	514	0.80
German	7,065	11.03
Greek	476	0.74
Guyanese	45	0.07
Hawaii Native/Pacific Islander:	122	0.19
Micronesian: (6)	15	0.02
Guamanian/Chamorro (4)	13	0.02
Other Micronesian (2)	2	0.00
Polynesian: (16)	34	0.05
Native Hawaiian (13)	27	0.04
Samoan (3)	7	0.01
Other Pac. Isl., specified	10	0.02
Other Pac. Isl., not spec. (17)	63	0.10
Hispanic or Latino:	2,232	3.48

Notes: 1. Figures in the "Number" column do not add up to the total population due to: a) Ancestry/Race overlap — e.g. persons can report being both White and Irish, b) persons of Hispanic origin can report being any race, c) persons reporting two ancestries are counted in both categories. 2. Numbers in parentheses indicate the number of persons reporting this ancestry/race alone, not in combination with any other ancestry/race. 3. Refer to the User's Guide in the front of the book for more detailed information.

Central American:	98	0.15
Costa Rican	12	0.02
Guatemalan	9	0.01
Honduran	21	0.03
Nicaraguan	20	0.03
Panamanian	15	0.02
Salvadoran	13	0.02
Other Central American	8	0.01
Cuban	160	0.25
Dominican Republic	32	0.05
Mexican	380	0.59
Puerto Rican	818	1.28
South American:	269	0.42
Argentinean	16	0.02
Bolivian	8	0.01
Chilean	36	0.06
Colombian	88	0.14
Ecuadorian	34	0.05
Peruvian	23	0.04
Uruguayan	11	0.02
Venezuelan	42	0.07
Other South American	11	0.02
Other Hispanic or Latino	475	0.74
Hungarian	372	0.58
Icelander	19	0.03
Iranian	42	0.07
Irish	6,659	10.39
Israeli	20	0.03
Italian	3,811	5.95
Latvian	13	0.02
Lithuanian	132	0.21
Maltese	7	0.01
Norwegian	387	0.60
Pennsylvania German	44	0.07
Polish	1,540	2.40
Portuguese	208	0.32
Romanian	86	0.13
Russian	355	0.55
Scandinavian	33	0.05
Scotch-Irish	857	1.34
Scottish	1,092	1.70
Serbian	22	0.03
Slavic	2	0.00
Slovak	80	0.12
Slovene	8	0.01
Swedish	733	1.14
Swiss	150	0.23
Turkish	53	0.08
Ukrainian	201	0.31
United States or American	3,311	5.17
Welsh	272	0.42
West Indian, excl. Hispanic:	867	1.35
Bahamian	113	0.18
British West Indian	53	0.08
Haitian	37	0.06
Jamaican	432	0.67
Trinidadian and Tobagonian	159	0.25
U.S. Virgin Islander	33	0.05
West Indian	40	0.06
White:	40,792	63.63
Not Hispanic (38,630)	39,365	61.40
Hispanic (1,333)	1,427	2.23
Yugoslavian	33	0.05

De Bary

Place Type: City
County: Volusia
Population: 15,559

Ancestry/Race	Number	%
African American/Black:	322	2.07
Not Hispanic (293)	308	1.98
Hispanic (3)	14	0.09
Alaska Native tribes, not specified	1	0.01
Am. Ind. or Alaska Nat., not spec.	27	0.17
American Indian tribes, specified:	51	0.33
Blackfeet (4)	5	0.03
Cherokee (8)	23	0.15
Chippewa (1)	2	0.01
Choctaw	2	0.01
Comanche	1	0.01
Creek (3)	3	0.02
Delaware	2	0.01
Iroquois (1)	2	0.01
Lumbee (1)	1	0.01
Seminole	2	0.01
Sioux	3	0.02
All other tribes (5)	5	0.03
American Indian tribes, not spec.	1	0.01
Arab:	53	0.34
Jordanian	10	0.06
Lebanese	28	0.18
Syrian	15	0.10
Armenian	8	0.05
Asian:	218	1.40
Chinese, ex. Taiwanese (34)	38	0.24
Filipino (34)	48	0.31
Indian (51)	58	0.37
Indonesian	2	0.01
Japanese (9)	18	0.12
Korean (11)	14	0.09
Laotian (3)	3	0.02
Pakistani (12)	15	0.10
Sri Lankan (2)	2	0.01
Thai (5)	5	0.03
Vietnamese (6)	6	0.04
Other Asian, not specified (8)	9	0.06
Austrian	39	0.25
Belgian	34	0.22
Brazilian	22	0.14
British	105	0.67
Canadian	131	0.83
Croatian	27	0.17
Czech	51	0.32
Czechoslovakian	77	0.49
Danish	64	0.41
Dutch	307	1.95
English	2,412	15.30
European	66	0.42
Finnish	34	0.22
French, except Basque	573	3.63
French Canadian	400	2.54
German	2,991	18.97
Greek	44	0.28
Hawaii Native/Pacific Islander:	8	0.05
Polynesian: (1)	3	0.02
Native Hawaiian (1)	3	0.02
Other Pac. Isl., not spec.	5	0.03
Hispanic or Latino:	645	4.15
Central American:	25	0.16
Costa Rican	4	0.03
Guatemalan	1	0.01
Honduran	3	0.02
Nicaraguan	9	0.06
Panamanian	7	0.04
Salvadoran	1	0.01
Cuban	64	0.41
Dominican Republic	12	0.08
Mexican	49	0.31
Puerto Rican	365	2.35
South American:	35	0.22
Argentinean	3	0.02
Chilean	2	0.01
Colombian	19	0.12
Ecuadorian	2	0.01
Peruvian	6	0.04
Venezuelan	3	0.02
Other Hispanic or Latino	95	0.61
Hungarian	88	0.56
Iranian	9	0.06
Irish	2,391	15.16
Italian	1,627	10.32
Lithuanian	65	0.41
Norwegian	162	1.03
Pennsylvania German	38	0.24
Polish	584	3.70
Portuguese	10	0.06
Romanian	22	0.14
Russian	52	0.33
Scotch-Irish	431	2.73
Scottish	464	2.94
Serbian	9	0.06
Slovak	82	0.52
Swedish	249	1.58
Swiss	39	0.25
Turkish	7	0.04
Ukrainian	42	0.27
United States or American	1,645	10.43
Welsh	173	1.10
West Indian, excl. Hispanic:	70	0.44
Bahamian	4	0.03
Jamaican	15	0.10
West Indian	33	0.21
Other West Indian	18	0.11
White:	14,904	95.79
Not Hispanic (14,295)	14,382	92.44
Hispanic (477)	522	3.35
Yugoslavian	21	0.13

De Land

Place Type: City
County: Volusia
Population: 20,904

Ancestry/Race	Number	%
African American/Black:	4,145	19.83
Not Hispanic (3,954)	4,072	19.48
Hispanic (56)	73	0.35
African, sub-Saharan:	229	1.09
African	229	1.09
Alaska Native tribes, specified:	1	0.00
Eskimo	1	0.00
Alaska Native tribes, not specified	1	0.00
Am. Ind. or Alaska Nat., not spec.	61	0.29
American Indian tribes, specified:	75	0.36
Apache (4)	4	0.02
Blackfeet (1)	2	0.01
Cherokee (9)	27	0.13
Chippewa (2)	4	0.02
Choctaw (3)	10	0.05
Creek (3)	5	0.02
Delaware (1)	1	0.00
Iroquois (1)	4	0.02
Latin American Indians (3)	6	0.03
Lumbee (1)	1	0.00
Osage	3	0.01
Ottawa (1)	1	0.00
Potawatomi	1	0.00
Seminole (1)	3	0.01
All other tribes (2)	3	0.01
American Indian tribes, not spec.	9	0.04
Arab:	39	0.19
Arab/Arabic	29	0.14
Lebanese	10	0.05
Asian:	256	1.22
Bangladeshi (6)	13	0.06
Chinese, ex. Taiwanese (30)	50	0.24
Filipino (36)	44	0.21
Indian (44)	75	0.36
Japanese (6)	16	0.08
Korean (6)	13	0.06
Laotian (5)	5	0.02
Pakistani (2)	2	0.01
Taiwanese (1)	2	0.01
Thai	2	0.01
Vietnamese (19)	22	0.11
Other Asian, not specified (7)	12	0.06
Austrian	71	0.34
Belgian	35	0.17
Brazilian	19	0.09
British	74	0.35
Bulgarian	31	0.15
Canadian	43	0.20
Czech	26	0.12
Czechoslovakian	55	0.26
Danish	71	0.34
Dutch	387	1.84
Eastern European	7	0.03
English	2,136	10.18
European	114	0.54
Finnish	9	0.04

Notes: 1. Figures in the "Number" column do not add up to the total population due to: a) Ancestry/Race overlap — e.g. persons can report being both White and Irish, b) persons of Hispanic origin can report being any race, c) persons reporting two ancestries are counted in both categories. 2. Numbers in parentheses indicate the number of persons reporting this ancestry/race alone, not in combination with any other ancestry/race. 3. Refer to the User's Guide in the front of the book for more detailed information.

French, except Basque	641	3.06
French Canadian	163	0.78
German	2,534	12.08
Greek	74	0.35
Hawaii Native/Pacific Islander:	15	0.07
Micronesian: (1)	2	0.01
Guamanian/Chamorro (1)	2	0.01
Polynesian: (2)	10	0.05
Native Hawaiian (1)	9	0.04
Samoan (1)	1	0.00
Other Pac. Isl., not spec.	3	0.01
Hispanic or Latino:	1,824	8.73
Central American:	21	0.10
Honduran	8	0.04
Nicaraguan	3	0.01
Panamanian	4	0.02
Salvadoran	6	0.03
Cuban	71	0.34
Dominican Republic	12	0.06
Mexican	1,060	5.07
Puerto Rican	441	2.11
South American:	34	0.16
Argentinean	10	0.05
Chilean	1	0.00
Colombian	13	0.06
Ecuadorian	1	0.00
Peruvian	2	0.01
Venezuelan	6	0.03
Other South American	1	0.00
Other Hispanic or Latino	185	0.88
Hungarian	118	0.56
Irish	2,191	10.44
Italian	1,085	5.17
Latvian	29	0.14
Lithuanian	23	0.11
Norwegian	193	0.92
Pennsylvania German	14	0.07
Polish	530	2.53
Portuguese	58	0.28
Romanian	15	0.07
Russian	69	0.33
Scandinavian	8	0.04
Scotch-Irish	458	2.18
Scottish	577	2.75
Serbian	26	0.12
Slovak	10	0.05
Swedish	139	0.66
Swiss	71	0.34
Turkish	33	0.16
Ukrainian	89	0.42
United States or American	1,468	7.00
Welsh	168	0.80
West Indian, excl. Hispanic:	194	0.92
Bahamian	13	0.06
Haitian	23	0.11
Jamaican	134	0.64
West Indian	8	0.04
Other West Indian	16	0.08
White:	15,973	76.41
Not Hispanic (14,633)	14,846	71.02
Hispanic (1,037)	1,127	5.39
Yugoslavian	5	0.02

Deerfield Beach

Place Type: City
County: Broward
Population: 64,583

Ancestry/Race	Number	%
African American/Black:	11,094	17.18
Not Hispanic (10,122)	10,807	16.73
Hispanic (217)	287	0.44
African, sub-Saharan:	407	0.63
African	173	0.27
Cape Verdean	7	0.01
Ghanian	105	0.16
Somalian	18	0.03
South African	104	0.16
Alaska Native tribes, specified:	4	0.01
Alaska Athabascan	1	0.00
Tlingit-Haida	3	0.00
Am. Ind. or Alaska Nat., not spec.	122	0.19
American Indian tribes, specified:	129	0.20
Apache (3)	3	0.00
Cherokee (21)	49	0.08
Chickasaw	1	0.00
Chippewa	3	0.00
Choctaw (1)	3	0.00
Cree (1)	1	0.00
Creek (2)	3	0.00
Iroquois (4)	6	0.01
Latin American Indians (17)	28	0.04
Menominee (2)	2	0.00
Navajo (1)	1	0.00
Potawatomi (1)	2	0.00
Pueblo	1	0.00
Shoshone	1	0.00
Sioux	3	0.00
Yakama	1	0.00
All other tribes (7)	21	0.03
American Indian tribes, not spec.	9	0.01
Arab:	430	0.66
Egyptian	44	0.07
Lebanese	214	0.33
Moroccan	53	0.08
Palestinian	9	0.01
Syrian	50	0.08
Other Arab	60	0.09
Armenian	58	0.09
Asian:	1,113	1.72
Bangladeshi (26)	34	0.05
Cambodian (15)	19	0.03
Chinese, ex. Taiwanese (194)	234	0.36
Filipino (109)	141	0.22
Indian (227)	262	0.41
Indonesian (1)	3	0.00
Japanese (38)	60	0.09
Korean (44)	57	0.09
Laotian (3)	3	0.00
Malaysian (5)	7	0.01
Pakistani (22)	38	0.06
Sri Lankan	2	0.00
Taiwanese (3)	4	0.01
Thai (28)	33	0.05
Vietnamese (132)	137	0.21
Other Asian, specified (8)	17	0.03
Other Asian, not specified (28)	62	0.10
Austrian	563	0.87
Basque	11	0.02
Belgian	55	0.08
Brazilian	2,307	3.56
British	266	0.41
Bulgarian	35	0.05
Canadian	708	1.09
Celtic	16	0.02
Croatian	35	0.05
Czech	230	0.36
Czechoslovakian	140	0.22
Danish	152	0.23
Dutch	683	1.06
Eastern European	132	0.20
English	4,659	7.20
European	249	0.38
Finnish	77	0.12
French, except Basque	1,569	2.42
French Canadian	783	1.21
German	6,223	9.62
Greek	440	0.68
Guyanese	33	0.05
Hawaii Native/Pacific Islander:	84	0.13
Micronesian: (5)	10	0.02
Guamanian/Chamorro (5)	10	0.02
Polynesian: (6)	20	0.03
Native Hawaiian (4)	16	0.02
Samoan (2)	4	0.01
Other Pac. Isl., specified	8	0.01
Other Pac. Isl., not spec. (8)	46	0.07
Hispanic or Latino:	5,643	8.74
Central American:	327	0.51
Costa Rican	84	0.13
Guatemalan	43	0.07
Honduran	79	0.12
Nicaraguan	35	0.05
Panamanian	44	0.07
Salvadoran	26	0.04
Other Central American	16	0.02
Cuban	661	1.02
Dominican Republic	298	0.46
Mexican	518	0.80
Puerto Rican	1,177	1.82
South American:	1,309	2.03
Argentinean	102	0.16
Bolivian	30	0.05
Chilean	50	0.08
Colombian	575	0.89
Ecuadorian	113	0.17
Paraguayan	1	0.00
Peruvian	197	0.31
Uruguayan	29	0.04
Venezuelan	158	0.24
Other South American	54	0.08
Other Hispanic or Latino	1,353	2.09
Hungarian	703	1.09
Iranian	26	0.04
Irish	6,957	10.75
Israeli	126	0.19
Italian	6,881	10.63
Latvian	55	0.08
Lithuanian	371	0.57
Luxemburger	11	0.02
Macedonian	14	0.02
Norwegian	439	0.68
Pennsylvania German	33	0.05
Polish	2,667	4.12
Portuguese	655	1.01
Romanian	307	0.47
Russian	2,147	3.32
Scandinavian	31	0.05
Scotch-Irish	535	0.83
Scottish	805	1.24
Slavic	10	0.02
Slovak	173	0.27
Slovene	16	0.02
Swedish	546	0.84
Swiss	116	0.18
Turkish	91	0.14
Ukrainian	277	0.43
United States or American	3,475	5.37
Welsh	196	0.30
West Indian, excl. Hispanic:	3,467	5.36
Bahamian	98	0.15
Barbadian	70	0.11
Belizean	9	0.01
British West Indian	177	0.27
Haitian	2,350	3.63
Jamaican	652	1.01
Trinidadian and Tobagonian	48	0.07
West Indian	63	0.10
White:	50,976	78.93
Not Hispanic (46,014)	46,730	72.36
Hispanic (3,880)	4,246	6.57
Yugoslavian	59	0.09

Delray Beach

Place Type: City
County: Palm Beach
Population: 60,020

Ancestry/Race	Number	%
Acadian/Cajun	8	0.01
African American/Black:	17,847	29.74
Not Hispanic (15,796)	17,609	29.34
Hispanic (185)	238	0.40
African, sub-Saharan:	431	0.72
African	320	0.53
Cape Verdean	19	0.03
Liberian	37	0.06
South African	38	0.06
Other sub-Saharan African	17	0.03
Alaska Native tribes, specified:	3	0.00
Tlingit-Haida	3	0.00
Am. Ind. or Alaska Nat., not spec.	115	0.19

Notes: 1. Figures in the "Number" column do not add up to the total population due to: a) Ancestry/Race overlap — e.g. persons can report being both White and Irish, b) persons of Hispanic origin can report being any race, c) persons reporting two ancestries are counted in both categories. 2. Numbers in parentheses indicate the number of persons reporting this ancestry/race alone, not in combination with any other ancestry/race. 3. Refer to the User's Guide in the front of the book for more detailed information.

Albanian	44	0.07
American Indian tribes, specified:	105	0.17
Apache (2)	2	0.00
Blackfeet (3)	6	0.01
Cherokee (13)	42	0.07
Chickasaw (2)	2	0.00
Chippewa (1)	7	0.01
Choctaw	1	0.00
Creek (3)	4	0.01
Delaware	1	0.00
Iroquois (9)	14	0.02
Latin American Indians (7)	12	0.02
Navajo (1)	2	0.00
Osage	1	0.00
Pueblo	1	0.00
Puget Sound Salish (1)	1	0.00
Sioux (1)	1	0.00
All other tribes (5)	8	0.01
American Indian tribes, not spec.	22	0.04
Arab:	336	0.56
Arab/Arabic	45	0.08
Egyptian	38	0.06
Jordanian	16	0.03
Lebanese	99	0.17
Moroccan	7	0.01
Palestinian	48	0.08
Syrian	56	0.09
Other Arab	27	0.05
Armenian	120	0.20
Asian:	906	1.51
Bangladeshi (16)	49	0.08
Cambodian	3	0.00
Chinese, ex. Taiwanese (125)	160	0.27
Filipino (95)	123	0.20
Indian (264)	339	0.56
Indonesian (4)	4	0.01
Japanese (31)	43	0.07
Korean (20)	26	0.04
Laotian	2	0.00
Malaysian (1)	2	0.00
Pakistani (2)	2	0.00
Sri Lankan (5)	6	0.01
Taiwanese (3)	3	0.00
Thai (11)	14	0.02
Vietnamese (45)	48	0.08
Other Asian, specified (1)	15	0.02
Other Asian, not specified (24)	67	0.11
Australian	16	0.03
Austrian	428	0.71
Basque	14	0.02
Belgian	77	0.13
Brazilian	156	0.26
British	330	0.55
Bulgarian	45	0.08
Canadian	278	0.46
Celtic	9	0.02
Croatian	54	0.09
Czech	151	0.25
Czechoslovakian	90	0.15
Danish	175	0.29
Dutch	747	1.25
Eastern European	123	0.21
English	4,856	8.10
Estonian	9	0.02
European	210	0.35
Finnish	98	0.16
French, except Basque	1,495	2.49
French Canadian	412	0.69
German	6,308	10.52
Greek	408	0.68
Hawaii Native/Pacific Islander:	255	0.42
Micronesian: (9)	11	0.02
Guamanian/Chamorro (9)	11	0.02
Polynesian: (34)	47	0.08
Native Hawaiian (12)	19	0.03
Samoan (21)	27	0.04
Other Polynesian (1)	1	0.00
Other Pac. Isl., specified	14	0.02
Other Pac. Isl., not spec. (6)	183	0.30
Hispanic or Latino:	4,184	6.97
Central American:	289	0.48
Costa Rican	24	0.04
Guatemalan	83	0.14
Honduran	48	0.08
Nicaraguan	42	0.07
Panamanian	21	0.03
Salvadoran	58	0.10
Other Central American	13	0.02
Cuban	465	0.77
Dominican Republic	63	0.10
Mexican	1,441	2.40
Puerto Rican	722	1.20
South American:	554	0.92
Argentinean	68	0.11
Bolivian	12	0.02
Chilean	39	0.06
Colombian	187	0.31
Ecuadorian	50	0.08
Paraguayan	13	0.02
Peruvian	75	0.12
Uruguayan	9	0.01
Venezuelan	72	0.12
Other South American	29	0.05
Other Hispanic or Latino	650	1.08
Hungarian	607	1.01
Iranian	9	0.02
Irish	6,173	10.30
Israeli	35	0.06
Italian	4,757	7.94
Latvian	64	0.11
Lithuanian	197	0.33
Northern European	29	0.05
Norwegian	381	0.64
Pennsylvania German	6	0.01
Polish	1,915	3.19
Portuguese	174	0.29
Romanian	281	0.47
Russian	2,001	3.34
Scandinavian	26	0.04
Scotch-Irish	608	1.01
Scottish	1,114	1.86
Serbian	15	0.03
Slavic	21	0.04
Slovak	92	0.15
Slovene	35	0.06
Swedish	745	1.24
Swiss	135	0.23
Turkish	80	0.13
Ukrainian	178	0.30
United States or American	3,128	5.22
Welsh	265	0.44
West Indian, excl. Hispanic:	7,220	12.05
Bahamian	286	0.48
Barbadian	66	0.11
Bermudan	7	0.01
British West Indian	50	0.08
Haitian	6,351	10.60
Jamaican	341	0.57
Trinidadian and Tobagonian	48	0.08
U.S. Virgin Islander	7	0.01
West Indian	51	0.09
Other West Indian	13	0.02
White:	40,506	67.49
Not Hispanic (37,074)	37,436	62.37
Hispanic (2,834)	3,070	5.11
Yugoslavian	67	0.11

Deltona

Place Type: City
County: Volusia
Population: 69,543

Ancestry/Race	Number	%
Acadian/Cajun	21	0.03
African American/Black:	5,345	7.69
Not Hispanic (4,478)	4,797	6.90
Hispanic (370)	548	0.79
African, sub-Saharan:	148	0.21
African	130	0.19
South African	18	0.03
Alaska Native tribes, specified:	3	0.00
Eskimo (1)	1	0.00
Tlingit-Haida (2)	2	0.00
Am. Ind. or Alaska Nat., not spec.	212	0.30
American Indian tribes, specified:	406	0.58
Apache	1	0.00
Blackfeet (2)	31	0.04
Cherokee (62)	188	0.27
Chickasaw (1)	1	0.00
Chippewa (6)	17	0.02
Choctaw (11)	15	0.02
Comanche (1)	1	0.00
Cree (1)	1	0.00
Creek (7)	10	0.01
Crow (1)	1	0.00
Delaware (2)	7	0.01
Iroquois (11)	27	0.04
Latin American Indians (14)	40	0.06
Navajo (1)	5	0.01
Osage (5)	5	0.01
Potawatomi (1)	1	0.00
Pueblo (4)	4	0.01
Seminole	7	0.01
Shoshone	1	0.00
Sioux (3)	9	0.01
Tohono O'Odham (3)	3	0.00
Yuman (1)	1	0.00
All other tribes (16)	30	0.04
American Indian tribes, not spec.	25	0.04
Arab:	141	0.20
Egyptian	23	0.03
Iraqi	6	0.01
Jordanian	25	0.04
Lebanese	52	0.07
Palestinian	23	0.03
Syrian	12	0.02
Asian:	888	1.28
Bangladeshi (1)	5	0.01
Cambodian (9)	9	0.01
Chinese, ex. Taiwanese (86)	123	0.18
Filipino (149)	226	0.32
Hmong	2	0.00
Indian (149)	190	0.27
Indonesian (6)	6	0.01
Japanese (26)	54	0.08
Korean (40)	56	0.08
Laotian (68)	73	0.10
Malaysian (5)	10	0.01
Pakistani (9)	11	0.02
Taiwanese	1	0.00
Thai (18)	23	0.03
Vietnamese (38)	50	0.07
Other Asian, specified	1	0.00
Other Asian, not specified (32)	48	0.07
Australian	16	0.02
Austrian	142	0.20
Belgian	98	0.14
Brazilian	57	0.08
British	305	0.44
Bulgarian	7	0.01
Canadian	261	0.37
Croatian	31	0.04
Czech	197	0.28
Czechoslovakian	117	0.17
Danish	307	0.44
Dutch	1,228	1.76
Eastern European	45	0.06
English	6,760	9.68
European	413	0.59
Finnish	110	0.16
French, except Basque	2,815	4.03
French Canadian	951	1.36
German	11,022	15.79
Greek	257	0.37
Guyanese	120	0.17
Hawaii Native/Pacific Islander:	82	0.12
Melanesian: (4)	4	0.01
Fijian (4)	4	0.01
Micronesian: (5)	8	0.01
Guamanian/Chamorro (5)	8	0.01
Polynesian: (18)	44	0.06
Native Hawaiian (5)	27	0.04
Samoan (5)	9	0.01

Notes: 1. Figures in the "Number" column do not add up to the total population due to: a) Ancestry/Race overlap — e.g. persons can report being both White and Irish, b) persons of Hispanic origin can report being any race, c) persons reporting two ancestries are counted in both categories. 2. Numbers in parentheses indicate the number of persons reporting this ancestry/race alone, not in combination with any other ancestry/race. 3. Refer to the User's Guide in the front of the book for more detailed information.

Tongan (6)	6	0.01
Other Polynesian (2)	2	0.00
Other Pac. Isl., specified	1	0.00
Other Pac. Isl., not spec. (9)	25	0.04
Hispanic or Latino:	12,747	18.33
Central American:	376	0.54
Costa Rican	32	0.05
Guatemalan	37	0.05
Honduran	75	0.11
Nicaraguan	35	0.05
Panamanian	101	0.15
Salvadoran	75	0.11
Other Central American	21	0.03
Cuban	543	0.78
Dominican Republic	281	0.40
Mexican	546	0.79
Puerto Rican	9,136	13.14
South American:	531	0.76
Argentinean	31	0.04
Bolivian	1	0.00
Chilean	16	0.02
Colombian	244	0.35
Ecuadorian	93	0.13
Paraguayan	5	0.01
Peruvian	62	0.09
Uruguayan	2	0.00
Venezuelan	49	0.07
Other South American	28	0.04
Other Hispanic or Latino	1,334	1.92
Hungarian	358	0.51
Iranian	44	0.06
Irish	10,116	14.49
Italian	6,827	9.78
Latvian	13	0.02
Lithuanian	93	0.13
Norwegian	634	0.91
Pennsylvania German	70	0.10
Polish	2,756	3.95
Portuguese	235	0.34
Romanian	50	0.07
Russian	532	0.76
Scandinavian	72	0.10
Scotch-Irish	1,189	1.70
Scottish	1,472	2.11
Serbian	46	0.07
Slavic	20	0.03
Slovak	127	0.18
Slovene	17	0.02
Swedish	894	1.28
Swiss	103	0.15
Turkish	31	0.04
Ukrainian	275	0.39
United States or American	4,543	6.51
Welsh	428	0.61
West Indian, excl. Hispanic:	915	1.31
Bahamian	18	0.03
Barbadian	18	0.03
Belizean	10	0.01
British West Indian	76	0.11
Haitian	163	0.23
Jamaican	407	0.58
Trinidadian and Tobagonian	30	0.04
U.S. Virgin Islander	123	0.18
West Indian	70	0.10
White:	60,029	86.32
Not Hispanic (50,540)	51,254	73.70
Hispanic (8,119)	8,775	12.62
Yugoslavian	41	0.06

Destin

Place Type: City
County: Okaloosa
Population: 11,119

Ancestry/Race	Number	%
Acadian/Cajun	16	0.14
African American/Black:	59	0.53
Not Hispanic (40)	53	0.48
Hispanic (1)	6	0.05
Alaska Native tribes, specified:	1	0.01
Eskimo (1)	1	0.01
Am. Ind. or Alaska Nat., not spec.	22	0.20
American Indian tribes, specified:	97	0.87
Apache (3)	7	0.06
Blackfeet (1)	3	0.03
Cherokee (8)	41	0.37
Chickasaw (1)	2	0.02
Choctaw (2)	10	0.09
Cree	3	0.03
Creek (4)	11	0.10
Iroquois	2	0.02
Kiowa (7)	8	0.07
Latin American Indians (1)	1	0.01
Lumbee (1)	3	0.03
Potawatomi	1	0.01
Pueblo	1	0.01
Seminole	1	0.01
Sioux	1	0.01
All other tribes (2)	2	0.02
American Indian tribes, not spec.	10	0.09
Arab:	65	0.58
Egyptian	9	0.08
Jordanian	8	0.07
Lebanese	48	0.43
Armenian	9	0.08
Asian:	170	1.53
Chinese, ex. Taiwanese (7)	10	0.09
Filipino (26)	42	0.38
Indian (9)	10	0.09
Japanese (6)	12	0.11
Korean (18)	26	0.23
Laotian (3)	3	0.03
Taiwanese (1)	2	0.02
Thai (14)	27	0.24
Vietnamese (21)	24	0.22
Other Asian, specified (2)	3	0.03
Other Asian, not specified (7)	11	0.10
Australian	21	0.19
Austrian	14	0.12
Belgian	45	0.40
Brazilian	16	0.14
British	53	0.47
Czech	43	0.38
Czechoslovakian	54	0.48
Danish	37	0.33
Dutch	218	1.94
English	1,663	14.79
European	67	0.60
Finnish	25	0.22
French, except Basque	519	4.61
French Canadian	52	0.46
German	1,864	16.57
Greek	121	1.08
Hawaii Native/Pacific Islander:	17	0.15
Micronesian: (2)	3	0.03
Guamanian/Chamorro (2)	3	0.03
Polynesian: (6)	10	0.09
Native Hawaiian (5)	9	0.08
Other Polynesian (1)	1	0.01
Other Pac. Isl., specified	1	0.01
Other Pac. Isl., not spec. (1)	3	0.03
Hispanic or Latino:	296	2.66
Central American:	11	0.10
Costa Rican	2	0.02
Nicaraguan	4	0.04
Panamanian	5	0.04
Cuban	27	0.24
Dominican Republic	2	0.02
Mexican	167	1.50
Puerto Rican	33	0.30
South American:	10	0.09
Chilean	2	0.02
Colombian	1	0.01
Ecuadorian	1	0.01
Peruvian	1	0.01
Venezuelan	5	0.04
Other Hispanic or Latino	46	0.41
Hungarian	48	0.43
Irish	1,411	12.55
Italian	625	5.56
Lithuanian	31	0.28
Norwegian	129	1.15
Pennsylvania German	9	0.08
Polish	370	3.29
Portuguese	18	0.16
Romanian	8	0.07
Russian	79	0.70
Scandinavian	9	0.08
Scotch-Irish	348	3.09
Scottish	477	4.24
Serbian	9	0.08
Slavic	11	0.10
Slovak	30	0.27
Swedish	121	1.08
Swiss	39	0.35
Ukrainian	25	0.22
United States or American	1,252	11.13
Welsh	108	0.96
White:	10,860	97.67
Not Hispanic (10,461)	10,606	95.39
Hispanic (237)	254	2.28
Yugoslavian	28	0.25

Doral

Place Type: Census Designated Place
County: Miami-Dade
Population: 20,438

Ancestry/Race	Number	%
African American/Black:	650	3.18
Not Hispanic (433)	470	2.30
Hispanic (110)	180	0.88
African, sub-Saharan:	62	0.30
African	35	0.17
South African	13	0.06
Other sub-Saharan African	14	0.07
Alaska Native tribes, specified:	1	0.00
Alaska Athabascan	1	0.00
Am. Ind. or Alaska Nat., not spec.	13	0.06
American Indian tribes, specified:	18	0.09
Blackfeet	2	0.01
Cherokee (2)	4	0.02
Chickasaw	1	0.00
Creek (1)	1	0.00
Latin American Indians (6)	7	0.03
Potawatomi (1)	1	0.00
Sioux (1)	2	0.01
American Indian tribes, not spec.	7	0.03
Arab:	283	1.38
Arab/Arabic	58	0.28
Lebanese	225	1.10
Asian:	1,168	5.71
Cambodian (1)	1	0.00
Chinese, ex. Taiwanese (361)	398	1.95
Filipino (46)	59	0.29
Indian (275)	289	1.41
Indonesian	3	0.01
Japanese (178)	193	0.94
Korean (109)	110	0.54
Laotian (2)	2	0.01
Pakistani (18)	36	0.18
Taiwanese (15)	19	0.09
Thai (16)	16	0.08
Vietnamese (6)	6	0.03
Other Asian, not specified (7)	36	0.18
Austrian	67	0.33
Basque	69	0.34
Brazilian	535	2.61
British	134	0.65
Canadian	27	0.13
Carpatho Rusyn	7	0.03
Czech	8	0.04
Czechoslovakian	41	0.20
Danish	20	0.10
Dutch	15	0.07
English	342	1.67
European	231	1.13
French, except Basque	271	1.32
French Canadian	25	0.12
German	502	2.45
Greek	57	0.28
Hawaii Native/Pacific Islander:	11	0.05

Notes: 1. Figures in the "Number" column do not add up to the total population due to: a) Ancestry/Race overlap — e.g. persons can report being both White and Irish, b) persons of Hispanic origin can report being any race, c) persons reporting two ancestries are counted in both categories. 2. Numbers in parentheses indicate the number of persons reporting this ancestry/race alone, not in combination with any other ancestry/race. 3. Refer to the User's Guide in the front of the book for more detailed information.

Micronesian: (3)	3	0.01
Guamanian/Chamorro (3)	3	0.01
Polynesian:	1	0.00
Samoan	1	0.00
Other Pac. Isl., not spec.	7	0.03
Hispanic or Latino:	13,784	67.44
Central American:	990	4.84
Costa Rican	66	0.32
Guatemalan	130	0.64
Honduran	135	0.66
Nicaraguan	346	1.69
Panamanian	192	0.94
Salvadoran	77	0.38
Other Central American	44	0.22
Cuban	3,106	15.20
Dominican Republic	540	2.64
Mexican	525	2.57
Puerto Rican	907	4.44
South American:	4,989	24.41
Argentinean	262	1.28
Bolivian	45	0.22
Chilean	224	1.10
Colombian	1,780	8.71
Ecuadorian	241	1.18
Paraguayan	21	0.10
Peruvian	602	2.95
Uruguayan	35	0.17
Venezuelan	1,680	8.22
Other South American	99	0.48
Other Hispanic or Latino	2,727	13.34
Hungarian	52	0.25
Iranian	91	0.44
Irish	518	2.53
Israeli	47	0.23
Italian	1,117	5.45
Lithuanian	23	0.11
Norwegian	46	0.22
Polish	116	0.57
Portuguese	259	1.26
Romanian	23	0.11
Russian	121	0.59
Scandinavian	9	0.04
Scotch-Irish	24	0.12
Scottish	122	0.59
Serbian	10	0.05
Slavic	12	0.06
Swedish	91	0.44
Swiss	57	0.28
Ukrainian	26	0.13
United States or American	685	3.34
Welsh	25	0.12
West Indian, excl. Hispanic:	170	0.83
Bahamian	13	0.06
Barbadian	17	0.08
British West Indian	39	0.19
Jamaican	87	0.42
Other West Indian	14	0.07
White:	17,849	87.33
Not Hispanic (4,912)	5,119	25.05
Hispanic (12,261)	12,730	62.29

Dunedin

Place Type: City
County: Pinellas
Population: 35,691

Ancestry/Race	Number	%
Acadian/Cajun	15	0.04
Afghan	31	0.09
African American/Black:	798	2.24
Not Hispanic (692)	755	2.12
Hispanic (22)	43	0.12
African, sub-Saharan:	41	0.11
African	15	0.04
Nigerian	8	0.02
South African	18	0.05
Alaska Native tribes, specified:	1	0.00
Eskimo (1)	1	0.00
Am. Ind. or Alaska Nat., not spec.	59	0.17
Albanian	199	0.55
American Indian tribes, specified:	128	0.36
Apache (1)	1	0.00
Blackfeet (3)	6	0.02
Cherokee (13)	58	0.16
Cheyenne (1)	3	0.01
Chippewa (3)	10	0.03
Choctaw (4)	4	0.01
Cree (1)	2	0.01
Creek (2)	3	0.01
Delaware	2	0.01
Iroquois (3)	8	0.02
Latin American Indians (2)	4	0.01
Lumbee (2)	3	0.01
Ottawa	1	0.00
Paiute (1)	1	0.00
Potawatomi	2	0.01
Seminole	2	0.01
Sioux (5)	7	0.02
All other tribes (3)	11	0.03
American Indian tribes, not spec.	11	0.03
Arab:	205	0.57
Arab/Arabic	7	0.02
Egyptian	5	0.01
Lebanese	134	0.37
Syrian	18	0.05
Other Arab	41	0.11
Armenian	40	0.11
Asian:	480	1.34
Cambodian (1)	1	0.00
Chinese, ex. Taiwanese (73)	80	0.22
Filipino (88)	109	0.31
Hmong	1	0.00
Indian (138)	150	0.42
Indonesian (1)	2	0.01
Japanese (19)	30	0.08
Korean (16)	26	0.07
Laotian (10)	10	0.03
Pakistani (2)	4	0.01
Taiwanese (8)	12	0.03
Thai (15)	23	0.06
Vietnamese (15)	16	0.04
Other Asian, specified (2)	2	0.01
Other Asian, not specified (3)	14	0.04
Australian	23	0.06
Austrian	145	0.40
Belgian	59	0.16
Brazilian	15	0.04
British	276	0.77
Bulgarian	45	0.13
Canadian	374	1.04
Celtic	16	0.04
Croatian	65	0.18
Czech	123	0.34
Czechoslovakian	97	0.27
Danish	162	0.45
Dutch	793	2.21
English	5,247	14.61
European	160	0.45
Finnish	58	0.16
French, except Basque	1,411	3.93
French Canadian	513	1.43
German	7,645	21.28
Greek	591	1.65
Guyanese	10	0.03
Hawaii Native/Pacific Islander:	27	0.08
Micronesian: (3)	3	0.01
Guamanian/Chamorro (3)	3	0.01
Polynesian: (6)	14	0.04
Native Hawaiian (2)	7	0.02
Samoan (2)	2	0.01
Tongan (2)	5	0.01
Other Pac. Isl., not spec. (3)	10	0.03
Hispanic or Latino:	1,192	3.34
Central American:	37	0.10
Costa Rican	11	0.03
Guatemalan	2	0.01
Honduran	4	0.01
Nicaraguan	9	0.03
Panamanian	7	0.02
Salvadoran	3	0.01
Other Central American	1	0.00
Cuban	148	0.41
Dominican Republic	26	0.07
Mexican	261	0.73
Puerto Rican	301	0.84
South American:	174	0.49
Argentinean	12	0.03
Bolivian	1	0.00
Chilean	6	0.02
Colombian	87	0.24
Ecuadorian	7	0.02
Paraguayan	1	0.00
Peruvian	24	0.07
Venezuelan	28	0.08
Other South American	8	0.02
Other Hispanic or Latino	245	0.69
Hungarian	344	0.96
Icelander	8	0.02
Irish	6,163	17.15
Israeli	10	0.03
Italian	3,677	10.23
Latvian	18	0.05
Lithuanian	103	0.29
Luxemburger	26	0.07
Northern European	69	0.19
Norwegian	427	1.19
Pennsylvania German	40	0.11
Polish	1,466	4.08
Portuguese	107	0.30
Romanian	81	0.23
Russian	438	1.22
Scandinavian	50	0.14
Scotch-Irish	946	2.63
Scottish	1,413	3.93
Serbian	27	0.08
Slavic	7	0.02
Slovak	170	0.47
Slovene	89	0.25
Swedish	677	1.88
Swiss	74	0.21
Turkish	64	0.18
Ukrainian	247	0.69
United States or American	1,627	4.53
Welsh	423	1.18
West Indian, excl. Hispanic:	254	0.71
Barbadian	16	0.04
British West Indian	46	0.13
Jamaican	156	0.43
Trinidadian and Tobagonian	14	0.04
West Indian	22	0.06
White:	34,223	95.89
Not Hispanic (32,996)	33,271	93.22
Hispanic (868)	952	2.67
Yugoslavian	38	0.11

East Lake

Place Type: Census Designated Place
County: Pinellas
Population: 29,394

Ancestry/Race	Number	%
Acadian/Cajun	7	0.02
African American/Black:	385	1.31
Not Hispanic (313)	363	1.23
Hispanic (14)	22	0.07
African, sub-Saharan:	36	0.12
African	8	0.03
South African	22	0.07
Other sub-Saharan African	6	0.02
Am. Ind. or Alaska Nat., not spec.	35	0.12
Alsatian	9	0.03
American Indian tribes, specified:	49	0.17
Apache (2)	2	0.01
Cherokee (5)	16	0.05
Chickasaw (1)	1	0.00
Chippewa (2)	4	0.01
Choctaw (4)	5	0.02
Comanche	1	0.00
Iroquois	2	0.01
Latin American Indians (1)	3	0.01
Lumbee (1)	1	0.00
Navajo (1)	1	0.00

Notes: 1. Figures in the "Number" column do not add up to the total population due to: a) Ancestry/Race overlap — e.g. persons can report being both White and Irish, b) persons of Hispanic origin can report being any race, c) persons reporting two ancestries are counted in both categories. 2. Numbers in parentheses indicate the number of persons reporting this ancestry/race alone, not in combination with any other ancestry/race. 3. Refer to the User's Guide in the front of the book for more detailed information.

Sioux (1)	1	0.00
All other tribes (3)	12	0.04
American Indian tribes, not spec.	8	0.03
Arab:	297	1.01
Arab/Arabic	36	0.12
Egyptian	43	0.15
Lebanese	92	0.31
Syrian	117	0.40
Other Arab	9	0.03
Armenian	89	0.30
Asian:	799	2.72
Bangladeshi (2)	2	0.01
Cambodian (6)	7	0.02
Chinese, ex. Taiwanese (83)	108	0.37
Filipino (96)	134	0.46
Indian (277)	294	1.00
Indonesian	1	0.00
Japanese (34)	49	0.17
Korean (56)	63	0.21
Laotian (1)	1	0.00
Pakistani (3)	3	0.01
Sri Lankan (1)	3	0.01
Taiwanese (13)	13	0.04
Thai (13)	14	0.05
Vietnamese (70)	75	0.26
Other Asian, specified (1)	1	0.00
Other Asian, not specified (15)	31	0.11
Assyrian/Chaldean/Syriac	5	0.02
Australian	37	0.13
Austrian	294	1.00
Belgian	31	0.11
Brazilian	45	0.15
British	144	0.49
Canadian	369	1.25
Celtic	11	0.04
Croatian	56	0.19
Czech	198	0.67
Czechoslovakian	77	0.26
Danish	90	0.31
Dutch	510	1.73
Eastern European	35	0.12
English	4,151	14.10
European	175	0.59
Finnish	85	0.29
French, except Basque	1,085	3.68
French Canadian	399	1.35
German	6,235	21.17
Greek	868	2.95
Hawaii Native/Pacific Islander:	15	0.05
Micronesian: (2)	2	0.01
Guamanian/Chamorro (2)	2	0.01
Polynesian:	8	0.03
Native Hawaiian	7	0.02
Samoan	1	0.00
Other Pac. Isl., not spec.	5	0.02
Hispanic or Latino:	1,094	3.72
Central American:	45	0.15
Costa Rican	9	0.03
Guatemalan	11	0.04
Honduran	1	0.00
Nicaraguan	7	0.02
Panamanian	11	0.04
Salvadoran	5	0.02
Other Central American	1	0.00
Cuban	133	0.45
Dominican Republic	18	0.06
Mexican	86	0.29
Puerto Rican	353	1.20
South American:	193	0.66
Argentinean	9	0.03
Bolivian	4	0.01
Chilean	9	0.03
Colombian	96	0.33
Ecuadorian	14	0.05
Paraguayan	1	0.00
Peruvian	23	0.08
Venezuelan	27	0.09
Other South American	10	0.03
Other Hispanic or Latino	266	0.90
Hungarian	420	1.43
Icelander	9	0.03
Iranian	30	0.10
Irish	4,913	16.68
Israeli	34	0.12
Italian	4,083	13.87
Lithuanian	144	0.49
Luxemburger	8	0.03
Macedonian	27	0.09
Northern European	124	0.42
Norwegian	428	1.45
Pennsylvania German	10	0.03
Polish	1,609	5.46
Portuguese	188	0.64
Romanian	56	0.19
Russian	584	1.98
Scandinavian	106	0.36
Scotch-Irish	634	2.15
Scottish	879	2.99
Slovak	181	0.61
Slovene	21	0.07
Swedish	733	2.49
Swiss	168	0.57
Ukrainian	193	0.66
United States or American	1,573	5.34
Welsh	200	0.68
West Indian, excl. Hispanic:	33	0.11
Bermudan	7	0.02
British West Indian	13	0.04
Jamaican	8	0.03
West Indian	5	0.02
White:	28,145	95.75
Not Hispanic (27,007)	27,214	92.58
Hispanic (879)	931	3.17
Yugoslavian	66	0.22

Edgewater

Place Type: City
County: Volusia
Population: 18,668

Ancestry/Race	Number	%
African American/Black:	321	1.72
Not Hispanic (261)	308	1.65
Hispanic (2)	13	0.07
Alaska Native tribes, specified:	2	0.01
Aleut	1	0.01
Eskimo	1	0.01
Am. Ind. or Alaska Nat., not spec.	38	0.20
Alsatian	10	0.05
American Indian tribes, specified:	89	0.48
Blackfeet	3	0.02
Cherokee (11)	33	0.18
Chippewa (3)	4	0.02
Choctaw (5)	13	0.07
Creek (2)	3	0.02
Delaware	2	0.01
Iroquois (8)	9	0.05
Latin American Indians	4	0.02
Navajo (1)	1	0.01
Ottawa (1)	1	0.01
Pueblo	3	0.02
Sioux	2	0.01
All other tribes (5)	11	0.06
Arab:	23	0.12
Lebanese	23	0.12
Asian:	149	0.80
Bangladeshi (1)	3	0.02
Cambodian (3)	3	0.02
Chinese, ex. Taiwanese (23)	31	0.17
Filipino (20)	33	0.18
Indian (30)	31	0.17
Indonesian	1	0.01
Japanese (5)	12	0.06
Korean (5)	12	0.06
Pakistani	1	0.01
Taiwanese (1)	2	0.01
Thai (1)	3	0.02
Vietnamese (3)	6	0.03
Other Asian, specified	1	0.01
Other Asian, not specified (6)	10	0.05
Australian	15	0.08
Austrian	96	0.51
Belgian	37	0.20
Brazilian	6	0.03
British	145	0.77
Canadian	107	0.57
Croatian	10	0.05
Czech	103	0.55
Czechoslovakian	64	0.34
Danish	54	0.29
Dutch	469	2.49
Eastern European	10	0.05
English	2,667	14.14
European	95	0.50
Finnish	14	0.07
French, except Basque	960	5.09
French Canadian	363	1.92
German	3,189	16.91
Greek	59	0.31
Hawaii Native/Pacific Islander:	9	0.05
Micronesian: (1)	2	0.01
Guamanian/Chamorro (1)	2	0.01
Polynesian: (1)	4	0.02
Native Hawaiian (1)	4	0.02
Other Pac. Isl., not spec.	3	0.02
Hispanic or Latino:	365	1.96
Central American:	7	0.04
Honduran	4	0.02
Panamanian	2	0.01
Other Central American	1	0.01
Cuban	31	0.17
Dominican Republic	3	0.02
Mexican	75	0.40
Puerto Rican	134	0.72
South American:	42	0.22
Argentinean	2	0.01
Colombian	17	0.09
Paraguayan	1	0.01
Peruvian	8	0.04
Uruguayan	2	0.01
Venezuelan	11	0.06
Other South American	1	0.01
Other Hispanic or Latino	73	0.39
Hungarian	169	0.90
Irish	3,115	16.52
Italian	1,872	9.93
Latvian	23	0.12
Lithuanian	147	0.78
New Zealander	7	0.04
Norwegian	245	1.30
Pennsylvania German	20	0.11
Polish	846	4.49
Portuguese	60	0.32
Russian	71	0.38
Scotch-Irish	465	2.47
Scottish	412	2.18
Serbian	8	0.04
Slovak	29	0.15
Slovene	15	0.08
Swedish	234	1.24
Swiss	67	0.36
Ukrainian	56	0.30
United States or American	1,541	8.17
Welsh	241	1.28
West Indian, excl. Hispanic:	23	0.12
Jamaican	6	0.03
Trinidadian and Tobagonian	17	0.09
White:	18,176	97.36
Not Hispanic (17,724)	17,874	95.75
Hispanic (263)	302	1.62
Yugoslavian	19	0.10

Egypt Lake-Leto

Place Type: Census Designated Place
County: Hillsborough
Population: 32,782

Ancestry/Race	Number	%
African American/Black:	2,952	9.00
Not Hispanic (2,251)	2,450	7.47
Hispanic (367)	502	1.53

Notes: 1. Figures in the "Number" column do not add up to the total population due to: a) Ancestry/Race overlap — e.g. persons can report being both White and Irish, b) persons of Hispanic origin can report being any race, c) persons reporting two ancestries are counted in both categories. 2. Numbers in parentheses indicate the number of persons reporting this ancestry/race alone, not in combination with any other ancestry/race. 3. Refer to the User's Guide in the front of the book for more detailed information.

African, sub-Saharan:	226	0.69
African	190	0.58
Ethiopian	26	0.08
Sierra Leonean	10	0.03
Alaska Native tribes, specified:	1	0.00
Aleut (1)	1	0.00
Am. Ind. or Alaska Nat., not spec.	122	0.37
Albanian	8	0.02
American Indian tribes, specified:	135	0.41
Apache (1)	1	0.00
Blackfeet (5)	12	0.04
Cherokee (19)	55	0.17
Cheyenne	1	0.00
Chippewa	3	0.01
Choctaw	2	0.01
Comanche	1	0.00
Cree (7)	8	0.02
Creek (3)	5	0.02
Delaware	2	0.01
Iroquois (2)	8	0.02
Latin American Indians (9)	22	0.07
Lumbee (1)	1	0.00
Seminole (4)	4	0.01
Sioux (1)	1	0.00
All other tribes (4)	9	0.03
American Indian tribes, not spec.	23	0.07
Arab:	259	0.79
Arab/Arabic	107	0.33
Egyptian	24	0.07
Lebanese	43	0.13
Palestinian	75	0.23
Syrian	10	0.03
Armenian	7	0.02
Asian:	1,325	4.04
Cambodian (1)	3	0.01
Chinese, ex. Taiwanese (98)	119	0.36
Filipino (120)	149	0.45
Hmong (1)	4	0.01
Indian (251)	291	0.89
Indonesian (3)	5	0.02
Japanese (24)	37	0.11
Korean (122)	140	0.43
Laotian (4)	6	0.02
Malaysian (1)	1	0.00
Pakistani (15)	21	0.06
Sri Lankan (4)	4	0.01
Taiwanese (1)	1	0.00
Thai (17)	20	0.06
Vietnamese (416)	458	1.40
Other Asian, specified (4)	4	0.01
Other Asian, not specified (12)	62	0.19
Austrian	46	0.14
Belgian	29	0.09
Brazilian	95	0.29
British	83	0.25
Bulgarian	8	0.02
Canadian	85	0.26
Croatian	8	0.02
Czech	50	0.15
Czechoslovakian	13	0.04
Danish	33	0.10
Dutch	216	0.66
Eastern European	12	0.04
English	1,726	5.26
European	50	0.15
Finnish	9	0.03
French, except Basque	692	2.11
French Canadian	130	0.40
German	2,492	7.60
Greek	63	0.19
Guyanese	29	0.09
Hawaii Native/Pacific Islander:	39	0.12
Micronesian: (3)	6	0.02
Guamanian/Chamorro (3)	6	0.02
Polynesian: (14)	16	0.05
Native Hawaiian (6)	8	0.02
Samoan (8)	8	0.02
Other Pac. Isl., not spec.	17	0.05
Hispanic or Latino:	15,015	45.80
Central American:	437	1.33
Costa Rican	71	0.22
Guatemalan	86	0.26
Honduran	74	0.23
Nicaraguan	59	0.18
Panamanian	73	0.22
Salvadoran	44	0.13
Other Central American	30	0.09
Cuban	5,977	18.23
Dominican Republic	471	1.44
Mexican	639	1.95
Puerto Rican	3,559	10.86
South American:	1,087	3.32
Argentinean	31	0.09
Bolivian	13	0.04
Chilean	28	0.09
Colombian	608	1.85
Ecuadorian	82	0.25
Peruvian	128	0.39
Uruguayan	9	0.03
Venezuelan	159	0.49
Other South American	29	0.09
Other Hispanic or Latino	2,845	8.68
Hungarian	150	0.46
Icelander	10	0.03
Iranian	4	0.01
Irish	2,224	6.78
Israeli	10	0.03
Italian	2,066	6.30
Latvian	6	0.02
Lithuanian	60	0.18
Northern European	13	0.04
Norwegian	176	0.54
Pennsylvania German	22	0.07
Polish	465	1.42
Portuguese	74	0.23
Romanian	21	0.06
Russian	210	0.64
Scotch-Irish	373	1.14
Scottish	354	1.08
Slovak	12	0.04
Swedish	163	0.50
Swiss	18	0.05
Turkish	89	0.27
Ukrainian	63	0.19
United States or American	1,802	5.50
Welsh	111	0.34
West Indian, excl. Hispanic:	442	1.35
Bahamian	12	0.04
British West Indian	44	0.13
Haitian	37	0.11
Jamaican	223	0.68
Trinidadian and Tobagonian	34	0.10
West Indian	92	0.28
White:	26,030	79.40
Not Hispanic (13,754)	14,187	43.28
Hispanic (11,192)	11,843	36.13
Yugoslavian	14	0.04

Elfers

Place Type: Census Designated Place
County: Pasco
Population: 13,161

Ancestry/Race	Number	%
African American/Black:	155	1.18
Not Hispanic (116)	140	1.06
Hispanic (10)	15	0.11
Alaska Native tribes, specified:	1	0.01
Eskimo	1	0.01
Am. Ind. or Alaska Nat., not spec.	33	0.25
American Indian tribes, specified:	92	0.70
Apache	7	0.05
Blackfeet	3	0.02
Cherokee (12)	43	0.33
Cheyenne (1)	1	0.01
Chippewa (2)	3	0.02
Choctaw	1	0.01
Cree	1	0.01
Creek (1)	2	0.02
Delaware (5)	5	0.04
Iroquois (1)	3	0.02
Latin American Indians (1)	1	0.01
Lumbee (3)	3	0.02
Osage	1	0.01
Seminole (1)	2	0.02
Sioux	3	0.02
All other tribes (7)	13	0.10
American Indian tribes, not spec.	4	0.03
Arab:	24	0.18
Arab/Arabic	8	0.06
Lebanese	7	0.05
Syrian	9	0.07
Asian:	163	1.24
Chinese, ex. Taiwanese (12)	13	0.10
Filipino (19)	32	0.24
Indian (30)	39	0.30
Japanese (3)	7	0.05
Korean (2)	7	0.05
Laotian (2)	4	0.03
Pakistani (1)	1	0.01
Thai (3)	6	0.05
Vietnamese (43)	45	0.34
Other Asian, not specified (4)	9	0.07
Austrian	37	0.28
Belgian	21	0.16
British	73	0.55
Bulgarian	5	0.04
Canadian	93	0.70
Czech	37	0.28
Czechoslovakian	21	0.16
Danish	59	0.45
Dutch	401	3.04
English	1,732	13.12
Estonian	8	0.06
European	50	0.38
Finnish	7	0.05
French, except Basque	686	5.20
French Canadian	173	1.31
German	2,320	17.57
Greek	196	1.48
Hawaii Native/Pacific Islander:	7	0.05
Polynesian: (3)	3	0.02
Samoan (3)	3	0.02
Other Pac. Isl., not spec. (1)	4	0.03
Hispanic or Latino:	595	4.52
Central American:	23	0.17
Costa Rican	1	0.01
Honduran	12	0.09
Nicaraguan	2	0.02
Panamanian	2	0.02
Salvadoran	6	0.05
Cuban	45	0.34
Dominican Republic	21	0.16
Mexican	85	0.65
Puerto Rican	258	1.96
South American:	42	0.32
Argentinean	4	0.03
Bolivian	3	0.02
Colombian	24	0.18
Ecuadorian	3	0.02
Peruvian	6	0.05
Other South American	2	0.02
Other Hispanic or Latino	121	0.92
Hungarian	123	0.93
Irish	2,160	16.36
Italian	1,772	13.42
Lithuanian	36	0.27
Macedonian	9	0.07
Maltese	7	0.05
Norwegian	168	1.27
Pennsylvania German	22	0.17
Polish	639	4.84
Portuguese	54	0.41
Romanian	10	0.08
Russian	105	0.80
Scandinavian	10	0.08
Scotch-Irish	212	1.61
Scottish	187	1.42
Serbian	33	0.25
Slavic	9	0.07
Slovak	71	0.54
Slovene	17	0.13
Swedish	164	1.24

Notes: 1. Figures in the "Number" column do not add up to the total population due to: a) Ancestry/Race overlap — e.g. persons can report being both White and Irish, b) persons of Hispanic origin can report being any race, c) persons reporting two ancestries are counted in both categories. 2. Numbers in parentheses indicate the number of persons reporting this ancestry/race alone, not in combination with any other ancestry/race. 3. Refer to the User's Guide in the front of the book for more detailed information.

Swiss	13	0.10
Turkish	10	0.08
Ukrainian	67	0.51
United States or American	1,067	8.08
Welsh	111	0.84
West Indian, excl. Hispanic:	14	0.11
Dutch West Indian	14	0.11
White:	12,725	96.69
Not Hispanic (12,124)	12,271	93.24
Hispanic (404)	454	3.45
Yugoslavian	36	0.27

Englewood

Place Type: Census Designated Place
County: Sarasota
Population: 16,196

Ancestry/Race	Number	%
African American/Black:	50	0.31
Not Hispanic (28)	47	0.29
Hispanic (2)	3	0.02
Am. Ind. or Alaska Nat., not spec.	28	0.17
Alsatian	9	0.06
American Indian tribes, specified:	47	0.29
Apache (1)	1	0.01
Blackfeet	2	0.01
Cherokee (9)	18	0.11
Chippewa (2)	2	0.01
Choctaw (1)	2	0.01
Iroquois (6)	7	0.04
Latin American Indians	1	0.01
Navajo	4	0.02
Osage (1)	1	0.01
Pueblo (1)	1	0.01
Sioux (1)	2	0.01
All other tribes (4)	6	0.04
American Indian tribes, not spec.	4	0.02
Armenian	18	0.11
Asian:	74	0.46
Cambodian (8)	8	0.05
Chinese, ex. Taiwanese (12)	15	0.09
Filipino (8)	11	0.07
Indian (12)	15	0.09
Japanese (6)	8	0.05
Korean (2)	5	0.03
Sri Lankan (3)	3	0.02
Taiwanese (1)	1	0.01
Thai (6)	6	0.04
Vietnamese (1)	1	0.01
Other Asian, specified	1	0.01
Assyrian/Chaldean/Syriac	9	0.06
Australian	7	0.04
Austrian	38	0.23
Belgian	76	0.47
Brazilian	15	0.09
British	66	0.41
Canadian	244	1.50
Croatian	8	0.05
Czech	43	0.26
Czechoslovakian	78	0.48
Danish	74	0.46
Dutch	564	3.47
English	3,140	19.32
European	53	0.33
Finnish	26	0.16
French, except Basque	813	5.00
French Canadian	280	1.72
German	3,952	24.32
Greek	32	0.20
Hawaii Native/Pacific Islander:	8	0.05
Polynesian: (2)	6	0.04
Native Hawaiian (2)	5	0.03
Samoan	1	0.01
Other Pac. Isl., specified	1	0.01
Other Pac. Isl., not spec.	1	0.01
Hispanic or Latino:	241	1.49
Central American:	3	0.02
Panamanian	2	0.01
Salvadoran	1	0.01
Cuban	9	0.06
Dominican Republic	1	0.01
Mexican	114	0.70
Puerto Rican	55	0.34
South American:	17	0.10
Colombian	4	0.02
Ecuadorian	3	0.02
Peruvian	7	0.04
Other South American	3	0.02
Other Hispanic or Latino	42	0.26
Hungarian	133	0.82
Iranian	8	0.05
Irish	2,362	14.54
Italian	1,025	6.31
Lithuanian	113	0.70
Luxemburger	9	0.06
Macedonian	4	0.02
Northern European	15	0.09
Norwegian	186	1.14
Pennsylvania German	16	0.10
Polish	892	5.49
Portuguese	59	0.36
Romanian	8	0.05
Russian	89	0.55
Scandinavian	19	0.12
Scotch-Irish	448	2.76
Scottish	569	3.50
Slovak	38	0.23
Swedish	462	2.84
Swiss	78	0.48
Turkish	11	0.07
Ukrainian	78	0.48
United States or American	1,060	6.52
Welsh	206	1.27
White:	15,995	98.76
Not Hispanic (15,752)	15,819	97.67
Hispanic (161)	176	1.09
Yugoslavian	9	0.06

Ensley

Place Type: Census Designated Place
County: Escambia
Population: 18,752

Ancestry/Race	Number	%
Acadian/Cajun	18	0.10
African American/Black:	5,432	28.97
Not Hispanic (5,304)	5,388	28.73
Hispanic (29)	44	0.23
African, sub-Saharan:	49	0.26
African	49	0.26
Am. Ind. or Alaska Nat., not spec.	97	0.52
American Indian tribes, specified:	248	1.32
Apache (1)	3	0.02
Blackfeet (1)	11	0.06
Cherokee (15)	62	0.33
Cheyenne	1	0.01
Chickasaw (1)	2	0.01
Chippewa (1)	4	0.02
Choctaw (4)	10	0.05
Comanche	1	0.01
Cree	1	0.01
Creek (73)	125	0.67
Crow	1	0.01
Houma	2	0.01
Iroquois (4)	5	0.03
Latin American Indians	1	0.01
Lumbee (8)	8	0.04
Navajo (1)	1	0.01
Osage	1	0.01
Ottawa (1)	1	0.01
Seminole (3)	3	0.02
Sioux (1)	2	0.01
All other tribes	3	0.02
American Indian tribes, not spec.	8	0.04
Arab:	10	0.05
Lebanese	10	0.05
Asian:	335	1.79
Cambodian (6)	6	0.03
Chinese, ex. Taiwanese (14)	26	0.14
Filipino (86)	133	0.71
Indian (10)	16	0.09
Indonesian (2)	2	0.01
Japanese (22)	42	0.22
Korean (14)	24	0.13
Thai (3)	12	0.06
Vietnamese (50)	56	0.30
Other Asian, specified	2	0.01
Other Asian, not specified (5)	16	0.09
British	71	0.38
Canadian	20	0.11
Croatian	16	0.09
Czech	39	0.21
Danish	32	0.17
Dutch	154	0.83
Eastern European	16	0.09
English	1,481	7.97
European	43	0.23
Finnish	23	0.12
French, except Basque	336	1.81
French Canadian	94	0.51
German	1,657	8.92
Greek	51	0.27
Hawaii Native/Pacific Islander:	18	0.10
Micronesian: (6)	9	0.05
Guamanian/Chamorro (6)	8	0.04
Other Micronesian	1	0.01
Polynesian: (1)	3	0.02
Native Hawaiian	1	0.01
Tongan (1)	2	0.01
Other Pac. Isl., specified	1	0.01
Other Pac. Isl., not spec. (2)	5	0.03
Hispanic or Latino:	390	2.08
Central American:	17	0.09
Guatemalan	2	0.01
Honduran	8	0.04
Nicaraguan	3	0.02
Panamanian	4	0.02
Cuban	19	0.10
Dominican Republic	6	0.03
Mexican	148	0.79
Puerto Rican	78	0.42
South American:	22	0.12
Argentinean	2	0.01
Colombian	13	0.07
Peruvian	3	0.02
Venezuelan	2	0.01
Other South American	2	0.01
Other Hispanic or Latino	100	0.53
Hungarian	74	0.40
Iranian	14	0.08
Irish	1,787	9.61
Italian	496	2.67
Lithuanian	7	0.04
Norwegian	68	0.37
Pennsylvania German	23	0.12
Polish	251	1.35
Portuguese	30	0.16
Russian	27	0.15
Scandinavian	19	0.10
Scotch-Irish	469	2.52
Scottish	293	1.58
Slavic	15	0.08
Slovak	15	0.08
Swedish	71	0.38
Swiss	11	0.06
Ukrainian	4	0.02
United States or American	2,112	11.36
Welsh	36	0.19
White:	12,846	68.50
Not Hispanic (12,336)	12,606	67.22
Hispanic (210)	240	1.28

Eustis

Place Type: City
County: Lake
Population: 15,106

Ancestry/Race	Number	%
African American/Black:	2,932	19.41
Not Hispanic (2,829)	2,886	19.10
Hispanic (38)	46	0.30

Notes: 1. Figures in the "Number" column do not add up to the total population due to: a) Ancestry/Race overlap — e.g. persons can report being both White and Irish, b) persons of Hispanic origin can report being any race, c) persons reporting two ancestries are counted in both categories. 2. Numbers in parentheses indicate the number of persons reporting this ancestry/race alone, not in combination with any other ancestry/race. 3. Refer to the User's Guide in the front of the book for more detailed information.

African, sub-Saharan:	43	0.28
African	43	0.28
Am. Ind. or Alaska Nat., not spec.	32	0.21
American Indian tribes, specified:	84	0.56
Blackfeet (1)	2	0.01
Cherokee (21)	37	0.24
Chippewa (4)	6	0.04
Choctaw (8)	9	0.06
Creek	1	0.01
Delaware	1	0.01
Iroquois (2)	4	0.03
Latin American Indians (1)	9	0.06
Lumbee	2	0.01
Seminole	2	0.01
Sioux (3)	4	0.03
Yakama (1)	1	0.01
All other tribes (3)	6	0.04
American Indian tribes, not spec.	4	0.03
Arab:	88	0.57
Egyptian	62	0.40
Lebanese	26	0.17
Armenian	17	0.11
Asian:	111	0.73
Chinese, ex. Taiwanese (15)	17	0.11
Filipino (23)	25	0.17
Indian (22)	25	0.17
Indonesian	2	0.01
Japanese (3)	3	0.02
Korean (7)	8	0.05
Malaysian	1	0.01
Sri Lankan (2)	2	0.01
Vietnamese (22)	22	0.15
Other Asian, specified (1)	1	0.01
Other Asian, not specified	5	0.03
Australian	10	0.07
Austrian	11	0.07
Belgian	10	0.07
British	84	0.55
Canadian	22	0.14
Croatian	18	0.12
Czech	72	0.47
Czechoslovakian	18	0.12
Danish	41	0.27
Dutch	216	1.41
Eastern European	9	0.06
English	2,232	14.54
European	34	0.22
Finnish	15	0.10
French, except Basque	394	2.57
French Canadian	123	0.80
German	2,079	13.54
Greek	15	0.10
Hawaii Native/Pacific Islander:	22	0.15
Polynesian: (6)	7	0.05
Native Hawaiian (2)	3	0.02
Samoan (4)	4	0.03
Other Pac. Isl., not spec. (8)	15	0.10
Hispanic or Latino:	962	6.37
Central American:	29	0.19
Costa Rican	1	0.01
Guatemalan	9	0.06
Nicaraguan	3	0.02
Panamanian	4	0.03
Salvadoran	11	0.07
Other Central American	1	0.01
Cuban	35	0.23
Dominican Republic	2	0.01
Mexican	576	3.81
Puerto Rican	192	1.27
South American:	28	0.19
Argentinean	4	0.03
Chilean	1	0.01
Colombian	9	0.06
Peruvian	11	0.07
Uruguayan	1	0.01
Venezuelan	2	0.01
Other Hispanic or Latino	100	0.66
Hungarian	31	0.20
Irish	1,852	12.06
Italian	723	4.71
Latvian	8	0.05
Lithuanian	11	0.07
Northern European	21	0.14
Norwegian	76	0.50
Polish	454	2.96
Romanian	21	0.14
Russian	17	0.11
Scandinavian	41	0.27
Scotch-Irish	291	1.90
Scottish	341	2.22
Serbian	8	0.05
Slovak	9	0.06
Slovene	11	0.07
Swedish	137	0.89
Swiss	38	0.25
Ukrainian	70	0.46
United States or American	1,487	9.69
Welsh	115	0.75
West Indian, excl. Hispanic:	123	0.80
Bahamian	67	0.44
Barbadian	6	0.04
Haitian	7	0.05
Jamaican	43	0.28
White:	11,758	77.84
Not Hispanic (11,040)	11,142	73.76
Hispanic (576)	616	4.08
Yugoslavian	15	0.10

Fairview Shores

Place Type: Census Designated Place
County: Orange
Population: 13,898

Ancestry/Race	Number	%
African American/Black:	1,960	14.10
Not Hispanic (1,809)	1,909	13.74
Hispanic (37)	51	0.37
African, sub-Saharan:	79	0.59
African	29	0.22
Ethiopian	50	0.37
Alaska Native tribes, specified:	1	0.01
Eskimo	1	0.01
Am. Ind. or Alaska Nat., not spec.	44	0.32
American Indian tribes, specified:	74	0.53
Apache (1)	2	0.01
Blackfeet	2	0.01
Cherokee (8)	33	0.24
Chippewa (5)	5	0.04
Choctaw	1	0.01
Creek (1)	3	0.02
Delaware (1)	2	0.01
Iroquois (3)	5	0.04
Latin American Indians (1)	3	0.02
Lumbee	1	0.01
Pueblo	1	0.01
Seminole (3)	4	0.03
Sioux (2)	4	0.03
All other tribes (2)	8	0.06
American Indian tribes, not spec.	11	0.08
Arab:	45	0.34
Arab/Arabic	8	0.06
Lebanese	15	0.11
Moroccan	10	0.07
Syrian	6	0.04
Other Arab	6	0.04
Asian:	459	3.30
Chinese, ex. Taiwanese (30)	41	0.30
Filipino (60)	68	0.49
Indian (9)	17	0.12
Japanese (4)	13	0.09
Korean (39)	51	0.37
Laotian (7)	8	0.06
Pakistani (10)	13	0.09
Thai (9)	13	0.09
Vietnamese (190)	213	1.53
Other Asian, not specified (5)	22	0.16
Australian	30	0.22
Austrian	21	0.16
Belgian	17	0.13
Brazilian	27	0.20
British	60	0.45
Bulgarian	9	0.07
Canadian	49	0.37
Croatian	11	0.08
Czech	28	0.21
Czechoslovakian	14	0.10
Danish	62	0.46
Dutch	229	1.71
English	1,567	11.69
European	55	0.41
Finnish	13	0.10
French, except Basque	428	3.19
French Canadian	203	1.52
German	2,008	14.99
Greek	19	0.14
Hawaii Native/Pacific Islander:	34	0.24
Melanesian: (3)	3	0.02
Other Melanesian (3)	3	0.02
Micronesian:	5	0.04
Guamanian/Chamorro	4	0.03
Other Micronesian	1	0.01
Polynesian: (11)	16	0.12
Native Hawaiian (9)	12	0.09
Samoan (2)	4	0.03
Other Pac. Isl., not spec. (1)	10	0.07
Hispanic or Latino:	1,310	9.43
Central American:	36	0.26
Costa Rican	2	0.01
Guatemalan	5	0.04
Honduran	7	0.05
Nicaraguan	8	0.06
Panamanian	11	0.08
Salvadoran	3	0.02
Cuban	128	0.92
Dominican Republic	62	0.45
Mexican	160	1.15
Puerto Rican	607	4.37
South American:	90	0.65
Argentinean	4	0.03
Bolivian	1	0.01
Chilean	3	0.02
Colombian	51	0.37
Ecuadorian	12	0.09
Peruvian	9	0.06
Uruguayan	3	0.02
Other South American	7	0.05
Other Hispanic or Latino	227	1.63
Hungarian	43	0.32
Irish	1,515	11.31
Italian	679	5.07
Latvian	10	0.07
Lithuanian	26	0.19
Norwegian	128	0.96
Polish	272	2.03
Portuguese	55	0.41
Romanian	31	0.23
Russian	89	0.66
Scandinavian	11	0.08
Scotch-Irish	341	2.54
Scottish	329	2.46
Serbian	5	0.04
Slavic	8	0.06
Slovak	26	0.19
Slovene	7	0.05
Swedish	105	0.78
Swiss	24	0.18
Turkish	4	0.03
Ukrainian	33	0.25
United States or American	1,026	7.66
Welsh	88	0.66
West Indian, excl. Hispanic:	156	1.16
Bahamian	12	0.09
Barbadian	27	0.20
Haitian	12	0.09
Jamaican	65	0.49
Trinidadian and Tobagonian	24	0.18
West Indian	16	0.12
White:	11,091	79.80
Not Hispanic (10,082)	10,263	73.85
Hispanic (771)	828	5.96

Notes: 1. Figures in the "Number" column do not add up to the total population due to: a) Ancestry/Race overlap — e.g. persons can report being both White and Irish, b) persons of Hispanic origin can report being any race, c) persons reporting two ancestries are counted in both categories. 2. Numbers in parentheses indicate the number of persons reporting this ancestry/race alone, not in combination with any other ancestry/race. 3. Refer to the User's Guide in the front of the book for more detailed information.

Fernandina Beach

Place Type: City
County: Nassau
Population: 10,549

Ancestry/Race	Number	%
African American/Black:	1,726	16.36
Not Hispanic (1,698)	1,714	16.25
Hispanic (10)	12	0.11
African, sub-Saharan:	4	0.04
African	4	0.04
Alaska Native tribes, specified:	5	0.05
Eskimo (1)	4	0.04
Tlingit-Haida (1)	1	0.01
Am. Ind. or Alaska Nat., not spec.	18	0.17
American Indian tribes, specified:	39	0.37
Cherokee (9)	18	0.17
Choctaw (1)	1	0.01
Creek (1)	5	0.05
Iroquois (1)	3	0.03
Latin American Indians (5)	5	0.05
Ottawa	1	0.01
Potawatomi	1	0.01
Seminole	1	0.01
Shoshone	2	0.02
Sioux	1	0.01
All other tribes	1	0.01
American Indian tribes, not spec.	2	0.02
Arab:	14	0.14
Lebanese	14	0.14
Asian:	84	0.80
Chinese, ex. Taiwanese (13)	15	0.14
Filipino (22)	32	0.30
Indian (5)	7	0.07
Japanese (7)	12	0.11
Korean (8)	9	0.09
Laotian (1)	1	0.01
Thai (2)	3	0.03
Vietnamese (2)	2	0.02
Other Asian, specified	1	0.01
Other Asian, not specified (1)	2	0.02
Austrian	48	0.47
Basque	14	0.14
Belgian	18	0.18
British	32	0.31
Canadian	10	0.10
Celtic	6	0.06
Czech	17	0.17
Czechoslovakian	32	0.31
Danish	8	0.08
Dutch	157	1.53
English	1,675	16.35
European	97	0.95
Finnish	43	0.42
French, except Basque	463	4.52
French Canadian	72	0.70
German	1,164	11.36
Greek	64	0.62
Hawaii Native/Pacific Islander:	13	0.12
Micronesian: (2)	2	0.02
Guamanian/Chamorro (2)	2	0.02
Polynesian: (3)	10	0.09
Native Hawaiian (3)	7	0.07
Samoan	3	0.03
Other Pac. Isl., specified	1	0.01
Hispanic or Latino:	246	2.33
Central American:	26	0.25
Costa Rican	9	0.09
Guatemalan	8	0.08
Honduran	8	0.08
Nicaraguan	1	0.01
Cuban	20	0.19
Dominican Republic	1	0.01
Mexican	91	0.86
Puerto Rican	29	0.27
South American:	20	0.19
Argentinean	1	0.01
Colombian	10	0.09
Ecuadorian	1	0.01
Peruvian	1	0.01
Venezuelan	7	0.07
Other Hispanic or Latino	59	0.56
Hungarian	17	0.17
Icelander	8	0.08
Irish	1,273	12.43
Italian	390	3.81
Lithuanian	40	0.39
Northern European	23	0.22
Norwegian	119	1.16
Polish	257	2.51
Portuguese	29	0.28
Romanian	23	0.22
Russian	59	0.58
Scandinavian	9	0.09
Scotch-Irish	279	2.72
Scottish	272	2.66
Slavic	10	0.10
Slovak	9	0.09
Swedish	128	1.25
Swiss	7	0.07
Ukrainian	18	0.18
United States or American	1,372	13.40
Welsh	64	0.62
West Indian, excl. Hispanic:	81	0.79
Bahamian	15	0.15
British West Indian	15	0.15
Haitian	44	0.43
Jamaican	7	0.07
White:	8,685	82.33
Not Hispanic (8,434)	8,499	80.57
Hispanic (168)	186	1.76
Yugoslavian	13	0.13

Ferry Pass

Place Type: Census Designated Place
County: Escambia
Population: 27,176

Ancestry/Race	Number	%
Acadian/Cajun	25	0.09
African American/Black:	3,010	11.08
Not Hispanic (2,852)	2,968	10.92
Hispanic (30)	42	0.15
African, sub-Saharan:	15	0.06
African	11	0.04
Nigerian	4	0.01
Alaska Native tribes, specified:	1	0.00
Tlingit-Haida (1)	1	0.00
Am. Ind. or Alaska Nat., not spec.	75	0.28
Albanian	8	0.03
American Indian tribes, specified:	270	0.99
Apache (3)	5	0.02
Blackfeet	7	0.03
Cherokee (35)	76	0.28
Chickasaw	1	0.00
Chippewa	2	0.01
Choctaw (5)	15	0.06
Comanche	1	0.00
Cree	4	0.01
Creek (60)	108	0.40
Delaware (1)	1	0.00
Houma (2)	2	0.01
Iroquois (1)	1	0.00
Latin American Indians (6)	11	0.04
Lumbee (2)	5	0.02
Navajo (1)	2	0.01
Osage (2)	2	0.01
Paiute	1	0.00
Potawatomi (1)	1	0.00
Puget Sound Salish	1	0.00
Seminole (2)	8	0.03
Sioux (1)	3	0.01
Ute	1	0.00
All other tribes (4)	12	0.04
American Indian tribes, not spec.	15	0.06
Arab:	146	0.54
Arab/Arabic	43	0.16
Egyptian	7	0.03
Jordanian	55	0.20
Lebanese	21	0.08
Syrian	13	0.05
Other Arab	7	0.03
Asian:	757	2.79
Cambodian (2)	3	0.01
Chinese, ex. Taiwanese (67)	97	0.36
Filipino (135)	221	0.81
Indian (63)	73	0.27
Indonesian (6)	9	0.03
Japanese (45)	88	0.32
Korean (43)	53	0.20
Malaysian (1)	1	0.00
Pakistani (11)	12	0.04
Sri Lankan	1	0.00
Taiwanese (7)	10	0.04
Thai (6)	9	0.03
Vietnamese (107)	119	0.44
Other Asian, specified	5	0.02
Other Asian, not specified (19)	56	0.21
Assyrian/Chaldean/Syriac	14	0.05
Australian	47	0.17
Austrian	29	0.11
Belgian	34	0.13
Brazilian	37	0.14
British	253	0.93
Bulgarian	22	0.08
Canadian	76	0.28
Croatian	8	0.03
Czech	86	0.32
Czechoslovakian	62	0.23
Danish	114	0.42
Dutch	395	1.45
English	2,970	10.93
European	203	0.75
Finnish	36	0.13
French, except Basque	1,012	3.72
French Canadian	194	0.71
German	3,630	13.36
Greek	81	0.30
Hawaii Native/Pacific Islander:	40	0.15
Melanesian:	1	0.00
Other Melanesian	1	0.00
Micronesian: (6)	14	0.05
Guamanian/Chamorro (4)	12	0.04
Other Micronesian (2)	2	0.01
Polynesian: (6)	13	0.05
Native Hawaiian (3)	7	0.03
Samoan (3)	6	0.02
Other Pac. Isl., specified	1	0.00
Other Pac. Isl., not spec.	11	0.04
Hispanic or Latino:	740	2.72
Central American:	37	0.14
Costa Rican	5	0.02
Guatemalan	3	0.01
Honduran	4	0.01
Panamanian	17	0.06
Salvadoran	5	0.02
Other Central American	3	0.01
Cuban	65	0.24
Dominican Republic	2	0.01
Mexican	219	0.81
Puerto Rican	177	0.65
South American:	62	0.23
Argentinean	3	0.01
Colombian	30	0.11
Ecuadorian	9	0.03
Peruvian	11	0.04
Venezuelan	5	0.02
Other South American	4	0.01
Other Hispanic or Latino	178	0.65
Hungarian	75	0.28
Iranian	30	0.11
Irish	3,001	11.04
Italian	1,149	4.23
Latvian	8	0.03
Lithuanian	64	0.24
Maltese	12	0.04
Northern European	8	0.03
Norwegian	208	0.77
Pennsylvania German	15	0.06
Polish	363	1.34
Portuguese	23	0.08
Romanian	11	0.04

Notes: 1. Figures in the "Number" column do not add up to the total population due to: a) Ancestry/Race overlap — e.g. persons can report being both White and Irish, b) persons of Hispanic origin can report being any race, c) persons reporting two ancestries are counted in both categories. 2. Numbers in parentheses indicate the number of persons reporting this ancestry/race alone, not in combination with any other ancestry/race. 3. Refer to the User's Guide in the front of the book for more detailed information.

Russian	180	0.66
Scandinavian	28	0.10
Scotch-Irish	951	3.50
Scottish	624	2.30
Slavic	8	0.03
Slovak	31	0.11
Slovene	7	0.03
Swedish	262	0.96
Swiss	79	0.29
Ukrainian	25	0.09
United States or American	3,297	12.13
Welsh	138	0.51
West Indian, excl. Hispanic:	69	0.25
Bahamian	8	0.03
Haitian	44	0.16
Jamaican	17	0.06
White:	23,310	85.77
Not Hispanic (22,322)	22,791	83.86
Hispanic (449)	519	1.91
Yugoslavian	12	0.04

Florida Ridge

Place Type: Census Designated Place
County: Indian River
Population: 15,217

Ancestry/Race	Number	%
Acadian/Cajun	7	0.05
African American/Black:	1,794	11.79
Not Hispanic (1,676)	1,780	11.70
Hispanic (13)	14	0.09
African, sub-Saharan:	58	0.38
African	44	0.29
Nigerian	14	0.09
Am. Ind. or Alaska Nat., not spec.	22	0.14
American Indian tribes, specified:	50	0.33
Apache	1	0.01
Blackfeet (1)	3	0.02
Cherokee (10)	28	0.18
Chippewa	2	0.01
Choctaw (1)	2	0.01
Cree	1	0.01
Creek	1	0.01
Houma (1)	1	0.01
Latin American Indians (1)	1	0.01
Lumbee (3)	3	0.02
Navajo (1)	1	0.01
Osage	3	0.02
Potawatomi (1)	1	0.01
All other tribes (1)	2	0.01
American Indian tribes, not spec.	2	0.01
Arab:	12	0.08
Lebanese	6	0.04
Syrian	6	0.04
Armenian	7	0.05
Asian:	138	0.91
Cambodian (1)	3	0.02
Chinese, ex. Taiwanese (25)	29	0.19
Filipino (14)	25	0.16
Indian (17)	22	0.14
Japanese (3)	7	0.05
Korean (9)	9	0.06
Pakistani	4	0.03
Taiwanese	2	0.01
Thai (5)	5	0.03
Vietnamese (20)	23	0.15
Other Asian, specified	2	0.01
Other Asian, not specified (6)	7	0.05
Australian	8	0.05
Austrian	41	0.27
Belgian	6	0.04
British	83	0.54
Canadian	79	0.52
Croatian	11	0.07
Czech	53	0.35
Czechoslovakian	40	0.26
Danish	30	0.20
Dutch	296	1.93
Eastern European	7	0.05
English	2,361	15.41
European	31	0.20
Finnish	6	0.04
French, except Basque	613	4.00
French Canadian	186	1.21
German	2,206	14.40
Greek	53	0.35
Hawaii Native/Pacific Islander:	12	0.08
Micronesian: (1)	1	0.01
Guamanian/Chamorro (1)	1	0.01
Polynesian: (1)	2	0.01
Native Hawaiian (1)	2	0.01
Other Pac. Isl., specified	1	0.01
Other Pac. Isl., not spec.	8	0.05
Hispanic or Latino:	620	4.07
Central American:	21	0.14
Costa Rican	2	0.01
Guatemalan	5	0.03
Honduran	3	0.02
Panamanian	7	0.05
Salvadoran	4	0.03
Cuban	68	0.45
Dominican Republic	4	0.03
Mexican	217	1.43
Puerto Rican	116	0.76
South American:	79	0.52
Argentinean	1	0.01
Bolivian	1	0.01
Chilean	4	0.03
Colombian	42	0.28
Ecuadorian	9	0.06
Peruvian	10	0.07
Uruguayan	2	0.01
Venezuelan	7	0.05
Other South American	3	0.02
Other Hispanic or Latino	115	0.76
Hungarian	136	0.89
Iranian	6	0.04
Irish	2,456	16.03
Italian	1,134	7.40
Latvian	13	0.08
Lithuanian	44	0.29
Macedonian	7	0.05
Norwegian	76	0.50
Pennsylvania German	8	0.05
Polish	617	4.03
Portuguese	50	0.33
Russian	82	0.54
Scandinavian	29	0.19
Scotch-Irish	285	1.86
Scottish	267	1.74
Slovak	47	0.31
Swedish	192	1.25
Swiss	45	0.29
Ukrainian	49	0.32
United States or American	1,275	8.32
Welsh	135	0.88
West Indian, excl. Hispanic:	177	1.16
Bahamian	86	0.56
British West Indian	6	0.04
Haitian	62	0.40
Jamaican	23	0.15
White:	13,167	86.53
Not Hispanic (12,592)	12,707	83.51
Hispanic (425)	460	3.02

Forest City

Place Type: Census Designated Place
County: Seminole
Population: 12,612

Ancestry/Race	Number	%
African American/Black:	717	5.69
Not Hispanic (578)	655	5.19
Hispanic (35)	62	0.49
African, sub-Saharan:	49	0.39
African	26	0.20
Kenyan	23	0.18
Am. Ind. or Alaska Nat., not spec.	17	0.13
American Indian tribes, specified:	56	0.44
Apache	2	0.02
Cherokee (9)	19	0.15
Cheyenne	1	0.01
Chippewa	1	0.01
Choctaw	2	0.02
Creek (1)	1	0.01
Delaware	1	0.01
Iroquois (3)	3	0.02
Latin American Indians (9)	14	0.11
Menominee	1	0.01
Potawatomi (1)	1	0.01
Seminole (1)	3	0.02
Sioux	4	0.03
All other tribes (2)	3	0.02
American Indian tribes, not spec.	10	0.08
Arab:	82	0.65
Arab/Arabic	53	0.42
Lebanese	18	0.14
Palestinian	11	0.09
Asian:	480	3.81
Chinese, ex. Taiwanese (48)	51	0.40
Filipino (39)	49	0.39
Indian (105)	128	1.01
Indonesian (4)	4	0.03
Japanese (13)	21	0.17
Korean (161)	163	1.29
Pakistani (13)	13	0.10
Taiwanese (2)	2	0.02
Thai (2)	3	0.02
Vietnamese (30)	31	0.25
Other Asian, not specified (11)	15	0.12
Austrian	7	0.06
Brazilian	12	0.09
British	64	0.50
Bulgarian	20	0.16
Canadian	74	0.58
Czech	7	0.06
Czechoslovakian	6	0.05
Danish	27	0.21
Dutch	229	1.80
Eastern European	8	0.06
English	1,461	11.49
European	77	0.61
Finnish	32	0.25
French, except Basque	418	3.29
French Canadian	155	1.22
German	1,931	15.19
Greek	74	0.58
Guyanese	18	0.14
Hawaii Native/Pacific Islander:	7	0.06
Melanesian: (1)	1	0.01
Fijian (1)	1	0.01
Polynesian: (4)	6	0.05
Native Hawaiian (4)	6	0.05
Hispanic or Latino:	1,964	15.57
Central American:	85	0.67
Costa Rican	10	0.08
Guatemalan	7	0.06
Honduran	14	0.11
Nicaraguan	24	0.19
Panamanian	14	0.11
Salvadoran	8	0.06
Other Central American	8	0.06
Cuban	416	3.30
Dominican Republic	88	0.70
Mexican	84	0.67
Puerto Rican	735	5.83
South American:	230	1.82
Argentinean	2	0.02
Bolivian	3	0.02
Chilean	9	0.07
Colombian	82	0.65
Ecuadorian	24	0.19
Peruvian	62	0.49
Venezuelan	35	0.28
Other South American	13	0.10
Other Hispanic or Latino	326	2.58
Hungarian	95	0.75
Icelander	7	0.06
Iranian	11	0.09
Irish	1,761	13.85
Italian	927	7.29

Notes: 1. Figures in the "Number" column do not add up to the total population due to: a) Ancestry/Race overlap — e.g. persons can report being both White and Irish, b) persons of Hispanic origin can report being any race, c) persons reporting two ancestries are counted in both categories. 2. Numbers in parentheses indicate the number of persons reporting this ancestry/race alone, not in combination with any other ancestry/race. 3. Refer to the User's Guide in the front of the book for more detailed information.

Lithuanian	46	0.36
Norwegian	135	1.06
Pennsylvania German	13	0.10
Polish	335	2.64
Portuguese	71	0.56
Romanian	17	0.13
Russian	131	1.03
Scandinavian	14	0.11
Scotch-Irish	193	1.52
Scottish	294	2.31
Slovak	80	0.63
Slovene	12	0.09
Swedish	228	1.79
Swiss	54	0.42
Turkish	39	0.31
Ukrainian	47	0.37
United States or American	859	6.76
Welsh	76	0.60
West Indian, excl. Hispanic:	270	2.12
Dutch West Indian	37	0.29
Haitian	67	0.53
Jamaican	126	0.99
West Indian	40	0.31
White:	11,010	87.30
Not Hispanic (9,386)	9,534	75.59
Hispanic (1,375)	1,476	11.70
Yugoslavian	23	0.18

Fort Lauderdale

Place Type: City
County: Broward
Population: 152,397

Ancestry/Race	Number	%
Afghan	7	0.00
African American/Black:	48,033	31.52
Not Hispanic (43,441)	47,272	31.02
Hispanic (569)	761	0.50
African, sub-Saharan:	1,802	1.18
African	1,594	1.05
Cape Verdean	11	0.01
Ethiopian	6	0.00
Nigerian	7	0.00
South African	120	0.08
Sudanese	8	0.01
Ugandan	13	0.01
Zimbabwean	36	0.02
Other sub-Saharan African	7	0.00
Alaska Native tribes, specified:	25	0.02
Alaska Athabascan	1	0.00
Aleut (2)	3	0.00
Eskimo (1)	5	0.00
Tlingit-Haida (1)	16	0.01
Am. Ind. or Alaska Nat., not spec.	325	0.21
Albanian	158	0.10
Alsatian	10	0.01
American Indian tribes, specified:	412	0.27
Apache (6)	9	0.01
Blackfeet (8)	19	0.01
Cherokee (50)	157	0.10
Chickasaw (3)	5	0.00
Chippewa (10)	15	0.01
Choctaw (9)	22	0.01
Comanche (1)	1	0.00
Cree (1)	1	0.00
Creek (3)	5	0.00
Delaware	3	0.00
Iroquois (13)	23	0.02
Kiowa (1)	1	0.00
Latin American Indians (39)	67	0.04
Lumbee (4)	4	0.00
Navajo (2)	4	0.00
Ottawa	1	0.00
Paiute	1	0.00
Pueblo	3	0.00
Seminole (13)	16	0.01
Shoshone (1)	1	0.00
Sioux (4)	12	0.01
Yaqui	1	0.00
Yuman	1	0.00
All other tribes (14)	40	0.03
American Indian tribes, not spec.	54	0.04
Arab:	723	0.48
Arab/Arabic	38	0.02
Egyptian	97	0.06
Iraqi	16	0.01
Jordanian	44	0.03
Lebanese	365	0.24
Moroccan	30	0.02
Palestinian	54	0.04
Syrian	26	0.02
Other Arab	53	0.03
Armenian	171	0.11
Asian:	2,194	1.44
Bangladeshi (9)	34	0.02
Cambodian (1)	1	0.00
Chinese, ex. Taiwanese (264)	337	0.22
Filipino (224)	298	0.20
Indian (536)	770	0.51
Indonesian (10)	12	0.01
Japanese (109)	156	0.10
Korean (73)	91	0.06
Laotian (1)	3	0.00
Malaysian (2)	6	0.00
Pakistani (33)	56	0.04
Sri Lankan (9)	10	0.01
Taiwanese (10)	11	0.01
Thai (88)	104	0.07
Vietnamese (100)	115	0.08
Other Asian, specified (4)	14	0.01
Other Asian, not specified (53)	176	0.12
Australian	94	0.06
Austrian	816	0.54
Basque	59	0.04
Belgian	153	0.10
Brazilian	917	0.60
British	882	0.58
Bulgarian	85	0.06
Canadian	655	0.43
Carpatho Rusyn	10	0.01
Celtic	19	0.01
Croatian	110	0.07
Cypriot	14	0.01
Czech	508	0.33
Czechoslovakian	167	0.11
Danish	570	0.37
Dutch	1,580	1.04
Eastern European	211	0.14
English	12,456	8.19
Estonian	9	0.01
European	615	0.40
Finnish	200	0.13
French, except Basque	4,153	2.73
French Canadian	1,163	0.76
German	15,857	10.42
Greek	1,038	0.68
Guyanese	46	0.03
Hawaii Native/Pacific Islander:	274	0.18
Melanesian: (1)	1	0.00
Fijian (1)	1	0.00
Micronesian: (19)	35	0.02
Guamanian/Chamorro (19)	34	0.02
Other Micronesian	1	0.00
Polynesian: (41)	81	0.05
Native Hawaiian (20)	50	0.03
Samoan (16)	20	0.01
Other Polynesian (5)	11	0.01
Other Pac. Isl., specified	8	0.01
Other Pac. Isl., not spec. (13)	149	0.10
Hispanic or Latino:	14,406	9.45
Central American:	1,927	1.26
Costa Rican	93	0.06
Guatemalan	477	0.31
Honduran	381	0.25
Nicaraguan	139	0.09
Panamanian	92	0.06
Salvadoran	674	0.44
Other Central American	71	0.05
Cuban	2,576	1.69
Dominican Republic	272	0.18
Mexican	1,404	0.92
Puerto Rican	2,801	1.84
South American:	2,449	1.61
Argentinean	289	0.19
Bolivian	25	0.02
Chilean	97	0.06
Colombian	988	0.65
Ecuadorian	125	0.08
Paraguayan	13	0.01
Peruvian	476	0.31
Uruguayan	54	0.04
Venezuelan	315	0.21
Other South American	67	0.04
Other Hispanic or Latino	2,977	1.95
Hungarian	1,161	0.76
Icelander	23	0.02
Iranian	101	0.07
Irish	15,639	10.28
Israeli	94	0.06
Italian	11,512	7.57
Latvian	64	0.04
Lithuanian	386	0.25
Luxemburger	26	0.02
Macedonian	66	0.04
Maltese	29	0.02
New Zealander	59	0.04
Northern European	81	0.05
Norwegian	1,204	0.79
Pennsylvania German	93	0.06
Polish	4,344	2.86
Portuguese	468	0.31
Romanian	375	0.25
Russian	2,408	1.58
Scandinavian	106	0.07
Scotch-Irish	1,616	1.06
Scottish	2,689	1.77
Serbian	71	0.05
Slavic	53	0.03
Slovak	265	0.17
Slovene	113	0.07
Swedish	1,518	1.00
Swiss	339	0.22
Turkish	87	0.06
Ukrainian	467	0.31
United States or American	8,904	5.85
Welsh	1,050	0.69
West Indian, excl. Hispanic:	14,964	9.84
Bahamian	607	0.40
Barbadian	84	0.06
Belizean	8	0.01
British West Indian	209	0.14
Dutch West Indian	12	0.01
Haitian	10,869	7.14
Jamaican	2,726	1.79
Trinidadian and Tobagonian	233	0.15
U.S. Virgin Islander	55	0.04
West Indian	124	0.08
Other West Indian	37	0.02
White:	99,898	65.55
Not Hispanic (87,577)	88,757	58.24
Hispanic (10,364)	11,141	7.31
Yugoslavian	109	0.07

Fort Myers

Place Type: City
County: Lee
Population: 48,208

Ancestry/Race	Number	%
African American/Black:	16,989	35.24
Not Hispanic (15,751)	16,533	34.30
Hispanic (344)	456	0.95
African, sub-Saharan:	462	0.96
African	427	0.89
Cape Verdean	11	0.02
Kenyan	8	0.02
Other sub-Saharan African	16	0.03
Alaska Native tribes, specified:	3	0.01
Eskimo (2)	2	0.00
Tlingit-Haida	1	0.00
Am. Ind. or Alaska Nat., not spec.	120	0.25
Albanian	16	0.03

Notes: 1. Figures in the "Number" column do not add up to the total population due to: a) Ancestry/Race overlap — e.g. persons can report being both White and Irish, b) persons of Hispanic origin can report being any race, c) persons reporting two ancestries are counted in both categories. 2. Numbers in parentheses indicate the number of persons reporting this ancestry/race alone, not in combination with any other ancestry/race. 3. Refer to the User's Guide in the front of the book for more detailed information.

American Indian tribes, specified:	220	0.46
Apache (7)	10	0.02
Blackfeet (4)	9	0.02
Cherokee (20)	55	0.11
Cheyenne (1)	1	0.00
Chippewa (2)	3	0.01
Choctaw (5)	6	0.01
Cree (1)	1	0.00
Creek (3)	7	0.01
Iroquois (4)	11	0.02
Latin American Indians (39)	76	0.16
Navajo (1)	1	0.00
Osage	3	0.01
Potawatomi (2)	2	0.00
Seminole (3)	5	0.01
Sioux (3)	4	0.01
Tohono O'Odham	1	0.00
Yakama	6	0.01
All other tribes (7)	19	0.04
American Indian tribes, not spec.	18	0.04
Arab:	233	0.48
Arab/Arabic	49	0.10
Egyptian	9	0.02
Lebanese	83	0.17
Moroccan	16	0.03
Syrian	47	0.10
Other Arab	29	0.06
Armenian	10	0.02
Asian:	642	1.33
Bangladeshi (10)	11	0.02
Chinese, ex. Taiwanese (72)	92	0.19
Filipino (60)	91	0.19
Indian (197)	234	0.49
Indonesian (6)	8	0.02
Japanese (11)	22	0.05
Korean (31)	44	0.09
Laotian (9)	22	0.05
Pakistani (7)	11	0.02
Sri Lankan (10)	10	0.02
Taiwanese	1	0.00
Thai (7)	23	0.05
Vietnamese (27)	32	0.07
Other Asian, specified	9	0.02
Other Asian, not specified (18)	32	0.07
Austrian	82	0.17
Belgian	46	0.10
Brazilian	142	0.30
British	217	0.45
Canadian	105	0.22
Croatian	6	0.01
Czech	130	0.27
Czechoslovakian	31	0.06
Danish	62	0.13
Dutch	521	1.08
Eastern European	15	0.03
English	3,823	7.96
Estonian	11	0.02
European	244	0.51
Finnish	85	0.18
French, except Basque	1,064	2.21
French Canadian	235	0.49
German	5,138	10.69
Greek	222	0.46
Guyanese	72	0.15
Hawaii Native/Pacific Islander:	109	0.23
Micronesian: (35)	47	0.10
Guamanian/Chamorro (33)	43	0.09
Other Micronesian (2)	4	0.01
Polynesian: (6)	27	0.06
Native Hawaiian (3)	18	0.04
Samoan (3)	7	0.01
Tongan	1	0.00
Other Polynesian	1	0.00
Other Pac. Isl., specified	9	0.02
Other Pac. Isl., not spec. (7)	26	0.05
Hispanic or Latino:	6,984	14.49
Central American:	670	1.39
Costa Rican	28	0.06
Guatemalan	475	0.99
Honduran	92	0.19
Nicaraguan	20	0.04
Panamanian	21	0.04
Salvadoran	23	0.05
Other Central American	11	0.02
Cuban	261	0.54
Dominican Republic	79	0.16
Mexican	2,588	5.37
Puerto Rican	2,258	4.68
South American:	272	0.56
Argentinean	23	0.05
Bolivian	4	0.01
Chilean	9	0.02
Colombian	117	0.24
Ecuadorian	34	0.07
Paraguayan	2	0.00
Peruvian	28	0.06
Uruguayan	1	0.00
Venezuelan	39	0.08
Other South American	15	0.03
Other Hispanic or Latino	856	1.78
Hungarian	288	0.60
Icelander	10	0.02
Irish	3,718	7.74
Israeli	15	0.03
Italian	1,779	3.70
Latvian	15	0.03
Lithuanian	71	0.15
Macedonian	6	0.01
Northern European	15	0.03
Norwegian	416	0.87
Pennsylvania German	12	0.02
Polish	793	1.65
Portuguese	164	0.34
Romanian	19	0.04
Russian	205	0.43
Scandinavian	34	0.07
Scotch-Irish	533	1.11
Scottish	567	1.18
Serbian	9	0.02
Slavic	11	0.02
Slovak	73	0.15
Swedish	284	0.59
Swiss	68	0.14
Ukrainian	65	0.14
United States or American	3,068	6.39
Welsh	290	0.60
West Indian, excl. Hispanic:	2,509	5.22
Bahamian	14	0.03
Belizean	50	0.10
British West Indian	32	0.07
Haitian	2,202	4.58
Jamaican	150	0.31
Trinidadian and Tobagonian	39	0.08
West Indian	22	0.05
White:	27,877	57.83
Not Hispanic (23,700)	24,111	50.01
Hispanic (3,466)	3,766	7.81
Yugoslavian	32	0.07

Fort Pierce

Place Type: City
County: Saint Lucie
Population: 37,516

Ancestry/Race	Number	%
African American/Black:	16,042	42.76
Not Hispanic (15,109)	15,781	42.06
Hispanic (217)	261	0.70
African, sub-Saharan:	583	1.56
African	542	1.45
Nigerian	30	0.08
South African	11	0.03
Alaska Native tribes, specified:	3	0.01
Alaska Athabascan	1	0.00
Tlingit-Haida	2	0.01
Alaska Native tribes, not specified	1	0.00
Am. Ind. or Alaska Nat., not spec.	130	0.35
American Indian tribes, specified:	108	0.29
Blackfeet (1)	6	0.02
Cherokee (18)	40	0.11
Chippewa (1)	2	0.01
Choctaw (1)	2	0.01
Cree	2	0.01
Creek (3)	3	0.01
Crow (4)	5	0.01
Iroquois (1)	2	0.01
Latin American Indians (23)	23	0.06
Lumbee (1)	1	0.00
Navajo (2)	2	0.01
Pueblo	1	0.00
Seminole (3)	5	0.01
Shoshone	1	0.00
Sioux	1	0.00
Tohono O'Odham	2	0.01
All other tribes (3)	10	0.03
American Indian tribes, not spec.	7	0.02
Arab:	53	0.14
Lebanese	22	0.06
Palestinian	8	0.02
Syrian	8	0.02
Other Arab	15	0.04
Armenian	9	0.02
Asian:	394	1.05
Bangladeshi (7)	11	0.03
Cambodian (1)	2	0.01
Chinese, ex. Taiwanese (25)	31	0.08
Filipino (27)	40	0.11
Indian (121)	140	0.37
Indonesian (3)	3	0.01
Japanese (10)	13	0.03
Korean (31)	40	0.11
Pakistani (10)	11	0.03
Taiwanese (4)	4	0.01
Thai (1)	1	0.00
Vietnamese (37)	45	0.12
Other Asian, specified	2	0.01
Other Asian, not specified (18)	51	0.14
Austrian	6	0.02
Belgian	146	0.39
British	90	0.24
Canadian	86	0.23
Croatian	8	0.02
Czech	105	0.28
Czechoslovakian	29	0.08
Danish	38	0.10
Dutch	344	0.92
Eastern European	11	0.03
English	2,597	6.93
Estonian	11	0.03
European	70	0.19
Finnish	52	0.14
French, except Basque	510	1.36
French Canadian	208	0.55
German	2,971	7.92
Greek	112	0.30
Hawaii Native/Pacific Islander:	61	0.16
Melanesian:	1	0.00
Fijian	1	0.00
Micronesian: (6)	9	0.02
Guamanian/Chamorro (6)	9	0.02
Polynesian: (17)	23	0.06
Native Hawaiian (13)	15	0.04
Samoan (4)	8	0.02
Other Pac. Isl., specified	2	0.01
Other Pac. Isl., not spec. (7)	26	0.07
Hispanic or Latino:	5,629	15.00
Central American:	209	0.56
Costa Rican	3	0.01
Guatemalan	95	0.25
Honduran	70	0.19
Nicaraguan	8	0.02
Panamanian	4	0.01
Salvadoran	28	0.07
Other Central American	1	0.00
Cuban	130	0.35
Dominican Republic	21	0.06
Mexican	4,311	11.49
Puerto Rican	366	0.98
South American:	75	0.20
Argentinean	6	0.02
Bolivian	1	0.00
Chilean	2	0.01

Notes: 1. Figures in the "Number" column do not add up to the total population due to: a) Ancestry/Race overlap — e.g. persons can report being both White and Irish, b) persons of Hispanic origin can report being any race, c) persons reporting two ancestries are counted in both categories. 2. Numbers in parentheses indicate the number of persons reporting this ancestry/race alone, not in combination with any other ancestry/race. 3. Refer to the User's Guide in the front of the book for more detailed information.

Colombian	33	0.09
Ecuadorian	14	0.04
Paraguayan	1	0.00
Peruvian	8	0.02
Venezuelan	8	0.02
Other South American	2	0.01
Other Hispanic or Latino	517	1.38
Hungarian	130	0.35
Irish	3,084	8.23
Italian	1,171	3.12
Lithuanian	40	0.11
Macedonian	6	0.02
New Zealander	6	0.02
Norwegian	168	0.45
Polish	501	1.34
Portuguese	78	0.21
Romanian	5	0.01
Russian	147	0.39
Scandinavian	21	0.06
Scotch-Irish	381	1.02
Scottish	389	1.04
Slovak	29	0.08
Slovene	8	0.02
Swedish	184	0.49
Swiss	7	0.02
Ukrainian	24	0.06
United States or American	2,478	6.61
Welsh	213	0.57
West Indian, excl. Hispanic:	2,816	7.51
Bahamian	94	0.25
Barbadian	61	0.16
Belizean	9	0.02
Haitian	2,303	6.14
Jamaican	281	0.75
West Indian	68	0.18
White:	19,113	50.95
Not Hispanic (15,516)	15,732	41.93
Hispanic (3,069)	3,381	9.01
Yugoslavian	7	0.02

Fort Walton Beach

Place Type: City
County: Okaloosa
Population: 19,973

Ancestry/Race	Number	%
African American/Black:	2,861	14.32
Not Hispanic (2,641)	2,821	14.12
Hispanic (23)	40	0.20
African, sub-Saharan:	10	0.05
African	6	0.03
Nigerian	4	0.02
Alaska Native tribes, specified:	3	0.02
Eskimo (3)	3	0.02
Am. Ind. or Alaska Nat., not spec.	78	0.39
American Indian tribes, specified:	165	0.83
Apache	2	0.01
Blackfeet (2)	13	0.07
Cherokee (19)	73	0.37
Chickasaw (1)	1	0.01
Chippewa	3	0.02
Choctaw (4)	10	0.05
Creek (15)	31	0.16
Iroquois (2)	6	0.03
Latin American Indians (2)	2	0.01
Lumbee (4)	5	0.03
Navajo (2)	3	0.02
Osage	1	0.01
Potawatomi (1)	1	0.01
Seminole	1	0.01
Sioux (2)	2	0.01
Tohono O'Odham (1)	1	0.01
All other tribes (5)	10	0.05
American Indian tribes, not spec.	30	0.15
Arab:	20	0.10
Arab/Arabic	5	0.02
Lebanese	10	0.05
Other Arab	5	0.02
Armenian	13	0.06
Asian:	843	4.22
Cambodian (2)	6	0.03
Chinese, ex. Taiwanese (35)	54	0.27
Filipino (182)	302	1.51
Indian (29)	39	0.20
Japanese (43)	92	0.46
Korean (70)	99	0.50
Laotian (7)	7	0.04
Malaysian	1	0.01
Pakistani (1)	1	0.01
Taiwanese (3)	6	0.03
Thai (89)	133	0.67
Vietnamese (59)	65	0.33
Other Asian, specified	9	0.05
Other Asian, not specified (12)	29	0.15
Australian	9	0.04
Austrian	17	0.08
British	153	0.75
Canadian	65	0.32
Croatian	33	0.16
Czech	43	0.21
Czechoslovakian	6	0.03
Danish	102	0.50
Dutch	232	1.14
English	2,495	12.30
European	167	0.82
Finnish	36	0.18
French, except Basque	606	2.99
French Canadian	225	1.11
German	2,829	13.94
Greek	51	0.25
Hawaii Native/Pacific Islander:	68	0.34
Micronesian: (3)	6	0.03
Guamanian/Chamorro (2)	5	0.03
Other Micronesian (1)	1	0.01
Polynesian: (8)	21	0.11
Native Hawaiian (5)	17	0.09
Samoan (3)	3	0.02
Other Polynesian	1	0.01
Other Pac. Isl., specified	6	0.03
Other Pac. Isl., not spec. (5)	35	0.18
Hispanic or Latino:	807	4.04
Central American:	41	0.21
Costa Rican	2	0.01
Guatemalan	4	0.02
Honduran	7	0.04
Nicaraguan	1	0.01
Panamanian	25	0.13
Salvadoran	2	0.01
Cuban	51	0.26
Dominican Republic	5	0.03
Mexican	269	1.35
Puerto Rican	232	1.16
South American:	44	0.22
Argentinean	1	0.01
Chilean	7	0.04
Colombian	15	0.08
Ecuadorian	2	0.01
Paraguayan	1	0.01
Peruvian	12	0.06
Venezuelan	6	0.03
Other Hispanic or Latino	165	0.83
Hungarian	84	0.41
Icelander	11	0.05
Irish	1,970	9.71
Israeli	9	0.04
Italian	542	2.67
Lithuanian	6	0.03
Northern European	8	0.04
Norwegian	246	1.21
Pennsylvania German	8	0.04
Polish	399	1.97
Portuguese	55	0.27
Russian	77	0.38
Scandinavian	17	0.08
Scotch-Irish	490	2.42
Scottish	490	2.42
Serbian	17	0.08
Slovak	45	0.22
Slovene	17	0.08
Swedish	236	1.16
Swiss	34	0.17
Ukrainian	15	0.07
United States or American	1,881	9.27
Welsh	174	0.86
West Indian, excl. Hispanic:	43	0.21
Haitian	4	0.02
Jamaican	39	0.19
White:	16,300	81.61
Not Hispanic (15,274)	15,757	78.89
Hispanic (472)	543	2.72

Fountainbleau

Place Type: Census Designated Place
County: Miami-Dade
Population: 59,549

Ancestry/Race	Number	%
African American/Black:	1,444	2.42
Not Hispanic (611)	662	1.11
Hispanic (603)	782	1.31
African, sub-Saharan:	107	0.18
African	5	0.01
Ethiopian	7	0.01
Nigerian	95	0.16
Am. Ind. or Alaska Nat., not spec.	98	0.16
American Indian tribes, specified:	112	0.19
Cherokee (3)	10	0.02
Chippewa	1	0.00
Choctaw	1	0.00
Iroquois	4	0.01
Latin American Indians (38)	86	0.14
Pueblo	3	0.01
All other tribes (1)	7	0.01
American Indian tribes, not spec.	7	0.01
Arab:	412	0.69
Arab/Arabic	62	0.10
Egyptian	9	0.02
Lebanese	170	0.29
Palestinian	98	0.16
Syrian	73	0.12
Asian:	1,238	2.08
Bangladeshi (7)	7	0.01
Chinese, ex. Taiwanese (314)	382	0.64
Filipino (68)	87	0.15
Indian (448)	481	0.81
Indonesian	1	0.00
Japanese (36)	50	0.08
Korean (51)	54	0.09
Pakistani (48)	54	0.09
Taiwanese (9)	12	0.02
Thai (7)	7	0.01
Vietnamese (37)	38	0.06
Other Asian, specified (8)	9	0.02
Other Asian, not specified (20)	56	0.09
Austrian	14	0.02
Basque	12	0.02
Belgian	12	0.02
Brazilian	286	0.48
British	11	0.02
Canadian	42	0.07
Czech	7	0.01
Czechoslovakian	25	0.04
Danish	22	0.04
Dutch	100	0.17
Eastern European	10	0.02
English	222	0.37
European	126	0.21
Finnish	19	0.03
French, except Basque	293	0.49
French Canadian	9	0.02
German	487	0.82
Greek	93	0.16
Guyanese	11	0.02
Hawaii Native/Pacific Islander:	44	0.07
Melanesian:	1	0.00
Other Melanesian	1	0.00
Micronesian: (11)	13	0.02
Guamanian/Chamorro (11)	13	0.02
Polynesian: (5)	10	0.02
Native Hawaiian (1)	3	0.01
Samoan (4)	4	0.01
Other Polynesian	3	0.01
Other Pac. Isl., not spec. (1)	20	0.03

Notes: 1. Figures in the "Number" column do not add up to the total population due to: a) Ancestry/Race overlap — e.g. persons can report being both White and Irish, b) persons of Hispanic origin can report being any race, c) persons reporting two ancestries are counted in both categories. 2. Numbers in parentheses indicate the number of persons reporting this ancestry/race alone, not in combination with any other ancestry/race. 3. Refer to the User's Guide in the front of the book for more detailed information.

Hispanic or Latino:	51,948	87.24
Central American:	7,342	12.33
Costa Rican	153	0.26
Guatemalan	235	0.39
Honduran	650	1.09
Nicaraguan	5,624	9.44
Panamanian	293	0.49
Salvadoran	244	0.41
Other Central American	143	0.24
Cuban	22,206	37.29
Dominican Republic	1,779	2.99
Mexican	544	0.91
Puerto Rican	2,015	3.38
South American:	8,100	13.60
Argentinean	518	0.87
Bolivian	153	0.26
Chilean	550	0.92
Colombian	3,153	5.29
Ecuadorian	564	0.95
Paraguayan	23	0.04
Peruvian	1,044	1.75
Uruguayan	71	0.12
Venezuelan	1,868	3.14
Other South American	156	0.26
Other Hispanic or Latino	9,962	16.73
Hungarian	22	0.04
Iranian	11	0.02
Irish	327	0.55
Italian	992	1.67
Lithuanian	7	0.01
Norwegian	25	0.04
Polish	88	0.15
Portuguese	94	0.16
Russian	85	0.14
Scandinavian	11	0.02
Scotch-Irish	25	0.04
Scottish	54	0.09
Swedish	55	0.09
Swiss	10	0.02
Turkish	7	0.01
Ukrainian	10	0.02
United States or American	1,499	2.52
Welsh	28	0.05
West Indian, excl. Hispanic:	495	0.83
Bahamian	7	0.01
Barbadian	15	0.03
Belizean	33	0.06
British West Indian	32	0.05
Haitian	176	0.30
Jamaican	134	0.23
Trinidadian and Tobagonian	42	0.07
U.S. Virgin Islander	31	0.05
West Indian	25	0.04
White:	52,913	88.86
Not Hispanic (5,618)	5,802	9.74
Hispanic (45,114)	47,111	79.11

Fruit Cove

Place Type: Census Designated Place
County: Saint Johns
Population: 16,077

Ancestry/Race	Number	%
African American/Black:	359	2.23
Not Hispanic (326)	348	2.16
Hispanic (5)	11	0.07
Am. Ind. or Alaska Nat., not spec.	30	0.19
American Indian tribes, specified:	43	0.27
Apache	1	0.01
Blackfeet (2)	3	0.02
Cherokee (6)	16	0.10
Chippewa	1	0.01
Choctaw (1)	1	0.01
Comanche	2	0.01
Creek (2)	3	0.02
Crow	2	0.01
Iroquois (2)	6	0.04
Kiowa	2	0.01
Lumbee (1)	1	0.01
Navajo	1	0.01
Osage (1)	1	0.01
All other tribes (3)	3	0.02
American Indian tribes, not spec.	2	0.01
Armenian	24	0.15
Asian:	310	1.93
Cambodian (4)	4	0.02
Chinese, ex. Taiwanese (57)	65	0.40
Filipino (98)	114	0.71
Indian (42)	48	0.30
Japanese (14)	25	0.16
Korean (24)	32	0.20
Pakistani (4)	4	0.02
Thai (3)	3	0.02
Vietnamese (5)	5	0.03
Other Asian, specified (4)	4	0.02
Other Asian, not specified (3)	6	0.04
Austrian	34	0.21
Belgian	12	0.07
Brazilian	7	0.04
British	156	0.97
Canadian	20	0.12
Celtic	16	0.10
Croatian	16	0.10
Czech	72	0.45
Czechoslovakian	96	0.60
Danish	90	0.56
Dutch	402	2.50
Eastern European	17	0.11
English	2,367	14.75
European	202	1.26
Finnish	39	0.24
French, except Basque	653	4.07
French Canadian	130	0.81
German	3,040	18.94
Greek	92	0.57
Hawaii Native/Pacific Islander:	22	0.14
Micronesian: (15)	15	0.09
Guamanian/Chamorro (15)	15	0.09
Polynesian: (5)	5	0.03
Samoan (5)	5	0.03
Other Pac. Isl., not spec. (2)	2	0.01
Hispanic or Latino:	382	2.38
Central American:	11	0.07
Guatemalan	1	0.01
Honduran	2	0.01
Nicaraguan	3	0.02
Panamanian	4	0.02
Salvadoran	1	0.01
Cuban	36	0.22
Dominican Republic	14	0.09
Mexican	66	0.41
Puerto Rican	121	0.75
South American:	42	0.26
Argentinean	4	0.02
Bolivian	2	0.01
Chilean	7	0.04
Colombian	14	0.09
Ecuadorian	5	0.03
Peruvian	8	0.05
Uruguayan	1	0.01
Venezuelan	1	0.01
Other Hispanic or Latino	92	0.57
Hungarian	140	0.87
Irish	2,671	16.64
Israeli	7	0.04
Italian	1,269	7.91
Latvian	20	0.12
Lithuanian	53	0.33
Maltese	7	0.04
Northern European	10	0.06
Norwegian	186	1.16
Pennsylvania German	4	0.02
Polish	534	3.33
Portuguese	71	0.44
Romanian	9	0.06
Russian	126	0.78
Scotch-Irish	374	2.33
Scottish	399	2.49
Slavic	38	0.24
Slovak	54	0.34
Swedish	189	1.18
Swiss	20	0.12
Ukrainian	98	0.61
United States or American	1,672	10.42
Welsh	166	1.03
West Indian, excl. Hispanic:	52	0.32
Haitian	8	0.05
Jamaican	35	0.22
West Indian	9	0.06
White:	15,350	95.48
Not Hispanic (14,943)	15,047	93.59
Hispanic (292)	303	1.88

Fruitville

Place Type: Census Designated Place
County: Sarasota
Population: 12,741

Ancestry/Race	Number	%
African American/Black:	193	1.51
Not Hispanic (162)	182	1.43
Hispanic (5)	11	0.09
African, sub-Saharan:	38	0.29
African	18	0.14
Nigerian	20	0.16
Am. Ind. or Alaska Nat., not spec.	18	0.14
Albanian	40	0.31
American Indian tribes, specified:	34	0.27
Apache (1)	1	0.01
Blackfeet	2	0.02
Cherokee (1)	6	0.05
Chippewa (1)	1	0.01
Comanche	1	0.01
Creek	5	0.04
Delaware (1)	2	0.02
Iroquois (2)	2	0.02
Latin American Indians (1)	2	0.02
Navajo	1	0.01
Potawatomi (1)	2	0.02
Sioux	2	0.02
All other tribes (3)	7	0.05
American Indian tribes, not spec.	2	0.02
Arab:	123	0.95
Arab/Arabic	36	0.28
Lebanese	26	0.20
Palestinian	52	0.40
Other Arab	9	0.07
Asian:	179	1.40
Chinese, ex. Taiwanese (39)	41	0.32
Filipino (30)	41	0.32
Indian (28)	33	0.26
Japanese (10)	13	0.10
Korean (14)	15	0.12
Taiwanese (4)	4	0.03
Thai (2)	2	0.02
Vietnamese (18)	24	0.19
Other Asian, not specified (4)	6	0.05
Australian	9	0.07
Austrian	73	0.57
Belgian	14	0.11
Brazilian	15	0.12
British	72	0.56
Bulgarian	8	0.06
Canadian	61	0.47
Croatian	27	0.21
Czech	84	0.65
Czechoslovakian	40	0.31
Danish	39	0.30
Dutch	275	2.13
Eastern European	18	0.14
English	1,709	13.26
European	51	0.40
Finnish	37	0.29
French, except Basque	422	3.27
French Canadian	134	1.04
German	3,000	23.27
Greek	38	0.29
Guyanese	25	0.19
Hawaii Native/Pacific Islander:	2	0.02
Polynesian: (1)	1	0.01
Samoan (1)	1	0.01
Other Pac. Isl., not spec.	1	0.01

Notes: 1. Figures in the "Number" column do not add up to the total population due to: a) Ancestry/Race overlap — e.g. persons can report being both White and Irish, b) persons of Hispanic origin can report being any race, c) persons reporting two ancestries are counted in both categories. 2. Numbers in parentheses indicate the number of persons reporting this ancestry/race alone, not in combination with any other ancestry/race. 3. Refer to the User's Guide in the front of the book for more detailed information.

Hispanic or Latino:	519	4.07
Central American:	24	0.19
Honduran	6	0.05
Nicaraguan	3	0.02
Panamanian	5	0.04
Salvadoran	8	0.06
Other Central American	2	0.02
Cuban	89	0.70
Dominican Republic	5	0.04
Mexican	145	1.14
Puerto Rican	117	0.92
South American:	66	0.52
Argentinean	7	0.05
Chilean	2	0.02
Colombian	25	0.20
Peruvian	8	0.06
Venezuelan	17	0.13
Other South American	7	0.05
Other Hispanic or Latino	73	0.57
Hungarian	140	1.09
Irish	1,937	15.02
Italian	1,242	9.63
Lithuanian	34	0.26
Northern European	9	0.07
Norwegian	126	0.98
Polish	510	3.96
Portuguese	28	0.22
Romanian	20	0.16
Russian	196	1.52
Scotch-Irish	334	2.59
Scottish	394	3.06
Slovak	48	0.37
Slovene	8	0.06
Swedish	263	2.04
Swiss	108	0.84
Ukrainian	42	0.33
United States or American	1,149	8.91
Welsh	81	0.63
West Indian, excl. Hispanic:	40	0.31
Haitian	18	0.14
West Indian	22	0.17
White:	12,289	96.45
Not Hispanic (11,804)	11,882	93.26
Hispanic (381)	407	3.19
Yugoslavian	20	0.16

Gainesville

Place Type: City
County: Alachua
Population: 95,447

Ancestry/Race	Number	%
Acadian/Cajun	37	0.04
African American/Black:	22,929	24.02
Not Hispanic (21,931)	22,594	23.67
Hispanic (250)	335	0.35
African, sub-Saharan:	1,630	1.70
African	1,249	1.31
Ethiopian	135	0.14
Ghanian	7	0.01
Kenyan	30	0.03
Nigerian	74	0.08
South African	81	0.08
Zimbabwean	33	0.03
Other sub-Saharan African	21	0.02
Alaska Native tribes, specified:	3	0.00
Aleut (1)	1	0.00
Eskimo (1)	2	0.00
Alaska Native tribes, not specified	1	0.00
Am. Ind. or Alaska Nat., not spec.	197	0.21
Albanian	36	0.04
Alsatian	38	0.04
American Indian tribes, specified:	424	0.44
Apache (1)	9	0.01
Blackfeet (5)	24	0.03
Cherokee (43)	184	0.19
Chickasaw (3)	3	0.00
Chippewa (4)	5	0.01
Choctaw (5)	23	0.02
Comanche	1	0.00
Cree	2	0.00
Creek (10)	21	0.02
Delaware	4	0.00
Houma (5)	5	0.01
Iroquois (7)	20	0.02
Latin American Indians (14)	35	0.04
Lumbee (2)	3	0.00
Menominee	1	0.00
Navajo (5)	10	0.01
Osage	3	0.00
Ottawa (1)	1	0.00
Potawatomi	1	0.00
Pueblo (3)	9	0.01
Seminole (11)	21	0.02
Shoshone (1)	1	0.00
Sioux (4)	9	0.01
Yaqui (3)	3	0.00
All other tribes (10)	26	0.03
American Indian tribes, not spec.	65	0.07
Arab:	551	0.58
Arab/Arabic	95	0.10
Egyptian	53	0.06
Lebanese	188	0.20
Moroccan	13	0.01
Palestinian	48	0.05
Syrian	79	0.08
Other Arab	75	0.08
Armenian	58	0.06
Asian:	4,976	5.21
Bangladeshi (16)	16	0.02
Cambodian (22)	32	0.03
Chinese, ex. Taiwanese (1,303)	1,411	1.48
Filipino (377)	499	0.52
Indian (1,074)	1,185	1.24
Indonesian (16)	24	0.03
Japanese (203)	293	0.31
Korean (511)	564	0.59
Laotian (8)	10	0.01
Malaysian (14)	21	0.02
Pakistani (47)	58	0.06
Sri Lankan (10)	16	0.02
Taiwanese (69)	87	0.09
Thai (95)	121	0.13
Vietnamese (413)	449	0.47
Other Asian, specified (7)	23	0.02
Other Asian, not specified (60)	167	0.17
Australian	55	0.06
Austrian	271	0.28
Basque	11	0.01
Belgian	107	0.11
Brazilian	172	0.18
British	759	0.79
Bulgarian	80	0.08
Canadian	201	0.21
Celtic	86	0.09
Croatian	43	0.04
Czech	336	0.35
Czechoslovakian	139	0.15
Danish	257	0.27
Dutch	1,228	1.28
Eastern European	161	0.17
English	9,421	9.85
Estonian	13	0.01
European	1,024	1.07
Finnish	191	0.20
French, except Basque	2,862	2.99
French Canadian	821	0.86
German	12,020	12.57
German Russian	5	0.01
Greek	475	0.50
Guyanese	13	0.01
Hawaii Native/Pacific Islander:	128	0.13
Micronesian: (6)	7	0.01
Guamanian/Chamorro (6)	7	0.01
Polynesian: (21)	60	0.06
Native Hawaiian (10)	30	0.03
Samoan (11)	28	0.03
Tongan	2	0.00
Other Pac. Isl., specified	16	0.02
Other Pac. Isl., not spec. (3)	45	0.05
Hispanic or Latino:	6,112	6.40
Central American:	434	0.45
Costa Rican	56	0.06
Guatemalan	41	0.04
Honduran	57	0.06
Nicaraguan	143	0.15
Panamanian	81	0.08
Salvadoran	35	0.04
Other Central American	21	0.02
Cuban	1,278	1.34
Dominican Republic	138	0.14
Mexican	511	0.54
Puerto Rican	1,596	1.67
South American:	1,081	1.13
Argentinean	96	0.10
Bolivian	40	0.04
Chilean	94	0.10
Colombian	342	0.36
Ecuadorian	53	0.06
Paraguayan	4	0.00
Peruvian	153	0.16
Uruguayan	16	0.02
Venezuelan	244	0.26
Other South American	39	0.04
Other Hispanic or Latino	1,074	1.13
Hungarian	380	0.40
Icelander	13	0.01
Iranian	216	0.23
Irish	10,195	10.66
Israeli	75	0.08
Italian	4,654	4.87
Latvian	16	0.02
Lithuanian	211	0.22
Luxemburger	14	0.01
Macedonian	7	0.01
Maltese	14	0.01
New Zealander	7	0.01
Northern European	137	0.14
Norwegian	755	0.79
Polish	2,499	2.61
Portuguese	211	0.22
Romanian	184	0.19
Russian	1,458	1.53
Scandinavian	47	0.05
Scotch-Irish	2,223	2.33
Scottish	2,298	2.40
Serbian	41	0.04
Slavic	59	0.06
Slovak	97	0.10
Slovene	46	0.05
Swedish	1,241	1.30
Swiss	267	0.28
Turkish	163	0.17
Ukrainian	284	0.30
United States or American	5,380	5.63
Welsh	636	0.67
West Indian, excl. Hispanic:	1,025	1.07
Bahamian	61	0.06
Barbadian	8	0.01
Belizean	20	0.02
Bermudan	19	0.02
British West Indian	39	0.04
Dutch West Indian	10	0.01
Haitian	231	0.24
Jamaican	418	0.44
Trinidadian and Tobagonian	110	0.12
West Indian	100	0.10
Other West Indian	9	0.01
White:	66,916	70.11
Not Hispanic (61,156)	62,425	65.40
Hispanic (4,087)	4,491	4.71
Yugoslavian	63	0.07

Gladeview

Place Type: Census Designated Place
County: Miami-Dade
Population: 14,468

Ancestry/Race	Number	%
African American/Black:	11,323	78.26
Not Hispanic (10,967)	11,085	76.62
Hispanic (171)	238	1.65

Notes: 1. Figures in the "Number" column do not add up to the total population due to: a) Ancestry/Race overlap — e.g. persons can report being both White and Irish, b) persons of Hispanic origin can report being any race, c) persons reporting two ancestries are counted in both categories. 2. Numbers in parentheses indicate the number of persons reporting this ancestry/race alone, not in combination with any other ancestry/race. 3. Refer to the User's Guide in the front of the book for more detailed information.

African, sub-Saharan:	181	1.25
African	151	1.04
Nigerian	30	0.21
Am. Ind. or Alaska Nat., not spec.	38	0.26
American Indian tribes, specified:	14	0.10
Cherokee	2	0.01
Latin American Indians (6)	9	0.06
Pueblo	1	0.01
Seminole	1	0.01
All other tribes (1)	1	0.01
American Indian tribes, not spec.	3	0.02
Arab:	14	0.10
Lebanese	14	0.10
Asian:	51	0.35
Chinese, ex. Taiwanese (1)	4	0.03
Filipino (1)	2	0.01
Indian (17)	23	0.16
Other Asian, specified	2	0.01
Other Asian, not specified (5)	20	0.14
British	49	0.34
Dutch	7	0.05
English	63	0.44
French, except Basque	24	0.17
German	35	0.24
Hawaii Native/Pacific Islander:	35	0.24
Polynesian: (2)	5	0.03
Native Hawaiian (2)	2	0.01
Samoan	3	0.02
Other Pac. Isl., specified	2	0.01
Other Pac. Isl., not spec. (2)	28	0.19
Hispanic or Latino:	3,084	21.32
Central American:	876	6.05
Costa Rican	5	0.03
Guatemalan	48	0.33
Honduran	223	1.54
Nicaraguan	536	3.70
Panamanian	2	0.01
Salvadoran	15	0.10
Other Central American	47	0.32
Cuban	1,003	6.93
Dominican Republic	129	0.89
Mexican	113	0.78
Puerto Rican	197	1.36
South American:	52	0.36
Colombian	25	0.17
Ecuadorian	7	0.05
Peruvian	12	0.08
Venezuelan	6	0.04
Other South American	2	0.01
Other Hispanic or Latino	714	4.94
Hungarian	19	0.13
Irish	35	0.24
Italian	13	0.09
Polish	47	0.32
Russian	17	0.12
Scandinavian	22	0.15
Scottish	14	0.10
United States or American	318	2.20
West Indian, excl. Hispanic:	504	3.48
Bahamian	138	0.95
Haitian	221	1.53
Jamaican	74	0.51
Trinidadian and Tobagonian	60	0.41
West Indian	11	0.08
White:	2,759	19.07
Not Hispanic (256)	281	1.94
Hispanic (2,289)	2,478	17.13

Glenvar Heights

Place Type: Census Designated Place
County: Miami-Dade
Population: 16,243

Ancestry/Race	Number	%
African American/Black:	575	3.54
Not Hispanic (405)	472	2.91
Hispanic (83)	103	0.63
African, sub-Saharan:	28	0.17
African	20	0.12
South African	8	0.05
Am. Ind. or Alaska Nat., not spec.	23	0.14
American Indian tribes, specified:	34	0.21
Apache	6	0.04
Cherokee	9	0.06
Chickasaw	1	0.01
Chippewa	1	0.01
Creek (1)	1	0.01
Latin American Indians (9)	11	0.07
Sioux	2	0.01
All other tribes (1)	3	0.02
American Indian tribes, not spec.	10	0.06
Arab:	221	1.37
Arab/Arabic	51	0.32
Jordanian	10	0.06
Lebanese	100	0.62
Syrian	9	0.06
Other Arab	51	0.32
Asian:	575	3.54
Bangladeshi (3)	3	0.02
Chinese, ex. Taiwanese (184)	210	1.29
Filipino (43)	52	0.32
Indian (133)	160	0.99
Indonesian	1	0.01
Japanese (14)	19	0.12
Korean (11)	13	0.08
Laotian (2)	2	0.01
Malaysian (2)	2	0.01
Pakistani (25)	37	0.23
Sri Lankan (7)	7	0.04
Taiwanese	3	0.02
Thai (20)	22	0.14
Vietnamese (18)	19	0.12
Other Asian, not specified (1)	25	0.15
Assyrian/Chaldean/Syriac	2	0.01
Australian	11	0.07
Austrian	14	0.09
Basque	31	0.19
Belgian	33	0.20
Brazilian	100	0.62
British	79	0.49
Canadian	43	0.27
Croatian	34	0.21
Czech	17	0.11
Danish	23	0.14
Dutch	80	0.50
Eastern European	41	0.25
English	885	5.49
European	125	0.78
Finnish	26	0.16
French, except Basque	309	1.92
French Canadian	41	0.25
German	1,008	6.26
Greek	112	0.70
Guyanese	9	0.06
Hawaii Native/Pacific Islander:	19	0.12
Melanesian: (1)	1	0.01
Fijian (1)	1	0.01
Micronesian: (4)	5	0.03
Guamanian/Chamorro (4)	5	0.03
Polynesian: (2)	2	0.01
Native Hawaiian (2)	2	0.01
Other Pac. Isl., not spec. (2)	11	0.07
Hispanic or Latino:	9,008	55.46
Central American:	569	3.50
Costa Rican	52	0.32
Guatemalan	25	0.15
Honduran	102	0.63
Nicaraguan	274	1.69
Panamanian	46	0.28
Salvadoran	57	0.35
Other Central American	13	0.08
Cuban	4,693	28.89
Dominican Republic	160	0.99
Mexican	150	0.92
Puerto Rican	528	3.25
South American:	1,567	9.65
Argentinean	81	0.50
Bolivian	30	0.18
Chilean	116	0.71
Colombian	563	3.47
Ecuadorian	96	0.59
Paraguayan	4	0.02
Peruvian	292	1.80
Uruguayan	24	0.15
Venezuelan	332	2.04
Other South American	29	0.18
Other Hispanic or Latino	1,341	8.26
Hungarian	126	0.78
Iranian	28	0.17
Irish	763	4.73
Italian	673	4.18
Lithuanian	41	0.25
Macedonian	5	0.03
Norwegian	58	0.36
Pennsylvania German	11	0.07
Polish	218	1.35
Portuguese	50	0.31
Romanian	30	0.19
Russian	360	2.23
Scotch-Irish	114	0.71
Scottish	226	1.40
Serbian	8	0.05
Slavic	10	0.06
Slovak	14	0.09
Swedish	89	0.55
Swiss	58	0.36
Ukrainian	21	0.13
United States or American	652	4.05
Welsh	41	0.25
West Indian, excl. Hispanic:	215	1.33
Bahamian	44	0.27
Belizean	8	0.05
British West Indian	34	0.21
Haitian	32	0.20
Jamaican	54	0.34
Trinidadian and Tobagonian	31	0.19
West Indian	12	0.07
White:	14,613	89.96
Not Hispanic (6,162)	6,294	38.75
Hispanic (8,084)	8,319	51.22
Yugoslavian	8	0.05

Golden Gate

Place Type: Census Designated Place
County: Collier
Population: 20,951

Ancestry/Race	Number	%
Acadian/Cajun	13	0.06
African American/Black:	2,592	12.37
Not Hispanic (2,037)	2,445	11.67
Hispanic (89)	147	0.70
African, sub-Saharan:	62	0.30
African	54	0.26
Sierra Leonean	8	0.04
Am. Ind. or Alaska Nat., not spec.	31	0.15
American Indian tribes, specified:	88	0.42
Apache	2	0.01
Blackfeet	4	0.02
Cherokee (4)	10	0.05
Chippewa (3)	4	0.02
Creek (1)	2	0.01
Delaware	1	0.00
Iroquois	5	0.02
Latin American Indians (32)	44	0.21
Lumbee (1)	1	0.00
Menominee (1)	1	0.00
Seminole (4)	5	0.02
All other tribes (3)	9	0.04
American Indian tribes, not spec.	19	0.09
Arab:	41	0.20
Lebanese	41	0.20
Armenian	15	0.07
Asian:	198	0.95
Chinese, ex. Taiwanese (25)	30	0.14
Filipino (22)	38	0.18
Indian (50)	54	0.26
Indonesian	7	0.03
Japanese	2	0.01
Korean (7)	9	0.04
Thai (2)	2	0.01
Vietnamese (32)	36	0.17
Other Asian, specified (2)	3	0.01

Notes: 1. Figures in the "Number" column do not add up to the total population due to: a) Ancestry/Race overlap — e.g. persons can report being both White and Irish, b) persons of Hispanic origin can report being any race, c) persons reporting two ancestries are counted in both categories. 2. Numbers in parentheses indicate the number of persons reporting this ancestry/race alone, not in combination with any other ancestry/race. 3. Refer to the User's Guide in the front of the book for more detailed information.

Other Asian, not specified (8)	17	0.08
Brazilian	49	0.23
British	5	0.02
Canadian	57	0.27
Croatian	16	0.08
Czech	66	0.31
Czechoslovakian	13	0.06
Danish	115	0.55
Dutch	114	0.54
English	1,095	5.21
European	79	0.38
Finnish	5	0.02
French, except Basque	294	1.40
French Canadian	159	0.76
German	1,978	9.41
Greek	65	0.31
Guyanese	11	0.05
Hawaii Native/Pacific Islander:	46	0.22
Micronesian: (23)	31	0.15
Guamanian/Chamorro (23)	31	0.15
Polynesian: (1)	7	0.03
Native Hawaiian	6	0.03
Samoan (1)	1	0.00
Other Pac. Isl., not spec. (1)	8	0.04
Hispanic or Latino:	7,781	37.14
Central American:	428	2.04
Costa Rican	28	0.13
Guatemalan	102	0.49
Honduran	143	0.68
Nicaraguan	44	0.21
Panamanian	10	0.05
Salvadoran	83	0.40
Other Central American	18	0.09
Cuban	1,660	7.92
Dominican Republic	76	0.36
Mexican	3,529	16.84
Puerto Rican	765	3.65
South American:	500	2.39
Argentinean	22	0.11
Bolivian	20	0.10
Chilean	21	0.10
Colombian	240	1.15
Ecuadorian	47	0.22
Peruvian	98	0.47
Uruguayan	4	0.02
Venezuelan	32	0.15
Other South American	16	0.08
Other Hispanic or Latino	823	3.93
Hungarian	87	0.41
Irish	1,644	7.82
Italian	825	3.93
Lithuanian	40	0.19
Norwegian	66	0.31
Polish	407	1.94
Portuguese	54	0.26
Romanian	16	0.08
Russian	69	0.33
Scandinavian	7	0.03
Scotch-Irish	154	0.73
Scottish	240	1.14
Serbian	33	0.16
Slovak	10	0.05
Slovene	21	0.10
Swedish	137	0.65
Swiss	50	0.24
Ukrainian	8	0.04
United States or American	1,552	7.39
Welsh	81	0.39
West Indian, excl. Hispanic:	1,402	6.67
Bahamian	60	0.29
Haitian	1,228	5.84
Jamaican	100	0.48
Trinidadian and Tobagonian	8	0.04
West Indian	6	0.03
White:	16,607	79.27
Not Hispanic (10,402)	10,547	50.34
Hispanic (5,730)	6,060	28.92

Golden Glades

Place Type: Census Designated Place
County: Miami-Dade
Population: 32,623

Ancestry/Race	Number	%
African American/Black:	22,922	70.26
Not Hispanic (20,669)	22,079	67.68
Hispanic (630)	843	2.58
African, sub-Saharan:	400	1.24
African	267	0.83
Ghanian	7	0.02
Nigerian	118	0.37
Sierra Leonean	8	0.02
Alaska Native tribes, specified:	5	0.02
Tlingit-Haida (1)	5	0.02
Am. Ind. or Alaska Nat., not spec.	83	0.25
American Indian tribes, specified:	88	0.27
Cherokee (3)	25	0.08
Cree (1)	2	0.01
Creek (1)	1	0.00
Crow (1)	1	0.00
Latin American Indians (24)	39	0.12
Navajo (1)	1	0.00
Paiute	1	0.00
Pueblo (5)	6	0.02
Seminole	2	0.01
Shoshone (1)	1	0.00
Sioux	1	0.00
All other tribes (4)	8	0.02
American Indian tribes, not spec.	21	0.06
Arab:	25	0.08
Arab/Arabic	17	0.05
Lebanese	8	0.02
Asian:	761	2.33
Bangladeshi (12)	13	0.04
Cambodian (6)	6	0.02
Chinese, ex. Taiwanese (107)	126	0.39
Filipino (183)	199	0.61
Hmong	1	0.00
Indian (162)	256	0.78
Indonesian (5)	6	0.02
Japanese (3)	6	0.02
Korean (6)	6	0.02
Laotian (14)	16	0.05
Pakistani (26)	26	0.08
Sri Lankan (1)	4	0.01
Thai (9)	13	0.04
Vietnamese (34)	34	0.10
Other Asian, specified	1	0.00
Other Asian, not specified (12)	48	0.15
Austrian	45	0.14
Brazilian	20	0.06
British	87	0.27
Canadian	22	0.07
Croatian	8	0.02
Czech	7	0.02
Danish	10	0.03
Dutch	53	0.16
Eastern European	6	0.02
English	414	1.29
European	67	0.21
French, except Basque	199	0.62
French Canadian	63	0.20
German	621	1.93
Greek	54	0.17
Guyanese	96	0.30
Hawaii Native/Pacific Islander:	110	0.34
Micronesian: (5)	6	0.02
Guamanian/Chamorro (5)	6	0.02
Polynesian: (8)	11	0.03
Native Hawaiian (6)	7	0.02
Samoan (1)	3	0.01
Other Polynesian (1)	1	0.00
Other Pac. Isl., not spec. (11)	93	0.29
Hispanic or Latino:	5,753	17.63
Central American:	659	2.02
Costa Rican	32	0.10
Guatemalan	75	0.23
Honduran	199	0.61
Nicaraguan	219	0.67
Panamanian	66	0.20
Salvadoran	40	0.12
Other Central American	28	0.09
Cuban	1,317	4.04
Dominican Republic	560	1.72
Mexican	175	0.54
Puerto Rican	1,275	3.91
South American:	622	1.91
Argentinean	36	0.11
Bolivian	12	0.04
Chilean	15	0.05
Colombian	240	0.74
Ecuadorian	63	0.19
Paraguayan	2	0.01
Peruvian	189	0.58
Uruguayan	7	0.02
Venezuelan	48	0.15
Other South American	10	0.03
Other Hispanic or Latino	1,145	3.51
Hungarian	146	0.45
Iranian	7	0.02
Irish	474	1.47
Israeli	6	0.02
Italian	503	1.56
Lithuanian	15	0.05
Norwegian	20	0.06
Polish	208	0.65
Portuguese	45	0.14
Romanian	28	0.09
Russian	186	0.58
Scotch-Irish	42	0.13
Scottish	133	0.41
Swedish	45	0.14
Swiss	14	0.04
Ukrainian	44	0.14
United States or American	1,686	5.24
Welsh	7	0.02
West Indian, excl. Hispanic:	13,197	41.01
Bahamian	541	1.68
Barbadian	67	0.21
Belizean	25	0.08
Bermudan	8	0.02
British West Indian	197	0.61
Dutch West Indian	12	0.04
Haitian	10,284	31.95
Jamaican	1,739	5.40
Trinidadian and Tobagonian	119	0.37
U.S. Virgin Islander	33	0.10
West Indian	172	0.53
White:	8,169	25.04
Not Hispanic (3,948)	4,160	12.75
Hispanic (3,680)	4,009	12.29

Goldenrod

Place Type: Census Designated Place
County: Seminole
Population: 12,871

Ancestry/Race	Number	%
Acadian/Cajun	12	0.09
African American/Black:	859	6.67
Not Hispanic (648)	738	5.73
Hispanic (64)	121	0.94
African, sub-Saharan:	91	0.70
African	91	0.70
Am. Ind. or Alaska Nat., not spec.	28	0.22
American Indian tribes, specified:	98	0.76
Apache (1)	2	0.02
Blackfeet	3	0.02
Cherokee (19)	40	0.31
Chippewa (1)	2	0.02
Creek	2	0.02
Iroquois (2)	3	0.02
Latin American Indians (14)	23	0.18
Navajo	1	0.01
Ottawa	1	0.01
Potawatomi (3)	5	0.04
Pueblo	1	0.01
Seminole	1	0.01
Sioux (2)	3	0.02

Notes: 1. Figures in the "Number" column do not add up to the total population due to: a) Ancestry/Race overlap — e.g. persons can report being both White and Irish, b) persons of Hispanic origin can report being any race, c) persons reporting two ancestries are counted in both categories. 2. Numbers in parentheses indicate the number of persons reporting this ancestry/race alone, not in combination with any other ancestry/race. 3. Refer to the User's Guide in the front of the book for more detailed information.

All other tribes (5)	11	0.09
American Indian tribes, not spec.	9	0.07
Arab:	38	0.29
Arab/Arabic	11	0.08
Lebanese	16	0.12
Other Arab	11	0.08
Armenian	5	0.04
Asian:	462	3.59
Cambodian (2)	3	0.02
Chinese, ex. Taiwanese (78)	98	0.76
Filipino (45)	58	0.45
Indian (95)	109	0.85
Indonesian (1)	3	0.02
Japanese (22)	30	0.23
Korean (26)	34	0.26
Laotian (1)	2	0.02
Malaysian (1)	3	0.02
Pakistani (4)	4	0.03
Sri Lankan (1)	1	0.01
Taiwanese (1)	1	0.01
Thai (10)	13	0.10
Vietnamese (65)	75	0.58
Other Asian, specified (2)	2	0.02
Other Asian, not specified (9)	26	0.20
Austrian	38	0.29
Belgian	5	0.04
Brazilian	7	0.05
British	121	0.93
Canadian	26	0.20
Celtic	12	0.09
Croatian	9	0.07
Czech	77	0.59
Czechoslovakian	42	0.32
Danish	42	0.32
Dutch	221	1.69
Eastern European	7	0.05
English	1,559	11.92
Estonian	9	0.07
European	165	1.26
Finnish	19	0.15
French, except Basque	319	2.44
French Canadian	166	1.27
German	1,784	13.65
Greek	70	0.54
Hawaii Native/Pacific Islander:	30	0.23
Micronesian: (1)	4	0.03
Guamanian/Chamorro (1)	4	0.03
Polynesian: (8)	13	0.10
Native Hawaiian (6)	11	0.09
Samoan (2)	2	0.02
Other Pac. Isl., not spec. (3)	13	0.10
Hispanic or Latino:	2,295	17.83
Central American:	118	0.92
Costa Rican	11	0.09
Guatemalan	13	0.10
Honduran	16	0.12
Nicaraguan	8	0.06
Panamanian	21	0.16
Salvadoran	44	0.34
Other Central American	5	0.04
Cuban	195	1.52
Dominican Republic	55	0.43
Mexican	291	2.26
Puerto Rican	1,106	8.59
South American:	221	1.72
Argentinean	7	0.05
Bolivian	3	0.02
Chilean	4	0.03
Colombian	98	0.76
Ecuadorian	22	0.17
Peruvian	22	0.17
Venezuelan	57	0.44
Other South American	8	0.06
Other Hispanic or Latino	309	2.40
Hungarian	33	0.25
Icelander	7	0.05
Iranian	22	0.17
Irish	1,739	13.30
Israeli	18	0.14
Italian	895	6.85
Macedonian	8	0.06
Norwegian	57	0.44
Pennsylvania German	8	0.06
Polish	336	2.57
Portuguese	41	0.31
Romanian	30	0.23
Russian	33	0.25
Scotch-Irish	322	2.46
Scottish	362	2.77
Slovak	82	0.63
Swedish	143	1.09
Swiss	36	0.28
Turkish	10	0.08
Ukrainian	127	0.97
United States or American	827	6.33
Welsh	71	0.54
West Indian, excl. Hispanic:	166	1.27
Belizean	12	0.09
British West Indian	10	0.08
Jamaican	111	0.85
Trinidadian and Tobagonian	25	0.19
U.S. Virgin Islander	8	0.06
White:	10,953	85.10
Not Hispanic (9,237)	9,442	73.36
Hispanic (1,372)	1,511	11.74
Yugoslavian	16	0.12

Gonzalez

Place Type: Census Designated Place
County: Escambia
Population: 11,365

Ancestry/Race	Number	%
Acadian/Cajun	30	0.26
African American/Black:	907	7.98
Not Hispanic (862)	896	7.88
Hispanic (7)	11	0.10
Alaska Native tribes, specified:	1	0.01
Eskimo (1)	1	0.01
Am. Ind. or Alaska Nat., not spec.	41	0.36
American Indian tribes, specified:	148	1.30
Blackfeet	1	0.01
Cherokee (18)	40	0.35
Cheyenne (4)	4	0.04
Chickasaw	1	0.01
Chippewa	3	0.03
Choctaw (1)	5	0.04
Creek (41)	71	0.62
Latin American Indians	1	0.01
Lumbee (2)	6	0.05
Seminole (2)	2	0.02
Sioux (1)	10	0.09
All other tribes (3)	4	0.04
American Indian tribes, not spec.	2	0.02
Arab:	10	0.09
Lebanese	10	0.09
Asian:	222	1.95
Chinese, ex. Taiwanese (21)	24	0.21
Filipino (47)	74	0.65
Indian (7)	13	0.11
Indonesian	1	0.01
Japanese (6)	10	0.09
Korean (13)	23	0.20
Taiwanese (1)	1	0.01
Thai (1)	1	0.01
Vietnamese (68)	69	0.61
Other Asian, specified	1	0.01
Other Asian, not specified (3)	5	0.04
Austrian	11	0.09
Belgian	20	0.17
British	49	0.42
Canadian	37	0.32
Czech	62	0.53
Czechoslovakian	40	0.34
Danish	95	0.81
Dutch	170	1.46
English	1,006	8.62
European	67	0.57
French, except Basque	403	3.45
French Canadian	55	0.47
German	1,230	10.54
Greek	7	0.06
Hawaii Native/Pacific Islander:	11	0.10
Micronesian: (1)	7	0.06
Guamanian/Chamorro (1)	7	0.06
Polynesian: (1)	2	0.02
Samoan (1)	2	0.02
Other Pac. Isl., not spec.	2	0.02
Hispanic or Latino:	190	1.67
Central American:	17	0.15
Costa Rican	1	0.01
Guatemalan	7	0.06
Honduran	1	0.01
Panamanian	4	0.04
Salvadoran	3	0.03
Other Central American	1	0.01
Cuban	22	0.19
Mexican	52	0.46
Puerto Rican	40	0.35
South American:	11	0.10
Bolivian	5	0.04
Chilean	1	0.01
Colombian	5	0.04
Other Hispanic or Latino	48	0.42
Hungarian	38	0.33
Icelander	11	0.09
Iranian	63	0.54
Irish	1,184	10.14
Italian	454	3.89
Northern European	10	0.09
Norwegian	19	0.16
Pennsylvania German	9	0.08
Polish	177	1.52
Russian	46	0.39
Scandinavian	7	0.06
Scotch-Irish	266	2.28
Scottish	382	3.27
Serbian	17	0.15
Slovak	16	0.14
Swedish	56	0.48
Swiss	37	0.32
Turkish	8	0.07
Ukrainian	9	0.08
United States or American	1,540	13.19
Welsh	79	0.68
West Indian, excl. Hispanic:	12	0.10
Belizean	12	0.10
White:	10,169	89.48
Not Hispanic (9,874)	10,025	88.21
Hispanic (130)	144	1.27

Greater Carrollwood

Place Type: Census Designated Place
County: Hillsborough
Population: 33,519

Ancestry/Race	Number	%
African American/Black:	2,195	6.55
Not Hispanic (1,834)	1,981	5.91
Hispanic (126)	214	0.64
African, sub-Saharan:	185	0.55
African	106	0.32
Ethiopian	17	0.05
Liberian	12	0.04
South African	50	0.15
Am. Ind. or Alaska Nat., not spec.	59	0.18
American Indian tribes, specified:	131	0.39
Apache (5)	7	0.02
Blackfeet (1)	3	0.01
Cherokee (27)	58	0.17
Choctaw	1	0.00
Cree (1)	1	0.00
Creek	1	0.00
Delaware	2	0.01
Iroquois (2)	6	0.02
Latin American Indians (13)	29	0.09
Lumbee	4	0.01
Navajo (1)	1	0.00
Paiute	1	0.00
Pueblo (1)	2	0.01
Seminole	4	0.01
Sioux (1)	1	0.00

Notes: 1. Figures in the "Number" column do not add up to the total population due to: a) Ancestry/Race overlap — e.g. persons can report being both White and Irish, b) persons of Hispanic origin can report being any race, c) persons reporting two ancestries are counted in both categories. 2. Numbers in parentheses indicate the number of persons reporting this ancestry/race alone, not in combination with any other ancestry/race. 3. Refer to the User's Guide in the front of the book for more detailed information.

Tohono O'Odham (1)	1	0.00
All other tribes (6)	9	0.03
American Indian tribes, not spec.	11	0.03
Arab:	205	0.61
Arab/Arabic	9	0.03
Egyptian	23	0.07
Lebanese	115	0.34
Moroccan	19	0.06
Syrian	39	0.12
Armenian	23	0.07
Asian:	1,411	4.21
Cambodian (2)	4	0.01
Chinese, ex. Taiwanese (147)	192	0.57
Filipino (164)	212	0.63
Indian (421)	468	1.40
Indonesian (8)	10	0.03
Japanese (28)	48	0.14
Korean (151)	176	0.53
Laotian (1)	1	0.00
Malaysian (1)	1	0.00
Pakistani (12)	22	0.07
Sri Lankan (6)	9	0.03
Taiwanese (10)	10	0.03
Thai (30)	38	0.11
Vietnamese (155)	178	0.53
Other Asian, specified	1	0.00
Other Asian, not specified (13)	41	0.12
Australian	40	0.12
Austrian	79	0.24
Belgian	46	0.14
Brazilian	67	0.20
British	173	0.51
Bulgarian	129	0.38
Canadian	126	0.37
Croatian	44	0.13
Czech	173	0.51
Czechoslovakian	69	0.21
Danish	123	0.37
Dutch	493	1.47
Eastern European	140	0.42
English	3,432	10.21
European	83	0.25
Finnish	29	0.09
French, except Basque	1,252	3.72
French Canadian	231	0.69
German	4,675	13.91
Greek	256	0.76
Hawaii Native/Pacific Islander:	35	0.10
Micronesian: (1)	4	0.01
Guamanian/Chamorro (1)	2	0.01
Other Micronesian	2	0.01
Polynesian: (6)	10	0.03
Native Hawaiian (6)	10	0.03
Other Pac. Isl., specified	1	0.00
Other Pac. Isl., not spec. (10)	20	0.06
Hispanic or Latino:	6,131	18.29
Central American:	228	0.68
Costa Rican	31	0.09
Guatemalan	37	0.11
Honduran	45	0.13
Nicaraguan	19	0.06
Panamanian	73	0.22
Salvadoran	16	0.05
Other Central American	7	0.02
Cuban	1,128	3.37
Dominican Republic	138	0.41
Mexican	230	0.69
Puerto Rican	1,942	5.79
South American:	829	2.47
Argentinean	27	0.08
Bolivian	15	0.04
Chilean	26	0.08
Colombian	444	1.32
Ecuadorian	119	0.36
Paraguayan	2	0.01
Peruvian	67	0.20
Uruguayan	5	0.01
Venezuelan	104	0.31
Other South American	20	0.06
Other Hispanic or Latino	1,636	4.88
Hungarian	299	0.89
Iranian	119	0.35
Irish	4,281	12.73
Italian	2,992	8.90
Latvian	20	0.06
Lithuanian	45	0.13
Luxemburger	14	0.04
Norwegian	167	0.50
Pennsylvania German	10	0.03
Polish	962	2.86
Portuguese	111	0.33
Romanian	62	0.18
Russian	543	1.62
Scandinavian	35	0.10
Scotch-Irish	565	1.68
Scottish	798	2.37
Serbian	35	0.10
Slovak	124	0.37
Slovene	34	0.10
Swedish	340	1.01
Swiss	25	0.07
Turkish	14	0.04
Ukrainian	116	0.35
United States or American	2,306	6.86
Welsh	254	0.76
West Indian, excl. Hispanic:	390	1.16
Belizean	10	0.03
British West Indian	20	0.06
Haitian	45	0.13
Jamaican	244	0.73
Trinidadian and Tobagonian	67	0.20
West Indian	4	0.01
White:	29,006	86.54
Not Hispanic (23,808)	24,182	72.14
Hispanic (4,512)	4,824	14.39
Yugoslavian	16	0.05

Greater Northdale

Place Type: Census Designated Place
County: Hillsborough
Population: 20,461

Ancestry/Race	Number	%
African American/Black:	1,278	6.25
Not Hispanic (1,106)	1,197	5.85
Hispanic (43)	81	0.40
African, sub-Saharan:	61	0.30
African	41	0.20
Ethiopian	16	0.08
Nigerian	4	0.02
Am. Ind. or Alaska Nat., not spec.	37	0.18
American Indian tribes, specified:	59	0.29
Apache (2)	2	0.01
Blackfeet (4)	6	0.03
Cherokee (11)	19	0.09
Chippewa (2)	2	0.01
Choctaw (1)	2	0.01
Creek (1)	1	0.00
Latin American Indians	18	0.09
Osage (1)	1	0.00
Seminole	4	0.02
Sioux (2)	2	0.01
Ute (1)	1	0.00
All other tribes (1)	1	0.00
American Indian tribes, not spec.	11	0.05
Arab:	292	1.44
Arab/Arabic	42	0.21
Egyptian	8	0.04
Jordanian	7	0.03
Lebanese	132	0.65
Palestinian	55	0.27
Syrian	48	0.24
Asian:	917	4.48
Chinese, ex. Taiwanese (105)	139	0.68
Filipino (114)	141	0.69
Hmong (2)	2	0.01
Indian (256)	289	1.41
Indonesian (1)	3	0.01
Japanese (20)	40	0.20
Korean (126)	139	0.68
Laotian (8)	9	0.04
Pakistani (7)	8	0.04
Sri Lankan (7)	7	0.03
Taiwanese (12)	12	0.06
Thai (29)	29	0.14
Vietnamese (40)	42	0.21
Other Asian, specified (1)	5	0.02
Other Asian, not specified (15)	52	0.25
Austrian	68	0.34
Belgian	6	0.03
Brazilian	27	0.13
British	150	0.74
Canadian	99	0.49
Celtic	9	0.04
Croatian	24	0.12
Czech	33	0.16
Czechoslovakian	107	0.53
Danish	81	0.40
Dutch	357	1.76
Eastern European	10	0.05
English	2,328	11.48
Estonian	6	0.03
European	146	0.72
Finnish	30	0.15
French, except Basque	766	3.78
French Canadian	252	1.24
German	3,378	16.66
Greek	57	0.28
Guyanese	10	0.05
Hawaii Native/Pacific Islander:	29	0.14
Micronesian: (12)	12	0.06
Guamanian/Chamorro (12)	12	0.06
Polynesian: (4)	6	0.03
Native Hawaiian (4)	6	0.03
Other Pac. Isl., not spec. (2)	11	0.05
Hispanic or Latino:	3,074	15.02
Central American:	104	0.51
Costa Rican	18	0.09
Guatemalan	11	0.05
Honduran	31	0.15
Nicaraguan	9	0.04
Panamanian	20	0.10
Salvadoran	9	0.04
Other Central American	6	0.03
Cuban	731	3.57
Dominican Republic	62	0.30
Mexican	155	0.76
Puerto Rican	861	4.21
South American:	396	1.94
Argentinean	11	0.05
Bolivian	5	0.02
Chilean	6	0.03
Colombian	166	0.81
Ecuadorian	50	0.24
Peruvian	75	0.37
Uruguayan	5	0.02
Venezuelan	54	0.26
Other South American	24	0.12
Other Hispanic or Latino	765	3.74
Hungarian	137	0.68
Iranian	105	0.52
Irish	3,029	14.93
Israeli	8	0.04
Italian	2,223	10.96
Lithuanian	91	0.45
Macedonian	8	0.04
Maltese	8	0.04
Norwegian	162	0.80
Pennsylvania German	8	0.04
Polish	680	3.35
Portuguese	45	0.22
Romanian	35	0.17
Russian	193	0.95
Scandinavian	28	0.14
Scotch-Irish	252	1.24
Scottish	448	2.21
Slavic	9	0.04
Slovak	43	0.21
Slovene	10	0.05
Swedish	205	1.01
Swiss	60	0.30
Turkish	9	0.04
Ukrainian	62	0.31

Notes: 1. Figures in the "Number" column do not add up to the total population due to: a) Ancestry/Race overlap — e.g. persons can report being both White and Irish, b) persons of Hispanic origin can report being any race, c) persons reporting two ancestries are counted in both categories. 2. Numbers in parentheses indicate the number of persons reporting this ancestry/race alone, not in combination with any other ancestry/race. 3. Refer to the User's Guide in the front of the book for more detailed information.

United States or American	1,244	6.13
Welsh	203	1.00
West Indian, excl. Hispanic:	278	1.37
Barbadian	8	0.04
British West Indian	6	0.03
Haitian	25	0.12
Jamaican	137	0.68
Trinidadian and Tobagonian	13	0.06
West Indian	30	0.15
Other West Indian	59	0.29
White:	17,941	87.68
Not Hispanic (15,125)	15,372	75.13
Hispanic (2,408)	2,569	12.56

Greater Sun Center

Place Type: Census Designated Place
County: Hillsborough
Population: 16,321

Ancestry/Race	Number	%
African American/Black:	33	0.20
Not Hispanic (22)	32	0.20
Hispanic	1	0.01
African, sub-Saharan:	10	0.06
African	10	0.06
Am. Ind. or Alaska Nat., not spec.	5	0.03
Alsatian	8	0.05
American Indian tribes, specified:	19	0.12
Blackfeet	2	0.01
Cherokee (5)	10	0.06
Chippewa (1)	1	0.01
Choctaw	1	0.01
Iroquois (4)	4	0.02
Sioux (1)	1	0.01
American Indian tribes, not spec.	4	0.02
Arab:	7	0.04
Lebanese	7	0.04
Armenian	25	0.15
Asian:	72	0.44
Chinese, ex. Taiwanese (10)	12	0.07
Filipino (16)	18	0.11
Indian (4)	6	0.04
Indonesian (1)	1	0.01
Japanese (17)	17	0.10
Korean (4)	4	0.02
Vietnamese (13)	13	0.08
Other Asian, not specified	1	0.01
Assyrian/Chaldean/Syriac	8	0.05
Australian	17	0.10
Austrian	148	0.91
Belgian	25	0.15
Brazilian	9	0.06
British	108	0.66
Bulgarian	8	0.05
Canadian	113	0.69
Croatian	8	0.05
Czech	90	0.55
Czechoslovakian	84	0.52
Danish	100	0.61
Dutch	387	2.38
English	3,336	20.48
European	68	0.42
Finnish	24	0.15
French, except Basque	807	4.96
French Canadian	332	2.04
German	3,737	22.95
Greek	29	0.18
Hawaii Native/Pacific Islander:	11	0.07
Micronesian: (4)	4	0.02
Guamanian/Chamorro (2)	2	0.01
Other Micronesian (2)	2	0.01
Polynesian: (6)	6	0.04
Native Hawaiian (4)	4	0.02
Samoan (2)	2	0.01
Other Pac. Isl., not spec. (1)	1	0.01
Hispanic or Latino:	195	1.19
Central American:	5	0.03
Costa Rican	1	0.01
Guatemalan	2	0.01
Nicaraguan	1	0.01
Panamanian	1	0.01
Cuban	12	0.07
Dominican Republic	2	0.01
Mexican	43	0.26
Puerto Rican	65	0.40
South American:	8	0.05
Argentinean	1	0.01
Colombian	6	0.04
Other South American	1	0.01
Other Hispanic or Latino	60	0.37
Hungarian	186	1.14
Irish	2,386	14.65
Italian	817	5.02
Lithuanian	48	0.29
Macedonian	29	0.18
Norwegian	230	1.41
Pennsylvania German	30	0.18
Polish	739	4.54
Portuguese	17	0.10
Romanian	23	0.14
Russian	207	1.27
Scandinavian	15	0.09
Scotch-Irish	557	3.42
Scottish	672	4.13
Slovak	60	0.37
Slovene	23	0.14
Swedish	423	2.60
Swiss	142	0.87
Ukrainian	60	0.37
United States or American	922	5.66
Welsh	253	1.55
West Indian, excl. Hispanic:	8	0.05
Jamaican	8	0.05
White:	16,181	99.14
Not Hispanic (15,986)	16,012	98.11
Hispanic (166)	169	1.04
Yugoslavian	8	0.05

Greenacres

Place Type: City
County: Palm Beach
Population: 27,569

Ancestry/Race	Number	%
African American/Black:	2,007	7.28
Not Hispanic (1,673)	1,848	6.70
Hispanic (117)	159	0.58
African, sub-Saharan:	40	0.15
African	35	0.13
Sierra Leonean	5	0.02
Am. Ind. or Alaska Nat., not spec.	42	0.15
Albanian	9	0.03
Alsatian	30	0.11
American Indian tribes, specified:	111	0.40
Apache	5	0.02
Blackfeet (3)	7	0.03
Cherokee (9)	30	0.11
Cheyenne (1)	4	0.01
Chickasaw (2)	3	0.01
Chippewa	1	0.00
Choctaw (1)	9	0.03
Comanche (2)	2	0.01
Cree (1)	2	0.01
Iroquois (3)	3	0.01
Latin American Indians (12)	27	0.10
Navajo (1)	1	0.00
Paiute (1)	1	0.00
Pueblo (1)	1	0.00
Sioux (3)	4	0.01
Yaqui	2	0.01
All other tribes (6)	9	0.03
American Indian tribes, not spec.	17	0.06
Arab:	92	0.34
Arab/Arabic	67	0.25
Egyptian	6	0.02
Lebanese	19	0.07
Armenian	23	0.08
Asian:	640	2.32
Bangladeshi (19)	23	0.08
Chinese, ex. Taiwanese (95)	115	0.42
Filipino (81)	98	0.36
Indian (185)	222	0.81
Japanese (8)	17	0.06
Korean (25)	26	0.09
Pakistani (28)	42	0.15
Sri Lankan (2)	2	0.01
Thai (12)	15	0.05
Vietnamese (33)	35	0.13
Other Asian, specified (5)	9	0.03
Other Asian, not specified (10)	36	0.13
Austrian	223	0.82
Belgian	12	0.04
Brazilian	19	0.07
British	167	0.61
Canadian	145	0.53
Croatian	34	0.12
Czech	45	0.17
Czechoslovakian	44	0.16
Danish	66	0.24
Dutch	434	1.59
Eastern European	9	0.03
English	2,022	7.42
Estonian	22	0.08
European	84	0.31
Finnish	232	0.85
French, except Basque	737	2.70
French Canadian	151	0.55
German	3,266	11.98
Greek	151	0.55
Guyanese	23	0.08
Hawaii Native/Pacific Islander:	37	0.13
Micronesian: (3)	5	0.02
Guamanian/Chamorro (3)	5	0.02
Polynesian: (3)	8	0.03
Native Hawaiian (3)	8	0.03
Other Pac. Isl., not spec. (5)	24	0.09
Hispanic or Latino:	5,858	21.25
Central American:	517	1.88
Costa Rican	14	0.05
Guatemalan	111	0.40
Honduran	180	0.65
Nicaraguan	112	0.41
Panamanian	21	0.08
Salvadoran	66	0.24
Other Central American	13	0.05
Cuban	665	2.41
Dominican Republic	198	0.72
Mexican	1,439	5.22
Puerto Rican	1,169	4.24
South American:	893	3.24
Argentinean	69	0.25
Bolivian	26	0.09
Chilean	51	0.18
Colombian	461	1.67
Ecuadorian	82	0.30
Paraguayan	1	0.00
Peruvian	85	0.31
Uruguayan	48	0.17
Venezuelan	50	0.18
Other South American	20	0.07
Other Hispanic or Latino	977	3.54
Hungarian	229	0.84
Irish	2,972	10.90
Italian	3,581	13.13
Lithuanian	52	0.19
Norwegian	158	0.58
Pennsylvania German	41	0.15
Polish	912	3.34
Portuguese	156	0.57
Romanian	87	0.32
Russian	648	2.38
Scandinavian	49	0.18
Scotch-Irish	223	0.82
Scottish	318	1.17
Serbian	27	0.10
Slavic	14	0.05
Slovak	53	0.19
Slovene	10	0.04
Swedish	217	0.80
Swiss	73	0.27
Turkish	9	0.03
Ukrainian	109	0.40

Notes: 1. Figures in the "Number" column do not add up to the total population due to: a) Ancestry/Race overlap — e.g. persons can report being both White and Irish, b) persons of Hispanic origin can report being any race, c) persons reporting two ancestries are counted in both categories. 2. Numbers in parentheses indicate the number of persons reporting this ancestry/race alone, not in combination with any other ancestry/race. 3. Refer to the User's Guide in the front of the book for more detailed information.

United States or American	1,453	5.33
Welsh	187	0.69
West Indian, excl. Hispanic:	680	2.49
Bahamian	13	0.05
Barbadian	12	0.04
Haitian	299	1.10
Jamaican	285	1.05
Trinidadian and Tobagonian	61	0.22
West Indian	10	0.04
White:	23,425	84.97
Not Hispanic (19,066)	19,244	69.80
Hispanic (3,873)	4,181	15.17
Yugoslavian	13	0.05

Gulf Gate Estates

Place Type: Census Designated Place
County: Sarasota
Population: 11,647

Ancestry/Race	Number	%
African American/Black:	113	0.97
Not Hispanic (84)	105	0.90
Hispanic (7)	8	0.07
African, sub-Saharan:	25	0.22
African	7	0.06
South African	18	0.16
Am. Ind. or Alaska Nat., not spec.	15	0.13
Alsatian	11	0.10
American Indian tribes, specified:	39	0.33
Apache	4	0.03
Blackfeet (2)	4	0.03
Cherokee (2)	17	0.15
Cheyenne (1)	1	0.01
Choctaw	3	0.03
Comanche	1	0.01
Creek (1)	1	0.01
Iroquois	2	0.02
Latin American Indians (2)	2	0.02
Sioux (1)	2	0.02
Ute	1	0.01
All other tribes	1	0.01
American Indian tribes, not spec.	4	0.03
Arab:	63	0.55
Lebanese	47	0.41
Moroccan	6	0.05
Syrian	10	0.09
Asian:	127	1.09
Chinese, ex. Taiwanese (25)	30	0.26
Filipino (15)	19	0.16
Indian (21)	25	0.21
Indonesian (1)	1	0.01
Japanese (4)	10	0.09
Korean (11)	17	0.15
Laotian (7)	7	0.06
Pakistani (1)	1	0.01
Thai (2)	6	0.05
Vietnamese (2)	3	0.03
Other Asian, not specified (4)	8	0.07
Austrian	23	0.20
Belgian	17	0.15
Brazilian	54	0.47
British	129	1.12
Bulgarian	21	0.18
Canadian	64	0.55
Croatian	22	0.19
Czech	58	0.50
Czechoslovakian	31	0.27
Danish	30	0.26
Dutch	175	1.51
English	1,731	14.98
European	7	0.06
Finnish	57	0.49
French, except Basque	544	4.71
French Canadian	195	1.69
German	2,248	19.45
Greek	82	0.71
Hawaii Native/Pacific Islander:	4	0.03
Micronesian: (3)	3	0.03
Guamanian/Chamorro (2)	2	0.02
Other Micronesian (1)	1	0.01
Polynesian:	1	0.01
Native Hawaiian	1	0.01
Hispanic or Latino:	373	3.20
Central American:	11	0.09
Costa Rican	1	0.01
Guatemalan	1	0.01
Honduran	1	0.01
Nicaraguan	1	0.01
Panamanian	3	0.03
Other Central American	4	0.03
Cuban	51	0.44
Dominican Republic	11	0.09
Mexican	96	0.82
Puerto Rican	66	0.57
South American:	72	0.62
Argentinean	3	0.03
Bolivian	3	0.03
Chilean	2	0.02
Colombian	46	0.39
Ecuadorian	3	0.03
Peruvian	12	0.10
Venezuelan	2	0.02
Other South American	1	0.01
Other Hispanic or Latino	66	0.57
Hungarian	222	1.92
Icelander	12	0.10
Irish	1,606	13.90
Israeli	9	0.08
Italian	1,087	9.40
Lithuanian	15	0.13
Norwegian	166	1.44
Pennsylvania German	6	0.05
Polish	470	4.07
Portuguese	26	0.22
Romanian	32	0.28
Russian	259	2.24
Scandinavian	18	0.16
Scotch-Irish	250	2.16
Scottish	270	2.34
Serbian	9	0.08
Slovak	70	0.61
Swedish	155	1.34
Swiss	114	0.99
Ukrainian	13	0.11
United States or American	739	6.39
Welsh	151	1.31
West Indian, excl. Hispanic:	17	0.15
Jamaican	17	0.15
White:	11,333	97.30
Not Hispanic (10,967)	11,053	94.90
Hispanic (268)	280	2.40
Yugoslavian	121	1.05

Gulfport

Place Type: City
County: Pinellas
Population: 12,527

Ancestry/Race	Number	%
African American/Black:	948	7.57
Not Hispanic (861)	913	7.29
Hispanic (23)	35	0.28
African, sub-Saharan:	62	0.49
African	62	0.49
Alaska Native tribes, specified:	1	0.01
Alaska Athabascan (1)	1	0.01
Alaska Native tribes, not specified	1	0.01
Am. Ind. or Alaska Nat., not spec.	26	0.21
Alsatian	6	0.05
American Indian tribes, specified:	111	0.89
Apache	2	0.02
Blackfeet (2)	15	0.12
Cherokee (22)	54	0.43
Cheyenne	1	0.01
Chickasaw (1)	3	0.02
Chippewa (1)	2	0.02
Choctaw	4	0.03
Comanche (2)	3	0.02
Cree	1	0.01
Creek (1)	1	0.01
Delaware (2)	2	0.02
Iroquois (1)	3	0.02
Latin American Indians (1)	4	0.03
Pueblo (1)	1	0.01
Seminole	1	0.01
Sioux	2	0.02
All other tribes (2)	12	0.10
American Indian tribes, not spec.	9	0.07
Arab:	70	0.55
Arab/Arabic	22	0.17
Egyptian	12	0.10
Lebanese	20	0.16
Syrian	10	0.08
Other Arab	6	0.05
Armenian	7	0.06
Asian:	96	0.77
Cambodian	1	0.01
Chinese, ex. Taiwanese (4)	7	0.06
Filipino (18)	29	0.23
Indian (14)	18	0.14
Japanese (8)	10	0.08
Korean (4)	6	0.05
Laotian (1)	1	0.01
Thai (2)	2	0.02
Vietnamese (14)	15	0.12
Other Asian, specified	1	0.01
Other Asian, not specified (2)	6	0.05
Austrian	35	0.28
Belgian	7	0.06
British	103	0.82
Bulgarian	5	0.04
Canadian	56	0.44
Celtic	6	0.05
Croatian	13	0.10
Czech	23	0.18
Czechoslovakian	21	0.17
Danish	64	0.51
Dutch	260	2.06
English	1,621	12.84
European	57	0.45
Finnish	39	0.31
French, except Basque	533	4.22
French Canadian	111	0.88
German	2,189	17.34
German Russian	5	0.04
Greek	108	0.86
Hawaii Native/Pacific Islander:	11	0.09
Micronesian: (3)	3	0.02
Other Micronesian (3)	3	0.02
Polynesian: (5)	5	0.04
Native Hawaiian (1)	1	0.01
Samoan (4)	4	0.03
Other Pac. Isl., specified	1	0.01
Other Pac. Isl., not spec.	2	0.02
Hispanic or Latino:	435	3.47
Central American:	6	0.05
Costa Rican	3	0.02
Guatemalan	1	0.01
Honduran	1	0.01
Panamanian	1	0.01
Cuban	62	0.49
Dominican Republic	5	0.04
Mexican	72	0.57
Puerto Rican	134	1.07
South American:	39	0.31
Argentinean	6	0.05
Chilean	1	0.01
Colombian	21	0.17
Ecuadorian	5	0.04
Peruvian	2	0.02
Venezuelan	3	0.02
Other South American	1	0.01
Other Hispanic or Latino	117	0.93
Hungarian	194	1.54
Irish	1,683	13.33
Italian	1,042	8.25
Latvian	7	0.06
Lithuanian	115	0.91
Luxemburger	5	0.04
Maltese	8	0.06
Norwegian	194	1.54
Pennsylvania German	29	0.23
Polish	420	3.33

Notes: 1. Figures in the "Number" column do not add up to the total population due to: a) Ancestry/Race overlap — e.g. persons can report being both White and Irish, b) persons of Hispanic origin can report being any race, c) persons reporting two ancestries are counted in both categories. 2. Numbers in parentheses indicate the number of persons reporting this ancestry/race alone, not in combination with any other ancestry/race. 3. Refer to the User's Guide in the front of the book for more detailed information.

Portuguese	38	0.30
Romanian	48	0.38
Russian	196	1.55
Scotch-Irish	253	2.00
Scottish	417	3.30
Serbian	21	0.17
Slavic	11	0.09
Slovak	34	0.27
Slovene	11	0.09
Swedish	260	2.06
Swiss	74	0.59
Ukrainian	216	1.71
United States or American	980	7.76
Welsh	117	0.93
West Indian, excl. Hispanic:	55	0.44
Bahamian	4	0.03
Jamaican	30	0.24
Trinidadian and Tobagonian	14	0.11
West Indian	7	0.06
White:	11,401	91.01
Not Hispanic (10,917)	11,083	88.47
Hispanic (282)	318	2.54
Yugoslavian	12	0.10

Haines City

Place Type: City
County: Polk
Population: 13,174

Ancestry/Race	Number	%
African American/Black:	4,316	32.76
Not Hispanic (4,143)	4,253	32.28
Hispanic (54)	63	0.48
African, sub-Saharan:	184	1.40
African	184	1.40
Am. Ind. or Alaska Nat., not spec.	38	0.29
American Indian tribes, specified:	59	0.45
Apache	4	0.03
Blackfeet	2	0.02
Cherokee (2)	19	0.14
Choctaw (1)	1	0.01
Cree (1)	1	0.01
Iroquois (2)	2	0.02
Latin American Indians (18)	19	0.14
Lumbee	1	0.01
Potawatomi (1)	1	0.01
Pueblo	1	0.01
All other tribes (6)	8	0.06
American Indian tribes, not spec.	9	0.07
Asian:	69	0.52
Bangladeshi (6)	7	0.05
Cambodian	1	0.01
Chinese, ex. Taiwanese (2)	2	0.02
Filipino (7)	10	0.08
Indian (14)	20	0.15
Japanese (9)	10	0.08
Korean (2)	3	0.02
Thai (1)	1	0.01
Vietnamese (3)	4	0.03
Other Asian, specified	2	0.02
Other Asian, not specified (5)	9	0.07
Austrian	21	0.16
Belgian	7	0.05
British	40	0.30
Canadian	19	0.14
Czech	25	0.19
Czechoslovakian	7	0.05
Dutch	90	0.69
English	755	5.75
European	57	0.43
French, except Basque	186	1.42
French Canadian	88	0.67
German	1,157	8.81
Greek	7	0.05
Hawaii Native/Pacific Islander:	20	0.15
Micronesian: (2)	3	0.02
Guamanian/Chamorro (2)	3	0.02
Polynesian: (2)	3	0.02
Native Hawaiian (1)	2	0.02
Samoan (1)	1	0.01
Other Pac. Isl., specified	2	0.02
Other Pac. Isl., not spec. (1)	12	0.09
Hispanic or Latino:	3,074	23.33
Central American:	48	0.36
Costa Rican	2	0.02
Guatemalan	5	0.04
Honduran	6	0.05
Nicaraguan	22	0.17
Panamanian	6	0.05
Salvadoran	3	0.02
Other Central American	4	0.03
Cuban	21	0.16
Dominican Republic	25	0.19
Mexican	2,309	17.53
Puerto Rican	473	3.59
South American:	27	0.20
Argentinean	3	0.02
Colombian	5	0.04
Ecuadorian	10	0.08
Peruvian	8	0.06
Venezuelan	1	0.01
Other Hispanic or Latino	171	1.30
Hungarian	44	0.34
Irish	646	4.92
Italian	171	1.30
Lithuanian	62	0.47
Luxemburger	11	0.08
Norwegian	31	0.24
Polish	85	0.65
Russian	7	0.05
Scotch-Irish	106	0.81
Scottish	124	0.94
Serbian	26	0.20
Slovak	18	0.14
Swedish	83	0.63
Swiss	35	0.27
Ukrainian	7	0.05
United States or American	1,145	8.72
Welsh	51	0.39
West Indian, excl. Hispanic:	510	3.88
Haitian	359	2.73
Jamaican	151	1.15
White:	7,371	55.95
Not Hispanic (5,688)	5,753	43.67
Hispanic (1,541)	1,618	12.28

Hallandale

Place Type: City
County: Broward
Population: 34,282

Ancestry/Race	Number	%
African American/Black:	5,828	17.00
Not Hispanic (5,353)	5,644	16.46
Hispanic (140)	184	0.54
African, sub-Saharan:	153	0.44
African	119	0.34
South African	19	0.05
Ugandan	7	0.02
Other sub-Saharan African	8	0.02
Alaska Native tribes, specified:	1	0.00
Aleut (1)	1	0.00
Am. Ind. or Alaska Nat., not spec.	77	0.22
Albanian	10	0.03
American Indian tribes, specified:	78	0.23
Blackfeet	5	0.01
Cherokee (8)	20	0.06
Chickasaw	1	0.00
Chippewa	4	0.01
Delaware	2	0.01
Iroquois (4)	5	0.01
Latin American Indians (6)	17	0.05
Navajo (1)	1	0.00
Paiute (1)	1	0.00
Potawatomi (1)	2	0.01
Pueblo (1)	2	0.01
Yaqui (3)	3	0.01
All other tribes (6)	15	0.04
American Indian tribes, not spec.	11	0.03
Arab:	303	0.88
Arab/Arabic	9	0.03
Egyptian	37	0.11
Iraqi	19	0.05
Lebanese	61	0.18
Moroccan	72	0.21
Palestinian	7	0.02
Syrian	9	0.03
Other Arab	89	0.26
Armenian	19	0.05
Asian:	485	1.41
Bangladeshi	2	0.01
Chinese, ex. Taiwanese (87)	114	0.33
Filipino (19)	35	0.10
Indian (152)	188	0.55
Indonesian (8)	16	0.05
Japanese (14)	24	0.07
Korean (7)	14	0.04
Pakistani (9)	13	0.04
Taiwanese (4)	6	0.02
Thai (13)	13	0.04
Vietnamese (6)	7	0.02
Other Asian, specified (4)	10	0.03
Other Asian, not specified (10)	43	0.13
Austrian	490	1.42
Belgian	23	0.07
Brazilian	125	0.36
British	123	0.36
Bulgarian	9	0.03
Canadian	475	1.37
Croatian	18	0.05
Cypriot	11	0.03
Czech	65	0.19
Czechoslovakian	86	0.25
Danish	19	0.05
Dutch	145	0.42
Eastern European	46	0.13
English	948	2.74
European	112	0.32
Finnish	21	0.06
French, except Basque	482	1.40
French Canadian	934	2.70
German	2,037	5.90
German Russian	17	0.05
Greek	243	0.70
Guyanese	6	0.02
Hawaii Native/Pacific Islander:	57	0.17
Micronesian: (2)	3	0.01
Guamanian/Chamorro (2)	3	0.01
Polynesian: (7)	15	0.04
Native Hawaiian (2)	9	0.03
Samoan (5)	6	0.02
Other Pac. Isl., specified	5	0.01
Other Pac. Isl., not spec. (5)	34	0.10
Hispanic or Latino:	6,447	18.81
Central American:	459	1.34
Costa Rican	63	0.18
Guatemalan	27	0.08
Honduran	136	0.40
Nicaraguan	111	0.32
Panamanian	48	0.14
Salvadoran	51	0.15
Other Central American	23	0.07
Cuban	1,308	3.82
Dominican Republic	228	0.67
Mexican	348	1.02
Puerto Rican	1,027	3.00
South American:	1,731	5.05
Argentinean	205	0.60
Bolivian	7	0.02
Chilean	98	0.29
Colombian	669	1.95
Ecuadorian	121	0.35
Paraguayan	1	0.00
Peruvian	391	1.14
Uruguayan	28	0.08
Venezuelan	147	0.43
Other South American	64	0.19
Other Hispanic or Latino	1,346	3.93
Hungarian	644	1.86
Irish	1,589	4.60
Israeli	126	0.36
Italian	3,171	9.18

Notes: 1. Figures in the "Number" column do not add up to the total population due to: a) Ancestry/Race overlap — e.g. persons can report being both White and Irish, b) persons of Hispanic origin can report being any race, c) persons reporting two ancestries are counted in both categories. 2. Numbers in parentheses indicate the number of persons reporting this ancestry/race alone, not in combination with any other ancestry/race. 3. Refer to the User's Guide in the front of the book for more detailed information.

Latvian	18	0.05
Lithuanian	126	0.36
Luxemburger	9	0.03
Norwegian	46	0.13
Polish	1,573	4.55
Portuguese	47	0.14
Romanian	1,056	3.06
Russian	1,750	5.06
Scotch-Irish	145	0.42
Scottish	270	0.78
Serbian	39	0.11
Slovak	32	0.09
Swedish	209	0.60
Swiss	38	0.11
Turkish	97	0.28
Ukrainian	242	0.70
United States or American	1,874	5.42
Welsh	73	0.21
West Indian, excl. Hispanic:	1,623	4.70
Bahamian	210	0.61
Belizean	8	0.02
Bermudan	6	0.02
British West Indian	33	0.10
Haitian	849	2.46
Jamaican	464	1.34
Trinidadian and Tobagonian	21	0.06
U.S. Virgin Islander	6	0.02
West Indian	26	0.08
White:	27,105	79.06
Not Hispanic (21,456)	21,783	63.54
Hispanic (5,028)	5,322	15.52
Yugoslavian	85	0.25

Hamptons at Boca Raton

Place Type: Census Designated Place
County: Palm Beach
Population: 11,306

Ancestry/Race	Number	%
African American/Black:	230	2.03
Not Hispanic (186)	227	2.01
Hispanic (2)	3	0.03
Alaska Native tribes, specified:	2	0.02
Eskimo (1)	1	0.01
Tlingit-Haida (1)	1	0.01
Am. Ind. or Alaska Nat., not spec.	13	0.11
American Indian tribes, specified:	12	0.11
Apache (1)	1	0.01
Cherokee (1)	3	0.03
Sioux	5	0.04
All other tribes	3	0.03
American Indian tribes, not spec.	3	0.03
Arab:	48	0.42
Moroccan	20	0.18
Syrian	28	0.25
Asian:	210	1.86
Cambodian	1	0.01
Chinese, ex. Taiwanese (22)	28	0.25
Filipino (10)	18	0.16
Indian (76)	82	0.73
Indonesian (1)	1	0.01
Japanese (8)	11	0.10
Korean (4)	7	0.06
Pakistani (7)	7	0.06
Thai (12)	15	0.13
Vietnamese (23)	26	0.23
Other Asian, specified (2)	5	0.04
Other Asian, not specified (1)	9	0.08
Austrian	391	3.42
Belgian	8	0.07
Brazilian	49	0.43
British	22	0.19
Canadian	61	0.53
Croatian	19	0.17
Czech	35	0.31
Czechoslovakian	47	0.41
Danish	47	0.41
Dutch	49	0.43
Eastern European	28	0.25
English	340	2.98
European	106	0.93
Finnish	5	0.04
French, except Basque	104	0.91
French Canadian	82	0.72
German	592	5.18
Greek	69	0.60
Hawaii Native/Pacific Islander:	12	0.11
Polynesian: (1)	5	0.04
Native Hawaiian (1)	3	0.03
Samoan	1	0.01
Other Polynesian	1	0.01
Other Pac. Isl., specified	3	0.03
Other Pac. Isl., not spec.	4	0.04
Hispanic or Latino:	522	4.62
Central American:	26	0.23
Costa Rican	2	0.02
Guatemalan	4	0.04
Honduran	6	0.05
Nicaraguan	2	0.02
Panamanian	3	0.03
Salvadoran	9	0.08
Cuban	74	0.65
Dominican Republic	12	0.11
Mexican	44	0.39
Puerto Rican	104	0.92
South American:	158	1.40
Argentinean	33	0.29
Bolivian	4	0.04
Chilean	12	0.11
Colombian	60	0.53
Ecuadorian	9	0.08
Peruvian	15	0.13
Uruguayan	1	0.01
Venezuelan	13	0.11
Other South American	11	0.10
Other Hispanic or Latino	104	0.92
Hungarian	187	1.64
Iranian	32	0.28
Irish	786	6.88
Israeli	96	0.84
Italian	872	7.63
Latvian	46	0.40
Lithuanian	51	0.45
Norwegian	33	0.29
Polish	1,143	10.01
Portuguese	17	0.15
Romanian	183	1.60
Russian	1,035	9.06
Scotch-Irish	61	0.53
Scottish	124	1.09
Slavic	9	0.08
Slovak	19	0.17
Swedish	19	0.17
Swiss	65	0.57
Turkish	28	0.25
Ukrainian	93	0.81
United States or American	952	8.33
Welsh	25	0.22
West Indian, excl. Hispanic:	31	0.27
Haitian	31	0.27
White:	10,810	95.61
Not Hispanic (10,315)	10,380	91.81
Hispanic (403)	430	3.80

Hialeah Gardens

Place Type: City
County: Miami-Dade
Population: 19,297

Ancestry/Race	Number	%
African American/Black:	416	2.16
Not Hispanic (70)	79	0.41
Hispanic (278)	337	1.75
Am. Ind. or Alaska Nat., not spec.	15	0.08
American Indian tribes, specified:	27	0.14
Cherokee	1	0.01
Latin American Indians (9)	21	0.11
All other tribes	5	0.03
American Indian tribes, not spec.	2	0.01
Arab:	44	0.23
Jordanian	18	0.09
Lebanese	18	0.09
Syrian	8	0.04
Asian:	217	1.12
Chinese, ex. Taiwanese (88)	108	0.56
Filipino (2)	2	0.01
Indian (36)	45	0.23
Japanese (2)	7	0.04
Korean (5)	6	0.03
Pakistani (6)	10	0.05
Taiwanese (5)	5	0.03
Thai (1)	4	0.02
Vietnamese (3)	15	0.08
Other Asian, not specified	15	0.08
Dutch	13	0.07
English	65	0.34
French, except Basque	27	0.14
German	50	0.26
Greek	16	0.08
Hawaii Native/Pacific Islander:	12	0.06
Polynesian:	1	0.01
Native Hawaiian	1	0.01
Other Pac. Isl., not spec.	11	0.06
Hispanic or Latino:	17,324	89.78
Central American:	1,472	7.63
Costa Rican	30	0.16
Guatemalan	92	0.48
Honduran	223	1.16
Nicaraguan	939	4.87
Panamanian	54	0.28
Salvadoran	86	0.45
Other Central American	48	0.25
Cuban	10,480	54.31
Dominican Republic	551	2.86
Mexican	138	0.72
Puerto Rican	641	3.32
South American:	1,471	7.62
Argentinean	47	0.24
Bolivian	25	0.13
Chilean	43	0.22
Colombian	892	4.62
Ecuadorian	161	0.83
Paraguayan	1	0.01
Peruvian	146	0.76
Uruguayan	10	0.05
Venezuelan	138	0.72
Other South American	8	0.04
Other Hispanic or Latino	2,571	13.32
Iranian	19	0.10
Irish	30	0.16
Italian	220	1.14
Portuguese	39	0.20
Russian	20	0.10
Scotch-Irish	17	0.09
Scottish	10	0.05
Ukrainian	8	0.04
United States or American	364	1.89
West Indian, excl. Hispanic:	18	0.09
British West Indian	7	0.04
Haitian	11	0.06
White:	17,690	91.67
Not Hispanic (1,683)	1,736	9.00
Hispanic (15,377)	15,954	82.68

Hialeah

Place Type: City
County: Miami-Dade
Population: 226,419

Ancestry/Race	Number	%
African American/Black:	6,580	2.91
Not Hispanic (2,127)	2,259	1.00
Hispanic (3,326)	4,321	1.91
African, sub-Saharan:	197	0.09
African	197	0.09
Alaska Native tribes, specified:	3	0.00
Alaska Athabascan (2)	2	0.00
Eskimo	1	0.00
Alaska Native tribes, not specified	1	0.00
Am. Ind. or Alaska Nat., not spec.	327	0.14
American Indian tribes, specified:	235	0.10

Notes: 1. Figures in the "Number" column do not add up to the total population due to: a) Ancestry/Race overlap — e.g. persons can report being both White and Irish, b) persons of Hispanic origin can report being any race, c) persons reporting two ancestries are counted in both categories. 2. Numbers in parentheses indicate the number of persons reporting this ancestry/race alone, not in combination with any other ancestry/race. 3. Refer to the User's Guide in the front of the book for more detailed information.

Blackfeet	1	0.00
Cherokee (3)	15	0.01
Chippewa (5)	5	0.00
Choctaw (3)	3	0.00
Iroquois (2)	3	0.00
Latin American Indians (86)	178	0.08
Navajo (3)	3	0.00
Paiute	1	0.00
Pueblo (2)	10	0.00
Seminole	1	0.00
Sioux (1)	3	0.00
All other tribes (3)	12	0.01
American Indian tribes, not spec.	59	0.03
Arab:	669	0.30
Arab/Arabic	106	0.05
Egyptian	20	0.01
Jordanian	7	0.00
Lebanese	429	0.19
Palestinian	68	0.03
Syrian	19	0.01
Other Arab	20	0.01
Armenian	15	0.01
Asian:	1,290	0.57
Bangladeshi (4)	6	0.00
Chinese, ex. Taiwanese (345)	497	0.22
Filipino (85)	116	0.05
Indian (234)	315	0.14
Indonesian (1)	1	0.00
Japanese (34)	53	0.02
Korean (11)	17	0.01
Laotian (1)	1	0.00
Malaysian	3	0.00
Pakistani (84)	117	0.05
Sri Lankan	1	0.00
Thai (5)	9	0.00
Vietnamese (73)	78	0.03
Other Asian, not specified (9)	76	0.03
Assyrian/Chaldean/Syriac	10	0.00
Austrian	38	0.02
Basque	40	0.02
Brazilian	131	0.06
British	157	0.07
Canadian	27	0.01
Celtic	14	0.01
Croatian	21	0.01
Czech	7	0.00
Czechoslovakian	43	0.02
Danish	95	0.04
Dutch	151	0.07
Eastern European	8	0.00
English	907	0.40
European	227	0.10
Finnish	11	0.00
French, except Basque	807	0.36
French Canadian	34	0.02
German	1,344	0.59
Greek	42	0.02
Guyanese	25	0.01
Hawaii Native/Pacific Islander:	170	0.08
Melanesian: (2)	2	0.00
Fijian (2)	2	0.00
Micronesian: (10)	14	0.01
Guamanian/Chamorro (10)	14	0.01
Polynesian: (8)	22	0.01
Native Hawaiian (4)	9	0.00
Samoan (4)	12	0.01
Other Polynesian	1	0.00
Other Pac. Isl., not spec. (33)	132	0.06
Hispanic or Latino:	204,543	90.34
Central American:	14,668	6.48
Costa Rican	473	0.21
Guatemalan	823	0.36
Honduran	2,593	1.15
Nicaraguan	9,211	4.07
Panamanian	379	0.17
Salvadoran	763	0.34
Other Central American	426	0.19
Cuban	140,651	62.12
Dominican Republic	4,106	1.81
Mexican	1,719	0.76
Puerto Rican	6,584	2.91
South American:	12,510	5.53
Argentinean	632	0.28
Bolivian	113	0.05
Chilean	611	0.27
Colombian	7,152	3.16
Ecuadorian	1,159	0.51
Paraguayan	16	0.01
Peruvian	1,418	0.63
Uruguayan	118	0.05
Venezuelan	1,117	0.49
Other South American	174	0.08
Other Hispanic or Latino	24,305	10.73
Hungarian	82	0.04
Iranian	18	0.01
Irish	1,027	0.45
Italian	1,583	0.70
Latvian	16	0.01
Lithuanian	58	0.03
Norwegian	97	0.04
Pennsylvania German	7	0.00
Polish	334	0.15
Portuguese	183	0.08
Romanian	19	0.01
Russian	144	0.06
Scandinavian	5	0.00
Scotch-Irish	193	0.09
Scottish	147	0.06
Slovak	8	0.00
Swedish	26	0.01
Swiss	15	0.01
Turkish	22	0.01
Ukrainian	69	0.03
United States or American	5,822	2.57
Welsh	41	0.02
West Indian, excl. Hispanic:	803	0.35
Bahamian	57	0.03
Belizean	8	0.00
British West Indian	30	0.01
Dutch West Indian	8	0.00
Haitian	423	0.19
Jamaican	186	0.08
Trinidadian and Tobagonian	67	0.03
U.S. Virgin Islander	8	0.00
West Indian	16	0.01
White:	206,539	91.22
Not Hispanic (18,267)	18,674	8.25
Hispanic (181,009)	187,865	82.97
Yugoslavian	7	0.00

Hobe Sound

Place Type: Census Designated Place
County: Martin
Population: 11,376

Ancestry/Race	Number	%
African American/Black:	684	6.01
Not Hispanic (656)	679	5.97
Hispanic (3)	5	0.04
African, sub-Saharan:	26	0.23
African	26	0.23
Am. Ind. or Alaska Nat., not spec.	12	0.11
American Indian tribes, specified:	27	0.24
Apache	1	0.01
Blackfeet (1)	1	0.01
Cherokee (3)	10	0.09
Chippewa (2)	2	0.02
Comanche	1	0.01
Crow (1)	1	0.01
Iroquois (1)	2	0.02
Latin American Indians (5)	5	0.04
Seminole	1	0.01
Sioux	1	0.01
All other tribes	2	0.02
American Indian tribes, not spec.	1	0.01
Arab:	49	0.44
Lebanese	7	0.06
Moroccan	42	0.38
Armenian	7	0.06
Asian:	90	0.79
Chinese, ex. Taiwanese (23)	27	0.24
Filipino (11)	15	0.13
Indian (18)	23	0.20
Indonesian (1)	2	0.02
Japanese (2)	2	0.02
Korean (4)	5	0.04
Sri Lankan (2)	2	0.02
Taiwanese (2)	2	0.02
Thai (2)	2	0.02
Vietnamese (3)	4	0.04
Other Asian, not specified	6	0.05
Austrian	16	0.14
Belgian	34	0.30
British	36	0.32
Canadian	44	0.39
Carpatho Rusyn	15	0.13
Croatian	25	0.22
Czech	63	0.56
Czechoslovakian	18	0.16
Danish	82	0.73
Dutch	265	2.37
Eastern European	31	0.28
English	1,583	14.14
European	36	0.32
Finnish	64	0.57
French, except Basque	545	4.87
French Canadian	256	2.29
German	1,975	17.64
Greek	78	0.70
Hawaii Native/Pacific Islander:	14	0.12
Melanesian: (1)	6	0.05
Other Melanesian (1)	6	0.05
Micronesian: (1)	1	0.01
Guamanian/Chamorro (1)	1	0.01
Polynesian: (1)	1	0.01
Native Hawaiian (1)	1	0.01
Other Pac. Isl., not spec.	6	0.05
Hispanic or Latino:	253	2.22
Central American:	11	0.10
Costa Rican	1	0.01
Guatemalan	2	0.02
Salvadoran	3	0.03
Other Central American	5	0.04
Cuban	47	0.41
Dominican Republic	3	0.03
Mexican	64	0.56
Puerto Rican	69	0.61
South American:	22	0.19
Argentinean	4	0.04
Chilean	1	0.01
Colombian	6	0.05
Paraguayan	1	0.01
Peruvian	2	0.02
Venezuelan	2	0.02
Other South American	6	0.05
Other Hispanic or Latino	37	0.33
Hungarian	65	0.58
Irish	1,691	15.11
Italian	868	7.75
Lithuanian	73	0.65
Norwegian	112	1.00
Pennsylvania German	32	0.29
Polish	431	3.85
Portuguese	26	0.23
Romanian	7	0.06
Russian	26	0.23
Scandinavian	14	0.13
Scotch-Irish	270	2.41
Scottish	301	2.69
Serbian	19	0.17
Slovak	69	0.62
Swedish	166	1.48
Swiss	56	0.50
Ukrainian	66	0.59
United States or American	967	8.64
Welsh	57	0.51
West Indian, excl. Hispanic:	47	0.42
Bermudan	8	0.07
Haitian	31	0.28
Jamaican	8	0.07
White:	10,535	92.61
Not Hispanic (10,286)	10,349	90.97
Hispanic (178)	186	1.64

Notes: 1. Figures in the "Number" column do not add up to the total population due to: a) Ancestry/Race overlap — e.g. persons can report being both White and Irish, b) persons of Hispanic origin can report being any race, c) persons reporting two ancestries are counted in both categories. 2. Numbers in parentheses indicate the number of persons reporting this ancestry/race alone, not in combination with any other ancestry/race. 3. Refer to the User's Guide in the front of the book for more detailed information.

Yugoslavian	9	0.08

Holiday

Place Type: Census Designated Place
County: Pasco
Population: 21,904

Ancestry/Race	Number	%
African American/Black:	360	1.64
Not Hispanic (291)	326	1.49
Hispanic (18)	34	0.16
African, sub-Saharan:	17	0.08
African	6	0.03
South African	11	0.05
Am. Ind. or Alaska Nat., not spec.	36	0.16
Albanian	41	0.19
American Indian tribes, specified:	123	0.56
Apache (2)	2	0.01
Blackfeet	8	0.04
Cherokee (22)	54	0.25
Chippewa (13)	14	0.06
Choctaw (2)	2	0.01
Cree	1	0.00
Creek (1)	6	0.03
Iroquois (2)	6	0.03
Latin American Indians	6	0.03
Navajo (1)	5	0.02
Pueblo	6	0.03
Sioux (6)	7	0.03
All other tribes	6	0.03
American Indian tribes, not spec.	9	0.04
Arab:	194	0.89
Arab/Arabic	13	0.06
Lebanese	64	0.29
Syrian	117	0.53
Armenian	32	0.15
Asian:	270	1.23
Chinese, ex. Taiwanese (11)	20	0.09
Filipino (34)	56	0.26
Indian (34)	42	0.19
Japanese (10)	15	0.07
Korean (6)	10	0.05
Laotian (7)	7	0.03
Pakistani (2)	7	0.03
Thai (6)	10	0.05
Vietnamese (71)	79	0.36
Other Asian, specified	2	0.01
Other Asian, not specified (7)	22	0.10
Austrian	106	0.48
Belgian	25	0.11
Brazilian	8	0.04
British	115	0.52
Canadian	227	1.04
Croatian	39	0.18
Czech	129	0.59
Czechoslovakian	81	0.37
Danish	100	0.46
Dutch	427	1.95
Eastern European	8	0.04
English	2,402	10.96
European	94	0.43
Finnish	45	0.21
French, except Basque	889	4.06
French Canadian	388	1.77
German	4,074	18.59
Greek	1,247	5.69
Guyanese	22	0.10
Hawaii Native/Pacific Islander:	24	0.11
Micronesian: (5)	10	0.05
Guamanian/Chamorro	2	0.01
Other Micronesian (5)	8	0.04
Polynesian: (3)	3	0.01
Native Hawaiian (3)	3	0.01
Other Pac. Isl., specified	1	0.00
Other Pac. Isl., not spec. (4)	10	0.05
Hispanic or Latino:	883	4.03
Central American:	25	0.11
Costa Rican	5	0.02
Guatemalan	5	0.02
Honduran	10	0.05
Panamanian	3	0.01
Other Central American	2	0.01
Cuban	107	0.49
Dominican Republic	29	0.13
Mexican	121	0.55
Puerto Rican	394	1.80
South American:	45	0.21
Argentinean	4	0.02
Chilean	1	0.00
Colombian	18	0.08
Ecuadorian	6	0.03
Peruvian	9	0.04
Venezuelan	4	0.02
Other South American	3	0.01
Other Hispanic or Latino	162	0.74
Hungarian	258	1.18
Irish	3,711	16.93
Israeli	7	0.03
Italian	2,528	11.53
Lithuanian	122	0.56
Maltese	7	0.03
Northern European	7	0.03
Norwegian	273	1.25
Pennsylvania German	15	0.07
Polish	1,123	5.12
Portuguese	147	0.67
Romanian	9	0.04
Russian	176	0.80
Scandinavian	38	0.17
Scotch-Irish	303	1.38
Scottish	375	1.71
Slovak	101	0.46
Slovene	5	0.02
Swedish	420	1.92
Swiss	78	0.36
Ukrainian	59	0.27
United States or American	1,141	5.21
Welsh	147	0.67
West Indian, excl. Hispanic:	69	0.31
Bahamian	6	0.03
Barbadian	8	0.04
Jamaican	44	0.20
Trinidadian and Tobagonian	11	0.05
White:	21,098	96.32
Not Hispanic (20,227)	20,432	93.28
Hispanic (611)	666	3.04
Yugoslavian	61	0.28

Holly Hill

Place Type: City
County: Volusia
Population: 12,119

Ancestry/Race	Number	%
African American/Black:	1,146	9.46
Not Hispanic (1,063)	1,104	9.11
Hispanic (24)	42	0.35
African, sub-Saharan:	51	0.42
African	43	0.36
Nigerian	8	0.07
Alaska Native tribes, specified:	1	0.01
Alaska Athabascan (1)	1	0.01
Am. Ind. or Alaska Nat., not spec.	48	0.40
American Indian tribes, specified:	94	0.78
Apache	1	0.01
Blackfeet (1)	3	0.02
Cherokee (8)	43	0.35
Chickasaw	1	0.01
Chippewa (3)	8	0.07
Creek (3)	9	0.07
Iroquois	4	0.03
Kiowa (1)	1	0.01
Latin American Indians	3	0.02
Lumbee (1)	1	0.01
Navajo (1)	1	0.01
Seminole (2)	8	0.07
Sioux	2	0.02
All other tribes (2)	9	0.07
American Indian tribes, not spec.	11	0.09
Arab:	51	0.42
Lebanese	38	0.31
Palestinian	13	0.11
Asian:	147	1.21
Chinese, ex. Taiwanese (14)	18	0.15
Filipino (27)	33	0.27
Indian (36)	42	0.35
Japanese (4)	5	0.04
Korean (14)	21	0.17
Thai (2)	2	0.02
Vietnamese (20)	23	0.19
Other Asian, not specified	3	0.02
Austrian	46	0.38
Brazilian	10	0.08
British	77	0.64
Canadian	13	0.11
Celtic	18	0.15
Czech	11	0.09
Czechoslovakian	24	0.20
Danish	36	0.30
Dutch	230	1.90
English	1,418	11.73
European	52	0.43
Finnish	10	0.08
French, except Basque	412	3.41
French Canadian	111	0.92
German	1,659	13.73
Greek	30	0.25
Hawaii Native/Pacific Islander:	3	0.02
Micronesian: (1)	1	0.01
Guamanian/Chamorro (1)	1	0.01
Polynesian: (2)	2	0.02
Samoan (2)	2	0.02
Hispanic or Latino:	447	3.69
Central American:	16	0.13
Costa Rican	7	0.06
Honduran	4	0.03
Nicaraguan	1	0.01
Panamanian	2	0.02
Other Central American	2	0.02
Cuban	65	0.54
Dominican Republic	11	0.09
Mexican	107	0.88
Puerto Rican	129	1.06
South American:	50	0.41
Argentinean	2	0.02
Bolivian	1	0.01
Chilean	8	0.07
Colombian	20	0.17
Ecuadorian	5	0.04
Peruvian	2	0.02
Uruguayan	2	0.02
Venezuelan	8	0.07
Other South American	2	0.02
Other Hispanic or Latino	69	0.57
Hungarian	54	0.45
Irish	1,466	12.13
Italian	899	7.44
Latvian	14	0.12
Lithuanian	15	0.12
Norwegian	156	1.29
Polish	438	3.62
Portuguese	56	0.46
Russian	13	0.11
Scandinavian	35	0.29
Scotch-Irish	254	2.10
Scottish	230	1.90
Serbian	9	0.07
Slovak	6	0.05
Swedish	111	0.92
Swiss	14	0.12
Ukrainian	17	0.14
United States or American	1,366	11.30
Welsh	45	0.37
West Indian, excl. Hispanic:	44	0.36
Bahamian	7	0.06
Trinidadian and Tobagonian	29	0.24
West Indian	8	0.07
White:	10,734	88.57
Not Hispanic (10,282)	10,424	86.01
Hispanic (274)	310	2.56
Yugoslavian	23	0.19

Notes: 1. Figures in the "Number" column do not add up to the total population due to: a) Ancestry/Race overlap — e.g. persons can report being both White and Irish, b) persons of Hispanic origin can report being any race, c) persons reporting two ancestries are counted in both categories. 2. Numbers in parentheses indicate the number of persons reporting this ancestry/race alone, not in combination with any other ancestry/race. 3. Refer to the User's Guide in the front of the book for more detailed information.

Hollywood

Place Type: City
County: Broward
Population: 139,357

Ancestry/Race	Number	%
Acadian/Cajun	9	0.01
African American/Black:	18,405	13.21
Not Hispanic (15,972)	17,170	12.32
Hispanic (881)	1,235	0.89
African, sub-Saharan:	961	0.69
African	554	0.40
Cape Verdean	18	0.01
Liberian	37	0.03
Nigerian	285	0.20
South African	56	0.04
Other sub-Saharan African	11	0.01
Alaska Native tribes, specified:	2	0.00
Aleut (2)	2	0.00
Alaska Native tribes, not specified	2	0.00
Am. Ind. or Alaska Nat., not spec.	314	0.23
Albanian	20	0.01
Alsatian	9	0.01
American Indian tribes, specified:	483	0.35
Apache (5)	10	0.01
Blackfeet (3)	23	0.02
Cherokee (57)	159	0.11
Cheyenne	3	0.00
Chickasaw	1	0.00
Chippewa (10)	14	0.01
Choctaw (8)	21	0.02
Comanche (1)	2	0.00
Cree (4)	4	0.00
Creek (5)	8	0.01
Crow (4)	5	0.00
Delaware	2	0.00
Iroquois (10)	27	0.02
Latin American Indians (38)	99	0.07
Lumbee (2)	2	0.00
Navajo	3	0.00
Paiute	3	0.00
Pueblo	6	0.00
Seminole (33)	38	0.03
Sioux (10)	18	0.01
Tohono O'Odham (1)	1	0.00
Ute (1)	1	0.00
All other tribes (12)	33	0.02
American Indian tribes, not spec.	53	0.04
Arab:	1,183	0.85
Arab/Arabic	158	0.11
Egyptian	85	0.06
Iraqi	15	0.01
Jordanian	100	0.07
Lebanese	394	0.28
Moroccan	107	0.08
Palestinian	49	0.04
Syrian	186	0.13
Other Arab	89	0.06
Armenian	95	0.07
Asian:	3,469	2.49
Bangladeshi (15)	17	0.01
Cambodian (3)	4	0.00
Chinese, ex. Taiwanese (640)	778	0.56
Filipino (259)	355	0.25
Indian (1,168)	1,410	1.01
Indonesian (11)	17	0.01
Japanese (83)	129	0.09
Korean (164)	181	0.13
Laotian (9)	10	0.01
Malaysian (3)	7	0.01
Pakistani (117)	166	0.12
Sri Lankan (2)	2	0.00
Taiwanese (15)	18	0.01
Thai (33)	40	0.03
Vietnamese (152)	162	0.12
Other Asian, specified (1)	8	0.01
Other Asian, not specified (55)	165	0.12
Australian	61	0.04
Austrian	790	0.57
Basque	8	0.01
Belgian	57	0.04
Brazilian	731	0.52
British	564	0.40
Bulgarian	58	0.04
Canadian	1,156	0.83
Croatian	121	0.09
Czech	228	0.16
Czechoslovakian	330	0.24
Danish	293	0.21
Dutch	1,419	1.02
Eastern European	494	0.35
English	7,354	5.28
European	872	0.63
Finnish	180	0.13
French, except Basque	3,601	2.59
French Canadian	1,696	1.22
German	11,959	8.59
German Russian	20	0.01
Greek	1,097	0.79
Guyanese	281	0.20
Hawaii Native/Pacific Islander:	260	0.19
Micronesian: (18)	27	0.02
Guamanian/Chamorro (12)	19	0.01
Other Micronesian (6)	8	0.01
Polynesian: (60)	87	0.06
Native Hawaiian (28)	51	0.04
Samoan (11)	14	0.01
Tongan (18)	18	0.01
Other Polynesian (3)	4	0.00
Other Pac. Isl., specified	3	0.00
Other Pac. Isl., not spec. (39)	143	0.10
Hispanic or Latino:	31,392	22.53
Central American:	2,021	1.45
Costa Rican	256	0.18
Guatemalan	272	0.20
Honduran	418	0.30
Nicaraguan	501	0.36
Panamanian	241	0.17
Salvadoran	272	0.20
Other Central American	61	0.04
Cuban	5,891	4.23
Dominican Republic	1,681	1.21
Mexican	1,288	0.92
Puerto Rican	7,463	5.36
South American:	6,952	4.99
Argentinean	456	0.33
Bolivian	100	0.07
Chilean	302	0.22
Colombian	3,152	2.26
Ecuadorian	592	0.42
Paraguayan	15	0.01
Peruvian	1,466	1.05
Uruguayan	113	0.08
Venezuelan	568	0.41
Other South American	188	0.13
Other Hispanic or Latino	6,096	4.37
Hungarian	1,703	1.22
Iranian	76	0.05
Irish	12,650	9.08
Israeli	742	0.53
Italian	13,206	9.48
Latvian	89	0.06
Lithuanian	490	0.35
Luxemburger	18	0.01
Macedonian	73	0.05
Maltese	11	0.01
Northern European	33	0.02
Norwegian	677	0.49
Pennsylvania German	61	0.04
Polish	5,026	3.61
Portuguese	588	0.42
Romanian	1,613	1.16
Russian	4,464	3.21
Scandinavian	31	0.02
Scotch-Irish	1,311	0.94
Scottish	1,402	1.01
Serbian	117	0.08
Slavic	49	0.04
Slovak	181	0.13
Slovene	32	0.02
Swedish	861	0.62
Swiss	421	0.30
Turkish	218	0.16
Ukrainian	753	0.54
United States or American	9,762	7.01
Welsh	440	0.32
West Indian, excl. Hispanic:	7,171	5.15
Bahamian	435	0.31
Barbadian	86	0.06
Belizean	38	0.03
Bermudan	7	0.01
British West Indian	224	0.16
Haitian	2,140	1.54
Jamaican	3,105	2.23
Trinidadian and Tobagonian	727	0.52
U.S. Virgin Islander	67	0.05
West Indian	324	0.23
Other West Indian	18	0.01
White:	112,460	80.70
Not Hispanic (85,808)	87,426	62.74
Hispanic (23,382)	25,034	17.96
Yugoslavian	245	0.18

Homestead

Place Type: City
County: Miami-Dade
Population: 31,909

Ancestry/Race	Number	%
African American/Black:	7,977	25.00
Not Hispanic (6,886)	7,534	23.61
Hispanic (308)	443	1.39
African, sub-Saharan:	103	0.32
African	103	0.32
Alaska Native tribes, specified:	3	0.01
Alaska Athabascan	1	0.00
Eskimo (1)	1	0.00
Tlingit-Haida	1	0.00
Am. Ind. or Alaska Nat., not spec.	68	0.21
American Indian tribes, specified:	180	0.56
Blackfeet (3)	5	0.02
Cherokee (12)	28	0.09
Cheyenne	1	0.00
Choctaw (1)	7	0.02
Crow (1)	1	0.00
Iroquois	2	0.01
Kiowa (1)	1	0.00
Latin American Indians (82)	104	0.33
Lumbee	1	0.00
Navajo	2	0.01
Potawatomi (1)	1	0.00
Seminole	1	0.00
Sioux (5)	5	0.02
All other tribes (6)	21	0.07
American Indian tribes, not spec.	14	0.04
Arab:	22	0.07
Arab/Arabic	8	0.02
Egyptian	14	0.04
Armenian	21	0.07
Asian:	351	1.10
Bangladeshi (17)	18	0.06
Cambodian (9)	9	0.03
Chinese, ex. Taiwanese (35)	46	0.14
Filipino (27)	49	0.15
Indian (72)	94	0.29
Indonesian	4	0.01
Japanese (11)	21	0.07
Korean (12)	21	0.07
Pakistani	2	0.01
Taiwanese (4)	4	0.01
Thai (9)	11	0.03
Vietnamese (30)	32	0.10
Other Asian, specified (7)	7	0.02
Other Asian, not specified (10)	33	0.10
British	28	0.09
Canadian	24	0.07
Croatian	9	0.03
Czech	26	0.08
Czechoslovakian	26	0.08
Danish	20	0.06
Dutch	247	0.77
Eastern European	9	0.03

Notes: 1. Figures in the "Number" column do not add up to the total population due to: a) Ancestry/Race overlap — e.g. persons can report being both White and Irish, b) persons of Hispanic origin can report being any race, c) persons reporting two ancestries are counted in both categories. 2. Numbers in parentheses indicate the number of persons reporting this ancestry/race alone, not in combination with any other ancestry/race. 3. Refer to the User's Guide in the front of the book for more detailed information.

English	871	2.72
European	25	0.08
Finnish	16	0.05
French, except Basque	323	1.01
French Canadian	27	0.08
German	1,289	4.02
Greek	55	0.17
Guyanese	6	0.02
Hawaii Native/Pacific Islander:	82	0.26
Melanesian:	1	0.00
Fijian	1	0.00
Micronesian: (10)	12	0.04
Guamanian/Chamorro (10)	12	0.04
Polynesian: (11)	19	0.06
Native Hawaiian (8)	14	0.04
Samoan (3)	5	0.02
Other Pac. Isl., not spec. (6)	50	0.16
Hispanic or Latino:	16,537	51.83
Central American:	2,595	8.13
Costa Rican	47	0.15
Guatemalan	1,059	3.32
Honduran	343	1.07
Nicaraguan	228	0.71
Panamanian	39	0.12
Salvadoran	859	2.69
Other Central American	20	0.06
Cuban	2,171	6.80
Dominican Republic	263	0.82
Mexican	7,279	22.81
Puerto Rican	2,084	6.53
South American:	425	1.33
Argentinean	21	0.07
Bolivian	2	0.01
Chilean	11	0.03
Colombian	195	0.61
Ecuadorian	57	0.18
Peruvian	59	0.18
Uruguayan	2	0.01
Venezuelan	74	0.23
Other South American	4	0.01
Other Hispanic or Latino	1,720	5.39
Hungarian	98	0.31
Irish	1,336	4.17
Italian	579	1.81
Lithuanian	8	0.02
Norwegian	25	0.08
Polish	287	0.90
Portuguese	35	0.11
Romanian	16	0.05
Russian	63	0.20
Scotch-Irish	108	0.34
Scottish	208	0.65
Slavic	9	0.03
Slovak	9	0.03
Swedish	187	0.58
Swiss	36	0.11
Turkish	30	0.09
Ukrainian	37	0.12
United States or American	1,680	5.24
Welsh	60	0.19
West Indian, excl. Hispanic:	1,923	6.00
Bahamian	52	0.16
British West Indian	21	0.07
Haitian	1,531	4.78
Jamaican	229	0.71
Trinidadian and Tobagonian	75	0.23
West Indian	15	0.05
White:	20,447	64.08
Not Hispanic (7,295)	7,542	23.64
Hispanic (12,170)	12,905	40.44

Homosassa Springs

Place Type: Census Designated Place
County: Citrus
Population: 12,458

Ancestry/Race	Number	%
African American/Black:	130	1.04
Not Hispanic (108)	125	1.00
Hispanic (4)	5	0.04
African, sub-Saharan:	43	0.34
African	43	0.34
Am. Ind. or Alaska Nat., not spec.	48	0.39
American Indian tribes, specified:	117	0.94
Apache (1)	1	0.01
Blackfeet (1)	5	0.04
Cherokee (16)	53	0.43
Chippewa (5)	9	0.07
Comanche (1)	1	0.01
Creek (7)	8	0.06
Delaware (1)	1	0.01
Iroquois (3)	7	0.06
Lumbee (1)	1	0.01
Navajo (3)	3	0.02
Osage	1	0.01
Ottawa	1	0.01
Paiute (1)	1	0.01
Potawatomi (1)	1	0.01
Pueblo (1)	1	0.01
Seminole (1)	2	0.02
Sioux (3)	3	0.02
All other tribes (13)	18	0.14
American Indian tribes, not spec.	6	0.05
Arab:	35	0.27
Lebanese	35	0.27
Armenian	10	0.08
Asian:	96	0.77
Chinese, ex. Taiwanese (4)	8	0.06
Filipino (10)	25	0.20
Indian (33)	42	0.34
Japanese (5)	6	0.05
Korean (3)	8	0.06
Pakistani	1	0.01
Vietnamese (3)	3	0.02
Other Asian, not specified (1)	3	0.02
Austrian	10	0.08
Belgian	7	0.05
British	49	0.38
Canadian	35	0.27
Croatian	6	0.05
Czech	34	0.27
Danish	49	0.38
Dutch	413	3.24
English	1,936	15.18
European	41	0.32
Finnish	40	0.31
French, except Basque	546	4.28
French Canadian	141	1.11
German	2,692	21.11
Greek	47	0.37
Hawaii Native/Pacific Islander:	2	0.02
Micronesian: (1)	2	0.02
Guamanian/Chamorro (1)	2	0.02
Hispanic or Latino:	260	2.09
Central American:	6	0.05
Honduran	1	0.01
Nicaraguan	3	0.02
Panamanian	2	0.02
Cuban	36	0.29
Dominican Republic	1	0.01
Mexican	35	0.28
Puerto Rican	119	0.96
South American:	13	0.10
Colombian	2	0.02
Ecuadorian	4	0.03
Peruvian	2	0.02
Venezuelan	3	0.02
Other South American	2	0.02
Other Hispanic or Latino	50	0.40
Hungarian	101	0.79
Irish	2,223	17.44
Italian	877	6.88
Latvian	17	0.13
Northern European	28	0.22
Norwegian	54	0.42
Pennsylvania German	17	0.13
Polish	443	3.47
Portuguese	31	0.24
Russian	33	0.26
Scandinavian	47	0.37
Scotch-Irish	310	2.43
Scottish	409	3.21
Serbian	11	0.09
Slavic	7	0.05
Slovak	8	0.06
Swedish	201	1.58
Swiss	61	0.48
Ukrainian	44	0.35
United States or American	1,449	11.36
Welsh	142	1.11
West Indian, excl. Hispanic:	25	0.20
Bahamian	8	0.06
Jamaican	17	0.13
White:	12,170	97.69
Not Hispanic (11,822)	11,942	95.86
Hispanic (219)	228	1.83
Yugoslavian	22	0.17

Hudson

Place Type: Census Designated Place
County: Pasco
Population: 12,765

Ancestry/Race	Number	%
African American/Black:	65	0.51
Not Hispanic (44)	59	0.46
Hispanic (2)	6	0.05
Am. Ind. or Alaska Nat., not spec.	28	0.22
Alsatian	9	0.07
American Indian tribes, specified:	87	0.68
Apache (1)	1	0.01
Blackfeet (1)	5	0.04
Cherokee (9)	42	0.33
Cheyenne	1	0.01
Chickasaw	1	0.01
Chippewa (2)	4	0.03
Choctaw (1)	1	0.01
Comanche	1	0.01
Creek	4	0.03
Iroquois (2)	7	0.05
Kiowa (1)	1	0.01
Lumbee	2	0.02
Ottawa	4	0.03
Paiute (1)	1	0.01
Seminole (1)	5	0.04
Shoshone	1	0.01
Sioux	1	0.01
Yaqui	4	0.03
All other tribes	1	0.01
American Indian tribes, not spec.	5	0.04
Arab:	34	0.27
Egyptian	16	0.13
Lebanese	11	0.09
Syrian	7	0.06
Asian:	153	1.20
Chinese, ex. Taiwanese (27)	32	0.25
Filipino (26)	27	0.21
Hmong (1)	1	0.01
Indian (36)	47	0.37
Japanese (6)	11	0.09
Korean (5)	9	0.07
Laotian (1)	1	0.01
Malaysian	2	0.02
Pakistani	4	0.03
Taiwanese (1)	1	0.01
Thai (4)	5	0.04
Vietnamese (5)	9	0.07
Other Asian, not specified (1)	4	0.03
Austrian	51	0.40
Belgian	42	0.33
British	71	0.56
Canadian	149	1.17
Croatian	30	0.24
Czech	191	1.50
Czechoslovakian	66	0.52
Danish	74	0.58
Dutch	284	2.23
English	1,687	13.26
Estonian	8	0.06
European	7	0.06
Finnish	18	0.14
French, except Basque	638	5.01
French Canadian	218	1.71

Notes: 1. Figures in the "Number" column do not add up to the total population due to: a) Ancestry/Race overlap — e.g. persons can report being both White and Irish, b) persons of Hispanic origin can report being any race, c) persons reporting two ancestries are counted in both categories. 2. Numbers in parentheses indicate the number of persons reporting this ancestry/race alone, not in combination with any other ancestry/race. 3. Refer to the User's Guide in the front of the book for more detailed information.

German	2,536	19.93
Greek	169	1.33
Hawaii Native/Pacific Islander:	9	0.07
Micronesian: (2)	2	0.02
Guamanian/Chamorro (2)	2	0.02
Polynesian: (2)	7	0.05
Native Hawaiian (1)	5	0.04
Tongan (1)	2	0.02
Hispanic or Latino:	332	2.60
Central American:	13	0.10
Costa Rican	5	0.04
Guatemalan	1	0.01
Honduran	5	0.04
Panamanian	1	0.01
Other Central American	1	0.01
Cuban	29	0.23
Mexican	56	0.44
Puerto Rican	175	1.37
South American:	16	0.13
Chilean	3	0.02
Colombian	9	0.07
Ecuadorian	1	0.01
Peruvian	2	0.02
Venezuelan	1	0.01
Other Hispanic or Latino	43	0.34
Hungarian	112	0.88
Icelander	6	0.05
Irish	2,259	17.75
Italian	1,529	12.02
Latvian	14	0.11
Lithuanian	137	1.08
Macedonian	8	0.06
Norwegian	174	1.37
Pennsylvania German	16	0.13
Polish	744	5.85
Portuguese	81	0.64
Romanian	44	0.35
Russian	52	0.41
Scandinavian	20	0.16
Scotch-Irish	152	1.19
Scottish	284	2.23
Slavic	109	0.86
Slovak	47	0.37
Slovene	9	0.07
Swedish	333	2.62
Swiss	75	0.59
Ukrainian	106	0.83
United States or American	627	4.93
Welsh	137	1.08
White:	12,512	98.02
Not Hispanic (12,109)	12,232	95.82
Hispanic (256)	280	2.19

Immokalee

Place Type: Census Designated Place
County: Collier
Population: 19,763

Ancestry/Race	Number	%
African American/Black:	4,331	21.91
Not Hispanic (3,491)	4,218	21.34
Hispanic (73)	113	0.57
African, sub-Saharan:	67	0.35
African	60	0.31
Cape Verdean	7	0.04
Alaska Native tribes, specified:	2	0.01
Alaska Athabascan	1	0.01
Tlingit-Haida	1	0.01
Am. Ind. or Alaska Nat., not spec.	63	0.32
American Indian tribes, specified:	174	0.88
Cherokee (4)	8	0.04
Choctaw (3)	3	0.02
Latin American Indians (19)	31	0.16
Osage (1)	1	0.01
Seminole (117)	123	0.62
All other tribes (1)	8	0.04
American Indian tribes, not spec.	12	0.06
Arab:	7	0.04
Syrian	7	0.04
Asian:	79	0.40
Chinese, ex. Taiwanese	2	0.01
Indian (23)	35	0.18
Japanese (1)	3	0.02
Korean (2)	2	0.01
Thai	2	0.01
Vietnamese (2)	2	0.01
Other Asian, not specified (11)	33	0.17
Dutch	6	0.03
English	92	0.47
European	20	0.10
Finnish	21	0.11
French, except Basque	63	0.32
German	48	0.25
Hawaii Native/Pacific Islander:	49	0.25
Micronesian: (34)	41	0.21
Guamanian/Chamorro (34)	41	0.21
Polynesian: (2)	6	0.03
Native Hawaiian (2)	5	0.03
Samoan	1	0.01
Other Pac. Isl., not spec. (1)	2	0.01
Hispanic or Latino:	14,027	70.98
Central American:	930	4.71
Guatemalan	861	4.36
Honduran	38	0.19
Nicaraguan	6	0.03
Panamanian	1	0.01
Salvadoran	19	0.10
Other Central American	5	0.03
Cuban	40	0.20
Dominican Republic	8	0.04
Mexican	11,354	57.45
Puerto Rican	377	1.91
South American:	23	0.12
Colombian	2	0.01
Paraguayan	1	0.01
Peruvian	19	0.10
Venezuelan	1	0.01
Other Hispanic or Latino	1,295	6.55
Irish	165	0.85
Italian	32	0.16
Norwegian	10	0.05
Polish	8	0.04
Portuguese	17	0.09
Russian	7	0.04
Scotch-Irish	4	0.02
Scottish	8	0.04
United States or American	646	3.33
West Indian, excl. Hispanic:	2,135	11.00
Bahamian	15	0.08
Haitian	2,095	10.79
Trinidadian and Tobagonian	25	0.13
White:	8,084	40.90
Not Hispanic (1,254)	1,291	6.53
Hispanic (6,356)	6,793	34.37

Iona

Place Type: Census Designated Place
County: Lee
Population: 11,756

Ancestry/Race	Number	%
African American/Black:	62	0.53
Not Hispanic (43)	54	0.46
Hispanic (5)	8	0.07
Alaska Native tribes, specified:	2	0.02
Eskimo (2)	2	0.02
Am. Ind. or Alaska Nat., not spec.	11	0.09
American Indian tribes, specified:	28	0.24
Blackfeet (4)	4	0.03
Cherokee (2)	11	0.09
Chippewa	2	0.02
Choctaw (1)	1	0.01
Lumbee (3)	3	0.03
Ottawa (2)	2	0.02
Shoshone	3	0.03
All other tribes (1)	2	0.02
American Indian tribes, not spec.	4	0.03
Arab:	20	0.17
Lebanese	13	0.11
Syrian	7	0.06
Asian:	73	0.62
Chinese, ex. Taiwanese (9)	12	0.10
Filipino (8)	10	0.09
Indian (18)	19	0.16
Indonesian	2	0.02
Japanese (6)	8	0.07
Korean (5)	5	0.04
Malaysian	1	0.01
Thai	2	0.02
Vietnamese (2)	2	0.02
Other Asian, specified (8)	9	0.08
Other Asian, not specified	3	0.03
Austrian	63	0.53
Belgian	10	0.08
British	72	0.61
Canadian	71	0.60
Croatian	45	0.38
Czech	71	0.60
Czechoslovakian	28	0.24
Danish	77	0.65
Dutch	252	2.13
English	1,995	16.83
European	15	0.13
Finnish	26	0.22
French, except Basque	392	3.31
French Canadian	251	2.12
German	2,970	25.06
Greek	18	0.15
Hawaii Native/Pacific Islander:	4	0.03
Polynesian: (1)	1	0.01
Native Hawaiian (1)	1	0.01
Other Pac. Isl., specified	1	0.01
Other Pac. Isl., not spec.	2	0.02
Hispanic or Latino:	463	3.94
Central American:	5	0.04
Honduran	2	0.02
Nicaraguan	1	0.01
Salvadoran	1	0.01
Other Central American	1	0.01
Cuban	13	0.11
Dominican Republic	3	0.03
Mexican	314	2.67
Puerto Rican	54	0.46
South American:	24	0.20
Argentinean	7	0.06
Chilean	1	0.01
Colombian	4	0.03
Ecuadorian	4	0.03
Peruvian	1	0.01
Venezuelan	7	0.06
Other Hispanic or Latino	50	0.43
Hungarian	142	1.20
Irish	1,871	15.79
Italian	800	6.75
Lithuanian	47	0.40
Norwegian	167	1.41
Pennsylvania German	10	0.08
Polish	360	3.04
Portuguese	15	0.13
Russian	167	1.41
Scotch-Irish	323	2.73
Scottish	274	2.31
Serbian	11	0.09
Slavic	16	0.13
Slovak	76	0.64
Slovene	8	0.07
Swedish	289	2.44
Swiss	56	0.47
Ukrainian	77	0.65
United States or American	1,044	8.81
Welsh	110	0.93
White:	11,524	98.03
Not Hispanic (11,128)	11,166	94.98
Hispanic (331)	358	3.05
Yugoslavian	28	0.24

Ives Estates

Place Type: Census Designated Place
County: Miami-Dade
Population: 17,586

Ancestry/Race	Number	%

Notes: 1. Figures in the "Number" column do not add up to the total population due to: a) Ancestry/Race overlap — e.g. persons can report being both White and Irish, b) persons of Hispanic origin can report being any race, c) persons reporting two ancestries are counted in both categories. 2. Numbers in parentheses indicate the number of persons reporting this ancestry/race alone, not in combination with any other ancestry/race. 3. Refer to the User's Guide in the front of the book for more detailed information.

African American/Black:	6,714	38.18
Not Hispanic (5,957)	6,385	36.31
Hispanic (217)	329	1.87
African, sub-Saharan:	242	1.39
African	188	1.08
Kenyan	26	0.15
Nigerian	17	0.10
South African	11	0.06
Alaska Native tribes, specified:	2	0.01
Aleut	1	0.01
Tlingit-Haida	1	0.01
Am. Ind. or Alaska Nat., not spec.	41	0.23
American Indian tribes, specified:	36	0.20
Blackfeet	6	0.03
Cherokee (3)	16	0.09
Choctaw (1)	1	0.01
Latin American Indians (2)	6	0.03
Seminole	1	0.01
All other tribes (3)	6	0.03
American Indian tribes, not spec.	5	0.03
Arab:	297	1.71
Arab/Arabic	127	0.73
Iraqi	7	0.04
Lebanese	44	0.25
Moroccan	5	0.03
Palestinian	40	0.23
Syrian	74	0.42
Asian:	1,024	5.82
Bangladeshi (3)	3	0.02
Cambodian (4)	4	0.02
Chinese, ex. Taiwanese (220)	273	1.55
Filipino (97)	120	0.68
Indian (276)	337	1.92
Indonesian (12)	13	0.07
Japanese (13)	24	0.14
Korean (32)	33	0.19
Laotian (4)	4	0.02
Malaysian	1	0.01
Pakistani (80)	93	0.53
Taiwanese (4)	4	0.02
Thai (15)	15	0.09
Vietnamese (25)	30	0.17
Other Asian, specified	1	0.01
Other Asian, not specified (20)	69	0.39
Austrian	115	0.66
Brazilian	161	0.92
British	66	0.38
Canadian	47	0.27
Croatian	18	0.10
Czech	34	0.20
Danish	14	0.08
Dutch	121	0.69
Eastern European	39	0.22
English	309	1.77
European	79	0.45
Finnish	33	0.19
French, except Basque	163	0.94
French Canadian	13	0.07
German	592	3.40
Greek	84	0.48
Guyanese	76	0.44
Hawaii Native/Pacific Islander:	49	0.28
Polynesian: (7)	8	0.05
Samoan (7)	8	0.05
Other Pac. Isl., specified	1	0.01
Other Pac. Isl., not spec. (2)	40	0.23
Hispanic or Latino:	4,234	24.08
Central American:	420	2.39
Costa Rican	45	0.26
Guatemalan	46	0.26
Honduran	94	0.53
Nicaraguan	120	0.68
Panamanian	70	0.40
Salvadoran	35	0.20
Other Central American	10	0.06
Cuban	617	3.51
Dominican Republic	269	1.53
Mexican	71	0.40
Puerto Rican	695	3.95
South American:	1,175	6.68
Argentinean	183	1.04
Bolivian	5	0.03
Chilean	36	0.20
Colombian	486	2.76
Ecuadorian	63	0.36
Paraguayan	1	0.01
Peruvian	230	1.31
Uruguayan	25	0.14
Venezuelan	120	0.68
Other South American	26	0.15
Other Hispanic or Latino	987	5.61
Hungarian	95	0.55
Iranian	18	0.10
Irish	588	3.38
Israeli	116	0.67
Italian	639	3.67
Latvian	10	0.06
Lithuanian	14	0.08
Norwegian	14	0.08
Pennsylvania German	17	0.10
Polish	346	1.99
Portuguese	62	0.36
Romanian	99	0.57
Russian	707	4.06
Scandinavian	24	0.14
Scotch-Irish	83	0.48
Scottish	166	0.95
Slavic	18	0.10
Swedish	9	0.05
Swiss	11	0.06
Turkish	34	0.20
Ukrainian	52	0.30
United States or American	917	5.26
Welsh	32	0.18
West Indian, excl. Hispanic:	3,901	22.40
Bahamian	146	0.84
Barbadian	15	0.09
Belizean	7	0.04
British West Indian	43	0.25
Haitian	2,449	14.06
Jamaican	1,000	5.74
Trinidadian and Tobagonian	108	0.62
U.S. Virgin Islander	32	0.18
West Indian	101	0.58
White:	9,443	53.70
Not Hispanic (5,863)	6,117	34.78
Hispanic (3,123)	3,326	18.91
Yugoslavian	6	0.03

Jacksonville Beach

Place Type: City
County: Duval
Population: 20,990

Ancestry/Race	Number	%
African American/Black:	1,074	5.12
Not Hispanic (996)	1,045	4.98
Hispanic (15)	29	0.14
African, sub-Saharan:	120	0.57
African	103	0.49
Ghanian	7	0.03
South African	10	0.05
Alaska Native tribes, specified:	1	0.00
Aleut (1)	1	0.00
Am. Ind. or Alaska Nat., not spec.	50	0.24
American Indian tribes, specified:	89	0.42
Apache	1	0.00
Blackfeet	1	0.00
Cherokee (17)	47	0.22
Chickasaw (1)	1	0.00
Chippewa (4)	4	0.02
Choctaw (2)	3	0.01
Comanche (1)	2	0.01
Creek (4)	11	0.05
Delaware	2	0.01
Iroquois	2	0.01
Latin American Indians (1)	2	0.01
Lumbee (3)	3	0.01
Ottawa (1)	1	0.00
Seminole (1)	1	0.00
Sioux	3	0.01
All other tribes (2)	5	0.02
American Indian tribes, not spec.	4	0.02
Arab:	172	0.82
Arab/Arabic	62	0.30
Lebanese	88	0.42
Moroccan	10	0.05
Palestinian	12	0.06
Armenian	38	0.18
Asian:	482	2.30
Cambodian (8)	8	0.04
Chinese, ex. Taiwanese (18)	34	0.16
Filipino (204)	267	1.27
Indian (38)	44	0.21
Indonesian (2)	2	0.01
Japanese (21)	44	0.21
Korean (9)	16	0.08
Laotian (2)	3	0.01
Taiwanese (1)	1	0.00
Thai (8)	12	0.06
Vietnamese (12)	23	0.11
Other Asian, not specified (12)	28	0.13
Austrian	32	0.15
Belgian	12	0.06
British	180	0.86
Bulgarian	12	0.06
Canadian	45	0.21
Croatian	23	0.11
Czech	133	0.63
Czechoslovakian	39	0.19
Danish	35	0.17
Dutch	500	2.38
Eastern European	15	0.07
English	3,246	15.46
European	260	1.24
Finnish	59	0.28
French, except Basque	932	4.44
French Canadian	262	1.25
German	2,732	13.02
Greek	186	0.89
Hawaii Native/Pacific Islander:	20	0.10
Micronesian: (1)	2	0.01
Guamanian/Chamorro	1	0.00
Other Micronesian (1)	1	0.00
Polynesian: (6)	10	0.05
Native Hawaiian (4)	7	0.03
Samoan (1)	2	0.01
Other Polynesian (1)	1	0.00
Other Pac. Isl., not spec. (2)	8	0.04
Hispanic or Latino:	628	2.99
Central American:	25	0.12
Costa Rican	2	0.01
Guatemalan	4	0.02
Honduran	6	0.03
Nicaraguan	5	0.02
Panamanian	5	0.02
Salvadoran	1	0.00
Other Central American	2	0.01
Cuban	57	0.27
Dominican Republic	4	0.02
Mexican	161	0.77
Puerto Rican	160	0.76
South American:	66	0.31
Bolivian	2	0.01
Chilean	16	0.08
Colombian	13	0.06
Ecuadorian	3	0.01
Peruvian	20	0.10
Uruguayan	1	0.00
Venezuelan	9	0.04
Other South American	2	0.01
Other Hispanic or Latino	155	0.74
Hungarian	116	0.55
Irish	3,347	15.95
Italian	1,676	7.98
Lithuanian	106	0.51
Maltese	8	0.04
Norwegian	218	1.04
Pennsylvania German	22	0.10
Polish	733	3.49
Portuguese	62	0.30
Romanian	35	0.17
Russian	244	1.16

Notes: 1. Figures in the "Number" column do not add up to the total population due to: a) Ancestry/Race overlap — e.g. persons can report being both White and Irish, b) persons of Hispanic origin can report being any race, c) persons reporting two ancestries are counted in both categories. 2. Numbers in parentheses indicate the number of persons reporting this ancestry/race alone, not in combination with any other ancestry/race. 3. Refer to the User's Guide in the front of the book for more detailed information.

Scandinavian	11	0.05
Scotch-Irish	567	2.70
Scottish	783	3.73
Slavic	9	0.04
Slovak	54	0.26
Slovene	13	0.06
Swedish	158	0.75
Swiss	52	0.25
Turkish	28	0.13
Ukrainian	33	0.16
United States or American	1,356	6.46
Welsh	187	0.89
West Indian, excl. Hispanic:	9	0.04
Jamaican	9	0.04
White:	19,376	92.31
Not Hispanic (18,675)	18,924	90.16
Hispanic (414)	452	2.15
Yugoslavian	16	0.08

Jacksonville

Place Type: Special City
County: Duval
Population: 735,617

Ancestry/Race	Number	%
Acadian/Cajun	179	0.02
Afghan	205	0.03
African American/Black:	218,451	29.70
Not Hispanic (211,252)	215,484	29.29
Hispanic (2,262)	2,967	0.40
African, sub-Saharan:	8,010	1.09
African	6,995	0.95
Cape Verdean	72	0.01
Ethiopian	99	0.01
Ghanian	112	0.02
Kenyan	7	0.00
Liberian	10	0.00
Nigerian	281	0.04
Sierra Leonean	49	0.01
South African	154	0.02
Sudanese	64	0.01
Other sub-Saharan African	167	0.02
Alaska Native tribes, specified:	46	0.01
Alaska Athabascan (4)	5	0.00
Aleut (11)	11	0.00
Eskimo (7)	12	0.00
Tlingit-Haida (10)	17	0.00
All other tribes (1)	1	0.00
Alaska Native tribes, not specified	9	0.00
Am. Ind. or Alaska Nat., not spec.	1,954	0.27
Albanian	855	0.12
Alsatian	43	0.01
American Indian tribes, specified:	3,545	0.48
Apache (36)	97	0.01
Blackfeet (42)	186	0.03
Cherokee (615)	1,717	0.23
Cheyenne (7)	15	0.00
Chickasaw (15)	23	0.00
Chippewa (54)	97	0.01
Choctaw (60)	131	0.02
Colville (3)	3	0.00
Comanche (2)	12	0.00
Cree (5)	10	0.00
Creek (100)	188	0.03
Crow (2)	7	0.00
Delaware (8)	10	0.00
Houma (13)	14	0.00
Iroquois (65)	131	0.02
Kiowa (3)	6	0.00
Latin American Indians (60)	141	0.02
Lumbee (81)	108	0.01
Menominee (1)	1	0.00
Navajo (35)	64	0.01
Osage (3)	14	0.00
Ottawa (11)	12	0.00
Paiute (6)	6	0.00
Pima	2	0.00
Potawatomi (7)	11	0.00
Pueblo (1)	9	0.00
Seminole (46)	124	0.02
Shoshone (3)	7	0.00
Sioux (58)	108	0.01
Ute (1)	3	0.00
Yaqui (4)	12	0.00
Yuman	1	0.00
All other tribes (151)	275	0.04
American Indian tribes, not spec.	288	0.04
Arab:	5,861	0.80
Arab/Arabic	1,602	0.22
Egyptian	167	0.02
Iraqi	169	0.02
Jordanian	81	0.01
Lebanese	1,623	0.22
Moroccan	94	0.01
Palestinian	789	0.11
Syrian	1,182	0.16
Other Arab	154	0.02
Armenian	397	0.05
Asian:	25,465	3.46
Bangladeshi (11)	16	0.00
Cambodian (891)	1,064	0.14
Chinese, ex. Taiwanese (1,376)	1,879	0.26
Filipino (9,958)	12,295	1.67
Hmong (5)	10	0.00
Indian (2,758)	3,163	0.43
Indonesian (32)	44	0.01
Japanese (486)	930	0.13
Korean (1,085)	1,366	0.19
Laotian (227)	273	0.04
Malaysian (15)	56	0.01
Pakistani (108)	147	0.02
Sri Lankan (27)	27	0.00
Taiwanese (66)	96	0.01
Thai (177)	271	0.04
Vietnamese (2,324)	2,566	0.35
Other Asian, specified (61)	152	0.02
Other Asian, not specified (470)	1,110	0.15
Assyrian/Chaldean/Syriac	29	0.00
Australian	137	0.02
Austrian	1,086	0.15
Basque	49	0.01
Belgian	645	0.09
Brazilian	116	0.02
British	3,160	0.43
Bulgarian	26	0.00
Canadian	1,400	0.19
Carpatho Rusyn	8	0.00
Celtic	195	0.03
Croatian	659	0.09
Cypriot	35	0.00
Czech	1,244	0.17
Czechoslovakian	741	0.10
Danish	1,337	0.18
Dutch	7,635	1.04
Eastern European	323	0.04
English	62,798	8.54
Estonian	28	0.00
European	5,173	0.70
Finnish	665	0.09
French, except Basque	16,196	2.20
French Canadian	4,238	0.58
German	70,440	9.58
Greek	2,314	0.31
Guyanese	358	0.05
Hawaii Native/Pacific Islander:	1,290	0.18
Melanesian: (1)	1	0.00
Other Melanesian (1)	1	0.00
Micronesian: (169)	300	0.04
Guamanian/Chamorro (145)	263	0.04
Other Micronesian (24)	37	0.01
Polynesian: (176)	493	0.07
Native Hawaiian (111)	369	0.05
Samoan (57)	105	0.01
Tongan (2)	2	0.00
Other Polynesian (6)	17	0.00
Other Pac. Isl., specified	59	0.01
Other Pac. Isl., not spec. (100)	437	0.06
Hispanic or Latino:	30,594	4.16
Central American:	1,651	0.22
Costa Rican	259	0.04
Guatemalan	172	0.02
Honduran	267	0.04
Nicaraguan	263	0.04
Panamanian	461	0.06
Salvadoran	169	0.02
Other Central American	60	0.01
Cuban	3,229	0.44
Dominican Republic	601	0.08
Mexican	6,076	0.83
Puerto Rican	11,066	1.50
South American:	2,037	0.28
Argentinean	117	0.02
Bolivian	55	0.01
Chilean	117	0.02
Colombian	924	0.13
Ecuadorian	201	0.03
Paraguayan	6	0.00
Peruvian	303	0.04
Uruguayan	24	0.00
Venezuelan	209	0.03
Other South American	81	0.01
Other Hispanic or Latino	5,934	0.81
Hungarian	2,485	0.34
Icelander	64	0.01
Iranian	407	0.06
Irish	66,148	8.99
Israeli	97	0.01
Italian	25,385	3.45
Latvian	103	0.01
Lithuanian	1,014	0.14
Luxemburger	42	0.01
Macedonian	6	0.00
Maltese	8	0.00
New Zealander	31	0.00
Northern European	188	0.03
Norwegian	4,816	0.65
Pennsylvania German	217	0.03
Polish	10,500	1.43
Portuguese	1,184	0.16
Romanian	707	0.10
Russian	3,705	0.50
Scandinavian	560	0.08
Scotch-Irish	13,064	1.78
Scottish	13,558	1.84
Serbian	155	0.02
Slavic	227	0.03
Slovak	564	0.08
Slovene	163	0.02
Swedish	4,774	0.65
Swiss	1,064	0.14
Turkish	324	0.04
Ukrainian	1,294	0.18
United States or American	68,488	9.31
Welsh	3,699	0.50
West Indian, excl. Hispanic:	4,952	0.67
Bahamian	264	0.04
Barbadian	76	0.01
Belizean	122	0.02
Bermudan	90	0.01
British West Indian	161	0.02
Dutch West Indian	37	0.01
Haitian	996	0.14
Jamaican	2,010	0.27
Trinidadian and Tobagonian	297	0.04
U.S. Virgin Islander	107	0.01
West Indian	750	0.10
Other West Indian	42	0.01
White:	485,785	66.04
Not Hispanic (457,478)	467,111	63.50
Hispanic (16,829)	18,674	2.54
Yugoslavian	2,655	0.36

Jasmine Estates

Place Type: Census Designated Place
County: Pasco
Population: 18,213

Ancestry/Race	Number	%
Acadian/Cajun	11	0.06
African American/Black:	370	2.03
Not Hispanic (286)	344	1.89
Hispanic (10)	26	0.14

Notes: 1. Figures in the "Number" column do not add up to the total population due to: a) Ancestry/Race overlap — e.g. persons can report being both White and Irish, b) persons of Hispanic origin can report being any race, c) persons reporting two ancestries are counted in both categories. 2. Numbers in parentheses indicate the number of persons reporting this ancestry/race alone, not in combination with any other ancestry/race. 3. Refer to the User's Guide in the front of the book for more detailed information.

African, sub-Saharan:	16	0.09
Sudanese	16	0.09
Alaska Native tribes, specified:	3	0.02
Eskimo	3	0.02
Am. Ind. or Alaska Nat., not spec.	37	0.20
American Indian tribes, specified:	91	0.50
Blackfeet (2)	9	0.05
Cherokee (18)	43	0.24
Cheyenne	1	0.01
Chippewa (5)	5	0.03
Choctaw	4	0.02
Creek (1)	1	0.01
Crow (1)	1	0.01
Iroquois (1)	4	0.02
Latin American Indians (1)	9	0.05
Navajo (1)	2	0.01
Ottawa (3)	3	0.02
Seminole	2	0.01
Sioux	3	0.02
All other tribes (4)	4	0.02
American Indian tribes, not spec.	12	0.07
Arab:	8	0.04
Lebanese	8	0.04
Armenian	29	0.16
Asian:	226	1.24
Chinese, ex. Taiwanese (40)	46	0.25
Filipino (45)	58	0.32
Indian (24)	38	0.21
Indonesian	4	0.02
Japanese (3)	8	0.04
Korean (5)	9	0.05
Pakistani (3)	9	0.05
Thai (4)	7	0.04
Vietnamese (21)	23	0.13
Other Asian, specified (1)	4	0.02
Other Asian, not specified (7)	20	0.11
Austrian	142	0.79
British	34	0.19
Canadian	85	0.47
Croatian	16	0.09
Czech	143	0.79
Czechoslovakian	30	0.17
Danish	47	0.26
Dutch	226	1.25
English	1,434	7.94
European	49	0.27
Finnish	64	0.35
French, except Basque	812	4.50
French Canadian	168	0.93
German	2,968	16.44
Greek	222	1.23
Guyanese	31	0.17
Hawaii Native/Pacific Islander:	14	0.08
Micronesian: (2)	3	0.02
Guamanian/Chamorro (2)	3	0.02
Polynesian: (1)	6	0.03
Native Hawaiian (1)	6	0.03
Other Pac. Isl., specified	1	0.01
Other Pac. Isl., not spec.	4	0.02
Hispanic or Latino:	1,105	6.07
Central American:	22	0.12
Costa Rican	3	0.02
Guatemalan	1	0.01
Honduran	7	0.04
Nicaraguan	2	0.01
Panamanian	4	0.02
Salvadoran	4	0.02
Other Central American	1	0.01
Cuban	83	0.46
Dominican Republic	15	0.08
Mexican	114	0.63
Puerto Rican	608	3.34
South American:	66	0.36
Argentinean	4	0.02
Bolivian	2	0.01
Chilean	1	0.01
Colombian	24	0.13
Ecuadorian	8	0.04
Peruvian	9	0.05
Uruguayan	5	0.03
Venezuelan	5	0.03
Other South American	8	0.04
Other Hispanic or Latino	197	1.08
Hungarian	260	1.44
Irish	2,861	15.85
Italian	3,432	19.01
Lithuanian	66	0.37
Maltese	19	0.11
Norwegian	112	0.62
Pennsylvania German	21	0.12
Polish	1,287	7.13
Portuguese	76	0.42
Romanian	8	0.04
Russian	176	0.97
Scandinavian	43	0.24
Scotch-Irish	320	1.77
Scottish	412	2.28
Slovak	51	0.28
Swedish	234	1.30
Swiss	48	0.27
Ukrainian	144	0.80
United States or American	1,489	8.25
Welsh	68	0.38
West Indian, excl. Hispanic:	99	0.55
Dutch West Indian	11	0.06
Haitian	13	0.07
Jamaican	30	0.17
West Indian	45	0.25
White:	17,436	95.73
Not Hispanic (16,401)	16,583	91.05
Hispanic (803)	853	4.68
Yugoslavian	54	0.30

Jensen Beach

Place Type: Census Designated Place
County: Martin
Population: 11,100

Ancestry/Race	Number	%
Acadian/Cajun	5	0.05
African American/Black:	271	2.44
Not Hispanic (230)	248	2.23
Hispanic (20)	23	0.21
Am. Ind. or Alaska Nat., not spec.	18	0.16
Alsatian	9	0.08
American Indian tribes, specified:	36	0.32
Blackfeet	1	0.01
Cherokee (5)	15	0.14
Chippewa (1)	2	0.02
Iroquois	2	0.02
Latin American Indians (2)	2	0.02
Lumbee (1)	1	0.01
Navajo	1	0.01
Pueblo	4	0.04
Seminole	1	0.01
Sioux (1)	1	0.01
All other tribes (4)	6	0.05
American Indian tribes, not spec.	5	0.05
Arab:	15	0.14
Lebanese	15	0.14
Armenian	6	0.05
Asian:	73	0.66
Chinese, ex. Taiwanese (13)	17	0.15
Filipino (8)	14	0.13
Indian (10)	12	0.11
Japanese (2)	9	0.08
Korean (1)	1	0.01
Pakistani (3)	3	0.03
Thai (1)	1	0.01
Vietnamese (7)	10	0.09
Other Asian, specified (5)	5	0.05
Other Asian, not specified (1)	1	0.01
Austrian	87	0.78
Belgian	56	0.50
British	45	0.41
Canadian	33	0.30
Czech	52	0.47
Czechoslovakian	10	0.09
Danish	51	0.46
Dutch	283	2.55
English	1,914	17.24
Estonian	7	0.06
European	71	0.64
Finnish	29	0.26
French, except Basque	485	4.37
French Canadian	114	1.03
German	2,316	20.86
Greek	8	0.07
Hawaii Native/Pacific Islander:	11	0.10
Micronesian:	1	0.01
Guamanian/Chamorro	1	0.01
Polynesian: (4)	8	0.07
Native Hawaiian (2)	6	0.05
Samoan (2)	2	0.02
Other Pac. Isl., not spec.	2	0.02
Hispanic or Latino:	307	2.77
Central American:	13	0.12
Costa Rican	1	0.01
Guatemalan	4	0.04
Honduran	3	0.03
Panamanian	4	0.04
Salvadoran	1	0.01
Cuban	76	0.68
Dominican Republic	3	0.03
Mexican	69	0.62
Puerto Rican	59	0.53
South American:	31	0.28
Argentinean	1	0.01
Chilean	1	0.01
Colombian	14	0.13
Ecuadorian	3	0.03
Peruvian	5	0.05
Venezuelan	5	0.05
Other South American	2	0.02
Other Hispanic or Latino	56	0.50
Hungarian	71	0.64
Irish	2,214	19.94
Italian	1,422	12.81
Latvian	2	0.02
Lithuanian	61	0.55
Maltese	18	0.16
Norwegian	83	0.75
Pennsylvania German	8	0.07
Polish	553	4.98
Portuguese	40	0.36
Russian	109	0.98
Scotch-Irish	217	1.95
Scottish	360	3.24
Serbian	4	0.04
Slavic	8	0.07
Slovak	33	0.30
Slovene	37	0.33
Swedish	246	2.22
Swiss	46	0.41
Ukrainian	25	0.23
United States or American	734	6.61
Welsh	121	1.09
West Indian, excl. Hispanic:	97	0.87
British West Indian	10	0.09
Haitian	34	0.31
Jamaican	53	0.48
White:	10,726	96.63
Not Hispanic (10,414)	10,483	94.44
Hispanic (220)	243	2.19

Jupiter

Place Type: Town
County: Palm Beach
Population: 39,328

Ancestry/Race	Number	%
African American/Black:	555	1.41
Not Hispanic (461)	513	1.30
Hispanic (19)	42	0.11
African, sub-Saharan:	54	0.14
Nigerian	24	0.06
South African	25	0.06
Other sub-Saharan African	5	0.01
Am. Ind. or Alaska Nat., not spec.	39	0.10
Albanian	22	0.06
American Indian tribes, specified:	131	0.33

Notes: 1. Figures in the "Number" column do not add up to the total population due to: a) Ancestry/Race overlap — e.g. persons can report being both White and Irish, b) persons of Hispanic origin can report being any race, c) persons reporting two ancestries are counted in both categories. 2. Numbers in parentheses indicate the number of persons reporting this ancestry/race alone, not in combination with any other ancestry/race. 3. Refer to the User's Guide in the front of the book for more detailed information.

Apache (1)	3	0.01
Blackfeet (1)	4	0.01
Cherokee (11)	38	0.10
Chippewa (6)	6	0.02
Choctaw (7)	10	0.03
Delaware (1)	2	0.01
Iroquois (4)	15	0.04
Latin American Indians (11)	25	0.06
Lumbee (3)	3	0.01
Navajo (1)	2	0.01
Pueblo	1	0.00
Shoshone	3	0.01
Sioux (3)	6	0.02
Ute	1	0.00
All other tribes (3)	12	0.03
American Indian tribes, not spec.	8	0.02
Arab:	130	0.33
Arab/Arabic	7	0.02
Lebanese	87	0.22
Palestinian	13	0.03
Syrian	23	0.06
Armenian	77	0.20
Asian:	594	1.51
Bangladeshi (10)	10	0.03
Chinese, ex. Taiwanese (104)	148	0.38
Filipino (58)	91	0.23
Indian (155)	176	0.45
Japanese (16)	29	0.07
Korean (24)	37	0.09
Laotian (9)	9	0.02
Malaysian (1)	2	0.01
Pakistani (5)	7	0.02
Taiwanese (1)	3	0.01
Thai (15)	18	0.05
Vietnamese (29)	32	0.08
Other Asian, specified	3	0.01
Other Asian, not specified (6)	29	0.07
Assyrian/Chaldean/Syriac	16	0.04
Australian	6	0.02
Austrian	295	0.75
Belgian	49	0.12
Brazilian	36	0.09
British	254	0.65
Canadian	210	0.53
Celtic	7	0.02
Croatian	74	0.19
Cypriot	8	0.02
Czech	169	0.43
Czechoslovakian	85	0.22
Danish	137	0.35
Dutch	727	1.85
Eastern European	33	0.08
English	5,363	13.64
Estonian	8	0.02
European	283	0.72
Finnish	164	0.42
French, except Basque	1,651	4.20
French Canadian	382	0.97
German	7,055	17.95
Greek	293	0.75
Hawaii Native/Pacific Islander:	75	0.19
Micronesian: (34)	34	0.09
Guamanian/Chamorro (34)	34	0.09
Polynesian: (5)	24	0.06
Native Hawaiian (3)	19	0.05
Samoan (1)	2	0.01
Other Polynesian (1)	3	0.01
Other Pac. Isl., specified	3	0.01
Other Pac. Isl., not spec. (6)	14	0.04
Hispanic or Latino:	2,881	7.33
Central American:	501	1.27
Costa Rican	15	0.04
Guatemalan	427	1.09
Honduran	18	0.05
Nicaraguan	12	0.03
Panamanian	8	0.02
Salvadoran	21	0.05
Cuban	262	0.67
Dominican Republic	17	0.04
Mexican	912	2.32
Puerto Rican	362	0.92
South American:	285	0.72
Argentinean	33	0.08
Bolivian	6	0.02
Chilean	10	0.03
Colombian	106	0.27
Ecuadorian	14	0.04
Paraguayan	8	0.02
Peruvian	51	0.13
Uruguayan	7	0.02
Venezuelan	39	0.10
Other South American	11	0.03
Other Hispanic or Latino	542	1.38
Hungarian	547	1.39
Icelander	8	0.02
Iranian	6	0.02
Irish	7,303	18.58
Israeli	7	0.02
Italian	6,586	16.75
Latvian	65	0.17
Lithuanian	310	0.79
Luxemburger	8	0.02
Macedonian	10	0.03
Maltese	12	0.03
New Zealander	15	0.04
Northern European	13	0.03
Norwegian	473	1.20
Pennsylvania German	14	0.04
Polish	1,922	4.89
Portuguese	230	0.59
Romanian	127	0.32
Russian	1,088	2.77
Scandinavian	31	0.08
Scotch-Irish	700	1.78
Scottish	1,105	2.81
Serbian	15	0.04
Slovak	120	0.31
Slovene	20	0.05
Swedish	424	1.08
Swiss	181	0.46
Turkish	32	0.08
Ukrainian	223	0.57
United States or American	1,942	4.94
Welsh	323	0.82
West Indian, excl. Hispanic:	198	0.50
Bahamian	16	0.04
Jamaican	157	0.40
Trinidadian and Tobagonian	10	0.03
West Indian	6	0.02
Other West Indian	9	0.02
White:	37,690	95.84
Not Hispanic (35,152)	35,402	90.02
Hispanic (2,155)	2,288	5.82
Yugoslavian	141	0.36

Kendale Lakes

Place Type: Census Designated Place
County: Miami-Dade
Population: 56,901

Ancestry/Race	Number	%
African American/Black:	1,569	2.76
Not Hispanic (997)	1,112	1.95
Hispanic (315)	457	0.80
African, sub-Saharan:	56	0.10
African	16	0.03
Ethiopian	11	0.02
Sierra Leonean	29	0.05
Am. Ind. or Alaska Nat., not spec.	72	0.13
Albanian	8	0.01
American Indian tribes, specified:	63	0.11
Apache	1	0.00
Cherokee	3	0.01
Chippewa (5)	6	0.01
Comanche	1	0.00
Creek	1	0.00
Iroquois	1	0.00
Latin American Indians (15)	38	0.07
Lumbee (1)	2	0.00
Navajo (1)	2	0.00
Pueblo	3	0.01
All other tribes (4)	5	0.01
American Indian tribes, not spec.	15	0.03
Arab:	207	0.36
Arab/Arabic	12	0.02
Egyptian	22	0.04
Lebanese	137	0.24
Syrian	27	0.05
Other Arab	9	0.02
Armenian	57	0.10
Asian:	1,428	2.51
Bangladeshi (5)	5	0.01
Cambodian (2)	2	0.00
Chinese, ex. Taiwanese (455)	561	0.99
Filipino (94)	121	0.21
Indian (266)	351	0.62
Indonesian	2	0.00
Japanese (36)	62	0.11
Korean (13)	21	0.04
Laotian (1)	2	0.00
Pakistani (94)	158	0.28
Sri Lankan (5)	5	0.01
Taiwanese (11)	13	0.02
Thai (7)	7	0.01
Vietnamese (36)	52	0.09
Other Asian, not specified (25)	66	0.12
Austrian	169	0.30
Belgian	35	0.06
Brazilian	215	0.38
British	182	0.32
Canadian	43	0.08
Czech	20	0.04
Czechoslovakian	9	0.02
Danish	44	0.08
Dutch	88	0.15
Eastern European	6	0.01
English	978	1.72
European	191	0.34
Finnish	16	0.03
French, except Basque	590	1.04
French Canadian	95	0.17
German	1,017	1.79
Greek	62	0.11
Guyanese	27	0.05
Hawaii Native/Pacific Islander:	30	0.05
Polynesian: (2)	6	0.01
Native Hawaiian	3	0.01
Samoan (2)	3	0.01
Other Pac. Isl., not spec. (12)	24	0.04
Hispanic or Latino:	43,574	76.58
Central American:	3,640	6.40
Costa Rican	108	0.19
Guatemalan	143	0.25
Honduran	284	0.50
Nicaraguan	2,612	4.59
Panamanian	221	0.39
Salvadoran	182	0.32
Other Central American	90	0.16
Cuban	21,953	38.58
Dominican Republic	858	1.51
Mexican	573	1.01
Puerto Rican	1,995	3.51
South American:	7,076	12.44
Argentinean	346	0.61
Bolivian	96	0.17
Chilean	381	0.67
Colombian	3,619	6.36
Ecuadorian	372	0.65
Paraguayan	7	0.01
Peruvian	1,157	2.03
Uruguayan	100	0.18
Venezuelan	875	1.54
Other South American	123	0.22
Other Hispanic or Latino	7,479	13.14
Hungarian	76	0.13
Iranian	25	0.04
Irish	954	1.68
Israeli	9	0.02
Italian	1,298	2.28
Latvian	28	0.05
Lithuanian	50	0.09
Norwegian	56	0.10

Notes: 1. Figures in the "Number" column do not add up to the total population due to: a) Ancestry/Race overlap — e.g. persons can report being both White and Irish, b) persons of Hispanic origin can report being any race, c) persons reporting two ancestries are counted in both categories. 2. Numbers in parentheses indicate the number of persons reporting this ancestry/race alone, not in combination with any other ancestry/race. 3. Refer to the User's Guide in the front of the book for more detailed information.

Pennsylvania German	11	0.02
Polish	340	0.60
Portuguese	39	0.07
Romanian	39	0.07
Russian	559	0.98
Scotch-Irish	187	0.33
Scottish	118	0.21
Slavic	22	0.04
Slovak	16	0.03
Swedish	130	0.23
Ukrainian	27	0.05
United States or American	1,614	2.84
Welsh	180	0.32
West Indian, excl. Hispanic:	1,216	2.14
Bahamian	22	0.04
British West Indian	18	0.03
Dutch West Indian	40	0.07
Haitian	644	1.13
Jamaican	440	0.77
Trinidadian and Tobagonian	17	0.03
West Indian	35	0.06
White:	51,341	90.23
Not Hispanic (10,765)	11,092	19.49
Hispanic (38,727)	40,249	70.74
Yugoslavian	10	0.02

Kendall

Place Type: Census Designated Place
County: Miami-Dade
Population: 75,226

Ancestry/Race	Number	%
Acadian/Cajun	14	0.02
African American/Black:	3,906	5.19
Not Hispanic (3,030)	3,404	4.53
Hispanic (318)	502	0.67
African, sub-Saharan:	113	0.15
African	52	0.07
Ghanian	15	0.02
Nigerian	28	0.04
Other sub-Saharan African	18	0.02
Alaska Native tribes, specified:	2	0.00
Aleut (1)	1	0.00
Eskimo (1)	1	0.00
Am. Ind. or Alaska Nat., not spec.	110	0.15
Albanian	18	0.02
Alsatian	10	0.01
American Indian tribes, specified:	131	0.17
Apache (3)	4	0.01
Blackfeet	6	0.01
Cherokee (9)	32	0.04
Choctaw (1)	1	0.00
Creek	2	0.00
Iroquois (1)	1	0.00
Latin American Indians (19)	66	0.09
Navajo (1)	1	0.00
Pueblo	2	0.00
Seminole (3)	4	0.01
Sioux (1)	2	0.00
All other tribes (7)	10	0.01
American Indian tribes, not spec.	10	0.01
Arab:	1,315	1.75
Arab/Arabic	41	0.05
Egyptian	60	0.08
Lebanese	755	1.00
Moroccan	24	0.03
Palestinian	52	0.07
Syrian	335	0.45
Other Arab	48	0.06
Armenian	46	0.06
Asian:	2,810	3.74
Chinese, ex. Taiwanese (796)	990	1.32
Filipino (196)	253	0.34
Indian (597)	714	0.95
Indonesian (5)	10	0.01
Japanese (162)	196	0.26
Korean (162)	176	0.23
Laotian (7)	8	0.01
Malaysian (2)	7	0.01
Pakistani (112)	153	0.20
Sri Lankan (4)	4	0.01
Taiwanese (8)	11	0.01
Thai (43)	51	0.07
Vietnamese (87)	105	0.14
Other Asian, specified (9)	10	0.01
Other Asian, not specified (25)	122	0.16
Australian	21	0.03
Austrian	451	0.60
Basque	69	0.09
Belgian	55	0.07
Brazilian	680	0.90
British	312	0.41
Bulgarian	25	0.03
Canadian	229	0.30
Celtic	17	0.02
Croatian	52	0.07
Czech	204	0.27
Czechoslovakian	65	0.09
Danish	110	0.15
Dutch	503	0.67
Eastern European	316	0.42
English	3,469	4.61
European	450	0.60
Finnish	73	0.10
French, except Basque	1,363	1.81
French Canadian	240	0.32
German	4,256	5.65
Greek	256	0.34
Guyanese	42	0.06
Hawaii Native/Pacific Islander:	81	0.11
Melanesian: (3)	3	0.00
Fijian (3)	3	0.00
Micronesian: (3)	4	0.01
Guamanian/Chamorro (3)	4	0.01
Polynesian: (9)	22	0.03
Native Hawaiian (6)	16	0.02
Samoan (2)	3	0.00
Other Polynesian (1)	3	0.00
Other Pac. Isl., specified	1	0.00
Other Pac. Isl., not spec. (6)	51	0.07
Hispanic or Latino:	37,549	49.91
Central American:	3,310	4.40
Costa Rican	171	0.23
Guatemalan	199	0.26
Honduran	387	0.51
Nicaraguan	1,869	2.48
Panamanian	268	0.36
Salvadoran	337	0.45
Other Central American	79	0.11
Cuban	16,029	21.31
Dominican Republic	821	1.09
Mexican	582	0.77
Puerto Rican	2,298	3.05
South American:	7,961	10.58
Argentinean	605	0.80
Bolivian	170	0.23
Chilean	479	0.64
Colombian	3,429	4.56
Ecuadorian	415	0.55
Paraguayan	31	0.04
Peruvian	1,512	2.01
Uruguayan	65	0.09
Venezuelan	1,108	1.47
Other South American	147	0.20
Other Hispanic or Latino	6,548	8.70
Hungarian	575	0.76
Icelander	22	0.03
Iranian	167	0.22
Irish	3,776	5.02
Israeli	65	0.09
Italian	3,842	5.10
Latvian	39	0.05
Lithuanian	175	0.23
Macedonian	4	0.01
Northern European	50	0.07
Norwegian	383	0.51
Pennsylvania German	19	0.03
Polish	1,583	2.10
Portuguese	489	0.65
Romanian	230	0.31
Russian	2,409	3.20
Scandinavian	64	0.09
Scotch-Irish	566	0.75
Scottish	593	0.79
Serbian	14	0.02
Slavic	65	0.09
Slovak	83	0.11
Swedish	624	0.83
Swiss	199	0.26
Turkish	56	0.07
Ukrainian	205	0.27
United States or American	4,036	5.36
Welsh	221	0.29
West Indian, excl. Hispanic:	2,298	3.05
Bahamian	51	0.07
Barbadian	27	0.04
Belizean	16	0.02
British West Indian	32	0.04
Haitian	974	1.29
Jamaican	894	1.19
Trinidadian and Tobagonian	205	0.27
U.S. Virgin Islander	10	0.01
West Indian	81	0.11
Other West Indian	8	0.01
White:	66,968	89.02
Not Hispanic (31,270)	31,885	42.39
Hispanic (33,785)	35,083	46.64
Yugoslavian	64	0.09

Kendall West

Place Type: Census Designated Place
County: Miami-Dade
Population: 38,034

Ancestry/Race	Number	%
African American/Black:	1,877	4.94
Not Hispanic (1,232)	1,372	3.61
Hispanic (377)	505	1.33
African, sub-Saharan:	82	0.22
African	30	0.08
Nigerian	47	0.12
South African	5	0.01
Am. Ind. or Alaska Nat., not spec.	87	0.23
American Indian tribes, specified:	56	0.15
Blackfeet (1)	1	0.00
Cherokee (3)	12	0.03
Choctaw (3)	3	0.01
Cree	1	0.00
Latin American Indians (15)	33	0.09
Lumbee (2)	2	0.01
Pueblo (1)	2	0.01
Seminole	1	0.00
All other tribes	1	0.00
American Indian tribes, not spec.	13	0.03
Arab:	131	0.35
Arab/Arabic	27	0.07
Egyptian	22	0.06
Lebanese	82	0.22
Armenian	18	0.05
Asian:	757	1.99
Chinese, ex. Taiwanese (190)	251	0.66
Filipino (111)	138	0.36
Hmong	1	0.00
Indian (144)	198	0.52
Indonesian (1)	1	0.00
Japanese (19)	28	0.07
Korean (13)	13	0.03
Pakistani (14)	44	0.12
Sri Lankan (1)	5	0.01
Taiwanese (11)	11	0.03
Thai (18)	19	0.05
Vietnamese (11)	18	0.05
Other Asian, specified	1	0.00
Other Asian, not specified (4)	29	0.08
Austrian	16	0.04
Basque	31	0.08
Brazilian	137	0.36
British	52	0.14
Canadian	16	0.04
Croatian	6	0.02
Czech	10	0.03
Czechoslovakian	13	0.03
Danish	34	0.09

Notes: 1. Figures in the "Number" column do not add up to the total population due to: a) Ancestry/Race overlap — e.g. persons can report being both White and Irish, b) persons of Hispanic origin can report being any race, c) persons reporting two ancestries are counted in both categories. 2. Numbers in parentheses indicate the number of persons reporting this ancestry/race alone, not in combination with any other ancestry/race. 3. Refer to the User's Guide in the front of the book for more detailed information.

Dutch	33	0.09
English	448	1.18
European	124	0.33
Finnish	12	0.03
French, except Basque	171	0.45
French Canadian	42	0.11
German	604	1.59
German Russian	8	0.02
Greek	38	0.10
Guyanese	38	0.10
Hawaii Native/Pacific Islander:	35	0.09
Polynesian: (1)	3	0.01
Native Hawaiian (1)	1	0.00
Samoan	2	0.01
Other Pac. Isl., not spec. (12)	32	0.08
Hispanic or Latino:	30,060	79.03
Central American:	2,511	6.60
Costa Rican	105	0.28
Guatemalan	84	0.22
Honduran	259	0.68
Nicaraguan	1,670	4.39
Panamanian	143	0.38
Salvadoran	200	0.53
Other Central American	50	0.13
Cuban	11,092	29.16
Dominican Republic	982	2.58
Mexican	445	1.17
Puerto Rican	2,142	5.63
South American:	7,073	18.60
Argentinean	294	0.77
Bolivian	79	0.21
Chilean	249	0.65
Colombian	3,778	9.93
Ecuadorian	417	1.10
Paraguayan	6	0.02
Peruvian	1,084	2.85
Uruguayan	48	0.13
Venezuelan	1,015	2.67
Other South American	103	0.27
Other Hispanic or Latino	5,815	15.29
Hungarian	8	0.02
Irish	396	1.04
Israeli	26	0.07
Italian	802	2.11
Latvian	22	0.06
Lithuanian	5	0.01
Norwegian	15	0.04
Pennsylvania German	22	0.06
Polish	198	0.52
Portuguese	44	0.12
Romanian	4	0.01
Russian	156	0.41
Scandinavian	6	0.02
Scotch-Irish	64	0.17
Scottish	111	0.29
Swedish	39	0.10
Ukrainian	26	0.07
United States or American	944	2.49
Welsh	33	0.09
West Indian, excl. Hispanic:	948	2.50
Bahamian	9	0.02
Belizean	18	0.05
British West Indian	44	0.12
Haitian	336	0.89
Jamaican	389	1.02
Trinidadian and Tobagonian	59	0.16
West Indian	79	0.21
Other West Indian	14	0.04
White:	33,110	87.05
Not Hispanic (5,812)	5,969	15.69
Hispanic (25,896)	27,141	71.36
Yugoslavian	10	0.03

Key Biscayne

Place Type: Village
County: Miami-Dade
Population: 10,507

Ancestry/Race	Number	%
African American/Black:	65	0.62
Not Hispanic (28)	42	0.40
Hispanic (20)	23	0.22
African, sub-Saharan:	17	0.16
African	8	0.08
South African	9	0.09
Am. Ind. or Alaska Nat., not spec.	8	0.08
American Indian tribes, specified:	13	0.12
Cherokee (2)	4	0.04
Latin American Indians (4)	7	0.07
Pueblo	1	0.01
Sioux (1)	1	0.01
American Indian tribes, not spec.	5	0.05
Arab:	127	1.21
Arab/Arabic	16	0.15
Egyptian	25	0.24
Iraqi	3	0.03
Lebanese	63	0.60
Syrian	20	0.19
Asian:	135	1.28
Chinese, ex. Taiwanese (28)	38	0.36
Filipino (10)	14	0.13
Indian (27)	37	0.35
Indonesian (1)	1	0.01
Japanese (22)	34	0.32
Pakistani (1)	1	0.01
Sri Lankan (1)	1	0.01
Vietnamese (4)	5	0.05
Other Asian, not specified (2)	4	0.04
Australian	35	0.33
Austrian	74	0.71
Basque	35	0.33
Belgian	33	0.31
Brazilian	180	1.72
British	96	0.92
Canadian	69	0.66
Celtic	8	0.08
Croatian	20	0.19
Czech	41	0.39
Czechoslovakian	18	0.17
Danish	23	0.22
Dutch	163	1.56
English	722	6.89
European	124	1.18
Finnish	7	0.07
French, except Basque	483	4.61
French Canadian	62	0.59
German	985	9.40
Greek	88	0.84
Hawaii Native/Pacific Islander:	3	0.03
Polynesian:	3	0.03
Native Hawaiian	2	0.02
Other Polynesian	1	0.01
Hispanic or Latino:	5,231	49.79
Central American:	303	2.88
Costa Rican	30	0.29
Guatemalan	35	0.33
Honduran	32	0.30
Nicaraguan	107	1.02
Panamanian	15	0.14
Salvadoran	67	0.64
Other Central American	17	0.16
Cuban	1,632	15.53
Dominican Republic	12	0.11
Mexican	193	1.84
Puerto Rican	116	1.10
South American:	1,793	17.06
Argentinean	282	2.68
Bolivian	27	0.26
Chilean	76	0.72
Colombian	743	7.07
Ecuadorian	102	0.97
Paraguayan	13	0.12
Peruvian	261	2.48
Uruguayan	6	0.06
Venezuelan	248	2.36
Other South American	35	0.33
Other Hispanic or Latino	1,182	11.25
Hungarian	70	0.67
Icelander	9	0.09
Iranian	20	0.19
Irish	504	4.81
Israeli	7	0.07
Italian	626	5.97
Lithuanian	12	0.11
Norwegian	32	0.31
Polish	120	1.15
Portuguese	67	0.64
Romanian	11	0.10
Russian	285	2.72
Scotch-Irish	82	0.78
Scottish	183	1.75
Slovak	12	0.11
Slovene	10	0.10
Swedish	160	1.53
Swiss	104	0.99
Turkish	26	0.25
United States or American	421	4.02
Welsh	26	0.25
West Indian, excl. Hispanic:	67	0.64
Jamaican	67	0.64
White:	10,182	96.91
Not Hispanic (5,058)	5,122	48.75
Hispanic (4,972)	5,060	48.16
Yugoslavian	7	0.07

Key Largo

Place Type: Census Designated Place
County: Monroe
Population: 11,886

Ancestry/Race	Number	%
African American/Black:	278	2.34
Not Hispanic (227)	238	2.00
Hispanic (16)	40	0.34
African, sub-Saharan:	24	0.20
African	24	0.20
Am. Ind. or Alaska Nat., not spec.	34	0.29
American Indian tribes, specified:	54	0.45
Apache	1	0.01
Blackfeet (1)	8	0.07
Cherokee (7)	23	0.19
Chippewa	1	0.01
Choctaw (3)	3	0.03
Comanche (1)	1	0.01
Creek	1	0.01
Iroquois (2)	5	0.04
Latin American Indians (2)	4	0.03
Lumbee (1)	1	0.01
Sioux	2	0.02
All other tribes (3)	4	0.03
American Indian tribes, not spec.	11	0.09
Arab:	16	0.13
Lebanese	16	0.13
Armenian	39	0.33
Asian:	86	0.72
Chinese, ex. Taiwanese (15)	21	0.18
Filipino (3)	9	0.08
Indian (13)	13	0.11
Indonesian (2)	2	0.02
Japanese (3)	6	0.05
Korean (6)	7	0.06
Thai (4)	5	0.04
Vietnamese (2)	3	0.03
Other Asian, specified (6)	8	0.07
Other Asian, not specified (2)	12	0.10
Austrian	30	0.25
Belgian	9	0.08
British	77	0.64
Canadian	118	0.98
Czech	72	0.60
Czechoslovakian	46	0.38
Danish	44	0.37
Dutch	266	2.22
Eastern European	9	0.08
English	1,723	14.38
European	147	1.23
Finnish	37	0.31
French, except Basque	606	5.06
French Canadian	79	0.66
German	2,273	18.97
Greek	60	0.50

Notes: 1. Figures in the "Number" column do not add up to the total population due to: a) Ancestry/Race overlap — e.g. persons can report being both White and Irish, b) persons of Hispanic origin can report being any race, c) persons reporting two ancestries are counted in both categories. 2. Numbers in parentheses indicate the number of persons reporting this ancestry/race alone, not in combination with any other ancestry/race. 3. Refer to the User's Guide in the front of the book for more detailed information.

Hawaii Native/Pacific Islander:	4	0.03
Micronesian:	1	0.01
Guamanian/Chamorro	1	0.01
Other Pac. Isl., not spec.	3	0.03
Hispanic or Latino:	1,979	16.65
Central American:	99	0.83
Costa Rican	23	0.19
Guatemalan	9	0.08
Honduran	27	0.23
Nicaraguan	18	0.15
Panamanian	2	0.02
Salvadoran	20	0.17
Cuban	1,160	9.76
Dominican Republic	10	0.08
Mexican	444	3.74
Puerto Rican	91	0.77
South American:	93	0.78
Argentinean	1	0.01
Bolivian	4	0.03
Chilean	5	0.04
Colombian	59	0.50
Ecuadorian	2	0.02
Paraguayan	1	0.01
Peruvian	14	0.12
Uruguayan	1	0.01
Venezuelan	6	0.05
Other Hispanic or Latino	82	0.69
Hungarian	49	0.41
Irish	1,588	13.26
Italian	1,013	8.46
Lithuanian	51	0.43
Maltese	5	0.04
Norwegian	96	0.80
Polish	428	3.57
Portuguese	14	0.12
Romanian	39	0.33
Russian	30	0.25
Scandinavian	17	0.14
Scotch-Irish	257	2.15
Scottish	337	2.81
Serbian	20	0.17
Slavic	8	0.07
Slovak	17	0.14
Slovene	10	0.08
Swedish	197	1.64
Swiss	59	0.49
Ukrainian	12	0.10
United States or American	967	8.07
Welsh	77	0.64
West Indian, excl. Hispanic:	53	0.44
Bahamian	17	0.14
Jamaican	19	0.16
West Indian	17	0.14
White:	11,407	95.97
Not Hispanic (9,446)	9,564	80.46
Hispanic (1,772)	1,843	15.51

Key West

Place Type: City
County: Monroe
Population: 25,478

Ancestry/Race	Number	%
Acadian/Cajun	12	0.05
African American/Black:	2,552	10.02
Not Hispanic (2,237)	2,381	9.35
Hispanic (128)	171	0.67
African, sub-Saharan:	104	0.41
African	71	0.28
Nigerian	18	0.07
South African	8	0.03
Other sub-Saharan African	7	0.03
Alaska Native tribes, specified:	1	0.00
Eskimo (1)	1	0.00
Alaska Native tribes, not specified	1	0.00
Am. Ind. or Alaska Nat., not spec.	68	0.27
American Indian tribes, specified:	132	0.52
Apache (1)	1	0.00
Blackfeet (1)	6	0.02
Cherokee (22)	43	0.17
Cheyenne	1	0.00
Chippewa (5)	6	0.02
Choctaw (5)	6	0.02
Comanche	3	0.01
Cree	1	0.00
Creek (2)	3	0.01
Delaware (1)	2	0.01
Iroquois (2)	6	0.02
Latin American Indians (8)	17	0.07
Navajo	1	0.00
Ottawa (1)	1	0.00
Seminole (1)	4	0.02
Sioux (1)	7	0.03
All other tribes (12)	24	0.09
American Indian tribes, not spec.	12	0.05
Arab:	124	0.49
Egyptian	16	0.06
Lebanese	83	0.33
Moroccan	12	0.05
Syrian	13	0.05
Armenian	93	0.36
Asian:	458	1.80
Bangladeshi	11	0.04
Cambodian (2)	2	0.01
Chinese, ex. Taiwanese (54)	68	0.27
Filipino (92)	135	0.53
Indian (66)	87	0.34
Japanese (35)	49	0.19
Korean (26)	35	0.14
Laotian (1)	1	0.00
Malaysian (1)	5	0.02
Pakistani	1	0.00
Sri Lankan (2)	3	0.01
Taiwanese (7)	7	0.03
Thai (6)	12	0.05
Vietnamese (7)	12	0.05
Other Asian, specified (13)	14	0.05
Other Asian, not specified (8)	16	0.06
Austrian	127	0.50
Belgian	15	0.06
British	107	0.42
Bulgarian	10	0.04
Canadian	55	0.22
Celtic	16	0.06
Czech	170	0.67
Czechoslovakian	92	0.36
Danish	66	0.26
Dutch	276	1.08
Eastern European	10	0.04
English	3,158	12.39
European	196	0.77
Finnish	23	0.09
French, except Basque	927	3.64
French Canadian	361	1.42
German	3,106	12.19
Greek	198	0.78
Guyanese	9	0.04
Hawaii Native/Pacific Islander:	31	0.12
Melanesian: (1)	1	0.00
Fijian (1)	1	0.00
Micronesian: (6)	7	0.03
Guamanian/Chamorro (2)	3	0.01
Other Micronesian (4)	4	0.02
Polynesian: (5)	15	0.06
Native Hawaiian (4)	13	0.05
Samoan (1)	2	0.01
Other Pac. Isl., specified	1	0.00
Other Pac. Isl., not spec. (2)	7	0.03
Hispanic or Latino:	4,215	16.54
Central American:	459	1.80
Costa Rican	33	0.13
Guatemalan	34	0.13
Honduran	21	0.08
Nicaraguan	311	1.22
Panamanian	28	0.11
Salvadoran	29	0.11
Other Central American	3	0.01
Cuban	1,977	7.76
Dominican Republic	23	0.09
Mexican	371	1.46
Puerto Rican	284	1.11
South American:	168	0.66
Argentinean	26	0.10
Bolivian	12	0.05
Chilean	5	0.02
Colombian	59	0.23
Ecuadorian	6	0.02
Peruvian	35	0.14
Uruguayan	2	0.01
Venezuelan	20	0.08
Other South American	3	0.01
Other Hispanic or Latino	933	3.66
Hungarian	110	0.43
Iranian	13	0.05
Irish	2,869	11.26
Israeli	52	0.20
Italian	1,730	6.79
Latvian	6	0.02
Lithuanian	92	0.36
Luxemburger	16	0.06
New Zealander	12	0.05
Northern European	49	0.19
Norwegian	229	0.90
Pennsylvania German	49	0.19
Polish	890	3.49
Portuguese	80	0.31
Romanian	19	0.07
Russian	283	1.11
Scandinavian	26	0.10
Scotch-Irish	465	1.82
Scottish	700	2.75
Slavic	16	0.06
Slovak	136	0.53
Swedish	404	1.59
Swiss	109	0.43
Turkish	10	0.04
Ukrainian	126	0.49
United States or American	1,522	5.97
Welsh	159	0.62
West Indian, excl. Hispanic:	580	2.28
Bahamian	269	1.06
Barbadian	8	0.03
British West Indian	30	0.12
Haitian	130	0.51
Jamaican	100	0.39
Trinidadian and Tobagonian	9	0.04
West Indian	34	0.13
White:	22,084	86.68
Not Hispanic (18,195)	18,482	72.54
Hispanic (3,447)	3,602	14.14
Yugoslavian	28	0.11

Keystone

Place Type: Census Designated Place
County: Hillsborough
Population: 14,627

Ancestry/Race	Number	%
African American/Black:	562	3.84
Not Hispanic (489)	528	3.61
Hispanic (23)	34	0.23
African, sub-Saharan:	6	0.04
African	6	0.04
Am. Ind. or Alaska Nat., not spec.	33	0.23
American Indian tribes, specified:	62	0.42
Cherokee (11)	37	0.25
Chickasaw (3)	3	0.02
Chippewa (3)	4	0.03
Creek (2)	2	0.01
Iroquois (1)	1	0.01
Latin American Indians (5)	5	0.03
Sioux (1)	3	0.02
All other tribes (7)	7	0.05
American Indian tribes, not spec.	9	0.06
Arab:	26	0.18
Egyptian	7	0.05
Palestinian	6	0.04
Syrian	13	0.09
Asian:	439	3.00
Chinese, ex. Taiwanese (43)	62	0.42
Filipino (52)	72	0.49
Indian (141)	143	0.98

Notes: 1. Figures in the "Number" column do not add up to the total population due to: a) Ancestry/Race overlap — e.g. persons can report being both White and Irish, b) persons of Hispanic origin can report being any race, c) persons reporting two ancestries are counted in both categories. 2. Numbers in parentheses indicate the number of persons reporting this ancestry/race alone, not in combination with any other ancestry/race. 3. Refer to the User's Guide in the front of the book for more detailed information.

Indonesian	3	0.02
Japanese (6)	18	0.12
Korean (58)	68	0.46
Malaysian	1	0.01
Sri Lankan (1)	1	0.01
Taiwanese (12)	12	0.08
Thai (6)	8	0.05
Vietnamese (29)	31	0.21
Other Asian, specified (1)	3	0.02
Other Asian, not specified (4)	17	0.12
Australian	7	0.05
Austrian	69	0.47
Belgian	30	0.20
Brazilian	36	0.24
British	54	0.37
Canadian	54	0.37
Croatian	9	0.06
Czech	46	0.31
Czechoslovakian	6	0.04
Danish	82	0.56
Dutch	241	1.64
Eastern European	74	0.50
English	2,191	14.88
European	79	0.54
French, except Basque	397	2.70
French Canadian	139	0.94
German	3,009	20.43
Greek	213	1.45
Hawaii Native/Pacific Islander:	17	0.12
Micronesian: (7)	9	0.06
Guamanian/Chamorro (7)	9	0.06
Polynesian:	6	0.04
Native Hawaiian	6	0.04
Other Pac. Isl., not spec.	2	0.01
Hispanic or Latino:	1,240	8.48
Central American:	31	0.21
Costa Rican	5	0.03
Honduran	8	0.05
Nicaraguan	3	0.02
Panamanian	4	0.03
Salvadoran	8	0.05
Other Central American	3	0.02
Cuban	288	1.97
Dominican Republic	16	0.11
Mexican	78	0.53
Puerto Rican	342	2.34
South American:	137	0.94
Argentinean	13	0.09
Bolivian	1	0.01
Chilean	4	0.03
Colombian	69	0.47
Ecuadorian	16	0.11
Paraguayan	4	0.03
Peruvian	7	0.05
Venezuelan	8	0.05
Other South American	15	0.10
Other Hispanic or Latino	348	2.38
Hungarian	117	0.79
Iranian	73	0.50
Irish	2,050	13.92
Italian	1,786	12.13
Lithuanian	51	0.35
Luxemburger	22	0.15
Norwegian	259	1.76
Polish	551	3.74
Portuguese	44	0.30
Romanian	26	0.18
Russian	158	1.07
Scandinavian	39	0.26
Scotch-Irish	224	1.52
Scottish	571	3.88
Serbian	20	0.14
Slovak	16	0.11
Swedish	223	1.51
Swiss	22	0.15
Ukrainian	53	0.36
United States or American	1,232	8.37
Welsh	142	0.96
West Indian, excl. Hispanic:	63	0.43
Belizean	14	0.10
Haitian	7	0.05
Jamaican	28	0.19
West Indian	7	0.05
Other West Indian	7	0.05
White:	13,528	92.49
Not Hispanic (12,328)	12,457	85.16
Hispanic (1,027)	1,071	7.32

Kings Point

Place Type: Census Designated Place
County: Palm Beach
Population: 12,207

Ancestry/Race	Number	%
African American/Black:	41	0.34
Not Hispanic (32)	40	0.33
Hispanic (1)	1	0.01
Alaska Native tribes, specified:	1	0.01
Eskimo (1)	1	0.01
Am. Ind. or Alaska Nat., not spec.	18	0.15
Albanian	22	0.18
Alsatian	6	0.05
American Indian tribes, specified:	1	0.01
Chippewa	1	0.01
American Indian tribes, not spec.	4	0.03
Arab:	6	0.05
Lebanese	6	0.05
Armenian	32	0.26
Asian:	35	0.29
Chinese, ex. Taiwanese (14)	16	0.13
Filipino	2	0.02
Indian (1)	3	0.02
Japanese (1)	1	0.01
Korean (2)	2	0.02
Thai (1)	1	0.01
Vietnamese (3)	3	0.02
Other Asian, specified	5	0.04
Other Asian, not specified	2	0.02
Austrian	420	3.39
Belgian	15	0.12
British	16	0.13
Canadian	16	0.13
Czech	34	0.27
Czechoslovakian	44	0.36
Danish	24	0.19
Dutch	16	0.13
Eastern European	23	0.19
English	202	1.63
Estonian	16	0.13
European	37	0.30
French, except Basque	13	0.10
French Canadian	15	0.12
German	424	3.42
Greek	74	0.60
Hawaii Native/Pacific Islander:	8	0.07
Micronesian: (1)	2	0.02
Guamanian/Chamorro (1)	2	0.02
Other Pac. Isl., specified	5	0.04
Other Pac. Isl., not spec.	1	0.01
Hispanic or Latino:	138	1.13
Central American:	1	0.01
Salvadoran	1	0.01
Cuban	16	0.13
Dominican Republic	2	0.02
Mexican	6	0.05
Puerto Rican	41	0.34
South American:	28	0.23
Argentinean	4	0.03
Chilean	5	0.04
Colombian	16	0.13
Ecuadorian	2	0.02
Other South American	1	0.01
Other Hispanic or Latino	44	0.36
Hungarian	341	2.75
Iranian	8	0.06
Irish	146	1.18
Israeli	12	0.10
Italian	886	7.15
Latvian	16	0.13
Lithuanian	93	0.75
Norwegian	17	0.14
Polish	1,345	10.86
Romanian	239	1.93
Russian	2,005	16.19
Scotch-Irish	9	0.07
Scottish	14	0.11
Slovak	8	0.06
Turkish	85	0.69
Ukrainian	138	1.11
United States or American	1,208	9.75
Welsh	18	0.15
White:	12,134	99.40
Not Hispanic (11,976)	12,007	98.36
Hispanic (121)	127	1.04

Kissimmee

Place Type: City
County: Osceola
Population: 47,814

Ancestry/Race	Number	%
Acadian/Cajun	16	0.03
African American/Black:	5,423	11.34
Not Hispanic (4,074)	4,411	9.23
Hispanic (701)	1,012	2.12
African, sub-Saharan:	293	0.62
African	191	0.40
Cape Verdean	56	0.12
Other sub-Saharan African	46	0.10
Am. Ind. or Alaska Nat., not spec.	227	0.47
Albanian	10	0.02
American Indian tribes, specified:	249	0.52
Apache (7)	11	0.02
Blackfeet (3)	7	0.01
Cherokee (17)	60	0.13
Cheyenne	1	0.00
Chippewa (2)	8	0.02
Choctaw (4)	11	0.02
Comanche (2)	2	0.00
Creek	3	0.01
Delaware	2	0.00
Houma (1)	1	0.00
Iroquois (3)	16	0.03
Latin American Indians (31)	70	0.15
Lumbee (3)	3	0.01
Menominee (3)	3	0.01
Navajo (4)	7	0.01
Osage (3)	3	0.01
Potawatomi (1)	1	0.00
Pueblo (1)	2	0.00
Puget Sound Salish (1)	1	0.00
Seminole (5)	9	0.02
Shoshone (1)	2	0.00
Sioux (1)	6	0.01
Yaqui (1)	1	0.00
All other tribes (13)	19	0.04
American Indian tribes, not spec.	11	0.02
Arab:	684	1.44
Arab/Arabic	201	0.42
Egyptian	12	0.03
Jordanian	6	0.01
Lebanese	111	0.23
Moroccan	249	0.52
Palestinian	7	0.01
Syrian	48	0.10
Other Arab	50	0.11
Armenian	11	0.02
Asian:	1,998	4.18
Bangladeshi (24)	44	0.09
Cambodian (3)	3	0.01
Chinese, ex. Taiwanese (226)	258	0.54
Filipino (374)	452	0.95
Indian (560)	640	1.34
Indonesian (2)	3	0.01
Japanese (26)	42	0.09
Korean (45)	65	0.14
Laotian (4)	7	0.01
Malaysian	1	0.00
Pakistani (112)	178	0.37
Sri Lankan (13)	13	0.03
Taiwanese (11)	17	0.04
Thai (24)	33	0.07

Notes: 1. Figures in the "Number" column do not add up to the total population due to: a) Ancestry/Race overlap — e.g. persons can report being both White and Irish, b) persons of Hispanic origin can report being any race, c) persons reporting two ancestries are counted in both categories. 2. Numbers in parentheses indicate the number of persons reporting this ancestry/race alone, not in combination with any other ancestry/race. 3. Refer to the User's Guide in the front of the book for more detailed information.

Vietnamese (103)	120	0.25
Other Asian, specified (2)	6	0.01
Other Asian, not specified (46)	116	0.24
Austrian	168	0.35
Brazilian	291	0.61
British	196	0.41
Canadian	156	0.33
Celtic	18	0.04
Croatian	15	0.03
Czech	241	0.51
Czechoslovakian	80	0.17
Danish	45	0.09
Dutch	393	0.83
English	2,984	6.27
Estonian	10	0.02
European	152	0.32
Finnish	59	0.12
French, except Basque	888	1.87
French Canadian	390	0.82
German	4,202	8.84
Greek	159	0.33
Guyanese	120	0.25
Hawaii Native/Pacific Islander:	132	0.28
Melanesian: (2)	4	0.01
Fijian (2)	4	0.01
Micronesian: (8)	19	0.04
Guamanian/Chamorro (5)	14	0.03
Other Micronesian (3)	5	0.01
Polynesian: (17)	38	0.08
Native Hawaiian (12)	25	0.05
Samoan (5)	13	0.03
Other Pac. Isl., specified	4	0.01
Other Pac. Isl., not spec. (19)	67	0.14
Hispanic or Latino:	19,954	41.73
Central American:	853	1.78
Costa Rican	69	0.14
Guatemalan	89	0.19
Honduran	141	0.29
Nicaraguan	148	0.31
Panamanian	91	0.19
Salvadoran	276	0.58
Other Central American	39	0.08
Cuban	817	1.71
Dominican Republic	964	2.02
Mexican	1,573	3.29
Puerto Rican	11,312	23.66
South American:	2,047	4.28
Argentinean	63	0.13
Bolivian	15	0.03
Chilean	54	0.11
Colombian	960	2.01
Ecuadorian	179	0.37
Paraguayan	3	0.01
Peruvian	250	0.52
Uruguayan	22	0.05
Venezuelan	454	0.95
Other South American	47	0.10
Other Hispanic or Latino	2,388	4.99
Hungarian	233	0.49
Iranian	25	0.05
Irish	3,393	7.13
Israeli	8	0.02
Italian	2,483	5.22
Lithuanian	28	0.06
Luxemburger	8	0.02
Northern European	16	0.03
Norwegian	145	0.30
Pennsylvania German	48	0.10
Polish	1,057	2.22
Portuguese	120	0.25
Romanian	6	0.01
Russian	321	0.67
Scandinavian	26	0.05
Scotch-Irish	376	0.79
Scottish	520	1.09
Serbian	12	0.03
Slavic	6	0.01
Slovak	63	0.13
Swedish	282	0.59
Swiss	19	0.04
Turkish	6	0.01
Ukrainian	134	0.28
United States or American	3,005	6.32
Welsh	176	0.37
West Indian, excl. Hispanic:	929	1.95
Bahamian	16	0.03
Barbadian	43	0.09
Belizean	6	0.01
British West Indian	87	0.18
Haitian	272	0.57
Jamaican	302	0.64
Trinidadian and Tobagonian	95	0.20
West Indian	108	0.23
White:	33,855	70.81
Not Hispanic (20,887)	21,564	45.10
Hispanic (11,252)	12,291	25.71
Yugoslavian	5	0.01

Lady Lake

Place Type: Town
County: Lake
Population: 11,828

Ancestry/Race	Number	%
African American/Black:	389	3.29
Not Hispanic (375)	380	3.21
Hispanic (8)	9	0.08
Alaska Native tribes, specified:	1	0.01
Aleut (1)	1	0.01
Am. Ind. or Alaska Nat., not spec.	19	0.16
American Indian tribes, specified:	44	0.37
Apache (1)	1	0.01
Blackfeet (2)	3	0.03
Cherokee (4)	20	0.17
Chickasaw	2	0.02
Chippewa (1)	3	0.03
Choctaw	4	0.03
Iroquois	3	0.03
Sioux	6	0.05
All other tribes (1)	2	0.02
American Indian tribes, not spec.	2	0.02
Arab:	17	0.15
Lebanese	8	0.07
Syrian	9	0.08
Asian:	44	0.37
Chinese, ex. Taiwanese (13)	18	0.15
Filipino (4)	6	0.05
Indian (4)	4	0.03
Japanese (9)	9	0.08
Korean (1)	1	0.01
Thai (4)	4	0.03
Vietnamese (1)	1	0.01
Other Asian, not specified	1	0.01
Austrian	18	0.15
Belgian	17	0.15
Brazilian	4	0.03
British	49	0.42
Bulgarian	8	0.07
Canadian	40	0.34
Croatian	34	0.29
Czech	49	0.42
Czechoslovakian	35	0.30
Danish	80	0.69
Dutch	302	2.59
English	2,130	18.24
European	8	0.07
Finnish	8	0.07
French, except Basque	640	5.48
French Canadian	182	1.56
German	2,232	19.11
Greek	27	0.23
Hawaii Native/Pacific Islander:	9	0.08
Polynesian: (5)	7	0.06
Native Hawaiian (4)	6	0.05
Samoan (1)	1	0.01
Other Pac. Isl., not spec. (2)	2	0.02
Hispanic or Latino:	217	1.83
Central American:	4	0.03
Panamanian	3	0.03
Other Central American	1	0.01
Cuban	9	0.08
Dominican Republic	5	0.04
Mexican	74	0.63
Puerto Rican	59	0.50
South American:	8	0.07
Chilean	1	0.01
Colombian	7	0.06
Other Hispanic or Latino	58	0.49
Hungarian	37	0.32
Irish	1,778	15.23
Italian	873	7.48
Latvian	8	0.07
Lithuanian	39	0.33
Maltese	8	0.07
Northern European	8	0.07
Norwegian	153	1.31
Polish	504	4.32
Portuguese	8	0.07
Romanian	16	0.14
Russian	74	0.63
Scandinavian	9	0.08
Scotch-Irish	298	2.55
Scottish	411	3.52
Serbian	9	0.08
Slavic	8	0.07
Slovak	49	0.42
Slovene	17	0.15
Swedish	168	1.44
Swiss	47	0.40
Ukrainian	40	0.34
United States or American	1,186	10.16
Welsh	187	1.60
West Indian, excl. Hispanic:	23	0.20
Jamaican	23	0.20
White:	11,328	95.77
Not Hispanic (11,116)	11,161	94.36
Hispanic (158)	167	1.41
Yugoslavian	7	0.06

Lake Magdalene

Place Type: Census Designated Place
County: Hillsborough
Population: 28,755

Ancestry/Race	Number	%
African American/Black:	1,873	6.51
Not Hispanic (1,598)	1,723	5.99
Hispanic (100)	150	0.52
African, sub-Saharan:	131	0.45
African	69	0.24
Nigerian	7	0.02
Sierra Leonean	8	0.03
South African	47	0.16
Alaska Native tribes, specified:	1	0.00
Tlingit-Haida	1	0.00
Am. Ind. or Alaska Nat., not spec.	70	0.24
American Indian tribes, specified:	127	0.44
Apache (1)	4	0.01
Blackfeet (1)	8	0.03
Cherokee (32)	72	0.25
Chickasaw (1)	3	0.01
Choctaw (3)	4	0.01
Creek (1)	3	0.01
Delaware	1	0.00
Iroquois (1)	4	0.01
Latin American Indians (5)	12	0.04
Lumbee	1	0.00
Navajo (1)	1	0.00
Pueblo (2)	2	0.01
Seminole (1)	1	0.00
Sioux	1	0.00
All other tribes (9)	10	0.03
American Indian tribes, not spec.	16	0.06
Arab:	436	1.51
Arab/Arabic	100	0.35
Egyptian	25	0.09
Jordanian	29	0.10
Lebanese	235	0.82
Moroccan	26	0.09
Syrian	21	0.07
Asian:	842	2.93
Chinese, ex. Taiwanese (91)	125	0.43

Notes: 1. Figures in the "Number" column do not add up to the total population due to: a) Ancestry/Race overlap — e.g. persons can report being both White and Irish, b) persons of Hispanic origin can report being any race, c) persons reporting two ancestries are counted in both categories. 2. Numbers in parentheses indicate the number of persons reporting this ancestry/race alone, not in combination with any other ancestry/race. 3. Refer to the User's Guide in the front of the book for more detailed information.

Filipino (131)	171	0.59
Indian (242)	262	0.91
Indonesian	2	0.01
Japanese (24)	56	0.19
Korean (48)	60	0.21
Laotian (7)	7	0.02
Malaysian (2)	3	0.01
Pakistani (5)	5	0.02
Taiwanese (1)	1	0.00
Thai (25)	32	0.11
Vietnamese (73)	78	0.27
Other Asian, specified (5)	6	0.02
Other Asian, not specified (13)	34	0.12
Austrian	124	0.43
Basque	8	0.03
Belgian	27	0.09
Brazilian	42	0.15
British	316	1.10
Bulgarian	7	0.02
Canadian	112	0.39
Croatian	14	0.05
Czech	199	0.69
Czechoslovakian	52	0.18
Danish	94	0.33
Dutch	504	1.75
Eastern European	30	0.10
English	3,437	11.92
European	294	1.02
Finnish	48	0.17
French, except Basque	917	3.18
French Canadian	227	0.79
German	4,343	15.06
Greek	269	0.93
Guyanese	8	0.03
Hawaii Native/Pacific Islander:	35	0.12
Melanesian: (1)	1	0.00
Other Melanesian (1)	1	0.00
Polynesian: (6)	11	0.04
Native Hawaiian (4)	9	0.03
Samoan (2)	2	0.01
Other Pac. Isl., specified	1	0.00
Other Pac. Isl., not spec. (2)	22	0.08
Hispanic or Latino:	3,886	13.51
Central American:	179	0.62
Costa Rican	24	0.08
Guatemalan	17	0.06
Honduran	61	0.21
Nicaraguan	24	0.08
Panamanian	35	0.12
Salvadoran	12	0.04
Other Central American	6	0.02
Cuban	665	2.31
Dominican Republic	63	0.22
Mexican	217	0.75
Puerto Rican	1,313	4.57
South American:	309	1.07
Argentinean	10	0.03
Bolivian	2	0.01
Chilean	2	0.01
Colombian	146	0.51
Ecuadorian	31	0.11
Peruvian	62	0.22
Uruguayan	4	0.01
Venezuelan	35	0.12
Other South American	17	0.06
Other Hispanic or Latino	1,140	3.96
Hungarian	200	0.69
Iranian	69	0.24
Irish	3,895	13.51
Italian	2,400	8.32
Latvian	6	0.02
Lithuanian	119	0.41
Northern European	30	0.10
Norwegian	268	0.93
Polish	736	2.55
Portuguese	55	0.19
Romanian	31	0.11
Russian	277	0.96
Scandinavian	18	0.06
Scotch-Irish	638	2.21
Scottish	656	2.28
Slavic	18	0.06
Slovak	98	0.34
Slovene	14	0.05
Soviet Union	7	0.02
Swedish	542	1.88
Swiss	55	0.19
Ukrainian	88	0.31
United States or American	2,370	8.22
Welsh	224	0.78
West Indian, excl. Hispanic:	432	1.50
Bahamian	58	0.20
Barbadian	6	0.02
British West Indian	11	0.04
Haitian	74	0.26
Jamaican	190	0.66
Trinidadian and Tobagonian	72	0.25
U.S. Virgin Islander	11	0.04
Other West Indian	10	0.03
White:	25,403	88.34
Not Hispanic (22,079)	22,407	77.92
Hispanic (2,836)	2,996	10.42
Yugoslavian	38	0.13

Lake Mary

Place Type: City
County: Seminole
Population: 11,458

Ancestry/Race	Number	%
Afghan	8	0.07
African American/Black:	469	4.09
Not Hispanic (396)	450	3.93
Hispanic (17)	19	0.17
African, sub-Saharan:	50	0.44
African	29	0.26
South African	9	0.08
Other sub-Saharan African	12	0.11
Am. Ind. or Alaska Nat., not spec.	22	0.19
American Indian tribes, specified:	50	0.44
Blackfeet (1)	1	0.01
Cherokee (4)	23	0.20
Choctaw (4)	5	0.04
Creek (1)	6	0.05
Latin American Indians (5)	8	0.07
Osage (1)	1	0.01
Seminole (3)	4	0.03
All other tribes (2)	2	0.02
Arab:	104	0.92
Egyptian	15	0.13
Lebanese	76	0.67
Palestinian	13	0.12
Armenian	132	1.17
Asian:	491	4.29
Cambodian (5)	10	0.09
Chinese, ex. Taiwanese (62)	73	0.64
Filipino (83)	95	0.83
Indian (124)	130	1.13
Indonesian (10)	10	0.09
Japanese (13)	19	0.17
Korean (55)	56	0.49
Laotian (1)	1	0.01
Pakistani (15)	15	0.13
Taiwanese (8)	8	0.07
Thai (7)	8	0.07
Vietnamese (48)	53	0.46
Other Asian, not specified (2)	13	0.11
Australian	38	0.34
Belgian	54	0.48
British	41	0.36
Canadian	32	0.28
Celtic	7	0.06
Czech	69	0.61
Czechoslovakian	29	0.26
Danish	30	0.27
Dutch	142	1.26
English	1,627	14.41
European	48	0.43
Finnish	5	0.04
French, except Basque	368	3.26
French Canadian	155	1.37
German	2,528	22.39
Greek	57	0.50
Guyanese	12	0.11
Hawaii Native/Pacific Islander:	15	0.13
Micronesian: (1)	1	0.01
Guamanian/Chamorro (1)	1	0.01
Polynesian: (5)	8	0.07
Native Hawaiian (4)	7	0.06
Samoan (1)	1	0.01
Other Pac. Isl., not spec. (4)	6	0.05
Hispanic or Latino:	713	6.22
Central American:	25	0.22
Costa Rican	3	0.03
Guatemalan	2	0.02
Honduran	1	0.01
Nicaraguan	1	0.01
Panamanian	11	0.10
Salvadoran	7	0.06
Cuban	58	0.51
Dominican Republic	11	0.10
Mexican	72	0.63
Puerto Rican	331	2.89
South American:	113	0.99
Argentinean	14	0.12
Bolivian	3	0.03
Chilean	1	0.01
Colombian	65	0.57
Ecuadorian	3	0.03
Peruvian	14	0.12
Venezuelan	6	0.05
Other South American	7	0.06
Other Hispanic or Latino	103	0.90
Hungarian	86	0.76
Iranian	33	0.29
Irish	1,575	13.95
Italian	1,143	10.12
Lithuanian	17	0.15
Luxemburger	9	0.08
Norwegian	184	1.63
Pennsylvania German	8	0.07
Polish	388	3.44
Portuguese	60	0.53
Romanian	22	0.19
Russian	186	1.65
Scotch-Irish	249	2.21
Scottish	323	2.86
Slovak	85	0.75
Swedish	83	0.74
Swiss	22	0.19
Ukrainian	63	0.56
United States or American	1,024	9.07
Welsh	64	0.57
West Indian, excl. Hispanic:	143	1.27
Bahamian	25	0.22
Bermudan	46	0.41
Haitian	38	0.34
Jamaican	34	0.30
White:	10,359	90.41
Not Hispanic (9,734)	9,827	85.77
Hispanic (502)	532	4.64
Yugoslavian	36	0.32

Lake Wales

Place Type: City
County: Polk
Population: 10,194

Ancestry/Race	Number	%
African American/Black:	3,610	35.41
Not Hispanic (3,492)	3,569	35.01
Hispanic (34)	41	0.40
African, sub-Saharan:	45	0.44
African	37	0.36
Cape Verdean	8	0.08
Am. Ind. or Alaska Nat., not spec.	14	0.14
American Indian tribes, specified:	42	0.41
Blackfeet	1	0.01
Cherokee (3)	19	0.19
Chippewa (1)	1	0.01
Choctaw	2	0.02
Creek (2)	3	0.03

Notes: 1. Figures in the "Number" column do not add up to the total population due to: a) Ancestry/Race overlap — e.g. persons can report being both White and Irish, b) persons of Hispanic origin can report being any race, c) persons reporting two ancestries are counted in both categories. 2. Numbers in parentheses indicate the number of persons reporting this ancestry/race alone, not in combination with any other ancestry/race. 3. Refer to the User's Guide in the front of the book for more detailed information.

Latin American Indians (2)	5	0.05
Navajo (1)	1	0.01
Potawatomi (1)	1	0.01
Seminole (6)	6	0.06
Sioux (1)	1	0.01
All other tribes (1)	2	0.02
American Indian tribes, not spec.	1	0.01
Arab:	38	0.37
Egyptian	38	0.37
Asian:	60	0.59
Chinese, ex. Taiwanese (4)	5	0.05
Filipino (7)	8	0.08
Indian (19)	19	0.19
Indonesian (1)	1	0.01
Japanese (5)	7	0.07
Korean (1)	1	0.01
Taiwanese (5)	5	0.05
Thai (3)	3	0.03
Vietnamese (6)	6	0.06
Other Asian, not specified (1)	5	0.05
Austrian	25	0.24
Belgian	20	0.19
British	45	0.44
Canadian	15	0.15
Celtic	10	0.10
Czech	26	0.25
Czechoslovakian	10	0.10
Danish	59	0.57
Dutch	175	1.70
English	888	8.62
Finnish	8	0.08
French, except Basque	246	2.39
French Canadian	24	0.23
German	806	7.82
Hawaii Native/Pacific Islander:	15	0.15
Micronesian: (7)	7	0.07
Guamanian/Chamorro (7)	7	0.07
Polynesian: (2)	3	0.03
Native Hawaiian	1	0.01
Samoan (2)	2	0.02
Other Pac. Isl., not spec. (1)	5	0.05
Hispanic or Latino:	1,014	9.95
Central American:	24	0.24
Guatemalan	5	0.05
Honduran	1	0.01
Nicaraguan	8	0.08
Panamanian	5	0.05
Salvadoran	4	0.04
Other Central American	1	0.01
Cuban	36	0.35
Dominican Republic	9	0.09
Mexican	575	5.64
Puerto Rican	237	2.32
South American:	31	0.30
Argentinean	2	0.02
Colombian	1	0.01
Ecuadorian	14	0.14
Peruvian	9	0.09
Uruguayan	2	0.02
Venezuelan	3	0.03
Other Hispanic or Latino	102	1.00
Hungarian	6	0.06
Irish	793	7.70
Italian	255	2.48
Lithuanian	8	0.08
Norwegian	100	0.97
Polish	199	1.93
Russian	43	0.42
Scotch-Irish	127	1.23
Scottish	95	0.92
Swedish	79	0.77
United States or American	1,149	11.15
Welsh	45	0.44
West Indian, excl. Hispanic:	92	0.89
Bahamian	11	0.11
Haitian	16	0.16
Jamaican	65	0.63
White:	6,157	60.40
Not Hispanic (5,484)	5,550	54.44
Hispanic (580)	607	5.95

Lake Worth Corridor

Place Type: Census Designated Place
County: Palm Beach
Population: 18,663

Ancestry/Race	Number	%
African American/Black:	2,936	15.73
Not Hispanic (2,378)	2,714	14.54
Hispanic (164)	222	1.19
African, sub-Saharan:	133	0.72
African	133	0.72
Am. Ind. or Alaska Nat., not spec.	66	0.35
Albanian	49	0.27
American Indian tribes, specified:	126	0.68
Blackfeet (1)	4	0.02
Cherokee (11)	28	0.15
Cheyenne (1)	1	0.01
Chippewa (4)	4	0.02
Choctaw	4	0.02
Crow (4)	4	0.02
Iroquois	3	0.02
Latin American Indians (35)	64	0.34
Lumbee (1)	1	0.01
Navajo (1)	1	0.01
Pima (1)	1	0.01
Pueblo	2	0.01
Seminole	1	0.01
Sioux (1)	2	0.01
All other tribes (2)	6	0.03
American Indian tribes, not spec.	18	0.10
Arab:	17	0.09
Egyptian	9	0.05
Lebanese	8	0.04
Asian:	304	1.63
Bangladeshi (25)	44	0.24
Chinese, ex. Taiwanese (19)	25	0.13
Filipino (16)	22	0.12
Indian (88)	112	0.60
Indonesian (3)	5	0.03
Japanese (5)	7	0.04
Korean (9)	9	0.05
Pakistani (11)	20	0.11
Sri Lankan (1)	1	0.01
Thai (5)	5	0.03
Vietnamese (14)	21	0.11
Other Asian, specified	1	0.01
Other Asian, not specified (17)	32	0.17
Austrian	72	0.39
Belgian	23	0.13
Brazilian	25	0.14
British	13	0.07
Canadian	38	0.21
Croatian	6	0.03
Czech	30	0.16
Czechoslovakian	23	0.13
Danish	42	0.23
Dutch	80	0.44
English	827	4.50
Estonian	8	0.04
European	15	0.08
Finnish	109	0.59
French, except Basque	524	2.85
French Canadian	110	0.60
German	1,495	8.13
Greek	38	0.21
Guyanese	26	0.14
Hawaii Native/Pacific Islander:	71	0.38
Micronesian: (7)	22	0.12
Guamanian/Chamorro (7)	21	0.11
Other Micronesian	1	0.01
Polynesian: (1)	7	0.04
Native Hawaiian	3	0.02
Samoan (1)	3	0.02
Other Polynesian	1	0.01
Other Pac. Isl., not spec. (6)	42	0.23
Hispanic or Latino:	7,613	40.79
Central American:	1,051	5.63
Costa Rican	21	0.11
Guatemalan	459	2.46
Honduran	216	1.16
Nicaraguan	97	0.52
Panamanian	10	0.05
Salvadoran	235	1.26
Other Central American	13	0.07
Cuban	608	3.26
Dominican Republic	180	0.96
Mexican	3,032	16.25
Puerto Rican	1,356	7.27
South American:	368	1.97
Argentinean	32	0.17
Bolivian	33	0.18
Chilean	14	0.08
Colombian	142	0.76
Ecuadorian	42	0.23
Paraguayan	3	0.02
Peruvian	52	0.28
Uruguayan	13	0.07
Venezuelan	31	0.17
Other South American	6	0.03
Other Hispanic or Latino	1,018	5.45
Hungarian	58	0.32
Irish	1,727	9.39
Israeli	11	0.06
Italian	966	5.25
Lithuanian	7	0.04
Norwegian	57	0.31
Pennsylvania German	25	0.14
Polish	338	1.84
Portuguese	32	0.17
Romanian	101	0.55
Russian	121	0.66
Scandinavian	10	0.05
Scotch-Irish	332	1.81
Scottish	115	0.63
Slavic	10	0.05
Slovak	18	0.10
Swedish	134	0.73
Swiss	4	0.02
Ukrainian	49	0.27
United States or American	918	4.99
Welsh	151	0.82
West Indian, excl. Hispanic:	989	5.38
Bahamian	87	0.47
Barbadian	23	0.13
Haitian	627	3.41
Jamaican	166	0.90
Trinidadian and Tobagonian	63	0.34
West Indian	23	0.13
White:	12,403	66.46
Not Hispanic (7,837)	8,028	43.02
Hispanic (3,976)	4,375	23.44

Lake Worth

Place Type: City
County: Palm Beach
Population: 35,133

Ancestry/Race	Number	%
African American/Black:	7,476	21.28
Not Hispanic (6,320)	7,106	20.23
Hispanic (307)	370	1.05
African, sub-Saharan:	59	0.17
African	48	0.14
Ethiopian	11	0.03
Alaska Native tribes, specified:	1	0.00
Tlingit-Haida	1	0.00
Am. Ind. or Alaska Nat., not spec.	84	0.24
American Indian tribes, specified:	412	1.17
Apache	1	0.00
Blackfeet	6	0.02
Cherokee (12)	33	0.09
Chickasaw (1)	1	0.00
Chippewa	1	0.00
Choctaw (1)	2	0.01
Cree	1	0.00
Creek (1)	3	0.01
Crow	3	0.01
Delaware	1	0.00
Iroquois (1)	4	0.01
Latin American Indians (181)	318	0.91
Lumbee (2)	3	0.01

Notes: 1. Figures in the "Number" column do not add up to the total population due to: a) Ancestry/Race overlap — e.g. persons can report being both White and Irish, b) persons of Hispanic origin can report being any race, c) persons reporting two ancestries are counted in both categories. 2. Numbers in parentheses indicate the number of persons reporting this ancestry/race alone, not in combination with any other ancestry/race. 3. Refer to the User's Guide in the front of the book for more detailed information.

Navajo (2)	2	0.01
Ottawa (1)	2	0.01
Paiute	1	0.00
Pueblo (6)	7	0.02
Sioux (3)	5	0.01
All other tribes (2)	18	0.05
American Indian tribes, not spec.	18	0.05
Arab:	149	0.42
Arab/Arabic	28	0.08
Egyptian	13	0.04
Lebanese	87	0.25
Palestinian	15	0.04
Other Arab	6	0.02
Armenian	40	0.11
Asian:	399	1.14
Bangladeshi (6)	6	0.02
Cambodian (2)	2	0.01
Chinese, ex. Taiwanese (29)	43	0.12
Filipino (43)	66	0.19
Indian (97)	144	0.41
Indonesian (10)	10	0.03
Japanese (4)	9	0.03
Korean (8)	11	0.03
Laotian (1)	3	0.01
Malaysian (2)	2	0.01
Pakistani	1	0.00
Taiwanese	1	0.00
Thai (13)	17	0.05
Vietnamese (26)	35	0.10
Other Asian, not specified (14)	49	0.14
Australian	11	0.03
Austrian	115	0.33
Belgian	14	0.04
Brazilian	52	0.15
British	218	0.62
Canadian	199	0.56
Croatian	28	0.08
Czech	80	0.23
Czechoslovakian	45	0.13
Danish	62	0.18
Dutch	389	1.10
Eastern European	9	0.03
English	2,159	6.13
Estonian	5	0.01
European	80	0.23
Finnish	1,026	2.91
French, except Basque	895	2.54
French Canadian	342	0.97
German	3,083	8.75
Greek	142	0.40
Hawaii Native/Pacific Islander:	106	0.30
Micronesian: (20)	33	0.09
Guamanian/Chamorro (20)	33	0.09
Polynesian: (8)	11	0.03
Native Hawaiian (1)	3	0.01
Samoan (6)	7	0.02
Other Polynesian (1)	1	0.00
Other Pac. Isl., not spec. (9)	62	0.18
Hispanic or Latino:	10,437	29.71
Central American:	2,965	8.44
Costa Rican	51	0.15
Guatemalan	1,711	4.87
Honduran	559	1.59
Nicaraguan	122	0.35
Panamanian	14	0.04
Salvadoran	433	1.23
Other Central American	75	0.21
Cuban	1,218	3.47
Dominican Republic	172	0.49
Mexican	2,400	6.83
Puerto Rican	1,652	4.70
South American:	522	1.49
Argentinean	62	0.18
Bolivian	63	0.18
Chilean	19	0.05
Colombian	154	0.44
Ecuadorian	78	0.22
Peruvian	80	0.23
Uruguayan	28	0.08
Venezuelan	31	0.09
Other South American	7	0.02
Other Hispanic or Latino	1,508	4.29
Hungarian	243	0.69
Irish	2,985	8.47
Italian	1,594	4.52
Lithuanian	127	0.36
Luxemburger	10	0.03
Maltese	11	0.03
Norwegian	185	0.53
Pennsylvania German	41	0.12
Polish	691	1.96
Portuguese	84	0.24
Romanian	48	0.14
Russian	240	0.68
Scandinavian	17	0.05
Scotch-Irish	303	0.86
Scottish	478	1.36
Serbian	7	0.02
Slavic	25	0.07
Slovak	52	0.15
Swedish	157	0.45
Swiss	29	0.08
Ukrainian	43	0.12
United States or American	1,610	4.57
Welsh	226	0.64
West Indian, excl. Hispanic:	3,512	9.97
Bahamian	39	0.11
Belizean	46	0.13
British West Indian	110	0.31
Haitian	2,763	7.84
Jamaican	442	1.25
Trinidadian and Tobagonian	91	0.26
West Indian	21	0.06
White:	23,684	67.41
Not Hispanic (16,884)	17,188	48.92
Hispanic (5,993)	6,496	18.49
Yugoslavian	34	0.10

Lakeland Highlands

Place Type: Census Designated Place
County: Polk
Population: 12,557

Ancestry/Race	Number	%
African American/Black:	342	2.72
Not Hispanic (302)	330	2.63
Hispanic (8)	12	0.10
African, sub-Saharan:	63	0.49
African	7	0.05
Ghanian	12	0.09
South African	44	0.35
Alaska Native tribes, not specified	1	0.01
Am. Ind. or Alaska Nat., not spec.	9	0.07
American Indian tribes, specified:	42	0.33
Blackfeet (2)	2	0.02
Cherokee (4)	14	0.11
Choctaw (7)	7	0.06
Creek	3	0.02
Latin American Indians (1)	3	0.02
Lumbee (1)	3	0.02
Osage	1	0.01
Potawatomi (1)	1	0.01
Seminole	1	0.01
Sioux (3)	7	0.06
American Indian tribes, not spec.	2	0.02
Arab:	69	0.54
Arab/Arabic	50	0.39
Palestinian	9	0.07
Syrian	10	0.08
Asian:	255	2.03
Cambodian	2	0.02
Chinese, ex. Taiwanese (26)	39	0.31
Filipino (52)	57	0.45
Indian (57)	64	0.51
Indonesian (3)	3	0.02
Japanese (4)	8	0.06
Korean (23)	32	0.25
Laotian	1	0.01
Pakistani (5)	5	0.04
Taiwanese	4	0.03
Thai (8)	11	0.09
Vietnamese (20)	25	0.20
Other Asian, not specified (4)	4	0.03
Austrian	75	0.59
British	111	0.87
Canadian	85	0.67
Celtic	32	0.25
Croatian	10	0.08
Czech	28	0.22
Czechoslovakian	41	0.32
Danish	8	0.06
Dutch	300	2.35
English	1,690	13.26
European	119	0.93
Finnish	8	0.06
French, except Basque	366	2.87
French Canadian	200	1.57
German	2,211	17.35
Greek	17	0.13
Hawaii Native/Pacific Islander:	7	0.06
Polynesian: (1)	1	0.01
Samoan (1)	1	0.01
Other Pac. Isl., not spec. (1)	6	0.05
Hispanic or Latino:	484	3.85
Central American:	17	0.14
Costa Rican	2	0.02
Guatemalan	2	0.02
Honduran	1	0.01
Nicaraguan	3	0.02
Panamanian	9	0.07
Cuban	162	1.29
Dominican Republic	10	0.08
Mexican	40	0.32
Puerto Rican	108	0.86
South American:	33	0.26
Argentinean	3	0.02
Bolivian	1	0.01
Colombian	16	0.13
Peruvian	6	0.05
Other South American	7	0.06
Other Hispanic or Latino	114	0.91
Hungarian	45	0.35
Iranian	44	0.35
Irish	1,701	13.34
Italian	770	6.04
Latvian	9	0.07
Northern European	9	0.07
Norwegian	138	1.08
Pennsylvania German	18	0.14
Polish	376	2.95
Portuguese	54	0.42
Romanian	32	0.25
Russian	78	0.61
Scandinavian	15	0.12
Scotch-Irish	342	2.68
Scottish	392	3.08
Slavic	36	0.28
Slovak	11	0.09
Slovene	10	0.08
Swedish	164	1.29
Swiss	24	0.19
Ukrainian	19	0.15
United States or American	1,943	15.24
Welsh	127	1.00
West Indian, excl. Hispanic:	65	0.51
Belizean	17	0.13
Haitian	20	0.16
Jamaican	17	0.13
Trinidadian and Tobagonian	11	0.09
White:	11,927	94.98
Not Hispanic (11,444)	11,518	91.73
Hispanic (386)	409	3.26

Lakeland

Place Type: City
County: Polk
Population: 78,452

Ancestry/Race	Number	%
Acadian/Cajun	23	0.03
African American/Black:	17,316	22.07
Not Hispanic (16,500)	17,022	21.70

Notes: 1. Figures in the "Number" column do not add up to the total population due to: a) Ancestry/Race overlap — e.g. persons can report being both White and Irish, b) persons of Hispanic origin can report being any race, c) persons reporting two ancestries are counted in both categories. 2. Numbers in parentheses indicate the number of persons reporting this ancestry/race alone, not in combination with any other ancestry/race. 3. Refer to the User's Guide in the front of the book for more detailed information.

Hispanic (182)	294	0.37
African, sub-Saharan:	401	0.51
African	312	0.40
Cape Verdean	10	0.01
Nigerian	74	0.09
South African	5	0.01
Alaska Native tribes, specified:	5	0.01
Alaska Athabascan (1)	1	0.00
Aleut (1)	1	0.00
Eskimo (1)	3	0.00
Am. Ind. or Alaska Nat., not spec.	196	0.25
Albanian	47	0.06
Alsatian	15	0.02
American Indian tribes, specified:	268	0.34
Apache (4)	9	0.01
Blackfeet (7)	23	0.03
Cherokee (49)	124	0.16
Chickasaw	1	0.00
Chippewa (4)	10	0.01
Choctaw (4)	14	0.02
Comanche	1	0.00
Cree (1)	2	0.00
Creek (1)	7	0.01
Delaware	1	0.00
Houma (1)	1	0.00
Iroquois (1)	10	0.01
Latin American Indians (5)	12	0.02
Lumbee (2)	3	0.00
Menominee (1)	1	0.00
Navajo (1)	5	0.01
Potawatomi	1	0.00
Seminole (1)	8	0.01
Sioux (8)	12	0.02
Ute (1)	3	0.00
All other tribes (8)	20	0.03
American Indian tribes, not spec.	56	0.07
Arab:	131	0.17
Arab/Arabic	35	0.04
Egyptian	5	0.01
Jordanian	7	0.01
Lebanese	39	0.05
Moroccan	25	0.03
Syrian	20	0.03
Armenian	21	0.03
Asian:	1,349	1.72
Cambodian (10)	24	0.03
Chinese, ex. Taiwanese (157)	197	0.25
Filipino (125)	156	0.20
Indian (412)	476	0.61
Indonesian (12)	18	0.02
Japanese (66)	98	0.12
Korean (79)	110	0.14
Laotian (25)	33	0.04
Pakistani (3)	16	0.02
Sri Lankan (16)	16	0.02
Taiwanese (11)	13	0.02
Thai (24)	32	0.04
Vietnamese (49)	63	0.08
Other Asian, specified (2)	9	0.01
Other Asian, not specified (34)	88	0.11
Austrian	109	0.14
Belgian	42	0.05
Brazilian	33	0.04
British	394	0.50
Bulgarian	15	0.02
Canadian	206	0.26
Celtic	19	0.02
Croatian	52	0.07
Czech	141	0.18
Czechoslovakian	93	0.12
Danish	122	0.16
Dutch	1,389	1.78
English	8,672	11.09
European	442	0.57
Finnish	68	0.09
French, except Basque	2,478	3.17
French Canadian	579	0.74
German	9,773	12.50
Greek	285	0.36
Guyanese	12	0.02
Hawaii Native/Pacific Islander:	100	0.13
Micronesian: (4)	7	0.01
Guamanian/Chamorro (4)	7	0.01
Polynesian: (33)	40	0.05
Native Hawaiian (18)	23	0.03
Samoan (15)	17	0.02
Other Pac. Isl., not spec. (8)	53	0.07
Hispanic or Latino:	5,032	6.41
Central American:	164	0.21
Costa Rican	17	0.02
Guatemalan	18	0.02
Honduran	27	0.03
Nicaraguan	36	0.05
Panamanian	28	0.04
Salvadoran	24	0.03
Other Central American	14	0.02
Cuban	688	0.88
Dominican Republic	71	0.09
Mexican	1,279	1.63
Puerto Rican	1,852	2.36
South American:	247	0.31
Argentinean	16	0.02
Bolivian	7	0.01
Chilean	8	0.01
Colombian	95	0.12
Ecuadorian	13	0.02
Peruvian	48	0.06
Uruguayan	1	0.00
Venezuelan	40	0.05
Other South American	19	0.02
Other Hispanic or Latino	731	0.93
Hungarian	472	0.60
Iranian	7	0.01
Irish	8,027	10.27
Israeli	6	0.01
Italian	2,494	3.19
Latvian	24	0.03
Lithuanian	75	0.10
Northern European	92	0.12
Norwegian	594	0.76
Pennsylvania German	61	0.08
Polish	1,494	1.91
Portuguese	161	0.21
Romanian	79	0.10
Russian	327	0.42
Scandinavian	54	0.07
Scotch-Irish	1,645	2.10
Scottish	1,591	2.04
Serbian	4	0.01
Slavic	27	0.03
Slovak	125	0.16
Slovene	15	0.02
Swedish	779	1.00
Swiss	164	0.21
Turkish	35	0.04
Ukrainian	75	0.10
United States or American	7,715	9.87
Welsh	494	0.63
West Indian, excl. Hispanic:	838	1.07
Bahamian	19	0.02
British West Indian	10	0.01
Dutch West Indian	5	0.01
Haitian	214	0.27
Jamaican	438	0.56
Trinidadian and Tobagonian	17	0.02
U.S. Virgin Islander	8	0.01
West Indian	127	0.16
White:	58,683	74.80
Not Hispanic (54,555)	55,286	70.47
Hispanic (3,122)	3,397	4.33
Yugoslavian	57	0.07

Lakeside

Place Type: Census Designated Place
County: Clay
Population: 30,927

Ancestry/Race	Number	%
Acadian/Cajun	16	0.05
African American/Black:	2,389	7.72
Not Hispanic (2,149)	2,301	7.44
Hispanic (50)	88	0.28
African, sub-Saharan:	97	0.31
African	38	0.12
Ghanian	28	0.09
Liberian	6	0.02
South African	25	0.08
Am. Ind. or Alaska Nat., not spec.	91	0.29
American Indian tribes, specified:	219	0.71
Apache (2)	7	0.02
Blackfeet	5	0.02
Cherokee (34)	109	0.35
Cheyenne	1	0.00
Chickasaw (1)	2	0.01
Chippewa (4)	8	0.03
Choctaw (7)	12	0.04
Comanche	4	0.01
Cree	1	0.00
Creek (6)	8	0.03
Crow	1	0.00
Delaware	1	0.00
Houma (1)	1	0.00
Iroquois (3)	7	0.02
Kiowa (2)	2	0.01
Latin American Indians (2)	4	0.01
Lumbee (8)	10	0.03
Navajo (2)	8	0.03
Potawatomi	1	0.00
Seminole (4)	9	0.03
Shoshone (1)	1	0.00
Sioux (3)	3	0.01
All other tribes (3)	14	0.05
American Indian tribes, not spec.	11	0.04
Arab:	27	0.09
Palestinian	14	0.05
Syrian	13	0.04
Armenian	15	0.05
Asian:	1,144	3.70
Cambodian (16)	16	0.05
Chinese, ex. Taiwanese (68)	97	0.31
Filipino (501)	659	2.13
Indian (73)	92	0.30
Indonesian (1)	7	0.02
Japanese (36)	78	0.25
Korean (52)	57	0.18
Malaysian	2	0.01
Pakistani (9)	21	0.07
Sri Lankan (1)	1	0.00
Taiwanese (1)	2	0.01
Thai (16)	19	0.06
Vietnamese (53)	65	0.21
Other Asian, specified (1)	1	0.00
Other Asian, not specified (6)	27	0.09
Austrian	75	0.24
Belgian	58	0.19
Brazilian	9	0.03
British	184	0.60
Canadian	144	0.47
Celtic	10	0.03
Croatian	8	0.03
Czech	39	0.13
Danish	81	0.26
Dutch	560	1.82
English	3,362	10.90
European	238	0.77
Finnish	106	0.34
French, except Basque	1,122	3.64
French Canadian	269	0.87
German	4,529	14.68
Greek	133	0.43
Guyanese	8	0.03
Hawaii Native/Pacific Islander:	64	0.21
Micronesian: (10)	23	0.07
Guamanian/Chamorro (10)	23	0.07
Polynesian: (11)	26	0.08
Native Hawaiian (5)	18	0.06
Samoan (6)	8	0.03
Other Pac. Isl., not spec. (5)	15	0.05
Hispanic or Latino:	1,638	5.30
Central American:	103	0.33
Costa Rican	11	0.04
Guatemalan	15	0.05
Honduran	9	0.03

Notes: 1. Figures in the "Number" column do not add up to the total population due to: a) Ancestry/Race overlap — e.g. persons can report being both White and Irish, b) persons of Hispanic origin can report being any race, c) persons reporting two ancestries are counted in both categories. 2. Numbers in parentheses indicate the number of persons reporting this ancestry/race alone, not in combination with any other ancestry/race. 3. Refer to the User's Guide in the front of the book for more detailed information.

Nicaraguan	7	0.02
Panamanian	36	0.12
Salvadoran	19	0.06
Other Central American	6	0.02
Cuban	52	0.17
Dominican Republic	43	0.14
Mexican	321	1.04
Puerto Rican	627	2.03
South American:	141	0.46
Argentinean	7	0.02
Chilean	12	0.04
Colombian	61	0.20
Ecuadorian	28	0.09
Peruvian	14	0.05
Uruguayan	3	0.01
Venezuelan	15	0.05
Other South American	1	0.00
Other Hispanic or Latino	351	1.13
Hungarian	196	0.64
Iranian	11	0.04
Irish	3,828	12.41
Italian	1,810	5.87
Lithuanian	42	0.14
Macedonian	6	0.02
Northern European	7	0.02
Norwegian	304	0.99
Pennsylvania German	16	0.05
Polish	878	2.85
Portuguese	129	0.42
Romanian	9	0.03
Russian	109	0.35
Scandinavian	16	0.05
Scotch-Irish	783	2.54
Scottish	749	2.43
Slovak	17	0.06
Swedish	208	0.67
Swiss	44	0.14
Ukrainian	135	0.44
United States or American	3,658	11.86
Welsh	247	0.80
West Indian, excl. Hispanic:	227	0.74
Bahamian	6	0.02
Barbadian	5	0.02
Belizean	24	0.08
British West Indian	8	0.03
Haitian	124	0.40
Jamaican	35	0.11
Trinidadian and Tobagonian	18	0.06
West Indian	7	0.02
White:	27,132	87.73
Not Hispanic (25,536)	26,015	84.12
Hispanic (984)	1,117	3.61
Yugoslavian	25	0.08

Lakewood Park

Place Type: Census Designated Place
County: Saint Lucie
Population: 10,458

Ancestry/Race	Number	%
African American/Black:	595	5.69
Not Hispanic (542)	584	5.58
Hispanic (10)	11	0.11
Alaska Native tribes, specified:	3	0.03
Aleut (1)	1	0.01
All other tribes	2	0.02
Am. Ind. or Alaska Nat., not spec.	28	0.27
American Indian tribes, specified:	55	0.53
Apache	3	0.03
Blackfeet	1	0.01
Cherokee (13)	25	0.24
Chippewa (2)	3	0.03
Iroquois (1)	4	0.04
Latin American Indians (2)	4	0.04
Navajo (3)	7	0.07
All other tribes (5)	8	0.08
American Indian tribes, not spec.	1	0.01
Arab:	15	0.14
Lebanese	15	0.14
Armenian	9	0.09
Asian:	86	0.82
Chinese, ex. Taiwanese (7)	10	0.10
Filipino (8)	17	0.16
Indian (10)	17	0.16
Japanese (6)	6	0.06
Korean (11)	11	0.11
Pakistani (11)	11	0.11
Thai (1)	1	0.01
Vietnamese (9)	9	0.09
Other Asian, not specified (1)	4	0.04
Assyrian/Chaldean/Syriac	6	0.06
Australian	8	0.08
Austrian	57	0.55
Belgian	16	0.15
British	40	0.38
Canadian	48	0.46
Croatian	6	0.06
Czechoslovakian	13	0.12
Danish	62	0.60
Dutch	259	2.49
English	1,373	13.19
European	16	0.15
Finnish	34	0.33
French, except Basque	562	5.40
French Canadian	181	1.74
German	1,708	16.41
Greek	204	1.96
Hawaii Native/Pacific Islander:	14	0.13
Polynesian: (4)	6	0.06
Native Hawaiian (4)	6	0.06
Other Pac. Isl., not spec. (2)	8	0.08
Hispanic or Latino:	266	2.54
Central American:	7	0.07
Costa Rican	1	0.01
Guatemalan	1	0.01
Honduran	2	0.02
Panamanian	2	0.02
Other Central American	1	0.01
Cuban	24	0.23
Dominican Republic	2	0.02
Mexican	116	1.11
Puerto Rican	53	0.51
South American:	22	0.21
Bolivian	1	0.01
Chilean	2	0.02
Colombian	9	0.09
Peruvian	6	0.06
Venezuelan	4	0.04
Other Hispanic or Latino	42	0.40
Hungarian	130	1.25
Icelander	13	0.12
Iranian	10	0.10
Irish	1,760	16.91
Israeli	52	0.50
Italian	1,021	9.81
Lithuanian	47	0.45
Norwegian	34	0.33
Polish	248	2.38
Portuguese	106	1.02
Russian	61	0.59
Scandinavian	5	0.05
Scotch-Irish	296	2.84
Scottish	347	3.33
Slavic	8	0.08
Slovak	16	0.15
Slovene	6	0.06
Swedish	202	1.94
Swiss	32	0.31
Ukrainian	31	0.30
United States or American	1,132	10.88
Welsh	92	0.88
West Indian, excl. Hispanic:	76	0.73
Bahamian	8	0.08
Haitian	47	0.45
Jamaican	21	0.20
White:	9,709	92.84
Not Hispanic (9,428)	9,524	91.07
Hispanic (174)	185	1.77
Yugoslavian	39	0.37

Land O' Lakes

Place Type: Census Designated Place
County: Pasco
Population: 20,971

Ancestry/Race	Number	%
African American/Black:	524	2.50
Not Hispanic (408)	467	2.23
Hispanic (34)	57	0.27
Alaska Native tribes, specified:	1	0.00
Tlingit-Haida	1	0.00
Am. Ind. or Alaska Nat., not spec.	31	0.15
American Indian tribes, specified:	121	0.58
Apache (9)	9	0.04
Blackfeet (1)	7	0.03
Cherokee (15)	65	0.31
Chippewa (3)	5	0.02
Cree	2	0.01
Creek (4)	5	0.02
Iroquois (1)	6	0.03
Latin American Indians (1)	4	0.02
Menominee	2	0.01
Pueblo (2)	2	0.01
Seminole (1)	1	0.00
Sioux (1)	2	0.01
Ute (1)	1	0.00
All other tribes (5)	10	0.05
American Indian tribes, not spec.	6	0.03
Arab:	75	0.36
Lebanese	26	0.13
Moroccan	49	0.24
Armenian	19	0.09
Asian:	354	1.69
Chinese, ex. Taiwanese (46)	57	0.27
Filipino (82)	99	0.47
Indian (79)	86	0.41
Indonesian (6)	9	0.04
Japanese (8)	22	0.10
Korean (16)	25	0.12
Pakistani (5)	11	0.05
Taiwanese (2)	2	0.01
Thai (5)	5	0.02
Vietnamese (19)	19	0.09
Other Asian, not specified (10)	19	0.09
Australian	13	0.06
Austrian	91	0.44
Belgian	93	0.45
British	117	0.56
Bulgarian	10	0.05
Canadian	34	0.16
Croatian	54	0.26
Czech	139	0.67
Czechoslovakian	46	0.22
Danish	22	0.11
Dutch	453	2.18
Eastern European	8	0.04
English	2,862	13.76
Estonian	8	0.04
European	155	0.75
Finnish	32	0.15
French, except Basque	965	4.64
French Canadian	263	1.26
German	4,231	20.35
Greek	100	0.48
Hawaii Native/Pacific Islander:	13	0.06
Micronesian: (1)	2	0.01
Guamanian/Chamorro (1)	2	0.01
Polynesian:	6	0.03
Native Hawaiian	6	0.03
Other Pac. Isl., not spec.	5	0.02
Hispanic or Latino:	1,836	8.75
Central American:	65	0.31
Costa Rican	11	0.05
Guatemalan	5	0.02
Honduran	17	0.08
Nicaraguan	7	0.03
Panamanian	14	0.07
Salvadoran	10	0.05
Other Central American	1	0.00
Cuban	248	1.18

Notes: 1. Figures in the "Number" column do not add up to the total population due to: a) Ancestry/Race overlap — e.g. persons can report being both White and Irish, b) persons of Hispanic origin can report being any race, c) persons reporting two ancestries are counted in both categories. 2. Numbers in parentheses indicate the number of persons reporting this ancestry/race alone, not in combination with any other ancestry/race. 3. Refer to the User's Guide in the front of the book for more detailed information.

Dominican Republic	12	0.06
Mexican	134	0.64
Puerto Rican	863	4.12
South American:	84	0.40
Argentinean	1	0.00
Bolivian	2	0.01
Chilean	1	0.00
Colombian	42	0.20
Ecuadorian	15	0.07
Paraguayan	1	0.00
Peruvian	4	0.02
Uruguayan	1	0.00
Venezuelan	5	0.02
Other South American	12	0.06
Other Hispanic or Latino	430	2.05
Hungarian	164	0.79
Irish	3,064	14.74
Israeli	32	0.15
Italian	1,611	7.75
Lithuanian	40	0.19
Luxemburger	11	0.05
Maltese	6	0.03
Northern European	9	0.04
Norwegian	313	1.51
Pennsylvania German	24	0.12
Polish	741	3.56
Portuguese	69	0.33
Romanian	23	0.11
Russian	150	0.72
Scandinavian	9	0.04
Scotch-Irish	539	2.59
Scottish	544	2.62
Slovak	6	0.03
Slovene	9	0.04
Swedish	382	1.84
Swiss	69	0.33
Turkish	24	0.12
Ukrainian	67	0.32
United States or American	1,806	8.69
Welsh	281	1.35
West Indian, excl. Hispanic:	99	0.48
Jamaican	41	0.20
Trinidadian and Tobagonian	41	0.20
West Indian	17	0.08
White:	19,881	94.80
Not Hispanic (18,147)	18,334	87.43
Hispanic (1,483)	1,547	7.38
Yugoslavian	25	0.12

Largo

Place Type: City
County: Pinellas
Population: 69,371

Ancestry/Race	Number	%
Acadian/Cajun	17	0.02
African American/Black:	2,144	3.09
Not Hispanic (1,806)	2,042	2.94
Hispanic (63)	102	0.15
African, sub-Saharan:	182	0.26
African	137	0.20
Cape Verdean	41	0.06
Other sub-Saharan African	4	0.01
Alaska Native tribes, specified:	11	0.02
Alaska Athabascan (1)	2	0.00
Eskimo (6)	6	0.01
Tlingit-Haida (1)	2	0.00
All other tribes (1)	1	0.00
Alaska Native tribes, not specified	2	0.00
Am. Ind. or Alaska Nat., not spec.	182	0.26
Albanian	312	0.45
Alsatian	9	0.01
American Indian tribes, specified:	297	0.43
Apache (2)	5	0.01
Blackfeet (8)	19	0.03
Cherokee (49)	126	0.18
Cheyenne	1	0.00
Chippewa (16)	24	0.03
Choctaw (5)	8	0.01
Cree (1)	1	0.00
Creek (3)	8	0.01
Delaware (2)	2	0.00
Iroquois (18)	31	0.04
Latin American Indians (11)	15	0.02
Lumbee (5)	5	0.01
Navajo (2)	2	0.00
Potawatomi (1)	1	0.00
Pueblo (2)	2	0.00
Seminole (2)	8	0.01
Sioux (3)	7	0.01
Ute	1	0.00
All other tribes (18)	31	0.04
American Indian tribes, not spec.	35	0.05
Arab:	262	0.38
Arab/Arabic	49	0.07
Egyptian	29	0.04
Jordanian	10	0.01
Lebanese	88	0.13
Moroccan	37	0.05
Palestinian	24	0.03
Syrian	18	0.03
Other Arab	7	0.01
Armenian	84	0.12
Asian:	1,427	2.06
Bangladeshi (10)	29	0.04
Cambodian (10)	11	0.02
Chinese, ex. Taiwanese (98)	126	0.18
Filipino (286)	346	0.50
Hmong	1	0.00
Indian (341)	403	0.58
Indonesian (2)	4	0.01
Japanese (40)	69	0.10
Korean (53)	67	0.10
Laotian (28)	33	0.05
Malaysian	1	0.00
Pakistani (10)	11	0.02
Sri Lankan (3)	3	0.00
Taiwanese (11)	15	0.02
Thai (32)	49	0.07
Vietnamese (197)	213	0.31
Other Asian, specified (2)	2	0.00
Other Asian, not specified (26)	44	0.06
Australian	16	0.02
Austrian	191	0.27
Belgian	65	0.09
Brazilian	66	0.10
British	466	0.67
Canadian	699	1.01
Croatian	178	0.26
Czech	268	0.39
Czechoslovakian	195	0.28
Danish	379	0.55
Dutch	1,412	2.03
Eastern European	15	0.02
English	9,669	13.92
European	278	0.40
Finnish	195	0.28
French, except Basque	3,167	4.56
French Canadian	1,079	1.55
German	12,735	18.33
Greek	731	1.05
Guyanese	37	0.05
Hawaii Native/Pacific Islander:	113	0.16
Micronesian: (20)	28	0.04
Guamanian/Chamorro (6)	10	0.01
Other Micronesian (14)	18	0.03
Polynesian: (23)	64	0.09
Native Hawaiian (5)	15	0.02
Samoan (2)	13	0.02
Tongan (14)	24	0.03
Other Polynesian (2)	12	0.02
Other Pac. Isl., not spec. (10)	21	0.03
Hispanic or Latino:	2,902	4.18
Central American:	104	0.15
Costa Rican	21	0.03
Guatemalan	12	0.02
Honduran	19	0.03
Nicaraguan	6	0.01
Panamanian	20	0.03
Salvadoran	22	0.03
Other Central American	4	0.01
Cuban	190	0.27
Dominican Republic	50	0.07
Mexican	910	1.31
Puerto Rican	800	1.15
South American:	326	0.47
Argentinean	17	0.02
Bolivian	7	0.01
Chilean	7	0.01
Colombian	139	0.20
Ecuadorian	68	0.10
Peruvian	37	0.05
Uruguayan	4	0.01
Venezuelan	34	0.05
Other South American	13	0.02
Other Hispanic or Latino	522	0.75
Hungarian	597	0.86
Iranian	79	0.11
Irish	10,696	15.40
Israeli	25	0.04
Italian	6,661	9.59
Latvian	28	0.04
Lithuanian	269	0.39
Luxemburger	16	0.02
Macedonian	9	0.01
Maltese	17	0.02
Northern European	30	0.04
Norwegian	1,128	1.62
Pennsylvania German	45	0.06
Polish	2,980	4.29
Portuguese	393	0.57
Romanian	103	0.15
Russian	578	0.83
Scandinavian	105	0.15
Scotch-Irish	1,632	2.35
Scottish	2,040	2.94
Serbian	26	0.04
Slavic	34	0.05
Slovak	200	0.29
Slovene	52	0.07
Swedish	905	1.30
Swiss	180	0.26
Turkish	68	0.10
Ukrainian	340	0.49
United States or American	5,100	7.34
Welsh	596	0.86
West Indian, excl. Hispanic:	158	0.23
Bermudan	13	0.02
Haitian	31	0.04
Jamaican	69	0.10
Trinidadian and Tobagonian	16	0.02
U.S. Virgin Islander	4	0.01
West Indian	25	0.04
White:	65,198	93.98
Not Hispanic (62,359)	63,050	90.89
Hispanic (1,955)	2,148	3.10
Yugoslavian	106	0.15

Lauderdale Lakes

Place Type: City
County: Broward
Population: 31,705

Ancestry/Race	Number	%
African American/Black:	22,834	72.02
Not Hispanic (21,243)	22,531	71.06
Hispanic (233)	303	0.96
African, sub-Saharan:	390	1.24
African	382	1.21
Ghanian	8	0.03
Alaska Native tribes, specified:	6	0.02
Alaska Athabascan	3	0.01
Tlingit-Haida (1)	3	0.01
Am. Ind. or Alaska Nat., not spec.	69	0.22
Alsatian	14	0.04
American Indian tribes, specified:	55	0.17
Blackfeet (1)	2	0.01
Cherokee	9	0.03
Iroquois (3)	7	0.02
Latin American Indians (2)	21	0.07
Lumbee (2)	2	0.01

Notes: 1. Figures in the "Number" column do not add up to the total population due to: a) Ancestry/Race overlap — e.g. persons can report being both White and Irish, b) persons of Hispanic origin can report being any race, c) persons reporting two ancestries are counted in both categories. 2. Numbers in parentheses indicate the number of persons reporting this ancestry/race alone, not in combination with any other ancestry/race. 3. Refer to the User's Guide in the front of the book for more detailed information.

Osage (4)	4	0.01
Pueblo	1	0.00
Sioux (1)	1	0.00
Yakama	4	0.01
All other tribes	4	0.01
American Indian tribes, not spec.	5	0.02
Arab:	49	0.16
Egyptian	40	0.13
Jordanian	9	0.03
Asian:	473	1.49
Bangladeshi (3)	5	0.02
Cambodian (1)	2	0.01
Chinese, ex. Taiwanese (75)	102	0.32
Filipino (15)	19	0.06
Hmong	1	0.00
Indian (154)	216	0.68
Indonesian (2)	3	0.01
Japanese (8)	8	0.03
Korean (11)	15	0.05
Laotian	1	0.00
Pakistani (9)	11	0.03
Taiwanese	1	0.00
Thai (5)	7	0.02
Vietnamese (33)	33	0.10
Other Asian, specified	5	0.02
Other Asian, not specified (8)	44	0.14
Austrian	71	0.23
Brazilian	109	0.35
British	85	0.27
Bulgarian	7	0.02
Canadian	132	0.42
Croatian	32	0.10
Czechoslovakian	14	0.04
Danish	24	0.08
Dutch	56	0.18
English	372	1.18
European	143	0.45
Finnish	9	0.03
French, except Basque	172	0.55
French Canadian	473	1.50
German	701	2.22
Greek	61	0.19
Guyanese	163	0.52
Hawaii Native/Pacific Islander:	100	0.32
Micronesian: (1)	1	0.00
Guamanian/Chamorro (1)	1	0.00
Polynesian: (4)	10	0.03
Native Hawaiian (3)	6	0.02
Samoan (1)	4	0.01
Other Pac. Isl., specified	5	0.02
Other Pac. Isl., not spec. (14)	84	0.26
Hispanic or Latino:	1,755	5.54
Central American:	154	0.49
Costa Rican	8	0.03
Guatemalan	12	0.04
Honduran	49	0.15
Nicaraguan	12	0.04
Panamanian	32	0.10
Salvadoran	36	0.11
Other Central American	5	0.02
Cuban	155	0.49
Dominican Republic	84	0.26
Mexican	212	0.67
Puerto Rican	484	1.53
South American:	255	0.80
Argentinean	4	0.01
Bolivian	3	0.01
Chilean	14	0.04
Colombian	134	0.42
Ecuadorian	18	0.06
Peruvian	41	0.13
Uruguayan	3	0.01
Venezuelan	30	0.09
Other South American	8	0.03
Other Hispanic or Latino	411	1.30
Hungarian	77	0.24
Iranian	8	0.03
Irish	536	1.70
Italian	781	2.48
Latvian	10	0.03
Lithuanian	22	0.07
Norwegian	32	0.10
Polish	358	1.14
Portuguese	25	0.08
Romanian	38	0.12
Russian	323	1.02
Scotch-Irish	53	0.17
Scottish	142	0.45
Serbian	25	0.08
Slovak	8	0.03
Slovene	9	0.03
Swedish	41	0.13
Swiss	10	0.03
Turkish	41	0.13
Ukrainian	78	0.25
United States or American	1,801	5.71
Welsh	7	0.02
West Indian, excl. Hispanic:	11,455	36.35
Bahamian	291	0.92
Barbadian	22	0.07
British West Indian	238	0.76
Haitian	4,732	15.01
Jamaican	5,646	17.91
Trinidadian and Tobagonian	217	0.69
U.S. Virgin Islander	159	0.50
West Indian	141	0.45
Other West Indian	9	0.03
White:	7,956	25.09
Not Hispanic (6,726)	6,994	22.06
Hispanic (870)	962	3.03

Lauderhill

Place Type: City
County: Broward
Population: 57,585

Ancestry/Race	Number	%
African American/Black:	35,657	61.92
Not Hispanic (33,355)	35,041	60.85
Hispanic (485)	616	1.07
African, sub-Saharan:	668	1.17
African	638	1.11
Ethiopian	10	0.02
Ghanian	7	0.01
Nigerian	5	0.01
South African	8	0.01
Alaska Native tribes, specified:	6	0.01
Tlingit-Haida	6	0.01
Am. Ind. or Alaska Nat., not spec.	121	0.21
American Indian tribes, specified:	83	0.14
Apache (1)	1	0.00
Blackfeet (1)	2	0.00
Cherokee (2)	27	0.05
Chippewa (1)	5	0.01
Comanche (1)	1	0.00
Cree (1)	1	0.00
Creek (1)	1	0.00
Delaware (1)	1	0.00
Iroquois (2)	6	0.01
Latin American Indians (5)	16	0.03
Navajo	1	0.00
Seminole (1)	2	0.00
Shoshone	1	0.00
Sioux (5)	8	0.01
All other tribes (3)	10	0.02
American Indian tribes, not spec.	8	0.01
Arab:	280	0.49
Arab/Arabic	44	0.08
Lebanese	62	0.11
Moroccan	84	0.15
Palestinian	58	0.10
Syrian	21	0.04
Other Arab	11	0.02
Armenian	12	0.02
Asian:	1,254	2.18
Bangladeshi (4)	4	0.01
Chinese, ex. Taiwanese (224)	313	0.54
Filipino (106)	126	0.22
Indian (365)	493	0.86
Indonesian (1)	1	0.00
Japanese (21)	29	0.05
Korean (66)	72	0.13
Malaysian (1)	1	0.00
Pakistani (21)	27	0.05
Taiwanese (1)	3	0.01
Thai (8)	10	0.02
Vietnamese (60)	70	0.12
Other Asian, specified (1)	15	0.03
Other Asian, not specified (18)	90	0.16
Austrian	241	0.42
Belgian	4	0.01
Brazilian	143	0.25
British	195	0.34
Bulgarian	12	0.02
Canadian	251	0.44
Czech	45	0.08
Czechoslovakian	52	0.09
Danish	42	0.07
Dutch	160	0.28
Eastern European	116	0.20
English	1,104	1.93
European	116	0.20
Finnish	16	0.03
French, except Basque	372	0.65
French Canadian	444	0.78
German	1,947	3.40
German Russian	7	0.01
Greek	123	0.21
Guyanese	217	0.38
Hawaii Native/Pacific Islander:	189	0.33
Micronesian: (2)	4	0.01
Guamanian/Chamorro (2)	4	0.01
Polynesian: (11)	19	0.03
Native Hawaiian (5)	12	0.02
Samoan (6)	7	0.01
Other Pac. Isl., specified	14	0.02
Other Pac. Isl., not spec. (22)	152	0.26
Hispanic or Latino:	3,995	6.94
Central American:	284	0.49
Costa Rican	35	0.06
Guatemalan	29	0.05
Honduran	86	0.15
Nicaraguan	13	0.02
Panamanian	76	0.13
Salvadoran	33	0.06
Other Central American	12	0.02
Cuban	436	0.76
Dominican Republic	144	0.25
Mexican	199	0.35
Puerto Rican	1,028	1.79
South American:	1,006	1.75
Argentinean	73	0.13
Bolivian	13	0.02
Chilean	26	0.05
Colombian	497	0.86
Ecuadorian	85	0.15
Peruvian	140	0.24
Uruguayan	26	0.05
Venezuelan	111	0.19
Other South American	35	0.06
Other Hispanic or Latino	898	1.56
Hungarian	277	0.48
Iranian	64	0.11
Irish	1,544	2.70
Israeli	141	0.25
Italian	2,157	3.77
Latvian	16	0.03
Lithuanian	145	0.25
Norwegian	78	0.14
Pennsylvania German	11	0.02
Polish	1,257	2.20
Portuguese	85	0.15
Romanian	205	0.36
Russian	1,379	2.41
Scotch-Irish	222	0.39
Scottish	415	0.72
Slovak	43	0.08
Swedish	101	0.18
Swiss	44	0.08
Turkish	8	0.01
Ukrainian	77	0.13
United States or American	4,316	7.54
Welsh	195	0.34

Notes: 1. Figures in the "Number" column do not add up to the total population due to: a) Ancestry/Race overlap — e.g. persons can report being both White and Irish, b) persons of Hispanic origin can report being any race, c) persons reporting two ancestries are counted in both categories. 2. Numbers in parentheses indicate the number of persons reporting this ancestry/race alone, not in combination with any other ancestry/race. 3. Refer to the User's Guide in the front of the book for more detailed information.

West Indian, excl. Hispanic:	16,626	29.04
Bahamian	473	0.83
Barbadian	168	0.29
Belizean	33	0.06
British West Indian	254	0.44
Haitian	5,034	8.79
Jamaican	9,723	16.98
Trinidadian and Tobagonian	480	0.84
U.S. Virgin Islander	82	0.14
West Indian	365	0.64
Other West Indian	14	0.02
White:	20,153	35.00
Not Hispanic (17,014)	17,476	30.35
Hispanic (2,468)	2,677	4.65
Yugoslavian	25	0.04

Leesburg

Place Type: City
County: Lake
Population: 15,956

Ancestry/Race	Number	%
African American/Black:	4,728	29.63
Not Hispanic (4,609)	4,689	29.39
Hispanic (37)	39	0.24
African, sub-Saharan:	417	2.63
African	417	2.63
Am. Ind. or Alaska Nat., not spec.	48	0.30
American Indian tribes, specified:	77	0.48
Apache	3	0.02
Blackfeet (1)	5	0.03
Cherokee (12)	39	0.24
Chippewa (1)	2	0.01
Choctaw	2	0.01
Creek	5	0.03
Iroquois (1)	5	0.03
Latin American Indians	6	0.04
Potawatomi (1)	1	0.01
Seminole (1)	5	0.03
Sioux (3)	3	0.02
All other tribes	1	0.01
American Indian tribes, not spec.	2	0.01
Arab:	17	0.11
Egyptian	6	0.04
Lebanese	11	0.07
Asian:	245	1.54
Chinese, ex. Taiwanese (26)	32	0.20
Filipino (46)	50	0.31
Indian (76)	80	0.50
Indonesian	1	0.01
Japanese (3)	4	0.03
Korean (16)	17	0.11
Laotian (5)	5	0.03
Malaysian	1	0.01
Pakistani (2)	7	0.04
Taiwanese (2)	2	0.01
Thai (6)	6	0.04
Vietnamese (27)	27	0.17
Other Asian, specified	3	0.02
Other Asian, not specified (3)	10	0.06
Austrian	28	0.18
Basque	4	0.03
British	47	0.30
Canadian	66	0.42
Celtic	31	0.20
Croatian	17	0.11
Czech	31	0.20
Czechoslovakian	27	0.17
Danish	77	0.48
Dutch	194	1.22
English	1,878	11.82
European	81	0.51
Finnish	31	0.20
French, except Basque	561	3.53
French Canadian	133	0.84
German	1,872	11.79
German Russian	9	0.06
Greek	70	0.44
Guyanese	9	0.06
Hawaii Native/Pacific Islander:	10	0.06
Micronesian:	1	0.01
Guamanian/Chamorro	1	0.01
Polynesian: (1)	1	0.01
Native Hawaiian (1)	1	0.01
Other Pac. Isl., specified	3	0.02
Other Pac. Isl., not spec.	5	0.03
Hispanic or Latino:	657	4.12
Central American:	52	0.33
Costa Rican	1	0.01
Guatemalan	20	0.13
Honduran	7	0.04
Panamanian	13	0.08
Salvadoran	10	0.06
Other Central American	1	0.01
Cuban	47	0.29
Dominican Republic	3	0.02
Mexican	280	1.75
Puerto Rican	151	0.95
South American:	25	0.16
Argentinean	1	0.01
Colombian	15	0.09
Ecuadorian	1	0.01
Peruvian	4	0.03
Venezuelan	4	0.03
Other Hispanic or Latino	99	0.62
Hungarian	49	0.31
Irish	1,189	7.49
Italian	358	2.25
Latvian	10	0.06
Lithuanian	20	0.13
Norwegian	130	0.82
Pennsylvania German	10	0.06
Polish	216	1.36
Portuguese	46	0.29
Romanian	8	0.05
Russian	37	0.23
Scandinavian	35	0.22
Scotch-Irish	196	1.23
Scottish	309	1.95
Slovak	48	0.30
Swedish	108	0.68
Swiss	5	0.03
Ukrainian	8	0.05
United States or American	1,313	8.27
Welsh	73	0.46
West Indian, excl. Hispanic:	152	0.96
Bahamian	11	0.07
Haitian	24	0.15
Jamaican	117	0.74
White:	10,809	67.74
Not Hispanic (10,265)	10,408	65.23
Hispanic (362)	401	2.51
Yugoslavian	34	0.21

Lehigh Acres

Place Type: Census Designated Place
County: Lee
Population: 33,430

Ancestry/Race	Number	%
African American/Black:	3,192	9.55
Not Hispanic (2,835)	3,044	9.11
Hispanic (103)	148	0.44
African, sub-Saharan:	110	0.33
African	110	0.33
Alaska Native tribes, specified:	2	0.01
Eskimo	2	0.01
Am. Ind. or Alaska Nat., not spec.	84	0.25
American Indian tribes, specified:	114	0.34
Apache	5	0.01
Blackfeet (1)	3	0.01
Cherokee (13)	39	0.12
Chippewa (1)	5	0.01
Choctaw (1)	1	0.00
Comanche	2	0.01
Cree (1)	2	0.01
Creek (1)	2	0.01
Delaware (1)	1	0.00
Iroquois (18)	20	0.06
Latin American Indians (7)	14	0.04
Lumbee (1)	1	0.00
Navajo (2)	2	0.01
Ottawa (1)	2	0.01
Potawatomi	3	0.01
Seminole	1	0.00
Shoshone (1)	1	0.00
Sioux (1)	4	0.01
All other tribes (5)	6	0.02
American Indian tribes, not spec.	20	0.06
Arab:	64	0.19
Arab/Arabic	13	0.04
Egyptian	15	0.05
Lebanese	31	0.09
Syrian	5	0.02
Armenian	17	0.05
Asian:	402	1.20
Cambodian (2)	3	0.01
Chinese, ex. Taiwanese (64)	80	0.24
Filipino (59)	91	0.27
Indian (58)	84	0.25
Indonesian (2)	9	0.03
Japanese (12)	22	0.07
Korean (25)	38	0.11
Laotian (21)	21	0.06
Thai (3)	6	0.02
Vietnamese (21)	27	0.08
Other Asian, not specified (10)	21	0.06
Austrian	74	0.22
Belgian	61	0.18
British	120	0.36
Canadian	169	0.51
Croatian	21	0.06
Czech	85	0.26
Czechoslovakian	81	0.24
Danish	120	0.36
Dutch	410	1.24
English	3,514	10.60
European	50	0.15
Finnish	40	0.12
French, except Basque	932	2.81
French Canadian	393	1.19
German	4,991	15.06
Greek	112	0.34
Guyanese	50	0.15
Hawaii Native/Pacific Islander:	54	0.16
Melanesian: (1)	1	0.00
Fijian (1)	1	0.00
Micronesian: (1)	6	0.02
Guamanian/Chamorro (1)	6	0.02
Polynesian: (1)	16	0.05
Native Hawaiian	11	0.03
Samoan (1)	5	0.01
Other Pac. Isl., not spec. (3)	31	0.09
Hispanic or Latino:	4,466	13.36
Central American:	135	0.40
Costa Rican	22	0.07
Guatemalan	35	0.10
Honduran	22	0.07
Nicaraguan	12	0.04
Panamanian	26	0.08
Salvadoran	15	0.04
Other Central American	3	0.01
Cuban	239	0.71
Dominican Republic	38	0.11
Mexican	1,169	3.50
Puerto Rican	2,098	6.28
South American:	164	0.49
Argentinean	4	0.01
Chilean	8	0.02
Colombian	82	0.25
Ecuadorian	14	0.04
Paraguayan	10	0.03
Peruvian	23	0.07
Venezuelan	16	0.05
Other South American	7	0.02
Other Hispanic or Latino	623	1.86
Hungarian	207	0.62
Irish	4,115	12.42
Israeli	9	0.03
Italian	2,627	7.93
Lithuanian	24	0.07
Macedonian	4	0.01
Northern European	13	0.04

Notes: 1. Figures in the "Number" column do not add up to the total population due to: a) Ancestry/Race overlap — e.g. persons can report being both White and Irish, b) persons of Hispanic origin can report being any race, c) persons reporting two ancestries are counted in both categories. 2. Numbers in parentheses indicate the number of persons reporting this ancestry/race alone, not in combination with any other ancestry/race. 3. Refer to the User's Guide in the front of the book for more detailed information.

Norwegian	368	1.11
Pennsylvania German	44	0.13
Polish	976	2.94
Portuguese	159	0.48
Romanian	24	0.07
Russian	149	0.45
Scandinavian	18	0.05
Scotch-Irish	524	1.58
Scottish	747	2.25
Serbian	6	0.02
Slovak	116	0.35
Slovene	20	0.06
Swedish	304	0.92
Swiss	99	0.30
Turkish	33	0.10
Ukrainian	42	0.13
United States or American	3,935	11.87
Welsh	185	0.56
West Indian, excl. Hispanic:	962	2.90
Bahamian	20	0.06
Barbadian	6	0.02
British West Indian	61	0.18
Dutch West Indian	7	0.02
Haitian	285	0.86
Jamaican	545	1.64
Trinidadian and Tobagonian	10	0.03
West Indian	28	0.08
White:	28,699	85.85
Not Hispanic (25,287)	25,600	76.58
Hispanic (2,896)	3,099	9.27
Yugoslavian	18	0.05

Leisure City

Place Type: Census Designated Place
County: Miami-Dade
Population: 22,152

Ancestry/Race	Number	%
African American/Black:	4,278	19.31
Not Hispanic (3,769)	3,975	17.94
Hispanic (218)	303	1.37
African, sub-Saharan:	171	0.79
African	159	0.73
Cape Verdean	12	0.06
Am. Ind. or Alaska Nat., not spec.	45	0.20
American Indian tribes, specified:	59	0.27
Blackfeet	1	0.00
Cherokee (4)	21	0.09
Choctaw	1	0.00
Cree (1)	1	0.00
Iroquois	5	0.02
Latin American Indians (8)	21	0.09
Lumbee (1)	1	0.00
Seminole (2)	2	0.01
All other tribes (2)	6	0.03
American Indian tribes, not spec.	7	0.03
Arab:	13	0.06
Arab/Arabic	13	0.06
Asian:	276	1.25
Bangladeshi	3	0.01
Chinese, ex. Taiwanese (13)	21	0.09
Filipino (18)	37	0.17
Indian (32)	42	0.19
Japanese (11)	15	0.07
Korean (17)	30	0.14
Laotian (25)	25	0.11
Malaysian (1)	1	0.00
Pakistani (8)	8	0.04
Sri Lankan (1)	1	0.00
Taiwanese	7	0.03
Thai (29)	39	0.18
Vietnamese (16)	22	0.10
Other Asian, not specified (10)	25	0.11
Brazilian	10	0.05
British	26	0.12
Czechoslovakian	17	0.08
Dutch	96	0.44
English	261	1.20
European	22	0.10
Finnish	6	0.03
French, except Basque	166	0.76
French Canadian	40	0.18
German	629	2.89
Greek	12	0.06
Hawaii Native/Pacific Islander:	26	0.12
Micronesian: (1)	1	0.00
Guamanian/Chamorro (1)	1	0.00
Polynesian: (3)	6	0.03
Native Hawaiian (1)	3	0.01
Samoan (2)	3	0.01
Other Pac. Isl., not spec. (3)	19	0.09
Hispanic or Latino:	14,465	65.30
Central American:	1,154	5.21
Costa Rican	52	0.23
Guatemalan	236	1.07
Honduran	213	0.96
Nicaraguan	304	1.37
Panamanian	34	0.15
Salvadoran	286	1.29
Other Central American	29	0.13
Cuban	3,799	17.15
Dominican Republic	221	1.00
Mexican	5,259	23.74
Puerto Rican	1,960	8.85
South American:	464	2.09
Argentinean	11	0.05
Bolivian	23	0.10
Chilean	28	0.13
Colombian	224	1.01
Ecuadorian	55	0.25
Peruvian	65	0.29
Uruguayan	8	0.04
Venezuelan	40	0.18
Other South American	10	0.05
Other Hispanic or Latino	1,608	7.26
Hungarian	22	0.10
Irish	648	2.98
Italian	234	1.07
Norwegian	32	0.15
Polish	60	0.28
Portuguese	83	0.38
Russian	26	0.12
Scandinavian	7	0.03
Scotch-Irish	58	0.27
Scottish	89	0.41
Serbian	7	0.03
Slovak	6	0.03
Swedish	49	0.23
Swiss	5	0.02
United States or American	1,119	5.14
Welsh	13	0.06
West Indian, excl. Hispanic:	1,067	4.90
Bahamian	32	0.15
British West Indian	18	0.08
Dutch West Indian	9	0.04
Haitian	765	3.51
Jamaican	170	0.78
Trinidadian and Tobagonian	73	0.34
White:	15,146	68.37
Not Hispanic (3,356)	3,498	15.79
Hispanic (11,050)	11,648	52.58
Yugoslavian	23	0.11

Lighthouse Point

Place Type: City
County: Broward
Population: 10,767

Ancestry/Race	Number	%
African American/Black:	61	0.57
Not Hispanic (46)	61	0.57
Am. Ind. or Alaska Nat., not spec.	10	0.09
Alsatian	9	0.08
American Indian tribes, specified:	30	0.28
Blackfeet (1)	2	0.02
Cherokee (3)	11	0.10
Comanche	1	0.01
Cree (1)	1	0.01
Iroquois (2)	2	0.02
Potawatomi	1	0.01
Seminole	1	0.01
Sioux	5	0.05
Ute	1	0.01
All other tribes (2)	5	0.05
American Indian tribes, not spec.	6	0.06
Arab:	78	0.73
Egyptian	15	0.14
Iraqi	9	0.08
Jordanian	9	0.08
Lebanese	31	0.29
Syrian	14	0.13
Armenian	26	0.24
Asian:	116	1.08
Chinese, ex. Taiwanese (29)	33	0.31
Filipino (5)	17	0.16
Indian (9)	11	0.10
Japanese (2)	2	0.02
Korean (18)	21	0.20
Taiwanese (3)	3	0.03
Thai (8)	8	0.07
Vietnamese (9)	11	0.10
Other Asian, specified	1	0.01
Other Asian, not specified (2)	9	0.08
Austrian	87	0.82
Belgian	9	0.08
Brazilian	38	0.36
British	173	1.62
Bulgarian	9	0.08
Canadian	75	0.70
Croatian	14	0.13
Czech	23	0.22
Czechoslovakian	71	0.67
Danish	36	0.34
Dutch	154	1.44
Eastern European	18	0.17
English	1,600	15.00
European	88	0.82
Finnish	61	0.57
French, except Basque	429	4.02
French Canadian	152	1.42
German	1,771	16.60
Greek	115	1.08
Hawaii Native/Pacific Islander:	6	0.06
Micronesian:	3	0.03
Guamanian/Chamorro	3	0.03
Polynesian: (1)	3	0.03
Native Hawaiian (1)	2	0.02
Other Polynesian	1	0.01
Hispanic or Latino:	450	4.18
Central American:	24	0.22
Costa Rican	6	0.06
Guatemalan	2	0.02
Honduran	6	0.06
Nicaraguan	5	0.05
Panamanian	1	0.01
Salvadoran	1	0.01
Other Central American	3	0.03
Cuban	100	0.93
Dominican Republic	2	0.02
Mexican	34	0.32
Puerto Rican	87	0.81
South American:	103	0.96
Argentinean	18	0.17
Chilean	2	0.02
Colombian	45	0.42
Ecuadorian	7	0.07
Paraguayan	1	0.01
Peruvian	16	0.15
Uruguayan	1	0.01
Venezuelan	3	0.03
Other South American	10	0.09
Other Hispanic or Latino	100	0.93
Hungarian	148	1.39
Icelander	13	0.12
Irish	2,023	18.96
Israeli	45	0.42
Italian	1,891	17.73
Latvian	6	0.06
Lithuanian	73	0.68
Macedonian	9	0.08
Maltese	17	0.16
Norwegian	158	1.48

Notes: 1. Figures in the "Number" column do not add up to the total population due to: a) Ancestry/Race overlap — e.g. persons can report being both White and Irish, b) persons of Hispanic origin can report being any race, c) persons reporting two ancestries are counted in both categories. 2. Numbers in parentheses indicate the number of persons reporting this ancestry/race alone, not in combination with any other ancestry/race. 3. Refer to the User's Guide in the front of the book for more detailed information.

Polish	573	5.37
Portuguese	49	0.46
Romanian	31	0.29
Russian	228	2.14
Scandinavian	9	0.08
Scotch-Irish	258	2.42
Scottish	396	3.71
Slavic	13	0.12
Slovak	29	0.27
Slovene	23	0.22
Swedish	242	2.27
Swiss	45	0.42
Turkish	29	0.27
Ukrainian	39	0.37
United States or American	697	6.53
Welsh	104	0.97
West Indian, excl. Hispanic:	38	0.36
Bahamian	11	0.10
Jamaican	27	0.25
White:	10,562	98.10
Not Hispanic (10,071)	10,149	94.26
Hispanic (378)	413	3.84
Yugoslavian	17	0.16

Lockhart

Place Type: Census Designated Place
County: Orange
Population: 12,944

Ancestry/Race	Number	%
African American/Black:	2,230	17.23
Not Hispanic (2,010)	2,102	16.24
Hispanic (71)	128	0.99
African, sub-Saharan:	119	0.95
African	73	0.58
Nigerian	16	0.13
Other sub-Saharan African	30	0.24
Am. Ind. or Alaska Nat., not spec.	51	0.39
American Indian tribes, specified:	88	0.68
Blackfeet	1	0.01
Cherokee (13)	41	0.32
Chippewa (2)	4	0.03
Choctaw (2)	6	0.05
Cree (1)	1	0.01
Creek (5)	6	0.05
Iroquois (8)	9	0.07
Latin American Indians (6)	10	0.08
Navajo (6)	6	0.05
Yuman	1	0.01
All other tribes (2)	3	0.02
American Indian tribes, not spec.	16	0.12
Arab:	33	0.26
Lebanese	25	0.20
Syrian	8	0.06
Asian:	354	2.73
Chinese, ex. Taiwanese (23)	30	0.23
Filipino (91)	119	0.92
Indian (38)	43	0.33
Indonesian (6)	6	0.05
Japanese (11)	19	0.15
Korean (2)	8	0.06
Laotian	4	0.03
Sri Lankan (1)	1	0.01
Thai (3)	7	0.05
Vietnamese (107)	112	0.87
Other Asian, not specified (2)	5	0.04
Austrian	27	0.22
British	62	0.49
Celtic	21	0.17
Croatian	9	0.07
Czechoslovakian	51	0.41
Danish	24	0.19
Dutch	179	1.43
English	922	7.36
European	68	0.54
French, except Basque	389	3.10
French Canadian	132	1.05
German	1,600	12.77
Greek	17	0.14
Guyanese	51	0.41
Hawaii Native/Pacific Islander:	25	0.19
Micronesian: (1)	3	0.02
Other Micronesian (1)	3	0.02
Polynesian: (2)	6	0.05
Native Hawaiian (1)	5	0.04
Samoan (1)	1	0.01
Other Pac. Isl., not spec. (2)	16	0.12
Hispanic or Latino:	2,083	16.09
Central American:	60	0.46
Costa Rican	9	0.07
Guatemalan	3	0.02
Honduran	24	0.19
Nicaraguan	4	0.03
Panamanian	8	0.06
Salvadoran	4	0.03
Other Central American	8	0.06
Cuban	163	1.26
Dominican Republic	76	0.59
Mexican	256	1.98
Puerto Rican	1,123	8.68
South American:	135	1.04
Argentinean	3	0.02
Chilean	10	0.08
Colombian	53	0.41
Ecuadorian	19	0.15
Paraguayan	1	0.01
Peruvian	16	0.12
Uruguayan	1	0.01
Venezuelan	18	0.14
Other South American	14	0.11
Other Hispanic or Latino	270	2.09
Hungarian	68	0.54
Irish	1,320	10.53
Italian	540	4.31
Latvian	9	0.07
Lithuanian	12	0.10
Norwegian	84	0.67
Polish	247	1.97
Portuguese	42	0.34
Romanian	9	0.07
Russian	63	0.50
Scandinavian	9	0.07
Scotch-Irish	149	1.19
Scottish	289	2.31
Slovak	43	0.34
Swedish	83	0.66
Swiss	18	0.14
United States or American	1,317	10.51
Welsh	50	0.40
West Indian, excl. Hispanic:	394	3.14
British West Indian	9	0.07
Haitian	108	0.86
Jamaican	209	1.67
Trinidadian and Tobagonian	57	0.45
West Indian	11	0.09
White:	9,871	76.26
Not Hispanic (8,244)	8,432	65.14
Hispanic (1,308)	1,439	11.12
Yugoslavian	50	0.40

Longwood

Place Type: City
County: Seminole
Population: 13,745

Ancestry/Race	Number	%
African American/Black:	584	4.25
Not Hispanic (450)	514	3.74
Hispanic (45)	70	0.51
African, sub-Saharan:	37	0.27
African	31	0.23
South African	6	0.04
Am. Ind. or Alaska Nat., not spec.	40	0.29
American Indian tribes, specified:	90	0.65
Apache	2	0.01
Blackfeet (2)	3	0.02
Cherokee (8)	50	0.36
Chippewa (1)	1	0.01
Choctaw	2	0.01
Comanche	1	0.01
Cree	1	0.01
Creek (4)	6	0.04
Iroquois (1)	6	0.04
Latin American Indians (3)	6	0.04
Ottawa	2	0.01
Pueblo (1)	1	0.01
Shoshone	5	0.04
Sioux	2	0.01
All other tribes	2	0.01
American Indian tribes, not spec.	3	0.02
Arab:	132	0.96
Lebanese	56	0.41
Moroccan	7	0.05
Palestinian	21	0.15
Syrian	48	0.35
Asian:	426	3.10
Bangladeshi (13)	13	0.09
Chinese, ex. Taiwanese (44)	51	0.37
Filipino (38)	57	0.41
Hmong (6)	6	0.04
Indian (83)	114	0.83
Indonesian (1)	1	0.01
Japanese (2)	3	0.02
Korean (48)	52	0.38
Laotian (26)	28	0.20
Malaysian (5)	5	0.04
Taiwanese	4	0.03
Thai (4)	7	0.05
Vietnamese (61)	70	0.51
Other Asian, specified (1)	1	0.01
Other Asian, not specified (2)	14	0.10
Austrian	57	0.42
Basque	6	0.04
Belgian	49	0.36
Brazilian	43	0.31
British	44	0.32
Bulgarian	8	0.06
Canadian	127	0.93
Celtic	7	0.05
Croatian	17	0.12
Czech	60	0.44
Czechoslovakian	35	0.26
Danish	17	0.12
Dutch	349	2.55
English	1,808	13.19
European	77	0.56
Finnish	16	0.12
French, except Basque	438	3.19
French Canadian	91	0.66
German	2,474	18.04
Greek	61	0.44
Guyanese	7	0.05
Hawaii Native/Pacific Islander:	22	0.16
Polynesian: (1)	3	0.02
Native Hawaiian (1)	2	0.01
Samoan	1	0.01
Other Pac. Isl., not spec. (5)	19	0.14
Hispanic or Latino:	1,519	11.05
Central American:	86	0.63
Costa Rican	19	0.14
Guatemalan	6	0.04
Honduran	15	0.11
Nicaraguan	6	0.04
Panamanian	13	0.09
Salvadoran	24	0.17
Other Central American	3	0.02
Cuban	162	1.18
Dominican Republic	48	0.35
Mexican	145	1.05
Puerto Rican	653	4.75
South American:	152	1.11
Argentinean	10	0.07
Bolivian	1	0.01
Chilean	4	0.03
Colombian	72	0.52
Ecuadorian	23	0.17
Peruvian	23	0.17
Uruguayan	1	0.01
Venezuelan	6	0.04
Other South American	12	0.09
Other Hispanic or Latino	273	1.99
Hungarian	183	1.33

Notes: 1. Figures in the "Number" column do not add up to the total population due to: a) Ancestry/Race overlap — e.g. persons can report being both White and Irish, b) persons of Hispanic origin can report being any race, c) persons reporting two ancestries are counted in both categories. 2. Numbers in parentheses indicate the number of persons reporting this ancestry/race alone, not in combination with any other ancestry/race. 3. Refer to the User's Guide in the front of the book for more detailed information.

Icelander	35	0.26
Irish	2,192	15.99
Italian	1,255	9.15
Latvian	4	0.03
Lithuanian	42	0.31
Northern European	13	0.09
Norwegian	127	0.93
Pennsylvania German	7	0.05
Polish	456	3.33
Portuguese	92	0.67
Romanian	12	0.09
Russian	259	1.89
Scotch-Irish	190	1.39
Scottish	285	2.08
Serbian	22	0.16
Slovak	101	0.74
Slovene	9	0.07
Swedish	262	1.91
Swiss	64	0.47
Turkish	16	0.12
Ukrainian	6	0.04
United States or American	949	6.92
Welsh	72	0.53
West Indian, excl. Hispanic:	98	0.71
Belizean	20	0.15
Jamaican	33	0.24
Trinidadian and Tobagonian	45	0.33
White:	12,249	89.12
Not Hispanic (11,145)	11,294	82.17
Hispanic (854)	955	6.95

Lutz

Place Type: Census Designated Place
County: Hillsborough
Population: 17,081

Ancestry/Race	Number	%
African American/Black:	565	3.31
Not Hispanic (491)	527	3.09
Hispanic (21)	38	0.22
Alaska Native tribes, specified:	2	0.01
Alaska Athabascan (1)	1	0.01
Aleut (1)	1	0.01
Am. Ind. or Alaska Nat., not spec.	38	0.22
American Indian tribes, specified:	99	0.58
Apache	1	0.01
Blackfeet	4	0.02
Cherokee (13)	45	0.26
Cheyenne (1)	1	0.01
Chippewa (1)	1	0.01
Choctaw (2)	7	0.04
Creek (3)	5	0.03
Crow	2	0.01
Iroquois (2)	7	0.04
Latin American Indians	7	0.04
Lumbee (2)	2	0.01
Menominee (1)	1	0.01
Navajo (1)	1	0.01
Seminole (2)	2	0.01
Sioux (3)	5	0.03
All other tribes (2)	8	0.05
American Indian tribes, not spec.	5	0.03
Arab:	37	0.22
Arab/Arabic	12	0.07
Lebanese	16	0.09
Syrian	9	0.05
Armenian	13	0.08
Asian:	320	1.87
Chinese, ex. Taiwanese (32)	40	0.23
Filipino (58)	74	0.43
Indian (43)	63	0.37
Indonesian (2)	9	0.05
Japanese (13)	27	0.16
Korean (30)	36	0.21
Malaysian (1)	2	0.01
Taiwanese (5)	5	0.03
Thai (8)	14	0.08
Vietnamese (35)	37	0.22
Other Asian, specified (2)	2	0.01
Other Asian, not specified (9)	11	0.06
Austrian	22	0.13
Basque	9	0.05
Belgian	77	0.45
Brazilian	24	0.14
British	123	0.72
Canadian	32	0.19
Croatian	39	0.23
Czech	108	0.63
Czechoslovakian	48	0.28
Danish	83	0.49
Dutch	456	2.67
Eastern European	13	0.08
English	2,517	14.76
European	63	0.37
Finnish	53	0.31
French, except Basque	596	3.49
French Canadian	116	0.68
German	3,091	18.12
Greek	100	0.59
Hawaii Native/Pacific Islander:	14	0.08
Polynesian:	3	0.02
Native Hawaiian	3	0.02
Other Pac. Isl., not spec. (1)	11	0.06
Hispanic or Latino:	1,343	7.86
Central American:	40	0.23
Costa Rican	7	0.04
Honduran	9	0.05
Nicaraguan	8	0.05
Panamanian	12	0.07
Salvadoran	3	0.02
Other Central American	1	0.01
Cuban	255	1.49
Dominican Republic	18	0.11
Mexican	84	0.49
Puerto Rican	362	2.12
South American:	114	0.67
Argentinean	6	0.04
Bolivian	2	0.01
Colombian	55	0.32
Ecuadorian	14	0.08
Peruvian	15	0.09
Uruguayan	1	0.01
Venezuelan	18	0.11
Other South American	3	0.02
Other Hispanic or Latino	470	2.75
Hungarian	186	1.09
Irish	2,793	16.38
Italian	1,385	8.12
Lithuanian	131	0.77
Maltese	8	0.05
Norwegian	152	0.89
Pennsylvania German	29	0.17
Polish	524	3.07
Portuguese	135	0.79
Romanian	11	0.06
Russian	90	0.53
Scandinavian	24	0.14
Scotch-Irish	311	1.82
Scottish	488	2.86
Serbian	28	0.16
Slavic	7	0.04
Slovak	9	0.05
Slovene	20	0.12
Swedish	220	1.29
Swiss	34	0.20
Ukrainian	26	0.15
United States or American	1,714	10.05
Welsh	197	1.16
West Indian, excl. Hispanic:	88	0.52
Belizean	21	0.12
British West Indian	27	0.16
Jamaican	20	0.12
Trinidadian and Tobagonian	12	0.07
West Indian	8	0.05
White:	16,021	93.79
Not Hispanic (14,752)	14,917	87.33
Hispanic (1,042)	1,104	6.46
Yugoslavian	36	0.21

Lynn Haven

Place Type: City
County: Bay
Population: 12,451

Ancestry/Race	Number	%
Acadian/Cajun	11	0.09
African American/Black:	1,218	9.78
Not Hispanic (1,157)	1,208	9.70
Hispanic (7)	10	0.08
African, sub-Saharan:	22	0.18
African	22	0.18
Alaska Native tribes, specified:	3	0.02
Alaska Athabascan (1)	1	0.01
Aleut	1	0.01
Tlingit-Haida (1)	1	0.01
Am. Ind. or Alaska Nat., not spec.	30	0.24
American Indian tribes, specified:	119	0.96
Apache	2	0.02
Blackfeet (1)	1	0.01
Cherokee (22)	45	0.36
Chippewa (3)	3	0.02
Choctaw (2)	3	0.02
Cree (1)	1	0.01
Creek (26)	44	0.35
Crow (1)	1	0.01
Houma (2)	2	0.02
Latin American Indians (1)	1	0.01
Lumbee (5)	5	0.04
Sioux (8)	8	0.06
All other tribes (2)	3	0.02
American Indian tribes, not spec.	8	0.06
Arab:	75	0.61
Egyptian	11	0.09
Palestinian	9	0.07
Syrian	55	0.45
Asian:	258	2.07
Cambodian (8)	8	0.06
Chinese, ex. Taiwanese (17)	23	0.18
Filipino (48)	70	0.56
Indian (36)	40	0.32
Indonesian (1)	1	0.01
Japanese (9)	17	0.14
Korean (36)	41	0.33
Malaysian	1	0.01
Pakistani (7)	8	0.06
Taiwanese	1	0.01
Thai (3)	5	0.04
Vietnamese (17)	25	0.20
Other Asian, not specified (13)	18	0.14
Austrian	31	0.25
Belgian	8	0.06
British	69	0.56
Canadian	7	0.06
Czech	27	0.22
Danish	36	0.29
Dutch	272	2.20
English	1,433	11.60
European	141	1.14
Finnish	9	0.07
French, except Basque	426	3.45
French Canadian	47	0.38
German	1,598	12.94
Hawaii Native/Pacific Islander:	32	0.26
Micronesian: (3)	4	0.03
Guamanian/Chamorro (3)	4	0.03
Polynesian: (11)	26	0.21
Native Hawaiian (9)	23	0.18
Samoan	1	0.01
Other Polynesian (2)	2	0.02
Other Pac. Isl., not spec.	2	0.02
Hispanic or Latino:	202	1.62
Central American:	15	0.12
Costa Rican	9	0.07
Guatemalan	1	0.01
Honduran	1	0.01
Panamanian	4	0.03
Cuban	22	0.18
Dominican Republic	5	0.04
Mexican	51	0.41

Notes: 1. Figures in the "Number" column do not add up to the total population due to: a) Ancestry/Race overlap — e.g. persons can report being both White and Irish, b) persons of Hispanic origin can report being any race, c) persons reporting two ancestries are counted in both categories. 2. Numbers in parentheses indicate the number of persons reporting this ancestry/race alone, not in combination with any other ancestry/race. 3. Refer to the User's Guide in the front of the book for more detailed information.

Puerto Rican	63	0.51
South American:	5	0.04
Argentinean	1	0.01
Colombian	2	0.02
Peruvian	1	0.01
Venezuelan	1	0.01
Other Hispanic or Latino	41	0.33
Icelander	15	0.12
Irish	1,776	14.38
Italian	306	2.48
Lithuanian	9	0.07
Northern European	13	0.11
Norwegian	73	0.59
Polish	230	1.86
Portuguese	49	0.40
Russian	31	0.25
Scandinavian	44	0.36
Scotch-Irish	300	2.43
Scottish	294	2.38
Serbian	8	0.06
Slavic	23	0.19
Slovene	7	0.06
Swedish	97	0.79
United States or American	1,838	14.88
Welsh	33	0.27
West Indian, excl. Hispanic:	45	0.36
Bahamian	6	0.05
Trinidadian and Tobagonian	39	0.32
White:	10,913	87.65
Not Hispanic (10,604)	10,762	86.43
Hispanic (134)	151	1.21
Yugoslavian	5	0.04

Maitland

Place Type: City
County: Orange
Population: 12,019

Ancestry/Race	Number	%
African American/Black:	1,249	10.39
Not Hispanic (1,135)	1,202	10.00
Hispanic (34)	47	0.39
African, sub-Saharan:	100	0.84
African	78	0.65
Nigerian	22	0.18
Alaska Native tribes, specified:	1	0.01
Aleut (1)	1	0.01
Am. Ind. or Alaska Nat., not spec.	15	0.12
American Indian tribes, specified:	32	0.27
Apache	1	0.01
Cherokee (3)	13	0.11
Chippewa	1	0.01
Choctaw	1	0.01
Creek	6	0.05
Iroquois	1	0.01
Latin American Indians (1)	2	0.02
Lumbee (1)	1	0.01
Menominee	1	0.01
Seminole (1)	4	0.03
Sioux (1)	1	0.01
American Indian tribes, not spec.	2	0.02
Arab:	77	0.65
Arab/Arabic	8	0.07
Egyptian	24	0.20
Iraqi	9	0.08
Lebanese	14	0.12
Palestinian	8	0.07
Syrian	8	0.07
Other Arab	6	0.05
Armenian	20	0.17
Asian:	312	2.60
Bangladeshi (2)	2	0.02
Cambodian (1)	1	0.01
Chinese, ex. Taiwanese (39)	49	0.41
Filipino (16)	29	0.24
Indian (95)	104	0.87
Indonesian (1)	1	0.01
Japanese (8)	20	0.17
Korean (20)	21	0.17
Laotian (6)	6	0.05
Malaysian	1	0.01
Pakistani (1)	2	0.02
Thai (4)	8	0.07
Vietnamese (48)	50	0.42
Other Asian, specified (1)	1	0.01
Other Asian, not specified (14)	17	0.14
Australian	8	0.07
Austrian	50	0.42
Belgian	12	0.10
Brazilian	16	0.13
British	84	0.70
Bulgarian	30	0.25
Canadian	60	0.50
Croatian	19	0.16
Czech	45	0.38
Czechoslovakian	6	0.05
Danish	35	0.29
Dutch	75	0.63
Eastern European	88	0.74
English	1,988	16.66
Estonian	7	0.06
European	247	2.07
Finnish	29	0.24
French, except Basque	485	4.06
French Canadian	121	1.01
German	1,694	14.19
Greek	47	0.39
Guyanese	10	0.08
Hawaii Native/Pacific Islander:	8	0.07
Polynesian:	1	0.01
Native Hawaiian	1	0.01
Other Pac. Isl., not spec. (1)	7	0.06
Hispanic or Latino:	717	5.97
Central American:	17	0.14
Guatemalan	1	0.01
Honduran	1	0.01
Nicaraguan	3	0.02
Panamanian	11	0.09
Other Central American	1	0.01
Cuban	71	0.59
Dominican Republic	18	0.15
Mexican	45	0.37
Puerto Rican	328	2.73
South American:	105	0.87
Argentinean	19	0.16
Chilean	4	0.03
Colombian	44	0.37
Ecuadorian	14	0.12
Peruvian	7	0.06
Venezuelan	17	0.14
Other Hispanic or Latino	133	1.11
Hungarian	117	0.98
Icelander	10	0.08
Iranian	24	0.20
Irish	1,318	11.04
Italian	626	5.25
Latvian	7	0.06
Lithuanian	46	0.39
Northern European	14	0.12
Norwegian	131	1.10
Pennsylvania German	13	0.11
Polish	300	2.51
Portuguese	45	0.38
Romanian	68	0.57
Russian	300	2.51
Scandinavian	17	0.14
Scotch-Irish	377	3.16
Scottish	393	3.29
Serbian	7	0.06
Slovak	26	0.22
Slovene	29	0.24
Swedish	156	1.31
Swiss	11	0.09
Ukrainian	32	0.27
United States or American	900	7.54
Welsh	79	0.66
West Indian, excl. Hispanic:	115	0.96
Haitian	8	0.07
Jamaican	87	0.73
Trinidadian and Tobagonian	5	0.04
U.S. Virgin Islander	15	0.13
White:	10,395	86.49
Not Hispanic (9,732)	9,855	82.00
Hispanic (511)	540	4.49
Yugoslavian	39	0.33

Marathon

Place Type: City
County: Monroe
Population: 10,255

Ancestry/Race	Number	%
African American/Black:	529	5.16
Not Hispanic (449)	499	4.87
Hispanic (28)	30	0.29
African, sub-Saharan:	30	0.29
African	30	0.29
Am. Ind. or Alaska Nat., not spec.	24	0.23
American Indian tribes, specified:	43	0.42
Apache (2)	2	0.02
Blackfeet (3)	4	0.04
Cherokee (8)	18	0.18
Chickasaw	1	0.01
Chippewa (2)	2	0.02
Cree (1)	2	0.02
Creek (1)	1	0.01
Iroquois	3	0.03
Latin American Indians	2	0.02
Ottawa	1	0.01
Sioux (1)	4	0.04
All other tribes (2)	3	0.03
American Indian tribes, not spec.	5	0.05
Arab:	25	0.25
Lebanese	25	0.25
Armenian	7	0.07
Asian:	68	0.66
Cambodian (2)	4	0.04
Chinese, ex. Taiwanese (13)	17	0.17
Filipino (10)	14	0.14
Indian (8)	8	0.08
Japanese (2)	2	0.02
Korean (6)	6	0.06
Laotian	2	0.02
Thai (1)	3	0.03
Vietnamese (5)	5	0.05
Other Asian, not specified (1)	7	0.07
Austrian	27	0.26
Belgian	17	0.17
British	55	0.54
Bulgarian	37	0.36
Canadian	46	0.45
Croatian	14	0.14
Czech	42	0.41
Czechoslovakian	21	0.21
Danish	55	0.54
Dutch	106	1.04
English	1,293	12.68
European	101	0.99
Finnish	30	0.29
French, except Basque	454	4.45
French Canadian	111	1.09
German	1,752	17.19
Greek	16	0.16
Hawaii Native/Pacific Islander:	12	0.12
Micronesian:	2	0.02
Guamanian/Chamorro	2	0.02
Polynesian: (4)	4	0.04
Native Hawaiian (4)	4	0.04
Other Pac. Isl., not spec.	6	0.06
Hispanic or Latino:	2,095	20.43
Central American:	300	2.93
Costa Rican	9	0.09
Guatemalan	120	1.17
Honduran	31	0.30
Nicaraguan	133	1.30
Salvadoran	7	0.07
Cuban	1,212	11.82
Dominican Republic	24	0.23
Mexican	270	2.63
Puerto Rican	92	0.90
South American:	80	0.78
Argentinean	18	0.18
Bolivian	2	0.02

Notes: 1. Figures in the "Number" column do not add up to the total population due to: a) Ancestry/Race overlap — e.g. persons can report being both White and Irish, b) persons of Hispanic origin can report being any race, c) persons reporting two ancestries are counted in both categories. 2. Numbers in parentheses indicate the number of persons reporting this ancestry/race alone, not in combination with any other ancestry/race. 3. Refer to the User's Guide in the front of the book for more detailed information.

Chilean	1	0.01
Colombian	27	0.26
Ecuadorian	7	0.07
Peruvian	3	0.03
Uruguayan	1	0.01
Venezuelan	16	0.16
Other South American	5	0.05
Other Hispanic or Latino	117	1.14
Hungarian	35	0.34
Irish	1,600	15.70
Israeli	7	0.07
Italian	557	5.46
Latvian	10	0.10
Lithuanian	35	0.34
Macedonian	5	0.05
Northern European	10	0.10
Norwegian	54	0.53
Polish	396	3.88
Portuguese	11	0.11
Romanian	17	0.17
Russian	81	0.79
Scandinavian	9	0.09
Scotch-Irish	246	2.41
Scottish	363	3.56
Serbian	6	0.06
Slavic	8	0.08
Slovak	16	0.16
Slovene	19	0.19
Swedish	205	2.01
Swiss	54	0.53
Turkish	7	0.07
Ukrainian	45	0.44
United States or American	596	5.85
Welsh	76	0.75
West Indian, excl. Hispanic:	82	0.80
Bahamian	39	0.38
Belizean	13	0.13
Haitian	9	0.09
Jamaican	21	0.21
White:	9,432	91.97
Not Hispanic (7,513)	7,573	73.85
Hispanic (1,828)	1,859	18.13
Yugoslavian	7	0.07

Marco Island

Place Type: City
County: Collier
Population: 14,879

Ancestry/Race	Number	%
African American/Black:	42	0.28
Not Hispanic (35)	39	0.26
Hispanic	3	0.02
Alaska Native tribes, specified:	2	0.01
Tlingit-Haida (1)	2	0.01
Am. Ind. or Alaska Nat., not spec.	15	0.10
Alsatian	7	0.05
American Indian tribes, specified:	26	0.17
Apache (1)	2	0.01
Blackfeet (1)	1	0.01
Cherokee (3)	5	0.03
Latin American Indians (10)	10	0.07
Pueblo (1)	1	0.01
Sioux (2)	5	0.03
All other tribes (1)	2	0.01
American Indian tribes, not spec.	1	0.01
Arab:	106	0.71
Lebanese	52	0.35
Palestinian	49	0.33
Syrian	5	0.03
Armenian	51	0.34
Asian:	111	0.75
Chinese, ex. Taiwanese (18)	23	0.15
Filipino (22)	33	0.22
Indian (16)	18	0.12
Indonesian	2	0.01
Japanese (4)	4	0.03
Korean (11)	12	0.08
Pakistani (1)	1	0.01
Sri Lankan (1)	1	0.01
Taiwanese (1)	1	0.01
Vietnamese (10)	11	0.07
Other Asian, not specified (2)	5	0.03
Assyrian/Chaldean/Syriac	8	0.05
Australian	9	0.06
Austrian	107	0.71
Basque	19	0.13
Belgian	7	0.05
Brazilian	22	0.15
British	79	0.53
Canadian	117	0.78
Croatian	67	0.45
Czech	79	0.53
Czechoslovakian	67	0.45
Danish	137	0.91
Dutch	271	1.81
English	2,235	14.92
European	121	0.81
Finnish	127	0.85
French, except Basque	467	3.12
French Canadian	150	1.00
German	3,498	23.35
Greek	107	0.71
Hawaii Native/Pacific Islander:	3	0.02
Polynesian: (1)	1	0.01
Native Hawaiian (1)	1	0.01
Other Pac. Isl., not spec.	2	0.01
Hispanic or Latino:	608	4.09
Central American:	61	0.41
Costa Rican	9	0.06
Guatemalan	33	0.22
Honduran	4	0.03
Nicaraguan	1	0.01
Panamanian	2	0.01
Salvadoran	12	0.08
Cuban	157	1.06
Dominican Republic	6	0.04
Mexican	233	1.57
Puerto Rican	44	0.30
South American:	32	0.22
Argentinean	2	0.01
Colombian	17	0.11
Ecuadorian	4	0.03
Uruguayan	2	0.01
Venezuelan	6	0.04
Other South American	1	0.01
Other Hispanic or Latino	75	0.50
Hungarian	167	1.11
Iranian	8	0.05
Irish	2,892	19.31
Italian	2,014	13.44
Lithuanian	107	0.71
Luxemburger	6	0.04
Northern European	23	0.15
Norwegian	294	1.96
Polish	751	5.01
Portuguese	12	0.08
Romanian	37	0.25
Russian	216	1.44
Scandinavian	27	0.18
Scotch-Irish	350	2.34
Scottish	438	2.92
Slavic	25	0.17
Slovak	49	0.33
Slovene	9	0.06
Swedish	437	2.92
Swiss	109	0.73
Ukrainian	38	0.25
United States or American	758	5.06
Welsh	183	1.22
West Indian, excl. Hispanic:	10	0.07
British West Indian	10	0.07
White:	14,650	98.46
Not Hispanic (14,077)	14,125	94.93
Hispanic (517)	525	3.53
Yugoslavian	9	0.06

Margate

Place Type: City
County: Broward
Population: 53,909

Ancestry/Race	Number	%
African American/Black:	7,054	13.09
Not Hispanic (6,069)	6,760	12.54
Hispanic (199)	294	0.55
African, sub-Saharan:	286	0.53
African	232	0.43
Ethiopian	36	0.07
Nigerian	18	0.03
Alaska Native tribes, specified:	1	0.00
Tlingit-Haida (1)	1	0.00
Am. Ind. or Alaska Nat., not spec.	132	0.24
American Indian tribes, specified:	172	0.32
Apache (8)	10	0.02
Blackfeet	4	0.01
Cherokee (16)	62	0.12
Chippewa (2)	3	0.01
Choctaw (1)	5	0.01
Creek	4	0.01
Iroquois (4)	7	0.01
Latin American Indians (20)	42	0.08
Lumbee (4)	5	0.01
Navajo	4	0.01
Ottawa (1)	1	0.00
Seminole (1)	1	0.00
Sioux (1)	4	0.01
Tohono O'Odham	3	0.01
All other tribes (12)	17	0.03
American Indian tribes, not spec.	17	0.03
Arab:	250	0.46
Arab/Arabic	35	0.06
Egyptian	19	0.04
Jordanian	31	0.06
Lebanese	109	0.20
Moroccan	8	0.01
Palestinian	40	0.07
Syrian	8	0.01
Armenian	34	0.06
Asian:	1,916	3.55
Bangladeshi (17)	26	0.05
Cambodian (1)	2	0.00
Chinese, ex. Taiwanese (296)	386	0.72
Filipino (127)	186	0.35
Indian (550)	691	1.28
Indonesian (1)	1	0.00
Japanese (21)	40	0.07
Korean (43)	55	0.10
Laotian (2)	2	0.00
Malaysian (4)	4	0.01
Pakistani (23)	37	0.07
Taiwanese (2)	3	0.01
Thai (45)	49	0.09
Vietnamese (321)	345	0.64
Other Asian, specified	3	0.01
Other Asian, not specified (24)	86	0.16
Austrian	232	0.43
Belgian	13	0.02
Brazilian	258	0.48
British	205	0.38
Bulgarian	10	0.02
Canadian	272	0.51
Croatian	53	0.10
Czech	96	0.18
Czechoslovakian	104	0.19
Danish	122	0.23
Dutch	546	1.01
Eastern European	67	0.12
English	3,508	6.51
European	181	0.34
Finnish	73	0.14
French, except Basque	1,220	2.27
French Canadian	713	1.32
German	6,057	11.25
Greek	341	0.63
Guyanese	16	0.03
Hawaii Native/Pacific Islander:	118	0.22

Notes: 1. Figures in the "Number" column do not add up to the total population due to: a) Ancestry/Race overlap — e.g. persons can report being both White and Irish, b) persons of Hispanic origin can report being any race, c) persons reporting two ancestries are counted in both categories. 2. Numbers in parentheses indicate the number of persons reporting this ancestry/race alone, not in combination with any other ancestry/race. 3. Refer to the User's Guide in the front of the book for more detailed information.

Micronesian: (3)	6	0.01
Guamanian/Chamorro (3)	6	0.01
Polynesian: (9)	28	0.05
Native Hawaiian (4)	20	0.04
Samoan (2)	5	0.01
Tongan (1)	1	0.00
Other Polynesian (2)	2	0.00
Other Pac. Isl., specified	2	0.00
Other Pac. Isl., not spec. (19)	82	0.15
Hispanic or Latino:	8,238	15.28
Central American:	530	0.98
Costa Rican	36	0.07
Guatemalan	48	0.09
Honduran	104	0.19
Nicaraguan	62	0.12
Panamanian	37	0.07
Salvadoran	214	0.40
Other Central American	29	0.05
Cuban	796	1.48
Dominican Republic	247	0.46
Mexican	820	1.52
Puerto Rican	2,154	4.00
South American:	2,029	3.76
Argentinean	89	0.17
Bolivian	15	0.03
Chilean	51	0.09
Colombian	1,199	2.22
Ecuadorian	135	0.25
Paraguayan	5	0.01
Peruvian	315	0.58
Uruguayan	24	0.04
Venezuelan	136	0.25
Other South American	60	0.11
Other Hispanic or Latino	1,662	3.08
Hungarian	545	1.01
Iranian	26	0.05
Irish	6,034	11.20
Israeli	39	0.07
Italian	6,867	12.75
Latvian	27	0.05
Lithuanian	186	0.35
Luxemburger	8	0.01
Maltese	7	0.01
Norwegian	300	0.56
Pennsylvania German	23	0.04
Polish	2,393	4.44
Portuguese	189	0.35
Romanian	185	0.34
Russian	1,650	3.06
Scotch-Irish	440	0.82
Scottish	666	1.24
Slavic	35	0.06
Slovak	252	0.47
Swedish	400	0.74
Swiss	64	0.12
Turkish	27	0.05
Ukrainian	249	0.46
United States or American	3,332	6.19
Welsh	261	0.48
West Indian, excl. Hispanic:	4,094	7.60
Bahamian	33	0.06
Barbadian	35	0.06
Bermudan	10	0.02
British West Indian	25	0.05
Haitian	1,853	3.44
Jamaican	1,734	3.22
Trinidadian and Tobagonian	333	0.62
U.S. Virgin Islander	10	0.02
West Indian	61	0.11
White:	43,693	81.05
Not Hispanic (36,534)	37,165	68.94
Hispanic (5,944)	6,528	12.11
Yugoslavian	67	0.12

Meadow Woods

Place Type: Census Designated Place
County: Orange
Population: 11,286

Ancestry/Race	Number	%
African American/Black:	1,498	13.27
Not Hispanic (1,150)	1,241	11.00
Hispanic (199)	257	2.28
African, sub-Saharan:	49	0.43
African	24	0.21
Cape Verdean	16	0.14
Nigerian	9	0.08
Am. Ind. or Alaska Nat., not spec.	57	0.51
American Indian tribes, specified:	58	0.51
Blackfeet	3	0.03
Cherokee (12)	19	0.17
Choctaw (2)	4	0.04
Creek	1	0.01
Iroquois (1)	1	0.01
Latin American Indians (8)	22	0.19
Sioux (1)	1	0.01
All other tribes (2)	7	0.06
American Indian tribes, not spec.	5	0.04
Arab:	131	1.14
Arab/Arabic	30	0.26
Iraqi	30	0.26
Lebanese	9	0.08
Palestinian	44	0.38
Other Arab	18	0.16
Asian:	358	3.17
Bangladeshi (3)	3	0.03
Cambodian (2)	10	0.09
Chinese, ex. Taiwanese (58)	68	0.60
Filipino (79)	88	0.78
Indian (64)	77	0.68
Japanese (7)	15	0.13
Korean (12)	14	0.12
Laotian	2	0.02
Pakistani (9)	13	0.12
Taiwanese (11)	13	0.12
Thai (5)	8	0.07
Vietnamese (17)	19	0.17
Other Asian, specified	1	0.01
Other Asian, not specified (1)	27	0.24
British	54	0.47
Bulgarian	20	0.17
Canadian	34	0.30
Czech	20	0.17
Czechoslovakian	8	0.07
Danish	24	0.21
Dutch	58	0.51
English	492	4.28
European	31	0.27
Finnish	13	0.11
French, except Basque	164	1.43
French Canadian	47	0.41
German	796	6.93
Greek	44	0.38
Guyanese	28	0.24
Hawaii Native/Pacific Islander:	36	0.32
Polynesian: (12)	29	0.26
Native Hawaiian (8)	19	0.17
Samoan (1)	5	0.04
Tongan	1	0.01
Other Polynesian (3)	4	0.04
Other Pac. Isl., specified	1	0.01
Other Pac. Isl., not spec.	6	0.05
Hispanic or Latino:	5,964	52.84
Central American:	149	1.32
Costa Rican	19	0.17
Guatemalan	15	0.13
Honduran	7	0.06
Nicaraguan	24	0.21
Panamanian	44	0.39
Salvadoran	29	0.26
Other Central American	11	0.10
Cuban	225	1.99
Dominican Republic	228	2.02
Mexican	161	1.43
Puerto Rican	3,772	33.42
South American:	714	6.33
Argentinean	20	0.18
Bolivian	1	0.01
Chilean	7	0.06
Colombian	408	3.62
Ecuadorian	95	0.84
Peruvian	72	0.64
Uruguayan	8	0.07
Venezuelan	79	0.70
Other South American	24	0.21
Other Hispanic or Latino	715	6.34
Hungarian	29	0.25
Irish	747	6.50
Italian	623	5.42
Lithuanian	16	0.14
Northern European	10	0.09
Norwegian	7	0.06
Pennsylvania German	19	0.17
Polish	200	1.74
Russian	7	0.06
Scotch-Irish	94	0.82
Scottish	110	0.96
Slovak	57	0.50
Swedish	19	0.17
Swiss	30	0.26
Ukrainian	23	0.20
United States or American	412	3.59
Welsh	18	0.16
West Indian, excl. Hispanic:	482	4.20
Barbadian	41	0.36
Belizean	45	0.39
Haitian	130	1.13
Jamaican	145	1.26
Trinidadian and Tobagonian	28	0.24
West Indian	93	0.81
White:	7,947	70.41
Not Hispanic (3,592)	3,735	33.09
Hispanic (3,969)	4,212	37.32

Melbourne

Place Type: City
County: Brevard
Population: 71,382

Ancestry/Race	Number	%
African American/Black:	7,176	10.05
Not Hispanic (6,493)	6,920	9.69
Hispanic (165)	256	0.36
African, sub-Saharan:	438	0.61
African	299	0.42
Nigerian	124	0.17
Other sub-Saharan African	15	0.02
Alaska Native tribes, specified:	5	0.01
Aleut (1)	1	0.00
Eskimo (3)	4	0.01
Alaska Native tribes, not specified	4	0.01
Am. Ind. or Alaska Nat., not spec.	201	0.28
American Indian tribes, specified:	447	0.63
Apache (6)	8	0.01
Blackfeet (4)	22	0.03
Cherokee (69)	243	0.34
Cheyenne (7)	7	0.01
Chickasaw	1	0.00
Chippewa (12)	17	0.02
Choctaw (3)	16	0.02
Comanche (1)	1	0.00
Cree (2)	5	0.01
Creek (4)	9	0.01
Houma (1)	1	0.00
Iroquois (10)	14	0.02
Latin American Indians (3)	11	0.02
Lumbee (3)	3	0.00
Menominee	1	0.00
Navajo	3	0.00
Osage (1)	3	0.00
Ottawa	2	0.00
Potawatomi (1)	1	0.00
Pueblo (3)	6	0.01
Seminole (2)	10	0.01
Sioux (11)	25	0.04
Yaqui (2)	4	0.01
All other tribes (23)	34	0.05
American Indian tribes, not spec.	16	0.02
Arab:	486	0.68
Arab/Arabic	175	0.25
Egyptian	7	0.01
Lebanese	107	0.15
Moroccan	19	0.03

Notes: 1. Figures in the "Number" column do not add up to the total population due to: a) Ancestry/Race overlap — e.g. persons can report being both White and Irish, b) persons of Hispanic origin can report being any race, c) persons reporting two ancestries are counted in both categories. 2. Numbers in parentheses indicate the number of persons reporting this ancestry/race alone, not in combination with any other ancestry/race. 3. Refer to the User's Guide in the front of the book for more detailed information.

Palestinian	40	0.06
Syrian	44	0.06
Other Arab	94	0.13
Armenian	32	0.04
Asian:	2,188	3.07
Bangladeshi (2)	2	0.00
Cambodian (21)	25	0.04
Chinese, ex. Taiwanese (218)	274	0.38
Filipino (341)	471	0.66
Indian (393)	452	0.63
Indonesian (11)	18	0.03
Japanese (116)	177	0.25
Korean (130)	191	0.27
Laotian (5)	5	0.01
Malaysian	6	0.01
Pakistani (17)	24	0.03
Sri Lankan (1)	1	0.00
Taiwanese (12)	17	0.02
Thai (114)	158	0.22
Vietnamese (175)	214	0.30
Other Asian, specified (11)	14	0.02
Other Asian, not specified (55)	139	0.19
Australian	19	0.03
Austrian	259	0.36
Basque	9	0.01
Belgian	34	0.05
Brazilian	36	0.05
British	656	0.92
Bulgarian	9	0.01
Canadian	367	0.51
Celtic	44	0.06
Croatian	69	0.10
Czech	250	0.35
Czechoslovakian	199	0.28
Danish	294	0.41
Dutch	1,624	2.28
Eastern European	33	0.05
English	9,106	12.76
European	568	0.80
Finnish	221	0.31
French, except Basque	3,126	4.38
French Canadian	863	1.21
German	11,896	16.67
Greek	303	0.42
Guyanese	37	0.05
Hawaii Native/Pacific Islander:	113	0.16
Melanesian: (3)	4	0.01
Fijian (3)	4	0.01
Micronesian: (13)	17	0.02
Guamanian/Chamorro (13)	17	0.02
Polynesian: (18)	51	0.07
Native Hawaiian (14)	39	0.05
Samoan (2)	7	0.01
Other Polynesian (2)	5	0.01
Other Pac. Isl., specified	2	0.00
Other Pac. Isl., not spec. (10)	39	0.05
Hispanic or Latino:	3,958	5.54
Central American:	171	0.24
Costa Rican	25	0.04
Guatemalan	27	0.04
Honduran	40	0.06
Nicaraguan	8	0.01
Panamanian	58	0.08
Salvadoran	12	0.02
Other Central American	1	0.00
Cuban	332	0.47
Dominican Republic	95	0.13
Mexican	694	0.97
Puerto Rican	1,529	2.14
South American:	399	0.56
Argentinean	27	0.04
Bolivian	6	0.01
Chilean	28	0.04
Colombian	125	0.18
Ecuadorian	54	0.08
Paraguayan	2	0.00
Peruvian	52	0.07
Uruguayan	7	0.01
Venezuelan	68	0.10
Other South American	30	0.04
Other Hispanic or Latino	738	1.03
Hungarian	324	0.45
Icelander	10	0.01
Iranian	102	0.14
Irish	10,484	14.69
Israeli	17	0.02
Italian	5,842	8.19
Lithuanian	305	0.43
Luxemburger	19	0.03
Maltese	36	0.05
New Zealander	8	0.01
Northern European	46	0.06
Norwegian	786	1.10
Pennsylvania German	78	0.11
Polish	2,407	3.37
Portuguese	209	0.29
Romanian	46	0.06
Russian	597	0.84
Scandinavian	130	0.18
Scotch-Irish	1,357	1.90
Scottish	1,906	2.67
Serbian	15	0.02
Slavic	50	0.07
Slovak	171	0.24
Slovene	74	0.10
Swedish	834	1.17
Swiss	164	0.23
Turkish	30	0.04
Ukrainian	252	0.35
United States or American	5,124	7.18
Welsh	537	0.75
West Indian, excl. Hispanic:	504	0.71
Bahamian	23	0.03
Barbadian	14	0.02
Bermudan	6	0.01
British West Indian	59	0.08
Dutch West Indian	9	0.01
Haitian	18	0.03
Jamaican	284	0.40
Trinidadian and Tobagonian	40	0.06
U.S. Virgin Islander	15	0.02
West Indian	36	0.05
White:	61,652	86.37
Not Hispanic (57,600)	58,702	82.24
Hispanic (2,739)	2,950	4.13
Yugoslavian	40	0.06

Merritt Island

Place Type: Census Designated Place
County: Brevard
Population: 36,090

Ancestry/Race	Number	%
Acadian/Cajun	12	0.03
African American/Black:	2,068	5.73
Not Hispanic (1,871)	2,002	5.55
Hispanic (47)	66	0.18
African, sub-Saharan:	106	0.29
African	94	0.26
South African	12	0.03
Alaska Native tribes, specified:	7	0.02
Eskimo (2)	4	0.01
Tlingit-Haida (3)	3	0.01
Am. Ind. or Alaska Nat., not spec.	78	0.22
American Indian tribes, specified:	244	0.68
Apache (2)	3	0.01
Blackfeet (1)	12	0.03
Cherokee (26)	91	0.25
Chickasaw (3)	3	0.01
Chippewa (6)	11	0.03
Choctaw (2)	4	0.01
Cree	1	0.00
Creek (6)	10	0.03
Iroquois (10)	18	0.05
Kiowa (2)	2	0.01
Latin American Indians (6)	19	0.05
Lumbee (9)	9	0.02
Navajo	3	0.01
Osage (1)	1	0.00
Paiute (1)	1	0.00
Pueblo (7)	10	0.03
Seminole (1)	8	0.02
Sioux (4)	8	0.02
Tohono O'Odham (1)	4	0.01
Ute	1	0.00
All other tribes (9)	25	0.07
American Indian tribes, not spec.	10	0.03
Arab:	107	0.30
Egyptian	13	0.04
Jordanian	7	0.02
Lebanese	28	0.08
Moroccan	4	0.01
Palestinian	33	0.09
Syrian	22	0.06
Armenian	49	0.14
Asian:	784	2.17
Cambodian (4)	7	0.02
Chinese, ex. Taiwanese (73)	108	0.30
Filipino (101)	145	0.40
Indian (158)	180	0.50
Indonesian	1	0.00
Japanese (52)	81	0.22
Korean (48)	66	0.18
Laotian (2)	2	0.01
Malaysian	1	0.00
Pakistani (1)	1	0.00
Sri Lankan (1)	3	0.01
Taiwanese (11)	11	0.03
Thai (24)	28	0.08
Vietnamese (105)	125	0.35
Other Asian, specified (1)	3	0.01
Other Asian, not specified (10)	22	0.06
Australian	41	0.11
Austrian	117	0.32
Basque	5	0.01
Belgian	71	0.20
Brazilian	59	0.16
British	264	0.73
Canadian	198	0.55
Celtic	21	0.06
Croatian	16	0.04
Czech	266	0.74
Czechoslovakian	55	0.15
Danish	206	0.57
Dutch	752	2.08
Eastern European	12	0.03
English	5,788	16.04
Estonian	22	0.06
European	381	1.06
Finnish	106	0.29
French, except Basque	1,674	4.64
French Canadian	508	1.41
German	7,083	19.63
Greek	235	0.65
Hawaii Native/Pacific Islander:	60	0.17
Micronesian: (9)	10	0.03
Guamanian/Chamorro (9)	10	0.03
Polynesian: (11)	33	0.09
Native Hawaiian (9)	28	0.08
Samoan (2)	5	0.01
Other Pac. Isl., not spec. (1)	17	0.05
Hispanic or Latino:	1,381	3.83
Central American:	75	0.21
Costa Rican	10	0.03
Guatemalan	9	0.02
Honduran	16	0.04
Nicaraguan	7	0.02
Panamanian	23	0.06
Salvadoran	6	0.02
Other Central American	4	0.01
Cuban	221	0.61
Dominican Republic	24	0.07
Mexican	215	0.60
Puerto Rican	470	1.30
South American:	102	0.28
Argentinean	10	0.03
Bolivian	1	0.00
Chilean	10	0.03
Colombian	28	0.08
Ecuadorian	10	0.03
Peruvian	19	0.05
Venezuelan	8	0.02

Notes: 1. Figures in the "Number" column do not add up to the total population due to: a) Ancestry/Race overlap — e.g. persons can report being both White and Irish, b) persons of Hispanic origin can report being any race, c) persons reporting two ancestries are counted in both categories. 2. Numbers in parentheses indicate the number of persons reporting this ancestry/race alone, not in combination with any other ancestry/race. 3. Refer to the User's Guide in the front of the book for more detailed information.

Other South American	16	0.04
Other Hispanic or Latino	274	0.76
Hungarian	325	0.90
Irish	5,584	15.47
Israeli	19	0.05
Italian	3,137	8.69
Latvian	39	0.11
Lithuanian	86	0.24
Luxemburger	6	0.02
Maltese	7	0.02
New Zealander	11	0.03
Northern European	22	0.06
Norwegian	504	1.40
Pennsylvania German	44	0.12
Polish	1,108	3.07
Portuguese	178	0.49
Romanian	78	0.22
Russian	379	1.05
Scandinavian	55	0.15
Scotch-Irish	1,199	3.32
Scottish	964	2.67
Serbian	39	0.11
Slavic	33	0.09
Slovak	67	0.19
Slovene	15	0.04
Swedish	600	1.66
Swiss	231	0.64
Ukrainian	197	0.55
United States or American	2,391	6.62
Welsh	311	0.86
West Indian, excl. Hispanic:	110	0.30
Bahamian	18	0.05
Barbadian	7	0.02
British West Indian	4	0.01
Jamaican	12	0.03
Trinidadian and Tobagonian	26	0.07
West Indian	43	0.12
White:	33,076	91.65
Not Hispanic (31,565)	31,983	88.62
Hispanic (995)	1,093	3.03
Yugoslavian	35	0.10

Miami Beach

Place Type: City
County: Miami-Dade
Population: 87,933

Ancestry/Race	Number	%
African American/Black:	4,218	4.80
Not Hispanic (2,491)	2,762	3.14
Hispanic (1,057)	1,456	1.66
African, sub-Saharan:	351	0.40
African	256	0.29
Cape Verdean	21	0.02
Ghanian	9	0.01
Nigerian	19	0.02
Somalian	9	0.01
South African	19	0.02
Zairian	12	0.01
Other sub-Saharan African	6	0.01
Alaska Native tribes, specified:	4	0.00
Alaska Athabascan (3)	3	0.00
Tlingit-Haida	1	0.00
Alaska Native tribes, not specified	1	0.00
Am. Ind. or Alaska Nat., not spec.	206	0.23
Albanian	47	0.05
Alsatian	12	0.01
American Indian tribes, specified:	232	0.26
Apache (3)	9	0.01
Blackfeet	2	0.00
Cherokee (19)	47	0.05
Chippewa (1)	4	0.00
Choctaw (2)	2	0.00
Comanche (1)	1	0.00
Creek	1	0.00
Iroquois (1)	5	0.01
Latin American Indians (57)	124	0.14
Lumbee (1)	2	0.00
Navajo (1)	2	0.00
Pueblo (1)	6	0.01
Seminole	2	0.00
Sioux (2)	8	0.01
All other tribes (5)	17	0.02
American Indian tribes, not spec.	24	0.03
Arab:	934	1.06
Arab/Arabic	139	0.16
Egyptian	100	0.11
Iraqi	41	0.05
Lebanese	271	0.31
Moroccan	120	0.14
Palestinian	56	0.06
Syrian	69	0.08
Other Arab	138	0.16
Armenian	104	0.12
Asian:	1,639	1.86
Bangladeshi (20)	49	0.06
Cambodian (3)	3	0.00
Chinese, ex. Taiwanese (188)	277	0.32
Filipino (272)	315	0.36
Indian (386)	499	0.57
Indonesian (23)	28	0.03
Japanese (102)	134	0.15
Korean (49)	63	0.07
Laotian (1)	1	0.00
Malaysian (4)	4	0.00
Pakistani (19)	32	0.04
Sri Lankan (8)	9	0.01
Taiwanese	2	0.00
Thai (35)	50	0.06
Vietnamese (33)	46	0.05
Other Asian, specified (8)	12	0.01
Other Asian, not specified (24)	115	0.13
Australian	59	0.07
Austrian	816	0.93
Basque	77	0.09
Belgian	201	0.23
Brazilian	1,949	2.21
British	333	0.38
Bulgarian	91	0.10
Canadian	387	0.44
Celtic	12	0.01
Croatian	110	0.12
Czech	113	0.13
Czechoslovakian	106	0.12
Danish	85	0.10
Dutch	532	0.60
Eastern European	414	0.47
English	2,185	2.48
Estonian	8	0.01
European	988	1.12
Finnish	23	0.03
French, except Basque	1,704	1.94
French Canadian	184	0.21
German	3,811	4.33
Greek	379	0.43
Guyanese	30	0.03
Hawaii Native/Pacific Islander:	133	0.15
Melanesian:	1	0.00
Fijian	1	0.00
Micronesian: (4)	9	0.01
Guamanian/Chamorro (4)	9	0.01
Polynesian: (18)	40	0.05
Native Hawaiian (8)	21	0.02
Samoan (9)	17	0.02
Other Polynesian (1)	2	0.00
Other Pac. Isl., specified	3	0.00
Other Pac. Isl., not spec. (17)	80	0.09
Hispanic or Latino:	47,000	53.45
Central American:	3,096	3.52
Costa Rican	293	0.33
Guatemalan	328	0.37
Honduran	1,062	1.21
Nicaraguan	905	1.03
Panamanian	224	0.25
Salvadoran	201	0.23
Other Central American	83	0.09
Cuban	18,038	20.51
Dominican Republic	1,084	1.23
Mexican	1,183	1.35
Puerto Rican	3,596	4.09
South American:	11,589	13.18
Argentinean	2,680	3.05
Bolivian	176	0.20
Chilean	623	0.71
Colombian	3,872	4.40
Ecuadorian	493	0.56
Paraguayan	64	0.07
Peruvian	1,630	1.85
Uruguayan	222	0.25
Venezuelan	1,572	1.79
Other South American	257	0.29
Other Hispanic or Latino	8,414	9.57
Hungarian	897	1.02
Iranian	106	0.12
Irish	2,881	3.27
Israeli	237	0.27
Italian	4,441	5.04
Latvian	96	0.11
Lithuanian	263	0.30
New Zealander	11	0.01
Northern European	18	0.02
Norwegian	283	0.32
Pennsylvania German	7	0.01
Polish	2,533	2.88
Portuguese	655	0.74
Romanian	400	0.45
Russian	3,286	3.73
Scandinavian	40	0.05
Scotch-Irish	301	0.34
Scottish	611	0.69
Serbian	24	0.03
Slavic	20	0.02
Slovak	86	0.10
Slovene	6	0.01
Swedish	244	0.28
Swiss	116	0.13
Turkish	342	0.39
Ukrainian	460	0.52
United States or American	4,437	5.04
Welsh	227	0.26
West Indian, excl. Hispanic:	1,240	1.41
Bahamian	39	0.04
Belizean	21	0.02
British West Indian	36	0.04
Haitian	422	0.48
Jamaican	527	0.60
Trinidadian and Tobagonian	114	0.13
West Indian	52	0.06
Other West Indian	29	0.03
White:	78,945	89.78
Not Hispanic (35,959)	36,764	41.81
Hispanic (40,317)	42,181	47.97
Yugoslavian	135	0.15

Miami Lakes

Place Type: Census Designated Place
County: Miami-Dade
Population: 22,676

Ancestry/Race	Number	%
Acadian/Cajun	8	0.04
African American/Black:	729	3.21
Not Hispanic (530)	575	2.54
Hispanic (105)	154	0.68
African, sub-Saharan:	47	0.21
Nigerian	28	0.12
South African	19	0.08
Alaska Native tribes, specified:	2	0.01
Alaska Athabascan	1	0.00
Eskimo	1	0.00
Am. Ind. or Alaska Nat., not spec.	27	0.12
American Indian tribes, specified:	28	0.12
Cherokee (2)	7	0.03
Chickasaw	1	0.00
Creek (3)	3	0.01
Delaware	1	0.00
Latin American Indians (8)	11	0.05
Sioux (1)	1	0.00
All other tribes (1)	4	0.02
American Indian tribes, not spec.	4	0.02
Arab:	396	1.74

Notes: 1. Figures in the "Number" column do not add up to the total population due to: a) Ancestry/Race overlap — e.g. persons can report being both White and Irish, b) persons of Hispanic origin can report being any race, c) persons reporting two ancestries are counted in both categories. 2. Numbers in parentheses indicate the number of persons reporting this ancestry/race alone, not in combination with any other ancestry/race. 3. Refer to the User's Guide in the front of the book for more detailed information.

Arab/Arabic	261	1.15
Egyptian	8	0.04
Lebanese	86	0.38
Moroccan	7	0.03
Palestinian	23	0.10
Syrian	11	0.05
Armenian	6	0.03
Asian:	624	2.75
Chinese, ex. Taiwanese (164)	200	0.88
Filipino (62)	68	0.30
Indian (94)	121	0.53
Japanese (19)	27	0.12
Korean (72)	81	0.36
Pakistani (35)	60	0.26
Sri Lankan (3)	3	0.01
Taiwanese (11)	11	0.05
Thai (8)	9	0.04
Vietnamese (14)	15	0.07
Other Asian, not specified (6)	29	0.13
Austrian	19	0.08
Brazilian	133	0.59
British	34	0.15
Canadian	45	0.20
Croatian	16	0.07
Czech	67	0.29
Danish	16	0.07
Dutch	97	0.43
Eastern European	9	0.04
English	490	2.16
European	39	0.17
French, except Basque	282	1.24
French Canadian	11	0.05
German	862	3.79
Greek	41	0.18
Hawaii Native/Pacific Islander:	12	0.05
Polynesian: (5)	10	0.04
Native Hawaiian (3)	3	0.01
Samoan (2)	7	0.03
Other Pac. Isl., not spec. (1)	2	0.01
Hispanic or Latino:	15,083	66.52
Central American:	485	2.14
Costa Rican	37	0.16
Guatemalan	31	0.14
Honduran	70	0.31
Nicaraguan	243	1.07
Panamanian	68	0.30
Salvadoran	28	0.12
Other Central American	8	0.04
Cuban	9,588	42.28
Dominican Republic	375	1.65
Mexican	161	0.71
Puerto Rican	701	3.09
South American:	1,879	8.29
Argentinean	100	0.44
Bolivian	24	0.11
Chilean	95	0.42
Colombian	1,005	4.43
Ecuadorian	170	0.75
Paraguayan	1	0.00
Peruvian	215	0.95
Uruguayan	12	0.05
Venezuelan	240	1.06
Other South American	17	0.07
Other Hispanic or Latino	1,894	8.35
Hungarian	66	0.29
Iranian	18	0.08
Irish	987	4.34
Israeli	14	0.06
Italian	784	3.45
Lithuanian	53	0.23
Maltese	6	0.03
Norwegian	53	0.23
Polish	133	0.59
Portuguese	102	0.45
Romanian	15	0.07
Russian	87	0.38
Scotch-Irish	113	0.50
Scottish	143	0.63
Slavic	15	0.07
Slovak	33	0.15
Swedish	76	0.33
Swiss	35	0.15
Turkish	40	0.18
Ukrainian	23	0.10
United States or American	870	3.83
Welsh	28	0.12
West Indian, excl. Hispanic:	125	0.55
Bahamian	22	0.10
Dutch West Indian	14	0.06
Haitian	9	0.04
Jamaican	64	0.28
Trinidadian and Tobagonian	9	0.04
U.S. Virgin Islander	7	0.03
White:	20,791	91.69
Not Hispanic (6,362)	6,493	28.63
Hispanic (13,877)	14,298	63.05
Yugoslavian	13	0.06

Miami Shores

Place Type: Village
County: Miami-Dade
Population: 10,380

Ancestry/Race	Number	%
African American/Black:	2,816	27.13
Not Hispanic (2,440)	2,688	25.90
Hispanic (101)	128	1.23
African, sub-Saharan:	88	0.84
African	66	0.63
Kenyan	22	0.21
Am. Ind. or Alaska Nat., not spec.	8	0.08
Albanian	6	0.06
American Indian tribes, specified:	22	0.21
Apache	2	0.02
Cherokee	6	0.06
Choctaw	1	0.01
Creek (1)	1	0.01
Kiowa (1)	1	0.01
Latin American Indians (3)	6	0.06
Seminole (1)	3	0.03
Sioux	1	0.01
All other tribes	1	0.01
American Indian tribes, not spec.	1	0.01
Arab:	51	0.49
Arab/Arabic	5	0.05
Lebanese	28	0.27
Palestinian	7	0.07
Syrian	11	0.11
Armenian	32	0.31
Asian:	355	3.42
Chinese, ex. Taiwanese (48)	80	0.77
Filipino (86)	116	1.12
Indian (59)	70	0.67
Indonesian	2	0.02
Japanese (9)	23	0.22
Korean (8)	8	0.08
Pakistani (4)	4	0.04
Taiwanese (4)	9	0.09
Thai (16)	16	0.15
Vietnamese (5)	8	0.08
Other Asian, not specified (4)	19	0.18
Australian	13	0.12
Austrian	39	0.37
Basque	8	0.08
Belgian	10	0.10
Brazilian	47	0.45
British	36	0.34
Canadian	36	0.34
Cypriot	7	0.07
Czech	31	0.30
Czechoslovakian	16	0.15
Danish	44	0.42
Dutch	91	0.87
Eastern European	9	0.09
English	769	7.36
European	95	0.91
French, except Basque	274	2.62
French Canadian	112	1.07
German	963	9.22
Greek	41	0.39
Guyanese	11	0.11
Hawaii Native/Pacific Islander:	27	0.26
Polynesian: (2)	5	0.05
Native Hawaiian	1	0.01
Samoan (1)	2	0.02
Other Polynesian (1)	2	0.02
Other Pac. Isl., not spec. (6)	22	0.21
Hispanic or Latino:	2,257	21.74
Central American:	241	2.32
Costa Rican	19	0.18
Guatemalan	45	0.43
Honduran	64	0.62
Nicaraguan	76	0.73
Panamanian	24	0.23
Salvadoran	12	0.12
Other Central American	1	0.01
Cuban	651	6.27
Dominican Republic	133	1.28
Mexican	61	0.59
Puerto Rican	345	3.32
South American:	405	3.90
Argentinean	48	0.46
Bolivian	5	0.05
Chilean	27	0.26
Colombian	170	1.64
Ecuadorian	17	0.16
Paraguayan	1	0.01
Peruvian	67	0.65
Uruguayan	5	0.05
Venezuelan	51	0.49
Other South American	14	0.13
Other Hispanic or Latino	421	4.06
Hungarian	104	1.00
Irish	1,234	11.82
Italian	831	7.96
Latvian	7	0.07
Lithuanian	30	0.29
Northern European	11	0.11
Norwegian	17	0.16
Polish	308	2.95
Portuguese	66	0.63
Russian	81	0.78
Scotch-Irish	149	1.43
Scottish	212	2.03
Slavic	13	0.12
Slovak	13	0.12
Slovene	17	0.16
Swedish	186	1.78
Swiss	58	0.56
Ukrainian	20	0.19
United States or American	319	3.05
Welsh	51	0.49
West Indian, excl. Hispanic:	1,377	13.19
Bahamian	29	0.28
Barbadian	6	0.06
British West Indian	5	0.05
Dutch West Indian	14	0.13
Haitian	969	9.28
Jamaican	242	2.32
Trinidadian and Tobagonian	47	0.45
U.S. Virgin Islander	7	0.07
West Indian	58	0.56
White:	7,054	67.96
Not Hispanic (5,043)	5,185	49.95
Hispanic (1,710)	1,869	18.01

Miami Springs

Place Type: City
County: Miami-Dade
Population: 13,712

Ancestry/Race	Number	%
African American/Black:	335	2.44
Not Hispanic (163)	194	1.41
Hispanic (117)	141	1.03
African, sub-Saharan:	3	0.02
African	3	0.02
Am. Ind. or Alaska Nat., not spec.	24	0.18
American Indian tribes, specified:	44	0.32
Blackfeet (1)	1	0.01
Cherokee (11)	26	0.19
Chickasaw (1)	1	0.01

Notes: 1. Figures in the "Number" column do not add up to the total population due to: a) Ancestry/Race overlap — e.g. persons can report being both White and Irish, b) persons of Hispanic origin can report being any race, c) persons reporting two ancestries are counted in both categories. 2. Numbers in parentheses indicate the number of persons reporting this ancestry/race alone, not in combination with any other ancestry/race. 3. Refer to the User's Guide in the front of the book for more detailed information.

Chippewa (1)	2	0.01
Cree (1)	1	0.01
Creek	1	0.01
Latin American Indians (4)	10	0.07
All other tribes (1)	2	0.01
American Indian tribes, not spec.	9	0.07
Arab:	89	0.65
Iraqi	29	0.21
Lebanese	33	0.24
Palestinian	10	0.07
Syrian	17	0.12
Armenian	6	0.04
Asian:	228	1.66
Chinese, ex. Taiwanese (31)	43	0.31
Filipino (18)	26	0.19
Indian (61)	82	0.60
Indonesian	3	0.02
Japanese (10)	13	0.09
Korean (2)	3	0.02
Pakistani (20)	28	0.20
Sri Lankan	3	0.02
Taiwanese (1)	1	0.01
Thai (4)	5	0.04
Vietnamese (5)	9	0.07
Other Asian, not specified (5)	12	0.09
Australian	7	0.05
Austrian	45	0.33
Brazilian	62	0.45
British	97	0.71
Canadian	59	0.43
Croatian	12	0.09
Czech	84	0.61
Czechoslovakian	21	0.15
Danish	51	0.37
Dutch	74	0.54
Eastern European	8	0.06
English	800	5.85
European	14	0.10
Finnish	11	0.08
French, except Basque	221	1.62
French Canadian	57	0.42
German	955	6.98
Greek	39	0.29
Hawaii Native/Pacific Islander:	8	0.06
Micronesian: (4)	4	0.03
Guamanian/Chamorro (2)	2	0.01
Other Micronesian (2)	2	0.01
Polynesian: (1)	1	0.01
Native Hawaiian (1)	1	0.01
Other Pac. Isl., not spec.	3	0.02
Hispanic or Latino:	8,173	59.60
Central American:	643	4.69
Costa Rican	109	0.79
Guatemalan	39	0.28
Honduran	129	0.94
Nicaraguan	283	2.06
Panamanian	25	0.18
Salvadoran	46	0.34
Other Central American	12	0.09
Cuban	4,364	31.83
Dominican Republic	158	1.15
Mexican	110	0.80
Puerto Rican	500	3.65
South American:	1,228	8.96
Argentinean	73	0.53
Bolivian	31	0.23
Chilean	46	0.34
Colombian	533	3.89
Ecuadorian	101	0.74
Paraguayan	7	0.05
Peruvian	260	1.90
Uruguayan	9	0.07
Venezuelan	139	1.01
Other South American	29	0.21
Other Hispanic or Latino	1,170	8.53
Hungarian	74	0.54
Icelander	24	0.18
Irish	858	6.27
Israeli	7	0.05
Italian	447	3.27
Lithuanian	59	0.43
Maltese	12	0.09
Norwegian	33	0.24
Pennsylvania German	15	0.11
Polish	172	1.26
Portuguese	26	0.19
Romanian	7	0.05
Russian	70	0.51
Scandinavian	18	0.13
Scotch-Irish	108	0.79
Scottish	169	1.24
Slovak	7	0.05
Swedish	100	0.73
Swiss	51	0.37
Ukrainian	19	0.14
United States or American	592	4.33
Welsh	16	0.12
West Indian, excl. Hispanic:	126	0.92
Bahamian	16	0.12
Belizean	25	0.18
Haitian	19	0.14
Jamaican	31	0.23
Trinidadian and Tobagonian	21	0.15
West Indian	6	0.04
Other West Indian	8	0.06
White:	12,765	93.09
Not Hispanic (5,073)	5,151	37.57
Hispanic (7,379)	7,614	55.53

Miami

Place Type: City
County: Miami-Dade
Population: 362,470

Ancestry/Race	Number	%
African American/Black:	87,857	24.24
Not Hispanic (72,190)	77,247	21.31
Hispanic (8,668)	10,610	2.93
African, sub-Saharan:	2,816	0.78
African	2,661	0.73
Ethiopian	8	0.00
Ghanian	7	0.00
Liberian	9	0.00
Nigerian	99	0.03
Sudanese	6	0.00
Zairian	7	0.00
Zimbabwean	12	0.00
Other sub-Saharan African	7	0.00
Alaska Native tribes, specified:	11	0.00
Eskimo	5	0.00
Tlingit-Haida	6	0.00
Alaska Native tribes, not specified	1	0.00
Am. Ind. or Alaska Nat., not spec.	897	0.25
Albanian	38	0.01
Alsatian	11	0.00
American Indian tribes, specified:	825	0.23
Apache (1)	4	0.00
Blackfeet (1)	11	0.00
Cherokee (34)	93	0.03
Chickasaw (1)	1	0.00
Chippewa	2	0.00
Choctaw (1)	6	0.00
Comanche	1	0.00
Creek (1)	12	0.00
Delaware	1	0.00
Iroquois (3)	14	0.00
Kiowa	1	0.00
Latin American Indians (191)	535	0.15
Lumbee (4)	7	0.00
Menominee	1	0.00
Navajo (2)	3	0.00
Osage (1)	1	0.00
Pima	1	0.00
Pueblo (5)	42	0.01
Seminole (1)	4	0.00
Shoshone	6	0.00
Sioux (6)	8	0.00
Yakama	1	0.00
All other tribes (17)	70	0.02
American Indian tribes, not spec.	157	0.04
Arab:	1,864	0.51
Arab/Arabic	333	0.09
Egyptian	10	0.00
Iraqi	89	0.02
Jordanian	55	0.02
Lebanese	855	0.24
Moroccan	80	0.02
Palestinian	119	0.03
Syrian	236	0.07
Other Arab	87	0.02
Armenian	138	0.04
Asian:	3,238	0.89
Bangladeshi (11)	12	0.00
Cambodian (4)	4	0.00
Chinese, ex. Taiwanese (813)	1,021	0.28
Filipino (382)	454	0.13
Indian (629)	859	0.24
Indonesian (17)	39	0.01
Japanese (124)	156	0.04
Korean (83)	115	0.03
Laotian (2)	2	0.00
Malaysian (3)	7	0.00
Pakistani (36)	56	0.02
Sri Lankan (4)	7	0.00
Taiwanese (31)	33	0.01
Thai (20)	32	0.01
Vietnamese (90)	117	0.03
Other Asian, specified (2)	26	0.01
Other Asian, not specified (83)	298	0.08
Assyrian/Chaldean/Syriac	5	0.00
Australian	94	0.03
Austrian	421	0.12
Basque	118	0.03
Belgian	79	0.02
Brazilian	802	0.22
British	414	0.11
Bulgarian	74	0.02
Canadian	377	0.10
Celtic	7	0.00
Croatian	73	0.02
Czech	158	0.04
Czechoslovakian	109	0.03
Danish	242	0.07
Dutch	573	0.16
Eastern European	160	0.04
English	3,893	1.07
European	637	0.18
Finnish	37	0.01
French, except Basque	2,799	0.77
French Canadian	247	0.07
German	4,411	1.22
Greek	628	0.17
Guyanese	53	0.01
Hawaii Native/Pacific Islander:	681	0.19
Micronesian: (34)	48	0.01
Guamanian/Chamorro (34)	45	0.01
Other Micronesian	3	0.00
Polynesian: (40)	103	0.03
Native Hawaiian (19)	71	0.02
Samoan (15)	25	0.01
Tongan (5)	5	0.00
Other Polynesian (1)	2	0.00
Other Pac. Isl., specified	21	0.01
Other Pac. Isl., not spec. (55)	509	0.14
Hispanic or Latino:	238,351	65.76
Central American:	40,158	11.08
Costa Rican	775	0.21
Guatemalan	2,475	0.68
Honduran	12,118	3.34
Nicaraguan	20,543	5.67
Panamanian	657	0.18
Salvadoran	2,482	0.68
Other Central American	1,108	0.31
Cuban	123,763	34.14
Dominican Republic	6,370	1.76
Mexican	3,669	1.01
Puerto Rican	10,257	2.83
South American:	15,076	4.16
Argentinean	1,669	0.46
Bolivian	355	0.10
Chilean	939	0.26
Colombian	5,784	1.60
Ecuadorian	1,408	0.39

Notes: 1. Figures in the "Number" column do not add up to the total population due to: a) Ancestry/Race overlap — e.g. persons can report being both White and Irish, b) persons of Hispanic origin can report being any race, c) persons reporting two ancestries are counted in both categories. 2. Numbers in parentheses indicate the number of persons reporting this ancestry/race alone, not in combination with any other ancestry/race. 3. Refer to the User's Guide in the front of the book for more detailed information.

Paraguayan	45	0.01
Peruvian	2,447	0.68
Uruguayan	221	0.06
Venezuelan	1,959	0.54
Other South American	249	0.07
Other Hispanic or Latino	39,058	10.78
Hungarian	457	0.13
Icelander	36	0.01
Iranian	111	0.03
Irish	3,626	1.00
Israeli	142	0.04
Italian	5,169	1.43
Latvian	81	0.02
Lithuanian	233	0.06
Macedonian	20	0.01
Northern European	7	0.00
Norwegian	380	0.10
Pennsylvania German	11	0.00
Polish	1,492	0.41
Portuguese	488	0.13
Romanian	208	0.06
Russian	1,888	0.52
Scandinavian	63	0.02
Scotch-Irish	663	0.18
Scottish	1,019	0.28
Serbian	42	0.01
Slavic	35	0.01
Slovak	53	0.01
Swedish	389	0.11
Swiss	170	0.05
Turkish	160	0.04
Ukrainian	202	0.06
United States or American	11,317	3.12
Welsh	333	0.09
West Indian, excl. Hispanic:	22,904	6.32
Bahamian	1,470	0.41
Barbadian	13	0.00
Belizean	105	0.03
British West Indian	189	0.05
Dutch West Indian	27	0.01
Haitian	18,309	5.05
Jamaican	2,080	0.57
Trinidadian and Tobagonian	229	0.06
U.S. Virgin Islander	107	0.03
West Indian	350	0.10
Other West Indian	25	0.01
White:	251,993	69.52
Not Hispanic (42,897)	44,105	12.17
Hispanic (198,573)	207,888	57.35
Yugoslavian	91	0.03

Middleburg

Place Type: Census Designated Place
County: Clay
Population: 10,338

Ancestry/Race	Number	%
African American/Black:	371	3.59
Not Hispanic (329)	361	3.49
Hispanic (5)	10	0.10
African, sub-Saharan:	41	0.39
African	41	0.39
Am. Ind. or Alaska Nat., not spec.	25	0.24
American Indian tribes, specified:	145	1.40
Apache (3)	10	0.10
Blackfeet (4)	5	0.05
Cherokee (24)	77	0.74
Chickasaw (1)	1	0.01
Choctaw (1)	5	0.05
Creek	2	0.02
Crow	2	0.02
Delaware	1	0.01
Iroquois (2)	8	0.08
Latin American Indians (1)	1	0.01
Lumbee	1	0.01
Menominee (4)	4	0.04
Pueblo	1	0.01
Seminole	6	0.06
Sioux	5	0.05
All other tribes (10)	16	0.15
American Indian tribes, not spec.	7	0.07
Asian:	109	1.05
Bangladeshi (5)	5	0.05
Chinese, ex. Taiwanese (3)	3	0.03
Filipino (33)	60	0.58
Indian (2)	3	0.03
Japanese (6)	12	0.12
Korean (3)	6	0.06
Pakistani (8)	8	0.08
Vietnamese (2)	5	0.05
Other Asian, specified	4	0.04
Other Asian, not specified	3	0.03
Austrian	14	0.13
British	29	0.28
Canadian	29	0.28
Celtic	5	0.05
Czechoslovakian	10	0.10
Danish	79	0.76
Dutch	116	1.11
English	1,390	13.36
European	72	0.69
Finnish	42	0.40
French, except Basque	610	5.86
French Canadian	134	1.29
German	1,473	14.16
Greek	19	0.18
Hawaii Native/Pacific Islander:	20	0.19
Micronesian: (3)	3	0.03
Guamanian/Chamorro (1)	1	0.01
Other Micronesian (2)	2	0.02
Polynesian: (2)	10	0.10
Native Hawaiian (2)	10	0.10
Other Pac. Isl., specified	4	0.04
Other Pac. Isl., not spec.	3	0.03
Hispanic or Latino:	266	2.57
Central American:	10	0.10
Guatemalan	2	0.02
Honduran	3	0.03
Panamanian	4	0.04
Salvadoran	1	0.01
Cuban	19	0.18
Dominican Republic	4	0.04
Mexican	69	0.67
Puerto Rican	97	0.94
South American:	7	0.07
Chilean	5	0.05
Peruvian	2	0.02
Other Hispanic or Latino	60	0.58
Hungarian	27	0.26
Irish	1,367	13.14
Italian	439	4.22
Lithuanian	6	0.06
Norwegian	108	1.04
Polish	273	2.62
Portuguese	47	0.45
Romanian	25	0.24
Russian	38	0.37
Scotch-Irish	182	1.75
Scottish	174	1.67
Slavic	6	0.06
Slovak	35	0.34
Swedish	125	1.20
Ukrainian	8	0.08
United States or American	1,502	14.43
Welsh	43	0.41
White:	9,765	94.46
Not Hispanic (9,460)	9,579	92.66
Hispanic (172)	186	1.80
Yugoslavian	29	0.28

Miramar

Place Type: City
County: Broward
Population: 72,739

Ancestry/Race	Number	%
African American/Black:	33,627	46.23
Not Hispanic (30,561)	32,317	44.43
Hispanic (937)	1,310	1.80
African, sub-Saharan:	818	1.13
African	514	0.71
Nigerian	267	0.37
South African	16	0.02
Sudanese	16	0.02
Other sub-Saharan African	5	0.01
Alaska Native tribes, specified:	3	0.00
Aleut	1	0.00
Eskimo	1	0.00
Tlingit-Haida	1	0.00
Am. Ind. or Alaska Nat., not spec.	134	0.18
Albanian	9	0.01
American Indian tribes, specified:	163	0.22
Apache	3	0.00
Blackfeet	12	0.02
Cherokee (12)	49	0.07
Chippewa (3)	5	0.01
Choctaw (1)	2	0.00
Creek (2)	10	0.01
Iroquois	7	0.01
Latin American Indians (16)	46	0.06
Lumbee (1)	1	0.00
Pueblo	1	0.00
Seminole (1)	3	0.00
Shoshone (2)	2	0.00
Sioux (1)	3	0.00
All other tribes (5)	19	0.03
American Indian tribes, not spec.	23	0.03
Arab:	167	0.23
Arab/Arabic	76	0.10
Jordanian	12	0.02
Lebanese	36	0.05
Syrian	36	0.05
Other Arab	7	0.01
Armenian	14	0.02
Asian:	2,893	3.98
Bangladeshi (12)	12	0.02
Cambodian (10)	13	0.02
Chinese, ex. Taiwanese (413)	618	0.85
Filipino (526)	586	0.81
Indian (828)	1,055	1.45
Indonesian (3)	10	0.01
Japanese (28)	48	0.07
Korean (54)	69	0.09
Laotian	3	0.00
Pakistani (63)	125	0.17
Sri Lankan (2)	2	0.00
Taiwanese (4)	4	0.01
Thai (18)	26	0.04
Vietnamese (179)	198	0.27
Other Asian, specified (1)	4	0.01
Other Asian, not specified (36)	120	0.16
Australian	5	0.01
Austrian	129	0.18
Belgian	18	0.02
Brazilian	242	0.33
British	334	0.46
Bulgarian	7	0.01
Canadian	168	0.23
Croatian	7	0.01
Czech	69	0.09
Czechoslovakian	82	0.11
Danish	104	0.14
Dutch	258	0.36
Eastern European	39	0.05
English	1,704	2.34
European	90	0.12
Finnish	7	0.01
French, except Basque	688	0.95
French Canadian	276	0.38
German	2,838	3.91
Greek	128	0.18
Guyanese	469	0.65
Hawaii Native/Pacific Islander:	251	0.35
Micronesian: (4)	8	0.01
Guamanian/Chamorro (4)	5	0.01
Other Micronesian	3	0.00
Polynesian: (23)	34	0.05
Native Hawaiian (17)	23	0.03
Samoan (6)	9	0.01
Other Polynesian	2	0.00
Other Pac. Isl., not spec. (45)	209	0.29

Notes: 1. Figures in the "Number" column do not add up to the total population due to: a) Ancestry/Race overlap — e.g. persons can report being both White and Irish, b) persons of Hispanic origin can report being any race, c) persons reporting two ancestries are counted in both categories. 2. Numbers in parentheses indicate the number of persons reporting this ancestry/race alone, not in combination with any other ancestry/race. 3. Refer to the User's Guide in the front of the book for more detailed information.

Hispanic or Latino:	21,374	29.38
Central American:	1,622	2.23
Costa Rican	122	0.17
Guatemalan	130	0.18
Honduran	287	0.39
Nicaraguan	589	0.81
Panamanian	336	0.46
Salvadoran	86	0.12
Other Central American	72	0.10
Cuban	6,377	8.77
Dominican Republic	1,439	1.98
Mexican	469	0.64
Puerto Rican	3,800	5.22
South American:	3,696	5.08
Argentinean	149	0.20
Bolivian	16	0.02
Chilean	143	0.20
Colombian	1,827	2.51
Ecuadorian	297	0.41
Paraguayan	1	0.00
Peruvian	614	0.84
Uruguayan	45	0.06
Venezuelan	499	0.69
Other South American	105	0.14
Other Hispanic or Latino	3,971	5.46
Hungarian	271	0.37
Iranian	11	0.02
Irish	2,206	3.04
Israeli	28	0.04
Italian	2,795	3.85
Lithuanian	83	0.11
New Zealander	10	0.01
Norwegian	128	0.18
Polish	668	0.92
Portuguese	122	0.17
Romanian	222	0.31
Russian	340	0.47
Scandinavian	13	0.02
Scotch-Irish	324	0.45
Scottish	204	0.28
Slavic	8	0.01
Swedish	189	0.26
Swiss	43	0.06
Ukrainian	48	0.07
United States or American	3,565	4.91
Welsh	34	0.05
West Indian, excl. Hispanic:	18,445	25.38
Bahamian	578	0.80
Barbadian	139	0.19
Belizean	42	0.06
Bermudan	11	0.02
British West Indian	428	0.59
Dutch West Indian	10	0.01
Haitian	4,359	6.00
Jamaican	11,263	15.50
Trinidadian and Tobagonian	897	1.23
U.S. Virgin Islander	207	0.28
West Indian	493	0.68
Other West Indian	18	0.02
White:	33,571	46.15
Not Hispanic (15,716)	16,444	22.61
Hispanic (15,988)	17,127	23.55
Yugoslavian	48	0.07

Myrtle Grove

Place Type: Census Designated Place
County: Escambia
Population: 17,211

Ancestry/Race	Number	%
Acadian/Cajun	15	0.09
African American/Black:	2,489	14.46
Not Hispanic (2,282)	2,426	14.10
Hispanic (40)	63	0.37
African, sub-Saharan:	20	0.12
African	20	0.12
Alaska Native tribes, specified:	3	0.02
Alaska Athabascan (2)	2	0.01
Aleut (1)	1	0.01
Am. Ind. or Alaska Nat., not spec.	90	0.52
American Indian tribes, specified:	245	1.42
Apache (1)	4	0.02
Blackfeet (4)	9	0.05
Cherokee (24)	74	0.43
Chippewa (3)	6	0.03
Choctaw (1)	5	0.03
Comanche (3)	3	0.02
Creek (41)	76	0.44
Crow (1)	1	0.01
Houma (3)	3	0.02
Iroquois (2)	13	0.08
Kiowa	1	0.01
Latin American Indians (1)	6	0.03
Lumbee (1)	1	0.01
Menominee (1)	1	0.01
Navajo (6)	10	0.06
Osage	1	0.01
Potawatomi (1)	4	0.02
Pueblo	4	0.02
Seminole	4	0.02
Shoshone (1)	1	0.01
Sioux (2)	3	0.02
Tohono O'Odham	1	0.01
Yaqui	1	0.01
All other tribes (4)	13	0.08
American Indian tribes, not spec.	14	0.08
Arab:	76	0.44
Arab/Arabic	29	0.17
Lebanese	7	0.04
Other Arab	40	0.23
Asian:	1,107	6.43
Cambodian (1)	1	0.01
Chinese, ex. Taiwanese (35)	51	0.30
Filipino (527)	683	3.97
Indian (36)	45	0.26
Indonesian (2)	2	0.01
Japanese (42)	68	0.40
Korean (31)	43	0.25
Laotian (1)	1	0.01
Thai (6)	8	0.05
Vietnamese (162)	178	1.03
Other Asian, specified	3	0.02
Other Asian, not specified (7)	24	0.14
Austrian	20	0.12
Belgian	14	0.08
Brazilian	29	0.17
British	66	0.38
Canadian	34	0.20
Celtic	11	0.06
Croatian	6	0.03
Czech	21	0.12
Danish	19	0.11
Dutch	215	1.24
Eastern European	9	0.05
English	1,588	9.18
European	178	1.03
Finnish	35	0.20
French, except Basque	574	3.32
French Canadian	95	0.55
German	2,144	12.39
Greek	63	0.36
Hawaii Native/Pacific Islander:	102	0.59
Micronesian: (13)	31	0.18
Guamanian/Chamorro (12)	27	0.16
Other Micronesian (1)	4	0.02
Polynesian: (29)	48	0.28
Native Hawaiian (12)	23	0.13
Samoan (16)	23	0.13
Tongan (1)	1	0.01
Other Polynesian	1	0.01
Other Pac. Isl., not spec. (9)	23	0.13
Hispanic or Latino:	740	4.30
Central American:	41	0.24
Costa Rican	8	0.05
Guatemalan	1	0.01
Honduran	1	0.01
Nicaraguan	2	0.01
Panamanian	26	0.15
Salvadoran	3	0.02
Cuban	29	0.17
Dominican Republic	10	0.06
Mexican	316	1.84
Puerto Rican	169	0.98
South American:	26	0.15
Argentinean	2	0.01
Bolivian	2	0.01
Colombian	9	0.05
Ecuadorian	3	0.02
Uruguayan	1	0.01
Venezuelan	9	0.05
Other Hispanic or Latino	149	0.87
Hungarian	7	0.04
Irish	2,153	12.44
Israeli	5	0.03
Italian	691	3.99
Lithuanian	18	0.10
Northern European	24	0.14
Norwegian	216	1.25
Polish	286	1.65
Portuguese	109	0.63
Romanian	7	0.04
Russian	103	0.60
Scandinavian	13	0.08
Scotch-Irish	446	2.58
Scottish	376	2.17
Soviet Union	5	0.03
Swedish	184	1.06
Swiss	9	0.05
Ukrainian	39	0.23
United States or American	1,641	9.48
Welsh	87	0.50
West Indian, excl. Hispanic:	61	0.35
Bahamian	5	0.03
Barbadian	7	0.04
Haitian	8	0.05
Jamaican	32	0.18
West Indian	9	0.05
White:	13,428	78.02
Not Hispanic (12,631)	13,039	75.76
Hispanic (319)	389	2.26
Yugoslavian	12	0.07

Naples

Place Type: City
County: Collier
Population: 20,976

Ancestry/Race	Number	%
African American/Black:	1,310	6.25
Not Hispanic (953)	1,285	6.13
Hispanic (22)	25	0.12
African, sub-Saharan:	47	0.22
African	15	0.07
South African	32	0.15
Alaska Native tribes, specified:	2	0.01
Tlingit-Haida	1	0.00
All other tribes (1)	1	0.00
Am. Ind. or Alaska Nat., not spec.	37	0.18
Alsatian	14	0.07
American Indian tribes, specified:	29	0.14
Apache (1)	1	0.00
Blackfeet	1	0.00
Cherokee (7)	14	0.07
Chippewa (1)	3	0.01
Choctaw	1	0.00
Creek (1)	1	0.00
Iroquois	1	0.00
Latin American Indians (1)	1	0.00
Navajo	1	0.00
Yaqui	2	0.01
All other tribes (2)	3	0.01
American Indian tribes, not spec.	9	0.04
Arab:	58	0.28
Arab/Arabic	23	0.11
Lebanese	20	0.10
Syrian	15	0.07
Armenian	46	0.22
Asian:	95	0.45
Bangladeshi (1)	1	0.00
Cambodian (1)	1	0.00
Chinese, ex. Taiwanese (22)	25	0.12
Filipino (7)	13	0.06
Indian (14)	23	0.11

Notes: 1. Figures in the "Number" column do not add up to the total population due to: a) Ancestry/Race overlap — e.g. persons can report being both White and Irish, b) persons of Hispanic origin can report being any race, c) persons reporting two ancestries are counted in both categories. 2. Numbers in parentheses indicate the number of persons reporting this ancestry/race alone, not in combination with any other ancestry/race. 3. Refer to the User's Guide in the front of the book for more detailed information.

Indonesian (1)	1	0.00
Japanese (3)	6	0.03
Korean (15)	16	0.08
Thai (2)	3	0.01
Vietnamese (3)	4	0.02
Other Asian, not specified (1)	2	0.01
Australian	7	0.03
Austrian	128	0.61
Belgian	72	0.34
Brazilian	19	0.09
British	238	1.13
Canadian	143	0.68
Croatian	19	0.09
Czech	88	0.42
Czechoslovakian	38	0.18
Danish	168	0.80
Dutch	454	2.16
Eastern European	14	0.07
English	3,920	18.68
Estonian	10	0.05
European	154	0.73
Finnish	47	0.22
French, except Basque	888	4.23
French Canadian	188	0.90
German	4,191	19.97
Greek	141	0.67
Hawaii Native/Pacific Islander:	15	0.07
Micronesian: (1)	2	0.01
Guamanian/Chamorro (1)	2	0.01
Polynesian: (3)	5	0.02
Native Hawaiian (1)	2	0.01
Samoan (2)	2	0.01
Tongan	1	0.00
Other Pac. Isl., not spec. (1)	8	0.04
Hispanic or Latino:	467	2.23
Central American:	17	0.08
Costa Rican	4	0.02
Guatemalan	7	0.03
Honduran	1	0.00
Nicaraguan	2	0.01
Panamanian	2	0.01
Other Central American	1	0.00
Cuban	155	0.74
Dominican Republic	7	0.03
Mexican	87	0.41
Puerto Rican	49	0.23
South American:	44	0.21
Argentinean	10	0.05
Bolivian	2	0.01
Chilean	2	0.01
Colombian	15	0.07
Ecuadorian	1	0.00
Paraguayan	5	0.02
Peruvian	2	0.01
Uruguayan	3	0.01
Venezuelan	4	0.02
Other Hispanic or Latino	108	0.51
Hungarian	280	1.33
Irish	3,246	15.47
Italian	1,522	7.25
Lithuanian	102	0.49
Luxemburger	7	0.03
Maltese	12	0.06
Northern European	7	0.03
Norwegian	428	2.04
Pennsylvania German	14	0.07
Polish	625	2.98
Portuguese	46	0.22
Romanian	65	0.31
Russian	234	1.11
Scandinavian	31	0.15
Scotch-Irish	670	3.19
Scottish	921	4.39
Slovak	77	0.37
Swedish	654	3.12
Swiss	213	1.01
Ukrainian	93	0.44
United States or American	1,180	5.62
Welsh	303	1.44
West Indian, excl. Hispanic:	278	1.32
Bahamian	37	0.18
Haitian	234	1.11
Trinidadian and Tobagonian	7	0.03
White:	19,510	93.01
Not Hispanic (19,048)	19,131	91.20
Hispanic (354)	379	1.81
Yugoslavian	20	0.10

New Port Richey

Place Type: City
County: Pasco
Population: 16,117

Ancestry/Race	Number	%
African American/Black:	193	1.20
Not Hispanic (145)	173	1.07
Hispanic (16)	20	0.12
African, sub-Saharan:	15	0.10
African	15	0.10
Am. Ind. or Alaska Nat., not spec.	69	0.43
American Indian tribes, specified:	125	0.78
Apache (2)	2	0.01
Blackfeet (2)	15	0.09
Cherokee (18)	56	0.35
Chippewa (4)	6	0.04
Choctaw (2)	3	0.02
Creek	4	0.02
Delaware	3	0.02
Iroquois (2)	4	0.02
Latin American Indians (5)	5	0.03
Lumbee (1)	1	0.01
Menominee (3)	3	0.02
Navajo (2)	2	0.01
Ottawa (1)	1	0.01
Sioux (5)	8	0.05
All other tribes	12	0.07
American Indian tribes, not spec.	12	0.07
Arab:	23	0.15
Lebanese	23	0.15
Armenian	5	0.03
Asian:	231	1.43
Cambodian (1)	1	0.01
Chinese, ex. Taiwanese (20)	28	0.17
Filipino (42)	65	0.40
Indian (17)	25	0.16
Indonesian (1)	1	0.01
Japanese (5)	8	0.05
Korean (5)	5	0.03
Laotian (1)	5	0.03
Pakistani (1)	1	0.01
Thai	3	0.02
Vietnamese (56)	72	0.45
Other Asian, specified	1	0.01
Other Asian, not specified (2)	16	0.10
Austrian	50	0.32
British	32	0.20
Bulgarian	29	0.18
Canadian	37	0.24
Croatian	68	0.43
Czech	94	0.60
Czechoslovakian	17	0.11
Danish	69	0.44
Dutch	188	1.20
Eastern European	26	0.17
English	2,084	13.29
European	65	0.41
Finnish	35	0.22
French, except Basque	621	3.96
French Canadian	193	1.23
German	2,817	17.96
Greek	100	0.64
Hawaii Native/Pacific Islander:	20	0.12
Polynesian: (14)	17	0.11
Native Hawaiian (3)	6	0.04
Samoan (11)	11	0.07
Other Pac. Isl., specified	1	0.01
Other Pac. Isl., not spec.	2	0.01
Hispanic or Latino:	846	5.25
Central American:	34	0.21
Costa Rican	2	0.01
Guatemalan	7	0.04
Honduran	14	0.09
Nicaraguan	4	0.02
Panamanian	3	0.02
Salvadoran	2	0.01
Other Central American	2	0.01
Cuban	32	0.20
Dominican Republic	13	0.08
Mexican	279	1.73
Puerto Rican	332	2.06
South American:	63	0.39
Argentinean	2	0.01
Chilean	4	0.02
Colombian	24	0.15
Ecuadorian	13	0.08
Peruvian	13	0.08
Uruguayan	1	0.01
Other South American	6	0.04
Other Hispanic or Latino	93	0.58
Hungarian	113	0.72
Icelander	7	0.04
Irish	2,637	16.81
Italian	1,764	11.25
Lithuanian	31	0.20
Macedonian	10	0.06
Norwegian	167	1.06
Pennsylvania German	16	0.10
Polish	853	5.44
Portuguese	81	0.52
Romanian	18	0.11
Russian	134	0.85
Scandinavian	24	0.15
Scotch-Irish	204	1.30
Scottish	244	1.56
Serbian	35	0.22
Slavic	11	0.07
Slovak	61	0.39
Slovene	6	0.04
Swedish	274	1.75
Ukrainian	70	0.45
United States or American	1,433	9.14
Welsh	151	0.96
West Indian, excl. Hispanic:	86	0.55
Dutch West Indian	6	0.04
Haitian	36	0.23
Jamaican	44	0.28
White:	15,455	95.89
Not Hispanic (14,606)	14,865	92.23
Hispanic (559)	590	3.66
Yugoslavian	164	1.05

New Smyrna Beach

Place Type: City
County: Volusia
Population: 20,048

Ancestry/Race	Number	%
African American/Black:	1,331	6.64
Not Hispanic (1,250)	1,319	6.58
Hispanic (7)	12	0.06
African, sub-Saharan:	23	0.11
African	23	0.11
Alaska Native tribes, specified:	3	0.01
Eskimo	3	0.01
Am. Ind. or Alaska Nat., not spec.	33	0.16
American Indian tribes, specified:	115	0.57
Apache (1)	3	0.01
Blackfeet	5	0.02
Cherokee (11)	37	0.18
Cheyenne	1	0.00
Chippewa	7	0.03
Choctaw (2)	2	0.01
Comanche	4	0.02
Creek (2)	3	0.01
Delaware	1	0.00
Iroquois (10)	16	0.08
Kiowa (2)	2	0.01
Latin American Indians (2)	2	0.01
Lumbee (2)	3	0.01
Menominee (1)	1	0.00
Ottawa	1	0.00
Potawatomi (4)	4	0.02
Pueblo	1	0.00

Notes: 1. Figures in the "Number" column do not add up to the total population due to: a) Ancestry/Race overlap — e.g. persons can report being both White and Irish, b) persons of Hispanic origin can report being any race, c) persons reporting two ancestries are counted in both categories. 2. Numbers in parentheses indicate the number of persons reporting this ancestry/race alone, not in combination with any other ancestry/race. 3. Refer to the User's Guide in the front of the book for more detailed information.

Seminole (2)	2	0.01
Shoshone	4	0.02
Sioux (2)	2	0.01
Ute (3)	3	0.01
All other tribes (6)	11	0.05
American Indian tribes, not spec.	6	0.03
Arab:	117	0.58
Egyptian	42	0.21
Iraqi	8	0.04
Lebanese	56	0.28
Syrian	11	0.05
Asian:	122	0.61
Bangladeshi (3)	3	0.01
Chinese, ex. Taiwanese (27)	29	0.14
Filipino (15)	20	0.10
Indian (18)	22	0.11
Japanese (11)	18	0.09
Korean (16)	16	0.08
Laotian (1)	1	0.00
Thai (2)	2	0.01
Vietnamese (4)	5	0.02
Other Asian, not specified (2)	6	0.03
Australian	23	0.11
Austrian	83	0.41
Belgian	36	0.18
Brazilian	19	0.09
British	184	0.91
Canadian	62	0.31
Croatian	18	0.09
Czech	61	0.30
Czechoslovakian	50	0.25
Danish	156	0.77
Dutch	483	2.38
English	3,429	16.90
European	103	0.51
Finnish	53	0.26
French, except Basque	776	3.82
French Canadian	260	1.28
German	3,730	18.38
Greek	85	0.42
Hawaii Native/Pacific Islander:	10	0.05
Micronesian: (1)	1	0.00
Guamanian/Chamorro (1)	1	0.00
Polynesian: (4)	5	0.02
Native Hawaiian (3)	4	0.02
Samoan (1)	1	0.00
Other Pac. Isl., not spec. (2)	4	0.02
Hispanic or Latino:	301	1.50
Central American:	13	0.06
Costa Rican	4	0.02
Guatemalan	1	0.00
Honduran	3	0.01
Nicaraguan	2	0.01
Panamanian	3	0.01
Cuban	35	0.17
Dominican Republic	12	0.06
Mexican	79	0.39
Puerto Rican	73	0.36
South American:	44	0.22
Argentinean	5	0.02
Bolivian	4	0.02
Chilean	4	0.02
Colombian	20	0.10
Ecuadorian	1	0.00
Uruguayan	5	0.02
Venezuelan	5	0.02
Other Hispanic or Latino	45	0.22
Hungarian	127	0.63
Irish	3,317	16.34
Israeli	7	0.03
Italian	1,784	8.79
Latvian	27	0.13
Lithuanian	40	0.20
Norwegian	184	0.91
Pennsylvania German	38	0.19
Polish	671	3.31
Portuguese	58	0.29
Romanian	53	0.26
Russian	128	0.63
Scotch-Irish	561	2.76
Scottish	572	2.82
Slavic	9	0.04
Slovak	112	0.55
Slovene	39	0.19
Swedish	263	1.30
Swiss	99	0.49
Ukrainian	68	0.34
United States or American	1,721	8.48
Welsh	279	1.37
West Indian, excl. Hispanic:	68	0.34
Bahamian	13	0.06
Haitian	33	0.16
Jamaican	13	0.06
West Indian	9	0.04
White:	18,538	92.47
Not Hispanic (18,141)	18,303	91.30
Hispanic (217)	235	1.17

Niceville

Place Type: City
County: Okaloosa
Population: 11,684

Ancestry/Race	Number	%
Acadian/Cajun	21	0.18
African American/Black:	626	5.36
Not Hispanic (529)	608	5.20
Hispanic (6)	18	0.15
African, sub-Saharan:	12	0.10
Ghanian	12	0.10
Alaska Native tribes, specified:	5	0.04
Tlingit-Haida	5	0.04
Am. Ind. or Alaska Nat., not spec.	58	0.50
American Indian tribes, specified:	107	0.92
Apache	1	0.01
Blackfeet	2	0.02
Cherokee (34)	52	0.45
Chickasaw	1	0.01
Chippewa (5)	5	0.04
Choctaw (6)	10	0.09
Comanche	1	0.01
Creek (12)	18	0.15
Iroquois	1	0.01
Latin American Indians (1)	2	0.02
Lumbee (2)	2	0.02
Menominee	1	0.01
Navajo (1)	1	0.01
Potawatomi	3	0.03
Seminole (2)	2	0.02
Sioux	2	0.02
Ute (1)	1	0.01
All other tribes (2)	2	0.02
American Indian tribes, not spec.	1	0.01
Arab:	42	0.36
Arab/Arabic	6	0.05
Egyptian	10	0.08
Lebanese	26	0.22
Asian:	579	4.96
Cambodian (5)	5	0.04
Chinese, ex. Taiwanese (25)	40	0.34
Filipino (147)	224	1.92
Indian (10)	12	0.10
Indonesian (1)	1	0.01
Japanese (36)	69	0.59
Korean (67)	101	0.86
Laotian (1)	1	0.01
Pakistani (1)	1	0.01
Taiwanese (1)	8	0.07
Thai (39)	60	0.51
Vietnamese (24)	27	0.23
Other Asian, specified (1)	2	0.02
Other Asian, not specified (8)	28	0.24
Austrian	5	0.04
Belgian	29	0.25
Brazilian	16	0.14
British	81	0.69
Canadian	56	0.47
Croatian	61	0.52
Czech	40	0.34
Czechoslovakian	9	0.08
Danish	21	0.18
Dutch	259	2.20
English	1,347	11.42
European	251	2.13
Finnish	12	0.10
French, except Basque	424	3.59
French Canadian	96	0.81
German	1,697	14.39
Greek	56	0.47
Hawaii Native/Pacific Islander:	39	0.33
Micronesian: (2)	5	0.04
Guamanian/Chamorro (2)	5	0.04
Polynesian: (9)	18	0.15
Native Hawaiian (9)	17	0.15
Samoan	1	0.01
Other Pac. Isl., specified	1	0.01
Other Pac. Isl., not spec. (2)	15	0.13
Hispanic or Latino:	434	3.71
Central American:	18	0.15
Costa Rican	5	0.04
Guatemalan	1	0.01
Honduran	1	0.01
Panamanian	11	0.09
Cuban	20	0.17
Dominican Republic	10	0.09
Mexican	128	1.10
Puerto Rican	144	1.23
South American:	12	0.10
Argentinean	1	0.01
Bolivian	1	0.01
Colombian	2	0.02
Peruvian	8	0.07
Other Hispanic or Latino	102	0.87
Hungarian	19	0.16
Irish	1,523	12.91
Italian	392	3.32
Northern European	26	0.22
Norwegian	275	2.33
Pennsylvania German	12	0.10
Polish	238	2.02
Romanian	9	0.08
Russian	42	0.36
Scandinavian	7	0.06
Scotch-Irish	371	3.15
Scottish	244	2.07
Slovak	21	0.18
Swedish	269	2.28
Swiss	26	0.22
Ukrainian	47	0.40
United States or American	1,522	12.90
Welsh	80	0.68
West Indian, excl. Hispanic:	52	0.44
Jamaican	44	0.37
West Indian	8	0.07
White:	10,475	89.65
Not Hispanic (9,941)	10,181	87.14
Hispanic (253)	294	2.52

Norland

Place Type: Census Designated Place
County: Miami-Dade
Population: 22,995

Ancestry/Race	Number	%
African American/Black:	18,992	82.59
Not Hispanic (17,916)	18,523	80.55
Hispanic (369)	469	2.04
African, sub-Saharan:	531	2.31
African	487	2.12
Nigerian	44	0.19
Am. Ind. or Alaska Nat., not spec.	67	0.29
American Indian tribes, specified:	47	0.20
Blackfeet (1)	2	0.01
Cherokee (3)	17	0.07
Cree	3	0.01
Latin American Indians (4)	16	0.07
Pueblo	1	0.00
Seminole	2	0.01
All other tribes	6	0.03
American Indian tribes, not spec.	10	0.04
Arab:	16	0.07
Lebanese	11	0.05

Notes: 1. Figures in the "Number" column do not add up to the total population due to: a) Ancestry/Race overlap — e.g. persons can report being both White and Irish, b) persons of Hispanic origin can report being any race, c) persons reporting two ancestries are counted in both categories. 2. Numbers in parentheses indicate the number of persons reporting this ancestry/race alone, not in combination with any other ancestry/race. 3. Refer to the User's Guide in the front of the book for more detailed information.

Syrian	5	0.02
Asian:	358	1.56
Bangladeshi (7)	7	0.03
Chinese, ex. Taiwanese (55)	85	0.37
Filipino (36)	38	0.17
Indian (107)	150	0.65
Japanese (10)	17	0.07
Korean (1)	7	0.03
Laotian	1	0.00
Pakistani	1	0.00
Thai	1	0.00
Vietnamese (26)	32	0.14
Other Asian, specified	5	0.02
Other Asian, not specified (4)	14	0.06
Austrian	16	0.07
Belgian	10	0.04
Brazilian	10	0.04
British	51	0.22
Canadian	7	0.03
Croatian	9	0.04
Dutch	32	0.14
English	229	0.99
European	20	0.09
French, except Basque	129	0.56
French Canadian	9	0.04
German	170	0.74
Greek	41	0.18
Guyanese	33	0.14
Hawaii Native/Pacific Islander:	81	0.35
Micronesian:	4	0.02
Guamanian/Chamorro	4	0.02
Polynesian:	2	0.01
Native Hawaiian	1	0.00
Samoan	1	0.00
Other Pac. Isl., specified	5	0.02
Other Pac. Isl., not spec. (1)	70	0.30
Hispanic or Latino:	2,285	9.94
Central American:	352	1.53
Costa Rican	11	0.05
Guatemalan	27	0.12
Honduran	72	0.31
Nicaraguan	163	0.71
Panamanian	45	0.20
Salvadoran	5	0.02
Other Central American	29	0.13
Cuban	456	1.98
Dominican Republic	249	1.08
Mexican	54	0.23
Puerto Rican	473	2.06
South American:	186	0.81
Argentinean	10	0.04
Bolivian	5	0.02
Chilean	14	0.06
Colombian	96	0.42
Ecuadorian	9	0.04
Peruvian	27	0.12
Venezuelan	11	0.05
Other South American	14	0.06
Other Hispanic or Latino	515	2.24
Hungarian	20	0.09
Irish	203	0.88
Italian	223	0.97
Norwegian	16	0.07
Polish	68	0.30
Russian	44	0.19
Scotch-Irish	16	0.07
Scottish	88	0.38
United States or American	872	3.79
West Indian, excl. Hispanic:	8,976	38.98
Bahamian	513	2.23
Barbadian	57	0.25
Belizean	18	0.08
British West Indian	305	1.32
Dutch West Indian	19	0.08
Haitian	2,789	12.11
Jamaican	4,849	21.06
Trinidadian and Tobagonian	328	1.42
U.S. Virgin Islander	24	0.10
West Indian	66	0.29
Other West Indian	8	0.03
White:	3,310	14.39
Not Hispanic (1,764)	1,931	8.40
Hispanic (1,225)	1,379	6.00

North Fort Myers

Place Type: Census Designated Place
County: Lee
Population: 40,214

Ancestry/Race	Number	%
Acadian/Cajun	18	0.04
African American/Black:	438	1.09
Not Hispanic (341)	397	0.99
Hispanic (34)	41	0.10
African, sub-Saharan:	27	0.07
African	15	0.04
Cape Verdean	7	0.02
South African	5	0.01
Alaska Native tribes, specified:	3	0.01
Eskimo	3	0.01
Am. Ind. or Alaska Nat., not spec.	97	0.24
Alsatian	4	0.01
American Indian tribes, specified:	187	0.47
Apache (1)	6	0.01
Blackfeet (1)	8	0.02
Cherokee (26)	84	0.21
Cheyenne	1	0.00
Chickasaw	1	0.00
Chippewa (12)	16	0.04
Choctaw (2)	3	0.01
Creek (3)	4	0.01
Delaware (1)	1	0.00
Iroquois (5)	8	0.02
Latin American Indians (7)	10	0.02
Lumbee	2	0.00
Menominee	1	0.00
Navajo (1)	2	0.00
Osage (1)	2	0.00
Ottawa (2)	3	0.01
Paiute (1)	1	0.00
Potawatomi	3	0.01
Seminole	1	0.00
Sioux (4)	12	0.03
Yuman (2)	2	0.00
All other tribes (13)	16	0.04
American Indian tribes, not spec.	13	0.03
Arab:	50	0.12
Lebanese	31	0.08
Syrian	19	0.05
Armenian	58	0.14
Asian:	269	0.67
Chinese, ex. Taiwanese (29)	36	0.09
Filipino (32)	50	0.12
Indian (37)	46	0.11
Japanese (11)	23	0.06
Korean (17)	22	0.05
Laotian (36)	42	0.10
Malaysian	1	0.00
Pakistani (5)	5	0.01
Taiwanese (1)	1	0.00
Thai (13)	16	0.04
Vietnamese (8)	10	0.02
Other Asian, specified	2	0.00
Other Asian, not specified (5)	15	0.04
Australian	6	0.01
Austrian	110	0.27
Belgian	22	0.05
British	148	0.37
Bulgarian	4	0.01
Canadian	259	0.64
Croatian	90	0.22
Czech	239	0.59
Czechoslovakian	86	0.21
Danish	208	0.52
Dutch	1,098	2.72
Eastern European	13	0.03
English	6,343	15.73
Estonian	6	0.01
European	166	0.41
Finnish	117	0.29
French, except Basque	1,754	4.35
French Canadian	630	1.56
German	8,078	20.03
Greek	127	0.31
Hawaii Native/Pacific Islander:	43	0.11
Micronesian: (14)	15	0.04
Guamanian/Chamorro (3)	3	0.01
Other Micronesian (11)	12	0.03
Polynesian: (6)	7	0.02
Native Hawaiian (5)	6	0.01
Samoan (1)	1	0.00
Other Pac. Isl., not spec. (2)	21	0.05
Hispanic or Latino:	1,166	2.90
Central American:	42	0.10
Costa Rican	8	0.02
Guatemalan	10	0.02
Honduran	3	0.01
Nicaraguan	9	0.02
Panamanian	4	0.01
Salvadoran	7	0.02
Other Central American	1	0.00
Cuban	93	0.23
Dominican Republic	26	0.06
Mexican	348	0.87
Puerto Rican	446	1.11
South American:	28	0.07
Argentinean	6	0.01
Chilean	4	0.01
Colombian	13	0.03
Ecuadorian	1	0.00
Paraguayan	1	0.00
Venezuelan	2	0.00
Other South American	1	0.00
Other Hispanic or Latino	183	0.46
Hungarian	355	0.88
Icelander	8	0.02
Irish	5,653	14.02
Israeli	10	0.02
Italian	2,327	5.77
Lithuanian	92	0.23
Luxemburger	15	0.04
Norwegian	423	1.05
Pennsylvania German	66	0.16
Polish	1,375	3.41
Portuguese	199	0.49
Romanian	33	0.08
Russian	173	0.43
Scandinavian	42	0.10
Scotch-Irish	874	2.17
Scottish	1,071	2.66
Serbian	6	0.01
Slavic	20	0.05
Slovak	148	0.37
Slovene	47	0.12
Swedish	632	1.57
Swiss	144	0.36
Turkish	5	0.01
Ukrainian	103	0.26
United States or American	4,012	9.95
Welsh	414	1.03
West Indian, excl. Hispanic:	135	0.33
Bahamian	9	0.02
Barbadian	7	0.02
Bermudan	12	0.03
Haitian	70	0.17
Jamaican	16	0.04
Trinidadian and Tobagonian	9	0.02
West Indian	12	0.03
White:	39,104	97.24
Not Hispanic (38,078)	38,317	95.28
Hispanic (726)	787	1.96
Yugoslavian	24	0.06

North Lauderdale

Place Type: City
County: Broward
Population: 32,264

Ancestry/Race	Number	%
African American/Black:	12,345	38.26
Not Hispanic (11,050)	11,971	37.10
Hispanic (293)	374	1.16

Notes: 1. Figures in the "Number" column do not add up to the total population due to: a) Ancestry/Race overlap — e.g. persons can report being both White and Irish, b) persons of Hispanic origin can report being any race, c) persons reporting two ancestries are counted in both categories. 2. Numbers in parentheses indicate the number of persons reporting this ancestry/race alone, not in combination with any other ancestry/race. 3. Refer to the User's Guide in the front of the book for more detailed information.

African, sub-Saharan:	441	1.36
African	380	1.18
Cape Verdean	23	0.07
Liberian	8	0.02
Nigerian	24	0.07
South African	6	0.02
Am. Ind. or Alaska Nat., not spec.	84	0.26
American Indian tribes, specified:	91	0.28
Blackfeet (4)	7	0.02
Cherokee (14)	37	0.11
Chippewa (2)	4	0.01
Choctaw (1)	2	0.01
Comanche (1)	1	0.00
Creek (2)	2	0.01
Iroquois (2)	4	0.01
Latin American Indians (17)	29	0.09
Navajo (1)	1	0.00
Ottawa	2	0.01
Sioux (1)	1	0.00
All other tribes	1	0.00
American Indian tribes, not spec.	14	0.04
Arab:	115	0.36
Arab/Arabic	8	0.02
Egyptian	48	0.15
Lebanese	50	0.15
Palestinian	9	0.03
Asian:	1,273	3.95
Bangladeshi (7)	7	0.02
Chinese, ex. Taiwanese (116)	180	0.56
Filipino (54)	77	0.24
Indian (382)	472	1.46
Indonesian (1)	3	0.01
Japanese (11)	23	0.07
Korean (16)	23	0.07
Laotian (9)	16	0.05
Pakistani (26)	30	0.09
Taiwanese (3)	3	0.01
Thai (27)	31	0.10
Vietnamese (339)	360	1.12
Other Asian, specified	2	0.01
Other Asian, not specified (6)	46	0.14
Australian	10	0.03
Austrian	51	0.16
Brazilian	283	0.88
British	64	0.20
Bulgarian	7	0.02
Canadian	82	0.25
Celtic	8	0.02
Czech	44	0.14
Czechoslovakian	44	0.14
Danish	14	0.04
Dutch	167	0.52
Eastern European	11	0.03
English	1,115	3.45
European	61	0.19
Finnish	25	0.08
French, except Basque	609	1.88
French Canadian	177	0.55
German	1,824	5.64
Greek	28	0.09
Guyanese	84	0.26
Hawaii Native/Pacific Islander:	100	0.31
Micronesian:	6	0.02
Guamanian/Chamorro	5	0.02
Other Micronesian	1	0.00
Polynesian: (4)	6	0.02
Native Hawaiian	1	0.00
Samoan (4)	4	0.01
Other Polynesian	1	0.00
Other Pac. Isl., specified	1	0.00
Other Pac. Isl., not spec. (17)	87	0.27
Hispanic or Latino:	6,816	21.13
Central American:	721	2.23
Costa Rican	25	0.08
Guatemalan	74	0.23
Honduran	145	0.45
Nicaraguan	68	0.21
Panamanian	60	0.19
Salvadoran	336	1.04
Other Central American	13	0.04
Cuban	334	1.04
Dominican Republic	246	0.76
Mexican	811	2.51
Puerto Rican	1,552	4.81
South American:	1,713	5.31
Argentinean	72	0.22
Bolivian	13	0.04
Chilean	39	0.12
Colombian	1,071	3.32
Ecuadorian	115	0.36
Paraguayan	2	0.01
Peruvian	240	0.74
Uruguayan	13	0.04
Venezuelan	102	0.32
Other South American	46	0.14
Other Hispanic or Latino	1,439	4.46
Hungarian	74	0.23
Iranian	43	0.13
Irish	2,030	6.28
Israeli	14	0.04
Italian	2,234	6.91
Latvian	10	0.03
Lithuanian	37	0.11
Norwegian	94	0.29
Pennsylvania German	11	0.03
Polish	799	2.47
Portuguese	162	0.50
Romanian	27	0.08
Russian	351	1.09
Scandinavian	33	0.10
Scotch-Irish	144	0.45
Scottish	246	0.76
Slovak	20	0.06
Swedish	153	0.47
Turkish	13	0.04
Ukrainian	49	0.15
United States or American	2,601	8.05
Welsh	106	0.33
West Indian, excl. Hispanic:	6,828	21.12
Bahamian	70	0.22
Barbadian	7	0.02
Belizean	19	0.06
British West Indian	82	0.25
Dutch West Indian	10	0.03
Haitian	2,223	6.88
Jamaican	3,688	11.41
Trinidadian and Tobagonian	357	1.10
U.S. Virgin Islander	65	0.20
West Indian	307	0.95
White:	16,994	52.67
Not Hispanic (11,831)	12,228	37.90
Hispanic (4,306)	4,766	14.77
Yugoslavian	8	0.02

North Miami Beach

Place Type: City
County: Miami-Dade
Population: 40,786

Ancestry/Race	Number	%
African American/Black:	17,066	41.84
Not Hispanic (15,273)	16,218	39.76
Hispanic (622)	848	2.08
African, sub-Saharan:	344	0.85
African	249	0.61
Ghanian	26	0.06
Nigerian	43	0.11
Senegalese	6	0.01
Ugandan	20	0.05
Alaska Native tribes, specified:	3	0.01
Eskimo (1)	1	0.00
Tlingit-Haida	2	0.00
Am. Ind. or Alaska Nat., not spec.	116	0.28
American Indian tribes, specified:	101	0.25
Apache (1)	1	0.00
Blackfeet	3	0.01
Cherokee (11)	20	0.05
Chippewa	2	0.00
Choctaw	1	0.00
Latin American Indians (22)	46	0.11
Pueblo (1)	1	0.00
Seminole	2	0.00
All other tribes (5)	25	0.06
American Indian tribes, not spec.	17	0.04
Arab:	188	0.46
Arab/Arabic	37	0.09
Lebanese	55	0.14
Moroccan	76	0.19
Syrian	9	0.02
Other Arab	11	0.03
Armenian	20	0.05
Asian:	2,031	4.98
Bangladeshi (21)	36	0.09
Cambodian (1)	3	0.01
Chinese, ex. Taiwanese (606)	677	1.66
Filipino (261)	303	0.74
Indian (408)	528	1.29
Indonesian (5)	9	0.02
Japanese (31)	42	0.10
Korean (17)	18	0.04
Laotian (2)	2	0.00
Pakistani (73)	90	0.22
Taiwanese (4)	4	0.01
Thai (41)	67	0.16
Vietnamese (108)	112	0.27
Other Asian, specified (3)	12	0.03
Other Asian, not specified (33)	128	0.31
Assyrian/Chaldean/Syriac	75	0.18
Australian	4	0.01
Austrian	77	0.19
Belgian	9	0.02
Brazilian	335	0.82
British	76	0.19
Bulgarian	19	0.05
Canadian	71	0.17
Croatian	15	0.04
Czech	32	0.08
Czechoslovakian	45	0.11
Danish	16	0.04
Dutch	96	0.24
Eastern European	45	0.11
English	628	1.54
Estonian	26	0.06
European	122	0.30
French, except Basque	253	0.62
French Canadian	45	0.11
German	996	2.45
Greek	89	0.22
Guyanese	72	0.18
Hawaii Native/Pacific Islander:	142	0.35
Micronesian: (5)	5	0.01
Guamanian/Chamorro (5)	5	0.01
Polynesian: (16)	23	0.06
Native Hawaiian (6)	9	0.02
Samoan (9)	11	0.03
Tongan (1)	2	0.00
Other Polynesian	1	0.00
Other Pac. Isl., specified	4	0.01
Other Pac. Isl., not spec. (6)	110	0.27
Hispanic or Latino:	12,245	30.02
Central American:	1,253	3.07
Costa Rican	74	0.18
Guatemalan	202	0.50
Honduran	394	0.97
Nicaraguan	374	0.92
Panamanian	84	0.21
Salvadoran	74	0.18
Other Central American	51	0.13
Cuban	2,008	4.92
Dominican Republic	976	2.39
Mexican	207	0.51
Puerto Rican	1,789	4.39
South American:	2,936	7.20
Argentinean	304	0.75
Bolivian	34	0.08
Chilean	186	0.46
Colombian	1,154	2.83
Ecuadorian	171	0.42
Paraguayan	13	0.03
Peruvian	733	1.80
Uruguayan	40	0.10
Venezuelan	222	0.54
Other South American	79	0.19

Notes: 1. Figures in the "Number" column do not add up to the total population due to: a) Ancestry/Race overlap — e.g. persons can report being both White and Irish, b) persons of Hispanic origin can report being any race, c) persons reporting two ancestries are counted in both categories. 2. Numbers in parentheses indicate the number of persons reporting this ancestry/race alone, not in combination with any other ancestry/race. 3. Refer to the User's Guide in the front of the book for more detailed information.

Other Hispanic or Latino	3,076	7.54
Hungarian	180	0.44
Iranian	20	0.05
Irish	1,001	2.46
Israeli	128	0.31
Italian	1,203	2.96
Lithuanian	14	0.03
Norwegian	35	0.09
Polish	614	1.51
Portuguese	126	0.31
Romanian	54	0.13
Russian	726	1.78
Scotch-Irish	132	0.32
Scottish	123	0.30
Serbian	8	0.02
Swedish	78	0.19
Swiss	20	0.05
Turkish	130	0.32
Ukrainian	125	0.31
United States or American	2,446	6.01
Welsh	34	0.08
West Indian, excl. Hispanic:	11,041	27.15
Bahamian	441	1.08
Barbadian	17	0.04
Belizean	85	0.21
British West Indian	64	0.16
Haitian	7,864	19.33
Jamaican	2,178	5.35
Trinidadian and Tobagonian	215	0.53
U.S. Virgin Islander	35	0.09
West Indian	117	0.29
Other West Indian	25	0.06
White:	20,106	49.30
Not Hispanic (10,104)	10,494	25.73
Hispanic (8,936)	9,612	23.57
Yugoslavian	27	0.07

North Miami

Place Type: City
County: Miami-Dade
Population: 59,880

Ancestry/Race	Number	%
African American/Black:	34,778	58.08
Not Hispanic (31,758)	33,411	55.80
Hispanic (1,109)	1,367	2.28
African, sub-Saharan:	662	1.10
African	499	0.83
Cape Verdean	7	0.01
Ethiopian	36	0.06
Ghanian	8	0.01
Kenyan	8	0.01
Nigerian	82	0.14
South African	12	0.02
Sudanese	10	0.02
Alaska Native tribes, specified:	13	0.02
Tlingit-Haida (1)	13	0.02
Alaska Native tribes, not specified	1	0.00
Am. Ind. or Alaska Nat., not spec.	231	0.39
American Indian tribes, specified:	150	0.25
Apache (6)	7	0.01
Blackfeet	3	0.01
Cherokee (10)	29	0.05
Chickasaw	1	0.00
Choctaw (1)	6	0.01
Cree	3	0.01
Creek (1)	2	0.00
Houma	1	0.00
Iroquois	1	0.00
Latin American Indians (35)	55	0.09
Lumbee	1	0.00
Menominee (3)	3	0.01
Navajo (1)	1	0.00
Paiute (1)	1	0.00
Pima (1)	1	0.00
Pueblo	3	0.01
Seminole	8	0.01
Shoshone (2)	2	0.00
All other tribes (2)	22	0.04
American Indian tribes, not spec.	24	0.04
Arab:	231	0.38
Arab/Arabic	20	0.03
Egyptian	14	0.02
Iraqi	9	0.01
Lebanese	97	0.16
Moroccan	13	0.02
Syrian	15	0.02
Other Arab	63	0.10
Armenian	11	0.02
Asian:	1,597	2.67
Bangladeshi (8)	19	0.03
Chinese, ex. Taiwanese (199)	270	0.45
Filipino (317)	371	0.62
Hmong	3	0.01
Indian (333)	511	0.85
Indonesian (8)	10	0.02
Japanese (45)	52	0.09
Korean (55)	63	0.11
Laotian (7)	7	0.01
Malaysian (1)	2	0.00
Pakistani (44)	80	0.13
Sri Lankan (1)	1	0.00
Taiwanese (9)	12	0.02
Thai (17)	23	0.04
Vietnamese (28)	30	0.05
Other Asian, specified	4	0.01
Other Asian, not specified (53)	139	0.23
Australian	8	0.01
Austrian	139	0.23
Basque	12	0.02
Brazilian	276	0.46
British	84	0.14
Bulgarian	13	0.02
Canadian	144	0.24
Croatian	41	0.07
Czech	80	0.13
Czechoslovakian	23	0.04
Danish	16	0.03
Dutch	224	0.37
Eastern European	74	0.12
English	938	1.56
European	116	0.19
Finnish	21	0.03
French, except Basque	454	0.76
French Canadian	44	0.07
German	1,451	2.42
German Russian	6	0.01
Greek	160	0.27
Guyanese	116	0.19
Hawaii Native/Pacific Islander:	247	0.41
Melanesian: (1)	1	0.00
Fijian (1)	1	0.00
Micronesian: (1)	3	0.01
Guamanian/Chamorro (1)	2	0.00
Other Micronesian	1	0.00
Polynesian: (10)	30	0.05
Native Hawaiian (9)	21	0.04
Samoan (1)	4	0.01
Other Polynesian	5	0.01
Other Pac. Isl., specified	4	0.01
Other Pac. Isl., not spec. (16)	209	0.35
Hispanic or Latino:	13,869	23.16
Central American:	1,709	2.85
Costa Rican	115	0.19
Guatemalan	217	0.36
Honduran	565	0.94
Nicaraguan	553	0.92
Panamanian	97	0.16
Salvadoran	108	0.18
Other Central American	54	0.09
Cuban	2,655	4.43
Dominican Republic	1,032	1.72
Mexican	367	0.61
Puerto Rican	2,660	4.44
South American:	2,009	3.36
Argentinean	223	0.37
Bolivian	33	0.06
Chilean	74	0.12
Colombian	858	1.43
Ecuadorian	118	0.20
Paraguayan	9	0.02
Peruvian	384	0.64
Uruguayan	26	0.04
Venezuelan	215	0.36
Other South American	69	0.12
Other Hispanic or Latino	3,437	5.74
Hungarian	148	0.25
Iranian	35	0.06
Irish	1,263	2.10
Israeli	82	0.14
Italian	1,171	1.95
Latvian	89	0.15
Lithuanian	76	0.13
Northern European	44	0.07
Norwegian	72	0.12
Pennsylvania German	6	0.01
Polish	638	1.06
Portuguese	107	0.18
Romanian	108	0.18
Russian	576	0.96
Scandinavian	10	0.02
Scotch-Irish	99	0.16
Scottish	240	0.40
Serbian	9	0.01
Slovak	33	0.05
Slovene	19	0.03
Swedish	223	0.37
Swiss	42	0.07
Turkish	48	0.08
Ukrainian	69	0.11
United States or American	3,319	5.53
Welsh	70	0.12
West Indian, excl. Hispanic:	22,034	36.70
Bahamian	675	1.12
Barbadian	149	0.25
Belizean	56	0.09
British West Indian	246	0.41
Dutch West Indian	18	0.03
Haitian	18,656	31.07
Jamaican	1,837	3.06
Trinidadian and Tobagonian	267	0.44
U.S. Virgin Islander	32	0.05
West Indian	98	0.16
White:	21,977	36.70
Not Hispanic (10,860)	11,283	18.84
Hispanic (9,982)	10,694	17.86
Yugoslavian	40	0.07

North Palm Beach

Place Type: Village
County: Palm Beach
Population: 12,064

Ancestry/Race	Number	%
African American/Black:	126	1.04
Not Hispanic (108)	122	1.01
Hispanic (4)	4	0.03
African, sub-Saharan:	8	0.07
Other sub-Saharan African	8	0.07
Am. Ind. or Alaska Nat., not spec.	17	0.14
Albanian	10	0.08
Alsatian	7	0.06
American Indian tribes, specified:	21	0.17
Blackfeet (1)	2	0.02
Cherokee (3)	5	0.04
Cheyenne	1	0.01
Chippewa (1)	2	0.02
Creek (2)	2	0.02
Delaware	1	0.01
Iroquois	2	0.02
Latin American Indians (1)	1	0.01
Osage	1	0.01
Sioux	1	0.01
All other tribes	3	0.02
Armenian	32	0.26
Asian:	191	1.58
Chinese, ex. Taiwanese (30)	34	0.28
Filipino (5)	16	0.13
Indian (31)	36	0.30
Japanese (6)	9	0.07
Korean (6)	7	0.06
Laotian (1)	1	0.01

Notes: 1. Figures in the "Number" column do not add up to the total population due to: a) Ancestry/Race overlap — e.g. persons can report being both White and Irish, b) persons of Hispanic origin can report being any race, c) persons reporting two ancestries are counted in both categories. 2. Numbers in parentheses indicate the number of persons reporting this ancestry/race alone, not in combination with any other ancestry/race. 3. Refer to the User's Guide in the front of the book for more detailed information.

Thai (4)	5	0.04
Vietnamese (56)	63	0.52
Other Asian, not specified (8)	20	0.17
Australian	9	0.07
Austrian	80	0.66
Belgian	30	0.25
British	74	0.61
Canadian	153	1.26
Croatian	9	0.07
Czech	43	0.35
Czechoslovakian	14	0.12
Danish	85	0.70
Dutch	363	2.99
Eastern European	43	0.35
English	1,836	15.14
European	72	0.59
Finnish	84	0.69
French, except Basque	576	4.75
French Canadian	106	0.87
German	2,469	20.36
Greek	183	1.51
Hawaii Native/Pacific Islander:	9	0.07
Micronesian: (1)	1	0.01
Guamanian/Chamorro (1)	1	0.01
Polynesian: (1)	7	0.06
Native Hawaiian (1)	6	0.05
Other Polynesian	1	0.01
Other Pac. Isl., not spec. (1)	1	0.01
Hispanic or Latino:	426	3.53
Central American:	16	0.13
Guatemalan	3	0.02
Honduran	3	0.02
Nicaraguan	6	0.05
Panamanian	1	0.01
Salvadoran	3	0.02
Cuban	93	0.77
Dominican Republic	2	0.02
Mexican	46	0.38
Puerto Rican	93	0.77
South American:	82	0.68
Argentinean	6	0.05
Chilean	5	0.04
Colombian	33	0.27
Ecuadorian	14	0.12
Paraguayan	1	0.01
Peruvian	10	0.08
Uruguayan	2	0.02
Venezuelan	11	0.09
Other Hispanic or Latino	94	0.78
Hungarian	83	0.68
Iranian	9	0.07
Irish	2,686	22.15
Israeli	10	0.08
Italian	1,393	11.48
Lithuanian	61	0.50
Norwegian	117	0.96
Pennsylvania German	18	0.15
Polish	451	3.72
Portuguese	41	0.34
Romanian	41	0.34
Russian	327	2.70
Scandinavian	9	0.07
Scotch-Irish	345	2.84
Scottish	416	3.43
Serbian	11	0.09
Slavic	37	0.31
Slovak	15	0.12
Slovene	8	0.07
Swedish	154	1.27
Swiss	52	0.43
Turkish	46	0.38
Ukrainian	85	0.70
United States or American	810	6.68
Welsh	132	1.09
West Indian, excl. Hispanic:	109	0.90
Haitian	72	0.59
Jamaican	28	0.23
West Indian	9	0.07
White:	11,715	97.11
Not Hispanic (11,265)	11,344	94.03
Hispanic (343)	371	3.08
Yugoslavian	26	0.21

North Port

Place Type: City
County: Sarasota
Population: 22,797

Ancestry/Race	Number	%
African American/Black:	1,069	4.69
Not Hispanic (912)	1,005	4.41
Hispanic (42)	64	0.28
African, sub-Saharan:	58	0.26
African	58	0.26
Alaska Native tribes, specified:	2	0.01
Eskimo (1)	2	0.01
Am. Ind. or Alaska Nat., not spec.	54	0.24
American Indian tribes, specified:	108	0.47
Blackfeet	6	0.03
Cherokee (15)	56	0.25
Chickasaw (1)	1	0.00
Chippewa (3)	7	0.03
Choctaw	1	0.00
Creek	6	0.03
Iroquois	6	0.03
Latin American Indians (1)	3	0.01
Lumbee (1)	7	0.03
Pueblo	1	0.00
Seminole	1	0.00
Sioux	2	0.01
All other tribes (2)	11	0.05
American Indian tribes, not spec.	6	0.03
Arab:	138	0.61
Arab/Arabic	36	0.16
Jordanian	23	0.10
Lebanese	74	0.33
Syrian	5	0.02
Armenian	18	0.08
Asian:	207	0.91
Cambodian (1)	1	0.00
Chinese, ex. Taiwanese (6)	15	0.07
Filipino (37)	73	0.32
Indian (21)	32	0.14
Indonesian (1)	2	0.01
Japanese (12)	21	0.09
Korean (14)	16	0.07
Laotian (2)	2	0.01
Pakistani	3	0.01
Sri Lankan (1)	1	0.00
Thai (2)	2	0.01
Vietnamese (12)	13	0.06
Other Asian, not specified (1)	26	0.11
Austrian	23	0.10
Belgian	48	0.21
Brazilian	19	0.08
British	129	0.57
Canadian	144	0.63
Croatian	52	0.23
Czech	118	0.52
Czechoslovakian	40	0.18
Danish	112	0.49
Dutch	544	2.39
Eastern European	32	0.14
English	2,700	11.89
Estonian	8	0.04
European	111	0.49
Finnish	50	0.22
French, except Basque	1,112	4.90
French Canadian	326	1.44
German	4,955	21.81
Greek	121	0.53
Hawaii Native/Pacific Islander:	19	0.08
Polynesian: (2)	12	0.05
Native Hawaiian (1)	11	0.05
Samoan (1)	1	0.00
Other Pac. Isl., not spec. (1)	7	0.03
Hispanic or Latino:	739	3.24
Central American:	51	0.22
Costa Rican	2	0.01
Guatemalan	12	0.05
Honduran	8	0.04
Nicaraguan	8	0.04
Panamanian	13	0.06
Salvadoran	8	0.04
Cuban	91	0.40
Dominican Republic	8	0.04
Mexican	139	0.61
Puerto Rican	259	1.14
South American:	39	0.17
Argentinean	2	0.01
Chilean	8	0.04
Colombian	10	0.04
Ecuadorian	2	0.01
Peruvian	13	0.06
Uruguayan	1	0.00
Venezuelan	1	0.00
Other South American	2	0.01
Other Hispanic or Latino	152	0.67
Hungarian	238	1.05
Irish	3,596	15.83
Israeli	24	0.11
Italian	1,934	8.51
Latvian	8	0.04
Lithuanian	119	0.52
Northern European	9	0.04
Norwegian	165	0.73
Pennsylvania German	8	0.04
Polish	1,075	4.73
Portuguese	207	0.91
Romanian	15	0.07
Russian	346	1.52
Scandinavian	9	0.04
Scotch-Irish	319	1.40
Scottish	470	2.07
Serbian	47	0.21
Slavic	8	0.04
Slovak	65	0.29
Slovene	9	0.04
Swedish	270	1.19
Swiss	43	0.19
Turkish	13	0.06
Ukrainian	612	2.69
United States or American	1,870	8.23
Welsh	182	0.80
West Indian, excl. Hispanic:	434	1.91
British West Indian	59	0.26
Haitian	10	0.04
Jamaican	329	1.45
Trinidadian and Tobagonian	28	0.12
West Indian	8	0.04
White:	21,461	94.14
Not Hispanic (20,625)	20,908	91.71
Hispanic (502)	553	2.43
Yugoslavian	52	0.23

Oak Ridge

Place Type: Census Designated Place
County: Orange
Population: 22,349

Ancestry/Race	Number	%
Acadian/Cajun	9	0.04
African American/Black:	7,397	33.10
Not Hispanic (5,946)	6,791	30.39
Hispanic (411)	606	2.71
African, sub-Saharan:	275	1.23
African	252	1.12
Cape Verdean	9	0.04
Ethiopian	14	0.06
Alaska Native tribes, specified:	1	0.00
Tlingit-Haida	1	0.00
Am. Ind. or Alaska Nat., not spec.	117	0.52
American Indian tribes, specified:	74	0.33
Blackfeet (1)	3	0.01
Cherokee (6)	27	0.12
Cheyenne	1	0.00
Chickasaw	2	0.01
Chippewa (1)	2	0.01
Creek (1)	1	0.00
Crow	1	0.00
Delaware	1	0.00
Iroquois	1	0.00

Notes: 1. Figures in the "Number" column do not add up to the total population due to: a) Ancestry/Race overlap — e.g. persons can report being both White and Irish, b) persons of Hispanic origin can report being any race, c) persons reporting two ancestries are counted in both categories. 2. Numbers in parentheses indicate the number of persons reporting this ancestry/race alone, not in combination with any other ancestry/race. 3. Refer to the User's Guide in the front of the book for more detailed information.

Latin American Indians (17)	28	0.13
Potawatomi (1)	1	0.00
Pueblo (1)	2	0.01
Seminole	1	0.00
All other tribes	3	0.01
American Indian tribes, not spec.	12	0.05
Arab:	46	0.21
Arab/Arabic	17	0.08
Egyptian	29	0.13
Asian:	1,525	6.82
Bangladeshi (14)	25	0.11
Cambodian (34)	50	0.22
Chinese, ex. Taiwanese (111)	146	0.65
Filipino (74)	97	0.43
Indian (212)	285	1.28
Indonesian (3)	4	0.02
Japanese (12)	15	0.07
Korean (26)	32	0.14
Laotian (48)	52	0.23
Malaysian (4)	4	0.02
Pakistani (12)	32	0.14
Taiwanese	2	0.01
Thai (5)	7	0.03
Vietnamese (644)	706	3.16
Other Asian, not specified (24)	68	0.30
Austrian	19	0.08
Brazilian	161	0.72
British	9	0.04
Canadian	18	0.08
Czech	17	0.08
Czechoslovakian	23	0.10
Dutch	80	0.36
English	683	3.05
Estonian	8	0.04
European	7	0.03
French, except Basque	168	0.75
French Canadian	80	0.36
German	866	3.86
Greek	82	0.37
Guyanese	18	0.08
Hawaii Native/Pacific Islander:	141	0.63
Melanesian: (3)	3	0.01
Fijian (3)	3	0.01
Micronesian: (20)	20	0.09
Guamanian/Chamorro (9)	9	0.04
Other Micronesian (11)	11	0.05
Polynesian: (36)	65	0.29
Native Hawaiian (6)	21	0.09
Samoan (5)	7	0.03
Tongan (23)	31	0.14
Other Polynesian (2)	6	0.03
Other Pac. Isl., not spec. (5)	53	0.24
Hispanic or Latino:	9,257	41.42
Central American:	403	1.80
Costa Rican	28	0.13
Guatemalan	62	0.28
Honduran	107	0.48
Nicaraguan	59	0.26
Panamanian	38	0.17
Salvadoran	98	0.44
Other Central American	11	0.05
Cuban	707	3.16
Dominican Republic	677	3.03
Mexican	967	4.33
Puerto Rican	4,249	19.01
South American:	865	3.87
Argentinean	35	0.16
Bolivian	3	0.01
Chilean	42	0.19
Colombian	431	1.93
Ecuadorian	91	0.41
Peruvian	108	0.48
Uruguayan	8	0.04
Venezuelan	115	0.51
Other South American	32	0.14
Other Hispanic or Latino	1,389	6.22
Hungarian	65	0.29
Irish	778	3.47
Italian	389	1.74
Latvian	14	0.06
Lithuanian	9	0.04
Polish	151	0.67
Portuguese	56	0.25
Russian	90	0.40
Scotch-Irish	47	0.21
Scottish	100	0.45
Slavic	37	0.17
Slovak	24	0.11
Swedish	43	0.19
Swiss	4	0.02
United States or American	989	4.41
Welsh	46	0.21
West Indian, excl. Hispanic:	2,824	12.60
Bahamian	14	0.06
Barbadian	13	0.06
British West Indian	13	0.06
Dutch West Indian	5	0.02
Haitian	2,240	10.00
Jamaican	296	1.32
Trinidadian and Tobagonian	119	0.53
U.S. Virgin Islander	23	0.10
West Indian	101	0.45
White:	10,547	47.19
Not Hispanic (4,542)	4,901	21.93
Hispanic (5,086)	5,646	25.26
Yugoslavian	23	0.10

Oakland Park

Place Type: City
County: Broward
Population: 30,966

Ancestry/Race	Number	%
African American/Black:	7,783	25.13
Not Hispanic (6,858)	7,551	24.38
Hispanic (155)	232	0.75
African, sub-Saharan:	379	1.21
African	360	1.15
South African	19	0.06
Alaska Native tribes, specified:	3	0.01
Tlingit-Haida (1)	3	0.01
Am. Ind. or Alaska Nat., not spec.	69	0.22
Albanian	24	0.08
American Indian tribes, specified:	119	0.38
Apache (1)	1	0.00
Blackfeet	6	0.02
Cherokee (7)	42	0.14
Chippewa	4	0.01
Choctaw	7	0.02
Comanche	1	0.00
Creek (1)	1	0.00
Delaware	2	0.01
Iroquois (2)	6	0.02
Latin American Indians (10)	25	0.08
Ottawa (1)	1	0.00
Potawatomi	1	0.00
Pueblo (1)	2	0.01
Seminole (1)	1	0.00
Sioux (1)	5	0.02
Yaqui (1)	1	0.00
All other tribes (1)	13	0.04
American Indian tribes, not spec.	12	0.04
Arab:	108	0.35
Arab/Arabic	9	0.03
Egyptian	30	0.10
Lebanese	61	0.20
Palestinian	8	0.03
Armenian	31	0.10
Asian:	783	2.53
Bangladeshi (14)	26	0.08
Cambodian (1)	3	0.01
Chinese, ex. Taiwanese (133)	164	0.53
Filipino (32)	43	0.14
Indian (228)	286	0.92
Indonesian (2)	3	0.01
Japanese (38)	54	0.17
Korean (19)	23	0.07
Laotian (3)	6	0.02
Malaysian (1)	1	0.00
Pakistani (10)	22	0.07
Sri Lankan (1)	1	0.00
Taiwanese (1)	1	0.00
Thai (38)	46	0.15
Vietnamese (56)	61	0.20
Other Asian, specified (5)	7	0.02
Other Asian, not specified (5)	36	0.12
Australian	18	0.06
Austrian	123	0.39
Basque	16	0.05
Brazilian	704	2.26
British	131	0.42
Bulgarian	16	0.05
Canadian	138	0.44
Croatian	105	0.34
Cypriot	9	0.03
Czech	79	0.25
Czechoslovakian	38	0.12
Danish	52	0.17
Dutch	285	0.91
Eastern European	43	0.14
English	2,101	6.73
European	115	0.37
Finnish	18	0.06
French, except Basque	823	2.64
French Canadian	146	0.47
German	3,217	10.31
Greek	134	0.43
Guyanese	48	0.15
Hawaii Native/Pacific Islander:	110	0.36
Micronesian: (14)	18	0.06
Guamanian/Chamorro (14)	17	0.05
Other Micronesian	1	0.00
Polynesian: (16)	33	0.11
Native Hawaiian (10)	21	0.07
Samoan (3)	8	0.03
Other Polynesian (3)	4	0.01
Other Pac. Isl., not spec. (11)	59	0.19
Hispanic or Latino:	5,556	17.94
Central American:	846	2.73
Costa Rican	26	0.08
Guatemalan	122	0.39
Honduran	163	0.53
Nicaraguan	43	0.14
Panamanian	35	0.11
Salvadoran	425	1.37
Other Central American	32	0.10
Cuban	629	2.03
Dominican Republic	140	0.45
Mexican	861	2.78
Puerto Rican	1,038	3.35
South American:	930	3.00
Argentinean	34	0.11
Bolivian	15	0.05
Chilean	90	0.29
Colombian	347	1.12
Ecuadorian	51	0.16
Paraguayan	4	0.01
Peruvian	196	0.63
Uruguayan	43	0.14
Venezuelan	104	0.34
Other South American	46	0.15
Other Hispanic or Latino	1,112	3.59
Hungarian	244	0.78
Iranian	31	0.10
Irish	2,995	9.60
Israeli	24	0.08
Italian	2,508	8.04
Lithuanian	57	0.18
Maltese	10	0.03
Northern European	31	0.10
Norwegian	172	0.55
Pennsylvania German	7	0.02
Polish	859	2.75
Portuguese	243	0.78
Romanian	23	0.07
Russian	271	0.87
Scandinavian	15	0.05
Scotch-Irish	230	0.74
Scottish	388	1.24
Serbian	30	0.10
Slavic	6	0.02
Slovak	94	0.30
Slovene	14	0.04

Notes: 1. Figures in the "Number" column do not add up to the total population due to: a) Ancestry/Race overlap — e.g. persons can report being both White and Irish, b) persons of Hispanic origin can report being any race, c) persons reporting two ancestries are counted in both categories. 2. Numbers in parentheses indicate the number of persons reporting this ancestry/race alone, not in combination with any other ancestry/race. 3. Refer to the User's Guide in the front of the book for more detailed information.

Swedish	329	1.05
Swiss	85	0.27
Turkish	131	0.42
Ukrainian	93	0.30
United States or American	1,393	4.46
Welsh	219	0.70
West Indian, excl. Hispanic:	3,501	11.22
Bahamian	138	0.44
Barbadian	7	0.02
Belizean	46	0.15
British West Indian	70	0.22
Haitian	2,299	7.37
Jamaican	743	2.38
Trinidadian and Tobagonian	141	0.45
U.S. Virgin Islander	9	0.03
West Indian	48	0.15
White:	21,173	68.37
Not Hispanic (16,703)	17,108	55.25
Hispanic (3,729)	4,065	13.13
Yugoslavian	14	0.04

Ocala

Place Type: City
County: Marion
Population: 45,943

Ancestry/Race	Number	%
Acadian/Cajun	24	0.05
African American/Black:	10,408	22.65
Not Hispanic (10,055)	10,253	22.32
Hispanic (119)	155	0.34
African, sub-Saharan:	256	0.56
African	186	0.41
Ethiopian	17	0.04
Kenyan	53	0.12
Am. Ind. or Alaska Nat., not spec.	129	0.28
Alsatian	7	0.02
American Indian tribes, specified:	262	0.57
Apache	3	0.01
Blackfeet (6)	17	0.04
Cherokee (50)	143	0.31
Chickasaw (1)	1	0.00
Chippewa (2)	4	0.01
Choctaw (1)	5	0.01
Comanche (2)	2	0.00
Creek (6)	11	0.02
Crow	2	0.00
Iroquois (6)	9	0.02
Latin American Indians (13)	21	0.05
Lumbee (5)	10	0.02
Navajo (3)	4	0.01
Potawatomi (1)	1	0.00
Pueblo	1	0.00
Seminole	5	0.01
Sioux (3)	5	0.01
All other tribes (7)	18	0.04
American Indian tribes, not spec.	19	0.04
Arab:	412	0.90
Arab/Arabic	149	0.33
Egyptian	8	0.02
Jordanian	29	0.06
Lebanese	142	0.31
Palestinian	7	0.02
Syrian	57	0.12
Other Arab	20	0.04
Asian:	665	1.45
Chinese, ex. Taiwanese (56)	68	0.15
Filipino (84)	113	0.25
Indian (229)	249	0.54
Indonesian (1)	3	0.01
Japanese (35)	43	0.09
Korean (59)	71	0.15
Laotian (1)	2	0.00
Malaysian (1)	1	0.00
Pakistani (9)	13	0.03
Sri Lankan (1)	1	0.00
Taiwanese (10)	11	0.02
Thai (3)	6	0.01
Vietnamese (46)	51	0.11
Other Asian, not specified (21)	33	0.07
Australian	7	0.02
Austrian	117	0.26
Belgian	52	0.11
Brazilian	19	0.04
British	246	0.54
Bulgarian	9	0.02
Canadian	171	0.37
Celtic	15	0.03
Croatian	55	0.12
Czech	55	0.12
Czechoslovakian	64	0.14
Danish	55	0.12
Dutch	797	1.75
English	5,056	11.08
European	253	0.55
Finnish	69	0.15
French, except Basque	1,450	3.18
French Canadian	307	0.67
German	6,040	13.24
German Russian	6	0.01
Greek	164	0.36
Hawaii Native/Pacific Islander:	30	0.07
Micronesian: (1)	3	0.01
Guamanian/Chamorro (1)	3	0.01
Polynesian: (8)	21	0.05
Native Hawaiian (3)	10	0.02
Samoan (5)	11	0.02
Other Pac. Isl., not spec.	6	0.01
Hispanic or Latino:	2,636	5.74
Central American:	105	0.23
Costa Rican	9	0.02
Guatemalan	30	0.07
Honduran	12	0.03
Nicaraguan	5	0.01
Panamanian	43	0.09
Salvadoran	3	0.01
Other Central American	3	0.01
Cuban	193	0.42
Dominican Republic	36	0.08
Mexican	606	1.32
Puerto Rican	1,040	2.26
South American:	189	0.41
Argentinean	9	0.02
Bolivian	1	0.00
Chilean	10	0.02
Colombian	87	0.19
Ecuadorian	35	0.08
Peruvian	18	0.04
Uruguayan	7	0.02
Venezuelan	17	0.04
Other South American	5	0.01
Other Hispanic or Latino	467	1.02
Hungarian	77	0.17
Iranian	35	0.08
Irish	5,378	11.79
Italian	2,486	5.45
Latvian	11	0.02
Lithuanian	55	0.12
Macedonian	6	0.01
Norwegian	340	0.75
Pennsylvania German	26	0.06
Polish	1,009	2.21
Portuguese	135	0.30
Romanian	26	0.06
Russian	236	0.52
Scandinavian	65	0.14
Scotch-Irish	796	1.74
Scottish	1,122	2.46
Serbian	8	0.02
Slovak	49	0.11
Slovene	42	0.09
Swedish	441	0.97
Swiss	99	0.22
Turkish	15	0.03
Ukrainian	81	0.18
United States or American	3,084	6.76
Welsh	310	0.68
West Indian, excl. Hispanic:	285	0.62
Bahamian	24	0.05
British West Indian	18	0.04
Haitian	38	0.08
Jamaican	168	0.37
Trinidadian and Tobagonian	19	0.04
West Indian	18	0.04
White:	34,097	74.22
Not Hispanic (31,982)	32,415	70.55
Hispanic (1,492)	1,682	3.66
Yugoslavian	37	0.08

Ocoee

Place Type: City
County: Orange
Population: 24,391

Ancestry/Race	Number	%
African American/Black:	1,775	7.28
Not Hispanic (1,538)	1,686	6.91
Hispanic (69)	89	0.36
African, sub-Saharan:	26	0.11
African	10	0.04
Nigerian	16	0.07
Alaska Native tribes, specified:	1	0.00
Eskimo (1)	1	0.00
Am. Ind. or Alaska Nat., not spec.	53	0.22
American Indian tribes, specified:	139	0.57
Apache	4	0.02
Blackfeet	3	0.01
Cherokee (25)	58	0.24
Chippewa (1)	4	0.02
Choctaw (1)	5	0.02
Comanche (3)	3	0.01
Creek (5)	7	0.03
Crow	1	0.00
Iroquois	7	0.03
Latin American Indians (8)	10	0.04
Navajo (6)	6	0.02
Pueblo (3)	3	0.01
Seminole (7)	14	0.06
Shoshone	1	0.00
Sioux (6)	7	0.03
All other tribes	6	0.02
American Indian tribes, not spec.	6	0.02
Arab:	75	0.32
Arab/Arabic	17	0.07
Jordanian	32	0.14
Moroccan	20	0.08
Syrian	6	0.03
Asian:	883	3.62
Cambodian (2)	2	0.01
Chinese, ex. Taiwanese (61)	73	0.30
Filipino (111)	144	0.59
Indian (288)	368	1.51
Japanese (31)	40	0.16
Korean (67)	72	0.30
Laotian (4)	4	0.02
Pakistani (11)	14	0.06
Sri Lankan (2)	2	0.01
Taiwanese (1)	1	0.00
Thai (1)	1	0.00
Vietnamese (116)	123	0.50
Other Asian, specified	4	0.02
Other Asian, not specified (16)	35	0.14
Brazilian	7	0.03
British	113	0.48
Canadian	124	0.52
Celtic	6	0.03
Croatian	24	0.10
Czech	107	0.45
Czechoslovakian	24	0.10
Danish	124	0.52
Dutch	394	1.67
Eastern European	6	0.03
English	2,373	10.04
European	174	0.74
Finnish	31	0.13
French, except Basque	833	3.53
French Canadian	271	1.15
German	3,325	14.07
Greek	88	0.37
Guyanese	41	0.17
Hawaii Native/Pacific Islander:	41	0.17
Micronesian: (2)	2	0.01
Guamanian/Chamorro (2)	2	0.01

Notes: 1. Figures in the "Number" column do not add up to the total population due to: a) Ancestry/Race overlap — e.g. persons can report being both White and Irish, b) persons of Hispanic origin can report being any race, c) persons reporting two ancestries are counted in both categories. 2. Numbers in parentheses indicate the number of persons reporting this ancestry/race alone, not in combination with any other ancestry/race. 3. Refer to the User's Guide in the front of the book for more detailed information.

Polynesian: (9)	22	0.09
Native Hawaiian (5)	13	0.05
Samoan (4)	4	0.02
Other Polynesian	5	0.02
Other Pac. Isl., specified	4	0.02
Other Pac. Isl., not spec. (3)	13	0.05
Hispanic or Latino:	3,707	15.20
Central American:	130	0.53
Costa Rican	6	0.02
Guatemalan	79	0.32
Honduran	8	0.03
Nicaraguan	11	0.05
Panamanian	17	0.07
Salvadoran	4	0.02
Other Central American	5	0.02
Cuban	162	0.66
Dominican Republic	46	0.19
Mexican	1,753	7.19
Puerto Rican	1,013	4.15
South American:	234	0.96
Argentinean	10	0.04
Bolivian	3	0.01
Chilean	6	0.02
Colombian	127	0.52
Ecuadorian	17	0.07
Peruvian	21	0.09
Uruguayan	9	0.04
Venezuelan	32	0.13
Other South American	9	0.04
Other Hispanic or Latino	369	1.51
Hungarian	105	0.44
Icelander	6	0.03
Irish	2,666	11.28
Italian	1,595	6.75
Lithuanian	36	0.15
Norwegian	272	1.15
Pennsylvania German	8	0.03
Polish	654	2.77
Portuguese	232	0.98
Romanian	52	0.22
Russian	121	0.51
Scandinavian	31	0.13
Scotch-Irish	350	1.48
Scottish	540	2.29
Slovak	41	0.17
Swedish	284	1.20
Swiss	57	0.24
Ukrainian	56	0.24
United States or American	2,344	9.92
Welsh	105	0.44
West Indian, excl. Hispanic:	376	1.59
Bahamian	15	0.06
Barbadian	10	0.04
Dutch West Indian	8	0.03
Haitian	30	0.13
Jamaican	271	1.15
Trinidadian and Tobagonian	11	0.05
West Indian	31	0.13
White:	20,271	83.11
Not Hispanic (17,909)	18,132	74.34
Hispanic (1,962)	2,139	8.77

Ojus

Place Type: Census Designated Place
County: Miami-Dade
Population: 16,642

Ancestry/Race	Number	%
African American/Black:	1,274	7.66
Not Hispanic (1,066)	1,132	6.80
Hispanic (108)	142	0.85
African, sub-Saharan:	82	0.49
African	34	0.20
South African	36	0.22
Other sub-Saharan African	12	0.07
Am. Ind. or Alaska Nat., not spec.	25	0.15
American Indian tribes, specified:	29	0.17
Cherokee (1)	6	0.04
Latin American Indians (8)	19	0.11
Pueblo	1	0.01
Sioux (1)	1	0.01
All other tribes (1)	2	0.01
American Indian tribes, not spec.	3	0.02
Arab:	365	2.19
Arab/Arabic	9	0.05
Egyptian	164	0.98
Jordanian	91	0.55
Lebanese	44	0.26
Moroccan	28	0.17
Syrian	14	0.08
Other Arab	15	0.09
Armenian	9	0.05
Asian:	378	2.27
Chinese, ex. Taiwanese (105)	125	0.75
Filipino (38)	51	0.31
Indian (76)	103	0.62
Japanese (4)	8	0.05
Korean (14)	22	0.13
Laotian (2)	4	0.02
Pakistani (16)	22	0.13
Sri Lankan (2)	2	0.01
Thai (13)	15	0.09
Vietnamese (4)	7	0.04
Other Asian, not specified (11)	19	0.11
Austrian	169	1.01
Basque	5	0.03
Brazilian	268	1.61
British	63	0.38
Canadian	59	0.35
Czech	46	0.28
Czechoslovakian	43	0.26
Dutch	65	0.39
Eastern European	157	0.94
English	404	2.42
Estonian	6	0.04
European	320	1.92
French, except Basque	369	2.21
French Canadian	130	0.78
German	780	4.68
Greek	166	1.00
Guyanese	27	0.16
Hawaii Native/Pacific Islander:	13	0.08
Micronesian: (2)	2	0.01
Guamanian/Chamorro (2)	2	0.01
Polynesian: (1)	2	0.01
Native Hawaiian (1)	1	0.01
Other Polynesian	1	0.01
Other Pac. Isl., not spec. (4)	9	0.05
Hispanic or Latino:	5,093	30.60
Central American:	336	2.02
Costa Rican	34	0.20
Guatemalan	51	0.31
Honduran	91	0.55
Nicaraguan	93	0.56
Panamanian	28	0.17
Salvadoran	24	0.14
Other Central American	15	0.09
Cuban	1,126	6.77
Dominican Republic	237	1.42
Mexican	89	0.53
Puerto Rican	487	2.93
South American:	1,609	9.67
Argentinean	249	1.50
Bolivian	33	0.20
Chilean	51	0.31
Colombian	618	3.71
Ecuadorian	71	0.43
Paraguayan	1	0.01
Peruvian	381	2.29
Uruguayan	31	0.19
Venezuelan	131	0.79
Other South American	43	0.26
Other Hispanic or Latino	1,209	7.26
Hungarian	202	1.21
Iranian	27	0.16
Irish	421	2.52
Israeli	295	1.77
Italian	795	4.77
Latvian	13	0.08
Lithuanian	118	0.71
Northern European	8	0.05
Norwegian	38	0.23
Polish	830	4.98
Portuguese	58	0.35
Romanian	177	1.06
Russian	1,256	7.53
Scandinavian	9	0.05
Scotch-Irish	32	0.19
Scottish	60	0.36
Swedish	29	0.17
Turkish	132	0.79
Ukrainian	206	1.23
United States or American	1,171	7.02
Welsh	29	0.17
West Indian, excl. Hispanic:	836	5.01
Bahamian	18	0.11
Barbadian	9	0.05
British West Indian	8	0.05
Haitian	505	3.03
Jamaican	181	1.09
Trinidadian and Tobagonian	108	0.65
West Indian	7	0.04
White:	14,542	87.38
Not Hispanic (9,894)	10,059	60.44
Hispanic (4,267)	4,483	26.94

Oldsmar

Place Type: City
County: Pinellas
Population: 11,910

Ancestry/Race	Number	%
African American/Black:	417	3.50
Not Hispanic (338)	396	3.32
Hispanic (14)	21	0.18
African, sub-Saharan:	11	0.09
African	11	0.09
Alaska Native tribes, specified:	1	0.01
Tlingit-Haida	1	0.01
Am. Ind. or Alaska Nat., not spec.	19	0.16
Albanian	75	0.64
American Indian tribes, specified:	61	0.51
Apache (1)	1	0.01
Blackfeet (1)	1	0.01
Cherokee (2)	16	0.13
Cheyenne (2)	2	0.02
Chickasaw (1)	1	0.01
Chippewa (3)	4	0.03
Choctaw (1)	1	0.01
Creek	1	0.01
Delaware (1)	2	0.02
Iroquois (4)	7	0.06
Latin American Indians (7)	8	0.07
Lumbee (3)	3	0.03
Ottawa (1)	1	0.01
Seminole	2	0.02
Shoshone (2)	3	0.03
Sioux	1	0.01
All other tribes (1)	7	0.06
American Indian tribes, not spec.	2	0.02
Arab:	172	1.47
Arab/Arabic	44	0.37
Egyptian	25	0.21
Lebanese	15	0.13
Moroccan	14	0.12
Syrian	65	0.55
Other Arab	9	0.08
Armenian	9	0.08
Asian:	409	3.43
Chinese, ex. Taiwanese (47)	56	0.47
Filipino (65)	85	0.71
Indian (110)	120	1.01
Japanese (8)	12	0.10
Korean (18)	26	0.22
Laotian (7)	13	0.11
Malaysian (1)	1	0.01
Pakistani (2)	2	0.02
Taiwanese	4	0.03
Thai (6)	6	0.05
Vietnamese (58)	60	0.50
Other Asian, not specified (4)	24	0.20
Austrian	51	0.43
Belgian	12	0.10

Notes: 1. Figures in the "Number" column do not add up to the total population due to: a) Ancestry/Race overlap — e.g. persons can report being both White and Irish, b) persons of Hispanic origin can report being any race, c) persons reporting two ancestries are counted in both categories. 2. Numbers in parentheses indicate the number of persons reporting this ancestry/race alone, not in combination with any other ancestry/race. 3. Refer to the User's Guide in the front of the book for more detailed information.

Brazilian	7	0.06
British	43	0.37
Canadian	98	0.84
Croatian	65	0.55
Cypriot	25	0.21
Czech	85	0.72
Czechoslovakian	9	0.08
Danish	75	0.64
Dutch	253	2.16
English	1,420	12.10
European	51	0.43
Finnish	20	0.17
French, except Basque	584	4.98
French Canadian	220	1.87
German	2,641	22.50
Greek	79	0.67
Hawaii Native/Pacific Islander:	23	0.19
Micronesian: (5)	5	0.04
Guamanian/Chamorro (5)	5	0.04
Polynesian: (8)	10	0.08
Native Hawaiian (4)	5	0.04
Samoan (4)	5	0.04
Other Pac. Isl., not spec. (6)	8	0.07
Hispanic or Latino:	794	6.67
Central American:	21	0.18
Costa Rican	5	0.04
Guatemalan	3	0.03
Honduran	4	0.03
Nicaraguan	2	0.02
Panamanian	4	0.03
Salvadoran	2	0.02
Other Central American	1	0.01
Cuban	75	0.63
Dominican Republic	15	0.13
Mexican	117	0.98
Puerto Rican	287	2.41
South American:	118	0.99
Argentinean	8	0.07
Bolivian	3	0.03
Chilean	2	0.02
Colombian	43	0.36
Ecuadorian	23	0.19
Peruvian	23	0.19
Uruguayan	2	0.02
Venezuelan	13	0.11
Other South American	1	0.01
Other Hispanic or Latino	161	1.35
Hungarian	65	0.55
Irish	2,223	18.94
Italian	1,544	13.16
Latvian	41	0.35
Norwegian	75	0.64
Polish	556	4.74
Portuguese	131	1.12
Romanian	38	0.32
Russian	99	0.84
Scotch-Irish	153	1.30
Scottish	303	2.58
Slavic	10	0.09
Slovak	43	0.37
Swedish	100	0.85
Swiss	49	0.42
Turkish	16	0.14
Ukrainian	34	0.29
United States or American	812	6.92
Welsh	121	1.03
West Indian, excl. Hispanic:	52	0.44
Barbadian	17	0.14
British West Indian	8	0.07
Haitian	8	0.07
West Indian	19	0.16
White:	10,990	92.28
Not Hispanic (10,210)	10,367	87.04
Hispanic (561)	623	5.23
Yugoslavian	12	0.10

Olympia Heights

Place Type: Census Designated Place
County: Miami-Dade
Population: 13,452

Ancestry/Race	Number	%
African American/Black:	141	1.05
Not Hispanic (20)	25	0.19
Hispanic (92)	116	0.86
African, sub-Saharan:	10	0.07
African	10	0.07
Am. Ind. or Alaska Nat., not spec.	12	0.09
American Indian tribes, specified:	17	0.13
Cherokee (5)	9	0.07
Latin American Indians (4)	8	0.06
American Indian tribes, not spec.	3	0.02
Arab:	75	0.56
Arab/Arabic	20	0.15
Lebanese	29	0.21
Moroccan	7	0.05
Palestinian	19	0.14
Asian:	139	1.03
Chinese, ex. Taiwanese (70)	76	0.56
Filipino (2)	2	0.01
Indian (30)	30	0.22
Japanese (3)	3	0.02
Korean (3)	3	0.02
Pakistani (5)	14	0.10
Taiwanese (4)	5	0.04
Vietnamese (2)	2	0.01
Other Asian, not specified (3)	4	0.03
Austrian	52	0.39
Belgian	21	0.16
Brazilian	19	0.14
British	9	0.07
Croatian	6	0.04
Czech	8	0.06
Czechoslovakian	7	0.05
Dutch	16	0.12
English	351	2.60
European	19	0.14
French, except Basque	121	0.90
French Canadian	35	0.26
German	362	2.68
Greek	14	0.10
Hawaii Native/Pacific Islander:	2	0.01
Micronesian:	2	0.01
Guamanian/Chamorro	2	0.01
Hispanic or Latino:	10,268	76.33
Central American:	432	3.21
Costa Rican	22	0.16
Guatemalan	41	0.30
Honduran	63	0.47
Nicaraguan	242	1.80
Panamanian	16	0.12
Salvadoran	34	0.25
Other Central American	14	0.10
Cuban	7,755	57.65
Dominican Republic	118	0.88
Mexican	101	0.75
Puerto Rican	272	2.02
South American:	570	4.24
Argentinean	31	0.23
Bolivian	7	0.05
Chilean	41	0.30
Colombian	268	1.99
Ecuadorian	40	0.30
Paraguayan	1	0.01
Peruvian	101	0.75
Uruguayan	3	0.02
Venezuelan	67	0.50
Other South American	11	0.08
Other Hispanic or Latino	1,020	7.58
Hungarian	29	0.21
Irish	480	3.56
Italian	218	1.62
Lithuanian	49	0.36
Norwegian	10	0.07
Polish	65	0.48
Romanian	23	0.17
Russian	105	0.78
Scotch-Irish	118	0.87
Scottish	89	0.66
Swiss	6	0.04
Ukrainian	9	0.07
United States or American	397	2.94
Welsh	15	0.11
White:	12,860	95.60
Not Hispanic (2,997)	3,024	22.48
Hispanic (9,581)	9,836	73.12
Yugoslavian	7	0.05

Opa-locka

Place Type: City
County: Miami-Dade
Population: 14,951

Ancestry/Race	Number	%
African American/Black:	10,705	71.60
Not Hispanic (9,933)	10,127	67.73
Hispanic (479)	578	3.87
African, sub-Saharan:	202	1.33
African	193	1.27
Cape Verdean	9	0.06
Alaska Native tribes, specified:	2	0.01
Eskimo	2	0.01
Am. Ind. or Alaska Nat., not spec.	52	0.35
American Indian tribes, specified:	40	0.27
Cherokee (5)	7	0.05
Crow	1	0.01
Iroquois	1	0.01
Latin American Indians (12)	18	0.12
Navajo (3)	3	0.02
Pueblo	1	0.01
Sioux (1)	1	0.01
All other tribes (1)	8	0.05
American Indian tribes, not spec.	6	0.04
Arab:	15	0.10
Lebanese	15	0.10
Asian:	78	0.52
Chinese, ex. Taiwanese (7)	18	0.12
Filipino (1)	1	0.01
Indian (10)	30	0.20
Japanese (1)	3	0.02
Korean (2)	3	0.02
Pakistani	1	0.01
Thai (4)	4	0.03
Vietnamese (2)	2	0.01
Other Asian, not specified (4)	16	0.11
Brazilian	11	0.07
British	13	0.09
Canadian	6	0.04
Czech	6	0.04
Dutch	8	0.05
English	154	1.01
European	7	0.05
French, except Basque	23	0.15
German	93	0.61
Hawaii Native/Pacific Islander:	42	0.28
Micronesian: (1)	7	0.05
Guamanian/Chamorro (1)	7	0.05
Polynesian: (2)	5	0.03
Native Hawaiian (2)	3	0.02
Samoan	2	0.01
Other Pac. Isl., not spec.	30	0.20
Hispanic or Latino:	4,268	28.55
Central American:	594	3.97
Costa Rican	12	0.08
Guatemalan	56	0.37
Honduran	133	0.89
Nicaraguan	332	2.22
Panamanian	13	0.09
Salvadoran	29	0.19
Other Central American	19	0.13
Cuban	1,432	9.58
Dominican Republic	387	2.59
Mexican	152	1.02
Puerto Rican	707	4.73
South American:	219	1.46
Argentinean	1	0.01
Bolivian	7	0.05

Notes: 1. Figures in the "Number" column do not add up to the total population due to: a) Ancestry/Race overlap — e.g. persons can report being both White and Irish, b) persons of Hispanic origin can report being any race, c) persons reporting two ancestries are counted in both categories. 2. Numbers in parentheses indicate the number of persons reporting this ancestry/race alone, not in combination with any other ancestry/race. 3. Refer to the User's Guide in the front of the book for more detailed information.

Chilean	3	0.02
Colombian	124	0.83
Ecuadorian	48	0.32
Paraguayan	1	0.01
Peruvian	20	0.13
Uruguayan	1	0.01
Venezuelan	8	0.05
Other South American	6	0.04
Other Hispanic or Latino	777	5.20
Icelander	13	0.09
Irish	125	0.82
Italian	64	0.42
Norwegian	20	0.13
Polish	5	0.03
Scotch-Irish	8	0.05
United States or American	457	3.00
West Indian, excl. Hispanic:	1,079	7.08
Bahamian	79	0.52
Barbadian	7	0.05
Belizean	8	0.05
British West Indian	36	0.24
Dutch West Indian	28	0.18
Haitian	364	2.39
Jamaican	389	2.55
Trinidadian and Tobagonian	49	0.32
U.S. Virgin Islander	7	0.05
West Indian	105	0.69
Other West Indian	7	0.05
White:	3,664	24.51
Not Hispanic (469)	507	3.39
Hispanic (2,945)	3,157	21.12

Orlando

Place Type: City
County: Orange
Population: 185,951

Ancestry/Race	Number	%
Acadian/Cajun	20	0.01
African American/Black:	52,652	28.31
Not Hispanic (48,547)	50,745	27.29
Hispanic (1,386)	1,907	1.03
African, sub-Saharan:	1,786	0.96
African	1,598	0.86
Cape Verdean	84	0.05
Nigerian	25	0.01
Sierra Leonean	12	0.01
South African	16	0.01
Zairian	10	0.01
Zimbabwean	10	0.01
Other sub-Saharan African	31	0.02
Alaska Native tribes, specified:	8	0.00
Alaska Athabascan (2)	4	0.00
Eskimo (1)	1	0.00
Tlingit-Haida (1)	1	0.00
All other tribes	2	0.00
Alaska Native tribes, not specified	1	0.00
Am. Ind. or Alaska Nat., not spec.	499	0.27
Albanian	114	0.06
Alsatian	13	0.01
American Indian tribes, specified:	807	0.43
Apache (12)	24	0.01
Blackfeet (7)	41	0.02
Cherokee (122)	349	0.19
Cheyenne	2	0.00
Chickasaw (2)	5	0.00
Chippewa (14)	27	0.01
Choctaw (19)	32	0.02
Colville	2	0.00
Comanche (1)	3	0.00
Creek (3)	22	0.01
Crow	1	0.00
Delaware (2)	3	0.00
Iroquois (26)	41	0.02
Kiowa (1)	1	0.00
Latin American Indians (38)	91	0.05
Lumbee (1)	3	0.00
Menominee	2	0.00
Navajo (5)	6	0.00
Osage	1	0.00
Ottawa	2	0.00
Paiute (2)	3	0.00
Potawatomi (3)	4	0.00
Pueblo (3)	8	0.00
Seminole (7)	36	0.02
Shoshone	1	0.00
Sioux (10)	23	0.01
Yakama (1)	1	0.00
Yaqui (4)	6	0.00
All other tribes (25)	67	0.04
American Indian tribes, not spec.	102	0.05
Arab:	1,693	0.91
Arab/Arabic	254	0.14
Egyptian	85	0.05
Jordanian	25	0.01
Lebanese	587	0.32
Moroccan	272	0.15
Palestinian	169	0.09
Syrian	204	0.11
Other Arab	97	0.05
Armenian	126	0.07
Asian:	6,259	3.37
Bangladeshi (17)	17	0.01
Cambodian (27)	29	0.02
Chinese, ex. Taiwanese (683)	873	0.47
Filipino (876)	1,138	0.61
Hmong (2)	5	0.00
Indian (1,247)	1,464	0.79
Indonesian (11)	19	0.01
Japanese (328)	447	0.24
Korean (437)	524	0.28
Laotian (34)	42	0.02
Malaysian (4)	7	0.00
Pakistani (133)	190	0.10
Sri Lankan (20)	21	0.01
Taiwanese (26)	30	0.02
Thai (73)	112	0.06
Vietnamese (849)	939	0.50
Other Asian, specified (15)	34	0.02
Other Asian, not specified (92)	368	0.20
Assyrian/Chaldean/Syriac	5	0.00
Australian	63	0.03
Austrian	362	0.19
Basque	27	0.01
Belgian	144	0.08
Brazilian	1,355	0.73
British	1,080	0.58
Bulgarian	13	0.01
Canadian	457	0.25
Carpatho Rusyn	17	0.01
Celtic	6	0.00
Croatian	145	0.08
Czech	255	0.14
Czechoslovakian	197	0.11
Danish	514	0.28
Dutch	2,223	1.20
Eastern European	101	0.05
English	14,663	7.88
Estonian	38	0.02
European	1,110	0.60
Finnish	330	0.18
French, except Basque	4,327	2.33
French Canadian	1,240	0.67
German	18,259	9.82
German Russian	9	0.00
Greek	682	0.37
Guyanese	131	0.07
Hawaii Native/Pacific Islander:	487	0.26
Melanesian: (2)	3	0.00
Fijian (2)	3	0.00
Micronesian: (49)	71	0.04
Guamanian/Chamorro (22)	33	0.02
Other Micronesian (27)	38	0.02
Polynesian: (66)	149	0.08
Native Hawaiian (32)	103	0.06
Samoan (22)	28	0.02
Tongan (6)	6	0.00
Other Polynesian (6)	12	0.01
Other Pac. Isl., specified	13	0.01
Other Pac. Isl., not spec. (33)	251	0.13
Hispanic or Latino:	32,510	17.48
Central American:	1,183	0.64
Costa Rican	119	0.06
Guatemalan	179	0.10
Honduran	329	0.18
Nicaraguan	123	0.07
Panamanian	230	0.12
Salvadoran	132	0.07
Other Central American	71	0.04
Cuban	2,696	1.45
Dominican Republic	1,191	0.64
Mexican	2,279	1.23
Puerto Rican	17,029	9.16
South American:	3,494	1.88
Argentinean	179	0.10
Bolivian	38	0.02
Chilean	84	0.05
Colombian	1,663	0.89
Ecuadorian	376	0.20
Paraguayan	7	0.00
Peruvian	336	0.18
Uruguayan	18	0.01
Venezuelan	674	0.36
Other South American	119	0.06
Other Hispanic or Latino	4,638	2.49
Hungarian	912	0.49
Icelander	91	0.05
Iranian	104	0.06
Irish	16,241	8.73
Israeli	13	0.01
Italian	8,557	4.60
Latvian	47	0.03
Lithuanian	319	0.17
Luxemburger	10	0.01
Maltese	18	0.01
New Zealander	6	0.00
Northern European	89	0.05
Norwegian	1,225	0.66
Pennsylvania German	35	0.02
Polish	3,297	1.77
Portuguese	514	0.28
Romanian	121	0.07
Russian	1,178	0.63
Scandinavian	192	0.10
Scotch-Irish	2,634	1.42
Scottish	3,164	1.70
Serbian	105	0.06
Slavic	54	0.03
Slovak	246	0.13
Slovene	43	0.02
Swedish	1,552	0.83
Swiss	377	0.20
Turkish	47	0.03
Ukrainian	388	0.21
United States or American	12,426	6.68
Welsh	1,046	0.56
West Indian, excl. Hispanic:	6,955	3.74
Bahamian	207	0.11
Barbadian	156	0.08
Belizean	36	0.02
British West Indian	279	0.15
Haitian	3,514	1.89
Jamaican	1,955	1.05
Trinidadian and Tobagonian	236	0.13
U.S. Virgin Islander	166	0.09
West Indian	369	0.20
Other West Indian	37	0.02
White:	117,957	63.43
Not Hispanic (94,452)	96,921	52.12
Hispanic (19,159)	21,036	11.31
Yugoslavian	118	0.06

Ormond Beach

Place Type: City
County: Volusia
Population: 36,301

Ancestry/Race	Number	%
Acadian/Cajun	26	0.07
African American/Black:	1,067	2.94
Not Hispanic (990)	1,053	2.90
Hispanic (10)	14	0.04

Notes: 1. Figures in the "Number" column do not add up to the total population due to: a) Ancestry/Race overlap — e.g. persons can report being both White and Irish, b) persons of Hispanic origin can report being any race, c) persons reporting two ancestries are counted in both categories. 2. Numbers in parentheses indicate the number of persons reporting this ancestry/race alone, not in combination with any other ancestry/race. 3. Refer to the User's Guide in the front of the book for more detailed information.

African, sub-Saharan:	113	0.31
African	101	0.28
Cape Verdean	6	0.02
Nigerian	6	0.02
Am. Ind. or Alaska Nat., not spec.	60	0.17
Alsatian	7	0.02
American Indian tribes, specified:	116	0.32
Blackfeet (1)	5	0.01
Cherokee (13)	58	0.16
Cheyenne (1)	1	0.00
Chickasaw (1)	1	0.00
Chippewa (2)	3	0.01
Choctaw (1)	2	0.01
Comanche (1)	1	0.00
Cree (1)	1	0.00
Creek (2)	6	0.02
Delaware	4	0.01
Iroquois (6)	12	0.03
Latin American Indians (1)	1	0.00
Pima (1)	2	0.01
Potawatomi	3	0.01
Pueblo	1	0.00
Seminole	1	0.00
Shoshone	1	0.00
Sioux (2)	5	0.01
All other tribes (5)	8	0.02
American Indian tribes, not spec.	5	0.01
Arab:	269	0.74
Arab/Arabic	18	0.05
Egyptian	119	0.33
Jordanian	29	0.08
Lebanese	92	0.25
Other Arab	11	0.03
Armenian	50	0.14
Asian:	619	1.71
Bangladeshi (1)	1	0.00
Chinese, ex. Taiwanese (73)	84	0.23
Filipino (75)	107	0.29
Indian (231)	261	0.72
Indonesian (2)	2	0.01
Japanese (22)	39	0.11
Korean (42)	45	0.12
Malaysian (1)	1	0.00
Pakistani (12)	12	0.03
Sri Lankan (4)	4	0.01
Taiwanese (5)	5	0.01
Thai (4)	5	0.01
Vietnamese (28)	28	0.08
Other Asian, specified	1	0.00
Other Asian, not specified (15)	24	0.07
Austrian	171	0.47
Belgian	33	0.09
Brazilian	43	0.12
British	259	0.71
Bulgarian	13	0.04
Canadian	231	0.64
Celtic	5	0.01
Croatian	38	0.10
Czech	90	0.25
Czechoslovakian	98	0.27
Danish	106	0.29
Dutch	732	2.01
Eastern European	20	0.06
English	6,146	16.91
Estonian	25	0.07
European	108	0.30
Finnish	90	0.25
French, except Basque	1,329	3.66
French Canadian	361	0.99
German	6,400	17.61
Greek	343	0.94
Hawaii Native/Pacific Islander:	15	0.04
Polynesian: (7)	15	0.04
Native Hawaiian (3)	11	0.03
Samoan (4)	4	0.01
Hispanic or Latino:	797	2.20
Central American:	45	0.12
Costa Rican	20	0.06
Guatemalan	10	0.03
Honduran	7	0.02
Nicaraguan	1	0.00
Panamanian	3	0.01
Salvadoran	4	0.01
Cuban	101	0.28
Dominican Republic	11	0.03
Mexican	87	0.24
Puerto Rican	275	0.76
South American:	123	0.34
Argentinean	14	0.04
Bolivian	1	0.00
Chilean	7	0.02
Colombian	28	0.08
Ecuadorian	22	0.06
Peruvian	14	0.04
Uruguayan	9	0.02
Venezuelan	13	0.04
Other South American	15	0.04
Other Hispanic or Latino	155	0.43
Hungarian	365	1.00
Icelander	6	0.02
Iranian	137	0.38
Irish	5,394	14.84
Italian	3,451	9.49
Latvian	6	0.02
Lithuanian	196	0.54
Luxemburger	6	0.02
Maltese	87	0.24
Northern European	57	0.16
Norwegian	459	1.26
Pennsylvania German	7	0.02
Polish	1,515	4.17
Portuguese	132	0.36
Romanian	23	0.06
Russian	543	1.49
Scandinavian	89	0.24
Scotch-Irish	1,127	3.10
Scottish	1,142	3.14
Serbian	60	0.17
Slavic	41	0.11
Slovak	109	0.30
Slovene	55	0.15
Swedish	572	1.57
Swiss	111	0.31
Ukrainian	227	0.62
United States or American	3,522	9.69
Welsh	331	0.91
West Indian, excl. Hispanic:	51	0.14
Bahamian	29	0.08
Jamaican	14	0.04
Trinidadian and Tobagonian	8	0.02
White:	34,566	95.22
Not Hispanic (33,564)	33,863	93.28
Hispanic (659)	703	1.94
Yugoslavian	28	0.08

Oviedo

Place Type: City
County: Seminole
Population: 26,316

Ancestry/Race	Number	%
African American/Black:	2,491	9.47
Not Hispanic (2,242)	2,363	8.98
Hispanic (83)	128	0.49
African, sub-Saharan:	104	0.38
African	87	0.32
Other sub-Saharan African	17	0.06
Alaska Native tribes, specified:	2	0.01
Eskimo (1)	1	0.00
Tlingit-Haida (1)	1	0.00
Am. Ind. or Alaska Nat., not spec.	61	0.23
Albanian	7	0.03
American Indian tribes, specified:	102	0.39
Apache (1)	2	0.01
Cherokee (11)	47	0.18
Chickasaw (1)	1	0.00
Chippewa	5	0.02
Choctaw (4)	7	0.03
Creek (2)	6	0.02
Iroquois (1)	3	0.01
Latin American Indians (7)	20	0.08
Navajo	2	0.01
Osage (1)	1	0.00
Ottawa	1	0.00
Seminole	3	0.01
Sioux	2	0.01
All other tribes (2)	2	0.01
American Indian tribes, not spec.	20	0.08
Arab:	215	0.80
Egyptian	44	0.16
Jordanian	55	0.20
Lebanese	36	0.13
Palestinian	36	0.13
Syrian	35	0.13
Other Arab	9	0.03
Armenian	32	0.12
Asian:	839	3.19
Cambodian (7)	7	0.03
Chinese, ex. Taiwanese (97)	150	0.57
Filipino (111)	161	0.61
Indian (174)	205	0.78
Indonesian (2)	4	0.02
Japanese (39)	64	0.24
Korean (76)	90	0.34
Laotian (2)	2	0.01
Pakistani (2)	13	0.05
Taiwanese (3)	4	0.02
Thai (7)	8	0.03
Vietnamese (97)	102	0.39
Other Asian, not specified (14)	29	0.11
Australian	8	0.03
Austrian	91	0.34
Basque	8	0.03
Belgian	74	0.27
British	307	1.14
Canadian	73	0.27
Celtic	21	0.08
Croatian	9	0.03
Czech	81	0.30
Czechoslovakian	52	0.19
Danish	103	0.38
Dutch	468	1.73
English	3,175	11.75
European	191	0.71
Finnish	85	0.31
French, except Basque	796	2.95
French Canadian	260	0.96
German	4,890	18.10
Greek	104	0.38
Guyanese	51	0.19
Hawaii Native/Pacific Islander:	40	0.15
Micronesian: (7)	12	0.05
Guamanian/Chamorro (7)	12	0.05
Polynesian: (3)	13	0.05
Native Hawaiian (3)	13	0.05
Other Pac. Isl., not spec.	15	0.06
Hispanic or Latino:	3,209	12.19
Central American:	130	0.49
Costa Rican	22	0.08
Guatemalan	7	0.03
Honduran	19	0.07
Nicaraguan	11	0.04
Panamanian	43	0.16
Salvadoran	16	0.06
Other Central American	12	0.05
Cuban	220	0.84
Dominican Republic	50	0.19
Mexican	308	1.17
Puerto Rican	1,807	6.87
South American:	318	1.21
Argentinean	10	0.04
Bolivian	9	0.03
Chilean	7	0.03
Colombian	148	0.56
Ecuadorian	49	0.19
Paraguayan	1	0.00
Peruvian	45	0.17
Uruguayan	3	0.01
Venezuelan	42	0.16
Other South American	4	0.02
Other Hispanic or Latino	376	1.43
Hungarian	156	0.58

Notes: 1. Figures in the "Number" column do not add up to the total population due to: a) Ancestry/Race overlap — e.g. persons can report being both White and Irish, b) persons of Hispanic origin can report being any race, c) persons reporting two ancestries are counted in both categories. 2. Numbers in parentheses indicate the number of persons reporting this ancestry/race alone, not in combination with any other ancestry/race. 3. Refer to the User's Guide in the front of the book for more detailed information.

Irish	3,621	13.40
Italian	3,136	11.60
Lithuanian	33	0.12
Maltese	8	0.03
Northern European	77	0.28
Norwegian	291	1.08
Pennsylvania German	10	0.04
Polish	1,243	4.60
Portuguese	81	0.30
Romanian	42	0.16
Russian	170	0.63
Scandinavian	7	0.03
Scotch-Irish	599	2.22
Scottish	659	2.44
Serbian	10	0.04
Slavic	29	0.11
Slovak	123	0.46
Slovene	28	0.10
Swedish	244	0.90
Swiss	77	0.28
Turkish	26	0.10
Ukrainian	27	0.10
United States or American	1,575	5.83
Welsh	248	0.92
West Indian, excl. Hispanic:	528	1.95
Belizean	3	0.01
British West Indian	47	0.17
Haitian	192	0.71
Jamaican	219	0.81
Trinidadian and Tobagonian	24	0.09
U.S. Virgin Islander	14	0.05
West Indian	29	0.11
White:	22,450	85.31
Not Hispanic (19,734)	20,053	76.20
Hispanic (2,252)	2,397	9.11
Yugoslavian	22	0.08

Palatka

Place Type: City
County: Putnam
Population: 10,033

Ancestry/Race	Number	%
African American/Black:	4,907	48.91
Not Hispanic (4,840)	4,880	48.64
Hispanic (19)	27	0.27
African, sub-Saharan:	62	0.61
African	62	0.61
Am. Ind. or Alaska Nat., not spec.	27	0.27
American Indian tribes, specified:	37	0.37
Apache (1)	3	0.03
Blackfeet	4	0.04
Cherokee (3)	23	0.23
Cree	1	0.01
Iroquois	1	0.01
Latin American Indians	1	0.01
Seminole	4	0.04
American Indian tribes, not spec.	1	0.01
Armenian	12	0.12
Asian:	60	0.60
Chinese, ex. Taiwanese (3)	3	0.03
Filipino (5)	9	0.09
Indian (12)	12	0.12
Japanese (3)	5	0.05
Korean (1)	1	0.01
Pakistani (12)	15	0.15
Thai	2	0.02
Vietnamese (3)	3	0.03
Other Asian, not specified (5)	10	0.10
British	22	0.22
Canadian	16	0.16
Celtic	9	0.09
Croatian	21	0.21
Danish	12	0.12
Dutch	84	0.82
English	565	5.54
European	12	0.12
French, except Basque	85	0.83
French Canadian	14	0.14
German	453	4.44
Greek	7	0.07
Guyanese	10	0.10
Hawaii Native/Pacific Islander:	2	0.02
Polynesian: (1)	2	0.02
Native Hawaiian (1)	2	0.02
Hispanic or Latino:	284	2.83
Central American:	2	0.02
Nicaraguan	2	0.02
Cuban	21	0.21
Dominican Republic	2	0.02
Mexican	65	0.65
Puerto Rican	131	1.31
South American:	10	0.10
Argentinean	1	0.01
Colombian	4	0.04
Ecuadorian	1	0.01
Peruvian	3	0.03
Venezuelan	1	0.01
Other Hispanic or Latino	53	0.53
Hungarian	8	0.08
Irish	555	5.44
Italian	114	1.12
Lithuanian	11	0.11
Norwegian	29	0.28
Polish	97	0.95
Portuguese	57	0.56
Russian	5	0.05
Scandinavian	22	0.22
Scotch-Irish	193	1.89
Scottish	192	1.88
Serbian	11	0.11
Slovak	11	0.11
Swedish	46	0.45
United States or American	1,045	10.24
Welsh	27	0.26
West Indian, excl. Hispanic:	64	0.63
Haitian	37	0.36
Jamaican	27	0.26
White:	4,982	49.66
Not Hispanic (4,762)	4,822	48.06
Hispanic (147)	160	1.59
Yugoslavian	8	0.08

Palm Bay

Place Type: City
County: Brevard
Population: 79,413

Ancestry/Race	Number	%
Acadian/Cajun	22	0.03
African American/Black:	9,697	12.21
Not Hispanic (8,634)	9,186	11.57
Hispanic (349)	511	0.64
African, sub-Saharan:	450	0.57
African	399	0.50
Cape Verdean	39	0.05
South African	12	0.02
Alaska Native tribes, specified:	9	0.01
Aleut (1)	1	0.00
Eskimo (3)	6	0.01
Tlingit-Haida (1)	1	0.00
All other tribes	1	0.00
Am. Ind. or Alaska Nat., not spec.	197	0.25
Albanian	8	0.01
American Indian tribes, specified:	449	0.57
Apache (6)	12	0.02
Blackfeet (7)	35	0.04
Cherokee (67)	183	0.23
Cheyenne (1)	3	0.00
Chickasaw (3)	7	0.01
Chippewa (10)	18	0.02
Choctaw (5)	6	0.01
Comanche (2)	3	0.00
Cree	1	0.00
Creek (2)	9	0.01
Iroquois (19)	32	0.04
Kiowa (3)	3	0.00
Latin American Indians (21)	39	0.05
Lumbee (1)	1	0.00
Menominee	2	0.00
Navajo (5)	12	0.02
Potawatomi (3)	5	0.01
Pueblo	4	0.01
Puget Sound Salish	1	0.00
Seminole (2)	20	0.03
Sioux (5)	15	0.02
Yuman (1)	1	0.00
All other tribes (14)	37	0.05
American Indian tribes, not spec.	36	0.05
Arab:	598	0.75
Arab/Arabic	226	0.28
Egyptian	91	0.11
Lebanese	166	0.21
Moroccan	27	0.03
Syrian	24	0.03
Other Arab	64	0.08
Armenian	43	0.05
Asian:	1,888	2.38
Bangladeshi (10)	11	0.01
Cambodian (12)	13	0.02
Chinese, ex. Taiwanese (156)	230	0.29
Filipino (316)	458	0.58
Indian (362)	419	0.53
Indonesian (9)	19	0.02
Japanese (92)	171	0.22
Korean (126)	162	0.20
Laotian (1)	1	0.00
Malaysian (3)	3	0.00
Pakistani (12)	17	0.02
Sri Lankan	1	0.00
Taiwanese (16)	24	0.03
Thai (58)	87	0.11
Vietnamese (135)	165	0.21
Other Asian, specified (3)	6	0.01
Other Asian, not specified (29)	101	0.13
Australian	37	0.05
Austrian	236	0.30
Basque	19	0.02
Belgian	31	0.04
Brazilian	62	0.08
British	378	0.48
Canadian	261	0.33
Celtic	6	0.01
Croatian	62	0.08
Cypriot	16	0.02
Czech	304	0.38
Czechoslovakian	144	0.18
Danish	262	0.33
Dutch	1,671	2.10
Eastern European	7	0.01
English	8,038	10.12
European	454	0.57
Finnish	136	0.17
French, except Basque	3,337	4.20
French Canadian	1,257	1.58
German	14,240	17.92
German Russian	11	0.01
Greek	438	0.55
Guyanese	211	0.27
Hawaii Native/Pacific Islander:	133	0.17
Melanesian: (1)	3	0.00
Fijian (1)	3	0.00
Micronesian: (11)	18	0.02
Guamanian/Chamorro (11)	18	0.02
Polynesian: (16)	40	0.05
Native Hawaiian (12)	28	0.04
Samoan (1)	5	0.01
Tongan (2)	6	0.01
Other Polynesian (1)	1	0.00
Other Pac. Isl., not spec. (8)	72	0.09
Hispanic or Latino:	6,850	8.63
Central American:	312	0.39
Costa Rican	36	0.05
Guatemalan	35	0.04
Honduran	40	0.05
Nicaraguan	22	0.03
Panamanian	127	0.16
Salvadoran	40	0.05
Other Central American	12	0.02
Cuban	404	0.51
Dominican Republic	182	0.23
Mexican	549	0.69

Notes: 1. Figures in the "Number" column do not add up to the total population due to: a) Ancestry/Race overlap — e.g. persons can report being both White and Irish, b) persons of Hispanic origin can report being any race, c) persons reporting two ancestries are counted in both categories. 2. Numbers in parentheses indicate the number of persons reporting this ancestry/race alone, not in combination with any other ancestry/race. 3. Refer to the User's Guide in the front of the book for more detailed information.

Puerto Rican	3,767	4.74
South American:	489	0.62
Argentinean	32	0.04
Bolivian	8	0.01
Chilean	15	0.02
Colombian	211	0.27
Ecuadorian	39	0.05
Paraguayan	10	0.01
Peruvian	70	0.09
Uruguayan	3	0.00
Venezuelan	79	0.10
Other South American	22	0.03
Other Hispanic or Latino	1,147	1.44
Hungarian	499	0.63
Iranian	34	0.04
Irish	11,603	14.60
Israeli	9	0.01
Italian	7,318	9.21
Lithuanian	281	0.35
Luxemburger	4	0.01
Maltese	27	0.03
Northern European	5	0.01
Norwegian	731	0.92
Pennsylvania German	47	0.06
Polish	3,059	3.85
Portuguese	445	0.56
Romanian	25	0.03
Russian	440	0.55
Scandinavian	52	0.07
Scotch-Irish	1,317	1.66
Scottish	1,636	2.06
Serbian	21	0.03
Slavic	23	0.03
Slovak	187	0.24
Slovene	9	0.01
Swedish	1,042	1.31
Swiss	222	0.28
Turkish	50	0.06
Ukrainian	282	0.35
United States or American	6,286	7.91
Welsh	719	0.90
West Indian, excl. Hispanic:	2,785	3.51
Bahamian	11	0.01
Barbadian	92	0.12
Belizean	13	0.02
British West Indian	75	0.09
Dutch West Indian	59	0.07
Haitian	175	0.22
Jamaican	1,756	2.21
Trinidadian and Tobagonian	356	0.45
U.S. Virgin Islander	32	0.04
West Indian	197	0.25
Other West Indian	19	0.02
White:	66,399	83.61
Not Hispanic (60,549)	61,781	77.80
Hispanic (4,206)	4,618	5.82
Yugoslavian	10	0.01

Palm Beach Gardens

Place Type: City
County: Palm Beach
Population: 35,058

Ancestry/Race	Number	%
Acadian/Cajun	14	0.04
Afghan	14	0.04
African American/Black:	904	2.58
Not Hispanic (736)	816	2.33
Hispanic (70)	88	0.25
African, sub-Saharan:	51	0.15
African	32	0.09
South African	19	0.06
Alaska Native tribes, specified:	1	0.00
Aleut	1	0.00
Am. Ind. or Alaska Nat., not spec.	40	0.11
Albanian	24	0.07
American Indian tribes, specified:	47	0.13
Blackfeet (1)	2	0.01
Cherokee (6)	14	0.04
Chippewa	1	0.00
Choctaw	3	0.01
Creek	5	0.01
Iroquois (1)	3	0.01
Latin American Indians (3)	6	0.02
Lumbee (1)	1	0.00
Pueblo	1	0.00
Seminole	2	0.01
All other tribes (4)	9	0.03
American Indian tribes, not spec.	10	0.03
Arab:	301	0.87
Arab/Arabic	89	0.26
Iraqi	17	0.05
Lebanese	54	0.16
Palestinian	39	0.11
Syrian	102	0.30
Armenian	92	0.27
Asian:	868	2.48
Bangladeshi (13)	17	0.05
Chinese, ex. Taiwanese (135)	154	0.44
Filipino (45)	62	0.18
Indian (256)	286	0.82
Indonesian (2)	2	0.01
Japanese (38)	57	0.16
Korean (91)	98	0.28
Laotian (2)	2	0.01
Malaysian (1)	2	0.01
Pakistani (8)	13	0.04
Sri Lankan (1)	1	0.00
Thai (8)	11	0.03
Vietnamese (130)	135	0.39
Other Asian, specified	1	0.00
Other Asian, not specified (8)	27	0.08
Austrian	195	0.57
Belgian	56	0.16
Brazilian	8	0.02
British	199	0.58
Bulgarian	7	0.02
Canadian	199	0.58
Celtic	23	0.07
Croatian	10	0.03
Czech	170	0.49
Czechoslovakian	116	0.34
Danish	213	0.62
Dutch	503	1.46
Eastern European	169	0.49
English	4,579	13.28
European	458	1.33
Finnish	109	0.32
French, except Basque	1,441	4.18
French Canadian	413	1.20
German	5,937	17.22
Greek	481	1.40
Hawaii Native/Pacific Islander:	28	0.08
Micronesian: (8)	12	0.03
Guamanian/Chamorro (8)	12	0.03
Polynesian: (2)	9	0.03
Native Hawaiian (1)	6	0.02
Samoan (1)	3	0.01
Other Pac. Isl., not spec. (1)	7	0.02
Hispanic or Latino:	1,973	5.63
Central American:	129	0.37
Costa Rican	11	0.03
Guatemalan	41	0.12
Honduran	19	0.05
Nicaraguan	9	0.03
Panamanian	9	0.03
Salvadoran	32	0.09
Other Central American	8	0.02
Cuban	429	1.22
Dominican Republic	23	0.07
Mexican	137	0.39
Puerto Rican	345	0.98
South American:	448	1.28
Argentinean	39	0.11
Bolivian	3	0.01
Chilean	48	0.14
Colombian	150	0.43
Ecuadorian	49	0.14
Peruvian	93	0.27
Uruguayan	3	0.01
Venezuelan	45	0.13
Other South American	18	0.05
Other Hispanic or Latino	462	1.32
Hungarian	643	1.87
Iranian	65	0.19
Irish	5,248	15.22
Israeli	48	0.14
Italian	4,451	12.91
Latvian	46	0.13
Lithuanian	156	0.45
Maltese	9	0.03
Northern European	6	0.02
Norwegian	295	0.86
Pennsylvania German	20	0.06
Polish	1,952	5.66
Portuguese	164	0.48
Romanian	165	0.48
Russian	1,548	4.49
Scandinavian	36	0.10
Scotch-Irish	635	1.84
Scottish	796	2.31
Serbian	11	0.03
Slovak	168	0.49
Swedish	471	1.37
Swiss	122	0.35
Turkish	32	0.09
Ukrainian	185	0.54
United States or American	2,125	6.16
Welsh	308	0.89
West Indian, excl. Hispanic:	325	0.94
Bahamian	52	0.15
Barbadian	14	0.04
Bermudan	15	0.04
British West Indian	26	0.08
Haitian	95	0.28
Jamaican	80	0.23
Trinidadian and Tobagonian	43	0.12
White:	33,157	94.58
Not Hispanic (31,252)	31,461	89.74
Hispanic (1,626)	1,696	4.84
Yugoslavian	10	0.03

Palm Beach

Place Type: Town
County: Palm Beach
Population: 10,468

Ancestry/Race	Number	%
African American/Black:	285	2.72
Not Hispanic (262)	278	2.66
Hispanic (7)	7	0.07
Alaska Native tribes, specified:	1	0.01
Aleut (1)	1	0.01
Am. Ind. or Alaska Nat., not spec.	4	0.04
Albanian	13	0.13
American Indian tribes, specified:	6	0.06
Cherokee	1	0.01
Chickasaw	1	0.01
Chippewa (1)	1	0.01
Comanche	1	0.01
Latin American Indians (1)	1	0.01
All other tribes (1)	1	0.01
American Indian tribes, not spec.	9	0.09
Arab:	151	1.46
Arab/Arabic	11	0.11
Egyptian	5	0.05
Iraqi	21	0.20
Lebanese	62	0.60
Moroccan	12	0.12
Palestinian	14	0.13
Syrian	26	0.25
Armenian	19	0.18
Asian:	78	0.75
Chinese, ex. Taiwanese (9)	11	0.11
Filipino (22)	26	0.25
Indian (9)	9	0.09
Japanese (7)	23	0.22
Korean (5)	5	0.05
Thai (2)	2	0.02
Other Asian, specified (1)	1	0.01
Other Asian, not specified (1)	1	0.01

Notes: 1. Figures in the "Number" column do not add up to the total population due to: a) Ancestry/Race overlap — e.g. persons can report being both White and Irish, b) persons of Hispanic origin can report being any race, c) persons reporting two ancestries are counted in both categories. 2. Numbers in parentheses indicate the number of persons reporting this ancestry/race alone, not in combination with any other ancestry/race. 3. Refer to the User's Guide in the front of the book for more detailed information.

Australian	5	0.05
Austrian	224	2.16
Basque	4	0.04
Belgian	10	0.10
Brazilian	11	0.11
British	99	0.95
Bulgarian	6	0.06
Canadian	48	0.46
Czech	5	0.05
Czechoslovakian	12	0.12
Danish	34	0.33
Dutch	102	0.98
Eastern European	68	0.66
English	1,323	12.75
Estonian	9	0.09
European	110	1.06
Finnish	34	0.33
French, except Basque	472	4.55
French Canadian	73	0.70
German	1,198	11.55
Greek	147	1.42
Hawaii Native/Pacific Islander:	6	0.06
Micronesian:	2	0.02
Guamanian/Chamorro	2	0.02
Polynesian: (1)	1	0.01
Tongan (1)	1	0.01
Other Pac. Isl., not spec. (1)	3	0.03
Hispanic or Latino:	268	2.56
Central American:	20	0.19
Guatemalan	6	0.06
Honduran	6	0.06
Nicaraguan	5	0.05
Panamanian	2	0.02
Salvadoran	1	0.01
Cuban	82	0.78
Dominican Republic	9	0.09
Mexican	19	0.18
Puerto Rican	13	0.12
South American:	53	0.51
Argentinean	14	0.13
Bolivian	3	0.03
Chilean	3	0.03
Colombian	15	0.14
Ecuadorian	2	0.02
Paraguayan	3	0.03
Peruvian	5	0.05
Uruguayan	1	0.01
Venezuelan	5	0.05
Other South American	2	0.02
Other Hispanic or Latino	72	0.69
Hungarian	136	1.31
Iranian	16	0.15
Irish	904	8.71
Israeli	12	0.12
Italian	646	6.23
Latvian	19	0.18
Lithuanian	155	1.49
Luxemburger	9	0.09
Maltese	12	0.12
Northern European	7	0.07
Norwegian	48	0.46
Polish	531	5.12
Portuguese	33	0.32
Romanian	102	0.98
Russian	1,089	10.50
Scandinavian	13	0.13
Scotch-Irish	89	0.86
Scottish	190	1.83
Serbian	36	0.35
Slovak	8	0.08
Slovene	14	0.13
Swedish	51	0.49
Swiss	27	0.26
Ukrainian	82	0.79
United States or American	777	7.49
Welsh	54	0.52
West Indian, excl. Hispanic:	37	0.36
British West Indian	32	0.31
Haitian	5	0.05
White:	10,104	96.52
Not Hispanic (9,817)	9,859	94.18
Hispanic (232)	245	2.34

Palm City

Place Type: Census Designated Place
County: Martin
Population: 20,097

Ancestry/Race	Number	%
Acadian/Cajun	12	0.06
African American/Black:	249	1.24
Not Hispanic (207)	235	1.17
Hispanic (10)	14	0.07
African, sub-Saharan:	16	0.08
African	16	0.08
Am. Ind. or Alaska Nat., not spec.	27	0.13
American Indian tribes, specified:	46	0.23
Apache (1)	3	0.01
Cherokee (5)	16	0.08
Chippewa (1)	1	0.00
Choctaw	1	0.00
Iroquois (4)	8	0.04
Latin American Indians	8	0.04
Osage	1	0.00
Pueblo (3)	3	0.01
Sioux	2	0.01
All other tribes (2)	3	0.01
American Indian tribes, not spec.	3	0.01
Arab:	70	0.35
Lebanese	45	0.22
Moroccan	9	0.04
Syrian	16	0.08
Armenian	41	0.20
Asian:	276	1.37
Chinese, ex. Taiwanese (66)	85	0.42
Filipino (23)	40	0.20
Indian (65)	73	0.36
Japanese (10)	19	0.09
Korean (14)	18	0.09
Malaysian (1)	2	0.01
Sri Lankan (2)	2	0.01
Thai (5)	7	0.03
Vietnamese (9)	13	0.06
Other Asian, not specified (6)	17	0.08
Australian	7	0.03
Austrian	203	1.01
Belgian	14	0.07
British	153	0.76
Canadian	58	0.29
Croatian	44	0.22
Czech	38	0.19
Czechoslovakian	57	0.28
Danish	183	0.91
Dutch	365	1.82
Eastern European	63	0.31
English	3,372	16.77
European	97	0.48
Finnish	63	0.31
French, except Basque	749	3.72
French Canadian	382	1.90
German	3,836	19.08
Greek	165	0.82
Guyanese	18	0.09
Hawaii Native/Pacific Islander:	4	0.02
Polynesian: (1)	3	0.01
Native Hawaiian (1)	3	0.01
Other Pac. Isl., not spec.	1	0.00
Hispanic or Latino:	556	2.77
Central American:	19	0.09
Costa Rican	2	0.01
Guatemalan	10	0.05
Nicaraguan	1	0.00
Panamanian	1	0.00
Salvadoran	3	0.01
Other Central American	2	0.01
Cuban	88	0.44
Dominican Republic	6	0.03
Mexican	82	0.41
Puerto Rican	150	0.75
South American:	91	0.45
Argentinean	6	0.03
Bolivian	10	0.05
Chilean	2	0.01
Colombian	25	0.12
Ecuadorian	14	0.07
Peruvian	7	0.03
Venezuelan	15	0.07
Other South American	12	0.06
Other Hispanic or Latino	120	0.60
Hungarian	290	1.44
Irish	3,470	17.26
Italian	2,992	14.88
Latvian	18	0.09
Lithuanian	40	0.20
Norwegian	277	1.38
Pennsylvania German	10	0.05
Polish	1,037	5.16
Portuguese	70	0.35
Romanian	37	0.18
Russian	432	2.15
Scandinavian	70	0.35
Scotch-Irish	476	2.37
Scottish	497	2.47
Slavic	60	0.30
Slovak	60	0.30
Slovene	26	0.13
Swedish	542	2.70
Swiss	131	0.65
Turkish	9	0.04
Ukrainian	104	0.52
United States or American	1,566	7.79
Welsh	157	0.78
West Indian, excl. Hispanic:	103	0.51
Bahamian	19	0.09
Haitian	36	0.18
Jamaican	39	0.19
West Indian	9	0.04
White:	19,535	97.20
Not Hispanic (18,971)	19,073	94.90
Hispanic (435)	462	2.30
Yugoslavian	24	0.12

Palm Coast

Place Type: City
County: Flagler
Population: 32,732

Ancestry/Race	Number	%
Acadian/Cajun	6	0.02
African American/Black:	3,592	10.97
Not Hispanic (3,261)	3,451	10.54
Hispanic (99)	141	0.43
African, sub-Saharan:	82	0.24
African	79	0.24
Cape Verdean	3	0.01
Alaska Native tribes, specified:	4	0.01
Eskimo	1	0.00
Tlingit-Haida (3)	3	0.01
Am. Ind. or Alaska Nat., not spec.	74	0.23
American Indian tribes, specified:	135	0.41
Apache (2)	2	0.01
Blackfeet (4)	7	0.02
Cherokee (22)	63	0.19
Cheyenne (1)	2	0.01
Chippewa (1)	2	0.01
Choctaw (1)	8	0.02
Comanche (1)	3	0.01
Creek	10	0.03
Delaware (1)	2	0.01
Iroquois (1)	5	0.02
Latin American Indians (4)	8	0.02
Potawatomi	1	0.00
Sioux (3)	4	0.01
All other tribes (7)	18	0.05
American Indian tribes, not spec.	16	0.05
Arab:	68	0.20
Egyptian	23	0.07
Lebanese	45	0.13
Armenian	32	0.10
Asian:	618	1.89
Cambodian (13)	17	0.05
Chinese, ex. Taiwanese (60)	85	0.26

Notes: 1. Figures in the "Number" column do not add up to the total population due to: a) Ancestry/Race overlap — e.g. persons can report being both White and Irish, b) persons of Hispanic origin can report being any race, c) persons reporting two ancestries are counted in both categories. 2. Numbers in parentheses indicate the number of persons reporting this ancestry/race alone, not in combination with any other ancestry/race. 3. Refer to the User's Guide in the front of the book for more detailed information.

Filipino (259)	304	0.93
Indian (68)	84	0.26
Indonesian (2)	5	0.02
Japanese (14)	24	0.07
Korean (31)	36	0.11
Laotian	1	0.00
Malaysian	2	0.01
Pakistani (1)	6	0.02
Taiwanese (11)	12	0.04
Thai (9)	12	0.04
Vietnamese (16)	20	0.06
Other Asian, not specified (6)	10	0.03
Australian	7	0.02
Austrian	177	0.53
Belgian	37	0.11
Brazilian	9	0.03
British	205	0.61
Canadian	91	0.27
Celtic	11	0.03
Croatian	60	0.18
Czech	168	0.50
Czechoslovakian	98	0.29
Danish	96	0.29
Dutch	612	1.83
English	3,975	11.86
European	75	0.22
Finnish	109	0.33
French, except Basque	1,067	3.18
French Canadian	318	0.95
German	5,341	15.94
Greek	160	0.48
Guyanese	115	0.34
Hawaii Native/Pacific Islander:	35	0.11
Melanesian: (2)	2	0.01
Other Melanesian (2)	2	0.01
Micronesian: (1)	1	0.00
Guamanian/Chamorro (1)	1	0.00
Polynesian: (5)	12	0.04
Native Hawaiian	2	0.01
Samoan (5)	10	0.03
Other Pac. Isl., not spec. (1)	20	0.06
Hispanic or Latino:	2,196	6.71
Central American:	85	0.26
Costa Rican	4	0.01
Guatemalan	17	0.05
Honduran	15	0.05
Nicaraguan	5	0.02
Panamanian	28	0.09
Salvadoran	11	0.03
Other Central American	5	0.02
Cuban	249	0.76
Dominican Republic	36	0.11
Mexican	172	0.53
Puerto Rican	912	2.79
South American:	305	0.93
Argentinean	24	0.07
Bolivian	6	0.02
Chilean	6	0.02
Colombian	139	0.42
Ecuadorian	25	0.08
Peruvian	49	0.15
Uruguayan	22	0.07
Venezuelan	19	0.06
Other South American	15	0.05
Other Hispanic or Latino	437	1.34
Hungarian	254	0.76
Icelander	24	0.07
Iranian	24	0.07
Irish	5,666	16.91
Israeli	27	0.08
Italian	5,128	15.31
Lithuanian	105	0.31
Macedonian	13	0.04
Maltese	30	0.09
New Zealander	48	0.14
Norwegian	262	0.78
Pennsylvania German	33	0.10
Polish	1,633	4.87
Portuguese	486	1.45
Romanian	7	0.02
Russian	446	1.33
Scandinavian	30	0.09
Scotch-Irish	519	1.55
Scottish	804	2.40
Serbian	83	0.25
Slavic	38	0.11
Slovak	130	0.39
Slovene	13	0.04
Swedish	466	1.39
Swiss	92	0.27
Turkish	58	0.17
Ukrainian	307	0.92
United States or American	1,473	4.40
Welsh	352	1.05
West Indian, excl. Hispanic:	839	2.50
Bahamian	15	0.04
Barbadian	43	0.13
Belizean	24	0.07
Bermudan	8	0.02
British West Indian	19	0.06
Haitian	37	0.11
Jamaican	492	1.47
Trinidadian and Tobagonian	72	0.21
West Indian	129	0.39
White:	28,261	86.34
Not Hispanic (26,217)	26,532	81.06
Hispanic (1,617)	1,729	5.28
Yugoslavian	33	0.10

Palm Harbor

Place Type: Census Designated Place
County: Pinellas
Population: 59,248

Ancestry/Race	Number	%
Acadian/Cajun	53	0.09
African American/Black:	695	1.17
Not Hispanic (545)	648	1.09
Hispanic (29)	47	0.08
African, sub-Saharan:	125	0.21
African	72	0.12
Kenyan	5	0.01
South African	48	0.08
Alaska Native tribes, specified:	3	0.01
Eskimo (2)	2	0.00
Tlingit-Haida	1	0.00
Am. Ind. or Alaska Nat., not spec.	65	0.11
Albanian	105	0.18
American Indian tribes, specified:	189	0.32
Apache	3	0.01
Blackfeet (7)	13	0.02
Cherokee (25)	82	0.14
Chickasaw	1	0.00
Chippewa (5)	7	0.01
Choctaw (4)	4	0.01
Creek (3)	11	0.02
Crow	1	0.00
Delaware	1	0.00
Houma (1)	1	0.00
Iroquois (4)	16	0.03
Latin American Indians (7)	8	0.01
Navajo	1	0.00
Osage (1)	1	0.00
Ottawa	1	0.00
Potawatomi (1)	1	0.00
Seminole (2)	5	0.01
Sioux (5)	12	0.02
Yaqui	3	0.01
All other tribes (9)	17	0.03
American Indian tribes, not spec.	40	0.07
Arab:	572	0.97
Arab/Arabic	54	0.09
Egyptian	129	0.22
Iraqi	8	0.01
Lebanese	215	0.36
Palestinian	105	0.18
Syrian	50	0.08
Other Arab	11	0.02
Armenian	44	0.07
Asian:	930	1.57
Cambodian (6)	6	0.01
Chinese, ex. Taiwanese (126)	145	0.24
Filipino (120)	159	0.27
Indian (268)	285	0.48
Indonesian (7)	8	0.01
Japanese (59)	98	0.17
Korean (47)	69	0.12
Laotian (9)	9	0.02
Malaysian (1)	2	0.00
Pakistani (18)	21	0.04
Taiwanese (3)	4	0.01
Thai (13)	14	0.02
Vietnamese (59)	71	0.12
Other Asian, specified (5)	7	0.01
Other Asian, not specified (16)	32	0.05
Australian	48	0.08
Austrian	238	0.40
Belgian	66	0.11
Brazilian	51	0.09
British	432	0.73
Bulgarian	14	0.02
Canadian	438	0.74
Celtic	12	0.02
Croatian	216	0.37
Cypriot	30	0.05
Czech	366	0.62
Czechoslovakian	222	0.38
Danish	531	0.90
Dutch	1,377	2.33
Eastern European	20	0.03
English	8,244	13.94
European	365	0.62
Finnish	195	0.33
French, except Basque	2,569	4.35
French Canadian	639	1.08
German	11,510	19.47
Greek	1,707	2.89
Hawaii Native/Pacific Islander:	41	0.07
Micronesian: (2)	5	0.01
Guamanian/Chamorro (2)	5	0.01
Polynesian: (12)	24	0.04
Native Hawaiian (12)	21	0.04
Samoan	2	0.00
Tongan	1	0.00
Other Pac. Isl., not spec.	12	0.02
Hispanic or Latino:	2,047	3.45
Central American:	71	0.12
Costa Rican	20	0.03
Guatemalan	15	0.03
Honduran	3	0.01
Nicaraguan	7	0.01
Panamanian	10	0.02
Salvadoran	13	0.02
Other Central American	3	0.01
Cuban	240	0.41
Dominican Republic	46	0.08
Mexican	268	0.45
Puerto Rican	611	1.03
South American:	352	0.59
Argentinean	20	0.03
Bolivian	9	0.02
Chilean	8	0.01
Colombian	145	0.24
Ecuadorian	55	0.09
Paraguayan	1	0.00
Peruvian	49	0.08
Uruguayan	2	0.00
Venezuelan	47	0.08
Other South American	16	0.03
Other Hispanic or Latino	459	0.77
Hungarian	792	1.34
Icelander	26	0.04
Iranian	44	0.07
Irish	9,754	16.50
Israeli	37	0.06
Italian	7,548	12.77
Latvian	8	0.01
Lithuanian	313	0.53
Macedonian	9	0.02
Maltese	44	0.07
Northern European	51	0.09
Norwegian	604	1.02
Pennsylvania German	29	0.05

Notes: 1. Figures in the "Number" column do not add up to the total population due to: a) Ancestry/Race overlap — e.g. persons can report being both White and Irish, b) persons of Hispanic origin can report being any race, c) persons reporting two ancestries are counted in both categories. 2. Numbers in parentheses indicate the number of persons reporting this ancestry/race alone, not in combination with any other ancestry/race. 3. Refer to the User's Guide in the front of the book for more detailed information.

Polish	3,230	5.46
Portuguese	299	0.51
Romanian	173	0.29
Russian	849	1.44
Scandinavian	61	0.10
Scotch-Irish	1,226	2.07
Scottish	1,780	3.01
Serbian	19	0.03
Slavic	51	0.09
Slovak	137	0.23
Slovene	26	0.04
Swedish	1,264	2.14
Swiss	233	0.39
Turkish	15	0.03
Ukrainian	253	0.43
United States or American	3,674	6.21
Welsh	604	1.02
West Indian, excl. Hispanic:	97	0.16
Jamaican	97	0.16
White:	57,366	96.82
Not Hispanic (55,198)	55,679	93.98
Hispanic (1,582)	1,687	2.85
Yugoslavian	89	0.15

Palm River-Clair Mel

Place Type: Census Designated Place
County: Hillsborough
Population: 17,589

Ancestry/Race	Number	%
African American/Black:	6,282	35.72
Not Hispanic (5,933)	6,061	34.46
Hispanic (154)	221	1.26
African, sub-Saharan:	105	0.60
African	83	0.47
South African	22	0.13
Am. Ind. or Alaska Nat., not spec.	73	0.42
Albanian	6	0.03
American Indian tribes, specified:	127	0.72
Apache (4)	5	0.03
Blackfeet (2)	4	0.02
Cherokee (16)	55	0.31
Cheyenne (1)	2	0.01
Chippewa (5)	5	0.03
Choctaw (1)	5	0.03
Comanche (4)	4	0.02
Cree	1	0.01
Crow	1	0.01
Iroquois (5)	7	0.04
Latin American Indians (5)	16	0.09
Lumbee (1)	1	0.01
Navajo	1	0.01
Pueblo (3)	3	0.02
Seminole	4	0.02
Sioux (1)	4	0.02
Yakama	2	0.01
All other tribes (2)	7	0.04
American Indian tribes, not spec.	9	0.05
Arab:	58	0.33
Lebanese	7	0.04
Moroccan	7	0.04
Palestinian	27	0.15
Other Arab	17	0.10
Asian:	295	1.68
Chinese, ex. Taiwanese (4)	7	0.04
Filipino (59)	71	0.40
Indian (57)	71	0.40
Japanese (13)	18	0.10
Korean (7)	14	0.08
Pakistani (2)	2	0.01
Thai (21)	28	0.16
Vietnamese (43)	51	0.29
Other Asian, specified	1	0.01
Other Asian, not specified (5)	32	0.18
British	20	0.11
Canadian	72	0.41
Croatian	6	0.03
Czech	10	0.06
Dutch	107	0.61
English	885	5.03
European	57	0.32
French, except Basque	154	0.88
French Canadian	59	0.34
German	1,059	6.02
Greek	47	0.27
Hawaii Native/Pacific Islander:	22	0.13
Micronesian: (1)	4	0.02
Guamanian/Chamorro (1)	4	0.02
Polynesian: (1)	7	0.04
Native Hawaiian (1)	5	0.03
Samoan	2	0.01
Other Pac. Isl., specified	1	0.01
Other Pac. Isl., not spec. (2)	10	0.06
Hispanic or Latino:	3,958	22.50
Central American:	155	0.88
Costa Rican	43	0.24
Guatemalan	23	0.13
Honduran	30	0.17
Nicaraguan	15	0.09
Panamanian	15	0.09
Salvadoran	14	0.08
Other Central American	15	0.09
Cuban	914	5.20
Dominican Republic	113	0.64
Mexican	525	2.98
Puerto Rican	1,462	8.31
South American:	110	0.63
Argentinean	1	0.01
Chilean	3	0.02
Colombian	40	0.23
Ecuadorian	22	0.13
Peruvian	12	0.07
Uruguayan	1	0.01
Venezuelan	29	0.16
Other South American	2	0.01
Other Hispanic or Latino	679	3.86
Hungarian	43	0.24
Irish	920	5.23
Italian	508	2.89
Lithuanian	12	0.07
Norwegian	47	0.27
Polish	187	1.06
Portuguese	32	0.18
Scandinavian	28	0.16
Scotch-Irish	224	1.27
Scottish	112	0.64
Slavic	10	0.06
Swedish	69	0.39
Ukrainian	19	0.11
United States or American	1,684	9.57
Welsh	51	0.29
West Indian, excl. Hispanic:	500	2.84
Barbadian	12	0.07
British West Indian	10	0.06
Dutch West Indian	9	0.05
Haitian	208	1.18
Jamaican	158	0.90
Trinidadian and Tobagonian	41	0.23
West Indian	62	0.35
White:	9,938	56.50
Not Hispanic (7,095)	7,275	41.36
Hispanic (2,461)	2,663	15.14

Palm Springs

Place Type: Village
County: Palm Beach
Population: 11,699

Ancestry/Race	Number	%
African American/Black:	857	7.33
Not Hispanic (736)	798	6.82
Hispanic (45)	59	0.50
African, sub-Saharan:	56	0.47
African	56	0.47
Am. Ind. or Alaska Nat., not spec.	30	0.26
Albanian	8	0.07
American Indian tribes, specified:	28	0.24
Cherokee (7)	13	0.11
Chickasaw (1)	1	0.01
Choctaw (1)	1	0.01
Iroquois (1)	1	0.01
Latin American Indians (4)	6	0.05
Lumbee	1	0.01
Sioux	1	0.01
Yuman (1)	1	0.01
All other tribes (2)	3	0.03
American Indian tribes, not spec.	8	0.07
Arab:	71	0.60
Lebanese	71	0.60
Asian:	216	1.85
Bangladeshi (6)	6	0.05
Chinese, ex. Taiwanese (15)	18	0.15
Filipino (26)	30	0.26
Indian (43)	62	0.53
Japanese (3)	4	0.03
Korean (19)	23	0.20
Pakistani (1)	9	0.08
Sri Lankan (4)	4	0.03
Taiwanese (2)	2	0.02
Thai (17)	27	0.23
Vietnamese (13)	15	0.13
Other Asian, specified (9)	9	0.08
Other Asian, not specified (3)	7	0.06
Austrian	45	0.38
Brazilian	93	0.79
British	18	0.15
Bulgarian	35	0.30
Canadian	49	0.41
Croatian	5	0.04
Czech	71	0.60
Czechoslovakian	26	0.22
Danish	6	0.05
Dutch	141	1.19
English	1,109	9.38
European	34	0.29
Finnish	48	0.41
French, except Basque	363	3.07
French Canadian	111	0.94
German	1,328	11.23
Greek	74	0.63
Hawaii Native/Pacific Islander:	8	0.07
Micronesian: (1)	2	0.02
Guamanian/Chamorro (1)	2	0.02
Polynesian: (2)	2	0.02
Samoan (2)	2	0.02
Other Pac. Isl., not spec.	4	0.03
Hispanic or Latino:	2,929	25.04
Central American:	194	1.66
Costa Rican	8	0.07
Guatemalan	29	0.25
Honduran	87	0.74
Nicaraguan	29	0.25
Panamanian	6	0.05
Salvadoran	25	0.21
Other Central American	10	0.09
Cuban	891	7.62
Dominican Republic	140	1.20
Mexican	233	1.99
Puerto Rican	532	4.55
South American:	425	3.63
Argentinean	14	0.12
Bolivian	6	0.05
Chilean	22	0.19
Colombian	223	1.91
Ecuadorian	61	0.52
Peruvian	44	0.38
Uruguayan	14	0.12
Venezuelan	26	0.22
Other South American	15	0.13
Other Hispanic or Latino	514	4.39
Hungarian	26	0.22
Icelander	6	0.05
Irish	1,368	11.57
Israeli	8	0.07
Italian	1,015	8.59
Lithuanian	46	0.39
Norwegian	41	0.35
Polish	358	3.03
Portuguese	36	0.30
Romanian	46	0.39
Russian	90	0.76
Scotch-Irish	263	2.22

Notes: 1. Figures in the "Number" column do not add up to the total population due to: a) Ancestry/Race overlap — e.g. persons can report being both White and Irish, b) persons of Hispanic origin can report being any race, c) persons reporting two ancestries are counted in both categories. 2. Numbers in parentheses indicate the number of persons reporting this ancestry/race alone, not in combination with any other ancestry/race. 3. Refer to the User's Guide in the front of the book for more detailed information.

Scottish	210	1.78
Serbian	9	0.08
Slavic	9	0.08
Swedish	94	0.80
Swiss	11	0.09
Ukrainian	17	0.14
United States or American	802	6.78
Welsh	43	0.36
West Indian, excl. Hispanic:	575	4.86
Bahamian	7	0.06
Haitian	365	3.09
Jamaican	152	1.29
Trinidadian and Tobagonian	40	0.34
U.S. Virgin Islander	11	0.09
White:	10,088	86.23
Not Hispanic (7,679)	7,785	66.54
Hispanic (2,176)	2,303	19.69
Yugoslavian	8	0.07

Palm Valley

Place Type: Census Designated Place
County: Saint Johns
Population: 19,860

Ancestry/Race	Number	%
Acadian/Cajun	39	0.20
African American/Black:	291	1.47
Not Hispanic (245)	280	1.41
Hispanic (4)	11	0.06
African, sub-Saharan:	55	0.28
African	29	0.15
Cape Verdean	11	0.06
South African	15	0.08
Am. Ind. or Alaska Nat., not spec.	15	0.08
Albanian	8	0.04
American Indian tribes, specified:	57	0.29
Apache (1)	2	0.01
Blackfeet	1	0.01
Cherokee (9)	24	0.12
Chickasaw (1)	2	0.01
Chippewa (1)	1	0.01
Choctaw (1)	2	0.01
Creek (2)	5	0.03
Delaware	3	0.02
Iroquois (6)	6	0.03
Latin American Indians (4)	4	0.02
Navajo	1	0.01
Osage	1	0.01
Sioux (1)	1	0.01
All other tribes (3)	4	0.02
American Indian tribes, not spec.	1	0.01
Arab:	103	0.52
Arab/Arabic	14	0.07
Egyptian	10	0.05
Lebanese	35	0.18
Syrian	44	0.22
Armenian	33	0.17
Asian:	337	1.70
Chinese, ex. Taiwanese (73)	86	0.43
Filipino (52)	75	0.38
Indian (65)	72	0.36
Indonesian (1)	3	0.02
Japanese (19)	37	0.19
Korean (15)	22	0.11
Laotian (1)	1	0.01
Pakistani (3)	3	0.02
Sri Lankan (4)	4	0.02
Taiwanese (2)	3	0.02
Thai (2)	2	0.01
Vietnamese (3)	8	0.04
Other Asian, specified (10)	10	0.05
Other Asian, not specified (1)	11	0.06
Australian	41	0.21
Austrian	155	0.78
Belgian	8	0.04
Brazilian	8	0.04
British	192	0.97
Bulgarian	9	0.05
Canadian	37	0.19
Croatian	18	0.09
Czech	68	0.34
Czechoslovakian	40	0.20
Danish	74	0.37
Dutch	262	1.32
Eastern European	16	0.08
English	3,584	18.05
European	160	0.81
Finnish	74	0.37
French, except Basque	760	3.83
French Canadian	185	0.93
German	3,558	17.92
Greek	140	0.71
Hawaii Native/Pacific Islander:	15	0.08
Micronesian: (1)	2	0.01
Guamanian/Chamorro (1)	2	0.01
Polynesian: (3)	5	0.03
Native Hawaiian (2)	4	0.02
Samoan (1)	1	0.01
Other Pac. Isl., not spec. (1)	8	0.04
Hispanic or Latino:	557	2.80
Central American:	29	0.15
Costa Rican	4	0.02
Guatemalan	6	0.03
Honduran	1	0.01
Nicaraguan	3	0.02
Panamanian	8	0.04
Salvadoran	1	0.01
Other Central American	6	0.03
Cuban	92	0.46
Dominican Republic	3	0.02
Mexican	101	0.51
Puerto Rican	152	0.77
South American:	65	0.33
Argentinean	3	0.02
Bolivian	6	0.03
Chilean	8	0.04
Colombian	18	0.09
Ecuadorian	9	0.05
Peruvian	9	0.05
Uruguayan	3	0.02
Venezuelan	6	0.03
Other South American	3	0.02
Other Hispanic or Latino	115	0.58
Hungarian	286	1.44
Icelander	16	0.08
Iranian	37	0.19
Irish	3,379	17.02
Israeli	59	0.30
Italian	1,719	8.66
Latvian	8	0.04
Lithuanian	107	0.54
Northern European	19	0.10
Norwegian	275	1.39
Pennsylvania German	19	0.10
Polish	711	3.58
Portuguese	19	0.10
Romanian	50	0.25
Russian	251	1.26
Scandinavian	11	0.06
Scotch-Irish	521	2.62
Scottish	858	4.32
Serbian	43	0.22
Slovak	84	0.42
Slovene	26	0.13
Swedish	391	1.97
Swiss	92	0.46
Ukrainian	102	0.51
United States or American	1,572	7.92
Welsh	154	0.78
West Indian, excl. Hispanic:	17	0.09
Jamaican	17	0.09
White:	19,195	96.65
Not Hispanic (18,591)	18,741	94.37
Hispanic (443)	454	2.29

Palmetto Estates

Place Type: Census Designated Place
County: Miami-Dade
Population: 13,675

Ancestry/Race	Number	%
African American/Black:	7,082	51.79
Not Hispanic (6,405)	6,742	49.30
Hispanic (264)	340	2.49
African, sub-Saharan:	190	1.39
African	190	1.39
Am. Ind. or Alaska Nat., not spec.	21	0.15
American Indian tribes, specified:	35	0.26
Blackfeet	2	0.01
Cherokee (4)	10	0.07
Cheyenne	2	0.01
Iroquois (1)	1	0.01
Latin American Indians (13)	17	0.12
Navajo	1	0.01
Seminole	1	0.01
All other tribes	1	0.01
American Indian tribes, not spec.	6	0.04
Arab:	28	0.20
Arab/Arabic	28	0.20
Asian:	611	4.47
Chinese, ex. Taiwanese (75)	140	1.02
Filipino (54)	60	0.44
Indian (213)	301	2.20
Indonesian	2	0.01
Japanese (5)	6	0.04
Korean (7)	15	0.11
Laotian (4)	4	0.03
Pakistani (4)	16	0.12
Sri Lankan (2)	2	0.01
Thai (5)	7	0.05
Vietnamese (43)	43	0.31
Other Asian, not specified	15	0.11
Austrian	44	0.32
Brazilian	67	0.49
British	96	0.70
Canadian	9	0.07
Czech	24	0.18
Danish	19	0.14
Dutch	45	0.33
Eastern European	6	0.04
English	256	1.87
European	13	0.10
French, except Basque	101	0.74
French Canadian	23	0.17
German	433	3.17
Guyanese	113	0.83
Hawaii Native/Pacific Islander:	48	0.35
Polynesian: (2)	3	0.02
Native Hawaiian (2)	3	0.02
Other Pac. Isl., not spec.	45	0.33
Hispanic or Latino:	3,953	28.91
Central American:	673	4.92
Costa Rican	28	0.20
Guatemalan	30	0.22
Honduran	141	1.03
Nicaraguan	326	2.38
Panamanian	80	0.59
Salvadoran	49	0.36
Other Central American	19	0.14
Cuban	1,180	8.63
Dominican Republic	150	1.10
Mexican	68	0.50
Puerto Rican	592	4.33
South American:	501	3.66
Argentinean	44	0.32
Bolivian	4	0.03
Chilean	23	0.17
Colombian	258	1.89
Ecuadorian	34	0.25
Paraguayan	1	0.01
Peruvian	90	0.66
Uruguayan	5	0.04
Venezuelan	33	0.24
Other South American	9	0.07
Other Hispanic or Latino	789	5.77
Hungarian	13	0.10
Irish	391	2.86
Italian	264	1.93
Norwegian	34	0.25
Polish	153	1.12
Portuguese	65	0.48
Romanian	25	0.18

Notes: 1. Figures in the "Number" column do not add up to the total population due to: a) Ancestry/Race overlap — e.g. persons can report being both White and Irish, b) persons of Hispanic origin can report being any race, c) persons reporting two ancestries are counted in both categories. 2. Numbers in parentheses indicate the number of persons reporting this ancestry/race alone, not in combination with any other ancestry/race. 3. Refer to the User's Guide in the front of the book for more detailed information.

Russian	44	0.32
Scotch-Irish	92	0.67
Scottish	36	0.26
Swedish	31	0.23
Ukrainian	28	0.20
United States or American	566	4.14
Welsh	10	0.07
West Indian, excl. Hispanic:	3,497	25.57
Bahamian	97	0.71
Barbadian	50	0.37
Belizean	40	0.29
British West Indian	35	0.26
Haitian	469	3.43
Jamaican	2,359	17.25
Trinidadian and Tobagonian	413	3.02
West Indian	34	0.25
White:	5,507	40.27
Not Hispanic (2,311)	2,465	18.03
Hispanic (2,842)	3,042	22.24

Palmetto

Place Type: City
County: Manatee
Population: 12,571

Ancestry/Race	Number	%
African American/Black:	1,702	13.54
Not Hispanic (1,547)	1,611	12.82
Hispanic (60)	91	0.72
African, sub-Saharan:	30	0.24
African	21	0.17
Ethiopian	9	0.07
Alaska Native tribes, specified:	2	0.02
Alaska Athabascan	1	0.01
Eskimo	1	0.01
Am. Ind. or Alaska Nat., not spec.	59	0.47
American Indian tribes, specified:	55	0.44
Apache (1)	1	0.01
Blackfeet (9)	9	0.07
Cherokee (5)	15	0.12
Chippewa	1	0.01
Creek	4	0.03
Iroquois	3	0.02
Latin American Indians (5)	5	0.04
Lumbee (4)	4	0.03
Pueblo (5)	5	0.04
Seminole (4)	4	0.03
Sioux	2	0.02
All other tribes	2	0.02
American Indian tribes, not spec.	9	0.07
Arab:	24	0.19
Arab/Arabic	24	0.19
Armenian	6	0.05
Asian:	60	0.48
Chinese, ex. Taiwanese (8)	13	0.10
Filipino (17)	18	0.14
Indian (7)	8	0.06
Japanese (2)	3	0.02
Korean (1)	1	0.01
Thai (5)	6	0.05
Vietnamese (2)	3	0.02
Other Asian, specified	3	0.02
Other Asian, not specified (2)	5	0.04
Austrian	31	0.25
Belgian	8	0.06
British	7	0.06
Canadian	14	0.11
Celtic	12	0.10
Croatian	10	0.08
Czech	26	0.21
Czechoslovakian	16	0.13
Danish	82	0.66
Dutch	169	1.37
English	1,391	11.28
European	32	0.26
Finnish	10	0.08
French, except Basque	310	2.51
French Canadian	84	0.68
German	1,419	11.50
Greek	78	0.63
Hawaii Native/Pacific Islander:	26	0.21
Micronesian: (2)	2	0.02
Guamanian/Chamorro (2)	2	0.02
Polynesian: (11)	13	0.10
Native Hawaiian (10)	11	0.09
Samoan (1)	2	0.02
Other Pac. Isl., specified	2	0.02
Other Pac. Isl., not spec.	9	0.07
Hispanic or Latino:	3,358	26.71
Central American:	88	0.70
Guatemalan	37	0.29
Honduran	39	0.31
Nicaraguan	7	0.06
Salvadoran	5	0.04
Cuban	42	0.33
Dominican Republic	1	0.01
Mexican	2,821	22.44
Puerto Rican	100	0.80
South American:	22	0.18
Bolivian	1	0.01
Colombian	12	0.10
Peruvian	9	0.07
Other Hispanic or Latino	284	2.26
Hungarian	30	0.24
Irish	971	7.87
Israeli	2	0.02
Italian	311	2.52
Northern European	9	0.07
Norwegian	98	0.79
Polish	153	1.24
Portuguese	12	0.10
Russian	23	0.19
Scotch-Irish	167	1.35
Scottish	234	1.90
Slovak	16	0.13
Swedish	90	0.73
Swiss	32	0.26
Ukrainian	43	0.35
United States or American	1,244	10.09
Welsh	106	0.86
West Indian, excl. Hispanic:	93	0.75
Bahamian	3	0.02
Haitian	90	0.73
White:	9,688	77.07
Not Hispanic (7,449)	7,541	59.99
Hispanic (2,005)	2,147	17.08

Panama City

Place Type: City
County: Bay
Population: 36,417

Ancestry/Race	Number	%
African American/Black:	8,028	22.04
Not Hispanic (7,648)	7,819	21.47
Hispanic (165)	209	0.57
African, sub-Saharan:	136	0.37
African	120	0.33
Ethiopian	7	0.02
Nigerian	9	0.02
Alaska Native tribes, specified:	7	0.02
Alaska Athabascan (4)	6	0.02
Eskimo	1	0.00
Am. Ind. or Alaska Nat., not spec.	133	0.37
American Indian tribes, specified:	351	0.96
Apache (2)	4	0.01
Blackfeet (5)	16	0.04
Cherokee (69)	139	0.38
Cheyenne (1)	2	0.01
Chickasaw (1)	1	0.00
Chippewa (11)	12	0.03
Choctaw (5)	14	0.04
Comanche	1	0.00
Cree (3)	4	0.01
Creek (39)	87	0.24
Delaware (1)	1	0.00
Houma (2)	2	0.01
Iroquois (4)	7	0.02
Kiowa	1	0.00
Latin American Indians (4)	11	0.03
Lumbee (6)	6	0.02
Navajo (1)	1	0.00
Potawatomi	1	0.00
Pueblo	1	0.00
Puget Sound Salish (1)	3	0.01
Seminole (4)	8	0.02
Shoshone (1)	1	0.00
Sioux (5)	14	0.04
Ute	1	0.00
Yakama (1)	1	0.00
Yaqui (1)	1	0.00
All other tribes (7)	11	0.03
American Indian tribes, not spec.	26	0.07
Arab:	148	0.41
Arab/Arabic	40	0.11
Egyptian	53	0.15
Lebanese	35	0.10
Palestinian	20	0.05
Asian:	786	2.16
Chinese, ex. Taiwanese (53)	67	0.18
Filipino (90)	136	0.37
Indian (51)	83	0.23
Indonesian	1	0.00
Japanese (31)	58	0.16
Korean (29)	38	0.10
Laotian (3)	3	0.01
Pakistani (20)	27	0.07
Taiwanese (1)	1	0.00
Thai (27)	37	0.10
Vietnamese (231)	259	0.71
Other Asian, specified	6	0.02
Other Asian, not specified (18)	70	0.19
Australian	9	0.02
Austrian	35	0.10
British	198	0.54
Bulgarian	6	0.02
Canadian	100	0.27
Czech	115	0.32
Czechoslovakian	28	0.08
Danish	79	0.22
Dutch	476	1.31
English	3,294	9.06
Estonian	4	0.01
European	270	0.74
Finnish	46	0.13
French, except Basque	929	2.55
French Canadian	247	0.68
German	3,551	9.76
German Russian	7	0.02
Greek	134	0.37
Guyanese	12	0.03
Hawaii Native/Pacific Islander:	70	0.19
Micronesian: (9)	18	0.05
Guamanian/Chamorro (9)	18	0.05
Polynesian: (14)	30	0.08
Native Hawaiian (14)	27	0.07
Samoan	3	0.01
Other Pac. Isl., specified	6	0.02
Other Pac. Isl., not spec. (5)	16	0.04
Hispanic or Latino:	1,060	2.91
Central American:	50	0.14
Costa Rican	10	0.03
Guatemalan	2	0.01
Honduran	5	0.01
Nicaraguan	1	0.00
Panamanian	24	0.07
Salvadoran	7	0.02
Other Central American	1	0.00
Cuban	182	0.50
Dominican Republic	5	0.01
Mexican	300	0.82
Puerto Rican	287	0.79
South American:	34	0.09
Bolivian	2	0.01
Chilean	3	0.01
Colombian	4	0.01
Paraguayan	2	0.01
Peruvian	22	0.06
Venezuelan	1	0.00
Other Hispanic or Latino	202	0.55
Hungarian	107	0.29
Iranian	5	0.01

Notes: 1. Figures in the "Number" column do not add up to the total population due to: a) Ancestry/Race overlap — e.g. persons can report being both White and Irish, b) persons of Hispanic origin can report being any race, c) persons reporting two ancestries are counted in both categories. 2. Numbers in parentheses indicate the number of persons reporting this ancestry/race alone, not in combination with any other ancestry/race. 3. Refer to the User's Guide in the front of the book for more detailed information.

Irish	3,731	10.26
Italian	1,074	2.95
Lithuanian	45	0.12
Luxemburger	8	0.02
Northern European	70	0.19
Norwegian	293	0.81
Pennsylvania German	6	0.02
Polish	437	1.20
Portuguese	132	0.36
Russian	65	0.18
Scandinavian	9	0.02
Scotch-Irish	800	2.20
Scottish	875	2.41
Slavic	28	0.08
Slovak	39	0.11
Slovene	5	0.01
Swedish	279	0.77
Swiss	53	0.15
Turkish	4	0.01
Ukrainian	24	0.07
United States or American	4,695	12.91
Welsh	327	0.90
West Indian, excl. Hispanic:	67	0.18
Bahamian	7	0.02
Haitian	16	0.04
Jamaican	37	0.10
West Indian	7	0.02
White:	27,379	75.18
Not Hispanic (26,317)	26,803	73.60
Hispanic (502)	576	1.58
Yugoslavian	4	0.01

Parkland

Place Type: City
County: Broward
Population: 13,835

Ancestry/Race	Number	%
African American/Black:	478	3.46
Not Hispanic (420)	468	3.38
Hispanic (5)	10	0.07
African, sub-Saharan:	82	0.59
African	8	0.06
Liberian	24	0.17
Nigerian	19	0.14
South African	31	0.22
Alaska Native tribes, specified:	1	0.01
Tlingit-Haida (1)	1	0.01
Am. Ind. or Alaska Nat., not spec.	15	0.11
American Indian tribes, specified:	23	0.17
Apache	1	0.01
Cherokee (4)	13	0.09
Chickasaw (1)	1	0.01
Chippewa	2	0.01
Lumbee (1)	1	0.01
Pueblo	4	0.03
All other tribes (1)	1	0.01
Arab:	111	0.79
Egyptian	14	0.10
Iraqi	7	0.05
Lebanese	14	0.10
Moroccan	15	0.11
Palestinian	37	0.26
Syrian	24	0.17
Armenian	105	0.75
Asian:	521	3.77
Chinese, ex. Taiwanese (168)	189	1.37
Filipino (35)	51	0.37
Indian (158)	170	1.23
Indonesian (1)	1	0.01
Japanese (11)	18	0.13
Korean (25)	31	0.22
Pakistani (9)	10	0.07
Taiwanese (6)	10	0.07
Thai (6)	7	0.05
Vietnamese (13)	22	0.16
Other Asian, not specified (7)	12	0.09
Australian	9	0.06
Austrian	90	0.64
Brazilian	73	0.52
British	94	0.67
Canadian	41	0.29
Croatian	47	0.34
Czech	88	0.63
Czechoslovakian	7	0.05
Danish	32	0.23
Dutch	201	1.44
Eastern European	100	0.71
English	919	6.57
European	67	0.48
French, except Basque	418	2.99
French Canadian	70	0.50
German	1,809	12.93
Greek	116	0.83
Guyanese	57	0.41
Hawaii Native/Pacific Islander:	9	0.07
Polynesian: (1)	9	0.07
Native Hawaiian (1)	6	0.04
Samoan	3	0.02
Hispanic or Latino:	1,152	8.33
Central American:	46	0.33
Costa Rican	9	0.07
Guatemalan	3	0.02
Honduran	2	0.01
Nicaraguan	19	0.14
Panamanian	10	0.07
Salvadoran	3	0.02
Cuban	234	1.69
Dominican Republic	24	0.17
Mexican	98	0.71
Puerto Rican	207	1.50
South American:	348	2.52
Argentinean	14	0.10
Bolivian	10	0.07
Chilean	13	0.09
Colombian	148	1.07
Ecuadorian	35	0.25
Peruvian	68	0.49
Uruguayan	2	0.01
Venezuelan	46	0.33
Other South American	12	0.09
Other Hispanic or Latino	195	1.41
Hungarian	178	1.27
Iranian	167	1.19
Irish	1,751	12.52
Israeli	26	0.19
Italian	2,293	16.39
Lithuanian	109	0.78
Norwegian	84	0.60
Polish	877	6.27
Portuguese	54	0.39
Romanian	112	0.80
Russian	976	6.98
Scandinavian	43	0.31
Scotch-Irish	45	0.32
Scottish	176	1.26
Slovak	21	0.15
Swedish	130	0.93
Swiss	20	0.14
Turkish	45	0.32
Ukrainian	49	0.35
United States or American	1,306	9.34
Welsh	9	0.06
West Indian, excl. Hispanic:	204	1.46
Bahamian	23	0.16
Jamaican	162	1.16
Trinidadian and Tobagonian	10	0.07
Other West Indian	9	0.06
White:	12,780	92.37
Not Hispanic (11,638)	11,731	84.79
Hispanic (1,010)	1,049	7.58
Yugoslavian	34	0.24

Pembroke Pines

Place Type: City
County: Broward
Population: 137,427

Ancestry/Race	Number	%
African American/Black:	20,115	14.64
Not Hispanic (17,471)	19,021	13.84
Hispanic (739)	1,094	0.80
African, sub-Saharan:	642	0.47
African	278	0.20
Ghanian	69	0.05
Nigerian	188	0.14
Somalian	22	0.02
South African	24	0.02
Sudanese	44	0.03
Other sub-Saharan African	17	0.01
Alaska Native tribes, specified:	1	0.00
Alaska Athabascan (1)	1	0.00
Alaska Native tribes, not specified	1	0.00
Am. Ind. or Alaska Nat., not spec.	236	0.17
Albanian	53	0.04
Alsatian	9	0.01
American Indian tribes, specified:	306	0.22
Apache (2)	6	0.00
Blackfeet (3)	13	0.01
Cherokee (35)	93	0.07
Cheyenne	1	0.00
Chickasaw	1	0.00
Chippewa (3)	4	0.00
Choctaw (1)	7	0.01
Comanche	1	0.00
Creek (2)	3	0.00
Crow (1)	1	0.00
Delaware (2)	3	0.00
Iroquois (6)	11	0.01
Latin American Indians (46)	104	0.08
Lumbee (3)	5	0.00
Navajo (1)	8	0.01
Potawatomi (1)	1	0.00
Pueblo (1)	5	0.00
Seminole (13)	13	0.01
Sioux (6)	8	0.01
All other tribes (8)	18	0.01
American Indian tribes, not spec.	28	0.02
Arab:	1,230	0.90
Arab/Arabic	220	0.16
Egyptian	72	0.05
Iraqi	9	0.01
Jordanian	44	0.03
Lebanese	421	0.31
Moroccan	99	0.07
Palestinian	68	0.05
Syrian	155	0.11
Other Arab	142	0.10
Armenian	54	0.04
Asian:	6,553	4.77
Bangladeshi (13)	18	0.01
Cambodian (6)	6	0.00
Chinese, ex. Taiwanese (1,199)	1,622	1.18
Filipino (891)	1,062	0.77
Indian (1,851)	2,237	1.63
Indonesian (11)	17	0.01
Japanese (121)	188	0.14
Korean (369)	428	0.31
Laotian (8)	9	0.01
Malaysian (2)	3	0.00
Pakistani (197)	307	0.22
Taiwanese (35)	45	0.03
Thai (52)	76	0.06
Vietnamese (220)	253	0.18
Other Asian, specified (7)	14	0.01
Other Asian, not specified (93)	268	0.20
Australian	31	0.02
Austrian	837	0.61
Basque	30	0.02
Belgian	91	0.07
Brazilian	751	0.55
British	552	0.40
Bulgarian	33	0.02
Canadian	544	0.40
Croatian	111	0.08
Czech	241	0.18
Czechoslovakian	140	0.10
Danish	225	0.16
Dutch	836	0.61
Eastern European	224	0.16
English	6,310	4.60

Notes: 1. Figures in the "Number" column do not add up to the total population due to: a) Ancestry/Race overlap — e.g. persons can report being both White and Irish, b) persons of Hispanic origin can report being any race, c) persons reporting two ancestries are counted in both categories. 2. Numbers in parentheses indicate the number of persons reporting this ancestry/race alone, not in combination with any other ancestry/race. 3. Refer to the User's Guide in the front of the book for more detailed information.

Estonian	7	0.01
European	614	0.45
Finnish	148	0.11
French, except Basque	2,256	1.65
French Canadian	851	0.62
German	11,085	8.08
Greek	582	0.42
Guyanese	508	0.37
Hawaii Native/Pacific Islander:	228	0.17
Micronesian: (15)	21	0.02
Guamanian/Chamorro (11)	17	0.01
Other Micronesian (4)	4	0.00
Polynesian: (27)	59	0.04
Native Hawaiian (18)	41	0.03
Samoan (9)	15	0.01
Tongan	2	0.00
Other Polynesian	1	0.00
Other Pac. Isl., specified	3	0.00
Other Pac. Isl., not spec. (25)	145	0.11
Hispanic or Latino:	38,700	28.16
Central American:	1,896	1.38
Costa Rican	227	0.17
Guatemalan	214	0.16
Honduran	273	0.20
Nicaraguan	533	0.39
Panamanian	367	0.27
Salvadoran	234	0.17
Other Central American	48	0.03
Cuban	11,901	8.66
Dominican Republic	1,637	1.19
Mexican	960	0.70
Puerto Rican	6,887	5.01
South American:	8,292	6.03
Argentinean	463	0.34
Bolivian	66	0.05
Chilean	298	0.22
Colombian	4,124	3.00
Ecuadorian	734	0.53
Paraguayan	20	0.01
Peruvian	1,082	0.79
Uruguayan	78	0.06
Venezuelan	1,242	0.90
Other South American	185	0.13
Other Hispanic or Latino	7,127	5.19
Hungarian	1,052	0.77
Iranian	98	0.07
Irish	11,272	8.22
Israeli	94	0.07
Italian	12,850	9.37
Latvian	19	0.01
Lithuanian	390	0.28
Maltese	22	0.02
Northern European	9	0.01
Norwegian	523	0.38
Pennsylvania German	20	0.01
Polish	4,881	3.56
Portuguese	592	0.43
Romanian	684	0.50
Russian	4,179	3.05
Scandinavian	139	0.10
Scotch-Irish	944	0.69
Scottish	1,289	0.94
Serbian	37	0.03
Slavic	63	0.05
Slovak	162	0.12
Slovene	54	0.04
Swedish	821	0.60
Swiss	126	0.09
Turkish	136	0.10
Ukrainian	374	0.27
United States or American	8,380	6.11
Welsh	505	0.37
West Indian, excl. Hispanic:	12,327	8.99
Bahamian	518	0.38
Barbadian	49	0.04
Belizean	54	0.04
British West Indian	270	0.20
Dutch West Indian	22	0.02
Haitian	2,583	1.88
Jamaican	7,648	5.58
Trinidadian and Tobagonian	592	0.43
U.S. Virgin Islander	46	0.03
West Indian	522	0.38
Other West Indian	23	0.02
White:	107,142	77.96
Not Hispanic (72,464)	74,076	53.90
Hispanic (31,406)	33,066	24.06
Yugoslavian	93	0.07

Pensacola

Place Type: City
County: Escambia
Population: 56,255

Ancestry/Race	Number	%
Acadian/Cajun	59	0.10
African American/Black:	17,551	31.20
Not Hispanic (17,086)	17,393	30.92
Hispanic (117)	158	0.28
African, sub-Saharan:	411	0.73
African	368	0.65
Nigerian	43	0.08
Alaska Native tribes, specified:	2	0.00
Tlingit-Haida (2)	2	0.00
Am. Ind. or Alaska Nat., not spec.	186	0.33
Alsatian	12	0.02
American Indian tribes, specified:	454	0.81
Apache (1)	1	0.00
Blackfeet (3)	10	0.02
Cherokee (64)	184	0.33
Chickasaw (1)	2	0.00
Chippewa (1)	3	0.01
Choctaw (4)	15	0.03
Comanche	1	0.00
Cree (2)	2	0.00
Creek (87)	160	0.28
Delaware	3	0.01
Iroquois (6)	10	0.02
Latin American Indians (1)	5	0.01
Navajo (1)	3	0.01
Ottawa (2)	2	0.00
Potawatomi (2)	2	0.00
Pueblo (2)	2	0.00
Seminole (2)	10	0.02
Sioux (1)	5	0.01
Ute	1	0.00
All other tribes (16)	33	0.06
American Indian tribes, not spec.	29	0.05
Arab:	208	0.37
Arab/Arabic	49	0.09
Lebanese	85	0.15
Other Arab	74	0.13
Armenian	5	0.01
Asian:	1,289	2.29
Bangladeshi (5)	5	0.01
Cambodian (15)	22	0.04
Chinese, ex. Taiwanese (148)	169	0.30
Filipino (184)	288	0.51
Indian (106)	127	0.23
Indonesian (4)	4	0.01
Japanese (52)	95	0.17
Korean (67)	98	0.17
Laotian (4)	4	0.01
Malaysian	4	0.01
Pakistani	1	0.00
Sri Lankan	4	0.01
Taiwanese (14)	17	0.03
Thai (11)	16	0.03
Vietnamese (340)	377	0.67
Other Asian, specified	8	0.01
Other Asian, not specified (19)	50	0.09
Australian	29	0.05
Austrian	103	0.18
Basque	14	0.02
Belgian	35	0.06
Brazilian	16	0.03
British	498	0.88
Canadian	110	0.20
Celtic	10	0.02
Croatian	20	0.04
Czech	204	0.36
Czechoslovakian	71	0.13
Danish	166	0.29
Dutch	587	1.04
Eastern European	20	0.04
English	6,180	10.98
European	512	0.91
Finnish	93	0.17
French, except Basque	1,786	3.17
French Canadian	495	0.88
German	5,902	10.49
Greek	245	0.44
Hawaii Native/Pacific Islander:	90	0.16
Melanesian: (2)	2	0.00
Fijian (2)	2	0.00
Micronesian: (10)	18	0.03
Guamanian/Chamorro (10)	15	0.03
Other Micronesian	3	0.01
Polynesian: (11)	33	0.06
Native Hawaiian (8)	21	0.04
Samoan (3)	12	0.02
Other Pac. Isl., specified	7	0.01
Other Pac. Isl., not spec. (6)	30	0.05
Hispanic or Latino:	1,167	2.07
Central American:	54	0.10
Costa Rican	8	0.01
Guatemalan	12	0.02
Honduran	9	0.02
Nicaraguan	1	0.00
Panamanian	19	0.03
Salvadoran	5	0.01
Cuban	138	0.25
Dominican Republic	16	0.03
Mexican	358	0.64
Puerto Rican	254	0.45
South American:	68	0.12
Argentinean	16	0.03
Bolivian	7	0.01
Chilean	2	0.00
Colombian	21	0.04
Ecuadorian	2	0.00
Peruvian	10	0.02
Uruguayan	4	0.01
Venezuelan	4	0.01
Other South American	2	0.00
Other Hispanic or Latino	279	0.50
Hungarian	174	0.31
Icelander	8	0.01
Iranian	37	0.07
Irish	5,604	9.96
Israeli	8	0.01
Italian	1,728	3.07
Latvian	22	0.04
Lithuanian	38	0.07
Maltese	6	0.01
Northern European	68	0.12
Norwegian	428	0.76
Pennsylvania German	9	0.02
Polish	1,084	1.93
Portuguese	111	0.20
Romanian	46	0.08
Russian	262	0.47
Scandinavian	59	0.10
Scotch-Irish	1,609	2.86
Scottish	1,395	2.48
Serbian	4	0.01
Slavic	50	0.09
Slovak	34	0.06
Slovene	19	0.03
Swedish	497	0.88
Swiss	65	0.12
Ukrainian	80	0.14
United States or American	4,332	7.70
Welsh	358	0.64
West Indian, excl. Hispanic:	331	0.59
Bahamian	36	0.06
Belizean	50	0.09
Dutch West Indian	8	0.01
Haitian	15	0.03
Jamaican	101	0.18
Trinidadian and Tobagonian	49	0.09
West Indian	72	0.13
White:	37,212	66.15

Notes: 1. Figures in the "Number" column do not add up to the total population due to: a) Ancestry/Race overlap — e.g. persons can report being both White and Irish, b) persons of Hispanic origin can report being any race, c) persons reporting two ancestries are counted in both categories. 2. Numbers in parentheses indicate the number of persons reporting this ancestry/race alone, not in combination with any other ancestry/race. 3. Refer to the User's Guide in the front of the book for more detailed information.

Not Hispanic (35,824)	36,438	64.77
Hispanic (690)	774	1.38

Pine Hills

Place Type: Census Designated Place
County: Orange
Population: 41,764

Ancestry/Race	Number	%
African American/Black:	23,135	55.39
Not Hispanic (21,004)	22,486	53.84
Hispanic (469)	649	1.55
African, sub-Saharan:	964	2.30
African	903	2.15
Nigerian	45	0.11
South African	16	0.04
Alaska Native tribes, specified:	2	0.00
Tlingit-Haida (1)	2	0.00
Am. Ind. or Alaska Nat., not spec.	133	0.32
American Indian tribes, specified:	160	0.38
Apache	4	0.01
Blackfeet	8	0.02
Cherokee (17)	82	0.20
Chippewa (1)	3	0.01
Choctaw (1)	4	0.01
Cree (2)	4	0.01
Creek (4)	8	0.02
Iroquois (2)	7	0.02
Kiowa (1)	1	0.00
Latin American Indians (9)	16	0.04
Lumbee (2)	2	0.00
Pueblo	4	0.01
Seminole (1)	7	0.02
Sioux (2)	3	0.01
All other tribes (3)	7	0.02
American Indian tribes, not spec.	22	0.05
Arab:	26	0.06
Egyptian	18	0.04
Lebanese	8	0.02
Asian:	1,509	3.61
Chinese, ex. Taiwanese (57)	90	0.22
Filipino (57)	82	0.20
Indian (383)	497	1.19
Indonesian (1)	1	0.00
Japanese (4)	18	0.04
Korean (28)	37	0.09
Laotian (6)	9	0.02
Malaysian (2)	2	0.00
Pakistani (8)	10	0.02
Thai (9)	11	0.03
Vietnamese (606)	646	1.55
Other Asian, specified (1)	6	0.01
Other Asian, not specified (19)	100	0.24
Austrian	22	0.05
Belgian	8	0.02
Brazilian	18	0.04
British	120	0.29
Canadian	173	0.41
Croatian	14	0.03
Czech	51	0.12
Czechoslovakian	18	0.04
Danish	19	0.05
Dutch	363	0.86
English	1,641	3.91
European	60	0.14
Finnish	51	0.12
French, except Basque	477	1.14
French Canadian	181	0.43
German	2,024	4.82
Greek	36	0.09
Guyanese	385	0.92
Hawaii Native/Pacific Islander:	165	0.40
Micronesian: (10)	10	0.02
Guamanian/Chamorro (10)	10	0.02
Polynesian: (4)	13	0.03
Native Hawaiian (3)	12	0.03
Samoan (1)	1	0.00
Other Pac. Isl., specified	4	0.01
Other Pac. Isl., not spec. (9)	138	0.33
Hispanic or Latino:	5,875	14.07
Central American:	267	0.64
Costa Rican	7	0.02
Guatemalan	45	0.11
Honduran	86	0.21
Nicaraguan	34	0.08
Panamanian	34	0.08
Salvadoran	36	0.09
Other Central American	25	0.06
Cuban	221	0.53
Dominican Republic	412	0.99
Mexican	861	2.06
Puerto Rican	2,958	7.08
South American:	226	0.54
Argentinean	5	0.01
Bolivian	1	0.00
Chilean	11	0.03
Colombian	104	0.25
Ecuadorian	29	0.07
Peruvian	23	0.06
Uruguayan	1	0.00
Venezuelan	44	0.11
Other South American	8	0.02
Other Hispanic or Latino	930	2.23
Hungarian	77	0.18
Irish	1,754	4.18
Italian	694	1.65
Lithuanian	19	0.05
Northern European	18	0.04
Norwegian	56	0.13
Pennsylvania German	34	0.08
Polish	289	0.69
Portuguese	67	0.16
Romanian	42	0.10
Russian	54	0.13
Scandinavian	9	0.02
Scotch-Irish	370	0.88
Scottish	190	0.45
Slavic	7	0.02
Slovak	25	0.06
Swedish	214	0.51
Turkish	12	0.03
Ukrainian	27	0.06
United States or American	2,778	6.62
Welsh	74	0.18
West Indian, excl. Hispanic:	7,145	17.02
Bahamian	59	0.14
Barbadian	112	0.27
British West Indian	176	0.42
Haitian	4,817	11.47
Jamaican	1,472	3.51
Trinidadian and Tobagonian	134	0.32
U.S. Virgin Islander	100	0.24
West Indian	275	0.65
White:	15,008	35.94
Not Hispanic (11,591)	12,042	28.83
Hispanic (2,581)	2,966	7.10
Yugoslavian	9	0.02

Pinecrest

Place Type: Village
County: Miami-Dade
Population: 19,055

Ancestry/Race	Number	%
African American/Black:	409	2.15
Not Hispanic (295)	357	1.87
Hispanic (32)	52	0.27
African, sub-Saharan:	42	0.22
African	36	0.19
South African	6	0.03
Am. Ind. or Alaska Nat., not spec.	26	0.14
American Indian tribes, specified:	46	0.24
Blackfeet	1	0.01
Cherokee (1)	17	0.09
Choctaw	2	0.01
Creek (3)	3	0.02
Delaware	1	0.01
Latin American Indians (6)	10	0.05
Navajo (1)	1	0.01
Paiute (1)	1	0.01
Pueblo (1)	2	0.01
Sioux (1)	5	0.03
All other tribes	3	0.02
American Indian tribes, not spec.	4	0.02
Arab:	477	2.49
Arab/Arabic	72	0.38
Egyptian	74	0.39
Jordanian	17	0.09
Lebanese	209	1.09
Palestinian	7	0.04
Syrian	55	0.29
Other Arab	43	0.22
Armenian	19	0.10
Asian:	1,019	5.35
Chinese, ex. Taiwanese (339)	405	2.13
Filipino (55)	75	0.39
Indian (242)	278	1.46
Indonesian (1)	2	0.01
Japanese (31)	46	0.24
Korean (75)	79	0.41
Pakistani (16)	16	0.08
Taiwanese (23)	24	0.13
Thai (36)	42	0.22
Vietnamese (12)	14	0.07
Other Asian, not specified (20)	38	0.20
Austrian	351	1.83
Basque	16	0.08
Belgian	38	0.20
Brazilian	175	0.91
British	249	1.30
Canadian	58	0.30
Croatian	10	0.05
Czech	71	0.37
Czechoslovakian	46	0.24
Danish	150	0.78
Dutch	127	0.66
Eastern European	64	0.33
English	1,895	9.88
European	315	1.64
French, except Basque	444	2.31
French Canadian	75	0.39
German	1,651	8.61
Greek	217	1.13
Guyanese	16	0.08
Hawaii Native/Pacific Islander:	9	0.05
Polynesian: (1)	6	0.03
Native Hawaiian (1)	6	0.03
Other Pac. Isl., not spec. (1)	3	0.02
Hispanic or Latino:	5,652	29.66
Central American:	518	2.72
Costa Rican	45	0.24
Guatemalan	25	0.13
Honduran	83	0.44
Nicaraguan	228	1.20
Panamanian	39	0.20
Salvadoran	84	0.44
Other Central American	14	0.07
Cuban	2,613	13.71
Dominican Republic	73	0.38
Mexican	201	1.05
Puerto Rican	281	1.47
South American:	1,006	5.28
Argentinean	113	0.59
Bolivian	22	0.12
Chilean	119	0.62
Colombian	340	1.78
Ecuadorian	42	0.22
Paraguayan	8	0.04
Peruvian	173	0.91
Uruguayan	12	0.06
Venezuelan	156	0.82
Other South American	21	0.11
Other Hispanic or Latino	960	5.04
Hungarian	165	0.86
Irish	1,285	6.70
Italian	827	4.31
Lithuanian	115	0.60
New Zealander	9	0.05
Northern European	15	0.08
Norwegian	61	0.32
Polish	688	3.59
Portuguese	50	0.26
Romanian	127	0.66

Notes: 1. Figures in the "Number" column do not add up to the total population due to: a) Ancestry/Race overlap — e.g. persons can report being both White and Irish, b) persons of Hispanic origin can report being any race, c) persons reporting two ancestries are counted in both categories. 2. Numbers in parentheses indicate the number of persons reporting this ancestry/race alone, not in combination with any other ancestry/race. 3. Refer to the User's Guide in the front of the book for more detailed information.

Russian	1,331	6.94
Scandinavian	22	0.11
Scotch-Irish	228	1.19
Scottish	284	1.48
Slavic	9	0.05
Slovak	47	0.25
Swedish	221	1.15
Swiss	63	0.33
Turkish	5	0.03
Ukrainian	65	0.34
United States or American	1,199	6.25
Welsh	58	0.30
West Indian, excl. Hispanic:	248	1.29
Bahamian	9	0.05
Belizean	11	0.06
British West Indian	6	0.03
Haitian	116	0.60
Jamaican	52	0.27
Trinidadian and Tobagonian	54	0.28
White:	17,533	92.01
Not Hispanic (11,961)	12,158	63.80
Hispanic (5,245)	5,375	28.21
Yugoslavian	23	0.12

Pinellas Park

Place Type: City
County: Pinellas
Population: 45,658

Ancestry/Race	Number	%
African American/Black:	1,123	2.46
Not Hispanic (892)	1,036	2.27
Hispanic (60)	87	0.19
African, sub-Saharan:	99	0.22
African	99	0.22
Alaska Native tribes, specified:	2	0.00
Eskimo	1	0.00
Tlingit-Haida (1)	1	0.00
Am. Ind. or Alaska Nat., not spec.	124	0.27
Alsatian	6	0.01
American Indian tribes, specified:	362	0.79
Apache (3)	8	0.02
Blackfeet (3)	21	0.05
Cherokee (64)	172	0.38
Cheyenne	4	0.01
Chickasaw (1)	2	0.00
Chippewa (9)	12	0.03
Choctaw (7)	14	0.03
Cree	7	0.02
Creek (2)	4	0.01
Crow (1)	2	0.00
Delaware (1)	3	0.01
Iroquois (15)	31	0.07
Latin American Indians (6)	10	0.02
Lumbee (1)	1	0.00
Navajo (5)	5	0.01
Osage	4	0.01
Paiute (1)	2	0.00
Potawatomi	2	0.00
Seminole (3)	10	0.02
Shoshone	5	0.01
Sioux (1)	11	0.02
All other tribes (8)	32	0.07
American Indian tribes, not spec.	17	0.04
Arab:	111	0.24
Egyptian	6	0.01
Iraqi	20	0.04
Lebanese	61	0.13
Palestinian	6	0.01
Syrian	18	0.04
Armenian	28	0.06
Asian:	2,217	4.86
Bangladeshi (5)	7	0.02
Cambodian (47)	58	0.13
Chinese, ex. Taiwanese (150)	184	0.40
Filipino (309)	383	0.84
Indian (139)	162	0.35
Indonesian (2)	3	0.01
Japanese (27)	58	0.13
Korean (87)	100	0.22
Laotian (277)	296	0.65
Malaysian (1)	11	0.02
Pakistani (14)	19	0.04
Thai (28)	48	0.11
Vietnamese (788)	839	1.84
Other Asian, specified	2	0.00
Other Asian, not specified (29)	47	0.10
Australian	8	0.02
Austrian	101	0.22
Belgian	59	0.13
Brazilian	25	0.06
British	191	0.42
Bulgarian	15	0.03
Canadian	180	0.40
Celtic	14	0.03
Croatian	138	0.30
Czech	102	0.22
Czechoslovakian	105	0.23
Danish	242	0.53
Dutch	1,004	2.21
English	5,254	11.57
European	319	0.70
Finnish	57	0.13
French, except Basque	1,984	4.37
French Canadian	823	1.81
German	8,383	18.46
Greek	263	0.58
Guyanese	12	0.03
Hawaii Native/Pacific Islander:	28	0.06
Micronesian: (1)	1	0.00
Guamanian/Chamorro (1)	1	0.00
Polynesian: (6)	16	0.04
Native Hawaiian (5)	8	0.02
Samoan	3	0.01
Tongan (1)	5	0.01
Other Pac. Isl., specified	1	0.00
Other Pac. Isl., not spec. (1)	10	0.02
Hispanic or Latino:	2,856	6.26
Central American:	102	0.22
Costa Rican	14	0.03
Guatemalan	27	0.06
Honduran	16	0.04
Nicaraguan	4	0.01
Panamanian	16	0.04
Salvadoran	24	0.05
Other Central American	1	0.00
Cuban	262	0.57
Dominican Republic	78	0.17
Mexican	612	1.34
Puerto Rican	1,219	2.67
South American:	146	0.32
Argentinean	2	0.00
Bolivian	2	0.00
Chilean	2	0.00
Colombian	76	0.17
Ecuadorian	22	0.05
Peruvian	18	0.04
Uruguayan	1	0.00
Venezuelan	22	0.05
Other South American	1	0.00
Other Hispanic or Latino	437	0.96
Hungarian	311	0.68
Iranian	22	0.05
Irish	7,197	15.85
Italian	3,836	8.45
Latvian	15	0.03
Lithuanian	193	0.42
Northern European	39	0.09
Norwegian	385	0.85
Pennsylvania German	30	0.07
Polish	1,588	3.50
Portuguese	277	0.61
Romanian	84	0.18
Russian	211	0.46
Scandinavian	14	0.03
Scotch-Irish	795	1.75
Scottish	1,168	2.57
Serbian	94	0.21
Slavic	48	0.11
Slovak	101	0.22
Slovene	19	0.04
Swedish	691	1.52
Swiss	146	0.32
Turkish	7	0.02
Ukrainian	76	0.17
United States or American	3,765	8.29
Welsh	285	0.63
West Indian, excl. Hispanic:	85	0.19
Bermudan	13	0.03
British West Indian	12	0.03
Jamaican	40	0.09
Trinidadian and Tobagonian	20	0.04
White:	41,598	91.11
Not Hispanic (38,962)	39,734	87.03
Hispanic (1,690)	1,864	4.08
Yugoslavian	338	0.74

Pinewood

Place Type: Census Designated Place
County: Miami-Dade
Population: 16,523

Ancestry/Race	Number	%
African American/Black:	12,422	75.18
Not Hispanic (11,434)	12,043	72.89
Hispanic (305)	379	2.29
African, sub-Saharan:	152	0.90
African	133	0.79
Ethiopian	11	0.07
Nigerian	8	0.05
Alaska Native tribes, specified:	4	0.02
Eskimo	2	0.01
Tlingit-Haida (1)	2	0.01
Am. Ind. or Alaska Nat., not spec.	56	0.34
American Indian tribes, specified:	39	0.24
Apache (4)	4	0.02
Blackfeet	2	0.01
Cherokee (3)	6	0.04
Chippewa (2)	2	0.01
Iroquois (1)	1	0.01
Latin American Indians (1)	7	0.04
Lumbee (1)	1	0.01
Pueblo (5)	12	0.07
All other tribes	4	0.02
American Indian tribes, not spec.	3	0.02
Arab:	23	0.14
Arab/Arabic	23	0.14
Armenian	7	0.04
Asian:	111	0.67
Chinese, ex. Taiwanese (7)	10	0.06
Filipino (16)	24	0.15
Indian (17)	35	0.21
Japanese	1	0.01
Korean (2)	7	0.04
Thai (1)	1	0.01
Vietnamese (1)	5	0.03
Other Asian, specified	6	0.04
Other Asian, not specified (9)	22	0.13
Brazilian	9	0.05
Czech	75	0.45
Danish	8	0.05
English	52	0.31
French, except Basque	50	0.30
French Canadian	13	0.08
German	69	0.41
Greek	35	0.21
Guyanese	10	0.06
Hawaii Native/Pacific Islander:	56	0.34
Polynesian: (5)	8	0.05
Native Hawaiian	3	0.02
Samoan (5)	5	0.03
Other Pac. Isl., specified	2	0.01
Other Pac. Isl., not spec.	46	0.28
Hispanic or Latino:	3,775	22.85
Central American:	715	4.33
Costa Rican	17	0.10
Guatemalan	46	0.28
Honduran	276	1.67
Nicaraguan	331	2.00
Panamanian	7	0.04
Salvadoran	20	0.12
Other Central American	18	0.11
Cuban	881	5.33

Notes: 1. Figures in the "Number" column do not add up to the total population due to: a) Ancestry/Race overlap — e.g. persons can report being both White and Irish, b) persons of Hispanic origin can report being any race, c) persons reporting two ancestries are counted in both categories. 2. Numbers in parentheses indicate the number of persons reporting this ancestry/race alone, not in combination with any other ancestry/race. 3. Refer to the User's Guide in the front of the book for more detailed information.

Dominican Republic	254	1.54
Mexican	95	0.57
Puerto Rican	894	5.41
South American:	111	0.67
Argentinean	5	0.03
Chilean	2	0.01
Colombian	40	0.24
Ecuadorian	31	0.19
Peruvian	13	0.08
Venezuelan	15	0.09
Other South American	5	0.03
Other Hispanic or Latino	825	4.99
Irish	22	0.13
Italian	59	0.35
Polish	20	0.12
Scottish	12	0.07
Swedish	12	0.07
Ukrainian	7	0.04
United States or American	920	5.47
West Indian, excl. Hispanic:	5,402	32.12
Bahamian	304	1.81
British West Indian	65	0.39
Haitian	4,315	25.66
Jamaican	576	3.42
Trinidadian and Tobagonian	59	0.35
U.S. Virgin Islander	14	0.08
West Indian	50	0.30
Other West Indian	19	0.11
White:	3,442	20.83
Not Hispanic (588)	628	3.80
Hispanic (2,594)	2,814	17.03

Plant City

Place Type: City
County: Hillsborough
Population: 29,915

Ancestry/Race	Number	%
Acadian/Cajun	25	0.08
African American/Black:	4,959	16.58
Not Hispanic (4,751)	4,858	16.24
Hispanic (82)	101	0.34
African, sub-Saharan:	99	0.33
African	89	0.30
Sudanese	10	0.03
Am. Ind. or Alaska Nat., not spec.	89	0.30
American Indian tribes, specified:	110	0.37
Blackfeet (1)	4	0.01
Cherokee (23)	54	0.18
Chippewa (1)	1	0.00
Choctaw	1	0.00
Comanche	2	0.01
Cree	2	0.01
Creek (1)	1	0.00
Crow	1	0.00
Houma (1)	1	0.00
Iroquois (2)	2	0.01
Latin American Indians (13)	15	0.05
Lumbee (4)	4	0.01
Navajo	1	0.00
Potawatomi	2	0.01
Pueblo (1)	1	0.00
Seminole (2)	5	0.02
Sioux (2)	2	0.01
All other tribes (5)	11	0.04
American Indian tribes, not spec.	20	0.07
Arab:	72	0.24
Arab/Arabic	27	0.09
Lebanese	27	0.09
Syrian	18	0.06
Armenian	16	0.05
Asian:	374	1.25
Chinese, ex. Taiwanese (22)	23	0.08
Filipino (31)	40	0.13
Indian (111)	139	0.46
Indonesian (1)	1	0.00
Japanese (8)	23	0.08
Korean (13)	21	0.07
Laotian (1)	1	0.00
Pakistani (10)	22	0.07
Taiwanese (4)	4	0.01
Thai (19)	20	0.07
Vietnamese (35)	42	0.14
Other Asian, specified	5	0.02
Other Asian, not specified (9)	33	0.11
Austrian	42	0.14
Belgian	7	0.02
Brazilian	7	0.02
British	145	0.48
Canadian	36	0.12
Czech	55	0.18
Danish	67	0.22
Dutch	379	1.26
Eastern European	9	0.03
English	3,215	10.68
Estonian	7	0.02
European	74	0.25
Finnish	36	0.12
French, except Basque	750	2.49
French Canadian	223	0.74
German	3,310	10.99
Greek	36	0.12
Hawaii Native/Pacific Islander:	44	0.15
Micronesian: (1)	12	0.04
Guamanian/Chamorro (1)	12	0.04
Polynesian: (11)	15	0.05
Native Hawaiian (8)	11	0.04
Samoan (3)	3	0.01
Other Polynesian	1	0.00
Other Pac. Isl., specified	5	0.02
Other Pac. Isl., not spec. (1)	12	0.04
Hispanic or Latino:	5,211	17.42
Central American:	148	0.49
Costa Rican	7	0.02
Guatemalan	76	0.25
Honduran	47	0.16
Nicaraguan	4	0.01
Panamanian	9	0.03
Salvadoran	5	0.02
Cuban	133	0.44
Dominican Republic	28	0.09
Mexican	3,681	12.30
Puerto Rican	635	2.12
South American:	74	0.25
Argentinean	8	0.03
Bolivian	1	0.00
Chilean	2	0.01
Colombian	25	0.08
Ecuadorian	12	0.04
Peruvian	19	0.06
Venezuelan	4	0.01
Other South American	3	0.01
Other Hispanic or Latino	512	1.71
Hungarian	154	0.51
Irish	3,393	11.27
Italian	911	3.03
Lithuanian	28	0.09
Macedonian	8	0.03
Norwegian	121	0.40
Pennsylvania German	10	0.03
Polish	499	1.66
Portuguese	175	0.58
Romanian	20	0.07
Russian	84	0.28
Scandinavian	43	0.14
Scotch-Irish	427	1.42
Scottish	653	2.17
Serbian	7	0.02
Slovak	81	0.27
Slovene	7	0.02
Swedish	143	0.47
Swiss	14	0.05
Ukrainian	78	0.26
United States or American	2,763	9.18
Welsh	143	0.47
West Indian, excl. Hispanic:	216	0.72
Dutch West Indian	16	0.05
Haitian	51	0.17
Jamaican	115	0.38
Trinidadian and Tobagonian	28	0.09
West Indian	6	0.02
White:	21,838	73.00
Not Hispanic (19,250)	19,471	65.09
Hispanic (2,190)	2,367	7.91
Yugoslavian	33	0.11

Plantation

Place Type: City
County: Broward
Population: 82,934

Ancestry/Race	Number	%
Acadian/Cajun	16	0.02
African American/Black:	12,497	15.07
Not Hispanic (11,101)	12,053	14.53
Hispanic (325)	444	0.54
African, sub-Saharan:	684	0.82
African	465	0.56
Kenyan	28	0.03
Nigerian	50	0.06
South African	119	0.14
Sudanese	10	0.01
Other sub-Saharan African	12	0.01
Alaska Native tribes, specified:	4	0.00
Alaska Athabascan	1	0.00
Tlingit-Haida (3)	3	0.00
Am. Ind. or Alaska Nat., not spec.	129	0.16
Albanian	26	0.03
American Indian tribes, specified:	188	0.23
Apache	8	0.01
Blackfeet	8	0.01
Cherokee (29)	74	0.09
Cheyenne (3)	3	0.00
Chickasaw (1)	1	0.00
Chippewa (6)	7	0.01
Choctaw (6)	9	0.01
Comanche (3)	3	0.00
Creek	2	0.00
Crow	1	0.00
Delaware (1)	1	0.00
Iroquois (2)	8	0.01
Latin American Indians (7)	32	0.04
Lumbee (2)	2	0.00
Navajo (2)	6	0.01
Potawatomi (1)	1	0.00
Seminole (2)	5	0.01
Sioux (1)	3	0.00
All other tribes (3)	14	0.02
American Indian tribes, not spec.	15	0.02
Arab:	703	0.84
Arab/Arabic	132	0.16
Egyptian	51	0.06
Iraqi	9	0.01
Jordanian	25	0.03
Lebanese	159	0.19
Moroccan	56	0.07
Palestinian	156	0.19
Syrian	29	0.03
Other Arab	86	0.10
Armenian	107	0.13
Asian:	3,021	3.64
Bangladeshi (19)	30	0.04
Cambodian (1)	1	0.00
Chinese, ex. Taiwanese (488)	646	0.78
Filipino (268)	351	0.42
Indian (1,090)	1,230	1.48
Indonesian (6)	14	0.02
Japanese (65)	106	0.13
Korean (123)	153	0.18
Laotian (3)	10	0.01
Malaysian (4)	4	0.00
Pakistani (86)	111	0.13
Sri Lankan	1	0.00
Taiwanese (28)	30	0.04
Thai (25)	33	0.04
Vietnamese (116)	139	0.17
Other Asian, specified (12)	16	0.02
Other Asian, not specified (28)	146	0.18
Australian	12	0.01
Austrian	735	0.88
Belgian	21	0.03
Brazilian	349	0.42
British	449	0.54

Notes: 1. Figures in the "Number" column do not add up to the total population due to: a) Ancestry/Race overlap — e.g. persons can report being both White and Irish, b) persons of Hispanic origin can report being any race, c) persons reporting two ancestries are counted in both categories. 2. Numbers in parentheses indicate the number of persons reporting this ancestry/race alone, not in combination with any other ancestry/race. 3. Refer to the User's Guide in the front of the book for more detailed information.

Bulgarian	8	0.01
Canadian	528	0.63
Croatian	111	0.13
Czech	311	0.37
Czechoslovakian	216	0.26
Danish	231	0.28
Dutch	687	0.82
Eastern European	525	0.63
English	5,894	7.08
Estonian	11	0.01
European	834	1.00
Finnish	25	0.03
French, except Basque	1,928	2.32
French Canadian	562	0.67
German	8,959	10.76
German Russian	14	0.02
Greek	776	0.93
Guyanese	158	0.19
Hawaii Native/Pacific Islander:	132	0.16
Micronesian: (5)	11	0.01
Guamanian/Chamorro (4)	10	0.01
Other Micronesian (1)	1	0.00
Polynesian: (14)	30	0.04
Native Hawaiian (8)	20	0.02
Samoan (1)	2	0.00
Other Polynesian (5)	8	0.01
Other Pac. Isl., specified	4	0.00
Other Pac. Isl., not spec. (18)	87	0.10
Hispanic or Latino:	10,860	13.09
Central American:	621	0.75
Costa Rican	55	0.07
Guatemalan	80	0.10
Honduran	135	0.16
Nicaraguan	90	0.11
Panamanian	100	0.12
Salvadoran	142	0.17
Other Central American	19	0.02
Cuban	2,043	2.46
Dominican Republic	387	0.47
Mexican	559	0.67
Puerto Rican	1,915	2.31
South American:	3,137	3.78
Argentinean	177	0.21
Bolivian	25	0.03
Chilean	72	0.09
Colombian	1,502	1.81
Ecuadorian	256	0.31
Paraguayan	8	0.01
Peruvian	484	0.58
Uruguayan	50	0.06
Venezuelan	468	0.56
Other South American	95	0.11
Other Hispanic or Latino	2,198	2.65
Hungarian	1,070	1.28
Iranian	149	0.18
Irish	8,473	10.17
Israeli	439	0.53
Italian	7,382	8.86
Latvian	39	0.05
Lithuanian	188	0.23
Macedonian	45	0.05
Northern European	48	0.06
Norwegian	553	0.66
Pennsylvania German	12	0.01
Polish	3,518	4.22
Portuguese	454	0.55
Romanian	469	0.56
Russian	3,428	4.12
Scandinavian	97	0.12
Scotch-Irish	1,054	1.27
Scottish	1,234	1.48
Serbian	30	0.04
Slavic	7	0.01
Slovak	79	0.09
Slovene	45	0.05
Swedish	707	0.85
Swiss	160	0.19
Turkish	62	0.07
Ukrainian	258	0.31
United States or American	6,631	7.96
Welsh	426	0.51
West Indian, excl. Hispanic:	7,276	8.74
Bahamian	223	0.27
Barbadian	55	0.07
Belizean	91	0.11
Bermudan	11	0.01
British West Indian	58	0.07
Dutch West Indian	50	0.06
Haitian	2,307	2.77
Jamaican	3,657	4.39
Trinidadian and Tobagonian	461	0.55
U.S. Virgin Islander	56	0.07
West Indian	288	0.35
Other West Indian	19	0.02
White:	66,357	80.01
Not Hispanic (56,411)	57,301	69.09
Hispanic (8,556)	9,056	10.92
Yugoslavian	65	0.08

Poinciana

Place Type: Census Designated Place
County: Osceola
Population: 13,647

Ancestry/Race	Number	%
African American/Black:	2,759	20.22
Not Hispanic (2,178)	2,405	17.62
Hispanic (242)	354	2.59
African, sub-Saharan:	155	1.14
African	65	0.48
Cape Verdean	90	0.66
Alaska Native tribes, specified:	6	0.04
Eskimo (2)	6	0.04
Am. Ind. or Alaska Nat., not spec.	49	0.36
Albanian	11	0.08
American Indian tribes, specified:	61	0.45
Apache (1)	2	0.01
Blackfeet (1)	4	0.03
Cherokee (6)	18	0.13
Cheyenne	1	0.01
Choctaw (1)	2	0.01
Delaware	2	0.01
Iroquois (2)	2	0.01
Latin American Indians (4)	15	0.11
Navajo (2)	2	0.01
Pueblo	3	0.02
Sioux (2)	3	0.02
Tohono O'Odham	3	0.02
Ute	3	0.02
All other tribes	1	0.01
American Indian tribes, not spec.	17	0.12
Arab:	81	0.60
Egyptian	29	0.21
Lebanese	13	0.10
Moroccan	39	0.29
Asian:	270	1.98
Chinese, ex. Taiwanese (20)	53	0.39
Filipino (52)	69	0.51
Indian (46)	82	0.60
Japanese	7	0.05
Korean (6)	13	0.10
Laotian (3)	3	0.02
Pakistani (3)	3	0.02
Thai (1)	1	0.01
Vietnamese (4)	18	0.13
Other Asian, not specified (2)	21	0.15
Australian	22	0.16
Austrian	35	0.26
Belgian	20	0.15
Brazilian	19	0.14
British	111	0.82
Canadian	8	0.06
Czech	13	0.10
Czechoslovakian	22	0.16
Dutch	206	1.52
English	598	4.40
European	93	0.68
Finnish	13	0.10
French, except Basque	538	3.96
French Canadian	165	1.21
German	1,335	9.83
Greek	18	0.13
Guyanese	70	0.52
Hawaii Native/Pacific Islander:	55	0.40
Micronesian: (1)	2	0.01
Guamanian/Chamorro (1)	2	0.01
Polynesian: (12)	23	0.17
Native Hawaiian (2)	8	0.06
Samoan (5)	9	0.07
Tongan (5)	5	0.04
Other Polynesian	1	0.01
Other Pac. Isl., not spec.	30	0.22
Hispanic or Latino:	5,393	39.52
Central American:	196	1.44
Costa Rican	18	0.13
Guatemalan	25	0.18
Honduran	27	0.20
Nicaraguan	23	0.17
Panamanian	58	0.43
Salvadoran	35	0.26
Other Central American	10	0.07
Cuban	135	0.99
Dominican Republic	217	1.59
Mexican	136	1.00
Puerto Rican	3,789	27.76
South American:	301	2.21
Argentinean	22	0.16
Bolivian	4	0.03
Chilean	13	0.10
Colombian	147	1.08
Ecuadorian	43	0.32
Peruvian	16	0.12
Uruguayan	3	0.02
Venezuelan	26	0.19
Other South American	27	0.20
Other Hispanic or Latino	619	4.54
Hungarian	118	0.87
Irish	1,164	8.57
Italian	979	7.21
Luxemburger	8	0.06
Norwegian	71	0.52
Pennsylvania German	10	0.07
Polish	355	2.61
Portuguese	87	0.64
Romanian	46	0.34
Russian	100	0.74
Scotch-Irish	62	0.46
Scottish	83	0.61
Slovak	25	0.18
Swedish	71	0.52
Swiss	9	0.07
Ukrainian	12	0.09
United States or American	424	3.12
Welsh	6	0.04
West Indian, excl. Hispanic:	1,088	8.01
Barbadian	44	0.32
British West Indian	20	0.15
Haitian	195	1.44
Jamaican	545	4.01
Trinidadian and Tobagonian	102	0.75
U.S. Virgin Islander	8	0.06
West Indian	162	1.19
Other West Indian	12	0.09
White:	9,382	68.75
Not Hispanic (5,450)	5,609	41.10
Hispanic (3,434)	3,773	27.65
Yugoslavian	9	0.07

Pompano Beach

Place Type: City
County: Broward
Population: 78,191

Ancestry/Race	Number	%
African American/Black:	21,687	27.74
Not Hispanic (19,520)	21,238	27.16
Hispanic (377)	449	0.57
African, sub-Saharan:	401	0.51
African	303	0.39
Kenyan	29	0.04
Nigerian	22	0.03
Senegalese	24	0.03
South African	23	0.03

Notes: 1. Figures in the "Number" column do not add up to the total population due to: a) Ancestry/Race overlap — e.g. persons can report being both White and Irish, b) persons of Hispanic origin can report being any race, c) persons reporting two ancestries are counted in both categories. 2. Numbers in parentheses indicate the number of persons reporting this ancestry/race alone, not in combination with any other ancestry/race. 3. Refer to the User's Guide in the front of the book for more detailed information.

Alaska Native tribes, specified:	7	0.01
Alaska Athabascan	2	0.00
Aleut (1)	3	0.00
Eskimo (1)	2	0.00
Am. Ind. or Alaska Nat., not spec.	173	0.22
American Indian tribes, specified:	194	0.25
Apache	2	0.00
Blackfeet (1)	6	0.01
Cherokee (24)	71	0.09
Chippewa (7)	7	0.01
Choctaw (5)	10	0.01
Cree (1)	1	0.00
Creek	3	0.00
Delaware (3)	3	0.00
Iroquois (7)	11	0.01
Kiowa (1)	1	0.00
Latin American Indians (32)	43	0.05
Navajo (1)	1	0.00
Pueblo (1)	1	0.00
Seminole (3)	7	0.01
Sioux (2)	4	0.01
Ute	1	0.00
All other tribes (6)	22	0.03
American Indian tribes, not spec.	29	0.04
Arab:	398	0.51
Arab/Arabic	24	0.03
Egyptian	37	0.05
Jordanian	10	0.01
Lebanese	149	0.19
Moroccan	29	0.04
Palestinian	30	0.04
Syrian	71	0.09
Other Arab	48	0.06
Armenian	75	0.10
Asian:	1,016	1.30
Bangladeshi (23)	32	0.04
Cambodian (3)	3	0.00
Chinese, ex. Taiwanese (103)	144	0.18
Filipino (77)	136	0.17
Indian (270)	377	0.48
Indonesian (1)	2	0.00
Japanese (28)	66	0.08
Korean (37)	61	0.08
Laotian (1)	1	0.00
Malaysian (1)	1	0.00
Pakistani (8)	10	0.01
Sri Lankan (1)	2	0.00
Thai (16)	17	0.02
Vietnamese (29)	46	0.06
Other Asian, specified (2)	14	0.02
Other Asian, not specified (13)	104	0.13
Assyrian/Chaldean/Syriac	12	0.02
Australian	44	0.06
Austrian	413	0.53
Belgian	67	0.09
Brazilian	919	1.17
British	506	0.65
Bulgarian	28	0.04
Canadian	516	0.66
Croatian	61	0.08
Czech	171	0.22
Czechoslovakian	82	0.10
Danish	197	0.25
Dutch	940	1.20
Eastern European	70	0.09
English	5,122	6.54
Estonian	20	0.03
European	339	0.43
Finnish	73	0.09
French, except Basque	2,105	2.69
French Canadian	964	1.23
German	7,615	9.73
Greek	523	0.67
Guyanese	25	0.03
Hawaii Native/Pacific Islander:	133	0.17
Micronesian: (3)	14	0.02
Guamanian/Chamorro (3)	14	0.02
Polynesian: (13)	41	0.05
Native Hawaiian (8)	32	0.04
Samoan (4)	8	0.01
Other Polynesian (1)	1	0.00
Other Pac. Isl., specified	9	0.01
Other Pac. Isl., not spec. (6)	69	0.09
Hispanic or Latino:	7,770	9.94
Central American:	342	0.44
Costa Rican	43	0.05
Guatemalan	72	0.09
Honduran	105	0.13
Nicaraguan	34	0.04
Panamanian	18	0.02
Salvadoran	63	0.08
Other Central American	7	0.01
Cuban	562	0.72
Dominican Republic	84	0.11
Mexican	2,795	3.57
Puerto Rican	1,275	1.63
South American:	1,461	1.87
Argentinean	81	0.10
Bolivian	27	0.03
Chilean	56	0.07
Colombian	479	0.61
Ecuadorian	82	0.10
Paraguayan	4	0.01
Peruvian	156	0.20
Uruguayan	25	0.03
Venezuelan	496	0.63
Other South American	55	0.07
Other Hispanic or Latino	1,251	1.60
Hungarian	781	1.00
Iranian	35	0.04
Irish	7,578	9.68
Israeli	36	0.05
Italian	6,975	8.91
Latvian	70	0.09
Lithuanian	295	0.38
Macedonian	8	0.01
New Zealander	22	0.03
Northern European	8	0.01
Norwegian	475	0.61
Pennsylvania German	61	0.08
Polish	2,624	3.35
Portuguese	333	0.43
Romanian	293	0.37
Russian	2,066	2.64
Scandinavian	37	0.05
Scotch-Irish	774	0.99
Scottish	1,246	1.59
Serbian	30	0.04
Slavic	40	0.05
Slovak	92	0.12
Slovene	32	0.04
Swedish	888	1.13
Swiss	188	0.24
Turkish	165	0.21
Ukrainian	335	0.43
United States or American	4,633	5.92
Welsh	325	0.42
West Indian, excl. Hispanic:	5,453	6.96
Bahamian	110	0.14
Barbadian	10	0.01
Belizean	21	0.03
British West Indian	91	0.12
Haitian	4,718	6.03
Jamaican	402	0.51
Trinidadian and Tobagonian	49	0.06
West Indian	52	0.07
White:	54,200	69.32
Not Hispanic (47,549)	48,331	61.81
Hispanic (5,440)	5,869	7.51
Yugoslavian	76	0.10

Port Charlotte

Place Type: Census Designated Place
County: Charlotte
Population: 46,451

Ancestry/Race	Number	%
African American/Black:	3,320	7.15
Not Hispanic (2,895)	3,128	6.73
Hispanic (138)	192	0.41
African, sub-Saharan:	160	0.34
African	150	0.32
Cape Verdean	10	0.02
Alaska Native tribes, specified:	1	0.00
Tlingit-Haida (1)	1	0.00
Alaska Native tribes, not specified	1	0.00
Am. Ind. or Alaska Nat., not spec.	95	0.20
American Indian tribes, specified:	223	0.48
Apache (2)	3	0.01
Blackfeet (5)	7	0.02
Cherokee (33)	92	0.20
Cheyenne	2	0.00
Chickasaw (2)	2	0.00
Chippewa (16)	26	0.06
Choctaw	4	0.01
Creek (1)	3	0.01
Crow (1)	2	0.00
Delaware (1)	1	0.00
Iroquois (9)	20	0.04
Latin American Indians (4)	20	0.04
Navajo (2)	3	0.01
Osage	1	0.00
Potawatomi	1	0.00
Pueblo	2	0.00
Seminole (4)	6	0.01
Sioux (2)	12	0.03
All other tribes (7)	16	0.03
American Indian tribes, not spec.	18	0.04
Arab:	239	0.51
Arab/Arabic	70	0.15
Egyptian	55	0.12
Lebanese	30	0.06
Palestinian	69	0.15
Syrian	15	0.03
Armenian	13	0.03
Asian:	701	1.51
Cambodian (1)	1	0.00
Chinese, ex. Taiwanese (90)	117	0.25
Filipino (136)	198	0.43
Indian (135)	174	0.37
Indonesian (1)	4	0.01
Japanese (26)	35	0.08
Korean (27)	32	0.07
Laotian (5)	5	0.01
Malaysian	3	0.01
Pakistani (10)	10	0.02
Sri Lankan (2)	2	0.00
Thai (21)	30	0.06
Vietnamese (48)	54	0.12
Other Asian, specified (1)	9	0.02
Other Asian, not specified (13)	27	0.06
Assyrian/Chaldean/Syriac	8	0.02
Austrian	147	0.32
Belgian	62	0.13
Brazilian	28	0.06
British	270	0.58
Bulgarian	6	0.01
Canadian	257	0.55
Celtic	20	0.04
Croatian	87	0.19
Czech	305	0.66
Czechoslovakian	117	0.25
Danish	178	0.38
Dutch	869	1.87
Eastern European	7	0.02
English	5,833	12.55
Estonian	8	0.02
European	229	0.49
Finnish	227	0.49
French, except Basque	2,390	5.14
French Canadian	580	1.25
German	8,981	19.33
Greek	193	0.42
Guyanese	125	0.27
Hawaii Native/Pacific Islander:	80	0.17
Micronesian: (4)	6	0.01
Guamanian/Chamorro (4)	6	0.01
Polynesian: (16)	34	0.07
Native Hawaiian (5)	19	0.04
Samoan (11)	13	0.03
Other Polynesian	2	0.00
Other Pac. Isl., specified	7	0.02

Notes: 1. Figures in the "Number" column do not add up to the total population due to: a) Ancestry/Race overlap — e.g. persons can report being both White and Irish, b) persons of Hispanic origin can report being any race, c) persons reporting two ancestries are counted in both categories. 2. Numbers in parentheses indicate the number of persons reporting this ancestry/race alone, not in combination with any other ancestry/race. 3. Refer to the User's Guide in the front of the book for more detailed information.

Other Pac. Isl., not spec. (2)	33	0.07
Hispanic or Latino:	2,395	5.16
Central American:	93	0.20
Costa Rican	15	0.03
Guatemalan	11	0.02
Honduran	14	0.03
Nicaraguan	10	0.02
Panamanian	29	0.06
Salvadoran	6	0.01
Other Central American	8	0.02
Cuban	322	0.69
Dominican Republic	62	0.13
Mexican	367	0.79
Puerto Rican	870	1.87
South American:	215	0.46
Argentinean	14	0.03
Chilean	2	0.00
Colombian	108	0.23
Ecuadorian	27	0.06
Peruvian	36	0.08
Uruguayan	4	0.01
Venezuelan	16	0.03
Other South American	8	0.02
Other Hispanic or Latino	466	1.00
Hungarian	450	0.97
Icelander	11	0.02
Irish	7,395	15.91
Israeli	9	0.02
Italian	4,833	10.40
Latvian	11	0.02
Lithuanian	177	0.38
Maltese	30	0.06
Northern European	9	0.02
Norwegian	409	0.88
Pennsylvania German	48	0.10
Polish	2,063	4.44
Portuguese	298	0.64
Romanian	63	0.14
Russian	325	0.70
Scandinavian	68	0.15
Scotch-Irish	757	1.63
Scottish	1,239	2.67
Serbian	40	0.09
Slavic	22	0.05
Slovak	161	0.35
Slovene	8	0.02
Swedish	648	1.39
Swiss	109	0.23
Ukrainian	310	0.67
United States or American	3,368	7.25
Welsh	441	0.95
West Indian, excl. Hispanic:	1,537	3.31
Barbadian	39	0.08
Belizean	12	0.03
British West Indian	18	0.04
Haitian	391	0.84
Jamaican	820	1.76
Trinidadian and Tobagonian	71	0.15
U.S. Virgin Islander	9	0.02
West Indian	177	0.38
White:	41,988	90.39
Not Hispanic (39,890)	40,298	86.75
Hispanic (1,558)	1,690	3.64
Yugoslavian	36	0.08

Port Orange

Place Type: City
County: Volusia
Population: 45,823

Ancestry/Race	Number	%
Acadian/Cajun	16	0.04
African American/Black:	800	1.75
Not Hispanic (695)	769	1.68
Hispanic (27)	31	0.07
African, sub-Saharan:	132	0.29
African	54	0.12
Cape Verdean	33	0.07
Ghanian	9	0.02
South African	9	0.02
Other sub-Saharan African	27	0.06
Alaska Native tribes, specified:	1	0.00
Eskimo	1	0.00
Am. Ind. or Alaska Nat., not spec.	59	0.13
Albanian	6	0.01
American Indian tribes, specified:	193	0.42
Apache	2	0.00
Blackfeet (5)	12	0.03
Cherokee (28)	73	0.16
Cheyenne	2	0.00
Chickasaw (2)	3	0.01
Chippewa (3)	4	0.01
Choctaw	2	0.00
Cree	1	0.00
Creek (2)	7	0.02
Delaware (4)	7	0.02
Iroquois (12)	29	0.06
Latin American Indians (5)	5	0.01
Lumbee (8)	9	0.02
Navajo	1	0.00
Pueblo (1)	1	0.00
Seminole (5)	7	0.02
Shoshone	1	0.00
Sioux (3)	3	0.01
Tohono O'Odham	1	0.00
All other tribes (11)	23	0.05
American Indian tribes, not spec.	13	0.03
Arab:	352	0.78
Arab/Arabic	55	0.12
Egyptian	73	0.16
Lebanese	95	0.21
Syrian	98	0.22
Other Arab	31	0.07
Armenian	25	0.06
Asian:	650	1.42
Cambodian	1	0.00
Chinese, ex. Taiwanese (91)	111	0.24
Filipino (103)	131	0.29
Indian (139)	151	0.33
Indonesian (4)	5	0.01
Japanese (24)	31	0.07
Korean (67)	84	0.18
Pakistani (12)	19	0.04
Taiwanese (2)	2	0.00
Thai (10)	13	0.03
Vietnamese (46)	56	0.12
Other Asian, specified	1	0.00
Other Asian, not specified (18)	45	0.10
Australian	7	0.02
Austrian	124	0.27
Belgian	73	0.16
Brazilian	9	0.02
British	191	0.42
Bulgarian	9	0.02
Canadian	225	0.50
Celtic	8	0.02
Croatian	131	0.29
Czech	174	0.38
Czechoslovakian	75	0.17
Danish	117	0.26
Dutch	906	2.00
Eastern European	17	0.04
English	6,354	14.00
European	218	0.48
Finnish	71	0.16
French, except Basque	1,850	4.08
French Canadian	792	1.75
German	8,246	18.18
Greek	353	0.78
Hawaii Native/Pacific Islander:	27	0.06
Micronesian: (3)	5	0.01
Guamanian/Chamorro (3)	3	0.01
Other Micronesian	2	0.00
Polynesian: (4)	17	0.04
Native Hawaiian (1)	8	0.02
Samoan (3)	8	0.02
Other Polynesian	1	0.00
Other Pac. Isl., not spec. (3)	5	0.01
Hispanic or Latino:	1,151	2.51
Central American:	36	0.08
Costa Rican	7	0.02
Guatemalan	6	0.01
Nicaraguan	5	0.01
Panamanian	11	0.02
Salvadoran	5	0.01
Other Central American	2	0.00
Cuban	94	0.21
Dominican Republic	16	0.03
Mexican	157	0.34
Puerto Rican	441	0.96
South American:	152	0.33
Argentinean	19	0.04
Bolivian	5	0.01
Chilean	8	0.02
Colombian	55	0.12
Ecuadorian	22	0.05
Peruvian	2	0.00
Uruguayan	7	0.02
Venezuelan	23	0.05
Other South American	11	0.02
Other Hispanic or Latino	255	0.56
Hungarian	254	0.56
Iranian	41	0.09
Irish	7,137	15.73
Italian	5,028	11.08
Latvian	8	0.02
Lithuanian	160	0.35
Luxemburger	17	0.04
Macedonian	13	0.03
New Zealander	8	0.02
Norwegian	319	0.70
Pennsylvania German	43	0.09
Polish	1,986	4.38
Portuguese	159	0.35
Romanian	45	0.10
Russian	360	0.79
Scandinavian	15	0.03
Scotch-Irish	997	2.20
Scottish	1,094	2.41
Serbian	28	0.06
Slavic	36	0.08
Slovak	224	0.49
Slovene	21	0.05
Swedish	648	1.43
Swiss	162	0.36
Turkish	10	0.02
Ukrainian	186	0.41
United States or American	3,612	7.96
Welsh	461	1.02
West Indian, excl. Hispanic:	144	0.32
Barbadian	9	0.02
British West Indian	8	0.02
Dutch West Indian	11	0.02
Haitian	71	0.16
Jamaican	34	0.07
Trinidadian and Tobagonian	6	0.01
West Indian	5	0.01
White:	44,167	96.39
Not Hispanic (42,941)	43,260	94.41
Hispanic (862)	907	1.98
Yugoslavian	45	0.10

Port Saint John

Place Type: Census Designated Place
County: Brevard
Population: 12,112

Ancestry/Race	Number	%
African American/Black:	659	5.44
Not Hispanic (593)	640	5.28
Hispanic (14)	19	0.16
Am. Ind. or Alaska Nat., not spec.	42	0.35
American Indian tribes, specified:	110	0.91
Apache	3	0.02
Blackfeet (1)	4	0.03
Cherokee (23)	61	0.50
Chickasaw (1)	1	0.01
Chippewa (1)	6	0.05
Choctaw	5	0.04
Creek (2)	4	0.03
Latin American Indians (1)	1	0.01
Lumbee (1)	1	0.01
Navajo (2)	2	0.02

Notes: 1. Figures in the "Number" column do not add up to the total population due to: a) Ancestry/Race overlap — e.g. persons can report being both White and Irish, b) persons of Hispanic origin can report being any race, c) persons reporting two ancestries are counted in both categories. 2. Numbers in parentheses indicate the number of persons reporting this ancestry/race alone, not in combination with any other ancestry/race. 3. Refer to the User's Guide in the front of the book for more detailed information.

Potawatomi (1)	1	0.01
Pueblo	1	0.01
Puget Sound Salish	1	0.01
Seminole (1)	2	0.02
Sioux (4)	7	0.06
All other tribes (5)	10	0.08
American Indian tribes, not spec.	1	0.01
Armenian	31	0.26
Asian:	174	1.44
Chinese, ex. Taiwanese (5)	5	0.04
Filipino (39)	57	0.47
Indian (20)	26	0.21
Indonesian (1)	1	0.01
Japanese (12)	37	0.31
Korean (7)	16	0.13
Malaysian (1)	1	0.01
Thai (6)	7	0.06
Vietnamese (11)	13	0.11
Other Asian, not specified (7)	11	0.09
Austrian	45	0.38
Belgian	62	0.52
Brazilian	18	0.15
British	11	0.09
Canadian	4	0.03
Cypriot	8	0.07
Czech	27	0.23
Czechoslovakian	30	0.25
Danish	35	0.29
Dutch	286	2.39
English	1,623	13.56
European	87	0.73
Finnish	11	0.09
French, except Basque	575	4.80
French Canadian	192	1.60
German	2,103	17.57
Greek	86	0.72
Hawaii Native/Pacific Islander:	33	0.27
Micronesian: (15)	21	0.17
Guamanian/Chamorro (14)	18	0.15
Other Micronesian (1)	3	0.02
Polynesian: (6)	10	0.08
Native Hawaiian (1)	5	0.04
Samoan (5)	5	0.04
Other Pac. Isl., not spec.	2	0.02
Hispanic or Latino:	397	3.28
Central American:	21	0.17
Costa Rican	3	0.02
Guatemalan	3	0.02
Honduran	3	0.02
Nicaraguan	2	0.02
Panamanian	8	0.07
Salvadoran	2	0.02
Cuban	31	0.26
Dominican Republic	4	0.03
Mexican	88	0.73
Puerto Rican	166	1.37
South American:	28	0.23
Argentinean	4	0.03
Colombian	13	0.11
Peruvian	4	0.03
Venezuelan	7	0.06
Other Hispanic or Latino	59	0.49
Hungarian	22	0.18
Irish	1,954	16.33
Italian	857	7.16
Latvian	8	0.07
Lithuanian	19	0.16
Norwegian	96	0.80
Pennsylvania German	16	0.13
Polish	318	2.66
Portuguese	8	0.07
Russian	58	0.48
Scandinavian	23	0.19
Scotch-Irish	297	2.48
Scottish	403	3.37
Slavic	12	0.10
Swedish	180	1.50
Swiss	29	0.24
Turkish	32	0.27
Ukrainian	37	0.31
United States or American	1,216	10.16
Welsh	65	0.54
West Indian, excl. Hispanic:	103	0.86
Bahamian	16	0.13
Jamaican	46	0.38
Trinidadian and Tobagonian	20	0.17
West Indian	21	0.18
White:	11,182	92.32
Not Hispanic (10,712)	10,893	89.94
Hispanic (273)	289	2.39

Port Saint Lucie

Place Type: City
County: Saint Lucie
Population: 88,769

Ancestry/Race	Number	%
Acadian/Cajun	7	0.01
African American/Black:	6,848	7.71
Not Hispanic (6,035)	6,509	7.33
Hispanic (260)	339	0.38
African, sub-Saharan:	282	0.32
African	220	0.25
Ghanian	16	0.02
Nigerian	12	0.01
South African	26	0.03
Zimbabwean	8	0.01
Alaska Native tribes, specified:	8	0.01
Eskimo (1)	1	0.00
Tlingit-Haida (1)	7	0.01
Am. Ind. or Alaska Nat., not spec.	171	0.19
American Indian tribes, specified:	378	0.43
Apache (6)	12	0.01
Blackfeet (2)	32	0.04
Cherokee (38)	149	0.17
Cheyenne (2)	4	0.00
Chickasaw (8)	12	0.01
Chippewa (6)	22	0.02
Choctaw	3	0.00
Comanche (1)	1	0.00
Cree (1)	1	0.00
Creek (1)	2	0.00
Delaware	3	0.00
Iroquois (11)	31	0.03
Latin American Indians (9)	26	0.03
Lumbee (1)	1	0.00
Menominee (1)	1	0.00
Navajo (1)	3	0.00
Osage (2)	4	0.00
Pueblo	2	0.00
Seminole (13)	17	0.02
Sioux (5)	12	0.01
All other tribes (9)	40	0.05
American Indian tribes, not spec.	24	0.03
Arab:	380	0.43
Arab/Arabic	136	0.15
Jordanian	21	0.02
Lebanese	121	0.14
Moroccan	7	0.01
Palestinian	11	0.01
Syrian	50	0.06
Other Arab	34	0.04
Armenian	17	0.02
Asian:	1,437	1.62
Bangladeshi (2)	9	0.01
Cambodian (40)	44	0.05
Chinese, ex. Taiwanese (230)	275	0.31
Filipino (285)	372	0.42
Indian (247)	323	0.36
Indonesian (7)	8	0.01
Japanese (40)	82	0.09
Korean (72)	96	0.11
Laotian (2)	2	0.00
Malaysian (5)	5	0.01
Pakistani (37)	38	0.04
Sri Lankan (4)	4	0.00
Taiwanese (1)	9	0.01
Thai (25)	33	0.04
Vietnamese (57)	62	0.07
Other Asian, specified (1)	2	0.00
Other Asian, not specified (25)	73	0.08
Australian	7	0.01
Austrian	392	0.44
Basque	45	0.05
Belgian	71	0.08
Brazilian	81	0.09
British	307	0.35
Bulgarian	19	0.02
Canadian	268	0.30
Carpatho Rusyn	16	0.02
Celtic	7	0.01
Croatian	71	0.08
Czech	260	0.29
Czechoslovakian	167	0.19
Danish	256	0.29
Dutch	1,624	1.83
Eastern European	33	0.04
English	10,173	11.46
Estonian	14	0.02
European	286	0.32
Finnish	201	0.23
French, except Basque	3,402	3.83
French Canadian	1,357	1.53
German	14,983	16.87
German Russian	11	0.01
Greek	524	0.59
Guyanese	57	0.06
Hawaii Native/Pacific Islander:	104	0.12
Micronesian: (10)	16	0.02
Guamanian/Chamorro (9)	15	0.02
Other Micronesian (1)	1	0.00
Polynesian: (16)	44	0.05
Native Hawaiian (10)	36	0.04
Samoan (5)	7	0.01
Other Polynesian (1)	1	0.00
Other Pac. Isl., specified	1	0.00
Other Pac. Isl., not spec. (5)	43	0.05
Hispanic or Latino:	6,677	7.52
Central American:	378	0.43
Costa Rican	24	0.03
Guatemalan	110	0.12
Honduran	91	0.10
Nicaraguan	32	0.04
Panamanian	80	0.09
Salvadoran	27	0.03
Other Central American	14	0.02
Cuban	786	0.89
Dominican Republic	193	0.22
Mexican	648	0.73
Puerto Rican	2,811	3.17
South American:	634	0.71
Argentinean	36	0.04
Bolivian	4	0.00
Chilean	30	0.03
Colombian	280	0.32
Ecuadorian	112	0.13
Paraguayan	1	0.00
Peruvian	83	0.09
Uruguayan	13	0.01
Venezuelan	51	0.06
Other South American	24	0.03
Other Hispanic or Latino	1,227	1.38
Hungarian	973	1.10
Icelander	7	0.01
Iranian	16	0.02
Irish	15,466	17.42
Israeli	6	0.01
Italian	13,966	15.73
Latvian	37	0.04
Lithuanian	342	0.39
Maltese	14	0.02
Norwegian	977	1.10
Pennsylvania German	57	0.06
Polish	4,487	5.05
Portuguese	537	0.60
Romanian	69	0.08
Russian	1,082	1.22
Scandinavian	168	0.19
Scotch-Irish	1,167	1.31
Scottish	1,916	2.16
Slavic	50	0.06
Slovak	429	0.48
Slovene	63	0.07

Notes: 1. Figures in the "Number" column do not add up to the total population due to: a) Ancestry/Race overlap — e.g. persons can report being both White and Irish, b) persons of Hispanic origin can report being any race, c) persons reporting two ancestries are counted in both categories. 2. Numbers in parentheses indicate the number of persons reporting this ancestry/race alone, not in combination with any other ancestry/race. 3. Refer to the User's Guide in the front of the book for more detailed information.

Swedish	1,129	1.27
Swiss	199	0.22
Turkish	38	0.04
Ukrainian	382	0.43
United States or American	5,962	6.71
Welsh	360	0.41
West Indian, excl. Hispanic:	2,798	3.15
Bahamian	130	0.15
Barbadian	38	0.04
British West Indian	48	0.05
Haitian	702	0.79
Jamaican	1,584	1.78
Trinidadian and Tobagonian	165	0.19
West Indian	131	0.15
White:	79,199	89.22
Not Hispanic (73,489)	74,290	83.69
Hispanic (4,522)	4,909	5.53
Yugoslavian	83	0.09

Port Salerno

Place Type: Census Designated Place
County: Martin
Population: 10,141

Ancestry/Race	Number	%
African American/Black:	755	7.45
Not Hispanic (694)	742	7.32
Hispanic (11)	13	0.13
Am. Ind. or Alaska Nat., not spec.	10	0.10
American Indian tribes, specified:	32	0.32
Blackfeet (1)	2	0.02
Cherokee (1)	11	0.11
Chippewa (1)	3	0.03
Cree (1)	1	0.01
Creek	1	0.01
Iroquois (3)	5	0.05
Latin American Indians (2)	4	0.04
Navajo (1)	1	0.01
Seminole	1	0.01
Shoshone	1	0.01
All other tribes	2	0.02
American Indian tribes, not spec.	3	0.03
Asian:	87	0.86
Chinese, ex. Taiwanese (15)	16	0.16
Filipino (13)	21	0.21
Indian (16)	17	0.17
Indonesian	2	0.02
Japanese	4	0.04
Korean (5)	5	0.05
Laotian (8)	8	0.08
Pakistani (2)	3	0.03
Sri Lankan (5)	5	0.05
Thai (1)	2	0.02
Vietnamese (3)	3	0.03
Other Asian, not specified (1)	1	0.01
Australian	10	0.10
Austrian	41	0.41
Belgian	11	0.11
British	61	0.60
Canadian	21	0.21
Croatian	7	0.07
Czech	39	0.39
Danish	24	0.24
Dutch	274	2.71
English	1,541	15.25
European	40	0.40
Finnish	18	0.18
French, except Basque	389	3.85
French Canadian	179	1.77
German	1,881	18.62
Greek	18	0.18
Hawaii Native/Pacific Islander:	17	0.17
Melanesian: (3)	3	0.03
Fijian (3)	3	0.03
Micronesian: (5)	6	0.06
Guamanian/Chamorro (5)	6	0.06
Polynesian: (4)	6	0.06
Native Hawaiian (3)	5	0.05
Samoan (1)	1	0.01
Other Pac. Isl., not spec.	2	0.02
Hispanic or Latino:	827	8.16
Central American:	96	0.95
Costa Rican	2	0.02
Guatemalan	63	0.62
Honduran	12	0.12
Panamanian	4	0.04
Salvadoran	13	0.13
Other Central American	2	0.02
Cuban	36	0.35
Dominican Republic	8	0.08
Mexican	359	3.54
Puerto Rican	195	1.92
South American:	29	0.29
Bolivian	1	0.01
Colombian	11	0.11
Ecuadorian	4	0.04
Paraguayan	4	0.04
Peruvian	6	0.06
Venezuelan	3	0.03
Other Hispanic or Latino	104	1.03
Hungarian	25	0.25
Irish	1,723	17.05
Italian	956	9.46
Lithuanian	31	0.31
Northern European	20	0.20
Norwegian	120	1.19
Polish	309	3.06
Portuguese	49	0.48
Russian	38	0.38
Scotch-Irish	254	2.51
Scottish	317	3.14
Serbian	11	0.11
Slovak	7	0.07
Swedish	137	1.36
Swiss	58	0.57
Ukrainian	31	0.31
United States or American	865	8.56
Welsh	35	0.35
West Indian, excl. Hispanic:	79	0.78
Bahamian	7	0.07
Haitian	65	0.64
Jamaican	7	0.07
White:	9,093	89.67
Not Hispanic (8,440)	8,519	84.01
Hispanic (535)	574	5.66

Princeton

Place Type: Census Designated Place
County: Miami-Dade
Population: 10,090

Ancestry/Race	Number	%
African American/Black:	3,433	34.02
Not Hispanic (3,143)	3,242	32.13
Hispanic (140)	191	1.89
African, sub-Saharan:	194	1.91
African	194	1.91
Alaska Native tribes, specified:	1	0.01
Tlingit-Haida (1)	1	0.01
Am. Ind. or Alaska Nat., not spec.	17	0.17
American Indian tribes, specified:	54	0.54
Blackfeet	13	0.13
Cherokee (2)	14	0.14
Chippewa (1)	1	0.01
Latin American Indians (21)	24	0.24
Puget Sound Salish	1	0.01
All other tribes (1)	1	0.01
American Indian tribes, not spec.	3	0.03
Asian:	227	2.25
Cambodian (1)	2	0.02
Chinese, ex. Taiwanese (27)	55	0.55
Filipino (13)	25	0.25
Indian (27)	40	0.40
Japanese (7)	15	0.15
Korean (14)	27	0.27
Laotian (11)	14	0.14
Pakistani (5)	7	0.07
Taiwanese (1)	4	0.04
Thai (11)	12	0.12
Vietnamese (14)	17	0.17
Other Asian, not specified (3)	9	0.09
Brazilian	27	0.27
British	32	0.32
Canadian	31	0.31
Czech	43	0.42
Dutch	8	0.08
English	120	1.18
French, except Basque	102	1.01
French Canadian	62	0.61
German	377	3.72
Greek	15	0.15
Hawaii Native/Pacific Islander:	19	0.19
Micronesian: (3)	6	0.06
Guamanian/Chamorro (3)	6	0.06
Polynesian: (3)	6	0.06
Native Hawaiian (2)	5	0.05
Samoan (1)	1	0.01
Other Pac. Isl., not spec.	7	0.07
Hispanic or Latino:	4,792	47.49
Central American:	533	5.28
Costa Rican	30	0.30
Guatemalan	79	0.78
Honduran	96	0.95
Nicaraguan	217	2.15
Panamanian	35	0.35
Salvadoran	54	0.54
Other Central American	22	0.22
Cuban	1,306	12.94
Dominican Republic	134	1.33
Mexican	844	8.36
Puerto Rican	1,009	10.00
South American:	345	3.42
Argentinean	16	0.16
Bolivian	3	0.03
Chilean	14	0.14
Colombian	179	1.77
Ecuadorian	30	0.30
Peruvian	48	0.48
Uruguayan	12	0.12
Venezuelan	36	0.36
Other South American	7	0.07
Other Hispanic or Latino	621	6.15
Hungarian	25	0.25
Irish	277	2.73
Italian	274	2.70
Lithuanian	7	0.07
Norwegian	16	0.16
Polish	69	0.68
Portuguese	11	0.11
Scotch-Irish	19	0.19
Scottish	31	0.31
Swedish	16	0.16
Turkish	5	0.05
Ukrainian	7	0.07
United States or American	282	2.78
Welsh	17	0.17
West Indian, excl. Hispanic:	414	4.08
Bahamian	61	0.60
Dutch West Indian	20	0.20
Haitian	75	0.74
Jamaican	171	1.69
Trinidadian and Tobagonian	80	0.79
West Indian	7	0.07
White:	5,736	56.85
Not Hispanic (1,811)	1,887	18.70
Hispanic (3,615)	3,849	38.15

Punta Gorda

Place Type: City
County: Charlotte
Population: 14,344

Ancestry/Race	Number	%
African American/Black:	489	3.41
Not Hispanic (447)	471	3.28
Hispanic (7)	18	0.13
African, sub-Saharan:	19	0.13
African	10	0.07
Liberian	9	0.06
Am. Ind. or Alaska Nat., not spec.	12	0.08
Albanian	9	0.06
American Indian tribes, specified:	40	0.28
Blackfeet	4	0.03

Notes: 1. Figures in the "Number" column do not add up to the total population due to: a) Ancestry/Race overlap — e.g. persons can report being both White and Irish, b) persons of Hispanic origin can report being any race, c) persons reporting two ancestries are counted in both categories. 2. Numbers in parentheses indicate the number of persons reporting this ancestry/race alone, not in combination with any other ancestry/race. 3. Refer to the User's Guide in the front of the book for more detailed information.

Cherokee (9)	12	0.08
Chippewa (5)	8	0.06
Creek	1	0.01
Iroquois (1)	1	0.01
Osage (1)	1	0.01
Ottawa (1)	5	0.03
Sioux (1)	2	0.01
All other tribes (2)	6	0.04
American Indian tribes, not spec.	1	0.01
Arab:	69	0.48
Arab/Arabic	20	0.14
Palestinian	39	0.27
Syrian	10	0.07
Asian:	134	0.93
Chinese, ex. Taiwanese (12)	16	0.11
Filipino (33)	42	0.29
Indian (35)	39	0.27
Japanese (4)	4	0.03
Korean (7)	7	0.05
Laotian	1	0.01
Malaysian	1	0.01
Taiwanese (2)	2	0.01
Thai (3)	3	0.02
Vietnamese (11)	11	0.08
Other Asian, not specified (4)	8	0.06
Austrian	132	0.91
Belgian	27	0.19
British	176	1.22
Canadian	129	0.89
Croatian	9	0.06
Czech	61	0.42
Czechoslovakian	50	0.35
Danish	150	1.04
Dutch	321	2.22
English	2,556	17.71
European	104	0.72
Finnish	48	0.33
French, except Basque	442	3.06
French Canadian	184	1.27
German	3,419	23.69
Greek	95	0.66
Guyanese	22	0.15
Hawaii Native/Pacific Islander:	10	0.07
Micronesian: (2)	3	0.02
Guamanian/Chamorro (2)	3	0.02
Polynesian: (2)	3	0.02
Native Hawaiian (2)	2	0.01
Samoan	1	0.01
Other Pac. Isl., not spec.	4	0.03
Hispanic or Latino:	285	1.99
Central American:	5	0.03
Costa Rican	5	0.03
Cuban	52	0.36
Mexican	47	0.33
Puerto Rican	120	0.84
South American:	12	0.08
Argentinean	2	0.01
Chilean	3	0.02
Colombian	2	0.01
Ecuadorian	2	0.01
Peruvian	1	0.01
Venezuelan	1	0.01
Other South American	1	0.01
Other Hispanic or Latino	49	0.34
Hungarian	183	1.27
Irish	2,430	16.84
Italian	1,244	8.62
Latvian	23	0.16
Lithuanian	86	0.60
Maltese	11	0.08
Northern European	16	0.11
Norwegian	316	2.19
Pennsylvania German	9	0.06
Polish	674	4.67
Portuguese	43	0.30
Romanian	48	0.33
Russian	158	1.09
Scandinavian	15	0.10
Scotch-Irish	320	2.22
Scottish	469	3.25
Slovak	64	0.44
Swedish	301	2.09
Swiss	164	1.14
Ukrainian	8	0.06
United States or American	809	5.61
Welsh	139	0.96
West Indian, excl. Hispanic:	83	0.58
Bermudan	24	0.17
Haitian	19	0.13
Jamaican	14	0.10
West Indian	26	0.18
White:	13,649	95.15
Not Hispanic (13,373)	13,449	93.76
Hispanic (196)	200	1.39
Yugoslavian	40	0.28

Richmond West

Place Type: Census Designated Place
County: Miami-Dade
Population: 28,082

Ancestry/Race	Number	%
African American/Black:	2,735	9.74
Not Hispanic (2,042)	2,237	7.97
Hispanic (349)	498	1.77
African, sub-Saharan:	223	0.80
African	123	0.44
Nigerian	91	0.32
Other sub-Saharan African	9	0.03
Am. Ind. or Alaska Nat., not spec.	32	0.11
American Indian tribes, specified:	66	0.24
Blackfeet (1)	4	0.01
Cherokee (1)	4	0.01
Comanche	1	0.00
Creek	1	0.00
Iroquois (2)	2	0.01
Latin American Indians (25)	40	0.14
All other tribes (3)	14	0.05
American Indian tribes, not spec.	1	0.00
Arab:	141	0.50
Arab/Arabic	11	0.04
Lebanese	76	0.27
Palestinian	54	0.19
Armenian	10	0.04
Asian:	893	3.18
Chinese, ex. Taiwanese (216)	322	1.15
Filipino (143)	161	0.57
Indian (148)	206	0.73
Indonesian (4)	6	0.02
Japanese (8)	19	0.07
Korean (9)	25	0.09
Laotian (1)	3	0.01
Malaysian (1)	1	0.00
Pakistani (30)	49	0.17
Thai (18)	24	0.09
Vietnamese (33)	41	0.15
Other Asian, specified (1)	1	0.00
Other Asian, not specified (8)	35	0.12
Austrian	19	0.07
Basque	17	0.06
Brazilian	43	0.15
British	142	0.51
Czechoslovakian	7	0.02
Dutch	112	0.40
English	362	1.29
European	78	0.28
Finnish	9	0.03
French, except Basque	162	0.58
French Canadian	38	0.14
German	469	1.67
Greek	48	0.17
Guyanese	139	0.50
Hawaii Native/Pacific Islander:	43	0.15
Micronesian: (6)	6	0.02
Guamanian/Chamorro (6)	6	0.02
Polynesian: (1)	5	0.02
Native Hawaiian	4	0.01
Other Polynesian (1)	1	0.00
Other Pac. Isl., not spec. (11)	32	0.11
Hispanic or Latino:	19,663	70.02
Central American:	1,963	6.99
Costa Rican	82	0.29
Guatemalan	80	0.28
Honduran	229	0.82
Nicaraguan	1,178	4.19
Panamanian	210	0.75
Salvadoran	121	0.43
Other Central American	63	0.22
Cuban	8,227	29.30
Dominican Republic	696	2.48
Mexican	269	0.96
Puerto Rican	2,045	7.28
South American:	2,906	10.35
Argentinean	111	0.40
Bolivian	38	0.14
Chilean	129	0.46
Colombian	1,441	5.13
Ecuadorian	197	0.70
Paraguayan	5	0.02
Peruvian	506	1.80
Uruguayan	14	0.05
Venezuelan	381	1.36
Other South American	84	0.30
Other Hispanic or Latino	3,557	12.67
Hungarian	67	0.24
Irish	615	2.20
Italian	750	2.68
Lithuanian	10	0.04
Norwegian	76	0.27
Polish	247	0.88
Portuguese	59	0.21
Romanian	9	0.03
Russian	118	0.42
Scotch-Irish	70	0.25
Scottish	153	0.55
Swedish	12	0.04
Turkish	6	0.02
United States or American	1,521	5.43
Welsh	14	0.05
West Indian, excl. Hispanic:	1,635	5.84
Bahamian	21	0.07
Barbadian	9	0.03
British West Indian	57	0.20
Haitian	415	1.48
Jamaican	947	3.38
Trinidadian and Tobagonian	177	0.63
West Indian	9	0.03
White:	22,930	81.65
Not Hispanic (5,269)	5,476	19.50
Hispanic (16,727)	17,454	62.15
Yugoslavian	8	0.03

Riverview

Place Type: Census Designated Place
County: Hillsborough
Population: 12,035

Ancestry/Race	Number	%
African American/Black:	1,081	8.98
Not Hispanic (958)	1,014	8.43
Hispanic (44)	67	0.56
African, sub-Saharan:	77	0.64
African	62	0.52
Sierra Leonean	15	0.12
Am. Ind. or Alaska Nat., not spec.	51	0.42
Albanian	10	0.08
American Indian tribes, specified:	86	0.71
Apache	3	0.02
Blackfeet	1	0.01
Cherokee (9)	35	0.29
Chickasaw	1	0.01
Chippewa (1)	3	0.02
Comanche	3	0.02
Creek (3)	4	0.03
Crow	2	0.02
Iroquois (2)	3	0.02
Latin American Indians (1)	1	0.01
Pueblo	3	0.02
Seminole (3)	7	0.06
Sioux (6)	7	0.06
Yakama	1	0.01
All other tribes (4)	12	0.10
American Indian tribes, not spec.	7	0.06

Notes: 1. Figures in the "Number" column do not add up to the total population due to: a) Ancestry/Race overlap — e.g. persons can report being both White and Irish, b) persons of Hispanic origin can report being any race, c) persons reporting two ancestries are counted in both categories. 2. Numbers in parentheses indicate the number of persons reporting this ancestry/race alone, not in combination with any other ancestry/race. 3. Refer to the User's Guide in the front of the book for more detailed information.

Arab:	47	0.39
Lebanese	47	0.39
Armenian	9	0.07
Asian:	228	1.89
Chinese, ex. Taiwanese (30)	34	0.28
Filipino (42)	53	0.44
Hmong (4)	6	0.05
Indian (22)	32	0.27
Japanese (5)	14	0.12
Korean (23)	34	0.28
Taiwanese (1)	1	0.01
Thai (3)	9	0.07
Vietnamese (17)	22	0.18
Other Asian, specified (2)	2	0.02
Other Asian, not specified (9)	21	0.17
Austrian	16	0.13
Belgian	8	0.07
British	55	0.46
Canadian	17	0.14
Croatian	15	0.12
Czechoslovakian	17	0.14
Danish	62	0.52
Dutch	243	2.02
Eastern European	8	0.07
English	1,327	11.06
Estonian	11	0.09
European	86	0.72
Finnish	42	0.35
French, except Basque	480	4.00
French Canadian	123	1.02
German	2,149	17.90
Greek	20	0.17
Guyanese	33	0.27
Hawaii Native/Pacific Islander:	19	0.16
Micronesian:	1	0.01
Guamanian/Chamorro	1	0.01
Polynesian: (5)	7	0.06
Native Hawaiian (5)	7	0.06
Other Pac. Isl., not spec. (3)	11	0.09
Hispanic or Latino:	1,085	9.02
Central American:	58	0.48
Costa Rican	2	0.02
Guatemalan	13	0.11
Honduran	5	0.04
Nicaraguan	1	0.01
Panamanian	32	0.27
Salvadoran	5	0.04
Cuban	130	1.08
Dominican Republic	10	0.08
Mexican	165	1.37
Puerto Rican	427	3.55
South American:	36	0.30
Argentinean	4	0.03
Chilean	1	0.01
Colombian	11	0.09
Ecuadorian	2	0.02
Venezuelan	15	0.12
Other South American	3	0.02
Other Hispanic or Latino	259	2.15
Hungarian	19	0.16
Irish	1,317	10.97
Italian	685	5.71
New Zealander	10	0.08
Northern European	21	0.17
Norwegian	79	0.66
Pennsylvania German	23	0.19
Polish	245	2.04
Portuguese	26	0.22
Russian	46	0.38
Scandinavian	51	0.42
Scotch-Irish	231	1.92
Scottish	288	2.40
Slovak	15	0.12
Swedish	105	0.87
Swiss	7	0.06
Ukrainian	7	0.06
United States or American	1,239	10.32
Welsh	73	0.61
West Indian, excl. Hispanic:	180	1.50
Barbadian	7	0.06
Bermudan	8	0.07
British West Indian	8	0.07
Haitian	8	0.07
Jamaican	143	1.19
West Indian	6	0.05
White:	10,521	87.42
Not Hispanic (9,562)	9,709	80.67
Hispanic (765)	812	6.75
Yugoslavian	8	0.07

Riviera Beach

Place Type: City
County: Palm Beach
Population: 29,884

Ancestry/Race	Number	%
African American/Black:	20,735	69.38
Not Hispanic (20,066)	20,476	68.52
Hispanic (198)	259	0.87
African, sub-Saharan:	344	1.13
African	313	1.03
Kenyan	7	0.02
Nigerian	2	0.01
South African	8	0.03
Other sub-Saharan African	14	0.05
Alaska Native tribes, not specified	1	0.00
Am. Ind. or Alaska Nat., not spec.	64	0.21
Albanian	13	0.04
Alsatian	4	0.01
American Indian tribes, specified:	68	0.23
Blackfeet (1)	1	0.00
Cherokee (5)	23	0.08
Chickasaw	3	0.01
Choctaw	1	0.00
Creek (1)	1	0.00
Iroquois (2)	2	0.01
Latin American Indians (3)	22	0.07
Paiute (1)	1	0.00
Pima (1)	2	0.01
Seminole	2	0.01
Sioux (1)	3	0.01
All other tribes (3)	7	0.02
American Indian tribes, not spec.	11	0.04
Arab:	68	0.22
Egyptian	8	0.03
Lebanese	39	0.13
Syrian	13	0.04
Other Arab	8	0.03
Armenian	8	0.03
Asian:	365	1.22
Bangladeshi (3)	3	0.01
Chinese, ex. Taiwanese (41)	53	0.18
Filipino (47)	53	0.18
Indian (78)	103	0.34
Japanese (8)	9	0.03
Korean (38)	41	0.14
Pakistani (2)	2	0.01
Taiwanese (1)	1	0.00
Thai (12)	14	0.05
Vietnamese (58)	63	0.21
Other Asian, specified	8	0.03
Other Asian, not specified (6)	15	0.05
Austrian	73	0.24
Basque	13	0.04
British	44	0.14
Bulgarian	9	0.03
Canadian	109	0.36
Croatian	3	0.01
Czech	53	0.17
Czechoslovakian	11	0.04
Danish	26	0.09
Dutch	108	0.36
Eastern European	8	0.03
English	1,244	4.09
European	48	0.16
Finnish	7	0.02
French, except Basque	374	1.23
French Canadian	142	0.47
German	1,331	4.38
Greek	80	0.26
Hawaii Native/Pacific Islander:	49	0.16
Micronesian: (8)	10	0.03
Guamanian/Chamorro (7)	9	0.03
Other Micronesian (1)	1	0.00
Polynesian: (3)	7	0.02
Native Hawaiian (3)	5	0.02
Other Polynesian	2	0.01
Other Pac. Isl., specified	8	0.03
Other Pac. Isl., not spec. (4)	24	0.08
Hispanic or Latino:	1,348	4.51
Central American:	176	0.59
Costa Rican	7	0.02
Guatemalan	98	0.33
Honduran	12	0.04
Nicaraguan	37	0.12
Panamanian	12	0.04
Salvadoran	8	0.03
Other Central American	2	0.01
Cuban	171	0.57
Dominican Republic	26	0.09
Mexican	182	0.61
Puerto Rican	341	1.14
South American:	125	0.42
Argentinean	12	0.04
Bolivian	3	0.01
Chilean	3	0.01
Colombian	61	0.20
Ecuadorian	8	0.03
Peruvian	17	0.06
Uruguayan	1	0.00
Venezuelan	9	0.03
Other South American	11	0.04
Other Hispanic or Latino	327	1.09
Hungarian	65	0.21
Iranian	21	0.07
Irish	1,150	3.78
Israeli	21	0.07
Italian	752	2.47
Lithuanian	43	0.14
Norwegian	136	0.45
Pennsylvania German	6	0.02
Polish	389	1.28
Portuguese	71	0.23
Romanian	6	0.02
Russian	200	0.66
Scotch-Irish	154	0.51
Scottish	239	0.79
Serbian	21	0.07
Slavic	18	0.06
Slovak	34	0.11
Slovene	4	0.01
Swedish	189	0.62
Swiss	30	0.10
Turkish	7	0.02
Ukrainian	48	0.16
United States or American	1,032	3.39
Welsh	94	0.31
West Indian, excl. Hispanic:	1,533	5.04
Bahamian	151	0.50
Barbadian	17	0.06
Belizean	27	0.09
British West Indian	40	0.13
Haitian	582	1.91
Jamaican	646	2.12
Trinidadian and Tobagonian	34	0.11
U.S. Virgin Islander	22	0.07
West Indian	14	0.05
White:	8,520	28.51
Not Hispanic (7,586)	7,729	25.86
Hispanic (711)	791	2.65
Yugoslavian	16	0.05

Rockledge

Place Type: City
County: Brevard
Population: 20,170

Ancestry/Race	Number	%
Acadian/Cajun	47	0.23
African American/Black:	3,073	15.24
Not Hispanic (2,928)	3,041	15.08
Hispanic (24)	32	0.16
African, sub-Saharan:	178	0.88

Notes: 1. Figures in the "Number" column do not add up to the total population due to: a) Ancestry/Race overlap — e.g. persons can report being both White and Irish, b) persons of Hispanic origin can report being any race, c) persons reporting two ancestries are counted in both categories. 2. Numbers in parentheses indicate the number of persons reporting this ancestry/race alone, not in combination with any other ancestry/race. 3. Refer to the User's Guide in the front of the book for more detailed information.

African	63	0.31
Nigerian	115	0.57
Am. Ind. or Alaska Nat., not spec.	45	0.22
Albanian	6	0.03
American Indian tribes, specified:	80	0.40
Apache (2)	4	0.02
Blackfeet (3)	4	0.02
Cherokee (17)	39	0.19
Chickasaw (1)	1	0.00
Chippewa (1)	2	0.01
Choctaw	1	0.00
Creek	2	0.01
Iroquois (3)	9	0.04
Latin American Indians (1)	3	0.01
Lumbee (1)	1	0.00
Menominee	2	0.01
Navajo (3)	4	0.02
Seminole	1	0.00
Sioux (1)	3	0.01
All other tribes (3)	4	0.02
American Indian tribes, not spec.	5	0.02
Arab:	71	0.35
Lebanese	60	0.30
Syrian	11	0.05
Asian:	450	2.23
Chinese, ex. Taiwanese (51)	70	0.35
Filipino (63)	93	0.46
Indian (94)	105	0.52
Indonesian (4)	4	0.02
Japanese (18)	39	0.19
Korean (35)	57	0.28
Pakistani (7)	7	0.03
Taiwanese (1)	1	0.00
Thai (19)	22	0.11
Vietnamese (41)	42	0.21
Other Asian, not specified (2)	10	0.05
Assyrian/Chaldean/Syriac	8	0.04
Austrian	50	0.25
Belgian	14	0.07
Brazilian	34	0.17
British	46	0.23
Canadian	20	0.10
Celtic	8	0.04
Croatian	31	0.15
Czech	136	0.68
Czechoslovakian	76	0.38
Danish	91	0.45
Dutch	376	1.87
English	2,888	14.35
European	91	0.45
Finnish	22	0.11
French, except Basque	692	3.44
French Canadian	208	1.03
German	3,358	16.69
Greek	98	0.49
Guyanese	44	0.22
Hawaii Native/Pacific Islander:	34	0.17
Polynesian: (13)	21	0.10
Native Hawaiian (6)	14	0.07
Samoan (7)	7	0.03
Other Pac. Isl., not spec. (4)	13	0.06
Hispanic or Latino:	662	3.28
Central American:	47	0.23
Costa Rican	3	0.01
Guatemalan	15	0.07
Honduran	4	0.02
Nicaraguan	2	0.01
Panamanian	22	0.11
Salvadoran	1	0.00
Cuban	79	0.39
Dominican Republic	11	0.05
Mexican	176	0.87
Puerto Rican	203	1.01
South American:	39	0.19
Argentinean	8	0.04
Chilean	3	0.01
Colombian	11	0.05
Peruvian	7	0.03
Uruguayan	2	0.01
Venezuelan	4	0.02
Other South American	4	0.02
Other Hispanic or Latino	107	0.53
Hungarian	124	0.62
Iranian	25	0.12
Irish	2,764	13.74
Italian	1,389	6.90
Lithuanian	48	0.24
Luxemburger	5	0.02
Northern European	15	0.07
Norwegian	289	1.44
Pennsylvania German	16	0.08
Polish	599	2.98
Portuguese	139	0.69
Romanian	7	0.03
Russian	141	0.70
Scandinavian	9	0.04
Scotch-Irish	522	2.59
Scottish	439	2.18
Slavic	20	0.10
Slovak	29	0.14
Swedish	371	1.84
Swiss	104	0.52
Turkish	18	0.09
Ukrainian	43	0.21
United States or American	1,590	7.90
Welsh	198	0.98
West Indian, excl. Hispanic:	72	0.36
Barbadian	10	0.05
Haitian	36	0.18
Trinidadian and Tobagonian	10	0.05
West Indian	16	0.08
White:	16,610	82.35
Not Hispanic (15,885)	16,101	79.83
Hispanic (464)	509	2.52
Yugoslavian	16	0.08

Royal Palm Beach

Place Type: Village
County: Palm Beach
Population: 21,523

Ancestry/Race	Number	%
African American/Black:	3,256	15.13
Not Hispanic (2,990)	3,162	14.69
Hispanic (69)	94	0.44
African, sub-Saharan:	150	0.70
African	49	0.23
Cape Verdean	18	0.08
Liberian	61	0.28
Nigerian	22	0.10
Alaska Native tribes, specified:	2	0.01
Eskimo (2)	2	0.01
Am. Ind. or Alaska Nat., not spec.	42	0.20
American Indian tribes, specified:	52	0.24
Apache (1)	1	0.00
Blackfeet (3)	5	0.02
Cherokee (10)	20	0.09
Chippewa (5)	5	0.02
Delaware (1)	1	0.00
Iroquois (7)	7	0.03
Latin American Indians (2)	2	0.01
Navajo	2	0.01
Pueblo	5	0.02
Sioux (1)	1	0.00
All other tribes (2)	3	0.01
American Indian tribes, not spec.	2	0.01
Arab:	93	0.43
Arab/Arabic	23	0.11
Lebanese	37	0.17
Moroccan	7	0.03
Palestinian	10	0.05
Syrian	16	0.07
Armenian	14	0.06
Asian:	702	3.26
Cambodian (2)	2	0.01
Chinese, ex. Taiwanese (79)	100	0.46
Filipino (197)	215	1.00
Indian (165)	210	0.98
Japanese (8)	19	0.09
Korean (37)	46	0.21
Laotian (1)	2	0.01
Pakistani	5	0.02
Sri Lankan (3)	3	0.01
Thai (20)	26	0.12
Vietnamese (40)	46	0.21
Other Asian, not specified (10)	28	0.13
Austrian	65	0.30
Belgian	36	0.17
Brazilian	37	0.17
British	88	0.41
Canadian	90	0.42
Celtic	8	0.04
Croatian	8	0.04
Czech	146	0.68
Czechoslovakian	14	0.06
Danish	71	0.33
Dutch	225	1.04
Eastern European	18	0.08
English	1,699	7.88
European	125	0.58
Finnish	24	0.11
French, except Basque	604	2.80
French Canadian	252	1.17
German	3,011	13.96
Greek	72	0.33
Guyanese	13	0.06
Hawaii Native/Pacific Islander:	33	0.15
Micronesian: (2)	3	0.01
Guamanian/Chamorro (1)	2	0.01
Other Micronesian (1)	1	0.00
Polynesian: (6)	14	0.07
Native Hawaiian (5)	10	0.05
Samoan (1)	4	0.02
Other Pac. Isl., not spec. (1)	16	0.07
Hispanic or Latino:	2,546	11.83
Central American:	148	0.69
Costa Rican	20	0.09
Guatemalan	26	0.12
Honduran	21	0.10
Nicaraguan	33	0.15
Panamanian	15	0.07
Salvadoran	17	0.08
Other Central American	16	0.07
Cuban	635	2.95
Dominican Republic	63	0.29
Mexican	267	1.24
Puerto Rican	684	3.18
South American:	312	1.45
Argentinean	12	0.06
Bolivian	1	0.00
Chilean	4	0.02
Colombian	168	0.78
Ecuadorian	37	0.17
Paraguayan	1	0.00
Peruvian	40	0.19
Uruguayan	5	0.02
Venezuelan	34	0.16
Other South American	10	0.05
Other Hispanic or Latino	437	2.03
Hungarian	183	0.85
Irish	2,555	11.85
Israeli	8	0.04
Italian	2,858	13.25
Latvian	25	0.12
Lithuanian	64	0.30
Maltese	5	0.02
Norwegian	127	0.59
Pennsylvania German	21	0.10
Polish	841	3.90
Portuguese	92	0.43
Romanian	56	0.26
Russian	573	2.66
Scandinavian	22	0.10
Scotch-Irish	141	0.65
Scottish	300	1.39
Slovak	81	0.38
Slovene	9	0.04
Swedish	205	0.95
Swiss	52	0.24
Turkish	21	0.10
Ukrainian	94	0.44
United States or American	1,840	8.53

Notes: 1. Figures in the "Number" column do not add up to the total population due to: a) Ancestry/Race overlap — e.g. persons can report being both White and Irish, b) persons of Hispanic origin can report being any race, c) persons reporting two ancestries are counted in both categories. 2. Numbers in parentheses indicate the number of persons reporting this ancestry/race alone, not in combination with any other ancestry/race. 3. Refer to the User's Guide in the front of the book for more detailed information.

Welsh	120	0.56
West Indian, excl. Hispanic:	1,385	6.42
Bahamian	21	0.10
Barbadian	34	0.16
British West Indian	15	0.07
Dutch West Indian	42	0.19
Haitian	180	0.83
Jamaican	970	4.50
Trinidadian and Tobagonian	81	0.38
West Indian	42	0.19
White:	17,184	79.84
Not Hispanic (14,934)	15,170	70.48
Hispanic (1,887)	2,014	9.36
Yugoslavian	25	0.12

Safety Harbor

Place Type: City
County: Pinellas
Population: 17,203

Ancestry/Race	Number	%
Acadian/Cajun	8	0.05
African American/Black:	774	4.50
Not Hispanic (698)	739	4.30
Hispanic (14)	35	0.20
Am. Ind. or Alaska Nat., not spec.	29	0.17
Albanian	27	0.16
American Indian tribes, specified:	74	0.43
Blackfeet	4	0.02
Cherokee (11)	39	0.23
Choctaw (1)	1	0.01
Comanche	1	0.01
Creek (1)	1	0.01
Delaware	1	0.01
Iroquois (3)	4	0.02
Latin American Indians (4)	4	0.02
Lumbee	1	0.01
Navajo (1)	1	0.01
Sioux (5)	12	0.07
All other tribes (4)	5	0.03
American Indian tribes, not spec.	6	0.03
Arab:	193	1.13
Arab/Arabic	40	0.23
Egyptian	19	0.11
Lebanese	85	0.50
Palestinian	8	0.05
Syrian	41	0.24
Armenian	40	0.23
Asian:	339	1.97
Bangladeshi (4)	4	0.02
Cambodian (6)	10	0.06
Chinese, ex. Taiwanese (81)	93	0.54
Filipino (54)	66	0.38
Hmong (8)	8	0.05
Indian (64)	73	0.42
Indonesian (5)	7	0.04
Japanese (8)	14	0.08
Korean (24)	25	0.15
Laotian	2	0.01
Sri Lankan (1)	1	0.01
Taiwanese (2)	3	0.02
Thai (5)	5	0.03
Vietnamese (22)	22	0.13
Other Asian, specified	1	0.01
Other Asian, not specified	5	0.03
Australian	12	0.07
Austrian	128	0.75
Belgian	16	0.09
British	159	0.93
Bulgarian	15	0.09
Canadian	89	0.52
Croatian	48	0.28
Czech	53	0.31
Czechoslovakian	12	0.07
Danish	73	0.43
Dutch	338	1.98
Eastern European	22	0.13
English	2,127	12.45
Estonian	8	0.05
European	185	1.08
Finnish	37	0.22
French, except Basque	556	3.25
French Canadian	284	1.66
German	3,302	19.32
Greek	241	1.41
Hawaii Native/Pacific Islander:	22	0.13
Micronesian: (1)	4	0.02
Guamanian/Chamorro (1)	4	0.02
Polynesian: (7)	13	0.08
Native Hawaiian (4)	10	0.06
Samoan (3)	3	0.02
Other Pac. Isl., specified	1	0.01
Other Pac. Isl., not spec.	4	0.02
Hispanic or Latino:	628	3.65
Central American:	43	0.25
Costa Rican	3	0.02
Guatemalan	5	0.03
Honduran	4	0.02
Nicaraguan	6	0.03
Panamanian	17	0.10
Salvadoran	8	0.05
Cuban	75	0.44
Dominican Republic	8	0.05
Mexican	115	0.67
Puerto Rican	169	0.98
South American:	68	0.40
Argentinean	1	0.01
Colombian	35	0.20
Ecuadorian	10	0.06
Peruvian	9	0.05
Venezuelan	8	0.05
Other South American	5	0.03
Other Hispanic or Latino	150	0.87
Hungarian	141	0.83
Iranian	7	0.04
Irish	2,774	16.23
Israeli	14	0.08
Italian	1,660	9.71
Latvian	4	0.02
Lithuanian	16	0.09
Macedonian	4	0.02
Norwegian	212	1.24
Polish	896	5.24
Portuguese	67	0.39
Romanian	19	0.11
Russian	271	1.59
Scandinavian	62	0.36
Scotch-Irish	406	2.38
Scottish	506	2.96
Slavic	23	0.13
Slovak	70	0.41
Slovene	10	0.06
Swedish	235	1.38
Swiss	104	0.61
Turkish	32	0.19
Ukrainian	104	0.61
United States or American	1,312	7.68
Welsh	127	0.74
West Indian, excl. Hispanic:	123	0.72
Barbadian	9	0.05
Haitian	26	0.15
Jamaican	49	0.29
West Indian	39	0.23
White:	16,052	93.31
Not Hispanic (15,390)	15,531	90.28
Hispanic (477)	521	3.03
Yugoslavian	48	0.28

Saint Augustine

Place Type: City
County: Saint Johns
Population: 11,592

Ancestry/Race	Number	%
Acadian/Cajun	5	0.04
African American/Black:	1,797	15.50
Not Hispanic (1,741)	1,788	15.42
Hispanic (6)	9	0.08
African, sub-Saharan:	45	0.39
African	22	0.19
Ghanian	23	0.20
Alaska Native tribes, not specified	1	0.01
Am. Ind. or Alaska Nat., not spec.	24	0.21
American Indian tribes, specified:	99	0.85
Apache (9)	9	0.08
Blackfeet	2	0.02
Cherokee (10)	57	0.49
Chippewa (2)	2	0.02
Choctaw (2)	3	0.03
Cree (2)	2	0.02
Creek (1)	3	0.03
Delaware	1	0.01
Iroquois (2)	3	0.03
Latin American Indians	1	0.01
Navajo	1	0.01
Seminole (2)	2	0.02
Shoshone (1)	1	0.01
Sioux (2)	5	0.04
All other tribes (3)	7	0.06
American Indian tribes, not spec.	5	0.04
Arab:	44	0.38
Jordanian	7	0.06
Lebanese	21	0.18
Syrian	8	0.07
Other Arab	8	0.07
Armenian	26	0.23
Asian:	121	1.04
Chinese, ex. Taiwanese (10)	10	0.09
Filipino (25)	27	0.23
Indian (30)	43	0.37
Japanese (3)	9	0.08
Korean (4)	6	0.05
Taiwanese (1)	1	0.01
Thai	1	0.01
Vietnamese (6)	9	0.08
Other Asian, specified	2	0.02
Other Asian, not specified (4)	13	0.11
Australian	17	0.15
Austrian	62	0.54
Belgian	23	0.20
British	94	0.82
Celtic	31	0.27
Croatian	6	0.05
Czech	65	0.56
Czechoslovakian	23	0.20
Danish	44	0.38
Dutch	188	1.63
English	1,571	13.65
European	101	0.88
Finnish	24	0.21
French, except Basque	503	4.37
French Canadian	152	1.32
German	1,679	14.58
Greek	81	0.70
Hawaii Native/Pacific Islander:	17	0.15
Micronesian: (4)	4	0.03
Guamanian/Chamorro (4)	4	0.03
Polynesian: (5)	5	0.04
Native Hawaiian (1)	1	0.01
Samoan (4)	4	0.03
Other Pac. Isl., specified	2	0.02
Other Pac. Isl., not spec. (2)	6	0.05
Hispanic or Latino:	361	3.11
Central American:	28	0.24
Costa Rican	2	0.02
Guatemalan	12	0.10
Honduran	7	0.06
Panamanian	6	0.05
Salvadoran	1	0.01
Cuban	37	0.32
Dominican Republic	3	0.03
Mexican	75	0.65
Puerto Rican	103	0.89
South American:	24	0.21
Argentinean	5	0.04
Bolivian	1	0.01
Chilean	3	0.03
Colombian	7	0.06
Ecuadorian	1	0.01
Peruvian	1	0.01
Venezuelan	4	0.03
Other South American	2	0.02

Notes: 1. Figures in the "Number" column do not add up to the total population due to: a) Ancestry/Race overlap — e.g. persons can report being both White and Irish, b) persons of Hispanic origin can report being any race, c) persons reporting two ancestries are counted in both categories. 2. Numbers in parentheses indicate the number of persons reporting this ancestry/race alone, not in combination with any other ancestry/race. 3. Refer to the User's Guide in the front of the book for more detailed information.

Other Hispanic or Latino	91	0.79
Hungarian	66	0.57
Irish	1,586	13.78
Italian	682	5.92
Lithuanian	35	0.30
Luxemburger	17	0.15
New Zealander	7	0.06
Norwegian	142	1.23
Pennsylvania German	19	0.17
Polish	274	2.38
Portuguese	63	0.55
Romanian	6	0.05
Russian	140	1.22
Scandinavian	47	0.41
Scotch-Irish	407	3.54
Scottish	316	2.74
Slavic	35	0.30
Slovene	8	0.07
Swedish	182	1.58
Swiss	40	0.35
Ukrainian	26	0.23
United States or American	755	6.56
Welsh	100	0.87
West Indian, excl. Hispanic:	29	0.25
Jamaican	29	0.25
White:	9,563	82.50
Not Hispanic (9,193)	9,307	80.29
Hispanic (221)	256	2.21

Saint Cloud

Place Type: City
County: Osceola
Population: 20,074

Ancestry/Race	Number	%
African American/Black:	476	2.37
Not Hispanic (319)	366	1.82
Hispanic (96)	110	0.55
African, sub-Saharan:	30	0.15
African	21	0.10
South African	9	0.04
Alaska Native tribes, specified:	1	0.00
Alaska Athabascan (1)	1	0.00
Am. Ind. or Alaska Nat., not spec.	47	0.23
American Indian tribes, specified:	150	0.75
Apache (1)	9	0.04
Blackfeet (3)	8	0.04
Cherokee (19)	68	0.34
Chickasaw	1	0.00
Chippewa (2)	4	0.02
Choctaw	1	0.00
Creek	1	0.00
Delaware (2)	2	0.01
Iroquois (4)	6	0.03
Latin American Indians (10)	12	0.06
Lumbee (3)	6	0.03
Osage	1	0.00
Pueblo (1)	1	0.00
Seminole (7)	9	0.04
Sioux (1)	3	0.01
All other tribes (11)	18	0.09
American Indian tribes, not spec.	7	0.03
Armenian	9	0.04
Asian:	278	1.38
Cambodian	1	0.00
Chinese, ex. Taiwanese (14)	24	0.12
Filipino (45)	69	0.34
Indian (51)	67	0.33
Indonesian	1	0.00
Japanese (10)	20	0.10
Korean (9)	18	0.09
Malaysian (1)	2	0.01
Pakistani (16)	23	0.11
Taiwanese (2)	2	0.01
Thai (11)	14	0.07
Vietnamese (18)	19	0.09
Other Asian, specified (1)	4	0.02
Other Asian, not specified (9)	14	0.07
Austrian	65	0.32
Belgian	40	0.20
British	146	0.73
Canadian	49	0.24
Croatian	15	0.07
Czech	126	0.63
Czechoslovakian	25	0.12
Danish	48	0.24
Dutch	489	2.43
English	2,127	10.58
European	115	0.57
Finnish	44	0.22
French, except Basque	778	3.87
French Canadian	273	1.36
German	3,466	17.24
Greek	90	0.45
Guyanese	8	0.04
Hawaii Native/Pacific Islander:	35	0.17
Micronesian: (2)	10	0.05
Guamanian/Chamorro (2)	10	0.05
Polynesian: (4)	14	0.07
Native Hawaiian (2)	11	0.05
Samoan (1)	2	0.01
Tongan (1)	1	0.00
Other Pac. Isl., specified	1	0.00
Other Pac. Isl., not spec. (8)	10	0.05
Hispanic or Latino:	2,681	13.36
Central American:	91	0.45
Costa Rican	14	0.07
Guatemalan	13	0.06
Honduran	18	0.09
Nicaraguan	5	0.02
Panamanian	16	0.08
Salvadoran	18	0.09
Other Central American	7	0.03
Cuban	152	0.76
Dominican Republic	58	0.29
Mexican	247	1.23
Puerto Rican	1,653	8.23
South American:	172	0.86
Bolivian	9	0.04
Chilean	15	0.07
Colombian	89	0.44
Ecuadorian	22	0.11
Peruvian	12	0.06
Venezuelan	21	0.10
Other South American	4	0.02
Other Hispanic or Latino	308	1.53
Hungarian	178	0.89
Irish	3,294	16.39
Italian	1,455	7.24
Lithuanian	13	0.06
Norwegian	182	0.91
Pennsylvania German	53	0.26
Polish	703	3.50
Portuguese	23	0.11
Russian	87	0.43
Scandinavian	8	0.04
Scotch-Irish	502	2.50
Scottish	395	1.97
Serbian	15	0.07
Slovak	66	0.33
Swedish	156	0.78
Swiss	27	0.13
Turkish	8	0.04
Ukrainian	44	0.22
United States or American	1,773	8.82
Welsh	236	1.17
West Indian, excl. Hispanic:	132	0.66
Haitian	24	0.12
Jamaican	69	0.34
Trinidadian and Tobagonian	9	0.04
West Indian	30	0.15
White:	18,505	92.18
Not Hispanic (16,513)	16,755	83.47
Hispanic (1,608)	1,750	8.72
Yugoslavian	39	0.19

Saint Petersburg

Place Type: City
County: Pinellas
Population: 248,232

Ancestry/Race	Number	%
Acadian/Cajun	30	0.01
African American/Black:	57,483	23.16
Not Hispanic (54,884)	56,642	22.82
Hispanic (618)	841	0.34
African, sub-Saharan:	2,394	0.97
African	2,107	0.85
Cape Verdean	5	0.00
Ethiopian	15	0.01
Ghanian	22	0.01
Kenyan	9	0.00
Liberian	5	0.00
Nigerian	136	0.05
Sierra Leonean	7	0.00
South African	55	0.02
Sudanese	5	0.00
Zimbabwean	19	0.01
Other sub-Saharan African	9	0.00
Alaska Native tribes, specified:	7	0.00
Aleut (2)	2	0.00
Eskimo (4)	5	0.00
Alaska Native tribes, not specified	6	0.00
Am. Ind. or Alaska Nat., not spec.	709	0.29
Albanian	311	0.13
Alsatian	11	0.00
American Indian tribes, specified:	1,364	0.55
Apache (17)	28	0.01
Blackfeet (16)	76	0.03
Cherokee (162)	619	0.25
Cheyenne	4	0.00
Chickasaw (3)	6	0.00
Chippewa (33)	52	0.02
Choctaw (26)	52	0.02
Colville (1)	1	0.00
Comanche (8)	12	0.00
Cree (6)	10	0.00
Creek (13)	33	0.01
Crow (1)	5	0.00
Delaware (6)	12	0.00
Houma (2)	2	0.00
Iroquois (39)	67	0.03
Kiowa	3	0.00
Latin American Indians (35)	82	0.03
Lumbee (14)	22	0.01
Navajo (7)	9	0.00
Osage (4)	11	0.00
Ottawa (1)	1	0.00
Paiute (1)	2	0.00
Potawatomi (7)	8	0.00
Pueblo (2)	8	0.00
Seminole (11)	41	0.02
Shoshone (1)	1	0.00
Sioux (21)	53	0.02
Tohono O'Odham (1)	1	0.00
Yakama (1)	1	0.00
Yuman (1)	1	0.00
All other tribes (68)	141	0.06
American Indian tribes, not spec.	103	0.04
Arab:	1,229	0.50
Arab/Arabic	172	0.07
Egyptian	55	0.02
Iraqi	34	0.01
Lebanese	565	0.23
Moroccan	87	0.04
Palestinian	127	0.05
Syrian	153	0.06
Other Arab	36	0.01
Armenian	146	0.06
Asian:	8,101	3.26
Bangladeshi (9)	25	0.01
Cambodian (437)	538	0.22
Chinese, ex. Taiwanese (531)	723	0.29
Filipino (798)	1,030	0.41
Hmong (1)	1	0.00
Indian (867)	1,067	0.43

Notes: 1. Figures in the "Number" column do not add up to the total population due to: a) Ancestry/Race overlap — e.g. persons can report being both White and Irish, b) persons of Hispanic origin can report being any race, c) persons reporting two ancestries are counted in both categories. 2. Numbers in parentheses indicate the number of persons reporting this ancestry/race alone, not in combination with any other ancestry/race. 3. Refer to the User's Guide in the front of the book for more detailed information.

Indonesian (28)	40	0.02
Japanese (151)	296	0.12
Korean (317)	393	0.16
Laotian (1,052)	1,178	0.47
Malaysian (10)	12	0.00
Pakistani (27)	36	0.01
Sri Lankan (3)	4	0.00
Taiwanese (13)	18	0.01
Thai (132)	191	0.08
Vietnamese (1,910)	2,108	0.85
Other Asian, specified (5)	34	0.01
Other Asian, not specified (181)	407	0.16
Assyrian/Chaldean/Syriac	7	0.00
Australian	84	0.03
Austrian	931	0.38
Basque	42	0.02
Belgian	269	0.11
Brazilian	134	0.05
British	1,607	0.65
Bulgarian	268	0.11
Canadian	963	0.39
Celtic	41	0.02
Croatian	284	0.11
Czech	990	0.40
Czechoslovakian	493	0.20
Danish	906	0.37
Dutch	4,000	1.61
Eastern European	129	0.05
English	27,556	11.12
Estonian	16	0.01
European	1,372	0.55
Finnish	407	0.16
French, except Basque	9,438	3.81
French Canadian	2,528	1.02
German	36,327	14.66
Greek	1,436	0.58
Guyanese	161	0.06
Hawaii Native/Pacific Islander:	369	0.15
Melanesian: (6)	10	0.00
Fijian (6)	10	0.00
Micronesian: (14)	32	0.01
Guamanian/Chamorro (13)	30	0.01
Other Micronesian (1)	2	0.00
Polynesian: (78)	155	0.06
Native Hawaiian (27)	71	0.03
Samoan (13)	28	0.01
Tongan (23)	33	0.01
Other Polynesian (15)	23	0.01
Other Pac. Isl., specified	26	0.01
Other Pac. Isl., not spec. (27)	146	0.06
Hispanic or Latino:	10,502	4.23
Central American:	462	0.19
Costa Rican	88	0.04
Guatemalan	76	0.03
Honduran	72	0.03
Nicaraguan	54	0.02
Panamanian	115	0.05
Salvadoran	47	0.02
Other Central American	10	0.00
Cuban	1,560	0.63
Dominican Republic	229	0.09
Mexican	1,474	0.59
Puerto Rican	3,574	1.44
South American:	1,127	0.45
Argentinean	84	0.03
Bolivian	44	0.02
Chilean	52	0.02
Colombian	377	0.15
Ecuadorian	89	0.04
Paraguayan	3	0.00
Peruvian	137	0.06
Uruguayan	8	0.00
Venezuelan	284	0.11
Other South American	49	0.02
Other Hispanic or Latino	2,076	0.84
Hungarian	1,673	0.68
Icelander	29	0.01
Iranian	74	0.03
Irish	30,759	12.41
Israeli	63	0.03
Italian	16,736	6.75
Latvian	350	0.14
Lithuanian	873	0.35
Macedonian	23	0.01
Maltese	11	0.00
New Zealander	43	0.02
Northern European	111	0.04
Norwegian	2,489	1.00
Pennsylvania German	35	0.01
Polish	7,542	3.04
Portuguese	882	0.36
Romanian	273	0.11
Russian	2,236	0.90
Scandinavian	210	0.08
Scotch-Irish	4,625	1.87
Scottish	6,317	2.55
Serbian	206	0.08
Slavic	116	0.05
Slovak	530	0.21
Slovene	92	0.04
Swedish	3,150	1.27
Swiss	615	0.25
Turkish	129	0.05
Ukrainian	943	0.38
United States or American	14,062	5.67
Welsh	1,985	0.80
West Indian, excl. Hispanic:	3,261	1.32
Bahamian	49	0.02
Barbadian	240	0.10
Belizean	44	0.02
Bermudan	15	0.01
British West Indian	113	0.05
Haitian	339	0.14
Jamaican	1,649	0.67
Trinidadian and Tobagonian	273	0.11
U.S. Virgin Islander	197	0.08
West Indian	268	0.11
Other West Indian	74	0.03
White:	181,278	73.03
Not Hispanic (170,396)	173,878	70.05
Hispanic (6,737)	7,400	2.98
Yugoslavian	1,459	0.59

San Carlos Park

Place Type: Census Designated Place
County: Lee
Population: 16,317

Ancestry/Race	Number	%
Acadian/Cajun	15	0.09
African American/Black:	257	1.58
Not Hispanic (173)	221	1.35
Hispanic (32)	36	0.22
African, sub-Saharan:	4	0.02
African	4	0.02
Am. Ind. or Alaska Nat., not spec.	42	0.26
Albanian	17	0.11
American Indian tribes, specified:	90	0.55
Apache	3	0.02
Blackfeet	3	0.02
Cherokee (15)	38	0.23
Chickasaw (4)	4	0.02
Chippewa (1)	3	0.02
Choctaw (4)	5	0.03
Comanche	1	0.01
Cree	1	0.01
Iroquois (2)	2	0.01
Latin American Indians (2)	2	0.01
Menominee	1	0.01
Navajo	2	0.01
Potawatomi (1)	2	0.01
Pueblo	1	0.01
Seminole	2	0.01
Sioux	3	0.02
All other tribes (10)	17	0.10
American Indian tribes, not spec.	3	0.02
Arab:	7	0.04
Lebanese	7	0.04
Armenian	6	0.04
Asian:	168	1.03
Chinese, ex. Taiwanese (43)	52	0.32
Filipino (35)	59	0.36
Indian (6)	7	0.04
Indonesian (1)	1	0.01
Japanese (4)	8	0.05
Korean (10)	16	0.10
Laotian (1)	1	0.01
Thai (1)	2	0.01
Vietnamese (5)	9	0.06
Other Asian, not specified (9)	13	0.08
Austrian	45	0.28
Belgian	17	0.11
Brazilian	34	0.21
British	76	0.47
Canadian	67	0.42
Croatian	22	0.14
Czech	61	0.38
Danish	40	0.25
Dutch	363	2.25
Eastern European	11	0.07
English	1,652	10.25
European	68	0.42
Finnish	44	0.27
French, except Basque	721	4.47
French Canadian	228	1.41
German	4,108	25.48
Greek	118	0.73
Hawaii Native/Pacific Islander:	14	0.09
Micronesian:	4	0.02
Guamanian/Chamorro	4	0.02
Polynesian: (1)	7	0.04
Native Hawaiian	6	0.04
Samoan (1)	1	0.01
Other Pac. Isl., not spec.	3	0.02
Hispanic or Latino:	1,329	8.14
Central American:	50	0.31
Costa Rican	6	0.04
Guatemalan	3	0.02
Honduran	16	0.10
Nicaraguan	11	0.07
Panamanian	3	0.02
Salvadoran	9	0.06
Other Central American	2	0.01
Cuban	85	0.52
Dominican Republic	14	0.09
Mexican	547	3.35
Puerto Rican	417	2.56
South American:	61	0.37
Argentinean	5	0.03
Bolivian	10	0.06
Chilean	10	0.06
Colombian	14	0.09
Ecuadorian	7	0.04
Paraguayan	1	0.01
Peruvian	4	0.02
Uruguayan	2	0.01
Venezuelan	5	0.03
Other South American	3	0.02
Other Hispanic or Latino	155	0.95
Hungarian	193	1.20
Irish	2,823	17.51
Italian	1,788	11.09
Lithuanian	54	0.33
Luxemburger	10	0.06
Norwegian	217	1.35
Pennsylvania German	38	0.24
Polish	830	5.15
Portuguese	134	0.83
Romanian	22	0.14
Russian	128	0.79
Scotch-Irish	200	1.24
Scottish	420	2.61
Serbian	6	0.04
Slavic	28	0.17
Slovak	25	0.16
Swedish	185	1.15
Swiss	27	0.17
Turkish	37	0.23
Ukrainian	67	0.42
United States or American	1,189	7.38
Welsh	176	1.09
West Indian, excl. Hispanic:	23	0.14

Notes: 1. Figures in the "Number" column do not add up to the total population due to: a) Ancestry/Race overlap — e.g. persons can report being both White and Irish, b) persons of Hispanic origin can report being any race, c) persons reporting two ancestries are counted in both categories. 2. Numbers in parentheses indicate the number of persons reporting this ancestry/race alone, not in combination with any other ancestry/race. 3. Refer to the User's Guide in the front of the book for more detailed information.

Haitian	11	0.07
Jamaican	12	0.07
White:	15,530	95.18
Not Hispanic (14,457)	14,612	89.55
Hispanic (855)	918	5.63

Sandalfoot Cove

Place Type: Census Designated Place
County: Palm Beach
Population: 16,582

Ancestry/Race	Number	%
African American/Black:	761	4.59
Not Hispanic (628)	708	4.27
Hispanic (29)	53	0.32
African, sub-Saharan:	85	0.51
South African	85	0.51
Am. Ind. or Alaska Nat., not spec.	43	0.26
Albanian	8	0.05
American Indian tribes, specified:	43	0.26
Apache	1	0.01
Blackfeet	5	0.03
Cherokee (1)	10	0.06
Chippewa	1	0.01
Choctaw	5	0.03
Delaware (1)	1	0.01
Iroquois	1	0.01
Latin American Indians (1)	5	0.03
Lumbee (1)	1	0.01
Sioux (3)	4	0.02
All other tribes (3)	9	0.05
American Indian tribes, not spec.	3	0.02
Arab:	154	0.93
Egyptian	8	0.05
Lebanese	98	0.59
Moroccan	10	0.06
Syrian	38	0.23
Armenian	17	0.10
Asian:	577	3.48
Bangladeshi (14)	22	0.13
Chinese, ex. Taiwanese (149)	168	1.01
Filipino (28)	39	0.24
Indian (119)	133	0.80
Japanese (15)	23	0.14
Korean (39)	43	0.26
Pakistani (12)	14	0.08
Sri Lankan (6)	6	0.04
Taiwanese (3)	3	0.02
Thai (16)	19	0.11
Vietnamese (74)	76	0.46
Other Asian, specified (6)	6	0.04
Other Asian, not specified (7)	25	0.15
Austrian	210	1.27
Belgian	13	0.08
Brazilian	340	2.05
British	58	0.35
Canadian	56	0.34
Celtic	11	0.07
Croatian	10	0.06
Czech	54	0.33
Czechoslovakian	58	0.35
Danish	21	0.13
Dutch	74	0.45
Eastern European	129	0.78
English	999	6.02
European	134	0.81
Finnish	18	0.11
French, except Basque	497	3.00
French Canadian	61	0.37
German	1,769	10.66
Greek	171	1.03
Hawaii Native/Pacific Islander:	22	0.13
Melanesian: (1)	1	0.01
Fijian (1)	1	0.01
Micronesian: (2)	3	0.02
Guamanian/Chamorro (2)	2	0.01
Other Micronesian	1	0.01
Other Pac. Isl., not spec. (6)	18	0.11
Hispanic or Latino:	2,397	14.46
Central American:	117	0.71
Costa Rican	11	0.07
Guatemalan	22	0.13
Honduran	15	0.09
Nicaraguan	20	0.12
Panamanian	9	0.05
Salvadoran	26	0.16
Other Central American	14	0.08
Cuban	235	1.42
Dominican Republic	86	0.52
Mexican	195	1.18
Puerto Rican	414	2.50
South American:	729	4.40
Argentinean	49	0.30
Bolivian	1	0.01
Chilean	29	0.17
Colombian	324	1.95
Ecuadorian	98	0.59
Paraguayan	9	0.05
Peruvian	152	0.92
Uruguayan	16	0.10
Venezuelan	49	0.30
Other South American	2	0.01
Other Hispanic or Latino	621	3.75
Hungarian	154	0.93
Iranian	27	0.16
Irish	1,777	10.71
Israeli	48	0.29
Italian	2,489	15.00
Lithuanian	56	0.34
Norwegian	135	0.81
Polish	757	4.56
Portuguese	94	0.57
Romanian	75	0.45
Russian	558	3.36
Scotch-Irish	205	1.24
Scottish	254	1.53
Slovak	38	0.23
Slovene	8	0.05
Swedish	201	1.21
Swiss	11	0.07
Turkish	43	0.26
Ukrainian	77	0.46
United States or American	1,142	6.88
Welsh	95	0.57
West Indian, excl. Hispanic:	316	1.90
Bahamian	12	0.07
Barbadian	31	0.19
British West Indian	93	0.56
Haitian	18	0.11
Jamaican	91	0.55
Trinidadian and Tobagonian	11	0.07
West Indian	60	0.36
White:	14,782	89.14
Not Hispanic (12,671)	12,887	77.72
Hispanic (1,790)	1,895	11.43
Yugoslavian	12	0.07

Sanford

Place Type: City
County: Seminole
Population: 38,291

Ancestry/Race	Number	%
African American/Black:	12,686	33.13
Not Hispanic (12,167)	12,474	32.58
Hispanic (141)	212	0.55
African, sub-Saharan:	607	1.61
African	607	1.61
Am. Ind. or Alaska Nat., not spec.	139	0.36
American Indian tribes, specified:	250	0.65
Apache	2	0.01
Blackfeet (6)	17	0.04
Cherokee (30)	97	0.25
Cheyenne (1)	1	0.00
Chippewa (2)	5	0.01
Choctaw (3)	8	0.02
Cree	4	0.01
Creek (8)	12	0.03
Crow	3	0.01
Delaware	2	0.01
Iroquois (7)	18	0.05
Latin American Indians (15)	23	0.06
Lumbee	1	0.00
Menominee (1)	2	0.01
Navajo (1)	6	0.02
Ottawa (1)	2	0.01
Pueblo	1	0.00
Puget Sound Salish (1)	1	0.00
Seminole (4)	15	0.04
Sioux (5)	8	0.02
Yakama (3)	3	0.01
Yaqui	2	0.01
All other tribes (11)	17	0.04
American Indian tribes, not spec.	21	0.05
Arab:	105	0.28
Arab/Arabic	17	0.05
Lebanese	64	0.17
Moroccan	17	0.05
Syrian	7	0.02
Armenian	64	0.17
Asian:	558	1.46
Bangladeshi (1)	1	0.00
Cambodian (2)	2	0.01
Chinese, ex. Taiwanese (50)	74	0.19
Filipino (70)	98	0.26
Indian (108)	137	0.36
Indonesian (4)	7	0.02
Japanese (20)	46	0.12
Korean (10)	25	0.07
Laotian (33)	34	0.09
Malaysian (1)	1	0.00
Pakistani (9)	11	0.03
Sri Lankan (1)	2	0.01
Taiwanese (2)	2	0.01
Thai (13)	21	0.05
Vietnamese (51)	55	0.14
Other Asian, specified (4)	6	0.02
Other Asian, not specified (20)	36	0.09
Austrian	52	0.14
Belgian	8	0.02
Brazilian	11	0.03
British	123	0.33
Canadian	115	0.31
Croatian	17	0.05
Czech	40	0.11
Czechoslovakian	39	0.10
Danish	52	0.14
Dutch	391	1.04
Eastern European	10	0.03
English	3,439	9.15
European	139	0.37
Finnish	5	0.01
French, except Basque	949	2.52
French Canadian	282	0.75
German	4,032	10.72
Greek	46	0.12
Guyanese	49	0.13
Hawaii Native/Pacific Islander:	56	0.15
Micronesian: (8)	8	0.02
Guamanian/Chamorro (8)	8	0.02
Polynesian: (8)	22	0.06
Native Hawaiian (6)	15	0.04
Samoan (1)	4	0.01
Other Polynesian (1)	3	0.01
Other Pac. Isl., specified	2	0.01
Other Pac. Isl., not spec. (4)	24	0.06
Hispanic or Latino:	3,974	10.38
Central American:	192	0.50
Costa Rican	18	0.05
Guatemalan	12	0.03
Honduran	26	0.07
Nicaraguan	12	0.03
Panamanian	57	0.15
Salvadoran	49	0.13
Other Central American	18	0.05
Cuban	126	0.33
Dominican Republic	73	0.19
Mexican	868	2.27
Puerto Rican	1,974	5.16
South American:	266	0.69
Argentinean	18	0.05
Bolivian	6	0.02
Chilean	10	0.03

Notes: 1. Figures in the "Number" column do not add up to the total population due to: a) Ancestry/Race overlap — e.g. persons can report being both White and Irish, b) persons of Hispanic origin can report being any race, c) persons reporting two ancestries are counted in both categories. 2. Numbers in parentheses indicate the number of persons reporting this ancestry/race alone, not in combination with any other ancestry/race. 3. Refer to the User's Guide in the front of the book for more detailed information.

Colombian	118	0.31
Ecuadorian	39	0.10
Peruvian	28	0.07
Uruguayan	7	0.02
Venezuelan	28	0.07
Other South American	12	0.03
Other Hispanic or Latino	475	1.24
Hungarian	92	0.24
Icelander	8	0.02
Irish	3,441	9.15
Italian	1,733	4.61
Lithuanian	57	0.15
New Zealander	5	0.01
Northern European	14	0.04
Norwegian	220	0.59
Pennsylvania German	13	0.03
Polish	770	2.05
Portuguese	106	0.28
Romanian	35	0.09
Russian	206	0.55
Scandinavian	32	0.09
Scotch-Irish	487	1.30
Scottish	563	1.50
Serbian	13	0.03
Slavic	28	0.07
Slovak	26	0.07
Slovene	13	0.03
Swedish	243	0.65
Swiss	53	0.14
Ukrainian	36	0.10
United States or American	2,326	6.19
Welsh	172	0.46
West Indian, excl. Hispanic:	501	1.33
Bahamian	75	0.20
Barbadian	24	0.06
Bermudan	6	0.02
Haitian	103	0.27
Jamaican	248	0.66
Trinidadian and Tobagonian	25	0.07
U.S. Virgin Islander	8	0.02
West Indian	12	0.03
White:	23,563	61.54
Not Hispanic (20,911)	21,381	55.84
Hispanic (1,961)	2,182	5.70
Yugoslavian	9	0.02

Sarasota Springs

Place Type: Census Designated Place
County: Sarasota
Population: 15,875

Ancestry/Race	Number	%
African American/Black:	159	1.00
Not Hispanic (110)	153	0.96
Hispanic (6)	6	0.04
Am. Ind. or Alaska Nat., not spec.	32	0.20
American Indian tribes, specified:	54	0.34
Apache	2	0.01
Blackfeet (1)	1	0.01
Cherokee (5)	19	0.12
Chippewa (1)	3	0.02
Choctaw (1)	1	0.01
Iroquois (1)	4	0.03
Latin American Indians (4)	4	0.03
Lumbee (2)	3	0.02
Pueblo (2)	2	0.01
Seminole	4	0.03
Shoshone	1	0.01
Sioux (5)	6	0.04
All other tribes (2)	4	0.03
American Indian tribes, not spec.	7	0.04
Arab:	27	0.17
Iraqi	8	0.05
Lebanese	13	0.08
Palestinian	6	0.04
Armenian	44	0.28
Asian:	173	1.09
Chinese, ex. Taiwanese (20)	24	0.15
Filipino (20)	30	0.19
Indian (15)	18	0.11
Japanese (8)	18	0.11
Korean (9)	12	0.08
Laotian (1)	1	0.01
Thai (5)	11	0.07
Vietnamese (38)	43	0.27
Other Asian, specified (1)	1	0.01
Other Asian, not specified (1)	15	0.09
Austrian	81	0.51
Belgian	39	0.25
Brazilian	38	0.24
British	67	0.42
Canadian	89	0.56
Czech	100	0.63
Czechoslovakian	36	0.23
Danish	96	0.61
Dutch	262	1.65
English	2,056	12.97
European	132	0.83
Finnish	61	0.38
French, except Basque	754	4.76
French Canadian	183	1.15
German	3,520	22.21
Greek	71	0.45
Guyanese	18	0.11
Hawaii Native/Pacific Islander:	7	0.04
Micronesian:	2	0.01
Guamanian/Chamorro	2	0.01
Polynesian: (4)	4	0.03
Native Hawaiian (3)	3	0.02
Samoan (1)	1	0.01
Other Pac. Isl., not spec.	1	0.01
Hispanic or Latino:	759	4.78
Central American:	22	0.14
Guatemalan	6	0.04
Honduran	2	0.01
Nicaraguan	6	0.04
Panamanian	3	0.02
Salvadoran	4	0.03
Other Central American	1	0.01
Cuban	130	0.82
Dominican Republic	5	0.03
Mexican	263	1.66
Puerto Rican	106	0.67
South American:	107	0.67
Argentinean	7	0.04
Bolivian	4	0.03
Chilean	14	0.09
Colombian	55	0.35
Ecuadorian	1	0.01
Peruvian	17	0.11
Uruguayan	1	0.01
Venezuelan	8	0.05
Other Hispanic or Latino	126	0.79
Hungarian	194	1.22
Iranian	6	0.04
Irish	2,232	14.08
Italian	1,284	8.10
Lithuanian	27	0.17
Maltese	6	0.04
Norwegian	216	1.36
Pennsylvania German	18	0.11
Polish	624	3.94
Portuguese	105	0.66
Romanian	17	0.11
Russian	198	1.25
Scotch-Irish	353	2.23
Scottish	376	2.37
Serbian	17	0.11
Slavic	10	0.06
Slovak	97	0.61
Slovene	16	0.10
Swedish	469	2.96
Swiss	83	0.52
Ukrainian	39	0.25
United States or American	1,469	9.27
Welsh	187	1.18
White:	15,386	96.92
Not Hispanic (14,672)	14,827	93.40
Hispanic (513)	559	3.52
Yugoslavian	41	0.26

Sarasota

Place Type: City
County: Sarasota
Population: 52,715

Ancestry/Race	Number	%
African American/Black:	8,852	16.79
Not Hispanic (8,250)	8,566	16.25
Hispanic (197)	286	0.54
African, sub-Saharan:	407	0.77
African	345	0.66
Cape Verdean	10	0.02
Ethiopian	28	0.05
South African	24	0.05
Alaska Native tribes, specified:	4	0.01
Aleut	1	0.00
Eskimo	2	0.00
Tlingit-Haida (1)	1	0.00
Am. Ind. or Alaska Nat., not spec.	146	0.28
Albanian	33	0.06
Alsatian	11	0.02
American Indian tribes, specified:	322	0.61
Apache (4)	7	0.01
Blackfeet (3)	15	0.03
Cherokee (33)	121	0.23
Chippewa (7)	17	0.03
Choctaw (6)	9	0.02
Cree	3	0.01
Creek (3)	16	0.03
Crow	1	0.00
Delaware (1)	1	0.00
Iroquois (8)	14	0.03
Latin American Indians (28)	44	0.08
Lumbee (5)	5	0.01
Navajo (4)	9	0.02
Paiute	2	0.00
Potawatomi	2	0.00
Seminole (7)	11	0.02
Sioux (7)	17	0.03
Ute	1	0.00
All other tribes (13)	27	0.05
American Indian tribes, not spec.	27	0.05
Arab:	317	0.60
Arab/Arabic	12	0.02
Egyptian	16	0.03
Lebanese	96	0.18
Moroccan	128	0.24
Palestinian	39	0.07
Syrian	8	0.02
Other Arab	18	0.03
Armenian	84	0.16
Asian:	713	1.35
Bangladeshi (4)	4	0.01
Chinese, ex. Taiwanese (86)	115	0.22
Filipino (49)	76	0.14
Indian (113)	130	0.25
Indonesian (1)	4	0.01
Japanese (25)	43	0.08
Korean (30)	38	0.07
Laotian (19)	19	0.04
Malaysian (1)	2	0.00
Pakistani (3)	3	0.01
Taiwanese (1)	1	0.00
Thai (25)	30	0.06
Vietnamese (163)	184	0.35
Other Asian, specified	2	0.00
Other Asian, not specified (7)	62	0.12
Australian	55	0.10
Austrian	221	0.42
Basque	26	0.05
Belgian	59	0.11
Brazilian	69	0.13
British	328	0.62
Bulgarian	10	0.02
Canadian	204	0.39
Croatian	14	0.03
Czech	130	0.25
Czechoslovakian	81	0.15
Danish	198	0.38
Dutch	905	1.72

Notes: 1. Figures in the "Number" column do not add up to the total population due to: a) Ancestry/Race overlap — e.g. persons can report being both White and Irish, b) persons of Hispanic origin can report being any race, c) persons reporting two ancestries are counted in both categories. 2. Numbers in parentheses indicate the number of persons reporting this ancestry/race alone, not in combination with any other ancestry/race. 3. Refer to the User's Guide in the front of the book for more detailed information.

Eastern European	32	0.06
English	5,501	10.47
Estonian	8	0.02
European	304	0.58
Finnish	102	0.19
French, except Basque	1,707	3.25
French Canadian	415	0.79
German	7,341	13.97
Greek	165	0.31
Hawaii Native/Pacific Islander:	72	0.14
Melanesian: (1)	1	0.00
Fijian (1)	1	0.00
Micronesian: (11)	15	0.03
Guamanian/Chamorro (7)	10	0.02
Other Micronesian (4)	5	0.01
Polynesian: (14)	42	0.08
Native Hawaiian (12)	29	0.06
Samoan (2)	9	0.02
Tongan	3	0.01
Other Polynesian	1	0.00
Other Pac. Isl., not spec.	14	0.03
Hispanic or Latino:	6,283	11.92
Central American:	223	0.42
Costa Rican	18	0.03
Guatemalan	27	0.05
Honduran	73	0.14
Nicaraguan	45	0.09
Panamanian	29	0.06
Salvadoran	26	0.05
Other Central American	5	0.01
Cuban	656	1.24
Dominican Republic	69	0.13
Mexican	3,587	6.80
Puerto Rican	572	1.09
South American:	417	0.79
Argentinean	42	0.08
Bolivian	4	0.01
Chilean	10	0.02
Colombian	181	0.34
Ecuadorian	18	0.03
Paraguayan	3	0.01
Peruvian	102	0.19
Uruguayan	2	0.00
Venezuelan	50	0.09
Other South American	5	0.01
Other Hispanic or Latino	759	1.44
Hungarian	506	0.96
Icelander	10	0.02
Iranian	8	0.02
Irish	5,496	10.46
Israeli	6	0.01
Italian	2,923	5.56
Latvian	28	0.05
Lithuanian	158	0.30
Luxemburger	9	0.02
New Zealander	7	0.01
Norwegian	490	0.93
Pennsylvania German	72	0.14
Polish	1,550	2.95
Portuguese	55	0.10
Romanian	103	0.20
Russian	679	1.29
Scandinavian	126	0.24
Scotch-Irish	857	1.63
Scottish	1,208	2.30
Serbian	58	0.11
Slavic	27	0.05
Slovak	149	0.28
Slovene	15	0.03
Swedish	861	1.64
Swiss	280	0.53
Ukrainian	192	0.37
United States or American	3,256	6.20
Welsh	362	0.69
West Indian, excl. Hispanic:	347	0.66
Barbadian	7	0.01
Belizean	11	0.02
British West Indian	6	0.01
Haitian	89	0.17
Jamaican	181	0.34
Trinidadian and Tobagonian	6	0.01
U.S. Virgin Islander	14	0.03
West Indian	33	0.06
White:	41,325	78.39
Not Hispanic (36,786)	37,256	70.67
Hispanic (3,756)	4,069	7.72
Yugoslavian	49	0.09

Scott Lake

Place Type: Census Designated Place
County: Miami-Dade
Population: 14,401

Ancestry/Race	Number	%
African American/Black:	13,445	93.36
Not Hispanic (12,916)	13,177	91.50
Hispanic (217)	268	1.86
African, sub-Saharan:	189	1.31
African	158	1.10
Nigerian	31	0.22
Am. Ind. or Alaska Nat., not spec.	33	0.23
American Indian tribes, specified:	27	0.19
Apache (1)	1	0.01
Blackfeet (2)	5	0.03
Cherokee (1)	9	0.06
Chippewa	1	0.01
Latin American Indians (2)	2	0.01
Seminole	3	0.02
Sioux	2	0.01
All other tribes (1)	4	0.03
Arab:	18	0.13
Egyptian	7	0.05
Lebanese	11	0.08
Asian:	94	0.65
Chinese, ex. Taiwanese (21)	36	0.25
Filipino (9)	13	0.09
Indian (18)	27	0.19
Japanese (1)	1	0.01
Pakistani	1	0.01
Thai (1)	1	0.01
Vietnamese	1	0.01
Other Asian, not specified (8)	14	0.10
Brazilian	10	0.07
Canadian	16	0.11
Croatian	7	0.05
English	64	0.44
European	11	0.08
Finnish	5	0.03
German	27	0.19
Greek	27	0.19
Guyanese	5	0.03
Hawaii Native/Pacific Islander:	43	0.30
Micronesian: (1)	1	0.01
Other Micronesian (1)	1	0.01
Polynesian: (1)	6	0.04
Native Hawaiian	5	0.03
Samoan (1)	1	0.01
Other Pac. Isl., not spec. (4)	36	0.25
Hispanic or Latino:	789	5.48
Central American:	129	0.90
Costa Rican	5	0.03
Guatemalan	3	0.02
Honduran	15	0.10
Nicaraguan	74	0.51
Panamanian	21	0.15
Salvadoran	3	0.02
Other Central American	8	0.06
Cuban	221	1.53
Dominican Republic	52	0.36
Mexican	21	0.15
Puerto Rican	131	0.91
South American:	57	0.40
Argentinean	1	0.01
Bolivian	6	0.04
Chilean	3	0.02
Colombian	26	0.18
Ecuadorian	8	0.06
Peruvian	10	0.07
Venezuelan	2	0.01
Other South American	1	0.01
Other Hispanic or Latino	178	1.24
Iranian	6	0.04
Irish	40	0.28
Lithuanian	13	0.09
Norwegian	18	0.13
Polish	5	0.03
Russian	6	0.04
Scotch-Irish	5	0.03
Slavic	9	0.06
United States or American	317	2.20
West Indian, excl. Hispanic:	3,269	22.72
Bahamian	223	1.55
Barbadian	8	0.06
Belizean	15	0.10
British West Indian	134	0.93
Haitian	788	5.48
Jamaican	1,870	13.00
Trinidadian and Tobagonian	104	0.72
U.S. Virgin Islander	85	0.59
West Indian	42	0.29
White:	740	5.14
Not Hispanic (287)	323	2.24
Hispanic (383)	417	2.90

Sebastian

Place Type: City
County: Indian River
Population: 16,181

Ancestry/Race	Number	%
African American/Black:	574	3.55
Not Hispanic (503)	552	3.41
Hispanic (12)	22	0.14
African, sub-Saharan:	123	0.75
African	114	0.69
South African	9	0.05
Am. Ind. or Alaska Nat., not spec.	17	0.11
American Indian tribes, specified:	59	0.36
Apache	3	0.02
Blackfeet (1)	2	0.01
Cherokee (15)	34	0.21
Chickasaw	1	0.01
Chippewa (1)	2	0.01
Choctaw	1	0.01
Delaware (2)	3	0.02
Iroquois	2	0.01
Kiowa (1)	2	0.01
Latin American Indians (1)	1	0.01
Lumbee (1)	1	0.01
Navajo	2	0.01
Osage	1	0.01
Yakama (1)	1	0.01
All other tribes (2)	3	0.02
American Indian tribes, not spec.	11	0.07
Arab:	82	0.50
Lebanese	32	0.19
Syrian	50	0.30
Armenian	11	0.07
Asian:	164	1.01
Cambodian (3)	3	0.02
Chinese, ex. Taiwanese (5)	10	0.06
Filipino (25)	36	0.22
Indian (31)	42	0.26
Indonesian (1)	2	0.01
Japanese (8)	18	0.11
Korean (9)	10	0.06
Pakistani (1)	4	0.02
Taiwanese (4)	4	0.02
Thai (1)	3	0.02
Vietnamese (26)	26	0.16
Other Asian, not specified (5)	6	0.04
Australian	10	0.06
Austrian	71	0.43
Belgian	18	0.11
Brazilian	45	0.27
British	40	0.24
Canadian	132	0.80
Croatian	11	0.07
Czech	47	0.29
Czechoslovakian	16	0.10
Danish	109	0.66
Dutch	355	2.16
English	2,254	13.70

Notes: 1. Figures in the "Number" column do not add up to the total population due to: a) Ancestry/Race overlap — e.g. persons can report being both White and Irish, b) persons of Hispanic origin can report being any race, c) persons reporting two ancestries are counted in both categories. 2. Numbers in parentheses indicate the number of persons reporting this ancestry/race alone, not in combination with any other ancestry/race. 3. Refer to the User's Guide in the front of the book for more detailed information.

European	125	0.76
Finnish	156	0.95
French, except Basque	783	4.76
French Canadian	194	1.18
German	3,252	19.77
Greek	77	0.47
Hawaii Native/Pacific Islander:	13	0.08
Micronesian:	1	0.01
Other Micronesian	1	0.01
Polynesian:	5	0.03
Native Hawaiian	5	0.03
Other Pac. Isl., not spec.	7	0.04
Hispanic or Latino:	625	3.86
Central American:	14	0.09
Costa Rican	1	0.01
Guatemalan	3	0.02
Nicaraguan	5	0.03
Panamanian	5	0.03
Cuban	64	0.40
Dominican Republic	8	0.05
Mexican	199	1.23
Puerto Rican	174	1.08
South American:	59	0.36
Argentinean	1	0.01
Colombian	45	0.28
Ecuadorian	8	0.05
Peruvian	1	0.01
Venezuelan	3	0.02
Other South American	1	0.01
Other Hispanic or Latino	107	0.66
Hungarian	77	0.47
Irish	2,457	14.94
Italian	2,249	13.67
Lithuanian	85	0.52
Norwegian	158	0.96
Pennsylvania German	17	0.10
Polish	705	4.29
Portuguese	210	1.28
Romanian	23	0.14
Russian	209	1.27
Scandinavian	21	0.13
Scotch-Irish	420	2.55
Scottish	475	2.89
Serbian	16	0.10
Slavic	17	0.10
Slovak	41	0.25
Swedish	223	1.36
Swiss	28	0.17
Ukrainian	38	0.23
United States or American	1,143	6.95
Welsh	167	1.02
West Indian, excl. Hispanic:	161	0.98
Bahamian	25	0.15
Bermudan	12	0.07
British West Indian	9	0.05
Jamaican	115	0.70
White:	15,322	94.69
Not Hispanic (14,748)	14,866	91.87
Hispanic (407)	456	2.82
Yugoslavian	8	0.05

Seminole

Place Type: City
County: Pinellas
Population: 10,890

Ancestry/Race	Number	%
African American/Black:	69	0.63
Not Hispanic (47)	61	0.56
Hispanic (5)	8	0.07
Am. Ind. or Alaska Nat., not spec.	23	0.21
Albanian	19	0.18
American Indian tribes, specified:	58	0.53
Apache	1	0.01
Blackfeet (1)	2	0.02
Cherokee (10)	26	0.24
Chippewa	2	0.02
Choctaw	1	0.01
Cree	1	0.01
Delaware	1	0.01
Iroquois (3)	7	0.06
Latin American Indians	1	0.01
Osage	1	0.01
Seminole (1)	1	0.01
Sioux (1)	3	0.03
All other tribes (9)	11	0.10
American Indian tribes, not spec.	11	0.10
Armenian	18	0.17
Asian:	109	1.00
Bangladeshi	2	0.02
Chinese, ex. Taiwanese (7)	8	0.07
Filipino (39)	45	0.41
Indian (28)	30	0.28
Japanese (2)	2	0.02
Korean (6)	8	0.07
Laotian (4)	4	0.04
Taiwanese (1)	3	0.03
Vietnamese (3)	3	0.03
Other Asian, not specified (3)	4	0.04
Austrian	37	0.34
Belgian	8	0.07
Brazilian	8	0.07
British	51	0.47
Canadian	70	0.65
Croatian	42	0.39
Czech	35	0.32
Czechoslovakian	100	0.93
Danish	85	0.79
Dutch	331	3.07
Eastern European	8	0.07
English	1,570	14.57
European	12	0.11
Finnish	13	0.12
French, except Basque	439	4.07
French Canadian	64	0.59
German	2,397	22.24
Greek	95	0.88
Guyanese	6	0.06
Hawaii Native/Pacific Islander:	4	0.04
Micronesian: (1)	1	0.01
Guamanian/Chamorro (1)	1	0.01
Polynesian: (2)	2	0.02
Native Hawaiian (1)	1	0.01
Samoan (1)	1	0.01
Other Pac. Isl., not spec.	1	0.01
Hispanic or Latino:	245	2.25
Central American:	22	0.20
Costa Rican	1	0.01
Honduran	3	0.03
Nicaraguan	5	0.05
Panamanian	5	0.05
Salvadoran	8	0.07
Cuban	19	0.17
Dominican Republic	7	0.06
Mexican	47	0.43
Puerto Rican	88	0.81
South American:	9	0.08
Argentinean	1	0.01
Bolivian	1	0.01
Colombian	6	0.06
Ecuadorian	1	0.01
Other Hispanic or Latino	53	0.49
Hungarian	166	1.54
Iranian	5	0.05
Irish	1,712	15.89
Italian	1,031	9.57
Latvian	9	0.08
Lithuanian	30	0.28
Norwegian	153	1.42
Pennsylvania German	20	0.19
Polish	394	3.66
Portuguese	38	0.35
Romanian	24	0.22
Russian	107	0.99
Scotch-Irish	288	2.67
Scottish	248	2.30
Slavic	6	0.06
Slovak	83	0.77
Slovene	7	0.06
Swedish	240	2.23
Swiss	30	0.28
Ukrainian	74	0.69
United States or American	797	7.40
Welsh	81	0.75
West Indian, excl. Hispanic:	29	0.27
Barbadian	8	0.07
British West Indian	8	0.07
Jamaican	9	0.08
Trinidadian and Tobagonian	4	0.04
White:	10,652	97.81
Not Hispanic (10,340)	10,458	96.03
Hispanic (181)	194	1.78
Yugoslavian	25	0.23

South Bradenton

Place Type: Census Designated Place
County: Manatee
Population: 21,587

Ancestry/Race	Number	%
African American/Black:	1,110	5.14
Not Hispanic (904)	1,007	4.66
Hispanic (93)	103	0.48
African, sub-Saharan:	10	0.05
African	10	0.05
Am. Ind. or Alaska Nat., not spec.	35	0.16
Albanian	12	0.06
Alsatian	10	0.05
American Indian tribes, specified:	109	0.50
Blackfeet (4)	11	0.05
Cherokee (16)	44	0.20
Chickasaw (1)	1	0.00
Chippewa (3)	4	0.02
Comanche	2	0.01
Creek (1)	2	0.01
Iroquois (2)	3	0.01
Latin American Indians (5)	5	0.02
Lumbee (1)	1	0.00
Menominee (1)	1	0.00
Navajo	3	0.01
Paiute	1	0.00
Potawatomi (1)	1	0.00
Pueblo (3)	3	0.01
Seminole	1	0.00
Sioux (3)	3	0.01
All other tribes (5)	23	0.11
American Indian tribes, not spec.	10	0.05
Arab:	64	0.30
Egyptian	7	0.03
Lebanese	24	0.11
Moroccan	11	0.05
Syrian	8	0.04
Other Arab	14	0.07
Asian:	336	1.56
Cambodian (29)	30	0.14
Chinese, ex. Taiwanese (72)	79	0.37
Filipino (38)	57	0.26
Indian (61)	74	0.34
Japanese (11)	15	0.07
Korean (18)	20	0.09
Laotian (1)	1	0.00
Pakistani	2	0.01
Taiwanese (1)	1	0.00
Thai (8)	10	0.05
Vietnamese (31)	36	0.17
Other Asian, not specified (8)	11	0.05
Australian	12	0.06
Austrian	60	0.28
Belgian	15	0.07
Brazilian	7	0.03
British	68	0.32
Canadian	71	0.33
Croatian	22	0.10
Czech	94	0.44
Czechoslovakian	50	0.23
Danish	17	0.08
Dutch	591	2.76
English	3,007	14.04
European	32	0.15
Finnish	19	0.09
French, except Basque	811	3.79
French Canadian	245	1.14

Notes: 1. Figures in the "Number" column do not add up to the total population due to: a) Ancestry/Race overlap — e.g. persons can report being both White and Irish, b) persons of Hispanic origin can report being any race, c) persons reporting two ancestries are counted in both categories. 2. Numbers in parentheses indicate the number of persons reporting this ancestry/race alone, not in combination with any other ancestry/race. 3. Refer to the User's Guide in the front of the book for more detailed information.

German	3,510	16.38
Greek	84	0.39
Hawaii Native/Pacific Islander:	31	0.14
Micronesian: (6)	6	0.03
Guamanian/Chamorro (6)	6	0.03
Polynesian: (12)	13	0.06
Native Hawaiian (6)	6	0.03
Samoan (6)	7	0.03
Other Pac. Isl., not spec. (3)	12	0.06
Hispanic or Latino:	1,870	8.66
Central American:	159	0.74
Costa Rican	6	0.03
Guatemalan	24	0.11
Honduran	84	0.39
Nicaraguan	17	0.08
Panamanian	5	0.02
Salvadoran	12	0.06
Other Central American	11	0.05
Cuban	92	0.43
Dominican Republic	21	0.10
Mexican	976	4.52
Puerto Rican	302	1.40
South American:	67	0.31
Argentinean	4	0.02
Chilean	6	0.03
Colombian	33	0.15
Ecuadorian	6	0.03
Peruvian	10	0.05
Uruguayan	5	0.02
Venezuelan	3	0.01
Other Hispanic or Latino	253	1.17
Hungarian	204	0.95
Iranian	8	0.04
Irish	2,747	12.82
Italian	1,435	6.70
Lithuanian	73	0.34
Northern European	18	0.08
Norwegian	107	0.50
Pennsylvania German	20	0.09
Polish	571	2.67
Portuguese	47	0.22
Russian	200	0.93
Scandinavian	39	0.18
Scotch-Irish	336	1.57
Scottish	519	2.42
Serbian	11	0.05
Slovak	93	0.43
Slovene	12	0.06
Swedish	330	1.54
Swiss	84	0.39
Turkish	22	0.10
Ukrainian	59	0.28
United States or American	1,718	8.02
Welsh	164	0.77
West Indian, excl. Hispanic:	96	0.45
Haitian	82	0.38
West Indian	14	0.07
White:	19,695	91.24
Not Hispanic (18,208)	18,400	85.24
Hispanic (1,202)	1,295	6.00
Yugoslavian	18	0.08

South Daytona

Place Type: City
County: Volusia
Population: 13,177

Ancestry/Race	Number	%
African American/Black:	1,104	8.38
Not Hispanic (1,021)	1,088	8.26
Hispanic (13)	16	0.12
African, sub-Saharan:	95	0.72
African	95	0.72
Am. Ind. or Alaska Nat., not spec.	15	0.11
Albanian	9	0.07
American Indian tribes, specified:	52	0.39
Blackfeet	1	0.01
Cherokee (2)	16	0.12
Chickasaw	3	0.02
Chippewa	1	0.01
Creek	3	0.02
Delaware	1	0.01
Iroquois	8	0.06
Kiowa	1	0.01
Latin American Indians (4)	4	0.03
Seminole	1	0.01
Sioux (6)	9	0.07
All other tribes (3)	4	0.03
American Indian tribes, not spec.	4	0.03
Arab:	109	0.83
Arab/Arabic	24	0.18
Lebanese	13	0.10
Palestinian	53	0.40
Syrian	19	0.14
Armenian	12	0.09
Asian:	209	1.59
Chinese, ex. Taiwanese (18)	21	0.16
Filipino (21)	42	0.32
Indian (46)	51	0.39
Indonesian (1)	3	0.02
Japanese (11)	11	0.08
Korean (19)	23	0.17
Laotian (1)	1	0.01
Sri Lankan (3)	3	0.02
Taiwanese	1	0.01
Thai (2)	4	0.03
Vietnamese (31)	36	0.27
Other Asian, not specified (6)	13	0.10
Austrian	47	0.36
Belgian	24	0.18
Brazilian	7	0.05
British	82	0.62
Canadian	102	0.78
Celtic	6	0.05
Croatian	5	0.04
Czech	53	0.40
Czechoslovakian	28	0.21
Danish	60	0.46
Dutch	214	1.63
English	1,933	14.69
European	49	0.37
Finnish	31	0.24
French, except Basque	533	4.05
French Canadian	242	1.84
German	1,906	14.49
Greek	48	0.36
Hawaii Native/Pacific Islander:	26	0.20
Melanesian:	1	0.01
Other Melanesian	1	0.01
Micronesian: (5)	13	0.10
Guamanian/Chamorro (5)	13	0.10
Polynesian: (2)	8	0.06
Native Hawaiian (2)	8	0.06
Other Pac. Isl., not spec.	4	0.03
Hispanic or Latino:	381	2.89
Central American:	7	0.05
Honduran	2	0.02
Panamanian	2	0.02
Other Central American	3	0.02
Cuban	27	0.20
Dominican Republic	5	0.04
Mexican	51	0.39
Puerto Rican	166	1.26
South American:	36	0.27
Argentinean	8	0.06
Bolivian	2	0.02
Colombian	13	0.10
Ecuadorian	2	0.02
Paraguayan	1	0.01
Uruguayan	4	0.03
Venezuelan	4	0.03
Other South American	2	0.02
Other Hispanic or Latino	89	0.68
Hungarian	106	0.81
Irish	2,173	16.52
Italian	970	7.37
Lithuanian	63	0.48
Northern European	5	0.04
Norwegian	88	0.67
Pennsylvania German	32	0.24
Polish	440	3.34
Portuguese	29	0.22
Romanian	7	0.05
Russian	55	0.42
Scandinavian	31	0.24
Scotch-Irish	246	1.87
Scottish	301	2.29
Slavic	6	0.05
Slovak	33	0.25
Slovene	14	0.11
Swedish	139	1.06
Swiss	51	0.39
Turkish	7	0.05
Ukrainian	76	0.58
United States or American	1,418	10.78
Welsh	79	0.60
West Indian, excl. Hispanic:	158	1.20
Bahamian	10	0.08
Belizean	13	0.10
British West Indian	12	0.09
Dutch West Indian	6	0.05
Haitian	57	0.43
Jamaican	60	0.46
White:	11,876	90.13
Not Hispanic (11,407)	11,573	87.83
Hispanic (277)	303	2.30
Yugoslavian	42	0.32

South Miami Heights

Place Type: Census Designated Place
County: Miami-Dade
Population: 33,522

Ancestry/Race	Number	%
African American/Black:	10,786	32.18
Not Hispanic (9,507)	9,910	29.56
Hispanic (656)	876	2.61
African, sub-Saharan:	76	0.23
African	50	0.15
Nigerian	26	0.08
Alaska Native tribes, specified:	1	0.00
All other tribes (1)	1	0.00
Am. Ind. or Alaska Nat., not spec.	100	0.30
American Indian tribes, specified:	79	0.24
Blackfeet	1	0.00
Cherokee (2)	28	0.08
Chippewa (1)	1	0.00
Choctaw	2	0.01
Creek (2)	2	0.01
Crow (1)	1	0.00
Latin American Indians (15)	28	0.08
Lumbee (1)	1	0.00
Osage (1)	1	0.00
Pueblo	2	0.01
Sioux	2	0.01
All other tribes (2)	10	0.03
American Indian tribes, not spec.	32	0.10
Arab:	61	0.18
Arab/Arabic	33	0.10
Lebanese	9	0.03
Palestinian	10	0.03
Syrian	9	0.03
Asian:	828	2.47
Bangladeshi	1	0.00
Chinese, ex. Taiwanese (54)	116	0.35
Filipino (65)	94	0.28
Hmong	3	0.01
Indian (406)	511	1.52
Japanese (7)	12	0.04
Korean (4)	9	0.03
Laotian (4)	4	0.01
Malaysian (2)	2	0.01
Pakistani (13)	19	0.06
Thai (13)	14	0.04
Vietnamese (16)	17	0.05
Other Asian, not specified (15)	26	0.08
Austrian	19	0.06
Brazilian	26	0.08
British	69	0.21
Canadian	7	0.02
Croatian	9	0.03
Danish	19	0.06

Notes: 1. Figures in the "Number" column do not add up to the total population due to: a) Ancestry/Race overlap — e.g. persons can report being both White and Irish, b) persons of Hispanic origin can report being any race, c) persons reporting two ancestries are counted in both categories. 2. Numbers in parentheses indicate the number of persons reporting this ancestry/race alone, not in combination with any other ancestry/race. 3. Refer to the User's Guide in the front of the book for more detailed information.

Dutch	155	0.46
English	587	1.75
European	43	0.13
Finnish	10	0.03
French, except Basque	237	0.71
French Canadian	17	0.05
German	543	1.62
Greek	29	0.09
Guyanese	337	1.00
Hawaii Native/Pacific Islander:	75	0.22
Micronesian: (1)	5	0.01
Guamanian/Chamorro	3	0.01
Other Micronesian (1)	2	0.01
Polynesian: (2)	9	0.03
Native Hawaiian (2)	6	0.02
Samoan	2	0.01
Other Polynesian	1	0.00
Other Pac. Isl., not spec. (4)	61	0.18
Hispanic or Latino:	18,829	56.17
Central American:	1,868	5.57
Costa Rican	80	0.24
Guatemalan	147	0.44
Honduran	366	1.09
Nicaraguan	936	2.79
Panamanian	98	0.29
Salvadoran	218	0.65
Other Central American	23	0.07
Cuban	8,616	25.70
Dominican Republic	851	2.54
Mexican	867	2.59
Puerto Rican	2,285	6.82
South American:	1,441	4.30
Argentinean	60	0.18
Bolivian	1	0.00
Chilean	56	0.17
Colombian	798	2.38
Ecuadorian	127	0.38
Paraguayan	4	0.01
Peruvian	243	0.72
Uruguayan	22	0.07
Venezuelan	106	0.32
Other South American	24	0.07
Other Hispanic or Latino	2,901	8.65
Hungarian	30	0.09
Iranian	44	0.13
Irish	413	1.23
Italian	355	1.06
Maltese	11	0.03
Norwegian	39	0.12
Polish	155	0.46
Portuguese	13	0.04
Russian	23	0.07
Scotch-Irish	24	0.07
Scottish	56	0.17
Swedish	23	0.07
Ukrainian	16	0.05
United States or American	1,482	4.41
Welsh	11	0.03
West Indian, excl. Hispanic:	2,956	8.80
Bahamian	124	0.37
British West Indian	133	0.40
Haitian	403	1.20
Jamaican	1,909	5.69
Trinidadian and Tobagonian	229	0.68
U.S. Virgin Islander	33	0.10
West Indian	101	0.30
Other West Indian	24	0.07
White:	19,771	58.98
Not Hispanic (3,746)	3,964	11.83
Hispanic (14,848)	15,807	47.15

South Miami

Place Type: City
County: Miami-Dade
Population: 10,741

Ancestry/Race	Number	%
Acadian/Cajun	14	0.13
African American/Black:	2,716	25.29
Not Hispanic (2,589)	2,643	24.61
Hispanic (64)	73	0.68
African, sub-Saharan:	48	0.44
African	38	0.35
South African	10	0.09
Am. Ind. or Alaska Nat., not spec.	10	0.09
Albanian	7	0.06
American Indian tribes, specified:	22	0.20
Apache	1	0.01
Cherokee	5	0.05
Comanche	1	0.01
Iroquois	1	0.01
Latin American Indians (6)	10	0.09
Pueblo (1)	1	0.01
Sioux	1	0.01
All other tribes	2	0.02
American Indian tribes, not spec.	6	0.06
Arab:	115	1.05
Arab/Arabic	9	0.08
Jordanian	9	0.08
Lebanese	38	0.35
Moroccan	24	0.22
Syrian	24	0.22
Other Arab	11	0.10
Asian:	205	1.91
Chinese, ex. Taiwanese (49)	62	0.58
Filipino (12)	14	0.13
Indian (51)	64	0.60
Indonesian (4)	4	0.04
Japanese (8)	12	0.11
Korean (3)	10	0.09
Malaysian (4)	5	0.05
Pakistani (1)	7	0.07
Sri Lankan (2)	2	0.02
Thai (7)	8	0.07
Vietnamese (4)	6	0.06
Other Asian, specified (1)	1	0.01
Other Asian, not specified (2)	10	0.09
Australian	10	0.09
Austrian	25	0.23
Basque	10	0.09
Belgian	67	0.61
Brazilian	12	0.11
British	69	0.63
Bulgarian	18	0.16
Czechoslovakian	22	0.20
Danish	28	0.26
Dutch	120	1.10
Eastern European	54	0.49
English	650	5.94
European	30	0.27
Finnish	19	0.17
French, except Basque	143	1.31
French Canadian	33	0.30
German	665	6.08
Greek	40	0.37
Hawaii Native/Pacific Islander:	15	0.14
Micronesian:	1	0.01
Guamanian/Chamorro	1	0.01
Polynesian: (3)	4	0.04
Native Hawaiian (2)	2	0.02
Samoan (1)	2	0.02
Other Pac. Isl., not spec. (1)	10	0.09
Hispanic or Latino:	3,692	34.37
Central American:	245	2.28
Costa Rican	23	0.21
Guatemalan	18	0.17
Honduran	33	0.31
Nicaraguan	112	1.04
Panamanian	29	0.27
Salvadoran	28	0.26
Other Central American	2	0.02
Cuban	2,103	19.58
Dominican Republic	64	0.60
Mexican	116	1.08
Puerto Rican	190	1.77
South American:	448	4.17
Argentinean	33	0.31
Bolivian	6	0.06
Chilean	25	0.23
Colombian	190	1.77
Ecuadorian	19	0.18
Paraguayan	5	0.05
Peruvian	75	0.70
Uruguayan	10	0.09
Venezuelan	81	0.75
Other South American	4	0.04
Other Hispanic or Latino	526	4.90
Hungarian	58	0.53
Iranian	10	0.09
Irish	712	6.51
Israeli	13	0.12
Italian	453	4.14
Latvian	15	0.14
Lithuanian	18	0.16
Norwegian	45	0.41
Polish	217	1.98
Portuguese	8	0.07
Romanian	9	0.08
Russian	244	2.23
Scotch-Irish	90	0.82
Scottish	205	1.87
Serbian	13	0.12
Swedish	80	0.73
Swiss	26	0.24
Turkish	20	0.18
United States or American	495	4.53
Welsh	44	0.40
West Indian, excl. Hispanic:	462	4.22
Bahamian	50	0.46
Haitian	67	0.61
Jamaican	312	2.85
Trinidadian and Tobagonian	3	0.03
West Indian	30	0.27
White:	7,675	71.46
Not Hispanic (4,174)	4,243	39.50
Hispanic (3,328)	3,432	31.95
Yugoslavian	21	0.19

South Venice

Place Type: Census Designated Place
County: Sarasota
Population: 13,539

Ancestry/Race	Number	%
African American/Black:	70	0.52
Not Hispanic (44)	57	0.42
Hispanic (10)	13	0.10
Alaska Native tribes, specified:	2	0.01
Eskimo	2	0.01
Am. Ind. or Alaska Nat., not spec.	30	0.22
American Indian tribes, specified:	59	0.44
Blackfeet	4	0.03
Cherokee (6)	18	0.13
Cheyenne	1	0.01
Chippewa (2)	3	0.02
Choctaw (2)	3	0.02
Comanche	1	0.01
Iroquois (5)	6	0.04
Latin American Indians	5	0.04
Lumbee (2)	2	0.01
Osage	1	0.01
Puget Sound Salish	1	0.01
Seminole	1	0.01
Sioux (3)	6	0.04
All other tribes	7	0.05
American Indian tribes, not spec.	2	0.01
Arab:	21	0.16
Lebanese	21	0.16
Asian:	91	0.67
Cambodian (7)	11	0.08
Chinese, ex. Taiwanese (13)	17	0.13
Filipino (24)	30	0.22
Indian (3)	3	0.02
Indonesian (1)	1	0.01
Japanese (2)	3	0.02
Korean (8)	13	0.10
Laotian (1)	1	0.01
Malaysian (1)	1	0.01
Vietnamese (6)	6	0.04
Other Asian, not specified (2)	5	0.04
Austrian	50	0.37
Belgian	89	0.66
British	25	0.19

Notes: 1. Figures in the "Number" column do not add up to the total population due to: a) Ancestry/Race overlap — e.g. persons can report being both White and Irish, b) persons of Hispanic origin can report being any race, c) persons reporting two ancestries are counted in both categories. 2. Numbers in parentheses indicate the number of persons reporting this ancestry/race alone, not in combination with any other ancestry/race. 3. Refer to the User's Guide in the front of the book for more detailed information.

Canadian	41	0.30
Croatian	17	0.13
Czech	40	0.30
Czechoslovakian	48	0.36
Danish	81	0.60
Dutch	306	2.26
English	2,345	17.36
European	65	0.48
Finnish	29	0.21
French, except Basque	838	6.20
French Canadian	221	1.64
German	2,807	20.78
Greek	54	0.40
Hawaii Native/Pacific Islander:	7	0.05
Polynesian: (2)	4	0.03
Native Hawaiian	2	0.01
Samoan (2)	2	0.01
Other Pac. Isl., not spec.	3	0.02
Hispanic or Latino:	236	1.74
Central American:	10	0.07
Costa Rican	3	0.02
Guatemalan	4	0.03
Honduran	1	0.01
Nicaraguan	2	0.01
Cuban	22	0.16
Dominican Republic	1	0.01
Mexican	47	0.35
Puerto Rican	63	0.47
South American:	44	0.32
Argentinean	12	0.09
Bolivian	1	0.01
Chilean	2	0.01
Colombian	11	0.08
Peruvian	12	0.09
Venezuelan	4	0.03
Other South American	2	0.01
Other Hispanic or Latino	49	0.36
Hungarian	184	1.36
Irish	2,372	17.56
Italian	1,300	9.62
Lithuanian	26	0.19
Norwegian	174	1.29
Pennsylvania German	27	0.20
Polish	697	5.16
Portuguese	26	0.19
Romanian	45	0.33
Russian	83	0.61
Scotch-Irish	278	2.06
Scottish	357	2.64
Serbian	11	0.08
Slavic	24	0.18
Slovak	22	0.16
Slovene	16	0.12
Swedish	306	2.26
Swiss	100	0.74
Turkish	8	0.06
Ukrainian	91	0.67
United States or American	1,077	7.97
Welsh	159	1.18
West Indian, excl. Hispanic:	36	0.27
Haitian	24	0.18
Trinidadian and Tobagonian	12	0.09
White:	13,319	98.38
Not Hispanic (13,066)	13,140	97.05
Hispanic (157)	179	1.32
Yugoslavian	17	0.13

Spring Hill

Place Type: Census Designated Place
County: Hernando
Population: 69,078

Ancestry/Race	Number	%
African American/Black:	2,345	3.39
Not Hispanic (1,940)	2,146	3.11
Hispanic (133)	199	0.29
African, sub-Saharan:	86	0.12
African	53	0.08
Cape Verdean	33	0.05
Alaska Native tribes, specified:	4	0.01
Alaska Athabascan (4)	4	0.01
Am. Ind. or Alaska Nat., not spec.	113	0.16
Albanian	12	0.02
Alsatian	9	0.01
American Indian tribes, specified:	285	0.41
Apache (5)	10	0.01
Blackfeet (4)	20	0.03
Cherokee (25)	119	0.17
Chickasaw	1	0.00
Chippewa (12)	16	0.02
Choctaw (6)	6	0.01
Cree (2)	2	0.00
Creek (2)	7	0.01
Delaware	2	0.00
Iroquois (9)	25	0.04
Kiowa (1)	1	0.00
Latin American Indians (9)	18	0.03
Lumbee (2)	4	0.01
Navajo (1)	2	0.00
Potawatomi (1)	2	0.00
Pueblo (4)	5	0.01
Seminole (1)	6	0.01
Sioux (11)	12	0.02
All other tribes (13)	27	0.04
American Indian tribes, not spec.	28	0.04
Arab:	418	0.60
Arab/Arabic	111	0.16
Egyptian	28	0.04
Iraqi	8	0.01
Lebanese	17	0.02
Syrian	239	0.35
Other Arab	15	0.02
Armenian	84	0.12
Asian:	722	1.05
Cambodian	2	0.00
Chinese, ex. Taiwanese (100)	145	0.21
Filipino (151)	199	0.29
Indian (164)	188	0.27
Indonesian (2)	3	0.00
Japanese (25)	40	0.06
Korean (27)	39	0.06
Laotian	3	0.00
Pakistani (1)	1	0.00
Taiwanese (1)	1	0.00
Thai (10)	19	0.03
Vietnamese (34)	44	0.06
Other Asian, specified	1	0.00
Other Asian, not specified (14)	37	0.05
Assyrian/Chaldean/Syriac	9	0.01
Austrian	319	0.46
Belgian	128	0.18
Brazilian	50	0.07
British	276	0.40
Canadian	294	0.42
Carpatho Rusyn	7	0.01
Croatian	75	0.11
Czech	294	0.42
Czechoslovakian	327	0.47
Danish	223	0.32
Dutch	1,524	2.20
Eastern European	39	0.06
English	7,629	11.03
European	96	0.14
Finnish	118	0.17
French, except Basque	2,582	3.73
French Canadian	983	1.42
German	13,617	19.68
Greek	391	0.57
Guyanese	31	0.04
Hawaii Native/Pacific Islander:	49	0.07
Micronesian: (3)	7	0.01
Guamanian/Chamorro (3)	7	0.01
Polynesian: (11)	23	0.03
Native Hawaiian (5)	16	0.02
Samoan (5)	6	0.01
Tongan (1)	1	0.00
Other Pac. Isl., specified	1	0.00
Other Pac. Isl., not spec. (1)	18	0.03
Hispanic or Latino:	4,720	6.83
Central American:	139	0.20
Costa Rican	11	0.02
Guatemalan	15	0.02
Honduran	23	0.03
Nicaraguan	9	0.01
Panamanian	43	0.06
Salvadoran	30	0.04
Other Central American	8	0.01
Cuban	276	0.40
Dominican Republic	76	0.11
Mexican	310	0.45
Puerto Rican	3,067	4.44
South American:	224	0.32
Argentinean	13	0.02
Chilean	8	0.01
Colombian	118	0.17
Ecuadorian	21	0.03
Peruvian	21	0.03
Uruguayan	3	0.00
Venezuelan	20	0.03
Other South American	20	0.03
Other Hispanic or Latino	628	0.91
Hungarian	744	1.08
Irish	11,765	17.00
Italian	12,431	17.96
Latvian	47	0.07
Lithuanian	388	0.56
Luxemburger	7	0.01
Macedonian	25	0.04
Maltese	20	0.03
Northern European	19	0.03
Norwegian	694	1.00
Pennsylvania German	132	0.19
Polish	4,108	5.94
Portuguese	410	0.59
Romanian	85	0.12
Russian	635	0.92
Scandinavian	119	0.17
Scotch-Irish	1,214	1.75
Scottish	1,232	1.78
Serbian	25	0.04
Slavic	44	0.06
Slovak	320	0.46
Slovene	72	0.10
Swedish	1,131	1.63
Swiss	182	0.26
Turkish	10	0.01
Ukrainian	444	0.64
United States or American	3,631	5.25
Welsh	520	0.75
West Indian, excl. Hispanic:	431	0.62
Belizean	7	0.01
Bermudan	9	0.01
British West Indian	2	0.00
Haitian	25	0.04
Jamaican	253	0.37
Trinidadian and Tobagonian	53	0.08
West Indian	82	0.12
White:	65,304	94.54
Not Hispanic (61,097)	61,575	89.14
Hispanic (3,494)	3,729	5.40
Yugoslavian	9	0.01

Stuart

Place Type: City
County: Martin
Population: 14,633

Ancestry/Race	Number	%
African American/Black:	1,892	12.93
Not Hispanic (1,793)	1,848	12.63
Hispanic (11)	44	0.30
African, sub-Saharan:	36	0.24
African	25	0.17
Nigerian	11	0.07
Alaska Native tribes, specified:	2	0.01
Tlingit-Haida (2)	2	0.01
Am. Ind. or Alaska Nat., not spec.	33	0.23
American Indian tribes, specified:	59	0.40
Apache	1	0.01
Blackfeet	1	0.01
Cherokee (5)	21	0.14

Notes: 1. Figures in the "Number" column do not add up to the total population due to: a) Ancestry/Race overlap — e.g. persons can report being both White and Irish, b) persons of Hispanic origin can report being any race, c) persons reporting two ancestries are counted in both categories. 2. Numbers in parentheses indicate the number of persons reporting this ancestry/race alone, not in combination with any other ancestry/race. 3. Refer to the User's Guide in the front of the book for more detailed information.

Chippewa	1	0.01
Choctaw (2)	2	0.01
Comanche	1	0.01
Creek	3	0.02
Latin American Indians (15)	25	0.17
Seminole	1	0.01
All other tribes (3)	3	0.02
American Indian tribes, not spec.	1	0.01
Asian:	129	0.88
Chinese, ex. Taiwanese (20)	25	0.17
Filipino (16)	25	0.17
Indian (20)	27	0.18
Japanese (8)	16	0.11
Korean (13)	14	0.10
Pakistani	3	0.02
Taiwanese (1)	1	0.01
Thai (1)	1	0.01
Vietnamese (11)	11	0.08
Other Asian, not specified (1)	6	0.04
Austrian	68	0.46
Basque	8	0.05
Belgian	15	0.10
British	38	0.26
Canadian	40	0.27
Czech	48	0.33
Czechoslovakian	22	0.15
Danish	70	0.48
Dutch	194	1.32
English	2,095	14.23
European	26	0.18
Finnish	12	0.08
French, except Basque	615	4.18
French Canadian	297	2.02
German	2,164	14.70
Greek	30	0.20
Hawaii Native/Pacific Islander:	24	0.16
Micronesian: (3)	12	0.08
Guamanian/Chamorro (3)	12	0.08
Polynesian: (1)	6	0.04
Native Hawaiian	3	0.02
Samoan (1)	3	0.02
Other Pac. Isl., not spec. (1)	6	0.04
Hispanic or Latino:	920	6.29
Central American:	242	1.65
Costa Rican	2	0.01
Guatemalan	186	1.27
Honduran	41	0.28
Salvadoran	9	0.06
Other Central American	4	0.03
Cuban	98	0.67
Dominican Republic	13	0.09
Mexican	181	1.24
Puerto Rican	202	1.38
South American:	52	0.36
Argentinean	5	0.03
Chilean	4	0.03
Colombian	25	0.17
Ecuadorian	2	0.01
Peruvian	7	0.05
Uruguayan	2	0.01
Venezuelan	4	0.03
Other South American	3	0.02
Other Hispanic or Latino	132	0.90
Hungarian	149	1.01
Iranian	9	0.06
Irish	2,318	15.74
Israeli	9	0.06
Italian	1,464	9.94
Latvian	14	0.10
Lithuanian	63	0.43
Norwegian	135	0.92
Pennsylvania German	9	0.06
Polish	378	2.57
Portuguese	89	0.60
Romanian	6	0.04
Russian	116	0.79
Scandinavian	77	0.52
Scotch-Irish	363	2.47
Scottish	268	1.82
Serbian	9	0.06
Slovak	27	0.18
Slovene	25	0.17
Swedish	167	1.13
Swiss	91	0.62
Turkish	6	0.04
Ukrainian	72	0.49
United States or American	815	5.53
Welsh	218	1.48
West Indian, excl. Hispanic:	120	0.81
Bahamian	35	0.24
Haitian	36	0.24
Jamaican	29	0.20
Trinidadian and Tobagonian	12	0.08
West Indian	8	0.05
White:	12,331	84.27
Not Hispanic (11,659)	11,759	80.36
Hispanic (530)	572	3.91

Sunny Isles Beach

Place Type: City
County: Miami-Dade
Population: 15,315

Ancestry/Race	Number	%
African American/Black:	344	2.25
Not Hispanic (271)	293	1.91
Hispanic (40)	51	0.33
African, sub-Saharan:	169	1.11
African	107	0.70
Ethiopian	24	0.16
South African	38	0.25
Alaska Native tribes, specified:	1	0.01
Tlingit-Haida	1	0.01
Am. Ind. or Alaska Nat., not spec.	29	0.19
Albanian	24	0.16
American Indian tribes, specified:	14	0.09
Cherokee	1	0.01
Chippewa	2	0.01
Crow (1)	1	0.01
Iroquois (1)	1	0.01
Latin American Indians (3)	6	0.04
Seminole (1)	1	0.01
All other tribes	2	0.01
American Indian tribes, not spec.	7	0.05
Arab:	380	2.49
Arab/Arabic	88	0.58
Egyptian	87	0.57
Lebanese	28	0.18
Moroccan	108	0.71
Syrian	57	0.37
Other Arab	12	0.08
Asian:	272	1.78
Chinese, ex. Taiwanese (56)	73	0.48
Filipino (30)	33	0.22
Indian (37)	42	0.27
Indonesian (8)	9	0.06
Japanese (27)	31	0.20
Korean (13)	17	0.11
Malaysian	1	0.01
Pakistani (14)	14	0.09
Taiwanese (5)	5	0.03
Thai (3)	4	0.03
Vietnamese (6)	10	0.07
Other Asian, specified (1)	5	0.03
Other Asian, not specified (3)	28	0.18
Austrian	99	0.65
Belgian	11	0.07
Brazilian	222	1.45
British	189	1.24
Bulgarian	34	0.22
Canadian	123	0.81
Czech	31	0.20
Czechoslovakian	55	0.36
Dutch	52	0.34
Eastern European	55	0.36
English	322	2.11
Estonian	25	0.16
European	143	0.94
French, except Basque	238	1.56
French Canadian	177	1.16
German	419	2.74
Greek	82	0.54
Hawaii Native/Pacific Islander:	13	0.08
Micronesian:	1	0.01
Guamanian/Chamorro	1	0.01
Polynesian:	1	0.01
Samoan	1	0.01
Other Pac. Isl., specified	3	0.02
Other Pac. Isl., not spec. (1)	8	0.05
Hispanic or Latino:	5,607	36.61
Central American:	163	1.06
Costa Rican	31	0.20
Guatemalan	23	0.15
Honduran	19	0.12
Nicaraguan	39	0.25
Panamanian	18	0.12
Salvadoran	30	0.20
Other Central American	3	0.02
Cuban	1,493	9.75
Dominican Republic	83	0.54
Mexican	135	0.88
Puerto Rican	322	2.10
South American:	2,150	14.04
Argentinean	371	2.42
Bolivian	26	0.17
Chilean	93	0.61
Colombian	930	6.07
Ecuadorian	81	0.53
Paraguayan	12	0.08
Peruvian	271	1.77
Uruguayan	29	0.19
Venezuelan	300	1.96
Other South American	37	0.24
Other Hispanic or Latino	1,261	8.23
Hungarian	124	0.81
Iranian	30	0.20
Irish	450	2.95
Israeli	260	1.70
Italian	895	5.86
Latvian	39	0.26
Lithuanian	79	0.52
Norwegian	30	0.20
Polish	770	5.04
Portuguese	68	0.45
Romanian	219	1.43
Russian	1,447	9.47
Scotch-Irish	93	0.61
Scottish	52	0.34
Swedish	39	0.26
Swiss	67	0.44
Turkish	59	0.39
Ukrainian	203	1.33
United States or American	753	4.93
Welsh	12	0.08
West Indian, excl. Hispanic:	159	1.04
British West Indian	16	0.10
Haitian	92	0.60
Jamaican	51	0.33
White:	14,383	93.91
Not Hispanic (9,010)	9,167	59.86
Hispanic (5,057)	5,216	34.06
Yugoslavian	9	0.06

Sunrise

Place Type: City
County: Broward
Population: 85,779

Ancestry/Race	Number	%
African American/Black:	18,825	21.95
Not Hispanic (17,176)	18,258	21.28
Hispanic (381)	567	0.66
African, sub-Saharan:	331	0.39
African	231	0.27
Cape Verdean	23	0.03
Nigerian	31	0.04
South African	46	0.05
Alaska Native tribes, specified:	5	0.01
Alaska Athabascan (1)	1	0.00
Aleut (1)	1	0.00
Tlingit-Haida	3	0.00
Alaska Native tribes, not specified	2	0.00

Notes: 1. Figures in the "Number" column do not add up to the total population due to: a) Ancestry/Race overlap — e.g. persons can report being both White and Irish, b) persons of Hispanic origin can report being any race, c) persons reporting two ancestries are counted in both categories. 2. Numbers in parentheses indicate the number of persons reporting this ancestry/race alone, not in combination with any other ancestry/race. 3. Refer to the User's Guide in the front of the book for more detailed information.

Am. Ind. or Alaska Nat., not spec.	133	0.16
Albanian	40	0.05
American Indian tribes, specified:	177	0.21
Apache (5)	7	0.01
Blackfeet (1)	6	0.01
Cherokee (22)	57	0.07
Chickasaw (1)	1	0.00
Chippewa (7)	8	0.01
Cree	1	0.00
Creek	5	0.01
Delaware (2)	3	0.00
Iroquois (8)	13	0.02
Latin American Indians (16)	35	0.04
Lumbee	2	0.00
Navajo	1	0.00
Pueblo (1)	4	0.00
Seminole (5)	6	0.01
Sioux (1)	4	0.00
Ute	4	0.00
All other tribes (5)	20	0.02
American Indian tribes, not spec.	18	0.02
Arab:	602	0.70
Arab/Arabic	17	0.02
Egyptian	25	0.03
Jordanian	43	0.05
Lebanese	282	0.33
Moroccan	26	0.03
Palestinian	61	0.07
Syrian	123	0.14
Other Arab	25	0.03
Armenian	77	0.09
Asian:	3,294	3.84
Bangladeshi (15)	22	0.03
Cambodian (1)	3	0.00
Chinese, ex. Taiwanese (682)	832	0.97
Filipino (323)	396	0.46
Indian (1,037)	1,217	1.42
Indonesian (9)	19	0.02
Japanese (42)	81	0.09
Korean (109)	136	0.16
Laotian (5)	5	0.01
Pakistani (147)	187	0.22
Sri Lankan (5)	5	0.01
Taiwanese (6)	8	0.01
Thai (45)	67	0.08
Vietnamese (150)	158	0.18
Other Asian, specified (1)	10	0.01
Other Asian, not specified (36)	148	0.17
Australian	12	0.01
Austrian	573	0.67
Belgian	99	0.12
Brazilian	617	0.72
British	422	0.49
Bulgarian	7	0.01
Canadian	327	0.38
Croatian	99	0.12
Czech	210	0.25
Czechoslovakian	130	0.15
Danish	119	0.14
Dutch	602	0.70
Eastern European	91	0.11
English	3,779	4.41
Estonian	19	0.02
European	344	0.40
Finnish	13	0.02
French, except Basque	1,562	1.82
French Canadian	382	0.45
German	6,357	7.42
Greek	253	0.30
Guyanese	218	0.25
Hawaii Native/Pacific Islander:	228	0.27
Micronesian: (4)	11	0.01
Guamanian/Chamorro (3)	8	0.01
Other Micronesian (1)	3	0.00
Polynesian: (17)	39	0.05
Native Hawaiian (7)	21	0.02
Samoan (10)	18	0.02
Other Pac. Isl., specified	4	0.00
Other Pac. Isl., not spec. (40)	174	0.20
Hispanic or Latino:	14,655	17.08
Central American:	784	0.91
Costa Rican	97	0.11
Guatemalan	76	0.09
Honduran	142	0.17
Nicaraguan	132	0.15
Panamanian	135	0.16
Salvadoran	158	0.18
Other Central American	44	0.05
Cuban	1,965	2.29
Dominican Republic	573	0.67
Mexican	570	0.66
Puerto Rican	3,223	3.76
South American:	4,320	5.04
Argentinean	233	0.27
Bolivian	40	0.05
Chilean	134	0.16
Colombian	2,090	2.44
Ecuadorian	392	0.46
Paraguayan	3	0.00
Peruvian	688	0.80
Uruguayan	92	0.11
Venezuelan	543	0.63
Other South American	105	0.12
Other Hispanic or Latino	3,220	3.75
Hungarian	679	0.79
Iranian	252	0.29
Irish	6,368	7.44
Israeli	434	0.51
Italian	8,815	10.29
Latvian	39	0.05
Lithuanian	252	0.29
Luxemburger	37	0.04
Macedonian	13	0.02
Maltese	25	0.03
Norwegian	287	0.34
Pennsylvania German	13	0.02
Polish	3,758	4.39
Portuguese	397	0.46
Romanian	559	0.65
Russian	3,533	4.13
Scandinavian	106	0.12
Scotch-Irish	590	0.69
Scottish	865	1.01
Slovak	169	0.20
Slovene	31	0.04
Swedish	466	0.54
Swiss	70	0.08
Turkish	140	0.16
Ukrainian	372	0.43
United States or American	5,325	6.22
Welsh	217	0.25
West Indian, excl. Hispanic:	11,027	12.88
Bahamian	227	0.27
Barbadian	74	0.09
Belizean	21	0.02
Bermudan	30	0.04
British West Indian	172	0.20
Haitian	2,524	2.95
Jamaican	6,888	8.04
Trinidadian and Tobagonian	694	0.81
U.S. Virgin Islander	47	0.05
West Indian	337	0.39
Other West Indian	13	0.02
White:	61,323	71.49
Not Hispanic (48,863)	49,791	58.05
Hispanic (10,734)	11,532	13.44
Yugoslavian	74	0.09

Sunset

Place Type: Census Designated Place
County: Miami-Dade
Population: 17,150

Ancestry/Race	Number	%
African American/Black:	317	1.85
Not Hispanic (193)	215	1.25
Hispanic (66)	102	0.59
Am. Ind. or Alaska Nat., not spec.	25	0.15
American Indian tribes, specified:	22	0.13
Blackfeet	1	0.01
Cherokee (1)	4	0.02
Chippewa	1	0.01
Creek (5)	5	0.03
Crow	1	0.01
Iroquois	2	0.01
Latin American Indians (4)	8	0.05
American Indian tribes, not spec.	6	0.03
Arab:	230	1.34
Arab/Arabic	92	0.54
Lebanese	128	0.75
Palestinian	10	0.06
Asian:	513	2.99
Chinese, ex. Taiwanese (188)	230	1.34
Filipino (31)	55	0.32
Hmong (1)	1	0.01
Indian (105)	112	0.65
Japanese (8)	24	0.14
Korean (6)	7	0.04
Laotian (7)	8	0.05
Pakistani (9)	13	0.08
Sri Lankan (4)	4	0.02
Thai (10)	11	0.06
Vietnamese (30)	36	0.21
Other Asian, not specified (8)	12	0.07
Austrian	28	0.16
Basque	6	0.04
Belgian	18	0.11
Brazilian	55	0.32
British	88	0.51
Canadian	30	0.18
Croatian	7	0.04
Czech	16	0.09
Czechoslovakian	10	0.06
Danish	13	0.08
Dutch	117	0.68
English	552	3.23
European	20	0.12
French, except Basque	199	1.16
French Canadian	6	0.04
German	795	4.65
Greek	41	0.24
Hawaii Native/Pacific Islander:	8	0.05
Polynesian:	2	0.01
Native Hawaiian	1	0.01
Samoan	1	0.01
Other Pac. Isl., not spec.	6	0.03
Hispanic or Latino:	11,952	69.69
Central American:	644	3.76
Costa Rican	25	0.15
Guatemalan	32	0.19
Honduran	96	0.56
Nicaraguan	370	2.16
Panamanian	45	0.26
Salvadoran	56	0.33
Other Central American	20	0.12
Cuban	7,989	46.58
Dominican Republic	119	0.69
Mexican	220	1.28
Puerto Rican	432	2.52
South American:	1,162	6.78
Argentinean	88	0.51
Bolivian	37	0.22
Chilean	54	0.31
Colombian	459	2.68
Ecuadorian	88	0.51
Paraguayan	1	0.01
Peruvian	248	1.45
Uruguayan	9	0.05
Venezuelan	146	0.85
Other South American	32	0.19
Other Hispanic or Latino	1,386	8.08
Hungarian	145	0.85
Iranian	53	0.31
Irish	599	3.50
Italian	644	3.76
Latvian	4	0.02
Lithuanian	28	0.16
Norwegian	6	0.04
Polish	136	0.79
Romanian	22	0.13
Russian	171	1.00
Scotch-Irish	80	0.47
Scottish	182	1.06

Notes: 1. Figures in the "Number" column do not add up to the total population due to: a) Ancestry/Race overlap — e.g. persons can report being both White and Irish, b) persons of Hispanic origin can report being any race, c) persons reporting two ancestries are counted in both categories. 2. Numbers in parentheses indicate the number of persons reporting this ancestry/race alone, not in combination with any other ancestry/race. 3. Refer to the User's Guide in the front of the book for more detailed information.

Slovak	7	0.04
Swedish	47	0.27
Swiss	5	0.03
Turkish	6	0.04
Ukrainian	5	0.03
United States or American	588	3.44
Welsh	7	0.04
West Indian, excl. Hispanic:	102	0.60
Bahamian	4	0.02
Haitian	75	0.44
Jamaican	23	0.13
White:	15,991	93.24
Not Hispanic (4,468)	4,564	26.61
Hispanic (11,179)	11,427	66.63

Sweetwater

Place Type: City
County: Miami-Dade
Population: 14,226

Ancestry/Race	Number	%
African American/Black:	156	1.10
Not Hispanic (14)	15	0.11
Hispanic (112)	141	0.99
African, sub-Saharan:	56	0.39
African	4	0.03
Nigerian	52	0.36
Am. Ind. or Alaska Nat., not spec.	38	0.27
American Indian tribes, specified:	11	0.08
Choctaw	1	0.01
Latin American Indians (9)	9	0.06
Osage (1)	1	0.01
American Indian tribes, not spec.	1	0.01
Arab:	29	0.20
Jordanian	24	0.17
Lebanese	5	0.04
Asian:	41	0.29
Chinese, ex. Taiwanese (13)	18	0.13
Filipino (2)	8	0.06
Indian (5)	6	0.04
Korean (1)	2	0.01
Pakistani (7)	7	0.05
Canadian	29	0.20
English	51	0.36
French, except Basque	29	0.20
French Canadian	12	0.08
German	40	0.28
Greek	16	0.11
Hawaii Native/Pacific Islander:	6	0.04
Polynesian: (2)	2	0.01
Native Hawaiian (2)	2	0.01
Other Pac. Isl., not spec.	4	0.03
Hispanic or Latino:	13,253	93.16
Central American:	2,818	19.81
Costa Rican	33	0.23
Guatemalan	49	0.34
Honduran	187	1.31
Nicaraguan	2,366	16.63
Panamanian	41	0.29
Salvadoran	74	0.52
Other Central American	68	0.48
Cuban	7,101	49.92
Dominican Republic	133	0.93
Mexican	69	0.49
Puerto Rican	286	2.01
South American:	582	4.09
Argentinean	32	0.22
Bolivian	4	0.03
Chilean	50	0.35
Colombian	244	1.72
Ecuadorian	56	0.39
Paraguayan	2	0.01
Peruvian	92	0.65
Uruguayan	5	0.04
Venezuelan	89	0.63
Other South American	8	0.06
Other Hispanic or Latino	2,264	15.91
Irish	59	0.41
Italian	71	0.50
Polish	10	0.07
Swiss	13	0.09
United States or American	330	2.31
Welsh	9	0.06
West Indian, excl. Hispanic:	14	0.10
Haitian	14	0.10
White:	12,984	91.27
Not Hispanic (884)	928	6.52
Hispanic (11,514)	12,056	84.75

Tallahassee

Place Type: City
County: Leon
Population: 150,624

Ancestry/Race	Number	%
Acadian/Cajun	70	0.05
African American/Black:	52,611	34.93
Not Hispanic (51,025)	51,926	34.47
Hispanic (544)	685	0.45
African, sub-Saharan:	2,240	1.49
African	1,726	1.15
Cape Verdean	8	0.01
Ethiopian	28	0.02
Ghanian	82	0.05
Kenyan	8	0.01
Nigerian	250	0.17
South African	18	0.01
Other sub-Saharan African	120	0.08
Alaska Native tribes, specified:	14	0.01
Aleut (4)	4	0.00
Eskimo (2)	9	0.01
All other tribes (1)	1	0.00
Am. Ind. or Alaska Nat., not spec.	333	0.22
Albanian	6	0.00
Alsatian	8	0.01
American Indian tribes, specified:	595	0.40
Apache (10)	23	0.02
Blackfeet (3)	15	0.01
Cherokee (65)	237	0.16
Cheyenne (1)	2	0.00
Chickasaw (1)	4	0.00
Chippewa (3)	7	0.00
Choctaw (6)	17	0.01
Comanche (2)	5	0.00
Cree (1)	1	0.00
Creek (58)	107	0.07
Delaware (7)	9	0.01
Houma (2)	2	0.00
Iroquois (10)	23	0.02
Kiowa (2)	2	0.00
Latin American Indians (9)	34	0.02
Lumbee (7)	8	0.01
Menominee (2)	3	0.00
Navajo (4)	7	0.00
Osage (1)	1	0.00
Ottawa (1)	1	0.00
Potawatomi (2)	2	0.00
Pueblo (2)	6	0.00
Seminole (7)	22	0.01
Sioux (5)	21	0.01
All other tribes (11)	36	0.02
American Indian tribes, not spec.	58	0.04
Arab:	651	0.43
Arab/Arabic	135	0.09
Egyptian	51	0.03
Jordanian	16	0.01
Lebanese	303	0.20
Moroccan	18	0.01
Syrian	79	0.05
Other Arab	49	0.03
Armenian	29	0.02
Asian:	4,417	2.93
Bangladeshi (9)	14	0.01
Cambodian (17)	18	0.01
Chinese, ex. Taiwanese (983)	1,118	0.74
Filipino (345)	489	0.32
Hmong (4)	4	0.00
Indian (1,010)	1,098	0.73
Indonesian (12)	14	0.01
Japanese (183)	306	0.20
Korean (446)	508	0.34
Laotian (5)	5	0.00
Malaysian (4)	8	0.01
Pakistani (46)	61	0.04
Sri Lankan (5)	7	0.00
Taiwanese (75)	106	0.07
Thai (56)	81	0.05
Vietnamese (255)	305	0.20
Other Asian, specified (3)	38	0.03
Other Asian, not specified (127)	237	0.16
Australian	86	0.06
Austrian	292	0.19
Belgian	134	0.09
Brazilian	62	0.04
British	1,136	0.75
Bulgarian	52	0.03
Canadian	347	0.23
Carpatho Rusyn	8	0.01
Celtic	125	0.08
Croatian	94	0.06
Czech	228	0.15
Czechoslovakian	140	0.09
Danish	421	0.28
Dutch	1,586	1.05
Eastern European	149	0.10
English	13,888	9.22
Estonian	7	0.00
European	1,416	0.94
Finnish	130	0.09
French, except Basque	3,382	2.25
French Canadian	660	0.44
German	14,091	9.36
Greek	772	0.51
Guyanese	116	0.08
Hawaii Native/Pacific Islander:	224	0.15
Melanesian:	1	0.00
Other Melanesian	1	0.00
Micronesian: (24)	32	0.02
Guamanian/Chamorro (21)	29	0.02
Other Micronesian (3)	3	0.00
Polynesian: (40)	91	0.06
Native Hawaiian (16)	52	0.03
Samoan (20)	32	0.02
Tongan (2)	2	0.00
Other Polynesian (2)	5	0.00
Other Pac. Isl., specified	21	0.01
Other Pac. Isl., not spec. (18)	79	0.05
Hispanic or Latino:	6,309	4.19
Central American:	437	0.29
Costa Rican	51	0.03
Guatemalan	36	0.02
Honduran	60	0.04
Nicaraguan	97	0.06
Panamanian	130	0.09
Salvadoran	45	0.03
Other Central American	18	0.01
Cuban	1,338	0.89
Dominican Republic	131	0.09
Mexican	1,102	0.73
Puerto Rican	1,302	0.86
South American:	741	0.49
Argentinean	60	0.04
Bolivian	29	0.02
Chilean	28	0.02
Colombian	365	0.24
Ecuadorian	52	0.03
Paraguayan	12	0.01
Peruvian	83	0.06
Uruguayan	8	0.01
Venezuelan	92	0.06
Other South American	12	0.01
Other Hispanic or Latino	1,258	0.84
Hungarian	503	0.33
Icelander	90	0.06
Iranian	64	0.04
Irish	13,276	8.82
Israeli	79	0.05
Italian	5,035	3.34
Latvian	39	0.03
Lithuanian	201	0.13
Luxemburger	7	0.00
Maltese	19	0.01
New Zealander	4	0.00

Notes: 1. Figures in the "Number" column do not add up to the total population due to: a) Ancestry/Race overlap — e.g. persons can report being both White and Irish, b) persons of Hispanic origin can report being any race, c) persons reporting two ancestries are counted in both categories. 2. Numbers in parentheses indicate the number of persons reporting this ancestry/race alone, not in combination with any other ancestry/race. 3. Refer to the User's Guide in the front of the book for more detailed information.

Northern European	84	0.06
Norwegian	961	0.64
Pennsylvania German	16	0.01
Polish	2,264	1.50
Portuguese	221	0.15
Romanian	181	0.12
Russian	1,128	0.75
Scandinavian	189	0.13
Scotch-Irish	3,309	2.20
Scottish	3,513	2.33
Serbian	41	0.03
Slavic	11	0.01
Slovak	217	0.14
Slovene	19	0.01
Swedish	1,110	0.74
Swiss	339	0.23
Turkish	108	0.07
Ukrainian	294	0.20
United States or American	7,976	5.30
Welsh	1,061	0.70
West Indian, excl. Hispanic:	2,340	1.55
Bahamian	187	0.12
Barbadian	32	0.02
Belizean	26	0.02
Bermudan	13	0.01
British West Indian	111	0.07
Dutch West Indian	6	0.00
Haitian	512	0.34
Jamaican	1,045	0.69
Trinidadian and Tobagonian	105	0.07
U.S. Virgin Islander	153	0.10
West Indian	132	0.09
Other West Indian	18	0.01
White:	92,887	61.67
Not Hispanic (87,047)	88,527	58.77
Hispanic (3,960)	4,360	2.89
Yugoslavian	38	0.03

Tamarac

Place Type: City
County: Broward
Population: 55,588

Ancestry/Race	Number	%
African American/Black:	6,460	11.62
Not Hispanic (5,623)	6,150	11.06
Hispanic (222)	310	0.56
African, sub-Saharan:	333	0.59
African	333	0.59
Alaska Native tribes, specified:	3	0.01
Aleut (1)	1	0.00
Eskimo	2	0.00
Am. Ind. or Alaska Nat., not spec.	88	0.16
Albanian	7	0.01
American Indian tribes, specified:	113	0.20
Apache (4)	6	0.01
Blackfeet (2)	3	0.01
Cherokee (7)	41	0.07
Chippewa (2)	4	0.01
Choctaw	1	0.00
Crow (1)	1	0.00
Iroquois (1)	7	0.01
Latin American Indians (10)	22	0.04
Lumbee	1	0.00
Ottawa (3)	3	0.01
Pueblo (2)	5	0.01
Seminole (2)	3	0.01
Sioux (3)	4	0.01
All other tribes (7)	12	0.02
American Indian tribes, not spec.	11	0.02
Arab:	222	0.40
Egyptian	43	0.08
Lebanese	108	0.19
Moroccan	19	0.03
Palestinian	19	0.03
Syrian	9	0.02
Other Arab	24	0.04
Armenian	7	0.01
Asian:	1,076	1.94
Bangladeshi (5)	5	0.01
Chinese, ex. Taiwanese (241)	303	0.55
Filipino (87)	116	0.21
Indian (293)	370	0.67
Indonesian (4)	5	0.01
Japanese (19)	30	0.05
Korean (53)	55	0.10
Pakistani (12)	31	0.06
Sri Lankan (3)	3	0.01
Taiwanese (4)	4	0.01
Thai (9)	14	0.03
Vietnamese (65)	85	0.15
Other Asian, specified	4	0.01
Other Asian, not specified (10)	51	0.09
Australian	51	0.09
Austrian	862	1.54
Basque	25	0.04
Belgian	54	0.10
Brazilian	164	0.29
British	145	0.26
Canadian	282	0.50
Croatian	17	0.03
Czech	78	0.14
Czechoslovakian	78	0.14
Danish	91	0.16
Dutch	511	0.91
Eastern European	177	0.32
English	2,706	4.83
European	305	0.54
Finnish	22	0.04
French, except Basque	1,233	2.20
French Canadian	273	0.49
German	4,326	7.71
Greek	217	0.39
Guyanese	31	0.06
Hawaii Native/Pacific Islander:	103	0.19
Micronesian: (4)	5	0.01
Guamanian/Chamorro (4)	5	0.01
Polynesian: (13)	17	0.03
Native Hawaiian (7)	10	0.02
Samoan (6)	6	0.01
Other Polynesian	1	0.00
Other Pac. Isl., specified	3	0.01
Other Pac. Isl., not spec. (3)	78	0.14
Hispanic or Latino:	8,274	14.88
Central American:	408	0.73
Costa Rican	55	0.10
Guatemalan	36	0.06
Honduran	130	0.23
Nicaraguan	53	0.10
Panamanian	55	0.10
Salvadoran	61	0.11
Other Central American	18	0.03
Cuban	790	1.42
Dominican Republic	263	0.47
Mexican	507	0.91
Puerto Rican	1,955	3.52
South American:	2,496	4.49
Argentinean	112	0.20
Bolivian	9	0.02
Chilean	51	0.09
Colombian	1,523	2.74
Ecuadorian	155	0.28
Peruvian	342	0.62
Uruguayan	32	0.06
Venezuelan	195	0.35
Other South American	77	0.14
Other Hispanic or Latino	1,855	3.34
Hungarian	725	1.29
Iranian	76	0.14
Irish	4,432	7.90
Israeli	122	0.22
Italian	6,122	10.92
Latvian	49	0.09
Lithuanian	159	0.28
Macedonian	11	0.02
Norwegian	232	0.41
Pennsylvania German	22	0.04
Polish	2,795	4.98
Portuguese	159	0.28
Romanian	452	0.81
Russian	3,431	6.12
Scotch-Irish	345	0.62
Scottish	427	0.76
Serbian	22	0.04
Slavic	10	0.02
Slovak	157	0.28
Slovene	24	0.04
Swedish	324	0.58
Swiss	123	0.22
Turkish	65	0.12
Ukrainian	293	0.52
United States or American	5,079	9.06
Welsh	110	0.20
West Indian, excl. Hispanic:	3,834	6.84
Bahamian	58	0.10
Barbadian	16	0.03
Belizean	59	0.11
British West Indian	72	0.13
Haitian	809	1.44
Jamaican	2,398	4.28
Trinidadian and Tobagonian	271	0.48
West Indian	151	0.27
White:	46,694	84.00
Not Hispanic (39,688)	40,225	72.36
Hispanic (5,937)	6,469	11.64
Yugoslavian	96	0.17

Tamiami

Place Type: Census Designated Place
County: Miami-Dade
Population: 54,788

Ancestry/Race	Number	%
African American/Black:	599	1.09
Not Hispanic (189)	209	0.38
Hispanic (297)	390	0.71
African, sub-Saharan:	62	0.11
African	24	0.04
Nigerian	31	0.06
Other sub-Saharan African	7	0.01
Am. Ind. or Alaska Nat., not spec.	47	0.09
American Indian tribes, specified:	44	0.08
Cherokee (4)	6	0.01
Choctaw	1	0.00
Iroquois	2	0.00
Latin American Indians (14)	27	0.05
Paiute	1	0.00
Sioux (1)	1	0.00
All other tribes (1)	6	0.01
American Indian tribes, not spec.	15	0.03
Arab:	425	0.78
Arab/Arabic	74	0.14
Lebanese	229	0.42
Palestinian	27	0.05
Syrian	95	0.17
Armenian	11	0.02
Asian:	415	0.76
Bangladeshi	1	0.00
Chinese, ex. Taiwanese (122)	159	0.29
Filipino (45)	46	0.08
Indian (75)	97	0.18
Indonesian (1)	1	0.00
Japanese (11)	17	0.03
Korean (8)	8	0.01
Malaysian (3)	3	0.01
Pakistani (11)	17	0.03
Taiwanese (15)	24	0.04
Vietnamese (15)	17	0.03
Other Asian, specified (1)	1	0.00
Other Asian, not specified (10)	24	0.04
Austrian	30	0.05
Basque	14	0.03
Brazilian	91	0.17
British	47	0.09
Bulgarian	15	0.03
Canadian	43	0.08
Czech	12	0.02
Czechoslovakian	7	0.01
Danish	9	0.02
Dutch	44	0.08
English	466	0.85
European	120	0.22

Notes: 1. Figures in the "Number" column do not add up to the total population due to: a) Ancestry/Race overlap — e.g. persons can report being both White and Irish, b) persons of Hispanic origin can report being any race, c) persons reporting two ancestries are counted in both categories. 2. Numbers in parentheses indicate the number of persons reporting this ancestry/race alone, not in combination with any other ancestry/race. 3. Refer to the User's Guide in the front of the book for more detailed information.

French, except Basque	397	0.73
German	475	0.87
Greek	76	0.14
Guyanese	12	0.02
Hawaii Native/Pacific Islander:	18	0.03
Micronesian: (2)	2	0.00
Guamanian/Chamorro (2)	2	0.00
Other Pac. Isl., not spec. (8)	16	0.03
Hispanic or Latino:	47,654	86.98
Central American:	3,451	6.30
Costa Rican	97	0.18
Guatemalan	122	0.22
Honduran	358	0.65
Nicaraguan	2,551	4.66
Panamanian	142	0.26
Salvadoran	86	0.16
Other Central American	95	0.17
Cuban	31,029	56.63
Dominican Republic	836	1.53
Mexican	377	0.69
Puerto Rican	1,382	2.52
South American:	4,322	7.89
Argentinean	251	0.46
Bolivian	82	0.15
Chilean	262	0.48
Colombian	2,161	3.94
Ecuadorian	322	0.59
Paraguayan	7	0.01
Peruvian	526	0.96
Uruguayan	56	0.10
Venezuelan	583	1.06
Other South American	72	0.13
Other Hispanic or Latino	6,257	11.42
Hungarian	24	0.04
Iranian	27	0.05
Irish	483	0.88
Italian	733	1.34
Polish	89	0.16
Portuguese	89	0.16
Romanian	37	0.07
Russian	99	0.18
Scotch-Irish	56	0.10
Scottish	33	0.06
Slavic	10	0.02
Swedish	49	0.09
Swiss	41	0.07
Turkish	68	0.12
Ukrainian	9	0.02
United States or American	1,052	1.92
Welsh	14	0.03
West Indian, excl. Hispanic:	93	0.17
Belizean	5	0.01
Haitian	8	0.01
Jamaican	80	0.15
White:	51,161	93.38
Not Hispanic (6,445)	6,589	12.03
Hispanic (43,174)	44,572	81.35
Yugoslavian	7	0.01

Tampa

Place Type: City
County: Hillsborough
Population: 303,447

Ancestry/Race	Number	%
Acadian/Cajun	47	0.02
African American/Black:	82,470	27.18
Not Hispanic (76,711)	79,161	26.09
Hispanic (2,407)	3,309	1.09
African, sub-Saharan:	2,718	0.90
African	2,282	0.75
Ethiopian	106	0.03
Ghanian	126	0.04
Nigerian	20	0.01
Somalian	11	0.00
South African	139	0.05
Sudanese	7	0.00
Ugandan	22	0.01
Other sub-Saharan African	5	0.00
Alaska Native tribes, specified:	22	0.01
Alaska Athabascan (5)	7	0.00
Aleut	1	0.00
Eskimo (1)	12	0.00
Tlingit-Haida	1	0.00
All other tribes (1)	1	0.00
Alaska Native tribes, not specified	8	0.00
Am. Ind. or Alaska Nat., not spec.	1,030	0.34
Albanian	65	0.02
American Indian tribes, specified:	1,559	0.51
Apache (22)	66	0.02
Blackfeet (19)	86	0.03
Cherokee (189)	651	0.21
Cheyenne (2)	4	0.00
Chickasaw (4)	9	0.00
Chippewa (18)	36	0.01
Choctaw (15)	34	0.01
Colville	1	0.00
Comanche (2)	5	0.00
Cree (6)	9	0.00
Creek (33)	56	0.02
Delaware	3	0.00
Houma	5	0.00
Iroquois (39)	77	0.03
Latin American Indians (101)	226	0.07
Lumbee (15)	18	0.01
Menominee (1)	1	0.00
Navajo (9)	18	0.01
Osage (6)	14	0.00
Ottawa (1)	1	0.00
Pima	1	0.00
Potawatomi (1)	2	0.00
Pueblo (3)	11	0.00
Puget Sound Salish (5)	6	0.00
Seminole (33)	74	0.02
Shoshone	7	0.00
Sioux (19)	44	0.01
Tohono O'Odham (1)	1	0.00
Ute (1)	1	0.00
Yaqui	2	0.00
Yuman (3)	3	0.00
All other tribes (45)	87	0.03
American Indian tribes, not spec.	172	0.06
Arab:	1,118	0.37
Arab/Arabic	333	0.11
Egyptian	81	0.03
Iraqi	10	0.00
Jordanian	10	0.00
Lebanese	315	0.10
Moroccan	84	0.03
Palestinian	43	0.01
Syrian	111	0.04
Other Arab	131	0.04
Armenian	222	0.07
Asian:	8,363	2.76
Bangladeshi (20)	29	0.01
Cambodian (13)	16	0.01
Chinese, ex. Taiwanese (678)	895	0.29
Filipino (1,025)	1,450	0.48
Hmong (1)	1	0.00
Indian (1,707)	1,955	0.64
Indonesian (19)	41	0.01
Japanese (231)	410	0.14
Korean (612)	772	0.25
Laotian (17)	22	0.01
Malaysian (2)	4	0.00
Pakistani (103)	150	0.05
Sri Lankan (12)	13	0.00
Taiwanese (46)	66	0.02
Thai (248)	376	0.12
Vietnamese (1,512)	1,677	0.55
Other Asian, specified (12)	45	0.01
Other Asian, not specified (156)	441	0.15
Australian	64	0.02
Austrian	585	0.19
Basque	76	0.03
Belgian	127	0.04
Brazilian	366	0.12
British	1,535	0.51
Bulgarian	61	0.02
Canadian	531	0.17
Celtic	111	0.04
Croatian	247	0.08
Czech	592	0.20
Czechoslovakian	308	0.10
Danish	591	0.19
Dutch	3,035	1.00
Eastern European	206	0.07
English	23,319	7.68
Estonian	7	0.00
European	1,958	0.65
Finnish	227	0.07
French, except Basque	7,198	2.37
French Canadian	1,892	0.62
German	27,990	9.22
German Russian	6	0.00
Greek	1,022	0.34
Guyanese	220	0.07
Hawaii Native/Pacific Islander:	643	0.21
Melanesian:	1	0.00
Fijian	1	0.00
Micronesian: (126)	168	0.06
Guamanian/Chamorro (45)	72	0.02
Other Micronesian (81)	96	0.03
Polynesian: (112)	189	0.06
Native Hawaiian (65)	117	0.04
Samoan (44)	64	0.02
Tongan (1)	1	0.00
Other Polynesian (2)	7	0.00
Other Pac. Isl., specified	25	0.01
Other Pac. Isl., not spec. (42)	260	0.09
Hispanic or Latino:	58,522	19.29
Central American:	2,362	0.78
Costa Rican	233	0.08
Guatemalan	225	0.07
Honduran	778	0.26
Nicaraguan	267	0.09
Panamanian	407	0.13
Salvadoran	362	0.12
Other Central American	90	0.03
Cuban	14,674	4.84
Dominican Republic	1,397	0.46
Mexican	6,272	2.07
Puerto Rican	17,527	5.78
South American:	2,791	0.92
Argentinean	117	0.04
Bolivian	64	0.02
Chilean	68	0.02
Colombian	1,401	0.46
Ecuadorian	311	0.10
Paraguayan	7	0.00
Peruvian	365	0.12
Uruguayan	10	0.00
Venezuelan	353	0.12
Other South American	95	0.03
Other Hispanic or Latino	13,499	4.45
Hungarian	1,218	0.40
Icelander	17	0.01
Iranian	122	0.04
Irish	25,499	8.40
Israeli	42	0.01
Italian	17,096	5.63
Latvian	49	0.02
Lithuanian	365	0.12
Macedonian	8	0.00
Northern European	81	0.03
Norwegian	1,786	0.59
Pennsylvania German	92	0.03
Polish	5,130	1.69
Portuguese	618	0.20
Romanian	217	0.07
Russian	2,419	0.80
Scandinavian	294	0.10
Scotch-Irish	4,497	1.48
Scottish	5,312	1.75
Serbian	85	0.03
Slavic	114	0.04
Slovak	228	0.08
Slovene	54	0.02
Swedish	2,521	0.83
Swiss	549	0.18
Turkish	208	0.07
Ukrainian	551	0.18
United States or American	18,834	6.21

Notes: 1. Figures in the "Number" column do not add up to the total population due to: a) Ancestry/Race overlap — e.g. persons can report being both White and Irish, b) persons of Hispanic origin can report being any race, c) persons reporting two ancestries are counted in both categories. 2. Numbers in parentheses indicate the number of persons reporting this ancestry/race alone, not in combination with any other ancestry/race. 3. Refer to the User's Guide in the front of the book for more detailed information.

Welsh	1,346	0.44
West Indian, excl. Hispanic:	4,748	1.56
Bahamian	252	0.08
Barbadian	99	0.03
Belizean	38	0.01
British West Indian	106	0.03
Dutch West Indian	34	0.01
Haitian	1,619	0.53
Jamaican	1,680	0.55
Trinidadian and Tobagonian	359	0.12
U.S. Virgin Islander	108	0.04
West Indian	415	0.14
Other West Indian	38	0.01
White:	201,268	66.33
Not Hispanic (154,872)	158,426	52.21
Hispanic (39,999)	42,842	14.12
Yugoslavian	345	0.11

Tarpon Springs

Place Type: City
County: Pinellas
Population: 21,003

Ancestry/Race	Number	%
African American/Black:	1,378	6.56
Not Hispanic (1,265)	1,341	6.38
Hispanic (27)	37	0.18
African, sub-Saharan:	147	0.70
African	114	0.54
South African	33	0.16
Alaska Native tribes, specified:	2	0.01
Aleut	1	0.00
Tlingit-Haida (1)	1	0.00
Am. Ind. or Alaska Nat., not spec.	28	0.13
Albanian	36	0.17
Alsatian	8	0.04
American Indian tribes, specified:	81	0.39
Apache (1)	4	0.02
Blackfeet (5)	6	0.03
Cherokee (17)	39	0.19
Chippewa (5)	6	0.03
Choctaw	2	0.01
Comanche	1	0.00
Creek (2)	2	0.01
Houma (1)	1	0.00
Iroquois (2)	3	0.01
Kiowa	1	0.00
Latin American Indians (3)	7	0.03
Lumbee	1	0.00
Navajo (1)	1	0.00
Ottawa	1	0.00
Pueblo	1	0.00
Shoshone	1	0.00
All other tribes (2)	4	0.02
American Indian tribes, not spec.	5	0.02
Arab:	126	0.60
Egyptian	54	0.26
Lebanese	61	0.29
Syrian	11	0.05
Armenian	22	0.10
Asian:	293	1.40
Chinese, ex. Taiwanese (25)	28	0.13
Filipino (28)	45	0.21
Indian (37)	48	0.23
Indonesian (3)	6	0.03
Japanese (15)	25	0.12
Korean (14)	21	0.10
Laotian (5)	14	0.07
Pakistani (2)	2	0.01
Thai (11)	20	0.10
Vietnamese (64)	70	0.33
Other Asian, specified (3)	5	0.02
Other Asian, not specified	9	0.04
Australian	7	0.03
Austrian	102	0.48
Belgian	16	0.08
British	154	0.73
Bulgarian	4	0.02
Canadian	112	0.53
Croatian	19	0.09
Czech	160	0.76
Czechoslovakian	80	0.38
Danish	60	0.28
Dutch	458	2.17
Eastern European	16	0.08
English	2,588	12.29
Estonian	10	0.05
European	84	0.40
Finnish	15	0.07
French, except Basque	841	3.99
French Canadian	225	1.07
German	3,726	17.69
Greek	2,479	11.77
Hawaii Native/Pacific Islander:	28	0.13
Micronesian: (5)	8	0.04
Guamanian/Chamorro (5)	8	0.04
Polynesian: (6)	10	0.05
Native Hawaiian (5)	8	0.04
Samoan (1)	2	0.01
Other Pac. Isl., specified	2	0.01
Other Pac. Isl., not spec. (2)	8	0.04
Hispanic or Latino:	909	4.33
Central American:	24	0.11
Costa Rican	8	0.04
Guatemalan	1	0.00
Honduran	1	0.00
Nicaraguan	2	0.01
Panamanian	5	0.02
Salvadoran	3	0.01
Other Central American	4	0.02
Cuban	74	0.35
Dominican Republic	2	0.01
Mexican	181	0.86
Puerto Rican	366	1.74
South American:	97	0.46
Argentinean	1	0.00
Chilean	2	0.01
Colombian	45	0.21
Ecuadorian	16	0.08
Peruvian	19	0.09
Uruguayan	2	0.01
Venezuelan	7	0.03
Other South American	5	0.02
Other Hispanic or Latino	165	0.79
Hungarian	117	0.56
Irish	3,132	14.87
Italian	1,991	9.45
Latvian	5	0.02
Lithuanian	47	0.22
Macedonian	11	0.05
New Zealander	11	0.05
Norwegian	228	1.08
Pennsylvania German	34	0.16
Polish	837	3.97
Portuguese	121	0.57
Romanian	28	0.13
Russian	236	1.12
Scandinavian	15	0.07
Scotch-Irish	436	2.07
Scottish	629	2.99
Serbian	8	0.04
Slovak	61	0.29
Slovene	8	0.04
Swedish	333	1.58
Swiss	98	0.47
Turkish	6	0.03
Ukrainian	24	0.11
United States or American	895	4.25
Welsh	230	1.09
West Indian, excl. Hispanic:	103	0.49
Bahamian	8	0.04
British West Indian	13	0.06
Haitian	23	0.11
Jamaican	55	0.26
West Indian	4	0.02
White:	19,208	91.45
Not Hispanic (18,263)	18,505	88.11
Hispanic (655)	703	3.35
Yugoslavian	8	0.04

Temple Terrace

Place Type: City
County: Hillsborough
Population: 20,918

Ancestry/Race	Number	%
African American/Black:	2,497	11.94
Not Hispanic (2,267)	2,385	11.40
Hispanic (67)	112	0.54
African, sub-Saharan:	83	0.40
African	83	0.40
Am. Ind. or Alaska Nat., not spec.	43	0.21
American Indian tribes, specified:	131	0.63
Apache (4)	6	0.03
Blackfeet (5)	14	0.07
Cherokee (21)	52	0.25
Chickasaw	1	0.00
Chippewa	2	0.01
Choctaw (4)	4	0.02
Creek (2)	3	0.01
Iroquois (1)	4	0.02
Latin American Indians (8)	20	0.10
Navajo	1	0.00
Osage (1)	1	0.00
Potawatomi (1)	1	0.00
Seminole (4)	5	0.02
Sioux	2	0.01
All other tribes (8)	15	0.07
American Indian tribes, not spec.	3	0.01
Arab:	428	2.05
Arab/Arabic	231	1.11
Jordanian	8	0.04
Lebanese	16	0.08
Moroccan	8	0.04
Palestinian	35	0.17
Syrian	32	0.15
Other Arab	98	0.47
Armenian	5	0.02
Asian:	668	3.19
Bangladeshi (5)	10	0.05
Chinese, ex. Taiwanese (70)	89	0.43
Filipino (65)	89	0.43
Indian (243)	253	1.21
Indonesian (10)	14	0.07
Japanese (28)	49	0.23
Korean (36)	36	0.17
Malaysian (1)	1	0.00
Pakistani (16)	23	0.11
Taiwanese (25)	32	0.15
Thai (7)	9	0.04
Vietnamese (18)	25	0.12
Other Asian, specified (6)	7	0.03
Other Asian, not specified (8)	31	0.15
Australian	10	0.05
Austrian	90	0.43
Belgian	12	0.06
Brazilian	9	0.04
British	139	0.67
Canadian	106	0.51
Croatian	7	0.03
Czech	49	0.23
Czechoslovakian	25	0.12
Danish	102	0.49
Dutch	417	2.00
English	2,563	12.28
European	202	0.97
Finnish	52	0.25
French, except Basque	671	3.21
French Canadian	136	0.65
German	3,228	15.47
Greek	87	0.42
Guyanese	102	0.49
Hawaii Native/Pacific Islander:	52	0.25
Micronesian: (11)	14	0.07
Guamanian/Chamorro (11)	14	0.07
Polynesian: (6)	12	0.06
Native Hawaiian (4)	7	0.03
Samoan (2)	2	0.01
Other Polynesian	3	0.01
Other Pac. Isl., not spec. (11)	26	0.12

Notes: 1. Figures in the "Number" column do not add up to the total population due to: a) Ancestry/Race overlap — e.g. persons can report being both White and Irish, b) persons of Hispanic origin can report being any race, c) persons reporting two ancestries are counted in both categories. 2. Numbers in parentheses indicate the number of persons reporting this ancestry/race alone, not in combination with any other ancestry/race. 3. Refer to the User's Guide in the front of the book for more detailed information.

Hispanic or Latino:	2,373	11.34
Central American:	108	0.52
Costa Rican	25	0.12
Guatemalan	6	0.03
Honduran	26	0.12
Nicaraguan	12	0.06
Panamanian	23	0.11
Salvadoran	12	0.06
Other Central American	4	0.02
Cuban	302	1.44
Dominican Republic	43	0.21
Mexican	274	1.31
Puerto Rican	690	3.30
South American:	323	1.54
Argentinean	12	0.06
Bolivian	4	0.02
Chilean	4	0.02
Colombian	191	0.91
Ecuadorian	14	0.07
Peruvian	39	0.19
Uruguayan	2	0.01
Venezuelan	51	0.24
Other South American	6	0.03
Other Hispanic or Latino	633	3.03
Hungarian	224	1.07
Irish	2,469	11.83
Italian	1,739	8.33
Lithuanian	46	0.22
Northern European	7	0.03
Norwegian	214	1.03
Pennsylvania German	18	0.09
Polish	504	2.41
Portuguese	47	0.23
Romanian	29	0.14
Russian	234	1.12
Scandinavian	14	0.07
Scotch-Irish	549	2.63
Scottish	651	3.12
Serbian	22	0.11
Slovak	42	0.20
Swedish	199	0.95
Swiss	80	0.38
Ukrainian	14	0.07
United States or American	1,201	5.75
Welsh	229	1.10
West Indian, excl. Hispanic:	361	1.73
Bahamian	30	0.14
British West Indian	30	0.14
Dutch West Indian	9	0.04
Haitian	25	0.12
Jamaican	217	1.04
Trinidadian and Tobagonian	31	0.15
U.S. Virgin Islander	9	0.04
West Indian	10	0.05
White:	17,323	82.81
Not Hispanic (15,163)	15,505	74.12
Hispanic (1,668)	1,818	8.69
Yugoslavian	41	0.20

The Crossings

Place Type: Census Designated Place
County: Miami-Dade
Population: 23,557

Ancestry/Race	Number	%
African American/Black:	1,314	5.58
Not Hispanic (1,016)	1,198	5.09
Hispanic (78)	116	0.49
Am. Ind. or Alaska Nat., not spec.	33	0.14
American Indian tribes, specified:	31	0.13
Cherokee (4)	14	0.06
Chippewa	1	0.00
Crow	3	0.01
Latin American Indians (4)	9	0.04
Pueblo	2	0.01
All other tribes (1)	2	0.01
American Indian tribes, not spec.	4	0.02
Arab:	302	1.28
Arab/Arabic	73	0.31
Egyptian	50	0.21
Lebanese	155	0.66
Palestinian	7	0.03
Other Arab	17	0.07
Armenian	18	0.08
Asian:	1,060	4.50
Chinese, ex. Taiwanese (299)	382	1.62
Filipino (38)	51	0.22
Indian (224)	297	1.26
Indonesian (1)	1	0.00
Japanese (78)	91	0.39
Korean (29)	37	0.16
Laotian (1)	1	0.00
Malaysian	2	0.01
Pakistani (28)	64	0.27
Sri Lankan (2)	2	0.01
Taiwanese (9)	13	0.06
Thai (15)	18	0.08
Vietnamese (37)	39	0.17
Other Asian, not specified (12)	62	0.26
Australian	11	0.05
Austrian	162	0.69
Brazilian	362	1.54
British	104	0.44
Canadian	42	0.18
Czech	37	0.16
Czechoslovakian	50	0.21
Danish	45	0.19
Dutch	80	0.34
Eastern European	29	0.12
English	603	2.56
European	143	0.61
Finnish	8	0.03
French, except Basque	490	2.08
French Canadian	34	0.14
German	1,132	4.81
Greek	149	0.63
Hawaii Native/Pacific Islander:	30	0.13
Micronesian: (4)	4	0.02
Guamanian/Chamorro (4)	4	0.02
Polynesian: (4)	10	0.04
Native Hawaiian	5	0.02
Samoan (3)	3	0.01
Other Polynesian (1)	2	0.01
Other Pac. Isl., not spec. (3)	16	0.07
Hispanic or Latino:	13,219	56.11
Central American:	1,004	4.26
Costa Rican	46	0.20
Guatemalan	56	0.24
Honduran	98	0.42
Nicaraguan	592	2.51
Panamanian	88	0.37
Salvadoran	105	0.45
Other Central American	19	0.08
Cuban	4,821	20.47
Dominican Republic	371	1.57
Mexican	203	0.86
Puerto Rican	910	3.86
South American:	3,326	14.12
Argentinean	233	0.99
Bolivian	69	0.29
Chilean	212	0.90
Colombian	1,454	6.17
Ecuadorian	122	0.52
Paraguayan	18	0.08
Peruvian	634	2.69
Uruguayan	48	0.20
Venezuelan	453	1.92
Other South American	83	0.35
Other Hispanic or Latino	2,584	10.97
Hungarian	198	0.84
Iranian	202	0.86
Irish	1,092	4.64
Israeli	38	0.16
Italian	1,074	4.56
Latvian	10	0.04
Lithuanian	37	0.16
Norwegian	52	0.22
Polish	437	1.86
Portuguese	52	0.22
Romanian	39	0.17
Russian	496	2.11
Scotch-Irish	101	0.43
Scottish	230	0.98
Serbian	5	0.02
Slavic	15	0.06
Slovak	34	0.14
Swedish	111	0.47
Swiss	39	0.17
Turkish	8	0.03
Ukrainian	26	0.11
United States or American	823	3.50
Welsh	36	0.15
West Indian, excl. Hispanic:	907	3.85
Bahamian	8	0.03
Belizean	11	0.05
British West Indian	37	0.16
Dutch West Indian	10	0.04
Haitian	348	1.48
Jamaican	369	1.57
Trinidadian and Tobagonian	124	0.53
White:	20,705	87.89
Not Hispanic (8,001)	8,280	35.15
Hispanic (12,070)	12,425	52.74
Yugoslavian	47	0.20

The Hammocks

Place Type: Census Designated Place
County: Miami-Dade
Population: 47,379

Ancestry/Race	Number	%
African American/Black:	3,842	8.11
Not Hispanic (2,899)	3,364	7.10
Hispanic (360)	478	1.01
African, sub-Saharan:	178	0.38
African	92	0.19
Cape Verdean	6	0.01
Kenyan	5	0.01
Nigerian	10	0.02
South African	8	0.02
Other sub-Saharan African	57	0.12
Am. Ind. or Alaska Nat., not spec.	88	0.19
American Indian tribes, specified:	100	0.21
Apache	1	0.00
Blackfeet	6	0.01
Cherokee (12)	22	0.05
Chippewa (3)	3	0.01
Choctaw (1)	2	0.00
Comanche	2	0.00
Creek	1	0.00
Delaware (1)	1	0.00
Iroquois	1	0.00
Latin American Indians (18)	38	0.08
Navajo (1)	1	0.00
Seminole (5)	5	0.01
All other tribes (12)	17	0.04
American Indian tribes, not spec.	19	0.04
Arab:	671	1.41
Arab/Arabic	199	0.42
Iraqi	11	0.02
Lebanese	174	0.37
Palestinian	112	0.24
Syrian	84	0.18
Other Arab	91	0.19
Asian:	1,960	4.14
Bangladeshi (6)	6	0.01
Chinese, ex. Taiwanese (577)	764	1.61
Filipino (220)	250	0.53
Indian (400)	525	1.11
Indonesian (4)	4	0.01
Japanese (54)	70	0.15
Korean (48)	58	0.12
Laotian (4)	6	0.01
Malaysian	1	0.00
Pakistani (103)	120	0.25
Taiwanese (16)	21	0.04
Thai (22)	23	0.05
Vietnamese (39)	44	0.09
Other Asian, specified (2)	2	0.00
Other Asian, not specified (17)	66	0.14
Austrian	56	0.12
Basque	38	0.08
Belgian	12	0.03

Notes: 1. Figures in the "Number" column do not add up to the total population due to: a) Ancestry/Race overlap — e.g. persons can report being both White and Irish, b) persons of Hispanic origin can report being any race, c) persons reporting two ancestries are counted in both categories. 2. Numbers in parentheses indicate the number of persons reporting this ancestry/race alone, not in combination with any other ancestry/race. 3. Refer to the User's Guide in the front of the book for more detailed information.

Brazilian	206	0.43
British	127	0.27
Canadian	79	0.17
Croatian	66	0.14
Cypriot	10	0.02
Czech	41	0.09
Danish	22	0.05
Dutch	180	0.38
Eastern European	30	0.06
English	739	1.56
European	262	0.55
Finnish	15	0.03
French, except Basque	537	1.13
French Canadian	43	0.09
German	1,443	3.04
Greek	86	0.18
Guyanese	55	0.12
Hawaii Native/Pacific Islander:	81	0.17
Micronesian: (1)	10	0.02
Guamanian/Chamorro (1)	7	0.01
Other Micronesian	3	0.01
Polynesian: (15)	29	0.06
Native Hawaiian (12)	23	0.05
Samoan (3)	6	0.01
Other Pac. Isl., not spec. (11)	42	0.09
Hispanic or Latino:	30,953	65.33
Central American:	2,324	4.91
Costa Rican	126	0.27
Guatemalan	120	0.25
Honduran	233	0.49
Nicaraguan	1,364	2.88
Panamanian	226	0.48
Salvadoran	201	0.42
Other Central American	54	0.11
Cuban	8,334	17.59
Dominican Republic	1,167	2.46
Mexican	504	1.06
Puerto Rican	2,763	5.83
South American:	9,494	20.04
Argentinean	401	0.85
Bolivian	93	0.20
Chilean	409	0.86
Colombian	4,749	10.02
Ecuadorian	522	1.10
Paraguayan	5	0.01
Peruvian	1,591	3.36
Uruguayan	79	0.17
Venezuelan	1,488	3.14
Other South American	157	0.33
Other Hispanic or Latino	6,367	13.44
Hungarian	140	0.30
Iranian	94	0.20
Irish	1,316	2.77
Israeli	31	0.07
Italian	1,914	4.04
Lithuanian	53	0.11
Northern European	11	0.02
Norwegian	116	0.24
Polish	428	0.90
Portuguese	193	0.41
Romanian	32	0.07
Russian	263	0.55
Scandinavian	19	0.04
Scotch-Irish	156	0.33
Scottish	168	0.35
Slovak	3	0.01
Swedish	37	0.08
Swiss	85	0.18
Turkish	53	0.11
Ukrainian	16	0.03
United States or American	1,491	3.14
Welsh	46	0.10
West Indian, excl. Hispanic:	2,670	5.63
Bahamian	113	0.24
Barbadian	28	0.06
Belizean	34	0.07
British West Indian	77	0.16
Dutch West Indian	9	0.02
Haitian	861	1.82
Jamaican	1,410	2.97
Trinidadian and Tobagonian	99	0.21
West Indian	39	0.08
White:	38,875	82.05
Not Hispanic (10,913)	11,396	24.05
Hispanic (26,347)	27,479	58.00
Yugoslavian	9	0.02

Titusville

Place Type: City
County: Brevard
Population: 40,670

Ancestry/Race	Number	%
Afghan	8	0.02
African American/Black:	5,382	13.23
Not Hispanic (5,073)	5,289	13.00
Hispanic (69)	93	0.23
African, sub-Saharan:	515	1.27
African	504	1.24
Nigerian	6	0.01
Other sub-Saharan African	5	0.01
Alaska Native tribes, specified:	5	0.01
Aleut (3)	3	0.01
Eskimo (2)	2	0.00
Am. Ind. or Alaska Nat., not spec.	111	0.27
American Indian tribes, specified:	262	0.64
Apache (2)	6	0.01
Blackfeet (2)	12	0.03
Cherokee (34)	130	0.32
Cheyenne (1)	1	0.00
Chickasaw (4)	7	0.02
Chippewa (4)	5	0.01
Choctaw (1)	10	0.02
Comanche	1	0.00
Cree	1	0.00
Creek (6)	9	0.02
Crow	1	0.00
Delaware (2)	3	0.01
Iroquois (14)	24	0.06
Latin American Indians (1)	4	0.01
Lumbee (2)	2	0.00
Navajo (2)	2	0.00
Pueblo (7)	8	0.02
Seminole (1)	8	0.02
Sioux (4)	5	0.01
Yaqui	1	0.00
All other tribes (12)	22	0.05
American Indian tribes, not spec.	17	0.04
Arab:	91	0.22
Arab/Arabic	9	0.02
Jordanian	5	0.01
Lebanese	69	0.17
Syrian	8	0.02
Armenian	15	0.04
Asian:	526	1.29
Chinese, ex. Taiwanese (56)	78	0.19
Filipino (61)	105	0.26
Indian (143)	166	0.41
Indonesian (1)	2	0.00
Japanese (26)	41	0.10
Korean (30)	37	0.09
Malaysian (1)	1	0.00
Thai (22)	28	0.07
Vietnamese (28)	37	0.09
Other Asian, specified (1)	5	0.01
Other Asian, not specified (11)	26	0.06
Assyrian/Chaldean/Syriac	9	0.02
Australian	7	0.02
Austrian	50	0.12
Belgian	89	0.22
Brazilian	17	0.04
British	272	0.67
Bulgarian	8	0.02
Canadian	140	0.34
Celtic	16	0.04
Croatian	24	0.06
Czech	67	0.16
Czechoslovakian	69	0.17
Danish	181	0.45
Dutch	692	1.70
English	5,048	12.41
Estonian	9	0.02
European	356	0.88
Finnish	70	0.17
French, except Basque	1,409	3.47
French Canadian	466	1.15
German	6,797	16.72
German Russian	8	0.02
Greek	108	0.27
Hawaii Native/Pacific Islander:	41	0.10
Melanesian:	1	0.00
Fijian	1	0.00
Micronesian: (6)	12	0.03
Guamanian/Chamorro (5)	10	0.02
Other Micronesian (1)	2	0.00
Polynesian: (8)	15	0.04
Native Hawaiian (4)	9	0.02
Samoan (4)	6	0.01
Other Pac. Isl., specified	4	0.01
Other Pac. Isl., not spec. (2)	9	0.02
Hispanic or Latino:	1,430	3.52
Central American:	59	0.15
Costa Rican	4	0.01
Guatemalan	8	0.02
Honduran	7	0.02
Nicaraguan	13	0.03
Panamanian	21	0.05
Salvadoran	3	0.01
Other Central American	3	0.01
Cuban	179	0.44
Dominican Republic	16	0.04
Mexican	200	0.49
Puerto Rican	654	1.61
South American:	62	0.15
Argentinean	7	0.02
Chilean	3	0.01
Colombian	32	0.08
Ecuadorian	4	0.01
Peruvian	4	0.01
Venezuelan	11	0.03
Other South American	1	0.00
Other Hispanic or Latino	260	0.64
Hungarian	280	0.69
Iranian	22	0.05
Irish	5,448	13.40
Italian	2,242	5.51
Latvian	14	0.03
Lithuanian	107	0.26
Maltese	9	0.02
Northern European	77	0.19
Norwegian	416	1.02
Pennsylvania German	32	0.08
Polish	938	2.31
Portuguese	121	0.30
Romanian	14	0.03
Russian	184	0.45
Scandinavian	46	0.11
Scotch-Irish	1,012	2.49
Scottish	966	2.38
Slavic	20	0.05
Slovak	95	0.23
Slovene	26	0.06
Swedish	465	1.14
Swiss	184	0.45
Ukrainian	77	0.19
United States or American	3,621	8.91
Welsh	268	0.66
West Indian, excl. Hispanic:	483	1.19
Bahamian	7	0.02
Belizean	8	0.02
British West Indian	98	0.24
Haitian	54	0.13
Jamaican	224	0.55
Trinidadian and Tobagonian	8	0.02
West Indian	84	0.21
White:	34,587	85.04
Not Hispanic (33,058)	33,509	82.39
Hispanic (1,022)	1,078	2.65
Yugoslavian	23	0.06

Notes: 1. Figures in the "Number" column do not add up to the total population due to: a) Ancestry/Race overlap — e.g. persons can report being both White and Irish, b) persons of Hispanic origin can report being any race, c) persons reporting two ancestries are counted in both categories. 2. Numbers in parentheses indicate the number of persons reporting this ancestry/race alone, not in combination with any other ancestry/race. 3. Refer to the User's Guide in the front of the book for more detailed information.

Town 'n' Country

Place Type: Census Designated Place
County: Hillsborough
Population: 72,523

Ancestry/Race	Number	%
African American/Black:	6,321	8.72
Not Hispanic (5,225)	5,638	7.77
Hispanic (499)	683	0.94
African, sub-Saharan:	337	0.47
African	276	0.38
Ethiopian	28	0.04
Nigerian	33	0.05
Alaska Native tribes, specified:	2	0.00
Alaska Athabascan (1)	2	0.00
Am. Ind. or Alaska Nat., not spec.	173	0.24
Albanian	6	0.01
American Indian tribes, specified:	356	0.49
Apache (5)	8	0.01
Blackfeet (4)	21	0.03
Cherokee (51)	139	0.19
Chickasaw (1)	2	0.00
Chippewa (5)	8	0.01
Choctaw (4)	12	0.02
Comanche (1)	1	0.00
Cree	1	0.00
Creek (8)	11	0.02
Crow	1	0.00
Delaware (1)	4	0.01
Iroquois (8)	18	0.02
Kiowa (1)	1	0.00
Latin American Indians (28)	60	0.08
Lumbee (5)	5	0.01
Menominee (1)	1	0.00
Navajo (3)	5	0.01
Osage (1)	2	0.00
Potawatomi	6	0.01
Pueblo (2)	3	0.00
Seminole (3)	7	0.01
Shoshone (2)	3	0.00
Sioux (6)	13	0.02
Tohono O'Odham (1)	1	0.00
Ute	1	0.00
All other tribes (9)	22	0.03
American Indian tribes, not spec.	27	0.04
Arab:	332	0.46
Arab/Arabic	100	0.14
Egyptian	24	0.03
Lebanese	140	0.19
Moroccan	22	0.03
Palestinian	6	0.01
Syrian	40	0.06
Armenian	18	0.02
Asian:	2,878	3.97
Bangladeshi (2)	5	0.01
Cambodian (11)	12	0.02
Chinese, ex. Taiwanese (243)	326	0.45
Filipino (350)	435	0.60
Indian (415)	487	0.67
Indonesian (6)	9	0.01
Japanese (58)	104	0.14
Korean (381)	444	0.61
Laotian (1)	3	0.00
Malaysian (4)	5	0.01
Pakistani (3)	7	0.01
Sri Lankan (5)	5	0.01
Taiwanese (7)	16	0.02
Thai (60)	82	0.11
Vietnamese (720)	807	1.11
Other Asian, specified (8)	14	0.02
Other Asian, not specified (38)	117	0.16
Australian	15	0.02
Austrian	129	0.18
Basque	5	0.01
Belgian	86	0.12
Brazilian	106	0.15
British	315	0.44
Canadian	187	0.26
Croatian	42	0.06
Czech	255	0.35
Czechoslovakian	82	0.11
Danish	162	0.22
Dutch	749	1.03
Eastern European	10	0.01
English	5,928	8.19
Estonian	11	0.02
European	379	0.52
Finnish	132	0.18
French, except Basque	1,935	2.67
French Canadian	622	0.86
German	9,554	13.20
Greek	521	0.72
Guyanese	354	0.49
Hawaii Native/Pacific Islander:	112	0.15
Micronesian: (8)	11	0.02
Guamanian/Chamorro (8)	11	0.02
Polynesian: (34)	48	0.07
Native Hawaiian (23)	35	0.05
Samoan (8)	10	0.01
Tongan (1)	1	0.00
Other Polynesian (2)	2	0.00
Other Pac. Isl., specified	1	0.00
Other Pac. Isl., not spec. (18)	52	0.07
Hispanic or Latino:	21,010	28.97
Central American:	691	0.95
Costa Rican	91	0.13
Guatemalan	59	0.08
Honduran	135	0.19
Nicaraguan	123	0.17
Panamanian	132	0.18
Salvadoran	105	0.14
Other Central American	46	0.06
Cuban	5,146	7.10
Dominican Republic	876	1.21
Mexican	829	1.14
Puerto Rican	7,505	10.35
South American:	2,008	2.77
Argentinean	65	0.09
Bolivian	28	0.04
Chilean	32	0.04
Colombian	1,057	1.46
Ecuadorian	226	0.31
Paraguayan	3	0.00
Peruvian	356	0.49
Uruguayan	19	0.03
Venezuelan	160	0.22
Other South American	62	0.09
Other Hispanic or Latino	3,955	5.45
Hungarian	322	0.44
Irish	7,491	10.35
Israeli	10	0.01
Italian	5,259	7.26
Latvian	9	0.01
Lithuanian	279	0.39
Maltese	19	0.03
Northern European	9	0.01
Norwegian	334	0.46
Pennsylvania German	8	0.01
Polish	2,256	3.12
Portuguese	195	0.27
Romanian	84	0.12
Russian	380	0.52
Scandinavian	56	0.08
Scotch-Irish	949	1.31
Scottish	1,083	1.50
Serbian	16	0.02
Slavic	39	0.05
Slovak	118	0.16
Swedish	637	0.88
Swiss	146	0.20
Turkish	25	0.03
Ukrainian	152	0.21
United States or American	4,570	6.31
Welsh	469	0.65
West Indian, excl. Hispanic:	997	1.38
Bahamian	27	0.04
Belizean	2	0.00
British West Indian	163	0.23
Haitian	161	0.22
Jamaican	457	0.63
Trinidadian and Tobagonian	34	0.05
U.S. Virgin Islander	48	0.07
West Indian	98	0.14
Other West Indian	7	0.01
White:	58,591	80.79
Not Hispanic (42,405)	43,240	59.62
Hispanic (14,508)	15,351	21.17
Yugoslavian	73	0.10

Union Park

Place Type: Census Designated Place
County: Orange
Population: 10,191

Ancestry/Race	Number	%
African American/Black:	614	6.02
Not Hispanic (434)	498	4.89
Hispanic (69)	116	1.14
African, sub-Saharan:	82	0.80
African	82	0.80
Am. Ind. or Alaska Nat., not spec.	33	0.32
Albanian	10	0.10
American Indian tribes, specified:	54	0.53
Apache (1)	6	0.06
Blackfeet	3	0.03
Cherokee (6)	21	0.21
Creek (2)	5	0.05
Crow (1)	1	0.01
Delaware	5	0.05
Houma (1)	1	0.01
Iroquois (1)	1	0.01
Latin American Indians (2)	7	0.07
Seminole (1)	1	0.01
All other tribes (2)	3	0.03
American Indian tribes, not spec.	3	0.03
Arab:	25	0.25
Egyptian	7	0.07
Lebanese	12	0.12
Moroccan	6	0.06
Armenian	6	0.06
Asian:	436	4.28
Cambodian	1	0.01
Chinese, ex. Taiwanese (22)	29	0.28
Filipino (108)	151	1.48
Indian (71)	82	0.80
Indonesian (3)	6	0.06
Japanese (27)	36	0.35
Korean (16)	17	0.17
Pakistani (2)	3	0.03
Thai (12)	15	0.15
Vietnamese (79)	83	0.81
Other Asian, not specified (7)	13	0.13
Austrian	9	0.09
Belgian	25	0.25
Brazilian	24	0.24
British	74	0.73
Croatian	7	0.07
Czech	34	0.33
Czechoslovakian	23	0.23
Danish	5	0.05
Dutch	160	1.57
English	827	8.11
European	42	0.41
Finnish	16	0.16
French, except Basque	233	2.28
French Canadian	64	0.63
German	1,258	12.34
Greek	24	0.24
Guyanese	15	0.15
Hawaii Native/Pacific Islander:	32	0.31
Micronesian: (1)	3	0.03
Guamanian/Chamorro (1)	3	0.03
Polynesian: (2)	4	0.04
Native Hawaiian (2)	4	0.04
Other Pac. Isl., not spec. (3)	25	0.25
Hispanic or Latino:	2,657	26.07
Central American:	64	0.63
Costa Rican	5	0.05
Guatemalan	5	0.05
Honduran	9	0.09
Nicaraguan	11	0.11
Panamanian	15	0.15

Notes: 1. Figures in the "Number" column do not add up to the total population due to: a) Ancestry/Race overlap — e.g. persons can report being both White and Irish, b) persons of Hispanic origin can report being any race, c) persons reporting two ancestries are counted in both categories. 2. Numbers in parentheses indicate the number of persons reporting this ancestry/race alone, not in combination with any other ancestry/race. 3. Refer to the User's Guide in the front of the book for more detailed information.

Salvadoran	15	0.15
Other Central American	4	0.04
Cuban	160	1.57
Dominican Republic	110	1.08
Mexican	125	1.23
Puerto Rican	1,730	16.98
South American:	202	1.98
Argentinean	3	0.03
Bolivian	9	0.09
Chilean	2	0.02
Colombian	122	1.20
Ecuadorian	13	0.13
Peruvian	16	0.16
Uruguayan	1	0.01
Venezuelan	27	0.26
Other South American	9	0.09
Other Hispanic or Latino	266	2.61
Hungarian	16	0.16
Irish	1,066	10.45
Israeli	13	0.13
Italian	676	6.63
Lithuanian	78	0.76
Norwegian	107	1.05
Polish	324	3.18
Portuguese	9	0.09
Russian	36	0.35
Scandinavian	43	0.42
Scotch-Irish	131	1.28
Scottish	141	1.38
Slovak	12	0.12
Swedish	54	0.53
Swiss	10	0.10
Ukrainian	21	0.21
United States or American	693	6.80
Welsh	42	0.41
West Indian, excl. Hispanic:	120	1.18
Haitian	12	0.12
Jamaican	85	0.83
Trinidadian and Tobagonian	23	0.23
White:	8,281	81.26
Not Hispanic (6,508)	6,669	65.44
Hispanic (1,457)	1,612	15.82
Yugoslavian	11	0.11

University

Place Type: Census Designated Place
County: Hillsborough
Population: 30,736

Ancestry/Race	Number	%
African American/Black:	11,027	35.88
Not Hispanic (10,141)	10,575	34.41
Hispanic (328)	452	1.47
African, sub-Saharan:	574	1.87
African	439	1.43
Cape Verdean	18	0.06
Nigerian	108	0.35
Other sub-Saharan African	9	0.03
Alaska Native tribes, specified:	2	0.01
Alaska Athabascan	1	0.00
Tlingit-Haida (1)	1	0.00
Am. Ind. or Alaska Nat., not spec.	136	0.44
American Indian tribes, specified:	162	0.53
Apache (2)	6	0.02
Blackfeet (3)	14	0.05
Cherokee (22)	80	0.26
Chickasaw (1)	2	0.01
Chippewa	1	0.00
Choctaw (1)	2	0.01
Creek	2	0.01
Delaware (4)	4	0.01
Iroquois (3)	7	0.02
Latin American Indians (14)	22	0.07
Seminole (2)	4	0.01
Sioux	3	0.01
All other tribes (7)	15	0.05
American Indian tribes, not spec.	22	0.07
Arab:	322	1.05
Arab/Arabic	71	0.23
Egyptian	33	0.11
Jordanian	44	0.14
Lebanese	35	0.11
Moroccan	17	0.06
Palestinian	31	0.10
Syrian	41	0.13
Other Arab	50	0.16
Armenian	24	0.08
Asian:	1,335	4.34
Bangladeshi (4)	5	0.02
Cambodian (3)	5	0.02
Chinese, ex. Taiwanese (310)	342	1.11
Filipino (94)	122	0.40
Indian (419)	470	1.53
Indonesian (6)	11	0.04
Japanese (26)	43	0.14
Korean (51)	67	0.22
Laotian (5)	7	0.02
Malaysian (1)	1	0.00
Pakistani (14)	18	0.06
Sri Lankan (19)	19	0.06
Taiwanese (14)	15	0.05
Thai (15)	23	0.07
Vietnamese (103)	115	0.37
Other Asian, specified	3	0.01
Other Asian, not specified (16)	69	0.22
Austrian	14	0.05
Belgian	8	0.03
Brazilian	10	0.03
British	98	0.32
Bulgarian	8	0.03
Canadian	51	0.17
Celtic	23	0.07
Croatian	41	0.13
Czech	69	0.22
Czechoslovakian	27	0.09
Danish	44	0.14
Dutch	236	0.77
English	1,256	4.09
European	201	0.66
Finnish	38	0.12
French, except Basque	443	1.44
French Canadian	215	0.70
German	2,065	6.73
Greek	42	0.14
Guyanese	14	0.05
Hawaii Native/Pacific Islander:	80	0.26
Micronesian: (7)	14	0.05
Guamanian/Chamorro (7)	14	0.05
Polynesian: (9)	15	0.05
Native Hawaiian (3)	6	0.02
Samoan (6)	9	0.03
Other Pac. Isl., specified	2	0.01
Other Pac. Isl., not spec. (6)	49	0.16
Hispanic or Latino:	5,935	19.31
Central American:	386	1.26
Costa Rican	16	0.05
Guatemalan	22	0.07
Honduran	222	0.72
Nicaraguan	32	0.10
Panamanian	45	0.15
Salvadoran	37	0.12
Other Central American	12	0.04
Cuban	403	1.31
Dominican Republic	92	0.30
Mexican	1,224	3.98
Puerto Rican	2,699	8.78
South American:	277	0.90
Argentinean	21	0.07
Bolivian	6	0.02
Chilean	9	0.03
Colombian	129	0.42
Ecuadorian	26	0.08
Peruvian	42	0.14
Venezuelan	29	0.09
Other South American	15	0.05
Other Hispanic or Latino	854	2.78
Hungarian	73	0.24
Iranian	42	0.14
Irish	1,882	6.13
Italian	1,200	3.91
Lithuanian	16	0.05
Northern European	32	0.10
Norwegian	170	0.55
Polish	514	1.68
Portuguese	23	0.07
Romanian	23	0.07
Russian	140	0.46
Scandinavian	25	0.08
Scotch-Irish	368	1.20
Scottish	347	1.13
Slavic	9	0.03
Slovak	64	0.21
Slovene	16	0.05
Swedish	59	0.19
Swiss	62	0.20
Turkish	62	0.20
United States or American	1,381	4.50
Welsh	81	0.26
West Indian, excl. Hispanic:	1,344	4.38
Bahamian	71	0.23
Barbadian	25	0.08
Belizean	27	0.09
British West Indian	67	0.22
Dutch West Indian	12	0.04
Haitian	545	1.78
Jamaican	372	1.21
Trinidadian and Tobagonian	49	0.16
U.S. Virgin Islander	11	0.04
West Indian	133	0.43
Other West Indian	32	0.10
White:	16,667	54.23
Not Hispanic (12,488)	13,035	42.41
Hispanic (3,280)	3,632	11.82
Yugoslavian	44	0.14

University Park

Place Type: Census Designated Place
County: Miami-Dade
Population: 26,538

Ancestry/Race	Number	%
African American/Black:	978	3.69
Not Hispanic (717)	754	2.84
Hispanic (186)	224	0.84
African, sub-Saharan:	28	0.11
African	28	0.11
Am. Ind. or Alaska Nat., not spec.	17	0.06
Albanian	23	0.09
American Indian tribes, specified:	16	0.06
Apache (1)	1	0.00
Blackfeet	2	0.01
Cherokee (3)	6	0.02
Creek	1	0.00
Latin American Indians	3	0.01
Navajo	1	0.00
Sioux	1	0.00
All other tribes	1	0.00
American Indian tribes, not spec.	8	0.03
Arab:	214	0.81
Arab/Arabic	61	0.23
Lebanese	107	0.40
Syrian	46	0.17
Asian:	519	1.96
Bangladeshi (3)	3	0.01
Chinese, ex. Taiwanese (162)	201	0.76
Filipino (41)	46	0.17
Indian (93)	129	0.49
Indonesian (1)	1	0.00
Japanese (40)	43	0.16
Korean (12)	14	0.05
Pakistani (11)	20	0.08
Sri Lankan (6)	6	0.02
Taiwanese (7)	12	0.05
Thai (6)	6	0.02
Vietnamese (15)	15	0.06
Other Asian, specified (1)	1	0.00
Other Asian, not specified (4)	22	0.08
Belgian	8	0.03
Brazilian	83	0.31
British	19	0.07
Canadian	44	0.17
Croatian	8	0.03
Czech	11	0.04

Notes: 1. Figures in the "Number" column do not add up to the total population due to: a) Ancestry/Race overlap — e.g. persons can report being both White and Irish, b) persons of Hispanic origin can report being any race, c) persons reporting two ancestries are counted in both categories. 2. Numbers in parentheses indicate the number of persons reporting this ancestry/race alone, not in combination with any other ancestry/race. 3. Refer to the User's Guide in the front of the book for more detailed information.

Dutch	15	0.06
English	245	0.93
European	51	0.19
Finnish	9	0.03
French, except Basque	161	0.61
French Canadian	13	0.05
German	259	0.98
Greek	30	0.11
Guyanese	16	0.06
Hawaii Native/Pacific Islander:	18	0.07
Micronesian: (3)	4	0.02
Guamanian/Chamorro (3)	4	0.02
Polynesian: (2)	7	0.03
Native Hawaiian (1)	3	0.01
Samoan (1)	3	0.01
Other Polynesian	1	0.00
Other Pac. Isl., not spec.	7	0.03
Hispanic or Latino:	21,945	82.69
Central American:	1,240	4.67
Costa Rican	43	0.16
Guatemalan	70	0.26
Honduran	147	0.55
Nicaraguan	767	2.89
Panamanian	76	0.29
Salvadoran	114	0.43
Other Central American	23	0.09
Cuban	15,871	59.80
Dominican Republic	280	1.06
Mexican	168	0.63
Puerto Rican	573	2.16
South American:	1,560	5.88
Argentinean	126	0.47
Bolivian	38	0.14
Chilean	64	0.24
Colombian	701	2.64
Ecuadorian	91	0.34
Paraguayan	4	0.02
Peruvian	227	0.86
Uruguayan	27	0.10
Venezuelan	264	0.99
Other South American	18	0.07
Other Hispanic or Latino	2,253	8.49
Iranian	13	0.05
Irish	185	0.70
Italian	615	2.32
Polish	61	0.23
Portuguese	110	0.42
Russian	106	0.40
Scotch-Irish	29	0.11
Scottish	19	0.07
Swedish	20	0.08
Swiss	29	0.11
Turkish	14	0.05
Ukrainian	8	0.03
United States or American	378	1.43
West Indian, excl. Hispanic:	332	1.25
Bahamian	61	0.23
Belizean	6	0.02
British West Indian	13	0.05
Dutch West Indian	6	0.02
Haitian	37	0.14
Jamaican	145	0.55
Trinidadian and Tobagonian	43	0.16
West Indian	7	0.03
Other West Indian	14	0.05
White:	24,230	91.30
Not Hispanic (3,329)	3,405	12.83
Hispanic (20,301)	20,825	78.47

Upper Grand Lagoon

Place Type: Census Designated Place
County: Bay
Population: 10,889

Ancestry/Race	Number	%
African American/Black:	186	1.71
Not Hispanic (151)	180	1.65
Hispanic (3)	6	0.06
African, sub-Saharan:	28	0.25
Cape Verdean	28	0.25
Alaska Native tribes, specified:	2	0.02
Eskimo (1)	1	0.01
Tlingit-Haida (1)	1	0.01
Alaska Native tribes, not specified	1	0.01
Am. Ind. or Alaska Nat., not spec.	25	0.23
American Indian tribes, specified:	124	1.14
Apache (3)	5	0.05
Blackfeet	2	0.02
Cherokee (24)	51	0.47
Chippewa (8)	14	0.13
Choctaw (2)	6	0.06
Creek (22)	31	0.28
Iroquois (1)	2	0.02
Navajo	2	0.02
Seminole	5	0.05
Sioux	2	0.02
Ute (3)	3	0.03
All other tribes	1	0.01
American Indian tribes, not spec.	7	0.06
Arab:	49	0.45
Lebanese	7	0.06
Moroccan	9	0.08
Palestinian	7	0.06
Other Arab	26	0.24
Asian:	234	2.15
Cambodian	1	0.01
Chinese, ex. Taiwanese (15)	19	0.17
Filipino (36)	58	0.53
Indian (38)	42	0.39
Japanese (20)	26	0.24
Korean (22)	31	0.28
Sri Lankan (1)	1	0.01
Thai (3)	8	0.07
Vietnamese (34)	35	0.32
Other Asian, not specified (7)	13	0.12
Austrian	35	0.32
British	78	0.71
Canadian	24	0.22
Czech	31	0.28
Czechoslovakian	26	0.24
Danish	62	0.56
Dutch	218	1.98
Eastern European	10	0.09
English	1,732	15.77
European	88	0.80
French, except Basque	460	4.19
French Canadian	208	1.89
German	1,482	13.49
Greek	73	0.66
Hawaii Native/Pacific Islander:	21	0.19
Micronesian: (7)	14	0.13
Guamanian/Chamorro (7)	14	0.13
Polynesian: (3)	5	0.05
Native Hawaiian (1)	3	0.03
Samoan (2)	2	0.02
Other Pac. Isl., not spec.	2	0.02
Hispanic or Latino:	267	2.45
Central American:	11	0.10
Costa Rican	2	0.02
Nicaraguan	2	0.02
Panamanian	5	0.05
Salvadoran	2	0.02
Cuban	42	0.39
Dominican Republic	4	0.04
Mexican	69	0.63
Puerto Rican	93	0.85
South American:	7	0.06
Colombian	1	0.01
Peruvian	3	0.03
Venezuelan	3	0.03
Other Hispanic or Latino	41	0.38
Hungarian	64	0.58
Irish	1,649	15.01
Israeli	9	0.08
Italian	416	3.79
Lithuanian	10	0.09
Norwegian	45	0.41
Polish	306	2.79
Portuguese	8	0.07
Russian	95	0.86
Scandinavian	7	0.06
Scotch-Irish	373	3.40
Scottish	364	3.31
Slovak	47	0.43
Slovene	18	0.16
Swedish	164	1.49
Swiss	17	0.15
Turkish	35	0.32
Ukrainian	19	0.17
United States or American	1,822	16.59
Welsh	63	0.57
West Indian, excl. Hispanic:	46	0.42
Belizean	28	0.25
Jamaican	9	0.08
Other West Indian	9	0.08
White:	10,373	95.26
Not Hispanic (10,026)	10,177	93.46
Hispanic (173)	196	1.80

Venice

Place Type: City
County: Sarasota
Population: 17,764

Ancestry/Race	Number	%
African American/Black:	113	0.64
Not Hispanic (90)	102	0.57
Hispanic (7)	11	0.06
Am. Ind. or Alaska Nat., not spec.	8	0.05
American Indian tribes, specified:	40	0.23
Apache	1	0.01
Blackfeet (1)	1	0.01
Cherokee (12)	23	0.13
Chickasaw	2	0.01
Chippewa	1	0.01
Iroquois (2)	3	0.02
Navajo	1	0.01
Ottawa	1	0.01
Seminole	1	0.01
Sioux (1)	2	0.01
All other tribes	4	0.02
American Indian tribes, not spec.	3	0.02
Arab:	59	0.33
Lebanese	59	0.33
Armenian	20	0.11
Asian:	99	0.56
Chinese, ex. Taiwanese (12)	18	0.10
Filipino (15)	23	0.13
Indian (7)	15	0.08
Indonesian (2)	2	0.01
Japanese (6)	7	0.04
Korean (6)	8	0.05
Thai (1)	1	0.01
Vietnamese (23)	23	0.13
Other Asian, not specified	2	0.01
Austrian	122	0.68
British	153	0.86
Bulgarian	8	0.04
Canadian	179	1.00
Croatian	33	0.18
Czech	138	0.77
Czechoslovakian	46	0.26
Danish	92	0.52
Dutch	394	2.21
English	3,402	19.06
Estonian	16	0.09
European	124	0.69
Finnish	21	0.12
French, except Basque	867	4.86
French Canadian	182	1.02
German	3,705	20.76
Greek	103	0.58
Hawaii Native/Pacific Islander:	6	0.03
Micronesian: (1)	1	0.01
Guamanian/Chamorro (1)	1	0.01
Polynesian: (1)	3	0.02
Native Hawaiian	1	0.01
Samoan (1)	1	0.01
Other Polynesian	1	0.01
Other Pac. Isl., not spec. (2)	2	0.01
Hispanic or Latino:	195	1.10
Central American:	10	0.06

Notes: 1. Figures in the "Number" column do not add up to the total population due to: a) Ancestry/Race overlap — e.g. persons can report being both White and Irish, b) persons of Hispanic origin can report being any race, c) persons reporting two ancestries are counted in both categories. 2. Numbers in parentheses indicate the number of persons reporting this ancestry/race alone, not in combination with any other ancestry/race. 3. Refer to the User's Guide in the front of the book for more detailed information.

Costa Rican	1	0.01
Honduran	3	0.02
Nicaraguan	1	0.01
Panamanian	3	0.02
Salvadoran	2	0.01
Cuban	21	0.12
Dominican Republic	5	0.03
Mexican	60	0.34
Puerto Rican	34	0.19
South American:	17	0.10
Argentinean	1	0.01
Bolivian	1	0.01
Chilean	1	0.01
Colombian	1	0.01
Ecuadorian	2	0.01
Paraguayan	1	0.01
Peruvian	6	0.03
Venezuelan	2	0.01
Other South American	2	0.01
Other Hispanic or Latino	48	0.27
Hungarian	113	0.63
Irish	3,104	17.39
Italian	1,402	7.85
Latvian	13	0.07
Lithuanian	81	0.45
Luxemburger	19	0.11
Macedonian	9	0.05
Maltese	8	0.04
Norwegian	244	1.37
Pennsylvania German	8	0.04
Polish	883	4.95
Portuguese	74	0.41
Russian	103	0.58
Scandinavian	28	0.16
Scotch-Irish	517	2.90
Scottish	744	4.17
Slovak	37	0.21
Slovene	8	0.04
Swedish	307	1.72
Swiss	99	0.55
Ukrainian	92	0.52
United States or American	1,174	6.58
Welsh	140	0.78
White:	17,519	98.62
Not Hispanic (17,299)	17,360	97.73
Hispanic (134)	159	0.90
Yugoslavian	7	0.04

Vero Beach South

Place Type: Census Designated Place
County: Indian River
Population: 20,362

Ancestry/Race	Number	%
African American/Black:	533	2.62
Not Hispanic (460)	523	2.57
Hispanic (7)	10	0.05
African, sub-Saharan:	16	0.08
African	9	0.04
Kenyan	7	0.03
Am. Ind. or Alaska Nat., not spec.	53	0.26
American Indian tribes, specified:	98	0.48
Apache	3	0.01
Blackfeet	2	0.01
Cherokee (27)	52	0.26
Chippewa (2)	4	0.02
Choctaw (4)	8	0.04
Creek	2	0.01
Crow	3	0.01
Iroquois (1)	9	0.04
Latin American Indians	2	0.01
Lumbee	3	0.01
Potawatomi (2)	2	0.01
Pueblo	1	0.00
Seminole	1	0.00
All other tribes	6	0.03
American Indian tribes, not spec.	3	0.01
Arab:	73	0.36
Arab/Arabic	31	0.15
Lebanese	21	0.10
Syrian	6	0.03
Other Arab	15	0.07
Armenian	45	0.22
Asian:	269	1.32
Bangladeshi (2)	2	0.01
Chinese, ex. Taiwanese (19)	31	0.15
Filipino (26)	42	0.21
Indian (76)	89	0.44
Indonesian (1)	1	0.00
Japanese (11)	22	0.11
Korean (18)	19	0.09
Laotian (2)	3	0.01
Pakistani (6)	6	0.03
Sri Lankan (2)	2	0.01
Vietnamese (21)	22	0.11
Other Asian, specified (1)	1	0.00
Other Asian, not specified (5)	29	0.14
Austrian	84	0.41
Belgian	24	0.12
Brazilian	6	0.03
British	111	0.54
Canadian	58	0.28
Celtic	10	0.05
Croatian	10	0.05
Czech	101	0.50
Czechoslovakian	57	0.28
Danish	116	0.57
Dutch	469	2.30
English	3,209	15.75
European	67	0.33
Finnish	70	0.34
French, except Basque	812	3.99
French Canadian	296	1.45
German	3,521	17.28
Greek	130	0.64
Hawaii Native/Pacific Islander:	30	0.15
Micronesian: (8)	9	0.04
Guamanian/Chamorro (8)	9	0.04
Polynesian: (6)	14	0.07
Native Hawaiian (3)	9	0.04
Samoan (1)	1	0.00
Tongan (1)	1	0.00
Other Polynesian (1)	3	0.01
Other Pac. Isl., not spec. (1)	7	0.03
Hispanic or Latino:	686	3.37
Central American:	22	0.11
Costa Rican	7	0.03
Guatemalan	1	0.00
Honduran	4	0.02
Nicaraguan	1	0.00
Panamanian	4	0.02
Salvadoran	5	0.02
Cuban	97	0.48
Dominican Republic	3	0.01
Mexican	203	1.00
Puerto Rican	136	0.67
South American:	104	0.51
Argentinean	6	0.03
Chilean	9	0.04
Colombian	61	0.30
Ecuadorian	4	0.02
Peruvian	12	0.06
Venezuelan	3	0.01
Other South American	9	0.04
Other Hispanic or Latino	121	0.59
Hungarian	147	0.72
Irish	3,954	19.41
Italian	1,970	9.67
Latvian	5	0.02
Lithuanian	46	0.23
Maltese	5	0.02
New Zealander	8	0.04
Northern European	7	0.03
Norwegian	147	0.72
Pennsylvania German	24	0.12
Polish	590	2.90
Portuguese	81	0.40
Romanian	15	0.07
Russian	148	0.73
Scandinavian	78	0.38
Scotch-Irish	390	1.91
Scottish	592	2.91
Serbian	13	0.06
Slavic	36	0.18
Slovak	67	0.33
Slovene	15	0.07
Swedish	466	2.29
Swiss	58	0.28
Turkish	8	0.04
Ukrainian	63	0.31
United States or American	2,047	10.05
Welsh	247	1.21
West Indian, excl. Hispanic:	45	0.22
Haitian	8	0.04
Jamaican	37	0.18
White:	19,423	95.39
Not Hispanic (18,692)	18,901	92.82
Hispanic (485)	522	2.56

Vero Beach

Place Type: City
County: Indian River
Population: 17,705

Ancestry/Race	Number	%
African American/Black:	654	3.69
Not Hispanic (581)	627	3.54
Hispanic (25)	27	0.15
African, sub-Saharan:	80	0.45
African	60	0.34
South African	20	0.11
Alaska Native tribes, specified:	3	0.02
Aleut	1	0.01
Eskimo (1)	1	0.01
All other tribes (1)	1	0.01
Am. Ind. or Alaska Nat., not spec.	14	0.08
Alsatian	8	0.04
American Indian tribes, specified:	41	0.23
Apache (1)	1	0.01
Blackfeet	1	0.01
Cherokee (14)	23	0.13
Choctaw	1	0.01
Delaware	1	0.01
Houma	1	0.01
Iroquois	2	0.01
Latin American Indians (2)	2	0.01
Lumbee (1)	1	0.01
Seminole	1	0.01
All other tribes (5)	7	0.04
American Indian tribes, not spec.	2	0.01
Arab:	40	0.22
Arab/Arabic	14	0.08
Lebanese	12	0.07
Syrian	14	0.08
Armenian	6	0.03
Asian:	265	1.50
Bangladeshi (9)	9	0.05
Cambodian (1)	1	0.01
Chinese, ex. Taiwanese (48)	52	0.29
Filipino (22)	32	0.18
Indian (58)	64	0.36
Indonesian (1)	2	0.01
Japanese (9)	18	0.10
Korean (20)	21	0.12
Malaysian	1	0.01
Pakistani (8)	8	0.05
Taiwanese (1)	3	0.02
Thai (2)	4	0.02
Vietnamese (23)	27	0.15
Other Asian, specified (1)	1	0.01
Other Asian, not specified (11)	22	0.12
Australian	11	0.06
Austrian	102	0.57
Belgian	22	0.12
British	239	1.34
Canadian	105	0.59
Celtic	6	0.03
Czech	71	0.40
Czechoslovakian	4	0.02
Danish	52	0.29
Dutch	394	2.21
English	2,880	16.14
European	211	1.18

Notes: 1. Figures in the "Number" column do not add up to the total population due to: a) Ancestry/Race overlap — e.g. persons can report being both White and Irish, b) persons of Hispanic origin can report being any race, c) persons reporting two ancestries are counted in both categories. 2. Numbers in parentheses indicate the number of persons reporting this ancestry/race alone, not in combination with any other ancestry/race. 3. Refer to the User's Guide in the front of the book for more detailed information.

Finnish	81	0.45
French, except Basque	605	3.39
French Canadian	91	0.51
German	2,925	16.39
Greek	109	0.61
Hawaii Native/Pacific Islander:	12	0.07
Micronesian: (4)	4	0.02
Guamanian/Chamorro (3)	3	0.02
Other Micronesian (1)	1	0.01
Polynesian: (1)	5	0.03
Native Hawaiian (1)	4	0.02
Samoan	1	0.01
Other Pac. Isl., not spec.	3	0.02
Hispanic or Latino:	1,025	5.79
Central American:	89	0.50
Costa Rican	5	0.03
Guatemalan	11	0.06
Honduran	37	0.21
Nicaraguan	6	0.03
Panamanian	3	0.02
Salvadoran	24	0.14
Other Central American	3	0.02
Cuban	77	0.43
Dominican Republic	7	0.04
Mexican	410	2.32
Puerto Rican	146	0.82
South American:	144	0.81
Argentinean	13	0.07
Bolivian	4	0.02
Chilean	7	0.04
Colombian	72	0.41
Ecuadorian	10	0.06
Peruvian	22	0.12
Uruguayan	1	0.01
Venezuelan	12	0.07
Other South American	3	0.02
Other Hispanic or Latino	152	0.86
Hungarian	118	0.66
Irish	3,191	17.88
Israeli	18	0.10
Italian	1,555	8.71
Lithuanian	11	0.06
Macedonian	8	0.04
Maltese	9	0.05
New Zealander	3	0.02
Norwegian	221	1.24
Polish	691	3.87
Portuguese	32	0.18
Russian	135	0.76
Scandinavian	43	0.24
Scotch-Irish	513	2.87
Scottish	607	3.40
Slovak	18	0.10
Swedish	320	1.79
Swiss	60	0.34
Turkish	20	0.11
Ukrainian	74	0.41
United States or American	1,173	6.57
Welsh	216	1.21
West Indian, excl. Hispanic:	87	0.49
Bahamian	8	0.04
Haitian	46	0.26
Jamaican	33	0.18
White:	16,570	93.59
Not Hispanic (15,695)	15,807	89.28
Hispanic (723)	763	4.31
Yugoslavian	17	0.10

Villas

Place Type: Census Designated Place
County: Lee
Population: 11,346

Ancestry/Race	Number	%
Afghan	6	0.05
African American/Black:	239	2.11
Not Hispanic (161)	208	1.83
Hispanic (26)	31	0.27
African, sub-Saharan:	7	0.06
African	7	0.06
Alaska Native tribes, specified:	6	0.05
Aleut (2)	2	0.02
Eskimo	4	0.04
Alaska Native tribes, not specified	1	0.01
Am. Ind. or Alaska Nat., not spec.	12	0.11
American Indian tribes, specified:	19	0.17
Apache	1	0.01
Blackfeet	1	0.01
Cherokee (2)	7	0.06
Creek (2)	2	0.02
Iroquois (1)	2	0.02
Latin American Indians	2	0.02
Sioux (1)	1	0.01
All other tribes	3	0.03
American Indian tribes, not spec.	2	0.02
Arab:	31	0.28
Egyptian	18	0.16
Lebanese	13	0.12
Asian:	183	1.61
Cambodian	1	0.01
Chinese, ex. Taiwanese (20)	26	0.23
Filipino (26)	43	0.38
Indian (38)	48	0.42
Japanese (2)	7	0.06
Korean (11)	17	0.15
Pakistani (3)	4	0.04
Sri Lankan (2)	2	0.02
Thai (2)	2	0.02
Vietnamese (20)	25	0.22
Other Asian, not specified (4)	8	0.07
Austrian	26	0.23
Belgian	24	0.21
Brazilian	54	0.48
British	82	0.73
Bulgarian	6	0.05
Canadian	49	0.44
Croatian	23	0.21
Czech	53	0.47
Czechoslovakian	14	0.13
Danish	57	0.51
Dutch	286	2.56
English	1,927	17.25
European	61	0.55
Finnish	44	0.39
French, except Basque	571	5.11
French Canadian	128	1.15
German	2,283	20.44
Greek	139	1.24
Hawaii Native/Pacific Islander:	9	0.08
Polynesian: (5)	8	0.07
Native Hawaiian (5)	8	0.07
Other Pac. Isl., not spec.	1	0.01
Hispanic or Latino:	634	5.59
Central American:	36	0.32
Costa Rican	6	0.05
Guatemalan	5	0.04
Honduran	6	0.05
Nicaraguan	6	0.05
Panamanian	6	0.05
Salvadoran	4	0.04
Other Central American	3	0.03
Cuban	81	0.71
Dominican Republic	5	0.04
Mexican	206	1.82
Puerto Rican	151	1.33
South American:	70	0.62
Argentinean	10	0.09
Chilean	4	0.04
Colombian	28	0.25
Ecuadorian	4	0.04
Peruvian	10	0.09
Venezuelan	3	0.03
Other South American	11	0.10
Other Hispanic or Latino	85	0.75
Hungarian	106	0.95
Irish	1,711	15.32
Israeli	9	0.08
Italian	1,125	10.07
Latvian	18	0.16
Lithuanian	66	0.59
Norwegian	174	1.56
Pennsylvania German	26	0.23
Polish	526	4.71
Portuguese	35	0.31
Romanian	21	0.19
Russian	116	1.04
Scandinavian	9	0.08
Scotch-Irish	205	1.84
Scottish	357	3.20
Serbian	10	0.09
Slovak	51	0.46
Slovene	23	0.21
Swedish	169	1.51
Swiss	37	0.33
Turkish	7	0.06
Ukrainian	29	0.26
United States or American	638	5.71
Welsh	129	1.16
West Indian, excl. Hispanic:	72	0.64
Dutch West Indian	12	0.11
Haitian	30	0.27
Jamaican	30	0.27
White:	10,827	95.43
Not Hispanic (10,266)	10,367	91.37
Hispanic (425)	460	4.05

Warrington

Place Type: Census Designated Place
County: Escambia
Population: 15,207

Ancestry/Race	Number	%
Acadian/Cajun	18	0.12
African American/Black:	3,410	22.42
Not Hispanic (3,278)	3,383	22.25
Hispanic (21)	27	0.18
African, sub-Saharan:	54	0.36
African	54	0.36
Am. Ind. or Alaska Nat., not spec.	65	0.43
American Indian tribes, specified:	293	1.93
Apache (4)	12	0.08
Blackfeet (1)	8	0.05
Cherokee (36)	116	0.76
Chippewa (3)	4	0.03
Choctaw (5)	14	0.09
Colville (1)	1	0.01
Creek (58)	89	0.59
Houma (4)	5	0.03
Iroquois	1	0.01
Latin American Indians (1)	4	0.03
Lumbee (5)	7	0.05
Navajo (2)	2	0.01
Paiute (3)	3	0.02
Puget Sound Salish (1)	1	0.01
Seminole (3)	4	0.03
Sioux (2)	11	0.07
All other tribes (2)	11	0.07
American Indian tribes, not spec.	14	0.09
Arab:	16	0.11
Arab/Arabic	4	0.03
Lebanese	4	0.03
Syrian	8	0.05
Asian:	417	2.74
Cambodian (2)	4	0.03
Chinese, ex. Taiwanese (10)	18	0.12
Filipino (150)	204	1.34
Indian (9)	17	0.11
Japanese (14)	23	0.15
Korean (8)	11	0.07
Malaysian	1	0.01
Thai (4)	5	0.03
Vietnamese (111)	119	0.78
Other Asian, specified	3	0.02
Other Asian, not specified (1)	12	0.08
Australian	11	0.07
Austrian	16	0.11
Belgian	35	0.23
Brazilian	28	0.18
British	27	0.18
Canadian	34	0.22
Croatian	10	0.07

Notes: 1. Figures in the "Number" column do not add up to the total population due to: a) Ancestry/Race overlap — e.g. persons can report being both White and Irish, b) persons of Hispanic origin can report being any race, c) persons reporting two ancestries are counted in both categories. 2. Numbers in parentheses indicate the number of persons reporting this ancestry/race alone, not in combination with any other ancestry/race. 3. Refer to the User's Guide in the front of the book for more detailed information.

Danish	44	0.29
Dutch	283	1.86
English	1,372	9.04
European	53	0.35
Finnish	26	0.17
French, except Basque	619	4.08
French Canadian	152	1.00
German	1,561	10.28
Greek	46	0.30
Hawaii Native/Pacific Islander:	50	0.33
Micronesian: (13)	18	0.12
Guamanian/Chamorro (9)	13	0.09
Other Micronesian (4)	5	0.03
Polynesian: (8)	17	0.11
Native Hawaiian (4)	12	0.08
Samoan (4)	5	0.03
Other Pac. Isl., specified	3	0.02
Other Pac. Isl., not spec. (2)	12	0.08
Hispanic or Latino:	438	2.88
Central American:	17	0.11
Guatemalan	1	0.01
Honduran	7	0.05
Nicaraguan	1	0.01
Panamanian	7	0.05
Salvadoran	1	0.01
Cuban	32	0.21
Dominican Republic	2	0.01
Mexican	145	0.95
Puerto Rican	117	0.77
South American:	11	0.07
Bolivian	1	0.01
Chilean	3	0.02
Colombian	6	0.04
Venezuelan	1	0.01
Other Hispanic or Latino	114	0.75
Hungarian	76	0.50
Irish	1,451	9.56
Italian	457	3.01
Lithuanian	25	0.16
Luxemburger	10	0.07
Norwegian	75	0.49
Pennsylvania German	9	0.06
Polish	171	1.13
Portuguese	29	0.19
Russian	30	0.20
Scandinavian	16	0.11
Scotch-Irish	511	3.37
Scottish	245	1.61
Serbian	7	0.05
Slavic	10	0.07
Slovak	5	0.03
Slovene	7	0.05
Swedish	146	0.96
Swiss	26	0.17
Ukrainian	17	0.11
United States or American	2,204	14.51
Welsh	35	0.23
West Indian, excl. Hispanic:	42	0.28
Bahamian	8	0.05
Dutch West Indian	7	0.05
Jamaican	16	0.11
West Indian	11	0.07
White:	11,211	73.72
Not Hispanic (10,658)	10,957	72.05
Hispanic (225)	254	1.67

Wekiwa Springs

Place Type: Census Designated Place
County: Seminole
Population: 23,169

Ancestry/Race	Number	%
Acadian/Cajun	11	0.05
African American/Black:	386	1.67
Not Hispanic (330)	364	1.57
Hispanic (13)	22	0.09
African, sub-Saharan:	107	0.46
African	56	0.24
South African	43	0.18
Other sub-Saharan African	8	0.03
Am. Ind. or Alaska Nat., not spec.	19	0.08
American Indian tribes, specified:	74	0.32
Blackfeet	4	0.02
Cherokee (8)	31	0.13
Chickasaw (4)	4	0.02
Chippewa (1)	1	0.00
Comanche (1)	1	0.00
Creek (1)	2	0.01
Delaware	1	0.00
Iroquois	2	0.01
Latin American Indians (5)	11	0.05
Lumbee (1)	1	0.00
Potawatomi (4)	5	0.02
Pueblo (1)	1	0.00
Seminole	2	0.01
Sioux (1)	1	0.00
All other tribes (4)	7	0.03
American Indian tribes, not spec.	1	0.00
Arab:	220	0.95
Egyptian	5	0.02
Iraqi	9	0.04
Jordanian	6	0.03
Lebanese	107	0.46
Syrian	93	0.40
Armenian	12	0.05
Asian:	607	2.62
Chinese, ex. Taiwanese (65)	79	0.34
Filipino (40)	48	0.21
Indian (248)	269	1.16
Indonesian (1)	1	0.00
Japanese (17)	30	0.13
Korean (86)	96	0.41
Pakistani (11)	18	0.08
Taiwanese (3)	4	0.02
Thai (9)	9	0.04
Vietnamese (25)	29	0.13
Other Asian, not specified (9)	24	0.10
Australian	7	0.03
Austrian	212	0.91
Belgian	24	0.10
Brazilian	7	0.03
British	275	1.18
Canadian	128	0.55
Croatian	19	0.08
Czech	99	0.43
Czechoslovakian	69	0.30
Danish	208	0.89
Dutch	396	1.70
Eastern European	158	0.68
English	3,654	15.70
Estonian	9	0.04
European	378	1.62
Finnish	63	0.27
French, except Basque	930	4.00
French Canadian	219	0.94
German	4,525	19.44
Greek	178	0.76
Hawaii Native/Pacific Islander:	17	0.07
Micronesian: (3)	3	0.01
Guamanian/Chamorro (3)	3	0.01
Polynesian: (3)	7	0.03
Native Hawaiian (2)	6	0.03
Samoan (1)	1	0.00
Other Pac. Isl , not spec.	7	0.03
Hispanic or Latino:	1,139	4.92
Central American:	32	0.14
Costa Rican	3	0.01
Guatemalan	5	0.02
Honduran	1	0.00
Nicaraguan	1	0.00
Panamanian	9	0.04
Salvadoran	8	0.03
Other Central American	5	0.02
Cuban	205	0.88
Dominican Republic	24	0.10
Mexican	83	0.36
Puerto Rican	371	1.60
South American:	219	0.95
Argentinean	45	0.19
Bolivian	3	0.01
Chilean	5	0.02
Colombian	94	0.41
Ecuadorian	9	0.04
Peruvian	38	0.16
Uruguayan	1	0.00
Venezuelan	16	0.07
Other South American	8	0.03
Other Hispanic or Latino	205	0.88
Hungarian	264	1.13
Icelander	10	0.04
Iranian	69	0.30
Irish	3,458	14.86
Israeli	32	0.14
Italian	2,069	8.89
Latvian	15	0.06
Lithuanian	143	0.61
New Zealander	10	0.04
Northern European	55	0.24
Norwegian	346	1.49
Pennsylvania German	13	0.06
Polish	1,208	5.19
Portuguese	59	0.25
Romanian	123	0.53
Russian	730	3.14
Scandinavian	45	0.19
Scotch-Irish	482	2.07
Scottish	535	2.30
Slovak	65	0.28
Slovene	17	0.07
Swedish	466	2.00
Swiss	108	0.46
Ukrainian	61	0.26
United States or American	1,274	5.47
Welsh	215	0.92
West Indian, excl. Hispanic:	80	0.34
Jamaican	80	0.34
White:	22,085	95.32
Not Hispanic (20,924)	21,082	90.99
Hispanic (954)	1,003	4.33

Wellington

Place Type: Village
County: Palm Beach
Population: 38,216

Ancestry/Race	Number	%
African American/Black:	2,286	5.98
Not Hispanic (1,957)	2,158	5.65
Hispanic (100)	128	0.33
African, sub-Saharan:	234	0.62
African	206	0.54
Ghanian	28	0.07
Am. Ind. or Alaska Nat., not spec.	31	0.08
American Indian tribes, specified:	113	0.30
Apache (2)	2	0.01
Blackfeet (2)	11	0.03
Cherokee (10)	48	0.13
Chickasaw (1)	1	0.00
Chippewa (2)	11	0.03
Choctaw	1	0.00
Cree	1	0.00
Houma	3	0.01
Iroquois (4)	5	0.01
Latin American Indians (3)	11	0.03
Menominee	2	0.01
Navajo	1	0.00
Ottawa	1	0.00
Potawatomi (1)	1	0.00
Pueblo (3)	3	0.01
Seminole	1	0.00
Sioux (1)	5	0.01
All other tribes (3)	5	0.01
American Indian tribes, not spec.	7	0.02
Arab:	232	0.61
Arab/Arabic	45	0.12
Egyptian	18	0.05
Lebanese	93	0.24
Moroccan	6	0.02
Palestinian	53	0.14
Syrian	17	0.04
Armenian	51	0.13

Notes: 1. Figures in the "Number" column do not add up to the total population due to: a) Ancestry/Race overlap — e.g. persons can report being both White and Irish, b) persons of Hispanic origin can report being any race, c) persons reporting two ancestries are counted in both categories. 2. Numbers in parentheses indicate the number of persons reporting this ancestry/race alone, not in combination with any other ancestry/race. 3. Refer to the User's Guide in the front of the book for more detailed information.

Asian:	979	2.56
Bangladeshi (12)	17	0.04
Chinese, ex. Taiwanese (169)	208	0.54
Filipino (101)	143	0.37
Indian (285)	349	0.91
Indonesian (3)	5	0.01
Japanese (24)	36	0.09
Korean (44)	64	0.17
Pakistani (18)	22	0.06
Sri Lankan (10)	10	0.03
Taiwanese (1)	5	0.01
Thai (19)	27	0.07
Vietnamese (42)	50	0.13
Other Asian, specified (7)	8	0.02
Other Asian, not specified (13)	35	0.09
Australian	11	0.03
Austrian	202	0.53
Basque	32	0.08
Belgian	27	0.07
Brazilian	14	0.04
British	273	0.72
Bulgarian	16	0.04
Canadian	230	0.60
Celtic	16	0.04
Croatian	32	0.08
Cypriot	20	0.05
Czech	176	0.46
Czechoslovakian	67	0.18
Danish	98	0.26
Dutch	332	0.87
Eastern European	225	0.59
English	4,245	11.16
Estonian	49	0.13
European	336	0.88
Finnish	146	0.38
French, except Basque	1,384	3.64
French Canadian	434	1.14
German	5,175	13.61
Greek	235	0.62
Guyanese	58	0.15
Hawaii Native/Pacific Islander:	37	0.10
Melanesian: (2)	2	0.01
Fijian (2)	2	0.01
Micronesian: (1)	3	0.01
Guamanian/Chamorro (1)	3	0.01
Polynesian: (3)	10	0.03
Native Hawaiian (1)	3	0.01
Samoan (1)	3	0.01
Other Polynesian (1)	4	0.01
Other Pac. Isl., not spec. (4)	22	0.06
Hispanic or Latino:	4,395	11.50
Central American:	171	0.45
Costa Rican	29	0.08
Guatemalan	17	0.04
Honduran	30	0.08
Nicaraguan	36	0.09
Panamanian	28	0.07
Salvadoran	21	0.05
Other Central American	10	0.03
Cuban	1,248	3.27
Dominican Republic	146	0.38
Mexican	451	1.18
Puerto Rican	769	2.01
South American:	840	2.20
Argentinean	103	0.27
Bolivian	15	0.04
Chilean	31	0.08
Colombian	362	0.95
Ecuadorian	76	0.20
Paraguayan	8	0.02
Peruvian	73	0.19
Uruguayan	31	0.08
Venezuelan	117	0.31
Other South American	24	0.06
Other Hispanic or Latino	770	2.01
Hungarian	453	1.19
Iranian	6	0.02
Irish	5,728	15.06
Israeli	77	0.20
Italian	5,550	14.59
Latvian	56	0.15
Lithuanian	140	0.37
Luxemburger	7	0.02
Maltese	12	0.03
Norwegian	348	0.91
Pennsylvania German	41	0.11
Polish	1,769	4.65
Portuguese	204	0.54
Romanian	98	0.26
Russian	1,463	3.85
Scandinavian	27	0.07
Scotch-Irish	550	1.45
Scottish	723	1.90
Serbian	9	0.02
Slovak	98	0.26
Slovene	17	0.04
Swedish	389	1.02
Swiss	95	0.25
Turkish	15	0.04
Ukrainian	205	0.54
United States or American	2,588	6.80
Welsh	217	0.57
West Indian, excl. Hispanic:	879	2.31
Bahamian	9	0.02
British West Indian	12	0.03
Haitian	422	1.11
Jamaican	373	0.98
Trinidadian and Tobagonian	24	0.06
West Indian	39	0.10
White:	34,456	90.16
Not Hispanic (30,473)	30,836	80.69
Hispanic (3,445)	3,620	9.47
Yugoslavian	51	0.13

West Little River

Place Type: Census Designated Place
County: Miami-Dade
Population: 32,498

Ancestry/Race	Number	%
African American/Black:	19,129	58.86
Not Hispanic (17,819)	18,206	56.02
Hispanic (775)	923	2.84
African, sub-Saharan:	539	1.67
African	539	1.67
Am. Ind. or Alaska Nat., not spec.	125	0.38
American Indian tribes, specified:	58	0.18
Apache	2	0.01
Cherokee (1)	10	0.03
Creek	1	0.00
Iroquois	1	0.00
Latin American Indians (16)	34	0.10
Pueblo	2	0.01
Sioux	1	0.00
All other tribes (3)	7	0.02
American Indian tribes, not spec.	11	0.03
Arab:	27	0.08
Arab/Arabic	14	0.04
Lebanese	5	0.02
Other Arab	8	0.02
Asian:	141	0.43
Cambodian (6)	6	0.02
Chinese, ex. Taiwanese (9)	25	0.08
Filipino (12)	14	0.04
Indian (17)	55	0.17
Indonesian	1	0.00
Japanese	1	0.00
Korean (7)	8	0.02
Vietnamese (2)	3	0.01
Other Asian, specified	7	0.02
Other Asian, not specified (6)	21	0.06
Brazilian	5	0.02
British	11	0.03
Canadian	13	0.04
English	42	0.13
European	30	0.09
French, except Basque	26	0.08
French Canadian	11	0.03
German	42	0.13
Guyanese	9	0.03
Hawaii Native/Pacific Islander:	86	0.26
Micronesian: (3)	5	0.02
Guamanian/Chamorro (3)	5	0.02
Polynesian: (1)	5	0.02
Native Hawaiian (1)	2	0.01
Samoan	3	0.01
Other Pac. Isl., specified	7	0.02
Other Pac. Isl., not spec. (18)	69	0.21
Hispanic or Latino:	13,016	40.05
Central American:	2,528	7.78
Costa Rican	14	0.04
Guatemalan	391	1.20
Honduran	709	2.18
Nicaraguan	1,163	3.58
Panamanian	34	0.10
Salvadoran	127	0.39
Other Central American	90	0.28
Cuban	5,452	16.78
Dominican Republic	786	2.42
Mexican	187	0.58
Puerto Rican	1,117	3.44
South American:	429	1.32
Argentinean	32	0.10
Bolivian	2	0.01
Chilean	11	0.03
Colombian	186	0.57
Ecuadorian	71	0.22
Peruvian	77	0.24
Uruguayan	4	0.01
Venezuelan	42	0.13
Other South American	4	0.01
Other Hispanic or Latino	2,517	7.75
Iranian	40	0.12
Irish	87	0.27
Italian	51	0.16
Lithuanian	16	0.05
Polish	6	0.02
Russian	6	0.02
Scottish	10	0.03
Swedish	25	0.08
United States or American	1,527	4.73
Welsh	12	0.04
West Indian, excl. Hispanic:	2,654	8.22
Bahamian	339	1.05
Belizean	6	0.02
British West Indian	18	0.06
Haitian	1,687	5.23
Jamaican	565	1.75
Trinidadian and Tobagonian	21	0.07
U.S. Virgin Islander	8	0.02
West Indian	10	0.03
White:	11,461	35.27
Not Hispanic (1,089)	1,173	3.61
Hispanic (9,483)	10,288	31.66
Yugoslavian	15	0.05

West Palm Beach

Place Type: City
County: Palm Beach
Population: 82,103

Ancestry/Race	Number	%
Acadian/Cajun	4	0.00
African American/Black:	27,925	34.01
Not Hispanic (25,958)	27,307	33.26
Hispanic (488)	618	0.75
African, sub-Saharan:	779	0.96
African	705	0.86
South African	52	0.06
Zimbabwean	7	0.01
Other sub-Saharan African	15	0.02
Alaska Native tribes, specified:	5	0.01
Alaska Athabascan	1	0.00
Eskimo	2	0.00
Tlingit-Haida	2	0.00
Am. Ind. or Alaska Nat., not spec.	198	0.24
Albanian	33	0.04
American Indian tribes, specified:	446	0.54
Apache (3)	4	0.00
Blackfeet (1)	6	0.01
Cherokee (29)	74	0.09
Cheyenne (2)	2	0.00

Notes: 1. Figures in the "Number" column do not add up to the total population due to: a) Ancestry/Race overlap — e.g. persons can report being both White and Irish, b) persons of Hispanic origin can report being any race, c) persons reporting two ancestries are counted in both categories. 2. Numbers in parentheses indicate the number of persons reporting this ancestry/race alone, not in combination with any other ancestry/race. 3. Refer to the User's Guide in the front of the book for more detailed information.

Chippewa (4)	7	0.01
Choctaw (2)	6	0.01
Comanche	4	0.00
Delaware	2	0.00
Iroquois (16)	19	0.02
Kiowa	1	0.00
Latin American Indians (76)	265	0.32
Lumbee (1)	1	0.00
Navajo (6)	9	0.01
Ottawa (1)	1	0.00
Paiute (1)	1	0.00
Potawatomi (2)	2	0.00
Pueblo (4)	5	0.01
Seminole (2)	7	0.01
Shoshone (1)	1	0.00
Sioux	5	0.01
Tohono O'Odham	1	0.00
Yuman (1)	2	0.00
All other tribes (11)	21	0.03
American Indian tribes, not spec.	39	0.05
Arab:	839	1.03
Arab/Arabic	123	0.15
Egyptian	58	0.07
Iraqi	41	0.05
Jordanian	15	0.02
Lebanese	307	0.38
Moroccan	23	0.03
Palestinian	149	0.18
Syrian	70	0.09
Other Arab	53	0.06
Armenian	33	0.04
Asian:	1,516	1.85
Bangladeshi (12)	21	0.03
Cambodian (7)	9	0.01
Chinese, ex. Taiwanese (162)	203	0.25
Filipino (200)	239	0.29
Indian (382)	446	0.54
Indonesian (3)	4	0.00
Japanese (52)	75	0.09
Korean (107)	129	0.16
Laotian (1)	1	0.00
Malaysian (3)	4	0.00
Pakistani (10)	25	0.03
Sri Lankan (9)	9	0.01
Taiwanese (2)	4	0.00
Thai (56)	71	0.09
Vietnamese (130)	139	0.17
Other Asian, specified (8)	14	0.02
Other Asian, not specified (38)	123	0.15
Australian	64	0.08
Austrian	445	0.55
Basque	9	0.01
Belgian	127	0.16
Brazilian	174	0.21
British	384	0.47
Bulgarian	11	0.01
Canadian	338	0.41
Croatian	41	0.05
Czech	164	0.20
Czechoslovakian	104	0.13
Danish	176	0.22
Dutch	764	0.94
Eastern European	141	0.17
English	5,016	6.15
European	365	0.45
Finnish	104	0.13
French, except Basque	1,740	2.13
French Canadian	406	0.50
German	6,078	7.45
Greek	379	0.46
Guyanese	62	0.08
Hawaii Native/Pacific Islander:	262	0.32
Melanesian:	3	0.00
Other Melanesian	3	0.00
Micronesian: (84)	98	0.12
Guamanian/Chamorro (84)	98	0.12
Polynesian: (24)	54	0.07
Native Hawaiian (15)	26	0.03
Samoan (8)	25	0.03
Other Polynesian (1)	3	0.00
Other Pac. Isl., specified	6	0.01
Other Pac. Isl., not spec. (23)	101	0.12
Hispanic or Latino:	14,955	18.21
Central American:	2,745	3.34
Costa Rican	116	0.14
Guatemalan	1,841	2.24
Honduran	308	0.38
Nicaraguan	265	0.32
Panamanian	37	0.05
Salvadoran	111	0.14
Other Central American	67	0.08
Cuban	4,343	5.29
Dominican Republic	418	0.51
Mexican	1,975	2.41
Puerto Rican	2,130	2.59
South American:	1,171	1.43
Argentinean	72	0.09
Bolivian	18	0.02
Chilean	31	0.04
Colombian	587	0.71
Ecuadorian	130	0.16
Paraguayan	8	0.01
Peruvian	131	0.16
Uruguayan	56	0.07
Venezuelan	98	0.12
Other South American	40	0.05
Other Hispanic or Latino	2,173	2.65
Hungarian	576	0.71
Iranian	61	0.07
Irish	5,742	7.04
Israeli	24	0.03
Italian	4,034	4.95
Latvian	32	0.04
Lithuanian	168	0.21
Maltese	5	0.01
Norwegian	346	0.42
Pennsylvania German	21	0.03
Polish	1,834	2.25
Portuguese	334	0.41
Romanian	109	0.13
Russian	1,425	1.75
Scandinavian	31	0.04
Scotch-Irish	835	1.02
Scottish	1,041	1.28
Serbian	28	0.03
Slavic	7	0.01
Slovak	89	0.11
Slovene	8	0.01
Swedish	538	0.66
Swiss	94	0.12
Turkish	63	0.08
Ukrainian	218	0.27
United States or American	4,276	5.24
Welsh	324	0.40
West Indian, excl. Hispanic:	6,338	7.77
Bahamian	327	0.40
Barbadian	50	0.06
Belizean	17	0.02
Bermudan	11	0.01
British West Indian	106	0.13
Haitian	3,389	4.16
Jamaican	2,134	2.62
Trinidadian and Tobagonian	132	0.16
U.S. Virgin Islander	34	0.04
West Indian	119	0.15
Other West Indian	19	0.02
White:	49,003	59.68
Not Hispanic (37,771)	38,444	46.82
Hispanic (9,925)	10,559	12.86
Yugoslavian	26	0.03

West Pensacola

Place Type: Census Designated Place
County: Escambia
Population: 21,939

Ancestry/Race	Number	%
African American/Black:	7,584	34.57
Not Hispanic (7,339)	7,508	34.22
Hispanic (52)	76	0.35
African, sub-Saharan:	177	0.81
African	129	0.59
Cape Verdean	32	0.15
Ghanian	7	0.03
Nigerian	9	0.04
Alaska Native tribes, specified:	3	0.01
Aleut (2)	2	0.01
Eskimo	1	0.00
Alaska Native tribes, not specified	1	0.00
Am. Ind. or Alaska Nat., not spec.	130	0.59
American Indian tribes, specified:	370	1.69
Apache (5)	7	0.03
Blackfeet (3)	13	0.06
Cherokee (40)	112	0.51
Cheyenne (2)	2	0.01
Chippewa (3)	3	0.01
Choctaw (2)	9	0.04
Creek (94)	150	0.68
Delaware (1)	1	0.00
Houma (4)	4	0.02
Iroquois (1)	6	0.03
Kiowa (1)	1	0.00
Latin American Indians (5)	7	0.03
Lumbee	2	0.01
Navajo (1)	2	0.01
Ottawa	1	0.00
Paiute	3	0.01
Potawatomi	1	0.00
Seminole (6)	8	0.04
Sioux (8)	14	0.06
All other tribes (11)	24	0.11
American Indian tribes, not spec.	18	0.08
Arab:	14	0.06
Syrian	14	0.06
Armenian	27	0.12
Asian:	933	4.25
Cambodian (7)	7	0.03
Chinese, ex. Taiwanese (14)	24	0.11
Filipino (257)	344	1.57
Indian (19)	33	0.15
Indonesian	1	0.00
Japanese (26)	49	0.22
Korean (16)	21	0.10
Laotian (2)	4	0.02
Taiwanese (1)	1	0.00
Thai (3)	4	0.02
Vietnamese (389)	412	1.88
Other Asian, specified	1	0.00
Other Asian, not specified (7)	32	0.15
Australian	8	0.04
Austrian	40	0.18
Brazilian	34	0.15
British	104	0.47
Czech	7	0.03
Czechoslovakian	14	0.06
Danish	21	0.10
Dutch	170	0.77
English	1,217	5.54
European	165	0.75
French, except Basque	537	2.45
French Canadian	90	0.41
German	1,274	5.80
German Russian	6	0.03
Greek	103	0.47
Hawaii Native/Pacific Islander:	88	0.40
Micronesian: (21)	24	0.11
Guamanian/Chamorro (21)	24	0.11
Polynesian: (21)	50	0.23
Native Hawaiian (9)	33	0.15
Samoan (12)	17	0.08
Other Pac. Isl., specified	1	0.00
Other Pac. Isl., not spec.	13	0.06
Hispanic or Latino:	571	2.60
Central American:	17	0.08
Costa Rican	1	0.00
Guatemalan	4	0.02
Honduran	3	0.01
Panamanian	9	0.04
Cuban	35	0.16
Dominican Republic	11	0.05
Mexican	173	0.79
Puerto Rican	135	0.62
South American:	17	0.08

Notes: 1. Figures in the "Number" column do not add up to the total population due to: a) Ancestry/Race overlap — e.g. persons can report being both White and Irish, b) persons of Hispanic origin can report being any race, c) persons reporting two ancestries are counted in both categories. 2. Numbers in parentheses indicate the number of persons reporting this ancestry/race alone, not in combination with any other ancestry/race. 3. Refer to the User's Guide in the front of the book for more detailed information.

Bolivian	2	0.01
Colombian	7	0.03
Ecuadorian	3	0.01
Peruvian	3	0.01
Venezuelan	1	0.00
Other South American	1	0.00
Other Hispanic or Latino	183	0.83
Hungarian	45	0.20
Icelander	9	0.04
Irish	1,564	7.12
Israeli	13	0.06
Italian	471	2.15
Lithuanian	19	0.09
Norwegian	114	0.52
Polish	211	0.96
Portuguese	48	0.22
Scotch-Irish	427	1.94
Scottish	279	1.27
Swedish	139	0.63
Swiss	11	0.05
United States or American	2,240	10.20
Welsh	58	0.26
West Indian, excl. Hispanic:	175	0.80
Haitian	146	0.66
Jamaican	17	0.08
West Indian	12	0.05
White:	13,222	60.27
Not Hispanic (12,432)	12,864	58.64
Hispanic (305)	358	1.63

West and East Lealman

Place Type: Census Designated Place
County: Pinellas
Population: 21,753

Ancestry/Race	Number	%
African American/Black:	802	3.69
Not Hispanic (673)	750	3.45
Hispanic (28)	52	0.24
African, sub-Saharan:	13	0.06
African	13	0.06
Am. Ind. or Alaska Nat., not spec.	73	0.34
Albanian	9	0.04
Alsatian	8	0.04
American Indian tribes, specified:	222	1.02
Apache	7	0.03
Blackfeet (7)	16	0.07
Cherokee (29)	103	0.47
Chippewa (5)	9	0.04
Choctaw (3)	6	0.03
Comanche (2)	4	0.02
Creek (2)	3	0.01
Crow (1)	1	0.00
Iroquois (20)	37	0.17
Latin American Indians (7)	8	0.04
Lumbee (2)	2	0.01
Seminole (2)	3	0.01
Sioux	8	0.04
Ute	1	0.00
All other tribes (8)	14	0.06
American Indian tribes, not spec.	21	0.10
Arab:	38	0.17
Lebanese	31	0.14
Syrian	7	0.03
Asian:	1,025	4.71
Bangladeshi (2)	2	0.01
Cambodian (40)	65	0.30
Chinese, ex. Taiwanese (22)	30	0.14
Filipino (44)	64	0.29
Indian (33)	44	0.20
Indonesian (1)	1	0.00
Japanese (7)	17	0.08
Korean (29)	36	0.17
Laotian (110)	120	0.55
Taiwanese (2)	2	0.01
Thai (20)	23	0.11
Vietnamese (539)	584	2.68
Other Asian, not specified (7)	37	0.17
Austrian	37	0.17
Belgian	13	0.06
British	139	0.64
Bulgarian	6	0.03
Canadian	133	0.61
Croatian	5	0.02
Czech	76	0.35
Czechoslovakian	17	0.08
Danish	38	0.17
Dutch	542	2.48
English	2,726	12.47
European	127	0.58
Finnish	35	0.16
French, except Basque	1,045	4.78
French Canadian	353	1.62
German	3,706	16.96
Greek	92	0.42
Hawaii Native/Pacific Islander:	28	0.13
Polynesian: (4)	7	0.03
Native Hawaiian (3)	5	0.02
Tongan (1)	2	0.01
Other Pac. Isl., not spec. (12)	21	0.10
Hispanic or Latino:	1,067	4.91
Central American:	38	0.17
Costa Rican	8	0.04
Guatemalan	1	0.00
Honduran	10	0.05
Nicaraguan	3	0.01
Panamanian	9	0.04
Salvadoran	7	0.03
Cuban	122	0.56
Dominican Republic	14	0.06
Mexican	261	1.20
Puerto Rican	432	1.99
South American:	62	0.29
Argentinean	5	0.02
Bolivian	4	0.02
Chilean	5	0.02
Colombian	22	0.10
Ecuadorian	8	0.04
Peruvian	4	0.02
Venezuelan	3	0.01
Other South American	11	0.05
Other Hispanic or Latino	138	0.63
Hungarian	147	0.67
Irish	3,318	15.18
Italian	1,672	7.65
Lithuanian	54	0.25
Norwegian	100	0.46
Pennsylvania German	8	0.04
Polish	925	4.23
Portuguese	75	0.34
Romanian	7	0.03
Russian	125	0.57
Scandinavian	17	0.08
Scotch-Irish	509	2.33
Scottish	468	2.14
Serbian	28	0.13
Slovak	46	0.21
Swedish	289	1.32
Swiss	41	0.19
Ukrainian	37	0.17
United States or American	2,025	9.27
Welsh	156	0.71
West Indian, excl. Hispanic:	145	0.66
Haitian	70	0.32
Jamaican	9	0.04
Trinidadian and Tobagonian	55	0.25
West Indian	11	0.05
White:	19,605	90.13
Not Hispanic (18,581)	18,903	86.90
Hispanic (629)	702	3.23
Yugoslavian	94	0.43

Westchase

Place Type: Census Designated Place
County: Hillsborough
Population: 11,116

Ancestry/Race	Number	%
Acadian/Cajun	7	0.06
African American/Black:	607	5.46
Not Hispanic (551)	586	5.27
Hispanic (12)	21	0.19
African, sub-Saharan:	94	0.85
African	62	0.56
Other sub-Saharan African	32	0.29
Am. Ind. or Alaska Nat., not spec.	6	0.05
American Indian tribes, specified:	21	0.19
Blackfeet	2	0.02
Cherokee (1)	5	0.04
Cheyenne	1	0.01
Chippewa (1)	1	0.01
Choctaw	2	0.02
Delaware (1)	1	0.01
Latin American Indians (3)	3	0.03
Lumbee (1)	1	0.01
Ottawa (2)	2	0.02
Sioux	1	0.01
All other tribes (2)	2	0.02
Arab:	20	0.18
Lebanese	20	0.18
Asian:	526	4.73
Cambodian	1	0.01
Chinese, ex. Taiwanese (72)	96	0.86
Filipino (97)	115	1.03
Hmong (4)	4	0.04
Indian (110)	122	1.10
Japanese (17)	25	0.22
Korean (64)	69	0.62
Laotian (3)	3	0.03
Sri Lankan (1)	1	0.01
Thai (8)	9	0.08
Vietnamese (62)	64	0.58
Other Asian, specified (6)	9	0.08
Other Asian, not specified (6)	8	0.07
Austrian	44	0.40
Basque	7	0.06
Belgian	23	0.21
Brazilian	4	0.04
British	62	0.56
Canadian	46	0.41
Croatian	10	0.09
Czech	78	0.70
Czechoslovakian	14	0.13
Danish	39	0.35
Dutch	137	1.23
Eastern European	26	0.23
English	1,413	12.71
European	49	0.44
Finnish	45	0.40
French, except Basque	421	3.79
French Canadian	94	0.85
German	2,018	18.15
Greek	128	1.15
Hawaii Native/Pacific Islander:	11	0.10
Polynesian: (1)	5	0.04
Native Hawaiian	4	0.04
Samoan (1)	1	0.01
Other Pac. Isl., specified	1	0.01
Other Pac. Isl., not spec.	5	0.04
Hispanic or Latino:	1,322	11.89
Central American:	33	0.30
Costa Rican	3	0.03
Guatemalan	6	0.05
Honduran	1	0.01
Nicaraguan	3	0.03
Panamanian	7	0.06
Salvadoran	8	0.07
Other Central American	5	0.04
Cuban	290	2.61
Dominican Republic	29	0.26
Mexican	75	0.67
Puerto Rican	422	3.80
South American:	189	1.70
Argentinean	8	0.07
Bolivian	6	0.05
Chilean	5	0.04
Colombian	76	0.68
Ecuadorian	14	0.13
Peruvian	48	0.43
Uruguayan	1	0.01
Venezuelan	12	0.11
Other South American	19	0.17

Notes: 1. Figures in the "Number" column do not add up to the total population due to: a) Ancestry/Race overlap — e.g. persons can report being both White and Irish, b) persons of Hispanic origin can report being any race, c) persons reporting two ancestries are counted in both categories. 2. Numbers in parentheses indicate the number of persons reporting this ancestry/race alone, not in combination with any other ancestry/race. 3. Refer to the User's Guide in the front of the book for more detailed information.

Other Hispanic or Latino	284	2.55
Hungarian	97	0.87
Iranian	9	0.08
Irish	1,883	16.94
Italian	1,290	11.60
Latvian	8	0.07
Lithuanian	34	0.31
Luxemburger	7	0.06
Norwegian	81	0.73
Pennsylvania German	26	0.23
Polish	540	4.86
Portuguese	19	0.17
Romanian	16	0.14
Russian	168	1.51
Scotch-Irish	232	2.09
Scottish	386	3.47
Serbian	23	0.21
Swedish	222	2.00
Swiss	58	0.52
Turkish	6	0.05
Ukrainian	44	0.40
United States or American	592	5.33
Welsh	98	0.88
West Indian, excl. Hispanic:	49	0.44
Dutch West Indian	23	0.21
Jamaican	26	0.23
White:	9,827	88.40
Not Hispanic (8,650)	8,759	78.80
Hispanic (1,011)	1,068	9.61

Westchester

Place Type: Census Designated Place
County: Miami-Dade
Population: 30,271

Ancestry/Race	Number	%
Afghan	5	0.02
African American/Black:	292	0.96
Not Hispanic (53)	72	0.24
Hispanic (133)	220	0.73
African, sub-Saharan:	9	0.03
African	9	0.03
Am. Ind. or Alaska Nat., not spec.	26	0.09
American Indian tribes, specified:	20	0.07
Apache (1)	2	0.01
Cherokee	1	0.00
Iroquois	2	0.01
Latin American Indians (9)	11	0.04
All other tribes	4	0.01
American Indian tribes, not spec.	1	0.00
Arab:	158	0.52
Arab/Arabic	47	0.16
Lebanese	111	0.37
Armenian	7	0.02
Asian:	195	0.64
Chinese, ex. Taiwanese (72)	85	0.28
Filipino (3)	7	0.02
Indian (37)	52	0.17
Japanese (12)	13	0.04
Korean (6)	9	0.03
Pakistani (4)	6	0.02
Vietnamese (15)	15	0.05
Other Asian, not specified (2)	8	0.03
Austrian	6	0.02
Basque	32	0.11
Belgian	7	0.02
Brazilian	16	0.05
Canadian	10	0.03
Czech	19	0.06
Danish	9	0.03
Dutch	10	0.03
English	338	1.12
European	19	0.06
French, except Basque	275	0.91
French Canadian	81	0.27
German	290	0.96
Greek	47	0.16
Hawaii Native/Pacific Islander:	17	0.06
Micronesian:	4	0.01
Guamanian/Chamorro	4	0.01
Polynesian: (1)	5	0.02
Native Hawaiian (1)	5	0.02
Other Pac. Isl., not spec.	8	0.03
Hispanic or Latino:	25,824	85.31
Central American:	1,230	4.06
Costa Rican	68	0.22
Guatemalan	130	0.43
Honduran	159	0.53
Nicaraguan	682	2.25
Panamanian	58	0.19
Salvadoran	106	0.35
Other Central American	27	0.09
Cuban	19,886	65.69
Dominican Republic	317	1.05
Mexican	199	0.66
Puerto Rican	509	1.68
South American:	1,329	4.39
Argentinean	91	0.30
Bolivian	18	0.06
Chilean	74	0.24
Colombian	536	1.77
Ecuadorian	119	0.39
Paraguayan	7	0.02
Peruvian	236	0.78
Uruguayan	29	0.10
Venezuelan	182	0.60
Other South American	37	0.12
Other Hispanic or Latino	2,354	7.78
Hungarian	8	0.03
Irish	280	0.93
Italian	473	1.56
Lithuanian	12	0.04
Norwegian	46	0.15
Polish	162	0.54
Romanian	19	0.06
Russian	187	0.62
Scotch-Irish	50	0.17
Scottish	46	0.15
Swedish	10	0.03
Turkish	10	0.03
Ukrainian	23	0.08
United States or American	737	2.44
Welsh	16	0.05
West Indian, excl. Hispanic:	44	0.15
Bahamian	15	0.05
Haitian	22	0.07
Jamaican	7	0.02
White:	29,004	95.81
Not Hispanic (4,142)	4,231	13.98
Hispanic (24,247)	24,773	81.84
Yugoslavian	17	0.06

Weston

Place Type: City
County: Broward
Population: 49,286

Ancestry/Race	Number	%
Acadian/Cajun	49	0.10
Afghan	11	0.02
African American/Black:	2,085	4.23
Not Hispanic (1,699)	1,892	3.84
Hispanic (133)	193	0.39
African, sub-Saharan:	262	0.53
African	31	0.06
Ethiopian	21	0.04
South African	210	0.43
Alaska Native tribes, specified:	2	0.00
Alaska Athabascan (1)	1	0.00
Eskimo (1)	1	0.00
Am. Ind. or Alaska Nat., not spec.	40	0.08
Albanian	7	0.01
American Indian tribes, specified:	59	0.12
Apache	3	0.01
Blackfeet	2	0.00
Cherokee (4)	13	0.03
Chippewa (1)	1	0.00
Choctaw	1	0.00
Comanche (1)	1	0.00
Latin American Indians (20)	24	0.05
Osage (3)	3	0.01
Seminole (2)	2	0.00
Sioux	2	0.00
Tohono O'Odham (1)	1	0.00
All other tribes (3)	6	0.01
American Indian tribes, not spec.	7	0.01
Arab:	428	0.87
Arab/Arabic	8	0.02
Egyptian	20	0.04
Iraqi	7	0.01
Jordanian	6	0.01
Lebanese	309	0.63
Moroccan	24	0.05
Palestinian	17	0.03
Syrian	22	0.04
Other Arab	15	0.03
Armenian	78	0.16
Asian:	1,850	3.75
Cambodian (3)	3	0.01
Chinese, ex. Taiwanese (369)	458	0.93
Filipino (144)	184	0.37
Indian (540)	598	1.21
Indonesian (3)	8	0.02
Japanese (95)	130	0.26
Korean (248)	262	0.53
Laotian (1)	1	0.00
Pakistani (32)	44	0.09
Sri Lankan (2)	2	0.00
Taiwanese (16)	22	0.04
Thai (10)	13	0.03
Vietnamese (43)	52	0.11
Other Asian, not specified (33)	73	0.15
Australian	10	0.02
Austrian	305	0.62
Basque	10	0.02
Belgian	117	0.24
Brazilian	471	0.96
British	374	0.76
Bulgarian	40	0.08
Canadian	272	0.55
Celtic	10	0.02
Croatian	26	0.05
Czech	60	0.12
Czechoslovakian	58	0.12
Danish	212	0.43
Dutch	383	0.78
Eastern European	328	0.67
English	2,994	6.09
Estonian	7	0.01
European	392	0.80
Finnish	61	0.12
French, except Basque	1,177	2.40
French Canadian	159	0.32
German	4,526	9.21
Greek	242	0.49
Guyanese	27	0.05
Hawaii Native/Pacific Islander:	28	0.06
Melanesian:	1	0.00
Other Melanesian	1	0.00
Micronesian: (3)	3	0.01
Guamanian/Chamorro (2)	2	0.00
Other Micronesian (1)	1	0.00
Polynesian: (3)	10	0.02
Native Hawaiian (2)	9	0.02
Samoan (1)	1	0.00
Other Pac. Isl., not spec. (2)	14	0.03
Hispanic or Latino:	14,880	30.19
Central American:	427	0.87
Costa Rican	53	0.11
Guatemalan	62	0.13
Honduran	52	0.11
Nicaraguan	105	0.21
Panamanian	84	0.17
Salvadoran	50	0.10
Other Central American	21	0.04
Cuban	1,995	4.05
Dominican Republic	364	0.74
Mexican	594	1.21
Puerto Rican	1,632	3.31
South American:	6,620	13.43
Argentinean	306	0.62
Bolivian	34	0.07

Notes: 1. Figures in the "Number" column do not add up to the total population due to: a) Ancestry/Race overlap — e.g. persons can report being both White and Irish, b) persons of Hispanic origin can report being any race, c) persons reporting two ancestries are counted in both categories. 2. Numbers in parentheses indicate the number of persons reporting this ancestry/race alone, not in combination with any other ancestry/race. 3. Refer to the User's Guide in the front of the book for more detailed information.

Chilean	116	0.24
Colombian	3,052	6.19
Ecuadorian	319	0.65
Paraguayan	11	0.02
Peruvian	588	1.19
Uruguayan	44	0.09
Venezuelan	2,020	4.10
Other South American	130	0.26
Other Hispanic or Latino	3,248	6.59
Hungarian	401	0.82
Iranian	157	0.32
Irish	3,894	7.93
Israeli	63	0.13
Italian	4,837	9.84
Latvian	44	0.09
Lithuanian	134	0.27
Macedonian	7	0.01
Maltese	18	0.04
Northern European	8	0.02
Norwegian	261	0.53
Polish	2,345	4.77
Portuguese	151	0.31
Romanian	289	0.59
Russian	2,784	5.67
Scandinavian	76	0.15
Scotch-Irish	363	0.74
Scottish	679	1.38
Serbian	19	0.04
Slavic	25	0.05
Slovak	140	0.28
Slovene	9	0.02
Swedish	469	0.95
Swiss	136	0.28
Turkish	183	0.37
Ukrainian	207	0.42
United States or American	3,355	6.83
Welsh	112	0.23
West Indian, excl. Hispanic:	1,262	2.57
Bahamian	59	0.12
Barbadian	26	0.05
British West Indian	10	0.02
Haitian	136	0.28
Jamaican	944	1.92
Trinidadian and Tobagonian	79	0.16
West Indian	8	0.02
White:	44,202	89.68
Not Hispanic (30,465)	30,847	62.59
Hispanic (12,821)	13,355	27.10
Yugoslavian	86	0.18

Westwood Lakes

Place Type: Census Designated Place
County: Miami-Dade
Population: 12,005

Ancestry/Race	Number	%
African American/Black:	119	0.99
Not Hispanic (31)	34	0.28
Hispanic (64)	85	0.71
African, sub-Saharan:	7	0.06
African	7	0.06
Am. Ind. or Alaska Nat., not spec.	12	0.10
American Indian tribes, specified:	9	0.07
Cherokee	2	0.02
Iroquois (1)	1	0.01
Latin American Indians (3)	6	0.05
American Indian tribes, not spec.	1	0.01
Arab:	26	0.22
Arab/Arabic	16	0.13
Jordanian	10	0.08
Asian:	179	1.49
Chinese, ex. Taiwanese (37)	57	0.47
Filipino (3)	7	0.06
Hmong	1	0.01
Indian (16)	21	0.17
Japanese (1)	4	0.03
Korean (2)	3	0.02
Pakistani (21)	32	0.27
Thai	1	0.01
Vietnamese (34)	46	0.38
Other Asian, not specified (2)	7	0.06
Belgian	8	0.07
Canadian	21	0.17
Croatian	8	0.07
Czech	16	0.13
Danish	18	0.15
Dutch	39	0.32
English	308	2.57
French, except Basque	163	1.36
French Canadian	19	0.16
German	421	3.51
Greek	24	0.20
Hispanic or Latino:	9,164	76.33
Central American:	512	4.26
Costa Rican	37	0.31
Guatemalan	52	0.43
Honduran	54	0.45
Nicaraguan	305	2.54
Panamanian	14	0.12
Salvadoran	24	0.20
Other Central American	26	0.22
Cuban	6,730	56.06
Dominican Republic	65	0.54
Mexican	183	1.52
Puerto Rican	233	1.94
South American:	515	4.29
Argentinean	40	0.33
Bolivian	10	0.08
Chilean	28	0.23
Colombian	253	2.11
Ecuadorian	28	0.23
Peruvian	91	0.76
Uruguayan	9	0.07
Venezuelan	53	0.44
Other South American	3	0.02
Other Hispanic or Latino	926	7.71
Hungarian	42	0.35
Irish	440	3.67
Italian	282	2.35
Lithuanian	37	0.31
Norwegian	29	0.24
Polish	59	0.49
Russian	13	0.11
Scotch-Irish	10	0.08
Scottish	30	0.25
Swedish	69	0.57
Ukrainian	7	0.06
United States or American	511	4.26
Welsh	47	0.39
West Indian, excl. Hispanic:	35	0.29
Trinidadian and Tobagonian	35	0.29
White:	11,408	95.03
Not Hispanic (2,637)	2,667	22.22
Hispanic (8,522)	8,741	72.81

Wilton Manors

Place Type: City
County: Broward
Population: 12,697

Ancestry/Race	Number	%
Acadian/Cajun	20	0.16
African American/Black:	1,989	15.67
Not Hispanic (1,624)	1,930	15.20
Hispanic (50)	59	0.46
African, sub-Saharan:	68	0.54
African	68	0.54
Am. Ind. or Alaska Nat., not spec.	14	0.11
American Indian tribes, specified:	48	0.38
Apache	1	0.01
Blackfeet	3	0.02
Cherokee (11)	24	0.19
Chickasaw (1)	1	0.01
Chippewa (2)	2	0.02
Choctaw (1)	1	0.01
Iroquois (2)	3	0.02
Lumbee (1)	1	0.01
Navajo	1	0.01
Osage (1)	1	0.01
Ottawa (2)	2	0.02
Pueblo	1	0.01
Seminole (1)	1	0.01
Sioux (2)	4	0.03
All other tribes	2	0.02
American Indian tribes, not spec.	4	0.03
Arab:	49	0.39
Lebanese	40	0.32
Syrian	9	0.07
Asian:	273	2.15
Bangladeshi (3)	10	0.08
Cambodian	1	0.01
Chinese, ex. Taiwanese (39)	48	0.38
Filipino (18)	19	0.15
Indian (98)	119	0.94
Indonesian	1	0.01
Japanese (9)	14	0.11
Korean (6)	7	0.06
Laotian (1)	1	0.01
Pakistani (5)	5	0.04
Taiwanese (1)	1	0.01
Thai (20)	29	0.23
Vietnamese (1)	2	0.02
Other Asian, specified	7	0.06
Other Asian, not specified (2)	9	0.07
Austrian	39	0.31
Basque	14	0.11
Brazilian	51	0.40
British	93	0.73
Bulgarian	10	0.08
Canadian	29	0.23
Celtic	8	0.06
Czech	109	0.86
Czechoslovakian	8	0.06
Danish	44	0.35
Dutch	286	2.25
English	1,539	12.12
European	96	0.76
Finnish	20	0.16
French, except Basque	442	3.48
French Canadian	158	1.24
German	1,693	13.33
Greek	64	0.50
Guyanese	25	0.20
Hawaii Native/Pacific Islander:	22	0.17
Micronesian: (3)	3	0.02
Guamanian/Chamorro (3)	3	0.02
Polynesian: (4)	7	0.06
Native Hawaiian (2)	3	0.02
Samoan (2)	4	0.03
Other Pac. Isl., specified	5	0.04
Other Pac. Isl., not spec.	7	0.06
Hispanic or Latino:	1,228	9.67
Central American:	145	1.14
Costa Rican	7	0.06
Guatemalan	28	0.22
Honduran	37	0.29
Nicaraguan	11	0.09
Panamanian	7	0.06
Salvadoran	47	0.37
Other Central American	8	0.06
Cuban	201	1.58
Dominican Republic	25	0.20
Mexican	204	1.61
Puerto Rican	226	1.78
South American:	158	1.24
Argentinean	14	0.11
Chilean	11	0.09
Colombian	59	0.46
Ecuadorian	9	0.07
Peruvian	36	0.28
Uruguayan	1	0.01
Venezuelan	25	0.20
Other South American	3	0.02
Other Hispanic or Latino	269	2.12
Hungarian	79	0.62
Irish	1,791	14.11
Israeli	11	0.09
Italian	1,149	9.05
Lithuanian	25	0.20
Norwegian	168	1.32
Pennsylvania German	11	0.09
Polish	385	3.03

Notes: 1. Figures in the "Number" column do not add up to the total population due to: a) Ancestry/Race overlap — e.g. persons can report being both White and Irish, b) persons of Hispanic origin can report being any race, c) persons reporting two ancestries are counted in both categories. 2. Numbers in parentheses indicate the number of persons reporting this ancestry/race alone, not in combination with any other ancestry/race. 3. Refer to the User's Guide in the front of the book for more detailed information.

Portuguese	15	0.12
Romanian	8	0.06
Russian	118	0.93
Scandinavian	67	0.53
Scotch-Irish	268	2.11
Scottish	227	1.79
Serbian	7	0.06
Slavic	13	0.10
Slovak	53	0.42
Slovene	9	0.07
Swedish	195	1.54
Swiss	7	0.06
Turkish	10	0.08
Ukrainian	70	0.55
United States or American	567	4.47
Welsh	105	0.83
West Indian, excl. Hispanic:	1,082	8.52
Bahamian	53	0.42
Haitian	925	7.29
Jamaican	15	0.12
Trinidadian and Tobagonian	85	0.67
West Indian	4	0.03
White:	10,266	80.85
Not Hispanic (9,159)	9,289	73.16
Hispanic (899)	977	7.69
Yugoslavian	16	0.13

Winter Garden

Place Type: City
County: Orange
Population: 14,351

Ancestry/Race	Number	%
Acadian/Cajun	7	0.05
African American/Black:	2,003	13.96
Not Hispanic (1,846)	1,920	13.38
Hispanic (56)	83	0.58
African, sub-Saharan:	48	0.34
African	48	0.34
Alaska Native tribes, specified:	2	0.01
Alaska Athabascan (1)	1	0.01
Tlingit-Haida	1	0.01
Am. Ind. or Alaska Nat., not spec.	44	0.31
American Indian tribes, specified:	96	0.67
Apache (2)	5	0.03
Blackfeet	6	0.04
Cherokee (14)	46	0.32
Chickasaw	1	0.01
Choctaw (2)	8	0.06
Comanche	2	0.01
Cree	1	0.01
Creek (3)	8	0.06
Iroquois (2)	8	0.06
Latin American Indians (2)	2	0.01
Paiute (1)	1	0.01
Potawatomi (1)	1	0.01
Seminole (1)	4	0.03
Sioux (1)	1	0.01
Yakama	1	0.01
All other tribes	1	0.01
American Indian tribes, not spec.	5	0.03
Arab:	9	0.06
Lebanese	9	0.06
Armenian	26	0.19
Asian:	196	1.37
Chinese, ex. Taiwanese (14)	20	0.14
Filipino (15)	18	0.13
Indian (55)	87	0.61
Japanese (3)	8	0.06
Korean (24)	27	0.19
Laotian (7)	7	0.05
Pakistani	1	0.01
Taiwanese (3)	3	0.02
Thai (4)	5	0.03
Vietnamese (9)	9	0.06
Other Asian, specified (4)	4	0.03
Other Asian, not specified (3)	7	0.05
Brazilian	47	0.34
British	36	0.26
Bulgarian	33	0.24
Canadian	10	0.07
Carpatho Rusyn	7	0.05
Celtic	12	0.09
Czechoslovakian	14	0.10
Danish	29	0.21
Dutch	195	1.39
English	1,619	11.57
European	104	0.74
Finnish	29	0.21
French, except Basque	317	2.26
French Canadian	156	1.11
German	1,597	11.41
Greek	31	0.22
Hawaii Native/Pacific Islander:	33	0.23
Micronesian: (1)	4	0.03
Guamanian/Chamorro (1)	4	0.03
Polynesian: (5)	15	0.10
Native Hawaiian	3	0.02
Samoan (3)	7	0.05
Tongan (1)	1	0.01
Other Polynesian (1)	4	0.03
Other Pac. Isl., not spec. (1)	14	0.10
Hispanic or Latino:	2,511	17.50
Central American:	75	0.52
Costa Rican	8	0.06
Guatemalan	23	0.16
Honduran	12	0.08
Nicaraguan	13	0.09
Panamanian	6	0.04
Salvadoran	13	0.09
Cuban	114	0.79
Dominican Republic	40	0.28
Mexican	1,137	7.92
Puerto Rican	772	5.38
South American:	113	0.79
Argentinean	1	0.01
Bolivian	5	0.03
Colombian	58	0.40
Ecuadorian	12	0.08
Peruvian	17	0.12
Venezuelan	14	0.10
Other South American	6	0.04
Other Hispanic or Latino	260	1.81
Hungarian	35	0.25
Irish	1,395	9.96
Italian	699	4.99
Maltese	8	0.06
Norwegian	99	0.71
Pennsylvania German	4	0.03
Polish	168	1.20
Portuguese	12	0.09
Romanian	43	0.31
Scandinavian	13	0.09
Scotch-Irish	266	1.90
Scottish	367	2.62
Slovak	61	0.44
Slovene	7	0.05
Swedish	112	0.80
Swiss	21	0.15
United States or American	1,539	10.99
Welsh	37	0.26
West Indian, excl. Hispanic:	162	1.16
Haitian	15	0.11
Jamaican	84	0.60
Trinidadian and Tobagonian	34	0.24
West Indian	29	0.21
White:	11,235	78.29
Not Hispanic (9,587)	9,726	67.77
Hispanic (1,406)	1,509	10.51

Winter Haven

Place Type: City
County: Polk
Population: 26,487

Ancestry/Race	Number	%
African American/Black:	6,499	24.54
Not Hispanic (6,050)	6,382	24.09
Hispanic (84)	117	0.44
African, sub-Saharan:	277	1.07
African	270	1.04
Nigerian	7	0.03
Alaska Native tribes, specified:	1	0.00
Tlingit-Haida	1	0.00
Am. Ind. or Alaska Nat., not spec.	44	0.17
American Indian tribes, specified:	82	0.31
Apache (1)	1	0.00
Blackfeet (1)	2	0.01
Cherokee (18)	45	0.17
Chippewa (1)	1	0.00
Choctaw (1)	8	0.03
Creek	2	0.01
Iroquois (2)	4	0.02
Latin American Indians	1	0.00
Lumbee (3)	3	0.01
Ottawa (2)	2	0.01
Seminole (1)	5	0.02
Sioux (2)	3	0.01
All other tribes (3)	5	0.02
American Indian tribes, not spec.	8	0.03
Arab:	34	0.13
Lebanese	23	0.09
Syrian	11	0.04
Armenian	3	0.01
Asian:	364	1.37
Chinese, ex. Taiwanese (36)	47	0.18
Filipino (51)	69	0.26
Indian (71)	84	0.32
Japanese (7)	15	0.06
Korean (7)	8	0.03
Sri Lankan (3)	3	0.01
Taiwanese (5)	5	0.02
Thai (3)	4	0.02
Vietnamese (78)	86	0.32
Other Asian, specified	1	0.00
Other Asian, not specified (7)	42	0.16
Australian	17	0.07
Austrian	24	0.09
Belgian	17	0.07
Brazilian	4	0.02
British	122	0.47
Canadian	109	0.42
Croatian	28	0.11
Czech	8	0.03
Czechoslovakian	33	0.13
Danish	95	0.37
Dutch	361	1.39
English	2,749	10.60
European	99	0.38
Finnish	82	0.32
French, except Basque	553	2.13
French Canadian	191	0.74
German	2,978	11.48
Greek	63	0.24
Hawaii Native/Pacific Islander:	28	0.11
Micronesian: (1)	1	0.00
Guamanian/Chamorro (1)	1	0.00
Polynesian: (7)	10	0.04
Native Hawaiian (4)	5	0.02
Samoan (3)	5	0.02
Other Pac. Isl., specified	1	0.00
Other Pac. Isl., not spec. (2)	16	0.06
Hispanic or Latino:	1,309	4.94
Central American:	25	0.09
Costa Rican	5	0.02
Guatemalan	1	0.00
Honduran	2	0.01
Panamanian	13	0.05
Salvadoran	4	0.02
Cuban	84	0.32
Dominican Republic	11	0.04
Mexican	339	1.28
Puerto Rican	627	2.37
South American:	41	0.15
Argentinean	3	0.01
Colombian	8	0.03
Ecuadorian	14	0.05
Peruvian	5	0.02
Uruguayan	6	0.02
Venezuelan	5	0.02
Other Hispanic or Latino	182	0.69
Hungarian	51	0.20

Notes: 1. Figures in the "Number" column do not add up to the total population due to: a) Ancestry/Race overlap — e.g. persons can report being both White and Irish, b) persons of Hispanic origin can report being any race, c) persons reporting two ancestries are counted in both categories. 2. Numbers in parentheses indicate the number of persons reporting this ancestry/race alone, not in combination with any other ancestry/race. 3. Refer to the User's Guide in the front of the book for more detailed information.

Irish	2,454	9.46
Italian	650	2.51
Lithuanian	9	0.03
Norwegian	144	0.56
Pennsylvania German	25	0.10
Polish	563	2.17
Portuguese	117	0.45
Russian	64	0.25
Scotch-Irish	380	1.46
Scottish	399	1.54
Slavic	12	0.05
Slovak	71	0.27
Slovene	14	0.05
Swedish	349	1.35
Swiss	93	0.36
Ukrainian	30	0.12
United States or American	3,798	14.64
Welsh	176	0.68
West Indian, excl. Hispanic:	723	2.79
British West Indian	15	0.06
Dutch West Indian	7	0.03
Haitian	550	2.12
Jamaican	151	0.58
White:	19,216	72.55
Not Hispanic (18,299)	18,501	69.85
Hispanic (642)	715	2.70

Winter Park

Place Type: City
County: Orange
Population: 24,090

Ancestry/Race	Number	%
Acadian/Cajun	5	0.02
African American/Black:	2,627	10.90
Not Hispanic (2,513)	2,591	10.76
Hispanic (21)	36	0.15
African, sub-Saharan:	141	0.58
African	111	0.46
South African	30	0.12
Alaska Native tribes, specified:	3	0.01
Tlingit-Haida (3)	3	0.01
Am. Ind. or Alaska Nat., not spec.	40	0.17
Albanian	6	0.02
American Indian tribes, specified:	57	0.24
Apache (1)	2	0.01
Blackfeet	2	0.01
Cherokee (8)	26	0.11
Chippewa (1)	3	0.01
Choctaw	2	0.01
Creek	2	0.01
Crow	1	0.00
Delaware (2)	2	0.01
Iroquois	1	0.00
Latin American Indians (5)	6	0.02
Lumbee (2)	2	0.01
Seminole	1	0.00
Yaqui	1	0.00
All other tribes (2)	6	0.02
American Indian tribes, not spec.	5	0.02
Arab:	62	0.26
Iraqi	7	0.03
Lebanese	55	0.23
Armenian	5	0.02
Asian:	414	1.72
Chinese, ex. Taiwanese (79)	100	0.42
Filipino (35)	59	0.24
Indian (54)	69	0.29
Japanese (28)	43	0.18
Korean (26)	37	0.15
Laotian (1)	1	0.00
Sri Lankan (3)	5	0.02
Taiwanese (4)	4	0.02
Thai (8)	11	0.05
Vietnamese (71)	77	0.32
Other Asian, specified	1	0.00
Other Asian, not specified (3)	7	0.03
Assyrian/Chaldean/Syriac	5	0.02
Australian	24	0.10
Austrian	102	0.42
Basque	31	0.13
Belgian	20	0.08
Brazilian	19	0.08
British	348	1.44
Canadian	130	0.54
Croatian	32	0.13
Czech	82	0.34
Czechoslovakian	34	0.14
Danish	180	0.74
Dutch	311	1.28
Eastern European	22	0.09
English	4,347	17.94
Estonian	6	0.02
European	265	1.09
Finnish	35	0.14
French, except Basque	1,161	4.79
French Canadian	190	0.78
German	3,709	15.31
Greek	153	0.63
Hawaii Native/Pacific Islander:	18	0.07
Polynesian: (6)	17	0.07
Native Hawaiian (6)	16	0.07
Samoan	1	0.00
Other Pac. Isl., specified	1	0.00
Hispanic or Latino:	1,039	4.31
Central American:	42	0.17
Guatemalan	4	0.02
Honduran	6	0.02
Nicaraguan	6	0.02
Panamanian	18	0.07
Salvadoran	6	0.02
Other Central American	2	0.01
Cuban	145	0.60
Dominican Republic	21	0.09
Mexican	142	0.59
Puerto Rican	394	1.64
South American:	120	0.50
Argentinean	13	0.05
Bolivian	2	0.01
Chilean	6	0.02
Colombian	46	0.19
Ecuadorian	13	0.05
Peruvian	14	0.06
Venezuelan	24	0.10
Other South American	2	0.01
Other Hispanic or Latino	175	0.73
Hungarian	94	0.39
Iranian	19	0.08
Irish	2,937	12.12
Israeli	65	0.27
Italian	1,206	4.98
Latvian	15	0.06
Lithuanian	44	0.18
Northern European	82	0.34
Norwegian	319	1.32
Pennsylvania German	26	0.11
Polish	536	2.21
Portuguese	44	0.18
Romanian	52	0.21
Russian	362	1.49
Scandinavian	68	0.28
Scotch-Irish	667	2.75
Scottish	1,229	5.07
Serbian	27	0.11
Slavic	27	0.11
Slovak	57	0.24
Swedish	365	1.51
Swiss	115	0.47
Turkish	7	0.03
Ukrainian	136	0.56
United States or American	1,469	6.06
Welsh	309	1.28
West Indian, excl. Hispanic:	179	0.74
Bahamian	8	0.03
British West Indian	12	0.05
Haitian	56	0.23
Jamaican	91	0.38
West Indian	12	0.05
White:	20,908	86.79
Not Hispanic (19,940)	20,112	83.49
Hispanic (754)	796	3.30
Yugoslavian	71	0.29

Winter Springs

Place Type: City
County: Seminole
Population: 31,666

Ancestry/Race	Number	%
Acadian/Cajun	10	0.03
African American/Black:	1,635	5.16
Not Hispanic (1,363)	1,503	4.75
Hispanic (89)	132	0.42
African, sub-Saharan:	66	0.21
South African	66	0.21
Alaska Native tribes, specified:	4	0.01
Eskimo (1)	3	0.01
Tlingit-Haida	1	0.00
Am. Ind. or Alaska Nat., not spec.	49	0.15
American Indian tribes, specified:	138	0.44
Apache (1)	7	0.02
Blackfeet	5	0.02
Cherokee (16)	54	0.17
Chickasaw	1	0.00
Chippewa (1)	9	0.03
Choctaw (1)	2	0.01
Comanche (1)	3	0.01
Creek (4)	9	0.03
Houma	1	0.00
Iroquois (2)	8	0.03
Latin American Indians (3)	17	0.05
Lumbee (4)	4	0.01
Menominee	1	0.00
Navajo	1	0.00
Pueblo	1	0.00
Seminole (2)	4	0.01
Sioux (1)	1	0.00
All other tribes (2)	10	0.03
American Indian tribes, not spec.	4	0.01
Arab:	361	1.15
Arab/Arabic	40	0.13
Egyptian	65	0.21
Jordanian	42	0.13
Lebanese	157	0.50
Palestinian	14	0.04
Syrian	24	0.08
Other Arab	19	0.06
Armenian	17	0.05
Asian:	748	2.36
Bangladeshi (2)	2	0.01
Cambodian (3)	3	0.01
Chinese, ex. Taiwanese (123)	149	0.47
Filipino (98)	134	0.42
Hmong (4)	4	0.01
Indian (138)	152	0.48
Indonesian (1)	6	0.02
Japanese (28)	49	0.15
Korean (78)	87	0.27
Laotian (12)	14	0.04
Malaysian (1)	1	0.00
Pakistani (10)	12	0.04
Sri Lankan (4)	4	0.01
Taiwanese (2)	3	0.01
Thai (14)	15	0.05
Vietnamese (84)	88	0.28
Other Asian, specified	1	0.00
Other Asian, not specified (9)	24	0.08
Australian	7	0.02
Austrian	125	0.40
Basque	7	0.02
Belgian	37	0.12
British	330	1.05
Bulgarian	14	0.04
Canadian	101	0.32
Celtic	8	0.03
Croatian	62	0.20
Czech	137	0.44
Czechoslovakian	129	0.41
Danish	164	0.52
Dutch	623	1.98
Eastern European	9	0.03
English	4,028	12.82

Notes: 1. Figures in the "Number" column do not add up to the total population due to: a) Ancestry/Race overlap — e.g. persons can report being both White and Irish, b) persons of Hispanic origin can report being any race, c) persons reporting two ancestries are counted in both categories. 2. Numbers in parentheses indicate the number of persons reporting this ancestry/race alone, not in combination with any other ancestry/race. 3. Refer to the User's Guide in the front of the book for more detailed information.

European	359	1.14
Finnish	94	0.30
French, except Basque	1,056	3.36
French Canadian	436	1.39
German	5,722	18.21
Greek	191	0.61
Guyanese	45	0.14
Hawaii Native/Pacific Islander:	26	0.08
Micronesian: (8)	11	0.03
Guamanian/Chamorro (5)	8	0.03
Other Micronesian (3)	3	0.01
Polynesian: (5)	9	0.03
Native Hawaiian (3)	6	0.02
Samoan (2)	3	0.01
Other Pac. Isl., specified	1	0.00
Other Pac. Isl., not spec. (1)	5	0.02
Hispanic or Latino:	3,330	10.52
Central American:	100	0.32
Costa Rican	5	0.02
Guatemalan	21	0.07
Honduran	10	0.03
Nicaraguan	13	0.04
Panamanian	28	0.09
Salvadoran	16	0.05
Other Central American	7	0.02
Cuban	284	0.90
Dominican Republic	90	0.28
Mexican	219	0.69
Puerto Rican	1,762	5.56
South American:	338	1.07
Argentinean	30	0.09
Bolivian	2	0.01
Chilean	2	0.01
Colombian	173	0.55
Ecuadorian	34	0.11
Paraguayan	2	0.01
Peruvian	42	0.13
Uruguayan	5	0.02
Venezuelan	36	0.11
Other South American	12	0.04
Other Hispanic or Latino	537	1.70
Hungarian	268	0.85
Iranian	39	0.12
Irish	4,909	15.62
Israeli	5	0.02
Italian	3,399	10.82
Latvian	13	0.04
Lithuanian	163	0.52
Macedonian	20	0.06
Maltese	7	0.02
Northern European	9	0.03
Norwegian	333	1.06
Polish	1,275	4.06
Portuguese	100	0.32
Romanian	22	0.07
Russian	506	1.61
Scandinavian	38	0.12
Scotch-Irish	727	2.31
Scottish	953	3.03
Serbian	19	0.06
Slavic	19	0.06
Slovak	123	0.39
Slovene	33	0.11
Swedish	551	1.75
Swiss	125	0.40
Turkish	20	0.06
Ukrainian	107	0.34
United States or American	2,405	7.65
Welsh	295	0.94
West Indian, excl. Hispanic:	358	1.14
Bahamian	18	0.06
Belizean	17	0.05
Haitian	58	0.18
Jamaican	180	0.57
Trinidadian and Tobagonian	32	0.10
U.S. Virgin Islander	28	0.09
West Indian	25	0.08
White:	28,644	90.46
Not Hispanic (25,851)	26,189	82.70
Hispanic (2,247)	2,455	7.75
Yugoslavian	98	0.31

Wright

Place Type: Census Designated Place
County: Okaloosa
Population: 21,697

Ancestry/Race	Number	%
Acadian/Cajun	21	0.10
African American/Black:	3,355	15.46
Not Hispanic (2,993)	3,269	15.07
Hispanic (52)	86	0.40
African, sub-Saharan:	79	0.37
African	79	0.37
Alaska Native tribes, specified:	1	0.00
Alaska Athabascan (1)	1	0.00
Am. Ind. or Alaska Nat., not spec.	110	0.51
American Indian tribes, specified:	235	1.08
Apache (3)	6	0.03
Blackfeet (3)	19	0.09
Cherokee (46)	111	0.51
Cheyenne (2)	4	0.02
Chickasaw (1)	4	0.02
Chippewa (2)	6	0.03
Choctaw	4	0.02
Creek (6)	18	0.08
Delaware (1)	1	0.00
Iroquois (8)	15	0.07
Kiowa (1)	1	0.00
Latin American Indians (6)	8	0.04
Lumbee (1)	1	0.00
Navajo (1)	1	0.00
Osage	4	0.02
Ottawa (3)	3	0.01
Pueblo	1	0.00
Puget Sound Salish (1)	1	0.00
Seminole	4	0.02
Shoshone	1	0.00
Sioux (2)	6	0.03
All other tribes (4)	16	0.07
American Indian tribes, not spec.	8	0.04
Arab:	56	0.26
Lebanese	44	0.20
Syrian	6	0.03
Other Arab	6	0.03
Armenian	23	0.11
Asian:	1,162	5.36
Chinese, ex. Taiwanese (34)	62	0.29
Filipino (266)	418	1.93
Hmong (1)	1	0.00
Indian (11)	18	0.08
Indonesian (1)	6	0.03
Japanese (58)	118	0.54
Korean (127)	182	0.84
Laotian (6)	8	0.04
Malaysian	1	0.00
Pakistani	2	0.01
Sri Lankan (1)	1	0.00
Taiwanese (4)	6	0.03
Thai (115)	193	0.89
Vietnamese (68)	83	0.38
Other Asian, specified	2	0.01
Other Asian, not specified (32)	61	0.28
Australian	59	0.27
British	122	0.57
Canadian	8	0.04
Croatian	16	0.07
Czech	6	0.03
Czechoslovakian	45	0.21
Danish	55	0.26
Dutch	285	1.32
English	2,018	9.36
European	182	0.84
Finnish	12	0.06
French, except Basque	617	2.86
French Canadian	150	0.70
German	2,801	13.00
Greek	142	0.66
Hawaii Native/Pacific Islander:	102	0.47
Micronesian: (20)	33	0.15
Guamanian/Chamorro (18)	30	0.14
Other Micronesian (2)	3	0.01
Polynesian: (16)	42	0.19
Native Hawaiian (15)	39	0.18
Samoan (1)	3	0.01
Other Pac. Isl., not spec. (4)	27	0.12
Hispanic or Latino:	1,136	5.24
Central American:	147	0.68
Costa Rican	2	0.01
Guatemalan	20	0.09
Honduran	43	0.20
Nicaraguan	20	0.09
Panamanian	54	0.25
Salvadoran	6	0.03
Other Central American	2	0.01
Cuban	43	0.20
Dominican Republic	5	0.02
Mexican	404	1.86
Puerto Rican	265	1.22
South American:	35	0.16
Bolivian	3	0.01
Chilean	2	0.01
Colombian	15	0.07
Paraguayan	3	0.01
Peruvian	8	0.04
Other South American	4	0.02
Other Hispanic or Latino	237	1.09
Hungarian	47	0.22
Irish	2,653	12.31
Italian	922	4.28
Lithuanian	36	0.17
Norwegian	139	0.64
Pennsylvania German	42	0.19
Polish	361	1.67
Portuguese	70	0.32
Romanian	32	0.15
Russian	88	0.41
Scandinavian	13	0.06
Scotch-Irish	503	2.33
Scottish	677	3.14
Serbian	10	0.05
Slovak	47	0.22
Swedish	244	1.13
Swiss	33	0.15
Ukrainian	44	0.20
United States or American	2,020	9.37
Welsh	86	0.40
West Indian, excl. Hispanic:	120	0.56
Barbadian	9	0.04
Jamaican	90	0.42
Trinidadian and Tobagonian	9	0.04
West Indian	12	0.06
White:	17,229	79.41
Not Hispanic (15,861)	16,500	76.05
Hispanic (630)	729	3.36
Yugoslavian	10	0.05

Yeehaw Junction

Place Type: Census Designated Place
County: Osceola
Population: 21,778

Ancestry/Race	Number	%
African American/Black:	2,943	13.51
Not Hispanic (2,203)	2,393	10.99
Hispanic (362)	550	2.53
African, sub-Saharan:	50	0.23
African	50	0.23
Am. Ind. or Alaska Nat., not spec.	78	0.36
American Indian tribes, specified:	95	0.44
Apache	1	0.00
Cherokee (7)	20	0.09
Choctaw (1)	1	0.00
Cree (1)	1	0.00
Delaware (1)	1	0.00
Iroquois (4)	7	0.03
Latin American Indians (27)	50	0.23
Sioux (1)	3	0.01
All other tribes (5)	11	0.05
American Indian tribes, not spec.	11	0.05
Arab:	26	0.12
Moroccan	6	0.03
Syrian	20	0.09

Notes: 1. Figures in the "Number" column do not add up to the total population due to: a) Ancestry/Race overlap — e.g. persons can report being both White and Irish, b) persons of Hispanic origin can report being any race, c) persons reporting two ancestries are counted in both categories. 2. Numbers in parentheses indicate the number of persons reporting this ancestry/race alone, not in combination with any other ancestry/race. 3. Refer to the User's Guide in the front of the book for more detailed information.

Armenian	23	0.10
Asian:	767	3.52
Cambodian (3)	3	0.01
Chinese, ex. Taiwanese (62)	88	0.40
Filipino (234)	291	1.34
Indian (186)	231	1.06
Indonesian (5)	7	0.03
Japanese (22)	35	0.16
Korean (11)	14	0.06
Laotian (6)	7	0.03
Malaysian	3	0.01
Pakistani (6)	11	0.05
Taiwanese (7)	8	0.04
Thai (20)	20	0.09
Vietnamese (15)	20	0.09
Other Asian, not specified (3)	29	0.13
Austrian	25	0.11
Belgian	6	0.03
Brazilian	25	0.11
British	102	0.46
Canadian	72	0.32
Celtic	11	0.05
Czechoslovakian	10	0.05
Danish	24	0.11
Dutch	47	0.21
English	757	3.42
European	114	0.51
Finnish	10	0.05
French, except Basque	330	1.49
French Canadian	155	0.70
German	1,131	5.10
Guyanese	42	0.19
Hawaii Native/Pacific Islander:	55	0.25
Micronesian:	2	0.01
Guamanian/Chamorro	2	0.01
Polynesian: (17)	26	0.12
Native Hawaiian (7)	16	0.07
Samoan (10)	10	0.05
Other Pac. Isl., not spec. (3)	27	0.12
Hispanic or Latino:	11,898	54.63
Central American:	348	1.60
Costa Rican	36	0.17
Guatemalan	41	0.19
Honduran	47	0.22
Nicaraguan	68	0.31
Panamanian	33	0.15
Salvadoran	102	0.47
Other Central American	21	0.10
Cuban	420	1.93
Dominican Republic	609	2.80
Mexican	288	1.32
Puerto Rican	7,980	36.64
South American:	812	3.73
Argentinean	51	0.23
Bolivian	4	0.02
Chilean	7	0.03
Colombian	476	2.19
Ecuadorian	107	0.49
Peruvian	84	0.39
Uruguayan	5	0.02
Venezuelan	58	0.27
Other South American	20	0.09
Other Hispanic or Latino	1,441	6.62
Hungarian	49	0.22
Irish	1,247	5.63
Israeli	22	0.10
Italian	961	4.34
Lithuanian	43	0.19
Norwegian	56	0.25
Pennsylvania German	11	0.05
Polish	215	0.97
Portuguese	149	0.67
Romanian	9	0.04
Russian	37	0.17
Scandinavian	17	0.08
Scotch-Irish	156	0.70
Scottish	235	1.06
Slavic	11	0.05
Slovak	14	0.06
Swedish	87	0.39
Swiss	6	0.03
Ukrainian	53	0.24
United States or American	1,067	4.81
Welsh	101	0.46
West Indian, excl. Hispanic:	1,150	5.19
Barbadian	29	0.13
Belizean	25	0.11
British West Indian	18	0.08
Haitian	441	1.99
Jamaican	378	1.71
Trinidadian and Tobagonian	53	0.24
U.S. Virgin Islander	50	0.23
West Indian	156	0.70
White:	14,442	66.31
Not Hispanic (6,530)	6,796	31.21
Hispanic (7,117)	7,646	35.11

Zephyrhills

Place Type: City
County: Pasco
Population: 10,833

Ancestry/Race	Number	%
African American/Black:	340	3.14
Not Hispanic (288)	324	2.99
Hispanic (14)	16	0.15
African, sub-Saharan:	7	0.07
Nigerian	7	0.07
Alaska Native tribes, not specified	1	0.01
Am. Ind. or Alaska Nat., not spec.	23	0.21
American Indian tribes, specified:	78	0.72
Apache	5	0.05
Blackfeet (1)	9	0.08
Cherokee (6)	34	0.31
Chippewa (3)	5	0.05
Choctaw	1	0.01
Comanche	2	0.02
Creek (1)	6	0.06
Iroquois	3	0.03
Latin American Indians	3	0.03
Osage	4	0.04
Seminole (1)	1	0.01
Sioux (1)	1	0.01
All other tribes (2)	4	0.04
American Indian tribes, not spec.	6	0.06
Arab:	35	0.33
Lebanese	35	0.33
Armenian	8	0.07
Asian:	142	1.31
Chinese, ex. Taiwanese (12)	13	0.12
Filipino (43)	49	0.45
Indian (33)	34	0.31
Indonesian (4)	4	0.04
Japanese (1)	10	0.09
Korean (3)	4	0.04
Thai (1)	2	0.02
Vietnamese (15)	16	0.15
Other Asian, specified (1)	3	0.03
Other Asian, not specified (6)	7	0.06
Austrian	26	0.24
Belgian	55	0.51
British	28	0.26
Canadian	58	0.54
Croatian	11	0.10
Czech	32	0.30
Czechoslovakian	16	0.15
Danish	29	0.27
Dutch	330	3.09
English	1,775	16.60
European	18	0.17
Finnish	61	0.57
French, except Basque	449	4.20
French Canadian	177	1.66
German	2,056	19.23
Greek	24	0.22
Hawaii Native/Pacific Islander:	9	0.08
Micronesian:	2	0.02
Other Micronesian	2	0.02
Polynesian: (3)	6	0.06
Native Hawaiian (1)	3	0.03
Samoan (2)	3	0.03
Other Pac. Isl., specified	1	0.01
Hispanic or Latino:	545	5.03
Central American:	14	0.13
Costa Rican	2	0.02
Guatemalan	3	0.03
Nicaraguan	4	0.04
Other Central American	5	0.05
Cuban	32	0.30
Dominican Republic	5	0.05
Mexican	121	1.12
Puerto Rican	267	2.46
South American:	14	0.13
Argentinean	2	0.02
Chilean	2	0.02
Colombian	4	0.04
Ecuadorian	2	0.02
Peruvian	3	0.03
Venezuelan	1	0.01
Other Hispanic or Latino	92	0.85
Hungarian	100	0.94
Irish	1,346	12.59
Italian	610	5.71
Lithuanian	36	0.34
Norwegian	89	0.83
Pennsylvania German	18	0.17
Polish	233	2.18
Portuguese	34	0.32
Russian	22	0.21
Scandinavian	23	0.22
Scotch-Irish	214	2.00
Scottish	332	3.11
Slovak	34	0.32
Slovene	7	0.07
Swedish	116	1.09
Swiss	7	0.07
Ukrainian	9	0.08
United States or American	1,388	12.98
Welsh	148	1.38
West Indian, excl. Hispanic:	74	0.69
Haitian	62	0.58
U.S. Virgin Islander	12	0.11
White:	10,204	94.19
Not Hispanic (9,720)	9,838	90.82
Hispanic (315)	366	3.38

Notes: 1. Figures in the "Number" column do not add up to the total population due to: a) Ancestry/Race overlap — e.g. persons can report being both White and Irish, b) persons of Hispanic origin can report being any race, c) persons reporting two ancestries are counted in both categories. 2. Numbers in parentheses indicate the number of persons reporting this ancestry/race alone, not in combination with any other ancestry/race. 3. Refer to the User's Guide in the front of the book for more detailed information.

Acadian/Cajun

Top 10 Places Sorted by Number
Based on all places, regardless of population

Place (place type) County	Number	%
Jacksonville (special city) Duval	179	0.02
Tallahassee (city) Leon	70	0.05
Pensacola (city) Escambia	59	0.10
Palm Harbor (cdp) Pinellas	53	0.09
Weston (city) Broward	49	0.10
Rockledge (city) Brevard	47	0.23
Tampa (city) Hillsborough	47	0.02
Bellview (cdp) Escambia	42	0.20
Palm Valley (cdp) St. Johns	39	0.20
Gainesville (city) Alachua	37	0.04

Top 10 Places Sorted by Percent
Based on all places, regardless of population

Place (place type) County	Number	%
Southchase (cdp) Orange	33	0.73
Freeport (city) Walton	8	0.65
Sharpes (cdp) Brevard	20	0.57
Belleair Beach (city) Pinellas	9	0.54
Inglis (town) Levy	6	0.40
Southgate (cdp) Sarasota	29	0.39
Cedar Key (city) Levy	3	0.39
Harbor Bluffs (cdp) Pinellas	11	0.38
Zellwood (cdp) Orange	9	0.37
Plantation Mobile Home Park (cdp) Palm Beach	5	0.37

Top 10 Places Sorted by Percent
Based on places with populations of 10,000 or more

Place (place type) County	Number	%
Gonzalez (cdp) Escambia	30	0.26
Rockledge (city) Brevard	47	0.23
Bellview (cdp) Escambia	42	0.20
Palm Valley (cdp) St. Johns	39	0.20
Niceville (city) Okaloosa	21	0.18
Wilton Manors (city) Broward	20	0.16
Callaway (city) Bay	21	0.15
Destin (city) Okaloosa	16	0.14
South Miami (city) Miami-Dade	14	0.13
Casselberry (city) Seminole	27	0.12

Afghan

Top 10 Places Sorted by Number
Based on all places, regardless of population

Place (place type) County	Number	%
Jacksonville (special city) Duval	205	0.03
Dunedin (city) Pinellas	31	0.09
Bellair-Meadowbrook Terrace (cdp) Clay	14	0.08
Palm Beach Gardens (city) Palm Beach	14	0.04
Davie (town) Broward	13	0.02
Weston (city) Broward	11	0.02
Bonita Springs (city) Lee	10	0.03
Lake Mary (city) Seminole	8	0.07
Titusville (city) Brevard	8	0.02
Fort Lauderdale (city) Broward	7	0.00

Top 10 Places Sorted by Percent
Based on all places, regardless of population

Place (place type) County	Number	%
Royal Palm Estates (cdp) Palm Beach	6	0.17
Dunedin (city) Pinellas	31	0.09
Bellair-Meadowbrook Terrace (cdp) Clay	14	0.08
Lake Mary (city) Seminole	8	0.07
Villas (cdp) Lee	6	0.05
Doctor Phillips (cdp) Orange	5	0.05
Palm Beach Gardens (city) Palm Beach	14	0.04
Jacksonville (special city) Duval	205	0.03
Bonita Springs (city) Lee	10	0.03
Davie (town) Broward	13	0.02

Top 10 Places Sorted by Percent
Based on places with populations of 10,000 or more

Place (place type) County	Number	%
Dunedin (city) Pinellas	31	0.09
Bellair-Meadowbrook Terrace (cdp) Clay	14	0.08
Lake Mary (city) Seminole	8	0.07
Villas (cdp) Lee	6	0.05
Palm Beach Gardens (city) Palm Beach	14	0.04
Jacksonville (special city) Duval	205	0.03
Bonita Springs (city) Lee	10	0.03
Davie (town) Broward	13	0.02
Weston (city) Broward	11	0.02
Titusville (city) Brevard	8	0.02

African American/Black

Top 10 Places Sorted by Number
Based on all places, regardless of population

Place (place type) County	Number	%
Jacksonville (special city) Duval	218,451	29.70
Miami (city) Miami-Dade	87,857	24.24
Tampa (city) Hillsborough	82,470	27.18
St. Petersburg (city) Pinellas	57,483	23.16
Orlando (city) Orange	52,652	28.31
Tallahassee (city) Leon	52,611	34.93
Fort Lauderdale (city) Broward	48,033	31.52
Lauderhill (city) Broward	35,657	61.92
North Miami (city) Miami-Dade	34,778	58.08
Miramar (city) Broward	33,627	46.23

Top 10 Places Sorted by Percent
Based on all places, regardless of population

Place (place type) County	Number	%
Washington Park (cdp) Broward	1,250	99.44
Franklin Park (cdp) Broward	933	98.94
Roosevelt Gardens (cdp) Broward	1,894	98.49
West Ken-Lark (cdp) Broward	3,358	98.42
Broward Estates (cdp) Broward	3,360	98.36
St. George (cdp) Broward	2,405	98.16
Rock Island (cdp) Broward	3,000	97.53
Bunche Park (cdp) Miami-Dade	3,863	97.26
Carver Ranches (cdp) Broward	4,165	96.88
Golden Heights (cdp) Broward	485	96.81

Top 10 Places Sorted by Percent
Based on places with populations of 10,000 or more

Place (place type) County	Number	%
Scott Lake (cdp) Miami-Dade	13,445	93.36
Brownsville (cdp) Miami-Dade	13,249	92.05
Norland (cdp) Miami-Dade	18,992	82.59
Gladeview (cdp) Miami-Dade	11,323	78.26
Pinewood (cdp) Miami-Dade	12,422	75.18
Lauderdale Lakes (city) Broward	22,834	72.02
Opa-locka (city) Miami-Dade	10,705	71.60
Golden Glades (cdp) Miami-Dade	22,922	70.26
Riviera Beach (city) Palm Beach	20,735	69.38
Lauderhill (city) Broward	35,657	61.92

African American/Black: Not Hispanic

Top 10 Places Sorted by Number
Based on all places, regardless of population

Place (place type) County	Number	%
Jacksonville (special city) Duval	215,484	29.29
Tampa (city) Hillsborough	79,161	26.09
Miami (city) Miami-Dade	77,247	21.31
St. Petersburg (city) Pinellas	56,642	22.82
Tallahassee (city) Leon	51,926	34.47
Orlando (city) Orange	50,745	27.29
Fort Lauderdale (city) Broward	47,272	31.02
Lauderhill (city) Broward	35,041	60.85
North Miami (city) Miami-Dade	33,411	55.80
Miramar (city) Broward	32,317	44.43

Top 10 Places Sorted by Percent
Based on all places, regardless of population

Place (place type) County	Number	%
Washington Park (cdp) Broward	1,243	98.89
Roosevelt Gardens (cdp) Broward	1,891	98.34
Franklin Park (cdp) Broward	924	97.99
St. George (cdp) Broward	2,394	97.71
Broward Estates (cdp) Broward	3,335	97.63
West Ken-Lark (cdp) Broward	3,329	97.57
Rock Island (cdp) Broward	2,990	97.20
Carver Ranches (cdp) Broward	4,146	96.44
Golden Heights (cdp) Broward	483	96.41
Bunche Park (cdp) Miami-Dade	3,820	96.17

Top 10 Places Sorted by Percent
Based on places with populations of 10,000 or more

Place (place type) County	Number	%
Scott Lake (cdp) Miami-Dade	13,177	91.50
Brownsville (cdp) Miami-Dade	13,069	90.80
Norland (cdp) Miami-Dade	18,523	80.55
Gladeview (cdp) Miami-Dade	11,085	76.62
Pinewood (cdp) Miami-Dade	12,043	72.89
Lauderdale Lakes (city) Broward	22,531	71.06
Riviera Beach (city) Palm Beach	20,476	68.52
Opa-locka (city) Miami-Dade	10,127	67.73
Golden Glades (cdp) Miami-Dade	22,079	67.68
Lauderhill (city) Broward	35,041	60.85

African American/Black: Hispanic

Top 10 Places Sorted by Number
Based on all places, regardless of population

Place (place type) County	Number	%
Miami (city) Miami-Dade	10,610	2.93
Hialeah (city) Miami-Dade	4,321	1.91
Tampa (city) Hillsborough	3,309	1.09
Jacksonville (special city) Duval	2,967	0.40
Orlando (city) Orange	1,907	1.03
Carol City (cdp) Miami-Dade	1,882	3.17
Miami Beach (city) Miami-Dade	1,456	1.66
North Miami (city) Miami-Dade	1,367	2.28
Miramar (city) Broward	1,310	1.80
Hollywood (city) Broward	1,235	0.89

Top 10 Places Sorted by Percent
Based on all places, regardless of population

Place (place type) County	Number	%
Opa-locka (city) Miami-Dade	578	3.87
Carol City (cdp) Miami-Dade	1,882	3.17
Homestead Base (cdp) Miami-Dade	14	3.14
Cloud Lake (town) Palm Beach	5	2.99
Miami (city) Miami-Dade	10,610	2.93
Miami Gardens (cdp) Broward	79	2.92
Stacey Street (cdp) Palm Beach	28	2.92
West Little River (cdp) Miami-Dade	923	2.84
El Portal (village) Miami-Dade	70	2.79
Oak Ridge (cdp) Orange	606	2.71

Top 10 Places Sorted by Percent
Based on places with populations of 10,000 or more

Place (place type) County	Number	%
Opa-locka (city) Miami-Dade	578	3.87
Carol City (cdp) Miami-Dade	1,882	3.17
Miami (city) Miami-Dade	10,610	2.93
West Little River (cdp) Miami-Dade	923	2.84
Oak Ridge (cdp) Orange	606	2.71
South Miami Heights (cdp) Miami-Dade	876	2.61
Poinciana (cdp) Osceola	354	2.59
Golden Glades (cdp) Miami-Dade	843	2.58
Yeehaw Junction (cdp) Osceola	550	2.53
Palmetto Estates (cdp) Miami-Dade	340	2.49

Notes: (cdp) census designated place; Refer to the User's Guide in the front of the book for more detailed information.

African, sub-Saharan

Top 10 Places Sorted by Number
Based on all places, regardless of population

Place (place type) County	Number	%
Jacksonville (special city) Duval	8,010	1.09
Miami (city) Miami-Dade	2,816	0.78
Tampa (city) Hillsborough	2,718	0.90
St. Petersburg (city) Pinellas	2,394	0.97
Tallahassee (city) Leon	2,240	1.49
Fort Lauderdale (city) Broward	1,802	1.18
Orlando (city) Orange	1,786	0.96
Gainesville (city) Alachua	1,630	1.70
Pine Hills (cdp) Orange	964	2.30
Hollywood (city) Broward	961	0.69

Top 10 Places Sorted by Percent
Based on all places, regardless of population

Place (place type) County	Number	%
Lake Harbor (cdp) Palm Beach	29	31.18
Century (town) Escambia	162	9.41
Fort Pierce North (cdp) St. Lucie	673	9.17
Tildenville (cdp) Orange	34	6.85
South Brooksville (cdp) Hernando	85	6.35
Franklin Park (cdp) Broward	56	5.10
Coleman (city) Sumter	32	4.59
Penney Farms (town) Clay	23	4.28
South Apopka (cdp) Orange	259	4.26
Graceville (city) Jackson	103	4.24

Top 10 Places Sorted by Percent
Based on places with populations of 10,000 or more

Place (place type) County	Number	%
Leesburg (city) Lake	417	2.63
Norland (cdp) Miami-Dade	531	2.31
Pine Hills (cdp) Orange	964	2.30
Brownsville (cdp) Miami-Dade	307	2.12
Princeton (cdp) Miami-Dade	194	1.91
University (cdp) Hillsborough	574	1.87
Gainesville (city) Alachua	1,630	1.70
West Little River (cdp) Miami-Dade	539	1.67
Crestview (city) Okaloosa	247	1.67
Sanford (city) Seminole	607	1.61

African, Subsaharan: African

Top 10 Places Sorted by Number
Based on all places, regardless of population

Place (place type) County	Number	%
Jacksonville (special city) Duval	6,995	0.95
Miami (city) Miami-Dade	2,661	0.73
Tampa (city) Hillsborough	2,282	0.75
St. Petersburg (city) Pinellas	2,107	0.85
Tallahassee (city) Leon	1,726	1.15
Orlando (city) Orange	1,598	0.86
Fort Lauderdale (city) Broward	1,594	1.05
Gainesville (city) Alachua	1,249	1.31
Pine Hills (cdp) Orange	903	2.15
West Palm Beach (city) Palm Beach	705	0.86

Top 10 Places Sorted by Percent
Based on all places, regardless of population

Place (place type) County	Number	%
Lake Harbor (cdp) Palm Beach	29	31.18
Century (town) Escambia	162	9.41
Fort Pierce North (cdp) St. Lucie	673	9.17
Tildenville (cdp) Orange	34	6.85
Franklin Park (cdp) Broward	56	5.10
Coleman (city) Sumter	32	4.59
Penney Farms (town) Clay	23	4.28
South Apopka (cdp) Orange	259	4.26
Graceville (city) Jackson	103	4.24
Goulding (cdp) Escambia	176	3.94

Top 10 Places Sorted by Percent
Based on places with populations of 10,000 or more

Place (place type) County	Number	%
Leesburg (city) Lake	417	2.63
Pine Hills (cdp) Orange	903	2.15
Norland (cdp) Miami-Dade	487	2.12
Brownsville (cdp) Miami-Dade	307	2.12
Princeton (cdp) Miami-Dade	194	1.91
West Little River (cdp) Miami-Dade	539	1.67
Crestview (city) Okaloosa	247	1.67
Sanford (city) Seminole	607	1.61
Fort Pierce (city) St. Lucie	542	1.45
University (cdp) Hillsborough	439	1.43

African, Subsaharan: Cape Verdean

Top 10 Places Sorted by Number
Based on all places, regardless of population

Place (place type) County	Number	%
Poinciana (cdp) Osceola	90	0.66
Orlando (city) Orange	84	0.05
Jacksonville (special city) Duval	72	0.01
Coral Springs (city) Broward	66	0.06
Kissimmee (city) Osceola	56	0.12
Bloomingdale (cdp) Hillsborough	53	0.27
Coconut Creek (city) Broward	52	0.12
Largo (city) Pinellas	41	0.06
Palm Bay (city) Brevard	39	0.05
Citrus Park (cdp) Hillsborough	35	0.17

Top 10 Places Sorted by Percent
Based on all places, regardless of population

Place (place type) County	Number	%
Poinciana (cdp) Osceola	90	0.66
Kendall Green (cdp) Broward	9	0.29
Chambers Estates (cdp) Broward	10	0.28
Bloomingdale (cdp) Hillsborough	53	0.27
Charlotte Park (cdp) Charlotte	6	0.26
Upper Grand Lagoon (cdp) Bay	28	0.25
Micco (cdp) Brevard	22	0.23
Richmond Heights (cdp) Miami-Dade	15	0.18
Citrus Park (cdp) Hillsborough	35	0.17
West Pensacola (cdp) Escambia	32	0.15

Top 10 Places Sorted by Percent
Based on places with populations of 10,000 or more

Place (place type) County	Number	%
Poinciana (cdp) Osceola	90	0.66
Bloomingdale (cdp) Hillsborough	53	0.27
Upper Grand Lagoon (cdp) Bay	28	0.25
Citrus Park (cdp) Hillsborough	35	0.17
West Pensacola (cdp) Escambia	32	0.15
Meadow Woods (cdp) Orange	16	0.14
Kissimmee (city) Osceola	56	0.12
Coconut Creek (city) Broward	52	0.12
Royal Palm Beach (village) Palm Beach	18	0.08
Lake Wales (city) Polk	8	0.08

African, Subsaharan: Ethiopian

Top 10 Places Sorted by Number
Based on all places, regardless of population

Place (place type) County	Number	%
Gainesville (city) Alachua	135	0.14
Tampa (city) Hillsborough	106	0.03
Jacksonville (special city) Duval	99	0.01
Boca Raton (city) Palm Beach	55	0.07
Fairview Shores (cdp) Orange	50	0.37
Tangelo Park (cdp) Orange	46	1.99
Margate (city) Broward	36	0.07
North Miami (city) Miami-Dade	36	0.06
Sarasota (city) Sarasota	28	0.05
Town 'n' Country (cdp) Hillsborough	28	0.04

Top 10 Places Sorted by Percent
Based on all places, regardless of population

Place (place type) County	Number	%
Tangelo Park (cdp) Orange	46	1.99
Esto (town) Holmes	3	0.86
Fairview Shores (cdp) Orange	50	0.37
Sunny Isles Beach (city) Miami-Dade	24	0.16
Gainesville (city) Alachua	135	0.14
Pine Castle (cdp) Orange	9	0.11
Thonotosassa (cdp) Hillsborough	6	0.10
Egypt Lake-Leto (cdp) Hillsborough	26	0.08
Greater Northdale (cdp) Hillsborough	16	0.08
Boca Raton (city) Palm Beach	55	0.07

Top 10 Places Sorted by Percent
Based on places with populations of 10,000 or more

Place (place type) County	Number	%
Fairview Shores (cdp) Orange	50	0.37
Sunny Isles Beach (city) Miami-Dade	24	0.16
Gainesville (city) Alachua	135	0.14
Egypt Lake-Leto (cdp) Hillsborough	26	0.08
Greater Northdale (cdp) Hillsborough	16	0.08
Boca Raton (city) Palm Beach	55	0.07
Margate (city) Broward	36	0.07
Pinewood (cdp) Miami-Dade	11	0.07
Palmetto (city) Manatee	9	0.07
North Miami (city) Miami-Dade	36	0.06

African, Subsaharan: Ghanian

Top 10 Places Sorted by Number
Based on all places, regardless of population

Place (place type) County	Number	%
Tampa (city) Hillsborough	126	0.04
Jacksonville (special city) Duval	112	0.02
Deerfield Beach (city) Broward	105	0.16
Tallahassee (city) Leon	82	0.05
Pembroke Pines (city) Broward	69	0.05
Lakeside (cdp) Clay	28	0.09
Wellington (village) Palm Beach	28	0.07
North Miami Beach (city) Miami-Dade	26	0.06
St. Augustine (city) St. Johns	23	0.20
St. Petersburg (city) Pinellas	22	0.01

Top 10 Places Sorted by Percent
Based on all places, regardless of population

Place (place type) County	Number	%
Mangonia Park (town) Palm Beach	8	0.62
Tedder (cdp) Broward	7	0.35
Pebble Creek (cdp) Hillsborough	10	0.21
St. Augustine (city) St. Johns	23	0.20
Deerfield Beach (city) Broward	105	0.16
Doctor Phillips (cdp) Orange	11	0.11
Niceville (city) Okaloosa	12	0.10
Lakeside (cdp) Clay	28	0.09
Lakeland Highlands (cdp) Polk	12	0.09
Wellington (village) Palm Beach	28	0.07

Top 10 Places Sorted by Percent
Based on places with populations of 10,000 or more

Place (place type) County	Number	%
St. Augustine (city) St. Johns	23	0.20
Deerfield Beach (city) Broward	105	0.16
Niceville (city) Okaloosa	12	0.10
Lakeside (cdp) Clay	28	0.09
Lakeland Highlands (cdp) Polk	12	0.09
Wellington (village) Palm Beach	28	0.07
North Miami Beach (city) Miami-Dade	26	0.06
Tallahassee (city) Leon	82	0.05
Pembroke Pines (city) Broward	69	0.05
Tampa (city) Hillsborough	126	0.04

Notes: (cdp) census designated place; Refer to the User's Guide in the front of the book for more detailed information.

African, Subsaharan: Kenyan

Top 10 Places Sorted by Number
Based on all places, regardless of population

Place (place type) County	Number	%
Ocala (city) Marion	53	0.12
Gainesville (city) Alachua	30	0.03
Pompano Beach (city) Broward	29	0.04
Plantation (city) Broward	28	0.03
Ives Estates (cdp) Miami-Dade	26	0.15
Forest City (cdp) Seminole	23	0.18
Miami Shores (village) Miami-Dade	22	0.21
Heathrow (cdp) Seminole	15	0.38
Daytona Beach (city) Volusia	10	0.02
Clearwater (city) Pinellas	10	0.01

Top 10 Places Sorted by Percent
Based on all places, regardless of population

Place (place type) County	Number	%
Heathrow (cdp) Seminole	15	0.38
Stacey Street (cdp) Palm Beach	2	0.24
Miami Shores (village) Miami-Dade	22	0.21
Forest City (cdp) Seminole	23	0.18
Ives Estates (cdp) Miami-Dade	26	0.15
Ocala (city) Marion	53	0.12
Lantana (town) Palm Beach	7	0.07
Pompano Beach (city) Broward	29	0.04
Gainesville (city) Alachua	30	0.03
Plantation (city) Broward	28	0.03

Top 10 Places Sorted by Percent
Based on places with populations of 10,000 or more

Place (place type) County	Number	%
Miami Shores (village) Miami-Dade	22	0.21
Forest City (cdp) Seminole	23	0.18
Ives Estates (cdp) Miami-Dade	26	0.15
Ocala (city) Marion	53	0.12
Pompano Beach (city) Broward	29	0.04
Gainesville (city) Alachua	30	0.03
Plantation (city) Broward	28	0.03
Vero Beach South (cdp) Indian River	7	0.03
Daytona Beach (city) Volusia	10	0.02
Fort Myers (city) Lee	8	0.02

African, Subsaharan: Liberian

Top 10 Places Sorted by Number
Based on all places, regardless of population

Place (place type) County	Number	%
Boynton Beach (city) Palm Beach	85	0.14
Royal Palm Beach (village) Palm Beach	61	0.28
Daytona Beach (city) Volusia	41	0.06
Delray Beach (city) Palm Beach	37	0.06
Hollywood (city) Broward	37	0.03
Parkland (city) Broward	24	0.17
Cape Coral (city) Lee	22	0.02
Greater Carrollwood (cdp) Hillsborough	12	0.04
Jacksonville (special city) Duval	10	0.00
Punta Gorda (city) Charlotte	9	0.06

Top 10 Places Sorted by Percent
Based on all places, regardless of population

Place (place type) County	Number	%
Royal Palm Beach (village) Palm Beach	61	0.28
Parkland (city) Broward	24	0.17
Boynton Beach (city) Palm Beach	85	0.14
Daytona Beach (city) Volusia	41	0.06
Delray Beach (city) Palm Beach	37	0.06
Punta Gorda (city) Charlotte	9	0.06
Greater Carrollwood (cdp) Hillsborough	12	0.04
Hollywood (city) Broward	37	0.03
Cape Coral (city) Lee	22	0.02
North Lauderdale (city) Broward	8	0.02

Top 10 Places Sorted by Percent
Based on places with populations of 10,000 or more

Place (place type) County	Number	%
Royal Palm Beach (village) Palm Beach	61	0.28
Parkland (city) Broward	24	0.17
Boynton Beach (city) Palm Beach	85	0.14
Daytona Beach (city) Volusia	41	0.06
Delray Beach (city) Palm Beach	37	0.06
Punta Gorda (city) Charlotte	9	0.06
Greater Carrollwood (cdp) Hillsborough	12	0.04
Hollywood (city) Broward	37	0.03
Cape Coral (city) Lee	22	0.02
North Lauderdale (city) Broward	8	0.02

African, Subsaharan: Nigerian

Top 10 Places Sorted by Number
Based on all places, regardless of population

Place (place type) County	Number	%
Hollywood (city) Broward	285	0.20
Jacksonville (special city) Duval	281	0.04
Miramar (city) Broward	267	0.37
Tallahassee (city) Leon	250	0.17
Pembroke Pines (city) Broward	188	0.14
St. Petersburg (city) Pinellas	136	0.05
Melbourne (city) Brevard	124	0.17
Golden Glades (cdp) Miami-Dade	118	0.37
Rockledge (city) Brevard	115	0.57
University (cdp) Hillsborough	108	0.35

Top 10 Places Sorted by Percent
Based on all places, regardless of population

Place (place type) County	Number	%
South Brooksville (cdp) Hernando	77	5.75
Homestead Base (cdp) Miami-Dade	12	2.96
Tangelo Park (cdp) Orange	33	1.42
Wesley Chapel (cdp) Pasco	65	1.10
Heathrow (cdp) Seminole	39	1.00
Country Walk (cdp) Miami-Dade	81	0.76
Andover (cdp) Miami-Dade	62	0.72
Rockledge (city) Brevard	115	0.57
Eatonville (town) Orange	12	0.50
Wimauma (cdp) Hillsborough	19	0.45

Top 10 Places Sorted by Percent
Based on places with populations of 10,000 or more

Place (place type) County	Number	%
Country Walk (cdp) Miami-Dade	81	0.76
Rockledge (city) Brevard	115	0.57
Cooper City (city) Broward	107	0.39
Miramar (city) Broward	267	0.37
Golden Glades (cdp) Miami-Dade	118	0.37
Sweetwater (city) Miami-Dade	52	0.36
University (cdp) Hillsborough	108	0.35
Richmond West (cdp) Miami-Dade	91	0.32
Scott Lake (cdp) Miami-Dade	31	0.22
Gladeview (cdp) Miami-Dade	30	0.21

African, Subsaharan: Senegalese

Top 10 Places Sorted by Number
Based on all places, regardless of population

Place (place type) County	Number	%
Coconut Creek (city) Broward	32	0.07
Pompano Beach (city) Broward	24	0.03
North Miami Beach (city) Miami-Dade	6	0.01

Top 10 Places Sorted by Percent
Based on all places, regardless of population

Place (place type) County	Number	%
Coconut Creek (city) Broward	32	0.07
Pompano Beach (city) Broward	24	0.03
North Miami Beach (city) Miami-Dade	6	0.01

Top 10 Places Sorted by Percent
Based on places with populations of 10,000 or more

Place (place type) County	Number	%
Coconut Creek (city) Broward	32	0.07
Pompano Beach (city) Broward	24	0.03
North Miami Beach (city) Miami-Dade	6	0.01

African, Subsaharan: Sierra Leonean

Top 10 Places Sorted by Number
Based on all places, regardless of population

Place (place type) County	Number	%
Jacksonville (special city) Duval	49	0.01
Kendale Lakes (cdp) Miami-Dade	29	0.05
Riverview (cdp) Hillsborough	15	0.12
Orlando (city) Orange	12	0.01
Egypt Lake-Leto (cdp) Hillsborough	10	0.03
Wedgefield (cdp) Orange	8	0.28
Golden Gate (cdp) Collier	8	0.04
Lake Magdalene (cdp) Hillsborough	8	0.03
Golden Glades (cdp) Miami-Dade	8	0.02
St. Petersburg (city) Pinellas	7	0.00

Top 10 Places Sorted by Percent
Based on all places, regardless of population

Place (place type) County	Number	%
Wedgefield (cdp) Orange	8	0.28
Riverview (cdp) Hillsborough	15	0.12
Kendale Lakes (cdp) Miami-Dade	29	0.05
Golden Gate (cdp) Collier	8	0.04
Egypt Lake-Leto (cdp) Hillsborough	10	0.03
Lake Magdalene (cdp) Hillsborough	8	0.03
Country Walk (cdp) Miami-Dade	3	0.03
Golden Glades (cdp) Miami-Dade	8	0.02
Greenacres (city) Palm Beach	5	0.02
Jacksonville (special city) Duval	49	0.01

Top 10 Places Sorted by Percent
Based on places with populations of 10,000 or more

Place (place type) County	Number	%
Riverview (cdp) Hillsborough	15	0.12
Kendale Lakes (cdp) Miami-Dade	29	0.05
Golden Gate (cdp) Collier	8	0.04
Egypt Lake-Leto (cdp) Hillsborough	10	0.03
Lake Magdalene (cdp) Hillsborough	8	0.03
Country Walk (cdp) Miami-Dade	3	0.03
Golden Glades (cdp) Miami-Dade	8	0.02
Greenacres (city) Palm Beach	5	0.02
Jacksonville (special city) Duval	49	0.01
Orlando (city) Orange	12	0.01

African, Subsaharan: Somalian

Top 10 Places Sorted by Number
Based on all places, regardless of population

Place (place type) County	Number	%
Pembroke Pines (city) Broward	22	0.02
Deerfield Beach (city) Broward	18	0.03
Tampa (city) Hillsborough	11	0.00
Miami Beach (city) Miami-Dade	9	0.01

Top 10 Places Sorted by Percent
Based on all places, regardless of population

Place (place type) County	Number	%
Deerfield Beach (city) Broward	18	0.03
Pembroke Pines (city) Broward	22	0.02
Miami Beach (city) Miami-Dade	9	0.01
Tampa (city) Hillsborough	11	0.00

Notes: (cdp) census designated place; Refer to the User's Guide in the front of the book for more detailed information.

Top 10 Places Sorted by Percent
Based on places with populations of 10,000 or more

Place (place type) County	Number	%
Deerfield Beach (city) Broward	18	0.03
Pembroke Pines (city) Broward	22	0.02
Miami Beach (city) Miami-Dade	9	0.01
Tampa (city) Hillsborough	11	0.00

African, Subsaharan: South African

Top 10 Places Sorted by Number
Based on all places, regardless of population

Place (place type) County	Number	%
Weston (city) Broward	210	0.43
Boca Raton (city) Palm Beach	163	0.22
Jacksonville (special city) Duval	154	0.02
Tampa (city) Hillsborough	139	0.05
Fort Lauderdale (city) Broward	120	0.08
Plantation (city) Broward	119	0.14
Coral Springs (city) Broward	114	0.10
Deerfield Beach (city) Broward	104	0.16
Boca Del Mar (cdp) Palm Beach	89	0.42
Aventura (city) Miami-Dade	88	0.35

Top 10 Places Sorted by Percent
Based on all places, regardless of population

Place (place type) County	Number	%
Gotha (cdp) Orange	31	4.14
Melbourne Beach (town) Brevard	41	1.24
Harbor Bluffs (cdp) Pinellas	21	0.73
Wesley Chapel South (cdp) Pasco	18	0.55
Three Oaks (cdp) Lee	12	0.53
Sandalfoot Cove (cdp) Palm Beach	85	0.51
Big Coppitt Key (cdp) Monroe	13	0.50
Chuluota (cdp) Seminole	9	0.45
North Andrews Gardens (cdp) Broward	42	0.44
Weston (city) Broward	210	0.43

Top 10 Places Sorted by Percent
Based on places with populations of 10,000 or more

Place (place type) County	Number	%
Sandalfoot Cove (cdp) Palm Beach	85	0.51
Weston (city) Broward	210	0.43
Boca Del Mar (cdp) Palm Beach	89	0.42
Aventura (city) Miami-Dade	88	0.35
Lakeland Highlands (cdp) Polk	44	0.35
Sunny Isles Beach (city) Miami-Dade	38	0.25
Boca Raton (city) Palm Beach	163	0.22
Ojus (cdp) Miami-Dade	36	0.22
Parkland (city) Broward	31	0.22
Winter Springs (city) Seminole	66	0.21

African, Subsaharan: Sudanese

Top 10 Places Sorted by Number
Based on all places, regardless of population

Place (place type) County	Number	%
Jacksonville (special city) Duval	64	0.01
Pembroke Pines (city) Broward	44	0.03
Clearwater (city) Pinellas	19	0.02
Jasmine Estates (cdp) Pasco	16	0.09
Miramar (city) Broward	16	0.02
Plant City (city) Hillsborough	10	0.03
North Miami (city) Miami-Dade	10	0.02
Plantation (city) Broward	10	0.01
Fort Lauderdale (city) Broward	8	0.01
Tampa (city) Hillsborough	7	0.00

Top 10 Places Sorted by Percent
Based on all places, regardless of population

Place (place type) County	Number	%
Jasmine Estates (cdp) Pasco	16	0.09
Pembroke Pines (city) Broward	44	0.03
Plant City (city) Hillsborough	10	0.03
Clearwater (city) Pinellas	19	0.02
Miramar (city) Broward	16	0.02
North Miami (city) Miami-Dade	10	0.02
Jacksonville (special city) Duval	64	0.01
Plantation (city) Broward	10	0.01
Fort Lauderdale (city) Broward	8	0.01
Tampa (city) Hillsborough	7	0.00

Top 10 Places Sorted by Percent
Based on places with populations of 10,000 or more

Place (place type) County	Number	%
Jasmine Estates (cdp) Pasco	16	0.09
Pembroke Pines (city) Broward	44	0.03
Plant City (city) Hillsborough	10	0.03
Clearwater (city) Pinellas	19	0.02
Miramar (city) Broward	16	0.02
North Miami (city) Miami-Dade	10	0.02
Jacksonville (special city) Duval	64	0.01
Plantation (city) Broward	10	0.01
Fort Lauderdale (city) Broward	8	0.01
Tampa (city) Hillsborough	7	0.00

African, Subsaharan: Ugandan

Top 10 Places Sorted by Number
Based on all places, regardless of population

Place (place type) County	Number	%
Tampa (city) Hillsborough	22	0.01
North Miami Beach (city) Miami-Dade	20	0.05
Fort Lauderdale (city) Broward	13	0.01
Hallandale (city) Broward	7	0.02

Top 10 Places Sorted by Percent
Based on all places, regardless of population

Place (place type) County	Number	%
North Miami Beach (city) Miami-Dade	20	0.05
Hallandale (city) Broward	7	0.02
Tampa (city) Hillsborough	22	0.01
Fort Lauderdale (city) Broward	13	0.01

Top 10 Places Sorted by Percent
Based on places with populations of 10,000 or more

Place (place type) County	Number	%
North Miami Beach (city) Miami-Dade	20	0.05
Hallandale (city) Broward	7	0.02
Tampa (city) Hillsborough	22	0.01
Fort Lauderdale (city) Broward	13	0.01

African, Subsaharan: Zairian

Top 10 Places Sorted by Number
Based on all places, regardless of population

Place (place type) County	Number	%
Miami Beach (city) Miami-Dade	12	0.01
Orlando (city) Orange	10	0.01
Miami (city) Miami-Dade	7	0.00

Top 10 Places Sorted by Percent
Based on all places, regardless of population

Place (place type) County	Number	%
Miami Beach (city) Miami-Dade	12	0.01
Orlando (city) Orange	10	0.01
Miami (city) Miami-Dade	7	0.00

Top 10 Places Sorted by Percent
Based on places with populations of 10,000 or more

Place (place type) County	Number	%
Miami Beach (city) Miami-Dade	12	0.01
Orlando (city) Orange	10	0.01
Miami (city) Miami-Dade	7	0.00

African, Subsaharan: Zimbabwean

Top 10 Places Sorted by Number
Based on all places, regardless of population

Place (place type) County	Number	%
Fort Lauderdale (city) Broward	36	0.02
Gainesville (city) Alachua	33	0.03
St. Petersburg (city) Pinellas	19	0.01
Bradenton (city) Manatee	14	0.03
Miami (city) Miami-Dade	12	0.00
Hunters Creek (cdp) Orange	10	0.11
Bloomingdale (cdp) Hillsborough	10	0.05
Orlando (city) Orange	10	0.01
Port St. Lucie (city) St. Lucie	8	0.01
West Palm Beach (city) Palm Beach	7	0.01

Top 10 Places Sorted by Percent
Based on all places, regardless of population

Place (place type) County	Number	%
Layton (city) Monroe	4	1.67
Hunters Creek (cdp) Orange	10	0.11
Bloomingdale (cdp) Hillsborough	10	0.05
Gainesville (city) Alachua	33	0.03
Bradenton (city) Manatee	14	0.03
Fort Lauderdale (city) Broward	36	0.02
St. Petersburg (city) Pinellas	19	0.01
Orlando (city) Orange	10	0.01
Port St. Lucie (city) St. Lucie	8	0.01
West Palm Beach (city) Palm Beach	7	0.01

Top 10 Places Sorted by Percent
Based on places with populations of 10,000 or more

Place (place type) County	Number	%
Bloomingdale (cdp) Hillsborough	10	0.05
Gainesville (city) Alachua	33	0.03
Bradenton (city) Manatee	14	0.03
Fort Lauderdale (city) Broward	36	0.02
St. Petersburg (city) Pinellas	19	0.01
Orlando (city) Orange	10	0.01
Port St. Lucie (city) St. Lucie	8	0.01
West Palm Beach (city) Palm Beach	7	0.01
Miami (city) Miami-Dade	12	0.00

African, Subsaharan: Other

Top 10 Places Sorted by Number
Based on all places, regardless of population

Place (place type) County	Number	%
Jacksonville (special city) Duval	167	0.02
Tallahassee (city) Leon	120	0.08
The Hammocks (cdp) Miami-Dade	57	0.12
Kissimmee (city) Osceola	46	0.10
Daytona Beach (city) Volusia	36	0.06
Clearwater (city) Pinellas	34	0.03
Westchase (cdp) Hillsborough	32	0.29
Orlando (city) Orange	31	0.02
Lockhart (cdp) Orange	30	0.24
Coral Springs (city) Broward	28	0.02

Top 10 Places Sorted by Percent
Based on all places, regardless of population

Place (place type) County	Number	%
Tedder (cdp) Broward	14	0.70
Westchase (cdp) Hillsborough	32	0.29
Plantation Mobile Home Park (cdp) Palm Beach	4	0.29
Pebble Creek (cdp) Hillsborough	13	0.27
Broward Estates (cdp) Broward	9	0.26
Lockhart (cdp) Orange	30	0.24
South Patrick Shores (cdp) Brevard	17	0.18
The Hammocks (cdp) Miami-Dade	57	0.12
Lake Mary (city) Seminole	12	0.11
Kissimmee (city) Osceola	46	0.10

Notes: (cdp) census designated place; Refer to the User's Guide in the front of the book for more detailed information.

Top 10 Places Sorted by Percent
Based on places with populations of 10,000 or more

Place (place type) County	Number	%
Westchase (cdp) Hillsborough	32	0.29
Lockhart (cdp) Orange	30	0.24
The Hammocks (cdp) Miami-Dade	57	0.12
Lake Mary (city) Seminole	12	0.11
Kissimmee (city) Osceola	46	0.10
Tallahassee (city) Leon	120	0.08
Doral (cdp) Miami-Dade	14	0.07
Ojus (cdp) Miami-Dade	12	0.07
North Palm Beach (village) Palm Beach	8	0.07
Daytona Beach (city) Volusia	36	0.06

Alaska Native tribes, specified

Top 10 Places Sorted by Number
Based on all places, regardless of population

Place (place type) County	Number	%
Jacksonville (special city) Duval	46	0.01
Fort Lauderdale (city) Broward	25	0.02
Tampa (city) Hillsborough	22	0.01
Tallahassee (city) Leon	14	0.01
North Miami (city) Miami-Dade	13	0.02
Largo (city) Pinellas	11	0.02
Miami (city) Miami-Dade	11	0.00
Palm Bay (city) Brevard	9	0.01
Port St. Lucie (city) St. Lucie	8	0.01
Orlando (city) Orange	8	0.00

Top 10 Places Sorted by Percent
Based on all places, regardless of population

Place (place type) County	Number	%
Three Oaks (cdp) Lee	3	0.13
Grand Ridge (town) Jackson	1	0.13
Palm Shores (town) Brevard	1	0.13
El Portal (village) Miami-Dade	3	0.12
Watertown (cdp) Columbia	3	0.11
North River Shores (cdp) Martin	3	0.10
Feather Sound (cdp) Pinellas	3	0.08
Crystal Lake (cdp) Polk	4	0.07
Palm Springs North (cdp) Miami-Dade	4	0.07
Mary Esther (city) Okaloosa	3	0.07

Top 10 Places Sorted by Percent
Based on places with populations of 10,000 or more

Place (place type) County	Number	%
Villas (cdp) Lee	6	0.05
Fernandina Beach (city) Nassau	5	0.05
Bartow (city) Polk	6	0.04
Poinciana (cdp) Osceola	6	0.04
Niceville (city) Okaloosa	5	0.04
Lakewood Park (cdp) St. Lucie	3	0.03
Fort Lauderdale (city) Broward	25	0.02
North Miami (city) Miami-Dade	13	0.02
Largo (city) Pinellas	11	0.02
Merritt Island (cdp) Brevard	7	0.02

Alaska Native: Alaska Athabascan

Top 10 Places Sorted by Number
Based on all places, regardless of population

Place (place type) County	Number	%
Tampa (city) Hillsborough	7	0.00
Panama City (city) Bay	6	0.02
Jacksonville (special city) Duval	5	0.00
Spring Hill (cdp) Hernando	4	0.01
Orlando (city) Orange	4	0.00
Watertown (cdp) Columbia	3	0.11
Lauderdale Lakes (city) Broward	3	0.01
Miami Beach (city) Miami-Dade	3	0.00
Bay Pines (cdp) Pinellas	2	0.07
Pretty Bayou (cdp) Bay	2	0.06

Top 10 Places Sorted by Percent
Based on all places, regardless of population

Place (place type) County	Number	%
Watertown (cdp) Columbia	3	0.11
Bay Pines (cdp) Pinellas	2	0.07
North Brooksville (cdp) Hernando	1	0.07
South Brooksville (cdp) Hernando	1	0.07
Pretty Bayou (cdp) Bay	2	0.06
Eastpoint (cdp) Franklin	1	0.05
Gibsonia (cdp) Polk	2	0.04
Ocean City (cdp) Okaloosa	2	0.04
Apollo Beach (cdp) Hillsborough	2	0.03
Panama City (city) Bay	6	0.02

Top 10 Places Sorted by Percent
Based on places with populations of 10,000 or more

Place (place type) County	Number	%
Panama City (city) Bay	6	0.02
Spring Hill (cdp) Hernando	4	0.01
Lauderdale Lakes (city) Broward	3	0.01
Myrtle Grove (cdp) Escambia	2	0.01
Callaway (city) Bay	1	0.01
Gulfport (city) Pinellas	1	0.01
Holly Hill (city) Volusia	1	0.01
Immokalee (cdp) Collier	1	0.01
Lutz (cdp) Hillsborough	1	0.01
Lynn Haven (city) Bay	1	0.01

Alaska Native: Aleut

Top 10 Places Sorted by Number
Based on all places, regardless of population

Place (place type) County	Number	%
Jacksonville (special city) Duval	11	0.00
Tallahassee (city) Leon	4	0.00
Three Oaks (cdp) Lee	3	0.13
North River Shores (cdp) Martin	3	0.10
Feather Sound (cdp) Pinellas	3	0.08
Rotonda (cdp) Charlotte	3	0.05
Collier Manor-Cresthaven (cdp) Broward	3	0.04
Titusville (city) Brevard	3	0.01
Fort Lauderdale (city) Broward	3	0.00
Pompano Beach (city) Broward	3	0.00

Top 10 Places Sorted by Percent
Based on all places, regardless of population

Place (place type) County	Number	%
Three Oaks (cdp) Lee	3	0.13
North River Shores (cdp) Martin	3	0.10
Feather Sound (cdp) Pinellas	3	0.08
Rotonda (cdp) Charlotte	3	0.05
Collier Manor-Cresthaven (cdp) Broward	3	0.04
Graceville (city) Jackson	1	0.04
Villas (cdp) Lee	2	0.02
Clewiston (city) Hendry	1	0.02
Palm Springs North (cdp) Miami-Dade	1	0.02
Sky Lake (cdp) Orange	1	0.02

Top 10 Places Sorted by Percent
Based on places with populations of 10,000 or more

Place (place type) County	Number	%
Villas (cdp) Lee	2	0.02
Titusville (city) Brevard	3	0.01
West Pensacola (cdp) Escambia	2	0.01
Bartow (city) Polk	1	0.01
Belle Glade (city) Palm Beach	1	0.01
Conway (cdp) Orange	1	0.01
Edgewater (city) Volusia	1	0.01
Ives Estates (cdp) Miami-Dade	1	0.01
Lady Lake (town) Lake	1	0.01
Lakewood Park (cdp) St. Lucie	1	0.01

Alaska Native: Eskimo

Top 10 Places Sorted by Number
Based on all places, regardless of population

Place (place type) County	Number	%
Jacksonville (special city) Duval	12	0.00
Tampa (city) Hillsborough	12	0.00
Tallahassee (city) Leon	9	0.01
Poinciana (cdp) Osceola	6	0.04
Largo (city) Pinellas	6	0.01
Palm Bay (city) Brevard	6	0.01
Bartow (city) Polk	5	0.03
Davie (town) Broward	5	0.01
Fort Lauderdale (city) Broward	5	0.00
Miami (city) Miami-Dade	5	0.00

Top 10 Places Sorted by Percent
Based on all places, regardless of population

Place (place type) County	Number	%
Laguna Beach (cdp) Bay	2	0.07
Five Points (cdp) Columbia	1	0.07
Anna Maria (city) Manatee	1	0.06
Gandy (cdp) Pinellas	1	0.05
Poinciana (cdp) Osceola	6	0.04
Fernandina Beach (city) Nassau	4	0.04
Villas (cdp) Lee	4	0.04
Combee Settlement (cdp) Polk	2	0.04
Bartow (city) Polk	5	0.03
High Springs (city) Alachua	1	0.03

Top 10 Places Sorted by Percent
Based on places with populations of 10,000 or more

Place (place type) County	Number	%
Poinciana (cdp) Osceola	6	0.04
Fernandina Beach (city) Nassau	4	0.04
Villas (cdp) Lee	4	0.04
Bartow (city) Polk	5	0.03
Fort Walton Beach (city) Okaloosa	3	0.02
Jasmine Estates (cdp) Pasco	3	0.02
Iona (cdp) Lee	2	0.02
Tallahassee (city) Leon	9	0.01
Largo (city) Pinellas	6	0.01
Palm Bay (city) Brevard	6	0.01

Alaska Native: Tlingit-Haida

Top 10 Places Sorted by Number
Based on all places, regardless of population

Place (place type) County	Number	%
Jacksonville (special city) Duval	17	0.00
Fort Lauderdale (city) Broward	16	0.01
North Miami (city) Miami-Dade	13	0.02
Port St. Lucie (city) St. Lucie	7	0.01
Lauderhill (city) Broward	6	0.01
Miami (city) Miami-Dade	6	0.00
Niceville (city) Okaloosa	5	0.04
Golden Glades (cdp) Miami-Dade	5	0.02
Bradenton (city) Manatee	4	0.01
El Portal (village) Miami-Dade	3	0.12

Top 10 Places Sorted by Percent
Based on all places, regardless of population

Place (place type) County	Number	%
Grand Ridge (town) Jackson	1	0.13
El Portal (village) Miami-Dade	3	0.12
Mary Esther (city) Okaloosa	3	0.07
Palm Springs North (cdp) Miami-Dade	3	0.05
Niceville (city) Okaloosa	5	0.04
Boyette (cdp) Hillsborough	2	0.03
Lake Lorraine (cdp) Okaloosa	2	0.03
Sharpes (cdp) Brevard	1	0.03
West Ken-Lark (cdp) Broward	1	0.03
North Miami (city) Miami-Dade	13	0.02

Notes: (cdp) census designated place; Refer to the User's Guide in the front of the book for more detailed information.

Top 10 Places Sorted by Percent
Based on places with populations of 10,000 or more

Place (place type) County	Number	%
Niceville (city) Okaloosa	5	0.04
North Miami (city) Miami-Dade	13	0.02
Golden Glades (cdp) Miami-Dade	5	0.02
Cypress Lake (cdp) Lee	2	0.02
Fort Lauderdale (city) Broward	16	0.01
Port St. Lucie (city) St. Lucie	7	0.01
Lauderhill (city) Broward	6	0.01
Bradenton (city) Manatee	4	0.01
Lauderdale Lakes (city) Broward	3	0.01
Merritt Island (cdp) Brevard	3	0.01

Alaska Native: All other tribes

Top 10 Places Sorted by Number
Based on all places, regardless of population

Place (place type) County	Number	%
Crystal Lake (cdp) Polk	3	0.06
Azalea Park (cdp) Orange	2	0.02
Lakewood Park (cdp) St. Lucie	2	0.02
Orlando (city) Orange	2	0.00
Palm Shores (town) Brevard	1	0.13
Wedgefield (cdp) Orange	1	0.04
Vero Beach (city) Indian River	1	0.01
Brent (cdp) Escambia	1	0.00
Jacksonville (special city) Duval	1	0.00
Largo (city) Pinellas	1	0.00

Top 10 Places Sorted by Percent
Based on all places, regardless of population

Place (place type) County	Number	%
Palm Shores (town) Brevard	1	0.13
Crystal Lake (cdp) Polk	3	0.06
Wedgefield (cdp) Orange	1	0.04
Azalea Park (cdp) Orange	2	0.02
Lakewood Park (cdp) St. Lucie	2	0.02
Vero Beach (city) Indian River	1	0.01
Orlando (city) Orange	2	0.00
Brent (cdp) Escambia	1	0.00
Jacksonville (special city) Duval	1	0.00
Largo (city) Pinellas	1	0.00

Top 10 Places Sorted by Percent
Based on places with populations of 10,000 or more

Place (place type) County	Number	%
Azalea Park (cdp) Orange	2	0.02
Lakewood Park (cdp) St. Lucie	2	0.02
Vero Beach (city) Indian River	1	0.01
Orlando (city) Orange	2	0.00
Brent (cdp) Escambia	1	0.00
Jacksonville (special city) Duval	1	0.00
Largo (city) Pinellas	1	0.00
Naples (city) Collier	1	0.00
Palm Bay (city) Brevard	1	0.00
South Miami Heights (cdp) Miami-Dade	1	0.00

Alaska Native tribes, not specified

Top 10 Places Sorted by Number
Based on all places, regardless of population

Place (place type) County	Number	%
Jacksonville (special city) Duval	9	0.00
Tampa (city) Hillsborough	8	0.00
St. Petersburg (city) Pinellas	6	0.00
Orange Park (town) Clay	4	0.04
Daytona Beach (city) Volusia	4	0.01
Melbourne (city) Brevard	4	0.01
Combee Settlement (cdp) Polk	2	0.04
Williamsburg (cdp) Orange	2	0.03
Hollywood (city) Broward	2	0.00
Largo (city) Pinellas	2	0.00

Top 10 Places Sorted by Percent
Based on all places, regardless of population

Place (place type) County	Number	%
Grand Ridge (town) Jackson	1	0.13
North Brooksville (cdp) Hernando	1	0.07
South Brooksville (cdp) Hernando	1	0.07
Chuluota (cdp) Seminole	1	0.05
Orange Park (town) Clay	4	0.04
Combee Settlement (cdp) Polk	2	0.04
Tyndall AFB (cdp) Bay	1	0.04
Williamsburg (cdp) Orange	2	0.03
Pretty Bayou (cdp) Bay	1	0.03
Dade City (city) Pasco	1	0.02

Top 10 Places Sorted by Percent
Based on places with populations of 10,000 or more

Place (place type) County	Number	%
Daytona Beach (city) Volusia	4	0.01
Melbourne (city) Brevard	4	0.01
De Bary (city) Volusia	1	0.01
Gulfport (city) Pinellas	1	0.01
Lakeland Highlands (cdp) Polk	1	0.01
St. Augustine (city) St. Johns	1	0.01
Upper Grand Lagoon (cdp) Bay	1	0.01
Villas (cdp) Lee	1	0.01
Zephyrhills (city) Pasco	1	0.01
Jacksonville (special city) Duval	9	0.00

American Indian or Alaska Native, not specified

Top 10 Places Sorted by Number
Based on all places, regardless of population

Place (place type) County	Number	%
Jacksonville (special city) Duval	1,954	0.27
Tampa (city) Hillsborough	1,030	0.34
Miami (city) Miami-Dade	897	0.25
St. Petersburg (city) Pinellas	709	0.29
Orlando (city) Orange	499	0.27
Tallahassee (city) Leon	333	0.22
Hialeah (city) Miami-Dade	327	0.14
Fort Lauderdale (city) Broward	325	0.21
Hollywood (city) Broward	314	0.23
Clearwater (city) Pinellas	260	0.24

Top 10 Places Sorted by Percent
Based on all places, regardless of population

Place (place type) County	Number	%
Hillsboro Ranches (cdp) Broward	1	2.13
Istachatta (cdp) Hernando	1	1.54
Caryville (town) Washington	3	1.38
Waldo (city) Alachua	11	1.34
Center Hill (city) Sumter	11	1.21
Vernon (city) Washington	9	1.21
Ebro (town) Washington	3	1.20
Esto (town) Holmes	4	1.12
St. Marks (city) Wakulla	3	1.10
Gotha (cdp) Orange	8	1.09

Top 10 Places Sorted by Percent
Based on places with populations of 10,000 or more

Place (place type) County	Number	%
West Pensacola (cdp) Escambia	130	0.59
Oak Ridge (cdp) Orange	117	0.52
Ensley (cdp) Escambia	97	0.52
Myrtle Grove (cdp) Escambia	90	0.52
Wright (cdp) Okaloosa	110	0.51
Bellview (cdp) Escambia	109	0.51
Meadow Woods (cdp) Orange	57	0.51
Niceville (city) Okaloosa	58	0.50
Cocoa (city) Brevard	79	0.48
Kissimmee (city) Osceola	227	0.47

Albanian

Top 10 Places Sorted by Number
Based on all places, regardless of population

Place (place type) County	Number	%
Jacksonville (special city) Duval	855	0.12
Largo (city) Pinellas	312	0.45
St. Petersburg (city) Pinellas	311	0.13
Clearwater (city) Pinellas	211	0.20
Dunedin (city) Pinellas	199	0.55
Fort Lauderdale (city) Broward	158	0.10
Orlando (city) Orange	114	0.06
Palm Harbor (cdp) Pinellas	105	0.18
Oldsmar (city) Pinellas	75	0.64
Tampa (city) Hillsborough	65	0.02

Top 10 Places Sorted by Percent
Based on all places, regardless of population

Place (place type) County	Number	%
Green Meadow (cdp) Broward	14	0.76
Cudjoe Key (cdp) Monroe	13	0.75
Oldsmar (city) Pinellas	75	0.64
Dunedin (city) Pinellas	199	0.55
Buckingham (cdp) Lee	20	0.51
Briny Breezes (town) Palm Beach	2	0.48
Largo (city) Pinellas	312	0.45
Islamorada (village) Monroe	29	0.42
South Pasadena (city) Pinellas	24	0.41
Atlantis (city) Palm Beach	8	0.38

Top 10 Places Sorted by Percent
Based on places with populations of 10,000 or more

Place (place type) County	Number	%
Oldsmar (city) Pinellas	75	0.64
Dunedin (city) Pinellas	199	0.55
Largo (city) Pinellas	312	0.45
Fruitville (cdp) Sarasota	40	0.31
Lake Worth Corridor (cdp) Palm Beach	49	0.27
Clearwater (city) Pinellas	211	0.20
Holiday (cdp) Pasco	41	0.19
Palm Harbor (cdp) Pinellas	105	0.18
Kings Point (cdp) Palm Beach	22	0.18
Seminole (city) Pinellas	19	0.18

Alsatian

Top 10 Places Sorted by Number
Based on all places, regardless of population

Place (place type) County	Number	%
Jacksonville (special city) Duval	43	0.01
Gainesville (city) Alachua	38	0.04
Greenacres (city) Palm Beach	30	0.11
Altamonte Springs (city) Seminole	23	0.06
Boynton Beach (city) Palm Beach	21	0.04
Boca Raton (city) Palm Beach	19	0.03
Coral Springs (city) Broward	17	0.01
Cape Coral (city) Lee	16	0.02
Lakeland (city) Polk	15	0.02
Naples (city) Collier	14	0.07

Top 10 Places Sorted by Percent
Based on all places, regardless of population

Place (place type) County	Number	%
Placid Lakes (cdp) Highlands	11	0.36
North Redington Beach (town) Pinellas	4	0.29
Sharpes (cdp) Brevard	9	0.25
Howey-in-the-Hills (town) Lake	2	0.20
Holmes Beach (city) Manatee	9	0.18
West Bradenton (cdp) Manatee	7	0.16
North Sarasota (cdp) Sarasota	10	0.14
Pelican Bay (cdp) Collier	8	0.14
Fort Myers Beach (town) Lee	8	0.12
Greenacres (city) Palm Beach	30	0.11

Notes: (cdp) census designated place; Refer to the User's Guide in the front of the book for more detailed information.

Top 10 Places Sorted by Percent

Based on places with populations of 10,000 or more

Place (place type) County	Number	%
Greenacres (city) Palm Beach	30	0.11
Gulf Gate Estates (cdp) Sarasota	11	0.10
Jensen Beach (cdp) Martin	9	0.08
Lighthouse Point (city) Broward	9	0.08
Naples (city) Collier	14	0.07
Atlantic Beach (city) Duval	9	0.07
Hudson (cdp) Pasco	9	0.07
Altamonte Springs (city) Seminole	23	0.06
Englewood (cdp) Sarasota	9	0.06
North Palm Beach (village) Palm Beach	7	0.06

American Indian tribes, specified

Top 10 Places Sorted by Number

Based on all places, regardless of population

Place (place type) County	Number	%
Jacksonville (special city) Duval	3,545	0.48
Tampa (city) Hillsborough	1,559	0.51
St. Petersburg (city) Pinellas	1,364	0.55
Miami (city) Miami-Dade	825	0.23
Orlando (city) Orange	807	0.43
Tallahassee (city) Leon	595	0.40
Clearwater (city) Pinellas	494	0.45
Hollywood (city) Broward	483	0.35
Brandon (cdp) Hillsborough	471	0.60
Pensacola (city) Escambia	454	0.81

Top 10 Places Sorted by Percent

Based on all places, regardless of population

Place (place type) County	Number	%
Ebro (town) Washington	48	19.20
Esto (town) Holmes	16	4.49
Waldo (city) Alachua	36	4.38
Vernon (city) Washington	28	3.77
Freeport (city) Walton	40	3.36
Ponce de Leon (town) Holmes	14	3.06
Lacoochee (cdp) Pasco	41	3.05
Bagdad (cdp) Santa Rosa	45	3.02
Paxton (town) Walton	19	2.90
Indiantown (cdp) Martin	160	2.86

Top 10 Places Sorted by Percent

Based on places with populations of 10,000 or more

Place (place type) County	Number	%
Warrington (cdp) Escambia	293	1.93
West Pensacola (cdp) Escambia	370	1.69
Bellview (cdp) Escambia	327	1.54
Myrtle Grove (cdp) Escambia	245	1.42
Middleburg (cdp) Clay	145	1.40
Ensley (cdp) Escambia	248	1.32
Gonzalez (cdp) Escambia	148	1.30
Lake Worth (city) Palm Beach	412	1.17
Upper Grand Lagoon (cdp) Bay	124	1.14
Brent (cdp) Escambia	246	1.11

American Indian: Apache

Top 10 Places Sorted by Number

Based on all places, regardless of population

Place (place type) County	Number	%
Jacksonville (special city) Duval	97	0.01
Tampa (city) Hillsborough	66	0.02
St. Petersburg (city) Pinellas	28	0.01
Orlando (city) Orange	24	0.01
Tallahassee (city) Leon	23	0.02
Clearwater (city) Pinellas	20	0.02
Warrington (cdp) Escambia	12	0.08
Palm Bay (city) Brevard	12	0.02
Cape Coral (city) Lee	12	0.01
Port St. Lucie (city) St. Lucie	12	0.01

Top 10 Places Sorted by Percent

Based on all places, regardless of population

Place (place type) County	Number	%
Esto (town) Holmes	4	1.12
Cottondale (town) Jackson	5	0.58
North Redington Beach (town) Pinellas	6	0.41
St. Marks (city) Wakulla	1	0.37
Lee (town) Madison	1	0.28
Cinco Bayou (town) Okaloosa	1	0.27
Jennings (town) Hamilton	2	0.24
Molino (cdp) Escambia	3	0.23
Rolling Oaks (cdp) Broward	3	0.23
East Bronson (cdp) Levy	2	0.19

Top 10 Places Sorted by Percent

Based on places with populations of 10,000 or more

Place (place type) County	Number	%
Middleburg (cdp) Clay	10	0.10
Warrington (cdp) Escambia	12	0.08
St. Augustine (city) St. Johns	9	0.08
Destin (city) Okaloosa	7	0.06
Union Park (cdp) Orange	6	0.06
Bayonet Point (cdp) Pasco	11	0.05
Elfers (cdp) Pasco	7	0.05
Upper Grand Lagoon (cdp) Bay	5	0.05
Zephyrhills (city) Pasco	5	0.05
Land O' Lakes (cdp) Pasco	9	0.04

American Indian: Blackfeet

Top 10 Places Sorted by Number

Based on all places, regardless of population

Place (place type) County	Number	%
Jacksonville (special city) Duval	186	0.03
Tampa (city) Hillsborough	86	0.03
St. Petersburg (city) Pinellas	76	0.03
Orlando (city) Orange	41	0.02
Palm Bay (city) Brevard	35	0.04
Port St. Lucie (city) St. Lucie	32	0.04
Davie (town) Broward	31	0.04
Deltona (city) Volusia	31	0.04
Clearwater (city) Pinellas	28	0.03
Brandon (cdp) Hillsborough	26	0.03

Top 10 Places Sorted by Percent

Based on all places, regardless of population

Place (place type) County	Number	%
Branford (town) Suwannee	6	0.86
Otter Creek (town) Levy	1	0.83
Edgewater (cdp) Broward	4	0.50
North Beach (cdp) Indian River	1	0.41
Lake Mack-Forest Hills (cdp) Lake	4	0.40
Ebro (town) Washington	1	0.40
South Brooksville (cdp) Hernando	5	0.36
Zephyrhills South (cdp) Pasco	13	0.29
Lee (town) Madison	1	0.28
Suncoast Estates (cdp) Lee	11	0.23

Top 10 Places Sorted by Percent

Based on places with populations of 10,000 or more

Place (place type) County	Number	%
Princeton (cdp) Miami-Dade	13	0.13
Gulfport (city) Pinellas	15	0.12
Callaway (city) Bay	14	0.10
Wright (cdp) Okaloosa	19	0.09
New Port Richey (city) Pasco	15	0.09
Zephyrhills (city) Pasco	9	0.08
West and East Lealman (cdp) Pinellas	16	0.07
Temple Terrace (city) Hillsborough	14	0.07
Fort Walton Beach (city) Okaloosa	13	0.07
Palmetto (city) Manatee	9	0.07

American Indian: Cherokee

Top 10 Places Sorted by Number

Based on all places, regardless of population

Place (place type) County	Number	%
Jacksonville (special city) Duval	1,717	0.23
Tampa (city) Hillsborough	651	0.21
St. Petersburg (city) Pinellas	619	0.25
Orlando (city) Orange	349	0.19
Melbourne (city) Brevard	243	0.34
Tallahassee (city) Leon	237	0.16
Brandon (cdp) Hillsborough	219	0.28
Deltona (city) Volusia	188	0.27
Pensacola (city) Escambia	184	0.33
Gainesville (city) Alachua	184	0.19

Top 10 Places Sorted by Percent

Based on all places, regardless of population

Place (place type) County	Number	%
Waldo (city) Alachua	33	4.02
Ebro (town) Washington	7	2.80
Golden Heights (cdp) Broward	10	2.00
Bagdad (cdp) Santa Rosa	23	1.54
Greenwood (town) Jackson	10	1.36
Callahan (town) Nassau	12	1.25
Vernon (city) Washington	9	1.21
Cottondale (town) Jackson	10	1.15
Esto (town) Holmes	4	1.12
Lake Mack-Forest Hills (cdp) Lake	11	1.11

Top 10 Places Sorted by Percent

Based on places with populations of 10,000 or more

Place (place type) County	Number	%
Warrington (cdp) Escambia	116	0.76
Middleburg (cdp) Clay	77	0.74
West Pensacola (cdp) Escambia	112	0.51
Wright (cdp) Okaloosa	111	0.51
Port St. John (cdp) Brevard	61	0.50
St. Augustine (city) St. Johns	57	0.49
Bellair-Meadowbrook Terrace (cdp) Clay	80	0.48
West and East Lealman (cdp) Pinellas	103	0.47
Upper Grand Lagoon (cdp) Bay	51	0.47
Niceville (city) Okaloosa	52	0.45

American Indian: Cheyenne

Top 10 Places Sorted by Number

Based on all places, regardless of population

Place (place type) County	Number	%
Jacksonville (special city) Duval	15	0.00
Melbourne (city) Brevard	7	0.01
Desoto Lakes (cdp) Sarasota	4	0.13
Gonzalez (cdp) Escambia	4	0.04
Wright (cdp) Okaloosa	4	0.02
Daytona Beach (city) Volusia	4	0.01
Greenacres (city) Palm Beach	4	0.01
Pinellas Park (city) Pinellas	4	0.01
Port St. Lucie (city) St. Lucie	4	0.00
St. Petersburg (city) Pinellas	4	0.00

Top 10 Places Sorted by Percent

Based on all places, regardless of population

Place (place type) County	Number	%
McIntosh (town) Marion	1	0.22
Desoto Lakes (cdp) Sarasota	4	0.13
Waldo (city) Alachua	1	0.12
Estates of Fort Lauderdale (cdp) Broward	2	0.11
Boulevard Gardens (cdp) Broward	1	0.07
Gonzalez (cdp) Escambia	4	0.04
Ocean City (cdp) Okaloosa	2	0.04
Big Coppitt Key (cdp) Monroe	1	0.04
Placid Lakes (cdp) Highlands	1	0.03
Wright (cdp) Okaloosa	4	0.02

Notes: (cdp) census designated place; Refer to the User's Guide in the front of the book for more detailed information.

Top 10 Places Sorted by Percent
Based on places with populations of 10,000 or more

Place (place type) County	Number	%
Gonzalez (cdp) Escambia	4	0.04
Wright (cdp) Okaloosa	4	0.02
Oldsmar (city) Pinellas	2	0.02
Melbourne (city) Brevard	7	0.01
Daytona Beach (city) Volusia	4	0.01
Greenacres (city) Palm Beach	4	0.01
Pinellas Park (city) Pinellas	4	0.01
Dunedin (city) Pinellas	3	0.01
Bayshore Gardens (cdp) Manatee	2	0.01
Callaway (city) Bay	2	0.01

American Indian: Chickasaw

Top 10 Places Sorted by Number
Based on all places, regardless of population

Place (place type) County	Number	%
Jacksonville (special city) Duval	23	0.00
Port St. Lucie (city) St. Lucie	12	0.01
Tampa (city) Hillsborough	9	0.00
Titusville (city) Brevard	7	0.02
Palm Bay (city) Brevard	7	0.01
Clearwater (city) Pinellas	6	0.01
St. Petersburg (city) Pinellas	6	0.00
Cypress Quarters (cdp) Okeechobee	5	0.43
Bellair-Meadowbrook Terrace (cdp) Clay	5	0.03
Altamonte Springs (city) Seminole	5	0.01

Top 10 Places Sorted by Percent
Based on all places, regardless of population

Place (place type) County	Number	%
Lazy Lake (village) Broward	1	2.63
Cypress Quarters (cdp) Okeechobee	5	0.43
Lely Resort (cdp) Collier	4	0.28
Sneads (town) Jackson	3	0.16
Bagdad (cdp) Santa Rosa	2	0.13
Chipley (city) Washington	3	0.08
Taft (cdp) Orange	1	0.05
Panama City Beach (city) Bay	3	0.04
Asbury Lake (cdp) Clay	1	0.04
Groveland (city) Lake	1	0.04

Top 10 Places Sorted by Percent
Based on places with populations of 10,000 or more

Place (place type) County	Number	%
Bellair-Meadowbrook Terrace (cdp) Clay	5	0.03
Titusville (city) Brevard	7	0.02
San Carlos Park (cdp) Lee	4	0.02
Wekiwa Springs (cdp) Seminole	4	0.02
Wright (cdp) Okaloosa	4	0.02
Gulfport (city) Pinellas	3	0.02
Keystone (cdp) Hillsborough	3	0.02
South Daytona (city) Volusia	3	0.02
Destin (city) Okaloosa	2	0.02
Lady Lake (town) Lake	2	0.02

American Indian: Chippewa

Top 10 Places Sorted by Number
Based on all places, regardless of population

Place (place type) County	Number	%
Jacksonville (special city) Duval	97	0.01
St. Petersburg (city) Pinellas	52	0.02
Tampa (city) Hillsborough	36	0.01
Orlando (city) Orange	27	0.01
Port Charlotte (cdp) Charlotte	26	0.06
Cape Coral (city) Lee	26	0.03
Largo (city) Pinellas	24	0.03
Port St. Lucie (city) St. Lucie	22	0.02
Palm Bay (city) Brevard	18	0.02
Sarasota (city) Sarasota	17	0.03

Top 10 Places Sorted by Percent
Based on all places, regardless of population

Place (place type) County	Number	%
Pine Island Center (cdp) Lee	6	0.35
Crooked Lake Park (cdp) Polk	4	0.24
Lochmoor Waterway Estates (cdp) Lee	8	0.21
Weeki Wachee Gardens (cdp) Hernando	2	0.18
Samsula-Spruce Creek (cdp) Volusia	8	0.16
Yankeetown (town) Levy	1	0.16
Micanopy (town) Alachua	1	0.15
Inverness Highlands North (cdp) Citrus	2	0.14
Loughman (cdp) Polk	2	0.14
Branford (town) Suwannee	1	0.14

Top 10 Places Sorted by Percent
Based on places with populations of 10,000 or more

Place (place type) County	Number	%
Upper Grand Lagoon (cdp) Bay	14	0.13
Homosassa Springs (cdp) Citrus	9	0.07
Holly Hill (city) Volusia	8	0.07
Port Charlotte (cdp) Charlotte	26	0.06
Holiday (cdp) Pasco	14	0.06
Conway (cdp) Orange	8	0.06
Punta Gorda (city) Charlotte	8	0.06
Port St. John (cdp) Brevard	6	0.05
Zephyrhills (city) Pasco	5	0.05
North Fort Myers (cdp) Lee	16	0.04

American Indian: Choctaw

Top 10 Places Sorted by Number
Based on all places, regardless of population

Place (place type) County	Number	%
Jacksonville (special city) Duval	131	0.02
St. Petersburg (city) Pinellas	52	0.02
Tampa (city) Hillsborough	34	0.01
Orlando (city) Orange	32	0.02
Clearwater (city) Pinellas	23	0.02
Gainesville (city) Alachua	23	0.02
Brandon (cdp) Hillsborough	22	0.03
Cape Coral (city) Lee	22	0.02
Fort Lauderdale (city) Broward	22	0.01
Hollywood (city) Broward	21	0.02

Top 10 Places Sorted by Percent
Based on all places, regardless of population

Place (place type) County	Number	%
Cypress Quarters (cdp) Okeechobee	5	0.43
Lacoochee (cdp) Pasco	5	0.37
Micanopy (town) Alachua	2	0.31
Woodville (cdp) Leon	7	0.23
Tavernier (cdp) Monroe	5	0.23
Cottondale (town) Jackson	2	0.23
Sopchoppy (city) Wakulla	1	0.23
North Redington Beach (town) Pinellas	3	0.20
Hernando Beach (cdp) Hernando	4	0.18
Laurel Hill (city) Okaloosa	1	0.18

Top 10 Places Sorted by Percent
Based on places with populations of 10,000 or more

Place (place type) County	Number	%
Bellview (cdp) Escambia	20	0.09
Warrington (cdp) Escambia	14	0.09
Destin (city) Okaloosa	10	0.09
Niceville (city) Okaloosa	10	0.09
Brent (cdp) Escambia	16	0.07
Edgewater (city) Volusia	13	0.07
Ferry Pass (cdp) Escambia	15	0.06
Eustis (city) Lake	9	0.06
Winter Garden (city) Orange	8	0.06
Lakeland Highlands (cdp) Polk	7	0.06

American Indian: Colville

Top 10 Places Sorted by Number
Based on all places, regardless of population

Place (place type) County	Number	%
Jacksonville (special city) Duval	3	0.00
Orlando (city) Orange	2	0.00
North Sarasota (cdp) Sarasota	1	0.01
Warrington (cdp) Escambia	1	0.01
Bellview (cdp) Escambia	1	0.00
St. Petersburg (city) Pinellas	1	0.00
Tampa (city) Hillsborough	1	0.00

Top 10 Places Sorted by Percent
Based on all places, regardless of population

Place (place type) County	Number	%
North Sarasota (cdp) Sarasota	1	0.01
Warrington (cdp) Escambia	1	0.01
Jacksonville (special city) Duval	3	0.00
Orlando (city) Orange	2	0.00
Bellview (cdp) Escambia	1	0.00
St. Petersburg (city) Pinellas	1	0.00
Tampa (city) Hillsborough	1	0.00

Top 10 Places Sorted by Percent
Based on places with populations of 10,000 or more

Place (place type) County	Number	%
Warrington (cdp) Escambia	1	0.01
Jacksonville (special city) Duval	3	0.00
Orlando (city) Orange	2	0.00
Bellview (cdp) Escambia	1	0.00
St. Petersburg (city) Pinellas	1	0.00
Tampa (city) Hillsborough	1	0.00

American Indian: Comanche

Top 10 Places Sorted by Number
Based on all places, regardless of population

Place (place type) County	Number	%
Jacksonville (special city) Duval	12	0.00
St. Petersburg (city) Pinellas	12	0.00
Tallahassee (city) Leon	5	0.00
Tampa (city) Hillsborough	5	0.00
Mango (cdp) Hillsborough	4	0.05
Atlantic Beach (city) Duval	4	0.03
Dania Beach (city) Broward	4	0.02
New Smyrna Beach (city) Volusia	4	0.02
Palm River-Clair Mel (cdp) Hillsborough	4	0.02
West and East Lealman (cdp) Pinellas	4	0.02

Top 10 Places Sorted by Percent
Based on all places, regardless of population

Place (place type) County	Number	%
Masaryktown (cdp) Hernando	1	0.11
Geneva (cdp) Seminole	2	0.08
Rolling Oaks (cdp) Broward	1	0.08
St. Augustine Beach (city) St. Johns	3	0.06
Baldwin (town) Duval	1	0.06
Mango (cdp) Hillsborough	4	0.05
Dunnellon (city) Marion	1	0.05
Bithlo (cdp) Orange	2	0.04
Parker (city) Bay	2	0.04
Mount Plymouth (cdp) Lake	1	0.04

Top 10 Places Sorted by Percent
Based on places with populations of 10,000 or more

Place (place type) County	Number	%
Atlantic Beach (city) Duval	4	0.03
Dania Beach (city) Broward	4	0.02
New Smyrna Beach (city) Volusia	4	0.02
Palm River-Clair Mel (cdp) Hillsborough	4	0.02
West and East Lealman (cdp) Pinellas	4	0.02
Conway (cdp) Orange	3	0.02

Place (place type) County	Number	%
Gulfport (city) Pinellas	3	0.02
Myrtle Grove (cdp) Escambia	3	0.02
Riverview (cdp) Hillsborough	3	0.02
Zephyrhills (city) Pasco	2	0.02

American Indian: Cree

Top 10 Places Sorted by Number

Based on all places, regardless of population

Place (place type) County	Number	%
Jacksonville (special city) Duval	10	0.00
St. Petersburg (city) Pinellas	10	0.00
Tampa (city) Hillsborough	9	0.00
Egypt Lake-Leto (cdp) Hillsborough	8	0.02
Pinellas Park (city) Pinellas	7	0.02
Lake Lorraine (cdp) Okaloosa	6	0.08
Cape Coral (city) Lee	6	0.01
Melbourne (city) Brevard	5	0.01
Pace (cdp) Santa Rosa	4	0.05
Daytona Beach (city) Volusia	4	0.01

Top 10 Places Sorted by Percent

Based on all places, regardless of population

Place (place type) County	Number	%
Micanopy (town) Alachua	2	0.31
Juno Ridge (cdp) Palm Beach	1	0.13
Blountstown (city) Calhoun	3	0.12
Dover (cdp) Hillsborough	3	0.11
Mexico Beach (city) Bay	1	0.10
Weeki Wachee Gardens (cdp) Hernando	1	0.09
Lake Lorraine (cdp) Okaloosa	6	0.08
Lower Grand Lagoon (cdp) Bay	3	0.07
Pace (cdp) Santa Rosa	4	0.05
Belle Isle (city) Orange	2	0.04

Top 10 Places Sorted by Percent

Based on places with populations of 10,000 or more

Place (place type) County	Number	%
Destin (city) Okaloosa	3	0.03
Egypt Lake-Leto (cdp) Hillsborough	8	0.02
Pinellas Park (city) Pinellas	7	0.02
Marathon (city) Monroe	2	0.02
St. Augustine (city) St. Johns	2	0.02
Cape Coral (city) Lee	6	0.01
Melbourne (city) Brevard	5	0.01
Daytona Beach (city) Volusia	4	0.01
Ferry Pass (cdp) Escambia	4	0.01
Panama City (city) Bay	4	0.01

American Indian: Creek

Top 10 Places Sorted by Number

Based on all places, regardless of population

Place (place type) County	Number	%
Jacksonville (special city) Duval	188	0.03
Pensacola (city) Escambia	160	0.28
West Pensacola (cdp) Escambia	150	0.68
Bellview (cdp) Escambia	135	0.64
Ensley (cdp) Escambia	125	0.67
Ferry Pass (cdp) Escambia	108	0.40
Tallahassee (city) Leon	107	0.07
Brent (cdp) Escambia	98	0.44
Warrington (cdp) Escambia	89	0.59
Pace (cdp) Santa Rosa	88	1.19

Top 10 Places Sorted by Percent

Based on all places, regardless of population

Place (place type) County	Number	%
Ebro (town) Washington	37	14.80
Freeport (city) Walton	34	2.86
Ponce de Leon (town) Holmes	9	1.97
Esto (town) Holmes	7	1.97
Vernon (city) Washington	14	1.88
Paxton (town) Walton	12	1.83
Pittman (cdp) Lake	3	1.56
Grand Ridge (town) Jackson	12	1.52
Wausau (town) Washington	5	1.26
Pace (cdp) Santa Rosa	88	1.19

Top 10 Places Sorted by Percent

Based on places with populations of 10,000 or more

Place (place type) County	Number	%
West Pensacola (cdp) Escambia	150	0.68
Ensley (cdp) Escambia	125	0.67
Bellview (cdp) Escambia	135	0.64
Gonzalez (cdp) Escambia	71	0.62
Warrington (cdp) Escambia	89	0.59
Brent (cdp) Escambia	98	0.44
Myrtle Grove (cdp) Escambia	76	0.44
Ferry Pass (cdp) Escambia	108	0.40
Lynn Haven (city) Bay	44	0.35
Pensacola (city) Escambia	160	0.28

American Indian: Crow

Top 10 Places Sorted by Number

Based on all places, regardless of population

Place (place type) County	Number	%
Jacksonville (special city) Duval	7	0.00
Lake City (city) Columbia	5	0.05
Fort Pierce (city) St. Lucie	5	0.01
Hollywood (city) Broward	5	0.00
St. Petersburg (city) Pinellas	5	0.00
Lake Worth Corridor (cdp) Palm Beach	4	0.02
Lake Worth (city) Palm Beach	3	0.01
Sanford (city) Seminole	3	0.01
The Crossings (cdp) Miami-Dade	3	0.01
Vero Beach South (cdp) Indian River	3	0.01

Top 10 Places Sorted by Percent

Based on all places, regardless of population

Place (place type) County	Number	%
Oak Hill (city) Volusia	1	0.07
Lake City (city) Columbia	5	0.05
Pine Manor (cdp) Lee	2	0.05
Fish Hawk (cdp) Hillsborough	1	0.05
Tedder (cdp) Broward	1	0.05
Fort Pierce South (cdp) St. Lucie	2	0.04
Harlem (cdp) Hendry	1	0.04
Lake Worth Corridor (cdp) Palm Beach	4	0.02
Hernando (cdp) Citrus	2	0.02
Middleburg (cdp) Clay	2	0.02

Top 10 Places Sorted by Percent

Based on places with populations of 10,000 or more

Place (place type) County	Number	%
Lake Worth Corridor (cdp) Palm Beach	4	0.02
Middleburg (cdp) Clay	2	0.02
Riverview (cdp) Hillsborough	2	0.02
Fort Pierce (city) St. Lucie	5	0.01
Lake Worth (city) Palm Beach	3	0.01
Sanford (city) Seminole	3	0.01
The Crossings (cdp) Miami-Dade	3	0.01
Vero Beach South (cdp) Indian River	3	0.01
Bellair-Meadowbrook Terrace (cdp) Clay	2	0.01
Fruit Cove (cdp) St. Johns	2	0.01

American Indian: Delaware

Top 10 Places Sorted by Number

Based on all places, regardless of population

Place (place type) County	Number	%
St. Petersburg (city) Pinellas	12	0.00
Jacksonville (special city) Duval	10	0.00
Tallahassee (city) Leon	9	0.01
Port Orange (city) Volusia	7	0.02
Deltona (city) Volusia	7	0.01
Union Park (cdp) Orange	5	0.05
Elfers (cdp) Pasco	5	0.04
Cape Coral (city) Lee	5	0.00
Tyndall AFB (cdp) Bay	4	0.15
Cape Canaveral (city) Brevard	4	0.05

Top 10 Places Sorted by Percent

Based on all places, regardless of population

Place (place type) County	Number	%
Tyndall AFB (cdp) Bay	4	0.15
Hilliard (town) Nassau	3	0.11
Gandy (cdp) Pinellas	2	0.10
Big Coppitt Key (cdp) Monroe	2	0.08
Astatula (town) Lake	1	0.08
Inverness Highlands North (cdp) Citrus	1	0.07
Pompano Estates (cdp) Broward	2	0.06
Sharpes (cdp) Brevard	2	0.06
Union Park (cdp) Orange	5	0.05
Cape Canaveral (city) Brevard	4	0.05

Top 10 Places Sorted by Percent

Based on places with populations of 10,000 or more

Place (place type) County	Number	%
Union Park (cdp) Orange	5	0.05
Elfers (cdp) Pasco	5	0.04
Port Orange (city) Volusia	7	0.02
New Port Richey (city) Pasco	3	0.02
Palm Valley (cdp) St. Johns	3	0.02
Sebastian (city) Indian River	3	0.02
Fruitville (cdp) Sarasota	2	0.02
Gulfport (city) Pinellas	2	0.02
Oldsmar (city) Pinellas	2	0.02
Tallahassee (city) Leon	9	0.01

American Indian: Houma

Top 10 Places Sorted by Number

Based on all places, regardless of population

Place (place type) County	Number	%
Jacksonville (special city) Duval	14	0.00
Bellview (cdp) Escambia	11	0.05
Warrington (cdp) Escambia	5	0.03
Gainesville (city) Alachua	5	0.01
Tampa (city) Hillsborough	5	0.00
Auburndale (city) Polk	4	0.04
Brent (cdp) Escambia	4	0.02
West Pensacola (cdp) Escambia	4	0.02
Riverland Village (cdp) Broward	3	0.14
Panama City Beach (city) Bay	3	0.04

Top 10 Places Sorted by Percent

Based on all places, regardless of population

Place (place type) County	Number	%
Riverland Village (cdp) Broward	3	0.14
North De Land (cdp) Volusia	1	0.08
Bellview (cdp) Escambia	11	0.05
Auburndale (city) Polk	4	0.04
Panama City Beach (city) Bay	3	0.04
Villano Beach (cdp) St. Johns	1	0.04
Warrington (cdp) Escambia	5	0.03
High Point (cdp) Hernando	1	0.03
Wesley Chapel South (cdp) Pasco	1	0.03
Brent (cdp) Escambia	4	0.02

Top 10 Places Sorted by Percent

Based on places with populations of 10,000 or more

Place (place type) County	Number	%
Bellview (cdp) Escambia	11	0.05
Auburndale (city) Polk	4	0.04
Warrington (cdp) Escambia	5	0.03
Brent (cdp) Escambia	4	0.02
West Pensacola (cdp) Escambia	4	0.02
Myrtle Grove (cdp) Escambia	3	0.02

Notes: (cdp) census designated place; Refer to the User's Guide in the front of the book for more detailed information.

Place (place type) County	Number	%
Lynn Haven (city) Bay	2	0.02
Gainesville (city) Alachua	5	0.01
Wellington (village) Palm Beach	3	0.01
Bayonet Point (cdp) Pasco	2	0.01

American Indian: Iroquois

Top 10 Places Sorted by Number

Based on all places, regardless of population

Place (place type) County	Number	%
Jacksonville (special city) Duval	131	0.02
Tampa (city) Hillsborough	77	0.03
St. Petersburg (city) Pinellas	67	0.03
Orlando (city) Orange	41	0.02
Cape Coral (city) Lee	38	0.04
West and East Lealman (cdp) Pinellas	37	0.17
Clearwater (city) Pinellas	36	0.03
Palm Bay (city) Brevard	32	0.04
Pinellas Park (city) Pinellas	31	0.07
Largo (city) Pinellas	31	0.04

Top 10 Places Sorted by Percent

Based on all places, regardless of population

Place (place type) County	Number	%
East Williston (cdp) Levy	10	1.04
Ebro (town) Washington	1	0.40
Big Coppitt Key (cdp) Monroe	9	0.35
Mexico Beach (city) Bay	3	0.29
Webster (city) Sumter	2	0.25
Lake Panasoffkee (cdp) Sumter	8	0.23
Fruitland Park (city) Lake	7	0.22
South Brooksville (cdp) Hernando	3	0.22
Lake Mack-Forest Hills (cdp) Lake	2	0.20
Redington Beach (town) Pinellas	3	0.19

Top 10 Places Sorted by Percent

Based on places with populations of 10,000 or more

Place (place type) County	Number	%
West and East Lealman (cdp) Pinellas	37	0.17
New Smyrna Beach (city) Volusia	16	0.08
Myrtle Grove (cdp) Escambia	13	0.08
Middleburg (cdp) Clay	8	0.08
Pinellas Park (city) Pinellas	31	0.07
Wright (cdp) Okaloosa	15	0.07
Lockhart (cdp) Orange	9	0.07
Port Orange (city) Volusia	29	0.06
Titusville (city) Brevard	24	0.06
Lehigh Acres (cdp) Lee	20	0.06

American Indian: Kiowa

Top 10 Places Sorted by Number

Based on all places, regardless of population

Place (place type) County	Number	%
Destin (city) Okaloosa	8	0.07
Jacksonville (special city) Duval	6	0.00
Orlovista (cdp) Orange	3	0.05
Palm Bay (city) Brevard	3	0.00
St. Petersburg (city) Pinellas	3	0.00
Citrus Park (cdp) Hillsborough	2	0.01
Fruit Cove (cdp) St. Johns	2	0.01
Lakeside (cdp) Clay	2	0.01
Merritt Island (cdp) Brevard	2	0.01
New Smyrna Beach (city) Volusia	2	0.01

Top 10 Places Sorted by Percent

Based on all places, regardless of population

Place (place type) County	Number	%
Destin (city) Okaloosa	8	0.07
Orlovista (cdp) Orange	3	0.05
Charlotte Harbor (cdp) Charlotte	1	0.03
Woodville (cdp) Leon	1	0.03
Live Oak (city) Suwannee	1	0.02
Citrus Park (cdp) Hillsborough	2	0.01
Fruit Cove (cdp) St. Johns	2	0.01
Lakeside (cdp) Clay	2	0.01
Merritt Island (cdp) Brevard	2	0.01
New Smyrna Beach (city) Volusia	2	0.01

Top 10 Places Sorted by Percent

Based on places with populations of 10,000 or more

Place (place type) County	Number	%
Destin (city) Okaloosa	8	0.07
Citrus Park (cdp) Hillsborough	2	0.01
Fruit Cove (cdp) St. Johns	2	0.01
Lakeside (cdp) Clay	2	0.01
Merritt Island (cdp) Brevard	2	0.01
New Smyrna Beach (city) Volusia	2	0.01
Sebastian (city) Indian River	2	0.01
Holly Hill (city) Volusia	1	0.01
Hudson (cdp) Pasco	1	0.01
Miami Shores (village) Miami-Dade	1	0.01

American Indian: Latin American Indians

Top 10 Places Sorted by Number

Based on all places, regardless of population

Place (place type) County	Number	%
Miami (city) Miami-Dade	535	0.15
Lake Worth (city) Palm Beach	318	0.91
West Palm Beach (city) Palm Beach	265	0.32
Tampa (city) Hillsborough	226	0.07
Hialeah (city) Miami-Dade	178	0.08
Indiantown (cdp) Martin	156	2.79
Jacksonville (special city) Duval	141	0.02
Miami Beach (city) Miami-Dade	124	0.14
Southeast Arcadia (cdp) De Soto	118	1.95
Homestead (city) Miami-Dade	104	0.33

Top 10 Places Sorted by Percent

Based on all places, regardless of population

Place (place type) County	Number	%
Indiantown (cdp) Martin	156	2.79
Southeast Arcadia (cdp) De Soto	118	1.95
Lake Worth (city) Palm Beach	318	0.91
Eagle Lake (city) Polk	22	0.88
Wimauma (cdp) Hillsborough	31	0.73
Tice (cdp) Lee	30	0.66
Wabasso (cdp) Indian River	6	0.65
Dover (cdp) Hillsborough	18	0.64
North De Land (cdp) Volusia	7	0.53
Lacoochee (cdp) Pasco	7	0.52

Top 10 Places Sorted by Percent

Based on places with populations of 10,000 or more

Place (place type) County	Number	%
Lake Worth (city) Palm Beach	318	0.91
Lake Worth Corridor (cdp) Palm Beach	64	0.34
Homestead (city) Miami-Dade	104	0.33
West Palm Beach (city) Palm Beach	265	0.32
Princeton (cdp) Miami-Dade	24	0.24
Yeehaw Junction (cdp) Osceola	50	0.23
Golden Gate (cdp) Collier	44	0.21
Meadow Woods (cdp) Orange	22	0.19
Goldenrod (cdp) Seminole	23	0.18
Stuart (city) Martin	25	0.17

American Indian: Lumbee

Top 10 Places Sorted by Number

Based on all places, regardless of population

Place (place type) County	Number	%
Jacksonville (special city) Duval	108	0.01
St. Petersburg (city) Pinellas	22	0.01
Tampa (city) Hillsborough	18	0.01
Lakeside (cdp) Clay	10	0.03
Ocala (city) Marion	10	0.02
Merritt Island (cdp) Brevard	9	0.02
Port Orange (city) Volusia	9	0.02
Cocoa (city) Brevard	8	0.05
Ensley (cdp) Escambia	8	0.04
Clearwater (city) Pinellas	8	0.01

Top 10 Places Sorted by Percent

Based on all places, regardless of population

Place (place type) County	Number	%
Winter Beach (cdp) Indian River	4	0.41
Lake Placid (town) Highlands	6	0.36
Davenport (city) Polk	6	0.31
Branford (town) Suwannee	2	0.29
Webster (city) Sumter	2	0.25
Placid Lakes (cdp) Highlands	5	0.16
Pine Lakes (cdp) Lake	1	0.13
Woodville (cdp) Leon	3	0.10
East Lake-Orient Park (cdp) Hillsborough	5	0.09
Newberry (city) Alachua	3	0.09

Top 10 Places Sorted by Percent

Based on places with populations of 10,000 or more

Place (place type) County	Number	%
Cocoa (city) Brevard	8	0.05
Warrington (cdp) Escambia	7	0.05
Gonzalez (cdp) Escambia	6	0.05
Ensley (cdp) Escambia	8	0.04
Lynn Haven (city) Bay	5	0.04
Lakeside (cdp) Clay	10	0.03
North Port (city) Sarasota	7	0.03
St. Cloud (city) Osceola	6	0.03
Fort Walton Beach (city) Okaloosa	5	0.03
Palmetto (city) Manatee	4	0.03

American Indian: Menominee

Top 10 Places Sorted by Number

Based on all places, regardless of population

Place (place type) County	Number	%
Gibsonton (cdp) Hillsborough	5	0.06
Middleburg (cdp) Clay	4	0.04
New Port Richey (city) Pasco	3	0.02
Kissimmee (city) Osceola	3	0.01
North Miami (city) Miami-Dade	3	0.01
Tallahassee (city) Leon	3	0.00
Land O' Lakes (cdp) Pasco	2	0.01
Rockledge (city) Brevard	2	0.01
Sanford (city) Seminole	2	0.01
Wellington (village) Palm Beach	2	0.01

Top 10 Places Sorted by Percent

Based on all places, regardless of population

Place (place type) County	Number	%
Gibsonton (cdp) Hillsborough	5	0.06
Anna Maria (city) Manatee	1	0.06
Middleburg (cdp) Clay	4	0.04
High Springs (city) Alachua	1	0.03
New Port Richey (city) Pasco	3	0.02
Butler Beach (cdp) St. Johns	1	0.02
Floral City (cdp) Citrus	1	0.02
June Park (cdp) Brevard	1	0.02
Zephyrhills West (cdp) Pasco	1	0.02
Kissimmee (city) Osceola	3	0.01

Top 10 Places Sorted by Percent

Based on places with populations of 10,000 or more

Place (place type) County	Number	%
Middleburg (cdp) Clay	4	0.04
New Port Richey (city) Pasco	3	0.02
Kissimmee (city) Osceola	3	0.01
North Miami (city) Miami-Dade	3	0.01
Land O' Lakes (cdp) Pasco	2	0.01
Rockledge (city) Brevard	2	0.01

Notes: (cdp) census designated place; Refer to the User's Guide in the front of the book for more detailed information.

Sanford (city) Seminole	2	0.01
Wellington (village) Palm Beach	2	0.01
Azalea Park (cdp) Orange	1	0.01
Forest City (cdp) Seminole	1	0.01

American Indian: Navajo

Top 10 Places Sorted by Number
Based on all places, regardless of population

Place (place type) County	Number	%
Jacksonville (special city) Duval	64	0.01
Tampa (city) Hillsborough	18	0.01
Bellair-Meadowbrook Terrace (cdp) Clay	12	0.07
Palm Bay (city) Brevard	12	0.02
Myrtle Grove (cdp) Escambia	10	0.06
Gainesville (city) Alachua	10	0.01
Sarasota (city) Sarasota	9	0.02
West Palm Beach (city) Palm Beach	9	0.01
St. Petersburg (city) Pinellas	9	0.00
Bellview (cdp) Escambia	8	0.04

Top 10 Places Sorted by Percent
Based on all places, regardless of population

Place (place type) County	Number	%
Pine Manor (cdp) Lee	4	0.11
Bronson (town) Levy	1	0.10
Schall Circle (cdp) Palm Beach	1	0.10
Eglin AFB (cdp) Okaloosa	7	0.09
Leisureville (cdp) Broward	1	0.09
Chipley (city) Washington	3	0.08
Lauderdale-by-the-Sea (town) Broward	2	0.08
Molino (cdp) Escambia	1	0.08
Bellair-Meadowbrook Terrace (cdp) Clay	12	0.07
Lakewood Park (cdp) St. Lucie	7	0.07

Top 10 Places Sorted by Percent
Based on places with populations of 10,000 or more

Place (place type) County	Number	%
Bellair-Meadowbrook Terrace (cdp) Clay	12	0.07
Lakewood Park (cdp) St. Lucie	7	0.07
Myrtle Grove (cdp) Escambia	10	0.06
Lockhart (cdp) Orange	6	0.05
Bellview (cdp) Escambia	8	0.04
Callaway (city) Bay	5	0.04
Lakeside (cdp) Clay	8	0.03
Brent (cdp) Escambia	6	0.03
Bartow (city) Polk	5	0.03
Palm Bay (city) Brevard	12	0.02

American Indian: Osage

Top 10 Places Sorted by Number
Based on all places, regardless of population

Place (place type) County	Number	%
Jacksonville (special city) Duval	14	0.00
Tampa (city) Hillsborough	14	0.00
St. Petersburg (city) Pinellas	11	0.00
Deltona (city) Volusia	5	0.01
Zephyrhills (city) Pasco	4	0.04
Wright (cdp) Okaloosa	4	0.02
Lauderdale Lakes (city) Broward	4	0.01
Pinellas Park (city) Pinellas	4	0.01
Port St. Lucie (city) St. Lucie	4	0.00
Nassau Village-Ratliff (cdp) Nassau	3	0.06

Top 10 Places Sorted by Percent
Based on all places, regardless of population

Place (place type) County	Number	%
Captiva (cdp) Lee	1	0.26
Greenwood (town) Jackson	1	0.14
Gun Club Estates (cdp) Palm Beach	1	0.14
Nassau Village-Ratliff (cdp) Nassau	3	0.06
Riverland Village (cdp) Broward	1	0.05
Zephyrhills (city) Pasco	4	0.04
South Patrick Shores (cdp) Brevard	3	0.03
Longboat Key (town) Sarasota	2	0.03
Milton (city) Santa Rosa	2	0.03
Indian River Shores (town) Indian River	1	0.03

Top 10 Places Sorted by Percent
Based on places with populations of 10,000 or more

Place (place type) County	Number	%
Zephyrhills (city) Pasco	4	0.04
Wright (cdp) Okaloosa	4	0.02
Florida Ridge (cdp) Indian River	3	0.02
Cocoa Beach (city) Brevard	2	0.02
Deltona (city) Volusia	5	0.01
Lauderdale Lakes (city) Broward	4	0.01
Pinellas Park (city) Pinellas	4	0.01
De Land (city) Volusia	3	0.01
Fort Myers (city) Lee	3	0.01
Kissimmee (city) Osceola	3	0.01

American Indian: Ottawa

Top 10 Places Sorted by Number
Based on all places, regardless of population

Place (place type) County	Number	%
Jacksonville (special city) Duval	12	0.00
Clearwater (city) Pinellas	8	0.01
Frostproof (city) Polk	5	0.17
Punta Gorda (city) Charlotte	5	0.03
Tyndall AFB (cdp) Bay	4	0.15
Inverness Highlands South (cdp) Citrus	4	0.07
Hudson (cdp) Pasco	4	0.03
Valparaiso (city) Okaloosa	3	0.05
Jasmine Estates (cdp) Pasco	3	0.02
Apopka (city) Orange	3	0.01

Top 10 Places Sorted by Percent
Based on all places, regardless of population

Place (place type) County	Number	%
Matlacha Isles-Matlacha Shores (cdp) Lee	1	0.33
Frostproof (city) Polk	5	0.17
Tyndall AFB (cdp) Bay	4	0.15
Gotha (cdp) Orange	1	0.14
Lake Kathryn (cdp) Lake	1	0.12
Eagle Lake (city) Polk	2	0.08
Seminole Manor (cdp) Palm Beach	2	0.08
Inverness Highlands South (cdp) Citrus	4	0.07
Belleair Beach (city) Pinellas	1	0.06
Valparaiso (city) Okaloosa	3	0.05

Top 10 Places Sorted by Percent
Based on places with populations of 10,000 or more

Place (place type) County	Number	%
Punta Gorda (city) Charlotte	5	0.03
Hudson (cdp) Pasco	4	0.03
Jasmine Estates (cdp) Pasco	3	0.02
Iona (cdp) Lee	2	0.02
Westchase (cdp) Hillsborough	2	0.02
Wilton Manors (city) Broward	2	0.02
Clearwater (city) Pinellas	8	0.01
Apopka (city) Orange	3	0.01
North Fort Myers (cdp) Lee	3	0.01
Tamarac (city) Broward	3	0.01

American Indian: Paiute

Top 10 Places Sorted by Number
Based on all places, regardless of population

Place (place type) County	Number	%
Jacksonville (special city) Duval	6	0.00
Bellview (cdp) Escambia	4	0.02
Warrington (cdp) Escambia	3	0.02
West Pensacola (cdp) Escambia	3	0.01
Hollywood (city) Broward	3	0.00
Orlando (city) Orange	3	0.00
Davie (town) Broward	2	0.00
Pinellas Park (city) Pinellas	2	0.00
St. Petersburg (city) Pinellas	2	0.00
Sarasota (city) Sarasota	2	0.00

Top 10 Places Sorted by Percent
Based on all places, regardless of population

Place (place type) County	Number	%
Malone (town) Jackson	1	0.05
Bellview (cdp) Escambia	4	0.02
Warrington (cdp) Escambia	3	0.02
Sky Lake (cdp) Orange	1	0.02
Vamo (cdp) Sarasota	1	0.02
West Pensacola (cdp) Escambia	3	0.01
Callaway (city) Bay	1	0.01
Cutler (cdp) Miami-Dade	1	0.01
Homosassa Springs (cdp) Citrus	1	0.01
Hudson (cdp) Pasco	1	0.01

Top 10 Places Sorted by Percent
Based on places with populations of 10,000 or more

Place (place type) County	Number	%
Bellview (cdp) Escambia	4	0.02
Warrington (cdp) Escambia	3	0.02
West Pensacola (cdp) Escambia	3	0.01
Callaway (city) Bay	1	0.01
Cutler (cdp) Miami-Dade	1	0.01
Homosassa Springs (cdp) Citrus	1	0.01
Hudson (cdp) Pasco	1	0.01
Pinecrest (village) Miami-Dade	1	0.01
Winter Garden (city) Orange	1	0.01
Jacksonville (special city) Duval	6	0.00

American Indian: Pima

Top 10 Places Sorted by Number
Based on all places, regardless of population

Place (place type) County	Number	%
Goulding (cdp) Escambia	3	0.07
Auburndale (city) Polk	3	0.03
Big Coppitt Key (cdp) Monroe	2	0.08
Ormond Beach (city) Volusia	2	0.01
Riviera Beach (city) Palm Beach	2	0.01
Jacksonville (special city) Duval	2	0.00
Indian River Estates (cdp) St. Lucie	1	0.02
Lake Worth Corridor (cdp) Palm Beach	1	0.01
Miami (city) Miami-Dade	1	0.00
North Miami (city) Miami-Dade	1	0.00

Top 10 Places Sorted by Percent
Based on all places, regardless of population

Place (place type) County	Number	%
Big Coppitt Key (cdp) Monroe	2	0.08
Goulding (cdp) Escambia	3	0.07
Auburndale (city) Polk	3	0.03
Indian River Estates (cdp) St. Lucie	1	0.02
Ormond Beach (city) Volusia	2	0.01
Riviera Beach (city) Palm Beach	2	0.01
Lake Worth Corridor (cdp) Palm Beach	1	0.01
Jacksonville (special city) Duval	2	0.00
Miami (city) Miami-Dade	1	0.00
North Miami (city) Miami-Dade	1	0.00

Top 10 Places Sorted by Percent
Based on places with populations of 10,000 or more

Place (place type) County	Number	%
Auburndale (city) Polk	3	0.03
Ormond Beach (city) Volusia	2	0.01
Riviera Beach (city) Palm Beach	2	0.01
Lake Worth Corridor (cdp) Palm Beach	1	0.01
Jacksonville (special city) Duval	2	0.00
Miami (city) Miami-Dade	1	0.00

Place (place type) County	Number	%
North Miami (city) Miami-Dade	1	0.00
Tampa (city) Hillsborough	1	0.00

American Indian: Potawatomi

Top 10 Places Sorted by Number

Based on all places, regardless of population

Place (place type) County	Number	%
Cape Coral (city) Lee	13	0.01
Jacksonville (special city) Duval	11	0.00
St. Petersburg (city) Pinellas	8	0.00
Town 'n' Country (cdp) Hillsborough	6	0.01
Goldenrod (cdp) Seminole	5	0.04
Wekiwa Springs (cdp) Seminole	5	0.02
Palm Bay (city) Brevard	5	0.01
Sorrento (cdp) Lake	4	0.52
Beacon Square (cdp) Pasco	4	0.06
Southgate (cdp) Sarasota	4	0.05

Top 10 Places Sorted by Percent

Based on all places, regardless of population

Place (place type) County	Number	%
Sorrento (cdp) Lake	4	0.52
Three Oaks (cdp) Lee	3	0.13
Palm Shores (town) Brevard	1	0.13
Chuluota (cdp) Seminole	2	0.10
De Land Southwest (cdp) Volusia	1	0.09
Freeport (city) Walton	1	0.08
Zephyrhills South (cdp) Pasco	3	0.07
Frostproof (city) Polk	2	0.07
Beacon Square (cdp) Pasco	4	0.06
Odessa (cdp) Hillsborough	2	0.06

Top 10 Places Sorted by Percent

Based on places with populations of 10,000 or more

Place (place type) County	Number	%
Goldenrod (cdp) Seminole	5	0.04
Niceville (city) Okaloosa	3	0.03
Wekiwa Springs (cdp) Seminole	5	0.02
Bellair-Meadowbrook Terrace (cdp) Clay	4	0.02
Myrtle Grove (cdp) Escambia	4	0.02
New Smyrna Beach (city) Volusia	4	0.02
Fruitville (cdp) Sarasota	2	0.02
Cape Coral (city) Lee	13	0.01
Town 'n' Country (cdp) Hillsborough	6	0.01
Palm Bay (city) Brevard	5	0.01

American Indian: Pueblo

Top 10 Places Sorted by Number

Based on all places, regardless of population

Place (place type) County	Number	%
Miami (city) Miami-Dade	42	0.01
Pinewood (cdp) Miami-Dade	12	0.07
Tampa (city) Hillsborough	11	0.00
Merritt Island (cdp) Brevard	10	0.03
Hialeah (city) Miami-Dade	10	0.00
Gainesville (city) Alachua	9	0.01
Jacksonville (special city) Duval	9	0.00
Titusville (city) Brevard	8	0.02
Orlando (city) Orange	8	0.00
St. Petersburg (city) Pinellas	8	0.00

Top 10 Places Sorted by Percent

Based on all places, regardless of population

Place (place type) County	Number	%
Homestead Base (cdp) Miami-Dade	1	0.22
Lacoochee (cdp) Pasco	2	0.15
Bithlo (cdp) Orange	5	0.11
Sharpes (cdp) Brevard	3	0.09
St. Augustine South (cdp) St. Johns	4	0.08
Pinewood (cdp) Miami-Dade	12	0.07
Westgate-Belvedere Homes (cdp) Palm Beach	5	0.06
Century (town) Escambia	1	0.06
Roseland (cdp) Indian River	1	0.06
West Samoset (cdp) Manatee	3	0.05

Top 10 Places Sorted by Percent

Based on places with populations of 10,000 or more

Place (place type) County	Number	%
Pinewood (cdp) Miami-Dade	12	0.07
Palmetto (city) Manatee	5	0.04
Jensen Beach (cdp) Martin	4	0.04
Merritt Island (cdp) Brevard	10	0.03
Holiday (cdp) Pasco	6	0.03
Parkland (city) Broward	4	0.03
Titusville (city) Brevard	8	0.02
Lake Worth (city) Palm Beach	7	0.02
Golden Glades (cdp) Miami-Dade	6	0.02
Royal Palm Beach (village) Palm Beach	5	0.02

American Indian: Puget Sound Salish

Top 10 Places Sorted by Number

Based on all places, regardless of population

Place (place type) County	Number	%
Bellview (cdp) Escambia	6	0.03
Bloomingdale (cdp) Hillsborough	6	0.03
Tampa (city) Hillsborough	6	0.00
Panama City (city) Bay	3	0.01
Odessa (cdp) Hillsborough	2	0.06
Eglin AFB (cdp) Okaloosa	2	0.02
Brent (cdp) Escambia	2	0.01
Altamonte Springs (city) Seminole	2	0.00
Cape Coral (city) Lee	2	0.00
Daytona Beach (city) Volusia	2	0.00

Top 10 Places Sorted by Percent

Based on all places, regardless of population

Place (place type) County	Number	%
Odessa (cdp) Hillsborough	2	0.06
Lake Helen (city) Volusia	1	0.04
Bellview (cdp) Escambia	6	0.03
Bloomingdale (cdp) Hillsborough	6	0.03
Eglin AFB (cdp) Okaloosa	2	0.02
Starke (city) Bradford	1	0.02
Panama City (city) Bay	3	0.01
Brent (cdp) Escambia	2	0.01
Port St. John (cdp) Brevard	1	0.01
Princeton (cdp) Miami-Dade	1	0.01

Top 10 Places Sorted by Percent

Based on places with populations of 10,000 or more

Place (place type) County	Number	%
Bellview (cdp) Escambia	6	0.03
Bloomingdale (cdp) Hillsborough	6	0.03
Panama City (city) Bay	3	0.01
Brent (cdp) Escambia	2	0.01
Port St. John (cdp) Brevard	1	0.01
Princeton (cdp) Miami-Dade	1	0.01
South Venice (cdp) Sarasota	1	0.01
Warrington (cdp) Escambia	1	0.01
Tampa (city) Hillsborough	6	0.00
Altamonte Springs (city) Seminole	2	0.00

American Indian: Seminole

Top 10 Places Sorted by Number

Based on all places, regardless of population

Place (place type) County	Number	%
Jacksonville (special city) Duval	124	0.02
Immokalee (cdp) Collier	123	0.62
Tampa (city) Hillsborough	74	0.02
St. Petersburg (city) Pinellas	41	0.02
Hollywood (city) Broward	38	0.03
Orlando (city) Orange	36	0.02
East Lake-Orient Park (cdp) Hillsborough	35	0.61
Davie (town) Broward	27	0.04
Brandon (cdp) Hillsborough	26	0.03
Okeechobee (city) Okeechobee	22	0.41

Top 10 Places Sorted by Percent

Based on all places, regardless of population

Place (place type) County	Number	%
La Crosse (town) Alachua	1	0.70
Immokalee (cdp) Collier	123	0.62
East Lake-Orient Park (cdp) Hillsborough	35	0.61
Reddick (town) Marion	3	0.53
Okeechobee (city) Okeechobee	22	0.41
Paisley (cdp) Lake	3	0.41
St. Lucie (village) St. Lucie	2	0.33
Bell (town) Gilchrist	1	0.29
East Bronson (cdp) Levy	3	0.28
Vernon (city) Washington	2	0.27

Top 10 Places Sorted by Percent

Based on places with populations of 10,000 or more

Place (place type) County	Number	%
Immokalee (cdp) Collier	123	0.62
Holly Hill (city) Volusia	8	0.07
Ocoee (city) Orange	14	0.06
Riverview (cdp) Hillsborough	7	0.06
Lake Wales (city) Polk	6	0.06
Middleburg (cdp) Clay	6	0.06
Cocoa Beach (city) Brevard	6	0.05
Upper Grand Lagoon (cdp) Bay	5	0.05
Davie (town) Broward	27	0.04
Sanford (city) Seminole	15	0.04

American Indian: Shoshone

Top 10 Places Sorted by Number

Based on all places, regardless of population

Place (place type) County	Number	%
Jacksonville (special city) Duval	7	0.00
Tampa (city) Hillsborough	7	0.00
Miami (city) Miami-Dade	6	0.00
Longwood (city) Seminole	5	0.04
Pinellas Park (city) Pinellas	5	0.01
Mount Plymouth (cdp) Lake	4	0.14
New Smyrna Beach (city) Volusia	4	0.02
Iona (cdp) Lee	3	0.03
Oldsmar (city) Pinellas	3	0.03
Jupiter (town) Palm Beach	3	0.01

Top 10 Places Sorted by Percent

Based on all places, regardless of population

Place (place type) County	Number	%
Webster (city) Sumter	2	0.25
Page Park (cdp) Lee	1	0.19
Mount Plymouth (cdp) Lake	4	0.14
Hawthorne (city) Alachua	2	0.14
Andrews (cdp) Levy	1	0.14
Christmas (cdp) Orange	1	0.09
Dunnellon (city) Marion	1	0.05
Taft (cdp) Orange	1	0.05
Longwood (city) Seminole	5	0.04
Iona (cdp) Lee	3	0.03

Top 10 Places Sorted by Percent

Based on places with populations of 10,000 or more

Place (place type) County	Number	%
Longwood (city) Seminole	5	0.04
Iona (cdp) Lee	3	0.03
Oldsmar (city) Pinellas	3	0.03
New Smyrna Beach (city) Volusia	4	0.02
Cypress Lake (cdp) Lee	2	0.02
Fernandina Beach (city) Nassau	2	0.02
Pinellas Park (city) Pinellas	5	0.01
Jupiter (town) Palm Beach	3	0.01

Notes: (cdp) census designated place; Refer to the User's Guide in the front of the book for more detailed information.

Place (place type) County	Number	%
Citrus Ridge (cdp) Lake	1	0.01
Conway (cdp) Orange	1	0.01

American Indian: Sioux

Top 10 Places Sorted by Number

Based on all places, regardless of population

Place (place type) County	Number	%
Jacksonville (special city) Duval	108	0.01
St. Petersburg (city) Pinellas	53	0.02
Tampa (city) Hillsborough	44	0.01
Cape Coral (city) Lee	32	0.03
Brandon (cdp) Hillsborough	28	0.04
Melbourne (city) Brevard	25	0.04
Orlando (city) Orange	23	0.01
Tallahassee (city) Leon	21	0.01
Hollywood (city) Broward	18	0.01
Sarasota (city) Sarasota	17	0.03

Top 10 Places Sorted by Percent

Based on all places, regardless of population

Place (place type) County	Number	%
Caryville (town) Washington	2	0.92
Christmas (cdp) Orange	4	0.34
Dunes Road (cdp) Palm Beach	1	0.26
Ponce de Leon (town) Holmes	1	0.22
Paxton (town) Walton	1	0.15
Pretty Bayou (cdp) Bay	5	0.14
Greenwood (town) Jackson	1	0.14
Matlacha (cdp) Lee	1	0.14
Apalachicola (city) Franklin	3	0.13
Pine Lakes (cdp) Lake	1	0.13

Top 10 Places Sorted by Percent

Based on places with populations of 10,000 or more

Place (place type) County	Number	%
Gonzalez (cdp) Escambia	10	0.09
Safety Harbor (city) Pinellas	12	0.07
Warrington (cdp) Escambia	11	0.07
South Daytona (city) Volusia	9	0.07
West Pensacola (cdp) Escambia	14	0.06
Lynn Haven (city) Bay	8	0.06
Lakeland Highlands (cdp) Polk	7	0.06
Port St. John (cdp) Brevard	7	0.06
Riverview (cdp) Hillsborough	7	0.06
Bellview (cdp) Escambia	10	0.05

American Indian: Tohono O'Odham

Top 10 Places Sorted by Number

Based on all places, regardless of population

Place (place type) County	Number	%
Big Coppitt Key (cdp) Monroe	7	0.27
Merritt Island (cdp) Brevard	4	0.01
Poinciana (cdp) Osceola	3	0.02
Margate (city) Broward	3	0.01
Deltona (city) Volusia	3	0.00
Fort Pierce (city) St. Lucie	2	0.01
Plantation Mobile Home Park (cdp) Palm Beach	1	0.08
Lakeside Green (cdp) Palm Beach	1	0.03
Fort Walton Beach (city) Okaloosa	1	0.01
Lake Park (town) Palm Beach	1	0.01

Top 10 Places Sorted by Percent

Based on all places, regardless of population

Place (place type) County	Number	%
Big Coppitt Key (cdp) Monroe	7	0.27
Plantation Mobile Home Park (cdp) Palm Beach	1	0.08
Lakeside Green (cdp) Palm Beach	1	0.03
Poinciana (cdp) Osceola	3	0.02
Merritt Island (cdp) Brevard	4	0.01
Margate (city) Broward	3	0.01
Fort Pierce (city) St. Lucie	2	0.01
Fort Walton Beach (city) Okaloosa	1	0.01
Lake Park (town) Palm Beach	1	0.01
Myrtle Grove (cdp) Escambia	1	0.01

Top 10 Places Sorted by Percent

Based on places with populations of 10,000 or more

Place (place type) County	Number	%
Poinciana (cdp) Osceola	3	0.02
Merritt Island (cdp) Brevard	4	0.01
Margate (city) Broward	3	0.01
Fort Pierce (city) St. Lucie	2	0.01
Fort Walton Beach (city) Okaloosa	1	0.01
Myrtle Grove (cdp) Escambia	1	0.01
Deltona (city) Volusia	3	0.00
Bonita Springs (city) Lee	1	0.00
Brandon (cdp) Hillsborough	1	0.00
Fort Myers (city) Lee	1	0.00

American Indian: Ute

Top 10 Places Sorted by Number

Based on all places, regardless of population

Place (place type) County	Number	%
Sunrise (city) Broward	4	0.00
Upper Grand Lagoon (cdp) Bay	3	0.03
Poinciana (cdp) Osceola	3	0.02
New Smyrna Beach (city) Volusia	3	0.01
Jacksonville (special city) Duval	3	0.00
Lakeland (city) Polk	3	0.00
Cutler Ridge (cdp) Miami-Dade	2	0.01
Daytona Beach (city) Volusia	2	0.00
Bushnell (city) Sumter	1	0.05
Asbury Lake (cdp) Clay	1	0.04

Top 10 Places Sorted by Percent

Based on all places, regardless of population

Place (place type) County	Number	%
Bushnell (city) Sumter	1	0.05
Asbury Lake (cdp) Clay	1	0.04
Blountstown (city) Calhoun	1	0.04
Upper Grand Lagoon (cdp) Bay	3	0.03
Poinciana (cdp) Osceola	3	0.02
New Smyrna Beach (city) Volusia	3	0.01
Cutler Ridge (cdp) Miami-Dade	2	0.01
Crestview (city) Okaloosa	1	0.01
Gulf Gate Estates (cdp) Sarasota	1	0.01
Lighthouse Point (city) Broward	1	0.01

Top 10 Places Sorted by Percent

Based on places with populations of 10,000 or more

Place (place type) County	Number	%
Upper Grand Lagoon (cdp) Bay	3	0.03
Poinciana (cdp) Osceola	3	0.02
New Smyrna Beach (city) Volusia	3	0.01
Cutler Ridge (cdp) Miami-Dade	2	0.01
Crestview (city) Okaloosa	1	0.01
Gulf Gate Estates (cdp) Sarasota	1	0.01
Lighthouse Point (city) Broward	1	0.01
Niceville (city) Okaloosa	1	0.01
Sunrise (city) Broward	4	0.00
Jacksonville (special city) Duval	3	0.00

American Indian: Yakama

Top 10 Places Sorted by Number

Based on all places, regardless of population

Place (place type) County	Number	%
Fort Myers (city) Lee	6	0.01
Lauderdale Lakes (city) Broward	4	0.01
Sanford (city) Seminole	3	0.01
Palm River-Clair Mel (cdp) Hillsborough	2	0.01
Masaryktown (cdp) Hernando	1	0.11
Hilliard (town) Nassau	1	0.04
Eustis (city) Lake	1	0.01
Riverview (cdp) Hillsborough	1	0.01
Sebastian (city) Indian River	1	0.01
Springfield (city) Bay	1	0.01

Top 10 Places Sorted by Percent

Based on all places, regardless of population

Place (place type) County	Number	%
Masaryktown (cdp) Hernando	1	0.11
Hilliard (town) Nassau	1	0.04
Fort Myers (city) Lee	6	0.01
Lauderdale Lakes (city) Broward	4	0.01
Sanford (city) Seminole	3	0.01
Palm River-Clair Mel (cdp) Hillsborough	2	0.01
Eustis (city) Lake	1	0.01
Riverview (cdp) Hillsborough	1	0.01
Sebastian (city) Indian River	1	0.01
Springfield (city) Bay	1	0.01

Top 10 Places Sorted by Percent

Based on places with populations of 10,000 or more

Place (place type) County	Number	%
Fort Myers (city) Lee	6	0.01
Lauderdale Lakes (city) Broward	4	0.01
Sanford (city) Seminole	3	0.01
Palm River-Clair Mel (cdp) Hillsborough	2	0.01
Eustis (city) Lake	1	0.01
Riverview (cdp) Hillsborough	1	0.01
Sebastian (city) Indian River	1	0.01
Winter Garden (city) Orange	1	0.01
Daytona Beach (city) Volusia	1	0.00
Deerfield Beach (city) Broward	1	0.00

American Indian: Yaqui

Top 10 Places Sorted by Number

Based on all places, regardless of population

Place (place type) County	Number	%
Jacksonville (special city) Duval	12	0.00
Casselberry (city) Seminole	11	0.05
West Vero Corridor (cdp) Indian River	6	0.08
Orlando (city) Orange	6	0.00
Hudson (cdp) Pasco	4	0.03
Daytona Beach (city) Volusia	4	0.01
Melbourne (city) Brevard	4	0.01
St. Augustine Shores (cdp) St. Johns	3	0.06
Eglin AFB (cdp) Okaloosa	3	0.04
Hallandale (city) Broward	3	0.01

Top 10 Places Sorted by Percent

Based on all places, regardless of population

Place (place type) County	Number	%
West Vero Corridor (cdp) Indian River	6	0.08
Laguna Beach (cdp) Bay	2	0.07
St. Augustine Shores (cdp) St. Johns	3	0.06
Casselberry (city) Seminole	11	0.05
Eglin AFB (cdp) Okaloosa	3	0.04
Hudson (cdp) Pasco	4	0.03
Medulla (cdp) Polk	2	0.03
Bay Hill (cdp) Orange	1	0.02
Labelle (city) Hendry	1	0.02
North Weeki Wachee (cdp) Hernando	1	0.02

Top 10 Places Sorted by Percent

Based on places with populations of 10,000 or more

Place (place type) County	Number	%
Casselberry (city) Seminole	11	0.05
Hudson (cdp) Pasco	4	0.03
Daytona Beach (city) Volusia	4	0.01
Melbourne (city) Brevard	4	0.01
Hallandale (city) Broward	3	0.01
Palm Harbor (cdp) Pinellas	3	0.01
Greenacres (city) Palm Beach	2	0.01
Naples (city) Collier	2	0.01

Place (place type) County	Number	%
Sanford (city) Seminole	2	0.01
Azalea Park (cdp) Orange	1	0.01

American Indian: Yuman

Top 10 Places Sorted by Number
Based on all places, regardless of population

Place (place type) County	Number	%
Tampa (city) Hillsborough	3	0.00
Ebro (town) Washington	2	0.80
North Fort Myers (cdp) Lee	2	0.00
West Palm Beach (city) Palm Beach	2	0.00
St. Augustine South (cdp) St. Johns	1	0.02
Cape Canaveral (city) Brevard	1	0.01
Fern Park (cdp) Seminole	1	0.01
Indian Harbour Beach (city) Brevard	1	0.01
Lockhart (cdp) Orange	1	0.01
Palm Springs (village) Palm Beach	1	0.01

Top 10 Places Sorted by Percent
Based on all places, regardless of population

Place (place type) County	Number	%
Ebro (town) Washington	2	0.80
St. Augustine South (cdp) St. Johns	1	0.02
Cape Canaveral (city) Brevard	1	0.01
Fern Park (cdp) Seminole	1	0.01
Indian Harbour Beach (city) Brevard	1	0.01
Lockhart (cdp) Orange	1	0.01
Palm Springs (village) Palm Beach	1	0.01
Tampa (city) Hillsborough	3	0.00
North Fort Myers (cdp) Lee	2	0.00
West Palm Beach (city) Palm Beach	2	0.00

Top 10 Places Sorted by Percent
Based on places with populations of 10,000 or more

Place (place type) County	Number	%
Lockhart (cdp) Orange	1	0.01
Palm Springs (village) Palm Beach	1	0.01
Tampa (city) Hillsborough	3	0.00
North Fort Myers (cdp) Lee	2	0.00
West Palm Beach (city) Palm Beach	2	0.00
Clearwater (city) Pinellas	1	0.00
Coconut Creek (city) Broward	1	0.00
Deltona (city) Volusia	1	0.00
Fort Lauderdale (city) Broward	1	0.00
Jacksonville (special city) Duval	1	0.00

American Indian: All other tribes

Top 10 Places Sorted by Number
Based on all places, regardless of population

Place (place type) County	Number	%
Jacksonville (special city) Duval	275	0.04
St. Petersburg (city) Pinellas	141	0.06
Tampa (city) Hillsborough	87	0.03
Miami (city) Miami-Dade	70	0.02
Orlando (city) Orange	67	0.04
Brandon (cdp) Hillsborough	42	0.05
Port St. Lucie (city) St. Lucie	40	0.05
Fort Lauderdale (city) Broward	40	0.03
Palm Bay (city) Brevard	37	0.05
Clearwater (city) Pinellas	36	0.03

Top 10 Places Sorted by Percent
Based on all places, regardless of population

Place (place type) County	Number	%
Beverly Beach (town) Flagler	3	0.55
Wausau (town) Washington	2	0.50
Williston (city) Levy	10	0.44
Ponce de Leon (town) Holmes	2	0.44
Crescent Beach (cdp) St. Johns	4	0.41
South Brooksville (cdp) Hernando	5	0.36
Mary Esther (city) Okaloosa	14	0.35
Chula Vista (cdp) Broward	2	0.35
Interlachen (town) Putnam	5	0.34
Crooked Lake Park (cdp) Polk	5	0.30

Top 10 Places Sorted by Percent
Based on places with populations of 10,000 or more

Place (place type) County	Number	%
Middleburg (cdp) Clay	16	0.15
Homosassa Springs (cdp) Citrus	18	0.14
Bloomingdale (cdp) Hillsborough	25	0.13
West Pensacola (cdp) Escambia	24	0.11
South Bradenton (cdp) Manatee	23	0.11
Callaway (city) Bay	15	0.11
San Carlos Park (cdp) Lee	17	0.10
Elfers (cdp) Pasco	13	0.10
Gulfport (city) Pinellas	12	0.10
Riverview (cdp) Hillsborough	12	0.10

American Indian tribes, not specified

Top 10 Places Sorted by Number
Based on all places, regardless of population

Place (place type) County	Number	%
Jacksonville (special city) Duval	288	0.04
Tampa (city) Hillsborough	172	0.06
Miami (city) Miami-Dade	157	0.04
St. Petersburg (city) Pinellas	103	0.04
Orlando (city) Orange	102	0.05
Gainesville (city) Alachua	65	0.07
Hialeah (city) Miami-Dade	59	0.03
Tallahassee (city) Leon	58	0.04
Lakeland (city) Polk	56	0.07
Fort Lauderdale (city) Broward	54	0.04

Top 10 Places Sorted by Percent
Based on all places, regardless of population

Place (place type) County	Number	%
Noma (town) Holmes	3	1.41
Glen Ridge (town) Palm Beach	3	1.09
Lawtey (city) Bradford	7	1.07
Chokoloskee (cdp) Collier	4	0.99
Beverly Beach (town) Flagler	4	0.73
Fort White (town) Columbia	3	0.73
Bristol (city) Liberty	6	0.71
Lake Kathryn (cdp) Lake	4	0.47
Alva (cdp) Lee	10	0.46
Glen St. Mary (town) Baker	2	0.42

Top 10 Places Sorted by Percent
Based on places with populations of 10,000 or more

Place (place type) County	Number	%
Brent (cdp) Escambia	43	0.19
Fort Walton Beach (city) Okaloosa	30	0.15
Callaway (city) Bay	18	0.13
Poinciana (cdp) Osceola	17	0.12
Lockhart (cdp) Orange	16	0.12
South Miami Heights (cdp) Miami-Dade	32	0.10
West and East Lealman (cdp) Pinellas	21	0.10
Lake Worth Corridor (cdp) Palm Beach	18	0.10
Seminole (city) Pinellas	11	0.10
Golden Gate (cdp) Collier	19	0.09

Arab

Top 10 Places Sorted by Number
Based on all places, regardless of population

Place (place type) County	Number	%
Jacksonville (special city) Duval	5,861	0.80
Miami (city) Miami-Dade	1,864	0.51
Orlando (city) Orange	1,693	0.91
Kendall (cdp) Miami-Dade	1,315	1.75
Coral Springs (city) Broward	1,247	1.06
Pembroke Pines (city) Broward	1,230	0.90
St. Petersburg (city) Pinellas	1,229	0.50
Hollywood (city) Broward	1,183	0.85
Tampa (city) Hillsborough	1,118	0.37
Miami Beach (city) Miami-Dade	934	1.06

Top 10 Places Sorted by Percent
Based on all places, regardless of population

Place (place type) County	Number	%
Dunes Road (cdp) Palm Beach	104	21.99
Cloud Lake (town) Palm Beach	5	4.07
Belleair Beach (city) Pinellas	65	3.88
Lake Belvedere Estates (cdp) Palm Beach	49	3.28
Tierra Verde (cdp) Pinellas	116	3.27
Gulf Stream (town) Palm Beach	22	3.18
Wesley Chapel (cdp) Pasco	186	3.16
Doctor Phillips (cdp) Orange	302	3.13
Gateway (cdp) Lee	82	2.70
Surfside (town) Miami-Dade	128	2.50

Top 10 Places Sorted by Percent
Based on places with populations of 10,000 or more

Place (place type) County	Number	%
Pinecrest (village) Miami-Dade	477	2.49
Sunny Isles Beach (city) Miami-Dade	380	2.49
Ojus (cdp) Miami-Dade	365	2.19
Temple Terrace (city) Hillsborough	428	2.05
Aventura (city) Miami-Dade	505	2.00
Kendall (cdp) Miami-Dade	1,315	1.75
Miami Lakes (cdp) Miami-Dade	396	1.74
Ives Estates (cdp) Miami-Dade	297	1.71
Azalea Park (cdp) Orange	189	1.70
Lake Magdalene (cdp) Hillsborough	436	1.51

Arab: Arab/Arabic

Top 10 Places Sorted by Number
Based on all places, regardless of population

Place (place type) County	Number	%
Jacksonville (special city) Duval	1,602	0.22
Tampa (city) Hillsborough	333	0.11
Miami (city) Miami-Dade	333	0.09
Miami Lakes (cdp) Miami-Dade	261	1.15
Orlando (city) Orange	254	0.14
Temple Terrace (city) Hillsborough	231	1.11
Palm Bay (city) Brevard	226	0.28
Pembroke Pines (city) Broward	220	0.16
Kissimmee (city) Osceola	201	0.42
The Hammocks (cdp) Miami-Dade	199	0.42

Top 10 Places Sorted by Percent
Based on all places, regardless of population

Place (place type) County	Number	%
Port La Belle (cdp) Hendry	58	1.79
Wesley Chapel (cdp) Pasco	86	1.46
Palm Shores (town) Brevard	11	1.39
Placid Lakes (cdp) Highlands	35	1.16
Gulf Stream (town) Palm Beach	8	1.16
Miami Lakes (cdp) Miami-Dade	261	1.15
Gateway (cdp) Lee	35	1.15
Shady Hills (cdp) Pasco	87	1.12
Temple Terrace (city) Hillsborough	231	1.11
Haverhill (town) Palm Beach	15	0.98

Top 10 Places Sorted by Percent
Based on places with populations of 10,000 or more

Place (place type) County	Number	%
Miami Lakes (cdp) Miami-Dade	261	1.15
Temple Terrace (city) Hillsborough	231	1.11
Belle Glade (city) Palm Beach	115	0.77
Ives Estates (cdp) Miami-Dade	127	0.73
Sunny Isles Beach (city) Miami-Dade	88	0.58
Sunset (cdp) Miami-Dade	92	0.54
Conway (cdp) Orange	70	0.49
Cooper City (city) Broward	127	0.46

Notes: (cdp) census designated place; Refer to the User's Guide in the front of the book for more detailed information.

Place (place type) County	Number	%
Kissimmee (city) Osceola	201	0.42
The Hammocks (cdp) Miami-Dade	199	0.42

Arab: Egyptian

Top 10 Places Sorted by Number
Based on all places, regardless of population

Place (place type) County	Number	%
Altamonte Springs (city) Seminole	204	0.49
Coral Springs (city) Broward	189	0.16
Jacksonville (special city) Duval	167	0.02
Ojus (cdp) Miami-Dade	164	0.98
Palm Harbor (cdp) Pinellas	129	0.22
Ormond Beach (city) Volusia	119	0.33
Clearwater (city) Pinellas	119	0.11
Cocoa Beach (city) Brevard	103	0.83
Miami Beach (city) Miami-Dade	100	0.11
Fort Lauderdale (city) Broward	97	0.06

Top 10 Places Sorted by Percent
Based on all places, regardless of population

Place (place type) County	Number	%
Belleair Beach (city) Pinellas	46	2.75
Rolling Oaks (cdp) Broward	23	1.62
Manalapan (town) Palm Beach	5	1.55
Butler Beach (cdp) St. Johns	63	1.39
Ojus (cdp) Miami-Dade	164	0.98
Tierra Verde (cdp) Pinellas	34	0.96
Fern Park (cdp) Seminole	79	0.95
Redington Beach (town) Pinellas	15	0.91
Kendall Green (cdp) Broward	27	0.86
Cocoa Beach (city) Brevard	103	0.83

Top 10 Places Sorted by Percent
Based on places with populations of 10,000 or more

Place (place type) County	Number	%
Ojus (cdp) Miami-Dade	164	0.98
Cocoa Beach (city) Brevard	103	0.83
Sunny Isles Beach (city) Miami-Dade	87	0.57
Altamonte Springs (city) Seminole	204	0.49
Eustis (city) Lake	62	0.40
Pinecrest (village) Miami-Dade	74	0.39
Lake Wales (city) Polk	38	0.37
Cypress Lake (cdp) Lee	44	0.36
Ormond Beach (city) Volusia	119	0.33
Atlantic Beach (city) Duval	44	0.33

Arab: Iraqi

Top 10 Places Sorted by Number
Based on all places, regardless of population

Place (place type) County	Number	%
Jacksonville (special city) Duval	169	0.02
Miami (city) Miami-Dade	89	0.02
Cocoa Beach (city) Brevard	41	0.33
Miami Beach (city) Miami-Dade	41	0.05
West Palm Beach (city) Palm Beach	41	0.05
Clearwater (city) Pinellas	36	0.03
St. Petersburg (city) Pinellas	34	0.01
Cooper City (city) Broward	32	0.12
Meadow Woods (cdp) Orange	30	0.26
Miami Springs (city) Miami-Dade	29	0.21

Top 10 Places Sorted by Percent
Based on all places, regardless of population

Place (place type) County	Number	%
Sea Ranch Lakes (village) Broward	5	0.36
Cocoa Beach (city) Brevard	41	0.33
Meadow Woods (cdp) Orange	30	0.26
Miami Springs (city) Miami-Dade	29	0.21
Palm Beach (town) Palm Beach	21	0.20
Golden Beach (town) Miami-Dade	2	0.19
Cooper City (city) Broward	32	0.12
Fort Myers Beach (town) Lee	8	0.12
Aventura (city) Miami-Dade	27	0.11
Dania Beach (city) Broward	22	0.11

Top 10 Places Sorted by Percent
Based on places with populations of 10,000 or more

Place (place type) County	Number	%
Cocoa Beach (city) Brevard	41	0.33
Meadow Woods (cdp) Orange	30	0.26
Miami Springs (city) Miami-Dade	29	0.21
Palm Beach (town) Palm Beach	21	0.20
Cooper City (city) Broward	32	0.12
Aventura (city) Miami-Dade	27	0.11
Dania Beach (city) Broward	22	0.11
Cocoa (city) Brevard	16	0.10
Lighthouse Point (city) Broward	9	0.08
Maitland (city) Orange	9	0.08

Arab: Jordanian

Top 10 Places Sorted by Number
Based on all places, regardless of population

Place (place type) County	Number	%
Hollywood (city) Broward	100	0.07
Ojus (cdp) Miami-Dade	91	0.55
Jacksonville (special city) Duval	81	0.01
Lakes by the Bay (cdp) Miami-Dade	64	0.71
Ferry Pass (cdp) Escambia	55	0.20
Oviedo (city) Seminole	55	0.20
Miami (city) Miami-Dade	55	0.02
Coral Springs (city) Broward	53	0.05
University (cdp) Hillsborough	44	0.14
Fort Lauderdale (city) Broward	44	0.03

Top 10 Places Sorted by Percent
Based on all places, regardless of population

Place (place type) County	Number	%
Lake Belvedere Estates (cdp) Palm Beach	35	2.34
Lakes by the Bay (cdp) Miami-Dade	64	0.71
Gulf Stream (town) Palm Beach	4	0.58
Ojus (cdp) Miami-Dade	91	0.55
Golden Lakes (cdp) Palm Beach	22	0.33
Wahneta (cdp) Polk	13	0.27
Ferry Pass (cdp) Escambia	55	0.20
Oviedo (city) Seminole	55	0.20
Sweetwater (city) Miami-Dade	24	0.17
Bay Hill (cdp) Orange	8	0.15

Top 10 Places Sorted by Percent
Based on places with populations of 10,000 or more

Place (place type) County	Number	%
Ojus (cdp) Miami-Dade	91	0.55
Ferry Pass (cdp) Escambia	55	0.20
Oviedo (city) Seminole	55	0.20
Sweetwater (city) Miami-Dade	24	0.17
University (cdp) Hillsborough	44	0.14
Ocoee (city) Orange	32	0.14
Winter Springs (city) Seminole	42	0.13
New Port Richey East (cdp) Pasco	12	0.12
Lake Magdalene (cdp) Hillsborough	29	0.10
North Port (city) Sarasota	23	0.10

Arab: Lebanese

Top 10 Places Sorted by Number
Based on all places, regardless of population

Place (place type) County	Number	%
Jacksonville (special city) Duval	1,623	0.22
Miami (city) Miami-Dade	855	0.24
Kendall (cdp) Miami-Dade	755	1.00
Orlando (city) Orange	587	0.32
St. Petersburg (city) Pinellas	565	0.23
Coral Springs (city) Broward	511	0.43
Hialeah (city) Miami-Dade	429	0.19
Pembroke Pines (city) Broward	421	0.31
Coral Gables (city) Miami-Dade	402	0.95
Hollywood (city) Broward	394	0.28

Top 10 Places Sorted by Percent
Based on all places, regardless of population

Place (place type) County	Number	%
Cloud Lake (town) Palm Beach	5	4.07
Leisureville (cdp) Broward	25	2.31
Tierra Verde (cdp) Pinellas	74	2.09
Biscayne Park (village) Miami-Dade	62	1.87
Chula Vista (cdp) Broward	9	1.54
Ocean Ridge (town) Palm Beach	24	1.47
Gulf Stream (town) Palm Beach	10	1.45
Vineyards (cdp) Collier	32	1.41
Wabasso Beach (cdp) Indian River	15	1.34
Shalimar (town) Okaloosa	8	1.13

Top 10 Places Sorted by Percent
Based on places with populations of 10,000 or more

Place (place type) County	Number	%
Doral (cdp) Miami-Dade	225	1.10
Pinecrest (village) Miami-Dade	209	1.09
Kendall (cdp) Miami-Dade	755	1.00
Coral Gables (city) Miami-Dade	402	0.95
Lake Magdalene (cdp) Hillsborough	235	0.82
Sunset (cdp) Miami-Dade	128	0.75
Azalea Park (cdp) Orange	79	0.71
Lake Mary (city) Seminole	76	0.67
The Crossings (cdp) Miami-Dade	155	0.66
Greater Northdale (cdp) Hillsborough	132	0.65

Arab: Moroccan

Top 10 Places Sorted by Number
Based on all places, regardless of population

Place (place type) County	Number	%
Orlando (city) Orange	272	0.15
Kissimmee (city) Osceola	249	0.52
Sarasota (city) Sarasota	128	0.24
Miami Beach (city) Miami-Dade	120	0.14
Sunny Isles Beach (city) Miami-Dade	108	0.71
Hollywood (city) Broward	107	0.08
Pembroke Pines (city) Broward	99	0.07
Clearwater (city) Pinellas	96	0.09
Jacksonville (special city) Duval	94	0.01
St. Petersburg (city) Pinellas	87	0.04

Top 10 Places Sorted by Percent
Based on all places, regardless of population

Place (place type) County	Number	%
Williamsburg (cdp) Orange	76	1.10
Bay Harbor Islands (town) Miami-Dade	41	0.80
Sunny Isles Beach (city) Miami-Dade	108	0.71
Hastings (town) St. Johns	3	0.64
Indian Harbour Beach (city) Brevard	49	0.60
Kissimmee (city) Osceola	249	0.52
Bal Harbour (village) Miami-Dade	17	0.51
St. Leo (town) Pasco	3	0.49
Three Lakes (cdp) Miami-Dade	27	0.39
Hobe Sound (cdp) Martin	42	0.38

Top 10 Places Sorted by Percent
Based on places with populations of 10,000 or more

Place (place type) County	Number	%
Sunny Isles Beach (city) Miami-Dade	108	0.71
Kissimmee (city) Osceola	249	0.52
Hobe Sound (cdp) Martin	42	0.38
Country Walk (cdp) Miami-Dade	41	0.38
Aventura (city) Miami-Dade	76	0.30
Poinciana (cdp) Osceola	39	0.29
Sarasota (city) Sarasota	128	0.24
Land O' Lakes (cdp) Pasco	49	0.24

Notes: (cdp) census designated place; Refer to the User's Guide in the front of the book for more detailed information.

Citrus Ridge (cdp) Lake	27	0.24
South Miami (city) Miami-Dade	24	0.22

Arab: Palestinian

Top 10 Places Sorted by Number
Based on all places, regardless of population

Place (place type) County	Number	%
Jacksonville (special city) Duval	789	0.11
Orlando (city) Orange	169	0.09
Plantation (city) Broward	156	0.19
Brandon (cdp) Hillsborough	149	0.19
West Palm Beach (city) Palm Beach	149	0.18
St. Petersburg (city) Pinellas	127	0.05
Miami (city) Miami-Dade	119	0.03
The Hammocks (cdp) Miami-Dade	112	0.24
Palm Harbor (cdp) Pinellas	105	0.18
Dunes Road (cdp) Palm Beach	104	21.99

Top 10 Places Sorted by Percent
Based on all places, regardless of population

Place (place type) County	Number	%
Dunes Road (cdp) Palm Beach	104	21.99
Molino (cdp) Escambia	18	1.27
Doctor Phillips (cdp) Orange	80	0.83
Wesley Chapel (cdp) Pasco	48	0.82
Bay Hill (cdp) Orange	38	0.71
Bay Pines (cdp) Pinellas	21	0.63
Surfside (town) Miami-Dade	27	0.53
Holden Heights (cdp) Orange	17	0.44
South Daytona (city) Volusia	53	0.40
Fruitville (cdp) Sarasota	52	0.40

Top 10 Places Sorted by Percent
Based on places with populations of 10,000 or more

Place (place type) County	Number	%
South Daytona (city) Volusia	53	0.40
Fruitville (cdp) Sarasota	52	0.40
Meadow Woods (cdp) Orange	44	0.38
Marco Island (city) Collier	49	0.33
Coral Terrace (cdp) Miami-Dade	69	0.28
Greater Northdale (cdp) Hillsborough	55	0.27
Punta Gorda (city) Charlotte	39	0.27
Parkland (city) Broward	37	0.26
The Hammocks (cdp) Miami-Dade	112	0.24
Egypt Lake-Leto (cdp) Hillsborough	75	0.23

Arab: Syrian

Top 10 Places Sorted by Number
Based on all places, regardless of population

Place (place type) County	Number	%
Jacksonville (special city) Duval	1,182	0.16
Kendall (cdp) Miami-Dade	335	0.45
Spring Hill (cdp) Hernando	239	0.35
Miami (city) Miami-Dade	236	0.07
Orlando (city) Orange	204	0.11
Hollywood (city) Broward	186	0.13
Aventura (city) Miami-Dade	182	0.72
Pembroke Pines (city) Broward	155	0.11
St. Petersburg (city) Pinellas	153	0.06
Sunrise (city) Broward	123	0.14

Top 10 Places Sorted by Percent
Based on all places, regardless of population

Place (place type) County	Number	%
Atlantis (city) Palm Beach	28	1.32
Surfside (town) Miami-Dade	50	0.98
Manalapan (town) Palm Beach	3	0.93
Polk City (town) Polk	13	0.87
Gateway (cdp) Lee	25	0.82
Briny Breezes (town) Palm Beach	3	0.73
Aventura (city) Miami-Dade	182	0.72
Bonnie Lock-Woodsetter North (cdp) Broward	28	0.65
Belleair Beach (city) Pinellas	10	0.60
East Palatka (cdp) Putnam	10	0.58

Top 10 Places Sorted by Percent
Based on places with populations of 10,000 or more

Place (place type) County	Number	%
Aventura (city) Miami-Dade	182	0.72
Oldsmar (city) Pinellas	65	0.55
Holiday (cdp) Pasco	117	0.53
Kendall (cdp) Miami-Dade	335	0.45
Lynn Haven (city) Bay	55	0.45
Ives Estates (cdp) Miami-Dade	74	0.42
East Lake (cdp) Pinellas	117	0.40
Wekiwa Springs (cdp) Seminole	93	0.40
Sunny Isles Beach (city) Miami-Dade	57	0.37
Spring Hill (cdp) Hernando	239	0.35

Arab: Other

Top 10 Places Sorted by Number
Based on all places, regardless of population

Place (place type) County	Number	%
Jacksonville (special city) Duval	154	0.02
Pembroke Pines (city) Broward	142	0.10
Miami Beach (city) Miami-Dade	138	0.16
Tampa (city) Hillsborough	131	0.04
Coral Springs (city) Broward	111	0.09
Temple Terrace (city) Hillsborough	98	0.47
Orlando (city) Orange	97	0.05
Melbourne (city) Brevard	94	0.13
The Hammocks (cdp) Miami-Dade	91	0.19
Hallandale (city) Broward	89	0.26

Top 10 Places Sorted by Percent
Based on all places, regardless of population

Place (place type) County	Number	%
Golden Beach (town) Miami-Dade	12	1.14
Yankeetown (town) Levy	4	0.62
Cypress Lakes (cdp) Palm Beach	7	0.51
Temple Terrace (city) Hillsborough	98	0.47
Azalea Park (cdp) Orange	46	0.41
Glenvar Heights (cdp) Miami-Dade	51	0.32
South Beach (cdp) Indian River	11	0.32
Live Oak (city) Suwannee	19	0.29
Feather Sound (cdp) Pinellas	11	0.27
Hallandale (city) Broward	89	0.26

Top 10 Places Sorted by Percent
Based on places with populations of 10,000 or more

Place (place type) County	Number	%
Temple Terrace (city) Hillsborough	98	0.47
Azalea Park (cdp) Orange	46	0.41
Glenvar Heights (cdp) Miami-Dade	51	0.32
Hallandale (city) Broward	89	0.26
Upper Grand Lagoon (cdp) Bay	26	0.24
Boca Del Mar (cdp) Palm Beach	49	0.23
Myrtle Grove (cdp) Escambia	40	0.23
Pinecrest (village) Miami-Dade	43	0.22
The Hammocks (cdp) Miami-Dade	91	0.19
Belle Glade (city) Palm Beach	26	0.17

Armenian

Top 10 Places Sorted by Number
Based on all places, regardless of population

Place (place type) County	Number	%
Jacksonville (special city) Duval	397	0.05
Tampa (city) Hillsborough	222	0.07
Coral Springs (city) Broward	191	0.16
Fort Lauderdale (city) Broward	171	0.11
Clearwater (city) Pinellas	152	0.14
St. Petersburg (city) Pinellas	146	0.06
Miami (city) Miami-Dade	138	0.04
Lake Mary (city) Seminole	132	1.17
Boca Raton (city) Palm Beach	132	0.17
Orlando (city) Orange	126	0.07

Top 10 Places Sorted by Percent
Based on all places, regardless of population

Place (place type) County	Number	%
Lake Mary (city) Seminole	132	1.17
Punta Rassa (cdp) Lee	19	1.13
Hillcrest Heights (town) Polk	3	1.11
Terra Mar (cdp) Broward	29	1.08
Yankeetown (town) Levy	6	0.93
Pine Ridge (cdp) Collier	15	0.81
Parkland (city) Broward	105	0.75
Pine Island Ridge (cdp) Broward	39	0.73
West Bradenton (cdp) Manatee	32	0.71
Bay Harbor Islands (town) Miami-Dade	36	0.70

Top 10 Places Sorted by Percent
Based on places with populations of 10,000 or more

Place (place type) County	Number	%
Lake Mary (city) Seminole	132	1.17
Parkland (city) Broward	105	0.75
Key West (city) Monroe	93	0.36
Marco Island (city) Collier	51	0.34
Key Largo (cdp) Monroe	39	0.33
Miami Shores (village) Miami-Dade	32	0.31
East Lake (cdp) Pinellas	89	0.30
Sarasota Springs (cdp) Sarasota	44	0.28
Palm Beach Gardens (city) Palm Beach	92	0.27
Kings Point (cdp) Palm Beach	32	0.26

Asian

Top 10 Places Sorted by Number
Based on all places, regardless of population

Place (place type) County	Number	%
Jacksonville (special city) Duval	25,465	3.46
Tampa (city) Hillsborough	8,363	2.76
St. Petersburg (city) Pinellas	8,101	3.26
Pembroke Pines (city) Broward	6,553	4.77
Orlando (city) Orange	6,259	3.37
Gainesville (city) Alachua	4,976	5.21
Coral Springs (city) Broward	4,925	4.19
Tallahassee (city) Leon	4,417	2.93
Hollywood (city) Broward	3,469	2.49
Sunrise (city) Broward	3,294	3.84

Top 10 Places Sorted by Percent
Based on all places, regardless of population

Place (place type) County	Number	%
Bay Hill (cdp) Orange	560	10.82
Southchase (cdp) Orange	493	10.64
Doctor Phillips (cdp) Orange	909	9.52
Ivanhoe Estates (cdp) Broward	26	9.32
Wedgefield (cdp) Orange	236	8.74
Hunters Creek (cdp) Orange	771	8.23
Cloud Lake (town) Palm Beach	13	7.78
Pebble Creek (cdp) Hillsborough	344	7.13
Oak Ridge (cdp) Orange	1,525	6.82
Myrtle Grove (cdp) Escambia	1,107	6.43

Top 10 Places Sorted by Percent
Based on places with populations of 10,000 or more

Place (place type) County	Number	%
Oak Ridge (cdp) Orange	1,525	6.82
Myrtle Grove (cdp) Escambia	1,107	6.43
Ives Estates (cdp) Miami-Dade	1,024	5.82
Doral (cdp) Miami-Dade	1,168	5.71
Wright (cdp) Okaloosa	1,162	5.36
Pinecrest (village) Miami-Dade	1,019	5.35
Gainesville (city) Alachua	4,976	5.21
North Miami Beach (city) Miami-Dade	2,031	4.98

Notes: (cdp) census designated place; Refer to the User's Guide in the front of the book for more detailed information.

Niceville (city) Okaloosa	579	4.96
Callaway (city) Bay	701	4.93

Asian: Bangladeshi

Top 10 Places Sorted by Number
Based on all places, regardless of population

Place (place type) County	Number	%
Boynton Beach (city) Palm Beach	50	0.08
Delray Beach (city) Palm Beach	49	0.08
Miami Beach (city) Miami-Dade	49	0.06
Lake Worth Corridor (cdp) Palm Beach	44	0.24
Kissimmee (city) Osceola	44	0.09
North Miami Beach (city) Miami-Dade	36	0.09
Deerfield Beach (city) Broward	34	0.05
Fort Lauderdale (city) Broward	34	0.02
Pompano Beach (city) Broward	32	0.04
Plantation (city) Broward	30	0.04

Top 10 Places Sorted by Percent
Based on all places, regardless of population

Place (place type) County	Number	%
North Brooksville (cdp) Hernando	5	0.34
Pompano Beach Highlands (cdp) Broward	19	0.29
Loch Lomond (cdp) Broward	10	0.28
Twin Lakes (cdp) Broward	5	0.27
Lake Worth Corridor (cdp) Palm Beach	44	0.24
Chambers Estates (cdp) Broward	8	0.22
Broadview-Pompano Park (cdp) Broward	11	0.21
Edgewood (city) Orange	4	0.21
Hypoluxo (town) Palm Beach	4	0.20
Dover (cdp) Hillsborough	5	0.18

Top 10 Places Sorted by Percent
Based on places with populations of 10,000 or more

Place (place type) County	Number	%
Lake Worth Corridor (cdp) Palm Beach	44	0.24
Sandalfoot Cove (cdp) Palm Beach	22	0.13
Oak Ridge (cdp) Orange	25	0.11
Kissimmee (city) Osceola	44	0.09
North Miami Beach (city) Miami-Dade	36	0.09
Longwood (city) Seminole	13	0.09
Country Walk (cdp) Miami-Dade	10	0.09
Boynton Beach (city) Palm Beach	50	0.08
Delray Beach (city) Palm Beach	49	0.08
Oakland Park (city) Broward	26	0.08

Asian: Cambodian

Top 10 Places Sorted by Number
Based on all places, regardless of population

Place (place type) County	Number	%
Jacksonville (special city) Duval	1,064	0.14
St. Petersburg (city) Pinellas	538	0.22
West and East Lealman (cdp) Pinellas	65	0.30
Pinellas Park (city) Pinellas	58	0.13
Oak Ridge (cdp) Orange	50	0.22
Port St. Lucie (city) St. Lucie	44	0.05
Brent (cdp) Escambia	41	0.18
Gainesville (city) Alachua	32	0.03
South Bradenton (cdp) Manatee	30	0.14
Orlando (city) Orange	29	0.02

Top 10 Places Sorted by Percent
Based on all places, regardless of population

Place (place type) County	Number	%
Kenneth City (town) Pinellas	26	0.59
West and East Lealman (cdp) Pinellas	65	0.30
Southchase (cdp) Orange	12	0.26
Williamsburg (cdp) Orange	17	0.25
St. Petersburg (city) Pinellas	538	0.22
Oak Ridge (cdp) Orange	50	0.22
Brent (cdp) Escambia	41	0.18
Goulding (cdp) Escambia	7	0.16
Jacksonville (special city) Duval	1,064	0.14
South Bradenton (cdp) Manatee	30	0.14

Top 10 Places Sorted by Percent
Based on places with populations of 10,000 or more

Place (place type) County	Number	%
West and East Lealman (cdp) Pinellas	65	0.30
St. Petersburg (city) Pinellas	538	0.22
Oak Ridge (cdp) Orange	50	0.22
Brent (cdp) Escambia	41	0.18
Jacksonville (special city) Duval	1,064	0.14
South Bradenton (cdp) Manatee	30	0.14
Pinellas Park (city) Pinellas	58	0.13
Bayshore Gardens (cdp) Manatee	21	0.12
Lake Mary (city) Seminole	10	0.09
Meadow Woods (cdp) Orange	10	0.09

Asian: Chinese, except Taiwanese

Top 10 Places Sorted by Number
Based on all places, regardless of population

Place (place type) County	Number	%
Jacksonville (special city) Duval	1,879	0.26
Pembroke Pines (city) Broward	1,622	1.18
Gainesville (city) Alachua	1,411	1.48
Tallahassee (city) Leon	1,118	0.74
Coral Springs (city) Broward	1,092	0.93
Miami (city) Miami-Dade	1,021	0.28
Kendall (cdp) Miami-Dade	990	1.32
Tampa (city) Hillsborough	895	0.29
Orlando (city) Orange	873	0.47
Sunrise (city) Broward	832	0.97

Top 10 Places Sorted by Percent
Based on all places, regardless of population

Place (place type) County	Number	%
Godfrey Road (cdp) Broward	5	2.91
Ivanhoe Estates (cdp) Broward	8	2.87
Pinecrest (village) Miami-Dade	405	2.13
Doral (cdp) Miami-Dade	398	1.95
Country Walk (cdp) Miami-Dade	198	1.86
Pebble Creek (cdp) Hillsborough	83	1.72
Three Lakes (cdp) Miami-Dade	119	1.71
Doctor Phillips (cdp) Orange	162	1.70
North Miami Beach (city) Miami-Dade	677	1.66
The Crossings (cdp) Miami-Dade	382	1.62

Top 10 Places Sorted by Percent
Based on places with populations of 10,000 or more

Place (place type) County	Number	%
Pinecrest (village) Miami-Dade	405	2.13
Doral (cdp) Miami-Dade	398	1.95
Country Walk (cdp) Miami-Dade	198	1.86
North Miami Beach (city) Miami-Dade	677	1.66
The Crossings (cdp) Miami-Dade	382	1.62
The Hammocks (cdp) Miami-Dade	764	1.61
Cutler (cdp) Miami-Dade	271	1.56
Ives Estates (cdp) Miami-Dade	273	1.55
Gainesville (city) Alachua	1,411	1.48
Parkland (city) Broward	189	1.37

Asian: Filipino

Top 10 Places Sorted by Number
Based on all places, regardless of population

Place (place type) County	Number	%
Jacksonville (special city) Duval	12,295	1.67
Tampa (city) Hillsborough	1,450	0.48
Orlando (city) Orange	1,138	0.61
Pembroke Pines (city) Broward	1,062	0.77
St. Petersburg (city) Pinellas	1,030	0.41
Myrtle Grove (cdp) Escambia	683	3.97
Lakeside (cdp) Clay	659	2.13
Brandon (cdp) Hillsborough	602	0.77
Miramar (city) Broward	586	0.81
Bellview (cdp) Escambia	585	2.76

Top 10 Places Sorted by Percent
Based on all places, regardless of population

Place (place type) County	Number	%
Wedgefield (cdp) Orange	165	6.11
Myrtle Grove (cdp) Escambia	683	3.97
Highland Park (village) Polk	8	3.28
Southchase (cdp) Orange	146	3.15
Eglin AFB (cdp) Okaloosa	242	2.99
Bellview (cdp) Escambia	585	2.76
Tyndall AFB (cdp) Bay	75	2.72
Bellair-Meadowbrook Terrace (cdp) Clay	436	2.64
Lakeside (cdp) Clay	659	2.13
Mary Esther (city) Okaloosa	86	2.12

Top 10 Places Sorted by Percent
Based on places with populations of 10,000 or more

Place (place type) County	Number	%
Myrtle Grove (cdp) Escambia	683	3.97
Bellview (cdp) Escambia	585	2.76
Bellair-Meadowbrook Terrace (cdp) Clay	436	2.64
Lakeside (cdp) Clay	659	2.13
Wright (cdp) Okaloosa	418	1.93
Niceville (city) Okaloosa	224	1.92
Callaway (city) Bay	257	1.81
Crestview (city) Okaloosa	249	1.69
Jacksonville (special city) Duval	12,295	1.67
Atlantic Beach (city) Duval	221	1.65

Asian: Hmong

Top 10 Places Sorted by Number
Based on all places, regardless of population

Place (place type) County	Number	%
Clearwater (city) Pinellas	27	0.02
South Highpoint (cdp) Pinellas	14	0.16
Fort Myers Beach (town) Lee	10	0.15
Jacksonville (special city) Duval	10	0.00
Safety Harbor (city) Pinellas	8	0.05
Riverview (cdp) Hillsborough	6	0.05
Longwood (city) Seminole	6	0.04
Bloomingdale (cdp) Hillsborough	6	0.03
Orlando (city) Orange	5	0.00
Westchase (cdp) Hillsborough	4	0.04

Top 10 Places Sorted by Percent
Based on all places, regardless of population

Place (place type) County	Number	%
South Highpoint (cdp) Pinellas	14	0.16
Fort Myers Beach (town) Lee	10	0.15
Safety Harbor (city) Pinellas	8	0.05
Riverview (cdp) Hillsborough	6	0.05
Longwood (city) Seminole	6	0.04
Westchase (cdp) Hillsborough	4	0.04
Bloomingdale (cdp) Hillsborough	6	0.03
Dade City North (cdp) Pasco	1	0.03
Clearwater (city) Pinellas	27	0.02
Jan Phyl Village (cdp) Polk	1	0.02

Top 10 Places Sorted by Percent
Based on places with populations of 10,000 or more

Place (place type) County	Number	%
Safety Harbor (city) Pinellas	8	0.05
Riverview (cdp) Hillsborough	6	0.05
Longwood (city) Seminole	6	0.04
Westchase (cdp) Hillsborough	4	0.04
Bloomingdale (cdp) Hillsborough	6	0.03
Clearwater (city) Pinellas	27	0.02
Egypt Lake-Leto (cdp) Hillsborough	4	0.01
Winter Springs (city) Seminole	4	0.01

Notes: (cdp) census designated place; Refer to the User's Guide in the front of the book for more detailed information.

Place (place type) County	Number	%
North Miami (city) Miami-Dade	3	0.01
South Miami Heights (cdp) Miami-Dade	3	0.01

Asian: Indian

Top 10 Places Sorted by Number

Based on all places, regardless of population

Place (place type) County	Number	%
Jacksonville (special city) Duval	3,163	0.43
Pembroke Pines (city) Broward	2,237	1.63
Coral Springs (city) Broward	2,149	1.83
Tampa (city) Hillsborough	1,955	0.64
Orlando (city) Orange	1,464	0.79
Hollywood (city) Broward	1,410	1.01
Plantation (city) Broward	1,230	1.48
Sunrise (city) Broward	1,217	1.42
Gainesville (city) Alachua	1,185	1.24
Tallahassee (city) Leon	1,098	0.73

Top 10 Places Sorted by Percent

Based on all places, regardless of population

Place (place type) County	Number	%
Cloud Lake (town) Palm Beach	12	7.19
Bay Hill (cdp) Orange	303	5.85
Ivanhoe Estates (cdp) Broward	14	5.02
Golden Heights (cdp) Broward	20	3.99
Doctor Phillips (cdp) Orange	375	3.93
Black Diamond (cdp) Citrus	25	3.60
Gotha (cdp) Orange	23	3.15
Lake Harbor (cdp) Palm Beach	6	3.08
Hunters Creek (cdp) Orange	244	2.60
Southchase (cdp) Orange	107	2.31

Top 10 Places Sorted by Percent

Based on places with populations of 10,000 or more

Place (place type) County	Number	%
Palmetto Estates (cdp) Miami-Dade	301	2.20
Cooper City (city) Broward	545	1.95
Ives Estates (cdp) Miami-Dade	337	1.92
Coral Springs (city) Broward	2,149	1.83
Pembroke Pines (city) Broward	2,237	1.63
University (cdp) Hillsborough	470	1.53
South Miami Heights (cdp) Miami-Dade	511	1.52
Ocoee (city) Orange	368	1.51
Plantation (city) Broward	1,230	1.48
North Lauderdale (city) Broward	472	1.46

Asian: Indonesian

Top 10 Places Sorted by Number

Based on all places, regardless of population

Place (place type) County	Number	%
Jacksonville (special city) Duval	44	0.01
Tampa (city) Hillsborough	41	0.01
St. Petersburg (city) Pinellas	40	0.02
Miami (city) Miami-Dade	39	0.01
Miami Beach (city) Miami-Dade	28	0.03
Gainesville (city) Alachua	24	0.03
Coral Springs (city) Broward	24	0.02
Brandon (cdp) Hillsborough	19	0.02
Palm Bay (city) Brevard	19	0.02
Sunrise (city) Broward	19	0.02

Top 10 Places Sorted by Percent

Based on all places, regardless of population

Place (place type) County	Number	%
Leisureville (cdp) Broward	3	0.26
Ravenswood Estates (cdp) Broward	2	0.21
Green Meadow (cdp) Broward	3	0.16
Pine Manor (cdp) Lee	5	0.13
Sawgrass (cdp) St. Johns	6	0.12
Live Oak (city) Suwannee	7	0.11
Lake Mary (city) Seminole	10	0.09
Lely (cdp) Collier	3	0.08
Brent (cdp) Escambia	16	0.07
Temple Terrace (city) Hillsborough	14	0.07

Top 10 Places Sorted by Percent

Based on places with populations of 10,000 or more

Place (place type) County	Number	%
Lake Mary (city) Seminole	10	0.09
Brent (cdp) Escambia	16	0.07
Temple Terrace (city) Hillsborough	14	0.07
Ives Estates (cdp) Miami-Dade	13	0.07
Sunny Isles Beach (city) Miami-Dade	9	0.06
Union Park (cdp) Orange	6	0.06
Hallandale (city) Broward	16	0.05
Lutz (cdp) Hillsborough	9	0.05
Lockhart (cdp) Orange	6	0.05
University (cdp) Hillsborough	11	0.04

Asian: Japanese

Top 10 Places Sorted by Number

Based on all places, regardless of population

Place (place type) County	Number	%
Jacksonville (special city) Duval	930	0.13
Orlando (city) Orange	447	0.24
Tampa (city) Hillsborough	410	0.14
Tallahassee (city) Leon	306	0.20
St. Petersburg (city) Pinellas	296	0.12
Gainesville (city) Alachua	293	0.31
Kendall (cdp) Miami-Dade	196	0.26
Doral (cdp) Miami-Dade	193	0.94
Pembroke Pines (city) Broward	188	0.14
Melbourne (city) Brevard	177	0.25

Top 10 Places Sorted by Percent

Based on all places, regardless of population

Place (place type) County	Number	%
Fisher Island (cdp) Miami-Dade	6	1.28
Tyndall AFB (cdp) Bay	28	1.02
Doral (cdp) Miami-Dade	193	0.94
Westville (town) Holmes	2	0.90
Highland Park (village) Polk	2	0.82
North Beach (cdp) Indian River	2	0.82
Mary Esther (city) Okaloosa	32	0.79
Williamsburg (cdp) Orange	49	0.73
Eglin AFB (cdp) Okaloosa	53	0.66
Mission Bay (cdp) Palm Beach	19	0.65

Top 10 Places Sorted by Percent

Based on places with populations of 10,000 or more

Place (place type) County	Number	%
Doral (cdp) Miami-Dade	193	0.94
Niceville (city) Okaloosa	69	0.59
Wright (cdp) Okaloosa	118	0.54
Fort Walton Beach (city) Okaloosa	92	0.46
Callaway (city) Bay	58	0.41
Myrtle Grove (cdp) Escambia	68	0.40
The Crossings (cdp) Miami-Dade	91	0.39
Bellair-Meadowbrook Terrace (cdp) Clay	61	0.37
Union Park (cdp) Orange	36	0.35
Bellview (cdp) Escambia	73	0.34

Asian: Korean

Top 10 Places Sorted by Number

Based on all places, regardless of population

Place (place type) County	Number	%
Jacksonville (special city) Duval	1,366	0.19
Tampa (city) Hillsborough	772	0.25
Gainesville (city) Alachua	564	0.59
Orlando (city) Orange	524	0.28
Tallahassee (city) Leon	508	0.34
Town 'n' Country (cdp) Hillsborough	444	0.61
Pembroke Pines (city) Broward	428	0.31
St. Petersburg (city) Pinellas	393	0.16
Coral Springs (city) Broward	357	0.30
Brandon (cdp) Hillsborough	313	0.40

Top 10 Places Sorted by Percent

Based on all places, regardless of population

Place (place type) County	Number	%
Royal Palm Ranches (cdp) Broward	4	1.36
Forest City (cdp) Seminole	163	1.29
Tyndall AFB (cdp) Bay	33	1.20
Lake Lorraine (cdp) Okaloosa	75	1.06
Heathrow (cdp) Seminole	41	1.01
Bay Hill (cdp) Orange	48	0.93
Callaway (city) Bay	125	0.88
Niceville (city) Okaloosa	101	0.86
Black Diamond (cdp) Citrus	6	0.86
Wright (cdp) Okaloosa	182	0.84

Top 10 Places Sorted by Percent

Based on places with populations of 10,000 or more

Place (place type) County	Number	%
Forest City (cdp) Seminole	163	1.29
Callaway (city) Bay	125	0.88
Niceville (city) Okaloosa	101	0.86
Wright (cdp) Okaloosa	182	0.84
Citrus Park (cdp) Hillsborough	142	0.70
Greater Northdale (cdp) Hillsborough	139	0.68
Westchase (cdp) Hillsborough	69	0.62
Town 'n' Country (cdp) Hillsborough	444	0.61
Gainesville (city) Alachua	564	0.59
Crestview (city) Okaloosa	87	0.59

Asian: Laotian

Top 10 Places Sorted by Number

Based on all places, regardless of population

Place (place type) County	Number	%
St. Petersburg (city) Pinellas	1,178	0.47
Pinellas Park (city) Pinellas	296	0.65
Jacksonville (special city) Duval	273	0.04
West and East Lealman (cdp) Pinellas	120	0.55
Deltona (city) Volusia	73	0.10
Lake Park (town) Palm Beach	55	0.63
Oak Ridge (cdp) Orange	52	0.23
Clearwater (city) Pinellas	52	0.05
Bartow (city) Polk	42	0.27
North Fort Myers (cdp) Lee	42	0.10

Top 10 Places Sorted by Percent

Based on all places, regardless of population

Place (place type) County	Number	%
Pinellas Park (city) Pinellas	296	0.65
Lake Park (town) Palm Beach	55	0.63
West and East Lealman (cdp) Pinellas	120	0.55
St. Petersburg (city) Pinellas	1,178	0.47
South Highpoint (cdp) Pinellas	40	0.45
Fort Myers Shores (cdp) Lee	21	0.36
Olga (cdp) Lee	5	0.36
De Leon Springs (cdp) Volusia	8	0.34
Three Oaks (cdp) Lee	7	0.31
Crescent City (city) Putnam	5	0.28

Top 10 Places Sorted by Percent

Based on places with populations of 10,000 or more

Place (place type) County	Number	%
Pinellas Park (city) Pinellas	296	0.65
West and East Lealman (cdp) Pinellas	120	0.55
St. Petersburg (city) Pinellas	1,178	0.47
Bartow (city) Polk	42	0.27
Oak Ridge (cdp) Orange	52	0.23
Longwood (city) Seminole	28	0.20
Princeton (cdp) Miami-Dade	14	0.14
Leisure City (cdp) Miami-Dade	25	0.11

Notes: (cdp) census designated place; Refer to the User's Guide in the front of the book for more detailed information.

Place (place type) County	Number	%
Oldsmar (city) Pinellas	13	0.11
Deltona (city) Volusia	73	0.10

Asian: Malaysian

Top 10 Places Sorted by Number

Based on all places, regardless of population

Place (place type) County	Number	%
Jacksonville (special city) Duval	56	0.01
Gainesville (city) Alachua	21	0.02
St. Petersburg (city) Pinellas	12	0.00
Pinellas Park (city) Pinellas	11	0.02
Deltona (city) Volusia	10	0.01
Bellview (cdp) Escambia	9	0.04
Atlantic Beach (city) Duval	8	0.06
Tallahassee (city) Leon	8	0.01
Deerfield Beach (city) Broward	7	0.01
Hollywood (city) Broward	7	0.01

Top 10 Places Sorted by Percent

Based on all places, regardless of population

Place (place type) County	Number	%
Page Park (cdp) Lee	1	0.19
Wedgefield (cdp) Orange	4	0.15
Broadview Park (cdp) Broward	6	0.09
Bay Hill (cdp) Orange	4	0.08
Atlantic Beach (city) Duval	8	0.06
Gibsonton (cdp) Hillsborough	5	0.06
Arcadia (city) De Soto	4	0.06
Biscayne Park (village) Miami-Dade	2	0.06
Pompano Estates (cdp) Broward	2	0.06
South Miami (city) Miami-Dade	5	0.05

Top 10 Places Sorted by Percent

Based on places with populations of 10,000 or more

Place (place type) County	Number	%
Atlantic Beach (city) Duval	8	0.06
South Miami (city) Miami-Dade	5	0.05
Bellview (cdp) Escambia	9	0.04
Longwood (city) Seminole	5	0.04
Gainesville (city) Alachua	21	0.02
Pinellas Park (city) Pinellas	11	0.02
Key West (city) Monroe	5	0.02
Oak Ridge (cdp) Orange	4	0.02
Goldenrod (cdp) Seminole	3	0.02
Cocoa Beach (city) Brevard	2	0.02

Asian: Pakistani

Top 10 Places Sorted by Number

Based on all places, regardless of population

Place (place type) County	Number	%
Pembroke Pines (city) Broward	307	0.22
Coral Springs (city) Broward	239	0.20
Orlando (city) Orange	190	0.10
Sunrise (city) Broward	187	0.22
Kissimmee (city) Osceola	178	0.37
Hollywood (city) Broward	166	0.12
Kendale Lakes (cdp) Miami-Dade	158	0.28
Davie (town) Broward	155	0.20
Kendall (cdp) Miami-Dade	153	0.20
Tampa (city) Hillsborough	150	0.05

Top 10 Places Sorted by Percent

Based on all places, regardless of population

Place (place type) County	Number	%
Jupiter Island (town) Martin	8	1.29
Bay Hill (cdp) Orange	62	1.20
Roseland (cdp) Indian River	16	0.90
Doctor Phillips (cdp) Orange	53	0.56
Ives Estates (cdp) Miami-Dade	93	0.53
Green Meadow (cdp) Broward	10	0.53
Hunters Creek (cdp) Orange	48	0.51
Southchase (cdp) Orange	20	0.43
Ravenswood Estates (cdp) Broward	4	0.42
Kissimmee (city) Osceola	178	0.37

Top 10 Places Sorted by Percent

Based on places with populations of 10,000 or more

Place (place type) County	Number	%
Ives Estates (cdp) Miami-Dade	93	0.53
Kissimmee (city) Osceola	178	0.37
Kendale Lakes (cdp) Miami-Dade	158	0.28
The Crossings (cdp) Miami-Dade	64	0.27
Westwood Lakes (cdp) Miami-Dade	32	0.27
Miami Lakes (cdp) Miami-Dade	60	0.26
The Hammocks (cdp) Miami-Dade	120	0.25
Country Club (cdp) Miami-Dade	89	0.25
Glenvar Heights (cdp) Miami-Dade	37	0.23
Pembroke Pines (city) Broward	307	0.22

Asian: Sri Lankan

Top 10 Places Sorted by Number

Based on all places, regardless of population

Place (place type) County	Number	%
Jacksonville (special city) Duval	27	0.00
Orlando (city) Orange	21	0.01
University (cdp) Hillsborough	19	0.06
Daytona Beach (city) Volusia	19	0.03
Coral Springs (city) Broward	18	0.02
Boca Raton (city) Palm Beach	17	0.02
Gainesville (city) Alachua	16	0.02
Lakeland (city) Polk	16	0.02
Kissimmee (city) Osceola	13	0.03
Tampa (city) Hillsborough	13	0.00

Top 10 Places Sorted by Percent

Based on all places, regardless of population

Place (place type) County	Number	%
Hillsboro Pines (cdp) Broward	1	0.25
Pebble Creek (cdp) Hillsborough	8	0.17
Bonnie Lock-Woodsetter North (cdp) Broward	7	0.16
Tedder (cdp) Broward	3	0.14
Juno Ridge (cdp) Palm Beach	1	0.13
Babson Park (cdp) Polk	1	0.08
Osprey (cdp) Sarasota	3	0.07
Ramblewood East (cdp) Broward	1	0.07
University (cdp) Hillsborough	19	0.06
South Beach (cdp) Indian River	2	0.06

Top 10 Places Sorted by Percent

Based on places with populations of 10,000 or more

Place (place type) County	Number	%
University (cdp) Hillsborough	19	0.06
Port Salerno (cdp) Martin	5	0.05
Bellair-Meadowbrook Terrace (cdp) Clay	7	0.04
Glenvar Heights (cdp) Miami-Dade	7	0.04
Sandalfoot Cove (cdp) Palm Beach	6	0.04
Atlantic Beach (city) Duval	5	0.04
Daytona Beach (city) Volusia	19	0.03
Kissimmee (city) Osceola	13	0.03
Wellington (village) Palm Beach	10	0.03
Greater Carrollwood (cdp) Hillsborough	9	0.03

Asian: Taiwanese

Top 10 Places Sorted by Number

Based on all places, regardless of population

Place (place type) County	Number	%
Tallahassee (city) Leon	106	0.07
Jacksonville (special city) Duval	96	0.01
Gainesville (city) Alachua	87	0.09
Tampa (city) Hillsborough	66	0.02
Coral Springs (city) Broward	47	0.04
Davie (town) Broward	45	0.06
Pembroke Pines (city) Broward	45	0.03
Miami (city) Miami-Dade	33	0.01
Temple Terrace (city) Hillsborough	32	0.15
Plantation (city) Broward	30	0.04

Top 10 Places Sorted by Percent

Based on all places, regardless of population

Place (place type) County	Number	%
Godfrey Road (cdp) Broward	2	1.16
Cinco Bayou (town) Okaloosa	2	0.53
Hunters Creek (cdp) Orange	23	0.25
Carrabelle (city) Franklin	3	0.23
Mission Bay (cdp) Palm Beach	6	0.21
Bagdad (cdp) Santa Rosa	3	0.20
Wesley Chapel (cdp) Pasco	11	0.19
Big Coppitt Key (cdp) Monroe	5	0.19
Pebble Creek (cdp) Hillsborough	8	0.17
Green Meadow (cdp) Broward	3	0.16

Top 10 Places Sorted by Percent

Based on places with populations of 10,000 or more

Place (place type) County	Number	%
Temple Terrace (city) Hillsborough	32	0.15
Pinecrest (village) Miami-Dade	24	0.13
Conway (cdp) Orange	19	0.13
Meadow Woods (cdp) Orange	13	0.12
Gainesville (city) Alachua	87	0.09
Doral (cdp) Miami-Dade	19	0.09
Miami Shores (village) Miami-Dade	9	0.09
Keystone (cdp) Hillsborough	12	0.08
Citrus Ridge (cdp) Lake	10	0.08
Tallahassee (city) Leon	106	0.07

Asian: Thai

Top 10 Places Sorted by Number

Based on all places, regardless of population

Place (place type) County	Number	%
Tampa (city) Hillsborough	376	0.12
Jacksonville (special city) Duval	271	0.04
Wright (cdp) Okaloosa	193	0.89
St. Petersburg (city) Pinellas	191	0.08
Melbourne (city) Brevard	158	0.22
Brandon (cdp) Hillsborough	140	0.18
Fort Walton Beach (city) Okaloosa	133	0.67
Gainesville (city) Alachua	121	0.13
Orlando (city) Orange	112	0.06
Fort Lauderdale (city) Broward	104	0.07

Top 10 Places Sorted by Percent

Based on all places, regardless of population

Place (place type) County	Number	%
Ocean City (cdp) Okaloosa	64	1.14
Wright (cdp) Okaloosa	193	0.89
Mary Esther (city) Okaloosa	31	0.76
Fort Walton Beach (city) Okaloosa	133	0.67
Palm Shores (town) Brevard	5	0.63
Springfield (city) Bay	48	0.54
Callaway (city) Bay	76	0.53
Lake Lorraine (cdp) Okaloosa	38	0.53
Cinco Bayou (town) Okaloosa	2	0.53
Niceville (city) Okaloosa	60	0.51

Top 10 Places Sorted by Percent

Based on places with populations of 10,000 or more

Place (place type) County	Number	%
Wright (cdp) Okaloosa	193	0.89
Fort Walton Beach (city) Okaloosa	133	0.67
Callaway (city) Bay	76	0.53
Niceville (city) Okaloosa	60	0.51
Crestview (city) Okaloosa	36	0.24
Destin (city) Okaloosa	27	0.24
Wilton Manors (city) Broward	29	0.23
Palm Springs (village) Palm Beach	27	0.23

Notes: (cdp) census designated place; Refer to the User's Guide in the front of the book for more detailed information.

Melbourne (city) Brevard	158	0.22
Pinecrest (village) Miami-Dade	42	0.22

Asian: Vietnamese

Top 10 Places Sorted by Number
Based on all places, regardless of population

Place (place type) County	Number	%
Jacksonville (special city) Duval	2,566	0.35
St. Petersburg (city) Pinellas	2,108	0.85
Tampa (city) Hillsborough	1,677	0.55
Orlando (city) Orange	939	0.50
Pinellas Park (city) Pinellas	839	1.84
Town 'n' Country (cdp) Hillsborough	807	1.11
Oak Ridge (cdp) Orange	706	3.16
Pine Hills (cdp) Orange	646	1.55
West and East Lealman (cdp) Pinellas	584	2.68
Egypt Lake-Leto (cdp) Hillsborough	458	1.40

Top 10 Places Sorted by Percent
Based on all places, regardless of population

Place (place type) County	Number	%
Oak Ridge (cdp) Orange	706	3.16
Springfield (city) Bay	254	2.88
Kenneth City (town) Pinellas	124	2.82
West and East Lealman (cdp) Pinellas	584	2.68
Village Park (cdp) Broward	22	2.46
Southchase (cdp) Orange	97	2.09
West Pensacola (cdp) Escambia	412	1.88
South Highpoint (cdp) Pinellas	164	1.86
Pinellas Park (city) Pinellas	839	1.84
Orlovista (cdp) Orange	97	1.60

Top 10 Places Sorted by Percent
Based on places with populations of 10,000 or more

Place (place type) County	Number	%
Oak Ridge (cdp) Orange	706	3.16
West and East Lealman (cdp) Pinellas	584	2.68
West Pensacola (cdp) Escambia	412	1.88
Pinellas Park (city) Pinellas	839	1.84
Azalea Park (cdp) Orange	174	1.57
Pine Hills (cdp) Orange	646	1.55
Fairview Shores (cdp) Orange	213	1.53
Egypt Lake-Leto (cdp) Hillsborough	458	1.40
North Lauderdale (city) Broward	360	1.12
Town 'n' Country (cdp) Hillsborough	807	1.11

Asian: Other Asian, specified

Top 10 Places Sorted by Number
Based on all places, regardless of population

Place (place type) County	Number	%
Jacksonville (special city) Duval	152	0.02
Tampa (city) Hillsborough	45	0.01
Tallahassee (city) Leon	38	0.03
Orlando (city) Orange	34	0.02
St. Petersburg (city) Pinellas	34	0.01
Miami (city) Miami-Dade	26	0.01
Gainesville (city) Alachua	23	0.02
Coral Springs (city) Broward	19	0.02
Deerfield Beach (city) Broward	17	0.03
Plantation (city) Broward	16	0.02

Top 10 Places Sorted by Percent
Based on all places, regardless of population

Place (place type) County	Number	%
De Leon Springs (cdp) Volusia	6	0.25
Willow Oak (cdp) Polk	10	0.20
West De Land (cdp) Volusia	7	0.20
Manattee Road (cdp) Levy	3	0.15
North Brooksville (cdp) Hernando	2	0.14
Lake Clarke Shores (town) Palm Beach	4	0.12
El Portal (village) Miami-Dade	3	0.12
Malabar (town) Brevard	3	0.11
Wabasso (cdp) Indian River	1	0.11
Southeast Arcadia (cdp) De Soto	6	0.10

Top 10 Places Sorted by Percent
Based on places with populations of 10,000 or more

Place (place type) County	Number	%
Iona (cdp) Lee	9	0.08
Palm Springs (village) Palm Beach	9	0.08
Westchase (cdp) Hillsborough	9	0.08
Key Largo (cdp) Monroe	8	0.07
Wilton Manors (city) Broward	7	0.06
Key West (city) Monroe	14	0.05
Palm Valley (cdp) St. Johns	10	0.05
Fort Walton Beach (city) Okaloosa	9	0.05
Jensen Beach (cdp) Martin	5	0.05
Cocoa (city) Brevard	7	0.04

Asian: Other Asian, not specified

Top 10 Places Sorted by Number
Based on all places, regardless of population

Place (place type) County	Number	%
Jacksonville (special city) Duval	1,110	0.15
Tampa (city) Hillsborough	441	0.15
St. Petersburg (city) Pinellas	407	0.16
Orlando (city) Orange	368	0.20
Miami (city) Miami-Dade	298	0.08
Pembroke Pines (city) Broward	268	0.20
Tallahassee (city) Leon	237	0.16
Fort Lauderdale (city) Broward	176	0.12
Coral Springs (city) Broward	175	0.15
Gainesville (city) Alachua	167	0.17

Top 10 Places Sorted by Percent
Based on all places, regardless of population

Place (place type) County	Number	%
Lake Harbor (cdp) Palm Beach	2	1.03
Hillcrest Heights (town) Polk	2	0.75
Glen Ridge (town) Palm Beach	2	0.72
Doctor Phillips (cdp) Orange	65	0.68
Homestead Base (cdp) Miami-Dade	3	0.67
Fisher Island (cdp) Miami-Dade	3	0.64
Windermere (town) Orange	11	0.58
Midway (cdp) Seminole	10	0.58
Christmas (cdp) Orange	6	0.52
Leisureville (cdp) Broward	6	0.52

Top 10 Places Sorted by Percent
Based on places with populations of 10,000 or more

Place (place type) County	Number	%
Ives Estates (cdp) Miami-Dade	69	0.39
North Miami Beach (city) Miami-Dade	128	0.31
Oak Ridge (cdp) Orange	68	0.30
Bellair-Meadowbrook Terrace (cdp) Clay	49	0.30
Wright (cdp) Okaloosa	61	0.28
The Crossings (cdp) Miami-Dade	62	0.26
Greater Northdale (cdp) Hillsborough	52	0.25
Kissimmee (city) Osceola	116	0.24
Pine Hills (cdp) Orange	100	0.24
Altamonte Springs (city) Seminole	99	0.24

Assyrian/Chaldean/Syriac

Top 10 Places Sorted by Number
Based on all places, regardless of population

Place (place type) County	Number	%
North Miami Beach (city) Miami-Dade	75	0.18
Big Pine Key (cdp) Monroe	38	0.75
Jacksonville (special city) Duval	29	0.00
St. Augustine Shores (cdp) St. Johns	18	0.35
Jupiter (town) Palm Beach	16	0.04
Ferry Pass (cdp) Escambia	14	0.05
Pompano Beach (city) Broward	12	0.02
Hialeah (city) Miami-Dade	10	0.00
Englewood (cdp) Sarasota	9	0.06
Titusville (city) Brevard	9	0.02

Top 10 Places Sorted by Percent
Based on all places, regardless of population

Place (place type) County	Number	%
Big Pine Key (cdp) Monroe	38	0.75
St. Augustine Shores (cdp) St. Johns	18	0.35
North Miami Beach (city) Miami-Dade	75	0.18
Juno Beach (town) Palm Beach	5	0.16
Ponce Inlet (town) Volusia	4	0.16
Perry (city) Taylor	7	0.10
Gifford (cdp) Indian River	7	0.09
Englewood (cdp) Sarasota	9	0.06
Lakewood Park (cdp) St. Lucie	6	0.06
Ferry Pass (cdp) Escambia	14	0.05

Top 10 Places Sorted by Percent
Based on places with populations of 10,000 or more

Place (place type) County	Number	%
North Miami Beach (city) Miami-Dade	75	0.18
Englewood (cdp) Sarasota	9	0.06
Lakewood Park (cdp) St. Lucie	6	0.06
Ferry Pass (cdp) Escambia	14	0.05
Greater Sun Center (cdp) Hillsborough	8	0.05
Marco Island (city) Collier	8	0.05
Jupiter (town) Palm Beach	16	0.04
Rockledge (city) Brevard	8	0.04
Pompano Beach (city) Broward	12	0.02
Titusville (city) Brevard	9	0.02

Australian

Top 10 Places Sorted by Number
Based on all places, regardless of population

Place (place type) County	Number	%
Jacksonville (special city) Duval	137	0.02
Fort Lauderdale (city) Broward	94	0.06
Miami (city) Miami-Dade	94	0.03
Tallahassee (city) Leon	86	0.06
St. Petersburg (city) Pinellas	84	0.03
Clearwater (city) Pinellas	70	0.06
West Palm Beach (city) Palm Beach	64	0.08
Tampa (city) Hillsborough	64	0.02
Orlando (city) Orange	63	0.03
Hollywood (city) Broward	61	0.04

Top 10 Places Sorted by Percent
Based on all places, regardless of population

Place (place type) County	Number	%
Molino (cdp) Escambia	23	1.62
Atlantis (city) Palm Beach	26	1.22
Cudjoe Key (cdp) Monroe	21	1.21
Tyndall AFB (cdp) Bay	23	0.83
Sunshine Acres (cdp) Broward	8	0.76
Tierra Verde (cdp) Pinellas	22	0.62
North Key Largo (cdp) Monroe	6	0.59
Fort Myers Shores (cdp) Lee	33	0.57
Apollo Beach (cdp) Hillsborough	41	0.55
Samsula-Spruce Creek (cdp) Volusia	23	0.47

Top 10 Places Sorted by Percent
Based on places with populations of 10,000 or more

Place (place type) County	Number	%
Lake Mary (city) Seminole	38	0.34
Key Biscayne (village) Miami-Dade	35	0.33
Wright (cdp) Okaloosa	59	0.27
Fairview Shores (cdp) Orange	30	0.22
Palm Valley (cdp) St. Johns	41	0.21
Destin (city) Okaloosa	21	0.19
Ferry Pass (cdp) Escambia	47	0.17
Poinciana (cdp) Osceola	22	0.16

Notes: (cdp) census designated place; Refer to the User's Guide in the front of the book for more detailed information.

St. Augustine (city) St. Johns	17	0.15
East Lake (cdp) Pinellas	37	0.13

Austrian

Top 10 Places Sorted by Number

Based on all places, regardless of population

Place (place type) County	Number	%
Jacksonville (special city) Duval	1,086	0.15
St. Petersburg (city) Pinellas	931	0.38
Tamarac (city) Broward	862	1.54
Pembroke Pines (city) Broward	837	0.61
Coral Springs (city) Broward	821	0.70
Miami Beach (city) Miami-Dade	816	0.93
Fort Lauderdale (city) Broward	816	0.54
Hollywood (city) Broward	790	0.57
Boca Raton (city) Palm Beach	786	1.04
Plantation (city) Broward	735	0.88

Top 10 Places Sorted by Percent

Based on all places, regardless of population

Place (place type) County	Number	%
Indian Creek (village) Miami-Dade	2	5.88
Oak Point (cdp) Broward	9	5.70
Highland Beach (town) Palm Beach	152	4.21
Golf (village) Palm Beach	10	4.18
High Point (cdp) Palm Beach	83	3.76
Villages of Oriole (cdp) Palm Beach	174	3.67
Hamptons at Boca Raton (cdp) Palm Beach	391	3.42
Kings Point (cdp) Palm Beach	420	3.39
Boca Pointe (cdp) Palm Beach	106	3.21
Burnt Store Marina (cdp) Lee	34	2.81

Top 10 Places Sorted by Percent

Based on places with populations of 10,000 or more

Place (place type) County	Number	%
Hamptons at Boca Raton (cdp) Palm Beach	391	3.42
Kings Point (cdp) Palm Beach	420	3.39
Palm Beach (town) Palm Beach	224	2.16
Pinecrest (village) Miami-Dade	351	1.83
Aventura (city) Miami-Dade	422	1.67
Tamarac (city) Broward	862	1.54
Hallandale (city) Broward	490	1.42
Boca Del Mar (cdp) Palm Beach	281	1.31
Sandalfoot Cove (cdp) Palm Beach	210	1.27
Coconut Creek (city) Broward	491	1.13

Basque

Top 10 Places Sorted by Number

Based on all places, regardless of population

Place (place type) County	Number	%
Miami (city) Miami-Dade	118	0.03
Cutler (cdp) Miami-Dade	96	0.54
Coral Gables (city) Miami-Dade	82	0.19
Miami Beach (city) Miami-Dade	77	0.09
Tampa (city) Hillsborough	76	0.03
Doral (cdp) Miami-Dade	69	0.34
Kendall (cdp) Miami-Dade	69	0.09
Fort Lauderdale (city) Broward	59	0.04
Jacksonville (special city) Duval	49	0.01
Port St. Lucie (city) St. Lucie	45	0.05

Top 10 Places Sorted by Percent

Based on all places, regardless of population

Place (place type) County	Number	%
Fisher Island (cdp) Miami-Dade	6	1.77
Madison (city) Madison	20	0.61
Cutler (cdp) Miami-Dade	96	0.54
Ocean Ridge (town) Palm Beach	6	0.37
Doral (cdp) Miami-Dade	69	0.34
Key Biscayne (village) Miami-Dade	35	0.33
Lake Clarke Shores (town) Palm Beach	11	0.31
Three Lakes (cdp) Miami-Dade	16	0.23
Belleview (city) Marion	8	0.23
Harbour Heights (cdp) Charlotte	7	0.23

Top 10 Places Sorted by Percent

Based on places with populations of 10,000 or more

Place (place type) County	Number	%
Cutler (cdp) Miami-Dade	96	0.54
Doral (cdp) Miami-Dade	69	0.34
Key Biscayne (village) Miami-Dade	35	0.33
Coral Gables (city) Miami-Dade	82	0.19
Glenvar Heights (cdp) Miami-Dade	31	0.19
Fernandina Beach (city) Nassau	14	0.14
Winter Park (city) Orange	31	0.13
Marco Island (city) Collier	19	0.13
Westchester (cdp) Miami-Dade	32	0.11
Wilton Manors (city) Broward	14	0.11

Belgian

Top 10 Places Sorted by Number

Based on all places, regardless of population

Place (place type) County	Number	%
Jacksonville (special city) Duval	645	0.09
St. Petersburg (city) Pinellas	269	0.11
Miami Beach (city) Miami-Dade	201	0.23
Cape Coral (city) Lee	160	0.16
Fort Lauderdale (city) Broward	153	0.10
Fort Pierce (city) St. Lucie	146	0.39
Orlando (city) Orange	144	0.08
Tallahassee (city) Leon	134	0.09
Brandon (cdp) Hillsborough	132	0.17
Spring Hill (cdp) Hernando	128	0.18

Top 10 Places Sorted by Percent

Based on all places, regardless of population

Place (place type) County	Number	%
Sunshine Acres (cdp) Broward	25	2.38
Riverland Village (cdp) Broward	30	1.46
Lochmoor Waterway Estates (cdp) Lee	49	1.27
Weeki Wachee Gardens (cdp) Hernando	13	1.12
Celebration (cdp) Osceola	27	0.98
Estates of Fort Lauderdale (cdp) Broward	18	0.98
Ocean Breeze Park (town) Martin	4	0.89
Cudjoe Key (cdp) Monroe	15	0.86
Palmona Park (cdp) Lee	10	0.78
Osprey (cdp) Sarasota	31	0.75

Top 10 Places Sorted by Percent

Based on places with populations of 10,000 or more

Place (place type) County	Number	%
South Venice (cdp) Sarasota	89	0.66
South Miami (city) Miami-Dade	67	0.61
Cypress Lake (cdp) Lee	73	0.60
Atlantic Beach (city) Duval	77	0.57
Port St. John (cdp) Brevard	62	0.52
Zephyrhills (city) Pasco	55	0.51
Jensen Beach (cdp) Martin	56	0.50
Lake Mary (city) Seminole	54	0.48
Englewood (cdp) Sarasota	76	0.47
Land O' Lakes (cdp) Pasco	93	0.45

Brazilian

Top 10 Places Sorted by Number

Based on all places, regardless of population

Place (place type) County	Number	%
Deerfield Beach (city) Broward	2,307	3.56
Miami Beach (city) Miami-Dade	1,949	2.21
Orlando (city) Orange	1,355	0.73
Pompano Beach (city) Broward	919	1.17
Fort Lauderdale (city) Broward	917	0.60
Coral Springs (city) Broward	901	0.77
Miami (city) Miami-Dade	802	0.22
Boca Raton (city) Palm Beach	788	1.04
Pembroke Pines (city) Broward	751	0.55
Hollywood (city) Broward	731	0.52

Top 10 Places Sorted by Percent

Based on all places, regardless of population

Place (place type) County	Number	%
Loch Lomond (cdp) Broward	469	14.12
Indian Creek (village) Miami-Dade	4	11.76
North Bay Village (city) Miami-Dade	419	6.22
Bonnie Lock-Woodsetter North (cdp) Broward	238	5.52
Deerfield Beach (city) Broward	2,307	3.56
Pompano Beach Highlands (cdp) Broward	178	2.74
Doral (cdp) Miami-Dade	535	2.61
Palm Aire (cdp) Broward	34	2.60
Country Estates (cdp) Broward	48	2.58
Kendall Green (cdp) Broward	73	2.32

Top 10 Places Sorted by Percent

Based on places with populations of 10,000 or more

Place (place type) County	Number	%
Deerfield Beach (city) Broward	2,307	3.56
Doral (cdp) Miami-Dade	535	2.61
Oakland Park (city) Broward	704	2.26
Miami Beach (city) Miami-Dade	1,949	2.21
Sandalfoot Cove (cdp) Palm Beach	340	2.05
Aventura (city) Miami-Dade	463	1.83
Key Biscayne (village) Miami-Dade	180	1.72
Ojus (cdp) Miami-Dade	268	1.61
The Crossings (cdp) Miami-Dade	362	1.54
Sunny Isles Beach (city) Miami-Dade	222	1.45

British

Top 10 Places Sorted by Number

Based on all places, regardless of population

Place (place type) County	Number	%
Jacksonville (special city) Duval	3,160	0.43
St. Petersburg (city) Pinellas	1,607	0.65
Tampa (city) Hillsborough	1,535	0.51
Tallahassee (city) Leon	1,136	0.75
Orlando (city) Orange	1,080	0.58
Fort Lauderdale (city) Broward	882	0.58
Clearwater (city) Pinellas	877	0.81
Gainesville (city) Alachua	759	0.79
Melbourne (city) Brevard	656	0.92
Coral Springs (city) Broward	653	0.56

Top 10 Places Sorted by Percent

Based on all places, regardless of population

Place (place type) County	Number	%
Pineland (cdp) Lee	26	5.49
Jupiter Island (town) Martin	26	4.19
Indian River Shores (town) Indian River	133	4.04
Golf (village) Palm Beach	9	3.77
Taft (cdp) Orange	64	3.34
Homosassa (cdp) Citrus	75	3.31
Wabasso Beach (cdp) Indian River	35	3.13
La Crosse (town) Alachua	4	3.08
Cedar Key (city) Levy	23	2.97
Belleair (town) Pinellas	114	2.80

Top 10 Places Sorted by Percent

Based on places with populations of 10,000 or more

Place (place type) County	Number	%
Lighthouse Point (city) Broward	173	1.62
Citrus Ridge (cdp) Lake	175	1.53
Winter Park (city) Orange	348	1.44
Vero Beach (city) Indian River	239	1.34
Pinecrest (village) Miami-Dade	249	1.30
Sunny Isles Beach (city) Miami-Dade	189	1.24
Punta Gorda (city) Charlotte	176	1.22
Wekiwa Springs (cdp) Seminole	275	1.18

Notes: (cdp) census designated place; Refer to the User's Guide in the front of the book for more detailed information.

Oviedo (city) Seminole	307	1.14
Naples (city) Collier	238	1.13

Bulgarian

Top 10 Places Sorted by Number

Based on all places, regardless of population

Place (place type) County	Number	%
St. Petersburg (city) Pinellas	268	0.11
Greater Carrollwood (cdp) Hillsborough	129	0.38
Miami Beach (city) Miami-Dade	91	0.10
Fort Lauderdale (city) Broward	85	0.06
Gainesville (city) Alachua	80	0.08
Boca Raton (city) Palm Beach	75	0.10
Miami (city) Miami-Dade	74	0.02
Tampa (city) Hillsborough	61	0.02
Clearwater (city) Pinellas	58	0.05
Hollywood (city) Broward	58	0.04

Top 10 Places Sorted by Percent

Based on all places, regardless of population

Place (place type) County	Number	%
Chambers Estates (cdp) Broward	42	1.18
Burnt Store Marina (cdp) Lee	11	0.91
Solana (cdp) Charlotte	6	0.61
Manattee Road (cdp) Levy	10	0.47
Country Estates (cdp) Broward	8	0.43
Trinity (cdp) Pasco	19	0.42
Greater Carrollwood (cdp) Hillsborough	129	0.38
Marathon (city) Monroe	37	0.36
Bal Harbour (village) Miami-Dade	12	0.36
North Redington Beach (town) Pinellas	5	0.36

Top 10 Places Sorted by Percent

Based on places with populations of 10,000 or more

Place (place type) County	Number	%
Greater Carrollwood (cdp) Hillsborough	129	0.38
Marathon (city) Monroe	37	0.36
Palm Springs (village) Palm Beach	35	0.30
Maitland (city) Orange	30	0.25
Winter Garden (city) Orange	33	0.24
Sunny Isles Beach (city) Miami-Dade	34	0.22
Apopka (city) Orange	55	0.21
New Port Richey (city) Pasco	29	0.18
Gulf Gate Estates (cdp) Sarasota	21	0.18
Meadow Woods (cdp) Orange	20	0.17

Canadian

Top 10 Places Sorted by Number

Based on all places, regardless of population

Place (place type) County	Number	%
Jacksonville (special city) Duval	1,400	0.19
Hollywood (city) Broward	1,156	0.83
St. Petersburg (city) Pinellas	963	0.39
Deerfield Beach (city) Broward	708	1.09
Largo (city) Pinellas	699	1.01
Fort Lauderdale (city) Broward	655	0.43
Coral Springs (city) Broward	599	0.51
Boca Raton (city) Palm Beach	582	0.77
Clearwater (city) Pinellas	570	0.53
Pembroke Pines (city) Broward	544	0.40

Top 10 Places Sorted by Percent

Based on all places, regardless of population

Place (place type) County	Number	%
Ravenswood Estates (cdp) Broward	100	10.72
Village Park (cdp) Broward	82	7.56
North Beach (cdp) Indian River	12	5.43
Dunes Road (cdp) Palm Beach	20	4.23
Estates of Fort Lauderdale (cdp) Broward	66	3.58
Andrews (cdp) Levy	23	3.05
Pembroke Park (town) Broward	191	3.01
Hypoluxo (town) Palm Beach	58	2.87
Orangetree (cdp) Collier	27	2.62
Layton (city) Monroe	6	2.50

Top 10 Places Sorted by Percent

Based on places with populations of 10,000 or more

Place (place type) County	Number	%
Englewood (cdp) Sarasota	244	1.50
Hallandale (city) Broward	475	1.37
North Palm Beach (village) Palm Beach	153	1.26
East Lake (cdp) Pinellas	369	1.25
Hudson (cdp) Pasco	149	1.17
Deerfield Beach (city) Broward	708	1.09
Dunedin (city) Pinellas	374	1.04
Holiday (cdp) Pasco	227	1.04
Largo (city) Pinellas	699	1.01
Venice (city) Sarasota	179	1.00

Carpatho Rusyn

Top 10 Places Sorted by Number

Based on all places, regardless of population

Place (place type) County	Number	%
Orlando (city) Orange	17	0.01
Port St. Lucie (city) St. Lucie	16	0.02
Hobe Sound (cdp) Martin	15	0.13
Roseland (cdp) Indian River	11	0.61
Coral Springs (city) Broward	11	0.01
Fort Lauderdale (city) Broward	10	0.01
Country Club (cdp) Miami-Dade	9	0.02
Gifford (cdp) Indian River	8	0.11
Tallahassee (city) Leon	8	0.01
Jacksonville (special city) Duval	8	0.00

Top 10 Places Sorted by Percent

Based on all places, regardless of population

Place (place type) County	Number	%
Roseland (cdp) Indian River	11	0.61
Briny Breezes (town) Palm Beach	2	0.48
Hobe Sound (cdp) Martin	15	0.13
Gifford (cdp) Indian River	8	0.11
Winter Garden (city) Orange	7	0.05
Doral (cdp) Miami-Dade	7	0.03
Port St. Lucie (city) St. Lucie	16	0.02
Country Club (cdp) Miami-Dade	9	0.02
Orlando (city) Orange	17	0.01
Coral Springs (city) Broward	11	0.01

Top 10 Places Sorted by Percent

Based on places with populations of 10,000 or more

Place (place type) County	Number	%
Hobe Sound (cdp) Martin	15	0.13
Winter Garden (city) Orange	7	0.05
Doral (cdp) Miami-Dade	7	0.03
Port St. Lucie (city) St. Lucie	16	0.02
Country Club (cdp) Miami-Dade	9	0.02
Orlando (city) Orange	17	0.01
Coral Springs (city) Broward	11	0.01
Fort Lauderdale (city) Broward	10	0.01
Tallahassee (city) Leon	8	0.01
Spring Hill (cdp) Hernando	7	0.01

Celtic

Top 10 Places Sorted by Number

Based on all places, regardless of population

Place (place type) County	Number	%
Jacksonville (special city) Duval	195	0.03
Tallahassee (city) Leon	125	0.08
Tampa (city) Hillsborough	111	0.04
Gainesville (city) Alachua	86	0.09
Callaway (city) Bay	64	0.45
Chuluota (cdp) Seminole	58	2.92
Melbourne (city) Brevard	44	0.06
West Bradenton (cdp) Manatee	41	0.91
St. Petersburg (city) Pinellas	41	0.02
Clearwater (city) Pinellas	39	0.04

Top 10 Places Sorted by Percent

Based on all places, regardless of population

Place (place type) County	Number	%
Chuluota (cdp) Seminole	58	2.92
St. Leo (town) Pasco	12	1.97
Jay (town) Santa Rosa	6	1.10
South Beach (cdp) Indian River	32	0.94
West Bradenton (cdp) Manatee	41	0.91
Melbourne Village (town) Brevard	6	0.89
St. George (cdp) Broward	19	0.79
Bradenton Beach (city) Manatee	9	0.61
Manasota Key (cdp) Charlotte	8	0.61
North Key Largo (cdp) Monroe	5	0.49

Top 10 Places Sorted by Percent

Based on places with populations of 10,000 or more

Place (place type) County	Number	%
Callaway (city) Bay	64	0.45
St. Augustine (city) St. Johns	31	0.27
Lakeland Highlands (cdp) Polk	32	0.25
Leesburg (city) Lake	31	0.20
Lockhart (cdp) Orange	21	0.17
Holly Hill (city) Volusia	18	0.15
Fruit Cove (cdp) St. Johns	16	0.10
Palmetto (city) Manatee	12	0.10
Lake Wales (city) Polk	10	0.10
Gainesville (city) Alachua	86	0.09

Croatian

Top 10 Places Sorted by Number

Based on all places, regardless of population

Place (place type) County	Number	%
Jacksonville (special city) Duval	659	0.09
Cape Coral (city) Lee	298	0.29
St. Petersburg (city) Pinellas	284	0.11
Tampa (city) Hillsborough	247	0.08
Palm Harbor (cdp) Pinellas	216	0.37
Largo (city) Pinellas	178	0.26
Orlando (city) Orange	145	0.08
Pinellas Park (city) Pinellas	138	0.30
Port Orange (city) Volusia	131	0.29
Hollywood (city) Broward	121	0.09

Top 10 Places Sorted by Percent

Based on all places, regardless of population

Place (place type) County	Number	%
North Redington Beach (town) Pinellas	24	1.75
Feather Sound (cdp) Pinellas	51	1.24
Harbour Heights (cdp) Charlotte	31	1.04
Pine Castle (cdp) Orange	77	0.94
Terra Mar (cdp) Broward	23	0.86
Holmes Beach (city) Manatee	42	0.85
Rio (cdp) Martin	9	0.85
Bay Hill (cdp) Orange	41	0.76
Lecanto (cdp) Citrus	33	0.70
Palmona Park (cdp) Lee	9	0.70

Top 10 Places Sorted by Percent

Based on places with populations of 10,000 or more

Place (place type) County	Number	%
Oldsmar (city) Pinellas	65	0.55
Niceville (city) Okaloosa	61	0.52
Marco Island (city) Collier	67	0.45
New Port Richey (city) Pasco	68	0.43
Seminole (city) Pinellas	42	0.39
Iona (cdp) Lee	45	0.38
Palm Harbor (cdp) Pinellas	216	0.37
Cypress Lake (cdp) Lee	44	0.36

Notes: (cdp) census designated place; Refer to the User's Guide in the front of the book for more detailed information.

Oakland Park (city) Broward	105	0.34
Bloomingdale (cdp) Hillsborough	68	0.34

Cypriot

Top 10 Places Sorted by Number
Based on all places, regardless of population

Place (place type) County	Number	%
Boca Raton (city) Palm Beach	52	0.07
Jacksonville (special city) Duval	35	0.00
Palm Harbor (cdp) Pinellas	30	0.05
Oldsmar (city) Pinellas	25	0.21
Wellington (village) Palm Beach	20	0.05
Brandon (cdp) Hillsborough	17	0.02
Palm Bay (city) Brevard	16	0.02
Fort Lauderdale (city) Broward	14	0.01
Boca Del Mar (cdp) Palm Beach	12	0.06
Bonita Springs (city) Lee	12	0.04

Top 10 Places Sorted by Percent
Based on all places, regardless of population

Place (place type) County	Number	%
Osprey (cdp) Sarasota	11	0.27
Oldsmar (city) Pinellas	25	0.21
Boca Raton (city) Palm Beach	52	0.07
Port St. John (cdp) Brevard	8	0.07
Miami Shores (village) Miami-Dade	7	0.07
Boca Del Mar (cdp) Palm Beach	12	0.06
Palm Harbor (cdp) Pinellas	30	0.05
Wellington (village) Palm Beach	20	0.05
Bonita Springs (city) Lee	12	0.04
Hallandale (city) Broward	11	0.03

Top 10 Places Sorted by Percent
Based on places with populations of 10,000 or more

Place (place type) County	Number	%
Oldsmar (city) Pinellas	25	0.21
Boca Raton (city) Palm Beach	52	0.07
Port St. John (cdp) Brevard	8	0.07
Miami Shores (village) Miami-Dade	7	0.07
Boca Del Mar (cdp) Palm Beach	12	0.06
Palm Harbor (cdp) Pinellas	30	0.05
Wellington (village) Palm Beach	20	0.05
Bonita Springs (city) Lee	12	0.04
Hallandale (city) Broward	11	0.03
Oakland Park (city) Broward	9	0.03

Czech

Top 10 Places Sorted by Number
Based on all places, regardless of population

Place (place type) County	Number	%
Jacksonville (special city) Duval	1,244	0.17
St. Petersburg (city) Pinellas	990	0.40
Tampa (city) Hillsborough	592	0.20
Cape Coral (city) Lee	509	0.50
Fort Lauderdale (city) Broward	508	0.33
Clearwater (city) Pinellas	489	0.45
Coral Springs (city) Broward	441	0.38
Boca Raton (city) Palm Beach	396	0.52
Daytona Beach (city) Volusia	393	0.61
Palm Harbor (cdp) Pinellas	366	0.62

Top 10 Places Sorted by Percent
Based on all places, regardless of population

Place (place type) County	Number	%
Goodland (cdp) Collier	25	11.31
Pine Island (cdp) Hernando	5	9.09
Anna Maria (city) Manatee	83	4.55
Solana (cdp) Charlotte	26	2.63
Cloud Lake (town) Palm Beach	3	2.44
Juno Ridge (cdp) Palm Beach	14	1.86
Wabasso Beach (cdp) Indian River	20	1.79
Jupiter Island (town) Martin	11	1.77
Duck Key (cdp) Monroe	9	1.66
High Point (cdp) Hernando	50	1.65

Top 10 Places Sorted by Percent
Based on places with populations of 10,000 or more

Place (place type) County	Number	%
Hudson (cdp) Pasco	191	1.50
Wilton Manors (city) Broward	109	0.86
Bonita Springs (city) Lee	276	0.84
Jasmine Estates (cdp) Pasco	143	0.79
Venice (city) Sarasota	138	0.77
Tarpon Springs (city) Pinellas	160	0.76
Merritt Island (cdp) Brevard	266	0.74
Oldsmar (city) Pinellas	85	0.72
Westchase (cdp) Hillsborough	78	0.70
Lake Magdalene (cdp) Hillsborough	199	0.69

Czechoslovakian

Top 10 Places Sorted by Number
Based on all places, regardless of population

Place (place type) County	Number	%
Jacksonville (special city) Duval	741	0.10
St. Petersburg (city) Pinellas	493	0.20
Hollywood (city) Broward	330	0.24
Spring Hill (cdp) Hernando	327	0.47
Tampa (city) Hillsborough	308	0.10
Clearwater (city) Pinellas	289	0.27
Cape Coral (city) Lee	239	0.23
Palm Harbor (cdp) Pinellas	222	0.38
Plantation (city) Broward	216	0.26
Melbourne (city) Brevard	199	0.28

Top 10 Places Sorted by Percent
Based on all places, regardless of population

Place (place type) County	Number	%
Dunes Road (cdp) Palm Beach	62	13.11
Lazy Lake (village) Broward	2	5.13
Goodland (cdp) Collier	11	4.98
Black Diamond (cdp) Citrus	30	4.60
Okahumpka (cdp) Lake	9	4.41
Ferndale (cdp) Lake	12	4.17
Cloud Lake (town) Palm Beach	5	4.07
Juno Ridge (cdp) Palm Beach	14	1.86
Lely Resort (cdp) Collier	24	1.68
Matlacha (cdp) Lee	13	1.64

Top 10 Places Sorted by Percent
Based on places with populations of 10,000 or more

Place (place type) County	Number	%
Seminole (city) Pinellas	100	0.93
Lighthouse Point (city) Broward	71	0.67
Fruit Cove (cdp) St. Johns	96	0.60
Greater Northdale (cdp) Hillsborough	107	0.53
Boca Del Mar (cdp) Palm Beach	112	0.52
Greater Sun Center (cdp) Hillsborough	84	0.52
Hudson (cdp) Pasco	66	0.52
De Bary (city) Volusia	77	0.49
Englewood (cdp) Sarasota	78	0.48
Cocoa Beach (city) Brevard	59	0.48

Danish

Top 10 Places Sorted by Number
Based on all places, regardless of population

Place (place type) County	Number	%
Jacksonville (special city) Duval	1,337	0.18
St. Petersburg (city) Pinellas	906	0.37
Tampa (city) Hillsborough	591	0.19
Fort Lauderdale (city) Broward	570	0.37
Palm Harbor (cdp) Pinellas	531	0.90
Orlando (city) Orange	514	0.28
Cape Coral (city) Lee	473	0.46
Tallahassee (city) Leon	421	0.28
Clearwater (city) Pinellas	405	0.38
Largo (city) Pinellas	379	0.55

Top 10 Places Sorted by Percent
Based on all places, regardless of population

Place (place type) County	Number	%
North Beach (cdp) Indian River	6	2.71
Burnt Store Marina (cdp) Lee	26	2.15
Loughman (cdp) Polk	27	2.11
Melbourne Village (town) Brevard	14	2.08
June Park (cdp) Brevard	97	2.07
Matlacha (cdp) Lee	16	2.02
Laguna Beach (cdp) Bay	56	1.90
Butler Beach (cdp) St. Johns	85	1.88
Matlacha Isles-Matlacha Shores (cdp) Lee	5	1.85
Worthington Springs (town) Union	3	1.81

Top 10 Places Sorted by Percent
Based on places with populations of 10,000 or more

Place (place type) County	Number	%
Punta Gorda (city) Charlotte	150	1.04
Palm City (cdp) Martin	183	0.91
Marco Island (city) Collier	137	0.91
Palm Harbor (cdp) Pinellas	531	0.90
Wekiwa Springs (cdp) Seminole	208	0.89
Gonzalez (cdp) Escambia	95	0.81
Naples (city) Collier	168	0.80
Seminole (city) Pinellas	85	0.79
Pinecrest (village) Miami-Dade	150	0.78
New Smyrna Beach (city) Volusia	156	0.77

Dutch

Top 10 Places Sorted by Number
Based on all places, regardless of population

Place (place type) County	Number	%
Jacksonville (special city) Duval	7,635	1.04
St. Petersburg (city) Pinellas	4,000	1.61
Tampa (city) Hillsborough	3,035	1.00
Orlando (city) Orange	2,223	1.20
Cape Coral (city) Lee	1,991	1.95
Clearwater (city) Pinellas	1,684	1.56
Palm Bay (city) Brevard	1,671	2.10
Melbourne (city) Brevard	1,624	2.28
Port St. Lucie (city) St. Lucie	1,624	1.83
Tallahassee (city) Leon	1,586	1.05

Top 10 Places Sorted by Percent
Based on all places, regardless of population

Place (place type) County	Number	%
Islandia (city) Miami-Dade	3	50.00
Indian Creek (village) Miami-Dade	7	20.59
Pine Island (cdp) Hernando	11	20.00
Lazy Lake (village) Broward	6	15.38
Solana (cdp) Charlotte	84	8.50
North De Land (cdp) Volusia	106	7.79
Matlacha Isles-Matlacha Shores (cdp) Lee	21	7.75
Hillsboro Pines (cdp) Broward	32	6.60
Duck Key (cdp) Monroe	35	6.47
Gotha (cdp) Orange	45	6.01

Top 10 Places Sorted by Percent
Based on places with populations of 10,000 or more

Place (place type) County	Number	%
Englewood (cdp) Sarasota	564	3.47
Homosassa Springs (cdp) Citrus	413	3.24
Zephyrhills (city) Pasco	330	3.09
Seminole (city) Pinellas	331	3.07
Elfers (cdp) Pasco	401	3.04
North Palm Beach (village) Palm Beach	363	2.99
South Bradenton (cdp) Manatee	591	2.76
North Fort Myers (cdp) Lee	1,098	2.72

Notes: (cdp) census designated place; Refer to the User's Guide in the front of the book for more detailed information.

Port Salerno (cdp) Martin	274	2.71
Lutz (cdp) Hillsborough	456	2.67

Eastern European

Top 10 Places Sorted by Number

Based on all places, regardless of population

Place (place type) County	Number	%
Plantation (city) Broward	525	0.63
Boca Raton (city) Palm Beach	518	0.69
Coral Springs (city) Broward	508	0.43
Hollywood (city) Broward	494	0.35
Miami Beach (city) Miami-Dade	414	0.47
Weston (city) Broward	328	0.67
Jacksonville (special city) Duval	323	0.04
Kendall (cdp) Miami-Dade	316	0.42
Aventura (city) Miami-Dade	297	1.18
Boca Del Mar (cdp) Palm Beach	250	1.17

Top 10 Places Sorted by Percent

Based on all places, regardless of population

Place (place type) County	Number	%
Mission Bay (cdp) Palm Beach	70	2.28
Celebration (cdp) Osceola	48	1.75
Boca Pointe (cdp) Palm Beach	55	1.67
Odessa (cdp) Hillsborough	46	1.38
Bay Harbor Islands (town) Miami-Dade	65	1.26
Whisper Walk (cdp) Palm Beach	62	1.21
Chambers Estates (cdp) Broward	43	1.21
Aventura (city) Miami-Dade	297	1.18
Boca Del Mar (cdp) Palm Beach	250	1.17
Ojus (cdp) Miami-Dade	157	0.94

Top 10 Places Sorted by Percent

Based on places with populations of 10,000 or more

Place (place type) County	Number	%
Aventura (city) Miami-Dade	297	1.18
Boca Del Mar (cdp) Palm Beach	250	1.17
Ojus (cdp) Miami-Dade	157	0.94
Sandalfoot Cove (cdp) Palm Beach	129	0.78
Cutler (cdp) Miami-Dade	132	0.75
Maitland (city) Orange	88	0.74
Cooper City (city) Broward	202	0.73
Parkland (city) Broward	100	0.71
Boca Raton (city) Palm Beach	518	0.69
Wekiwa Springs (cdp) Seminole	158	0.68

English

Top 10 Places Sorted by Number

Based on all places, regardless of population

Place (place type) County	Number	%
Jacksonville (special city) Duval	62,798	8.54
St. Petersburg (city) Pinellas	27,556	11.12
Tampa (city) Hillsborough	23,319	7.68
Orlando (city) Orange	14,663	7.88
Tallahassee (city) Leon	13,888	9.22
Clearwater (city) Pinellas	12,820	11.88
Fort Lauderdale (city) Broward	12,456	8.19
Cape Coral (city) Lee	12,127	11.87
Port St. Lucie (city) St. Lucie	10,173	11.46
Largo (city) Pinellas	9,669	13.92

Top 10 Places Sorted by Percent

Based on all places, regardless of population

Place (place type) County	Number	%
Bayport (cdp) Hernando	16	66.67
Golf (village) Palm Beach	91	38.08
Captiva (cdp) Lee	140	35.71
Layton (city) Monroe	83	34.58
North Key Largo (cdp) Monroe	317	31.36
Orchid (town) Indian River	42	30.43
Punta Rassa (cdp) Lee	502	29.97
Jupiter Inlet Colony (town) Palm Beach	115	29.79
Penney Farms (town) Clay	155	28.86
Jupiter Island (town) Martin	177	28.50

Top 10 Places Sorted by Percent

Based on places with populations of 10,000 or more

Place (place type) County	Number	%
Greater Sun Center (cdp) Hillsborough	3,336	20.48
Englewood (cdp) Sarasota	3,140	19.32
Venice (city) Sarasota	3,402	19.06
Naples (city) Collier	3,920	18.68
Lady Lake (town) Lake	2,130	18.24
Palm Valley (cdp) St. Johns	3,584	18.05
Winter Park (city) Orange	4,347	17.94
Punta Gorda (city) Charlotte	2,556	17.71
Cypress Lake (cdp) Lee	2,121	17.53
South Venice (cdp) Sarasota	2,345	17.36

Estonian

Top 10 Places Sorted by Number

Based on all places, regardless of population

Place (place type) County	Number	%
Wellington (village) Palm Beach	49	0.13
Dania Beach (city) Broward	43	0.21
Orlando (city) Orange	38	0.02
Jacksonville (special city) Duval	28	0.00
North Miami Beach (city) Miami-Dade	26	0.06
Sunny Isles Beach (city) Miami-Dade	25	0.16
Ormond Beach (city) Volusia	25	0.07
Greenacres (city) Palm Beach	22	0.08
Merritt Island (cdp) Brevard	22	0.06
Boca Raton (city) Palm Beach	21	0.03

Top 10 Places Sorted by Percent

Based on all places, regardless of population

Place (place type) County	Number	%
East Palatka (cdp) Putnam	6	0.35
Lower Grand Lagoon (cdp) Bay	13	0.32
Carrabelle (city) Franklin	4	0.31
Orlovista (cdp) Orange	16	0.26
St. James City (cdp) Lee	9	0.22
Dania Beach (city) Broward	43	0.21
Baldwin (town) Duval	3	0.18
Osprey (cdp) Sarasota	7	0.17
Sunny Isles Beach (city) Miami-Dade	25	0.16
Cypress Lake (cdp) Lee	18	0.15

Top 10 Places Sorted by Percent

Based on places with populations of 10,000 or more

Place (place type) County	Number	%
Dania Beach (city) Broward	43	0.21
Sunny Isles Beach (city) Miami-Dade	25	0.16
Cypress Lake (cdp) Lee	18	0.15
Wellington (village) Palm Beach	49	0.13
Kings Point (cdp) Palm Beach	16	0.13
Venice (city) Sarasota	16	0.09
Riverview (cdp) Hillsborough	11	0.09
Palm Beach (town) Palm Beach	9	0.09
Greenacres (city) Palm Beach	22	0.08
Ormond Beach (city) Volusia	25	0.07

European

Top 10 Places Sorted by Number

Based on all places, regardless of population

Place (place type) County	Number	%
Jacksonville (special city) Duval	5,173	0.70
Tampa (city) Hillsborough	1,958	0.65
Tallahassee (city) Leon	1,416	0.94
St. Petersburg (city) Pinellas	1,372	0.55
Orlando (city) Orange	1,110	0.60
Gainesville (city) Alachua	1,024	1.07
Miami Beach (city) Miami-Dade	988	1.12
Coral Springs (city) Broward	944	0.80
Hollywood (city) Broward	872	0.63
Brandon (cdp) Hillsborough	856	1.10

Top 10 Places Sorted by Percent

Based on all places, regardless of population

Place (place type) County	Number	%
Edgewater (cdp) Broward	78	11.00
Ivanhoe Estates (cdp) Broward	19	7.51
San Antonio (city) Pasco	39	6.34
Fisher Island (cdp) Miami-Dade	20	5.90
Wewahitchka (city) Gulf	102	5.86
Worthington Springs (town) Union	7	4.22
Indialantic (town) Brevard	107	3.64
North Brooksville (cdp) Hernando	52	3.52
Geneva (cdp) Seminole	98	3.49
Lake Lorraine (cdp) Okaloosa	230	3.24

Top 10 Places Sorted by Percent

Based on places with populations of 10,000 or more

Place (place type) County	Number	%
Niceville (city) Okaloosa	251	2.13
Maitland (city) Orange	247	2.07
Ojus (cdp) Miami-Dade	320	1.92
Cutler (cdp) Miami-Dade	319	1.81
Pinecrest (village) Miami-Dade	315	1.64
Wekiwa Springs (cdp) Seminole	378	1.62
Palm Beach Gardens (city) Palm Beach	458	1.33
Fruit Cove (cdp) St. Johns	202	1.26
Goldenrod (cdp) Seminole	165	1.26
Jacksonville Beach (city) Duval	260	1.24

Finnish

Top 10 Places Sorted by Number

Based on all places, regardless of population

Place (place type) County	Number	%
Lake Worth (city) Palm Beach	1,026	2.91
Jacksonville (special city) Duval	665	0.09
Lantana (town) Palm Beach	570	5.97
St. Petersburg (city) Pinellas	407	0.16
Orlando (city) Orange	330	0.18
Clearwater (city) Pinellas	317	0.29
Cape Coral (city) Lee	315	0.31
Greenacres (city) Palm Beach	232	0.85
Port Charlotte (cdp) Charlotte	227	0.49
Tampa (city) Hillsborough	227	0.07

Top 10 Places Sorted by Percent

Based on all places, regardless of population

Place (place type) County	Number	%
Lantana (town) Palm Beach	570	5.97
South Palm Beach (town) Palm Beach	30	4.14
Hypoluxo (town) Palm Beach	77	3.81
Lake Worth (city) Palm Beach	1,026	2.91
Manalapan (town) Palm Beach	9	2.79
Riverland Village (cdp) Broward	32	1.55
Wabasso (cdp) Indian River	12	1.44
Bokeelia (cdp) Lee	24	1.24
Melbourne Village (town) Brevard	8	1.19
Hutchinson Island South (cdp) St. Lucie	56	1.18

Top 10 Places Sorted by Percent

Based on places with populations of 10,000 or more

Place (place type) County	Number	%
Lake Worth (city) Palm Beach	1,026	2.91
Sebastian (city) Indian River	156	0.95
Greenacres (city) Palm Beach	232	0.85
Marco Island (city) Collier	127	0.85
North Palm Beach (village) Palm Beach	84	0.69
Lake Worth Corridor (cdp) Palm Beach	109	0.59
Hobe Sound (cdp) Martin	64	0.57
Lighthouse Point (city) Broward	61	0.57

Notes: (cdp) census designated place; Refer to the User's Guide in the front of the book for more detailed information.

Zephyrhills (city) Pasco	61	0.57
Port Charlotte (cdp) Charlotte	227	0.49

French, except Basque

Top 10 Places Sorted by Number
Based on all places, regardless of population

Place (place type) County	Number	%
Jacksonville (special city) Duval	16,196	2.20
St. Petersburg (city) Pinellas	9,438	3.81
Tampa (city) Hillsborough	7,198	2.37
Orlando (city) Orange	4,327	2.33
Cape Coral (city) Lee	4,300	4.21
Fort Lauderdale (city) Broward	4,153	2.73
Clearwater (city) Pinellas	3,814	3.53
Hollywood (city) Broward	3,601	2.59
Port St. Lucie (city) St. Lucie	3,402	3.83
Tallahassee (city) Leon	3,382	2.25

Top 10 Places Sorted by Percent
Based on all places, regardless of population

Place (place type) County	Number	%
Bay Lake (city) Orange	14	35.90
Glen Ridge (town) Palm Beach	47	17.34
Layton (city) Monroe	41	17.08
Lake Buena Vista (city) Orange	2	12.50
Hampton (city) Bradford	57	11.59
Weeki Wachee (city) Hernando	1	11.11
Page Park (cdp) Lee	60	10.70
Matlacha Isles-Matlacha Shores (cdp) Lee	29	10.70
Ravenswood Estates (cdp) Broward	98	10.50
Belleview (city) Marion	358	10.07

Top 10 Places Sorted by Percent
Based on places with populations of 10,000 or more

Place (place type) County	Number	%
South Venice (cdp) Sarasota	838	6.20
Middleburg (cdp) Clay	610	5.86
Lady Lake (town) Lake	640	5.48
Lakewood Park (cdp) St. Lucie	562	5.40
Cocoa Beach (city) Brevard	648	5.22
Elfers (cdp) Pasco	686	5.20
Port Charlotte (cdp) Charlotte	2,390	5.14
Villas (cdp) Lee	571	5.11
Edgewater (city) Volusia	960	5.09
Key Largo (cdp) Monroe	606	5.06

French Canadian

Top 10 Places Sorted by Number
Based on all places, regardless of population

Place (place type) County	Number	%
Jacksonville (special city) Duval	4,238	0.58
St. Petersburg (city) Pinellas	2,528	1.02
Tampa (city) Hillsborough	1,892	0.62
Hollywood (city) Broward	1,696	1.22
Port St. Lucie (city) St. Lucie	1,357	1.53
Clearwater (city) Pinellas	1,290	1.20
Palm Bay (city) Brevard	1,257	1.58
Orlando (city) Orange	1,240	0.67
Fort Lauderdale (city) Broward	1,163	0.76
Largo (city) Pinellas	1,079	1.55

Top 10 Places Sorted by Percent
Based on all places, regardless of population

Place (place type) County	Number	%
Godfrey Road (cdp) Broward	18	8.45
Matlacha Isles-Matlacha Shores (cdp) Lee	15	5.54
Hypoluxo (town) Palm Beach	101	4.99
Crescent Beach (cdp) St. Johns	39	4.91
Pembroke Park (town) Broward	296	4.67
Rio (cdp) Martin	49	4.60
Ridge Manor (cdp) Hernando	176	4.27
Ravenswood Estates (cdp) Broward	38	4.07
Highland Park (village) Polk	9	3.81
East Bronson (cdp) Levy	38	3.57

Top 10 Places Sorted by Percent
Based on places with populations of 10,000 or more

Place (place type) County	Number	%
Hallandale (city) Broward	934	2.70
De Bary (city) Volusia	400	2.54
Dania Beach (city) Broward	491	2.44
Hobe Sound (cdp) Martin	256	2.29
Iona (cdp) Lee	251	2.12
Greater Sun Center (cdp) Hillsborough	332	2.04
Stuart (city) Martin	297	2.02
Edgewater (city) Volusia	363	1.92
Palm City (cdp) Martin	382	1.90
Upper Grand Lagoon (cdp) Bay	208	1.89

German

Top 10 Places Sorted by Number
Based on all places, regardless of population

Place (place type) County	Number	%
Jacksonville (special city) Duval	70,440	9.58
St. Petersburg (city) Pinellas	36,327	14.66
Tampa (city) Hillsborough	27,990	9.22
Cape Coral (city) Lee	21,385	20.92
Orlando (city) Orange	18,259	9.82
Clearwater (city) Pinellas	18,191	16.86
Fort Lauderdale (city) Broward	15,857	10.42
Port St. Lucie (city) St. Lucie	14,983	16.87
Palm Bay (city) Brevard	14,240	17.92
Tallahassee (city) Leon	14,091	9.36

Top 10 Places Sorted by Percent
Based on all places, regardless of population

Place (place type) County	Number	%
Pine Island (cdp) Hernando	28	50.91
Islandia (city) Miami-Dade	3	50.00
Dunes Road (cdp) Palm Beach	228	48.20
Bayport (cdp) Hernando	10	41.67
Lake Buena Vista (city) Orange	6	37.50
Istachatta (cdp) Hernando	22	36.07
Matlacha Isles-Matlacha Shores (cdp) Lee	94	34.69
Royal Palm Ranches (cdp) Broward	97	32.23
Captiva (cdp) Lee	118	30.10
Matlacha (cdp) Lee	234	29.55

Top 10 Places Sorted by Percent
Based on places with populations of 10,000 or more

Place (place type) County	Number	%
San Carlos Park (cdp) Lee	4,108	25.48
Iona (cdp) Lee	2,970	25.06
Englewood (cdp) Sarasota	3,952	24.32
Punta Gorda (city) Charlotte	3,419	23.69
Marco Island (city) Collier	3,498	23.35
Fruitville (cdp) Sarasota	3,000	23.27
Cypress Lake (cdp) Lee	2,793	23.08
Greater Sun Center (cdp) Hillsborough	3,737	22.95
Oldsmar (city) Pinellas	2,641	22.50
Lake Mary (city) Seminole	2,528	22.39

German Russian

Top 10 Places Sorted by Number
Based on all places, regardless of population

Place (place type) County	Number	%
Melrose Park (cdp) Broward	29	0.41
Hollywood (city) Broward	20	0.01
Hallandale (city) Broward	17	0.05
Plantation (city) Broward	14	0.02
Palm Bay (city) Brevard	11	0.01
Port St. Lucie (city) St. Lucie	11	0.01
Leesburg (city) Lake	9	0.06
Orlando (city) Orange	9	0.00
Kendall West (cdp) Miami-Dade	8	0.02
Titusville (city) Brevard	8	0.02

Top 10 Places Sorted by Percent
Based on all places, regardless of population

Place (place type) County	Number	%
Melrose Park (cdp) Broward	29	0.41
Leesburg (city) Lake	9	0.06
Hallandale (city) Broward	17	0.05
Gulfport (city) Pinellas	5	0.04
Bayshore Gardens (cdp) Manatee	6	0.03
West Pensacola (cdp) Escambia	6	0.03
Plantation (city) Broward	14	0.02
Kendall West (cdp) Miami-Dade	8	0.02
Titusville (city) Brevard	8	0.02
Panama City (city) Bay	7	0.02

Top 10 Places Sorted by Percent
Based on places with populations of 10,000 or more

Place (place type) County	Number	%
Leesburg (city) Lake	9	0.06
Hallandale (city) Broward	17	0.05
Gulfport (city) Pinellas	5	0.04
Bayshore Gardens (cdp) Manatee	6	0.03
West Pensacola (cdp) Escambia	6	0.03
Plantation (city) Broward	14	0.02
Kendall West (cdp) Miami-Dade	8	0.02
Titusville (city) Brevard	8	0.02
Panama City (city) Bay	7	0.02
Hollywood (city) Broward	20	0.01

Greek

Top 10 Places Sorted by Number
Based on all places, regardless of population

Place (place type) County	Number	%
Tarpon Springs (city) Pinellas	2,479	11.77
Jacksonville (special city) Duval	2,314	0.31
Clearwater (city) Pinellas	1,934	1.79
Palm Harbor (cdp) Pinellas	1,707	2.89
St. Petersburg (city) Pinellas	1,436	0.58
Holiday (cdp) Pasco	1,247	5.69
Hollywood (city) Broward	1,097	0.79
Boca Raton (city) Palm Beach	1,065	1.41
Fort Lauderdale (city) Broward	1,038	0.68
Tampa (city) Hillsborough	1,022	0.34

Top 10 Places Sorted by Percent
Based on all places, regardless of population

Place (place type) County	Number	%
Tarpon Springs (city) Pinellas	2,479	11.77
Holiday (cdp) Pasco	1,247	5.69
Fisher Island (cdp) Miami-Dade	18	5.31
East Lake (cdp) Pinellas	868	2.95
Beacon Square (cdp) Pasco	212	2.92
Palm Harbor (cdp) Pinellas	1,707	2.89
Twin Lakes (cdp) Broward	47	2.75
Miramar Beach (cdp) Walton	56	2.30
Indian Rocks Beach (city) Pinellas	109	2.15
Sea Ranch Lakes (village) Broward	28	2.03

Top 10 Places Sorted by Percent
Based on places with populations of 10,000 or more

Place (place type) County	Number	%
Tarpon Springs (city) Pinellas	2,479	11.77
Holiday (cdp) Pasco	1,247	5.69
East Lake (cdp) Pinellas	868	2.95
Palm Harbor (cdp) Pinellas	1,707	2.89
Lakewood Park (cdp) St. Lucie	204	1.96
New Port Richey East (cdp) Pasco	188	1.86
Clearwater (city) Pinellas	1,934	1.79
Dunedin (city) Pinellas	591	1.65

Notes: (cdp) census designated place; Refer to the User's Guide in the front of the book for more detailed information.

North Palm Beach (village) Palm Beach	183	1.51
Elfers (cdp) Pasco	196	1.48

Guyanese

Top 10 Places Sorted by Number
Based on all places, regardless of population

Place (place type) County	Number	%
Pembroke Pines (city) Broward	508	0.37
Miramar (city) Broward	469	0.65
Pine Hills (cdp) Orange	385	0.92
Jacksonville (special city) Duval	358	0.05
Town 'n' Country (cdp) Hillsborough	354	0.49
South Miami Heights (cdp) Miami-Dade	337	1.00
Hollywood (city) Broward	281	0.20
Tampa (city) Hillsborough	220	0.07
Sunrise (city) Broward	218	0.25
Lauderhill (city) Broward	217	0.38

Top 10 Places Sorted by Percent
Based on all places, regardless of population

Place (place type) County	Number	%
Wedgefield (cdp) Orange	91	3.23
Broadview-Pompano Park (cdp) Broward	72	1.40
Pine Castle (cdp) Orange	100	1.22
Southchase (cdp) Orange	54	1.19
South Miami Heights (cdp) Miami-Dade	337	1.00
Riverland Village (cdp) Broward	20	0.97
Pine Hills (cdp) Orange	385	0.92
Melrose Park (cdp) Broward	65	0.92
Silver Springs Shores (cdp) Marion	60	0.92
Palmetto Estates (cdp) Miami-Dade	113	0.83

Top 10 Places Sorted by Percent
Based on places with populations of 10,000 or more

Place (place type) County	Number	%
South Miami Heights (cdp) Miami-Dade	337	1.00
Pine Hills (cdp) Orange	385	0.92
Palmetto Estates (cdp) Miami-Dade	113	0.83
Miramar (city) Broward	469	0.65
Lauderdale Lakes (city) Broward	163	0.52
Citrus Park (cdp) Hillsborough	105	0.52
Poinciana (cdp) Osceola	70	0.52
Richmond West (cdp) Miami-Dade	139	0.50
Town 'n' Country (cdp) Hillsborough	354	0.49
Temple Terrace (city) Hillsborough	102	0.49

Hawaii Native/Pacific Islander

Top 10 Places Sorted by Number
Based on all places, regardless of population

Place (place type) County	Number	%
Jacksonville (special city) Duval	1,290	0.18
Miami (city) Miami-Dade	681	0.19
Tampa (city) Hillsborough	643	0.21
Orlando (city) Orange	487	0.26
St. Petersburg (city) Pinellas	369	0.15
Fort Lauderdale (city) Broward	274	0.18
West Palm Beach (city) Palm Beach	262	0.32
Hollywood (city) Broward	260	0.19
Delray Beach (city) Palm Beach	255	0.42
Miramar (city) Broward	251	0.35

Top 10 Places Sorted by Percent
Based on all places, regardless of population

Place (place type) County	Number	%
Ebro (town) Washington	5	2.00
Pine Island (cdp) Hernando	1	1.56
Center Hill (city) Sumter	12	1.32
Sky Lake (cdp) Orange	64	1.13
Webster (city) Sumter	9	1.12
Indiantown (cdp) Martin	62	1.11
Lake Harbor (cdp) Palm Beach	2	1.03
Hillsboro Pines (cdp) Broward	4	0.99
Gun Club Estates (cdp) Palm Beach	7	0.98
Belle Glade (city) Palm Beach	145	0.97

Top 10 Places Sorted by Percent
Based on places with populations of 10,000 or more

Place (place type) County	Number	%
Belle Glade (city) Palm Beach	145	0.97
Oak Ridge (cdp) Orange	141	0.63
Myrtle Grove (cdp) Escambia	102	0.59
Wright (cdp) Okaloosa	102	0.47
Brent (cdp) Escambia	103	0.46
Delray Beach (city) Palm Beach	255	0.42
North Miami (city) Miami-Dade	247	0.41
Pine Hills (cdp) Orange	165	0.40
West Pensacola (cdp) Escambia	88	0.40
Poinciana (cdp) Osceola	55	0.40

Hawaii Native/Pacific Islander: Melanesian

Top 10 Places Sorted by Number
Based on all places, regardless of population

Place (place type) County	Number	%
St. Petersburg (city) Pinellas	10	0.00
Hobe Sound (cdp) Martin	6	0.05
Deltona (city) Volusia	4	0.01
Kissimmee (city) Osceola	4	0.01
Melbourne (city) Brevard	4	0.01
Sky Lake (cdp) Orange	3	0.05
Port Salerno (cdp) Martin	3	0.03
Fairview Shores (cdp) Orange	3	0.02
Boca Del Mar (cdp) Palm Beach	3	0.01
Brent (cdp) Escambia	3	0.01

Top 10 Places Sorted by Percent
Based on all places, regardless of population

Place (place type) County	Number	%
Hobe Sound (cdp) Martin	6	0.05
Sky Lake (cdp) Orange	3	0.05
Port Salerno (cdp) Martin	3	0.03
Charlotte Harbor (cdp) Charlotte	1	0.03
Fairview Shores (cdp) Orange	3	0.02
Eglin AFB (cdp) Okaloosa	2	0.02
Mount Dora (city) Lake	2	0.02
Bay Hill (cdp) Orange	1	0.02
Deltona (city) Volusia	4	0.01
Kissimmee (city) Osceola	4	0.01

Top 10 Places Sorted by Percent
Based on places with populations of 10,000 or more

Place (place type) County	Number	%
Hobe Sound (cdp) Martin	6	0.05
Port Salerno (cdp) Martin	3	0.03
Fairview Shores (cdp) Orange	3	0.02
Deltona (city) Volusia	4	0.01
Kissimmee (city) Osceola	4	0.01
Melbourne (city) Brevard	4	0.01
Boca Del Mar (cdp) Palm Beach	3	0.01
Brent (cdp) Escambia	3	0.01
Oak Ridge (cdp) Orange	3	0.01
Palm Coast (city) Flagler	2	0.01

Hawaii Native/Pacific Islander: Fijian

Top 10 Places Sorted by Number
Based on all places, regardless of population

Place (place type) County	Number	%
St. Petersburg (city) Pinellas	10	0.00
Deltona (city) Volusia	4	0.01
Kissimmee (city) Osceola	4	0.01
Melbourne (city) Brevard	4	0.01
Sky Lake (cdp) Orange	3	0.05
Port Salerno (cdp) Martin	3	0.03
Boca Del Mar (cdp) Palm Beach	3	0.01
Oak Ridge (cdp) Orange	3	0.01
Kendall (cdp) Miami-Dade	3	0.00
Orlando (city) Orange	3	0.00

Top 10 Places Sorted by Percent
Based on all places, regardless of population

Place (place type) County	Number	%
Sky Lake (cdp) Orange	3	0.05
Port Salerno (cdp) Martin	3	0.03
Charlotte Harbor (cdp) Charlotte	1	0.03
Eglin AFB (cdp) Okaloosa	2	0.02
Deltona (city) Volusia	4	0.01
Kissimmee (city) Osceola	4	0.01
Melbourne (city) Brevard	4	0.01
Boca Del Mar (cdp) Palm Beach	3	0.01
Oak Ridge (cdp) Orange	3	0.01
Wellington (village) Palm Beach	2	0.01

Top 10 Places Sorted by Percent
Based on places with populations of 10,000 or more

Place (place type) County	Number	%
Port Salerno (cdp) Martin	3	0.03
Deltona (city) Volusia	4	0.01
Kissimmee (city) Osceola	4	0.01
Melbourne (city) Brevard	4	0.01
Boca Del Mar (cdp) Palm Beach	3	0.01
Oak Ridge (cdp) Orange	3	0.01
Wellington (village) Palm Beach	2	0.01
Forest City (cdp) Seminole	1	0.01
Glenvar Heights (cdp) Miami-Dade	1	0.01
Sandalfoot Cove (cdp) Palm Beach	1	0.01

Hawaii Native/Pacific Islander: Other Melanesian

Top 10 Places Sorted by Number
Based on all places, regardless of population

Place (place type) County	Number	%
Hobe Sound (cdp) Martin	6	0.05
Fairview Shores (cdp) Orange	3	0.02
Brent (cdp) Escambia	3	0.01
West Palm Beach (city) Palm Beach	3	0.00
Mount Dora (city) Lake	2	0.02
Palm Coast (city) Flagler	2	0.01
Bay Hill (cdp) Orange	1	0.02
Sebring (city) Highlands	1	0.01
South Daytona (city) Volusia	1	0.01
Ferry Pass (cdp) Escambia	1	0.00

Top 10 Places Sorted by Percent
Based on all places, regardless of population

Place (place type) County	Number	%
Hobe Sound (cdp) Martin	6	0.05
Fairview Shores (cdp) Orange	3	0.02
Mount Dora (city) Lake	2	0.02
Bay Hill (cdp) Orange	1	0.02
Brent (cdp) Escambia	3	0.01
Palm Coast (city) Flagler	2	0.01
Sebring (city) Highlands	1	0.01
South Daytona (city) Volusia	1	0.01
West Palm Beach (city) Palm Beach	3	0.00
Ferry Pass (cdp) Escambia	1	0.00

Top 10 Places Sorted by Percent
Based on places with populations of 10,000 or more

Place (place type) County	Number	%
Hobe Sound (cdp) Martin	6	0.05
Fairview Shores (cdp) Orange	3	0.02
Brent (cdp) Escambia	3	0.01
Palm Coast (city) Flagler	2	0.01
South Daytona (city) Volusia	1	0.01
West Palm Beach (city) Palm Beach	3	0.00
Ferry Pass (cdp) Escambia	1	0.00

Notes: (cdp) census designated place; Refer to the User's Guide in the front of the book for more detailed information.

Place (place type) County	Number	%
Fountainbleau (cdp) Miami-Dade	1	0.00
Jacksonville (special city) Duval	1	0.00
Lake Magdalene (cdp) Hillsborough	1	0.00

Hawaii Native/Pacific Islander: Micronesian

Top 10 Places Sorted by Number

Based on all places, regardless of population

Place (place type) County	Number	%
Jacksonville (special city) Duval	300	0.04
Tampa (city) Hillsborough	168	0.06
West Palm Beach (city) Palm Beach	98	0.12
Orlando (city) Orange	71	0.04
Brent (cdp) Escambia	64	0.29
Indiantown (cdp) Martin	55	0.98
Miami (city) Miami-Dade	48	0.01
Fort Myers (city) Lee	47	0.10
Immokalee (cdp) Collier	41	0.21
Cocoa (city) Brevard	38	0.23

Top 10 Places Sorted by Percent

Based on all places, regardless of population

Place (place type) County	Number	%
Pine Island (cdp) Hernando	1	1.56
Ebro (town) Washington	3	1.20
Indiantown (cdp) Martin	55	0.98
Noma (town) Holmes	2	0.94
Palm Shores (town) Brevard	6	0.76
Paradise Heights (cdp) Orange	9	0.69
Juno Ridge (cdp) Palm Beach	4	0.54
Chula Vista (cdp) Broward	3	0.52
Broadview Park (cdp) Broward	34	0.50
Center Hill (city) Sumter	4	0.44

Top 10 Places Sorted by Percent

Based on places with populations of 10,000 or more

Place (place type) County	Number	%
Brent (cdp) Escambia	64	0.29
Cocoa (city) Brevard	38	0.23
Immokalee (cdp) Collier	41	0.21
Myrtle Grove (cdp) Escambia	31	0.18
Port St. John (cdp) Brevard	21	0.17
Wright (cdp) Okaloosa	33	0.15
Golden Gate (cdp) Collier	31	0.15
Upper Grand Lagoon (cdp) Bay	14	0.13
West Palm Beach (city) Palm Beach	98	0.12
Lake Worth Corridor (cdp) Palm Beach	22	0.12

Hawaii Native/Pacific Islander: Guamanian or Chamorro

Top 10 Places Sorted by Number

Based on all places, regardless of population

Place (place type) County	Number	%
Jacksonville (special city) Duval	263	0.04
West Palm Beach (city) Palm Beach	98	0.12
Tampa (city) Hillsborough	72	0.02
Indiantown (cdp) Martin	55	0.98
Miami (city) Miami-Dade	45	0.01
Brent (cdp) Escambia	44	0.20
Fort Myers (city) Lee	43	0.09
Immokalee (cdp) Collier	41	0.21
Cocoa (city) Brevard	38	0.23
Broadview Park (cdp) Broward	34	0.50

Top 10 Places Sorted by Percent

Based on all places, regardless of population

Place (place type) County	Number	%
Pine Island (cdp) Hernando	1	1.56
Ebro (town) Washington	3	1.20
Indiantown (cdp) Martin	55	0.98
Noma (town) Holmes	2	0.94
Palm Shores (town) Brevard	6	0.76
Paradise Heights (cdp) Orange	9	0.69
Juno Ridge (cdp) Palm Beach	4	0.54
Chula Vista (cdp) Broward	3	0.52
Broadview Park (cdp) Broward	34	0.50
Center Hill (city) Sumter	4	0.44

Top 10 Places Sorted by Percent

Based on places with populations of 10,000 or more

Place (place type) County	Number	%
Cocoa (city) Brevard	38	0.23
Immokalee (cdp) Collier	41	0.21
Brent (cdp) Escambia	44	0.20
Myrtle Grove (cdp) Escambia	27	0.16
Golden Gate (cdp) Collier	31	0.15
Port St. John (cdp) Brevard	18	0.15
Wright (cdp) Okaloosa	30	0.14
Upper Grand Lagoon (cdp) Bay	14	0.13
West Palm Beach (city) Palm Beach	98	0.12
Bellview (cdp) Escambia	24	0.11

Hawaii Native/Pacific Islander: Other Micronesian

Top 10 Places Sorted by Number

Based on all places, regardless of population

Place (place type) County	Number	%
Tampa (city) Hillsborough	96	0.03
Orlando (city) Orange	38	0.02
Jacksonville (special city) Duval	37	0.01
Brent (cdp) Escambia	20	0.09
Largo (city) Pinellas	18	0.03
North Fort Myers (cdp) Lee	12	0.03
Oak Ridge (cdp) Orange	11	0.05
Holiday (cdp) Pasco	8	0.04
Hollywood (city) Broward	8	0.01
Osprey (cdp) Sarasota	5	0.12

Top 10 Places Sorted by Percent

Based on all places, regardless of population

Place (place type) County	Number	%
Edgewater (cdp) Broward	2	0.25
Reddick (town) Marion	1	0.18
Osprey (cdp) Sarasota	5	0.12
Brent (cdp) Escambia	20	0.09
Minneola (city) Lake	5	0.09
Freeport (city) Walton	1	0.08
Southchase (cdp) Orange	3	0.06
Oak Ridge (cdp) Orange	11	0.05
Kensington Park (cdp) Sarasota	2	0.05
Holiday (cdp) Pasco	8	0.04

Top 10 Places Sorted by Percent

Based on places with populations of 10,000 or more

Place (place type) County	Number	%
Brent (cdp) Escambia	20	0.09
Oak Ridge (cdp) Orange	11	0.05
Holiday (cdp) Pasco	8	0.04
Tampa (city) Hillsborough	96	0.03
Largo (city) Pinellas	18	0.03
North Fort Myers (cdp) Lee	12	0.03
Warrington (cdp) Escambia	5	0.03
Orlando (city) Orange	38	0.02
Dania Beach (city) Broward	4	0.02
Key West (city) Monroe	4	0.02

Hawaii Native/Pacific Islander: Polynesian

Top 10 Places Sorted by Number

Based on all places, regardless of population

Place (place type) County	Number	%
Jacksonville (special city) Duval	493	0.07
Tampa (city) Hillsborough	189	0.06
St. Petersburg (city) Pinellas	155	0.06
Orlando (city) Orange	149	0.08
Miami (city) Miami-Dade	103	0.03
Tallahassee (city) Leon	91	0.06
Hollywood (city) Broward	87	0.06
Fort Lauderdale (city) Broward	81	0.05
Cape Coral (city) Lee	69	0.07
Brandon (cdp) Hillsborough	66	0.08

Top 10 Places Sorted by Percent

Based on all places, regardless of population

Place (place type) County	Number	%
Webster (city) Sumter	8	0.99
Pine Lakes (cdp) Lake	7	0.93
Charleston Park (cdp) Lee	3	0.73
Sky Lake (cdp) Orange	40	0.71
Hastings (town) St. Johns	3	0.58
Mexico Beach (city) Bay	5	0.49
Eglin AFB (cdp) Okaloosa	39	0.48
Taft (cdp) Orange	7	0.36
Plantation Mobile Home Park (cdp) Palm Beach	4	0.33
Matlacha Isles-Matlacha Shores (cdp) Lee	1	0.33

Top 10 Places Sorted by Percent

Based on places with populations of 10,000 or more

Place (place type) County	Number	%
Oak Ridge (cdp) Orange	65	0.29
Myrtle Grove (cdp) Escambia	48	0.28
Meadow Woods (cdp) Orange	29	0.26
West Pensacola (cdp) Escambia	50	0.23
Lynn Haven (city) Bay	26	0.21
Wright (cdp) Okaloosa	42	0.19
Crestview (city) Okaloosa	25	0.17
Poinciana (cdp) Osceola	23	0.17
Callaway (city) Bay	23	0.16
Niceville (city) Okaloosa	18	0.15

Hawaii Native/Pacific Islander: Native Hawaiian

Top 10 Places Sorted by Number

Based on all places, regardless of population

Place (place type) County	Number	%
Jacksonville (special city) Duval	369	0.05
Tampa (city) Hillsborough	117	0.04
Orlando (city) Orange	103	0.06
St. Petersburg (city) Pinellas	71	0.03
Miami (city) Miami-Dade	71	0.02
Cape Coral (city) Lee	62	0.06
Tallahassee (city) Leon	52	0.03
Hollywood (city) Broward	51	0.04
Fort Lauderdale (city) Broward	50	0.03
Clearwater (city) Pinellas	41	0.04

Top 10 Places Sorted by Percent

Based on all places, regardless of population

Place (place type) County	Number	%
Webster (city) Sumter	8	0.99
Pine Lakes (cdp) Lake	6	0.79
Mexico Beach (city) Bay	5	0.49
Eglin AFB (cdp) Okaloosa	32	0.40
Sky Lake (cdp) Orange	22	0.39
Plantation Mobile Home Park (cdp) Palm Beach	4	0.33
Howey-in-the-Hills (town) Lake	3	0.31
Manalapan (town) Palm Beach	1	0.31
Keystone Heights (city) Clay	4	0.30
Bowling Green (city) Hardee	8	0.28

Top 10 Places Sorted by Percent

Based on places with populations of 10,000 or more

Place (place type) County	Number	%
Wright (cdp) Okaloosa	39	0.18
Lynn Haven (city) Bay	23	0.18
Crestview (city) Okaloosa	25	0.17

Notes: (cdp) census designated place; Refer to the User's Guide in the front of the book for more detailed information.

Place (place type) County	Number	%
Meadow Woods (cdp) Orange	19	0.17
West Pensacola (cdp) Escambia	33	0.15
Callaway (city) Bay	21	0.15
Niceville (city) Okaloosa	17	0.15
Myrtle Grove (cdp) Escambia	23	0.13
Bellair-Meadowbrook Terrace (cdp) Clay	21	0.13
Bellview (cdp) Escambia	23	0.11

Hawaii Native/Pacific Islander: Samoan

Top 10 Places Sorted by Number

Based on all places, regardless of population

Place (place type) County	Number	%
Jacksonville (special city) Duval	105	0.01
Tampa (city) Hillsborough	64	0.02
Tallahassee (city) Leon	32	0.02
Gainesville (city) Alachua	28	0.03
Orlando (city) Orange	28	0.02
St. Petersburg (city) Pinellas	28	0.01
Delray Beach (city) Palm Beach	27	0.04
West Palm Beach (city) Palm Beach	25	0.03
Miami (city) Miami-Dade	25	0.01
Myrtle Grove (cdp) Escambia	23	0.13

Top 10 Places Sorted by Percent

Based on all places, regardless of population

Place (place type) County	Number	%
Hastings (town) St. Johns	3	0.58
Matlacha Isles-Matlacha Shores (cdp) Lee	1	0.33
St. Leo (town) Pasco	1	0.17
Myrtle Grove (cdp) Escambia	23	0.13
Pine Lakes (cdp) Lake	1	0.13
Lake Forest (cdp) Broward	6	0.12
Zolfo Springs (town) Hardee	2	0.12
Sky Lake (cdp) Orange	6	0.11
South Highpoint (cdp) Pinellas	9	0.10
Pine Ridge (cdp) Collier	2	0.10

Top 10 Places Sorted by Percent

Based on places with populations of 10,000 or more

Place (place type) County	Number	%
Myrtle Grove (cdp) Escambia	23	0.13
West Pensacola (cdp) Escambia	17	0.08
Brent (cdp) Escambia	16	0.07
New Port Richey (city) Pasco	11	0.07
Poinciana (cdp) Osceola	9	0.07
Bartow (city) Polk	9	0.06
Yeehaw Junction (cdp) Osceola	10	0.05
Ives Estates (cdp) Miami-Dade	8	0.05
Winter Garden (city) Orange	7	0.05
Delray Beach (city) Palm Beach	27	0.04

Hawaii Native/Pacific Islander: Tongan

Top 10 Places Sorted by Number

Based on all places, regardless of population

Place (place type) County	Number	%
St. Petersburg (city) Pinellas	33	0.01
Oak Ridge (cdp) Orange	31	0.14
Largo (city) Pinellas	24	0.03
Hollywood (city) Broward	18	0.01
Pine Castle (cdp) Orange	9	0.10
Deltona (city) Volusia	6	0.01
Palm Bay (city) Brevard	6	0.01
Orlando (city) Orange	6	0.00
Poinciana (cdp) Osceola	5	0.04
Bradenton (city) Manatee	5	0.01

Top 10 Places Sorted by Percent

Based on all places, regardless of population

Place (place type) County	Number	%
Page Park (cdp) Lee	1	0.19
Oak Ridge (cdp) Orange	31	0.14
Pine Castle (cdp) Orange	9	0.10
Lochmoor Waterway Estates (cdp) Lee	4	0.10
Gandy (cdp) Pinellas	2	0.10
Holden Heights (cdp) Orange	3	0.08
Carrabelle (city) Franklin	1	0.08
Citrus Springs (cdp) Citrus	3	0.07
Port Richey (city) Pasco	2	0.07
North Redington Beach (town) Pinellas	1	0.07

Top 10 Places Sorted by Percent

Based on places with populations of 10,000 or more

Place (place type) County	Number	%
Oak Ridge (cdp) Orange	31	0.14
Poinciana (cdp) Osceola	5	0.04
Largo (city) Pinellas	24	0.03
Hudson (cdp) Pasco	2	0.02
St. Petersburg (city) Pinellas	33	0.01
Hollywood (city) Broward	18	0.01
Deltona (city) Volusia	6	0.01
Palm Bay (city) Brevard	6	0.01
Bradenton (city) Manatee	5	0.01
Dunedin (city) Pinellas	5	0.01

Hawaii Native/Pacific Islander: Other Polynesian

Top 10 Places Sorted by Number

Based on all places, regardless of population

Place (place type) County	Number	%
St. Petersburg (city) Pinellas	23	0.01
Jacksonville (special city) Duval	17	0.00
Largo (city) Pinellas	12	0.02
Orlando (city) Orange	12	0.01
Sky Lake (cdp) Orange	11	0.19
Fort Lauderdale (city) Broward	11	0.01
Brandon (cdp) Hillsborough	10	0.01
Coral Springs (city) Broward	9	0.01
Plantation (city) Broward	8	0.01
Tampa (city) Hillsborough	7	0.00

Top 10 Places Sorted by Percent

Based on all places, regardless of population

Place (place type) County	Number	%
Charleston Park (cdp) Lee	3	0.73
Sky Lake (cdp) Orange	11	0.19
Pine Castle (cdp) Orange	4	0.05
Doctor Phillips (cdp) Orange	4	0.04
Meadow Woods (cdp) Orange	4	0.04
Tavares (city) Lake	4	0.04
Golden Lakes (cdp) Palm Beach	3	0.04
Malabar (town) Brevard	1	0.04
Oak Ridge (cdp) Orange	6	0.03
Winter Garden (city) Orange	4	0.03

Top 10 Places Sorted by Percent

Based on places with populations of 10,000 or more

Place (place type) County	Number	%
Meadow Woods (cdp) Orange	4	0.04
Oak Ridge (cdp) Orange	6	0.03
Winter Garden (city) Orange	4	0.03
Azalea Park (cdp) Orange	3	0.03
Largo (city) Pinellas	12	0.02
Ocoee (city) Orange	5	0.02
Bayshore Gardens (cdp) Manatee	4	0.02
Cutler Ridge (cdp) Miami-Dade	4	0.02
Lynn Haven (city) Bay	2	0.02
Miami Shores (village) Miami-Dade	2	0.02

Hawaii Native/Pacific Islander: Other Pacific Islander, specified

Top 10 Places Sorted by Number

Based on all places, regardless of population

Place (place type) County	Number	%
Jacksonville (special city) Duval	59	0.01
St. Petersburg (city) Pinellas	26	0.01
Tampa (city) Hillsborough	25	0.01
Miami (city) Miami-Dade	21	0.01
Tallahassee (city) Leon	21	0.01
Gainesville (city) Alachua	16	0.02
Delray Beach (city) Palm Beach	14	0.02
Lauderhill (city) Broward	14	0.02
Orlando (city) Orange	13	0.01
Willow Oak (cdp) Polk	10	0.20

Top 10 Places Sorted by Percent

Based on all places, regardless of population

Place (place type) County	Number	%
De Leon Springs (cdp) Volusia	6	0.25
Willow Oak (cdp) Polk	10	0.20
Manattee Road (cdp) Levy	3	0.15
North Brooksville (cdp) Hernando	2	0.14
Southeast Arcadia (cdp) De Soto	6	0.10
Perry (city) Taylor	6	0.09
Goulding (cdp) Escambia	4	0.09
Williston (city) Levy	2	0.09
Graceville (city) Jackson	2	0.08
Ridgecrest (cdp) Pinellas	2	0.08

Top 10 Places Sorted by Percent

Based on places with populations of 10,000 or more

Place (place type) County	Number	%
Kings Point (cdp) Palm Beach	5	0.04
Wilton Manors (city) Broward	5	0.04
Middleburg (cdp) Clay	4	0.04
Riviera Beach (city) Palm Beach	8	0.03
Fort Walton Beach (city) Okaloosa	6	0.03
Hamptons at Boca Raton (cdp) Palm Beach	3	0.03
Gainesville (city) Alachua	16	0.02
Delray Beach (city) Palm Beach	14	0.02
Lauderhill (city) Broward	14	0.02
Daytona Beach (city) Volusia	10	0.02

Hawaii Native/Pacific Islander: Other Pacific Islander, not specified

Top 10 Places Sorted by Number

Based on all places, regardless of population

Place (place type) County	Number	%
Miami (city) Miami-Dade	509	0.14
Jacksonville (special city) Duval	437	0.06
Tampa (city) Hillsborough	260	0.09
Orlando (city) Orange	251	0.13
North Miami (city) Miami-Dade	209	0.35
Miramar (city) Broward	209	0.29
Delray Beach (city) Palm Beach	183	0.30
Sunrise (city) Broward	174	0.20
Lauderhill (city) Broward	152	0.26
Fort Lauderdale (city) Broward	149	0.10

Top 10 Places Sorted by Percent

Based on all places, regardless of population

Place (place type) County	Number	%
Lake Harbor (cdp) Palm Beach	2	1.03
Hillsboro Pines (cdp) Broward	4	0.99
Gun Club Estates (cdp) Palm Beach	7	0.98
Belle Glade (city) Palm Beach	138	0.93
Center Hill (city) Sumter	8	0.88
Ebro (town) Washington	2	0.80
Sunshine Acres (cdp) Broward	6	0.73
St. Leo (town) Pasco	3	0.50
Watertown (cdp) Columbia	14	0.49

Notes: (cdp) census designated place; Refer to the User's Guide in the front of the book for more detailed information.

Tangerine (cdp) Orange	4	0.48

Top 10 Places Sorted by Percent
Based on places with populations of 10,000 or more

Place (place type) County	Number	%
Belle Glade (city) Palm Beach	138	0.93
North Miami (city) Miami-Dade	209	0.35
Pine Hills (cdp) Orange	138	0.33
Palmetto Estates (cdp) Miami-Dade	45	0.33
Delray Beach (city) Palm Beach	183	0.30
Norland (cdp) Miami-Dade	70	0.30
Miramar (city) Broward	209	0.29
Golden Glades (cdp) Miami-Dade	93	0.29
Pinewood (cdp) Miami-Dade	46	0.28
North Miami Beach (city) Miami-Dade	110	0.27

Hispanic or Latino

Top 10 Places Sorted by Number
Based on all places, regardless of population

Place (place type) County	Number	%
Miami (city) Miami-Dade	238,351	65.76
Hialeah (city) Miami-Dade	204,543	90.34
Tampa (city) Hillsborough	58,522	19.29
Fountainbleau (cdp) Miami-Dade	51,948	87.24
Tamiami (cdp) Miami-Dade	47,654	86.98
Miami Beach (city) Miami-Dade	47,000	53.45
Kendale Lakes (cdp) Miami-Dade	43,574	76.58
Pembroke Pines (city) Broward	38,700	28.16
Kendall (cdp) Miami-Dade	37,549	49.91
Orlando (city) Orange	32,510	17.48

Top 10 Places Sorted by Percent
Based on all places, regardless of population

Place (place type) County	Number	%
Sweetwater (city) Miami-Dade	13,253	93.16
Hialeah (city) Miami-Dade	204,543	90.34
Hialeah Gardens (city) Miami-Dade	17,324	89.78
Fountainbleau (cdp) Miami-Dade	51,948	87.24
Tamiami (cdp) Miami-Dade	47,654	86.98
Westchester (cdp) Miami-Dade	25,824	85.31
West Miami (city) Miami-Dade	4,927	84.04
University Park (cdp) Miami-Dade	21,945	82.69
Coral Terrace (cdp) Miami-Dade	20,015	82.10
Kendall West (cdp) Miami-Dade	30,060	79.03

Top 10 Places Sorted by Percent
Based on places with populations of 10,000 or more

Place (place type) County	Number	%
Sweetwater (city) Miami-Dade	13,253	93.16
Hialeah (city) Miami-Dade	204,543	90.34
Hialeah Gardens (city) Miami-Dade	17,324	89.78
Fountainbleau (cdp) Miami-Dade	51,948	87.24
Tamiami (cdp) Miami-Dade	47,654	86.98
Westchester (cdp) Miami-Dade	25,824	85.31
University Park (cdp) Miami-Dade	21,945	82.69
Coral Terrace (cdp) Miami-Dade	20,015	82.10
Kendall West (cdp) Miami-Dade	30,060	79.03
Kendale Lakes (cdp) Miami-Dade	43,574	76.58

Hispanic: Central American

Top 10 Places Sorted by Number
Based on all places, regardless of population

Place (place type) County	Number	%
Miami (city) Miami-Dade	40,158	11.08
Hialeah (city) Miami-Dade	14,668	6.48
Fountainbleau (cdp) Miami-Dade	7,342	12.33
Kendale Lakes (cdp) Miami-Dade	3,640	6.40
Tamiami (cdp) Miami-Dade	3,451	6.30
Kendall (cdp) Miami-Dade	3,310	4.40
Miami Beach (city) Miami-Dade	3,096	3.52
Lake Worth (city) Palm Beach	2,965	8.44
Sweetwater (city) Miami-Dade	2,818	19.81
West Palm Beach (city) Palm Beach	2,745	3.34

Top 10 Places Sorted by Percent
Based on all places, regardless of population

Place (place type) County	Number	%
Sweetwater (city) Miami-Dade	2,818	19.81
Indiantown (cdp) Martin	985	17.63
Fountainbleau (cdp) Miami-Dade	7,342	12.33
Miami (city) Miami-Dade	40,158	11.08
Canal Point (cdp) Palm Beach	50	9.52
Lake Worth (city) Palm Beach	2,965	8.44
Homestead (city) Miami-Dade	2,595	8.13
West Little River (cdp) Miami-Dade	2,528	7.78
Hialeah Gardens (city) Miami-Dade	1,472	7.63
Broadview Park (cdp) Broward	481	7.08

Top 10 Places Sorted by Percent
Based on places with populations of 10,000 or more

Place (place type) County	Number	%
Sweetwater (city) Miami-Dade	2,818	19.81
Fountainbleau (cdp) Miami-Dade	7,342	12.33
Miami (city) Miami-Dade	40,158	11.08
Lake Worth (city) Palm Beach	2,965	8.44
Homestead (city) Miami-Dade	2,595	8.13
West Little River (cdp) Miami-Dade	2,528	7.78
Hialeah Gardens (city) Miami-Dade	1,472	7.63
Richmond West (cdp) Miami-Dade	1,963	6.99
Kendall West (cdp) Miami-Dade	2,511	6.60
Hialeah (city) Miami-Dade	14,668	6.48

Hispanic: Costa Rican

Top 10 Places Sorted by Number
Based on all places, regardless of population

Place (place type) County	Number	%
Miami (city) Miami-Dade	775	0.21
Hialeah (city) Miami-Dade	473	0.21
Miami Beach (city) Miami-Dade	293	0.33
Jacksonville (special city) Duval	259	0.04
Hollywood (city) Broward	256	0.18
Tampa (city) Hillsborough	233	0.08
Pembroke Pines (city) Broward	227	0.17
Kendall (cdp) Miami-Dade	171	0.23
Fountainbleau (cdp) Miami-Dade	153	0.26
Carol City (cdp) Miami-Dade	128	0.22

Top 10 Places Sorted by Percent
Based on all places, regardless of population

Place (place type) County	Number	%
Medley (town) Miami-Dade	10	0.91
Miami Springs (city) Miami-Dade	109	0.79
Virginia Gardens (village) Miami-Dade	18	0.77
Golden Beach (town) Miami-Dade	7	0.76
Hillcrest Heights (town) Polk	2	0.75
Callahan (town) Nassau	7	0.73
Naples Park (cdp) Collier	33	0.49
Utopia (cdp) Broward	3	0.42
North Beach (cdp) Indian River	1	0.41
El Portal (village) Miami-Dade	10	0.40

Top 10 Places Sorted by Percent
Based on places with populations of 10,000 or more

Place (place type) County	Number	%
Miami Springs (city) Miami-Dade	109	0.79
Miami Beach (city) Miami-Dade	293	0.33
Doral (cdp) Miami-Dade	66	0.32
Glenvar Heights (cdp) Miami-Dade	52	0.32
Westwood Lakes (cdp) Miami-Dade	37	0.31
Princeton (cdp) Miami-Dade	30	0.30
Richmond West (cdp) Miami-Dade	82	0.29
Key Biscayne (village) Miami-Dade	30	0.29
Kendall West (cdp) Miami-Dade	105	0.28
The Hammocks (cdp) Miami-Dade	126	0.27

Hispanic: Guatemalan

Top 10 Places Sorted by Number
Based on all places, regardless of population

Place (place type) County	Number	%
Miami (city) Miami-Dade	2,475	0.68
West Palm Beach (city) Palm Beach	1,841	2.24
Lake Worth (city) Palm Beach	1,711	4.87
Homestead (city) Miami-Dade	1,059	3.32
Indiantown (cdp) Martin	923	16.52
Immokalee (cdp) Collier	861	4.36
Hialeah (city) Miami-Dade	823	0.36
Fort Lauderdale (city) Broward	477	0.31
Fort Myers (city) Lee	475	0.99
Lake Worth Corridor (cdp) Palm Beach	459	2.46

Top 10 Places Sorted by Percent
Based on all places, regardless of population

Place (place type) County	Number	%
Indiantown (cdp) Martin	923	16.52
Lake Worth (city) Palm Beach	1,711	4.87
Immokalee (cdp) Collier	861	4.36
Tice (cdp) Lee	191	4.21
Mangonia Park (town) Palm Beach	49	3.82
Homestead (city) Miami-Dade	1,059	3.32
Westgate-Belvedere Homes (cdp) Palm Beach	265	3.26
Jennings (town) Hamilton	25	3.00
Lake Worth Corridor (cdp) Palm Beach	459	2.46
Fanning Springs (city) Levy	17	2.31

Top 10 Places Sorted by Percent
Based on places with populations of 10,000 or more

Place (place type) County	Number	%
Lake Worth (city) Palm Beach	1,711	4.87
Immokalee (cdp) Collier	861	4.36
Homestead (city) Miami-Dade	1,059	3.32
Lake Worth Corridor (cdp) Palm Beach	459	2.46
West Palm Beach (city) Palm Beach	1,841	2.24
Stuart (city) Martin	186	1.27
Bonita Springs (city) Lee	393	1.20
West Little River (cdp) Miami-Dade	391	1.20
Marathon (city) Monroe	120	1.17
Jupiter (town) Palm Beach	427	1.09

Hispanic: Honduran

Top 10 Places Sorted by Number
Based on all places, regardless of population

Place (place type) County	Number	%
Miami (city) Miami-Dade	12,118	3.34
Hialeah (city) Miami-Dade	2,593	1.15
Miami Beach (city) Miami-Dade	1,062	1.21
Tampa (city) Hillsborough	778	0.26
West Little River (cdp) Miami-Dade	709	2.18
Fountainbleau (cdp) Miami-Dade	650	1.09
North Miami (city) Miami-Dade	565	0.94
Lake Worth (city) Palm Beach	559	1.59
Carol City (cdp) Miami-Dade	428	0.72
Hollywood (city) Broward	418	0.30

Top 10 Places Sorted by Percent
Based on all places, regardless of population

Place (place type) County	Number	%
Loch Lomond (cdp) Broward	128	3.62
Miami (city) Miami-Dade	12,118	3.34
Broadview Park (cdp) Broward	182	2.68
Canal Point (cdp) Palm Beach	13	2.48
West Little River (cdp) Miami-Dade	709	2.18
Bonnie Lock-Woodsetter North (cdp) Broward	73	1.71
Pinewood (cdp) Miami-Dade	276	1.67
Lake Worth (city) Palm Beach	559	1.59
Medley (town) Miami-Dade	17	1.55
Gladeview (cdp) Miami-Dade	223	1.54

Notes: (cdp) census designated place; Refer to the User's Guide in the front of the book for more detailed information.

Top 10 Places Sorted by Percent
Based on places with populations of 10,000 or more

Place (place type) County	Number	%
Miami (city) Miami-Dade	12,118	3.34
West Little River (cdp) Miami-Dade	709	2.18
Pinewood (cdp) Miami-Dade	276	1.67
Lake Worth (city) Palm Beach	559	1.59
Gladeview (cdp) Miami-Dade	223	1.54
Sweetwater (city) Miami-Dade	187	1.31
Miami Beach (city) Miami-Dade	1,062	1.21
Hialeah Gardens (city) Miami-Dade	223	1.16
Lake Worth Corridor (cdp) Palm Beach	216	1.16
Hialeah (city) Miami-Dade	2,593	1.15

Hispanic: Nicaraguan

Top 10 Places Sorted by Number
Based on all places, regardless of population

Place (place type) County	Number	%
Miami (city) Miami-Dade	20,543	5.67
Hialeah (city) Miami-Dade	9,211	4.07
Fountainbleau (cdp) Miami-Dade	5,624	9.44
Kendale Lakes (cdp) Miami-Dade	2,612	4.59
Tamiami (cdp) Miami-Dade	2,551	4.66
Sweetwater (city) Miami-Dade	2,366	16.63
Kendall (cdp) Miami-Dade	1,869	2.48
Kendall West (cdp) Miami-Dade	1,670	4.39
The Hammocks (cdp) Miami-Dade	1,364	2.88
Carol City (cdp) Miami-Dade	1,305	2.20

Top 10 Places Sorted by Percent
Based on all places, regardless of population

Place (place type) County	Number	%
Sweetwater (city) Miami-Dade	2,366	16.63
Fountainbleau (cdp) Miami-Dade	5,624	9.44
Canal Point (cdp) Palm Beach	32	6.10
Miami (city) Miami-Dade	20,543	5.67
Hialeah Gardens (city) Miami-Dade	939	4.87
Tamiami (cdp) Miami-Dade	2,551	4.66
Kendale Lakes (cdp) Miami-Dade	2,612	4.59
Kendall West (cdp) Miami-Dade	1,670	4.39
Richmond West (cdp) Miami-Dade	1,178	4.19
Hialeah (city) Miami-Dade	9,211	4.07

Top 10 Places Sorted by Percent
Based on places with populations of 10,000 or more

Place (place type) County	Number	%
Sweetwater (city) Miami-Dade	2,366	16.63
Fountainbleau (cdp) Miami-Dade	5,624	9.44
Miami (city) Miami-Dade	20,543	5.67
Hialeah Gardens (city) Miami-Dade	939	4.87
Tamiami (cdp) Miami-Dade	2,551	4.66
Kendale Lakes (cdp) Miami-Dade	2,612	4.59
Kendall West (cdp) Miami-Dade	1,670	4.39
Richmond West (cdp) Miami-Dade	1,178	4.19
Hialeah (city) Miami-Dade	9,211	4.07
Gladeview (cdp) Miami-Dade	536	3.70

Hispanic: Panamanian

Top 10 Places Sorted by Number
Based on all places, regardless of population

Place (place type) County	Number	%
Miami (city) Miami-Dade	657	0.18
Jacksonville (special city) Duval	461	0.06
Tampa (city) Hillsborough	407	0.13
Hialeah (city) Miami-Dade	379	0.17
Pembroke Pines (city) Broward	367	0.27
Miramar (city) Broward	336	0.46
Fountainbleau (cdp) Miami-Dade	293	0.49
Kendall (cdp) Miami-Dade	268	0.36
Hollywood (city) Broward	241	0.17
Country Club (cdp) Miami-Dade	240	0.66

Top 10 Places Sorted by Percent
Based on all places, regardless of population

Place (place type) County	Number	%
Indian Creek (village) Miami-Dade	1	3.03
Lisbon (cdp) Lake	5	1.83
Miami Gardens (cdp) Broward	29	1.07
Doral (cdp) Miami-Dade	192	0.94
Richmond West (cdp) Miami-Dade	210	0.75
Lakes by the Bay (cdp) Miami-Dade	65	0.72
Tyndall AFB (cdp) Bay	19	0.69
Country Club (cdp) Miami-Dade	240	0.66
Palmetto Estates (cdp) Miami-Dade	80	0.59
Eglin AFB (cdp) Okaloosa	41	0.51

Top 10 Places Sorted by Percent
Based on places with populations of 10,000 or more

Place (place type) County	Number	%
Doral (cdp) Miami-Dade	192	0.94
Richmond West (cdp) Miami-Dade	210	0.75
Country Club (cdp) Miami-Dade	240	0.66
Palmetto Estates (cdp) Miami-Dade	80	0.59
Fountainbleau (cdp) Miami-Dade	293	0.49
The Hammocks (cdp) Miami-Dade	226	0.48
Miramar (city) Broward	336	0.46
Poinciana (cdp) Osceola	58	0.43
Ives Estates (cdp) Miami-Dade	70	0.40
Country Walk (cdp) Miami-Dade	43	0.40

Hispanic: Salvadoran

Top 10 Places Sorted by Number
Based on all places, regardless of population

Place (place type) County	Number	%
Miami (city) Miami-Dade	2,482	0.68
Homestead (city) Miami-Dade	859	2.69
Hialeah (city) Miami-Dade	763	0.34
Fort Lauderdale (city) Broward	674	0.44
Lake Worth (city) Palm Beach	433	1.23
Oakland Park (city) Broward	425	1.37
Tampa (city) Hillsborough	362	0.12
Kendall (cdp) Miami-Dade	337	0.45
North Lauderdale (city) Broward	336	1.04
Leisure City (cdp) Miami-Dade	286	1.29

Top 10 Places Sorted by Percent
Based on all places, regardless of population

Place (place type) County	Number	%
Clewiston (city) Hendry	200	3.10
Homestead (city) Miami-Dade	859	2.69
Belle Glade Camp (cdp) Palm Beach	20	1.75
Florida City (city) Miami-Dade	129	1.64
North Andrews Gardens (cdp) Broward	157	1.63
Greensboro (town) Gadsden	10	1.62
Quincy (city) Gadsden	110	1.58
Caryville (town) Washington	3	1.38
Oakland Park (city) Broward	425	1.37
Leisure City (cdp) Miami-Dade	286	1.29

Top 10 Places Sorted by Percent
Based on places with populations of 10,000 or more

Place (place type) County	Number	%
Homestead (city) Miami-Dade	859	2.69
Oakland Park (city) Broward	425	1.37
Leisure City (cdp) Miami-Dade	286	1.29
Lake Worth Corridor (cdp) Palm Beach	235	1.26
Lake Worth (city) Palm Beach	433	1.23
North Lauderdale (city) Broward	336	1.04
Miami (city) Miami-Dade	2,482	0.68
South Miami Heights (cdp) Miami-Dade	218	0.65
Key Biscayne (village) Miami-Dade	67	0.64
Kissimmee (city) Osceola	276	0.58

Hispanic: Other Central American

Top 10 Places Sorted by Number
Based on all places, regardless of population

Place (place type) County	Number	%
Miami (city) Miami-Dade	1,108	0.31
Hialeah (city) Miami-Dade	426	0.19
Fountainbleau (cdp) Miami-Dade	143	0.24
Tamiami (cdp) Miami-Dade	95	0.17
West Little River (cdp) Miami-Dade	90	0.28
Kendale Lakes (cdp) Miami-Dade	90	0.16
Tampa (city) Hillsborough	90	0.03
Miami Beach (city) Miami-Dade	83	0.09
Kendall (cdp) Miami-Dade	79	0.11
Lake Worth (city) Palm Beach	75	0.21

Top 10 Places Sorted by Percent
Based on all places, regardless of population

Place (place type) County	Number	%
Godfrey Road (cdp) Broward	1	0.58
Village Park (cdp) Broward	5	0.56
Broadview Park (cdp) Broward	36	0.53
Sweetwater (city) Miami-Dade	68	0.48
Homestead Base (cdp) Miami-Dade	2	0.45
Miami Gardens (cdp) Broward	12	0.44
Belle Glade Camp (cdp) Palm Beach	5	0.44
Indiantown (cdp) Martin	23	0.41
Mangonia Park (town) Palm Beach	5	0.39
Loch Lomond (cdp) Broward	13	0.37

Top 10 Places Sorted by Percent
Based on places with populations of 10,000 or more

Place (place type) County	Number	%
Sweetwater (city) Miami-Dade	68	0.48
Gladeview (cdp) Miami-Dade	47	0.32
Miami (city) Miami-Dade	1,108	0.31
West Little River (cdp) Miami-Dade	90	0.28
Hialeah Gardens (city) Miami-Dade	48	0.25
Fountainbleau (cdp) Miami-Dade	143	0.24
Richmond West (cdp) Miami-Dade	63	0.22
Doral (cdp) Miami-Dade	44	0.22
Westwood Lakes (cdp) Miami-Dade	26	0.22
Princeton (cdp) Miami-Dade	22	0.22

Hispanic: Cuban

Top 10 Places Sorted by Number
Based on all places, regardless of population

Place (place type) County	Number	%
Hialeah (city) Miami-Dade	140,651	62.12
Miami (city) Miami-Dade	123,763	34.14
Tamiami (cdp) Miami-Dade	31,029	56.63
Fountainbleau (cdp) Miami-Dade	22,206	37.29
Kendale Lakes (cdp) Miami-Dade	21,953	38.58
Westchester (cdp) Miami-Dade	19,886	65.69
Miami Beach (city) Miami-Dade	18,038	20.51
Kendall (cdp) Miami-Dade	16,029	21.31
University Park (cdp) Miami-Dade	15,871	59.80
Coral Terrace (cdp) Miami-Dade	15,084	61.87

Top 10 Places Sorted by Percent
Based on all places, regardless of population

Place (place type) County	Number	%
Westchester (cdp) Miami-Dade	19,886	65.69
Hialeah (city) Miami-Dade	140,651	62.12
Coral Terrace (cdp) Miami-Dade	15,084	61.87
West Miami (city) Miami-Dade	3,612	61.61
University Park (cdp) Miami-Dade	15,871	59.80
Olympia Heights (cdp) Miami-Dade	7,755	57.65
Tamiami (cdp) Miami-Dade	31,029	56.63
Westwood Lakes (cdp) Miami-Dade	6,730	56.06
Hialeah Gardens (city) Miami-Dade	10,480	54.31
Medley (town) Miami-Dade	570	51.91

Notes: (cdp) census designated place; Refer to the User's Guide in the front of the book for more detailed information.

Top 10 Places Sorted by Percent
Based on places with populations of 10,000 or more

Place (place type) County	Number	%
Westchester (cdp) Miami-Dade	19,886	65.69
Hialeah (city) Miami-Dade	140,651	62.12
Coral Terrace (cdp) Miami-Dade	15,084	61.87
University Park (cdp) Miami-Dade	15,871	59.80
Olympia Heights (cdp) Miami-Dade	7,755	57.65
Tamiami (cdp) Miami-Dade	31,029	56.63
Westwood Lakes (cdp) Miami-Dade	6,730	56.06
Hialeah Gardens (city) Miami-Dade	10,480	54.31
Sweetwater (city) Miami-Dade	7,101	49.92
Sunset (cdp) Miami-Dade	7,989	46.58

Hispanic: Dominican Republic

Top 10 Places Sorted by Number
Based on all places, regardless of population

Place (place type) County	Number	%
Miami (city) Miami-Dade	6,370	1.76
Hialeah (city) Miami-Dade	4,106	1.81
Carol City (cdp) Miami-Dade	1,785	3.00
Fountainbleau (cdp) Miami-Dade	1,779	2.99
Hollywood (city) Broward	1,681	1.21
Pembroke Pines (city) Broward	1,637	1.19
Miramar (city) Broward	1,439	1.98
Tampa (city) Hillsborough	1,397	0.46
Country Club (cdp) Miami-Dade	1,309	3.61
Orlando (city) Orange	1,191	0.64

Top 10 Places Sorted by Percent
Based on all places, regardless of population

Place (place type) County	Number	%
Miami Gardens (cdp) Broward	125	4.62
Lake Forest (cdp) Broward	198	3.96
Country Club (cdp) Miami-Dade	1,309	3.61
Oak Ridge (cdp) Orange	677	3.03
Carol City (cdp) Miami-Dade	1,785	3.00
Fountainbleau (cdp) Miami-Dade	1,779	2.99
Hialeah Gardens (city) Miami-Dade	551	2.86
Yeehaw Junction (cdp) Osceola	609	2.80
Doral (cdp) Miami-Dade	540	2.64
Opa-locka (city) Miami-Dade	387	2.59

Top 10 Places Sorted by Percent
Based on places with populations of 10,000 or more

Place (place type) County	Number	%
Country Club (cdp) Miami-Dade	1,309	3.61
Oak Ridge (cdp) Orange	677	3.03
Carol City (cdp) Miami-Dade	1,785	3.00
Fountainbleau (cdp) Miami-Dade	1,779	2.99
Hialeah Gardens (city) Miami-Dade	551	2.86
Yeehaw Junction (cdp) Osceola	609	2.80
Doral (cdp) Miami-Dade	540	2.64
Opa-locka (city) Miami-Dade	387	2.59
Kendall West (cdp) Miami-Dade	982	2.58
South Miami Heights (cdp) Miami-Dade	851	2.54

Hispanic: Mexican

Top 10 Places Sorted by Number
Based on all places, regardless of population

Place (place type) County	Number	%
Immokalee (cdp) Collier	11,354	57.45
Homestead (city) Miami-Dade	7,279	22.81
Tampa (city) Hillsborough	6,272	2.07
Jacksonville (special city) Duval	6,076	0.83
Leisure City (cdp) Miami-Dade	5,259	23.74
Clearwater (city) Pinellas	4,771	4.39
Fort Pierce (city) St. Lucie	4,311	11.49
Bonita Springs (city) Lee	3,955	12.06
Plant City (city) Hillsborough	3,681	12.30
Miami (city) Miami-Dade	3,669	1.01

Top 10 Places Sorted by Percent
Based on all places, regardless of population

Place (place type) County	Number	%
Fellsmere (city) Indian River	2,585	67.79
Wimauma (cdp) Hillsborough	2,816	66.32
Pierson (town) Volusia	1,593	61.36
Immokalee (cdp) Collier	11,354	57.45
Naples Manor (cdp) Collier	2,601	50.15
Dade City North (cdp) Pasco	1,616	48.69
Wahneta (cdp) Polk	2,028	42.87
Zolfo Springs (town) Hardee	702	42.78
Southeast Arcadia (cdp) De Soto	2,542	41.92
Dover (cdp) Hillsborough	1,162	41.53

Top 10 Places Sorted by Percent
Based on places with populations of 10,000 or more

Place (place type) County	Number	%
Immokalee (cdp) Collier	11,354	57.45
Leisure City (cdp) Miami-Dade	5,259	23.74
Homestead (city) Miami-Dade	7,279	22.81
Palmetto (city) Manatee	2,821	22.44
Haines City (city) Polk	2,309	17.53
Golden Gate (cdp) Collier	3,529	16.84
Lake Worth Corridor (cdp) Palm Beach	3,032	16.25
Belle Glade (city) Palm Beach	2,302	15.44
Plant City (city) Hillsborough	3,681	12.30
Bonita Springs (city) Lee	3,955	12.06

Hispanic: Puerto Rican

Top 10 Places Sorted by Number
Based on all places, regardless of population

Place (place type) County	Number	%
Tampa (city) Hillsborough	17,527	5.78
Orlando (city) Orange	17,029	9.16
Kissimmee (city) Osceola	11,312	23.66
Jacksonville (special city) Duval	11,066	1.50
Miami (city) Miami-Dade	10,257	2.83
Deltona (city) Volusia	9,136	13.14
Yeehaw Junction (cdp) Osceola	7,980	36.64
Town 'n' Country (cdp) Hillsborough	7,505	10.35
Hollywood (city) Broward	7,463	5.36
Pembroke Pines (city) Broward	6,887	5.01

Top 10 Places Sorted by Percent
Based on all places, regardless of population

Place (place type) County	Number	%
Harlem Heights (cdp) Lee	396	37.18
Yeehaw Junction (cdp) Osceola	7,980	36.64
Meadow Woods (cdp) Orange	3,772	33.42
Poinciana (cdp) Osceola	3,789	27.76
Azalea Park (cdp) Orange	2,745	24.79
Kissimmee (city) Osceola	11,312	23.66
Oak Ridge (cdp) Orange	4,249	19.01
Southchase (cdp) Orange	880	18.99
Interlachen (town) Putnam	252	17.08
Union Park (cdp) Orange	1,730	16.98

Top 10 Places Sorted by Percent
Based on places with populations of 10,000 or more

Place (place type) County	Number	%
Yeehaw Junction (cdp) Osceola	7,980	36.64
Meadow Woods (cdp) Orange	3,772	33.42
Poinciana (cdp) Osceola	3,789	27.76
Azalea Park (cdp) Orange	2,745	24.79
Kissimmee (city) Osceola	11,312	23.66
Oak Ridge (cdp) Orange	4,249	19.01
Union Park (cdp) Orange	1,730	16.98
Deltona (city) Volusia	9,136	13.14
Egypt Lake-Leto (cdp) Hillsborough	3,559	10.86
Town 'n' Country (cdp) Hillsborough	7,505	10.35

Hispanic: South American

Top 10 Places Sorted by Number
Based on all places, regardless of population

Place (place type) County	Number	%
Miami (city) Miami-Dade	15,076	4.16
Hialeah (city) Miami-Dade	12,510	5.53
Miami Beach (city) Miami-Dade	11,589	13.18
The Hammocks (cdp) Miami-Dade	9,494	20.04
Pembroke Pines (city) Broward	8,292	6.03
Fountainbleau (cdp) Miami-Dade	8,100	13.60
Kendall (cdp) Miami-Dade	7,961	10.58
Kendale Lakes (cdp) Miami-Dade	7,076	12.44
Kendall West (cdp) Miami-Dade	7,073	18.60
Hollywood (city) Broward	6,952	4.99

Top 10 Places Sorted by Percent
Based on all places, regardless of population

Place (place type) County	Number	%
Doral (cdp) Miami-Dade	4,989	24.41
The Hammocks (cdp) Miami-Dade	9,494	20.04
Kendall West (cdp) Miami-Dade	7,073	18.60
Key Biscayne (village) Miami-Dade	1,793	17.06
North Bay Village (city) Miami-Dade	1,087	16.14
Virginia Gardens (village) Miami-Dade	345	14.69
The Crossings (cdp) Miami-Dade	3,326	14.12
Sunny Isles Beach (city) Miami-Dade	2,150	14.04
Fountainbleau (cdp) Miami-Dade	8,100	13.60
Bay Harbor Islands (town) Miami-Dade	699	13.58

Top 10 Places Sorted by Percent
Based on places with populations of 10,000 or more

Place (place type) County	Number	%
Doral (cdp) Miami-Dade	4,989	24.41
The Hammocks (cdp) Miami-Dade	9,494	20.04
Kendall West (cdp) Miami-Dade	7,073	18.60
Key Biscayne (village) Miami-Dade	1,793	17.06
The Crossings (cdp) Miami-Dade	3,326	14.12
Sunny Isles Beach (city) Miami-Dade	2,150	14.04
Fountainbleau (cdp) Miami-Dade	8,100	13.60
Weston (city) Broward	6,620	13.43
Country Club (cdp) Miami-Dade	4,843	13.34
Miami Beach (city) Miami-Dade	11,589	13.18

Hispanic: Argentinean

Top 10 Places Sorted by Number
Based on all places, regardless of population

Place (place type) County	Number	%
Miami Beach (city) Miami-Dade	2,680	3.05
Miami (city) Miami-Dade	1,669	0.46
Hialeah (city) Miami-Dade	632	0.28
Kendall (cdp) Miami-Dade	605	0.80
Fountainbleau (cdp) Miami-Dade	518	0.87
Coral Springs (city) Broward	498	0.42
Pembroke Pines (city) Broward	463	0.34
Hollywood (city) Broward	456	0.33
Aventura (city) Miami-Dade	424	1.68
The Hammocks (cdp) Miami-Dade	401	0.85

Top 10 Places Sorted by Percent
Based on all places, regardless of population

Place (place type) County	Number	%
North Bay Village (city) Miami-Dade	252	3.74
Miami Beach (city) Miami-Dade	2,680	3.05
Bay Harbor Islands (town) Miami-Dade	157	3.05
Key Biscayne (village) Miami-Dade	282	2.68
Sunny Isles Beach (city) Miami-Dade	371	2.42
Surfside (town) Miami-Dade	117	2.38
Bal Harbour (village) Miami-Dade	74	2.24
Fisher Island (cdp) Miami-Dade	8	1.71
Aventura (city) Miami-Dade	424	1.68
Biscayne Park (village) Miami-Dade	52	1.59

Notes: (cdp) census designated place; Refer to the User's Guide in the front of the book for more detailed information.

Top 10 Places Sorted by Percent

Based on places with populations of 10,000 or more

Place (place type) County	Number	%
Miami Beach (city) Miami-Dade	2,680	3.05
Key Biscayne (village) Miami-Dade	282	2.68
Sunny Isles Beach (city) Miami-Dade	371	2.42
Aventura (city) Miami-Dade	424	1.68
Ojus (cdp) Miami-Dade	249	1.50
Doral (cdp) Miami-Dade	262	1.28
Ives Estates (cdp) Miami-Dade	183	1.04
The Crossings (cdp) Miami-Dade	233	0.99
Fountainbleau (cdp) Miami-Dade	518	0.87
The Hammocks (cdp) Miami-Dade	401	0.85

Hispanic: Bolivian

Top 10 Places Sorted by Number

Based on all places, regardless of population

Place (place type) County	Number	%
Miami (city) Miami-Dade	355	0.10
Miami Beach (city) Miami-Dade	176	0.20
Kendall (cdp) Miami-Dade	170	0.23
Fountainbleau (cdp) Miami-Dade	153	0.26
Hialeah (city) Miami-Dade	113	0.05
Hollywood (city) Broward	100	0.07
Kendale Lakes (cdp) Miami-Dade	96	0.17
The Hammocks (cdp) Miami-Dade	93	0.20
Tamiami (cdp) Miami-Dade	82	0.15
Kendall West (cdp) Miami-Dade	79	0.21

Top 10 Places Sorted by Percent

Based on all places, regardless of population

Place (place type) County	Number	%
North Bay Village (city) Miami-Dade	31	0.46
Medley (town) Miami-Dade	5	0.46
Lely Resort (cdp) Collier	5	0.35
Golden Beach (town) Miami-Dade	3	0.33
Naples Park (cdp) Collier	21	0.31
The Crossings (cdp) Miami-Dade	69	0.29
Fountainbleau (cdp) Miami-Dade	153	0.26
Key Biscayne (village) Miami-Dade	27	0.26
Bay Harbor Islands (town) Miami-Dade	13	0.25
Kendall (cdp) Miami-Dade	170	0.23

Top 10 Places Sorted by Percent

Based on places with populations of 10,000 or more

Place (place type) County	Number	%
The Crossings (cdp) Miami-Dade	69	0.29
Fountainbleau (cdp) Miami-Dade	153	0.26
Key Biscayne (village) Miami-Dade	27	0.26
Kendall (cdp) Miami-Dade	170	0.23
Miami Springs (city) Miami-Dade	31	0.23
Doral (cdp) Miami-Dade	45	0.22
Sunset (cdp) Miami-Dade	37	0.22
Kendall West (cdp) Miami-Dade	79	0.21
Miami Beach (city) Miami-Dade	176	0.20
The Hammocks (cdp) Miami-Dade	93	0.20

Hispanic: Chilean

Top 10 Places Sorted by Number

Based on all places, regardless of population

Place (place type) County	Number	%
Miami (city) Miami-Dade	939	0.26
Miami Beach (city) Miami-Dade	623	0.71
Hialeah (city) Miami-Dade	611	0.27
Fountainbleau (cdp) Miami-Dade	550	0.92
Kendall (cdp) Miami-Dade	479	0.64
The Hammocks (cdp) Miami-Dade	409	0.86
Kendale Lakes (cdp) Miami-Dade	381	0.67
Hollywood (city) Broward	302	0.22
Pembroke Pines (city) Broward	298	0.22
Tamiami (cdp) Miami-Dade	262	0.48

Top 10 Places Sorted by Percent

Based on all places, regardless of population

Place (place type) County	Number	%
Doral (cdp) Miami-Dade	224	1.10
North Bay Village (city) Miami-Dade	68	1.01
Fountainbleau (cdp) Miami-Dade	550	0.92
The Crossings (cdp) Miami-Dade	212	0.90
Chula Vista (cdp) Broward	5	0.87
The Hammocks (cdp) Miami-Dade	409	0.86
Country Walk (cdp) Miami-Dade	83	0.78
Cutler (cdp) Miami-Dade	129	0.74
Key Biscayne (village) Miami-Dade	76	0.72
Miami Beach (city) Miami-Dade	623	0.71

Top 10 Places Sorted by Percent

Based on places with populations of 10,000 or more

Place (place type) County	Number	%
Doral (cdp) Miami-Dade	224	1.10
Fountainbleau (cdp) Miami-Dade	550	0.92
The Crossings (cdp) Miami-Dade	212	0.90
The Hammocks (cdp) Miami-Dade	409	0.86
Country Walk (cdp) Miami-Dade	83	0.78
Cutler (cdp) Miami-Dade	129	0.74
Key Biscayne (village) Miami-Dade	76	0.72
Miami Beach (city) Miami-Dade	623	0.71
Glenvar Heights (cdp) Miami-Dade	116	0.71
Kendale Lakes (cdp) Miami-Dade	381	0.67

Hispanic: Colombian

Top 10 Places Sorted by Number

Based on all places, regardless of population

Place (place type) County	Number	%
Hialeah (city) Miami-Dade	7,152	3.16
Miami (city) Miami-Dade	5,784	1.60
The Hammocks (cdp) Miami-Dade	4,749	10.02
Pembroke Pines (city) Broward	4,124	3.00
Miami Beach (city) Miami-Dade	3,872	4.40
Kendall West (cdp) Miami-Dade	3,778	9.93
Kendale Lakes (cdp) Miami-Dade	3,619	6.36
Kendall (cdp) Miami-Dade	3,429	4.56
Fountainbleau (cdp) Miami-Dade	3,153	5.29
Hollywood (city) Broward	3,152	2.26

Top 10 Places Sorted by Percent

Based on all places, regardless of population

Place (place type) County	Number	%
The Hammocks (cdp) Miami-Dade	4,749	10.02
Kendall West (cdp) Miami-Dade	3,778	9.93
Doral (cdp) Miami-Dade	1,780	8.71
Country Club (cdp) Miami-Dade	3,134	8.63
Virginia Gardens (village) Miami-Dade	168	7.16
Key Biscayne (village) Miami-Dade	743	7.07
Kendale Lakes (cdp) Miami-Dade	3,619	6.36
Weston (city) Broward	3,052	6.19
The Crossings (cdp) Miami-Dade	1,454	6.17
Sunny Isles Beach (city) Miami-Dade	930	6.07

Top 10 Places Sorted by Percent

Based on places with populations of 10,000 or more

Place (place type) County	Number	%
The Hammocks (cdp) Miami-Dade	4,749	10.02
Kendall West (cdp) Miami-Dade	3,778	9.93
Doral (cdp) Miami-Dade	1,780	8.71
Country Club (cdp) Miami-Dade	3,134	8.63
Key Biscayne (village) Miami-Dade	743	7.07
Kendale Lakes (cdp) Miami-Dade	3,619	6.36
Weston (city) Broward	3,052	6.19
The Crossings (cdp) Miami-Dade	1,454	6.17
Sunny Isles Beach (city) Miami-Dade	930	6.07
Country Walk (cdp) Miami-Dade	594	5.58

Hispanic: Ecuadorian

Top 10 Places Sorted by Number

Based on all places, regardless of population

Place (place type) County	Number	%
Miami (city) Miami-Dade	1,408	0.39
Hialeah (city) Miami-Dade	1,159	0.51
Pembroke Pines (city) Broward	734	0.53
Hollywood (city) Broward	592	0.42
Fountainbleau (cdp) Miami-Dade	564	0.95
The Hammocks (cdp) Miami-Dade	522	1.10
Miami Beach (city) Miami-Dade	493	0.56
Coral Springs (city) Broward	441	0.38
Kendall West (cdp) Miami-Dade	417	1.10
Kendall (cdp) Miami-Dade	415	0.55

Top 10 Places Sorted by Percent

Based on all places, regardless of population

Place (place type) County	Number	%
Virginia Gardens (village) Miami-Dade	31	1.32
Doral (cdp) Miami-Dade	241	1.18
The Hammocks (cdp) Miami-Dade	522	1.10
Kendall West (cdp) Miami-Dade	417	1.10
Key Biscayne (village) Miami-Dade	102	0.97
Fountainbleau (cdp) Miami-Dade	564	0.95
Country Club (cdp) Miami-Dade	326	0.90
Country Walk (cdp) Miami-Dade	93	0.87
Sunshine Acres (cdp) Broward	7	0.85
Meadow Woods (cdp) Orange	95	0.84

Top 10 Places Sorted by Percent

Based on places with populations of 10,000 or more

Place (place type) County	Number	%
Doral (cdp) Miami-Dade	241	1.18
The Hammocks (cdp) Miami-Dade	522	1.10
Kendall West (cdp) Miami-Dade	417	1.10
Key Biscayne (village) Miami-Dade	102	0.97
Fountainbleau (cdp) Miami-Dade	564	0.95
Country Club (cdp) Miami-Dade	326	0.90
Country Walk (cdp) Miami-Dade	93	0.87
Meadow Woods (cdp) Orange	95	0.84
Hialeah Gardens (city) Miami-Dade	161	0.83
Miami Lakes (cdp) Miami-Dade	170	0.75

Hispanic: Paraguayan

Top 10 Places Sorted by Number

Based on all places, regardless of population

Place (place type) County	Number	%
Miami Beach (city) Miami-Dade	64	0.07
Miami (city) Miami-Dade	45	0.01
Kendall (cdp) Miami-Dade	31	0.04
Coral Gables (city) Miami-Dade	26	0.06
Fountainbleau (cdp) Miami-Dade	23	0.04
Doral (cdp) Miami-Dade	21	0.10
Pembroke Pines (city) Broward	20	0.01
The Crossings (cdp) Miami-Dade	18	0.08
Hialeah (city) Miami-Dade	16	0.01
Hollywood (city) Broward	15	0.01

Top 10 Places Sorted by Percent

Based on all places, regardless of population

Place (place type) County	Number	%
Fisher Island (cdp) Miami-Dade	3	0.64
Golden Beach (town) Miami-Dade	5	0.54
Ramblewood East (cdp) Broward	7	0.50
Hypoluxo (town) Palm Beach	3	0.15
North Bay Village (city) Miami-Dade	9	0.13
Key Biscayne (village) Miami-Dade	13	0.12
Village Park (cdp) Broward	1	0.11
Doral (cdp) Miami-Dade	21	0.10
Harbour Heights (cdp) Charlotte	3	0.10
Bal Harbour (village) Miami-Dade	3	0.09

Notes: (cdp) census designated place; Refer to the User's Guide in the front of the book for more detailed information.

Top 10 Places Sorted by Percent

Based on places with populations of 10,000 or more

Place (place type) County	Number	%
Key Biscayne (village) Miami-Dade	13	0.12
Doral (cdp) Miami-Dade	21	0.10
The Crossings (cdp) Miami-Dade	18	0.08
Sunny Isles Beach (city) Miami-Dade	12	0.08
Miami Beach (city) Miami-Dade	64	0.07
Coral Gables (city) Miami-Dade	26	0.06
Cutler Ridge (cdp) Miami-Dade	12	0.05
Sandalfoot Cove (cdp) Palm Beach	9	0.05
Miami Springs (city) Miami-Dade	7	0.05
South Miami (city) Miami-Dade	5	0.05

Hispanic: Peruvian

Top 10 Places Sorted by Number

Based on all places, regardless of population

Place (place type) County	Number	%
Miami (city) Miami-Dade	2,447	0.68
Miami Beach (city) Miami-Dade	1,630	1.85
The Hammocks (cdp) Miami-Dade	1,591	3.36
Kendall (cdp) Miami-Dade	1,512	2.01
Hollywood (city) Broward	1,466	1.05
Hialeah (city) Miami-Dade	1,418	0.63
Kendale Lakes (cdp) Miami-Dade	1,157	2.03
Kendall West (cdp) Miami-Dade	1,084	2.85
Pembroke Pines (city) Broward	1,082	0.79
Fountainbleau (cdp) Miami-Dade	1,044	1.75

Top 10 Places Sorted by Percent

Based on all places, regardless of population

Place (place type) County	Number	%
The Hammocks (cdp) Miami-Dade	1,591	3.36
Virginia Gardens (village) Miami-Dade	76	3.24
Bay Harbor Islands (town) Miami-Dade	160	3.11
Doral (cdp) Miami-Dade	602	2.95
Kendall West (cdp) Miami-Dade	1,084	2.85
The Crossings (cdp) Miami-Dade	634	2.69
Key Biscayne (village) Miami-Dade	261	2.48
Ojus (cdp) Miami-Dade	381	2.29
North Bay Village (city) Miami-Dade	146	2.17
Kendale Lakes (cdp) Miami-Dade	1,157	2.03

Top 10 Places Sorted by Percent

Based on places with populations of 10,000 or more

Place (place type) County	Number	%
The Hammocks (cdp) Miami-Dade	1,591	3.36
Doral (cdp) Miami-Dade	602	2.95
Kendall West (cdp) Miami-Dade	1,084	2.85
The Crossings (cdp) Miami-Dade	634	2.69
Key Biscayne (village) Miami-Dade	261	2.48
Ojus (cdp) Miami-Dade	381	2.29
Kendale Lakes (cdp) Miami-Dade	1,157	2.03
Kendall (cdp) Miami-Dade	1,512	2.01
Miami Springs (city) Miami-Dade	260	1.90
Miami Beach (city) Miami-Dade	1,630	1.85

Hispanic: Uruguayan

Top 10 Places Sorted by Number

Based on all places, regardless of population

Place (place type) County	Number	%
Miami Beach (city) Miami-Dade	222	0.25
Miami (city) Miami-Dade	221	0.06
Hialeah (city) Miami-Dade	118	0.05
Hollywood (city) Broward	113	0.08
Kendale Lakes (cdp) Miami-Dade	100	0.18
Coral Springs (city) Broward	99	0.08
North Andrews Gardens (cdp) Broward	93	0.96
Sunrise (city) Broward	92	0.11
The Hammocks (cdp) Miami-Dade	79	0.17
Pembroke Pines (city) Broward	78	0.06

Top 10 Places Sorted by Percent

Based on all places, regardless of population

Place (place type) County	Number	%
Cloud Lake (town) Palm Beach	2	1.20
North Andrews Gardens (cdp) Broward	93	0.96
Twin Lakes (cdp) Broward	10	0.53
Golden Beach (town) Miami-Dade	4	0.44
Sunshine Acres (cdp) Broward	3	0.36
Glen Ridge (town) Palm Beach	1	0.36
North Bay Village (city) Miami-Dade	22	0.33
Bay Harbor Islands (town) Miami-Dade	17	0.33
Palm Aire (cdp) Broward	4	0.26
Miami Beach (city) Miami-Dade	222	0.25

Top 10 Places Sorted by Percent

Based on places with populations of 10,000 or more

Place (place type) County	Number	%
Miami Beach (city) Miami-Dade	222	0.25
The Crossings (cdp) Miami-Dade	48	0.20
Ojus (cdp) Miami-Dade	31	0.19
Sunny Isles Beach (city) Miami-Dade	29	0.19
Kendale Lakes (cdp) Miami-Dade	100	0.18
The Hammocks (cdp) Miami-Dade	79	0.17
Greenacres (city) Palm Beach	48	0.17
Doral (cdp) Miami-Dade	35	0.17
Country Club (cdp) Miami-Dade	56	0.15
Glenvar Heights (cdp) Miami-Dade	24	0.15

Hispanic: Venezuelan

Top 10 Places Sorted by Number

Based on all places, regardless of population

Place (place type) County	Number	%
Weston (city) Broward	2,020	4.10
Miami (city) Miami-Dade	1,959	0.54
Fountainbleau (cdp) Miami-Dade	1,868	3.14
Doral (cdp) Miami-Dade	1,680	8.22
Miami Beach (city) Miami-Dade	1,572	1.79
The Hammocks (cdp) Miami-Dade	1,488	3.14
Pembroke Pines (city) Broward	1,242	0.90
Hialeah (city) Miami-Dade	1,117	0.49
Kendall (cdp) Miami-Dade	1,108	1.47
Kendall West (cdp) Miami-Dade	1,015	2.67

Top 10 Places Sorted by Percent

Based on all places, regardless of population

Place (place type) County	Number	%
Doral (cdp) Miami-Dade	1,680	8.22
Weston (city) Broward	2,020	4.10
Fisher Island (cdp) Miami-Dade	19	4.07
Fountainbleau (cdp) Miami-Dade	1,868	3.14
The Hammocks (cdp) Miami-Dade	1,488	3.14
Kendall West (cdp) Miami-Dade	1,015	2.67
Lazy Lake (village) Broward	1	2.63
Key Biscayne (village) Miami-Dade	248	2.36
North Bay Village (city) Miami-Dade	145	2.15
Glenvar Heights (cdp) Miami-Dade	332	2.04

Top 10 Places Sorted by Percent

Based on places with populations of 10,000 or more

Place (place type) County	Number	%
Doral (cdp) Miami-Dade	1,680	8.22
Weston (city) Broward	2,020	4.10
Fountainbleau (cdp) Miami-Dade	1,868	3.14
The Hammocks (cdp) Miami-Dade	1,488	3.14
Kendall West (cdp) Miami-Dade	1,015	2.67
Key Biscayne (village) Miami-Dade	248	2.36
Glenvar Heights (cdp) Miami-Dade	332	2.04
Sunny Isles Beach (city) Miami-Dade	300	1.96
The Crossings (cdp) Miami-Dade	453	1.92
Miami Beach (city) Miami-Dade	1,572	1.79

Hispanic: Other South American

Top 10 Places Sorted by Number

Based on all places, regardless of population

Place (place type) County	Number	%
Miami Beach (city) Miami-Dade	257	0.29
Miami (city) Miami-Dade	249	0.07
Hollywood (city) Broward	188	0.13
Pembroke Pines (city) Broward	185	0.13
Hialeah (city) Miami-Dade	174	0.08
The Hammocks (cdp) Miami-Dade	157	0.33
Fountainbleau (cdp) Miami-Dade	156	0.26
Coral Springs (city) Broward	156	0.13
Kendall (cdp) Miami-Dade	147	0.20
Weston (city) Broward	130	0.26

Top 10 Places Sorted by Percent

Based on all places, regardless of population

Place (place type) County	Number	%
Surfside (town) Miami-Dade	30	0.61
Village Park (cdp) Broward	5	0.56
Doral (cdp) Miami-Dade	99	0.48
Biscayne Park (village) Miami-Dade	14	0.43
The Crossings (cdp) Miami-Dade	83	0.35
The Hammocks (cdp) Miami-Dade	157	0.33
Key Biscayne (village) Miami-Dade	35	0.33
Bay Harbor Islands (town) Miami-Dade	17	0.33
Bronson (town) Levy	3	0.31
Richmond West (cdp) Miami-Dade	84	0.30

Top 10 Places Sorted by Percent

Based on places with populations of 10,000 or more

Place (place type) County	Number	%
Doral (cdp) Miami-Dade	99	0.48
The Crossings (cdp) Miami-Dade	83	0.35
The Hammocks (cdp) Miami-Dade	157	0.33
Key Biscayne (village) Miami-Dade	35	0.33
Richmond West (cdp) Miami-Dade	84	0.30
Miami Beach (city) Miami-Dade	257	0.29
Kendall West (cdp) Miami-Dade	103	0.27
Fountainbleau (cdp) Miami-Dade	156	0.26
Weston (city) Broward	130	0.26
Ojus (cdp) Miami-Dade	43	0.26

Hispanic: Other

Top 10 Places Sorted by Number

Based on all places, regardless of population

Place (place type) County	Number	%
Miami (city) Miami-Dade	39,058	10.78
Hialeah (city) Miami-Dade	24,305	10.73
Tampa (city) Hillsborough	13,499	4.45
Fountainbleau (cdp) Miami-Dade	9,962	16.73
Miami Beach (city) Miami-Dade	8,414	9.57
Kendale Lakes (cdp) Miami-Dade	7,479	13.14
Pembroke Pines (city) Broward	7,127	5.19
Kendall (cdp) Miami-Dade	6,548	8.70
The Hammocks (cdp) Miami-Dade	6,367	13.44
Tamiami (cdp) Miami-Dade	6,257	11.42

Top 10 Places Sorted by Percent

Based on all places, regardless of population

Place (place type) County	Number	%
Fountainbleau (cdp) Miami-Dade	9,962	16.73
Sweetwater (city) Miami-Dade	2,264	15.91
Kendall West (cdp) Miami-Dade	5,815	15.29
The Hammocks (cdp) Miami-Dade	6,367	13.44
Doral (cdp) Miami-Dade	2,727	13.34
Hialeah Gardens (city) Miami-Dade	2,571	13.32
Kendale Lakes (cdp) Miami-Dade	7,479	13.14
Richmond West (cdp) Miami-Dade	3,557	12.67
Virginia Gardens (village) Miami-Dade	297	12.65
Country Club (cdp) Miami-Dade	4,563	12.57

Notes: (cdp) census designated place; Refer to the User's Guide in the front of the book for more detailed information.

Top 10 Places Sorted by Percent
Based on places with populations of 10,000 or more

Place (place type) County	Number	%
Fountainbleau (cdp) Miami-Dade	9,962	16.73
Sweetwater (city) Miami-Dade	2,264	15.91
Kendall West (cdp) Miami-Dade	5,815	15.29
The Hammocks (cdp) Miami-Dade	6,367	13.44
Doral (cdp) Miami-Dade	2,727	13.34
Hialeah Gardens (city) Miami-Dade	2,571	13.32
Kendale Lakes (cdp) Miami-Dade	7,479	13.14
Richmond West (cdp) Miami-Dade	3,557	12.67
Country Club (cdp) Miami-Dade	4,563	12.57
Tamiami (cdp) Miami-Dade	6,257	11.42

Hungarian

Top 10 Places Sorted by Number
Based on all places, regardless of population

Place (place type) County	Number	%
Jacksonville (special city) Duval	2,485	0.34
Hollywood (city) Broward	1,703	1.22
St. Petersburg (city) Pinellas	1,673	0.68
Tampa (city) Hillsborough	1,218	0.40
Fort Lauderdale (city) Broward	1,161	0.76
Coral Springs (city) Broward	1,134	0.97
Plantation (city) Broward	1,070	1.28
Boca Raton (city) Palm Beach	1,054	1.39
Pembroke Pines (city) Broward	1,052	0.77
Port St. Lucie (city) St. Lucie	973	1.10

Top 10 Places Sorted by Percent
Based on all places, regardless of population

Place (place type) County	Number	%
Godfrey Road (cdp) Broward	38	17.84
Layton (city) Monroe	24	10.00
Indian Creek (village) Miami-Dade	2	5.88
Boca Pointe (cdp) Palm Beach	149	4.52
Yalaha (cdp) Lake	46	4.14
Chokoloskee (cdp) Collier	18	3.50
Cypress Lakes (cdp) Palm Beach	48	3.48
South Palm Beach (town) Palm Beach	24	3.31
Century Village (cdp) Palm Beach	246	3.24
Lakeside Green (cdp) Palm Beach	113	3.19

Top 10 Places Sorted by Percent
Based on places with populations of 10,000 or more

Place (place type) County	Number	%
Kings Point (cdp) Palm Beach	341	2.75
Gulf Gate Estates (cdp) Sarasota	222	1.92
Palm Beach Gardens (city) Palm Beach	643	1.87
Hallandale (city) Broward	644	1.86
Boca Del Mar (cdp) Palm Beach	382	1.78
Hamptons at Boca Raton (cdp) Palm Beach	187	1.64
Gulfport (city) Pinellas	194	1.54
Seminole (city) Pinellas	166	1.54
Aventura (city) Miami-Dade	378	1.50
Cooper City (city) Broward	411	1.48

Icelander

Top 10 Places Sorted by Number
Based on all places, regardless of population

Place (place type) County	Number	%
Orlando (city) Orange	91	0.05
Tallahassee (city) Leon	90	0.06
Jacksonville (special city) Duval	64	0.01
Miami (city) Miami-Dade	36	0.01
Longwood (city) Seminole	35	0.26
Placid Lakes (cdp) Highlands	34	1.13
St. Petersburg (city) Pinellas	29	0.01
Palm Harbor (cdp) Pinellas	26	0.04
Miami Springs (city) Miami-Dade	24	0.18
Palm Coast (city) Flagler	24	0.07

Top 10 Places Sorted by Percent
Based on all places, regardless of population

Place (place type) County	Number	%
Placid Lakes (cdp) Highlands	34	1.13
Southchase (cdp) Orange	22	0.48
Callahan (town) Nassau	3	0.32
Zephyrhills South (cdp) Pasco	14	0.30
Longwood (city) Seminole	35	0.26
Cape Canaveral (city) Brevard	23	0.26
West De Land (cdp) Volusia	8	0.23
Lake Butter (cdp) Orange	15	0.21
Miami Springs (city) Miami-Dade	24	0.18
Warm Mineral Springs (cdp) Sarasota	9	0.18

Top 10 Places Sorted by Percent
Based on places with populations of 10,000 or more

Place (place type) County	Number	%
Longwood (city) Seminole	35	0.26
Miami Springs (city) Miami-Dade	24	0.18
Lynn Haven (city) Bay	15	0.12
Lakewood Park (cdp) St. Lucie	13	0.12
Lighthouse Point (city) Broward	13	0.12
Gulf Gate Estates (cdp) Sarasota	12	0.10
Opa-locka (city) Miami-Dade	13	0.09
Gonzalez (cdp) Escambia	11	0.09
Key Biscayne (village) Miami-Dade	9	0.09
Palm Valley (cdp) St. Johns	16	0.08

Iranian

Top 10 Places Sorted by Number
Based on all places, regardless of population

Place (place type) County	Number	%
Jacksonville (special city) Duval	407	0.06
Sunrise (city) Broward	252	0.29
Coral Springs (city) Broward	247	0.21
Gainesville (city) Alachua	216	0.23
The Crossings (cdp) Miami-Dade	202	0.86
Boca Raton (city) Palm Beach	202	0.27
Parkland (city) Broward	167	1.19
Kendall (cdp) Miami-Dade	167	0.22
Weston (city) Broward	157	0.32
Plantation (city) Broward	149	0.18

Top 10 Places Sorted by Percent
Based on all places, regardless of population

Place (place type) County	Number	%
Fisher Island (cdp) Miami-Dade	30	8.85
Naranja (cdp) Miami-Dade	63	1.50
Pebble Creek (cdp) Hillsborough	61	1.26
Parkland (city) Broward	167	1.19
Malabar (town) Brevard	31	1.10
Hillsboro Beach (town) Broward	20	0.92
Hunters Creek (cdp) Orange	81	0.91
The Crossings (cdp) Miami-Dade	202	0.86
Cutler (cdp) Miami-Dade	132	0.75
Heathrow (cdp) Seminole	25	0.64

Top 10 Places Sorted by Percent
Based on places with populations of 10,000 or more

Place (place type) County	Number	%
Parkland (city) Broward	167	1.19
The Crossings (cdp) Miami-Dade	202	0.86
Cutler (cdp) Miami-Dade	132	0.75
Gonzalez (cdp) Escambia	63	0.54
Greater Northdale (cdp) Hillsborough	105	0.52
Keystone (cdp) Hillsborough	73	0.50
Doral (cdp) Miami-Dade	91	0.44
Ormond Beach (city) Volusia	137	0.38
Greater Carrollwood (cdp) Hillsborough	119	0.35
Lakeland Highlands (cdp) Polk	44	0.35

Irish

Top 10 Places Sorted by Number
Based on all places, regardless of population

Place (place type) County	Number	%
Jacksonville (special city) Duval	66,148	8.99
St. Petersburg (city) Pinellas	30,759	12.41
Tampa (city) Hillsborough	25,499	8.40
Cape Coral (city) Lee	16,271	15.92
Orlando (city) Orange	16,241	8.73
Fort Lauderdale (city) Broward	15,639	10.28
Port St. Lucie (city) St. Lucie	15,466	17.42
Clearwater (city) Pinellas	14,935	13.84
Tallahassee (city) Leon	13,276	8.82
Coral Springs (city) Broward	13,257	11.28

Top 10 Places Sorted by Percent
Based on all places, regardless of population

Place (place type) County	Number	%
Bay Lake (city) Orange	23	58.97
Godfrey Road (cdp) Broward	70	32.86
Lake Kathryn (cdp) Lake	215	30.63
Istachatta (cdp) Hernando	18	29.51
Lazy Lake (village) Broward	11	28.21
Three Oaks (cdp) Lee	607	26.93
Duck Key (cdp) Monroe	143	26.43
Cloud Lake (town) Palm Beach	30	24.39
Cudjoe Key (cdp) Monroe	415	23.89
Golf (village) Palm Beach	57	23.85

Top 10 Places Sorted by Percent
Based on places with populations of 10,000 or more

Place (place type) County	Number	%
North Palm Beach (village) Palm Beach	2,686	22.15
Jensen Beach (cdp) Martin	2,214	19.94
Vero Beach South (cdp) Indian River	3,954	19.41
Marco Island (city) Collier	2,892	19.31
Lighthouse Point (city) Broward	2,023	18.96
Oldsmar (city) Pinellas	2,223	18.94
Jupiter (town) Palm Beach	7,303	18.58
Cocoa Beach (city) Brevard	2,300	18.53
Vero Beach (city) Indian River	3,191	17.88
Hudson (cdp) Pasco	2,259	17.75

Israeli

Top 10 Places Sorted by Number
Based on all places, regardless of population

Place (place type) County	Number	%
Hollywood (city) Broward	742	0.53
Aventura (city) Miami-Dade	580	2.30
Plantation (city) Broward	439	0.53
Sunrise (city) Broward	434	0.51
Coral Springs (city) Broward	320	0.27
Ojus (cdp) Miami-Dade	295	1.77
Sunny Isles Beach (city) Miami-Dade	260	1.70
Boca Raton (city) Palm Beach	237	0.31
Miami Beach (city) Miami-Dade	237	0.27
Cooper City (city) Broward	233	0.84

Top 10 Places Sorted by Percent
Based on all places, regardless of population

Place (place type) County	Number	%
Golden Beach (town) Miami-Dade	46	4.39
Estates of Fort Lauderdale (cdp) Broward	61	3.31
Aventura (city) Miami-Dade	580	2.30
Ojus (cdp) Miami-Dade	295	1.77
Sunny Isles Beach (city) Miami-Dade	260	1.70
Mission Bay (cdp) Palm Beach	50	1.63
Cooper City (city) Broward	233	0.84
Hamptons at Boca Raton (cdp) Palm Beach	96	0.84
Ramblewood East (cdp) Broward	9	0.71
Ives Estates (cdp) Miami-Dade	116	0.67

Notes: (cdp) census designated place; Refer to the User's Guide in the front of the book for more detailed information.

Top 10 Places Sorted by Percent
Based on places with populations of 10,000 or more

Place (place type) County	Number	%
Aventura (city) Miami-Dade	580	2.30
Ojus (cdp) Miami-Dade	295	1.77
Sunny Isles Beach (city) Miami-Dade	260	1.70
Cooper City (city) Broward	233	0.84
Hamptons at Boca Raton (cdp) Palm Beach	96	0.84
Ives Estates (cdp) Miami-Dade	116	0.67
Hollywood (city) Broward	742	0.53
Plantation (city) Broward	439	0.53
Sunrise (city) Broward	434	0.51
Lakewood Park (cdp) St. Lucie	52	0.50

Italian

Top 10 Places Sorted by Number
Based on all places, regardless of population

Place (place type) County	Number	%
Jacksonville (special city) Duval	25,385	3.45
Tampa (city) Hillsborough	17,096	5.63
St. Petersburg (city) Pinellas	16,736	6.75
Coral Springs (city) Broward	16,709	14.22
Port St. Lucie (city) St. Lucie	13,966	15.73
Cape Coral (city) Lee	13,437	13.15
Hollywood (city) Broward	13,206	9.48
Pembroke Pines (city) Broward	12,850	9.37
Spring Hill (cdp) Hernando	12,431	17.96
Fort Lauderdale (city) Broward	11,512	7.57

Top 10 Places Sorted by Percent
Based on all places, regardless of population

Place (place type) County	Number	%
Hillsboro Pines (cdp) Broward	149	30.72
Godfrey Road (cdp) Broward	56	26.29
Estates of Fort Lauderdale (cdp) Broward	398	21.57
Cypress Lakes (cdp) Palm Beach	296	21.48
Trinity (cdp) Pasco	902	20.12
Dunes Road (cdp) Palm Beach	93	19.66
Jasmine Estates (cdp) Pasco	3,432	19.01
Ferndale (cdp) Lake	53	18.40
Inverness Highlands South (cdp) Citrus	1,057	18.29
Ivanhoe Estates (cdp) Broward	46	18.18

Top 10 Places Sorted by Percent
Based on places with populations of 10,000 or more

Place (place type) County	Number	%
Jasmine Estates (cdp) Pasco	3,432	19.01
Spring Hill (cdp) Hernando	12,431	17.96
Lighthouse Point (city) Broward	1,891	17.73
Jupiter (town) Palm Beach	6,586	16.75
Parkland (city) Broward	2,293	16.39
Bayonet Point (cdp) Pasco	3,823	16.15
Port St. Lucie (city) St. Lucie	13,966	15.73
Palm Coast (city) Flagler	5,128	15.31
Sandalfoot Cove (cdp) Palm Beach	2,489	15.00
Palm City (cdp) Martin	2,992	14.88

Latvian

Top 10 Places Sorted by Number
Based on all places, regardless of population

Place (place type) County	Number	%
St. Petersburg (city) Pinellas	350	0.14
Jacksonville (special city) Duval	103	0.01
Coral Springs (city) Broward	99	0.08
St. Pete Beach (city) Pinellas	97	0.98
Miami Beach (city) Miami-Dade	96	0.11
North Miami (city) Miami-Dade	89	0.15
Hollywood (city) Broward	89	0.06
Miami (city) Miami-Dade	81	0.02
Davie (town) Broward	79	0.10
Boca Raton (city) Palm Beach	72	0.10

Top 10 Places Sorted by Percent
Based on all places, regardless of population

Place (place type) County	Number	%
Orchid (town) Indian River	3	2.17
Palm Beach Shores (town) Palm Beach	13	1.07
St. Pete Beach (city) Pinellas	97	0.98
Longboat Key (town) Sarasota	49	0.65
Cypress Lakes (cdp) Palm Beach	9	0.65
Pine Island Ridge (cdp) Broward	32	0.60
Surfside (town) Miami-Dade	25	0.49
Villages of Oriole (cdp) Palm Beach	23	0.49
South Pasadena (city) Pinellas	27	0.46
St. Augustine South (cdp) St. Johns	22	0.44

Top 10 Places Sorted by Percent
Based on places with populations of 10,000 or more

Place (place type) County	Number	%
Hamptons at Boca Raton (cdp) Palm Beach	46	0.40
Oldsmar (city) Pinellas	41	0.35
Sunny Isles Beach (city) Miami-Dade	39	0.26
Palm Beach (town) Palm Beach	19	0.18
Jupiter (town) Palm Beach	65	0.17
Punta Gorda (city) Charlotte	23	0.16
Villas (cdp) Lee	18	0.16
North Miami (city) Miami-Dade	89	0.15
Wellington (village) Palm Beach	56	0.15
St. Petersburg (city) Pinellas	350	0.14

Lithuanian

Top 10 Places Sorted by Number
Based on all places, regardless of population

Place (place type) County	Number	%
Jacksonville (special city) Duval	1,014	0.14
St. Petersburg (city) Pinellas	873	0.35
Hollywood (city) Broward	490	0.35
Coral Springs (city) Broward	450	0.38
Clearwater (city) Pinellas	446	0.41
Cape Coral (city) Lee	398	0.39
Pembroke Pines (city) Broward	390	0.28
Spring Hill (cdp) Hernando	388	0.56
Fort Lauderdale (city) Broward	386	0.25
St. Pete Beach (city) Pinellas	375	3.78

Top 10 Places Sorted by Percent
Based on all places, regardless of population

Place (place type) County	Number	%
Juno Ridge (cdp) Palm Beach	41	5.44
Pine Lakes (cdp) Lake	23	3.85
St. Pete Beach (city) Pinellas	375	3.78
Paisley (cdp) Lake	22	3.26
Pineland (cdp) Lee	14	2.95
Royal Palm Ranches (cdp) Broward	8	2.66
Belleview (city) Marion	75	2.11
Sea Ranch Lakes (village) Broward	28	2.03
Juno Beach (town) Palm Beach	59	1.89
North Key Largo (cdp) Monroe	19	1.88

Top 10 Places Sorted by Percent
Based on places with populations of 10,000 or more

Place (place type) County	Number	%
Palm Beach (town) Palm Beach	155	1.49
Hudson (cdp) Pasco	137	1.08
Gulfport (city) Pinellas	115	0.91
Jupiter (town) Palm Beach	310	0.79
Edgewater (city) Volusia	147	0.78
Parkland (city) Broward	109	0.78
Lutz (cdp) Hillsborough	131	0.77
Union Park (cdp) Orange	78	0.76
Kings Point (cdp) Palm Beach	93	0.75
Boca Del Mar (cdp) Palm Beach	155	0.72

Luxemburger

Top 10 Places Sorted by Number
Based on all places, regardless of population

Place (place type) County	Number	%
Clearwater (city) Pinellas	122	0.11
Bee Ridge (cdp) Sarasota	47	0.53
Coral Gables (city) Miami-Dade	47	0.11
Jacksonville (special city) Duval	42	0.01
Sunrise (city) Broward	37	0.04
Dunedin (city) Pinellas	26	0.07
Fort Lauderdale (city) Broward	26	0.02
Keystone (cdp) Hillsborough	22	0.15
Venice (city) Sarasota	19	0.11
Melbourne (city) Brevard	19	0.03

Top 10 Places Sorted by Percent
Based on all places, regardless of population

Place (place type) County	Number	%
Howey-in-the-Hills (town) Lake	7	0.70
Bee Ridge (cdp) Sarasota	47	0.53
Charlotte Park (cdp) Charlotte	7	0.31
Kensington Park (cdp) Sarasota	11	0.30
Brookridge (cdp) Hernando	9	0.29
Lake Lorraine (cdp) Okaloosa	16	0.23
Heathrow (cdp) Seminole	9	0.23
Indian Shores (town) Pinellas	4	0.23
St. Augustine Beach (city) St. Johns	8	0.17
Warm Mineral Springs (cdp) Sarasota	8	0.16

Top 10 Places Sorted by Percent
Based on places with populations of 10,000 or more

Place (place type) County	Number	%
Keystone (cdp) Hillsborough	22	0.15
St. Augustine (city) St. Johns	17	0.15
Clearwater (city) Pinellas	122	0.11
Coral Gables (city) Miami-Dade	47	0.11
Venice (city) Sarasota	19	0.11
Palm Beach (town) Palm Beach	9	0.09
Haines City (city) Polk	11	0.08
Lake Mary (city) Seminole	9	0.08
Dunedin (city) Pinellas	26	0.07
Warrington (cdp) Escambia	10	0.07

Macedonian

Top 10 Places Sorted by Number
Based on all places, regardless of population

Place (place type) County	Number	%
Hollywood (city) Broward	73	0.05
Boca Raton (city) Palm Beach	70	0.09
Fort Lauderdale (city) Broward	66	0.04
Plantation (city) Broward	45	0.05
Clearwater (city) Pinellas	37	0.03
Boynton Beach (city) Palm Beach	34	0.06
Cooper City (city) Broward	30	0.11
Greater Sun Center (cdp) Hillsborough	29	0.18
East Lake (cdp) Pinellas	27	0.09
Spring Hill (cdp) Hernando	25	0.04

Top 10 Places Sorted by Percent
Based on all places, regardless of population

Place (place type) County	Number	%
Pine Ridge (cdp) Collier	14	0.75
Belleair Bluffs (city) Pinellas	8	0.36
Redington Beach (town) Pinellas	4	0.24
Greater Sun Center (cdp) Hillsborough	29	0.18
Pelican Bay (cdp) Collier	10	0.18
West Melbourne (city) Brevard	15	0.15
Indian River Estates (cdp) St. Lucie	8	0.14
Sawgrass (cdp) St. Johns	7	0.14
Cooper City (city) Broward	30	0.11
Doctor Phillips (cdp) Orange	10	0.10

Notes: (cdp) census designated place; Refer to the User's Guide in the front of the book for more detailed information.

Top 10 Places Sorted by Percent
Based on places with populations of 10,000 or more

Place (place type) County	Number	%
Greater Sun Center (cdp) Hillsborough	29	0.18
Cooper City (city) Broward	30	0.11
Boca Raton (city) Palm Beach	70	0.09
East Lake (cdp) Pinellas	27	0.09
Dania Beach (city) Broward	18	0.09
Lighthouse Point (city) Broward	9	0.08
Boca Del Mar (cdp) Palm Beach	15	0.07
Elfers (cdp) Pasco	9	0.07
Boynton Beach (city) Palm Beach	34	0.06
Winter Springs (city) Seminole	20	0.06

Maltese

Top 10 Places Sorted by Number
Based on all places, regardless of population

Place (place type) County	Number	%
Cape Coral (city) Lee	141	0.14
Ormond Beach (city) Volusia	87	0.24
Shady Hills (cdp) Pasco	57	0.73
Clearwater (city) Pinellas	53	0.05
Coconut Creek (city) Broward	49	0.11
Boca Raton (city) Palm Beach	45	0.06
Palm Harbor (cdp) Pinellas	44	0.07
Coral Springs (city) Broward	37	0.03
Melbourne (city) Brevard	36	0.05
Bayonet Point (cdp) Pasco	34	0.14

Top 10 Places Sorted by Percent
Based on all places, regardless of population

Place (place type) County	Number	%
Shady Hills (cdp) Pasco	57	0.73
Sawgrass (cdp) St. Johns	28	0.57
Pebble Creek (cdp) Hillsborough	25	0.52
North De Land (cdp) Volusia	6	0.44
Country Estates (cdp) Broward	8	0.43
North Weeki Wachee (cdp) Hernando	12	0.29
Lochmoor Waterway Estates (cdp) Lee	11	0.29
Nokomis (cdp) Sarasota	9	0.27
Naples Park (cdp) Collier	18	0.26
Holden Heights (cdp) Orange	10	0.26

Top 10 Places Sorted by Percent
Based on places with populations of 10,000 or more

Place (place type) County	Number	%
Ormond Beach (city) Volusia	87	0.24
Cutler (cdp) Miami-Dade	31	0.18
Jensen Beach (cdp) Martin	18	0.16
Lighthouse Point (city) Broward	17	0.16
Cape Coral (city) Lee	141	0.14
Bayonet Point (cdp) Pasco	34	0.14
Palm Beach (town) Palm Beach	12	0.12
Coconut Creek (city) Broward	49	0.11
Jasmine Estates (cdp) Pasco	19	0.11
Dania Beach (city) Broward	21	0.10

New Zealander

Top 10 Places Sorted by Number
Based on all places, regardless of population

Place (place type) County	Number	%
Fort Lauderdale (city) Broward	59	0.04
Palm Coast (city) Flagler	48	0.14
St. Petersburg (city) Pinellas	43	0.02
Jacksonville (special city) Duval	31	0.00
Cape Coral (city) Lee	23	0.02
Pompano Beach (city) Broward	22	0.03
Coral Springs (city) Broward	19	0.02
Treasure Island (city) Pinellas	18	0.24
Surfside (town) Miami-Dade	17	0.33
St. Pete Beach (city) Pinellas	17	0.17

Top 10 Places Sorted by Percent
Based on all places, regardless of population

Place (place type) County	Number	%
Chokoloskee (cdp) Collier	8	1.55
Surfside (town) Miami-Dade	17	0.33
Nokomis (cdp) Sarasota	10	0.30
Biscayne Park (village) Miami-Dade	9	0.27
Treasure Island (city) Pinellas	18	0.24
Thonotosassa (cdp) Hillsborough	12	0.20
St. Pete Beach (city) Pinellas	17	0.17
Bay Harbor Islands (town) Miami-Dade	9	0.17
Palm Coast (city) Flagler	48	0.14
Inverness (city) Citrus	7	0.10

Top 10 Places Sorted by Percent
Based on places with populations of 10,000 or more

Place (place type) County	Number	%
Palm Coast (city) Flagler	48	0.14
Riverview (cdp) Hillsborough	10	0.08
St. Augustine (city) St. Johns	7	0.06
Key West (city) Monroe	12	0.05
Tarpon Springs (city) Pinellas	11	0.05
Pinecrest (village) Miami-Dade	9	0.05
Fort Lauderdale (city) Broward	59	0.04
Jupiter (town) Palm Beach	15	0.04
Wekiwa Springs (cdp) Seminole	10	0.04
Vero Beach South (cdp) Indian River	8	0.04

Northern European

Top 10 Places Sorted by Number
Based on all places, regardless of population

Place (place type) County	Number	%
Jacksonville (special city) Duval	188	0.03
Gainesville (city) Alachua	137	0.14
East Lake (cdp) Pinellas	124	0.42
St. Petersburg (city) Pinellas	111	0.04
Lakeland (city) Polk	92	0.12
Orlando (city) Orange	89	0.05
Tallahassee (city) Leon	84	0.06
Winter Park (city) Orange	82	0.34
Fort Lauderdale (city) Broward	81	0.05
Tampa (city) Hillsborough	81	0.03

Top 10 Places Sorted by Percent
Based on all places, regardless of population

Place (place type) County	Number	%
McIntosh (town) Marion	8	1.86
Trinity (cdp) Pasco	47	1.05
Tedder (cdp) Broward	18	0.91
Edgewood (city) Orange	13	0.71
Pine Ridge (cdp) Collier	13	0.70
Orange Park (town) Clay	62	0.69
Ridge Wood Heights (cdp) Sarasota	33	0.64
South Pasadena (city) Pinellas	30	0.51
Boyette (cdp) Hillsborough	29	0.47
East Lake (cdp) Pinellas	124	0.42

Top 10 Places Sorted by Percent
Based on places with populations of 10,000 or more

Place (place type) County	Number	%
East Lake (cdp) Pinellas	124	0.42
Winter Park (city) Orange	82	0.34
Oviedo (city) Seminole	77	0.28
Crestview (city) Okaloosa	42	0.28
Wekiwa Springs (cdp) Seminole	55	0.24
Homosassa Springs (cdp) Citrus	28	0.22
Niceville (city) Okaloosa	26	0.22
Fernandina Beach (city) Nassau	23	0.22
Port Salerno (cdp) Martin	20	0.20
Titusville (city) Brevard	77	0.19

Norwegian

Top 10 Places Sorted by Number
Based on all places, regardless of population

Place (place type) County	Number	%
Jacksonville (special city) Duval	4,816	0.65
St. Petersburg (city) Pinellas	2,489	1.00
Tampa (city) Hillsborough	1,786	0.59
Cape Coral (city) Lee	1,299	1.27
Clearwater (city) Pinellas	1,234	1.14
Orlando (city) Orange	1,225	0.66
Fort Lauderdale (city) Broward	1,204	0.79
Largo (city) Pinellas	1,128	1.62
Port St. Lucie (city) St. Lucie	977	1.10
Tallahassee (city) Leon	961	0.64

Top 10 Places Sorted by Percent
Based on all places, regardless of population

Place (place type) County	Number	%
Islandia (city) Miami-Dade	1	16.67
Lake Lindsey (cdp) Hernando	7	15.91
North Beach (cdp) Indian River	24	10.86
Nobleton (cdp) Hernando	9	6.82
Orchid (town) Indian River	9	6.52
Otter Creek (town) Levy	6	5.50
Beverly Beach (town) Flagler	27	5.49
Plantation Island (cdp) Collier	9	4.23
Duck Key (cdp) Monroe	22	4.07
Goodland (cdp) Collier	9	4.07

Top 10 Places Sorted by Percent
Based on places with populations of 10,000 or more

Place (place type) County	Number	%
Niceville (city) Okaloosa	275	2.33
Punta Gorda (city) Charlotte	316	2.19
Naples (city) Collier	428	2.04
Marco Island (city) Collier	294	1.96
Azalea Park (cdp) Orange	204	1.83
Keystone (cdp) Hillsborough	259	1.76
Lake Mary (city) Seminole	184	1.63
Largo (city) Pinellas	1,128	1.62
Cocoa Beach (city) Brevard	198	1.60
Villas (cdp) Lee	174	1.56

Pennsylvania German

Top 10 Places Sorted by Number
Based on all places, regardless of population

Place (place type) County	Number	%
Jacksonville (special city) Duval	217	0.03
Clearwater (city) Pinellas	134	0.12
Spring Hill (cdp) Hernando	132	0.19
Cape Coral (city) Lee	110	0.11
Bradenton (city) Manatee	109	0.22
Fort Lauderdale (city) Broward	93	0.06
Tampa (city) Hillsborough	92	0.03
Melbourne (city) Brevard	78	0.11
Sarasota (city) Sarasota	72	0.14
Deltona (city) Volusia	70	0.10

Top 10 Places Sorted by Percent
Based on all places, regardless of population

Place (place type) County	Number	%
Nobleton (cdp) Hernando	7	5.30
Matlacha Isles-Matlacha Shores (cdp) Lee	6	2.21
Sorrento (cdp) Lake	15	2.02
Ellenton (cdp) Manatee	61	1.98
Matlacha (cdp) Lee	15	1.89
Plantation Mobile Home Park (cdp) Palm Beach	25	1.84
Beverly Beach (town) Flagler	9	1.83
Dunnellon (city) Marion	23	1.20
Orangetree (cdp) Collier	12	1.16
Odessa (cdp) Hillsborough	27	0.81

Notes: (cdp) census designated place; Refer to the User's Guide in the front of the book for more detailed information.

Top 10 Places Sorted by Percent
Based on places with populations of 10,000 or more

Place (place type) County	Number	%
Hobe Sound (cdp) Martin	32	0.29
St. Cloud (city) Osceola	53	0.26
Citrus Ridge (cdp) Lake	29	0.25
De Bary (city) Volusia	38	0.24
San Carlos Park (cdp) Lee	38	0.24
South Daytona (city) Volusia	32	0.24
Gulfport (city) Pinellas	29	0.23
Villas (cdp) Lee	26	0.23
Westchase (cdp) Hillsborough	26	0.23
Bradenton (city) Manatee	109	0.22

Polish

Top 10 Places Sorted by Number
Based on all places, regardless of population

Place (place type) County	Number	%
Jacksonville (special city) Duval	10,500	1.43
St. Petersburg (city) Pinellas	7,542	3.04
Coral Springs (city) Broward	6,741	5.74
Tampa (city) Hillsborough	5,130	1.69
Cape Coral (city) Lee	5,055	4.95
Hollywood (city) Broward	5,026	3.61
Pembroke Pines (city) Broward	4,881	3.56
Boca Raton (city) Palm Beach	4,521	5.98
Port St. Lucie (city) St. Lucie	4,487	5.05
Fort Lauderdale (city) Broward	4,344	2.86

Top 10 Places Sorted by Percent
Based on all places, regardless of population

Place (place type) County	Number	%
Hillsboro Pines (cdp) Broward	57	11.75
Villages of Oriole (cdp) Palm Beach	553	11.68
Whisper Walk (cdp) Palm Beach	573	11.16
Boca Pointe (cdp) Palm Beach	359	10.88
Kings Point (cdp) Palm Beach	1,345	10.86
Spring Lake (cdp) Hernando	29	10.82
Hernando Beach (cdp) Hernando	231	10.74
Oak Point (cdp) Broward	16	10.13
Hamptons at Boca Raton (cdp) Palm Beach	1,143	10.01
Century Village (cdp) Palm Beach	705	9.29

Top 10 Places Sorted by Percent
Based on places with populations of 10,000 or more

Place (place type) County	Number	%
Kings Point (cdp) Palm Beach	1,345	10.86
Hamptons at Boca Raton (cdp) Palm Beach	1,143	10.01
Aventura (city) Miami-Dade	1,893	7.49
Boca Del Mar (cdp) Palm Beach	1,604	7.49
Jasmine Estates (cdp) Pasco	1,287	7.13
Coconut Creek (city) Broward	2,954	6.82
Bayonet Point (cdp) Pasco	1,492	6.30
Parkland (city) Broward	877	6.27
Boca Raton (city) Palm Beach	4,521	5.98
Spring Hill (cdp) Hernando	4,108	5.94

Portuguese

Top 10 Places Sorted by Number
Based on all places, regardless of population

Place (place type) County	Number	%
Jacksonville (special city) Duval	1,184	0.16
St. Petersburg (city) Pinellas	882	0.36
Coral Springs (city) Broward	848	0.72
Deerfield Beach (city) Broward	655	1.01
Miami Beach (city) Miami-Dade	655	0.74
Tampa (city) Hillsborough	618	0.20
Pembroke Pines (city) Broward	592	0.43
Hollywood (city) Broward	588	0.42
Port St. Lucie (city) St. Lucie	537	0.60
Cape Coral (city) Lee	536	0.52

Top 10 Places Sorted by Percent
Based on all places, regardless of population

Place (place type) County	Number	%
Pine Lakes (cdp) Lake	44	7.36
Jupiter Island (town) Martin	35	5.64
Sunshine Ranches (cdp) Broward	77	4.24
Bokeelia (cdp) Lee	52	2.69
Citrus Hills (cdp) Citrus	99	2.45
Ivanhoe Estates (cdp) Broward	6	2.37
Chambers Estates (cdp) Broward	82	2.30
Ravenswood Estates (cdp) Broward	21	2.25
High Point (cdp) Hernando	53	1.75
Chula Vista (cdp) Broward	10	1.71

Top 10 Places Sorted by Percent
Based on places with populations of 10,000 or more

Place (place type) County	Number	%
Palm Coast (city) Flagler	486	1.45
Sebastian (city) Indian River	210	1.28
Doral (cdp) Miami-Dade	259	1.26
Oldsmar (city) Pinellas	131	1.12
Lakewood Park (cdp) St. Lucie	106	1.02
Deerfield Beach (city) Broward	655	1.01
Ocoee (city) Orange	232	0.98
North Port (city) Sarasota	207	0.91
Citrus Ridge (cdp) Lake	102	0.89
San Carlos Park (cdp) Lee	134	0.83

Romanian

Top 10 Places Sorted by Number
Based on all places, regardless of population

Place (place type) County	Number	%
Hollywood (city) Broward	1,613	1.16
Hallandale (city) Broward	1,056	3.06
Jacksonville (special city) Duval	707	0.10
Pembroke Pines (city) Broward	684	0.50
Coral Springs (city) Broward	611	0.52
Sunrise (city) Broward	559	0.65
Plantation (city) Broward	469	0.56
Tamarac (city) Broward	452	0.81
Aventura (city) Miami-Dade	446	1.77
Davie (town) Broward	407	0.54

Top 10 Places Sorted by Percent
Based on all places, regardless of population

Place (place type) County	Number	%
Hallandale (city) Broward	1,056	3.06
Fisher Island (cdp) Miami-Dade	8	2.36
Villages of Oriole (cdp) Palm Beach	107	2.26
Century Village (cdp) Palm Beach	159	2.10
Kings Point (cdp) Palm Beach	239	1.93
Whisper Walk (cdp) Palm Beach	99	1.93
Aventura (city) Miami-Dade	446	1.77
Boca Pointe (cdp) Palm Beach	57	1.73
Hamptons at Boca Raton (cdp) Palm Beach	183	1.60
Sunny Isles Beach (city) Miami-Dade	219	1.43

Top 10 Places Sorted by Percent
Based on places with populations of 10,000 or more

Place (place type) County	Number	%
Hallandale (city) Broward	1,056	3.06
Kings Point (cdp) Palm Beach	239	1.93
Aventura (city) Miami-Dade	446	1.77
Hamptons at Boca Raton (cdp) Palm Beach	183	1.60
Sunny Isles Beach (city) Miami-Dade	219	1.43
Hollywood (city) Broward	1,613	1.16
Cutler (cdp) Miami-Dade	201	1.14
Ojus (cdp) Miami-Dade	177	1.06
Palm Beach (town) Palm Beach	102	0.98
Boca Del Mar (cdp) Palm Beach	208	0.97

Russian

Top 10 Places Sorted by Number
Based on all places, regardless of population

Place (place type) County	Number	%
Coral Springs (city) Broward	5,710	4.86
Hollywood (city) Broward	4,464	3.21
Pembroke Pines (city) Broward	4,179	3.05
Boca Raton (city) Palm Beach	4,066	5.38
Jacksonville (special city) Duval	3,705	0.50
Sunrise (city) Broward	3,533	4.13
Tamarac (city) Broward	3,431	6.12
Plantation (city) Broward	3,428	4.12
Miami Beach (city) Miami-Dade	3,286	3.73
Aventura (city) Miami-Dade	2,998	11.87

Top 10 Places Sorted by Percent
Based on all places, regardless of population

Place (place type) County	Number	%
Marineland (town) Flagler	5	71.43
Boca Pointe (cdp) Palm Beach	584	17.70
Villages of Oriole (cdp) Palm Beach	829	17.50
Duck Key (cdp) Monroe	94	17.38
Kings Point (cdp) Palm Beach	2,005	16.19
Fisher Island (cdp) Miami-Dade	54	15.93
High Point (cdp) Palm Beach	330	14.97
Century Village (cdp) Palm Beach	1,129	14.88
Oak Point (cdp) Broward	22	13.92
Ramblewood East (cdp) Broward	165	13.01

Top 10 Places Sorted by Percent
Based on places with populations of 10,000 or more

Place (place type) County	Number	%
Kings Point (cdp) Palm Beach	2,005	16.19
Aventura (city) Miami-Dade	2,998	11.87
Palm Beach (town) Palm Beach	1,089	10.50
Sunny Isles Beach (city) Miami-Dade	1,447	9.47
Boca Del Mar (cdp) Palm Beach	2,027	9.46
Hamptons at Boca Raton (cdp) Palm Beach	1,035	9.06
Ojus (cdp) Miami-Dade	1,256	7.53
Parkland (city) Broward	976	6.98
Pinecrest (village) Miami-Dade	1,331	6.94
Coconut Creek (city) Broward	2,804	6.47

Scandinavian

Top 10 Places Sorted by Number
Based on all places, regardless of population

Place (place type) County	Number	%
Jacksonville (special city) Duval	560	0.08
Tampa (city) Hillsborough	294	0.10
Clearwater (city) Pinellas	226	0.21
St. Petersburg (city) Pinellas	210	0.08
Orlando (city) Orange	192	0.10
Tallahassee (city) Leon	189	0.13
Port St. Lucie (city) St. Lucie	168	0.19
Coral Springs (city) Broward	152	0.13
Cape Coral (city) Lee	144	0.14
Pembroke Pines (city) Broward	139	0.10

Top 10 Places Sorted by Percent
Based on all places, regardless of population

Place (place type) County	Number	%
Cloud Lake (town) Palm Beach	3	2.44
Masaryktown (cdp) Hernando	15	1.70
Pine Island Ridge (cdp) Broward	86	1.61
Crescent Beach (cdp) St. Johns	11	1.39
Lochmoor Waterway Estates (cdp) Lee	46	1.19
Indian River Shores (town) Indian River	37	1.12
Inwood (cdp) Polk	75	1.11
Geneva (cdp) Seminole	29	1.03
Gibsonia (cdp) Polk	48	0.99
Ellenton (cdp) Manatee	28	0.91

Notes: (cdp) census designated place; Refer to the User's Guide in the front of the book for more detailed information.

Top 10 Places Sorted by Percent

Based on places with populations of 10,000 or more

Place (place type) County	Number	%
Wilton Manors (city) Broward	67	0.53
Stuart (city) Martin	77	0.52
Riverview (cdp) Hillsborough	51	0.42
Union Park (cdp) Orange	43	0.42
St. Augustine (city) St. Johns	47	0.41
Vero Beach South (cdp) Indian River	78	0.38
Homosassa Springs (cdp) Citrus	47	0.37
East Lake (cdp) Pinellas	106	0.36
Safety Harbor (city) Pinellas	62	0.36
Lynn Haven (city) Bay	44	0.36

Scotch-Irish

Top 10 Places Sorted by Number

Based on all places, regardless of population

Place (place type) County	Number	%
Jacksonville (special city) Duval	13,064	1.78
St. Petersburg (city) Pinellas	4,625	1.87
Tampa (city) Hillsborough	4,497	1.48
Tallahassee (city) Leon	3,309	2.20
Orlando (city) Orange	2,634	1.42
Gainesville (city) Alachua	2,223	2.33
Clearwater (city) Pinellas	2,091	1.94
Cape Coral (city) Lee	1,735	1.70
Lakeland (city) Polk	1,645	2.10
Largo (city) Pinellas	1,632	2.35

Top 10 Places Sorted by Percent

Based on all places, regardless of population

Place (place type) County	Number	%
Bayport (cdp) Hernando	6	25.00
Lee (town) Madison	31	8.86
Matlacha Isles-Matlacha Shores (cdp) Lee	18	6.64
Highland Park (village) Polk	15	6.36
Pineland (cdp) Lee	30	6.33
Country Estates (cdp) Broward	116	6.24
Silver Lake (cdp) Lake	116	6.21
Penney Farms (town) Clay	33	6.15
Chuluota (cdp) Seminole	120	6.05
Yankeetown (town) Levy	39	6.03

Top 10 Places Sorted by Percent

Based on places with populations of 10,000 or more

Place (place type) County	Number	%
Cocoa Beach (city) Brevard	471	3.79
St. Augustine (city) St. Johns	407	3.54
Ferry Pass (cdp) Escambia	951	3.50
Greater Sun Center (cdp) Hillsborough	557	3.42
Upper Grand Lagoon (cdp) Bay	373	3.40
Warrington (cdp) Escambia	511	3.37
Merritt Island (cdp) Brevard	1,199	3.32
Naples (city) Collier	670	3.19
Maitland (city) Orange	377	3.16
Niceville (city) Okaloosa	371	3.15

Scottish

Top 10 Places Sorted by Number

Based on all places, regardless of population

Place (place type) County	Number	%
Jacksonville (special city) Duval	13,558	1.84
St. Petersburg (city) Pinellas	6,317	2.55
Tampa (city) Hillsborough	5,312	1.75
Tallahassee (city) Leon	3,513	2.33
Orlando (city) Orange	3,164	1.70
Fort Lauderdale (city) Broward	2,689	1.77
Clearwater (city) Pinellas	2,555	2.37
Gainesville (city) Alachua	2,298	2.40
Largo (city) Pinellas	2,040	2.94
Cape Coral (city) Lee	2,012	1.97

Top 10 Places Sorted by Percent

Based on all places, regardless of population

Place (place type) County	Number	%
Highland Park (village) Polk	32	13.56
Golf (village) Palm Beach	25	10.46
Lazy Lake (village) Broward	4	10.26
Manasota Key (cdp) Charlotte	134	10.24
Captiva (cdp) Lee	38	9.69
Pine Island (cdp) Hernando	5	9.09
Punta Rassa (cdp) Lee	149	8.90
Lake Harbor (cdp) Palm Beach	8	8.60
Crescent Beach (cdp) St. Johns	61	7.68
Goodland (cdp) Collier	16	7.24

Top 10 Places Sorted by Percent

Based on places with populations of 10,000 or more

Place (place type) County	Number	%
Winter Park (city) Orange	1,229	5.07
Atlantic Beach (city) Duval	613	4.55
Naples (city) Collier	921	4.39
Palm Valley (cdp) St. Johns	858	4.32
Destin (city) Okaloosa	477	4.24
Venice (city) Sarasota	744	4.17
Greater Sun Center (cdp) Hillsborough	672	4.13
Dunedin (city) Pinellas	1,413	3.93
Keystone (cdp) Hillsborough	571	3.88
Jacksonville Beach (city) Duval	783	3.73

Serbian

Top 10 Places Sorted by Number

Based on all places, regardless of population

Place (place type) County	Number	%
St. Petersburg (city) Pinellas	206	0.08
Jacksonville (special city) Duval	155	0.02
Hollywood (city) Broward	117	0.08
Orlando (city) Orange	105	0.06
Cape Coral (city) Lee	101	0.10
Pinellas Park (city) Pinellas	94	0.21
Warm Mineral Springs (cdp) Sarasota	90	1.83
Tampa (city) Hillsborough	85	0.03
Palm Coast (city) Flagler	83	0.25
Coral Springs (city) Broward	78	0.07

Top 10 Places Sorted by Percent

Based on all places, regardless of population

Place (place type) County	Number	%
Warm Mineral Springs (cdp) Sarasota	90	1.83
Edgewater (cdp) Broward	6	0.85
Ramblewood East (cdp) Broward	10	0.79
Macclenny (city) Baker	33	0.75
Howey-in-the-Hills (town) Lake	7	0.70
Doctor Phillips (cdp) Orange	66	0.68
Alva (cdp) Lee	13	0.64
Belleair Beach (city) Pinellas	10	0.60
Brooker (town) Bradford	2	0.58
Tequesta (village) Palm Beach	28	0.54

Top 10 Places Sorted by Percent

Based on places with populations of 10,000 or more

Place (place type) County	Number	%
Palm Beach (town) Palm Beach	36	0.35
Palm Coast (city) Flagler	83	0.25
Elfers (cdp) Pasco	33	0.25
Casselberry (city) Seminole	49	0.22
Palm Valley (cdp) St. Johns	43	0.22
New Port Richey (city) Pasco	35	0.22
Pinellas Park (city) Pinellas	94	0.21
North Port (city) Sarasota	47	0.21
Westchase (cdp) Hillsborough	23	0.21
Haines City (city) Polk	26	0.20

Slavic

Top 10 Places Sorted by Number

Based on all places, regardless of population

Place (place type) County	Number	%
Jacksonville (special city) Duval	227	0.03
St. Petersburg (city) Pinellas	116	0.05
Tampa (city) Hillsborough	114	0.04
Hudson (cdp) Pasco	109	0.86
Neptune Beach (city) Duval	90	1.24
Kendall (cdp) Miami-Dade	65	0.09
Coral Springs (city) Broward	65	0.06
Pembroke Pines (city) Broward	63	0.05
Palm City (cdp) Martin	60	0.30
Gainesville (city) Alachua	59	0.06

Top 10 Places Sorted by Percent

Based on all places, regardless of population

Place (place type) County	Number	%
Fisher Island (cdp) Miami-Dade	11	3.24
Matlacha Isles-Matlacha Shores (cdp) Lee	6	2.21
Wedgefield (cdp) Orange	48	1.71
Neptune Beach (city) Duval	90	1.24
Hudson (cdp) Pasco	109	0.86
South Palm Beach (town) Palm Beach	6	0.83
Glencoe (cdp) Volusia	18	0.71
Naples Park (cdp) Collier	44	0.65
Indian River Estates (cdp) St. Lucie	35	0.60
Tierra Verde (cdp) Pinellas	20	0.56

Top 10 Places Sorted by Percent

Based on places with populations of 10,000 or more

Place (place type) County	Number	%
Hudson (cdp) Pasco	109	0.86
North Palm Beach (village) Palm Beach	37	0.31
Palm City (cdp) Martin	60	0.30
St. Augustine (city) St. Johns	35	0.30
Lakeland Highlands (cdp) Polk	36	0.28
Fruit Cove (cdp) St. Johns	38	0.24
Boca Del Mar (cdp) Palm Beach	40	0.19
Lynn Haven (city) Bay	23	0.19
Vero Beach South (cdp) Indian River	36	0.18
South Venice (cdp) Sarasota	24	0.18

Slovak

Top 10 Places Sorted by Number

Based on all places, regardless of population

Place (place type) County	Number	%
Jacksonville (special city) Duval	564	0.08
St. Petersburg (city) Pinellas	530	0.21
Cape Coral (city) Lee	529	0.52
Port St. Lucie (city) St. Lucie	429	0.48
Spring Hill (cdp) Hernando	320	0.46
Clearwater (city) Pinellas	280	0.26
Fort Lauderdale (city) Broward	265	0.17
Margate (city) Broward	252	0.47
Orlando (city) Orange	246	0.13
Tampa (city) Hillsborough	228	0.08

Top 10 Places Sorted by Percent

Based on all places, regardless of population

Place (place type) County	Number	%
Winter Beach (cdp) Indian River	59	5.26
Matlacha (cdp) Lee	33	4.17
Masaryktown (cdp) Hernando	35	3.97
Layton (city) Monroe	5	2.08
Ponce Inlet (town) Volusia	49	1.95
Jupiter Island (town) Martin	12	1.93
Edgewood (city) Orange	33	1.80
Crescent Beach (cdp) St. Johns	13	1.64
Desoto Lakes (cdp) Sarasota	51	1.57
Olga (cdp) Lee	23	1.56

Notes: (cdp) census designated place; Refer to the User's Guide in the front of the book for more detailed information.

Top 10 Places Sorted by Percent
Based on places with populations of 10,000 or more

Place (place type) County	Number	%
Seminole (city) Pinellas	83	0.77
Lake Mary (city) Seminole	85	0.75
Longwood (city) Seminole	101	0.74
Iona (cdp) Lee	76	0.64
Goldenrod (cdp) Seminole	82	0.63
Forest City (cdp) Seminole	80	0.63
Hobe Sound (cdp) Martin	69	0.62
East Lake (cdp) Pinellas	181	0.61
Sarasota Springs (cdp) Sarasota	97	0.61
Gulf Gate Estates (cdp) Sarasota	70	0.61

Slovene

Top 10 Places Sorted by Number
Based on all places, regardless of population

Place (place type) County	Number	%
Jacksonville (special city) Duval	163	0.02
Cape Coral (city) Lee	138	0.14
Fort Lauderdale (city) Broward	113	0.07
St. Petersburg (city) Pinellas	92	0.04
Dunedin (city) Pinellas	89	0.25
Melbourne (city) Brevard	74	0.10
Spring Hill (cdp) Hernando	72	0.10
Samsula-Spruce Creek (cdp) Volusia	67	1.35
Port St. Lucie (city) St. Lucie	63	0.07
Ormond Beach (city) Volusia	55	0.15

Top 10 Places Sorted by Percent
Based on all places, regardless of population

Place (place type) County	Number	%
Samsula-Spruce Creek (cdp) Volusia	67	1.35
Lely (cdp) Collier	34	0.89
Palm Beach Shores (town) Palm Beach	9	0.74
Crooked Lake Park (cdp) Polk	12	0.65
Hernando (cdp) Citrus	49	0.58
Charlotte Park (cdp) Charlotte	13	0.57
Umatilla (city) Lake	12	0.55
Country Estates (cdp) Broward	10	0.54
Hernando Beach (cdp) Hernando	11	0.51
North Redington Beach (town) Pinellas	7	0.51

Top 10 Places Sorted by Percent
Based on places with populations of 10,000 or more

Place (place type) County	Number	%
Jensen Beach (cdp) Martin	37	0.33
Dunedin (city) Pinellas	89	0.25
Maitland (city) Orange	29	0.24
Lighthouse Point (city) Broward	23	0.22
Villas (cdp) Lee	23	0.21
New Smyrna Beach (city) Volusia	39	0.19
Marathon (city) Monroe	19	0.19
Stuart (city) Martin	25	0.17
Bellair-Meadowbrook Terrace (cdp) Clay	26	0.16
Upper Grand Lagoon (cdp) Bay	18	0.16

Soviet Union

Top 10 Places Sorted by Number
Based on all places, regardless of population

Place (place type) County	Number	%
Boca Del Mar (cdp) Palm Beach	15	0.07
Cocoa Beach (city) Brevard	10	0.08
Aventura (city) Miami-Dade	7	0.03
Lake Magdalene (cdp) Hillsborough	7	0.02
St. Pete Beach (city) Pinellas	5	0.05
Myrtle Grove (cdp) Escambia	5	0.03

Top 10 Places Sorted by Percent
Based on all places, regardless of population

Place (place type) County	Number	%
Cocoa Beach (city) Brevard	10	0.08
Boca Del Mar (cdp) Palm Beach	15	0.07
St. Pete Beach (city) Pinellas	5	0.05
Aventura (city) Miami-Dade	7	0.03
Myrtle Grove (cdp) Escambia	5	0.03
Lake Magdalene (cdp) Hillsborough	7	0.02

Top 10 Places Sorted by Percent
Based on places with populations of 10,000 or more

Place (place type) County	Number	%
Cocoa Beach (city) Brevard	10	0.08
Boca Del Mar (cdp) Palm Beach	15	0.07
Aventura (city) Miami-Dade	7	0.03
Myrtle Grove (cdp) Escambia	5	0.03
Lake Magdalene (cdp) Hillsborough	7	0.02

Swedish

Top 10 Places Sorted by Number
Based on all places, regardless of population

Place (place type) County	Number	%
Jacksonville (special city) Duval	4,774	0.65
St. Petersburg (city) Pinellas	3,150	1.27
Tampa (city) Hillsborough	2,521	0.83
Clearwater (city) Pinellas	1,863	1.73
Cape Coral (city) Lee	1,598	1.56
Orlando (city) Orange	1,552	0.83
Fort Lauderdale (city) Broward	1,518	1.00
Coral Springs (city) Broward	1,324	1.13
Palm Harbor (cdp) Pinellas	1,264	2.14
Gainesville (city) Alachua	1,241	1.30

Top 10 Places Sorted by Percent
Based on all places, regardless of population

Place (place type) County	Number	%
Pine Island (cdp) Hernando	12	21.82
Plantation Island (cdp) Collier	15	7.04
Reddick (town) Marion	36	6.35
Pineland (cdp) Lee	28	5.91
Lake Kathryn (cdp) Lake	40	5.70
Royal Palm Ranches (cdp) Broward	16	5.32
Briny Breezes (town) Palm Beach	21	5.08
Homosassa (cdp) Citrus	109	4.82
Hillsboro Pines (cdp) Broward	23	4.74
Celebration (cdp) Osceola	120	4.37

Top 10 Places Sorted by Percent
Based on places with populations of 10,000 or more

Place (place type) County	Number	%
Naples (city) Collier	654	3.12
Sarasota Springs (cdp) Sarasota	469	2.96
Marco Island (city) Collier	437	2.92
Englewood (cdp) Sarasota	462	2.84
Palm City (cdp) Martin	542	2.70
Hudson (cdp) Pasco	333	2.62
Greater Sun Center (cdp) Hillsborough	423	2.60
East Lake (cdp) Pinellas	733	2.49
Iona (cdp) Lee	289	2.44
Vero Beach South (cdp) Indian River	466	2.29

Swiss

Top 10 Places Sorted by Number
Based on all places, regardless of population

Place (place type) County	Number	%
Jacksonville (special city) Duval	1,064	0.14
St. Petersburg (city) Pinellas	615	0.25
Tampa (city) Hillsborough	549	0.18
Hollywood (city) Broward	421	0.30
Clearwater (city) Pinellas	414	0.38
Orlando (city) Orange	377	0.20
Tallahassee (city) Leon	339	0.23
Fort Lauderdale (city) Broward	339	0.22
Cape Coral (city) Lee	336	0.33
Sarasota (city) Sarasota	280	0.53

Top 10 Places Sorted by Percent
Based on all places, regardless of population

Place (place type) County	Number	%
Pittman (cdp) Lake	11	14.10
Lazy Lake (village) Broward	4	10.26
Crescent Beach (cdp) St. Johns	27	3.40
Highland Park (village) Polk	7	2.97
Orangetree (cdp) Collier	29	2.81
Punta Rassa (cdp) Lee	41	2.45
Vineyards (cdp) Collier	55	2.42
Williston Highlands (cdp) Levy	31	2.33
Samsula-Spruce Creek (cdp) Volusia	106	2.14
Wausau (town) Washington	8	2.02

Top 10 Places Sorted by Percent
Based on places with populations of 10,000 or more

Place (place type) County	Number	%
Punta Gorda (city) Charlotte	164	1.14
Naples (city) Collier	213	1.01
Cypress Lake (cdp) Lee	122	1.01
Gulf Gate Estates (cdp) Sarasota	114	0.99
Key Biscayne (village) Miami-Dade	104	0.99
Greater Sun Center (cdp) Hillsborough	142	0.87
Fruitville (cdp) Sarasota	108	0.84
South Venice (cdp) Sarasota	100	0.74
Marco Island (city) Collier	109	0.73
Palm City (cdp) Martin	131	0.65

Turkish

Top 10 Places Sorted by Number
Based on all places, regardless of population

Place (place type) County	Number	%
Miami Beach (city) Miami-Dade	342	0.39
Jacksonville (special city) Duval	324	0.04
Hollywood (city) Broward	218	0.16
Tampa (city) Hillsborough	208	0.07
Coral Springs (city) Broward	192	0.16
Coconut Creek (city) Broward	186	0.43
Weston (city) Broward	183	0.37
Pompano Beach (city) Broward	165	0.21
Gainesville (city) Alachua	163	0.17
Miami (city) Miami-Dade	160	0.04

Top 10 Places Sorted by Percent
Based on all places, regardless of population

Place (place type) County	Number	%
Royal Palm Ranches (cdp) Broward	14	4.65
Palm Shores (town) Brevard	15	1.90
Bay Harbor Islands (town) Miami-Dade	70	1.36
Highland Beach (town) Palm Beach	44	1.22
Matlacha (cdp) Lee	7	0.88
Ojus (cdp) Miami-Dade	132	0.79
Kings Point (cdp) Palm Beach	85	0.69
Cudjoe Key (cdp) Monroe	10	0.58
Madeira Beach (city) Pinellas	25	0.56
Aventura (city) Miami-Dade	140	0.55

Top 10 Places Sorted by Percent
Based on places with populations of 10,000 or more

Place (place type) County	Number	%
Ojus (cdp) Miami-Dade	132	0.79
Kings Point (cdp) Palm Beach	85	0.69
Aventura (city) Miami-Dade	140	0.55
Coconut Creek (city) Broward	186	0.43
Oakland Park (city) Broward	131	0.42
Miami Beach (city) Miami-Dade	342	0.39
Sunny Isles Beach (city) Miami-Dade	59	0.39

Notes: (cdp) census designated place; Refer to the User's Guide in the front of the book for more detailed information.

North Palm Beach (village) Palm Beach	46	0.38
Weston (city) Broward	183	0.37
Cutler (cdp) Miami-Dade	65	0.37

Ukrainian

Top 10 Places Sorted by Number

Based on all places, regardless of population

Place (place type) County	Number	%
Jacksonville (special city) Duval	1,294	0.18
St. Petersburg (city) Pinellas	943	0.38
Hollywood (city) Broward	753	0.54
North Port (city) Sarasota	612	2.69
Tampa (city) Hillsborough	551	0.18
Clearwater (city) Pinellas	507	0.47
Fort Lauderdale (city) Broward	467	0.31
Miami Beach (city) Miami-Dade	460	0.52
Spring Hill (cdp) Hernando	444	0.64
Coral Springs (city) Broward	428	0.36

Top 10 Places Sorted by Percent

Based on all places, regardless of population

Place (place type) County	Number	%
Oak Point (cdp) Broward	40	25.32
North Beach (cdp) Indian River	17	7.69
Paisley (cdp) Lake	23	3.41
Warm Mineral Springs (cdp) Sarasota	139	2.83
North Port (city) Sarasota	612	2.69
Ferndale (cdp) Lake	7	2.43
Pine Ridge (cdp) Collier	45	2.42
Ponce Inlet (town) Volusia	55	2.19
St. Leo (town) Pasco	12	1.97
Plantation (cdp) Sarasota	77	1.94

Top 10 Places Sorted by Percent

Based on places with populations of 10,000 or more

Place (place type) County	Number	%
North Port (city) Sarasota	612	2.69
Gulfport (city) Pinellas	216	1.71
Sunny Isles Beach (city) Miami-Dade	203	1.33
Ojus (cdp) Miami-Dade	206	1.23
Boca Del Mar (cdp) Palm Beach	244	1.14
Kings Point (cdp) Palm Beach	138	1.11
Goldenrod (cdp) Seminole	127	0.97
Palm Coast (city) Flagler	307	0.92
Hudson (cdp) Pasco	106	0.83
Hamptons at Boca Raton (cdp) Palm Beach	93	0.81

United States or American

Top 10 Places Sorted by Number

Based on all places, regardless of population

Place (place type) County	Number	%
Jacksonville (special city) Duval	68,488	9.31
Tampa (city) Hillsborough	18,834	6.21
St. Petersburg (city) Pinellas	14,062	5.67
Orlando (city) Orange	12,426	6.68
Miami (city) Miami-Dade	11,317	3.12
Hollywood (city) Broward	9,762	7.01
Fort Lauderdale (city) Broward	8,904	5.85
Pembroke Pines (city) Broward	8,380	6.11
Tallahassee (city) Leon	7,976	5.30
Cape Coral (city) Lee	7,841	7.67

Top 10 Places Sorted by Percent

Based on all places, regardless of population

Place (place type) County	Number	%
Chokoloskee (cdp) Collier	259	50.29
Westville (town) Holmes	95	41.13
Jay (town) Santa Rosa	218	40.07
Bristol (city) Liberty	319	39.73
Altha (town) Calhoun	212	39.70
Nassau Village-Ratliff (cdp) Nassau	1,631	35.74
Glen St. Mary (town) Baker	155	34.44
Islandia (city) Miami-Dade	2	33.33
Sneads (town) Jackson	613	31.65
Kathleen (cdp) Polk	1,061	31.44

Top 10 Places Sorted by Percent

Based on places with populations of 10,000 or more

Place (place type) County	Number	%
Auburndale (city) Polk	1,984	17.69
Upper Grand Lagoon (cdp) Bay	1,822	16.59
Lakeland Highlands (cdp) Polk	1,943	15.24
Lynn Haven (city) Bay	1,838	14.88
Winter Haven (city) Polk	3,798	14.64
Warrington (cdp) Escambia	2,204	14.51
Middleburg (cdp) Clay	1,502	14.43
Crestview (city) Okaloosa	2,121	14.31
Callaway (city) Bay	1,977	13.87
Bellview (cdp) Escambia	2,863	13.59

Welsh

Top 10 Places Sorted by Number

Based on all places, regardless of population

Place (place type) County	Number	%
Jacksonville (special city) Duval	3,699	0.50
St. Petersburg (city) Pinellas	1,985	0.80
Tampa (city) Hillsborough	1,346	0.44
Tallahassee (city) Leon	1,061	0.70
Fort Lauderdale (city) Broward	1,050	0.69
Orlando (city) Orange	1,046	0.56
Cape Coral (city) Lee	773	0.76
Palm Bay (city) Brevard	719	0.90
Gainesville (city) Alachua	636	0.67
Clearwater (city) Pinellas	616	0.57

Top 10 Places Sorted by Percent

Based on all places, regardless of population

Place (place type) County	Number	%
Marineland (town) Flagler	2	28.57
Matlacha (cdp) Lee	45	5.68
Penney Farms (town) Clay	25	4.66
Pine Lakes (cdp) Lake	26	4.35
Indialantic (town) Brevard	108	3.67
Sorrento (cdp) Lake	27	3.64
Goodland (cdp) Collier	8	3.62
Chokoloskee (cdp) Collier	16	3.11
Hillcrest Heights (town) Polk	8	2.95
North Key Largo (cdp) Monroe	29	2.87

Top 10 Places Sorted by Percent

Based on places with populations of 10,000 or more

Place (place type) County	Number	%
Lady Lake (town) Lake	187	1.60
Greater Sun Center (cdp) Hillsborough	253	1.55
Stuart (city) Martin	218	1.48
Bellair-Meadowbrook Terrace (cdp) Clay	241	1.45
Naples (city) Collier	303	1.44
Zephyrhills (city) Pasco	148	1.38
New Smyrna Beach (city) Volusia	279	1.37
Land O' Lakes (cdp) Pasco	281	1.35
Gulf Gate Estates (cdp) Sarasota	151	1.31
Winter Park (city) Orange	309	1.28

West Indian, excluding Hispanic

Top 10 Places Sorted by Number

Based on all places, regardless of population

Place (place type) County	Number	%
Miami (city) Miami-Dade	22,904	6.32
North Miami (city) Miami-Dade	22,034	36.70
Miramar (city) Broward	18,445	25.38
Lauderhill (city) Broward	16,626	29.04
Fort Lauderdale (city) Broward	14,964	9.84
Golden Glades (cdp) Miami-Dade	13,197	41.01
Pembroke Pines (city) Broward	12,327	8.99
Lauderdale Lakes (city) Broward	11,455	36.35
North Miami Beach (city) Miami-Dade	11,041	27.15
Sunrise (city) Broward	11,027	12.88

Top 10 Places Sorted by Percent

Based on all places, regardless of population

Place (place type) County	Number	%
Melrose Park (cdp) Broward	2,918	41.17
Golden Glades (cdp) Miami-Dade	13,197	41.01
Norland (cdp) Miami-Dade	8,976	38.98
North Miami (city) Miami-Dade	22,034	36.70
Lauderdale Lakes (city) Broward	11,455	36.35
Pompano Estates (cdp) Broward	1,172	33.82
El Portal (village) Miami-Dade	813	32.30
Pinewood (cdp) Miami-Dade	5,402	32.12
Lauderhill (city) Broward	16,626	29.04
Belle Glade Camp (cdp) Palm Beach	355	28.09

Top 10 Places Sorted by Percent

Based on places with populations of 10,000 or more

Place (place type) County	Number	%
Golden Glades (cdp) Miami-Dade	13,197	41.01
Norland (cdp) Miami-Dade	8,976	38.98
North Miami (city) Miami-Dade	22,034	36.70
Lauderdale Lakes (city) Broward	11,455	36.35
Pinewood (cdp) Miami-Dade	5,402	32.12
Lauderhill (city) Broward	16,626	29.04
North Miami Beach (city) Miami-Dade	11,041	27.15
Palmetto Estates (cdp) Miami-Dade	3,497	25.57
Miramar (city) Broward	18,445	25.38
Scott Lake (cdp) Miami-Dade	3,269	22.72

West Indian: Bahamian, excluding Hispanic

Top 10 Places Sorted by Number

Based on all places, regardless of population

Place (place type) County	Number	%
Miami (city) Miami-Dade	1,470	0.41
North Miami (city) Miami-Dade	675	1.12
Fort Lauderdale (city) Broward	607	0.40
Miramar (city) Broward	578	0.80
Golden Glades (cdp) Miami-Dade	541	1.68
Pembroke Pines (city) Broward	518	0.38
Norland (cdp) Miami-Dade	513	2.23
Lauderhill (city) Broward	473	0.83
North Miami Beach (city) Miami-Dade	441	1.08
Carol City (cdp) Miami-Dade	437	0.74

Top 10 Places Sorted by Percent

Based on all places, regardless of population

Place (place type) County	Number	%
Stacey Street (cdp) Palm Beach	50	6.02
Andover (cdp) Miami-Dade	295	3.41
Bunche Park (cdp) Miami-Dade	131	3.29
Lake Lucerne (cdp) Miami-Dade	237	2.59
Carver Ranches (cdp) Broward	109	2.54
Norland (cdp) Miami-Dade	513	2.23
El Portal (village) Miami-Dade	53	2.11
Brownsville (cdp) Miami-Dade	279	1.93
Lake Forest (cdp) Broward	92	1.85
Goulds (cdp) Miami-Dade	140	1.84

Top 10 Places Sorted by Percent

Based on places with populations of 10,000 or more

Place (place type) County	Number	%
Norland (cdp) Miami-Dade	513	2.23
Brownsville (cdp) Miami-Dade	279	1.93
Pinewood (cdp) Miami-Dade	304	1.81
Golden Glades (cdp) Miami-Dade	541	1.68
Scott Lake (cdp) Miami-Dade	223	1.55
North Miami (city) Miami-Dade	675	1.12

Notes: (cdp) census designated place; Refer to the User's Guide in the front of the book for more detailed information.

North Miami Beach (city) Miami-Dade	441	1.08
Key West (city) Monroe	269	1.06
West Little River (cdp) Miami-Dade	339	1.05
Gladeview (cdp) Miami-Dade	138	0.95

West Indian: Barbadian, excluding Hispanic

Top 10 Places Sorted by Number

Based on all places, regardless of population

Place (place type) County	Number	%
St. Petersburg (city) Pinellas	240	0.10
Lauderhill (city) Broward	168	0.29
Orlando (city) Orange	156	0.08
North Miami (city) Miami-Dade	149	0.25
Miramar (city) Broward	139	0.19
Pine Hills (cdp) Orange	112	0.27
Tampa (city) Hillsborough	99	0.03
Palm Bay (city) Brevard	92	0.12
Hollywood (city) Broward	86	0.06
Fort Lauderdale (city) Broward	84	0.06

Top 10 Places Sorted by Percent

Based on all places, regardless of population

Place (place type) County	Number	%
Harlem (cdp) Hendry	34	1.20
St. George (cdp) Broward	24	1.00
Mangonia Park (town) Palm Beach	11	0.85
Melrose Park (cdp) Broward	54	0.76
Belle Glade Camp (cdp) Palm Beach	8	0.63
Samsula-Spruce Creek (cdp) Volusia	30	0.61
De Land Southwest (cdp) Volusia	6	0.53
Three Lakes (cdp) Miami-Dade	31	0.44
Waverly (cdp) Polk	8	0.43
Indiantown (cdp) Martin	22	0.41

Top 10 Places Sorted by Percent

Based on places with populations of 10,000 or more

Place (place type) County	Number	%
Azalea Park (cdp) Orange	45	0.40
Palmetto Estates (cdp) Miami-Dade	50	0.37
Meadow Woods (cdp) Orange	41	0.36
Poinciana (cdp) Osceola	44	0.32
Lauderhill (city) Broward	168	0.29
Pine Hills (cdp) Orange	112	0.27
North Miami (city) Miami-Dade	149	0.25
Norland (cdp) Miami-Dade	57	0.25
Golden Glades (cdp) Miami-Dade	67	0.21
Fairview Shores (cdp) Orange	27	0.20

West Indian: Belizean, excluding Hispanic

Top 10 Places Sorted by Number

Based on all places, regardless of population

Place (place type) County	Number	%
Jacksonville (special city) Duval	122	0.02
Pine Manor (cdp) Lee	119	3.06
Miami (city) Miami-Dade	105	0.03
Plantation (city) Broward	91	0.11
North Miami Beach (city) Miami-Dade	85	0.21
Carol City (cdp) Miami-Dade	85	0.14
Tamarac (city) Broward	59	0.11
North Miami (city) Miami-Dade	56	0.09
Collier Manor-Cresthaven (cdp) Broward	55	0.69
Pembroke Pines (city) Broward	54	0.04

Top 10 Places Sorted by Percent

Based on all places, regardless of population

Place (place type) County	Number	%
Pine Manor (cdp) Lee	119	3.06
Royal Palm Estates (cdp) Palm Beach	45	1.30
Collier Manor-Cresthaven (cdp) Broward	55	0.69
Rock Island (cdp) Broward	17	0.54
Roosevelt Gardens (cdp) Broward	10	0.54
Bithlo (cdp) Orange	20	0.45
Golden Lakes (cdp) Palm Beach	28	0.42
Washington Park (cdp) Broward	5	0.40
Meadow Woods (cdp) Orange	45	0.39
Tangelo Park (cdp) Orange	7	0.30

Top 10 Places Sorted by Percent

Based on places with populations of 10,000 or more

Place (place type) County	Number	%
Meadow Woods (cdp) Orange	45	0.39
Palmetto Estates (cdp) Miami-Dade	40	0.29
Upper Grand Lagoon (cdp) Bay	28	0.25
Brownsville (cdp) Miami-Dade	33	0.23
North Miami Beach (city) Miami-Dade	85	0.21
Casselberry (city) Seminole	39	0.18
Miami Springs (city) Miami-Dade	25	0.18
Oakland Park (city) Broward	46	0.15
Longwood (city) Seminole	20	0.15
Carol City (cdp) Miami-Dade	85	0.14

West Indian: Bermudan, excluding Hispanic

Top 10 Places Sorted by Number

Based on all places, regardless of population

Place (place type) County	Number	%
Jacksonville (special city) Duval	90	0.01
Lake Mary (city) Seminole	46	0.41
Fern Park (cdp) Seminole	38	0.46
Sunrise (city) Broward	30	0.04
Celebration (cdp) Osceola	24	0.87
Punta Gorda (city) Charlotte	24	0.17
Springfield (city) Bay	20	0.22
Gainesville (city) Alachua	19	0.02
Cape Coral (city) Lee	17	0.02
Casselberry (city) Seminole	16	0.07

Top 10 Places Sorted by Percent

Based on all places, regardless of population

Place (place type) County	Number	%
Celebration (cdp) Osceola	24	0.87
Lawtey (city) Bradford	3	0.53
Fern Park (cdp) Seminole	38	0.46
Lake Mary (city) Seminole	46	0.41
Springfield (city) Bay	20	0.22
Pompano Estates (cdp) Broward	7	0.20
Port La Belle (cdp) Hendry	6	0.19
Punta Gorda (city) Charlotte	24	0.17
South Bay (city) Palm Beach	5	0.13
Live Oak (city) Suwannee	7	0.11

Top 10 Places Sorted by Percent

Based on places with populations of 10,000 or more

Place (place type) County	Number	%
Lake Mary (city) Seminole	46	0.41
Punta Gorda (city) Charlotte	24	0.17
Casselberry (city) Seminole	16	0.07
Sebastian (city) Indian River	12	0.07
Hobe Sound (cdp) Martin	8	0.07
Riverview (cdp) Hillsborough	8	0.07
Sunrise (city) Broward	30	0.04
Palm Beach Gardens (city) Palm Beach	15	0.04
Pinellas Park (city) Pinellas	13	0.03
North Fort Myers (cdp) Lee	12	0.03

West Indian: British West Indian, excluding Hispanic

Top 10 Places Sorted by Number

Based on all places, regardless of population

Place (place type) County	Number	%
Miramar (city) Broward	428	0.59
Carol City (cdp) Miami-Dade	327	0.55
Norland (cdp) Miami-Dade	305	1.32
Orlando (city) Orange	279	0.15
Pembroke Pines (city) Broward	270	0.20
Lauderhill (city) Broward	254	0.44
North Miami (city) Miami-Dade	246	0.41
Lauderdale Lakes (city) Broward	238	0.76
Hollywood (city) Broward	224	0.16
Fort Lauderdale (city) Broward	209	0.14

Top 10 Places Sorted by Percent

Based on all places, regardless of population

Place (place type) County	Number	%
Utopia (cdp) Broward	29	4.00
Bunche Park (cdp) Miami-Dade	63	1.58
Royal Palm Estates (cdp) Palm Beach	46	1.33
Norland (cdp) Miami-Dade	305	1.32
Pembroke Park (town) Broward	66	1.04
Scott Lake (cdp) Miami-Dade	134	0.93
Golden Lakes (cdp) Palm Beach	56	0.84
Loch Lomond (cdp) Broward	26	0.78
Lake Lucerne (cdp) Miami-Dade	70	0.77
Lauderdale Lakes (city) Broward	238	0.76

Top 10 Places Sorted by Percent

Based on places with populations of 10,000 or more

Place (place type) County	Number	%
Norland (cdp) Miami-Dade	305	1.32
Scott Lake (cdp) Miami-Dade	134	0.93
Lauderdale Lakes (city) Broward	238	0.76
Golden Glades (cdp) Miami-Dade	197	0.61
Miramar (city) Broward	428	0.59
Sandalfoot Cove (cdp) Palm Beach	93	0.56
Carol City (cdp) Miami-Dade	327	0.55
Lauderhill (city) Broward	254	0.44
Pine Hills (cdp) Orange	176	0.42
North Miami (city) Miami-Dade	246	0.41

West Indian: Dutch West Indian, excluding Hispanic

Top 10 Places Sorted by Number

Based on all places, regardless of population

Place (place type) County	Number	%
Palm Bay (city) Brevard	59	0.07
Plantation (city) Broward	50	0.06
Royal Palm Beach (village) Palm Beach	42	0.19
Kendale Lakes (cdp) Miami-Dade	40	0.07
Forest City (cdp) Seminole	37	0.29
Jacksonville (special city) Duval	37	0.01
Tampa (city) Hillsborough	34	0.01
Brandon (cdp) Hillsborough	32	0.04
Opa-locka (city) Miami-Dade	28	0.18
Miami (city) Miami-Dade	27	0.01

Top 10 Places Sorted by Percent

Based on all places, regardless of population

Place (place type) County	Number	%
Edgewood (city) Orange	6	0.33
Forest City (cdp) Seminole	37	0.29
Samoset (cdp) Manatee	8	0.24
Chambers Estates (cdp) Broward	8	0.22
Westchase (cdp) Hillsborough	23	0.21
Daytona Beach Shores (city) Volusia	9	0.21
Princeton (cdp) Miami-Dade	20	0.20
Royal Palm Beach (village) Palm Beach	42	0.19
Opa-locka (city) Miami-Dade	28	0.18
Boyette (cdp) Hillsborough	10	0.16

Top 10 Places Sorted by Percent

Based on places with populations of 10,000 or more

Place (place type) County	Number	%
Forest City (cdp) Seminole	37	0.29
Westchase (cdp) Hillsborough	23	0.21

Princeton (cdp) Miami-Dade	20	0.20
Royal Palm Beach (village) Palm Beach	42	0.19
Opa-locka (city) Miami-Dade	28	0.18
Miami Shores (village) Miami-Dade	14	0.13
Elfers (cdp) Pasco	14	0.11
Villas (cdp) Lee	12	0.11
Norland (cdp) Miami-Dade	19	0.08
Palm Bay (city) Brevard	59	0.07

West Indian: Haitian, excluding Hispanic

Top 10 Places Sorted by Number

Based on all places, regardless of population

Place (place type) County	Number	%
North Miami (city) Miami-Dade	18,656	31.07
Miami (city) Miami-Dade	18,309	5.05
Fort Lauderdale (city) Broward	10,869	7.14
Golden Glades (cdp) Miami-Dade	10,284	31.95
North Miami Beach (city) Miami-Dade	7,864	19.33
Delray Beach (city) Palm Beach	6,351	10.60
Lauderhill (city) Broward	5,034	8.79
Pine Hills (cdp) Orange	4,817	11.47
Lauderdale Lakes (city) Broward	4,732	15.01
Pompano Beach (city) Broward	4,718	6.03

Top 10 Places Sorted by Percent

Based on all places, regardless of population

Place (place type) County	Number	%
Golden Glades (cdp) Miami-Dade	10,284	31.95
Pompano Estates (cdp) Broward	1,083	31.26
North Miami (city) Miami-Dade	18,656	31.07
Pinewood (cdp) Miami-Dade	4,315	25.66
Tedder (cdp) Broward	499	25.11
Kendall Green (cdp) Broward	724	23.04
Belle Glade Camp (cdp) Palm Beach	284	22.47
El Portal (village) Miami-Dade	556	22.09
Bonnie Lock-Woodsetter North (cdp) Broward	872	20.24
North Miami Beach (city) Miami-Dade	7,864	19.33

Top 10 Places Sorted by Percent

Based on places with populations of 10,000 or more

Place (place type) County	Number	%
Golden Glades (cdp) Miami-Dade	10,284	31.95
North Miami (city) Miami-Dade	18,656	31.07
Pinewood (cdp) Miami-Dade	4,315	25.66
North Miami Beach (city) Miami-Dade	7,864	19.33
Lauderdale Lakes (city) Broward	4,732	15.01
Ives Estates (cdp) Miami-Dade	2,449	14.06
Norland (cdp) Miami-Dade	2,789	12.11
Pine Hills (cdp) Orange	4,817	11.47
Immokalee (cdp) Collier	2,095	10.79
Delray Beach (city) Palm Beach	6,351	10.60

West Indian: Jamaican, excluding Hispanic

Top 10 Places Sorted by Number

Based on all places, regardless of population

Place (place type) County	Number	%
Miramar (city) Broward	11,263	15.50
Lauderhill (city) Broward	9,723	16.98
Pembroke Pines (city) Broward	7,648	5.58
Sunrise (city) Broward	6,888	8.04
Lauderdale Lakes (city) Broward	5,646	17.91
Norland (cdp) Miami-Dade	4,849	21.06
North Lauderdale (city) Broward	3,688	11.41
Plantation (city) Broward	3,657	4.39
Carol City (cdp) Miami-Dade	3,111	5.23
Hollywood (city) Broward	3,105	2.23

Top 10 Places Sorted by Percent

Based on all places, regardless of population

Place (place type) County	Number	%
Melrose Park (cdp) Broward	1,596	22.52
Norland (cdp) Miami-Dade	4,849	21.06
Lauderdale Lakes (city) Broward	5,646	17.91
Palmetto Estates (cdp) Miami-Dade	2,359	17.25
Lauderhill (city) Broward	9,723	16.98
Andover (cdp) Miami-Dade	1,433	16.55
Miramar (city) Broward	11,263	15.50
Scott Lake (cdp) Miami-Dade	1,870	13.00
Utopia (cdp) Broward	91	12.55
North Lauderdale (city) Broward	3,688	11.41

Top 10 Places Sorted by Percent

Based on places with populations of 10,000 or more

Place (place type) County	Number	%
Norland (cdp) Miami-Dade	4,849	21.06
Lauderdale Lakes (city) Broward	5,646	17.91
Palmetto Estates (cdp) Miami-Dade	2,359	17.25
Lauderhill (city) Broward	9,723	16.98
Miramar (city) Broward	11,263	15.50
Scott Lake (cdp) Miami-Dade	1,870	13.00
North Lauderdale (city) Broward	3,688	11.41
Sunrise (city) Broward	6,888	8.04
Ives Estates (cdp) Miami-Dade	1,000	5.74
South Miami Heights (cdp) Miami-Dade	1,909	5.69

West Indian: Trinidadian and Tobagonian, excluding Hispanic

Top 10 Places Sorted by Number

Based on all places, regardless of population

Place (place type) County	Number	%
Miramar (city) Broward	897	1.23
Hollywood (city) Broward	727	0.52
Sunrise (city) Broward	694	0.81
Pembroke Pines (city) Broward	592	0.43
Lauderhill (city) Broward	480	0.84
Plantation (city) Broward	461	0.55
Coral Springs (city) Broward	433	0.37
Palmetto Estates (cdp) Miami-Dade	413	3.02
Tampa (city) Hillsborough	359	0.12
North Lauderdale (city) Broward	357	1.10

Top 10 Places Sorted by Percent

Based on all places, regardless of population

Place (place type) County	Number	%
Palmetto Estates (cdp) Miami-Dade	413	3.02
Naranja (cdp) Miami-Dade	105	2.50
West Perrine (cdp) Miami-Dade	207	2.41
Loch Lomond (cdp) Broward	63	1.90
Country Walk (cdp) Miami-Dade	190	1.78
East Perrine (cdp) Miami-Dade	121	1.77
Ramblewood East (cdp) Broward	21	1.66
Bonnie Lock-Woodsetter North (cdp) Broward	65	1.51
Norland (cdp) Miami-Dade	328	1.42
Surfside (town) Miami-Dade	73	1.42

Top 10 Places Sorted by Percent

Based on places with populations of 10,000 or more

Place (place type) County	Number	%
Palmetto Estates (cdp) Miami-Dade	413	3.02
Country Walk (cdp) Miami-Dade	190	1.78
Norland (cdp) Miami-Dade	328	1.42
Miramar (city) Broward	897	1.23
North Lauderdale (city) Broward	357	1.10
Lauderhill (city) Broward	480	0.84
Sunrise (city) Broward	694	0.81
Princeton (cdp) Miami-Dade	80	0.79
Poinciana (cdp) Osceola	102	0.75
Scott Lake (cdp) Miami-Dade	104	0.72

West Indian: U.S. Virgin Islander, excluding Hispanic

Top 10 Places Sorted by Number

Based on all places, regardless of population

Place (place type) County	Number	%
Miramar (city) Broward	207	0.28
St. Petersburg (city) Pinellas	197	0.08
Orlando (city) Orange	166	0.09
Lauderdale Lakes (city) Broward	159	0.50
Tallahassee (city) Leon	153	0.10
Deltona (city) Volusia	123	0.18
Tampa (city) Hillsborough	108	0.04
Miami (city) Miami-Dade	107	0.03
Jacksonville (special city) Duval	107	0.01
Pine Hills (cdp) Orange	100	0.24

Top 10 Places Sorted by Percent

Based on all places, regardless of population

Place (place type) County	Number	%
Utopia (cdp) Broward	15	2.07
Opa-locka North (cdp) Miami-Dade	94	1.51
Silver Springs Shores (cdp) Marion	40	0.61
Scott Lake (cdp) Miami-Dade	85	0.59
Pembroke Park (town) Broward	36	0.57
Golden Lakes (cdp) Palm Beach	34	0.51
Lauderdale Lakes (city) Broward	159	0.50
Naples Manor (cdp) Collier	22	0.43
Westview (cdp) Miami-Dade	39	0.41
Lake Lucerne (cdp) Miami-Dade	36	0.39

Top 10 Places Sorted by Percent

Based on places with populations of 10,000 or more

Place (place type) County	Number	%
Scott Lake (cdp) Miami-Dade	85	0.59
Lauderdale Lakes (city) Broward	159	0.50
Miramar (city) Broward	207	0.28
Pine Hills (cdp) Orange	100	0.24
Yeehaw Junction (cdp) Osceola	50	0.23
North Lauderdale (city) Broward	65	0.20
Deltona (city) Volusia	123	0.18
Ives Estates (cdp) Miami-Dade	32	0.18
Lauderhill (city) Broward	82	0.14
Country Club (cdp) Miami-Dade	52	0.14

West Indian: West Indian, excluding Hispanic

Top 10 Places Sorted by Number

Based on all places, regardless of population

Place (place type) County	Number	%
Jacksonville (special city) Duval	750	0.10
Pembroke Pines (city) Broward	522	0.38
Miramar (city) Broward	493	0.68
Tampa (city) Hillsborough	415	0.14
Orlando (city) Orange	369	0.20
Lauderhill (city) Broward	365	0.64
Miami (city) Miami-Dade	350	0.10
Sunrise (city) Broward	337	0.39
Hollywood (city) Broward	324	0.23
North Lauderdale (city) Broward	307	0.95

Top 10 Places Sorted by Percent

Based on all places, regardless of population

Place (place type) County	Number	%
Gun Club Estates (cdp) Palm Beach	92	10.86
Chula Vista (cdp) Broward	20	3.42
Lake Belvedere Estates (cdp) Palm Beach	27	1.81
St. Leo (town) Pasco	10	1.64
Orlovista (cdp) Orange	95	1.56
East Perrine (cdp) Miami-Dade	102	1.49
Roosevelt Gardens (cdp) Broward	26	1.39
Sky Lake (cdp) Orange	81	1.37
Loch Lomond (cdp) Broward	41	1.23

Notes: (cdp) census designated place; Refer to the User's Guide in the front of the book for more detailed information.

Place (place type) County	Number	%
Poinciana (cdp) Osceola	162	1.19

Top 10 Places Sorted by Percent
Based on places with populations of 10,000 or more

Place (place type) County	Number	%
Poinciana (cdp) Osceola	162	1.19
North Lauderdale (city) Broward	307	0.95
Meadow Woods (cdp) Orange	93	0.81
Yeehaw Junction (cdp) Osceola	156	0.70
Opa-locka (city) Miami-Dade	105	0.69
Miramar (city) Broward	493	0.68
Pine Hills (cdp) Orange	275	0.65
Lauderhill (city) Broward	365	0.64
Apopka (city) Orange	165	0.63
Ives Estates (cdp) Miami-Dade	101	0.58

West Indian: Other, excluding Hispanic

Top 10 Places Sorted by Number
Based on all places, regardless of population

Place (place type) County	Number	%
St. Petersburg (city) Pinellas	74	0.03
Greater Northdale (cdp) Hillsborough	59	0.29
Davie (town) Broward	42	0.06
Jacksonville (special city) Duval	42	0.01
Tampa (city) Hillsborough	38	0.01
Fort Lauderdale (city) Broward	37	0.02
Orlando (city) Orange	37	0.02
Carol City (cdp) Miami-Dade	34	0.06
University (cdp) Hillsborough	32	0.10
Miami Beach (city) Miami-Dade	29	0.03

Top 10 Places Sorted by Percent
Based on all places, regardless of population

Place (place type) County	Number	%
Seffner (cdp) Hillsborough	28	0.50
Fussels Corner (cdp) Polk	16	0.31
Greater Northdale (cdp) Hillsborough	59	0.29
Madeira Beach (city) Pinellas	10	0.22
East Perrine (cdp) Miami-Dade	12	0.18
Flagler Beach (city) Flagler	9	0.18
Pinewood (cdp) Miami-Dade	19	0.11
De Bary (city) Volusia	18	0.11
University (cdp) Hillsborough	32	0.10
Atlantic Beach (city) Duval	13	0.10

Top 10 Places Sorted by Percent
Based on places with populations of 10,000 or more

Place (place type) County	Number	%
Greater Northdale (cdp) Hillsborough	59	0.29
Pinewood (cdp) Miami-Dade	19	0.11
De Bary (city) Volusia	18	0.11
University (cdp) Hillsborough	32	0.10
Atlantic Beach (city) Duval	13	0.10
Poinciana (cdp) Osceola	12	0.09
De Land (city) Volusia	16	0.08
Upper Grand Lagoon (cdp) Bay	9	0.08
South Miami Heights (cdp) Miami-Dade	24	0.07
Citrus Park (cdp) Hillsborough	15	0.07

White

Top 10 Places Sorted by Number
Based on all places, regardless of population

Place (place type) County	Number	%
Jacksonville (special city) Duval	485,785	66.04
Miami (city) Miami-Dade	251,993	69.52
Hialeah (city) Miami-Dade	206,539	91.22
Tampa (city) Hillsborough	201,268	66.33
St. Petersburg (city) Pinellas	181,278	73.03
Orlando (city) Orange	117,957	63.43
Hollywood (city) Broward	112,460	80.70
Pembroke Pines (city) Broward	107,142	77.96
Fort Lauderdale (city) Broward	99,898	65.55
Coral Springs (city) Broward	97,897	83.28

Top 10 Places Sorted by Percent
Based on all places, regardless of population

Place (place type) County	Number	%
Plantation Island (cdp) Collier	202	100.00
Nobleton (cdp) Hernando	160	100.00
Orchid (town) Indian River	140	100.00
Bascom (town) Jackson	106	100.00
Lake Lindsey (cdp) Hernando	49	100.00
Indian Creek (village) Miami-Dade	33	100.00
Lake Buena Vista (city) Orange	16	100.00
Weeki Wachee (city) Hernando	12	100.00
Islandia (city) Miami-Dade	6	100.00
Marineland (town) Flagler	6	100.00

Top 10 Places Sorted by Percent
Based on places with populations of 10,000 or more

Place (place type) County	Number	%
Kings Point (cdp) Palm Beach	12,134	99.40
Greater Sun Center (cdp) Hillsborough	16,181	99.14
Englewood (cdp) Sarasota	15,995	98.76
Venice (city) Sarasota	17,519	98.62
Marco Island (city) Collier	14,650	98.46
South Venice (cdp) Sarasota	13,319	98.38
Lighthouse Point (city) Broward	10,562	98.10
Iona (cdp) Lee	11,524	98.03
Hudson (cdp) Pasco	12,512	98.02
Seminole (city) Pinellas	10,652	97.81

White: Not Hispanic

Top 10 Places Sorted by Number
Based on all places, regardless of population

Place (place type) County	Number	%
Jacksonville (special city) Duval	467,111	63.50
St. Petersburg (city) Pinellas	173,878	70.05
Tampa (city) Hillsborough	158,426	52.21
Orlando (city) Orange	96,921	52.12
Cape Coral (city) Lee	90,436	88.41
Fort Lauderdale (city) Broward	88,757	58.24
Tallahassee (city) Leon	88,527	58.77
Hollywood (city) Broward	87,426	62.74
Clearwater (city) Pinellas	86,260	79.29
Coral Springs (city) Broward	83,258	70.83

Top 10 Places Sorted by Percent
Based on all places, regardless of population

Place (place type) County	Number	%
Bascom (town) Jackson	106	100.00
Lake Lindsey (cdp) Hernando	49	100.00
Lake Buena Vista (city) Orange	16	100.00
Weeki Wachee (city) Hernando	12	100.00
Islandia (city) Miami-Dade	6	100.00
Marineland (town) Flagler	6	100.00
Jupiter Inlet Colony (town) Palm Beach	367	99.73
Orchid (town) Indian River	139	99.29
Punta Rassa (cdp) Lee	1,715	99.08
Briny Breezes (town) Palm Beach	407	99.03

Top 10 Places Sorted by Percent
Based on places with populations of 10,000 or more

Place (place type) County	Number	%
Kings Point (cdp) Palm Beach	12,007	98.36
Greater Sun Center (cdp) Hillsborough	16,012	98.11
Venice (city) Sarasota	17,360	97.73
Englewood (cdp) Sarasota	15,819	97.67
South Venice (cdp) Sarasota	13,140	97.05
Seminole (city) Pinellas	10,458	96.03
Homosassa Springs (cdp) Citrus	11,942	95.86
Hudson (cdp) Pasco	12,232	95.82
Edgewater (city) Volusia	17,874	95.75
Cocoa Beach (city) Brevard	11,911	95.43

White: Hispanic

Top 10 Places Sorted by Number
Based on all places, regardless of population

Place (place type) County	Number	%
Miami (city) Miami-Dade	207,888	57.35
Hialeah (city) Miami-Dade	187,865	82.97
Fountainbleau (cdp) Miami-Dade	47,111	79.11
Tamiami (cdp) Miami-Dade	44,572	81.35
Tampa (city) Hillsborough	42,842	14.12
Miami Beach (city) Miami-Dade	42,181	47.97
Kendale Lakes (cdp) Miami-Dade	40,249	70.74
Kendall (cdp) Miami-Dade	35,083	46.64
Pembroke Pines (city) Broward	33,066	24.06
The Hammocks (cdp) Miami-Dade	27,479	58.00

Top 10 Places Sorted by Percent
Based on all places, regardless of population

Place (place type) County	Number	%
Sweetwater (city) Miami-Dade	12,056	84.75
Hialeah (city) Miami-Dade	187,865	82.97
Hialeah Gardens (city) Miami-Dade	15,954	82.68
Westchester (cdp) Miami-Dade	24,773	81.84
Tamiami (cdp) Miami-Dade	44,572	81.35
West Miami (city) Miami-Dade	4,660	79.48
Fountainbleau (cdp) Miami-Dade	47,111	79.11
University Park (cdp) Miami-Dade	20,825	78.47
Coral Terrace (cdp) Miami-Dade	19,121	78.43
Olympia Heights (cdp) Miami-Dade	9,836	73.12

Top 10 Places Sorted by Percent
Based on places with populations of 10,000 or more

Place (place type) County	Number	%
Sweetwater (city) Miami-Dade	12,056	84.75
Hialeah (city) Miami-Dade	187,865	82.97
Hialeah Gardens (city) Miami-Dade	15,954	82.68
Westchester (cdp) Miami-Dade	24,773	81.84
Tamiami (cdp) Miami-Dade	44,572	81.35
Fountainbleau (cdp) Miami-Dade	47,111	79.11
University Park (cdp) Miami-Dade	20,825	78.47
Coral Terrace (cdp) Miami-Dade	19,121	78.43
Olympia Heights (cdp) Miami-Dade	9,836	73.12
Westwood Lakes (cdp) Miami-Dade	8,741	72.81

Yugoslavian

Top 10 Places Sorted by Number
Based on all places, regardless of population

Place (place type) County	Number	%
Jacksonville (special city) Duval	2,655	0.36
St. Petersburg (city) Pinellas	1,459	0.59
Clearwater (city) Pinellas	585	0.54
Tampa (city) Hillsborough	345	0.11
Pinellas Park (city) Pinellas	338	0.74
Hollywood (city) Broward	245	0.18
Coral Springs (city) Broward	183	0.16
New Port Richey (city) Pasco	164	1.05
Jupiter (town) Palm Beach	141	0.36
Miami Beach (city) Miami-Dade	135	0.15

Top 10 Places Sorted by Percent
Based on all places, regardless of population

Place (place type) County	Number	%
Goodland (cdp) Collier	11	4.98
Plantation Island (cdp) Collier	8	3.76
Cudjoe Key (cdp) Monroe	27	1.55
New Port Richey (city) Pasco	164	1.05
Gulf Gate Estates (cdp) Sarasota	121	1.05
Pine Castle (cdp) Orange	78	0.95
Wewahitchka (city) Gulf	14	0.80
Pinellas Park (city) Pinellas	338	0.74
Desoto Lakes (cdp) Sarasota	24	0.74
South Sarasota (cdp) Sarasota	35	0.68

Notes: (cdp) census designated place; Refer to the User's Guide in the front of the book for more detailed information.

Top 10 Places Sorted by Percent

Based on places with populations of 10,000 or more

Place (place type) County	Number	%
New Port Richey (city) Pasco	164	1.05
Gulf Gate Estates (cdp) Sarasota	121	1.05
Pinellas Park (city) Pinellas	338	0.74
St. Petersburg (city) Pinellas	1,459	0.59
Clearwater (city) Pinellas	585	0.54
Casselberry (city) Seminole	110	0.50
West and East Lealman (cdp) Pinellas	94	0.43
Lockhart (cdp) Orange	50	0.40
Lakewood Park (cdp) St. Lucie	39	0.37
Jacksonville (special city) Duval	2,655	0.36

Notes: (cdp) census designated place; Refer to the User's Guide in the front of the book for more detailed information.

Population

(Universe: Total Population)

Place	Total population	Total Hispanic population	Argentinian	Bolivian	Central American[1]	Chilean	Colombian	Costa Rican	Cuban	Dominican	Ecuadorian	Guatemalan	Honduran	Mexican	Nicaraguan	Panamanian	Paraguayan	Peruvian	Puerto Rican	Salvadoran	South American[2]	Spaniard	Uruguayan	Venezuelan	Other Hisp.
UNITED STATES	281,421,906	35,238,481 12.52	107,275 0.30 0.04	45,188 0.13 0.02	1,811,676 5.14 0.64	73,951 0.21 0.03	496,748 1.41 0.18	72,175 0.20 0.03	1,249,820 3.55 0.44	799,768 2.27 0.28	273,013 0.77 0.10	407,127 1.16 0.14	237,431 0.67 0.08	20,900,102 59.31 7.43	194,493 0.55 0.07	98,475 0.28 0.03	8,929 0.03 <0.01	247,601 0.70 0.09	3,403,510 9.66 1.21	708,741 2.01 0.25	1,419,979 4.03 0.50	112,999 0.32 0.04	20,242 0.06 0.01	96,091 0.27 0.03	5,540,627 15.72 1.97
FLORIDA	15,982,378	2,680,314 16.77	23,825 0.89 0.15	4,406 0.16 0.03	218,696 8.16 1.37	13,423 0.50 0.08	147,404 5.50 0.92	12,109 0.45 0.08	846,080 31.57 5.29	75,539 2.82 0.47	25,973 0.97 0.16	31,657 1.18 0.20	44,949 1.68 0.28	358,123 13.36 2.24	86,750 3.24 0.54	17,008 0.63 0.11	927 0.03 0.01	46,902 1.75 0.29	481,337 17.96 3.01	21,217 0.79 0.13	316,368 11.80 1.98	15,320 0.57 0.10	4,434 0.17 0.03	42,526 1.59 0.27	368,851 13.76 2.31
Alachua County	217,955	12,333 5.66	-	-	620 5.03 0.28	-	637 5.17 0.29	-	2,441 19.79 1.12	-	-	-	-	1,327 10.76 0.61	-	-	-	-	3,268 26.50 1.50	-	2,020 16.38 0.93	-	-	-	2,238 18.15 1.03
Gainesville (city)	95,605	5,962 6.24	-	-	-	-	-	-	1,141 19.14 1.19	-	-	-	-	442 7.41 0.46	-	-	-	-	1,844 30.93 1.93	-	1,091 18.30 1.14	-	-	-	999 16.76 1.04
Bay County	148,217	3,534 2.38	-	-	-	-	-	-	-	-	-	-	-	1,203 34.04 0.81	-	-	-	-	1,017 28.78 0.69	-	-	-	-	-	422 11.94 0.28
Brevard County	476,230	21,902 4.60	-	-	1,226 5.60 0.26	-	710 3.24 0.15	-	2,111 9.64 0.44	371 1.69 0.08	-	-	-	3,664 16.73 0.77	-	398 1.82 0.08	-	-	9,231 42.15 1.94	-	1,719 7.85 0.36	-	-	-	3,365 15.36 0.71
Melbourne (city)	71,371	3,807 5.33	-	-	-	-	-	-	-	-	-	-	-	845 22.20 1.18	-	-	-	-	1,545 40.58 2.16	-	-	-	-	-	482 12.66 0.68
Palm Bay (city)	79,455	6,968 8.77	-	-	-	-	-	-	-	-	-	-	-	721 10.35 0.91	-	-	-	-	3,961 56.85 4.99	-	529 7.59 0.67	-	-	-	1,035 14.85 1.30
Broward County	1,623,018	271,523 16.73	4,060 1.50 0.25	698 0.26 0.04	20,002 7.37 1.23	2,092 0.77 0.13	30,925 11.39 1.91	1,922 0.71 0.12	53,150 19.57 3.27	10,709 3.94 0.66	5,333 1.96 0.33	2,872 1.06 0.18	4,149 1.53 0.26	18,614 6.86 1.15	3,566 1.31 0.22	2,486 0.92 0.15	-	11,320 4.17 0.70	54,184 19.96 3.34	4,469 1.65 0.28	65,798 24.23 4.05	2,314 0.85 0.14	960 0.35 0.06	9,039 3.33 0.56	46,752 17.22 2.88
Coral Springs (city)	117,482	18,279 15.56	-	-	827 4.52 0.70	-	2,294 12.55 1.95	-	2,019 11.05 1.72	533 2.92 0.45	942 5.15 0.80	-	-	1,595 8.73 1.36	-	-	-	953 5.21 0.81	4,029 22.04 3.43	-	5,526 30.23 4.70	-	-	496 2.71 0.42	3,458 18.92 2.94
Davie (town)	75,685	14,384 19.01	-	-	1,088 7.56 1.44	-	1,214 8.44 1.60	-	3,440 23.92 4.55	-	-	-	-	712 4.95 0.94	-	-	-	646 4.49 0.85	3,432 23.86 4.53	-	2,990 20.79 3.95	-	-	-	2,181 15.16 2.88
Deerfield Beach (city)	64,716	5,517 8.52	-	-	494 8.95 0.76	-	705 12.78 1.09	-	772 13.99 1.19	-	-	-	-	469 8.50 0.72	-	-	-	-	1,307 23.69 2.02	-	1,408 25.52 2.18	-	-	-	837 15.17 1.29
Fort Lauderdale (city)	152,125	13,894 9.13	-	-	1,783 12.83 1.17	-	1,304 9.39 0.86	-	2,702 19.45 1.78	-	-	371 2.67 0.24	-	1,232 8.87 0.81	-	-	-	474 3.41 0.31	2,431 17.50 1.60	664 4.78 0.44	2,980 21.45 1.96	-	-	-	2,415 17.38 1.59
Hollywood (city)	139,261	31,380 22.53	559 1.78 0.40	-	2,262 7.21 1.62	377 1.20 0.27	3,312 10.55 2.38	-	6,012 19.16 4.32	1,688 5.38 1.21	628 2.00 0.45	-	444 1.41 0.32	1,203 3.83 0.86	601 1.92 0.43	-	-	1,337 4.26 0.96	6,955 22.16 4.99	-	7,347 23.41 5.28	-	-	654 2.08 0.47	5,716 18.22 4.10

Notes: Please refer to the User's Guide for an explanation of data; data is arranged alphabetically by state, then county, then city within each county and only includes counties with populations > 99,999 and cities with populations > 49,999; (1) Includes Costa Rican, Guatemalan, Honduran, Nicaraguan, Panamanian, Salvadoran, and other Central American; (2) Includes Argentinian, Bolivian, Chilean, Colombian, Ecuadorian, Paraguayan, Peruvian, Uruguayan, Venezuelan, and other South American

Place	Total population	Total Hispanic population	Argentinian	Bolivian	Central American[1]	Chilean	Colombian	Costa Rican	Cuban	Dominican	Ecuadorian	Guatelmalan	Honduran	Mexican	Nicaraguan	Panamanian	Paraguayan	Peruvian	Puerto Rican	Salvadoran	South American[2]	Spaniard	Uruguayan	Venezuelan	Other Hisp.
Lauderhill (city)	57,254	3,915 6.84	-	-	-	-	473 12.08 0.83	-	-	-	-	-	-	-	-	-	-	-	910 23.24 1.59	-	1,058 27.02 1.85	-	-	-	820 20.95 1.43
Margate (city)	53,852	8,222 15.27	-	-	549 6.68 1.02	-	1,134 13.79 2.11	-	691 8.40 1.28	-	-	-	-	836 10.17 1.55	-	-	-	-	2,203 26.79 4.09	-	2,015 24.51 3.74	-	-	-	1,583 19.25 2.94
Miramar (city)	72,674	21,536 29.63	-	-	1,682 7.81 2.31	-	1,982 9.20 2.73	-	6,539 30.36 9.00	1,412 6.56 1.94	-	-	-	574 2.67 0.79	645 2.99 0.89	367 1.70 0.50	-	662 3.07 0.91	3,533 16.41 4.86	-	3,746 17.39 5.15	-	-	-	3,914 18.17 5.39
Pembroke Pines (city)	137,112	38,348 27.97	-	-	1,928 5.03 1.41	-	3,463 9.03 2.53	-	12,401 32.34 9.04	1,809 4.72 1.32	486 1.27 0.35	-	-	934 2.44 0.68	-	-	-	1,505 3.92 1.10	7,370 19.22 5.38	-	7,815 20.38 5.70	-	-	1,480 3.86 1.08	5,783 15.08 4.22
Plantation (city)	83,274	10,999 13.21	-	-	725 6.59 0.87	-	2,138 19.44 2.57	-	1,984 18.04 2.38	-	-	-	-	652 5.93 0.78	-	-	-	505 4.59 0.61	1,612 14.66 1.94	-	3,882 35.29 4.66	-	-	538 4.89 0.65	1,703 15.48 2.05
Pompano Beach (city)	78,301	7,710 9.85	-	-	-	-	558 7.24 0.71	-	652 8.46 0.83	-	-	-	-	2,577 33.42 3.29	-	-	-	-	1,150 14.92 1.47	-	1,454 18.86 1.86	-	-	-	1,260 16.34 1.61
Sunrise (city)	85,636	14,542 16.98	-	-	753 5.18 0.88	-	2,460 16.92 2.87	-	2,069 14.23 2.42	734 5.05 0.86	529 3.64 0.62	-	-	844 5.80 0.99	-	-	-	594 4.08 0.69	2,902 19.96 3.39	-	4,573 31.45 5.34	-	-	-	2,584 17.77 3.02
Tamarac (city)	56,081	7,969 14.21	-	-	-	-	1,255 15.75 2.24	-	853 10.70 1.52	-	-	-	-	-	-	-	-	-	1,931 24.23 3.44	-	2,238 28.08 3.99	-	-	-	1,890 23.72 3.37
Charlotte County	141,627	4,585 3.24	-	-	-	-	-	-	594 12.96 0.42	-	-	-	-	968 21.11 0.68	-	-	-	-	1,447 31.56 1.02	-	-	-	-	-	852 18.58 0.60
Citrus County	118,085	3,058 2.59	-	-	-	-	-	-	-	-	-	-	-	510 16.68 0.43	-	-	-	-	1,249 40.84 1.06	-	-	-	-	-	627 20.50 0.53
Clay County	140,814	6,181 4.39	-	-	-	-	-	-	-	-	-	-	-	1,194 19.32 0.85	-	-	-	-	2,457 39.75 1.74	-	-	-	-	-	1,360 22.00 0.97
Collier County	251,377	49,252 19.59	-	-	3,373 6.85 1.34	-	1,156 2.35 0.46	-	7,278 14.78 2.90	502 1.02 0.20	-	1,573 3.19 0.63	723 1.47 0.29	28,230 57.32 11.23	-	-	-	-	3,145 6.39 1.25	-	2,185 4.44 0.87	-	-	-	4,381 8.90 1.74
Duval County	778,879	31,809 4.08	-	-	1,820 5.72 0.23	-	1,430 4.50 0.18	-	3,332 10.48 0.43	670 2.11 0.09	-	-	-	5,909 18.58 0.76	-	598 1.88 0.08	-	482 1.52 0.06	11,377 35.77 1.46	-	2,774 8.72 0.36	-	-	-	5,667 17.82 0.73
Jacksonville (city)	735,503	30,414 4.14	-	-	1,802 5.92 0.25	-	1,373 4.51 0.19	-	3,250 10.69 0.44	670 2.20 0.09	-	-	-	5,521 18.15 0.75	-	581 1.91 0.08	-	-	10,924 35.92 1.49	-	2,601 8.55 0.35	-	-	-	5,400 17.75 0.73
Escambia County	294,410	7,816 2.65	-	-	538 6.88 0.18	-	-	-	736 9.42 0.25	-	-	-	-	2,710 34.67 0.92	-	-	-	-	1,713 21.92 0.58	-	448 5.73 0.15	-	-	-	1,575 20.15 0.53

Notes: Please refer to the User's Guide for an explanation of data; data is arranged alphabetically by state, then county, then city within each county and only includes counties with populations > 99,999 and cities with populations > 49,999; (1) Includes Costa Rican, Guatemalan, Honduran, Nicaraguan, Panamanian, Salvadoran, and other Central American; (2) Includes Argentinian, Bolivian, Chilean, Colombian, Ecuadorian, Paraguayan, Peruvian, Uruguayan, Venezuelan, and other South American

Place	Total population	Total Hispanic population	Argentinian	Bolivian	Central American[1]	Chilean	Colombian	Costa Rican	Cuban	Dominican	Ecuadorian	Guatelmalan	Honduran	Mexican	Nicaraguan	Panamanian	Paraguayan	Peruvian	Puerto Rican	Salvadoran	South American[2]	Spaniard	Uruguayan	Venezuelan	Other Hisp.
Pensacola (city)	56,288	1,198 2.13	-	-	-	-	-	-	-	-	-	-	-	-	-	-	-	-	-	-	-	-	-	-	-
Hernando County	130,802	6,717 5.14	-	-	-	-	-	-	623 9.27 0.48	-	-	-	-	975 14.52 0.75	-	-	-	-	3,812 56.75 2.91	-	-	-	-	-	818 12.18 0.63
Spring Hill (cdp)	69,196	4,911 7.10	-	-	-	-	-	-	409 8.33 0.59	-	-	-	-	-	-	-	-	-	3,084 62.80 4.46	-	-	-	-	-	614 12.50 0.89
Hillsborough County	998,948	179,637 17.98	-	-	7,922 4.41 0.79	-	6,053 3.37 0.61	960 0.53 0.10	34,877 19.42 3.49	3,882 2.16 0.39	1,282 0.71 0.13	1,056 0.59 0.11	2,243 1.25 0.22	36,549 20.35 3.66	1,017 0.57 0.10	1,646 0.92 0.16	-	1,816 1.01 0.18	50,246 27.97 5.03	752 0.42 0.08	12,290 6.84 1.23	1,830 1.02 0.18	-	1,771 0.99 0.18	32,041 17.84 3.21
Brandon (cdp)	77,732	10,068 12.95	-	-	538 5.34 0.69	-	-	-	1,087 10.80 1.40	-	-	-	-	1,062 10.55 1.37	-	-	-	-	4,847 48.14 6.24	-	606 6.02 0.78	-	-	-	1,567 15.56 2.02
Tampa (city)	303,512	58,571 19.30	-	-	3,229 5.51 1.06	-	1,704 2.91 0.56	-	14,268 24.36 4.70	1,426 2.43 0.47	418 0.71 0.14	-	894 1.53 0.29	7,216 12.32 2.38	468 0.80 0.15	632 1.08 0.21	-	-	15,837 27.04 5.22	-	3,596 6.14 1.18	733 1.25 0.24	-	624 1.07 0.21	12,266 20.94 4.04
Town 'n' Country (cdp)	72,397	20,662 28.54	-	-	857 4.15 1.18	-	1,264 6.12 1.75	-	4,748 22.98 6.56	750 3.63 1.04	-	-	-	1,094 5.29 1.51	-	-	-	-	7,453 36.07 10.29	-	2,117 10.25 2.92	-	-	-	3,442 16.66 4.75
Indian River County	112,947	7,300 6.46	-	-	342 4.68 0.30	-	-	-	366 5.01 0.32	-	-	-	-	4,482 61.40 3.97	-	-	-	-	684 9.37 0.61	-	515 7.05 0.46	-	-	-	889 12.18 0.79
Lake County	210,528	11,836 5.62	-	-	500 4.22 0.24	-	-	-	763 6.45 0.36	-	-	-	-	5,391 45.55 2.56	-	-	-	-	2,917 24.65 1.39	-	559 4.72 0.27	-	-	-	1,591 13.44 0.76
Lee County	440,888	41,993 9.52	-	-	3,017 7.18 0.68	-	1,022 2.43 0.23	-	3,366 8.02 0.76	1,067 2.54 0.24	-	1,407 3.35 0.32	496 1.18 0.11	15,020 35.77 3.41	-	-	-	-	11,828 28.17 2.68	-	2,460 5.86 0.56	-	-	-	5,142 12.24 1.17
Cape Coral (city)	102,206	8,355 8.17	-	-	-	-	581 6.95 0.57	-	1,582 18.93 1.55	582 6.97 0.57	-	-	-	1,335 15.98 1.31	-	-	-	-	2,176 26.04 2.13	-	1,062 12.71 1.04	-	-	-	1,258 15.06 1.23
Leon County	239,452	8,220 3.43	-	-	-	-	-	-	1,905 23.18 0.80	-	-	-	-	1,431 17.41 0.60	-	-	-	-	1,579 19.21 0.66	-	1,033 12.57 0.43	-	-	-	1,631 19.84 0.68
Tallahassee (city)	150,581	6,077 4.04	-	-	-	-	-	-	1,454 23.93 0.97	-	-	-	-	905 14.89 0.60	-	-	-	-	1,153 18.97 0.77	-	802 13.20 0.53	-	-	-	1,242 20.44 0.82
Manatee County	264,002	24,501 9.28	-	-	1,470 6.00 0.56	-	-	-	1,187 4.84 0.45	-	-	-	-	15,049 61.42 5.70	-	-	-	-	3,221 13.15 1.22	-	937 3.82 0.35	-	-	-	2,421 9.88 0.92
Marion County	258,916	15,535 6.00	-	-	543 3.50 0.21	-	563 3.62 0.22	-	1,233 7.94 0.48	-	-	-	-	3,345 21.53 1.29	-	-	-	-	6,951 44.74 2.68	-	1,091 7.02 0.42	-	-	-	2,079 13.38 0.80

Notes: Please refer to the User's Guide for an explanation of data; data is arranged alphabetically by state, then county, then city within each county and only includes counties with populations > 99,999 and cities with populations > 49,999; (1) Includes Costa Rican, Guatemalan, Honduran, Nicaraguan, Panamanian, Salvadoran, and other Central American; (2) Includes Argentinian, Bolivian, Chilean, Colombian, Ecuadorian, Paraguayan, Peruvian, Uruguayan, Venezuelan, and other South American

Place	Total population	Total Hispanic population	Argentinian	Bolivian	Central American[1]	Chilean	Colombian	Costa Rican	Cuban	Dominican	Ecuadorian	Guatelmalan	Honduran	Mexican	Nicaraguan	Panamanian	Paraguayan	Peruvian	Puerto Rican	Salvadoran	South American[2]	Spaniard	Uruguayan	Venezuelan	Other Hisp.
Martin County	126,731	9,490 7.49	-	-	2,379 25.07 1.88	-	-	-	802 8.45 0.63	-	-	2,021 21.30 1.59	-	3,860 40.67 3.05	-	-	-	-	1,421 14.97 1.12	-	-	-	-	-	703 7.41 0.55
Miami-Dade County	2,253,362	1,291,681 57.32	14,181 1.10 0.63	2,292 0.18 0.10	138,710 10.74 6.16	8,033 0.62 0.36	75,009 5.81 3.33	4,631 0.36 0.21	656,751 50.84 29.15	39,888 3.09 1.77	11,555 0.89 0.51	10,647 0.82 0.47	29,007 2.25 1.29	37,390 2.89 1.66	75,466 5.84 3.35	6,750 0.52 0.30	-	23,793 1.84 1.06	79,813 6.18 3.54	9,575 0.74 0.42	162,329 12.57 7.20	6,197 0.48 0.28	1,971 0.15 0.09	22,596 1.75 1.00	170,603 13.21 7.57
Carol City (cdp)	59,443	24,973 42.01	-	-	2,642 10.58 4.44	-	1,466 5.87 2.47	-	11,216 44.91 18.87	1,883 7.54 3.17	-	-	518 2.07 0.87	-	1,448 5.80 2.44	-	-	-	2,790 11.17 4.69	-	2,534 10.15 4.26	-	-	-	3,486 13.96 5.86
Fountainbleau (cdp)	59,518	51,833 87.09	440 0.85 0.74	-	8,161 15.74 13.71	703 1.36 1.18	2,781 5.37 4.67	-	22,301 43.02 37.47	1,928 3.72 3.24	799 1.54 1.34	-	642 1.24 1.08	482 0.93 0.81	6,120 11.81 10.28	522 1.01 0.88	-	1,181 2.28 1.98	1,883 3.63 3.16	-	8,376 16.16 14.07	-	-	2,084 4.02 3.50	8,566 16.53 14.39
Hialeah (city)	226,411	204,808 90.46	429 0.21 0.19	-	15,904 7.77 7.02	750 0.37 0.33	7,715 3.77 3.41	523 0.26 0.23	141,302 68.99 62.41	4,886 2.39 2.16	1,233 0.60 0.54	842 0.41 0.37	2,651 1.29 1.17	1,608 0.79 0.71	10,161 4.96 4.49	-	-	1,459 0.71 0.64	6,971 3.40 3.08	950 0.46 0.42	12,903 6.30 5.70	509 0.25 0.22	-	955 0.47 0.42	20,725 10.12 9.15
Kendale Lakes (cdp)	56,886	43,588 76.62	-	-	4,079 9.36 7.17	-	4,003 9.18 7.04	-	22,057 50.60 38.77	843 1.93 1.48	-	-	557 1.28 0.98	583 1.34 1.02	2,847 6.53 5.00	-	-	967 2.22 1.70	1,644 3.77 2.89	-	7,318 16.79 12.86	-	-	871 2.00 1.53	6,905 15.84 12.14
Kendall (cdp)	75,279	37,640 50.00	655 1.74 0.87	-	3,845 10.22 5.11	480 1.28 0.64	4,130 10.97 5.49	-	15,868 42.16 21.08	799 2.12 1.06	-	-	-	-	2,232 5.93 2.96	-	-	1,370 3.64 1.82	2,245 5.96 2.98	-	8,700 23.11 11.56	-	-	1,453 3.86 1.93	5,387 14.31 7.16
Miami Beach (city)	88,061	46,980 53.35	3,031 6.45 3.44	-	2,823 6.01 3.21	739 1.57 0.84	4,493 9.56 5.10	-	18,241 38.83 20.71	1,396 2.97 1.59	662 1.41 0.75	-	810 1.72 0.92	986 2.10 1.12	992 2.11 1.13	-	-	1,898 4.04 2.16	3,552 7.56 4.03	-	12,984 27.64 14.74	573 1.22 0.65	-	1,456 3.10 1.65	6,425 13.68 7.30
Miami (city)	362,563	238,461 65.77	2,029 0.85 0.56	-	43,925 18.42 12.12	897 0.38 0.25	6,006 2.52 1.66	816 0.34 0.23	124,734 52.31 34.40	7,270 3.05 2.01	1,755 0.74 0.48	2,851 1.20 0.79	13,660 5.73 3.77	3,167 1.33 0.87	22,571 9.47 6.23	883 0.37 0.24	-	2,767 1.16 0.76	10,138 4.25 2.80	2,394 1.00 0.66	15,956 6.69 4.40	951 0.40 0.26	-	1,760 0.74 0.49	32,320 13.55 8.91
North Miami (city)	60,036	14,311 23.84	-	-	1,759 12.29 2.93	-	1,025 7.16 1.71	-	2,823 19.73 4.70	1,098 7.67 1.83	-	-	590 4.12 0.98	-	716 5.00 1.19	-	-	-	2,797 19.54 4.66	-	2,075 14.50 3.46	-	-	-	3,271 22.86 5.45
Tamiami (cdp)	54,745	47,691 87.11	-	-	3,850 8.07 7.03	-	2,031 4.26 3.71	-	32,381 67.90 59.15	667 1.40 1.22	-	-	453 0.95 0.83	541 1.13 0.99	2,757 5.78 5.04	-	-	-	1,083 2.27 1.98	-	3,974 8.33 7.26	-	-	545 1.14 1.00	5,016 10.52 9.16
Okaloosa County	170,498	6,901 4.05	-	-	362 5.25 0.21	-	-	-	577 8.36 0.34	-	-	-	-	2,377 34.44 1.39	-	-	-	-	1,517 21.98 0.89	-	-	-	-	-	1,550 22.46 0.91
Orange County	896,344	168,191 18.76	702 0.42 0.08	-	5,786 3.44 0.65	459 0.27 0.05	7,698 4.58 0.86	596 0.35 0.07	13,232 7.87 1.48	6,195 3.68 0.69	1,772 1.05 0.20	1,033 0.61 0.12	1,240 0.74 0.14	19,951 11.86 2.23	885 0.53 0.10	951 0.57 0.11	-	1,767 1.05 0.20	86,266 51.29 9.62	943 0.56 0.11	15,806 9.40 1.76	671 0.40 0.07	-	2,616 1.56 0.29	20,284 12.06 2.26
Orlando (city)	185,984	32,897 17.69	-	-	1,375 4.18 0.74	-	1,773 5.39 0.95	-	2,981 9.06 1.60	1,241 3.77 0.67	-	-	-	2,320 7.05 1.25	-	-	-	455 1.38 0.24	16,701 50.77 8.98	-	3,955 12.02 2.13	-	-	781 2.37 0.42	4,197 12.76 2.26
Osceola County	172,493	50,742 29.42	-	-	1,938 3.82 1.12	-	1,942 3.83 1.13	-	1,839 3.62 1.07	2,468 4.86 1.43	444 0.88 0.26	-	-	3,438 6.78 1.99	-	-	-	-	32,630 64.31 18.92	539 1.06 0.31	3,639 7.17 2.11	-	-	526 1.04 0.30	4,586 9.04 2.66

Notes: Please refer to the User's Guide for an explanation of data; data is arranged alphabetically by state, then county, then city within each county and only includes counties with populations > 99,999 and cities with populations > 49,999; (1) Includes Costa Rican, Guatemalan, Honduran, Nicaraguan, Panamanian, Salvadoran, and other Central American; (2) Includes Argentinian, Bolivian, Chilean, Colombian, Ecuadorian, Paraguayan, Peruvian, Uruguayan, Venezuelan, and other South American

Place	Total population	Total Hispanic population	Argentinian	Bolivian	Central American[1]	Chilean	Colombian	Costa Rican	Cuban	Dominican	Ecuadorian	Guatemalan	Honduran	Mexican	Nicaraguan	Panamanian	Paraguayan	Peruvian	Puerto Rican	Salvadoran	South American[2]	Spaniard	Uruguayan	Venezuelan	Other Hisp.
Palm Beach County	1,131,184	140,568 12.43	1,855 1.32 0.16	-	15,539 11.05 1.37	685 0.49 0.06	9,525 6.78 0.84	843 0.60 0.07	26,157 18.61 2.31	3,589 2.55 0.32	1,991 1.42 0.18	6,914 4.92 0.61	3,270 2.33 0.29	29,583 21.05 2.62	2,105 1.50 0.19	432 0.31 0.04	-	2,483 1.77 0.22	24,774 17.62 2.19	1,661 1.18 0.15	20,252 14.41 1.79	469 0.33 0.04	810 0.58 0.07	1,778 1.26 0.16	20,205 14.37 1.79
Boca Raton (city)	75,594	6,368 8.42	-	-	-	-	870 13.66 1.15	-	917 14.40 1.21	-	-	-	-	833 13.08 1.10	-	-	-	-	840 13.19 1.11	-	2,085 32.74 2.76	-	-	-	1,231 19.33 1.63
Boynton Beach (city)	59,951	5,000 8.34	-	-	586 11.72 0.98	-	-	-	576 11.52 0.96	-	-	-	-	840 16.80 1.40	-	-	-	-	1,447 28.94 2.41	-	748 14.96 1.25	-	-	-	684 13.68 1.14
Delray Beach (city)	59,941	4,165 6.95	-	-	-	-	-	-	-	-	-	-	-	1,460 35.05 2.44	-	-	-	-	733 17.60 1.22	-	599 14.38 1.00	-	-	-	485 11.64 0.81
West Palm Beach (city)	81,539	15,007 18.40	-	-	2,801 18.66 3.44	-	741 4.94 0.91	-	4,406 29.36 5.40	390 2.60 0.48	-	2,060 13.73 2.53	-	1,976 13.17 2.42	-	-	-	-	1,866 12.43 2.29	-	1,591 10.60 1.95	-	-	-	1,948 12.98 2.39
Pasco County	344,765	19,555 5.67	-	-	637 3.26 0.18	-	-	-	1,814 9.28 0.53	-	-	-	-	5,981 30.59 1.73	-	-	-	-	6,963 35.61 2.02	-	863 4.41 0.25	-	-	-	2,884 14.75 0.84
Pinellas County	921,482	42,128 4.57	-	-	1,396 3.31 0.15	-	1,883 4.47 0.20	-	4,727 11.22 0.51	904 2.15 0.10	403 0.96 0.04	-	-	10,292 24.43 1.12	-	-	-	793 1.88 0.09	13,138 31.19 1.43	-	4,789 11.37 0.52	515 1.22 0.06	-	877 2.08 0.10	6,367 15.11 0.69
Clearwater (city)	107,925	9,615 8.91	-	-	-	-	390 4.06 0.36	-	571 5.94 0.53	-	-	-	-	4,211 43.80 3.90	-	-	-	-	2,256 23.46 2.09	-	1,045 10.87 0.97	-	-	-	1,092 11.36 1.01
Largo (city)	69,470	2,849 4.10	-	-	-	-	-	-	-	-	-	-	-	554 19.45 0.80	-	-	-	-	779 27.34 1.12	-	-	-	-	-	-
Palm Harbor (cdp)	59,123	1,939 3.28	-	-	-	-	-	-	-	-	-	-	-	-	-	-	-	-	818 42.19 1.38	-	-	-	-	-	-
St. Petersburg (city)	247,793	9,878 3.99	-	-	-	-	-	-	1,657 16.77 0.67	-	-	-	-	1,670 16.91 0.67	-	-	-	-	3,250 32.90 1.31	-	1,177 11.92 0.47	-	-	-	1,460 14.78 0.59
Polk County	483,924	45,650 9.43	-	-	1,217 2.67 0.25	-	-	-	2,508 5.49 0.52	466 1.02 0.10	-	-	-	24,388 53.42 5.04	-	-	-	-	11,359 24.88 2.35	-	994 2.18 0.21	-	-	-	4,533 9.93 0.94
Lakeland (city)	78,162	5,050 6.46	-	-	-	-	-	-	644 12.75 0.82	-	-	-	-	944 18.69 1.21	-	-	-	-	2,003 39.66 2.56	-	-	-	-	-	811 16.06 1.04
St. Johns County	123,135	3,596 2.92	-	-	-	-	-	-	-	-	-	-	-	950 26.42 0.77	-	-	-	-	881 24.50 0.72	-	-	-	-	-	609 16.94 0.49
St. Lucie County	192,695	16,004 8.31	-	-	1,027 6.42 0.53	-	421 2.63 0.22	-	1,067 6.67 0.55	-	-	-	-	7,213 45.07 3.74	-	-	-	-	3,707 23.16 1.92	-	1,010 6.31 0.52	-	-	-	1,520 9.50 0.79

Notes: Please refer to the User's Guide for an explanation of data; data is arranged alphabetically by state, then county, then city within each county and only includes counties with populations > 99,999 and cities with populations > 49,999; (1) Includes Costa Rican, Guatemalan, Honduran, Nicaraguan, Panamanian, Salvadoran, and other Central American; (2) Includes Argentinian, Bolivian, Chilean, Colombian, Ecuadorian, Paraguayan, Peruvian, Uruguayan, Venezuelan, and other South American

Place	Total population	Total Hispanic population	Argentinian	Bolivian	Central American[1]	Chilean	Colombian	Costa Rican	Cuban	Dominican	Ecuadorian	Guatelmalan	Honduran	Mexican	Nicaraguan	Panamanian	Paraguayan	Peruvian	Puerto Rican	Salvadoran	South American[2]	Spaniard	Uruguayan	Venezuelan	Other Hisp.
Port St. Lucie (city)	88,796	6,822 7.68	-	-	-	-	-	-	721 10.57 0.81	-	-	-	-	1,114 16.33 1.25	-	-	-	-	2,621 38.42 2.95	-	697 10.22 0.78	-	-	-	883 12.94 0.99
Santa Rosa County	117,743	2,821 2.40	-	-	-	-	-	-	-	-	-	-	-	838 29.71 0.71	-	-	-	-	771 27.33 0.65	-	-	-	-	-	525 18.61 0.45
Sarasota County	325,957	14,373 4.41	-	-	632 4.40 0.19	-	875 6.09 0.27	-	1,931 13.43 0.59	-	-	-	-	5,956 41.44 1.83	-	-	-	-	1,715 11.93 0.53	-	1,865 12.98 0.57	-	-	-	1,962 13.65 0.60
Sarasota (city)	52,537	6,390 12.16	-	-	-	-	-	-	667 10.44 1.27	-	-	-	-	3,545 55.48 6.75	-	-	-	-	424 6.64 0.81	-	647 10.13 1.23	-	-	-	699 10.94 1.33
Seminole County	365,196	40,656 11.13	444 1.09 0.12	-	2,017 4.96 0.55	-	2,244 5.52 0.61	-	3,747 9.22 1.03	1,165 2.87 0.32	486 1.20 0.13	-	-	3,545 8.72 0.97	-	547 1.35 0.15	-	540 1.33 0.15	19,734 48.54 5.40	-	4,536 11.16 1.24	-	-	439 1.08 0.12	5,699 14.02 1.56
Volusia County	443,343	29,273 6.60	-	-	789 2.70 0.18	-	677 2.31 0.15	-	1,359 4.64 0.31	588 2.01 0.13	-	-	-	8,060 27.53 1.82	-	-	-	-	13,952 47.66 3.15	-	1,609 5.50 0.36	-	-	-	2,764 9.44 0.62
Daytona Beach (city)	64,070	2,275 3.55	-	-	-	-	-	-	-	-	-	-	-	-	-	-	-	-	902 39.65 1.41	-	-	-	-	-	402 17.67 0.63
Deltona (city)	69,818	12,855 18.41	-	-	-	-	-	-	558 4.34 0.80	-	-	-	-	670 5.21 0.96	-	-	-	-	9,488 73.81 13.59	-	621 4.83 0.89	-	-	-	982 7.64 1.41

Notes: Please refer to the User's Guide for an explanation of data: data is arranged alphabetically by state, then county, then city within each county and only includes counties with populations > 99,999 and cities with populations > 49,999; (1) Includes Costa Rican, Guatemalan, Honduran, Nicaraguan, Panamanian, Salvadoran, and other Central American; (2) Includes Argentinian, Bolivian, Chilean, Colombian, Ecuadorian, Paraguayan, Peruvian, Uruguayan, Venezuelan, and other South American

Median Age

(Universe: Total Population)

Place	Total population	Total Hispanic population	Argentinian	Bolivian	Central American[1]	Chilean	Colombian	Costa Rican	Cuban	Dominican	Ecuadorian	Guatelmalan	Honduran	Mexican	Nicaraguan	Panamanian	Paraguayan	Peruvian	Puerto Rican	Salvadoran	South American[2]	Spaniard	Uruguayan	Venezuelan	Other Hisp.
UNITED STATES	35.4	26.0	35.6	31.3	29.0	34.1	33.6	30.9	40.3	29.6	31.3	27.8	28.4	24.4	31.3	32.6	25.2	33.6	27.7	28.6	33.0	35.8	37.3	29.8	24.8
FLORIDA	38.8	32.8	35.4	33.5	30.4	35.0	34.5	32.2	41.8	32.9	34.5	27.1	30.3	23.9	31.3	33.1	34.9	34.2	30.4	30.0	34.0	41.8	39.7	30.4	25.1
Alachua County	29.0	22.7	-	-	22.3	-	22.8	-	22.3	-	-	-	-	20.9	-	-	-	-	24.6	-	24.0	-	-	-	21.8
Gainesville (city)	26.5	22.5	-	-	-	-	-	-	21.7	-	-	-	-	22.2	-	-	-	-	23.2	-	23.4	-	-	-	21.5
Bay County	37.5	29.3	-	-	-	-	-	-	-	-	-	-	-	25.5	-	-	-	-	25.2	-	-	-	-	-	26.9
Brevard County	41.6	30.6	-	-	32.6	-	35.3	-	35.6	34.0	-	-	-	26.6	-	33.6	-	-	31.0	-	34.3	-	-	-	27.8
Melbourne (city)	39.8	29.4	-	-	-	-	-	-	-	-	-	-	-	22.9	-	-	-	-	31.9	-	-	-	-	-	28.1
Palm Bay (city)	37.2	31.1	-	-	-	-	-	-	-	-	-	-	-	26.4	-	-	-	-	31.0	-	38.2	-	-	-	27.4
Broward County	37.9	32.1	36.2	35.3	30.6	35.1	34.4	33.2	36.8	33.9	33.1	29.8	29.4	26.3	31.2	35.0	-	33.7	31.3	29.1	33.7	38.0	34.3	31.0	25.9
Coral Springs (city)	34.0	29.7	-	-	30.3	-	33.1	-	34.7	37.1	32.4	-	-	24.1	-	-	-	31.6	28.6	-	32.3	-	-	32.4	20.9
Davie (town)	35.9	32.2	-	-	28.3	-	38.1	-	36.1	-	-	-	-	25.0	-	-	-	36.5	28.6	-	35.7	-	-	-	24.9
Deerfield Beach (city)	44.2	32.3	-	-	35.3	-	32.7	-	35.3	-	-	-	-	30.5	-	-	-	-	30.7	-	33.4	-	-	-	29.6
Fort Lauderdale (city)	39.6	33.2	-	-	30.0	-	35.1	-	44.6	-	-	30.0	-	28.5	-	-	-	37.1	31.1	26.2	35.2	-	-	-	27.5
Hollywood (city)	39.2	32.8	35.9	-	32.2	42.1	35.4	-	36.8	33.5	33.1	-	35.8	30.9	31.4	-	-	34.1	30.3	-	34.5	-	-	29.8	27.6
Lauderhill (city)	35.2	31.7	-	-	-	-	34.9	-	-	-	-	-	-	-	-	-	-	-	27.6	-	33.5	-	-	-	29.4
Margate (city)	40.9	31.4	-	-	29.1	-	37.4	-	36.8	-	-	-	-	27.1	-	-	-	-	35.4	-	35.1	-	-	-	26.0
Miramar (city)	32.0	32.2	-	-	31.8	-	33.8	-	34.4	35.0	-	-	-	29.1	31.8	32.1	-	32.4	32.2	-	34.1	-	-	-	20.2
Pembroke Pines (city)	36.7	33.5	-	-	32.9	-	33.9	-	36.3	32.7	36.1	-	-	33.1	-	-	-	31.3	33.2	-	33.1	-	-	31.3	22.5
Plantation (city)	37.9	33.1	-	-	33.3	-	37.0	-	37.7	-	-	-	-	28.4	-	-	-	33.3	30.3	-	35.4	-	-	25.5	20.2
Pompano Beach (city)	42.0	29.0	-	-	-	-	30.8	-	38.2	-	-	-	-	23.8	-	-	-	-	28.9	-	32.9	-	-	-	36.4
Sunrise (city)	36.8	31.3	-	-	31.3	-	32.3	-	32.7	32.1	30.5	-	-	28.0	-	-	-	36.4	33.1	-	33.1	-	-	-	27.0
Tamarac (city)	51.9	33.5	-	-	-	-	34.7	-	41.1	-	-	-	-	-	-	-	-	-	37.0	-	34.6	-	-	-	29.4
Charlotte County	54.2	33.1	-	-	-	-	-	-	45.9	-	-	-	-	25.5	-	-	-	-	34.9	-	-	-	-	-	35.1
Citrus County	52.6	40.3	-	-	-	-	-	-	-	-	-	-	-	24.8	-	-	-	-	48.1	-	-	-	-	-	44.5
Clay County	35.9	25.7	-	-	-	-	-	-	-	-	-	-	-	24.7	-	-	-	-	25.0	-	-	-	-	-	22.8
Collier County	44.1	26.3	-	-	26.7	-	36.6	-	35.6	30.7	-	26.3	25.7	23.8	-	-	-	-	31.8	-	35.8	-	-	-	22.9
Duval County	34.2	28.1	-	-	28.4	-	32.0	-	37.2	26.6	-	-	-	25.5	-	28.4	-	34.1	26.2	-	33.2	-	-	-	24.9
Jacksonville (city)	33.9	27.9	-	-	28.3	-	32.5	-	37.3	26.6	-	-	-	25.2	-	28.4	-	-	25.9	-	33.4	-	-	-	24.8
Escambia County	35.5	27.2	-	-	22.5	-	-	-	39.0	-	-	-	-	21.9	-	-	-	-	27.8	-	29.3	-	-	-	31.7
Pensacola (city)	39.3	31.1	-	-	-	-	-	-	-	-	-	-	-	-	-	-	-	-	-	-	-	-	-	-	-
Hernando County	49.2	35.0	-	-	-	-	-	-	37.8	-	-	-	-	26.0	-	-	-	-	37.7	-	-	-	-	-	41.9
Spring Hill (cdp)	47.5	37.1	-	-	-	-	-	-	37.2	-	-	-	-	-	-	-	-	-	39.0	-	-	-	-	-	38.7
Hillsborough County	35.2	29.6	-	-	30.4	-	33.3	31.8	37.8	31.1	36.3	29.9	28.8	22.4	31.7	31.7	-	31.1	29.1	32.2	33.8	45.4	-	29.4	29.2

Notes: Please refer to the User's Guide for an explanation of data: data is arranged alphabetically by state, then county, then city within each county and only includes counties with populations > 99,999 and cities with populations > 49,999; (1) Includes Costa Rican, Guatemalan, Honduran, Nicaraguan, Panamanian, Salvadoran, and other Central American; (2) Includes Argentinian, Bolivian, Chilean, Colombian, Ecuadorian, Paraguayan, Peruvian, Uruguayan, Venezuelan, and other South American

Place	Total population	Total Hispanic population	Argentinian	Bolivian	Central American[1]	Chilean	Colombian	Costa Rican	Cuban	Dominican	Ecuadorian	Guatemalan	Honduran	Mexican	Nicaraguan	Panamanian	Paraguayan	Peruvian	Puerto Rican	Salvadoran	South American[2]	Spaniard	Uruguayan	Venezuelan	Other Hisp.
Brandon (cdp)	34.3	28.9	-	-	31.5	-	-	-	29.9	-	-	-	-	23.3	-	-	-	-	30.1	-	31.3	-	-	-	27.6
Tampa (city)	34.7	32.5	-	-	30.9	-	31.9	-	41.6	27.8	38.5	-	29.0	24.4	31.1	31.5	-	-	29.2	-	32.2	54.5	-	28.2	35.5
Town 'n' Country (cdp)	35.3	31.8	-	-	30.4	-	33.7	-	38.5	31.5	-	-	-	27.1	-	-	-	-	28.7	-	35.7	-	-	-	22.7
Indian River County	46.9	25.3	-	-	24.1	-	-	-	34.5	-	-	-	-	23.7	-	-	-	-	31.5	-	38.8	-	-	-	26.4
Lake County	44.9	26.3	-	-	39.3	-	-	-	36.7	-	-	-	-	23.8	-	-	-	-	30.2	-	32.0	-	-	-	20.4
Lee County	45.1	25.8	-	-	26.4	-	38.4	-	35.1	33.4	-	24.7	29.7	23.4	-	-	-	-	28.5	-	34.1	-	-	-	21.9
Cape Coral (city)	41.5	32.0	-	-	-	-	36.1	-	37.3	37.4	-	-	-	27.1	-	-	-	-	33.5	-	34.7	-	-	-	20.8
Leon County	29.6	24.0	-	-	-	-	-	-	22.2	-	-	-	-	23.5	-	-	-	-	23.8	-	25.3	-	-	-	28.3
Tallahassee (city)	26.4	23.4	-	-	-	-	-	-	21.9	-	-	-	-	23.3	-	-	-	-	23.7	-	25.2	-	-	-	27.0
Manatee County	43.6	24.4	-	-	26.6	-	-	-	36.1	-	-	-	-	22.2	-	-	-	-	28.4	-	32.6	-	-	-	25.0
Marion County	43.8	30.3	-	-	36.3	-	35.8	-	34.9	-	-	-	-	22.0	-	-	-	-	32.1	-	35.2	-	-	-	29.7
Martin County	47.3	24.8	-	-	21.3	-	-	-	38.3	-	-	20.8	-	22.9	-	-	-	-	32.7	-	-	-	-	-	30.6
Miami-Dade County	35.8	36.9	34.6	36.8	31.6	36.1	35.2	32.6	43.8	33.5	34.9	30.6	31.3	25.5	31.6	34.9	-	34.9	32.7	30.6	34.5	44.7	43.2	30.4	24.6
Carol City (cdp)	32.5	36.0	-	-	33.6	-	36.4	-	42.0	34.5	-	-	34.1	-	33.2	-	-	-	33.2	-	35.1	-	-	-	19.3
Fountainbleau (cdp)	35.3	36.8	33.6	-	32.5	33.7	34.2	-	47.8	32.5	28.5	-	30.0	30.6	32.4	33.0	-	36.0	32.9	-	31.9	-	-	28.1	24.8
Hialeah (city)	37.6	38.8	35.0	-	30.2	36.4	37.2	30.6	43.6	34.7	40.7	30.4	29.2	29.1	30.2	-	-	34.9	34.2	29.5	36.3	55.3	-	25.0	21.6
Kendale Lakes (cdp)	35.8	36.4	-	-	33.0	-	36.8	-	40.0	32.9	-	-	29.7	27.5	32.9	-	-	35.2	36.9	-	35.8	-	-	32.7	25.9
Kendall (cdp)	37.2	35.6	34.8	-	32.8	35.5	36.0	-	39.1	30.9	-	-	-	-	32.3	-	-	32.1	34.9	-	34.3	-	-	30.4	25.3
Miami Beach (city)	39.3	39.6	29.4	-	33.3	36.0	36.5	-	54.6	36.4	34.4	-	32.4	32.9	34.3	-	-	37.0	31.9	-	33.9	40.5	-	31.1	35.4
Miami (city)	37.7	40.0	33.6	-	31.7	40.8	36.1	31.3	52.8	34.8	37.4	32.6	31.7	28.9	31.4	36.3	-	36.8	33.0	31.3	36.4	54.0	-	35.1	26.7
North Miami (city)	31.8	33.9	-	-	33.2	-	35.7	-	42.9	27.5	-	-	32.4	-	33.7	-	-	-	32.1	-	35.8	-	-	-	27.4
Tamiami (cdp)	36.8	38.1	-	-	30.9	-	36.5	-	41.8	36.9	-	-	31.8	32.3	30.1	-	-	-	35.4	-	36.6	-	-	31.1	24.5
Okaloosa County	36.2	28.1	-	-	27.8	-	-	-	37.8	-	-	-	-	23.9	-	-	-	-	26.7	-	-	-	-	-	29.1
Orange County	33.6	28.7	37.3	-	30.2	28.4	31.6	29.4	36.2	32.0	33.1	32.6	29.6	25.0	29.1	34.7	-	34.5	29.1	29.1	31.6	34.1	-	27.7	20.8
Orlando (city)	33.2	29.2	-	-	27.8	-	32.6	-	38.8	31.4	-	-	-	26.9	-	-	-	32.8	28.2	-	31.1	-	-	27.2	24.4
Osceola County	34.7	28.5	-	-	31.1	-	31.8	-	39.2	32.5	36.7	-	-	24.6	-	-	-	-	28.4	30.5	32.8	-	-	31.1	18.9
Palm Beach County	41.8	29.7	36.2	-	26.2	32.3	34.3	29.2	38.1	31.6	34.2	24.6	27.0	24.5	27.3	33.6	-	34.9	31.3	30.0	34.7	44.5	37.4	33.3	24.3
Boca Raton (city)	42.8	32.5	-	-	-	-	30.3	-	39.8	-	-	-	-	24.9	-	-	-	-	27.4	-	33.8	-	-	-	36.7
Boynton Beach (city)	41.5	29.4	-	-	24.4	-	-	-	34.4	-	-	-	-	24.2	-	-	-	-	31.5	-	36.1	-	-	-	23.9
Delray Beach (city)	44.0	30.3	-	-	-	-	-	-	-	-	-	-	-	25.3	-	-	-	-	31.5	-	37.6	-	-	-	26.9
West Palm Beach (city)	37.1	30.8	-	-	24.9	-	34.2	-	45.4	34.8	-	24.3	-	24.3	-	-	-	-	32.2	-	32.9	-	-	-	23.7
Pasco County	44.8	29.3	-	-	27.6	-	-	-	36.6	-	-	-	-	23.8	-	-	-	-	30.9	-	38.1	-	-	-	29.5
Pinellas County	43.1	29.7	-	-	31.2	-	30.6	-	39.2	28.8	35.5	-	-	24.6	-	-	-	36.4	29.6	-	32.9	42.7	-	28.7	30.8
Clearwater (city)	41.6	26.3	-	-	-	-	30.7	-	52.6	-	-	-	-	23.6	-	-	-	-	27.7	-	30.6	-	-	-	27.0
Largo (city)	47.5	30.3	-	-	-	-	-	-	-	-	-	-	-	33.1	-	-	-	-	30.7	-	-	-	-	-	-
Palm Harbor (cdp)	43.3	35.8	-	-	-	-	-	-	-	-	-	-	-	-	-	-	-	-	34.0	-	-	-	-	-	-
St. Petersburg (city)	39.5	31.5	-	-	-	-	-	-	38.9	-	-	-	-	27.1	-	-	-	-	29.2	-	36.2	-	-	-	30.7

Notes: Please refer to the User's Guide for an explanation of data: data is arranged alphabetically by state, then county, then city within each county and only includes counties with populations > 99,999 and cities with populations > 49,999; (1) Includes Costa Rican, Guatemalan, Honduran, Nicaraguan, Panamanian, Salvadoran, and other Central American; (2) Includes Argentinian, Bolivian, Chilean, Colombian, Ecuadorian, Paraguayan, Peruvian, Uruguayan, Venezuelan, and other South American

Place	Total population	Total Hispanic population	Argentinian	Bolivian	Central American[1]	Chilean	Colombian	Costa Rican	Cuban	Dominican	Ecuadorian	Guatelmalan	Honduran	Mexican	Nicaraguan	Panamanian	Paraguayan	Peruvian	Puerto Rican	Salvadoran	South American[2]	Spaniard	Uruguayan	Venezuelan	Other Hisp.
Polk County	38.6	24.6	-	-	29.2	-	-	-	37.6	31.9	-	-	-	22.6	-	-	-	-	28.3	-	27.6	-	-	-	21.9
Lakeland (city)	39.8	30.4	-	-	-	-	-	-	38.4	-	-	-	-	24.3	-	-	-	-	29.8	-	-	-	-	-	31.1
St. Johns County	40.9	30.7	-	-	-	-	-	-	-	-	-	-	-	20.6	-	-	-	-	31.5	-	-	-	-	-	31.2
St. Lucie County	42.1	26.3	-	-	28.1	-	30.1	-	41.7	-	-	-	-	22.6	-	-	-	-	33.2	-	33.6	-	-	-	24.1
Port St. Lucie (city)	39.9	32.7	-	-	-	-	-	-	43.9	-	-	-	-	23.9	-	-	-	-	34.2	-	33.9	-	-	-	16.8
Santa Rosa County	36.8	27.7	-	-	-	-	-	-	-	-	-	-	-	24.7	-	-	-	-	27.1	-	-	-	-	-	32.1
Sarasota County	50.4	29.8	-	-	33.5	-	37.7	-	38.0	-	-	-	-	25.3	-	-	-	-	40.2	-	36.4	-	-	-	26.9
Sarasota (city)	41.2	26.6	-	-	-	-	-	-	36.9	-	-	-	-	24.3	-	-	-	-	37.5	-	39.0	-	-	-	21.4
Seminole County	36.3	31.1	36.2	-	29.4	-	34.5	-	36.1	33.0	34.9	-	-	26.8	-	29.0	-	30.3	31.6	-	34.5	-	-	35.6	23.9
Volusia County	42.4	29.4	-	-	32.8	-	32.0	-	41.6	33.9	-	-	-	23.5	-	-	-	-	33.1	-	34.8	-	-	-	28.1
Daytona Beach (city)	37.4	25.7	-	-	-	-	-	-	-	-	-	-	-	-	-	-	-	-	24.5	-	-	-	-	-	28.7
Deltona (city)	37.0	33.3	-	-	-	-	-	-	42.6	-	-	-	-	26.2	-	-	-	-	33.8	-	37.0	-	-	-	18.3

Notes: Please refer to the User's Guide for an explanation of data; data is arranged alphabetically by state, then county, then city within each county and only includes counties with populations > 99,999 and cities with populations > 49,999; (1) Includes Costa Rican, Guatemalan, Honduran, Nicaraguan, Panamanian, Salvadoran, and other Central American; (2) Includes Argentinian, Bolivian, Chilean, Colombian, Ecuadorian, Paraguayan, Peruvian, Uruguayan, Venezuelan, and other South American

Average Household Size

(Universe: Households)

Place	All households	Hispanic households	Argentinian	Bolivian	Central American[1]	Chilean	Colombian	Costa Rican	Cuban	Dominican	Ecuadorian	Guatemalan	Honduran	Mexican	Nicaraguan	Panamanian	Paraguayan	Peruvian	Puerto Rican	Salvadoran	South American[2]	Spaniard	Uruguayan	Venezuelan	Other Hisp.
UNITED STATES	2.59	3.59	2.75	3.54	3.89	2.91	3.21	3.15	2.76	3.61	3.71	4.08	3.72	3.90	3.79	2.83	3.05	3.36	2.97	4.14	3.24	2.59	2.92	2.83	3.29
FLORIDA	2.46	3.10	2.82	3.19	3.66	3.06	3.24	3.15	2.83	3.44	3.32	3.96	3.54	3.95	3.90	2.85	3.02	3.22	2.98	3.62	3.13	2.49	2.86	2.93	3.01
Alachua County	2.34	2.42	-	-	2.34	-	2.18	-	2.19	-	-	-	-	3.07	-	-	-	-	2.51	-	2.17	-	-	-	2.58
Gainesville (city)	2.25	2.29	-	-	-	-	-	-	2.07	-	-	-	-	2.44	-	-	-	-	2.64	-	2.08	-	-	-	2.10
Bay County	2.43	2.54	-	-	-	-	-	-	-	-	-	-	-	2.91	-	-	-	-	2.73	-	-	-	-	-	2.28
Brevard County	2.35	2.81	-	-	3.24	-	3.02	-	2.57	3.01	-	-	-	2.91	-	2.54	-	-	2.84	-	2.93	-	-	-	2.64
Melbourne (city)	2.22	2.57	-	-	-	-	-	-	-	-	-	-	-	2.95	-	-	-	-	2.66	-	-	-	-	-	1.85
Palm Bay (city)	2.60	3.08	-	-	-	-	-	-	-	-	-	-	-	3.40	-	-	-	-	3.11	-	3.59	-	-	-	2.65
Broward County	2.45	3.08	2.91	3.48	3.34	3.01	3.30	3.17	2.95	3.53	3.48	3.56	3.38	3.55	3.28	2.84	-	3.35	2.85	3.61	3.21	2.68	3.00	3.02	2.99
Coral Springs (city)	2.96	3.38	-	-	3.12	-	3.54	-	3.24	3.42	4.05	-	-	3.86	-	-	-	3.72	3.16	-	3.61	-	-	3.68	3.34
Davie (town)	2.64	3.20	-	-	3.87	-	3.12	-	3.09	-	-	-	-	3.52	-	-	-	3.09	3.10	-	3.32	-	-	-	3.04
Deerfield Beach (city)	2.02	2.81	-	-	3.84	-	3.69	-	2.70	-	-	-	-	2.71	-	-	-	-	2.56	-	3.10	-	-	-	2.44
Fort Lauderdale (city)	2.14	2.56	-	-	3.23	-	2.70	-	2.41	-	-	3.61	-	2.87	-	-	-	2.51	2.31	3.79	2.59	-	-	-	2.53
Hollywood (city)	2.31	2.93	3.31	-	2.95	3.31	3.14	-	2.76	3.30	3.26	-	3.34	3.09	2.74	-	-	3.03	2.81	-	3.06	-	-	2.39	2.98
Lauderhill (city)	2.49	2.65	-	-	-	-	3.06	-	-	-	-	-	-	-	-	-	-	-	2.78	-	2.93	-	-	-	2.54
Margate (city)	2.35	3.28	-	-	3.83	-	3.50	-	3.18	-	-	-	-	3.49	-	-	-	-	2.92	-	3.48	-	-	-	3.04
Miramar (city)	3.16	3.49	-	-	3.73	-	3.66	-	3.38	4.12	-	-	-	3.09	4.28	3.15	-	4.36	3.15	-	3.72	-	-	-	3.58
Pembroke Pines (city)	2.61	3.12	-	-	3.16	-	3.48	-	2.99	3.66	3.38	-	-	3.22	-	-	-	3.48	3.01	-	3.36	-	-	3.16	3.10
Plantation (city)	2.48	3.04	-	-	3.47	-	3.29	-	3.01	-	-	-	-	3.04	-	-	-	3.09	2.73	-	3.19	-	-	3.48	2.93
Pompano Beach (city)	2.13	2.82	-	-	-	-	2.02	-	2.06	-	-	-	-	3.94	-	-	-	-	2.54	-	2.21	-	-	-	2.46
Sunrise (city)	2.54	2.97	-	-	2.78	-	3.34	-	2.78	3.84	3.39	-	-	3.11	-	-	-	3.47	2.63	-	3.24	-	-	-	2.89
Tamarac (city)	2.00	2.76	-	-	-	-	3.17	-	2.45	-	-	-	-	-	-	-	-	-	2.48	-	2.96	-	-	-	2.85
Charlotte County	2.17	2.80	-	-	-	-	-	-	2.22	-	-	-	-	3.51	-	-	-	-	2.78	-	-	-	-	-	2.52
Citrus County	2.20	2.37	-	-	-	-	-	-	-	-	-	-	-	2.94	-	-	-	-	2.37	-	-	-	-	-	1.96
Clay County	2.76	3.31	-	-	-	-	-	-	-	-	-	-	-	3.71	-	-	-	-	3.25	-	-	-	-	-	3.01
Collier County	2.39	3.90	-	-	4.84	-	2.93	-	3.09	4.03	-	5.65	4.27	4.45	-	-	-	-	3.28	-	2.94	-	-	-	3.52
Duval County	2.51	2.87	-	-	3.01	-	2.97	-	2.63	2.59	-	-	-	2.97	-	2.77	-	2.87	2.95	-	2.98	-	-	-	2.70
Jacksonville (city)	2.53	2.86	-	-	2.99	-	2.98	-	2.62	2.59	-	-	-	2.96	-	2.72	-	-	2.95	-	2.98	-	-	-	2.68
Escambia County	2.45	2.68	-	-	3.19	-	-	-	2.32	-	-	-	-	3.01	-	-	-	-	2.84	-	2.40	-	-	-	2.34
Pensacola (city)	2.28	2.50	-	-	-	-	-	-	-	-	-	-	-	-	-	-	-	-	-	-	-	-	-	-	-
Hernando County	2.32	2.93	-	-	-	-	-	-	2.68	-	-	-	-	3.69	-	-	-	-	2.98	-	-	-	-	-	2.29
Spring Hill (cdp)	2.39	2.91	-	-	-	-	-	-	2.85	-	-	-	-	-	-	-	-	-	2.96	-	-	-	-	-	2.48
Hillsborough County	2.51	3.01	-	-	3.24	-	3.06	3.27	2.71	3.39	2.97	3.67	3.35	4.12	3.06	2.73	-	2.99	2.94	3.43	3.00	2.15	-	3.19	2.61

Notes: Please refer to the User's Guide for an explanation of data; data is arranged alphabetically by state, then county, then city within each county and only includes counties with populations > 99,999 and cities with populations > 49,999; (1) Includes Costa Rican, Guatemalan, Honduran, Nicaraguan, Panamanian, Salvadoran, and other Central American; (2) Includes Argentinian, Bolivian, Chilean, Colombian, Ecuadorian, Paraguayan, Peruvian, Uruguayan, Venezuelan, and other South American

Place	All households	Hispanic households	Argentinian	Bolivian	Central American[1]	Chilean	Colombian	Costa Rican	Cuban	Dominican	Ecuadorian	Guatelmalan	Honduran	Mexican	Nicaraguan	Panamanian	Paraguayan	Peruvian	Puerto Rican	Salvadoran	South American[2]	Spaniard	Uruguayan	Venezuelan	Other Hisp.
Brandon (cdp)	2.68	3.12	-	-	3.56	-	-	-	3.20	-	-	-	-	3.80	-	-	-	-	3.06	-	3.52	-	-	-	2.76
Tampa (city)	2.36	2.66	-	-	3.05	-	2.93	-	2.40	3.21	2.72	-	3.13	3.74	2.98	2.57	-	-	2.80	-	2.91	1.69	-	3.19	2.30
Town 'n' Country (cdp)	2.50	3.10	-	-	3.77	-	3.39	-	2.89	3.71	-	-	-	3.01	-	-	-	-	3.13	-	3.26	-	-	-	3.04
Indian River County	2.25	3.80	-	-	3.55	-	-	-	3.54	-	-	-	-	4.49	-	-	-	-	3.02	-	2.45	-	-	-	3.21
Lake County	2.34	3.45	-	-	3.33	-	-	-	3.22	-	-	-	-	3.90	-	-	-	-	3.09	-	3.10	-	-	-	2.97
Lee County	2.31	3.47	-	-	3.87	-	3.66	-	2.63	3.35	-	4.49	3.94	4.14	-	-	-	-	3.10	-	3.57	-	-	-	3.33
Cape Coral (city)	2.49	3.05	-	-	-	-	3.83	-	2.58	3.16	-	-	-	3.47	-	-	-	-	2.96	-	3.58	-	-	-	3.05
Leon County	2.34	2.39	-	-	-	-	-	-	2.50	-	-	-	-	2.69	-	-	-	-	2.51	-	2.46	-	-	-	2.07
Tallahassee (city)	2.18	2.33	-	-	-	-	-	-	2.42	-	-	-	-	2.52	-	-	-	-	2.41	-	2.43	-	-	-	2.09
Manatee County	2.29	3.72	-	-	3.31	-	-	-	2.51	-	-	-	-	4.46	-	-	-	-	3.18	-	2.57	-	-	-	3.14
Marion County	2.36	3.04	-	-	3.16	-	3.45	-	2.87	-	-	-	-	3.16	-	-	-	-	3.09	-	3.46	-	-	-	2.49
Martin County	2.23	3.87	-	-	4.95	-	-	-	2.98	-	-	5.05	-	4.26	-	-	-	-	3.17	-	-	-	-	-	3.02
Miami-Dade County	2.84	3.03	2.77	3.29	3.74	3.15	3.26	3.25	2.84	3.47	3.37	3.56	3.59	3.78	3.97	3.02	-	3.21	2.96	3.55	3.13	2.65	2.84	2.85	3.23
Carol City (cdp)	3.57	3.71	-	-	4.16	-	4.20	-	3.48	4.13	-	-	3.71	-	4.48	-	-	-	3.72	-	4.30	-	-	-	3.75
Fountainbleau (cdp)	2.84	2.90	2.67	-	3.98	3.71	3.19	-	2.49	3.33	4.32	-	4.40	3.36	4.15	2.83	-	3.00	2.58	-	3.23	-	-	3.09	3.23
Hialeah (city)	3.15	3.21	3.71	-	3.92	3.10	3.64	3.98	3.06	3.63	3.64	3.59	3.72	3.69	4.08	-	-	4.01	3.31	3.20	3.60	3.36	-	3.07	3.61
Kendale Lakes (cdp)	3.14	3.32	-	-	3.87	-	4.03	-	3.16	3.81	-	-	4.09	3.20	3.94	-	-	3.19	2.79	-	3.63	-	-	2.71	3.55
Kendall (cdp)	2.62	2.88	2.82	-	3.31	3.05	3.04	-	2.74	3.27	-	-	-	-	3.76	-	-	3.68	2.39	-	3.03	-	-	2.90	3.19
Miami Beach (city)	1.88	2.06	2.34	-	2.54	1.87	2.45	-	1.86	2.45	2.15	-	2.43	2.18	2.70	-	-	2.33	2.03	-	2.24	2.35	-	1.67	2.10
Miami (city)	2.61	2.70	2.57	-	3.54	3.30	2.69	2.46	2.41	3.35	2.88	3.37	3.50	2.77	3.78	2.61	-	2.77	2.73	2.96	2.69	2.22	-	2.22	3.25
North Miami (city)	2.88	2.95	-	-	3.50	-	2.50	-	2.67	3.70	-	-	3.41	-	3.69	-	-	-	3.04	-	2.40	-	-	-	3.07
Tamiami (cdp)	3.33	3.36	-	-	4.02	-	3.69	-	3.24	3.39	-	-	3.49	3.86	4.19	-	-	-	3.40	-	3.69	-	-	4.17	3.65
Okaloosa County	2.49	2.89	-	-	2.28	-	-	-	2.91	-	-	-	-	3.18	-	-	-	-	3.03	-	-	-	-	-	2.30
Orange County	2.61	3.12	2.88	-	3.57	2.96	3.26	3.27	2.78	3.67	3.35	4.10	3.39	3.56	3.31	2.77	-	3.47	3.05	4.62	3.24	2.57	-	3.15	2.93
Orlando (city)	2.25	2.68	-	-	3.32	-	2.92	-	2.38	3.41	-	-	-	2.33	-	-	-	2.95	2.65	-	2.90	-	-	3.02	2.59
Osceola County	2.79	3.32	-	-	3.54	-	3.65	-	2.79	3.42	3.23	-	-	3.65	-	-	-	-	3.31	3.71	3.48	-	-	3.10	3.11
Palm Beach County	2.34	3.30	3.11	-	4.06	3.41	3.28	2.97	2.82	3.09	3.27	4.43	4.18	4.12	4.20	2.53	-	3.24	3.03	3.63	3.20	2.61	2.91	2.83	3.06
Boca Raton (city)	2.27	2.84	-	-	-	-	3.36	-	2.67	-	-	-	-	3.72	-	-	-	-	2.72	-	3.07	-	-	-	2.50
Boynton Beach (city)	2.26	3.13	-	-	3.70	-	-	-	2.76	-	-	-	-	3.70	-	-	-	-	3.08	-	2.54	-	-	-	3.35
Delray Beach (city)	2.21	3.05	-	-	-	-	-	-	-	-	-	-	-	4.01	-	-	-	-	2.63	-	2.43	-	-	-	3.14
West Palm Beach (city)	2.25	3.10	-	-	4.64	-	3.34	-	2.51	3.16	-	5.27	-	3.80	-	-	-	-	2.88	-	3.07	-	-	-	2.89
Pasco County	2.30	3.09	-	-	3.25	-	-	-	2.77	-	-	-	-	4.01	-	-	-	-	2.81	-	2.84	-	-	-	2.78
Pinellas County	2.16	2.70	-	-	3.05	-	2.87	-	2.28	2.66	2.22	-	-	3.22	-	-	-	2.51	2.78	-	2.64	2.01	-	2.80	2.34
Clearwater (city)	2.16	3.31	-	-	-	-	2.64	-	2.86	-	-	-	-	4.01	-	-	-	-	2.97	-	2.65	-	-	-	2.70
Largo (city)	1.99	2.39	-	-	-	-	-	-	-	-	-	-	-	2.11	-	-	-	-	2.69	-	-	-	-	-	-
Palm Harbor (cdp)	2.28	2.61	-	-	-	-	-	-	-	-	-	-	-	-	-	-	-	-	2.95	-	-	-	-	-	-
St. Petersburg (city)	2.20	2.36	-	-	-	-	-	-	1.95	-	-	-	-	2.37	-	-	-	-	2.71	-	2.69	-	-	-	1.99

Notes: Please refer to the User's Guide for an explanation of data; data is arranged alphabetically by state, then county, then city within each county and only includes counties with populations > 99,999 and cities with populations > 49,999; (1) Includes Costa Rican, Guatemalan, Honduran, Nicaraguan, Panamanian, Salvadoran, and other Central American; (2) Includes Argentinian, Bolivian, Chilean, Colombian, Ecuadorian, Paraguayan, Peruvian, Uruguayan, Venezuelan, and other South American

Place	All households	Hispanic households	Argentinian	Bolivian	Central American[1]	Chilean	Colombian	Costa Rican	Cuban	Dominican	Ecuadorian	Guatelmalan	Honduran	Mexican	Nicaraguan	Panamanian	Paraguayan	Peruvian	Puerto Rican	Salvadoran	South American[2]	Spaniard	Uruguayan	Venezuelan	Other Hisp.
Polk County	2.52	3.65	-	-	4.00	-	-	-	2.82	3.02	-	-	-	4.27	-	-	-	-	3.11	-	3.20	-	-	-	3.04
Lakeland (city)	2.22	2.68	-	-	-	-	-	-	2.86	-	-	-	-	2.77	-	-	-	-	2.61	-	-	-	-	-	2.42
St. Johns County	2.44	2.73	-	-	-	-	-	-	-	-	-	-	-	3.13	-	-	-	-	2.85	-	-	-	-	-	2.61
St. Lucie County	2.47	3.65	-	-	4.25	-	3.49	-	3.07	-	-	-	-	4.65	-	-	-	-	2.91	-	3.45	-	-	-	2.69
Port St. Lucie (city)	2.60	3.25	-	-	-	-	-	-	3.07	-	-	-	-	4.59	-	-	-	-	3.00	-	3.61	-	-	-	2.90
Santa Rosa County	2.63	3.06	-	-	-	-	-	-	-	-	-	-	-	3.97	-	-	-	-	3.15	-	-	-	-	-	2.31
Sarasota County	2.13	3.19	-	-	2.64	-	2.98	-	2.87	-	-	-	-	3.85	-	-	-	-	2.54	-	2.95	-	-	-	2.93
Sarasota (city)	2.10	3.55	-	-	-	-	-	-	2.81	-	-	-	-	4.40	-	-	-	-	2.31	-	3.26	-	-	-	2.95
Seminole County	2.59	3.09	2.65	-	3.07	-	3.33	-	2.92	3.60	3.54	-	-	3.39	-	3.35	-	3.69	3.07	-	3.23	-	-	3.44	2.96
Volusia County	2.32	3.20	-	-	3.11	-	2.99	-	2.50	3.19	-	-	-	4.33	-	-	-	-	3.03	-	2.80	-	-	-	2.68
Daytona Beach (city)	2.06	2.33	-	-	-	-	-	-	-	-	-	-	-	-	-	-	-	-	2.56	-	-	-	-	-	2.01
Deltona (city)	2.80	3.24	-	-	-	-	-	-	3.16	-	-	-	-	3.13	-	-	-	-	3.27	-	2.94	-	-	-	3.18

Notes: Please refer to the User's Guide for an explanation of data: data is arranged alphabetically by state, then county, then city within each county and only includes counties with populations > 99,999 and cities with populations > 49,999; (1) Includes Costa Rican, Guatemalan, Honduran, Nicaraguan, Panamanian, Salvadoran, and other Central American; (2) Includes Argentinian, Bolivian, Chilean, Colombian, Ecuadorian, Paraguayan, Peruvan, Uruguayan, Venezuelan, and other South American

Language Spoken at Home: English Only

(Universe: Population 5 Years and Over)

Place	Total population 5 years and over who speak English-only at home	Hispanic population 5 years and over	Hispanics 5 years and over who speak English-only at home	Argentinian	Bolivian	Central American[1]	Chilean	Colombian	Costa Rican	Cuban	Dominican	Ecuadorian	Guatelmalan	Honduran	Mexican	Nicaraguan	Panamanian	Paraguayan	Peruvian	Puerto Rican	Salvadoran	South American[2]	Spaniard	Uruguayan	Venezuelan	Other Hisp.
UNITED STATES	215,423,557	31,569,576	6,764,744	12,450	5,010	143,333	11,727	45,499	11,495	162,947	52,501	20,088	25,800	19,020	3,923,681	15,359	24,158	2,365	23,383	761,550	39,275	140,497	42,386	1,688	9,590	1,537,849
	82.11		21.43	12.18	11.79	8.54	16.75	9.67	17.04	13.70	7.10	7.85	6.89	8.64	21.19	8.34	26.19	28.17	9.99	24.64	6.02	10.47	40.08	8.71	10.55	31.32
				0.18	0.07	2.12	0.17	0.67	0.17	2.41	0.78	0.30	0.38	0.28	58.00	0.23	0.36	0.03	0.35	11.26	0.58	2.08	0.63	0.02	0.14	22.73
			21.43	0.04	0.02	0.45	0.04	0.14	0.04	0.52	0.17	0.06	0.08	0.06	12.43	0.05	0.08	0.01	0.07	2.41	0.12	0.45	0.13	0.01	0.03	4.87
			3.14	0.01	<0.01	0.07	0.01	0.02	0.01	0.08	0.02	0.01	0.01	0.01	1.82	0.01	0.01	<0.01	0.01	0.35	0.02	0.07	0.02	<0.01	<0.01	0.71
FLORIDA	11,569,739	2,489,063	290,650	1,540	321	13,914	1,125	7,468	1,268	63,584	4,184	1,727	1,551	2,725	53,558	4,047	2,545	85	2,625	77,288	1,324	17,775	3,744	232	2,045	56,603
	76.91		11.68	6.75	7.54	6.74	8.78	5.33	11.03	7.85	5.84	6.97	5.31	6.46	16.92	4.88	15.82	9.63	5.90	17.41	6.65	5.91	25.70	5.42	5.08	17.40
				0.53	0.11	4.79	0.39	2.57	0.44	21.88	1.44	0.59	0.53	0.94	18.43	1.39	0.88	0.03	0.90	26.59	0.46	6.12	1.29	0.08	0.70	19.47
			11.68	0.06	0.01	0.56	0.05	0.30	0.05	2.55	0.17	0.07	0.06	0.11	2.15	0.16	0.10	<0.01	0.11	3.11	0.05	0.71	0.15	0.01	0.08	2.27
			2.51	0.01	<0.01	0.12	0.01	0.06	0.01	0.55	0.04	0.01	0.01	0.02	0.46	0.03	0.02	<0.01	0.02	0.67	0.01	0.15	0.03	<0.01	0.02	0.49
Alachua County	183,049	11,656	3,551	-	-	142	-	160	-	812	-	-	-	-	506	-	-	-	-	756	-	366	-	-	-	871
	88.49		30.46			23.87		25.68		33.68					39.91					24.80		18.57				44.08
						4.00		4.51		22.87					14.25					21.29		10.31				24.53
			30.46			1.22		1.37		6.97					4.34					6.49		3.14				7.47
			1.94			0.08		0.09		0.44					0.28					0.41		0.20				0.48
Gainesville (city)	78,746	5,649	1,573	-	-	-	-	-	-	407	-	-	-	-	209	-	-	-	-	346	-	160	-	-	-	329
	86.29		27.85							36.31					47.29					20.20		15.14				36.80
										25.87					13.29					22.00		10.17				20.92
			27.85							7.20					3.70					6.12		2.83				5.82
			2.00							0.52					0.27					0.44		0.20				0.42
Bay County	130,288	3,184	1,419	-	-	-	-	-	-	-	-	-	-	-	613	-	-	-	-	361	-	-	-	-	-	240
	93.59		44.57												60.33					39.07						62.50
															43.20					25.44						16.91
			44.57												19.25					11.34						7.54
			1.09												0.47					0.28						0.18
Brevard County	412,102	20,164	6,681	-	-	181	-	135	-	662	44	-	-	-	1,702	-	85	-	-	2,593	-	419	-	-	-	1,019
	91.26		33.13			16.47		19.85		34.12	12.26				51.92		23.55			30.47		25.61				32.59
						2.71		2.02		9.91	0.66				25.48		1.27			38.81		6.27				15.25
			33.13			0.90		0.67		3.28	0.22				8.44		0.42			12.86		2.08				5.05
			1.62			0.04		0.03		0.16	0.01				0.41		0.02			0.63		0.10				0.25
Melbourne (city)	60,520	3,428	1,058	-	-	-	-	-	-	-	-	-	-	-	244	-	-	-	-	453	-	-	-	-	-	152
	89.52		30.86												33.33					32.24						35.43
															23.06					42.82						14.37
			30.86												7.12					13.21						4.43
			1.75												0.40					0.75						0.25
Palm Bay (city)	65,200	6,438	1,720	-	-	-	-	-	-	-	-	-	-	-	338	-	-	-	-	862	-	126	-	-	-	262
	87.49		26.72												51.29					23.50		25.40				27.70
															19.65					50.12		7.33				15.23
			26.72												5.25					13.39		1.96				4.07
			2.64												0.52					1.32		0.19				0.40
Broward County	1,083,041	251,327	33,072	449	55	1,627	212	1,515	230	6,860	657	337	149	333	3,274	273	404	-	632	10,556	189	3,825	624	76	447	5,649
	71.21		13.16	11.65	8.17	8.66	10.70	5.17	12.41	13.77	6.49	6.69	5.37	8.59	19.68	8.27	17.51		5.94	21.00	4.50	6.15	28.78	8.33	5.30	13.67
				1.36	0.17	4.92	0.64	4.58	0.70	20.74	1.99	1.02	0.45	1.01	9.90	0.83	1.22		1.91	31.92	0.57	11.57	1.89	0.23	1.35	17.08
			13.16	0.18	0.02	0.65	0.08	0.60	0.09	2.73	0.26	0.13	0.06	0.13	1.30	0.11	0.16		0.25	4.20	0.08	1.52	0.25	0.03	0.18	2.25
			3.05	0.04	0.01	0.15	0.02	0.14	0.02	0.63	0.06	0.03	0.01	0.03	0.30	0.03	0.04		0.06	0.97	0.02	0.35	0.06	0.01	0.04	0.52

Notes: Please refer to the User's Guide for an explanation of data; data is arranged alphabetically by state, then county, then city within each county and only includes counties with populations > 99,999 and cities with populations > 49,999; (1) Includes Costa Rican, Guatemalan, Honduran, Nicaraguan, Panamanian, Salvadoran, and other Central American; (2) Includes Argentinian, Bolivian, Chilean, Colombian, Ecuadorian, Paraguayan, Peruvian, Uruguayan, Venezuelan, and other South American

Place	Total population 5 years and over who speak English-only at home	Hispanic population 5 years and over	Hispanics 5 years and over who speak English-only at home	Argentinian	Bolivian	Central American[1]	Chilean	Colombian	Costa Rican	Cuban	Dominican	Ecuadorian	Guatemalan	Honduran	Mexican	Nicaraguan	Panamanian	Paraguayan	Peruvian	Puerto Rican	Salvadoran	South American[2]	Spaniard	Uruguayan	Venezuelan	Other Hisp.
	80,884	16,926	2,634	-	-	101	-	31	-	420	57	67	-	-	323	-	-	-	18	982	-	267	-	-	62	430
	73.97		15.56			13.36		1.44		22.01	10.78	7.49			21.68				1.99	26.48		5.13			12.89	14.05
Coral Springs (city)						3.83		1.18		15.95	2.16	2.54			12.26				0.68	37.28		10.14			2.35	16.32
			15.56			0.60		0.18		2.48	0.34	0.40			1.91				0.11	5.80		1.58			0.37	2.54
			3.26			0.12		0.04		0.52	0.07	0.08			0.40				0.02	1.21		0.33			0.08	0.53
	52,660	13,367	2,124	-	-	93	-	78	-	693	-	-	-	-	99	-	-	-	43	567	-	153	-	-	-	398
	74.65		15.89			8.95		6.63		22.08					14.10				7.18	17.90		5.42				20.00
Davie (town)						4.38		3.67		32.63					4.66				2.02	26.69		7.20				18.74
			15.89			0.70		0.58		5.18					0.74				0.32	4.24		1.14				2.98
			4.03			0.18		0.15		1.32					0.19				0.08	1.08		0.29				0.76
	46,032	5,120	653	-	-	25	-	0	-	88	-	-	-	-	100	-	-	-	-	233	-	45	-	-	-	130
	74.74		12.75			5.34		0.00		12.26					22.52					18.84		3.39				18.52
Deerfield Beach (city)						3.83		0.00		13.48					15.31					35.68		6.89				19.91
			12.75			0.49		0.00		1.72					1.95					4.55		0.88				2.54
			1.42			0.05		0.00		0.19					0.22					0.51		0.10				0.28
	108,442	13,104	2,088	-	-	120	-	109	-	437	-	-	8	-	338	-	-	-	39	460	23	309	-	-	-	385
	75.14		15.93			6.94		8.85		16.66			2.22		30.84				8.97	20.10	3.57	10.86				17.56
Fort Lauderdale (city)						5.75		5.22		20.93			0.38		16.19				1.87	22.03	1.10	14.80				18.44
			15.93			0.92		0.83		3.33			0.06		2.58				0.30	3.51	0.18	2.36				2.94
			1.93			0.11		0.10		0.40			0.01		0.31				0.04	0.42	0.02	0.28				0.36
	87,182	29,277	3,667	36	-	150	7	205	-	815	118	54	-	14	256	30	-	-	96	1,198	-	443	-	-	41	631
	66.49		12.53	6.56		7.06	1.99	6.47		14.11	7.41	8.87		3.48	22.86	5.34			7.74	18.88		6.36			7.00	12.21
Hollywood (city)				0.98		4.09	0.19	5.59		22.23	3.22	1.47		0.38	6.98	0.82			2.62	32.67		12.08			1.12	17.21
			12.53	0.12		0.51	0.02	0.70		2.78	0.40	0.18		0.05	0.87	0.10			0.33	4.09		1.51			0.14	2.16
			4.21	0.04		0.17	0.01	0.24		0.93	0.14	0.06		0.02	0.29	0.03			0.11	1.37		0.51			0.05	0.72
	41,341	3,528	543	-	-	-	-	7	-	-	-	-	-	-	-	-	-	-	-	159	-	88	-	-	-	114
	78.15		15.39					1.57												19.65		9.15				15.45
Lauderhill (city)								1.29												29.28		16.21				20.99
			15.39					0.20												4.51		2.49				3.23
			1.31					0.02												0.38		0.21				0.28
	38,001	7,688	1,400	-	-	71	-	82	-	150	-	-	-	-	146	-	-	-	-	545	-	165	-	-	-	287
	74.77		18.21			13.35		7.56		22.76					19.52					25.54		8.63				20.96
Margate (city)						5.07		5.86		10.71					10.43					38.93		11.79				20.50
			18.21			0.92		1.07		1.95					1.90					7.09		2.15				3.73
			3.68			0.19		0.22		0.39					0.38					1.43		0.43				0.76
	39,331	19,713	2,028	-	-	150	-	64	-	583	32	-	-	-	103	39	81	-	31	540	-	179	-	-	-	422
	59.36		10.29			9.68		3.52		9.52	2.43				20.12	6.57	23.48		4.98	16.58		5.14				12.59
Miramar (city)						7.40		3.16		28.75	1.58				5.08	1.92	3.99		1.53	26.63		8.83				20.81
			10.29			0.76		0.32		2.96	0.16				0.52	0.20	0.41		0.16	2.74		0.91				2.14
			5.16			0.38		0.16		1.48	0.08				0.26	0.10	0.21		0.08	1.37		0.46				1.07
	79,783	35,369	4,010	-	-	156	-	179	-	1,143	52	23	-	-	223	-	-	-	98	1,302	-	439	-	-	35	619
	62.55		11.34			8.39		5.49		9.92	3.08	4.79			26.52				7.19	18.96		6.03			2.60	12.32
Pembroke Pines (city)						3.89		4.46		28.50	1.30	0.57			5.56				2.44	32.47		10.95			0.87	15.44
			11.34			0.44		0.51		3.23	0.15	0.07			0.63				0.28	3.68		1.24			0.10	1.75
			5.03			0.20		0.22		1.43	0.07	0.03			0.28				0.12	1.63		0.55			0.04	0.78
	60,475	10,096	1,769	-	-	143	-	175	-	293	-	-	-	-	268	-	-	-	8	483	-	294	-	-	37	201
	77.16		17.52			23.06		8.50		15.69					42.88				1.77	32.70		7.96			7.58	14.59
Plantation (city)						8.08		9.89		16.56					15.15				0.45	27.30		16.62			2.09	11.36
			17.52			1.42		1.73		2.90					2.65				0.08	4.78		2.91			0.37	1.99
			2.93			0.24		0.29		0.48					0.44				0.01	0.80		0.49			0.06	0.33

Notes: Please refer to the User's Guide for an explanation of data; data is arranged alphabetically by state, then county, then city within each county and only includes counties with populations > 99,999 and cities with populations > 49,999; (1) Includes Costa Rican, Guatemalan, Honduran, Nicaraguan, Panamanian, Salvadoran, and other Central American; (2) Includes Argentinian, Bolivian, Chilean, Colombian, Ecuadorian, Paraguayan, Peruvian, Uruguayan, Venezuelan, and other South American

Place	Total population 5 years and over who speak English-only at home	Hispanic population 5 years and over	Hispanics 5 years and over who speak English-only at home	Argentinian	Bolivian	Central American[1]	Chilean	Colombian	Costa Rican	Cuban	Dominican	Ecuadorian	Guatemalan	Honduran	Mexican	Nicaraguan	Panamanian	Paraguayan	Peruvian	Puerto Rican	Salvadoran	South American[2]	Spaniard	Uruguayan	Venezuelan	Other Hisp.
Pompano Beach (city)	56,257 75.72	7,030	1,083 15.41 15.41 1.93	-	-	-	-	67 12.34 6.19 0.95 0.12	-	172 28.81 15.88 2.45 0.31	-	-	-	-	255 11.39 23.55 3.63 0.45	-	-	-	-	377 34.84 34.81 5.36 0.67	-	90 6.56 8.31 1.28 0.16	-	-	-	155 13.08 14.31 2.20 0.28
Sunrise (city)	57,283 71.46	13,427	1,802 13.42 13.42 3.15	-	-	47 7.13 2.61 0.35 0.08	-	73 3.16 4.05 0.54 0.13	-	333 17.72 18.48 2.48 0.58	41 6.09 2.28 0.31 0.07	29 5.75 1.61 0.22 0.05	-	-	223 29.77 12.38 1.66 0.39	-	-	-	36 6.38 2.00 0.27 0.06	609 22.56 33.80 4.54 1.06	-	215 4.97 11.93 1.60 0.38	-	-	-	310 13.14 17.20 2.31 0.54
Tamarac (city)	41,355 77.16	7,434	939 12.63 12.63 2.27	-	-	-	-	31 2.54 3.30 0.42 0.07	-	42 5.29 4.47 0.56 0.10	-	-	-	-	-	-	-	-	-	423 23.05 45.05 5.69 1.02	-	110 5.13 11.71 1.48 0.27	-	-	-	167 9.96 17.78 2.25 0.40
Charlotte County	125,400 91.76	4,272	1,235 28.91 28.91 0.98	-	-	-	-	-	-	140 24.60 11.34 3.28 0.11	-	-	-	-	336 38.62 27.21 7.87 0.27	-	-	-	-	396 29.95 32.06 9.27 0.32	-	-	-	-	-	220 26.80 17.81 5.15 0.18
Citrus County	106,153 93.41	2,845	906 31.85 31.85 0.85	-	-	-	-	-	-	-	-	-	-	-	212 49.07 23.40 7.45 0.20	-	-	-	-	284 23.61 31.35 9.98 0.27	-	-	-	-	-	277 44.82 30.57 9.74 0.26
Clay County	121,540 92.27	5,530	1,751 31.66 31.66 1.44	-	-	-	-	-	-	-	-	-	-	-	407 40.02 23.24 7.36 0.33	-	-	-	-	657 29.33 37.52 11.88 0.54	-	-	-	-	-	434 37.41 24.79 7.85 0.36
Collier County	178,413 74.94	44,418	5,091 11.46 11.46 2.85	-	-	167 5.39 3.28 0.38 0.09	-	53 4.86 1.04 0.12 0.03	-	750 11.10 14.73 1.69 0.42	58 11.67 1.14 0.13 0.03	-	123 8.75 2.42 0.28 0.07	26 3.78 0.51 0.06 0.01	2,667 10.63 52.39 6.00 1.49	-	-	-	-	621 21.44 12.20 1.40 0.35	-	168 8.05 3.30 0.38 0.09	-	-	-	603 15.66 11.84 1.36 0.34
Duval County	654,825 90.55	28,733	8,852 30.81 30.81 1.35	-	-	353 20.72 3.99 1.23 0.05	-	191 14.49 2.16 0.66 0.03	-	700 22.35 7.91 2.44 0.11	51 8.24 0.58 0.18 0.01	-	-	-	2,693 51.55 30.42 9.37 0.41	-	153 25.98 1.73 0.53 0.02	-	18 3.94 0.20 0.06 <0.01	2,569 24.85 29.02 8.94 0.39	-	354 13.72 4.00 1.23 0.05	-	-	-	1,974 40.24 22.30 6.87 0.30
Jacksonville (city)	616,988 90.45	27,470	8,444 30.74 30.74 1.37	-	-	348 20.64 4.12 1.27 0.06	-	167 13.15 1.98 0.61 0.03	-	657 21.48 7.78 2.39 0.11	51 8.24 0.60 0.19 0.01	-	-	-	2,601 53.17 30.80 9.47 0.42	-	149 26.05 1.76 0.54 0.02	-	-	2,459 24.84 29.12 8.95 0.40	-	310 12.80 3.67 1.13 0.05	-	-	-	1,868 39.99 22.12 6.80 0.30
Escambia County	257,796 93.19	7,142	2,972 41.61 41.61 1.15	-	-	136 27.25 4.58 1.90 0.05	-	-	-	116 16.38 3.90 1.62 0.04	-	-	-	-	1,186 48.55 39.91 16.61 0.46	-	-	-	-	591 37.86 19.89 8.27 0.23	-	34 8.02 1.14 0.48 0.01	-	-	-	898 63.15 30.22 12.57 0.35

Notes: Please refer to the User's Guide for an explanation of data: data is arranged alphabetically by state, then county, then city within each county and only includes counties with populations > 99,999 and cities with populations > 49,999; (1) Includes Costa Rican, Guatemalan, Honduran, Nicaraguan, Panamanian, Salvadoran, and other Central American; (2) Includes Argentinian, Bolivian, Chilean, Colombian, Ecuadorian, Paraguayan, Peruvian, Uruguayan, Venezuelan, and other South American

Place	Total population 5 years and over who speak English-only at home	Hispanic population 5 years and over	Hispanics 5 years and over who speak English-only at home	Argentinian	Bolivian	Central American[1]	Chilean	Colombian	Costa Rican	Cuban	Dominican	Ecuadorian	Guatelmalan	Honduran	Mexican	Nicaraguan	Panamanian	Paraguayan	Peruvian	Puerto Rican	Salvadoran	South American[2]	Spaniard	Uruguayan	Venezuelan	Other Hisp.
Pensacola (city)	49,659	1,046	439	-	-	-	-	-	-	-	-	-	-	-	-	-	-	-	-	-	-	-	-	-	-	-
	93.77		41.97																							
			41.97																							
			0.88																							
Hernando County	113,262	6,223	1,940	-	-	-	-	-	-	150	-	-	-	-	361	-	-	-	-	982	-	-	-	-	-	326
	90.67		31.17							26.98					41.45					27.51						42.45
										7.73					18.61					50.62						16.80
			31.17							2.41					5.80					15.78						5.24
			1.71							0.13					0.32					0.87						0.29
Spring Hill (cdp)	58,162	4,625	1,418	-	-	-	-	-	-	96	-	-	-	-	-	-	-	-	-	781	-	-	-	-	-	229
	87.96		30.66							26.09										26.82						39.76
										6.77										55.08						16.15
			30.66							2.08										16.89						4.95
			2.44							0.17										1.34						0.39
Hillsborough County	736,750	163,887	30,977	-	-	1,166	-	323	97	5,524	214	81	54	309	4,844	183	325	-	131	7,779	125	846	720	-	125	9,884
	79.11		18.90			15.68		5.70	10.65	16.88	5.84	6.60	5.35	15.05	15.24	18.64	21.02		7.70	16.91	17.88	7.29	42.03		7.49	34.11
						3.76		1.04	0.31	17.83	0.69	0.26	0.17	1.00	15.64	0.59	1.05		0.42	25.11	0.40	2.73	2.32		0.40	31.91
			18.90			0.71		0.20	0.06	3.37	0.13	0.05	0.03	0.19	2.96	0.11	0.20		0.08	4.75	0.08	0.52	0.44		0.08	6.03
			4.20			0.16		0.04	0.01	0.75	0.03	0.01	0.01	0.04	0.66	0.02	0.04		0.02	1.06	0.02	0.11	0.10		0.02	1.34
Brandon (cdp)	60,947	9,253	2,304	-	-	124	-	-	-	333	-	-	-	-	269	-	-	-	-	893	-	62	-	-	-	569
	84.33		24.90			25.41				32.71					30.12					19.70		11.11				40.21
						5.38				14.45					11.68					38.76		2.69				24.70
			24.90			1.34				3.60					2.91					9.65		0.67				6.15
			3.78			0.20				0.55					0.44					1.47		0.10				0.93
Tampa (city)	218,362	54,047	10,107	-	-	638	-	126	-	1,971	50	34	-	168	1,251	119	170	-	-	2,273	-	273	185	-	87	3,466
	77.14		18.70			21.03		7.88		14.52	3.93	8.85		20.82	19.57	26.21	27.91			15.81		8.16	26.43		15.59	30.54
						6.31		1.25		19.50	0.49	0.34		1.66	12.38	1.18	1.68			22.49		2.70	1.83		0.86	34.29
			18.70			1.18		0.23		3.65	0.09	0.06		0.31	2.31	0.22	0.31			4.21		0.51	0.34		0.16	6.41
			4.63			0.29		0.06		0.90	0.02	0.02		0.08	0.57	0.05	0.08			1.04		0.13	0.08		0.04	1.59
Town 'n' Country (cdp)	45,703	19,035	2,658	-	-	48	-	36	-	519	40	-	-	-	172	-	-	-	-	1,008	-	76	-	-	-	766
	67.36		13.96			5.99		3.12		11.54	5.57				17.77					14.72		3.82				25.34
						1.81		1.35		19.53	1.50				6.47					37.92		2.86				28.82
			13.96			0.25		0.19		2.73	0.21				0.90					5.30		0.40				4.02
			5.82			0.11		0.08		1.14	0.09				0.38					2.21		0.17				1.68
Indian River County	96,498	6,551	1,050	-	-	37	-	-	-	68	-	-	-	-	390	-	-	-	-	205	-	77	-	-	-	265
	89.56		16.03			11.08				20.00					9.98					31.78		14.95				33.67
						3.52				6.48					37.14					19.52		7.33				25.24
			16.03			0.56				1.04					5.95					3.13		1.18				4.05
			1.09			0.04				0.07					0.40					0.21		0.08				0.27
Lake County	182,724	10,610	2,074	-	-	76	-	-	-	229	-	-	-	-	618	-	-	-	-	563	-	64	-	-	-	515
	91.56		19.55			16.41				31.76					13.00					21.38		11.72				37.37
						3.66				11.04					29.80					27.15		3.09				24.83
			19.55			0.72				2.16					5.82					5.31		0.60				4.85
			1.14			0.04				0.13					0.34					0.31		0.04				0.28
Lee County	361,208	37,471	6,334	-	-	326	-	117	-	643	65	-	36	61	1,634	-	-	-	-	2,197	-	288	-	-	-	1,151
	86.46		16.90			11.93		12.00		20.39	6.53		2.97	13.26	12.42					20.65		12.52				26.07
						5.15		1.85		10.15	1.03		0.57	0.96	25.80					34.69		4.55				18.17
			16.90			0.87		0.31		1.72	0.17		0.10	0.16	4.36					5.86		0.77				3.07
			1.75			0.09		0.03		0.18	0.02		0.01	0.02	0.45					0.61		0.08				0.32

Notes: Please refer to the User's Guide for an explanation of data; data is arranged alphabetically by state, then county, then city within each county and only includes counties with populations > 99,999 and cities with populations > 49,999; (1) Includes Costa Rican, Guatemalan, Honduran, Nicaraguan, Panamanian, Salvadoran, and other Central American; (2) Includes Argentinian, Bolivian, Chilean, Colombian, Ecuadorian, Paraguayan, Peruvian, Uruguayan, Venezuelan, and other South American

Place	Total population 5 years and over who speak English-only at home	Hispanic population 5 years and over	Hispanics 5 years and over who speak English-only at home	Argentinian	Bolivian	Central American[1]	Chilean	Colombian	Costa Rican	Cuban	Dominican	Ecuadorian	Guatemalan	Honduran	Mexican	Nicaraguan	Panamanian	Paraguayan	Peruvian	Puerto Rican	Salvadoran	South American[2]	Spaniard	Uruguayan	Venezuelan	Other Hisp.
Cape Coral (city)	83,549	7,677	1,755	-	-	-	-	60	-	297	27	-	-	-	370	-	-	-	-	608	-	96	-	-	-	258
	86.56		22.86					11.11		19.99	5.03				30.88					30.51		9.45				23.29
								3.42		16.92	1.54				21.08					34.64		5.47				14.70
			22.86					0.78		3.87	0.35				4.82					7.92		1.25				3.36
			2.10					0.07		0.36	0.03				0.44					0.73		0.11				0.31
Leon County	208,570	7,821	3,065	-	-	-	-	-	-	449	-	-	-	-	618	-	-	-	-	639	-	382	-	-	-	764
	92.40		39.19							24.13					46.26					42.12		38.70				51.66
										14.65					20.16					20.85		12.46				24.93
			39.19							5.74					7.90					8.17		4.88				9.77
			1.47							0.22					0.30					0.31		0.18				0.37
Tallahassee (city)	130,526	5,819	2,319	-	-	-	-	-	-	364	-	-	-	-	387	-	-	-	-	478	-	324	-	-	-	566
	91.37		39.85							25.60					44.74					42.41		42.13				50.76
										15.70					16.69					20.61		13.97				24.41
			39.85							6.26					6.65					8.21		5.57				9.73
			1.78							0.28					0.30					0.37		0.25				0.43
Manatee County	218,481	21,417	4,390	-	-	221	-	-	-	339	-	-	-	-	2,178	-	-	-	-	841	-	48	-	-	-	708
	87.74		20.50			16.42				30.54					16.96					28.91		5.57				32.84
						5.03				7.72					49.61					19.16		1.09				16.13
			20.50			1.03				1.58					10.17					3.93		0.22				3.31
			2.01			0.10				0.16					1.00					0.38		0.02				0.32
Marion County	224,174	14,165	3,194	-	-	74	-	81	-	380	-	-	-	-	711	-	-	-	-	1,175	-	207	-	-	-	597
	91.19		22.55			14.62		14.89		33.69					24.26					18.39		19.87				31.81
						2.32		2.54		11.90					22.26					36.79		6.48				18.69
			22.55			0.52		0.57		2.68					5.02					8.30		1.46				4.21
			1.42			0.03		0.04		0.17					0.32					0.52		0.09				0.27
Martin County	107,584	8,447	1,193	-	-	75	-	-	-	208	-	-	55	-	398	-	-	-	-	215	-	-	-	-	-	269
	88.71		14.12			3.60				27.40			3.12		11.91					16.10						42.43
						6.29				17.44			4.61		33.36					18.02						22.55
			14.12			0.89				2.46			0.65		4.71					2.55						3.18
			1.11			0.07				0.19			0.05		0.37					0.20						0.25
Miami-Dade County	676,347	1,221,202	67,855	417	159	5,700	389	2,664	186	33,187	1,567	547	384	1,197	3,231	2,924	406	-	790	7,414	394	5,823	462	49	708	10,471
	32.08		5.56	3.06	7.18	4.31	5.10	3.72	4.16	5.26	4.13	4.92	3.84	4.35	9.61	4.05	6.22		3.48	9.89	4.39	3.75	7.75	2.51	3.29	6.98
				0.61	0.23	8.40	0.57	3.93	0.27	48.91	2.31	0.81	0.57	1.76	4.76	4.31	0.60		1.16	10.93	0.58	8.58	0.68	0.07	1.04	15.43
			5.56	0.03	0.01	0.47	0.03	0.22	0.02	2.72	0.13	0.04	0.03	0.10	0.26	0.24	0.03		0.06	0.61	0.03	0.48	0.04	<0.01	0.06	0.86
			10.03	0.06	0.02	0.84	0.06	0.39	0.03	4.91	0.23	0.08	0.06	0.18	0.48	0.43	0.06		0.12	1.10	0.06	0.86	0.07	0.01	0.10	1.55
Carol City (cdp)	29,525	23,504	1,442	-	-	118	-	44	-	567	79	-	-	33	-	77	-	-	-	312	-	60	-	-	-	246
	53.43		6.14			4.66		3.09		5.30	4.43			6.55		5.61				11.99		2.46				8.04
						8.18		3.05		39.32	5.48			2.29		5.34				21.64		4.16				17.06
			6.14			0.50		0.19		2.41	0.34			0.14		0.33				1.33		0.26				1.05
			4.88			0.40		0.15		1.92	0.27			0.11		0.26				1.06		0.20				0.83
Fountainbleau (cdp)	3,448	49,241	1,641	6	-	378	0	117	-	746	6	24	-	15	7	310	36	-	22	76	-	176	-	-	0	252
	6.19		3.33	1.39		4.81	0.00	4.38		3.43	0.33	3.12		2.40	1.79	5.26	7.05		1.95	4.41		2.20			0.00	3.32
				0.37		23.03	0.00	7.13		45.46	0.37	1.46		0.91	0.43	18.89	2.19		1.34	4.63		10.73			0.00	15.36
			3.33	0.01		0.77	0.00	0.24		1.51	0.01	0.05		0.03	0.01	0.63	0.07		0.04	0.15		0.36			0.00	0.51
			47.59	0.17		10.96	0.00	3.39		21.64	0.17	0.70		0.44	0.20	8.99	1.04		0.64	2.20		5.10			0.00	7.31
Hialeah (city)	15,691	194,772	8,606	0	-	460	67	212	0	6,190	109	33	0	67	83	316	-	-	0	382	9	334	25	-	22	1,023
	7.36		4.42	0.00		3.01	8.93	2.83	0.00	4.55	2.32	2.75	0.00	2.64	5.61	3.24			0.00	5.88	1.01	2.67	5.10		2.37	5.70
				0.00		5.35	0.78	2.46	0.00	71.93	1.27	0.38	0.00	0.78	0.96	3.67			0.00	4.44	0.10	3.88	0.29		0.26	11.89
			4.42	0.00		0.24	0.03	0.11	0.00	3.18	0.06	0.02	0.00	0.03	0.04	0.16			0.00	0.20	<0.01	0.17	0.01		0.01	0.53
			54.85	0.00		2.93	0.43	1.35	0.00	39.45	0.69	0.21	0.00	0.43	0.53	2.01			0.00	2.43	0.06	2.13	0.16		0.14	6.52

Notes: Please refer to the User's Guide for an explanation of data; data is arranged alphabetically by state, then county, then city within each county and only includes counties with populations > 99,999 and cities with populations > 49,999; (1) Includes Costa Rican, Guatemalan, Honduran, Nicaraguan, Panamanian, Salvadoran, and other Central American; (2) Includes Argentinian, Bolivian, Chilean, Colombian, Ecuadorian, Paraguayan, Peruvian, Uruguayan, Venezuelan, and other South American

Place	Total population 5 years and over who speak English-only at home	Hispanic population 5 years and over	Hispanics 5 years and over who speak English-only at home	Argentinian	Bolivian	Central American[1]	Chilean	Colombian	Costa Rican	Cuban	Dominican	Ecuadorian	Guatemalan	Honduran	Mexican	Nicaraguan	Panamanian	Paraguayan	Peruvian	Puerto Rican	Salvadoran	South American[2]	Spaniard	Uruguayan	Venezuelan	Other Hisp.
Kendale Lakes (cdp)	7,981 14.97	41,279	1,557 3.77 3.77 19.51	-	-	103 2.66 6.62 0.25 1.29	-	63 1.66 4.05 0.15 0.79	-	868 4.13 55.75 2.10 10.88	12 1.42 0.77 0.03 0.15	-	-	8 1.58 0.51 0.02 0.10	78 14.29 5.01 0.19 0.98	95 3.50 6.10 0.23 1.19	-	-	70 7.51 4.50 0.17 0.88	72 4.51 4.62 0.17 0.90	-	186 2.63 11.95 0.45 2.33	-	-	29 3.38 1.86 0.07 0.36	229 3.69 14.71 0.55 2.87
Kendall (cdp)	28,297 39.94	35,482	2,704 7.62 7.62 9.56	35 5.55 1.29 0.10 0.12	-	252 6.79 9.32 0.71 0.89	38 8.12 1.41 0.11 0.13	124 3.15 4.59 0.35 0.44	-	1,179 7.83 43.60 3.32 4.17	32 4.20 1.18 0.09 0.11	-	-	-	-	102 4.81 3.77 0.29 0.36	-	-	72 5.75 2.66 0.20 0.25	283 13.26 10.47 0.80 1.00	-	384 4.64 14.20 1.08 1.36	-	-	77 5.60 2.85 0.22 0.27	455 9.48 16.83 1.28 1.61
Miami Beach (city)	27,554 32.46	45,437	3,150 6.93 6.93 11.43	84 2.87 2.67 0.18 0.30	-	176 6.38 5.59 0.39 0.64	104 14.40 3.30 0.23 0.38	236 5.42 7.49 0.52 0.86	-	1,325 7.41 42.06 2.92 4.81	45 3.30 1.43 0.10 0.16	46 7.13 1.46 0.10 0.17	-	33 4.27 1.05 0.07 0.12	100 10.66 3.17 0.22 0.36	110 11.17 3.49 0.24 0.40	-	-	46 2.53 1.46 0.10 0.17	449 12.99 14.25 0.99 1.63	-	608 4.84 19.30 1.34 2.21	36 6.41 1.14 0.08 0.13	-	40 2.84 1.27 0.09 0.15	411 6.95 13.05 0.90 1.49
Miami (city)	86,669 25.40	227,443	12,945 5.69 5.69 14.94	75 3.93 0.58 0.03 0.09	-	1,726 4.14 13.33 0.76 1.99	26 2.96 0.20 0.01 0.03	255 4.42 1.97 0.11 0.29	57 7.17 0.44 0.03 0.07	6,769 5.57 52.29 2.98 7.81	482 7.01 3.72 0.21 0.56	134 7.92 1.04 0.06 0.15	140 5.24 1.08 0.06 0.16	581 4.49 4.49 0.26 0.67	338 11.29 2.61 0.15 0.39	758 3.53 5.86 0.33 0.87	10 1.17 0.08 <0.01 0.01	-	104 3.93 0.80 0.05 0.12	844 8.83 6.52 0.37 0.97	123 5.40 0.95 0.05 0.14	713 4.66 5.51 0.31 0.82	37 3.98 0.29 0.02 0.04	-	81 4.80 0.63 0.04 0.09	2,036 7.15 15.73 0.90 2.35
North Miami (city)	19,252 34.89	13,316	846 6.35 6.35 4.39	-	-	87 5.18 10.28 0.65 0.45	-	63 6.38 7.45 0.47 0.33	-	171 6.45 20.21 1.28 0.89	31 3.14 3.66 0.23 0.16	-	-	34 5.92 4.02 0.26 0.18	-	53 7.81 6.26 0.40 0.28	-	-	-	210 8.25 24.82 1.58 1.09	-	89 4.40 10.52 0.67 0.46	-	-	-	145 4.89 17.14 1.09 0.75
Tamiami (cdp)	3,587 6.95	45,478	1,678 3.69 3.69 46.78	-	-	107 2.95 6.38 0.24 2.98	-	34 1.72 2.03 0.07 0.95	-	1,136 3.64 67.70 2.50 31.67	26 3.95 1.55 0.06 0.72	-	-	0 0.00 0.00 0.00 0.00	73 14.54 4.35 0.16 2.04	67 2.60 3.99 0.15 1.87	-	-	-	17 1.61 1.01 0.04 0.47	-	102 2.67 6.08 0.22 2.84	-	-	0 0.00 0.00 0.00 0.00	217 4.88 12.93 0.48 6.05
Okaloosa County	147,138 92.11	6,296	2,815 44.71 44.71 1.91	-	-	55 18.21 1.95 0.87 0.04	-	-	-	132 23.91 4.69 2.10 0.09	-	-	-	-	1,170 54.02 41.56 18.58 0.80	-	-	-	-	507 37.67 18.01 8.05 0.34	-	-	-	-	-	824 57.54 29.27 13.09 0.56
Orange County	622,997 74.58	153,771	21,054 13.69 13.69 3.38	61 8.80 0.29 0.04 0.01	-	698 12.65 3.32 0.45 0.11	37 8.11 0.18 0.02 0.01	320 4.42 1.52 0.21 0.05	111 19.30 0.53 0.07 0.02	2,196 17.73 10.43 1.43 0.35	410 6.88 1.95 0.27 0.07	152 9.11 0.72 0.10 0.02	106 10.74 0.50 0.07 0.02	120 10.26 0.57 0.08 0.02	3,654 20.75 17.36 2.38 0.59	74 8.58 0.35 0.05 0.01	131 14.41 0.62 0.09 0.02	-	165 9.85 0.78 0.11 0.03	9,689 12.21 46.02 6.30 1.56	156 17.51 0.74 0.10 0.03	1,032 6.91 4.90 0.67 0.17	225 36.35 1.07 0.15 0.04	-	163 6.69 0.77 0.11 0.03	3,150 18.13 14.96 2.05 0.51
Orlando (city)	130,439 75.04	30,074	4,005 13.32 13.32 3.07	-	-	133 10.14 3.32 0.44 0.10	-	92 5.37 2.30 0.31 0.07	-	493 17.84 12.31 1.64 0.38	106 9.15 2.65 0.35 0.08	-	-	-	531 25.14 13.26 1.77 0.41	-	-	-	39 9.07 0.97 0.13 0.03	1,824 11.87 45.54 6.07 1.40	-	229 6.06 5.72 0.76 0.18	-	-	38 5.19 0.95 0.13 0.03	655 18.81 16.35 2.18 0.50
Osceola County	107,397 66.70	46,598	5,240 11.25 11.25 4.88	-	-	171 9.32 3.26 0.37 0.16	-	81 4.29 1.55 0.17 0.08	-	201 11.38 3.84 0.43 0.19	87 3.70 1.66 0.19 0.08	0 0.00 0.00 0.00 0.00	-	-	624 20.25 11.91 1.34 0.58	-	-	-	-	3,313 11.04 63.23 7.11 3.08	32 5.94 0.61 0.07 0.03	136 3.90 2.60 0.29 0.13	-	-	9 1.84 0.17 0.02 0.01	675 17.24 12.88 1.45 0.63

Notes: Please refer to the User's Guide for an explanation of data; data is arranged alphabetically by state, then county, then city within each county and only includes counties with populations > 99,999 and cities with populations > 49,999; (1) Includes Costa Rican, Guatemalan, Honduran, Nicaraguan, Panamanian, Salvadoran, and other Central American; (2) Includes Argentinian, Bolivian, Chilean, Colombian, Ecuadorian, Paraguayan, Peruvian, Uruguayan, Venezuelan, and other South American

Place	Total population 5 years and over who speak English-only at home	Hispanic population 5 years and over	Hispanics 5 years and over who speak English-only at home	Argentinian	Bolivian	Central American[1]	Chilean	Colombian	Costa Rican	Cuban	Dominican	Ecuadorian	Guatelmalan	Honduran	Mexican	Nicaraguan	Panamanian	Paraguayan	Peruvian	Puerto Rican	Salvadoran	South American[2]	Spaniard	Uruguayan	Venezuelan	Other Hisp.
Palm Beach County	837,066	128,500	16,884	151	-	856	39	584	31	3,064	210	127	239	216	3,448	161	121	-	154	4,966	82	1,224	129	19	125	2,987
	78.28		13.14	8.56		6.06	5.89	6.58	3.93	12.39	6.29	6.79	3.84	7.52	13.12	8.07	28.54		6.46	21.70	5.34	6.43	27.86	2.49	7.40	16.95
				0.89		5.07	0.23	3.46	0.18	18.15	1.24	0.75	1.42	1.28	20.42	0.95	0.72		0.91	29.41	0.49	7.25	0.76	0.11	0.74	17.69
			13.14	0.12		0.67	0.03	0.45	0.02	2.38	0.16	0.10	0.19	0.17	2.68	0.13	0.09		0.12	3.86	0.06	0.95	0.10	0.01	0.10	2.32
			2.02	0.02		0.10	<0.01	0.07	<0.01	0.37	0.03	0.02	0.03	0.03	0.41	0.02	0.01		0.02	0.59	0.01	0.15	0.02	<0.01	0.01	0.36
Boca Raton (city)	57,156	6,020	852	-	-	-	-	31	-	155	-	-	-	-	98	-	-	-	-	306	-	74	-	-	-	180
	79.21		14.15					3.82		17.86					12.61					39.43		3.74				15.33
								3.64		18.19					11.50					35.92		8.69				21.13
			14.15					0.51		2.57					1.63					5.08		1.23				2.99
			1.49					0.05		0.27					0.17					0.54		0.13				0.31
Boynton Beach (city)	44,651	4,424	898	-	-	67	-	-	-	100	-	-	-	-	211	-	-	-	-	348	-	24	-	-	-	107
	79.08		20.30			12.67				20.37					29.35					26.42		3.48				18.80
						7.46				11.14					23.50					38.75		2.67				11.92
			20.30			1.51				2.26					4.77					7.87		0.54				2.42
			2.01			0.15				0.22					0.47					0.78		0.05				0.24
Delray Beach (city)	42,558	3,817	584	-	-	-	-	-	-	-	-	-	-	-	170	-	-	-	-	159	-	73	-	-	-	54
	74.51		15.30												13.36					23.49		12.56				12.36
															29.11					27.23		12.50				9.25
			15.30												4.45					4.17		1.91				1.41
			1.37												0.40					0.37		0.17				0.13
West Palm Beach (city)	55,174	13,900	1,226	-	-	148	-	44	-	284	32	-	134	-	178	-	-	-	-	226	-	137	-	-	-	216
	71.71		8.82			5.71		6.60		6.70	8.56		6.99		10.27					13.10		9.07				12.72
						12.07		3.59		23.16	2.61		10.93		14.52					18.43		11.17				17.62
			8.82			1.06		0.32		2.04	0.23		0.96		1.28					1.63		0.99				1.55
			2.22			0.27		0.08		0.51	0.06		0.24		0.32					0.41		0.25				0.39
Pasco County	293,294	17,792	5,425	-	-	131	-	-	-	596	-	-	-	-	997	-	-	-	-	1,967	-	91	-	-	-	1,495
	89.72		30.49			25.05				35.08					18.76					30.54		11.08				57.74
						2.41				10.99					18.38					36.26		1.68				27.56
			30.49			0.74				3.35					5.60					11.06		0.51				8.40
			1.85			0.04				0.20					0.34					0.67		0.03				0.51
Pinellas County	771,726	38,440	10,484	-	-	291	-	253	-	1,002	105	47	-	-	2,702	-	-	-	174	3,376	-	638	186	-	48	2,184
	88.04		27.27			22.11		14.32		22.06	12.88	11.66			29.24				23.02	28.74		14.05	36.12		5.83	38.14
						2.78		2.41		9.56	1.00	0.45			25.77				1.66	32.20		6.09	1.77		0.46	20.83
			27.27			0.76		0.66		2.61	0.27	0.12			7.03				0.45	8.78		1.66	0.48		0.12	5.68
			1.36			0.04		0.03		0.13	0.01	0.01			0.35				0.02	0.44		0.08	0.02		0.01	0.28
Clearwater (city)	85,394	8,713	1,515	-	-	-	-	20	-	117	-	-	-	-	555	-	-	-	-	421	-	72	-	-	-	312
	83.41		17.39					5.67		20.89					14.92					20.20		7.39				32.70
								1.32		7.72					36.63					27.79		4.75				20.59
			17.39					0.23		1.34					6.37					4.83		0.83				3.58
			1.77					0.02		0.14					0.65					0.49		0.08				0.37
Largo (city)	59,429	2,628	784	-	-	-	-	-	-	-	-	-	-	-	253	-	-	-	-	239	-	-	-	-	-	-
	89.40		29.83												52.27					32.61						
															32.27					30.48						
			29.83												9.63					9.09						
			1.32												0.43					0.40						
Palm Harbor (cdp)	49,972	1,749	572	-	-	-	-	-	-	-	-	-	-	-	-	-	-	-	-	184	-	-	-	-	-	-
	88.60		32.70																	25.52						
																				32.17						
			32.70																	10.52						
			1.14																	0.37						

Notes: Please refer to the User's Guide for an explanation of data; data is arranged alphabetically by state, then county, then city within each county and only includes counties with populations > 99,999 and cities with populations > 49,999; (1) Includes Costa Rican, Guatemalan, Honduran, Nicaraguan, Panamanian, Salvadoran, and other Central American; (2) Includes Argentinian, Bolivian, Chilean, Colombian, Ecuadorian, Paraguayan, Peruvian, Uruguayan, Venezuelan, and other South American

Place	Total population 5 years and over who speak English-only at home	Hispanic population 5 years and over	Hispanics 5 years and over who speak English-only at home	Argentinian	Bolivian	Central American[1]	Chilean	Colombian	Costa Rican	Cuban	Dominican	Ecuadorian	Guatemalan	Honduran	Mexican	Nicaraguan	Panamanian	Paraguayan	Peruvian	Puerto Rican	Salvadoran	South American[2]	Spaniard	Uruguayan	Venezuelan	Other Hisp.
St. Petersburg (city)	206,489 88.26	9,153	2,724 29.76 29.76 1.32	-	-	-	-	-	-	263 16.66 9.65 2.87 0.13	-	-	-	-	740 47.04 27.17 8.08 0.36	-	-	-	-	838 28.87 30.76 9.16 0.41	-	134 11.82 4.92 1.46 0.06	-	-	-	581 44.18 21.33 6.35 0.28
Polk County	398,332 87.90	40,881	6,521 15.95 15.95 1.64	-	-	96 8.28 1.47 0.23 0.02	-	-	-	536 22.68 8.22 1.31 0.13	62 13.54 0.95 0.15 0.02	-	-	-	2,410 11.23 36.96 5.90 0.61	-	-	-	-	1,860 18.06 28.52 4.55 0.47	-	136 14.48 2.09 0.33 0.03	-	-	-	1,327 32.99 20.35 3.25 0.33
Lakeland (city)	65,999 89.92	4,550	853 18.75 18.75 1.29	-	-	-	-	-	-	91 14.65 10.67 2.00 0.14	-	-	-	-	150 19.61 17.58 3.30 0.23	-	-	-	-	281 15.16 32.94 6.18 0.43	-	-	-	-	-	212 30.90 24.85 4.66 0.32
St. Johns County	108,870 93.28	3,349	1,559 46.55 46.55 1.43	-	-	-	-	-	-	-	-	-	-	-	566 63.67 36.31 16.90 0.52	-	-	-	-	256 32.12 16.42 7.64 0.24	-	-	-	-	-	332 55.70 21.30 9.91 0.30
St. Lucie County	156,941 86.22	14,555	2,734 18.78 18.78 1.74	-	-	87 8.74 3.18 0.60 0.06	-	21 5.65 0.77 0.14 0.01	-	191 18.99 6.99 1.31 0.12	-	-	-	-	810 12.59 29.63 5.57 0.52	-	-	-	-	995 28.82 36.39 6.84 0.63	-	88 9.46 3.22 0.60 0.06	-	-	-	454 35.25 16.61 3.12 0.29
Port St. Lucie (city)	73,071 87.44	6,329	1,670 26.39 26.39 2.29	-	-	-	-	-	-	150 21.37 8.98 2.37 0.21	-	-	-	-	402 40.85 24.07 6.35 0.55	-	-	-	-	715 28.60 42.81 11.30 0.98	-	55 8.40 3.29 0.87 0.08	-	-	-	206 28.49 12.34 3.25 0.28
Santa Rosa County	104,132 94.69	2,541	1,253 49.31 49.31 1.20	-	-	-	-	-	-	-	-	-	-	-	455 61.32 36.31 17.91 0.44	-	-	-	-	314 45.77 25.06 12.36 0.30	-	-	-	-	-	282 60.39 22.51 11.10 0.27
Sarasota County	280,340 89.47	13,114	2,733 20.84 20.84 0.97	-	-	93 15.37 3.40 0.71 0.03	-	83 10.39 3.04 0.63 0.03	-	259 14.05 9.48 1.97 0.09	-	-	-	-	650 12.34 23.78 4.96 0.23	-	-	-	-	602 37.81 22.03 4.59 0.21	-	226 12.81 8.27 1.72 0.08	-	-	-	797 45.99 29.16 6.08 0.28
Sarasota (city)	41,115 82.41	5,753	573 9.96 9.96 1.39	-	-	-	-	-	-	86 13.98 15.01 1.49 0.21	-	-	-	-	143 4.54 24.96 2.49 0.35	-	-	-	-	104 26.00 18.15 1.81 0.25	-	10 1.58 1.75 0.17 0.02	-	-	-	211 37.21 36.82 3.67 0.51
Seminole County	288,646 84.41	37,260	7,159 19.21 19.21 2.48	69 16.43 0.96 0.19 0.02	-	403 20.88 5.63 1.08 0.14	-	128 5.99 1.79 0.34 0.04	-	1,000 28.51 13.97 2.68 0.35	147 13.76 2.05 0.39 0.05	8 1.77 0.11 0.02 <0.01	-	-	971 32.11 13.56 2.61 0.34	-	170 33.46 2.37 0.46 0.06	-	61 12.01 0.85 0.16 0.02	3,123 17.15 43.62 8.38 1.08	-	332 7.72 4.64 0.89 0.12	-	-	19 4.38 0.27 0.05 0.01	1,115 22.17 15.57 2.99 0.39

Notes: Please refer to the User's Guide for an explanation of data; data is arranged alphabetically by state, then county, then city within each county and only includes counties with populations > 99,999 and cities with populations > 49,999; (1) Includes Costa Rican, Guatemalan, Honduran, Nicaraguan, Panamanian, Salvadoran, and other Central American; (2) Includes Argentinian, Bolivian, Chilean, Colombian, Ecuadorian, Paraguayan, Peruvian, Uruguayan, Venezuelan, and other South American

Place	Total population 5 years and over who speak English-only at home	Hispanic population 5 years and over	Hispanics 5 years and over who speak English-only at home	Argentinian	Bolivian	Central American[1]	Chilean	Colombian	Costa Rican	Cuban	Dominican	Ecuadorian	Guatelmalan	Honduran	Mexican	Nicaraguan	Panamanian	Paraguayan	Peruvian	Puerto Rican	Salvadoran	South American[2]	Spaniard	Uruguayan	Venezuelan	Other Hisp.
Volusia County	376,145 89.23	26,511	5,711 21.54 21.54 1.52	-	-	132 18.88 2.31 0.50 0.04	-	101 15.88 1.77 0.38 0.03	-	410 31.32 7.18 1.55 0.11	85 15.51 1.49 0.32 0.02	-	-	-	1,426 20.16 24.97 5.38 0.38	-	-	-	-	2,448 19.09 42.86 9.23 0.65	-	278 18.52 4.87 1.05 0.07	-	-	-	887 36.62 15.53 3.35 0.24
Daytona Beach (city)	54,341 89.20	2,046	518 25.32 25.32 0.95	-	-	-	-	-	-	-	-	-	-	-	-	-	-	-	-	155 19.82 29.92 7.58 0.29	-	-	-	-	-	91 24.14 17.57 4.45 0.17
Deltona (city)	52,695 80.55	11,881	2,314 19.48 19.48 4.39	-	-	-	-	-	-	78 14.47 3.37 0.66 0.15	-	-	-	-	224 39.44 9.68 1.89 0.43	-	-	-	-	1,502 17.01 64.91 12.64 2.85	-	130 21.92 5.62 1.09 0.25	-	-	-	295 34.26 12.75 2.48 0.56

Notes: Please refer to the User's Guide for an explanation of data; data is arranged alphabetically by state, then county, then city within each county and only includes counties with populations > 99,999 and cities with populations > 49,999; (1) Includes Costa Rican, Guatemalan, Honduran, Nicaraguan, Panamanian, Salvadoran, and other Central American; (2) Includes Argentinian, Bolivian, Chilean, Colombian, Ecuadorian, Paraguayan, Peruvan, Uruguayan, Venezuelan, and other South American

Language Spoken at Home: Spanish

(Universe: Population 5 Years and Over)

Place	Total population 5 years and over who speak Spanish at home	Hispanic population 5 years and over	Hispanics 5 years and over who speak Spanish at home	Argentinian	Bolivian	Central American[1]	Chilean	Colombian	Costa Rican	Cuban	Dominican	Ecuadorian	Guatemalan	Honduran	Mexican	Nicaraguan	Panamanian	Paraguayan	Peruvian	Puerto Rican	Salvadoran	South American[2]	Spaniard	Uruguayan	Venezuelan	Other Hisp.
UNITED STATES	28,101,052	31,569,576	24,636,215	87,146	37,010	1,524,108	57,375	422,348	55,603	1,020,786	684,822	234,688	343,035	200,033	14,539,577	168,157	67,454	5,718	208,704	2,315,342	611,687	1,187,834	59,758	17,332	79,623	3,303,988
	10.71		78.04	85.27	87.08	90.84	81.96	89.80	82.42	85.82	92.61	91.77	91.66	90.90	78.53	91.27	73.13	68.12	89.20	74.90	93.78	88.53	56.50	89.47	87.62	67.28
				0.35	0.15	6.19	0.23	1.71	0.23	4.14	2.78	0.95	1.39	0.81	59.02	0.68	0.27	0.02	0.85	9.40	2.48	4.82	0.24	0.07	0.32	13.41
			78.04	0.28	0.12	4.83	0.18	1.34	0.18	3.23	2.17	0.74	1.09	0.63	46.06	0.53	0.21	0.02	0.66	7.33	1.94	3.76	0.19	0.05	0.25	10.47
			87.67	0.31	0.13	5.42	0.20	1.50	0.20	3.63	2.44	0.84	1.22	0.71	51.74	0.60	0.24	0.02	0.74	8.24	2.18	4.23	0.21	0.06	0.28	11.76
FLORIDA	2,476,528	2,489,063	2,179,438	20,858	3,888	190,254	11,503	132,035	10,146	743,713	67,047	22,995	26,111	39,316	261,433	78,572	13,485	790	41,579	365,217	18,532	280,840	10,522	4,030	37,693	260,412
	16.46		87.56	91.41	91.35	92.15	89.83	94.25	88.26	91.87	93.59	92.77	89.38	93.15	82.57	94.82	83.85	89.47	93.47	82.26	93.11	93.32	72.24	94.16	93.71	80.05
				0.96	0.18	8.73	0.53	6.06	0.47	34.12	3.08	1.06	1.20	1.80	12.00	3.61	0.62	0.04	1.91	16.76	0.85	12.89	0.48	0.18	1.73	11.95
			87.56	0.84	0.16	7.64	0.46	5.30	0.41	29.88	2.69	0.92	1.05	1.58	10.50	3.16	0.54	0.03	1.67	14.67	0.74	11.28	0.42	0.16	1.51	10.46
			88.00	0.84	0.16	7.68	0.46	5.33	0.41	30.03	2.71	0.93	1.05	1.59	10.56	3.17	0.54	0.03	1.68	14.75	0.75	11.34	0.42	0.16	1.52	10.52
Alachua County	11,438	11,656	7,923	-	-	453	-	456	-	1,580	-	-	-	-	762	-	-	-	-	2,272	-	1,523	-	-	-	1,055
	5.53		67.97			76.13		73.19		65.53					60.09					74.54		77.27				53.39
						5.72		5.76		19.94					9.62					28.68		19.22				13.32
			67.97			3.89		3.91		13.56					6.54					19.49		13.07				9.05
			69.27			3.96		3.99		13.81					6.66					19.86		13.32				9.22
Gainesville (city)	5,706	5,649	3,972	-	-	-	-	-	-	695	-	-	-	-	233	-	-	-	-	1,360	-	838	-	-	-	546
	6.25		70.31							62.00					52.71					79.39		79.28				61.07
										17.50					5.87					34.24		21.10				13.75
			70.31							12.30					4.12					24.08		14.83				9.67
			69.61							12.18					4.08					23.83		14.69				9.57
Bay County	3,542	3,184	1,749	-	-	-	-	-	-	-	-	-	-	-	403	-	-	-	-	556	-	-	-	-	-	135
	2.54		54.93												39.67					60.17						35.16
															23.04					31.79						7.72
			54.93												12.66					17.46						4.24
			49.38												11.38					15.70						3.81
Brevard County	18,320	20,164	13,236	-	-	886	-	538	-	1,272	315	-	-	-	1,557	-	268	-	-	5,889	-	1,177	-	-	-	1,997
	4.06		65.64			80.62		79.12		65.57	87.74				47.50		74.24			69.20		71.94				63.86
						6.69		4.06		9.61	2.38				11.76		2.02			44.49		8.89				15.09
			65.64			4.39		2.67		6.31	1.56				7.72		1.33			29.21		5.84				9.90
			72.25			4.84		2.94		6.94	1.72				8.50		1.46			32.15		6.42				10.90
Melbourne (city)	3,144	3,428	2,362	-	-	-	-	-	-	-	-	-	-	-	488	-	-	-	-	952	-	-	-	-	-	277
	4.65		68.90												66.67					67.76						64.57
															20.66					40.30						11.73
			68.90												14.24					27.77						8.08
			75.13												15.52					30.28						8.81
Palm Bay (city)	5,491	6,438	4,627	-	-	-	-	-	-	-	-	-	-	-	309	-	-	-	-	2,796	-	356	-	-	-	629
	7.37		71.87												46.89					76.23		71.77				66.49
															6.68					60.43		7.69				13.59
			71.87												4.80					43.43		5.53				9.77
			84.27												5.63					50.92		6.48				11.46
Broward County	248,207	251,327	215,199	3,332	618	16,983	1,761	27,636	1,603	42,815	9,398	4,697	2,529	3,522	13,232	3,017	1,880	-	9,880	39,467	4,001	57,866	1,524	836	7,902	33,914
	16.32		85.63	86.46	91.83	90.40	88.85	94.33	86.51	85.92	92.79	93.18	91.20	90.84	79.52	91.42	81.49		92.92	78.52	95.33	93.07	70.30	91.67	93.76	82.04
				1.55	0.29	7.89	0.82	12.84	0.74	19.90	4.37	2.18	1.18	1.64	6.15	1.40	0.87		4.59	18.34	1.86	26.89	0.71	0.39	3.67	15.76
			85.63	1.33	0.25	6.76	0.70	11.00	0.64	17.04	3.74	1.87	1.01	1.40	5.26	1.20	0.75		3.93	15.70	1.59	23.02	0.61	0.33	3.14	13.49
			86.70	1.34	0.25	6.84	0.71	11.13	0.65	17.25	3.79	1.89	1.02	1.42	5.33	1.22	0.76		3.98	15.90	1.61	23.31	0.61	0.34	3.18	13.66

Notes: Please refer to the User's Guide for an explanation of data; data is arranged alphabetically by state, then county, then city within each county and only includes counties with populations > 99,999 and cities with populations > 49,999; (1) Includes Costa Rican, Guatemalan, Honduran, Nicaraguan, Panamanian, Salvadoran, and other Central American; (2) Includes Argentinian, Bolivian, Chilean, Colombian, Ecuadorian, Paraguayan, Peruvian, Uruguayan, Venezuelan, and other South American

Place	Total population 5 years and over who speak Spanish at home	Hispanic population 5 years and over	Hispanics 5 years and over who speak Spanish at home	Argentinian	Bolivian	Central American[1]	Chilean	Colombian	Costa Rican	Cuban	Dominican	Ecuadorian	Guatemalan	Honduran	Mexican	Nicaraguan	Panamanian	Paraguayan	Peruvian	Puerto Rican	Salvadoran	South American[2]	Spaniard	Uruguayan	Venezuelan	Other Hisp.
Coral Springs (city)	16,280	16,926	14,053	-	-	655	-	2,093	-	1,481	472	827	-	-	1,167	-	-	-	851	2,707	-	4,856	-	-	419	2,496
	14.89		83.03			86.64		97.21		77.62	89.22	92.51			78.32				94.03	73.00		93.35			87.11	81.57
						4.66		14.89		10.54	3.36	5.88			8.30				6.06	19.26		34.55			2.98	17.76
			83.03			3.87		12.37		8.75	2.79	4.89			6.89				5.03	15.99		28.69			2.48	14.75
			86.32			4.02		12.86		9.10	2.90	5.08			7.17				5.23	16.63		29.83			2.57	15.33
Davie (town)	13,076	13,367	11,134	-	-	946	-	1,098	-	2,420	-	-	-	-	603	-	-	-	541	2,589	-	2,653	-	-	-	1,534
	18.54		83.29			91.05		93.37		77.12					85.90				90.32	81.75		94.04				77.09
						8.50		9.86		21.74					5.42				4.86	23.25		23.83				13.78
			83.29			7.08		8.21		18.10					4.51				4.05	19.37		19.85				11.48
			85.15			7.23		8.40		18.51					4.61				4.14	19.80		20.29				11.73
Deerfield Beach (city)	5,311	5,120	4,324	-	-	426	-	656	-	620	-	-	-	-	327	-	-	-	-	1,004	-	1,250	-	-	-	505
	8.62		84.45			91.03		100.00		86.35					73.65					81.16		94.20				71.94
						9.85		15.17		14.34					7.56					23.22		28.91				11.68
			84.45			8.32		12.81		12.11					6.39					19.61		24.41				9.86
			81.42			8.02		12.35		11.67					6.16					18.90		23.54				9.51
Fort Lauderdale (city)	13,523	13,104	10,831	-	-	1,605	-	1,115	-	2,182	-	-	353	-	750	-	-	-	389	1,828	622	2,521	-	-	-	1,654
	9.37		82.65			92.77		90.50		83.19			97.78		68.43				89.43	79.90	96.43	88.61				75.46
						14.82		10.29		20.15			3.26		6.92				3.59	16.88	5.74	23.28				15.27
			82.65			12.25		8.51		16.65			2.69		5.72				2.97	13.95	4.75	19.24				12.62
			80.09			11.87		8.25		16.14			2.61		5.55				2.88	13.52	4.60	18.64				12.23
Hollywood (city)	28,163	29,277	25,439	496	-	1,961	345	2,960	-	4,949	1,475	555	-	375	857	532	-	-	1,145	5,146	-	6,494	-	-	545	4,426
	21.48		86.89	90.35		92.33	98.01	93.40		85.68	92.59	91.13		93.28	76.52	94.66			92.26	81.12		93.22			93.00	85.66
				1.95		7.71	1.36	11.64		19.45	5.80	2.18		1.47	3.37	2.09			4.50	20.23		25.53			2.14	17.40
			86.89	1.69		6.70	1.18	10.11		16.90	5.04	1.90		1.28	2.93	1.82			3.91	17.58		22.18			1.86	15.12
			90.33	1.76		6.96	1.23	10.51		17.57	5.24	1.97		1.33	3.04	1.89			4.07	18.27		23.06			1.94	15.72
Lauderhill (city)	3,613	3,528	2,839	-	-	-	-	417	-	-	-	-	-	-	-	-	-	-	-	589	-	845	-	-	-	575
	6.83		80.47					93.50												72.81		87.84				77.91
								14.69												20.75		29.76				20.25
			80.47					11.82												16.70		23.95				16.30
			78.58					11.54												16.30		23.39				15.91
Margate (city)	6,903	7,688	6,236	-	-	454	-	1,002	-	509	-	-	-	-	602	-	-	-	-	1,583	-	1,748	-	-	-	1,043
	13.58		81.11			85.34		92.44		77.24					80.48					74.18		91.37				76.19
						7.28		16.07		8.16					9.65					25.38		28.03				16.73
			81.11			5.91		13.03		6.62					7.83					20.59		22.74				13.57
			90.34			6.58		14.52		7.37					8.72					22.93		25.32				15.11
Miramar (city)	19,631	19,713	17,548	-	-	1,400	-	1,753	-	5,524	1,276	-	-	-	400	555	264	-	591	2,717	-	3,267	-	-	-	2,863
	29.63		89.02			90.32		96.48		90.23	97.03				78.13	93.43	76.52		95.02	83.42		93.77				85.39
						7.98		9.99		31.48	7.27				2.28	3.16	1.50		3.37	15.48		18.62				16.32
			89.02			7.10		8.89		28.02	6.47				2.03	2.82	1.34		3.00	13.78		16.57				14.52
			89.39			7.13		8.93		28.14	6.50				2.04	2.83	1.34		3.01	13.84		16.64				14.58
Pembroke Pines (city)	35,320	35,369	31,076	-	-	1,704	-	3,083	-	10,368	1,608	457	-	-	610	-	-	-	1,265	5,539	-	6,811	-	-	1,283	4,220
	27.69		87.86			91.61		94.51		89.99	95.37	95.21			72.53				92.81	80.67		93.58			95.32	83.98
						5.48		9.92		33.36	5.17	1.47			1.96				4.07	17.82		21.92			4.13	13.58
			87.86			4.82		8.72		29.31	4.55	1.29			1.72				3.58	15.66		19.26			3.63	11.93
			87.98			4.82		8.73		29.35	4.55	1.29			1.73				3.58	15.68		19.28			3.63	11.95
Plantation (city)	10,085	10,096	8,191	-	-	468	-	1,874	-	1,565	-	-	-	-	347	-	-	-	443	967	-	3,390	-	-	451	1,135
	12.87		81.13			75.48		91.06		83.82					55.52				98.23	65.47		91.80			92.42	82.37
						5.71		22.88		19.11					4.24				5.41	11.81		41.39			5.51	13.86
			81.13			4.64		18.56		15.50					3.44				4.39	9.58		33.58			4.47	11.24
			81.22			4.64		18.58		15.52					3.44				4.39	9.59		33.61			4.47	11.25

Notes: Please refer to the User's Guide for an explanation of data; data is arranged alphabetically by state, then county, then city within each county and only includes counties with populations > 99,999 and cities with populations > 49,999; (1) Includes Costa Rican, Guatemalan, Honduran, Nicaraguan, Panamanian, Salvadoran, and other Central American; (2) Includes Argentinian, Bolivian, Chilean, Colombian, Ecuadorian, Paraguayan, Peruvian, Uruguayan, Venezuelan, and other South American

Place	Total population 5 years and over who speak Spanish at home	Hispanic population 5 years and over	Hispanics 5 years and over who speak Spanish at home	Argentinian	Bolivian	Central American[1]	Chilean	Colombian	Costa Rican	Cuban	Dominican	Ecuadorian	Guatemalan	Honduran	Mexican	Nicaraguan	Panamanian	Paraguayan	Peruvian	Puerto Rican	Salvadoran	South American[2]	Spaniard	Uruguayan	Venezuelan	Other Hisp.
Pompano Beach (city)	6,881 9.26	7,030	5,780 82.22 82.22 84.00	-	-	-	-	476 87.66 8.24 6.77 6.92	-	425 71.19 7.35 6.05 6.18	-	-	-	-	1,944 86.86 33.63 27.65 28.25	-	-	-	-	705 65.16 12.20 10.03 10.25	-	1,233 89.93 21.33 17.54 17.92	-	-	-	950 80.17 16.44 13.51 13.81
Sunrise (city)	13,346 16.65	13,427	11,528 85.86 85.86 86.38	-	-	612 92.87 5.31 4.56 4.59	-	2,233 96.62 19.37 16.63 16.73	-	1,546 82.28 13.41 11.51 11.58	632 93.91 5.48 4.71 4.74	475 94.25 4.12 3.54 3.56	-	-	519 69.29 4.50 3.87 3.89	-	-	-	518 91.84 4.49 3.86 3.88	2,065 76.48 17.91 15.38 15.47	-	4,076 94.24 35.36 30.36 30.54	-	-	-	2,019 85.59 17.51 15.04 15.13
Tamarac (city)	7,264 13.55	7,434	6,415 86.29 86.29 88.31	-	-	-	-	1,188 97.46 18.52 15.98 16.35	-	746 93.95 11.63 10.03 10.27	-	-	-	-	-	-	-	-	-	1,403 76.46 21.87 18.87 19.31	-	2,036 94.87 31.74 27.39 28.03	-	-	-	1,444 86.16 22.51 19.42 19.88
Charlotte County	4,011 2.94	4,272	2,821 66.03 66.03 70.33	-	-	-	-	-	-	339 59.58 12.02 7.94 8.45	-	-	-	-	534 61.38 18.93 12.50 13.31	-	-	-	-	918 69.44 32.54 21.49 22.89	-	-	-	-	-	499 60.78 17.69 11.68 12.44
Citrus County	3,185 2.80	2,845	1,924 67.63 67.63 60.41	-	-	-	-	-	-	-	-	-	-	-	220 50.93 11.43 7.73 6.91	-	-	-	-	919 76.39 47.77 32.30 28.85	-	-	-	-	-	332 53.72 17.26 11.67 10.42
Clay County	5,467 4.15	5,530	3,725 67.36 67.36 68.14	-	-	-	-	-	-	-	-	-	-	-	600 59.00 16.11 10.85 10.97	-	-	-	-	1,583 70.67 42.50 28.63 28.96	-	-	-	-	-	688 59.31 18.47 12.44 12.58
Collier County	42,158 17.71	44,418	38,977 87.75 87.75 92.45	-	-	2,834 91.54 7.27 6.38 6.72	-	1,037 95.14 2.66 2.33 2.46	-	6,001 88.80 15.40 13.51 14.23	428 86.12 1.10 0.96 1.02	-	1,188 84.50 3.05 2.67 2.82	662 96.22 1.70 1.49 1.57	22,256 88.75 57.10 50.11 52.79	-	-	-	-	2,276 78.56 5.84 5.12 5.40	-	1,919 91.95 4.92 4.32 4.55	-	-	-	3,165 82.21 8.12 7.13 7.51
Duval County	29,719 4.11	28,733	19,601 68.22 68.22 65.95	-	-	1,351 79.28 6.89 4.70 4.55	-	1,127 85.51 5.75 3.92 3.79	-	2,395 76.47 12.22 8.34 8.06	552 89.18 2.82 1.92 1.86	-	-	-	2,492 47.70 12.71 8.67 8.39	-	436 74.02 2.22 1.52 1.47	-	419 91.68 2.14 1.46 1.41	7,711 74.59 39.34 26.84 25.95	-	2,178 84.42 11.11 7.58 7.33	-	-	-	2,849 58.08 14.53 9.92 9.59
Jacksonville (city)	28,171 4.13	27,470	18,771 68.33 68.33 66.63	-	-	1,338 79.36 7.13 4.87 4.75	-	1,103 86.85 5.88 4.02 3.92	-	2,364 77.31 12.59 8.61 8.39	552 89.18 2.94 2.01 1.96	-	-	-	2,266 46.32 12.07 8.25 8.04	-	423 73.95 2.25 1.54 1.50	-	-	7,382 74.57 39.33 26.87 26.20	-	2,064 85.22 11.00 7.51 7.33	-	-	-	2,732 58.49 14.55 9.95 9.70
Escambia County	7,669 2.77	7,142	4,009 56.13 56.13 52.28	-	-	363 72.75 9.05 5.08 4.73	-	-	-	554 78.25 13.82 7.76 7.22	-	-	-	-	1,205 49.32 30.06 16.87 15.71	-	-	-	-	941 60.28 23.47 13.18 12.27	-	390 91.98 9.73 5.46 5.09	-	-	-	482 33.90 12.02 6.75 6.29

Notes: Please refer to the User's Guide for an explanation of data; data is arranged alphabetically by state, then county, then city within each county and only includes counties with populations > 99,999 and cities with populations > 49,999; (1) Includes Costa Rican, Guatemalan, Honduran, Nicaraguan, Panamanian, Salvadoran, and other Central American; (2) Includes Argentinian, Bolivian, Chilean, Colombian, Ecuadorian, Paraguayan, Peruvian, Uruguayan, Venezuelan, and other South American

Place	Total population 5 years and over who speak Spanish at home	Hispanic population 5 years and over	Hispanics 5 years and over who speak Spanish at home	Argentinian	Bolivian	Central American[1]	Chilean	Colombian	Costa Rican	Cuban	Dominican	Ecuadorian	Guatemalan	Honduran	Mexican	Nicaraguan	Panamanian	Paraguayan	Peruvian	Puerto Rican	Salvadoran	South American[2]	Spaniard	Uruguayan	Venezuelan	Other Hisp.
Pensacola (city)	1,272 2.40	1,046	599 57.27 57.27 47.09	-	-	-	-	-	-	-	-	-	-	-	-	-	-	-	-	-	-	-	-	-	-	-
Hernando County	5,624 4.50	6,223	4,248 68.26 68.26 75.53	-	-	-	-	-	-	406 73.02 9.56 6.52 7.22	-	-	-	-	489 56.14 11.51 7.86 8.69	-	-	-	-	2,579 72.24 60.71 41.44 45.86	-	-	-	-	-	437 56.90 10.29 7.02 7.77
Spring Hill (cdp)	3,912 5.92	4,625	3,172 68.58 68.58 81.08	-	-	-	-	-	-	272 73.91 8.58 5.88 6.95	-	-	-	-	-	-	-	-	-	2,122 72.87 66.90 45.88 54.24	-	-	-	-	-	342 59.38 10.78 7.39 8.74
Hillsborough County	149,070 16.01	163,887	132,102 80.61 80.61 88.62	-	-	6,261 84.22 4.74 3.82 4.20	-	5,345 94.30 4.05 3.26 3.59	814 89.35 0.62 0.50 0.55	27,127 82.89 20.53 16.55 18.20	3,448 94.16 2.61 2.10 2.31	1,134 92.35 0.86 0.69 0.76	956 94.65 0.72 0.58 0.64	1,737 84.61 1.31 1.06 1.17	26,830 84.43 20.31 16.37 18.00	799 81.36 0.60 0.49 0.54	1,221 78.98 0.92 0.75 0.82	-	1,570 92.30 1.19 0.96 1.05	38,123 82.90 28.86 23.26 25.57	574 82.12 0.43 0.35 0.39	10,707 92.25 8.11 6.53 7.18	954 55.69 0.72 0.58 0.64	-	1,544 92.51 1.17 0.94 1.04	18,652 64.36 14.12 11.38 12.51
Brandon (cdp)	7,919 10.96	9,253	6,931 74.91 74.91 87.52	-	-	364 74.59 5.25 3.93 4.60	-	-	-	685 67.29 9.88 7.40 8.65	-	-	-	-	624 69.88 9.00 6.74 7.88	-	-	-	-	3,640 80.30 52.52 39.34 45.97	-	496 88.89 7.16 5.36 6.26	-	-	-	828 58.52 11.95 8.95 10.46
Tampa (city)	50,106 17.70	54,047	43,611 80.69 80.69 87.04	-	-	2,396 78.97 5.49 4.43 4.78	-	1,473 92.12 3.38 2.73 2.94	-	11,550 85.10 26.48 21.37 23.05	1,223 96.07 2.80 2.26 2.44	337 87.76 0.77 0.62 0.67	-	639 79.18 1.47 1.18 1.28	5,120 80.10 11.74 9.47 10.22	335 73.79 0.77 0.62 0.67	439 72.09 1.01 0.81 0.88	-	-	12,075 83.96 27.69 22.34 24.10	-	3,054 91.27 7.00 5.65 6.10	506 72.29 1.16 0.94 1.01	-	471 84.41 1.08 0.87 0.94	7,687 67.74 17.63 14.22 15.34
Town 'n' Country (cdp)	17,988 26.51	19,035	16,309 85.68 85.68 90.67	-	-	754 94.01 4.62 3.96 4.19	-	1,117 96.88 6.85 5.87 6.21	-	3,977 88.46 24.39 20.89 22.11	678 94.43 4.16 3.56 3.77	-	-	-	796 82.23 4.88 4.18 4.43	-	-	-	-	5,835 85.18 35.78 30.65 32.44	-	1,903 95.63 11.67 10.00 10.58	-	-	-	2,207 73.01 13.53 11.59 12.27
Indian River County	6,925 6.43	6,551	5,469 83.48 83.48 78.97	-	-	297 88.92 5.43 4.53 4.29	-	-	-	272 80.00 4.97 4.15 3.93	-	-	-	-	3,510 89.82 64.18 53.58 50.69	-	-	-	-	440 68.22 8.05 6.72 6.35	-	438 85.05 8.01 6.69 6.32	-	-	-	498 63.28 9.11 7.60 7.19
Lake County	11,262 5.64	10,610	8,491 80.03 80.03 75.40	-	-	387 83.59 4.56 3.65 3.44	-	-	-	492 68.24 5.79 4.64 4.37	-	-	-	-	4,131 86.90 48.65 38.93 36.68	-	-	-	-	2,070 78.62 24.38 19.51 18.38	-	476 87.18 5.61 4.49 4.23	-	-	-	829 60.16 9.76 7.81 7.36
Lee County	36,086 8.64	37,471	30,791 82.17 82.17 85.33	-	-	2,273 83.20 7.38 6.07 6.30	-	858 88.00 2.79 2.29 2.38	-	2,461 78.03 7.99 6.57 6.82	931 93.47 3.02 2.48 2.58	-	1,059 87.38 3.44 2.83 2.93	399 86.74 1.30 1.06 1.11	11,472 87.18 37.26 30.62 31.79	-	-	-	-	8,441 79.35 27.41 22.53 23.39	-	1,971 85.66 6.40 5.26 5.46	-	-	-	3,196 72.39 10.38 8.53 8.86

Notes: Please refer to the User's Guide for an explanation of data; data is arranged alphabetically by state, then county, then city within each county and only includes counties with populations > 99,999 and cities with populations > 49,999; (1) Includes Costa Rican, Guatemalan, Honduran, Nicaraguan, Panamanian, Salvadoran, and other Central American; (2) Includes Argentinian, Bolivian, Chilean, Colombian, Ecuadorian, Paraguayan, Peruvian, Uruguayan, Venezuelan, and other South American

Place	Total population 5 years and over who speak Spanish at home	Hispanic population 5 years and over	Hispanics 5 years and over who speak Spanish at home	Argentinian	Bolivian	Central American[1]	Chilean	Colombian	Costa Rican	Cuban	Dominican	Ecuadorian	Guatelmalan	Honduran	Mexican	Nicaraguan	Panamanian	Paraguayan	Peruvian	Puerto Rican	Salvadoran	South American[2]	Spaniard	Uruguayan	Venezuelan	Other Hisp.
Cape Coral (city)	7,295	7,677	5,862	-	-	-	-	480	-	1,152	510	-	-	-	828	-	-	-	-	1,385	-	914	-	-	-	833
	7.56		76.36					88.89		77.52	94.97				69.12					69.49		89.96				75.18
								8.19		19.65	8.70				14.12					23.63		15.59				14.21
			76.36					6.25		15.01	6.64				10.79					18.04		11.91				10.85
			80.36					6.58		15.79	6.99				11.35					18.99		12.53				11.42
Leon County	8,248	7,821	4,691	-	-	-	-	-	-	1,412	-	-	-	-	718	-	-	-	-	855	-	598	-	-	-	690
	3.65		59.98							75.87					53.74					56.36		60.59				46.65
										30.10					15.31					18.23		12.75				14.71
			59.98							18.05					9.18					10.93		7.65				8.82
			56.87							17.12					8.71					10.37		7.25				8.37
Tallahassee (city)	5,838	5,819	3,476	-	-	-	-	-	-	1,058	-	-	-	-	478	-	-	-	-	649	-	438	-	-	-	532
	4.09		59.74							74.40					55.26					57.59		56.96				47.71
										30.44					13.75					18.67		12.60				15.30
			59.74							18.18					8.21					11.15		7.53				9.14
			59.54							18.12					8.19					11.12		7.50				9.11
Manatee County	19,924	21,417	16,925	-	-	1,125	-	-	-	763	-	-	-	-	10,609	-	-	-	-	2,036	-	813	-	-	-	1,440
	8.00		79.03			83.58				68.74					82.62					69.99		94.43				66.79
						6.65				4.51					62.68					12.03		4.80				8.51
			79.03			5.25				3.56					49.54					9.51		3.80				6.72
			84.95			5.65				3.83					53.25					10.22		4.08				7.23
Marion County	13,815	14,165	10,841	-	-	432	-	458	-	722	-	-	-	-	2,191	-	-	-	-	5,191	-	830	-	-	-	1,241
	5.62		76.53			85.38		84.19		64.01					74.75					81.26		79.65				66.12
						3.98		4.22		6.66					20.21					47.88		7.66				11.45
			76.53			3.05		3.23		5.10					15.47					36.65		5.86				8.76
			78.47			3.13		3.32		5.23					15.86					37.58		6.01				8.98
Martin County	8,139	8,447	6,548	-	-	1,322	-	-	-	551	-	-	1,090	-	2,944	-	-	-	-	1,106	-	-	-	-	-	358
	6.71		77.52			63.50				72.60			61.90		88.09					82.85						56.47
						20.19				8.41			16.65		44.96					16.89						5.47
			77.52			15.65				6.52			12.90		34.85					13.09						4.24
			80.45			16.24				6.77			13.39		36.17					13.59						4.40
Miami-Dade County	1,248,616	1,221,202	1,146,845	12,970	2,026	126,027	7,153	68,725	4,241	596,678	36,222	10,553	9,601	26,188	30,172	69,055	6,098	-	21,839	67,296	8,548	148,421	5,406	1,894	20,564	136,623
	59.22		93.91	95.24	91.51	95.36	93.75	95.89	94.90	94.52	95.51	95.00	95.94	95.25	89.78	95.65	93.44		96.12	89.77	95.30	95.59	90.74	96.98	95.53	91.07
				1.13	0.18	10.99	0.62	5.99	0.37	52.03	3.16	0.92	0.84	2.28	2.63	6.02	0.53		1.90	5.87	0.75	12.94	0.47	0.17	1.79	11.91
			93.91	1.06	0.17	10.32	0.59	5.63	0.35	48.86	2.97	0.86	0.79	2.14	2.47	5.65	0.50		1.79	5.51	0.70	12.15	0.44	0.16	1.68	11.19
			91.85	1.04	0.16	10.09	0.57	5.50	0.34	47.79	2.90	0.85	0.77	2.10	2.42	5.53	0.49		1.75	5.39	0.68	11.89	0.43	0.15	1.65	10.94
Carol City (cdp)	23,720	23,504	21,927	-	-	2,394	-	1,378	-	10,091	1,677	-	-	462	-	1,285	-	-	-	2,283	-	2,381	-	-	-	2,774
	42.92		93.29			94.55		96.91		94.31	94.05			91.67		93.59				87.71		97.54				90.71
						10.92		6.28		46.02	7.65			2.11		5.86				10.41		10.86				12.65
			93.29			10.19		5.86		42.93	7.13			1.97		5.47				9.71		10.13				11.80
			92.44			10.09		5.81		42.54	7.07			1.95		5.42				9.62		10.04				11.69
Fountainbleau (cdp)	50,247	49,241	47,278	402	-	7,389	626	2,544	-	20,915	1,821	746	-	610	376	5,503	475	-	1,109	1,647	-	7,745	-	-	1,970	7,249
	90.14		96.01	93.27		94.09	98.12	95.25		96.26	99.24	96.88		97.60	96.41	93.29	92.95		98.05	95.59		96.95			98.85	95.53
				0.85		15.63	1.32	5.38		44.24	3.85	1.58		1.29	0.80	11.64	1.00		2.35	3.48		16.38			4.17	15.33
			96.01	0.82		15.01	1.27	5.17		42.47	3.70	1.51		1.24	0.76	11.18	0.96		2.25	3.34		15.73			4.00	14.72
			94.09	0.80		14.71	1.25	5.06		41.62	3.62	1.48		1.21	0.75	10.95	0.95		2.21	3.28		15.41			3.92	14.43
Hialeah (city)	195,884	194,772	185,933	389	-	14,810	683	7,273	515	129,600	4,582	1,167	819	2,474	1,396	9,424	-	-	1,386	6,105	881	12,158	465	-	908	16,817
	91.88		95.46	100.00		96.99	91.07	97.17	100.00	95.37	97.68	97.25	100.00	97.36	94.39	96.76			100.00	93.95	98.99	97.25	94.90		97.63	93.71
				0.21		7.97	0.37	3.91	0.28	69.70	2.46	0.63	0.44	1.33	0.75	5.07			0.75	3.28	0.47	6.54	0.25		0.49	9.04
			95.46	0.20		7.60	0.35	3.73	0.26	66.54	2.35	0.60	0.42	1.27	0.72	4.84			0.71	3.13	0.45	6.24	0.24		0.47	8.63
			94.92	0.20		7.56	0.35	3.71	0.26	66.16	2.34	0.60	0.42	1.26	0.71	4.81			0.71	3.12	0.45	6.21	0.24		0.46	8.59

Notes: Please refer to the User's Guide for an explanation of data; data is arranged alphabetically by state, then county, then city within each county and only includes counties with populations > 99,999 and cities with populations > 49,999; (1) Includes Costa Rican, Guatemalan, Honduran, Nicaraguan, Panamanian, Salvadoran, and other Central American; (2) Includes Argentinian, Bolivian, Chilean, Colombian, Ecuadorian, Paraguayan, Peruvian, Uruguayan, Venezuelan, and other South American

Place	Total population 5 years and over who speak Spanish at home	Hispanic population 5 years and over	Hispanics 5 years and over who speak Spanish at home	Argentinian	Bolivian	Central American[1]	Chilean	Colombian	Costa Rican	Cuban	Dominican	Ecuadorian	Guatelmalan	Honduran	Mexican	Nicaraguan	Panamanian	Paraguayan	Peruvian	Puerto Rican	Salvadoran	South American[2]	Spaniard	Uruguayan	Venezuelan	Other Hisp.
Kendale Lakes (cdp)	43,425	41,279	39,673	-	-	3,776	-	3,743	-	20,107	831	-	-	498	468	2,619	-	-	862	1,524	-	6,876	-	-	828	5,941
	81.46		96.11			97.34		98.34		95.78	98.58			98.42	85.71	96.50			92.49	95.49		97.37			96.62	95.81
						9.52		9.43		50.68	2.09			1.26	1.18	6.60			2.17	3.84		17.33			2.09	14.97
			96.11			9.15		9.07		48.71	2.01			1.21	1.13	6.34			2.09	3.69		16.66			2.01	14.39
			91.36			8.70		8.62		46.30	1.91			1.15	1.08	6.03			1.99	3.51		15.83			1.91	13.68
Kendall (cdp)	36,760	35,482	32,456	587	-	3,425	424	3,795	-	13,857	730	-	-	-	-	2,020	-	-	1,180	1,831	-	7,847	-	-	1,287	4,136
	51.88		91.47	93.03		92.34	90.60	96.39		92.04	95.80					95.19			94.25	85.80		94.84			93.67	86.20
				1.81		10.55	1.31	11.69		42.69	2.25					6.22			3.64	5.64		24.18			3.97	12.74
			91.47	1.65		9.65	1.19	10.70		39.05	2.06					5.69			3.33	5.16		22.12			3.63	11.66
			88.29	1.60		9.32	1.15	10.32		37.70	1.99					5.50			3.21	4.98		21.35			3.50	11.25
Miami Beach (city)	46,174	45,437	41,617	2,783	-	2,546	618	4,050	-	16,439	1,317	599	-	740	838	854	-	-	1,754	2,986	-	11,781	526	-	1,344	5,184
	54.40		91.59	95.15		92.28	85.60	93.02		91.93	96.70	92.87		95.73	89.34	86.70			96.32	86.40		93.79	93.59		95.39	87.61
				6.69		6.12	1.48	9.73		39.50	3.16	1.44		1.78	2.01	2.05			4.21	7.17		28.31	1.26		3.23	12.46
			91.59	6.12		5.60	1.36	8.91		36.18	2.90	1.32		1.63	1.84	1.88			3.86	6.57		25.93	1.16		2.96	11.41
			90.13	6.03		5.51	1.34	8.77		35.60	2.85	1.30		1.60	1.81	1.85			3.80	6.47		25.51	1.14		2.91	11.23
Miami (city)	227,293	227,443	213,295	1,810	-	39,899	843	5,496	728	114,426	6,386	1,558	2,534	12,285	2,634	20,705	848	-	2,506	8,662	2,155	14,456	888	-	1,549	25,944
	66.61		93.78	94.96		95.63	95.90	95.27	91.57	94.10	92.90	92.08	94.76	95.03	88.01	96.36	98.83		94.78	90.58	94.60	94.43	95.48		91.82	91.17
				0.85		18.71	0.40	2.58	0.34	53.65	2.99	0.73	1.19	5.76	1.23	9.71	0.40		1.17	4.06	1.01	6.78	0.42		0.73	12.16
			93.78	0.80		17.54	0.37	2.42	0.32	50.31	2.81	0.69	1.11	5.40	1.16	9.10	0.37		1.10	3.81	0.95	6.36	0.39		0.68	11.41
			93.84	0.80		17.55	0.37	2.42	0.32	50.34	2.81	0.69	1.11	5.40	1.16	9.11	0.37		1.10	3.81	0.95	6.36	0.39		0.68	11.41
North Miami (city)	13,501	13,316	12,002	-	-	1,551	-	925	-	2,445	931	-	-	513	-	612	-	-	-	2,313	-	1,923	-	-	-	2,508
	24.47		90.13			92.38		93.62		92.19	94.23			89.37		90.13				90.85		95.15				84.59
						12.92		7.71		20.37	7.76			4.27		5.10				19.27		16.02				20.90
			90.13			11.65		6.95		18.36	6.99			3.85		4.60				17.37		14.44				18.83
			88.90			11.49		6.85		18.11	6.90			3.80		4.53				17.13		14.24				18.58
Tamiami (cdp)	47,435	45,478	43,701	-	-	3,520	-	1,947	-	30,022	632	-	-	430	429	2,514	-	-	-	1,039	-	3,684	-	-	533	4,196
	91.91		96.09			97.05		98.28		96.26	96.05			100.00	85.46	97.40				98.39		96.31			100.00	94.44
						8.05		4.46		68.70	1.45			0.98	0.98	5.75				2.38		8.43			1.22	9.60
			96.09			7.74		4.28		66.01	1.39			0.95	0.94	5.53				2.28		8.10			1.17	9.23
			92.13			7.42		4.10		63.29	1.33			0.91	0.90	5.30				2.19		7.77			1.12	8.85
Okaloosa County	5,577	6,296	3,388	-	-	247	-	-	-	420	-	-	-	-	957	-	-	-	-	828	-	-	-	-	-	565
	3.49		53.81			81.79				76.09					44.18					61.52						39.46
						7.29				12.40					28.25					24.44						16.68
			53.81			3.92				6.67					15.20					13.15						8.97
			60.75			4.43				7.53					17.16					14.85						10.13
Orange County	144,579	153,771	131,435	608	-	4,771	419	6,874	454	10,130	5,512	1,506	852	1,040	13,891	788	778	-	1,505	69,483	735	13,720	381	-	2,230	13,547
	17.31		85.47	87.73		86.46	91.89	95.02	78.96	81.81	92.44	90.29	86.32	88.89	78.89	91.42	85.59		89.85	87.54	82.49	91.87	61.55		91.51	77.97
				0.46		3.63	0.32	5.23	0.35	7.71	4.19	1.15	0.65	0.79	10.57	0.60	0.59		1.15	52.86	0.56	10.44	0.29		1.70	10.31
			85.47	0.40		3.10	0.27	4.47	0.30	6.59	3.58	0.98	0.55	0.68	9.03	0.51	0.51		0.98	45.19	0.48	8.92	0.25		1.45	8.81
			90.91	0.42		3.30	0.29	4.75	0.31	7.01	3.81	1.04	0.59	0.72	9.61	0.55	0.54		1.04	48.06	0.51	9.49	0.26		1.54	9.37
Orlando (city)	28,710	30,074	25,783	-	-	1,150	-	1,621	-	2,265	1,036	-	-	-	1,574	-	-	-	386	13,487	-	3,521	-	-	676	2,683
	16.52		85.73			87.65		94.63		81.95	89.46				74.53				89.77	87.77		93.17			92.35	77.05
						4.46		6.29		8.78	4.02				6.10				1.50	52.31		13.66			2.62	10.41
			85.73			3.82		5.39		7.53	3.44				5.23				1.28	44.85		11.71			2.25	8.92
			89.80			4.01		5.65		7.89	3.61				5.48				1.34	46.98		12.26			2.35	9.35
Osceola County	43,861	46,598	41,159	-	-	1,657	-	1,807	-	1,560	2,265	444	-	-	2,458	-	-	-	-	26,630	507	3,326	-	-	457	3,135
	27.24		88.33			90.35		95.71		88.29	96.30	100.00			79.75					88.76	94.06	95.41			93.27	80.08
						4.03		4.39		3.79	5.50	1.08			5.97					64.70	1.23	8.08			1.11	7.62
			88.33			3.56		3.88		3.35	4.86	0.95			5.27					57.15	1.09	7.14			0.98	6.73
			93.84			3.78		4.12		3.56	5.16	1.01			5.60					60.71	1.16	7.58			1.04	7.15

Notes: Please refer to the User's Guide for an explanation of data; data is arranged alphabetically by state, then county, then city within each county and only includes counties with populations > 99,999 and cities with populations > 49,999; (1) Includes Costa Rican, Guatemalan, Honduran, Nicaraguan, Panamanian, Salvadoran, and other Central American; (2) Includes Argentinian, Bolivian, Chilean, Colombian, Ecuadorian, Paraguayan, Peruvian, Uruguayan, Venezuelan, and other South American

Place	Total population 5 years and over who speak Spanish at home	Hispanic population 5 years and over	Hispanics 5 years and over who speak Spanish at home	Argentinian	Bolivian	Central American[1]	Chilean	Colombian	Costa Rican	Cuban	Dominican	Ecuadorian	Guatelmalan	Honduran	Mexican	Nicaraguan	Panamanian	Paraguayan	Peruvian	Puerto Rican	Salvadoran	South American[2]	Spaniard	Uruguayan	Venezuelan	Other Hisp.
	127,084	128,500	109,921	1,608	-	12,690	623	8,275	757	21,584	3,094	1,729	5,441	2,649	22,759	1,833	303	-	2,217	17,879	1,453	17,742	303	744	1,539	13,870
	11.89		85.54	91.10		89.77	94.11	93.19	96.07	87.29	92.69	92.46	87.34	92.20	86.59	91.93	71.46		92.99	78.13	94.66	93.13	65.44	97.51	91.07	78.73
Palm Beach County				1.46		11.54	0.57	7.53	0.69	19.64	2.81	1.57	4.95	2.41	20.70	1.67	0.28		2.02	16.27	1.32	16.14	0.28	0.68	1.40	12.62
			85.54	1.25		9.88	0.48	6.44	0.59	16.80	2.41	1.35	4.23	2.06	17.71	1.43	0.24		1.73	13.91	1.13	13.81	0.24	0.58	1.20	10.79
			86.49	1.27		9.99	0.49	6.51	0.60	16.98	2.43	1.36	4.28	2.08	17.91	1.44	0.24		1.74	14.07	1.14	13.96	0.24	0.59	1.21	10.91
	6,646	6,020	5,028	-	-	-	-	780	-	713	-	-	-	-	657	-	-	-	-	470	-	1,898	-	-	-	899
	9.21		83.52					96.18		82.14					84.56					60.57		95.91				76.58
Boca Raton (city)								15.51		14.18					13.07					9.35		37.75				17.88
			83.52					12.96		11.84					10.91					7.81		31.53				14.93
			75.65					11.74		10.73					9.89					7.07		28.56				13.53
	4,072	4,424	3,506	-	-	462	-	-	-	391	-	-	-	-	508	-	-	-	-	969	-	662	-	-	-	446
	7.21		79.25			87.33				79.63					70.65					73.58		95.94				78.38
Boynton Beach (city)						13.18				11.15					14.49					27.64		18.88				12.72
			79.25			10.44				8.84					11.48					21.90		14.96				10.08
			86.10			11.35				9.60					12.48					23.80		16.26				10.95
	3,954	3,817	3,152	-	-	-	-	-	-	-	-	-	-	-	1,098	-	-	-	-	518	-	508	-	-	-	306
	6.92		82.58												86.32					76.51		87.44				70.02
Delray Beach (city)															34.84					16.43		16.12				9.71
			82.58												28.77					13.57		13.31				8.02
			79.72												27.77					13.10		12.85				7.74
	13,476	13,900	12,303	-	-	2,209	-	623	-	3,938	342	-	1,548	-	1,555	-	-	-	-	1,493	-	1,359	-	-	-	1,383
	17.52		88.51			85.19		93.40		92.94	91.44		80.71		89.73					86.55		89.94				81.45
West Palm Beach (city)						17.95		5.06		32.01	2.78		12.58		12.64					12.14		11.05				11.24
			88.51			15.89		4.48		28.33	2.46		11.14		11.19					10.74		9.78				9.95
			91.30			16.39		4.62		29.22	2.54		11.49		11.54					11.08		10.08				10.26
	15,411	17,792	12,179	-	-	392	-	-	-	1,078	-	-	-	-	4,295	-	-	-	-	4,442	-	722	-	-	-	1,034
	4.71		68.45			74.95				63.45					80.82					68.98		87.94				39.94
Pasco County						3.22				8.85					35.27					36.47		5.93				8.49
			68.45			2.20				6.06					24.14					24.97		4.06				5.81
			79.03			2.54				7.00					27.87					28.82		4.68				6.71
	39,287	38,440	27,353	-	-	1,013	-	1,455	-	3,521	675	356	-	-	6,375	-	-	-	582	8,312	-	3,777	293	-	760	3,387
	4.48		71.16			76.98		82.34		77.52	82.82	88.34			68.99				76.98	70.77		83.18	56.89		92.35	59.15
Pinellas County						3.70		5.32		12.87	2.47	1.30			23.31				2.13	30.39		13.81	1.07		2.78	12.38
			71.16			2.64		3.79		9.16	1.76	0.93			16.58				1.51	21.62		9.83	0.76		1.98	8.81
			69.62			2.58		3.70		8.96	1.72	0.91			16.23				1.48	21.16		9.61	0.75		1.93	8.62
	8,674	8,713	7,101	-	-	-	-	333	-	430	-	-	-	-	3,117	-	-	-	-	1,654	-	902	-	-	-	619
	8.47		81.50					94.33		76.79					83.81					79.37		92.61				64.88
Clearwater (city)								4.69		6.06					43.90					23.29		12.70				8.72
			81.50					3.82		4.94					35.77					18.98		10.35				7.10
			81.87					3.84		4.96					35.93					19.07		10.40				7.14
	2,636	2,628	1,770	-	-	-	-	-	-	-	-	-	-	-	223	-	-	-	-	471	-	-	-	-	-	-
	3.97		67.35												46.07					64.26						
Largo (city)															12.60					26.61						
			67.35												8.49					17.92						
			67.15												8.46					17.87						
	1,903	1,749	1,138	-	-	-	-	-	-	-	-	-	-	-	-	-	-	-	-	537	-	-	-	-	-	-
	3.37		65.07																	74.48						
Palm Harbor (cdp)																				47.19						
			65.07																	30.70						
			59.80																	28.22						

Notes: Please refer to the User's Guide for an explanation of data; data is arranged alphabetically by state, then county, then city within each county and only includes counties with populations > 99,999 and cities with populations > 49,999; (1) Includes Costa Rican, Guatemalan, Honduran, Nicaraguan, Panamanian, Salvadoran, and other Central American; (2) Includes Argentinian, Bolivian, Chilean, Colombian, Ecuadorian, Paraguayan, Peruvian, Uruguayan, Venezuelan, and other South American

Place	Total population 5 years and over who speak Spanish at home	Hispanic population 5 years and over	Hispanics 5 years and over who speak Spanish at home	Argentinian	Bolivian	Central American[1]	Chilean	Colombian	Costa Rican	Cuban	Dominican	Ecuadorian	Guatemalan	Honduran	Mexican	Nicaraguan	Panamanian	Paraguayan	Peruvian	Puerto Rican	Salvadoran	South American[2]	Spaniard	Uruguayan	Venezuelan	Other Hisp.
St. Petersburg (city)	10,331	9,153	6,342	-	-	-	-	-	-	1,316	-	-	-	-	791	-	-	-	-	2,065	-	1,000	-	-	-	706
	4.42		69.29							83.34					50.29					71.13		88.18				53.69
										20.75					12.47					32.56		15.77				11.13
			69.29							14.38					8.64					22.56		10.93				7.71
			61.39							12.74					7.66					19.99		9.68				6.83
Polk County	40,178	40,881	34,199	-	-	1,053	-	-	-	1,822	389	-	-	-	19,035	-	-	-	-	8,398	-	798	-	-	-	2,613
	8.87		83.65			90.85				77.11	84.93				88.72					81.54		84.98				64.95
						3.08				5.33	1.14				55.66					24.56		2.33				7.64
			83.65			2.58				4.46	0.95				46.56					20.54		1.95				6.39
			85.12			2.62				4.53	0.97				47.38					20.90		1.99				6.50
Lakeland (city)	4,673	4,550	3,658	-	-	-	-	-	-	530	-	-	-	-	615	-	-	-	-	1,550	-	-	-	-	-	458
	6.37		80.40							85.35					80.39					83.60						66.76
										14.49					16.81					42.37						12.52
			80.40							11.65					13.52					34.07						10.07
			78.28							11.34					13.16					33.17						9.80
St. Johns County	3,572	3,349	1,772	-	-	-	-	-	-	-	-	-	-	-	323	-	-	-	-	523	-	-	-	-	-	264
	3.06		52.91												36.33					65.62						44.30
															18.23					29.51						14.90
			52.91												9.64					15.62						7.88
			49.61												9.04					14.64						7.39
St. Lucie County	13,807	14,555	11,660	-	-	900	-	351	-	799	-	-	-	-	5,557	-	-	-	-	2,443	-	829	-	-	-	791
	7.59		80.11			90.45		94.35		79.42					86.37					70.77		89.14				61.41
						7.72		3.01		6.85					47.66					20.95		7.11				6.78
			80.11			6.18		2.41		5.49					38.18					16.78		5.70				5.43
			84.45			6.52		2.54		5.79					40.25					17.69		6.00				5.73
Port St. Lucie (city)	5,470	6,329	4,598	-	-	-	-	-	-	544	-	-	-	-	582	-	-	-	-	1,771	-	587	-	-	-	499
	6.55		72.65							77.49					59.15					70.84		89.62				69.02
										11.83					12.66					38.52		12.77				10.85
			72.65							8.60					9.20					27.98		9.27				7.88
			84.06							9.95					10.64					32.38		10.73				9.12
Santa Rosa County	2,704	2,541	1,249	-	-	-	-	-	-	-	-	-	-	-	287	-	-	-	-	345	-	-	-	-	-	185
	2.46		49.15												38.68					50.29						39.61
															22.98					27.62						14.81
			49.15												11.29					13.58						7.28
			46.19												10.61					12.76						6.84
Sarasota County	13,751	13,114	10,197	-	-	512	-	716	-	1,558	-	-	-	-	4,591	-	-	-	-	968	-	1,538	-	-	-	827
	4.39		77.76			84.63		89.61		84.54					87.15					60.80		87.19				47.72
						5.02		7.02		15.28					45.02					9.49		15.08				8.11
			77.76			3.90		5.46		11.88					35.01					7.38		11.73				6.31
			74.15			3.72		5.21		11.33					33.39					7.04		11.18				6.01
Sarasota (city)	5,957	5,753	5,142	-	-	-	-	-	-	516	-	-	-	-	3,005	-	-	-	-	296	-	621	-	-	-	331
	11.94		89.38							83.90					95.46					74.00		98.42				58.38
										10.04					58.44					5.76		12.08				6.44
			89.38							8.97					52.23					5.15		10.79				5.75
			86.32							8.66					50.44					4.97		10.42				5.56
Seminole County	35,438	37,260	29,791	351	-	1,527	-	1,994	-	2,497	921	443	-	-	2,024	-	338	-	447	15,013	-	3,957	-	-	415	3,726
	10.36		79.95	83.57		79.12		93.35		71.20	86.24	98.23			66.93		66.54		87.99	82.47		91.96			95.62	74.09
				1.18		5.13		6.69		8.38	3.09	1.49			6.79		1.13		1.50	50.39		13.28			1.39	12.51
			79.95	0.94		4.10		5.35		6.70	2.47	1.19			5.43		0.91		1.20	40.29		10.62			1.11	10.00
			84.07	0.99		4.31		5.63		7.05	2.60	1.25			5.71		0.95		1.26	42.36		11.17			1.17	10.51

Notes: Please refer to the User's Guide for an explanation of data; data is arranged alphabetically by state, then county, then city within each county and only includes counties with populations > 99,999 and cities with populations > 49,999; (1) Includes Costa Rican, Guatemalan, Honduran, Nicaraguan, Panamanian, Salvadoran, and other Central American; (2) Includes Argentinian, Bolivian, Chilean, Colombian, Ecuadorian, Paraguayan, Peruvian, Uruguayan, Venezuelan, and other South American

Place	Total population 5 years and over who speak Spanish at home	Hispanic population 5 years and over	Hispanics 5 years and over who speak Spanish at home	Argentinian	Bolivian	Central American[1]	Chilean	Colombian	Costa Rican	Cuban	Dominican	Ecuadorian	Guatemalan	Honduran	Mexican	Nicaraguan	Panamanian	Paraguayan	Peruvian	Puerto Rican	Salvadoran	South American[2]	Spaniard	Uruguayan	Venezuelan	Other Hisp.
Volusia County	26,190	26,511	20,648	-	-	554	-	535	-	896	463	-	-	-	5,641	-	-	-	-	10,351	-	1,208	-	-	-	1,472
	6.21		77.88			79.26		84.12		68.45	84.49				79.75					80.70		80.48				60.78
						2.68		2.59		4.34	2.24				27.32					50.13		5.85				7.13
			77.88			2.09		2.02		3.38	1.75				21.28					39.04		4.56				5.55
			78.84			2.12		2.04		3.42	1.77				21.54					39.52		4.61				5.62
Daytona Beach (city)	2,409	2,046	1,468	-	-	-	-	-	-	-	-	-	-	-	-	-	-	-	-	619	-	-	-	-	-	278
	3.95		71.75																	79.16						73.74
																				42.17						18.94
			71.75																	30.25						13.59
			60.94																	25.70						11.54
Deltona (city)	10,259	11,881	9,548	-	-	-	-	-	-	461	-	-	-	-	344	-	-	-	-	7,308	-	463	-	-	-	566
	15.68		80.36							85.53					60.56					82.77		78.08				65.74
										4.83					3.60					76.54		4.85				5.93
			80.36							3.88					2.90					61.51		3.90				4.76
			93.07							4.49					3.35					71.24		4.51				5.52

Notes: Please refer to the User's Guide for an explanation of data: data is arranged alphabetically by state, then county, then city within each county and only includes counties with populations > 99,999 and cities with populations > 49,999; (1) Includes Costa Rican, Guatemalan, Honduran, Nicaraguan, Panamanian, Salvadoran, and other Central American; (2) Includes Argentinian, Bolivian, Chilean, Colombian, Ecuadorian, Paraguayan, Peruvan, Uruguayan, Venezuelan, and other South American

Foreign Born

(Universe: Total Population)

Place	Total foreign-born population	Total Hispanic population	Hispanics who are foreign born	Argentinian	Bolivian	Central American[1]	Chilean	Colombian	Costa Rican	Cuban	Dominican	Ecuadorian	Guatelmalan	Honduran	Mexican	Nicaraguan	Panamanian	Paraguayan	Peruvian	Puerto Rican	Salvadoran	South American[2]	Spaniard	Uruguayan	Venezuelan	Other Hisp.
UNITED STATES	31,107,889	35,238,481	14,157,817	82,281	34.263	1,372,428	55.410	378.260	50,920	855,907	545.262	207,701	317,531	186.511	8,677,303	150,502	61,179	6,979	193,139	47,128	536,162	1,087,398	45,421	16,191	76,981	1,526,970
	11.05		40.18	76.70	75.82	75.75	74.93	76.15	70.55	68.48	68.18	76.08	77.99	78.55	41.52	77.38	62.13	78.16	78.00	1.38	75.65	76.58	40.20	79.99	80.11	27.56
				0.58	0.24	9.69	0.39	2.67	0.36	6.05	3.85	1.47	2.24	1.32	61.29	1.06	0.43	0.05	1.36	0.33	3.79	7.68	0.32	0.11	0.54	10.79
			40.18	0.23	0.10	3.89	0.16	1.07	0.14	2.43	1.55	0.59	0.90	0.53	24.62	0.43	0.17	0.02	0.55	0.13	1.52	3.09	0.13	0.05	0.22	4.33
			45.51	0.26	0.11	4.41	0.18	1.22	0.16	2.75	1.75	0.67	1.02	0.60	27.89	0.48	0.20	0.02	0.62	0.15	1.72	3.50	0.15	0.05	0.25	4.91
FLORIDA	2,670,828	2,680,314	1,484,673	20,097	3,594	176,811	11,077	117,518	9,085	634,281	53,154	20,085	24,702	37,386	184,715	73,328	11,683	725	38,743	7,166	16,710	256,891	8,877	3,702	36,296	162,778
	16.71		55.39	84.35	81.57	80.85	82.52	79.73	75.03	74.97	70.37	77.33	78.03	83.17	51.58	84.53	68.69	78.21	82.60	1.49	78.76	81.20	57.94	83.49	85.35	44.13
				1.35	0.24	11.91	0.75	7.92	0.61	42.72	3.58	1.35	1.66	2.52	12.44	4.94	0.79	0.05	2.61	0.48	1.13	17.30	0.60	0.25	2.44	10.96
			55.39	0.75	0.13	6.60	0.41	4.38	0.34	23.66	1.98	0.75	0.92	1.39	6.89	2.74	0.44	0.03	1.45	0.27	0.62	9.58	0.33	0.14	1.35	6.07
			55.59	0.75	0.13	6.62	0.41	4.40	0.34	23.75	1.99	0.75	0.92	1.40	6.92	2.75	0.44	0.03	1.45	0.27	0.63	9.62	0.33	0.14	1.36	6.09
Alachua County	15,895	12,333	3,464	-	-	390	-	346	-	524	-	-	-	-	439	-	-	-	-	39	-	1,169	-	-	-	699
	7.29		28.09			62.90		54.32		21.47					33.08					1.19		57.87				31.23
						11.26		9.99		15.13					12.67					1.13		33.75				20.18
			28.09			3.16		2.81		4.25					3.56					0.32		9.48				5.67
			21.79			2.45		2.18		3.30					2.76					0.25		7.35				4.40
Gainesville (city)	8,320	5,962	1,519	-	-	-	-	-	-	173	-	-	-	-	104	-	-	-	-	13	-	631	-	-	-	370
	8.70		25.48							15.16					23.53					0.70		57.84				37.04
										11.39					6.85					0.86		41.54				24.36
			25.48							2.90					1.74					0.22		10.58				6.21
			18.26							2.08					1.25					0.16		7.58				4.45
Bay County	5,382	3,534	703	-	-	-	-	-	-	-	-	-	-	-	218	-	-	-	-	9	-	-	-	-	-	92
	3.63		19.89												18.12					0.88						21.80
															31.01					1.28						13.09
			19.89												6.17					0.25						2.60
			13.06												4.05					0.17						1.71
Brevard County	31,001	21,902	5,588	-	-	881	-	410	-	926	238	-	-	-	955	-	278	-	-	102	-	1,133	-	-	-	1,234
	6.51		25.51			71.86		57.75		43.87	64.15				26.06		69.85			1.10		65.91				36.67
						15.77		7.34		16.57	4.26				17.09		4.97			1.83		20.28				22.08
			25.51			4.02		1.87		4.23	1.09				4.36		1.27			0.47		5.17				5.63
			18.03			2.84		1.32		2.99	0.77				3.08		0.90			0.33		3.65				3.98
Melbourne (city)	5,593	3,807	1,037	-	-	-	-	-	-	-	-	-	-	-	325	-	-	-	-	9	-	-	-	-	-	192
	7.84		27.24												38.46					0.58						39.83
															31.34					0.87						18.51
			27.24												8.54					0.24						5.04
			18.54												5.81					0.16						3.43
Palm Bay (city)	7,584	6,968	1,447	-	-	-	-	-	-	-	-	-	-	-	227	-	-	-	-	21	-	382	-	-	-	372
	9.55		20.77												31.48					0.53		72.21				35.94
															15.69					1.45		26.40				25.71
			20.77												3.26					0.30		5.48				5.34
			19.08												2.99					0.28		5.04				4.91
Broward County	410,387	271,523	145,126	3,240	551	15,949	1,676	24,653	1,491	32,127	7,123	3,999	2,390	3,347	10,540	2,895	1,896	-	9,362	998	3,512	53,044	1,356	710	7,849	23,989
	25.29		53.45	79.80	78.94	79.74	80.11	79.72	77.58	60.45	66.51	74.99	83.22	80.67	56.62	81.18	76.27		82.70	1.84	78.59	80.62	58.60	73.96	86.83	51.31
				2.23	0.38	10.99	1.15	16.99	1.03	22.14	4.91	2.76	1.65	2.31	7.26	1.99	1.31		6.45	0.69	2.42	36.55	0.93	0.49	5.41	16.53
			53.45	1.19	0.20	5.87	0.62	9.08	0.55	11.83	2.62	1.47	0.88	1.23	3.88	1.07	0.70		3.45	0.37	1.29	19.54	0.50	0.26	2.89	8.83
			35.36	0.79	0.13	3.89	0.41	6.01	0.36	7.83	1.74	0.97	0.58	0.82	2.57	0.71	0.46		2.28	0.24	0.86	12.93	0.33	0.17	1.91	5.85

Notes: Please refer to the User's Guide for an explanation of data; data is arranged alphabetically by state, then county, then city within each county and only includes counties with populations > 99,999 and cities with populations > 49,999; (1) Includes Costa Rican, Guatemalan, Honduran, Nicaraguan, Panamanian, Salvadoran, and other Central American; (2) Includes Argentinian, Bolivian, Chilean, Colombian, Ecuadorian, Paraguayan, Peruvian, Uruguayan, Venezuelan, and other South American

Place	Total foreign-born population	Total Hispanic population	Hispanics who are foreign born	Argentinian	Bolivian	Central American[1]	Chilean	Colombian	Costa Rican	Cuban	Dominican	Ecuadorian	Guatemalan	Honduran	Mexican	Nicaraguan	Panamanian	Paraguayan	Peruvian	Puerto Rican	Salvadoran	South American[2]	Spaniard	Uruguayan	Venezuelan	Other Hisp.
Coral Springs (city)	24,979	18,279	9,287	-	-	620	-	1,817	-	1,057	325	673	-	-	861	-	-	-	870	17	-	4,362	-	-	363	1,840
	21.26		50.81			74.97		79.21		52.35	60.98	71.44			53.98				91.29	0.42		78.94			73.19	53.21
						6.68		19.56		11.38	3.50	7.25			9.27				9.37	0.18		46.97			3.91	19.81
			50.81			3.39		9.94		5.78	1.78	3.68			4.71				4.76	0.09		23.86			1.99	10.07
			37.18			2.48		7.27		4.23	1.30	2.69			3.45				3.48	0.07		17.46			1.45	7.37
Davie (town)	13,277	14,384	6,974	-	-	853	-	966	-	1,880	-	-	-	-	395	-	-	-	553	52	-	2,361	-	-	-	1,095
	17.54		48.48			78.40		79.57		54.65					55.48				85.60	1.52		78.96				50.21
						12.23		13.85		26.96					5.66				7.93	0.75		33.85				15.70
			48.48			5.93		6.72		13.07					2.75				3.84	0.36		16.41				7.61
			52.53			6.42		7.28		14.16					2.98				4.17	0.39		17.78				8.25
Deerfield Beach (city)	14,678	5,517	3,070	-	-	444	-	649	-	425	-	-	-	-	250	-	-	-	-	50	-	1,286	-	-	-	461
	22.68		55.65			89.88		92.06		55.05					53.30					3.83		91.34				55.08
						14.46		21.14		13.84					8.14					1.63		41.89				15.02
			55.65			8.05		11.76		7.70					4.53					0.91		23.31				8.36
			20.92			3.02		4.42		2.90					1.70					0.34		8.76				3.14
Fort Lauderdale (city)	32,938	13,894	8,097	-	-	1,458	-	984	-	1,985	-	-	331	-	625	-	-	-	407	112	529	2,360	-	-	-	1,308
	21.65		58.28			81.77		75.46		73.46			89.22		50.73				85.86	4.61	79.67	79.19				54.16
						18.01		12.15		24.52			4.09		7.72				5.03	1.38	6.53	29.15				16.15
			58.28			10.49		7.08		14.29			2.38		4.50				2.93	0.81	3.81	16.99				9.41
			24.58			4.43		2.99		6.03			1.00		1.90				1.24	0.34	1.61	7.16				3.97
Hollywood (city)	36,562	31,380	16,492	491	-	1,697	320	2,681	-	3,881	998	443	-	351	675	502	-	-	1,052	97	-	5,885	-	-	516	3,150
	26.25		52.56	87.84		75.02	84.88	80.95		64.55	59.12	70.54		79.05	56.11	83.53			78.68	1.39		80.10			78.90	55.11
				2.98		10.29	1.94	16.26		23.53	6.05	2.69		2.13	4.09	3.04			6.38	0.59		35.68			3.13	19.10
			52.56	1.56		5.41	1.02	8.54		12.37	3.18	1.41		1.12	2.15	1.60			3.35	0.31		18.75			1.64	10.04
			45.11	1.34		4.64	0.88	7.33		10.61	2.73	1.21		0.96	1.85	1.37			2.88	0.27		16.10			1.41	8.62
Lauderhill (city)	19,380	3,915	2,110	-	-	-	-	375	-	-	-	-	-	-	-	-	-	-	-	54	-	808	-	-	-	461
	33.85		53.90					79.28												5.93		76.37				56.22
								17.77												2.56		38.29				21.85
			53.90					9.58												1.38		20.64				11.78
			10.89					1.93												0.28		4.17				2.38
Margate (city)	11,850	8,222	4,208	-	-	481	-	871	-	420	-	-	-	-	580	-	-	-	-	66	-	1,552	-	-	-	864
	22.00		51.18			87.61		76.81		60.78					69.38					3.00		77.02				54.58
						11.43		20.70		9.98					13.78					1.57		36.88				20.53
			51.18			5.85		10.59		5.11					7.05					0.80		18.88				10.51
			35.51			4.06		7.35		3.54					4.89					0.56		13.10				7.29
Miramar (city)	29,580	21,536	11,412	-	-	1,439	-	1,543	-	4,004	997	-	-	-	280	590	288	-	546	67	-	2,968	-	-	-	1,595
	40.70		52.99			85.55		77.85		61.23	70.61				48.78	91.47	78.47		82.48	1.90		79.23				40.75
						12.61		13.52		35.09	8.74				2.45	5.17	2.52		4.78	0.59		26.01				13.98
			52.99			6.68		7.16		18.59	4.63				1.30	2.74	1.34		2.54	0.31		13.78				7.41
			38.58			4.86		5.22		13.54	3.37				0.95	1.99	0.97		1.85	0.23		10.03				5.39
Pembroke Pines (city)	39,727	38,348	19,189	-	-	1,487	-	2,699	-	7,105	1,072	396	-	-	414	-	-	-	1,060	85	-	6,074	-	-	1,292	2,763
	28.97		50.04			77.13		77.94		57.29	59.26	81.48			44.33				70.43	1.15		77.72			87.30	47.78
						7.75		14.07		37.03	5.59	2.06			2.16				5.52	0.44		31.65			6.73	14.40
			50.04			3.88		7.04		18.53	2.80	1.03			1.08				2.76	0.22		15.84			3.37	7.21
			48.30			3.74		6.79		17.88	2.70	1.00			1.04				2.67	0.21		15.29			3.25	6.95
Plantation (city)	18,632	10,999	6,025	-	-	464	-	1,762	-	1,129	-	-	-	-	306	-	-	-	409	67	-	3,131	-	-	453	642
	22.37		54.78			64.00		82.41		56.91					46.93				80.99	4.16		80.65			84.20	37.70
						7.70		29.24		18.74					5.08				6.79	1.11		51.97			7.52	10.66
			54.78			4.22		16.02		10.26					2.78				3.72	0.61		28.47			4.12	5.84
			32.34			2.49		9.46		6.06					1.64				2.20	0.36		16.80			2.43	3.45

Notes: Please refer to the User's Guide for an explanation of data; data is arranged alphabetically by state, then county, then city within each county and only includes counties with populations > 99,999 and cities with populations > 49,999; (1) Includes Costa Rican, Guatemalan, Honduran, Nicaraguan, Panamanian, Salvadoran, and other Central American; (2) Includes Argentinian, Bolivian, Chilean, Colombian, Ecuadorian, Paraguayan, Peruvan, Uruguayan, Venezuelan, and other South American

Place	Total foreign-born population	Total Hispanic population	Hispanics who are foreign born	Argentinian	Bolivian	Central American[1]	Chilean	Colombian	Costa Rican	Cuban	Dominican	Ecuadorian	Guatelmalan	Honduran	Mexican	Nicaraguan	Panamanian	Paraguayan	Peruvian	Puerto Rican	Salvadoran	South American[2]	Spaniard	Uruguayan	Venezuelan	Other Hisp.
Pompano Beach (city)	15,876	7,710	4,449	-	-	-	-	414	-	381	-	-	-	-	1,535	-	-	-	-	33	-	1,223	-	-	-	794
	20.28		57.70					74.19		58.44					59.57					2.87		84.11				63.02
								9.31		8.56					34.50					0.74		27.49				17.85
			57.70					5.37		4.94					19.91					0.43		15.86				10.30
			28.02					2.61		2.40					9.67					0.21		7.70				5.00
Sunrise (city)	24,099	14,542	7,683	-	-	563	-	1,870	-	1,057	473	386	-	-	443	-	-	-	488	46	-	3,574	-	-	-	1,494
	28.14		52.83			74.77		76.02		51.09	64.44	72.97			52.49				82.15	1.59		78.15				57.82
						7.33		24.34		13.76	6.16	5.02			5.77				6.35	0.60		46.52				19.45
			52.83			3.87		12.86		7.27	3.25	2.65			3.05				3.36	0.32		24.58				10.27
			31.88			2.34		7.76		4.39	1.96	1.60			1.84				2.02	0.19		14.83				6.20
Tamarac (city)	11,935	7,969	4,388	-	-	-	-	1,135	-	608	-	-	-	-	-	-	-	-	-	47	-	1,947	-	-	-	1,081
	21.28		55.06					90.44		71.28										2.43		87.00				57.20
								25.87		13.86										1.07		44.37				24.64
			55.06					14.24		7.63										0.59		24.43				13.57
			36.77					9.51		5.09										0.39		16.31				9.06
Charlotte County	11,292	4,585	1,480	-	-	-	-	-	-	351	-	-	-	-	298	-	-	-	-	9	-	-	-	-	-	271
	7.97		32.28							59.09					30.79					0.62						31.81
										23.72					20.14					0.61						18.31
			32.28							7.66					6.50					0.20						5.91
			13.11							3.11					2.64					0.08						2.40
Citrus County	5,742	3,058	632	-	-	-	-	-	-	-	-	-	-	-	30	-	-	-	-	0	-	-	-	-	-	185
	4.86		20.67												5.88					0.00						29.51
															4.75					0.00						29.27
			20.67												0.98					0.00						6.05
			11.01												0.52					0.00						3.22
Clay County	6,356	6,181	1,538	-	-	-	-	-	-	-	-	-	-	-	338	-	-	-	-	34	-	-	-	-	-	449
	4.51		24.88												28.31					1.38						33.01
															21.98					2.21						29.19
			24.88												5.47					0.55						7.26
			24.20												5.32					0.53						7.06
Collier County	46,071	49,252	27,806	-	-	2,685	-	963	-	5,195	445	-	1,168	641	15,988	-	-	-	-	23	-	1,855	-	-	-	1,558
	18.33		56.46			79.60		83.30		71.38	88.65		74.25	88.66	56.63					0.73		84.90				35.56
						9.66		3.46		18.68	1.60		4.20	2.31	57.50					0.08		6.67				5.60
			56.46			5.45		1.96		10.55	0.90		2.37	1.30	32.46					0.05		3.77				3.16
			60.35			5.83		2.09		11.28	0.97		2.54	1.39	34.70					0.05		4.03				3.38
Duval County	45,651	31,809	8,464	-	-	1,121	-	950	-	1,810	405	-	-	-	1,351	-	302	-	414	167	-	1,957	-	-	-	1,563
	5.86		26.61			61.59		66.43		54.32	60.45				22.86		50.50		85.89	1.47		70.55				27.58
						13.24		11.22		21.38	4.78				15.96		3.57		4.89	1.97		23.12				18.47
			26.61			3.52		2.99		5.69	1.27				4.25		0.95		1.30	0.53		6.15				4.91
			18.54			2.46		2.08		3.96	0.89				2.96		0.66		0.91	0.37		4.29				3.42
Jacksonville (city)	43,661	30,414	8,121	-	-	1,108	-	926	-	1,785	405	-	-	-	1,182	-	290	-	-	167	-	1,866	-	-	-	1,526
	5.94		26.70			61.49		67.44		54.92	60.45				21.41		49.91			1.53		71.74				28.26
						13.64		11.40		21.98	4.99				14.55		3.57			2.06		22.98				18.79
			26.70			3.64		3.04		5.87	1.33				3.89		0.95			0.55		6.14				5.02
			18.60			2.54		2.12		4.09	0.93				2.71		0.66			0.38		4.27				3.50
Escambia County	10,821	7,816	1,760	-	-	318	-	-	-	409	-	-	-	-	486	-	-	-	-	20	-	284	-	-	-	182
	3.68		22.52			59.11				55.57					17.93					1.17		63.39				11.56
						18.07				23.24					27.61					1.14		16.14				10.34
			22.52			4.07				5.23					6.22					0.26		3.63				2.33
			16.26			2.94				3.78					4.49					0.18		2.62				1.68

Notes: Please refer to the User's Guide for an explanation of data; data is arranged alphabetically by state, then county, then city within each county and only includes counties with populations > 99,999 and cities with populations > 49,999; (1) Includes Costa Rican, Guatemalan, Honduran, Nicaraguan, Panamanian, Salvadoran, and other Central American; (2) Includes Argentinian, Bolivian, Chilean, Colombian, Ecuadorian, Paraguayan, Peruvan, Uruguayan, Venezuelan, and other South American

Place	Total foreign-born population	Total Hispanic population	Hispanics who are foreign born	Argentinian	Bolivian	Central American[1]	Chilean	Colombian	Costa Rican	Cuban	Dominican	Ecuadorian	Guatelmalan	Honduran	Mexican	Nicaraguan	Panamanian	Paraguayan	Peruvian	Puerto Rican	Salvadoran	South American[2]	Spaniard	Uruguayan	Venezuelan	Other Hisp.
Pensacola (city)	2,054 3.65	1,198	296 24.71 24.71 14.41	-	-	-	-	-	-	-	-	-	-	-	-	-	-	-	-	-	-	-	-	-	-	-
Hernando County	6,942 5.31	6,717	1,044 15.54 15.54 15.04	-	-	-	-	-	-	244 39.17 23.37 3.63 3.51	-	-	-	-	259 26.56 24.81 3.86 3.73	-	-	-	-	26 0.68 2.49 0.39 0.37	-	-	-	-	-	230 28.12 22.03 3.42 3.31
Spring Hill (cdp)	4,652 6.72	4,911	693 14.11 14.11 14.90	-	-	-	-	-	-	194 47.43 27.99 3.95 4.17	-	-	-	-	-	-	-	-	-	26 0.84 3.75 0.53 0.56	-	-	-	-	-	203 33.06 29.29 4.13 4.36
Hillsborough County	115,151 11.53	179,637	63,978 35.62 35.62 55.56	-	-	5,490 69.30 8.58 3.06 4.77	-	4,486 74.11 7.01 2.50 3.90	699 72.81 1.09 0.39 0.61	20,757 59.51 32.44 11.55 18.03	2,574 66.31 4.02 1.43 2.24	976 76.13 1.53 0.54 0.85	779 73.77 1.22 0.43 0.68	1,622 72.31 2.54 0.90 1.41	17,393 47.59 27.19 9.68 15.10	744 73.16 1.16 0.41 0.65	902 54.80 1.41 0.50 0.78	-	1,360 74.89 2.13 0.76 1.18	887 1.77 1.39 0.49 0.77	569 75.66 0.89 0.32 0.49	9,313 75.78 14.56 5.18 8.09	455 24.86 0.71 0.25 0.40	-	1,461 82.50 2.28 0.81 1.27	7,109 22.19 11.11 3.96 6.17
Brandon (cdp)	5,932 7.63	10,068	1,948 19.35 19.35 32.84	-	-	351 65.24 18.02 3.49 5.92	-	-	-	327 30.08 16.79 3.25 5.51	-	-	-	-	271 25.52 13.91 2.69 4.57	-	-	-	-	56 1.16 2.87 0.56 0.94	-	389 64.19 19.97 3.86 6.56	-	-	-	341 21.76 17.51 3.39 5.75
Tampa (city)	37,027 12.20	58,571	21,240 36.26 36.26 57.36	-	-	2,175 67.36 10.24 3.71 5.87	-	1,166 68.43 5.49 1.99 3.15	-	8,798 61.66 41.42 15.02 23.76	935 65.57 4.40 1.60 2.53	338 80.86 1.59 0.58 0.91	-	639 71.48 3.01 1.09 1.73	3,769 52.23 17.74 6.43 10.18	263 56.20 1.24 0.45 0.71	344 54.43 1.62 0.59 0.93	-	-	192 1.21 0.90 0.33 0.52	-	2,708 75.31 12.75 4.62 7.31	191 26.06 0.90 0.33 0.52	-	547 87.66 2.58 0.93 1.48	2,472 20.15 11.64 4.22 6.68
Town 'n' Country (cdp)	12,774 17.64	20,662	7,942 38.44 38.44 62.17	-	-	639 74.56 8.05 3.09 5.00	-	990 78.32 12.47 4.79 7.75	-	3,178 66.93 40.02 15.38 24.88	507 67.60 6.38 2.45 3.97	-	-	-	479 43.78 6.03 2.32 3.75	-	-	-	-	232 3.11 2.92 1.12 1.82	-	1,704 80.49 21.46 8.25 13.34	-	-	-	1,136 33.00 14.30 5.50 8.89
Indian River County	9,151 8.10	7,300	3,942 54.00 54.00 43.08	-	-	240 70.18 6.09 3.29 2.62	-	-	-	215 58.74 5.45 2.95 2.35	-	-	-	-	2,626 58.59 66.62 35.97 28.70	-	-	-	-	4 0.58 0.10 0.05 0.04	-	456 88.54 11.57 6.25 4.98	-	-	-	379 42.63 9.61 5.19 4.14
Lake County	10,820 5.14	11,836	4,459 37.67 37.67 41.21	-	-	398 79.60 8.93 3.36 3.68	-	-	-	364 47.71 8.16 3.08 3.36	-	-	-	-	2,754 51.09 61.76 23.27 25.45	-	-	-	-	18 0.62 0.40 0.15 0.17	-	457 81.75 10.25 3.86 4.22	-	-	-	399 25.08 8.95 3.37 3.69
Lee County	40,362 9.15	41,993	16,793 39.99 39.99 41.61	-	-	2,317 76.80 13.80 5.52 5.74	-	744 72.80 4.43 1.77 1.84	-	1,791 53.21 10.67 4.26 4.44	698 65.42 4.16 1.66 1.73	-	1,083 76.97 6.45 2.58 2.68	415 83.67 2.47 0.99 1.03	8,355 55.63 49.75 19.90 20.70	-	-	-	-	96 0.81 0.57 0.23 0.24	-	1,774 72.11 10.56 4.22 4.40	-	-	-	1,733 33.70 10.32 4.13 4.29

Notes: Please refer to the User's Guide for an explanation of data: data is arranged alphabetically by state, then county, then city within each county and only includes counties with populations > 99,999 and cities with populations > 49,999; (1) Includes Costa Rican, Guatemalan, Honduran, Nicaraguan, Panamanian, Salvadoran, and other Central American; (2) Includes Argentinian, Bolivian, Chilean, Colombian, Ecuadorian, Paraguayan, Peruvian, Uruguayan, Venezuelan, and other South American

Place	Total foreign-born population	Total Hispanic population	Hispanics who are foreign born	Argentinian	Bolivian	Central American[1]	Chilean	Colombian	Costa Rican	Cuban	Dominican	Ecuadorian	Guatelmalan	Honduran	Mexican	Nicaraguan	Panamanian	Paraguayan	Peruvian	Puerto Rican	Salvadoran	South American[2]	Spaniard	Uruguayan	Venezuelan	Other Hisp.
Cape Coral (city)	8,920	8,355	3,238	-	-	-	-	394	-	968	358	-	-	-	457	-	-	-	-	42	-	774	-	-	-	371
	8.73		38.76					67.81		61.19	61.51				34.23					1.93		72.88				29.49
								12.17		29.89	11.06				14.11					1.30		23.90				11.46
			38.76					4.72		11.59	4.28				5.47					0.50		9.26				4.44
			36.30					4.42		10.85	4.01				5.12					0.47		8.68				4.16
Leon County	11,345	8,220	2,026	-	-	-	-	-	-	458	-	-	-	-	425	-	-	-	-	17	-	446	-	-	-	318
	4.74		24.65							24.04					29.70					1.08		43.18				19.50
										22.61					20.98					0.84		22.01				15.70
			24.65							5.57					5.17					0.21		5.43				3.87
			17.86							4.04					3.75					0.15		3.93				2.80
Tallahassee (city)	8,283	6,077	1,354	-	-	-	-	-	-	274	-	-	-	-	267	-	-	-	-	17	-	330	-	-	-	199
	5.50		22.28							18.84					29.50					1.47		41.15				16.02
										20.24					19.72					1.26		24.37				14.70
			22.28							4.51					4.39					0.28		5.43				3.27
			16.35							3.31					3.22					0.21		3.98				2.40
Manatee County	22,235	24,501	10,340	-	-	965	-	-	-	653	-	-	-	-	6,871	-	-	-	-	41	-	716	-	-	-	994
	8.42		42.20			65.65				55.01					45.66					1.27		76.41				41.06
						9.33				6.32					66.45					0.40		6.92				9.61
			42.20			3.94				2.67					28.04					0.17		2.92				4.06
			46.50			4.34				2.94					30.90					0.18		3.22				4.47
Marion County	13,352	15,535	4,258	-	-	430	-	437	-	542	-	-	-	-	1,622	-	-	-	-	89	-	745	-	-	-	676
	5.16		27.41			79.19		77.62		43.96					48.49					1.28		68.29				32.52
						10.10		10.26		12.73					38.09					2.09		17.50				15.88
			27.41			2.77		2.81		3.49					10.44					0.57		4.80				4.35
			31.89			3.22		3.27		4.06					12.15					0.67		5.58				5.06
Martin County	10,318	9,490	4,684	-	-	1,629	-	-	-	367	-	-	1,374	-	2,143	-	-	-	-	0	-	-	-	-	-	327
	8.14		49.36			68.47				45.76			67.99		55.52					0.00						46.51
						34.78				7.84			29.33		45.75					0.00						6.98
			49.36			17.17				3.87			14.48		22.58					0.00						3.45
			45.40			15.79				3.56			13.32		20.77					0.00						3.17
Miami-Dade County	1,147,765	1,291,681	922,819	12,484	1,895	117,195	7,019	61,930	3,688	520,614	29,881	9,443	8,606	25,008	20,240	64,588	5,344	-	20,335	1,970	7,855	137,029	5,047	1,768	19,698	90,843
	50.94		71.44	88.03	82.68	84.49	87.38	82.56	79.64	79.27	74.91	81.72	80.83	86.21	54.13	85.59	79.17		85.47	2.47	82.04	84.41	81.44	89.70	87.17	53.25
				1.35	0.21	12.70	0.76	6.71	0.40	56.42	3.24	1.02	0.93	2.71	2.19	7.00	0.58		2.20	0.21	0.85	14.85	0.55	0.19	2.13	9.84
			71.44	0.97	0.15	9.07	0.54	4.79	0.29	40.31	2.31	0.73	0.67	1.94	1.57	5.00	0.41		1.57	0.15	0.61	10.61	0.39	0.14	1.52	7.03
			80.40	1.09	0.17	10.21	0.61	5.40	0.32	45.36	2.60	0.82	0.75	2.18	1.76	5.63	0.47		1.77	0.17	0.68	11.94	0.44	0.15	1.72	7.91
Carol City (cdp)	22,102	24,973	16,553	-	-	2,130	-	1,167	-	9,107	1,274	-	-	402	-	1,193	-	-	-	140	-	2,042	-	-	-	1,645
	37.18		66.28			80.62		79.60		81.20	67.66			77.61		82.39				5.02		80.58				47.19
						12.87		7.05		55.02	7.70			2.43		7.21				0.85		12.34				9.94
			66.28			8.53		4.67		36.47	5.10			1.61		4.78				0.56		8.18				6.59
			74.89			9.64		5.28		41.20	5.76			1.82		5.40				0.63		9.24				7.44
Fountainbleau (cdp)	43,496	51,833	41,125	360	-	6,984	638	2,458	-	19,287	1,568	635	-	585	356	5,271	396	-	1,036	41	-	7,308	-	-	1,876	5,455
	73.08		79.34	81.82		85.58	90.75	88.39		86.48	81.33	79.47		91.12	73.86	86.13	75.86		87.72	2.18		87.25			90.02	63.68
				0.88		16.98	1.55	5.98		46.90	3.81	1.54		1.42	0.87	12.82	0.96		2.52	0.10		17.77			4.56	13.26
			79.34	0.69		13.47	1.23	4.74		37.21	3.03	1.23		1.13	0.69	10.17	0.76		2.00	0.08		14.10			3.62	10.52
			94.55	0.83		16.06	1.47	5.65		44.34	3.60	1.46		1.34	0.82	12.12	0.91		2.38	0.09		16.80			4.31	12.54
Hialeah (city)	163,256	204,808	160,779	395	-	13,832	722	6,687	451	119,595	3,813	1,076	682	2,290	1,068	8,960	-	-	1,280	197	765	11,377	410	-	876	10,487
	72.11		78.50	92.07		86.97	96.27	86.68	86.23	84.64	78.04	87.27	81.00	86.38	66.42	88.18			87.73	2.83	80.53	88.17	80.55		91.73	50.60
				0.25		8.60	0.45	4.16	0.28	74.38	2.37	0.67	0.42	1.42	0.66	5.57			0.80	0.12	0.48	7.08	0.26		0.54	6.52
			78.50	0.19		6.75	0.35	3.27	0.22	58.39	1.86	0.53	0.33	1.12	0.52	4.37			0.62	0.10	0.37	5.55	0.20		0.43	5.12
			98.48	0.24		8.47	0.44	4.10	0.28	73.26	2.34	0.66	0.42	1.40	0.65	5.49			0.78	0.12	0.47	6.97	0.25		0.54	6.42

Notes: Please refer to the User's Guide for an explanation of data; data is arranged alphabetically by state, then county, then city within each county and only includes counties with populations > 99,999 and cities with populations > 49,999; (1) Includes Costa Rican, Guatemalan, Honduran, Nicaraguan, Panamanian, Salvadoran, and other Central American; (2) Includes Argentinian, Bolivian, Chilean, Colombian, Ecuadorian, Paraguayan, Peruvian, Uruguayan, Venezuelan, and other South American

Place	Total foreign-born population	Total Hispanic population	Hispanics who are foreign born	Argentinian	Bolivian	Central American[1]	Chilean	Colombian	Costa Rican	Cuban	Dominican	Ecuadorian	Guatelmalan	Honduran	Mexican	Nicaraguan	Panamanian	Paraguayan	Peruvian	Puerto Rican	Salvadoran	South American[2]	Spaniard	Uruguayan	Venezuelan	Other Hisp.
Kendale Lakes (cdp)	33,460	43,588	30,802	-	-	3,409	-	3,204	-	16,265	613	-	-	444	355	2,384	-	-	805	57	-	6,097	-	-	782	3,847
	58.82		70.67			83.57		80.04		73.74	72.72			79.71	60.89	83.74			83.25	3.47		83.32			89.78	55.71
						11.07		10.40		52.81	1.99			1.44	1.15	7.74			2.61	0.19		19.79			2.54	12.49
			70.67			7.82		7.35		37.32	1.41			1.02	0.81	5.47			1.85	0.13		13.99			1.79	8.83
			92.06			10.19		9.58		48.61	1.83			1.33	1.06	7.12			2.41	0.17		18.22			2.34	11.50
Kendall (cdp)	32,059	37,640	24,625	547	-	3,037	435	3,491	-	10,264	574	-	-	-	-	1,752	-	-	1,105	27	-	7,294	-	-	1,212	2,833
	42.59		65.42	83.51		78.99	90.63	84.53		64.68	71.84					78.49			80.66	1.20		83.84			83.41	52.59
				2.22		12.33	1.77	14.18		41.68	2.33					7.11			4.49	0.11		29.62			4.92	11.50
			65.42	1.45		8.07	1.16	9.27		27.27	1.52					4.65			2.94	0.07		19.38			3.22	7.53
			76.81	1.71		9.47	1.36	10.89		32.02	1.79					5.46			3.45	0.08		22.75			3.78	8.84
Miami Beach (city)	48,852	46,980	36,211	2,809	-	2,478	612	3,937	-	15,214	1,212	514	-	739	673	898	-	-	1,704	57	-	11,585	498	-	1,331	4,494
	55.48		77.08	92.68		87.78	82.81	87.63		83.41	86.82	77.64		91.23	68.26	90.52			89.78	1.60		89.23	86.91		91.41	69.95
				7.76		6.84	1.69	10.87		42.01	3.35	1.42		2.04	1.86	2.48			4.71	0.16		31.99	1.38		3.68	12.41
			77.08	5.98		5.27	1.30	8.38		32.38	2.58	1.09		1.57	1.43	1.91			3.63	0.12		24.66	1.06		2.83	9.57
			74.12	5.75		5.07	1.25	8.06		31.14	2.48	1.05		1.51	1.38	1.84			3.49	0.12		23.71	1.02		2.72	9.20
Miami (city)	215,739	238,461	188,008	1,801	-	38,302	811	5,243	667	108,492	5,723	1,459	2,400	12,099	2,109	19,647	759	-	2,373	335	2,130	13,962	819	-	1,619	18,266
	59.50		78.84	88.76		87.20	90.41	87.30	81.74	86.98	78.72	83.13	84.18	88.57	66.59	87.05	85.96		85.76	3.30	88.97	87.50	86.12		91.99	56.52
				0.96		20.37	0.43	2.79	0.35	57.71	3.04	0.78	1.28	6.44	1.12	10.45	0.40		1.26	0.18	1.13	7.43	0.44		0.86	9.72
			78.84	0.76		16.06	0.34	2.20	0.28	45.50	2.40	0.61	1.01	5.07	0.88	8.24	0.32		1.00	0.14	0.89	5.86	0.34		0.68	7.66
			87.15	0.83		17.75	0.38	2.43	0.31	50.29	2.65	0.68	1.11	5.61	0.98	9.11	0.35		1.10	0.16	0.99	6.47	0.38		0.75	8.47
North Miami (city)	29,144	14,311	8,370	-	-	1,560	-	850	-	2,087	777	-	-	532	-	613	-	-	-	39	-	1,756	-	-	-	1,879
	48.54		58.49			88.69		82.93		73.93	70.77			90.17		85.61				1.39		84.63				57.44
						18.64		10.16		24.93	9.28			6.36		7.32				0.47		20.98				22.45
			58.49			10.90		5.94		14.58	5.43			3.72		4.28				0.27		12.27				13.13
			28.72			5.35		2.92		7.16	2.67			1.83		2.10				0.13		6.03				6.45
Tamiami (cdp)	35,850	47,691	34,857	-	-	3,130	-	1,723	-	24,750	473	-	-	391	287	2,184	-	-	-	37	-	3,447	-	-	512	2,578
	65.49		73.09			81.30		84.84		76.43	70.91			86.31	53.05	79.22				3.42		86.74			93.94	51.40
						8.98		4.94		71.00	1.36			1.12	0.82	6.27				0.11		9.89			1.47	7.40
			73.09			6.56		3.61		51.90	0.99			0.82	0.60	4.58				0.08		7.23			1.07	5.41
			97.23			8.73		4.81		69.04	1.32			1.09	0.80	6.09				0.10		9.62			1.43	7.19
Okaloosa County	8,984	6,901	1,529	-	-	210	-	-	-	290	-	-	-	-	412	-	-	-	-	19	-	-	-	-	-	267
	5.27		22.16			58.01				50.26					17.33					1.25						17.23
						13.73				18.97					26.95					1.24						17.46
			22.16			3.04				4.20					5.97					0.28						3.87
			17.02			2.34				3.23					4.59					0.21						2.97
Orange County	128,904	168,191	48,031	532	-	4,025	385	5,882	379	8,392	3,854	1,257	812	992	10,912	590	639	-	1,369	946	498	12,324	292	-	2,262	7,286
	14.38		28.56	75.78		69.56	83.88	76.41	63.59	63.42	62.21	70.94	78.61	80.00	54.69	66.67	67.19		77.48	1.10	52.81	77.97	43.52		86.47	35.92
				1.11		8.38	0.80	12.25	0.79	17.47	8.02	2.62	1.69	2.07	22.72	1.23	1.33		2.85	1.97	1.04	25.66	0.61		4.71	15.17
			28.56	0.32		2.39	0.23	3.50	0.23	4.99	2.29	0.75	0.48	0.59	6.49	0.35	0.38		0.81	0.56	0.30	7.33	0.17		1.34	4.33
			37.26	0.41		3.12	0.30	4.56	0.29	6.51	2.99	0.98	0.63	0.77	8.47	0.46	0.50		1.06	0.73	0.39	9.56	0.23		1.75	5.65
Orlando (city)	26,741	32,897	10,097	-	-	913	-	1,470	-	1,989	755	-	-	-	1,165	-	-	-	327	219	-	3,231	-	-	708	1,759
	14.38		30.69			66.40		82.91		66.72	60.84				50.22				71.87	1.31		81.69			90.65	41.91
						9.04		14.56		19.70	7.48				11.54				3.24	2.17		32.00			7.01	17.42
			30.69			2.78		4.47		6.05	2.30				3.54				0.99	0.67		9.82			2.15	5.35
			37.76			3.41		5.50		7.44	2.82				4.36				1.22	0.82		12.08			2.65	6.58
Osceola County	24,110	50,742	11,372	-	-	1,480	-	1,627	-	1,227	1,786	394	-	-	1,705	-	-	-	-	265	449	3,019	-	-	442	1,829
	13.98		22.41			76.37		83.78		66.72	72.37	88.74			49.59					0.81	83.30	82.96			84.03	39.88
						13.01		14.31		10.79	15.71	3.46			14.99					2.33	3.95	26.55			3.89	16.08
			22.41			2.92		3.21		2.42	3.52	0.78			3.36					0.52	0.88	5.95			0.87	3.60
			47.17			6.14		6.75		5.09	7.41	1.63			7.07					1.10	1.86	12.52			1.83	7.59

Notes: Please refer to the User's Guide for an explanation of data; data is arranged alphabetically by state, then county, then city within each county and only includes counties with populations > 99,999 and cities with populations > 49,999; (1) Includes Costa Rican, Guatemalan, Honduran, Nicaraguan, Panamanian, Salvadoran, and other Central American; (2) Includes Argentinian, Bolivian, Chilean, Colombian, Ecuadorian, Paraguayan, Peruvian, Uruguayan, Venezuelan, and other South American

Place	Total foreign-born population	Total Hispanic population	Hispanics who are foreign born	Argentinian	Bolivian	Central American[1]	Chilean	Colombian	Costa Rican	Cuban	Dominican	Ecuadorian	Guatelmalan	Honduran	Mexican	Nicaraguan	Panamanian	Paraguayan	Peruvian	Puerto Rican	Salvadoran	South American[2]	Spaniard	Uruguayan	Venezuelan	Other Hisp.
Palm Beach County	196,852 17.40	140,568	75,965 54.04 54.04 38.59	1,626 87.65 2.14 1.16 0.83	-	12,130 78.06 15.97 8.63 6.16	564 82.34 0.74 0.40 0.29	7,271 76.34 9.57 5.17 3.69	657 77.94 0.86 0.47 0.33	18,569 70.99 24.44 13.21 9.43	2,370 66.04 3.12 1.69 1.20	1,576 79.16 2.07 1.12 0.80	5,439 78.67 7.16 3.87 2.76	2,500 76.45 3.29 1.78 1.27	16,433 55.55 21.63 11.69 8.35	1,659 78.81 2.18 1.18 0.84	286 66.20 0.38 0.20 0.15	-	1,953 78.65 2.57 1.39 0.99	622 2.51 0.82 0.44 0.32	1,343 80.85 1.77 0.96 0.68	15,948 78.75 20.99 11.35 8.10	267 56.93 0.35 0.19 0.14	693 85.56 0.91 0.49 0.35	1,431 80.48 1.88 1.02 0.73	9,626 47.64 12.67 6.85 4.89
Boca Raton (city)	13,601 17.99	6,368	4,094 64.29 64.29 30.10	-	-	-	-	702 80.69 17.15 11.02 5.16	-	599 65.32 14.63 9.41 4.40	-	-	-	-	579 69.51 14.14 9.09 4.26	-	-	-	-	42 5.00 1.03 0.66 0.31	-	1,768 84.80 43.19 27.76 13.00	-	-	-	766 62.23 18.71 12.03 5.63
Boynton Beach (city)	10,408 17.36	5,000	1,928 38.56 38.56 18.52	-	-	457 77.99 23.70 9.14 4.39	-	-	-	260 45.14 13.49 5.20 2.50	-	-	-	-	257 30.60 13.33 5.14 2.47	-	-	-	-	26 1.80 1.35 0.52 0.25	-	583 77.94 30.24 11.66 5.60	-	-	-	304 44.44 15.77 6.08 2.92
Delray Beach (city)	12,888 21.50	4,165	2,203 52.89 52.89 17.09	-	-	-	-	-	-	-	-	-	-	-	758 51.92 34.41 18.20 5.88	-	-	-	-	48 6.55 2.18 1.15 0.37	-	510 85.14 23.15 12.24 3.96	-	-	-	334 68.87 15.16 8.02 2.59
West Palm Beach (city)	20,152 24.71	15,007	9,923 66.12 66.12 49.24	-	-	2,397 85.58 24.16 15.97 11.89	-	642 86.64 6.47 4.28 3.19	-	3,622 82.21 36.50 24.14 17.97	275 70.51 2.77 1.83 1.36	-	1,781 86.46 17.95 11.87 8.84	-	1,271 64.32 12.81 8.47 6.31	-	-	-	-	46 2.47 0.46 0.31 0.23	-	1,307 82.15 13.17 8.71 6.49	-	-	-	981 50.36 9.89 6.54 4.87
Pasco County	24,129 7.00	19,555	5,280 27.00 27.00 21.88	-	-	403 63.27 7.63 2.06 1.67	-	-	-	806 44.43 15.27 4.12 3.34	-	-	-	-	2,615 43.72 49.53 13.37 10.84	-	-	-	-	57 0.82 1.08 0.29 0.24	-	749 86.79 14.19 3.83 3.10	-	-	-	517 17.93 9.79 2.64 2.14
Pinellas County	87,685 9.52	42,128	15,589 37.00 37.00 17.78	-	-	928 66.48 5.95 2.20 1.06	-	1,422 75.52 9.12 3.38 1.62	-	2,703 57.18 17.34 6.42 3.08	579 64.05 3.71 1.37 0.66	303 75.19 1.94 0.72 0.35	-	-	5,517 53.60 35.39 13.10 6.29	-	-	-	628 79.19 4.03 1.49 0.72	110 0.84 0.71 0.26 0.13	-	3,581 74.78 22.97 8.50 4.08	220 42.72 1.41 0.52 0.25	-	603 68.76 3.87 1.43 0.69	1,951 30.64 12.52 4.63 2.23
Clearwater (city)	14,280 13.23	9,615	4,863 50.58 50.58 34.05	-	-	-	-	285 73.08 5.86 2.96 2.00	-	338 59.19 6.95 3.52 2.37	-	-	-	-	2,953 70.13 60.72 30.71 20.68	-	-	-	-	5 0.22 0.10 0.05 0.04	-	818 78.28 16.82 8.51 5.73	-	-	-	386 35.35 7.94 4.01 2.70
Largo (city)	6,509 9.37	2,849	1,089 38.22 38.22 16.73	-	-	-	-	-	-	-	-	-	-	-	224 40.43 20.57 7.86 3.44	-	-	-	-	35 4.49 3.21 1.23 0.54	-	-	-	-	-	-
Palm Harbor (cdp)	4,949 8.37	1,939	564 29.09 29.09 11.40	-	-	-	-	-	-	-	-	-	-	-	-	-	-	-	-	10 1.22 1.77 0.52 0.20	-	-	-	-	-	-

Notes: Please refer to the User's Guide for an explanation of data; data is arranged alphabetically by state, then county, then city within each county and only includes counties with populations > 99,999 and cities with populations > 49,999; (1) Includes Costa Rican, Guatemalan, Honduran, Nicaraguan, Panamanian, Salvadoran, and other Central American; (2) Includes Argentinian, Bolivian, Chilean, Colombian, Ecuadorian, Paraguayan, Peruvian, Uruguayan, Venezuelan, and other South American

Place	Total foreign-born population	Total Hispanic population	Hispanics who are foreign born	Argentinian	Bolivian	Central American[1]	Chilean	Colombian	Costa Rican	Cuban	Dominican	Ecuadorian	Guatemalan	Honduran	Mexican	Nicaraguan	Panamanian	Paraguayan	Peruvian	Puerto Rican	Salvadoran	South American[2]	Spaniard	Uruguayan	Venezuelan	Other Hisp.
St. Petersburg (city)	22,635 9.13	9,878	3,384 34.26 34.26 14.95	-	-	-	-	-	-	1,109 66.93 32.77 11.23 4.90	-	-	-	-	621 37.19 18.35 6.29 2.74	-	-	-	-	0 0.00 0.00 0.00 0.00	-	903 76.72 26.68 9.14 3.99	-	-	-	367 25.14 10.85 3.72 1.62
Polk County	33,519 6.93	45,650	17,832 39.06 39.06 53.20	-	-	963 79.13 5.40 2.11 2.87	-	-	-	1,384 55.18 7.76 3.03 4.13	278 59.66 1.56 0.61 0.83	-	-	-	13,077 53.62 73.33 28.65 39.01	-	-	-	-	172 1.51 0.96 0.38 0.51	-	706 71.03 3.96 1.55 2.11	-	-	-	1,224 27.00 6.86 2.68 3.65
Lakeland (city)	4,424 5.66	5,050	1,454 28.79 28.79 32.87	-	-	-	-	-	-	417 64.75 28.68 8.26 9.43	-	-	-	-	431 45.66 29.64 8.53 9.74	-	-	-	-	52 2.60 3.58 1.03 1.18	-	-	-	-	-	178 21.95 12.24 3.52 4.02
St. Johns County	6,038 4.90	3,596	867 24.11 24.11 14.36	-	-	-	-	-	-	-	-	-	-	-	142 14.95 16.38 3.95 2.35	-	-	-	-	0 0.00 0.00 0.00 0.00	-	-	-	-	-	173 28.41 19.95 4.81 2.87
St. Lucie County	20,165 10.46	16,004	7,460 46.61 46.61 36.99	-	-	806 78.48 10.80 5.04 4.00	-	351 83.37 4.71 2.19 1.74	-	616 57.73 8.26 3.85 3.05	-	-	-	-	4,493 62.29 60.23 28.07 22.28	-	-	-	-	42 1.13 0.56 0.26 0.21	-	827 81.88 11.09 5.17 4.10	-	-	-	479 31.51 6.42 2.99 2.38
Port St. Lucie (city)	8,516 9.59	6,822	2,214 32.45 32.45 26.00	-	-	-	-	-	-	412 57.14 18.61 6.04 4.84	-	-	-	-	469 42.10 21.18 6.87 5.51	-	-	-	-	8 0.31 0.36 0.12 0.09	-	592 84.94 26.74 8.68 6.95	-	-	-	311 35.22 14.05 4.56 3.65
Santa Rosa County	3,549 3.01	2,821	513 18.19 18.19 14.45	-	-	-	-	-	-	-	-	-	-	-	126 15.04 24.56 4.47 3.55	-	-	-	-	0 0.00 0.00 0.00 0.00	-	-	-	-	-	77 14.67 15.01 2.73 2.17
Sarasota County	30,416 9.33	14,373	8,130 56.56 56.56 26.73	-	-	461 72.94 5.67 3.21 1.52	-	688 78.63 8.46 4.79 2.26	-	1,285 66.55 15.81 8.94 4.22	-	-	-	-	4,118 69.14 50.65 28.65 13.54	-	-	-	-	27 1.57 0.33 0.19 0.09	-	1,463 78.45 18.00 10.18 4.81	-	-	-	538 27.42 6.62 3.74 1.77
Sarasota (city)	7,289 13.87	6,390	4,359 68.22 68.22 59.80	-	-	-	-	-	-	463 69.42 10.62 7.25 6.35	-	-	-	-	2,776 78.31 63.68 43.44 38.08	-	-	-	-	0 0.00 0.00 0.00 0.00	-	565 87.33 12.96 8.84 7.75	-	-	-	209 29.90 4.79 3.27 2.87
Seminole County	33,285 9.11	40,656	11,152 27.43 27.43 33.50	318 71.62 2.85 0.78 0.96	-	1,327 65.79 11.90 3.26 3.99	-	1,655 73.75 14.84 4.07 4.97	-	2,034 54.28 18.24 5.00 6.11	731 62.75 6.55 1.80 2.20	306 62.96 2.74 0.75 0.92	-	-	1,417 39.97 12.71 3.49 4.26	-	249 45.52 2.23 0.61 0.75	-	411 76.11 3.69 1.01 1.23	168 0.85 1.51 0.41 0.50	-	3,295 72.64 29.55 8.10 9.90	-	-	348 79.27 3.12 0.86 1.05	2,081 36.52 18.66 5.12 6.25

Notes: Please refer to the User's Guide for an explanation of data; data is arranged alphabetically by state, then county, then city within each county and only includes counties with populations > 99,999 and cities with populations > 49,999; (1) Includes Costa Rican, Guatemalan, Honduran, Nicaraguan, Panamanian, Salvadoran, and other Central American; (2) Includes Argentinian, Bolivian, Chilean, Colombian, Ecuadorian, Paraguayan, Peruvian, Uruguayan, Venezuelan, and other South American

Place	Total foreign-born population	Total Hispanic population	Hispanics who are foreign born	Argentinian	Bolivian	Central American[1]	Chilean	Colombian	Costa Rican	Cuban	Dominican	Ecuadorian	Guatelmalan	Honduran	Mexican	Nicaraguan	Panamanian	Paraguayan	Peruvian	Puerto Rican	Salvadoran	South American[2]	Spaniard	Uruguayan	Venezuelan	Other Hisp.
	28,353	29,273	7,536	-	-	566	-	512	-	828	368	-	-	-	3,609	-	-	-	-	96	-	1,163	-	-	-	822
	6.40		25.74			71.74		75.63		60.93	62.59				44.78					0.69		72.28				29.74
Volusia County						7.51		6.79		10.99	4.88				47.89					1.27		15.43				10.91
			25.74			1.93		1.75		2.83	1.26				12.33					0.33		3.97				2.81
			26.58			2.00		1.81		2.92	1.30				12.73					0.34		4.10				2.90
	4,925	2,275	700	-	-	-	-	-	-	-	-	-	-	-	-	-	-	-	-	7	-	-	-	-	-	177
	7.69		30.77																	0.78						44.03
Daytona Beach (city)																				1.00						25.29
			30.77																	0.31						7.78
			14.21																	0.14						3.59
	4,977	12,855	1,742	-	-	-	-	-	-	401	-	-	-	-	217	-	-	-	-	86	-	441	-	-	-	228
	7.13		13.55							71.86					32.39					0.91		71.01				23.22
Deltona (city)										23.02					12.46					4.94		25.32				13.09
			13.55							3.12					1.69					0.67		3.43				1.77
			35.00							8.06					4.36					1.73		8.86				4.58

Notes: Please refer to the User's Guide for an explanation of data; data is arranged alphabetically by state, then county, then city within each county and only includes counties with populations > 99,999 and cities with populations > 49,999; (1) Includes Costa Rican, Guatemalan, Honduran, Nicaraguan, Panamanian, Salvadoran, and other Central American; (2) Includes Argentinian, Bolivian, Chilean, Colombian, Ecuadorian, Paraguayan, Peruvan, Uruguayan, Venezuelan, and other South American

Foreign-Born Naturalized Citizens

(Universe: Total Population)

Place	Total foreign-born naturalized citizens	Total Hispanic population	Hispanics who are foreign-born naturalized citizens	Argentinian	Bolivian	Central American[1]	Chilean	Colombian	Costa Rican	Cuban	Dominican	Ecuadorian	Guatelmalan	Honduran	Mexican	Nicaraguan	Panamanian	Paraguayan	Peruvian	Puerto Rican	Salvadoran	South American[2]	Spaniard	Uruguayan	Venezuelan	Other Hisp.
UNITED STATES	12,542,626	35,238,481	3,939,732	35,511	11,585	359,574	21,008	149,331	17,874	517,386	198,903	67,659	67,865	42,864	1,929,928	45,738	32,813	3,486	69,482	20,062	129,989	399,506	16,856	7,675	15,899	497,517
	4.46		11.18	33.10	25.64	19.85	28.41	30.06	24.76	41.40	24.87	24.78	16.67	18.05	9.23	23.52	33.32	39.04	28.06	0.59	18.34	28.13	14.92	37.92	16.55	8.98
				0.90	0.29	9.13	0.53	3.79	0.45	13.13	5.05	1.72	1.72	1.09	48.99	1.16	0.83	0.09	1.76	0.51	3.30	10.14	0.43	0.19	0.40	12.63
			11.18	0.10	0.03	1.02	0.06	0.42	0.05	1.47	0.56	0.19	0.19	0.12	5.48	0.13	0.09	0.01	0.20	0.06	0.37	1.13	0.05	0.02	0.05	1.41
			31.41	0.28	0.09	2.87	0.17	1.19	0.14	4.13	1.59	0.54	0.54	0.34	15.39	0.36	0.26	0.03	0.55	0.16	1.04	3.19	0.13	0.06	0.13	3.97
FLORIDA	1,207,502	2,680,314	629,436	6,855	1,158	45,013	3,770	43,240	3,526	371,126	25,035	8,495	4,986	8,619	32,223	16,545	5,278	290	13,102	3,511	4,657	87,642	3,830	1,711	6,560	61,056
	7.56		23.48	28.77	26.28	20.58	28.09	29.33	29.12	43.86	33.14	32.71	15.75	19.18	9.00	19.07	31.03	31.28	27.93	0.73	21.95	27.70	25.00	38.59	15.43	16.55
				1.09	0.18	7.15	0.60	6.87	0.56	58.96	3.98	1.35	0.79	1.37	5.12	2.63	0.84	0.05	2.08	0.56	0.74	13.92	0.61	0.27	1.04	9.70
			23.48	0.26	0.04	1.68	0.14	1.61	0.13	13.85	0.93	0.32	0.19	0.32	1.20	0.62	0.20	0.01	0.49	0.13	0.17	3.27	0.14	0.06	0.24	2.28
			52.13	0.57	0.10	3.73	0.31	3.58	0.29	30.74	2.07	0.70	0.41	0.71	2.67	1.37	0.44	0.02	1.09	0.29	0.39	7.26	0.32	0.14	0.54	5.06
Alachua County	5,956	12,333	1,266	-	-	186	-	141	-	366	-	-	-	-	89	-	-	-	-	20	-	304	-	-	-	220
	2.73		10.27			30.00		22.14		14.99					6.71					0.61		15.05				9.83
						14.69		11.14		28.91					7.03					1.58		24.01				17.38
			10.27			1.51		1.14		2.97					0.72					0.16		2.46				1.78
			21.26			3.12		2.37		6.15					1.49					0.34		5.10				3.69
Gainesville (city)	2,832	5,962	522	-	-	-	-	-	-	118	-	-	-	-	26	-	-	-	-	13	-	156	-	-	-	129
	2.96		8.76							10.34					5.88					0.70		14.30				12.91
										22.61					4.98					2.49		29.89				24.71
			8.76							1.98					0.44					0.22		2.62				2.16
			18.43							4.17					0.92					0.46		5.51				4.56
Bay County	2,885	3,534	374	-	-	-	-	-	-	-	-	-	-	-	61	-	-	-	-	9	-	-	-	-	-	76
	1.95		10.58												5.07					0.88						18.01
															16.31					2.41						20.32
			10.58												1.73					0.25						2.15
			12.96												2.11					0.31						2.63
Brevard County	18,374	21,902	3,032	-	-	416	-	235	-	764	139	-	-	-	297	-	162	-	-	53	-	603	-	-	-	698
	3.86		13.84			33.93		33.10		36.19	37.47				8.11		40.70			0.57		35.08				20.74
						13.72		7.75		25.20	4.58				9.80		5.34			1.75		19.89				23.02
			13.84			1.90		1.07		3.49	0.63				1.36		0.74			0.24		2.75				3.19
			16.50			2.26		1.28		4.16	0.76				1.62		0.88			0.29		3.28				3.80
Melbourne (city)	2,567	3,807	443	-	-	-	-	-	-	-	-	-	-	-	59	-	-	-	-	0	-	-	-	-	-	59
	3.60		11.64												6.98					0.00						12.24
															13.32					0.00						13.32
			11.64												1.55					0.00						1.55
			17.26												2.30					0.00						2.30
Palm Bay (city)	4,910	6,968	846	-	-	-	-	-	-	-	-	-	-	-	60	-	-	-	-	6	-	176	-	-	-	291
	6.18		12.14												8.32					0.15		33.27				28.12
															7.09					0.71		20.80				34.40
			12.14												0.86					0.09		2.53				4.18
			17.23												1.22					0.12		3.58				5.93
Broward County	183,641	271,523	60,513	1,223	134	4,573	547	8,355	546	22,731	3,680	1,824	641	810	2,188	857	687	-	3,104	482	858	17,231	601	305	1,205	9,027
	11.31		22.29	30.12	19.20	22.86	26.15	27.02	28.41	42.77	34.36	34.20	22.32	19.52	11.75	24.03	27.63		27.42	0.89	19.20	26.19	25.97	31.77	13.33	19.31
				2.02	0.22	7.56	0.90	13.81	0.90	37.56	6.08	3.01	1.06	1.34	3.62	1.42	1.14		5.13	0.80	1.42	28.47	0.99	0.50	1.99	14.92
			22.29	0.45	0.05	1.68	0.20	3.08	0.20	8.37	1.36	0.67	0.24	0.30	0.81	0.32	0.25		1.14	0.18	0.32	6.35	0.22	0.11	0.44	3.32
			32.95	0.67	0.07	2.49	0.30	4.55	0.30	12.38	2.00	0.99	0.35	0.44	1.19	0.47	0.37		1.69	0.26	0.47	9.38	0.33	0.17	0.66	4.92

Notes: Please refer to the User's Guide for an explanation of data; data is arranged alphabetically by state, then county, then city within each county and only includes counties with populations > 99,999 and cities with populations > 49,999; (1) Includes Costa Rican, Guatemalan, Honduran, Nicaraguan, Panamanian, Salvadoran, and other Central American; (2) Includes Argentinian, Bolivian, Chilean, Colombian, Ecuadorian, Paraguayan, Peruvian, Uruguayan, Venezuelan, and other South American

Place	Total foreign-born naturalized citizens	Total Hispanic population	Hispanics who are foreign-born naturalized citizens	Argentinian	Bolivian	Central American[1]	Chilean	Colombian	Costa Rican	Cuban	Dominican	Ecuadorian	Guatelmalan	Honduran	Mexican	Nicaraguan	Panamanian	Paraguayan	Peruvian	Puerto Rican	Salvadoran	South American[2]	Spaniard	Uruguayan	Venezuelan	Other Hisp.
Coral Springs (city)	10,248	18,279	3,268	-	-	196	-	598	-	883	179	278	-	-	110	-	-	-	144	10	-	1,361	-	-	89	448
	8.72		17.88			23.70		26.07		43.73	33.58	29.51			6.90				15.11	0.25		24.63			17.94	12.96
						6.00		18.30		27.02	5.48	8.51			3.37				4.41	0.31		41.65			2.72	13.71
			17.88			1.07		3.27		4.83	0.98	1.52			0.60				0.79	0.05		7.45			0.49	2.45
			31.89			1.91		5.84		8.62	1.75	2.71			1.07				1.41	0.10		13.28			0.87	4.37
Davie (town)	6,440	14,384	3,209	-	-	234	-	354	-	1,286	-	-	-	-	119	-	-	-	143	10	-	907	-	-	-	462
	8.51		22.31			21.51		29.16		37.38					16.71				22.14	0.29		30.33				21.18
						7.29		11.03		40.07					3.71				4.46	0.31		28.26				14.40
			22.31			1.63		2.46		8.94					0.83				0.99	0.07		6.31				3.21
			49.83			3.63		5.50		19.97					1.85				2.22	0.16		14.08				7.17
Deerfield Beach (city)	6,008	5,517	973	-	-	75	-	142	-	281	-	-	-	-	59	-	-	-	-	30	-	328	-	-	-	120
	9.28		17.64			15.18		20.14		36.40					12.58					2.30		23.30				14.34
						7.71		14.59		28.88					6.06					3.08		33.71				12.33
			17.64			1.36		2.57		5.09					1.07					0.54		5.95				2.18
			16.20			1.25		2.36		4.68					0.98					0.50		5.46				2.00
Fort Lauderdale (city)	12,469	13,894	3,151	-	-	386	-	348	-	1,206	-	-	86	-	148	-	-	-	117	30	120	791	-	-	-	446
	8.20		22.68			21.65		26.69		44.63			23.18		12.01				24.68	1.23	18.07	26.54				18.47
						12.25		11.04		38.27			2.73		4.70				3.71	0.95	3.81	25.10				14.15
			22.68			2.78		2.50		8.68			0.62		1.07				0.84	0.22	0.86	5.69				3.21
			25.27			3.10		2.79		9.67			0.69		1.19				0.94	0.24	0.96	6.34				3.58
Hollywood (city)	16,136	31,380	6,562	120	-	477	91	917	-	2,406	513	189	-	109	146	96	-	-	288	13	-	1,814	-	-	105	1,132
	11.59		20.91	21.47		21.09	24.14	27.69		40.02	30.39	30.10		24.55	12.14	15.97			21.54	0.19		24.69			16.06	19.80
				1.83		7.27	1.39	13.97		36.67	7.82	2.88		1.66	2.22	1.46			4.39	0.20		27.64			1.60	17.25
			20.91	0.38		1.52	0.29	2.92		7.67	1.63	0.60		0.35	0.47	0.31			0.92	0.04		5.78			0.33	3.61
			40.67	0.74		2.96	0.56	5.68		14.91	3.18	1.17		0.68	0.90	0.59			1.78	0.08		11.24			0.65	7.02
Lauderhill (city)	7,773	3,915	900	-	-	-	-	134	-	-	-	-	-	-	-	-	-	-	-	40	-	244	-	-	-	236
	13.58		22.99					28.33												4.40		23.06				28.78
								14.89												4.44		27.11				26.22
			22.99					3.42												1.02		6.23				6.03
			11.58					1.72												0.51		3.14				3.04
Margate (city)	5,804	8,222	1,678	-	-	105	-	357	-	288	-	-	-	-	145	-	-	-	-	35	-	541	-	-	-	442
	10.78		20.41			19.13		31.48		41.68					17.34					1.59		26.85				27.92
						6.26		21.28		17.16					8.64					2.09		32.24				26.34
			20.41			1.28		4.34		3.50					1.76					0.43		6.58				5.38
			28.91			1.81		6.15		4.96					2.50					0.60		9.32				7.62
Miramar (city)	14,675	21,536	5,621	-	-	568	-	566	-	2,521	498	-	-	-	53	216	94	-	248	45	-	1,166	-	-	-	748
	20.19		26.10			33.77		28.56		38.55	35.27				9.23	33.49	25.61		37.46	1.27		31.13				19.11
						10.10		10.07		44.85	8.86				0.94	3.84	1.67		4.41	0.80		20.74				13.31
			26.10			2.64		2.63		11.71	2.31				0.25	1.00	0.44		1.15	0.21		5.41				3.47
			38.30			3.87		3.86		17.18	3.39				0.36	1.47	0.64		1.69	0.31		7.95				5.10
Pembroke Pines (city)	22,597	38,348	10,874	-	-	702	-	1,114	-	5,844	638	302	-	-	125	-	-	-	425	75	-	2,334	-	-	186	1,079
	16.48		28.36			36.41		32.17		47.13	35.27	62.14			13.38				28.24	1.02		29.87			12.57	18.66
						6.46		10.24		53.74	5.87	2.78			1.15				3.91	0.69		21.46			1.71	9.92
			28.36			1.83		2.90		15.24	1.66	0.79			0.33				1.11	0.20		6.09			0.49	2.81
			48.12			3.11		4.93		25.86	2.82	1.34			0.55				1.88	0.33		10.33			0.82	4.77
Plantation (city)	9,272	10,999	2,802	-	-	143	-	724	-	983	-	-	-	-	136	-	-	-	154	41	-	1,081	-	-	52	223
	11.13		25.48			19.72		33.86		49.55					20.86				30.50	2.54		27.85			9.67	13.09
						5.10		25.84		35.08					4.85				5.50	1.46		38.58			1.86	7.96
			25.48			1.30		6.58		8.94					1.24				1.40	0.37		9.83			0.47	2.03
			30.22			1.54		7.81		10.60					1.47				1.66	0.44		11.66			0.56	2.41

Notes: Please refer to the User's Guide for an explanation of data; data is arranged alphabetically by state, then county, then city within each county and only includes counties with populations > 99,999 and cities with populations > 49,999; (1) Includes Costa Rican, Guatemalan, Honduran, Nicaraguan, Panamanian, Salvadoran, and other Central American; (2) Includes Argentinian, Bolivian, Chilean, Colombian, Ecuadorian, Paraguayan, Peruvian, Uruguayan, Venezuelan, and other South American

Place	Total foreign-born naturalized citizens	Total Hispanic population	Hispanics who are foreign-born naturalized citizens	Argentinian	Bolivian	Central American[1]	Chilean	Colombian	Costa Rican	Cuban	Dominican	Ecuadorian	Guatemalan	Honduran	Mexican	Nicaraguan	Panamanian	Paraguayan	Peruvian	Puerto Rican	Salvadoran	South American[2]	Spaniard	Uruguayan	Venezuelan	Other Hisp.
Pompano Beach (city)	5,225 6.67	7,710	1,163 15.08 15.08 22.26	-	-	-	-	112 20.07 9.63 1.45 2.14	-	265 40.64 22.79 3.44 5.07	-	-	-	-	175 6.79 15.05 2.27 3.35	-	-	-	-	21 1.83 1.81 0.27 0.40	-	336 23.11 28.89 4.36 6.43	-	-	-	288 22.86 24.76 3.74 5.51
Sunrise (city)	12,272 14.33	14,542	3,317 22.81 22.81 27.03	-	-	171 22.71 5.16 1.18 1.39	-	638 25.93 19.23 4.39 5.20	-	822 39.73 24.78 5.65 6.70	246 33.51 7.42 1.69 2.00	191 36.11 5.76 1.31 1.56	-	-	116 13.74 3.50 0.80 0.95	-	-	-	265 44.61 7.99 1.82 2.16	38 1.31 1.15 0.26 0.31	-	1,332 29.13 40.16 9.16 10.85	-	-	-	592 22.91 17.85 4.07 4.82
Tamarac (city)	5,883 10.49	7,969	1,737 21.80 21.80 29.53	-	-	-	-	379 30.20 21.82 4.76 6.44	-	476 55.80 27.40 5.97 8.09	-	-	-	-	-	-	-	-	-	19 0.98 1.09 0.24 0.32	-	616 27.52 35.46 7.73 10.47	-	-	-	366 19.37 21.07 4.59 6.22
Charlotte County	6,815 4.81	4,585	828 18.06 18.06 12.15	-	-	-	-	-	-	287 48.32 34.66 6.26 4.21	-	-	-	-	85 8.78 10.27 1.85 1.25	-	-	-	-	0 0.00 0.00 0.00 0.00	-	-	-	-	-	162 19.01 19.57 3.53 2.38
Citrus County	3,861 3.27	3,058	356 11.64 11.64 9.22	-	-	-	-	-	-	-	-	-	-	-	11 2.16 3.09 0.36 0.28	-	-	-	-	0 0.00 0.00 0.00 0.00	-	-	-	-	-	99 15.79 27.81 3.24 2.56
Clay County	3,472 2.47	6,181	691 11.18 11.18 19.90	-	-	-	-	-	-	-	-	-	-	-	68 5.70 9.84 1.10 1.96	-	-	-	-	18 0.73 2.60 0.29 0.52	-	-	-	-	-	171 12.57 24.75 2.77 4.93
Collier County	14,194 5.65	49,252	6,008 12.20 12.20 42.33	-	-	347 10.29 5.78 0.70 2.44	-	328 28.37 5.46 0.67 2.31	-	2,140 29.40 35.62 4.35 15.08	74 14.74 1.23 0.15 0.52	-	78 4.96 1.30 0.16 0.55	52 7.19 0.87 0.11 0.37	2,383 8.44 39.66 4.84 16.79	-	-	-	-	16 0.51 0.27 0.03 0.11	-	586 26.82 9.75 1.19 4.13	-	-	-	437 9.97 7.27 0.89 3.08
Duval County	21,813 2.80	31,809	3,957 12.44 12.44 18.14	-	-	456 25.05 11.52 1.43 2.09	-	443 30.98 11.20 1.39 2.03	-	1,146 34.39 28.96 3.60 5.25	286 42.69 7.23 0.90 1.31	-	-	-	412 6.97 10.41 1.30 1.89	-	156 26.09 3.94 0.49 0.72	-	202 41.91 5.10 0.64 0.93	62 0.54 1.57 0.19 0.28	-	905 32.62 22.87 2.85 4.15	-	-	-	650 11.47 16.43 2.04 2.98
Jacksonville (city)	20,786 2.83	30,414	3,838 12.62 12.62 18.46	-	-	444 24.64 11.57 1.46 2.14	-	443 32.27 11.54 1.46 2.13	-	1,121 34.49 29.21 3.69 5.39	286 42.69 7.45 0.94 1.38	-	-	-	355 6.43 9.25 1.17 1.71	-	144 24.78 3.75 0.47 0.69	-	-	62 0.57 1.62 0.20 0.30	-	880 33.83 22.93 2.89 4.23	-	-	-	650 12.04 16.94 2.14 3.13
Escambia County	6,088 2.07	7,816	816 10.44 10.44 13.40	-	-	145 26.95 17.77 1.86 2.38	-	-	-	278 37.77 34.07 3.56 4.57	-	-	-	-	165 6.09 20.22 2.11 2.71	-	-	-	-	4 0.23 0.49 0.05 0.07	-	115 25.67 14.09 1.47 1.89	-	-	-	71 4.51 8.70 0.91 1.17

Notes: Please refer to the User's Guide for an explanation of data. data is arranged alphabetically by state. then county. then city within each county and only includes counties with populations > 99.999 and cities with populations > 49.999; (1) Includes Costa Rican. Guatemalan. Honduran, Nicaraguan, Panamanian, Salvadoran. and other Central American; (2) Includes Argentinian, Bolivian, Chilean, Colombian, Ecuadorian, Paraguayan, Peruvian, Uruguayan, Venezuelan. and other South American

Place	Total foreign-born naturalized citizens	Total Hispanic population	Hispanics who are foreign-born naturalized citizens	Argentinian	Bolivian	Central American[1]	Chilean	Colombian	Costa Rican	Cuban	Dominican	Ecuadorian	Guatelmalan	Honduran	Mexican	Nicaraguan	Panamanian	Paraguayan	Peruvian	Puerto Rican	Salvadoran	South American[2]	Spaniard	Uruguayan	Venezuelan	Other Hisp.
Pensacola (city)	1,176 2.09	1,198	169 14.11 14.11 14.37	-	-	-	-	-	-	-	-	-	-	-	-	-	-	-	-	-	-	-	-	-	-	-
Hernando County	4,701 3.59	6,717	501 7.46 7.46 10.66	-	-	-	-	-	-	131 21.03 26.15 1.95 2.79	-	-	-	-	77 7.90 15.37 1.15 1.64	-	-	-	-	26 0.68 5.19 0.39 0.55	-	-	-	-	-	94 11.49 18.76 1.40 2.00
Spring Hill (cdp)	3,195 4.62	4,911	352 7.17 7.17 11.02	-	-	-	-	-	-	91 22.25 25.85 1.85 2.85	-	-	-	-	-	-	-	-	-	26 0.84 7.39 0.53 0.81	-	-	-	-	-	67 10.91 19.03 1.36 2.10
Hillsborough County	47,127 4.72	179,637	23,768 13.23 13.23 50.43	-	-	1,916 24.19 8.06 1.07 4.07	-	1,678 27.72 7.06 0.93 3.56	136 14.17 0.57 0.08 0.29	10,283 29.48 43.26 5.72 21.82	1,292 33.28 5.44 0.72 2.74	508 39.63 2.14 0.28 1.08	209 19.79 0.88 0.12 0.44	532 23.72 2.24 0.30 1.13	3,118 8.53 13.12 1.74 6.62	308 30.29 1.30 0.17 0.65	462 28.07 1.94 0.26 0.98	-	500 27.53 2.10 0.28 1.06	401 0.80 1.69 0.22 0.85	160 21.28 0.67 0.09 0.34	3,680 29.94 15.48 2.05 7.81	218 11.91 0.92 0.12 0.46	-	458 25.86 1.93 0.25 0.97	2,860 8.93 12.03 1.59 6.07
Brandon (cdp)	2,958 3.81	10,068	901 8.95 8.95 30.46	-	-	171 31.78 18.98 1.70 5.78	-	-	-	141 12.97 15.65 1.40 4.77	-	-	-	-	117 11.02 12.99 1.16 3.96	-	-	-	-	25 0.52 2.77 0.25 0.85	-	163 26.90 18.09 1.62 5.51	-	-	-	192 12.25 21.31 1.91 6.49
Tampa (city)	14,683 4.84	58,571	8,147 13.91 13.91 55.49	-	-	715 22.14 8.78 1.22 4.87	-	391 22.95 4.80 0.67 2.66	-	4,192 29.38 51.45 7.16 28.55	330 23.14 4.05 0.56 2.25	213 50.96 2.61 0.36 1.45	-	206 23.04 2.53 0.35 1.40	637 8.83 7.82 1.09 4.34	123 26.28 1.51 0.21 0.84	149 23.58 1.83 0.25 1.01	-	-	71 0.45 0.87 0.12 0.48	-	1,102 30.65 13.53 1.88 7.51	78 10.64 0.96 0.13 0.53	-	199 31.89 2.44 0.34 1.36	1,022 8.33 12.54 1.74 6.96
Town 'n' Country (cdp)	5,679 7.84	20,662	3,470 16.79 16.79 61.10	-	-	203 23.69 5.85 0.98 3.57	-	269 21.28 7.75 1.30 4.74	-	1,703 35.87 49.08 8.24 29.99	346 46.13 9.97 1.67 6.09	-	-	-	115 10.51 3.31 0.56 2.03	-	-	-	-	105 1.41 3.03 0.51 1.85	-	541 25.56 15.59 2.62 9.53	-	-	-	424 12.32 12.22 2.05 7.47
Indian River County	4,120 3.65	7,300	867 11.88 11.88 21.04	-	-	40 11.70 4.61 0.55 0.97	-	-	-	76 20.77 8.77 1.04 1.84	-	-	-	-	361 8.05 41.64 4.95 8.76	-	-	-	-	4 0.58 0.46 0.05 0.10	-	237 46.02 27.34 3.25 5.75	-	-	-	135 15.19 15.57 1.85 3.28
Lake County	5,084 2.41	11,836	1,418 11.98 11.98 27.89	-	-	136 27.20 9.59 1.15 2.68	-	-	-	303 39.71 21.37 2.56 5.96	-	-	-	-	551 10.22 38.86 4.66 10.84	-	-	-	-	14 0.48 0.99 0.12 0.28	-	200 35.78 14.10 1.69 3.93	-	-	-	166 10.43 11.71 1.40 3.27
Lee County	15,380 3.49	41,993	4,133 9.84 9.84 26.87	-	-	407 13.49 9.85 0.97 2.65	-	279 27.30 6.75 0.66 1.81	-	1,068 31.73 25.84 2.54 6.94	293 27.46 7.09 0.70 1.91	-	75 5.33 1.81 0.18 0.49	98 19.76 2.37 0.23 0.64	1,143 7.61 27.66 2.72 7.43	-	-	-	-	41 0.35 0.99 0.10 0.27	-	634 25.77 15.34 1.51 4.12	-	-	-	544 10.58 13.16 1.30 3.54

Notes: Please refer to the User's Guide for an explanation of data: data is arranged alphabetically by state, then county, then city within each county and only includes counties with populations > 99,999 and cities with populations > 49,999; (1) Includes Costa Rican, Guatemalan, Honduran, Nicaraguan, Panamanian, Salvadoran, and other Central American; (2) Includes Argentinian, Bolivian, Chilean, Colombian, Ecuadorian, Paraguayan, Peruvian, Uruguayan, Venezuelan, and other South American

Place	Total foreign-born naturalized citizens	Total Hispanic population	Hispanics who are foreign-born naturalized citizens	Argentinian	Bolivian	Central American[1]	Chilean	Colombian	Costa Rican	Cuban	Dominican	Ecuadorian	Guatelmalan	Honduran	Mexican	Nicaraguan	Panamanian	Paraguayan	Peruvian	Puerto Rican	Salvadoran	South American[2]	Spaniard	Uruguayan	Venezuelan	Other Hisp.
Cape Coral (city)	4,610	8,355	1,675	-	-	-	-	143	-	651	216	-	-	-	67	-	-	-	-	32	-	350	-	-	-	239
	4.51		20.05					24.61		41.15	37.11				5.02					1.47		32.96				19.00
								8.54		38.87	12.90				4.00					1.91		20.90				14.27
			20.05					1.71		7.79	2.59				0.80					0.38		4.19				2.86
			36.33					3.10		14.12	4.69				1.45					0.69		7.59				5.18
Leon County	4,776	8,220	790	-	-	-	-	-	-	328	-	-	-	-	53	-	-	-	-	0	-	144	-	-	-	117
	1.99		9.61							17.22					3.70					0.00		13.94				7.17
										41.52					6.71					0.00		18.23				14.81
			9.61							3.99					0.64					0.00		1.75				1.42
			16.54							6.87					1.11					0.00		3.02				2.45
Tallahassee (city)	3,038	6,077	420	-	-	-	-	-	-	176	-	-	-	-	16	-	-	-	-	0	-	91	-	-	-	55
	2.02		6.91							12.10					1.77					0.00		11.35				4.43
										41.90					3.81					0.00		21.67				13.10
			6.91							2.90					0.26					0.00		1.50				0.91
			13.82							5.79					0.53					0.00		3.00				1.81
Manatee County	8,466	24,501	2,440	-	-	143	-	-	-	380	-	-	-	-	1,244	-	-	-	-	21	-	284	-	-	-	313
	3.21		9.96			9.73				32.01					8.27					0.65		30.31				12.93
						5.86				15.57					50.98					0.86		11.64				12.83
			9.96			0.58				1.55					5.08					0.09		1.16				1.28
			28.82			1.69				4.49					14.69					0.25		3.35				3.70
Marion County	7,516	15,535	1,545	-	-	221	-	198	-	279	-	-	-	-	224	-	-	-	-	25	-	339	-	-	-	384
	2.90		9.95			40.70		35.17		22.63					6.70					0.36		31.07				18.47
						14.30		12.82		18.06					14.50					1.62		21.94				24.85
			9.95			1.42		1.27		1.80					1.44					0.16		2.18				2.47
			20.56			2.94		2.63		3.71					2.98					0.33		4.51				5.11
Martin County	4,482	9,490	1,091	-	-	312	-	-	-	271	-	-	203	-	310	-	-	-	-	0	-	-	-	-	-	93
	3.54		11.50			13.11				33.79			10.04		8.03					0.00						13.23
						28.60				24.84			18.61		28.41					0.00						8.52
			11.50			3.29				2.86			2.14		3.27					0.00						0.98
			24.34			6.96				6.05			4.53		6.92					0.00						2.07
Miami-Dade County	535,080	1,291,681	431,262	3,728	692	28,372	2,322	22,937	1,525	303,693	13,352	3,764	2,255	5,546	4,205	14,027	2,178	-	6,463	1,123	2,146	45,395	2,195	826	3,591	32,927
	23.75		33.39	26.29	30.19	20.45	28.91	30.58	32.93	46.24	33.47	32.57	21.18	19.12	11.25	18.59	32.27		27.16	1.41	22.41	27.96	35.42	41.91	15.89	19.30
				0.86	0.16	6.58	0.54	5.32	0.35	70.42	3.10	0.87	0.52	1.29	0.98	3.25	0.51		1.50	0.26	0.50	10.53	0.51	0.19	0.83	7.64
			33.39	0.29	0.05	2.20	0.18	1.78	0.12	23.51	1.03	0.29	0.17	0.43	0.33	1.09	0.17		0.50	0.09	0.17	3.51	0.17	0.06	0.28	2.55
			80.60	0.70	0.13	5.30	0.43	4.29	0.29	56.76	2.50	0.70	0.42	1.04	0.79	2.62	0.41		1.21	0.21	0.40	8.48	0.41	0.15	0.67	6.15
Carol City (cdp)	11,019	24,973	7,852	-	-	676	-	632	-	4,749	617	-	-	163	-	261	-	-	-	105	-	901	-	-	-	723
	18.54		31.44			25.59		43.11		42.34	32.77			31.47		18.02				3.76		35.56				20.74
						8.61		8.05		60.48	7.86			2.08		3.32				1.34		11.47				9.21
			31.44			2.71		2.53		19.02	2.47			0.65		1.05				0.42		3.61				2.90
			71.26			6.13		5.74		43.10	5.60			1.48		2.37				0.95		8.18				6.56
Fountainbleau (cdp)	18,348	51,833	17,610	136	-	1,921	159	753	-	11,226	717	166	-	123	78	1,414	99	-	329	12	-	1,906	-	-	258	1,673
	30.83		33.97	30.91		23.54	22.62	27.08		50.34	37.19	20.78		19.16	16.18	23.10	18.97		27.86	0.64		22.76			12.38	19.53
				0.77		10.91	0.90	4.28		63.75	4.07	0.94		0.70	0.44	8.03	0.56		1.87	0.07		10.82			1.47	9.50
			33.97	0.26		3.71	0.31	1.45		21.66	1.38	0.32		0.24	0.15	2.73	0.19		0.63	0.02		3.68			0.50	3.23
			95.98	0.74		10.47	0.87	4.10		61.18	3.91	0.90		0.67	0.43	7.71	0.54		1.79	0.07		10.39			1.41	9.12
Hialeah (city)	70,331	204,808	69,014	84	-	2,654	213	2,567	179	56,623	1,718	465	160	465	248	1,484	-	-	393	73	208	4,027	220	-	181	3,451
	31.06		33.70	19.58		16.69	28.40	33.27	34.23	40.07	35.16	37.71	19.00	17.54	15.42	14.60			26.94	1.05	21.89	31.21	43.22		18.95	16.65
				0.12		3.85	0.31	3.72	0.26	82.05	2.49	0.67	0.23	0.67	0.36	2.15			0.57	0.11	0.30	5.84	0.32		0.26	5.00
			33.70	0.04		1.30	0.10	1.25	0.09	27.65	0.84	0.23	0.08	0.23	0.12	0.72			0.19	0.04	0.10	1.97	0.11		0.09	1.68
			98.13	0.12		3.77	0.30	3.65	0.25	80.51	2.44	0.66	0.23	0.66	0.35	2.11			0.56	0.10	0.30	5.73	0.31		0.26	4.91

Notes: Please refer to the User's Guide for an explanation of data; data is arranged alphabetically by state, then county, then city within each county and only includes counties with populations > 99,999 and cities with populations > 49,999; (1) Includes Costa Rican, Guatemalan, Honduran, Nicaraguan, Panamanian, Salvadoran, and other Central American; (2) Includes Argentinian, Bolivian, Chilean, Colombian, Ecuadorian, Paraguayan, Peruvian, Uruguayan, Venezuelan, and other South American

Place	Total foreign-born naturalized citizens	Total Hispanic population	Hispanics who are foreign-born naturalized citizens	Argentinian	Bolivian	Central American[1]	Chilean	Colombian	Costa Rican	Cuban	Dominican	Ecuadorian	Guatelmalan	Honduran	Mexican	Nicaraguan	Panamanian	Paraguayan	Peruvian	Puerto Rican	Salvadoran	South American[2]	Spaniard	Uruguayan	Venezuelan	Other Hisp.
Kendale Lakes (cdp)	17,856	43,588	16,336	-	-	1,132	-	1,233	-	10,627	359	-	-	137	133	780	-	-	351	45	-	2,444	-	-	165	1,523
	31.39		37.48			27.75		30.80		48.18	42.59			24.60	22.81	27.40			36.30	2.74		33.40			18.94	22.06
						6.93		7.55		65.05	2.20			0.84	0.81	4.77			2.15	0.28		14.96			1.01	9.32
			37.48			2.60		2.83		24.38	0.82			0.31	0.31	1.79			0.81	0.10		5.61			0.38	3.49
			91.49			6.34		6.91		59.52	2.01			0.77	0.74	4.37			1.97	0.25		13.69			0.92	8.53
Kendall (cdp)	16,474	37,640	13,071	211	-	1,231	216	1,173	-	7,647	228	-	-	-	-	769	-	-	234	27	-	2,258	-	-	217	1,420
	21.88		34.73	32.21		32.02	45.00	28.40		48.19	28.54					34.45			17.08	1.20		25.95			14.93	26.36
				1.61		9.42	1.65	8.97		58.50	1.74					5.88			1.79	0.21		17.27			1.66	10.86
			34.73	0.56		3.27	0.57	3.12		20.32	0.61					2.04			0.62	0.07		6.00			0.58	3.77
			79.34	1.28		7.47	1.31	7.12		46.42	1.38					4.67			1.42	0.16		13.71			1.32	8.62
Miami Beach (city)	21,744	46,980	16,432	548	-	756	206	1,151	-	10,266	490	197	-	177	193	351	-	-	434	32	-	3,005	137	-	202	1,553
	24.69		34.98	18.08		26.78	27.88	25.62		56.28	35.10	29.76		21.85	19.57	35.38			22.87	0.90		23.14	23.91		13.87	24.17
				3.33		4.60	1.25	7.00		62.48	2.98	1.20		1.08	1.17	2.14			2.64	0.19		18.29	0.83		1.23	9.45
			34.98	1.17		1.61	0.44	2.45		21.85	1.04	0.42		0.38	0.41	0.75			0.92	0.07		6.40	0.29		0.43	3.31
			75.57	2.52		3.48	0.95	5.29		47.21	2.25	0.91		0.81	0.89	1.61			2.00	0.15		13.82	0.63		0.93	7.14
Miami (city)	89,727	238,461	79,264	473	-	5,529	202	1,681	193	61,227	2,182	559	533	1.767	272	2,209	255	-	756	228	407	4,188	450	-	243	5.188
	24.75		33.24	23.31		12.59	22.52	27.99	23.65	49.09	30.01	31.85	18.70	12.94	8.59	9.79	28.88		27.32	2.25	17.00	26.25	47.32		13.81	16.05
				0.60		6.98	0.25	2.12	0.24	77.24	2.75	0.71	0.67	2.23	0.34	2.79	0.32		0.95	0.29	0.51	5.28	0.57		0.31	6.55
			33.24	0.20		2.32	0.08	0.70	0.08	25.68	0.92	0.23	0.22	0.74	0.11	0.93	0.11		0.32	0.10	0.17	1.76	0.19		0.10	2.18
			88.34	0.53		6.16	0.23	1.87	0.22	68.24	2.43	0.62	0.59	1.97	0.30	2.46	0.28		0.84	0.25	0.45	4.67	0.50		0.27	5.78
North Miami (city)	12,035	14,311	3,799	-	-	540	-	343	-	1,374	298	-	-	208	-	155	-	-	-	34	-	634	-	-	-	843
	20.05		26.55			30.70		33.46		48.67	27.14			35.25		21.65				1.22		30.55				25.77
						14.21		9.03		36.17	7.84			5.48		4.08				0.89		16.69				22.19
			26.55			3.77		2.40		9.60	2.08			1.45		1.08				0.24		4.43				5.89
			31.57			4.49		2.85		11.42	2.48			1.73		1.29				0.28		5.27				7.00
Tamiami (cdp)	20,633	47,691	20,107	-	-	1,215	-	758	-	15,736	400	-	-	165	104	728	-	-	-	37	-	1,256	-	-	68	1,246
	37.69		42.16			31.56		37.32		48.60	59.97			36.42	19.22	26.41				3.42		31.61			12.48	24.84
						6.04		3.77		78.26	1.99			0.82	0.52	3.62				0.18		6.25			0.34	6.20
			42.16			2.55		1.59		33.00	0.84			0.35	0.22	1.53				0.08		2.63			0.14	2.61
			97.45			5.89		3.67		76.27	1.94			0.80	0.50	3.53				0.18		6.09			0.33	6.04
Okaloosa County	5,715	6,901	824	-	-	93	-	-	-	201	-	-	-	-	111	-	-	-	-	19	-	-	-	-	-	207
	3.35		11.94			25.69				34.84					4.67					1.25						13.35
						11.29				24.39					13.47					2.31						25.12
			11.94			1.35				2.91					1.61					0.28						3.00
			14.42			1.63				3.52					1.94					0.33						3.62
Orange County	53,651	168,191	17,503	213	-	1,407	57	2,195	130	4,568	2,007	594	266	243	2,070	123	294	-	541	413	267	4,169	110	-	328	2,759
	5.99		10.41	30.34		24.32	12.42	28.51	21.81	34.52	32.40	33.52	25.75	19.60	10.38	13.90	30.91		30.62	0.48	28.31	26.38	16.39		12.54	13.60
				1.22		8.04	0.33	12.54	0.74	26.10	11.47	3.39	1.52	1.39	11.83	0.70	1.68		3.09	2.36	1.53	23.82	0.63		1.87	15.76
			10.41	0.13		0.84	0.03	1.31	0.08	2.72	1.19	0.35	0.16	0.14	1.23	0.07	0.17		0.32	0.25	0.16	2.48	0.07		0.20	1.64
			32.62	0.40		2.62	0.11	4.09	0.24	8.51	3.74	1.11	0.50	0.45	3.86	0.23	0.55		1.01	0.77	0.50	7.77	0.21		0.61	5.14
Orlando (city)	9,667	32,897	3,434	-	-	247	-	545	-	1,184	386	-	-	-	213	-	-	-	112	42	-	855	-	-	49	483
	5.20		10.44			17.96		30.74		39.72	31.10				9.18				24.62	0.25		21.62			6.27	11.51
						7.19		15.87		34.48	11.24				6.20				3.26	1.22		24.90			1.43	14.07
			10.44			0.75		1.66		3.60	1.17				0.65				0.34	0.13		2.60			0.15	1.47
			35.52			2.56		5.64		12.25	3.99				2.20				1.16	0.43		8.84			0.51	5.00
Osceola County	9,514	50,742	3,900	-	-	424	-	464	-	668	835	169	-	-	335	-	-	-	-	99	78	907	-	-	93	622
	5.52		7.69			21.88		23.89		36.32	33.83	38.06			9.74					0.30	14.47	24.92			17.68	13.56
						10.87		11.90		17.13	21.41	4.33			8.59					2.54	2.00	23.26			2.38	15.95
			7.69			0.84		0.91		1.32	1.65	0.33			0.66					0.20	0.15	1.79			0.18	1.23
			40.99			4.46		4.88		7.02	8.78	1.78			3.52					1.04	0.82	9.53			0.98	6.54

Notes: Please refer to the User's Guide for an explanation of data; data is arranged alphabetically by state, then county, then city within each county and only includes counties with populations > 99,999 and cities with populations > 49,999; (1) Includes Costa Rican, Guatemalan, Honduran, Nicaraguan, Panamanian, Salvadoran, and other Central American; (2) Includes Argentinian, Bolivian, Chilean, Colombian, Ecuadorian, Paraguayan, Peruvian, Uruguayan, Venezuelan, and other South American

Place	Total foreign-born naturalized citizens	Total Hispanic population	Hispanics who are foreign-born naturalized citizens	Argentinian	Bolivian	Central American[1]	Chilean	Colombian	Costa Rican	Cuban	Dominican	Ecuadorian	Guatemalan	Honduran	Mexican	Nicaraguan	Panamanian	Paraguayan	Peruvian	Puerto Rican	Salvadoran	South American[2]	Spaniard	Uruguayan	Venezuelan	Other Hisp.
Palm Beach County	83,681 7.40	140,568	26,374 18.76 18.76 31.52	625 33.69 2.37 0.44 0.75	-	2,196 14.13 8.33 1.56 2.62	148 21.61 0.56 0.11 0.18	2,647 27.79 10.04 1.88 3.16	217 25.74 0.82 0.15 0.26	10,325 39.47 39.15 7.35 12.34	1,256 35.00 4.76 0.89 1.50	551 27.67 2.09 0.39 0.66	478 6.91 1.81 0.34 0.57	465 14.22 1.76 0.33 0.56	2,819 9.53 10.69 2.01 3.37	484 22.99 1.84 0.34 0.58	158 36.57 0.60 0.11 0.19	-	762 30.69 2.89 0.54 0.91	220 0.89 0.83 0.16 0.26	329 19.81 1.25 0.23 0.39	5,678 28.04 21.53 4.04 6.79	115 24.52 0.44 0.08 0.14	345 42.59 1.31 0.25 0.41	247 13.89 0.94 0.18 0.30	3,765 18.63 14.28 2.68 4.50
Boca Raton (city)	5,638 7.46	6,368	1,487 23.35 23.35 26.37	-	-	-	-	215 24.71 14.46 3.38 3.81	-	464 50.60 31.20 7.29 8.23	-	-	-	-	79 9.48 5.31 1.24 1.40	-	-	-	-	7 0.83 0.47 0.11 0.12	-	471 22.59 31.67 7.40 8.35	-	-	-	301 24.45 20.24 4.73 5.34
Boynton Beach (city)	4,289 7.15	5,000	755 15.10 15.10 17.60	-	-	121 20.65 16.03 2.42 2.82	-	-	-	193 33.51 25.56 3.86 4.50	-	-	-	-	100 11.90 13.25 2.00 2.33	-	-	-	-	17 1.17 2.25 0.34 0.40	-	223 29.81 29.54 4.46 5.20	-	-	-	71 10.38 9.40 1.42 1.66
Delray Beach (city)	4,137 6.90	4,165	773 18.56 18.56 18.69	-	-	-	-	-	-	-	-	-	-	-	89 6.10 11.51 2.14 2.15	-	-	-	-	44 6.00 5.69 1.06 1.06	-	229 38.23 29.62 5.50 5.54	-	-	-	109 22.47 14.10 2.62 2.63
West Palm Beach (city)	7,116 8.73	15,007	2,872 19.14 19.14 40.36	-	-	139 4.96 4.84 0.93 1.95	-	205 27.67 7.14 1.37 2.88	-	1,647 37.38 57.35 10.97 23.15	152 38.97 5.29 1.01 2.14	-	46 2.23 1.60 0.31 0.65	-	124 6.28 4.32 0.83 1.74	-	-	-	-	0 0.00 0.00 0.00 0.00	-	468 29.42 16.30 3.12 6.58	-	-	-	335 17.20 11.66 2.23 4.71
Pasco County	13,303 3.86	19,555	2,081 10.64 10.64 15.64	-	-	132 20.72 6.34 0.68 0.99	-	-	-	580 31.97 27.87 2.97 4.36	-	-	-	-	613 10.25 29.46 3.13 4.61	-	-	-	-	29 0.42 1.39 0.15 0.22	-	329 38.12 15.81 1.68 2.47	-	-	-	346 12.00 16.63 1.77 2.60
Pinellas County	40,786 4.43	42,128	5,397 12.81 12.81 13.23	-	-	415 29.73 7.69 0.99 1.02	-	482 25.60 8.93 1.14 1.18	-	1,834 38.80 33.98 4.35 4.50	262 28.98 4.85 0.62 0.64	117 29.03 2.17 0.28 0.29	-	-	841 8.17 15.58 2.00 2.06	-	-	-	265 33.42 4.91 0.63 0.65	48 0.37 0.89 0.11 0.12	-	1,187 24.79 21.99 2.82 2.91	39 7.57 0.72 0.09 0.10	-	69 7.87 1.28 0.16 0.17	771 12.11 14.29 1.83 1.89
Clearwater (city)	4,901 4.54	9,615	1,007 10.47 10.47 20.55	-	-	-	-	74 18.97 7.35 0.77 1.51	-	289 50.61 28.70 3.01 5.90	-	-	-	-	292 6.93 29.00 3.04 5.96	-	-	-	-	5 0.22 0.50 0.05 0.10	-	197 18.85 19.56 2.05 4.02	-	-	-	131 12.00 13.01 1.36 2.67
Largo (city)	2,815 4.05	2,849	379 13.30 13.30 13.46	-	-	-	-	-	-	-	-	-	-	-	56 10.11 14.78 1.97 1.99	-	-	-	-	5 0.64 1.32 0.18 0.18	-	-	-	-	-	-
Palm Harbor (cdp)	2,721 4.60	1,939	316 16.30 16.30 11.61	-	-	-	-	-	-	-	-	-	-	-	-	-	-	-	-	10 1.22 3.16 0.52 0.37	-	-	-	-	-	-

Notes: Please refer to the User's Guide for an explanation of data; data is arranged alphabetically by state, then county, then city within each county and only includes counties with populations > 99,999 and cities with populations > 49,999; (1) Includes Costa Rican, Guatemalan, Honduran, Nicaraguan, Panamanian, Salvadoran, and other Central American; (2) Includes Argentinian, Bolivian, Chilean, Colombian, Ecuadorian, Paraguayan, Peruvan, Uruguayan, Venezuelan, and other South American

Place	Total foreign-born naturalized citizens	Total Hispanic population	Hispanics who are foreign-born naturalized citizens	Argentinian	Bolivian	Central American[1]	Chilean	Colombian	Costa Rican	Cuban	Dominican	Ecuadorian	Guatemalan	Honduran	Mexican	Nicaraguan	Panamanian	Paraguayan	Peruvian	Puerto Rican	Salvadoran	South American[2]	Spaniard	Uruguayan	Venezuelan	Other Hisp.
	9,924	9,878	1,408	-	-	-	-	-	-	655	-	-	-	-	131	-	-	-	-	0	-	330	-	-	-	154
	4.00		14.25							39.53					7.84					0.00		28.04				10.55
St. Petersburg (city)										46.52					9.30					0.00		23.44				10.94
			14.25							6.63					1.33					0.00		3.34				1.56
			14.19							6.60					1.32					0.00		3.33				1.55
	11,908	45,650	4,519	-	-	232	-	-	-	799	157	-	-	-	2,588	-	-	-	-	72	-	217	-	-	-	442
	2.46		9.90			19.06				31.86	33.69				10.61					0.63		21.83				9.75
Polk County						5.13				17.68	3.47				57.27					1.59		4.80				9.78
			9.90			0.51				1.75	0.34				5.67					0.16		0.48				0.97
			37.95			1.95				6.71	1.32				21.73					0.60		1.82				3.71
	1,944	5,050	651	-	-	-	-	-	-	282	-	-	-	-	79	-	-	-	-	37	-	-	-	-	-	71
	2.49		12.89							43.79					8.37					1.85						8.75
Lakeland (city)										43.32					12.14					5.68						10.91
			12.89							5.58					1.56					0.73						1.41
			33.49							14.51					4.06					1.90						3.65
	3,604	3,596	543	-	-	-	-	-	-	-	-	-	-	-	71	-	-	-	-	0	-	-	-	-	-	112
	2.93		15.10												7.47					0.00						18.39
St. Johns County															13.08					0.00						20.63
			15.10												1.97					0.00						3.11
			15.07												1.97					0.00						3.11
	8,746	16,004	2,093	-	-	256	-	147	-	503	-	-	-	-	590	-	-	-	-	37	-	372	-	-	-	188
	4.54		13.08			24.93		34.92		47.14					8.18					1.00		36.83				12.37
St. Lucie County						12.23		7.02		24.03					28.19					1.77		17.77				8.98
			13.08			1.60		0.92		3.14					3.69					0.23		2.32				1.17
			23.93			2.93		1.68		5.75					6.75					0.42		4.25				2.15
	4,946	6,822	1,170	-	-	-	-	-	-	384	-	-	-	-	80	-	-	-	-	8	-	276	-	-	-	136
	5.57		17.15							53.26					7.18					0.31		39.60				15.40
Port St. Lucie (city)										32.82					6.84					0.68		23.59				11.62
			17.15							5.63					1.17					0.12		4.05				1.99
			23.66							7.76					1.62					0.16		5.58				2.75
	2,065	2,821	284	-	-	-	-	-	-	-	-	-	-	-	57	-	-	-	-	0	-	-	-	-	-	41
	1.75		10.07												6.80					0.00						7.81
Santa Rosa County															20.07					0.00						14.44
			10.07												2.02					0.00						1.45
			13.75												2.76					0.00						1.99
	14,642	14,373	2,233	-	-	185	-	232	-	718	-	-	-	-	563	-	-	-	-	27	-	467	-	-	-	193
	4.49		15.54			29.27		26.51		37.18					9.45					1.57		25.04				9.84
Sarasota County						8.28		10.39		32.15					25.21					1.21		20.91				8.64
			15.54			1.29		1.61		5.00					3.92					0.19		3.25				1.34
			15.25			1.26		1.58		4.90					3.85					0.18		3.19				1.32
	2,328	6,390	701	-	-	-	-	-	-	190	-	-	-	-	288	-	-	-	-	0	-	92	-	-	-	43
	4.43		10.97							28.49					8.12					0.00		14.22				6.15
Sarasota (city)										27.10					41.08					0.00		13.12				6.13
			10.97							2.97					4.51					0.00		1.44				0.67
			30.11							8.16					12.37					0.00		3.95				1.85
	16,507	40,656	5,138	120	-	488	-	713	-	1,358	388	159	-	-	328	-	90	-	130	123	-	1,377	-	-	74	1,022
	4.52		12.64	27.03		24.19		31.77		36.24	33.30	32.72			9.25		16.45		24.07	0.62		30.36			16.86	17.93
Seminole County				2.34		9.50		13.88		26.43	7.55	3.09			6.38		1.75		2.53	2.39		26.80			1.44	19.89
			12.64	0.30		1.20		1.75		3.34	0.95	0.39			0.81		0.22		0.32	0.30		3.39			0.18	2.51
			31.13	0.73		2.96		4.32		8.23	2.35	0.96			1.99		0.55		0.79	0.75		8.34			0.45	6.19

Notes: Please refer to the User's Guide for an explanation of data: data is arranged alphabetically by state, then county, then city within each county and only includes counties with populations > 99,999 and cities with populations > 49,999; (1) Includes Costa Rican, Guatemalan, Honduran, Nicaraguan, Panamanian, Salvadoran, and other Central American; (2) Includes Argentinian, Bolivian, Chilean, Colombian, Ecuadorian, Paraguayan, Peruvian, Uruguayan, Venezuelan, and other South American

Place	Total foreign-born naturalized citizens	Total Hispanic population	Hispanics who are foreign-born naturalized citizens	Argentinian	Bolivian	Central American[1]	Chilean	Colombian	Costa Rican	Cuban	Dominican	Ecuadorian	Guatemalan	Honduran	Mexican	Nicaraguan	Panamanian	Paraguayan	Peruvian	Puerto Rican	Salvadoran	South American[2]	Spaniard	Uruguayan	Venezuelan	Other Hisp.
Volusia County	14,955 3.37	29,273	2,708 9.25 9.25 18.11	-	-	348 44.11 12.85 1.19 2.33	-	237 35.01 8.75 0.81 1.58	-	555 40.84 20.49 1.90 3.71	172 29.25 6.35 0.59 1.15	-	-	-	560 6.95 20.68 1.91 3.74	-	-	-	-	69 0.49 2.55 0.24 0.46	-	551 34.24 20.35 1.88 3.68	-	-	-	386 13.97 14.25 1.32 2.58
Daytona Beach (city)	2,227 3.48	2,275	224 9.85 9.85 10.06	-	-	-	-	-	-	-	-	-	-	-	-	-	-	-	-	0 0.00 0.00 0.00 0.00	-	-	-	-	-	73 18.16 32.59 3.21 3.28
Deltona (city)	2,811 4.03	12,855	946 7.36 7.36 33.65	-	-	-	-	-	-	207 37.10 21.88 1.61 7.36	-	-	-	-	58 8.66 6.13 0.45 2.06	-	-	-	-	69 0.73 7.29 0.54 2.45	-	235 37.84 24.84 1.83 8.36	-	-	-	122 12.42 12.90 0.95 4.34

Notes: Please refer to the User's Guide for an explanation of data: data is arranged alphabetically by state, then county, then city within each county and only includes counties with populations > 99,999 and cities with populations > 49,999; (1) Includes Costa Rican, Guatemalan, Honduran, Nicaraguan, Panamanian, Salvadoran, and other Central American; (2) Includes Argentinian, Bolivian, Chilean, Colombian, Ecuadorian, Paraguayan, Peruvian, Uruguayan, Venezuelan, and other South American

Educational Attainment: High School Grads

(Universe: Population 25 Years and Over)

Place	Total population 25 years and over who are High School graduates	Hispanic population 25 years and over	Hispanics 25 years and over who are High School graduates	Argentinian	Bolivian	Central American[1]	Chilean	Colombian	Costa Rican	Cuban	Dominican	Ecuadorian	Guatelmalan	Honduran	Mexican	Nicaraguan	Panamanian	Paraguayan	Peruvian	Puerto Rican	Salvadoran	South American[2]	Spaniard	Uruguayan	Venezuelan	Other Hisp.
UNITED STATES	146,496,014	18,270,377	9,577,031	61,857	23,864	497,990	41,451	243,908	32,927	588,278	236,324	112,858	90,521	63,882	4,662,491	76,084	54,475	3,324	136,832	1,166,324	150,547	715,472	60,310	10,690	52,212	1,649,842
	80.40		52.42	80.44	84.59	46.03	83.07	74.45	72.56	62.95	51.08	63.61	38.79	45.28	45.81	62.91	84.87	74.06	82.53	63.29	36.07	76.11	77.04	70.91	87.99	59.95
				0.65	0.25	5.20	0.43	2.55	0.34	6.14	2.47	1.18	0.95	0.67	48.68	0.79	0.57	0.03	1.43	12.18	1.57	7.47	0.63	0.11	0.55	17.23
			52.42	0.34	0.13	2.73	0.23	1.33	0.18	3.22	1.29	0.62	0.50	0.35	25.52	0.42	0.30	0.02	0.75	6.38	0.82	3.92	0.33	0.06	0.29	9.03
			6.54	0.04	0.02	0.34	0.03	0.17	0.02	0.40	0.16	0.08	0.06	0.04	3.18	0.05	0.04	<0.01	0.09	0.80	0.10	0.49	0.04	0.01	0.04	1.13
FLORIDA	8,804,697	1,695,497	1,073,491	13,628	2,549	78,257	7,686	77,739	5,647	387,039	30,993	13,929	7,200	14,423	66,522	32,982	9,796	534	27,862	202,296	6,413	173,733	8,942	2,269	23,550	125,709
	79.86		63.31	80.40	88.75	57.55	82.72	77.98	72.63	59.65	64.66	77.96	40.68	50.04	39.37	61.10	86.72	86.41	87.16	71.47	48.50	81.15	75.68	65.58	88.68	68.02
				1.27	0.24	7.29	0.72	7.24	0.53	36.05	2.89	1.30	0.67	1.34	6.20	3.07	0.91	0.05	2.60	18.84	0.60	16.18	0.83	0.21	2.19	11.71
			63.31	0.80	0.15	4.62	0.45	4.59	0.33	22.83	1.83	0.82	0.42	0.85	3.92	1.95	0.58	0.03	1.64	11.93	0.38	10.25	0.53	0.13	1.39	7.41
			12.19	0.15	0.03	0.89	0.09	0.88	0.06	4.40	0.35	0.16	0.08	0.16	0.76	0.37	0.11	0.01	0.32	2.30	0.07	1.97	0.10	0.03	0.27	1.43
Alachua County	108,766	5,108	4,559	-	-	209	-	208	-	752	-	-	-	-	415	-	-	-	-	1,403	-	847	-	-	-	787
	88.05		89.25			90.87		95.85		88.99					82.50					87.63		97.24				88.43
						4.58		4.56		16.49					9.10					30.77		18.58				17.26
			89.25			4.09		4.07		14.72					8.12					27.47		16.58				15.41
			4.19			0.19		0.19		0.69					0.38					1.29		0.78				0.72
Gainesville (city)	44,391	2,325	2,098	-	-	-	-	-	-	338	-	-	-	-	145	-	-	-	-	740	-	410	-	-	-	310
	87.77		90.24							92.10					86.31					87.26		94.47				87.82
										16.11					6.91					35.27		19.54				14.78
			90.24							14.54					6.24					31.83		17.63				13.33
			4.73							0.76					0.33					1.67		0.92				0.70
Bay County	80,855	2,011	1,556	-	-	-	-	-	-	-	-	-	-	-	486	-	-	-	-	449	-	-	-	-	-	198
	81.04		77.37												78.39					87.35						86.84
															31.23					28.86						12.72
			77.37												24.17					22.33						9.85
			1.92												0.60					0.56						0.24
Brevard County	293,322	12,809	10,269	-	-	636	-	377	-	1,097	214	-	-	-	1,387	-	267	-	-	4,333	-	1,017	-	-	-	1,446
	86.34		80.17			75.71		90.84		82.11	81.37				72.43		95.36			81.45		90.97				78.12
						6.19		3.67		10.68	2.08				13.51		2.60			42.19		9.90				14.08
			80.17			4.97		2.94		8.56	1.67				10.83		2.08			33.83		7.94				11.29
			3.50			0.22		0.13		0.37	0.07				0.47		0.09			1.48		0.35				0.49
Melbourne (city)	42,590	2,183	1,703	-	-	-	-	-	-	-	-	-	-	-	235	-	-	-	-	777	-	-	-	-	-	212
	85.29		78.01												62.33					84.00						78.52
															13.80					45.63						12.45
			78.01												10.77					35.59						9.71
			4.00												0.55					1.82						0.50
Palm Bay (city)	43,755	4,054	3,177	-	-	-	-	-	-	-	-	-	-	-	307	-	-	-	-	1,762	-	314	-	-	-	386
	83.65		78.37												79.95					78.14		88.45				68.81
															9.66					55.46		9.88				12.15
			78.37												7.57					43.46		7.75				9.52
			7.26												0.70					4.03		0.72				0.88
Broward County	923,268	171,046	129,557	2,326	380	7,980	1,236	17,022	961	28,873	4,786	3,119	965	1,579	5,905	1,549	1,465	-	6,983	24,814	1,240	37,819	1,332	487	5,353	18,048
	81.96		75.74	83.16	89.20	62.25	83.51	81.62	75.43	75.44	69.13	86.78	55.56	59.95	59.33	67.73	82.86		90.85	74.70	45.26	85.34	79.33	67.36	93.34	75.63
				1.80	0.29	6.16	0.95	13.14	0.74	22.29	3.69	2.41	0.74	1.22	4.56	1.20	1.13		5.39	19.15	0.96	29.19	1.03	0.38	4.13	13.93
			75.74	1.36	0.22	4.67	0.72	9.95	0.56	16.88	2.80	1.82	0.56	0.92	3.45	0.91	0.86		4.08	14.51	0.72	22.11	0.78	0.28	3.13	10.55
			14.03	0.25	0.04	0.86	0.13	1.84	0.10	3.13	0.52	0.34	0.10	0.17	0.64	0.17	0.16		0.76	2.69	0.13	4.10	0.14	0.05	0.58	1.95

Notes: Please refer to the User's Guide for an explanation of data; data is arranged alphabetically by state, then county, then city within each county and only includes counties with populations > 99,999 and cities with populations > 49,999; (1) Includes Costa Rican, Guatemalan, Honduran, Nicaraguan, Panamanian, Salvadoran, and other Central American; (2) Includes Argentinian, Bolivian, Chilean, Colombian, Ecuadorian, Paraguayan, Peruvian, Uruguayan, Venezuelan, and other South American

Place	Total population 25 years and over who are High School graduates	Hispanic population 25 years and over	Hispanics 25 years and over who are High School graduates	Argentinian	Bolivian	Central American[1]	Chilean	Colombian	Costa Rican	Cuban	Dominican	Ecuadorian	Guatemalan	Honduran	Mexican	Nicaraguan	Panamanian	Paraguayan	Peruvian	Puerto Rican	Salvadoran	South American[2]	Spaniard	Uruguayan	Venezuelan	Other Hisp.
Coral Springs (city)	64,781	10,412	8,705	-	-	395	-	1,283	-	1,235	318	511	-	-	435	-	-	-	518	1,806	-	2,998	-	-	249	1,356
	89.56		83.61			75.38		88.97		89.43	83.68	83.50			59.26				94.01	82.24		88.59			89.89	83.50
						4.54		14.74		14.19	3.65	5.87			5.00				5.95	20.75		34.44			2.86	15.58
			83.61			3.79		12.32		11.86	3.05	4.91			4.18				4.98	17.35		28.79			2.39	13.02
			13.44			0.61		1.98		1.91	0.49	0.79			0.67				0.80	2.79		4.63			0.38	2.09
Davie (town)	42,058	8,725	6,494	-	-	486	-	655	-	1,906	-	-	-	-	246	-	-	-	454	1,246	-	1,605	-	-	-	727
	84.45		74.43			72.97		78.35		81.35					69.30				91.35	66.35		81.06				66.76
						7.48		10.09		29.35					3.79				6.99	19.19		24.72				11.19
			74.43			5.57		7.51		21.85					2.82				5.20	14.28		18.40				8.33
			15.44			1.16		1.56		4.53					0.58				1.08	2.96		3.82				1.73
Deerfield Beach (city)	40,122	3,779	2,726	-	-	223	-	391	-	336	-	-	-	-	169	-	-	-	-	667	-	827	-	-	-	398
	79.32		72.14			65.01		82.32		61.99					62.83					72.42		83.70				76.54
						8.18		14.34		12.33					6.20					24.47		30.34				14.60
			72.14			5.90		10.35		8.89					4.47					17.65		21.88				10.53
			6.79			0.56		0.97		0.84					0.42					1.66		2.06				0.99
Fort Lauderdale (city)	87,921	9,340	6,381	-	-	457	-	685	-	1,510	-	-	63	-	522	-	-	-	320	1,056	102	1,753	-	-	-	851
	78.99		68.32			41.21		78.74		68.17			30.29		69.41				91.43	68.44	29.91	83.52				62.80
						7.16		10.73		23.66			0.99		8.18				5.01	16.55	1.60	27.47				13.34
			68.32			4.89		7.33		16.17			0.67		5.59				3.43	11.31	1.09	18.77				9.11
			7.26			0.52		0.78		1.72			0.07		0.59				0.36	1.20	0.12	1.99				0.97
Hollywood (city)	79,650	19,957	14,128	298	-	1,098	191	1,752	-	2,934	726	325	-	233	457	302	-	-	784	2,749	-	3,982	-	-	384	2,096
	79.64		70.79	77.40		73.40	67.25	76.24		68.42	69.61	87.84		67.34	58.22	79.89			85.59	66.47		78.91			88.07	69.63
				2.11		7.77	1.35	12.40		20.77	5.14	2.30		1.65	3.23	2.14			5.55	19.46		28.19			2.72	14.84
			70.79	1.49		5.50	0.96	8.78		14.70	3.64	1.63		1.17	2.29	1.51			3.93	13.77		19.95			1.92	10.50
			17.74	0.37		1.38	0.24	2.20		3.68	0.91	0.41		0.29	0.57	0.38			0.98	3.45		5.00			0.48	2.63
Lauderhill (city)	28,217	2,509	1,839	-	-	-	-	269	-	-	-	-	-	-	-	-	-	-	-	405	-	588	-	-	-	309
	75.87		73.30					80.54												81.65		79.25				66.88
								14.63												22.02		31.97				16.80
			73.30					10.72												16.14		23.44				12.32
			6.52					0.95												1.44		2.08				1.10
Margate (city)	31,658	5,145	3,627	-	-	143	-	531	-	360	-	-	-	-	307	-	-	-	-	1,133	-	1,013	-	-	-	577
	80.24		70.50			45.11		70.52		71.71					67.77					74.10		75.82				71.59
						3.94		14.64		9.93					8.46					31.24		27.93				15.91
			70.50			2.78		10.32		7.00					5.97					22.02		19.69				11.21
			11.46			0.45		1.68		1.14					0.97					3.58		3.20				1.82
Miramar (city)	36,237	13,625	10,369	-	-	750	-	1,016	-	3,443	642	-	-	-	231	274	171	-	346	1,820	-	2,040	-	-	-	1,345
	82.29		76.10			66.79		76.51		75.26	70.24				73.80	63.57	72.77		85.01	79.62		80.92				75.18
						7.23		9.80		33.20	6.19				2.23	2.64	1.65		3.34	17.55		19.67				12.97
			76.10			5.50		7.46		25.27	4.71				1.70	2.01	1.26		2.54	13.36		14.97				9.87
			28.61			2.07		2.80		9.50	1.77				0.64	0.76	0.47		0.95	5.02		5.63				3.71
Pembroke Pines (city)	82,419	24,734	21,009	-	-	1,091	-	2,040	-	7,255	916	365	-	-	511	-	-	-	890	3,956	-	4,740	-	-	893	2,383
	88.05		84.94			79.81		89.32		81.66	82.97	97.33			84.18				93.88	85.81		91.49			94.30	85.50
						5.19		9.71		34.53	4.36	1.74			2.43				4.24	18.83		22.56			4.25	11.34
			84.94			4.41		8.25		29.33	3.70	1.48			2.07				3.60	15.99		19.16			3.61	9.63
			25.49			1.32		2.48		8.80	1.11	0.44			0.62				1.08	4.80		5.75			1.08	2.89
Plantation (city)	53,217	7,163	6,056	-	-	386	-	1,314	-	1,116	-	-	-	-	269	-	-	-	341	904	-	2,442	-	-	256	661
	90.97		84.55			88.74		81.46		79.43					74.31				96.60	85.36		87.78			92.09	82.21
						6.37		21.70		18.43					4.44				5.63	14.93		40.32			4.23	10.91
			84.55			5.39		18.34		15.58					3.76				4.76	12.62		34.09			3.57	9.23
			11.38			0.73		2.47		2.10					0.51				0.64	1.70		4.59			0.48	1.24

Notes: Please refer to the User's Guide for an explanation of data; data is arranged alphabetically by state, then county, then city within each county and only includes counties with populations > 99,999 and cities with populations > 49,999; (1) Includes Costa Rican, Guatemalan, Honduran, Nicaraguan, Panamanian, Salvadoran, and other Central American; (2) Includes Argentinian, Bolivian, Chilean, Colombian, Ecuadorian, Paraguayan, Peruvian, Uruguayan, Venezuelan, and other South American

Place	Total population 25 years and over who are High School graduates	Hispanic population 25 years and over	Hispanics 25 years and over who are High School graduates	Argentinian	Bolivian	Central American¹	Chilean	Colombian	Costa Rican	Cuban	Dominican	Ecuadorian	Guatelmalan	Honduran	Mexican	Nicaraguan	Panamanian	Paraguayan	Peruvian	Puerto Rican	Salvadoran	South American²	Spaniard	Uruguayan	Venezuelan	Other Hisp.
Pompano Beach (city)	45,333	4,553	2,991	-	-	-	-	270	-	348	-	-	-	-	373	-	-	-	-	425	-	887	-	-	-	744
	77.19		65.69					69.59		73.42					33.13					64.49		86.12				80.43
								9.03		11.63					12.47					14.21		29.66				24.87
			65.69					5.93		7.64					8.19					9.33		19.48				16.34
			6.60					0.60		0.77					0.82					0.94		1.96				1.64
Sunrise (city)	48,685	9,173	7,467	-	-	365	-	1,343	-	1,142	267	346	-	-	328	-	-	-	396	1,442	-	2,758	-	-	-	1,117
	83.67		81.40			72.28		85.76		81.81	59.47	89.41			72.25				93.84	77.61		89.23				82.07
						4.89		17.99		15.29	3.58	4.63			4.39				5.30	19.31		36.94				14.96
			81.40			3.98		14.64		12.45	2.91	3.77			3.58				4.32	15.72		30.07				12.18
			15.34			0.75		2.76		2.35	0.55	0.71			0.67				0.81	2.96		5.66				2.29
Tamarac (city)	38,059	5,445	4,043	-	-	-	-	750	-	468	-	-	-	-	-	-	-	-	-	973	-	1,284	-	-	-	790
	83.52		74.25					79.70		66.20										71.23		82.63				72.21
								18.55		11.58										24.07		31.76				19.54
			74.25					13.77		8.60										17.87		23.58				14.51
			10.62					1.97		1.23										2.56		3.37				2.08
Charlotte County	92,886	2,908	1,978	-	-	-	-	-	-	286	-	-	-	-	260	-	-	-	-	683	-	-	-	-	-	383
	82.15		68.02							62.04					53.06					74.00						70.15
										14.46					13.14					34.53						19.36
			68.02							9.83					8.94					23.49						13.17
			2.13							0.31					0.28					0.74						0.41
Citrus County	72,516	2,007	1,390	-	-	-	-	-	-	-	-	-	-	-	156	-	-	-	-	581	-	-	-	-	-	311
	78.32		69.26												61.66					67.79						68.65
															11.22					41.80						22.37
			69.26												7.77					28.95						15.50
			1.92												0.22					0.80						0.43
Clay County	78,085	3,170	2,550	-	-	-	-	-	-	-	-	-	-	-	390	-	-	-	-	1,017	-	-	-	-	-	528
	86.39		80.44												67.13					82.62						82.24
															15.29					39.88						20.71
			80.44												12.30					32.08						16.66
			3.27												0.50					1.30						0.68
Collier County	151,535	26,077	10,625	-	-	610	-	677	-	3,062	169	-	169	136	3,339	-	-	-	-	1,073	-	1,238	-	-	-	1,082
	81.75		40.74			33.06		84.41		59.72	52.32		19.88	35.98	25.22					58.38		79.51				52.78
						5.74		6.37		28.82	1.59		1.59	1.28	31.43					10.10		11.65				10.18
			40.74			2.34		2.60		11.74	0.65		0.65	0.52	12.80					4.11		4.75				4.15
			7.01			0.40		0.45		2.02	0.11		0.11	0.09	2.20					0.71		0.82				0.71
Duval County	413,266	17,615	13,912	-	-	900	-	781	-	1,816	284	-	-	-	2,213	-	335	-	308	4,624	-	1,642	-	-	-	2,282
	82.72		78.98			78.53		89.16		76.21	78.24				73.40		96.82		94.19	78.17		90.82				80.78
						6.47		5.61		13.05	2.04				15.91		2.41		2.21	33.24		11.80				16.40
			78.98			5.11		4.43		10.31	1.61				12.56		1.90		1.75	26.25		9.32				12.95
			3.37			0.22		0.19		0.44	0.07				0.54		0.08		0.07	1.12		0.40				0.55
Jacksonville (city)	385,300	16,739	13,219	-	-	887	-	745	-	1,752	284	-	-	-	2,066	-	323	-	-	4,413	-	1,523	-	-	-	2,151
	82.27		78.97			78.29		88.69		75.55	78.24				74.32		96.71			78.38		90.17				80.47
						6.71		5.64		13.25	2.15				15.63		2.44			33.38		11.52				16.27
			78.97			5.30		4.45		10.47	1.70				12.34		1.93			26.36		9.10				12.85
			3.43			0.23		0.19		0.45	0.07				0.54		0.08			1.15		0.40				0.56
Escambia County	155,668	4,250	3,399	-	-	213	-	-	-	465	-	-	-	-	884	-	-	-	-	775	-	217	-	-	-	797
	82.06		79.98			83.86				79.76					77.82					80.14		76.14				82.08
						6.27				13.68					26.01					22.80		6.38				23.45
			79.98			5.01				10.94					20.80					18.24		5.11				18.75
			2.18			0.14				0.30					0.57					0.50		0.14				0.51

Notes: Please refer to the User's Guide for an explanation of data; data is arranged alphabetically by state, then county, then city within each county and only includes counties with populations > 99,999 and cities with populations > 49,999; (1) Includes Costa Rican, Guatemalan, Honduran, Nicaraguan, Panamanian, Salvadoran, and other Central American; (2) Includes Argentinian, Bolivian, Chilean, Colombian, Ecuadorian, Paraguayan, Peruvian, Uruguayan, Venezuelan, and other South American

Place	Total population 25 years and over who are High School graduates	Hispanic population 25 years and over	Hispanics 25 years and over who are High School graduates	Argentinian	Bolivian	Central American[1]	Chilean	Colombian	Costa Rican	Cuban	Dominican	Ecuadorian	Guatelmalan	Honduran	Mexican	Nicaraguan	Panamanian	Paraguayan	Peruvian	Puerto Rican	Salvadoran	South American[2]	Spaniard	Uruguayan	Venezuelan	Other Hisp.
Pensacola (city)	32,366	754	640	-	-	-	-	-	-	-	-	-	-	-	-	-	-	-	-	-	-	-	-	-	-	-
	84.55		84.88																							
			84.88																							
			1.98																							
Hernando County	77,747	4,174	2,865	-	-	-	-	-	-	274	-	-	-	-	258	-	-	-	-	1,765	-	-	-	-	-	357
	78.47		68.64							69.19					50.99					71.08						70.14
										9.56					9.01					61.61						12.46
			68.64							6.56					6.18					42.29						8.55
			3.69							0.35					0.33					2.27						0.46
Spring Hill (cdp)	40,768	3,074	2,114	-	-	-	-	-	-	168	-	-	-	-	-	-	-	-	-	1,400	-	-	-	-	-	270
	78.75		68.77							68.57										68.49						76.27
										7.95										66.23						12.77
			68.77							5.47										45.54						8.78
			5.19							0.41										3.43						0.66
Hillsborough County	528,058	103,423	65,990	-	-	3,091	-	2,920	465	15,389	1,510	743	343	612	6,066	436	862	-	975	19,545	273	6,347	1,168	-	804	12,874
	80.76		63.81			63.68		74.91	73.23	61.45	64.78	76.28	52.29	45.60	38.11	76.76	83.69		86.51	69.36	56.29	79.15	82.84		80.24	72.86
						4.68		4.42	0.70	23.32	2.29	1.13	0.52	0.93	9.19	0.66	1.31		1.48	29.62	0.41	9.62	1.77		1.22	19.51
			63.81			2.99		2.82	0.45	14.88	1.46	0.72	0.33	0.59	5.87	0.42	0.83		0.94	18.90	0.26	6.14	1.13		0.78	12.45
			12.50			0.59		0.55	0.09	2.91	0.29	0.14	0.06	0.12	1.15	0.08	0.16		0.18	3.70	0.05	1.20	0.22		0.15	2.44
Brandon (cdp)	44,737	5,664	4,502	-	-	284	-	-	-	620	-	-	-	-	317	-	-	-	-	2,156	-	249	-	-	-	705
	89.18		79.48			90.45				91.31					65.23					78.34		74.33				81.41
						6.31				13.77					7.04					47.89		5.53				15.66
			79.48			5.01				10.95					5.60					38.06		4.40				12.45
			10.06			0.63				1.39					0.71					4.82		0.56				1.58
Tampa (city)	153,114	36,559	22,246	-	-	1,258	-	756	-	5,867	473	268	-	235	1,801	177	367	-	-	5,350	-	1,739	518	-	271	5,240
	77.06		60.85			61.22		71.66		54.28	58.04	80.00		40.94	51.69	71.37	84.17			60.38		77.60	81.57		84.16	68.40
						5.65		3.40		26.37	2.13	1.20		1.06	8.10	0.80	1.65			24.05		7.82	2.33		1.22	23.55
			60.85			3.44		2.07		16.05	1.29	0.73		0.64	4.93	0.48	1.00			14.63		4.76	1.42		0.74	14.33
			14.53			0.82		0.49		3.83	0.31	0.18		0.15	1.18	0.12	0.24			3.49		1.14	0.34		0.18	3.42
Town 'n' Country (cdp)	40,492	12,620	8,914	-	-	368	-	573	-	2,282	358	-	-	-	352	-	-	-	-	3,089	-	1,108	-	-	-	1,221
	82.67		70.63			67.03		74.80		63.39	76.17				57.80					73.71		78.53				75.70
						4.13		6.43		25.60	4.02				3.95					34.65		12.43				13.70
			70.63			2.92		4.54		18.08	2.84				2.79					24.48		8.78				9.68
			22.01			0.91		1.42		5.64	0.88				0.87					7.63		2.74				3.02
Indian River County	68,940	3,716	1,464	-	-	89	-	-	-	203	-	-	-	-	352	-	-	-	-	239	-	307	-	-	-	265
	81.56		39.40			55.28				79.61					17.18					63.23		79.33				57.11
						6.08				13.87					24.04					16.33		20.97				18.10
			39.40			2.40				5.46					9.47					6.43		8.26				7.13
			2.12			0.13				0.29					0.51					0.35		0.45				0.38
Lake County	124,090	6,248	3,543	-	-	239	-	-	-	452	-	-	-	-	694	-	-	-	-	1,334	-	293	-	-	-	478
	79.76		56.71			66.02				83.39					27.87					78.61		83.00				64.95
						6.75				12.76					19.59					37.65		8.27				13.49
			56.71			3.83				7.23					11.11					21.35		4.69				7.65
			2.86			0.19				0.36					0.56					1.08		0.24				0.39
Lee County	269,652	21,755	11,435	-	-	668	-	581	-	1,669	375	-	159	109	2,318	-	-	-	-	3,763	-	1,286	-	-	-	1,324
	82.29		52.56			40.73		83.00		71.94	58.59		23.42	37.72	34.19					57.62		83.18				59.03
						5.84		5.08		14.60	3.28		1.39	0.95	20.27					32.91		11.25				11.58
			52.56			3.07		2.67		7.67	1.72		0.73	0.50	10.66					17.30		5.91				6.09
			4.24			0.25		0.22		0.62	0.14		0.06	0.04	0.86					1.40		0.48				0.49

Notes: Please refer to the User's Guide for an explanation of data; data is arranged alphabetically by state, then county, then city within each county and only includes counties with populations > 99,999 and cities with populations > 49,999; (1) Includes Costa Rican, Guatemalan, Honduran, Nicaraguan, Panamanian, Salvadoran, and other Central American; (2) Includes Argentinian, Bolivian, Chilean, Colombian, Ecuadorian, Paraguayan, Peruvian, Uruguayan, Venezuelan, and other South American

Place	Total population 25 years and over who are High School graduates	Hispanic population 25 years and over	Hispanics 25 years and over who are High School graduates	Argentinian	Bolivian	Central American[1]	Chilean	Colombian	Costa Rican	Cuban	Dominican	Ecuadorian	Guatemalan	Honduran	Mexican	Nicaraguan	Panamanian	Paraguayan	Peruvian	Puerto Rican	Salvadoran	South American[2]	Spaniard	Uruguayan	Venezuelan	Other Hisp.
Cape Coral (city)	62,780	5,032	3,607	-	-	-	-	284	-	793	190	-	-	-	476	-	-	-	-	1,025	-	552	-	-	-	415
	85.47		71.68					80.23		69.50	54.60				66.67					76.10		79.31				75.73
								7.87		21.99	5.27				13.20					28.42		15.30				11.51
			71.68					5.64		15.76	3.78				9.46					20.37		10.97				8.25
			5.75					0.45		1.26	0.30				0.76					1.63		0.88				0.66
Leon County	122,570	3,872	3,375	-	-	-	-	-	-	652	-	-	-	-	484	-	-	-	-	641	-	537	-	-	-	766
	89.12		87.16							87.05					75.51					92.10		99.08				82.54
										19.32					14.34					18.99		15.91				22.70
			87.16							16.84					12.50					16.55		13.87				19.78
			2.75							0.53					0.39					0.52		0.44				0.62
Tallahassee (city)	71,754	2,626	2,239	-	-	-	-	-	-	396	-	-	-	-	250	-	-	-	-	450	-	408	-	-	-	532
	89.85		85.26							82.33					66.14					92.59		98.79				80.61
										17.69					11.17					20.10		18.22				23.76
			85.26							15.08					9.52					17.14		15.54				20.26
			3.12							0.55					0.35					0.63		0.57				0.74
Manatee County	157,012	11,913	5,041	-	-	282	-	-	-	614	-	-	-	-	1,818	-	-	-	-	1,126	-	478	-	-	-	660
	81.44		42.32			33.37				71.15					27.80					64.38		81.71				54.55
						5.59				12.18					36.06					22.34		9.48				13.09
			42.32			2.37				5.15					15.26					9.45		4.01				5.54
			3.21			0.18				0.39					1.16					0.72		0.30				0.42
Marion County	146,374	8,790	5,330	-	-	253	-	190	-	553	-	-	-	-	562	-	-	-	-	2,543	-	477	-	-	-	783
	78.20		60.64			63.73		54.76		68.87					39.55					61.34		71.73				68.93
						4.75		3.56		10.38					10.54					47.71		8.95				14.69
			60.64			2.88		2.16		6.29					6.39					28.93		5.43				8.91
			3.64			0.17		0.13		0.38					0.38					1.74		0.33				0.53
Martin County	82,284	4,721	2,218	-	-	158	-	-	-	426	-	-	94	-	703	-	-	-	-	451	-	-	-	-	-	237
	85.30		46.98			16.70				78.89			12.01		41.09					55.61						53.26
						7.12				19.21			4.24		31.70					20.33						10.69
			46.98			3.35				9.02			1.99		14.89					9.55						5.02
			2.70			0.19				0.52			0.11		0.85					0.55						0.29
Miami-Dade County	1,012,436	900,566	551,256	8,012	1,439	51,128	4,578	39,784	2,175	294,726	15,893	5,892	3,404	8,960	9,029	28,436	4,134	-	13,949	34,721	3,082	88,878	3,436	1,038	12,489	53,445
	67.87		61.21	79.30	89.27	57.59	79.62	76.41	69.82	57.29	61.77	73.83	50.62	46.79	47.04	60.23	88.09		84.67	68.17	50.20	79.27	68.79	65.04	86.95	63.38
				1.45	0.26	9.27	0.83	7.22	0.39	53.46	2.88	1.07	0.62	1.63	1.64	5.16	0.75		2.53	6.30	0.56	16.12	0.62	0.19	2.27	9.70
			61.21	0.89	0.16	5.68	0.51	4.42	0.24	32.73	1.76	0.65	0.38	0.99	1.00	3.16	0.46		1.55	3.86	0.34	9.87	0.38	0.12	1.39	5.93
			54.45	0.79	0.14	5.05	0.45	3.93	0.21	29.11	1.57	0.58	0.34	0.88	0.89	2.81	0.41		1.38	3.43	0.30	8.78	0.34	0.10	1.23	5.28
Carol City (cdp)	21,583	16,481	7,796	-	-	980	-	668	-	3,461	527	-	-	107	-	520	-	-	-	960	-	1,077	-	-	-	718
	61.03		47.30			58.68		68.16		40.03	42.92			33.86		58.17				55.85		66.73				51.47
						12.57		8.57		44.39	6.76			1.37		6.67				12.31		13.81				9.21
			47.30			5.95		4.05		21.00	3.20			0.65		3.16				5.82		6.53				4.36
			36.12			4.54		3.10		16.04	2.44			0.50		2.41				4.45		4.99				3.33
Fountainbleau (cdp)	28,166	36,399	24,867	278	-	3,896	346	1,403	-	11,258	914	423	-	278	222	2,750	369	-	796	948	-	4,585	-	-	1,117	2,973
	70.21		68.32	76.16		73.11	73.31	72.85		61.43	75.98	87.58		70.74	75.51	69.50	92.95		89.04	77.32		81.25			89.94	69.81
				1.12		15.67	1.39	5.64		45.27	3.68	1.70		1.12	0.89	11.06	1.48		3.20	3.81		18.44			4.49	11.96
			68.32	0.76		10.70	0.95	3.85		30.93	2.51	1.16		0.76	0.61	7.56	1.01		2.19	2.60		12.60			3.07	8.17
			88.29	0.99		13.83	1.23	4.98		39.97	3.25	1.50		0.99	0.79	9.76	1.31		2.83	3.37		16.28			3.97	10.56
Hialeah (city)	77,548	146,118	70,397	180	-	4,920	358	3,604	167	49,639	1,952	525	245	783	358	3,100	-	-	754	2,621	317	5,994	144	-	408	4,769
	49.84		48.18	61.64		51.59	66.92	65.22	54.93	45.36	62.07	61.40	49.70	48.85	39.87	51.44			74.21	59.19	53.55	66.82	36.09		85.53	51.30
				0.26		6.99	0.51	5.12	0.24	70.51	2.77	0.75	0.35	1.11	0.51	4.40			1.07	3.72	0.45	8.51	0.20		0.58	6.77
			48.18	0.12		3.37	0.25	2.47	0.11	33.97	1.34	0.36	0.17	0.54	0.25	2.12			0.52	1.79	0.22	4.10	0.10		0.28	3.26
			90.78	0.23		6.34	0.46	4.65	0.22	64.01	2.52	0.68	0.32	1.01	0.46	4.00			0.97	3.38	0.41	7.73	0.19		0.53	6.15

Notes: Please refer to the User's Guide for an explanation of data; data is arranged alphabetically by state, then county, then city within each county and only includes counties with populations > 99,999 and cities with populations > 49,999; (1) Includes Costa Rican, Guatemalan, Honduran, Nicaraguan, Panamanian, Salvadoran, and other Central American; (2) Includes Argentinian, Bolivian, Chilean, Colombian, Ecuadorian, Paraguayan, Peruvian, Uruguayan, Venezuelan, and other South American

Place	Total population 25 years and over who are High School graduates	Hispanic population 25 years and over	Hispanics 25 years and over who are High School graduates	Argentinian	Bolivian	Central American[1]	Chilean	Colombian	Costa Rican	Cuban	Dominican	Ecuadorian	Guatemalan	Honduran	Mexican	Nicaraguan	Panamanian	Paraguayan	Peruvian	Puerto Rican	Salvadoran	South American[2]	Spaniard	Uruguayan	Venezuelan	Other Hisp.
	29,137	29,518	22,385	-	-	2,117	-	2,110	-	11,881	352	-	-	226	210	1,493	-	-	578	959	-	4,052	-	-	464	2,699
	78.53		75.84			79.44		81.15		72.55	67.05			69.54	62.13	80.75			95.22	84.20		84.50			83.15	76.50
Kendale Lakes (cdp)						9.46		9.43		53.08	1.57			1.01	0.94	6.67			2.58	4.28		18.10			2.07	12.06
			75.84			7.17		7.15		40.25	1.19			0.77	0.71	5.06			1.96	3.25		13.73			1.57	9.14
			76.83			7.27		7.24		40.78	1.21			0.78	0.72	5.12			1.98	3.29		13.91			1.59	9.26
	45,626	25,692	21,481	461	-	2,098	301	2,372	-	9,687	338	-	-	-	-	1,150	-	-	849	1,344	-	5,284	-	-	906	2,220
	88.53		83.61	93.70		81.60	100.00	83.64		82.13	66.54					80.48			95.18	87.67		88.48			93.79	82.01
Kendall (cdp)				2.15		9.77	1.40	11.04		45.10	1.57					5.35			3.95	6.26		24.60			4.22	10.33
			83.61	1.79		8.17	1.17	9.23		37.70	1.32					4.48			3.30	5.23		20.57			3.53	8.64
			47.08	1.01		4.60	0.66	5.20		21.23	0.74					2.52			1.86	2.95		11.58			1.99	4.87
	54,590	36,891	25,722	1,670	-	1,542	488	2,614	-	9,885	770	422	-	373	576	591	-	-	1,159	1,906	-	7,679	414	-	907	2,950
	78.78		69.72	80.02		75.74	85.76	79.28		61.19	71.90	80.38		63.76	68.98	85.78			82.90	76.09		81.11	86.97		90.43	67.88
Miami Beach (city)				6.49		5.99	1.90	10.16		38.43	2.99	1.64		1.45	2.24	2.30			4.51	7.41		29.85	1.61		3.53	11.47
			69.72	4.53		4.18	1.32	7.09		26.80	2.09	1.14		1.01	1.56	1.60			3.14	5.17		20.82	1.12		2.46	8.00
			47.12	3.06		2.82	0.89	4.79		18.11	1.41	0.77		0.68	1.06	1.08			2.12	3.49		14.07	0.76		1.66	5.40
	133,069	176,590	83,405	1,063	-	11,896	521	3,124	380	48,348	2,196	719	677	3,353	1,007	6,285	449	-	1,471	3,366	528	8,224	408	-	912	7,960
	52.70		47.23	73.41		41.74	72.26	68.25	64.08	45.95	45.46	57.94	34.49	35.81	51.38	45.62	73.73		73.48	51.60	31.41	69.60	49.94		72.79	47.03
Miami (city)				1.27		14.26	0.62	3.75	0.46	57.97	2.63	0.86	0.81	4.02	1.21	7.54	0.54		1.76	4.04	0.63	9.86	0.49		1.09	9.54
			47.23	0.60		6.74	0.30	1.77	0.22	27.38	1.24	0.41	0.38	1.90	0.57	3.56	0.25		0.83	1.91	0.30	4.66	0.23		0.52	4.51
			62.68	0.80		8.94	0.39	2.35	0.29	36.33	1.65	0.54	0.51	2.52	0.76	4.72	0.34		1.11	2.53	0.40	6.18	0.31		0.69	5.98
	24,357	9,277	5,911	-	-	707	-	575	-	1,428	393	-	-	207	-	283	-	-	-	1,023	-	1,111	-	-	-	1,030
	66.99		63.72			60.27		76.06		64.21	63.80			54.91		63.03				59.62		73.04				60.20
North Miami (city)						11.96		9.73		24.16	6.65			3.50		4.79				17.31		18.80				17.43
			63.72			7.62		6.20		15.39	4.24			2.23		3.05				11.03		11.98				11.10
			24.27			2.90		2.36		5.86	1.61			0.85		1.16				4.20		4.56				4.23
	25,941	33,730	23,414	-	-	1,846	-	1,081	-	16,494	359	-	-	224	179	1,221	-	-	-	668	-	2,133	-	-	298	1,636
	70.82		69.42			76.44		76.56		67.52	78.21			72.03	56.47	73.87				81.66		80.25			90.03	66.37
Tamiami (cdp)						7.88		4.62		70.45	1.53			0.96	0.76	5.21				2.85		9.11			1.27	6.99
			69.42			5.47		3.20		48.90	1.06			0.66	0.53	3.62				1.98		6.32			0.88	4.85
			90.26			7.12		4.17		63.58	1.38			0.86	0.69	4.71				2.58		8.22			1.15	6.31
	98,958	3,850	3,153	-	-	172	-	-	-	337	-	-	-	-	904	-	-	-	-	704	-	-	-	-	-	695
	88.02		81.90			80.37				75.90					79.44					87.24						81.86
Okaloosa County						5.46				10.69					28.67					22.33						22.04
			81.90			4.47				8.75					23.48					18.29						18.05
			3.19			0.17				0.34					0.91					0.71						0.70
	469,510	95,505	67,763	463	-	2,561	266	3,984	308	6,398	2,618	887	405	521	4,708	328	576	-	1,107	36,489	367	8,337	340	-	1,200	6,312
	81.78		70.95	84.80		69.18	92.68	80.02	86.03	68.24	70.55	73.92	58.78	61.01	47.33	64.69	86.10		88.84	74.10	68.47	81.88	70.25		82.93	71.27
Orange County				0.68		3.78	0.39	5.88	0.45	9.44	3.86	1.31	0.60	0.77	6.95	0.48	0.85		1.63	53.85	0.54	12.30	0.50		1.77	9.31
			70.95	0.48		2.68	0.28	4.17	0.32	6.70	2.74	0.93	0.42	0.55	4.93	0.34	0.60		1.16	38.21	0.38	8.73	0.36		1.26	6.61
			14.43	0.10		0.55	0.06	0.85	0.07	1.36	0.56	0.19	0.09	0.11	1.00	0.07	0.12		0.24	7.77	0.08	1.78	0.07		0.26	1.34
	103,129	19,606	14,472	-	-	541	-	1,018	-	1,519	537	-	-	-	796	-	-	-	263	7,158	-	2,278	-	-	392	1,561
	82.19		73.81			62.91		81.57		66.51	73.97				59.09				84.84	75.20		83.60			85.22	75.89
Orlando (city)						3.74		7.03		10.50	3.71				5.50				1.82	49.46		15.74			2.71	10.79
			73.81			2.76		5.19		7.75	2.74				4.06				1.34	36.51		11.62			2.00	7.96
			14.03			0.52		0.99		1.47	0.52				0.77				0.26	6.94		2.21			0.38	1.51
	87,512	28,364	20,117	-	-	666	-	935	-	995	1,069	271	-	-	886	-	-	-	-	13,188	89	1,919	-	-	310	1,310
	79.12		70.92			57.66		77.92		70.82	66.36	74.04			52.68					72.79	29.37	81.38			95.98	68.87
Osceola County						3.31		4.65		4.95	5.31	1.35			4.40					65.56	0.44	9.54			1.54	6.51
			70.92			2.35		3.30		3.51	3.77	0.96			3.12					46.50	0.31	6.77			1.09	4.62
			22.99			0.76		1.07		1.14	1.22	0.31			1.01					15.07	0.10	2.19			0.35	1.50

Notes: Please refer to the User's Guide for an explanation of data; data is arranged alphabetically by state, then county, then city within each county and only includes counties with populations > 99,999 and cities with populations > 49,999; (1) Includes Costa Rican, Guatemalan, Honduran, Nicaraguan, Panamanian, Salvadoran, and other Central American; (2) Includes Argentinian, Bolivian, Chilean, Colombian, Ecuadorian, Paraguayan, Peruvian, Uruguayan, Venezuelan, and other South American

Place	Total population 25 years and over who are High School graduates	Hispanic population 25 years and over	Hispanics 25 years and over who are High School graduates	Argentinian	Bolivian	Central American[1]	Chilean	Colombian	Costa Rican	Cuban	Dominican	Ecuadorian	Guatelmalan	Honduran	Mexican	Nicaraguan	Panamanian	Paraguayan	Peruvian	Puerto Rican	Salvadoran	South American[2]	Spaniard	Uruguayan	Venezuelan	Other Hisp.
Palm Beach County	683,553	82,887	49,934	897	-	3,431	397	4,734	316	12,614	1,522	1,012	642	960	5,192	710	278	-	1,533	9,533	421	10,684	307	350	1,051	6,651
	83.57		60.24	71.82		41.44	92.76	75.90	62.70	65.65	64.33	76.78	19.15	52.86	35.91	62.39	100.00		91.25	64.82	42.10	79.05	80.58	54.26	91.23	66.74
				1.80		6.87	0.80	9.48	0.63	25.26	3.05	2.03	1.29	1.92	10.40	1.42	0.56		3.07	19.09	0.84	21.40	0.61	0.70	2.10	13.32
			60.24	1.08		4.14	0.48	5.71	0.38	15.22	1.84	1.22	0.77	1.16	6.26	0.86	0.34		1.85	11.50	0.51	12.89	0.37	0.42	1.27	8.02
			7.31	0.13		0.50	0.06	0.69	0.05	1.85	0.22	0.15	0.09	0.14	0.76	0.10	0.04		0.22	1.39	0.06	1.56	0.04	0.05	0.15	0.97
Boca Raton (city)	50,705	4,054	3,244	-	-	-	-	369	-	566	-	-	-	-	239	-	-	-	-	406	-	1,086	-	-	-	721
	91.96		80.02					72.21		80.06					58.15					89.04		82.46				82.12
								11.37		17.45					7.37					12.52		33.48				22.23
			80.02					9.10		13.96					5.90					10.01		26.79				17.78
			6.40					0.73		1.12					0.47					0.80		2.14				1.42
Boynton Beach (city)	35,896	2,966	1,927	-	-	134	-	-	-	317	-	-	-	-	203	-	-	-	-	606	-	391	-	-	-	188
	80.55		64.97			47.52				79.25					50.75					68.71		68.96				55.46
						6.95				16.45					10.53					31.45		20.29				9.76
			64.97			4.52				10.69					6.84					20.43		13.18				6.34
			5.37			0.37				0.88					0.57					1.69		1.09				0.52
Delray Beach (city)	36,838	2,543	1,674	-	-	-	-	-	-	-	-	-	-	-	275	-	-	-	-	274	-	399	-	-	-	207
	81.01		65.83												36.96					60.75		88.27				73.93
															16.43					16.37		23.84				12.37
			65.83												10.81					10.77		15.69				8.14
			4.54												0.75					0.74		1.08				0.56
West Palm Beach (city)	42,701	9,257	4,577	-	-	390	-	406	-	1,796	104	-	141	-	355	-	-	-	-	626	-	739	-	-	-	554
	75.51		49.44			28.08		83.37		51.20	41.43		14.49		37.97					51.14		75.41				58.56
						8.52		8.87		39.24	2.27		3.08		7.76					13.68		16.15				12.10
			49.44			4.21		4.39		19.40	1.12		1.52		3.83					6.76		7.98				5.98
			10.72			0.91		0.95		4.21	0.24		0.33		0.83					1.47		1.73				1.30
Pasco County	198,175	11,046	7,234	-	-	281	-	-	-	951	-	-	-	-	1,081	-	-	-	-	2,984	-	499	-	-	-	1,190
	77.57		65.49			69.55				77.19					38.76					70.85		82.07				78.19
						3.88				13.15					14.94					41.25		6.90				16.45
			65.49			2.54				8.61					9.79					27.01		4.52				10.77
			3.65			0.14				0.48					0.55					1.51		0.25				0.60
Pinellas County	576,396	25,032	18,442	-	-	608	-	980	-	2,725	369	263	-	-	2,935	-	-	-	553	5,610	-	2,848	360	-	521	2,987
	84.01		73.67			71.03		81.60		74.86	70.42	79.22			58.59				91.86	74.02		86.59	82.57		98.30	80.75
						3.30		5.31		14.78	2.00	1.43			15.91				3.00	30.42		15.44	1.95		2.83	16.20
			73.67			2.43		3.91		10.89	1.47	1.05			11.72				2.21	22.41		11.38	1.44		2.08	11.93
			3.20			0.11		0.17		0.47	0.06	0.05			0.51				0.10	0.97		0.49	0.06		0.09	0.52
Clearwater (city)	66,707	5,129	3,382	-	-	-	-	262	-	356	-	-	-	-	955	-	-	-	-	775	-	702	-	-	-	416
	84.39		65.94					95.97		73.10					52.65					63.16		96.96				71.11
								7.75		10.53					28.24					22.92		20.76				12.30
			65.94					5.11		6.94					18.62					15.11		13.69				8.11
			5.07					0.39		0.53					1.43					1.16		1.05				0.62
Largo (city)	45,562	1,814	1,351	-	-	-	-	-	-	-	-	-	-	-	282	-	-	-	-	362	-	-	-	-	-	-
	83.38		74.48												82.70					72.98						
															20.87					26.79						
			74.48												15.55					19.96						
			2.97												0.62					0.79						
Palm Harbor (cdp)	39,579	1,266	1,072	-	-	-	-	-	-	-	-	-	-	-	-	-	-	-	-	411	-	-	-	-	-	-
	90.23		84.68																	84.74						
																				38.34						
			84.68																	32.46						
			2.71																	1.04						

Notes: Please refer to the User's Guide for an explanation of data; data is arranged alphabetically by state, then county, then city within each county and only includes counties with populations > 99,999 and cities with populations > 49,999; (1) Includes Costa Rican, Guatemalan, Honduran, Nicaraguan, Panamanian, Salvadoran, and other Central American; (2) Includes Argentinian, Bolivian, Chilean, Colombian, Ecuadorian, Paraguayan, Peruvian, Uruguayan, Venezuelan, and other South American

Place	Total population 25 years and over who are High School graduates	Hispanic population 25 years and over	Hispanics 25 years and over who are High School graduates	Argentinian	Bolivian	Central American[1]	Chilean	Colombian	Costa Rican	Cuban	Dominican	Ecuadorian	Guatelmalan	Honduran	Mexican	Nicaraguan	Panamanian	Paraguayan	Peruvian	Puerto Rican	Salvadoran	South American[2]	Spaniard	Uruguayan	Venezuelan	Other Hisp.
St. Petersburg (city)	143,458 81.86	6,189	4,781 77.25 77.25 3.33	-	-	-	-	-	-	1,007 79.17 21.06 16.27 0.70	-	-	-	-	601 67.68 12.57 9.71 0.42	-	-	-	-	1,404 74.29 29.37 22.69 0.98	-	694 77.80 14.52 11.21 0.48	-	-	-	751 88.46 15.71 12.13 0.52
Polk County	243,868 74.76	22,407	10,254 45.76 45.76 4.20	-	-	418 61.83 4.08 1.87 0.17	-	-	-	1,198 68.61 11.68 5.35 0.49	131 50.00 1.28 0.58 0.05	-	-	-	2,666 24.88 26.00 11.90 1.09	-	-	-	-	4,101 65.23 39.99 18.30 1.68	-	409 74.91 3.99 1.83 0.17	-	-	-	1,214 59.98 11.84 5.42 0.50
Lakeland (city)	42,397 79.18	2,925	1,939 66.29 66.29 4.57	-	-	-	-	-	-	270 62.50 13.92 9.23 0.64	-	-	-	-	207 46.94 10.68 7.08 0.49	-	-	-	-	832 70.63 42.91 28.44 1.96	-	-	-	-	-	301 67.49 15.52 10.29 0.71
St. Johns County	75,162 87.20	2,111	1,806 85.55 85.55 2.40	-	-	-	-	-	-	-	-	-	-	-	300 73.17 16.61 14.21 0.40	-	-	-	-	491 90.93 27.19 23.26 0.65	-	-	-	-	-	318 92.98 17.61 15.06 0.42
St. Lucie County	105,985 77.67	8,403	4,694 55.86 55.86 4.43	-	-	364 65.82 7.75 4.33 0.34	-	220 89.07 4.69 2.62 0.21	-	538 69.69 11.46 6.40 0.51	-	-	-	-	876 28.11 18.66 10.42 0.83	-	-	-	-	1,676 74.16 35.71 19.95 1.58	-	561 82.87 11.95 6.68 0.53	-	-	-	455 61.49 9.69 5.41 0.43
Port St. Lucie (city)	51,886 83.68	4,057	2,975 73.33 73.33 5.73	-	-	-	-	-	-	359 67.61 12.07 8.85 0.69	-	-	-	-	276 51.78 9.28 6.80 0.53	-	-	-	-	1,239 76.81 41.65 30.54 2.39	-	446 91.02 14.99 10.99 0.86	-	-	-	286 69.42 9.61 7.05 0.55
Santa Rosa County	66,781 85.43	1,637	1,364 83.32 83.32 2.04	-	-	-	-	-	-	-	-	-	-	-	323 78.02 23.68 19.73 0.48	-	-	-	-	378 84.56 27.71 23.09 0.57	-	-	-	-	-	246 81.19 18.04 15.03 0.37
Sarasota County	223,638 87.09	8,535	5,513 64.59 64.59 2.47	-	-	300 67.57 5.44 3.51 0.13	-	370 65.60 6.71 4.34 0.17	-	921 63.65 16.71 10.79 0.41	-	-	-	-	1,406 46.25 25.50 16.47 0.63	-	-	-	-	908 79.03 16.47 10.64 0.41	-	999 80.11 18.12 11.70 0.45	-	-	-	846 82.70 15.35 9.91 0.38
Sarasota (city)	30,697 80.10	3,481	1,654 47.52 47.52 5.39	-	-	-	-	-	-	210 42.68 12.70 6.03 0.68	-	-	-	-	618 36.40 37.36 17.75 2.01	-	-	-	-	190 71.16 11.49 5.46 0.62	-	271 59.96 16.38 7.79 0.88	-	-	-	199 63.99 12.03 5.72 0.65
Seminole County	215,693 88.68	24,165	19,094 79.02 79.02 8.85	278 85.28 1.46 1.15 0.13	-	920 74.07 4.82 3.81 0.43	-	1,156 80.33 6.05 4.78 0.54	-	1,822 73.65 9.54 7.54 0.84	576 74.90 3.02 2.38 0.27	255 81.73 1.34 1.06 0.12	-	-	1,274 67.09 6.67 5.27 0.59	-	301 89.58 1.58 1.25 0.14	-	289 96.98 1.51 1.20 0.13	9,703 81.51 50.82 40.15 4.50	-	2,449 84.10 12.83 10.13 1.14	-	-	283 94.97 1.48 1.17 0.13	2,180 78.00 11.42 9.02 1.01

Notes: Please refer to the User's Guide for an explanation of data; data is arranged alphabetically by state, then county, then city within each county and only includes counties with populations > 99,999 and cities with populations > 49,999; (1) Includes Costa Rican, Guatemalan, Honduran, Nicaraguan, Panamanian, Salvadoran, and other Central American; (2) Includes Argentinian, Bolivian, Chilean, Colombian, Ecuadorian, Paraguayan, Peruvian, Uruguayan, Venezuelan, and other South American

Place	Total population 25 years and over who are High School graduates	Hispanic population 25 years and over	Hispanics 25 years and over who are High School graduates	Argentinian	Bolivian	Central American[1]	Chilean	Colombian	Costa Rican	Cuban	Dominican	Ecuadorian	Guatemalan	Honduran	Mexican	Nicaraguan	Panamanian	Paraguayan	Peruvian	Puerto Rican	Salvadoran	South American[2]	Spaniard	Uruguayan	Venezuelan	Other Hisp.
Volusia County	260,243	16,659	10,457	-	-	433	-	324	-	687	219	-	-	-	1,067	-	-	-	-	5,961	-	851	-	-	-	1,152
	82.04		62.77			79.74		68.35		65.30	63.48				29.44					70.54		78.07				79.83
						4.14		3.10		6.57	2.09				10.20					57.00		8.14				11.02
			62.77			2.60		1.94		4.12	1.31				6.40					35.78		5.11				6.92
			4.02			0.17		0.12		0.26	0.08				0.41					2.29		0.33				0.44
Daytona Beach (city)	33,414	1,209	954	-	-	-	-	-	-	-	-	-	-	-	-	-	-	-	-	370	-	-	-	-	-	205
	79.57		78.91																	83.90						89.52
																				38.78						21.49
			78.91																	30.60						16.96
			2.86																	1.11						0.61
Deltona (city)	37,763	7,858	5,501	-	-	-	-	-	-	236	-	-	-	-	197	-	-	-	-	4,070	-	377	-	-	-	332
	82.50		70.01							55.01					56.94					69.96		82.86				80.00
										4.29					3.58					73.99		6.85				6.04
			70.01							3.00					2.51					51.79		4.80				4.22
			14.57							0.62					0.52					10.78		1.00				0.88

Notes: Please refer to the User's Guide for an explanation of data; data is arranged alphabetically by state, then county, then city within each county and only includes counties with populations > 99,999 and cities with populations > 49,999; (1) Includes Costa Rican, Guatemalan, Honduran, Nicaraguan, Panamanian, Salvadoran, and other Central American; (2) Includes Argentinian, Bolivian, Chilean, Colombian, Ecuadorian, Paraguayan, Peruvan, Uruguayan, Venezuelan, and other South American

Educational Attainment: 4-Year College Grads

(Universe: Population 25 Years and Over)

Place	Total population 25 years and over who are 4-year college graduates	Hispanic population 25 years and over	Hispanics 25 years and over who are 4-year college graduates	Argentinian	Bolivian	Central American[1]	Chilean	Colombian	Costa Rican	Cuban	Dominican	Ecuadorian	Guatemalan	Honduran	Mexican	Nicaraguan	Panamanian	Paraguayan	Peruvian	Puerto Rican	Salvadoran	South American[2]	Spaniard	Uruguayan	Venezuelan	Other Hisp.
UNITED STATES	44,462,605	18,270,377	1,908,039	27,118	8,127	102,929	15,495	77,720	9,537	197,694	50,410	25,785	16,083	12,250	759,375	19,131	16,241	1,114	41,325	230,181	22,958	236,699	23,414	3,087	26,159	307,337
	24.40		10.44	35.26	28.81	9.51	31.05	23.72	21.02	21.15	10.90	14.53	6.89	8.68	7.46	15.82	25.30	24.82	24.93	12.49	5.50	25.18	29.91	20.48	44.08	11.17
				1.42	0.43	5.39	0.81	4.07	0.50	10.36	2.64	1.35	0.84	0.64	39.80	1.00	0.85	0.06	2.17	12.06	1.20	12.41	1.23	0.16	1.37	16.11
			10.44	0.15	0.04	0.56	0.08	0.43	0.05	1.08	0.28	0.14	0.09	0.07	4.16	0.10	0.09	0.01	0.23	1.26	0.13	1.30	0.13	0.02	0.14	1.68
			4.29	0.06	0.02	0.23	0.03	0.17	0.02	0.44	0.11	0.06	0.04	0.03	1.71	0.04	0.04	<0.01	0.09	0.52	0.05	0.53	0.05	0.01	0.06	0.69
FLORIDA	2,462,328	1,695,497	296,452	4,546	792	18,404	2,113	24,400	1,487	119,089	7,335	3,456	1,517	2,581	12,848	8,026	2,851	210	8,779	45,299	1,375	56,877	3,396	475	10,597	33,204
	22.33		17.48	26.82	27.58	13.53	22.74	24.47	19.13	18.35	15.30	19.34	8.57	8.95	7.60	14.87	25.24	33.98	27.46	16.00	10.40	26.57	28.74	13.73	39.90	17.97
				1.53	0.27	6.21	0.71	8.23	0.50	40.17	2.47	1.17	0.51	0.87	4.33	2.71	0.96	0.07	2.96	15.28	0.46	19.19	1.15	0.16	3.57	11.20
			17.48	0.27	0.05	1.09	0.12	1.44	0.09	7.02	0.43	0.20	0.09	0.15	0.76	0.47	0.17	0.01	0.52	2.67	0.08	3.35	0.20	0.03	0.63	1.96
			12.04	0.18	0.03	0.75	0.09	0.99	0.06	4.84	0.30	0.14	0.06	0.10	0.52	0.33	0.12	0.01	0.36	1.84	0.06	2.31	0.14	0.02	0.43	1.35
Alachua County	47,803	5,108	2,401	-	-	99	-	140	-	433	-	-	-	-	245	-	-	-	-	645	-	499	-	-	-	378
	38.70		47.00			43.04		64.52		51.24					48.71					40.29		57.29				42.47
						4.12		5.83		18.03					10.20					26.86		20.78				15.74
			47.00			1.94		2.74		8.48					4.80					12.63		9.77				7.40
			5.02			0.21		0.29		0.91					0.51					1.35		1.04				0.79
Gainesville (city)	21,653	2,325	1,091	-	-	-	-	-	-	183	-	-	-	-	89	-	-	-	-	327	-	236	-	-	-	160
	42.81		46.92							49.86					52.98					38.56		54.38				45.33
										16.77					8.16					29.97		21.63				14.67
			46.92							7.87					3.83					14.06		10.15				6.88
			5.04							0.85					0.41					1.51		1.09				0.74
Bay County	17,636	2,011	382	-	-	-	-	-	-	-	-	-	-	-	99	-	-	-	-	123	-	-	-	-	-	63
	17.68		19.00												15.97					23.93						27.63
															25.92					32.20						16.49
			19.00												4.92					6.12						3.13
			2.17												0.56					0.70						0.36
Brevard County	80,020	12,809	2,935	-	-	208	-	139	-	444	86	-	-	-	412	-	109	-	-	943	-	347	-	-	-	450
	23.55		22.91			24.76		33.49		33.23	32.70				21.51		38.93			17.73		31.04				24.31
						7.09		4.74		15.13	2.93				14.04		3.71			32.13		11.82				15.33
			22.91			1.62		1.09		3.47	0.67				3.22		0.85			7.36		2.71				3.51
			3.67			0.26		0.17		0.55	0.11				0.51		0.14			1.18		0.43				0.56
Melbourne (city)	10,635	2,183	437	-	-	-	-	-	-	-	-	-	-	-	116	-	-	-	-	94	-	-	-	-	-	61
	21.30		20.02												30.77					10.16						22.59
															26.54					21.51						13.96
			20.02												5.31					4.31						2.79
			4.11												1.09					0.88						0.57
Palm Bay (city)	8,735	4,054	736	-	-	-	-	-	-	-	-	-	-	-	72	-	-	-	-	307	-	136	-	-	-	96
	16.70		18.15												18.75					13.61		38.31				17.11
															9.78					41.71		18.48				13.04
			18.15												1.78					7.57		3.35				2.37
			8.43												0.82					3.51		1.56				1.10
Broward County	276,527	171,046	39,336	753	115	1,987	356	5,822	240	9,365	1,302	847	265	322	1,423	421	433	-	2,223	6,571	221	13,221	512	116	2,649	4,955
	24.55		23.00	26.92	27.00	15.50	24.05	27.92	18.84	24.47	18.81	23.57	15.26	12.22	14.30	18.41	24.49		28.92	19.78	8.07	29.83	30.49	16.04	46.19	20.76
				1.91	0.29	5.05	0.91	14.80	0.61	23.81	3.31	2.15	0.67	0.82	3.62	1.07	1.10		5.65	16.70	0.56	33.61	1.30	0.29	6.73	12.60
			23.00	0.44	0.07	1.16	0.21	3.40	0.14	5.48	0.76	0.50	0.15	0.19	0.83	0.25	0.25		1.30	3.84	0.13	7.73	0.30	0.07	1.55	2.90
			14.23	0.27	0.04	0.72	0.13	2.11	0.09	3.39	0.47	0.31	0.10	0.12	0.51	0.15	0.16		0.80	2.38	0.08	4.78	0.19	0.04	0.96	1.79

Notes: Please refer to the User's Guide for an explanation of data; data is arranged alphabetically by state, then county, then city within each county and only includes counties with populations > 99,999 and cities with populations > 49,999; (1) Includes Costa Rican, Guatemalan, Honduran, Nicaraguan, Panamanian, Salvadoran, and other Central American; (2) Includes Argentinian, Bolivian, Chilean, Colombian, Ecuadorian, Paraguayan, Peruvian, Uruguayan, Venezuelan, and other South American

Place	Total population 25 years and over who are 4-year college graduates	Hispanic population 25 years and over	Hispanics 25 years and over who are 4-year college graduates	Argentinian	Bolivian	Central American[1]	Chilean	Colombian	Costa Rican	Cuban	Dominican	Ecuadorian	Guatelmalan	Honduran	Mexican	Nicaraguan	Panamanian	Paraguayan	Peruvian	Puerto Rican	Salvadoran	South American[2]	Spaniard	Uruguayan	Venezuelan	Other Hisp.
	24,489	10,412	2,819	-	-	138	-	418	-	458	55	176	-	-	42	-	-	-	155	742	-	983	-	-	139	345
	33.86		27.07			26.34		28.99		33.16	14.47	28.76			5.72				28.13	33.79		29.05			50.18	21.24
Coral Springs (city)						4.90		14.83		16.25	1.95	6.24			1.49				5.50	26.32		34.87			4.93	12.24
			27.07			1.33		4.01		4.40	0.53	1.69			0.40				1.49	7.13		9.44			1.33	3.31
			11.51			0.56		1.71		1.87	0.22	0.72			0.17				0.63	3.03		4.01			0.57	1.41
	12,850	8,725	1,993	-	-	157	-	235	-	647	-	-	-	-	46	-	-	-	136	336	-	457	-	-	-	247
	25.80		22.84			23.57		28.11		27.61					12.96				27.36	17.89		23.08				22.68
Davie (town)						7.88		11.79		32.46					2.31				6.82	16.86		22.93				12.39
			22.84			1.80		2.69		7.42					0.53				1.56	3.85		5.24				2.83
			15.51			1.22		1.83		5.04					0.36				1.06	2.61		3.56				1.92
	10,705	3,779	778	-	-	42	-	105	-	89	-	-	-	-	31	-	-	-	-	268	-	258	-	-	-	38
	21.16		20.59			12.24		22.11		16.42					11.52					29.10		26.11				7.31
Deerfield Beach (city)						5.40		13.50		11.44					3.98					34.45		33.16				4.88
			20.59			1.11		2.78		2.36					0.82					7.09		6.83				1.01
			7.27			0.39		0.98		0.83					0.29					2.50		2.41				0.35
	31,059	9,340	2,124	-	-	98	-	272	-	579	-	-	0	-	152	-	-	-	103	247	14	680	-	-	-	257
	27.91		22.74			8.84		31.26		26.14			0.00		20.21				29.43	16.01	4.11	32.40				18.97
Fort Lauderdale (city)						4.61		12.81		27.26			0.00		7.16				4.85	11.63	0.66	32.02				12.10
			22.74			1.05		2.91		6.20			0.00		1.63				1.10	2.64	0.15	7.28				2.75
			6.84			0.32		0.88		1.86			0.00		0.49				0.33	0.80	0.05	2.19				0.83
	21,870	19,957	3,178	67	-	212	42	480	-	781	156	56	-	40	51	63	-	-	176	481	-	1,076	-	-	174	402
	21.87		15.92	17.40		14.17	14.79	20.89		18.21	14.96	15.14		11.56	6.50	16.67			19.21	11.63		21.32			39.91	13.36
Hollywood (city)				2.11		6.67	1.32	15.10		24.58	4.91	1.76		1.26	1.60	1.98			5.54	15.14		33.86			5.48	12.65
			15.92	0.34		1.06	0.21	2.41		3.91	0.78	0.28		0.20	0.26	0.32			0.88	2.41		5.39			0.87	2.01
			14.53	0.31		0.97	0.19	2.19		3.57	0.71	0.26		0.18	0.23	0.29			0.80	2.20		4.92			0.80	1.84
	6,037	2,509	464	-	-	-	-	81	-	-	-	-	-	-	-	-	-	-	-	80	-	168	-	-	-	118
	16.23		18.49					24.25												16.13		22.64				25.54
Lauderhill (city)								17.46												17.24		36.21				25.43
			18.49					3.23												3.19		6.70				4.70
			7.69					1.34												1.33		2.78				1.95
	6,710	5,145	690	-	-	55	-	92	-	101	-	-	-	-	11	-	-	-	-	176	-	230	-	-	-	102
	17.01		13.41			17.35		12.22		20.12					2.43					11.51		17.22				12.66
Margate (city)						7.97		13.33		14.64					1.59					25.51		33.33				14.78
			13.41			1.07		1.79		1.96					0.21					3.42		4.47				1.98
			10.28			0.82		1.37		1.51					0.16					2.62		3.43				1.52
	9,095	13,625	2,652	-	-	177	-	295	-	873	123	-	-	-	75	53	27	-	92	451	-	607	-	-	-	327
	20.65		19.46			15.76		22.21		19.08	13.46				23.96	12.30	11.49		22.60	19.73		24.08				18.28
Miramar (city)						6.67		11.12		32.92	4.64				2.83	2.00	1.02		3.47	17.01		22.89				12.33
			19.46			1.30		2.17		6.41	0.90				0.55	0.39	0.20		0.68	3.31		4.46				2.40
			29.16			1.95		3.24		9.60	1.35				0.82	0.58	0.30		1.01	4.96		6.67				3.60
	26,847	24,734	7,101	-	-	355	-	762	-	2,349	353	107	-	-	156	-	-	-	403	1,165	-	1,921	-	-	468	761
	28.68		28.71			25.97		33.36		26.44	31.97	28.53			25.70				42.51	25.27		37.08			49.42	27.31
Pembroke Pines (city)						5.00		10.73		33.08	4.97	1.51			2.20				5.68	16.41		27.05			6.59	10.72
			28.71			1.44		3.08		9.50	1.43	0.43			0.63				1.63	4.71		7.77			1.89	3.08
			26.45			1.32		2.84		8.75	1.31	0.40			0.58				1.50	4.34		7.16			1.74	2.83
	21,462	7,163	2,452	-	-	134	-	531	-	497	-	-	-	-	89	-	-	-	157	381	-	1,065	-	-	109	217
	36.69		34.23			30.80		32.92		35.37					24.59				44.48	35.98		38.28			39.21	26.99
Plantation (city)						5.46		21.66		20.27					3.63				6.40	15.54		43.43			4.45	8.85
			34.23			1.87		7.41		6.94					1.24				2.19	5.32		14.87			1.52	3.03
			11.42			0.62		2.47		2.32					0.41				0.73	1.78		4.96			0.51	1.01

Notes: Please refer to the User's Guide for an explanation of data; data is arranged alphabetically by state, then county, then city within each county and only includes counties with populations > 99,999 and cities with populations > 49,999; (1) Includes Costa Rican, Guatemalan, Honduran, Nicaraguan, Panamanian, Salvadoran, and other Central American; (2) Includes Argentinian, Bolivian, Chilean, Colombian, Ecuadorian, Paraguayan, Peruvian, Uruguayan, Venezuelan, and other South American

Place	Total population 25 years and over who are 4-year college graduates	Hispanic population 25 years and over	Hispanics 25 years and over who are 4-year college graduates	Argentinian	Bolivian	Central American[1]	Chilean	Colombian	Costa Rican	Cuban	Dominican	Ecuadorian	Guatemalan	Honduran	Mexican	Nicaraguan	Panamanian	Paraguayan	Peruvian	Puerto Rican	Salvadoran	South American[2]	Spaniard	Uruguayan	Venezuelan	Other Hisp.
Pompano Beach (city)	12,704 21.63	4,553	1,009 22.16 22.16 7.94	-	-	-	-	79 20.36 7.83 1.74 0.62	-	143 30.17 14.17 3.14 1.13	-	-	-	-	58 5.15 5.75 1.27 0.46	-	-	-	-	100 15.17 9.91 2.20 0.79	-	368 35.73 36.47 8.08 2.90	-	-	-	224 24.22 22.20 4.92 1.76
Sunrise (city)	11,615 19.96	9,173	1,955 21.31 21.31 16.83	-	-	91 18.02 4.65 0.99 0.78	-	348 22.22 17.80 3.79 3.00	-	274 19.63 14.02 2.99 2.36	64 14.25 3.27 0.70 0.55	42 10.85 2.15 0.46 0.36	-	-	106 23.35 5.42 1.16 0.91	-	-	-	121 28.67 6.19 1.32 1.04	220 11.84 11.25 2.40 1.89	-	754 24.39 38.57 8.22 6.49	-	-	-	431 31.67 22.05 4.70 3.71
Tamarac (city)	7,870 17.27	5,445	854 15.68 15.68 10.85	-	-	-	-	225 23.91 26.35 4.13 2.86	-	105 14.85 12.30 1.93 1.33	-	-	-	-	-	-	-	-	-	140 10.25 16.39 2.57 1.78	-	348 22.39 40.75 6.39 4.42	-	-	-	168 15.36 19.67 3.09 2.13
Charlotte County	19,875 17.58	2,908	503 17.30 17.30 2.53	-	-	-	-	-	-	100 21.69 19.88 3.44 0.50	-	-	-	-	37 7.55 7.36 1.27 0.19	-	-	-	-	204 22.10 40.56 7.02 1.03	-	-	-	-	-	85 15.57 16.90 2.92 0.43
Citrus County	12,177 13.15	2,007	221 11.01 11.01 1.81	-	-	-	-	-	-	-	-	-	-	-	5 1.98 2.26 0.25 0.04	-	-	-	-	65 7.58 29.41 3.24 0.53	-	-	-	-	-	72 15.89 32.58 3.59 0.59
Clay County	18,159 20.09	3,170	569 17.95 17.95 3.13	-	-	-	-	-	-	-	-	-	-	-	36 6.20 6.33 1.14 0.20	-	-	-	-	268 21.77 47.10 8.45 1.48	-	-	-	-	-	95 14.80 16.70 3.00 0.52
Collier County	51,757 27.92	26,077	1,848 7.09 7.09 3.57	-	-	80 4.34 4.33 0.31 0.15	-	172 21.45 9.31 0.66 0.33	-	656 12.80 35.50 2.52 1.27	65 20.12 3.52 0.25 0.13	-	7 0.82 0.38 0.03 0.01	22 5.82 1.19 0.08 0.04	398 3.01 21.54 1.53 0.77	-	-	-	-	122 6.64 6.60 0.47 0.24	-	303 19.46 16.40 1.16 0.59	-	-	-	224 10.93 12.12 0.86 0.43
Duval County	109,473 21.91	17,615	3,848 21.85 21.85 3.52	-	-	216 18.85 5.61 1.23 0.20	-	281 32.08 7.30 1.60 0.26	-	818 34.33 21.26 4.64 0.75	54 14.88 1.40 0.31 0.05	-	-	-	444 14.73 11.54 2.52 0.41	-	52 15.03 1.35 0.30 0.05	-	116 35.47 3.01 0.66 0.11	1,045 17.67 27.16 5.93 0.95	-	581 32.13 15.10 3.30 0.53	-	-	-	638 22.58 16.58 3.62 0.58
Jacksonville (city)	98,991 21.14	16,739	3,662 21.88 21.88 3.70	-	-	208 18.36 5.68 1.24 0.21	-	267 31.79 7.29 1.60 0.27	-	789 34.02 21.55 4.71 0.80	54 14.88 1.47 0.32 0.05	-	-	-	436 15.68 11.91 2.60 0.44	-	44 13.17 1.20 0.26 0.04	-	-	978 17.37 26.71 5.84 0.99	-	550 32.56 15.02 3.29 0.56	-	-	-	595 22.26 16.25 3.55 0.60
Escambia County	39,789 20.97	4,250	970 22.82 22.82 2.44	-	-	81 31.89 8.35 1.91 0.20	-	-	-	147 25.21 15.15 3.46 0.37	-	-	-	-	228 20.07 23.51 5.36 0.57	-	-	-	-	206 21.30 21.24 4.85 0.52	-	127 44.56 13.09 2.99 0.32	-	-	-	170 17.51 17.53 4.00 0.43

Notes: Please refer to the User's Guide for an explanation of data; data is arranged alphabetically by state, then county, then city within each county and only includes counties with populations > 99,999 and cities with populations > 49,999; (1) Includes Costa Rican, Guatemalan, Honduran, Nicaraguan, Panamanian, Salvadoran, and other Central American; (2) Includes Argentinian, Bolivian, Chilean, Colombian, Ecuadorian, Paraguayan, Peruvian, Uruguayan, Venezuelan, and other South American

Place	Total population 25 years and over who are 4-year college graduates	Hispanic population 25 years and over	Hispanics 25 years and over who are 4-year college graduates	Argentinian	Bolivian	Central American[1]	Chilean	Colombian	Costa Rican	Cuban	Dominican	Ecuadorian	Guatelmalan	Honduran	Mexican	Nicaraguan	Panamanian	Paraguayan	Peruvian	Puerto Rican	Salvadoran	South American[2]	Spaniard	Uruguayan	Venezuelan	Other Hisp.
Pensacola (city)	12,391 32.37	754	263 34.88 34.88 2.12	-	-	-	-	-	-	-	-	-	-	-	-	-	-	-	-	-	-	-	-	-	-	-
Hernando County	12,615 12.73	4,174	372 8.91 8.91 2.95	-	-	-	-	-	-	32 8.08 8.60 0.77 0.25	-	-	-	-	29 5.73 7.80 0.69 0.23	-	-	-	-	222 8.94 59.68 5.32 1.76	-	-	-	-	-	28 5.50 7.53 0.67 0.22
Spring Hill (cdp)	5,988 11.57	3,074	284 9.24 9.24 4.74	-	-	-	-	-	-	22 8.98 7.75 0.72 0.37	-	-	-	-	-	-	-	-	-	188 9.20 66.20 6.12 3.14	-	-	-	-	-	21 5.93 7.39 0.68 0.35
Hillsborough County	164,109 25.10	103,423	16,278 15.74 15.74 9.92	-	-	707 14.57 4.34 0.68 0.43	-	910 23.35 5.59 0.88 0.55	161 25.35 0.99 0.16 0.10	4,130 16.49 25.37 3.99 2.52	268 11.50 1.65 0.26 0.16	177 18.17 1.09 0.17 0.11	30 4.57 0.18 0.03 0.02	103 7.68 0.63 0.10 0.06	1,205 7.57 7.40 1.17 0.73	147 25.88 0.90 0.14 0.09	146 14.17 0.90 0.14 0.09	-	377 33.45 2.32 0.36 0.23	4,010 14.23 24.63 3.88 2.44	94 19.38 0.58 0.09 0.06	2,214 27.61 13.60 2.14 1.35	512 36.31 3.15 0.50 0.31	-	459 45.81 2.82 0.44 0.28	3,232 18.29 19.86 3.13 1.97
Brandon (cdp)	12,811 25.54	5,664	1,079 19.05 19.05 8.42	-	-	28 8.92 2.59 0.49 0.22	-	-	-	157 23.12 14.55 2.77 1.23	-	-	-	-	26 5.35 2.41 0.46 0.20	-	-	-	-	529 19.22 49.03 9.34 4.13	-	107 31.94 9.92 1.89 0.84	-	-	-	187 21.59 17.33 3.30 1.46
Tampa (city)	50,471 25.40	36,559	5,390 14.74 14.74 10.68	-	-	260 12.65 4.82 0.71 0.52	-	204 19.34 3.78 0.56 0.40	-	1,547 14.31 28.70 4.23 3.07	99 12.15 1.84 0.27 0.20	83 24.78 1.54 0.23 0.16	-	26 4.53 0.48 0.07 0.05	393 11.28 7.29 1.07 0.78	36 14.52 0.67 0.10 0.07	52 11.93 0.96 0.14 0.10	-	-	902 10.18 16.73 2.47 1.79	-	585 26.10 10.85 1.60 1.16	244 38.43 4.53 0.67 0.48	-	147 45.65 2.73 0.40 0.29	1,360 17.75 25.23 3.72 2.69
Town 'n' Country (cdp)	11,423 23.32	12,620	1,837 14.56 14.56 16.08	-	-	92 16.76 5.01 0.73 0.81	-	126 16.45 6.86 1.00 1.10	-	587 16.31 31.95 4.65 5.14	56 11.91 3.05 0.44 0.49	-	-	-	119 19.54 6.48 0.94 1.04	-	-	-	-	488 11.64 26.57 3.87 4.27	-	266 18.85 14.48 2.11 2.33	-	-	-	196 12.15 10.67 1.55 1.72
Indian River County	19,533 23.11	3,716	337 9.07 9.07 1.73	-	-	31 19.25 9.20 0.83 0.16	-	-	-	75 29.41 22.26 2.02 0.38	-	-	-	-	24 1.17 7.12 0.65 0.12	-	-	-	-	32 8.47 9.50 0.86 0.16	-	103 26.61 30.56 2.77 0.53	-	-	-	72 15.52 21.36 1.94 0.37
Lake County	25,811 16.59	6,248	907 14.52 14.52 3.51	-	-	81 22.38 8.93 1.30 0.31	-	-	-	151 27.86 16.65 2.42 0.59	-	-	-	-	113 4.54 12.46 1.81 0.44	-	-	-	-	319 18.80 35.17 5.11 1.24	-	105 29.75 11.58 1.68 0.41	-	-	-	131 17.80 14.44 2.10 0.51
Lee County	69,153 21.10	21,755	1,943 8.93 8.93 2.81	-	-	172 10.49 8.85 0.79 0.25	-	134 19.14 6.90 0.62 0.19	-	406 17.50 20.90 1.87 0.59	51 7.97 2.62 0.23 0.07	-	28 4.12 1.44 0.13 0.04	34 11.76 1.75 0.16 0.05	202 2.98 10.40 0.93 0.29	-	-	-	-	550 8.42 28.31 2.53 0.80	-	297 19.21 15.29 1.37 0.43	-	-	-	259 11.55 13.33 1.19 0.37

Notes: Please refer to the User's Guide for an explanation of data: data is arranged alphabetically by state, then county, then city within each county and only includes counties with populations > 99,999 and cities with populations > 49,999; (1) Includes Costa Rican, Guatemalan, Honduran, Nicaraguan, Panamanian, Salvadoran, and other Central American; (2) Includes Argentinian, Bolivian, Chilean, Colombian, Ecuadorian, Paraguayan, Peruvian, Uruguayan, Venezuelan, and other South American

Place	Total population 25 years and over who are 4-year college graduates	Hispanic population 25 years and over	Hispanics 25 years and over who are 4-year college graduates	Argentinian	Bolivian	Central American[1]	Chilean	Colombian	Costa Rican	Cuban	Dominican	Ecuadorian	Guatemalan	Honduran	Mexican	Nicaraguan	Panamanian	Paraguayan	Peruvian	Puerto Rican	Salvadoran	South American[2]	Spaniard	Uruguayan	Venezuelan	Other Hisp.
Cape Coral (city)	12,871	5,032	600	-	-	-	-	66	-	151	38	-	-	-	58	-	-	-	-	152	-	126	-	-	-	63
	17.52		11.92					18.64		13.23	10.92				8.12					11.28		18.10				11.50
								11.00		25.17	6.33				9.67					25.33		21.00				10.50
			11.92					1.31		3.00	0.76				1.15					3.02		2.50				1.25
			4.66					0.51		1.17	0.30				0.45					1.18		0.98				0.49
Leon County	57,396	3,872	1,481	-	-	-	-	-	-	333	-	-	-	-	173	-	-	-	-	340	-	213	-	-	-	265
	41.73		38.25							44.46					26.99					48.85		39.30				28.56
										22.48					11.68					22.96		14.38				17.89
			38.25							8.60					4.47					8.78		5.50				6.84
			2.58							0.58					0.30					0.59		0.37				0.46
Tallahassee (city)	35,901	2,626	989	-	-	-	-	-	-	216	-	-	-	-	98	-	-	-	-	210	-	171	-	-	-	186
	44.96		37.66							44.91					25.93					43.21		41.40				28.18
										21.84					9.91					21.23		17.29				18.81
			37.66							8.23					3.73					8.00		6.51				7.08
			2.75							0.60					0.27					0.58		0.48				0.52
Manatee County	40,059	11,913	992	-	-	88	-	-	-	212	-	-	-	-	216	-	-	-	-	258	-	113	-	-	-	102
	20.78		8.33			10.41				24.57					3.30					14.75		19.32				8.43
						8.87				21.37					21.77					26.01		11.39				10.28
			8.33			0.74				1.78					1.81					2.17		0.95				0.86
			2.48			0.22				0.53					0.54					0.64		0.28				0.25
Marion County	25,626	8,790	831	-	-	41	-	29	-	150	-	-	-	-	68	-	-	-	-	356	-	72	-	-	-	116
	13.69		9.45			10.33		8.36		18.68					4.79					8.59		10.83				10.21
						4.93		3.49		18.05					8.18					42.84		8.66				13.96
			9.45			0.47		0.33		1.71					0.77					4.05		0.82				1.32
			3.24			0.16		0.11		0.59					0.27					1.39		0.28				0.45
Martin County	25,413	4,721	667	-	-	20	-	-	-	188	-	-	20	-	166	-	-	-	-	65	-	-	-	-	-	94
	26.34		14.13			2.11				34.81			2.55		9.70					8.01						21.12
						3.00				28.19			3.00		24.89					9.75						14.09
			14.13			0.42				3.98			0.42		3.52					1.38						1.99
			2.62			0.08				0.74			0.08		0.65					0.26						0.37
Miami-Dade County	323,399	900,566	163,132	2,754	423	11,911	1,157	12,382	581	90,700	3,869	1,410	676	1,465	2,714	6,756	1,373	-	4,341	9,224	780	28,718	1,406	196	5,458	14,590
	21.68		18.11	27.26	26.24	13.42	20.12	23.78	18.65	17.63	15.04	17.67	10.05	7.65	14.14	14.31	29.26		26.35	18.11	12.71	25.61	28.15	12.28	38.00	17.30
				1.69	0.26	7.30	0.71	7.59	0.36	55.60	2.37	0.86	0.41	0.90	1.66	4.14	0.84		2.66	5.65	0.48	17.60	0.86	0.12	3.35	8.94
			18.11	0.31	0.05	1.32	0.13	1.37	0.06	10.07	0.43	0.16	0.08	0.16	0.30	0.75	0.15		0.48	1.02	0.09	3.19	0.16	0.02	0.61	1.62
			50.44	0.85	0.13	3.68	0.36	3.83	0.18	28.05	1.20	0.44	0.21	0.45	0.84	2.09	0.42		1.34	2.85	0.24	8.88	0.43	0.06	1.69	4.51
Carol City (cdp)	3,413	16,481	1,238	-	-	115	-	85	-	656	58	-	-	22	-	68	-	-	-	128	-	176	-	-	-	93
	9.65		7.51			6.89		8.67		7.59	4.72			6.96		7.61				7.45		10.90				6.67
						9.29		6.87		52.99	4.68			1.78		5.49				10.34		14.22				7.51
			7.51			0.70		0.52		3.98	0.35			0.13		0.41				0.78		1.07				0.56
			36.27			3.37		2.49		19.22	1.70			0.64		1.99				3.75		5.16				2.72
Fountainbleau (cdp)	8,970	36,399	7,698	54	-	966	107	458	-	3,668	341	97	-	46	65	697	103	-	280	353	-	1,478	-	-	408	827
	22.36		21.15	14.79		18.13	22.67	23.78		20.01	28.35	20.08		11.70	22.11	17.61	25.94		31.32	28.79		26.19			32.85	19.42
				0.70		12.55	1.39	5.95		47.65	4.43	1.26		0.60	0.84	9.05	1.34		3.64	4.59		19.20			5.30	10.74
			21.15	0.15		2.65	0.29	1.26		10.08	0.94	0.27		0.13	0.18	1.91	0.28		0.77	0.97		4.06			1.12	2.27
			85.82	0.60		10.77	1.19	5.11		40.89	3.80	1.08		0.51	0.72	7.77	1.15		3.12	3.94		16.48			4.55	9.22
Hialeah (city)	16,117	146,118	14,660	57	-	875	45	611	21	10,997	402	118	17	92	29	661	-	-	146	393	9	1,106	8	-	104	850
	10.36		10.03	19.52		9.17	8.41	11.06	6.91	10.05	12.78	13.80	3.45	5.74	3.23	10.97			14.37	8.88	1.52	12.33	2.01		21.80	9.14
				0.39		5.97	0.31	4.17	0.14	75.01	2.74	0.80	0.12	0.63	0.20	4.51			1.00	2.68	0.06	7.54	0.05		0.71	5.80
			10.03	0.04		0.60	0.03	0.42	0.01	7.53	0.28	0.08	0.01	0.06	0.02	0.45			0.10	0.27	0.01	0.76	0.01		0.07	0.58
			90.96	0.35		5.43	0.28	3.79	0.13	68.23	2.49	0.73	0.11	0.57	0.18	4.10			0.91	2.44	0.06	6.86	0.05		0.65	5.27

Notes: Please refer to the User's Guide for an explanation of data; data is arranged alphabetically by state, then county, then city within each county and only includes counties with populations > 99,999 and cities with populations > 49,999; (1) Includes Costa Rican, Guatemalan, Honduran, Nicaraguan, Panamanian, Salvadoran, and other Central American; (2) Includes Argentinian, Bolivian, Chilean, Colombian, Ecuadorian, Paraguayan, Peruvian, Uruguayan, Venezuelan, and other South American

Place	Total population 25 years and over who are 4-year college graduates	Hispanic population 25 years and over	Hispanics 25 years and over who are 4-year college graduates	Argentinian	Bolivian	Central American[1]	Chilean	Colombian	Costa Rican	Cuban	Dominican	Ecuadorian	Guatelmalan	Honduran	Mexican	Nicaraguan	Panamanian	Paraguayan	Peruvian	Puerto Rican	Salvadoran	South American[2]	Spaniard	Uruguayan	Venezuelan	Other Hisp.
Kendale Lakes (cdp)	8,523	29,518	6,174	-	-	537	-	533	-	3,310	102	-	-	36	80	379	-	-	177	271	-	1,073	-	-	184	758
	22.97		20.92			20.15		20.50		20.21	19.43			11.08	23.67	20.50			29.16	23.79		22.38			32.97	21.49
						8.70		8.63		53.61	1.65			0.58	1.30	6.14			2.87	4.39		17.38			2.98	12.28
			20.92			1.82		1.81		11.21	0.35			0.12	0.27	1.28			0.60	0.92		3.64			0.62	2.57
			72.44			6.30		6.25		38.84	1.20			0.42	0.94	4.45			2.08	3.18		12.59			2.16	8.89
Kendall (cdp)	21,045	25,692	8,729	205	-	687	74	991	-	4,215	110	-	-	-	-	342	-	-	383	533	-	2,238	-	-	484	750
	40.84		33.98	41.67		26.72	24.58	34.94		35.74	21.65					23.93			42.94	34.77		37.47			50.10	27.71
				2.35		7.87	0.85	11.35		48.29	1.26					3.92			4.39	6.11		25.64			5.54	8.59
			33.98	0.80		2.67	0.29	3.86		16.41	0.43					1.33			1.49	2.07		8.71			1.88	2.92
			41.48	0.97		3.26	0.35	4.71		20.03	0.52					1.63			1.82	2.53		10.63			2.30	3.56
Miami Beach (city)	23,205	36,891	9,176	604	-	417	117	1,027	-	3,847	241	165	-	82	211	156	-	-	277	604	-	2,651	228	-	338	977
	33.49		24.87	28.94		20.48	20.56	31.15		23.81	22.50	31.43		14.02	25.27	22.64			19.81	24.11		28.00	47.90		33.70	22.48
				6.58		4.54	1.28	11.19		41.92	2.63	1.80		0.89	2.30	1.70			3.02	6.58		28.89	2.48		3.68	10.65
			24.87	1.64		1.13	0.32	2.78		10.43	0.65	0.45		0.22	0.57	0.42			0.75	1.64		7.19	0.62		0.92	2.65
			39.54	2.60		1.80	0.50	4.43		16.58	1.04	0.71		0.35	0.91	0.67			1.19	2.60		11.42	0.98		1.46	4.21
Miami (city)	41,004	176,590	23,714	433	-	2,228	147	1,060	77	14,926	428	213	140	468	401	1,247	121	-	464	964	128	2,864	164	-	378	1,739
	16.24		13.43	29.90		7.82	20.39	23.16	12.98	14.19	8.86	17.16	7.13	5.00	20.46	9.05	19.87		23.18	14.78	7.61	24.24	20.07		30.17	10.27
				1.83		9.40	0.62	4.47	0.32	62.94	1.80	0.90	0.59	1.97	1.69	5.26	0.51		1.96	4.07	0.54	12.08	0.69		1.59	7.33
			13.43	0.25		1.26	0.08	0.60	0.04	8.45	0.24	0.12	0.08	0.27	0.23	0.71	0.07		0.26	0.55	0.07	1.62	0.09		0.21	0.98
			57.83	1.06		5.43	0.36	2.59	0.19	36.40	1.04	0.52	0.34	1.14	0.98	3.04	0.30		1.13	2.35	0.31	6.98	0.40		0.92	4.24
North Miami (city)	5,751	9,277	1,247	-	-	124	-	154	-	396	44	-	-	5	-	88	-	-	-	138	-	270	-	-	-	243
	15.82		13.44			10.57		20.37		17.81	7.14			1.33		19.60				8.04		17.75				14.20
						9.94		12.35		31.76	3.53			0.40		7.06				11.07		21.65				19.49
			13.44			1.34		1.66		4.27	0.47			0.05		0.95				1.49		2.91				2.62
			21.68			2.16		2.68		6.89	0.77			0.09		1.53				2.40		4.69				4.23
Tamiami (cdp)	7,820	33,730	7,028	-	-	491	-	324	-	5,056	91	-	-	50	48	316	-	-	-	169	-	733	-	-	151	413
	21.35		20.84			20.33		22.95		20.70	19.83			16.08	15.14	19.12				20.66		27.58			45.62	16.75
						6.99		4.61		71.94	1.29			0.71	0.68	4.50				2.40		10.43			2.15	5.88
			20.84			1.46		0.96		14.99	0.27			0.15	0.14	0.94				0.50		2.17			0.45	1.22
			89.87			6.28		4.14		64.65	1.16			0.64	0.61	4.04				2.16		9.37			1.93	5.28
Okaloosa County	27,250	3,850	753	-	-	31	-	-	-	120	-	-	-	-	141	-	-	-	-	172	-	-	-	-	-	171
	24.24		19.56			14.49				27.03					12.39					21.31						20.14
						4.12				15.94					18.73					22.84						22.71
			19.56			0.81				3.12					3.66					4.47						4.44
			2.76			0.11				0.44					0.52					0.63						0.63
Orange County	150,009	95,505	16,194	172	-	616	102	1,115	84	2,092	497	163	90	132	1,021	59	199	-	323	7,692	40	2,543	150	-	477	1,583
	26.13		16.96	31.50		16.64	35.54	22.39	23.46	22.31	13.39	13.58	13.06	15.46	10.26	11.64	29.75		25.92	15.62	7.46	24.98	30.99		32.96	17.87
				1.06		3.80	0.63	6.89	0.52	12.92	3.07	1.01	0.56	0.82	6.30	0.36	1.23		1.99	47.50	0.25	15.70	0.93		2.95	9.78
			16.96	0.18		0.64	0.11	1.17	0.09	2.19	0.52	0.17	0.09	0.14	1.07	0.06	0.21		0.34	8.05	0.04	2.66	0.16		0.50	1.66
			10.80	0.11		0.41	0.07	0.74	0.06	1.39	0.33	0.11	0.06	0.09	0.68	0.04	0.13		0.22	5.13	0.03	1.70	0.10		0.32	1.06
Orlando (city)	35,396	19,606	3,667	-	-	131	-	324	-	569	92	-	-	-	271	-	-	-	50	1,395	-	733	-	-	192	434
	28.21		18.70			15.23		25.96		24.91	12.67				20.12				16.13	14.66		26.90			41.74	21.10
						3.57		8.84		15.52	2.51				7.39				1.36	38.04		19.99			5.24	11.84
			18.70			0.67		1.65		2.90	0.47				1.38				0.26	7.12		3.74			0.98	2.21
			10.36			0.37		0.92		1.61	0.26				0.77				0.14	3.94		2.07			0.54	1.23
Osceola County	17,416	28,364	3,552	-	-	104	-	224	-	253	144	48	-	-	129	-	-	-	-	2,188	0	434	-	-	108	267
	15.75		12.52			9.00		18.67		18.01	8.94	13.11			7.67					12.08	0.00	18.41			33.44	14.04
						2.93		6.31		7.12	4.05	1.35			3.63					61.60	0.00	12.22			3.04	7.52
			12.52			0.37		0.79		0.89	0.51	0.17			0.45					7.71	0.00	1.53			0.38	0.94
			20.40			0.60		1.29		1.45	0.83	0.28			0.74					12.56	0.00	2.49			0.62	1.53

Notes: Please refer to the User's Guide for an explanation of data; data is arranged alphabetically by state, then county, then city within each county and only includes counties with populations > 99,999 and cities with populations > 49,999; (1) Includes Costa Rican, Guatemalan, Honduran, Nicaraguan, Panamanian, Salvadoran, and other Central American; (2) Includes Argentinian, Bolivian, Chilean, Colombian, Ecuadorian, Paraguayan, Peruvian, Uruguayan, Venezuelan, and other South American

Place	Total population 25 years and over who are 4-year college graduates	Hispanic population 25 years and over	Hispanics 25 years and over who are 4-year college graduates	Argentinian	Bolivian	Central American[1]	Chilean	Colombian	Costa Rican	Cuban	Dominican	Ecuadorian	Guatelmalan	Honduran	Mexican	Nicaraguan	Panamanian	Paraguayan	Peruvian	Puerto Rican	Salvadoran	South American[2]	Spaniard	Uruguayan	Venezuelan	Other Hisp.
Palm Beach County	226,615 27.71	82,887	12,708 15.33 15.33 5.61	291 23.30 2.29 0.35 0.13	-	726 8.77 5.71 0.88 0.32	87 20.33 0.68 0.10 0.04	1,314 21.07 10.34 1.59 0.58	79 15.67 0.62 0.10 0.03	3,880 20.19 30.53 4.68 1.71	378 15.98 2.97 0.46 0.17	278 21.09 2.19 0.34 0.12	115 3.43 0.90 0.14 0.05	106 5.84 0.83 0.13 0.05	825 5.71 6.49 1.00 0.36	163 14.32 1.28 0.20 0.07	102 36.69 0.80 0.12 0.05	-	504 30.00 3.97 0.61 0.22	1,731 11.77 13.62 2.09 0.76	98 9.80 0.77 0.12 0.04	3,278 24.25 25.79 3.95 1.45	60 15.75 0.47 0.07 0.03	66 10.23 0.52 0.08 0.03	454 39.41 3.57 0.55 0.20	1,830 18.36 14.40 2.21 0.81
Boca Raton (city)	24,362 44.18	4,054	1,257 31.01 31.01 5.16	-	-	-	-	107 20.94 8.51 2.64 0.44	-	272 38.47 21.64 6.71 1.12	-	-	-	-	76 18.49 6.05 1.87 0.31	-	-	-	-	118 25.88 9.39 2.91 0.48	-	471 35.76 37.47 11.62 1.93	-	-	-	249 28.36 19.81 6.14 1.02
Boynton Beach (city)	9,215 20.68	2,966	482 16.25 16.25 5.23	-	-	34 12.06 7.05 1.15 0.37	-	-	-	174 43.50 36.10 5.87 1.89	-	-	-	-	13 3.25 2.70 0.44 0.14	-	-	-	-	66 7.48 13.69 2.23 0.72	-	136 23.99 28.22 4.59 1.48	-	-	-	59 17.40 12.24 1.99 0.64
Delray Beach (city)	13,329 29.31	2,543	514 20.21 20.21 3.86	-	-	-	-	-	-	-	-	-	-	-	39 5.24 7.59 1.53 0.29	-	-	-	-	44 9.76 8.56 1.73 0.33	-	177 39.16 34.44 6.96 1.33	-	-	-	77 27.50 14.98 3.03 0.58
West Palm Beach (city)	15,187 26.86	9,257	1,161 12.54 12.54 7.64	-	-	84 6.05 7.24 0.91 0.55	-	104 21.36 8.96 1.12 0.68	-	505 14.40 43.50 5.46 3.33	12 4.78 1.03 0.13 0.08	-	15 1.54 1.29 0.16 0.10	-	73 7.81 6.29 0.79 0.48	-	-	-	-	123 10.05 10.59 1.33 0.81	-	210 21.43 18.09 2.27 1.38	-	-	-	154 16.28 13.26 1.66 1.01
Pasco County	33,548 13.13	11,046	1,568 14.20 14.20 4.67	-	-	80 19.80 5.10 0.72 0.24	-	-	-	272 22.08 17.35 2.46 0.81	-	-	-	-	111 3.98 7.08 1.00 0.33	-	-	-	-	649 15.41 41.39 5.88 1.93	-	157 25.82 10.01 1.42 0.47	-	-	-	234 15.37 14.92 2.12 0.70
Pinellas County	157,235 22.92	25,032	5,002 19.98 19.98 3.18	-	-	170 19.86 3.40 0.68 0.11	-	285 23.73 5.70 1.14 0.18	-	947 26.02 18.93 3.78 0.60	131 25.00 2.62 0.52 0.08	71 21.39 1.42 0.28 0.05	-	-	581 11.60 11.62 2.32 0.37	-	-	-	154 25.58 3.08 0.62 0.10	1,201 15.85 24.01 4.80 0.76	-	943 28.67 18.85 3.77 0.60	107 24.54 2.14 0.43 0.07	-	217 40.94 4.34 0.87 0.14	922 24.93 18.43 3.68 0.59
Clearwater (city)	18,858 23.86	5,129	796 15.52 15.52 4.22	-	-	-	-	92 33.70 11.56 1.79 0.49	-	118 24.23 14.82 2.30 0.63	-	-	-	-	183 10.09 22.99 3.57 0.97	-	-	-	-	97 7.91 12.19 1.89 0.51	-	210 29.01 26.38 4.09 1.11	-	-	-	133 22.74 16.71 2.59 0.71
Largo (city)	8,982 16.44	1,814	366 20.18 20.18 4.07	-	-	-	-	-	-	-	-	-	-	-	79 23.17 21.58 4.36 0.88	-	-	-	-	77 15.52 21.04 4.24 0.86	-	-	-	-	-	-
Palm Harbor (cdp)	12,386 28.24	1,266	355 28.04 28.04 2.87	-	-	-	-	-	-	-	-	-	-	-	-	-	-	-	-	121 24.95 34.08 9.56 0.98	-	-	-	-	-	-

Notes: Please refer to the User's Guide for an explanation of data; data is arranged alphabetically by state, then county, then city within each county and only includes counties with populations > 99,999 and cities with populations > 49,999; (1) Includes Costa Rican, Guatemalan, Honduran, Nicaraguan, Panamanian, Salvadoran, and other Central American; (2) Includes Argentinian, Bolivian, Chilean, Colombian, Ecuadorian, Paraguayan, Peruvan, Uruguayan, Venezuelan, and other South American

Place	Total population 25 years and over who are 4-year college graduates	Hispanic population 25 years and over	Hispanics 25 years and over who are 4-year college graduates	Argentinian	Bolivian	Central American[1]	Chilean	Colombian	Costa Rican	Cuban	Dominican	Ecuadorian	Guatemalan	Honduran	Mexican	Nicaraguan	Panamanian	Paraguayan	Peruvian	Puerto Rican	Salvadoran	South American[2]	Spaniard	Uruguayan	Venezuelan	Other Hisp.
St. Petersburg (city)	39,987 22.82	6,189	1,252 20.23 20.23 3.13	-	-	-	-	-	-	301 23.66 24.04 4.86 0.75	-	-	-	-	79 8.90 6.31 1.28 0.20	-	-	-	-	308 16.30 24.60 4.98 0.77	-	319 35.76 25.48 5.15 0.80	-	-	-	182 21.44 14.54 2.94 0.46
Polk County	48,669 14.92	22,407	1,935 8.64 8.64 3.98	-	-	98 14.50 5.06 0.44 0.20	-	-	-	388 22.22 20.05 1.73 0.80	27 10.31 1.40 0.12 0.06	-	-	-	321 3.00 16.59 1.43 0.66	-	-	-	-	660 10.50 34.11 2.95 1.36	-	160 29.30 8.27 0.71 0.33	-	-	-	242 11.96 12.51 1.08 0.50
Lakeland (city)	11,168 20.86	2,925	460 15.73 15.73 4.12	-	-	-	-	-	-	78 18.06 16.96 2.67 0.70	-	-	-	-	34 7.71 7.39 1.16 0.30	-	-	-	-	152 12.90 33.04 5.20 1.36	-	-	-	-	-	76 17.04 16.52 2.60 0.68
St. Johns County	28,560 33.13	2,111	547 25.91 25.91 1.92	-	-	-	-	-	-	-	-	-	-	-	56 13.66 10.24 2.65 0.20	-	-	-	-	119 22.04 21.76 5.64 0.42	-	-	-	-	-	90 26.32 16.45 4.26 0.32
St. Lucie County	20,562 15.07	8,403	970 11.54 11.54 4.72	-	-	91 16.46 9.38 1.08 0.44	-	93 37.65 9.59 1.11 0.45	-	147 19.04 15.15 1.75 0.71	-	-	-	-	113 3.63 11.65 1.34 0.55	-	-	-	-	293 12.96 30.21 3.49 1.42	-	150 22.16 15.46 1.79 0.73	-	-	-	141 19.05 14.54 1.68 0.69
Port St. Lucie (city)	9,276 14.96	4,057	685 16.88 16.88 7.38	-	-	-	-	-	-	71 13.37 10.36 1.75 0.77	-	-	-	-	34 6.38 4.96 0.84 0.37	-	-	-	-	242 15.00 35.33 5.96 2.61	-	142 28.98 20.73 3.50 1.53	-	-	-	93 22.57 13.58 2.29 1.00
Santa Rosa County	17,881 22.88	1,637	391 23.89 23.89 2.19	-	-	-	-	-	-	-	-	-	-	-	66 15.94 16.88 4.03 0.37	-	-	-	-	83 18.57 21.23 5.07 0.46	-	-	-	-	-	97 32.01 24.81 5.93 0.54
Sarasota County	70,446 27.43	8,535	1,666 19.52 19.52 2.36	-	-	50 11.26 3.00 0.59 0.07	-	205 36.35 12.30 2.40 0.29	-	317 21.91 19.03 3.71 0.45	-	-	-	-	269 8.85 16.15 3.15 0.38	-	-	-	-	268 23.32 16.09 3.14 0.38	-	435 34.88 26.11 5.10 0.62	-	-	-	261 25.51 15.67 3.06 0.37
Sarasota (city)	9,842 25.68	3,481	321 9.22 9.22 3.26	-	-	-	-	-	-	51 10.37 15.89 1.47 0.52	-	-	-	-	96 5.65 29.91 2.76 0.98	-	-	-	-	44 16.48 13.71 1.26 0.45	-	62 13.72 19.31 1.78 0.63	-	-	-	46 14.79 14.33 1.32 0.47
Seminole County	75,491 31.04	24,165	5,625 23.28 23.28 7.45	104 31.90 1.85 0.43 0.14	-	227 18.28 4.04 0.94 0.30	-	336 23.35 5.97 1.39 0.45	-	749 30.27 13.32 3.10 0.99	90 11.70 1.60 0.37 0.12	39 12.50 0.69 0.16 0.05	-	-	338 17.80 6.01 1.40 0.45	-	90 26.79 1.60 0.37 0.12	-	97 32.55 1.72 0.40 0.13	2,856 23.99 50.77 11.82 3.78	-	754 25.89 13.40 3.12 1.00	-	-	102 34.23 1.81 0.42 0.14	574 20.54 10.20 2.38 0.76

Notes: Please refer to the User's Guide for an explanation of data: data is arranged alphabetically by state, then county, then city within each county and only includes counties with populations > 99,999 and cities with populations > 49,999; (1) Includes Costa Rican, Guatemalan, Honduran, Nicaraguan, Panamanian, Salvadoran, and other Central American; (2) Includes Argentinian, Bolivian, Chilean, Colombian, Ecuadorian, Paraguayan, Peruvian, Uruguayan, Venezuelan, and other South American

Place	Total population 25 years and over who are 4-year college graduates	Hispanic population 25 years and over	Hispanics 25 years and over who are 4-year college graduates	Argentinian	Bolivian	Central American[1]	Chilean	Colombian	Costa Rican	Cuban	Dominican	Ecuadorian	Guatelmalan	Honduran	Mexican	Nicaraguan	Panamanian	Paraguayan	Peruvian	Puerto Rican	Salvadoran	South American[2]	Spaniard	Uruguayan	Venezuelan	Other Hisp.
Volusia County	55,961 17.64	16,659	1,954 11.73 11.73 3.49	-	-	96 17.68 4.91 0.58 0.17	-	61 12.87 3.12 0.37 0.11	-	166 15.78 8.50 1.00 0.30	30 8.70 1.54 0.18 0.05	-	-	-	157 4.33 8.03 0.94 0.28	-	-	-	-	990 11.71 50.67 5.94 1.77	-	256 23.49 13.10 1.54 0.46	-	-	-	225 15.59 11.51 1.35 0.40
Daytona Beach (city)	7,910 18.84	1,209	189 15.63 15.63 2.39	-	-	-	-	-	-	-	-	-	-	-	-	-	-	-	-	92 20.86 48.68 7.61 1.16	-	-	-	-	-	23 10.04 12.17 1.90 0.29
Deltona (city)	6,128 13.39	7,858	880 11.20 11.20 14.36	-	-	-	-	-	-	40 9.32 4.55 0.51 0.65	-	-	-	-	26 7.51 2.95 0.33 0.42	-	-	-	-	589 10.12 66.93 7.50 9.61	-	95 20.88 10.80 1.21 1.55	-	-	-	75 18.07 8.52 0.95 1.22

Notes: Please refer to the User's Guide for an explanation of data: data is arranged alphabetically by state, then county, then city within each county and only includes counties with populations > 99,999 and cities with populations > 49,999; (1) Includes Costa Rican, Guatemalan, Honduran, Nicaraguan, Panamanian, Salvadoran, and other Central American; (2) Includes Argentinian, Bolivian, Chilean, Colombian, Ecuadorian, Paraguayan, Peruvan, Uruguayan, Venezuelan, and other South American

Median Household Income

(Universe: Households)

Place	All households	Hispanic households	Argentinian	Bolivian	Central American[1]	Chilean	Colombian	Costa Rican	Cuban	Dominican	Ecuadorian	Guatelmalan	Honduran	Mexican	Nicaraguan	Panamanian	Paraguayan	Peruvian	Puerto Rican	Salvadoran	South American[2]	Spaniard	Uruguayan	Venezuelan	Other Hisp.
UNITED STATES	41,994	33,676	46,091	47,245	35,517	42,311	38,514	40,041	36,671	29,099	40,924	34,255	31,601	33,621	38,952	39,321	38,551	42,333	30,644	35,366	41,132	45,174	44,458	39,977	32,916
FLORIDA	38,819	34,333	39,486	37,460	33,817	36,598	34,036	34,446	35,133	32,772	36,655	33,733	29,964	32,335	36,089	37,388	31,583	37,976	33,696	32,411	36,011	40,307	37,395	36,530	33,735
Alachua County	31,426	21,434	-	-	10,536	-	19,135	-	18,750	-	-	-	-	25,655	-	-	-	-	22,106	-	20,974	-	-	-	25,350
Gainesville (city)	28,164	18,813	-	-	-	-	-	-	14,146	-	-	-	-	14,130	-	-	-	-	19,545	-	21,893	-	-	-	21,957
Bay County	36,092	32,404	-	-	-	-	-	-	-	-	-	-	-	32,548	-	-	-	-	31,528	-	-	-	-	-	22,708
Brevard County	40,099	36,890	-	-	39,881	-	50,081	-	43,537	40,938	-	-	-	37,646	-	83,204	-	-	35,517	-	31,352	-	-	-	39,952
Melbourne (city)	34,571	31,492	-	-	-	-	-	-	-	-	-	-	-	30,972	-	-	-	-	35,388	-	-	-	-	-	23,750
Palm Bay (city)	36,508	35,781	-	-	-	-	-	-	-	-	-	-	-	39,615	-	-	-	-	35,584	-	24,632	-	-	-	40,139
Broward County	41,691	42,225	45,357	37,778	38,892	40,900	37,664	41,023	52,047	38,982	48,542	40,293	32,421	37,409	43,185	40,957	-	40,926	41,123	35,087	40,490	46,654	37,043	41,105	39,087
Coral Springs (city)	58,459	46,985	-	-	52,961	-	40,208	-	64,097	37,857	69,444	-	-	38,917	-	-	-	31,677	50,218	-	46,170	-	-	46,719	37,981
Davie (town)	47,014	43,737	-	-	36,940	-	40,863	-	59,500	-	-	-	-	50,662	-	-	-	33,558	33,826	-	41,676	-	-	-	46,250
Deerfield Beach (city)	34,041	36,250	-	-	40,938	-	38,818	-	27,222	-	-	-	-	22,621	-	-	-	-	45,463	-	37,957	-	-	-	32,250
Fort Lauderdale (city)	37,887	30,957	-	-	30,795	-	26,603	-	34,323	-	-	31,250	-	35,000	-	-	-	40,882	24,978	29,792	29,853	-	-	-	34,792
Hollywood (city)	36,714	33,649	27,857	-	35,200	36,667	30,122	-	41,061	31,685	37,578	-	33,929	43,864	39,219	-	-	32,404	31,390	-	31,424	-	-	31,071	31,856
Lauderhill (city)	32,515	33,179	-	-	-	-	34,000	-	-	-	-	-	-	-	-	-	-	-	32,031	-	35,556	-	-	-	18,594
Margate (city)	38,722	41,755	-	-	45,000	-	36,888	-	57,727	-	-	-	-	42,778	-	-	-	-	41,250	-	40,119	-	-	-	41,125
Miramar (city)	50,289	54,945	-	-	54,671	-	45,199	-	63,663	43,000	-	-	-	56,339	58,935	35,855	-	56,591	50,429	-	47,394	-	-	-	54,330
Pembroke Pines (city)	52,629	56,223	-	-	60,969	-	48,672	-	61,895	52,050	58,333	-	-	73,047	-	-	-	56,808	52,860	-	52,219	-	-	42,386	47,667
Plantation (city)	53,746	50,583	-	-	60,139	-	50,263	-	68,167	-	-	-	-	43,750	-	-	-	37,917	42,574	-	48,295	-	-	55,227	45,811
Pompano Beach (city)	36,073	28,984	-	-	-	-	28,088	-	25,268	-	-	-	-	25,984	-	-	-	-	36,167	-	28,085	-	-	-	36,719
Sunrise (city)	40,998	42,609	-	-	26,528	-	40,577	-	51,300	50,375	37,250	-	-	52,308	-	-	-	44,821	41,786	-	41,604	-	-	-	37,989
Tamarac (city)	34,290	37,372	-	-	-	-	30,160	-	40,455	-	-	-	-	-	-	-	-	-	36,250	-	33,690	-	-	-	41,756
Charlotte County	36,379	34,201	-	-	-	-	-	-	29,958	-	-	-	-	27,303	-	-	-	-	41,800	-	-	-	-	-	38,387
Citrus County	31,001	24,649	-	-	-	-	-	-	-	-	-	-	-	29,688	-	-	-	-	18,450	-	-	-	-	-	30,114
Clay County	48,854	38,922	-	-	-	-	-	-	-	-	-	-	-	37,083	-	-	-	-	36,970	-	-	-	-	-	39,663
Collier County	48,289	35,941	-	-	38,304	-	22,198	-	38,892	43,688	-	35,208	34,779	34,479	-	-	-	-	36,235	-	33,795	-	-	-	36,758
Duval County	40,703	37,497	-	-	47,024	-	37,393	-	44,375	27,171	-	-	-	38,263	-	48,594	-	46,458	34,643	-	44,963	-	-	-	33,917
Jacksonville (city)	40,316	37,497	-	-	46,845	-	37,214	-	42,016	27,171	-	-	-	39,367	-	47,969	-	-	33,929	-	44,743	-	-	-	33,683
Escambia County	35,234	32,407	-	-	45,625	-	-	-	24,922	-	-	-	-	33,561	-	-	-	-	35,203	-	25,417	-	-	-	32,014
Pensacola (city)	34,779	32,750	-	-	-	-	-	-	-	-	-	-	-	-	-	-	-	-	-	-	-	-	-	-	-
Hernando County	32,572	29,744	-	-	-	-	-	-	22,688	-	-	-	-	30,781	-	-	-	-	29,980	-	-	-	-	-	31,875
Spring Hill (cdp)	32,861	28,561	-	-	-	-	-	-	22,031	-	-	-	-	-	-	-	-	-	28,620	-	-	-	-	-	37,386
Hillsborough County	40,663	32,462	-	-	30,903	-	31,410	34,750	33,641	35,143	31,172	42,250	30,330	32,313	32,557	32,599	-	41,987	31,008	29,632	33,416	42,083	-	37,554	35,006

Notes: Please refer to the User's Guide for an explanation of data; data is arranged alphabetically by state, then county, then city within each county and only includes counties with populations > 99,999 and cities with populations > 49,999; (1) Includes Costa Rican, Guatemalan, Honduran, Nicaraguan, Panamanian, Salvadoran, and other Central American; (2) Includes Argentinian, Bolivian, Chilean, Colombian, Ecuadorian, Paraguayan, Peruvian, Uruguayan, Venezuelan, and other South American

Place	All households	Hispanic households	Argentinian	Bolivian	Central American[1]	Chilean	Colombian	Costa Rican	Cuban	Dominican	Ecuadorian	Guatemalan	Honduran	Mexican	Nicaraguan	Panamanian	Paraguayan	Peruvian	Puerto Rican	Salvadoran	South American[2]	Spaniard	Uruguayan	Venezuelan	Other Hisp.
Brandon (cdp)	51,639	45,119	-	-	38,542	-	-	-	57,321	-	-	-	-	45,500	-	-	-	-	41,285	-	43,750	-	-	-	46,574
Tampa (city)	34,415	27,393	-	-	28,850	-	29,545	-	25,443	28,816	20,294	-	26,324	35,348	29,440	24,671	-	-	23,477	-	27,650	31,625	-	13,468	28,905
Town 'n' Country (cdp)	42,415	37,698	-	-	35,500	-	32,411	-	38,878	40,536	-	-	-	41,591	-	-	-	-	36,935	-	34,769	-	-	-	35,399
Indian River County	39,635	32,011	-	-	12,438	-	-	-	29,375	-	-	-	-	31,054	-	-	-	-	37,750	-	33,000	-	-	-	29,196
Lake County	36,903	36,137	-	-	32,292	-	-	-	67,679	-	-	-	-	35,107	-	-	-	-	35,465	-	43,438	-	-	-	32,083
Lee County	40,319	32,749	-	-	33,784	-	33,672	-	36,618	29,750	-	34,688	33,750	33,294	-	-	-	-	29,588	-	41,417	-	-	-	31,211
Cape Coral (city)	43,410	34,237	-	-	-	-	38,352	-	31,500	31,136	-	-	-	38,844	-	-	-	-	35,792	-	39,741	-	-	-	32,115
Leon County	37,517	27,844	-	-	-	-	-	-	29,375	-	-	-	-	30,172	-	-	-	-	39,779	-	27,386	-	-	-	17,429
Tallahassee (city)	30,571	23,789	-	-	-	-	-	-	22,000	-	-	-	-	30,433	-	-	-	-	32,885	-	24,886	-	-	-	16,500
Manatee County	38,673	30,670	-	-	33,875	-	-	-	37,902	-	-	-	-	28,185	-	-	-	-	32,170	-	26,855	-	-	-	32,617
Marion County	31,944	28,573	-	-	31,633	-	28,167	-	33,083	-	-	-	-	25,703	-	-	-	-	27,500	-	31,848	-	-	-	29,911
Martin County	43,083	29,757	-	-	26,303	-	-	-	48,750	-	-	25,667	-	27,208	-	-	-	-	29,421	-	-	-	-	-	40,150
Miami-Dade County	35,966	33,536	36,458	43,553	32,319	36,674	33,456	34,236	33,427	32,286	31,822	30,836	27,397	33,178	35,059	36,371	-	36,796	34,854	29,824	35,048	40,582	36,861	36,549	32,715
Carol City (cdp)	38,652	35,139	-	-	36,466	-	43,836	-	31,761	38,777	-	-	35,063	-	38,750	-	-	-	36,280	-	43,836	-	-	-	35,714
Fountainbleau (cdp)	35,509	34,643	31,944	-	40,868	40,395	30,969	-	31,426	37,857	32,426	-	45,500	33,929	39,923	55,231	-	34,896	43,292	-	33,836	-	-	33,576	35,054
Hialeah (city)	29,492	29,179	39,688	-	30,714	25,195	30,776	25,769	28,369	30,889	35,169	24,189	30,958	28,393	31,181	-	-	34,893	32,198	21,500	32,336	38,359	-	39,000	32,702
Kendale Lakes (cdp)	44,156	42,109	-	-	41,793	-	36,914	-	44,293	43,259	-	-	21,625	39,773	44,047	-	-	34,534	38,214	-	37,031	-	-	37,150	37,736
Kendall (cdp)	51,330	44,992	40,938	-	45,089	36,719	35,378	-	51,720	30,469	-	-	-	-	49,375	-	-	32,167	39,920	-	36,754	-	-	47,216	39,767
Miami Beach (city)	27,322	22,245	22,154	-	28,056	21,875	21,650	-	20,758	23,438	24,375	-	20,781	27,614	33,389	-	-	22,864	23,257	-	22,437	43,906	-	24,219	21,798
Miami (city)	23,483	22,209	36,289	-	24,941	28,667	25,445	28,405	20,615	23,066	25,664	28,583	23,233	31,250	25,628	32,054	-	30,912	20,995	21,797	26,949	25,134	-	27,813	26,149
North Miami (city)	29,778	31,655	-	-	36,099	-	26,989	-	34,167	31,731	-	-	35,699	-	37,969	-	-	-	36,429	-	27,179	-	-	-	29,697
Tamiami (cdp)	47,503	46,835	-	-	50,469	-	40,104	-	48,805	41,429	-	-	26,667	38,162	52,188	-	-	-	53,702	-	41,023	-	-	43,864	39,965
Okaloosa County	41,474	34,964	-	-	23,000	-	-	-	56,071	-	-	-	-	38,190	-	-	-	-	29,524	-	-	-	-	-	33,063
Orange County	41,311	33,474	47,292	-	39,722	32,411	32,122	31,875	37,619	29,776	33,810	48,633	33,750	35,339	40,750	40,179	-	40,789	33,019	41,595	34,042	33,571	-	32,175	31,015
Orlando (city)	35,732	29,347	-	-	33,750	-	27,338	-	33,214	26,875	-	-	-	27,917	-	-	-	35,119	27,243	-	31,613	-	-	30,169	26,729
Osceola County	38,214	31,538	-	-	34,938	-	26,863	-	32,875	30,304	34,545	-	-	32,894	-	-	-	-	31,731	34,375	27,733	-	-	23,333	31,280
Palm Beach County	45,062	36,539	38,011	-	36,331	41,563	36,319	30,197	41,056	35,429	37,243	34,578	37,050	34,779	45,921	36,538	-	40,303	34,318	28,333	38,819	57,885	40,625	39,358	35,560
Boca Raton (city)	60,248	38,826	-	-	-	-	36,500	-	42,500	-	-	-	-	34,180	-	-	-	-	31,250	-	40,795	-	-	-	44,393
Boynton Beach (city)	39,845	37,451	-	-	42,581	-	-	-	30,521	-	-	-	-	31,510	-	-	-	-	39,917	-	36,848	-	-	-	29,792
Delray Beach (city)	43,371	39,621	-	-	-	-	-	-	-	-	-	-	-	41,667	-	-	-	-	28,359	-	36,161	-	-	-	37,143
West Palm Beach (city)	36,774	30,529	-	-	32,841	-	34,167	-	25,683	25,962	-	37,313	-	32,467	-	-	-	-	32,805	-	34,079	-	-	-	25,170
Pasco County	32,969	35,827	-	-	40,625	-	-	-	43,611	-	-	-	-	27,467	-	-	-	-	35,673	-	38,320	-	-	-	37,188
Pinellas County	37,111	34,172	-	-	35,375	-	28,819	-	33,424	36,339	26,912	-	-	33,525	-	-	-	36,607	34,651	-	30,553	45,833	-	30,000	35,398
Clearwater (city)	36,494	31,173	-	-	-	-	31,250	-	32,083	-	-	-	-	38,355	-	-	-	-	27,857	-	28,864	-	-	-	24,828
Largo (city)	32,217	25,598	-	-	-	-	-	-	-	-	-	-	-	22,177	-	-	-	-	28,690	-	-	-	-	-	-
Palm Harbor (cdp)	45,404	41,528	-	-	-	-	-	-	-	-	-	-	-	-	-	-	-	-	43,636	-	-	-	-	-	-
St. Petersburg (city)	34,597	34,554	-	-	-	-	-	-	30,951	-	-	-	-	30,625	-	-	-	-	34,583	-	37,500	-	-	-	37,390

Notes: Please refer to the User's Guide for an explanation of data; data is arranged alphabetically by state, then county, then city within each county and only includes counties with populations > 99,999 and cities with populations > 49,999; (1) Includes Costa Rican, Guatemalan, Honduran, Nicaraguan, Panamanian, Salvadoran, and other Central American; (2) Includes Argentinian, Bolivian, Chilean, Colombian, Ecuadorian, Paraguayan, Peruvian, Uruguayan, Venezuelan, and other South American

Place	All households	Hispanic households	Argentinian	Bolivian	Central American[1]	Chilean	Colombian	Costa Rican	Cuban	Dominican	Ecuadorian	Guatelmalan	Honduran	Mexican	Nicaraguan	Panamanian	Paraguayan	Peruvian	Puerto Rican	Salvadoran	South American[2]	Spaniard	Uruguayan	Venezuelan	Other Hisp.
Polk County	36,036	31,101	-	-	35,817	-	-	-	36,810	21,607	-	-	-	31,060	-	-	-	-	30,346	-	38,073	-	-	-	29,583
Lakeland (city)	33,119	29,554	-	-	-	-	-	-	37,059	-	-	-	-	27,148	-	-	-	-	29,207	-	-	-	-	-	27,760
St. Johns County	50,099	36,088	-	-	-	-	-	-	-	-	-	-	-	33,000	-	-	-	-	31,576	-	-	-	-	-	41,389
St. Lucie County	36,363	32,293	-	-	42,798	-	19,405	-	31,742	-	-	-	-	31,521	-	-	-	-	32,535	-	40,263	-	-	-	27,125
Port St. Lucie (city)	40,509	37,357	-	-	-	-	-	-	28,750	-	-	-	-	43,750	-	-	-	-	42,375	-	38,750	-	-	-	28,594
Santa Rosa County	41,881	37,465	-	-	-	-	-	-	-	-	-	-	-	43,929	-	-	-	-	33,688	-	-	-	-	-	29,118
Sarasota County	41,957	35,285	-	-	26,875	-	34,132	-	33,906	-	-	-	-	36,507	-	-	-	-	38,036	-	34,572	-	-	-	28,811
Sarasota (city)	34,077	29,974	-	-	-	-	-	-	30,972	-	-	-	-	32,500	-	-	-	-	31,923	-	33,185	-	-	-	21,250
Seminole County	49,326	39,590	68,500	-	40,583	-	36,364	-	41,982	36,583	49,583	-	-	43,262	-	43,250	-	30,694	39,023	-	39,279	-	-	37,563	38,140
Volusia County	35,219	32,296	-	-	28,846	-	30,469	-	29,722	31,615	-	-	-	26,429	-	-	-	-	34,145	-	30,880	-	-	-	33,807
Daytona Beach (city)	25,439	23,953	-	-	-	-	-	-	-	-	-	-	-	-	-	-	-	-	25,451	-	-	-	-	-	11,458
Deltona (city)	39,736	36,062	-	-	-	-	-	-	29,500	-	-	-	-	34,857	-	-	-	-	36,566	-	20,250	-	-	-	41,154

Notes: Please refer to the User's Guide for an explanation of data: data is arranged alphabetically by state, then county, then city within each county and only includes counties with populations > 99,999 and cities with populations > 49,999; (1) Includes Costa Rican, Guatemalan, Honduran, Nicaraguan, Panamanian, Salvadoran, and other Central American; (2) Includes Argentinian, Bolivian, Chilean, Colombian, Ecuadorian, Paraguayan, Peruvian, Uruguayan, Venezuelan, and other South American

Per Capita Income

(Universe: Total Population)

Place	Total population	Total Hispanic population	Argentinian	Bolivian	Central American[1]	Chilean	Colombian	Costa Rican	Cuban	Dominican	Ecuadorian	Guatemalan	Honduran	Mexican	Nicaraguan	Panamanian	Paraguayan	Peruvian	Puerto Rican	Salvadoran	South American[2]	Spaniard	Uruguayan	Venezuelan	Other Hisp.
UNITED STATES	21,587	12,111	26,121	17,438	13,012	20,502	16,428	16,197	20,451	11,773	15,042	12,083	11,629	10,918	14,194	18,518	13,525	17,366	13,518	12,349	17,645	23,046	22,870	17,997	11,981
FLORIDA	21,557	15,198	21,391	16,239	12,809	18,506	15,583	14,959	19,044	13,872	15,202	11,596	11,438	10,569	12,625	17,610	14,742	16,455	14,350	12,702	16,509	23,079	20,762	16,294	12,211
Alachua County	18,465	11,467	-	-	9,842	-	10,464	-	11,753	-	-	-	-	8,700	-	-	-	-	13,428	-	11,816	-	-	-	10,337
Gainesville (city)	16,779	9,704	-	-	-	-	-	-	8,317	-	-	-	-	6,456	-	-	-	-	11,890	-	9,780	-	-	-	8,893
Bay County	18,700	14,970	-	-	-	-	-	-	-	-	-	-	-	15,772	-	-	-	-	14,023	-	-	-	-	-	14,437
Brevard County	21,484	15,872	-	-	16,737	-	15,007	-	23,091	21,476	-	-	-	15,488	-	26,053	-	-	14,108	-	15,070	-	-	-	15,882
Melbourne (city)	19,175	15,557	-	-	-	-	-	-	-	-	-	-	-	19,303	-	-	-	-	14,165	-	-	-	-	-	12,648
Palm Bay (city)	16,992	12,762	-	-	-	-	-	-	-	-	-	-	-	12,276	-	-	-	-	12,321	-	13,471	-	-	-	13,751
Broward County	23,170	17,854	22,450	14,769	15,164	25,921	16,127	16,875	25,277	15,021	17,422	16,069	13,124	14,364	16,357	19,214	-	14,852	18,091	12,544	17,024	28,004	19,328	17,806	12,992
Coral Springs (city)	25,282	18,029	-	-	18,668	-	16,576	-	30,053	19,051	19,023	-	-	16,129	-	-	-	11,818	19,199	-	16,483	-	-	18,516	12,569
Davie (town)	23,271	18,267	-	-	14,185	-	16,193	-	27,634	-	-	-	-	15,366	-	-	-	15,105	15,649	-	15,890	-	-	-	14,266
Deerfield Beach (city)	23,296	20,742	-	-	10,762	-	32,633	-	17,997	-	-	-	-	12,200	-	-	-	-	29,214	-	24,204	-	-	-	14,287
Fort Lauderdale (city)	27,798	18,544	-	-	12,122	-	14,672	-	24,990	-	-	11,372	-	17,108	-	-	-	16,036	17,559	10,466	19,564	-	-	-	11,780
Hollywood (city)	22,097	14,796	14,713	-	14,782	41,421	12,471	-	18,411	12,869	12,036	-	15,868	14,556	16,534	-	-	12,447	16,170	-	14,434	-	-	13,517	10,430
Lauderhill (city)	17,243	15,060	-	-	-	-	13,187	-	-	-	-	-	-	-	-	-	-	-	13,405	-	13,982	-	-	-	12,175
Margate (city)	20,308	14,269	-	-	16,121	-	12,258	-	20,218	-	-	-	-	14,256	-	-	-	-	16,027	-	12,994	-	-	-	10,788
Miramar (city)	18,462	19,626	-	-	16,568	-	16,766	-	27,121	13,445	-	-	-	17,715	19,507	11,234	-	14,034	19,936	-	17,321	-	-	-	12,915
Pembroke Pines (city)	23,843	21,162	-	-	20,872	-	17,853	-	26,262	16,807	25,478	-	-	24,223	-	-	-	16,043	20,309	-	18,958	-	-	20,022	15,279
Plantation (city)	28,250	21,113	-	-	24,614	-	18,299	-	30,139	-	-	-	-	21,763	-	-	-	20,234	21,168	-	18,576	-	-	10,441	13,604
Pompano Beach (city)	23,938	13,710	-	-	-	-	16,872	-	20,844	-	-	-	-	8,461	-	-	-	-	15,706	-	16,166	-	-	-	16,494
Sunrise (city)	18,713	16,774	-	-	14,088	-	13,472	-	22,735	14,445	16,225	-	-	17,747	-	-	-	15,779	16,786	-	14,984	-	-	-	15,682
Tamarac (city)	22,243	15,554	-	-	-	-	12,934	-	18,979	-	-	-	-	-	-	-	-	-	18,040	-	12,682	-	-	-	12,910
Charlotte County	21,806	14,912	-	-	-	-	-	-	24,353	-	-	-	-	11,296	-	-	-	-	14,343	-	-	-	-	-	15,476
Citrus County	18,585	13,165	-	-	-	-	-	-	-	-	-	-	-	10,690	-	-	-	-	10,180	-	-	-	-	-	18,071
Clay County	20,868	13,082	-	-	-	-	-	-	-	-	-	-	-	10,526	-	-	-	-	12,559	-	-	-	-	-	12,098
Collier County	31,195	11,638	-	-	12,650	-	16,683	-	16,772	16,283	-	10,950	11,029	9,166	-	-	-	-	12,140	-	16,670	-	-	-	15,004
Duval County	20,753	16,963	-	-	14,957	-	24,928	-	28,806	13,649	-	-	-	16,257	-	15,417	-	19,098	14,155	-	22,728	-	-	-	14,382
Jacksonville (city)	20,337	16,964	-	-	14,994	-	25,440	-	28,682	13,649	-	-	-	16,540	-	15,532	-	-	14,029	-	22,895	-	-	-	14,315
Escambia County	18,641	14,708	-	-	13,244	-	-	-	15,394	-	-	-	-	13,614	-	-	-	-	16,395	-	11,609	-	-	-	15,993
Pensacola (city)	21,438	16,249	-	-	-	-	-	-	-	-	-	-	-	-	-	-	-	-	-	-	-	-	-	-	-
Hernando County	18,321	11,527	-	-	-	-	-	-	12,264	-	-	-	-	9,442	-	-	-	-	11,529	-	-	-	-	-	12,410
Spring Hill (cdp)	17,184	11,546	-	-	-	-	-	-	11,921	-	-	-	-	-	-	-	-	-	11,558	-	-	-	-	-	12,682
Hillsborough County	21,812	14,545	-	-	13,454	-	17,420	12,911	18,476	16,072	15,084	13,366	12,137	10,111	15,733	12,904	-	14,084	13,140	13,939	16,781	26,340	-	14,448	16,081

Notes: Please refer to the User's Guide for an explanation of data; data is arranged alphabetically by state, then county, then city within each county and only includes counties with populations > 99,999 and cities with populations > 49,999; (1) Includes Costa Rican, Guatemalan, Honduran, Nicaraguan, Panamanian, Salvadoran, and other Central American; (2) Includes Argentinian, Bolivian, Chilean, Colombian, Ecuadorian, Paraguayan, Peruvian, Uruguayan, Venezuelan, and other South American

Place	Total population	Total Hispanic population	Argentinian	Bolivian	Central American[1]	Chilean	Colombian	Costa Rican	Cuban	Dominican	Ecuadorian	Guatemalan	Honduran	Mexican	Nicaraguan	Panamanian	Paraguayan	Peruvian	Puerto Rican	Salvadoran	South American[2]	Spaniard	Uruguayan	Venezuelan	Other Hisp.
Brandon (cdp)	22,080	15,619	-	-	13,516	-	-	-	21,928	-	-	-	-	13,160	-	-	-	-	14,554	-	11,292	-	-	-	17,701
Tampa (city)	21,953	14,684	-	-	13,230	-	13,886	-	17,550	15,739	10,737	-	11,016	13,098	17,344	11,665	-	-	10,738	-	14,822	26,392	-	10,264	16,898
Town 'n' Country (cdp)	21,346	14,498	-	-	15,678	-	13,557	-	18,489	14,740	-	-	-	15,691	-	-	-	-	12,750	-	14,682	-	-	-	11,127
Indian River County	27,227	11,566	-	-	8,986	-	-	-	11,300	-	-	-	-	8,728	-	-	-	-	14,959	-	30,244	-	-	-	11,484
Lake County	20,199	12,830	-	-	21,327	-	-	-	23,044	-	-	-	-	10,347	-	-	-	-	13,994	-	15,785	-	-	-	10,876
Lee County	24,542	11,122	-	-	12,404	-	12,053	-	15,979	10,953	-	9,708	17,696	9,323	-	-	-	-	11,621	-	14,478	-	-	-	9,663
Cape Coral (city)	21,021	12,640	-	-	-	-	11,324	-	13,288	13,312	-	-	-	10,872	-	-	-	-	13,265	-	15,108	-	-	-	9,855
Leon County	21,024	14,933	-	-	-	-	-	-	17,362	-	-	-	-	13,201	-	-	-	-	19,132	-	11,708	-	-	-	12,462
Tallahassee (city)	18,981	13,856	-	-	-	-	-	-	15,392	-	-	-	-	14,350	-	-	-	-	16,637	-	10,437	-	-	-	12,197
Manatee County	22,388	11,483	-	-	12,222	-	-	-	17,387	-	-	-	-	10,287	-	-	-	-	13,174	-	16,791	-	-	-	11,365
Marion County	17,848	13,246	-	-	12,388	-	13,361	-	15,220	-	-	-	-	18,269	-	-	-	-	11,222	-	15,784	-	-	-	9,905
Martin County	29,584	12,095	-	-	7,454	-	-	-	35,406	-	-	7,334	-	8,709	-	-	-	-	11,310	-	-	-	-	-	12,966
Miami-Dade County	18,497	16,194	20,512	17,941	12,392	17,112	15,737	15,371	18,559	13,519	14,391	11,888	10,463	11,881	12,199	20,265	-	16,772	16,070	12,562	16,605	22,820	20,398	16,723	11,180
Carol City (cdp)	12,600	11,464	-	-	12,303	-	12,725	-	12,436	10,699	-	-	14,697	-	11,498	-	-	-	12,213	-	11,871	-	-	-	7,478
Fountainbleau (cdp)	14,716	14,708	15,238	-	13,319	11,869	12,494	-	17,050	13,715	10,453	-	10,874	16,258	13,026	17,102	-	16,513	18,113	-	12,940	-	-	12,249	10,925
Hialeah (city)	12,402	12,577	14,892	-	10,658	11,676	11,052	10,481	13,385	11,417	13,189	7,641	10,504	10,984	11,026	-	-	16,658	12,420	9,042	12,269	13,312	-	10,517	9,161
Kendale Lakes (cdp)	17,592	16,936	-	-	14,991	-	13,404	-	20,200	14,156	-	-	8,129	13,705	16,729	-	-	22,421	16,773	-	15,160	-	-	11,288	10,064
Kendall (cdp)	27,914	22,492	21,551	-	18,632	18,805	14,982	-	29,833	13,772	-	-	-	-	16,571	-	-	13,814	20,432	-	16,952	-	-	16,144	14,656
Miami Beach (city)	27,853	19,644	17,211	-	14,415	16,063	15,128	-	25,069	14,357	17,788	-	12,407	19,765	14,632	-	-	12,561	16,493	-	16,587	25,841	-	24,212	15,037
Miami (city)	15,128	13,305	20,737	-	9,637	16,787	16,984	11,901	15,008	10,722	14,825	10,887	9,228	16,034	9,037	23,014	-	19,081	11,975	10,207	18,023	17,083	-	19,488	10,008
North Miami (city)	14,581	14,580	-	-	11,093	-	12,418	-	20,735	14,268	-	-	9,015	-	11,195	-	-	-	13,723	-	14,494	-	-	-	12,218
Tamiami (cdp)	17,601	18,240	-	-	15,421	-	15,682	-	19,996	18,429	-	-	11,964	14,380	13,848	-	-	-	19,310	-	15,099	-	-	12,506	11,559
Okaloosa County	20,918	14,926	-	-	12,346	-	-	-	19,130	-	-	-	-	12,386	-	-	-	-	14,968	-	-	-	-	-	18,473
Orange County	20,916	13,574	20,438	-	15,421	16,975	13,728	12,790	19,598	13,207	13,201	17,378	12,295	12,235	19,956	17,801	-	20,313	13,299	12,649	14,904	19,968	-	14,110	10,466
Orlando (city)	21,216	13,660	-	-	13,368	-	13,181	-	19,929	10,912	-	-	-	20,044	-	-	-	22,045	12,316	-	15,297	-	-	13,127	10,311
Osceola County	17,022	11,782	-	-	17,676	-	10,440	-	16,734	11,519	14,111	-	-	10,753	-	-	-	-	11,713	12,158	11,612	-	-	11,912	8,918
Palm Beach County	28,801	14,653	25,191	-	10,948	15,230	14,545	12,165	21,192	14,335	15,472	8,904	11,261	10,511	13,204	21,031	-	21,014	14,883	11,860	17,131	19,539	20,062	17,633	12,281
Boca Raton (city)	45,628	25,476	-	-	-	-	15,239	-	42,127	-	-	-	-	11,052	-	-	-	-	19,481	-	26,302	-	-	-	28,953
Boynton Beach (city)	22,573	15,458	-	-	11,508	-	-	-	22,305	-	-	-	-	12,668	-	-	-	-	14,413	-	19,436	-	-	-	14,091
Delray Beach (city)	29,350	16,370	-	-	-	-	-	-	-	-	-	-	-	10,242	-	-	-	-	13,257	-	28,413	-	-	-	15,035
West Palm Beach (city)	23,188	13,094	-	-	9,824	-	12,353	-	17,906	10,243	-	9,018	-	10,366	-	-	-	-	12,810	-	16,122	-	-	-	8,066
Pasco County	18,439	13,962	-	-	17,018	-	-	-	22,077	-	-	-	-	9,643	-	-	-	-	14,500	-	14,074	-	-	-	14,768
Pinellas County	23,497	15,517	-	-	16,029	-	14,833	-	20,872	16,063	17,609	-	-	11,689	-	-	-	16,464	15,169	-	15,330	26,143	-	12,391	17,536
Clearwater (city)	22,786	11,646	-	-	-	-	14,436	-	19,854	-	-	-	-	9,670	-	-	-	-	11,008	-	14,407	-	-	-	10,430
Largo (city)	20,848	14,063	-	-	-	-	-	-	-	-	-	-	-	14,567	-	-	-	-	14,651	-	-	-	-	-	-
Palm Harbor (cdp)	26,470	17,923	-	-	-	-	-	-	-	-	-	-	-	-	-	-	-	-	16,471	-	-	-	-	-	-
St. Petersburg (city)	21,107	16,926	-	-	-	-	-	-	19,103	-	-	-	-	13,800	-	-	-	-	14,881	-	18,614	-	-	-	17,764

Notes: Please refer to the User's Guide for an explanation of data; data is arranged alphabetically by state, then county, then city within each county and only includes counties with populations > 99,999 and cities with populations > 49,999; (1) Includes Costa Rican, Guatemalan, Honduran, Nicaraguan, Panamanian, Salvadoran, and other Central American; (2) Includes Argentinian, Bolivian, Chilean, Colombian, Ecuadorian, Paraguayan, Peruvian, Uruguayan, Venezuelan, and other South American

Place	Total population	Total Hispanic population	Argentinian	Bolivian	Central American[1]	Chilean	Colombian	Costa Rican	Cuban	Dominican	Ecuadorian	Guatelmalan	Honduran	Mexican	Nicaraguan	Panamanian	Paraguayan	Peruvian	Puerto Rican	Salvadoran	South American[2]	Spaniard	Uruguayan	Venezuelan	Other Hisp.
Polk County	18,302	10,603	-	-	12,686	-	-	-	19,330	11,625	-	-	-	9,039	-	-	-	-	11,436	-	13,582	-	-	-	10,566
Lakeland (city)	19,760	13,168	-	-	-	-	-	-	16,151	-	-	-	-	11,177	-	-	-	-	12,039	-	-	-	-	-	13,539
St. Johns County	28,674	18,279	-	-	-	-	-	-	-	-	-	-	-	9,561	-	-	-	-	17,019	-	-	-	-	-	15,397
St. Lucie County	18,790	10,980	-	-	11,838	-	11,369	-	16,201	-	-	-	-	8,490	-	-	-	-	13,221	-	13,898	-	-	-	10,417
Port St. Lucie (city)	18,059	13,098	-	-	-	-	-	-	13,326	-	-	-	-	10,454	-	-	-	-	14,545	-	15,251	-	-	-	8,629
Santa Rosa County	20,089	17,048	-	-	-	-	-	-	-	-	-	-	-	23,032	-	-	-	-	12,297	-	-	-	-	-	14,645
Sarasota County	28,326	15,097	-	-	11,745	-	14,102	-	21,617	-	-	-	-	10,710	-	-	-	-	20,990	-	15,211	-	-	-	14,449
Sarasota (city)	23,197	11,461	-	-	-	-	-	-	13,070	-	-	-	-	9,176	-	-	-	-	18,224	-	10,477	-	-	-	9,282
Seminole County	24,591	16,764	28,529	-	19,261	-	17,739	-	20,868	15,909	15,541	-	-	16,855	-	23,699	-	15,669	16,416	-	17,911	-	-	13,644	13,124
Volusia County	19,664	12,652	-	-	13,554	-	13,293	-	21,236	9,476	-	-	-	9,670	-	-	-	-	13,197	-	13,784	-	-	-	14,039
Daytona Beach (city)	17,530	13,780	-	-	-	-	-	-	-	-	-	-	-	-	-	-	-	-	11,775	-	-	-	-	-	10,358
Deltona (city)	16,648	12,812	-	-	-	-	-	-	14,228	-	-	-	-	14,108	-	-	-	-	12,417	-	12,264	-	-	-	14,579

Notes: Please refer to the User's Guide for an explanation of data; data is arranged alphabetically by state, then county, then city within each county and only includes counties with populations > 99,999 and cities with populations > 49,999; (1) Includes Costa Rican, Guatemalan, Honduran, Nicaraguan, Panamanian, Salvadoran, and other Central American; (2) Includes Argentinian, Bolivian, Chilean, Colombian, Ecuadorian, Paraguayan, Peruvan, Uruguayan, Venezuelan, and other South American

Poverty Status

(Universe: Population for Whom Poverty Status is Determined)

Place	Total population with income below poverty level	Hispanic pop. for whom poverty status is determined	Hispanics with income below poverty level	Argentinian	Bolivian	Central American[1]	Chilean	Colombian	Costa Rican	Cuban	Dominican	Ecuadorian	Guatelmalan	Honduran	Mexican	Nicaraguan	Panamanian	Paraguayan	Peruvian	Puerto Rican	Salvadoran	South American[2]	Spaniard	Uruguayan	Venezuelan	Other Hisp.
UNITED STATES	33,899,812	34,450,868	7,797,874	14,584	5,823	355,028	8,980	81,486	11,397	177,935	215,854	44,109	88,004	56,782	4,814,500	31,334	12,473	1,011	29,866	853,443	138,706	210,017	14,141	2,229	16,375	1,156,956
	12.38		22.63	13.78	13.11	19.89	12.35	16.78	16.06	14.56	27.52	16.37	21.93	24.35	23.51	16.30	13.00	11.50	12.23	25.84	19.85	15.05	12.75	11.22	17.35	21.54
				0.19	0.07	4.55	0.12	1.04	0.15	2.28	2.77	0.57	1.13	0.73	61.74	0.40	0.16	0.01	0.38	10.94	1.78	2.69	0.18	0.03	0.21	14.84
			22.63	0.04	0.02	1.03	0.03	0.24	0.03	0.52	0.63	0.13	0.26	0.16	13.97	0.09	0.04	<0.01	0.09	2.48	0.40	0.61	0.04	0.01	0.05	3.36
			23.00	0.04	0.02	1.05	0.03	0.24	0.03	0.52	0.64	0.13	0.26	0.17	14.20	0.09	0.04	<0.01	0.09	2.52	0.41	0.62	0.04	0.01	0.05	3.41
FLORIDA	1,952,629	2,633,991	472,975	4,559	554	42,455	1,947	27,913	1,770	123,181	13,138	3,517	8,059	9,440	93,971	15,392	2,412	181	6,743	82,067	4,491	54,744	1,849	632	7,987	61,570
	12.51		17.96	19.26	12.71	19.62	14.61	19.23	14.77	14.80	17.58	13.68	25.89	21.27	26.84	17.86	14.41	19.67	14.49	17.38	21.41	17.51	12.29	14.55	18.95	17.06
				0.96	0.12	8.98	0.41	5.90	0.37	26.04	2.78	0.74	1.70	2.00	19.87	3.25	0.51	0.04	1.43	17.35	0.95	11.57	0.39	0.13	1.69	13.02
			17.96	0.17	0.02	1.61	0.07	1.06	0.07	4.68	0.50	0.13	0.31	0.36	3.57	0.58	0.09	0.01	0.26	3.12	0.17	2.08	0.07	0.02	0.30	2.34
			24.22	0.23	0.03	2.17	0.10	1.43	0.09	6.31	0.67	0.18	0.41	0.48	4.81	0.79	0.12	0.01	0.35	4.20	0.23	2.80	0.09	0.03	0.41	3.15
Alachua County	46,939	11,248	3,749	-	-	206	-	241	-	880	-	-	-	-	399	-	-	-	-	860	-	667	-	-	-	564
	22.76		33.33			35.89		41.62		41.33					31.89					29.05		35.94				27.10
						5.49		6.43		23.47					10.64					22.94		17.79				15.04
			33.33			1.83		2.14		7.82					3.55					7.65		5.93				5.01
			7.99			0.44		0.51		1.87					0.85					1.83		1.42				1.20
Gainesville (city)	22,559	4,887	1,859	-	-	-	-	-	-	365	-	-	-	-	182	-	-	-	-	585	-	308	-	-	-	248
	26.69		38.04							44.03					49.73					38.09		33.23				29.11
										19.63					9.79					31.47		16.57				13.34
			38.04							7.47					3.72					11.97		6.30				5.07
			8.24							1.62					0.81					2.59		1.37				1.10
Bay County	18,882	3,307	717	-	-	-	-	-	-	-	-	-	-	-	260	-	-	-	-	252	-	-	-	-	-	121
	13.04		21.68												22.24					25.85						28.67
															36.26					35.15						16.88
			21.68												7.86					7.62						3.66
			3.80												1.38					1.33						0.64
Brevard County	44,218	21,323	3,099	-	-	107	-	44	-	189	91	-	-	-	720	-	27	-	-	1,236	-	168	-	-	-	530
	9.47		14.53			9.21		6.29		9.16	25.71				19.93		7.22			13.77		10.13				16.16
						3.45		1.42		6.10	2.94				23.23		0.87			39.88		5.42				17.10
			14.53			0.50		0.21		0.89	0.43				3.38		0.13			5.80		0.79				2.49
			7.01			0.24		0.10		0.43	0.21				1.63		0.06			2.80		0.38				1.20
Melbourne (city)	7,843	3,640	681	-	-	-	-	-	-	-	-	-	-	-	191	-	-	-	-	279	-	-	-	-	-	70
	11.48		18.71												23.07					18.67						16.09
															28.05					40.97						10.28
			18.71												5.25					7.66						1.92
			8.68												2.44					3.56						0.89
Palm Bay (city)	7,471	6,919	978	-	-	-	-	-	-	-	-	-	-	-	83	-	-	-	-	565	-	60	-	-	-	175
	9.47		14.13												11.51					14.39		11.34				17.04
															8.49					57.77		6.13				17.89
			14.13												1.20					8.17		0.87				2.53
			13.09												1.11					7.56		0.80				2.34
Broward County	184,589	269,562	35,664	716	129	3,130	200	5,256	224	3,896	1,309	461	330	574	3,556	669	376	-	1,692	7,300	859	10,348	219	116	1,600	5,906
	11.51		13.23	17.66	18.48	15.77	9.56	17.09	11.73	7.38	12.25	8.68	11.58	13.90	19.28	18.85	15.30		14.97	13.60	19.47	15.79	9.46	12.45	17.72	12.77
				2.01	0.36	8.78	0.56	14.74	0.63	10.92	3.67	1.29	0.93	1.61	9.97	1.88	1.05		4.74	20.47	2.41	29.02	0.61	0.33	4.49	16.56
			13.23	0.27	0.05	1.16	0.07	1.95	0.08	1.45	0.49	0.17	0.12	0.21	1.32	0.25	0.14		0.63	2.71	0.32	3.84	0.08	0.04	0.59	2.19
			19.32	0.39	0.07	1.70	0.11	2.85	0.12	2.11	0.71	0.25	0.18	0.31	1.93	0.36	0.20		0.92	3.95	0.47	5.61	0.12	0.06	0.87	3.20

Notes: Please refer to the User's Guide for an explanation of data: data is arranged alphabetically by state, then county, then city within each county and only includes counties with populations > 99,999 and cities with populations > 49,999; (1) Includes Costa Rican, Guatemalan, Honduran, Nicaraguan, Panamanian, Salvadoran, and other Central American; (2) Includes Argentinian, Bolivian, Chilean, Colombian, Ecuadorian, Paraguayan, Peruvian, Uruguayan, Venezuelan, and other South American

Place	Total population with income below poverty level	Hispanic pop. for whom poverty status is determined	Hispanics with income below poverty level	Argentinian	Bolivian	Central American[1]	Chilean	Colombian	Costa Rican	Cuban	Dominican	Ecuadorian	Guatelmalan	Honduran	Mexican	Nicaraguan	Panamanian	Paraguayan	Peruvian	Puerto Rican	Salvadoran	South American[2]	Spaniard	Uruguayan	Venezuelan	Other Hisp.
Coral Springs (city)	9,366	18,134	2,510	-	-	112	-	228	-	89	47	19	-	-	466	-	-	-	166	458	-	649	-	-	92	636
	8.03		13.84			13.68		10.08		4.41	8.82	2.02			29.48				17.42	11.55		11.82			18.55	18.52
						4.46		9.08		3.55	1.87	0.76			18.57				6.61	18.25		25.86			3.67	25.34
			13.84			0.62		1.26		0.49	0.26	0.10			2.57				0.92	2.53		3.58			0.51	3.51
			26.80			1.20		2.43		0.95	0.50	0.20			4.98				1.77	4.89		6.93			0.98	6.79
Davie (town)	7,424	14,353	2,265	-	-	287	-	337	-	315	-	-	-	-	106	-	-	-	77	598	-	550	-	-	-	339
	9.85		15.78			26.38		27.76		9.16					14.89				11.92	17.42		18.39				15.77
						12.67		14.88		13.91					4.68				3.40	26.40		24.28				14.97
			15.78			2.00		2.35		2.19					0.74				0.54	4.17		3.83				2.36
			30.51			3.87		4.54		4.24					1.43				1.04	8.05		7.41				4.57
Deerfield Beach (city)	7,984	5,489	919	-	-	132	-	108	-	183	-	-	-	-	91	-	-	-	-	142	-	214	-	-	-	126
	12.48		16.74			26.72		15.32		23.70					20.09					10.86		15.20				15.27
						14.36		11.75		19.91					9.90					15.45		23.29				13.71
			16.74			2.40		1.97		3.33					1.66					2.59		3.90				2.30
			11.51			1.65		1.35		2.29					1.14					1.78		2.68				1.58
Fort Lauderdale (city)	26,158	13,525	2,499	-	-	395	-	199	-	277	-	-	124	-	165	-	-	-	81	641	127	541	-	-	-	432
	17.74		18.48			22.51		15.88		10.57			33.42		13.65				17.09	27.81	19.54	18.51				18.29
						15.81		7.96		11.08			4.96		6.60				3.24	25.65	5.08	21.65				17.29
			18.48			2.92		1.47		2.05			0.92		1.22				0.60	4.74	0.94	4.00				3.19
			9.55			1.51		0.76		1.06			0.47		0.63				0.31	2.45	0.49	2.07				1.65
Hollywood (city)	18,222	31,197	4,910	207	-	251	41	746	-	475	311	44	-	35	271	68	-	-	281	1,206	-	1,545	-	-	153	799
	13.22		15.74	37.03		11.18	10.88	22.59		7.93	18.42	7.01		7.99	22.53	11.43			21.02	17.53		21.06			23.39	14.13
				4.22		5.11	0.84	15.19		9.67	6.33	0.90		0.71	5.52	1.38			5.72	24.56		31.47			3.12	16.27
			15.74	0.66		0.80	0.13	2.39		1.52	1.00	0.14		0.11	0.87	0.22			0.90	3.87		4.95			0.49	2.56
			26.95	1.14		1.38	0.23	4.09		2.61	1.71	0.24		0.19	1.49	0.37			1.54	6.62		8.48			0.84	4.38
Lauderhill (city)	10,101	3,872	637	-	-	-	-	104	-	-	-	-	-	-	-	-	-	-	-	233	-	167	-	-	-	113
	17.78		16.45					21.99												25.60		15.89				14.02
								16.33												36.58		26.22				17.74
			16.45					2.69												6.02		4.31				2.92
			6.31					1.03												2.31		1.65				1.12
Margate (city)	4,457	8,175	747	-	-	36	-	199	-	22	-	-	-	-	67	-	-	-	-	129	-	341	-	-	-	86
	8.35		9.14			6.70		17.55		3.24					8.01					5.88		16.97				5.46
						4.82		26.64		2.95					8.97					17.27		45.65				11.51
			9.14			0.44		2.43		0.27					0.82					1.58		4.17				1.05
			16.76			0.81		4.46		0.49					1.50					2.89		7.65				1.93
Miramar (city)	5,912	21,453	1,602	-	-	184	-	253	-	371	88	-	-	-	51	102	46	-	0	246	-	341	-	-	-	309
	8.17		7.47			10.94		12.76		5.71	6.23				8.95	15.81	12.53		0.00	6.99		9.10				7.95
						11.49		15.79		23.16	5.49				3.18	6.37	2.87		0.00	15.36		21.29				19.29
			7.47			0.86		1.18		1.73	0.41				0.24	0.48	0.21		0.00	1.15		1.59				1.44
			27.10			3.11		4.28		6.28	1.49				0.86	1.73	0.78		0.00	4.16		5.77				5.23
Pembroke Pines (city)	7,291	38,031	2,390	-	-	148	-	455	-	412	114	18	-	-	88	-	-	-	66	604	-	709	-	-	149	307
	5.38		6.28			7.72		13.20		3.35	6.38	3.70			9.58				4.41	8.27		9.14			10.13	5.34
						6.19		19.04		17.24	4.77	0.75			3.68				2.76	25.27		29.67			6.23	12.85
			6.28			0.39		1.20		1.08	0.30	0.05			0.23				0.17	1.59		1.86			0.39	0.81
			32.78			2.03		6.24		5.65	1.56	0.25			1.21				0.91	8.28		9.72			2.04	4.21
Plantation (city)	5,309	10,926	1,178	-	-	36	-	337	-	114	-	-	-	-	70	-	-	-	70	182	-	564	-	-	117	178
	6.42		10.78			4.97		15.88		5.76					10.74				13.86	11.29		14.59			21.75	10.78
						3.06		28.61		9.68					5.94				5.94	15.45		47.88			9.93	15.11
			10.78			0.33		3.08		1.04					0.64				0.64	1.67		5.16			1.07	1.63
			22.19			0.68		6.35		2.15					1.32				1.32	3.43		10.62			2.20	3.35

Notes: Please refer to the User's Guide for an explanation of data; data is arranged alphabetically by state, then county, then city within each county and only includes counties with populations > 99,999 and cities with populations > 49,999; (1) Includes Costa Rican, Guatemalan, Honduran, Nicaraguan, Panamanian, Salvadoran, and other Central American; (2) Includes Argentinian, Bolivian, Chilean, Colombian, Ecuadorian, Paraguayan, Peruvian, Uruguayan, Venezuelan, and other South American

Place	Total population with income below poverty level	Hispanic pop. for whom poverty status is determined	Hispanics with income below poverty level	Argentinian	Bolivian	Central American[1]	Chilean	Colombian	Costa Rican	Cuban	Dominican	Ecuadorian	Guatelmalan	Honduran	Mexican	Nicaraguan	Panamanian	Paraguayan	Peruvian	Puerto Rican	Salvadoran	South American[2]	Spaniard	Uruguayan	Venezuelan	Other Hisp.
	12,796	7,457	1,700	-	-	-	-	121	-	64	-	-	-	-	891	-	-	-	-	166	-	269	-	-	-	198
	16.97		22.80					22.12		10.26					35.22					15.87		18.64				16.38
Pompano Beach (city)								7.12		3.76					52.41					9.76		15.82				11.65
			22.80					1.62		0.86					11.95					2.23		3.61				2.66
			13.29					0.95		0.50					6.96					1.30		2.10				1.55
	8,173	14,492	1,717	-	-	117	-	315	-	161	62	29	-	-	90	-	-	-	90	356	-	622	-	-	-	309
	9.66		11.85			15.73		12.80		7.80	8.45	5.48			10.71				15.15	12.29		13.60				12.08
Sunrise (city)						6.81		18.35		9.38	3.61	1.69			5.24				5.24	20.73		36.23				18.00
			11.85			0.81		2.17		1.11	0.43	0.20			0.62				0.62	2.46		4.29				2.13
			21.01			1.43		3.85		1.97	0.76	0.35			1.10				1.10	4.36		7.61				3.78
	4,935	7,911	967	-	-	-	-	203	-	61	-	-	-	-	-	-	-	-	-	95	-	464	-	-	-	209
	8.88		12.22					16.28		7.24										4.92		20.81				11.23
Tamarac (city)								20.99		6.31										9.82		47.98				21.61
			12.22					2.57		0.77										1.20		5.87				2.64
			19.59					4.11		1.24										1.93		9.40				4.24
	11,419	4,411	592	-	-	-	-	-	-	91	-	-	-	-	174	-	-	-	-	107	-	-	-	-	-	78
	8.23		13.42							16.79					18.39					7.73						9.50
Charlotte County										15.37					29.39					18.07						13.18
			13.42							2.06					3.94					2.43						1.77
			5.18							0.80					1.52					0.94						0.68
	13,541	2,983	547	-	-	-	-	-	-	-	-	-	-	-	31	-	-	-	-	322	-	-	-	-	-	105
	11.68		18.34												6.15					26.31						17.13
Citrus County															5.67					58.87						19.20
			18.34												1.04					10.79						3.52
			4.04												0.23					2.38						0.78
	9,437	6,062	708	-	-	-	-	-	-	-	-	-	-	-	185	-	-	-	-	311	-	-	-	-	-	128
	6.78		11.68												15.96					12.91						9.65
Clay County															26.13					43.93						18.08
			11.68												3.05					5.13						2.11
			7.50												1.96					3.30						1.36
	25,449	48,380	11,350	-	-	898	-	278	-	875	75	-	718	99	7,798	-	-	-	-	524	-	381	-	-	-	770
	10.26		23.46			27.25		24.05		12.13	14.94		47.87	13.77	28.26					16.81		17.44				17.83
Collier County						7.91		2.45		7.71	0.66		6.33	0.87	68.70					4.62		3.36				6.78
			23.46			1.86		0.57		1.81	0.16		1.48	0.20	16.12					1.08		0.79				1.59
			44.60			3.53		1.09		3.44	0.29		2.82	0.39	30.64					2.06		1.50				3.03
	90,828	30,897	4,290	-	-	163	-	167	-	431	80	-	-	-	763	-	81	-	0	1,819	-	250	-	-	-	759
	11.91		13.88			9.17		11.79		13.01	13.27				13.49		13.92		0.00	16.43		9.34				13.69
Duval County						3.80		3.89		10.05	1.86				17.79		1.89		0.00	42.40		5.83				17.69
			13.88			0.53		0.54		1.39	0.26				2.47		0.26		0.00	5.89		0.81				2.46
			4.72			0.18		0.18		0.47	0.09				0.84		0.09		0.00	2.00		0.28				0.84
	87,691	29,519	4,124	-	-	163	-	167	-	431	80	-	-	-	672	-	81	-	-	1,766	-	250	-	-	-	743
	12.18		13.97			9.26		12.28		13.34	13.27				12.73		14.34			16.64		9.99				14.06
Jacksonville (city)						3.95		4.05		10.45	1.94				16.29		1.96			42.82		6.06				18.02
			13.97			0.55		0.57		1.46	0.27				2.28		0.27			5.98		0.85				2.52
			4.70			0.19		0.19		0.49	0.09				0.77		0.09			2.01		0.29				0.85
	41,978	6,349	1,285	-	-	101	-	-	-	51	-	-	-	-	380	-	-	-	-	314	-	104	-	-	-	335
	15.44		20.24			20.87				10.39					17.98					23.00		27.01				23.18
Escambia County						7.86				3.97					29.57					24.44		8.09				26.07
			20.24			1.59				0.80					5.99					4.95		1.64				5.28
			3.06			0.24				0.12					0.91					0.75		0.25				0.80

Notes: Please refer to the User's Guide for an explanation of data; data is arranged alphabetically by state, then county, then city within each county and only includes counties with populations > 99,999 and cities with populations > 49,999; (1) Includes Costa Rican, Guatemalan, Honduran, Nicaraguan, Panamanian, Salvadoran, and other Central American; (2) Includes Argentinian, Bolivian, Chilean, Colombian, Ecuadorian, Paraguayan, Peruvian, Uruguayan, Venezuelan, and other South American

Place	Total population with income below poverty level	Hispanic pop. for whom poverty status is determined	Hispanics with income below poverty level	Argentinian	Bolivian	Central American[1]	Chilean	Colombian	Costa Rican	Cuban	Dominican	Ecuadorian	Guatelmalan	Honduran	Mexican	Nicaraguan	Panamanian	Paraguayan	Peruvian	Puerto Rican	Salvadoran	South American[2]	Spaniard	Uruguayan	Venezuelan	Other Hisp.
Pensacola (city)	8,964 16.09	1,180	197 16.69 16.69 2.20	-	-	-	-	-	-	-	-	-	-	-	-	-	-	-	-	-	-	-	-	-	-	-
Hernando County	13,307 10.33	6,521	1,278 19.60 19.60 9.60	-	-	-	-	-	-	150 24.88 11.74 2.30 1.13	-	-	-	-	234 24.76 18.31 3.59 1.76	-	-	-	-	639 17.18 50.00 9.80 4.80	-	-	-	-	-	159 20.81 12.44 2.44 1.19
Spring Hill (cdp)	6,443 9.49	4,777	969 20.28 20.28 15.04	-	-	-	-	-	-	91 23.39 9.39 1.90 1.41	-	-	-	-	-	-	-	-	-	599 19.97 61.82 12.54 9.30	-	-	-	-	-	110 17.92 11.35 2.30 1.71
Hillsborough County	122,872 12.51	177,498	34,239 19.29 19.29 27.87	-	-	1,334 16.94 3.90 0.75 1.09	-	1,069 17.81 3.12 0.60 0.87	143 15.43 0.42 0.08 0.12	5,096 14.80 14.88 2.87 4.15	732 18.97 2.14 0.41 0.60	150 11.79 0.44 0.08 0.12	302 28.60 0.88 0.17 0.25	429 19.18 1.25 0.24 0.35	10,169 28.15 29.70 5.73 8.28	56 5.51 0.16 0.03 0.05	174 10.61 0.51 0.10 0.14	-	303 16.72 0.88 0.17 0.25	10,137 20.40 29.61 5.71 8.25	230 30.59 0.67 0.13 0.19	2,176 17.80 6.36 1.23 1.77	109 5.99 0.32 0.06 0.09	-	474 26.76 1.38 0.27 0.39	4,486 14.26 13.10 2.53 3.65
Brandon (cdp)	4,132 5.36	10,018	987 9.85 9.85 23.89	-	-	76 14.13 7.70 0.76 1.84	-	-	-	32 2.98 3.24 0.32 0.77	-	-	-	-	100 9.42 10.13 1.00 2.42	-	-	-	-	574 11.92 58.16 5.73 13.89	-	82 13.53 8.31 0.82 1.98	-	-	-	103 6.59 10.44 1.03 2.49
Tampa (city)	53,425 18.12	57,579	13,275 23.06 23.06 24.85	-	-	684 21.35 5.15 1.19 1.28	-	322 19.06 2.43 0.56 0.60	-	2,906 20.69 21.89 5.05 5.44	277 19.63 2.09 0.48 0.52	78 18.66 0.59 0.14 0.15	-	352 39.37 2.65 0.61 0.66	1,925 27.04 14.50 3.34 3.60	40 8.55 0.30 0.07 0.07	93 14.72 0.70 0.16 0.17	-	-	4,353 27.85 32.79 7.56 8.15	-	948 26.47 7.14 1.65 1.77	87 11.87 0.66 0.15 0.16	-	346 55.45 2.61 0.60 0.65	2,095 17.67 15.78 3.64 3.92
Town 'n' Country (cdp)	6,177 8.60	20,500	2,414 11.78 11.78 39.08	-	-	43 5.06 1.78 0.21 0.70	-	220 17.52 9.11 1.07 3.56	-	504 10.67 20.88 2.46 8.16	209 27.87 8.66 1.02 3.38	-	-	-	120 10.97 4.97 0.59 1.94	-	-	-	-	819 11.09 33.93 4.00 13.26	-	312 14.82 12.92 1.52 5.05	-	-	-	395 11.65 16.36 1.93 6.39
Indian River County	10,325 9.30	7,042	1,632 23.18 23.18 15.81	-	-	73 22.96 4.47 1.04 0.71	-	-	-	23 6.63 1.41 0.33 0.22	-	-	-	-	1,192 27.61 73.04 16.93 11.54	-	-	-	-	86 13.40 5.27 1.22 0.83	-	50 9.71 3.06 0.71 0.48	-	-	-	208 23.61 12.75 2.95 2.01
Lake County	19,907 9.63	11,686	2,177 18.63 18.63 10.94	-	-	57 11.40 2.62 0.49 0.29	-	-	-	21 2.80 0.96 0.18 0.11	-	-	-	-	1,124 21.15 51.63 9.62 5.65	-	-	-	-	478 16.54 21.96 4.09 2.40	-	164 29.34 7.53 1.40 0.82	-	-	-	333 21.39 15.30 2.85 1.67
Lee County	42,316 9.73	41,430	8,522 20.57 20.57 20.14	-	-	678 22.65 7.96 1.64 1.60	-	197 19.49 2.31 0.48 0.47	-	461 13.74 5.41 1.11 1.09	268 25.12 3.14 0.65 0.63	-	406 29.17 4.76 0.98 0.96	94 18.95 1.10 0.23 0.22	3,307 22.51 38.81 7.98 7.82	-	-	-	-	2,421 20.68 28.41 5.84 5.72	-	260 10.62 3.05 0.63 0.61	-	-	-	1,127 22.21 13.22 2.72 2.66

Notes: Please refer to the User's Guide for an explanation of data; data is arranged alphabetically by state, then county, then city within each county and only includes counties with populations > 99,999 and cities with populations > 49,999; (1) Includes Costa Rican, Guatemalan, Honduran, Nicaraguan, Panamanian, Salvadoran, and other Central American; (2) Includes Argentinian, Bolivian, Chilean, Colombian, Ecuadorian, Paraguayan, Peruvan, Uruguayan, Venezuelan, and other South American

Place	Total population with income below poverty level	Hispanic pop. for whom poverty status is determined	Hispanics with income below poverty level	Argentinian	Bolivian	Central American[1]	Chilean	Colombian	Costa Rican	Cuban	Dominican	Ecuadorian	Guatelmalan	Honduran	Mexican	Nicaraguan	Panamanian	Paraguayan	Peruvian	Puerto Rican	Salvadoran	South American[2]	Spaniard	Uruguayan	Venezuelan	Other Hisp.
Cape Coral (city)	7,097 7.00	8,313	1,114 13.40 13.40 15.70	-	-	-	-	140 24.10 12.57 1.68 1.97	-	204 12.97 18.31 2.45 2.87	90 15.46 8.08 1.08 1.27	-	-	-	140 10.53 12.57 1.68 1.97	-	-	-	-	307 14.29 27.56 3.69 4.33	-	173 16.29 15.53 2.08 2.44	-	-	-	178 14.15 15.98 2.14 2.51
Leon County	41,078 18.19	7,357	2,189 29.75 29.75 5.33	-	-	-	-	-	-	589 34.01 26.91 8.01 1.43	-	-	-	-	388 28.26 17.72 5.27 0.94	-	-	-	-	344 22.41 15.71 4.68 0.84	-	233 27.80 10.64 3.17 0.57	-	-	-	390 29.93 17.82 5.30 0.95
Tallahassee (city)	33,978 24.70	5,218	1,831 35.09 35.09 5.39	-	-	-	-	-	-	488 38.10 26.65 9.35 1.44	-	-	-	-	237 27.98 12.94 4.54 0.70	-	-	-	-	331 29.85 18.08 6.34 0.97	-	224 36.90 12.23 4.29 0.66	-	-	-	322 35.08 17.59 6.17 0.95
Manatee County	26,104 10.08	23,372	6,131 26.23 26.23 23.49	-	-	356 25.48 5.81 1.52 1.36	-	-	-	175 16.48 2.85 0.75 0.67	-	-	-	-	4,246 29.84 69.25 18.17 16.27	-	-	-	-	680 21.77 11.09 2.91 2.60	-	144 15.37 2.35 0.62 0.55	-	-	-	484 20.11 7.89 2.07 1.85
Marion County	32,918 13.08	15,116	3,479 23.02 23.02 10.57	-	-	126 23.20 3.62 0.83 0.38	-	64 11.37 1.84 0.42 0.19	-	252 21.88 7.24 1.67 0.77	-	-	-	-	945 29.28 27.16 6.25 2.87	-	-	-	-	1,403 20.64 40.33 9.28 4.26	-	195 18.14 5.61 1.29 0.59	-	-	-	448 22.08 12.88 2.96 1.36
Martin County	10,844 8.77	9,320	2,620 28.11 28.11 24.16	-	-	662 28.56 25.27 7.10 6.10	-	-	-	37 4.77 1.41 0.40 0.34	-	-	546 27.55 20.84 5.86 5.04	-	1,447 37.67 55.23 15.53 13.34	-	-	-	-	258 18.87 9.85 2.77 2.38	-	-	-	-	-	195 28.10 7.44 2.09 1.80
Miami-Dade County	396,995 17.97	1,274,511	223,335 17.52 17.52 56.26	3,058 21.68 1.37 0.24 0.77	247 10.85 0.11 0.02 0.06	27,325 19.86 12.23 2.14 6.88	1,402 17.55 0.63 0.11 0.35	15,076 20.32 6.75 1.18 3.80	747 16.32 0.33 0.06 0.19	101,285 15.63 45.35 7.95 25.51	7,551 19.13 3.38 0.59 1.90	1,926 16.76 0.86 0.15 0.49	2,248 21.27 1.01 0.18 0.57	6,591 22.99 2.95 0.52 1.66	9,628 26.30 4.31 0.76 2.43	13,819 18.42 6.19 1.08 3.48	1,111 16.65 0.50 0.09 0.28	-	3,675 15.53 1.65 0.29 0.93	15,538 19.87 6.96 1.22 3.91	2,181 23.01 0.98 0.17 0.55	30,235 18.78 13.54 2.37 7.62	900 14.84 0.40 0.07 0.23	344 17.62 0.15 0.03 0.09	4,202 18.76 1.88 0.33 1.06	30,873 18.43 13.82 2.42 7.78
Carol City (cdp)	9,697 16.53	24,787	4,044 16.32 16.32 41.70	-	-	323 12.29 7.99 1.30 3.33	-	235 16.03 5.81 0.95 2.42	-	1,892 17.04 46.79 7.63 19.51	262 13.91 6.48 1.06 2.70	-	-	47 9.07 1.16 0.19 0.48	-	209 14.49 5.17 0.84 2.16	-	-	-	464 16.66 11.47 1.87 4.78	-	334 13.30 8.26 1.35 3.44	-	-	-	647 18.73 16.00 2.61 6.67
Fountainbleau (cdp)	8,428 14.19	51,729	7,568 14.63 14.63 89.80	106 24.09 1.40 0.20 1.26	-	794 9.75 10.49 1.53 9.42	147 20.91 1.94 0.28 1.74	629 22.66 8.31 1.22 7.46	-	3,214 14.42 42.47 6.21 38.13	241 12.50 3.18 0.47 2.86	102 12.77 1.35 0.20 1.21	-	129 20.35 1.70 0.25 1.53	89 18.46 1.18 0.17 1.06	401 6.57 5.30 0.78 4.76	68 13.03 0.90 0.13 0.81	-	158 13.38 2.09 0.31 1.87	391 20.76 5.17 0.76 4.64	-	1,521 18.24 20.10 2.94 18.05	-	-	342 16.66 4.52 0.66 4.06	1,300 15.24 17.18 2.51 15.42
Hialeah (city)	41,537 18.62	202,369	38,013 18.78 18.78 91.52	70 16.75 0.18 0.03 0.17	-	2,956 18.71 7.78 1.46 7.12	112 15.20 0.29 0.06 0.27	1,489 19.60 3.92 0.74 3.58	83 15.87 0.22 0.04 0.20	25,322 18.14 66.61 12.51 60.96	991 20.42 2.61 0.49 2.39	147 11.92 0.39 0.07 0.35	204 24.58 0.54 0.10 0.49	438 16.84 1.15 0.22 1.05	394 25.63 1.04 0.19 0.95	1,803 17.83 4.74 0.89 4.34	-	-	246 16.97 0.65 0.12 0.59	1,337 19.78 3.52 0.66 3.22	247 26.00 0.65 0.12 0.59	2,347 18.41 6.17 1.16 5.65	78 15.60 0.21 0.04 0.19	-	257 26.91 0.68 0.13 0.62	4,588 22.27 12.07 2.27 11.05

Notes: Please refer to the User's Guide for an explanation of data; data is arranged alphabetically by state, then county, then city within each county and only includes counties with populations > 99,999 and cities with populations > 49,999; (1) Includes Costa Rican, Guatemalan, Honduran, Nicaraguan, Panamanian, Salvadoran, and other Central American; (2) Includes Argentinian, Bolivian, Chilean, Colombian, Ecuadorian, Paraguayan, Peruvian, Uruguayan, Venezuelan, and other South American

Place	Total population with income below poverty level	Hispanic pop. for whom poverty status is determined	Hispanics with income below poverty level	Argentinian	Bolivian	Central American[1]	Chilean	Colombian	Costa Rican	Cuban	Dominican	Ecuadorian	Guatelmalan	Honduran	Mexican	Nicaraguan	Panamanian	Paraguayan	Peruvian	Puerto Rican	Salvadoran	South American[2]	Spaniard	Uruguayan	Venezuelan	Other Hisp.
Kendale Lakes (cdp)	5,811	43,444	4,679	-	-	356	-	781	-	1,965	178	-	-	50	119	186	-	-	108	110	-	1,124	-	-	89	816
	10.26		10.77			8.74		19.63		8.94	21.12			8.98	20.41	6.54			11.29	6.69		15.46			10.31	11.85
						7.61		16.69		42.00	3.80			1.07	2.54	3.98			2.31	2.35		24.02			1.90	17.44
			10.77			0.82		1.80		4.52	0.41			0.12	0.27	0.43			0.25	0.25		2.59			0.20	1.88
			80.52			6.13		13.44		33.82	3.06			0.86	2.05	3.20			1.86	1.89		19.34			1.53	14.04
Kendall (cdp)	6,431	37,427	3,727	106	-	276	64	913	-	905	79	-	-	-	-	110	-	-	122	207	-	1,488	-	-	207	651
	8.60		9.96	16.72		7.19	13.33	22.14		5.76	9.96					4.93			8.91	9.25		17.16			14.25	12.12
				2.84		7.41	1.72	24.50		24.28	2.12					2.95			3.27	5.55		39.92			5.55	17.47
			9.96	0.28		0.74	0.17	2.44		2.42	0.21					0.29			0.33	0.55		3.98			0.55	1.74
			57.95	1.65		4.29	1.00	14.20		14.07	1.23					1.71			1.90	3.22		23.14			3.22	10.12
Miami Beach (city)	19,003	46,603	12,069	1,029	-	691	226	1,471	-	4,465	314	102	-	199	166	207	-	-	617	742	-	3,940	88	-	370	1,663
	21.84		25.90	33.95		24.56	30.58	32.89		24.85	22.59	15.41		24.84	16.84	20.87			32.58	21.04		30.40	15.36		25.41	26.05
				8.53		5.73	1.87	12.19		37.00	2.60	0.85		1.65	1.38	1.72			5.11	6.15		32.65	0.73		3.07	13.78
			25.90	2.21		1.48	0.48	3.16		9.58	0.67	0.22		0.43	0.36	0.44			1.32	1.59		8.45	0.19		0.79	3.57
			63.51	5.41		3.64	1.19	7.74		23.50	1.65	0.54		1.05	0.87	1.09			3.25	3.90		20.73	0.46		1.95	8.75
Miami (city)	100,405	233,984	62,475	672	-	12,437	220	1,751	263	30,214	1,959	441	686	4,077	812	6,476	199	-	650	3,783	484	4,425	175	-	496	8,670
	28.45		26.70	33.37		28.54	24.53	29.56	32.23	24.55	27.21	25.23	24.15	30.03	26.90	28.94	22.74		23.75	38.57	20.62	28.01	18.98		28.59	28.35
				1.08		19.91	0.35	2.80	0.42	48.36	3.14	0.71	1.10	6.53	1.30	10.37	0.32		1.04	6.06	0.77	7.08	0.28		0.79	13.88
			26.70	0.29		5.32	0.09	0.75	0.11	12.91	0.84	0.19	0.29	1.74	0.35	2.77	0.09		0.28	1.62	0.21	1.89	0.07		0.21	3.71
			62.22	0.67		12.39	0.22	1.74	0.26	30.09	1.95	0.44	0.68	4.06	0.81	6.45	0.20		0.65	3.77	0.48	4.41	0.17		0.49	8.64
North Miami (city)	14,055	14,088	2,581	-	-	294	-	232	-	555	121	-	-	63	-	135	-	-	-	478	-	423	-	-	-	582
	23.92		18.32			17.30		22.97		20.04	11.11			11.31		19.34				17.29		20.81				17.93
						11.39		8.99		21.50	4.69			2.44		5.23				18.52		16.39				22.55
			18.32			2.09		1.65		3.94	0.86			0.45		0.96				3.39		3.00				4.13
			18.36			2.09		1.65		3.95	0.86			0.45		0.96				3.40		3.01				4.14
Tamiami (cdp)	5,091	47,107	4,445	-	-	278	-	258	-	2,923	20	-	-	74	0	185	-	-	-	102	-	680	-	-	105	442
	9.40		9.44			7.27		13.02		9.14	3.00			16.70	0.00	6.73				9.71		17.33			19.27	8.89
						6.25		5.80		65.76	0.45			1.66	0.00	4.16				2.29		15.30			2.36	9.94
			9.44			0.59		0.55		6.21	0.04			0.16	0.00	0.39				0.22		1.44			0.22	0.94
			87.31			5.46		5.07		57.42	0.39			1.45	0.00	3.63				2.00		13.36			2.06	8.68
Okaloosa County	14,562	6,298	658	-	-	52	-	-	-	13	-	-	-	-	255	-	-	-	-	168	-	-	-	-	-	101
	8.84		10.45			15.16				2.91					11.07					12.79						7.13
						7.90				1.98					38.75					25.53						15.35
			10.45			0.83				0.21					4.05					2.67						1.60
			4.52			0.36				0.09					1.75					1.15						0.69
Orange County	106,233	166,629	27,435	66	-	676	50	1,689	125	1,658	1,058	197	64	262	3,934	50	86	-	155	13,691	75	2,770	48	-	573	3,600
	12.11		16.46	9.40		11.82	10.89	22.07	20.97	12.68	17.22	11.12	6.37	21.13	19.95	5.70	9.26		8.82	16.01	8.03	17.62	7.40		22.15	17.95
				0.24		2.46	0.18	6.16	0.46	6.04	3.86	0.72	0.23	0.95	14.34	0.18	0.31		0.56	49.90	0.27	10.10	0.17		2.09	13.12
			16.46	0.04		0.41	0.03	1.01	0.08	1.00	0.63	0.12	0.04	0.16	2.36	0.03	0.05		0.09	8.22	0.05	1.66	0.03		0.34	2.16
			25.83	0.06		0.64	0.05	1.59	0.12	1.56	1.00	0.19	0.06	0.25	3.70	0.05	0.08		0.15	12.89	0.07	2.61	0.05		0.54	3.39
Orlando (city)	29,029	32,658	6,545	-	-	214	-	425	-	334	339	-	-	-	472	-	-	-	76	3,339	-	791	-	-	239	1,030
	15.88		20.04			15.90		23.97		11.24	27.43				20.67				16.70	20.17		20.06			31.08	24.54
						3.27		6.49		5.10	5.18				7.21				1.16	51.02		12.09			3.65	15.74
			20.04			0.66		1.30		1.02	1.04				1.45				0.23	10.22		2.42			0.73	3.15
			22.55			0.74		1.46		1.15	1.17				1.63				0.26	11.50		2.72			0.82	3.55
Osceola County	19,532	50,087	8,245	-	-	240	-	398	-	254	435	67	-	-	528	-	-	-	-	5,274	90	735	-	-	156	741
	11.52		16.46			12.44		20.90		13.91	17.70	15.09			15.58					16.40	16.70	20.41			29.66	16.33
						2.91		4.83		3.08	5.28	0.81			6.40					63.97	1.09	8.91			1.89	8.99
			16.46			0.48		0.79		0.51	0.87	0.13			1.05					10.53	0.18	1.47			0.31	1.48
			42.21			1.23		2.04		1.30	2.23	0.34			2.70					27.00	0.46	3.76			0.80	3.79

Notes: Please refer to the User's Guide for an explanation of data; data is arranged alphabetically by state, then county, then city within each county and only includes counties with populations > 99,999 and cities with populations > 49,999; (1) Includes Costa Rican, Guatemalan, Honduran, Nicaraguan, Panamanian, Salvadoran, and other Central American; (2) Includes Argentinian, Bolivian, Chilean, Colombian, Ecuadorian, Paraguayan, Peruvan, Uruguayan, Venezuelan, and other South American

Place	Total population with income below poverty level	Hispanic pop. for whom poverty status is determined	Hispanics with income below poverty level	Argentinian	Bolivian	Central American[1]	Chilean	Colombian	Costa Rican	Cuban	Dominican	Ecuadorian	Guatelmalan	Honduran	Mexican	Nicaraguan	Panamanian	Paraguayan	Peruvian	Puerto Rican	Salvadoran	South American[2]	Spaniard	Uruguayan	Venezuelan	Other Hisp.
Palm Beach County	110,430 9.92	138,665	23,797 17.16 17.16 21.55	340 18.45 1.43 0.25 0.31	-	3.901 25.33 16.39 2.81 3.53	6 0.88 0.03 <0.01 0.01	1,288 13.82 5.41 0.93 1.17	74 8.78 0.31 0.05 0.07	2,701 10.49 11.35 1.95 2.45	512 14.33 2.15 0.37 0.46	305 15.70 1.28 0.22 0.28	2,462 36.09 10.35 1.78 2.23	561 17.36 2.36 0.40 0.51	6.759 23.16 28.40 4.87 6.12	310 14.73 1.30 0.22 0.28	45 10.42 0.19 0.03 0.04	-	150 6.08 0.63 0.11 0.14	4,436 18.17 18.64 3.20 4.02	425 25.66 1.79 0.31 0.38	2,529 12.70 10.63 1.82 2.29	41 8.74 0.17 0.03 0.04	76 9.49 0.32 0.05 0.07	205 11.87 0.86 0.15 0.19	2,918 14.61 12.26 2.10 2.64
Boca Raton (city)	4,886 6.69	6,154	697 11.33 11.33 14.27	-	-	-	-	95 11.22 13.63 1.54 1.94	-	81 9.10 11.62 1.32 1.66	-	-	-	-	207 24.85 29.70 3.36 4.24	-	-	-	-	23 2.87 3.30 0.37 0.47	-	194 9.79 27.83 3.15 3.97	-	-	-	146 12.16 20.95 2.37 2.99
Boynton Beach (city)	5,976 10.16	4,938	737 14.93 14.93 12.33	-	-	42 7.17 5.70 0.85 0.70	-	-	-	151 26.49 20.49 3.06 2.53	-	-	-	-	96 11.58 13.03 1.94 1.61	-	-	-	-	206 14.56 27.95 4.17 3.45	-	107 14.30 14.52 2.17 1.79	-	-	-	127 18.93 17.23 2.57 2.13
Delray Beach (city)	7,012 11.80	4,165	435 10.44 10.44 6.20	-	-	-	-	-	-	-	-	-	-	-	235 16.10 54.02 5.64 3.35	-	-	-	-	89 12.14 20.46 2.14 1.27	-	42 7.01 9.66 1.01 0.60	-	-	-	41 8.45 9.43 0.98 0.58
West Palm Beach (city)	14,933 18.85	14,824	3,574 24.11 24.11 23.93	-	-	1,013 36.41 28.34 6.83 6.78	-	228 31.02 6.38 1.54 1.53	-	812 18.54 22.72 5.48 5.44	58 15.14 1.62 0.39 0.39	-	831 40.56 23.25 5.61 5.56	-	420 21.47 11.75 2.83 2.81	-	-	-	-	472 25.89 13.21 3.18 3.16	-	333 21.32 9.32 2.25 2.23	-	-	-	455 23.83 12.73 3.07 3.05
Pasco County	36,201 10.67	19,255	3,483 18.09 18.09 9.62	-	-	53 8.60 1.52 0.28 0.15	-	-	-	174 9.69 5.00 0.90 0.48	-	-	-	-	1,816 30.52 52.14 9.43 5.02	-	-	-	-	1,012 14.82 29.06 5.26 2.80	-	167 20.17 4.79 0.87 0.46	-	-	-	257 9.04 7.38 1.33 0.71
Pinellas County	90.059 9.97	41,369	7,003 16.93 16.93 7.78	-	-	266 19.39 3.80 0.64 0.30	-	536 29.26 7.65 1.30 0.60	-	444 9.56 6.34 1.07 0.49	89 9.89 1.27 0.22 0.10	80 20.94 1.14 0.19 0.09	-	-	1,989 19.59 28.40 4.81 2.21	-	-	-	78 9.84 1.11 0.19 0.09	2,478 19.11 35.38 5.99 2.75	-	978 20.84 13.97 2.36 1.09	54 10.74 0.77 0.13 0.06	-	146 16.88 2.08 0.35 0.16	705 11.49 10.07 1.70 0.78
Clearwater (city)	13,043 12.35	9,502	2,203 23.18 23.18 16.89	-	-	-	-	136 35.42 6.17 1.43 1.04	-	94 16.46 4.27 0.99 0.72	-	-	-	-	824 19.88 37.40 8.67 6.32	-	-	-	-	725 32.48 32.91 7.63 5.56	-	243 23.39 11.03 2.56 1.86	-	-	-	212 19.70 9.62 2.23 1.63
Largo (city)	6.221 9.10	2,821	488 17.30 17.30 7.84	-	-	-	-	-	-	-	-	-	-	-	73 13.18 14.96 2.59 1.17	-	-	-	-	55 7.16 11.27 1.95 0.88	-	-	-	-	-	-
Palm Harbor (cdp)	3,219 5.54	1,939	184 9.49 9.49 5.72	-	-	-	-	-	-	-	-	-	-	-	-	-	-	-	-	75 9.17 40.76 3.87 2.33	-	-	-	-	-	-

Notes: Please refer to the User's Guide for an explanation of data: data is arranged alphabetically by state, then county, then city within each county and only includes counties with populations > 99.999 and cities with populations > 49.999; (1) Includes Costa Rican, Guatemalan, Honduran, Nicaraguan, Panamanian, Salvadoran, and other Central American; (2) Includes Argentinian, Bolivian, Chilean, Colombian, Ecuadorian, Paraguayan, Peruvian, Uruguayan, Venezuelan, and other South American

Place	Total population with income below poverty level	Hispanic pop. for whom poverty status is determined	Hispanics with income below poverty level	Argentinian	Bolivian	Central American[1]	Chilean	Colombian	Costa Rican	Cuban	Dominican	Ecuadorian	Guatemalan	Honduran	Mexican	Nicaraguan	Panamanian	Paraguayan	Peruvian	Puerto Rican	Salvadoran	South American[2]	Spaniard	Uruguayan	Venezuelan	Other Hisp.
St. Petersburg (city)	32,127	9,697	1,351	-	-	-	-	-	-	133	-	-	-	-	250	-	-	-	-	616	-	181	-	-	-	140
	13.26		13.93							8.13					15.41					19.27		15.54				9.76
										9.84					18.50					45.60		13.40				10.36
			13.93							1.37					2.58					6.35		1.87				1.44
			4.21							0.41					0.78					1.92		0.56				0.44
Polk County	60,953	44,696	11,030	-	-	156	-	-	-	214	109	-	-	-	6,938	-	-	-	-	2,487	-	164	-	-	-	947
	12.94		24.68			12.99				8.85	23.85				28.94					22.42		16.96				21.46
						1.41				1.94	0.99				62.90					22.55		1.49				8.59
			24.68			0.35				0.48	0.24				15.52					5.56		0.37				2.12
			18.10			0.26				0.35	0.18				11.38					4.08		0.27				1.55
Lakeland (city)	11,228	4,930	1,076	-	-	-	-	-	-	42	-	-	-	-	282	-	-	-	-	517	-	-	-	-	-	100
	15.03		21.83							6.56					30.16					26.38						12.76
										3.90					26.21					48.05						9.29
			21.83							0.85					5.72					10.49						2.03
			9.58							0.37					2.51					4.60						0.89
St. Johns County	9,698	3,535	389	-	-	-	-	-	-	-	-	-	-	-	134	-	-	-	-	122	-	-	-	-	-	38
	8.02		11.00												14.11					13.99						6.82
															34.45					31.36						9.77
			11.00												3.79					3.45						1.07
			4.01												1.38					1.26						0.39
St. Lucie County	25,464	15,600	3,685	-	-	250	-	55	-	157	-	-	-	-	2,152	-	-	-	-	613	-	62	-	-	-	380
	13.40		23.62			25.30		13.06		15.00					30.83					16.75		6.19				25.94
						6.78		1.49		4.26					58.40					16.64		1.68				10.31
			23.62			1.60		0.35		1.01					13.79					3.93		0.40				2.44
			14.47			0.98		0.22		0.62					8.45					2.41		0.24				1.49
Port St. Lucie (city)	6,957	6,778	807	-	-	-	-	-	-	93	-	-	-	-	117	-	-	-	-	232	-	24	-	-	-	243
	7.90		11.91							12.90					10.56					8.88		3.44				28.45
										11.52					14.50					28.75		2.97				30.11
			11.91							1.37					1.73					3.42		0.35				3.59
			11.60							1.34					1.68					3.33		0.34				3.49
Santa Rosa County	11,282	2,623	228	-	-	-	-	-	-	-	-	-	-	-	28	-	-	-	-	87	-	-	-	-	-	75
	9.83		8.69												3.35					12.59						16.03
															12.28					38.16						32.89
			8.69												1.07					3.32						2.86
			2.02												0.25					0.77						0.66
Sarasota County	24,817	14,256	2,730	-	-	152	-	207	-	132	-	-	-	-	1,518	-	-	-	-	184	-	308	-	-	-	380
	7.77		19.15			24.05		23.66		6.84					25.94					10.80		16.51				19.37
						5.57		7.58		4.84					55.60					6.74		11.28				13.92
			19.15			1.07		1.45		0.93					10.65					1.29		2.16				2.67
			11.00			0.61		0.83		0.53					6.12					0.74		1.24				1.53
Sarasota (city)	8,271	6,304	1,617	-	-	-	-	-	-	83	-	-	-	-	1,005	-	-	-	-	45	-	88	-	-	-	267
	16.70		25.65							12.44					29.00					10.77		13.60				38.20
										5.13					62.15					2.78		5.44				16.51
			25.65							1.32					15.94					0.71		1.40				4.24
			19.55							1.00					12.15					0.54		1.06				3.23
Seminole County	26,804	40,376	4,746	96	-	214	-	449	-	453	98	9	-	-	408	-	29	-	86	2,091	-	774	-	-	114	700
	7.41		11.75	21.82		10.68		20.19		12.31	8.44	1.98			11.71		5.36		15.93	10.63		17.28			25.97	12.30
				2.02		4.51		9.46		9.54	2.06	0.19			8.60		0.61		1.81	44.06		16.31			2.40	14.75
			11.75	0.24		0.53		1.11		1.12	0.24	0.02			1.01		0.07		0.21	5.18		1.92			0.28	1.73
			17.71	0.36		0.80		1.68		1.69	0.37	0.03			1.52		0.11		0.32	7.80		2.89			0.43	2.61

Notes: Please refer to the User's Guide for an explanation of data; data is arranged alphabetically by state, then county, then city within each county and only includes counties with populations > 99,999 and cities with populations > 49,999; (1) Includes Costa Rican, Guatemalan, Honduran, Nicaraguan, Panamanian, Salvadoran, and other Central American; (2) Includes Argentinian, Bolivian, Chilean, Colombian, Ecuadorian, Paraguayan, Peruvian, Uruguayan, Venezuelan, and other South American

Place	Total population with income below poverty level	Hispanic pop. for whom poverty status is determined	Hispanics with income below poverty level	Argentinian	Bolivian	Central American[1]	Chilean	Colombian	Costa Rican	Cuban	Dominican	Ecuadorian	Guatelmalan	Honduran	Mexican	Nicaraguan	Panamanian	Paraguayan	Peruvian	Puerto Rican	Salvadoran	South American[2]	Spaniard	Uruguayan	Venezuelan	Other Hisp.
Volusia County	49,907 11.62	28,677	5,318 18.54 18.54 10.66	-	-	105 13.31 1.97 0.37 0.21	-	98 14.94 1.84 0.34 0.20	-	118 8.96 2.22 0.41 0.24	61 10.82 1.15 0.21 0.12	-	-	-	2,625 33.08 49.36 9.15 5.26	-	-	-	-	1,738 12.69 32.68 6.06 3.48	-	254 16.27 4.78 0.89 0.51	-	-	-	417 15.69 7.84 1.45 0.84
Daytona Beach (city)	13,954 23.61	2,055	537 26.13 26.13 3.85	-	-	-	-	-	-	-	-	-	-	-	-	-	-	-	-	206 24.44 38.36 10.02 1.48	-	-	-	-	-	125 35.92 23.28 6.08 0.90
Deltona (city)	5,608 8.10	12,779	1,318 10.31 10.31 23.50	-	-	-	-	-	-	49 8.91 3.72 0.38 0.87	-	-	-	-	68 10.30 5.16 0.53 1.21	-	-	-	-	1,010 10.69 76.63 7.90 18.01	-	97 15.77 7.36 0.76 1.73	-	-	-	51 5.19 3.87 0.40 0.91

Notes: Please refer to the User's Guide for an explanation of data; data is arranged alphabetically by state, then county, then city within each county and only includes counties with populations > 99,999 and cities with populations > 49,999; (1) Includes Costa Rican, Guatemalan, Honduran, Nicaraguan, Panamanian, Salvadoran, and other Central American; (2) Includes Argentinian, Bolivian, Chilean, Colombian, Ecuadorian, Paraguayan, Peruvian, Uruguayan, Venezuelan, and other South American

Homeownership

(Universe: Occupied Housing Units)

Place	All owner-occupied housing units	Hispanic-occupied housing units	Hispanics who own and occupy their own homes	Argentinian	Bolivian	Central American[1]	Chilean	Colombian	Costa Rican	Cuban	Dominican	Ecuadorian	Guatemalan	Honduran	Mexican	Nicaraguan	Panamanian	Paraguayan	Peruvian	Puerto Rican	Salvadoran	South American[2]	Spaniard	Uruguayan	Venezuelan	Other Hisp.
UNITED STATES	69,816,513 66.19	9,179,764	4,190,613 45.65 45.65 6.00	21,662 51.91 0.52 0.24 0.03	6,244 48.13 0.15 0.07 0.01	158,749 31.66 3.79 1.73 0.23	10,934 45.67 0.26 0.12 0.02	60,772 40.16 1.45 0.66 0.09	8,365 38.82 0.20 0.09 0.01	275,106 57.59 6.56 3.00 0.39	47,905 20.22 1.14 0.52 0.07	24,481 31.27 0.58 0.27 0.04	29,308 26.79 0.70 0.32 0.04	15,386 24.41 0.37 0.17 0.02	2,424,171 48.41 57.85 26.41 3.47	20,916 38.65 0.50 0.23 0.03	13,524 41.59 0.32 0.15 0.02	795 38.97 0.02 0.01 <0.01	31,653 41.74 0.76 0.34 0.05	369,181 34.35 8.81 4.02 0.53	60,862 31.72 1.45 0.66 0.09	182,350 41.17 4.35 1.99 0.26	23,152 56.78 0.55 0.25 0.03	3,921 49.46 0.09 0.04 0.01	12,952 42.52 0.31 0.14 0.02	709,999 50.81 16.94 7.73 1.02
FLORIDA	4,441,711 70.08	844,253	471,112 55.80 55.80 10.61	5,411 55.92 1.15 0.64 0.12	810 53.86 0.17 0.10 0.02	24,818 40.86 5.27 2.94 0.56	2,594 53.10 0.55 0.31 0.06	24,354 52.85 5.17 2.88 0.55	1,745 48.77 0.37 0.21 0.04	202,458 62.60 42.97 23.98 4.56	12,692 51.99 2.69 1.50 0.29	4,733 56.68 1.00 0.56 0.11	3,012 36.15 0.64 0.36 0.07	4,077 33.13 0.87 0.48 0.09	35,214 43.52 7.47 4.17 0.79	9,555 40.95 2.03 1.13 0.22	2,896 54.81 0.61 0.34 0.07	155 55.96 0.03 0.02 <0.01	7,736 52.63 1.64 0.92 0.17	87,974 56.02 18.67 10.42 1.98	2,790 44.45 0.59 0.33 0.06	55,220 53.33 11.72 6.54 1.24	4,156 67.27 0.88 0.49 0.09	1,107 56.94 0.23 0.13 0.02	6,704 49.23 1.42 0.79 0.15	48,580 55.19 10.31 5.75 1.09
Alachua County	48,084 54.95	4,278	1,408 32.91 32.91 2.93	-	-	84 33.07 5.97 1.96 0.17	-	42 21.21 2.98 0.98 0.09	-	269 29.56 19.11 6.29 0.56	-	-	-	-	124 34.64 8.81 2.90 0.26	-	-	-	-	475 40.74 33.74 11.10 0.99	-	185 23.18 13.14 4.32 0.38	-	-	-	245 35.77 17.40 5.73 0.51
Gainesville (city)	17,791 47.73	1,902	572 30.07 30.07 3.22	-	-	-	-	-	-	98 27.76 17.13 5.15 0.55	-	-	-	-	52 37.41 9.09 2.73 0.29	-	-	-	-	205 37.07 35.84 10.78 1.15	-	86 21.72 15.03 4.52 0.48	-	-	-	74 25.69 12.94 3.89 0.42
Bay County	40,892 68.61	1,128	549 48.67 48.67 1.34	-	-	-	-	-	-	-	-	-	-	-	118 33.91 21.49 10.46 0.29	-	-	-	-	167 47.99 30.42 14.80 0.41	-	-	-	-	-	76 52.78 13.84 6.74 0.19
Brevard County	147,878 74.61	6,591	4,095 62.13 62.13 2.77	-	-	229 70.03 5.59 3.47 0.15	-	129 66.84 3.15 1.96 0.09	-	462 66.28 11.28 7.01 0.31	64 59.81 1.56 0.97 0.04	-	-	-	442 47.27 10.79 6.71 0.30	-	36 51.43 0.88 0.55 0.02	-	-	1,958 65.18 47.81 29.71 1.32	-	299 58.17 7.30 4.54 0.20	-	-	-	563 62.91 13.75 8.54 0.38
Melbourne (city)	19,108 62.05	1,233	556 45.09 45.09 2.91	-	-	-	-	-	-	-	-	-	-	-	80 39.02 14.39 6.49 0.42	-	-	-	-	289 49.07 51.98 23.44 1.51	-	-	-	-	-	46 40.00 8.27 3.73 0.24
Palm Bay (city)	22,874 75.36	2,105	1,446 68.69 68.69 6.32	-	-	-	-	-	-	-	-	-	-	-	60 32.79 4.15 2.85 0.26	-	-	-	-	954 77.18 65.98 45.32 4.17	-	128 74.85 8.85 6.08 0.56	-	-	-	154 58.11 10.65 7.32 0.67
Broward County	454,625 69.47	86,014	53,705 62.44 62.44 11.81	1,018 66.02 1.90 1.18 0.22	116 51.33 0.22 0.13 0.03	2,921 49.34 5.44 3.40 0.64	465 64.40 0.87 0.54 0.10	5,582 57.23 10.39 6.49 1.23	346 60.07 0.64 0.40 0.08	15,478 78.35 28.82 17.99 3.40	2,129 61.51 3.96 2.48 0.47	1,130 66.24 2.10 1.31 0.25	442 47.53 0.82 0.51 0.10	407 40.58 0.76 0.47 0.09	2,125 43.94 3.96 2.47 0.47	575 53.00 1.07 0.67 0.13	458 53.32 0.85 0.53 0.10	-	1,748 52.52 3.25 2.03 0.38	10,980 59.44 20.45 12.77 2.42	588 47.53 1.09 0.68 0.13	12,516 58.63 23.31 14.55 2.75	588 63.91 1.09 0.68 0.13	288 65.60 0.54 0.33 0.06	1,761 58.68 3.28 2.05 0.39	6,968 61.64 12.97 8.10 1.53

Notes: Please refer to the User's Guide for an explanation of data; data is arranged alphabetically by state, then county, then city within each county and only includes counties with populations > 99,999 and cities with populations > 49,999; (1) Includes Costa Rican, Guatemalan, Honduran, Nicaraguan, Panamanian, Salvadoran, and other Central American; (2) Includes Argentinian, Bolivian, Chilean, Colombian, Ecuadorian, Paraguayan, Peruvian, Uruguayan, Venezuelan, and other South American

Place	All owner-occupied housing units	Hispanic-occupied housing units	Hispanics who own and occupy their own homes	Argentinian	Bolivian	Central American[1]	Chilean	Colombian	Costa Rican	Cuban	Dominican	Ecuadorian	Guatelmalan	Honduran	Mexican	Nicaraguan	Panamanian	Paraguayan	Peruvian	Puerto Rican	Salvadoran	South American[2]	Spaniard	Uruguayan	Venezuelan	Other Hisp.
Coral Springs (city)	25,668	5,200	2,673	-	-	106	-	347	-	544	107	129	-	-	60	-	-	-	86	609	-	814	-	-	80	378
	64.99		51.40			53.00		54.65		70.19	50.47	56.83			17.44				31.05	50.04		50.37			47.06	49.41
						3.97		12.98		20.35	4.00	4.83			2.24				3.22	22.78		30.45			2.99	14.14
			51.40			2.04		6.67		10.46	2.06	2.48			1.15				1.65	11.71		15.65			1.54	7.27
			10.41			0.41		1.35		2.12	0.42	0.50			0.23				0.34	2.37		3.17			0.31	1.47
Davie (town)	21,836	4,361	3,087	-	-	169	-	272	-	934	-	-	-	-	121	-	-	-	106	675	-	638	-	-	-	415
	76.35		70.79			53.48		68.00		79.90					71.18				54.92	65.47		68.53				80.43
						5.47		8.81		30.26					3.92				3.43	21.87		20.67				13.44
			70.79			3.88		6.24		21.42					2.77				2.43	15.48		14.63				9.52
			14.14			0.77		1.25		4.28					0.55				0.49	3.09		2.92				1.90
Deerfield Beach (city)	22,070	1,877	867	-	-	38	-	37	-	170	-	-	-	-	91	-	-	-	-	227	-	164	-	-	-	100
	70.26		46.19			33.63		18.88		62.73					60.26					45.13		34.17				40.32
						4.38		4.27		19.61					10.50					26.18		18.92				11.53
			46.19			2.02		1.97		9.06					4.85					12.09		8.74				5.33
			3.93			0.17		0.17		0.77					0.41					1.03		0.74				0.45
Fort Lauderdale (city)	37,927	5,028	1,972	-	-	169	-	164	-	679	-	-	37	-	147	-	-	-	59	284	35	431	-	-	-	236
	55.41		39.22			30.18		37.53		57.69			25.00		35.68				39.07	32.20	22.29	39.91				31.85
						8.57		8.32		34.43			1.88		7.45				2.99	14.40	1.77	21.86				11.97
			39.22			3.36		3.26		13.50			0.74		2.92				1.17	5.65	0.70	8.57				4.69
			5.20			0.45		0.43		1.79			0.10		0.39				0.16	0.75	0.09	1.14				0.62
Hollywood (city)	37,102	10,659	5,521	83	-	333	89	568	-	1,482	337	101	-	32	177	66	-	-	153	1,214	-	1,195	-	-	123	767
	62.22		51.80	47.43		42.53	60.54	50.27		65.11	50.52	61.59		32.65	44.70	30.70			33.63	47.76		47.31			42.12	54.51
				1.50		6.03	1.61	10.29		26.84	6.10	1.83		0.58	3.21	1.20			2.77	21.99		21.64			2.23	13.89
			51.80	0.78		3.12	0.83	5.33		13.90	3.16	0.95		0.30	1.66	0.62			1.44	11.39		11.21			1.15	7.20
			14.88	0.22		0.90	0.24	1.53		3.99	0.91	0.27		0.09	0.48	0.18			0.41	3.27		3.22			0.33	2.07
Lauderhill (city)	13,511	1,293	785	-	-	-	-	117	-	-	-	-	-	-	-	-	-	-	-	176	-	242	-	-	-	142
	59.46		60.71					74.52												54.32		66.85				63.11
								14.90												22.42		30.83				18.09
			60.71					9.05												13.61		18.72				10.98
			5.81					0.87												1.30		1.79				1.05
Margate (city)	18,173	2,569	1,766	-	-	57	-	299	-	212	-	-	-	-	85	-	-	-	-	544	-	511	-	-	-	238
	80.01		68.74			38.51		75.51		74.39					47.49					73.32		72.07				68.39
						3.23		16.93		12.00					4.81					30.80		28.94				13.48
			68.74			2.22		11.64		8.25					3.31					21.18		19.89				9.26
			9.72			0.31		1.65		1.17					0.47					2.99		2.81				1.31
Miramar (city)	18,538	6,381	5,354	-	-	397	-	472	-	1,949	339	-	-	-	115	186	68	-	115	985	-	907	-	-	-	630
	80.40		83.91			78.00		76.62		91.46	80.71				65.34	88.15	52.31		89.15	83.83		79.35				80.87
						7.42		8.82		36.40	6.33				2.15	3.47	1.27		2.15	18.40		16.94				11.77
			83.91			6.22		7.40		30.54	5.31				1.80	2.91	1.07		1.80	15.44		14.21				9.87
			28.88			2.14		2.55		10.51	1.83				0.62	1.00	0.37		0.62	5.31		4.89				3.40
Pembroke Pines (city)	41,636	12,171	9,565	-	-	369	-	758	-	4,094	381	171	-	-	165	-	-	-	321	1,783	-	1,850	-	-	328	868
	80.10		78.59			70.69		70.71		87.89	75.90	73.39			66.27				86.52	72.63		75.70			69.49	68.62
						3.86		7.92		42.80	3.98	1.79			1.73				3.36	18.64		19.34			3.43	9.07
			78.59			3.03		6.23		33.64	3.13	1.40			1.36				2.64	14.65		15.20			2.69	7.13
			22.97			0.89		1.82		9.83	0.92	0.41			0.40				0.77	4.28		4.44			0.79	2.08
Plantation (city)	23,829	3,591	2,196	-	-	150	-	370	-	613	-	-	-	-	109	-	-	-	89	322	-	662	-	-	64	246
	71.46		61.15			70.09		57.10		79.82					52.91				42.58	60.07		51.40			45.71	57.61
						6.83		16.85		27.91					4.96				4.05	14.66		30.15			2.91	11.20
			61.15			4.18		10.30		17.07					3.04				2.48	8.97		18.43			1.78	6.85
			9.22			0.63		1.55		2.57					0.46				0.37	1.35		2.78			0.27	1.03

Notes: Please refer to the User's Guide for an explanation of data; data is arranged alphabetically by state, then county, then city within each county and only includes counties with populations > 99,999 and cities with populations > 49,999; (1) Includes Costa Rican, Guatemalan, Honduran, Nicaraguan, Panamanian, Salvadoran, and other Central American; (2) Includes Argentinian, Bolivian, Chilean, Colombian, Ecuadorian, Paraguayan, Peruvian, Uruguayan, Venezuelan, and other South American

Place	All owner-occupied housing units	Hispanic-occupied housing units	Hispanics who own and occupy their own homes	Argentinian	Bolivian	Central American[1]	Chilean	Colombian	Costa Rican	Cuban	Dominican	Ecuadorian	Guatemalan	Honduran	Mexican	Nicaraguan	Panamanian	Paraguayan	Peruvian	Puerto Rican	Salvadoran	South American[2]	Spaniard	Uruguayan	Venezuelan	Other Hisp.
Pompano Beach (city)	21,993 62.53	2,414	1,007 41.71 41.71 4.58	-	-	-	-	102 50.75 10.13 4.23 0.46	-	135 64.90 13.41 5.59 0.61	-	-	-	-	76 11.99 7.55 3.15 0.35	-	-	-	-	161 47.08 15.99 6.67 0.73	-	316 56.63 31.38 13.09 1.44	-	-	-	247 55.88 24.53 10.23 1.12
Sunrise (city)	24,624 73.99	4,697	3,039 64.70 64.70 12.34	-	-	117 50.43 3.85 2.49 0.48	-	478 62.08 15.73 10.18 1.94	-	609 75.75 20.04 12.97 2.47	127 58.26 4.18 2.70 0.52	100 60.98 3.29 2.13 0.41	-	-	124 60.78 4.08 2.64 0.50	-	-	-	131 66.84 4.31 2.79 0.53	724 65.52 23.82 15.41 2.94	-	903 60.77 29.71 19.23 3.67	-	-	-	415 66.94 13.66 8.84 1.69
Tamarac (city)	21,946 80.04	2,700	1,633 60.48 60.48 7.44	-	-	-	-	152 41.08 9.31 5.63 0.69	-	305 76.63 18.68 11.30 1.39	-	-	-	-	-	-	-	-	-	463 60.76 28.35 17.15 2.11	-	373 50.82 22.84 13.81 1.70	-	-	-	324 67.50 19.84 12.00 1.48
Charlotte County	53,444 83.68	1,456	1,057 72.60 72.60 1.98	-	-	-	-	-	-	168 90.81 15.89 11.54 0.31	-	-	-	-	115 51.57 10.88 7.90 0.22	-	-	-	-	389 70.22 36.80 26.72 0.73	-	-	-	-	-	197 74.34 18.64 13.53 0.37
Citrus County	45,047 85.59	908	736 81.06 81.06 1.63	-	-	-	-	-	-	-	-	-	-	-	95 87.16 12.91 10.46 0.21	-	-	-	-	318 79.30 43.21 35.02 0.71	-	-	-	-	-	156 73.93 21.20 17.18 0.35
Clay County	39,120 77.86	1,633	1,016 62.22 62.22 2.60	-	-	-	-	-	-	-	-	-	-	-	196 67.82 19.29 12.00 0.50	-	-	-	-	383 52.97 37.70 23.45 0.98	-	-	-	-	-	215 71.67 21.16 13.17 0.55
Collier County	77,829 75.58	11,521	5,526 47.96 47.96 7.10	-	-	203 28.96 3.67 1.76 0.26	-	74 22.36 1.34 0.64 0.10	-	1,489 62.51 26.95 12.92 1.91	104 68.42 1.88 0.90 0.13	-	55 21.24 1.00 0.48 0.07	45 28.30 0.81 0.39 0.06	2,392 42.78 43.29 20.76 3.07	-	-	-	-	522 55.36 9.45 4.53 0.67	-	268 37.75 4.85 2.33 0.34	-	-	-	504 50.50 9.12 4.37 0.65
Duval County	191,722 63.12	10,056	4,853 48.26 48.26 2.53	-	-	250 43.03 5.15 2.49 0.13	-	185 40.84 3.81 1.84 0.10	-	789 59.91 16.26 7.85 0.41	36 18.18 0.74 0.36 0.02	-	-	-	737 42.63 15.19 7.33 0.38	-	100 50.76 2.06 0.99 0.05	-	50 34.01 1.03 0.50 0.03	1,771 48.23 36.49 17.61 0.92	-	410 46.91 8.45 4.08 0.21	-	-	-	796 49.78 16.40 7.92 0.42
Jacksonville (city)	179,782 63.19	9,559	4,627 48.40 48.40 2.57	-	-	238 41.98 5.14 2.49 0.13	-	178 39.91 3.85 1.86 0.10	-	756 59.06 16.34 7.91 0.42	36 18.18 0.78 0.38 0.02	-	-	-	705 45.11 15.24 7.38 0.39	-	88 47.57 1.90 0.92 0.05	-	-	1,677 47.82 36.24 17.54 0.93	-	398 47.61 8.60 4.16 0.22	-	-	-	758 49.64 16.38 7.93 0.42
Escambia County	74,690 67.26	2,017	980 48.59 48.59 1.31	-	-	32 29.63 3.27 1.59 0.04	-	-	-	64 32.99 6.53 3.17 0.09	-	-	-	-	308 52.03 31.43 15.27 0.41	-	-	-	-	176 39.82 17.96 8.73 0.24	-	39 31.71 3.98 1.93 0.05	-	-	-	347 65.35 35.41 17.20 0.46

Notes: Please refer to the User's Guide for an explanation of data: data is arranged alphabetically by state, then county, then city within each county and only includes counties with populations > 99,999 and cities with populations > 49,999; (1) Includes Costa Rican, Guatemalan, Honduran, Nicaraguan, Panamanian, Salvadoran, and other Central American; (2) Includes Argentinian, Bolivian, Chilean, Colombian, Ecuadorian, Paraguayan, Peruvian, Uruguayan, Venezuelan, and other South American

Place	All owner-occupied housing units	Hispanic-occupied housing units	Hispanics who own and occupy their own homes	Argentinian	Bolivian	Central American[1]	Chilean	Colombian	Costa Rican	Cuban	Dominican	Ecuadorian	Guatelmalan	Honduran	Mexican	Nicaraguan	Panamanian	Paraguayan	Peruvian	Puerto Rican	Salvadoran	South American[2]	Spaniard	Uruguayan	Venezuelan	Other Hisp.
Pensacola (city)	15,524	447	213	-	-	-	-	-	-	-	-	-	-	-	-	-	-	-	-	-	-	-	-	-	-	-
	63.52		47.65																							
			47.65																							
			1.37																							
Hernando County	47,954	1,972	1,595	-	-	-	-	-	-	129	-	-	-	-	122	-	-	-	-	1,040	-	-	-	-	-	212
	86.52		80.88							73.30					64.55					82.41						94.64
										8.09					7.65					65.20						13.29
			80.88							6.54					6.19					52.74						10.75
			3.33							0.27					0.25					2.17						0.44
Spring Hill (cdp)	24,396	1,486	1,200	-	-	-	-	-	-	63	-	-	-	-	-	-	-	-	-	857	-	-	-	-	-	162
	86.24		80.75							61.76										81.77						96.43
										5.25										71.42						13.50
			80.75							4.24										57.67						10.90
			4.92							0.26										3.51						0.66
Hillsborough County	251,023	56,858	31,644	-	-	1,071	-	920	132	8,801	724	228	175	269	3,402	92	216	-	244	8,453	148	2,005	572	-	265	6,616
	64.14		55.65			44.98		48.68	59.73	67.10	50.10	50.67	62.06	38.21	41.99	27.14	50.35		43.03	49.83	47.28	50.24	68.83		48.27	65.97
						3.38		2.91	0.42	27.81	2.29	0.72	0.55	0.85	10.75	0.29	0.68		0.77	26.71	0.47	6.34	1.81		0.84	20.91
			55.65			1.88		1.62	0.23	15.48	1.27	0.40	0.31	0.47	5.98	0.16	0.38		0.43	14.87	0.26	3.53	1.01		0.47	11.64
			12.61			0.43		0.37	0.05	3.51	0.29	0.09	0.07	0.11	1.36	0.04	0.09		0.10	3.37	0.06	0.80	0.23		0.11	2.64
Brandon (cdp)	20,618	3,007	1,932	-	-	64	-	-	-	254	-	-	-	-	96	-	-	-	-	1,033	-	89	-	-	-	315
	71.85		64.25			44.14				78.64					40.68					65.55		64.96				66.04
						3.31				13.15					4.97					53.47		4.61				16.30
			64.25			2.13				8.45					3.19					34.35		2.96				10.48
			9.37			0.31				1.23					0.47					5.01		0.43				1.53
Tampa (city)	68,753	20,896	10,742	-	-	442	-	170	-	3,331	214	84	-	110	719	39	87	-	-	2,288	-	434	295	-	46	3,019
	55.10		51.41			43.72		34.00		55.99	38.15	50.91		38.87	40.62	26.17	46.28			41.38		39.13	74.68		33.33	66.03
						4.11		1.58		31.01	1.99	0.78		1.02	6.69	0.36	0.81			21.30		4.04	2.75		0.43	28.10
			51.41			2.12		0.81		15.94	1.02	0.40		0.53	3.44	0.19	0.42			10.95		2.08	1.41		0.22	14.45
			15.62			0.64		0.25		4.84	0.31	0.12		0.16	1.05	0.06	0.13			3.33		0.63	0.43		0.07	4.39
Town 'n' Country (cdp)	18,683	6,660	4,357	-	-	147	-	230	-	1,466	193	-	-	-	177	-	-	-	-	1,370	-	380	-	-	-	534
	64.89		65.42			56.11		60.85		82.22	67.25				49.72					57.98		51.84				71.11
						3.37		5.28		33.65	4.43				4.06					31.44		8.72				12.26
			65.42			2.21		3.45		22.01	2.90				2.66					20.57		5.71				8.02
			23.32			0.79		1.23		7.85	1.03				0.95					7.33		2.03				2.86
Indian River County	38,119	1,812	950	-	-	36	-	-	-	37	-	-	-	-	437	-	-	-	-	136	-	137	-	-	-	152
	77.58		52.43			66.67				56.92					46.44					54.62		59.83				58.69
						3.79				3.89					46.00					14.32		14.42				16.00
			52.43			1.99				2.04					24.12					7.51		7.56				8.39
			2.49			0.09				0.10					1.15					0.36		0.36				0.40
Lake County	72,047	3,244	1,996	-	-	101	-	-	-	226	-	-	-	-	666	-	-	-	-	629	-	131	-	-	-	232
	81.49		61.53			64.33				88.98					50.84					64.78		70.43				66.67
						5.06				11.32					33.37					31.51		6.56				11.62
			61.53			3.11				6.97					20.53					19.39		4.04				7.15
			2.77			0.14				0.31					0.92					0.87		0.18				0.32
Lee County	144,256	11,080	5,580	-	-	283	-	174	-	800	174	-	74	59	1,328	-	-	-	-	1,895	-	473	-	-	-	593
	76.49		50.36			33.02		55.95		66.17	51.79		21.76	38.82	41.31					53.80		62.32				51.66
						5.07		3.12		14.34	3.12		1.33	1.06	23.80					33.96		8.48				10.63
			50.36			2.55		1.57		7.22	1.57		0.67	0.53	11.99					17.10		4.27				5.35
			3.87			0.20		0.12		0.55	0.12		0.05	0.04	0.92					1.31		0.33				0.41

Notes: Please refer to the User's Guide for an explanation of data; data is arranged alphabetically by state, then county, then city within each county and only includes counties with populations > 99,999 and cities with populations > 49,999; (1) Includes Costa Rican, Guatemalan, Honduran, Nicaraguan, Panamanian, Salvadoran, and other Central American; (2) Includes Argentinian, Bolivian, Chilean, Colombian, Ecuadorian, Paraguayan, Peruvian, Uruguayan, Venezuelan, and other South American

Place	All owner-occupied housing units	Hispanic-occupied housing units	Hispanics who own and occupy their own homes	Argentinian	Bolivian	Central American[1]	Chilean	Colombian	Costa Rican	Cuban	Dominican	Ecuadorian	Guatemalan	Honduran	Mexican	Nicaraguan	Panamanian	Paraguayan	Peruvian	Puerto Rican	Salvadoran	South American[2]	Spaniard	Uruguayan	Venezuelan	Other Hisp.
Cape Coral (city)	32,663	2,425	1,629	-	-	-	-	97	-	440	112	-	-	-	160	-	-	-	-	407	-	244	-	-	-	198
	79.95		67.18					58.08		76.39	62.22				56.54					65.54		67.97				64.92
								5.95		27.01	6.88				9.82					24.98		14.98				12.15
			67.18					4.00		18.14	4.62				6.60					16.78		10.06				8.16
			4.99					0.30		1.35	0.34				0.49					1.25		0.75				0.61
Leon County	55,014	2,573	922	-	-	-	-	-	-	211	-	-	-	-	159	-	-	-	-	219	-	121	-	-	-	153
	57.00		35.83							38.22					39.16					39.96		36.67				32.35
										22.89					17.25					23.75		13.12				16.59
			35.83							8.20					6.18					8.51		4.70				5.95
			1.68							0.38					0.29					0.40		0.22				0.28
Tallahassee (city)	27,737	2,031	472	-	-	-	-	-	-	135	-	-	-	-	72	-	-	-	-	113	-	68	-	-	-	63
	43.91		23.24							28.72					26.09					26.22		25.37				17.50
										28.60					15.25					23.94		14.41				13.35
			23.24							6.65					3.55					5.56		3.35				3.10
			1.70							0.49					0.26					0.41		0.25				0.23
Manatee County	82,936	5,310	2,196	-	-	155	-	-	-	254	-	-	-	-	921	-	-	-	-	440	-	96	-	-	-	273
	73.75		41.36			48.29				65.63					34.09					46.41		34.78				45.96
						7.06				11.57					41.94					20.04		4.37				12.43
			41.36			2.92				4.78					17.34					8.29		1.81				5.14
			2.65			0.19				0.31					1.11					0.53		0.12				0.33
Marion County	85,171	4,676	3,028	-	-	138	-	133	-	286	-	-	-	-	345	-	-	-	-	1,500	-	252	-	-	-	426
	79.78		64.76			67.65		71.51		66.20					39.93					70.32		69.42				74.61
						4.56		4.39		9.45					11.39					49.54		8.32				14.07
			64.76			2.95		2.84		6.12					7.38					32.08		5.39				9.11
			3.56			0.16		0.16		0.34					0.41					1.76		0.30				0.50
Martin County	44,131	2,223	1,016	-	-	124	-	-	-	194	-	-	111	-	389	-	-	-	-	181	-	-	-	-	-	85
	79.82		45.70			25.67				71.59			26.62		46.14					48.40						47.22
						12.20				19.09			10.93		38.29					17.81						8.37
			45.70			5.58				8.73			4.99		17.50					8.14						3.82
			2.30			0.28				0.44			0.25		0.88					0.41						0.19
Miami-Dade County	449,333	438,356	242,535	3,025	476	14,918	1,500	12,418	603	155,265	6,153	1,950	1,249	2,389	3,592	8,023	1,255	-	3,901	14,501	1,106	27,812	1,720	419	3,536	18,574
	57.85		55.33	51.67	59.87	38.69	49.75	51.52	43.60	60.93	47.76	52.24	38.80	29.77	39.18	40.13	53.00		49.62	51.29	39.81	50.87	64.01	46.76	47.92	49.81
				1.25	0.20	6.15	0.62	5.12	0.25	64.02	2.54	0.80	0.51	0.99	1.48	3.31	0.52		1.61	5.98	0.46	11.47	0.71	0.17	1.46	7.66
			55.33	0.69	0.11	3.40	0.34	2.83	0.14	35.42	1.40	0.44	0.28	0.54	0.82	1.83	0.29		0.89	3.31	0.25	6.34	0.39	0.10	0.81	4.24
			53.98	0.67	0.11	3.32	0.33	2.76	0.13	34.55	1.37	0.43	0.28	0.53	0.80	1.79	0.28		0.87	3.23	0.25	6.19	0.38	0.09	0.79	4.13
Carol City (cdp)	13,583	6,912	5,867	-	-	566	-	304	-	3,181	387	-	-	126	-	300	-	-	-	637	-	517	-	-	-	514
	82.81		84.88			85.89		83.06		87.06	77.71			84.56		87.21				76.56		83.79				89.70
						9.65		5.18		54.22	6.60			2.15		5.11				10.86		8.81				8.76
			84.88			8.19		4.40		46.02	5.60			1.82		4.34				9.22		7.48				7.44
			43.19			4.17		2.24		23.42	2.85			0.93		2.21				4.69		3.81				3.78
Fountainbleau (cdp)	10,781	18,606	9,941	52	-	1,092	67	339	-	6,416	284	96	-	52	71	809	103	-	180	254	-	897	-	-	127	867
	51.52		53.43	27.08		48.43	28.39	35.06		64.61	41.22	48.00		44.83	44.65	48.44	49.05		41.76	33.47		32.12			19.66	44.71
				0.52		10.98	0.67	3.41		64.54	2.86	0.97		0.52	0.71	8.14	1.04		1.81	2.56		9.02			1.28	8.72
			53.43	0.28		5.87	0.36	1.82		34.48	1.53	0.52		0.28	0.38	4.35	0.55		0.97	1.37		4.82			0.68	4.66
			92.21	0.48		10.13	0.62	3.14		59.51	2.63	0.89		0.48	0.66	7.50	0.96		1.67	2.36		8.32			1.18	8.04
Hialeah (city)	35,963	66,891	33,368	108	-	1,226	143	1,082	69	26,589	628	212	100	185	133	727	-	-	241	1,048	57	1,943	114	-	88	1,687
	50.82		49.88	70.59		29.71	45.83	47.33	52.67	52.58	40.97	49.07	40.00	25.55	33.25	28.59			45.82	47.10	23.55	47.92	84.44		42.11	43.81
				0.32		3.67	0.43	3.24	0.21	79.68	1.88	0.64	0.30	0.55	0.40	2.18			0.72	3.14	0.17	5.82	0.34		0.26	5.06
			49.88	0.16		1.83	0.21	1.62	0.10	39.75	0.94	0.32	0.15	0.28	0.20	1.09			0.36	1.57	0.09	2.90	0.17		0.13	2.52
			92.78	0.30		3.41	0.40	3.01	0.19	73.93	1.75	0.59	0.28	0.51	0.37	2.02			0.67	2.91	0.16	5.40	0.32		0.24	4.69

Notes: Please refer to the User's Guide for an explanation of data; data is arranged alphabetically by state, then county, then city within each county and only includes counties with populations > 99,999 and cities with populations > 49,999; (1) Includes Costa Rican, Guatemalan, Honduran, Nicaraguan, Panamanian, Salvadoran, and other Central American; (2) Includes Argentinian, Bolivian, Chilean, Colombian, Ecuadorian, Paraguayan, Peruvan, Uruguayan, Venezuelan, and other South American

Place	All owner-occupied housing units	Hispanic-occupied housing units	Hispanics who own and occupy their own homes	Argentinian	Bolivian	Central American[1]	Chilean	Colombian	Costa Rican	Cuban	Dominican	Ecuadorian	Guatemalan	Honduran	Mexican	Nicaraguan	Panamanian	Paraguayan	Peruvian	Puerto Rican	Salvadoran	South American[2]	Spaniard	Uruguayan	Venezuelan	Other Hisp.
Kendale Lakes (cdp)	14,271	14,039	10,917	-	-	780	-	714	-	6,799	153	-	-	79	99	543	-	-	214	465	-	1,498	-	-	135	1,058
	78.94		77.76			69.27		65.03		83.26	62.96			78.22	79.20	69.44			57.37	75.49		66.55			61.64	74.14
						7.14		6.54		62.28	1.40			0.72	0.91	4.97			1.96	4.26		13.72			1.24	9.69
			77.76			5.56		5.09		48.43	1.09			0.56	0.71	3.87			1.52	3.31		10.67			0.96	7.54
			76.50			5.47		5.00		47.64	1.07			0.55	0.69	3.80			1.50	3.26		10.50			0.95	7.41
Kendall (cdp)	19,032	13,256	8,115	191	-	559	89	582	-	4,472	125	-	-	-	-	320	-	-	209	508	-	1,447	-	-	282	796
	66.86		61.22	57.01		50.00	58.55	44.29		69.35	45.96					52.03			57.42	59.00		50.00			58.51	57.47
				2.35		6.89	1.10	7.17		55.11	1.54					3.94			2.58	6.26		17.83			3.48	9.81
			61.22	1.44		4.22	0.67	4.39		33.74	0.94					2.41			1.58	3.83		10.92			2.13	6.00
			42.64	1.00		2.94	0.47	3.06		23.50	0.66					1.68			1.10	2.67		7.60			1.48	4.18
Miami Beach (city)	16,930	23,289	7,288	405	-	182	119	548	-	4,204	103	64	-	27	83	65	-	-	158	384	-	1,503	150	-	168	679
	36.63		31.29	28.76		15.65	32.16	28.32		40.19	17.25	19.16		8.65	18.36	15.97			21.38	19.89		25.77	47.02		22.46	26.80
				5.56		2.50	1.63	7.52		57.68	1.41	0.88		0.37	1.14	0.89			2.17	5.27		20.62	2.06		2.31	9.32
			31.29	1.74		0.78	0.51	2.35		18.05	0.44	0.27		0.12	0.36	0.28			0.68	1.65		6.45	0.64		0.72	2.92
			43.05	2.39		1.08	0.70	3.24		24.83	0.61	0.38		0.16	0.49	0.38			0.93	2.27		8.88	0.89		0.99	4.01
Miami (city)	46,847	89,745	29,933	306	-	1,802	132	670	59	22,008	658	202	136	498	225	802	89	-	210	1,168	177	1,824	251	-	222	1,997
	34.87		33.35	39.08		14.11	31.28	31.95	22.52	39.31	25.64	31.08	14.20	12.47	21.45	13.07	24.45		22.36	29.55	22.26	31.23	54.09		34.91	28.06
				1.02		6.02	0.44	2.24	0.20	73.52	2.20	0.67	0.45	1.66	0.75	2.68	0.30		0.70	3.90	0.59	6.09	0.84		0.74	6.67
			33.35	0.34		2.01	0.15	0.75	0.07	24.52	0.73	0.23	0.15	0.55	0.25	0.89	0.10		0.23	1.30	0.20	2.03	0.28		0.25	2.23
			63.90	0.65		3.85	0.28	1.43	0.13	46.98	1.40	0.43	0.29	1.06	0.48	1.71	0.19		0.45	2.49	0.38	3.89	0.54		0.47	4.26
North Miami (city)	10,302	4,800	2,566	-	-	265	-	258	-	737	156	-	-	57	-	125	-	-	-	422	-	460	-	-	-	466
	50.20		53.46			50.00		60.99		67.86	48.30			33.53		65.10				47.31		53.06				51.15
						10.33		10.05		28.72	6.08			2.22		4.87				16.45		17.93				18.16
			53.46			5.52		5.38		15.35	3.25			1.19		2.60				8.79		9.58				9.71
			24.91			2.57		2.50		7.15	1.51			0.55		1.21				4.10		4.47				4.52
Tamiami (cdp)	13,661	14,915	12,432	-	-	666	-	474	-	9,444	175	-	-	53	74	453	-	-	-	330	-	918	-	-	124	743
	83.90		83.35			71.92		82.01		85.54	77.43			55.21	60.66	72.36				74.32		80.95			85.52	80.15
						5.36		3.81		75.97	1.41			0.43	0.60	3.64				2.65		7.38			1.00	5.98
			83.35			4.47		3.18		63.32	1.17			0.36	0.50	3.04				2.21		6.15			0.83	4.98
			91.00			4.88		3.47		69.13	1.28			0.39	0.54	3.32				2.42		6.72			0.91	5.44
Okaloosa County	43,972	1,879	906	-	-	20	-	-	-	84	-	-	-	-	287	-	-	-	-	229	-	-	-	-	-	211
	66.35		48.22			22.47				54.55					42.90					51.46						53.96
						2.21				9.27					31.68					25.28						23.29
			48.22			1.06				4.47					15.27					12.19						11.23
			2.06			0.05				0.19					0.65					0.52						0.48
Orange County	204,230	51,400	26,441	162	-	859	30	1,154	72	3,092	1,063	235	169	158	1,990	100	171	-	373	14,855	152	2,352	117	-	275	2,113
	60.73		51.44	56.45		49.25	19.23	45.81	33.33	60.97	53.04	43.93	55.59	42.82	39.98	43.86	55.88		65.78	53.21	55.88	46.51	53.92		37.77	47.89
				0.61		3.25	0.11	4.36	0.27	11.69	4.02	0.89	0.64	0.60	7.53	0.38	0.65		1.41	56.18	0.57	8.90	0.44		1.04	7.99
			51.44	0.32		1.67	0.06	2.25	0.14	6.02	2.07	0.46	0.33	0.31	3.87	0.19	0.33		0.73	28.90	0.30	4.58	0.23		0.54	4.11
			12.95	0.08		0.42	0.01	0.57	0.04	1.51	0.52	0.12	0.08	0.08	0.97	0.05	0.08		0.18	7.27	0.07	1.15	0.06		0.13	1.03
Orlando (city)	33,052	11,763	3,337	-	-	93	-	204	-	623	129	-	-	-	109	-	-	-	62	1,718	-	386	-	-	47	267
	40.79		28.37			23.91		28.14		45.98	29.45				13.51				40.52	27.97		25.48			17.80	24.61
						2.79		6.11		18.67	3.87				3.27				1.86	51.48		11.57			1.41	8.00
			28.37			0.79		1.73		5.30	1.10				0.93				0.53	14.61		3.28			0.40	2.27
			10.10			0.28		0.62		1.88	0.39				0.33				0.19	5.20		1.17			0.14	0.81
Osceola County	41,315	14,738	8,265	-	-	293	-	263	-	395	503	78	-	-	285	-	-	-	-	5,616	70	586	-	-	84	561
	67.76		56.08			52.23		42.49		59.40	59.81	58.65			32.76					59.02	49.65	49.62			43.08	53.79
						3.55		3.18		4.78	6.09	0.94			3.45					67.95	0.85	7.09			1.02	6.79
			56.08			1.99		1.78		2.68	3.41	0.53			1.93					38.11	0.47	3.98			0.57	3.81
			20.00			0.71		0.64		0.96	1.22	0.19			0.69					13.59	0.17	1.42			0.20	1.36

Notes: Please refer to the User's Guide for an explanation of data; data is arranged alphabetically by state, then county, then city within each county and only includes counties with populations > 99,999 and cities with populations > 49,999; (1) Includes Costa Rican, Guatemalan, Honduran, Nicaraguan, Panamanian, Salvadoran, and other Central American; (2) Includes Argentinian, Bolivian, Chilean, Colombian, Ecuadorian, Paraguayan, Peruvian, Uruguayan, Venezuelan, and other South American

Place	All owner-occupied housing units	Hispanic-occupied housing units	Hispanics who own and occupy their own homes	Argentinian	Bolivian	Central American[1]	Chilean	Colombian	Costa Rican	Cuban	Dominican	Ecuadorian	Guatelmalan	Honduran	Mexican	Nicaraguan	Panamanian	Paraguayan	Peruvian	Puerto Rican	Salvadoran	South American[2]	Spaniard	Uruguayan	Venezuelan	Other Hisp.
Palm Beach County	354,024 74.66	40,581	23,036 56.77 56.77 6.51	419 58.44 1.82 1.03 0.12	-	1,310 33.57 5.69 3.23 0.37	137 76.54 0.59 0.34 0.04	1,684 63.14 7.31 4.15 0.48	143 49.14 0.62 0.35 0.04	6,528 68.71 28.34 16.09 1.84	720 63.44 3.13 1.77 0.20	381 62.36 1.65 0.94 0.11	261 17.13 1.13 0.64 0.07	246 34.12 1.07 0.61 0.07	3,099 44.52 13.45 7.64 0.88	290 50.97 1.26 0.71 0.08	81 52.94 0.35 0.20 0.02	-	557 76.51 2.42 1.37 0.16	4,530 57.07 19.66 11.16 1.28	225 41.13 0.98 0.55 0.06	3,943 64.15 17.12 9.72 1.11	151 78.24 0.66 0.37 0.04	238 69.59 1.03 0.59 0.07	255 51.41 1.11 0.63 0.07	2,755 57.35 11.96 6.79 0.78
Boca Raton (city)	24,212 75.69	1,989	1,117 56.16 56.16 4.61	-	-	-	-	141 70.50 12.62 7.09 0.58	-	264 73.33 23.63 13.27 1.09	-	-	-	-	77 33.19 6.89 3.87 0.32	-	-	-	-	155 57.20 13.88 7.79 0.64	-	359 62.00 32.14 18.05 1.48	-	-	-	216 49.77 19.34 10.86 0.89
Boynton Beach (city)	18,931 72.79	1,509	820 54.34 54.34 4.33	-	-	59 40.14 7.20 3.91 0.31	-	-	-	134 55.14 16.34 8.88 0.71	-	-	-	-	90 39.82 10.98 5.96 0.48	-	-	-	-	270 65.69 32.93 17.89 1.43	-	170 66.15 20.73 11.27 0.90	-	-	-	75 38.86 9.15 4.97 0.40
Delray Beach (city)	18,596 69.50	1,233	689 55.88 55.88 3.71	-	-	-	-	-	-	-	-	-	-	-	159 50.64 23.08 12.90 0.86	-	-	-	-	153 58.85 22.21 12.41 0.82	-	154 58.11 22.35 12.49 0.83	-	-	-	72 63.72 10.45 5.84 0.39
West Palm Beach (city)	18,056 52.12	4,769	2,102 44.08 44.08 11.64	-	-	121 17.51 5.76 2.54 0.67	-	134 57.76 6.37 2.81 0.74	-	942 52.86 44.81 19.75 5.22	82 55.78 3.90 1.72 0.45	-	32 6.91 1.52 0.67 0.18	-	176 32.84 8.37 3.69 0.97	-	-	-	-	258 39.03 12.27 5.41 1.43	-	274 56.73 13.04 5.75 1.52	-	-	-	249 54.25 11.85 5.22 1.38
Pasco County	121,548 82.37	5,354	3,790 70.79 70.79 3.12	-	-	174 78.73 4.59 3.25 0.14	-	-	-	575 89.70 15.17 10.74 0.47	-	-	-	-	647 49.39 17.07 12.08 0.53	-	-	-	-	1,541 72.89 40.66 28.78 1.27	-	206 77.74 5.44 3.85 0.17	-	-	-	545 78.99 14.38 10.18 0.45
Pinellas County	293,869 70.82	13,142	6,417 48.83 48.83 2.18	-	-	152 43.80 2.37 1.16 0.05	-	263 54.45 4.10 2.00 0.09	-	1,241 65.77 19.34 9.44 0.42	133 41.69 2.07 1.01 0.05	80 44.44 1.25 0.61 0.03	-	-	850 32.64 13.25 6.47 0.29	-	-	-	128 65.98 1.99 0.97 0.04	2,220 49.76 34.60 16.89 0.76	-	702 49.79 10.94 5.34 0.24	154 80.63 2.40 1.17 0.05	-	67 29.52 1.04 0.51 0.02	965 50.18 15.04 7.34 0.33
Clearwater (city)	29,938 62.04	2,612	850 32.54 32.54 2.84	-	-	-	-	44 48.89 5.18 1.68 0.15	-	155 56.99 18.24 5.93 0.52	-	-	-	-	135 14.58 15.88 5.17 0.45	-	-	-	-	218 33.33 25.65 8.35 0.73	-	146 47.56 17.18 5.59 0.49	-	-	-	116 36.71 13.65 4.44 0.39
Largo (city)	23,069 67.82	925	396 42.81 42.81 1.72	-	-	-	-	-	-	-	-	-	-	-	93 50.54 23.48 10.05 0.40	-	-	-	-	141 44.48 35.61 15.24 0.61	-	-	-	-	-	-
Palm Harbor (cdp)	19,854 78.19	573	449 78.36 78.36 2.26	-	-	-	-	-	-	-	-	-	-	-	-	-	-	-	-	163 69.07 36.30 28.45 0.82	-	-	-	-	-	-

Notes: Please refer to the User's Guide for an explanation of data; data is arranged alphabetically by state, then county, then city within each county and only includes counties with populations > 99,999 and cities with populations > 49,999; (1) Includes Costa Rican, Guatemalan, Honduran, Nicaraguan, Panamanian, Salvadoran, and other Central American; (2) Includes Argentinian, Bolivian, Chilean, Colombian, Ecuadorian, Paraguayan, Peruvan, Uruguayan, Venezuelan, and other South American

Place	All owner-occupied housing units	Hispanic-occupied housing units	Hispanics who own and occupy their own homes	Argentinian	Bolivian	Central American[1]	Chilean	Colombian	Costa Rican	Cuban	Dominican	Ecuadorian	Guatelmalan	Honduran	Mexican	Nicaraguan	Panamanian	Paraguayan	Peruvian	Puerto Rican	Salvadoran	South American[2]	Spaniard	Uruguayan	Venezuelan	Other Hisp.
St. Petersburg (city)	69,697	3,456	1,710	-	-	-	-	-	-	381	-	-	-	-	190	-	-	-	-	636	-	168	-	-	-	257
	63.64		49.48							58.35					35.98					54.87		44.68				45.73
										22.28					11.11					37.19		9.82				15.03
			49.48							11.02					5.50					18.40		4.86				7.44
			2.45							0.55					0.27					0.91		0.24				0.37
Polk County	137,373	11,208	6.032	-	-	141	-	-	-	587	71	-	-	-	2,649	-	-	-	-	1,848	-	159	-	-	-	539
	73.37		53.82			39.94				65.59	44.38				49.66					56.84		57.19				60.43
						2.34				9.73	1.18				43.92					30.64		2.64				8.94
			53.82			1.26				5.24	0.63				23.63					16.49		1.42				4.81
			4.39			0.10				0.43	0.05				1.93					1.35		0.12				0.39
Lakeland (city)	20,053	1,666	686	-	-	-	-	-	-	167	-	-	-	-	99	-	-	-	-	247	-	-	-	-	-	92
	59.95		41.18							60.95					35.23					35.75						43.19
										24.34					14.43					36.01						13.41
			41.18							10.02					5.94					14.83						5.52
			3.42							0.83					0.49					1.23						0.46
St. Johns County	37,889	948	647	-	-	-	-	-	-	-	-	-	-	-	72	-	-	-	-	162	-	-	-	-	-	111
	76.37		68.25												50.00					62.31						68.94
															11.13					25.04						17.16
			68.25												7.59					17.09						11.71
			1.71												0.19					0.43						0.29
St. Lucie County	60,035	4,177	2,535	-	-	107	-	45	-	378	-	-	-	-	705	-	-	-	-	861	-	161	-	-	-	205
	78.04		60.69			55.15		42.45		75.90					47.25					70.81		57.30				61.38
						4.22		1.78		14.91					27.81					33.96		6.35				8.09
			60.69			2.56		1.08		9.05					16.88					20.61		3.85				4.91
			4.22			0.18		0.07		0.63					1.17					1.43		0.27				0.34
Port St. Lucie (city)	28,114	2,076	1,531	-	-	-	-	-	-	286	-	-	-	-	136	-	-	-	-	690	-	103	-	-	-	129
	82.93		73.75							84.87					58.12					76.16		54.21				70.11
										18.68					8.88					45.07		6.73				8.43
			73.75							13.78					6.55					33.24		4.96				6.21
			5.45							1.02					0.48					2.45		0.37				0.46
Santa Rosa County	35,198	736	573	-	-	-	-	-	-	-	-	-	-	-	107	-	-	-	-	180	-	-	-	-	-	131
	80.37		77.85												61.14					80.36						81.37
															18.67					31.41						22.86
			77.85												14.54					24.46						17.80
			1.63												0.30					0.51						0.37
Sarasota County	118,538	4,287	2,285	-	-	121	-	106	-	529	-	-	-	-	594	-	-	-	-	402	-	305	-	-	-	299
	79.06		53.30			61.42		50.96		72.66					39.73					60.82		55.56				52.27
						5.30		4.64		23.15					26.00					17.59		13.35				13.09
			53.30			2.82		2.47		12.34					13.86					9.38		7.11				6.97
			1.93			0.10		0.09		0.45					0.50					0.34		0.26				0.25
Sarasota (city)	13,728	1,798	620	-	-	-	-	-	-	146	-	-	-	-	204	-	-	-	-	86	-	86	-	-	-	55
	58.62		34.48							62.39					25.15					40.57		43.65				23.01
										23.55					32.90					13.87		13.87				8.87
			34.48							8.12					11.35					4.78		4.78				3.06
			4.52							1.06					1.49					0.63		0.63				0.40
Seminole County	96,956	12,503	7,353	118	-	296	-	370	-	886	188	95	-	-	450	-	64	-	80	3,870	-	836	-	-	69	747
	69.47		58.81	63.10		48.05		56.84		69.33	50.40	70.37			49.45		49.61		57.55	60.84		58.83			44.81	52.27
				1.60		4.03		5.03		12.05	2.56	1.29			6.12		0.87		1.09	52.63		11.37			0.94	10.16
			58.81	0.94		2.37		2.96		7.09	1.50	0.76			3.60		0.51		0.64	30.95		6.69			0.55	5.97
			7.58	0.12		0.31		0.38		0.91	0.19	0.10			0.46		0.07		0.08	3.99		0.86			0.07	0.77

Notes: Please refer to the User's Guide for an explanation of data; data is arranged alphabetically by state, then county, then city within each county and only includes counties with populations > 99,999 and cities with populations > 49,999; (1) Includes Costa Rican, Guatemalan, Honduran, Nicaraguan, Panamanian, Salvadoran, and other Central American; (2) Includes Argentinian, Bolivian, Chilean, Colombian, Ecuadorian, Paraguayan, Peruvian, Uruguayan, Venezuelan, and other South American

Place	All owner-occupied housing units	Hispanic-occupied housing units	Hispanics who own and occupy their own homes	Argentinian	Bolivian	Central American[1]	Chilean	Colombian	Costa Rican	Cuban	Dominican	Ecuadorian	Guatelmalan	Honduran	Mexican	Nicaraguan	Panamanian	Paraguayan	Peruvian	Puerto Rican	Salvadoran	South American[2]	Spaniard	Uruguayan	Venezuelan	Other Hisp.
Volusia County	139,037	8,217	5,591	-	-	154	-	101	-	296	85	-	-	-	799	-	-	-	-	3,392	-	339	-	-	-	470
	75.27		68.04			66.09		56.74		60.53	52.15				51.32					76.11		65.32				63.26
						2.75		1.81		5.29	1.52				14.29					60.67		6.06				8.41
			68.04			1.87		1.23		3.60	1.03				9.72					41.28		4.13				5.72
			4.02			0.11		0.07		0.21	0.06				0.57					2.44		0.24				0.34
Daytona Beach (city)	13,539	831	289	-	-	-	-	-	-	-	-	-	-	-	-	-	-	-	-	91	-	-	-	-	-	55
	47.28		34.78																	27.25						39.29
																				31.49						19.03
			34.78																	10.95						6.62
			2.13																	0.67						0.41
Deltona (city)	21,715	3,935	3,261	-	-	-	-	-	-	131	-	-	-	-	147	-	-	-	-	2,523	-	106	-	-	-	181
	87.19		82.87							78.92					72.06					85.73		60.23				81.17
										4.02					4.51					77.37		3.25				5.55
			82.87							3.33					3.74					64.12		2.69				4.60
			15.02							0.60					0.68					11.62		0.49				0.83

Notes: Please refer to the User's Guide for an explanation of data; data is arranged alphabetically by state, then county, then city within each county and only includes counties with populations > 99,999 and cities with populations > 49,999; (1) Includes Costa Rican, Guatemalan, Honduran, Nicaraguan, Panamanian, Salvadoran, and other Central American; (2) Includes Argentinian, Bolivian, Chilean, Colombian, Ecuadorian, Paraguayan, Peruvian, Uruguayan, Venezuelan, and other South American

Median Gross Rent

(Universe: Specified Renter-Occupied Housing Units Paying Cash Rent)

Place	All specified renter-occupied housing units	Specified housing units rented by Hispanics	Argentinian	Bolivian	Central American[1]	Chilean	Colombian	Costa Rican	Cuban	Dominican	Ecuadorian	Guatelmalan	Honduran	Mexican	Nicaraguan	Panamanian	Paraguayan	Peruvian	Puerto Rican	Salvadoran	South American[2]	Spaniard	Uruguayan	Venezuelan	Other Hisp.
UNITED STATES	602	604	771	797	645	763	750	714	614	646	732	635	608	583	678	663	779	758	596	648	751	717	747	752	603
FLORIDA	641	643	752	735	639	716	753	720	604	672	730	618	601	568	658	705	800	725	659	626	748	727	703	776	667
Alachua County	553	567	-	-	559	-	500	-	602	-	-	-	-	601	-	-	-	-	555	-	535	-	-	-	613
Gainesville (city)	540	531	-	-	-	-	-	-	528	-	-	-	-	607	-	-	-	-	507	-	557	-	-	-	519
Bay County	536	562	-	-	-	-	-	-	-	-	-	-	-	573	-	-	-	-	703	-	-	-	-	-	531
Brevard County	604	605	-	-	667	-	600	-	607	728	-	-	-	614	-	692	-	-	603	-	597	-	-	-	598
Melbourne (city)	588	562	-	-	-	-	-	-	-	-	-	-	-	624	-	-	-	-	483	-	-	-	-	-	564
Palm Bay (city)	633	637	-	-	-	-	-	-	-	-	-	-	-	568	-	-	-	-	651	-	684	-	-	-	598
Broward County	757	763	846	900	708	739	840	789	762	738	879	712	693	707	746	727	-	769	743	686	830	890	811	866	751
Coral Springs (city)	899	859	-	-	823	-	904	-	869	772	953	-	-	847	-	-	-	907	827	-	921	-	-	1,058	793
Davie (town)	792	724	-	-	763	-	728	-	723	-	-	-	-	595	-	-	-	704	742	-	698	-	-	-	701
Deerfield Beach (city)	790	814	-	-	832	-	836	-	793	-	-	-	-	672	-	-	-	-	829	-	825	-	-	-	732
Fort Lauderdale (city)	641	633	-	-	591	-	617	-	590	-	-	630	-	623	-	-	-	617	618	576	680	-	-	-	640
Hollywood (city)	685	671	741	-	652	715	720	-	731	635	698	-	664	693	760	-	-	618	647	-	689	-	-	699	656
Lauderhill (city)	687	660	-	-	-	-	697	-	-	-	-	-	-	-	-	-	-	-	590	-	730	-	-	-	588
Margate (city)	805	852	-	-	770	-	870	-	910	-	-	-	-	775	-	-	-	-	719	-	895	-	-	-	884
Miramar (city)	784	766	-	-	834	-	852	-	728	699	-	-	-	771	894	829	-	1,219	687	-	879	-	-	-	677
Pembroke Pines (city)	945	969	-	-	903	-	981	-	955	962	1,053	-	-	1,149	-	-	-	1,000	965	-	988	-	-	996	984
Plantation (city)	938	941	-	-	814	-	970	-	910	-	-	-	-	1,023	-	-	-	995	929	-	973	-	-	970	1,028
Pompano Beach (city)	707	687	-	-	-	-	760	-	774	-	-	-	-	613	-	-	-	-	642	-	791	-	-	-	738
Sunrise (city)	849	877	-	-	831	-	939	-	969	849	853	-	-	904	-	-	-	766	850	-	894	-	-	-	861
Tamarac (city)	789	783	-	-	-	-	815	-	760	-	-	-	-	-	-	-	-	-	827	-	793	-	-	-	744
Charlotte County	626	601	-	-	-	-	-	-	894	-	-	-	-	608	-	-	-	-	598	-	-	-	-	-	662
Citrus County	478	406	-	-	-	-	-	-	-	-	-	-	-	611	-	-	-	-	378	-	-	-	-	-	513
Clay County	668	681	-	-	-	-	-	-	-	-	-	-	-	683	-	-	-	-	683	-	-	-	-	-	625
Collier County	753	659	-	-	670	-	779	-	719	769	-	587	693	579	-	-	-	-	684	-	799	-	-	-	729
Duval County	604	633	-	-	626	-	674	-	610	652	-	-	-	644	-	732	-	702	617	-	700	-	-	-	640
Jacksonville (city)	598	631	-	-	626	-	674	-	609	652	-	-	-	641	-	732	-	-	615	-	694	-	-	-	639
Escambia County	533	556	-	-	570	-	-	-	588	-	-	-	-	673	-	-	-	-	516	-	608	-	-	-	481
Pensacola (city)	536	544	-	-	-	-	-	-	-	-	-	-	-	-	-	-	-	-	-	-	-	-	-	-	-
Hernando County	550	568	-	-	-	-	-	-	497	-	-	-	-	479	-	-	-	-	593	-	-	-	-	-	575
Spring Hill (cdp)	613	600	-	-	-	-	-	-	472	-	-	-	-	-	-	-	-	-	608	-	-	-	-	-	625
Hilisborough County	623	583	-	-	585	-	629	595	539	616	585	584	571	526	608	589	-	666	604	574	646	663	-	705	608

Notes: Please refer to the User's Guide for an explanation of data; data is arranged alphabetically by state, then county, then city within each county and only includes counties with populations > 99,999 and cities with populations > 49,999; (1) Includes Costa Rican, Guatemalan, Honduran, Nicaraguan, Panamanian, Salvadoran, and other Central American; (2) Includes Argentinian, Bolivian, Chilean, Colombian, Ecuadorian, Paraguayan, Peruvian, Uruguayan, Venezuelan, and other South American

Place	All specified renter-occupied housing units	Specified housing units rented by Hispanics	Argentinian	Bolivian	Central American[1]	Chilean	Colombian	Costa Rican	Cuban	Dominican	Ecuadorian	Guatemalan	Honduran	Mexican	Nicaraguan	Panamanian	Paraguayan	Peruvian	Puerto Rican	Salvadoran	South American[2]	Spaniard	Uruguayan	Venezuelan	Other Hisp.
Brandon (cdp)	721	686	-	-	721	-	-	-	709	-	-	-	-	683	-	-	-	-	690	-	620	-	-	-	654
Tampa (city)	577	543	-	-	549	-	596	-	470	587	439	-	548	580	543	568	-	-	541	-	618	573	-	698	564
Town 'n' Country (cdp)	722	712	-	-	788	-	703	-	648	785	-	-	-	692	-	-	-	-	710	-	668	-	-	-	734
Indian River County	615	531	-	-	475	-	-	-	825	-	-	-	-	495	-	-	-	-	605	-	596	-	-	-	581
Lake County	534	547	-	-	642	-	-	-	739	-	-	-	-	510	-	-	-	-	665	-	608	-	-	-	525
Lee County	646	599	-	-	604	-	677	-	711	579	-	588	662	597	-	-	-	-	577	-	682	-	-	-	581
Cape Coral (city)	696	624	-	-	-	-	681	-	711	571	-	-	-	612	-	-	-	-	603	-	691	-	-	-	679
Leon County	606	595	-	-	-	-	-	-	593	-	-	-	-	551	-	-	-	-	682	-	699	-	-	-	579
Tallahassee (city)	605	599	-	-	-	-	-	-	596	-	-	-	-	566	-	-	-	-	676	-	690	-	-	-	590
Manatee County	637	566	-	-	515	-	-	-	588	-	-	-	-	540	-	-	-	-	620	-	689	-	-	-	623
Marion County	513	491	-	-	621	-	458	-	525	-	-	-	-	444	-	-	-	-	531	-	522	-	-	-	456
Martin County	633	594	-	-	581	-	-	-	703	-	-	564	-	562	-	-	-	-	632	-	-	-	-	-	618
Miami-Dade County	647	640	755	829	634	729	751	721	597	660	714	598	585	615	657	748	-	725	670	600	747	756	670	769	678
Carol City (cdp)	747	764	-	-	835	-	1,015	-	701	768	-	-	823	-	888	-	-	-	813	-	879	-	-	-	695
Fountainbleau (cdp)	791	786	800	-	803	831	813	-	743	813	833	-	855	775	806	775	-	789	848	-	815	-	-	820	805
Hialeah (city)	614	613	819	-	665	647	710	713	589	694	711	638	698	670	662	-	-	676	641	623	700	671	-	666	659
Kendale Lakes (cdp)	865	861	-	-	841	-	895	-	858	791	-	-	1,125	813	845	-	-	854	876	-	879	-	-	748	843
Kendall (cdp)	780	758	807	-	786	843	794	-	727	740	-	-	-	-	790	-	-	759	702	-	796	-	-	813	716
Miami Beach (city)	632	593	632	-	614	676	642	-	536	618	558	-	589	591	624	-	-	611	597	-	633	703	-	652	604
Miami (city)	535	543	769	-	568	693	618	666	513	556	581	530	547	613	592	545	-	634	570	534	645	509	-	664	574
North Miami (city)	613	650	-	-	636	-	649	-	593	666	-	-	658	-	588	-	-	-	650	-	665	-	-	-	648
Tamiami (cdp)	854	850	-	-	787	-	848	-	866	1,065	-	-	749	878	781	-	-	-	948	-	797	-	-	1,031	827
Okaloosa County	601	593	-	-	510	-	-	-	789	-	-	-	-	610	-	-	-	-	569	-	-	-	-	-	629
Orange County	699	686	727	-	692	729	718	724	650	719	757	689	663	643	713	674	-	801	687	700	728	710	-	739	696
Orlando (city)	700	695	-	-	749	-	727	-	654	733	-	-	-	692	-	-	-	709	675	-	738	-	-	751	700
Osceola County	714	705	-	-	721	-	776	-	698	725	817	-	-	694	-	-	-	-	705	761	758	-	-	732	677
Palm Beach County	739	674	873	-	641	721	827	733	636	715	812	644	631	637	644	769	-	767	694	611	827	1,125	750	886	719
Boca Raton (city)	847	781	-	-	-	-	792	-	738	-	-	-	-	762	-	-	-	-	805	-	826	-	-	-	771
Boynton Beach (city)	787	746	-	-	608	-	-	-	732	-	-	-	-	806	-	-	-	-	739	-	842	-	-	-	725
Delray Beach (city)	807	711	-	-	-	-	-	-	-	-	-	-	-	673	-	-	-	-	595	-	920	-	-	-	706
West Palm Beach (city)	664	618	-	-	645	-	735	-	524	677	-	639	-	645	-	-	-	-	616	-	609	-	-	-	681
Pasco County	518	479	-	-	342	-	-	-	590	-	-	-	-	412	-	-	-	-	543	-	485	-	-	-	579
Pinellas County	616	604	-	-	661	-	773	-	519	539	635	-	-	599	-	-	-	625	594	-	677	585	-	680	615
Clearwater (city)	637	623	-	-	-	-	818	-	496	-	-	-	-	635	-	-	-	-	613	-	691	-	-	-	602
Largo (city)	625	605	-	-	-	-	-	-	-	-	-	-	-	675	-	-	-	-	583	-	-	-	-	-	-
Palm Harbor (cdp)	786	797	-	-	-	-	-	-	-	-	-	-	-	-	-	-	-	-	795	-	-	-	-	-	-
St. Petersburg (city)	567	562	-	-	-	-	-	-	494	-	-	-	-	525	-	-	-	-	540	-	658	-	-	-	630

Notes: Please refer to the User's Guide for an explanation of data; data is arranged alphabetically by state, then county, then city within each county and only includes counties with populations > 99,999 and cities with populations > 49,999; (1) Includes Costa Rican, Guatemalan, Honduran, Nicaraguan, Panamanian, Salvadoran, and other Central American; (2) Includes Argentinian, Bolivian, Chilean, Colombian, Ecuadorian, Paraguayan, Peruvian, Uruguayan, Venezuelan, and other South American

Place	All specified renter-occupied housing units	Specified housing units rented by Hispanics	Argentinian	Bolivian	Central American[1]	Chilean	Colombian	Costa Rican	Cuban	Dominican	Ecuadorian	Guatelmalan	Honduran	Mexican	Nicaraguan	Panamanian	Paraguayan	Peruvian	Puerto Rican	Salvadoran	South American[2]	Spaniard	Uruguayan	Venezuelan	Other Hisp.
Polk County	501	466	-	-	499	-	-	-	566	370	-	-	-	440	-	-	-	-	515	-	496	-	-	-	476
Lakeland (city)	528	518	-	-	-	-	-	-	581	-	-	-	-	558	-	-	-	-	516	-	-	-	-	-	446
St. Johns County	724	691	-	-	-	-	-	-	-	-	-	-	-	671	-	-	-	-	656	-	-	-	-	-	838
St. Lucie County	621	625	-	-	518	-	794	-	677	-	-	-	-	571	-	-	-	-	681	-	775	-	-	-	596
Port St. Lucie (city)	741	711	-	-	-	-	-	-	725	-	-	-	-	677	-	-	-	-	705	-	817	-	-	-	707
Santa Rosa County	540	618	-	-	-	-	-	-	-	-	-	-	-	603	-	-	-	-	825	-	-	-	-	-	527
Sarasota County	711	627	-	-	592	-	648	-	589	-	-	-	-	623	-	-	-	-	633	-	651	-	-	-	639
Sarasota (city)	648	606	-	-	-	-	-	-	558	-	-	-	-	630	-	-	-	-	620	-	657	-	-	-	584
Seminole County	731	703	640	-	701	-	713	-	664	736	619	-	-	751	-	703	-	746	686	-	721	-	-	773	721
Volusia County	597	588	-	-	594	-	602	-	565	638	-	-	-	521	-	-	-	-	620	-	570	-	-	-	652
Daytona Beach (city)	530	580	-	-	-	-	-	-	-	-	-	-	-	-	-	-	-	-	611	-	-	-	-	-	532
Deltona (city)	708	672	-	-	-	-	-	-	653	-	-	-	-	635	-	-	-	-	672	-	580	-	-	-	709

Notes: Please refer to the User's Guide for an explanation of data; data is arranged alphabetically by state, then county, then city within each county and only includes counties with populations > 99,999 and cities with populations > 49,999; (1) Includes Costa Rican, Guatemalan, Honduran, Nicaraguan, Panamanian, Salvadoran, and other Central American; (2) Includes Argentinian, Bolivian, Chilean, Colombian, Ecuadorian, Paraguayan, Peruvan, Uruguayan, Venezuelan, and other South American

Median Home Value

(Universe: Specified Owner-Occupied Housing Units)

Place	All specified owner-occupied housing units	Specified housing units owned and occup. by Hispanics	Argentinian	Bolivian	Central American[1]	Chilean	Colombian	Costa Rican	Cuban	Dominican	Ecuadorian	Guatelmalan	Honduran	Mexican	Nicaraguan	Panamanian	Paraguayan	Peruvian	Puerto Rican	Salvadoran	South American[2]	Spaniard	Uruguayan	Venezuelan	Other Hisp.
UNITED STATES	119,600	105,600	180,000	169,900	131,400	157,700	142,400	138,800	135,700	130,300	155,900	133,000	106,300	95,300	128,200	134,800	177,300	151,100	112,500	132,700	153,100	162,100	150,500	146,600	100,700
FLORIDA	105,500	113,000	140,900	136,400	102,400	127,500	116,700	107,600	129,000	102,900	110,800	100,000	96,200	80,600	105,800	109,800	107,700	120,000	95,200	98,300	121,900	127,800	120,000	140,500	104,900
Alachua County	97,300	98,400	-	-	67,700	-	65,800	-	98,000	-	-	-	-	93,900	-	-	-	-	106,000	-	91,700	-	-	-	115,200
Gainesville (city)	86,300	83,400	-	-	-	-	-	-	84,400	-	-	-	-	93,200	-	-	-	-	84,500	-	76,700	-	-	-	92,100
Bay County	93,500	88,800	-	-	-	-	-	-	-	-	-	-	-	83,800	-	-	-	-	87,500	-	-	-	-	-	73,100
Brevard County	94,400	87,600	-	-	81,700	-	112,500	-	94,700	76,400	-	-	-	86,700	-	88,300	-	-	85,200	-	87,200	-	-	-	94,600
Melbourne (city)	85,400	84,000	-	-	-	-	-	-	-	-	-	-	-	80,000	-	-	-	-	87,400	-	-	-	-	-	80,000
Palm Bay (city)	78,300	79,500	-	-	-	-	-	-	-	-	-	-	-	70,000	-	-	-	-	78,100	-	77,300	-	-	-	86,500
Broward County	128,600	127,100	145,000	138,600	109,500	137,500	124,700	112,500	141,900	111,100	121,000	104,900	93,300	113,300	116,700	132,900	-	118,900	117,200	106,000	130,100	153,800	114,800	154,400	122,200
Coral Springs (city)	175,500	159,900	-	-	158,400	-	167,600	-	171,400	127,700	148,500	-	-	159,300	-	-	-	134,100	158,500	-	158,700	-	-	189,600	141,600
Davie (town)	151,900	142,900	-	-	149,500	-	150,000	-	159,500	-	-	-	-	124,100	-	-	-	115,900	129,300	-	148,900	-	-	-	128,700
Deerfield Beach (city)	118,600	112,800	-	-	135,400	-	151,600	-	87,800	-	-	-	-	130,000	-	-	-	-	113,400	-	112,900	-	-	-	106,300
Fort Lauderdale (city)	150,100	111,300	-	-	111,000	-	124,100	-	103,400	-	-	85,000	-	88,800	-	-	-	105,400	92,500	66,300	180,900	-	-	-	111,800
Hollywood (city)	109,000	97,300	85,400	-	87,600	92,000	97,200	-	103,400	89,000	92,500	-	78,600	103,600	86,800	-	-	111,900	96,700	-	98,000	-	-	162,200	95,600
Lauderhill (city)	111,000	127,200	-	-	-	-	113,500	-	-	-	-	-	-	-	-	-	-	-	107,700	-	125,300	-	-	-	132,700
Margate (city)	109,500	108,500	-	-	104,000	-	117,500	-	122,100	-	-	-	-	85,500	-	-	-	-	106,700	-	113,000	-	-	-	89,300
Miramar (city)	116,200	135,100	-	-	119,000	-	131,900	-	153,100	107,600	-	-	-	104,500	133,400	137,500	-	158,600	125,600	-	143,000	-	-	-	126,800
Pembroke Pines (city)	143,200	145,700	-	-	122,500	-	144,800	-	151,900	138,000	136,700	-	-	144,100	-	-	-	137,100	141,800	-	144,800	-	-	152,800	139,400
Plantation (city)	158,000	147,000	-	-	159,600	-	138,700	-	159,200	-	-	-	-	152,500	-	-	-	128,000	134,600	-	137,800	-	-	135,900	149,400
Pompano Beach (city)	135,700	130,700	-	-	-	-	-	-	173,900	-	-	-	-	117,200	-	-	-	-	84,500	-	139,100	-	-	-	134,200
Sunrise (city)	111,900	109,600	-	-	110,800	-	101,700	-	116,700	101,300	105,600	-	-	108,500	-	-	-	111,500	109,300	-	106,400	-	-	-	119,100
Tamarac (city)	95,200	95,400	-	-	-	-	86,800	-	101,600	-	-	-	-	-	-	-	-	-	95,200	-	89,900	-	-	-	95,700
Charlotte County	97,000	87,100	-	-	-	-	-	-	112,500	-	-	-	-	116,700	-	-	-	-	78,100	-	-	-	-	-	91,900
Citrus County	84,400	78,000	-	-	-	-	-	-	-	-	-	-	-	62,400	-	-	-	-	78,700	-	-	-	-	-	93,900
Clay County	108,400	95,300	-	-	-	-	-	-	-	-	-	-	-	94,100	-	-	-	-	93,100	-	-	-	-	-	100,500
Collier County	168,000	103,100	-	-	108,100	-	136,800	-	122,000	98,300	-	101,300	139,600	86,100	-	-	-	-	123,300	-	126,400	-	-	-	100,900
Duval County	89,600	94,000	-	-	89,100	-	89,900	-	107,800	90,000	-	-	-	96,500	-	84,600	-	99,000	89,400	-	100,000	-	-	-	97,000
Jacksonville (city)	87,800	93,800	-	-	89,300	-	105,800	-	105,900	90,000	-	-	-	97,500	-	80,000	-	-	89,300	-	100,600	-	-	-	96,000
Escambia County	85,700	83,000	-	-	107,500	-	-	-	133,900	-	-	-	-	81,000	-	-	-	-	102,200	-	85,200	-	-	-	76,300
Pensacola (city)	93,400	82,000	-	-	-	-	-	-	-	-	-	-	-	-	-	-	-	-	-	-	-	-	-	-	-
Hernando County	87,300	81,100	-	-	-	-	-	-	77,900	-	-	-	-	79,300	-	-	-	-	83,100	-	-	-	-	-	74,100
Spring Hill (cdp)	84,700	80,200	-	-	-	-	-	-	79,600	-	-	-	-	-	-	-	-	-	81,600	-	-	-	-	-	73,100
Hillsborough County	97,700	85,100	-	-	77,300	-	95,000	94,900	84,200	84,500	84,800	76,000	74,700	72,300	75,000	72,300	-	98,300	86,300	89,500	92,400	96,800	-	90,800	86,000

Notes: Please refer to the User's Guide for an explanation of data: data is arranged alphabetically by state, then county, then city within each county and only includes counties with populations > 99,999 and cities with populations > 49,999; (1) Includes Costa Rican, Guatemalan, Honduran, Nicaraguan, Panamanian, Salvadoran, and other Central American; (2) Includes Argentinian, Bolivian, Chilean, Colombian, Ecuadorian, Paraguayan, Peruvan, Uruguayan, Venezuelan, and other South American

Place	All specified owner-occupied housing units	Specified housing units owned and occup. by Hispanics	Argentinian	Bolivian	Central American[1]	Chilean	Colombian	Costa Rican	Cuban	Dominican	Ecuadorian	Guatemalan	Honduran	Mexican	Nicaraguan	Panamanian	Paraguayan	Peruvian	Puerto Rican	Salvadoran	South American[2]	Spaniard	Uruguayan	Venezuelan	Other Hisp.
Brandon (cdp)	101,500	99,600	-	-	85,600	-	-	-	110,300	-	-	-	-	87,700	-	-	-	-	101,800	-	97,500	-	-	-	107,000
Tampa (city)	81,500	73,600	-	-	70,800	-	84,800	-	75,200	56,800	70,000	-	70,500	65,000	81,000	67,900	-	-	70,600	-	89,500	83,300	-	88,800	75,200
Town 'n' Country (cdp)	91,800	81,900	-	-	74,800	-	90,800	-	82,800	83,100	-	-	-	75,300	-	-	-	-	81,900	-	87,100	-	-	-	82,000
Indian River County	104,000	82,300	-	-	83,300	-	-	-	80,400	-	-	-	-	65,800	-	-	-	-	87,300	-	110,100	-	-	-	97,800
Lake County	100,600	102,700	-	-	110,300	-	-	-	139,400	-	-	-	-	74,800	-	-	-	-	104,200	-	124,300	-	-	-	97,200
Lee County	112,900	83,500	-	-	78,800	-	98,500	-	94,500	85,100	-	60,800	118,800	74,900	-	-	-	-	78,500	-	106,200	-	-	-	84,600
Cape Coral (city)	110,800	97,900	-	-	-	-	97,300	-	98,800	88,900	-	-	-	113,700	-	-	-	-	95,100	-	97,400	-	-	-	97,800
Leon County	110,900	107,500	-	-	-	-	-	-	136,600	-	-	-	-	82,800	-	-	-	-	109,200	-	92,400	-	-	-	108,800
Tallahassee (city)	102,500	100,700	-	-	-	-	-	-	135,300	-	-	-	-	81,300	-	-	-	-	102,000	-	95,300	-	-	-	110,000
Manatee County	119,400	85,100	-	-	90,800	-	-	-	147,700	-	-	-	-	72,200	-	-	-	-	92,800	-	128,100	-	-	-	99,200
Marion County	81,300	77,200	-	-	69,600	-	63,400	-	87,800	-	-	-	-	85,500	-	-	-	-	74,400	-	92,500	-	-	-	83,300
Martin County	152,400	89,200	-	-	95,800	-	-	-	185,800	-	-	100,800	-	82,400	-	-	-	-	89,000	-	-	-	-	-	98,300
Miami-Dade County	124,000	128,100	152,700	137,100	109,600	135,200	122,600	120,600	132,900	110,800	119,000	111,000	102,900	98,800	108,200	120,700	-	130,300	111,600	111,000	129,800	142,600	135,600	140,200	119,100
Carol City (cdp)	87,700	91,800	-	-	91,800	-	88,100	-	93,500	93,400	-	-	87,300	-	89,200	-	-	-	91,300	-	89,600	-	-	-	85,600
Fountainbleau (cdp)	107,700	107,000	100,000	-	97,400	122,900	97,000	-	111,300	106,300	89,100	-	99,500	130,500	98,100	94,300	-	104,200	106,300	-	99,300	-	-	96,200	108,000
Hialeah (city)	113,900	114,000	88,400	-	99,900	99,300	101,400	111,900	116,200	110,600	111,800	96,400	87,800	120,000	99,400	-	-	109,700	104,500	87,700	105,000	109,500	-	103,600	103,400
Kendale Lakes (cdp)	119,600	119,200	-	-	97,600	-	104,900	-	126,400	113,000	-	-	135,200	108,100	96,400	-	-	101,500	123,100	-	111,100	-	-	120,800	99,400
Kendall (cdp)	175,700	168,700	150,600	-	145,800	165,300	144,900	-	186,000	118,500	-	-	-	-	138,900	-	-	147,700	158,300	-	150,600	-	-	141,100	150,400
Miami Beach (city)	334,400	246,600	384,400	-	445,200	531,300	403,800	-	231,300	371,400	450,000	-	450,000	104,700	-	-	-	175,000	161,800	-	376,400	190,600	-	365,400	210,000
Miami (city)	120,100	124,000	145,800	-	110,700	149,200	129,900	136,700	126,000	117,100	154,700	116,000	100,000	134,600	116,100	126,300	-	143,300	95,900	122,800	141,300	119,100	-	182,500	116,700
North Miami (city)	91,400	90,400	-	-	88,100	-	82,000	-	92,300	90,900	-	-	87,400	-	85,500	-	-	-	86,700	-	97,900	-	-	-	87,000
Tamiami (cdp)	141,200	141,400	-	-	130,600	-	144,400	-	143,200	138,700	-	-	92,900	132,600	129,300	-	-	-	138,500	-	136,400	-	-	121,300	133,900
Okaloosa County	101,200	94,300	-	-	127,100	-	-	-	157,800	-	-	-	-	85,900	-	-	-	-	87,800	-	-	-	-	-	117,900
Orange County	107,500	96,100	132,800	-	94,800	205,000	112,000	100,000	100,300	93,000	109,600	106,400	99,200	82,700	76,800	101,000	-	103,100	94,700	83,600	111,700	118,100	-	108,600	97,900
Orlando (city)	103,200	89,400	-	-	77,600	-	107,900	-	92,500	89,300	-	-	-	107,100	-	-	-	81,100	85,500	-	104,900	-	-	99,500	89,600
Osceola County	99,300	95,800	-	-	103,200	-	86,000	-	101,400	100,000	101,300	-	-	95,100	-	-	-	-	95,700	100,500	90,800	-	-	115,300	90,900
Palm Beach County	135,200	100,100	130,200	-	90,400	99,200	99,500	97,500	106,500	98,600	110,300	89,200	87,000	85,400	88,800	99,700	-	127,000	97,500	84,400	113,800	95,000	106,300	143,900	106,300
Boca Raton (city)	230,200	180,000	-	-	-	-	159,000	-	167,300	-	-	-	-	181,700	-	-	-	-	177,500	-	233,800	-	-	-	168,200
Boynton Beach (city)	96,100	91,300	-	-	111,700	-	-	-	112,900	-	-	-	-	85,100	-	-	-	-	75,800	-	98,600	-	-	-	87,600
Delray Beach (city)	127,700	97,000	-	-	-	-	-	-	-	-	-	-	-	63,000	-	-	-	-	87,100	-	137,500	-	-	-	129,500
West Palm Beach (city)	98,000	82,900	-	-	86,300	-	81,200	-	81,900	76,000	-	69,400	-	72,900	-	-	-	-	81,500	-	88,200	-	-	-	89,200
Pasco County	79,600	87,200	-	-	87,900	-	-	-	109,400	-	-	-	-	55,400	-	-	-	-	89,300	-	73,000	-	-	-	94,800
Pinellas County	96,500	89,200	-	-	118,200	-	101,000	-	90,500	76,800	91,300	-	-	81,200	-	-	-	89,800	86,200	-	99,400	132,100	-	87,600	97,800
Clearwater (city)	100,500	88,200	-	-	-	-	75,000	-	107,800	-	-	-	-	71,800	-	-	-	-	91,100	-	74,400	-	-	-	96,800
Largo (city)	88,800	81,100	-	-	-	-	-	-	-	-	-	-	-	84,000	-	-	-	-	78,000	-	-	-	-	-	-
Palm Harbor (cdp)	124,700	111,400	-	-	-	-	-	-	-	-	-	-	-	-	-	-	-	-	109,800	-	-	-	-	-	-
St. Petersburg (city)	81,000	78,800	-	-	-	-	-	-	74,200	-	-	-	-	68,600	-	-	-	-	79,100	-	85,900	-	-	-	79,000

Notes: Please refer to the User's Guide for an explanation of data: data is arranged alphabetically by state, then county, then city within each county and only includes counties with populations > 99,999 and cities with populations > 49,999; (1) Includes Costa Rican, Guatemalan, Honduran, Nicaraguan, Panamanian, Salvadoran, and other Central American; (2) Includes Argentinian, Bolivian, Chilean, Colombian, Ecuadorian, Paraguayan, Peruvian, Uruguayan, Venezuelan, and other South American

Place	All specified owner-occupied housing units	Specified housing units owned and occup. by Hispanics	Argentinian	Bolivian	Central American[1]	Chilean	Colombian	Costa Rican	Cuban	Dominican	Ecuadorian	Guatelmalan	Honduran	Mexican	Nicaraguan	Panamanian	Paraguayan	Peruvian	Puerto Rican	Salvadoran	South American[2]	Spaniard	Uruguayan	Venezuelan	Other Hisp.
Polk County	83,300	72,200	-	-	84,000	-	-	-	103,500	81,200	-	-	-	52,800	-	-	-	-	82,600	-	85,500	-	-	-	91,000
Lakeland (city)	81,100	72,100	-	-	-	-	-	-	87,100	-	-	-	-	55,400	-	-	-	-	65,600	-	-	-	-	-	78,600
St. Johns County	158,400	174,300	-	-	-	-	-	-	-	-	-	-	-	98,200	-	-	-	-	148,500	-	-	-	-	-	182,500
St. Lucie County	86,100	76,600	-	-	97,900	-	69,400	-	82,800	-	-	-	-	56,200	-	-	-	-	84,700	-	83,100	-	-	-	79,100
Port St. Lucie (city)	88,700	85,400	-	-	-	-	-	-	83,500	-	-	-	-	75,200	-	-	-	-	87,000	-	86,900	-	-	-	82,900
Santa Rosa County	106,000	106,500	-	-	-	-	-	-	-	-	-	-	-	97,800	-	-	-	-	110,600	-	-	-	-	-	106,500
Sarasota County	122,000	96,200	-	-	94,300	-	117,500	-	94,500	-	-	-	-	93,800	-	-	-	-	107,200	-	106,500	-	-	-	97,700
Sarasota (city)	96,000	84,800	-	-	-	-	-	-	74,000	-	-	-	-	85,100	-	-	-	-	103,600	-	87,500	-	-	-	76,400
Seminole County	119,900	104,700	152,800	-	99,800	-	116,900	-	112,300	100,200	99,100	-	-	108,600	-	95,000	-	116,400	102,200	-	117,800	-	-	109,700	97,800
Volusia County	87,300	83,500	-	-	75,300	-	84,000	-	81,800	77,000	-	-	-	73,100	-	-	-	-	84,000	-	85,900	-	-	-	97,800
Daytona Beach (city)	79,700	84,100	-	-	-	-	-	-	-	-	-	-	-	-	-	-	-	-	78,600	-	-	-	-	-	94,400
Deltona (city)	82,200	83,800	-	-	-	-	-	-	73,800	-	-	-	-	94,400	-	-	-	-	83,500	-	92,400	-	-	-	88,800

Notes: Please refer to the User's Guide for an explanation of data; data is arranged alphabetically by state, then county, then city within each county and only includes counties with populations > 99,999 and cities with populations > 49,999; (1) Includes Costa Rican, Guatemalan, Honduran, Nicaraguan, Panamanian, Salvadoran, and other Central American; (2) Includes Argentinian, Bolivian, Chilean, Colombian, Ecuadorian, Paraguayan, Peruvian, Uruguayan, Venezuelan, and other South American

Population

Total Population
Top 10 Places Sorted by Number

Place (place type) County	Number
Jacksonville (city) Duval	735,503
Miami (city) Miami-Dade	362,563
Tampa (city) Hillsborough	303,512
St. Petersburg (city) Pinellas	247,793
Hialeah (city) Miami-Dade	226,411
Orlando (city) Orange	185,984
Fort Lauderdale (city) Broward	152,125
Tallahassee (city) Leon	150,581
Hollywood (city) Broward	139,261
Pembroke Pines (city) Broward	137,112

Hispanic
Top 10 Places Sorted by Number

Place (place type) County	Number
Miami (city) Miami-Dade	238,461
Hialeah (city) Miami-Dade	204,808
Tampa (city) Hillsborough	58,571
Fountainbleau (cdp) Miami-Dade	51,833
Tamiami (cdp) Miami-Dade	47,691
Miami Beach (city) Miami-Dade	46,980
Kendale Lakes (cdp) Miami-Dade	43,588
Pembroke Pines (city) Broward	38,348
Kendall (cdp) Miami-Dade	37,640
Orlando (city) Orange	32,897

Hispanic
Top 10 Places Sorted by Percent of Total Population

Place (place type) County	Percent
Sweetwater (city) Miami-Dade	93.61
Hialeah (city) Miami-Dade	90.46
Hialeah Gardens (city) Miami-Dade	90.13
Tamiami (cdp) Miami-Dade	87.11
Fountainbleau (cdp) Miami-Dade	87.09
Westchester (cdp) Miami-Dade	85.43
University Park (cdp) Miami-Dade	82.77
Coral Terrace (cdp) Miami-Dade	81.92
Kendall West (cdp) Miami-Dade	79.15
Kendale Lakes (cdp) Miami-Dade	76.62

Argentinian
Top 10 Places Sorted by Number

Place (place type) County	Number
Miami Beach (city) Miami-Dade	3,031
Miami (city) Miami-Dade	2,029
Kendall (cdp) Miami-Dade	655
Sunny Isles Beach (city) Miami-Dade	571
Hollywood (city) Broward	559
Fountainbleau (cdp) Miami-Dade	440
Hialeah (city) Miami-Dade	429

Argentinian
Top 10 Places Sorted by Percent of Hispanic Population

Place (place type) County	Percent
Sunny Isles Beach (city) Miami-Dade	10.19
Miami Beach (city) Miami-Dade	6.45
Hollywood (city) Broward	1.78
Kendall (cdp) Miami-Dade	1.74
Fountainbleau (cdp) Miami-Dade	0.85
Miami (city) Miami-Dade	0.85
Hialeah (city) Miami-Dade	0.21

Argentinian
Top 10 Places Sorted by Percent of Total Population

Place (place type) County	Percent
Sunny Isles Beach (city) Miami-Dade	3.74
Miami Beach (city) Miami-Dade	3.44
Kendall (cdp) Miami-Dade	0.87
Fountainbleau (cdp) Miami-Dade	0.74
Miami (city) Miami-Dade	0.56
Hollywood (city) Broward	0.40
Hialeah (city) Miami-Dade	0.19

Bolivian
Top 10 Places Sorted by Number

Place (place type) County	Number

No places met population threshold.

Bolivian
Top 10 Places Sorted by Percent of Hispanic Population

Place (place type) County	Percent

No places met population threshold.

Bolivian
Top 10 Places Sorted by Percent of Total Population

Place (place type) County	Percent

No places met population threshold.

Central American
Top 10 Places Sorted by Number

Place (place type) County	Number
Miami (city) Miami-Dade	43,925
Hialeah (city) Miami-Dade	15,904
Fountainbleau (cdp) Miami-Dade	8,161
Kendale Lakes (cdp) Miami-Dade	4,079
Tamiami (cdp) Miami-Dade	3,850
Kendall (cdp) Miami-Dade	3,845
Homestead (city) Miami-Dade	3,418
Tampa (city) Hillsborough	3,229
Lake Worth (city) Palm Beach	3,204
Miami Beach (city) Miami-Dade	2,823

Central American
Top 10 Places Sorted by Percent of Hispanic Population

Place (place type) County	Percent
Gladeview (cdp) Miami-Dade	33.13
Lake Worth (city) Palm Beach	30.78
Brownsville (cdp) Miami-Dade	29.13
Palmetto Estates (cdp) Miami-Dade	23.77
Oakland Park (city) Broward	21.52
Homestead (city) Miami-Dade	19.95
Pinewood (cdp) Miami-Dade	19.77
West Little River (cdp) Miami-Dade	19.30
Sweetwater (city) Miami-Dade	19.19
West Palm Beach (city) Palm Beach	18.66

Central American
Top 10 Places Sorted by Percent of Total Population

Place (place type) County	Percent
Sweetwater (city) Miami-Dade	17.97
Fountainbleau (cdp) Miami-Dade	13.71
Miami (city) Miami-Dade	12.12
Homestead (city) Miami-Dade	10.67
Lake Worth (city) Palm Beach	9.09
West Little River (cdp) Miami-Dade	7.74
Kendale Lakes (cdp) Miami-Dade	7.17
Gladeview (cdp) Miami-Dade	7.03
Tamiami (cdp) Miami-Dade	7.03
Hialeah (city) Miami-Dade	7.02

Chilean
Top 10 Places Sorted by Number

Place (place type) County	Number
Miami (city) Miami-Dade	897
Hialeah (city) Miami-Dade	750
Miami Beach (city) Miami-Dade	739
Fountainbleau (cdp) Miami-Dade	703
Kendall (cdp) Miami-Dade	480
Hollywood (city) Broward	377

Chilean
Top 10 Places Sorted by Percent of Hispanic Population

Place (place type) County	Percent
Miami Beach (city) Miami-Dade	1.57
Fountainbleau (cdp) Miami-Dade	1.36
Kendall (cdp) Miami-Dade	1.28
Hollywood (city) Broward	1.20
Miami (city) Miami-Dade	0.38
Hialeah (city) Miami-Dade	0.37

Chilean
Top 10 Places Sorted by Percent of Total Population

Place (place type) County	Percent
Fountainbleau (cdp) Miami-Dade	1.18
Miami Beach (city) Miami-Dade	0.84
Kendall (cdp) Miami-Dade	0.64
Hialeah (city) Miami-Dade	0.33
Hollywood (city) Broward	0.27
Miami (city) Miami-Dade	0.25

Columbian
Top 10 Places Sorted by Number

Place (place type) County	Number
Hialeah (city) Miami-Dade	7,715
Miami (city) Miami-Dade	6,006
The Hammocks (cdp) Miami-Dade	4,988
Miami Beach (city) Miami-Dade	4,493
Kendall West (cdp) Miami-Dade	4,368
Kendall (cdp) Miami-Dade	4,130
Kendale Lakes (cdp) Miami-Dade	4,003
Country Club (cdp) Miami-Dade	3,669
Pembroke Pines (city) Broward	3,463
Hollywood (city) Broward	3,312

Columbian
Top 10 Places Sorted by Percent of Hispanic Population

Place (place type) County	Percent
Weston (city) Broward	19.92
Aventura (city) Miami-Dade	19.46
Plantation (city) Broward	19.44
Sandalfoot Cove (cdp) Palm Beach	17.24
Sunrise (city) Broward	16.92
Country Club (cdp) Miami-Dade	16.61
The Hammocks (cdp) Miami-Dade	16.07
Tamarac (city) Broward	15.75
Key Biscayne (village) Miami-Dade	15.34
Sunny Isles Beach (city) Miami-Dade	15.02

Columbian
Top 10 Places Sorted by Percent of Total Population

Place (place type) County	Percent
Kendall West (cdp) Miami-Dade	11.51
The Hammocks (cdp) Miami-Dade	10.52
Country Club (cdp) Miami-Dade	10.08
Doral (cdp) Miami-Dade	7.74
The Crossings (cdp) Miami-Dade	7.72
Key Biscayne (village) Miami-Dade	7.64
Kendale Lakes (cdp) Miami-Dade	7.04
Weston (city) Broward	6.11
Sunny Isles Beach (city) Miami-Dade	5.51
Kendall (cdp) Miami-Dade	5.49

Costa Rican
Top 10 Places Sorted by Number

Place (place type) County	Number
Miami (city) Miami-Dade	816
Hialeah (city) Miami-Dade	523

Costa Rican
Top 10 Places Sorted by Percent of Hispanic Population

Place (place type) County	Percent
Miami (city) Miami-Dade	0.34
Hialeah (city) Miami-Dade	0.26

Notes: Please refer to the User's Guide for an explanation of data; tables include places with populations > 9,999 and reflect only those areas that meet Summary File 4 population thresholds, therefore there may be less than 10 places listed

Costa Rican
Top 10 Places Sorted by Percent of Total Population

Place (place type) County	Percent
Hialeah (city) Miami-Dade	0.23
Miami (city) Miami-Dade	0.23

Cuban
Top 10 Places Sorted by Number

Place (place type) County	Number
Hialeah (city) Miami-Dade	141,302
Miami (city) Miami-Dade	124,734
Tamiami (cdp) Miami-Dade	32,381
Fountainbleau (cdp) Miami-Dade	22,301
Kendale Lakes (cdp) Miami-Dade	22,057
Westchester (cdp) Miami-Dade	20,420
Miami Beach (city) Miami-Dade	18,241
Kendall (cdp) Miami-Dade	15,868
University Park (cdp) Miami-Dade	15,699
Coral Terrace (cdp) Miami-Dade	15,063

Cuban
Top 10 Places Sorted by Percent of Hispanic Population

Place (place type) County	Percent
Westchester (cdp) Miami-Dade	78.98
Coral Terrace (cdp) Miami-Dade	75.48
Olympia Heights (cdp) Miami-Dade	75.21
Westwood Lakes (cdp) Miami-Dade	74.82
University Park (cdp) Miami-Dade	71.64
Sunset (cdp) Miami-Dade	69.36
Hialeah (city) Miami-Dade	68.99
Tamiami (cdp) Miami-Dade	67.90
Miami Lakes (cdp) Miami-Dade	63.74
Key Largo (cdp) Monroe	63.33

Cuban
Top 10 Places Sorted by Percent of Total Population

Place (place type) County	Percent
Westchester (cdp) Miami-Dade	67.48
Hialeah (city) Miami-Dade	62.41
Coral Terrace (cdp) Miami-Dade	61.84
University Park (cdp) Miami-Dade	59.30
Tamiami (cdp) Miami-Dade	59.15
Olympia Heights (cdp) Miami-Dade	57.28
Westwood Lakes (cdp) Miami-Dade	57.26
Hialeah Gardens (city) Miami-Dade	57.02
Sweetwater (city) Miami-Dade	53.92
Sunset (cdp) Miami-Dade	48.24

Dominican
Top 10 Places Sorted by Number

Place (place type) County	Number
Miami (city) Miami-Dade	7,270
Hialeah (city) Miami-Dade	4,886
Fountainbleau (cdp) Miami-Dade	1,928
Carol City (cdp) Miami-Dade	1,883
Pembroke Pines (city) Broward	1,809
Hollywood (city) Broward	1,688
The Hammocks (cdp) Miami-Dade	1,519
Tampa (city) Hillsborough	1,426
Miramar (city) Broward	1,412
Miami Beach (city) Miami-Dade	1,396

Dominican
Top 10 Places Sorted by Percent of Hispanic Population

Place (place type) County	Percent
Golden Glades (cdp) Miami-Dade	10.41
West Little River (cdp) Miami-Dade	7.74
North Miami (city) Miami-Dade	7.67
North Miami Beach (city) Miami-Dade	7.59
Carol City (cdp) Miami-Dade	7.54
Cape Coral (city) Lee	6.97
Oak Ridge (cdp) Orange	6.85
Miramar (city) Broward	6.56
Country Club (cdp) Miami-Dade	6.20
Kissimmee (city) Osceola	5.88

Dominican
Top 10 Places Sorted by Percent of Total Population

Place (place type) County	Percent
Country Club (cdp) Miami-Dade	3.76
Hialeah Gardens (city) Miami-Dade	3.45
Fountainbleau (cdp) Miami-Dade	3.24
The Hammocks (cdp) Miami-Dade	3.20
Carol City (cdp) Miami-Dade	3.17
Richmond West (cdp) Miami-Dade	3.14
West Little River (cdp) Miami-Dade	3.10
South Miami Heights (cdp) Miami-Dade	2.91
Oak Ridge (cdp) Orange	2.87
Yeehaw Junction (cdp) Osceola	2.64

Ecuadorian
Top 10 Places Sorted by Number

Place (place type) County	Number
Miami (city) Miami-Dade	1,755
Hialeah (city) Miami-Dade	1,233
Coral Springs (city) Broward	942
Fountainbleau (cdp) Miami-Dade	799
Miami Beach (city) Miami-Dade	662
Hollywood (city) Broward	628
Sunrise (city) Broward	529
Pembroke Pines (city) Broward	486
Tampa (city) Hillsborough	418

Ecuadorian
Top 10 Places Sorted by Percent of Hispanic Population

Place (place type) County	Percent
Coral Springs (city) Broward	5.15
Sunrise (city) Broward	3.64
Hollywood (city) Broward	2.00
Fountainbleau (cdp) Miami-Dade	1.54
Miami Beach (city) Miami-Dade	1.41
Pembroke Pines (city) Broward	1.27
Miami (city) Miami-Dade	0.74
Tampa (city) Hillsborough	0.71
Hialeah (city) Miami-Dade	0.60

Ecuadorian
Top 10 Places Sorted by Percent of Total Population

Place (place type) County	Percent
Fountainbleau (cdp) Miami-Dade	1.34
Coral Springs (city) Broward	0.80
Miami Beach (city) Miami-Dade	0.75
Sunrise (city) Broward	0.62
Hialeah (city) Miami-Dade	0.54
Miami (city) Miami-Dade	0.48
Hollywood (city) Broward	0.45
Pembroke Pines (city) Broward	0.35
Tampa (city) Hillsborough	0.14

Guatelmalan
Top 10 Places Sorted by Number

Place (place type) County	Number
Miami (city) Miami-Dade	2,851
West Palm Beach (city) Palm Beach	2,060
Lake Worth (city) Palm Beach	1,966
Homestead (city) Miami-Dade	1,435
Immokalee (cdp) Collier	1,154
Hialeah (city) Miami-Dade	842
Fort Myers (city) Lee	393
Fort Lauderdale (city) Broward	371
Bonita Springs (city) Lee	369

Guatelmalan
Top 10 Places Sorted by Percent of Hispanic Population

Place (place type) County	Percent
Lake Worth (city) Palm Beach	18.89
West Palm Beach (city) Palm Beach	13.73
Immokalee (cdp) Collier	8.44
Homestead (city) Miami-Dade	8.37
Bonita Springs (city) Lee	6.53
Fort Myers (city) Lee	5.75
Fort Lauderdale (city) Broward	2.67
Miami (city) Miami-Dade	1.20
Hialeah (city) Miami-Dade	0.41

Guatelmalan
Top 10 Places Sorted by Percent of Total Population

Place (place type) County	Percent
Immokalee (cdp) Collier	5.95
Lake Worth (city) Palm Beach	5.58
Homestead (city) Miami-Dade	4.48
West Palm Beach (city) Palm Beach	2.53
Bonita Springs (city) Lee	1.12
Fort Myers (city) Lee	0.82
Miami (city) Miami-Dade	0.79
Hialeah (city) Miami-Dade	0.37
Fort Lauderdale (city) Broward	0.24

Honduran
Top 10 Places Sorted by Number

Place (place type) County	Number
Miami (city) Miami-Dade	13,660
Hialeah (city) Miami-Dade	2,651
West Little River (cdp) Miami-Dade	975
Tampa (city) Hillsborough	894
Miami Beach (city) Miami-Dade	810
Fountainbleau (cdp) Miami-Dade	642
North Miami (city) Miami-Dade	590
Kendale Lakes (cdp) Miami-Dade	557
Carol City (cdp) Miami-Dade	518
North Miami Beach (city) Miami-Dade	509

Honduran
Top 10 Places Sorted by Percent of Hispanic Population

Place (place type) County	Percent
West Little River (cdp) Miami-Dade	7.53
Miami (city) Miami-Dade	5.73
Lake Worth (city) Palm Beach	4.65
North Miami Beach (city) Miami-Dade	4.13
North Miami (city) Miami-Dade	4.12
Carol City (cdp) Miami-Dade	2.07
Miami Beach (city) Miami-Dade	1.72
Tampa (city) Hillsborough	1.53
Hollywood (city) Broward	1.41
Hialeah (city) Miami-Dade	1.29

Honduran
Top 10 Places Sorted by Percent of Total Population

Place (place type) County	Percent
Miami (city) Miami-Dade	3.77
West Little River (cdp) Miami-Dade	3.02
Lake Worth (city) Palm Beach	1.37
North Miami Beach (city) Miami-Dade	1.25
Hialeah (city) Miami-Dade	1.17
Fountainbleau (cdp) Miami-Dade	1.08
Kendale Lakes (cdp) Miami-Dade	0.98
North Miami (city) Miami-Dade	0.98
Miami Beach (city) Miami-Dade	0.92
Carol City (cdp) Miami-Dade	0.87

Mexican
Top 10 Places Sorted by Number

Place (place type) County	Number
Immokalee (cdp) Collier	10,817
Tampa (city) Hillsborough	7,216
Homestead (city) Miami-Dade	7,106
Jacksonville (city) Duval	5,521
Leisure City (cdp) Miami-Dade	5,441
Clearwater (city) Pinellas	4,211
Fort Pierce (city) Saint Lucie	4,177
Golden Gate (cdp) Collier	3,689
Bradenton (city) Manatee	3,625
Sarasota (city) Sarasota	3,545

Notes: Please refer to the User's Guide for an explanation of data; tables include places with populations > 9,999 and reflect only those areas that meet Summary File 4 population thresholds, therefore there may be less than 10 places listed

Mexican

Top 10 Places Sorted by Percent of Hispanic Population

Place (place type) County	Percent
Palmetto (city) Manatee	80.37
Immokalee (cdp) Collier	79.13
Haines City (city) Polk	75.16
Auburndale (city) Polk	74.73
Fort Pierce (city) Saint Lucie	71.81
Plant City (city) Hillsborough	67.40
Bradenton (city) Manatee	64.52
Lake Wales (city) Polk	64.31
Bonita Springs (city) Lee	59.18
De Land (city) Volusia	58.30

Mexican

Top 10 Places Sorted by Percent of Total Population

Place (place type) County	Percent
Immokalee (cdp) Collier	55.73
Leisure City (cdp) Miami-Dade	24.99
Homestead (city) Miami-Dade	22.17
Palmetto (city) Manatee	20.97
Lake Worth Corridor (cdp) Palm Beach	17.58
Golden Gate (cdp) Collier	17.56
Haines City (city) Polk	17.49
Belle Glade (city) Palm Beach	15.47
Plant City (city) Hillsborough	11.61
Fort Pierce (city) Saint Lucie	11.14

Nicaraguan

Top 10 Places Sorted by Number

Place (place type) County	Number
Miami (city) Miami-Dade	22,571
Hialeah (city) Miami-Dade	10,161
Fountainbleau (cdp) Miami-Dade	6,120
Kendale Lakes (cdp) Miami-Dade	2,847
Tamiami (cdp) Miami-Dade	2,757
Sweetwater (city) Miami-Dade	2,404
Kendall (cdp) Miami-Dade	2,232
Kendall West (cdp) Miami-Dade	1,598
The Hammocks (cdp) Miami-Dade	1,526
Carol City (cdp) Miami-Dade	1,448

Nicaraguan

Top 10 Places Sorted by Percent of Hispanic Population

Place (place type) County	Percent
Gladeview (cdp) Miami-Dade	26.78
Sweetwater (city) Miami-Dade	18.00
Pinewood (cdp) Miami-Dade	15.00
Fountainbleau (cdp) Miami-Dade	11.81
Palmetto Estates (cdp) Miami-Dade	11.63
Miami (city) Miami-Dade	9.47
West Little River (cdp) Miami-Dade	8.75
Kendale Lakes (cdp) Miami-Dade	6.53
Richmond West (cdp) Miami-Dade	6.17
Kendall (cdp) Miami-Dade	5.93

Nicaraguan

Top 10 Places Sorted by Percent of Total Population

Place (place type) County	Percent
Sweetwater (city) Miami-Dade	16.85
Fountainbleau (cdp) Miami-Dade	10.28
Miami (city) Miami-Dade	6.23
Gladeview (cdp) Miami-Dade	5.69
Tamiami (cdp) Miami-Dade	5.04
Kendale Lakes (cdp) Miami-Dade	5.00
Hialeah (city) Miami-Dade	4.49
Hialeah Gardens (city) Miami-Dade	4.38
Richmond West (cdp) Miami-Dade	4.32
Kendall West (cdp) Miami-Dade	4.21

Panamanian

Top 10 Places Sorted by Number

Place (place type) County	Number
Miami (city) Miami-Dade	883
Tampa (city) Hillsborough	632
Jacksonville (city) Duval	581
Fountainbleau (cdp) Miami-Dade	522
Miramar (city) Broward	367

Panamanian

Top 10 Places Sorted by Percent of Hispanic Population

Place (place type) County	Percent
Jacksonville (city) Duval	1.91
Miramar (city) Broward	1.70
Tampa (city) Hillsborough	1.08
Fountainbleau (cdp) Miami-Dade	1.01
Miami (city) Miami-Dade	0.37

Panamanian

Top 10 Places Sorted by Percent of Total Population

Place (place type) County	Percent
Fountainbleau (cdp) Miami-Dade	0.88
Miramar (city) Broward	0.50
Miami (city) Miami-Dade	0.24
Tampa (city) Hillsborough	0.21
Jacksonville (city) Duval	0.08

Paraguayan

Top 10 Places Sorted by Number

Place (place type) County	Number

No places met population threshold.

Paraguayan

Top 10 Places Sorted by Percent of Hispanic Population

Place (place type) County	Percent

No places met population threshold.

Paraguayan

Top 10 Places Sorted by Percent of Total Population

Place (place type) County	Percent

No places met population threshold.

Peruvian

Top 10 Places Sorted by Number

Place (place type) County	Number
Miami (city) Miami-Dade	2,767
Miami Beach (city) Miami-Dade	1,898
The Hammocks (cdp) Miami-Dade	1,821
Pembroke Pines (city) Broward	1,505
Hialeah (city) Miami-Dade	1,459
Kendall (cdp) Miami-Dade	1,370
Hollywood (city) Broward	1,337
Fountainbleau (cdp) Miami-Dade	1,181
Kendall West (cdp) Miami-Dade	1,147
Kendale Lakes (cdp) Miami-Dade	967

Peruvian

Top 10 Places Sorted by Percent of Hispanic Population

Place (place type) County	Percent
North Lauderdale (city) Broward	7.92
North Miami Beach (city) Miami-Dade	6.36
The Hammocks (cdp) Miami-Dade	5.87
Coral Springs (city) Broward	5.21
Weston (city) Broward	4.79
Plantation (city) Broward	4.59
Davie (town) Broward	4.49
The Crossings (cdp) Miami-Dade	4.48
Hollywood (city) Broward	4.26
Sunrise (city) Broward	4.08

Peruvian

Top 10 Places Sorted by Percent of Total Population

Place (place type) County	Percent
The Hammocks (cdp) Miami-Dade	3.84
Kendall West (cdp) Miami-Dade	3.02
Doral (cdp) Miami-Dade	2.66
The Crossings (cdp) Miami-Dade	2.55
Miami Beach (city) Miami-Dade	2.16
Fountainbleau (cdp) Miami-Dade	1.98
North Miami Beach (city) Miami-Dade	1.93
Richmond West (cdp) Miami-Dade	1.86
Kendall (cdp) Miami-Dade	1.82
North Lauderdale (city) Broward	1.72

Puerto Rican

Top 10 Places Sorted by Number

Place (place type) County	Number
Orlando (city) Orange	16,701
Tampa (city) Hillsborough	15,837
Kissimmee (city) Osceola	12,079
Jacksonville (city) Duval	10,924
Miami (city) Miami-Dade	10,138
Deltona (city) Volusia	9,488
Yeehaw Junction (cdp) Osceola	8,357
Town 'n' Country (cdp) Hillsborough	7,453
Pembroke Pines (city) Broward	7,370
Hialeah (city) Miami-Dade	6,971

Puerto Rican

Top 10 Places Sorted by Percent of Hispanic Population

Place (place type) County	Percent
Poinciana (cdp) Osceola	78.45
Deltona (city) Volusia	73.81
Zephyrhills (city) Pasco	72.73
Yeehaw Junction (cdp) Osceola	68.99
St. Cloud (city) Osceola	66.40
Lockhart (cdp) Orange	65.55
Spring Hill (cdp) Hernando	62.80
Meadow Woods (cdp) Orange	62.60
Azalea Park (cdp) Orange	61.54
Kissimmee (city) Osceola	61.46

Puerto Rican

Top 10 Places Sorted by Percent of Total Population

Place (place type) County	Percent
Yeehaw Junction (cdp) Osceola	37.71
Meadow Woods (cdp) Orange	33.14
Poinciana (cdp) Osceola	31.19
Kissimmee (city) Osceola	25.40
Azalea Park (cdp) Orange	23.90
Oak Ridge (cdp) Orange	17.35
Union Park (cdp) Orange	16.24
Deltona (city) Volusia	13.59
Egypt Lake-Leto (cdp) Hillsborough	10.35
Town 'n' Country (cdp) Hillsborough	10.29

Salvadoran

Top 10 Places Sorted by Number

Place (place type) County	Number
Miami (city) Miami-Dade	2,394
Homestead (city) Miami-Dade	1,120
Hialeah (city) Miami-Dade	950
Oakland Park (city) Broward	775
Fort Lauderdale (city) Broward	664
Lake Worth (city) Palm Beach	527

Salvadoran

Top 10 Places Sorted by Percent of Hispanic Population

Place (place type) County	Percent
Oakland Park (city) Broward	13.79
Homestead (city) Miami-Dade	6.54
Lake Worth (city) Palm Beach	5.06
Fort Lauderdale (city) Broward	4.78
Miami (city) Miami-Dade	1.00
Hialeah (city) Miami-Dade	0.46

Salvadoran

Top 10 Places Sorted by Percent of Total Population

Place (place type) County	Percent
Homestead (city) Miami-Dade	3.49
Oakland Park (city) Broward	2.48
Lake Worth (city) Palm Beach	1.50

Notes: Please refer to the User's Guide for an explanation of data; tables include places with populations > 9,999 and reflect only those areas that meet Summary File 4 population thresholds, therefore there may be less than 10 places listed

Miami (city) Miami-Dade	0.66
Fort Lauderdale (city) Broward	0.44
Hialeah (city) Miami-Dade	0.42

South American
Top 10 Places Sorted by Number

Place (place type) County	Number
Miami (city) Miami-Dade	15,956
Miami Beach (city) Miami-Dade	12,984
Hialeah (city) Miami-Dade	12,903
The Hammocks (cdp) Miami-Dade	9,791
Kendall (cdp) Miami-Dade	8,700
Fountainbleau (cdp) Miami-Dade	8,376
Pembroke Pines (city) Broward	7,815
Kendall West (cdp) Miami-Dade	7,733
Hollywood (city) Broward	7,347
Kendale Lakes (cdp) Miami-Dade	7,318

South American
Top 10 Places Sorted by Percent of Hispanic Population

Place (place type) County	Percent
Aventura (city) Miami-Dade	45.30
Weston (city) Broward	43.67
Sunny Isles Beach (city) Miami-Dade	40.74
Doral (cdp) Miami-Dade	37.28
Sandalfoot Cove (cdp) Palm Beach	35.73
Plantation (city) Broward	35.29
Ojus (cdp) Miami-Dade	34.77
Key Biscayne (village) Miami-Dade	34.75
Boca Raton (city) Palm Beach	32.74
The Hammocks (cdp) Miami-Dade	31.54

South American
Top 10 Places Sorted by Percent of Total Population

Place (place type) County	Percent
Doral (cdp) Miami-Dade	24.76
The Hammocks (cdp) Miami-Dade	20.64
Kendall West (cdp) Miami-Dade	20.37
Key Biscayne (village) Miami-Dade	17.30
The Crossings (cdp) Miami-Dade	16.83
Sunny Isles Beach (city) Miami-Dade	14.95
Country Club (cdp) Miami-Dade	14.78
Miami Beach (city) Miami-Dade	14.74
Fountainbleau (cdp) Miami-Dade	14.07
Weston (city) Broward	13.39

Spaniard
Top 10 Places Sorted by Number

Place (place type) County	Number
Miami (city) Miami-Dade	951
Tampa (city) Hillsborough	733
Miami Beach (city) Miami-Dade	573
Hialeah (city) Miami-Dade	509

Spaniard
Top 10 Places Sorted by Percent of Hispanic Population

Place (place type) County	Percent
Tampa (city) Hillsborough	1.25
Miami Beach (city) Miami-Dade	1.22
Miami (city) Miami-Dade	0.40
Hialeah (city) Miami-Dade	0.25

Spaniard
Top 10 Places Sorted by Percent of Total Population

Place (place type) County	Percent
Miami Beach (city) Miami-Dade	0.65
Miami (city) Miami-Dade	0.26
Tampa (city) Hillsborough	0.24
Hialeah (city) Miami-Dade	0.22

Uruguayan
Top 10 Places Sorted by Number

Place (place type) County	Number

No places met population threshold.

Uruguayan
Top 10 Places Sorted by Percent of Hispanic Population

Place (place type) County	Percent

No places met population threshold.

Uruguayan
Top 10 Places Sorted by Percent of Total Population

Place (place type) County	Percent

No places met population threshold.

Venezuelan
Top 10 Places Sorted by Number

Place (place type) County	Number
Fountainbleau (cdp) Miami-Dade	2,084
Weston (city) Broward	1,969
Doral (cdp) Miami-Dade	1,841
Miami (city) Miami-Dade	1,760
The Hammocks (cdp) Miami-Dade	1,668
Pembroke Pines (city) Broward	1,480
Miami Beach (city) Miami-Dade	1,456
Kendall (cdp) Miami-Dade	1,453
Kendall West (cdp) Miami-Dade	1,160
Hialeah (city) Miami-Dade	955

Venezuelan
Top 10 Places Sorted by Percent of Hispanic Population

Place (place type) County	Percent
Doral (cdp) Miami-Dade	13.51
Weston (city) Broward	13.07
The Hammocks (cdp) Miami-Dade	5.37
Plantation (city) Broward	4.89
The Crossings (cdp) Miami-Dade	4.64
Fountainbleau (cdp) Miami-Dade	4.02
Kendall (cdp) Miami-Dade	3.86
Kendall West (cdp) Miami-Dade	3.86
Pembroke Pines (city) Broward	3.86
Richmond West (cdp) Miami-Dade	3.12

Venezuelan
Top 10 Places Sorted by Percent of Total Population

Place (place type) County	Percent
Doral (cdp) Miami-Dade	8.97
Weston (city) Broward	4.01
The Hammocks (cdp) Miami-Dade	3.52
Fountainbleau (cdp) Miami-Dade	3.50
Kendall West (cdp) Miami-Dade	3.06
The Crossings (cdp) Miami-Dade	2.64
Richmond West (cdp) Miami-Dade	2.18
Kendall (cdp) Miami-Dade	1.93
Miami Beach (city) Miami-Dade	1.65
Kendale Lakes (cdp) Miami-Dade	1.53

Other Hispanic
Top 10 Places Sorted by Number

Place (place type) County	Number
Miami (city) Miami-Dade	32,320
Hialeah (city) Miami-Dade	20,725
Tampa (city) Hillsborough	12,266
Fountainbleau (cdp) Miami-Dade	8,566
Kendale Lakes (cdp) Miami-Dade	6,905
Miami Beach (city) Miami-Dade	6,425
Pembroke Pines (city) Broward	5,783
The Hammocks (cdp) Miami-Dade	5,769
Hollywood (city) Broward	5,716
Jacksonville (city) Duval	5,400

Other Hispanic
Top 10 Places Sorted by Percent of Hispanic Population

Place (place type) County	Percent
Lake Magdalene (cdp) Hillsborough	24.72
Lakeside (cdp) Clay	24.42
Sandalfoot Cove (cdp) Palm Beach	24.04
Tamarac (city) Broward	23.72
Greater Northdale (cdp) Hillsborough	23.07
North Miami (city) Miami-Dade	22.86
Greater Carrollwood (cdp) Hillsborough	22.34
North Miami Beach (city) Miami-Dade	21.59
Country Walk (cdp) Miami-Dade	21.57
Norland (cdp) Miami-Dade	21.46

Other Hispanic
Top 10 Places Sorted by Percent of Total Population

Place (place type) County	Percent
Fountainbleau (cdp) Miami-Dade	14.39
Sweetwater (city) Miami-Dade	12.97
Kendall West (cdp) Miami-Dade	12.57
Richmond West (cdp) Miami-Dade	12.25
Country Walk (cdp) Miami-Dade	12.17
The Hammocks (cdp) Miami-Dade	12.16
Kendale Lakes (cdp) Miami-Dade	12.14
Doral (cdp) Miami-Dade	11.84
Hialeah Gardens (city) Miami-Dade	11.17
Country Club (cdp) Miami-Dade	10.98

Median Age

Total Population
Top 10 Places Sorted by Number

Place (place type) County	Years
Hamptons at Boca Raton (cdp) Palm Beach	73.0
Naples (city) Collier	60.6
North Fort Myers (cdp) Lee	60.3
Marco Island (city) Collier	59.5
Bayonet Point (cdp) Pasco	57.9
Cypress Lake (cdp) Lee	56.5
Bonita Springs (city) Lee	53.8
Aventura (city) Miami-Dade	52.8
Hallandale (city) Broward	52.8
Tamarac (city) Broward	51.9

Hispanic
Top 10 Places Sorted by Number

Place (place type) County	Years
Palm Coast (city) Flagler	45.4
Westchester (cdp) Miami-Dade	44.4
University Park (cdp) Miami-Dade	43.2
Coral Terrace (cdp) Miami-Dade	42.6
Naples (city) Collier	42.1
Lakeland Highlands (cdp) Polk	41.3
Olympia Heights (cdp) Miami-Dade	41.3
Sunny Isles Beach (city) Miami-Dade	40.2
Miami (city) Miami-Dade	40.0
Coral Gables (city) Miami-Dade	39.7

Argentinian
Top 10 Places Sorted by Number

Place (place type) County	Years
Sunny Isles Beach (city) Miami-Dade	43.3
Hollywood (city) Broward	35.9
Hialeah (city) Miami-Dade	35.0
Kendall (cdp) Miami-Dade	34.8
Fountainbleau (cdp) Miami-Dade	33.6
Miami (city) Miami-Dade	33.6
Miami Beach (city) Miami-Dade	29.4

Bolivian
Top 10 Places Sorted by Number

Place (place type) County	Years

No places met population threshold.

Central American
Top 10 Places Sorted by Number

Place (place type) County	Years
The Crossings (cdp) Miami-Dade	37.2
Pinecrest (village) Miami-Dade	37.1
Doral (cdp) Miami-Dade	35.7
Deerfield Beach (city) Broward	35.3
Cutler Ridge (cdp) Miami-Dade	34.7

Notes: Please refer to the User's Guide for an explanation of data; tables include places with populations > 9,999 and reflect only those areas that meet Summary File 4 population thresholds, therefore there may be less than 10 places listed

Glenvar Heights (cdp) Miami-Dade	34.6
Sunset (cdp) Miami-Dade	34.6
University Park (cdp) Miami-Dade	34.5
Coral Gables (city) Miami-Dade	34.2
Carol City (cdp) Miami-Dade	33.6

Chilean

Top 10 Places Sorted by Number

Place (place type) County	Years
Hollywood (city) Broward	42.1
Miami (city) Miami-Dade	40.8
Hialeah (city) Miami-Dade	36.4
Miami Beach (city) Miami-Dade	36.0
Kendall (cdp) Miami-Dade	35.5
Fountainbleau (cdp) Miami-Dade	33.7

Columbian

Top 10 Places Sorted by Number

Place (place type) County	Years
Cutler Ridge (cdp) Miami-Dade	40.8
Westchester (cdp) Miami-Dade	40.2
University Park (cdp) Miami-Dade	38.5
Davie (town) Broward	38.1
Miami Springs (city) Miami-Dade	38.1
Margate (city) Broward	37.4
Hialeah (city) Miami-Dade	37.2
Plantation (city) Broward	37.0
Cooper City (city) Broward	36.9
Greater Carrollwood (cdp) Hillsborough	36.8

Costa Rican

Top 10 Places Sorted by Number

Place (place type) County	Years
Miami (city) Miami-Dade	31.3
Hialeah (city) Miami-Dade	30.6

Cuban

Top 10 Places Sorted by Number

Place (place type) County	Years
Sunny Isles Beach (city) Miami-Dade	59.2
Miami Beach (city) Miami-Dade	54.6
Miami (city) Miami-Dade	52.8
Clearwater (city) Pinellas	52.6
Aventura (city) Miami-Dade	50.7
Hallandale (city) Broward	49.8
Key Biscayne (village) Miami-Dade	49.8
Opa-locka (city) Miami-Dade	49.4
University Park (cdp) Miami-Dade	48.6
Brownsville (cdp) Miami-Dade	48.3

Dominican

Top 10 Places Sorted by Number

Place (place type) County	Years
South Miami Heights (cdp) Miami-Dade	38.1
Cape Coral (city) Lee	37.4
Coral Springs (city) Broward	37.1
Tamiami (cdp) Miami-Dade	36.9
Miami Beach (city) Miami-Dade	36.4
Golden Glades (cdp) Miami-Dade	35.1
Hialeah Gardens (city) Miami-Dade	35.0
Miramar (city) Broward	35.0
Miami (city) Miami-Dade	34.8
West Palm Beach (city) Palm Beach	34.8

Ecuadorian

Top 10 Places Sorted by Number

Place (place type) County	Years
Hialeah (city) Miami-Dade	40.7
Tampa (city) Hillsborough	38.5
Miami (city) Miami-Dade	37.4
Pembroke Pines (city) Broward	36.1
Miami Beach (city) Miami-Dade	34.4
Hollywood (city) Broward	33.1
Coral Springs (city) Broward	32.4
Sunrise (city) Broward	30.5
Fountainbleau (cdp) Miami-Dade	28.5

Guatelmalan

Top 10 Places Sorted by Number

Place (place type) County	Years
Miami (city) Miami-Dade	32.6
Hialeah (city) Miami-Dade	30.4
Fort Lauderdale (city) Broward	30.0
Immokalee (cdp) Collier	26.0
Homestead (city) Miami-Dade	24.5
Bonita Springs (city) Lee	24.3
West Palm Beach (city) Palm Beach	24.3
Fort Myers (city) Lee	22.9
Lake Worth (city) Palm Beach	22.3

Honduran

Top 10 Places Sorted by Number

Place (place type) County	Years
Hollywood (city) Broward	35.8
Carol City (cdp) Miami-Dade	34.1
Miami Beach (city) Miami-Dade	32.4
North Miami (city) Miami-Dade	32.4
Tamiami (cdp) Miami-Dade	31.8
Miami (city) Miami-Dade	31.7
Fountainbleau (cdp) Miami-Dade	30.0
North Miami Beach (city) Miami-Dade	29.8
Kendale Lakes (cdp) Miami-Dade	29.7
Hialeah (city) Miami-Dade	29.2

Mexican

Top 10 Places Sorted by Number

Place (place type) County	Years
Doral (cdp) Miami-Dade	33.1
Largo (city) Pinellas	33.1
Pembroke Pines (city) Broward	33.1
Miami Beach (city) Miami-Dade	32.9
Tamiami (cdp) Miami-Dade	32.3
The Hammocks (cdp) Miami-Dade	31.4
Hollywood (city) Broward	30.9
Fountainbleau (cdp) Miami-Dade	30.6
Deerfield Beach (city) Broward	30.5
Hialeah (city) Miami-Dade	29.1

Nicaraguan

Top 10 Places Sorted by Number

Place (place type) County	Years
The Crossings (cdp) Miami-Dade	37.3
Coral Gables (city) Miami-Dade	35.8
Miami Springs (city) Miami-Dade	34.9
University Park (cdp) Miami-Dade	34.8
Miami Beach (city) Miami-Dade	34.3
Pinewood (cdp) Miami-Dade	34.2
North Miami (city) Miami-Dade	33.7
Carol City (cdp) Miami-Dade	33.2
Kendale Lakes (cdp) Miami-Dade	32.9
Coral Terrace (cdp) Miami-Dade	32.5

Panamanian

Top 10 Places Sorted by Number

Place (place type) County	Years
Miami (city) Miami-Dade	36.3
Fountainbleau (cdp) Miami-Dade	33.0
Miramar (city) Broward	32.1
Tampa (city) Hillsborough	31.5
Jacksonville (city) Duval	28.4

Paraguayan

Top 10 Places Sorted by Number

Place (place type) County	Years

No places met population threshold.

Peruvian

Top 10 Places Sorted by Number

Place (place type) County	Years
Fort Lauderdale (city) Broward	37.1
Miami Beach (city) Miami-Dade	37.0
Miami (city) Miami-Dade	36.8
Davie (town) Broward	36.5
Sunrise (city) Broward	36.4
The Crossings (cdp) Miami-Dade	36.3
Fountainbleau (cdp) Miami-Dade	36.0
Kendale Lakes (cdp) Miami-Dade	35.2
Richmond West (cdp) Miami-Dade	35.2
Hialeah (city) Miami-Dade	34.9

Puerto Rican

Top 10 Places Sorted by Number

Place (place type) County	Years
Ojus (cdp) Miami-Dade	40.4
Westchester (cdp) Miami-Dade	39.6
Coral Terrace (cdp) Miami-Dade	39.5
Land O' Lakes (cdp) Pasco	39.2
Spring Hill (cdp) Hernando	39.0
Palm Coast (city) Flagler	38.5
Forest City (cdp) Seminole	38.1
Miami Lakes (cdp) Miami-Dade	37.8
Jupiter (town) Palm Beach	37.7
Sarasota (city) Sarasota	37.5

Salvadoran

Top 10 Places Sorted by Number

Place (place type) County	Years
Miami (city) Miami-Dade	31.3
Hialeah (city) Miami-Dade	29.5
Oakland Park (city) Broward	26.5
Fort Lauderdale (city) Broward	26.2
Homestead (city) Miami-Dade	24.7
Lake Worth (city) Palm Beach	24.0

South American

Top 10 Places Sorted by Number

Place (place type) County	Years
Westwood Lakes (cdp) Miami-Dade	40.6
Olympia Heights (cdp) Miami-Dade	40.3
West Little River (cdp) Miami-Dade	40.0
Sweetwater (city) Miami-Dade	39.6
Parkland (city) Broward	39.4
Coral Terrace (cdp) Miami-Dade	39.3
Sarasota (city) Sarasota	39.0
Palm Bay (city) Brevard	38.2
Cutler Ridge (cdp) Miami-Dade	37.6
Delray Beach (city) Palm Beach	37.6

Spaniard

Top 10 Places Sorted by Number

Place (place type) County	Years
Hialeah (city) Miami-Dade	55.3
Tampa (city) Hillsborough	54.5
Miami (city) Miami-Dade	54.0
Miami Beach (city) Miami-Dade	40.5

Uruguayan

Top 10 Places Sorted by Number

Place (place type) County	Years

No places met population threshold.

Venezuelan

Top 10 Places Sorted by Number

Place (place type) County	Years
Miami (city) Miami-Dade	35.1
Kendale Lakes (cdp) Miami-Dade	32.7
Coral Springs (city) Broward	32.4
Kendall West (cdp) Miami-Dade	32.4
Weston (city) Broward	32.4
Pembroke Pines (city) Broward	31.3

Notes: Please refer to the User's Guide for an explanation of data; tables include places with populations > 9,999 and reflect only those areas that meet Summary File 4 population thresholds, therefore there may be less than 10 places listed

Miami Beach (city) Miami-Dade	31.1
Tamiami (cdp) Miami-Dade	31.1
Coral Gables (city) Miami-Dade	30.5
Doral (cdp) Miami-Dade	30.5

Other Hispanic

Top 10 Places Sorted by Number

Place (place type) County	Years
Key West (city) Monroe	40.3
Aventura (city) Miami-Dade	39.3
Spring Hill (cdp) Hernando	38.7
Hallandale (city) Broward	36.8
Boca Raton (city) Palm Beach	36.7
Pompano Beach (city) Broward	36.4
Ojus (cdp) Miami-Dade	35.8
Tampa (city) Hillsborough	35.5
Miami Beach (city) Miami-Dade	35.4
Sunny Isles Beach (city) Miami-Dade	35.0

Average Household Size

Total Population

Top 10 Places Sorted by Number

Place (place type) County	Number
Immokalee (cdp) Collier	3.90
Leisure City (cdp) Miami-Dade	3.65
Princeton (cdp) Miami-Dade	3.60
Scott Lake (cdp) Miami-Dade	3.58
Carol City (cdp) Miami-Dade	3.57
Richmond West (cdp) Miami-Dade	3.57
Westwood Lakes (cdp) Miami-Dade	3.42
Hialeah Gardens (city) Miami-Dade	3.38
West Little River (cdp) Miami-Dade	3.38
Palmetto Estates (cdp) Miami-Dade	3.35

Hispanic

Top 10 Places Sorted by Number

Place (place type) County	Number
Scott Lake (cdp) Miami-Dade	4.60
Fort Pierce (city) Saint Lucie	4.37
Immokalee (cdp) Collier	4.36
Palmetto (city) Manatee	4.34
De Land (city) Volusia	4.33
Zephyrhills (city) Pasco	4.11
Bonita Springs (city) Lee	4.07
Golden Gate (cdp) Collier	4.06
Lake Worth Corridor (cdp) Palm Beach	4.05
Eustis (city) Lake	4.02

Argentinian

Top 10 Places Sorted by Number

Place (place type) County	Number
Hialeah (city) Miami-Dade	3.71
Hollywood (city) Broward	3.31
Kendall (cdp) Miami-Dade	2.82
Fountainbleau (cdp) Miami-Dade	2.67
Miami (city) Miami-Dade	2.57
Miami Beach (city) Miami-Dade	2.34
Sunny Isles Beach (city) Miami-Dade	2.24

Bolivian

Top 10 Places Sorted by Number

Place (place type) County	Number

No places met population threshold.

Central American

Top 10 Places Sorted by Number

Place (place type) County	Number
Immokalee (cdp) Collier	6.66
Palmetto Estates (cdp) Miami-Dade	4.94
Coral Terrace (cdp) Miami-Dade	4.81
West Palm Beach (city) Palm Beach	4.64
Lake Worth Corridor (cdp) Palm Beach	4.52
South Miami Heights (cdp) Miami-Dade	4.42
West Little River (cdp) Miami-Dade	4.39
Fort Myers (city) Lee	4.35
Pinewood (cdp) Miami-Dade	4.34
Princeton (cdp) Miami-Dade	4.33

Chilean

Top 10 Places Sorted by Number

Place (place type) County	Number
Fountainbleau (cdp) Miami-Dade	3.71
Hollywood (city) Broward	3.31
Miami (city) Miami-Dade	3.30
Hialeah (city) Miami-Dade	3.10
Kendall (cdp) Miami-Dade	3.05
Miami Beach (city) Miami-Dade	1.87

Columbian

Top 10 Places Sorted by Number

Place (place type) County	Number
Meadow Woods (cdp) Orange	4.69
South Miami Heights (cdp) Miami-Dade	4.61
Yeehaw Junction (cdp) Osceola	4.53
Richmond West (cdp) Miami-Dade	4.42
Carol City (cdp) Miami-Dade	4.20
Sandalfoot Cove (cdp) Palm Beach	4.12
Kendale Lakes (cdp) Miami-Dade	4.03
Cutler Ridge (cdp) Miami-Dade	3.99
Cape Coral (city) Lee	3.83
Hialeah Gardens (city) Miami-Dade	3.81

Costa Rican

Top 10 Places Sorted by Number

Place (place type) County	Number
Hialeah (city) Miami-Dade	3.98
Miami (city) Miami-Dade	2.46

Cuban

Top 10 Places Sorted by Number

Place (place type) County	Number
Westwood Lakes (cdp) Miami-Dade	3.68
Pinecrest (village) Miami-Dade	3.56
Cooper City (city) Broward	3.55
Princeton (cdp) Miami-Dade	3.53
Carol City (cdp) Miami-Dade	3.48
Citrus Park (cdp) Hillsborough	3.48
West Little River (cdp) Miami-Dade	3.48
Golden Gate (cdp) Collier	3.47
Cutler (cdp) Miami-Dade	3.44
Greater Northdale (cdp) Hillsborough	3.43

Dominican

Top 10 Places Sorted by Number

Place (place type) County	Number
Weston (city) Broward	4.27
Carol City (cdp) Miami-Dade	4.13
Hialeah Gardens (city) Miami-Dade	4.13
Miramar (city) Broward	4.12
South Miami Heights (cdp) Miami-Dade	4.01
Kendall West (cdp) Miami-Dade	3.98
The Hammocks (cdp) Miami-Dade	3.97
West Little River (cdp) Miami-Dade	3.93
North Miami Beach (city) Miami-Dade	3.85
Richmond West (cdp) Miami-Dade	3.84

Ecuadorian

Top 10 Places Sorted by Number

Place (place type) County	Number
Fountainbleau (cdp) Miami-Dade	4.32
Coral Springs (city) Broward	4.05
Hialeah (city) Miami-Dade	3.64
Sunrise (city) Broward	3.39
Pembroke Pines (city) Broward	3.38
Hollywood (city) Broward	3.26
Miami (city) Miami-Dade	2.88
Tampa (city) Hillsborough	2.72
Miami Beach (city) Miami-Dade	2.15

Guatelmalan

Top 10 Places Sorted by Number

Place (place type) County	Number
Immokalee (cdp) Collier	7.17
West Palm Beach (city) Palm Beach	5.27
Fort Myers (city) Lee	4.96
Lake Worth (city) Palm Beach	4.41
Homestead (city) Miami-Dade	4.17
Bonita Springs (city) Lee	4.02
Fort Lauderdale (city) Broward	3.61
Hialeah (city) Miami-Dade	3.59
Miami (city) Miami-Dade	3.37

Honduran

Top 10 Places Sorted by Number

Place (place type) County	Number
Fountainbleau (cdp) Miami-Dade	4.40
West Little River (cdp) Miami-Dade	4.24
North Miami Beach (city) Miami-Dade	4.17
Kendale Lakes (cdp) Miami-Dade	4.09
Lake Worth (city) Palm Beach	3.93
Hialeah (city) Miami-Dade	3.72
Carol City (cdp) Miami-Dade	3.71
Miami (city) Miami-Dade	3.50
Tamiami (cdp) Miami-Dade	3.49
North Miami (city) Miami-Dade	3.41

Mexican

Top 10 Places Sorted by Number

Place (place type) County	Number
De Land (city) Volusia	5.23
Golden Gate (cdp) Collier	5.18
Lake Worth Corridor (cdp) Palm Beach	5.00
South Miami Heights (cdp) Miami-Dade	4.97
North Lauderdale (city) Broward	4.86
Fort Pierce (city) Saint Lucie	4.84
Palmetto (city) Manatee	4.76
Leisure City (cdp) Miami-Dade	4.75
Apopka (city) Orange	4.65
Coconut Creek (city) Broward	4.59

Nicaraguan

Top 10 Places Sorted by Number

Place (place type) County	Number
Palmetto Estates (cdp) Miami-Dade	5.38
Coral Terrace (cdp) Miami-Dade	5.10
South Miami Heights (cdp) Miami-Dade	4.67
West Little River (cdp) Miami-Dade	4.57
Pinewood (cdp) Miami-Dade	4.53
Carol City (cdp) Miami-Dade	4.48
Sweetwater (city) Miami-Dade	4.46
Richmond West (cdp) Miami-Dade	4.29
Miramar (city) Broward	4.28
Tamiami (cdp) Miami-Dade	4.19

Panamanian

Top 10 Places Sorted by Number

Place (place type) County	Number
Miramar (city) Broward	3.15
Fountainbleau (cdp) Miami-Dade	2.83
Jacksonville (city) Duval	2.72
Miami (city) Miami-Dade	2.61
Tampa (city) Hillsborough	2.57

Paraguayan

Top 10 Places Sorted by Number

Place (place type) County	Number

No places met population threshold.

Notes: Please refer to the User's Guide for an explanation of data; tables include places with populations > 9,999 and reflect only those areas that meet Summary File 4 population thresholds, therefore there may be less than 10 places listed

Peruvian

Top 10 Places Sorted by Number

Place (place type) County	Number
Miramar (city) Broward	4.36
Richmond West (cdp) Miami-Dade	4.10
Hialeah (city) Miami-Dade	4.01
The Hammocks (cdp) Miami-Dade	3.97
Kendall West (cdp) Miami-Dade	3.95
North Lauderdale (city) Broward	3.95
Coral Springs (city) Broward	3.72
Kendall (cdp) Miami-Dade	3.68
Pembroke Pines (city) Broward	3.48
Sunrise (city) Broward	3.47

Puerto Rican

Top 10 Places Sorted by Number

Place (place type) County	Number
Forest City (cdp) Seminole	4.27
West Little River (cdp) Miami-Dade	4.25
Zephyrhills (city) Pasco	4.20
Pinewood (cdp) Miami-Dade	4.08
University Park (cdp) Miami-Dade	4.05
Poinciana (cdp) Osceola	3.93
Palmetto Estates (cdp) Miami-Dade	3.87
Oviedo (city) Seminole	3.79
Longwood (city) Seminole	3.73
Carol City (cdp) Miami-Dade	3.72

Salvadoran

Top 10 Places Sorted by Number

Place (place type) County	Number
Homestead (city) Miami-Dade	4.13
Fort Lauderdale (city) Broward	3.79
Oakland Park (city) Broward	3.52
Lake Worth (city) Palm Beach	3.38
Hialeah (city) Miami-Dade	3.20
Miami (city) Miami-Dade	2.96

South American

Top 10 Places Sorted by Number

Place (place type) County	Number
Meadow Woods (cdp) Orange	4.79
Leisure City (cdp) Miami-Dade	4.60
West Little River (cdp) Miami-Dade	4.43
Carol City (cdp) Miami-Dade	4.30
Yeehaw Junction (cdp) Osceola	4.20
Richmond West (cdp) Miami-Dade	4.18
Pinecrest (village) Miami-Dade	4.17
Westwood Lakes (cdp) Miami-Dade	4.14
Sweetwater (city) Miami-Dade	4.10
Sandalfoot Cove (cdp) Palm Beach	3.95

Spaniard

Top 10 Places Sorted by Number

Place (place type) County	Number
Hialeah (city) Miami-Dade	3.36
Miami Beach (city) Miami-Dade	2.35
Miami (city) Miami-Dade	2.22
Tampa (city) Hillsborough	1.69

Uruguayan

Top 10 Places Sorted by Number

Place (place type) County	Number

No places met population threshold.

Venezuelan

Top 10 Places Sorted by Number

Place (place type) County	Number
Tamiami (cdp) Miami-Dade	4.17
Richmond West (cdp) Miami-Dade	3.93
Coral Springs (city) Broward	3.68
Plantation (city) Broward	3.48
The Crossings (cdp) Miami-Dade	3.45
Kendall West (cdp) Miami-Dade	3.37
Weston (city) Broward	3.28
Tampa (city) Hillsborough	3.19
Doral (cdp) Miami-Dade	3.18
Pembroke Pines (city) Broward	3.16

Other Hispanic

Top 10 Places Sorted by Number

Place (place type) County	Number
Leisure City (cdp) Miami-Dade	5.58
Immokalee (cdp) Collier	4.61
Opa-locka (city) Miami-Dade	4.46
West Little River (cdp) Miami-Dade	4.32
Olympia Heights (cdp) Miami-Dade	4.30
Bonita Springs (city) Lee	4.17
Richmond West (cdp) Miami-Dade	4.08
Gladeview (cdp) Miami-Dade	3.88
Plant City (city) Hillsborough	3.84
Hialeah Gardens (city) Miami-Dade	3.82

Language Spoken at Home: English Only

Total Population 5 Years and Over Who Speak English-Only at Home

Top 10 Places Sorted by Number

Place (place type) County	Number
Jacksonville (city) Duval	616,988
Tampa (city) Hillsborough	218,362
St. Petersburg (city) Pinellas	206,489
Tallahassee (city) Leon	130,526
Orlando (city) Orange	130,439
Fort Lauderdale (city) Broward	108,442
Hollywood (city) Broward	87,182
Miami (city) Miami-Dade	86,669
Clearwater (city) Pinellas	85,394
Cape Coral (city) Lee	83,549

Total Population 5 Years and Over Who Speak English-Only at Home

Top 10 Places Sorted by Percent

Place (place type) County	Percent
Port St. John (cdp) Brevard	95.01
North Fort Myers (cdp) Lee	94.07
Pensacola (city) Escambia	93.77
Bellview (cdp) Escambia	93.50
Jensen Beach (cdp) Martin	93.45
Titusville (city) Brevard	93.44
Leesburg (city) Lake	93.42
Jacksonville Beach (city) Duval	93.08
Rockledge (city) Brevard	92.94
Ferry Pass (cdp) Escambia	92.93

Hispanics 5 Years and Over Who Speak English-Only at Home

Top 10 Places Sorted by Number

Place (place type) County	Number
Miami (city) Miami-Dade	12,945
Tampa (city) Hillsborough	10,107
Hialeah (city) Miami-Dade	8,606
Jacksonville (city) Duval	8,444
Pembroke Pines (city) Broward	4,010
Orlando (city) Orange	4,005
Hollywood (city) Broward	3,667
Miami Beach (city) Miami-Dade	3,150
St. Petersburg (city) Pinellas	2,724
Kendall (cdp) Miami-Dade	2,704

Hispanics 5 Years and Over Who Speak English-Only at Home

Top 10 Places Sorted by Percent

Place (place type) County	Percent
Callaway (city) Bay	61.01
Port St. John (cdp) Brevard	59.24
Wright (cdp) Okaloosa	56.56
Warrington (cdp) Escambia	53.30
Bayonet Point (cdp) Pasco	50.77
Myrtle Grove (cdp) Escambia	49.57
Titusville (city) Brevard	47.39
Ferry Pass (cdp) Escambia	46.36
West Pensacola (cdp) Escambia	42.83
Pensacola (city) Escambia	41.97

Argentinians 5 Years and Over Who Speak English-Only at Home

Top 10 Places Sorted by Number

Place (place type) County	Number
Miami Beach (city) Miami-Dade	84
Miami (city) Miami-Dade	75
Sunny Isles Beach (city) Miami-Dade	51
Hollywood (city) Broward	36
Kendall (cdp) Miami-Dade	35
Fountainbleau (cdp) Miami-Dade	6
Hialeah (city) Miami-Dade	0

Argentinians 5 Years and Over Who Speak English-Only at Home

Top 10 Places Sorted by Percent

Place (place type) County	Percent
Sunny Isles Beach (city) Miami-Dade	9.17
Hollywood (city) Broward	6.56
Kendall (cdp) Miami-Dade	5.55
Miami (city) Miami-Dade	3.93
Miami Beach (city) Miami-Dade	2.87
Fountainbleau (cdp) Miami-Dade	1.39
Hialeah (city) Miami-Dade	0.00

Bolivians 5 Years and Over Who Speak English-Only at Home

Top 10 Places Sorted by Number

Place (place type) County	Number

No places met population threshold.

Bolivians 5 Years and Over Who Speak English-Only at Home

Top 10 Places Sorted by Percent

Place (place type) County	Percent

No places met population threshold.

Central Americans 5 Years and Over Who Speak English-Only at Home

Top 10 Places Sorted by Number

Place (place type) County	Number
Miami (city) Miami-Dade	1,726
Tampa (city) Hillsborough	638
Hialeah (city) Miami-Dade	460
Fountainbleau (cdp) Miami-Dade	378
Jacksonville (city) Duval	348
Kendall (cdp) Miami-Dade	252
Homestead (city) Miami-Dade	204
Miami Beach (city) Miami-Dade	176
Pembroke Pines (city) Broward	156
Hollywood (city) Broward	150

Central Americans 5 Years and Over Who Speak English-Only at Home

Top 10 Places Sorted by Percent

Place (place type) County	Percent
Brandon (cdp) Hillsborough	25.41
Plantation (city) Broward	23.06
Tampa (city) Hillsborough	21.03
Jacksonville (city) Duval	20.64
Yeehaw Junction (cdp) Osceola	14.32
Coral Springs (city) Broward	13.36
Margate (city) Broward	13.35
Boynton Beach (city) Palm Beach	12.67
Opa-locka (city) Miami-Dade	12.58
Bonita Springs (city) Lee	11.42

Notes: Please refer to the User's Guide for an explanation of data; tables include places with populations > 9,999 and reflect only those areas that meet Summary File 4 population thresholds, therefore there may be less than 10 places listed

Chileans 5 Years and Over Who Speak English-Only at Home

Top 10 Places Sorted by Number

Place (place type) County	Number
Miami Beach (city) Miami-Dade	104
Hialeah (city) Miami-Dade	67
Kendall (cdp) Miami-Dade	38
Miami (city) Miami-Dade	26
Hollywood (city) Broward	7
Fountainbleau (cdp) Miami-Dade	0

Chileans 5 Years and Over Who Speak English-Only at Home

Top 10 Places Sorted by Percent

Place (place type) County	Percent
Miami Beach (city) Miami-Dade	14.40
Hialeah (city) Miami-Dade	8.93
Kendall (cdp) Miami-Dade	8.12
Miami (city) Miami-Dade	2.96
Hollywood (city) Broward	1.99
Fountainbleau (cdp) Miami-Dade	0.00

Columbians 5 Years and Over Who Speak English-Only at Home

Top 10 Places Sorted by Number

Place (place type) County	Number
Miami (city) Miami-Dade	255
Miami Beach (city) Miami-Dade	236
Hialeah (city) Miami-Dade	212
Hollywood (city) Broward	205
Pembroke Pines (city) Broward	179
Plantation (city) Broward	175
Jacksonville (city) Duval	167
Tampa (city) Hillsborough	126
Kendall (cdp) Miami-Dade	124
Fountainbleau (cdp) Miami-Dade	117

Columbians 5 Years and Over Who Speak English-Only at Home

Top 10 Places Sorted by Percent

Place (place type) County	Percent
Cooper City (city) Broward	20.70
Jacksonville (city) Duval	13.15
Pompano Beach (city) Broward	12.34
Cape Coral (city) Lee	11.11
Sandalfoot Cove (cdp) Palm Beach	10.38
University Park (cdp) Miami-Dade	8.96
Fort Lauderdale (city) Broward	8.85
Plantation (city) Broward	8.50
Coconut Creek (city) Broward	8.26
Cutler Ridge (cdp) Miami-Dade	8.21

Costa Ricans 5 Years and Over Who Speak English-Only at Home

Top 10 Places Sorted by Number

Place (place type) County	Number
Miami (city) Miami-Dade	57
Hialeah (city) Miami-Dade	0

Costa Ricans 5 Years and Over Who Speak English-Only at Home

Top 10 Places Sorted by Percent

Place (place type) County	Percent
Miami (city) Miami-Dade	7.17
Hialeah (city) Miami-Dade	0.00

Cubans 5 Years and Over Who Speak English-Only at Home

Top 10 Places Sorted by Number

Place (place type) County	Number
Miami (city) Miami-Dade	6,769
Hialeah (city) Miami-Dade	6,190
Tampa (city) Hillsborough	1,971
Miami Beach (city) Miami-Dade	1,325
Kendall (cdp) Miami-Dade	1,179
Pembroke Pines (city) Broward	1,143
Tamiami (cdp) Miami-Dade	1,136
Westchester (cdp) Miami-Dade	912
Kendale Lakes (cdp) Miami-Dade	868
Hollywood (city) Broward	815

Cubans 5 Years and Over Who Speak English-Only at Home

Top 10 Places Sorted by Percent

Place (place type) County	Percent
Gainesville (city) Alachua	36.31
Brandon (cdp) Hillsborough	32.71
Lake Magdalene (cdp) Hillsborough	31.81
Pompano Beach (city) Broward	28.81
Spring Hill (cdp) Hernando	26.09
Tallahassee (city) Leon	25.60
Greater Northdale (cdp) Hillsborough	25.24
Royal Palm Beach (village) Palm Beach	24.89
Weston (city) Broward	24.77
Key West (city) Monroe	23.54

Dominicans 5 Years and Over Who Speak English-Only at Home

Top 10 Places Sorted by Number

Place (place type) County	Number
Miami (city) Miami-Dade	482
Hollywood (city) Broward	118
Hialeah (city) Miami-Dade	109
Orlando (city) Orange	106
Carol City (cdp) Miami-Dade	79
Kissimmee (city) Osceola	63
The Hammocks (cdp) Miami-Dade	60
Coral Springs (city) Broward	57
Weston (city) Broward	54
Pembroke Pines (city) Broward	52

Dominicans 5 Years and Over Who Speak English-Only at Home

Top 10 Places Sorted by Percent

Place (place type) County	Percent
Weston (city) Broward	14.10
Coral Springs (city) Broward	10.78
Orlando (city) Orange	9.15
Egypt Lake-Leto (cdp) Hillsborough	8.92
West Palm Beach (city) Palm Beach	8.56
Jacksonville (city) Duval	8.24
Hollywood (city) Broward	7.41
Miami (city) Miami-Dade	7.01
Sunrise (city) Broward	6.09
Kissimmee (city) Osceola	5.83

Ecuadorians 5 Years and Over Who Speak English-Only at Home

Top 10 Places Sorted by Number

Place (place type) County	Number
Miami (city) Miami-Dade	134
Coral Springs (city) Broward	67
Hollywood (city) Broward	54
Miami Beach (city) Miami-Dade	46
Tampa (city) Hillsborough	34
Hialeah (city) Miami-Dade	33
Sunrise (city) Broward	29
Fountainbleau (cdp) Miami-Dade	24
Pembroke Pines (city) Broward	23

Ecuadorians 5 Years and Over Who Speak English-Only at Home

Top 10 Places Sorted by Percent

Place (place type) County	Percent
Hollywood (city) Broward	8.87
Tampa (city) Hillsborough	8.85
Miami (city) Miami-Dade	7.92
Coral Springs (city) Broward	7.49
Miami Beach (city) Miami-Dade	7.13
Sunrise (city) Broward	5.75
Pembroke Pines (city) Broward	4.79
Fountainbleau (cdp) Miami-Dade	3.12
Hialeah (city) Miami-Dade	2.75

Guatelmalans 5 Years and Over Who Speak English-Only at Home

Top 10 Places Sorted by Number

Place (place type) County	Number
Miami (city) Miami-Dade	140
West Palm Beach (city) Palm Beach	134
Immokalee (cdp) Collier	99
Homestead (city) Miami-Dade	77
Lake Worth (city) Palm Beach	35
Fort Myers (city) Lee	21
Fort Lauderdale (city) Broward	8
Bonita Springs (city) Lee	0
Hialeah (city) Miami-Dade	0

Guatelmalans 5 Years and Over Who Speak English-Only at Home

Top 10 Places Sorted by Percent

Place (place type) County	Percent
Immokalee (cdp) Collier	9.45
West Palm Beach (city) Palm Beach	6.99
Fort Myers (city) Lee	6.02
Homestead (city) Miami-Dade	5.77
Miami (city) Miami-Dade	5.24
Fort Lauderdale (city) Broward	2.22
Lake Worth (city) Palm Beach	2.05
Bonita Springs (city) Lee	0.00
Hialeah (city) Miami-Dade	0.00

Hondurans 5 Years and Over Who Speak English-Only at Home

Top 10 Places Sorted by Number

Place (place type) County	Number
Miami (city) Miami-Dade	581
Tampa (city) Hillsborough	168
Hialeah (city) Miami-Dade	67
North Miami Beach (city) Miami-Dade	49
North Miami (city) Miami-Dade	34
Carol City (cdp) Miami-Dade	33
Miami Beach (city) Miami-Dade	33
Fountainbleau (cdp) Miami-Dade	15
Hollywood (city) Broward	14
West Little River (cdp) Miami-Dade	14

Hondurans 5 Years and Over Who Speak English-Only at Home

Top 10 Places Sorted by Percent

Place (place type) County	Percent
Tampa (city) Hillsborough	20.82
North Miami Beach (city) Miami-Dade	9.90
Carol City (cdp) Miami-Dade	6.55
North Miami (city) Miami-Dade	5.92
Miami (city) Miami-Dade	4.49
Miami Beach (city) Miami-Dade	4.27
Hollywood (city) Broward	3.48
Hialeah (city) Miami-Dade	2.64
Fountainbleau (cdp) Miami-Dade	2.40
Kendale Lakes (cdp) Miami-Dade	1.58

Mexicans 5 Years and Over Who Speak English-Only at Home

Top 10 Places Sorted by Number

Place (place type) County	Number
Jacksonville (city) Duval	2,601
Tampa (city) Hillsborough	1,251
Immokalee (cdp) Collier	803
St. Petersburg (city) Pinellas	740
Golden Gate (cdp) Collier	559
Clearwater (city) Pinellas	555
Orlando (city) Orange	531
Bradenton (city) Manatee	495
Palmetto (city) Manatee	466
Port St. Lucie (city) Saint Lucie	402

Notes: Please refer to the User's Guide for an explanation of data; tables include places with populations > 9,999 and reflect only those areas that meet Summary File 4 population thresholds, therefore there may be less than 10 places listed

Mexicans 5 Years and Over Who Speak English-Only at Home

Top 10 Places Sorted by Percent

Place (place type) County	Percent
Wright (cdp) Okaloosa	62.57
Panama City (city) Bay	56.02
Jacksonville (city) Duval	53.17
Largo (city) Pinellas	52.27
Palm Bay (city) Brevard	51.29
Gainesville (city) Alachua	47.29
St. Petersburg (city) Pinellas	47.04
Tallahassee (city) Leon	44.74
Plantation (city) Broward	42.88
Port St. Lucie (city) Saint Lucie	40.85

Nicaraguans 5 Years and Over Who Speak English-Only at Home

Top 10 Places Sorted by Number

Place (place type) County	Number
Miami (city) Miami-Dade	758
Hialeah (city) Miami-Dade	316
Fountainbleau (cdp) Miami-Dade	310
Tampa (city) Hillsborough	119
Miami Beach (city) Miami-Dade	110
Kendall (cdp) Miami-Dade	102
Kendale Lakes (cdp) Miami-Dade	95
Sweetwater (city) Miami-Dade	81
Carol City (cdp) Miami-Dade	77
Kendall West (cdp) Miami-Dade	76

Nicaraguans 5 Years and Over Who Speak English-Only at Home

Top 10 Places Sorted by Percent

Place (place type) County	Percent
Tampa (city) Hillsborough	26.21
Miami Beach (city) Miami-Dade	11.17
North Miami (city) Miami-Dade	7.81
Miramar (city) Broward	6.57
Carol City (cdp) Miami-Dade	5.61
Coral Terrace (cdp) Miami-Dade	5.53
Pinewood (cdp) Miami-Dade	5.36
Hollywood (city) Broward	5.34
Fountainbleau (cdp) Miami-Dade	5.26
South Miami Heights (cdp) Miami-Dade	5.04

Panamanians 5 Years and Over Who Speak English-Only at Home

Top 10 Places Sorted by Number

Place (place type) County	Number
Tampa (city) Hillsborough	170
Jacksonville (city) Duval	149
Miramar (city) Broward	81
Fountainbleau (cdp) Miami-Dade	36
Miami (city) Miami-Dade	10

Panamanians 5 Years and Over Who Speak English-Only at Home

Top 10 Places Sorted by Percent

Place (place type) County	Percent
Tampa (city) Hillsborough	27.91
Jacksonville (city) Duval	26.05
Miramar (city) Broward	23.48
Fountainbleau (cdp) Miami-Dade	7.05
Miami (city) Miami-Dade	1.17

Paraguayans 5 Years and Over Who Speak English-Only at Home

Top 10 Places Sorted by Number

Place (place type) County	Number

No places met population threshold.

Paraguayans 5 Years and Over Who Speak English-Only at Home

Top 10 Places Sorted by Percent

Place (place type) County	Percent

No places met population threshold.

Peruvians 5 Years and Over Who Speak English-Only at Home

Top 10 Places Sorted by Number

Place (place type) County	Number
Miami (city) Miami-Dade	104
Pembroke Pines (city) Broward	98
Hollywood (city) Broward	96
Kendall (cdp) Miami-Dade	72
Kendale Lakes (cdp) Miami-Dade	70
Kendall West (cdp) Miami-Dade	59
Miami Beach (city) Miami-Dade	46
North Lauderdale (city) Broward	44
Weston (city) Broward	44
Davie (town) Broward	43

Peruvians 5 Years and Over Who Speak English-Only at Home

Top 10 Places Sorted by Percent

Place (place type) County	Percent
Orlando (city) Orange	9.07
Fort Lauderdale (city) Broward	8.97
North Lauderdale (city) Broward	8.09
Hollywood (city) Broward	7.74
Richmond West (cdp) Miami-Dade	7.61
Kendale Lakes (cdp) Miami-Dade	7.51
Pembroke Pines (city) Broward	7.19
Davie (town) Broward	7.18
Sunrise (city) Broward	6.38
Weston (city) Broward	6.25

Puerto Ricans 5 Years and Over Who Speak English-Only at Home

Top 10 Places Sorted by Number

Place (place type) County	Number
Jacksonville (city) Duval	2,459
Tampa (city) Hillsborough	2,273
Orlando (city) Orange	1,824
Deltona (city) Volusia	1,502
Pembroke Pines (city) Broward	1,302
Kissimmee (city) Osceola	1,293
Hollywood (city) Broward	1,198
Town 'n' Country (cdp) Hillsborough	1,008
Coral Springs (city) Broward	982
Brandon (cdp) Hillsborough	893

Puerto Ricans 5 Years and Over Who Speak English-Only at Home

Top 10 Places Sorted by Percent

Place (place type) County	Percent
Dunedin (city) Pinellas	46.39
Titusville (city) Brevard	42.76
Tallahassee (city) Leon	42.41
Lakeside (cdp) Clay	42.01
Jasmine Estates (cdp) Pasco	41.72
Port Orange (city) Volusia	39.79
Merritt Island (cdp) Brevard	39.51
Boca Raton (city) Palm Beach	39.43
North Fort Myers (cdp) Lee	36.53
Pompano Beach (city) Broward	34.84

Salvadorans 5 Years and Over Who Speak English-Only at Home

Top 10 Places Sorted by Number

Place (place type) County	Number
Miami (city) Miami-Dade	123
Homestead (city) Miami-Dade	42
Fort Lauderdale (city) Broward	23
Hialeah (city) Miami-Dade	9
Lake Worth (city) Palm Beach	0
Oakland Park (city) Broward	0

Salvadorans 5 Years and Over Who Speak English-Only at Home

Top 10 Places Sorted by Percent

Place (place type) County	Percent
Miami (city) Miami-Dade	5.40
Homestead (city) Miami-Dade	4.45
Fort Lauderdale (city) Broward	3.57
Hialeah (city) Miami-Dade	1.01
Lake Worth (city) Palm Beach	0.00
Oakland Park (city) Broward	0.00

South Americans 5 Years and Over Who Speak English-Only at Home

Top 10 Places Sorted by Number

Place (place type) County	Number
Miami (city) Miami-Dade	713
Miami Beach (city) Miami-Dade	608
Hollywood (city) Broward	443
Pembroke Pines (city) Broward	439
Kendall (cdp) Miami-Dade	384
Hialeah (city) Miami-Dade	334
Tallahassee (city) Leon	324
Jacksonville (city) Duval	310
Fort Lauderdale (city) Broward	309
Plantation (city) Broward	294

South Americans 5 Years and Over Who Speak English-Only at Home

Top 10 Places Sorted by Percent

Place (place type) County	Percent
Tallahassee (city) Leon	42.13
Palm Bay (city) Brevard	25.40
Deltona (city) Volusia	21.92
Cooper City (city) Broward	19.14
Gainesville (city) Alachua	15.14
Jacksonville (city) Duval	12.80
Delray Beach (city) Palm Beach	12.56
St. Petersburg (city) Pinellas	11.82
Brandon (cdp) Hillsborough	11.11
Coconut Creek (city) Broward	10.95

Spaniards 5 Years and Over Who Speak English-Only at Home

Top 10 Places Sorted by Number

Place (place type) County	Number
Tampa (city) Hillsborough	185
Miami (city) Miami-Dade	37
Miami Beach (city) Miami-Dade	36
Hialeah (city) Miami-Dade	25

Spaniards 5 Years and Over Who Speak English-Only at Home

Top 10 Places Sorted by Percent

Place (place type) County	Percent
Tampa (city) Hillsborough	26.43
Miami Beach (city) Miami-Dade	6.41
Hialeah (city) Miami-Dade	5.10
Miami (city) Miami-Dade	3.98

Uruguayans 5 Years and Over Who Speak English-Only at Home

Top 10 Places Sorted by Number

Place (place type) County	Number

No places met population threshold.

Uruguayans 5 Years and Over Who Speak English-Only at Home

Top 10 Places Sorted by Percent

Place (place type) County	Percent

No places met population threshold.

Notes: Please refer to the User's Guide for an explanation of data; tables include places with populations > 9,999 and reflect only those areas that meet Summary File 4 population thresholds, therefore there may be less than 10 places listed

Venezuelans 5 Years and Over Who Speak English-Only at Home
Top 10 Places Sorted by Number

Place (place type) County	Number
Tampa (city) Hillsborough	87
Miami (city) Miami-Dade	81
Kendall (cdp) Miami-Dade	77
Coral Springs (city) Broward	62
The Hammocks (cdp) Miami-Dade	61
Hollywood (city) Broward	41
Miami Beach (city) Miami-Dade	40
Orlando (city) Orange	38
Plantation (city) Broward	37
Pembroke Pines (city) Broward	35

Venezuelans 5 Years and Over Who Speak English-Only at Home
Top 10 Places Sorted by Percent

Place (place type) County	Percent
Tampa (city) Hillsborough	15.59
Coral Springs (city) Broward	12.89
Plantation (city) Broward	7.58
Hollywood (city) Broward	7.00
Kendall (cdp) Miami-Dade	5.60
Orlando (city) Orange	5.19
Miami (city) Miami-Dade	4.80
The Hammocks (cdp) Miami-Dade	3.90
Kendale Lakes (cdp) Miami-Dade	3.38
Miami Beach (city) Miami-Dade	2.84

Other Hispanics 5 Years and Over Who Speak English-Only at Home
Top 10 Places Sorted by Number

Place (place type) County	Number
Tampa (city) Hillsborough	3,466
Miami (city) Miami-Dade	2,036
Jacksonville (city) Duval	1,868
Hialeah (city) Miami-Dade	1,023
Town 'n' Country (cdp) Hillsborough	766
Orlando (city) Orange	655
Hollywood (city) Broward	631
Pembroke Pines (city) Broward	619
Egypt Lake-Leto (cdp) Hillsborough	609
St. Petersburg (city) Pinellas	581

Other Hispanics 5 Years and Over Who Speak English-Only at Home
Top 10 Places Sorted by Percent

Place (place type) County	Percent
Tallahassee (city) Leon	50.76
Greater Northdale (cdp) Hillsborough	48.37
St. Petersburg (city) Pinellas	44.18
Greater Carrollwood (cdp) Hillsborough	42.83
Apopka (city) Orange	40.29
Brandon (cdp) Hillsborough	40.21
Jacksonville (city) Duval	39.99
Spring Hill (cdp) Hernando	39.76
University (cdp) Hillsborough	39.05
Key West (city) Monroe	38.60

Language Spoken at Home: Spanish

Total Population 5 Years and Over Who Speak Spanish at Home
Top 10 Places Sorted by Number

Place (place type) County	Number
Miami (city) Miami-Dade	227,293
Hialeah (city) Miami-Dade	195,884
Fountainbleau (cdp) Miami-Dade	50,247
Tampa (city) Hillsborough	50,106
Tamiami (cdp) Miami-Dade	47,435
Miami Beach (city) Miami-Dade	46,174
Kendale Lakes (cdp) Miami-Dade	43,425
Kendall (cdp) Miami-Dade	36,760
Pembroke Pines (city) Broward	35,320
The Hammocks (cdp) Miami-Dade	30,890

Total Population 5 Years and Over Who Speak Spanish at Home
Top 10 Places Sorted by Percent

Place (place type) County	Percent
Hialeah Gardens (city) Miami-Dade	95.13
Sweetwater (city) Miami-Dade	92.39
Tamiami (cdp) Miami-Dade	91.91
Hialeah (city) Miami-Dade	91.88
Fountainbleau (cdp) Miami-Dade	90.14
Westchester (cdp) Miami-Dade	87.99
University Park (cdp) Miami-Dade	85.61
Coral Terrace (cdp) Miami-Dade	84.04
Kendall West (cdp) Miami-Dade	83.05
Kendale Lakes (cdp) Miami-Dade	81.46

Hispanics 5 Years and Over Who Speak Spanish at Home
Top 10 Places Sorted by Number

Place (place type) County	Number
Miami (city) Miami-Dade	213,295
Hialeah (city) Miami-Dade	185,933
Fountainbleau (cdp) Miami-Dade	47,278
Tamiami (cdp) Miami-Dade	43,701
Tampa (city) Hillsborough	43,611
Miami Beach (city) Miami-Dade	41,617
Kendale Lakes (cdp) Miami-Dade	39,673
Kendall (cdp) Miami-Dade	32,456
Pembroke Pines (city) Broward	31,076
The Hammocks (cdp) Miami-Dade	27,580

Hispanics 5 Years and Over Who Speak Spanish at Home
Top 10 Places Sorted by Percent

Place (place type) County	Percent
Hialeah Gardens (city) Miami-Dade	97.34
Kendale Lakes (cdp) Miami-Dade	96.11
Tamiami (cdp) Miami-Dade	96.09
Fountainbleau (cdp) Miami-Dade	96.01
Olympia Heights (cdp) Miami-Dade	95.49
Hialeah (city) Miami-Dade	95.46
Westchester (cdp) Miami-Dade	95.22
University Park (cdp) Miami-Dade	95.20
Country Club (cdp) Miami-Dade	94.95
Doral (cdp) Miami-Dade	94.91

Argentinians 5 Years and Over Who Speak Spanish at Home
Top 10 Places Sorted by Number

Place (place type) County	Number
Miami Beach (city) Miami-Dade	2,783
Miami (city) Miami-Dade	1,810
Kendall (cdp) Miami-Dade	587
Sunny Isles Beach (city) Miami-Dade	505
Hollywood (city) Broward	496
Fountainbleau (cdp) Miami-Dade	402
Hialeah (city) Miami-Dade	389

Argentinians 5 Years and Over Who Speak Spanish at Home
Top 10 Places Sorted by Percent

Place (place type) County	Percent
Hialeah (city) Miami-Dade	100.00
Miami Beach (city) Miami-Dade	95.15
Miami (city) Miami-Dade	94.96
Fountainbleau (cdp) Miami-Dade	93.27
Kendall (cdp) Miami-Dade	93.03
Sunny Isles Beach (city) Miami-Dade	90.83
Hollywood (city) Broward	90.35

Bolivians 5 Years and Over Who Speak Spanish at Home
Top 10 Places Sorted by Number

Place (place type) County	Number

No places met population threshold.

Bolivians 5 Years and Over Who Speak Spanish at Home
Top 10 Places Sorted by Percent

Place (place type) County	Percent

No places met population threshold.

Central Americans 5 Years and Over Who Speak Spanish at Home
Top 10 Places Sorted by Number

Place (place type) County	Number
Miami (city) Miami-Dade	39,899
Hialeah (city) Miami-Dade	14,810
Fountainbleau (cdp) Miami-Dade	7,389
Kendale Lakes (cdp) Miami-Dade	3,776
Tamiami (cdp) Miami-Dade	3,520
Kendall (cdp) Miami-Dade	3,425
Homestead (city) Miami-Dade	2,908
Miami Beach (city) Miami-Dade	2,546
Lake Worth (city) Palm Beach	2,428
Kendall West (cdp) Miami-Dade	2,403

Central Americans 5 Years and Over Who Speak Spanish at Home
Top 10 Places Sorted by Percent

Place (place type) County	Percent
Hialeah Gardens (city) Miami-Dade	98.75
Country Walk (cdp) Miami-Dade	98.21
University Park (cdp) Miami-Dade	98.09
The Hammocks (cdp) Miami-Dade	98.03
Bradenton (city) Manatee	97.97
Country Club (cdp) Miami-Dade	97.57
West Little River (cdp) Miami-Dade	97.46
Kendale Lakes (cdp) Miami-Dade	97.34
Gladeview (cdp) Miami-Dade	97.24
Lake Worth Corridor (cdp) Palm Beach	97.08

Chileans 5 Years and Over Who Speak Spanish at Home
Top 10 Places Sorted by Number

Place (place type) County	Number
Miami (city) Miami-Dade	843
Hialeah (city) Miami-Dade	683
Fountainbleau (cdp) Miami-Dade	626
Miami Beach (city) Miami-Dade	618
Kendall (cdp) Miami-Dade	424
Hollywood (city) Broward	345

Chileans 5 Years and Over Who Speak Spanish at Home
Top 10 Places Sorted by Percent

Place (place type) County	Percent
Fountainbleau (cdp) Miami-Dade	98.12
Hollywood (city) Broward	98.01
Miami (city) Miami-Dade	95.90
Hialeah (city) Miami-Dade	91.07
Kendall (cdp) Miami-Dade	90.60
Miami Beach (city) Miami-Dade	85.60

Columbians 5 Years and Over Who Speak Spanish at Home
Top 10 Places Sorted by Number

Place (place type) County	Number
Hialeah (city) Miami-Dade	7,273
Miami (city) Miami-Dade	5,496
The Hammocks (cdp) Miami-Dade	4,684
Miami Beach (city) Miami-Dade	4,050
Kendall West (cdp) Miami-Dade	3,963
Kendall (cdp) Miami-Dade	3,795
Kendale Lakes (cdp) Miami-Dade	3,743

Notes: Please refer to the User's Guide for an explanation of data; tables include places with populations > 9,999 and reflect only those areas that meet Summary File 4 population thresholds, therefore there may be less than 10 places listed

Country Club (cdp) Miami-Dade	3,401
Pembroke Pines (city) Broward	3,083
Hollywood (city) Broward	2,960

Columbians 5 Years and Over Who Speak Spanish at Home

Top 10 Places Sorted by Percent

Place (place type) County	Percent
Deerfield Beach (city) Broward	100.00
Oak Ridge (cdp) Orange	100.00
Doral (cdp) Miami-Dade	98.50
Kendale Lakes (cdp) Miami-Dade	98.34
Tamiami (cdp) Miami-Dade	98.28
Sunset (cdp) Miami-Dade	98.27
The Hammocks (cdp) Miami-Dade	97.77
Aventura (city) Miami-Dade	97.71
Country Club (cdp) Miami-Dade	97.48
Tamarac (city) Broward	97.46

Costa Ricans 5 Years and Over Who Speak Spanish at Home

Top 10 Places Sorted by Number

Place (place type) County	Number
Miami (city) Miami-Dade	728
Hialeah (city) Miami-Dade	515

Costa Ricans 5 Years and Over Who Speak Spanish at Home

Top 10 Places Sorted by Percent

Place (place type) County	Percent
Hialeah (city) Miami-Dade	100.00
Miami (city) Miami-Dade	91.57

Cubans 5 Years and Over Who Speak Spanish at Home

Top 10 Places Sorted by Number

Place (place type) County	Number
Hialeah (city) Miami-Dade	129,600
Miami (city) Miami-Dade	114,426
Tamiami (cdp) Miami-Dade	30,022
Fountainbleau (cdp) Miami-Dade	20,915
Kendale Lakes (cdp) Miami-Dade	20,107
Westchester (cdp) Miami-Dade	18,859
Miami Beach (city) Miami-Dade	16,439
University Park (cdp) Miami-Dade	14,574
Kendall (cdp) Miami-Dade	13,857
Coral Terrace (cdp) Miami-Dade	13,775

Cubans 5 Years and Over Who Speak Spanish at Home

Top 10 Places Sorted by Percent

Place (place type) County	Percent
Hialeah Gardens (city) Miami-Dade	97.83
Fountainbleau (cdp) Miami-Dade	96.26
Tamiami (cdp) Miami-Dade	96.26
Glenvar Heights (cdp) Miami-Dade	96.20
South Miami Heights (cdp) Miami-Dade	96.02
Kendale Lakes (cdp) Miami-Dade	95.78
Olympia Heights (cdp) Miami-Dade	95.60
University Park (cdp) Miami-Dade	95.40
West Little River (cdp) Miami-Dade	95.38
Hialeah (city) Miami-Dade	95.37

Dominicans 5 Years and Over Who Speak Spanish at Home

Top 10 Places Sorted by Number

Place (place type) County	Number
Miami (city) Miami-Dade	6,386
Hialeah (city) Miami-Dade	4,582
Fountainbleau (cdp) Miami-Dade	1,821
Carol City (cdp) Miami-Dade	1,677
Pembroke Pines (city) Broward	1,608
Hollywood (city) Broward	1,475
The Hammocks (cdp) Miami-Dade	1,343
Miami Beach (city) Miami-Dade	1,317
Miramar (city) Broward	1,276
Country Club (cdp) Miami-Dade	1,255

Dominicans 5 Years and Over Who Speak Spanish at Home

Top 10 Places Sorted by Percent

Place (place type) County	Percent
Country Club (cdp) Miami-Dade	100.00
Fountainbleau (cdp) Miami-Dade	99.24
Hialeah Gardens (city) Miami-Dade	99.08
Kendale Lakes (cdp) Miami-Dade	98.58
Kendall West (cdp) Miami-Dade	98.15
North Miami Beach (city) Miami-Dade	97.94
Hialeah (city) Miami-Dade	97.68
Yeehaw Junction (cdp) Osceola	97.66
Miramar (city) Broward	97.03
Oak Ridge (cdp) Orange	96.93

Ecuadorians 5 Years and Over Who Speak Spanish at Home

Top 10 Places Sorted by Number

Place (place type) County	Number
Miami (city) Miami-Dade	1,558
Hialeah (city) Miami-Dade	1,167
Coral Springs (city) Broward	827
Fountainbleau (cdp) Miami-Dade	746
Miami Beach (city) Miami-Dade	599
Hollywood (city) Broward	555
Sunrise (city) Broward	475
Pembroke Pines (city) Broward	457
Tampa (city) Hillsborough	337

Ecuadorians 5 Years and Over Who Speak Spanish at Home

Top 10 Places Sorted by Percent

Place (place type) County	Percent
Hialeah (city) Miami-Dade	97.25
Fountainbleau (cdp) Miami-Dade	96.88
Pembroke Pines (city) Broward	95.21
Sunrise (city) Broward	94.25
Miami Beach (city) Miami-Dade	92.87
Coral Springs (city) Broward	92.51
Miami (city) Miami-Dade	92.08
Hollywood (city) Broward	91.13
Tampa (city) Hillsborough	87.76

Guatelmalans 5 Years and Over Who Speak Spanish at Home

Top 10 Places Sorted by Number

Place (place type) County	Number
Miami (city) Miami-Dade	2,534
West Palm Beach (city) Palm Beach	1,548
Lake Worth (city) Palm Beach	1,367
Homestead (city) Miami-Dade	1,244
Immokalee (cdp) Collier	902
Hialeah (city) Miami-Dade	819
Fort Lauderdale (city) Broward	353
Fort Myers (city) Lee	292
Bonita Springs (city) Lee	233

Guatelmalans 5 Years and Over Who Speak Spanish at Home

Top 10 Places Sorted by Percent

Place (place type) County	Percent
Hialeah (city) Miami-Dade	100.00
Fort Lauderdale (city) Broward	97.78
Miami (city) Miami-Dade	94.76
Homestead (city) Miami-Dade	93.18
Immokalee (cdp) Collier	86.07
Fort Myers (city) Lee	83.67
West Palm Beach (city) Palm Beach	80.71
Lake Worth (city) Palm Beach	80.13
Bonita Springs (city) Lee	79.79

Hondurans 5 Years and Over Who Speak Spanish at Home

Top 10 Places Sorted by Number

Place (place type) County	Number
Miami (city) Miami-Dade	12,285
Hialeah (city) Miami-Dade	2,474
West Little River (cdp) Miami-Dade	872
Miami Beach (city) Miami-Dade	740
Tampa (city) Hillsborough	639
Fountainbleau (cdp) Miami-Dade	610
North Miami (city) Miami-Dade	513
Kendale Lakes (cdp) Miami-Dade	498
Carol City (cdp) Miami-Dade	462
North Miami Beach (city) Miami-Dade	446

Hondurans 5 Years and Over Who Speak Spanish at Home

Top 10 Places Sorted by Percent

Place (place type) County	Percent
Lake Worth (city) Palm Beach	100.00
Tamiami (cdp) Miami-Dade	100.00
Kendale Lakes (cdp) Miami-Dade	98.42
West Little River (cdp) Miami-Dade	98.42
Fountainbleau (cdp) Miami-Dade	97.60
Hialeah (city) Miami-Dade	97.36
Miami Beach (city) Miami-Dade	95.73
Miami (city) Miami-Dade	95.03
Hollywood (city) Broward	93.28
Carol City (cdp) Miami-Dade	91.67

Mexicans 5 Years and Over Who Speak Spanish at Home

Top 10 Places Sorted by Number

Place (place type) County	Number
Immokalee (cdp) Collier	8,739
Homestead (city) Miami-Dade	5,717
Tampa (city) Hillsborough	5,120
Leisure City (cdp) Miami-Dade	4,443
Fort Pierce (city) Saint Lucie	3,484
Clearwater (city) Pinellas	3,117
Sarasota (city) Sarasota	3,005
Golden Gate (cdp) Collier	2,788
Bonita Springs (city) Lee	2,742
Plant City (city) Hillsborough	2,718

Mexicans 5 Years and Over Who Speak Spanish at Home

Top 10 Places Sorted by Percent

Place (place type) County	Percent
Fountainbleau (cdp) Miami-Dade	96.41
Doral (cdp) Miami-Dade	96.33
Sarasota (city) Sarasota	95.46
De Land (city) Volusia	94.90
Bonita Springs (city) Lee	94.72
The Hammocks (cdp) Miami-Dade	94.48
Fort Pierce (city) Saint Lucie	94.39
Hialeah (city) Miami-Dade	94.39
Homestead (city) Miami-Dade	94.05
Auburndale (city) Polk	93.90

Nicaraguans 5 Years and Over Who Speak Spanish at Home

Top 10 Places Sorted by Number

Place (place type) County	Number
Miami (city) Miami-Dade	20,705
Hialeah (city) Miami-Dade	9,424
Fountainbleau (cdp) Miami-Dade	5,503
Kendale Lakes (cdp) Miami-Dade	2,619
Tamiami (cdp) Miami-Dade	2,514
Sweetwater (city) Miami-Dade	2,196
Kendall (cdp) Miami-Dade	2,020
Kendall West (cdp) Miami-Dade	1,486
The Hammocks (cdp) Miami-Dade	1,444
Carol City (cdp) Miami-Dade	1,285

Notes: Please refer to the User's Guide for an explanation of data; tables include places with populations > 9,999 and reflect only those areas that meet Summary File 4 population thresholds, therefore there may be less than 10 places listed

Nicaraguans 5 Years and Over Who Speak Spanish at Home

Top 10 Places Sorted by Percent

Place (place type) County	Percent
The Crossings (cdp) Miami-Dade	100.00
Hialeah Gardens (city) Miami-Dade	99.25
The Hammocks (cdp) Miami-Dade	98.37
West Little River (cdp) Miami-Dade	98.36
Country Club (cdp) Miami-Dade	97.92
Tamiami (cdp) Miami-Dade	97.40
Palmetto Estates (cdp) Miami-Dade	97.16
University Park (cdp) Miami-Dade	97.12
Coral Gables (city) Miami-Dade	96.81
Hialeah (city) Miami-Dade	96.76

Panamanians 5 Years and Over Who Speak Spanish at Home

Top 10 Places Sorted by Number

Place (place type) County	Number
Miami (city) Miami-Dade	848
Fountainbleau (cdp) Miami-Dade	475
Tampa (city) Hillsborough	439
Jacksonville (city) Duval	423
Miramar (city) Broward	264

Panamanians 5 Years and Over Who Speak Spanish at Home

Top 10 Places Sorted by Percent

Place (place type) County	Percent
Miami (city) Miami-Dade	98.83
Fountainbleau (cdp) Miami-Dade	92.95
Miramar (city) Broward	76.52
Jacksonville (city) Duval	73.95
Tampa (city) Hillsborough	72.09

Paraguayans 5 Years and Over Who Speak Spanish at Home

Top 10 Places Sorted by Number

Place (place type) County	Number

No places met population threshold.

Paraguayans 5 Years and Over Who Speak Spanish at Home

Top 10 Places Sorted by Percent

Place (place type) County	Percent

No places met population threshold.

Peruvians 5 Years and Over Who Speak Spanish at Home

Top 10 Places Sorted by Number

Place (place type) County	Number
Miami (city) Miami-Dade	2,506
Miami Beach (city) Miami-Dade	1,754
The Hammocks (cdp) Miami-Dade	1,712
Hialeah (city) Miami-Dade	1,386
Pembroke Pines (city) Broward	1,265
Kendall (cdp) Miami-Dade	1,180
Hollywood (city) Broward	1,145
Fountainbleau (cdp) Miami-Dade	1,109
Kendall West (cdp) Miami-Dade	1,049
Kendale Lakes (cdp) Miami-Dade	862

Peruvians 5 Years and Over Who Speak Spanish at Home

Top 10 Places Sorted by Percent

Place (place type) County	Percent
Hialeah (city) Miami-Dade	100.00
North Miami Beach (city) Miami-Dade	100.00
Plantation (city) Broward	98.23
Fountainbleau (cdp) Miami-Dade	98.05
The Hammocks (cdp) Miami-Dade	98.05
Doral (cdp) Miami-Dade	96.99
Miami Beach (city) Miami-Dade	96.32
Miramar (city) Broward	95.02
The Crossings (cdp) Miami-Dade	94.97
Miami (city) Miami-Dade	94.78

Puerto Ricans 5 Years and Over Who Speak Spanish at Home

Top 10 Places Sorted by Number

Place (place type) County	Number
Orlando (city) Orange	13,487
Tampa (city) Hillsborough	12,075
Kissimmee (city) Osceola	9,753
Miami (city) Miami-Dade	8,662
Jacksonville (city) Duval	7,382
Deltona (city) Volusia	7,308
Yeehaw Junction (cdp) Osceola	6,972
Hialeah (city) Miami-Dade	6,105
Town 'n' Country (cdp) Hillsborough	5,835
Pembroke Pines (city) Broward	5,539

Puerto Ricans 5 Years and Over Who Speak Spanish at Home

Top 10 Places Sorted by Percent

Place (place type) County	Percent
Opa-locka (city) Miami-Dade	98.68
Tamiami (cdp) Miami-Dade	98.39
Doral (cdp) Miami-Dade	97.61
The Crossings (cdp) Miami-Dade	96.99
West Little River (cdp) Miami-Dade	96.46
Fountainbleau (cdp) Miami-Dade	95.59
Kendale Lakes (cdp) Miami-Dade	95.49
University Park (cdp) Miami-Dade	95.43
Hialeah Gardens (city) Miami-Dade	94.68
Meadow Woods (cdp) Orange	93.98

Salvadorans 5 Years and Over Who Speak Spanish at Home

Top 10 Places Sorted by Number

Place (place type) County	Number
Miami (city) Miami-Dade	2,155
Homestead (city) Miami-Dade	902
Hialeah (city) Miami-Dade	881
Oakland Park (city) Broward	739
Fort Lauderdale (city) Broward	622
Lake Worth (city) Palm Beach	493

Salvadorans 5 Years and Over Who Speak Spanish at Home

Top 10 Places Sorted by Percent

Place (place type) County	Percent
Lake Worth (city) Palm Beach	100.00
Oakland Park (city) Broward	100.00
Hialeah (city) Miami-Dade	98.99
Fort Lauderdale (city) Broward	96.43
Homestead (city) Miami-Dade	95.55
Miami (city) Miami-Dade	94.60

South Americans 5 Years and Over Who Speak Spanish at Home

Top 10 Places Sorted by Number

Place (place type) County	Number
Miami (city) Miami-Dade	14,456
Hialeah (city) Miami-Dade	12,158
Miami Beach (city) Miami-Dade	11,781
The Hammocks (cdp) Miami-Dade	9,112
Kendall (cdp) Miami-Dade	7,847
Fountainbleau (cdp) Miami-Dade	7,745
Kendall West (cdp) Miami-Dade	7,122
Kendale Lakes (cdp) Miami-Dade	6,876
Pembroke Pines (city) Broward	6,811
Hollywood (city) Broward	6,494

South Americans 5 Years and Over Who Speak Spanish at Home

Top 10 Places Sorted by Percent

Place (place type) County	Percent
Olympia Heights (cdp) Miami-Dade	100.00
Palm Beach Gardens (city) Palm Beach	100.00
Altamonte Springs (city) Seminole	99.12
West Little River (cdp) Miami-Dade	98.77
Sarasota (city) Sarasota	98.42
Westchester (cdp) Miami-Dade	98.07
Doral (cdp) Miami-Dade	97.97
Golden Glades (cdp) Miami-Dade	97.72
Hialeah Gardens (city) Miami-Dade	97.70
Greater Carrollwood (cdp) Hillsborough	97.66

Spaniards 5 Years and Over Who Speak Spanish at Home

Top 10 Places Sorted by Number

Place (place type) County	Number
Miami (city) Miami-Dade	888
Miami Beach (city) Miami-Dade	526
Tampa (city) Hillsborough	506
Hialeah (city) Miami-Dade	465

Spaniards 5 Years and Over Who Speak Spanish at Home

Top 10 Places Sorted by Percent

Place (place type) County	Percent
Miami (city) Miami-Dade	95.48
Hialeah (city) Miami-Dade	94.90
Miami Beach (city) Miami-Dade	93.59
Tampa (city) Hillsborough	72.29

Uruguayans 5 Years and Over Who Speak Spanish at Home

Top 10 Places Sorted by Number

Place (place type) County	Number

No places met population threshold.

Uruguayans 5 Years and Over Who Speak Spanish at Home

Top 10 Places Sorted by Percent

Place (place type) County	Percent

No places met population threshold.

Venezuelans 5 Years and Over Who Speak Spanish at Home

Top 10 Places Sorted by Number

Place (place type) County	Number
Fountainbleau (cdp) Miami-Dade	1,970
Weston (city) Broward	1,860
Doral (cdp) Miami-Dade	1,649
Miami (city) Miami-Dade	1,549
The Hammocks (cdp) Miami-Dade	1,471
Miami Beach (city) Miami-Dade	1,344
Kendall (cdp) Miami-Dade	1,287
Pembroke Pines (city) Broward	1,283
Kendall West (cdp) Miami-Dade	1,114
Hialeah (city) Miami-Dade	908

Venezuelans 5 Years and Over Who Speak Spanish at Home

Top 10 Places Sorted by Percent

Place (place type) County	Percent
Tamiami (cdp) Miami-Dade	100.00
The Crossings (cdp) Miami-Dade	100.00
Weston (city) Broward	99.04
Fountainbleau (cdp) Miami-Dade	98.85
Kendall West (cdp) Miami-Dade	97.72
Hialeah (city) Miami-Dade	97.63
Richmond West (cdp) Miami-Dade	97.36
Doral (cdp) Miami-Dade	97.23
Kendale Lakes (cdp) Miami-Dade	96.62
Miami Beach (city) Miami-Dade	95.39

Other Hispanics 5 Years and Over Who Speak Spanish at Home

Top 10 Places Sorted by Number

Place (place type) County	Number
Miami (city) Miami-Dade	25,944
Hialeah (city) Miami-Dade	16,817

Notes: Please refer to the User's Guide for an explanation of data; tables include places with populations > 9,999 and reflect only those areas that meet Summary File 4 population thresholds, therefore there may be less than 10 places listed

Tampa (city) Hillsborough	7,687
Fountainbleau (cdp) Miami-Dade	7,249
Kendale Lakes (cdp) Miami-Dade	5,941
Miami Beach (city) Miami-Dade	5,184
The Hammocks (cdp) Miami-Dade	4,598
Hollywood (city) Broward	4,426
Pembroke Pines (city) Broward	4,220
Tamiami (cdp) Miami-Dade	4,196

Other Hispanics 5 Years and Over Who Speak Spanish at Home

Top 10 Places Sorted by Percent

Place (place type) County	Percent
Sunny Isles Beach (city) Miami-Dade	99.16
Olympia Heights (cdp) Miami-Dade	97.04
Kendale Lakes (cdp) Miami-Dade	95.81
Fountainbleau (cdp) Miami-Dade	95.53
Poinciana (cdp) Osceola	95.44
Gladeview (cdp) Miami-Dade	94.76
Ives Estates (cdp) Miami-Dade	94.67
Sweetwater (city) Miami-Dade	94.52
Tamiami (cdp) Miami-Dade	94.44
Palmetto Estates (cdp) Miami-Dade	94.11

Foreign Born

Total Population

Top 10 Places Sorted by Number

Place (place type) County	Number
Miami (city) Miami-Dade	215,739
Hialeah (city) Miami-Dade	163,256
Miami Beach (city) Miami-Dade	48,852
Jacksonville (city) Duval	43,661
Fountainbleau (cdp) Miami-Dade	43,496
Pembroke Pines (city) Broward	39,727
Tampa (city) Hillsborough	37,027
Hollywood (city) Broward	36,562
Tamiami (cdp) Miami-Dade	35,850
Kendale Lakes (cdp) Miami-Dade	33,460

Total Population

Top 10 Places Sorted by Percent

Place (place type) County	Percent
Sweetwater (city) Miami-Dade	74.68
Fountainbleau (cdp) Miami-Dade	73.08
Hialeah (city) Miami-Dade	72.11
Hialeah Gardens (city) Miami-Dade	70.11
Westchester (cdp) Miami-Dade	69.00
University Park (cdp) Miami-Dade	66.62
Coral Terrace (cdp) Miami-Dade	66.12
Tamiami (cdp) Miami-Dade	65.49
Doral (cdp) Miami-Dade	62.55
Miami (city) Miami-Dade	59.50

Hispanic

Top 10 Places Sorted by Number

Place (place type) County	Number
Miami (city) Miami-Dade	188,008
Hialeah (city) Miami-Dade	160,779
Fountainbleau (cdp) Miami-Dade	41,125
Miami Beach (city) Miami-Dade	36,211
Tamiami (cdp) Miami-Dade	34,857
Kendale Lakes (cdp) Miami-Dade	30,802
Kendall (cdp) Miami-Dade	24,625
Tampa (city) Hillsborough	21,240
Kendall West (cdp) Miami-Dade	20,522
Westchester (cdp) Miami-Dade	20,394

Hispanic

Top 10 Places Sorted by Percent

Place (place type) County	Percent
Marco Island (city) Collier	82.30
Aventura (city) Miami-Dade	81.08
Sunny Isles Beach (city) Miami-Dade	80.73
Fountainbleau (cdp) Miami-Dade	79.34
Westchester (cdp) Miami-Dade	78.88
Miami (city) Miami-Dade	78.84
Sweetwater (city) Miami-Dade	78.51
Hialeah (city) Miami-Dade	78.50
Coral Terrace (cdp) Miami-Dade	77.22
Miami Beach (city) Miami-Dade	77.08

Argentinian

Top 10 Places Sorted by Number

Place (place type) County	Number
Miami Beach (city) Miami-Dade	2,809
Miami (city) Miami-Dade	1,801
Kendall (cdp) Miami-Dade	547
Sunny Isles Beach (city) Miami-Dade	543
Hollywood (city) Broward	491
Hialeah (city) Miami-Dade	395
Fountainbleau (cdp) Miami-Dade	360

Argentinian

Top 10 Places Sorted by Percent

Place (place type) County	Percent
Sunny Isles Beach (city) Miami-Dade	95.10
Miami Beach (city) Miami-Dade	92.68
Hialeah (city) Miami-Dade	92.07
Miami (city) Miami-Dade	88.76
Hollywood (city) Broward	87.84
Kendall (cdp) Miami-Dade	83.51
Fountainbleau (cdp) Miami-Dade	81.82

Bolivian

Top 10 Places Sorted by Number

Place (place type) County	Number

No places met population threshold.

Bolivian

Top 10 Places Sorted by Percent

Place (place type) County	Percent

No places met population threshold.

Central American

Top 10 Places Sorted by Number

Place (place type) County	Number
Miami (city) Miami-Dade	38,302
Hialeah (city) Miami-Dade	13,832
Fountainbleau (cdp) Miami-Dade	6,984
Kendale Lakes (cdp) Miami-Dade	3,409
Tamiami (cdp) Miami-Dade	3,130
Kendall (cdp) Miami-Dade	3,037
Homestead (city) Miami-Dade	2,836
Miami Beach (city) Miami-Dade	2,478
Lake Worth (city) Palm Beach	2,403
West Palm Beach (city) Palm Beach	2,397

Central American

Top 10 Places Sorted by Percent

Place (place type) County	Percent
Deerfield Beach (city) Broward	89.88
Gladeview (cdp) Miami-Dade	89.88
Golden Gate (cdp) Collier	89.07
North Miami (city) Miami-Dade	88.69
Opa-locka (city) Miami-Dade	88.46
Jupiter (town) Palm Beach	88.00
Miami Beach (city) Miami-Dade	87.78
Pinewood (cdp) Miami-Dade	87.67
Margate (city) Broward	87.61
Coral Gables (city) Miami-Dade	87.57

Chilean

Top 10 Places Sorted by Number

Place (place type) County	Number
Miami (city) Miami-Dade	811
Hialeah (city) Miami-Dade	722
Fountainbleau (cdp) Miami-Dade	638
Miami Beach (city) Miami-Dade	612
Kendall (cdp) Miami-Dade	435
Hollywood (city) Broward	320

Chilean

Top 10 Places Sorted by Percent

Place (place type) County	Percent
Hialeah (city) Miami-Dade	96.27
Fountainbleau (cdp) Miami-Dade	90.75
Kendall (cdp) Miami-Dade	90.63
Miami (city) Miami-Dade	90.41
Hollywood (city) Broward	84.88
Miami Beach (city) Miami-Dade	82.81

Columbian

Top 10 Places Sorted by Number

Place (place type) County	Number
Hialeah (city) Miami-Dade	6,687
Miami (city) Miami-Dade	5,243
The Hammocks (cdp) Miami-Dade	4,210
Miami Beach (city) Miami-Dade	3,937
Kendall West (cdp) Miami-Dade	3,541
Kendall (cdp) Miami-Dade	3,491
Kendale Lakes (cdp) Miami-Dade	3,204
Country Club (cdp) Miami-Dade	2,962
Pembroke Pines (city) Broward	2,699
Hollywood (city) Broward	2,681

Columbian

Top 10 Places Sorted by Percent

Place (place type) County	Percent
Deerfield Beach (city) Broward	92.06
Sunny Isles Beach (city) Miami-Dade	90.50
University Park (cdp) Miami-Dade	90.50
Tamarac (city) Broward	90.44
Glenvar Heights (cdp) Miami-Dade	89.04
Fountainbleau (cdp) Miami-Dade	88.39
Kissimmee (city) Osceola	88.03
Doral (cdp) Miami-Dade	87.78
Miami Beach (city) Miami-Dade	87.63
Miami (city) Miami-Dade	87.30

Costa Rican

Top 10 Places Sorted by Number

Place (place type) County	Number
Miami (city) Miami-Dade	667
Hialeah (city) Miami-Dade	451

Costa Rican

Top 10 Places Sorted by Percent

Place (place type) County	Percent
Hialeah (city) Miami-Dade	86.23
Miami (city) Miami-Dade	81.74

Cuban

Top 10 Places Sorted by Number

Place (place type) County	Number
Hialeah (city) Miami-Dade	119,595
Miami (city) Miami-Dade	108,492
Tamiami (cdp) Miami-Dade	24,750
Fountainbleau (cdp) Miami-Dade	19,287
Westchester (cdp) Miami-Dade	16,690
Kendale Lakes (cdp) Miami-Dade	16,265
Miami Beach (city) Miami-Dade	15,214
University Park (cdp) Miami-Dade	12,655
Coral Terrace (cdp) Miami-Dade	12,393
Kendall (cdp) Miami-Dade	10,264

Cuban

Top 10 Places Sorted by Percent

Place (place type) County	Percent
Sunny Isles Beach (city) Miami-Dade	89.81
Brownsville (cdp) Miami-Dade	88.68
Miami (city) Miami-Dade	86.98
Fountainbleau (cdp) Miami-Dade	86.48

Notes: Please refer to the User's Guide for an explanation of data; tables include places with populations > 9,999 and reflect only those areas that meet Summary File 4 population thresholds, therefore there may be less than 10 places listed

Hialeah (city) Miami-Dade	84.64
Golden Gate (cdp) Collier	84.34
Pinewood (cdp) Miami-Dade	83.89
Miami Beach (city) Miami-Dade	83.41
Belle Glade (city) Palm Beach	83.13
Hialeah Gardens (city) Miami-Dade	82.92

Dominican
Top 10 Places Sorted by Number

Place (place type) County	Number
Miami (city) Miami-Dade	5,723
Hialeah (city) Miami-Dade	3,813
Fountainbleau (cdp) Miami-Dade	1,568
Carol City (cdp) Miami-Dade	1,274
Miami Beach (city) Miami-Dade	1,212
The Hammocks (cdp) Miami-Dade	1,130
Pembroke Pines (city) Broward	1,072
Hollywood (city) Broward	998
Miramar (city) Broward	997
Country Club (cdp) Miami-Dade	951

Dominican
Top 10 Places Sorted by Percent

Place (place type) County	Percent
Hialeah Gardens (city) Miami-Dade	92.01
Miami Beach (city) Miami-Dade	86.82
Doral (cdp) Miami-Dade	83.02
Fountainbleau (cdp) Miami-Dade	81.33
Miami (city) Miami-Dade	78.72
Hialeah (city) Miami-Dade	78.04
West Little River (cdp) Miami-Dade	75.85
The Hammocks (cdp) Miami-Dade	74.39
North Miami Beach (city) Miami-Dade	72.91
Golden Glades (cdp) Miami-Dade	72.83

Ecuadorian
Top 10 Places Sorted by Number

Place (place type) County	Number
Miami (city) Miami-Dade	1,459
Hialeah (city) Miami-Dade	1,076
Coral Springs (city) Broward	673
Fountainbleau (cdp) Miami-Dade	635
Miami Beach (city) Miami-Dade	514
Hollywood (city) Broward	443
Pembroke Pines (city) Broward	396
Sunrise (city) Broward	386
Tampa (city) Hillsborough	338

Ecuadorian
Top 10 Places Sorted by Percent

Place (place type) County	Percent
Hialeah (city) Miami-Dade	87.27
Miami (city) Miami-Dade	83.13
Pembroke Pines (city) Broward	81.48
Tampa (city) Hillsborough	80.86
Fountainbleau (cdp) Miami-Dade	79.47
Miami Beach (city) Miami-Dade	77.64
Sunrise (city) Broward	72.97
Coral Springs (city) Broward	71.44
Hollywood (city) Broward	70.54

Guatelmalan
Top 10 Places Sorted by Number

Place (place type) County	Number
Miami (city) Miami-Dade	2,400
West Palm Beach (city) Palm Beach	1,781
Lake Worth (city) Palm Beach	1,382
Homestead (city) Miami-Dade	1,224
Immokalee (cdp) Collier	833
Hialeah (city) Miami-Dade	682
Fort Lauderdale (city) Broward	331
Fort Myers (city) Lee	309
Bonita Springs (city) Lee	281

Guatelmalan
Top 10 Places Sorted by Percent

Place (place type) County	Percent
Fort Lauderdale (city) Broward	89.22
West Palm Beach (city) Palm Beach	86.46
Homestead (city) Miami-Dade	85.30
Miami (city) Miami-Dade	84.18
Hialeah (city) Miami-Dade	81.00
Fort Myers (city) Lee	78.63
Bonita Springs (city) Lee	76.15
Immokalee (cdp) Collier	72.18
Lake Worth (city) Palm Beach	70.30

Honduran
Top 10 Places Sorted by Number

Place (place type) County	Number
Miami (city) Miami-Dade	12,099
Hialeah (city) Miami-Dade	2,290
West Little River (cdp) Miami-Dade	797
Miami Beach (city) Miami-Dade	739
Tampa (city) Hillsborough	639
Fountainbleau (cdp) Miami-Dade	585
North Miami (city) Miami-Dade	532
Kendale Lakes (cdp) Miami-Dade	444
North Miami Beach (city) Miami-Dade	415
Lake Worth (city) Palm Beach	404

Honduran
Top 10 Places Sorted by Percent

Place (place type) County	Percent
Miami Beach (city) Miami-Dade	91.23
Fountainbleau (cdp) Miami-Dade	91.12
North Miami (city) Miami-Dade	90.17
Miami (city) Miami-Dade	88.57
Hialeah (city) Miami-Dade	86.38
Tamiami (cdp) Miami-Dade	86.31
Lake Worth (city) Palm Beach	83.47
West Little River (cdp) Miami-Dade	81.74
North Miami Beach (city) Miami-Dade	81.53
Kendale Lakes (cdp) Miami-Dade	79.71

Mexican
Top 10 Places Sorted by Number

Place (place type) County	Number
Immokalee (cdp) Collier	5,667
Tampa (city) Hillsborough	3,769
Homestead (city) Miami-Dade	3,731
Clearwater (city) Pinellas	2,953
Fort Pierce (city) Saint Lucie	2,925
Sarasota (city) Sarasota	2,776
Golden Gate (cdp) Collier	2,760
Leisure City (cdp) Miami-Dade	2,572
Bonita Springs (city) Lee	2,191
Lake Worth Corridor (cdp) Palm Beach	2,128

Mexican
Top 10 Places Sorted by Percent

Place (place type) County	Percent
Oak Ridge (cdp) Orange	79.70
Kendall West (cdp) Miami-Dade	78.41
Sarasota (city) Sarasota	78.31
Doral (cdp) Miami-Dade	76.29
Golden Gate (cdp) Collier	74.82
Fountainbleau (cdp) Miami-Dade	73.86
Oakland Park (city) Broward	72.87
Clearwater (city) Pinellas	70.13
Fort Pierce (city) Saint Lucie	70.03
Boca Raton (city) Palm Beach	69.51

Nicaraguan
Top 10 Places Sorted by Number

Place (place type) County	Number
Miami (city) Miami-Dade	19,647
Hialeah (city) Miami-Dade	8,960
Fountainbleau (cdp) Miami-Dade	5,271
Kendale Lakes (cdp) Miami-Dade	2,384
Tamiami (cdp) Miami-Dade	2,184
Sweetwater (city) Miami-Dade	2,071
Kendall (cdp) Miami-Dade	1,752
Kendall West (cdp) Miami-Dade	1,426
The Hammocks (cdp) Miami-Dade	1,322
Carol City (cdp) Miami-Dade	1,193

Nicaraguan
Top 10 Places Sorted by Percent

Place (place type) County	Percent
Palmetto Estates (cdp) Miami-Dade	92.78
Miramar (city) Broward	91.47
Miami Beach (city) Miami-Dade	90.52
Pinewood (cdp) Miami-Dade	90.36
West Little River (cdp) Miami-Dade	90.29
Gladeview (cdp) Miami-Dade	90.16
Kendall West (cdp) Miami-Dade	89.24
Coral Terrace (cdp) Miami-Dade	89.11
The Crossings (cdp) Miami-Dade	88.49
Hialeah (city) Miami-Dade	88.18

Panamanian
Top 10 Places Sorted by Number

Place (place type) County	Number
Miami (city) Miami-Dade	759
Fountainbleau (cdp) Miami-Dade	396
Tampa (city) Hillsborough	344
Jacksonville (city) Duval	290
Miramar (city) Broward	288

Panamanian
Top 10 Places Sorted by Percent

Place (place type) County	Percent
Miami (city) Miami-Dade	85.96
Miramar (city) Broward	78.47
Fountainbleau (cdp) Miami-Dade	75.86
Tampa (city) Hillsborough	54.43
Jacksonville (city) Duval	49.91

Paraguayan
Top 10 Places Sorted by Number

Place (place type) County	Number

No places met population threshold.

Paraguayan
Top 10 Places Sorted by Percent

Place (place type) County	Percent

No places met population threshold.

Peruvian
Top 10 Places Sorted by Number

Place (place type) County	Number
Miami (city) Miami-Dade	2,373
Miami Beach (city) Miami-Dade	1,704
The Hammocks (cdp) Miami-Dade	1,423
Hialeah (city) Miami-Dade	1,280
Kendall (cdp) Miami-Dade	1,105
Pembroke Pines (city) Broward	1,060
Hollywood (city) Broward	1,052
Kendall West (cdp) Miami-Dade	1,049
Fountainbleau (cdp) Miami-Dade	1,036
Coral Springs (city) Broward	870

Peruvian
Top 10 Places Sorted by Percent

Place (place type) County	Percent
Doral (cdp) Miami-Dade	91.74
Kendall West (cdp) Miami-Dade	91.46
Coral Springs (city) Broward	91.29
Miami Beach (city) Miami-Dade	89.78
The Crossings (cdp) Miami-Dade	89.68
North Miami Beach (city) Miami-Dade	89.66
Hialeah (city) Miami-Dade	87.73

Notes: Please refer to the User's Guide for an explanation of data; tables include places with populations > 9,999 and reflect only those areas that meet Summary File 4 population thresholds, therefore there may be less than 10 places listed

Fountainbleau (cdp) Miami-Dade	87.72
Weston (city) Broward	87.66
Richmond West (cdp) Miami-Dade	86.18

Puerto Rican
Top 10 Places Sorted by Number

Place (place type) County	**Number**
Miami (city) Miami-Dade	335
Town 'n' Country (cdp) Hillsborough	232
Orlando (city) Orange	219
Hialeah (city) Miami-Dade	197
Tampa (city) Hillsborough	192
Kissimmee (city) Osceola	175
Jacksonville (city) Duval	167
Carol City (cdp) Miami-Dade	140
Fort Lauderdale (city) Broward	112
Cutler Ridge (cdp) Miami-Dade	101

Puerto Rican
Top 10 Places Sorted by Percent

Place (place type) County	**Percent**
Miami Springs (city) Miami-Dade	12.41
Westchester (cdp) Miami-Dade	12.00
Glenvar Heights (cdp) Miami-Dade	10.66
Wekiwa Springs (cdp) Seminole	7.46
Delray Beach (city) Palm Beach	6.55
Lake Worth Corridor (cdp) Palm Beach	6.28
Cutler Ridge (cdp) Miami-Dade	6.25
Lauderhill (city) Broward	5.93
Hallandale (city) Broward	5.90
Hialeah Gardens (city) Miami-Dade	5.19

Salvadoran
Top 10 Places Sorted by Number

Place (place type) County	**Number**
Miami (city) Miami-Dade	2,130
Homestead (city) Miami-Dade	908
Hialeah (city) Miami-Dade	765
Oakland Park (city) Broward	626
Fort Lauderdale (city) Broward	529
Lake Worth (city) Palm Beach	444

Salvadoran
Top 10 Places Sorted by Percent

Place (place type) County	**Percent**
Miami (city) Miami-Dade	88.97
Lake Worth (city) Palm Beach	84.25
Homestead (city) Miami-Dade	81.07
Oakland Park (city) Broward	80.77
Hialeah (city) Miami-Dade	80.53
Fort Lauderdale (city) Broward	79.67

South American
Top 10 Places Sorted by Number

Place (place type) County	**Number**
Miami (city) Miami-Dade	13,962
Miami Beach (city) Miami-Dade	11,585
Hialeah (city) Miami-Dade	11,377
The Hammocks (cdp) Miami-Dade	8,110
Fountainbleau (cdp) Miami-Dade	7,308
Kendall (cdp) Miami-Dade	7,294
Kendall West (cdp) Miami-Dade	6,484
Kendale Lakes (cdp) Miami-Dade	6,097
Pembroke Pines (city) Broward	6,074
Hollywood (city) Broward	5,885

South American
Top 10 Places Sorted by Percent

Place (place type) County	**Percent**
Oakland Park (city) Broward	93.30
Sunny Isles Beach (city) Miami-Dade	93.12
Oak Ridge (cdp) Orange	92.67
Deerfield Beach (city) Broward	91.34
Doral (cdp) Miami-Dade	89.88
Miami Beach (city) Miami-Dade	89.23
Pinecrest (village) Miami-Dade	88.84
Hialeah (city) Miami-Dade	88.17
Sunset (cdp) Miami-Dade	88.15
Aventura (city) Miami-Dade	87.89

Spaniard
Top 10 Places Sorted by Number

Place (place type) County	**Number**
Miami (city) Miami-Dade	819
Miami Beach (city) Miami-Dade	498
Hialeah (city) Miami-Dade	410
Tampa (city) Hillsborough	191

Spaniard
Top 10 Places Sorted by Percent

Place (place type) County	**Percent**
Miami Beach (city) Miami-Dade	86.91
Miami (city) Miami-Dade	86.12
Hialeah (city) Miami-Dade	80.55
Tampa (city) Hillsborough	26.06

Uruguayan
Top 10 Places Sorted by Number

Place (place type) County	**Number**
No places met population threshold.	

Uruguayan
Top 10 Places Sorted by Percent

Place (place type) County	**Percent**
No places met population threshold.	

Venezuelan
Top 10 Places Sorted by Number

Place (place type) County	**Number**
Fountainbleau (cdp) Miami-Dade	1,876
Weston (city) Broward	1,779
Doral (cdp) Miami-Dade	1,685
Miami (city) Miami-Dade	1,619
The Hammocks (cdp) Miami-Dade	1,413
Miami Beach (city) Miami-Dade	1,331
Pembroke Pines (city) Broward	1,292
Kendall (cdp) Miami-Dade	1,212
Kendall West (cdp) Miami-Dade	982
Hialeah (city) Miami-Dade	876

Venezuelan
Top 10 Places Sorted by Percent

Place (place type) County	**Percent**
Tamiami (cdp) Miami-Dade	93.94
Miami (city) Miami-Dade	91.99
Hialeah (city) Miami-Dade	91.73
Doral (cdp) Miami-Dade	91.53
Miami Beach (city) Miami-Dade	91.41
Orlando (city) Orange	90.65
Weston (city) Broward	90.35
Fountainbleau (cdp) Miami-Dade	90.02
Kendale Lakes (cdp) Miami-Dade	89.78
Tampa (city) Hillsborough	87.66

Other Hispanic
Top 10 Places Sorted by Number

Place (place type) County	**Number**
Miami (city) Miami-Dade	18,266
Hialeah (city) Miami-Dade	10,487
Fountainbleau (cdp) Miami-Dade	5,455
Miami Beach (city) Miami-Dade	4,494
Kendale Lakes (cdp) Miami-Dade	3,847
Hollywood (city) Broward	3,150
The Hammocks (cdp) Miami-Dade	2,910
Kendall (cdp) Miami-Dade	2,833
Pembroke Pines (city) Broward	2,763
Kendall West (cdp) Miami-Dade	2,708

Other Hispanic
Top 10 Places Sorted by Percent

Place (place type) County	**Percent**
Aventura (city) Miami-Dade	83.65
Gladeview (cdp) Miami-Dade	73.99
Key Biscayne (village) Miami-Dade	71.48
Miami Beach (city) Miami-Dade	69.95
Doral (cdp) Miami-Dade	68.95
Delray Beach (city) Palm Beach	68.87
Ojus (cdp) Miami-Dade	68.08
Golden Gate (cdp) Collier	66.18
Jupiter (town) Palm Beach	64.27
Fountainbleau (cdp) Miami-Dade	63.68

Foreign-Born Naturalized Citizens

Total Population
Top 10 Places Sorted by Number

Place (place type) County	**Number**
Miami (city) Miami-Dade	89,727
Hialeah (city) Miami-Dade	70,331
Pembroke Pines (city) Broward	22,597
Miami Beach (city) Miami-Dade	21,744
Jacksonville (city) Duval	20,786
Tamiami (cdp) Miami-Dade	20,633
Fountainbleau (cdp) Miami-Dade	18,348
Kendale Lakes (cdp) Miami-Dade	17,856
Kendall (cdp) Miami-Dade	16,474
Hollywood (city) Broward	16,136

Total Population
Top 10 Places Sorted by Percent

Place (place type) County	**Percent**
Westchester (cdp) Miami-Dade	41.34
University Park (cdp) Miami-Dade	40.38
Tamiami (cdp) Miami-Dade	37.69
Coral Terrace (cdp) Miami-Dade	36.41
Olympia Heights (cdp) Miami-Dade	36.14
Westwood Lakes (cdp) Miami-Dade	33.37
Sunset (cdp) Miami-Dade	32.98
Miami Lakes (cdp) Miami-Dade	32.32
Kendale Lakes (cdp) Miami-Dade	31.39
Hialeah (city) Miami-Dade	31.06

Hispanic
Top 10 Places Sorted by Number

Place (place type) County	**Number**
Miami (city) Miami-Dade	79,264
Hialeah (city) Miami-Dade	69,014
Tamiami (cdp) Miami-Dade	20,107
Fountainbleau (cdp) Miami-Dade	17,610
Miami Beach (city) Miami-Dade	16,432
Kendale Lakes (cdp) Miami-Dade	16,336
Kendall (cdp) Miami-Dade	13,071
Westchester (cdp) Miami-Dade	12,212
Pembroke Pines (city) Broward	10,874
University Park (cdp) Miami-Dade	10,263

Hispanic
Top 10 Places Sorted by Percent

Place (place type) County	**Percent**
Westchester (cdp) Miami-Dade	47.23
University Park (cdp) Miami-Dade	46.83
Coral Gables (city) Miami-Dade	45.23
Olympia Heights (cdp) Miami-Dade	45.19
Miami Lakes (cdp) Miami-Dade	44.06
Sunset (cdp) Miami-Dade	43.93
Coral Terrace (cdp) Miami-Dade	42.28
Westwood Lakes (cdp) Miami-Dade	42.22
Tamiami (cdp) Miami-Dade	42.16
South Miami (city) Miami-Dade	38.70

Notes: Please refer to the User's Guide for an explanation of data; tables include places with populations > 9,999 and reflect only those areas that meet Summary File 4 population thresholds, therefore there may be less than 10 places listed

Argentinian
Top 10 Places Sorted by Number

Place (place type) County	Number
Miami Beach (city) Miami-Dade	548
Miami (city) Miami-Dade	473
Kendall (cdp) Miami-Dade	211
Sunny Isles Beach (city) Miami-Dade	166
Fountainbleau (cdp) Miami-Dade	136
Hollywood (city) Broward	120
Hialeah (city) Miami-Dade	84

Argentinian
Top 10 Places Sorted by Percent

Place (place type) County	Percent
Kendall (cdp) Miami-Dade	32.21
Fountainbleau (cdp) Miami-Dade	30.91
Sunny Isles Beach (city) Miami-Dade	29.07
Miami (city) Miami-Dade	23.31
Hollywood (city) Broward	21.47
Hialeah (city) Miami-Dade	19.58
Miami Beach (city) Miami-Dade	18.08

Bolivian
Top 10 Places Sorted by Number

Place (place type) County	Number

No places met population threshold.

Bolivian
Top 10 Places Sorted by Percent

Place (place type) County	Percent

No places met population threshold.

Central American
Top 10 Places Sorted by Number

Place (place type) County	Number
Miami (city) Miami-Dade	5,529
Hialeah (city) Miami-Dade	2,654
Fountainbleau (cdp) Miami-Dade	1,921
Kendall (cdp) Miami-Dade	1,231
Tamiami (cdp) Miami-Dade	1,215
Kendale Lakes (cdp) Miami-Dade	1,132
The Hammocks (cdp) Miami-Dade	823
Miami Beach (city) Miami-Dade	756
Tampa (city) Hillsborough	715
Pembroke Pines (city) Broward	702

Central American
Top 10 Places Sorted by Percent

Place (place type) County	Percent
Gladeview (cdp) Miami-Dade	42.73
The Crossings (cdp) Miami-Dade	41.07
Sunset (cdp) Miami-Dade	39.92
Pembroke Pines (city) Broward	36.41
Richmond West (cdp) Miami-Dade	34.85
Egypt Lake-Leto (cdp) Hillsborough	34.31
Miramar (city) Broward	33.77
The Hammocks (cdp) Miami-Dade	33.35
North Miami Beach (city) Miami-Dade	33.21
Doral (cdp) Miami-Dade	33.06

Chilean
Top 10 Places Sorted by Number

Place (place type) County	Number
Kendall (cdp) Miami-Dade	216
Hialeah (city) Miami-Dade	213
Miami Beach (city) Miami-Dade	206
Miami (city) Miami-Dade	202
Fountainbleau (cdp) Miami-Dade	159
Hollywood (city) Broward	91

Chilean
Top 10 Places Sorted by Percent

Place (place type) County	Percent
Kendall (cdp) Miami-Dade	45.00
Hialeah (city) Miami-Dade	28.40
Miami Beach (city) Miami-Dade	27.88
Hollywood (city) Broward	24.14
Fountainbleau (cdp) Miami-Dade	22.62
Miami (city) Miami-Dade	22.52

Columbian
Top 10 Places Sorted by Number

Place (place type) County	Number
Hialeah (city) Miami-Dade	2,567
Miami (city) Miami-Dade	1,681
The Hammocks (cdp) Miami-Dade	1,537
Kendall West (cdp) Miami-Dade	1,237
Kendale Lakes (cdp) Miami-Dade	1,233
Kendall (cdp) Miami-Dade	1,173
Miami Beach (city) Miami-Dade	1,151
Pembroke Pines (city) Broward	1,114
Country Club (cdp) Miami-Dade	994
Hollywood (city) Broward	917

Columbian
Top 10 Places Sorted by Percent

Place (place type) County	Percent
Carol City (cdp) Miami-Dade	43.11
Miami Springs (city) Miami-Dade	42.57
Greater Carrollwood (cdp) Hillsborough	39.23
Coral Gables (city) Miami-Dade	38.52
Westchester (cdp) Miami-Dade	38.43
University Park (cdp) Miami-Dade	37.63
Tamiami (cdp) Miami-Dade	37.32
Hallandale (city) Broward	37.06
Country Walk (cdp) Miami-Dade	36.03
The Crossings (cdp) Miami-Dade	34.12

Costa Rican
Top 10 Places Sorted by Number

Place (place type) County	Number
Miami (city) Miami-Dade	193
Hialeah (city) Miami-Dade	179

Costa Rican
Top 10 Places Sorted by Percent

Place (place type) County	Percent
Hialeah (city) Miami-Dade	34.23
Miami (city) Miami-Dade	23.65

Cuban
Top 10 Places Sorted by Number

Place (place type) County	Number
Miami (city) Miami-Dade	61,227
Hialeah (city) Miami-Dade	56,623
Tamiami (cdp) Miami-Dade	15,736
Fountainbleau (cdp) Miami-Dade	11,226
Westchester (cdp) Miami-Dade	10,668
Kendale Lakes (cdp) Miami-Dade	10,627
Miami Beach (city) Miami-Dade	10,266
University Park (cdp) Miami-Dade	8,683
Kendall (cdp) Miami-Dade	7,647
Coral Terrace (cdp) Miami-Dade	7,193

Cuban
Top 10 Places Sorted by Percent

Place (place type) County	Percent
Sunny Isles Beach (city) Miami-Dade	67.92
Key Biscayne (village) Miami-Dade	60.99
Hallandale (city) Broward	58.80
Coral Gables (city) Miami-Dade	58.04
Miami Lakes (cdp) Miami-Dade	57.06
Aventura (city) Miami-Dade	56.98
Miami Beach (city) Miami-Dade	56.28
Tamarac (city) Broward	55.80
University Park (cdp) Miami-Dade	55.31
Port St. Lucie (city) Saint Lucie	53.26

Dominican
Top 10 Places Sorted by Number

Place (place type) County	Number
Miami (city) Miami-Dade	2,182
Hialeah (city) Miami-Dade	1,718
Fountainbleau (cdp) Miami-Dade	717
Pembroke Pines (city) Broward	638
Carol City (cdp) Miami-Dade	617
The Hammocks (cdp) Miami-Dade	584
Hollywood (city) Broward	513
Miramar (city) Broward	498
Miami Beach (city) Miami-Dade	490
Country Club (cdp) Miami-Dade	401

Dominican
Top 10 Places Sorted by Percent

Place (place type) County	Percent
Tamiami (cdp) Miami-Dade	59.97
Town 'n' Country (cdp) Hillsborough	46.13
Jacksonville (city) Duval	42.69
Kendale Lakes (cdp) Miami-Dade	42.59
Hialeah Gardens (city) Miami-Dade	39.82
West Palm Beach (city) Palm Beach	38.97
The Hammocks (cdp) Miami-Dade	38.45
Fountainbleau (cdp) Miami-Dade	37.19
Cape Coral (city) Lee	37.11
Weston (city) Broward	36.61

Ecuadorian
Top 10 Places Sorted by Number

Place (place type) County	Number
Miami (city) Miami-Dade	559
Hialeah (city) Miami-Dade	465
Pembroke Pines (city) Broward	302
Coral Springs (city) Broward	278
Tampa (city) Hillsborough	213
Miami Beach (city) Miami-Dade	197
Sunrise (city) Broward	191
Hollywood (city) Broward	189
Fountainbleau (cdp) Miami-Dade	166

Ecuadorian
Top 10 Places Sorted by Percent

Place (place type) County	Percent
Pembroke Pines (city) Broward	62.14
Tampa (city) Hillsborough	50.96
Hialeah (city) Miami-Dade	37.71
Sunrise (city) Broward	36.11
Miami (city) Miami-Dade	31.85
Hollywood (city) Broward	30.10
Miami Beach (city) Miami-Dade	29.76
Coral Springs (city) Broward	29.51
Fountainbleau (cdp) Miami-Dade	20.78

Guatelmalan
Top 10 Places Sorted by Number

Place (place type) County	Number
Miami (city) Miami-Dade	533
Hialeah (city) Miami-Dade	160
Lake Worth (city) Palm Beach	90
Fort Lauderdale (city) Broward	86
West Palm Beach (city) Palm Beach	46
Homestead (city) Miami-Dade	38
Immokalee (cdp) Collier	33
Bonita Springs (city) Lee	11
Fort Myers (city) Lee	6

Notes: Please refer to the User's Guide for an explanation of data; tables include places with populations > 9,999 and reflect only those areas that meet Summary File 4 population thresholds, therefore there may be less than 10 places listed

Guatelmalan

Top 10 Places Sorted by Percent

Place (place type) County	Percent
Fort Lauderdale (city) Broward	23.18
Hialeah (city) Miami-Dade	19.00
Miami (city) Miami-Dade	18.70
Lake Worth (city) Palm Beach	4.58
Bonita Springs (city) Lee	2.98
Immokalee (cdp) Collier	2.86
Homestead (city) Miami-Dade	2.65
West Palm Beach (city) Palm Beach	2.23
Fort Myers (city) Lee	1.53

Honduran

Top 10 Places Sorted by Number

Place (place type) County	Number
Miami (city) Miami-Dade	1,767
Hialeah (city) Miami-Dade	465
North Miami (city) Miami-Dade	208
Tampa (city) Hillsborough	206
West Little River (cdp) Miami-Dade	191
Miami Beach (city) Miami-Dade	177
Tamiami (cdp) Miami-Dade	165
Carol City (cdp) Miami-Dade	163
Kendale Lakes (cdp) Miami-Dade	137
Fountainbleau (cdp) Miami-Dade	123

Honduran

Top 10 Places Sorted by Percent

Place (place type) County	Percent
Tamiami (cdp) Miami-Dade	36.42
North Miami (city) Miami-Dade	35.25
Carol City (cdp) Miami-Dade	31.47
Kendale Lakes (cdp) Miami-Dade	24.60
Hollywood (city) Broward	24.55
Tampa (city) Hillsborough	23.04
Miami Beach (city) Miami-Dade	21.85
North Miami Beach (city) Miami-Dade	20.04
West Little River (cdp) Miami-Dade	19.59
Fountainbleau (cdp) Miami-Dade	19.16

Mexican

Top 10 Places Sorted by Number

Place (place type) County	Number
Immokalee (cdp) Collier	1,030
Tampa (city) Hillsborough	637
Bradenton (city) Manatee	478
Leisure City (cdp) Miami-Dade	427
Homestead (city) Miami-Dade	359
Plant City (city) Hillsborough	358
Jacksonville (city) Duval	355
Fort Pierce (city) Saint Lucie	345
Haines City (city) Polk	340
Clearwater (city) Pinellas	292

Mexican

Top 10 Places Sorted by Percent

Place (place type) County	Percent
Kendale Lakes (cdp) Miami-Dade	22.81
San Carlos Park (cdp) Lee	22.41
Plantation (city) Broward	20.86
Miami Beach (city) Miami-Dade	19.57
Tamiami (cdp) Miami-Dade	19.22
Margate (city) Broward	17.34
Ocoee (city) Orange	17.09
Davie (town) Broward	16.71
Fountainbleau (cdp) Miami-Dade	16.18
Hialeah (city) Miami-Dade	15.42

Nicaraguan

Top 10 Places Sorted by Number

Place (place type) County	Number
Miami (city) Miami-Dade	2,209
Hialeah (city) Miami-Dade	1,484
Fountainbleau (cdp) Miami-Dade	1,414
Kendale Lakes (cdp) Miami-Dade	780
Kendall (cdp) Miami-Dade	769
Tamiami (cdp) Miami-Dade	728
The Hammocks (cdp) Miami-Dade	459
Sweetwater (city) Miami-Dade	409
Kendall West (cdp) Miami-Dade	363
Gladeview (cdp) Miami-Dade	355

Nicaraguan

Top 10 Places Sorted by Percent

Place (place type) County	Percent
The Crossings (cdp) Miami-Dade	48.11
Gladeview (cdp) Miami-Dade	43.13
Miami Beach (city) Miami-Dade	35.38
Kendall (cdp) Miami-Dade	34.45
Miramar (city) Broward	33.49
The Hammocks (cdp) Miami-Dade	30.08
Palmetto Estates (cdp) Miami-Dade	28.88
Richmond West (cdp) Miami-Dade	27.87
Kendale Lakes (cdp) Miami-Dade	27.40
Tamiami (cdp) Miami-Dade	26.41

Panamanian

Top 10 Places Sorted by Number

Place (place type) County	Number
Miami (city) Miami-Dade	255
Tampa (city) Hillsborough	149
Jacksonville (city) Duval	144
Fountainbleau (cdp) Miami-Dade	99
Miramar (city) Broward	94

Panamanian

Top 10 Places Sorted by Percent

Place (place type) County	Percent
Miami (city) Miami-Dade	28.88
Miramar (city) Broward	25.61
Jacksonville (city) Duval	24.78
Tampa (city) Hillsborough	23.58
Fountainbleau (cdp) Miami-Dade	18.97

Paraguayan

Top 10 Places Sorted by Number

Place (place type) County	Number
No places met population threshold.	

Paraguayan

Top 10 Places Sorted by Percent

Place (place type) County	Percent
No places met population threshold.	

Peruvian

Top 10 Places Sorted by Number

Place (place type) County	Number
Miami (city) Miami-Dade	756
The Hammocks (cdp) Miami-Dade	448
Miami Beach (city) Miami-Dade	434
Pembroke Pines (city) Broward	425
Hialeah (city) Miami-Dade	393
Kendale Lakes (cdp) Miami-Dade	351
Fountainbleau (cdp) Miami-Dade	329
Hollywood (city) Broward	288
Sunrise (city) Broward	265
Miramar (city) Broward	248

Peruvian

Top 10 Places Sorted by Percent

Place (place type) County	Percent
Sunrise (city) Broward	44.61
Miramar (city) Broward	37.46
Kendale Lakes (cdp) Miami-Dade	36.30
The Crossings (cdp) Miami-Dade	35.44
Weston (city) Broward	32.18
Richmond West (cdp) Miami-Dade	31.09
Plantation (city) Broward	30.50
North Lauderdale (city) Broward	29.50
Pembroke Pines (city) Broward	28.24
Fountainbleau (cdp) Miami-Dade	27.86

Puerto Rican

Top 10 Places Sorted by Number

Place (place type) County	Number
Miami (city) Miami-Dade	228
Carol City (cdp) Miami-Dade	105
Town 'n' Country (cdp) Hillsborough	105
Pembroke Pines (city) Broward	75
Hialeah (city) Miami-Dade	73
Tampa (city) Hillsborough	71
Deltona (city) Volusia	69
Egypt Lake-Leto (cdp) Hillsborough	64
Jacksonville (city) Duval	62
Kendale Lakes (cdp) Miami-Dade	45

Puerto Rican

Top 10 Places Sorted by Percent

Place (place type) County	Percent
Westchester (cdp) Miami-Dade	8.47
Glenvar Heights (cdp) Miami-Dade	8.45
Delray Beach (city) Palm Beach	6.00
The Crossings (cdp) Miami-Dade	4.45
Lauderhill (city) Broward	4.40
Carol City (cdp) Miami-Dade	3.76
Hialeah Gardens (city) Miami-Dade	3.76
Miami Springs (city) Miami-Dade	3.42
Tamiami (cdp) Miami-Dade	3.42
Hallandale (city) Broward	3.34

Salvadoran

Top 10 Places Sorted by Number

Place (place type) County	Number
Miami (city) Miami-Dade	407
Hialeah (city) Miami-Dade	208
Fort Lauderdale (city) Broward	120
Oakland Park (city) Broward	62
Lake Worth (city) Palm Beach	52
Homestead (city) Miami-Dade	38

Salvadoran

Top 10 Places Sorted by Percent

Place (place type) County	Percent
Hialeah (city) Miami-Dade	21.89
Fort Lauderdale (city) Broward	18.07
Miami (city) Miami-Dade	17.00
Lake Worth (city) Palm Beach	9.87
Oakland Park (city) Broward	8.00
Homestead (city) Miami-Dade	3.39

South American

Top 10 Places Sorted by Number

Place (place type) County	Number
Miami (city) Miami-Dade	4,188
Hialeah (city) Miami-Dade	4,027
Miami Beach (city) Miami-Dade	3,005
The Hammocks (cdp) Miami-Dade	2,614
Kendale Lakes (cdp) Miami-Dade	2,444
Pembroke Pines (city) Broward	2,334
Kendall (cdp) Miami-Dade	2,258
Kendall West (cdp) Miami-Dade	1,910
Fountainbleau (cdp) Miami-Dade	1,906
Hollywood (city) Broward	1,814

South American

Top 10 Places Sorted by Percent

Place (place type) County	Percent
Citrus Park (cdp) Hillsborough	47.65
Golden Glades (cdp) Miami-Dade	46.42
Palm Beach Gardens (city) Palm Beach	43.15
Parkland (city) Broward	39.89
Sweetwater (city) Miami-Dade	39.77

Notes: Please refer to the User's Guide for an explanation of data; tables include places with populations > 9,999 and reflect only those areas that meet Summary File 4 population thresholds, therefore there may be less than 10 places listed

Cutler (cdp) Miami-Dade	39.75
Port St. Lucie (city) Saint Lucie	39.60
Olympia Heights (cdp) Miami-Dade	39.30
South Miami (city) Miami-Dade	39.05
Delray Beach (city) Palm Beach	38.23

Spaniard
Top 10 Places Sorted by Number

Place (place type) County	Number
Miami (city) Miami-Dade	450
Hialeah (city) Miami-Dade	220
Miami Beach (city) Miami-Dade	137
Tampa (city) Hillsborough	78

Spaniard
Top 10 Places Sorted by Percent

Place (place type) County	Percent
Miami (city) Miami-Dade	47.32
Hialeah (city) Miami-Dade	43.22
Miami Beach (city) Miami-Dade	23.91
Tampa (city) Hillsborough	10.64

Uruguayan
Top 10 Places Sorted by Number

Place (place type) County	Number

No places met population threshold.

Uruguayan
Top 10 Places Sorted by Percent

Place (place type) County	Percent

No places met population threshold.

Venezuelan
Top 10 Places Sorted by Number

Place (place type) County	Number
Fountainbleau (cdp) Miami-Dade	258
Miami (city) Miami-Dade	243
The Hammocks (cdp) Miami-Dade	241
Kendall (cdp) Miami-Dade	217
Miami Beach (city) Miami-Dade	202
Tampa (city) Hillsborough	199
Pembroke Pines (city) Broward	186
Hialeah (city) Miami-Dade	181
Kendall West (cdp) Miami-Dade	180
Kendale Lakes (cdp) Miami-Dade	165

Venezuelan
Top 10 Places Sorted by Percent

Place (place type) County	Percent
Tampa (city) Hillsborough	31.89
Richmond West (cdp) Miami-Dade	24.02
Hialeah (city) Miami-Dade	18.95
Kendale Lakes (cdp) Miami-Dade	18.94
Coral Springs (city) Broward	17.94
The Crossings (cdp) Miami-Dade	17.52
Coral Gables (city) Miami-Dade	17.30
Hollywood (city) Broward	16.06
Kendall West (cdp) Miami-Dade	15.52
Kendall (cdp) Miami-Dade	14.93

Other Hispanic
Top 10 Places Sorted by Number

Place (place type) County	Number
Miami (city) Miami-Dade	5,188
Hialeah (city) Miami-Dade	3,451
Fountainbleau (cdp) Miami-Dade	1,673
Miami Beach (city) Miami-Dade	1,553
Kendale Lakes (cdp) Miami-Dade	1,523
Kendall (cdp) Miami-Dade	1,420
Tamiami (cdp) Miami-Dade	1,246
Hollywood (city) Broward	1,132
Pembroke Pines (city) Broward	1,079
The Hammocks (cdp) Miami-Dade	1,051

Other Hispanic
Top 10 Places Sorted by Percent

Place (place type) County	Percent
Norland (cdp) Miami-Dade	40.51
Ojus (cdp) Miami-Dade	34.31
Hallandale (city) Broward	30.16
Lauderhill (city) Broward	28.78
Palm Bay (city) Brevard	28.12
Margate (city) Broward	27.92
Coral Terrace (cdp) Miami-Dade	27.19
Kendall (cdp) Miami-Dade	26.36
Palm Springs (village) Palm Beach	26.21
Coral Gables (city) Miami-Dade	26.12

Educational Attainment: High School Graduates

Total Population 25 Years and Over Who are High School Graduates
Top 10 Places Sorted by Number

Place (place type) County	Number
Jacksonville (city) Duval	385,300
Tampa (city) Hillsborough	153,114
St. Petersburg (city) Pinellas	143,458
Miami (city) Miami-Dade	133,069
Orlando (city) Orange	103,129
Fort Lauderdale (city) Broward	87,921
Pembroke Pines (city) Broward	82,419
Hollywood (city) Broward	79,650
Hialeah (city) Miami-Dade	77,548
Tallahassee (city) Leon	71,754

Total Population 25 Years and Over Who are High School Graduates
Top 10 Places Sorted by Percent

Place (place type) County	Percent
Westchase (cdp) Hillsborough	96.62
Wekiwa Springs (cdp) Seminole	96.03
Weston (city) Broward	95.47
Key Biscayne (village) Miami-Dade	94.99
Boca Del Mar (cdp) Palm Beach	94.88
Keystone (cdp) Hillsborough	94.87
Bloomingdale (cdp) Hillsborough	94.79
Pinecrest (village) Miami-Dade	94.24
Parkland (city) Broward	94.07
Palm Beach Gardens (city) Palm Beach	94.03

Hispanics 25 Years and Over Who are High School Graduates
Top 10 Places Sorted by Number

Place (place type) County	Number
Miami (city) Miami-Dade	83,405
Hialeah (city) Miami-Dade	70,397
Miami Beach (city) Miami-Dade	25,722
Fountainbleau (cdp) Miami-Dade	24,867
Tamiami (cdp) Miami-Dade	23,414
Kendale Lakes (cdp) Miami-Dade	22,385
Tampa (city) Hillsborough	22,246
Kendall (cdp) Miami-Dade	21,481
Pembroke Pines (city) Broward	21,009
The Hammocks (cdp) Miami-Dade	16,989

Hispanics 25 Years and Over Who are High School Graduates
Top 10 Places Sorted by Percent

Place (place type) County	Percent
East Lake (cdp) Pinellas	97.21
Westchase (cdp) Hillsborough	96.16
Weston (city) Broward	92.90
Boca Del Mar (cdp) Palm Beach	92.71
Key Biscayne (village) Miami-Dade	92.16
Keystone (cdp) Hillsborough	91.80
Land O' Lakes (cdp) Pasco	91.23
Parkland (city) Broward	90.60
Gainesville (city) Alachua	90.24
Callaway (city) Bay	90.11

Argentinians 25 Years and Over Who are High School Graduates
Top 10 Places Sorted by Number

Place (place type) County	Number
Miami Beach (city) Miami-Dade	1,670
Miami (city) Miami-Dade	1,063
Kendall (cdp) Miami-Dade	461
Sunny Isles Beach (city) Miami-Dade	375
Hollywood (city) Broward	298
Fountainbleau (cdp) Miami-Dade	278
Hialeah (city) Miami-Dade	180

Argentinians 25 Years and Over Who are High School Graduates
Top 10 Places Sorted by Percent

Place (place type) County	Percent
Kendall (cdp) Miami-Dade	93.70
Miami Beach (city) Miami-Dade	80.02
Sunny Isles Beach (city) Miami-Dade	77.96
Hollywood (city) Broward	77.40
Fountainbleau (cdp) Miami-Dade	76.16
Miami (city) Miami-Dade	73.41
Hialeah (city) Miami-Dade	61.64

Bolivians 25 Years and Over Who are High School Graduates
Top 10 Places Sorted by Number

Place (place type) County	Number

No places met population threshold.

Bolivians 25 Years and Over Who are High School Graduates
Top 10 Places Sorted by Percent

Place (place type) County	Percent

No places met population threshold.

Central Americans 25 Years and Over Who are High School Graduates
Top 10 Places Sorted by Number

Place (place type) County	Number
Miami (city) Miami-Dade	11,896
Hialeah (city) Miami-Dade	4,920
Fountainbleau (cdp) Miami-Dade	3,896
Kendale Lakes (cdp) Miami-Dade	2,117
Kendall (cdp) Miami-Dade	2,098
Tamiami (cdp) Miami-Dade	1,846
The Hammocks (cdp) Miami-Dade	1,589
Miami Beach (city) Miami-Dade	1,542
Kendall West (cdp) Miami-Dade	1,268
Tampa (city) Hillsborough	1,258

Central Americans 25 Years and Over Who are High School Graduates
Top 10 Places Sorted by Percent

Place (place type) County	Percent
Doral (cdp) Miami-Dade	94.66
Brandon (cdp) Hillsborough	90.45
The Hammocks (cdp) Miami-Dade	90.34
The Crossings (cdp) Miami-Dade	90.15
Country Walk (cdp) Miami-Dade	88.81
Plantation (city) Broward	88.74
Kendall (cdp) Miami-Dade	81.60
Pembroke Pines (city) Broward	79.81
Coral Gables (city) Miami-Dade	79.50
Kendale Lakes (cdp) Miami-Dade	79.44

Chileans 25 Years and Over Who are High School Graduates
Top 10 Places Sorted by Number

Place (place type) County	Number
Miami (city) Miami-Dade	521
Miami Beach (city) Miami-Dade	488
Hialeah (city) Miami-Dade	358

Notes: Please refer to the User's Guide for an explanation of data; tables include places with populations > 9,999 and reflect only those areas that meet Summary File 4 population thresholds, therefore there may be less than 10 places listed

Fountainbleau (cdp) Miami-Dade	346
Kendall (cdp) Miami-Dade	301
Hollywood (city) Broward	191

Chileans 25 Years and Over Who are High School Graduates

Top 10 Places Sorted by Percent

Place (place type) County	Percent
Kendall (cdp) Miami-Dade	100.00
Miami Beach (city) Miami-Dade	85.76
Fountainbleau (cdp) Miami-Dade	73.31
Miami (city) Miami-Dade	72.26
Hollywood (city) Broward	67.25
Hialeah (city) Miami-Dade	66.92

Columbians 25 Years and Over Who are High School Graduates

Top 10 Places Sorted by Number

Place (place type) County	Number
Hialeah (city) Miami-Dade	3,604
Miami (city) Miami-Dade	3,124
The Hammocks (cdp) Miami-Dade	2,697
Miami Beach (city) Miami-Dade	2,614
Kendall (cdp) Miami-Dade	2,372
Kendale Lakes (cdp) Miami-Dade	2,110
Pembroke Pines (city) Broward	2,040
Kendall West (cdp) Miami-Dade	2,013
Country Club (cdp) Miami-Dade	1,947
Hollywood (city) Broward	1,752

Columbians 25 Years and Over Who are High School Graduates

Top 10 Places Sorted by Percent

Place (place type) County	Percent
Clearwater (city) Pinellas	95.97
The Crossings (cdp) Miami-Dade	94.83
Weston (city) Broward	93.55
Key Biscayne (village) Miami-Dade	91.18
Sandalfoot Cove (cdp) Palm Beach	91.04
Country Walk (cdp) Miami-Dade	90.91
Doral (cdp) Miami-Dade	90.17
Aventura (city) Miami-Dade	89.68
Pembroke Pines (city) Broward	89.32
Coral Springs (city) Broward	88.97

Costa Ricans 25 Years and Over Who are High School Graduates

Top 10 Places Sorted by Number

Place (place type) County	Number
Miami (city) Miami-Dade	380
Hialeah (city) Miami-Dade	167

Costa Ricans 25 Years and Over Who are High School Graduates

Top 10 Places Sorted by Percent

Place (place type) County	Percent
Miami (city) Miami-Dade	64.08
Hialeah (city) Miami-Dade	54.93

Cubans 25 Years and Over Who are High School Graduates

Top 10 Places Sorted by Number

Place (place type) County	Number
Hialeah (city) Miami-Dade	49,639
Miami (city) Miami-Dade	48,348
Tamiami (cdp) Miami-Dade	16,494
Kendale Lakes (cdp) Miami-Dade	11,881
Fountainbleau (cdp) Miami-Dade	11,258
Westchester (cdp) Miami-Dade	10,120
Miami Beach (city) Miami-Dade	9,885
Kendall (cdp) Miami-Dade	9,687
Coral Gables (city) Miami-Dade	8,336
University Park (cdp) Miami-Dade	8,150

Cubans 25 Years and Over Who are High School Graduates

Top 10 Places Sorted by Percent

Place (place type) County	Percent
Weston (city) Broward	92.88
Key Biscayne (village) Miami-Dade	92.49
Gainesville (city) Alachua	92.10
Pinecrest (village) Miami-Dade	91.83
Cutler (cdp) Miami-Dade	91.77
Brandon (cdp) Hillsborough	91.31
Miami Shores (village) Miami-Dade	89.97
Coral Springs (city) Broward	89.43
Doral (cdp) Miami-Dade	87.30
Coral Gables (city) Miami-Dade	87.28

Dominicans 25 Years and Over Who are High School Graduates

Top 10 Places Sorted by Number

Place (place type) County	Number
Miami (city) Miami-Dade	2,196
Hialeah (city) Miami-Dade	1,952
Pembroke Pines (city) Broward	916
Fountainbleau (cdp) Miami-Dade	914
The Hammocks (cdp) Miami-Dade	862
Miami Beach (city) Miami-Dade	770
Hollywood (city) Broward	726
Miramar (city) Broward	642
Country Club (cdp) Miami-Dade	616
Orlando (city) Orange	537

Dominicans 25 Years and Over Who are High School Graduates

Top 10 Places Sorted by Percent

Place (place type) County	Percent
Weston (city) Broward	87.90
The Hammocks (cdp) Miami-Dade	86.81
Doral (cdp) Miami-Dade	85.15
Coral Springs (city) Broward	83.68
Pembroke Pines (city) Broward	82.97
Kendall West (cdp) Miami-Dade	80.19
Jacksonville (city) Duval	78.24
Tamiami (cdp) Miami-Dade	78.21
Richmond West (cdp) Miami-Dade	76.28
Town 'n' Country (cdp) Hillsborough	76.17

Ecuadorians 25 Years and Over Who are High School Graduates

Top 10 Places Sorted by Number

Place (place type) County	Number
Miami (city) Miami-Dade	719
Hialeah (city) Miami-Dade	525
Coral Springs (city) Broward	511
Fountainbleau (cdp) Miami-Dade	423
Miami Beach (city) Miami-Dade	422
Pembroke Pines (city) Broward	365
Sunrise (city) Broward	346
Hollywood (city) Broward	325
Tampa (city) Hillsborough	268

Ecuadorians 25 Years and Over Who are High School Graduates

Top 10 Places Sorted by Percent

Place (place type) County	Percent
Pembroke Pines (city) Broward	97.33
Sunrise (city) Broward	89.41
Hollywood (city) Broward	87.84
Fountainbleau (cdp) Miami-Dade	87.58
Coral Springs (city) Broward	83.50
Miami Beach (city) Miami-Dade	80.38
Tampa (city) Hillsborough	80.00
Hialeah (city) Miami-Dade	61.40
Miami (city) Miami-Dade	57.94

Guatelmalans 25 Years and Over Who are High School Graduates

Top 10 Places Sorted by Number

Place (place type) County	Number
Miami (city) Miami-Dade	677
Hialeah (city) Miami-Dade	245
West Palm Beach (city) Palm Beach	141
Lake Worth (city) Palm Beach	113
Immokalee (cdp) Collier	68
Fort Lauderdale (city) Broward	63
Homestead (city) Miami-Dade	40
Bonita Springs (city) Lee	32
Fort Myers (city) Lee	0

Guatelmalans 25 Years and Over Who are High School Graduates

Top 10 Places Sorted by Percent

Place (place type) County	Percent
Hialeah (city) Miami-Dade	49.70
Miami (city) Miami-Dade	34.49
Fort Lauderdale (city) Broward	30.29
Bonita Springs (city) Lee	21.19
West Palm Beach (city) Palm Beach	14.49
Lake Worth (city) Palm Beach	13.12
Immokalee (cdp) Collier	11.35
Homestead (city) Miami-Dade	5.86
Fort Myers (city) Lee	0.00

Hondurans 25 Years and Over Who are High School Graduates

Top 10 Places Sorted by Number

Place (place type) County	Number
Miami (city) Miami-Dade	3,353
Hialeah (city) Miami-Dade	783
Miami Beach (city) Miami-Dade	373
Fountainbleau (cdp) Miami-Dade	278
West Little River (cdp) Miami-Dade	239
Tampa (city) Hillsborough	235
Hollywood (city) Broward	233
Kendale Lakes (cdp) Miami-Dade	226
Tamiami (cdp) Miami-Dade	224
North Miami (city) Miami-Dade	207

Hondurans 25 Years and Over Who are High School Graduates

Top 10 Places Sorted by Percent

Place (place type) County	Percent
Tamiami (cdp) Miami-Dade	72.03
Fountainbleau (cdp) Miami-Dade	70.74
Kendale Lakes (cdp) Miami-Dade	69.54
North Miami Beach (city) Miami-Dade	67.60
Hollywood (city) Broward	67.34
Miami Beach (city) Miami-Dade	63.76
North Miami (city) Miami-Dade	54.91
Hialeah (city) Miami-Dade	48.85
West Little River (cdp) Miami-Dade	46.50
Tampa (city) Hillsborough	40.94

Mexicans 25 Years and Over Who are High School Graduates

Top 10 Places Sorted by Number

Place (place type) County	Number
Jacksonville (city) Duval	2,066
Tampa (city) Hillsborough	1,801
Miami (city) Miami-Dade	1,007
Clearwater (city) Pinellas	955
Immokalee (cdp) Collier	867
Orlando (city) Orange	796
Sarasota (city) Sarasota	618
St. Petersburg (city) Pinellas	601
Miami Beach (city) Miami-Dade	576
Homestead (city) Miami-Dade	573

Notes: Please refer to the User's Guide for an explanation of data; tables include places with populations > 9,999 and reflect only those areas that meet Summary File 4 population thresholds, therefore there may be less than 10 places listed

Mexicans 25 Years and Over Who are High School Graduates

Top 10 Places Sorted by Percent

Place (place type) County	Percent
The Hammocks (cdp) Miami-Dade	94.70
Doral (cdp) Miami-Dade	94.31
Gainesville (city) Alachua	86.31
Pembroke Pines (city) Broward	84.18
Panama City (city) Bay	84.03
Largo (city) Pinellas	82.70
Weston (city) Broward	82.13
Wright (cdp) Okaloosa	81.50
Palm Bay (city) Brevard	79.95
Fountainbleau (cdp) Miami-Dade	75.51

Nicaraguans 25 Years and Over Who are High School Graduates

Top 10 Places Sorted by Number

Place (place type) County	Number
Miami (city) Miami-Dade	6,285
Hialeah (city) Miami-Dade	3,100
Fountainbleau (cdp) Miami-Dade	2,750
Kendale Lakes (cdp) Miami-Dade	1,493
Tamiami (cdp) Miami-Dade	1,221
Kendall (cdp) Miami-Dade	1,150
The Hammocks (cdp) Miami-Dade	1,039
Sweetwater (city) Miami-Dade	906
Kendall West (cdp) Miami-Dade	759
Richmond West (cdp) Miami-Dade	607

Nicaraguans 25 Years and Over Who are High School Graduates

Top 10 Places Sorted by Percent

Place (place type) County	Percent
The Hammocks (cdp) Miami-Dade	91.06
The Crossings (cdp) Miami-Dade	89.42
Miami Beach (city) Miami-Dade	85.78
Coral Gables (city) Miami-Dade	84.59
Kendale Lakes (cdp) Miami-Dade	80.75
Kendall (cdp) Miami-Dade	80.48
Hollywood (city) Broward	79.89
University Park (cdp) Miami-Dade	79.16
Tamiami (cdp) Miami-Dade	73.87
Kendall West (cdp) Miami-Dade	73.83

Panamanians 25 Years and Over Who are High School Graduates

Top 10 Places Sorted by Number

Place (place type) County	Number
Miami (city) Miami-Dade	449
Fountainbleau (cdp) Miami-Dade	369
Tampa (city) Hillsborough	367
Jacksonville (city) Duval	323
Miramar (city) Broward	171

Panamanians 25 Years and Over Who are High School Graduates

Top 10 Places Sorted by Percent

Place (place type) County	Percent
Jacksonville (city) Duval	96.71
Fountainbleau (cdp) Miami-Dade	92.95
Tampa (city) Hillsborough	84.17
Miami (city) Miami-Dade	73.73
Miramar (city) Broward	72.77

Paraguayans 25 Years and Over Who are High School Graduates

Top 10 Places Sorted by Number

Place (place type) County	Number

No places met population threshold.

Paraguayans 25 Years and Over Who are High School Graduates

Top 10 Places Sorted by Percent

Place (place type) County	Percent

No places met population threshold.

Peruvians 25 Years and Over Who are High School Graduates

Top 10 Places Sorted by Number

Place (place type) County	Number
Miami (city) Miami-Dade	1,471
The Hammocks (cdp) Miami-Dade	1,201
Miami Beach (city) Miami-Dade	1,159
Pembroke Pines (city) Broward	890
Kendall (cdp) Miami-Dade	849
Fountainbleau (cdp) Miami-Dade	796
Hollywood (city) Broward	784
Hialeah (city) Miami-Dade	754
Kendall West (cdp) Miami-Dade	714
Kendale Lakes (cdp) Miami-Dade	578

Peruvians 25 Years and Over Who are High School Graduates

Top 10 Places Sorted by Percent

Place (place type) County	Percent
Plantation (city) Broward	96.60
Weston (city) Broward	95.95
Kendale Lakes (cdp) Miami-Dade	95.22
Kendall (cdp) Miami-Dade	95.18
Richmond West (cdp) Miami-Dade	94.82
The Hammocks (cdp) Miami-Dade	94.34
Coral Springs (city) Broward	94.01
Pembroke Pines (city) Broward	93.88
Sunrise (city) Broward	93.84
North Lauderdale (city) Broward	92.47

Puerto Ricans 25 Years and Over Who are High School Graduates

Top 10 Places Sorted by Number

Place (place type) County	Number
Orlando (city) Orange	7,158
Tampa (city) Hillsborough	5,350
Kissimmee (city) Osceola	4,774
Jacksonville (city) Duval	4,413
Deltona (city) Volusia	4,070
Pembroke Pines (city) Broward	3,956
Yeehaw Junction (cdp) Osceola	3,409
Miami (city) Miami-Dade	3,366
Town 'n' Country (cdp) Hillsborough	3,089
Hollywood (city) Broward	2,749

Puerto Ricans 25 Years and Over Who are High School Graduates

Top 10 Places Sorted by Percent

Place (place type) County	Percent
Coral Gables (city) Miami-Dade	96.22
Weston (city) Broward	95.68
Wekiwa Springs (cdp) Seminole	94.09
Cooper City (city) Broward	93.17
Tallahassee (city) Leon	92.59
Longwood (city) Seminole	91.34
Oviedo (city) Seminole	91.23
Doral (cdp) Miami-Dade	90.94
The Hammocks (cdp) Miami-Dade	90.78
Port Orange (city) Volusia	89.93

Salvadorans 25 Years and Over Who are High School Graduates

Top 10 Places Sorted by Number

Place (place type) County	Number
Miami (city) Miami-Dade	528
Hialeah (city) Miami-Dade	317
Fort Lauderdale (city) Broward	102
Oakland Park (city) Broward	84
Lake Worth (city) Palm Beach	83
Homestead (city) Miami-Dade	31

Salvadorans 25 Years and Over Who are High School Graduates

Top 10 Places Sorted by Percent

Place (place type) County	Percent
Hialeah (city) Miami-Dade	53.55
Lake Worth (city) Palm Beach	34.73
Miami (city) Miami-Dade	31.41
Fort Lauderdale (city) Broward	29.91
Oakland Park (city) Broward	19.91
Homestead (city) Miami-Dade	5.66

South Americans 25 Years and Over Who are High School Graduates

Top 10 Places Sorted by Number

Place (place type) County	Number
Miami (city) Miami-Dade	8,224
Miami Beach (city) Miami-Dade	7,679
Hialeah (city) Miami-Dade	5,994
The Hammocks (cdp) Miami-Dade	5,653
Kendall (cdp) Miami-Dade	5,284
Pembroke Pines (city) Broward	4,740
Fountainbleau (cdp) Miami-Dade	4,585
Kendale Lakes (cdp) Miami-Dade	4,052
Hollywood (city) Broward	3,982
Weston (city) Broward	3,957

South Americans 25 Years and Over Who are High School Graduates

Top 10 Places Sorted by Percent

Place (place type) County	Percent
Tallahassee (city) Leon	98.79
Clearwater (city) Pinellas	96.96
Weston (city) Broward	95.17
Gainesville (city) Alachua	94.47
Key Biscayne (village) Miami-Dade	93.79
South Miami (city) Miami-Dade	93.03
Aventura (city) Miami-Dade	92.40
Sandalfoot Cove (cdp) Palm Beach	92.34
Pembroke Pines (city) Broward	91.49
Coconut Creek (city) Broward	91.20

Spaniards 25 Years and Over Who are High School Graduates

Top 10 Places Sorted by Number

Place (place type) County	Number
Tampa (city) Hillsborough	518
Miami Beach (city) Miami-Dade	414
Miami (city) Miami-Dade	408
Hialeah (city) Miami-Dade	144

Spaniards 25 Years and Over Who are High School Graduates

Top 10 Places Sorted by Percent

Place (place type) County	Percent
Miami Beach (city) Miami-Dade	86.97
Tampa (city) Hillsborough	81.57
Miami (city) Miami-Dade	49.94
Hialeah (city) Miami-Dade	36.09

Uruguayans 25 Years and Over Who are High School Graduates

Top 10 Places Sorted by Number

Place (place type) County	Number

No places met population threshold.

Uruguayans 25 Years and Over Who are High School Graduates

Top 10 Places Sorted by Percent

Place (place type) County	Percent

No places met population threshold.

Notes: Please refer to the User's Guide for an explanation of data; tables include places with populations > 9,999 and reflect only those areas that meet Summary File 4 population thresholds, therefore there may be less than 10 places listed

Venezuelans 25 Years and Over Who are High School Graduates

Top 10 Places Sorted by Number

Place (place type) County	Number
Weston (city) Broward	1,221
Fountainbleau (cdp) Miami-Dade	1,117
Doral (cdp) Miami-Dade	1,115
Miami (city) Miami-Dade	912
Miami Beach (city) Miami-Dade	907
Kendall (cdp) Miami-Dade	906
The Hammocks (cdp) Miami-Dade	906
Pembroke Pines (city) Broward	893
Kendall West (cdp) Miami-Dade	580
Kendale Lakes (cdp) Miami-Dade	464

Venezuelans 25 Years and Over Who are High School Graduates

Top 10 Places Sorted by Percent

Place (place type) County	Percent
The Crossings (cdp) Miami-Dade	98.03
Weston (city) Broward	96.45
Coral Gables (city) Miami-Dade	95.27
Pembroke Pines (city) Broward	94.30
Kendall (cdp) Miami-Dade	93.79
Doral (cdp) Miami-Dade	93.70
Plantation (city) Broward	92.09
Richmond West (cdp) Miami-Dade	91.67
Miami Beach (city) Miami-Dade	90.43
Tamiami (cdp) Miami-Dade	90.03

Other Hispanics 25 Years and Over Who are High School Graduates

Top 10 Places Sorted by Number

Place (place type) County	Number
Miami (city) Miami-Dade	7,960
Tampa (city) Hillsborough	5,240
Hialeah (city) Miami-Dade	4,769
Fountainbleau (cdp) Miami-Dade	2,973
Miami Beach (city) Miami-Dade	2,950
Kendale Lakes (cdp) Miami-Dade	2,699
Pembroke Pines (city) Broward	2,383
Kendall (cdp) Miami-Dade	2,220
Jacksonville (city) Duval	2,151
Hollywood (city) Broward	2,096

Other Hispanics 25 Years and Over Who are High School Graduates

Top 10 Places Sorted by Percent

Place (place type) County	Percent
Key Biscayne (village) Miami-Dade	94.55
Greater Northdale (cdp) Hillsborough	93.00
Lake Magdalene (cdp) Hillsborough	92.20
Lakeside (cdp) Clay	91.83
Glenvar Heights (cdp) Miami-Dade	89.80
Daytona Beach (city) Volusia	89.52
Weston (city) Broward	88.83
Country Walk (cdp) Miami-Dade	88.64
St. Petersburg (city) Pinellas	88.46
Gainesville (city) Alachua	87.82

Educational Attainment: Four-Year College Graduates

Total Population 25 Years and Over Who are Four-Year College Graduates

Top 10 Places Sorted by Number

Place (place type) County	Number
Jacksonville (city) Duval	98,991
Tampa (city) Hillsborough	50,471
Miami (city) Miami-Dade	41,004
St. Petersburg (city) Pinellas	39,987
Tallahassee (city) Leon	35,901
Orlando (city) Orange	35,396
Fort Lauderdale (city) Broward	31,059
Pembroke Pines (city) Broward	26,847
Coral Springs (city) Broward	24,489
Boca Raton (city) Palm Beach	24,362

Total Population 25 Years and Over Who are Four-Year College Graduates

Top 10 Places Sorted by Percent

Place (place type) County	Percent
Key Biscayne (village) Miami-Dade	64.95
Pinecrest (village) Miami-Dade	61.56
Coral Gables (city) Miami-Dade	58.28
Cutler (cdp) Miami-Dade	55.75
Parkland (city) Broward	52.79
Maitland (city) Orange	51.78
Weston (city) Broward	50.87
Winter Park (city) Orange	50.14
Wekiwa Springs (cdp) Seminole	49.62
Westchase (cdp) Hillsborough	49.04

Hispanics 25 Years and Over Who are Four-Year College Graduates

Top 10 Places Sorted by Number

Place (place type) County	Number
Miami (city) Miami-Dade	23,714
Hialeah (city) Miami-Dade	14,660
Miami Beach (city) Miami-Dade	9,176
Kendall (cdp) Miami-Dade	8,729
Coral Gables (city) Miami-Dade	7,706
Fountainbleau (cdp) Miami-Dade	7,698
Pembroke Pines (city) Broward	7,101
Tamiami (cdp) Miami-Dade	7,028
Kendale Lakes (cdp) Miami-Dade	6,174
The Hammocks (cdp) Miami-Dade	5,424

Hispanics 25 Years and Over Who are Four-Year College Graduates

Top 10 Places Sorted by Percent

Place (place type) County	Percent
Key Biscayne (village) Miami-Dade	60.96
Parkland (city) Broward	56.93
Coral Gables (city) Miami-Dade	52.09
Pinecrest (village) Miami-Dade	50.38
Gainesville (city) Alachua	46.92
Weston (city) Broward	46.16
Cutler (cdp) Miami-Dade	44.95
Wekiwa Springs (cdp) Seminole	44.31
Aventura (city) Miami-Dade	44.24
Doral (cdp) Miami-Dade	44.17

Argentinians 25 Years and Over Who are Four-Year College Graduates

Top 10 Places Sorted by Number

Place (place type) County	Number
Miami Beach (city) Miami-Dade	604
Miami (city) Miami-Dade	433
Kendall (cdp) Miami-Dade	205
Sunny Isles Beach (city) Miami-Dade	73
Hollywood (city) Broward	67
Hialeah (city) Miami-Dade	57
Fountainbleau (cdp) Miami-Dade	54

Argentinians 25 Years and Over Who are Four-Year College Graduates

Top 10 Places Sorted by Percent

Place (place type) County	Percent
Kendall (cdp) Miami-Dade	41.67
Miami (city) Miami-Dade	29.90
Miami Beach (city) Miami-Dade	28.94
Hialeah (city) Miami-Dade	19.52
Hollywood (city) Broward	17.40
Sunny Isles Beach (city) Miami-Dade	15.18
Fountainbleau (cdp) Miami-Dade	14.79

Bolivians 25 Years and Over Who are Four-Year College Graduates

Top 10 Places Sorted by Number

Place (place type) County	Number
No places met population threshold.	

Bolivians 25 Years and Over Who are Four-Year College Graduates

Top 10 Places Sorted by Percent

Place (place type) County	Percent
No places met population threshold.	

Central Americans 25 Years and Over Who are Four-Year College Graduates

Top 10 Places Sorted by Number

Place (place type) County	Number
Miami (city) Miami-Dade	2,228
Fountainbleau (cdp) Miami-Dade	966
Hialeah (city) Miami-Dade	875
Kendall (cdp) Miami-Dade	687
Kendale Lakes (cdp) Miami-Dade	537
Tamiami (cdp) Miami-Dade	491
The Hammocks (cdp) Miami-Dade	483
Miami Beach (city) Miami-Dade	417
Pembroke Pines (city) Broward	355
Kendall West (cdp) Miami-Dade	343

Central Americans 25 Years and Over Who are Four-Year College Graduates

Top 10 Places Sorted by Percent

Place (place type) County	Percent
Doral (cdp) Miami-Dade	51.55
Coral Gables (city) Miami-Dade	40.72
Pinecrest (village) Miami-Dade	37.85
The Crossings (cdp) Miami-Dade	32.88
Plantation (city) Broward	30.80
The Hammocks (cdp) Miami-Dade	27.46
Glenvar Heights (cdp) Miami-Dade	27.00
Kendall (cdp) Miami-Dade	26.72
Coral Springs (city) Broward	26.34
Pembroke Pines (city) Broward	25.97

Chileans 25 Years and Over Who are Four-Year College Graduates

Top 10 Places Sorted by Number

Place (place type) County	Number
Miami (city) Miami-Dade	147
Miami Beach (city) Miami-Dade	117
Fountainbleau (cdp) Miami-Dade	107
Kendall (cdp) Miami-Dade	74
Hialeah (city) Miami-Dade	45
Hollywood (city) Broward	42

Chileans 25 Years and Over Who are Four-Year College Graduates

Top 10 Places Sorted by Percent

Place (place type) County	Percent
Kendall (cdp) Miami-Dade	24.58
Fountainbleau (cdp) Miami-Dade	22.67
Miami Beach (city) Miami-Dade	20.56
Miami (city) Miami-Dade	20.39
Hollywood (city) Broward	14.79
Hialeah (city) Miami-Dade	8.41

Columbians 25 Years and Over Who are Four-Year College Graduates

Top 10 Places Sorted by Number

Place (place type) County	Number
Miami (city) Miami-Dade	1,060
Weston (city) Broward	1,058
Miami Beach (city) Miami-Dade	1,027
Kendall (cdp) Miami-Dade	991
The Hammocks (cdp) Miami-Dade	886
Pembroke Pines (city) Broward	762
Doral (cdp) Miami-Dade	623

Notes: Please refer to the User's Guide for an explanation of data; tables include places with populations > 9,999 and reflect only those areas that meet Summary File 4 population thresholds, therefore there may be less than 10 places listed

Hialeah (city) Miami-Dade		611
Kendale Lakes (cdp) Miami-Dade		533
Plantation (city) Broward		531

Columbians 25 Years and Over Who are Four-Year College Graduates

Top 10 Places Sorted by Percent

Place (place type) County	Percent
Key Biscayne (village) Miami-Dade	63.04
Weston (city) Broward	57.85
Doral (cdp) Miami-Dade	56.18
Aventura (city) Miami-Dade	53.00
Coral Gables (city) Miami-Dade	47.35
Glenvar Heights (cdp) Miami-Dade	34.94
Kendall (cdp) Miami-Dade	34.94
Cooper City (city) Broward	33.97
Clearwater (city) Pinellas	33.70
Pembroke Pines (city) Broward	33.36

Costa Ricans 25 Years and Over Who are Four-Year College Graduates

Top 10 Places Sorted by Number

Place (place type) County	Number
Miami (city) Miami-Dade	77
Hialeah (city) Miami-Dade	21

Costa Ricans 25 Years and Over Who are Four-Year College Graduates

Top 10 Places Sorted by Percent

Place (place type) County	Percent
Miami (city) Miami-Dade	12.98
Hialeah (city) Miami-Dade	6.91

Cubans 25 Years and Over Who are Four-Year College Graduates

Top 10 Places Sorted by Number

Place (place type) County	Number
Miami (city) Miami-Dade	14,926
Hialeah (city) Miami-Dade	10,997
Tamiami (cdp) Miami-Dade	5,056
Coral Gables (city) Miami-Dade	5,031
Kendall (cdp) Miami-Dade	4,215
Miami Beach (city) Miami-Dade	3,847
Fountainbleau (cdp) Miami-Dade	3,668
Westchester (cdp) Miami-Dade	3,462
Kendale Lakes (cdp) Miami-Dade	3,310
University Park (cdp) Miami-Dade	2,916

Cubans 25 Years and Over Who are Four-Year College Graduates

Top 10 Places Sorted by Percent

Place (place type) County	Percent
Key Biscayne (village) Miami-Dade	58.47
Pinecrest (village) Miami-Dade	57.56
Coral Gables (city) Miami-Dade	52.68
Gainesville (city) Alachua	49.86
Miami Shores (village) Miami-Dade	47.04
Tallahassee (city) Leon	44.91
Cutler (cdp) Miami-Dade	44.58
Boynton Beach (city) Palm Beach	43.50
Weston (city) Broward	42.81
Boca Raton (city) Palm Beach	38.47

Dominicans 25 Years and Over Who are Four-Year College Graduates

Top 10 Places Sorted by Number

Place (place type) County	Number
Miami (city) Miami-Dade	428
Hialeah (city) Miami-Dade	402
Pembroke Pines (city) Broward	353
Fountainbleau (cdp) Miami-Dade	341
The Hammocks (cdp) Miami-Dade	308
Miami Beach (city) Miami-Dade	241
Doral (cdp) Miami-Dade	186
Hollywood (city) Broward	156
Country Club (cdp) Miami-Dade	127
Miramar (city) Broward	123

Dominicans 25 Years and Over Who are Four-Year College Graduates

Top 10 Places Sorted by Percent

Place (place type) County	Percent
Doral (cdp) Miami-Dade	52.10
Weston (city) Broward	37.50
Pembroke Pines (city) Broward	31.97
The Hammocks (cdp) Miami-Dade	31.02
Fountainbleau (cdp) Miami-Dade	28.35
Richmond West (cdp) Miami-Dade	23.72
Miami Beach (city) Miami-Dade	22.50
Kendall (cdp) Miami-Dade	21.65
Tamiami (cdp) Miami-Dade	19.83
Kendale Lakes (cdp) Miami-Dade	19.43

Ecuadorians 25 Years and Over Who are Four-Year College Graduates

Top 10 Places Sorted by Number

Place (place type) County	Number
Miami (city) Miami-Dade	213
Coral Springs (city) Broward	176
Miami Beach (city) Miami-Dade	165
Hialeah (city) Miami-Dade	118
Pembroke Pines (city) Broward	107
Fountainbleau (cdp) Miami-Dade	97
Tampa (city) Hillsborough	83
Hollywood (city) Broward	56
Sunrise (city) Broward	42

Ecuadorians 25 Years and Over Who are Four-Year College Graduates

Top 10 Places Sorted by Percent

Place (place type) County	Percent
Miami Beach (city) Miami-Dade	31.43
Coral Springs (city) Broward	28.76
Pembroke Pines (city) Broward	28.53
Tampa (city) Hillsborough	24.78
Fountainbleau (cdp) Miami-Dade	20.08
Miami (city) Miami-Dade	17.16
Hollywood (city) Broward	15.14
Hialeah (city) Miami-Dade	13.80
Sunrise (city) Broward	10.85

Guatelmalans 25 Years and Over Who are Four-Year College Graduates

Top 10 Places Sorted by Number

Place (place type) County	Number
Miami (city) Miami-Dade	140
Lake Worth (city) Palm Beach	42
Hialeah (city) Miami-Dade	17
West Palm Beach (city) Palm Beach	15
Bonita Springs (city) Lee	5
Fort Lauderdale (city) Broward	0
Fort Myers (city) Lee	0
Homestead (city) Miami-Dade	0
Immokalee (cdp) Collier	0

Guatelmalans 25 Years and Over Who are Four-Year College Graduates

Top 10 Places Sorted by Percent

Place (place type) County	Percent
Miami (city) Miami-Dade	7.13
Lake Worth (city) Palm Beach	4.88
Hialeah (city) Miami-Dade	3.45
Bonita Springs (city) Lee	3.31
West Palm Beach (city) Palm Beach	1.54
Fort Lauderdale (city) Broward	0.00
Fort Myers (city) Lee	0.00
Homestead (city) Miami-Dade	0.00
Immokalee (cdp) Collier	0.00

Hondurans 25 Years and Over Who are Four-Year College Graduates

Top 10 Places Sorted by Number

Place (place type) County	Number
Miami (city) Miami-Dade	468
Hialeah (city) Miami-Dade	92
Miami Beach (city) Miami-Dade	82
Tamiami (cdp) Miami-Dade	50
Fountainbleau (cdp) Miami-Dade	46
Hollywood (city) Broward	40
Kendale Lakes (cdp) Miami-Dade	36
Tampa (city) Hillsborough	26
Carol City (cdp) Miami-Dade	22
Lake Worth (city) Palm Beach	22

Hondurans 25 Years and Over Who are Four-Year College Graduates

Top 10 Places Sorted by Percent

Place (place type) County	Percent
Tamiami (cdp) Miami-Dade	16.08
Miami Beach (city) Miami-Dade	14.02
Fountainbleau (cdp) Miami-Dade	11.70
Hollywood (city) Broward	11.56
Kendale Lakes (cdp) Miami-Dade	11.08
Lake Worth (city) Palm Beach	8.59
Carol City (cdp) Miami-Dade	6.96
Hialeah (city) Miami-Dade	5.74
Miami (city) Miami-Dade	5.00
Tampa (city) Hillsborough	4.53

Mexicans 25 Years and Over Who are Four-Year College Graduates

Top 10 Places Sorted by Number

Place (place type) County	Number
Jacksonville (city) Duval	436
Miami (city) Miami-Dade	401
Tampa (city) Hillsborough	393
Doral (cdp) Miami-Dade	287
Orlando (city) Orange	271
Miami Beach (city) Miami-Dade	211
Clearwater (city) Pinellas	183
Pembroke Pines (city) Broward	156
The Hammocks (cdp) Miami-Dade	153
Fort Lauderdale (city) Broward	152

Mexicans 25 Years and Over Who are Four-Year College Graduates

Top 10 Places Sorted by Percent

Place (place type) County	Percent
Doral (cdp) Miami-Dade	65.38
Gainesville (city) Alachua	52.98
The Hammocks (cdp) Miami-Dade	47.66
Weston (city) Broward	45.36
Melbourne (city) Brevard	30.77
Tallahassee (city) Leon	25.93
Pembroke Pines (city) Broward	25.70
Miami Beach (city) Miami-Dade	25.27
Plantation (city) Broward	24.59
Miramar (city) Broward	23.96

Nicaraguans 25 Years and Over Who are Four-Year College Graduates

Top 10 Places Sorted by Number

Place (place type) County	Number
Miami (city) Miami-Dade	1,247
Fountainbleau (cdp) Miami-Dade	697
Hialeah (city) Miami-Dade	661
Kendale Lakes (cdp) Miami-Dade	379
Kendall (cdp) Miami-Dade	342
Tamiami (cdp) Miami-Dade	316
The Hammocks (cdp) Miami-Dade	272
Sweetwater (city) Miami-Dade	228
Kendall West (cdp) Miami-Dade	193
Richmond West (cdp) Miami-Dade	160

Notes: Please refer to the User's Guide for an explanation of data; tables include places with populations > 9,999 and reflect only those areas that meet Summary File 4 population thresholds, therefore there may be less than 10 places listed

Nicaraguans 25 Years and Over Who are Four-Year College Graduates

Top 10 Places Sorted by Percent

Place (place type) County	Percent
Coral Gables (city) Miami-Dade	34.05
The Crossings (cdp) Miami-Dade	30.48
Kendall (cdp) Miami-Dade	23.93
The Hammocks (cdp) Miami-Dade	23.84
Miami Beach (city) Miami-Dade	22.64
Kendale Lakes (cdp) Miami-Dade	20.50
Hialeah Gardens (city) Miami-Dade	20.36
North Miami (city) Miami-Dade	19.60
Tamiami (cdp) Miami-Dade	19.12
Richmond West (cdp) Miami-Dade	19.09

Panamanians 25 Years and Over Who are Four-Year College Graduates

Top 10 Places Sorted by Number

Place (place type) County	Number
Miami (city) Miami-Dade	121
Fountainbleau (cdp) Miami-Dade	103
Tampa (city) Hillsborough	52
Jacksonville (city) Duval	44
Miramar (city) Broward	27

Panamanians 25 Years and Over Who are Four-Year College Graduates

Top 10 Places Sorted by Percent

Place (place type) County	Percent
Fountainbleau (cdp) Miami-Dade	25.94
Miami (city) Miami-Dade	19.87
Jacksonville (city) Duval	13.17
Tampa (city) Hillsborough	11.93
Miramar (city) Broward	11.49

Paraguayans 25 Years and Over Who are Four-Year College Graduates

Top 10 Places Sorted by Number

Place (place type) County	Number
No places met population threshold.	

Paraguayans 25 Years and Over Who are Four-Year College Graduates

Top 10 Places Sorted by Percent

Place (place type) County	Percent
No places met population threshold.	

Peruvians 25 Years and Over Who are Four-Year College Graduates

Top 10 Places Sorted by Number

Place (place type) County	Number
Miami (city) Miami-Dade	464
Pembroke Pines (city) Broward	403
Kendall (cdp) Miami-Dade	383
The Hammocks (cdp) Miami-Dade	330
Fountainbleau (cdp) Miami-Dade	280
Miami Beach (city) Miami-Dade	277
Weston (city) Broward	201
Kendall West (cdp) Miami-Dade	191
Kendale Lakes (cdp) Miami-Dade	177
Hollywood (city) Broward	176

Peruvians 25 Years and Over Who are Four-Year College Graduates

Top 10 Places Sorted by Percent

Place (place type) County	Percent
Plantation (city) Broward	44.48
Kendall (cdp) Miami-Dade	42.94
Pembroke Pines (city) Broward	42.51
Weston (city) Broward	38.73
Doral (cdp) Miami-Dade	34.48
Fountainbleau (cdp) Miami-Dade	31.32
Fort Lauderdale (city) Broward	29.43
Kendale Lakes (cdp) Miami-Dade	29.16
Sunrise (city) Broward	28.67
Coral Springs (city) Broward	28.13

Puerto Ricans 25 Years and Over Who are Four-Year College Graduates

Top 10 Places Sorted by Number

Place (place type) County	Number
Orlando (city) Orange	1,395
Pembroke Pines (city) Broward	1,165
Jacksonville (city) Duval	978
Miami (city) Miami-Dade	964
Tampa (city) Hillsborough	902
Kissimmee (city) Osceola	744
Coral Springs (city) Broward	742
Yeehaw Junction (cdp) Osceola	647
Weston (city) Broward	616
Miami Beach (city) Miami-Dade	604

Puerto Ricans 25 Years and Over Who are Four-Year College Graduates

Top 10 Places Sorted by Percent

Place (place type) County	Percent
Coral Gables (city) Miami-Dade	63.52
Glenvar Heights (cdp) Miami-Dade	57.33
Weston (city) Broward	53.20
Doral (cdp) Miami-Dade	45.31
Tallahassee (city) Leon	43.21
Wekiwa Springs (cdp) Seminole	42.73
Gainesville (city) Alachua	38.56
Miami Lakes (cdp) Miami-Dade	37.18
Cooper City (city) Broward	36.12
Plantation (city) Broward	35.98

Salvadorans 25 Years and Over Who are Four-Year College Graduates

Top 10 Places Sorted by Number

Place (place type) County	Number
Miami (city) Miami-Dade	128
Fort Lauderdale (city) Broward	14
Oakland Park (city) Broward	14
Lake Worth (city) Palm Beach	13
Homestead (city) Miami-Dade	12
Hialeah (city) Miami-Dade	9

Salvadorans 25 Years and Over Who are Four-Year College Graduates

Top 10 Places Sorted by Percent

Place (place type) County	Percent
Miami (city) Miami-Dade	7.61
Lake Worth (city) Palm Beach	5.44
Fort Lauderdale (city) Broward	4.11
Oakland Park (city) Broward	3.32
Homestead (city) Miami-Dade	2.19
Hialeah (city) Miami-Dade	1.52

South Americans 25 Years and Over Who are Four-Year College Graduates

Top 10 Places Sorted by Number

Place (place type) County	Number
Miami (city) Miami-Dade	2,864
Miami Beach (city) Miami-Dade	2,651
Kendall (cdp) Miami-Dade	2,238
Weston (city) Broward	2,127
Pembroke Pines (city) Broward	1,921
The Hammocks (cdp) Miami-Dade	1,729
Doral (cdp) Miami-Dade	1,497
Fountainbleau (cdp) Miami-Dade	1,478
Hialeah (city) Miami-Dade	1,106
Hollywood (city) Broward	1,076

South Americans 25 Years and Over Who are Four-Year College Graduates

Top 10 Places Sorted by Percent

Place (place type) County	Percent
Key Biscayne (village) Miami-Dade	59.61
Parkland (city) Broward	54.84
Gainesville (city) Alachua	54.38
Coral Gables (city) Miami-Dade	53.13
Aventura (city) Miami-Dade	52.13
Weston (city) Broward	51.15
Pinecrest (village) Miami-Dade	48.18
South Miami (city) Miami-Dade	45.30
Doral (cdp) Miami-Dade	43.98
Tallahassee (city) Leon	41.40

Spaniards 25 Years and Over Who are Four-Year College Graduates

Top 10 Places Sorted by Number

Place (place type) County	Number
Tampa (city) Hillsborough	244
Miami Beach (city) Miami-Dade	228
Miami (city) Miami-Dade	164
Hialeah (city) Miami-Dade	8

Spaniards 25 Years and Over Who are Four-Year College Graduates

Top 10 Places Sorted by Percent

Place (place type) County	Percent
Miami Beach (city) Miami-Dade	47.90
Tampa (city) Hillsborough	38.43
Miami (city) Miami-Dade	20.07
Hialeah (city) Miami-Dade	2.01

Uruguayans 25 Years and Over Who are Four-Year College Graduates

Top 10 Places Sorted by Number

Place (place type) County	Number
No places met population threshold.	

Uruguayans 25 Years and Over Who are Four-Year College Graduates

Top 10 Places Sorted by Percent

Place (place type) County	Percent
No places met population threshold.	

Venezuelans 25 Years and Over Who are Four-Year College Graduates

Top 10 Places Sorted by Number

Place (place type) County	Number
Weston (city) Broward	656
Doral (cdp) Miami-Dade	582
Kendall (cdp) Miami-Dade	484
Pembroke Pines (city) Broward	468
Fountainbleau (cdp) Miami-Dade	408
Miami (city) Miami-Dade	378
The Hammocks (cdp) Miami-Dade	348
Miami Beach (city) Miami-Dade	338
Coral Gables (city) Miami-Dade	214
Orlando (city) Orange	192

Venezuelans 25 Years and Over Who are Four-Year College Graduates

Top 10 Places Sorted by Percent

Place (place type) County	Percent
Coral Gables (city) Miami-Dade	63.31
Weston (city) Broward	51.82
Coral Springs (city) Broward	50.18
Kendall (cdp) Miami-Dade	50.10
Pembroke Pines (city) Broward	49.42
Doral (cdp) Miami-Dade	48.91
Tampa (city) Hillsborough	45.65
Tamiami (cdp) Miami-Dade	45.62
Richmond West (cdp) Miami-Dade	43.01
Orlando (city) Orange	41.74

Other Hispanics 25 Years and Over Who are Four-Year College Graduates

Top 10 Places Sorted by Number

Place (place type) County	Number
Miami (city) Miami-Dade	1,739
Tampa (city) Hillsborough	1,360

Notes: Please refer to the User's Guide for an explanation of data; tables include places with populations > 9,999 and reflect only those areas that meet Summary File 4 population thresholds, therefore there may be less than 10 places listed

Miami Beach (city) Miami-Dade	977
Hialeah (city) Miami-Dade	850
Fountainbleau (cdp) Miami-Dade	827
Pembroke Pines (city) Broward	761
Kendale Lakes (cdp) Miami-Dade	758
Kendall (cdp) Miami-Dade	750
Doral (cdp) Miami-Dade	637
Jacksonville (city) Duval	595

Other Hispanics 25 Years and Over Who are Four-Year College Graduates

Top 10 Places Sorted by Percent

Place (place type) County	Percent
Key Biscayne (village) Miami-Dade	66.46
Cutler (cdp) Miami-Dade	54.55
Doral (cdp) Miami-Dade	45.37
Gainesville (city) Alachua	45.33
Coral Gables (city) Miami-Dade	43.41
Temple Terrace (city) Hillsborough	42.65
Aventura (city) Miami-Dade	38.61
Greater Carrollwood (cdp) Hillsborough	36.53
Sandalfoot Cove (cdp) Palm Beach	35.51
Cooper City (city) Broward	35.02

Median Household Income

Total Population

Top 10 Places Sorted by Number

Place (place type) County	Dollars
Pinecrest (village) Miami-Dade	107,507
Cutler (cdp) Miami-Dade	106,432
Parkland (city) Broward	102,624
Key Biscayne (village) Miami-Dade	86,599
Weston (city) Broward	80,920
Keystone (cdp) Hillsborough	80,677
Westchase (cdp) Hillsborough	79,561
Cooper City (city) Broward	75,166
Wekiwa Springs (cdp) Seminole	71,839
Wellington (village) Palm Beach	70,271

Hispanic

Top 10 Places Sorted by Number

Place (place type) County	Dollars
Cutler (cdp) Miami-Dade	109,352
Pinecrest (village) Miami-Dade	97,084
Lake Mary (city) Seminole	91,247
Wekiwa Springs (cdp) Seminole	90,000
Parkland (city) Broward	89,876
Key Biscayne (village) Miami-Dade	83,752
Westchase (cdp) Hillsborough	76,380
Cooper City (city) Broward	74,952
Keystone (cdp) Hillsborough	72,083
Bloomingdale (cdp) Hillsborough	66,500

Argentinian

Top 10 Places Sorted by Number

Place (place type) County	Dollars
Kendall (cdp) Miami-Dade	40,938
Hialeah (city) Miami-Dade	39,688
Miami (city) Miami-Dade	36,289
Fountainbleau (cdp) Miami-Dade	31,944
Hollywood (city) Broward	27,857
Sunny Isles Beach (city) Miami-Dade	23,750
Miami Beach (city) Miami-Dade	22,154

Bolivian

Top 10 Places Sorted by Number

Place (place type) County	Dollars

No places met population threshold.

Central American

Top 10 Places Sorted by Number

Place (place type) County	Dollars
Country Walk (cdp) Miami-Dade	72,396
Sunset (cdp) Miami-Dade	64,821
Pembroke Pines (city) Broward	60,969
Plantation (city) Broward	60,139
The Crossings (cdp) Miami-Dade	60,114
Jupiter (town) Palm Beach	57,500
Richmond West (cdp) Miami-Dade	57,250
The Hammocks (cdp) Miami-Dade	55,882
Doral (cdp) Miami-Dade	55,000
Miramar (city) Broward	54,671

Chilean

Top 10 Places Sorted by Number

Place (place type) County	Dollars
Fountainbleau (cdp) Miami-Dade	40,395
Kendall (cdp) Miami-Dade	36,719
Hollywood (city) Broward	36,667
Miami (city) Miami-Dade	28,667
Hialeah (city) Miami-Dade	25,195
Miami Beach (city) Miami-Dade	21,875

Columbian

Top 10 Places Sorted by Number

Place (place type) County	Dollars
Meadow Woods (cdp) Orange	60,880
Cooper City (city) Broward	60,476
Miami Lakes (cdp) Miami-Dade	57,422
Key Biscayne (village) Miami-Dade	55,469
Wellington (village) Palm Beach	55,441
Richmond West (cdp) Miami-Dade	54,286
South Miami Heights (cdp) Miami-Dade	53,092
Sunset (cdp) Miami-Dade	52,115
Coral Gables (city) Miami-Dade	51,118
Plantation (city) Broward	50,263

Costa Rican

Top 10 Places Sorted by Number

Place (place type) County	Dollars
Miami (city) Miami-Dade	28,405
Hialeah (city) Miami-Dade	25,769

Cuban

Top 10 Places Sorted by Number

Place (place type) County	Dollars
Pinecrest (village) Miami-Dade	136,566
Cutler (cdp) Miami-Dade	125,198
Key Biscayne (village) Miami-Dade	97,344
Weston (city) Broward	94,463
Cooper City (city) Broward	88,617
Coral Gables (city) Miami-Dade	73,830
Wellington (village) Palm Beach	68,438
Plantation (city) Broward	68,167
Miami Lakes (cdp) Miami-Dade	67,143
Miami Shores (village) Miami-Dade	64,750

Dominican

Top 10 Places Sorted by Number

Place (place type) County	Dollars
The Hammocks (cdp) Miami-Dade	57,228
Weston (city) Broward	57,014
Pembroke Pines (city) Broward	52,050
Sunrise (city) Broward	50,375
Kendale Lakes (cdp) Miami-Dade	43,259
Miramar (city) Broward	43,000
Richmond West (cdp) Miami-Dade	42,414
Tamiami (cdp) Miami-Dade	41,429
Town 'n' Country (cdp) Hillsborough	40,536
Hialeah Gardens (city) Miami-Dade	40,313

Ecuadorian

Top 10 Places Sorted by Number

Place (place type) County	Dollars
Coral Springs (city) Broward	69,444
Pembroke Pines (city) Broward	58,333
Hollywood (city) Broward	37,578
Sunrise (city) Broward	37,250
Hialeah (city) Miami-Dade	35,169
Fountainbleau (cdp) Miami-Dade	32,426
Miami (city) Miami-Dade	25,664
Miami Beach (city) Miami-Dade	24,375
Tampa (city) Hillsborough	20,294

Guatelmalan

Top 10 Places Sorted by Number

Place (place type) County	Dollars
Immokalee (cdp) Collier	47,679
Fort Myers (city) Lee	45,625
West Palm Beach (city) Palm Beach	37,313
Lake Worth (city) Palm Beach	32,292
Bonita Springs (city) Lee	32,222
Fort Lauderdale (city) Broward	31,250
Miami (city) Miami-Dade	28,583
Homestead (city) Miami-Dade	25,657
Hialeah (city) Miami-Dade	24,189

Honduran

Top 10 Places Sorted by Number

Place (place type) County	Dollars
Fountainbleau (cdp) Miami-Dade	45,500
Lake Worth (city) Palm Beach	40,750
North Miami (city) Miami-Dade	35,699
Carol City (cdp) Miami-Dade	35,063
Hollywood (city) Broward	33,929
Hialeah (city) Miami-Dade	30,958
Tamiami (cdp) Miami-Dade	26,667
West Little River (cdp) Miami-Dade	26,667
Tampa (city) Hillsborough	26,324
Miami (city) Miami-Dade	23,233

Mexican

Top 10 Places Sorted by Number

Place (place type) County	Dollars
Doral (cdp) Miami-Dade	76,197
Pembroke Pines (city) Broward	73,047
Weston (city) Broward	71,538
Key West (city) Monroe	58,333
Miramar (city) Broward	56,339
Sunrise (city) Broward	52,308
The Hammocks (cdp) Miami-Dade	51,250
Davie (town) Broward	50,662
South Miami Heights (cdp) Miami-Dade	46,000
Brandon (cdp) Hillsborough	45,500

Nicaraguan

Top 10 Places Sorted by Number

Place (place type) County	Dollars
The Crossings (cdp) Miami-Dade	59,821
Miramar (city) Broward	58,935
The Hammocks (cdp) Miami-Dade	58,347
Richmond West (cdp) Miami-Dade	57,344
Coral Gables (city) Miami-Dade	53,917
Tamiami (cdp) Miami-Dade	52,188
Kendall (cdp) Miami-Dade	49,375
Palmetto Estates (cdp) Miami-Dade	46,250
South Miami Heights (cdp) Miami-Dade	44,318
Kendale Lakes (cdp) Miami-Dade	44,047

Panamanian

Top 10 Places Sorted by Number

Place (place type) County	Dollars
Fountainbleau (cdp) Miami-Dade	55,231
Jacksonville (city) Duval	47,969
Miramar (city) Broward	35,855
Miami (city) Miami-Dade	32,054
Tampa (city) Hillsborough	24,671

Notes: Please refer to the User's Guide for an explanation of data; tables include places with populations > 9,999 and reflect only those areas that meet Summary File 4 population thresholds, therefore there may be less than 10 places listed

Paraguayan

Top 10 Places Sorted by Number

Place (place type) County	Dollars

No places met population threshold.

Peruvian

Top 10 Places Sorted by Number

Place (place type) County	Dollars
The Crossings (cdp) Miami-Dade	64,000
Weston (city) Broward	58,750
Doral (cdp) Miami-Dade	58,077
Pembroke Pines (city) Broward	56,808
Miramar (city) Broward	56,591
The Hammocks (cdp) Miami-Dade	55,917
Richmond West (cdp) Miami-Dade	53,000
Sunrise (city) Broward	44,821
Kendall West (cdp) Miami-Dade	41,932
Fort Lauderdale (city) Broward	40,882

Puerto Rican

Top 10 Places Sorted by Number

Place (place type) County	Dollars
Wekiwa Springs (cdp) Seminole	86,365
Weston (city) Broward	70,703
Richmond West (cdp) Miami-Dade	67,279
Coral Gables (city) Miami-Dade	65,720
Cooper City (city) Broward	64,259
Coconut Creek (city) Broward	61,250
Royal Palm Beach (village) Palm Beach	60,417
Palmetto Estates (cdp) Miami-Dade	59,716
The Crossings (cdp) Miami-Dade	58,750
Miami Lakes (cdp) Miami-Dade	58,438

Salvadoran

Top 10 Places Sorted by Number

Place (place type) County	Dollars
Homestead (city) Miami-Dade	32,639
Fort Lauderdale (city) Broward	29,792
Oakland Park (city) Broward	25,542
Lake Worth (city) Palm Beach	24,615
Miami (city) Miami-Dade	21,797
Hialeah (city) Miami-Dade	21,500

South American

Top 10 Places Sorted by Number

Place (place type) County	Dollars
Cutler (cdp) Miami-Dade	85,412
Parkland (city) Broward	65,417
Cooper City (city) Broward	61,190
Meadow Woods (cdp) Orange	60,909
Key Biscayne (village) Miami-Dade	60,000
Weston (city) Broward	55,945
Wellington (village) Palm Beach	55,737
Miami Lakes (cdp) Miami-Dade	55,481
Richmond West (cdp) Miami-Dade	54,663
Coral Terrace (cdp) Miami-Dade	52,946

Spaniard

Top 10 Places Sorted by Number

Place (place type) County	Dollars
Miami Beach (city) Miami-Dade	43,906
Hialeah (city) Miami-Dade	38,359
Tampa (city) Hillsborough	31,625
Miami (city) Miami-Dade	25,134

Uruguayan

Top 10 Places Sorted by Number

Place (place type) County	Dollars

No places met population threshold.

Venezuelan

Top 10 Places Sorted by Number

Place (place type) County	Dollars
Richmond West (cdp) Miami-Dade	60,658
Coral Gables (city) Miami-Dade	56,875
Weston (city) Broward	55,513
Plantation (city) Broward	55,227
Kendall (cdp) Miami-Dade	47,216
Coral Springs (city) Broward	46,719
Tamiami (cdp) Miami-Dade	43,864
Pembroke Pines (city) Broward	42,386
Doral (cdp) Miami-Dade	41,333
The Hammocks (cdp) Miami-Dade	41,094

Other Hispanic

Top 10 Places Sorted by Number

Place (place type) County	Dollars
Cooper City (city) Broward	77,028
Greater Northdale (cdp) Hillsborough	59,583
Temple Terrace (city) Hillsborough	59,286
Miami Lakes (cdp) Miami-Dade	57,083
Richmond West (cdp) Miami-Dade	56,767
Key Biscayne (village) Miami-Dade	56,071
Miami Shores (village) Miami-Dade	55,972
Coral Terrace (cdp) Miami-Dade	55,694
Country Walk (cdp) Miami-Dade	54,948
Miramar (city) Broward	54,330

Per Capita Income

Total Population

Top 10 Places Sorted by Number

Place (place type) County	Dollars
Naples (city) Collier	61,141
Key Biscayne (village) Miami-Dade	54,213
Pinecrest (village) Miami-Dade	51,181
Coral Gables (city) Miami-Dade	46,163
Boca Raton (city) Palm Beach	45,628
Cutler (cdp) Miami-Dade	42,986
Palm Beach Gardens (city) Palm Beach	42,975
Marco Island (city) Collier	42,875
Parkland (city) Broward	41,896
Aventura (city) Miami-Dade	41,092

Hispanic

Top 10 Places Sorted by Number

Place (place type) County	Dollars
Key Biscayne (village) Miami-Dade	46,682
Coral Gables (city) Miami-Dade	41,997
Westchase (cdp) Hillsborough	41,823
Pinecrest (village) Miami-Dade	40,784
Cutler (cdp) Miami-Dade	36,802
Parkland (city) Broward	36,728
Lake Mary (city) Seminole	32,302
Aventura (city) Miami-Dade	31,980
Maitland (city) Orange	27,579
Miami Lakes (cdp) Miami-Dade	27,543

Argentinian

Top 10 Places Sorted by Number

Place (place type) County	Dollars
Kendall (cdp) Miami-Dade	21,551
Miami (city) Miami-Dade	20,737
Miami Beach (city) Miami-Dade	17,211
Sunny Isles Beach (city) Miami-Dade	16,962
Fountainbleau (cdp) Miami-Dade	15,238
Hialeah (city) Miami-Dade	14,892
Hollywood (city) Broward	14,713

Bolivian

Top 10 Places Sorted by Number

Place (place type) County	Dollars

No places met population threshold.

Central American

Top 10 Places Sorted by Number

Place (place type) County	Dollars
Pinecrest (village) Miami-Dade	32,446
Kissimmee (city) Osceola	30,814
Coral Gables (city) Miami-Dade	27,046
Doral (cdp) Miami-Dade	26,410
Plantation (city) Broward	24,614
The Crossings (cdp) Miami-Dade	22,224
Pembroke Pines (city) Broward	20,872
Richmond West (cdp) Miami-Dade	19,882
The Hammocks (cdp) Miami-Dade	18,882
Coral Springs (city) Broward	18,668

Chilean

Top 10 Places Sorted by Number

Place (place type) County	Dollars
Hollywood (city) Broward	41,421
Kendall (cdp) Miami-Dade	18,805
Miami (city) Miami-Dade	16,787
Miami Beach (city) Miami-Dade	16,063
Fountainbleau (cdp) Miami-Dade	11,869
Hialeah (city) Miami-Dade	11,676

Columbian

Top 10 Places Sorted by Number

Place (place type) County	Dollars
Greater Carrollwood (cdp) Hillsborough	39,919
Key Biscayne (village) Miami-Dade	39,675
Miami Lakes (cdp) Miami-Dade	34,692
Deerfield Beach (city) Broward	32,633
Coral Gables (city) Miami-Dade	31,909
Doral (cdp) Miami-Dade	30,236
Aventura (city) Miami-Dade	26,011
Jacksonville (city) Duval	25,440
Ojus (cdp) Miami-Dade	24,060
Weston (city) Broward	21,914

Costa Rican

Top 10 Places Sorted by Number

Place (place type) County	Dollars
Miami (city) Miami-Dade	11,901
Hialeah (city) Miami-Dade	10,481

Cuban

Top 10 Places Sorted by Number

Place (place type) County	Dollars
Key Biscayne (village) Miami-Dade	65,854
Pinecrest (village) Miami-Dade	53,282
Coral Gables (city) Miami-Dade	48,094
Cutler (cdp) Miami-Dade	47,146
Boca Raton (city) Palm Beach	42,127
Weston (city) Broward	37,503
Lake Magdalene (cdp) Hillsborough	37,023
Glenvar Heights (cdp) Miami-Dade	36,948
Altamonte Springs (city) Seminole	33,321
Doral (cdp) Miami-Dade	32,899

Dominican

Top 10 Places Sorted by Number

Place (place type) County	Dollars
The Hammocks (cdp) Miami-Dade	19,896
Weston (city) Broward	19,856
Coral Springs (city) Broward	19,051
Tamiami (cdp) Miami-Dade	18,429
Doral (cdp) Miami-Dade	17,829
Pembroke Pines (city) Broward	16,807
Tampa (city) Hillsborough	15,739
Richmond West (cdp) Miami-Dade	14,875
Town 'n' Country (cdp) Hillsborough	14,740
Hialeah Gardens (city) Miami-Dade	14,546

Notes: Please refer to the User's Guide for an explanation of data; tables include places with populations > 9,999 and reflect only those areas that meet Summary File 4 population thresholds, therefore there may be less than 10 places listed

Ecuadorian

Top 10 Places Sorted by Number

Place (place type) County	Dollars
Pembroke Pines (city) Broward	25,478
Coral Springs (city) Broward	19,023
Miami Beach (city) Miami-Dade	17,788
Sunrise (city) Broward	16,225
Miami (city) Miami-Dade	14,825
Hialeah (city) Miami-Dade	13,189
Hollywood (city) Broward	12,036
Tampa (city) Hillsborough	10,737
Fountainbleau (cdp) Miami-Dade	10,453

Guatelmalan

Top 10 Places Sorted by Number

Place (place type) County	Dollars
Fort Lauderdale (city) Broward	11,372
Miami (city) Miami-Dade	10,887
Immokalee (cdp) Collier	10,409
West Palm Beach (city) Palm Beach	9,018
Bonita Springs (city) Lee	8,989
Fort Myers (city) Lee	8,650
Hialeah (city) Miami-Dade	7,641
Homestead (city) Miami-Dade	7,234
Lake Worth (city) Palm Beach	7,210

Honduran

Top 10 Places Sorted by Number

Place (place type) County	Dollars
Hollywood (city) Broward	15,868
Carol City (cdp) Miami-Dade	14,697
Miami Beach (city) Miami-Dade	12,407
Tamiami (cdp) Miami-Dade	11,964
Tampa (city) Hillsborough	11,016
Fountainbleau (cdp) Miami-Dade	10,874
Hialeah (city) Miami-Dade	10,504
North Miami Beach (city) Miami-Dade	9,819
Lake Worth (city) Palm Beach	9,633
Miami (city) Miami-Dade	9,228

Mexican

Top 10 Places Sorted by Number

Place (place type) County	Dollars
Doral (cdp) Miami-Dade	27,236
Pembroke Pines (city) Broward	24,223
Plantation (city) Broward	21,763
Weston (city) Broward	20,312
Orlando (city) Orange	20,044
Miami Beach (city) Miami-Dade	19,765
Melbourne (city) Brevard	19,303
The Hammocks (cdp) Miami-Dade	18,123
Sunrise (city) Broward	17,747
Miramar (city) Broward	17,715

Nicaraguan

Top 10 Places Sorted by Number

Place (place type) County	Dollars
The Crossings (cdp) Miami-Dade	23,575
Coral Gables (city) Miami-Dade	21,491
The Hammocks (cdp) Miami-Dade	20,046
Miramar (city) Broward	19,507
Tampa (city) Hillsborough	17,344
Richmond West (cdp) Miami-Dade	17,110
Kendale Lakes (cdp) Miami-Dade	16,729
Kendall (cdp) Miami-Dade	16,571
Hollywood (city) Broward	16,534
Miami Beach (city) Miami-Dade	14,632

Panamanian

Top 10 Places Sorted by Number

Place (place type) County	Dollars
Miami (city) Miami-Dade	23,014
Fountainbleau (cdp) Miami-Dade	17,102
Jacksonville (city) Duval	15,532
Tampa (city) Hillsborough	11,665
Miramar (city) Broward	11,234

Paraguayan

Top 10 Places Sorted by Number

Place (place type) County	Dollars

No places met population threshold.

Peruvian

Top 10 Places Sorted by Number

Place (place type) County	Dollars
Weston (city) Broward	24,906
Kendale Lakes (cdp) Miami-Dade	22,421
Orlando (city) Orange	22,045
Plantation (city) Broward	20,234
The Hammocks (cdp) Miami-Dade	20,131
The Crossings (cdp) Miami-Dade	20,023
Miami (city) Miami-Dade	19,081
Doral (cdp) Miami-Dade	17,508
Hialeah (city) Miami-Dade	16,658
Fountainbleau (cdp) Miami-Dade	16,513

Puerto Rican

Top 10 Places Sorted by Number

Place (place type) County	Dollars
Coral Gables (city) Miami-Dade	42,008
Weston (city) Broward	29,363
Deerfield Beach (city) Broward	29,214
Miami Lakes (cdp) Miami-Dade	27,535
Wekiwa Springs (cdp) Seminole	27,388
Lake Magdalene (cdp) Hillsborough	26,128
The Crossings (cdp) Miami-Dade	26,066
Glenvar Heights (cdp) Miami-Dade	25,124
Doral (cdp) Miami-Dade	23,838
Coconut Creek (city) Broward	23,518

Salvadoran

Top 10 Places Sorted by Number

Place (place type) County	Dollars
Fort Lauderdale (city) Broward	10,466
Miami (city) Miami-Dade	10,207
Oakland Park (city) Broward	10,067
Homestead (city) Miami-Dade	9,794
Lake Worth (city) Palm Beach	9,326
Hialeah (city) Miami-Dade	9,042

South American

Top 10 Places Sorted by Number

Place (place type) County	Dollars
Cutler (cdp) Miami-Dade	37,651
Key Biscayne (village) Miami-Dade	36,450
Coral Gables (city) Miami-Dade	32,634
Aventura (city) Miami-Dade	29,891
Delray Beach (city) Palm Beach	28,413
Miami Lakes (cdp) Miami-Dade	28,403
Greater Carrollwood (cdp) Hillsborough	27,633
Boca Raton (city) Palm Beach	26,302
Deerfield Beach (city) Broward	24,204
Doral (cdp) Miami-Dade	23,359

Spaniard

Top 10 Places Sorted by Number

Place (place type) County	Dollars
Tampa (city) Hillsborough	26,392
Miami Beach (city) Miami-Dade	25,841
Miami (city) Miami-Dade	17,083
Hialeah (city) Miami-Dade	13,312

Uruguayan

Top 10 Places Sorted by Number

Place (place type) County	Dollars

No places met population threshold.

Venezuelan

Top 10 Places Sorted by Number

Place (place type) County	Dollars
Coral Gables (city) Miami-Dade	36,827
Weston (city) Broward	24,539
Miami Beach (city) Miami-Dade	24,212
The Crossings (cdp) Miami-Dade	21,774
Pembroke Pines (city) Broward	20,022
Doral (cdp) Miami-Dade	19,591
Miami (city) Miami-Dade	19,488
Coral Springs (city) Broward	18,516
Kendall (cdp) Miami-Dade	16,144
Richmond West (cdp) Miami-Dade	15,721

Other Hispanic

Top 10 Places Sorted by Number

Place (place type) County	Dollars
Golden Gate (cdp) Collier	30,936
Key Biscayne (village) Miami-Dade	30,118
Aventura (city) Miami-Dade	29,609
Greater Carrollwood (cdp) Hillsborough	29,288
Boca Raton (city) Palm Beach	28,953
Temple Terrace (city) Hillsborough	28,529
Coral Gables (city) Miami-Dade	27,641
Pinecrest (village) Miami-Dade	23,213
Greater Northdale (cdp) Hillsborough	20,999
Key West (city) Monroe	19,820

Poverty Status

Total Population with Income Below Poverty Level

Top 10 Places Sorted by Number

Place (place type) County	Number
Miami (city) Miami-Dade	100,405
Jacksonville (city) Duval	87,691
Tampa (city) Hillsborough	53,425
Hialeah (city) Miami-Dade	41,537
Tallahassee (city) Leon	33,978
St. Petersburg (city) Pinellas	32,127
Orlando (city) Orange	29,029
Fort Lauderdale (city) Broward	26,158
Gainesville (city) Alachua	22,559
Miami Beach (city) Miami-Dade	19,003

Total Population with Income Below Poverty Level

Top 10 Places Sorted by Percent

Place (place type) County	Percent
Gladeview (cdp) Miami-Dade	52.77
Brownsville (cdp) Miami-Dade	42.71
Immokalee (cdp) Collier	39.84
Opa-locka (city) Miami-Dade	35.20
Pinewood (cdp) Miami-Dade	33.46
Belle Glade (city) Palm Beach	32.87
Homestead (city) Miami-Dade	31.77
University (cdp) Hillsborough	31.34
Fort Pierce (city) Saint Lucie	30.91
West Little River (cdp) Miami-Dade	29.04

Hispanics with Income Below Poverty Level

Top 10 Places Sorted by Number

Place (place type) County	Number
Miami (city) Miami-Dade	62,475
Hialeah (city) Miami-Dade	38,013
Tampa (city) Hillsborough	13,275
Miami Beach (city) Miami-Dade	12,069
Fountainbleau (cdp) Miami-Dade	7,568
Orlando (city) Orange	6,545
Homestead (city) Miami-Dade	5,795
Kendall West (cdp) Miami-Dade	5,128
Immokalee (cdp) Collier	5,062
Hollywood (city) Broward	4,910

Notes: Please refer to the User's Guide for an explanation of data; tables include places with populations > 9,999 and reflect only those areas that meet Summary File 4 population thresholds, therefore there may be less than 10 places listed

Hispanics with Income Below Poverty Level
Top 10 Places Sorted by Percent

Place (place type) County	Percent
Gladeview (cdp) Miami-Dade	60.15
West Pensacola (cdp) Escambia	44.07
Auburndale (city) Polk	41.95
Brownsville (cdp) Miami-Dade	40.05
University (cdp) Hillsborough	39.56
De Land (city) Volusia	39.05
Fort Pierce (city) Saint Lucie	38.51
Immokalee (cdp) Collier	38.08
Gainesville (city) Alachua	38.04
Brent (cdp) Escambia	36.47

Argentinians with Income Below Poverty Level
Top 10 Places Sorted by Number

Place (place type) County	Number
Miami Beach (city) Miami-Dade	1,029
Miami (city) Miami-Dade	672
Hollywood (city) Broward	207
Sunny Isles Beach (city) Miami-Dade	121
Fountainbleau (cdp) Miami-Dade	106
Kendall (cdp) Miami-Dade	106
Hialeah (city) Miami-Dade	70

Argentinians with Income Below Poverty Level
Top 10 Places Sorted by Percent

Place (place type) County	Percent
Hollywood (city) Broward	37.03
Miami Beach (city) Miami-Dade	33.95
Miami (city) Miami-Dade	33.37
Fountainbleau (cdp) Miami-Dade	24.09
Sunny Isles Beach (city) Miami-Dade	21.19
Hialeah (city) Miami-Dade	16.75
Kendall (cdp) Miami-Dade	16.72

Bolivians with Income Below Poverty Level
Top 10 Places Sorted by Number

Place (place type) County	Number

No places met population threshold.

Bolivians with Income Below Poverty Level
Top 10 Places Sorted by Percent

Place (place type) County	Percent

No places met population threshold.

Central Americans with Income Below Poverty Level
Top 10 Places Sorted by Number

Place (place type) County	Number
Miami (city) Miami-Dade	12,437
Hialeah (city) Miami-Dade	2,956
West Palm Beach (city) Palm Beach	1,013
Lake Worth (city) Palm Beach	1,002
Homestead (city) Miami-Dade	922
Fountainbleau (cdp) Miami-Dade	794
West Little River (cdp) Miami-Dade	789
Miami Beach (city) Miami-Dade	691
Tampa (city) Hillsborough	684
Kendall West (cdp) Miami-Dade	655

Central Americans with Income Below Poverty Level
Top 10 Places Sorted by Percent

Place (place type) County	Percent
Gladeview (cdp) Miami-Dade	57.17
Immokalee (cdp) Collier	54.24
Leisure City (cdp) Miami-Dade	36.48
West Palm Beach (city) Palm Beach	36.41
Oakland Park (city) Broward	35.60
Pinewood (cdp) Miami-Dade	34.82
Brownsville (cdp) Miami-Dade	32.83
Lake Worth (city) Palm Beach	32.09
Bonita Springs (city) Lee	32.07
West Little River (cdp) Miami-Dade	31.85

Chileans with Income Below Poverty Level
Top 10 Places Sorted by Number

Place (place type) County	Number
Miami Beach (city) Miami-Dade	226
Miami (city) Miami-Dade	220
Fountainbleau (cdp) Miami-Dade	147
Hialeah (city) Miami-Dade	112
Kendall (cdp) Miami-Dade	64
Hollywood (city) Broward	41

Chileans with Income Below Poverty Level
Top 10 Places Sorted by Percent

Place (place type) County	Percent
Miami Beach (city) Miami-Dade	30.58
Miami (city) Miami-Dade	24.53
Fountainbleau (cdp) Miami-Dade	20.91
Hialeah (city) Miami-Dade	15.20
Kendall (cdp) Miami-Dade	13.33
Hollywood (city) Broward	10.88

Columbians with Income Below Poverty Level
Top 10 Places Sorted by Number

Place (place type) County	Number
Miami (city) Miami-Dade	1,751
Hialeah (city) Miami-Dade	1,489
Miami Beach (city) Miami-Dade	1,471
Kendall West (cdp) Miami-Dade	1,291
The Hammocks (cdp) Miami-Dade	983
Kendall (cdp) Miami-Dade	913
Kendale Lakes (cdp) Miami-Dade	781
Hollywood (city) Broward	746
Country Club (cdp) Miami-Dade	694
Fountainbleau (cdp) Miami-Dade	629

Columbians with Income Below Poverty Level
Top 10 Places Sorted by Percent

Place (place type) County	Percent
Oak Ridge (cdp) Orange	43.90
Egypt Lake-Leto (cdp) Hillsborough	38.10
Clearwater (city) Pinellas	35.42
Sunny Isles Beach (city) Miami-Dade	33.37
Miami Beach (city) Miami-Dade	32.89
West Palm Beach (city) Palm Beach	31.02
Kendall West (cdp) Miami-Dade	29.77
Miami (city) Miami-Dade	29.56
Kissimmee (city) Osceola	27.93
Davie (town) Broward	27.76

Costa Ricans with Income Below Poverty Level
Top 10 Places Sorted by Number

Place (place type) County	Number
Miami (city) Miami-Dade	263
Hialeah (city) Miami-Dade	83

Costa Ricans with Income Below Poverty Level
Top 10 Places Sorted by Percent

Place (place type) County	Percent
Miami (city) Miami-Dade	32.23
Hialeah (city) Miami-Dade	15.87

Cubans with Income Below Poverty Level
Top 10 Places Sorted by Number

Place (place type) County	Number
Miami (city) Miami-Dade	30,214
Hialeah (city) Miami-Dade	25,322
Miami Beach (city) Miami-Dade	4,465
Fountainbleau (cdp) Miami-Dade	3,214
Tamiami (cdp) Miami-Dade	2,923
Tampa (city) Hillsborough	2,906
Westchester (cdp) Miami-Dade	2,326
Kendale Lakes (cdp) Miami-Dade	1,965
Carol City (cdp) Miami-Dade	1,892
University Park (cdp) Miami-Dade	1,836

Cubans with Income Below Poverty Level
Top 10 Places Sorted by Percent

Place (place type) County	Percent
Gladeview (cdp) Miami-Dade	65.72
Gainesville (city) Alachua	44.03
Brownsville (cdp) Miami-Dade	43.22
Tallahassee (city) Leon	38.10
Homestead (city) Miami-Dade	32.94
Pinewood (cdp) Miami-Dade	31.90
Opa-locka (city) Miami-Dade	31.06
Boynton Beach (city) Palm Beach	26.49
West Little River (cdp) Miami-Dade	26.33
Miami Beach (city) Miami-Dade	24.85

Dominicans with Income Below Poverty Level
Top 10 Places Sorted by Number

Place (place type) County	Number
Miami (city) Miami-Dade	1,959
Hialeah (city) Miami-Dade	991
West Little River (cdp) Miami-Dade	377
Orlando (city) Orange	339
Miami Beach (city) Miami-Dade	314
Hollywood (city) Broward	311
Tampa (city) Hillsborough	277
Carol City (cdp) Miami-Dade	262
South Miami Heights (cdp) Miami-Dade	250
Fountainbleau (cdp) Miami-Dade	241

Dominicans with Income Below Poverty Level
Top 10 Places Sorted by Percent

Place (place type) County	Percent
West Little River (cdp) Miami-Dade	37.97
Oak Ridge (cdp) Orange	30.32
Egypt Lake-Leto (cdp) Hillsborough	28.26
Town 'n' Country (cdp) Hillsborough	27.87
Orlando (city) Orange	27.43
Miami (city) Miami-Dade	27.21
Hialeah Gardens (city) Miami-Dade	26.95
Golden Glades (cdp) Miami-Dade	26.06
South Miami Heights (cdp) Miami-Dade	25.83
Miami Beach (city) Miami-Dade	22.59

Ecuadorians with Income Below Poverty Level
Top 10 Places Sorted by Number

Place (place type) County	Number
Miami (city) Miami-Dade	441
Hialeah (city) Miami-Dade	147
Fountainbleau (cdp) Miami-Dade	102
Miami Beach (city) Miami-Dade	102
Tampa (city) Hillsborough	78
Hollywood (city) Broward	44
Sunrise (city) Broward	29
Coral Springs (city) Broward	19
Pembroke Pines (city) Broward	18

Ecuadorians with Income Below Poverty Level
Top 10 Places Sorted by Percent

Place (place type) County	Percent
Miami (city) Miami-Dade	25.23
Tampa (city) Hillsborough	18.66
Miami Beach (city) Miami-Dade	15.41
Fountainbleau (cdp) Miami-Dade	12.77
Hialeah (city) Miami-Dade	11.92
Hollywood (city) Broward	7.01
Sunrise (city) Broward	5.48
Pembroke Pines (city) Broward	3.70
Coral Springs (city) Broward	2.02

Guatelmalans with Income Below Poverty Level
Top 10 Places Sorted by Number

Place (place type) County	Number
West Palm Beach (city) Palm Beach	831
Lake Worth (city) Palm Beach	779
Miami (city) Miami-Dade	686
Immokalee (cdp) Collier	592

Notes: Please refer to the User's Guide for an explanation of data; tables include places with populations > 9,999 and reflect only those areas that meet Summary File 4 population thresholds, therefore there may be less than 10 places listed

Homestead (city) Miami-Dade	433
Hialeah (city) Miami-Dade	204
Bonita Springs (city) Lee	188
Fort Lauderdale (city) Broward	124
Fort Myers (city) Lee	68

Guatelmalans with Income Below Poverty Level
Top 10 Places Sorted by Percent

Place (place type) County	Percent
Immokalee (cdp) Collier	53.87
Bonita Springs (city) Lee	50.95
Lake Worth (city) Palm Beach	40.96
West Palm Beach (city) Palm Beach	40.56
Fort Lauderdale (city) Broward	33.42
Homestead (city) Miami-Dade	30.17
Hialeah (city) Miami-Dade	24.58
Miami (city) Miami-Dade	24.15
Fort Myers (city) Lee	17.85

Hondurans with Income Below Poverty Level
Top 10 Places Sorted by Number

Place (place type) County	Number
Miami (city) Miami-Dade	4,077
Hialeah (city) Miami-Dade	438
Tampa (city) Hillsborough	352
West Little River (cdp) Miami-Dade	287
Miami Beach (city) Miami-Dade	199
Fountainbleau (cdp) Miami-Dade	129
Lake Worth (city) Palm Beach	78
Tamiami (cdp) Miami-Dade	74
North Miami Beach (city) Miami-Dade	70
North Miami (city) Miami-Dade	63

Hondurans with Income Below Poverty Level
Top 10 Places Sorted by Percent

Place (place type) County	Percent
Tampa (city) Hillsborough	39.37
Miami (city) Miami-Dade	30.03
West Little River (cdp) Miami-Dade	29.71
Miami Beach (city) Miami-Dade	24.84
Fountainbleau (cdp) Miami-Dade	20.35
Hialeah (city) Miami-Dade	16.84
Lake Worth (city) Palm Beach	16.74
Tamiami (cdp) Miami-Dade	16.70
North Miami Beach (city) Miami-Dade	13.86
North Miami (city) Miami-Dade	11.31

Mexicans with Income Below Poverty Level
Top 10 Places Sorted by Number

Place (place type) County	Number
Immokalee (cdp) Collier	3,982
Homestead (city) Miami-Dade	2,590
Tampa (city) Hillsborough	1,925
Fort Pierce (city) Saint Lucie	1,451
Leisure City (cdp) Miami-Dade	1,429
Bradenton (city) Manatee	1,127
Sarasota (city) Sarasota	1,005
Lake Worth (city) Palm Beach	912
Pompano Beach (city) Broward	891
Clearwater (city) Pinellas	824

Mexicans with Income Below Poverty Level
Top 10 Places Sorted by Percent

Place (place type) County	Percent
Gainesville (city) Alachua	49.73
University (cdp) Hillsborough	45.87
De Land (city) Volusia	44.01
Ocala (city) Marion	42.48
Auburndale (city) Polk	41.71
Kendall West (cdp) Miami-Dade	41.33
Immokalee (cdp) Collier	37.94
Homestead (city) Miami-Dade	36.55
Fort Pierce (city) Saint Lucie	35.63
Pompano Beach (city) Broward	35.22

Nicaraguans with Income Below Poverty Level
Top 10 Places Sorted by Number

Place (place type) County	Number
Miami (city) Miami-Dade	6,476
Hialeah (city) Miami-Dade	1,803
Gladeview (cdp) Miami-Dade	476
Fountainbleau (cdp) Miami-Dade	401
Sweetwater (city) Miami-Dade	399
West Little River (cdp) Miami-Dade	347
Kendall West (cdp) Miami-Dade	344
Pinewood (cdp) Miami-Dade	220
Carol City (cdp) Miami-Dade	209
Miami Beach (city) Miami-Dade	207

Nicaraguans with Income Below Poverty Level
Top 10 Places Sorted by Percent

Place (place type) County	Percent
Gladeview (cdp) Miami-Dade	57.84
Pinewood (cdp) Miami-Dade	39.29
West Little River (cdp) Miami-Dade	30.98
Miami (city) Miami-Dade	28.94
Kendall West (cdp) Miami-Dade	21.53
Miami Beach (city) Miami-Dade	20.87
North Miami (city) Miami-Dade	19.34
Hialeah (city) Miami-Dade	17.83
Westchester (cdp) Miami-Dade	16.73
Sweetwater (city) Miami-Dade	16.60

Panamanians with Income Below Poverty Level
Top 10 Places Sorted by Number

Place (place type) County	Number
Miami (city) Miami-Dade	199
Tampa (city) Hillsborough	93
Jacksonville (city) Duval	81
Fountainbleau (cdp) Miami-Dade	68
Miramar (city) Broward	46

Panamanians with Income Below Poverty Level
Top 10 Places Sorted by Percent

Place (place type) County	Percent
Miami (city) Miami-Dade	22.74
Tampa (city) Hillsborough	14.72
Jacksonville (city) Duval	14.34
Fountainbleau (cdp) Miami-Dade	13.03
Miramar (city) Broward	12.53

Paraguayans with Income Below Poverty Level
Top 10 Places Sorted by Number

Place (place type) County	Number
No places met population threshold.	

Paraguayans with Income Below Poverty Level
Top 10 Places Sorted by Percent

Place (place type) County	Percent
No places met population threshold.	

Peruvians with Income Below Poverty Level
Top 10 Places Sorted by Number

Place (place type) County	Number
Miami (city) Miami-Dade	650
Miami Beach (city) Miami-Dade	617
Hollywood (city) Broward	281
North Lauderdale (city) Broward	266
Hialeah (city) Miami-Dade	246
Kendall West (cdp) Miami-Dade	192
Coral Springs (city) Broward	166
Fountainbleau (cdp) Miami-Dade	158
The Hammocks (cdp) Miami-Dade	133
North Miami Beach (city) Miami-Dade	128

Peruvians with Income Below Poverty Level
Top 10 Places Sorted by Percent

Place (place type) County	Percent
North Lauderdale (city) Broward	47.84
Miami Beach (city) Miami-Dade	32.58
Miami (city) Miami-Dade	23.75
Hollywood (city) Broward	21.02
Coral Springs (city) Broward	17.42
Fort Lauderdale (city) Broward	17.09
Hialeah (city) Miami-Dade	16.97
Kendall West (cdp) Miami-Dade	16.74
Orlando (city) Orange	16.70
North Miami Beach (city) Miami-Dade	16.35

Puerto Ricans with Income Below Poverty Level
Top 10 Places Sorted by Number

Place (place type) County	Number
Tampa (city) Hillsborough	4,353
Miami (city) Miami-Dade	3,783
Orlando (city) Orange	3,339
Kissimmee (city) Osceola	2,507
Jacksonville (city) Duval	1,766
Hialeah (city) Miami-Dade	1,337
University (cdp) Hillsborough	1,302
Hollywood (city) Broward	1,206
Deltona (city) Volusia	1,010
Yeehaw Junction (cdp) Osceola	983

Puerto Ricans with Income Below Poverty Level
Top 10 Places Sorted by Percent

Place (place type) County	Percent
Fort Pierce (city) Saint Lucie	59.47
University (cdp) Hillsborough	46.63
Winter Haven (city) Polk	39.14
Miami (city) Miami-Dade	38.57
Gainesville (city) Alachua	38.09
West Little River (cdp) Miami-Dade	37.38
Homestead (city) Miami-Dade	37.29
Lake Worth Corridor (cdp) Palm Beach	36.87
Lake Worth (city) Palm Beach	36.04
West and East Lealman (cdp) Pinellas	35.01

Salvadorans with Income Below Poverty Level
Top 10 Places Sorted by Number

Place (place type) County	Number
Miami (city) Miami-Dade	484
Homestead (city) Miami-Dade	323
Hialeah (city) Miami-Dade	247
Oakland Park (city) Broward	233
Lake Worth (city) Palm Beach	145
Fort Lauderdale (city) Broward	127

Salvadorans with Income Below Poverty Level
Top 10 Places Sorted by Percent

Place (place type) County	Percent
Oakland Park (city) Broward	30.06
Homestead (city) Miami-Dade	29.07
Lake Worth (city) Palm Beach	27.51
Hialeah (city) Miami-Dade	26.00
Miami (city) Miami-Dade	20.62
Fort Lauderdale (city) Broward	19.54

South Americans with Income Below Poverty Level
Top 10 Places Sorted by Number

Place (place type) County	Number
Miami (city) Miami-Dade	4,425
Miami Beach (city) Miami-Dade	3,940
Hialeah (city) Miami-Dade	2,347
Kendall West (cdp) Miami-Dade	1,816
The Hammocks (cdp) Miami-Dade	1,557
Hollywood (city) Broward	1,545
Fountainbleau (cdp) Miami-Dade	1,521
Kendall (cdp) Miami-Dade	1,488
Kendale Lakes (cdp) Miami-Dade	1,124
Doral (cdp) Miami-Dade	1,098

Notes: Please refer to the User's Guide for an explanation of data; tables include places with populations > 9,999 and reflect only those areas that meet Summary File 4 population thresholds, therefore there may be less than 10 places listed

South Americans with Income Below Poverty Level
Top 10 Places Sorted by Percent

Place (place type) County	Percent
Tallahassee (city) Leon	36.90
Homestead (city) Miami-Dade	35.75
Egypt Lake-Leto (cdp) Hillsborough	35.36
Gainesville (city) Alachua	33.23
Oak Ridge (cdp) Orange	32.79
Altamonte Springs (city) Seminole	30.81
Miami Beach (city) Miami-Dade	30.40
Dania Beach (city) Broward	29.04
Miami (city) Miami-Dade	28.01
Tampa (city) Hillsborough	26.47

Spaniards with Income Below Poverty Level
Top 10 Places Sorted by Number

Place (place type) County	Number
Miami (city) Miami-Dade	175
Miami Beach (city) Miami-Dade	88
Tampa (city) Hillsborough	87
Hialeah (city) Miami-Dade	78

Spaniards with Income Below Poverty Level
Top 10 Places Sorted by Percent

Place (place type) County	Percent
Miami (city) Miami-Dade	18.98
Hialeah (city) Miami-Dade	15.60
Miami Beach (city) Miami-Dade	15.36
Tampa (city) Hillsborough	11.87

Uruguayans with Income Below Poverty Level
Top 10 Places Sorted by Number

Place (place type) County	Number

No places met population threshold.

Uruguayans with Income Below Poverty Level
Top 10 Places Sorted by Percent

Place (place type) County	Percent

No places met population threshold.

Venezuelans with Income Below Poverty Level
Top 10 Places Sorted by Number

Place (place type) County	Number
Miami (city) Miami-Dade	496
Doral (cdp) Miami-Dade	401
Miami Beach (city) Miami-Dade	370
The Hammocks (cdp) Miami-Dade	347
Tampa (city) Hillsborough	346
Fountainbleau (cdp) Miami-Dade	342
Weston (city) Broward	263
Hialeah (city) Miami-Dade	257
Orlando (city) Orange	239
Kendall (cdp) Miami-Dade	207

Venezuelans with Income Below Poverty Level
Top 10 Places Sorted by Percent

Place (place type) County	Percent
Tampa (city) Hillsborough	55.45
Orlando (city) Orange	31.08
Miami (city) Miami-Dade	28.59
Hialeah (city) Miami-Dade	26.91
Miami Beach (city) Miami-Dade	25.41
Hollywood (city) Broward	23.39
Doral (cdp) Miami-Dade	21.78
Plantation (city) Broward	21.75
The Hammocks (cdp) Miami-Dade	20.93
Tamiami (cdp) Miami-Dade	19.27

Other Hispanics with Income Below Poverty Level
Top 10 Places Sorted by Number

Place (place type) County	Number
Miami (city) Miami-Dade	8,670
Hialeah (city) Miami-Dade	4,588
Tampa (city) Hillsborough	2,095
Miami Beach (city) Miami-Dade	1,663
Fountainbleau (cdp) Miami-Dade	1,300
Orlando (city) Orange	1,030
Kendale Lakes (cdp) Miami-Dade	816
Hollywood (city) Broward	799
Jacksonville (city) Duval	743
Country Club (cdp) Miami-Dade	660

Other Hispanics with Income Below Poverty Level
Top 10 Places Sorted by Percent

Place (place type) County	Percent
Gladeview (cdp) Miami-Dade	48.75
Plant City (city) Hillsborough	42.02
Pine Hills (cdp) Orange	39.53
Sarasota (city) Sarasota	38.20
Daytona Beach (city) Volusia	35.92
Tallahassee (city) Leon	35.08
Homestead (city) Miami-Dade	34.34
Lake Worth Corridor (cdp) Palm Beach	32.90
Immokalee (cdp) Collier	30.31
Lake Worth (city) Palm Beach	29.98

Homeownership

Total Population Who Own Their Own Homes
Top 10 Places Sorted by Number

Place (place type) County	Number
Jacksonville (city) Duval	179,782
St. Petersburg (city) Pinellas	69,697
Tampa (city) Hillsborough	68,753
Miami (city) Miami-Dade	46,847
Pembroke Pines (city) Broward	41,636
Fort Lauderdale (city) Broward	37,927
Hollywood (city) Broward	37,102
Hialeah (city) Miami-Dade	35,963
Orlando (city) Orange	33,052
Cape Coral (city) Lee	32,663

Total Population Who Own Their Own Homes
Top 10 Places Sorted by Percent

Place (place type) County	Percent
Keystone (cdp) Hillsborough	94.74
Richmond West (cdp) Miami-Dade	93.84
Lakeland Highlands (cdp) Polk	92.63
Cooper City (city) Broward	92.24
Country Walk (cdp) Miami-Dade	92.05
Cutler (cdp) Miami-Dade	88.65
Miami Shores (village) Miami-Dade	88.63
De Bary (city) Volusia	88.33
Royal Palm Beach (village) Palm Beach	88.31
Westchase (cdp) Hillsborough	88.29

Hispanics Who Own Their Own Homes
Top 10 Places Sorted by Number

Place (place type) County	Number
Hialeah (city) Miami-Dade	33,368
Miami (city) Miami-Dade	29,933
Tamiami (cdp) Miami-Dade	12,432
Kendale Lakes (cdp) Miami-Dade	10,917
Tampa (city) Hillsborough	10,742
Fountainbleau (cdp) Miami-Dade	9,941
Pembroke Pines (city) Broward	9,565
Kendall (cdp) Miami-Dade	8,115
Miami Beach (city) Miami-Dade	7,288
The Hammocks (cdp) Miami-Dade	6,353

Hispanics Who Own Their Own Homes
Top 10 Places Sorted by Percent

Place (place type) County	Percent
Lakeland Highlands (cdp) Polk	100.00
Keystone (cdp) Hillsborough	97.59
Hamptons at Boca Raton (cdp) Palm Beach	96.07
Land O' Lakes (cdp) Pasco	95.35
Richmond West (cdp) Miami-Dade	94.10
Country Walk (cdp) Miami-Dade	93.37
Palm Coast (city) Flagler	89.94
Cooper City (city) Broward	89.41
Royal Palm Beach (village) Palm Beach	88.18
Bloomingdale (cdp) Hillsborough	87.31

Argentinians Who Own Their Own Homes
Top 10 Places Sorted by Number

Place (place type) County	Number
Miami Beach (city) Miami-Dade	405
Miami (city) Miami-Dade	306
Kendall (cdp) Miami-Dade	191
Sunny Isles Beach (city) Miami-Dade	110
Hialeah (city) Miami-Dade	108
Hollywood (city) Broward	83
Fountainbleau (cdp) Miami-Dade	52

Argentinians Who Own Their Own Homes
Top 10 Places Sorted by Percent

Place (place type) County	Percent
Hialeah (city) Miami-Dade	70.59
Kendall (cdp) Miami-Dade	57.01
Sunny Isles Beach (city) Miami-Dade	49.33
Hollywood (city) Broward	47.43
Miami (city) Miami-Dade	39.08
Miami Beach (city) Miami-Dade	28.76
Fountainbleau (cdp) Miami-Dade	27.08

Bolivians Who Own Their Own Homes
Top 10 Places Sorted by Number

Place (place type) County	Number

No places met population threshold.

Bolivians Who Own Their Own Homes
Top 10 Places Sorted by Percent

Place (place type) County	Percent

No places met population threshold.

Central Americans Who Own Their Own Homes
Top 10 Places Sorted by Number

Place (place type) County	Number
Miami (city) Miami-Dade	1,802
Hialeah (city) Miami-Dade	1,226
Fountainbleau (cdp) Miami-Dade	1,092
Kendale Lakes (cdp) Miami-Dade	780
Tamiami (cdp) Miami-Dade	666
Richmond West (cdp) Miami-Dade	581
Carol City (cdp) Miami-Dade	566
Kendall (cdp) Miami-Dade	559
Tampa (city) Hillsborough	442
Kendall West (cdp) Miami-Dade	413

Central Americans Who Own Their Own Homes
Top 10 Places Sorted by Percent

Place (place type) County	Percent
Richmond West (cdp) Miami-Dade	97.32
Country Walk (cdp) Miami-Dade	94.59
Palmetto Estates (cdp) Miami-Dade	86.21
Carol City (cdp) Miami-Dade	85.89
Miramar (city) Broward	78.00
South Miami Heights (cdp) Miami-Dade	77.80
The Crossings (cdp) Miami-Dade	73.56
Tamiami (cdp) Miami-Dade	71.92
Pembroke Pines (city) Broward	70.69
Princeton (cdp) Miami-Dade	70.64

Chileans Who Own Their Own Homes
Top 10 Places Sorted by Number

Place (place type) County	Number
Hialeah (city) Miami-Dade	143
Miami (city) Miami-Dade	132
Miami Beach (city) Miami-Dade	119
Hollywood (city) Broward	89

Notes: Please refer to the User's Guide for an explanation of data; tables include places with populations > 9,999 and reflect only those areas that meet Summary File 4 population thresholds, therefore there may be less than 10 places listed

Kendall (cdp) Miami-Dade	89
Fountainbleau (cdp) Miami-Dade	67

Chileans Who Own Their Own Homes
Top 10 Places Sorted by Percent

Place (place type) County	Percent
Hollywood (city) Broward	60.54
Kendall (cdp) Miami-Dade	58.55
Hialeah (city) Miami-Dade	45.83
Miami Beach (city) Miami-Dade	32.16
Miami (city) Miami-Dade	31.28
Fountainbleau (cdp) Miami-Dade	28.39

Columbians Who Own Their Own Homes
Top 10 Places Sorted by Number

Place (place type) County	Number
Hialeah (city) Miami-Dade	1,082
The Hammocks (cdp) Miami-Dade	856
Pembroke Pines (city) Broward	758
Kendale Lakes (cdp) Miami-Dade	714
Miami (city) Miami-Dade	670
Kendall West (cdp) Miami-Dade	613
Kendall (cdp) Miami-Dade	582
Country Club (cdp) Miami-Dade	574
Hollywood (city) Broward	568
Miami Beach (city) Miami-Dade	548

Columbians Who Own Their Own Homes
Top 10 Places Sorted by Percent

Place (place type) County	Percent
Country Walk (cdp) Miami-Dade	93.42
Richmond West (cdp) Miami-Dade	91.40
Carol City (cdp) Miami-Dade	83.06
Tamiami (cdp) Miami-Dade	82.01
Miramar (city) Broward	76.62
South Miami Heights (cdp) Miami-Dade	76.56
Margate (city) Broward	75.51
Lauderhill (city) Broward	74.52
Cooper City (city) Broward	73.33
University Park (cdp) Miami-Dade	72.53

Costa Ricans Who Own Their Own Homes
Top 10 Places Sorted by Number

Place (place type) County	Number
Hialeah (city) Miami-Dade	69
Miami (city) Miami-Dade	59

Costa Ricans Who Own Their Own Homes
Top 10 Places Sorted by Percent

Place (place type) County	Percent
Hialeah (city) Miami-Dade	52.67
Miami (city) Miami-Dade	22.52

Cubans Who Own Their Own Homes
Top 10 Places Sorted by Number

Place (place type) County	Number
Hialeah (city) Miami-Dade	26,589
Miami (city) Miami-Dade	22,008
Tamiami (cdp) Miami-Dade	9,444
Kendale Lakes (cdp) Miami-Dade	6,799
Fountainbleau (cdp) Miami-Dade	6,416
Westchester (cdp) Miami-Dade	4,956
Kendall (cdp) Miami-Dade	4,472
Miami Beach (city) Miami-Dade	4,204
Pembroke Pines (city) Broward	4,094
University Park (cdp) Miami-Dade	4,012

Cubans Who Own Their Own Homes
Top 10 Places Sorted by Percent

Place (place type) County	Percent
Royal Palm Beach (village) Palm Beach	100.00
Country Walk (cdp) Miami-Dade	94.23
Cooper City (city) Broward	93.32
Richmond West (cdp) Miami-Dade	93.31
Miramar (city) Broward	91.46
Palm River-Clair Mel (cdp) Hillsborough	90.79
Cutler (cdp) Miami-Dade	90.00
Pinecrest (village) Miami-Dade	89.30
The Crossings (cdp) Miami-Dade	88.58
Weston (city) Broward	88.55

Dominicans Who Own Their Own Homes
Top 10 Places Sorted by Number

Place (place type) County	Number
Miami (city) Miami-Dade	658
Hialeah (city) Miami-Dade	628
Carol City (cdp) Miami-Dade	387
Pembroke Pines (city) Broward	381
Miramar (city) Broward	339
Hollywood (city) Broward	337
The Hammocks (cdp) Miami-Dade	335
Fountainbleau (cdp) Miami-Dade	284
South Miami Heights (cdp) Miami-Dade	245
Richmond West (cdp) Miami-Dade	222

Dominicans Who Own Their Own Homes
Top 10 Places Sorted by Percent

Place (place type) County	Percent
Weston (city) Broward	91.96
Richmond West (cdp) Miami-Dade	88.45
Yeehaw Junction (cdp) Osceola	82.63
Miramar (city) Broward	80.71
Carol City (cdp) Miami-Dade	77.71
Tamiami (cdp) Miami-Dade	77.43
Pembroke Pines (city) Broward	75.90
The Hammocks (cdp) Miami-Dade	72.20
South Miami Heights (cdp) Miami-Dade	71.22
Kendall West (cdp) Miami-Dade	67.96

Ecuadorians Who Own Their Own Homes
Top 10 Places Sorted by Number

Place (place type) County	Number
Hialeah (city) Miami-Dade	212
Miami (city) Miami-Dade	202
Pembroke Pines (city) Broward	171
Coral Springs (city) Broward	129
Hollywood (city) Broward	101
Sunrise (city) Broward	100
Fountainbleau (cdp) Miami-Dade	96
Tampa (city) Hillsborough	84
Miami Beach (city) Miami-Dade	64

Ecuadorians Who Own Their Own Homes
Top 10 Places Sorted by Percent

Place (place type) County	Percent
Pembroke Pines (city) Broward	73.39
Hollywood (city) Broward	61.59
Sunrise (city) Broward	60.98
Coral Springs (city) Broward	56.83
Tampa (city) Hillsborough	50.91
Hialeah (city) Miami-Dade	49.07
Fountainbleau (cdp) Miami-Dade	48.00
Miami (city) Miami-Dade	31.08
Miami Beach (city) Miami-Dade	19.16

Guatelmalans Who Own Their Own Homes
Top 10 Places Sorted by Number

Place (place type) County	Number
Miami (city) Miami-Dade	136
Hialeah (city) Miami-Dade	100
Fort Lauderdale (city) Broward	37
Lake Worth (city) Palm Beach	36
West Palm Beach (city) Palm Beach	32
Homestead (city) Miami-Dade	31
Immokalee (cdp) Collier	18
Bonita Springs (city) Lee	11
Fort Myers (city) Lee	5

Guatelmalans Who Own Their Own Homes
Top 10 Places Sorted by Percent

Place (place type) County	Percent
Hialeah (city) Miami-Dade	40.00
Fort Lauderdale (city) Broward	25.00
Miami (city) Miami-Dade	14.20
Bonita Springs (city) Lee	12.09
Immokalee (cdp) Collier	11.76
Lake Worth (city) Palm Beach	8.98
Homestead (city) Miami-Dade	8.59
West Palm Beach (city) Palm Beach	6.91
Fort Myers (city) Lee	5.56

Hondurans Who Own Their Own Homes
Top 10 Places Sorted by Number

Place (place type) County	Number
Miami (city) Miami-Dade	498
Hialeah (city) Miami-Dade	185
Carol City (cdp) Miami-Dade	126
West Little River (cdp) Miami-Dade	112
Tampa (city) Hillsborough	110
North Miami Beach (city) Miami-Dade	84
Kendale Lakes (cdp) Miami-Dade	79
North Miami (city) Miami-Dade	57
Tamiami (cdp) Miami-Dade	53
Fountainbleau (cdp) Miami-Dade	52

Hondurans Who Own Their Own Homes
Top 10 Places Sorted by Percent

Place (place type) County	Percent
Carol City (cdp) Miami-Dade	84.56
Kendale Lakes (cdp) Miami-Dade	78.22
North Miami Beach (city) Miami-Dade	55.63
Tamiami (cdp) Miami-Dade	55.21
West Little River (cdp) Miami-Dade	46.09
Fountainbleau (cdp) Miami-Dade	44.83
Tampa (city) Hillsborough	38.87
North Miami (city) Miami-Dade	33.53
Hollywood (city) Broward	32.65
Hialeah (city) Miami-Dade	25.55

Mexicans Who Own Their Own Homes
Top 10 Places Sorted by Number

Place (place type) County	Number
Immokalee (cdp) Collier	939
Tampa (city) Hillsborough	719
Jacksonville (city) Duval	705
Leisure City (cdp) Miami-Dade	503
Fort Pierce (city) Saint Lucie	392
Bonita Springs (city) Lee	336
Plant City (city) Hillsborough	280
Haines City (city) Polk	267
Ocoee (city) Orange	248
Belle Glade (city) Palm Beach	247

Mexicans Who Own Their Own Homes
Top 10 Places Sorted by Percent

Place (place type) County	Percent
Weston (city) Broward	93.53
Lehigh Acres (cdp) Lee	83.26
Kendale Lakes (cdp) Miami-Dade	79.20
Deltona (city) Volusia	72.06
Davie (town) Broward	71.18
Ocoee (city) Orange	69.66
Pembroke Pines (city) Broward	66.27
Miramar (city) Broward	65.34
Coconut Creek (city) Broward	63.58
Apopka (city) Orange	60.81

Nicaraguans Who Own Their Own Homes
Top 10 Places Sorted by Number

Place (place type) County	Number
Fountainbleau (cdp) Miami-Dade	809
Miami (city) Miami-Dade	802
Hialeah (city) Miami-Dade	727

Notes: Please refer to the User's Guide for an explanation of data; tables include places with populations > 9,999 and reflect only those areas that meet Summary File 4 population thresholds, therefore there may be less than 10 places listed

Kendale Lakes (cdp) Miami-Dade	543
Tamiami (cdp) Miami-Dade	453
Kendall (cdp) Miami-Dade	320
Richmond West (cdp) Miami-Dade	308
Carol City (cdp) Miami-Dade	300
Kendall West (cdp) Miami-Dade	299
The Hammocks (cdp) Miami-Dade	291

Nicaraguans Who Own Their Own Homes
Top 10 Places Sorted by Percent

Place (place type) County	Percent
Richmond West (cdp) Miami-Dade	97.16
Miramar (city) Broward	88.15
Carol City (cdp) Miami-Dade	87.21
South Miami Heights (cdp) Miami-Dade	79.51
The Crossings (cdp) Miami-Dade	78.57
Palmetto Estates (cdp) Miami-Dade	73.08
Tamiami (cdp) Miami-Dade	72.36
Kendale Lakes (cdp) Miami-Dade	69.44
North Miami (city) Miami-Dade	65.10
Hialeah Gardens (city) Miami-Dade	62.65

Panamanians Who Own Their Own Homes
Top 10 Places Sorted by Number

Place (place type) County	Number
Fountainbleau (cdp) Miami-Dade	103
Miami (city) Miami-Dade	89
Jacksonville (city) Duval	88
Tampa (city) Hillsborough	87
Miramar (city) Broward	68

Panamanians Who Own Their Own Homes
Top 10 Places Sorted by Percent

Place (place type) County	Percent
Miramar (city) Broward	52.31
Fountainbleau (cdp) Miami-Dade	49.05
Jacksonville (city) Duval	47.57
Tampa (city) Hillsborough	46.28
Miami (city) Miami-Dade	24.45

Paraguayans Who Own Their Own Homes
Top 10 Places Sorted by Number

Place (place type) County	Number

No places met population threshold.

Paraguayans Who Own Their Own Homes
Top 10 Places Sorted by Percent

Place (place type) County	Percent

No places met population threshold.

Peruvians Who Own Their Own Homes
Top 10 Places Sorted by Number

Place (place type) County	Number
The Hammocks (cdp) Miami-Dade	357
Pembroke Pines (city) Broward	321
Hialeah (city) Miami-Dade	241
Kendale Lakes (cdp) Miami-Dade	214
Miami (city) Miami-Dade	210
Kendall (cdp) Miami-Dade	209
Fountainbleau (cdp) Miami-Dade	180
Miami Beach (city) Miami-Dade	158
North Miami Beach (city) Miami-Dade	157
Kendall West (cdp) Miami-Dade	155

Peruvians Who Own Their Own Homes
Top 10 Places Sorted by Percent

Place (place type) County	Percent
Miramar (city) Broward	89.15
Pembroke Pines (city) Broward	86.52
Richmond West (cdp) Miami-Dade	84.21
The Crossings (cdp) Miami-Dade	73.62
Weston (city) Broward	69.10
The Hammocks (cdp) Miami-Dade	66.85
Sunrise (city) Broward	66.84

Doral (cdp) Miami-Dade	61.19
Kendall (cdp) Miami-Dade	57.42
Kendale Lakes (cdp) Miami-Dade	57.37

Puerto Ricans Who Own Their Own Homes
Top 10 Places Sorted by Number

Place (place type) County	Number
Deltona (city) Volusia	2,523
Tampa (city) Hillsborough	2,288
Pembroke Pines (city) Broward	1,783
Yeehaw Junction (cdp) Osceola	1,737
Orlando (city) Orange	1,718
Jacksonville (city) Duval	1,677
Kissimmee (city) Osceola	1,465
Town 'n' Country (cdp) Hillsborough	1,370
Hollywood (city) Broward	1,214
Miami (city) Miami-Dade	1,168

Puerto Ricans Who Own Their Own Homes
Top 10 Places Sorted by Percent

Place (place type) County	Percent
Richmond West (cdp) Miami-Dade	100.00
Land O' Lakes (cdp) Pasco	96.88
Country Walk (cdp) Miami-Dade	94.12
Oviedo (city) Seminole	94.10
Wekiwa Springs (cdp) Seminole	90.91
Palm Coast (city) Flagler	89.84
Longwood (city) Seminole	89.41
Cooper City (city) Broward	86.92
Deltona (city) Volusia	85.73
Meadow Woods (cdp) Orange	85.46

Salvadorans Who Own Their Own Homes
Top 10 Places Sorted by Number

Place (place type) County	Number
Miami (city) Miami-Dade	177
Homestead (city) Miami-Dade	58
Hialeah (city) Miami-Dade	57
Oakland Park (city) Broward	57
Lake Worth (city) Palm Beach	38
Fort Lauderdale (city) Broward	35

Salvadorans Who Own Their Own Homes
Top 10 Places Sorted by Percent

Place (place type) County	Percent
Oakland Park (city) Broward	28.08
Lake Worth (city) Palm Beach	23.90
Hialeah (city) Miami-Dade	23.55
Fort Lauderdale (city) Broward	22.29
Miami (city) Miami-Dade	22.26
Homestead (city) Miami-Dade	18.83

South Americans Who Own Their Own Homes
Top 10 Places Sorted by Number

Place (place type) County	Number
Hialeah (city) Miami-Dade	1,943
Pembroke Pines (city) Broward	1,850
Miami (city) Miami-Dade	1,824
The Hammocks (cdp) Miami-Dade	1,720
Miami Beach (city) Miami-Dade	1,503
Kendale Lakes (cdp) Miami-Dade	1,498
Kendall (cdp) Miami-Dade	1,447
Weston (city) Broward	1,300
Hollywood (city) Broward	1,195
Kendall West (cdp) Miami-Dade	1,148

South Americans Who Own Their Own Homes
Top 10 Places Sorted by Percent

Place (place type) County	Percent
Citrus Park (cdp) Hillsborough	91.45
Richmond West (cdp) Miami-Dade	91.27
Country Walk (cdp) Miami-Dade	91.25
Olympia Heights (cdp) Miami-Dade	83.81
Carol City (cdp) Miami-Dade	83.79

West Little River (cdp) Miami-Dade	82.48
Parkland (city) Broward	81.13
Tamiami (cdp) Miami-Dade	80.95
Cooper City (city) Broward	80.20
Miramar (city) Broward	79.35

Spaniards Who Own Their Own Homes
Top 10 Places Sorted by Number

Place (place type) County	Number
Tampa (city) Hillsborough	295
Miami (city) Miami-Dade	251
Miami Beach (city) Miami-Dade	150
Hialeah (city) Miami-Dade	114

Spaniards Who Own Their Own Homes
Top 10 Places Sorted by Percent

Place (place type) County	Percent
Hialeah (city) Miami-Dade	84.44
Tampa (city) Hillsborough	74.68
Miami (city) Miami-Dade	54.09
Miami Beach (city) Miami-Dade	47.02

Uruguayans Who Own Their Own Homes
Top 10 Places Sorted by Number

Place (place type) County	Number

No places met population threshold.

Uruguayans Who Own Their Own Homes
Top 10 Places Sorted by Percent

Place (place type) County	Percent

No places met population threshold.

Venezuelans Who Own Their Own Homes
Top 10 Places Sorted by Number

Place (place type) County	Number
Weston (city) Broward	487
Doral (cdp) Miami-Dade	361
Pembroke Pines (city) Broward	328
Kendall (cdp) Miami-Dade	282
Miami (city) Miami-Dade	222
The Hammocks (cdp) Miami-Dade	215
Miami Beach (city) Miami-Dade	168
Kendall West (cdp) Miami-Dade	166
The Crossings (cdp) Miami-Dade	154
Kendale Lakes (cdp) Miami-Dade	135

Venezuelans Who Own Their Own Homes
Top 10 Places Sorted by Percent

Place (place type) County	Percent
Richmond West (cdp) Miami-Dade	92.25
Tamiami (cdp) Miami-Dade	85.52
Weston (city) Broward	71.20
Pembroke Pines (city) Broward	69.49
The Crossings (cdp) Miami-Dade	63.11
Kendale Lakes (cdp) Miami-Dade	61.64
Kendall (cdp) Miami-Dade	58.51
Doral (cdp) Miami-Dade	56.94
Kendall West (cdp) Miami-Dade	47.16
Coral Springs (city) Broward	47.06

Other Hispanics Who Own Their Own Homes
Top 10 Places Sorted by Number

Place (place type) County	Number
Tampa (city) Hillsborough	3,019
Miami (city) Miami-Dade	1,997
Hialeah (city) Miami-Dade	1,687
Kendale Lakes (cdp) Miami-Dade	1,058
Pembroke Pines (city) Broward	868
Fountainbleau (cdp) Miami-Dade	867
Kendall (cdp) Miami-Dade	796
The Hammocks (cdp) Miami-Dade	770
Hollywood (city) Broward	767
Jacksonville (city) Duval	758

Notes: Please refer to the User's Guide for an explanation of data; tables include places with populations > 9,999 and reflect only those areas that meet Summary File 4 population thresholds, therefore there may be less than 10 places listed

Other Hispanics Who Own Their Own Homes
Top 10 Places Sorted by Percent

Place (place type) County	Percent
Miami Shores (village) Miami-Dade	100.00
Spring Hill (cdp) Hernando	96.43
Richmond West (cdp) Miami-Dade	93.71
Country Walk (cdp) Miami-Dade	93.48
Palmetto Estates (cdp) Miami-Dade	92.23
Carol City (cdp) Miami-Dade	89.70
Cooper City (city) Broward	88.33
Ojus (cdp) Miami-Dade	85.86
Citrus Park (cdp) Hillsborough	84.88
Poinciana (cdp) Osceola	84.62

Median Gross Rent

All Specified Renter-Occupied Housing Units
Top 10 Places Sorted by Number

Place (place type) County	Dollars/Month
Key Biscayne (village) Miami-Dade	1,674
Aventura (city) Miami-Dade	1,256
Parkland (city) Broward	1,128
Richmond West (cdp) Miami-Dade	1,084
Weston (city) Broward	1,084
Country Walk (cdp) Miami-Dade	1,017
Wekiwa Springs (cdp) Seminole	1,014
Boca Del Mar (cdp) Palm Beach	1,010
Sandalfoot Cove (cdp) Palm Beach	996
Wellington (village) Palm Beach	989

Specified Housing Units Rented by Hispanics
Top 10 Places Sorted by Number

Place (place type) County	Dollars/Month
Key Biscayne (village) Miami-Dade	1,822
Aventura (city) Miami-Dade	1,261
Land O' Lakes (cdp) Pasco	1,250
Parkland (city) Broward	1,169
Richmond West (cdp) Miami-Dade	1,056
Weston (city) Broward	1,028
Wekiwa Springs (cdp) Seminole	990
Pembroke Pines (city) Broward	969
Wellington (village) Palm Beach	965
Westwood Lakes (cdp) Miami-Dade	959

Specified Housing Units Rented by Argentinians
Top 10 Places Sorted by Number

Place (place type) County	Dollars/Month
Sunny Isles Beach (city) Miami-Dade	870
Hialeah (city) Miami-Dade	819
Kendall (cdp) Miami-Dade	807
Fountainbleau (cdp) Miami-Dade	800
Miami (city) Miami-Dade	769
Hollywood (city) Broward	741
Miami Beach (city) Miami-Dade	632

Specified Housing Units Rented by Bolivians
Top 10 Places Sorted by Number

Place (place type) County	Dollars/Month

Specified Housing Units Rented by Central Americans
Top 10 Places Sorted by Number

Place (place type) County	Dollars/Month
Richmond West (cdp) Miami-Dade	1,278
Doral (cdp) Miami-Dade	1,071
Country Walk (cdp) Miami-Dade	950
The Crossings (cdp) Miami-Dade	922
Pembroke Pines (city) Broward	903
The Hammocks (cdp) Miami-Dade	895
Coral Terrace (cdp) Miami-Dade	868
Princeton (cdp) Miami-Dade	850
Kendale Lakes (cdp) Miami-Dade	841
Carol City (cdp) Miami-Dade	835

Specified Housing Units Rented by Chileans
Top 10 Places Sorted by Number

Place (place type) County	Dollars/Month
Kendall (cdp) Miami-Dade	843
Fountainbleau (cdp) Miami-Dade	831
Hollywood (city) Broward	715
Miami (city) Miami-Dade	693
Miami Beach (city) Miami-Dade	676
Hialeah (city) Miami-Dade	647

Specified Housing Units Rented by Columbians
Top 10 Places Sorted by Number

Place (place type) County	Dollars/Month
Key Biscayne (village) Miami-Dade	2,001
Aventura (city) Miami-Dade	1,190
Meadow Woods (cdp) Orange	1,139
Cooper City (city) Broward	1,100
Weston (city) Broward	1,068
Wellington (village) Palm Beach	1,048
Carol City (cdp) Miami-Dade	1,015
Sandalfoot Cove (cdp) Palm Beach	989
Pembroke Pines (city) Broward	981
Plantation (city) Broward	970

Specified Housing Units Rented by Costa Ricans
Top 10 Places Sorted by Number

Place (place type) County	Dollars/Month
Hialeah (city) Miami-Dade	713
Miami (city) Miami-Dade	666

Specified Housing Units Rented by Cubans
Top 10 Places Sorted by Number

Place (place type) County	Dollars/Month
Key Biscayne (village) Miami-Dade	1,736
Aventura (city) Miami-Dade	1,236
Country Walk (cdp) Miami-Dade	1,167
Weston (city) Broward	1,114
Richmond West (cdp) Miami-Dade	1,085
Westwood Lakes (cdp) Miami-Dade	1,002
Sunrise (city) Broward	969
The Crossings (cdp) Miami-Dade	969
Wellington (village) Palm Beach	964
Pembroke Pines (city) Broward	955

Specified Housing Units Rented by Dominicans
Top 10 Places Sorted by Number

Place (place type) County	Dollars/Month
Doral (cdp) Miami-Dade	1,174
Tamiami (cdp) Miami-Dade	1,065
Richmond West (cdp) Miami-Dade	1,059
Pembroke Pines (city) Broward	962
Weston (city) Broward	850
Sunrise (city) Broward	849
The Hammocks (cdp) Miami-Dade	830
Fountainbleau (cdp) Miami-Dade	813
Country Club (cdp) Miami-Dade	804
Kendale Lakes (cdp) Miami-Dade	791

Specified Housing Units Rented by Ecuadorians
Top 10 Places Sorted by Number

Place (place type) County	Dollars/Month
Pembroke Pines (city) Broward	1,053
Coral Springs (city) Broward	953
Sunrise (city) Broward	853
Fountainbleau (cdp) Miami-Dade	833
Hialeah (city) Miami-Dade	711
Hollywood (city) Broward	698
Miami (city) Miami-Dade	581
Miami Beach (city) Miami-Dade	558
Tampa (city) Hillsborough	439

Specified Housing Units Rented by Guatelmalans
Top 10 Places Sorted by Number

Place (place type) County	Dollars/Month
Bonita Springs (city) Lee	690
West Palm Beach (city) Palm Beach	639
Hialeah (city) Miami-Dade	638
Fort Lauderdale (city) Broward	630
Lake Worth (city) Palm Beach	615
Homestead (city) Miami-Dade	605
Immokalee (cdp) Collier	580
Fort Myers (city) Lee	556
Miami (city) Miami-Dade	530

Specified Housing Units Rented by Hondurans
Top 10 Places Sorted by Number

Place (place type) County	Dollars/Month
Kendale Lakes (cdp) Miami-Dade	1,125
Fountainbleau (cdp) Miami-Dade	855
Carol City (cdp) Miami-Dade	823
Tamiami (cdp) Miami-Dade	749
Hialeah (city) Miami-Dade	698
North Miami Beach (city) Miami-Dade	667
Hollywood (city) Broward	664
North Miami (city) Miami-Dade	658
Lake Worth (city) Palm Beach	609
Miami Beach (city) Miami-Dade	589

Specified Housing Units Rented by Mexicans
Top 10 Places Sorted by Number

Place (place type) County	Dollars/Month
Doral (cdp) Miami-Dade	1,155
Pembroke Pines (city) Broward	1,149
Plantation (city) Broward	1,023
Weston (city) Broward	950
Key West (city) Monroe	933
Sunrise (city) Broward	904
Tamiami (cdp) Miami-Dade	878
Coral Springs (city) Broward	847
Coconut Creek (city) Broward	822
Kendale Lakes (cdp) Miami-Dade	813

Specified Housing Units Rented by Nicaraguans
Top 10 Places Sorted by Number

Place (place type) County	Dollars/Month
Richmond West (cdp) Miami-Dade	1,375
South Miami Heights (cdp) Miami-Dade	929
The Crossings (cdp) Miami-Dade	922
The Hammocks (cdp) Miami-Dade	900
Miramar (city) Broward	894
Carol City (cdp) Miami-Dade	888
Coral Terrace (cdp) Miami-Dade	877
Kendale Lakes (cdp) Miami-Dade	845
Fountainbleau (cdp) Miami-Dade	806
Kendall West (cdp) Miami-Dade	805

Specified Housing Units Rented by Panamanians
Top 10 Places Sorted by Number

Place (place type) County	Dollars/Month
Miramar (city) Broward	829
Fountainbleau (cdp) Miami-Dade	775
Jacksonville (city) Duval	732
Tampa (city) Hillsborough	568
Miami (city) Miami-Dade	545

Specified Housing Units Rented by Paraguayans
Top 10 Places Sorted by Number

Place (place type) County	Dollars/Month

Specified Housing Units Rented by Peruvians
Top 10 Places Sorted by Number

Place (place type) County	Dollars/Month
Miramar (city) Broward	1,219
Weston (city) Broward	1,146
Richmond West (cdp) Miami-Dade	1,125

Notes: Please refer to the User's Guide for an explanation of data; tables include places with populations > 9,999 and reflect only those areas that meet Summary File 4 population thresholds, therefore there may be less than 10 places listed

Pembroke Pines (city) Broward	1,000
Plantation (city) Broward	995
Doral (cdp) Miami-Dade	959
The Hammocks (cdp) Miami-Dade	952
Coral Springs (city) Broward	907
North Lauderdale (city) Broward	890
Kendale Lakes (cdp) Miami-Dade	854

Specified Housing Units Rented by Puerto Ricans

Top 10 Places Sorted by Number

Place (place type) County	Dollars/Month
Wellington (village) Palm Beach	1,054
Pembroke Pines (city) Broward	965
Wekiwa Springs (cdp) Seminole	950
Tamiami (cdp) Miami-Dade	948
The Crossings (cdp) Miami-Dade	947
Miami Lakes (cdp) Miami-Dade	938
Plantation (city) Broward	929
Weston (city) Broward	897
Coconut Creek (city) Broward	886
Doral (cdp) Miami-Dade	878

Specified Housing Units Rented by Salvadorans

Top 10 Places Sorted by Number

Place (place type) County	Dollars/Month
Oakland Park (city) Broward	670
Hialeah (city) Miami-Dade	623
Fort Lauderdale (city) Broward	576
Lake Worth (city) Palm Beach	547
Homestead (city) Miami-Dade	542
Miami (city) Miami-Dade	534

Specified Housing Units Rented by South Americans

Top 10 Places Sorted by Number

Place (place type) County	Dollars/Month
Key Biscayne (village) Miami-Dade	1,736
Aventura (city) Miami-Dade	1,316
Parkland (city) Broward	1,179
Meadow Woods (cdp) Orange	1,135
Cooper City (city) Broward	1,100
Richmond West (cdp) Miami-Dade	1,063
Weston (city) Broward	1,047
Sandalfoot Cove (cdp) Palm Beach	1,030
Wellington (village) Palm Beach	1,030
Pembroke Pines (city) Broward	988

Specified Housing Units Rented by Spaniards

Top 10 Places Sorted by Number

Place (place type) County	Dollars/Month
Miami Beach (city) Miami-Dade	703
Hialeah (city) Miami-Dade	671
Tampa (city) Hillsborough	573
Miami (city) Miami-Dade	509

Specified Housing Units Rented by Uruguayans

Top 10 Places Sorted by Number

Place (place type) County	Dollars/Month

Specified Housing Units Rented by Venezuelans

Top 10 Places Sorted by Number

Place (place type) County	Dollars/Month
Richmond West (cdp) Miami-Dade	1,375
Coral Springs (city) Broward	1,058
Tamiami (cdp) Miami-Dade	1,031
Weston (city) Broward	1,017
Pembroke Pines (city) Broward	996
The Crossings (cdp) Miami-Dade	979
Plantation (city) Broward	970
Doral (cdp) Miami-Dade	937
The Hammocks (cdp) Miami-Dade	846
Fountainbleau (cdp) Miami-Dade	820

Specified Housing Units Rented by Other Hispanics

Top 10 Places Sorted by Number

Place (place type) County	Dollars/Month
Cooper City (city) Broward	2,001
Key Biscayne (village) Miami-Dade	2,001
Aventura (city) Miami-Dade	1,267
Palmetto Estates (cdp) Miami-Dade	1,125
Plantation (city) Broward	1,028
Doral (cdp) Miami-Dade	988
The Crossings (cdp) Miami-Dade	988
Pembroke Pines (city) Broward	984
Weston (city) Broward	958
Wellington (village) Palm Beach	956

Median Home Value

All Specified Owner-Occupied Housing Units

Top 10 Places Sorted by Number

Place (place type) County	Dollars
Key Biscayne (village) Miami-Dade	615,500
Naples (city) Collier	416,000
Pinecrest (village) Miami-Dade	393,900
Coral Gables (city) Miami-Dade	336,800
Miami Beach (city) Miami-Dade	334,400
Parkland (city) Broward	309,700
Sunny Isles Beach (city) Miami-Dade	298,400
Marco Island (city) Collier	291,100
Cutler (cdp) Miami-Dade	266,800
Key West (city) Monroe	265,800

Specified Housing Units Owned and Occupied by Hispanics

Top 10 Places Sorted by Number

Place (place type) County	Dollars
Key Biscayne (village) Miami-Dade	612,400
Sunny Isles Beach (city) Miami-Dade	426,900
Pinecrest (village) Miami-Dade	418,100
Coral Gables (city) Miami-Dade	319,100
Cutler (cdp) Miami-Dade	283,800
Key West (city) Monroe	255,100
Miami Beach (city) Miami-Dade	246,600
Parkland (city) Broward	239,400
Glenvar Heights (cdp) Miami-Dade	238,600
East Lake (cdp) Pinellas	215,200

Specified Housing Units Owned and Occupied by Argentinians

Top 10 Places Sorted by Number

Place (place type) County	Dollars
Miami Beach (city) Miami-Dade	384,400
Sunny Isles Beach (city) Miami-Dade	272,700
Kendall (cdp) Miami-Dade	150,600
Miami (city) Miami-Dade	145,800
Fountainbleau (cdp) Miami-Dade	100,000
Hialeah (city) Miami-Dade	88,400
Hollywood (city) Broward	85,400

Specified Housing Units Owned and Occupied by Bolivians

Top 10 Places Sorted by Number

Place (place type) County	Dollars

No places met population threshold.

Specified Housing Units Owned and Occupied by Central Americans

Top 10 Places Sorted by Number

Place (place type) County	Dollars
Miami Beach (city) Miami-Dade	445,200
Key West (city) Monroe	337,500
Coral Gables (city) Miami-Dade	325,000
Pinecrest (village) Miami-Dade	297,200
Glenvar Heights (cdp) Miami-Dade	180,900
Westchester (cdp) Miami-Dade	164,400
Plantation (city) Broward	159,600
Coral Springs (city) Broward	158,400
Doral (cdp) Miami-Dade	155,700
Sunset (cdp) Miami-Dade	153,100

Specified Housing Units Owned and Occupied by Chileans

Top 10 Places Sorted by Number

Place (place type) County	Dollars
Miami Beach (city) Miami-Dade	531,300
Kendall (cdp) Miami-Dade	165,300
Miami (city) Miami-Dade	149,200
Fountainbleau (cdp) Miami-Dade	122,900
Hialeah (city) Miami-Dade	99,300
Hollywood (city) Broward	92,000

Specified Housing Units Owned and Occupied by Columbians

Top 10 Places Sorted by Number

Place (place type) County	Dollars
Key Biscayne (village) Miami-Dade	875,000
Miami Beach (city) Miami-Dade	403,800
Aventura (city) Miami-Dade	350,000
Coral Gables (city) Miami-Dade	319,700
Ojus (cdp) Miami-Dade	240,600
Doral (cdp) Miami-Dade	171,900
Weston (city) Broward	171,300
Miami Springs (city) Miami-Dade	168,800
Coral Springs (city) Broward	167,600
Miami Lakes (cdp) Miami-Dade	167,200

Specified Housing Units Owned and Occupied by Costa Ricans

Top 10 Places Sorted by Number

Place (place type) County	Dollars
Miami (city) Miami-Dade	136,700
Hialeah (city) Miami-Dade	111,900

Specified Housing Units Owned and Occupied by Cubans

Top 10 Places Sorted by Number

Place (place type) County	Dollars
Key Biscayne (village) Miami-Dade	601,400
Sunny Isles Beach (city) Miami-Dade	517,900
Pinecrest (village) Miami-Dade	412,000
Coral Gables (city) Miami-Dade	316,300
Cutler (cdp) Miami-Dade	271,900
Key West (city) Monroe	268,000
Glenvar Heights (cdp) Miami-Dade	263,700
Miami Beach (city) Miami-Dade	231,300
Miami Shores (village) Miami-Dade	216,700
Weston (city) Broward	207,400

Specified Housing Units Owned and Occupied by Dominicans

Top 10 Places Sorted by Number

Place (place type) County	Dollars
Miami Beach (city) Miami-Dade	371,400
Weston (city) Broward	169,800
Doral (cdp) Miami-Dade	141,800
Tamiami (cdp) Miami-Dade	138,700
Pembroke Pines (city) Broward	138,000
The Hammocks (cdp) Miami-Dade	128,700
Coral Springs (city) Broward	127,700
Richmond West (cdp) Miami-Dade	125,300
Kendall (cdp) Miami-Dade	118,500
Miami (city) Miami-Dade	117,100

Specified Housing Units Owned and Occupied by Ecuadorians

Top 10 Places Sorted by Number

Place (place type) County	Dollars
Miami Beach (city) Miami-Dade	450,000
Miami (city) Miami-Dade	154,700
Coral Springs (city) Broward	148,500
Pembroke Pines (city) Broward	136,700
Hialeah (city) Miami-Dade	111,800

Notes: Please refer to the User's Guide for an explanation of data; tables include places with populations > 9,999 and reflect only those areas that meet Summary File 4 population thresholds, therefore there may be less than 10 places listed

Sunrise (city) Broward	105,600
Hollywood (city) Broward	92,500
Fountainbleau (cdp) Miami-Dade	89,100
Tampa (city) Hillsborough	70,000

Specified Housing Units Owned and Occupied by Guatelmalans

Top 10 Places Sorted by Number

Place (place type) County	Dollars
Miami (city) Miami-Dade	116,000
Bonita Springs (city) Lee	112,500
Hialeah (city) Miami-Dade	96,400
Fort Lauderdale (city) Broward	85,000
Homestead (city) Miami-Dade	78,100
West Palm Beach (city) Palm Beach	69,400
Fort Myers (city) Lee	65,000
Immokalee (cdp) Collier	65,000
Lake Worth (city) Palm Beach	54,100

Specified Housing Units Owned and Occupied by Hondurans

Top 10 Places Sorted by Number

Place (place type) County	Dollars
Miami Beach (city) Miami-Dade	450,000
Kendale Lakes (cdp) Miami-Dade	135,200
Miami (city) Miami-Dade	100,000
Fountainbleau (cdp) Miami-Dade	99,500
North Miami Beach (city) Miami-Dade	98,900
Tamiami (cdp) Miami-Dade	92,900
Hialeah (city) Miami-Dade	87,800
North Miami (city) Miami-Dade	87,400
Carol City (cdp) Miami-Dade	87,300
Hollywood (city) Broward	78,600

Specified Housing Units Owned and Occupied by Mexicans

Top 10 Places Sorted by Number

Place (place type) County	Dollars
Weston (city) Broward	192,100
Boca Raton (city) Palm Beach	181,700
Doral (cdp) Miami-Dade	172,800
Coral Springs (city) Broward	159,300
Plantation (city) Broward	152,500
Pembroke Pines (city) Broward	144,100
Coconut Creek (city) Broward	139,500
Auburndale (city) Polk	137,500
The Hammocks (cdp) Miami-Dade	135,600
Miami (city) Miami-Dade	134,600

Specified Housing Units Owned and Occupied by Nicaraguans

Top 10 Places Sorted by Number

Place (place type) County	Dollars
Coral Gables (city) Miami-Dade	234,500
Westchester (cdp) Miami-Dade	185,700
Miami Springs (city) Miami-Dade	154,700
Kendall (cdp) Miami-Dade	138,900
Miramar (city) Broward	133,400
The Hammocks (cdp) Miami-Dade	132,600
Tamiami (cdp) Miami-Dade	129,300
Coral Terrace (cdp) Miami-Dade	128,900
Kendall West (cdp) Miami-Dade	127,300
The Crossings (cdp) Miami-Dade	126,400

Specified Housing Units Owned and Occupied by Panamanians

Top 10 Places Sorted by Number

Place (place type) County	Dollars
Miramar (city) Broward	137,500
Miami (city) Miami-Dade	126,300
Fountainbleau (cdp) Miami-Dade	94,300
Jacksonville (city) Duval	80,000
Tampa (city) Hillsborough	67,900

Specified Housing Units Owned and Occupied by Paraguayans

Top 10 Places Sorted by Number

Place (place type) County	Dollars

No places met population threshold.

Specified Housing Units Owned and Occupied by Peruvians

Top 10 Places Sorted by Number

Place (place type) County	Dollars
Weston (city) Broward	220,000
Doral (cdp) Miami-Dade	190,900
Miami Beach (city) Miami-Dade	175,000
Miramar (city) Broward	158,600
Kendall (cdp) Miami-Dade	147,700
Miami (city) Miami-Dade	143,300
Richmond West (cdp) Miami-Dade	139,400
The Hammocks (cdp) Miami-Dade	137,300
Pembroke Pines (city) Broward	137,100
Coral Springs (city) Broward	134,100

Specified Housing Units Owned and Occupied by Puerto Ricans

Top 10 Places Sorted by Number

Place (place type) County	Dollars
Coral Gables (city) Miami-Dade	313,300
Doral (cdp) Miami-Dade	186,900
Boca Raton (city) Palm Beach	177,500
Weston (city) Broward	177,000
Miami Lakes (cdp) Miami-Dade	169,600
Miami Beach (city) Miami-Dade	161,800
Coral Springs (city) Broward	158,500
Kendall (cdp) Miami-Dade	158,300
Wellington (village) Palm Beach	150,800
Coconut Creek (city) Broward	147,300

Specified Housing Units Owned and Occupied by Salvadorans

Top 10 Places Sorted by Number

Place (place type) County	Dollars
Miami (city) Miami-Dade	122,800
Oakland Park (city) Broward	112,500
Hialeah (city) Miami-Dade	87,700
Lake Worth (city) Palm Beach	74,400
Fort Lauderdale (city) Broward	66,300
Homestead (city) Miami-Dade	66,100

Specified Housing Units Owned and Occupied by South Americans

Top 10 Places Sorted by Number

Place (place type) County	Dollars
Key Biscayne (village) Miami-Dade	564,300
Pinecrest (village) Miami-Dade	541,700
Miami Beach (city) Miami-Dade	376,400
Coral Gables (city) Miami-Dade	329,200
Cutler (cdp) Miami-Dade	301,300
Sunny Isles Beach (city) Miami-Dade	295,500
Parkland (city) Broward	260,000
Boca Raton (city) Palm Beach	233,800
Ojus (cdp) Miami-Dade	209,400
Aventura (city) Miami-Dade	188,900

Specified Housing Units Owned and Occupied by Spaniards

Top 10 Places Sorted by Number

Place (place type) County	Dollars
Miami Beach (city) Miami-Dade	190,600
Miami (city) Miami-Dade	119,100
Hialeah (city) Miami-Dade	109,500
Tampa (city) Hillsborough	83,300

Specified Housing Units Owned and Occupied by Uruguayans

Top 10 Places Sorted by Number

Place (place type) County	Dollars

No places met population threshold.

Specified Housing Units Owned and Occupied by Venezuelans

Top 10 Places Sorted by Number

Place (place type) County	Dollars
Coral Gables (city) Miami-Dade	420,000
Miami Beach (city) Miami-Dade	365,400
Coral Springs (city) Broward	189,600
Miami (city) Miami-Dade	182,500
Weston (city) Broward	174,500
Doral (cdp) Miami-Dade	170,800
Hollywood (city) Broward	162,200
Pembroke Pines (city) Broward	152,800
The Hammocks (cdp) Miami-Dade	146,200
The Crossings (cdp) Miami-Dade	144,600

Specified Housing Units Owned and Occupied by Other Hispanics

Top 10 Places Sorted by Number

Place (place type) County	Dollars
Key Biscayne (village) Miami-Dade	666,700
Pinecrest (village) Miami-Dade	386,400
Coral Gables (city) Miami-Dade	298,900
Cutler (cdp) Miami-Dade	271,700
Key West (city) Monroe	210,500
Miami Beach (city) Miami-Dade	210,000
Glenvar Heights (cdp) Miami-Dade	201,400
Miami Lakes (cdp) Miami-Dade	194,000
Weston (city) Broward	175,900
Aventura (city) Miami-Dade	172,900

Notes: Please refer to the User's Guide for an explanation of data; tables include places with populations > 9,999 and reflect only those areas that meet Summary File 4 population thresholds, therefore there may be less than 10 places listed

Asian and NHPI Population

(Universe: Total Population)

Place	Total population	Total Asian population	Total NHPI[1] population	Asian Indian	Bangladeshi	Cambodian	Chinese[2]	Fijian	Filipino	Guamanian[3]	Hawaiian, Native	Hmong	Indonesian	Japanese	Korean	Laotian	Malaysian	Pakistani	Samoan	Sri Lankan	Taiwanese	Thai	Tongan	Vietnamese
UNITED STATES	281,421,906	10,171,820 3.61	378,782 0.13	1,645,510 16.18 0.58	41,428 0.41 0.01	178,043 1.75 0.06	2,300,219 22.61 0.82	10,265 2.71 <0.01	1,864,120 18.33 0.66	55,130 14.55 0.02	139,495 36.83 0.05	170,049 1.67 0.06	37,167 0.37 0.01	795,051 7.82 0.28	1,072,682 10.55 0.38	167,792 1.65 0.06	10,711 0.11 <0.01	155,909 1.53 0.06	85,243 22.50 0.03	19,078 0.19 0.01	122,751 1.21 0.04	110,851 1.09 0.04	27,686 7.31 0.01	1,110,207 10.91 0.39
FLORIDA	15,982,378	264,377 1.65	6,812 0.04	67,790 25.64 0.42	1,260 0.48 0.01	2,762 1.04 0.02	44,867 16.97 0.28	-	54,332 20.55 0.34	2,020 29.65 0.01	1,971 28.93 0.01	-	894 0.34 0.01	11,346 4.29 0.07	19,077 7.22 0.12	4,031 1.52 0.03	-	5,446 2.06 0.03	849 12.46 0.01	402 0.15 <0.01	2,027 0.77 0.01	6,572 2.49 0.04	-	33,391 12.63 0.21
Alachua County	217,955	7,858 3.61	-	1,949 24.80 0.89	-	-	2,135 27.17 0.98	-	1,046 13.31 0.48	-	-	-	-	433 5.51 0.20	1,005 12.79 0.46	-	-	-	-	-	-	-	-	617 7.85 0.28
Gainesville (city)	95,605	4,399 4.60	-	1,056 24.01 1.10	-	-	1,456 33.10 1.52	-	-	-	-	-	-	-	501 11.39 0.52	-	-	-	-	-	-	-	-	-
Bay County	148,217	2,369 1.60	-	-	-	-	-	-	484 20.43 0.33	-	-	-	-	-	-	-	-	-	-	-	-	-	-	666 28.11 0.45
Callaway (city)	14,253	530 3.72	-	-	-	-	-	-	-	-	-	-	-	-	-	-	-	-	-	-	-	-	-	-
Brevard County	476,230	7,122 1.50	-	1,971 27.67 0.41	-	-	892 12.52 0.19	-	1,537 21.58 0.32	-	-	-	-	525 7.37 0.11	621 8.72 0.13	-	-	-	-	-	-	-	-	763 10.71 0.16
Broward County	1,623,018	36,505 2.25	645 0.04	13,009 35.64 0.80	-	-	8,556 23.44 0.53	-	4,870 13.34 0.30	-	-	-	-	1,045 2.86 0.06	2,260 6.19 0.14	-	-	1,097 3.01 0.07	-	-	-	599 1.64 0.04	-	2,867 7.85 0.18
Cooper City (city)	27,685	1,241 4.48	-	593 47.78 2.14	-	-	-	-	-	-	-	-	-	-	-	-	-	-	-	-	-	-	-	-
Pembroke Pines (city)	137,112	5,004 3.65	-	1,752 35.01 1.28	-	-	1,153 23.04 0.84	-	927 18.53 0.68	-	-	-	-	-	-	-	-	-	-	-	-	-	-	-
Charlotte County	141,627	872 0.62	-	-	-	-	-	-	-	-	-	-	-	-	-	-	-	-	-	-	-	-	-	-
Citrus County	118,085	1,145 0.97	-	-	-	-	-	-	-	-	-	-	-	-	-	-	-	-	-	-	-	-	-	-
Clay County	140,814	2,901 2.06	-	-	-	-	-	-	1,724 59.43 1.22	-	-	-	-	-	-	-	-	-	-	-	-	-	-	-
Bellair-Meadowbrook Ter. (cdp)	16,565	635 3.83	-	-	-	-	-	-	-	-	-	-	-	-	-	-	-	-	-	-	-	-	-	-

Notes: Please refer to the User's Guide for an explanation of data; data is arranged alphabetically by state, then county, then city within each county; table includes counties with populations greater than 49,999 unless noted and cities with populations greater than 9,999 whose Asian and/or NHPI population rates are greater than the national average; (1) Native Hawaiian and other Pacific Islander; (2) excludes Taiwanese; (3) includes Chamorro; (4) county does not meet population thresnold but is shown in order to allow inclusion of city

Place	Total population	Total Asian population	Total NHPI[1] population	Asian Indian	Bangladeshi	Cambodian	Chinese[2]	Fijian	Filipino	Guamanian[3]	Hawaiian, Native	Hmong	Indonesian	Japanese	Korean	Laotian	Malaysian	Pakistani	Samoan	Sri Lankan	Taiwanese	Thai	Tongan	Vietnamese
Collier County	251,377	1,200 0.48	-	-	-	-	-	-	-	-	-	-	-	-	-	-	-	-	-	-	-	-	-	-
Columbia County	56,513	386 0.68	-	-	-	-	-	-	-	-	-	-	-	-	-	-	-	-	-	-	-	-	-	-
Duval County	778,879	20,554 2.64	507 0.07	2,767 13.46 0.36	-	1,001 4.87 0.13	1,642 7.99 0.21	-	10,206 49.65 1.31	-	-	-	-	550 2.68 0.07	967 4.70 0.12	-	-	-	-	-	-	-	-	2,112 10.28 0.27
Escambia County	294,410	6,565 2.23	-	516 7.86 0.18	-	-	587 8.94 0.20	-	2,717 41.39 0.92	-	-	-	-	-	-	-	-	-	-	-	-	-	-	1,597 24.33 0.54
Bellview (cdp)	21,067	787 3.74	-	-	-	-	-	-	412 52.35 1.96	-	-	-	-	-	-	-	-	-	-	-	-	-	-	-
Myrtle Grove (cdp)	17,307	812 4.69	-	-	-	-	-	-	471 58.00 2.72	-	-	-	-	-	-	-	-	-	-	-	-	-	-	-
Hernando County	130,802	773 0.59	-	-	-	-	-	-	-	-	-	-	-	-	-	-	-	-	-	-	-	-	-	-
Highlands County	87,366	964 1.10	-	-	-	-	-	-	447 46.37 0.51	-	-	-	-	-	-	-	-	-	-	-	-	-	-	-
Hillsborough County	998,948	21,571 2.16	540 0.05	5,901 27.36 0.59	-	-	2,679 12.42 0.27	-	3,203 14.85 0.32	-	-	-	-	863 4.00 0.09	2,718 12.60 0.27	-	-	-	-	-	-	676 3.13 0.07	-	3,993 18.51 0.40
Westchase (cdp)	11,116	508 4.57	-	-	-	-	-	-	-	-	-	-	-	-	-	-	-	-	-	-	-	-	-	-
Indian River County	112,947	864 0.76	-	-	-	-	-	-	-	-	-	-	-	-	-	-	-	-	-	-	-	-	-	-
Lake County	210,528	1,422 0.68	-	-	-	-	-	-	-	-	-	-	-	-	-	-	-	-	-	-	-	-	-	-
Lee County	440,888	3,159 0.72	-	669 21.18 0.15	-	-	596 18.87 0.14	-	1,104 34.95 0.25	-	-	-	-	-	-	-	-	-	-	-	-	-	-	-
Leon County	239,452	4,858 2.03	-	1,508 31.04 0.63	-	-	1,085 22.33 0.45	-	526 10.83 0.22	-	-	-	-	-	446 9.18 0.19	-	-	-	-	-	-	-	-	-
Manatee County	264,002	2,237 0.85	-	-	-	-	-	-	538 24.05 0.20	-	-	-	-	-	-	-	-	-	-	-	-	-	-	-

Notes: Please refer to the User's Guide for an explanation of data; data is arranged alphabetically by state, then county, then city within each county; table includes counties with populations greater than 49,999 unless noted and cities with populations greater than 9,999 whose Asian and/or NHPI population rates are greater than the national average; (1) Native Hawaiian and other Pacific Islander; (2) excludes Taiwanese; (3) includes Chamorro; (4) county does not meet population threshold but is shown in order to allow inclusion of city

Place	Total population	Total Asian population	Total NHPI[1] population	Asian Indian	Bangladeshi	Cambodian	Chinese[2]	Fijian	Filipino	Guamanian[3]	Hawaiian, Native	Hmong	Indonesian	Japanese	Korean	Laotian	Malaysian	Pakistani	Samoan	Sri Lankan	Taiwanese	Thai	Tongan	Vietnamese
Marion County	258,916	2,221 0.86	-	949 42.73 0.37	-	-	-	-	-	-	-	-	-	-	-	-	-	-	-	-	-	-	-	-
Martin County	126,731	701 0.55	-	-	-	-	-	-	-	-	-	-	-	-	-	-	-	-	-	-	-	-	-	-
Miami-Dade County	2,253,362	30,692 1.36	605 0.03	8,938 29.12 0.40	-	-	8,889 28.96 0.39	-	4,521 14.73 0.20	-	-	-	-	1,404 4.57 0.06	1,336 4.35 0.06	-	-	794 2.59 0.04	-	-	-	882 2.87 0.04	-	1,595 5.20 0.07
Doral (cdp)	20,513	1,186 5.78	-	-	-	-	-	-	-	-	-	-	-	-	-	-	-	-	-	-	-	-	-	-
Ives Estates (cdp)	17,417	831 4.77	-	-	-	-	-	-	-	-	-	-	-	-	-	-	-	-	-	-	-	-	-	-
North Miami Beach (city)	40,673	1,706 4.19	-	396 23.21 0.97	-	-	741 43.43 1.82	-	-	-	-	-	-	-	-	-	-	-	-	-	-	-	-	-
Pinecrest (village)	19,181	884 4.61	-	-	-	-	-	-	-	-	-	-	-	-	-	-	-	-	-	-	-	-	-	-
Monroe County	79,589	566 0.71	-	-	-	-	-	-	-	-	-	-	-	-	-	-	-	-	-	-	-	-	-	-
Nassau County	57,663	422 0.73	-	-	-	-	-	-	-	-	-	-	-	-	-	-	-	-	-	-	-	-	-	-
Okaloosa County	170,498	4,432 2.60	-	-	-	-	-	-	1,742 39.31 1.02	-	-	-	-	-	720 16.25 0.42	-	-	-	-	-	-	624 14.08 0.37	-	400 9.03 0.23
Wright (cdp)	21,553	825 3.83	-	-	-	-	-	-	-	-	-	-	-	-	-	-	-	-	-	-	-	-	-	-
Orange County	896,344	28,748 3.21	853 0.10	7,651 26.61 0.85	-	-	3,992 13.89 0.45	-	4,524 15.74 0.50	-	-	-	-	1,200 4.17 0.13	2,145 7.46 0.24	-	-	901 3.13 0.10	-	-	-	-	-	6,357 22.11 0.71
Oak Ridge (cdp)	22,407	1,306 5.83	-	-	-	-	-	-	-	-	-	-	-	-	-	-	-	-	-	-	-	-	-	527 40.35 2.35
Osceola County	172,493	3,642 2.11	-	966 26.52 0.56	-	-	584 16.04 0.34	-	883 24.24 0.51	-	-	-	-	-	-	-	-	-	-	-	-	-	-	-
Palm Beach County	1,131,184	16,895 1.49	423 0.04	5,098 30.17 0.45	-	-	3,641 21.55 0.32	-	2,238 13.25 0.20	-	-	-	-	574 3.40 0.05	932 5.52 0.08	-	-	-	-	-	-	760 4.50 0.07	-	1,994 11.80 0.18

Notes: Please refer to the User's Guide for an explanation of data; data is arranged alphabetically by state, then county, then city within each county; table includes counties with populations greater than 49,999 unless noted and cities with populations greater than 9,999 whose Asian and/or NHPI population rates are greater than the national average; (1) Native Hawaiian and other Pacific Islander; (2) excludes Taiwanese; (3) includes Chamorro; (4) county does not meet population threshold but is shown in order to allow inclusion of city

Place	Total population	Total Asian population	Total NHPI[1] population	Asian Indian	Bangladeshi	Cambodian	Chinese[2]	Fijian	Filipino	Guamanian[3]	Hawaiian, Native	Hmong	Indonesian	Japanese	Korean	Laotian	Malaysian	Pakistani	Samoan	Sri Lankan	Taiwanese	Thai	Tongan	Vietnamese
Pasco County	344,765	3,489 1.01	-	993 28.46 0.29	-	-	504 14.45 0.15	-	994 28.49 0.29	-	-	-	-	-	-	-	-	-	-	-	-	-	-	-
Pinellas County	921,482	18,783 2.04	-	3,648 19.42 0.40	-	718 3.82 0.08	2,085 11.10 0.23	-	3,034 16.15 0.33	-	-	-	-	568 3.02 0.06	854 4.55 0.09	1,855 9.88 0.20	-	-	-	-	-	488 2.60 0.05	-	4,234 22.54 0.46
Pinellas Park (city)	45,414	1,811 3.99	-	-	-	-	-	-	-	-	-	-	-	-	-	-	-	-	-	-	-	-	-	526 29.04 1.16
Polk County	483,924	5,805 1.20	-	1,717 29.58 0.35	-	-	595 10.25 0.12	-	902 15.54 0.19	-	-	-	-	-	-	401 6.91 0.08	-	-	-	-	-	-	-	872 15.02 0.18
Putnam County	70,423	291 0.41	-	-	-	-	-	-	-	-	-	-	-	-	-	-	-	-	-	-	-	-	-	-
St. Johns County	123,135	1,244 1.01	-	-	-	-	-	-	-	-	-	-	-	-	-	-	-	-	-	-	-	-	-	-
St. Lucie County	192,695	1,885 0.98	-	-	-	-	-	-	-	-	-	-	-	-	-	-	-	-	-	-	-	-	-	-
Santa Rosa County	117,743	1,608 1.37	-	-	-	-	-	-	707 43.97 0.60	-	-	-	-	-	-	-	-	-	-	-	-	-	-	-
Sarasota County	325,957	2,624 0.81	-	-	-	-	426 16.23 0.13	-	540 20.58 0.17	-	-	-	-	-	-	-	-	-	-	-	-	-	-	683 26.03 0.21
Seminole County	365,196	8,682 2.38	-	2,781 32.03 0.76	-	-	1,385 15.95 0.38	-	1,313 15.12 0.36	-	-	-	-	-	976 11.24 0.27	-	-	-	-	-	-	-	-	1,064 12.26 0.29
Volusia County	443,343	4,812 1.09	-	1,590 33.04 0.36	-	-	658 13.67 0.15	-	881 18.31 0.20	-	-	-	-	-	462 9.60 0.10	-	-	-	-	-	-	-	-	-

Notes: Please refer to the User's Guide for an explanation of data; data is arranged alphabetically by state, then county, then city within each county; table includes counties with populations greater than 49,999 unless noted and cities with populations greater than 9,999 whose Asian and/or NHPI population rates are greater than the national average; (1) Native Hawaiian and other Pacific Islander; (2) excludes Taiwanese; (3) includes Chamorro; (4) county does not meet population threshold but is shown in order to allow inclusion of city

Median Age

(Universe: Total Population)

Place	Total population	Total Asian population	Total NHPI[1] population	Asian Indian	Bangladeshi	Cambodian	Chinese[2]	Fijian	Filipino	Guamanian[3]	Hawaiian, Native	Hmong	Indonesian	Japanese	Korean	Laotian	Malaysian	Pakistani	Samoan	Sri Lankan	Taiwanese	Thai	Tongan	Vietnamese
UNITED STATES	35.4	33.0	27.6	30.3	29.7	23.8	35.6	29.3	35.5	29.3	31.8	16.3	30.1	42.6	32.7	26.1	29.2	28.7	24.4	35.8	32.8	34.7	23.2	30.5
FLORIDA	38.8	34.1	29.6	32.1	33.0	29.5	36.4	-	36.3	29.1	33.6	-	40.0	41.0	35.8	29.5	-	32.4	28.9	39.4	36.2	39.1	-	30.5
Alachua County	29.0	25.9	-	23.9	-	-	27.4	-	30.1	-	-	-	-	32.1	28.8	-	-	-	-	-	-	-	-	25.3
Gainesville (city)	26.5	25.7	-	23.2	-	-	27.5	-	-	-	-	-	-	-	28.8	-	-	-	-	-	-	-	-	-
Bay County	37.5	35.2	-	-	-	-	-	-	35.1	-	-	-	-	-	-	-	-	-	-	-	-	-	-	27.5
Callaway (city)	33.2	35.9	-	-	-	-	-	-	-	-	-	-	-	-	-	-	-	-	-	-	-	-	-	-
Brevard County	41.6	38.3	-	34.9	-	-	38.4	-	38.4	-	-	-	-	45.0	43.2	-	-	-	-	-	-	-	-	36.3
Broward County	37.9	35.0	35.5	33.5	-	-	37.3	-	37.6	-	-	-	-	39.7	32.7	-	-	31.0	-	-	-	36.9	-	30.0
Cooper City (city)	37.2	38.0	-	38.5	-	-	-	-	-	-	-	-	-	-	-	-	-	-	-	-	-	-	-	-
Pembroke Pines (city)	36.7	35.9	-	31.8	-	-	37.7	-	39.9	-	-	-	-	-	-	-	-	-	-	-	-	-	-	-
Charlotte County	54.2	40.9	-	-	-	-	-	-	-	-	-	-	-	-	-	-	-	-	-	-	-	-	-	-
Citrus County	52.6	39.2	-	-	-	-	-	-	-	-	-	-	-	-	-	-	-	-	-	-	-	-	-	-
Clay County	35.9	38.2	-	-	-	-	-	-	41.2	-	-	-	-	-	-	-	-	-	-	-	-	-	-	-
Bellair-Meadowbrook Ter. (cdp)	32.9	39.5	-	-	-	-	-	-	-	-	-	-	-	-	-	-	-	-	-	-	-	-	-	-
Collier County	44.1	31.8	-	-	-	-	-	-	-	-	-	-	-	-	-	-	-	-	-	-	-	-	-	-
Columbia County	37.4	31.9	-	-	-	-	-	-	-	-	-	-	-	-	-	-	-	-	-	-	-	-	-	-
Duval County	34.2	33.1	25.8	30.8	-	28.9	36.2	-	35.2	-	-	-	-	36.7	36.5	-	-	-	-	-	-	-	-	29.3
Escambia County	35.5	32.2	-	29.0	-	-	34.5	-	34.8	-	-	-	-	-	-	-	-	-	-	-	-	-	-	24.3
Bellview (cdp)	36.2	34.8	-	-	-	-	-	-	41.6	-	-	-	-	-	-	-	-	-	-	-	-	-	-	-
Myrtle Grove (cdp)	32.3	32.8	-	-	-	-	-	-	36.9	-	-	-	-	-	-	-	-	-	-	-	-	-	-	-
Hernando County	49.2	40.0	-	-	-	-	-	-	-	-	-	-	-	-	-	-	-	-	-	-	-	-	-	-
Highlands County	50.0	36.9	-	-	-	-	-	-	40.2	-	-	-	-	-	-	-	-	-	-	-	-	-	-	-
Hillsborough County	35.2	32.4	27.9	29.7	-	-	34.3	-	31.8	-	-	-	-	43.5	37.2	-	-	-	-	-	-	35.4	-	31.1
Westchase (cdp)	34.0	32.0	-	-	-	-	-	-	-	-	-	-	-	-	-	-	-	-	-	-	-	-	-	-
Indian River County	46.9	33.9	-	-	-	-	-	-	-	-	-	-	-	-	-	-	-	-	-	-	-	-	-	-
Lake County	44.9	33.8	-	-	-	-	-	-	-	-	-	-	-	-	-	-	-	-	-	-	-	-	-	-
Lee County	45.1	37.2	-	33.6	-	-	35.3	-	39.4	-	-	-	-	-	-	-	-	-	-	-	-	-	-	-
Leon County	29.6	30.9	-	29.4	-	-	31.6	-	30.2	-	-	-	-	-	32.6	-	-	-	-	-	-	-	-	-
Manatee County	43.6	36.4	-	-	-	-	-	-	35.3	-	-	-	-	-	-	-	-	-	-	-	-	-	-	-
Marion County	43.8	37.9	-	32.9	-	-	-	-	-	-	-	-	-	-	-	-	-	-	-	-	-	-	-	-
Martin County	47.3	36.6	-	-	-	-	-	-	-	-	-	-	-	-	-	-	-	-	-	-	-	-	-	-
Miami-Dade County	35.8	34.9	31.6	31.4	-	-	38.2	-	38.5	-	-	-	-	38.4	37.0	-	-	36.3	-	-	-	37.6	-	27.5
Doral (cdp)	32.8	32.3	-	-	-	-	-	-	-	-	-	-	-	-	-	-	-	-	-	-	-	-	-	-
Ives Estates (cdp)	34.6	32.4	-	-	-	-	-	-	-	-	-	-	-	-	-	-	-	-	-	-	-	-	-	-

Notes: Please refer to the User's Guide for an explanation of data; data is arranged alphabetically by state, then county, then city within each county; table includes counties with populations greater than 49,999 unless noted and cities with populations greater than 9,999 whose Asian and/or NHPI population rates are greater than the national average; (1) Native Hawaiian and other Pacific Islander; (2) excludes Taiwanese; (3) includes Chamorro; (4) county does not meet population threshold but is shown in order to allow inclusion of city

Place	Total population	Total Asian population	Total NHPI[1] population	Asian Indian	Bangladeshi	Cambodian	Chinese[2]	Fijian	Filipino	Guamanian[3]	Hawaiian, Native	Hmong	Indonesian	Japanese	Korean	Laotian	Malaysian	Pakistani	Samoan	Sri Lankan	Taiwanese	Thai	Tongan	Vietnamese
North Miami Beach (city)	35.1	37.0	-	32.7	-	-	41.0	-	-	-	-	-	-	-	-	-	-	-	-	-	-	-	-	-
Pinecrest (village)	38.3	38.6	-	-	-	-	-	-	-	-	-	-	-	-	-	-	-	-	-	-	-	-	-	-
Monroe County	42.6	38.1	-	-	-	-	-	-	-	-	-	-	-	-	-	-	-	-	-	-	-	-	-	-
Nassau County	38.3	36.2	-	-	-	-	-	-	-	-	-	-	-	-	-	-	-	-	-	-	-	-	-	-
Okaloosa County	36.2	38.0	-	-	-	-	-	-	34.6	-	-	-	-	-	38.4	-	-	-	-	-	-	48.7	-	30.3
Wright (cdp)	34.0	40.9	-	-	-	-	-	-	-	-	-	-	-	-	-	-	-	-	-	-	-	-	-	-
Orange County	33.6	33.0	24.7	32.8	-	-	36.2	-	33.5	-	-	-	-	35.3	35.2	-	-	32.6	-	-	-	-	-	30.4
Oak Ridge (cdp)	29.1	31.9	-	-	-	-	-	-	-	-	-	-	-	-	-	-	-	-	-	-	-	-	-	31.2
Osceola County	34.7	37.3	-	29.4	-	-	44.1	-	40.8	-	-	-	-	-	-	-	-	-	-	-	-	-	-	-
Palm Beach County	41.8	35.4	33.2	33.6	-	-	36.4	-	36.5	-	-	-	-	47.1	39.3	-	-	-	-	-	-	38.3	-	32.9
Pasco County	44.8	37.2	-	33.4	-	-	39.0	-	38.5	-	-	-	-	-	-	-	-	-	-	-	-	-	-	-
Pinellas County	43.1	33.7	-	34.0	-	25.4	38.5	-	35.3	-	-	-	-	39.8	38.8	29.5	-	-	-	-	-	37.2	-	31.9
Pinellas Park (city)	40.2	34.4	-	-	-	-	-	-	-	-	-	-	-	-	-	-	-	-	-	-	-	-	-	30.8
Polk County	38.6	33.0	-	34.2	-	-	34.3	-	38.3	-	-	-	-	-	-	27.7	-	-	-	-	-	-	-	27.7
Putnam County	40.5	39.4	-	-	-	-	-	-	-	-	-	-	-	-	-	-	-	-	-	-	-	-	-	-
St. Johns County	40.9	36.6	-	-	-	-	-	-	-	-	-	-	-	-	-	-	-	-	-	-	-	-	-	-
St. Lucie County	42.1	38.4	-	-	-	-	-	-	-	-	-	-	-	-	-	-	-	-	-	-	-	-	-	-
Santa Rosa County	36.8	38.2	-	-	-	-	-	-	39.9	-	-	-	-	-	-	-	-	-	-	-	-	-	-	-
Sarasota County	50.4	35.8	-	-	-	-	26.8	-	41.1	-	-	-	-	-	-	-	-	-	-	-	-	-	-	32.9
Seminole County	36.3	34.8	-	34.6	-	-	36.6	-	33.9	-	-	-	-	-	34.0	-	-	-	-	-	-	-	-	33.5
Volusia County	42.4	35.4	-	35.6	-	-	36.3	-	37.4	-	-	-	-	-	29.7	-	-	-	-	-	-	-	-	-

Notes: Please refer to the User's Guide for an explanation of data; data is arranged alphabetically by state, then county, then city within each county; table includes counties with populations greater than 49,999 unless noted and cities with populations greater than 9,999 whose Asian and/or NHPI population rates are greater than the national average; (1) Native Hawaiian and other Pacific Islander; (2) excludes Taiwanese; (3) includes Chamorro; (4) county does not meet population threshold but is shown in order to allow inclusion of city

Average Household Size

(Universe: Households)

Place	All households	Asian households	NHPI[1] households	Asian Indian	Bangladeshi	Cambodian	Chinese[2]	Fijian	Filipino	Guamanian[3]	Hawaiian, Native	Hmong	Indonesian	Japanese	Korean	Laotian	Malaysian	Pakistani	Samoan	Sri Lankan	Taiwanese	Thai	Tongan	Vietnamese
UNITED STATES	2.59	3.08	3.60	3.06	3.67	4.41	2.91	3.72	3.41	3.31	3.21	6.14	2.67	2.25	2.76	4.23	2.61	3.80	4.33	2.86	2.85	2.64	5.31	3.70
FLORIDA	2.46	2.91	2.91	2.97	3.40	3.82	2.71	-	2.93	3.41	2.54	-	2.29	2.10	2.59	3.62	-	3.74	2.60	2.23	2.60	2.51	-	3.42
Alachua County	2.34	2.23	-	2.33	-	-	2.17	-	2.72	-	-	-	-	1.71	2.32	-	-	-	-	-	-	-	-	2.11
Gainesville (city)	2.25	2.07	-	2.08	-	-	2.04	-	-	-	-	-	-	-	2.15	-	-	-	-	-	-	-	-	-
Bay County	2.43	2.68	-	-	-	-	-	-	2.54	-	-	-	-	-	-	-	-	-	-	-	-	-	-	3.46
Callaway (city)	2.58	3.09	-	-	-	-	-	-	-	-	-	-	-	-	-	-	-	-	-	-	-	-	-	-
Brevard County	2.35	2.72	-	3.13	-	-	2.40	-	3.03	-	-	-	-	1.85	2.23	-	-	-	-	-	-	-	-	2.85
Broward County	2.45	2.96	2.25	3.00	-	-	2.87	-	3.20	-	-	-	-	2.15	2.69	-	-	3.48	-	-	-	3.01	-	3.14
Cooper City (city)	3.06	3.58	-	3.41	-	-	-	-	-	-	-	-	-	-	-	-	-	-	-	-	-	-	-	-
Pembroke Pines (city)	2.61	2.93	-	3.05	-	-	2.89	-	3.17	-	-	-	-	-	-	-	-	-	-	-	-	-	-	-
Charlotte County	2.17	2.80	-	-	-	-	-	-	-	-	-	-	-	-	-	-	-	-	-	-	-	-	-	-
Citrus County	2.20	2.73	-	-	-	-	-	-	-	-	-	-	-	-	-	-	-	-	-	-	-	-	-	-
Clay County	2.76	3.20	-	-	-	-	-	-	3.17	-	-	-	-	-	-	-	-	-	-	-	-	-	-	-
Bellair-Meadowbrook Ter. (cdp)	2.53	3.05	-	-	-	-	-	-	-	-	-	-	-	-	-	-	-	-	-	-	-	-	-	-
Collier County	2.39	2.45	-	-	-	-	-	-	-	-	-	-	-	-	-	-	-	-	-	-	-	-	-	-
Columbia County	2.56	2.34	-	-	-	-	-	-	-	-	-	-	-	-	-	-	-	-	-	-	-	-	-	-
Duval County	2.51	3.01	3.10	2.64	-	4.11	2.66	-	3.18	-	-	-	-	1.90	2.74	-	-	-	-	-	-	-	-	3.27
Escambia County	2.45	3.15	-	3.94	-	-	2.80	-	2.89	-	-	-	-	-	-	-	-	-	-	-	-	-	-	3.82
Bellview (cdp)	2.61	3.35	-	-	-	-	-	-	3.13	-	-	-	-	-	-	-	-	-	-	-	-	-	-	-
Myrtle Grove (cdp)	2.49	2.83	-	-	-	-	-	-	2.56	-	-	-	-	-	-	-	-	-	-	-	-	-	-	-
Hernando County	2.32	3.00	-	-	-	-	-	-	-	-	-	-	-	-	-	-	-	-	-	-	-	-	-	-
Highlands County	2.29	3.17	-	-	-	-	-	-	3.53	-	-	-	-	-	-	-	-	-	-	-	-	-	-	-
Hillsborough County	2.51	2.88	3.23	2.86	-	-	2.67	-	2.53	-	-	-	-	1.85	2.95	-	-	-	-	-	-	2.62	-	3.76
Westchase (cdp)	2.66	3.07	-	-	-	-	-	-	-	-	-	-	-	-	-	-	-	-	-	-	-	-	-	-
Indian River County	2.25	3.04	-	-	-	-	-	-	-	-	-	-	-	-	-	-	-	-	-	-	-	-	-	-
Lake County	2.34	2.94	-	-	-	-	-	-	-	-	-	-	-	-	-	-	-	-	-	-	-	-	-	-
Lee County	2.31	2.60	-	2.99	-	-	2.62	-	2.57	-	-	-	-	-	-	-	-	-	-	-	-	-	-	-
Leon County	2.34	2.48	-	2.60	-	-	2.36	-	2.76	-	-	-	-	-	2.00	-	-	-	-	-	-	-	-	-
Manatee County	2.29	2.83	-	-	-	-	-	-	2.10	-	-	-	-	-	-	-	-	-	-	-	-	-	-	-
Marion County	2.36	3.02	-	3.30	-	-	-	-	-	-	-	-	-	-	-	-	-	-	-	-	-	-	-	-
Martin County	2.23	2.23	-	-	-	-	-	-	-	-	-	-	-	-	-	-	-	-	-	-	-	-	-	-
Miami-Dade County	2.84	2.79	3.07	2.85	-	-	2.69	-	2.77	-	-	-	-	2.20	2.78	-	-	3.64	-	-	-	2.72	-	3.24
Doral (cdp)	2.65	2.54	-	-	-	-	-	-	-	-	-	-	-	-	-	-	-	-	-	-	-	-	-	-
Ives Estates (cdp)	2.55	2.66	-	-	-	-	-	-	-	-	-	-	-	-	-	-	-	-	-	-	-	-	-	-

Notes: Please refer to the User's Guide for an explanation of data; data is arranged alphabetically by state, then county, then city within each county; table includes counties with populations greater than 49,999 unless noted and cities with populations greater than 9,999 whose Asian and/or NHPI population rates are greater than the national average; (1) Native Hawaiian and other Pacific Islander; (2) excludes Taiwanese; (3) includes Chamorro; (4) county does not meet population threshold but is shown in order to allow inclusion of city

Place	All households	Asian households	NHPI[1] households	Asian Indian	Bangladeshi	Cambodian	Chinese[2]	Fijian	Filipino	Guamanian[3]	Hawaiian, Native	Hmong	Indonesian	Japanese	Korean	Laotian	Malaysian	Pakistani	Samoan	Sri Lankan	Taiwanese	Thai	Tongan	Vietnamese
North Miami Beach (city)	2.87	3.11	-	2.67	-	-	3.29	-	-	-	-	-	-	-	-	-	-	-	-	-	-	-	-	-
Pinecrest (village)	3.06	3.21	-	-	-	-	-	-	-	-	-	-	-	-	-	-	-	-	-	-	-	-	-	-
Monroe County	2.23	2.52	-	-	-	-	-	-	-	-	-	-	-	-	-	-	-	-	-	-	-	-	-	-
Nassau County	2.60	2.91	-	-	-	-	-	-	-	-	-	-	-	-	-	-	-	-	-	-	-	-	-	-
Okaloosa County	2.49	2.51	-	-	-	-	-	-	2.68	-	-	-	-	-	2.35	-	-	-	-	-	-	2.00	-	3.61
Wright (cdp)	2.32	2.60	-	-	-	-	-	-	-	-	-	-	-	-	-	-	-	-	-	-	-	-	-	-
Orange County	2.61	3.05	3.04	2.99	-	-	2.91	-	3.07	-	-	-	-	2.24	2.73	-	-	4.09	-	-	-	-	-	3.50
Oak Ridge (cdp)	3.01	3.30	-	-	-	-	-	-	-	-	-	-	-	-	-	-	-	-	-	-	-	-	-	3.65
Osceola County	2.79	3.20	-	3.96	-	-	2.66	-	3.31	-	-	-	-	-	-	-	-	-	-	-	-	-	-	-
Palm Beach County	2.34	2.92	3.16	2.96	-	-	2.77	-	2.85	-	-	-	-	2.02	2.34	-	-	-	-	-	-	2.89	-	3.39
Pasco County	2.30	3.14	-	3.73	-	-	2.81	-	2.75	-	-	-	-	-	-	-	-	-	-	-	-	-	-	-
Pinellas County	2.16	3.08	-	3.13	-	3.91	2.64	-	2.79	-	-	-	-	2.08	2.35	3.99	-	-	-	-	-	3.24	-	3.49
Pinellas Park (city)	2.30	3.37	-	-	-	-	-	-	-	-	-	-	-	-	-	-	-	-	-	-	-	-	-	3.23
Polk County	2.52	3.25	-	3.33	-	-	2.98	-	3.29	-	-	-	-	-	-	3.98	-	-	-	-	-	-	-	4.00
Putnam County	2.48	3.37	-	-	-	-	-	-	-	-	-	-	-	-	-	-	-	-	-	-	-	-	-	-
St. Johns County	2.44	2.68	-	-	-	-	-	-	-	-	-	-	-	-	-	-	-	-	-	-	-	-	-	-
St. Lucie County	2.47	3.22	-	-	-	-	-	-	-	-	-	-	-	-	-	-	-	-	-	-	-	-	-	-
Santa Rosa County	2.63	3.08	-	-	-	-	-	-	2.76	-	-	-	-	-	-	-	-	-	-	-	-	-	-	-
Sarasota County	2.13	2.94	-	-	-	-	2.62	-	2.76	-	-	-	-	-	-	-	-	-	-	-	-	-	-	3.99
Seminole County	2.59	3.06	-	3.22	-	-	2.99	-	2.83	-	-	-	-	-	2.88	-	-	-	-	-	-	-	-	3.88
Volusia County	2.32	2.67	-	3.18	-	-	2.16	-	3.05	-	-	-	-	-	2.20	-	-	-	-	-	-	-	-	-

Notes: Please refer to the User's Guide for an explanation of data; data is arranged alphabetically by state, then county, then city within each county; table includes counties with populations greater than 49,999 unless noted and cities with populations greater than 9,999 whose Asian and/or NHPI population rates are greater than the national average; (1) Native Hawaiian and other Pacific Islander; (2) excludes Taiwanese; (3) includes Chamorro; (4) county does not meet population threshold but is shown in order to allow inclusion of city

Language Spoken at Home: English Only

(Universe: Population 5 Years and Over)

Place	Total population 5 years and over who speak English-only at home	Asian population 5 years and over	Asians 5 years and over who speak English-only at home	NHPI[1] population 5 years and over	NHPIs[1] 5 years and over who speak English-only at home	Asian Indian	Bangladeshi	Cambodian	Chinese[2]	Fijian	Filipino	Guamanian[3]	Hawaiian, Native	Hmong	Indonesian	Japanese	Korean	Laotian	Malaysian	Pakistani	Samoan	Sri Lankan	Taiwanese	Thai	Tongan	Vietnamese
UNITED STATES	215,423,557	9,520,205	2,003,642	347,400	195,395	292,374	1,536	13,874	322,586	1,565	517,234	28,796	108,611	6,566	5,855	405,791	183,215	11,151	1,960	10,887	27,622	4,553	9,368	20,712	4,175	71,438
	82.11		21.05		56.24	19.30	4.09	8.43	14.95	16.31	29.31	56.44	83.03	4.39	16.71	52.73	18.06	7.18	19.18	7.73	35.88	25.34	7.99	19.23	17.04	6.94
						14.59	0.08	0.69	16.10	0.80	25.81	14.74	55.59	0.33	0.29	20.25	9.14	0.56	0.10	0.54	14.14	0.23	0.47	1.03	2.14	3.57
			21.05		56.24	3.07	0.02	0.15	3.39	0.45	5.43	8.29	31.26	0.07	0.06	4.26	1.92	0.12	0.02	0.11	7.95	0.05	0.10	0.22	1.20	0.75
			0.93		0.09	0.14	<0.01	0.01	0.15	<0.01	0.24	0.01	0.05	<0.01	<0.01	0.19	0.09	0.01	<0.01	0.01	0.01	<0.01	<0.01	0.01	<0.01	0.03
FLORIDA	11,569,739	248,294	65,032	6,416	3,558	21,428	32	351	9,153	-	16,338	829	1,519	-	126	4,185	4,264	382	-	483	359	114	393	1,593	-	2,713
	76.91		26.19		55.46	34.05	2.80	13.36	21.90		31.41	43.86	81.54		14.96	38.08	23.55	10.07		9.69	45.79	29.84	20.01	25.02		8.73
						32.95	0.05	0.54	14.07		25.12	23.30	42.69		0.19	6.44	6.56	0.59		0.74	10.09	0.18	0.60	2.45		4.17
			26.19		55.46	8.63	0.01	0.14	3.69		6.58	12.92	23.68		0.05	1.69	1.72	0.15		0.19	5.60	0.05	0.16	0.64		1.09
			0.56		0.03	0.19	<0.01	<0.01	0.08		0.14	0.01	0.01		<0.01	0.04	0.04	<0.01		<0.01	<0.01	<0.01	<0.01	0.01		0.02
Alachua County	183,049	7,539	1,753	-	-	544	-	-	177	-	505	-	-	-	-	147	95	-	-	-	-	-	-	-	-	114
	88.49		23.25			28.44			8.77		49.90					36.12	10.17									18.87
						31.03			10.10		28.81					8.39	5.42									6.50
			23.25			7.22			2.35		6.70					1.95	1.26									1.51
			0.96			0.30			0.10		0.28					0.08	0.05									0.06
Gainesville (city)	78,746	4,202	854	-	-	290	-	-	110	-	-	-	-	-	-	-	48	-	-	-	-	-	-	-	-	-
	86.29		20.32			27.94			7.99								10.55									
						33.96			12.88								5.62									
			20.32			6.90			2.62								1.14									
			1.08			0.37			0.14								0.06									
Bay County	130,288	2,236	582	-	-	-	-	-	-	-	150	-	-	-	-	-	-	-	-	-	-	-	-	-	-	80
	93.59		26.03								32.61															13.31
											25.77															13.75
			26.03								6.71															3.58
			0.45								0.12															0.06
Callaway (city)	12,151	485	156	-	-	-	-	-	-	-	-	-	-	-	-	-	-	-	-	-	-	-	-	-	-	-
	92.05		32.16																							
			32.16																							
			1.28																							
Brevard County	412,102	6,768	1,937	-	-	515	-	-	225	-	494	-	-	-	-	275	121	-	-	-	-	-	-	-	-	116
	91.26		28.62			28.31			27.08		33.86					52.38	19.64									15.68
						26.59			11.62		25.50					14.20	6.25									5.99
			28.62			7.61			3.32		7.30					4.06	1.79									1.71
			0.47			0.12			0.05		0.12					0.07	0.03									0.03
Broward County	1,083,041	33,911	11,197	602	390	5,904	-	-	1,848	-	1,494	-	-	-	-	396	523	-	-	85	-	-	-	170	-	262
	71.21		33.02		64.78	48.99			23.34		31.98					38.56	24.94			8.23				29.57		10.16
						52.73			16.50		13.34					3.54	4.67			0.76				1.52		2.34
			33.02		64.78	17.41			5.45		4.41					1.17	1.54			0.25				0.50		0.77
			1.03		0.04	0.55			0.17		0.14					0.04	0.05			0.01				0.02		0.02
Cooper City (city)	19,666	1,204	249	-	-	126	-	-	-	-	-	-	-	-	-	-	-	-	-	-	-	-	-	-	-	-
	75.27		20.68			22.66																				
						50.60																				
			20.68			10.47																				
			1.27			0.64																				

Notes: Please refer to the User's Guide for an explanation of data; data is arranged alphabetically by state, then county, then city within each county; table includes counties with populations greater than 49,999 unless noted and cities with populations greater than 9,999 whose Asian and/or NHPI population rates are greater than the national average; (1) Native Hawaiian and other Pacific Islander; (2) excludes Taiwanese; (3) includes Chamorro; (4) county does not meet population threshold but is shown in order to allow inclusion of city

Place	Total population 5 years and over who speak English-only at home	Asian population 5 years and over	Asians 5 years and over who speak English-only at home	NHPI[1] population 5 years and over	NHPIs[1] 5 years and over who speak English-only at home	Asian Indian	Bangladeshi	Cambodian	Chinese[2]	Fijian	Filipino	Guamanian[3]	Hawaiian, Native	Hmong	Indonesian	Japanese	Korean	Laotian	Malaysian	Pakistani	Samoan	Sri Lankan	Taiwanese	Thai	Tongan	Vietnamese
Pembroke Pines (city)	79,783 62.55	4,512	1,377 30.52 30.52 1.73	-	-	665 42.63 48.29 14.74 0.83	-	-	288 27.88 20.92 6.38 0.36	-	216 24.41 15.69 4.79 0.27	-	-	-	-	-	-	-	-	-	-	-	-	-	-	-
Charlotte County	125,400 91.76	855	138 16.14 16.14 0.11	-	-	-	-	-	-	-	-	-	-	-	-	-	-	-	-	-	-	-	-	-	-	-
Citrus County	106,153 93.41	1,086	275 25.32 25.32 0.26	-	-	-	-	-	-	-	-	-	-	-	-	-	-	-	-	-	-	-	-	-	-	-
Clay County	121,540 92.27	2,731	829 30.36 30.36 0.68	-	-	-	-	-	-	-	465 27.91 56.09 17.03 0.38	-	-	-	-	-	-	-	-	-	-	-	-	-	-	-
Bellair-Meadowbrook Ter. (cdp)	13,670 88.27	608	137 22.53 22.53 1.00	-	-	-	-	-	-	-	-	-	-	-	-	-	-	-	-	-	-	-	-	-	-	-
Collier County	178,413 74.94	1,093	471 43.09 43.09 0.26	-	-	-	-	-	-	-	-	-	-	-	-	-	-	-	-	-	-	-	-	-	-	-
Columbia County	50,221 94.93	373	91 24.40 24.40 0.18	-	-	-	-	-	-	-	-	-	-	-	-	-	-	-	-	-	-	-	-	-	-	-
Duval County	654,825 90.55	19,316	4,871 25.22 25.22 0.74	427	260 60.89 60.89 0.04	438 17.77 8.99 2.27 0.07	-	106 11.22 2.18 0.55 0.02	217 14.11 4.45 1.12 0.03	-	3,303 33.84 67.81 17.10 0.50	-	-	-	-	224 41.79 4.60 1.16 0.03	147 16.33 3.02 0.76 0.02	-	-	-	-	-	-	-	-	126 6.54 2.59 0.65 0.02
Escambia County	257,796 93.19	6,215	1,704 27.42 27.42 0.66	-	-	111 24.61 6.51 1.79 0.04	-	-	75 13.49 4.40 1.21 0.03	-	1,011 37.96 59.33 16.27 0.39	-	-	-	-	-	-	-	-	-	-	-	-	-	-	123 8.52 7.22 1.98 0.05
Bellview (cdp)	18,455 93.50	747	266 35.61 35.61 1.44	-	-	-	-	-	-	-	155 38.37 58.27 20.75 0.84	-	-	-	-	-	-	-	-	-	-	-	-	-	-	-

Notes: Please refer to the User's Guide for an explanation of data; data is arranged alphabetically by state, then county, then city within each county; table includes counties with populations greater than 49,999 unless noted and cities with populations greater than 9,999 whose Asian and/or NHPI population rates are greater than the national average; (1) Native Hawaiian and other Pacific Islander; (2) excludes Taiwanese; (3) includes Chamorro; (4) county does not meet population threshold but is shown in order to allow inclusion of city

Place	Total population 5 years and over who speak English-only at home	Asian population 5 years and over	Asians 5 years and over who speak English-only at home	NHPI[1] population 5 years and over	NHPIs[1] 5 years and over who speak English-only at home	Asian Indian	Bangladeshi	Cambodian	Chinese[2]	Fijian	Filipino	Guamanian[3]	Hawaiian, Native	Hmong	Indonesian	Japanese	Korean	Laotian	Malaysian	Pakistani	Samoan	Sri Lankan	Taiwanese	Thai	Tongan	Vietnamese
Myrtle Grove (cdp)	14,689 90.63	775	237 30.58 30.58 1.61	-	-	-	-	-	-	-	175 37.88 73.84 22.58 1.19	-	-	-	-	-	-	-	-	-	-	-	-	-	-	-
Hernando County	113,262 90.67	704	200 28.41 28.41 0.18	-	-	-	-	-	-	-	-	-	-	-	-	-	-	-	-	-	-	-	-	-	-	-
Highlands County	71,297 86.12	892	143 16.03 16.03 0.20	-	-	-	-	-	-	-	87 20.76 60.84 9.75 0.12	-	-	-	-	-	-	-	-	-	-	-	-	-	-	-
Hillsborough County	736,750 79.11	20,228	4,820 23.83 23.83 0.65	523	433 82.79 82.79 0.06	1,358 25.15 28.17 6.71 0.18	-	-	607 24.48 12.59 3.00 0.08	-	1,013 33.12 21.02 5.01 0.14	-	-	-	-	382 45.42 7.93 1.89 0.05	537 20.77 11.14 2.65 0.07	-	-	-	-	-	-	156 23.93 3.24 0.77 0.02	-	299 7.90 6.20 1.48 0.04
Westchase (cdp)	8,301 83.51	475	170 35.79 35.79 2.05	-	-	-	-	-	-	-	-	-	-	-	-	-	-	-	-	-	-	-	-	-	-	-
Indian River County	96,498 89.56	806	213 26.43 26.43 0.22	-	-	-	-	-	-	-	-	-	-	-	-	-	-	-	-	-	-	-	-	-	-	-
Lake County	182,724 91.56	1,308	329 25.15 25.15 0.18	-	-	-	-	-	-	-	-	-	-	-	-	-	-	-	-	-	-	-	-	-	-	-
Lee County	361,208 86.46	2,970	878 29.56 29.56 0.24	-	-	138 23.27 15.72 4.65 0.04	-	-	216 38.85 24.60 7.27 0.06	-	278 26.55 31.66 9.36 0.08	-	-	-	-	-	-	-	-	-	-	-	-	-	-	-
Leon County	208,570 92.40	4,470	1,343 30.04 30.04 0.64	-	-	576 41.26 42.89 12.89 0.28	-	-	188 19.85 14.00 4.21 0.09	-	189 38.10 14.07 4.23 0.09	-	-	-	-	-	75 18.89 5.58 1.68 0.04	-	-	-	-	-	-	-	-	-
Manatee County	218,481 87.74	2,173	524 24.11 24.11 0.24	-	-	-	-	-	-	-	121 22.49 23.09 5.57 0.06	-	-	-	-	-	-	-	-	-	-	-	-	-	-	-

Notes: Please refer to the User's Guide for an explanation of data; data is arranged alphabetically by state, then county, then city within each county; table includes counties with populations greater than 49,999 unless noted and cities with populations greater than 9,999 whose Asian and/or NHPI population rates are greater than the national average; (1) Native Hawaiian and other Pacific Islander; (2) excludes Taiwanese; (3) includes Chamorro; (4) county does not meet population threshold but is shown in order to allow inclusion of city

Place	Total population 5 years and over who speak English-only at home	Asian population 5 years and over	Asians 5 years and over who speak English-only at home	NHPI[1] population 5 years and over	NHPIs[1] 5 years and over who speak English-only at home	Asian Indian	Bangladeshi	Cambodian	Chinese[2]	Fijian	Filipino	Guamanian[3]	Hawaiian, Native	Hmong	Indonesian	Japanese	Korean	Laotian	Malaysian	Pakistani	Samoan	Sri Lankan	Taiwanese	Thai	Tongan	Vietnamese
Marion County	224,174 91.19	2,044	710 34.74 34.74 0.32	-	-	342 39.63 48.17 16.73 0.15	-	-	-	-	-	-	-	-	-	-	-	-	-	-	-	-	-	-	-	-
Martin County	107,584 88.71	690	286 41.45 41.45 0.27	-	-	-	-	-	-	-	-	-	-	-	-	-	-	-	-	-	-	-	-	-	-	-
Miami-Dade County	676,347 32.08	28,911	7,409 25.63 25.63 1.10	599	264 44.07 44.07 0.04	3,346 39.94 45.16 11.57 0.49	-	-	1,993 23.81 26.90 6.89 0.29	-	746 17.36 10.07 2.58 0.11	-	-	-	-	231 17.04 3.12 0.80 0.03	210 16.50 2.83 0.73 0.03	-	-	23 3.16 0.31 0.08 <0.01	-	-	-	168 19.47 2.27 0.58 0.02	-	191 13.19 2.58 0.66 0.03
Doral (cdp)	2,898 15.64	1,047	74 7.07 7.07 2.55	-	-	-	-	-	-	-	-	-	-	-	-	-	-	-	-	-	-	-	-	-	-	-
Ives Estates (cdp)	8,535 52.60	756	131 17.33 17.33 1.53	-	-	-	-	-	-	-	-	-	-	-	-	-	-	-	-	-	-	-	-	-	-	-
North Miami Beach (city)	14,349 37.82	1,632	292 17.89 17.89 2.03	-	-	159 44.29 54.45 9.74 1.11	-	-	67 9.12 22.95 4.11 0.47	-	-	-	-	-	-	-	-	-	-	-	-	-	-	-	-	-
Pinecrest (village)	10,057 56.03	818	127 15.53 15.53 1.26	-	-	-	-	-	-	-	-	-	-	-	-	-	-	-	-	-	-	-	-	-	-	-
Monroe County	59,964 78.59	528	165 31.25 31.25 0.28	-	-	-	-	-	-	-	-	-	-	-	-	-	-	-	-	-	-	-	-	-	-	-
Nassau County	52,061 96.15	401	203 50.62 50.62 0.39	-	-	-	-	-	-	-	-	-	-	-	-	-	-	-	-	-	-	-	-	-	-	-
Okaloosa County	147,138 92.11	4,218	1,330 31.53 31.53 0.90	-	-	-	-	-	-	-	588 36.18 44.21 13.94 0.40	-	-	-	-	-	126 18.42 9.47 2.99 0.09	-	-	-	-	-	-	183 29.66 13.76 4.34 0.12	-	66 17.28 4.96 1.56 0.04

Notes: Please refer to the User's Guide for an explanation of data; data is arranged alphabetically by state, then county, then city within each county; table includes counties with populations greater than 49,999 unless noted and cities with populations greater than 9,999 whose Asian and/or NHPI population rates are greater than the national average; (1) Native Hawaiian and other Pacific Islander; (2) excludes Taiwanese; (3) includes Chamorro; (4) county does not meet population threshold but is shown in order to allow inclusion of city

Place	Total population 5 years and over who speak English-only at home	Asian population 5 years and over	Asians 5 years and over who speak English-only at home	NHPI[1] population 5 years and over	NHPIs[1] 5 years and over who speak English-only at home	Asian Indian	Bangladeshi	Cambodian	Chinese[2]	Fijian	Filipino	Guamanian[3]	Hawaiian, Native	Hmong	Indonesian	Japanese	Korean	Laotian	Malaysian	Pakistani	Samoan	Sri Lankan	Taiwanese	Thai	Tongan	Vietnamese
Wright (cdp)	18,487 91.42	786	230 29.26 29.26 1.24	-	-	-	-	-	-	-	-	-	-	-	-	-	-	-	-	-	-	-	-	-	-	-
Orange County	622,997 74.58	27,026	6,439 23.83 23.83 1.03	784	315 40.18 40.18 0.05	2,591 35.89 40.24 9.59 0.42	-	-	646 17.42 10.03 2.39 0.10	-	1,529 35.30 23.75 5.66 0.25	-	-	-	-	349 30.80 5.42 1.29 0.06	332 16.14 5.16 1.23 0.05	-	-	93 11.51 1.44 0.34 0.01	-	-	-	-	-	421 7.09 6.54 1.56 0.07
Oak Ridge (cdp)	8,435 41.16	1,169	138 11.80 11.80 1.64	-	-	-	-	-	-	-	-	-	-	-	-	-	-	-	-	-	-	-	-	-	-	7 1.51 5.07 0.60 0.08
Osceola County	107,397 66.70	3,401	744 21.88 21.88 0.69	-	-	246 28.47 33.06 7.23 0.23	-	-	76 13.36 10.22 2.23 0.07	-	248 28.94 33.33 7.29 0.23	-	-	-	-	-	-	-	-	-	-	-	-	-	-	-
Palm Beach County	837,066 78.28	15,958	4,085 25.60 25.60 0.49	396	215 54.29 54.29 0.03	1,549 32.26 37.92 9.71 0.19	-	-	701 20.44 17.16 4.39 0.08	-	593 27.74 14.52 3.72 0.07	-	-	-	-	179 32.78 4.38 1.12 0.02	309 33.99 7.56 1.94 0.04	-	-	-	-	-	-	159 22.08 3.89 1.00 0.02	-	209 11.02 5.12 1.31 0.02
Pasco County	293,294 89.72	3,260	854 26.20 26.20 0.29	-	-	196 21.63 22.95 6.01 0.07	-	-	66 14.35 7.73 2.02 0.02	-	316 32.58 37.00 9.69 0.11	-	-	-	-	-	-	-	-	-	-	-	-	-	-	-
Pinellas County	771,726 88.04	17,689	3,363 19.01 19.01 0.44	-	-	894 26.03 26.58 5.05 0.12	-	49 7.18 1.46 0.28 0.01	384 19.82 11.42 2.17 0.05	-	761 26.77 22.63 4.30 0.10	-	-	-	-	157 27.94 4.67 0.89 0.02	280 34.57 8.33 1.58 0.04	108 6.17 3.21 0.61 0.01	-	-	-	-	-	168 35.74 5.00 0.95 0.02	-	238 5.97 7.08 1.35 0.03
Pinellas Park (city)	37,192 87.10	1,680	200 11.90 11.90 0.54	-	-	-	-	-	-	-	-	-	-	-	-	-	-	-	-	-	-	-	-	-	-	26 5.32 13.00 1.55 0.07
Polk County	398,332 87.90	5,315	1,074 20.21 20.21 0.27	-	-	212 13.70 19.74 3.99 0.05	-	-	148 27.61 13.78 2.78 0.04	-	175 20.11 16.29 3.29 0.04	-	-	-	-	-	-	71 19.19 6.61 1.34 0.02	-	-	-	-	-	-	-	94 12.45 8.75 1.77 0.02
Putnam County	61,253 92.75	284	99 34.86 34.86 0.16	-	-	-	-	-	-	-	-	-	-	-	-	-	-	-	-	-	-	-	-	-	-	-

Notes: Please refer to the User's Guide for an explanation of data; data is arranged alphabetically by state, then county, then city within each county; table includes counties with populations greater than 49,999 unless noted and cities with populations greater than 9,999 whose Asian and/or NHPI population rates are greater than the national average; (1) Native Hawaiian and other Pacific Islander; (2) excludes Taiwanese; (3) includes Chamorro; (4) county does not meet population threshold but is shown in order to allow inclusion of city

Place	Total population 5 years and over who speak English-only at home	Asian population 5 years and over	Asians 5 years and over who speak English-only at home	NHPI[1] population 5 years and over	NHPIs[1] 5 years and over who speak English-only at home	Asian Indian	Bangladeshi	Cambodian	Chinese[2]	Fijian	Filipino	Guamanian[3]	Hawaiian, Native	Hmong	Indonesian	Japanese	Korean	Laotian	Malaysian	Pakistani	Samoan	Sri Lankan	Taiwanese	Thai	Tongan	Vietnamese
St. Johns County	108,870 93.28	1,168	411 35.19 35.19 0.38	-	-	-	-	-	-	-	-	-	-	-	-	-	-	-	-	-	-	-	-	-	-	-
St. Lucie County	156,941 86.22	1,758	366 20.82 20.82 0.23	-	-	-	-	-	-	-	-	-	-	-	-	-	-	-	-	-	-	-	-	-	-	-
Santa Rosa County	104,132 94.69	1,537	417 27.13 27.13 0.40	-	-	-	-	-	-	-	220 32.21 52.76 14.31 0.21	-	-	-	-	-	-	-	-	-	-	-	-	-	-	-
Sarasota County	280,340 89.47	2,502	698 27.90 27.90 0.25	-	-	-	-	-	87 23.97 12.46 3.48 0.03	-	230 42.59 32.95 9.19 0.08	-	-	-	-	-	-	-	-	-	-	-	-	-	-	55 8.38 7.88 2.20 0.02
Seminole County	288,646 84.41	8,122	1,965 24.19 24.19 0.68	-	-	743 28.47 37.81 9.15 0.26	-	-	313 24.40 15.93 3.85 0.11	-	426 34.47 21.68 5.25 0.15	-	-	-	-	-	123 13.53 6.26 1.51 0.04	-	-	-	-	-	-	-	-	83 8.38 4.22 1.02 0.03
Volusia County	376,145 89.23	4,589	1,337 29.13 29.13 0.36	-	-	432 28.37 32.31 9.41 0.11	-	-	136 22.19 10.17 2.96 0.04	-	263 32.00 19.67 5.73 0.07	-	-	-	-	-	127 28.93 9.50 2.77 0.03	-	-	-	-	-	-	-	-	-

Notes: Please refer to the User's Guide for an explanation of data; data is arranged alphabetically by state, then county, then city within each county; table includes counties with populations greater than 49,999 unless noted and cities with populations greater than 9,999 whose Asian and/or NHPI population rates are greater than the national average; (1) Native Hawaiian and other Pacific Islander; (2) excludes Taiwanese; (3) includes Chamorro; (4) county does not meet population threshold but is shown in order to allow inclusion of city

Foreign Born

(Universe: Total Population)

Place	Total foreign-born population	Total Asian population	Asians who are foreign born	Total NHPI[1] population	NHPIs[1] who are foreign born	Asian Indian	Bangladeshi	Cambodian	Chinese[2]	Fijian	Filipino	Guamanian[3]	Hawaiian, Native	Hmong	Indonesian	Japanese	Korean	Laotian	Malaysian	Pakistani	Samoan	Sri Lankan	Taiwanese	Thai	Tongan	Vietnamese
	31,107,889	10,171,820	7,012,202	378,782	75,477	1,240,755	34,353	117,164	1,621,997	7,968	1,261,611	6,842	3,019	94,583	30,788	314,178	833,454	114,300	9,510	117,723	17,858	15,767	94,685	86,242	14,221	844,893
	11.05		68.94		19.93	75.40	82.92	65.81	70.51	77.62	67.68	12.41	2.16	55.62	82.84	39.52	77.70	68.12	88.79	75.51	20.95	82.64	77.14	77.80	51.37	76.10
UNITED STATES						17.69	0.49	1.67	23.13	10.56	17.99	9.07	4.00	1.35	0.44	4.48	11.89	1.63	0.14	1.68	23.66	0.22	1.35	1.23	18.84	12.05
			68.94		19.93	12.20	0.34	1.15	15.95	2.10	12.40	1.81	0.80	0.93	0.30	3.09	8.19	1.12	0.09	1.16	4.71	0.16	0.93	0.85	3.75	8.31
			22.54		0.24	3.99	0.11	0.38	5.21	0.03	4.06	0.02	0.01	0.30	0.10	1.01	2.68	0.37	0.03	0.38	0.06	0.05	0.30	0.28	0.05	2.72
	2,670,828	264,377	196,638	6,812	1,771	51,515	1,060	2,118	33,776	-	39,071	534	98	-	801	7,916	15,001	2,992	-	3,953	246	326	1,529	5,353	-	25,753
	16.71		74.38		26.00	75.99	84.13	76.68	75.28		71.91	26.44	4.97		89.60	69.77	78.63	74.22		72.59	28.98	81.09	75.43	81.45		77.13
FLORIDA						26.20	0.54	1.08	17.18		19.87	30.15	5.53		0.41	4.03	7.63	1.52		2.01	13.89	0.17	0.78	2.72		13.10
			74.38		26.00	19.49	0.40	0.80	12.78		14.78	7.84	1.44		0.30	2.99	5.67	1.13		1.50	3.61	0.12	0.58	2.02		9.74
			7.36		0.07	1.93	0.04	0.08	1.26		1.46	0.02	<0.01		0.03	0.30	0.56	0.11		0.15	0.01	0.01	0.06	0.20		0.96
	15,895	7,858	5,532	-	-	1,264	-	-	1,604	-	640	-	-	-	-	306	833	-	-	-	-	-	-	-	-	453
	7.29		70.40			64.85			75.13		61.19					70.67	82.89									73.42
Alachua County						22.85			28.99		11.57					5.53	15.06									8.19
			70.40			16.09			20.41		8.14					3.89	10.60									5.76
			34.80			7.95			10.09		4.03					1.93	5.24									2.85
	8,320	4,399	3,191	-	-	692	-	-	1,193	-	-	-	-	-	-	-	388	-	-	-	-	-	-	-	-	-
	8.70		72.54			65.53			81.94								77.45									
Gainesville (city)						21.69			37.39								12.16									
			72.54			15.73			27.12								8.82									
			38.35			8.32			14.34								4.66									
	5,382	2,369	1,615	-	-	-	-	-	-	-	357	-	-	-	-	-	-	-	-	-	-	-	-	-	-	390
	3.63		68.17								73.76															58.56
Bay County											22.11															24.15
			68.17								15.07															16.46
			30.01								6.63															7.25
	848	530	318	-	-	-	-	-	-	-	-	-	-	-	-	-	-	-	-	-	-	-	-	-	-	-
	5.95		60.00																							
Callaway (city)																										
			60.00																							
			37.50																							
	31,001	7,122	5,383	-	-	1,577	-	-	698	-	1,088	-	-	-	-	293	538	-	-	-	-	-	-	-	-	561
	6.51		75.58			80.01			78.25		70.79					55.81	86.63									73.53
Brevard County						29.30			12.97		20.21					5.44	9.99									10.42
			75.58			22.14			9.80		15.28					4.11	7.55									7.88
			17.36			5.09			2.25		3.51					0.95	1.74									1.81
	410,387	36,505	27,766	645	239	10,283	-	-	6,404	-	3,609	-	-	-	-	725	1,727	-	-	837	-	-	-	470	-	2,211
	25.29		76.06		37.05	79.05			74.85		74.11					69.38	76.42			76.30				78.46		77.12
Broward County						37.03			23.06		13.00					2.61	6.22			3.01				1.69		7.96
			76.06		37.05	28.17			17.54		9.89					1.99	4.73			2.29				1.29		6.06
			6.77		0.06	2.51			1.56		0.88					0.18	0.42			0.20				0.11		0.54
	4,684	1,241	936	-	-	481	-	-	-	-	-	-	-	-	-	-	-	-	-	-	-	-	-	-	-	-
	16.92		75.42			81.11																				
Cooper City (city)						51.39																				
			75.42			38.76																				
			19.98			10.27																				

Notes: Please refer to the User's Guide for an explanation of data; data is arranged alphabetically by state, then county, then city within each county; table includes counties with populations greater than 49,999 unless noted and cities with populations greater than 9,999 whose Asian and/or NHPI population rates are greater than the national average; (1) Native Hawaiian and other Pacific Islander; (2) excludes Taiwanese; (3) includes Chamorro; (4) county does not meet population threshold but is shown in order to allow inclusion of city

Place	Total foreign-born population	Total Asian population	Asians who are foreign born	Total NHPI[1] population	NHPIs[1] who are foreign born	Asian Indian	Bangladeshi	Cambodian	Chinese[2]	Fijian	Filipino	Guamanian[3]	Hawaiian, Native	Hmong	Indonesian	Japanese	Korean	Laotian	Malaysian	Pakistani	Samoan	Sri Lankan	Taiwanese	Thai	Tongan	Vietnamese
Pembroke Pines (city)	39,727 28.97	5,004	3,758 75.10 75.10 9.46	-	-	1,346 76.83 35.82 26.90 3.39	-	-	847 73.46 22.54 16.93 2.13	-	754 81.34 20.06 15.07 1.90	-	-	-	-	-	-	-	-	-	-	-	-	-	-	-
Charlotte County	11,292 7.97	872	734 84.17 84.17 6.50	-	-	-	-	-	-	-	-	-	-	-	-	-	-	-	-	-	-	-	-	-	-	-
Citrus County	5,742 4.86	1,145	836 73.01 73.01 14.56	-	-	-	-	-	-	-	-	-	-	-	-	-	-	-	-	-	-	-	-	-	-	-
Clay County	6,356 4.51	2,901	2,198 75.77 75.77 34.58	-	-	-	-	-	-	-	1,356 78.65 61.69 46.74 21.33	-	-	-	-	-	-	-	-	-	-	-	-	-	-	-
Bellair-Meadowbrook Ter. (cdp)	1,063 6.42	635	526 82.83 82.83 49.48	-	-	-	-	-	-	-	-	-	-	-	-	-	-	-	-	-	-	-	-	-	-	-
Collier County	46,071 18.33	1,200	889 74.08 74.08 1.93	-	-	-	-	-	-	-	-	-	-	-	-	-	-	-	-	-	-	-	-	-	-	-
Columbia County	1,316 2.33	386	277 71.76 71.76 21.05	-	-	-	-	-	-	-	-	-	-	-	-	-	-	-	-	-	-	-	-	-	-	-
Duval County	45,651 5.86	20,554	14,268 69.42 69.42 31.25	507	36 7.10 7.10 0.08	2,086 75.39 14.62 10.15 4.57	-	725 72.43 5.08 3.53 1.59	1,097 66.81 7.69 5.34 2.40	-	6,796 66.59 47.63 33.06 14.89	-	-	-	-	362 65.82 2.54 1.76 0.79	798 82.52 5.59 3.88 1.75	-	-	-	-	-	-	-	-	1,570 74.34 11.00 7.64 3.44
Escambia County	10,821 3.68	6,565	4,291 65.36 65.36 39.65	-	-	356 68.99 8.30 5.42 3.29	-	-	400 68.14 9.32 6.09 3.70	-	1,759 64.74 40.99 26.79 16.26	-	-	-	-	-	-	-	-	-	-	-	-	-	-	1,053 65.94 24.54 16.04 9.73
Bellview (cdp)	874 4.15	787	467 59.34 59.34 53.43	-	-	-	-	-	-	-	266 64.56 56.96 33.80 30.43	-	-	-	-	-	-	-	-	-	-	-	-	-	-	-

Notes: Please refer to the User's Guide for an explanation of data; data is arranged alphabetically by state, then county, then city within each county; table includes counties with populations greater than 49,999 unless noted and cities with populations greater than 9,999 whose Asian and/or NHPI population rates are greater than the national average; (1) Native Hawaiian and other Pacific Islander; (2) excludes Taiwanese; (3) includes Chamorro; (4) county does not meet population threshold but is shown in order to allow inclusion of city

Place	Total foreign-born population	Total Asian population	Asians who are foreign born	Total NHPI[1] population	NHPIs[1] who are foreign born	Asian Indian	Bangladeshi	Cambodian	Chinese[2]	Fijian	Filipino	Guamanian[3]	Hawaiian, Native	Hmong	Indonesian	Japanese	Korean	Laotian	Malaysian	Pakistani	Samoan	Sri Lankan	Taiwanese	Thai	Tongan	Vietnamese
Myrtle Grove (cdp)	960 5.55	812	526 64.78 64.78 54.79	-	-	-	-	-	-	-	317 67.30 60.27 39.04 33.02	-	-	-	-	-	-	-	-	-	-	-	-	-	-	-
Hernando County	6,942 5.31	773	623 80.60 80.60 8.97	-	-	-	-	-	-	-	-	-	-	-	-	-	-	-	-	-	-	-	-	-	-	-
Highlands County	7,912 9.06	964	733 76.04 76.04 9.26	-	-	-	-	-	-	-	316 70.69 43.11 32.78 3.99	-	-	-	-	-	-	-	-	-	-	-	-	-	-	-
Hillsborough County	115,151 11.53	21,571	15,847 73.46 73.46 13.76	540	77 14.26 14.26 0.07	4,182 70.87 26.39 19.39 3.63	-	-	1,987 74.17 12.54 9.21 1.73	-	2,268 70.81 14.31 10.51 1.97	-	-	-	-	541 62.69 3.41 2.51 0.47	2,087 76.78 13.17 9.68 1.81	-	-	-	-	-	-	561 82.99 3.54 2.60 0.49	-	3,230 80.89 20.38 14.97 2.81
Westchase (cdp)	1,070 9.63	508	333 65.55 65.55 31.12	-	-	-	-	-	-	-	-	-	-	-	-	-	-	-	-	-	-	-	-	-	-	-
Indian River County	9,151 8.10	864	635 73.50 73.50 6.94	-	-	-	-	-	-	-	-	-	-	-	-	-	-	-	-	-	-	-	-	-	-	-
Lake County	10,820 5.14	1,422	1,035 72.78 72.78 9.57	-	-	-	-	-	-	-	-	-	-	-	-	-	-	-	-	-	-	-	-	-	-	-
Lee County	40,362 9.15	3,159	2,414 76.42 76.42 5.98	-	-	534 79.82 22.12 16.90 1.32	-	-	418 70.13 17.32 13.23 1.04	-	815 73.82 33.76 25.80 2.02	-	-	-	-	-	-	-	-	-	-	-	-	-	-	-
Leon County	11,345 4.74	4,858	3,578 73.65 73.65 31.54	-	-	1,140 75.60 31.86 23.47 10.05	-	-	816 75.21 22.81 16.80 7.19	-	302 57.41 8.44 6.22 2.66	-	-	-	-	-	354 79.37 9.89 7.29 3.12	-	-	-	-	-	-	-	-	-
Manatee County	22,235 8.42	2,237	1,791 80.06 80.06 8.05	-	-	-	-	-	-	-	472 87.73 26.35 21.10 2.12	-	-	-	-	-	-	-	-	-	-	-	-	-	-	-

Notes: Please refer to the User's Guide for an explanation of data; data is arranged alphabetically by state, then county, then city within each county; table includes counties with populations greater than 49,999 unless noted and cities with populations greater than 9,999 whose Asian and/or NHPI population rates are greater than the national average; (1) Native Hawaiian and other Pacific Islander; (2) excludes Taiwanese; (3) includes Chamorro; (4) county does not meet population threshold but is shown in order to allow inclusion of city

Place	Total foreign-born population	Total Asian population	Asians who are foreign born	Total NHPI[1] population	NHPIs[1] who are foreign born	Asian Indian	Bangladeshi	Cambodian	Chinese[2]	Fijian	Filipino	Guamanian[3]	Hawaiian, Native	Hmong	Indonesian	Japanese	Korean	Laotian	Malaysian	Pakistani	Samoan	Sri Lankan	Taiwanese	Thai	Tongan	Vietnamese
Marion County	13,352 5.16	2,221	1,526 68.71 68.71 11.43	-	-	643 67.76 42.14 28.95 4.82	-	-	-	-	-	-	-	-	-	-	-	-	-	-	-	-	-	-	-	-
Martin County	10,318 8.14	701	549 78.32 78.32 5.32	-	-	-	-	-	-	-	-	-	-	-	-	-	-	-	-	-	-	-	-	-	-	-
Miami-Dade County	1,147,765 50.94	30,692	23,901 77.87 77.87 2.08	605	394 65.12 65.12 0.03	6,825 76.36 28.56 22.24 0.59	-	-	6,951 78.20 29.08 22.65 0.61	-	3,586 79.32 15.00 11.68 0.31	-	-	-	-	1,180 84.05 4.94 3.84 0.10	1,008 75.45 4.22 3.28 0.09	-	-	685 86.27 2.87 2.23 0.06	-	-	-	734 83.22 3.07 2.39 0.06	-	1,281 80.31 5.36 4.17 0.11
Doral (cdp)	12,831 62.55	1,186	1,010 85.16 85.16 7.87	-	-	-	-	-	-	-	-	-	-	-	-	-	-	-	-	-	-	-	-	-	-	-
Ives Estates (cdp)	7,092 40.72	831	646 77.74 77.74 9.11	-	-	-	-	-	-	-	-	-	-	-	-	-	-	-	-	-	-	-	-	-	-	-
North Miami Beach (city)	20,201 49.67	1,706	1,374 80.54 80.54 6.80	-	-	307 77.53 22.34 18.00 1.52	-	-	591 79.76 43.01 34.64 2.93	-	-	-	-	-	-	-	-	-	-	-	-	-	-	-	-	-
Pinecrest (village)	5,302 27.64	884	684 77.38 77.38 12.90	-	-	-	-	-	-	-	-	-	-	-	-	-	-	-	-	-	-	-	-	-	-	-
Monroe County	11,732 14.74	566	407 71.91 71.91 3.47	-	-	-	-	-	-	-	-	-	-	-	-	-	-	-	-	-	-	-	-	-	-	-
Nassau County	1,541 2.67	422	346 81.99 81.99 22.45	-	-	-	-	-	-	-	-	-	-	-	-	-	-	-	-	-	-	-	-	-	-	-
Okaloosa County	8,984 5.27	4,432	3,036 68.50 68.50 33.79	-	-	-	-	-	-	-	1,183 67.91 38.97 26.69 13.17	-	-	-	-	-	581 80.69 19.14 13.11 6.47	-	-	-	-	-	-	518 83.01 17.06 11.69 5.77	-	225 56.25 7.41 5.08 2.50

Notes: Please refer to the User's Guide for an explanation of data; data is arranged alphabetically by state, then county, then city within each county; table includes counties with populations greater than 49,999 unless noted and cities with populations greater than 9,999 whose Asian and/or NHPI population rates are greater than the national average; (1) Native Hawaiian and other Pacific Islander; (2) excludes Taiwanese; (3) includes Chamorro; (4) county does not meet population threshold but is shown in order to allow inclusion of city

Place	Total foreign-born population	Total Asian population	Asians who are foreign born	Total NHPI[1] population	NHPIs[1] who are foreign born	Asian Indian	Bangladeshi	Cambodian	Chinese[2]	Fijian	Filipino	Guamanian[3]	Hawaiian, Native	Hmong	Indonesian	Japanese	Korean	Laotian	Malaysian	Pakistani	Samoan	Sri Lankan	Taiwanese	Thai	Tongan	Vietnamese
Wright (cdp)	1,542 7.15	825	580 70.30 70.30 37.61	-	-	-	-	-	-	-	-	-	-	-	-	-	-	-	-	-	-	-	-	-	-	-
Orange County	128,904 14.38	28,748	21,638 75.27 75.27 16.79	853	166 19.46 19.46 0.13	5,793 75.72 26.77 20.15 4.49	-	-	2,976 74.55 13.75 10.35 2.31	-	3,087 68.24 14.27 10.74 2.39	-	-	-	-	911 75.92 4.21 3.17 0.71	1,664 77.58 7.69 5.79 1.29	-	-	614 68.15 2.84 2.14 0.48	-	-	-	-	-	5,267 82.85 24.34 18.32 4.09
Oak Ridge (cdp)	7,957 35.51	1,306	974 74.58 74.58 12.24	-	-	-	-	-	-	-	-	-	-	-	-	-	-	-	-	-	-	-	-	-	-	450 85.39 46.20 34.46 5.66
Osceola County	24,110 13.98	3,642	2,712 74.46 74.46 11.25	-	-	731 75.67 26.95 20.07 3.03	-	-	459 78.60 16.92 12.60 1.90	-	626 70.89 23.08 17.19 2.60	-	-	-	-	-	-	-	-	-	-	-	-	-	-	-
Palm Beach County	196,852 17.40	16,895	12,934 76.56 76.56 6.57	423	94 22.22 22.22 0.05	4,074 79.91 31.50 24.11 2.07	-	-	2,808 77.12 21.71 16.62 1.43	-	1,666 74.44 12.88 9.86 0.85	-	-	-	-	400 69.69 3.09 2.37 0.20	728 78.11 5.63 4.31 0.37	-	-	-	-	-	-	617 81.18 4.77 3.65 0.31	-	1,550 77.73 11.98 9.17 0.79
Pasco County	24,129 7.00	3,489	2,553 73.17 73.17 10.58	-	-	764 76.94 29.93 21.90 3.17	-	-	350 69.44 13.71 10.03 1.45	-	771 77.57 30.20 22.10 3.20	-	-	-	-	-	-	-	-	-	-	-	-	-	-	-
Pinellas County	87,685 9.52	18,783	14,421 76.78 76.78 16.45	-	-	2,873 78.76 19.92 15.30 3.28	-	532 74.09 3.69 2.83 0.61	1,661 79.66 11.52 8.84 1.89	-	2,270 74.82 15.74 12.09 2.59	-	-	-	-	444 78.17 3.08 2.36 0.51	712 83.37 4.94 3.79 0.81	1,388 74.82 9.62 7.39 1.58	-	-	-	-	-	376 77.05 2.61 2.00 0.43	-	3,298 77.89 22.87 17.56 3.76
Pinellas Park (city)	4,295 9.46	1,811	1,425 78.69 78.69 33.18	-	-	-	-	-	-	-	-	-	-	-	-	-	-	-	-	-	-	-	-	-	-	391 74.33 27.44 21.59 9.10
Polk County	33,519 6.93	5,805	4,103 70.68 70.68 12.24	-	-	1,243 72.39 30.29 21.41 3.71	-	-	433 72.77 10.55 7.46 1.29	-	680 75.39 16.57 11.71 2.03	-	-	-	-	-	-	273 68.08 6.65 4.70 0.81	-	-	-	-	-	-	-	569 65.25 13.87 9.80 1.70
Putnam County	2,371 3.37	291	209 71.82 71.82 8.81	-	-	-	-	-	-	-	-	-	-	-	-	-	-	-	-	-	-	-	-	-	-	-

Notes: Please refer to the User's Guide for an explanation of data; data is arranged alphabetically by state, then county, then city within each county; table includes counties with populations greater than 49,999 unless noted and cities with populations greater than 9,999 whose Asian and/or NHPI population rates are greater than the national average; (1) Native Hawaiian and other Pacific Islander; (2) excludes Taiwanese; (3) includes Chamorro; (4) county does not meet population threshold but is shown in order to allow inclusion of city

Place	Total foreign-born population	Total Asian population	Asians who are foreign born	Total NHPI[1] population	NHPIs[1] who are foreign born	Asian Indian	Bangladeshi	Cambodian	Chinese[2]	Fijian	Filipino	Guamanian[3]	Hawaiian, Native	Hmong	Indonesian	Japanese	Korean	Laotian	Malaysian	Pakistani	Samoan	Sri Lankan	Taiwanese	Thai	Tongan	Vietnamese
St. Johns County	6,038 4.90	1,244	900 72.35 72.35 14.91	-	-	-	-	-	-	-	-	-	-	-	-	-	-	-	-	-	-	-	-	-	-	-
St. Lucie County	20,165 10.46	1,885	1,348 71.51 71.51 6.68	-	-	-	-	-	-	-	-	-	-	-	-	-	-	-	-	-	-	-	-	-	-	-
Santa Rosa County	3,549 3.01	1,608	1,259 78.30 78.30 35.47	-	-	-	-	-	-	-	585 82.74 46.47 36.38 16.48	-	-	-	-	-	-	-	-	-	-	-	-	-	-	-
Sarasota County	30,416 9.33	2,624	1,920 73.17 73.17 6.31	-	-	-	-	-	321 75.35 16.72 12.23 1.06	-	412 76.30 21.46 15.70 1.35	-	-	-	-	-	-	-	-	-	-	-	-	-	-	511 74.82 26.61 19.47 1.68
Seminole County	33,285 9.11	8,682	6,381 73.50 73.50 19.17	-	-	2,074 74.58 32.50 23.89 6.23	-	-	970 70.04 15.20 11.17 2.91	-	946 72.05 14.83 10.90 2.84	-	-	-	-	-	761 77.97 11.93 8.77 2.29	-	-	-	-	-	-	-	-	758 71.24 11.88 8.73 2.28
Volusia County	28,353 6.40	4,812	3,543 73.63 73.63 12.50	-	-	1,204 75.72 33.98 25.02 4.25	-	-	481 73.10 13.58 10.00 1.70	-	714 81.04 20.15 14.84 2.52	-	-	-	-	-	352 76.19 9.94 7.32 1.24	-	-	-	-	-	-	-	-	-

Notes: Please refer to the User's Guide for an explanation of data; data is arranged alphabetically by state, then county, then city within each county; table includes counties with populations greater than 49,999 unless noted and cities with populations greater than 9,999 whose Asian and/or NHPI population rates are greater than the national average; (1) Native Hawaiian and other Pacific Islander; (2) excludes Taiwanese; (3) includes Chamorro; (4) county does not meet population threshold but is shown in order to allow inclusion of city

Foreign-Born Naturalized Citizens

(Universe: Total Population)

Place	Total foreign-born naturalized citizens	Total Asian population	Asians who are foreign-born naturalized citizens	Total NHPI[1] population	NHPIs[1] who are foreign-born naturalized citizens	Asian Indian	Bangladeshi	Cambodian	Chinese[2]	Fijian	Filipino	Guamanian[3]	Hawaiian, Native	Hmong	Indonesian	Japanese	Korean	Laotian	Malaysian	Pakistani	Samoan	Sri Lankan	Taiwanese	Thai	Tongan	Vietnamese
UNITED STATES	12,542,626	10,171,820	3,502,021	378,782	30,284	487,795	10,515	53,496	857,071	2,901	775,400	2,308	1,459	29,664	7,646	80,119	423,393	55,076	1,391	47,923	10,283	5,950	52,483	36,227	5,434	488,874
	4.46		34.43		8.00	29.64	25.38	30.05	37.26	28.26	41.60	4.19	1.05	17.44	20.57	10.08	39.47	32.82	12.99	30.74	12.06	31.19	42.76	32.68	19.63	44.03
						13.93	0.30	1.53	24.47	9.58	22.14	7.62	4.82	0.85	0.22	2.29	12.09	1.57	0.04	1.37	33.96	0.17	1.50	1.03	17.94	13.96
			34.43		8.00	4.80	0.10	0.53	8.43	0.77	7.62	0.61	0.39	0.29	0.08	0.79	4.16	0.54	0.01	0.47	2.71	0.06	0.52	0.36	1.43	4.81
			27.92		0.24	3.89	0.08	0.43	6.83	0.02	6.18	0.02	0.01	0.24	0.06	0.64	3.38	0.44	0.01	0.38	0.08	0.05	0.42	0.29	0.04	3.90
FLORIDA	1,207,502	264,377	99,107	6,812	700	21,913	328	1,171	17,580	-	23,541	66	41	-	346	2,972	8,158	1,438	-	1,810	190	155	988	2,470	-	13,645
	7.56		37.49		10.28	32.32	26.03	42.40	39.18		43.33	3.27	2.08		38.70	26.19	42.76	35.67		33.24	22.38	38.56	48.74	37.58		40.86
						22.11	0.33	1.18	17.74		23.75	9.43	5.86		0.35	3.00	8.23	1.45		1.83	27.14	0.16	1.00	2.49		13.77
			37.49		10.28	8.29	0.12	0.44	6.65		8.90	0.97	0.60		0.13	1.12	3.09	0.54		0.68	2.79	0.06	0.37	0.93		5.16
			8.21		0.06	1.81	0.03	0.10	1.46		1.95	0.01	<0.01		0.03	0.25	0.68	0.12		0.15	0.02	0.01	0.08	0.20		1.13
Alachua County	5,956	7,858	2,010	-	-	562	-	-	367	-	386	-	-	-	-	91	132	-	-	-	-	-	-	-	-	294
	2.73		25.58			28.84			17.19		36.90					21.02	13.13									47.65
						27.96			18.26		19.20					4.53	6.57									14.63
			25.58			7.15			4.67		4.91					1.16	1.68									3.74
			33.75			9.44			6.16		6.48					1.53	2.22									4.94
Gainesville (city)	2,832	4,399	897	-	-	201	-	-	215	-	-	-	-	-	-	-	53	-	-	-	-	-	-	-	-	-
	2.96		20.39			19.03			14.77								10.58									
						22.41			23.97								5.91									
			20.39			4.57			4.89								1.20									
			31.67			7.10			7.59								1.87									
Bay County	2,885	2,369	944	-	-	-	-	-	-	-	201	-	-	-	-	-	-	-	-	-	-	-	-	-	-	252
	1.95		39.85								41.53															37.84
											21.29															26.69
			39.85								8.48															10.64
			32.72								6.97															8.73
Callaway (city)	500	530	217	-	-	-	-	-	-	-	-	-	-	-	-	-	-	-	-	-	-	-	-	-	-	-
	3.51		40.94																							
			40.94																							
			43.40																							
Brevard County	18,374	7,122	2,983	-	-	683	-	-	344	-	769	-	-	-	-	131	312	-	-	-	-	-	-	-	-	406
	3.86		41.88			34.65			38.57		50.03					24.95	50.24									53.21
						22.90			11.53		25.78					4.39	10.46									13.61
			41.88			9.59			4.83		10.80					1.84	4.38									5.70
			16.23			3.72			1.87		4.19					0.71	1.70									2.21
Broward County	183,641	36,505	13,921	645	176	4,500	-	-	3,658	-	2,112	-	-	-	-	205	916	-	-	287	-	-	-	154	-	1,353
	11.31		38.13		27.29	34.59			42.75		43.37					19.62	40.53			26.16				25.71		47.19
						32.33			26.28		15.17					1.47	6.58			2.06				1.11		9.72
			38.13		27.29	12.33			10.02		5.79					0.56	2.51			0.79				0.42		3.71
			7.58		0.10	2.45			1.99		1.15					0.11	0.50			0.16				0.08		0.74
Cooper City (city)	3,037	1,241	587	-	-	303	-	-	-	-	-	-	-	-	-	-	-	-	-	-	-	-	-	-	-	-
	10.97		47.30			51.10																				
						51.62																				
			47.30			24.42																				
			19.33			9.98																				

Notes: Please refer to the User's Guide for an explanation of data; data is arranged alphabetically by state, then county, then city within each county; table includes counties with populations greater than 49,999 unless noted and cities with populations greater than 9,999 whose Asian and/or NHPI population rates are greater than the national average; (1) Native Hawaiian and other Pacific Islander; (2) excludes Taiwanese; (3) includes Chamorro; (4) county does not meet population threshold but is shown in order to allow inclusion of city

Place	Total foreign-born naturalized citizens	Total Asian population	Asians who are foreign-born naturalized citizens	Total NHPI[1] population	NHPIs[1] who are foreign-born naturalized citizens	Asian Indian	Bangladeshi	Cambodian	Chinese[2]	Fijian	Filipino	Guamanian[3]	Hawaiian, Native	Hmong	Indonesian	Japanese	Korean	Laotian	Malaysian	Pakistani	Samoan	Sri Lankan	Taiwanese	Thai	Tongan	Vietnamese
Pembroke Pines (city)	22,597 16.48	5,004	2,069 41.35 41.35 9.16	-	-	683 38.98 33.01 13.65 3.02	-	-	497 43.10 24.02 9.93 2.20	-	460 49.62 22.23 9.19 2.04	-	-	-	-	-	-	-	-	-	-	-	-	-	-	-
Charlotte County	6,815 4.81	872	382 43.81 43.81 5.61	-	-	-	-	-	-	-	-	-	-	-	-	-	-	-	-	-	-	-	-	-	-	-
Citrus County	3,861 3.27	1,145	508 44.37 44.37 13.16	-	-	-	-	-	-	-	-	-	-	-	-	-	-	-	-	-	-	-	-	-	-	-
Clay County	3,472 2.47	2,901	1,206 41.57 41.57 34.74	-	-	-	-	-	-	-	867 50.29 71.89 29.89 24.97	-	-	-	-	-	-	-	-	-	-	-	-	-	-	-
Bellair-Meadowbrook Ter. (cdp)	526 3.18	635	277 43.62 43.62 52.66	-	-	-	-	-	-	-	-	-	-	-	-	-	-	-	-	-	-	-	-	-	-	-
Collier County	14,194 5.65	1,200	526 43.83 43.83 3.71	-	-	-	-	-	-	-	-	-	-	-	-	-	-	-	-	-	-	-	-	-	-	-
Columbia County	779 1.38	386	177 45.85 45.85 22.72	-	-	-	-	-	-	-	-	-	-	-	-	-	-	-	-	-	-	-	-	-	-	-
Duval County	21,813 2.80	20,554	7,933 38.60 38.60 36.37	507	15 2.96 2.96 0.07	674 24.36 8.50 3.28 3.09	-	349 34.87 4.40 1.70 1.60	645 39.28 8.13 3.14 2.96	-	4,580 44.88 57.73 22.28 21.00	-	-	-	-	163 29.64 2.05 0.79 0.75	416 43.02 5.24 2.02 1.91	-	-	-	-	-	-	-	-	714 33.81 9.00 3.47 3.27
Escambia County	6,088 2.07	6,565	2,693 41.02 41.02 44.23	-	-	199 38.57 7.39 3.03 3.27	-	-	202 34.41 7.50 3.08 3.32	-	1,258 46.30 46.71 19.16 20.66	-	-	-	-	-	-	-	-	-	-	-	-	-	-	578 36.19 21.46 8.80 9.49
Bellview (cdp)	590 2.80	787	323 41.04 41.04 54.75	-	-	-	-	-	-	-	205 49.76 63.47 26.05 34.75	-	-	-	-	-	-	-	-	-	-	-	-	-	-	-

Notes: Please refer to the User's Guide for an explanation of data; data is arranged alphabetically by state, then county, then city within each county; table includes counties with populations greater than 49,999 unless noted and cities with populations greater than 9,999 whose Asian and/or NHPI population rates are greater than the national average; (1) Native Hawaiian and other Pacific Islander; (2) excludes Taiwanese; (3) includes Chamorro; (4) county does not meet population threshold but is shown in order to allow inclusion of city

Place	Total foreign-born naturalized citizens	Total Asian population	Asians who are foreign-born naturalized citizens	Total NHPI[1] population	NHPIs[1] who are foreign-born naturalized citizens	Asian Indian	Bangladeshi	Cambodian	Chinese[2]	Fijian	Filipino	Guamanian[3]	Hawaiian, Native	Hmong	Indonesian	Japanese	Korean	Laotian	Malaysian	Pakistani	Samoan	Sri Lankan	Taiwanese	Thai	Tongan	Vietnamese
Myrtle Grove (cdp)	565 3.26	812	332 40.89 40.89 58.76	-	-	-	-	-	-	-	239 50.74 71.99 29.43 42.30	-	-	-	-	-	-	-	-	-	-	-	-	-	-	-
Hernando County	4,701 3.59	773	298 38.55 38.55 6.34	-	-	-	-	-	-	-	-	-	-	-	-	-	-	-	-	-	-	-	-	-	-	-
Highlands County	2,795 3.20	964	320 33.20 33.20 11.45	-	-	-	-	-	-	-	156 34.90 48.75 16.18 5.58	-	-	-	-	-	-	-	-	-	-	-	-	-	-	-
Hillsborough County	47,127 4.72	21,571	7,068 32.77 32.77 15.00	540	34 6.30 6.30 0.07	1,558 26.40 22.04 7.22 3.31	-	-	749 27.96 10.60 3.47 1.59	-	1,172 36.59 16.58 5.43 2.49	-	-	-	-	285 33.02 4.03 1.32 0.60	951 34.99 13.46 4.41 2.02	-	-	-	-	-	-	264 39.05 3.74 1.22 0.56	-	1,556 38.97 22.01 7.21 3.30
Westchase (cdp)	577 5.19	508	176 34.65 34.65 30.50	-	-	-	-	-	-	-	-	-	-	-	-	-	-	-	-	-	-	-	-	-	-	-
Indian River County	4,120 3.65	864	358 41.44 41.44 8.69	-	-	-	-	-	-	-	-	-	-	-	-	-	-	-	-	-	-	-	-	-	-	-
Lake County	5,084 2.41	1,422	566 39.80 39.80 11.13	-	-	-	-	-	-	-	-	-	-	-	-	-	-	-	-	-	-	-	-	-	-	-
Lee County	15,380 3.49	3,159	1,359 43.02 43.02 8.84	-	-	257 38.42 18.91 8.14 1.67	-	-	297 49.83 21.85 9.40 1.93	-	456 41.30 33.55 14.43 2.96	-	-	-	-	-	-	-	-	-	-	-	-	-	-	-
Leon County	4,776 1.99	4,858	1,560 32.11 32.11 32.66	-	-	516 34.22 33.08 10.62 10.80	-	-	274 25.25 17.56 5.64 5.74	-	169 32.13 10.83 3.48 3.54	-	-	-	-	-	165 37.00 10.58 3.40 3.45	-	-	-	-	-	-	-	-	-
Manatee County	8,466 3.21	2,237	1,050 46.94 46.94 12.40	-	-	-	-	-	-	-	227 42.19 21.62 10.15 2.68	-	-	-	-	-	-	-	-	-	-	-	-	-	-	-

Notes: Please refer to the User's Guide for an explanation of data; data is arranged alphabetically by state, then county, then city within each county; table includes counties with populations greater than 49,999 unless noted and cities with populations greater than 9,999 whose Asian and/or NHPI population rates are greater than the national average; (1) Native Hawaiian and other Pacific Islander; (2) excludes Taiwanese; (3) includes Chamorro; (4) county does not meet population threshold but is shown in order to allow inclusion of city

Place	Total foreign-born naturalized citizens	Total Asian population	Asians who are foreign-born naturalized citizens	Total NHPI[1] population	NHPIs[1] who are foreign-born naturalized citizens	Asian Indian	Bangladeshi	Cambodian	Chinese[2]	Fijian	Filipino	Guamanian[3]	Hawaiian, Native	Hmong	Indonesian	Japanese	Korean	Laotian	Malaysian	Pakistani	Samoan	Sri Lankan	Taiwanese	Thai	Tongan	Vietnamese
Marion County	7,516 2.90	2,221	840 37.82 37.82 11.18	-	-	305 32.14 36.31 13.73 4.06	-	-	-	-	-	-	-	-	-	-	-	-	-	-	-	-	-	-	-	-
Martin County	4,482 3.54	701	364 51.93 51.93 8.12	-	-	-	-	-	-	-	-	-	-	-	-	-	-	-	-	-	-	-	-	-	-	-
Miami-Dade County	535,080 23.75	30,692	11,851 38.61 38.61 2.21	605	220 36.36 36.36 0.04	2,962 33.14 24.99 9.65 0.55	-	-	4,020 45.22 33.92 13.10 0.75	-	1,874 41.45 15.81 6.11 0.35	-	-	-	-	218 15.53 1.84 0.71 0.04	600 44.91 5.06 1.95 0.11	-	-	357 44.96 3.01 1.16 0.07	-	-	-	256 29.02 2.16 0.83 0.05	-	702 44.01 5.92 2.29 0.13
Doral (cdp)	3,753 18.30	1,186	186 15.68 15.68 4.96	-	-	-	-	-	-	-	-	-	-	-	-	-	-	-	-	-	-	-	-	-	-	-
Ives Estates (cdp)	3,439 19.75	831	381 45.85 45.85 11.08	-	-	-	-	-	-	-	-	-	-	-	-	-	-	-	-	-	-	-	-	-	-	-
North Miami Beach (city)	8,469 20.82	1,706	607 35.58 35.58 7.17	-	-	103 26.01 16.97 6.04 1.22	-	-	360 48.58 59.31 21.10 4.25	-	-	-	-	-	-	-	-	-	-	-	-	-	-	-	-	-
Pinecrest (village)	2,830 14.75	884	364 41.18 41.18 12.86	-	-	-	-	-	-	-	-	-	-	-	-	-	-	-	-	-	-	-	-	-	-	-
Monroe County	5,004 6.29	566	185 32.69 32.69 3.70	-	-	-	-	-	-	-	-	-	-	-	-	-	-	-	-	-	-	-	-	-	-	-
Nassau County	666 1.15	422	177 41.94 41.94 26.58	-	-	-	-	-	-	-	-	-	-	-	-	-	-	-	-	-	-	-	-	-	-	-
Okaloosa County	5,715 3.35	4,432	2,115 47.72 47.72 37.01	-	-	-	-	-	-	-	748 42.94 35.37 16.88 13.09	-	-	-	-	-	392 54.44 18.53 8.84 6.86	-	-	-	-	-	-	389 62.34 18.39 8.78 6.81	-	181 45.25 8.56 4.08 3.17

Notes: Please refer to the User's Guide for an explanation of data; data is arranged alphabetically by state, then county, then city within each county; table includes counties with populations greater than 49,999 unless noted and cities with populations greater than 9,999 whose Asian and/or NHPI population rates are greater than the national average; (1) Native Hawaiian and other Pacific Islander; (2) excludes Taiwanese; (3) includes Chamorro; (4) county does not meet population threshold but is shown in order to allow inclusion of city

Place	Total foreign-born naturalized citizens	Total Asian population	Asians who are foreign-born naturalized citizens	Total NHPI[1] population	NHPIs[1] who are foreign-born naturalized citizens	Asian Indian	Bangladeshi	Cambodian	Chinese[2]	Fijian	Filipino	Guamanian[3]	Hawaiian, Native	Hmong	Indonesian	Japanese	Korean	Laotian	Malaysian	Pakistani	Samoan	Sri Lankan	Taiwanese	Thai	Tongan	Vietnamese
Wright (cdp)	964 4.47	825	385 46.67 46.67 39.94	-	-	-	-	-	-	-	-	-	-	-	-	-	-	-	-	-	-	-	-	-	-	-
Orange County	53,651 5.99	28,748	10,922 37.99 37.99 20.36	853	53 6.21 6.21 0.10	2,510 32.81 22.98 8.73 4.68	-	-	1,479 37.05 13.54 5.14 2.76	-	1,835 40.56 16.80 6.38 3.42	-	-	-	-	271 22.58 2.48 0.94 0.51	872 40.65 7.98 3.03 1.63	-	-	285 31.63 2.61 0.99 0.53	-	-	-	-	-	2,892 45.49 26.48 10.06 5.39
Oak Ridge (cdp)	2,133 9.52	1,306	465 35.60 35.60 21.80	-	-	-	-	-	-	-	-	-	-	-	-	-	-	-	-	-	-	-	-	-	-	226 42.88 48.60 17.30 10.60
Osceola County	9,514 5.52	3,642	1,480 40.64 40.64 15.56	-	-	241 24.95 16.28 6.62 2.53	-	-	286 48.97 19.32 7.85 3.01	-	440 49.83 29.73 12.08 4.62	-	-	-	-	-	-	-	-	-	-	-	-	-	-	-
Palm Beach County	83,681 7.40	16,895	6,076 35.96 35.96 7.26	423	17 4.02 4.02 0.02	1,577 30.93 25.95 9.33 1.88	-	-	1,380 37.90 22.71 8.17 1.65	-	889 39.72 14.63 5.26 1.06	-	-	-	-	179 31.18 2.95 1.06 0.21	403 43.24 6.63 2.39 0.48	-	-	-	-	-	-	257 33.82 4.23 1.52 0.31	-	841 42.18 13.84 4.98 1.01
Pasco County	13,303 3.86	3,489	1,432 41.04 41.04 10.76	-	-	247 24.87 17.25 7.08 1.86	-	-	226 44.84 15.78 6.48 1.70	-	481 48.39 33.59 13.79 3.62	-	-	-	-	-	-	-	-	-	-	-	-	-	-	-
Pinellas County	40,786 4.43	18,783	6,215 33.09 33.09 15.24	-	-	1,211 33.20 19.49 6.45 2.97	-	203 28.27 3.27 1.08 0.50	793 38.03 12.76 4.22 1.94	-	1,026 33.82 16.51 5.46 2.52	-	-	-	-	125 22.01 2.01 0.67 0.31	419 49.06 6.74 2.23 1.03	624 33.64 10.04 3.32 1.53	-	-	-	-	-	97 19.88 1.56 0.52 0.24	-	1,356 32.03 21.82 7.22 3.32
Pinellas Park (city)	1,901 4.19	1,811	595 32.85 32.85 31.30	-	-	-	-	-	-	-	-	-	-	-	-	-	-	-	-	-	-	-	-	-	-	159 30.23 26.72 8.78 8.36
Polk County	11,908 2.46	5,805	1,942 33.45 33.45 16.31	-	-	507 29.53 26.11 8.73 4.26	-	-	180 30.25 9.27 3.10 1.51	-	427 47.34 21.99 7.36 3.59	-	-	-	-	-	-	84 20.95 4.33 1.45 0.71	-	-	-	-	-	-	-	330 37.84 16.99 5.68 2.77
Putnam County	986 1.40	291	142 48.80 48.80 14.40	-	-	-	-	-	-	-	-	-	-	-	-	-	-	-	-	-	-	-	-	-	-	-

Notes: Please refer to the User's Guide for an explanation of data; data is arranged alphabetically by state, then county, then city within each county; table includes counties with populations greater than 49,999 unless noted and cities with populations greater than 9,999 whose Asian and/or NHPI population rates are greater than the national average; (1) Native Hawaiian and other Pacific Islander; (2) excludes Taiwanese; (3) includes Chamorro; (4) county does not meet population threshold but is shown in order to allow inclusion of city

Place	Total foreign-born naturalized citizens	Total Asian population	Asians who are foreign-born naturalized citizens	Total NHPI[1] population	NHPIs[1] who are foreign-born naturalized citizens	Asian Indian	Bangladeshi	Cambodian	Chinese[2]	Fijian	Filipino	Guamanian[3]	Hawaiian, Native	Hmong	Indonesian	Japanese	Korean	Laotian	Malaysian	Pakistani	Samoan	Sri Lankan	Taiwanese	Thai	Tongan	Vietnamese
St. Johns County	3,604 2.93	1,244	563 45.26 45.26 15.62	-	-	-	-	-	-	-	-	-	-	-	-	-	-	-	-	-	-	-	-	-	-	-
St. Lucie County	8,746 4.54	1,885	693 36.76 36.76 7.92	-	-	-	-	-	-	-	-	-	-	-	-	-	-	-	-	-	-	-	-	-	-	-
Santa Rosa County	2,065 1.75	1,608	853 53.05 53.05 41.31	-	-	-	-	-	-	-	410 57.99 48.07 25.50 19.85	-	-	-	-	-	-	-	-	-	-	-	-	-	-	-
Sarasota County	14,642 4.49	2,624	918 34.98 34.98 6.27	-	-	-	-	-	127 29.81 13.83 4.84 0.87	-	264 48.89 28.76 10.06 1.80	-	-	-	-	-	-	-	-	-	-	-	-	-	-	200 29.28 21.79 7.62 1.37
Seminole County	16,507 4.52	8,682	3,298 37.99 37.99 19.98	-	-	1,038 37.32 31.47 11.96 6.29	-	-	502 36.25 15.22 5.78 3.04	-	521 39.68 15.80 6.00 3.16	-	-	-	-	-	365 37.40 11.07 4.20 2.21	-	-	-	-	-	-	-	-	523 49.15 15.86 6.02 3.17
Volusia County	14,955 3.37	4,812	1,962 40.77 40.77 13.12	-	-	593 37.30 30.22 12.32 3.97	-	-	299 45.44 15.24 6.21 2.00	-	460 52.21 23.45 9.56 3.08	-	-	-	-	-	204 44.16 10.40 4.24 1.36	-	-	-	-	-	-	-	-	-

Notes: Please refer to the User's Guide for an explanation of data; data is arranged alphabetically by state, then county, then city within each county; table includes counties with populations greater than 49,999 unless noted and cities with populations greater than 9,999 whose Asian and/or NHPI population rates are greater than the national average; (1) Native Hawaiian and other Pacific Islander; (2) excludes Taiwanese; (3) includes Chamorro; (4) county does not meet population threshold but is shown in order to allow inclusion of city

Educational Attainment: High School Graduates

(Universe: Population 25 Years and Over)

Place	Total population 25 years and over who are high school graduates	Asian population 25 years and over	Asians 25 years and over who are high school graduates	NHPI[1] population 25 years and over	NHPIs[1] 25 years and over who are high school graduates	Asian Indian	Bangladeshi	Cambodian	Chinese[2]	Fijian	Filipino	Guamanian[3]	Hawaiian, Native	Hmong	Indonesian	Japanese	Korean	Laotian	Malaysian	Pakistani	Samoan	Sri Lankan	Taiwanese	Thai	Tongan	Vietnamese
UNITED STATES	146,496,014	6,640,671	5,340,921	206,675	161,732	906,483	19,556	40,287	1,205,190	3,914	1,097,808	25,286	70,074	21,922	21,566	577,286	599,278	43,977	6,004	71,715	31,625	11,612	75,069	62,006	8,559	429,134
	80.40		80.43		78.25	86.69	78.22	46.66	76.20	66.84	87.34	77.85	83.17	40.40	92.60	91.12	86.31	50.40	89.05	82.03	75.81	86.55	93.01	79.12	65.27	61.88
						16.97	0.37	0.75	22.57	2.42	20.55	15.63	43.33	0.41	0.40	10.81	11.22	0.82	0.11	1.34	19.55	0.22	1.41	1.16	5.29	8.03
			80.43		78.25	13.65	0.29	0.61	18.15	1.89	16.53	12.23	33.91	0.33	0.32	8.69	9.02	0.66	0.09	1.08	15.30	0.17	1.13	0.93	4.14	6.46
			3.65		0.11	0.62	0.01	0.03	0.82	<0.01	0.75	0.02	0.05	0.01	0.01	0.39	0.41	0.03	<0.01	0.05	0.02	0.01	0.05	0.04	0.01	0.29
FLORIDA	8,804,697	177,289	143,001	4,096	2,930	37,097	678	823	24,216	-	33,761	745	1,010	-	647	8,143	10,830	1,443	-	2,797	376	268	1,289	3,625	-	13,059
	79.86		80.66		71.53	85.72	80.43	53.55	77.01		88.44	62.87	76.05		93.63	88.12	82.56	59.36		84.60	75.35	93.06	92.80	71.27		61.58
						25.94	0.47	0.58	16.93		23.61	25.43	34.47		0.45	5.69	7.57	1.01		1.96	12.83	0.19	0.90	2.53		9.13
			80.66		71.53	20.92	0.38	0.46	13.66		19.04	18.19	24.66		0.36	4.59	6.11	0.81		1.58	9.18	0.15	0.73	2.04		7.37
			1.62		0.03	0.42	0.01	0.01	0.28		0.38	0.01	0.01		0.01	0.09	0.12	0.02		0.03	<0.01	<0.01	0.01	0.04		0.15
Alachua County	108,766	4,231	4,096	-	-	831	-	-	1,268	-	586	-	-	-	-	288	569	-	-	-	-	-	-	-	-	271
	88.05		96.81			96.63			98.68		98.16					96.64	98.27									84.42
						20.29			30.96		14.31					7.03	13.89									6.62
			96.81			19.64			29.97		13.85					6.81	13.45									6.41
			3.77			0.76			1.17		0.54					0.26	0.52									0.25
Gainesville (city)	44,391	2,330	2,232	-	-	407	-	-	874	-	-	-	-	-	-	-	270	-	-	-	-	-	-	-	-	-
	87.77		95.79			96.90			98.09								96.43									
						18.23			39.16								12.10									
			95.79			17.47			37.51								11.59									
			5.03			0.92			1.97								0.61									
Bay County	80,855	1,586	1,020	-	-	-	-	-	-	-	238	-	-	-	-	-	-	-	-	-	-	-	-	-	-	153
	81.04		64.31								73.46															42.27
											23.33															15.00
			64.31								15.01															9.65
			1.26								0.29															0.19
Callaway (city)	7,267	355	231	-	-	-	-	-	-	-	-	-	-	-	-	-	-	-	-	-	-	-	-	-	-	-
	83.25		65.07																							
			65.07																							
			3.18																							
Brevard County	293,322	5,153	4,249	-	-	1,125	-	-	533	-	973	-	-	-	-	415	385	-	-	-	-	-	-	-	-	394
	86.34		82.46			87.07			75.60		84.61					94.32	73.33									81.24
						26.48			12.54		22.90					9.77	9.06									9.27
			82.46			21.83			10.34		18.88					8.05	7.47									7.65
			1.45			0.38			0.18		0.33					0.14	0.13									0.13
Broward County	923,268	24,543	19,872	439	346	7,050	-	-	4,202	-	3,117	-	-	-	-	805	1,367	-	-	580	-	-	-	384	-	1,219
	81.96		80.97		78.82	83.63			70.30		90.03					93.28	91.74			87.75				78.85		65.43
						35.48			21.15		15.69					4.05	6.88			2.92				1.93		6.13
			80.97		78.82	28.73			17.12		12.70					3.28	5.57			2.36				1.56		4.97
			2.15		0.04	0.76			0.46		0.34					0.09	0.15			0.06				0.04		0.13
Cooper City (city)	15,873	735	648	-	-	328	-	-	-	-	-	-	-	-	-	-	-	-	-	-	-	-	-	-	-	-
	92.14		88.16			90.86																				
						50.62																				
			88.16			44.63																				
			4.08			2.07																				

Notes: Please refer to the User's Guide for an explanation of data; data is arranged alphabetically by state, then county, then city within each county; table includes counties with populations greater than 49,999 unless noted and cities with populations greater than 9,999 whose Asian and/or NHPI population rates are greater than the national average; (1) Native Hawaiian and other Pacific Islander; (2) excludes Taiwanese; (3) includes Chamorro; (4) county does not meet population threshold but is shown in order to allow inclusion of city

Place	Total population 25 years and over who are high school graduates	Asian population 25 years and over	Asians 25 years and over who are high school graduates	NHPI[1] population 25 years and over	NHPIs[1] 25 years and over who are high school graduates	Asian Indian	Bangladeshi	Cambodian	Chinese[2]	Fijian	Filipino	Guamanian[3]	Hawaiian, Native	Hmong	Indonesian	Japanese	Korean	Laotian	Malaysian	Pakistani	Samoan	Sri Lankan	Taiwanese	Thai	Tongan	Vietnamese
Pembroke Pines (city)	82,419 88.05	3,411	2,957 86.69 86.69 3.59	-	-	1,059 91.85 35.81 31.05 1.28	-	-	532 69.00 17.99 15.60 0.65	-	655 93.57 22.15 19.20 0.79	-	-	-	-	-	-	-	-	-	-	-	-	-	-	-
Charlotte County	92,886 82.15	674	573 85.01 85.01 0.62	-	-	-	-	-	-	-	-	-	-	-	-	-	-	-	-	-	-	-	-	-	-	-
Citrus County	72,516 78.32	834	684 82.01 82.01 0.94	-	-	-	-	-	-	-	-	-	-	-	-	-	-	-	-	-	-	-	-	-	-	-
Clay County	78,085 86.39	2,076	1,709 82.32 82.32 2.19	-	-	-	-	-	-	-	1,117 86.52 65.36 53.81 1.43	-	-	-	-	-	-	-	-	-	-	-	-	-	-	-
Bellair-Meadowbrook Ter. (cdp)	9,192 87.09	517	439 84.91 84.91 4.78	-	-	-	-	-	-	-	-	-	-	-	-	-	-	-	-	-	-	-	-	-	-	-
Collier County	151,535 81.75	876	762 86.99 86.99 0.50	-	-	-	-	-	-	-	-	-	-	-	-	-	-	-	-	-	-	-	-	-	-	-
Columbia County	27,547 74.69	249	202 81.12 81.12 0.73	-	-	-	-	-	-	-	-	-	-	-	-	-	-	-	-	-	-	-	-	-	-	-
Duval County	413,266 82.72	13,470	10,931 81.15 81.15 2.65	286	220 76.92 76.92 0.05	1,684 91.92 15.41 12.50 0.41	-	249 46.89 2.28 1.85 0.06	877 83.05 8.02 6.51 0.21	-	6,003 87.62 54.92 44.57 1.45	-	-	-	-	382 83.22 3.49 2.84 0.09	497 75.19 4.55 3.69 0.12	-	-	-	-	-	-	-	-	611 48.11 5.59 4.54 0.15
Escambia County	155,668 82.06	4,153	3,073 73.99 73.99 1.97	-	-	300 88.24 9.76 7.22 0.19	-	-	253 67.29 8.23 6.09 0.16	-	1,546 83.79 50.31 37.23 0.99	-	-	-	-	-	-	-	-	-	-	-	-	-	-	326 41.69 10.61 7.85 0.21
Bellview (cdp)	11,439 83.36	518	391 75.48 75.48 3.42	-	-	-	-	-	-	-	245 83.33 62.66 47.30 2.14	-	-	-	-	-	-	-	-	-	-	-	-	-	-	-

Notes: Please refer to the User's Guide for an explanation of data; data is arranged alphabetically by state, then county, then city within each county; table includes counties with populations greater than 49,999 unless noted and cities with populations greater than 9,999 whose Asian and/or NHPI population rates are greater than the national average; (1) Native Hawaiian and other Pacific Islander; (2) excludes Taiwanese; (3) includes Chamorro; (4) county does not meet population threshold but is shown in order to allow inclusion of city

Place	Total population 25 years and over who are high school graduates	Asian population 25 years and over	Asians 25 years and over who are high school graduates	NHPI[1] population 25 years and over	NHPIs[1] 25 years and over who are high school graduates	Asian Indian	Bangladeshi	Cambodian	Chinese[2]	Fijian	Filipino	Guamanian[3]	Hawaiian, Native	Hmong	Indonesian	Japanese	Korean	Laotian	Malaysian	Pakistani	Samoan	Sri Lankan	Taiwanese	Thai	Tongan	Vietnamese
Myrtle Grove (cdp)	8,947 84.09	521	373 71.59 71.59 4.17	-	-	-	-	-	-	-	275 81.12 73.73 52.78 3.07	-	-	-	-	-	-	-	-	-	-	-	-	-	-	-
Hernando County	77,747 78.47	545	423 77.61 77.61 0.54	-	-	-	-	-	-	-	-	-	-	-	-	-	-	-	-	-	-	-	-	-	-	-
Highlands County	48,500 74.52	648	522 80.56 80.56 1.08	-	-	-	-	-	-	-	268 87.30 51.34 41.36 0.55	-	-	-	-	-	-	-	-	-	-	-	-	-	-	-
Hillsborough County	528,058 80.76	14,352	11,689 81.45 81.45 2.21	325	237 72.92 72.92 0.04	3,170 88.08 27.12 22.09 0.60	-	-	1,464 80.97 12.52 10.20 0.28	-	2,031 93.98 17.38 14.15 0.38	-	-	-	-	619 82.86 5.30 4.31 0.12	1,554 82.48 13.29 10.83 0.29	-	-	-	-	-	-	426 78.74 3.64 2.97 0.08	-	1,628 61.57 13.93 11.34 0.31
Westchase (cdp)	7,377 96.62	341	289 84.75 84.75 3.92	-	-	-	-	-	-	-	-	-	-	-	-	-	-	-	-	-	-	-	-	-	-	-
Indian River County	68,940 81.56	592	521 88.01 88.01 0.76	-	-	-	-	-	-	-	-	-	-	-	-	-	-	-	-	-	-	-	-	-	-	-
Lake County	124,090 79.76	1,000	798 79.80 79.80 0.64	-	-	-	-	-	-	-	-	-	-	-	-	-	-	-	-	-	-	-	-	-	-	-
Lee County	269,652 82.29	2,321	1,921 82.77 82.77 0.71	-	-	377 86.07 19.63 16.24 0.14	-	-	332 80.98 17.28 14.30 0.12	-	755 87.89 39.30 32.53 0.28	-	-	-	-	-	-	-	-	-	-	-	-	-	-	-
Leon County	122,570 89.12	3,165	2,909 91.91 91.91 2.37	-	-	894 96.13 30.73 28.25 0.73	-	-	726 96.41 24.96 22.94 0.59	-	305 95.31 10.48 9.64 0.25	-	-	-	-	-	298 91.41 10.24 9.42 0.24	-	-	-	-	-	-	-	-	-
Manatee County	157,012 81.44	1,589	1,164 73.25 73.25 0.74	-	-	-	-	-	-	-	279 76.65 23.97 17.56 0.18	-	-	-	-	-	-	-	-	-	-	-	-	-	-	-

Notes: Please refer to the User's Guide for an explanation of data; data is arranged alphabetically by state, then county, then city within each county; table includes counties with populations greater than 49,999 unless noted and cities with populations greater than 9,999 whose Asian and/or NHPI population rates are greater than the national average; (1) Native Hawaiian and other Pacific Islander; (2) excludes Taiwanese; (3) includes Chamorro; (4) county does not meet population threshold but is shown in order to allow inclusion of city

Place	Total population 25 years and over who are high school graduates	Asian population 25 years and over	Asians 25 years and over who are high school graduates	NHPI[1] population 25 years and over	NHPIs[1] 25 years and over who are high school graduates	Asian Indian	Bangladeshi	Cambodian	Chinese[2]	Fijian	Filipino	Guamanian[3]	Hawaiian, Native	Hmong	Indonesian	Japanese	Korean	Laotian	Malaysian	Pakistani	Samoan	Sri Lankan	Taiwanese	Thai	Tongan	Vietnamese
Marion County	146,374 78.20	1,485	1,149 77.37 77.37 0.78	-	-	489 83.16 42.56 32.93 0.33	-	-	-	-	-	-	-	-	-	-	-	-	-	-	-	-	-	-	-	-
Martin County	82,284 85.30	509	453 89.00 89.00 0.55	-	-	-	-	-	-	-	-	-	-	-	-	-	-	-	-	-	-	-	-	-	-	-
Miami-Dade County	1,012,436 67.87	20,980	16,886 80.49 80.49 1.67	384	252 65.63 65.63 0.02	4,621 81.36 27.37 22.03 0.46	-	-	4,825 74.38 28.57 23.00 0.48	-	2,972 90.91 17.60 14.17 0.29	-	-	-	-	964 91.29 5.71 4.59 0.10	823 87.65 4.87 3.92 0.08	-	-	446 81.83 2.64 2.13 0.04	-	-	-	571 82.75 3.38 2.72 0.06	-	610 64.35 3.61 2.91 0.06
Doral (cdp)	12,631 91.29	789	662 83.90 83.90 5.24	-	-	-	-	-	-	-	-	-	-	-	-	-	-	-	-	-	-	-	-	-	-	-
Ives Estates (cdp)	9,869 85.07	561	465 82.89 82.89 4.71	-	-	-	-	-	-	-	-	-	-	-	-	-	-	-	-	-	-	-	-	-	-	-
North Miami Beach (city)	17,683 68.34	1,087	737 67.80 67.80 4.17	-	-	188 78.66 25.51 17.30 1.06	-	-	249 50.92 33.79 22.91 1.41	-	-	-	-	-	-	-	-	-	-	-	-	-	-	-	-	-
Pinecrest (village)	11,395 94.24	587	509 86.71 86.71 4.47	-	-	-	-	-	-	-	-	-	-	-	-	-	-	-	-	-	-	-	-	-	-	-
Monroe County	51,929 84.91	432	325 75.23 75.23 0.63	-	-	-	-	-	-	-	-	-	-	-	-	-	-	-	-	-	-	-	-	-	-	-
Nassau County	31,574 81.02	278	214 76.98 76.98 0.68	-	-	-	-	-	-	-	-	-	-	-	-	-	-	-	-	-	-	-	-	-	-	-
Okaloosa County	98,958 88.02	3,161	2,139 67.67 67.67 2.16	-	-	-	-	-	-	-	877 72.48 41.00 27.74 0.89	-	-	-	-	-	349 66.48 16.32 11.04 0.35	-	-	-	-	-	-	230 43.40 10.75 7.28 0.23	-	141 62.39 6.59 4.46 0.14

Notes: Please refer to the User's Guide for an explanation of data; data is arranged alphabetically by state, then county, then city within each county; table includes counties with populations greater than 49,999 unless noted and cities with populations greater than 9,999 whose Asian and/or NHPI population rates are greater than the national average; (1) Native Hawaiian and other Pacific Islander; (2) excludes Taiwanese; (3) includes Chamorro; (4) county does not meet population threshold but is shown in order to allow inclusion of city

Place	Total population 25 years and over who are high school graduates	Asian population 25 years and over	Asians 25 years and over who are high school graduates	NHPI[1] population 25 years and over	NHPIs[1] 25 years and over who are high school graduates	Asian Indian	Bangladeshi	Cambodian	Chinese[2]	Fijian	Filipino	Guamanian[3]	Hawaiian, Native	Hmong	Indonesian	Japanese	Korean	Laotian	Malaysian	Pakistani	Samoan	Sri Lankan	Taiwanese	Thai	Tongan	Vietnamese
Wright (cdp)	12,248 87.70	604	382 63.25 63.25 3.12	-	-	-	-	-	-	-	-	-	-	-	-	-	-	-	-	-	-	-	-	-	-	-
Orange County	469,510 81.78	19,367	15,500 80.03 80.03 3.30	411	327 79.56 79.56 0.07	4,011 82.45 25.88 20.71 0.85	-	-	2,318 82.02 14.95 11.97 0.49	-	2,796 92.00 18.04 14.44 0.60	-	-	-	-	921 93.12 5.94 4.76 0.20	1,298 88.72 8.37 6.70 0.28	-	-	480 87.43 3.10 2.48 0.10	-	-	-	-	-	2,713 62.90 17.50 14.01 0.58
Oak Ridge (cdp)	8,738 67.13	864	469 54.28 54.28 5.37	-	-	-	-	-	-	-	-	-	-	-	-	-	-	-	-	-	-	-	-	-	-	154 38.21 32.84 17.82 1.76
Osceola County	87,512 79.12	2,425	2,031 83.75 83.75 2.32	-	-	442 85.83 21.76 18.23 0.51	-	-	387 82.87 19.05 15.96 0.44	-	540 91.22 26.59 22.27 0.62	-	-	-	-	-	-	-	-	-	-	-	-	-	-	-
Palm Beach County	683,553 83.57	11,637	9,680 83.18 83.18 1.42	270	147 54.44 54.44 0.02	2,938 85.71 30.35 25.25 0.43	-	-	1,993 77.01 20.59 17.13 0.29	-	1,569 94.35 16.21 13.48 0.23	-	-	-	-	405 84.91 4.18 3.48 0.06	600 87.46 6.20 5.16 0.09	-	-	-	-	-	-	438 83.11 4.52 3.76 0.06	-	994 77.54 10.27 8.54 0.15
Pasco County	198,175 77.57	2,251	1,922 85.38 85.38 0.97	-	-	525 87.35 27.32 23.32 0.26	-	-	212 73.61 11.03 9.42 0.11	-	612 87.06 31.84 27.19 0.31	-	-	-	-	-	-	-	-	-	-	-	-	-	-	-
Pinellas County	576,396 84.01	12,435	9,148 73.57 73.57 1.59	-	-	2,150 88.04 23.50 17.29 0.37	-	161 44.35 1.76 1.29 0.03	1,213 76.53 13.26 9.75 0.21	-	1,826 84.62 19.96 14.68 0.32	-	-	-	-	439 92.81 4.80 3.53 0.08	488 80.00 5.33 3.92 0.08	531 49.72 5.80 4.27 0.09	-	-	-	-	-	265 76.81 2.90 2.13 0.05	-	1,523 55.28 16.65 12.25 0.26
Pinellas Park (city)	26,327 80.19	1,175	855 72.77 72.77 3.25	-	-	-	-	-	-	-	-	-	-	-	-	-	-	-	-	-	-	-	-	-	-	278 75.75 32.51 23.66 1.06
Polk County	243,868 74.76	3,533	2,669 75.54 75.54 1.09	-	-	901 82.43 33.76 25.50 0.37	-	-	259 70.00 9.70 7.33 0.11	-	513 88.75 19.22 14.52 0.21	-	-	-	-	-	-	132 59.46 4.95 3.74 0.05	-	-	-	-	-	-	-	225 46.49 8.43 6.37 0.09
Putnam County	33,601 70.35	208	124 59.62 59.62 0.37	-	-	-	-	-	-	-	-	-	-	-	-	-	-	-	-	-	-	-	-	-	-	-

Notes: Please refer to the User's Guide for an explanation of data; data is arranged alphabetically by state, then county, then city within each county; table includes counties with populations greater than 49,999 unless noted and cities with populations greater than 9,999 whose Asian and/or NHPI population rates are greater than the national average; (1) Native Hawaiian and other Pacific Islander; (2) excludes Taiwanese; (3) includes Chamorro; (4) county does not meet population threshold but is shown in order to allow inclusion of city

Place	Total population 25 years and over who are high school graduates	Asian population 25 years and over	Asians 25 years and over who are high school graduates	NHPI[1] population 25 years and over	NHPIs[1] 25 years and over who are high school graduates	Asian Indian	Bangladeshi	Cambodian	Chinese[2]	Fijian	Filipino	Guamanian[3]	Hawaiian, Native	Hmong	Indonesian	Japanese	Korean	Laotian	Malaysian	Pakistani	Samoan	Sri Lankan	Taiwanese	Thai	Tongan	Vietnamese
St. Johns County	75,162 87.20	862	753 87.35 87.35 1.00	-	-	-	-	-	-	-	-	-	-	-	-	-	-	-	-	-	-	-	-	-	-	-
St. Lucie County	105,985 77.67	1,269	970 76.44 76.44 0.92	-	-	-	-	-	-	-	-	-	-	-	-	-	-	-	-	-	-	-	-	-	-	-
Santa Rosa County	66,781 85.43	1,232	924 75.00 75.00 1.38	-	-	-	-	-	-	-	446 79.93 48.27 36.20 0.67	-	-	-	-	-	-	-	-	-	-	-	-	-	-	-
Sarasota County	223,638 87.09	1,694	1,270 74.97 74.97 0.57	-	-	-	-	-	146 63.48 11.50 8.62 0.07	-	316 79.40 24.88 18.65 0.14	-	-	-	-	-	-	-	-	-	-	-	-	-	-	252 60.87 19.84 14.88 0.11
Seminole County	215,693 88.68	5,863	5,225 89.12 89.12 2.42	-	-	1,661 92.07 31.79 28.33 0.77	-	-	798 80.36 15.27 13.61 0.37	-	888 94.77 17.00 15.15 0.41	-	-	-	-	-	583 94.18 11.16 9.94 0.27	-	-	-	-	-	-	-	-	603 85.29 11.54 10.28 0.28
Volusia County	260,243 82.04	3,243	2,711 83.60 83.60 1.04	-	-	867 84.50 31.98 26.73 0.33	-	-	364 79.48 13.43 11.22 0.14	-	591 90.23 21.80 18.22 0.23	-	-	-	-	-	246 85.12 9.07 7.59 0.09	-	-	-	-	-	-	-	-	-

Notes: Please refer to the User's Guide for an explanation of data: data is arranged alphabetically by state, then county, then city within each county: table includes counties with populations greater than 49,999 unless noted and cities with populations greater than 9,999 whose Asian and/or NHPI population rates are greater than the national average; (1) Native Hawaiian and other Pacific Islander; (2) excludes Taiwanese; (3) includes Chamorro; (4) county does not meet population threshold but is shown in order to allow inclusion of city

Educational Attainment: 4-Year College Graduates

(Universe: Population 25 Years and Over)

Place	Total population 25 years and over who are 4-year college graduates	Asian population 25 years and over	Asians 25 years and over who are 4-year college graduates	NHPI[1] population 25 years and over	NHPIs[1] 25 years and over who are 4-year college graduates	Asian Indian	Bangladeshi	Cambodian	Chinese[2]	Fijian	Filipino	Guamanian[3]	Hawaiian, Native	Hmong	Indonesian	Japanese	Korean	Laotian	Malaysian	Pakistani	Samoan	Sri Lankan	Taiwanese	Thai	Tongan	Vietnamese
UNITED STATES	44,462,605	6,640,671	2,925,743	206,675	28,498	668,029	12,355	7,943	744,668	514	550,230	4,635	12,843	4,053	10,852	265,248	304,272	6,722	3,607	47,470	4,369	6,849	54,160	30,219	1,133	134,820
	24.40		44.06		13.79	63.89	49.42	9.20	47.08	8.78	43.77	14.27	15.24	7.47	46.60	41.87	43.82	7.70	53.50	54.30	10.47	51.05	67.11	38.56	8.64	19.44
						22.83	0.42	0.27	25.45	1.80	18.81	16.26	45.07	0.14	0.37	9.07	10.40	0.23	0.12	1.62	15.33	0.23	1.85	1.03	3.98	4.61
			44.06		13.79	10.06	0.19	0.12	11.21	0.25	8.29	2.24	6.21	0.06	0.16	3.99	4.58	0.10	0.05	0.71	2.11	0.10	0.82	0.46	0.55	2.03
			6.58		0.06	1.50	0.03	0.02	1.67	<0.01	1.24	0.01	0.03	0.01	0.02	0.60	0.68	0.02	0.01	0.11	0.01	0.02	0.12	0.07	<0.01	0.30
FLORIDA	2,462,328	177,289	72,564	4,096	615	22,389	364	111	13,959	-	17,128	172	158	-	269	2,928	4,715	262	-	1,784	72	194	821	1,336	-	4,165
	22.33		40.93		15.01	51.73	43.18	7.22	44.39		44.87	14.51	11.90		38.93	31.68	35.94	10.78		53.96	14.43	67.36	59.11	26.27		19.64
						30.85	0.50	0.15	19.24		23.60	27.97	25.69		0.37	4.04	6.50	0.36		2.46	11.71	0.27	1.13	1.84		5.74
			40.93		15.01	12.63	0.21	0.06	7.87		9.66	4.20	3.86		0.15	1.65	2.66	0.15		1.01	1.76	0.11	0.46	0.75		2.35
			2.95		0.02	0.91	0.01	<0.01	0.57		0.70	0.01	0.01		0.01	0.12	0.19	0.01		0.07	<0.01	0.01	0.03	0.05		0.17
Alachua County	47,803	4,231	3,333	-	-	717	-	-	1,177	-	441	-	-	-	-	149	425	-	-	-	-	-	-	-	-	211
	38.70		78.78			83.37			91.60		73.87					50.00	73.40									65.73
						21.51			35.31		13.23					4.47	12.75									6.33
			78.78			16.95			27.82		10.42					3.52	10.04									4.99
			6.97			1.50			2.46		0.92					0.31	0.89									0.44
Gainesville (city)	21,653	2,330	1,874	-	-	361	-	-	825	-	-	-	-	-	-	-	215	-	-	-	-	-	-	-	-	-
	42.81		80.43			85.95			92.59								76.79									
						19.26			44.02								11.47									
			80.43			15.49			35.41								9.23									
			8.65			1.67			3.81								0.99									
Bay County	17,636	1,586	364	-	-	-	-	-	-	-	81	-	-	-	-	-	-	-	-	-	-	-	-	-	-	19
	17.68		22.95								25.00															5.25
											22.25															5.22
			22.95								5.11															1.20
			2.06								0.46															0.11
Callaway (city)	1,226	355	28	-	-	-	-	-	-	-	-	-	-	-	-	-	-	-	-	-	-	-	-	-	-	-
	14.05		7.89																							
			7.89																							
			2.28																							
Brevard County	80,020	5,153	1,946	-	-	700	-	-	319	-	398	-	-	-	-	117	122	-	-	-	-	-	-	-	-	128
	23.55		37.76			54.18			45.25		34.61					26.59	23.24									26.39
						35.97			16.39		20.45					6.01	6.27									6.58
			37.76			13.58			6.19		7.72					2.27	2.37									2.48
			2.43			0.87			0.40		0.50					0.15	0.15									0.16
Broward County	276,527	24,543	9,524	439	60	3,340	-	-	1,960	-	1,835	-	-	-	-	300	612	-	-	355	-	-	-	168	-	440
	24.55		38.81		13.67	39.62			32.79		53.00					34.76	41.07			53.71				34.50		23.62
						35.07			20.58		19.27					3.15	6.43			3.73				1.76		4.62
			38.81		13.67	13.61			7.99		7.48					1.22	2.49			1.45				0.68		1.79
			3.44		0.02	1.21			0.71		0.66					0.11	0.22			0.13				0.06		0.16
Cooper City (city)	6,575	735	392	-	-	210	-	-	-	-	-	-	-	-	-	-	-	-	-	-	-	-	-	-	-	-
	38.17		53.33			58.17																				
						53.57																				
			53.33			28.57																				
			5.96			3.19																				

Notes: Please refer to the User's Guide for an explanation of data; data is arranged alphabetically by state, then county, then city within each county; table includes counties with populations greater than 49,999 unless noted and cities with populations greater than 9,999 whose Asian and/or NHPI population rates are greater than the national average; (1) Native Hawaiian and other Pacific Islander; (2) excludes Taiwanese; (3) includes Chamorro; (4) county does not meet population threshold but is shown in order to allow inclusion of city

Place	Total population 25 years and over who are 4-year college graduates	Asian population 25 years and over	Asians 25 years and over who are 4-year college graduates	NHPI[1] population 25 years and over	NHPIs[1] 25 years and over who are 4-year college graduates	Asian Indian	Bangladeshi	Cambodian	Chinese[2]	Fijian	Filipino	Guamanian[3]	Hawaiian, Native	Hmong	Indonesian	Japanese	Korean	Laotian	Malaysian	Pakistani	Samoan	Sri Lankan	Taiwanese	Thai	Tongan	Vietnamese
Pembroke Pines (city)	26,847 28.68	3,411	1,762 51.66 51.66 6.56	-	-	653 56.63 37.06 19.14 2.43	-	-	262 33.98 14.87 7.68 0.98	-	411 58.71 23.33 12.05 1.53	-	-	-	-	-	-	-	-	-	-	-	-	-	-	-
Charlotte County	19,875 17.58	674	289 42.88 42.88 1.45	-	-	-	-	-	-	-	-	-	-	-	-	-	-	-	-	-	-	-	-	-	-	-
Citrus County	12,177 13.15	834	351 42.09 42.09 2.88	-	-	-	-	-	-	-	-	-	-	-	-	-	-	-	-	-	-	-	-	-	-	-
Clay County	18,159 20.09	2,076	654 31.50 31.50 3.60	-	-	-	-	-	-	-	437 33.85 66.82 21.05 2.41	-	-	-	-	-	-	-	-	-	-	-	-	-	-	-
Bellair-Meadowbrook Ter. (cdp)	1,887 17.88	517	180 34.82 34.82 9.54	-	-	-	-	-	-	-	-	-	-	-	-	-	-	-	-	-	-	-	-	-	-	-
Collier County	51,757 27.92	876	432 49.32 49.32 0.83	-	-	-	-	-	-	-	-	-	-	-	-	-	-	-	-	-	-	-	-	-	-	-
Columbia County	4,028 10.92	249	131 52.61 52.61 3.25	-	-	-	-	-	-	-	-	-	-	-	-	-	-	-	-	-	-	-	-	-	-	-
Duval County	109,473 21.91	13,470	4,638 34.43 34.43 4.24	286	42 14.69 14.69 0.04	1,267 69.16 27.32 9.41 1.16	-	32 6.03 0.69 0.24 0.03	458 43.37 9.87 3.40 0.42	-	2,178 31.79 46.96 16.17 1.99	-	-	-	-	47 10.24 1.01 0.35 0.04	107 16.19 2.31 0.79 0.10	-	-	-	-	-	-	-	-	218 17.17 4.70 1.62 0.20
Escambia County	39,789 20.97	4,153	970 23.36 23.36 2.44	-	-	125 36.76 12.89 3.01 0.31	-	-	97 25.80 10.00 2.34 0.24	-	438 23.74 45.15 10.55 1.10	-	-	-	-	-	-	-	-	-	-	-	-	-	-	50 6.39 5.15 1.20 0.13
Bellview (cdp)	1,866 13.60	518	89 17.18 17.18 4.77	-	-	-	-	-	-	-	51 17.35 57.30 9.85 2.73	-	-	-	-	-	-	-	-	-	-	-	-	-	-	-

Notes: Please refer to the User's Guide for an explanation of data: data is arranged alphabetically by state, then county, then city within each county; table includes counties with populations greater than 49,999 unless noted and cities with populations greater than 9,999 whose Asian and/or NHPI population rates are greater than the national average; (1) Native Hawaiian and other Pacific Islander; (2) excludes Taiwanese; (3) includes Chamorro; (4) county does not meet population threshold but is shown in order to allow inclusion of city

Place	Total population 25 years and over who are 4-year college graduates	Asian population 25 years and over	Asians 25 years and over who are 4-year college graduates	NHPI[1] population 25 years and over	NHPIs[1] 25 years and over who are 4-year college graduates	Asian Indian	Bangladeshi	Cambodian	Chinese[2]	Fijian	Filipino	Guamanian[3]	Hawaiian, Native	Hmong	Indonesian	Japanese	Korean	Laotian	Malaysian	Pakistani	Samoan	Sri Lankan	Taiwanese	Thai	Tongan	Vietnamese
Myrtle Grove (cdp)	1,928 18.12	521	70 13.44 13.44 3.63	-	-	-	-	-	-	-	47 13.86 67.14 9.02 2.44	-	-	-	-	-	-	-	-	-	-	-	-	-	-	-
Hernando County	12,615 12.73	545	155 28.44 28.44 1.23	-	-	-	-	-	-	-	-	-	-	-	-	-	-	-	-	-	-	-	-	-	-	-
Highlands County	8,837 13.58	648	314 48.46 48.46 3.55	-	-	-	-	-	-	-	191 62.21 60.83 29.48 2.16	-	-	-	-	-	-	-	-	-	-	-	-	-	-	-
Hillsborough County	164,109 25.10	14,352	6,188 43.12 43.12 3.77	325	77 23.69 23.69 0.05	2,119 58.88 34.24 14.76 1.29	-	-	980 54.20 15.84 6.83 0.60	-	1,114 51.55 18.00 7.76 0.68	-	-	-	-	249 33.33 4.02 1.73 0.15	768 40.76 12.41 5.35 0.47	-	-	-	-	-	-	221 40.85 3.57 1.54 0.13	-	341 12.90 5.51 2.38 0.21
Westchase (cdp)	3,744 49.04	341	135 39.59 39.59 3.61	-	-	-	-	-	-	-	-	-	-	-	-	-	-	-	-	-	-	-	-	-	-	-
Indian River County	19,533 23.11	592	279 47.13 47.13 1.43	-	-	-	-	-	-	-	-	-	-	-	-	-	-	-	-	-	-	-	-	-	-	-
Lake County	25,811 16.59	1,000	338 33.80 33.80 1.31	-	-	-	-	-	-	-	-	-	-	-	-	-	-	-	-	-	-	-	-	-	-	-
Lee County	69,153 21.10	2,321	982 42.31 42.31 1.42	-	-	257 58.68 26.17 11.07 0.37	-	-	196 47.80 19.96 8.44 0.28	-	390 45.40 39.71 16.80 0.56	-	-	-	-	-	-	-	-	-	-	-	-	-	-	-
Leon County	57,396 41.73	3,165	2,092 66.10 66.10 3.64	-	-	710 76.34 33.94 22.43 1.24	-	-	582 77.29 27.82 18.39 1.01	-	203 63.44 9.70 6.41 0.35	-	-	-	-	-	185 56.75 8.84 5.85 0.32	-	-	-	-	-	-	-	-	-
Manatee County	40,059 20.78	1,589	530 33.35 33.35 1.32	-	-	-	-	-	-	-	169 46.43 31.89 10.64 0.42	-	-	-	-	-	-	-	-	-	-	-	-	-	-	-

Notes: Please refer to the User's Guide for an explanation of data; data is arranged alphabetically by state, then county, then city within each county; table includes counties with populations greater than 49,999 unless noted and cities with populations greater than 9,999 whose Asian and/or NHPI population rates are greater than the national average; (1) Native Hawaiian and other Pacific Islander; (2) excludes Taiwanese; (3) includes Chamorro; (4) county does not meet population threshold but is shown in order to allow inclusion of city

Place	Total population 25 years and over who are 4-year college graduates	Asian population 25 years and over	Asians 25 years and over who are 4-year college graduates	NHPI[1] population 25 years and over	NHPIs[1] 25 years and over who are 4-year college graduates	Asian Indian	Bangladeshi	Cambodian	Chinese[2]	Fijian	Filipino	Guamanian[3]	Hawaiian, Native	Hmong	Indonesian	Japanese	Korean	Laotian	Malaysian	Pakistani	Samoan	Sri Lankan	Taiwanese	Thai	Tongan	Vietnamese
Marion County	25,626 13.69	1,485	513 34.55 34.55 2.00	-	-	302 51.36 58.87 20.34 1.18	-	-	-	-	-	-	-	-	-	-	-	-	-	-	-	-	-	-	-	-
Martin County	25,413 26.34	509	231 45.38 45.38 0.91	-	-	-	-	-	-	-	-	-	-	-	-	-	-	-	-	-	-	-	-	-	-	-
Miami-Dade County	323,399 21.68	20,980	9,467 45.12 45.12 2.93	384	88 22.92 22.92 0.03	2,676 47.11 28.27 12.76 0.83	-	-	2,581 39.79 27.26 12.30 0.80	-	1,904 58.24 20.11 9.08 0.59	-	-	-	-	511 48.39 5.40 2.44 0.16	441 46.96 4.66 2.10 0.14	-	-	308 56.51 3.25 1.47 0.10	-	-	-	280 40.58 2.96 1.33 0.09	-	232 24.47 2.45 1.11 0.07
Doral (cdp)	6,587 47.61	789	465 58.94 58.94 7.06	-	-	-	-	-	-	-	-	-	-	-	-	-	-	-	-	-	-	-	-	-	-	-
Ives Estates (cdp)	3,062 26.39	561	305 54.37 54.37 9.96	-	-	-	-	-	-	-	-	-	-	-	-	-	-	-	-	-	-	-	-	-	-	-
North Miami Beach (city)	3,671 14.19	1,087	266 24.47 24.47 7.25	-	-	62 25.94 23.31 5.70 1.69	-	-	61 12.47 22.93 5.61 1.66	-	-	-	-	-	-	-	-	-	-	-	-	-	-	-	-	-
Pinecrest (village)	7,444 61.56	587	347 59.11 59.11 4.66	-	-	-	-	-	-	-	-	-	-	-	-	-	-	-	-	-	-	-	-	-	-	-
Monroe County	15,583 25.48	432	221 51.16 51.16 1.42	-	-	-	-	-	-	-	-	-	-	-	-	-	-	-	-	-	-	-	-	-	-	-
Nassau County	7,364 18.90	278	74 26.62 26.62 1.00	-	-	-	-	-	-	-	-	-	-	-	-	-	-	-	-	-	-	-	-	-	-	-
Okaloosa County	27,250 24.24	3,161	460 14.55 14.55 1.69	-	-	-	-	-	-	-	188 15.54 40.87 5.95 0.69	-	-	-	-	-	101 19.24 21.96 3.20 0.37	-	-	-	-	-	-	10 1.89 2.17 0.32 0.04	-	66 29.20 14.35 2.09 0.24

Notes: Please refer to the User's Guide for an explanation of data; data is arranged alphabetically by state, then county, then city within each county; table includes counties with populations greater than 49,999 unless noted and cities with populations greater than 9,999 whose Asian and/or NHPI population rates are greater than the national average; (1) Native Hawaiian and other Pacific Islander; (2) excludes Taiwanese; (3) includes Chamorro; (4) county does not meet population threshold but is shown in order to allow inclusion of city

Place	Total population 25 years and over who are 4-year college graduates	Asian population 25 years and over	Asians 25 years and over who are 4-year college graduates	NHPI[1] population 25 years and over	NHPIs[1] 25 years and over who are 4-year college graduates	Asian Indian	Bangladeshi	Cambodian	Chinese[2]	Fijian	Filipino	Guamanian[3]	Hawaiian, Native	Hmong	Indonesian	Japanese	Korean	Laotian	Malaysian	Pakistani	Samoan	Sri Lankan	Taiwanese	Thai	Tongan	Vietnamese
Wright (cdp)	2,960 21.20	604	58 9.60 9.60 1.96	-	-	-	-	-	-	-	-	-	-	-	-	-	-	-	-	-	-	-	-	-	-	-
Orange County	150,009 26.13	19,367	7,945 41.02 41.02 5.30	411	76 18.49 18.49 0.05	2,243 46.10 28.23 11.58 1.50	-	-	1,489 52.69 18.74 7.69 0.99	-	1,546 50.87 19.46 7.98 1.03	-	-	-	-	337 34.07 4.24 1.74 0.22	543 37.12 6.83 2.80 0.36	-	-	326 59.38 4.10 1.68 0.22	-	-	-	-	-	998 23.14 12.56 5.15 0.67
Oak Ridge (cdp)	1,364 10.48	864	100 11.57 11.57 7.33	-	-	-	-	-	-	-	-	-	-	-	-	-	-	-	-	-	-	-	-	-	-	9 2.23 9.00 1.04 0.66
Osceola County	17,416 15.75	2,425	997 41.11 41.11 5.72	-	-	216 41.94 21.66 8.91 1.24	-	-	156 33.40 15.65 6.43 0.90	-	319 53.89 32.00 13.15 1.83	-	-	-	-	-	-	-	-	-	-	-	-	-	-	-
Palm Beach County	226,615 27.71	11,637	5,612 48.23 48.23 2.48	270	16 5.93 5.93 0.01	1,902 55.48 33.89 16.34 0.84	-	-	1,293 49.96 23.04 11.11 0.57	-	1,076 64.70 19.17 9.25 0.47	-	-	-	-	154 32.29 2.74 1.32 0.07	231 33.67 4.12 1.99 0.10	-	-	-	-	-	-	140 26.57 2.49 1.20 0.06	-	404 31.51 7.20 3.47 0.18
Pasco County	33,548 13.13	2,251	1,041 46.25 46.25 3.10	-	-	283 47.09 27.19 12.57 0.84	-	-	85 29.51 8.17 3.78 0.25	-	392 55.76 37.66 17.41 1.17	-	-	-	-	-	-	-	-	-	-	-	-	-	-	-
Pinellas County	157,235 22.92	12,435	4,198 33.76 33.76 2.67	-	-	1,519 62.20 36.18 12.22 0.97	-	6 1.65 0.14 0.05 <0.01	599 37.79 14.27 4.82 0.38	-	893 41.38 21.27 7.18 0.57	-	-	-	-	160 33.83 3.81 1.29 0.10	240 39.34 5.72 1.93 0.15	47 4.40 1.12 0.38 0.03	-	-	-	-	-	85 24.64 2.02 0.68 0.05	-	311 11.29 7.41 2.50 0.20
Pinellas Park (city)	3,897 11.87	1,175	262 22.30 22.30 6.72	-	-	-	-	-	-	-	-	-	-	-	-	-	-	-	-	-	-	-	-	-	-	29 7.90 11.07 2.47 0.74
Polk County	48,669 14.92	3,533	1,446 40.93 40.93 2.97	-	-	527 48.22 36.45 14.92 1.08	-	-	169 45.68 11.69 4.78 0.35	-	372 64.36 25.73 10.53 0.76	-	-	-	-	-	-	23 10.36 1.59 0.65 0.05	-	-	-	-	-	-	-	94 19.42 6.50 2.66 0.19
Putnam County	4,507 9.44	208	51 24.52 24.52 1.13	-	-	-	-	-	-	-	-	-	-	-	-	-	-	-	-	-	-	-	-	-	-	-

Notes: Please refer to the User's Guide for an explanation of data; data is arranged alphabetically by state, then county, then city within each county; table includes counties with populations greater than 49,999 unless noted and cities with populations greater than 9,999 whose Asian and/or NHPI population rates are greater than the national average; (1) Native Hawaiian and other Pacific Islander; (2) excludes Taiwanese; (3) includes Chamorro; (4) county does not meet population threshold but is shown in order to allow inclusion of city

Place	Total population 25 years and over who are 4-year college graduates	Asian population 25 years and over	Asians 25 years and over who are 4-year college graduates	NHPI[1] population 25 years and over	NHPIs[1] 25 years and over who are 4-year college graduates	Asian Indian	Bangladeshi	Cambodian	Chinese[2]	Fijian	Filipino	Guamanian[3]	Hawaiian, Native	Hmong	Indonesian	Japanese	Korean	Laotian	Malaysian	Pakistani	Samoan	Sri Lankan	Taiwanese	Thai	Tongan	Vietnamese
St. Johns County	28,560 33.13	862	510 59.16 59.16 1.79	-	-	-	-	-	-	-	-	-	-	-	-	-	-	-	-	-	-	-	-	-	-	-
St. Lucie County	20,562 15.07	1,269	389 30.65 30.65 1.89	-	-	-	-	-	-	-	-	-	-	-	-	-	-	-	-	-	-	-	-	-	-	-
Santa Rosa County	17,881 22.88	1,232	360 29.22 29.22 2.01	-	-	-	-	-	-	-	152 27.24 42.22 12.34 0.85	-	-	-	-	-	-	-	-	-	-	-	-	-	-	-
Sarasota County	70,446 27.43	1,694	584 34.47 34.47 0.83	-	-	-	-	-	61 26.52 10.45 3.60 0.09	-	209 52.51 35.79 12.34 0.30	-	-	-	-	-	-	-	-	-	-	-	-	-	-	79 19.08 13.53 4.66 0.11
Seminole County	75,491 31.04	5,863	2,838 48.41 48.41 3.76	-	-	1,192 66.08 42.00 20.33 1.58	-	-	490 49.35 17.27 8.36 0.65	-	423 45.14 14.90 7.21 0.56	-	-	-	-	-	208 33.60 7.33 3.55 0.28	-	-	-	-	-	-	-	-	198 28.01 6.98 3.38 0.26
Volusia County	55,961 17.64	3,243	1,190 36.69 36.69 2.13	-	-	414 40.35 34.79 12.77 0.74	-	-	171 37.34 14.37 5.27 0.31	-	351 53.59 29.50 10.82 0.63	-	-	-	-	-	46 15.92 3.87 1.42 0.08	-	-	-	-	-	-	-	-	-

Notes: Please refer to the User's Guide for an explanation of data; data is arranged alphabetically by state, then county, then city within each county; table includes counties with populations greater than 49,999 unless noted and cities with populations greater than 9,999 whose Asian and/or NHPI population rates are greater than the national average; (1) Native Hawaiian and other Pacific Islander; (2) excludes Taiwanese; (3) includes Chamorro; (4) county does not meet population threshold but is shown in order to allow inclusion of city

Median Household Income

(Universe: Households)

Place	All households	Asian households	NHPI[1] households	Asian Indian	Bangladeshi	Cambodian	Chinese[2]	Fijian	Filipino	Guamanian[3]	Hawaiian, Native	Hmong	Indonesian	Japanese	Korean	Laotian	Malaysian	Pakistani	Samoan	Sri Lankan	Taiwanese	Thai	Tongan	Vietnamese
UNITED STATES	41,994	51,908	42,717	63,669	39,321	36,155	51,321	45,420	60,570	46,306	44,554	32,076	38,175	52,060	40,037	42,978	35,767	47,241	40,620	52,661	54,928	40,329	45,700	45,085
FLORIDA	38,819	44,780	39,050	50,390	36,570	40,345	40,680	-	52,039	39,929	34,479	-	38,167	34,663	36,368	42,808	-	50,150	40,956	23,750	45,583	37,139	-	38,877
Alachua County	31,426	18,082	-	26,250	-	-	18,549	-	41,250	-	-	-	-	8,750	12,330	-	-	-	-	-	-	-	-	17,917
Gainesville (city)	28,164	15,551	-	14,550	-	-	17,708	-	-	-	-	-	-	-	11,506	-	-	-	-	-	-	-	-	-
Bay County	36,092	32,420	-	-	-	-	-	-	40,682	-	-	-	-	-	-	-	-	-	-	-	-	-	-	30,435
Callaway (city)	36,064	31,016	-	-	-	-	-	-	-	-	-	-	-	-	-	-	-	-	-	-	-	-	-	-
Brevard County	40,099	42,278	-	59,107	-	-	38,015	-	41,821	-	-	-	-	28,958	30,455	-	-	-	-	-	-	-	-	46,103
Broward County	41,691	47,731	40,819	49,518	-	-	41,049	-	69,201	-	-	-	-	52,917	36,121	-	-	41,875	-	-	-	46,058	-	41,333
Cooper City (city)	75,166	61,806	-	57,750	-	-	-	-	-	-	-	-	-	-	-	-	-	-	-	-	-	-	-	-
Pembroke Pines (city)	52,629	60,089	-	60,294	-	-	50,469	-	68,906	-	-	-	-	-	-	-	-	-	-	-	-	-	-	-
Charlotte County	36,379	61,000	-	-	-	-	-	-	-	-	-	-	-	-	-	-	-	-	-	-	-	-	-	-
Citrus County	31,001	44,375	-	-	-	-	-	-	-	-	-	-	-	-	-	-	-	-	-	-	-	-	-	-
Clay County	48,854	55,822	-	-	-	-	-	-	62,888	-	-	-	-	-	-	-	-	-	-	-	-	-	-	-
Bellair-Meadowbrook Ter. (cdp)	42,426	52,875	-	-	-	-	-	-	-	-	-	-	-	-	-	-	-	-	-	-	-	-	-	-
Collier County	48,289	62,742	-	-	-	-	-	-	-	-	-	-	-	-	-	-	-	-	-	-	-	-	-	-
Columbia County	30,881	40,139	-	-	-	-	-	-	-	-	-	-	-	-	-	-	-	-	-	-	-	-	-	-
Duval County	40,703	51,603	40,294	58,892	-	42,292	48,472	-	54,076	-	-	-	-	35,063	39,688	-	-	-	-	-	-	-	-	31,842
Escambia County	35,234	36,726	-	48,750	-	-	46,071	-	37,835	-	-	-	-	-	-	-	-	-	-	-	-	-	-	27,118
Bellview (cdp)	38,725	43,750	-	-	-	-	-	-	47,083	-	-	-	-	-	-	-	-	-	-	-	-	-	-	-
Myrtle Grove (cdp)	33,601	27,750	-	-	-	-	-	-	29,167	-	-	-	-	-	-	-	-	-	-	-	-	-	-	-
Hernando County	32,572	51,583	-	-	-	-	-	-	-	-	-	-	-	-	-	-	-	-	-	-	-	-	-	-
Highlands County	30,160	56,354	-	-	-	-	-	-	91,662	-	-	-	-	-	-	-	-	-	-	-	-	-	-	-
Hillsborough County	40,663	46,081	44,531	52,464	-	-	42,656	-	45,919	-	-	-	-	32,188	49,722	-	-	-	-	-	-	30,972	-	38,750
Westchase (cdp)	79,561	54,375	-	-	-	-	-	-	-	-	-	-	-	-	-	-	-	-	-	-	-	-	-	-
Indian River County	39,635	51,111	-	-	-	-	-	-	-	-	-	-	-	-	-	-	-	-	-	-	-	-	-	-
Lake County	36,903	45,083	-	-	-	-	-	-	-	-	-	-	-	-	-	-	-	-	-	-	-	-	-	-
Lee County	40,319	40,382	-	37,750	-	-	46,406	-	46,029	-	-	-	-	-	-	-	-	-	-	-	-	-	-	-
Leon County	37,517	40,531	-	56,574	-	-	41,779	-	33,047	-	-	-	-	-	30,952	-	-	-	-	-	-	-	-	-
Manatee County	38,673	52,539	-	-	-	-	-	-	56,484	-	-	-	-	-	-	-	-	-	-	-	-	-	-	-
Marion County	31,944	38,589	-	41,579	-	-	-	-	-	-	-	-	-	-	-	-	-	-	-	-	-	-	-	-
Martin County	43,083	36,250	-	-	-	-	-	-	-	-	-	-	-	-	-	-	-	-	-	-	-	-	-	-
Miami-Dade County	35,966	42,961	56,719	43,600	-	-	36,386	-	59,049	-	-	-	-	41,630	47,130	-	-	42,917	-	-	-	41,699	-	32,447
Doral (cdp)	53,060	55,909	-	-	-	-	-	-	-	-	-	-	-	-	-	-	-	-	-	-	-	-	-	-
Ives Estates (cdp)	40,717	40,556	-	-	-	-	-	-	-	-	-	-	-	-	-	-	-	-	-	-	-	-	-	-

Notes: Please refer to the User's Guide for an explanation of data; data is arranged alphabetically by state, then county, then city within each county; table includes counties with populations greater than 49,999 unless noted and cities with populations greater than 9,999 whose Asian and/or NHPI population rates are greater than the national average; (1) Native Hawaiian and other Pacific Islander; (2) excludes Taiwanese; (3) includes Chamorro; (4) county does not meet population threshold but is shown in order to allow inclusion of city

Place	All households	Asian households	NHPI[1] households	Asian Indian	Bangladeshi	Cambodian	Chinese[2]	Fijian	Filipino	Guamanian[3]	Hawaiian, Native	Hmong	Indonesian	Japanese	Korean	Laotian	Malaysian	Pakistani	Samoan	Sri Lankan	Taiwanese	Thai	Tongan	Vietnamese
North Miami Beach (city)	31,377	21,696	-	17,500	-	-	26,389	-	-	-	-	-	-	-	-	-	-	-	-	-	-	-	-	-
Pinecrest (village)	107,507	68,913	-	-	-	-	-	-	-	-	-	-	-	-	-	-	-	-	-	-	-	-	-	-
Monroe County	42,283	47,188	-	-	-	-	-	-	-	-	-	-	-	-	-	-	-	-	-	-	-	-	-	-
Nassau County	46,022	55,268	-	-	-	-	-	-	-	-	-	-	-	-	-	-	-	-	-	-	-	-	-	-
Okaloosa County	41,474	36,458	-	-	-	-	-	-	35,221	-	-	-	-	-	32,396	-	-	-	-	-	-	34,464	-	55,795
Wright (cdp)	36,940	38,889	-	-	-	-	-	-	-	-	-	-	-	-	-	-	-	-	-	-	-	-	-	-
Orange County	41,311	45,409	42,609	45,961	-	-	50,000	-	55,833	-	-	-	-	32,308	32,875	-	-	65,515	-	-	-	-	-	40,761
Oak Ridge (cdp)	30,290	34,500	-	-	-	-	-	-	-	-	-	-	-	-	-	-	-	-	-	-	-	-	-	39,293
Osceola County	38,214	41,840	-	32,143	-	-	52,120	-	53,864	-	-	-	-	-	-	-	-	-	-	-	-	-	-	-
Palm Beach County	45,062	47,829	48,750	55,041	-	-	45,927	-	56,354	-	-	-	-	41,071	40,042	-	-	-	-	-	-	33,750	-	43,533
Pasco County	32,969	51,761	-	65,163	-	-	34,464	-	57,976	-	-	-	-	-	-	-	-	-	-	-	-	-	-	-
Pinellas County	37,111	43,313	-	60,488	-	34,602	39,569	-	40,375	-	-	-	-	18,281	42,548	43,561	-	-	-	-	-	41,250	-	39,527
Pinellas Park (city)	35,048	34,856	-	-	-	-	-	-	-	-	-	-	-	-	-	-	-	-	-	-	-	-	-	34,196
Polk County	36,036	51,344	-	57,823	-	-	35,900	-	56,563	-	-	-	-	-	-	61,150	-	-	-	-	-	-	-	50,662
Putnam County	28,180	63,542	-	-	-	-	-	-	-	-	-	-	-	-	-	-	-	-	-	-	-	-	-	-
St. Johns County	50,099	53,500	-	-	-	-	-	-	-	-	-	-	-	-	-	-	-	-	-	-	-	-	-	-
St. Lucie County	36,363	39,728	-	-	-	-	-	-	-	-	-	-	-	-	-	-	-	-	-	-	-	-	-	-
Santa Rosa County	41,881	40,030	-	-	-	-	-	-	34,224	-	-	-	-	-	-	-	-	-	-	-	-	-	-	-
Sarasota County	41,957	42,813	-	-	-	-	37,656	-	36,579	-	-	-	-	-	-	-	-	-	-	-	-	-	-	50,313
Seminole County	49,326	56,111	-	65,292	-	-	46,528	-	64,792	-	-	-	-	-	45,625	-	-	-	-	-	-	-	-	70,521
Volusia County	35,219	31,528	-	37,206	-	-	31,842	-	39,083	-	-	-	-	-	29,375	-	-	-	-	-	-	-	-	-

Notes: Please refer to the User's Guide for an explanation of data; data is arranged alphabetically by state, then county, then city within each county; table includes counties with populations greater than 49,999 unless noted and cities with populations greater than 9,999 whose Asian and/or NHPI population rates are greater than the national average; (1) Native Hawaiian and other Pacific Islander; (2) excludes Taiwanese; (3) includes Chamorro; (4) county does not meet population threshold but is shown in order to allow inclusion of city

Per Capita Income

(Universe: Total Population)

Place	Total population	Total Asian population	Total NHPI[1] population	Asian Indian	Bangladeshi	Cambodian	Chinese[2]	Fijian	Filipino	Guamanian[3]	Hawaiian, Native	Hmong	Indonesian	Japanese	Korean	Laotian	Malaysian	Pakistani	Samoan	Sri Lankan	Taiwanese	Thai	Tongan	Vietnamese
UNITED STATES	21,587	21,823	15,054	27,514	13,971	10,366	23,642	14,745	21,267	17,583	17,697	6,600	18,932	30,075	18,805	11,830	19,895	18,096	12,160	27,478	25,890	19,066	10,680	15,655
FLORIDA	21,557	20,429	15,251	24,363	11,343	12,325	21,313	-	20,901	14,108	16,057	-	20,935	22,113	16,577	13,014	-	20,603	15,628	43,144	40,339	17,104	-	14,962
Alachua County	18,465	16,659	-	19,398	-	-	14,240	-	19,853	-	-	-	-	18,282	8,958	-	-	-	-	-	-	-	-	15,805
Gainesville (city)	16,779	12,149	-	14,123	-	-	10,383	-	-	-	-	-	-	-	7,384	-	-	-	-	-	-	-	-	-
Bay County	18,700	13,995	-	-	-	-	-	-	11,480	-	-	-	-	-	-	-	-	-	-	-	-	-	-	8,841
Callaway (city)	16,102	9,226	-	-	-	-	-	-	-	-	-	-	-	-	-	-	-	-	-	-	-	-	-	-
Brevard County	21,484	19,087	-	23,246	-	-	17,910	-	16,420	-	-	-	-	17,682	18,074	-	-	-	-	-	-	-	-	17,474
Broward County	23,170	20,147	19,375	20,230	-	-	21,094	-	24,606	-	-	-	-	24,222	15,533	-	-	13,943	-	-	-	16,263	-	18,109
Cooper City (city)	27,474	22,066	-	22,102	-	-	-	-	-	-	-	-	-	-	-	-	-	-	-	-	-	-	-	-
Pembroke Pines (city)	23,843	21,611	-	22,365	-	-	18,843	-	25,764	-	-	-	-	-	-	-	-	-	-	-	-	-	-	-
Charlotte County	21,806	20,973	-	-	-	-	-	-	-	-	-	-	-	-	-	-	-	-	-	-	-	-	-	-
Citrus County	18,585	34,576	-	-	-	-	-	-	-	-	-	-	-	-	-	-	-	-	-	-	-	-	-	-
Clay County	20,868	18,699	-	-	-	-	-	-	20,396	-	-	-	-	-	-	-	-	-	-	-	-	-	-	-
Bellair-Meadowbrook Ter. (cdp)	21,095	23,173	-	-	-	-	-	-	-	-	-	-	-	-	-	-	-	-	-	-	-	-	-	-
Collier County	31,195	33,926	-	-	-	-	-	-	-	-	-	-	-	-	-	-	-	-	-	-	-	-	-	-
Columbia County	14,598	19,896	-	-	-	-	-	-	-	-	-	-	-	-	-	-	-	-	-	-	-	-	-	-
Duval County	20,753	19,721	15,447	29,720	-	11,706	22,730	-	19,817	-	-	-	-	14,698	14,941	-	-	-	-	-	-	-	-	13,540
Escambia County	18,641	15,540	-	19,732	-	-	23,954	-	15,163	-	-	-	-	-	-	-	-	-	-	-	-	-	-	9,134
Bellview (cdp)	18,173	12,806	-	-	-	-	-	-	15,612	-	-	-	-	-	-	-	-	-	-	-	-	-	-	-
Myrtle Grove (cdp)	18,268	11,260	-	-	-	-	-	-	13,996	-	-	-	-	-	-	-	-	-	-	-	-	-	-	-
Hernando County	18,321	23,110	-	-	-	-	-	-	-	-	-	-	-	-	-	-	-	-	-	-	-	-	-	-
Highlands County	17,222	25,879	-	-	-	-	-	-	31,556	-	-	-	-	-	-	-	-	-	-	-	-	-	-	-
Hillsborough County	21,812	20,690	17,270	28,174	-	-	21,060	-	20,375	-	-	-	-	19,906	18,563	-	-	-	-	-	-	17,085	-	12,130
Westchase (cdp)	37,630	19,745	-	-	-	-	-	-	-	-	-	-	-	-	-	-	-	-	-	-	-	-	-	-
Indian River County	27,227	28,557	-	-	-	-	-	-	-	-	-	-	-	-	-	-	-	-	-	-	-	-	-	-
Lake County	20,199	21,089	-	-	-	-	-	-	-	-	-	-	-	-	-	-	-	-	-	-	-	-	-	-
Lee County	24,542	17,908	-	22,339	-	-	19,205	-	18,579	-	-	-	-	-	-	-	-	-	-	-	-	-	-	-
Leon County	21,024	22,009	-	30,481	-	-	24,031	-	13,619	-	-	-	-	-	16,709	-	-	-	-	-	-	-	-	-
Manatee County	22,388	18,041	-	-	-	-	-	-	21,237	-	-	-	-	-	-	-	-	-	-	-	-	-	-	-
Marion County	17,848	19,852	-	25,928	-	-	-	-	-	-	-	-	-	-	-	-	-	-	-	-	-	-	-	-
Martin County	29,584	18,328	-	-	-	-	-	-	-	-	-	-	-	-	-	-	-	-	-	-	-	-	-	-
Miami-Dade County	18,497	21,336	16,570	20,039	-	-	20,553	-	23,913	-	-	-	-	47,220	19,982	-	-	19,747	-	-	-	19,015	-	16,236
Doral (cdp)	27,705	23,653	-	-	-	-	-	-	-	-	-	-	-	-	-	-	-	-	-	-	-	-	-	-
Ives Estates (cdp)	19,118	18,795	-	-	-	-	-	-	-	-	-	-	-	-	-	-	-	-	-	-	-	-	-	-

Notes: Please refer to the User's Guide for an explanation of data: data is arranged alphabetically by state, then county, then city within each county; table includes counties with populations greater than 49,999 unless noted and cities with populations greater than 9,999 whose Asian and/or NHPI population rates are greater than the national average; (1) Native Hawaiian and other Pacific Islander; (2) excludes Taiwanese; (3) includes Chamorro; (4) county does not meet population threshold but is shown in order to allow inclusion of city

Place	Total population	Total Asian population	Total NHPI[1] population	Asian Indian	Bangladeshi	Cambodian	Chinese[2]	Fijian	Filipino	Guamanian[3]	Hawaiian, Native	Hmong	Indonesian	Japanese	Korean	Laotian	Malaysian	Pakistani	Samoan	Sri Lankan	Taiwanese	Thai	Tongan	Vietnamese
North Miami Beach (city)	14,699	14,597	-	8,817	-	-	19,120	-	-	-	-	-	-	-	-	-	-	-	-	-	-	-	-	-
Pinecrest (village)	51,181	58,647	-	-	-	-	-	-	-	-	-	-	-	-	-	-	-	-	-	-	-	-	-	-
Monroe County	26,102	21,969	-	-	-	-	-	-	-	-	-	-	-	-	-	-	-	-	-	-	-	-	-	-
Nassau County	22,836	13,991	-	-	-	-	-	-	-	-	-	-	-	-	-	-	-	-	-	-	-	-	-	-
Okaloosa County	20,918	15,213	-	-	-	-	-	-	14,849	-	-	-	-	-	13,818	-	-	-	-	-	-	11,397	-	17,425
Wright (cdp)	18,746	15,114	-	-	-	-	-	-	-	-	-	-	-	-	-	-	-	-	-	-	-	-	-	-
Orange County	20,916	20,259	13,933	23,770	-	-	20,860	-	19,048	-	-	-	-	18,295	18,071	-	-	23,458	-	-	-	-	-	17,443
Oak Ridge (cdp)	12,347	11,530	-	-	-	-	-	-	-	-	-	-	-	-	-	-	-	-	-	-	-	-	-	11,864
Osceola County	17,022	19,318	-	9,148	-	-	33,080	-	23,791	-	-	-	-	-	-	-	-	-	-	-	-	-	-	-
Palm Beach County	28,801	23,964	17,329	26,198	-	-	22,400	-	26,303	-	-	-	-	20,400	22,165	-	-	-	-	-	-	14,587	-	16,834
Pasco County	18,439	21,713	-	25,124	-	-	16,405	-	21,928	-	-	-	-	-	-	-	-	-	-	-	-	-	-	-
Pinellas County	23,497	19,028	-	31,591	-	10,582	19,729	-	19,797	-	-	-	-	17,260	16,234	11,534	-	-	-	-	-	16,847	-	14,143
Pinellas Park (city)	18,701	14,175	-	-	-	-	-	-	-	-	-	-	-	-	-	-	-	-	-	-	-	-	-	15,915
Polk County	18,302	18,106	-	18,923	-	-	17,818	-	25,142	-	-	-	-	-	-	16,796	-	-	-	-	-	-	-	12,065
Putnam County	15,603	32,782	-	-	-	-	-	-	-	-	-	-	-	-	-	-	-	-	-	-	-	-	-	-
St. Johns County	28,674	40,366	-	-	-	-	-	-	-	-	-	-	-	-	-	-	-	-	-	-	-	-	-	-
St. Lucie County	18,790	19,054	-	-	-	-	-	-	-	-	-	-	-	-	-	-	-	-	-	-	-	-	-	-
Santa Rosa County	20,089	22,558	-	-	-	-	-	-	11,037	-	-	-	-	-	-	-	-	-	-	-	-	-	-	-
Sarasota County	28,326	19,140	-	-	-	-	22,142	-	18,028	-	-	-	-	-	-	-	-	-	-	-	-	-	-	12,661
Seminole County	24,591	24,961	-	31,121	-	-	23,797	-	25,876	-	-	-	-	-	16,430	-	-	-	-	-	-	-	-	21,038
Volusia County	19,664	20,853	-	25,792	-	-	18,972	-	22,985	-	-	-	-	-	13,006	-	-	-	-	-	-	-	-	-

Notes: Please refer to the User's Guide for an explanation of data; data is arranged alphabetically by state, then county, then city within each county; table includes counties with populations greater than 49,999 unless noted and cities with populations greater than 9,999 whose Asian and/or NHPI population rates are greater than the national average; (1) Native Hawaiian and other Pacific Islander; (2) excludes Taiwanese; (3) includes Chamorro; (4) county does not meet population threshold but is shown in order to allow inclusion of city

Poverty Status

(Universe: Population for Whom Poverty Status is Determined)

Place	Total population with income below poverty level	Asian population for whom poverty status is determined	Asians with income below poverty level	NHPI[1] population for whom poverty status is determined	NHPIs[1] with income below poverty level	Asian Indian	Bangladeshi	Cambodian	Chinese[2]	Fijian	Filipino	Guamanian[3]	Hawaiian, Native	Hmong	Indonesian	Japanese	Korean	Laotian	Malaysian	Pakistani	Samoan	Sri Lankan	Taiwanese	Thai	Tongan	Vietnamese
UNITED STATES	33,899,812	9,979,963	1,257,237	364,909	64,558	157,516	8,734	51,240	303,054	1,066	114,849	7,292	20,840	63,633	7,650	75,540	154,688	30,604	2,618	25,406	16,629	1,933	17,523	15,548	5,310	175,924
	12.38		12.60		17.69	9.75	21.29	29.28	13.43	10.47	6.25	13.75	15.58	37.78	20.92	9.72	14.77	18.51	25.04	16.47	20.18	10.36	14.73	14.35	19.48	16.05
						12.53	0.69	4.08	24.10	1.65	9.14	11.30	32.28	5.06	0.61	6.01	12.30	2.43	0.21	2.02	25.76	0.15	1.39	1.24	8.23	13.99
			12.60		17.69	1.58	0.09	0.51	3.04	0.29	1.15	2.00	5.71	0.64	0.08	0.76	1.55	0.31	0.03	0.25	4.56	0.02	0.18	0.16	1.46	1.76
			3.71		0.19	0.46	0.03	0.15	0.89	<0.01	0.34	0.02	0.06	0.19	0.02	0.22	0.46	0.09	0.01	0.07	0.05	0.01	0.05	0.05	0.02	0.52
FLORIDA	1,952,629	261,321	31,860	6,440	1,131	8,515	266	247	6,167	-	3,518	497	228	-	86	1,493	3,025	337	-	856	108	77	328	709	-	4,824
	12.51		12.19		17.56	12.72	21.25	9.13	13.86		6.56	25.33	12.50		9.62	13.29	16.05	8.37		15.81	14.12	19.54	16.34	10.87		14.59
						26.73	0.83	0.78	19.36		11.04	43.94	20.16		0.27	4.69	9.49	1.06		2.69	9.55	0.24	1.03	2.23		15.14
			12.19		17.56	3.26	0.10	0.09	2.36		1.35	7.72	3.54		0.03	0.57	1.16	0.13		0.33	1.68	0.03	0.13	0.27		1.85
			1.63		0.06	0.44	0.01	0.01	0.32		0.18	0.03	0.01		<0.01	0.08	0.15	0.02		0.04	0.01	<0.01	0.02	0.04		0.25
Alachua County	46,939	7,360	2,478	-	-	660	-	-	624	-	183	-	-	-	-	155	441	-	-	-	-	-	-	-	-	179
	22.76		33.67			37.39			31.04		18.47					36.38	45.23									31.85
						26.63			25.18		7.38					6.26	17.80									7.22
			33.67			8.97			8.48		2.49					2.11	5.99									2.43
			5.28			1.41			1.33		0.39					0.33	0.94									0.38
Gainesville (city)	22,559	3,901	1,476	-	-	362	-	-	462	-	-	-	-	-	-	-	243	-	-	-	-	-	-	-	-	-
	26.69		37.84			41.51			34.71								51.59									
						24.53			31.30								16.46									
			37.84			9.28			11.84								6.23									
			6.54			1.60			2.05								1.08									
Bay County	18,882	2,369	299	-	-	-	-	-	-	-	13	-	-	-	-	-	-	-	-	-	-	-	-	-	-	167
	13.04		12.62								2.69															25.08
											4.35															55.85
			12.62								0.55															7.05
			1.58								0.07															0.88
Callaway (city)	1,645	530	71	-	-	-	-	-	-	-	-	-	-	-	-	-	-	-	-	-	-	-	-	-	-	-
	11.57		13.40																							
			13.40																							
			4.32																							
Brevard County	44,218	7,043	826	-	-	250	-	-	156	-	50	-	-	-	-	77	98	-	-	-	-	-	-	-	-	63
	9.47		11.73			13.00			17.59		3.25					14.67	15.99									8.32
						30.27			18.89		6.05					9.32	11.86									7.63
			11.73			3.55			2.21		0.71					1.09	1.39									0.89
			1.87			0.57			0.35		0.11					0.17	0.22									0.14
Broward County	184,589	36,431	3,857	639	66	1,333	-	-	1,123	-	231	-	-	-	-	93	444	-	-	79	-	-	-	98	-	281
	11.51		10.59		10.33	10.25			13.18		4.76					8.90	19.75			7.20				16.36		9.81
						34.56			29.12		5.99					2.41	11.51			2.05				2.54		7.29
			10.59		10.33	3.66			3.08		0.63					0.26	1.22			0.22				0.27		0.77
			2.09		0.04	0.72			0.61		0.13					0.05	0.24			0.04				0.05		0.15
Cooper City (city)	888	1,241	75	-	-	75	-	-	-	-	-	-	-	-	-	-	-	-	-	-	-	-	-	-	-	-
	3.21		6.04			12.65																				
						100.00																				
			6.04			6.04																				
			8.45			8.45																				

Notes: Please refer to the User's Guide for an explanation of data; data is arranged alphabetically by state, then county, then city within each county; table includes counties with populations greater than 49,999 unless noted and cities with populations greater than 9,999 whose Asian and/or NHPI population rates are greater than the national average; (1) Native Hawaiian and other Pacific Islander; (2) excludes Taiwanese; (3) includes Chamorro; (4) county does not meet population threshold but is shown in order to allow inclusion of city

Place	Total population with income below poverty level	Asian population for whom poverty status is determined	Asians with income below poverty level	NHPI[1] population for whom poverty status is determined	NHPIs[1] with income below poverty level	Asian Indian	Bangladeshi	Cambodian	Chinese[2]	Fijian	Filipino	Guamanian[3]	Hawaiian, Native	Hmong	Indonesian	Japanese	Korean	Laotian	Malaysian	Pakistani	Samoan	Sri Lankan	Taiwanese	Thai	Tongan	Vietnamese
Pembroke Pines (city)	7,291 5.38	5,004	356 7.11 7.11 4.88	-	-	119 6.79 33.43 2.38 1.63	-	-	132 11.45 37.08 2.64 1.81	-	71 7.66 19.94 1.42 0.97	-	-	-	-	-	-	-	-	-	-	-	-	-	-	-
Charlotte County	11,419 8.23	849	99 11.66 11.66 0.87	-	-	-	-	-	-	-	-	-	-	-	-	-	-	-	-	-	-	-	-	-	-	-
Citrus County	13,541 11.68	1,116	118 10.57 10.57 0.87	-	-	-	-	-	-	-	-	-	-	-	-	-	-	-	-	-	-	-	-	-	-	-
Clay County	9,437 6.78	2,893	258 8.92 8.92 2.73	-	-	-	-	-	-	-	28 1.63 10.85 0.97 0.30	-	-	-	-	-	-	-	-	-	-	-	-	-	-	-
Bellair-Meadowbrook Ter. (cdp)	1,218 7.51	627	33 5.26 5.26 2.71	-	-	-	-	-	-	-	-	-	-	-	-	-	-	-	-	-	-	-	-	-	-	-
Collier County	25,449 10.26	1,200	116 9.67 9.67 0.46	-	-	-	-	-	-	-	-	-	-	-	-	-	-	-	-	-	-	-	-	-	-	-
Columbia County	8,027 15.01	386	31 8.03 8.03 0.39	-	-	-	-	-	-	-	-	-	-	-	-	-	-	-	-	-	-	-	-	-	-	-
Duval County	90,828 11.91	20,258	1,669 8.24 8.24 1.84	481	47 9.77 9.77 0.05	220 7.98 13.18 1.09 0.24	-	69 6.93 4.13 0.34 0.08	191 11.75 11.44 0.94 0.21	-	557 5.55 33.37 2.75 0.61	-	-	-	-	72 13.36 4.31 0.36 0.08	102 10.90 6.11 0.50 0.11	-	-	-	-	-	-	-	-	370 17.70 22.17 1.83 0.41
Escambia County	41,978 15.44	6,222	873 14.03 14.03 2.08	-	-	75 14.94 8.59 1.21 0.18	-	-	67 11.53 7.67 1.08 0.16	-	195 7.58 22.34 3.13 0.46	-	-	-	-	-	-	-	-	-	-	-	-	-	-	449 29.02 51.43 7.22 1.07
Bellview (cdp)	2,125 10.17	787	105 13.34 13.34 4.94	-	-	-	-	-	-	-	24 5.83 22.86 3.05 1.13	-	-	-	-	-	-	-	-	-	-	-	-	-	-	-

Notes: Please refer to the User's Guide for an explanation of data; data is arranged alphabetically by state, then county, then city within each county; table includes counties with populations greater than 49,999 unless noted and cities with populations greater than 9,999 whose Asian and/or NHPI population rates are greater than the national average; (1) Native Hawaiian and other Pacific Islander; (2) excludes Taiwanese; (3) includes Chamorro; (4) county does not meet population threshold but is shown in order to allow inclusion of city

Place	Total population with income below poverty level	Asian population for whom poverty status is determined	Asians with income below poverty level	NHPI[1] population for whom poverty status is determined	NHPIs[1] with income below poverty level	Asian Indian	Bangladeshi	Cambodian	Chinese[2]	Fijian	Filipino	Guamanian[3]	Hawaiian, Native	Hmong	Indonesian	Japanese	Korean	Laotian	Malaysian	Pakistani	Samoan	Sri Lankan	Taiwanese	Thai	Tongan	Vietnamese
Myrtle Grove (cdp)	2,174 14.24	753	139 18.46 18.46 6.39	-	-	-	-	-	-	-	6 1.38 4.32 0.80 0.28	-	-	-	-	-	-	-	-	-	-	-	-	-	-	-
Hernando County	13,307 10.33	766	72 9.40 9.40 0.54	-	-	-	-	-	-	-	-	-	-	-	-	-	-	-	-	-	-	-	-	-	-	-
Highlands County	13,065 15.22	964	98 10.17 10.17 0.75	-	-	-	-	-	-	-	0 0.00 0.00 0.00 0.00	-	-	-	-	-	-	-	-	-	-	-	-	-	-	-
Hillsborough County	122,872 12.51	21,431	2,536 11.83 11.83 2.06	428	32 7.48 7.48 0.03	640 10.91 25.24 2.99 0.52	-	-	323 12.06 12.74 1.51 0.26	-	163 5.17 6.43 0.76 0.13	-	-	-	-	127 14.92 5.01 0.59 0.10	401 14.75 15.81 1.87 0.33	-	-	-	-	-	-	74 10.95 2.92 0.35 0.06	-	690 17.28 27.21 3.22 0.56
Westchase (cdp)	261 2.35	508	26 5.12 5.12 9.96	-	-	-	-	-	-	-	-	-	-	-	-	-	-	-	-	-	-	-	-	-	-	-
Indian River County	10,325 9.30	821	148 18.03 18.03 1.43	-	-	-	-	-	-	-	-	-	-	-	-	-	-	-	-	-	-	-	-	-	-	-
Lake County	19,907 9.63	1,415	54 3.82 3.82 0.27	-	-	-	-	-	-	-	-	-	-	-	-	-	-	-	-	-	-	-	-	-	-	-
Lee County	42,316 9.73	3,144	371 11.80 11.80 0.88	-	-	81 12.11 21.83 2.58 0.19	-	-	64 10.74 17.25 2.04 0.15	-	136 12.49 36.66 4.33 0.32	-	-	-	-	-	-	-	-	-	-	-	-	-	-	-
Leon County	41,078 18.19	4,722	732 15.50 15.50 1.78	-	-	152 10.27 20.77 3.22 0.37	-	-	81 7.62 11.07 1.72 0.20	-	89 17.28 12.16 1.88 0.22	-	-	-	-	-	136 30.49 18.58 2.88 0.33	-	-	-	-	-	-	-	-	-
Manatee County	26,104 10.08	2,217	192 8.66 8.66 0.74	-	-	-	-	-	-	-	43 7.99 22.40 1.94 0.16	-	-	-	-	-	-	-	-	-	-	-	-	-	-	-

Notes: Please refer to the User's Guide for an explanation of data; data is arranged alphabetically by state, then county, then city within each county; table includes counties with populations greater than 49,999 unless noted and cities with populations greater than 9,999 whose Asian and/or NHPI population rates are greater than the national average; (1) Native Hawaiian and other Pacific Islander; (2) excludes Taiwanese; (3) includes Chamorro; (4) county does not meet population threshold but is shown in order to allow inclusion of city

Place	Total population with income below poverty level	Asian population for whom poverty status is determined	Asians with income below poverty level	NHPI[1] population for whom poverty status is determined	NHPIs[1] with income below poverty level	Asian Indian	Bangladeshi	Cambodian	Chinese[2]	Fijian	Filipino	Guamanian[3]	Hawaiian, Native	Hmong	Indonesian	Japanese	Korean	Laotian	Malaysian	Pakistani	Samoan	Sri Lankan	Taiwanese	Thai	Tongan	Vietnamese
Marion County	32,918 13.08	2,185	302 13.82 13.82 0.92	-	-	150 15.81 49.67 6.86 0.46	-	-	-	-	-	-	-	-	-	-	-	-	-	-	-	-	-	-	-	-
Martin County	10,844 8.77	697	36 5.16 5.16 0.33	-	-	-	-	-	-	-	-	-	-	-	-	-	-	-	-	-	-	-	-	-	-	-
Miami-Dade County	396,995 17.97	30,177	4,192 13.89 13.89 1.06	582	85 14.60 14.60 0.02	1,340 15.52 31.97 4.44 0.34	-	-	1,432 16.21 34.16 4.75 0.36	-	330 7.41 7.87 1.09 0.08	-	-	-	-	90 6.48 2.15 0.30 0.02	148 11.45 3.53 0.49 0.04	-	-	167 21.03 3.98 0.55 0.04	-	-	-	89 10.09 2.12 0.29 0.02	-	290 18.51 6.92 0.96 0.07
Doral (cdp)	2,404 11.74	1,186	120 10.12 10.12 4.99	-	-	-	-	-	-	-	-	-	-	-	-	-	-	-	-	-	-	-	-	-	-	-
Ives Estates (cdp)	1,487 8.57	831	68 8.18 8.18 4.57	-	-	-	-	-	-	-	-	-	-	-	-	-	-	-	-	-	-	-	-	-	-	-
North Miami Beach (city)	8,230 20.52	1,681	537 31.95 31.95 6.52	-	-	175 44.19 32.59 10.41 2.13	-	-	160 21.80 29.80 9.52 1.94	-	-	-	-	-	-	-	-	-	-	-	-	-	-	-	-	-
Pinecrest (village)	780 4.07	884	89 10.07 10.07 11.41	-	-	-	-	-	-	-	-	-	-	-	-	-	-	-	-	-	-	-	-	-	-	-
Monroe County	7,977 10.18	549	51 9.29 9.29 0.64	-	-	-	-	-	-	-	-	-	-	-	-	-	-	-	-	-	-	-	-	-	-	-
Nassau County	5,192 9.15	422	113 26.78 26.78 2.18	-	-	-	-	-	-	-	-	-	-	-	-	-	-	-	-	-	-	-	-	-	-	-
Okaloosa County	14,562 8.84	4,368	376 8.61 8.61 2.58	-	-	-	-	-	-	-	126 7.38 33.51 2.88 0.87	-	-	-	-	-	68 9.44 18.09 1.56 0.47	-	-	-	-	-	-	50 8.14 13.30 1.14 0.34	-	43 11.03 11.44 0.98 0.30

Notes: Please refer to the User's Guide for an explanation of data; data is arranged alphabetically by state, then county, then city within each county; table includes counties with populations greater than 49,999 unless noted and cities with populations greater than 9,999 whose Asian and/or NHPI population rates are greater than the national average; (1) Native Hawaiian and other Pacific Islander; (2) excludes Taiwanese; (3) includes Chamorro; (4) county does not meet population threshold but is shown in order to allow inclusion of city

Place	Total population with income below poverty level	Asian population for whom poverty status is determined	Asians with income below poverty level	NHPI[1] population for whom poverty status is determined	NHPIs[1] with income below poverty level	Asian Indian	Bangladeshi	Cambodian	Chinese[2]	Fijian	Filipino	Guamanian[3]	Hawaiian, Native	Hmong	Indonesian	Japanese	Korean	Laotian	Malaysian	Pakistani	Samoan	Sri Lankan	Taiwanese	Thai	Tongan	Vietnamese
Wright (cdp)	2,291 10.93	825	83 10.06 10.06 3.62	-	-	-	-	-	-	-	-	-	-	-	-	-	-	-	-	-	-	-	-	-	-	-
Orange County	106,233 12.11	28,640	3,323 11.60 11.60 3.13	823	136 16.52 16.52 0.13	969 12.70 29.16 3.38 0.91	-	-	367 9.22 11.04 1.28 0.35	-	371 8.29 11.16 1.30 0.35	-	-	-	-	242 20.17 7.28 0.84 0.23	440 20.51 13.24 1.54 0.41	-	-	119 13.21 3.58 0.42 0.11	-	-	-	-	-	602 9.47 18.12 2.10 0.57
Oak Ridge (cdp)	4,357 19.57	1,306	200 15.31 15.31 4.59	-	-	-	-	-	-	-	-	-	-	-	-	-	-	-	-	-	-	-	-	-	-	41 7.78 20.50 3.14 0.94
Osceola County	19,532 11.52	3,635	573 15.76 15.76 2.93	-	-	272 28.16 47.47 7.48 1.39	-	-	39 6.68 6.81 1.07 0.20	-	61 6.91 10.65 1.68 0.31	-	-	-	-	-	-	-	-	-	-	-	-	-	-	-
Palm Beach County	110,430 9.92	16,813	1,911 11.37 11.37 1.73	407	81 19.90 19.90 0.07	618 12.15 32.34 3.68 0.56	-	-	407 11.20 21.30 2.42 0.37	-	129 5.80 6.75 0.77 0.12	-	-	-	-	69 12.39 3.61 0.41 0.06	24 2.61 1.26 0.14 0.02	-	-	-	-	-	-	68 9.01 3.56 0.40 0.06	-	190 9.56 9.94 1.13 0.17
Pasco County	36,201 10.67	3,482	307 8.82 8.82 0.85	-	-	138 14.00 44.95 3.96 0.38	-	-	99 19.64 32.25 2.84 0.27	-	11 1.11 3.58 0.32 0.03	-	-	-	-	-	-	-	-	-	-	-	-	-	-	-
Pinellas County	90,059 9.97	18,677	1,992 10.67 10.67 2.21	-	-	351 9.65 17.62 1.88 0.39	-	98 14.16 4.92 0.52 0.11	197 9.47 9.89 1.05 0.22	-	342 11.30 17.17 1.83 0.38	-	-	-	-	104 18.74 5.22 0.56 0.12	104 12.18 5.22 0.56 0.12	141 7.60 7.08 0.75 0.16	-	-	-	-	-	36 7.38 1.81 0.19 0.04	-	437 10.38 21.94 2.34 0.49
Pinellas Park (city)	4,178 9.34	1,791	190 10.61 10.61 4.55	-	-	-	-	-	-	-	-	-	-	-	-	-	-	-	-	-	-	-	-	-	-	84 15.97 44.21 4.69 2.01
Polk County	60,953 12.94	5,762	762 13.22 13.22 1.25	-	-	108 6.36 14.17 1.87 0.18	-	-	84 14.12 11.02 1.46 0.14	-	20 2.22 2.62 0.35 0.03	-	-	-	-	-	-	36 8.98 4.72 0.62 0.06	-	-	-	-	-	-	-	168 19.47 22.05 2.92 0.28
Putnam County	14,449 20.87	291	36 12.37 12.37 0.25	-	-	-	-	-	-	-	-	-	-	-	-	-	-	-	-	-	-	-	-	-	-	-

Notes: Please refer to the User's Guide for an explanation of data; data is arranged alphabetically by state, then county, then city within each county; table includes counties with populations greater than 49,999 unless noted and cities with populations greater than 9,999 whose Asian and/or NHPI population rates are greater than the national average; (1) Native Hawaiian and other Pacific Islander; (2) excludes Taiwanese; (3) includes Chamorro; (4) county does not meet population threshold but is shown in order to allow inclusion of city

Place	Total population with income below poverty level	Asian population for whom poverty status is determined	Asians with income below poverty level	NHPI[1] population for whom poverty status is determined	NHPIs[1] with income below poverty level	Asian Indian	Bangladeshi	Cambodian	Chinese[2]	Fijian	Filipino	Guamanian[3]	Hawaiian, Native	Hmong	Indonesian	Japanese	Korean	Laotian	Malaysian	Pakistani	Samoan	Sri Lankan	Taiwanese	Thai	Tongan	Vietnamese
St. Johns County	9,698 8.02	1,244	110 8.84 8.84 1.13	-	-	-	-	-	-	-	-	-	-	-	-	-	-	-	-	-	-	-	-	-	-	-
St. Lucie County	25,464 13.40	1,879	214 11.39 11.39 0.84	-	-	-	-	-	-	-	-	-	-	-	-	-	-	-	-	-	-	-	-	-	-	-
Santa Rosa County	11,282 9.83	1,585	98 6.18 6.18 0.87	-	-	-	-	-	-	-	11 1.56 11.22 0.69 0.10	-	-	-	-	-	-	-	-	-	-	-	-	-	-	-
Sarasota County	24,817 7.77	2,560	415 16.21 16.21 1.67	-	-	-	-	-	104 24.41 25.06 4.06 0.42	-	16 2.96 3.86 0.63 0.06	-	-	-	-	-	-	-	-	-	-	-	-	-	-	166 25.70 40.00 6.48 0.67
Seminole County	26,804 7.41	8,682	833 9.59 9.59 3.11	-	-	285 10.25 34.21 3.28 1.06	-	-	188 13.57 22.57 2.17 0.70	-	80 6.09 9.60 0.92 0.30	-	-	-	-	-	130 13.32 15.61 1.50 0.49	-	-	-	-	-	-	-	-	72 6.77 8.64 0.83 0.27
Volusia County	49,907 11.62	4,676	814 17.41 17.41 1.63	-	-	330 21.50 40.54 7.06 0.66	-	-	128 19.72 15.72 2.74 0.26	-	46 5.22 5.65 0.98 0.09	-	-	-	-	-	103 23.68 12.65 2.20 0.21	-	-	-	-	-	-	-	-	-

Notes: Please refer to the User's Guide for an explanation of data; data is arranged alphabetically by state, then county, then city within each county; table includes counties with populations greater than 49,999 unless noted and cities with populations greater than 9,999 whose Asian and/or NHPI population rates are greater than the national average; (1) Native Hawaiian and other Pacific Islander; (2) excludes Taiwanese; (3) includes Chamorro; (4) county does not meet population threshold but is shown in order to allow inclusion of city

Homeownership

(Universe: Occupied Housing Units)

Place	All owner-occupied housing units	Asian-occupied housing units	Asians who own and occupy their own homes	NHPI[1]-occupied housing units	NHPIs[1] who own and occupy their own homes	Asian Indian	Bangladeshi	Cambodian	Chinese[2]	Fijian	Filipino	Guamanian[3]	Hawaiian, Native	Hmong	Indonesian	Japanese	Korean	Laotian	Malaysian	Pakistani	Samoan	Sri Lankan	Taiwanese	Thai	Tongan	Vietnamese
UNITED STATES	69,816,513	3,117,356	1,659,794	98,739	44,896	247,650	3,171	17,134	441,852	1,389	307,810	7,536	21,581	10,419	4,977	204,997	134,736	20,717	1,092	17,306	6,585	3,424	26,324	16,556	2,465	155,325
	66.19		53.24		45.47	46.87	28.17	43.59	58.08	50.38	59.98	47.57	52.22	38.74	38.55	60.84	40.08	52.37	29.70	41.65	34.36	51.07	64.75	48.06	48.14	53.22
						14.92	0.19	1.03	26.62	3.09	18.55	16.79	48.07	0.63	0.30	12.35	8.12	1.25	0.07	1.04	14.67	0.21	1.59	1.00	5.49	9.36
			53.24		45.47	7.94	0.10	0.55	14.17	1.41	9.87	7.63	21.86	0.33	0.16	6.58	4.32	0.66	0.04	0.56	6.67	0.11	0.84	0.53	2.50	4.98
			2.38		0.06	0.35	<0.01	0.02	0.63	<0.01	0.44	0.01	0.03	0.01	0.01	0.29	0.19	0.03	<0.01	0.02	0.01	<0.01	0.04	0.02	<0.01	0.22
FLORIDA	4,441,711	82,089	49,897	1,914	919	12,490	134	547	10,446	-	10,160	249	315	-	218	2,368	2,661	766	-	905	94	110	528	1,069	-	5,870
	70.08		60.78		48.01	55.38	33.84	78.59	65.96		66.89	44.86	48.69		53.69	58.05	47.95	68.82		55.62	47.24	62.50	71.45	56.62		63.81
						25.03	0.27	1.10	20.94		20.36	27.09	34.28		0.44	4.75	5.33	1.54		1.81	10.23	0.22	1.06	2.14		11.76
			60.78		48.01	15.22	0.16	0.67	12.73		12.38	13.01	16.46		0.27	2.88	3.24	0.93		1.10	4.91	0.13	0.64	1.30		7.15
			1.12		0.02	0.28	<0.01	0.01	0.24		0.23	0.01	0.01		<0.01	0.05	0.06	0.02		0.02	<0.01	<0.01	0.01	0.02		0.13
Alachua County	48,084	3,104	939	-	-	299	-	-	237	-	138	-	-	-	-	26	56	-	-	-	-	-	-	-	-	76
	54.95		30.25			38.48			25.93		42.86					15.48	13.93									33.93
						31.84			25.24		14.70					2.77	5.96									8.09
			30.25			9.63			7.64		4.45					0.84	1.80									2.45
			1.95			0.62			0.49		0.29					0.05	0.12									0.16
Gainesville (city)	17,791	1,765	426	-	-	135	-	-	91	-	-	-	-	-	-	-	31	-	-	-	-	-	-	-	-	-
	47.73		24.14			33.67			15.17								14.90									
						31.69			21.36								7.28									
			24.14			7.65			5.16								1.76									
			2.39			0.76			0.51								0.17									
Bay County	40,892	663	348	-	-	-	-	-	-	-	38	-	-	-	-	-	-	-	-	-	-	-	-	-	-	111
	68.61		52.49								43.68															58.12
											10.92															31.90
			52.49								5.73															16.74
			0.85								0.09															0.27
Callaway (city)	3,565	158	87	-	-	-	-	-	-	-	-	-	-	-	-	-	-	-	-	-	-	-	-	-	-	-
	63.88		55.06																							
			55.06																							
			2.44																							
Brevard County	147,878	2,252	1,379	-	-	379	-	-	182	-	299	-	-	-	-	112	116	-	-	-	-	-	-	-	-	156
	74.61		61.23			58.85			55.83		62.82					53.85	67.05									75.73
						27.48			13.20		21.68					8.12	8.41									11.31
			61.23			16.83			8.08		13.28					4.97	5.15									6.93
			0.93			0.26			0.12		0.20					0.08	0.08									0.11
Broward County	454,625	11,261	7,555	206	106	2,666	-	-	2,240	-	862	-	-	-	-	275	310	-	-	135	-	-	-	123	-	550
	69.47		67.09		51.46	63.80			80.87		71.48					69.27	43.12			40.42				63.08		63.44
						35.29			29.65		11.41					3.64	4.10			1.79				1.63		7.28
			67.09		51.46	23.67			19.89		7.65					2.44	2.75			1.20				1.09		4.88
			1.66		0.02	0.59			0.49		0.19					0.06	0.07			0.03				0.03		0.12
Cooper City (city)	8,381	337	301	-	-	135	-	-	-	-	-	-	-	-	-	-	-	-	-	-	-	-	-	-	-	-
	92.24		89.32			78.95																				
						44.85																				
			89.32			40.06																				
			3.59			1.61																				

Notes: Please refer to the User's Guide for an explanation of data; data is arranged alphabetically by state, then county, then city within each county; table includes counties with populations greater than 49,999 unless noted and cities with populations greater than 9,999 whose Asian and/or NHPI population rates are greater than the national average; (1) Native Hawaiian and other Pacific Islander; (2) excludes Taiwanese; (3) includes Chamorro; (4) county does not meet population threshold but is shown in order to allow inclusion of city

Place	All owner-occupied housing units	Asian-occupied housing units	Asians who own and occupy their own homes	NHPI[1]-occupied housing units	NHPIs[1] who own and occupy their own homes	Asian Indian	Bangladeshi	Cambodian	Chinese[2]	Fijian	Filipino	Guamanian[3]	Hawaiian, Native	Hmong	Indonesian	Japanese	Korean	Laotian	Malaysian	Pakistani	Samoan	Sri Lankan	Taiwanese	Thai	Tongan	Vietnamese
Pembroke Pines (city)	41,636 80.10	1,515	1,099 72.54 72.54 2.64	-	-	345 65.84 31.39 22.77 0.83	-	-	286 78.36 26.02 18.88 0.69	-	244 85.92 22.20 16.11 0.59	-	-	-	-	-	-	-	-	-	-	-	-	-	-	-
Charlotte County	53,444 83.68	220	168 76.36 76.36 0.31	-	-	-	-	-	-	-	-	-	-	-	-	-	-	-	-	-	-	-	-	-	-	-
Citrus County	45,047 85.59	353	223 63.17 63.17 0.50	-	-	-	-	-	-	-	-	-	-	-	-	-	-	-	-	-	-	-	-	-	-	-
Clay County	39,120 77.86	691	562 81.33 81.33 1.44	-	-	-	-	-	-	-	317 81.91 56.41 45.88 0.81	-	-	-	-	-	-	-	-	-	-	-	-	-	-	-
Bellair-Meadowbrook Ter. (cdp)	3,400 52.56	187	139 74.33 74.33 4.09	-	-	-	-	-	-	-	-	-	-	-	-	-	-	-	-	-	-	-	-	-	-	-
Collier County	77,829 75.58	362	156 43.09 43.09 0.20	-	-	-	-	-	-	-	-	-	-	-	-	-	-	-	-	-	-	-	-	-	-	-
Columbia County	16,137 77.12	125	75 60.00 60.00 0.46	-	-	-	-	-	-	-	-	-	-	-	-	-	-	-	-	-	-	-	-	-	-	-
Duval County	191,722 63.12	6,151	3,898 63.37 63.37 2.03	154	68 44.16 44.16 0.04	399 38.00 10.24 6.49 0.21	-	172 74.14 4.41 2.80 0.09	312 53.06 8.00 5.07 0.16	-	2,230 77.94 57.21 36.25 1.16	-	-	-	-	115 64.97 2.95 1.87 0.06	144 55.17 3.69 2.34 0.08	-	-	-	-	-	-	-	-	274 46.76 7.03 4.45 0.14
Escambia County	74,690 67.26	1,800	1,127 62.61 62.61 1.51	-	-	92 67.65 8.16 5.11 0.12	-	-	115 61.83 10.20 6.39 0.15	-	480 64.52 42.59 26.67 0.64	-	-	-	-	-	-	-	-	-	-	-	-	-	-	240 57.28 21.30 13.33 0.32
Bellview (cdp)	6,082 75.17	210	146 69.52 69.52 2.40	-	-	-	-	-	-	-	88 73.95 60.27 41.90 1.45	-	-	-	-	-	-	-	-	-	-	-	-	-	-	-

Notes: Please refer to the User's Guide for an explanation of data; data is arranged alphabetically by state, then county, then city within each county; table includes counties with populations greater than 49,999 unless noted and cities with populations greater than 9,999 whose Asian and/or NHPI population rates are greater than the national average; (1) Native Hawaiian and other Pacific Islander; (2) excludes Taiwanese; (3) includes Chamorro; (4) county does not meet population threshold but is shown in order to allow inclusion of city

Place	All owner-occupied housing units	Asian-occupied housing units	Asians who own and occupy their own homes	NHPI[1]-occupied housing units	NHPIs[1] who own and occupy their own homes	Asian Indian	Bangladeshi	Cambodian	Chinese[2]	Fijian	Filipino	Guamanian[3]	Hawaiian, Native	Hmong	Indonesian	Japanese	Korean	Laotian	Malaysian	Pakistani	Samoan	Sri Lankan	Taiwanese	Thai	Tongan	Vietnamese
Myrtle Grove (cdp)	3,700 58.91	258	126 48.84 48.84 3.41	-	-	-	-	-	-	-	101 58.72 80.16 39.15 2.73	-	-	-	-	-	-	-	-	-	-	-	-	-	-	-
Hernando County	47,954 86.52	237	179 75.53 75.53 0.37	-	-	-	-	-	-	-	-	-	-	-	-	-	-	-	-	-	-	-	-	-	-	-
Highlands County	29,854 79.67	293	195 66.55 66.55 0.65	-	-	-	-	-	-	-	88 70.97 45.13 30.03 0.29	-	-	-	-	-	-	-	-	-	-	-	-	-	-	-
Hillsborough County	251,023 64.14	6,599	3,573 54.14 54.14 1.42	120	76 63.33 63.33 0.03	944 46.53 26.42 14.31 0.38	-	-	527 55.07 14.75 7.99 0.21	-	500 56.88 13.99 7.58 0.20	-	-	-	-	190 56.72 5.32 2.88 0.08	402 55.91 11.25 6.09 0.16	-	-	-	-	-	-	144 62.07 4.03 2.18 0.06	-	576 58.54 16.12 8.73 0.23
Westchase (cdp)	3,688 88.29	148	130 87.84 87.84 3.52	-	-	-	-	-	-	-	-	-	-	-	-	-	-	-	-	-	-	-	-	-	-	-
Indian River County	38,119 77.58	237	158 66.67 66.67 0.41	-	-	-	-	-	-	-	-	-	-	-	-	-	-	-	-	-	-	-	-	-	-	-
Lake County	72,047 81.49	414	293 70.77 70.77 0.41	-	-	-	-	-	-	-	-	-	-	-	-	-	-	-	-	-	-	-	-	-	-	-
Lee County	144,256 76.49	952	588 61.76 61.76 0.41	-	-	131 57.46 22.28 13.76 0.09	-	-	178 82.79 30.27 18.70 0.12	-	203 70.73 34.52 21.32 0.14	-	-	-	-	-	-	-	-	-	-	-	-	-	-	-
Leon County	55,014 57.00	1,774	806 45.43 45.43 1.47	-	-	308 52.56 38.21 17.36 0.56	-	-	174 44.05 21.59 9.81 0.32	-	59 37.11 7.32 3.33 0.11	-	-	-	-	-	52 27.66 6.45 2.93 0.09	-	-	-	-	-	-	-	-	-
Manatee County	82,936 73.75	691	518 74.96 74.96 0.62	-	-	-	-	-	-	-	105 81.40 20.27 15.20 0.13	-	-	-	-	-	-	-	-	-	-	-	-	-	-	-

Notes: Please refer to the User's Guide for an explanation of data; data is arranged alphabetically by state, then county, then city within each county; table includes counties with populations greater than 49,999 unless noted and cities with populations greater than 9,999 whose Asian and/or NHPI population rates are greater than the national average; (1) Native Hawaiian and other Pacific Islander; (2) excludes Taiwanese; (3) includes Chamorro; (4) county does not meet population threshold but is shown in order to allow inclusion of city

Place	All owner-occupied housing units	Asian-occupied housing units	Asians who own and occupy their own homes	NHPI[1]-occupied housing units	NHPIs[1] who own and occupy their own homes	Asian Indian	Bangladeshi	Cambodian	Chinese[2]	Fijian	Filipino	Guamanian[3]	Hawaiian, Native	Hmong	Indonesian	Japanese	Korean	Laotian	Malaysian	Pakistani	Samoan	Sri Lankan	Taiwanese	Thai	Tongan	Vietnamese
Marion County	85,171 79.78	631	460 72.90 72.90 0.54	-	-	175 62.72 38.04 27.73 0.21	-	-	-	-	-	-	-	-	-	-	-	-	-	-	-	-	-	-	-	-
Martin County	44,131 79.82	205	100 48.78 48.78 0.23	-	-	-	-	-	-	-	-	-	-	-	-	-	-	-	-	-	-	-	-	-	-	-
Miami-Dade County	449,333 57.85	10,275	6,017 58.56 58.56 1.34	133	81 60.90 60.90 0.02	1,537 50.96 25.54 14.96 0.34	-	-	2,181 68.93 36.25 21.23 0.49	-	888 59.60 14.76 8.64 0.20	-	-	-	-	271 52.02 4.50 2.64 0.06	278 60.30 4.62 2.71 0.06	-	-	166 55.33 2.76 1.62 0.04	-	-	-	123 54.42 2.04 1.20 0.03	-	186 39.41 3.09 1.81 0.04
Doral (cdp)	4,382 56.44	390	219 56.15 56.15 5.00	-	-	-	-	-	-	-	-	-	-	-	-	-	-	-	-	-	-	-	-	-	-	-
Ives Estates (cdp)	5,294 77.22	265	168 63.40 63.40 3.17	-	-	-	-	-	-	-	-	-	-	-	-	-	-	-	-	-	-	-	-	-	-	-
North Miami Beach (city)	8,688 62.11	506	314 62.06 62.06 3.61	-	-	60 46.88 19.11 11.86 0.69	-	-	175 79.55 55.73 34.58 2.01	-	-	-	-	-	-	-	-	-	-	-	-	-	-	-	-	-
Pinecrest (village)	5,186 83.02	224	107 47.77 47.77 2.06	-	-	-	-	-	-	-	-	-	-	-	-	-	-	-	-	-	-	-	-	-	-	-
Monroe County	21,900 62.42	206	119 57.77 57.77 0.54	-	-	-	-	-	-	-	-	-	-	-	-	-	-	-	-	-	-	-	-	-	-	-
Nassau County	17,732 80.67	95	61 64.21 64.21 0.34	-	-	-	-	-	-	-	-	-	-	-	-	-	-	-	-	-	-	-	-	-	-	-
Okaloosa County	43,972 66.35	1,059	609 57.51 57.51 1.38	-	-	-	-	-	-	-	219 52.64 35.96 20.68 0.50	-	-	-	-	-	64 51.20 10.51 6.04 0.15	-	-	-	-	-	-	69 65.71 11.33 6.52 0.16	-	68 62.39 11.17 6.42 0.15

Notes: Please refer to the User's Guide for an explanation of data; data is arranged alphabetically by state, then county, then city within each county; table includes counties with populations greater than 49,999 unless noted and cities with populations greater than 9,999 whose Asian and/or NHPI population rates are greater than the national average; (1) Native Hawaiian and other Pacific Islander; (2) excludes Taiwanese; (3) includes Chamorro; (4) county does not meet population threshold but is shown in order to allow inclusion of city

Place	All owner-occupied housing units	Asian-occupied housing units	Asians who own and occupy their own homes	NHPI[1]-occupied housing units	NHPIs[1] who own and occupy their own homes	Asian Indian	Bangladeshi	Cambodian	Chinese[2]	Fijian	Filipino	Guamanian[3]	Hawaiian, Native	Hmong	Indonesian	Japanese	Korean	Laotian	Malaysian	Pakistani	Samoan	Sri Lankan	Taiwanese	Thai	Tongan	Vietnamese
Wright (cdp)	4,973 54.47	218	128 58.72 58.72 2.57	-	-	-	-	-	-	-	-	-	-	-	-	-	-	-	-	-	-	-	-	-	-	-
Orange County	204,230 60.73	8,969	5,346 59.61 59.61 2.62	180	100 55.56 55.56 0.05	1,382 55.84 25.85 15.41 0.68	-	-	863 61.55 16.14 9.62 0.42	-	833 66.91 15.58 9.29 0.41	-	-	-	-	196 42.89 3.67 2.19 0.10	344 43.22 6.43 3.84 0.17	-	-	153 59.53 2.86 1.71 0.07	-	-	-	-	-	1,225 71.14 22.91 13.66 0.60
Oak Ridge (cdp)	2,776 37.47	409	228 55.75 55.75 8.21	-	-	-	-	-	-	-	-	-	-	-	-	-	-	-	-	-	-	-	-	-	-	129 88.97 56.58 31.54 4.65
Osceola County	41,315 67.76	1,171	731 62.43 62.43 1.77	-	-	149 52.28 20.38 12.72 0.36	-	-	193 73.11 26.40 16.48 0.47	-	213 78.60 29.14 18.19 0.52	-	-	-	-	-	-	-	-	-	-	-	-	-	-	-
Palm Beach County	354,024 74.66	5,569	3,626 65.11 65.11 1.02	80	15 18.75 18.75 <0.01	970 55.88 26.75 17.42 0.27	-	-	971 75.15 26.78 17.44 0.27	-	414 58.23 11.42 7.43 0.12	-	-	-	-	171 77.38 4.72 3.07 0.05	115 43.56 3.17 2.07 0.03	-	-	-	-	-	-	135 62.50 3.72 2.42 0.04	-	424 73.23 11.69 7.61 0.12
Pasco County	121,548 82.37	1,034	821 79.40 79.40 0.68	-	-	199 72.36 24.24 19.25 0.16	-	-	132 82.50 16.08 12.77 0.11	-	229 76.59 27.89 22.15 0.19	-	-	-	-	-	-	-	-	-	-	-	-	-	-	-
Pinellas County	293,869 70.82	5,901	3,528 59.79 59.79 1.20	-	-	641 51.78 18.17 10.86 0.22	-	161 81.31 4.56 2.73 0.05	546 63.56 15.48 9.25 0.19	-	539 56.15 15.28 9.13 0.18	-	-	-	-	110 44.72 3.12 1.86 0.04	172 63.00 4.88 2.91 0.06	328 71.62 9.30 5.56 0.11	-	-	-	-	-	53 40.77 1.50 0.90 0.02	-	846 69.46 23.98 14.34 0.29
Pinellas Park (city)	14,530 74.65	552	387 70.11 70.11 2.66	-	-	-	-	-	-	-	-	-	-	-	-	-	-	-	-	-	-	-	-	-	-	158 80.61 40.83 28.62 1.09
Polk County	137,373 73.37	1,524	943 61.88 61.88 0.69	-	-	290 57.88 30.75 19.03 0.21	-	-	98 53.55 10.39 6.43 0.07	-	155 74.16 16.44 10.17 0.11	-	-	-	-	-	-	86 100.00 9.12 5.64 0.06	-	-	-	-	-	-	-	142 71.00 15.06 9.32 0.10
Putnam County	22,265 79.98	81	56 69.14 69.14 0.25	-	-	-	-	-	-	-	-	-	-	-	-	-	-	-	-	-	-	-	-	-	-	-

Notes: Please refer to the User's Guide for an explanation of data; data is arranged alphabetically by state, then county, then city within each county; table includes counties with populations greater than 49,999 unless noted and cities with populations greater than 9,999 whose Asian and/or NHPI population rates are greater than the national average; (1) Native Hawaiian and other Pacific Islander; (2) excludes Taiwanese; (3) includes Chamorro; (4) county does not meet population threshold but is shown in order to allow inclusion of city

Place	All owner-occupied housing units	Asian-occupied housing units	Asians who own and occupy their own homes	NHPI[1]-occupied housing units	NHPIs[1] who own and occupy their own homes	Asian Indian	Bangladeshi	Cambodian	Chinese[2]	Fijian	Filipino	Guamanian[3]	Hawaiian, Native	Hmong	Indonesian	Japanese	Korean	Laotian	Malaysian	Pakistani	Samoan	Sri Lankan	Taiwanese	Thai	Tongan	Vietnamese
St. Johns County	37,889 76.37	380	221 58.16 58.16 0.58	-	-	-	-	-	-	-	-	-	-	-	-	-	-	-	-	-	-	-	-	-	-	-
St. Lucie County	60,035 78.04	568	405 71.30 71.30 0.67	-	-	-	-	-	-	-	-	-	-	-	-	-	-	-	-	-	-	-	-	-	-	-
Santa Rosa County	35,198 80.37	331	208 62.84 62.84 0.59	-	-	-	-	-	-	-	90 62.50 43.27 27.19 0.26	-	-	-	-	-	-	-	-	-	-	-	-	-	-	-
Sarasota County	118,538 79.06	719	501 69.68 69.68 0.42	-	-	-	-	-	94 66.67 18.76 13.07 0.08	-	51 68.00 10.18 7.09 0.04	-	-	-	-	-	-	-	-	-	-	-	-	-	-	107 69.03 21.36 14.88 0.09
Seminole County	96,956 69.47	2,770	1,821 65.74 65.74 1.88	-	-	623 67.06 34.21 22.49 0.64	-	-	326 73.59 17.90 11.77 0.34	-	282 76.63 15.49 10.18 0.29	-	-	-	-	-	85 29.82 4.67 3.07 0.09	-	-	-	-	-	-	-	-	250 81.17 13.73 9.03 0.26
Volusia County	139,037 75.27	1,478	903 61.10 61.10 0.65	-	-	285 59.87 31.56 19.28 0.20	-	-	156 56.73 17.28 10.55 0.11	-	170 71.13 18.83 11.50 0.12	-	-	-	-	-	47 41.96 5.20 3.18 0.03	-	-	-	-	-	-	-	-	-

Notes: Please refer to the User's Guide for an explanation of data: data is arranged alphabetically by state, then county, then city within each county; table includes counties with populations greater than 49,999 unless noted and cities with populations greater than 9,999 whose Asian and/or NHPI population rates are greater than the national average; (1) Native Hawaiian and other Pacific Islander; (2) excludes Taiwanese; (3) includes Chamorro; (4) county does not meet population threshold but is shown in order to allow inclusion of city

Median Gross Rent

(Universe: Specified Renter-Occupied Housing Units Paying Cash Rent)

Place	All specified renter-occupied	Specified housing units rented by	Specified housing units rented by	Asian Indian	Bangladeshi	Cambodian	Chinese[2]	Fijian	Filipino	Guamanian[3]	Hawaiian, Native	Hmong	Indonesian	Japanese	Korean	Laotian	Malaysian	Pakistani	Samoan	Sri Lankan	Taiwanese	Thai	Tongan	Vietnamese
UNITED STATES	602	734	690	793	721	582	689	740	730	673	687	517	722	825	796	564	662	763	701	722	763	671	740	653
FLORIDA	641	685	653	740	656	448	654	-	637	635	628	-	573	706	740	688	-	781	585	775	589	686	-	594
Alachua County	553	534	-	642	-	-	421	-	525	-	-	-	-	714	569	-	-	-	-	-	-	-	-	529
Gainesville (city)	540	460	-	572	-	-	402	-	-	-	-	-	-	-	488	-	-	-	-	-	-	-	-	-
Bay County	536	556	-	-	-	-	-	-	561	-	-	-	-	-	-	-	-	-	-	-	-	-	-	497
Callaway (city)	536	548	-	-	-	-	-	-	-	-	-	-	-	-	-	-	-	-	-	-	-	-	-	-
Brevard County	604	595	-	592	-	-	588	-	580	-	-	-	-	661	629	-	-	-	-	-	-	-	-	575
Broward County	757	811	753	781	-	-	849	-	788	-	-	-	-	756	897	-	-	865	-	-	-	838	-	788
Cooper City (city)	988	750	-	750	-	-	-	-	-	-	-	-	-	-	-	-	-	-	-	-	-	-	-	-
Pembroke Pines (city)	945	913	-	922	-	-	945	-	859	-	-	-	-	-	-	-	-	-	-	-	-	-	-	-
Charlotte County	626	1,534	-	-	-	-	-	-	-	-	-	-	-	-	-	-	-	-	-	-	-	-	-	-
Citrus County	478	632	-	-	-	-	-	-	-	-	-	-	-	-	-	-	-	-	-	-	-	-	-	-
Clay County	668	559	-	-	-	-	-	-	552	-	-	-	-	-	-	-	-	-	-	-	-	-	-	-
Bellair-Meadowbrook Ter. (cdp)	706	560	-	-	-	-	-	-	-	-	-	-	-	-	-	-	-	-	-	-	-	-	-	-
Collier County	753	778	-	-	-	-	-	-	-	-	-	-	-	-	-	-	-	-	-	-	-	-	-	-
Columbia County	448	623	-	-	-	-	-	-	-	-	-	-	-	-	-	-	-	-	-	-	-	-	-	-
Duval County	604	635	575	750	-	384	663	-	627	-	-	-	-	464	631	-	-	-	-	-	-	-	-	474
Escambia County	533	493	-	623	-	-	453	-	518	-	-	-	-	-	-	-	-	-	-	-	-	-	-	474
Bellview (cdp)	585	647	-	-	-	-	-	-	665	-	-	-	-	-	-	-	-	-	-	-	-	-	-	-
Myrtle Grove (cdp)	576	520	-	-	-	-	-	-	496	-	-	-	-	-	-	-	-	-	-	-	-	-	-	-
Hernando County	550	756	-	-	-	-	-	-	-	-	-	-	-	-	-	-	-	-	-	-	-	-	-	-
Highlands County	479	565	-	-	-	-	-	-	639	-	-	-	-	-	-	-	-	-	-	-	-	-	-	-
Hillsborough County	623	640	735	656	-	-	591	-	654	-	-	-	-	796	659	-	-	-	-	-	-	628	-	557
Westchase (cdp)	934	982	-	-	-	-	-	-	-	-	-	-	-	-	-	-	-	-	-	-	-	-	-	-
Indian River County	615	826	-	-	-	-	-	-	-	-	-	-	-	-	-	-	-	-	-	-	-	-	-	-
Lake County	534	619	-	-	-	-	-	-	-	-	-	-	-	-	-	-	-	-	-	-	-	-	-	-
Lee County	646	616	-	576	-	-	678	-	635	-	-	-	-	-	-	-	-	-	-	-	-	-	-	-
Leon County	606	554	-	541	-	-	481	-	625	-	-	-	-	-	600	-	-	-	-	-	-	-	-	-
Manatee County	637	561	-	-	-	-	-	-	613	-	-	-	-	-	-	-	-	-	-	-	-	-	-	-
Marion County	513	742	-	824	-	-	-	-	-	-	-	-	-	-	-	-	-	-	-	-	-	-	-	-
Martin County	633	664	-	-	-	-	-	-	-	-	-	-	-	-	-	-	-	-	-	-	-	-	-	-
Miami-Dade County	647	749	683	795	-	-	733	-	711	-	-	-	-	842	910	-	-	725	-	-	-	790	-	682
Doral (cdp)	968	873	-	-	-	-	-	-	-	-	-	-	-	-	-	-	-	-	-	-	-	-	-	-
Ives Estates (cdp)	776	735	-	-	-	-	-	-	-	-	-	-	-	-	-	-	-	-	-	-	-	-	-	-

Notes: Please refer to the User's Guide for an explanation of data; data is arranged alphabetically by state, then county, then city within each county; table includes counties with populations greater than 49,999 unless noted and cities with populations greater than 9,999 whose Asian and/or NHPI population rates are greater than the national average; (1) Native Hawaiian and other Pacific Islander; (2) excludes Taiwanese; (3) includes Chamorro; (4) county does not meet population threshold but is shown in order to allow inclusion of city

Place	All specified renter-occupied	Specified housing units rented by	Specified housing units rented by	Asian Indian	Bangladeshi	Cambodian	Chinese[2]	Fijian	Filipino	Guamanian[3]	Hawaiian, Native	Hmong	Indonesian	Japanese	Korean	Laotian	Malaysian	Pakistani	Samoan	Sri Lankan	Taiwanese	Thai	Tongan	Vietnamese
North Miami Beach (city)	643	672	-	830	-	-	653	-	-	-	-	-	-	-	-	-	-	-	-	-	-	-	-	-
Pinecrest (village)	775	734	-	-	-	-	-	-	-	-	-	-	-	-	-	-	-	-	-	-	-	-	-	-
Monroe County	820	825	-	-	-	-	-	-	-	-	-	-	-	-	-	-	-	-	-	-	-	-	-	-
Nassau County	553	660	-	-	-	-	-	-	-	-	-	-	-	-	-	-	-	-	-	-	-	-	-	-
Okaloosa County	601	561	-	-	-	-	-	-	518	-	-	-	-	-	626	-	-	-	-	-	-	771	-	584
Wright (cdp)	595	758	-	-	-	-	-	-	-	-	-	-	-	-	-	-	-	-	-	-	-	-	-	-
Orange County	699	726	688	777	-	-	694	-	722	-	-	-	-	735	808	-	-	689	-	-	-	-	-	622
Oak Ridge (cdp)	671	666	-	-	-	-	-	-	-	-	-	-	-	-	-	-	-	-	-	-	-	-	-	600
Osceola County	714	712	-	675	-	-	675	-	693	-	-	-	-	-	-	-	-	-	-	-	-	-	-	-
Palm Beach County	739	764	845	830	-	-	731	-	762	-	-	-	-	566	841	-	-	-	-	-	-	850	-	595
Pasco County	518	528	-	600	-	-	423	-	452	-	-	-	-	-	-	-	-	-	-	-	-	-	-	-
Pinellas County	616	617	-	662	-	444	644	-	580	-	-	-	-	568	603	650	-	-	-	-	-	714	-	472
Pinellas Park (city)	614	605	-	-	-	-	-	-	-	-	-	-	-	-	-	-	-	-	-	-	-	-	-	603
Polk County	501	538	-	562	-	-	496	-	520	-	-	-	-	-	-	0	-	-	-	-	-	-	-	491
Putnam County	384	920	-	-	-	-	-	-	-	-	-	-	-	-	-	-	-	-	-	-	-	-	-	-
St. Johns County	724	751	-	-	-	-	-	-	-	-	-	-	-	-	-	-	-	-	-	-	-	-	-	-
St. Lucie County	621	713	-	-	-	-	-	-	-	-	-	-	-	-	-	-	-	-	-	-	-	-	-	-
Santa Rosa County	540	628	-	-	-	-	-	-	432	-	-	-	-	-	-	-	-	-	-	-	-	-	-	-
Sarasota County	711	644	-	-	-	-	622	-	597	-	-	-	-	-	-	-	-	-	-	-	-	-	-	586
Seminole County	731	782	-	839	-	-	628	-	604	-	-	-	-	-	857	-	-	-	-	-	-	-	-	742
Volusia County	597	634	-	736	-	-	578	-	632	-	-	-	-	-	640	-	-	-	-	-	-	-	-	-

Notes: Please refer to the User's Guide for an explanation of data; data is arranged alphabetically by state, then county, then city within each county; table includes counties with populations greater than 49,999 unless noted and cities with populations greater than 9,999 whose Asian and/or NHPI population rates are greater than the national average; (1) Native Hawaiian and other Pacific Islander; (2) excludes Taiwanese; (3) includes Chamorro; (4) county does not meet population threshold but is shown in order to allow inclusion of city

Median Home Value

(Universe: Specified Owner-Occupied Housing Units)

Place	All specified owner-occupied	Specified housing units owned and	Specified housing units owned and	Asian Indian	Bangladeshi	Cambodian	Chinese[2]	Fijian	Filipino	Guamanian[3]	Hawaiian, Native	Hmong	Indonesian	Japanese	Korean	Laotian	Malaysian	Pakistani	Samoan	Sri Lankan	Taiwanese	Thai	Tongan	Vietnamese
UNITED STATES	119,600	199,300	160,500	210,200	171,000	120,800	230,700	181,000	188,100	143,500	177,100	92,600	186,300	238,300	209,500	100,500	169,700	181,400	153,200	202,000	260,700	160,900	149,100	151,400
FLORIDA	105,500	119,700	92,000	142,500	117,900	88,800	131,600	-	110,400	96,800	92,600	-	112,900	114,100	135,300	77,800	-	143,200	78,000	151,000	189,600	94,400	-	91,500
Alachua County	97,300	133,700	-	130,700	-	-	131,500	-	151,600	-	-	-	-	157,000	118,400	-	-	-	-	-	-	-	-	90,000
Gainesville (city)	86,300	99,200	-	96,300	-	-	134,700	-	-	-	-	-	-	-	137,500	-	-	-	-	-	-	-	-	-
Bay County	93,500	83,500	-	-	-	-	-	-	86,500	-	-	-	-	-	-	-	-	-	-	-	-	-	-	64,100
Callaway (city)	93,100	91,900	-	-	-	-	-	-	-	-	-	-	-	-	-	-	-	-	-	-	-	-	-	-
Brevard County	94,400	107,000	-	140,700	-	-	130,200	-	87,100	-	-	-	-	101,000	88,200	-	-	-	-	-	-	-	-	98,300
Broward County	128,600	137,400	108,000	137,400	-	-	134,800	-	150,600	-	-	-	-	142,100	155,000	-	-	140,900	-	-	-	115,200	-	111,800
Cooper City (city)	154,200	156,700	-	156,700	-	-	-	-	-	-	-	-	-	-	-	-	-	-	-	-	-	-	-	-
Pembroke Pines (city)	143,200	155,500	-	146,000	-	-	159,000	-	167,400	-	-	-	-	-	-	-	-	-	-	-	-	-	-	-
Charlotte County	97,000	98,900	-	-	-	-	-	-	-	-	-	-	-	-	-	-	-	-	-	-	-	-	-	-
Citrus County	84,400	106,500	-	-	-	-	-	-	-	-	-	-	-	-	-	-	-	-	-	-	-	-	-	-
Clay County	108,400	115,600	-	-	-	-	-	-	116,500	-	-	-	-	-	-	-	-	-	-	-	-	-	-	-
Bellair-Meadowbrook Ter. (cdp)	86,400	98,200	-	-	-	-	-	-	-	-	-	-	-	-	-	-	-	-	-	-	-	-	-	-
Collier County	168,000	223,800	-	-	-	-	-	-	-	-	-	-	-	-	-	-	-	-	-	-	-	-	-	-
Columbia County	73,600	88,600	-	-	-	-	-	-	-	-	-	-	-	-	-	-	-	-	-	-	-	-	-	-
Duval County	89,600	104,100	81,100	162,000	-	83,900	134,300	-	99,600	-	-	-	-	100,500	125,300	-	-	-	-	-	-	-	-	72,900
Escambia County	85,700	82,000	-	101,600	-	-	133,700	-	80,700	-	-	-	-	-	-	-	-	-	-	-	-	-	-	66,900
Bellview (cdp)	80,300	81,600	-	-	-	-	-	-	87,800	-	-	-	-	-	-	-	-	-	-	-	-	-	-	-
Myrtle Grove (cdp)	78,800	77,900	-	-	-	-	-	-	80,900	-	-	-	-	-	-	-	-	-	-	-	-	-	-	-
Hernando County	87,300	89,300	-	-	-	-	-	-	-	-	-	-	-	-	-	-	-	-	-	-	-	-	-	-
Highlands County	72,800	99,700	-	-	-	-	-	-	110,400	-	-	-	-	-	-	-	-	-	-	-	-	-	-	-
Hillsborough County	97,700	120,400	106,900	150,200	-	-	136,200	-	105,400	-	-	-	-	104,900	133,400	-	-	-	-	-	-	83,900	-	85,000
Westchase (cdp)	173,800	223,100	-	-	-	-	-	-	-	-	-	-	-	-	-	-	-	-	-	-	-	-	-	-
Indian River County	104,000	89,100	-	-	-	-	-	-	-	-	-	-	-	-	-	-	-	-	-	-	-	-	-	-
Lake County	100,600	127,900	-	-	-	-	-	-	-	-	-	-	-	-	-	-	-	-	-	-	-	-	-	-
Lee County	112,900	121,500	-	123,300	-	-	145,400	-	100,900	-	-	-	-	-	-	-	-	-	-	-	-	-	-	-
Leon County	110,900	137,300	-	161,400	-	-	163,300	-	79,700	-	-	-	-	-	148,800	-	-	-	-	-	-	-	-	-
Manatee County	119,400	120,500	-	-	-	-	-	-	114,300	-	-	-	-	-	-	-	-	-	-	-	-	-	-	-
Marion County	81,300	111,900	-	160,300	-	-	-	-	-	-	-	-	-	-	-	-	-	-	-	-	-	-	-	-
Martin County	152,400	210,200	-	-	-	-	-	-	-	-	-	-	-	-	-	-	-	-	-	-	-	-	-	-
Miami-Dade County	124,000	132,300	97,100	142,600	-	-	134,300	-	127,500	-	-	-	-	133,200	133,100	-	-	122,200	-	-	-	122,700	-	118,100
Doral (cdp)	178,500	159,400	-	-	-	-	-	-	-	-	-	-	-	-	-	-	-	-	-	-	-	-	-	-
Ives Estates (cdp)	102,400	101,600	-	-	-	-	-	-	-	-	-	-	-	-	-	-	-	-	-	-	-	-	-	-

Notes: Please refer to the User's Guide for an explanation of data; data is arranged alphabetically by state, then county, then city within each county: table includes counties with populations greater than 49,999 unless noted and cities with populations greater than 9,999 whose Asian and/or NHPI population rates are greater than the national average; (1) Native Hawaiian and other Pacific Islander; (2) excludes Taiwanese; (3) includes Chamorro; (4) county does not meet population threshold but is shown in order to allow inclusion of city

Place	All specified owner-occupied	Specified housing units owned and	Specified housing units owned and	Asian Indian	Bangladeshi	Cambodian	Chinese[2]	Fijian	Filipino	Guamanian[3]	Hawaiian, Native	Hmong	Indonesian	Japanese	Korean	Laotian	Malaysian	Pakistani	Samoan	Sri Lankan	Taiwanese	Thai	Tongan	Vietnamese
North Miami Beach (city)	93,000	88,200	-	82,100	-	-	86,700	-	-	-	-	-	-	-	-	-	-	-	-	-	-	-	-	-
Pinecrest (village)	393,900	202,800	-	-	-	-	-	-	-	-	-	-	-	-	-	-	-	-	-	-	-	-	-	-
Monroe County	241,200	129,900	-	-	-	-	-	-	-	-	-	-	-	-	-	-	-	-	-	-	-	-	-	-
Nassau County	126,700	97,900	-	-	-	-	-	-	-	-	-	-	-	-	-	-	-	-	-	-	-	-	-	-
Okaloosa County	101,200	97,400	-	-	-	-	-	-	91,800	-	-	-	-	-	125,000	-	-	-	-	-	-	90,000	-	148,300
Wright (cdp)	94,500	108,900	-	-	-	-	-	-	-	-	-	-	-	-	-	-	-	-	-	-	-	-	-	-
Orange County	107,500	123,900	85,600	141,800	-	-	134,300	-	122,100	-	-	-	-	109,300	174,200	-	-	182,000	-	-	-	-	-	95,700
Oak Ridge (cdp)	81,100	83,700	-	-	-	-	-	-	-	-	-	-	-	-	-	-	-	-	-	-	-	-	-	85,900
Osceola County	99,300	112,500	-	97,600	-	-	119,900	-	111,400	-	-	-	-	-	-	-	-	-	-	-	-	-	-	-
Palm Beach County	135,200	141,000	117,000	153,300	-	-	155,900	-	143,100	-	-	-	-	154,600	154,200	-	-	-	-	-	-	104,700	-	113,100
Pasco County	79,600	117,400	-	149,300	-	-	90,000	-	118,500	-	-	-	-	-	-	-	-	-	-	-	-	-	-	-
Pinellas County	96,500	86,600	-	175,000	-	75,700	109,100	-	85,100	-	-	-	-	140,000	76,800	68,700	-	-	-	-	-	77,900	-	75,300
Pinellas Park (city)	75,500	77,900	-	-	-	-	-	-	-	-	-	-	-	-	-	-	-	-	-	-	-	-	-	80,300
Polk County	83,300	96,500	-	111,300	-	-	87,800	-	103,100	-	-	-	-	-	-	62,900	-	-	-	-	-	-	-	62,900
Putnam County	68,500	112,500	-	-	-	-	-	-	-	-	-	-	-	-	-	-	-	-	-	-	-	-	-	-
St. Johns County	158,400	155,900	-	-	-	-	-	-	-	-	-	-	-	-	-	-	-	-	-	-	-	-	-	-
St. Lucie County	86,100	94,800	-	-	-	-	-	-	-	-	-	-	-	-	-	-	-	-	-	-	-	-	-	-
Santa Rosa County	106,000	121,500	-	-	-	-	-	-	77,800	-	-	-	-	-	-	-	-	-	-	-	-	-	-	-
Sarasota County	122,000	97,800	-	-	-	-	101,000	-	102,800	-	-	-	-	-	-	-	-	-	-	-	-	-	-	79,400
Seminole County	119,900	135,000	-	163,800	-	-	136,500	-	125,400	-	-	-	-	-	171,900	-	-	-	-	-	-	-	-	118,400
Volusia County	87,300	98,800	-	114,300	-	-	109,200	-	107,100	-	-	-	-	-	88,000	-	-	-	-	-	-	-	-	-

Notes: Please refer to the User's Guide for an explanation of data; data is arranged alphabetically by state, then county, then city within each county; table includes counties with populations greater than 49,999 unless noted and cities with populations greater than 9,999 whose Asian and/or NHPI population rates are greater than the national average; (1) Native Hawaiian and other Pacific Islander; (2) excludes Taiwanese; (3) includes Chamorro; (4) county does not meet population threshold but is shown in order to allow inclusion of city

Population

Total Population

Top 10 Places Sorted by Number

Place (place type) County	Number
Jacksonville (city) Duval	735,503
Miami (city) Miami-Dade	362,563
Tampa (city) Hillsborough	303,512
St. Petersburg (city) Pinellas	247,793
Hialeah (city) Miami-Dade	226,411
Orlando (city) Orange	185,984
Fort Lauderdale (city) Broward	152,125
Tallahassee (city) Leon	150,581
Hollywood (city) Broward	139,261
Pembroke Pines (city) Broward	137,112

Asian

Top 10 Places Sorted by Number

Place (place type) County	Number
Jacksonville (city) Duval	19,838
St. Petersburg (city) Pinellas	6,729
Tampa (city) Hillsborough	6,415
Pembroke Pines (city) Broward	5,004
Orlando (city) Orange	4,823
Gainesville (city) Alachua	4,399
Coral Springs (city) Broward	3,985
Tallahassee (city) Leon	3,466
Hollywood (city) Broward	2,940
Sunrise (city) Broward	2,915

Asian

Top 10 Places Sorted by Percent of Total Population

Place (place type) County	Percent
Hunters Creek (cdp) Orange	8.61
Doctor Phillips (cdp) Orange	7.99
Oak Ridge (cdp) Orange	5.83
Springfield (city) Bay	5.81
Doral (cdp) Miami-Dade	5.78
Ives Estates (cdp) Miami-Dade	4.77
Myrtle Grove (cdp) Escambia	4.69
Pinecrest (village) Miami-Dade	4.61
Gainesville (city) Alachua	4.60
Westchase (cdp) Hillsborough	4.57

Native Hawaiian and Other Pacific Islander

Top 10 Places Sorted by Number

Place (place type) County	Number
Jacksonville (city) Duval	497

Native Hawaiian and Other Pacific Islander

Top 10 Places Sorted by Percent of Asian Population

Place (place type) County	Percent
Jacksonville (city) Duval	100.00

Native Hawaiian and Other Pacific Islander

Top 10 Places Sorted by Percent of Total Population

Place (place type) County	Percent
Jacksonville (city) Duval	0.07

Asian Indian

Top 10 Places Sorted by Number

Place (place type) County	Number
Jacksonville (city) Duval	2,730
Coral Springs (city) Broward	1,855
Pembroke Pines (city) Broward	1,752
Orlando (city) Orange	1,460
Tampa (city) Hillsborough	1,408
Hollywood (city) Broward	1,269
Tallahassee (city) Leon	1,109
Plantation (city) Broward	1,105
Gainesville (city) Alachua	1,056
Sunrise (city) Broward	990

Asian Indian

Top 10 Places Sorted by Percent of Asian Population

Place (place type) County	Percent
East Lake (cdp) Pinellas	66.57
Plantation (city) Broward	49.86
West Palm Beach (city) Palm Beach	48.62
Cooper City (city) Broward	47.78
Coral Springs (city) Broward	46.55
Altamonte Springs (city) Seminole	46.35
Doctor Phillips (cdp) Orange	45.01
Hollywood (city) Broward	43.16
Lakeland (city) Polk	42.42
Miami (city) Miami-Dade	39.79

Asian Indian

Top 10 Places Sorted by Percent of Total Population

Place (place type) County	Percent
Doctor Phillips (cdp) Orange	3.60
Cooper City (city) Broward	2.14
East Lake (cdp) Pinellas	1.60
Coral Springs (city) Broward	1.58
Altamonte Springs (city) Seminole	1.38
Plantation (city) Broward	1.33
Pembroke Pines (city) Broward	1.28
Sunrise (city) Broward	1.16
Weston (city) Broward	1.13
Gainesville (city) Alachua	1.10

Bangladeshi

Top 10 Places Sorted by Number

Place (place type) County	Number
No places met population threshold.	

Bangladeshi

Top 10 Places Sorted by Percent of Asian Population

Place (place type) County	Percent
No places met population threshold.	

Bangladeshi

Top 10 Places Sorted by Percent of Total Population

Place (place type) County	Percent
No places met population threshold.	

Cambodian

Top 10 Places Sorted by Number

Place (place type) County	Number
Jacksonville (city) Duval	1,001
St. Petersburg (city) Pinellas	516

Cambodian

Top 10 Places Sorted by Percent of Asian Population

Place (place type) County	Percent
St. Petersburg (city) Pinellas	7.67
Jacksonville (city) Duval	5.05

Cambodian

Top 10 Places Sorted by Percent of Total Population

Place (place type) County	Percent
St. Petersburg (city) Pinellas	0.21
Jacksonville (city) Duval	0.14

Chinese (except Taiwanese)

Top 10 Places Sorted by Number

Place (place type) County	Number
Jacksonville (city) Duval	1,629
Gainesville (city) Alachua	1,456
Pembroke Pines (city) Broward	1,153
Sunrise (city) Broward	903
Coral Springs (city) Broward	893
Tallahassee (city) Leon	753
North Miami Beach (city) Miami-Dade	741
St. Petersburg (city) Pinellas	731
Tampa (city) Hillsborough	672
Hollywood (city) Broward	649

Chinese (except Taiwanese)

Top 10 Places Sorted by Percent of Asian Population

Place (place type) County	Percent
North Miami Beach (city) Miami-Dade	43.43
Gainesville (city) Alachua	33.10
Margate (city) Broward	32.13
Sunrise (city) Broward	30.98
Davie (town) Broward	30.37
The Hammocks (cdp) Miami-Dade	28.62
Kendall (cdp) Miami-Dade	26.75
Miramar (city) Broward	24.14
Pembroke Pines (city) Broward	23.04
Miami (city) Miami-Dade	22.74

Chinese (except Taiwanese)

Top 10 Places Sorted by Percent of Total Population

Place (place type) County	Percent
North Miami Beach (city) Miami-Dade	1.82
Gainesville (city) Alachua	1.52
Sunrise (city) Broward	1.05
Margate (city) Broward	1.01
The Hammocks (cdp) Miami-Dade	0.89
Pembroke Pines (city) Broward	0.84
Davie (town) Broward	0.83
Kendall (cdp) Miami-Dade	0.83
Coral Springs (city) Broward	0.76
Miramar (city) Broward	0.70

Fijian

Top 10 Places Sorted by Number

Place (place type) County	Number
No places met population threshold.	

Fijian

Top 10 Places Sorted by Percent of Asian Population

Place (place type) County	Percent
No places met population threshold.	

Fijian

Top 10 Places Sorted by Percent of Total Population

Place (place type) County	Percent
No places met population threshold.	

Filipino

Top 10 Places Sorted by Number

Place (place type) County	Number
Jacksonville (city) Duval	9,783
Tampa (city) Hillsborough	970
Pembroke Pines (city) Broward	927
St. Petersburg (city) Pinellas	870
Orlando (city) Orange	724
Cape Coral (city) Lee	683
Lakeside (cdp) Clay	571
Miramar (city) Broward	476
Myrtle Grove (cdp) Escambia	471
Clearwater (city) Pinellas	451

Filipino

Top 10 Places Sorted by Percent of Asian Population

Place (place type) County	Percent
Lakeside (cdp) Clay	73.39
Cape Coral (city) Lee	59.70
Yeehaw Junction (cdp) Osceola	59.10
Myrtle Grove (cdp) Escambia	58.00
Bellview (cdp) Escambia	52.35
Jacksonville (city) Duval	49.31
Clearwater (city) Pinellas	28.47
Miramar (city) Broward	22.53
Pembroke Pines (city) Broward	18.53
Tampa (city) Hillsborough	15.12

Notes: Please refer to the User's Guide for an explanation of data; tables include places with populations > 9,999 and reflect only those areas that meet Summary File 4 population thresholds, therefore there may be less than 10 places listed

Filipino
Top 10 Places Sorted by Percent of Total Population

Place (place type) County	Percent
Myrtle Grove (cdp) Escambia	2.72
Bellview (cdp) Escambia	1.96
Lakeside (cdp) Clay	1.85
Yeehaw Junction (cdp) Osceola	1.54
Jacksonville (city) Duval	1.33
Pembroke Pines (city) Broward	0.68
Cape Coral (city) Lee	0.67
Miramar (city) Broward	0.65
Clearwater (city) Pinellas	0.42
Orlando (city) Orange	0.39

Guamanian or Chamorro
Top 10 Places Sorted by Number

Place (place type) County	Number

No places met population threshold.

Guamanian or Chamorro
Top 10 Places Sorted by Percent of Asian Population

Place (place type) County	Percent

No places met population threshold.

Guamanian or Chamorro
Top 10 Places Sorted by Percent of Total Population

Place (place type) County	Percent

No places met population threshold.

Hawaiian, Native
Top 10 Places Sorted by Number

Place (place type) County	Number

No places met population threshold.

Hawaiian, Native
Top 10 Places Sorted by Percent of Asian Population

Place (place type) County	Percent

No places met population threshold.

Hawaiian, Native
Top 10 Places Sorted by Percent of Total Population

Place (place type) County	Percent

No places met population threshold.

Hmong
Top 10 Places Sorted by Number

Place (place type) County	Number

No places met population threshold.

Hmong
Top 10 Places Sorted by Percent of Asian Population

Place (place type) County	Percent

No places met population threshold.

Hmong
Top 10 Places Sorted by Percent of Total Population

Place (place type) County	Percent

No places met population threshold.

Indonesian
Top 10 Places Sorted by Number

Place (place type) County	Number

No places met population threshold.

Indonesian
Top 10 Places Sorted by Percent of Asian Population

Place (place type) County	Percent

No places met population threshold.

Indonesian
Top 10 Places Sorted by Percent of Total Population

Place (place type) County	Percent

No places met population threshold.

Japanese
Top 10 Places Sorted by Number

Place (place type) County	Number
Jacksonville (city) Duval	531

Japanese
Top 10 Places Sorted by Percent of Asian Population

Place (place type) County	Percent
Jacksonville (city) Duval	2.68

Japanese
Top 10 Places Sorted by Percent of Total Population

Place (place type) County	Percent
Jacksonville (city) Duval	0.07

Korean
Top 10 Places Sorted by Number

Place (place type) County	Number
Tampa (city) Hillsborough	963
Jacksonville (city) Duval	940
Orlando (city) Orange	550
Gainesville (city) Alachua	501

Korean
Top 10 Places Sorted by Percent of Asian Population

Place (place type) County	Percent
Tampa (city) Hillsborough	15.01
Orlando (city) Orange	11.40
Gainesville (city) Alachua	11.39
Jacksonville (city) Duval	4.74

Korean
Top 10 Places Sorted by Percent of Total Population

Place (place type) County	Percent
Gainesville (city) Alachua	0.52
Tampa (city) Hillsborough	0.32
Orlando (city) Orange	0.30
Jacksonville (city) Duval	0.13

Laotian
Top 10 Places Sorted by Number

Place (place type) County	Number
St. Petersburg (city) Pinellas	1,133

Laotian
Top 10 Places Sorted by Percent of Asian Population

Place (place type) County	Percent
St. Petersburg (city) Pinellas	16.84

Laotian
Top 10 Places Sorted by Percent of Total Population

Place (place type) County	Percent
St. Petersburg (city) Pinellas	0.46

Malaysian
Top 10 Places Sorted by Number

Place (place type) County	Number

No places met population threshold.

Malaysian
Top 10 Places Sorted by Percent of Asian Population

Place (place type) County	Percent

No places met population threshold.

Malaysian
Top 10 Places Sorted by Percent of Total Population

Place (place type) County	Percent

No places met population threshold.

Pakistani
Top 10 Places Sorted by Number

Place (place type) County	Number

No places met population threshold.

Pakistani
Top 10 Places Sorted by Percent of Asian Population

Place (place type) County	Percent

No places met population threshold.

Pakistani
Top 10 Places Sorted by Percent of Total Population

Place (place type) County	Percent

No places met population threshold.

Samoan
Top 10 Places Sorted by Number

Place (place type) County	Number

No places met population threshold.

Samoan
Top 10 Places Sorted by Percent of Asian Population

Place (place type) County	Percent

No places met population threshold.

Samoan
Top 10 Places Sorted by Percent of Total Population

Place (place type) County	Percent

No places met population threshold.

Sri Lankan
Top 10 Places Sorted by Number

Place (place type) County	Number

No places met population threshold.

Sri Lankan
Top 10 Places Sorted by Percent of Asian Population

Place (place type) County	Percent

No places met population threshold.

Sri Lankan
Top 10 Places Sorted by Percent of Total Population

Place (place type) County	Percent

No places met population threshold.

Taiwanese
Top 10 Places Sorted by Number

Place (place type) County	Number

No places met population threshold.

Taiwanese
Top 10 Places Sorted by Percent of Asian Population

Place (place type) County	Percent

No places met population threshold.

Taiwanese
Top 10 Places Sorted by Percent of Total Population

Place (place type) County	Percent

No places met population threshold.

Thai
Top 10 Places Sorted by Number

Place (place type) County	Number

No places met population threshold.

Notes: Please refer to the User's Guide for an explanation of data; tables include places with populations > 9,999 and reflect only those areas that meet Summary File 4 population thresholds, therefore there may be less than 10 places listed

Thai
Top 10 Places Sorted by Percent of Asian Population

Place (place type) County	Percent

No places met population threshold.

Thai
Top 10 Places Sorted by Percent of Total Population

Place (place type) County	Percent

No places met population threshold.

Tongan
Top 10 Places Sorted by Number

Place (place type) County	Number

No places met population threshold.

Tongan
Top 10 Places Sorted by Percent of Asian Population

Place (place type) County	Percent

No places met population threshold.

Tongan
Top 10 Places Sorted by Percent of Total Population

Place (place type) County	Percent

No places met population threshold.

Vietnamese
Top 10 Places Sorted by Number

Place (place type) County	Number
Jacksonville (city) Duval	2,051
St. Petersburg (city) Pinellas	1,610
Tampa (city) Hillsborough	1,379
Orlando (city) Orange	694
Town 'n' Country (cdp) Hillsborough	686
Pine Hills (cdp) Orange	641
Oak Ridge (cdp) Orange	527
Pinellas Park (city) Pinellas	526
West and East Lealman (cdp) Pinellas	457

Vietnamese
Top 10 Places Sorted by Percent of Asian Population

Place (place type) County	Percent
West and East Lealman (cdp) Pinellas	58.59
Pine Hills (cdp) Orange	54.79
Oak Ridge (cdp) Orange	40.35
Town 'n' Country (cdp) Hillsborough	30.10
Pinellas Park (city) Pinellas	29.04
St. Petersburg (city) Pinellas	23.93
Tampa (city) Hillsborough	21.50
Orlando (city) Orange	14.39
Jacksonville (city) Duval	10.34

Vietnamese
Top 10 Places Sorted by Percent of Total Population

Place (place type) County	Percent
Oak Ridge (cdp) Orange	2.35
West and East Lealman (cdp) Pinellas	2.09
Pine Hills (cdp) Orange	1.53
Pinellas Park (city) Pinellas	1.16
Town 'n' Country (cdp) Hillsborough	0.95
St. Petersburg (city) Pinellas	0.65
Tampa (city) Hillsborough	0.45
Orlando (city) Orange	0.37
Jacksonville (city) Duval	0.28

Median Age

Total Population
Top 10 Places Sorted by Number

Place (place type) County	Years
Tamarac (city) Broward	51.9
Palm Coast (city) Flagler	50.7
Ormond Beach (city) Volusia	47.6
Largo (city) Pinellas	47.5
Spring Hill (cdp) Hernando	47.5
Palm Beach Gardens (city) Palm Beach	44.7
Deerfield Beach (city) Broward	44.2
Delray Beach (city) Palm Beach	44.0
Palm Harbor (cdp) Pinellas	43.3
Merritt Island (cdp) Brevard	42.9

Asian
Top 10 Places Sorted by Number

Place (place type) County	Years
Hialeah (city) Miami-Dade	45.3
Kendale Lakes (cdp) Miami-Dade	42.9
Lakeside (cdp) Clay	42.6
Fort Walton Beach (city) Okaloosa	42.4
Niceville (city) Okaloosa	41.8
Wright (cdp) Okaloosa	40.9
Golden Glades (cdp) Miami-Dade	40.3
Bellair-Meadowbrook Terrace (cdp) Clay	39.5
Titusville (city) Brevard	39.5
Cape Coral (city) Lee	39.4

Native Hawaiian and Other Pacific Islander
Top 10 Places Sorted by Number

Place (place type) County	Years
Jacksonville (city) Duval	25.7

Asian Indian
Top 10 Places Sorted by Number

Place (place type) County	Years
Doctor Phillips (cdp) Orange	39.6
Cooper City (city) Broward	38.5
Lakeland (city) Polk	38.1
Sunrise (city) Broward	37.6
Davie (town) Broward	35.6
The Hammocks (cdp) Miami-Dade	35.5
Coral Springs (city) Broward	35.4
Hollywood (city) Broward	35.4
Boca Raton (city) Palm Beach	34.5
Miramar (city) Broward	34.3

Bangladeshi
Top 10 Places Sorted by Number

Place (place type) County	Years

No places met population threshold.

Cambodian
Top 10 Places Sorted by Number

Place (place type) County	Years
Jacksonville (city) Duval	28.9
St. Petersburg (city) Pinellas	21.4

Chinese (except Taiwanese)
Top 10 Places Sorted by Number

Place (place type) County	Years
Miami (city) Miami-Dade	52.2
North Miami Beach (city) Miami-Dade	41.0
Coral Springs (city) Broward	39.8
The Hammocks (cdp) Miami-Dade	39.7
Pembroke Pines (city) Broward	37.7
Sunrise (city) Broward	37.7
Orlando (city) Orange	37.6
Davie (town) Broward	37.0
Hollywood (city) Broward	37.0
Kendall (cdp) Miami-Dade	36.8

Fijian
Top 10 Places Sorted by Number

Place (place type) County	Years

No places met population threshold.

Filipino
Top 10 Places Sorted by Number

Place (place type) County	Years
Lakeside (cdp) Clay	43.5
Bellview (cdp) Escambia	41.6
Cape Coral (city) Lee	40.3
Pembroke Pines (city) Broward	39.9
Yeehaw Junction (cdp) Osceola	38.4
Myrtle Grove (cdp) Escambia	36.9
Miramar (city) Broward	36.0
St. Petersburg (city) Pinellas	35.5
Jacksonville (city) Duval	35.2
Tampa (city) Hillsborough	35.1

Guamanian or Chamorro
Top 10 Places Sorted by Number

Place (place type) County	Years

No places met population threshold.

Hawaiian, Native
Top 10 Places Sorted by Number

Place (place type) County	Years

No places met population threshold.

Hmong
Top 10 Places Sorted by Number

Place (place type) County	Years

No places met population threshold.

Indonesian
Top 10 Places Sorted by Number

Place (place type) County	Years

No places met population threshold.

Japanese
Top 10 Places Sorted by Number

Place (place type) County	Years
Jacksonville (city) Duval	36.5

Korean
Top 10 Places Sorted by Number

Place (place type) County	Years
Jacksonville (city) Duval	37.1
Tampa (city) Hillsborough	37.0
Orlando (city) Orange	33.4
Gainesville (city) Alachua	28.8

Laotian
Top 10 Places Sorted by Number

Place (place type) County	Years
St. Petersburg (city) Pinellas	30.3

Malaysian
Top 10 Places Sorted by Number

Place (place type) County	Years

No places met population threshold.

Pakistani
Top 10 Places Sorted by Number

Place (place type) County	Years

No places met population threshold.

Samoan
Top 10 Places Sorted by Number

Place (place type) County	Years

No places met population threshold.

Notes: Please refer to the User's Guide for an explanation of data; tables include places with populations > 9,999 and reflect only those areas that meet Summary File 4 population thresholds, therefore there may be less than 10 places listed

Sri Lankan
Top 10 Places Sorted by Number

Place (place type) County	Years

No places met population threshold.

Taiwanese
Top 10 Places Sorted by Number

Place (place type) County	Years

No places met population threshold.

Thai
Top 10 Places Sorted by Number

Place (place type) County	Years

No places met population threshold.

Tongan
Top 10 Places Sorted by Number

Place (place type) County	Years

No places met population threshold.

Vietnamese
Top 10 Places Sorted by Number

Place (place type) County	Years
Orlando (city) Orange	35.4
Town 'n' Country (cdp) Hillsborough	34.6
St. Petersburg (city) Pinellas	33.3
Oak Ridge (cdp) Orange	31.2
Pinellas Park (city) Pinellas	30.8
West and East Lealman (cdp) Pinellas	30.5
Pine Hills (cdp) Orange	29.9
Jacksonville (city) Duval	29.5
Tampa (city) Hillsborough	29.5

Average Household Size

Total Population
Top 10 Places Sorted by Number

Place (place type) County	Number
Richmond West (cdp) Miami-Dade	3.57
South Miami Heights (cdp) Miami-Dade	3.34
Golden Glades (cdp) Miami-Dade	3.23
Kendall West (cdp) Miami-Dade	3.22
Yeehaw Junction (cdp) Osceola	3.17
Miramar (city) Broward	3.16
Hialeah (city) Miami-Dade	3.15
Kendale Lakes (cdp) Miami-Dade	3.14
Oviedo (city) Seminole	3.11
Pine Hills (cdp) Orange	3.10

Asian
Top 10 Places Sorted by Number

Place (place type) County	Number
Sunset (cdp) Miami-Dade	3.98
East Lake (cdp) Pinellas	3.93
Springfield (city) Bay	3.79
Weston (city) Broward	3.79
Greater Northdale (cdp) Hillsborough	3.72
Doctor Phillips (cdp) Orange	3.62
West and East Lealman (cdp) Pinellas	3.61
Cooper City (city) Broward	3.58
Pensacola (city) Escambia	3.52
Brandon (cdp) Hillsborough	3.51

Native Hawaiian and Other Pacific Islander
Top 10 Places Sorted by Number

Place (place type) County	Number
Jacksonville (city) Duval	3.24

Asian Indian
Top 10 Places Sorted by Number

Place (place type) County	Number
East Lake (cdp) Pinellas	4.18
Weston (city) Broward	4.16
The Hammocks (cdp) Miami-Dade	3.89
Cooper City (city) Broward	3.41
Sunrise (city) Broward	3.29
Coral Springs (city) Broward	3.25
Doctor Phillips (cdp) Orange	3.22
Miramar (city) Broward	3.19
West Palm Beach (city) Palm Beach	3.17
Hollywood (city) Broward	3.14

Bangladeshi
Top 10 Places Sorted by Number

Place (place type) County	Number

No places met population threshold.

Cambodian
Top 10 Places Sorted by Number

Place (place type) County	Number
Jacksonville (city) Duval	4.11
St. Petersburg (city) Pinellas	3.95

Chinese (except Taiwanese)
Top 10 Places Sorted by Number

Place (place type) County	Number
Sunrise (city) Broward	3.64
Margate (city) Broward	3.37
North Miami Beach (city) Miami-Dade	3.29
Davie (town) Broward	3.26
Miramar (city) Broward	3.22
Pembroke Pines (city) Broward	2.89
Jacksonville (city) Duval	2.68
St. Petersburg (city) Pinellas	2.64
Coral Springs (city) Broward	2.51
Hollywood (city) Broward	2.50

Fijian
Top 10 Places Sorted by Number

Place (place type) County	Number

No places met population threshold.

Filipino
Top 10 Places Sorted by Number

Place (place type) County	Number
Miramar (city) Broward	4.04
Yeehaw Junction (cdp) Osceola	3.71
Cape Coral (city) Lee	3.23
Lakeside (cdp) Clay	3.23
Jacksonville (city) Duval	3.20
Pembroke Pines (city) Broward	3.17
Bellview (cdp) Escambia	3.13
Clearwater (city) Pinellas	2.83
Orlando (city) Orange	2.65
St. Petersburg (city) Pinellas	2.65

Guamanian or Chamorro
Top 10 Places Sorted by Number

Place (place type) County	Number

No places met population threshold.

Hawaiian, Native
Top 10 Places Sorted by Number

Place (place type) County	Number

No places met population threshold.

Hmong
Top 10 Places Sorted by Number

Place (place type) County	Number

No places met population threshold.

Indonesian
Top 10 Places Sorted by Number

Place (place type) County	Number

No places met population threshold.

Japanese
Top 10 Places Sorted by Number

Place (place type) County	Number
Jacksonville (city) Duval	1.96

Korean
Top 10 Places Sorted by Number

Place (place type) County	Number
Tampa (city) Hillsborough	2.82
Jacksonville (city) Duval	2.74
Orlando (city) Orange	2.54
Gainesville (city) Alachua	2.15

Laotian
Top 10 Places Sorted by Number

Place (place type) County	Number
St. Petersburg (city) Pinellas	4.23

Malaysian
Top 10 Places Sorted by Number

Place (place type) County	Number

No places met population threshold.

Pakistani
Top 10 Places Sorted by Number

Place (place type) County	Number

No places met population threshold.

Samoan
Top 10 Places Sorted by Number

Place (place type) County	Number

No places met population threshold.

Sri Lankan
Top 10 Places Sorted by Number

Place (place type) County	Number

No places met population threshold.

Taiwanese
Top 10 Places Sorted by Number

Place (place type) County	Number

No places met population threshold.

Thai
Top 10 Places Sorted by Number

Place (place type) County	Number

No places met population threshold.

Tongan
Top 10 Places Sorted by Number

Place (place type) County	Number

No places met population threshold.

Vietnamese
Top 10 Places Sorted by Number

Place (place type) County	Number
Town 'n' Country (cdp) Hillsborough	5.26
Oak Ridge (cdp) Orange	3.65
West and East Lealman (cdp) Pinellas	3.58
St. Petersburg (city) Pinellas	3.48
Tampa (city) Hillsborough	3.26
Jacksonville (city) Duval	3.24
Pinellas Park (city) Pinellas	3.23
Pine Hills (cdp) Orange	3.18
Orlando (city) Orange	2.97

Notes: Please refer to the User's Guide for an explanation of data; tables include places with populations > 9,999 and reflect only those areas that meet Summary File 4 population thresholds, therefore there may be less than 10 places listed

Language Spoken at Home: English Only

Total Populations 5 Years and Over Who Speak English-Only at Home

Top 10 Places Sorted by Number

Place (place type) County	Number
Jacksonville (city) Duval	616,988
Tampa (city) Hillsborough	218,362
St. Petersburg (city) Pinellas	206,489
Tallahassee (city) Leon	130,526
Orlando (city) Orange	130,439
Fort Lauderdale (city) Broward	108,442
Hollywood (city) Broward	87,182
Miami (city) Miami-Dade	86,669
Clearwater (city) Pinellas	85,394
Cape Coral (city) Lee	83,549

Total Populations 5 Years and Over Who Speak English-Only at Home

Top 10 Places Sorted by Percent

Place (place type) County	Percent
Ensley (cdp) Escambia	95.13
Pensacola (city) Escambia	93.77
Bellview (cdp) Escambia	93.50
Titusville (city) Brevard	93.44
Jacksonville Beach (city) Duval	93.08
Ferry Pass (cdp) Escambia	92.93
Panama City (city) Bay	92.78
West Pensacola (cdp) Escambia	92.54
Callaway (city) Bay	92.05
Merritt Island (cdp) Brevard	91.84

Asians 5 Years and Over Who Speak English-Only at Home

Top 10 Places Sorted by Number

Place (place type) County	Number
Jacksonville (city) Duval	4,610
Pembroke Pines (city) Broward	1,377
Tampa (city) Hillsborough	1,286
Coral Springs (city) Broward	1,223
Hollywood (city) Broward	1,205
Orlando (city) Orange	1,157
St. Petersburg (city) Pinellas	1,025
Tallahassee (city) Leon	889
Gainesville (city) Alachua	854
Plantation (city) Broward	833

Asians 5 Years and Over Who Speak English-Only at Home

Top 10 Places Sorted by Percent

Place (place type) County	Percent
South Miami Heights (cdp) Miami-Dade	95.38
Richmond West (cdp) Miami-Dade	49.51
Jacksonville Beach (city) Duval	45.86
Lake Magdalene (cdp) Hillsborough	44.72
Hollywood (city) Broward	44.58
Sanford (city) Seminole	42.70
Tamarac (city) Broward	42.69
Deltona (city) Volusia	42.37
Coconut Creek (city) Broward	41.32
Pompano Beach (city) Broward	41.09

Native Hawaiian and Other Pacific Islanders 5 Years and Over Who Speak English-Only at Home

Top 10 Places Sorted by Number

Place (place type) County	Number
Jacksonville (city) Duval	250

Native Hawaiian and Other Pacific Islanders 5 Years and Over Who Speak English-Only at Home

Top 10 Places Sorted by Percent

Place (place type) County	Percent
Jacksonville (city) Duval	59.95

Asian Indians 5 Years and Over Who Speak English-Only at Home

Top 10 Places Sorted by Number

Place (place type) County	Number
Hollywood (city) Broward	765
Coral Springs (city) Broward	750
Pembroke Pines (city) Broward	665
Plantation (city) Broward	583
Sunrise (city) Broward	481
Jacksonville (city) Duval	436
Tallahassee (city) Leon	420
Miramar (city) Broward	332
Miami (city) Miami-Dade	311
Tampa (city) Hillsborough	307

Asian Indians 5 Years and Over Who Speak English-Only at Home

Top 10 Places Sorted by Percent

Place (place type) County	Percent
Hollywood (city) Broward	67.94
Miramar (city) Broward	60.04
Plantation (city) Broward	55.47
Sunrise (city) Broward	51.50
Kendall (cdp) Miami-Dade	45.13
North Miami Beach (city) Miami-Dade	44.29
The Hammocks (cdp) Miami-Dade	43.91
Coral Springs (city) Broward	43.71
Fort Lauderdale (city) Broward	42.86
Pembroke Pines (city) Broward	42.63

Bangladeshis 5 Years and Over Who Speak English-Only at Home

Top 10 Places Sorted by Number

Place (place type) County	Number

No places met population threshold.

Bangladeshis 5 Years and Over Who Speak English-Only at Home

Top 10 Places Sorted by Percent

Place (place type) County	Percent

No places met population threshold.

Cambodians 5 Years and Over Who Speak English-Only at Home

Top 10 Places Sorted by Number

Place (place type) County	Number
Jacksonville (city) Duval	106
St. Petersburg (city) Pinellas	41

Cambodians 5 Years and Over Who Speak English-Only at Home

Top 10 Places Sorted by Percent

Place (place type) County	Percent
Jacksonville (city) Duval	11.22
St. Petersburg (city) Pinellas	8.22

Chinese (except Taiwanese)s 5 Years and Over Who Speak English-Only at Home

Top 10 Places Sorted by Number

Place (place type) County	Number
Kendall (cdp) Miami-Dade	299
Pembroke Pines (city) Broward	288
Miramar (city) Broward	211
Jacksonville (city) Duval	210
Coral Springs (city) Broward	177
Hollywood (city) Broward	153
Sunrise (city) Broward	143
Tampa (city) Hillsborough	134
Gainesville (city) Alachua	110
Orlando (city) Orange	95

Chinese (except Taiwanese)s 5 Years and Over Who Speak English-Only at Home

Top 10 Places Sorted by Percent

Place (place type) County	Percent
Kendall (cdp) Miami-Dade	48.54
Miramar (city) Broward	45.38
Pembroke Pines (city) Broward	27.88
Hollywood (city) Broward	24.52
Coral Springs (city) Broward	20.97
Tampa (city) Hillsborough	20.71
The Hammocks (cdp) Miami-Dade	20.10
Orlando (city) Orange	19.59
Margate (city) Broward	18.75
Sunrise (city) Broward	17.25

Fijians 5 Years and Over Who Speak English-Only at Home

Top 10 Places Sorted by Number

Place (place type) County	Number

No places met population threshold.

Fijians 5 Years and Over Who Speak English-Only at Home

Top 10 Places Sorted by Percent

Place (place type) County	Percent

No places met population threshold.

Filipinos 5 Years and Over Who Speak English-Only at Home

Top 10 Places Sorted by Number

Place (place type) County	Number
Jacksonville (city) Duval	3,124
Tampa (city) Hillsborough	285
Orlando (city) Orange	274
Pembroke Pines (city) Broward	216
St. Petersburg (city) Pinellas	183
Myrtle Grove (cdp) Escambia	175
Cape Coral (city) Lee	169
Bellview (cdp) Escambia	155
Lakeside (cdp) Clay	155
Clearwater (city) Pinellas	142

Filipinos 5 Years and Over Who Speak English-Only at Home

Top 10 Places Sorted by Percent

Place (place type) County	Percent
Bellview (cdp) Escambia	38.37
Orlando (city) Orange	38.06
Myrtle Grove (cdp) Escambia	37.88
Jacksonville (city) Duval	33.40
Clearwater (city) Pinellas	33.02
Miramar (city) Broward	30.92
Tampa (city) Hillsborough	30.06
Yeehaw Junction (cdp) Osceola	28.88
Lakeside (cdp) Clay	27.43
Cape Coral (city) Lee	26.16

Guamanian or Chamorros 5 Years and Over Who Speak English-Only at Home

Top 10 Places Sorted by Number

Place (place type) County	Number

No places met population threshold.

Guamanian or Chamorros 5 Years and Over Who Speak English-Only at Home

Top 10 Places Sorted by Percent

Place (place type) County	Percent

No places met population threshold.

Hawaiian, Natives 5 Years and Over Who Speak English-Only at Home

Top 10 Places Sorted by Number

Place (place type) County	Number

No places met population threshold.

Notes: Please refer to the User's Guide for an explanation of data; tables include places with populations > 9,999 and reflect only those areas that meet Summary File 4 population thresholds, therefore there may be less than 10 places listed

Hawaiian, Natives 5 Years and Over Who Speak English-Only at Home
Top 10 Places Sorted by Percent

Place (place type) County	Percent

No places met population threshold.

Hmongs 5 Years and Over Who Speak English-Only at Home
Top 10 Places Sorted by Number

Place (place type) County	Number

No places met population threshold.

Hmongs 5 Years and Over Who Speak English-Only at Home
Top 10 Places Sorted by Percent

Place (place type) County	Percent

No places met population threshold.

Indonesians 5 Years and Over Who Speak English-Only at Home
Top 10 Places Sorted by Number

Place (place type) County	Number

No places met population threshold.

Indonesians 5 Years and Over Who Speak English-Only at Home
Top 10 Places Sorted by Percent

Place (place type) County	Percent

No places met population threshold.

Japaneses 5 Years and Over Who Speak English-Only at Home
Top 10 Places Sorted by Number

Place (place type) County	Number
Jacksonville (city) Duval	224

Japaneses 5 Years and Over Who Speak English-Only at Home
Top 10 Places Sorted by Percent

Place (place type) County	Percent
Jacksonville (city) Duval	43.33

Koreans 5 Years and Over Who Speak English-Only at Home
Top 10 Places Sorted by Number

Place (place type) County	Number
Jacksonville (city) Duval	147
Tampa (city) Hillsborough	144
Orlando (city) Orange	122
Gainesville (city) Alachua	48

Koreans 5 Years and Over Who Speak English-Only at Home
Top 10 Places Sorted by Percent

Place (place type) County	Percent
Orlando (city) Orange	24.02
Jacksonville (city) Duval	16.42
Tampa (city) Hillsborough	15.43
Gainesville (city) Alachua	10.55

Laotians 5 Years and Over Who Speak English-Only at Home
Top 10 Places Sorted by Number

Place (place type) County	Number
St. Petersburg (city) Pinellas	36

Laotians 5 Years and Over Who Speak English-Only at Home
Top 10 Places Sorted by Percent

Place (place type) County	Percent
St. Petersburg (city) Pinellas	3.34

Malaysians 5 Years and Over Who Speak English-Only at Home
Top 10 Places Sorted by Number

Place (place type) County	Number

No places met population threshold.

Malaysians 5 Years and Over Who Speak English-Only at Home
Top 10 Places Sorted by Percent

Place (place type) County	Percent

No places met population threshold.

Pakistanis 5 Years and Over Who Speak English-Only at Home
Top 10 Places Sorted by Number

Place (place type) County	Number

No places met population threshold.

Pakistanis 5 Years and Over Who Speak English-Only at Home
Top 10 Places Sorted by Percent

Place (place type) County	Percent

No places met population threshold.

Samoans 5 Years and Over Who Speak English-Only at Home
Top 10 Places Sorted by Number

Place (place type) County	Number

No places met population threshold.

Samoans 5 Years and Over Who Speak English-Only at Home
Top 10 Places Sorted by Percent

Place (place type) County	Percent

No places met population threshold.

Sri Lankans 5 Years and Over Who Speak English-Only at Home
Top 10 Places Sorted by Number

Place (place type) County	Number

No places met population threshold.

Sri Lankans 5 Years and Over Who Speak English-Only at Home
Top 10 Places Sorted by Percent

Place (place type) County	Percent

No places met population threshold.

Taiwaneses 5 Years and Over Who Speak English-Only at Home
Top 10 Places Sorted by Number

Place (place type) County	Number

No places met population threshold.

Taiwaneses 5 Years and Over Who Speak English-Only at Home
Top 10 Places Sorted by Percent

Place (place type) County	Percent

No places met population threshold.

Thais 5 Years and Over Who Speak English-Only at Home
Top 10 Places Sorted by Number

Place (place type) County	Number

No places met population threshold.

Thais 5 Years and Over Who Speak English-Only at Home
Top 10 Places Sorted by Percent

Place (place type) County	Percent

No places met population threshold.

Tongans 5 Years and Over Who Speak English-Only at Home
Top 10 Places Sorted by Number

Place (place type) County	Number

No places met population threshold.

Tongans 5 Years and Over Who Speak English-Only at Home
Top 10 Places Sorted by Percent

Place (place type) County	Percent

No places met population threshold.

Vietnamese 5 Years and Over Who Speak English-Only at Home
Top 10 Places Sorted by Number

Place (place type) County	Number
Jacksonville (city) Duval	123
Orlando (city) Orange	85
Tampa (city) Hillsborough	83
St. Petersburg (city) Pinellas	76
West and East Lealman (cdp) Pinellas	63
Town 'n' Country (cdp) Hillsborough	55
Pine Hills (cdp) Orange	51
Pinellas Park (city) Pinellas	26
Oak Ridge (cdp) Orange	7

Vietnamese 5 Years and Over Who Speak English-Only at Home
Top 10 Places Sorted by Percent

Place (place type) County	Percent
West and East Lealman (cdp) Pinellas	14.52
Orlando (city) Orange	12.96
Pine Hills (cdp) Orange	8.59
Town 'n' Country (cdp) Hillsborough	8.12
Jacksonville (city) Duval	6.57
Tampa (city) Hillsborough	6.39
Pinellas Park (city) Pinellas	5.32
St. Petersburg (city) Pinellas	4.96
Oak Ridge (cdp) Orange	1.51

Foreign Born

Total Population
Top 10 Places Sorted by Number

Place (place type) County	Number
Miami (city) Miami-Dade	215,739
Hialeah (city) Miami-Dade	163,256
Miami Beach (city) Miami-Dade	48,852
Jacksonville (city) Duval	43,661
Fountainbleau (cdp) Miami-Dade	43,496
Pembroke Pines (city) Broward	39,727
Tampa (city) Hillsborough	37,027
Hollywood (city) Broward	36,562
Kendale Lakes (cdp) Miami-Dade	33,460
Fort Lauderdale (city) Broward	32,938

Total Population
Top 10 Places Sorted by Percent

Place (place type) County	Percent
Fountainbleau (cdp) Miami-Dade	73.08
Hialeah (city) Miami-Dade	72.11
Doral (cdp) Miami-Dade	62.55
Miami (city) Miami-Dade	59.50
Kendall West (cdp) Miami-Dade	59.41
Kendale Lakes (cdp) Miami-Dade	58.82
Miami Beach (city) Miami-Dade	55.48
The Hammocks (cdp) Miami-Dade	52.44
Sunset (cdp) Miami-Dade	50.66
North Miami Beach (city) Miami-Dade	49.67

Asian
Top 10 Places Sorted by Number

Place (place type) County	Number
Jacksonville (city) Duval	13,857

Notes: Please refer to the User's Guide for an explanation of data; tables include places with populations > 9,999 and reflect only those areas that meet Summary File 4 population thresholds, therefore there may be less than 10 places listed

Place (place type) County	Number
St. Petersburg (city) Pinellas	5,185
Tampa (city) Hillsborough	5,046
Pembroke Pines (city) Broward	3,758
Orlando (city) Orange	3,740
Gainesville (city) Alachua	3,191
Coral Springs (city) Broward	3,064
Tallahassee (city) Leon	2,632
Sunrise (city) Broward	2,268
Hollywood (city) Broward	2,218

Asian
Top 10 Places Sorted by Percent

Place (place type) County	Percent
Pine Hills (cdp) Orange	88.55
Sunset (cdp) Miami-Dade	86.31
Doral (cdp) Miami-Dade	85.16
Boca Raton (city) Palm Beach	84.33
Fountainbleau (cdp) Miami-Dade	84.22
Palm Bay (city) Brevard	83.20
Deerfield Beach (city) Broward	83.07
Bellair-Meadowbrook Terrace (cdp) Clay	82.83
Kendall (cdp) Miami-Dade	82.35
University (cdp) Hillsborough	82.24

Native Hawaiian and Other Pacific Islander
Top 10 Places Sorted by Number

Place (place type) County	Number
Jacksonville (city) Duval	36

Native Hawaiian and Other Pacific Islander
Top 10 Places Sorted by Percent

Place (place type) County	Percent
Jacksonville (city) Duval	7.24

Asian Indian
Top 10 Places Sorted by Number

Place (place type) County	Number
Jacksonville (city) Duval	2,055
Coral Springs (city) Broward	1,422
Pembroke Pines (city) Broward	1,346
Orlando (city) Orange	1,198
Tampa (city) Hillsborough	1,039
Hollywood (city) Broward	1,003
Plantation (city) Broward	853
Tallahassee (city) Leon	852
Sunrise (city) Broward	815
St. Petersburg (city) Pinellas	723

Asian Indian
Top 10 Places Sorted by Percent

Place (place type) County	Percent
Boca Raton (city) Palm Beach	94.23
Lakeland (city) Polk	87.86
Melbourne (city) Brevard	86.78
Fort Lauderdale (city) Broward	82.77
Kendall (cdp) Miami-Dade	82.76
Sunrise (city) Broward	82.32
Orlando (city) Orange	82.05
Cooper City (city) Broward	81.11
St. Petersburg (city) Pinellas	80.60
West Palm Beach (city) Palm Beach	79.38

Bangladeshi
Top 10 Places Sorted by Number

Place (place type) County	Number

No places met population threshold.

Bangladeshi
Top 10 Places Sorted by Percent

Place (place type) County	Percent

No places met population threshold.

Cambodian
Top 10 Places Sorted by Number

Place (place type) County	Number
Jacksonville (city) Duval	725
St. Petersburg (city) Pinellas	369

Cambodian
Top 10 Places Sorted by Percent

Place (place type) County	Percent
Jacksonville (city) Duval	72.43
St. Petersburg (city) Pinellas	71.51

Chinese (except Taiwanese)
Top 10 Places Sorted by Number

Place (place type) County	Number
Gainesville (city) Alachua	1,193
Jacksonville (city) Duval	1,091
Pembroke Pines (city) Broward	847
Coral Springs (city) Broward	695
Sunrise (city) Broward	655
St. Petersburg (city) Pinellas	608
Tallahassee (city) Leon	602
North Miami Beach (city) Miami-Dade	591
Kendall (cdp) Miami-Dade	538
Tampa (city) Hillsborough	496

Chinese (except Taiwanese)
Top 10 Places Sorted by Percent

Place (place type) County	Percent
Kendall (cdp) Miami-Dade	85.94
Orlando (city) Orange	85.57
St. Petersburg (city) Pinellas	83.17
Gainesville (city) Alachua	81.94
Tallahassee (city) Leon	79.95
North Miami Beach (city) Miami-Dade	79.76
Coral Springs (city) Broward	77.83
Miami (city) Miami-Dade	77.19
Miramar (city) Broward	77.06
Davie (town) Broward	76.36

Fijian
Top 10 Places Sorted by Number

Place (place type) County	Number

No places met population threshold.

Fijian
Top 10 Places Sorted by Percent

Place (place type) County	Percent

No places met population threshold.

Filipino
Top 10 Places Sorted by Number

Place (place type) County	Number
Jacksonville (city) Duval	6,587
Tampa (city) Hillsborough	783
Pembroke Pines (city) Broward	754
St. Petersburg (city) Pinellas	647
Cape Coral (city) Lee	490
Orlando (city) Orange	471
Lakeside (cdp) Clay	463
Clearwater (city) Pinellas	317
Myrtle Grove (cdp) Escambia	317
Miramar (city) Broward	311

Filipino
Top 10 Places Sorted by Percent

Place (place type) County	Percent
Pembroke Pines (city) Broward	81.34
Lakeside (cdp) Clay	81.09
Tampa (city) Hillsborough	80.72
St. Petersburg (city) Pinellas	74.37
Yeehaw Junction (cdp) Osceola	72.43
Cape Coral (city) Lee	71.74
Clearwater (city) Pinellas	70.29
Jacksonville (city) Duval	67.33
Myrtle Grove (cdp) Escambia	67.30
Miramar (city) Broward	65.34

Guamanian or Chamorro
Top 10 Places Sorted by Number

Place (place type) County	Number

No places met population threshold.

Guamanian or Chamorro
Top 10 Places Sorted by Percent

Place (place type) County	Percent

No places met population threshold.

Hawaiian, Native
Top 10 Places Sorted by Number

Place (place type) County	Number

No places met population threshold.

Hawaiian, Native
Top 10 Places Sorted by Percent

Place (place type) County	Percent

No places met population threshold.

Hmong
Top 10 Places Sorted by Number

Place (place type) County	Number

No places met population threshold.

Hmong
Top 10 Places Sorted by Percent

Place (place type) County	Percent

No places met population threshold.

Indonesian
Top 10 Places Sorted by Number

Place (place type) County	Number

No places met population threshold.

Indonesian
Top 10 Places Sorted by Percent

Place (place type) County	Percent

No places met population threshold.

Japanese
Top 10 Places Sorted by Number

Place (place type) County	Number
Jacksonville (city) Duval	343

Japanese
Top 10 Places Sorted by Percent

Place (place type) County	Percent
Jacksonville (city) Duval	64.60

Korean
Top 10 Places Sorted by Number

Place (place type) County	Number
Jacksonville (city) Duval	771
Tampa (city) Hillsborough	737
Orlando (city) Orange	416
Gainesville (city) Alachua	388

Korean
Top 10 Places Sorted by Percent

Place (place type) County	Percent
Jacksonville (city) Duval	82.02
Gainesville (city) Alachua	77.45
Tampa (city) Hillsborough	76.53
Orlando (city) Orange	75.64

Notes: Please refer to the User's Guide for an explanation of data; tables include places with populations > 9,999 and reflect only those areas that meet Summary File 4 population thresholds, therefore there may be less than 10 places listed

Laotian
Top 10 Places Sorted by Number

Place (place type) County	Number
St. Petersburg (city) Pinellas	898

Laotian
Top 10 Places Sorted by Percent

Place (place type) County	Percent
St. Petersburg (city) Pinellas	79.26

Malaysian
Top 10 Places Sorted by Number

Place (place type) County	Number

No places met population threshold.

Malaysian
Top 10 Places Sorted by Percent

Place (place type) County	Percent

No places met population threshold.

Pakistani
Top 10 Places Sorted by Number

Place (place type) County	Number

No places met population threshold.

Pakistani
Top 10 Places Sorted by Percent

Place (place type) County	Percent

No places met population threshold.

Samoan
Top 10 Places Sorted by Number

Place (place type) County	Number

No places met population threshold.

Samoan
Top 10 Places Sorted by Percent

Place (place type) County	Percent

No places met population threshold.

Sri Lankan
Top 10 Places Sorted by Number

Place (place type) County	Number

No places met population threshold.

Sri Lankan
Top 10 Places Sorted by Percent

Place (place type) County	Percent

No places met population threshold.

Taiwanese
Top 10 Places Sorted by Number

Place (place type) County	Number

No places met population threshold.

Taiwanese
Top 10 Places Sorted by Percent

Place (place type) County	Percent

No places met population threshold.

Thai
Top 10 Places Sorted by Number

Place (place type) County	Number

No places met population threshold.

Thai
Top 10 Places Sorted by Percent

Place (place type) County	Percent

No places met population threshold.

Tongan
Top 10 Places Sorted by Number

Place (place type) County	Number

No places met population threshold.

Tongan
Top 10 Places Sorted by Percent

Place (place type) County	Percent

No places met population threshold.

Vietnamese
Top 10 Places Sorted by Number

Place (place type) County	Number
Jacksonville (city) Duval	1,535
St. Petersburg (city) Pinellas	1,248
Tampa (city) Hillsborough	1,244
Town 'n' Country (cdp) Hillsborough	595
Pine Hills (cdp) Orange	569
Orlando (city) Orange	568
Oak Ridge (cdp) Orange	450
Pinellas Park (city) Pinellas	391
West and East Lealman (cdp) Pinellas	365

Vietnamese
Top 10 Places Sorted by Percent

Place (place type) County	Percent
Tampa (city) Hillsborough	90.21
Pine Hills (cdp) Orange	88.77
Town 'n' Country (cdp) Hillsborough	86.73
Oak Ridge (cdp) Orange	85.39
Orlando (city) Orange	81.84
West and East Lealman (cdp) Pinellas	79.87
St. Petersburg (city) Pinellas	77.52
Jacksonville (city) Duval	74.84
Pinellas Park (city) Pinellas	74.33

Foreign-Born Naturalized Citizens

Total Population
Top 10 Places Sorted by Number

Place (place type) County	Number
Miami (city) Miami-Dade	89,727
Hialeah (city) Miami-Dade	70,331
Pembroke Pines (city) Broward	22,597
Miami Beach (city) Miami-Dade	21,744
Jacksonville (city) Duval	20,786
Fountainbleau (cdp) Miami-Dade	18,348
Kendale Lakes (cdp) Miami-Dade	17,856
Kendall (cdp) Miami-Dade	16,474
Hollywood (city) Broward	16,136
Tampa (city) Hillsborough	14,683

Total Population
Top 10 Places Sorted by Percent

Place (place type) County	Percent
Sunset (cdp) Miami-Dade	32.98
Miami Lakes (cdp) Miami-Dade	32.32
Kendale Lakes (cdp) Miami-Dade	31.39
Hialeah (city) Miami-Dade	31.06
Fountainbleau (cdp) Miami-Dade	30.83
Miami (city) Miami-Dade	24.75
Miami Beach (city) Miami-Dade	24.69
Kendall West (cdp) Miami-Dade	24.63
Coral Gables (city) Miami-Dade	24.38
The Hammocks (cdp) Miami-Dade	24.16

Asian
Top 10 Places Sorted by Number

Place (place type) County	Number
Jacksonville (city) Duval	7,673
St. Petersburg (city) Pinellas	2,206
Tampa (city) Hillsborough	2,080
Pembroke Pines (city) Broward	2,069
Orlando (city) Orange	1,750
Coral Springs (city) Broward	1,392
Sunrise (city) Broward	1,184
Hollywood (city) Broward	1,034
Tallahassee (city) Leon	977
Gainesville (city) Alachua	897

Asian
Top 10 Places Sorted by Percent

Place (place type) County	Percent
Kendale Lakes (cdp) Miami-Dade	54.45
Ferry Pass (cdp) Escambia	54.19
Yeehaw Junction (cdp) Osceola	49.74
North Lauderdale (city) Broward	49.70
South Miami Heights (cdp) Miami-Dade	49.42
Royal Palm Beach (village) Palm Beach	49.24
Lakeside (cdp) Clay	49.10
Niceville (city) Okaloosa	48.78
Doctor Phillips (cdp) Orange	48.77
Fort Walton Beach (city) Okaloosa	48.72

Native Hawaiian and Other Pacific Islander
Top 10 Places Sorted by Number

Place (place type) County	Number
Jacksonville (city) Duval	15

Native Hawaiian and Other Pacific Islander
Top 10 Places Sorted by Percent

Place (place type) County	Percent
Jacksonville (city) Duval	3.02

Asian Indian
Top 10 Places Sorted by Number

Place (place type) County	Number
Pembroke Pines (city) Broward	683
Jacksonville (city) Duval	660
Orlando (city) Orange	593
Coral Springs (city) Broward	549
Sunrise (city) Broward	357
Hollywood (city) Broward	346
Plantation (city) Broward	331
Tallahassee (city) Leon	318
Tampa (city) Hillsborough	313
Kendall (cdp) Miami-Dade	308

Asian Indian
Top 10 Places Sorted by Percent

Place (place type) County	Percent
Cooper City (city) Broward	51.10
Davie (town) Broward	46.78
Altamonte Springs (city) Seminole	46.76
Doctor Phillips (cdp) Orange	43.23
Melbourne (city) Brevard	42.22
Kendall (cdp) Miami-Dade	42.13
Orlando (city) Orange	40.62
Fort Lauderdale (city) Broward	40.07
Pembroke Pines (city) Broward	38.98
East Lake (cdp) Pinellas	36.17

Bangladeshi
Top 10 Places Sorted by Number

Place (place type) County	Number

No places met population threshold.

Bangladeshi
Top 10 Places Sorted by Percent

Place (place type) County	Percent

No places met population threshold.

Cambodian
Top 10 Places Sorted by Number

Place (place type) County	Number
Jacksonville (city) Duval	349

Notes: Please refer to the User's Guide for an explanation of data; tables include places with populations > 9,999 and reflect only those areas that meet Summary File 4 population thresholds, therefore there may be less than 10 places listed

St. Petersburg (city) Pinellas	136

Cambodian
Top 10 Places Sorted by Percent

Place (place type) County	Percent
Jacksonville (city) Duval	34.87
St. Petersburg (city) Pinellas	26.36

Chinese (except Taiwanese)
Top 10 Places Sorted by Number

Place (place type) County	Number
Jacksonville (city) Duval	639
Pembroke Pines (city) Broward	497
Sunrise (city) Broward	427
Coral Springs (city) Broward	376
North Miami Beach (city) Miami-Dade	360
Kendall (cdp) Miami-Dade	306
Hollywood (city) Broward	296
Miami (city) Miami-Dade	272
Margate (city) Broward	263
Tampa (city) Hillsborough	237

Chinese (except Taiwanese)
Top 10 Places Sorted by Percent

Place (place type) County	Percent
Miami (city) Miami-Dade	55.40
Kendall (cdp) Miami-Dade	48.88
North Miami Beach (city) Miami-Dade	48.58
Margate (city) Broward	48.43
Sunrise (city) Broward	47.29
Miramar (city) Broward	45.88
Hollywood (city) Broward	45.61
Pembroke Pines (city) Broward	43.10
Coral Springs (city) Broward	42.11
Orlando (city) Orange	40.68

Fijian
Top 10 Places Sorted by Number

Place (place type) County	Number

No places met population threshold.

Fijian
Top 10 Places Sorted by Percent

Place (place type) County	Percent

No places met population threshold.

Filipino
Top 10 Places Sorted by Number

Place (place type) County	Number
Jacksonville (city) Duval	4,406
Pembroke Pines (city) Broward	460
Tampa (city) Hillsborough	365
St. Petersburg (city) Pinellas	363
Lakeside (cdp) Clay	318
Orlando (city) Orange	265
Cape Coral (city) Lee	261
Myrtle Grove (cdp) Escambia	239
Bellview (cdp) Escambia	205
Miramar (city) Broward	203

Filipino
Top 10 Places Sorted by Percent

Place (place type) County	Percent
Lakeside (cdp) Clay	55.69
Myrtle Grove (cdp) Escambia	50.74
Bellview (cdp) Escambia	49.76
Pembroke Pines (city) Broward	49.62
Yeehaw Junction (cdp) Osceola	48.97
Jacksonville (city) Duval	45.04
Miramar (city) Broward	42.65
St. Petersburg (city) Pinellas	41.72
Cape Coral (city) Lee	38.21
Tampa (city) Hillsborough	37.63

Guamanian or Chamorro
Top 10 Places Sorted by Number

Place (place type) County	Number

No places met population threshold.

Guamanian or Chamorro
Top 10 Places Sorted by Percent

Place (place type) County	Percent

No places met population threshold.

Hawaiian, Native
Top 10 Places Sorted by Number

Place (place type) County	Number

No places met population threshold.

Hawaiian, Native
Top 10 Places Sorted by Percent

Place (place type) County	Percent

No places met population threshold.

Hmong
Top 10 Places Sorted by Number

Place (place type) County	Number

No places met population threshold.

Hmong
Top 10 Places Sorted by Percent

Place (place type) County	Percent

No places met population threshold.

Indonesian
Top 10 Places Sorted by Number

Place (place type) County	Number

No places met population threshold.

Indonesian
Top 10 Places Sorted by Percent

Place (place type) County	Percent

No places met population threshold.

Japanese
Top 10 Places Sorted by Number

Place (place type) County	Number
Jacksonville (city) Duval	154

Japanese
Top 10 Places Sorted by Percent

Place (place type) County	Percent
Jacksonville (city) Duval	29.00

Korean
Top 10 Places Sorted by Number

Place (place type) County	Number
Jacksonville (city) Duval	416
Tampa (city) Hillsborough	252
Orlando (city) Orange	126
Gainesville (city) Alachua	53

Korean
Top 10 Places Sorted by Percent

Place (place type) County	Percent
Jacksonville (city) Duval	44.26
Tampa (city) Hillsborough	26.17
Orlando (city) Orange	22.91
Gainesville (city) Alachua	10.58

Laotian
Top 10 Places Sorted by Number

Place (place type) County	Number
St. Petersburg (city) Pinellas	377

Laotian
Top 10 Places Sorted by Percent

Place (place type) County	Percent
St. Petersburg (city) Pinellas	33.27

Malaysian
Top 10 Places Sorted by Number

Place (place type) County	Number

No places met population threshold.

Malaysian
Top 10 Places Sorted by Percent

Place (place type) County	Percent

No places met population threshold.

Pakistani
Top 10 Places Sorted by Number

Place (place type) County	Number

No places met population threshold.

Pakistani
Top 10 Places Sorted by Percent

Place (place type) County	Percent

No places met population threshold.

Samoan
Top 10 Places Sorted by Number

Place (place type) County	Number

No places met population threshold.

Samoan
Top 10 Places Sorted by Percent

Place (place type) County	Percent

No places met population threshold.

Sri Lankan
Top 10 Places Sorted by Number

Place (place type) County	Number

No places met population threshold.

Sri Lankan
Top 10 Places Sorted by Percent

Place (place type) County	Percent

No places met population threshold.

Taiwanese
Top 10 Places Sorted by Number

Place (place type) County	Number

No places met population threshold.

Taiwanese
Top 10 Places Sorted by Percent

Place (place type) County	Percent

No places met population threshold.

Thai
Top 10 Places Sorted by Number

Place (place type) County	Number

No places met population threshold.

Thai
Top 10 Places Sorted by Percent

Place (place type) County	Percent

No places met population threshold.

Tongan
Top 10 Places Sorted by Number

Place (place type) County	Number

No places met population threshold.

Notes: Please refer to the User's Guide for an explanation of data; tables include places with populations > 9,999 and reflect only those areas that meet Summary File 4 population thresholds, therefore there may be less than 10 places listed

Tongan

Top 10 Places Sorted by Percent

Place (place type) County	Percent

No places met population threshold.

Vietnamese

Top 10 Places Sorted by Number

Place (place type) County	Number
Jacksonville (city) Duval	714
Tampa (city) Hillsborough	521
St. Petersburg (city) Pinellas	500
Town 'n' Country (cdp) Hillsborough	296
Orlando (city) Orange	295
Oak Ridge (cdp) Orange	226
Pinellas Park (city) Pinellas	159
Pine Hills (cdp) Orange	142
West and East Lealman (cdp) Pinellas	108

Vietnamese

Top 10 Places Sorted by Percent

Place (place type) County	Percent
Town 'n' Country (cdp) Hillsborough	43.15
Oak Ridge (cdp) Orange	42.88
Orlando (city) Orange	42.51
Tampa (city) Hillsborough	37.78
Jacksonville (city) Duval	34.81
St. Petersburg (city) Pinellas	31.06
Pinellas Park (city) Pinellas	30.23
West and East Lealman (cdp) Pinellas	23.63
Pine Hills (cdp) Orange	22.15

Educational Attainment: High School Graduates

Total Populations 25 Years and Over Who are High School Graduates

Top 10 Places Sorted by Number

Place (place type) County	Number
Jacksonville (city) Duval	385,300
Tampa (city) Hillsborough	153,114
St. Petersburg (city) Pinellas	143,458
Miami (city) Miami-Dade	133,069
Orlando (city) Orange	103,129
Fort Lauderdale (city) Broward	87,921
Pembroke Pines (city) Broward	82,419
Hollywood (city) Broward	79,650
Hialeah (city) Miami-Dade	77,548
Tallahassee (city) Leon	71,754

Total Populations 25 Years and Over Who are High School Graduates

Top 10 Places Sorted by Percent

Place (place type) County	Percent
Westchase (cdp) Hillsborough	96.62
Wekiwa Springs (cdp) Seminole	96.03
Weston (city) Broward	95.47
Pinecrest (village) Miami-Dade	94.24
Palm Beach Gardens (city) Palm Beach	94.03
East Lake (cdp) Pinellas	93.96
Doctor Phillips (cdp) Orange	93.86
Oviedo (city) Seminole	93.33
Hunters Creek (cdp) Orange	93.32
Wellington (village) Palm Beach	92.16

Asians 25 Years and Over Who are High School Graduates

Top 10 Places Sorted by Number

Place (place type) County	Number
Jacksonville (city) Duval	10,604
Tampa (city) Hillsborough	3,596
Orlando (city) Orange	3,005
Pembroke Pines (city) Broward	2,957
St. Petersburg (city) Pinellas	2,903
Gainesville (city) Alachua	2,232
Coral Springs (city) Broward	2,215
Tallahassee (city) Leon	2,108
Hollywood (city) Broward	1,496
Sunrise (city) Broward	1,373

Asians 25 Years and Over Who are High School Graduates

Top 10 Places Sorted by Percent

Place (place type) County	Percent
Oviedo (city) Seminole	97.65
Gainesville (city) Alachua	95.79
Temple Terrace (city) Hillsborough	93.75
University (cdp) Hillsborough	93.57
Palm Harbor (cdp) Pinellas	92.42
Tamarac (city) Broward	92.10
Citrus Park (cdp) Hillsborough	92.05
Royal Palm Beach (village) Palm Beach	91.93
Tallahassee (city) Leon	91.61
Weston (city) Broward	91.14

Native Hawaiian and Other Pacific Islanders 25 Years and Over Who are High School Graduates

Top 10 Places Sorted by Number

Place (place type) County	Number
Jacksonville (city) Duval	210

Native Hawaiian and Other Pacific Islanders 25 Years and Over Who are High School Graduates

Top 10 Places Sorted by Percent

Place (place type) County	Percent
Jacksonville (city) Duval	76.09

Asian Indians 25 Years and Over Who are High School Graduates

Top 10 Places Sorted by Number

Place (place type) County	Number
Jacksonville (city) Duval	1,661
Pembroke Pines (city) Broward	1,059
Coral Springs (city) Broward	1,018
Orlando (city) Orange	951
Tampa (city) Hillsborough	747
Tallahassee (city) Leon	664
Hollywood (city) Broward	575
St. Petersburg (city) Pinellas	572
Plantation (city) Broward	541
Miami (city) Miami-Dade	526

Asian Indians 25 Years and Over Who are High School Graduates

Top 10 Places Sorted by Percent

Place (place type) County	Percent
Gainesville (city) Alachua	96.90
Lakeland (city) Polk	96.10
Davie (town) Broward	96.08
Tallahassee (city) Leon	95.68
Kendall (cdp) Miami-Dade	93.57
Orlando (city) Orange	92.51
St. Petersburg (city) Pinellas	92.26
Jacksonville (city) Duval	91.97
Pembroke Pines (city) Broward	91.85
Weston (city) Broward	91.40

Bangladeshis 25 Years and Over Who are High School Graduates

Top 10 Places Sorted by Number

Place (place type) County	Number

No places met population threshold.

Bangladeshis 25 Years and Over Who are High School Graduates

Top 10 Places Sorted by Percent

Place (place type) County	Percent

No places met population threshold.

Cambodians 25 Years and Over Who are High School Graduates

Top 10 Places Sorted by Number

Place (place type) County	Number
Jacksonville (city) Duval	249
St. Petersburg (city) Pinellas	103

Cambodians 25 Years and Over Who are High School Graduates

Top 10 Places Sorted by Percent

Place (place type) County	Percent
Jacksonville (city) Duval	46.89
St. Petersburg (city) Pinellas	42.39

Chinese (except Taiwanese)s 25 Years and Over Who are High School Graduates

Top 10 Places Sorted by Number

Place (place type) County	Number
Gainesville (city) Alachua	874
Jacksonville (city) Duval	870
Tallahassee (city) Leon	551
Pembroke Pines (city) Broward	532
Coral Springs (city) Broward	516
Tampa (city) Hillsborough	427
Kendall (cdp) Miami-Dade	400
St. Petersburg (city) Pinellas	396
Orlando (city) Orange	342
Sunrise (city) Broward	334

Chinese (except Taiwanese)s 25 Years and Over Who are High School Graduates

Top 10 Places Sorted by Percent

Place (place type) County	Percent
Gainesville (city) Alachua	98.09
Tallahassee (city) Leon	97.35
Miramar (city) Broward	92.07
Tampa (city) Hillsborough	85.06
Jacksonville (city) Duval	83.41
Orlando (city) Orange	82.21
Kendall (cdp) Miami-Dade	82.14
Davie (town) Broward	77.92
Margate (city) Broward	77.78
Coral Springs (city) Broward	77.01

Fijians 25 Years and Over Who are High School Graduates

Top 10 Places Sorted by Number

Place (place type) County	Number

No places met population threshold.

Fijians 25 Years and Over Who are High School Graduates

Top 10 Places Sorted by Percent

Place (place type) County	Percent

No places met population threshold.

Filipinos 25 Years and Over Who are High School Graduates

Top 10 Places Sorted by Number

Place (place type) County	Number
Jacksonville (city) Duval	5,771
Pembroke Pines (city) Broward	655
Tampa (city) Hillsborough	583
St. Petersburg (city) Pinellas	542
Orlando (city) Orange	464
Cape Coral (city) Lee	420
Lakeside (cdp) Clay	394
Myrtle Grove (cdp) Escambia	275
Miramar (city) Broward	272
Clearwater (city) Pinellas	267

Notes: Please refer to the User's Guide for an explanation of data; tables include places with populations > 9,999 and reflect only those areas that meet Summary File 4 population thresholds, therefore there may be less than 10 places listed

Filipinos 25 Years and Over Who are High School Graduates

Top 10 Places Sorted by Percent

Place (place type) County	Percent
Orlando (city) Orange	95.47
Yeehaw Junction (cdp) Osceola	94.20
Pembroke Pines (city) Broward	93.57
Tampa (city) Hillsborough	89.55
Miramar (city) Broward	88.60
Clearwater (city) Pinellas	88.41
Jacksonville (city) Duval	88.11
Lakeside (cdp) Clay	86.40
Cape Coral (city) Lee	84.34
St. Petersburg (city) Pinellas	84.03

Guamanian or Chamorros 25 Years and Over Who are High School Graduates

Top 10 Places Sorted by Number

Place (place type) County	Number

No places met population threshold.

Guamanian or Chamorros 25 Years and Over Who are High School Graduates

Top 10 Places Sorted by Percent

Place (place type) County	Percent

No places met population threshold.

Hawaiian, Natives 25 Years and Over Who are High School Graduates

Top 10 Places Sorted by Number

Place (place type) County	Number

No places met population threshold.

Hawaiian, Natives 25 Years and Over Who are High School Graduates

Top 10 Places Sorted by Percent

Place (place type) County	Percent

No places met population threshold.

Hmongs 25 Years and Over Who are High School Graduates

Top 10 Places Sorted by Number

Place (place type) County	Number

No places met population threshold.

Hmongs 25 Years and Over Who are High School Graduates

Top 10 Places Sorted by Percent

Place (place type) County	Percent

No places met population threshold.

Indonesians 25 Years and Over Who are High School Graduates

Top 10 Places Sorted by Number

Place (place type) County	Number

No places met population threshold.

Indonesians 25 Years and Over Who are High School Graduates

Top 10 Places Sorted by Percent

Place (place type) County	Percent

No places met population threshold.

Japaneses 25 Years and Over Who are High School Graduates

Top 10 Places Sorted by Number

Place (place type) County	Number
Jacksonville (city) Duval	371

Japaneses 25 Years and Over Who are High School Graduates

Top 10 Places Sorted by Percent

Place (place type) County	Percent
Jacksonville (city) Duval	84.32

Koreans 25 Years and Over Who are High School Graduates

Top 10 Places Sorted by Number

Place (place type) County	Number
Tampa (city) Hillsborough	539
Jacksonville (city) Duval	497
Orlando (city) Orange	341
Gainesville (city) Alachua	270

Koreans 25 Years and Over Who are High School Graduates

Top 10 Places Sorted by Percent

Place (place type) County	Percent
Gainesville (city) Alachua	96.43
Orlando (city) Orange	86.33
Tampa (city) Hillsborough	82.67
Jacksonville (city) Duval	75.76

Laotians 25 Years and Over Who are High School Graduates

Top 10 Places Sorted by Number

Place (place type) County	Number
St. Petersburg (city) Pinellas	343

Laotians 25 Years and Over Who are High School Graduates

Top 10 Places Sorted by Percent

Place (place type) County	Percent
St. Petersburg (city) Pinellas	51.89

Malaysians 25 Years and Over Who are High School Graduates

Top 10 Places Sorted by Number

Place (place type) County	Number

No places met population threshold.

Malaysians 25 Years and Over Who are High School Graduates

Top 10 Places Sorted by Percent

Place (place type) County	Percent

No places met population threshold.

Pakistanis 25 Years and Over Who are High School Graduates

Top 10 Places Sorted by Number

Place (place type) County	Number

No places met population threshold.

Pakistanis 25 Years and Over Who are High School Graduates

Top 10 Places Sorted by Percent

Place (place type) County	Percent

No places met population threshold.

Samoans 25 Years and Over Who are High School Graduates

Top 10 Places Sorted by Number

Place (place type) County	Number

No places met population threshold.

Samoans 25 Years and Over Who are High School Graduates

Top 10 Places Sorted by Percent

Place (place type) County	Percent

No places met population threshold.

Sri Lankans 25 Years and Over Who are High School Graduates

Top 10 Places Sorted by Number

Place (place type) County	Number

No places met population threshold.

Sri Lankans 25 Years and Over Who are High School Graduates

Top 10 Places Sorted by Percent

Place (place type) County	Percent

No places met population threshold.

Taiwaneses 25 Years and Over Who are High School Graduates

Top 10 Places Sorted by Number

Place (place type) County	Number

No places met population threshold.

Taiwaneses 25 Years and Over Who are High School Graduates

Top 10 Places Sorted by Percent

Place (place type) County	Percent

No places met population threshold.

Thais 25 Years and Over Who are High School Graduates

Top 10 Places Sorted by Number

Place (place type) County	Number

No places met population threshold.

Thais 25 Years and Over Who are High School Graduates

Top 10 Places Sorted by Percent

Place (place type) County	Percent

No places met population threshold.

Tongans 25 Years and Over Who are High School Graduates

Top 10 Places Sorted by Number

Place (place type) County	Number

No places met population threshold.

Tongans 25 Years and Over Who are High School Graduates

Top 10 Places Sorted by Percent

Place (place type) County	Percent

No places met population threshold.

Vietnamese 25 Years and Over Who are High School Graduates

Top 10 Places Sorted by Number

Place (place type) County	Number
Tampa (city) Hillsborough	677
Jacksonville (city) Duval	608
St. Petersburg (city) Pinellas	505
Orlando (city) Orange	329
Town 'n' Country (cdp) Hillsborough	327
Pinellas Park (city) Pinellas	278
Pine Hills (cdp) Orange	242
Oak Ridge (cdp) Orange	154
West and East Lealman (cdp) Pinellas	86

Vietnamese 25 Years and Over Who are High School Graduates

Top 10 Places Sorted by Percent

Place (place type) County	Percent
Pinellas Park (city) Pinellas	75.75
Tampa (city) Hillsborough	70.08
Town 'n' Country (cdp) Hillsborough	68.55
Orlando (city) Orange	66.87
Pine Hills (cdp) Orange	58.03
St. Petersburg (city) Pinellas	50.45
Jacksonville (city) Duval	48.76

Notes: Please refer to the User's Guide for an explanation of data; tables include places with populations > 9,999 and reflect only those areas that meet Summary File 4 population thresholds, therefore there may be less than 10 places listed

Oak Ridge (cdp) Orange	38.21
West and East Lealman (cdp) Pinellas	29.86

Educational Attainment: Four-Year College Graduates

Total Populations 25 Years and Over Who are Four-Year College Graduates
Top 10 Places Sorted by Number

Place (place type) County	Number
Jacksonville (city) Duval	98,991
Tampa (city) Hillsborough	50,471
Miami (city) Miami-Dade	41,004
St. Petersburg (city) Pinellas	39,987
Tallahassee (city) Leon	35,901
Orlando (city) Orange	35,396
Fort Lauderdale (city) Broward	31,059
Pembroke Pines (city) Broward	26,847
Coral Springs (city) Broward	24,489
Boca Raton (city) Palm Beach	24,362

Total Populations 25 Years and Over Who are Four-Year College Graduates
Top 10 Places Sorted by Percent

Place (place type) County	Percent
Pinecrest (village) Miami-Dade	61.56
Coral Gables (city) Miami-Dade	58.28
Weston (city) Broward	50.87
Wekiwa Springs (cdp) Seminole	49.62
Doctor Phillips (cdp) Orange	49.54
Westchase (cdp) Hillsborough	49.04
Doral (cdp) Miami-Dade	47.61
Hunters Creek (cdp) Orange	44.99
Tallahassee (city) Leon	44.96
Boca Raton (city) Palm Beach	44.18

Asians 25 Years and Over Who are Four-Year College Graduates
Top 10 Places Sorted by Number

Place (place type) County	Number
Jacksonville (city) Duval	4,517
Gainesville (city) Alachua	1,874
Pembroke Pines (city) Broward	1,762
Tampa (city) Hillsborough	1,756
Tallahassee (city) Leon	1,540
Orlando (city) Orange	1,465
St. Petersburg (city) Pinellas	1,069
Coral Springs (city) Broward	1,026
Kendall (cdp) Miami-Dade	856
Miami (city) Miami-Dade	721

Asians 25 Years and Over Who are Four-Year College Graduates
Top 10 Places Sorted by Percent

Place (place type) County	Percent
Gainesville (city) Alachua	80.43
University (cdp) Hillsborough	75.64
Tallahassee (city) Leon	66.93
Temple Terrace (city) Hillsborough	65.28
Weston (city) Broward	61.48
Glenvar Heights (cdp) Miami-Dade	61.32
Country Club (cdp) Miami-Dade	60.78
Fountainbleau (cdp) Miami-Dade	59.71
Coral Gables (city) Miami-Dade	59.63
Palm Harbor (cdp) Pinellas	59.57

Native Hawaiian and Other Pacific Islanders 25 Years and Over Who are Four-Year College Graduates
Top 10 Places Sorted by Number

Place (place type) County	Number
Jacksonville (city) Duval	42

Native Hawaiian and Other Pacific Islanders 25 Years and Over Who are Four-Year College Graduates
Top 10 Places Sorted by Percent

Place (place type) County	Percent
Jacksonville (city) Duval	15.22

Asian Indians 25 Years and Over Who are Four-Year College Graduates
Top 10 Places Sorted by Number

Place (place type) County	Number
Jacksonville (city) Duval	1,245
Pembroke Pines (city) Broward	653
Tallahassee (city) Leon	552
Orlando (city) Orange	543
Tampa (city) Hillsborough	491
Coral Springs (city) Broward	471
Gainesville (city) Alachua	361
St. Petersburg (city) Pinellas	341
Plantation (city) Broward	331
Miami (city) Miami-Dade	305

Asian Indians 25 Years and Over Who are Four-Year College Graduates
Top 10 Places Sorted by Percent

Place (place type) County	Percent
Gainesville (city) Alachua	85.95
Tallahassee (city) Leon	79.54
Lakeland (city) Polk	69.16
Jacksonville (city) Duval	68.94
Town 'n' Country (cdp) Hillsborough	67.35
Altamonte Springs (city) Seminole	64.96
Kendall (cdp) Miami-Dade	64.30
Davie (town) Broward	60.84
Cooper City (city) Broward	58.17
Melbourne (city) Brevard	56.75

Bangladeshis 25 Years and Over Who are Four-Year College Graduates
Top 10 Places Sorted by Number

Place (place type) County	Number

No places met population threshold.

Bangladeshis 25 Years and Over Who are Four-Year College Graduates
Top 10 Places Sorted by Percent

Place (place type) County	Percent

No places met population threshold.

Cambodians 25 Years and Over Who are Four-Year College Graduates
Top 10 Places Sorted by Number

Place (place type) County	Number
Jacksonville (city) Duval	32
St. Petersburg (city) Pinellas	6

Cambodians 25 Years and Over Who are Four-Year College Graduates
Top 10 Places Sorted by Percent

Place (place type) County	Percent
Jacksonville (city) Duval	6.03
St. Petersburg (city) Pinellas	2.47

Chinese (except Taiwanese)s 25 Years and Over Who are Four-Year College Graduates
Top 10 Places Sorted by Number

Place (place type) County	Number
Gainesville (city) Alachua	825
Jacksonville (city) Duval	458
Tallahassee (city) Leon	448
Pembroke Pines (city) Broward	262
Coral Springs (city) Broward	253
Tampa (city) Hillsborough	248
Kendall (cdp) Miami-Dade	242
Orlando (city) Orange	218
St. Petersburg (city) Pinellas	173
Davie (town) Broward	165

Chinese (except Taiwanese)s 25 Years and Over Who are Four-Year College Graduates
Top 10 Places Sorted by Percent

Place (place type) County	Percent
Gainesville (city) Alachua	92.59
Tallahassee (city) Leon	79.15
The Hammocks (cdp) Miami-Dade	54.76
Orlando (city) Orange	52.40
Kendall (cdp) Miami-Dade	49.69
Tampa (city) Hillsborough	49.40
Jacksonville (city) Duval	43.91
Davie (town) Broward	42.86
Coral Springs (city) Broward	37.76
Pembroke Pines (city) Broward	33.98

Fijians 25 Years and Over Who are Four-Year College Graduates
Top 10 Places Sorted by Number

Place (place type) County	Number

No places met population threshold.

Fijians 25 Years and Over Who are Four-Year College Graduates
Top 10 Places Sorted by Percent

Place (place type) County	Percent

No places met population threshold.

Filipinos 25 Years and Over Who are Four-Year College Graduates
Top 10 Places Sorted by Number

Place (place type) County	Number
Jacksonville (city) Duval	2,111
Pembroke Pines (city) Broward	411
Tampa (city) Hillsborough	305
St. Petersburg (city) Pinellas	263
Cape Coral (city) Lee	229
Orlando (city) Orange	202
Lakeside (cdp) Clay	152
Miramar (city) Broward	141
Yeehaw Junction (cdp) Osceola	128
Clearwater (city) Pinellas	127

Filipinos 25 Years and Over Who are Four-Year College Graduates
Top 10 Places Sorted by Percent

Place (place type) County	Percent
Yeehaw Junction (cdp) Osceola	61.84
Pembroke Pines (city) Broward	58.71
Tampa (city) Hillsborough	46.85
Cape Coral (city) Lee	45.98
Miramar (city) Broward	45.93
Clearwater (city) Pinellas	42.05
Orlando (city) Orange	41.56
St. Petersburg (city) Pinellas	40.78
Lakeside (cdp) Clay	33.33
Jacksonville (city) Duval	32.23

Guamanian or Chamorros 25 Years and Over Who are Four-Year College Graduates
Top 10 Places Sorted by Number

Place (place type) County	Number

No places met population threshold.

Guamanian or Chamorros 25 Years and Over Who are Four-Year College Graduates
Top 10 Places Sorted by Percent

Place (place type) County	Percent

No places met population threshold.

Notes: Please refer to the User's Guide for an explanation of data; tables include places with populations > 9,999 and reflect only those areas that meet Summary File 4 population thresholds, therefore there may be less than 10 places listed

Hawaiian, Natives 25 Years and Over Who are Four-Year College Graduates
Top 10 Places Sorted by Number

Place (place type) County	Number
No places met population threshold.	

Hawaiian, Natives 25 Years and Over Who are Four-Year College Graduates
Top 10 Places Sorted by Percent

Place (place type) County	Percent
No places met population threshold.	

Hmongs 25 Years and Over Who are Four-Year College Graduates
Top 10 Places Sorted by Number

Place (place type) County	Number
No places met population threshold.	

Hmongs 25 Years and Over Who are Four-Year College Graduates
Top 10 Places Sorted by Percent

Place (place type) County	Percent
No places met population threshold.	

Indonesians 25 Years and Over Who are Four-Year College Graduates
Top 10 Places Sorted by Number

Place (place type) County	Number
No places met population threshold.	

Indonesians 25 Years and Over Who are Four-Year College Graduates
Top 10 Places Sorted by Percent

Place (place type) County	Percent
No places met population threshold.	

Japaneses 25 Years and Over Who are Four-Year College Graduates
Top 10 Places Sorted by Number

Place (place type) County	Number
Jacksonville (city) Duval	47

Japaneses 25 Years and Over Who are Four-Year College Graduates
Top 10 Places Sorted by Percent

Place (place type) County	Percent
Jacksonville (city) Duval	10.68

Koreans 25 Years and Over Who are Four-Year College Graduates
Top 10 Places Sorted by Number

Place (place type) County	Number
Tampa (city) Hillsborough	319
Gainesville (city) Alachua	215
Orlando (city) Orange	133
Jacksonville (city) Duval	107

Koreans 25 Years and Over Who are Four-Year College Graduates
Top 10 Places Sorted by Percent

Place (place type) County	Percent
Gainesville (city) Alachua	76.79
Tampa (city) Hillsborough	48.93
Orlando (city) Orange	33.67
Jacksonville (city) Duval	16.31

Laotians 25 Years and Over Who are Four-Year College Graduates
Top 10 Places Sorted by Number

Place (place type) County	Number
St. Petersburg (city) Pinellas	26

Laotians 25 Years and Over Who are Four-Year College Graduates
Top 10 Places Sorted by Percent

Place (place type) County	Percent
St. Petersburg (city) Pinellas	3.93

Malaysians 25 Years and Over Who are Four-Year College Graduates
Top 10 Places Sorted by Number

Place (place type) County	Number
No places met population threshold.	

Malaysians 25 Years and Over Who are Four-Year College Graduates
Top 10 Places Sorted by Percent

Place (place type) County	Percent
No places met population threshold.	

Pakistanis 25 Years and Over Who are Four-Year College Graduates
Top 10 Places Sorted by Number

Place (place type) County	Number
No places met population threshold.	

Pakistanis 25 Years and Over Who are Four-Year College Graduates
Top 10 Places Sorted by Percent

Place (place type) County	Percent
No places met population threshold.	

Samoans 25 Years and Over Who are Four-Year College Graduates
Top 10 Places Sorted by Number

Place (place type) County	Number
No places met population threshold.	

Samoans 25 Years and Over Who are Four-Year College Graduates
Top 10 Places Sorted by Percent

Place (place type) County	Percent
No places met population threshold.	

Sri Lankans 25 Years and Over Who are Four-Year College Graduates
Top 10 Places Sorted by Number

Place (place type) County	Number
No places met population threshold.	

Sri Lankans 25 Years and Over Who are Four-Year College Graduates
Top 10 Places Sorted by Percent

Place (place type) County	Percent
No places met population threshold.	

Taiwaneses 25 Years and Over Who are Four-Year College Graduates
Top 10 Places Sorted by Number

Place (place type) County	Number
No places met population threshold.	

Taiwaneses 25 Years and Over Who are Four-Year College Graduates
Top 10 Places Sorted by Percent

Place (place type) County	Percent
No places met population threshold.	

Thais 25 Years and Over Who are Four-Year College Graduates
Top 10 Places Sorted by Number

Place (place type) County	Number
No places met population threshold.	

Thais 25 Years and Over Who are Four-Year College Graduates
Top 10 Places Sorted by Percent

Place (place type) County	Percent
No places met population threshold.	

Tongans 25 Years and Over Who are Four-Year College Graduates
Top 10 Places Sorted by Number

Place (place type) County	Number
No places met population threshold.	

Tongans 25 Years and Over Who are Four-Year College Graduates
Top 10 Places Sorted by Percent

Place (place type) County	Percent
No places met population threshold.	

Vietnamese 25 Years and Over Who are Four-Year College Graduates
Top 10 Places Sorted by Number

Place (place type) County	Number
Jacksonville (city) Duval	215
Tampa (city) Hillsborough	163
Orlando (city) Orange	137
St. Petersburg (city) Pinellas	50
West and East Lealman (cdp) Pinellas	44
Town 'n' Country (cdp) Hillsborough	42
Pine Hills (cdp) Orange	41
Pinellas Park (city) Pinellas	29
Oak Ridge (cdp) Orange	9

Vietnamese 25 Years and Over Who are Four-Year College Graduates
Top 10 Places Sorted by Percent

Place (place type) County	Percent
Orlando (city) Orange	27.85
Jacksonville (city) Duval	17.24
Tampa (city) Hillsborough	16.87
West and East Lealman (cdp) Pinellas	15.28
Pine Hills (cdp) Orange	9.83
Town 'n' Country (cdp) Hillsborough	8.81
Pinellas Park (city) Pinellas	7.90
St. Petersburg (city) Pinellas	5.00
Oak Ridge (cdp) Orange	2.23

Median Household Income

Total Population
Top 10 Places Sorted by Number

Place (place type) County	Dollars
Pinecrest (village) Miami-Dade	107,507
Weston (city) Broward	80,920
Westchase (cdp) Hillsborough	79,561
Cooper City (city) Broward	75,166
Wekiwa Springs (cdp) Seminole	71,839
Doctor Phillips (cdp) Orange	70,754
Wellington (village) Palm Beach	70,271
Hunters Creek (cdp) Orange	67,775
East Lake (cdp) Pinellas	67,546
Coral Gables (city) Miami-Dade	66,839

Asian
Top 10 Places Sorted by Number

Place (place type) County	Dollars
East Lake (cdp) Pinellas	91,877
Hunters Creek (cdp) Orange	83,827
Weston (city) Broward	82,682
Ocoee (city) Orange	80,085
Ormond Beach (city) Volusia	76,832
Wellington (village) Palm Beach	76,445
Wekiwa Springs (cdp) Seminole	75,783
Oviedo (city) Seminole	75,244
Richmond West (cdp) Miami-Dade	75,190

Notes: Please refer to the User's Guide for an explanation of data; tables include places with populations > 9,999 and reflect only those areas that meet Summary File 4 population thresholds, therefore there may be less than 10 places listed

Place (place type) County	Dollars
Citrus Park (cdp) Hillsborough	72,022

Native Hawaiian and Other Pacific Islander
Top 10 Places Sorted by Number

Place (place type) County	Dollars
Jacksonville (city) Duval	38,750

Asian Indian
Top 10 Places Sorted by Number

Place (place type) County	Dollars
East Lake (cdp) Pinellas	100,000
Davie (town) Broward	69,083
Doctor Phillips (cdp) Orange	68,571
Altamonte Springs (city) Seminole	62,143
Weston (city) Broward	61,042
Pembroke Pines (city) Broward	60,294
Sunrise (city) Broward	60,144
Jacksonville (city) Duval	58,835
Lakeland (city) Polk	58,750
The Hammocks (cdp) Miami-Dade	58,214

Bangladeshi
Top 10 Places Sorted by Number

Place (place type) County	Dollars

No places met population threshold.

Cambodian
Top 10 Places Sorted by Number

Place (place type) County	Dollars
Jacksonville (city) Duval	42,292
St. Petersburg (city) Pinellas	34,261

Chinese (except Taiwanese)
Top 10 Places Sorted by Number

Place (place type) County	Dollars
Kendall (cdp) Miami-Dade	53,750
Pembroke Pines (city) Broward	50,469
Jacksonville (city) Duval	49,306
Miramar (city) Broward	46,111
St. Petersburg (city) Pinellas	45,199
Davie (town) Broward	42,045
Coral Springs (city) Broward	40,417
Hollywood (city) Broward	38,125
Sunrise (city) Broward	36,434
Orlando (city) Orange	35,347

Fijian
Top 10 Places Sorted by Number

Place (place type) County	Dollars

No places met population threshold.

Filipino
Top 10 Places Sorted by Number

Place (place type) County	Dollars
Miramar (city) Broward	88,334
Pembroke Pines (city) Broward	68,906
Yeehaw Junction (cdp) Osceola	68,882
Lakeside (cdp) Clay	63,365
Jacksonville (city) Duval	54,035
Bellview (cdp) Escambia	47,083
Orlando (city) Orange	46,607
Cape Coral (city) Lee	45,417
Tampa (city) Hillsborough	40,662
St. Petersburg (city) Pinellas	36,667

Guamanian or Chamorro
Top 10 Places Sorted by Number

Place (place type) County	Dollars

No places met population threshold.

Hawaiian, Native
Top 10 Places Sorted by Number

Place (place type) County	Dollars

No places met population threshold.

Hmong
Top 10 Places Sorted by Number

Place (place type) County	Dollars

No places met population threshold.

Indonesian
Top 10 Places Sorted by Number

Place (place type) County	Dollars

No places met population threshold.

Japanese
Top 10 Places Sorted by Number

Place (place type) County	Dollars
Jacksonville (city) Duval	35,375

Korean
Top 10 Places Sorted by Number

Place (place type) County	Dollars
Jacksonville (city) Duval	39,688
Tampa (city) Hillsborough	31,500
Orlando (city) Orange	20,833
Gainesville (city) Alachua	11,506

Laotian
Top 10 Places Sorted by Number

Place (place type) County	Dollars
St. Petersburg (city) Pinellas	48,092

Malaysian
Top 10 Places Sorted by Number

Place (place type) County	Dollars

No places met population threshold.

Pakistani
Top 10 Places Sorted by Number

Place (place type) County	Dollars

No places met population threshold.

Samoan
Top 10 Places Sorted by Number

Place (place type) County	Dollars

No places met population threshold.

Sri Lankan
Top 10 Places Sorted by Number

Place (place type) County	Dollars

No places met population threshold.

Taiwanese
Top 10 Places Sorted by Number

Place (place type) County	Dollars

No places met population threshold.

Thai
Top 10 Places Sorted by Number

Place (place type) County	Dollars

No places met population threshold.

Tongan
Top 10 Places Sorted by Number

Place (place type) County	Dollars

No places met population threshold.

Vietnamese
Top 10 Places Sorted by Number

Place (place type) County	Dollars
Town 'n' Country (cdp) Hillsborough	56,250
St. Petersburg (city) Pinellas	41,154
Orlando (city) Orange	40,278
Oak Ridge (cdp) Orange	39,293
West and East Lealman (cdp) Pinellas	38,281
Pinellas Park (city) Pinellas	34,196
Jacksonville (city) Duval	31,842
Pine Hills (cdp) Orange	26,853
Tampa (city) Hillsborough	25,789

Per Capita Income

Total Population
Top 10 Places Sorted by Number

Place (place type) County	Dollars
Pinecrest (village) Miami-Dade	51,181
Coral Gables (city) Miami-Dade	46,163
Boca Raton (city) Palm Beach	45,628
Palm Beach Gardens (city) Palm Beach	42,975
Westchase (cdp) Hillsborough	37,630
East Lake (cdp) Pinellas	36,206
Wekiwa Springs (cdp) Seminole	36,196
Weston (city) Broward	35,490
Jupiter (town) Palm Beach	35,088
Doctor Phillips (cdp) Orange	31,197

Asian
Top 10 Places Sorted by Number

Place (place type) County	Dollars
Pinecrest (village) Miami-Dade	58,647
Ormond Beach (city) Volusia	46,372
Wellington (village) Palm Beach	37,821
Wekiwa Springs (cdp) Seminole	36,200
East Lake (cdp) Pinellas	34,938
Greater Carrollwood (cdp) Hillsborough	34,513
Palm Beach Gardens (city) Palm Beach	34,389
Palm Harbor (cdp) Pinellas	30,541
Jupiter (town) Palm Beach	29,586
Coral Gables (city) Miami-Dade	29,400

Native Hawaiian and Other Pacific Islander
Top 10 Places Sorted by Number

Place (place type) County	Dollars
Jacksonville (city) Duval	14,953

Asian Indian
Top 10 Places Sorted by Number

Place (place type) County	Dollars
Doctor Phillips (cdp) Orange	39,901
East Lake (cdp) Pinellas	35,452
Tallahassee (city) Leon	31,654
Town 'n' Country (cdp) Hillsborough	30,345
Jacksonville (city) Duval	29,608
Kendall (cdp) Miami-Dade	27,955
St. Petersburg (city) Pinellas	27,702
Tampa (city) Hillsborough	26,153
Davie (town) Broward	25,698
West Palm Beach (city) Palm Beach	23,139

Bangladeshi
Top 10 Places Sorted by Number

Place (place type) County	Dollars

No places met population threshold.

Cambodian
Top 10 Places Sorted by Number

Place (place type) County	Dollars
Jacksonville (city) Duval	11,706
St. Petersburg (city) Pinellas	9,283

Notes: Please refer to the User's Guide for an explanation of data; tables include places with populations > 9,999 and reflect only those areas that meet Summary File 4 population thresholds, therefore there may be less than 10 places listed

Chinese (except Taiwanese)
Top 10 Places Sorted by Number

Place (place type) County	Dollars
Hollywood (city) Broward	39,812
Coral Springs (city) Broward	29,188
Orlando (city) Orange	27,271
Kendall (cdp) Miami-Dade	26,510
Tampa (city) Hillsborough	23,278
Jacksonville (city) Duval	22,836
St. Petersburg (city) Pinellas	22,766
The Hammocks (cdp) Miami-Dade	21,633
Davie (town) Broward	20,205
Tallahassee (city) Leon	19,956

Fijian
Top 10 Places Sorted by Number

Place (place type) County	Dollars

No places met population threshold.

Filipino
Top 10 Places Sorted by Number

Place (place type) County	Dollars
Pembroke Pines (city) Broward	25,764
St. Petersburg (city) Pinellas	24,537
Miramar (city) Broward	22,974
Yeehaw Junction (cdp) Osceola	21,033
Jacksonville (city) Duval	19,773
Tampa (city) Hillsborough	18,175
Orlando (city) Orange	18,137
Lakeside (cdp) Clay	17,771
Clearwater (city) Pinellas	16,165
Bellview (cdp) Escambia	15,612

Guamanian or Chamorro
Top 10 Places Sorted by Number

Place (place type) County	Dollars

No places met population threshold.

Hawaiian, Native
Top 10 Places Sorted by Number

Place (place type) County	Dollars

No places met population threshold.

Hmong
Top 10 Places Sorted by Number

Place (place type) County	Dollars

No places met population threshold.

Indonesian
Top 10 Places Sorted by Number

Place (place type) County	Dollars

No places met population threshold.

Japanese
Top 10 Places Sorted by Number

Place (place type) County	Dollars
Jacksonville (city) Duval	14,228

Korean
Top 10 Places Sorted by Number

Place (place type) County	Dollars
Tampa (city) Hillsborough	15,615
Jacksonville (city) Duval	15,344
Orlando (city) Orange	13,416
Gainesville (city) Alachua	7,384

Laotian
Top 10 Places Sorted by Number

Place (place type) County	Dollars
St. Petersburg (city) Pinellas	12,356

Malaysian
Top 10 Places Sorted by Number

Place (place type) County	Dollars

No places met population threshold.

Pakistani
Top 10 Places Sorted by Number

Place (place type) County	Dollars

No places met population threshold.

Samoan
Top 10 Places Sorted by Number

Place (place type) County	Dollars

No places met population threshold.

Sri Lankan
Top 10 Places Sorted by Number

Place (place type) County	Dollars

No places met population threshold.

Taiwanese
Top 10 Places Sorted by Number

Place (place type) County	Dollars

No places met population threshold.

Thai
Top 10 Places Sorted by Number

Place (place type) County	Dollars

No places met population threshold.

Tongan
Top 10 Places Sorted by Number

Place (place type) County	Dollars

No places met population threshold.

Vietnamese
Top 10 Places Sorted by Number

Place (place type) County	Dollars
Orlando (city) Orange	20,441
Pinellas Park (city) Pinellas	15,915
Jacksonville (city) Duval	13,762
St. Petersburg (city) Pinellas	13,092
Town 'n' Country (cdp) Hillsborough	12,451
Tampa (city) Hillsborough	12,346
Oak Ridge (cdp) Orange	11,864
West and East Lealman (cdp) Pinellas	10,405
Pine Hills (cdp) Orange	9,166

Poverty Status

Total Populations with Income Below Poverty Level
Top 10 Places Sorted by Number

Place (place type) County	Number
Miami (city) Miami-Dade	100,405
Jacksonville (city) Duval	87,691
Tampa (city) Hillsborough	53,425
Hialeah (city) Miami-Dade	41,537
Tallahassee (city) Leon	33,978
St. Petersburg (city) Pinellas	32,127
Orlando (city) Orange	29,029
Fort Lauderdale (city) Broward	26,158
Gainesville (city) Alachua	22,559
Miami Beach (city) Miami-Dade	19,003

Total Populations with Income Below Poverty Level
Top 10 Places Sorted by Percent

Place (place type) County	Percent
University (cdp) Hillsborough	31.34
Miami (city) Miami-Dade	28.45
Gainesville (city) Alachua	26.69
West Pensacola (cdp) Escambia	25.33
Tallahassee (city) Leon	24.70
North Miami (city) Miami-Dade	23.92
Daytona Beach (city) Volusia	23.61
Miami Beach (city) Miami-Dade	21.84
Fort Myers (city) Lee	21.77
Springfield (city) Bay	21.49

Asians with Income Below Poverty Level
Top 10 Places Sorted by Number

Place (place type) County	Number
Jacksonville (city) Duval	1,585
Gainesville (city) Alachua	1,476
Tampa (city) Hillsborough	1,145
Tallahassee (city) Leon	629
Orlando (city) Orange	582
North Miami Beach (city) Miami-Dade	537
Miami (city) Miami-Dade	525
Coral Springs (city) Broward	512
St. Petersburg (city) Pinellas	500
Hollywood (city) Broward	356

Asians with Income Below Poverty Level
Top 10 Places Sorted by Percent

Place (place type) County	Percent
Ocala (city) Marion	37.93
Gainesville (city) Alachua	37.84
South Miami Heights (cdp) Miami-Dade	34.62
University (cdp) Hillsborough	32.59
North Miami Beach (city) Miami-Dade	31.95
Daytona Beach (city) Volusia	28.77
Oakland Park (city) Broward	28.10
Miami Beach (city) Miami-Dade	26.58
Ensley (cdp) Escambia	24.69
Miami (city) Miami-Dade	24.43

Native Hawaiian and Other Pacific Islanders with Income Below Poverty Level
Top 10 Places Sorted by Number

Place (place type) County	Number
Jacksonville (city) Duval	47

Native Hawaiian and Other Pacific Islanders with Income Below Poverty Level
Top 10 Places Sorted by Percent

Place (place type) County	Percent
Jacksonville (city) Duval	9.98

Asian Indians with Income Below Poverty Level
Top 10 Places Sorted by Number

Place (place type) County	Number
Gainesville (city) Alachua	362
Jacksonville (city) Duval	220
Miami (city) Miami-Dade	209
North Miami Beach (city) Miami-Dade	175
Tampa (city) Hillsborough	169
Coral Springs (city) Broward	162
Hollywood (city) Broward	156
East Lake (cdp) Pinellas	153
Fort Lauderdale (city) Broward	143
Plantation (city) Broward	131

Asian Indians with Income Below Poverty Level
Top 10 Places Sorted by Percent

Place (place type) County	Percent
North Miami Beach (city) Miami-Dade	44.19
Gainesville (city) Alachua	41.51
East Lake (cdp) Pinellas	32.55
Fort Lauderdale (city) Broward	26.78
Miami (city) Miami-Dade	24.33
Boca Raton (city) Palm Beach	23.18
West Palm Beach (city) Palm Beach	16.56
Kendall (cdp) Miami-Dade	15.87
Miramar (city) Broward	15.45
Melbourne (city) Brevard	13.55

Notes: Please refer to the User's Guide for an explanation of data; tables include places with populations > 9,999 and reflect only those areas that meet Summary File 4 population thresholds, therefore there may be less than 10 places listed

Bangladeshis with Income Below Poverty Level
Top 10 Places Sorted by Number

Place (place type) County	Number

No places met population threshold.

Bangladeshis with Income Below Poverty Level
Top 10 Places Sorted by Percent

Place (place type) County	Percent

No places met population threshold.

Cambodians with Income Below Poverty Level
Top 10 Places Sorted by Number

Place (place type) County	Number
St. Petersburg (city) Pinellas	81
Jacksonville (city) Duval	69

Cambodians with Income Below Poverty Level
Top 10 Places Sorted by Percent

Place (place type) County	Percent
St. Petersburg (city) Pinellas	16.53
Jacksonville (city) Duval	6.93

Chinese (except Taiwanese)s with Income Below Poverty Level
Top 10 Places Sorted by Number

Place (place type) County	Number
Gainesville (city) Alachua	462
Sunrise (city) Broward	205
Jacksonville (city) Duval	191
Coral Springs (city) Broward	188
North Miami Beach (city) Miami-Dade	160
Miami (city) Miami-Dade	157
Pembroke Pines (city) Broward	132
Hollywood (city) Broward	130
Tampa (city) Hillsborough	123
The Hammocks (cdp) Miami-Dade	86

Chinese (except Taiwanese)s with Income Below Poverty Level
Top 10 Places Sorted by Percent

Place (place type) County	Percent
Gainesville (city) Alachua	34.71
Miami (city) Miami-Dade	31.98
Sunrise (city) Broward	22.70
North Miami Beach (city) Miami-Dade	21.80
Coral Springs (city) Broward	21.05
The Hammocks (cdp) Miami-Dade	20.67
Hollywood (city) Broward	20.03
Tampa (city) Hillsborough	18.30
Margate (city) Broward	15.65
Jacksonville (city) Duval	11.85

Fijians with Income Below Poverty Level
Top 10 Places Sorted by Number

Place (place type) County	Number

No places met population threshold.

Fijians with Income Below Poverty Level
Top 10 Places Sorted by Percent

Place (place type) County	Percent

No places met population threshold.

Filipinos with Income Below Poverty Level
Top 10 Places Sorted by Number

Place (place type) County	Number
Jacksonville (city) Duval	543
Tampa (city) Hillsborough	86
Cape Coral (city) Lee	81
Orlando (city) Orange	78
Pembroke Pines (city) Broward	71
St. Petersburg (city) Pinellas	71
Clearwater (city) Pinellas	38
Bellview (cdp) Escambia	24
Yeehaw Junction (cdp) Osceola	7
Myrtle Grove (cdp) Escambia	6

Filipinos with Income Below Poverty Level
Top 10 Places Sorted by Percent

Place (place type) County	Percent
Cape Coral (city) Lee	11.86
Orlando (city) Orange	11.13
Tampa (city) Hillsborough	9.18
Clearwater (city) Pinellas	8.43
St. Petersburg (city) Pinellas	8.16
Pembroke Pines (city) Broward	7.66
Bellview (cdp) Escambia	5.83
Jacksonville (city) Duval	5.65
Yeehaw Junction (cdp) Osceola	2.05
Myrtle Grove (cdp) Escambia	1.38

Guamanian or Chamorros with Income Below Poverty Level
Top 10 Places Sorted by Number

Place (place type) County	Number

No places met population threshold.

Guamanian or Chamorros with Income Below Poverty Level
Top 10 Places Sorted by Percent

Place (place type) County	Percent

No places met population threshold.

Hawaiian, Natives with Income Below Poverty Level
Top 10 Places Sorted by Number

Place (place type) County	Number

No places met population threshold.

Hawaiian, Natives with Income Below Poverty Level
Top 10 Places Sorted by Percent

Place (place type) County	Percent

No places met population threshold.

Hmongs with Income Below Poverty Level
Top 10 Places Sorted by Number

Place (place type) County	Number

No places met population threshold.

Hmongs with Income Below Poverty Level
Top 10 Places Sorted by Percent

Place (place type) County	Percent

No places met population threshold.

Indonesians with Income Below Poverty Level
Top 10 Places Sorted by Number

Place (place type) County	Number

No places met population threshold.

Indonesians with Income Below Poverty Level
Top 10 Places Sorted by Percent

Place (place type) County	Percent

No places met population threshold.

Japaneses with Income Below Poverty Level
Top 10 Places Sorted by Number

Place (place type) County	Number
Jacksonville (city) Duval	72

Japaneses with Income Below Poverty Level
Top 10 Places Sorted by Percent

Place (place type) County	Percent
Jacksonville (city) Duval	13.85

Koreans with Income Below Poverty Level
Top 10 Places Sorted by Number

Place (place type) County	Number
Tampa (city) Hillsborough	291
Gainesville (city) Alachua	243
Orlando (city) Orange	107
Jacksonville (city) Duval	102

Koreans with Income Below Poverty Level
Top 10 Places Sorted by Percent

Place (place type) County	Percent
Gainesville (city) Alachua	51.59
Tampa (city) Hillsborough	30.22
Orlando (city) Orange	19.45
Jacksonville (city) Duval	11.22

Laotians with Income Below Poverty Level
Top 10 Places Sorted by Number

Place (place type) County	Number
St. Petersburg (city) Pinellas	49

Laotians with Income Below Poverty Level
Top 10 Places Sorted by Percent

Place (place type) County	Percent
St. Petersburg (city) Pinellas	4.32

Malaysians with Income Below Poverty Level
Top 10 Places Sorted by Number

Place (place type) County	Number

No places met population threshold.

Malaysians with Income Below Poverty Level
Top 10 Places Sorted by Percent

Place (place type) County	Percent

No places met population threshold.

Pakistanis with Income Below Poverty Level
Top 10 Places Sorted by Number

Place (place type) County	Number

No places met population threshold.

Pakistanis with Income Below Poverty Level
Top 10 Places Sorted by Percent

Place (place type) County	Percent

No places met population threshold.

Samoans with Income Below Poverty Level
Top 10 Places Sorted by Number

Place (place type) County	Number

No places met population threshold.

Samoans with Income Below Poverty Level
Top 10 Places Sorted by Percent

Place (place type) County	Percent

No places met population threshold.

Sri Lankans with Income Below Poverty Level
Top 10 Places Sorted by Number

Place (place type) County	Number

No places met population threshold.

Sri Lankans with Income Below Poverty Level
Top 10 Places Sorted by Percent

Place (place type) County	Percent

No places met population threshold.

Taiwaneses with Income Below Poverty Level
Top 10 Places Sorted by Number

Place (place type) County	Number

No places met population threshold.

Notes: Please refer to the User's Guide for an explanation of data; tables include places with populations > 9,999 and reflect only those areas that meet Summary File 4 population thresholds, therefore there may be less than 10 places listed

Taiwaneses with Income Below Poverty Level
Top 10 Places Sorted by Percent

Place (place type) County	Percent

No places met population threshold.

Thais with Income Below Poverty Level
Top 10 Places Sorted by Number

Place (place type) County	Number

No places met population threshold.

Thais with Income Below Poverty Level
Top 10 Places Sorted by Percent

Place (place type) County	Percent

No places met population threshold.

Tongans with Income Below Poverty Level
Top 10 Places Sorted by Number

Place (place type) County	Number

No places met population threshold.

Tongans with Income Below Poverty Level
Top 10 Places Sorted by Percent

Place (place type) County	Percent

No places met population threshold.

Vietnamese with Income Below Poverty Level
Top 10 Places Sorted by Number

Place (place type) County	Number
Jacksonville (city) Duval	347
Tampa (city) Hillsborough	322
St. Petersburg (city) Pinellas	110
Pinellas Park (city) Pinellas	84
West and East Lealman (cdp) Pinellas	70
Pine Hills (cdp) Orange	65
Orlando (city) Orange	59
Oak Ridge (cdp) Orange	41
Town 'n' Country (cdp) Hillsborough	14

Vietnamese with Income Below Poverty Level
Top 10 Places Sorted by Percent

Place (place type) County	Percent
Tampa (city) Hillsborough	23.35
Jacksonville (city) Duval	17.10
Pinellas Park (city) Pinellas	15.97
West and East Lealman (cdp) Pinellas	15.35
Pine Hills (cdp) Orange	10.14
Orlando (city) Orange	8.50
Oak Ridge (cdp) Orange	7.78
St. Petersburg (city) Pinellas	6.90
Town 'n' Country (cdp) Hillsborough	2.04

Homeownership

Total Populations Who Own Their Own Homes
Top 10 Places Sorted by Number

Place (place type) County	Number
Jacksonville (city) Duval	179,782
St. Petersburg (city) Pinellas	69,697
Tampa (city) Hillsborough	68,753
Miami (city) Miami-Dade	46,847
Pembroke Pines (city) Broward	41,636
Fort Lauderdale (city) Broward	37,927
Hollywood (city) Broward	37,102
Hialeah (city) Miami-Dade	35,963
Orlando (city) Orange	33,052
Cape Coral (city) Lee	32,663

Total Populations Who Own Their Own Homes
Top 10 Places Sorted by Percent

Place (place type) County	Percent
Richmond West (cdp) Miami-Dade	93.84
Cooper City (city) Broward	92.24
Royal Palm Beach (village) Palm Beach	88.31
Westchase (cdp) Hillsborough	88.29
Deltona (city) Volusia	87.19
Palm Coast (city) Flagler	86.37
Spring Hill (cdp) Hernando	86.24
Oviedo (city) Seminole	85.75
Ocoee (city) Orange	84.30
East Lake (cdp) Pinellas	83.68

Asians Who Own Their Own Homes
Top 10 Places Sorted by Number

Place (place type) County	Number
Jacksonville (city) Duval	3,753
St. Petersburg (city) Pinellas	1,299
Pembroke Pines (city) Broward	1,099
Tampa (city) Hillsborough	864
Coral Springs (city) Broward	813
Orlando (city) Orange	654
Sunrise (city) Broward	609
Hollywood (city) Broward	568
Kendall (cdp) Miami-Dade	516
Miramar (city) Broward	493

Asians Who Own Their Own Homes
Top 10 Places Sorted by Percent

Place (place type) County	Percent
Ocoee (city) Orange	93.26
Deltona (city) Volusia	93.15
Richmond West (cdp) Miami-Dade	92.27
Royal Palm Beach (village) Palm Beach	89.68
Cooper City (city) Broward	89.32
Westchase (cdp) Hillsborough	87.84
Oviedo (city) Seminole	86.67
Merritt Island (cdp) Brevard	86.16
Miramar (city) Broward	85.00
Palm Coast (city) Flagler	84.11

Native Hawaiian and Other Pacific Islanders Who Own Their Own Homes
Top 10 Places Sorted by Number

Place (place type) County	Number
Jacksonville (city) Duval	63

Native Hawaiian and Other Pacific Islanders Who Own Their Own Homes
Top 10 Places Sorted by Percent

Place (place type) County	Percent
Jacksonville (city) Duval	42.28

Asian Indians Who Own Their Own Homes
Top 10 Places Sorted by Number

Place (place type) County	Number
Coral Springs (city) Broward	400
Jacksonville (city) Duval	397
Pembroke Pines (city) Broward	345
Sunrise (city) Broward	251
Orlando (city) Orange	216
Hollywood (city) Broward	212
Kendall (cdp) Miami-Dade	201
Tallahassee (city) Leon	192
Plantation (city) Broward	179
Miramar (city) Broward	162

Asian Indians Who Own Their Own Homes
Top 10 Places Sorted by Percent

Place (place type) County	Percent
Miramar (city) Broward	86.63
Davie (town) Broward	83.15
Weston (city) Broward	83.15
Cooper City (city) Broward	78.95
Sunrise (city) Broward	78.68
Coral Springs (city) Broward	77.37
Doctor Phillips (cdp) Orange	75.45
Pembroke Pines (city) Broward	65.84
Kendall (cdp) Miami-Dade	63.61
The Hammocks (cdp) Miami-Dade	63.48

Bangladeshis Who Own Their Own Homes
Top 10 Places Sorted by Number

Place (place type) County	Number

No places met population threshold.

Bangladeshis Who Own Their Own Homes
Top 10 Places Sorted by Percent

Place (place type) County	Percent

No places met population threshold.

Cambodians Who Own Their Own Homes
Top 10 Places Sorted by Number

Place (place type) County	Number
Jacksonville (city) Duval	172
St. Petersburg (city) Pinellas	118

Cambodians Who Own Their Own Homes
Top 10 Places Sorted by Percent

Place (place type) County	Percent
St. Petersburg (city) Pinellas	82.52
Jacksonville (city) Duval	74.14

Chinese (except Taiwanese)s Who Own Their Own Homes
Top 10 Places Sorted by Number

Place (place type) County	Number
Jacksonville (city) Duval	307
Pembroke Pines (city) Broward	286
Coral Springs (city) Broward	249
Sunrise (city) Broward	212
Kendall (cdp) Miami-Dade	182
St. Petersburg (city) Pinellas	182
Hollywood (city) Broward	179
North Miami Beach (city) Miami-Dade	175
Margate (city) Broward	151
Tampa (city) Hillsborough	133

Chinese (except Taiwanese)s Who Own Their Own Homes
Top 10 Places Sorted by Percent

Place (place type) County	Percent
Miramar (city) Broward	91.61
Sunrise (city) Broward	89.83
Margate (city) Broward	87.79
Coral Springs (city) Broward	80.32
North Miami Beach (city) Miami-Dade	79.55
Pembroke Pines (city) Broward	78.36
Davie (town) Broward	75.64
Hollywood (city) Broward	73.97
Kendall (cdp) Miami-Dade	67.66
The Hammocks (cdp) Miami-Dade	65.92

Fijians Who Own Their Own Homes
Top 10 Places Sorted by Number

Place (place type) County	Number

No places met population threshold.

Fijians Who Own Their Own Homes
Top 10 Places Sorted by Percent

Place (place type) County	Percent

No places met population threshold.

Filipinos Who Own Their Own Homes
Top 10 Places Sorted by Number

Place (place type) County	Number
Jacksonville (city) Duval	2,124
Pembroke Pines (city) Broward	244
St. Petersburg (city) Pinellas	203
Tampa (city) Hillsborough	128
Cape Coral (city) Lee	108
Myrtle Grove (cdp) Escambia	101

Notes: Please refer to the User's Guide for an explanation of data; tables include places with populations > 9,999 and reflect only those areas that meet Summary File 4 population thresholds, therefore there may be less than 10 places listed

Lakeside (cdp) Clay	95
Miramar (city) Broward	95
Bellview (cdp) Escambia	88
Orlando (city) Orange	80

Filipinos Who Own Their Own Homes
Top 10 Places Sorted by Percent

Place (place type) County	Percent
Miramar (city) Broward	95.00
Pembroke Pines (city) Broward	85.92
Yeehaw Junction (cdp) Osceola	85.11
Jacksonville (city) Duval	77.83
Cape Coral (city) Lee	76.06
Lakeside (cdp) Clay	76.00
Bellview (cdp) Escambia	73.95
St. Petersburg (city) Pinellas	61.89
Myrtle Grove (cdp) Escambia	58.72
Tampa (city) Hillsborough	46.21

Guamanian or Chamorros Who Own Their Own Homes
Top 10 Places Sorted by Number

Place (place type) County	Number

No places met population threshold.

Guamanian or Chamorros Who Own Their Own Homes
Top 10 Places Sorted by Percent

Place (place type) County	Percent

No places met population threshold.

Hawaiian, Natives Who Own Their Own Homes
Top 10 Places Sorted by Number

Place (place type) County	Number

No places met population threshold.

Hawaiian, Natives Who Own Their Own Homes
Top 10 Places Sorted by Percent

Place (place type) County	Percent

No places met population threshold.

Hmongs Who Own Their Own Homes
Top 10 Places Sorted by Number

Place (place type) County	Number

No places met population threshold.

Hmongs Who Own Their Own Homes
Top 10 Places Sorted by Percent

Place (place type) County	Percent

No places met population threshold.

Indonesians Who Own Their Own Homes
Top 10 Places Sorted by Number

Place (place type) County	Number

No places met population threshold.

Indonesians Who Own Their Own Homes
Top 10 Places Sorted by Percent

Place (place type) County	Percent

No places met population threshold.

Japaneses Who Own Their Own Homes
Top 10 Places Sorted by Number

Place (place type) County	Number
Jacksonville (city) Duval	102

Japaneses Who Own Their Own Homes
Top 10 Places Sorted by Percent

Place (place type) County	Percent
Jacksonville (city) Duval	62.20

Koreans Who Own Their Own Homes
Top 10 Places Sorted by Number

Place (place type) County	Number
Jacksonville (city) Duval	144
Tampa (city) Hillsborough	129
Orlando (city) Orange	60
Gainesville (city) Alachua	31

Koreans Who Own Their Own Homes
Top 10 Places Sorted by Percent

Place (place type) County	Percent
Jacksonville (city) Duval	55.17
Tampa (city) Hillsborough	44.95
Orlando (city) Orange	27.27
Gainesville (city) Alachua	14.90

Laotians Who Own Their Own Homes
Top 10 Places Sorted by Number

Place (place type) County	Number
St. Petersburg (city) Pinellas	219

Laotians Who Own Their Own Homes
Top 10 Places Sorted by Percent

Place (place type) County	Percent
St. Petersburg (city) Pinellas	79.64

Malaysians Who Own Their Own Homes
Top 10 Places Sorted by Number

Place (place type) County	Number

No places met population threshold.

Malaysians Who Own Their Own Homes
Top 10 Places Sorted by Percent

Place (place type) County	Percent

No places met population threshold.

Pakistanis Who Own Their Own Homes
Top 10 Places Sorted by Number

Place (place type) County	Number

No places met population threshold.

Pakistanis Who Own Their Own Homes
Top 10 Places Sorted by Percent

Place (place type) County	Percent

No places met population threshold.

Samoans Who Own Their Own Homes
Top 10 Places Sorted by Number

Place (place type) County	Number

No places met population threshold.

Samoans Who Own Their Own Homes
Top 10 Places Sorted by Percent

Place (place type) County	Percent

No places met population threshold.

Sri Lankans Who Own Their Own Homes
Top 10 Places Sorted by Number

Place (place type) County	Number

No places met population threshold.

Sri Lankans Who Own Their Own Homes
Top 10 Places Sorted by Percent

Place (place type) County	Percent

No places met population threshold.

Taiwaneses Who Own Their Own Homes
Top 10 Places Sorted by Number

Place (place type) County	Number

No places met population threshold.

Taiwaneses Who Own Their Own Homes
Top 10 Places Sorted by Percent

Place (place type) County	Percent

No places met population threshold.

Thais Who Own Their Own Homes
Top 10 Places Sorted by Number

Place (place type) County	Number

No places met population threshold.

Thais Who Own Their Own Homes
Top 10 Places Sorted by Percent

Place (place type) County	Percent

No places met population threshold.

Tongans Who Own Their Own Homes
Top 10 Places Sorted by Number

Place (place type) County	Number

No places met population threshold.

Tongans Who Own Their Own Homes
Top 10 Places Sorted by Percent

Place (place type) County	Percent

No places met population threshold.

Vietnamese Who Own Their Own Homes
Top 10 Places Sorted by Number

Place (place type) County	Number
Jacksonville (city) Duval	274
St. Petersburg (city) Pinellas	273
Pinellas Park (city) Pinellas	158
Tampa (city) Hillsborough	143
Town 'n' Country (cdp) Hillsborough	137
Oak Ridge (cdp) Orange	129
Orlando (city) Orange	112
Pine Hills (cdp) Orange	100
West and East Lealman (cdp) Pinellas	82

Vietnamese Who Own Their Own Homes
Top 10 Places Sorted by Percent

Place (place type) County	Percent
Town 'n' Country (cdp) Hillsborough	89.54
Oak Ridge (cdp) Orange	88.97
Pinellas Park (city) Pinellas	80.61
West and East Lealman (cdp) Pinellas	67.77
St. Petersburg (city) Pinellas	63.05
Pine Hills (cdp) Orange	60.61
Jacksonville (city) Duval	48.32
Orlando (city) Orange	41.79
Tampa (city) Hillsborough	38.75

Median Gross Rent

All Specified Renter-Occupied Housing Units
Top 10 Places Sorted by Number

Place (place type) County	Dollars/Month
Doctor Phillips (cdp) Orange	1,150
Richmond West (cdp) Miami-Dade	1,084
Weston (city) Broward	1,084
Wekiwa Springs (cdp) Seminole	1,014
Wellington (village) Palm Beach	989
Cooper City (city) Broward	988
Hunters Creek (cdp) Orange	972
Doral (cdp) Miami-Dade	968
Pembroke Pines (city) Broward	945
Palm Beach Gardens (city) Palm Beach	939

Specified Housing Units Rented by Asians
Top 10 Places Sorted by Number

Place (place type) County	Dollars/Month
Hunters Creek (cdp) Orange	1,139
Kendale Lakes (cdp) Miami-Dade	1,139

Notes: Please refer to the User's Guide for an explanation of data; tables include places with populations > 9,999 and reflect only those areas that meet Summary File 4 population thresholds, therefore there may be less than 10 places listed

Doctor Phillips (cdp) Orange	1,060
Jupiter (town) Palm Beach	1,031
Palm Coast (city) Flagler	1,014
Richmond West (cdp) Miami-Dade	1,014
Wellington (village) Palm Beach	989
Westchase (cdp) Hillsborough	982
Weston (city) Broward	969
Royal Palm Beach (village) Palm Beach	950

Specified Housing Units Rented by Native Hawaiian and Other Pacific Islanders

Top 10 Places Sorted by Number

Place (place type) County	Dollars/Month
Jacksonville (city) Duval	575

Specified Housing Units Rented by Asian Indians

Top 10 Places Sorted by Number

Place (place type) County	Dollars/Month
Doctor Phillips (cdp) Orange	1,125
Pembroke Pines (city) Broward	922
Plantation (city) Broward	921
Coral Springs (city) Broward	919
Weston (city) Broward	841
North Miami Beach (city) Miami-Dade	830
Boca Raton (city) Palm Beach	815
West Palm Beach (city) Palm Beach	793
Orlando (city) Orange	772
Miramar (city) Broward	767

Specified Housing Units Rented by Bangladeshis

Top 10 Places Sorted by Number

Place (place type) County	Dollars/Month

Specified Housing Units Rented by Cambodians

Top 10 Places Sorted by Number

Place (place type) County	Dollars/Month
St. Petersburg (city) Pinellas	467
Jacksonville (city) Duval	384

Specified Housing Units Rented by Chinese (except Taiwanese)s

Top 10 Places Sorted by Number

Place (place type) County	Dollars/Month
Pembroke Pines (city) Broward	945
Coral Springs (city) Broward	910
The Hammocks (cdp) Miami-Dade	873
Miramar (city) Broward	850
Hollywood (city) Broward	819
Davie (town) Broward	808
Orlando (city) Orange	769
Margate (city) Broward	740
Kendall (cdp) Miami-Dade	701
Sunrise (city) Broward	680

Specified Housing Units Rented by Fijians

Top 10 Places Sorted by Number

Place (place type) County	Dollars/Month

Specified Housing Units Rented by Filipinos

Top 10 Places Sorted by Number

Place (place type) County	Dollars/Month
Miramar (city) Broward	1,375
Pembroke Pines (city) Broward	859
Yeehaw Junction (cdp) Osceola	750
Orlando (city) Orange	697
Cape Coral (city) Lee	694
Bellview (cdp) Escambia	665
Jacksonville (city) Duval	642
St. Petersburg (city) Pinellas	586
Tampa (city) Hillsborough	585
Clearwater (city) Pinellas	565

Specified Housing Units Rented by Guamanian or Chamorros

Top 10 Places Sorted by Number

Place (place type) County	Dollars/Month

Specified Housing Units Rented by Hawaiian, Natives

Top 10 Places Sorted by Number

Place (place type) County	Dollars/Month

Specified Housing Units Rented by Hmongs

Top 10 Places Sorted by Number

Place (place type) County	Dollars/Month

Specified Housing Units Rented by Indonesians

Top 10 Places Sorted by Number

Place (place type) County	Dollars/Month

Specified Housing Units Rented by Japaneses

Top 10 Places Sorted by Number

Place (place type) County	Dollars/Month
Jacksonville (city) Duval	464

Specified Housing Units Rented by Koreans

Top 10 Places Sorted by Number

Place (place type) County	Dollars/Month
Orlando (city) Orange	811
Jacksonville (city) Duval	631
Tampa (city) Hillsborough	489
Gainesville (city) Alachua	488

Specified Housing Units Rented by Laotians

Top 10 Places Sorted by Number

Place (place type) County	Dollars/Month
St. Petersburg (city) Pinellas	708

Specified Housing Units Rented by Malaysians

Top 10 Places Sorted by Number

Place (place type) County	Dollars/Month

Specified Housing Units Rented by Pakistanis

Top 10 Places Sorted by Number

Place (place type) County	Dollars/Month

Specified Housing Units Rented by Samoans

Top 10 Places Sorted by Number

Place (place type) County	Dollars/Month

Specified Housing Units Rented by Sri Lankans

Top 10 Places Sorted by Number

Place (place type) County	Dollars/Month

Specified Housing Units Rented by Taiwaneses

Top 10 Places Sorted by Number

Place (place type) County	Dollars/Month

Specified Housing Units Rented by Thais

Top 10 Places Sorted by Number

Place (place type) County	Dollars/Month

Specified Housing Units Rented by Tongans

Top 10 Places Sorted by Number

Place (place type) County	Dollars/Month

Specified Housing Units Rented by Vietnamese

Top 10 Places Sorted by Number

Place (place type) County	Dollars/Month
Orlando (city) Orange	630
Pinellas Park (city) Pinellas	603
Oak Ridge (cdp) Orange	600
Town 'n' Country (cdp) Hillsborough	536
Tampa (city) Hillsborough	517
Jacksonville (city) Duval	495
Pine Hills (cdp) Orange	489
West and East Lealman (cdp) Pinellas	473
St. Petersburg (city) Pinellas	407

Median Home Value

All Specified Owner-Occupied Housing Units

Top 10 Places Sorted by Number

Place (place type) County	Dollars
Pinecrest (village) Miami-Dade	393,900
Coral Gables (city) Miami-Dade	336,800
Miami Beach (city) Miami-Dade	334,400
Boca Raton (city) Palm Beach	230,200
Glenvar Heights (cdp) Miami-Dade	215,000
Weston (city) Broward	202,000
East Lake (cdp) Pinellas	197,700
Doral (cdp) Miami-Dade	178,500
Kendall (cdp) Miami-Dade	175,700
Coral Springs (city) Broward	175,500

Specified Housing Units Owned and Occupied by Asians

Top 10 Places Sorted by Number

Place (place type) County	Dollars
Miami Beach (city) Miami-Dade	440,000
East Lake (cdp) Pinellas	254,800
Westchase (cdp) Hillsborough	223,100
Weston (city) Broward	215,600
Pinecrest (village) Miami-Dade	202,800
Coral Gables (city) Miami-Dade	200,000
Ormond Beach (city) Volusia	200,000
Hunters Creek (cdp) Orange	186,700
Doctor Phillips (cdp) Orange	186,400
Wekiwa Springs (cdp) Seminole	186,100

Specified Housing Units Owned and Occupied by Native Hawaiian and Other Pacific Islanders

Top 10 Places Sorted by Number

Place (place type) County	Dollars
Jacksonville (city) Duval	68,300

Specified Housing Units Owned and Occupied by Asian Indians

Top 10 Places Sorted by Number

Place (place type) County	Dollars
East Lake (cdp) Pinellas	288,600
Davie (town) Broward	229,300
Weston (city) Broward	221,900
Kendall (cdp) Miami-Dade	214,000
Orlando (city) Orange	191,100
Doctor Phillips (cdp) Orange	184,600
Plantation (city) Broward	179,800
Miami (city) Miami-Dade	169,100
Tampa (city) Hillsborough	163,800
Jacksonville (city) Duval	162,000

Specified Housing Units Owned and Occupied by Bangladeshis

Top 10 Places Sorted by Number

Place (place type) County	Dollars

No places met population threshold.

Specified Housing Units Owned and Occupied by Cambodians

Top 10 Places Sorted by Number

Place (place type) County	Dollars
Jacksonville (city) Duval	83,900
St. Petersburg (city) Pinellas	72,700

Notes: Please refer to the User's Guide for an explanation of data; tables include places with populations > 9,999 and reflect only those areas that meet Summary File 4 population thresholds, therefore there may be less than 10 places listed

Specified Housing Units Owned and Occupied by Chinese (except Taiwanese)s

Top 10 Places Sorted by Number

Place (place type) County	Dollars
Miami (city) Miami-Dade	225,000
Pembroke Pines (city) Broward	159,000
Tallahassee (city) Leon	158,300
Davie (town) Broward	157,600
Coral Springs (city) Broward	141,000
Orlando (city) Orange	136,700
Jacksonville (city) Duval	135,900
Gainesville (city) Alachua	134,700
Miramar (city) Broward	130,800
The Hammocks (cdp) Miami-Dade	128,800

Specified Housing Units Owned and Occupied by Fijians

Top 10 Places Sorted by Number

Place (place type) County	Dollars

No places met population threshold.

Specified Housing Units Owned and Occupied by Filipinos

Top 10 Places Sorted by Number

Place (place type) County	Dollars
Pembroke Pines (city) Broward	167,400
Miramar (city) Broward	143,800
Yeehaw Junction (cdp) Osceola	133,200
Clearwater (city) Pinellas	130,000
Orlando (city) Orange	125,000
Cape Coral (city) Lee	113,700
Jacksonville (city) Duval	100,900
Tampa (city) Hillsborough	89,300
Bellview (cdp) Escambia	87,800
Myrtle Grove (cdp) Escambia	80,900

Specified Housing Units Owned and Occupied by Guamanian or Chamorros

Top 10 Places Sorted by Number

Place (place type) County	Dollars

No places met population threshold.

Specified Housing Units Owned and Occupied by Hawaiian, Natives

Top 10 Places Sorted by Number

Place (place type) County	Dollars

No places met population threshold.

Specified Housing Units Owned and Occupied by Hmongs

Top 10 Places Sorted by Number

Place (place type) County	Dollars

No places met population threshold.

Specified Housing Units Owned and Occupied by Indonesians

Top 10 Places Sorted by Number

Place (place type) County	Dollars

No places met population threshold.

Specified Housing Units Owned and Occupied by Japaneses

Top 10 Places Sorted by Number

Place (place type) County	Dollars
Jacksonville (city) Duval	85,000

Specified Housing Units Owned and Occupied by Koreans

Top 10 Places Sorted by Number

Place (place type) County	Dollars
Orlando (city) Orange	173,500
Tampa (city) Hillsborough	154,200
Gainesville (city) Alachua	137,500
Jacksonville (city) Duval	125,300

Specified Housing Units Owned and Occupied by Laotians

Top 10 Places Sorted by Number

Place (place type) County	Dollars
St. Petersburg (city) Pinellas	68,400

Specified Housing Units Owned and Occupied by Malaysians

Top 10 Places Sorted by Number

Place (place type) County	Dollars

No places met population threshold.

Specified Housing Units Owned and Occupied by Pakistanis

Top 10 Places Sorted by Number

Place (place type) County	Dollars

No places met population threshold.

Specified Housing Units Owned and Occupied by Samoans

Top 10 Places Sorted by Number

Place (place type) County	Dollars

No places met population threshold.

Specified Housing Units Owned and Occupied by Sri Lankans

Top 10 Places Sorted by Number

Place (place type) County	Dollars

No places met population threshold.

Specified Housing Units Owned and Occupied by Taiwaneses

Top 10 Places Sorted by Number

Place (place type) County	Dollars

No places met population threshold.

Specified Housing Units Owned and Occupied by Thais

Top 10 Places Sorted by Number

Place (place type) County	Dollars

No places met population threshold.

Specified Housing Units Owned and Occupied by Tongans

Top 10 Places Sorted by Number

Place (place type) County	Dollars

No places met population threshold.

Specified Housing Units Owned and Occupied by Vietnamese

Top 10 Places Sorted by Number

Place (place type) County	Dollars
Orlando (city) Orange	93,300
Oak Ridge (cdp) Orange	85,900
Pine Hills (cdp) Orange	84,100
Town 'n' Country (cdp) Hillsborough	81,600
Pinellas Park (city) Pinellas	80,300
West and East Lealman (cdp) Pinellas	75,000
Jacksonville (city) Duval	72,900
Tampa (city) Hillsborough	68,200
St. Petersburg (city) Pinellas	64,500

Notes: Please refer to the User's Guide for an explanation of data; tables include places with populations > 9,999 and reflect only those areas that meet Summary File 4 population thresholds, therefore there may be less than 10 places listed

PHYSICAL FEATURES. Florida, situated between latitudes 24° 30' and 31° N., and longitudes 80° and 87° 30' W., is largely a lowland peninsula comprising about 54,100 square miles of land area and is surrounded on three sides by the waters of the Atlantic Ocean and the Gulf of Mexico. Countless shallow lakes, which exist particularly on the peninsula and range in size from small cypress ponds to that of Lake Okeechobee, account for approximately 4,400 square miles of additional water area.

No point in the State is more than 70 miles from salt water, and the highest natural land in the Northwest Division is only 345 feet above sea level. Coastal areas are low and flat and are indented by many small bays or inlets. Many small islands dot the shorelines. The elevation of most of the interior ranges from 50 to 100 feet above sea level, though gentle hills in the interior of the peninsula and across the northern and western portions of the State rise above 200 feet.

A large portion of the southern one-third of the peninsula is the swampland known as the Everglades. An ill-defined divide of low, rolling hills, extending north-to-south near the middle of the peninsula and terminating north of Lake Okeechobee, gives rise to most peninsula streams, chains of lakes, and many springs. Stream gradients are slight and often insufficient to handle the runoff following heavy rainfall. Consequently, there are sizable areas of swamp and marshland near these streams.

GENERAL CLIMATE. Climate is probably Florida's greatest natural resource. General climatic conditions range from a zone of transition between temperate and subtropical conditions in the extreme northern interior portion of the State to the tropical conditions found on the Florida Keys. The chief factors of climatic control are: latitude, proximity to the Atlantic Ocean and Gulf of Mexico, and numerous inland lakes.

Summers throughout the State are long, warm, and relatively humid; winters, although punctuated with periodic invasions of cool to occasionally cold air from the north, are mild because of the southern latitude and relatively warm adjacent ocean waters. The Gulf Stream, which flows around the western tip of Cuba, through the Straits of Florida, and northward along the lower east coast, exerts a warming influence to the southern east coast largely because the predominate wind direction is from the east. Coastal weather stations throughout the State average slightly warmer in winter and cooler in summer than do inland weather stations at the same latitude.

Florida enjoys abundant rainfall. Except for the northwestern portion of the State, the average year can be divided into two seasons—the so-called "rainy season" and the long, relatively dry season. On the peninsula, generally more than one-half of the precipitation for an average year can be expected to fall during the four-month period, June through September. In northwest Florida, there is a secondary rainfall maximum in late winter and in early spring.

The summer heat is tempered by sea breezes along the coast and by frequent afternoon or early evening thunderstorms in all areas. During the warm season, sea breezes are felt almost daily within several miles of the coast and occasionally 20 to 30 miles inland. Thundershowers, which on the average occur about one-half of the days in summer, frequently are accompanied by as much as a rapid 10 to 20°F. drop in temperature, resulting in comfortable weather for the remainder of the day. Gentle breezes occur almost daily in all areas and serve to mitigate further the oppressiveness that otherwise would accompany the prevailing summer temperature and humidity conditions. Because most of the large-scale wind patterns affecting Florida have passed over water surfaces, hot drying winds seldom occur.

Most of the summer rainfall is derived from "local" showers or thundershowers. Many weather stations average more than 80 thundershowers per year, and some average more than 100. Showers are often heavy, usually lasting only one or two hours, and generally occur near the hottest part of the day. The more severe thundershowers are occasionally attended by hail or locally strong winds which may inflict serious local damage to crops and property. Day-long summer rains are usually associated with tropical disturbances and are infrequent. Even in the wet season, the rainfall duration is generally less than 10 percent of the time.

DROUGHTS. Florida is not immune from drought, even though annual rainfall amounts are relatively large. Prolonged periods of deficient rainfall are occasionally experienced even during the time of the expected rainy season. Several such dry periods, in the course of one or two years, can lead to significantly lowered water tables and lake levels which, in turn, may cause serious water shortages for those communities that depend upon lakes and shallow wells for their water supply. Statewide droughts during summer are rare, but it is not unusual during a drought in one portion of the State for other portions to receive generous rainfall. In a few instances, individual weather stations have experienced periods of a month or more without rainfall.

SNOW. Snowfall in Florida is unusual, although measurable amounts have fallen in the northern portions at irregular intervals, and a trace of snow has been recorded as far south as Fort Myers.

WIND. Prevailing winds over the southern peninsula are southeast and east. Over the remainder of the State, wind directions are influenced locally by convectional forces inland and by the land-and-sea-breeze-effect near the coast. Consequently, prevailing directions are somewhat erratic, but, in general, follow a pattern from the north in winter and from the south in summer. The windiest months are March and April. High local winds of short duration occur occasionally in connection with thunderstorms in summer and with cold fronts moving across the State in other seasons. Tornadoes, funnel clouds, and waterspouts also occur, averaging 10 to 15 in a year. Tornadoes have occurred in all seasons, but are most frequent in spring; they also occur in connection with tropical storms. Generally, tornado paths in Florida are short. Occasionally, waterspouts come inland, but they usually dissipate soon after reaching land and affect only very small areas.

TROPICAL STORMS. Storms that produce high winds and are often destructive are usually tropical in origin. Florida, jutting out into the ocean between the subtropical Atlantic and the Gulf of Mexico, is the most exposed of all States to these storms. In particular, hurricanes can approach from the Atlantic Ocean to the east, from the Caribbean Sea to the south, and from the Gulf of Mexico to the west.

The vulnerability of the State to tropical storms varies with the progress of the hurricane season. In August and early September, tropical storms normally approach the State from the east or southeast, but as the season progresses into late September and October, the region of maximum hurricane activity (insofar as Florida is concerned) shifts to the western Caribbean. Most of those storms that move into Florida approach the State from the south or southwest, entering the Keys, the Miami area, or along the west coast. Some of the world's heaviest rainfalls have occurred within tropical cyclones. Rainfall over 20 inches in 24 hours is not uncommon. The intensity of the rainfall, however, does not seem to bear any relation to the intensity of the wind circulation.

OTHER CLIMATIC ELEMENTS. The climate of Florida is humid. Inland areas with greater temperature extremes enjoy slightly lower relative humidity, especially during times of hot weather. On the average, variations in relative humidity from one place to another are small; humidities range from about 50 to 65 percent during the afternoon hours to about 85 to 95 percent during the night and early morning hours.

Heavy fogs are usually confined to the night and early morning hours in the late fall, winter, and early spring months. On the average, they occur about 35 to 40 days in a year over the extreme northern portion; about 25 to 30 days in a year over the central portion; and less than 10 days in a year over the extreme southern portion of the State. These fogs usually dissipate or thin soon after sunrise; heavy daytime fog is seldom observed in Florida.

Florida has been nicknamed the Sunshine State. Sunshine measurements made at widely separated stations in the State indicate the sun shines about two-thirds of the possible sunlight hours during the year, ranging from slightly more than 60 percent of possible in December and January to more than 70 percent of possible in April and May. In general, southern Florida enjoys a higher percentage of possible sunshine hours than does northern Florida. The length of day operates to Florida's advantage. In winter, when sunshine is highly valued, the sun can shine longer in Florida than in the more northern latitudes. In summer, the situation reverses itself with longer days returning to the north.

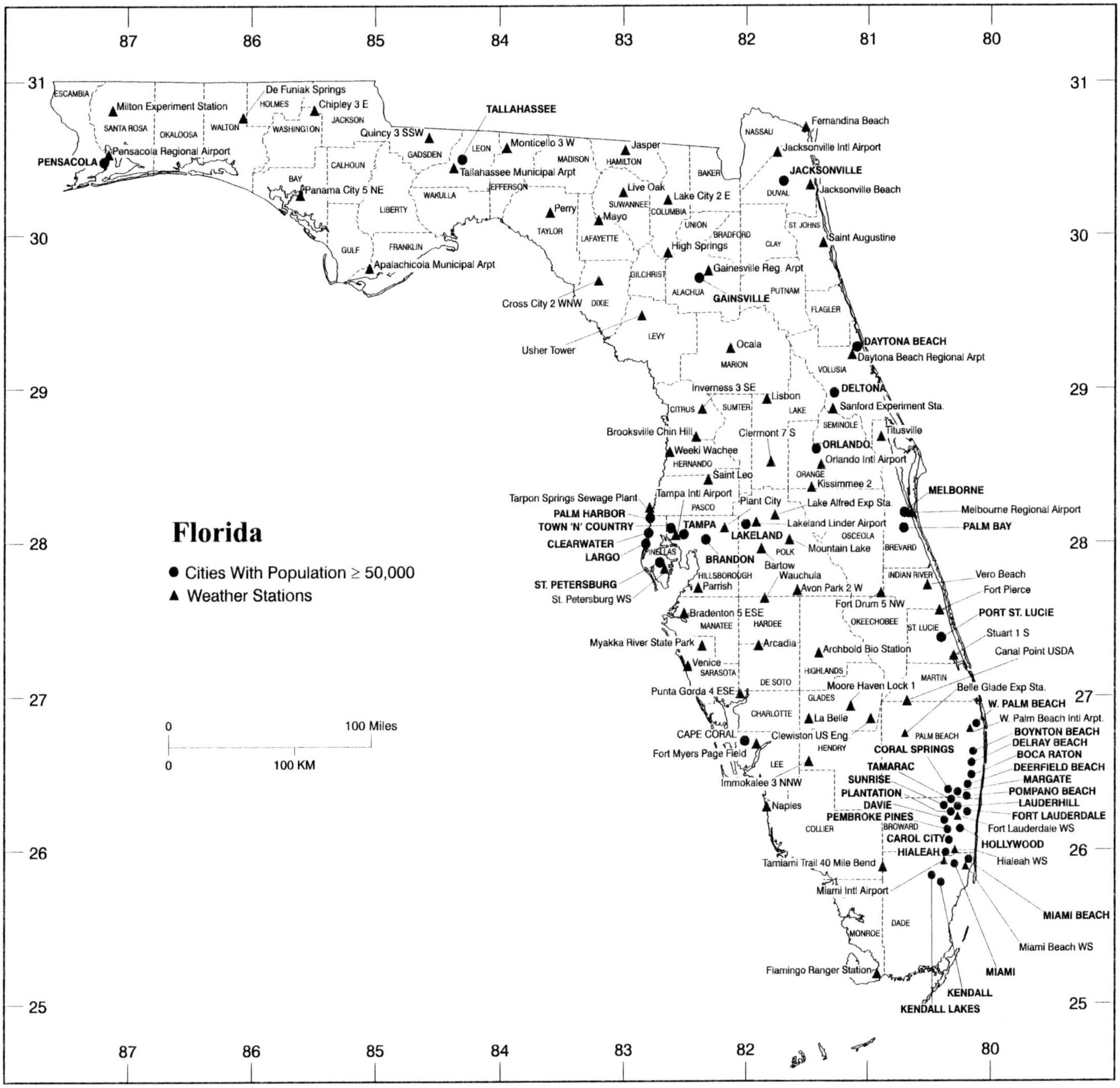
87
86
85
84
83
82
81
80
31
30
29
28
27
26
25
Florida
● Cities With Population ≥ 50,000
▲ Weather Stations
0
100 Miles
0
100 KM
ESCAMBIA
Milton Experiment Station
SANTA ROSA
OKALOOSA
WALTON
De Funiak Springs
HOLMES
Chipley 3 E
JACKSON
WASHINGTON
PENSACOLA
Pensacola Regional Airport
BAY
Panama City 5 NE
CALHOUN
LIBERTY
GULF
FRANKLIN
Apalachicola Municipal Arpt
Quincy 3 SSW
GADSDEN
TALLAHASSEE
LEON
Tallahassee Municipal Arpt
WAKULLA
Monticello 3 W
JEFFERSON
MADISON
Jasper
HAMILTON
Live Oak
SUWANNEE
Perry
TAYLOR
Mayo
LAFAYETTE
Cross City 2 WNW
DIXIE
Usher Tower
LEVY
GILCHRIST
High Springs
Lake City 2 E
COLUMBIA
UNION
BRADFORD
BAKER
NASSAU
Fernandina Beach
Jacksonville Intl Airport
JACKSONVILLE
DUVAL
Jacksonville Beach
ST. JOHNS
Saint Augustine
CLAY
Gainesville Reg. Arpt
ALACHUA
GAINSVILLE
PUTNAM
FLAGLER
DAYTONA BEACH
Daytona Beach Regional Arpt
VOLUSIA
Ocala
MARION
Inverness 3 SE
Lisbon
DELTONA
CITRUS
SUMTER
LAKE
Sanford Experiment Sta.
SEMINOLE
Titusville
Brooksville Chin Hill
Clermont 7 S
ORLANDO
Weeki Wachee
HERNANDO
Orlando Intl Airport
ORANGE
Saint Leo
Kissimmee 2
Tarpon Springs Sewage Plant
Tampa Intl Airport
PASCO
Plant City
Lake Alfred Exp Sta.
MELBORNE
Melbourne Regional Airport
PALM HARBOR
TOWN 'N' COUNTRY
TAMPA
LAKELAND
Lakeland Linder Airport
PALM BAY
OSCEOLA
CLEARWATER
LARGO
PINELLAS
BRANDON
POLK
Mountain Lake
BREVARD
Bartow
ST. PETERSBURG
St. Petersburg WS
HILLSBOROUGH
Parrish
Wauchula
Avon Park 2 W
INDIAN RIVER
Vero Beach
Fort Pierce
Fort Drum 5 NW
Bradenton 5 ESE
MANATEE
HARDEE
OKEECHOBEE
ST. LUCIE
PORT ST. LUCIE
Stuart 1 S
Myakka River State Park
Arcadia
Archbold Bio Station
Canal Point USDA
Venice
SARASOTA
HIGHLANDS
MARTIN
DE SOTO
Belle Glade Exp Sta.
Punta Gorda 4 ESE
Moore Haven Lock 1
GLADES
W. PALM BEACH
CHARLOTTE
La Belle
W. Palm Beach Intl Arpt.
CAPE CORAL
Clewiston US Eng.
PALM BEACH
BOYNTON BEACH
DELRAY BEACH
Fort Myers Page Field
HENDRY
CORAL SPRINGS
BOCA RATON
LEE
TAMARAC
DEERFIELD BEACH
Immokalee 3 NNW
SUNRISE
MARGATE
PLANTATION
POMPANO BEACH
Naples
DAVIE
LAUDERHILL
PEMBROKE PINES
FORT LAUDERDALE
COLLIER
BROWARD
Fort Lauderdale WS
CAROL CITY
HOLLYWOOD
HIALEAH
Hialeah WS
Tamiami Trail 40 Mile Bend
Miami Intl Airport
MIAMI BEACH
DADE
MONROE
Miami Beach WS
Flamingo Ranger Station
MIAMI
KENDALL
KENDALL LAKES

Florida Weather Stations by County

County	Station Name
Alachua	Gainesville Regional Airport High Springs
Bay	Panama City 5 NE
Brevard	Melbourne Regional Airport Titusville
Broward	Fort Lauderdale
Charlotte	Punta Gorda 4 ESE
Citrus	Inverness 3 SE
Collier	Immokalee 3 NNW Naples
Columbia	Lake City 2 E
Dade	Hialeah Miami Beach Miami Int'l Airport Tamiami Trail 40 Mile Bend
Desoto	Arcadia
Dixie	Cross City 2 WNW
Duval	Jacksonville Beach Jacksonville Int'l Airport
Escambia	Pensacola Regional Airport
Franklin	Apalachicola Municipal Airport
Gadsden	Quincy 3 SSW
Glades	Moore Haven Lock 1
Hamilton	Jasper
Hardee	Wauchula
Hendry	Clewiston U.S. Engineers La Belle
Hernando	Brooksville Chin Hill Weeki Wachee
Highlands	Archbold Bio Station Avon Park 2 W
Hillsborough	Plant City Tampa Int'l Airport
Indian River	Vero Beach
Jefferson	Monticello 3 W
Lafayette	Mayo
Lake	Clermont 7 S Lisbon
Lee	Fort Myers Page Field
Leon	Tallahassee Municipal Airport
Levy	Usher Tower
Manatee	Bradenton 5 ESE Parrish
Marion	Ocala
Martin	Stuart 1 S
Monroe	Flamingo Ranger Station Key West Int'l Airport Tavernier
Nassau	Fernandina Beach
Okeechobee	Fort Drum 5 NW
Orange	Orlando Int'l Airport
Osceola	Kissimmee 2
Palm Beach	Belle Glade Exp. Station Canal Point USDA West Palm Beach Int'l Airport
Pasco	Saint Leo
Pinellas	Saint Petersburg Tarpon Springs Sewage Plant
Polk	Bartow Lake Alfred Exp. Station Lakeland Linder Airport Mountain Lake
Santa Rosa	Milton Experiment Station
Sarasota	Myakka River State Park Venice
Seminole	Sanford Experiment Station
St. Johns	Saint Augustine
St. Lucie	Fort Pierce
Suwannee	Live Oak
Taylor	Perry
Volusia	Daytona Beach Regional Airport
Walton	De Funiak Springs
Washington	Chipley 3 E

Florida Weather Stations by City

City	Station Name	Miles
Boca Raton	Fort Lauderdale	19
Boynton Beach	West Palm Beach Int'l Airport	11
Brandon	Plant City	11
	Tampa Int'l Airport	15
Cape Coral	Fort Myers Page Field	6
Carol City	Fort Lauderdale	12
	Hialeah	8
	Miami Beach	14
	Miami Int'l Airport	9
Clearwater	Saint Petersburg	17
	Tampa Int'l Airport	14
	Tarpon Springs Sewage Plant	12
Coral Springs	Fort Lauderdale	12
Davie	Fort Lauderdale	5
	Hialeah	17
	Miami Int'l Airport	18
Daytona Beach	Daytona Beach Reg Airport	2
Deerfield Beach	Fort Lauderdale	15
Delray Beach	West Palm Beach Int'l Airport	16
Deltona	Sanford Experiment Station	7
Fort Lauderdale	Fort Lauderdale	5
Gainesville	High Springs	19
	Gainesville Regional Airport	4
Hialeah	Fort Lauderdale	18
	Hialeah	2
	Miami Beach	12
	Miami Int'l Airport	3
Hollywood	Fort Lauderdale	6
	Hialeah	14
	Miami Beach	17
	Miami Int'l Airport	16
Jacksonville	Jacksonville Int'l Airport	14
	Jacksonville Beach	15
Kendale Lakes	Hialeah	12
	Miami Beach	18
	Miami Int'l Airport	10
Kendall	Hialeah	12
	Miami Beach	15
	Miami Int'l Airport	10
Lakeland	Bartow	11
	Lake Alfred Exp. Station	15
	Lakeland Linder Airport	0
	Plant City	11
Largo	Saint Petersburg	13
Largo *(cont.)*	Tampa Int'l Airport	16
	Tarpon Springs Sewage Plant	17
Lauderhill	Fort Lauderdale	5
Margate	Fort Lauderdale	10
Melbourne	Melbourne Regional Airport	1
Miami	Hialeah	5
	Miami Beach	6
	Miami Int'l Airport	5
Miami Beach	Hialeah	9
	Miami Beach	2
	Miami Int'l Airport	10
Orlando	Kissimmee 2	18
	Orlando Int'l Airport	7
Palm Bay	Melbourne Regional Airport	7
Palm Harbor	Tampa Int'l Airport	15
	Tarpon Springs Sewage Plant	5
Pembroke Pines	Fort Lauderdale	8
	Hialeah	12
	Miami Beach	18
	Miami Int'l Airport	14
Pensacola	Pensacola Regional Airport	2
Plantation	Fort Lauderdale	4
Pompano Beach	Fort Lauderdale	10
Port St. Lucie	Fort Pierce	13
	Stuart 1 S	10
St. Petersburg	Saint Petersburg	2
	Tampa Int'l Airport	15
Sunrise	Fort Lauderdale	6
Tallahassee	Quincy 3 SSW	19
	Tallahassee Municipal Airport	6
Tamarac	Fort Lauderdale	8
Tampa	Saint Petersburg	17
	Tampa Int'l Airport	4
Town 'n' Country	Saint Petersburg	17
	Tampa Int'l Airport	4
	Tarpon Springs Sewage Plant	14
West Palm Beach	West Palm Beach Int'l Airport	3

Note: Miles is the distance between the geographic center of the city and the weather station.

Florida Weather Stations by Elevation

Feet	Station Name
242	Quincy 3 SSW
239	Brooksville Chin Hill
229	De Funiak Springs
216	Milton Experiment Station
209	Lakeland Linder Airport
193	Lake City 2 E
187	Saint Leo
150	Avon Park 2 W
144	Jasper
144	Monticello 3 W
137	Archbold Bio Station
137	Lake Alfred Exp. Station
131	Gainesville Regional Airport
127	Chipley 3 E
124	Bartow
124	Mountain Lake
118	Live Oak
118	Plant City
111	Pensacola Regional Airport
108	Clermont 7 S
95	Orlando Int'l Airport
72	Ocala
68	Fort Drum 5 NW
65	Lisbon
62	Arcadia
62	High Springs
62	Mayo
59	Kissimmee 2
59	Parrish
59	Wauchula
52	Tallahassee Municipal Airport
42	Perry
39	Cross City 2 WNW
39	Inverness 3 SE
32	Immokalee 3 NNW
32	Melbourne Regional Airport
32	Miami Int'l Airport
32	Moore Haven Lock 1
32	Usher Tower
29	Canal Point USDA
29	Panama City 5 NE
29	Titusville
26	Daytona Beach Regional Airport
22	Fort Pierce
22	Jacksonville Int'l Airport
19	Apalachicola Municipal Airport
19	Bradenton 5 ESE
19	Clewiston U.S. Engineers
19	Myakka River State Park
19	Punta Gorda 4 ESE
19	Vero Beach
19	Weeki Wachee
16	Tampa Int'l Airport
16	West Palm Beach Int'l Airport
13	Belle Glade Exp. Station

Feet	Station Name
13	Fernandina Beach
13	Fort Lauderdale
13	Fort Myers Page Field
13	La Belle
13	Sanford Experiment Station
13	Tamiami Trail 40 Mile Bend
9	Hialeah
9	Jacksonville Beach
9	Stuart 1 S
6	Saint Augustine
6	Saint Petersburg
6	Tarpon Springs Sewage Plant
6	Tavernier
6	Venice
3	Key West Int'l Airport
3	Miami Beach
3	Naples
0	Flamingo Ranger Station

Apalachicola Municipal Airport

Apalachicola is located in a coastal area that is low and flat and bordered by the Gulf of Mexico from the east-northeast through the south to the west-southwest. There are many rivers, creeks, lakes, and bays to the north. Apalachicola is situated at the mouth of the Apalachicola River and on the Apalachicola Bay. Several islands to the east and south offer very good protection from the occasionally rough seas of the Gulf. The land area is generally sandy, and is heavily covered with pine and cypress forests and scattered palmetto palms.

The climate of this locality is typical of that experienced on the northern Gulf of Mexico. Because of the moderating effect of the surrounding Gulf, temperatures are usually mild and subtropical in nature, but are subject to occasional wide winter variations.

Average annual rainfall is about 57 inches, but actual monthly and yearly totals vary widely. Sandy soil and generally adequate drainage allow rapid absorption and runoff during occasional tropical downpours. Thunderstorms occur in all months. About three-fourths of the average annual number occur during the summer months. Very few tropical storms affect Apalachicola.

Hail has fallen on occasions, but averages less than one occurrence a year. There is no record of sleet or glaze. Snow has fallen on rare occasions, but generally melted as it fell. A measurable amount of snow is rare.

Apalachicola Municipal Airport *Franklin Co.* Elevation: 19 ft. Latitude: 29° 44' N Longitude: 85° 02' W

	JAN	FEB	MAR	APR	MAY	JUN	JUL	AUG	SEP	OCT	NOV	DEC	YEAR
Mean Maximum Temp. (°F)	62.1	64.6	69.9	76.1	83.1	88.2	89.7	89.3	86.9	79.9	71.9	65.1	77.2
Mean Temp. (°F)	53.1	55.6	61.1	67.1	74.3	80.1	81.9	81.8	79.2	70.6	62.4	55.9	68.6
Mean Minimum Temp. (°F)	44.1	46.6	52.4	58.0	65.5	71.9	74.2	74.1	71.3	61.3	52.8	46.6	59.9
Extreme Maximum Temp. (°F)	80	80	85	90	98	100	101	103	97	92	85	83	103
Extreme Minimum Temp. (°F)	9	19	22	36	47	48	63	62	52	33	27	14	9
Days Maximum Temp. ≥ 90°F	0	0	0	0	2	10	16	14	7	1	0	0	50
Days Maximum Temp. ® 32°F	0	0	0	0	0	0	0	0	0	0	0	0	0
Days Minimum Temp. ® 32°F	5	2	0	0	0	0	0	0	0	0	0	3	10
Days Minimum Temp. ® 0°F	0	0	0	0	0	0	0	0	0	0	0	0	0
Heating Degree Days (base 65°F)	368	268	151	40	1	0	0	0	0	20	135	294	1,277
Cooling Degree Days (base 65°F)	6	11	39	105	300	462	542	534	427	208	67	20	2,721
Mean Precipitation (in.)	4.92	3.82	5.00	3.05	2.86	4.26	7.10	7.89	6.59	4.39	3.45	3.58	56.91
Maximum Precipitation (in.)	20.8	8.9	13.5	12.1	12.1	18.3	18.1	21.1	18.3	11.2	6.7	9.7	88.2
Minimum Precipitation (in.)	0.8	0.5	0.7	0.1	0.3	0.3	0.8	2.3	0.6	0.1	0.5	0.9	38.1
Maximum 24-hr. Precipitation (in.)	4.0	4.4	8.2	6.2	6.8	4.2	6.3	5.4	7.7	6.2	4.2	3.6	8.2
Days With ≥ 0.1" Precipitation	7	5	6	4	3	6	9	9	8	4	5	6	72
Days With ≥ 1.0" Precipitation	2	1	2	1	1	1	1	2	2	1	1	1	17
Mean Snowfall (in.)	trace	trace	trace	0.0	0.0	0.0	0.0	0.0	0.0	0.0	0.0	trace	trace
Maximum Snowfall (in.)	trace	trace	trace	0	0	0	0	0	0	0	0	trace	trace
Maximum 24-hr. Snowfall (in.)	trace	trace	trace	0	0	0	0	0	0	0	0	trace	trace
Days With ≥ 1.0" Snow Depth	0	0	0	0	0	0	0	0	0	0	0	0	0
Thunderstorm Days	2	3	4	3	5	11	17	17	10	2	2	2	78
Foggy Days	17	15	17	14	12	8	7	8	9	11	13	16	147
Predominant Sky Cover	OVR	OVR	OVR	CLR	SCT	SCT	SCT	SCT	SCT	CLR	CLR	OVR	OVR
Mean Relative Humidity 7am (%)	83	86	88	87	87	87	89	91	89	86	86	85	87
Mean Relative Humidity 4pm (%)	62	64	66	62	65	67	70	69	67	60	64	65	65
Mean Dewpoint (°F)	42	47	53	58	66	71	74	74	70	60	54	47	60
Prevailing Wind Direction	N	SE	SE	SE	S	SW	SW	SE	NE	NE	NE	N	SE
Prevailing Wind Speed (mph)	10	9	10	10	8	8	7	9	8	8	8	10	9
Maximum Wind Gust (mph)	41	49	41	43	61	38	41	68	68	44	85	47	85

Daytona Beach Regional Airport

Daytona Beach is located on the Atlantic Ocean. The Halifax River, part of the Florida Inland Waterway, runs through the city. The terrain in the area is flat and the soil is mostly sandy. Elevations in the area range from three to 15 feet above mean sea level near the ocean to about 31 feet at the airport and on a ridge running along the western city limits.

Nearness to the ocean results in a climate tempered by the effect of land and sea breezes. In the summer, while maximum temperatures reach 90 degrees or above during the late morning or early afternoon, the number of hours of 90 degrees or above is relatively small due to the beginning of the sea breeze near midday and the occurrence of local afternoon convective thunderstorms which lower the temperature to the comfortable 80s. Winters, although subject to invasions of cold air, are relatively mild due to the nearness of the ocean and latitudinal location.

The rainy season from June through mid-October produces 60 percent of the annual rainfall. The major portion of the summer rainfall occurs in the form of local convective thunderstorms which are occasionally heavy and produce as much as two or three inches of rain. The more severe thunderstorms may be attended by strong gusty winds. Almost all rainfall during the winter months is associated with frontal passages.

Long periods of cloudiness and rain are infrequent, usually not lasting over two or three days. These periods are usually associated with a stationary front, a so-called northeaster, or a tropical disturbance.

Tropical disturbances or hurricanes are not considered a great threat to this area of the state. Generally hurricanes in this latitude tend to pass well offshore or lose much of their intensity while crossing the state before reaching this area. Only in gusts have hurricane-force winds been recorded at this station.

Heavy fog occurs mostly during the winter and early spring. These fogs usually form by radiational cooling at night and dissipate soon after sunrise. On rare occasions sea fog moves in from the ocean and persists for two or three days. There is no significant source in the area for air pollution.

Daytona Beach Regional Airport *Volusia Co.* Elevation: 26 ft. Latitude: 29° 11' N Longitude: 81° 04' W

	JAN	FEB	MAR	APR	MAY	JUN	JUL	AUG	SEP	OCT	NOV	DEC	YEAR
Mean Maximum Temp. (°F)	68.7	70.4	75.2	79.7	84.7	88.5	90.5	89.6	87.3	82.0	76.0	70.9	80.3
Mean Temp. (°F)	58.2	59.9	64.6	69.2	74.9	79.8	81.6	81.3	79.7	73.9	66.6	60.8	70.9
Mean Minimum Temp. (°F)	47.5	49.2	54.1	58.7	65.0	71.0	72.7	73.0	72.0	65.7	57.2	50.6	61.4
Extreme Maximum Temp. (°F)	87	89	92	94	97	101	102	100	96	93	88	88	102
Extreme Minimum Temp. (°F)	15	26	26	36	44	52	60	65	53	41	30	19	15
Days Maximum Temp. ≥ 90°F	0	0	0	2	5	11	19	15	7	1	0	0	60
Days Maximum Temp. ® 32°F	0	0	0	0	0	0	0	0	0	0	0	0	0
Days Minimum Temp. ® 32°F	2	1	0	0	0	0	0	0	0	0	0	1	4
Days Minimum Temp. ® 0°F	0	0	0	0	0	0	0	0	0	0	0	0	0
Heating Degree Days (base 65°F)	242	181	95	26	1	0	0	0	0	6	67	179	797
Cooling Degree Days (base 65°F)	31	45	83	149	308	450	525	517	439	288	127	53	3,015
Mean Precipitation (in.)	3.20	2.84	3.68	2.57	3.18	5.67	5.12	6.10	6.28	4.58	3.00	2.70	48.92
Maximum Precipitation (in.)	7.2	9.1	8.1	7.1	12.3	15.2	14.4	19.9	15.2	13.0	12.9	12.0	79.3
Minimum Precipitation (in.)	0.1	0.6	0.3	trace	0.1	1.0	0.2	2.0	0.4	0.2	trace	0.1	31.4
Maximum 24-hr. Precipitation (in.)	5.7	3.6	5.0	4.0	4.0	6.1	3.3	4.4	6.2	9.1	9.0	3.6	9.1
Days With ≥ 0.1" Precipitation	5	5	5	3	5	8	8	10	8	6	4	5	72
Days With ≥ 1.0" Precipitation	1	1	1	1	1	2	1	2	2	1	1	1	15
Mean Snowfall (in.)	trace	0.0	trace	0.0	0.0	trace	0.0	trace	0.0	0.0	0.0	trace	trace
Maximum Snowfall (in.)	trace	trace	0	0	0	0	0	0	0	0	0	trace	trace
Maximum 24-hr. Snowfall (in.)	trace	trace	0	0	0	0	0	0	0	0	0	trace	trace
Days With ≥ 1.0" Snow Depth	0	0	0	0	0	0	0	0	0	0	0	0	0
Thunderstorm Days	1	2	3	4	8	14	17	15	9	3	1	1	78
Foggy Days	15	12	12	10	10	10	8	9	8	9	12	14	129
Predominant Sky Cover	OVR	OVR	CLR	CLR	SCT	SCT	SCT	SCT	SCT	SCT	CLR	OVR	SCT
Mean Relative Humidity 7am (%)	87	86	86	85	85	87	89	91	90	87	87	87	87
Mean Relative Humidity 4pm (%)	61	59	57	56	61	68	69	71	71	66	64	63	64
Mean Dewpoint (°F)	49	50	54	58	65	70	72	73	71	65	57	52	61
Prevailing Wind Direction	NW	N	WSW	ESE	ESE	E	SW	E	ENE	ENE	NW	NW	E
Prevailing Wind Speed (mph)	9	12	12	12	12	10	7	10	12	12	8	8	10
Maximum Wind Gust (mph)	62	58	77	58	69	74	67	68	55	56	55	60	77

Fort Myers Page Field

Located on the south bank of the Caloosahatchee River, about 15 miles from the Gulf of Mexico, Fort Myers has a climate characterized as subtropical, with temperature extremes of both summer and winter tempered by the marine influence of the Gulf.

Temperatures generally range from the low 60s in winter to the low 80s in summer. Winters are mild, with many bright, warm days and moderately cool nights. Occasional cold snaps bring temperatures in the 30s, but only rarely do temperatures drop into the 20s. Frost occurs in the farming areas on only a few occasions each year, and usually is light and scattered. In the summer, temperatures have reached 100 degrees, but these occurrences are very rare.

About two-thirds of annual precipitation occurs during June through September. There are frequent long periods during the winter when only very light, or no rain falls. Most rain during the summer occurs as late afternoon or early evening thunderstorms, which bring welcome cooling on hot summer days. These showers seldom last long, even though they yield large amounts of rain. Exceptions are during the late summer or fall when tropical storms or hurricanes may pass near the Fort Myers area. These may result in heavy downpours that may reach torrential proportions. 24 hour amounts of from six to over 10 inches may occur.

The prevailing wind direction is east and, except during the passage of tropical storms, high velocities are not experienced. During winter and spring there are usually a few days with 20 to 30 mph winds and thunderstorms are sometimes accompanied by strong gusts for brief periods. Winds approximating 100 mph have been experienced with the passage of hurricanes during the fall months.

Thunderstorms have occurred during every month, but are infrequent from November to April. From June through September they occur on 2 out of every 3 days on an average, and as a general rule, in the late afternoons or early evenings. Heavy fog is rather infrequent, occurring mostly in winter during the early mornings. There is seldom a day without sunshine at some time.

Relative humidity is high during the night, dropping off in the middle of the day.

Fort Myers Page Field *Lee County* Elevation: 13 ft. Latitude: 26° 35' N Longitude: 81° 52' W

	JAN	FEB	MAR	APR	MAY	JUN	JUL	AUG	SEP	OCT	NOV	DEC	YEAR
Mean Maximum Temp. (°F)	74.8	76.1	80.2	84.6	88.8	91.1	91.7	91.7	90.3	86.4	81.4	76.7	84.5
Mean Temp. (°F)	64.5	65.5	69.5	73.6	78.5	82.1	83.1	83.3	82.2	77.6	71.8	66.4	74.9
Mean Minimum Temp. (°F)	54.1	54.9	58.9	62.7	68.0	73.2	74.5	74.8	74.2	68.8	62.2	56.2	65.2
Extreme Maximum Temp. (°F)	88	91	93	96	99	103	98	98	96	95	95	***90***	***103***
Extreme Minimum Temp. (°F)	28	32	33	42	52	60	67	69	64	48	34	***27***	***27***
Days Maximum Temp. ≥ 90°F	0	0	1	4	14	21	25	25	20	7	1	0	118
Days Maximum Temp. ® 32°F	0	0	0	0	0	0	0	0	0	0	0	0	0
Days Minimum Temp. ® 32°F	0	0	0	0	0	0	0	0	0	0	0	0	0
Days Minimum Temp. ® 0°F	0	0	0	0	0	0	0	0	0	0	0	0	0
Heating Degree Days (base 65°F)	107	76	26	3	0	0	0	0	0	1	17	73	303
Cooling Degree Days (base 65°F)	93	112	176	275	434	539	578	582	532	410	239	***128***	***4,098***
Mean Precipitation (in.)	2.36	2.12	3.27	1.62	3.56	9.68	9.00	9.58	7.80	2.49	1.79	1.59	54.86
Maximum Precipitation (in.)	7.9	10.8	18.6	5.7	10.3	20.1	16.7	16.7	16.6	11.9	8.1	5.2	74.8
Minimum Precipitation (in.)	0	0.1	trace	trace	0.3	2.0	2.3	4.0	1.9	0	trace	trace	32.8
Maximum 24-hr. Precipitation (in.)	2.6	2.6	5.6	3.8	7.8	5.7	7.3	5.1	5.5	6.2	3.6	3.0	7.8
Days With ≥ 0.1" Precipitation	3	3	4	3	5	11	13	13	11	4	3	3	76
Days With ≥ 1.0" Precipitation	1	1	1	0	1	3	3	3	2	1	0	0	16
Mean Snowfall (in.)	0.0	0.0	0.0	0.0	0.0	0.0	0.0	0.0	0.0	***0.0***	***0.0***	***0.0***	***0.0***
Maximum Snowfall (in.)	0	0	0	0	0	0	0	0	0	0	0	0	0
Maximum 24-hr. Snowfall (in.)	0	0	0	0	0	0	0	0	0	0	0	0	0
Days With ≥ 1.0" Snow Depth	0	0	0	0	0	0	0	0	0	***0***	***0***	***0***	***0***
Thunderstorm Days	1	1	2	3	6	16	22	21	14	4	1	1	92
Foggy Days	15	12	13	10	9	6	3	3	4	8	11	13	107
Predominant Sky Cover	CLR	CLR	CLR	CLR	SCT	SCT	BRK	BRK	SCT	SCT	SCT	CLR	SCT
Mean Relative Humidity 7am (%)	90	89	89	88	87	89	90	91	92	90	90	90	90
Mean Relative Humidity 4pm (%)	56	54	52	50	53	64	68	67	66	59	58	57	59
Mean Dewpoint (°F)	55	55	58	61	66	72	73	74	73	67	61	57	64
Prevailing Wind Direction	NE	NE	ENE	E	E	E	E	E	ENE	NE	NE	NE	ENE
Prevailing Wind Speed (mph)	8	9	9	9	8	7	7	7	7	9	8	8	8
Maximum Wind Gust (mph)	45	46	39	38	45	71	45	48	41	40	37	47	71

Gainesville Regional Airport

Gainsville lies in the north central part of the Florida peninsula, almost midway between the coasts of the Atlantic Ocean and the Gulf of Mexico. The terrain is fairly level with several nearby lakes to the east and south. Due to its centralized location, maritime influences are somewhat less than they would be along coastlines at the same latitude.

Maximum temperatures in summer average slightly more than 90 degrees. From June to September, the number of days when temperatures exceed 89 degrees is 84 on average. Record high temperatures are in excess of 100 degrees. Minimum temperatures in winter average a little more than 44 degrees. The average number of days per year when temperatures are freezing or below is 18. Record lows occur in the teens. Low temperatures are a consequence of cold winds from the north or nighttime radiational cooling of the ground in contact with rather calm air.

Rainfall is appreciable in every month but is most abundant from showers and thunderstorms in summer. The average number of thunderstorm hours yearly is approximately 160. In winter, large-scale cyclone and frontal activity is responsible for some of the precipitation. Monthly average values range from about two inches in November to about eight inches in August. Snowfall is practically unknown.

Because of its inland location, Gainesville does not have serious problems with hurricanes. An occasional hurricane will cross the Gulf or Atlantic coast and head toward Gainesville, but before it arrives it is weakened by surface friction and a depletion of water vapor.

Gainesville Regional Airport *Alachua Co.* Elevation: 131 ft. Latitude: 29° 42' N Longitude: 82° 17' W

	JAN	FEB	MAR	APR	MAY	JUN	JUL	AUG	SEP	OCT	NOV	DEC	YEAR
Mean Maximum Temp. (°F)	na	na	na	na	na	na	na	na	na	na	na	na	na
Mean Temp. (°F)	na	na	na	na	na	na	na	na	na	na	na	na	na
Mean Minimum Temp. (°F)	na	na	na	na	na	na	na	na	na	na	na	na	na
Extreme Maximum Temp. (°F)	na	na	na	na	na	na	na	na	na	na	na	na	na
Extreme Minimum Temp. (°F)	na	na	na	na	na	na	na	na	na	na	na	na	na
Days Maximum Temp. ≥ 90°F	na	na	na	na	na	na	na	na	na	na	na	na	na
Days Maximum Temp. ® 32°F	na	na	na	na	na	na	na	na	na	na	na	na	na
Days Minimum Temp. ® 32°F	na	na	na	na	na	na	na	na	na	na	na	na	na
Days Minimum Temp. ® 0°F	na	na	na	na	na	na	na	na	na	na	na	na	na
Heating Degree Days (base 65°F)	na	na	na	na	na	na	na	na	na	na	na	na	na
Cooling Degree Days (base 65°F)	***17***	***29***	***63***	***130***	***312***	***443***	***511***	***497***	***405***	***214***	***83***	***25***	***2,729***
Mean Precipitation (in.)	na	na	na	na	na	na	na	na	na	na	na	na	na
Maximum Precipitation (in.)	9.0	6.9	9.8	6.0	7.2	14.8	12.2	15.8	12.0	8.0	4.5	6.4	70.8
Minimum Precipitation (in.)	0.5	0.3	0.7	0.4	0.2	2.2	1.5	2.5	1.9	trace	0.3	0.2	40.5
Maximum 24-hr. Precipitation (in.)	2.2	2.6	3.3	2.8	3.5	4.3	3.2	3.8	6.2	5.1	2.0	2.3	6.2
Days With ≥ 0.1" Precipitation	na	na	na	na	na	na	na	na	na	na	na	na	na
Days With ≥ 1.0" Precipitation	na	na	na	na	na	na	na	na	na	na	na	na	na
Mean Snowfall (in.)	na	na	na	na	na	na	na	na	na	na	na	na	na
Maximum Snowfall (in.)	0	trace	0	0	0	0	0	0	0	0	0	trace	trace
Maximum 24-hr. Snowfall (in.)	0	trace	0	0	0	0	0	0	0	0	0	trace	trace
Days With ≥ 1.0" Snow Depth	na	na	na	na	na	na	na	na	na	na	na	na	na
Thunderstorm Days	1	2	3	3	6	13	20	17	8	3	1	1	78
Foggy Days	19	17	20	21	22	23	21	24	23	21	21	19	251
Predominant Sky Cover	OVR	OVR	CLR	CLR	SCT	BRK	SCT	BRK	SCT	CLR	CLR	OVR	SCT
Mean Relative Humidity 7am (%)	90	90	92	92	91	93	94	96	96	94	94	92	93
Mean Relative Humidity 4pm (%)	60	55	52	50	51	61	67	67	67	63	63	61	60
Mean Dewpoint (°F)	47	49	53	56	63	70	73	73	70	63	57	49	60
Prevailing Wind Direction	WNW	W	W	W	ESE	WSW	WSW	E	E	NE	NE	NW	E
Prevailing Wind Speed (mph)	9	10	10	9	9	9	9	7	8	9	9	8	9
Maximum Wind Gust (mph)	na	na	na	na	na	na	na	na	na	na	na	na	na

Jacksonville Int'l Airport

Jacksonville, a very large metropolitan area covering 840 square miles, extends from the Atlantic Ocean to about 40 miles inland. Downtown Jacksonville is located some 16 miles inland on the St. Johns River. The surrounding terrain is level. Easterly winds blowing about 40 percent of the time produce a maritime influence that modifies to some extent the heat of summer and the cold of winter. Summers are long, warm and relatively humid. Winters, although punctuated with periodic invasions of cool to occasionally cold air from the north, are mild because of the southern latitude and the proximity to the warm Atlantic Ocean waters. Because of the nearness to the ocean, climatic features across the city vary. For example, during the summer months temperatures at Jacksonville International Airport, located 17 miles inland, usually reach into the low and mid-90s before being tempered by sea breezes. Temperatures along the beaches rarely exceed 90 degrees. Summer thunderstorms usually occur before the noon hour along the beaches, while afternoon thunderstorms are the rule inland.

The annual temperature for Jacksonville is between 68 and 69 degrees. June, July, and August are the hottest months, with temperatures averaging near 80 degrees. December, January, and February are the coolest months, with temperatures near the middle 50s. Temperatures exceed 95 degrees only about ten times a year. Night temperatures in summer are usually comfortable, rarely failing to drop below 80 degrees.

The greatest rainfall, mostly in the form of local thundershowers, occurs during the summer months when a measurable amount can be expected one day in two. Rainfall of one inch or more in 24 hours normally occurs about fourteen times a year, and very infrequently heavy rains, associated with tropical storms, reach amounts of several inches with durations of more than 24 hours.

The atmosphere is moist, with an average relative humidity of about 75 percent, ranging from about 90 percent in early morning hours to about 55 percent during the afternoon.

Prevailing winds are northeasterly in the fall and winter months, and southwesterly in spring and summer. Wind movement, which averages slightly less than nine mph, is two to three mph higher in the early afternoon than the early morning hours, and slightly higher in spring than in other seasons of the year. Although this area is in the Hurricane Belt, this section of the coast has been very fortunate in escaping hurricane-force winds. Most hurricanes reaching this latitude have tended to move parallel to the coastline, keeping well out to sea.

Jacksonville Int'l Airport *Duval County* Elevation: 22 ft. Latitude: 30° 30' N Longitude: 81° 42' W

	JAN	FEB	MAR	APR	MAY	JUN	JUL	AUG	SEP	OCT	NOV	DEC	YEAR
Mean Maximum Temp. (°F)	64.6	67.7	73.9	79.5	85.1	89.7	92.1	90.6	87.4	80.2	73.4	66.9	79.3
Mean Temp. (°F)	53.2	56.0	61.9	67.2	73.8	79.6	82.3	81.5	78.5	70.1	62.1	55.7	68.5
Mean Minimum Temp. (°F)	41.8	44.3	49.9	55.0	62.5	69.4	72.5	72.3	69.4	59.9	50.8	44.4	57.7
Extreme Maximum Temp. (°F)	84	86	91	94	98	103	103	102	98	94	88	84	103
Extreme Minimum Temp. (°F)	7	19	23	34	45	47	61	63	48	36	21	11	7
Days Maximum Temp. ≥ 90°F	0	0	0	1	6	16	24	20	10	1	0	0	78
Days Maximum Temp. ® 32°F	0	0	0	0	0	0	0	0	0	0	0	0	0
Days Minimum Temp. ® 32°F	7	4	1	0	0	0	0	0	0	0	1	5	18
Days Minimum Temp. ® 0°F	0	0	0	0	0	0	0	0	0	0	0	0	0
Heating Degree Days (base 65°F)	373	269	150	51	4	0	0	0	0	27	146	305	1,325
Cooling Degree Days (base 65°F)	12	25	60	125	289	459	557	528	405	198	70	22	2,750
Mean Precipitation (in.)	3.73	3.40	4.21	3.11	3.51	5.37	6.04	6.99	7.62	3.98	2.28	2.64	52.88
Maximum Precipitation (in.)	10.2	8.8	10.2	11.6	10.4	14.0	16.2	16.2	19.4	13.4	5.0	7.1	79.6
Minimum Precipitation (in.)	0.1	0.5	0.7	0.1	0.2	1.6	2.0	2.2	1.0	0.3	trace	trace	31.2
Maximum 24-hr. Precipitation (in.)	2.9	4.9	7.1	7.3	5.4	5.9	7.3	7.8	10.+	7.8	2.8	2.9	10.+
Days With ≥ 0.1" Precipitation	6	5	6	4	5	9	10	10	9	5	4	5	78
Days With ≥ 1.0" Precipitation	1	1	1	1	1	1	2	2	2	1	1	1	15
Mean Snowfall (in.)	trace	trace	trace	trace	0.0	trace	trace	0.0	0.0	0.0	0.0	trace	trace
Maximum Snowfall (in.)	trace	2	1	0	0	0	0	0	0	0	0	1	2
Maximum 24-hr. Snowfall (in.)	trace	2	1	0	0	0	0	0	0	0	0	1	2
Days With ≥ 1.0" Snow Depth	0	0	0	0	0	0	0	0	0	0	0	0	0
Thunderstorm Days	1	2	3	4	6	11	16	13	7	2	1	1	67
Foggy Days	18	14	15	13	14	13	11	15	16	17	16	17	179
Predominant Sky Cover	OVR	OVR	OVR	CLR	SCT	BRK	BRK	SCT	SCT	CLR	CLR	OVR	OVR
Mean Relative Humidity 7am (%)	87	86	87	87	87	88	89	92	92	91	90	88	89
Mean Relative Humidity 4pm (%)	57	53	50	49	54	61	64	66	67	62	59	59	58
Mean Dewpoint (°F)	44	46	50	56	63	70	72	73	70	62	53	47	59
Prevailing Wind Direction	NW	NW	WSW	SE	SE	SW	SW	SW	NE	NE	NW	NW	SW
Prevailing Wind Speed (mph)	9	10	10	10	10	8	7	7	10	12	8	9	9
Maximum Wind Gust (mph)	64	62	66	67	71	67	69	66	59	43	49	61	71

Key West Int'l Airport

Key West is located at the end of the Overseas Highway and near the western end of the Florida Keys, which are a chain of islands swinging in a southwesterly arc from the southeast coast of the Florida peninsula. The nearest point of the mainland is about 60 statute miles to the northeast, while Cuba at its closest point is 98 miles south. The city occupies the island of the same name which is three and a half miles long and one mile wide. Its mean elevation is around eight feet. The maximum elevation of 18 feet covers only about one acre in the western portion. Soil is a thin layer of sand, or marlfill, overlying a stratum of Oolitic limestone. Vegetation on the eastern end of the island is scanty, chiefly of low growth. The western end, where settlement and landscaping are older, has a little heavier growth. The airport and Weather Service Office are located on the southeast shore on partially filled mangrove swamp.

The waters surrounding the key are quite shallow up to the mainland on the northeast and for six miles to the reef on the south. There is little wave action because the reef disrupts any established wave pattern.

Because of the nearness of the Gulf Stream in the Straits of Florida, about 12 miles south and southeast, and the tempering effects of the Gulf of Mexico to the west and north, Key West has a notably mild, tropical-maritime climate in which the average temperatures during the winter are about 14 degrees lower than in summer. Cold fronts are strongly modified by the warm water as they move in from northerly quadrants in winter. There is no known record of frost, ice, sleet, or snow in Key West. Prevailing easterly tradewinds and sea breezes suppress the usual summertime heating. Diurnal variations throughout the year average only about 10 degrees.

Precipitation is characterized by dry and wet seasons. The period of December through April receives abundant sunshine and slightly less than 25 percent of the annual rainfall. This rainfall usually occurs in advance of cold fronts in a few heavy showers, or occasionally five to eight light showers per month. June through October is normally the wet season, receiving approximately 53 percent of the yearly total in numerous showers and thunderstorms. Early morning is the favored time for diurnal showers. Easterly waves during this season occasionally bring excessive rainfall, while infrequent hurricanes may be accompanied by unusually heavy amounts. Humidity remains relatively high during the entire year.

Key West Int'l Airport *Monroe County* Elevation: 3 ft. Latitude: 24° 33' N Longitude: 81° 45' W

	JAN	FEB	MAR	APR	MAY	JUN	JUL	AUG	SEP	OCT	NOV	DEC	YEAR
Mean Maximum Temp. (°F)	75.2	75.8	78.7	81.9	85.3	88.0	89.3	89.4	88.1	84.7	80.5	76.8	82.8
Mean Temp. (°F)	70.2	70.7	73.7	77.1	80.6	83.4	84.5	84.3	83.3	80.3	76.2	72.1	78.0
Mean Minimum Temp. (°F)	65.1	65.6	68.8	72.3	75.9	78.7	79.6	79.2	78.4	75.7	71.9	67.3	73.2
Extreme Maximum Temp. (°F)	86	85	88	90	91	93	94	98	93	91	89	86	98
Extreme Minimum Temp. (°F)	41	45	47	48	64	70	71	71	69	65	50	44	41
Days Maximum Temp. ≥ 90°F	0	0	0	0	1	7	15	16	7	0	0	0	46
Days Maximum Temp. ® 32°F	0	0	0	0	0	0	0	0	0	0	0	0	0
Days Minimum Temp. ® 32°F	0	0	0	0	0	0	0	0	0	0	0	0	0
Days Minimum Temp. ® 0°F	0	0	0	0	0	0	0	0	0	0	0	0	0
Heating Degree Days (base 65°F)	25	17	6	0	0	0	0	0	0	0	0	13	61
Cooling Degree Days (base 65°F)	186	199	272	363	491	566	616	612	557	482	348	234	4,926
Mean Precipitation (in.)	2.47	1.56	1.88	1.99	3.52	4.52	3.53	5.24	5.50	4.40	2.63	2.08	39.32
Maximum Precipitation (in.)	17.6	4.5	9.7	10.6	12.9	14.4	11.7	10.4	18.4	21.6	27.7	11.2	62.9
Minimum Precipitation (in.)	trace	trace	trace	0	0.3	0.3	0.4	2.2	1.7	0.7	trace	0.1	20.0
Maximum 24-hr. Precipitation (in.)	6.4	2.5	5.3	6.2	7.2	5.1	3.0	3.3	6.1	6.5	23.+	6.7	23.+
Days With ≥ 0.1" Precipitation	4	3	3	3	4	7	7	9	10	6	3	3	62
Days With ≥ 1.0" Precipitation	1	0	0	1	1	1	1	2	1	1	1	1	11
Mean Snowfall (in.)	0.0	0.0	0.0	0.0	0.0	0.0	0.0	0.0	0.0	0.0	0.0	0.0	0.0
Maximum Snowfall (in.)	0	0	0	0	0	0	0	0	0	0	0	0	0
Maximum 24-hr. Snowfall (in.)	0	0	0	0	0	0	0	0	0	0	0	0	0
Days With ≥ 1.0" Snow Depth	0	0	0	0	0	0	0	0	0	0	0	0	0
Thunderstorm Days	1	1	2	2	4	10	13	15	12	4	1	1	66
Foggy Days	3	1	1	< 1	< 1	< 1	< 1	< 1	< 1	< 1	1	1	7
Predominant Sky Cover	SCT	SCT	SCT	SCT	SCT	SCT	SCT	SCT	SCT	SCT	SCT	SCT	SCT
Mean Relative Humidity 7am (%)	82	81	79	76	76	78	76	78	81	82	83	82	79
Mean Relative Humidity 4pm (%)	69	67	66	63	65	68	66	67	69	69	70	70	68
Mean Dewpoint (°F)	62	62	64	66	70	74	74	75	74	71	67	63	69
Prevailing Wind Direction	NE	NE	SE	ESE	ESE	SE	ESE	ESE	ESE	ENE	NE	NE	ESE
Prevailing Wind Speed (mph)	12	12	13	14	13	10	12	12	12	13	13	12	12
Maximum Wind Gust (mph)	58	55	75	78	53	70	67	56	87	90	69	54	90

Miami Int'l Airport

Miami is located on the lower east coast of Florida. To the east of the city lies Biscayne Bay, an arm of the ocean, about 15 miles long and three miles wide. East of the bay is the island of Miami Beach, a mile or less wide and about 10 miles long, and beyond Miami Beach is the Atlantic Ocean. The surrounding countryside is level and sparsely wooded.

The climate of Miami is essentially subtropical marine, featured by a long and warm summer, with abundant rainfall, followed by a mild, dry winter. The marine influence is evidenced by the low daily range of temperature and the rapid warming of cold air masses which pass to the east of the state. The Miami area is subject to winds from the east or southeast about half the time, and in several specific respects has a climate whose features differ from those farther inland.

One of these features is the annual precipitation for the area. During the early morning hours more rainfall occurs at Miami Beach than at the airport, while during the afternoon the reverse is true. The airport office is about nine miles inland.

An even more striking difference appears in the annual number of days with temperatures reaching 90 degrees or higher, with inland stations having about four times more than the beach. Minimum temperature contrasts also are particularly marked under proper conditions, with the difference between inland locations and the Miami Beach station frequently reaching to 15 degrees or more, especially in winter.

Freezing temperatures occur occasionally in the suburbs and farming districts southwest, west, and northwest of the city, but rarely near the ocean.

Hurricanes occasionally affect the area. The months of greatest frequency are September and October. Destructive tornadoes are very rare. Funnel clouds are occasionally sighted and a few touch the ground briefly but significant damage is seldom reported. Waterspouts are often visible from the beaches during the summer months, however, significant damage is seldom reported. June, July, and August have the highest frequency of dangerous lightning events.

Miami Int'l Airport *Miami-Dade County* Elevation: 32 ft. Latitude: 25° 49' N Longitude: 80° 18' W

	JAN	FEB	MAR	APR	MAY	JUN	JUL	AUG	SEP	OCT	NOV	DEC	YEAR
Mean Maximum Temp. (°F)	75.9	76.8	79.6	82.8	86.0	88.4	89.7	89.7	88.3	85.1	80.9	77.4	83.4
Mean Temp. (°F)	68.0	69.0	72.1	75.6	79.3	82.0	83.3	83.4	82.3	79.0	74.4	70.1	76.6
Mean Minimum Temp. (°F)	60.1	61.1	64.7	68.4	72.5	75.6	76.9	77.0	76.2	72.8	67.9	62.8	69.7
Extreme Maximum Temp. (°F)	88	89	92	96	96	98	98	98	97	95	89	87	98
Extreme Minimum Temp. (°F)	30	37	32	46	56	60	69	69	68	53	40	30	30
Days Maximum Temp. ≥ 90°F	0	0	0	2	5	11	17	17	11	3	0	0	66
Days Maximum Temp. ® 32°F	0	0	0	0	0	0	0	0	0	0	0	0	0
Days Minimum Temp. ® 32°F	0	0	0	0	0	0	0	0	0	0	0	0	0
Days Minimum Temp. ® 0°F	0	0	0	0	0	0	0	0	0	0	0	0	0
Heating Degree Days (base 65°F)	58	37	14	1	0	0	0	0	0	0	5	36	151
Cooling Degree Days (base 65°F)	157	170	237	321	454	530	590	589	533	455	306	201	4,543
Mean Precipitation (in.)	1.95	2.09	2.64	3.28	5.82	8.55	5.77	8.51	8.32	5.67	3.42	1.98	58.00
Maximum Precipitation (in.)	6.7	8.1	10.6	10.2	18.5	22.4	11.2	16.6	24.4	21.6	13.8	6.4	89.3
Minimum Precipitation (in.)	trace	0.1	trace	0	0.4	2.0	1.8	1.6	2.6	1.3	0.1	0.1	37.0
Maximum 24-hr. Precipitation (in.)	2.4	4.5	7.1	7.3	12.+	6.6	4.5	6.6	6.1	9.9	7.6	4.4	12.+
Days With ≥ 0.1" Precipitation	4	4	4	4	8	11	11	12	12	8	5	3	86
Days With ≥ 1.0" Precipitation	0	0	1	1	2	3	2	2	3	2	1	0	17
Mean Snowfall (in.)	0.0	0.0	0.0	0.0	trace	0.0	0.0	0.0	0.0	0.0	0.0	0.0	trace
Maximum Snowfall (in.)	0	0	0	0	0	0	0	0	0	0	0	0	0
Maximum 24-hr. Snowfall (in.)	0	0	0	0	0	0	0	0	0	0	0	0	0
Days With ≥ 1.0" Snow Depth	0	0	0	0	0	0	0	0	0	0	0	0	0
Thunderstorm Days	1	1	2	3	6	12	15	16	12	5	1	1	75
Foggy Days	7	5	4	3	3	1	1	1	1	3	5	6	40
Predominant Sky Cover	SCT	SCT	SCT	SCT	SCT	SCT	SCT	SCT	SCT	SCT	SCT	SCT	SCT
Mean Relative Humidity 7am (%)	85	84	82	80	81	84	84	86	88	87	85	84	84
Mean Relative Humidity 4pm (%)	60	58	57	57	61	68	66	67	69	65	63	60	63
Mean Dewpoint (°F)	58	58	60	63	68	72	73	74	73	69	64	59	66
Prevailing Wind Direction	NNW	ESE	SE	ESE	ESE	ESE	ESE	ESE	E	ENE	ENE	NNW	ESE
Prevailing Wind Speed (mph)	9	12	12	12	10	10	9	9	9	12	13	9	10
Maximum Wind Gust (mph)	58	61	60	78	62	68	56	115	94	125	53	46	125

Orlando Int'l Airport

Orlando is located in the central section of the Florida peninsula, surrounded by many lakes. Relative humidities remain high the year-round, with values near 90 percent at night and 40 to 50 percent in the afternoon. On some winter days, the humidity may drop to 20 percent.

The rainy season extends from June through September, sometimes through October when tropical storms are near. During this period, scattered afternoon thunderstorms are an almost daily occurrence, and these bring a drop in temperature to make the climate bearable. Summer temperatures above 95 degrees are rather rare. There is usually a breeze which contributes to the general comfort.

During the winter months rainfall is light. While temperatures, on infrequent occasion, may drop at night to near freezing, they rise rapidly during the day and, in brilliant sunshine, afternoons are pleasant.

Frozen precipitation in the form of snowflakes, snow pellets, or sleet is rare. However, hail is occasionally reported during thunderstorms.

Hurricanes are usually not considered a great threat to Orlando, since, to reach this area, they must pass over a substantial stretch of land and, in so doing, lose much of their punch. Sustained hurricane winds of 75 mph or higher rarely occur. Orlando, being inland, is relatively safe from high water, although heavy rains sometimes briefly flood sections of the city.

Orlando Int'l Airport *Orange County* Elevation: 95 ft. Latitude: 28° 26' N Longitude: 81° 20' W

	JAN	FEB	MAR	APR	MAY	JUN	JUL	AUG	SEP	OCT	NOV	DEC	YEAR
Mean Maximum Temp. (°F)	***70.9***	73.8	78.3	82.8	87.9	90.8	91.9	91.6	89.8	84.5	78.6	72.9	***82.8***
Mean Temp. (°F)	***59.9***	62.6	67.0	71.4	77.1	81.3	82.6	82.7	81.2	75.2	68.7	62.5	***72.7***
Mean Minimum Temp. (°F)	***48.9***	51.3	55.7	59.9	66.2	71.8	73.3	73.8	72.5	65.8	58.6	52.2	***62.5***
Extreme Maximum Temp. (°F)	***87***	89	92	95	97	100	101	100	98	95	89	90	***101***
Extreme Minimum Temp. (°F)	***19***	26	25	38	48	53	64	65	57	44	35	20	***19***
Days Maximum Temp. ≥ 90°F	0	0	0	3	12	20	25	25	19	4	0	0	108
Days Maximum Temp. ® 32°F	0	0	0	0	0	0	0	0	0	0	0	0	0
Days Minimum Temp. ® 32°F	***2***	1	0	0	0	0	0	0	0	0	0	1	***4***
Days Minimum Temp. ® 0°F	0	0	0	0	0	0	0	0	0	0	0	0	0
Heating Degree Days (base 65°F)	***197***	126	59	9	1	0	0	0	0	3	42	141	***578***
Cooling Degree Days (base 65°F)	50	67	124	203	382	498	559	562	491	336	160	75	3,507
Mean Precipitation (in.)	***2.51***	2.43	3.70	2.51	3.85	7.42	7.36	6.38	5.89	2.87	2.44	2.34	***49.70***
Maximum Precipitation (in.)	7.2	8.3	11.4	9.1	10.4	15.3	13.3	11.6	10.3	5.6	10.3	5.3	67.8
Minimum Precipitation (in.)	0.2	0.1	1.1	0.1	0.5	3.5	2.6	2.9	2.5	0.4	0.2	0.2	31.7
Maximum 24-hr. Precipitation (in.)	4.2	2.4	4.1	5.1	3.1	4.4	4.1	3.0	3.6	2.4	3.8	2.8	5.1
Days With ≥ 0.1" Precipitation	***4***	4	5	3	6	10	11	11	9	5	4	4	***76***
Days With ≥ 1.0" Precipitation	***1***	1	1	1	1	2	2	2	2	1	1	1	***16***
Mean Snowfall (in.)	trace	0.0	trace	trace	trace	0.0	trace	trace	0.0	0.0	0.0	0.0	trace
Maximum Snowfall (in.)	trace	0	0	0	0	0	0	0	0	0	0	0	trace
Maximum 24-hr. Snowfall (in.)	trace	0	0	0	0	0	0	0	0	0	0	0	trace
Days With ≥ 1.0" Snow Depth	***0***	0	0	0	0	0	0	0	0	0	0	0	***0***
Thunderstorm Days	1	2	3	3	8	16	19	19	11	3	1	1	87
Foggy Days	16	14	15	13	13	12	10	9	11	14	16	17	160
Predominant Sky Cover	OVR	OVR	OVR	CLR	SCT	BRK	BRK	BRK	BRK	SCT	OVR	OVR	BRK
Mean Relative Humidity 7am (%)	88	89	90	88	89	91	91	93	93	91	91	90	90
Mean Relative Humidity 4pm (%)	54	50	48	47	51	61	64	66	65	59	58	58	57
Mean Dewpoint (°F)	50	51	55	58	65	71	72	73	72	65	59	53	62
Prevailing Wind Direction	N	N	S	E	E	S	S	E	NE	N	N	N	N
Prevailing Wind Speed (mph)	9	9	10	9	9	8	8	8	8	8	9	9	9
Maximum Wind Gust (mph)	48	51	62	56	68	62	74	62	56	40	49	44	74

Pensacola Regional Airport

Pensacola is situated on a somewhat hilly, sandy slope which borders Pensacola Bay, an expanse of deep water several miles in width. The bay is separated from the Gulf of Mexico by a long, narrow island that forms a natural breakwater for the harbor. Elevations in the city range from a few feet above sea level to more than 100 feet in portions of the residential sections, and most of the city is well above storm tides.

The Gulf of Mexico, about six miles distant, moderates the climate of Pensacola by tempering the cold Northers of winter and causing cool and refreshing sea breezes during the daytime in summer.

The average temperature for the summer months is around 80 degrees with an average daily range of 12.5 degrees. Temperatures of 90 degrees or higher occur on the average of 39 times yearly. A temperature of 100 degrees or higher occurs occasionally. The average winter temperature is in the low to mid 50s with an average daily range of 15.7 degrees. On the average, the temperature falls to freezing or below on only nine days of the year. The average occurrence of the last temperature as low as 32 degrees in spring is mid-February, and the average earliest occurrence in autumn is early December, making the average growing season 292 days. Severe cold waves are rather infrequent.

Rainfall is usually well distributed through the year with the greatest frequency normally being in July and August. The greatest monthly rainfall occurs, on average, in July and least in October. Much of the rainfall in summer occurs during the daylight hours and comes in the form of thunderstorms, often producing excessive amounts. Winter rains are frequently lighter, but extend over longer periods. Snow has occurred in about 30 percent of the winters but measurable amounts are less frequent.

A moderate sea breeze usually blows off the Gulf of Mexico during most of the day in summer. Seriously destructive hurricanes are occasionally experienced in this vicinity but loss of life is rare. Hurricanes have occurred from early July to mid-October.

Pensacola Regional Airport *Escambia Co.* Elevation: 111 ft. Latitude: 30° 29' N Longitude: 87° 11' W

	JAN	FEB	MAR	APR	MAY	JUN	JUL	AUG	SEP	OCT	NOV	DEC	YEAR
Mean Maximum Temp. (°F)	60.8	64.1	70.0	76.3	83.4	89.0	90.5	90.0	87.1	79.3	70.3	63.6	77.0
Mean Temp. (°F)	51.7	54.6	60.9	67.1	74.6	80.6	82.5	82.1	78.9	69.6	60.7	54.3	68.1
Mean Minimum Temp. (°F)	42.6	45.1	51.7	57.9	65.8	72.1	74.5	74.2	70.6	59.8	51.0	45.0	59.2
Extreme Maximum Temp. (°F)	80	82	86	96	98	101	106	104	98	92	85	81	106
Extreme Minimum Temp. (°F)	5	15	22	33	48	56	66	62	49	32	25	11	5
Days Maximum Temp. ≥ 90°F	0	0	0	0	3	13	19	18	10	0	0	0	63
Days Maximum Temp. ® 32°F	0	0	0	0	0	0	0	0	0	0	0	0	0
Days Minimum Temp. ® 32°F	6	3	1	0	0	0	0	0	0	0	1	4	15
Days Minimum Temp. ® 0°F	0	0	0	0	0	0	0	0	0	0	0	0	0
Heating Degree Days (base 65°F)	415	297	166	44	1	0	0	0	1	32	172	344	1,472
Cooling Degree Days (base 65°F)	6	11	41	106	302	473	552	541	413	179	48	18	2,690
Mean Precipitation (in.)	5.44	4.90	6.53	3.90	4.65	6.59	8.03	7.01	5.57	4.35	4.23	3.98	65.18
Maximum Precipitation (in.)	18.8	11.7	13.0	15.5	10.3	21.1	20.4	14.1	15.7	14.8	12.0	15.3	92.7
Minimum Precipitation (in.)	0.6	0.5	0.8	0.4	0.1	0.3	1.7	0.9	0.4	0	0.3	0.6	28.5
Maximum 24-hr. Precipitation (in.)	5.4	4.7	11.+	5.9	4.9	6.4	5.1	6.3	9.3	5.0	3.3	3.5	11.+
Days With ≥ 0.1" Precipitation	7	6	7	5	5	7	10	9	6	4	5	6	77
Days With ≥ 1.0" Precipitation	2	1	2	1	2	2	2	2	2	1	1	1	19
Mean Snowfall (in.)	trace	trace	trace	0.0	0.0	0.0	trace	0.0	0.0	0.0	0.0	trace	trace
Maximum Snowfall (in.)	3	2	2	0	0	0	0	0	0	0	0	trace	3
Maximum 24-hr. Snowfall (in.)	2	2	2	0	0	0	0	0	0	0	0	trace	2
Days With ≥ 1.0" Snow Depth	0	0	0	0	0	0	0	0	0	0	0	0	0
Thunderstorm Days	2	3	4	4	5	10	15	14	7	2	2	1	69
Foggy Days	18	15	18	16	15	13	12	15	14	14	14	17	181
Predominant Sky Cover	OVR	OVR	OVR	CLR	SCT	SCT	SCT	SCT	SCT	CLR	CLR	OVR	SCT
Mean Relative Humidity 7am (%)	84	84	82	80	78	79	81	83	83	81	83	85	82
Mean Relative Humidity 4pm (%)	64	62	60	59	61	63	67	67	64	59	63	67	63
Mean Dewpoint (°F)	44	47	50	56	65	71	73	73	68	59	51	46	58
Prevailing Wind Direction	NNW	N	NNW	SE	SSE	SSW	SW	NE	N	N	NNW	N	N
Prevailing Wind Speed (mph)	10	10	12	12	10	9	8	7	8	8	10	9	9
Maximum Wind Gust (mph)	na	na	na	na	na	na	na	na	na	na	na	na	na

Tallahassee Municipal Airport

Located about 20 miles from the Gulf of Mexico, Tallahassee has a mild, moist climate of the Gulf States. In contrast to the southern part of the Florida Peninsula, there is a definite march of the four seasons with considerable winter rainfall and quite a bit less winter sunshine. The annual average temperature is about 68 degrees.

During the winter, topographic effects and cold air drainage into lower elevations produce a wide variation of low temperatures on cold, clear and calm nights. Freezing temperatures at the airport and surrounding suburban areas average about thirty-six occurrences each winter, but freezing temperatures in the city are about half that number. Temperatures of 25 degrees or lower in the suburban areas average about twelve times per winter, with temperatures dropping into the teens on occasions. Below zero temperatures are rarely recorded. Snow in Tallahassee is infrequent. The date for the last occurrence of 32 degrees is February 28, but has been as late as April 8. The date of the first occurrence of 32 degrees in the fall is November 25, but has been as early as October 18. This gives an average growing season of some 270 days.

Summer is the least pleasant time of the year. Thunderstorms occur every other day. Rather high temperatures and very high humidities cause considerable discomfort. Occurrences of temperatures of 90 degrees or higher average about 90 days per year, but only about 22 of these days have readings as high as 95 degrees. Temperatures reach 100 degrees once or twice in less than half the years. In general, summertime cloudiness holds the high temperatures about 90 degrees.

July is the wettest month followed by August, September, and June. The driest months are October, November, and April.

Extended droughts are infrequent, shorter droughts are rather common, but both are significant. Droughts, or rainfall deficiencies, when extended over months or years, cause the disappearance of large lakes and cypress ponds. Droughts of shorter duration create fire danger in the nearby forests.

High winds are infrequent and of short duration, usually associated with strong cold fronts in the late winter and early spring months. The likelihood of a hurricane occurrence in our coastal area is about once every 17 years with fringe effects felt about once every five years.

Tallahassee Municipal Airport *Leon County* Elevation: 52 ft. Latitude: 30° 24' N Longitude: 84° 21' W

	JAN	FEB	MAR	APR	MAY	JUN	JUL	AUG	SEP	OCT	NOV	DEC	YEAR
Mean Maximum Temp. (°F)	63.5	67.2	73.8	80.1	86.3	90.8	91.8	91.3	88.7	81.2	72.9	66.1	79.5
Mean Temp. (°F)	51.3	54.2	60.5	66.0	73.6	79.6	81.6	81.4	78.4	68.7	60.0	53.6	67.4
Mean Minimum Temp. (°F)	39.1	41.1	47.1	51.8	60.9	68.4	71.3	71.4	68.1	56.3	47.0	41.2	55.3
Extreme Maximum Temp. (°F)	82	85	89	95	99	103	103	103	99	94	87	84	103
Extreme Minimum Temp. (°F)	6	14	20	29	34	46	59	57	45	30	13	13	6
Days Maximum Temp. ≥ 90°F	0	0	0	1	8	19	24	23	16	2	0	0	93
Days Maximum Temp. ® 32°F	0	0	0	0	0	0	0	0	0	0	0	0	0
Days Minimum Temp. ® 32°F	11	7	3	0	0	0	0	0	0	0	4	9	34
Days Minimum Temp. ® 0°F	0	0	0	0	0	0	0	0	0	0	0	0	0
Heating Degree Days (base 65°F)	427	312	180	67	5	0	0	0	1	45	193	362	1,592
Cooling Degree Days (base 65°F)	6	15	46	101	288	457	533	526	406	181	53	15	2,627
Mean Precipitation (in.)	5.49	4.74	6.74	3.67	5.09	6.99	8.41	7.06	4.78	3.38	3.84	4.12	64.31
Maximum Precipitation (in.)	18.9	11.5	16.5	13.1	11.7	17.4	20.1	15.7	20.3	12.3	10.4	12.6	104.
Minimum Precipitation (in.)	0.2	0.8	1.0	0.3	trace	2.1	2.3	2.4	0.1	trace	0.4	0.9	31.0
Maximum 24-hr. Precipitation (in.)	4.9	5.6	7.1	4.9	5.1	6.7	8.2	7.1	8.9	6.6	4.9	5.0	8.9
Days With ≥ 0.1" Precipitation	7	6	6	4	6	9	11	10	7	4	4	6	80
Days With ≥ 1.0" Precipitation	2	2	2	1	2	2	2	2	1	1	1	1	19
Mean Snowfall (in.)	trace	trace	trace	0.0	***0.0***	trace	trace	0.0	trace	0.0	0.0	trace	***trace***
Maximum Snowfall (in.)	trace	3	trace	0	0	0	0	0	0	0	0	1	3
Maximum 24-hr. Snowfall (in.)	trace	2	trace	0	0	0	0	0	0	0	0	1	2
Days With ≥ 1.0" Snow Depth	0	0	0	0	0	0	0	0	0	0	0	0	0
Thunderstorm Days	2	2	4	4	8	14	19	16	8	2	2	2	83
Foggy Days	17	16	18	17	19	18	17	19	18	16	16	17	208
Predominant Sky Cover	OVR	OVR	OVR	CLR	SCT	SCT	BRK	SCT	SCT	CLR	CLR	OVR	OVR
Mean Relative Humidity 7am (%)	87	87	88	89	89	91	93	94	92	90	89	87	90
Mean Relative Humidity 4pm (%)	54	51	49	46	50	58	66	64	60	51	52	55	55
Mean Dewpoint (°F)	42	44	49	55	62	69	72	72	69	58	49	44	57
Prevailing Wind Direction	N	N	S	S	S	S	S	E	ENE	N	N	N	N
Prevailing Wind Speed (mph)	8	9	10	10	9	8	7	6	8	7	8	8	8
Maximum Wind Gust (mph)	53	51	53	54	81	76	67	64	83	58	68	43	83

Tampa Int'l Airport

Tampa is on west central coast of the Florida Peninsula. Very near the Gulf of Mexico at the upper end of Tampa Bay, land and sea breezes modify the subtropical climate. Major rivers flowing into the area are the Hillsborough, the Alafia, and the Little Manatee.

Winters are mild. Summers are long, rather warm, and humid. Low temperatures are about 50 degrees in the winter and 70 degrees during the summer. Afternoon highs range from the low 70s in the winter to around 90 degrees from June through September. Invasions of cold northern air produce an occasional cool winter morning. Freezing temperatures occur on one or two mornings per year during December, January, and February. In some years no freezing temperatures occur. Temperatures rarely fail to recover to the 60s on the cooler winter days. Temperatures above the low 90s are uncommon because of the afternoon sea breezes and thunderstorms. An outstanding feature of the Tampa climate is the summer thunderstorm season. Most of the thunderstorms occur in the late afternoon hours from June through September. The resulting sudden drop in temperature from about 90 degrees to around 70 degrees makes for a pleasant change. Between a dry spring and a dry fall, some 30 inches of rain, about 60 percent of the annual total, falls during the summer months. Snowfall is very rare.

A large part of the generally flat sandy land near the coast has an elevation of under 15 feet above sea level. This does make the area vulnerable to tidal surges. Tropical storms threaten the area on a few occasions most years. The greatest risk of hurricanes has been during the months of June and October. Many hurricanes, by replenishing the soil moisture and raising the water table, do far more good than harm. The heaviest rains in a 24-hour period, around 12 inches, have been associated with hurricanes.

Fittingly named the Suncoast, the sun shines more than 65 percent of the possible, with the sunniest months being April and May. Afternoon humidities are usually 60 percent or higher in the summer months, but range from 50 to 60 percent the remainder of the year.

Night ground fogs occur frequently during the cooler winter months. Prevailing winds are easterly, but westerly afternoon and early evening sea breezes occur most months of the year. Winds in excess of 25 mph are not common and usually occur only with thunderstorms or tropical disturbances.

Based on the 1951-1980 period, the average first occurrence of 32 degrees Fahrenheit in the fall is December 26 and the average last occurrence in the spring is February 3.

Tampa Int'l Airport *Hillsborough County* Elevation: 16 ft. Latitude: 27° 58' N Longitude: 82° 32' W

	JAN	FEB	MAR	APR	MAY	JUN	JUL	AUG	SEP	OCT	NOV	DEC	YEAR
Mean Maximum Temp. (°F)	70.5	72.2	76.9	81.5	87.2	89.9	90.7	90.6	89.3	84.4	78.2	72.6	82.0
Mean Temp. (°F)	60.6	62.2	67.0	71.5	77.6	81.7	82.8	82.8	81.3	75.4	68.5	62.8	72.8
Mean Minimum Temp. (°F)	50.6	52.1	56.9	61.4	68.0	73.5	74.8	74.8	73.3	66.3	58.8	53.0	63.6
Extreme Maximum Temp. (°F)	86	88	89	93	98	99	97	98	96	94	90	86	99
Extreme Minimum Temp. (°F)	21	25	29	40	49	53	63	67	57	44	23	19	19
Days Maximum Temp. ≥ 90°F	0	0	0	1	8	17	22	22	17	3	0	0	90
Days Maximum Temp. ® 32°F	0	0	0	0	0	0	0	0	0	0	0	0	0
Days Minimum Temp. ® 32°F	1	1	0	0	0	0	0	0	0	0	0	1	3
Days Minimum Temp. ® 0°F	0	0	0	0	0	0	0	0	0	0	0	0	0
Heating Degree Days (base 65°F)	187	134	61	11	0	0	0	0	0	3	47	139	582
Cooling Degree Days (base 65°F)	54	70	124	209	405	513	561	562	494	337	166	80	3,575
Mean Precipitation (in.)	2.31	2.80	3.03	1.81	2.99	5.42	6.31	7.70	6.50	2.32	1.59	2.29	45.07
Maximum Precipitation (in.)	8.0	7.9	12.6	6.6	17.6	13.8	20.6	18.6	14.0	7.4	6.1	6.7	76.6
Minimum Precipitation (in.)	trace	0.2	0.1	trace	0.1	1.9	1.6	2.3	1.3	0.1	trace	0.1	28.9
Maximum 24-hr. Precipitation (in.)	3.3	3.1	4.3	3.3	11.+	5.5	9.1	4.9	4.4	2.7	3.8	2.7	11.+
Days With ≥ 0.1" Precipitation	4	4	4	3	4	8	10	11	8	4	3	4	67
Days With ≥ 1.0" Precipitation	1	1	1	0	1	2	2	3	2	1	0	1	15
Mean Snowfall (in.)	trace	0.0	trace	trace	0.0	0.0	trace	0.0	0.0	0.0	0.0	trace	trace
Maximum Snowfall (in.)	trace	trace	trace	0	0	0	0	0	0	0	0	trace	trace
Maximum 24-hr. Snowfall (in.)	trace	trace	trace	0	0	0	0	0	0	0	0	trace	trace
Days With ≥ 1.0" Snow Depth	0	0	0	0	0	0	0	0	0	0	0	0	0
Thunderstorm Days	1	2	3	3	5	14	21	20	12	3	1	1	86
Foggy Days	15	13	13	10	10	8	6	8	9	9	12	14	127
Predominant Sky Cover	OVR	OVR	SCT	CLR	SCT	SCT	BRK	BRK	SCT	SCT	CLR	CLR	SCT
Mean Relative Humidity 7am (%)	87	87	87	86	85	86	88	90	91	89	88	87	88
Mean Relative Humidity 4pm (%)	57	55	54	51	52	60	65	66	64	57	56	58	58
Mean Dewpoint (°F)	51	52	56	60	65	71	73	73	72	65	58	53	62
Prevailing Wind Direction	NE	E	E	E	E	W	E	E	ENE	NE	NE	NE	ENE
Prevailing Wind Speed (mph)	8	8	8	9	9	10	7	7	8	9	8	8	8
Maximum Wind Gust (mph)	55	73	58	56	99	78	67	59	75	53	54	60	99

Vero Beach

Vero Beach is located on the southeast coast of Florida, separated from the Atlantic Ocean by the Inland Waterway and a narrow island offshore. Its climate is strongly influenced by this maritime location. Temperatures in summer rarely reach 100 degrees. The average maximum temperature in July and August is about 90 degrees. In winter the average minimum temperature is slightly above 50 degrees with record lows near 20 degrees. On average, only one day a year experiences freezing temperatures, usually in January.

Rainfall occurs in all seasons but most abundantly in summer when showers are common. Thunderstorms are present approximately 70 to 80 days a year. Monthly precipitation amounts in winter are about half those in summer, and are due in part to cold frontal systems traversing the region. Throughout the year, relative humidity at 7 A.M. tends to range from 80 to 90 percent. The 1 P.M. humidity ranges from 60 to 70 percent with lower values occurring in midafternoon when temperatures are the highest.

Vero Beach lies at the northern boundary of a tropical rainy region. Within that region during summer and fall there may be hurricane activity. Of those hurricanes that pass close to Vero Beach, many move northward offshore, some cross the peninsula of Florida moving generally eastward but being weakened by their passage over land, and some enter the coastal area from the Atlantic Ocean. The frequency of the latter group has been small, about five in 114 years.

Vero Beach *Indian River County* Elevation: 19 ft. Latitude: 27° 38' N Longitude: 80° 27' W

	JAN	FEB	MAR	APR	MAY	JUN	JUL	AUG	SEP	OCT	NOV	DEC	YEAR
Mean Maximum Temp. (°F)	73.1	74.1	77.9	81.5	85.6	88.6	90.4	90.3	88.6	84.5	79.5	74.8	82.4
Mean Temp. (°F)	61.9	63.0	67.1	70.8	75.6	79.5	81.1	81.2	80.1	75.5	69.7	64.1	72.5
Mean Minimum Temp. (°F)	50.6	51.8	56.2	60.1	65.5	70.4	71.7	72.1	71.5	66.5	59.9	53.5	62.5
Extreme Maximum Temp. (°F)	86	89	92	95	97	98	99	97	96	93	90	87	99
Extreme Minimum Temp. (°F)	23	29	26	37	46	56	62	63	63	44	31	24	23
Days Maximum Temp. ≥ 90°F	0	0	0	2	5	13	21	21	13	2	0	0	77
Days Maximum Temp. ® 32°F	0	0	0	0	0	0	0	0	0	0	0	0	0
Days Minimum Temp. ® 32°F	1	1	0	0	0	0	0	0	0	0	0	0	2
Days Minimum Temp. ® 0°F	0	0	0	0	0	0	0	0	0	0	0	0	0
Heating Degree Days (base 65°F)	152	117	55	13	1	0	0	0	0	2	32	107	479
Cooling Degree Days (base 65°F)	61	73	123	188	334	448	515	516	459	342	185	89	3,333
Mean Precipitation (in.)	2.79	2.98	3.96	2.49	4.46	6.94	6.18	6.95	7.24	5.61	3.83	2.28	55.71
Maximum Precipitation (in.)	8.9	6.8	12.8	8.8	5.8	10.8	11.1	11.7	15.4	12.4	11.8	5.9	66.7
Minimum Precipitation (in.)	0.3	0.3	0.2	trace	0.3	1.5	2.9	2.0	1.7	0.8	0.3	0.2	35.2
Maximum 24-hr. Precipitation (in.)	2.8	2.5	6.8	4.1	2.7	2.6	3.4	6.4	7.2	4.5	4.8	2.6	7.2
Days With ≥ 0.1" Precipitation	5	5	5	5	7	9	10	10	11	8	5	4	84
Days With ≥ 1.0" Precipitation	1	1	1	1	1	2	2	2	2	1	1	0	15
Mean Snowfall (in.)	trace	0.0	0.0	0.0	0.0	0.0	0.0	0.0	0.0	0.0	0.0	0.0	trace
Maximum Snowfall (in.)	0	0	0	0	0	0	0	0	0	0	0	0	0
Maximum 24-hr. Snowfall (in.)	0	0	0	0	0	0	0	0	0	0	0	0	0
Days With ≥ 1.0" Snow Depth	0	0	0	0	0	0	0	0	0	0	0	0	0
Thunderstorm Days	1	1	3	4	6	12	16	15	10	4	1	< 1	73
Foggy Days	12	12	12	10	10	8	7	9	7	9	11	12	119
Predominant Sky Cover	SCT	SCT	SCT	SCT	SCT	SCT	SCT	SCT	SCT	SCT	SCT	SCT	SCT
Mean Relative Humidity 7am (%)	89	88	86	84	83	86	88	90	90	87	87	88	87
Mean Relative Humidity 4pm (%)	63	60	59	58	62	69	69	70	70	68	66	64	65
Mean Dewpoint (°F)	56	56	58	61	67	72	73	74	73	68	62	56	65
Prevailing Wind Direction	NW	ESE	SE	ESE	ESE	ESE	ESE	ESE	ENE	NE	NW	NW	ESE
Prevailing Wind Speed (mph)	10	12	14	12	12	12	10	10	10	12	9	9	12
Maximum Wind Gust (mph)	na	na	na	na	na	na	na	na	na	na	na	na	na

West Palm Beach Int'l Airport

West Palm Beach and Palm Beach, both located on the coastal sand ridge of southeastern Florida, are separated by Lake Worth, a portion of the Inland Waterway. The entire coastal ridge is only about five miles wide and in early times the Everglades reached to its western edge. Now most of the swampland has been drained and is devoted to agriculture, the peat-like muck soil being very fertile when fortified with certain lacking minerals. The Atlantic Ocean forms the eastern edge of Palm Beach, and the Gulf Stream flows northward about two miles offshore, its nearest approach to the Florida coast.

Because of its southerly location and marine influences, the Palm Beach area has a notably equable climate. Cold continental air must either travel over water or flow down the Florida Peninsula to reach the area, and in either case its cold is appreciably modified. Actually, the coldest weather, with infrequent frosts, is experienced the second or third night after the arrival of the cold air, due to the loss of heat through radiation cooling. The frequency of temperatures as low as the freezing mark is about one per three years at the National Weather Service Office, but in the farmlands farther from the coast the frequency of light freezes is much higher.

Summer temperatures are tempered by the ocean breeze, and by the frequent formation of cumulus clouds, which shade the land somewhat without completely obscuring the sun. Temperatures of 89 degrees or higher have occurred in all months of the year, but the 100 degree mark has rarely occurred. August is the warmest month and has an average maximum temperature of about 90 degrees. The occurrence of 90 degree temperatures in August is so common that such can be expected on more than two-thirds of the days. However, temperatures as high as 100 degrees rarely occur.

The moist, unstable air in this area results in frequent showers, usually of short duration. Thunderstorms are frequent during the summer, occurring every other day. Rainfall is heaviest during the summer and fall, the fall rainfall occurring from occasional heavy rains accompanying tropical disturbances. High winds, associated with hurricanes, have been estimated at about 140 mph in the city.

Flying weather is usually very good in this area, with instrument weather occurring only rarely. Heavy fog occurs on an average of only one morning a month in the winter and spring, and almost never in the summer and fall.

W. Palm Beach Int'l Airport *Palm Beach Co.* Elevation: 16 ft. Latitude: 26° 41' N Longitude: 80° 06' W

	JAN	FEB	MAR	APR	MAY	JUN	JUL	AUG	SEP	OCT	NOV	DEC	YEAR
Mean Maximum Temp. (°F)	75.0	76.1	79.0	82.2	85.8	88.6	90.1	90.1	88.6	85.1	80.4	76.6	83.1
Mean Temp. (°F)	66.1	67.1	70.4	73.8	78.2	81.1	82.6	82.8	81.6	78.2	73.0	68.3	75.3
Mean Minimum Temp. (°F)	57.1	58.0	61.8	65.5	70.5	73.7	75.0	75.4	74.7	71.3	65.6	60.0	67.4
Extreme Maximum Temp. (°F)	87	89	94	99	96	98	99	97	95	95	91	88	99
Extreme Minimum Temp. (°F)	27	32	30	43	51	61	68	69	67	48	37	28	27
Days Maximum Temp. ≥ 90°F	0	0	0	2	4	11	19	20	11	2	0	0	69
Days Maximum Temp. ≤ 32°F	0	0	0	0	0	0	0	0	0	0	0	0	0
Days Minimum Temp. ≤ 32°F	0	0	0	0	0	0	0	0	0	0	0	0	0
Days Minimum Temp. ≤ 0°F	0	0	0	0	0	0	0	0	0	0	0	0	0
Heating Degree Days (base 65°F)	84	59	26	3	0	0	0	0	0	0	11	55	238
Cooling Degree Days (base 65°F)	122	137	196	274	416	501	561	564	512	426	266	164	4,139
Mean Precipitation (in.)	3.86	2.63	4.01	3.47	5.57	7.75	5.86	6.73	8.12	5.37	5.38	3.06	61.81
Maximum Precipitation (in.)	11.0	8.7	16.8	12.6	15.2	17.9	13.3	20.1	24.9	18.7	14.6	11.7	85.9
Minimum Precipitation (in.)	0.2	0.3	0.3	trace	0.4	1.1	1.2	1.7	1.8	1.2	0.2	0.1	37.3
Maximum 24-hr. Precipitation (in.)	6.8	2.9	5.6	6.5	7.0	4.9	5.3	8.0	5.7	7.1	7.4	6.4	8.0
Days With ≥ 0.1" Precipitation	5	5	5	4	7	11	10	11	12	8	6	5	89
Days With ≥ 1.0" Precipitation	1	1	1	1	2	3	1	2	3	1	2	1	19
Mean Snowfall (in.)	trace	0.0	trace	0.0	0.0	0.0	0.0	trace	0.0	0.0	0.0	0.0	trace
Maximum Snowfall (in.)	trace	0	0	0	0	0	0	0	0	0	0	0	trace
Maximum 24-hr. Snowfall (in.)	trace	0	0	0	0	0	0	0	0	0	0	0	trace
Days With ≥ 1.0" Snow Depth	0	0	0	0	0	0	0	0	0	0	0	0	0
Thunderstorm Days	1	1	3	4	7	13	16	16	11	4	2	1	79
Foggy Days	7	6	6	4	3	3	2	2	2	4	5	6	50
Predominant Sky Cover	SCT	SCT	SCT	SCT	SCT	SCT	SCT	SCT	SCT	SCT	SCT	SCT	SCT
Mean Relative Humidity 7am (%)	84	84	83	79	80	84	85	86	87	85	84	84	84
Mean Relative Humidity 4pm (%)	61	59	58	58	63	69	68	68	70	66	64	62	64
Mean Dewpoint (°F)	56	57	59	62	67	72	73	73	73	68	63	58	65
Prevailing Wind Direction	NW	NW	SE	SE	ESE	ESE	ESE	ESE	E	ENE	E	NW	E
Prevailing Wind Speed (mph)	10	10	13	13	12	10	10	10	12	14	14	10	12
Maximum Wind Gust (mph)	62	52	74	63	74	92	59	66	75	49	47	53	92

Arcadia *Desoto County* Elevation: 62 ft. Latitude: 27° 14' N Longitude: 81° 51' W

	JAN	FEB	MAR	APR	MAY	JUN	JUL	AUG	SEP	OCT	NOV	DEC	YEAR
Mean Maximum Temp. (°F)	73.8	75.4	80.1	84.3	89.2	91.1	91.8	91.5	89.8	85.5	79.8	75.1	83.9
Mean Temp. (°F)	61.4	62.6	67.2	70.9	76.4	79.9	81.3	81.3	80.0	74.9	68.5	63.4	72.3
Mean Minimum Temp. (°F)	49.0	49.6	54.2	57.4	63.3	68.7	70.7	71.1	70.2	64.4	57.0	51.7	60.6
Extreme Maximum Temp. (°F)	88	92	94	98	100	104	100	98	97	98	92	89	104
Extreme Minimum Temp. (°F)	18	24	26	32	43	52	61	62	56	41	23	22	18
Days Maximum Temp. ≥ 90°F	0	0	1	5	16	22	26	26	19	5	0	0	120
Days Maximum Temp. ≤ 32°F	0	0	0	0	0	0	0	0	0	0	0	0	0
Days Minimum Temp. ≤ 32°F	3	2	0	0	0	0	0	0	0	0	0	2	7
Days Minimum Temp. ≤ 0°F	0	0	0	0	0	0	0	0	0	0	0	0	0
Heating Degree Days (base 65°F)	164	124	56	14	0	0	0	0	0	3	40	122	523
Cooling Degree Days (base 65°F)	51	***64***	121	189	364	460	519	515	457	326	154	79	***3,299***
Mean Precipitation (in.)	2.20	2.55	3.28	1.74	4.15	8.04	7.39	6.96	6.75	2.85	2.11	1.80	49.82
Days With ≥ 0.1" Precipitation	3	3	4	3	5	9	10	10	9	4	3	3	66
Days With ≥ 1.0" Precipitation	1	1	1	1	1	3	2	2	2	1	1	1	17
Mean Snowfall (in.)	0.0	0.0	0.0	0.0	0.0	0.0	0.0	0.0	0.0	0.0	0.0	0.0	0.0
Days With ≥ 1.0" Snow Depth	0	0	0	0	0	0	0	0	0	0	0	0	0

Archbold Bio Station *Highlands County* Elevation: 137 ft. Latitude: 27° 11' N Longitude: 81° 21' W

	JAN	FEB	MAR	APR	MAY	JUN	JUL	AUG	SEP	OCT	NOV	DEC	YEAR
Mean Maximum Temp. (°F)	74.3	76.3	80.8	85.3	89.8	91.9	93.0	92.8	91.0	86.6	81.0	75.8	84.9
Mean Temp. (°F)	61.0	62.3	66.8	70.5	75.7	79.6	80.7	81.1	79.9	74.8	68.9	63.2	72.0
Mean Minimum Temp. (°F)	47.6	48.3	52.7	55.6	61.6	67.2	68.4	69.2	68.7	63.0	56.8	50.5	59.1
Extreme Maximum Temp. (°F)	87	91	94	98	100	102	103	99	98	96	96	90	103
Extreme Minimum Temp. (°F)	13	21	24	27	36	50	58	60	56	38	28	18	13
Days Maximum Temp. ≥ 90°F	0	0	2	7	17	23	28	28	23	8	1	0	137
Days Maximum Temp. ≤ 32°F	0	0	0	0	0	0	0	0	0	0	0	0	0
Days Minimum Temp. ≤ 32°F	4	3	1	0	0	0	0	0	0	0	0	2	10
Days Minimum Temp. ≤ 0°F	0	0	0	0	0	0	0	0	0	0	0	0	0
Heating Degree Days (base 65°F)	177	136	67	23	1	0	0	0	0	4	40	129	577
Cooling Degree Days (base 65°F)	58	72	125	189	337	451	501	511	451	319	163	79	3,256
Mean Precipitation (in.)	2.44	2.48	3.48	2.28	4.11	7.90	7.79	7.50	6.40	3.06	2.06	1.94	51.44
Days With ≥ 0.1" Precipitation	4	4	4	4	6	11	11	11	10	5	3	3	76
Days With ≥ 1.0" Precipitation	1	1	1	1	2	3	3	2	2	1	1	1	19
Mean Snowfall (in.)	trace	0.0	0.0	0.0	0.0	0.0	0.0	0.0	0.0	0.0	0.0	0.0	trace
Days With ≥ 1.0" Snow Depth	0	0	0	0	0	0	0	0	0	0	0	0	0

Avon Park 2 W *Highlands County* Elevation: 150 ft. Latitude: 27° 36' N Longitude: 81° 32' W

	JAN	FEB	MAR	APR	MAY	JUN	JUL	AUG	SEP	OCT	NOV	DEC	YEAR
Mean Maximum Temp. (°F)	72.3	75.1	79.2	83.8	88.5	90.8	91.8	91.6	89.9	85.2	79.4	74.5	83.5
Mean Temp. (°F)	60.0	62.7	67.0	71.5	76.7	80.4	81.7	81.7	80.3	74.9	68.3	62.9	72.3
Mean Minimum Temp. (°F)	47.7	50.3	54.7	59.1	64.9	70.0	71.5	71.8	70.7	64.5	57.3	51.3	61.1
Extreme Maximum Temp. (°F)	88	92	93	95	98	101	100	99	99	96	92	88	101
Extreme Minimum Temp. (°F)	18	26	23	34	44	50	62	59	58	43	29	23	18
Days Maximum Temp. ≥ 90°F	0	0	0	4	13	21	26	25	19	5	0	0	113
Days Maximum Temp. ≤ 32°F	0	0	0	0	0	0	0	0	0	0	0	0	0
Days Minimum Temp. ≤ 32°F	3	1	0	0	0	0	0	0	0	0	0	1	5
Days Minimum Temp. ≤ 0°F	0	0	0	0	0	0	0	0	0	0	0	0	0
Heating Degree Days (base 65°F)	201	126	62	14	1	0	0	0	0	4	45	137	590
Cooling Degree Days (base 65°F)	49	74	122	203	366	470	526	526	462	319	149	75	3,341
Mean Precipitation (in.)	2.57	2.47	3.16	2.16	3.75	8.23	7.10	7.21	5.99	3.10	2.28	1.84	49.86
Days With ≥ 0.1" Precipitation	4	4	4	3	6	10	11	11	9	5	3	3	73
Days With ≥ 1.0" Precipitation	1	1	1	1	1	3	2	2	2	1	1	1	17
Mean Snowfall (in.)	trace	0.0	0.0	0.0	0.0	0.0	0.0	0.0	0.0	0.0	0.0	0.0	trace
Days With ≥ 1.0" Snow Depth	0	0	0	0	0	0	0	0	0	0	0	0	0

Bartow *Polk County* Elevation: 124 ft. Latitude: 27° 54' N Longitude: 81° 51' W

	JAN	FEB	MAR	APR	MAY	JUN	JUL	AUG	SEP	OCT	NOV	DEC	YEAR
Mean Maximum Temp. (°F)	73.4	75.2	80.0	84.3	88.9	91.4	92.3	92.3	90.4	85.4	79.7	74.7	84.0
Mean Temp. (°F)	61.8	63.4	67.9	72.2	77.5	81.3	82.4	82.5	81.0	75.2	69.2	63.5	73.2
Mean Minimum Temp. (°F)	50.1	51.6	55.8	60.1	66.0	71.2	72.4	72.7	71.5	64.9	58.6	52.2	62.3
Extreme Maximum Temp. (°F)	86	89	93	96	98	103	101	99	96	94	93	90	103
Extreme Minimum Temp. (°F)	20	23	23	39	49	59	63	63	56	42	32	22	20
Days Maximum Temp. ≥ 90°F	0	0	1	4	14	23	27	27	21	4	0	0	121
Days Maximum Temp. ≤ 32°F	0	0	0	0	0	0	0	0	0	0	0	0	0
Days Minimum Temp. ≤ 32°F	2	1	0	0	0	0	0	0	0	0	0	1	4
Days Minimum Temp. ≤ 0°F	0	0	0	0	0	0	0	0	0	0	0	0	0
Heating Degree Days (base 65°F)	158	112	47	7	0	0	0	0	0	2	36	121	483
Cooling Degree Days (base 65°F)	62	85	143	232	402	510	563	568	496	339	176	83	3,659
Mean Precipitation (in.)	2.58	2.89	3.31	2.54	3.95	6.76	8.44	6.56	6.62	2.74	2.17	2.38	50.94
Days With ≥ 0.1" Precipitation	4	4	5	4	5	9	12	11	9	5	4	4	76
Days With ≥ 1.0" Precipitation	1	1	1	1	1	2	3	2	2	1	1	1	17
Mean Snowfall (in.)	0.0	0.0	0.0	0.0	0.0	0.0	0.0	0.0	0.0	0.0	0.0	0.0	0.0
Days With ≥ 1.0" Snow Depth	0	0	0	0	0	0	0	0	0	0	0	0	0

Belle Glade Exp. Station *Palm Beach County* Elevation: 13 ft. Latitude: 26° 39' N Longitude: 80° 38' W

	JAN	FEB	MAR	APR	MAY	JUN	JUL	AUG	SEP	OCT	NOV	DEC	YEAR
Mean Maximum Temp. (°F)	75.0	76.4	79.9	83.6	87.3	89.8	91.2	91.2	89.7	85.9	80.9	76.5	84.0
Mean Temp. (°F)	63.5	64.5	68.2	71.5	76.1	79.9	81.2	81.3	80.1	75.8	70.4	65.5	73.2
Mean Minimum Temp. (°F)	51.9	52.5	56.6	59.4	64.9	70.0	71.1	71.3	70.5	65.6	60.0	54.4	62.3
Extreme Maximum Temp. (°F)	88	90	92	95	97	98	97	98	97	96	91	89	98
Extreme Minimum Temp. (°F)	21	29	29	34	45	55	64	65	60	39	36	24	21
Days Maximum Temp. ≥ 90°F	0	0	1	3	8	17	24	25	18	5	0	0	101
Days Maximum Temp. ≤ 32°F	0	0	0	0	0	0	0	0	0	0	0	0	0
Days Minimum Temp. ≤ 32°F	1	0	0	0	0	0	0	0	0	0	0	1	2
Days Minimum Temp. ≤ 0°F	0	0	0	0	0	0	0	0	0	0	0	0	0
Heating Degree Days (base 65°F)	124	93	41	11	0	0	0	0	0	2	22	87	380
Cooling Degree Days (base 65°F)	80	93	144	210	350	464	516	519	460	351	196	107	3,490
Mean Precipitation (in.)	2.58	1.93	3.07	2.17	5.16	7.40	7.44	7.44	7.13	3.50	2.78	1.81	52.41
Days With ≥ 0.1" Precipitation	4	4	4	4	7	10	11	11	11	6	4	3	79
Days With ≥ 1.0" Precipitation	1	0	1	1	2	2	2	2	2	1	1	0	15
Mean Snowfall (in.)	trace	0.0	0.0	0.0	0.0	0.0	0.0	0.0	0.0	0.0	0.0	0.0	trace
Days With ≥ 1.0" Snow Depth	0	0	0	0	0	0	0	0	0	0	0	0	0

Bradenton 5 ESE *Manatee County* Elevation: 19 ft. Latitude: 27° 27' N Longitude: 82° 28' W

	JAN	FEB	MAR	APR	MAY	JUN	JUL	AUG	SEP	OCT	NOV	DEC	YEAR
Mean Maximum Temp. (°F)	72.5	74.0	78.1	82.3	87.4	90.3	91.5	91.5	90.0	85.3	79.5	74.3	83.1
Mean Temp. (°F)	61.3	62.8	67.0	70.9	76.3	80.5	82.0	82.2	80.9	75.2	68.9	63.3	72.6
Mean Minimum Temp. (°F)	50.0	51.5	55.9	59.4	65.1	70.6	72.3	72.9	71.8	65.1	58.2	52.3	62.1
Extreme Maximum Temp. (°F)	89	88	90	94	95	100	100	99	97	95	90	89	100
Extreme Minimum Temp. (°F)	23	24	30	38	46	52	62	60	59	44	29	20	20
Days Maximum Temp. ≥ 90°F	0	0	0	1	10	20	25	25	19	5	0	0	105
Days Maximum Temp. ≤ 32°F	0	0	0	0	0	0	0	0	0	0	0	0	0
Days Minimum Temp. ≤ 32°F	1	1	0	0	0	0	0	0	0	0	0	1	3
Days Minimum Temp. ≤ 0°F	0	0	0	0	0	0	0	0	0	0	0	0	0
Heating Degree Days (base 65°F)	173	125	59	14	0	0	0	0	0	3	42	128	544
Cooling Degree Days (base 65°F)	62	78	129	202	368	486	548	554	489	341	175	86	3,518
Mean Precipitation (in.)	2.99	2.72	3.52	1.79	2.96	7.42	8.50	9.43	7.17	2.99	2.34	2.44	54.27
Days With ≥ 0.1" Precipitation	4	4	4	3	4	9	12	13	10	4	3	4	74
Days With ≥ 1.0" Precipitation	1	1	1	0	1	3	3	3	2	1	1	1	18
Mean Snowfall (in.)	0.0	0.0	0.0	0.0	0.0	0.0	0.0	0.0	0.0	0.0	0.0	0.0	0.0
Days With ≥ 1.0" Snow Depth	0	0	0	0	0	0	0	0	0	0	0	0	0

Brooksville Chin Hill *Hernando County* Elevation: 239 ft. Latitude: 28° 37' N Longitude: 82° 22' W

	JAN	FEB	MAR	APR	MAY	JUN	JUL	AUG	SEP	OCT	NOV	DEC	YEAR
Mean Maximum Temp. (°F)	70.8	72.7	78.2	82.3	***87.6***	89.9	90.7	90.2	89.1	83.9	77.9	72.5	***82.1***
Mean Temp. (°F)	59.7	61.2	66.5	70.7	***76.3***	80.0	81.2	81.1	79.8	73.9	67.1	61.7	***71.6***
Mean Minimum Temp. (°F)	48.5	49.6	54.8	59.2	***64.8***	70.1	71.7	71.8	70.4	63.9	56.3	50.8	***61.0***
Extreme Maximum Temp. (°F)	89	89	90	96	100	104	100	99	96	94	89	86	104
Extreme Minimum Temp. (°F)	13	21	20	36	48	55	61	62	55	40	22	15	13
Days Maximum Temp. ≥ 90°F	0	0	0	2	9	***17***	21	21	15	2	0	0	***87***
Days Maximum Temp. ≤ 32°F	0	0	0	0	0	0	0	0	0	0	0	0	0
Days Minimum Temp. ≤ 32°F	2	1	0	0	0	0	0	0	0	0	0	1	4
Days Minimum Temp. ≤ 0°F	0	0	0	0	0	0	0	0	0	0	0	0	0
Heating Degree Days (base 65°F)	209	150	62	15	***1***	0	0	0	0	4	57	157	***655***
Cooling Degree Days (base 65°F)	45	53	109	187	***361***	458	513	***511***	449	290	131	60	***3,167***
Mean Precipitation (in.)	3.36	3.36	4.36	2.65	3.44	7.04	6.86	8.47	6.13	2.44	2.36	2.47	52.94
Days With ≥ 0.1" Precipitation	5	4	5	3	5	9	10	11	8	4	3	4	71
Days With ≥ 1.0" Precipitation	1	1	1	1	1	2	2	3	2	1	1	1	17
Mean Snowfall (in.)	0.0	0.0	0.0	0.0	0.0	0.0	0.0	0.0	0.0	0.0	0.0	0.0	0.0
Days With ≥ 1.0" Snow Depth	0	0	0	0	0	0	0	0	0	0	0	0	0

Canal Point USDA *Palm Beach County* Elevation: 29 ft. Latitude: 26° 52' N Longitude: 80° 37' W

	JAN	FEB	MAR	APR	MAY	JUN	JUL	AUG	SEP	OCT	NOV	DEC	YEAR
Mean Maximum Temp. (°F)	74.4	75.7	79.8	84.1	87.9	90.3	91.8	91.6	90.3	86.4	81.0	76.1	84.1
Mean Temp. (°F)	63.7	64.9	68.8	72.5	76.8	80.3	81.4	81.5	80.6	76.9	71.3	65.9	73.7
Mean Minimum Temp. (°F)	52.9	54.1	57.8	60.9	65.6	70.2	71.0	71.4	70.8	67.2	61.4	55.8	63.3
Extreme Maximum Temp. (°F)	89	90	92	95	97	98	100	98	98	96	91	89	100
Extreme Minimum Temp. (°F)	25	29	31	41	48	54	62	61	60	42	39	25	25
Days Maximum Temp. ≥ 90°F	0	0	1	3	11	20	26	26	21	7	0	0	115
Days Maximum Temp. ≤ 32°F	0	0	0	0	0	0	0	0	0	0	0	0	0
Days Minimum Temp. ≤ 32°F	0	0	0	0	0	0	0	0	0	0	0	0	0
Days Minimum Temp. ≤ 0°F	0	0	0	0	0	0	0	0	0	0	0	0	0
Heating Degree Days (base 65°F)	108	79	30	4	0	0	0	0	0	1	14	72	308
Cooling Degree Days (base 65°F)	73	96	158	238	376	473	524	527	478	385	218	111	3,657
Mean Precipitation (in.)	2.68	2.34	3.83	2.18	4.80	7.46	6.27	7.00	7.04	3.94	2.94	2.05	52.53
Days With ≥ 0.1" Precipitation	4	4	5	3	6	10	10	11	10	6	4	4	77
Days With ≥ 1.0" Precipitation	1	1	1	1	2	2	2	2	2	1	1	1	17
Mean Snowfall (in.)	0.0	0.0	0.0	0.0	0.0	0.0	0.0	0.0	0.0	0.0	0.0	0.0	0.0
Days With ≥ 1.0" Snow Depth	0	0	0	0	0	0	0	0	0	0	0	0	0

Chipley 3 E *Washington County* Elevation: 127 ft. Latitude: 30° 47' N Longitude: 85° 29' W

	JAN	FEB	MAR	APR	MAY	JUN	JUL	AUG	SEP	OCT	NOV	DEC	YEAR
Mean Maximum Temp. (°F)	60.2	64.5	71.7	78.4	85.1	89.7	91.4	90.8	87.6	79.7	70.7	63.5	77.8
Mean Temp. (°F)	48.9	52.5	59.4	65.6	72.9	78.7	81.1	80.5	76.7	66.8	58.1	51.7	66.1
Mean Minimum Temp. (°F)	37.6	40.4	47.0	52.7	60.6	67.8	70.7	70.1	65.8	53.9	45.5	39.9	54.3
Extreme Maximum Temp. (°F)	81	83	88	94	100	104	104	102	98	94	88	85	104
Extreme Minimum Temp. (°F)	2	13	20	31	39	47	61	55	43	29	17	10	2
Days Maximum Temp. ≥ 90°F	0	0	0	1	6	16	22	21	13	1	0	0	80
Days Maximum Temp. ≤ 32°F	0	0	0	0	0	0	0	0	0	0	0	0	0
Days Minimum Temp. ≤ 32°F	11	7	2	0	0	0	0	0	0	0	3	10	33
Days Minimum Temp. ≤ 0°F	0	0	0	0	0	0	0	0	0	0	0	0	0
Heating Degree Days (base 65°F)	499	358	206	75	6	0	0	0	2	66	234	421	1,867
Cooling Degree Days (base 65°F)	5	12	35	92	260	421	509	488	344	133	33	13	2,345
Mean Precipitation (in.)	6.11	5.04	6.18	3.80	4.31	5.32	6.88	5.47	4.62	3.11	3.93	3.84	58.61
Days With ≥ 0.1" Precipitation	8	6	7	5	6	8	10	8	6	4	5	6	79
Days With ≥ 1.0" Precipitation	2	2	2	1	1	2	2	2	1	1	1	1	18
Mean Snowfall (in.)	trace	0.0	0.0	0.0	0.0	0.0	0.0	0.0	0.0	0.0	0.0	0.0	trace
Days With ≥ 1.0" Snow Depth	0	0	0	0	0	0	0	0	0	0	0	0	0

Clermont 7 S *Lake County* Elevation: 108 ft. Latitude: 28° 27' N Longitude: 81° 45' W

	JAN	FEB	MAR	APR	MAY	JUN	JUL	AUG	SEP	OCT	NOV	DEC	YEAR
Mean Maximum Temp. (°F)	70.3	72.9	78.2	83.0	87.6	90.1	91.6	91.0	88.9	83.3	77.1	71.8	82.2
Mean Temp. (°F)	59.9	61.8	66.8	71.1	76.3	80.3	81.8	81.8	80.2	74.3	67.5	61.8	71.9
Mean Minimum Temp. (°F)	49.3	50.6	55.4	59.1	65.0	70.4	71.9	72.5	71.4	65.2	57.8	51.7	61.7
Extreme Maximum Temp. (°F)	86	89	91	94	99	101	101	98	96	94	88	87	101
Extreme Minimum Temp. (°F)	18	27	25	39	49	51	62	64	55	41	28	19	18
Days Maximum Temp. ≥ 90°F	0	0	0	3	10	17	24	21	15	2	0	0	92
Days Maximum Temp. ≤ 32°F	0	0	0	0	0	0	0	0	0	0	0	0	0
Days Minimum Temp. ≤ 32°F	2	1	0	0	0	0	0	0	0	0	0	1	4
Days Minimum Temp. ≤ 0°F	0	0	0	0	0	0	0	0	0	0	0	0	0
Heating Degree Days (base 65°F)	199	139	61	13	0	0	0	0	0	4	51	150	617
Cooling Degree Days (base 65°F)	43	60	115	189	351	463	531	528	453	301	139	59	3,232
Mean Precipitation (in.)	3.15	2.73	3.96	2.17	3.76	7.91	6.76	6.85	5.75	2.48	2.37	2.43	50.32
Days With ≥ 0.1" Precipitation	5	5	5	3	5	10	11	11	8	4	3	4	74
Days With ≥ 1.0" Precipitation	1	1	1	1	1	2	2	2	1	1	1	1	15
Mean Snowfall (in.)	trace	trace	0.0	0.0	0.0	0.0	0.0	0.0	0.0	0.0	0.0	0.0	trace
Days With ≥ 1.0" Snow Depth	0	0	0	0	0	0	0	0	0	0	0	0	0

Clewiston U.S. Engineers *Hendry County* Elevation: 19 ft. Latitude: 26° 45' N Longitude: 80° 55' W

	JAN	FEB	MAR	APR	MAY	JUN	JUL	AUG	SEP	OCT	NOV	DEC	YEAR
Mean Maximum Temp. (°F)	73.4	75.3	79.8	83.7	87.6	90.1	91.8	91.3	89.8	***85.2***	***80.0***	***74.9***	***83.6***
Mean Temp. (°F)	63.8	65.4	69.6	73.3	77.7	81.0	82.2	82.3	81.5	***77.3***	***71.9***	***66.1***	***74.3***
Mean Minimum Temp. (°F)	54.2	55.6	59.2	62.9	67.8	71.9	72.5	73.1	73.1	***69.4***	***63.7***	57.4	***65.1***
Extreme Maximum Temp. (°F)	90	92	95	98	98	101	101	101	98	97	93	90	101
Extreme Minimum Temp. (°F)	26	32	29	40	51	62	66	67	65	49	35	26	26
Days Maximum Temp. ≥ 90°F	0	0	2	4	9	17	24	23	17	4	1	0	101
Days Maximum Temp. ≤ 32°F	0	0	0	0	0	0	0	0	0	0	0	0	0
Days Minimum Temp. ≤ 32°F	1	0	0	0	0	0	0	0	0	0	0	0	1
Days Minimum Temp. ≤ 0°F	0	0	0	0	0	0	0	0	0	0	0	0	0
Heating Degree Days (base 65°F)	120	81	31	6	0	0	0	0	0	***1***	***17***	***79***	***335***
Cooling Degree Days (base 65°F)	***84***	114	***176***	***260***	410	***500***	***548***	***551***	***501***	***397***	***245***	***119***	***3,905***
Mean Precipitation (in.)	2.18	2.07	3.02	2.13	4.65	7.19	6.53	6.36	4.93	2.97	2.25	1.51	45.79
Days With ≥ 0.1" Precipitation	4	4	4	3	5	9	9	10	8	4	3	3	66
Days With ≥ 1.0" Precipitation	1	1	1	1	1	2	2	2	1	1	1	0	14
Mean Snowfall (in.)	0.0	0.0	0.0	0.0	0.0	0.0	0.0	0.0	0.0	0.0	0.0	0.0	0.0
Days With ≥ 1.0" Snow Depth	0	0	0	0	0	0	0	0	0	0	0	0	0

Cross City 2 WNW *Dixie County* Elevation: 39 ft. Latitude: 29° 39' N Longitude: 83° 10' W

	JAN	FEB	MAR	APR	MAY	JUN	JUL	AUG	SEP	OCT	NOV	DEC	YEAR
Mean Maximum Temp. (°F)	65.1	67.9	73.9	79.2	85.5	89.5	***90.4***	***90.1***	88.0	81.8	***74.3***	67.7	***79.4***
Mean Temp. (°F)	52.6	55.4	61.3	66.3	73.0	78.5	***80.4***	***80.2***	77.8	***69.8***	***62.0***	55.3	***67.7***
Mean Minimum Temp. (°F)	39.8	42.9	48.7	53.4	60.5	67.4	***70.3***	70.4	67.7	57.4	49.2	42.4	***55.8***
Extreme Maximum Temp. (°F)	84	84	90	92	100	100	101	100	96	96	89	85	101
Extreme Minimum Temp. (°F)	10	16	20	31	38	50	57	55	49	31	15	13	10
Days Maximum Temp. ≥ 90°F	0	0	0	0	5	16	***20***	***19***	13	2	0	0	***75***
Days Maximum Temp. ≤ 32°F	0	0	0	0	0	0	0	0	0	0	0	0	0
Days Minimum Temp. ≤ 32°F	9	5	1	0	0	0	0	0	0	0	2	7	24
Days Minimum Temp. ≤ 0°F	0	0	0	0	0	0	0	0	0	0	0	0	0
Heating Degree Days (base 65°F)	389	278	158	59	5	0	***0***	***0***	0	***33***	***150***	319	***1,391***
Cooling Degree Days (base 65°F)	9	18	49	96	264	416	***486***	***487***	385	198	70	21	***2,499***
Mean Precipitation (in.)	4.49	3.59	4.70	3.51	3.20	6.27	8.91	9.79	5.78	3.02	2.40	3.37	59.03
Days With ≥ 0.1" Precipitation	7	5	5	4	5	8	11	12	8	4	4	5	78
Days With ≥ 1.0" Precipitation	1	1	2	1	1	2	3	3	2	1	1	1	19
Mean Snowfall (in.)	0.0	0.0	0.0	0.0	0.0	0.0	0.0	0.0	0.0	0.0	0.0	0.0	0.0
Days With ≥ 1.0" Snow Depth	0	0	0	0	0	0	0	0	0	0	0	0	0

De Funiak Springs *Walton County* Elevation: 229 ft. Latitude: 30° 44' N Longitude: 86° 04' W

	JAN	FEB	MAR	APR	MAY	JUN	JUL	AUG	SEP	OCT	NOV	DEC	YEAR
Mean Maximum Temp. (°F)	62.5	66.0	72.7	79.2	85.6	90.4	91.8	91.2	88.1	80.5	71.3	64.5	78.6
Mean Temp. (°F)	50.4	53.5	59.9	65.7	73.0	78.7	81.0	80.4	76.8	67.2	58.2	52.6	66.4
Mean Minimum Temp. (°F)	38.2	40.9	47.1	52.2	60.3	67.0	70.1	69.5	65.4	53.9	45.1	40.6	54.2
Extreme Maximum Temp. (°F)	81	82	90	95	***99***	***104***	***105***	***101***	***99***	***93***	***88***	***83***	***105***
Extreme Minimum Temp. (°F)	3	12	19	28	***35***	***44***	***55***	***58***	***40***	***28***	***16***	***7***	***3***
Days Maximum Temp. ≥ 90°F	0	0	0	1	6	17	23	22	14	1	0	0	84
Days Maximum Temp. ≤ 32°F	0	0	0	0	0	0	0	0	0	0	0	0	0
Days Minimum Temp. ≤ 32°F	12	7	3	0	0	0	0	0	0	0	4	9	35
Days Minimum Temp. ≤ 0°F	0	0	0	0	0	0	0	0	0	0	0	0	0
Heating Degree Days (base 65°F)	455	330	191	69	5	0	0	0	2	55	228	395	1,730
Cooling Degree Days (base 65°F)	4	12	36	90	262	***425***	510	490	***353***	139	***29***	15	***2,365***
Mean Precipitation (in.)	5.39	5.75	6.40	3.96	5.03	6.93	7.95	7.04	5.91	3.60	4.68	4.42	67.06
Days With ≥ 0.1" Precipitation	7	7	7	5	6	10	12	10	7	3	5	6	85
Days With ≥ 1.0" Precipitation	2	2	3	1	1	2	2	2	2	1	2	1	21
Mean Snowfall (in.)	trace	trace	trace	0.0	0.0	0.0	0.0	0.0	0.0	0.0	0.0	0.0	trace
Days With ≥ 1.0" Snow Depth	0	0	0	0	0	0	0	0	0	0	0	0	0

Fernandina Beach *Nassau County* Elevation: 13 ft. Latitude: 30° 40' N Longitude: 81° 28' W

	JAN	FEB	MAR	APR	MAY	JUN	JUL	AUG	SEP	OCT	NOV	DEC	YEAR
Mean Maximum Temp. (°F)	62.2	65.1	70.9	76.6	82.5	87.4	89.9	88.5	85.5	78.5	71.4	65.1	77.0
Mean Temp. (°F)	52.7	55.5	61.2	67.1	73.7	79.3	81.9	81.1	78.6	71.1	62.9	56.1	68.4
Mean Minimum Temp. (°F)	43.2	45.9	51.4	57.6	65.0	71.2	73.7	73.7	71.6	63.7	54.4	47.1	59.9
Extreme Maximum Temp. (°F)	88	85	88	94	96	102	102	101	99	94	87	85	102
Extreme Minimum Temp. (°F)	4	20	22	37	40	51	63	61	52	41	24	12	4
Days Maximum Temp. ≥ 90°F	0	0	0	1	3	10	16	11	4	1	0	0	46
Days Maximum Temp. ≤ 32°F	0	0	0	0	0	0	0	0	0	0	0	0	0
Days Minimum Temp. ≤ 32°F	4	2	0	0	0	0	0	0	0	0	0	2	8
Days Minimum Temp. ≤ 0°F	0	0	0	0	0	0	0	0	0	0	0	0	0
Heating Degree Days (base 65°F)	383	276	156	49	3	0	0	0	0	17	125	288	1,297
Cooling Degree Days (base 65°F)	8	16	43	111	282	445	539	515	411	217	71	19	2,677
Mean Precipitation (in.)	3.85	3.32	4.17	2.78	2.98	5.31	5.92	5.46	7.37	4.45	2.52	2.74	50.87
Days With ≥ 0.1" Precipitation	7	6	6	4	5	8	9	8	9	5	4	5	76
Days With ≥ 1.0" Precipitation	1	1	1	1	1	1	2	2	2	1	1	1	15
Mean Snowfall (in.)	trace	trace	trace	0.0	0.0	0.0	0.0	0.0	0.0	0.0	0.0	0.0	trace
Days With ≥ 1.0" Snow Depth	0	0	0	0	0	0	0	0	0	0	0	0	0

Flamingo Ranger Station *Monroe County* Elevation: 0 ft. Latitude: 25° 09' N Longitude: 80° 55' W

	JAN	FEB	MAR	APR	MAY	JUN	JUL	AUG	SEP	OCT	NOV	DEC	YEAR
Mean Maximum Temp. (°F)	76.6	77.2	79.5	82.9	86.0	88.2	89.3	89.8	88.9	86.1	82.3	78.4	83.8
Mean Temp. (°F)	66.3	67.1	69.9	73.5	77.3	80.8	81.7	81.9	81.1	77.6	73.2	68.5	74.9
Mean Minimum Temp. (°F)	56.0	56.9	60.2	64.1	68.7	73.3	74.1	74.0	73.3	69.1	63.9	58.5	66.0
Extreme Maximum Temp. (°F)	88	92	88	94	96	104	100	97	101	99	91	89	104
Extreme Minimum Temp. (°F)	27	24	33	44	48	58	62	28	60	41	36	25	24
Days Maximum Temp. ≥ 90°F	0	0	0	0	3	9	16	19	13	2	0	0	62
Days Maximum Temp. ≤ 32°F	0	0	0	0	0	0	0	0	0	0	0	0	0
Days Minimum Temp. ≤ 32°F	0	0	0	0	0	0	0	0	0	0	0	0	0
Days Minimum Temp. ≤ 0°F	0	0	0	0	0	0	0	0	0	0	0	0	0
Heating Degree Days (base 65°F)	71	53	21	2	0	0	0	0	0	0	6	38	191
Cooling Degree Days (base 65°F)	117	132	180	268	396	489	535	535	490	410	265	160	3,977
Mean Precipitation (in.)	2.02	1.61	1.87	2.06	5.01	7.29	4.93	7.53	7.25	4.27	2.46	1.51	47.81
Days With ≥ 0.1" Precipitation	4	3	3	3	6	9	9	10	11	6	4	3	71
Days With ≥ 1.0" Precipitation	0	0	0	0	2	2	1	2	2	1	1	0	11
Mean Snowfall (in.)	0.0	0.0	0.0	0.0	0.0	0.0	0.0	0.0	0.0	0.0	0.0	0.0	0.0
Days With ≥ 1.0" Snow Depth	0	0	0	0	0	0	0	0	0	0	0	0	0

Fort Drum 5 NW *Okeechobee County* Elevation: 68 ft. Latitude: 27° 35' N Longitude: 80° 50' W

	JAN	FEB	MAR	APR	MAY	JUN	JUL	AUG	SEP	OCT	NOV	DEC	YEAR
Mean Maximum Temp. (°F)	74.7	75.9	79.7	83.7	87.8	90.4	***91.5***	91.5	89.8	***85.5***	80.4	75.6	***83.9***
Mean Temp. (°F)	62.4	63.4	67.2	70.9	75.7	79.9	***81.1***	81.5	80.1	***75.4***	69.4	64.0	***72.6***
Mean Minimum Temp. (°F)	50.1	51.0	54.7	58.0	63.5	69.3	***70.8***	71.5	70.4	***65.2***	58.5	52.3	***61.3***
Extreme Maximum Temp. (°F)	89	88	92	97	98	102	101	99	97	98	93	87	102
Extreme Minimum Temp. (°F)	17	20	27	32	42	55	60	62	60	41	24	22	17
Days Maximum Temp. ≥ 90°F	0	0	0	3	9	17	22	23	18	4	0	0	96
Days Maximum Temp. ≤ 32°F	0	0	0	0	0	0	0	0	0	0	0	0	0
Days Minimum Temp. ≤ 32°F	2	1	0	0	0	0	0	0	0	0	0	1	4
Days Minimum Temp. ≤ 0°F	0	0	0	0	0	0	0	0	0	0	0	0	0
Heating Degree Days (base 65°F)	139	108	48	10	0	0	***0***	0	0	***2***	30	109	***446***
Cooling Degree Days (base 65°F)	67	78	123	194	341	464	***522***	***530***	463	***345***	181	82	***3,390***
Mean Precipitation (in.)	2.35	2.51	3.89	2.38	4.53	8.06	7.78	7.16	6.71	3.65	2.31	1.89	53.22
Days With ≥ 0.1" Precipitation	2	4	3	3	5	9	8	8	8	4	3	3	60
Days With ≥ 1.0" Precipitation	0	1	1	1	1	3	3	2	2	1	1	0	16
Mean Snowfall (in.)	trace	0.0	0.0	0.0	0.0	0.0	0.0	0.0	0.0	0.0	0.0	0.0	trace
Days With ≥ 1.0" Snow Depth	0	0	0	0	0	0	0	0	0	0	0	0	0

Fort Lauderdale *Broward County* Elevation: 13 ft. Latitude: 26° 06' N Longitude: 80° 12' W

	JAN	FEB	MAR	APR	MAY	JUN	JUL	AUG	SEP	OCT	NOV	DEC	YEAR
Mean Maximum Temp. (°F)	76.2	76.8	79.4	82.5	85.6	88.3	89.5	89.8	88.6	85.5	81.1	77.6	83.4
Mean Temp. (°F)	67.4	67.9	71.1	74.4	78.2	81.2	82.4	82.8	81.7	78.5	73.8	69.4	75.7
Mean Minimum Temp. (°F)	58.6	59.0	62.7	66.3	70.7	74.1	75.3	75.6	74.8	71.6	66.4	61.3	68.0
Extreme Maximum Temp. (°F)	88	89	92	94	97	97	99	97	98	95	89	88	99
Extreme Minimum Temp. (°F)	28	34	32	42	54	63	64	66	65	47	36	30	28
Days Maximum Temp. ≥ 90°F	0	0	0	1	4	10	15	18	9	2	0	0	59
Days Maximum Temp. ≤ 32°F	0	0	0	0	0	0	0	0	0	0	0	0	0
Days Minimum Temp. ≤ 32°F	0	0	0	0	0	0	0	0	0	0	0	0	0
Days Minimum Temp. ≤ 0°F	0	0	0	0	0	0	0	0	0	0	0	0	0
Heating Degree Days (base 65°F)	62	45	17	2	0	0	0	0	0	0	7	39	172
Cooling Degree Days (base 65°F)	149	154	213	295	423	500	557	567	514	442	291	190	4,295
Mean Precipitation (in.)	3.03	2.79	3.02	3.77	6.43	9.92	6.59	6.95	8.34	6.21	4.55	2.53	64.13
Days With ≥ 0.1" Precipitation	5	4	4	4	8	11	10	11	12	9	6	4	88
Days With ≥ 1.0" Precipitation	1	1	1	1	2	3	2	2	2	2	1	1	19
Mean Snowfall (in.)	0.0	0.0	0.0	0.0	0.0	0.0	0.0	0.0	0.0	0.0	0.0	0.0	0.0
Days With ≥ 1.0" Snow Depth	0	0	0	0	0	0	0	0	0	0	0	0	0

Fort Pierce *St. Lucie County* Elevation: 22 ft. Latitude: 27° 28' N Longitude: 80° 21' W

	JAN	FEB	MAR	APR	MAY	JUN	JUL	AUG	SEP	OCT	NOV	DEC	YEAR
Mean Maximum Temp. (°F)	74.3	75.3	78.9	82.3	86.3	89.4	91.2	90.9	89.4	85.4	80.4	76.0	83.3
Mean Temp. (°F)	63.0	64.1	68.0	71.8	76.7	80.3	81.7	81.7	80.6	76.5	70.5	65.2	73.3
Mean Minimum Temp. (°F)	51.7	52.8	57.2	61.4	67.0	71.0	72.2	72.4	71.8	67.5	60.7	54.4	63.3
Extreme Maximum Temp. (°F)	89	89	92	97	98	100	101	98	99	96	92	88	101
Extreme Minimum Temp. (°F)	19	25	26	33	45	56	64	61	63	42	31	19	19
Days Maximum Temp. ≥ 90°F	0	0	1	2	6	14	24	24	16	4	0	0	91
Days Maximum Temp. ≤ 32°F	0	0	0	0	0	0	0	0	0	0	0	0	0
Days Minimum Temp. ≤ 32°F	1	0	0	0	0	0	0	0	0	0	0	1	2
Days Minimum Temp. ≤ 0°F	0	0	0	0	0	0	0	0	0	0	0	0	0
Heating Degree Days (base 65°F)	134	101	48	9	0	0	0	0	0	2	25	95	414
Cooling Degree Days (base 65°F)	73	87	140	213	371	471	533	528	474	365	199	105	3,559
Mean Precipitation (in.)	2.75	3.03	3.43	2.66	4.62	5.75	5.65	6.38	8.07	5.92	3.53	2.29	54.08
Days With ≥ 0.1" Precipitation	5	5	5	4	7	9	8	10	11	8	5	4	81
Days With ≥ 1.0" Precipitation	1	1	1	1	1	2	2	2	2	2	1	0	16
Mean Snowfall (in.)	trace	0.0	0.0	0.0	0.0	0.0	0.0	0.0	0.0	0.0	0.0	0.0	trace
Days With ≥ 1.0" Snow Depth	0	0	0	0	0	0	0	0	0	0	0	0	0

Hialeah *Dade County* Elevation: 9 ft. Latitude: 25° 50' N Longitude: 80° 17' W

	JAN	FEB	MAR	APR	MAY	JUN	JUL	AUG	SEP	OCT	NOV	DEC	YEAR
Mean Maximum Temp. (°F)	77.2	77.5	80.5	83.3	86.8	89.1	90.8	90.8	89.5	86.2	82.0	78.3	84.3
Mean Temp. (°F)	68.1	68.5	72.4	75.1	79.1	81.8	83.4	83.5	82.4	78.8	74.3	69.8	76.4
Mean Minimum Temp. (°F)	58.5	59.5	63.9	66.9	71.3	74.5	75.9	76.0	75.2	71.3	66.6	61.2	68.4
Extreme Maximum Temp. (°F)	89	90	92	95	97	99	100	99	97	95	91	90	100
Extreme Minimum Temp. (°F)	28	36	32	40	55	60	62	60	62	51	38	30	28
Days Maximum Temp. ≥ 90°F	0	0	0	2	7	14	22	23	16	5	0	0	89
Days Maximum Temp. ≤ 32°F	0	0	0	0	0	0	0	0	0	0	0	0	0
Days Minimum Temp. ≤ 32°F	0	0	0	0	0	0	0	0	0	0	0	0	0
Days Minimum Temp. ≤ 0°F	0	0	0	0	0	0	0	0	0	0	0	0	0
Heating Degree Days (base 65°F)	55	42	14	2	0	0	0	0	0	0	6	36	155
Cooling Degree Days (base 65°F)	166	169	255	320	458	527	595	597	539	448	307	205	4,586
Mean Precipitation (in.)	2.47	2.25	3.20	3.82	6.32	10.37	6.95	9.00	8.89	6.43	3.81	2.41	65.92
Days With ≥ 0.1" Precipitation	5	4	4	4	8	12	11	12	13	9	6	4	92
Days With ≥ 1.0" Precipitation	1	1	1	1	2	3	2	3	3	2	1	1	21
Mean Snowfall (in.)	0.0	0.0	0.0	0.0	0.0	0.0	0.0	0.0	0.0	0.0	0.0	0.0	0.0
Days With ≥ 1.0" Snow Depth	0	0	0	0	0	0	0	0	0	0	0	0	0

High Springs *Alachua County* Elevation: 62 ft. Latitude: 29° 50' N Longitude: 82° 36' W

	JAN	FEB	MAR	APR	MAY	JUN	JUL	AUG	SEP	OCT	NOV	DEC	YEAR
Mean Maximum Temp. (°F)	68.0	71.9	77.9	83.3	88.6	91.6	92.5	92.0	89.8	83.4	76.8	70.5	82.2
Mean Temp. (°F)	54.1	57.6	63.5	68.4	75.1	80.1	81.5	81.3	78.7	70.5	63.2	56.9	69.2
Mean Minimum Temp. (°F)	40.2	43.1	48.9	53.4	61.6	68.5	70.6	70.6	67.6	57.8	49.4	43.2	56.2
Extreme Maximum Temp. (°F)	87	88	92	96	101	104	107	104	99	99	90	89	107
Extreme Minimum Temp. (°F)	9	17	20	30	***41***	45	55	59	49	29	26	8	***8***
Days Maximum Temp. ≥ 90°F	0	0	0	4	***15***	***22***	25	24	18	3	0	0	***111***
Days Maximum Temp. ≤ 32°F	0	0	0	0	0	0	0	0	0	0	0	0	0
Days Minimum Temp. ≤ 32°F	9	5	1	0	0	0	0	0	0	0	2	6	23
Days Minimum Temp. ≤ 0°F	0	0	0	0	0	0	0	0	0	0	0	0	0
Heating Degree Days (base 65°F)	***344***	225	114	38	***1***	0	0	0	0	23	125	269	***1,139***
Cooling Degree Days (base 65°F)	13	27	68	135	327	461	528	523	413	203	79	24	2,801
Mean Precipitation (in.)	4.42	3.80	4.52	3.36	3.81	6.81	7.34	8.19	4.37	3.05	2.19	2.72	54.58
Days With ≥ 0.1" Precipitation	6	5	6	4	6	9	11	11	7	4	4	4	77
Days With ≥ 1.0" Precipitation	2	1	2	1	1	2	2	3	1	1	1	1	18
Mean Snowfall (in.)	trace	0.0	0.0	0.0	0.0	0.0	0.0	0.0	0.0	0.0	0.0	0.0	trace
Days With ≥ 1.0" Snow Depth	0	0	0	0	0	0	0	0	0	0	0	0	0

Immokalee 3 NNW *Collier County* Elevation: 32 ft. Latitude: 26° 28' N Longitude: 81° 26' W

	JAN	FEB	MAR	APR	MAY	JUN	JUL	AUG	SEP	OCT	NOV	DEC	YEAR
Mean Maximum Temp. (°F)	76.5	78.0	81.6	84.9	89.0	90.8	91.6	91.4	89.9	86.4	81.5	77.6	84.9
Mean Temp. (°F)	64.3	65.3	69.0	72.0	76.9	80.4	81.7	82.0	80.9	76.4	70.8	66.0	73.8
Mean Minimum Temp. (°F)	52.0	52.6	56.4	59.1	64.7	69.9	71.7	72.5	71.8	66.3	60.1	54.3	62.6
Extreme Maximum Temp. (°F)	88	90	99	96	99	101	98	100	96	94	91	89	101
Extreme Minimum Temp. (°F)	20	25	30	38	49	54	63	64	64	45	27	24	20
Days Maximum Temp. ≥ 90°F	0	0	1	5	14	20	26	25	19	6	0	0	116
Days Maximum Temp. ≤ 32°F	0	0	0	0	0	0	0	0	0	0	0	0	0
Days Minimum Temp. ≤ 32°F	1	1	0	0	0	0	0	0	0	0	0	1	3
Days Minimum Temp. ≤ 0°F	0	0	0	0	0	0	0	0	0	0	0	0	0
Heating Degree Days (base 65°F)	106	81	32	7	0	0	0	0	0	1	21	75	323
Cooling Degree Days (base 65°F)	86	104	162	226	374	479	529	539	483	366	210	113	3,671
Mean Precipitation (in.)	2.34	2.30	2.98	2.42	4.23	7.92	7.04	7.53	6.43	2.82	2.31	1.76	50.08
Days With ≥ 0.1" Precipitation	4	4	4	3	6	10	12	13	10	5	3	3	77
Days With ≥ 1.0" Precipitation	1	1	1	1	1	3	2	2	2	1	1	1	17
Mean Snowfall (in.)	0.0	0.0	0.0	0.0	0.0	0.0	0.0	0.0	0.0	0.0	0.0	0.0	0.0
Days With ≥ 1.0" Snow Depth	0	0	0	0	0	0	0	0	0	0	0	0	0

Inverness 3 SE *Citrus County* Elevation: 39 ft. Latitude: 28° 48' N Longitude: 82° 19' W

	JAN	FEB	MAR	APR	MAY	JUN	JUL	AUG	SEP	OCT	NOV	DEC	YEAR
Mean Maximum Temp. (°F)	69.6	71.7	77.2	82.1	87.6	90.5	91.7	91.1	89.6	83.7	77.3	72.1	82.0
Mean Temp. (°F)	56.9	58.7	64.2	69.2	75.4	80.2	81.6	81.4	79.6	72.7	65.2	59.4	70.4
Mean Minimum Temp. (°F)	44.1	45.6	51.2	56.3	63.1	69.7	71.4	71.6	69.6	61.6	53.1	46.6	58.7
Extreme Maximum Temp. (°F)	85	89	92	94	100	101	100	99	101	94	92	89	101
Extreme Minimum Temp. (°F)	15	21	24	32	42	52	61	61	51	33	24	15	15
Days Maximum Temp. ≥ 90°F	0	0	0	3	10	19	24	23	18	4	0	0	101
Days Maximum Temp. ≤ 32°F	0	0	0	0	0	0	0	0	0	0	0	0	0
Days Minimum Temp. ≤ 32°F	5	4	1	0	0	0	0	0	0	0	1	3	14
Days Minimum Temp. ≤ 0°F	0	0	0	0	0	0	0	0	0	0	0	0	0
Heating Degree Days (base 65°F)	277	207	106	29	1	0	0	0	0	11	89	209	929
Cooling Degree Days (base 65°F)	24	36	76	145	320	456	514	513	431	258	104	39	2,916
Mean Precipitation (in.)	3.61	3.08	4.26	2.41	3.48	7.30	6.90	7.76	5.89	2.73	2.26	2.56	52.24
Days With ≥ 0.1" Precipitation	5	4	5	3	5	9	11	12	9	4	4	4	75
Days With ≥ 1.0" Precipitation	1	1	1	1	1	2	2	2	2	1	1	1	16
Mean Snowfall (in.)	0.0	0.0	0.0	0.0	0.0	0.0	0.0	0.0	0.0	0.0	0.0	0.0	0.0
Days With ≥ 1.0" Snow Depth	0	0	0	0	0	0	0	0	0	0	0	0	0

Jacksonville Beach *Duval County* Elevation: 9 ft. Latitude: 30° 17' N Longitude: 81° 24' W

	JAN	FEB	MAR	APR	MAY	JUN	JUL	AUG	SEP	OCT	NOV	DEC	YEAR
Mean Maximum Temp. (°F)	63.8	65.9	71.4	76.9	82.7	87.1	89.8	88.5	86.0	79.8	***72.3***	66.5	***77.6***
Mean Temp. (°F)	54.9	57.0	62.5	68.1	74.5	79.5	81.7	81.3	79.4	72.7	***64.1***	58.1	***69.5***
Mean Minimum Temp. (°F)	46.0	48.0	53.6	59.3	66.2	71.7	73.7	74.1	72.9	65.5	***55.8***	49.6	***61.4***
Extreme Maximum Temp. (°F)	85	85	89	94	97	99	103	102	98	93	88	85	103
Extreme Minimum Temp. (°F)	14	21	24	37	50	55	63	64	53	40	25	15	14
Days Maximum Temp. ≥ 90°F	0	0	0	1	2	8	14	9	3	1	0	0	38
Days Maximum Temp. ≤ 32°F	0	0	0	0	0	0	0	0	0	0	0	0	0
Days Minimum Temp. ≤ 32°F	3	2	0	0	0	0	0	0	0	0	0	1	6
Days Minimum Temp. ≤ 0°F	0	0	0	0	0	0	0	0	0	0	0	0	0
Heating Degree Days (base 65°F)	320	238	123	31	1	0	0	0	0	9	***102***	235	***1,059***
Cooling Degree Days (base 65°F)	9	18	50	128	305	445	533	522	437	259	***76***	28	***2,810***
Mean Precipitation (in.)	3.66	3.04	4.11	2.84	3.09	5.69	5.18	6.10	7.06	5.17	2.30	2.77	51.01
Days With ≥ 0.1" Precipitation	6	5	6	4	5	8	8	8	9	6	4	5	74
Days With ≥ 1.0" Precipitation	1	1	1	1	1	2	2	2	2	1	1	1	16
Mean Snowfall (in.)	trace	trace	0.0	0.0	0.0	0.0	0.0	0.0	0.0	0.0	0.0	trace	trace
Days With ≥ 1.0" Snow Depth	0	0	0	0	0	0	0	0	0	0	0	0	0

Jasper *Hamilton County* Elevation: 144 ft. Latitude: 30° 31' N Longitude: 82° 57' W

	JAN	FEB	MAR	APR	MAY	JUN	JUL	AUG	SEP	OCT	NOV	DEC	YEAR
Mean Maximum Temp. (°F)	64.0	66.9	73.8	79.4	85.5	90.0	91.6	91.2	88.8	81.2	73.7	66.3	79.4
Mean Temp. (°F)	51.2	54.0	60.6	66.1	72.9	78.6	80.9	80.4	77.4	68.3	60.4	53.5	67.0
Mean Minimum Temp. (°F)	38.4	41.3	47.4	52.7	60.2	67.2	70.1	69.6	66.0	55.3	47.1	40.5	54.6
Extreme Maximum Temp. (°F)	83	84	90	93	97	103	102	103	102	94	89	86	103
Extreme Minimum Temp. (°F)	4	14	19	33	39	47	59	59	45	31	15	12	4
Days Maximum Temp. ≥ 90°F	0	0	0	1	6	18	24	22	15	2	0	0	88
Days Maximum Temp. ≤ 32°F	0	0	0	0	0	0	0	0	0	0	0	0	0
Days Minimum Temp. ≤ 32°F	11	6	2	0	0	0	0	0	0	0	3	9	31
Days Minimum Temp. ≤ 0°F	0	0	0	0	0	0	0	0	0	0	0	0	0
Heating Degree Days (base 65°F)	432	316	175	66	6	0	0	0	0	47	182	367	1,591
Cooling Degree Days (base 65°F)	6	14	45	101	260	421	506	489	368	160	54	16	2,440
Mean Precipitation (in.)	4.96	4.14	5.28	3.46	3.42	5.99	5.74	6.47	3.88	2.92	2.78	3.45	52.49
Days With ≥ 0.1" Precipitation	7	6	6	4	5	9	10	10	6	3	4	5	75
Days With ≥ 1.0" Precipitation	2	1	2	1	1	2	2	2	1	1	1	1	17
Mean Snowfall (in.)	trace	trace	trace	0.0	0.0	0.0	0.0	0.0	0.0	0.0	0.0	trace	trace
Days With ≥ 1.0" Snow Depth	0	0	0	0	0	0	0	0	0	0	0	0	0

Kissimmee 2 *Osceola County* Elevation: 59 ft. Latitude: 28° 17' N Longitude: 81° 25' W

	JAN	FEB	MAR	APR	MAY	JUN	JUL	AUG	SEP	OCT	NOV	DEC	YEAR
Mean Maximum Temp. (°F)	73.4	75.2	79.3	83.2	87.5	90.7	91.8	91.6	89.8	85.0	79.8	74.7	83.5
Mean Temp. (°F)	61.6	63.1	67.5	71.3	76.3	80.7	82.1	82.2	80.7	75.2	68.9	63.2	72.8
Mean Minimum Temp. (°F)	49.8	51.0	55.6	59.3	65.1	70.8	72.4	72.8	71.6	65.3	58.0	51.7	62.0
Extreme Maximum Temp. (°F)	85	89	91	98	97	101	101	100	97	95	89	88	101
Extreme Minimum Temp. (°F)	19	27	25	38	46	53	63	65	56	42	29	20	19
Days Maximum Temp. ≥ 90°F	0	0	0	2	9	20	26	25	18	4	0	0	104
Days Maximum Temp. ≤ 32°F	0	0	0	0	0	0	0	0	0	0	0	0	0
Days Minimum Temp. ≤ 32°F	2	1	0	0	0	0	0	0	0	0	0	1	4
Days Minimum Temp. ≤ 0°F	0	0	0	0	0	0	0	0	0	0	0	0	0
Heating Degree Days (base 65°F)	159	113	52	10	0	0	0	0	0	3	37	123	497
Cooling Degree Days (base 65°F)	57	72	130	201	360	484	550	551	478	335	168	77	3,463
Mean Precipitation (in.)	2.42	2.80	3.58	2.04	3.91	6.03	6.59	7.23	5.91	3.20	2.41	2.22	48.34
Days With ≥ 0.1" Precipitation	4	4	5	3	6	9	11	11	9	5	3	4	74
Days With ≥ 1.0" Precipitation	1	1	1	0	1	2	2	2	2	1	1	1	15
Mean Snowfall (in.)	0.0	0.0	0.0	0.0	0.0	0.0	0.0	0.0	0.0	0.0	0.0	0.0	0.0
Days With ≥ 1.0" Snow Depth	0	0	0	0	0	0	0	0	0	0	0	0	0

La Belle *Hendry County* Elevation: 13 ft. Latitude: 26° 45' N Longitude: 81° 26' W

	JAN	FEB	MAR	APR	MAY	JUN	JUL	AUG	SEP	OCT	NOV	DEC	YEAR
Mean Maximum Temp. (°F)	na	77.9	***81.8***	85.9	na	92.0	na	na	na	***87.0***	na	na	na
Mean Temp. (°F)	na	64.9	***68.5***	***72.2***	na	80.6	na	na	na	***76.1***	na	na	na
Mean Minimum Temp. (°F)	na	51.8	***55.0***	***58.6***	***63.8***	69.1	na	na	na	***65.2***	na	na	na
Extreme Maximum Temp. (°F)	90	92	95	98	104	102	101	***99***	97	96	94	90	***104***
Extreme Minimum Temp. (°F)	19	24	28	37	47	55	61	***62***	60	42	27	***24***	***19***
Days Maximum Temp. ≥ 90°F	0	1	3	7	14	22	23	***24***	19	8	1	0	***122***
Days Maximum Temp. ≤ 32°F	0	0	0	0	0	0	0	0	0	0	0	0	0
Days Minimum Temp. ≤ 32°F	1	1	0	0	0	0	0	0	0	0	0	1	3
Days Minimum Temp. ≤ 0°F	0	0	0	0	0	0	0	0	0	0	0	0	0
Heating Degree Days (base 65°F)	na	91	***45***	***9***	na	0	na	na	na	***1***	na	na	na
Cooling Degree Days (base 65°F)	na	103	na	229	na	485	na	na	***488***	***357***	na	na	na
Mean Precipitation (in.)	2.44	2.23	3.30	2.27	4.10	8.86	7.73	7.79	6.26	3.36	2.30	1.68	52.32
Days With ≥ 0.1" Precipitation	3	3	4	3	5	9	10	9	8	4	2	2	62
Days With ≥ 1.0" Precipitation	1	1	1	1	1	2	2	2	2	1	1	0	15
Mean Snowfall (in.)	trace	0.0	0.0	0.0	0.0	0.0	0.0	0.0	0.0	0.0	0.0	0.0	trace
Days With ≥ 1.0" Snow Depth	0	0	0	0	0	0	0	0	0	0	0	0	0

Lake Alfred Exp. Station *Polk County* Elevation: 137 ft. Latitude: 28° 06' N Longitude: 81° 43' W

	JAN	FEB	MAR	APR	MAY	JUN	JUL	AUG	SEP	OCT	NOV	DEC	YEAR
Mean Maximum Temp. (°F)	72.1	74.2	78.7	83.5	88.6	91.4	92.8	92.8	90.8	85.8	79.8	74.0	83.7
Mean Temp. (°F)	59.6	61.6	66.5	70.9	76.4	80.8	82.3	82.3	80.4	74.5	68.1	62.0	72.1
Mean Minimum Temp. (°F)	47.1	49.0	54.1	58.2	64.3	70.1	71.8	71.7	70.0	63.2	56.5	50.0	60.5
Extreme Maximum Temp. (°F)	88	89	93	96	99	104	103	101	98	95	90	88	104
Extreme Minimum Temp. (°F)	19	25	24	35	45	50	61	60	54	38	26	19	19
Days Maximum Temp. ≥ 90°F	0	0	1	4	14	22	27	27	21	6	0	0	122
Days Maximum Temp. ≤ 32°F	0	0	0	0	0	0	0	0	0	0	0	0	0
Days Minimum Temp. ≤ 32°F	3	1	0	0	0	0	0	0	0	0	0	2	6
Days Minimum Temp. ≤ 0°F	0	0	0	0	0	0	0	0	0	0	0	0	0
Heating Degree Days (base 65°F)	211	150	72	18	0	0	0	0	0	5	51	155	662
Cooling Degree Days (base 65°F)	46	66	119	196	366	484	551	548	466	317	157	72	3,388
Mean Precipitation (in.)	2.57	2.81	3.66	1.99	4.20	6.89	7.23	7.27	6.47	2.99	2.28	2.24	50.60
Days With ≥ 0.1" Precipitation	4	5	5	3	6	9	11	11	9	4	3	3	73
Days With ≥ 1.0" Precipitation	1	1	1	1	1	2	2	2	2	1	1	1	16
Mean Snowfall (in.)	trace	0.0	0.0	0.0	0.0	0.0	0.0	0.0	0.0	0.0	0.0	0.0	trace
Days With ≥ 1.0" Snow Depth	0	0	0	0	0	0	0	0	0	0	0	0	0

Lake City 2 E *Columbia County* Elevation: 193 ft. Latitude: 30° 11' N Longitude: 82° 36' W

	JAN	FEB	MAR	APR	MAY	JUN	JUL	AUG	SEP	OCT	NOV	DEC	YEAR
Mean Maximum Temp. (°F)	64.4	67.7	74.1	79.6	85.8	89.8	91.4	90.7	87.9	80.8	73.6	67.0	79.4
Mean Temp. (°F)	53.1	56.0	62.0	67.1	73.8	79.2	81.2	80.7	77.9	69.8	62.3	55.8	68.2
Mean Minimum Temp. (°F)	41.8	44.3	49.8	54.8	61.8	68.5	71.0	70.7	68.0	58.7	50.9	44.5	57.1
Extreme Maximum Temp. (°F)	84	88	89	96	96	104	102	104	97	93	87	91	104
Extreme Minimum Temp. (°F)	7	16	19	34	41	49	57	62	47	34	18	9	7
Days Maximum Temp. ≥ 90°F	0	0	0	1	7	17	23	22	13	1	0	0	84
Days Maximum Temp. ≤ 32°F	0	0	0	0	0	0	0	0	0	0	0	0	0
Days Minimum Temp. ≤ 32°F	8	4	1	0	0	0	0	0	0	0	2	5	20
Days Minimum Temp. ≤ 0°F	0	0	0	0	0	0	0	0	0	0	0	0	0
Heating Degree Days (base 65°F)	377	269	150	53	4	0	0	0	0	30	146	304	1,333
Cooling Degree Days (base 65°F)	13	23	62	125	295	448	522	507	390	190	76	26	2,677
Mean Precipitation (in.)	4.53	3.79	5.06	3.25	3.84	6.76	6.70	7.36	4.59	2.88	2.39	3.00	54.15
Days With ≥ 0.1" Precipitation	7	5	6	4	6	9	10	11	7	4	3	5	77
Days With ≥ 1.0" Precipitation	2	1	2	1	1	2	2	2	1	1	1	1	17
Mean Snowfall (in.)	trace	0.0	0.0	0.0	0.0	0.0	0.0	0.0	0.0	0.0	0.0	0.0	trace
Days With ≥ 1.0" Snow Depth	0	0	0	0	0	0	0	0	0	0	0	0	0

Lakeland Linder Airport *Polk County* Elevation: 209 ft. Latitude: 28° 02' N Longitude: 81° 57' W

	JAN	FEB	MAR	APR	MAY	JUN	JUL	AUG	SEP	OCT	NOV	DEC	YEAR
Mean Maximum Temp. (°F)	72.0	74.5	79.7	84.0	88.9	91.7	92.9	92.5	90.8	85.2	78.9	73.7	83.7
Mean Temp. (°F)	61.3	63.2	68.2	72.3	77.7	81.5	82.7	82.8	81.3	75.4	68.9	63.2	73.2
Mean Minimum Temp. (°F)	50.4	51.9	56.7	60.6	66.4	71.4	72.6	73.0	71.8	65.5	58.8	52.7	62.6
Extreme Maximum Temp. (°F)	87	90	92	95	103	105	100	100	98	96	93	87	105
Extreme Minimum Temp. (°F)	20	27	25	35	47	52	64	66	57	42	28	21	20
Days Maximum Temp. ≥ 90°F	0	0	1	4	14	22	26	26	20	5	0	0	118
Days Maximum Temp. ≤ 32°F	0	0	0	0	0	0	0	0	0	0	0	0	0
Days Minimum Temp. ≤ 32°F	1	1	0	0	0	0	0	0	0	0	0	1	3
Days Minimum Temp. ≤ 0°F	0	0	0	0	0	0	0	0	0	0	0	0	0
Heating Degree Days (base 65°F)	173	117	44	7	0	0	0	0	0	2	44	127	514
Cooling Degree Days (base 65°F)	62	86	154	237	419	523	578	579	508	351	184	81	3,762
Mean Precipitation (in.)	2.54	2.77	3.59	1.95	4.24	7.08	7.80	7.41	6.10	2.26	2.25	2.12	50.11
Days With ≥ 0.1" Precipitation	4	4	5	4	5	10	12	11	9	3	3	4	74
Days With ≥ 1.0" Precipitation	1	1	1	1	1	2	3	2	2	1	1	0	16
Mean Snowfall (in.)	trace	0.0	0.0	0.0	0.0	0.0	0.0	0.0	0.0	0.0	0.0	0.0	trace
Days With ≥ 1.0" Snow Depth	0	0	0	0	0	0	0	0	0	0	0	0	0

Lisbon *Lake County* Elevation: 65 ft. Latitude: 28° 52' N Longitude: 81° 47' W

	JAN	FEB	MAR	APR	MAY	JUN	JUL	AUG	SEP	OCT	NOV	DEC	YEAR
Mean Maximum Temp. (°F)	68.7	71.2	76.6	81.3	86.5	89.8	91.3	91.1	89.0	83.0	76.2	70.2	81.3
Mean Temp. (°F)	57.7	60.0	65.1	69.7	75.7	80.2	81.9	81.7	79.9	73.2	65.6	59.6	70.9
Mean Minimum Temp. (°F)	46.7	48.6	53.5	58.3	64.9	70.5	72.3	72.3	70.7	63.4	55.0	49.0	60.4
Extreme Maximum Temp. (°F)	86	89	91	95	98	100	100	101	100	97	89	86	101
Extreme Minimum Temp. (°F)	16	24	25	39	46	53	62	61	52	39	24	18	16
Days Maximum Temp. ≥ 90°F	0	0	0	1	8	17	23	23	15	2	0	0	89
Days Maximum Temp. ≤ 32°F	0	0	0	0	0	0	0	0	0	0	0	0	0
Days Minimum Temp. ≤ 32°F	3	2	0	0	0	0	0	0	0	0	0	2	7
Days Minimum Temp. ≤ 0°F	0	0	0	0	0	0	0	0	0	0	0	0	0
Heating Degree Days (base 65°F)	254	175	89	22	1	0	0	0	0	8	79	202	830
Cooling Degree Days (base 65°F)	26	41	84	159	336	468	539	536	446	265	100	36	3,036
Mean Precipitation (in.)	3.41	3.03	4.16	2.83	4.18	6.12	5.51	6.25	5.61	2.63	2.51	2.64	48.88
Days With ≥ 0.1" Precipitation	5	4	5	4	6	9	10	11	8	5	4	5	76
Days With ≥ 1.0" Precipitation	1	1	2	1	1	2	1	2	2	1	1	1	16
Mean Snowfall (in.)	trace	trace	0.0	0.0	0.0	0.0	0.0	0.0	0.0	0.0	0.0	0.0	trace
Days With ≥ 1.0" Snow Depth	0	0	0	0	0	0	0	0	0	0	0	0	0

Live Oak *Suwannee County* Elevation: 118 ft. Latitude: 30° 14' N Longitude: 82° 58' W

	JAN	FEB	MAR	APR	MAY	JUN	JUL	AUG	SEP	OCT	NOV	DEC	YEAR
Mean Maximum Temp. (°F)	67.1	70.5	76.7	82.2	88.3	91.9	93.1	92.4	89.9	83.1	75.8	69.0	81.7
Mean Temp. (°F)	54.7	57.4	63.2	68.5	75.2	80.2	82.2	81.7	79.0	70.8	63.2	56.6	69.4
Mean Minimum Temp. (°F)	42.1	44.1	49.7	54.7	62.0	68.5	71.1	70.9	68.0	58.5	50.5	44.2	57.0
Extreme Maximum Temp. (°F)	86	88	91	96	100	106	104	103	99	95	88	86	106
Extreme Minimum Temp. (°F)	6	16	19	31	40	47	60	60	46	29	15	13	6
Days Maximum Temp. ≥ 90°F	0	0	0	2	12	22	27	26	19	4	0	0	112
Days Maximum Temp. ≤ 32°F	0	0	0	0	0	0	0	0	0	0	0	0	0
Days Minimum Temp. ≤ 32°F	8	5	2	0	0	0	0	0	0	0	2	6	23
Days Minimum Temp. ≤ 0°F	0	0	0	0	0	0	0	0	0	0	0	0	0
Heating Degree Days (base 65°F)	335	237	123	39	2	0	0	0	0	25	131	281	1,173
Cooling Degree Days (base 65°F)	16	32	74	151	333	473	550	533	420	220	87	30	2,919
Mean Precipitation (in.)	5.00	3.98	5.42	3.47	3.33	6.08	6.54	6.63	4.33	3.32	2.43	3.09	53.62
Days With ≥ 0.1" Precipitation	7	5	6	4	5	9	9	9	6	3	4	5	72
Days With ≥ 1.0" Precipitation	2	1	2	1	1	2	2	2	1	1	1	1	17
Mean Snowfall (in.)	trace	trace	trace	0.0	0.0	0.0	0.0	0.0	0.0	0.0	0.0	0.1	0.1
Days With ≥ 1.0" Snow Depth	0	0	0	0	0	0	0	0	0	0	0	0	0

Mayo *Lafayette County* Elevation: 62 ft. Latitude: 30° 03' N Longitude: 83° 10' W

	JAN	FEB	MAR	APR	MAY	JUN	JUL	AUG	SEP	OCT	NOV	DEC	YEAR
Mean Maximum Temp. (°F)	65.1	68.6	75.2	80.8	87.0	90.8	92.2	91.7	89.3	82.3	74.7	67.4	80.4
Mean Temp. (°F)	52.7	55.7	62.2	67.4	74.4	79.7	81.8	81.3	78.5	69.5	61.9	54.9	68.3
Mean Minimum Temp. (°F)	40.2	42.7	49.1	54.0	61.7	68.6	71.3	70.8	67.6	56.7	49.2	42.4	56.2
Extreme Maximum Temp. (°F)	86	86	91	96	98	104	103	103	99	96	90	86	104
Extreme Minimum Temp. (°F)	7	12	19	32	41	47	60	60	46	32	25	12	7
Days Maximum Temp. ≥ 90°F	0	0	0	2	10	20	25	24	18	3	0	0	102
Days Maximum Temp. ≤ 32°F	0	0	0	0	0	0	0	0	0	0	0	0	0
Days Minimum Temp. ≤ 32°F	9	6	1	0	0	0	0	0	0	0	2	7	25
Days Minimum Temp. ≤ 0°F	0	0	0	0	0	0	0	0	0	0	0	0	0
Heating Degree Days (base 65°F)	390	277	148	52	4	0	0	0	0	38	156	329	1,394
Cooling Degree Days (base 65°F)	12	23	63	128	307	456	535	520	405	195	74	26	2,744
Mean Precipitation (in.)	5.01	3.74	5.14	3.16	3.23	5.86	7.67	8.12	4.73	3.05	2.57	3.31	55.59
Days With ≥ 0.1" Precipitation	6	6	6	4	5	9	11	11	7	3	4	5	77
Days With ≥ 1.0" Precipitation	2	1	2	1	1	2	3	2	1	1	1	1	18
Mean Snowfall (in.)	trace	0.0	0.0	0.0	0.0	0.0	0.0	0.0	0.0	0.0	0.0	0.0	trace
Days With ≥ 1.0" Snow Depth	0	0	0	0	0	0	0	0	0	0	0	0	0

Melbourne Regional Airport *Brevard County* Elevation: 32 ft. Latitude: 28° 07' N Longitude: 80° 39' W

	JAN	FEB	MAR	APR	MAY	JUN	JUL	AUG	SEP	OCT	NOV	DEC	YEAR
Mean Maximum Temp. (°F)	71.7	72.9	77.2	80.6	85.1	88.7	90.5	89.9	88.1	83.3	78.1	73.4	81.6
Mean Temp. (°F)	61.5	62.5	66.8	70.8	76.0	80.0	81.4	81.4	80.1	75.5	69.4	63.6	72.4
Mean Minimum Temp. (°F)	51.2	52.0	56.5	60.9	66.8	71.2	72.3	72.9	72.2	67.6	60.5	53.7	63.2
Extreme Maximum Temp. (°F)	88	88	93	97	97	101	102	101	98	93	91	89	102
Extreme Minimum Temp. (°F)	17	28	25	25	47	55	60	60	58	41	31	21	17
Days Maximum Temp. ≥ 90°F	0	0	1	2	5	12	19	17	9	2	0	0	67
Days Maximum Temp. ≤ 32°F	0	0	0	0	0	0	0	0	0	0	0	0	0
Days Minimum Temp. ≤ 32°F	1	1	0	0	0	0	0	0	0	0	0	1	3
Days Minimum Temp. ≤ 0°F	0	0	0	0	0	0	0	0	0	0	0	0	0
Heating Degree Days (base 65°F)	164	127	61	16	0	0	0	0	0	3	36	122	529
Cooling Degree Days (base 65°F)	56	70	115	187	346	464	521	520	461	347	178	83	3,348
Mean Precipitation (in.)	2.54	2.52	3.01	2.05	4.05	5.67	5.35	5.70	7.15	4.72	3.11	2.29	48.16
Days With ≥ 0.1" Precipitation	4	5	4	3	6	9	8	9	9	7	4	4	72
Days With ≥ 1.0" Precipitation	1	1	1	0	1	2	2	2	2	1	1	1	15
Mean Snowfall (in.)	0.0	0.0	0.0	0.0	0.0	0.0	0.0	0.0	0.0	0.0	0.0	0.0	0.0
Days With ≥ 1.0" Snow Depth	0	0	0	0	0	0	0	0	0	0	0	0	0

Miami Beach *Dade County* Elevation: 3 ft. Latitude: 25° 47' N Longitude: 80° 08' W

	JAN	FEB	MAR	APR	MAY	JUN	JUL	AUG	SEP	OCT	NOV	DEC	YEAR
Mean Maximum Temp. (°F)	74.2	74.8	76.7	79.4	82.7	85.8	87.4	87.6	86.3	83.2	79.1	75.7	81.1
Mean Temp. (°F)	68.6	69.2	71.8	74.9	78.4	81.3	82.9	83.1	82.0	79.0	74.8	70.7	76.4
Mean Minimum Temp. (°F)	63.0	63.5	66.8	70.2	74.0	76.7	78.4	78.5	77.7	74.8	70.5	65.6	71.6
Extreme Maximum Temp. (°F)	84	88	92	94	95	97	98	98	96	95	89	85	98
Extreme Minimum Temp. (°F)	32	37	32	46	58	66	66	67	67	54	39	32	32
Days Maximum Temp. ≥ 90°F	0	0	0	0	1	3	5	5	2	1	0	0	17
Days Maximum Temp. ≤ 32°F	0	0	0	0	0	0	0	0	0	0	0	0	0
Days Minimum Temp. ≤ 32°F	0	0	0	0	0	0	0	0	0	0	0	0	0
Days Minimum Temp. ≤ 0°F	0	0	0	0	0	0	0	0	0	0	0	0	0
Heating Degree Days (base 65°F)	48	32	14	2	0	0	0	0	0	0	4	30	130
Cooling Degree Days (base 65°F)	169	173	226	303	425	503	574	579	524	452	316	218	4,462
Mean Precipitation (in.)	2.49	2.18	2.20	2.66	5.04	6.91	3.31	5.24	6.85	4.57	3.35	1.95	46.75
Days With ≥ 0.1" Precipitation	4	4	4	4	6	9	7	9	9	7	5	3	71
Days With ≥ 1.0" Precipitation	1	1	1	1	2	2	1	1	2	1	1	1	15
Mean Snowfall (in.)	0.0	0.0	0.0	0.0	0.0	0.0	0.0	0.0	0.0	0.0	0.0	0.0	0.0
Days With ≥ 1.0" Snow Depth	0	0	0	0	0	0	0	0	0	0	0	0	0

Milton Experiment Stn. *Santa Rosa County* Elevation: 216 ft. Latitude: 30° 47' N Longitude: 87° 08' W

	JAN	FEB	MAR	APR	MAY	JUN	JUL	AUG	SEP	OCT	NOV	DEC	YEAR
Mean Maximum Temp. (°F)	61.0	64.9	71.6	78.2	85.0	90.1	91.5	91.4	88.3	80.4	71.1	63.9	78.1
Mean Temp. (°F)	50.1	53.3	60.1	66.1	73.5	79.4	81.4	81.0	77.4	67.8	59.2	52.8	66.8
Mean Minimum Temp. (°F)	39.1	41.6	48.6	54.0	61.9	68.7	71.2	70.6	66.5	55.1	47.2	41.7	55.5
Extreme Maximum Temp. (°F)	79	83	88	94	99	102	103	101	102	93	88	82	103
Extreme Minimum Temp. (°F)	3	12	20	30	39	50	61	57	45	31	19	8	3
Days Maximum Temp. ≥ 90°F	0	0	0	0	6	18	22	23	15	2	0	0	86
Days Maximum Temp. ≤ 32°F	0	0	0	0	0	0	0	0	0	0	0	0	0
Days Minimum Temp. ≤ 32°F	10	6	2	0	0	0	0	0	0	0	3	8	29
Days Minimum Temp. ≤ 0°F	0	0	0	0	0	0	0	0	0	0	0	0	0
Heating Degree Days (base 65°F)	465	335	186	65	4	0	0	0	2	56	208	389	1,710
Cooling Degree Days (base 65°F)	5	12	38	98	274	441	519	510	374	149	40	15	2,475
Mean Precipitation (in.)	6.40	5.14	7.37	4.31	5.08	7.39	8.12	6.70	6.08	4.02	5.22	4.37	70.20
Days With ≥ 0.1" Precipitation	8	6	7	5	6	8	11	10	7	4	6	6	84
Days With ≥ 1.0" Precipitation	2	2	2	1	1	2	2	2	2	1	2	1	20
Mean Snowfall (in.)	0.1	0.1	trace	0.0	0.0	0.0	0.0	0.0	0.0	0.0	0.0	0.0	0.2
Days With ≥ 1.0" Snow Depth	0	0	0	0	0	0	0	0	0	0	0	0	0

Monticello 3 W *Jefferson County* Elevation: 144 ft. Latitude: 30° 32' N Longitude: 83° 55' W

	JAN	FEB	MAR	APR	MAY	JUN	JUL	AUG	SEP	OCT	NOV	DEC	YEAR
Mean Maximum Temp. (°F)	61.7	65.9	72.3	78.2	84.5	89.3	90.6	89.9	87.2	79.7	71.8	64.8	78.0
Mean Temp. (°F)	49.8	53.2	59.9	65.3	72.3	78.2	80.2	79.7	76.4	66.8	59.0	52.4	66.1
Mean Minimum Temp. (°F)	37.8	40.5	47.4	52.4	60.1	67.1	69.9	69.4	65.6	53.9	46.1	39.9	54.2
Extreme Maximum Temp. (°F)	83	85	90	93	96	103	102	100	97	93	87	84	103
Extreme Minimum Temp. (°F)	4	14	18	31	38	44	58	58	43	31	13	11	4
Days Maximum Temp. ≥ 90°F	0	0	0	0	4	15	20	18	10	1	0	0	68
Days Maximum Temp. ≤ 32°F	0	0	0	0	0	0	0	0	0	0	0	0	0
Days Minimum Temp. ≤ 32°F	12	7	2	0	0	0	0	0	0	0	4	10	35
Days Minimum Temp. ≤ 0°F	0	0	0	0	0	0	0	0	0	0	0	0	0
Heating Degree Days (base 65°F)	471	338	193	77	8	0	0	0	2	64	216	398	1,767
Cooling Degree Days (base 65°F)	4	13	39	90	249	414	492	472	344	137	46	14	2,314
Mean Precipitation (in.)	5.63	4.62	6.02	3.63	4.06	5.71	6.65	6.75	4.47	3.41	3.57	3.89	58.41
Days With ≥ 0.1" Precipitation	7	5	6	4	6	8	10	10	6	4	4	5	75
Days With ≥ 1.0" Precipitation	2	1	2	1	1	2	2	2	1	1	1	1	17
Mean Snowfall (in.)	trace	trace	trace	0.0	0.0	0.0	0.0	0.0	0.0	0.0	0.0	trace	trace
Days With ≥ 1.0" Snow Depth	0	0	0	0	0	0	0	0	0	0	0	0	0

Moore Haven Lock 1 *Glades County* Elevation: 32 ft. Latitude: 26° 50' N Longitude: 81° 05' W

	JAN	FEB	MAR	APR	MAY	JUN	JUL	AUG	SEP	OCT	NOV	DEC	YEAR
Mean Maximum Temp. (°F)	74.0	75.6	79.5	83.4	87.7	90.4	91.7	91.3	89.5	85.2	79.9	75.4	83.6
Mean Temp. (°F)	62.8	63.9	68.1	72.0	76.8	80.6	81.9	82.0	80.9	76.2	70.2	64.8	73.4
Mean Minimum Temp. (°F)	51.6	52.3	56.5	60.6	65.8	70.7	72.1	72.6	72.3	67.2	60.5	54.2	63.0
Extreme Maximum Temp. (°F)	88	90	93	97	98	101	100	98	99	95	91	89	101
Extreme Minimum Temp. (°F)	23	29	26	39	44	57	62	63	62	45	32	23	23
Days Maximum Temp. ≥ 90°F	0	0	1	4	11	18	25	24	17	5	0	0	105
Days Maximum Temp. ≤ 32°F	0	0	0	0	0	0	0	0	0	0	0	0	0
Days Minimum Temp. ≤ 32°F	1	0	0	0	0	0	0	0	0	0	0	1	2
Days Minimum Temp. ≤ 0°F	0	0	0	0	0	0	0	0	0	0	0	0	0
Heating Degree Days (base 65°F)	138	104	46	9	0	0	0	0	0	1	27	99	424
Cooling Degree Days (base 65°F)	76	90	149	223	378	483	540	544	487	364	194	101	3,629
Mean Precipitation (in.)	2.13	2.12	3.29	2.21	3.78	7.15	6.71	6.94	6.13	3.06	1.90	1.63	47.05
Days With ≥ 0.1" Precipitation	4	3	4	4	6	11	10	11	8	5	3	3	72
Days With ≥ 1.0" Precipitation	1	1	1	1	1	2	2	2	2	1	0	0	14
Mean Snowfall (in.)	0.0	0.0	0.0	0.0	0.0	0.0	0.0	0.0	0.0	0.0	0.0	0.0	0.0
Days With ≥ 1.0" Snow Depth	0	0	0	0	0	0	0	0	0	0	0	0	0

Mountain Lake *Polk County* Elevation: 124 ft. Latitude: 27° 56' N Longitude: 81° 36' W

	JAN	FEB	MAR	APR	MAY	JUN	JUL	AUG	SEP	OCT	NOV	DEC	YEAR
Mean Maximum Temp. (°F)	73.8	76.0	80.6	84.9	89.5	92.0	92.8	92.5	90.5	85.7	79.7	75.1	84.4
Mean Temp. (°F)	61.4	63.1	67.7	71.8	76.9	80.8	81.8	82.0	80.5	74.8	68.3	63.1	72.7
Mean Minimum Temp. (°F)	49.0	50.1	54.7	58.6	64.2	69.6	70.8	71.5	70.4	63.9	56.9	51.2	60.9
Extreme Maximum Temp. (°F)	89	91	95	96	99	101	105	100	98	96	91	89	105
Extreme Minimum Temp. (°F)	16	24	25	34	44	50	53	62	57	40	24	19	16
Days Maximum Temp. ≥ 90°F	0	0	3	7	16	22	27	27	20	6	0	0	128
Days Maximum Temp. ≤ 32°F	0	0	0	0	0	0	0	0	0	0	0	0	0
Days Minimum Temp. ≤ 32°F	3	1	0	0	0	0	0	0	0	0	0	2	6
Days Minimum Temp. ≤ 0°F	0	0	0	0	0	0	0	0	0	0	0	0	0
Heating Degree Days (base 65°F)	169	120	53	10	0	0	0	0	0	3	44	127	526
Cooling Degree Days (base 65°F)	57	74	128	212	371	481	526	535	464	314	149	71	3,382
Mean Precipitation (in.)	2.44	2.49	3.27	2.02	4.02	7.47	7.52	6.61	5.81	2.51	2.22	2.14	48.52
Days With ≥ 0.1" Precipitation	4	4	5	3	6	10	12	10	8	5	4	4	75
Days With ≥ 1.0" Precipitation	1	1	1	1	1	2	2	2	2	1	1	1	16
Mean Snowfall (in.)	trace	0.0	0.0	0.0	0.0	0.0	0.0	0.0	0.0	0.0	0.0	0.0	trace
Days With ≥ 1.0" Snow Depth	0	0	0	0	0	0	0	0	0	0	0	0	0

Myakka River State Park *Sarasota County* Elevation: 19 ft. Latitude: 27° 14' N Longitude: 82° 19' W

	JAN	FEB	MAR	APR	MAY	JUN	JUL	AUG	SEP	OCT	NOV	DEC	YEAR
Mean Maximum Temp. (°F)	74.7	76.8	81.4	85.7	90.9	92.4	93.0	92.9	91.4	87.1	81.3	76.3	85.3
Mean Temp. (°F)	62.1	63.7	68.2	71.9	77.1	80.8	82.0	82.6	81.4	76.0	69.5	64.2	73.3
Mean Minimum Temp. (°F)	49.4	50.6	54.9	58.0	63.2	69.1	71.0	72.2	71.3	64.8	57.6	52.0	61.2
Extreme Maximum Temp. (°F)	89	91	93	98	104	105	101	104	103	97	95	90	105
Extreme Minimum Temp. (°F)	18	22	28	34	43	50	63	63	58	42	24	22	18
Days Maximum Temp. ≥ 90°F	0	0	2	8	21	25	28	28	23	11	1	0	147
Days Maximum Temp. ≤ 32°F	0	0	0	0	0	0	0	0	0	0	0	0	0
Days Minimum Temp. ≤ 32°F	2	1	0	0	0	0	0	0	0	0	0	1	4
Days Minimum Temp. ≤ 0°F	0	0	0	0	0	0	0	0	0	0	0	0	0
Heating Degree Days (base 65°F)	148	107	43	9	0	0	0	0	0	2	33	108	450
Cooling Degree Days (base 65°F)	66	90	148	223	388	493	542	562	501	360	183	96	3,652
Mean Precipitation (in.)	3.16	2.91	3.61	2.11	3.37	8.92	9.63	9.61	8.05	3.21	2.23	2.30	59.11
Days With ≥ 0.1" Precipitation	4	4	4	3	5	10	13	13	10	5	4	3	78
Days With ≥ 1.0" Precipitation	1	1	1	1	1	3	3	3	3	1	1	1	20
Mean Snowfall (in.)	0.0	0.0	0.0	0.0	0.0	0.0	0.0	0.0	0.0	0.0	0.0	trace	trace
Days With ≥ 1.0" Snow Depth	0	0	0	0	0	0	0	0	0	0	0	0	0

Naples *Collier County* Elevation: 3 ft. Latitude: 26° 10' N Longitude: 81° 47' W

	JAN	FEB	MAR	APR	MAY	JUN	JUL	AUG	SEP	OCT	NOV	DEC	YEAR
Mean Maximum Temp. (°F)	76.6	77.6	80.9	84.4	88.0	90.4	91.7	91.9	90.9	87.6	82.9	78.3	85.1
Mean Temp. (°F)	65.3	66.2	69.7	73.2	77.5	81.1	82.1	82.5	81.8	77.9	72.4	67.3	74.8
Mean Minimum Temp. (°F)	54.0	54.7	58.4	62.0	67.0	71.7	72.5	73.1	72.7	68.0	61.8	56.2	64.4
Extreme Maximum Temp. (°F)	88	89	91	93	95	98	98	97	99	95	91	89	99
Extreme Minimum Temp. (°F)	26	28	33	39	52	59	62	63	59	48	31	27	26
Days Maximum Temp. ≥ 90°F	0	0	0	2	9	20	27	28	24	9	1	0	120
Days Maximum Temp. ≤ 32°F	0	0	0	0	0	0	0	0	0	0	0	0	0
Days Minimum Temp. ≤ 32°F	1	0	0	0	0	0	0	0	0	0	0	0	1
Days Minimum Temp. ≤ 0°F	0	0	0	0	0	0	0	0	0	0	0	0	0
Heating Degree Days (base 65°F)	88	64	24	4	0	0	0	0	0	0	11	58	249
Cooling Degree Days (base 65°F)	100	114	175	257	399	497	546	557	512	416	243	137	3,953
Mean Precipitation (in.)	2.06	2.21	2.49	1.95	4.33	8.20	7.98	7.68	8.22	3.69	2.00	1.52	52.33
Days With ≥ 0.1" Precipitation	3	4	3	3	5	10	12	12	11	5	3	3	74
Days With ≥ 1.0" Precipitation	1	1	1	0	2	3	3	2	2	1	1	0	17
Mean Snowfall (in.)	0.0	0.0	0.0	0.0	0.0	0.0	0.0	0.0	0.0	0.0	0.0	0.0	0.0
Days With ≥ 1.0" Snow Depth	0	0	0	0	0	0	0	0	0	0	0	0	0

Ocala *Marion County* Elevation: 72 ft. Latitude: 29° 12' N Longitude: 82° 05' W

	JAN	FEB	MAR	APR	MAY	JUN	JUL	AUG	SEP	OCT	NOV	DEC	YEAR
Mean Maximum Temp. (°F)	70.3	72.8	78.3	83.0	88.3	91.1	92.3	91.7	89.9	84.2	77.5	72.0	82.6
Mean Temp. (°F)	57.9	59.9	65.3	69.6	75.7	80.2	81.7	81.3	79.4	72.8	65.7	59.7	70.8
Mean Minimum Temp. (°F)	45.6	46.9	52.3	56.2	63.0	69.2	71.1	70.8	68.7	61.3	53.6	47.4	58.8
Extreme Maximum Temp. (°F)	86	89	91	97	101	105	100	100	97	95	89	88	105
Extreme Minimum Temp. (°F)	11	20	23	33	45	48	58	60	45	32	23	15	11
Days Maximum Temp. ≥ 90°F	0	0	0	3	12	21	26	24	19	4	0	0	109
Days Maximum Temp. ≤ 32°F	0	0	0	0	0	0	0	0	0	0	0	0	0
Days Minimum Temp. ≤ 32°F	5	3	1	0	0	0	0	0	0	0	1	3	13
Days Minimum Temp. ≤ 0°F	0	0	0	0	0	0	0	0	0	0	0	0	0
Heating Degree Days (base 65°F)	250	181	90	25	1	0	0	0	0	11	81	202	841
Cooling Degree Days (base 65°F)	32	47	98	168	339	465	531	518	430	258	111	44	3,041
Mean Precipitation (in.)	3.64	3.28	4.18	2.87	3.81	7.11	6.39	6.05	5.46	2.77	2.43	2.69	50.68
Days With ≥ 0.1" Precipitation	6	5	6	4	5	9	11	12	8	4	4	4	78
Days With ≥ 1.0" Precipitation	1	1	1	1	1	2	2	1	2	1	1	1	15
Mean Snowfall (in.)	trace	trace	0.0	0.0	0.0	0.0	0.0	0.0	0.0	0.0	0.0	0.0	trace
Days With ≥ 1.0" Snow Depth	0	0	0	0	0	0	0	0	0	0	0	0	0

Panama City 5 NE *Bay County* Elevation: 29 ft. Latitude: 30° 13' N Longitude: 85° 36' W

	JAN	FEB	MAR	APR	MAY	JUN	JUL	AUG	SEP	OCT	NOV	DEC	YEAR
Mean Maximum Temp. (°F)	62.7	65.4	71.1	77.2	83.6	88.5	89.9	90.0	87.8	80.4	72.5	64.9	77.8
Mean Temp. (°F)	51.2	53.7	59.8	65.5	72.7	78.7	80.9	80.7	77.8	68.3	60.5	53.2	66.9
Mean Minimum Temp. (°F)	39.7	42.1	48.3	53.9	61.7	68.9	71.8	71.4	67.8	56.3	48.4	41.4	56.0
Extreme Maximum Temp. (°F)	80	82	87	93	100	100	101	100	98	93	91	82	101
Extreme Minimum Temp. (°F)	6	15	23	34	40	46	60	59	45	33	26	11	6
Days Maximum Temp. ≥ 90°F	0	0	0	0	3	13	18	19	12	1	0	0	66
Days Maximum Temp. ≤ 32°F	0	0	0	0	0	0	0	0	0	0	0	0	0
Days Minimum Temp. ≤ 32°F	10	6	2	0	0	0	0	0	0	0	2	8	28
Days Minimum Temp. ≤ 0°F	0	0	0	0	0	0	0	0	0	0	0	0	0
Heating Degree Days (base 65°F)	428	322	190	65	5	0	0	0	1	43	179	375	1,608
Cooling Degree Days (base 65°F)	5	12	32	82	249	416	498	497	384	162	47	15	2,399
Mean Precipitation (in.)	5.95	4.90	6.23	3.93	4.03	6.12	8.86	7.52	6.19	3.67	4.57	4.10	66.07
Days With ≥ 0.1" Precipitation	7	6	7	4	5	8	11	11	7	4	5	6	81
Days With ≥ 1.0" Precipitation	2	2	2	1	1	2	3	2	2	1	1	1	20
Mean Snowfall (in.)	trace	trace	0.0	0.0	0.0	0.0	0.0	0.0	0.0	0.0	0.0	0.0	trace
Days With ≥ 1.0" Snow Depth	0	0	0	0	0	0	0	0	0	0	0	0	0

Parrish *Manatee County* Elevation: 59 ft. Latitude: 27° 37' N Longitude: 82° 21' W

	JAN	FEB	MAR	APR	MAY	JUN	JUL	AUG	SEP	OCT	NOV	DEC	YEAR
Mean Maximum Temp. (°F)	72.9	74.4	78.4	82.7	87.6	90.2	91.2	91.1	89.9	85.4	79.6	74.5	83.2
Mean Temp. (°F)	61.5	62.6	66.8	70.7	75.9	80.2	81.6	81.8	80.6	75.1	68.8	63.3	72.4
Mean Minimum Temp. (°F)	50.0	50.8	55.1	58.7	64.2	70.2	72.0	72.4	71.3	64.8	57.9	52.0	61.6
Extreme Maximum Temp. (°F)	86	88	91	93	97	101	98	101	99	93	91	87	101
Extreme Minimum Temp. (°F)	18	24	29	36	41	51	62	64	57	44	25	23	18
Days Maximum Temp. ≥ 90°F	0	0	0	1	9	20	25	24	20	5	0	0	104
Days Maximum Temp. ≤ 32°F	0	0	0	0	0	0	0	0	0	0	0	0	0
Days Minimum Temp. ≤ 32°F	2	1	0	0	0	0	0	0	0	0	0	1	4
Days Minimum Temp. ≤ 0°F	0	0	0	0	0	0	0	0	0	0	0	0	0
Heating Degree Days (base 65°F)	167	125	61	16	1	0	0	0	0	4	40	129	543
Cooling Degree Days (base 65°F)	55	67	111	182	336	466	522	526	470	326	158	79	3,298
Mean Precipitation (in.)	2.85	3.19	3.23	2.03	3.18	7.15	7.45	8.68	7.39	2.86	2.31	2.26	52.58
Days With ≥ 0.1" Precipitation	4	4	4	3	4	9	11	12	9	4	3	3	70
Days With ≥ 1.0" Precipitation	1	1	1	1	1	3	2	3	2	1	1	1	18
Mean Snowfall (in.)	trace	0.0	0.0	0.0	0.0	0.0	0.0	0.0	0.0	0.0	0.0	0.0	trace
Days With ≥ 1.0" Snow Depth	0	0	0	0	0	0	0	0	0	0	0	0	0

Perry *Taylor County* Elevation: 42 ft. Latitude: 30° 06' N Longitude: 83° 34' W

	JAN	FEB	MAR	APR	MAY	JUN	JUL	AUG	SEP	OCT	NOV	DEC	YEAR
Mean Maximum Temp. (°F)	67.0	70.3	76.2	81.8	87.8	91.4	92.7	92.2	90.3	83.6	76.4	69.7	81.6
Mean Temp. (°F)	54.2	56.9	62.5	67.7	74.7	79.7	81.7	81.4	78.9	70.5	62.8	56.5	69.0
Mean Minimum Temp. (°F)	41.4	43.4	48.8	53.6	61.5	67.9	70.7	70.4	67.5	57.2	49.1	43.2	56.2
Extreme Maximum Temp. (°F)	85	87	90	94	99	103	104	102	99	94	90	86	104
Extreme Minimum Temp. (°F)	7	14	19	29	40	46	59	59	45	28	14	12	7
Days Maximum Temp. ≥ 90°F	0	0	0	2	11	22	26	25	20	4	0	0	110
Days Maximum Temp. ≤ 32°F	0	0	0	0	0	0	0	0	0	0	0	0	0
Days Minimum Temp. ≤ 32°F	8	5	2	0	0	0	0	0	0	0	3	7	25
Days Minimum Temp. ≤ 0°F	0	0	0	0	0	0	0	0	0	0	0	0	0
Heating Degree Days (base 65°F)	343	244	132	45	2	0	0	0	0	26	136	282	1,210
Cooling Degree Days (base 65°F)	12	25	60	126	309	446	526	518	414	208	80	27	2,751
Mean Precipitation (in.)	4.91	4.00	5.59	3.35	3.52	6.02	8.48	8.86	5.01	3.15	2.70	3.38	58.97
Days With ≥ 0.1" Precipitation	7	6	6	4	6	8	12	11	7	4	4	6	81
Days With ≥ 1.0" Precipitation	2	1	2	1	1	2	2	3	2	1	1	1	19
Mean Snowfall (in.)	trace	0.0	0.0	0.0	0.0	0.0	0.0	0.0	0.0	0.0	0.0	0.0	trace
Days With ≥ 1.0" Snow Depth	0	0	0	0	0	0	0	0	0	0	0	0	0

Plant City *Hillsborough County* Elevation: 118 ft. Latitude: 28° 01' N Longitude: 82° 08' W

	JAN	FEB	MAR	APR	MAY	JUN	JUL	AUG	SEP	OCT	NOV	DEC	YEAR
Mean Maximum Temp. (°F)	73.0	74.7	79.4	83.6	88.5	90.8	91.8	91.4	90.2	85.5	79.5	74.6	83.6
Mean Temp. (°F)	61.2	62.6	67.2	71.2	76.6	80.6	81.8	81.9	80.5	75.0	68.3	63.0	72.5
Mean Minimum Temp. (°F)	49.3	50.5	54.9	58.9	64.6	70.4	71.8	72.2	70.8	64.6	57.1	51.3	61.4
Extreme Maximum Temp. (°F)	87	89	91	96	99	102	102	99	98	94	92	89	102
Extreme Minimum Temp. (°F)	17	25	24	35	43	49	62	63	55	39	21	20	17
Days Maximum Temp. ≥ 90°F	0	0	1	3	12	21	26	25	20	5	0	0	113
Days Maximum Temp. ≤ 32°F	0	0	0	0	0	0	0	0	0	0	0	0	0
Days Minimum Temp. ≤ 32°F	2	1	0	0	0	0	0	0	0	0	0	1	4
Days Minimum Temp. ≤ 0°F	0	0	0	0	0	0	0	0	0	0	0	0	0
Heating Degree Days (base 65°F)	176	127	60	15	0	0	0	0	0	4	47	133	562
Cooling Degree Days (base 65°F)	56	76	126	203	370	483	535	536	468	321	155	75	3,404
Mean Precipitation (in.)	2.74	3.17	3.56	2.13	3.81	7.01	7.35	7.83	6.56	2.41	2.11	2.55	51.23
Days With ≥ 0.1" Precipitation	4	4	5	4	5	9	11	12	9	4	3	4	74
Days With ≥ 1.0" Precipitation	1	1	1	1	1	2	2	2	2	1	1	1	16
Mean Snowfall (in.)	0.0	0.0	0.0	0.0	0.0	0.0	0.0	0.0	0.0	0.0	0.0	0.0	0.0
Days With ≥ 1.0" Snow Depth	0	0	0	0	0	0	0	0	0	0	0	0	0

Punta Gorda 4 ESE *Charlotte County* Elevation: 19 ft. Latitude: 26° 55' N Longitude: 82° 00' W

	JAN	FEB	MAR	APR	MAY	JUN	JUL	AUG	SEP	OCT	NOV	DEC	YEAR
Mean Maximum Temp. (°F)	74.3	75.9	80.2	84.4	89.1	91.5	92.2	92.2	90.7	86.3	80.8	76.2	84.5
Mean Temp. (°F)	63.0	64.4	68.6	72.4	77.5	81.4	82.6	82.8	81.6	76.4	70.2	65.1	73.8
Mean Minimum Temp. (°F)	51.7	52.9	56.9	60.4	65.9	71.2	72.9	73.3	72.4	66.4	59.5	54.0	63.1
Extreme Maximum Temp. (°F)	89	92	91	94	98	101	99	97	95	94	93	89	101
Extreme Minimum Temp. (°F)	23	27	29	38	49	57	63	65	61	46	28	25	23
Days Maximum Temp. ≥ 90°F	0	0	1	3	14	23	27	27	22	6	0	0	123
Days Maximum Temp. ≤ 32°F	0	0	0	0	0	0	0	0	0	0	0	0	0
Days Minimum Temp. ≤ 32°F	1	0	0	0	0	0	0	0	0	0	0	1	2
Days Minimum Temp. ≤ 0°F	0	0	0	0	0	0	0	0	0	0	0	0	0
Heating Degree Days (base 65°F)	130	91	35	4	0	0	0	0	0	1	25	88	374
Cooling Degree Days (base 65°F)	79	94	154	241	401	512	566	571	510	375	197	105	3,805
Mean Precipitation (in.)	2.33	2.35	3.01	1.69	3.35	8.46	7.72	7.76	6.58	3.12	1.86	1.78	50.01
Days With ≥ 0.1" Precipitation	4	4	4	3	5	10	13	11	10	5	3	3	75
Days With ≥ 1.0" Precipitation	1	1	1	0	1	3	2	2	2	1	0	1	15
Mean Snowfall (in.)	0.0	0.0	0.0	0.0	0.0	0.0	0.0	0.0	0.0	0.0	0.0	0.0	0.0
Days With ≥ 1.0" Snow Depth	0	0	0	0	0	0	0	0	0	0	0	0	0

Quincy 3 SSW *Gadsden County* Elevation: 242 ft. Latitude: 30° 36' N Longitude: 84° 33' W

	JAN	FEB	MAR	APR	MAY	JUN	JUL	AUG	SEP	OCT	NOV	DEC	YEAR
Mean Maximum Temp. (°F)	61.7	65.7	72.1	78.4	84.9	89.4	90.7	90.0	87.4	79.8	71.7	65.0	78.1
Mean Temp. (°F)	50.8	53.9	60.3	66.1	73.3	79.1	80.8	80.4	77.3	68.3	60.3	53.9	67.0
Mean Minimum Temp. (°F)	39.8	42.0	48.6	53.7	61.6	68.5	70.9	70.7	67.1	56.7	48.8	42.7	55.9
Extreme Maximum Temp. (°F)	83	85	90	92	99	102	102	101	98	93	86	84	102
Extreme Minimum Temp. (°F)	4	0	19	33	36	49	62	59	48	33	20	12	0
Days Maximum Temp. ≥ 90°F	0	0	0	0	5	15	21	18	11	1	0	0	71
Days Maximum Temp. ≤ 32°F	0	0	0	0	0	0	0	0	0	0	0	0	0
Days Minimum Temp. ≤ 32°F	9	6	1	0	0	0	0	0	0	0	2	6	24
Days Minimum Temp. ≤ 0°F	0	0	0	0	0	0	0	0	0	0	0	0	0
Heating Degree Days (base 65°F)	442	320	183	67	6	0	0	0	1	44	183	356	1,602
Cooling Degree Days (base 65°F)	6	14	41	101	272	440	510	496	370	159	49	16	2,474
Mean Precipitation (in.)	5.68	4.49	6.21	3.64	4.81	5.59	6.85	5.64	3.74	3.43	3.53	3.59	57.20
Days With ≥ 0.1" Precipitation	7	6	7	4	6	8	10	9	6	4	4	6	77
Days With ≥ 1.0" Precipitation	2	1	2	1	2	2	2	1	1	1	1	1	17
Mean Snowfall (in.)	trace	trace	trace	0.0	0.0	0.0	0.0	0.0	0.0	0.0	0.0	0.0	trace
Days With ≥ 1.0" Snow Depth	0	0	0	0	0	0	0	0	0	0	0	0	0

Saint Augustine *St. Johns County* Elevation: 6 ft. Latitude: 29° 54' N Longitude: 81° 19' W

	JAN	FEB	MAR	APR	MAY	JUN	JUL	AUG	SEP	OCT	NOV	DEC	YEAR
Mean Maximum Temp. (°F)	***66.8***	69.2	73.6	78.7	83.9	88.1	90.6	89.2	86.5	80.7	74.6	68.3	***79.2***
Mean Temp. (°F)	***56.4***	58.5	63.3	68.4	74.4	79.4	81.5	80.8	78.9	72.4	65.4	58.6	***69.8***
Mean Minimum Temp. (°F)	***46.0***	47.8	52.9	58.0	64.9	70.5	72.4	72.4	71.2	64.0	56.1	48.8	***60.4***
Extreme Maximum Temp. (°F)	***86***	87	93	95	97	101	103	101	98	94	88	86	***103***
Extreme Minimum Temp. (°F)	***10***	21	23	34	45	52	59	61	51	36	31	16	***10***
Days Maximum Temp. ≥ 90°F	***0***	0	0	1	4	11	18	13	6	1	0	0	***54***
Days Maximum Temp. ≤ 32°F	***0***	0	0	0	0	0	0	0	0	0	0	0	***0***
Days Minimum Temp. ≤ 32°F	***3***	2	0	0	0	0	0	0	0	0	0	2	***7***
Days Minimum Temp. ≤ 0°F	***0***	0	0	0	0	0	0	0	0	0	0	0	***0***
Heating Degree Days (base 65°F)	***278***	202	109	29	1	0	0	0	0	9	81	224	***933***
Cooling Degree Days (base 65°F)	16	25	55	134	296	439	521	501	413	251	98	32	2,781
Mean Precipitation (in.)	3.21	2.96	***3.73***	2.69	3.17	5.24	4.57	5.92	6.57	4.58	2.27	2.90	***47.81***
Days With ≥ 0.1" Precipitation	***5***	5	***5***	4	5	8	7	9	9	6	4	5	***72***
Days With ≥ 1.0" Precipitation	***1***	1	***1***	1	1	1	1	2	2	1	0	1	***13***
Mean Snowfall (in.)	trace	0.0	trace	0.0	0.0	0.0	0.0	0.0	0.0	0.0	0.0	0.0	trace
Days With ≥ 1.0" Snow Depth	0	0	0	0	0	0	0	0	0	0	0	0	0

Saint Leo *Pasco County* Elevation: 187 ft. Latitude: 28° 20' N Longitude: 82° 16' W

	JAN	FEB	MAR	APR	MAY	JUN	JUL	AUG	SEP	OCT	NOV	DEC	YEAR
Mean Maximum Temp. (°F)	71.7	74.3	79.2	83.8	89.1	91.5	92.4	92.1	90.7	85.4	79.2	74.0	83.6
Mean Temp. (°F)	60.2	62.5	67.2	71.6	77.1	81.0	82.2	82.1	80.6	74.7	68.1	62.7	72.5
Mean Minimum Temp. (°F)	48.7	50.6	55.2	59.4	65.1	70.5	71.9	72.0	70.5	63.9	57.1	51.4	61.4
Extreme Maximum Temp. (°F)	87	90	92	95	99	103	100	99	98	96	92	88	103
Extreme Minimum Temp. (°F)	18	22	24	38	46	54	64	63	53	39	27	20	18
Days Maximum Temp. ≥ 90°F	0	0	1	4	16	22	27	26	21	6	0	0	123
Days Maximum Temp. ≤ 32°F	0	0	0	0	0	0	0	0	0	0	0	0	0
Days Minimum Temp. ≤ 32°F	2	1	0	0	0	0	0	0	0	0	0	1	4
Days Minimum Temp. ≤ 0°F	0	0	0	0	0	0	0	0	0	0	0	0	0
Heating Degree Days (base 65°F)	193	130	58	10	0	0	0	0	0	3	48	138	580
Cooling Degree Days (base 65°F)	53	75	130	215	395	497	551	547	476	316	157	75	3,487
Mean Precipitation (in.)	3.48	3.55	4.25	2.37	4.10	6.94	7.66	7.40	6.52	2.86	2.49	2.67	54.29
Days With ≥ 0.1" Precipitation	5	5	5	3	5	9	12	12	9	4	4	4	77
Days With ≥ 1.0" Precipitation	1	1	2	1	1	2	3	2	2	1	1	1	18
Mean Snowfall (in.)	trace	0.0	0.0	0.0	0.0	0.0	0.0	0.0	0.0	0.0	0.0	0.0	trace
Days With ≥ 1.0" Snow Depth	0	0	0	0	0	0	0	0	0	0	0	0	0

Saint Petersburg *Pinellas County* Elevation: 6 ft. Latitude: 27° 46' N Longitude: 82° 38' W

	JAN	FEB	MAR	APR	MAY	JUN	JUL	AUG	SEP	OCT	NOV	DEC	YEAR
Mean Maximum Temp. (°F)	70.0	71.6	76.0	80.8	86.2	89.5	90.6	90.2	88.7	83.7	77.3	72.0	81.4
Mean Temp. (°F)	62.2	63.6	68.2	73.0	78.6	82.4	83.7	83.4	82.1	76.9	70.1	64.4	74.1
Mean Minimum Temp. (°F)	54.3	55.6	60.3	65.2	71.0	75.4	76.7	76.6	75.6	70.1	62.9	56.8	66.7
Extreme Maximum Temp. (°F)	88	90	88	93	96	99	100	99	97	92	89	88	100
Extreme Minimum Temp. (°F)	27	28	34	46	55	61	69	67	61	51	35	24	24
Days Maximum Temp. ≥ 90°F	0	0	0	0	5	16	22	21	13	2	0	0	79
Days Maximum Temp. ≤ 32°F	0	0	0	0	0	0	0	0	0	0	0	0	0
Days Minimum Temp. ≤ 32°F	0	0	0	0	0	0	0	0	0	0	0	0	0
Days Minimum Temp. ≤ 0°F	0	0	0	0	0	0	0	0	0	0	0	0	0
Heating Degree Days (base 65°F)	140	97	38	4	0	0	0	0	0	1	26	97	403
Cooling Degree Days (base 65°F)	50	68	133	237	428	529	586	582	515	375	184	83	3,770
Mean Precipitation (in.)	2.78	2.99	3.52	1.92	2.90	5.99	6.25	8.09	7.51	2.69	2.03	2.62	49.29
Days With ≥ 0.1" Precipitation	5	4	5	3	4	7	10	11	9	4	3	4	69
Days With ≥ 1.0" Precipitation	1	1	1	0	1	2	2	3	2	1	1	1	16
Mean Snowfall (in.)	trace	0.0	0.0	0.0	0.0	0.0	0.0	0.0	0.0	0.0	0.0	0.0	trace
Days With ≥ 1.0" Snow Depth	0	0	0	0	0	0	0	0	0	0	0	0	0

Sanford Experiment Station *Seminole County* Elevation: 13 ft. Latitude: 28° 48' N Longitude: 81° 14' W

	JAN	FEB	MAR	APR	MAY	JUN	JUL	AUG	SEP	OCT	NOV	DEC	YEAR
Mean Maximum Temp. (°F)	70.4	72.2	77.1	81.6	87.0	90.5	92.0	91.6	89.2	83.6	77.6	72.0	82.1
Mean Temp. (°F)	59.1	60.7	65.6	69.7	75.3	80.1	81.8	81.8	80.0	74.0	67.4	61.5	71.4
Mean Minimum Temp. (°F)	47.7	49.1	54.0	57.8	63.6	69.6	71.6	72.0	70.7	64.3	57.2	50.8	60.7
Extreme Maximum Temp. (°F)	89	89	92	96	100	102	103	100	98	95	92	87	103
Extreme Minimum Temp. (°F)	19	26	27	36	45	52	60	65	52	39	30	19	19
Days Maximum Temp. ≥ 90°F	0	0	0	2	10	18	25	24	16	3	0	0	98
Days Maximum Temp. ≤ 32°F	0	0	0	0	0	0	0	0	0	0	0	0	0
Days Minimum Temp. ≤ 32°F	2	1	0	0	0	0	0	0	0	0	0	1	4
Days Minimum Temp. ≤ 0°F	0	0	0	0	0	0	0	0	0	0	0	0	0
Heating Degree Days (base 65°F)	220	161	79	22	1	0	0	0	0	5	54	162	704
Cooling Degree Days (base 65°F)	36	48	97	164	327	461	536	533	450	296	139	58	3,145
Mean Precipitation (in.)	3.01	3.07	3.92	2.57	3.64	6.46	6.80	7.35	5.72	3.65	2.96	2.58	51.73
Days With ≥ 0.1" Precipitation	4	4	5	3	5	9	9	10	7	6	3	4	69
Days With ≥ 1.0" Precipitation	1	1	1	1	1	2	2	2	2	1	1	1	16
Mean Snowfall (in.)	0.0	0.0	0.0	0.0	0.0	0.0	0.0	0.0	0.0	0.0	0.0	0.0	0.0
Days With ≥ 1.0" Snow Depth	0	0	0	0	0	0	0	0	0	0	0	0	0

Stuart 1 S *Martin County* Elevation: 9 ft. Latitude: 27° 10' N Longitude: 80° 14' W

	JAN	FEB	MAR	APR	MAY	JUN	JUL	AUG	SEP	OCT	NOV	DEC	YEAR
Mean Maximum Temp. (°F)	75.3	76.2	79.0	82.2	85.5	88.6	90.0	90.1	89.0	85.5	80.5	76.8	83.2
Mean Temp. (°F)	65.2	65.8	69.5	73.0	77.1	80.6	82.0	82.3	81.5	77.5	72.0	67.5	74.5
Mean Minimum Temp. (°F)	55.1	55.5	59.8	63.7	68.7	72.7	73.9	74.4	73.9	69.5	63.5	58.2	65.7
Extreme Maximum Temp. (°F)	89	89	93	95	96	98	101	99	97	96	89	89	101
Extreme Minimum Temp. (°F)	23	28	26	37	45	55	63	61	65	44	33	27	23
Days Maximum Temp. ≥ 90°F	0	0	0	2	5	11	17	18	13	3	0	0	69
Days Maximum Temp. ≤ 32°F	0	0	0	0	0	0	0	0	0	0	0	0	0
Days Minimum Temp. ≤ 32°F	1	0	0	0	0	0	0	0	0	0	0	0	1
Days Minimum Temp. ≤ 0°F	0	0	0	0	0	0	0	0	0	0	0	0	0
Heating Degree Days (base 65°F)	87	67	28	5	0	0	0	0	0	1	12	55	255
Cooling Degree Days (base 65°F)	105	109	170	252	395	489	550	558	511	411	246	148	3,944
Mean Precipitation (in.)	3.12	3.35	4.57	2.78	5.43	6.93	6.25	6.43	8.16	6.42	4.18	2.72	60.34
Days With ≥ 0.1" Precipitation	5	5	6	6	8	11	11	11	11	9	6	5	94
Days With ≥ 1.0" Precipitation	1	1	1	1	2	2	2	2	2	2	1	1	18
Mean Snowfall (in.)	0.0	0.0	0.0	0.0	0.0	0.0	0.0	0.0	0.0	0.0	0.0	0.0	0.0
Days With ≥ 1.0" Snow Depth	0	0	0	0	0	0	0	0	0	0	0	0	0

Tamiami Trail 40 Mile Bend *Dade County* Elevation: 13 ft. Latitude: 25° 46' N Longitude: 80° 49' W

	JAN	FEB	MAR	APR	MAY	JUN	JUL	AUG	SEP	OCT	NOV	DEC	YEAR
Mean Maximum Temp. (°F)	77.6	78.7	***82.0***	85.6	89.1	91.0	92.2	92.4	90.9	***87.1***	82.6	78.7	***85.7***
Mean Temp. (°F)	67.4	68.0	***70.9***	74.2	78.2	81.5	83.2	83.7	82.8	***79.1***	74.1	69.1	***76.0***
Mean Minimum Temp. (°F)	57.0	57.3	***59.8***	62.7	67.2	71.9	74.2	75.0	74.6	***71.1***	65.5	59.4	***66.3***
Extreme Maximum Temp. (°F)	89	90	92	98	98	102	99	101	97	97	93	95	102
Extreme Minimum Temp. (°F)	28	33	34	42	45	59	63	64	65	52	36	28	28
Days Maximum Temp. ≥ 90°F	0	0	1	6	14	22	27	27	***22***	9	1	0	***129***
Days Maximum Temp. ≤ 32°F	0	0	0	0	0	0	0	0	0	0	0	0	0
Days Minimum Temp. ≤ 32°F	0	0	0	0	0	0	0	0	0	0	0	0	0
Days Minimum Temp. ≤ 0°F	0	0	0	0	0	0	0	0	0	0	0	0	0
Heating Degree Days (base 65°F)	61	43	***16***	3	0	0	0	0	0	0	6	39	***168***
Cooling Degree Days (base 65°F)	140	153	216	298	427	513	588	603	545	***457***	295	177	***4,412***
Mean Precipitation (in.)	1.90	2.00	2.30	2.38	4.96	8.54	7.60	6.91	6.56	4.46	2.28	1.63	51.52
Days With ≥ 0.1" Precipitation	3	3	3	4	7	11	11	11	10	6	3	3	75
Days With ≥ 1.0" Precipitation	0	0	0	1	1	3	2	2	2	1	1	0	13
Mean Snowfall (in.)	0.0	0.0	0.0	0.0	0.0	0.0	0.0	0.0	0.0	0.0	0.0	0.0	0.0
Days With ≥ 1.0" Snow Depth	0	0	0	0	0	0	0	0	0	0	0	0	0

Tarpon Springs Sewage Plant *Pinellas County* Elevation: 6 ft. Latitude: 28° 09' N Longitude: 82° 45' W

	JAN	FEB	MAR	APR	MAY	JUN	JUL	AUG	SEP	OCT	NOV	DEC	YEAR
Mean Maximum Temp. (°F)	71.1	72.8	77.4	81.6	86.9	90.0	91.4	91.5	90.2	85.2	79.0	73.5	82.5
Mean Temp. (°F)	60.6	62.2	66.9	71.2	76.8	81.0	82.5	82.5	81.0	75.2	68.6	62.8	72.6
Mean Minimum Temp. (°F)	50.1	51.6	56.3	60.8	66.6	71.9	73.5	73.5	71.9	65.1	58.2	52.1	62.6
Extreme Maximum Temp. (°F)	87	88	89	92	97	100	102	99	97	93	90	87	102
Extreme Minimum Temp. (°F)	19	23	31	37	45	51	64	64	55	42	28	21	19
Days Maximum Temp. ≥ 90°F	0	0	0	1	8	18	24	24	19	5	0	0	99
Days Maximum Temp. ≤ 32°F	0	0	0	0	0	0	0	0	0	0	0	0	0
Days Minimum Temp. ≤ 32°F	2	1	0	0	0	0	0	0	0	0	0	1	4
Days Minimum Temp. ≤ 0°F	0	0	0	0	0	0	0	0	0	0	0	0	0
Heating Degree Days (base 65°F)	183	132	58	10	0	0	0	0	0	3	43	137	566
Cooling Degree Days (base 65°F)	56	69	123	208	388	501	562	566	497	338	173	82	3,563
Mean Precipitation (in.)	3.26	3.31	4.05	1.95	3.15	5.67	6.72	8.31	7.04	3.41	2.36	3.01	52.24
Days With ≥ 0.1" Precipitation	5	4	5	3	4	8	10	11	9	5	4	4	72
Days With ≥ 1.0" Precipitation	1	1	2	1	1	2	2	3	2	1	1	1	18
Mean Snowfall (in.)	0.0	0.0	0.0	0.0	0.0	0.0	0.0	0.0	0.0	0.0	0.0	0.0	0.0
Days With ≥ 1.0" Snow Depth	0	0	0	0	0	0	0	0	0	0	0	0	0

Tavernier *Monroe County* Elevation: 6 ft. Latitude: 25° 00' N Longitude: 80° 31' W

	JAN	FEB	MAR	APR	MAY	JUN	JUL	AUG	SEP	OCT	NOV	DEC	YEAR
Mean Maximum Temp. (°F)	76.6	77.5	80.5	83.6	86.7	88.8	***90.9***	90.4	89.0	85.7	81.5	77.9	***84.1***
Mean Temp. (°F)	70.0	70.7	73.8	77.0	80.3	***82.8***	***84.6***	84.2	83.0	79.9	75.9	71.8	***77.8***
Mean Minimum Temp. (°F)	63.3	63.8	67.0	70.3	73.9	***76.7***	***78.2***	77.9	77.0	74.1	70.2	65.7	***71.5***
Extreme Maximum Temp. (°F)	86	87	90	94	93	***96***	***97***	97	95	94	90	89	***97***
Extreme Minimum Temp. (°F)	35	39	40	51	62	***68***	***69***	69	66	57	42	35	***35***
Days Maximum Temp. ≥ 90°F	0	0	0	1	4	12	20	20	13	3	0	0	73
Days Maximum Temp. ≤ 32°F	0	0	0	0	0	0	0	0	0	0	0	0	0
Days Minimum Temp. ≤ 32°F	0	0	0	0	0	0	0	0	0	0	0	0	0
Days Minimum Temp. ≤ 0°F	0	0	0	0	0	0	0	0	0	0	0	0	0
Heating Degree Days (base 65°F)	33	19	7	0	0	0	***0***	0	0	0	2	20	***81***
Cooling Degree Days (base 65°F)	***191***	201	276	362	487	***552***	***622***	606	551	473	341	237	***4,899***
Mean Precipitation (in.)	2.50	1.97	2.26	1.94	3.91	6.80	3.25	5.11	6.74	5.36	2.99	1.99	44.82
Days With ≥ 0.1" Precipitation	3	3	3	3	5	***8***	5	8	9	7	4	3	***61***
Days With ≥ 1.0" Precipitation	1	1	1	1	1	2	1	1	2	1	1	1	14
Mean Snowfall (in.)	0.0	0.0	0.0	0.0	0.0	0.0	0.0	0.0	0.0	0.0	0.0	0.0	0.0
Days With ≥ 1.0" Snow Depth	0	0	0	0	0	0	0	0	0	0	0	0	0

Titusville *Brevard County* Elevation: 29 ft. Latitude: 28° 37' N Longitude: 80° 50' W

	JAN	FEB	MAR	APR	MAY	JUN	JUL	AUG	SEP	OCT	NOV	DEC	YEAR
Mean Maximum Temp. (°F)	70.4	72.3	77.3	81.2	86.3	89.6	91.5	91.1	88.7	83.4	77.5	72.5	81.8
Mean Temp. (°F)	59.4	61.1	66.3	70.2	75.8	79.9	81.7	81.5	79.9	74.3	67.7	62.0	71.6
Mean Minimum Temp. (°F)	48.3	49.8	55.1	59.1	65.2	70.2	71.7	71.9	71.0	65.2	57.8	51.4	61.4
Extreme Maximum Temp. (°F)	88	88	92	96	101	103	101	100	98	98	93	88	103
Extreme Minimum Temp. (°F)	19	23	26	35	45	56	62	62	57	40	30	19	19
Days Maximum Temp. ≥ 90°F	0	0	1	2	8	16	23	22	13	3	0	0	88
Days Maximum Temp. ≤ 32°F	0	0	0	0	0	0	0	0	0	0	0	0	0
Days Minimum Temp. ≤ 32°F	2	1	0	0	0	0	0	0	0	0	0	1	4
Days Minimum Temp. ≤ 0°F	0	0	0	0	0	0	0	0	0	0	0	0	0
Heating Degree Days (base 65°F)	212	153	71	18	0	0	0	0	0	4	52	153	663
Cooling Degree Days (base 65°F)	34	50	111	171	339	456	531	521	446	303	143	65	3,170
Mean Precipitation (in.)	2.54	2.81	3.80	2.81	3.66	6.17	7.27	7.52	6.80	4.40	3.47	2.54	53.79
Days With ≥ 0.1" Precipitation	4	5	5	4	6	10	10	11	10	7	5	5	82
Days With ≥ 1.0" Precipitation	1	1	1	1	1	2	3	2	2	1	1	1	17
Mean Snowfall (in.)	trace	0.0	0.0	0.0	0.0	0.0	0.0	0.0	0.0	0.0	0.0	0.0	trace
Days With ≥ 1.0" Snow Depth	0	0	0	0	0	0	0	0	0	0	0	0	0

Usher Tower *Levy County* Elevation: 32 ft. Latitude: 29° 25' N Longitude: 82° 49' W

	JAN	FEB	MAR	APR	MAY	JUN	JUL	AUG	SEP	OCT	NOV	DEC	YEAR
Mean Maximum Temp. (°F)	68.2	71.0	77.0	82.3	87.8	91.0	91.9	91.3	89.7	83.8	76.2	70.2	81.7
Mean Temp. (°F)	55.8	58.3	63.8	68.7	74.7	79.5	81.1	81.1	79.1	71.5	63.6	57.7	69.6
Mean Minimum Temp. (°F)	43.4	45.6	50.6	55.1	61.5	67.9	70.2	70.8	68.5	59.3	51.1	45.2	57.4
Extreme Maximum Temp. (°F)	87	86	92	96	102	105	102	100	99	96	92	86	105
Extreme Minimum Temp. (°F)	9	17	22	32	42	44	59	61	48	32	17	12	9
Days Maximum Temp. ≥ 90°F	0	0	0	2	11	21	25	23	18	3	0	0	103
Days Maximum Temp. ≤ 32°F	0	0	0	0	0	0	0	0	0	0	0	0	0
Days Minimum Temp. ≤ 32°F	6	4	1	0	0	0	0	0	0	0	1	5	17
Days Minimum Temp. ≤ 0°F	0	0	0	0	0	0	0	0	0	0	0	0	0
Heating Degree Days (base 65°F)	299	210	107	29	1	0	0	0	0	16	118	249	1,029
Cooling Degree Days (base 65°F)	17	30	75	149	313	445	515	511	424	233	90	32	2,834
Mean Precipitation (in.)	4.57	3.52	4.81	3.66	3.09	6.72	8.49	10.22	6.38	2.99	2.54	3.32	60.31
Days With ≥ 0.1" Precipitation	7	5	6	4	5	9	12	14	9	4	4	5	84
Days With ≥ 1.0" Precipitation	2	1	2	1	1	2	2	3	2	1	1	1	19
Mean Snowfall (in.)	0.0	trace	0.0	0.0	0.0	0.0	0.0	0.0	0.0	0.0	0.0	0.0	trace
Days With ≥ 1.0" Snow Depth	0	0	0	0	0	0	0	0	0	0	0	0	0

Venice *Sarasota County* Elevation: 6 ft. Latitude: 27° 06' N Longitude: 82° 26' W

	JAN	FEB	MAR	APR	MAY	JUN	JUL	AUG	SEP	OCT	NOV	DEC	YEAR
Mean Maximum Temp. (°F)	71.8	73.6	77.4	81.5	86.4	89.5	***91.0***	91.2	90.0	***85.6***	***79.8***	74.4	***82.7***
Mean Temp. (°F)	61.4	63.0	67.3	71.4	76.7	80.9	***82.2***	82.5	81.4	***75.9***	***69.5***	***64.4***	***73.1***
Mean Minimum Temp. (°F)	51.0	52.3	57.2	61.1	66.9	72.2	73.4	73.8	72.8	66.3	59.1	54.1	63.4
Extreme Maximum Temp. (°F)	89	***89***	90	95	***98***	100	***99***	99	99	***95***	***91***	***89***	***100***
Extreme Minimum Temp. (°F)	23	***26***	33	41	51	***56***	***62***	65	61	***45***	***29***	***24***	***23***
Days Maximum Temp. ≥ 90°F	0	0	0	1	***7***	14	***22***	***23***	***18***	***4***	***0***	***0***	***89***
Days Maximum Temp. ≤ 32°F	0	0	0	0	0	0	***0***	0	0	***0***	***0***	0	***0***
Days Minimum Temp. ≤ 32°F	1	0	0	0	0	0	***0***	0	0	***0***	***0***	***1***	***2***
Days Minimum Temp. ≤ 0°F	0	0	0	0	0	0	***0***	0	0	***0***	***0***	0	***0***
Heating Degree Days (base 65°F)	166	117	50	9	0	0	***0***	0	0	***2***	***31***	***115***	***490***
Cooling Degree Days (base 65°F)	***59***	***79***	133	205	374	498	***559***	***568***	513	***364***	***176***	***109***	***3,637***
Mean Precipitation (in.)	2.73	2.15	3.60	1.85	2.28	6.74	6.64	8.30	7.39	3.12	2.09	2.34	49.23
Days With ≥ 0.1" Precipitation	4	4	4	3	4	8	10	12	10	4	3	3	69
Days With ≥ 1.0" Precipitation	1	1	1	1	1	2	2	2	2	1	1	1	16
Mean Snowfall (in.)	trace	0.0	0.0	0.0	0.0	0.0	0.0	0.0	0.0	0.0	0.0	0.0	trace
Days With ≥ 1.0" Snow Depth	0	0	0	0	0	0	0	0	0	0	0	0	0

Wauchula *Hardee County* Elevation: 59 ft. Latitude: 27° 33' N Longitude: 81° 48' W

	JAN	FEB	MAR	APR	MAY	JUN	JUL	AUG	SEP	OCT	NOV	DEC	YEAR
Mean Maximum Temp. (°F)	74.1	75.9	80.3	84.4	89.1	91.3	92.4	92.3	90.7	85.9	80.2	75.4	84.3
Mean Temp. (°F)	61.9	63.3	67.4	71.2	76.6	80.6	81.9	82.2	80.8	75.3	68.8	63.6	72.8
Mean Minimum Temp. (°F)	49.7	50.6	54.5	57.9	64.1	69.8	71.4	72.0	70.7	64.5	57.3	51.7	61.2
Extreme Maximum Temp. (°F)	87	90	94	96	99	102	100	98	96	95	90	92	102
Extreme Minimum Temp. (°F)	20	25	23	35	44	51	62	64	58	39	26	22	20
Days Maximum Temp. ≥ 90°F	0	0	1	5	15	22	27	27	22	6	0	0	125
Days Maximum Temp. ≤ 32°F	0	0	0	0	0	0	0	0	0	0	0	0	0
Days Minimum Temp. ≤ 32°F	2	1	0	0	0	0	0	0	0	0	0	1	4
Days Minimum Temp. ≤ 0°F	0	0	0	0	0	0	0	0	0	0	0	0	0
Heating Degree Days (base 65°F)	157	117	55	12	0	0	0	0	0	3	40	121	505
Cooling Degree Days (base 65°F)	63	81	127	196	364	479	538	545	477	331	161	80	3,442
Mean Precipitation (in.)	2.41	2.71	3.47	2.33	4.00	8.01	8.07	7.32	6.03	2.73	2.08	1.98	51.14
Days With ≥ 0.1" Precipitation	4	4	5	3	5	10	11	12	9	4	3	3	73
Days With ≥ 1.0" Precipitation	1	1	1	1	1	2	3	2	2	1	0	1	16
Mean Snowfall (in.)	trace	0.0	0.0	0.0	0.0	0.0	0.0	0.0	0.0	0.0	0.0	0.0	trace
Days With ≥ 1.0" Snow Depth	0	0	0	0	0	0	0	0	0	0	0	0	0

Weeki Wachee *Hernando County* Elevation: 19 ft. Latitude: 28° 31' N Longitude: 82° 35' W

	JAN	FEB	MAR	APR	MAY	JUN	JUL	AUG	SEP	OCT	NOV	DEC	YEAR
Mean Maximum Temp. (°F)	70.3	72.2	77.2	82.2	87.1	90.2	91.6	91.5	90.3	85.0	78.7	72.8	82.4
Mean Temp. (°F)	57.4	59.2	64.3	69.1	74.8	79.8	81.2	81.1	79.6	73.1	66.1	59.6	70.4
Mean Minimum Temp. (°F)	44.5	46.1	51.4	55.9	62.4	69.2	70.8	70.7	68.8	61.0	53.3	46.4	58.4
Extreme Maximum Temp. (°F)	88	91	92	96	100	100	100	98	98	97	91	90	100
Extreme Minimum Temp. (°F)	13	22	21	34	44	47	60	63	48	36	23	19	13
Days Maximum Temp. ≥ 90°F	0	0	0	2	9	19	25	25	19	5	0	0	104
Days Maximum Temp. ≤ 32°F	0	0	0	0	0	0	0	0	0	0	0	0	0
Days Minimum Temp. ≤ 32°F	5	3	1	0	0	0	0	0	0	0	0	3	12
Days Minimum Temp. ≤ 0°F	0	0	0	0	0	0	0	0	0	0	0	0	0
Heating Degree Days (base 65°F)	264	197	106	30	1	0	0	0	0	9	76	208	891
Cooling Degree Days (base 65°F)	34	45	89	161	321	464	525	519	444	276	127	52	3,057
Mean Precipitation (in.)	3.84	3.20	4.24	2.51	2.95	5.92	8.31	7.60	6.46	2.29	2.12	2.50	51.94
Days With ≥ 0.1" Precipitation	5	4	4	3	4	7	11	10	7	3	3	4	65
Days With ≥ 1.0" Precipitation	1	1	1	1	1	2	3	2	2	1	1	1	17
Mean Snowfall (in.)	0.0	0.0	0.0	0.0	0.0	0.0	0.0	0.0	0.0	0.0	0.0	0.0	0.0
Days With ≥ 1.0" Snow Depth	0	0	0	0	0	0	0	0	0	0	0	0	0

Note: *See Appendix D for explanation of data.*

Annual Extreme Maximum Temperature

Highest

Rank	Station Name	°F
1	High Springs	107
2	Live Oak	106
2	Pensacola Regional Airport	106
4	De Funiak Springs	***105***
4	Lakeland Linder Airport	***105***
4	Mountain Lake	105
4	Myakka River State Park	105
4	Ocala	105
4	Usher Tower	105
10	Arcadia	104
10	Brooksville Chin Hill	104
10	Chipley 3 E	104
10	Flamingo Ranger Station	104
10	La Belle	***104***
10	Lake Alfred Exp. Station	104
10	Lake City 2 E	104
10	Mayo	104
10	Perry	104
19	Apalachicola Municipal Airport	103
19	Archbold Bio Station	103
19	Bartow	103
19	Fort Myers Page Field	***103***
19	Jacksonville Beach	103
19	Jacksonville Int'l Airport	103
19	Jasper	103

Lowest

Rank	Station Name	°F
1	Tavernier	***97***
2	Belle Glade Exp. Station	98
2	Key West Int'l Airport	98
2	Miami Beach	98
2	Miami Int'l Airport	98
6	Fort Lauderdale	99
6	Naples	99
6	Tampa Int'l Airport	99
6	Vero Beach	99
6	West Palm Beach Int'l Airport	99
11	Bradenton 5 ESE	100
11	Canal Point USDA	100
11	Hialeah	100
11	Saint Petersburg	100
11	Venice	***100***
11	Weeki Wachee	100
17	Avon Park 2 W	101
17	Clermont 7 S	101
17	Clewiston U.S. Engineers	101
17	Cross City 2 WNW	101
17	Fort Pierce	101
17	Immokalee 3 NNW	101
17	Inverness 3 SE	101
17	Kissimmee 2	101
17	Lisbon	101

Annual Mean Maximum Temperature

Highest

Rank	Station Name	°F
1	Tamiami Trail 40 Mile Bend	***85.7***
2	Myakka River State Park	85.3
3	Naples	85.1
4	Archbold Bio Station	84.9
4	Immokalee 3 NNW	84.9
6	Fort Myers Page Field	84.5
6	Punta Gorda 4 ESE	84.5
8	Mountain Lake	84.4
9	Hialeah	84.3
9	Wauchula	84.3
11	Canal Point USDA	84.1
11	Tavernier	***84.1***
13	Bartow	84.0
13	Belle Glade Exp. Station	84.0
15	Arcadia	83.9
15	Fort Drum 5 NW	***83.9***
17	Flamingo Ranger Station	83.8
18	Lake Alfred Exp. Station	83.7
18	Lakeland Linder Airport	***83.7***
20	Clewiston U.S. Engineers	***83.6***
20	Moore Haven Lock 1	83.6
20	Plant City	83.6
20	Saint Leo	83.6
24	Avon Park 2 W	83.5
24	Kissimmee 2	83.5

Lowest

Rank	Station Name	°F
1	Fernandina Beach	77.0
1	Pensacola Regional Airport	77.0
3	Apalachicola Municipal Airport	77.2
4	Jacksonville Beach	***77.6***
5	Chipley 3 E	77.8
5	Panama City 5 NE	77.8
7	Monticello 3 W	78.0
8	Milton Experiment Station	78.1
8	Quincy 3 SSW	78.1
10	De Funiak Springs	78.6
11	Saint Augustine	***79.2***
12	Jacksonville Int'l Airport	79.3
13	Cross City 2 WNW	***79.4***
13	Jasper	79.4
13	Lake City 2 E	79.4
16	Tallahassee Municipal Airport	79.5
17	Daytona Beach Regional Airport	80.3
18	Mayo	80.4
19	Miami Beach	81.1
20	Lisbon	81.3
21	Saint Petersburg	81.4
22	Melbourne Regional Airport	81.6
22	Perry	81.6
24	Live Oak	81.7
24	Usher Tower	81.7

Annual Mean Temperature

Highest			Lowest		
Rank	Station Name	°F	Rank	Station Name	°F
1	Key West Int'l Airport	78.0	1	Chipley 3 E	66.1
2	Tavernier	***77.8***	1	Monticello 3 W	66.1
3	Miami Int'l Airport	76.6	3	De Funiak Springs	66.4
4	Hialeah	76.4	4	Milton Experiment Station	66.8
4	Miami Beach	76.4	5	Panama City 5 NE	66.9
6	Tamiami Trail 40 Mile Bend	***76.0***	6	Jasper	67.0
7	Fort Lauderdale	75.7	6	Quincy 3 SSW	67.0
8	West Palm Beach Int'l Airport	75.3	8	Tallahassee Municipal Airport	67.4
9	Flamingo Ranger Station	74.9	9	Cross City 2 WNW	***67.7***
9	Fort Myers Page Field	74.9	10	Pensacola Regional Airport	68.1
11	Naples	74.8	11	Lake City 2 E	68.2
12	Stuart 1 S	74.5	12	Mayo	68.3
13	Clewiston U.S. Engineers	***74.3***	13	Fernandina Beach	68.4
14	Saint Petersburg	74.1	14	Jacksonville Int'l Airport	68.5
15	Immokalee 3 NNW	73.8	15	Apalachicola Municipal Airport	68.6
15	Punta Gorda 4 ESE	73.8	16	Perry	69.0
17	Canal Point USDA	73.7	17	High Springs	69.2
18	Moore Haven Lock 1	73.4	18	Live Oak	69.4
19	Fort Pierce	73.3	19	Jacksonville Beach	***69.5***
19	Myakka River State Park	73.3	20	Usher Tower	69.6
21	Bartow	73.2	21	Saint Augustine	***69.8***
21	Belle Glade Exp. Station	73.2	22	Inverness 3 SE	70.4
21	Lakeland Linder Airport	***73.2***	22	Weeki Wachee	70.4
24	Venice	***73.1***	24	Ocala	70.8
25	Kissimmee 2	72.8	25	Daytona Beach Regional Airport	70.9

Annual Mean Minimum Temperature

Highest			Lowest		
Rank	Station Name	°F	Rank	Station Name	°F
1	Key West Int'l Airport	73.2	1	De Funiak Springs	54.2
2	Miami Beach	71.6	1	Monticello 3 W	54.2
3	Tavernier	***71.5***	3	Chipley 3 E	54.3
4	Miami Int'l Airport	69.7	4	Jasper	54.6
5	Hialeah	68.4	5	Tallahassee Municipal Airport	55.3
6	Fort Lauderdale	68.0	6	Milton Experiment Station	55.5
7	West Palm Beach Int'l Airport	67.4	7	Cross City 2 WNW	***55.8***
8	Saint Petersburg	66.7	8	Quincy 3 SSW	55.9
9	Tamiami Trail 40 Mile Bend	***66.3***	9	Panama City 5 NE	56.0
10	Flamingo Ranger Station	66.0	10	High Springs	56.2
11	Stuart 1 S	65.7	10	Mayo	56.2
12	Fort Myers Page Field	65.2	10	Perry	56.2
13	Clewiston U.S. Engineers	***65.1***	13	Live Oak	57.0
14	Naples	64.4	14	Lake City 2 E	57.1
15	Tampa Int'l Airport	63.6	15	Usher Tower	57.4
16	Venice	***63.4***	16	Jacksonville Int'l Airport	57.7
17	Canal Point USDA	63.3	17	Weeki Wachee	58.4
17	Fort Pierce	63.3	18	Inverness 3 SE	58.7
19	Melbourne Regional Airport	63.2	19	Ocala	58.8
20	Punta Gorda 4 ESE	63.1	20	Archbold Bio Station	59.1
21	Moore Haven Lock 1	63.0	21	Pensacola Regional Airport	59.2
22	Immokalee 3 NNW	62.6	22	Apalachicola Municipal Airport	59.9
22	Lakeland Linder Airport	***62.6***	22	Fernandina Beach	59.9
22	Tarpon Springs Sewage Plant	62.6	24	Lisbon	60.4
25	Orlando Int'l Airport	***62.5***	24	Saint Augustine	***60.4***

Annual Extreme Minimum Temperature

Highest

Rank	Station Name	°F
1	Key West Int'l Airport	41
2	Tavernier	***35***
3	Miami Beach	32
4	Miami Int'l Airport	30
5	Fort Lauderdale	28
5	Hialeah	28
5	Tamiami Trail 40 Mile Bend	28
8	Fort Myers Page Field	***27***
8	West Palm Beach Int'l Airport	27
10	Clewiston U.S. Engineers	26
10	Naples	26
12	Canal Point USDA	25
13	Flamingo Ranger Station	24
13	Saint Petersburg	24
15	Moore Haven Lock 1	23
15	Punta Gorda 4 ESE	23
15	Stuart 1 S	23
15	Venice	***23***
15	Vero Beach	23
20	Belle Glade Exp. Station	21
21	Bartow	20
21	Bradenton 5 ESE	20
21	Immokalee 3 NNW	20
21	Lakeland Linder Airport	***20***
21	Wauchula	20

Lowest

Rank	Station Name	°F
1	Quincy 3 SSW	0
2	Chipley 3 E	2
3	De Funiak Springs	***3***
3	Milton Experiment Station	3
5	Fernandina Beach	4
5	Jasper	4
5	Monticello 3 W	4
8	Pensacola Regional Airport	5
9	Live Oak	6
9	Panama City 5 NE	6
9	Tallahassee Municipal Airport	6
12	Jacksonville Int'l Airport	7
12	Lake City 2 E	7
12	Mayo	7
12	Perry	7
16	High Springs	***8***
17	Apalachicola Municipal Airport	9
17	Usher Tower	9
19	Cross City 2 WNW	10
19	Saint Augustine	***10***
21	Ocala	11
22	Archbold Bio Station	13
22	Brooksville Chin Hill	13
22	Weeki Wachee	13
25	Jacksonville Beach	14

July Mean Maximum Temperature

Highest

Rank	Station Name	°F
1	Live Oak	93.1
2	Archbold Bio Station	93.0
2	Myakka River State Park	93.0
4	Lakeland Linder Airport	92.9
5	Lake Alfred Exp. Station	92.8
5	Mountain Lake	92.8
7	Perry	92.7
8	High Springs	92.5
9	Saint Leo	92.4
9	Wauchula	92.4
11	Bartow	92.3
11	Ocala	92.3
13	Mayo	92.2
13	Punta Gorda 4 ESE	92.2
13	Tamiami Trail 40 Mile Bend	92.2
16	Jacksonville Int'l Airport	92.1
17	Sanford Experiment Station	92.0
18	Orlando Int'l Airport	91.9
18	Usher Tower	91.9
20	Arcadia	91.8
20	Avon Park 2 W	91.8
20	Canal Point USDA	91.8
20	Clewiston U.S. Engineers	91.8
20	De Funiak Springs	91.8
20	Kissimmee 2	91.8

Lowest

Rank	Station Name	°F
1	Miami Beach	87.4
2	Flamingo Ranger Station	89.3
2	Key West Int'l Airport	89.3
4	Fort Lauderdale	89.5
5	Apalachicola Municipal Airport	89.7
5	Miami Int'l Airport	89.7
7	Jacksonville Beach	89.8
8	Fernandina Beach	89.9
8	Panama City 5 NE	89.9
10	Stuart 1 S	90.0
11	West Palm Beach Int'l Airport	90.1
12	Cross City 2 WNW	***90.4***
12	Vero Beach	90.4
14	Daytona Beach Regional Airport	90.5
14	Melbourne Regional Airport	90.5
14	Pensacola Regional Airport	90.5
17	Monticello 3 W	90.6
17	Saint Augustine	90.6
17	Saint Petersburg	90.6
20	Brooksville Chin Hill	90.7
20	Quincy 3 SSW	90.7
20	Tampa Int'l Airport	90.7
23	Hialeah	90.8
24	Tavernier	***90.9***
25	Venice	***91.0***

January Mean Minimum Temperature

Highest			Lowest		
Rank	Station Name	°F	Rank	Station Name	°F
1	Key West Int'l Airport	65.1	1	Chipley 3 E	37.6
2	Tavernier	63.3	2	Monticello 3 W	37.8
3	Miami Beach	63.0	3	De Funiak Springs	38.2
4	Miami Int'l Airport	60.1	4	Jasper	38.4
5	Fort Lauderdale	58.6	5	Milton Experiment Station	39.1
6	Hialeah	58.5	5	Tallahassee Municipal Airport	39.1
7	West Palm Beach Int'l Airport	57.1	7	Panama City 5 NE	39.7
8	Tamiami Trail 40 Mile Bend	57.0	8	Cross City 2 WNW	39.8
9	Flamingo Ranger Station	56.0	8	Quincy 3 SSW	39.8
10	Stuart 1 S	55.1	10	High Springs	40.2
11	Saint Petersburg	54.3	10	Mayo	40.2
12	Clewiston U.S. Engineers	54.2	12	Perry	41.4
13	Fort Myers Page Field	54.1	13	Jacksonville Int'l Airport	41.8
14	Naples	54.0	13	Lake City 2 E	41.8
15	Canal Point USDA	52.9	15	Live Oak	42.1
16	Immokalee 3 NNW	52.0	16	Pensacola Regional Airport	42.6
17	Belle Glade Exp. Station	51.9	17	Fernandina Beach	43.2
18	Fort Pierce	51.7	18	Usher Tower	43.4
18	Punta Gorda 4 ESE	51.7	19	Apalachicola Municipal Airport	44.1
20	Moore Haven Lock 1	51.6	19	Inverness 3 SE	44.1
21	Melbourne Regional Airport	51.2	21	Weeki Wachee	44.5
22	Venice	51.0	22	Ocala	45.6
23	Tampa Int'l Airport	50.6	23	Jacksonville Beach	46.0
23	Vero Beach	50.6	23	Saint Augustine	***46.0***
25	Lakeland Linder Airport	50.4	25	Lisbon	46.7

Number of Annual Heating Degree Days

Highest			Lowest		
Rank	Station Name	Num.	Rank	Station Name	Num.
1	Chipley 3 E	1,867	1	Key West Int'l Airport	61
2	Monticello 3 W	1,767	2	Tavernier	***81***
3	De Funiak Springs	1,730	3	Miami Beach	130
4	Milton Experiment Station	1,710	4	Miami Int'l Airport	151
5	Panama City 5 NE	1,608	5	Hialeah	155
6	Quincy 3 SSW	1,602	6	Tamiami Trail 40 Mile Bend	***168***
7	Tallahassee Municipal Airport	1,592	7	Fort Lauderdale	172
8	Jasper	1,591	8	Flamingo Ranger Station	191
9	Pensacola Regional Airport	1,472	9	West Palm Beach Int'l Airport	238
10	Mayo	1,394	10	Naples	249
11	Cross City 2 WNW	***1,391***	11	Stuart 1 S	255
12	Lake City 2 E	1,333	12	Fort Myers Page Field	303
13	Jacksonville Int'l Airport	1,325	13	Canal Point USDA	308
14	Fernandina Beach	1,297	14	Immokalee 3 NNW	323
15	Apalachicola Municipal Airport	1,277	15	Clewiston U.S. Engineers	***335***
16	Perry	1,210	16	Punta Gorda 4 ESE	374
17	Live Oak	1,173	17	Belle Glade Exp. Station	380
18	High Springs	***1,139***	18	Saint Petersburg	403
19	Jacksonville Beach	***1,059***	19	Fort Pierce	414
20	Usher Tower	1,029	20	Moore Haven Lock 1	424
21	Saint Augustine	***933***	21	Fort Drum 5 NW	***446***
22	Inverness 3 SE	929	22	Myakka River State Park	450
23	Weeki Wachee	891	23	Vero Beach	479
24	Ocala	841	24	Bartow	483
25	Lisbon	830	25	Venice	***490***

Number of Annual Cooling Degree Days

Highest

Rank	Station Name	Num.
1	Key West Int'l Airport	4,926
2	Tavernier	***4,899***
3	Hialeah	4,586
4	Miami Int'l Airport	4,543
5	Miami Beach	4,462
6	Tamiami Trail 40 Mile Bend	***4,412***
7	Fort Lauderdale	4,295
8	West Palm Beach Int'l Airport	4,139
9	Fort Myers Page Field	***4,098***
10	Flamingo Ranger Station	3,977
11	Naples	3,953
12	Stuart 1 S	3,944
13	Clewiston U.S. Engineers	***3,905***
14	Punta Gorda 4 ESE	3,805
15	Saint Petersburg	3,770
16	Lakeland Linder Airport	***3,762***
17	Immokalee 3 NNW	3,671
18	Bartow	3,659
19	Canal Point USDA	3,657
20	Myakka River State Park	3,652
21	Venice	***3,637***
22	Moore Haven Lock 1	3,629
23	Tampa Int'l Airport	3,575
24	Tarpon Springs Sewage Plant	3,563
25	Fort Pierce	3,559

Lowest

Rank	Station Name	Num.
1	Monticello 3 W	2,314
2	Chipley 3 E	2,345
3	De Funiak Springs	***2,365***
4	Panama City 5 NE	2,399
5	Jasper	2,440
6	Quincy 3 SSW	2,474
7	Milton Experiment Station	2,475
8	Cross City 2 WNW	***2,499***
9	Tallahassee Municipal Airport	2,627
10	Fernandina Beach	2,677
10	Lake City 2 E	2,677
12	Pensacola Regional Airport	2,690
13	Apalachicola Municipal Airport	2,721
14	Gainesville Regional Airport	***2,729***
15	Mayo	2,744
16	Jacksonville Int'l Airport	2,750
17	Perry	2,751
18	Saint Augustine	2,781
19	High Springs	2,801
20	Jacksonville Beach	***2,810***
21	Usher Tower	2,834
22	Inverness 3 SE	2,916
23	Live Oak	2,919
24	Daytona Beach Regional Airport	3,015
25	Lisbon	3,036

Annual Precipitation

Highest

Rank	Station Name	Inches
1	Milton Experiment Station	70.20
2	De Funiak Springs	67.06
3	Panama City 5 NE	66.07
4	Hialeah	65.92
5	Pensacola Regional Airport	65.18
6	Tallahassee Municipal Airport	64.31
7	Fort Lauderdale	64.13
8	West Palm Beach Int'l Airport	61.81
9	Stuart 1 S	60.34
10	Usher Tower	60.31
11	Myakka River State Park	59.11
12	Cross City 2 WNW	59.03
13	Perry	58.97
14	Chipley 3 E	58.61
15	Monticello 3 W	58.41
16	Miami Int'l Airport	58.00
17	Quincy 3 SSW	57.20
18	Apalachicola Municipal Airport	56.91
19	Vero Beach	55.71
20	Mayo	55.59
21	Fort Myers Page Field	54.86
22	High Springs	54.58
23	Saint Leo	54.29
24	Bradenton 5 ESE	54.27
25	Lake City 2 E	54.15

Lowest

Rank	Station Name	Inches
1	Key West Int'l Airport	39.32
2	Tavernier	44.82
3	Tampa Int'l Airport	45.07
4	Clewiston U.S. Engineers	45.79
5	Miami Beach	46.75
6	Moore Haven Lock 1	47.05
7	Flamingo Ranger Station	47.81
7	Saint Augustine	***47.81***
9	Melbourne Regional Airport	48.16
10	Kissimmee 2	48.34
11	Mountain Lake	48.52
12	Lisbon	48.88
13	Daytona Beach Regional Airport	48.92
14	Venice	49.23
15	Saint Petersburg	49.29
16	Orlando Int'l Airport	***49.70***
17	Arcadia	49.82
18	Avon Park 2 W	49.86
19	Punta Gorda 4 ESE	50.01
20	Immokalee 3 NNW	50.08
21	Lakeland Linder Airport	***50.11***
22	Clermont 7 S	50.32
23	Lake Alfred Exp. Station	50.60
24	Ocala	50.68
25	Fernandina Beach	50.87

Number of Days Annually With ≥ 0.1″ Precipitation

Highest			Lowest		
Rank	Station Name	Days	Rank	Station Name	Days
1	Stuart 1 S	94	1	Fort Drum 5 NW	60
2	Hialeah	92	2	Tavernier	***61***
3	West Palm Beach Int'l Airport	89	3	Key West Int'l Airport	62
4	Fort Lauderdale	88	3	La Belle	62
5	Miami Int'l Airport	86	5	Weeki Wachee	65
6	De Funiak Springs	85	6	Arcadia	66
7	Milton Experiment Station	84	6	Clewiston U.S. Engineers	66
7	Usher Tower	84	8	Tampa Int'l Airport	67
7	Vero Beach	84	9	Saint Petersburg	69
10	Titusville	82	9	Sanford Experiment Station	***69***
11	Fort Pierce	81	9	Venice	69
11	Panama City 5 NE	81	12	Parrish	70
11	Perry	81	13	Brooksville Chin Hill	71
14	Tallahassee Municipal Airport	80	13	Flamingo Ranger Station	71
15	Belle Glade Exp. Station	79	13	Miami Beach	71
15	Chipley 3 E	79	16	Apalachicola Municipal Airport	72
17	Cross City 2 WNW	78	16	Daytona Beach Regional Airport	72
17	Jacksonville Int'l Airport	78	16	Live Oak	72
17	Myakka River State Park	78	16	Melbourne Regional Airport	72
17	Ocala	78	16	Moore Haven Lock 1	72
21	Canal Point USDA	77	16	Saint Augustine	***72***
21	High Springs	77	16	Tarpon Springs Sewage Plant	72
21	Immokalee 3 NNW	77	23	Avon Park 2 W	73
21	Lake City 2 E	77	23	Lake Alfred Exp. Station	73
21	Mayo	77	23	Wauchula	73

Number of Days Annually With ≥ 0.1″ Precipitation

Highest			Lowest		
Rank	Station Name	Days	Rank	Station Name	Days
1	De Funiak Springs	21	1	Flamingo Ranger Station	11
1	Hialeah	21	1	Key West Int'l Airport	11
3	Milton Experiment Station	20	3	Saint Augustine	***13***
3	Myakka River State Park	20	3	Tamiami Trail 40 Mile Bend	13
3	Panama City 5 NE	20	5	Clewiston U.S. Engineers	14
6	Archbold Bio Station	19	5	Moore Haven Lock 1	14
6	Cross City 2 WNW	19	5	Tavernier	14
6	Fort Lauderdale	19	8	Belle Glade Exp. Station	15
6	Pensacola Regional Airport	19	8	Clermont 7 S	15
6	Perry	19	8	Daytona Beach Regional Airport	15
6	Tallahassee Municipal Airport	19	8	Fernandina Beach	15
6	Usher Tower	19	8	Jacksonville Int'l Airport	15
6	West Palm Beach Int'l Airport	19	8	Kissimmee 2	15
14	Bradenton 5 ESE	18	8	La Belle	15
14	Chipley 3 E	18	8	Melbourne Regional Airport	15
14	High Springs	18	8	Miami Beach	15
14	Mayo	18	8	Ocala	15
14	Parrish	18	8	Punta Gorda 4 ESE	15
14	Saint Leo	18	8	Tampa Int'l Airport	15
14	Stuart 1 S	18	8	Vero Beach	15
14	Tarpon Springs Sewage Plant	18	21	Fort Drum 5 NW	16
22	Apalachicola Municipal Airport	17	21	Fort Myers Page Field	16
22	Arcadia	17	21	Fort Pierce	16
22	Avon Park 2 W	17	21	Inverness 3 SE	16
22	Bartow	17	21	Jacksonville Beach	16

Annual Snowfall

Highest

Rank	Station Name	Inches
1	Milton Experiment Station	0.2
2	Live Oak	0.1
3	Apalachicola Municipal Airport	Trace
3	Archbold Bio Station	Trace
3	Avon Park 2 W	Trace
3	Belle Glade Exp. Station	Trace
3	Chipley 3 E	Trace
3	Clermont 7 S	Trace
3	Daytona Beach Regional Airport	Trace
3	De Funiak Springs	Trace
3	Fernandina Beach	Trace
3	Fort Drum 5 NW	Trace
3	Fort Pierce	Trace
3	High Springs	Trace
3	Jacksonville Beach	Trace
3	Jacksonville Int'l Airport	Trace
3	Jasper	Trace
3	La Belle	Trace
3	Lake Alfred Exp. Station	Trace
3	Lake City 2 E	Trace
3	Lakeland Linder Airport	***Trace***
3	Lisbon	Trace
3	Mayo	Trace
3	Miami Int'l Airport	Trace
3	Monticello 3 W	Trace

Lowest

Rank	Station Name	Inches
1	Arcadia	0.0
1	Bartow	0.0
1	Bradenton 5 ESE	0.0
1	Brooksville Chin Hill	0.0
1	Canal Point USDA	0.0
1	Clewiston U.S. Engineers	0.0
1	Cross City 2 WNW	0.0
1	Flamingo Ranger Station	0.0
1	Fort Lauderdale	0.0
1	Fort Myers Page Field	***0.0***
1	Hialeah	0.0
1	Immokalee 3 NNW	0.0
1	Inverness 3 SE	0.0
1	Key West Int'l Airport	0.0
1	Kissimmee 2	0.0
1	Melbourne Regional Airport	0.0
1	Miami Beach	0.0
1	Moore Haven Lock 1	0.0
1	Naples	0.0
1	Plant City	0.0
1	Punta Gorda 4 ESE	0.0
1	Sanford Experiment Station	0.0
1	Stuart 1 S	0.0
1	Tamiami Trail 40 Mile Bend	0.0
1	Tarpon Springs Sewage Plant	0.0

Note: *See User's Guide for explanation of data.*

Deadliest Storm Events in Florida: January 1995 - May 2005

Rank	Location or County	Date	Storm Event	Fatalities	Injuries	Property Damage ($mil.)	Crop Damage ($mil.)
1	Intercession City	2/23/1998	Tornado	25	145	50.0	0.0
2	Longwood	2/23/1998	Tornado	12	36	30.0	0.0
3	Escambia, Okaloosa, and Santa Rosa Counties	9/13/2004	Hurricane Ivan	7	0	4,000.0	25.0
4	Southwest and West Central Florida	8/13/2004	Hurricane Charlie	7	780	5,400.0	285.0
5	Inlet Beach	6/8/2003	Rip Current	6	0	0.0	0.0
6	Western Florida Panhandle	9/15/2004	Hurricane Ivan	6	16	90.4	0.0
7	Blountstown	9/15/2004	Tornado	4	5	2.5	0.0
8	Central Florida Coast	9/4/2004	Hurricane Frances	4	0	0.0	0.0
9	Orange, Osceola, and Seminole Counties	8/13/2004	High Wind (Hurricane Charlie)	4	0	1,300.0	0.0
10	Brevard, Osceola, Orange and Indian River Counties	8/2/1995	Hurricane Erin	3	0	0.0	130.0
11	Coastal Broward and Coastal Palm Beach Counties	11/11/2003	Heavy Surf/High Surf	3	0	0.0	0.0
12	Winter Garden	2/22/1998	Tornado	3	70	15.0	0.0
13	Boca Raton	9/1/2003	Rip Current	2	0	0.0	0.0
14	Charlotte Harbor	3/29/2001	Lightning	2	0	0.0	0.0
15	Coastal Miami-Dade County	7/10/1996	Hurricane	2	0	0.0	0.0
16	Coastal Palm Beach County	4/20/2003	Heavy Surf/High Surf	2	0	0.0	0.0
17	Coconut Creek	6/8/2000	Lightning	2	0	0.0	0.0
18	Crescent Beach	5/7/1995	Rip Current	2	0	0.0	0.0
19	Daytona Beach	6/7/2000	Rip Currents	2	0	0.0	0.0
20	Eastern Florida Panhandle	8/2/1995	Hurricane Erin	2	0	1.0	0.0
21	Fort Myers	3/28/1997	Rip Currents	2	0	0.0	0.0
22	Lake Okeechobee	12/26/1998	High Wind	2	0	0.0	0.0
23	Lakeland	7/6/1998	Lightning	2	0	0.0	0.0
24	Marco Island	9/27/1997	Rip Currents	2	0	0.0	0.0
25	Miami Beach	7/28/1996	Rip Currents	2	0	0.0	0.0
26	Naples Park	8/17/1996	Lightning	2	6	0.0	0.0
27	Navarre	6/6/2001	Rip Currents	2	2	0.0	0.0
28	North Naples	9/5/1995	Lightning	2	1	0.0	0.0
29	Orlando	8/16/1998	Lightning	2	0	0.0	0.0
30	Panama City Area	9/2/1998	Hurricane Earl	2	2	6.0	0.0
31	Panama City Beach	7/2/2003	Rip Current	2	0	0.0	0.0
32	Pensacola Beach	6/4/2000	Rip Currents	2	0	0.0	0.0
33	Pensacola Beach	9/8/2001	Lightning	2	0	0.0	0.0
34	Putnam County	11/12/2003	Dense Fog	2	7	0.1	0.0
35	South Columbia	8/2/1995	Wind	2	0	0.0	0.0
36	South Florida	11/4/1998	Tropical Storm Mitch	2	65	30.0	20.0
37	Tampa	8/23/1998	Rip Currents	2	0	0.0	0.0
38	Volusia County	8/13/2004	Hurricane Charlie	2	0	52.0	0.0

Most Destructive Storm Events in Florida: January 1995 - May 2005

Rank	Location or County	Date	Storm Event	Fatalities	Injuries	Property Damage ($mil.)	Crop Damage ($mil.)
1	Charlotte, De Soto, Lee, Manatee, Sarasota Counties	8/13/2004	Hurricane Charley	7	780	5,400.0	285.0
2	Brevard, Indian River, Martin, St. Lucie, Volusia Counties	9/4/2004	Hurricane Frances	0	0	4,800.0	93.2
3	Escambia, Okaloosa, and Santa Rosa Counties	9/13/2004	Hurricane Ivan	7	0	4,000.0	25.0
4	Orange, Osceola, and Seminole Counties	8/13/2004	High Wind (Hurricane Charley)	4	0	1,300.0	0.0
5	Northwest Florida	10/4/1995	Hurricane Opal	0	0	1,000.0	0.0
6	Hardee, Highlands, and Polk Counties	8/13/2004	High Wind (Hurricane Charley)	1	12	929.0	175.0
7	Highlands, and Polk Counties	9/25/2004	High Wind (Hurricane Jeanne)	0	0	702.0	0.0
8	Broward, Collier, Miami-Dade, Palm Beach, Glades, and Hendry Counties	9/4/2004	Hurricane Frances	0	0	621.0	90.0
9	Coastal Broward and Miami-Dade Counties	10/3/2000	Flood	0	0	450.0	500.0
10	Brevard, Indian River, Martin, St. Lucie, and Volusia Counties	9/25/2004	Hurricane Jeanne	0	0	379.9	8.7
11	Calhoun, Franklin, Gadsden, Gulf, Holmes, Jackson, Walton Counties	3/10/1998	Flood	0	0	367.0	0.0
12	Broward, Dade, Palm Beach, Glades, Hendry Counties	9/25/2004	Hurricane Jeanne	0	0	323.0	30.0
13	Coastal Broward, Miami-Dade, Palm Beach Counties	10/14/1999	Hurricane Irene	0	4	262.0	338.0
14	Coastal Miami-Dade, Monroe County/Lower Keys	9/25/1998	Hurricane Georges	0	0	255.0	15.0
15	Northwest Florida	8/3/1995	Hurricane Erin	0	0	230.0	5.0
16	Brevard County	7/1/1998	Wild/Forest Fire	0	52	200.0	0.0
17	Charlotte, Citrus, De Soto, Hernando, Hillsborough, Lee, Levy, Manatee, Pasco, and Pinellas Counties	9/5/2004	Tropical Storm Frances	1	0	179.4	0.0
18	Miami Int'l Airport	2/2/1998	Tornado	0	6	175.0	0.0
19	Volusia County	7/1/1998	Wild/Forest Fire	0	11	150.0	0.0
20	Escambia, Okaloosa, and Santa Rosa Counties	9/25/1998	Hurricane Georges	0	0	135.0	0.0
21	Charlotte, Citrus, De Soto, Hernando, Hillsborough, Lee, Levy, Manatee, Pasco, Pinellas, and Sarasota Counties	9/25/2004	Tropical Storm Jeanne	0	0	134.8	0.0
22	Hardee, Highlands, Polk, and Sumter Counties	9/5/2004	High Wind (Hurricane Frances)	0	0	127.2	0.0
23	Miami-Dade County, East Portion	10/15/1999	Flash Flood	0	0	100.0	200.0

FLORIDA - Core Based Statistical Areas and Counties

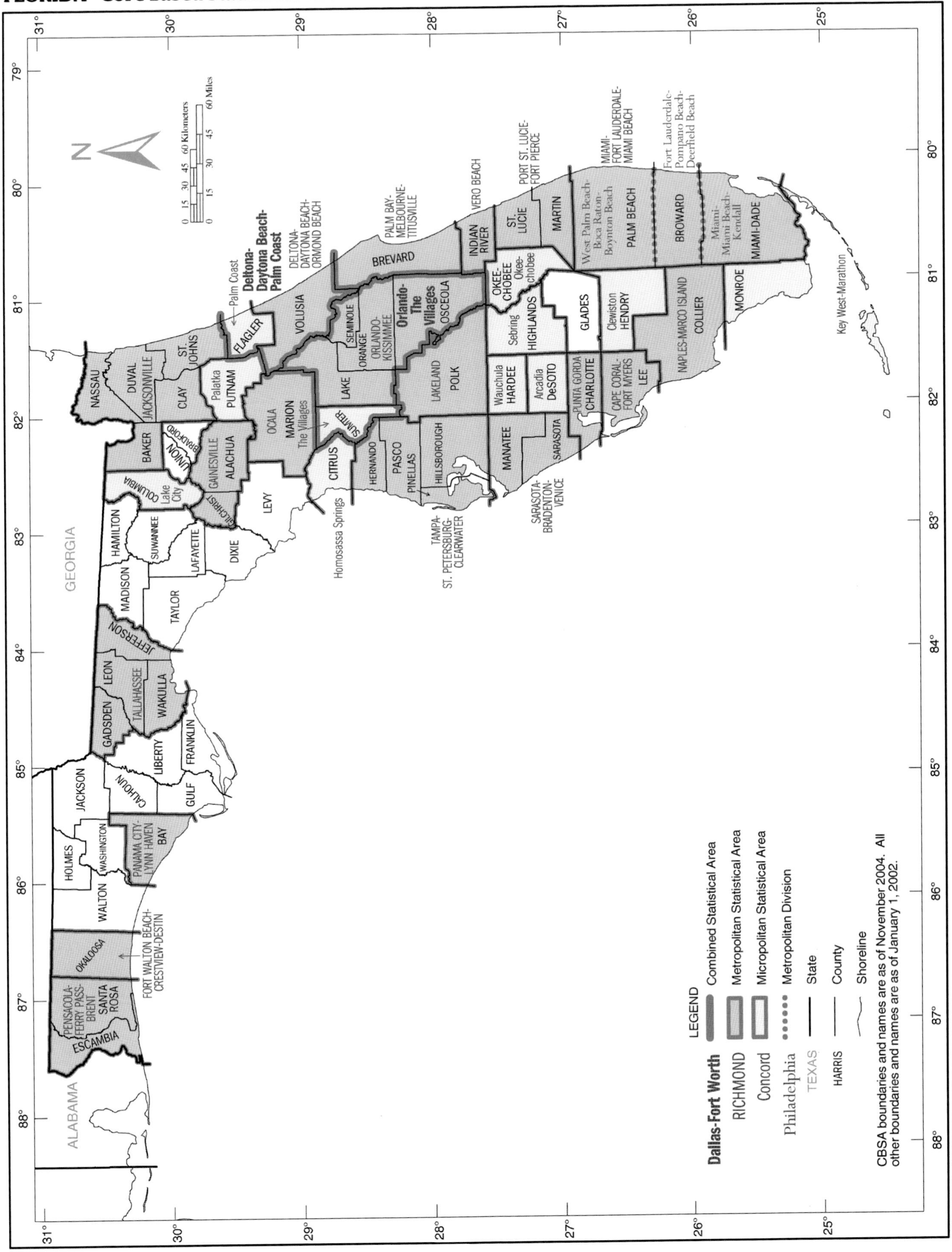

Florida Congressional Districts - 25 Districts Total

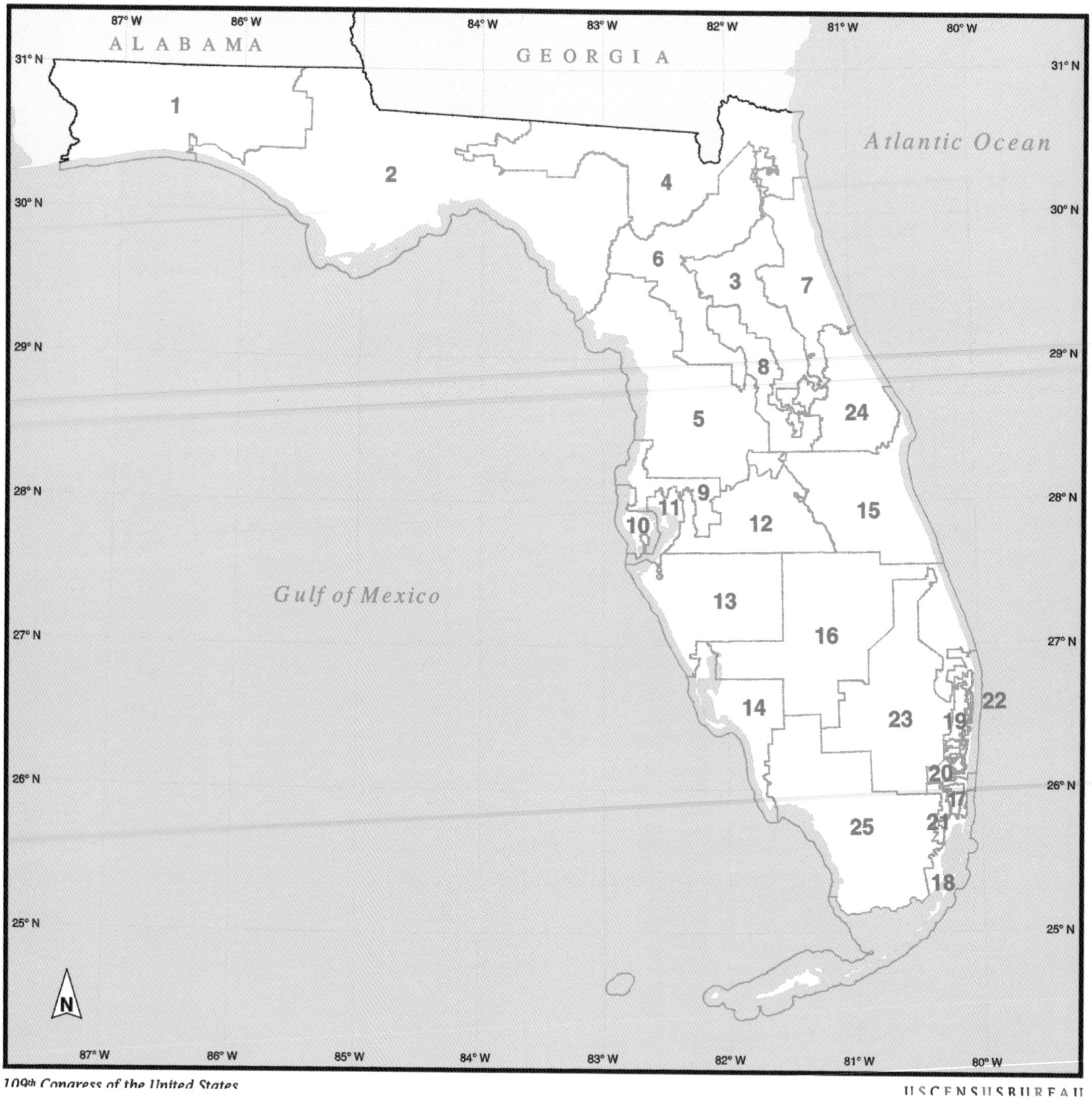

Population (2004)

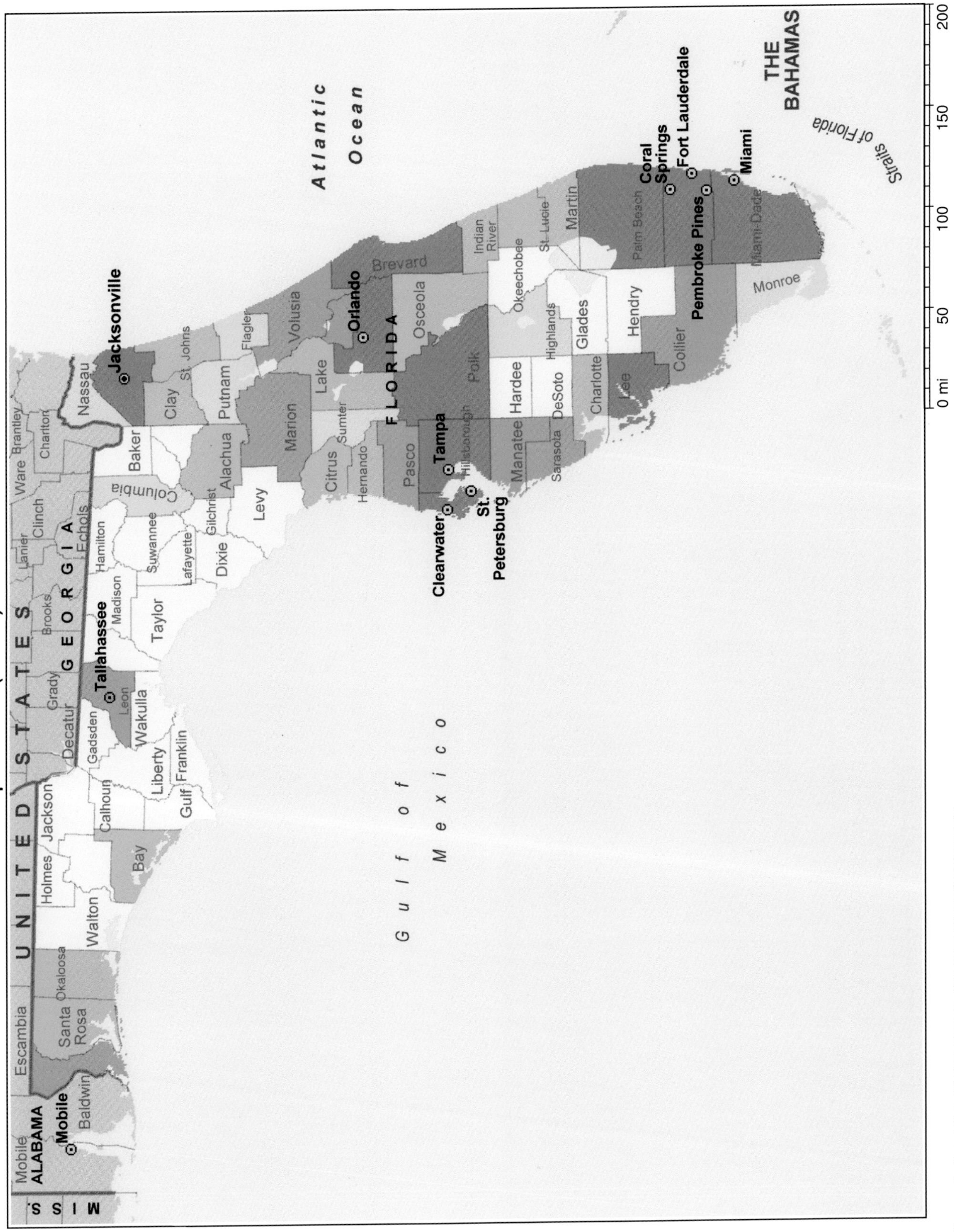

Legend
- 500,000 and Over
- 250,000 to 499,999
- 100,000 to 249,999
- 50,000 to 99,999
- Under 50,000

Percent White Alone (2004)

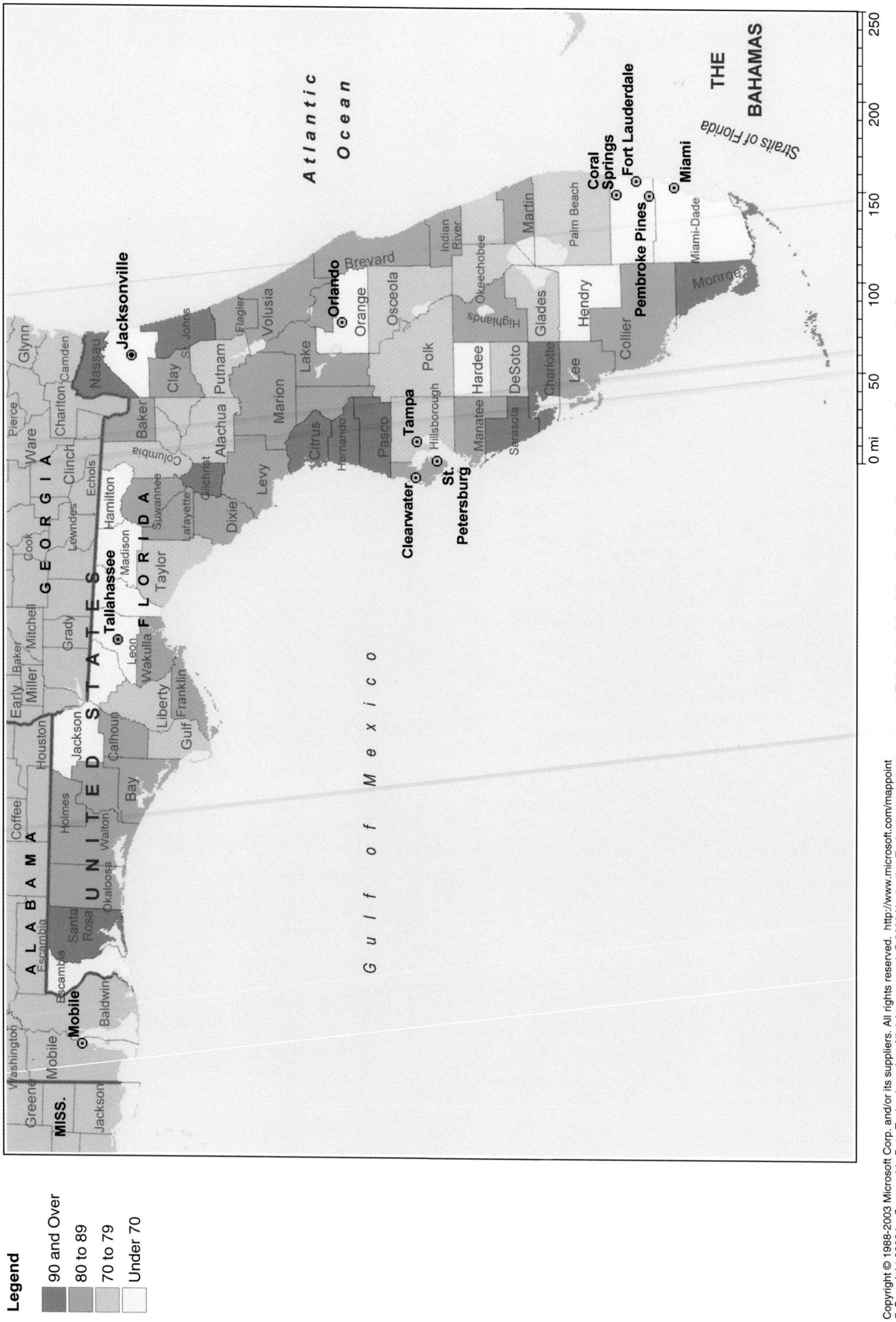
Legend
90 and Over
80 to 89
70 to 79
Under 70
Atlantic Ocean
Gulf of Mexico
Straits of Florida
THE BAHAMAS
UNITED STATES
FLORIDA
GEORGIA
ALABAMA
MISS.
Jacksonville
Tallahassee
Orlando
Tampa
Clearwater
St. Petersburg
Coral Springs
Fort Lauderdale
Pembroke Pines
Miami
Mobile
0 mi 50 100 150 200 250

Percent Black Alone (2004)

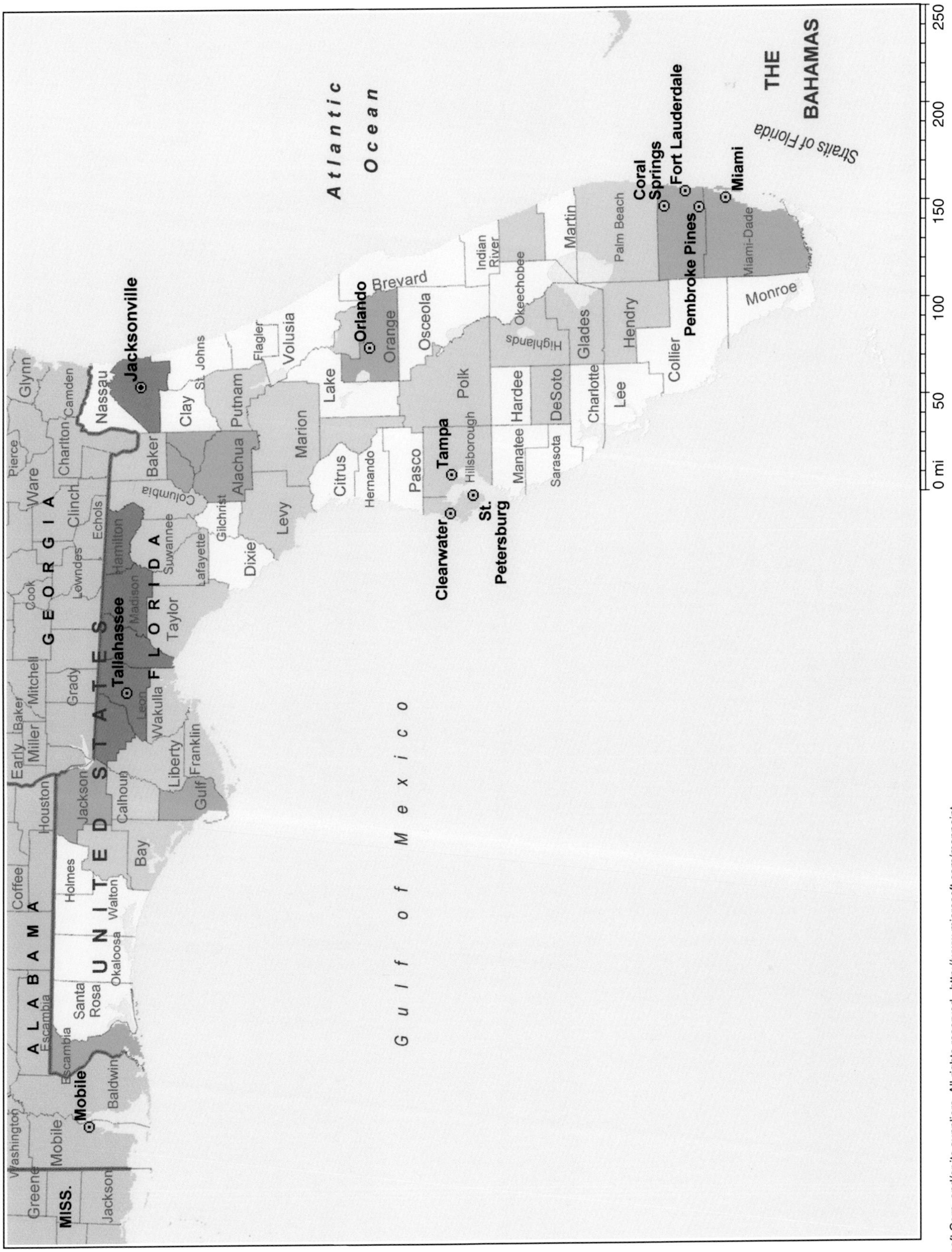

Legend

- 30 and Over
- 20 to 29
- 10 to 19
- Under 10

Percent Asian Alone (2004)

Legend

- 2.0 to 3.9
- 1.0 to 1.9
- 0.5 to 0.9
- Under 0.5

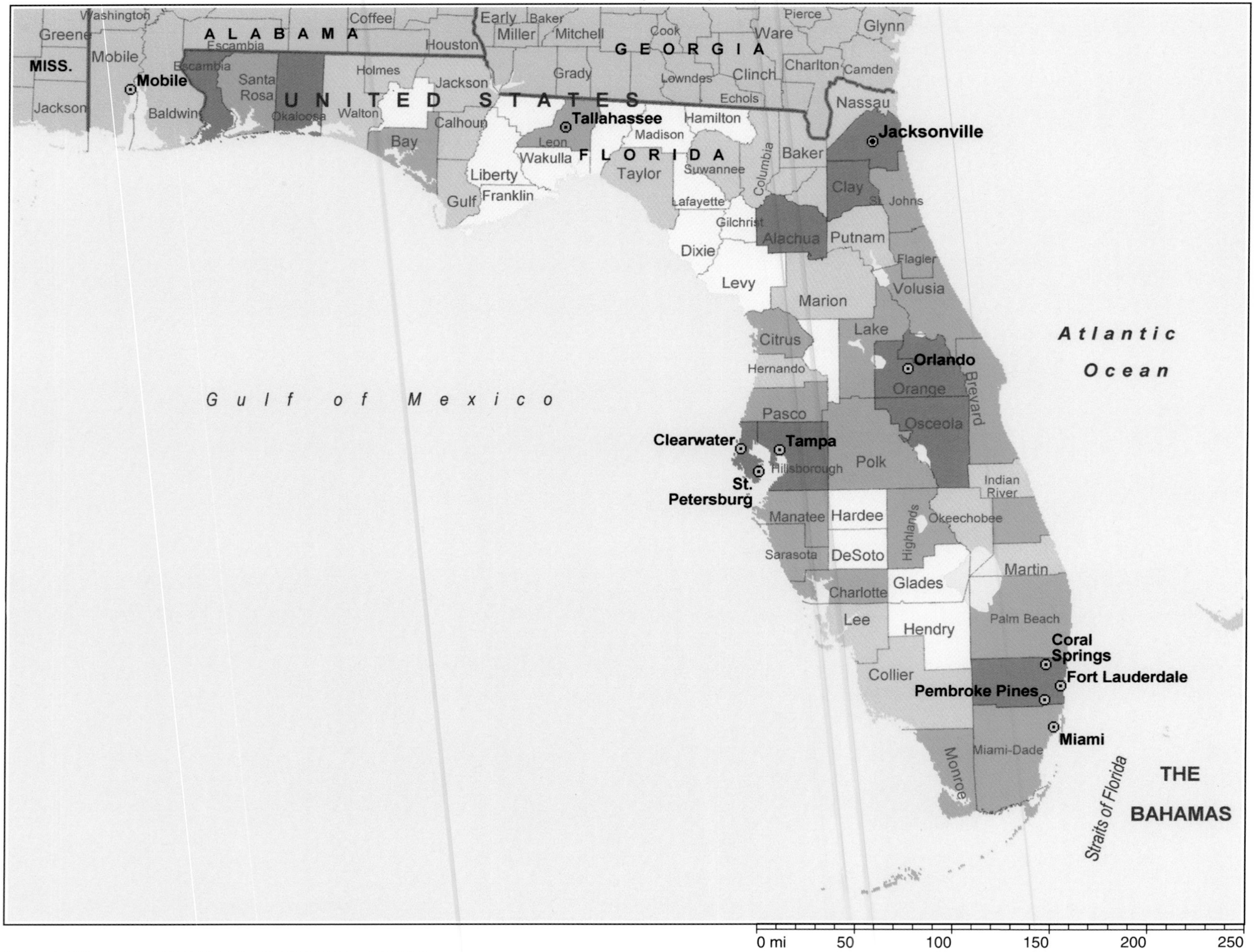

Percent Hispanic (2004)

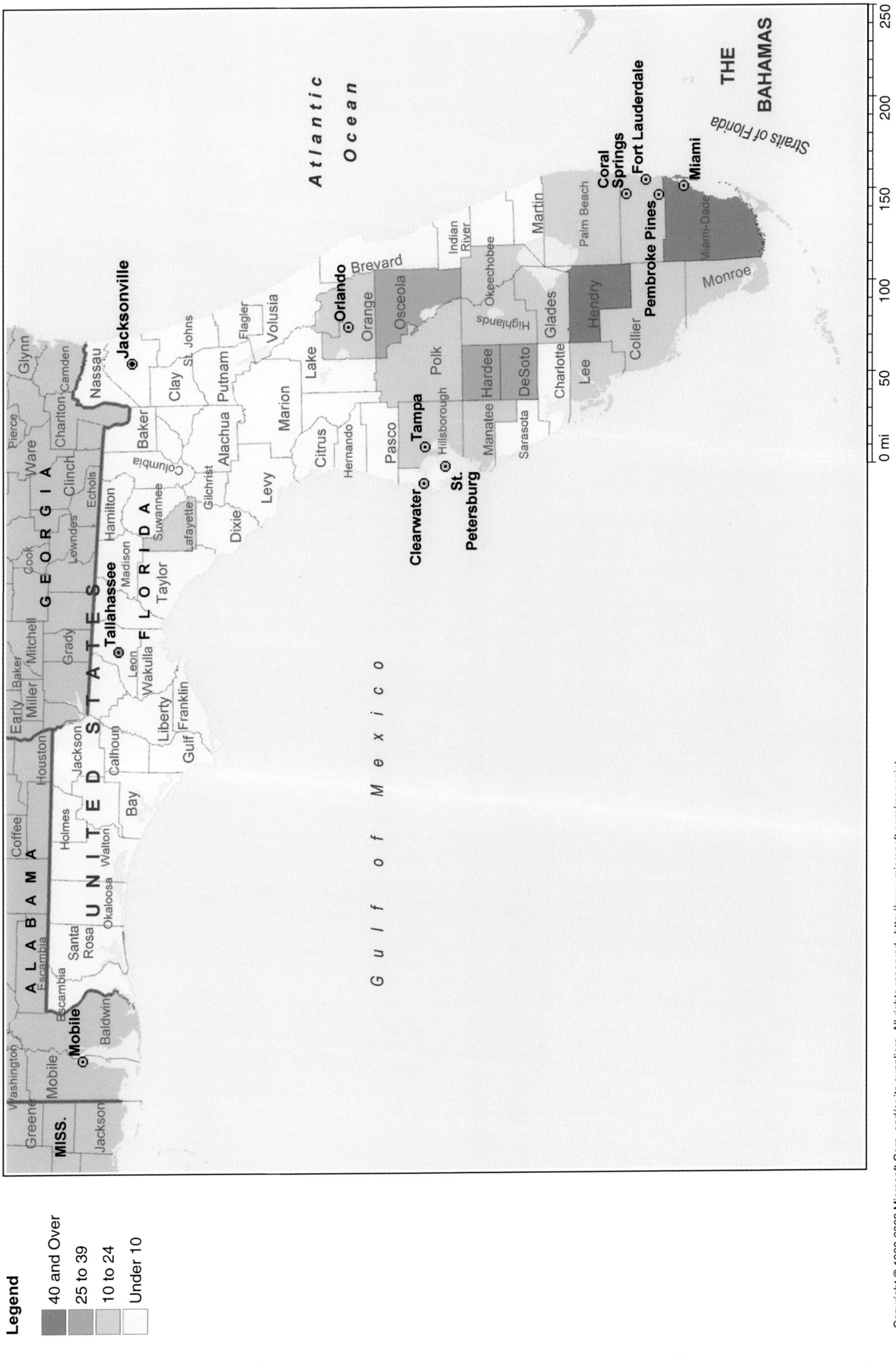

Average Household Size (2004)
Legend
2.82 to 4.15
2.60 to 2.81
2.41 to 2.59
2.17 to 2.40
Atlantic Ocean
Gulf of Mexico
Straits of Florida
THE BAHAMAS
UNITED STATES
FLORIDA
GEORGIA
ALABAMA
MISS.
Jacksonville
Tallahassee
Orlando
Tampa
Clearwater
St. Petersburg
Coral Springs
Fort Lauderdale
Pembroke Pines
Miami
Mobile
Escambia
Santa Rosa
Okaloosa
Walton
Holmes
Jackson
Washington
Bay
Calhoun
Gulf
Liberty
Franklin
Gadsden
Leon
Wakulla
Jefferson
Madison
Taylor
Hamilton
Suwannee
Lafayette
Dixie
Columbia
Baker
Union
Bradford
Nassau
Duval
Clay
St. Johns
Putnam
Alachua
Gilchrist
Levy
Marion
Flagler
Volusia
Lake
Sumter
Citrus
Hernando
Pasco
Hillsborough
Pinellas
Polk
Orange
Seminole
Osceola
Brevard
Indian River
Okeechobee
St. Lucie
Martin
Highlands
Hardee
Manatee
Sarasota
DeSoto
Charlotte
Glades
Lee
Hendry
Palm Beach
Collier
Broward
Miami-Dade
Monroe
Greene
Jackson
Mobile
Baldwin
Covington
Coffee
Houston
Early
Baker
Miller
Mitchell
Grady
Cook
Lowndes
Echols
Clinch
Ware
Pierce
Charlton
Glynn
0 mi
50
100
150
200
250

Median Age (2004)

Number of Males per 100 Females (2004)

Median Household Income (2004)

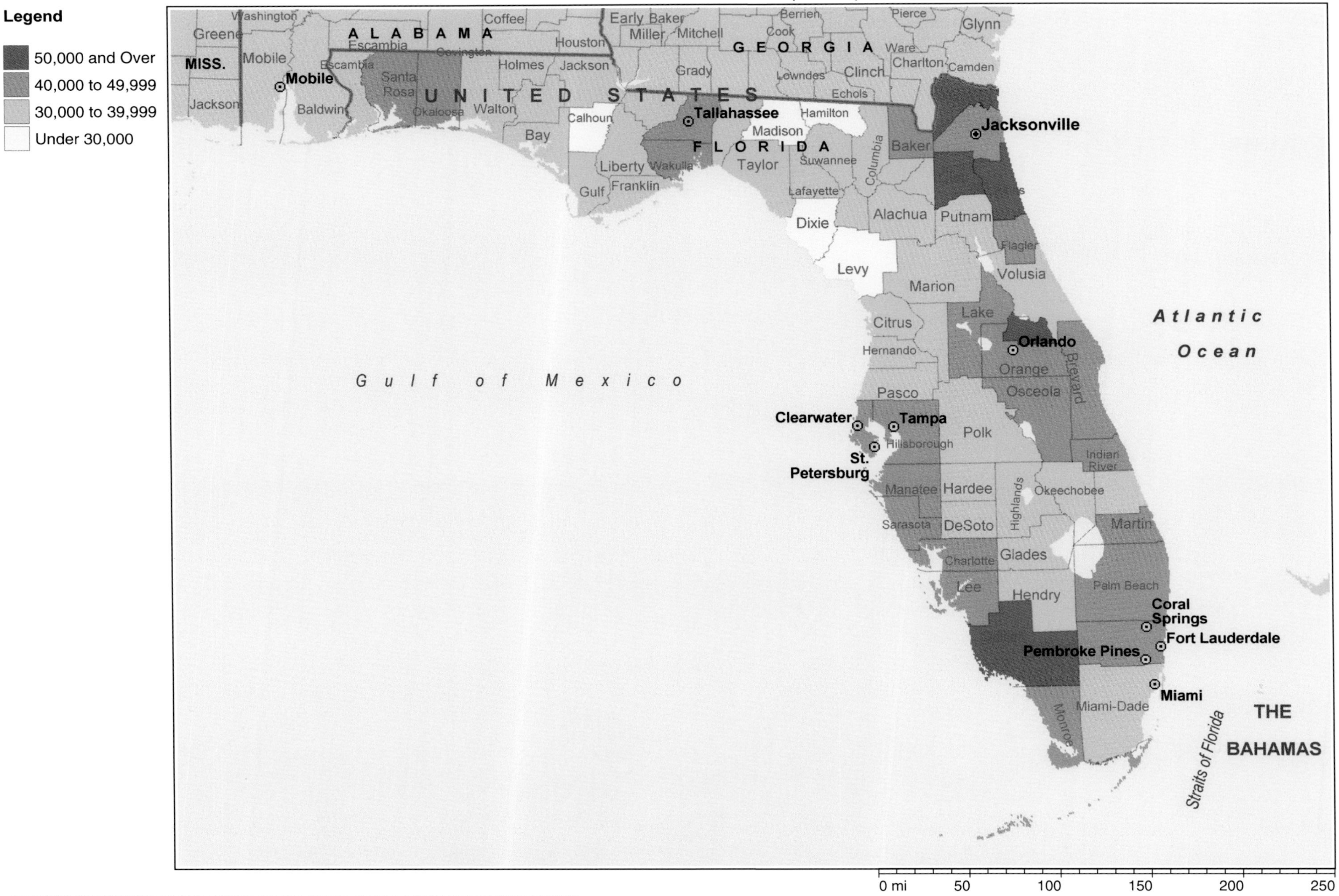

Percent in Poverty (2002)

Percent High School Graduates* (2004)

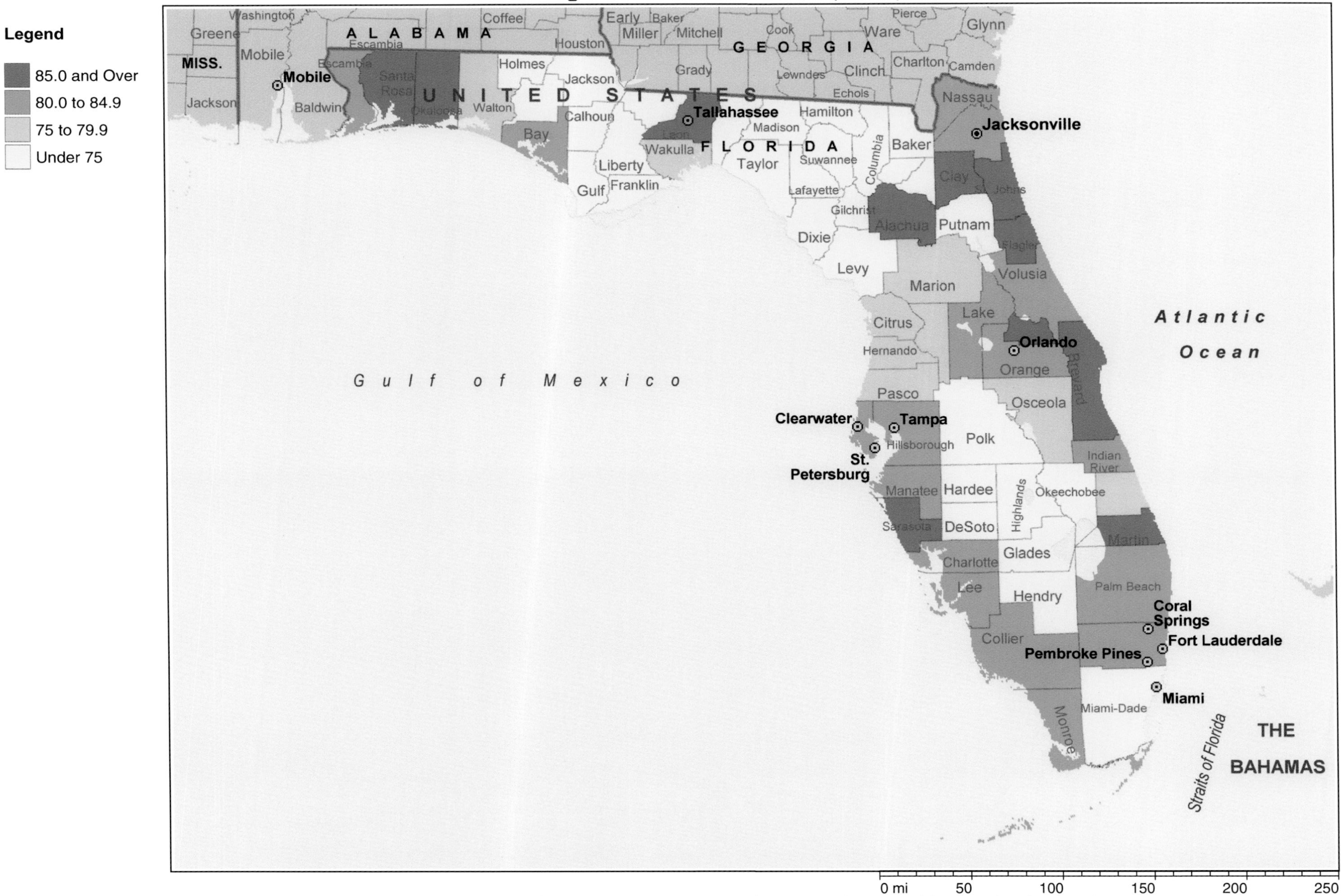

Note: *Percent of population age 25 and over with a high school diploma (including equivalency) or higher.

Percent College Graduates* (2004)

Note: *Percent of population age 25 and over with a Bachelor's degree or higher.

Percent of Population who Voted for George Bush in 2004 Presidential Election

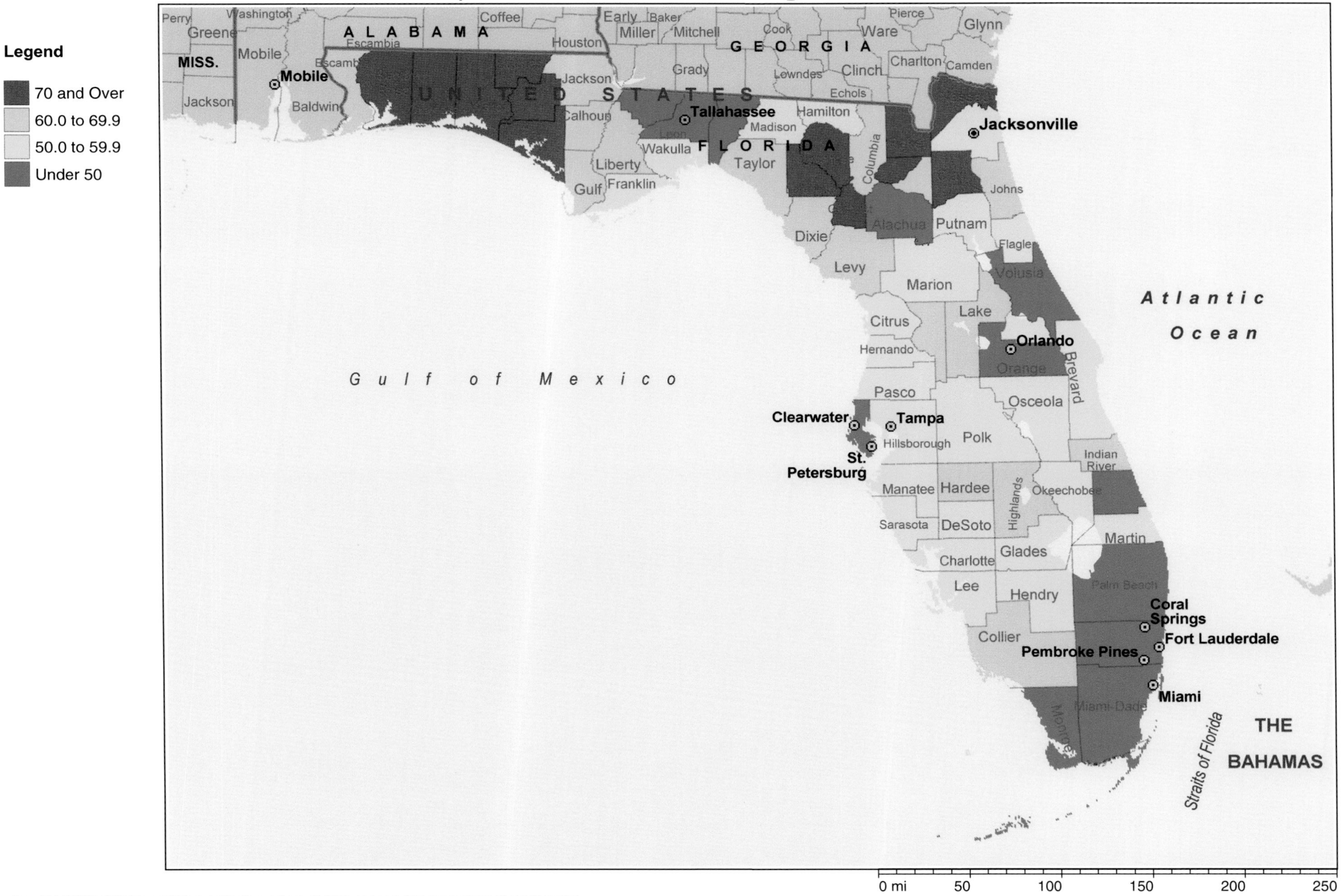

Percent of Population who Voted for John Kerry in 2004 Presidential Election

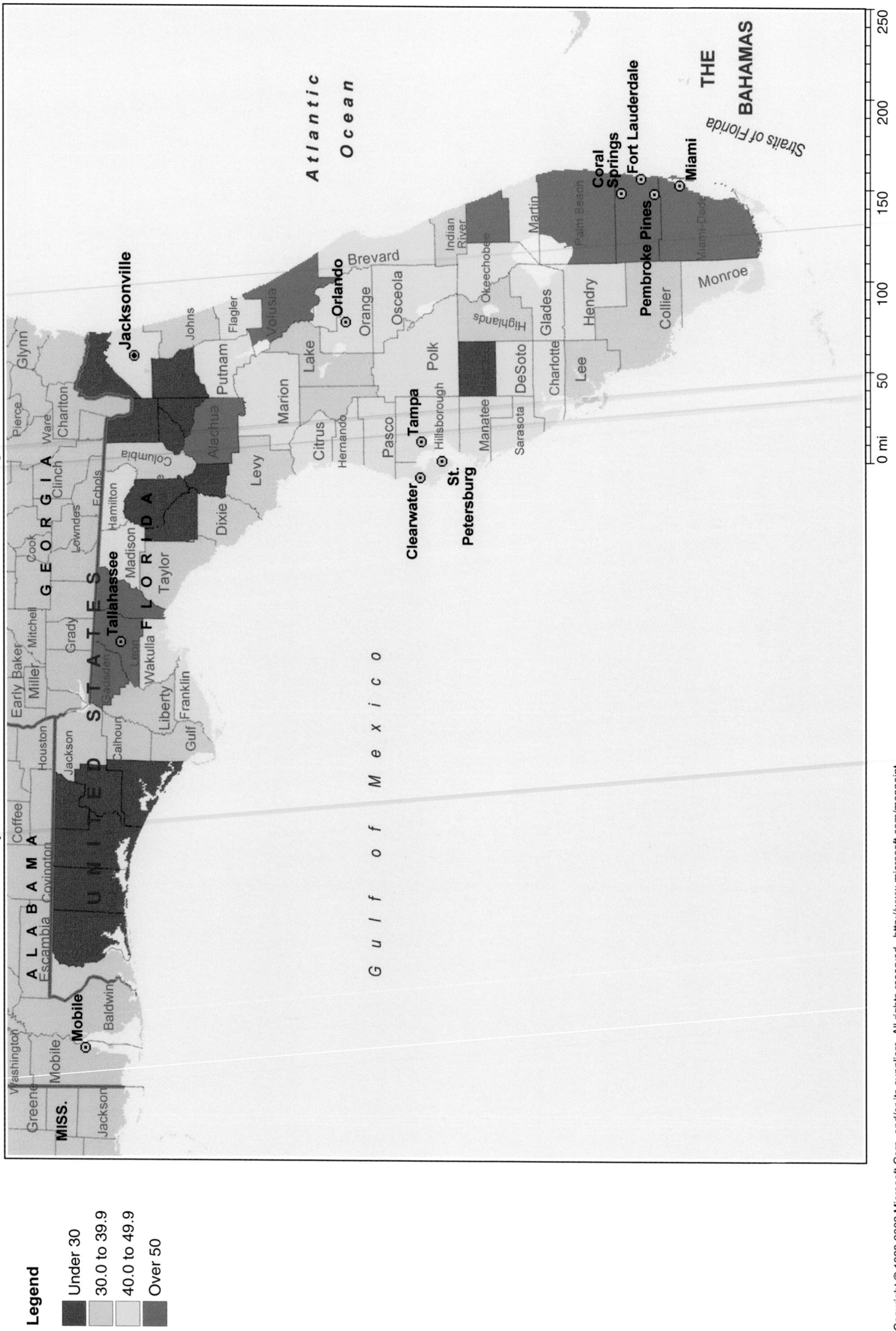

BLEED

PAGE

REMOVE

FLORIDA - Core Based Statistical Areas and Counties

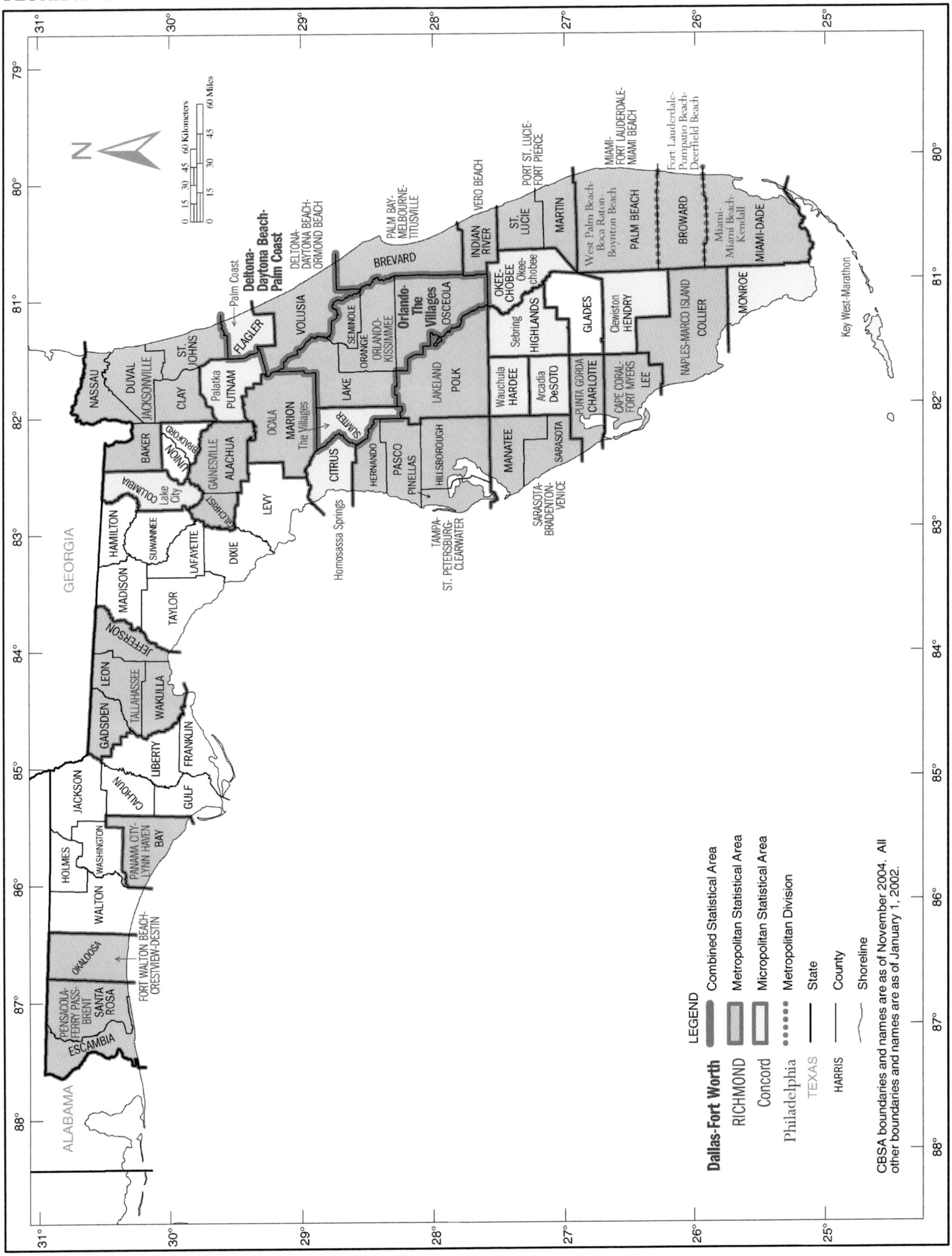

Florida Congressional Districts - 25 Districts Total

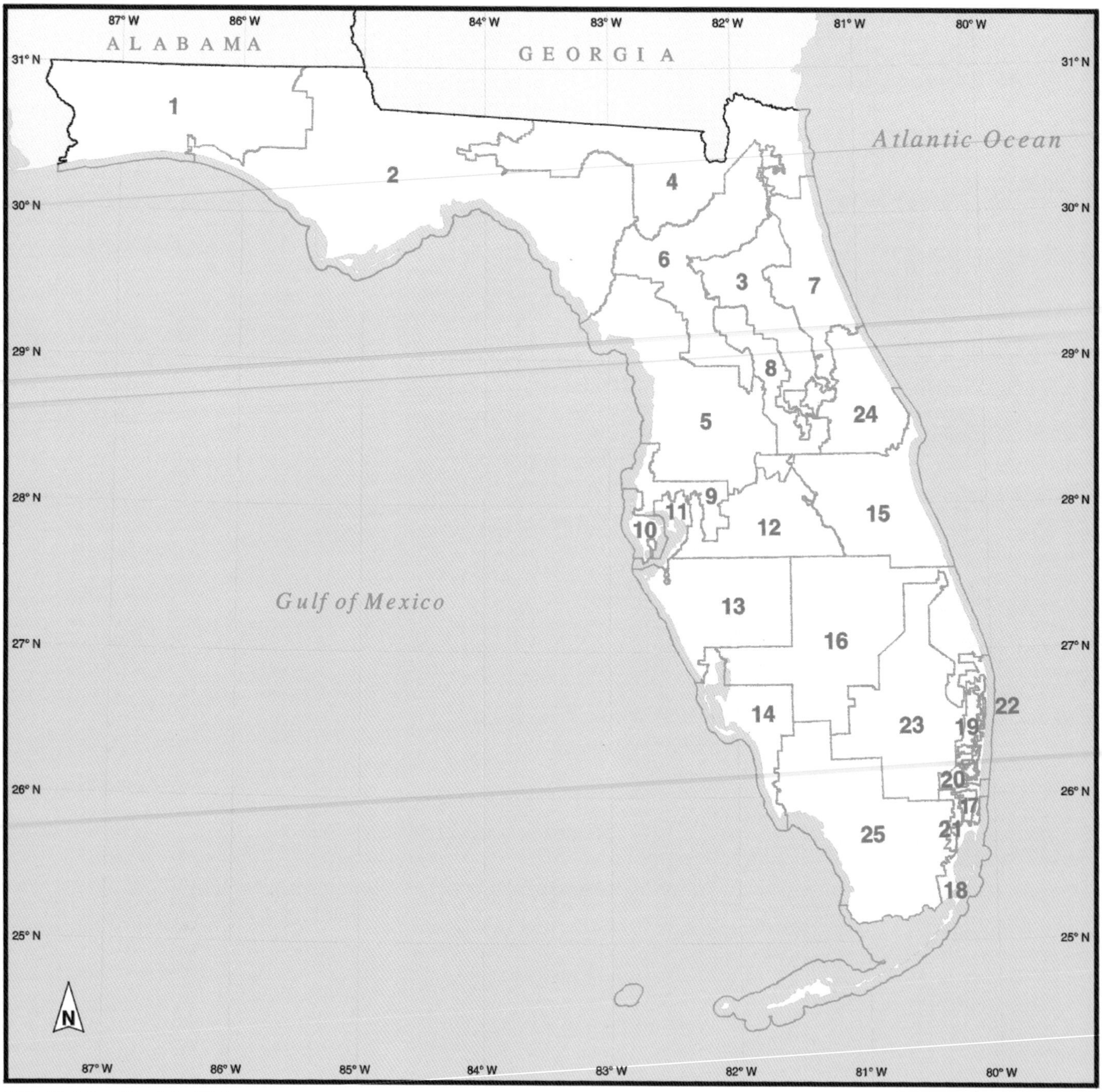

109th Congress of the United States

U S C E N S U S B U R E A U

Population (2004)

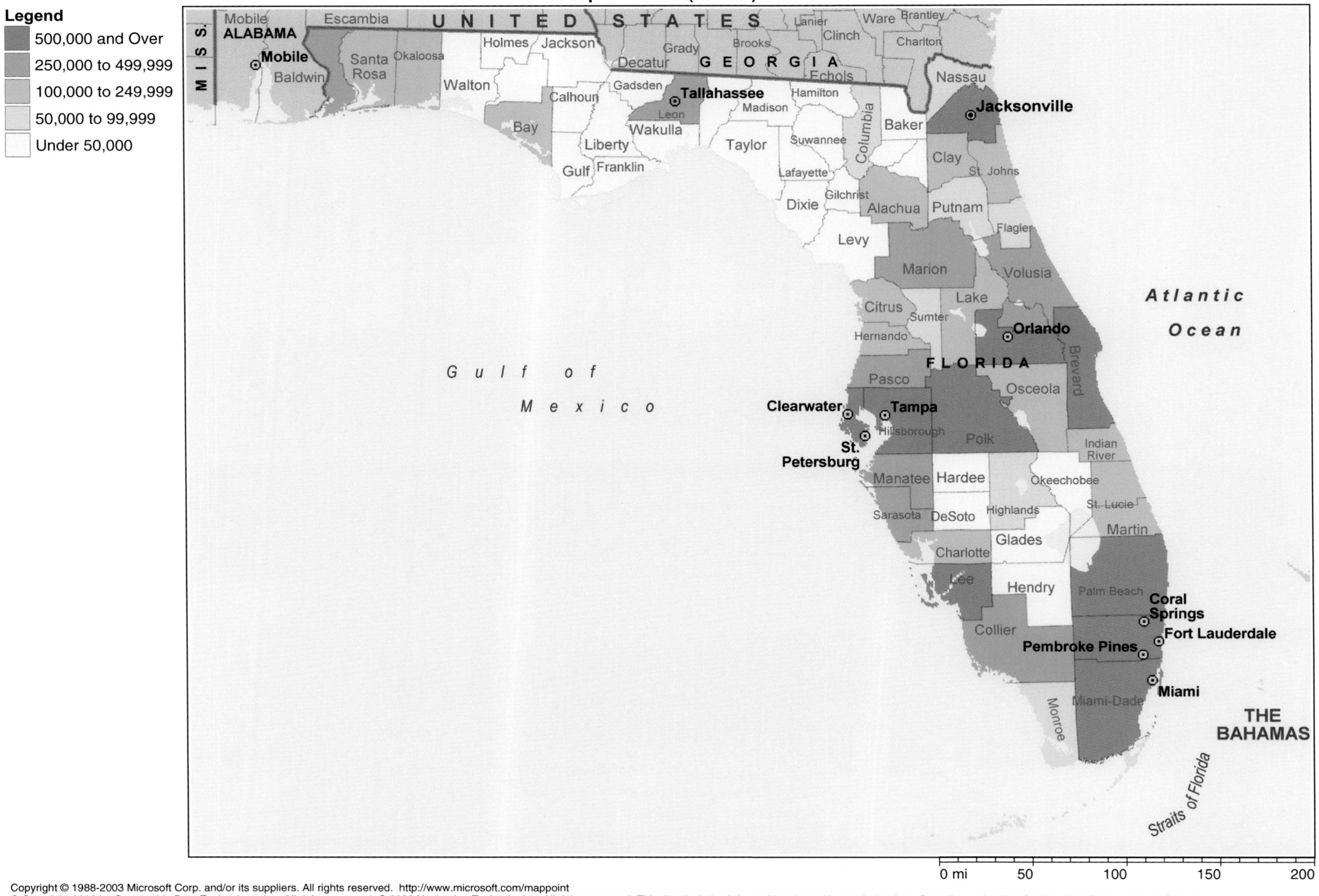

Percent White Alone (2004)

Legend

- 90 and Over
- 80 to 89
- 70 to 79
- Under 70

Percent Black Alone (2004)

Percent Asian Alone (2004)

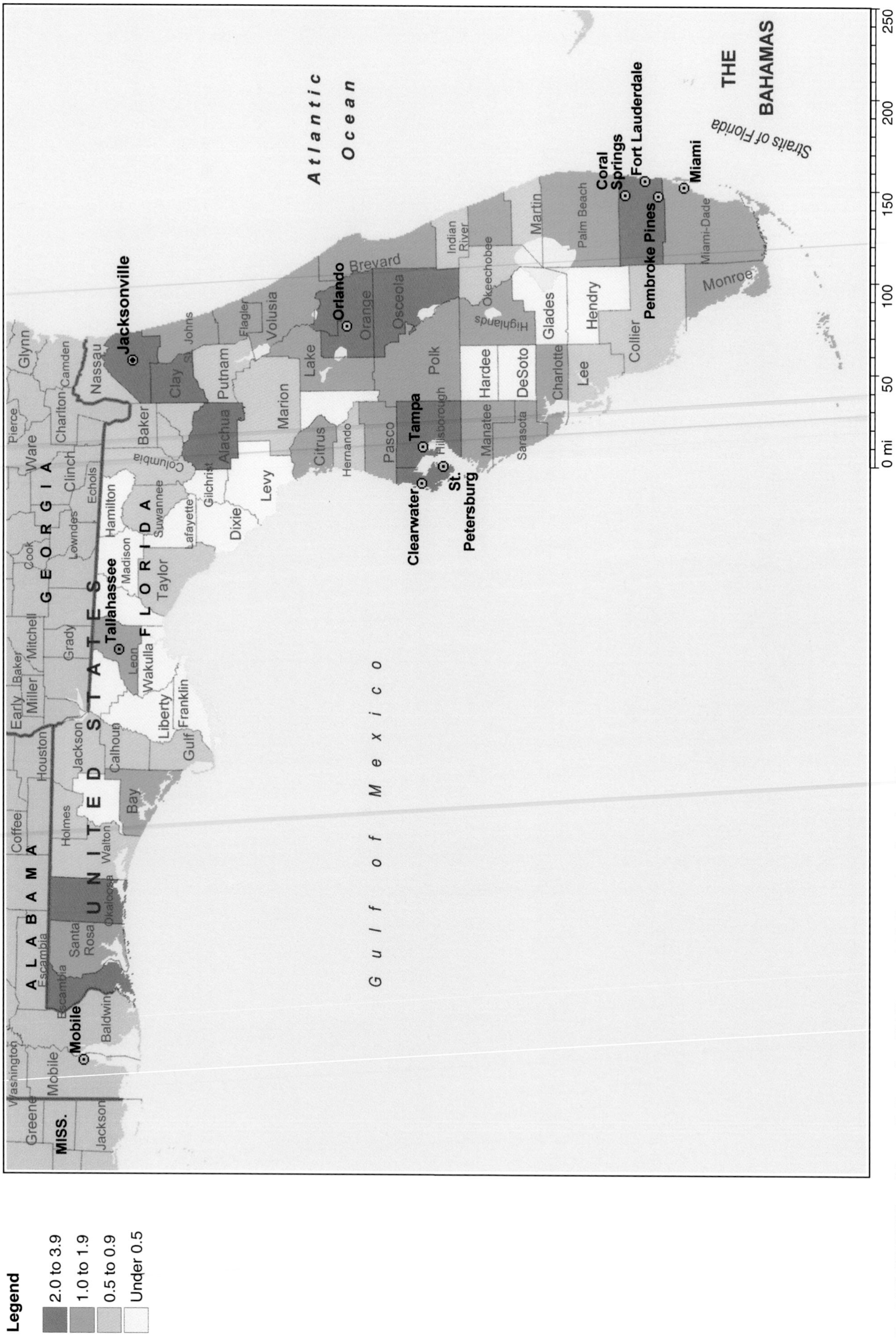

Percent Hispanic (2004)

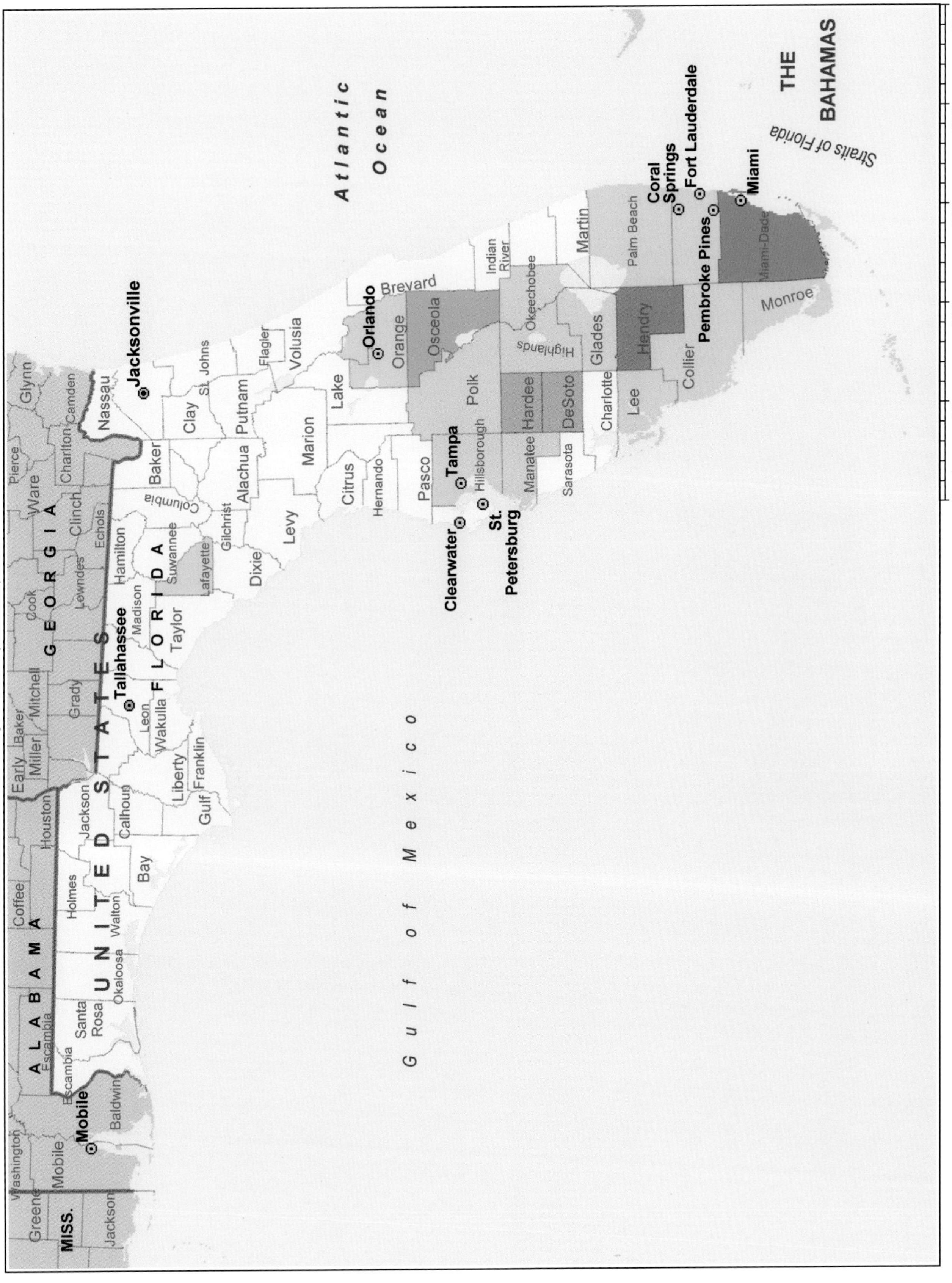

Legend

- 40 and Over
- 25 to 39
- 10 to 24
- Under 10

Average Household Size (2004)

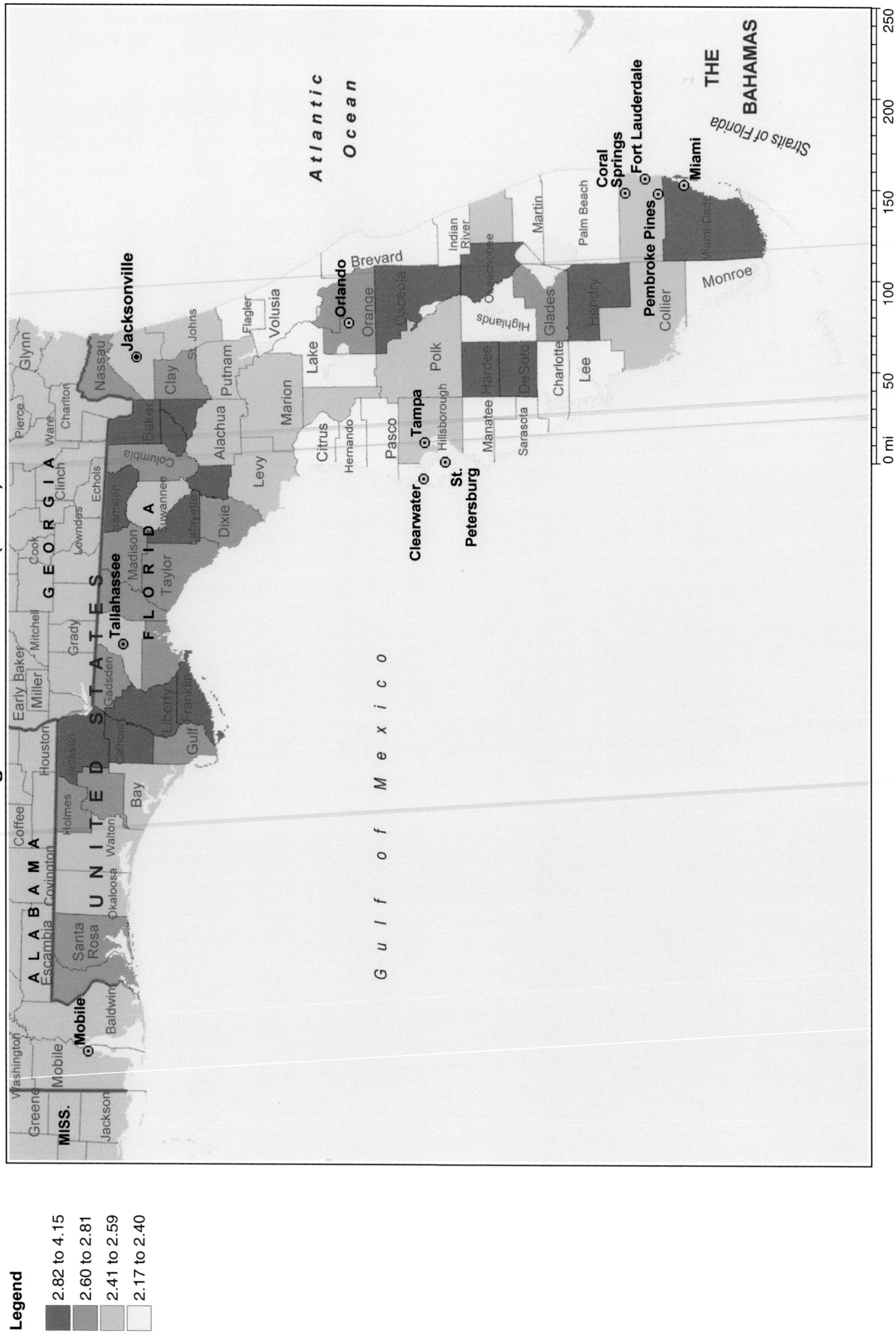

Median Age (2004)

Number of Males per 100 Females (2004)

Legend

- 115 and Over
- 100 to 114
- 95 to 99
- 90 to 94

Median Household Income (2004)

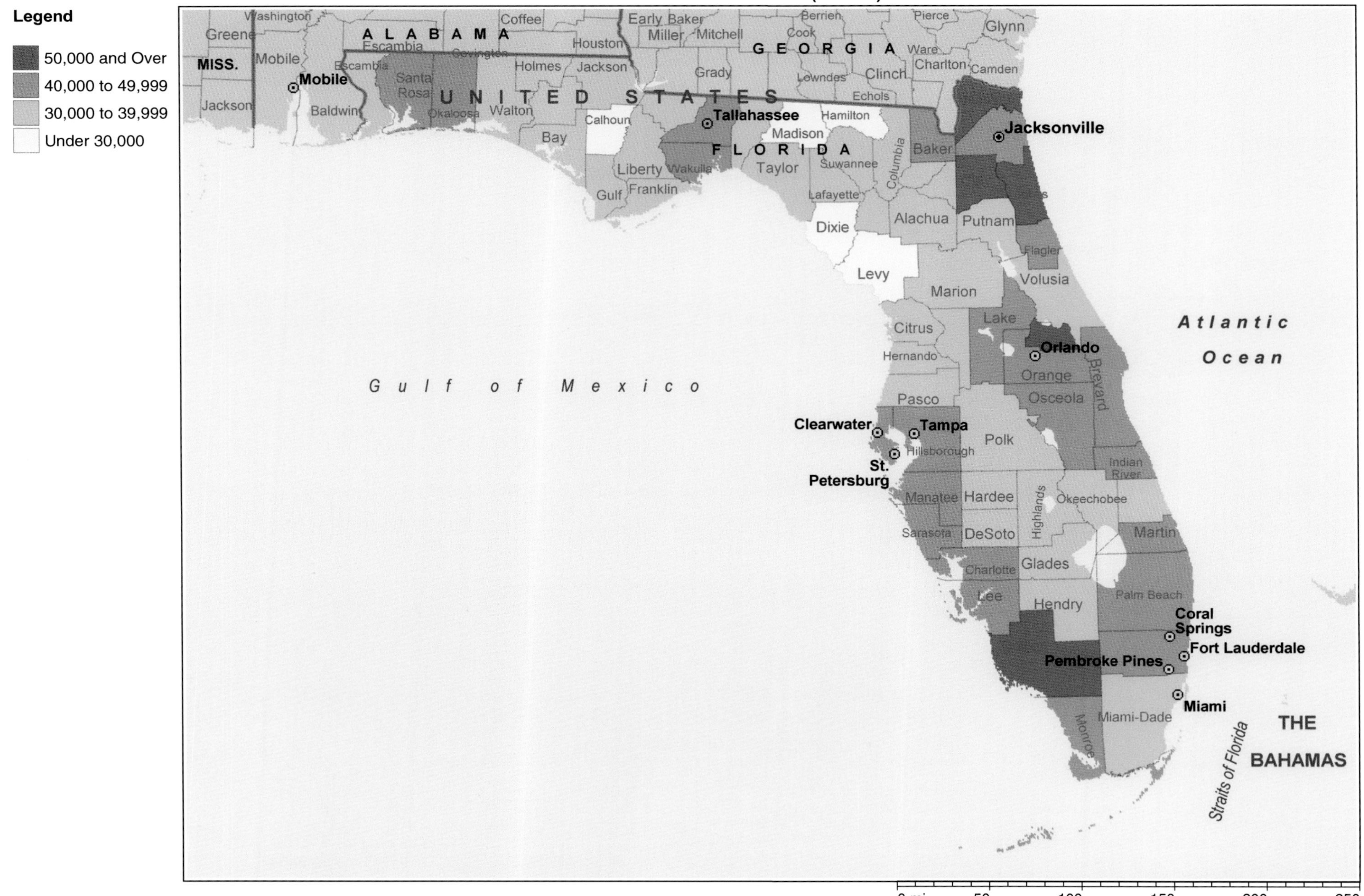

Percent in Poverty (2002)

Percent High School Graduates* (2004)

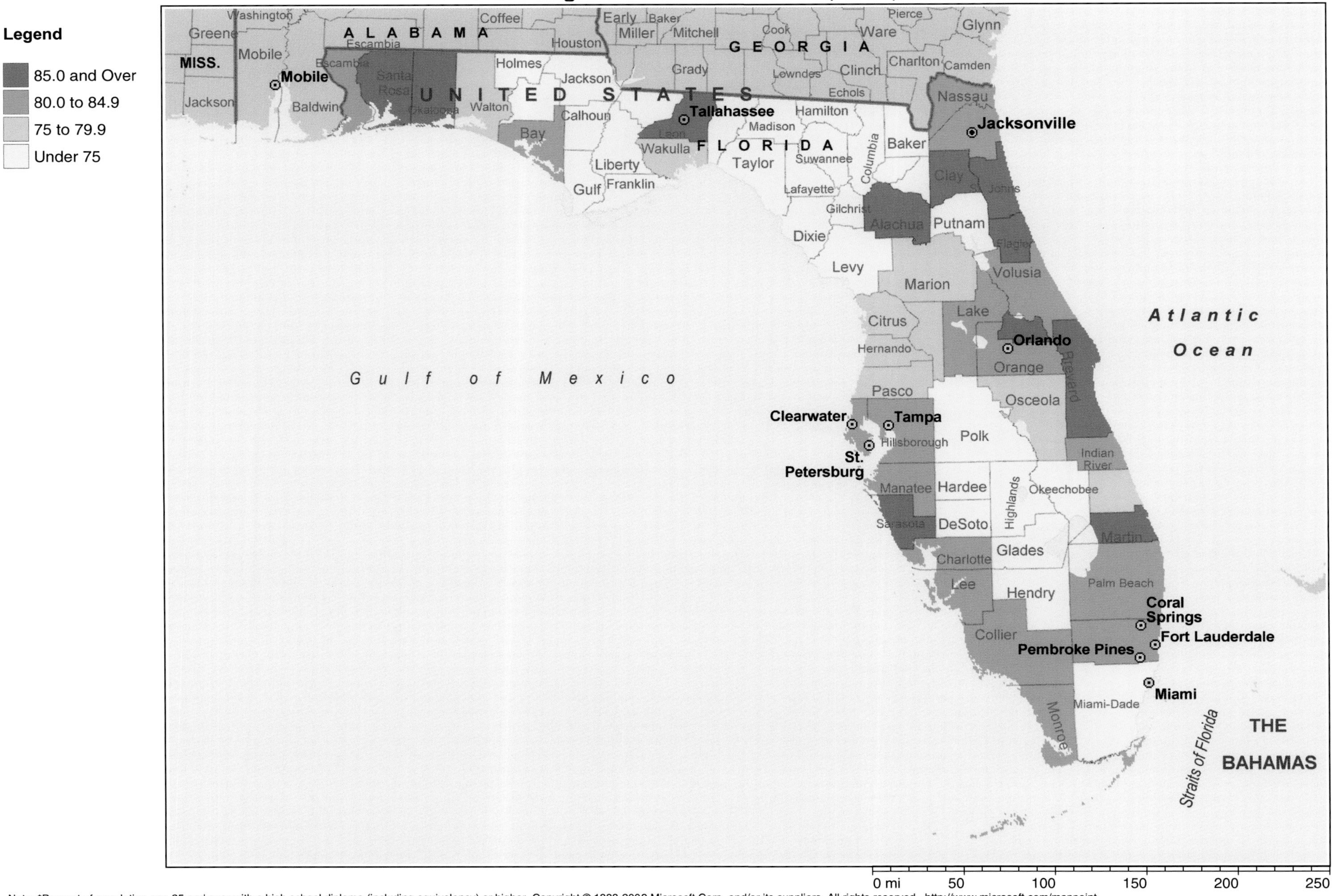

Note: *Percent of population age 25 and over with a high school diploma (including equivalency) or higher.

Percent College Graduates* (2004)

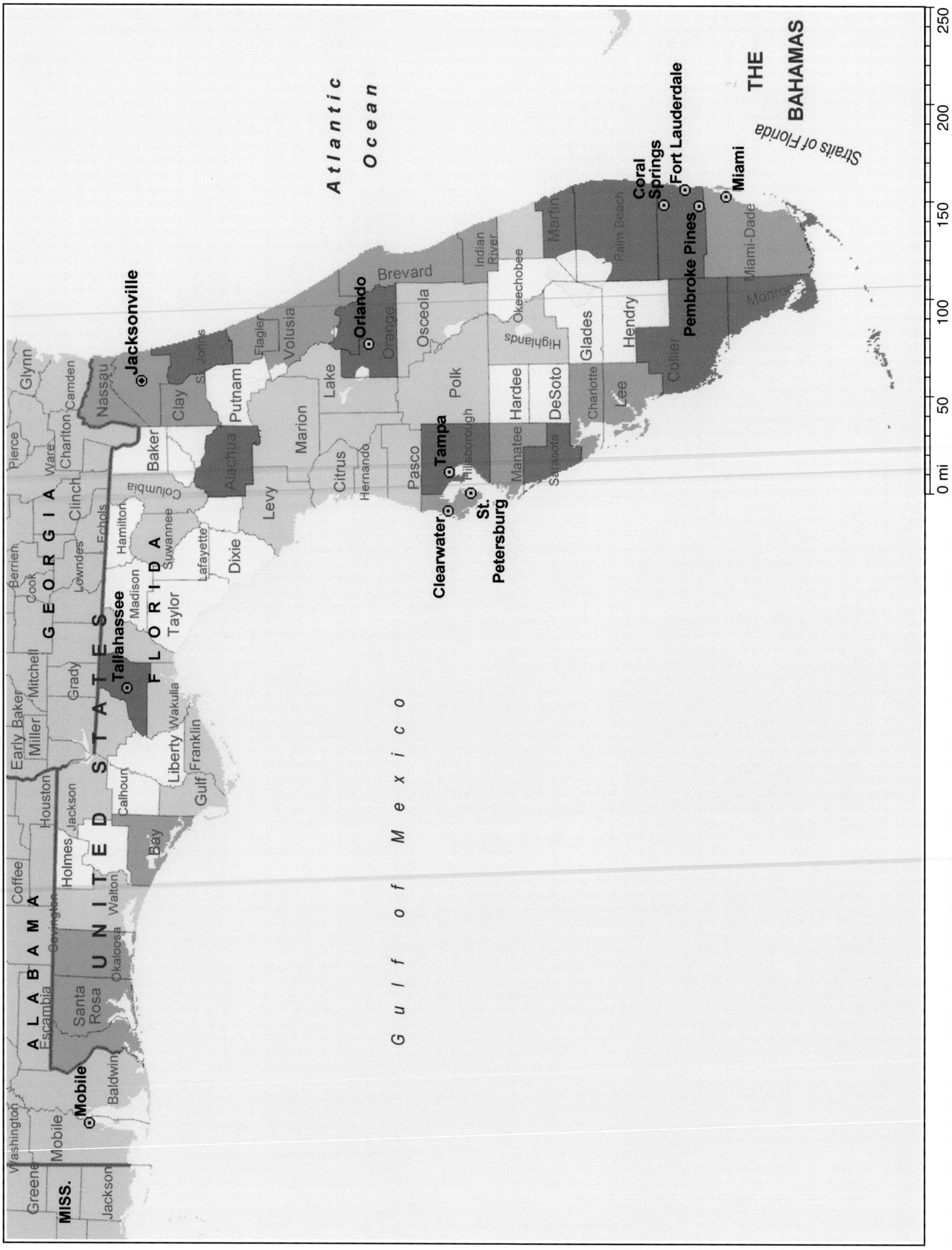

Legend

- 25.0 and Over
- 17.5 to 24.9
- 10.0 to 17.4
- Under 10.0

Note: *Percent of population age 25 and over with a Bachelor's degree or higher.

Percent of Population who Voted for George Bush in 2004 Presidential Election

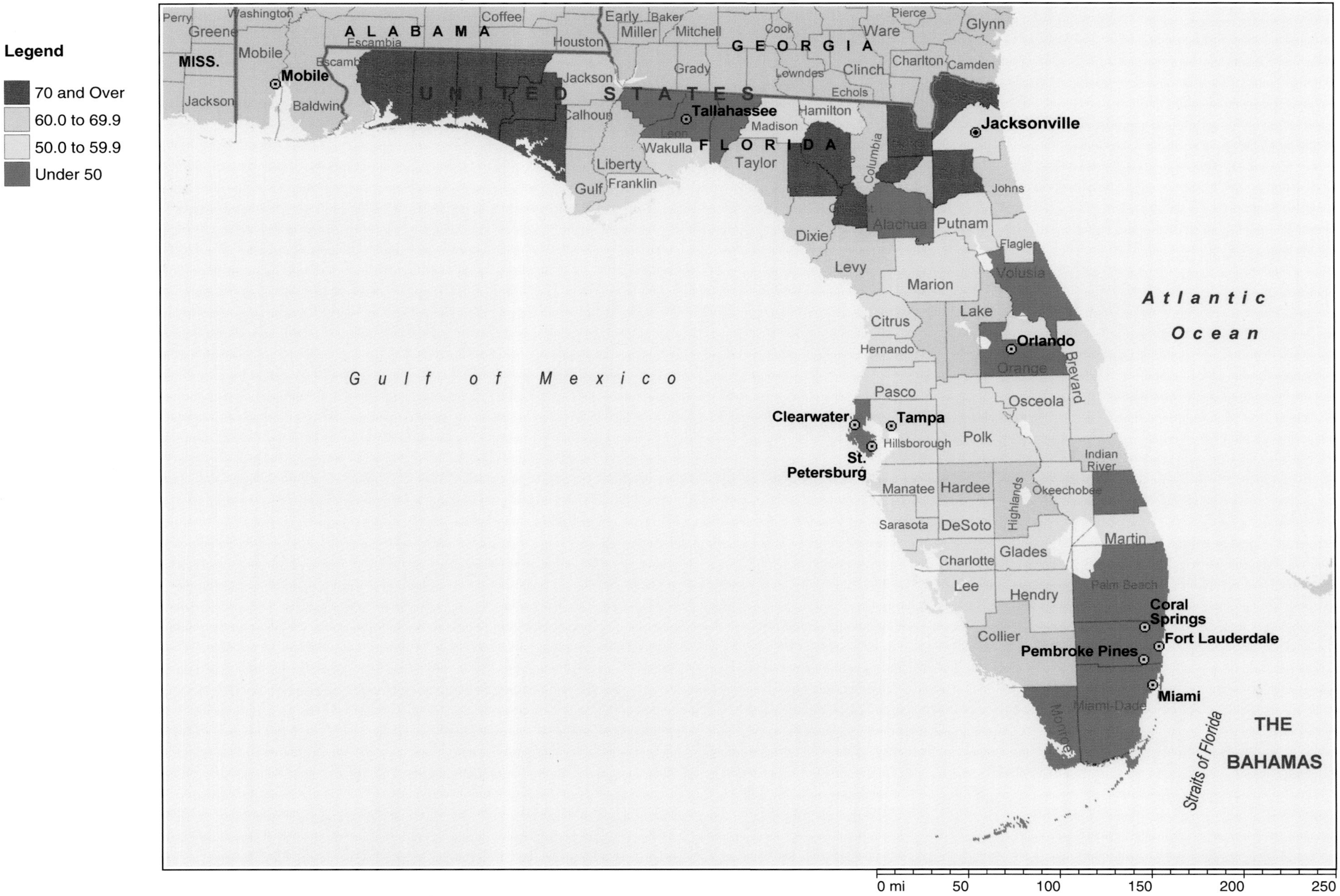

Percent of Population who Voted for John Kerry in 2004 Presidential Election

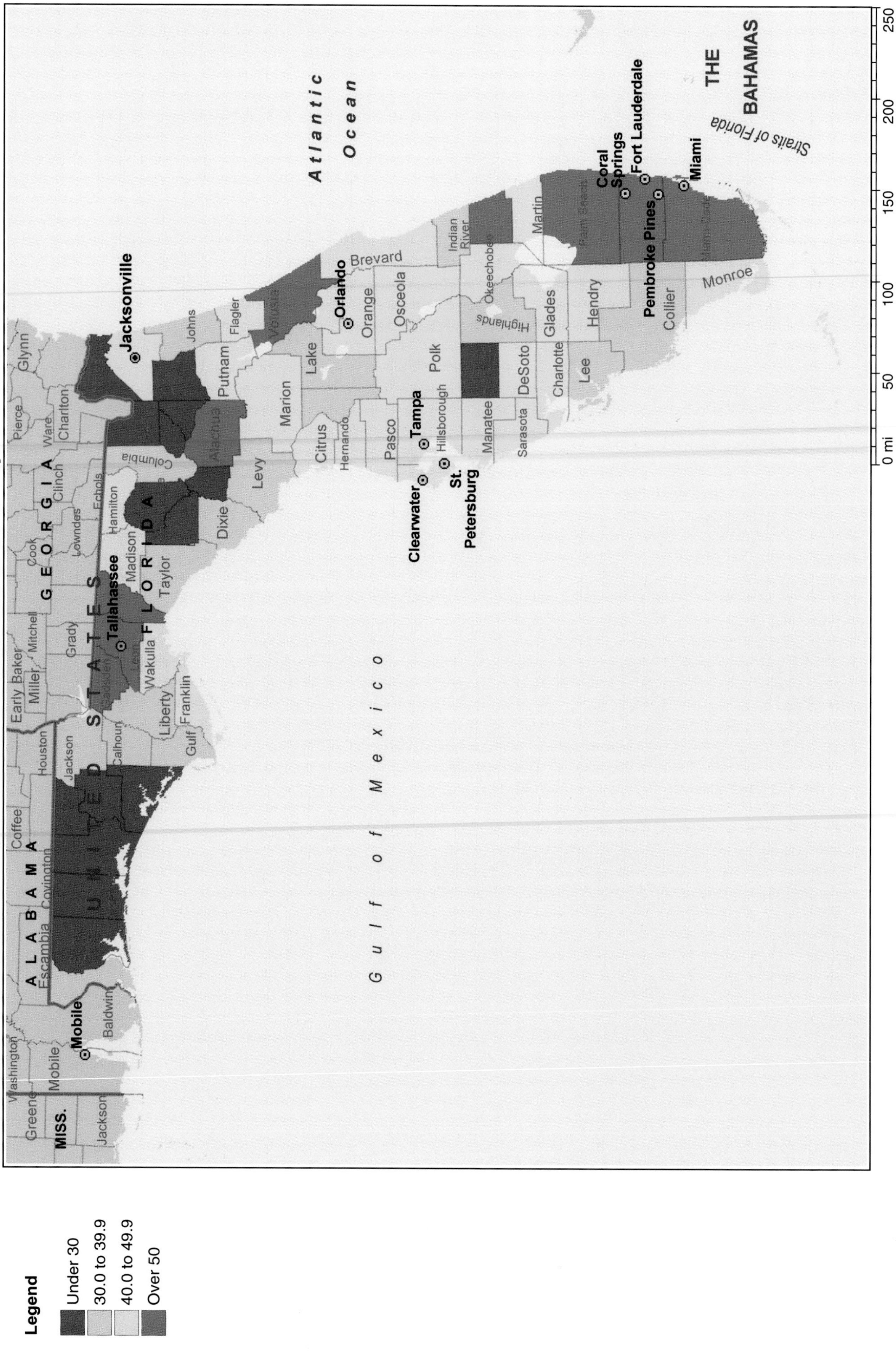

The Value of a Dollar 1860-2004, Third Edition

A guide to practical economy, *The Value of a Dollar* records the actual prices of thousands of items that consumers purchased from the Civil War to the present, along with facts about investment options and income opportunities. This brand new Third Edition boasts a brand new addition to each five-year chapter, a section on Trends. This informative section charts the change in price over time and provides added detail on the reasons prices changed within the time period, including industry developments, changes in consumer attitudes and important historical facts. Plus, a brand new chapter for 2000-2004 has been added. Each 5-year chapter includes a Historical Snapshot, Consumer Expenditures, Investments, Selected Income, Income/Standard Jobs, Food Basket, Standard Prices and Miscellany. This interesting and useful publication will be widely used in any reference collection.

"Recommended for high school, college and public libraries." –ARBA

600 pages; Hardcover ISBN 1-59237-074-8, $135.00

The Value of a Dollar 1600-1859, The Colonial Era to The Civil War

Following the format of the widely acclaimed, *The Value of a Dollar, 1860-2004, The Value of a Dollar 1600-1859, The Colonial Era to The Civil War* records the actual prices of thousands of items that consumers purchased from the Colonial Era to the Civil War. Our editorial department had been flooded with requests from users of our Value of a Dollar for the same type of information, just from an earlier time period. This new volume is just the answer – with pricing data from 1600 to 1859. Arranged into five-year chapters, each 5-year chapter includes a Historical Snapshot, Consumer Expenditures, Investments, Selected Income, Income/Standard Jobs, Food Basket, Standard Prices and Miscellany. There is also a section on Trends. This informative section charts the change in price over time and provides added detail on the reasons prices changed within the time period, including industry developments, changes in consumer attitudes and important historical facts. This fascinating survey will serve a wide range of research needs and will be useful in all high school, public and academic library reference collections.

600 pages; Hardcover ISBN 1-59237-094-2, $135.00

Working Americans 1880-1999
Volume I: The Working Class, Volume II: The Middle Class, Volume III: The Upper Class

Each of the volumes in the *Working Americans 1880-1999* series focuses on a particular class of Americans, The Working Class, The Middle Class and The Upper Class over the last 120 years. Chapters in each volume focus on one decade and profile three to five families. Family Profiles include real data on Income & Job Descriptions, Selected Prices of the Times, Annual Income, Annual Budgets, Family Finances, Life at Work, Life at Home, Life in the Community, Working Conditions, Cost of Living, Amusements and much more. Each chapter also contains an Economic Profile with Average Wages of other Professions, a selection of Typical Pricing, Key Events & Inventions, News Profiles, Articles from Local Media and Illustrations. The *Working Americans* series captures the lifestyles of each of the classes from the last twelve decades, covers a vast array of occupations and ethnic backgrounds and travels the entire nation. These interesting and useful compilations of portraits of the American Working, Middle and Upper Classes during the last 120 years will be an important addition to any high school, public or academic library reference collection.

"These interesting, unique compilations of economic and social facts, figures and graphs will support multiple research needs. They will engage and enlighten patrons in high school, public and academic library collections." –Booklist

Volume I: The Working Class ◆ 558 pages; Hardcover ISBN 1-891482-81-5, $145.00
Volume II: The Middle Class ◆ 591 pages; Hardcover ISBN 1-891482-72-6; $145.00
Volume III: The Upper Class ◆ 567 pages; Hardcover ISBN 1-930956-38-X, $145.00

Working Americans 1880-1999 Volume IV: Their Children

This Fourth Volume in the highly successful *Working Americans 1880-1999* series focuses on American children, decade by decade from 1880 to 1999. This interesting and useful volume introduces the reader to three children in each decade, one from each of the Working, Middle and Upper classes. Like the first three volumes in the series, the individual profiles are created from interviews, diaries, statistical studies, biographies and news reports. Profiles cover a broad range of ethnic backgrounds, geographic area and lifestyles – everything from an orphan in Memphis in 1882, following the Yellow Fever epidemic of 1878 to an eleven-year-old nephew of a beer baron and owner of the New York Yankees in New York City in 1921. Chapters also contain important supplementary materials including News Features as well as information on everything from Schools to Parks, Infectious Diseases to Childhood Fears along with Entertainment, Family Life and much more to provide an informative overview of the lifestyles of children from each decade. This interesting account of what life was like for Children in the Working, Middle and Upper Classes will be a welcome addition to the reference collection of any high school, public or academic library.

600 pages; Hardcover ISBN 1-930956-35-5, $145.00

Working Americans 1880-2003 Volume V: Americans At War

Working Americans 1880-2003 Volume V: Americans At War is divided into 11 chapters, each covering a decade from 1880-2003 and examines the lives of Americans during the time of war, including declared conflicts, one-time military actions, protests, and preparations for war. Each decade includes several personal profiles, whether on the battlefield or on the homefront, that tell the stories of civilians, soldiers, and officers during the decade. The profiles examine: Life at Home; Life at Work; and Life in the Community. Each decade also includes an Economic Profile with statistical comparisons, a Historical Snapshot, News Profiles, local News Articles, and Illustrations that provide a solid historical background to the decade being examined. Profiles range widely not only geographically, but also emotionally, from that of a girl whose leg was torn off in a blast during WWI, to the boredom of being stationed in the Dakotas as the Indian Wars were drawing to a close. As in previous volumes of the *Working Americans* series, information is presented in narrative form, but hard facts and real-life situations back up each story. The basis of the profiles come from diaries, private print books, personal interviews, family histories, estate documents and magazine articles. For easy reference, *Working Americans 1880-2003 Volume V: Americans At War* includes an in-depth Subject Index. The *Working Americans* series has become an important reference for public libraries, academic libraries and high school libraries. This fifth volume will be a welcome addition to all of these types of reference collections.

600 pages; Hardcover ISBN 1-59237-024-1; $145.00
Five Volume Set (Volumes I-V), Hardcover ISBN 1-59237-034-9, $675.00

Working Americans 1880-2005 Volume VI: Women at Work

Unlike any other volume in the *Working Americans* series, this Sixth Volume, is the first to focus on a particular gender of Americans. *Volume VI: Women at Work*, traces what life was like for working women from the 1860's to the present time. Beginning with the life of a maid in 1890 and a store clerk in 1900 and ending with the life and times of the modern working women, this text captures the struggle, strengths and changing perception of the American woman at work. Each chapter focuses on one decade and profiles three to five women with real data on Income & Job Descriptions, Selected Prices of the Times, Annual Income, Annual Budgets, Family Finances, Life at Work, Life at Home, Life in the Community, Working Conditions, Cost of Living, Amusements and much more. For even broader access to the events, economics and attitude towards women throughout the past 130 years, each chapter is supplemented with News Profiles, Articles from Local Media, Illustrations, Economic Profiles, Typical Pricing, Key Events, Inventions and more. This important volume illustrates what life was like for working women over time and allows the reader to develop an understanding of the changing role of women at work. These interesting and useful compilations of portraits of women at work will be an important addition to any high school, public or academic library reference collection.

600 pages; Hardcover ISBN 1-59237-063-2; $145.00
Six Volume Set (Volumes I-VI), Hardcover ISBN 1-59237-063-2, $810.00

The Comparative Guide to American Elementary & Secondary Schools, 2004/05

The only guide of its kind, this award winning compilation offers a snapshot profile of every public school district in the United States serving 1,500 or more students – more than 5,900 districts are covered. Organized alphabetically by district within state, each chapter begins with a Statistical Overview of the state. Each district listing includes contact information (name, address, phone number and web site) plus Grades Served, the Numbers of Students and Teachers and the Number of Regular, Special Education, Alternative and Vocational Schools in the district along with statistics on Student/Classroom Teacher Ratios, Drop Out Rates, Ethnicity, the Numbers of Librarians and Guidance Counselors and District Expenditures per student. As an added bonus, *The Comparative Guide to American Elementary and Secondary Schools* provides important ranking tables, both by state and nationally, for each data element. For easy navigation through this wealth of information, this handbook contains a useful City Index that lists all districts that operate schools within a city. These important comparative statistics are necessary for anyone considering relocation or doing comparative research on their own district and would be a perfect acquisition for any public library or school district library.

"This straightforward guide is an easy way to find general information. Valuable for academic and large public library collections." –ARBA

2,400 pages; Softcover ISBN 1-59237-047-0, $125.00

The American Tally: Statistics & Comparative Rankings for U.S. Cities with Populations over 10,000

This important statistical handbook compiles, all in one place, comparative statistics on all U.S. cities and towns with a 10,000+ population. *The American Tally* provides statistical details on over 4,000 cities and towns and profiles how they compare with one another in Population Characteristics, Education, Language & Immigration, Income & Employment and Housing. Each section begins with an alphabetical listing of cities by state, allowing for quick access to both the statistics and relative rankings of any city. Next, the highest and lowest cities are listed in each statistic. These important, informative lists provide quick reference to which cities are at both extremes of the spectrum for each statistic. Unlike any other reference, *The American Tally* provides quick, easy access to comparative statistics – a must-have for any reference collection.

"A solid library reference." -Bookwatch

500 pages; Softcover ISBN 1-930956-29-0, $125.00

To preview any of our Directories Risk-Free for 30 days, call (800) 562-2139 or fax to (518) 789-0556

Profiles of America: Facts, Figures & Statistics for Every Populated Place in the United States

Profiles of America is the only source that pulls together, in one place, statistical, historical and descriptive information about every place in the United States in an easy-to-use format. This award winning reference set, now in its second edition, compiles statistics and data from over 20 different sources – the latest census information has been included along with more than nine brand new statistical topics. This Four-Volume Set details over 40,000 places, from the biggest metropolis to the smallest unincorporated hamlet, and provides statistical details and information on over 50 different topics including Geography, Climate, Population, Vital Statistics, Economy, Income, Taxes, Education, Housing, Health & Environment, Public Safety, Newspapers, Transportation, Presidential Election Results and Information Contacts or Chambers of Commerce. Profiles are arranged, for ease-of-use, by state and then by county. Each county begins with a County-Wide Overview and is followed by information for each Community in that particular county. The Community Profiles within the county are arranged alphabetically. *Profiles of America* is a virtual snapshot of America at your fingertips and a unique compilation of information that will be widely used in any reference collection.

A Library Journal Best Reference Book "An outstanding compilation." –Library Journal

10,000 pages; Four Volume Set; Softcover ISBN 1-891482-80-7, $595.00

The Environmental Resource Handbook, 2005/06

The Environmental Resource Handbook is the most up-to-date and comprehensive source for Environmental Resources and Statistics. Section I: Resources provides detailed contact information for thousands of information sources, including Associations & Organizations, Awards & Honors, Conferences, Foundations & Grants, Environmental Health, Government Agencies, National Parks & Wildlife Refuges, Publications, Research Centers, Educational Programs, Green Product Catalogs, Consultants and much more. Section II: Statistics, provides statistics and rankings on hundreds of important topics, including Children's Environmental Index, Municipal Finances, Toxic Chemicals, Recycling, Climate, Air & Water Quality and more. This kind of up-to-date environmental data, all in one place, is not available anywhere else on the market place today. This vast compilation of resources and statistics is a must-have for all public and academic libraries as well as any organization with a primary focus on the environment.

"...the intrinsic value of the information make it worth consideration by libraries with environmental collections and environmentally concerned users." –Booklist

1,000 pages; Softcover ISBN 1-59237-090-X, $155.00 ◆ Online Database $300.00

Weather America, A Thirty-Year Summary of Statistical Weather Data and Rankings

This valuable resource provides extensive climatological data for over 4,000 National and Cooperative Weather Stations throughout the United States. *Weather America* begins with a new Major Storms section that details major storm events of the nation and a National Rankings section that details rankings for several data elements, such as Maximum Temperature and Precipitation. The main body of *Weather America* is organized into 50 state sections. Each section provides a Data Table on each Weather Station, organized alphabetically, that provides statistics on Maximum and Minimum Temperatures, Precipitation, Snowfall, Extreme Temperatures, Foggy Days, Humidity and more. State sections contain two brand new features in this edition – a City Index and a narrative Description of the climatic conditions of the state. Each section also includes a revised Map of the State that includes not only weather stations, but cities and towns.

"Best Reference Book of the Year." –Library Journal

2,013 pages; Softcover ISBN 1-891482-29-7, $175.00

Grey House Publishing
Business Directories

The Directory of Business Information Resources, 2006

With 100% verification, over 1,000 new listings and more than 12,000 updates, this 2006 edition of *The Directory of Business Information Resources* is the most up-to-date source for contacts in over 98 business areas – from advertising and agriculture to utilities and wholesalers. This carefully researched volume details: the Associations representing each industry; the Newsletters that keep members current; the Magazines and Journals - with their "Special Issues" - that are important to the trade, the Conventions that are "must attends," Databases, Directories and Industry Web Sites that provide access to must-have marketing resources. Includes contact names, phone & fax numbers, web sites and e-mail addresses. This one-volume resource is a gold mine of information and would be a welcome addition to any reference collection.

"This is a most useful and easy-to-use addition to any researcher's library." –The Information Professionals Institute

2,500 pages; Softcover ISBN 1-59237-078-0, $195.00 ◆ Online Database $495.00

Nations of the World, 2005 A Political, Economic and Business Handbook

This completely revised edition covers all the nations of the world in an easy-to-use, single volume. Each nation is profiled in a single chapter that includes Key Facts, Political & Economic Issues, a Country Profile and Business Information. In this fast-changing world, it is extremely important to make sure that the most up-to-date information is included in your reference collection. This 2005 edition is just the answer. Each of the 200+ country chapters have been carefully reviewed by a political expert to make sure that the text reflects the most current information on Politics, Travel Advisories, Economics and more. You'll find such vital information as a Country Map, Population Characteristics, Inflation, Agricultural Production, Foreign Debt, Political History, Foreign Policy, Regional Insecurity, Economics, Trade & Tourism, Historical Profile, Political Systems, Ethnicity, Languages, Media, Climate, Hotels, Chambers of Commerce, Banking, Travel Information and more. Five Regional Chapters follow the main text and include a Regional Map, an Introductory Article, Key Indicators and Currencies for the Region. New for 2004, an all-inclusive CD-ROM is available as a companion to the printed text. Noted for its sophisticated, up-to-date and reliable compilation of political, economic and business information, this brand new edition will be an important acquisition to any public, academic or special library reference collection.

"A useful addition to both general reference collections and business collections." –RUSQ

1,700 pages; Print Version Only Softcover ISBN 1-59237-051-9, $145.00 ◆ Print Version and CD-ROM $180.00

The Grey House Performing Arts Directory, 2005

The Grey House Performing Arts Directory is the most comprehensive resource covering the Performing Arts. This important directory provides current information on over 8,500 Dance Companies, Instrumental Music Programs, Opera Companies, Choral Groups, Theater Companies, Performing Arts Series and Performing Arts Facilities. Plus, this edition now contains a brand new section on Artist Management Groups. In addition to mailing address, phone & fax numbers, e-mail addresses and web sites, dozens of other fields of available information include mission statement, key contacts, facilities, seating capacity, season, attendance and more. This directory also provides an important Information Resources section that covers hundreds of Performing Arts Associations, Magazines, Newsletters, Trade Shows, Directories, Databases and Industry Web Sites. Five indexes provide immediate access to this wealth of information: Entry Name, Executive Name, Performance Facilities, Geographic and Information Resources. *The Grey House Performing Arts Directory* pulls together thousands of Performing Arts Organizations, Facilities and Information Resources into an easy-to-use source – this kind of comprehensiveness and extensive detail is not available in any resource on the market place today.

"Immensely useful and user-friendly ... recommended for public, academic and certain special library reference collections." –Booklist

1,500 pages; Softcover ISBN 1-59237-023-3, $185.00 ◆ Online Database $335.00

International Business and Trade Directories

Completely updated, the Third Edition of *International Business and Trade Directories* now contains more than 10,000 entries, over 2,000 more than the last edition, making this directory the most comprehensive resource of the worlds business and trade directories. Entries include content descriptions, price, publisher's name and address, web site and e-mail addresses, phone and fax numbers and editorial staff. Organized by industry group, and then by region, this resource puts over 10,000 industry-specific business and trade directories at the reader's fingertips. Three indexes are included for quick access to information: Geographic Index, Publisher Index and Title Index. Public, college and corporate libraries, as well as individuals and corporations seeking critical market information will want to add this directory to their marketing collection.

"Reasonably priced for a work of this type, this directory should appeal to larger academic, public and corporate libraries with an international focus." –Library Journal

1,800 pages; Softcover ISBN 1-930956-63-0, $225.00 ◆ Online Database (includes a free copy of the directory) $450.00

The Grey House Safety & Security Directory, 2005

The Grey House Safety & Security Directory is the most comprehensive reference tool and buyer's guide for the safety and security industry. Arranged by safety topic, each chapter begins with OSHA regulations for the topic, followed by Training Articles written by top professionals in the field and Self-Inspection Checklists. Next, each topic contains Buyer's Guide sections that feature related products and services. Topics include Administration, Insurance, Loss Control & Consulting, Protective Equipment & Apparel, Noise & Vibration, Facilities Monitoring & Maintenance, Employee Health Maintenance & Ergonomics, Retail Food Services, Machine Guards, Process Guidelines & Tool Handling, Ordinary Materials Handling, Hazardous Materials Handling, Workplace Preparation & Maintenance, Electrical Lighting & Safety, Fire & Rescue and Security. The Buyer's Guide sections are carefully indexed within each topic area to ensure that you can find the supplies needed to meet OSHA's regulations. This comprehensive, up-to-date reference will provide every tool necessary to make sure a business is in compliance with OSHA regulations and locate the products and services needed to meet those regulations.

"Presents industrial safety information for engineers, plant managers, risk managers, and construction site supervisors..." –Choice

1,500 pages, 2 Volume Set; Softcover ISBN 1-59237-067-5, $225.00

To preview any of our Directories Risk-Free for 30 days, call (800) 562-2139 or fax to (518) 789-0556

The Grey House Homeland Security Directory, 2005

This updated edition features the latest contact information for government and private organizations involved with Homeland Security along with the latest product information and provides detailed profiles of nearly 1,000 Federal & State Organizations & Agencies and over 3,000 Officials and Key Executives involved with Homeland Security. These listings are incredibly detailed and include Mailing Address, Phone & Fax Numbers, Email Addresses & Web Sites, a complete Description of the Agency and a complete list of the Officials and Key Executives associated with the Agency. Next, *The Grey House Homeland Security Directory* provides the go-to source for Homeland Security Products & Services. This section features over 2,000 Companies that provide Consulting, Products or Services. With this Buyer's Guide at their fingertips, users can locate suppliers of everything from Training Materials to Access Controls, from Perimeter Security to BioTerrorism Countermeasures and everything in between – complete with contact information and product descriptions. A handy Product Locator Index is provided to quickly and easily locate suppliers of a particular product. Lastly, an Information Resources Section provides immediate access to contact information for hundreds of Associations, Newsletters, Magazines, Trade Shows, Databases and Directories that focus on Homeland Security. This comprehensive, information-packed resource will be a welcome tool for any company or agency that is in need of Homeland Security information and will be a necessary acquisition for the reference collection of all public libraries and large school districts.

"Compiles this information in one place and is discerning in content. A useful purchase for public and academic libraries." –Booklist

800 pages; Softcover ISBN 1-59237-057-8, $195.00 ◆ Online Database (includes a free copy of the directory) $385.00

The Grey House Transportation Security Directory & Handbook, 2005

This brand new title is the only reference of its kind that brings together current data on Transportation Security. With information on everything from Regulatory Authorities to Security Equipment, this top-flight database brings together the relevant information necessary for creating and maintaining a security plan for a wide range of transportation facilities. With this current, comprehensive directory at the ready you'll have immediate access to: Regulatory Authorities & Legislation; Information Resources; Sample Security Plans & Checklists; Contact Data for Major Airports, Seaports, Railroads, Trucking Companies and Oil Pipelines; Security Service Providers; Recommended Equipment & Product Information and more. Using the *Grey House Transportation Security Directory & Handbook*, managers will be able to quickly and easily assess their current security plans; develop contacts to create and maintain new security procedures; and source the products and services necessary to adequately maintain a secure environment. This valuable resource is a must for all Security Managers at Airports, Seaports, Railroads, Trucking Companies and Oil Pipelines.

800 pages; Softcover ISBN 1-59237-075-6, $195

The Directory of Venture Capital & Private Equity Firms, 2005

This edition has been extensively updated and broadly expanded to offer direct access to over 2,800 Domestic and International Venture Capital Firms, including address, phone & fax numbers, e-mail addresses and web sites for both primary and branch locations. Entries include details on the firm's Mission Statement, Industry Group Preferences, Geographic Preferences, Average and Minimum Investments and Investment Criteria. You'll also find details that are available nowhere else, including the Firm's Portfolio Companies and extensive information on each of the firm's Managing Partners, such as Education, Professional Background and Directorships held, along with the Partner's E-mail Address. *The Directory of Venture Capital & Private Equity Firms* offers five important indexes: Geographic Index, Executive Name Index, Portfolio Company Index, Industry Preference Index and College & University Index. With its comprehensive coverage and detailed, extensive information on each company, *The Directory of Venture Capital & Private Equity Firms* is an important addition to any finance collection.

"The sheer number of listings, the descriptive information provided and the outstanding indexing make this directory a better value than its principal competitor, Pratt's Guide to Venture Capital Sources. Recommended for business collections in large public, academic and business libraries." –Choice

1,300 pages; Softcover ISBN 1-59237-062-4, $450.00 ◆ Online Database (includes a free copy of the directory) $889.00

The Directory of Mail Order Catalogs, 2005

Published since 1981, this 2005 edition features 100% verification of data and is the premier source of information on the mail order catalog industry. Details over 12,000 consumer catalog companies with 44 different product chapters from Animals to Toys & Games. Contains detailed contact information including e-mail addresses and web sites along with important business details such as employee size, years in business, sales volume, catalog size, number of catalogs mailed and more. Four indexes provide quick access to information: Catalog & Company Name Index, Geographic Index, Product Index and Web Sites Index.

"This is a godsend for those looking for information." –Reference Book Review

1,700 pages; Softcover ISBN 1-59237-066-7 $250.00 ◆ Online Database (includes a free copy of the directory) $495.00

Thomas Food and Beverage Market Place, 2005

Thomas Food and Beverage Market Place is bigger and better than ever with thousands of new companies, thousands of updates to existing companies and two revised and enhanced product category indexes. This comprehensive directory profiles over 18,000 Food & Beverage Manufacturers, 12,000 Equipment & Supply Companies, 2,200 Transportation & Warehouse Companies, 2,000 Brokers & Wholesalers, 8,000 Importers & Exporters, 900 Industry Resources and hundreds of Mail Order Catalogs. Listings include detailed Contact Information, Sales Volumes, Key Contacts, Brand & Product Information, Packaging Details and much more. *Thomas Food and Beverage Market Place* is available as a three-volume printed set, a subscription-based Online Database via the Internet, on CD-ROM, as well as mailing lists and a licensable database.

"An essential purchase for those in the food industry but will also be useful in public libraries where needed. Much of the information will be difficult and time consuming to locate without this handy three-volume ready-reference source." –ARBA

8,500 pages, 3 Volume Set; Softcover ISBN 1-59237-058-6, $495.00 ◆ CD-ROM $695.00 ◆
CD-ROM & 3 Volume Set Combo $895.00 ◆ Online Database $695.00 ◆ Online Database & 3 Volume Set Combo, $895.00

Sports Market Place Directory, 2005

For over 20 years, this comprehensive, up-to-date directory has offered direct access to the Who, What, When & Where of the Sports Industry. With over 20,000 updates and enhancements, the *Sports Market Place Directory* is the most detailed, comprehensive and current sports business reference source available. In 1,800 information-packed pages, *Sports Market Place Directory* profiles contact information and key executives for: Single Sport Organizations, Professional Leagues, Multi-Sport Organizations, Disabled Sports, High School & Youth Sports, Military Sports, Olympic Organizations, Media, Sponsors, Sponsorship & Marketing Event Agencies, Event & Meeting Calendars, Professional Services, College Sports, Manufacturers & Retailers, Facilities and much more. *The Sports Market Place Directory* provides organization's contact information with detailed descriptions including: Key Contacts, physical, mailing, email and web addresses plus phone and fax numbers. Plus, nine important indexes make sure that you can find the information you're looking for quickly and easily: Entry Index, Single Sport Index, Media Index, Sponsor Index, Agency Index, Manufacturers Index, Brand Name Index, Facilities Index and Executive/Geographic Index. For over twenty years, *The Sports Market Place Directory* has assisted thousands of individuals in their pursuit of a career in the sports industry. Why not use "THE SOURCE" that top recruiters, headhunters and career placement centers use to find information on or about sports organizations and key hiring contacts.

1,800 pages; Softcover ISBN 1-59237-077-2, $225.00 ◆ CD-ROM $479.00

New York State Directory, 2005/06

The New York State Directory, published annually since 1983, is a comprehensive and easy-to-use guide to accessing public officials and private sector organizations and individuals who influence public policy in the state of New York. *The New York State Directory* includes important information on all New York state legislators and congressional representatives, including biographies and key committee assignments. It also includes staff rosters for all branches of New York state government and for federal agencies and departments that impact the state policy process. Following the state government section are 25 chapters covering policy areas from agriculture through veterans' affairs. Each chapter identifies the state, local and federal agencies and officials that formulate or implement policy. In addition, each chapter contains a roster of private sector experts and advocates who influence the policy process. The directory also offers appendices that include statewide party officials; chambers of commerce; lobbying organizations; public and private universities and colleges; television, radio and print media; and local government agencies and officials.

New York State Directory - 800 pages; Softcover ISBN 1-59237-093-4; $129.00
New York State Directory with Profiles of New York – 2 volumes; 1,600 pages; Softcover ISBN 1-59237-095-0; $195

Older Americans Information Directory, 2004/05

Completely updated for 2004/05, this Fifth Edition has been completely revised and now contains 1,000 new listings, over 8,000 updates to existing listings and over 3,000 brand new e-mail addresses and web sites. You'll find important resources for Older Americans including National, Regional, State & Local Organizations, Government Agencies, Research Centers, Libraries & Information Centers, Legal Resources, Discount Travel Information, Continuing Education Programs, Disability Aids & Assistive Devices, Health, Print Media and Electronic Media. Three indexes: Entry Index, Subject Index and Geographic Index make it easy to find just the right source of information. This comprehensive guide to resources for Older Americans will be a welcome addition to any reference collection.

"Highly recommended for academic, public, health science and consumer libraries…" –Choice

1,200 pages; Softcover ISBN 1-59237-037-3, $165.00 ◆ Online Database $215.00 ◆ Online Database & Directory Combo $300.00

The Complete Directory for Pediatric Disorders, 2004/05

This important directory provides parents and caregivers with information about Pediatric Conditions, Disorders, Diseases and Disabilities, including Blood Disorders, Bone & Spinal Disorders, Brain Defects & Abnormalities, Chromosomal Disorders, Congenital Heart Defects, Movement Disorders, Neuromuscular Disorders and Pediatric Tumors & Cancers. This carefully written directory offers: understandable Descriptions of 15 major bodily systems; Descriptions of more than 200 Disorders and a Resources Section, detailing National Agencies & Associations, State Associations, Online Services, Libraries & Resource Centers, Research Centers, Support Groups & Hotlines, Camps, Books and Periodicals. This resource will provide immediate access to information crucial to families and caregivers when coping with children's illnesses.

"Recommended for public and consumer health libraries." –Library Journal

1,200 pages; Softcover ISBN 1-59237-045-4, $165.00 ◆ Online Database $215.00 ◆ Online Database & Directory Combo $300.00

The Complete Directory for People with Rare Disorders

This outstanding reference is produced in conjunction with the National Organization for Rare Disorders to provide comprehensive and needed access to important information on over 1,000 rare disorders, including Cancers and Muscular, Genetic and Blood Disorders. An informative Disorder Description is provided for each of the 1,100 disorders (rare Cancers and Muscular, Genetic and Blood Disorders) followed by information on National and State Organizations dealing with a particular disorder, Umbrella Organizations that cover a wide range of disorders, the Publications that can be useful when researching a disorder and the Government Agencies to contact. Detailed and up-to-date listings contain mailing address, phone and fax numbers, web sites and e-mail addresses along with a description. For quick, easy access to information, this directory contains two indexes: Entry Name Index and Acronym/Keyword Index along with an informative Guide for Rare Disorder Advocates. The Complete Directory for People with Rare Disorders will be an invaluable tool for the thousands of families that have been struck with a rare or "orphan" disease, who feel that they have no place to turn and will be a much-used addition to the reference collection of any public or academic library.

"Quick access to information… public libraries and hospital patient libraries will find this a useful resource in directing users to support groups or agencies dealing with a rare disorder." –Booklist

726 pages; Softcover ISBN 1-891482-18-1, $165.00

The Directory of Drug & Alcohol Residential Rehabilitation Facilities

This brand new directory is the first-ever resource to bring together, all in one place, data on the thousands of drug and alcohol residential rehabilitation facilities in the United States. *The Directory of Drug & Alcohol Residential Rehabilitation Facilities* covers over 1,000 facilities, with detailed contact information for each one, including mailing address, phone and fax numbers, email addresses and web sites, mission statement, type of treatment programs, cost, average length of stay, numbers of residents and counselors, accreditation, insurance plans accepted, type of environment, religious affiliation, education components and much more. It also contains a helpful chapter on General Resources that provides contact information for Associations, Print & Electronic Media, Support Groups and Conferences. Multiple indexes allow the user to pinpoint the facilities that meet very specific criteria. This time-saving tool is what so many counselors, parents and medical professionals have been asking for. *The Directory of Drug & Alcohol Residential Rehabilitation Facilities* will be a helpful tool in locating the right source for treatment for a wide range of individuals. This comprehensive directory will be an important acquisition for all reference collections: public and academic libraries, case managers, social workers, state agencies and many more.

"This is an excellent, much needed directory that fills an important gap…" –Booklist

300 pages; Softcover ISBN 1-59237-031-4, $135.00

The HMO/PPO Directory, 2005

The HMO/PPO Directory is a comprehensive source that provides detailed information about Health Maintenance Organizations and Preferred Provider Organizations nationwide. This comprehensive directory details more information about more managed health care organizations than ever before. Over 1,100 HMOs, PPOs and affiliated companies are listed, arranged alphabetically by state. Detailed listings include Key Contact Information, Prescription Drug Benefits, Enrollment, Geographical Areas served, Affiliated Physicians & Hospitals, Federal Qualifications, Status, Year Founded, Managed Care Partners, Employer References, Fees & Payment Information and more. Plus, five years of historical information is included related to Revenues, Net Income, Medical Loss Ratios, Membership Enrollment and Number of Patient Complaints. Five easy-to-use, cross-referenced indexes will put this vast array of information at your fingertips immediately: HMO Index, PPO Index, Other Providers Index, Personnel Index and Enrollment Index. *The HMO/PPO Directory* provides the most comprehensive information on the most companies available on the market place today.

"Helpful to individuals requesting certain HMO/PPO issues such as co-payment costs, subscription costs and patient complaints. Individuals concerned (or those with questions) about their insurance may find this text to be of use to them." -ARBA

600 pages; Softcover ISBN 1-59237-057-8, $275.00 • Online Database, $495.00 • Online Database & Directory Combo, $600.00

The Directory of Independent Ambulatory Care Centers

This first edition of *The Directory of Independent Ambulatory Care Centers* provides access to detailed information that, before now, could only be found scattered in hundreds of different sources. This comprehensive and up-to-date directory pulls together a vast array of contact information for over 7,200 Ambulatory Surgery Centers, Ambulatory General and Urgent Care Clinics, and Diagnostic Imaging Centers that are not affiliated with a hospital or major medical center. Detailed listings include Mailing Address, Phone & Fax Numbers, E-mail and Web Site addresses, Contact Name and Phone Numbers of the Medical Director and other Key Executives and Purchasing Agents, Specialties & Services Offered, Year Founded, Numbers of Employees and Surgeons, Number of Operating Rooms, Number of Cases seen per year, Overnight Options, Contracted Services and much more. Listings are arranged by State, by Center Category and then alphabetically by Organization Name. Two indexes provide quick and easy access to this wealth of information: Entry Name Index and Specialty/Service Index. *The Directory of Independent Ambulatory Care Centers* is a must-have resource for anyone marketing a product or service to this important industry and will be an invaluable tool for those searching for a local care center that will meet their specific needs.

"Among the numerous hospital directories, no other provides information on independent ambulatory centers. A handy, well-organized resource that would be useful in medical center libraries and public libraries." –Choice

986 pages; Softcover ISBN 1-930956-90-8, $185.00 • Online Database, $365.00 • Online Database & Directory Combo, $450.00

Sedgwick Press
Education Directories

Educators Resource Directory, 2005/06

Educators Resource Directory is a comprehensive resource that provides the educational professional with thousands of resources and statistical data for professional development. This directory saves hours of research time by providing immediate access to Associations & Organizations, Conferences & Trade Shows, Educational Research Centers, Employment Opportunities & Teaching Abroad, School Library Services, Scholarships, Financial Resources, Professional Consultants, Computer Software & Testing Resources and much more. Plus, this comprehensive directory also includes a section on Statistics and Rankings with over 100 tables, including statistics on Average Teacher Salaries, SAT/ACT scores, Revenues & Expenditures and more. These important statistics will allow the user to see how their school rates among others, make relocation decisions and so much more. For quick access to information, this directory contains four indexes: Entry & Publisher Index, Geographic Index, a Subject & Grade Index and Web Sites Index. *Educators Resource Directory* will be a well-used addition to the reference collection of any school district, education department or public library.

"Recommended for all collections that serve elementary and secondary school professionals." –Choice

1,000 pages; Softcover ISBN 1-59237-080-2, $145.00 • Online Database $195.00 • Online Database & Directory Combo $280.00